Coll
ENGLISH
THESAURUS

Published by Collins
An imprint of HarperCollins Publishers
Westerhill Road
Bishopbriggs
Glasgow G64 2QT

HarperCollins*Publishers*
1st Floor, Watermarque Building,
Ringsend Road, Dublin 4, Ireland

Paperback Eighth Edition 2019
ISBN 978-0-00-830945-9

Essential Second Edition 2019
ISBN 978-0-00-830944-2

10 9 8 7 6 5 4

www.collinsdictionary.com

Typeset by Davidson Publishing Solutions

Printed and bound in the UK using 100%
Renewable Electricity at CPI Group (UK) Ltd

A catalogue record for this book is
available from the British Library.

If you would like to comment on any
aspect of this book, please contact us at
the given address or online.
E-mail: dictionaries@harpercollins.co.uk
 facebook.com/collinsdictionary
 @collinsdict

Acknowledgements
We would like to thank those authors and
publishers who kindly gave permission
for copyright material to be used in the
Collins Corpus. We would also like to
thank Times Newspapers Ltd for
providing valuable data.

Contents

EDITORIAL STAFF
Rachel Fletcher
Mary O'Neill
Elizabeth Walter
Kate Woodford

WORDS FOR CRYPTIC CROSSWORDS
Michael Kindred and Derrick Knight

FOR THE PUBLISHER
Gerry Breslin
Kerry Ferguson

Using this thesaurus

Main Entry Words

Main entry words are printed in large bold type:

eagerness

Variant Spellings

Common acceptable variant spellings are shown in full:

email *or* **e-mail** NOUN

Fixed Phrases

Fixed phrases are printed in small bold type introduced by a circular bullet:

empathize VERB • **empathize with** = **identify with**, understand, relate to, feel for, sympathize with, have a rapport with, feel at one with, be on the same wavelength as

Parts of Speech

Parts of speech are shown in small capitals. Where a word has several senses for one part of speech, the senses are numbered:

edition NOUN **1** *a rare first edition of a Dickens novel* = **printing**, publication **2** *The Christmas edition of the catalogue is out now.* = **copy**, impression, number **3** = **version**, volume, issue **4** *We'll be back in our next edition in a week's time.* = **programme** (*TV & Radio*)

A change in part of speech is indicated by a solid arrow:

elbow NOUN *The boat was moored at the elbow of the river.* = **joint**, turn, corner, bend, angle, curve ▶ VERB *They elbowed me out of the way.* = **push**, force, crowd (*informal*), shoulder, knock, bump, shove, nudge, jostle, hustle

Alternatives

The key synonym for each sense is given in bold type, with other alternatives given in roman:

ear NOUN **1** *He has a fine ear for music.* = **sensitivity**, taste, discrimination, appreciation, musical perception

Using this thesaurus

Examples

Example sentences are given in italics:

> **eve** NOUN **1** *the eve of his 27th birthday*
> = **night before**, day before, vigil **2** *when*
> *Europe stood on the eve of war in 1914*
> = **brink**, point, edge, verge, threshold

Opposites

Opposites are given after the list of alternatives and are introduced by a solid square:

> **edible** ADJECTIVE = **safe to eat**, harmless,
> wholesome, palatable, digestible,
> eatable, comestible (*rare*), fit to eat,
> good ■ **OPPOSITE:** inedible

Related Words

Related words are introduced by a solid square:

> **sky** NOUN = **heavens**, firmament, upper
> atmosphere, azure (*poetic*), welkin
> (*archaic*), vault of heaven, rangi (*N.Z.*)
> ■ **RELATED WORD**: *adjective* celestial

Labels

Labels show the restricted region or register of a word or phrase:

> **evening** NOUN = **dusk** (*archaic*), night,
> sunset, twilight, sundown, eve, vesper
> (*archaic*), eventide (*archaic, poetic*),
> gloaming (*Scot., poetic*), e'en (*archaic,*
> *poetic*), close of day, crepuscule, even,
> evo (*Austral. slang*)

Usage Notes

Usage notes are introduced by the heading USAGE:

> **USAGE** The spelling of *elusive*, as in *a shy,*
> *elusive character*, should be noted. This
> adjective derives from the verb *elude*, and
> should not be confused with the rare
> word *illusive* meaning 'not real' or 'based
> on illusion'.

Cross References

Cross references refer the user to another entry where full information is given.

enquire *see* **inquire**

Abbreviations used in this thesaurus

AD	Anno Domini
Austral.	Australia/Australian
BC	before Christ
Brit.	British
Canad.	Canada/Canadian
cap.	capital
esp.	especially
etc.	et cetera
N.Z.	New Zealand
®	trademark
S.	South
Scot.	Scottish
U.S.	United States

Aa

aback ADVERB • **taken aback** = **surprised**, thrown, shocked, stunned, confused, astonished, staggered, startled, bewildered, astounded, disconcerted, bowled over (*informal*), stupefied, floored (*informal*), knocked for six, dumbfounded, left open-mouthed, nonplussed, flabbergasted (*informal*)

abandon VERB **1** *She claimed that her parents had abandoned her.* = **leave**, strand, ditch (*slang*), leave behind, walk out on, forsake, jilt, run out on, throw over, turn your back on, desert, dump, leave high and dry, leave in the lurch **2** *The authorities have abandoned any attempt to distribute food.* = **stop**, drop, give up, halt, cease, cut out, pack in (*Brit. informal*), discontinue, leave off, desist from ■ **OPPOSITE:** continue **3** *They were persuaded to abandon their lawsuit.* = **give up**, resign from, yield, surrender, relinquish, renounce, waive, cede, forgo, abdicate ■ **OPPOSITE:** keep ▶ NOUN *He has splashed money around with gay abandon.* = **recklessness**, dash, wildness, wantonness, unrestraint, careless freedom ■ **OPPOSITE:** restraint • **abandon ship** *The crew prepared to abandon ship.* = **evacuate**, quit, withdraw from, vacate, depart from

abandoned ADJECTIVE **1** *abandoned buildings that become a breeding ground for crime* = **unoccupied**, empty, deserted, vacant, derelict, uninhabited ■ **OPPOSITE:** occupied **2** *a newsreel of abandoned children suffering from cold and hunger* = **deserted**, dropped, rejected, neglected, stranded, ditched, discarded, relinquished, left, forsaken, cast off, jilted, cast aside, cast out, cast away **3** *people who enjoy a wild, abandoned lifestyle* = **uninhibited**, wild, uncontrolled, unbridled, unrestrained, unconstrained ■ **OPPOSITE:** inhibited

abandonment NOUN **1** *memories of her father's complete abandonment of her* = **desertion**, leaving, forsaking, jilting **2** *the abandonment of two North Sea oilfields* = **evacuation**, leaving, quitting, departure, withdrawal **3** *Rain forced the abandonment of the next day's competitions.* = **stopping**, cessation, discontinuation **4** *their*

abandonment of the policy = **renunciation**, giving up, surrender, waiver, abdication, cession, relinquishment

abate VERB **1** *The storms soon abated.* = **decrease**, decline, relax, ease, sink, fade, weaken, diminish, dwindle, lessen, slow, wane, subside, ebb, let up, slacken, attenuate, taper off ■ **OPPOSITE:** increase **2** *a government programme to abate greenhouse gas emissions* = **reduce**, slow, relax, ease, relieve, moderate, weaken, dull, diminish, decrease, lessen, alleviate, quell, mitigate, attenuate ■ **OPPOSITE:** increase

abatement NOUN **1** *Demand for the product shows no sign of abatement.* = **decrease**, slowing, decline, easing, sinking, fading, weakening, relaxation, dwindling, lessening, waning, subsiding, ebbing, cessation, let-up (*informal*), slackening, diminution, tapering off, attenuation **2** *noise abatement* = **reduction**, slowing, relief, easing, weakening, dulling, decrease, lessening, cutback, quelling, moderation, remission, slackening, mitigation, diminution, curtailment, alleviation, attenuation, extenuation

abattoir NOUN = **slaughterhouse**, shambles, butchery

abbey NOUN = **monastery**, convent, priory, cloister, nunnery, friary

abbreviate VERB = **shorten**, reduce, contract, trim, cut, prune, summarize, compress, condense, abridge ■ **OPPOSITE:** expand

abbreviated ADJECTIVE = **shortened**, shorter, reduced, brief, potted, trimmed, pruned, cut, summarized, compressed, concise, condensed, abridged ■ **OPPOSITE:** expanded

abbreviation NOUN = **shortening**, reduction, résumé, trimming, summary, contraction, compression, synopsis, précis, abridgment

abdicate VERB **1** *The last French king abdicated in 1848.* = **resign**, retire, quit, step down (*informal*) **2** *Edward chose to abdicate the throne, rather than give Mrs Simpson up.* = **give up**, yield, hand over, surrender, relinquish, renounce, waive, vacate, cede, abjure **3** *Many parents simply abdicate all responsibility for their children.* = **renounce**, give up, waive, abandon, surrender, relinquish, forgo, abnegate

abdication NOUN **1** *the abdication of Edward VIII* = **resignation**, quitting, retirement, retiral (*chiefly Scot.*) **2** *Edward was titled Duke of Windsor after his abdication of the throne.* = **giving up**, yielding, surrender, waiving, renunciation, cession, relinquishment, abjuration

a

abdomen NOUN = **stomach**, guts (slang), belly, tummy (informal), midriff, midsection, makutu (N.Z.), puku (N.Z.) ■ **RELATED WORD:** adjective abdominal

abdominal ADJECTIVE = **gastric**, intestinal, visceral

abduct VERB = **kidnap**, seize, carry off, run off with, run away with, make off with, snatch (slang)

abduction NOUN = **kidnapping**, seizure, carrying off

aberrant ADJECTIVE **1** His rages and aberrant behaviour worsened. = **abnormal**, odd, strange, extraordinary, curious, weird, peculiar, eccentric, queer, irregular, erratic, deviant, off-the-wall (slang), oddball (informal), anomalous, untypical, outré **2** cruel and aberrant acts = **depraved**, corrupt, perverted, perverse, degenerate, deviant, debased, debauched

aberration NOUN = **anomaly**, exception, defect, abnormality, inconsistency, deviation, quirk, peculiarity, divergence, departure, irregularity, incongruity

abet VERB **1** We shall strike hard at terrorists and those who abet them. = **help**, aid, encourage, sustain, assist, uphold, back, second, incite, egg on, succour **2** The media have abetted the feeling of unreality. = **encourage**, further, forward, promote, urge, boost, prompt, spur, foster, incite, connive at

abetting NOUN = **help**, backing, support, aid, assistance, encouragement, abetment, abettal

abeyance NOUN • **in abeyance** = **shelved**, pending, on ice (informal), in cold storage (informal), hanging fire, suspended

abhor VERB = **hate**, loathe, despise, detest, shrink from, shudder at, recoil from, be repelled by, have an aversion to, abominate, execrate, regard with repugnance or horror ■ **OPPOSITE:** love

abhorrent ADJECTIVE = **hateful**, hated, offensive, disgusting, horrible, revolting, obscene, distasteful, horrid, repellent, obnoxious, despicable, repulsive, heinous, odious, repugnant, loathsome, abominable, execrable, detestable

abide VERB **1** I can't abide people who can't make up their minds. = **tolerate**, suffer, accept, bear, endure, brook, hack (slang), put up with, take, stand, stomach, thole (Scot.) **2** to make moral judgements on the basis of what is eternal and abides = **last**, continue, remain, survive, carry on, endure, persist, keep on • **abide by something** They have got to abide by the rules. = **obey**, follow, agree to, carry out, observe, fulfil, stand by, act on, comply with, hold to, heed, submit to, conform to, keep to, adhere to, mind

abiding ADJECTIVE = **enduring**, lasting, continuing, remaining, surviving, permanent, constant, prevailing, persisting, persistent, eternal, tenacious, firm, fast, everlasting, unending, unchanging ■ **OPPOSITE:** brief

ability NOUN **1** No one had faith in his ability to do the job. = **capability**, power, potential, facility, capacity, qualification, competence, proficiency, competency, potentiality ■ **OPPOSITE:** inability **2** Her drama teacher spotted her ability. = **skill**, talent, know-how (informal), gift, expertise, faculty, flair, competence, energy, accomplishment, knack, aptitude, proficiency, dexterity, cleverness, potentiality, adroitness, adeptness

abject ADJECTIVE **1** Both of them died in abject poverty. = **wretched**, miserable, hopeless, dismal, outcast, pitiful, forlorn, deplorable, pitiable **2** He sounded abject and eager to please. = **servile**, humble, craven, cringing, fawning, submissive, grovelling, subservient, slavish, mean, low, obsequious ■ **OPPOSITE:** dignified **3** an abject traitor = **despicable**, base, degraded, worthless, vile, sordid, debased, reprehensible, contemptible, dishonourable, ignoble, detestable, scungy (Austral. & N.Z.)

ablaze ADJECTIVE **1** Shops, houses and vehicles were ablaze. = **on fire**, burning, flaming, blazing, fiery, alight, aflame, afire **2** The chamber was ablaze with light. = **bright**, brilliant, flashing, glowing, sparkling, illuminated, gleaming, radiant, luminous, incandescent, aglow **3** She was ablaze with enthusiasm. = **passionate**, excited, stimulated, fierce, enthusiastic, aroused, animated, frenzied, fervent, impassioned, fervid

able ADJECTIVE = **capable**, experienced, fit, skilled, expert, powerful, masterly, effective, qualified, talented, gifted, efficient, clever, practised, accomplished, competent, skilful, adept, masterful, strong, proficient, adroit, highly endowed ■ **OPPOSITE:** incapable

able-bodied ADJECTIVE = **strong**, firm, sound, fit, powerful, healthy, strapping, hardy, robust, vigorous, sturdy, hale (old-fashioned), stout, staunch, hearty, lusty, right as rain (Brit. informal), tough, capable, sturdy, Herculean, fighting fit, sinewy, fit as a fiddle

abnormal ADJECTIVE = **unusual**, different, odd, strange, surprising, extraordinary, remarkable, bizarre, unexpected, curious, weird, exceptional, peculiar, eccentric, unfamiliar, queer, irregular, phenomenal, uncommon, erratic, monstrous, singular, unnatural, deviant, unconventional, off-the-wall (slang), oddball (informal), out of the ordinary, left-field (informal), anomalous, atypical, aberrant, untypical, outré ■ **OPPOSITE:** normal

abnormality NOUN **1** *Further scans are required to confirm any abnormality.*
= **strangeness**, deviation, eccentricity, aberration, peculiarity, idiosyncrasy, irregularity, weirdness, singularity, oddness, waywardness, unorthodoxy, unexpectedness, queerness, unnaturalness, bizarreness, unusualness, extraordinariness, aberrance, atypicalness, uncommonness, untypicalness, curiousness **2** *Genetic abnormalities are usually associated with paternal DNA.*
= **anomaly**, flaw, rarity, deviation, oddity, aberration, exception, peculiarity, deformity, irregularity, malformation

abnormally ADVERB = **unusually**, oddly, strangely, extremely, exceptionally, extraordinarily, overly, excessively, peculiarly, particularly, bizarrely, disproportionately, singularly, fantastically, unnaturally, uncannily, inordinately, uncommonly, prodigiously, freakishly, atypically, subnormally, supernormally

abode NOUN = **home**, house, quarters, lodging, pad (slang), residence, habitat, dwelling (formal, literary), habitation (formal), domicile, dwelling place

abolish VERB = **do away with**, end, destroy, eliminate, shed, cancel, axe (informal), get rid of, ditch (slang), dissolve, junk (informal), suppress, overturn, throw out, discard, wipe out, overthrow, void, terminate, drop, trash (slang), repeal, eradicate, put an end to, quash, extinguish, dispense with, revoke, stamp out, obliterate, subvert, jettison, repudiate, annihilate, rescind, exterminate, invalidate, bring to an end, annul, nullify, blot out, expunge (formal), abrogate, vitiate, extirpate, kennet (Austral. slang), jeff (Austral. slang)
■ **OPPOSITE:** establish

abolition NOUN = **eradication**, ending, end, withdrawal, destruction, removal, overturning, wiping out, overthrow, voiding, extinction, repeal, elimination, cancellation, suppression, quashing, termination, stamping out, subversion, extermination, annihilation, blotting out, repudiation, erasure, annulment, obliteration, revocation, effacement, nullification, abrogation, rescission,

extirpation, invalidation, vitiation, expunction

abominable ADJECTIVE = **detestable**, shocking, terrible (informal), offensive, foul, disgusting, horrible, revolting, obscene, vile, horrid, repellent, atrocious (informal), obnoxious, despicable, repulsive, base, heinous, hellish (informal), odious, hateful, repugnant, reprehensible, loathsome, abhorrent, contemptible, villainous, nauseous, wretched, accursed, execrable, godawful (slang) ■ **OPPOSITE:** pleasant

abomination NOUN **1** *What is happening is an abomination.* = **outrage**, bête noire, horror, evil, shame, plague (informal), curse, disgrace, crime, atrocity, torment, anathema, barbarism, bugbear **2** *He had become an object of abomination.* = **hatred**, hate, horror, disgust, dislike, loathing, distaste, animosity, aversion, revulsion, antagonism, antipathy, enmity, ill will, animus, abhorrence, repugnance, odium (formal), detestation, execration

aboriginal ADJECTIVE = **indigenous**, first, earliest, original, primary, ancient, native, primitive, pristine, primordial, primeval, autochthonous

aborigine NOUN = **original inhabitant**, native, aboriginal, indigene

abort VERB *The take-off was aborted.* = **stop**, end, finish, check, arrest, halt, cease, bring or come to a halt or a standstill, axe (informal), pull up, terminate, call off, break off, cut short, pack in (Brit. informal), discontinue, desist

abortion NOUN **1** *Doctors advised her to have an abortion.* = **termination**, feticide, aborticide, miscarriage, deliberate miscarriage **2** *the abortion of the original nuclear project* = **failure**, disappointment, fiasco, misadventure, vain effort

abortive ADJECTIVE = **failed**, failing, useless, vain, unsuccessful, idle, ineffective, futile, fruitless, unproductive, ineffectual, miscarried, unavailing, bootless

abound VERB *Stories abound about when he was in charge.* = **be plentiful**, thrive, flourish, be numerous, proliferate, be abundant, be thick on the ground, superabound
• **abound with** *or* **in something** *Venice abounds in famous hotels.* = **overflow with**, be packed with, teem with, be crowded with, swell with, crawl with, swarm with, be jammed with, be infested with, be thronged with, luxuriate with

about PREPOSITION **1** *She knew a lot about food.* = **regarding**, on, re, concerning, touching, dealing with, respecting, referring to, relating to, concerned with, connected with, relative to, with respect to, as regards, anent (*Scot.*) **2** *For 18 years, he wandered about Germany, Switzerland and Italy.* = **around**, over, through, round, throughout, all over **3** *The restaurant is somewhere about here.* = **near**, around, close to, bordering, nearby, beside, close by, adjacent to, just round the corner from, in the neighbourhood of, alongside of, contiguous to, within sniffing distance of (*informal*), at close quarters to, a hop, skip and a jump away from (*informal*) ▶ ADVERB **1** *The rate of inflation is running at about 2.7 per cent.* = **approximately**, around, almost, nearing, nearly, approaching, close to, roughly, just about, more or less, in the region of, in the vicinity of, not far off **2** *The house isn't big enough with three children running about.* = **everywhere**, around, all over, here and there, on all sides, in all directions, to and fro, from place to place, hither and thither • **about to** *I think he's about to leave.* = **on the point of**, ready to, intending to, on the verge or brink of

about-turn NOUN *The decision was seen as an about-turn for the government.* = **change of direction**, reverse, reversal, turnaround, U-turn, right about (turn), about-face, volte-face, turnabout, paradigm shift ▶ VERB *She about-turned abruptly and left.* = **change direction**, reverse, about-face, volte-face, face the opposite direction, turn about or around, turn through 180 degrees, do or perform a U-turn or volte-face

above PREPOSITION **1** *He lifted his arms above his head.* = **over**, upon, beyond, on top of, exceeding, higher than, atop ■ OPPOSITE: under **2** *the people above you in the organization* = **senior to**, over, ahead of, in charge of, higher than, surpassing, superior to, more powerful than ■ OPPOSITE: subordinate to **3** *I want to be honest, above everything else.* = **before**, more than, rather than, beyond, instead of, sooner than, in preference to ▶ ADVERB *A long scream sounded from somewhere above.* = **overhead**, upward, in the sky, on high, in heaven, atop, aloft, up above, skyward ▶ ADJECTIVE *The department posted the above picture on its website.* = **preceding**, earlier, previous, prior, foregoing, aforementioned, aforesaid ■ RELATED WORDS: prefixes super-, supra-, sur-

abrasion NOUN **1** *He had severe abrasions to his right cheek.* = **graze**, scratch, trauma (*Pathology*), scrape, scuff, chafe, surface injury **2** *The sole of the shoe should be designed to take constant abrasion.* = **rubbing**, wear, scratching, scraping, grating, friction, scouring, attrition, corrosion, wearing down, erosion, scuffing, chafing, grinding down, wearing away, abrading

abrasive ADJECTIVE **1** *She was unrepentant about her abrasive remarks.* = **harsh**, cutting, biting, tough, sharp, severe, bitter, rough, hard, nasty, cruel, annoying, brutal, stern, irritating, unpleasant, grating, abusive, galling, unkind, hurtful, caustic, vitriolic, pitiless, unfeeling, comfortless **2** *an all-purpose non-abrasive cleaner* = **rough**, scratching, scraping, grating, scuffing, chafing, scratchy, frictional, erosive ▶ NOUN *Avoid abrasives, which can damage the tiles.* = **scourer**, grinder, burnisher, scarifier, abradant

abreast ADVERB *a group of youths riding four abreast* = **alongside**, level, beside, in a row, side by side, neck and neck, shoulder to shoulder • **abreast of** *or* **with** *We'll keep you abreast of developments.* = **informed about**, in touch with, familiar with, acquainted with, up to date with, knowledgeable about, conversant with, up to speed with (*informal*), in the picture about, *au courant* with, *au fait* with, keeping your finger on the pulse of

abridge VERB = **shorten**, reduce, contract, trim, clip, diminish, decrease, abstract, digest, cut down, cut back, cut, prune, concentrate, lessen, summarize, compress, curtail, condense, abbreviate, truncate, epitomize, downsize, précis, synopsize (*U.S.*) ■ OPPOSITE: expand

abridged ADJECTIVE = **shortened**, shorter, reduced, brief, potted (*informal*), trimmed, diminished, pruned, summarized, cut, compressed, curtailed, concise, condensed, abbreviated ■ OPPOSITE: expanded

abroad ADVERB **1** *About 65 per cent of our sales come from abroad.* = **overseas**, out of the country, beyond the sea, in foreign lands **2** *There is still a feeling abroad that this change must be recognized.* = **about**, everywhere, circulating, at large, here and there, current, all over, in circulation

abrupt ADJECTIVE **1** *His abrupt departure is bound to raise questions.* = **sudden**, unexpected, hurried, rapid, surprising, quick, swift, rash, precipitate, hasty, impulsive, headlong, unforeseen, unanticipated ■ OPPOSITE: slow **2** *He was abrupt to the point of rudeness.* = **curt**, direct, brief, sharp, rough, short, clipped, blunt, rude, tart, impatient, brisk, concise, snappy, terse, gruff, succinct, pithy, brusque, offhand, impolite, monosyllabic, ungracious, discourteous, uncivil, unceremonious, snappish

■ **OPPOSITE:** polite **3** *narrow valleys and abrupt hillsides* = **steep**, sharp, sheer, sudden, precipitous ■ **OPPOSITE:** gradual

abruptly ADVERB **1** *He stopped abruptly and looked my way.* = **suddenly**, short, unexpectedly, all of a sudden, hastily, precipitately, all at once, hurriedly ■ **OPPOSITE:** gradually **2** *'Good night then,' she said abruptly.* = **curtly**, bluntly, rudely, briskly, tersely, shortly, sharply, brusquely, gruffly, snappily ■ **OPPOSITE:** politely

abscess NOUN = **boil**, infection, swelling, blister, ulcer, inflammation, gathering (*informal*), whitlow, blain, carbuncle, pustule, bubo, furuncle (*Pathology*), gumboil, parulis (*Pathology*)

abscond VERB = **escape**, flee, get away, bolt, fly, disappear, skip, run off, slip away, clear out, flit (*informal*), make off, break free *or* out, decamp, hook it (*slang*), do a runner (*slang*), steal away, sneak away, do a bunk (*Brit. slang*), fly the coop (*U.S. & Canad. informal*), skedaddle (*informal*), take a powder (*U.S. & Canad. slang*), go on the lam (*U.S. & Canad. slang*), make your getaway, do a Skase (*Austral. informal*), make *or* effect your escape

absence NOUN **1** *I see you've been busy in my absence.* = **time off**, leave, break, vacation, recess, truancy, absenteeism, nonappearance, nonattendance **2** *In the absence of a will, the courts decide who the guardian is.* = **lack**, deficiency, deprivation, omission, scarcity, want, need, shortage, dearth, privation (*formal*), unavailability, nonexistence

absent ADJECTIVE **1** *He has been absent from his desk for two weeks.* = **away**, missing, gone, lacking, elsewhere, unavailable, not present, truant, nonexistent, nonattendant ■ **OPPOSITE:** present **2** *'Nothing,' she said in an absent way.* = **absent-minded**, blank, unconscious, abstracted, vague, distracted, unaware, musing, vacant, preoccupied, empty, absorbed, bemused, oblivious, dreamy, daydreaming, faraway, unthinking, heedless, inattentive, unheeding

■ **OPPOSITE:** alert • **absent yourself** *He pleaded guilty to absenting himself without leave.* = **stay away**, withdraw, depart, keep away, truant, abscond, play truant, slope off (*informal*), bunk off (*slang*), remove yourself

absentee NOUN = **nonattender**, stay-at-home, truant, no-show, stayaway

absent-minded ADJECTIVE = **forgetful**, absorbed, abstracted, vague, absent, distracted, unaware, musing, preoccupied, careless, bemused, oblivious, dreamy, faraway, engrossed, unthinking, neglectful, heedless, inattentive, unmindful, unheeding, apt to forget, in a brown study, ditzy *or* ditsy (*slang*) ■ **OPPOSITE:** alert

absolute ADJECTIVE **1** *A sick person needs to have absolute trust in a doctor.* = **complete**, total, perfect, entire, pure, sheer, utter, outright, thorough, downright, consummate, unqualified, full-on (*informal*), out-and-out, unadulterated, unmitigated, dyed-in-the-wool, thoroughgoing, unalloyed, unmixed, arrant, deep-dyed **2** *a ruler with absolute power* = **supreme**, sovereign, unlimited, ultimate, full, utmost, unconditional, unqualified, predominant, superlative, unrestricted, pre-eminent, unrestrained, tyrannical, peerless, unsurpassed, unquestionable, matchless, peremptory, unbounded **3** *the doctrine of absolute monarchy* = **autocratic**, supreme, unlimited, autonomous, arbitrary, dictatorial, all-powerful, imperious, domineering, tyrannical, despotic, absolutist, tyrannous, autarchical **4** *He brought the absolute proof that we needed.* = **definite**, sure, certain, positive, guaranteed, actual, assured, genuine, exact, precise, decisive, conclusive, unequivocal, unambiguous, infallible, categorical, unquestionable, dinkum (*Austral. & N.Z. informal*), nailed-on (*slang*)

absolutely ADVERB **1** *She is absolutely right.* = **completely**, totally, perfectly, quite, fully, entirely, purely, altogether, thoroughly, wholly, utterly, consummately, every inch, to the hilt, a hundred per cent, one hundred per cent, unmitigatedly, lock, stock and barrel ■ **OPPOSITE:** somewhat **2** *'It's worrying, isn't it?' 'Absolutely.'* = **definitely**, surely, certainly, clearly, obviously, plainly, truly, precisely, exactly, genuinely, positively, decidedly, decisively, without doubt, unquestionably, undeniably, categorically, without question, unequivocally, conclusively, unambiguously, beyond any doubt, infallibly

absolution NOUN = **forgiveness**, release, freedom, liberation, discharge, amnesty, mercy, pardon, indulgence, exemption, acquittal, remission, vindication, deliverance, dispensation, exoneration, exculpation, shriving, condonation

absolve VERB = **excuse**, free, clear, release, deliver, loose, forgive, discharge, liberate, pardon, exempt, acquit, vindicate, remit, let off, set free, exonerate, exculpate
■ **OPPOSITE:** condemn

a

absorb VERB 1 *Refined sugars are absorbed into the bloodstream very quickly.* = **soak up**, drink in, devour, suck up, receive, digest, imbibe, ingest, osmose 2 *a second career which absorbed her more completely than acting ever had* = **engross**, hold, involve, fill, arrest, fix, occupy, engage, fascinate, preoccupy, engulf, fill up, immerse, rivet, captivate, monopolize, enwrap

absorbed ADJECTIVE = **engrossed**, lost, involved, fixed, concentrating, occupied, engaged, gripped, fascinated, caught up, intrigued, wrapped up, preoccupied, immersed, dialed in, locked in, riveted, captivated, enthralled, rapt, up to your ears

absorbent ADJECTIVE = **porous**, receptive, imbibing, spongy, permeable, absorptive, blotting, penetrable, pervious, assimilative

absorbing ADJECTIVE = **fascinating**, interesting, engaging, gripping, arresting, compelling, intriguing, enticing, preoccupying, enchanting, seductive, riveting, captivating, alluring, bewitching, engrossing, spellbinding ■ OPPOSITE: boring

absorption NOUN 1 *Vitamin C increases absorption of iron.* = **soaking up**, consumption, digestion, sucking up, osmosis 2 *He was struck by the artists' total absorption in their work.* = **immersion**, holding, involvement, concentration, occupation, engagement, fascination, preoccupation, intentness, captivation, raptness

abstain from VERB = **refrain from**, avoid, decline, give up, stop, refuse, cease, do without, shun, renounce, eschew, leave off, keep from, forgo, withhold from, forbear, desist from, deny yourself, kick (*informal*) ■ OPPOSITE: abandon yourself

abstention NOUN 1 *Abstention is traditionally high in this region.* = **abstaining**, non-voting, refusal to vote 2 *a daylong abstention from food and water* = **abstinence**, refraining, avoidance, forbearance, eschewal, desistance, nonindulgence

abstinence NOUN = **abstention**, continence, temperance, self-denial, self-restraint, forbearance, refraining, avoidance, moderation, sobriety, asceticism, teetotalism, abstemiousness, soberness ■ OPPOSITE: self-indulgence

abstract ADJECTIVE *starting with a few abstract principles* = **theoretical**, general, complex, academic, intellectual, subtle, profound, philosophical, speculative, unrealistic, conceptual, indefinite, deep, separate, occult, hypothetical, generalized, impractical, arcane, notional, abstruse, recondite, theoretic, conjectural, unpractical, nonconcrete ■ OPPOSITE: actual ▶ NOUN *If you want to submit a paper, you must supply an abstract.* = **summary**, résumé, outline, extract, essence, summing-up, digest, epitome, rundown, condensation, compendium, synopsis, précis, recapitulation, review, abridgment ■ OPPOSITE: expansion ▶ VERB *The author has abstracted poems from earlier books.* = **extract**, draw, pull, remove, separate, withdraw, isolate, pull out, take out, take away, detach, dissociate, pluck out ■ OPPOSITE: add

abstracted ADJECTIVE = **preoccupied**, withdrawn, remote, absorbed, intent, absent, distracted, unaware, wrapped up, bemused, immersed, oblivious, dreamy, daydreaming, faraway, engrossed, rapt, absent-minded, heedless, inattentive, distrait, woolgathering

abstraction NOUN 1 *Is it worth fighting in the name of an abstraction?* = **concept**, thought, idea, view, theory, impression, formula, notion, hypothesis, generalization, theorem, generality 2 *He noticed her abstraction and asked, 'What's bothering you?'* = **absent-mindedness**, musing, preoccupation, daydreaming, vagueness, remoteness, absence, inattention, dreaminess, obliviousness, absence of mind, pensiveness, woolgathering, distractedness, bemusedness

absurd ADJECTIVE = **ridiculous**, crazy (*informal*), silly, incredible, outrageous, foolish, unbelievable, daft (*informal*), hilarious, ludicrous, meaningless, unreasonable, irrational, senseless, preposterous, laughable, funny, stupid, farcical, illogical, incongruous, comical, zany, idiotic, nonsensical, inane, dumb-ass (*slang*) ■ OPPOSITE: sensible

absurdity NOUN = **ridiculousness**, nonsense, malarkey, folly, stupidity, foolishness, silliness, idiocy, irrationality, incongruity, meaninglessness, daftness (*informal*), senselessness, illogicality, ludicrousness, unreasonableness, preposterousness, farcicality, craziness (*informal*), bêtise (*rare*), farcicalness, illogicalness

absurdly ADVERB = **ridiculously**, incredibly, unbelievably, foolishly, ludicrously, unreasonably, incongruously, laughably, irrationally, implausibly, preposterously, illogically, inanely, senselessly, idiotically, inconceivably, farcically

abundance NOUN 1 *a staggering abundance of food* = **plenty**, heap (*informal*), bounty, exuberance, profusion, plethora, affluence, fullness, opulence, plenitude, fruitfulness, copiousness, ampleness, cornucopia, plenteousness, plentifulness ■ **OPPOSITE:** shortage **2** *What customers want is a display of lushness and abundance.* = **wealth**, money, funds, capital, cash, riches, resources, assets, fortune, possessions, prosperity, big money, wad (*U.S. & Canad. slang*), affluence, big bucks (*informal, chiefly U.S.*), opulence, megabucks (*U.S. & Canad. slang*), tidy sum (*informal*), lucre, pretty penny (*informal*), pelf (*archaic*), top whack (*informal*)

abundant ADJECTIVE = **plentiful**, full, rich, liberal, generous, lavish, ample, infinite, overflowing, exuberant, teeming, copious, inexhaustible, bountiful, luxuriant, profuse, rank, well-provided, well-supplied, bounteous, plenteous ■ **OPPOSITE:** scarce

abundantly ADVERB = **plentifully**, greatly, freely, amply, richly, liberally, fully, thoroughly, substantially, lavishly, extensively, generously, profusely, copiously, exuberantly, in plentiful supply, luxuriantly, unstintingly, bountifully, bounteously, plenteously, in great or large numbers ■ **OPPOSITE:** sparsely

abuse NOUN **1** *an investigation into alleged child abuse* = **maltreatment**, wrong, damage, injury, hurt, harm, spoiling, bullying, oppression, imposition, mistreatment, manhandling, ill-treatment, rough handling **2** *A group of people started to heckle and shout abuse.* = **insults**, blame, slights, curses, put-downs, libel, censure, reproach, scolding, defamation, indignities, offence, tirade, derision, slander, rudeness, vilification, invective, swear words, opprobrium, insolence, upbraiding, aspersions, character assassination, disparagement, vituperation, castigation, contumely, revilement, traducement, calumniation **3** *an abuse of power* = **misuse**, corruption, perversion, misapplication, exploitation, misemployment, misusage ▶ VERB **1** *People responsible for abusing prisoners must be held accountable.* = **ill-treat**, wrong, damage, hurt, injure, harm, mar, oppress, maul, molest, impose upon, manhandle, rough up, brutalize, maltreat, handle roughly, knock about or around ■ **OPPOSITE:** care for **2** *He alleged that he was verbally abused by other soldiers.* = **insult**, injure, offend, curse, put down, smear, libel, slate (*informal, chiefly Brit.*), slag (off) (*slang*), malign, scold, swear at, disparage, castigate, revile, vilify, slander, defame, upbraid, slight, inveigh against, call names, traduce (*formal*), calumniate, vituperate ■ **OPPOSITE:** praise

abusive ADJECTIVE **1** *a cruel and abusive partner* = **violent**, wild, rough, cruel, savage, brutal, vicious, destructive, harmful, maddened, hurtful, unrestrained, impetuous, homicidal, intemperate, raging, furious, injurious, maniacal ■ **OPPOSITE:** kind **2** *He was alleged to have used abusive language.* = **insulting**, offensive, rude, degrading, scathing, maligning, scolding, affronting, contemptuous, disparaging, castigating, reviling, vilifying, invective, scurrilous, defamatory, insolent, derisive, censorious, slighting, libellous, upbraiding, vituperative, reproachful, slanderous, traducing, opprobrious, calumniating, contumelious ■ **OPPOSITE:** complimentary

abut VERB = **adjoin**, join, touch, border, neighbour, link to, attach to, combine with, connect with, couple with, communicate with, annex, meet, unite with, verge on, impinge, append (*formal*), affix to

abysmal ADJECTIVE = **dreadful**, bad, terrible (*informal*), awful, appalling, dismal, dire, ghastly, hideous, atrocious (*informal*), godawful (*informal*)

abyss NOUN = **chasm**, gulf, split, crack, gap, pit, opening, breach, hollow, void, gorge, crater, cavity, ravine, cleft, fissure, crevasse, bottomless depth, abysm

academic ADJECTIVE **1** *the country's richest and most famous academic institutions* = **scholastic**, school, university, college, educational, campus, collegiate **2** *The author has settled for a more academic approach.* = **scholarly**, learned, intellectual, literary, erudite, highbrow, studious, lettered **3** *These arguments are purely academic.* = **theoretical**, ideal, abstract, speculative, hypothetical, impractical, notional, conjectural ▶ NOUN *He is an academic who believes in winning through argument.* = **scholar**, intellectual, don, student, master, professor, fellow, pupil, lecturer, tutor, scholastic, bookworm, man or woman of letters, egghead (*informal*), savant, academician, acca (*Austral. slang*), bluestocking (*usually derogatory*), schoolman (*U.S., rare*)

academy NOUN = **college**, school, university, institution, institute, establishment, seminary, centre of learning, whare wananga (*N.Z.*)

accede to VERB **1** *Why didn't you accede to our demands at the outset?* = **agree to**, accept, grant, endorse, consent to, give in to, surrender to, yield to, concede to, acquiesce in, assent to, comply with, concur to **2** *when Henry VIII acceded to the*

a

throne = **inherit**, come to, assume, succeed, come into, attain, succeed to (*an heir*), enter upon, fall heir to

accelerate VERB **1** *Growth will accelerate to 2.9 per cent next year.* = **increase**, grow, advance, extend, expand, build up, strengthen, raise, swell, intensify, enlarge, escalate, multiply, inflate, magnify, proliferate, snowball ■ **OPPOSITE:** fall **2** *The government is to accelerate its privatisation programme.* = **expedite**, press, forward, promote, spur, further, stimulate, hurry, step up (*informal*), speed up, facilitate, hasten, precipitate, quicken ■ **OPPOSITE:** delay **3** *Suddenly the car accelerated.* = **speed up**, speed, advance, quicken, get under way, gather momentum, get moving, pick up speed, put your foot down (*informal*), open up the throttle, put on speed ■ **OPPOSITE:** slow down

acceleration NOUN = **hastening**, hurrying, stepping up (*informal*), expedition, speeding up, stimulation, advancement, promotion, spurring, quickening

accent NOUN *He has developed a slight American accent.* = **pronunciation**, tone, articulation, inflection, brogue, intonation, diction, modulation, elocution, enunciation, accentuation ▶ VERB *She had a round face accented by a little white cap.* = **emphasize**, stress, highlight, underline, bring home, underscore, accentuate, give emphasis to, call or draw attention to

accentuate VERB = **emphasize**, stress, highlight, accent, underline, bring home, underscore, foreground, give emphasis to, call or draw attention to ■ **OPPOSITE:** minimize

accept VERB **1** *All old clothes will be gratefully accepted by the organizers.* = **receive**, take, gain, pick up, secure, collect, have, get, obtain, acquire **2** *Everyone told me I should accept the job.* = **take on**, try, begin, attempt, bear, assume, tackle, acknowledge, undertake, embark on, set about, commence, avow, enter upon ■ **OPPOSITE:** reject **3** *I do not accept that there is any kind of crisis in the industry.* = **acknowledge**, believe, allow, admit, adopt, approve, recognize, yield, concede, swallow (*informal*), buy (*slang*), affirm, profess, consent to, buy into (*slang*), cooperate with, take on board, accede, acquiesce, concur with **4** *Urban dwellers have to accept noise as part of city life.* = **stand**, take, experience, suffer, bear, allow, weather, cope with, tolerate, sustain, put up with, wear (*Brit. slang*), stomach, endure, undergo, brook, hack (*slang*),

abide, withstand, bow to, yield to, countenance, like it or lump it (*informal*)

acceptability NOUN = **adequacy**, fitness, suitability, propriety, appropriateness, admissibility, permissibility, acceptableness, satisfactoriness ■ **OPPOSITE:** unacceptability

acceptable ADJECTIVE **1** *There was one restaurant that looked acceptable.* = **satisfactory**, fair, all right, suitable, sufficient, good enough, standard, adequate, so-so (*informal*), tolerable, up to scratch (*informal*), passable, up to the mark ■ **OPPOSITE:** unsatisfactory **2** *a most acceptable present* = **pleasant**, pleasing, welcome, satisfying, grateful, refreshing, delightful, gratifying, agreeable, pleasurable

acceptance NOUN **1** *The party is being downgraded by its acceptance of secret donations.* = **accepting**, taking, receiving, obtaining, acquiring, reception, receipt **2** *a theory that is steadily gaining acceptance* = **acknowledgement**, agreement, belief, approval, recognition, admission, consent, consensus, adoption, affirmation, assent, credence, accession, approbation, concurrence, accedence, stamp or seal of approval **3** *a letter of acceptance* = **taking on**, admission, assumption, acknowledgement, undertaking, avowal **4** *He thought about it for a moment, then nodded his reluctant acceptance.* = **submission**, yielding, resignation, concession, compliance, deference, passivity, acquiescence

accepted ADJECTIVE = **agreed**, received, common, standard, established, traditional, confirmed, regular, usual, approved, acknowledged, recognized, sanctioned, acceptable, universal, authorized, customary, agreed upon, time-honoured ■ **OPPOSITE:** unconventional

access NOUN **1** *The facilities have been adapted to give access to wheelchair users.* = **admission**, entry, passage, entrée, admittance, ingress **2** *a courtyard with a side access to the rear gardens* = **entrance**, road, door, approach, entry, path, gate, opening, way in, passage, avenue, doorway, gateway, portal (*literary*), passageway

accessibility NOUN **1** *the town's accessibility to the city* = **approachability**, availability, readiness, nearness, handiness **2** *growing fears about the cost and accessibility of health care* = **availability**, possibility, attainability, obtainability

accessible ADJECTIVE = **handy**, near, nearby, at hand, within reach, at your fingertips, reachable, achievable, get-at-able (*informal*), a hop, skip and a jump away ■ **OPPOSITE:** inaccessible

accession • **accession to** = **succession to**, attainment of, inheritance of, elevation to, taking up of, assumption of, taking over of, taking on of

accessory NOUN **1** *an exclusive range of bathroom accessories* = **extra**, addition, supplement, convenience, attachment, add-on, component, extension, adjunct, appendage, appurtenance **2** *She was charged with being an accessory to the embezzlement of funds.* = **accomplice**, partner, ally, associate, assistant, helper, colleague, collaborator, confederate, henchman or woman or person, abettor ▶ ADJECTIVE *Minerals are accessory food factors required in maintaining health.* = **supplementary**, extra, additional, accompanying, secondary, subordinate, complementary, auxiliary, abetting, supplemental, contributory, ancillary

accident NOUN **1** *She was involved in a serious car accident last week.* = **crash**, smash, wreck, collision, pile-up (*informal*), smash-up (*informal*) **2** *5,000 people die every year because of accidents in the home.* = **misfortune**, blow, disaster, tragedy, setback, calamity, mishap, misadventure, mischance, stroke of bad luck **3** *She discovered the problem by accident.* = **chance**, fortune, luck, fate, hazard, coincidence, fluke, fortuity

accidental ADJECTIVE **1** *The jury returned a verdict of accidental death.* = **unintentional**, unexpected, incidental, unforeseen, unintended, unplanned, unpremeditated ■ **OPPOSITE:** deliberate **2** *His hand brushed against hers; it could have been accidental.* = **chance**, random, casual, unintentional, unintended, unplanned, fortuitous, inadvertent, serendipitous, unlooked-for, uncalculated, contingent

accidentally ADVERB = **unintentionally**, casually, unexpectedly, incidentally, by accident, by chance, inadvertently, unwittingly, randomly, unconsciously, by mistake, haphazardly, fortuitously, adventitiously ■ **OPPOSITE:** deliberately

acclaim VERB *He was acclaimed as the country's greatest modern painter.* = **praise**, celebrate, honour, cheer, admire, hail, applaud, compliment, salute, approve, congratulate, clap, pay tribute to, commend, exalt, laud (*literary*), extol, crack up (*informal*), eulogize ▶ NOUN *She won critical acclaim for her performance.* = **praise**, honour, celebration, approval, tribute,

applause, cheering, clapping, ovation, accolades, plaudits, kudos, commendation, exaltation, approbation, acclamation, eulogizing, panegyric, encomium ■ **OPPOSITE:** criticism

acclaimed ADJECTIVE = **celebrated**, famous, acknowledged, praised, outstanding, distinguished, admired, renowned, noted, highly rated, eminent, revered, famed, illustrious, well received, much vaunted, highly esteemed, much touted, well thought of, lionized, highly thought of ■ **OPPOSITE:** criticized

accolade NOUN **1** *the ultimate accolade in the sciences* = **honour**, award, recognition, tribute **2** *We're always pleased to receive accolades from our guests.* = **praise**, approval, acclaim, applause, compliment, homage, laud (*literary*), eulogy, congratulation, commendation, acclamation (*formal*), recognition, tribute, ovation, plaudit

accommodate VERB **1** *Students are accommodated in homes nearby.* = **house**, put up, take in, lodge, board, quarter, shelter, entertain, harbour, cater for, billet **2** *He has never made an effort to accommodate photographers.* = **help**, support, aid, encourage, assist, befriend, cooperate with, abet, lend a hand to, lend a helping hand to, give a leg up to (*informal*) **3** *She walked slowly to accommodate herself to his pace.* = **adapt**, match, fit, fashion, settle, alter, adjust, modify, compose, comply, accustom, reconcile, harmonize

accommodating ADJECTIVE = **obliging**, willing, kind, friendly, helpful, polite, cooperative, agreeable, amiable, courteous, considerate, hospitable, unselfish, eager to please, complaisant ■ **OPPOSITE:** unhelpful

accommodation NOUN **1** *The government is to provide accommodation for 3,000 homeless people.* = **housing**, homes, houses, board, quartering, quarters, digs (*Brit. informal*), shelter, sheltering, lodging(s), dwellings **2** *Religions have to make accommodations with larger political structures.* = **adaptation**, change, settlement, compromise, composition, adjustment, transformation, reconciliation, compliance, modification, alteration, conformity

accompaniment NOUN **1** *He sang to the musical director's piano accompaniment.* = **backing music**, backing, support, obbligato **2** *The recipe makes a good accompaniment to ice-cream.* = **supplement**, extra, addition, extension, companion, accessory, complement, decoration, frill, adjunct, appendage, adornment

a

accompany VERB **1** *Ken agreed to accompany me on a trip to Africa.* = **go with**, lead, partner, protect, guide, attend, conduct, escort, shepherd, convoy, usher, chaperon **2** *This volume of essays was designed to accompany an exhibition.* = **occur with**, belong to, come with, supplement, coincide with, join with, coexist with, go together with, follow, go cheek by jowl with

accompanying ADJECTIVE = **additional**, added, extra, related, associate, associated, joint, fellow, connected, attached, accessory, attendant, complementary, supplementary, supplemental, concurrent, concomitant, appended

accomplice NOUN = **partner in crime**, ally, associate, assistant, companion, accessory, comrade, helper, colleague, collaborator, confederate, henchman *or* woman *or* person, coadjutor, abettor

accomplish VERB = **realize**, produce, effect, finish, complete, manage, achieve, perform, carry out, conclude, fulfil, execute, bring about, attain, consummate, bring off (*informal*), do, effectuate ■ **OPPOSITE:** fail

accomplished ADJECTIVE = **skilled**, able, professional, expert, masterly, talented, gifted, polished, practised, cultivated, skilful, adept, consummate, proficient ■ **OPPOSITE:** unskilled

accomplishment NOUN **1** *The accomplishments of the past year are quite extraordinary.* = **achievement**, feat, attainment, act, stroke, triumph, coup, exploit, deed **2** (*often plural*) *She can now add basketball to her list of accomplishments.* = **talent**, ability, skill, gift, achievement, craft, faculty, capability, forte, attainment, proficiency **3** *His function is vital to the accomplishment of the mission.* = **accomplishing**, effecting, finishing, carrying out, achievement, conclusion, bringing about, execution, completion, realization, fulfilment, attainment, consummation

accord NOUN **1** *The party was made legal under the 1991 peace accords.* = **treaty**, contract, agreement, arrangement, settlement, pact, deal (*informal*) **2** *I found myself in total accord.* = **sympathy**, agreement, concert, harmony, accordance, unison, rapport, conformity, assent, unanimity, concurrence ■ **OPPOSITE:** conflict ▶ VERB *On his return home, the government accorded him the rank of Colonel.* = **grant**, give, award, render, assign, present with, endow with,

bestow on, confer on, vouchsafe (*old-fashioned*), impart with ■ **OPPOSITE:** refuse
• **accord with something** *Such an approach accords with the principles of Socialist ideology.* = **agree with**, match, coincide with, fit with, square with, correspond with, conform with, concur with, tally with, be in tune with (*informal*), harmonize with, assent with

accordance NOUN • **in accordance with** = **in agreement with**, consistent with, in harmony with, in concert with, in sympathy with, in conformity with, in assent with, in congruence with

accordingly ADVERB **1** *We have different backgrounds. Accordingly we will have different futures.* = **consequently**, so, thus, therefore, hence, subsequently, in consequence, ergo, as a result **2** *It is a difficult job and they should be paid accordingly.* = **appropriately**, correspondingly, properly, suitably, fitly

accost VERB = **confront**, challenge, address, stop, approach, oppose, halt, greet, hail, buttonhole

account NOUN **1** *I gave a detailed account of what had happened that night.* = **description**, report, record, story, history, detail, statement, relation, version, tale, explanation, narrative, chronicle, portrayal, recital, depiction, narration **2** *These obscure little groups were of no account in national politics.* = **importance**, standing, concern, value, note, benefit, use, profit, worth, weight, advantage, rank, import (*formal*), honour, consequence, substance, merit, significance, distinction, esteem, usefulness, repute, momentousness **3** *a detailed account of all expenditures* = **ledger**, charge, bill, statement, balance, tally, invoice, computation ▶ VERB *The first day of the event was accounted a success.* = **consider**, rate, value, judge, estimate, think, hold, believe, count, reckon, assess, weigh, calculate, esteem (*formal*), deem, compute, gauge, appraise, regard as
• **account for something 1** *Computers account for 5% of the country's electricity consumption.* = **constitute**, make, make up, compose, comprise **2** *How do you account for the company's high staff turnover?* = **explain**, excuse, justify, clarify, give a reason for, give an explanation for, illuminate, clear up, answer for, rationalize, elucidate **3** *The squadron accounted for seven enemy aircraft in the first week.* = **put out of action**, kill (*informal*), destroy, put paid to, incapacitate
• **on account of** *He declined to give the speech on account of a sore throat.* = **by reason of**,

because of, owing to, on the basis of, for the sake of, on the grounds of

accountability NOUN = **responsibility**, liability, culpability, answerability, chargeability

accountable ADJECTIVE = **answerable**, subject, responsible, obliged, liable, amenable, obligated, chargeable

accountant NOUN = **auditor**, book-keeper, bean counter (*informal*)

accounting NOUN = **accountancy**, auditing, book-keeping

accoutrements PLURAL NOUN = **paraphernalia**, fittings, dress, material, clothing, stuff, equipment, tackle, gear, things, kit, outfit, trimmings, fixtures, array, decorations, baggage, apparatus, furnishings, trappings, garb, adornments, ornamentation, bells and whistles, impedimenta, appurtenances, equipage

accredit VERB 1 *The degree programme is fully accredited by the Institute of Engineers.* = **approve**, support, back, commission, champion, favour, guarantee, promote, recommend, appoint, recognize, sanction, advocate, license, endorse, warrant, authorize, ratify, empower, certify, entrust, vouch for, depute 2 *The discovery of runes is, in Norse mythology, accredited to Odin.* = **attribute**, credit, assign, ascribe, trace to, put down to, lay at the door of

accredited ADJECTIVE = **authorized**, official, commissioned, guaranteed, appointed, recognized, sanctioned, licensed, endorsed, empowered, certified, vouched for, deputed, deputized

accrue VERB = **accumulate**, issue, increase, grow, collect, gather, flow, build up, enlarge, follow, ensue, pile up, amass, spring up, stockpile

accumulate VERB = **build up**, increase, grow, be stored, collect, gather, pile up, amass, stockpile, hoard, accrue, cumulate ■ **OPPOSITE:** disperse

accumulation NOUN 1 *accumulations of dirt* = **collection**, increase, stock, store, mass, build-up, pile, stack, heap, rick, stockpile, hoard 2 *The rate of accumulation decreases with time.* = **growth**, collection, gathering, build-up, aggregation, conglomeration, augmentation

accuracy NOUN = **exactness**, precision, fidelity, authenticity, correctness, closeness, truth, verity, nicety, veracity, faithfulness, truthfulness, niceness, exactitude, strictness, meticulousness, carefulness, scrupulousness, preciseness, faultlessness, accurateness ■ **OPPOSITE:** inaccuracy

accurate ADJECTIVE 1 *a more accurate description of the terrain* = **precise**, right, close, regular, correct, careful, strict, exact, faithful, explicit, authentic, spot-on, just, clear-cut, meticulous, truthful, faultless, scrupulous, unerring, veracious ■ **OPPOSITE:** inaccurate 2 *Their prediction was accurate.* = **correct**, right, true, exact, faithful, spot-on (*Brit. informal*), faultless, on the money (*informal*)

accurately ADVERB 1 *The test can accurately predict what a bigger explosion would do.* = **precisely**, rightly, correctly, closely, carefully, truly, properly, strictly, literally, exactly, faithfully, meticulously, to the letter, justly, scrupulously, truthfully, authentically, unerringly, faultlessly, veraciously 2 *His concept of 'power' could be more accurately described as 'control'.* = **exactly**, rightly, closely, correctly, definitely, truly, properly, precisely, nicely, strictly, faithfully, explicitly, unequivocally, scrupulously, truthfully

accusation NOUN = **charge**, complaint, allegation, indictment, impeachment, recrimination, citation, denunciation, attribution, imputation, arraignment, incrimination

accuse VERB 1 *He accused me of being lazy.* = **point a** or **the finger at**, blame for, denounce, attribute to, hold responsible for, impute blame to ■ **OPPOSITE:** exonerate 2 *Her assistant was accused of theft and fraud by the police.* = **charge with**, indict for, impeach for, arraign for, cite, tax with, censure with, incriminate for, recriminate for ■ **OPPOSITE:** absolve

accustom VERB = **familiarize**, train, coach, discipline, adapt, instruct, make used, school, season, acquaint, inure, habituate, acclimatize, make conversant

accustomed ADJECTIVE 1 *I was accustomed to being the only child amongst adults.* = **used**, trained, familiar, disciplined, given to, adapted, acquainted, in the habit of, familiarized, seasoned, inured, habituated, exercised, acclimatized ■ **OPPOSITE:** unaccustomed 2 *He took up his accustomed position at the fire.* = **usual**, established, expected, general, common, standard, set, traditional, normal, fixed, regular, ordinary, familiar, conventional, routine, everyday, customary, habitual, wonted ■ **OPPOSITE:** unusual

ace NOUN 1 *the ace of hearts* = **one**, single point 2 *a first-world-war flying ace* = **expert**, star, champion, authority, winner, professional, master, pro (*informal*), specialist, genius, guru, buff (*informal*),

a

wizard (*informal*), whizz (*informal*), virtuoso, connoisseur, hotshot (*informal*), past master, dab hand (*Brit. informal*), maven (*U.S.*) ▶ ADJECTIVE *It's been a while since I've seen a really ace film.* = **great** (*informal*), good, brilliant, mean (*slang*), fine, champion, expert, masterly, wonderful, excellent, cracking (*Brit. informal*), outstanding, superb, fantastic (*informal*), tremendous (*informal*), marvellous (*informal*), terrific (*informal*), mega (*slang*), awesome (*slang*), dope (*slang*), sick (*slang*), admirable, virtuoso, first-rate, brill (*informal*), bitchin' (*U.S. slang*), chillin' (*U.S. slang*), booshit (*Austral. slang*), exo (*Austral. slang*), sik (*Austral. slang*), ka pai (*N.Z.*), rad (*informal*), phat (*slang*), schmick (*Austral. informal*), beaut (*informal*), barrie (*Scot. slang*), belting (*Brit. slang*), pearler (*Austral. slang*)

acerbic ADJECTIVE = **sharp**, cutting, biting, severe, acid, bitter, nasty, harsh, stern, rude, scathing, acrimonious, barbed, unkind, unfriendly, sarcastic, sardonic, caustic, churlish, vitriolic, trenchant, acrid, brusque, rancorous, mordant

ache VERB **1** *Her head was hurting and she ached all over.* = **hurt**, suffer, burn, pain, smart, sting, pound, throb, be tender, twinge, be sore **2** *It must have been hard to keep smiling when his heart was aching.* = **suffer**, hurt, grieve, sorrow, agonize, be in pain, go through the mill (*informal*), mourn, feel wretched ▶ NOUN **1** *You feel nausea and aches in your muscles.* = **pain**, discomfort, suffering, hurt, smart, smarting, cramp, throb, throbbing, irritation, tenderness, pounding, spasm, pang, twinge, soreness, throe (*rare*) **2** *Nothing could relieve the terrible ache of fear.* = **anguish**, suffering, pain, torture, distress, grief, misery, mourning, torment, sorrow, woe, heartache, heartbreak

achievable ADJECTIVE = **attainable**, obtainable, winnable, reachable, realizable, within your grasp, graspable, gettable, acquirable, possible, accessible, probable, feasible, practicable, accomplishable

achieve VERB = **accomplish**, reach, fulfil, finish, complete, gain, perform, earn, do, get, win, carry out, realize, obtain, conclude, acquire, execute, bring about, attain, consummate, procure, bring off (*informal*), effectuate, put the tin lid on

achievement NOUN **1** *a conference celebrating women's achievements* = **accomplishment**, effort, feat, deed, stroke, triumph, coup, exploit, act, attainment, feather in your cap **2** *It is the achievement of these goals that will bring lasting peace.* = **fulfilment**, effecting, performance, production, execution, implementation, completion, accomplishment, realization, attainment, acquirement, carrying out *or* through

achiever NOUN = **success**, winner, dynamo, high-flyer, doer, go-getter (*informal*), organizer, active person, overachiever, man *or* woman of action, wheeler-dealer (*informal*)

aching ADJECTIVE **1** *The aching joints and fever should last no longer than a few days.* = **painful**, suffering, hurting, tired, smarting, pounding, raw, tender, sore, throbbing, inflamed, excruciating, agonizing **2** *He has an aching need for love.* = **longing**, anxious, eager, pining, hungering, craving, yearning, languishing, thirsting, ardent, avid, wishful, wistful, hankering, desirous

acid ADJECTIVE **1** *These wines are rather hard, and somewhat acid.* = **sour**, sharp, tart, pungent, biting, acidic, acerbic, acrid, acetic, vinegary, acidulous, acidulated, vinegarish, acerb ■ OPPOSITE: sweet **2** *a comedy told with compassion and acid humour* = **sharp**, cutting, biting, severe, bitter, harsh, stinging, scathing, acrimonious, barbed, pungent, hurtful, sarcastic, sardonic, caustic, vitriolic, acerbic, trenchant, mordant, mordacious ■ OPPOSITE: kindly

acidity NOUN = **sourness**, bitterness, sharpness, pungency, tartness, acerbity, acridness, acidulousness, acridity, vinegariness, vinegarishness

acknowledge VERB **1** *I acknowledge that I made a mistake.* = **admit**, own up to, allow, accept, reveal, grant, declare, recognize, yield, concede, confess, disclose, affirm, profess, divulge, accede, acquiesce, fess up (*U.S. slang*) ■ OPPOSITE: deny **2** *He saw but refused to even acknowledge her.* = **greet**, address, notice, recognize, salute, nod to, accost, tip your hat to ■ OPPOSITE: snub **3** *They sent me a text acknowledging my request.* = **reply to**, answer, notice, recognize, respond to, come back to, react to, write back to, retort to ■ OPPOSITE: ignore

acknowledged ADJECTIVE = **accepted**, admitted, established, confirmed, declared, approved, recognized, well-known, sanctioned, confessed, authorized, professed, accredited, agreed upon

acknowledgment *or* **acknowledgement** NOUN **1** *He appreciated her acknowledgement of his maturity.* = **recognition**, allowing, understanding, yielding, profession, admission, awareness, acceptance, confession, realization, accession, acquiescence **2** *He smiled in acknowledgement and gave her a bow.* = **greeting**, welcome, notice, recognition, reception, hail, hailing, salute, salutation (*formal*) **3** *Grateful acknowledgement is made for permission to reprint.* = **appreciation**, answer, thanks, credit, response, reply, reaction, recognition, gratitude, indebtedness, thankfulness, gratefulness

acme NOUN = **height**, top, crown, summit, peak, climax, crest, optimum, high point, pinnacle, culmination, zenith, apex, apogee, vertex ■ **OPPOSITE:** depths

acolyte NOUN **1** *To his acolytes, he is known simply as 'The Boss'.* = **follower**, fan, supporter, pupil, convert, believer, admirer, backer, partisan, disciple, devotee, worshipper, apostle, cohort (*chiefly U.S.*), adherent, henchman, habitué, votary **2** *When they reached the shrine, acolytes removed the pall.* = **attendant**, assistant, follower, helper, altar boy *or* girl, altar server

acquaint VERB = **tell**, reveal, advise, inform, communicate, disclose, notify, enlighten, divulge, familiarize, apprise, let (someone) know

acquaintance NOUN **1** *I exchanged a few words with an old acquaintance.* = **associate**, contact, ally, colleague, comrade, confrère ■ **OPPOSITE:** intimate **2** *He becomes involved in a real murder mystery through his acquaintance with a police officer.* = **relationship**, association, exchange, connection, intimacy, fellowship, familiarity, companionship, social contact, cognizance, conversance, conversancy ■ **OPPOSITE:** unfamiliarity

acquainted ADJECTIVE • **acquainted with** = **familiar with**, aware of, in on, experienced in, conscious of, informed of, alive to, privy to, knowledgeable about, versed in, conversant with, apprised of, cognizant of, up to speed with, *au fait* with

acquiesce VERB = **submit**, agree, accept, approve, yield, bend, surrender, consent, tolerate, comply, give in, conform, succumb, go along with, bow to, cave in (*informal*), concur, assent, capitulate, accede, play ball (*informal*), toe the line, hoist the white flag ■ **OPPOSITE:** resist

acquiescence NOUN = **agreement**, yielding, approval, acceptance, consent, harmony, giving in, submission, compliance, obedience, conformity, assent, accession, concord, concurrence

acquire VERB = **get**, win, buy, receive, land (*informal*), score (*slang*), gain, achieve, earn,

pick up, bag, secure, collect, gather, realize, obtain, attain, amass, procure, come into possession of ■ **OPPOSITE:** lose

acquisition NOUN **1** *the President's recent acquisition of a helicopter* = **acquiring**, gaining, achievement, procurement, attainment, acquirement, obtainment **2** *her latest acquisition, a bright red dress* = **purchase**, buy, investment, property, gain, prize, asset, possession

acquisitive ADJECTIVE = **greedy**, grabbing, grasping, hungry, selfish, avid, predatory, rapacious, avaricious, desirous, covetous ■ **OPPOSITE:** generous

acquit VERB *He was acquitted of disorderly behaviour by magistrates.* = **clear**, free, release, deliver, excuse, relieve, discharge, liberate, vindicate, exonerate, absolve, exculpate ■ **OPPOSITE:** find guilty • **acquit yourself** *Most men acquitted themselves well throughout the action.* = **behave**, bear yourself, conduct yourself, comport yourself

acquittal NOUN = **clearance**, freeing, release, relief, liberation, discharge, pardon, setting free, vindication, deliverance, absolution, exoneration, exculpation

acrid ADJECTIVE **1** *The room filled with the acrid smell of tobacco.* = **pungent**, biting, strong, burning, sharp, acid, bitter, harsh, stinging, irritating, caustic, astringent, vitriolic, highly flavoured, acerb **2** *He is soured by acrid memories he has dredged up.* = **harsh**, cutting, biting, sharp, bitter, nasty, acrimonious, caustic, vitriolic, trenchant, mordant, mordacious

acrimonious ADJECTIVE = **bitter**, cutting, biting, sharp, severe, hostile, crabbed, sarcastic, embittered, caustic, petulant, spiteful, churlish, astringent, vitriolic, acerbic, trenchant, irascible, testy, censorious, rancorous, mordant, peevish, splenetic, mordacious ■ **OPPOSITE:** good-tempered

acrimony NOUN = **bitterness**, harshness, rancour, ill will, virulence, sarcasm, pungency, asperity, tartness, astringency, irascibility, peevishness, acerbity, churlishness, trenchancy, mordancy ■ **OPPOSITE:** goodwill

acrobat NOUN = **gymnast**, balancer, tumbler, tightrope walker, rope walker, funambulist

across PREPOSITION **1** *Anyone from the houses across the road could see him.* = **over**, on the other *or* far side of, past, beyond **2** *The film opens across America in December.* = **throughout**, over, all over, right through, all through, covering, straddling, everywhere in, through the whole of, from end to end of, over the length and breadth of ▶ ADVERB *Trim toenails straight across using nail clippers.* = **from side to side**, athwart, transversely, crossways or crosswise

across-the-board ADJECTIVE = **general**, full, complete, total, sweeping, broad, widespread, comprehensive, universal, blanket, thorough, wholesale, panoramic, indiscriminate, all-inclusive, wall-to-wall, all-embracing, overarching, all-encompassing, thoroughgoing, without exception or omission, one-size-fits-all
■ **OPPOSITE:** limited

act VERB **1** *I have no reason to doubt that the bank acted properly.* = **do something**, perform, move, function, go about, conduct yourself, undertake something **2** *They were just acting tough.* = **play**, seem to be, pose as, pretend to be, posture as, imitate, sham, feign, characterize, enact, personify, impersonate, play the part of **3** *She told her parents of her desire to act.* = **perform**, mimic, mime ▶ NOUN **1** *My insurance covers acts of sabotage.* = **deed**, action, step, performance, operation, doing, move, blow, achievement, stroke, undertaking, exploit, execution, feat, accomplishment, exertion **2** *His anger was real. It wasn't just an act.* = **pretence**, show, front, performance, display, attitude, pose, stance, fake, posture, façade, sham, veneer, counterfeit, feigning, affectation, dissimulation **3** *an Act of Parliament* = **law**, bill, measure, resolution, decree, statute, ordinance, enactment, edict **4** *Numerous bands are playing, as well as comedy acts.* = **performance**, show, turn, production, routine (*informal*), presentation, gig (*informal*), sketch • **act for someone** *Because we travel so much, we asked a broker to act for us.* = **stand in for**, serve, represent, replace, substitute for, cover for, take the place of, fill in for, deputize for, function in place of • **act on** or **upon something 1** *A patient will usually listen to the doctor's advice and act on it.* = **obey**, follow, carry out, observe, embrace, execute, comply with, heed, conform to, adhere to, abide by, yield to, act upon, be ruled by, act in accordance with, do what is expected **2** *The drug acts very fast on the central nervous system.* = **affect**, change, influence, impact, transform, alter, modify • **act up** *I could hear him acting up downstairs.* = **misbehave**, carry on (*informal*), cause trouble, mess about, be naughty, horse around (*informal*), give trouble, give someone grief (*Brit. & S. African*), give bother

acting NOUN *She has returned home to pursue her career in acting.* = **performance**, playing, performing, theatre, dramatics, portraying, enacting, portrayal, impersonation, characterization, stagecraft ▶ ADJECTIVE *The new acting President has a reputation for being independent.* = **temporary**, substitute, intervening, interim, provisional, surrogate, stopgap, pro tem

action NOUN **1** *He was the sort of person who didn't like his actions questioned.* = **deed**, move, act, performance, blow, exercise, achievement, stroke, undertaking, exploit, feat, accomplishment, exertion **2** *The government is taking emergency action to deal with the crisis.* = **measure**, act, step, operation, manoeuvre **3** *a libel action brought by one of the country's top bureaucrats* = **lawsuit**, case, cause, trial, suit, argument, proceeding, dispute, contest, prosecution, litigation **4** *Hollywood is where the action is now.* = **energy**, activity, spirit, force, vitality, vigour, liveliness, vim **5** *Her description of the action of poisons is very accurate.* = **effect**, working, work, force, power, process, effort, operation, activity, movement, influence, functioning, motion, exertion **6** *Ten soldiers were wounded in action.* = **battle**, war, fight, fighting, conflict, clash, contest, encounter, combat, engagement, hostilities, warfare, fray, skirmish, sortie, affray

activate VERB = **start**, move, trigger (off), stimulate, turn on, set off, initiate, switch on, propel, rouse, prod, get going, mobilize, kick-start (*informal*), set in motion, impel, galvanize, set going, actuate
■ **OPPOSITE:** stop

activation NOUN = **start**, triggering, turning on, switching on, animation, arousal, initiation, mobilization, setting in motion, actuation

active ADJECTIVE **1** *Having an active youngster about the house can be quite wearing.* = **busy**, involved, occupied, engaged, lively, energetic, bustling, restless, on the move, strenuous, tireless, on the go (*informal*)
■ **OPPOSITE:** sluggish **2** *the tragedy of an active mind trapped by failing physical health* = **energetic**, strong, spirited, quick, vital, alert, dynamic, lively, vigorous, potent, animated, vibrant, forceful, nimble, diligent, industrious, sprightly, vivacious, on the go (*informal*), alive and kicking, spry, full of beans (*informal*), bright-eyed and bushy-tailed (*informal*) ■ **OPPOSITE:** inactive **3** *Guerrilla groups are active in the province.* = **in operation**, working, live, running, moving,

acting, functioning, stirring, at work, in business, in action, operative, in force, effectual, astir

activist NOUN = **militant**, partisan, organizer, warrior

activity NOUN 1 *There is an extraordinary level of activity in the market.* = **action**, work, life, labour, movement, energy, exercise, spirit, enterprise, motion, bustle, animation, vigour, hustle, exertion, hurly-burly, liveliness, activeness ■ OPPOSITE: inaction 2 *Activities range from canoeing to birdwatching.* = **pursuit**, act, project, scheme, task, pleasure, interest, enterprise, undertaking, occupation, hobby, deed, endeavour, pastime, avocation

actor or **actress** NOUN *You have to be a very good actor to play that part.* = **performer**, player, artiste, leading man or lady, Thespian, luvvie (*informal*), trouper, thesp (*informal*), play-actor, dramatic artist, tragedian or tragedienne

> USAGE The use of *actress* is now very much on the decline, and women who work in the profession invariably prefer to be referred to as *actors*.

actual ADJECTIVE 1 *They are using local actors or the actual people involved.* = **genuine**, real, true, confirmed, authentic, verified, truthful, bona fide, dinkum (*Austral. & N.Z. informal*) ■ OPPOSITE: unreal 2 *She had written some notes, but she hadn't started the actual work.* = **real**, substantial (*formal*), concrete, definite, tangible ■ OPPOSITE: theoretical

> USAGE The words *actual* and *actually* are often used when speaking, but should only be used in writing where they add something to the meaning of a sentence. For example, in the sentence *he actually rather enjoyed the film*, the word *actually* is only needed if there was originally some doubt as to whether he would enjoy it.

actuality NOUN 1 *It exists in dreams rather than actuality.* = **reality**, truth, substance, verity, materiality, realness, substantiality, factuality, corporeality 2 *You may theorise, but we are concerned with actualities.* = **fact**, truth, reality, verity

actually ADVERB = **really**, in fact, indeed, essentially, truly, literally, genuinely, in reality, in truth, in actuality, in point of fact, veritably, as a matter of fact

acumen NOUN = **judgment**, intelligence, perception, wisdom, insight, wit, ingenuity, sharpness, cleverness, keenness, shrewdness, discernment, perspicacity (*formal*), sagacity, smartness, smarts (*slang,*

chiefly U.S.), astuteness, acuteness, perspicuity

acute ADJECTIVE 1 *The war aggravated an acute economic crisis.* = **serious**, important, dangerous, critical, crucial (*informal*), alarming, severe, grave, sudden, urgent, decisive 2 *His back is arched as if in acute pain.* = **sharp**, shooting, powerful, violent, severe, intense, overwhelming, distressing, stabbing, cutting, fierce, piercing, racking, exquisite, poignant, harrowing, overpowering, shrill, excruciating 3 *His relaxed exterior hides an extremely acute mind.* = **perceptive**, sharp, keen, smart, sensitive, clever, subtle, piercing, penetrating, discriminating, discerning, ingenious, astute, intuitive, canny, incisive, insightful, observant, perspicacious (*formal*)

adage NOUN = **saying**, motto, maxim, proverb, dictum, precept, by-word, saw (*old-fashioned*), axiom, aphorism, apophthegm

adamant ADJECTIVE = **determined**, firm, fixed, stiff, rigid, set, relentless, stubborn, uncompromising, insistent, resolute, inflexible, unrelenting, inexorable, unyielding, intransigent, immovable, unbending, obdurate, unshakable ■ OPPOSITE: flexible

adapt VERB 1 *Things will be different and we will have to adapt.* = **adjust**, change, match, alter, modify, accommodate, comply, conform, reconcile, harmonize, familiarize, habituate, acclimatize 2 *Shelves were built to adapt the library for use as an office.* = **convert**, change, prepare, fit, fashion, make, shape, suit, qualify, transform, alter, modify, tailor, remodel, tweak (*informal*), metamorphose, customize

adaptability NOUN = **flexibility**, versatility, resilience, variability, convertibility, plasticity, malleability, pliability, changeability, pliancy, adjustability, compliancy, modifiability, adaptableness, alterability

adaptable ADJECTIVE 1 *They are adaptable foragers that can survive on a wide range of foods.* = **flexible**, variable, versatile, resilient, easy-going, changeable, modifiable, conformable 2 *We hope to make the workforce more adaptable and skilled.* = **adjustable**, flexible, compliant, malleable, pliant, plastic, modifiable, alterable

adaptation NOUN 1 *Most creatures are capable of adaptation when necessary.* = **acclimatization**, naturalization, habituation, familiarization, accustomedness **2** *He won two awards for his screen adaptation of the play.* = **conversion**, change, shift, variation, adjustment, transformation, modification, alteration, remodelling, reworking, refitting

add VERB **1** *Banks add all the interest and other charges together.* = **count up**, total, reckon, sum up, compute, add up, tot up ■ **OPPOSITE:** take away **2** *She wants to add a huge sports complex to the hotel.* = **include**, attach, supplement, increase by, adjoin, annex, amplify, augment, affix, append (*formal*), enlarge by • **add to something** *Smiles and cheerful faces added to the general gaiety.* = **increase**, boost, expand, strengthen, enhance, step up (*informal*), intensify, raise, advance, spread, extend, heighten, enlarge, escalate, multiply, inflate, magnify, amplify, augment, proliferate • **add up 1** *Many of the children were not able to add up properly.* = **count up**, add, total, count, reckon, calculate, sum up, compute, tally, tot up, add together **2** *They arrested her because her statements did not add up.* = **make sense**, hold up, be reasonable, ring true, be plausible, stand to reason, hold water, bear examination, bear investigation • **add up to something** *All this adds up to very bad news for the car industry.* = **mean**, reveal, indicate, imply, amount to, signify

addict NOUN **1** *He's only 24 years old and a drug addict.* = abuser, user (*informal*), druggie (*informal*) **2** *She's a TV addict and watches as much as she can.* = **fan**, lover, nut (*slang*), follower, enthusiast, freak (*informal*), admirer, buff (*informal*), junkie (*informal*), devotee, fiend (*informal*), adherent, rooter (*U.S.*), zealot, groupie (*slang*), aficionado ■ **RELATED WORD:** suffix -holic

addicted ADJECTIVE = **hooked** (*informal*), dependent ■ **RELATED WORD:** suffix -holic

addiction NOUN **1** *She helped him fight his drug addiction.* = **dependence**, need, habit, weakness, obsession, attachment, craving, vulnerability, subordination, enslavement, subservience, overreliance **2** (*with* **to**) *I've developed an addiction to rollercoasters.* = **love of**, passion for, attachment to, fondness for, zeal for, fervour for, ardour for

addictive ADJECTIVE = **habit-forming**, compelling, compulsive, causing addiction or dependency, moreish or morish (*informal*)

addition NOUN **1** *This book is a worthy addition to the series.* = **extra**, supplement, complement, adjunct, increase, gain, bonus, extension, accessory, additive, appendix, increment, appendage, addendum **2** *It was completely refurbished*

with the addition of a picnic site. = **inclusion**, adding, increasing, extension, attachment, adjoining, insertion, incorporation, annexation, accession, affixing, augmentation ■ **OPPOSITE:** removal **3** *simple addition and subtraction problems* = **counting up**, totalling, reckoning, summing up, adding up, computation, totting up, summation ■ **OPPOSITE:** subtraction • **in addition to** *There's a postage and packing fee in addition to the repair charge.* = **as well as**, along with, on top of, besides, to boot, additionally, over and above, to say nothing of, into the bargain

additional ADJECTIVE = **extra**, more, new, other, added, increased, further, fresh, spare, supplementary, auxiliary, ancillary, appended

additive NOUN = **added ingredient**, artificial or synthetic ingredient, E number, extra, supplement

addled ADJECTIVE = **confused**, silly, foolish, at sea, bewildered, mixed-up, muddled, perplexed, flustered, befuddled

address NOUN **1** *The address on the envelope was illegible.* = **direction**, label, inscription, superscription **2** *We had turned up for the meeting at the wrong address.* = **location**, home, place, house, point, position, situation, site, spot, venue, lodging, pad (*slang*), residence, dwelling (*formal, literary*), whereabouts, abode, locus, locale, domicile **3** (*Computing*) = **URL**, website, addy (*informal*), IP address, web address **4** *The president had scheduled an address to the people for that evening.* = **speech**, talk, lecture, discourse, sermon, dissertation, harangue, homily, oration, spiel (*informal*), disquisition ▶ VERB **1** *She will address a conference on human rights next week.* = **give a speech to**, talk to, speak to, lecture, discourse, harangue, give a talk to, spout to, hold forth to, expound to, orate to, sermonize to **2** *The two ministers did not address each other directly.* = **speak to**, talk to, greet, hail, salute, invoke, communicate with, accost, approach, converse with, apostrophize, korero (*N.Z.*) • **address yourself to something** *We have addressed ourselves to the problem of ethics throughout.* = **concentrate on**, turn to, focus on, take up, look to, undertake, engage in, take care of, attend to, knuckle down to, devote yourself to, apply yourself to

adept ADJECTIVE *He is an adept guitar player.* = **skilful**, able, skilled, expert, masterly, practised, accomplished, versed, masterful, proficient, adroit, dexterous ■ **OPPOSITE:** unskilled ▶ NOUN *He was an* *adept at getting people to talk confidentially to him.* = **expert**, master, genius, buff (*informal*), whizz (*informal*), hotshot (*informal*), rocket scientist (*informal*), dab hand (*Brit. informal*), maven (*U.S.*)

adequacy NOUN = **sufficiency**, capability, competence, suitability, tolerability, fairness, commensurateness, requisiteness, satisfactoriness

adequate ADJECTIVE **1** *One in four people are without adequate homes.* = **passable**, acceptable, middling, average, fair, ordinary, moderate, satisfactory, competent, mediocre, so-so (*informal*), tolerable, up to scratch (*informal*), presentable, unexceptional ■ **OPPOSITE:** inadequate **2** *an amount adequate to purchase another house* = **sufficient**, enough, capable, suitable, requisite ■ **OPPOSITE:** insufficient

adherent NOUN *Communism was gaining adherents in Latin America.* = **supporter**, fan, advocate, follower, admirer, partisan, disciple, protagonist, devotee, henchman or woman or person, hanger-on, upholder, sectary ■ **OPPOSITE:** opponent ▶ ADJECTIVE *an adherent bandage* = **adhering**, holding, sticking, clinging, sticky, tacky, adhesive, tenacious, glutinous, gummy, gluey, mucilaginous

adhere to VERB **1** *All members adhere to a strict code of practice.* = **follow**, keep, maintain, respect, observe, be true, fulfil, obey, heed, keep to, abide by, be loyal, mind, be constant, be faithful **2** *He urged them to adhere to the values of Islam.* = **be faithful**, follow, support, respect, observe, be true, obey, be devoted, be attached, keep to, be loyal **3** *Small particles adhere to the seed.* = **stick to**, attach to, cling to, unite to, glue to, fix to, fasten to, hold fast to, paste to, cement to, cleave to, glue on to, stick fast to, cohere to

adhesion NOUN = **sticking**, grip, attachment, cohesion, coherence, adherence, adhesiveness

> **USAGE** *Adhesion* is preferred when talking about sticking or holding fast in a physical sense and a useful alternative that could be used here is *sticking*. The word *adherence*, although close in meaning, would be the preferred word when talking about principles, rules and values.

adhesive NOUN *Glue the mirror in with a strong adhesive.* = **glue**, cement, gum, paste, mucilage ▶ ADJECTIVE *adhesive tape* = **sticky**, holding, sticking, attaching, clinging, adhering, tacky, cohesive, tenacious, glutinous, gummy, gluey, mucilaginous

ad hoc ADJECTIVE *An ad hoc committee was set up to examine the problem.* = **makeshift**, emergency, improvised, impromptu, expedient, stopgap, jury-rigged (*chiefly Nautical*) ■ **OPPOSITE:** permanent

adjacent ADJECTIVE *The fire quickly spread to adjacent shops.* = **adjoining**, neighbouring, nearby, abutting ■ **OPPOSITE:** far away

adjoin VERB = **connect with** *or* **to**, join, neighbour (on), link with, attach to, combine with, couple with, communicate with, touch on, border on, annex, approximate, unite with, verge on, impinge on, append (*formal*), affix to, interconnect with

adjoining ADJECTIVE = **connecting**, nearby, joined, joining, touching, bordering, neighbouring, next door, adjacent, interconnecting, abutting, contiguous (*formal*)

adjourn VERB = **postpone**, delay, suspend, interrupt, put off, stay, defer, recess, discontinue, put on the back burner (*informal*), prorogue, take a rain check on (*U.S. & Canad. informal*) ■ **OPPOSITE:** continue

adjournment NOUN = **postponement**, delay, suspension, putting off, stay, recess, interruption, deferment, deferral, discontinuation, prorogation

adjudge VERB = **judge**, determine, declare, decide, assign, pronounce, decree, apportion, adjudicate

adjudicate VERB **1** = **decide**, judge, determine, settle, mediate, adjudge, arbitrate **2** = **judge**, referee, umpire

adjudication NOUN = **judgment**, finding, ruling, decision, settlement, conclusion, verdict, determination, arbitration, pronouncement, adjudgment

adjudicator NOUN = **judge**, referee, umpire, umpie (*Austral. slang*), arbiter, arbitrator, moderator

adjunct NOUN = **addition**, supplement, accessory, complement, auxiliary, add-on, appendage, addendum, appurtenance

adjust VERB **1** *I felt I had adjusted to the idea of being a mother very well.* = **adapt**, change, settle, convert, alter, accommodate, dispose, get used, accustom, conform, reconcile, harmonize, acclimatize, familiarize yourself, attune **2** *To attract investors the country has adjusted its tax laws.* = **change**, order, reform, fix, arrange, alter, adapt, revise, modify, set, regulate, amend, reconcile, remodel, redress, rectify, recast, customize, make conform **3** *Liz adjusted her mirror and edged the car out.* = **modify**, arrange, fix, tune (up), alter, adapt, remodel, tweak (*informal*), customize

a

adjustable ADJECTIVE = **alterable**, flexible, adaptable, malleable, movable, tractable, modifiable, mouldable

adjustment NOUN **1** *A technician made an adjustment to a smoke machine at the back.* = **alteration**, setting, change, ordering, fixing, arrangement, tuning, repair, conversion, modifying, adaptation, modification, remodelling, redress, refinement, rectification **2** *He will need a period of adjustment.* = **acclimatization**, settling in, orientation, familiarization, change, regulation, settlement, amendment, reconciliation, adaptation, accustoming, revision, modification, naturalization, acculturation, harmonization, habituation, acclimation, inurement

administer VERB **1** *Next summer's exams will be straightforward to administer.* = **manage**, run, control, rule, direct, handle, conduct, command, govern, oversee, supervise, preside over, be in charge of, superintend **2** *Sister came to watch the nurses administer the drugs.* = **dispense**, give, share, provide, apply, distribute, assign, allocate, allot, dole out, apportion, deal out **3** *He is shown administering most of the blows.* = **execute**, do, give, provide, apply, perform, carry out, impose, realize, implement, enforce, render, discharge, enact, dispense, mete out, bring off

administration NOUN **1** *Standards in the administration of justice have degenerated.* = **management**, government, running, control, performance, handling, direction, conduct, application, command, provision, distribution, governing, administering, execution, overseeing, supervision, manipulation, governance, dispensation, superintendence **2** *They would like the college administration to exert more control.* = **directors**, board, executive(s), bosses (*informal*), management, employers, directorate **3** *He served in posts in both the Ford and Carter administrations.* = **government**, authority, executive, leadership, ministry, regime, governing body

administrative ADJECTIVE = **managerial**, executive, management, directing, regulatory, governmental, organizational, supervisory, directorial, gubernatorial (*chiefly U.S.*)

administrator NOUN = **manager**, head, official, director, officer, executive, minister, boss (*informal*), agent, governor, controller, supervisor, bureaucrat, superintendent, gaffer (*informal,*

chiefly Brit.*), organizer, mandarin, functionary, overseer

admirable ADJECTIVE = **praiseworthy**, good, great (*informal*), fine, capital, noted, choice, champion, prime, select, wonderful, excellent, brilliant, rare, cracking (*Brit. informal*), outstanding, valuable, superb, distinguished, superior, sterling, worthy, first-class, notable, sovereign, dope (*slang*), world-class, exquisite, exemplary, first-rate, superlative, commendable, top-notch (*informal*), brill (*informal*), laudable, meritorious, estimable, tiptop, A1 or A-one (*informal*), bitchin' (*U.S. slang*), chillin' (*U.S. slang*), booshit (*Austral. slang*), exo (*Austral. slang*), sik (*Austral. slang*), ka pai (*N.Z.*), rad (*informal*), phat (*slang*), schmick (*Austral. informal*), beaut (*informal*), barrie (*Scot. slang*), belting (*Brit. slang*), pearler (*Austral. slang*) ■ OPPOSITE: deplorable

admiration NOUN = **regard**, surprise, wonder, respect, delight, pleasure, praise, approval, recognition, affection, esteem, appreciation, amazement, astonishment, reverence, deference, adoration, veneration, wonderment, approbation

admire VERB **1** *He admired the way she had coped with life.* = **respect**, value, prize, honour, praise, appreciate, esteem, approve of, revere, venerate, take your hat off to, have a good or high opinion of, think highly of ■ OPPOSITE: despise **2** *I admired her when I first met her and I still think she's marvellous.* = **adore**, like, love, desire, take to, go for, fancy (*Brit. informal*), treasure, worship, cherish, glorify, look up to, dote on, hold dear, be captivated by, have an eye for, find attractive, idolize, take a liking to, be infatuated with, be enamoured of, lavish affection on **3** *We took time to stop and admire the view.* = **marvel at**, look at, appreciate, delight in, gaze at, wonder at, be amazed by, take pleasure in, gape at, be awed by, goggle at, be filled with surprise by

admirer NOUN **1** *He was an admirer of her grandmother's paintings.* = **fan**, supporter, follower, enthusiast, partisan, disciple, buff (*informal*), protagonist, devotee, worshipper, adherent, votary **2** *Susie had caught the eye of many an admirer.* = **suitor**, lover, beau (*old-fashioned*), wooer

admissible ADJECTIVE = **permissible**, allowed, permitted, acceptable, tolerated, tolerable, passable, allowable ■ OPPOSITE: inadmissible

admission NOUN **1** *There have been increases in hospital admissions of children.* = **admittance**, access, entry, introduction, entrance, acceptance, initiation, entrée, ingress **2** *She wanted an admission of guilt from her father.* = **confession**, admitting, profession, declaration, revelation, concession, allowance, disclosure, acknowledgement, affirmation, unburdening, avowal, divulgence, unbosoming

admit VERB **1** *A huge proportion of them admit to regularly breaking the laws of the road.* = **confess**, own up, confide, profess, own up, come clean (*informal*), come out of the closet, sing (*slang, chiefly U.S.*), cough (*slang*), spill your guts (*slang*), fess up (*U.S. slang*) **2** *I am willing to admit that I do make mistakes.* = **allow**, agree, accept, reveal, grant, declare, acknowledge, recognize, concede, disclose, affirm, divulge ■ **OPPOSITE:** deny **3** *Security personnel refused to admit him or his wife.* = **let in**, allow, receive, accept, introduce, take in, initiate, give access to, allow to enter ■ **OPPOSITE:** keep out

admittance NOUN = **access**, entry, way in, passage, entrance, reception, acceptance

admittedly ADVERB = **it must be admitted**, certainly, undeniably, it must be said, to be fair or honest, avowedly, it cannot be denied, it must be allowed, confessedly, it must be confessed, allowedly

admonish VERB **1** *They admonished me for taking risks with my health.* = **reprimand**, caution, censure, rebuke, scold, berate, check, chide, tear into (*informal*), tell off (*informal*), reprove, upbraid, read the riot act to someone, carpet (*informal*), chew out (*U.S. & Canad. informal*), tear someone off a strip (*Brit. informal*), give someone a rocket (*Brit. & N.Z. informal*), slap someone on the wrist, rap someone over the knuckles ■ **OPPOSITE:** praise **2** *Your doctor may one day admonish you to improve your posture.* = **advise**, suggest, warn, urge, recommend, counsel, caution, prescribe, exhort (*formal*), enjoin, forewarn

admonition NOUN = **reprimand**, warning, advice, counsel, caution, rebuke, reproach, scolding, berating, chiding, telling off (*informal*), upbraiding, reproof, remonstrance (*formal*)

ado NOUN = **fuss**, to-do, trouble, delay, bother, stir, confusion, excitement, disturbance, bustle, flurry, agitation, commotion, pother (*literary*)

adolescence NOUN = **teens**, youth, minority, boyhood, girlhood, juvenescence

adolescent ADJECTIVE **1** *adolescent rebellion* = **young**, growing, junior, teenage, juvenile, youthful, childish, immature, boyish, undeveloped, girlish, puerile, in the springtime of life **2** *An adolescent boy should have an adult in whom he can confide.* = **immature**, young, teen (*informal*), juvenile, youthful ▶ NOUN *Adolescents are happiest with small groups of close friends.* = **teenager**, girl, boy, kid (*informal*), youth, lad, minor, young man, youngster, young woman, juvenile, young person, lass, young adult

adopt VERB **1** *Pupils should be helped to adopt a positive approach.* = **take on**, follow, support, choose, accept, maintain, assume, select, take over, approve, appropriate, take up, embrace, engage in, endorse, ratify, become involved in, espouse **2** *There are hundreds of people desperate to adopt a child.* = **take in**, raise, nurse, parent, rear, foster, bring up, take care of ■ **OPPOSITE:** abandon

adoption NOUN **1** *They gave their babies up for adoption.* = **fostering**, adopting, taking in, fosterage **2** *the adoption of Japanese management practices* = **embracing**, choice, taking on, taking up, support, taking over, selection, approval, following, assumption, maintenance, acceptance, endorsement, appropriation, ratification, approbation, espousal

adorable ADJECTIVE = **lovable**, pleasing, appealing, dear, sweet, attractive, charming, precious, darling, fetching (*informal*), delightful, cute, captivating, cutesy (*informal*) ■ **OPPOSITE:** hateful

adoration NOUN = **love**, honour, worship, worshipping, esteem, admiration, reverence, estimation, exaltation, veneration, glorification, idolatry, idolization

adore VERB = **love**, honour, admire, worship, esteem, cherish, bow to, revere, dote on, idolize ■ **OPPOSITE:** hate

adoring ADJECTIVE = **admiring**, loving, devoted, worshipping, fond, affectionate, ardent, doting, venerating, enamoured, reverential, reverent, idolizing, adulatory ■ **OPPOSITE:** hating

adorn VERB = **decorate**, enhance, deck, trim, grace, array, enrich, garnish, ornament, embellish, emblazon, festoon, bedeck, beautify, engarland

adornment NOUN **1** *a building without any adornment or decoration* = **decoration**, trimming, supplement, accessory, ornament, frill, festoon, embellishment, frippery **2** *Cosmetics are used for adornment.* = **beautification**, decorating, decoration, embellishment, ornamentation

adrift ADJECTIVE **1** *They were spotted adrift in a dinghy.* = **drifting**, afloat, cast off, unmoored, aweigh, unanchored **2** *She had the growing sense that she was adrift and isolated.* = **aimless**, goalless, directionless, purposeless ▶ ADVERB *They are trying to place the blame for a policy that has gone adrift.* = **wrong**, astray, off course, amiss, off target, wide of the mark

adroit ADJECTIVE = **skilful**, able, skilled, expert, bright (*informal*), clever, apt, cunning, ingenious, adept, deft, nimble, masterful, proficient, artful, quick-witted, dexterous ■ **OPPOSITE:** unskilful

adulation NOUN = **extravagant flattery**, worship, fawning, sycophancy, fulsome praise, blandishment, bootlicking (*informal*), servile flattery ■ **OPPOSITE:** ridicule

adult NOUN *Children under 14 must be accompanied by an adult.* = **grown-up**, mature person, person of mature age, grown or grown-up person, man or woman ▶ ADJECTIVE **1** *a pair of adult birds* = **fully grown**, mature, grown-up, of age, ripe, fully fledged, fully developed, full grown **2** *people working in the adult entertainment industry* = **pornographic**, blue, dirty, offensive, sexy, erotic, porn (*informal*), obscene, taboo, filthy, indecent, sensual, hard-core, lewd, carnal, porno (*informal*), X-rated (*informal*), salacious, prurient, smutty

adulterer or **adulteress** NOUN = **cheat** (*informal*), love rat (*slang*), love cheat (*slang*), fornicator

adulterous ADJECTIVE = **unfaithful**, cheating (*informal*), extramarital, fornicating, unchaste

adultery NOUN = **unfaithfulness**, infidelity, cheating (*informal*), fornication, playing the field (*slang*), extramarital sex, playing away from home (*slang*), illicit sex, unchastity, extramarital relations, extracurricular sex (*informal*), extramarital congress, having an affair or a fling ■ **OPPOSITE:** faithfulness

advance VERB **1** *Rebel forces are advancing on the capital.* = **progress**, proceed, go ahead, move up, come forward, go forward, press on, gain ground, make inroads, make headway, make your way, cover ground, make strides, move onward ■ **OPPOSITE:** retreat **2** *Too much protein in the diet may advance the ageing process.* = **accelerate**, speed, promote, hurry (up), step up (*informal*), hasten, precipitate, quicken, bring forward, push forward, expedite, send forward, crack on (*informal*)

3 *The country has advanced from a rural society to an industrial power.* = **improve**, rise, grow, develop, reform, pick up, progress, thrive, upgrade, multiply, prosper, make strides **4** *Many theories have been advanced as to why this is.* = **suggest**, offer, present, propose, allege, cite, advocate, submit, prescribe, put forward, proffer, adduce, offer as a suggestion ■ **OPPOSITE:** withhold **5** *I advanced him some money, which he promised to repay.* = **lend**, loan, accommodate someone with, supply on credit ■ **OPPOSITE:** withhold payment ▶ NOUN **1** *She was paid a £100,000 advance for her next two novels.* = **down payment**, credit, fee, deposit, retainer, prepayment, loan **2** *They simulated an advance on enemy positions.* = **attack**, charge, strike, rush, assault, raid, invasion, offensive, onslaught, advancement, foray, incursion, forward movement, onward movement **3** *These two vaccines are a huge advance for preventing cancer.* = **improvement**, development, gain, growth, breakthrough, advancement, step, headway, inroads, betterment, furtherance, forward movement, amelioration, onward movement ▶ ADJECTIVE *The event received little advance publicity.* = **prior**, early, previous, beforehand • **in advance** *The subject of the talk is announced a week in advance.* = **beforehand**, earlier, ahead, previously, pre-need, in the lead, in the forefront

advanced ADJECTIVE = **sophisticated**, foremost, modern, revolutionary, up-to-date, higher, leading, recent, prime, forward, ahead, supreme, extreme, principal, progressive, paramount, state-of-the-art, avant-garde, precocious, pre-eminent, up-to-the-minute, ahead of the times ■ **OPPOSITE:** backward

advancement NOUN **1** *He cared little for social advancement.* = **promotion**, rise, gain, growth, advance, progress, improvement, betterment, preferment, amelioration **2** *her work for the advancement of the status of women* = **progress**, advance, headway, forward movement, onward movement

advantage NOUN **1** *A good crowd will be a definite advantage to the team.* = **benefit**, use, start, help, service, aid, profit, favour, asset, assistance, blessing, utility, boon, ace in the hole, ace up your sleeve ■ **OPPOSITE:** disadvantage **2** *Men still have an economic position of advantage over women.* = **lead**, control, edge, sway, dominance, superiority, upper hand, precedence, primacy, pre-eminence **3** *The great* advantage of home-grown fruit is its magnificent flavour. = **superiority**, good, worth, gain, comfort, welfare, enjoyment, mileage (informal)

advantageous ADJECTIVE **1** Free exchange of goods was advantageous to all. = **beneficial**, useful, valuable, helpful, profitable, of service, convenient, worthwhile, expedient ■ OPPOSITE: unfavourable **2** She was determined to prise what she could from an advantageous situation. = **superior**, dominating, commanding, dominant, important, powerful, favourable, fortuitous

advent NOUN = **coming**, approach, appearance, arrival, entrance, onset, occurrence, visitation

adventure NOUN I set off for a new adventure in the US on the first day of the year. = **venture**, experience, chance, risk, incident, enterprise, speculation, undertaking, exploit, fling, hazard, occurrence, contingency, caper, escapade ▶ VERB The group has adventured as far as the Alps. = **venture**, risk, brave, dare

adventurer NOUN **1** ambitious political adventurers = **mercenary**, rogue, gambler, speculator, opportunist, charlatan, fortune-hunter **2** A round-the-world adventurer was killed when her plane crashed. = **venturer**, hero, traveller, heroine, wanderer, voyager, daredevil, soldier of fortune, swashbuckler, knight-errant

adventurous ADJECTIVE = **daring**, dangerous, enterprising, bold, risky, rash, have-a-go (informal), hazardous, reckless, audacious, intrepid, foolhardy, daredevil, headstrong, venturesome, adventuresome, temerarious (rare) ■ OPPOSITE: cautious

adversary NOUN = **opponent**, rival, opposer, enemy, competitor, foe (formal, literary), contestant, antagonist ■ OPPOSITE: ally

adverse ADJECTIVE **1** The decision would have no adverse effect on the investigation. = **harmful**, damaging, conflicting, dangerous, opposite, negative, destructive, detrimental, hurtful, antagonistic, injurious, inimical, inopportune, disadvantageous, unpropitious, inexpedient ■ OPPOSITE: beneficial **2** Despite the adverse conditions, the road was finished in just eight months. = **unfavourable**, bad, threatening, hostile, unfortunate, unlucky, ominous, unfriendly, untimely, unsuited, ill-suited, inopportune, disadvantageous, unseasonable **3** These drugs have received adverse publicity because of their side-effects. = **negative**, opposing,

reluctant, hostile, contrary, dissenting, unwilling, unfriendly, unsympathetic, ill-disposed

adversity NOUN = **hardship**, trouble, distress, suffering, trial, disaster, reverse, misery, hard times, catastrophe, sorrow, woe, misfortune, bad luck, deep water, calamity, mishap, affliction, wretchedness, ill-fortune, ill-luck

advert NOUN = **advertisement**, bill, notice, display, commercial, ad (informal), announcement, promotion, publicity, poster, plug (informal), puff, circular, placard, blurb, banner ad

advertise VERB = **publicize**, promote, plug (informal), announce, publish, push (informal), display, declare, broadcast, advise, inform, praise, proclaim, puff, hype, notify, tout, flaunt, crack up (informal), promulgate, make known, apprise, beat the drum (informal), blazon, bring to public notice

advertisement NOUN = **advert** (Brit.), bill, notice, display, commercial, ad (informal), announcement, promotion, publicity, poster, plug (informal), puff, circular, placard, blurb

advice NOUN **1** Don't be afraid to ask for advice when ordering a meal. = **guidance**, help, opinion, direction, suggestion, instruction, counsel, counselling, recommendation, injunction, admonition **2** Most have now left the country on the advice of their governments. = **instruction**, notification, view, information, warning, teaching, notice, word, intelligence

advisable ADJECTIVE = **wise**, seemly, sound, suggested, fitting, fit, politic, recommended, appropriate, suitable, sensible, proper, profitable, desirable, apt, prudent, expedient, judicious ■ OPPOSITE: unwise

advise VERB **1** I would strongly advise against it. = **recommend**, suggest, urge, counsel, advocate, caution, prescribe, commend, admonish, enjoin **2** I must advise you of my decision to retire. = **notify**, tell, report, announce, warn, declare, inform, acquaint, make known, apprise, let (someone) know

adviser NOUN = **counsellor**, authority, teacher, coach, guide, lawyer, consultant, solicitor, counsel, aide, tutor, guru, mentor, helper, confidant, right-hand man or woman or person, consigliere

advisory ADJECTIVE = **advising**, helping, recommending, counselling, consultative

advocacy NOUN = **recommendation**, support, defence, championing, backing, proposal, urging, promotion, campaigning for, upholding, encouragement, justification, argument for, advancement, pleading for, propagation, espousal, promulgation, boosterism, spokesmanship

advocate VERB *They advocate fewer government controls on business.* = **recommend**, support, champion, encourage, propose, favour, defend, promote, urge, advise, justify, endorse, campaign for, prescribe, speak for, uphold, press for, argue for, commend, plead for, espouse, countenance, hold a brief for (*informal*) ■ OPPOSITE: oppose ▶ NOUN **1** *He was a strong advocate of free market policies.* = **supporter**, spokesman or woman or person, champion, defender, speaker, pleader, campaigner, promoter, counsellor, backer, proponent, apostle, apologist, upholder, proposer **2** *When she became an advocate there were only a few women practising.* = **lawyer**, attorney, solicitor, counsel, barrister

aegis NOUN = **support**, backing, wing, favour, protection, shelter, sponsorship, patronage, advocacy, auspices, guardianship

aesthetic ADJECTIVE = **ornamental**, artistic, pleasing, pretty, fancy, enhancing, decorative, tasteful, beautifying, nonfunctional

affable ADJECTIVE = **friendly**, kindly, civil, warm, pleasant, mild, obliging, benign, gracious, benevolent, good-humoured, amiable, courteous, amicable, cordial, sociable, genial, congenial, urbane, approachable, good-natured ■ OPPOSITE: unfriendly

affair NOUN **1** *The government has mishandled the whole affair.* = **matter**, thing, business, question, issue, happening, concern, event, subject, project, activity, incident, proceeding, circumstance, episode, topic, undertaking, transaction, occurrence **2** *A supervisor was carrying on an affair with a colleague.* = **relationship**, romance, intrigue, fling, liaison, flirtation, amour, dalliance

affect¹ VERB **1** *Millions of people have been affected by the drought.* = **influence**, involve, concern, impact, transform, alter, modify, change, manipulate, act on, sway, prevail over, bear upon, impinge upon **2** *He loved his sister, and her loss clearly still affects him.* = **emotionally move**, touch, upset, overcome, stir, disturb, perturb, impress on, tug at your heartstrings (*often facetious*)

affect² VERB *He listened to them, affecting an amused interest.* = **put on**, assume, adopt, pretend, imitate, simulate, contrive, aspire to, sham, counterfeit, feign

affectation NOUN = **pretence**, show, posing, posturing, act, display, appearance, pose, façade, simulation, sham, pretension, veneer, artifice, mannerism, insincerity, pretentiousness, hokum (*slang, chiefly U.S. & Canad.*), artificiality, fakery, affectedness, assumed manners, false display, unnatural imitation

affected¹ ADJECTIVE *Staff at the hospital were deeply affected by the tragedy.* = **touched**, influenced, concerned, troubled, damaged, hurt, injured, upset, impressed, stirred, altered, changed, distressed, stimulated, melted, impaired, afflicted, deeply moved ■ OPPOSITE: untouched

affected² ADJECTIVE *She passed by with an affected air and a disdainful look.* = **pretended**, artificial, contrived, put-on, assumed, mannered, studied, precious, stiff, simulated, mincing, sham, unnatural, pompous, pretentious, counterfeit, feigned, spurious, conceited, insincere, camp (*informal*), la-di-da (*informal*), arty-farty (*informal*), phoney or phony (*informal*) ■ OPPOSITE: genuine

affecting ADJECTIVE = **emotionally moving**, touching, sad, pathetic, poignant, saddening, pitiful, pitiable, piteous

affection NOUN = **fondness**, liking, feeling, love, care, desire, passion, warmth, attachment, goodwill, devotion, kindness, inclination, tenderness, propensity, friendliness, amity (*formal*), aroha (*N.Z.*)

affectionate ADJECTIVE = **fond**, loving, kind, caring, warm, friendly, attached, devoted, tender, doting, warm-hearted ■ OPPOSITE: cool

affiliate VERB = **associate**, unite, join, link, ally, combine, connect, incorporate, annex, confederate, amalgamate, band together

affiliated ADJECTIVE = **associated**, united, joined, linked, allied, connected, incorporated, confederated, amalgamated, federated, conjoined

affiliation NOUN = **association**, union, joining, league, relationship, connection, alliance, combination, coalition, merging, confederation, incorporation, amalgamation, banding together

affinity NOUN **1** *There is a natural affinity between the two.* = **attraction**, liking, leaning, sympathy, inclination, rapport, fondness, partiality, aroha (*N.Z.*) ■ OPPOSITE: hostility **2** *The two plots share certain obvious affinities.* = **similarity**, relationship, relation, connection, alliance, correspondence, analogy, resemblance, closeness, likeness, compatibility, kinship ■ OPPOSITE: difference

affirm VERB **1** *'The place is a dump,' she affirmed.*
= **declare**, state, maintain, swear, assert,
testify, pronounce, certify, attest, avow,
aver, asseverate (*formal*), avouch
■ **OPPOSITE:** deny **2** *Everything I had*
accomplished seemed to affirm that opinion.
= **confirm**, prove, sanction, endorse, ratify,
verify, validate, bear out, substantiate,
corroborate, authenticate ■ **OPPOSITE:**
refute

affirmation NOUN **1** *The ministers issued a*
robust affirmation of their faith in the system.
= **declaration**, statement, assertion, oath,
certification, pronouncement, avowal,
asseveration (*formal*), averment **2** *The high*
turnout was an affirmation of the importance of
the election. = **confirmation**, testimony,
ratification, attestation, avouchment

affirmative ADJECTIVE = **agreeing**,
confirming, positive, approving, consenting,
favourable, concurring, assenting,
corroborative ■ **OPPOSITE:** negative

affix VERB = **attach**, add, join, stick on, bind,
put on, tag, glue, paste, tack, fasten,
annex, append (*formal*), subjoin
■ **OPPOSITE:** remove

afflict VERB = **torment**, trouble, pain, hurt,
wound, burden, distress, rack, try, plague,
grieve, harass, ail (*literary*), oppress, beset,
smite

affliction NOUN = **misfortune**, suffering,
trouble, trial, disease, pain, distress, grief,
misery, plague (*informal*), curse, ordeal,
sickness, torment, hardship, sorrow, woe,
adversity, calamity, scourge, tribulation,
wretchedness

affluence NOUN = **wealth**, riches, plenty,
fortune, prosperity, abundance, big money,
exuberance, profusion, big bucks (*informal,*
chiefly U.S.), opulence, megabucks (*U.S. &*
Canad. slang), pretty penny (*informal*), wad
(*U.S. & Canad. slang*)

affluent ADJECTIVE = **wealthy**, rich,
prosperous, loaded (*slang*), well-off,
opulent, well-heeled (*informal*),
well-to-do, moneyed, minted (*Brit. slang*)
■ **OPPOSITE:** poor

afford VERB **1** *The arts should be available at*
prices people can afford. = **have the money**
for, manage, bear, pay for, spare, stand,
stretch to **2** *We cannot afford to wait.* = **bear**,
stand, sustain, allow yourself **3** *The room*
afforded fine views of the city. = **give**, offer,
provide, produce, supply, grant, yield,
render, furnish, bestow, impart

affordable ADJECTIVE = **inexpensive**, fair,
cheap, reasonable, moderate, modest,
low-price, low-cost, economical
■ **OPPOSITE:** expensive

affront VERB *One example that particularly*
affronted him was at the world championships.
= **offend**, anger, provoke, outrage, insult,
annoy, vex, displease, pique, put *or* get your
back up, slight ▶ NOUN *She has taken my*
enquiry as a personal affront. = **insult**, wrong,
injury, abuse, offence, slight, outrage,
provocation, slur, indignity, slap in the face
(*informal*), vexation

affronted ADJECTIVE = **offended**, cross,
angry, upset, slighted, outraged, insulted,
annoyed, stung, incensed, indignant, irate,
miffed (*informal*), displeased, peeved
(*informal*), piqued, tooshie (*Austral. slang*)

afloat ADJECTIVE **1** *Three hours is a long time to*
try and stay afloat. = **floating**, on the
surface, buoyant, keeping your head above
water, unsubmerged ■ **OPPOSITE:** sunken
2 *Efforts were being made to keep the company*
afloat. = **solvent**, in business, above water
■ **OPPOSITE:** bankrupt

afoot ADJECTIVE = **going on**, happening,
current, operating, abroad, brewing,
hatching, circulating, up (*informal*), about,
in preparation, in progress, afloat, in the
wind, on the go (*informal*), astir

afraid ADJECTIVE **1** *She did not seem at all afraid.*
= **scared**, frightened, nervous, anxious,
terrified, shaken, alarmed, startled,
suspicious, intimidated, fearful, cowardly,
timid, apprehensive, petrified, panicky, panic-
stricken, timorous (*literary*), faint-hearted
■ **OPPOSITE:** unafraid **2** *He seems to live in an*
ivory tower, afraid to enter the real world.
= **reluctant**, slow, frightened, scared,
unwilling, backward, hesitant, recalcitrant,
loath, disinclined, unenthusiastic,
indisposed **3** *I'm afraid I can't help you.*
= **sorry**, apologetic, regretful, sad,
distressed, unhappy ■ **OPPOSITE:** pleased

afresh ADVERB = **again**, newly, once again,
once more, over again, anew

after PREPOSITION **1** *After breakfast she phoned*
for a taxi. = **at the end of**, following,
subsequent to ■ **OPPOSITE:** before **2** *People*
were after him for large amounts of money.
= **following**, chasing, pursuing, on the
hunt for, on the tail of (*informal*), on the
track of ▶ ADVERB *tomorrow, or the day after*
= **following**, later, next, succeeding,
afterwards, subsequently, thereafter
■ **RELATED WORD:** *prefix* post-

aftereffect NOUN (*usually plural*)
= **consequence**, wake, trail, aftermath,
hangover (*informal*), spin-off, repercussion,
afterglow, aftershock, delayed response

aftermath NOUN = **effects**, end, results,
wake, consequences, outcome, sequel, end
result, upshot, aftereffects

a

afterwards or **afterward** ADVERB = **later**, after, then, after that, subsequently, thereafter, following that, at a later date or time

again ADVERB 1 *He kissed her again.* = **once more**, another time, anew, afresh 2 *And again, that's probably part of the progress of technology.* = **also**, in addition, moreover, besides, furthermore • **there again** or **then again** *They may agree, but there again, they may not.* = **on the other hand**, in contrast, on the contrary, conversely

against PREPOSITION 1 *She leaned against him.* = **beside**, on, up against, in contact with, abutting, close up to 2 *She was very much against commencing the treatment.* = **opposed to**, anti (*informal*), opposing, counter, contra (*informal*), hostile to, in opposition to, averse to, opposite to, not in accord with 3 *swimming upstream against the current* = **in opposition to**, resisting, versus, counter to, in the opposite direction of 4 *You'll need insurance against fire, flood and breakage.* = **in preparation for**, in case of, in anticipation of, in expectation of, in provision for ■ **RELATED WORDS:** prefixes anti-, contra-, counter-

age NOUN 1 *She's very confident for her age.* = **years**, days, generation, lifetime, stage of life, length of life, length of existence 2 *Perhaps he has grown wiser with age.* = **old age**, experience, maturity, completion, seniority, fullness, majority, maturation, senility, decline, advancing years, declining years, senescence, full growth, matureness ■ **OPPOSITE:** youth 3 *the age of steam and steel* = **time**, day(s), period, generation, era, epoch ▶ PLURAL NOUN *The bus took ages to arrive.* = **a long time** or **while**, years, centuries, for ever (*informal*), aeons, donkey's years (*informal*), yonks (*informal*), a month of Sundays (*informal*), an age or eternity ▶ VERB 1 *He seemed to have aged in the last few months.* = **grow old**, decline, weather, fade, deteriorate, wither 2 *Whisky loses strength as it ages.* = **mature**, season, condition, soften, mellow, ripen

aged ADJECTIVE = **old**, getting on, grey, ancient, antique, elderly, past it (*informal*), age-old, antiquated, hoary, superannuated, senescent, cobwebby ■ **OPPOSITE:** young

ageing or **aging** ADJECTIVE *He lives with his ageing mother.* = **growing old** or **older**, declining, maturing, deteriorating, mellowing, in decline, senile, long in the tooth, senescent, getting on or past it (*informal*) ▶ NOUN *degenerative diseases and premature ageing* = **growing old**, decline,

decay, deterioration, degeneration, maturation, senility, senescence

ageless ADJECTIVE = **eternal**, enduring, abiding, perennial, timeless, immortal, unchanging, deathless, unfading ■ **OPPOSITE:** momentary

agency NOUN 1 *a successful advertising agency* = **business**, company, office, firm, department, organization, enterprise, establishment, bureau 2 *a negotiated settlement through the agency of the UN* = **medium**, work, means, force, power, action, operation, activity, influence, vehicle, instrument, intervention, mechanism, efficiency, mediation, auspices, intercession, instrumentality

agenda NOUN = **programme**, list, plan, schedule, diary, calendar, timetable

agent NOUN 1 *You are buying direct, rather than through an agent.* = **representative**, deputy, substitute, advocate, rep (*informal*), broker, delegate, factor (*Scot.*), negotiator, envoy, trustee, proxy, surrogate, go-between, emissary 2 *They regard themselves as the agents of change in society.* = **author**, officer, worker, actor, vehicle, instrument, operator, performer, operative, catalyst, executor, doer, perpetuator 3 *the bleaching agent in white flour* = **force**, means, power, cause, instrument

aggravate VERB 1 *Stress and lack of sleep can aggravate the situation.* = **make worse**, exaggerate, intensify, worsen, heighten, exacerbate, magnify, inflame, increase, add insult to injury, fan the flames of ■ **OPPOSITE:** improve 2 *What aggravates you most about this country?* = **annoy**, bother, provoke, needle (*informal*), irritate, tease, hassle (*informal*), gall, exasperate, nettle, pester, vex, irk, get under your skin (*informal*), get on your nerves (*informal*), nark (*Brit., Austral. & N.Z. slang*), get up your nose (*informal*), be on your back (*slang*), rub (someone) up the wrong way (*informal*), get in your hair (*informal*), get on your wick (*Brit. slang*), hack you off (*informal*) ■ **OPPOSITE:** please

aggravating ADJECTIVE 1 *You don't realise how aggravating you can be.* = **annoying**, provoking, irritating, teasing, galling, exasperating, vexing, irksome 2 *Stress is a frequent aggravating factor.* = **worsening**, exaggerating, intensifying, heightening, exacerbating, magnifying, inflaming

aggravation NOUN 1 *I just couldn't take the aggravation.* = **annoyance**, grief (*informal*), teasing, irritation, hassle (*informal*), provocation, gall, exasperation, vexation, irksomeness 2 *Any aggravations of the*

injury would keep him out of the match.
= **worsening**, heightening, inflaming,
exaggeration, intensification,
magnification, exacerbation

aggregate NOUN *society viewed as an
aggregate of individuals* = **total**, body, whole,
amount, collection, cluster, mass, sum,
combination, pile, mixture, bulk, lump,
heap, accumulation, assemblage,
agglomeration ▶ ADJECTIVE *the rate of
growth of aggregate demand* = **collective**,
added, mixed, combined, collected,
corporate, assembled, accumulated,
composite, cumulative ▶ VERB *We should
never aggregate votes to predict results under
another system.* = **combine**, mix, collect,
assemble, heap, accumulate, pile, amass

aggregation NOUN = **collection**, body,
mass, combination, pile, mixture, bulk,
lump, heap, accumulation, assemblage,
agglomeration

aggression NOUN 1 *Aggression is by no means
a male-only trait.* = **hostility**, malice,
antagonism, antipathy, aggressiveness,
ill will, belligerence, destructiveness,
malevolence, pugnacity 2 *the threat of
massive military aggression* = **attack**,
campaign, injury, assault, offence, raid,
invasion, offensive, onslaught, foray,
encroachment

aggressive ADJECTIVE 1 *Some children are
much more aggressive than others.* = **hostile**,
offensive, destructive, belligerent, unkind,
unfriendly, malevolent, contrary,
antagonistic, pugnacious, bellicose,
quarrelsome, aggro (*Austral. & N.Z.*), aggers
(*Austral. slang*), biffo (*Austral. slang*),
inimical, rancorous, ill-disposed
■ OPPOSITE: friendly 2 *a very competitive and
aggressive executive* = **forceful**, powerful,
convincing, effective, enterprising,
dynamic, bold, militant, pushing, vigorous,
energetic, persuasive, assertive, zealous,
pushy (*informal*), in-your-face (*slang*)
■ OPPOSITE: submissive

aggressor NOUN = **attacker**, assaulter,
invader, assailant

aggrieved ADJECTIVE = **hurt**, wronged,
injured, harmed, disturbed, distressed,
unhappy, afflicted, saddened, woeful,
peeved (*informal*), ill-used

aghast ADJECTIVE = **horrified**, shocked,
amazed, stunned, appalled, astonished,
startled, astounded, confounded,
awestruck, horror-struck, thunder-struck

agile ADJECTIVE 1 *He is not as strong and agile as
he was at 20.* = **nimble**, active, quick, lively,
swift, brisk, supple, sprightly, lithe, limber,
spry, lissom(e) ■ OPPOSITE: slow 2 *She was*

*quick-witted, and had an extraordinarily agile
mind.* = **acute**, sharp, quick, bright
(*informal*), prompt, alert, clever, lively,
nimble, quick-witted

agility NOUN 1 *She blinked in surprise at his
agility.* = **nimbleness**, activity, suppleness,
quickness, swiftness, liveliness, briskness,
litheness, sprightliness, spryness 2 *His
intellect and mental agility have never been in
doubt.* = **acuteness**, sharpness, alertness,
cleverness, quickness, liveliness,
promptness, quick-wittedness,
promptitude

agitate VERB 1 *Gently agitate the water with a
paintbrush.* = **stir**, beat, mix, shake, disturb,
toss, rouse, churn 2 *The thought of them
inheriting all these things agitated her.* = **upset**,
worry, trouble, disturb, excite, alarm,
stimulate, distract, rouse, ruffle, inflame,
incite, unnerve, disconcert, disquiet,
fluster, perturb, faze, work someone up,
give someone grief (*Brit. & S. African*)
■ OPPOSITE: calm

agitated ADJECTIVE = **upset**, worried,
troubled, disturbed, shaken, excited,
alarmed, nervous, anxious, distressed,
rattled (*informal*), distracted, uneasy,
unsettled, worked up, ruffled, unnerved,
disconcerted, disquieted, edgy, flustered,
perturbed, on edge, fazed, ill at ease, hot
under the collar (*informal*), in a flap
(*informal*), hot and bothered (*informal*),
antsy (*informal*), angsty, all of a flutter
(*informal*), discomposed ■ OPPOSITE: calm

agitation NOUN 1 *Temperature is a measure of
agitation of molecules.* = **turbulence**, rocking,
shaking, stirring, stir, tossing, disturbance,
upheaval, churning, convulsion 2 *She was in
a state of emotional agitation.* = **turmoil**,
worry, trouble, upset, alarm, confusion,
excitement, disturbance, distraction,
upheaval, stimulation, flurry, outcry,
clamour, arousal, ferment, disquiet,
commotion, fluster, lather (*informal*),
incitement, tumult, discomposure, tizzy,
tizz or tiz-woz (*informal*)

agitator NOUN = **troublemaker**,
revolutionary, inciter, firebrand, instigator,
demagogue, rabble-rouser, agent
provocateur, stirrer (*informal*)

ago ADVERB = **previously**, back, before,
since, earlier, formerly

> USAGE Although *since* can be used as a
> synonym of *ago* in certain contexts, the
> use of *ago* and *since* together, as in *it's ten
> years ago since he wrote that novel*, is
> redundant. Instead, it would be correct
> to use *it is ten years since he wrote that novel*,
> or *it is ten years ago that he wrote that novel*.

agonize VERB = **suffer**, labour, worry, struggle, strain, strive, writhe, be distressed, be in agony, go through the mill, be in anguish

agonized ADJECTIVE = **tortured**, suffering, wounded, distressed, racked, tormented, anguished, broken-hearted, grief-stricken, wretched

agonizing ADJECTIVE = **painful**, bitter, distressing, harrowing, heartbreaking, grievous, excruciating, hellish, heart-rending, gut-wrenching, torturous

agony NOUN = **suffering**, pain, distress, misery, torture, discomfort, torment, hardship, woe, anguish, pangs, affliction, throes

agrarian ADJECTIVE = **agricultural**, country, land, farming, rural, rustic, agrestic
■ **OPPOSITE:** urban

agree VERB 1 *I'm not sure I agree with you.* = **concur**, engage, be as one, sympathize, assent, see eye to eye, be of the same opinion, be of the same mind, be down with (*informal*) ■ **OPPOSITE:** disagree
2 *His second statement agrees with the facts.* = **correspond**, match, accord, answer, fit, suit, square, coincide, tally, conform, chime, harmonize • **agree on something** *The warring sides have agreed on a ceasefire.* = **shake hands on**, reach agreement on, settle on, negotiate, work out, arrive at, yield to, thrash out, accede to, concede to • **agree to something** *All 100 senators agreed to postponement.* = **consent to**, grant, approve, permit, accede to, assent to, acquiesce to, comply to, concur to • **agree with someone** *I don't think the food here agrees with me.* = **suit**, get on with, be good for, befit

agreeable ADJECTIVE 1 *more agreeable and better paid occupations* = **pleasant**, pleasing, satisfying, acceptable, delightful, enjoyable, gratifying, pleasurable, congenial, to your liking, to your taste, likable *or* likeable ■ **OPPOSITE:** unpleasant
2 *I've gone out of my way to be agreeable to his friends.* = **friendly**, pleasant, nice, sociable, affable, congenial, good-natured, likable *or* likeable 3 *She was agreeable to the project.* = **consenting**, willing, agreeing, approving, sympathetic, complying, responsive, concurring, amenable, in accord, well-disposed, acquiescent

agreed ADJECTIVE *There is a discount if goods do not arrive by the agreed time.* = **settled**, given, established, guaranteed, fixed, arranged, definite, stipulated, predetermined
■ **OPPOSITE:** indefinite ▶ INTERJECTION *That means we move out today. Agreed?* = **all right**, done, settled, it's a bargain *or* deal, O.K. *or* okay (*informal*), you're on (*informal*), ka pai (*N.Z.*)

agreement NOUN 1 *a new defence agreement* = **treaty**, contract, bond, arrangement, alliance, deal (*informal*), understanding, settlement, bargain, pact, compact, covenant, entente 2 *The talks ended in acrimony rather than agreement.* = **concurrence**, harmony, compliance, union, agreeing, concession, consent, unison, assent, concord, acquiescence
■ **OPPOSITE:** disagreement 3 *The results are generally in agreement with these figures.* = **correspondence**, agreeing, accord, similarity, consistency, analogy, accordance, correlation, affinity, conformity, compatibility, congruity, suitableness ■ **OPPOSITE:** difference

agricultural ADJECTIVE = **farming**, country, rural, rustic, agrarian, agronomic, agronomical, agrestic

agriculture NOUN = **farming**, culture, cultivation, husbandry, tillage, agronomy, agronomics

aground ADVERB = **beached**, grounded, stuck, shipwrecked, foundered, stranded, ashore, marooned, on the rocks, high and dry

ahead ADVERB 1 *He looked straight ahead.* = **in front**, on, forwards, in advance, onwards, towards the front, frontwards 2 *Children in smaller classes were 1.5 months ahead in reading.* = **at an advantage**, in advance, in the lead 3 *Australia were ahead throughout the game.* = **in the lead**, winning, leading, at the head, to the fore, at an advantage 4 *You go on ahead. I'll catch you up later.* = **in advance**, in front, before, onwards, in the lead, in the vanguard

aid NOUN 1 *He was forced to turn to his former enemy for aid.* = **help**, backing, support, benefit, favour, relief, promotion, assistance, encouragement, helping hand, succour ■ **OPPOSITE:** hindrance 2 *A young woman employed as an aid spoke.* = **helper**, supporter, assistant, aide, adjutant, aide-de-camp, second, abettor ▶ VERB 1 *a software system to aid managers in decision-making* = **help**, second, support, serve, sustain, assist, relieve, avail, subsidize, abet, succour, be of service to, lend a hand to, give a leg up to (*informal*)
■ **OPPOSITE:** hinder 2 *Calcium may aid the prevention of colon cancer.* = **promote**, help, further, forward, encourage, favour, facilitate, pave the way for, expedite, smooth the path of, assist the progress of

aide NOUN = **assistant**, supporter, deputy, attendant, helper, henchman *or* woman *or* person, right-hand man or woman or person, adjutant, second, helpmate, coadjutor (*rare*)

ail VERB **1** *a debate on what ails the industry* = **trouble**, worry, bother, distress, pain, upset, annoy, irritate, sicken, afflict, be the matter with **2** *He is said to be ailing at his home in the country.* = **be ill**, be sick, be unwell, feel unwell, be indisposed, be or feel off colour

ailing ADJECTIVE **1** *A rise in overseas sales is good news for the ailing economy.* = **weak**, failing, poor, flawed, unstable, feeble, unsatisfactory, deficient, unsound **2** *I stopped working to care for my ailing mother.* = **ill**, suffering, poorly (*informal*), diseased, sick, weak, crook (*Austral. & N.Z. informal*), feeble, invalid, debilitated, sickly, unwell, infirm, off colour, under the weather (*informal*), indisposed

ailment NOUN = **illness**, disease, complaint, disorder, sickness, affliction, malady, infirmity, lurgy (*informal*)

aim VERB **1** *He was aiming for the 100 metres world record.* = **try for**, want, seek, work for, plan for, strive, aspire to, wish for, have designs on, set your sights on **2** *He was aiming the rifle at me.* = **point**, level, train, direct, sight, take aim (at) ▶ NOUN *a research programme that has failed to achieve its aim* = **intention**, end, point, plan, course, mark, goal, design, target, wish, scheme, purpose, direction, desire, object, objective, ambition, intent, aspiration, Holy Grail (*informal*)

aimless ADJECTIVE = **purposeless**, random, stray, pointless, erratic, wayward, frivolous, chance, goalless, haphazard, vagrant, directionless, unguided, undirected ■ OPPOSITE: purposeful

air NOUN **1** *Draughts help to circulate air.* = **wind**, blast, breath, breeze, puff, whiff, draught, gust, waft, zephyr, air-current, current of air **2** *They fired their guns in the air.* = **atmosphere**, sky, heavens, aerosphere **3** *an old Irish air* = **tune**, song, theme, melody, strain, lay, aria **4** *The meal gave the occasion an almost festive air.* = **manner**, feeling, effect, style, quality, character, bearing, appearance, look, aspect, atmosphere, tone, mood, impression, flavour, aura, ambience, demeanour, vibe (*slang*) ▶ VERB **1** *The whole issue was thoroughly aired at the meeting.* = **publicize**, tell, reveal, exhibit, communicate, voice, express, display, declare, expose, disclose, proclaim, utter, circulate, make public, divulge, disseminate, ventilate, make known, give vent to, take the wraps off **2** *Make sure the room is properly cleaned and*

aired. = **ventilate**, expose, freshen, aerate
■ RELATED WORD: *adjective* aerial

airborne ADJECTIVE = **flying**, floating, soaring, in the air, hovering, gliding, in flight, on the wing, wind-borne, volitant

aircraft NOUN = **plane**, jet, aeroplane, airplane (*U.S. & Canad.*), airliner, kite (*Brit. slang*), flying machine

airfield NOUN = **airport**, airstrip, aerodrome, landing strip, air station, airdrome (*U.S.*)

airily ADVERB = **light-heartedly**, happily, blithely, gaily, animatedly, breezily, jauntily, buoyantly, high-spiritedly

airing NOUN **1** *Open the windows and give the bedroom a good airing.* = **ventilation**, drying, freshening, aeration **2** *The subject of money rarely gets an airing.* = **exposure**, display, expression, publicity, vent, utterance, dissemination

airless ADJECTIVE = **stuffy**, close, heavy, stifling, oppressive, stale, breathless, suffocating, sultry, muggy, unventilated ■ OPPOSITE: airy

airplane (*U.S. & Canad.*) NOUN = **plane**, aircraft, jet, aeroplane, airliner, kite (*Brit. slang*), flying machine

airport NOUN = **airfield**, aerodrome, airdrome (*U.S.*)

airs PLURAL NOUN *We're poor and we never put on airs.* = **affectation**, arrogance, pretensions, pomposity, swank (*informal*), hauteur, haughtiness, superciliousness, affectedness

airy ADJECTIVE **1** *The bathroom is light and airy.* = **well-ventilated**, open, light, fresh, spacious, windy, lofty, breezy, uncluttered, draughty, gusty, blowy ■ OPPOSITE: stuffy **2** *He sailed past, giving them an airy wave of the hand.* = **light-hearted**, light, happy, gay, lively, cheerful, animated, merry, upbeat (*informal*), buoyant, graceful, cheery, genial, high-spirited, jaunty, chirpy (*informal*), sprightly, debonair, nonchalant, blithe, frolicsome ■ OPPOSITE: gloomy **3** *'launch aid', an airy euphemism for more state handouts* = **insubstantial**, imaginary, visionary, flimsy, fanciful, ethereal, immaterial, illusory, wispy, weightless, incorporeal, vaporous ■ OPPOSITE: real

aisle NOUN = **passageway**, path, lane, passage, corridor, alley, gangway

ajar ADJECTIVE = **open**, gaping, agape, partly open, unclosed

akin ADJECTIVE • **akin to** = **similar to**, like, related to, corresponding to, parallel to, comparable to, allied with, analogous to, affiliated with, of a piece with, kin to, cognate with, congenial with, connected with or to

alacrity NOUN = **eagerness**, enthusiasm, willingness, readiness, speed, zeal, gaiety, alertness, hilarity, cheerfulness, quickness, liveliness, briskness, promptness, avidity, joyousness, sprightliness ■ **OPPOSITE:** reluctance

alarm NOUN **1** *The news was greeted with alarm by MPs.* = **fear**, horror, panic, anxiety, distress, terror, dread, dismay, fright, unease, apprehension, nervousness, consternation, trepidation (*formal*), uneasiness ■ **OPPOSITE:** calmness **2** *As soon as the door opened he heard the alarm go off.* = **danger signal**, warning, bell, alert, siren, alarm bell, hooter, distress signal, tocsin ▶ VERB *We could not see what had alarmed him.* = **frighten**, shock, scare, panic, distress, terrify, startle, rattle, dismay, daunt, unnerve, terrorize, put the wind up (*informal*), give (someone) a turn (*informal*), make (someone's) hair stand on end ■ **OPPOSITE:** calm

alarmed ADJECTIVE = **frightened**, troubled, shocked, scared, nervous, disturbed, anxious, distressed, terrified, startled, dismayed, uneasy, fearful, daunted, unnerved, apprehensive, in a panic ■ **OPPOSITE:** calm

alarming ADJECTIVE = **frightening**, shocking, scaring, disturbing, distressing, terrifying, appalling, startling, dreadful, horrifying, menacing, intimidating, dismaying, scary (*informal*), fearful, daunting, fearsome, unnerving, hair-raising, bloodcurdling

albeit CONJUNCTION = **even though**, though, although, even if, notwithstanding, tho'

album NOUN **1** *He has a large collection of blues albums.* = **record**, recording, CD, release, disc (*old-fashioned*), waxing (*old-fashioned*, *informal*), LP, vinyl, platter (*U.S., old-fashioned slang*) **2** *She showed me her photo album.* = **book**, collection, scrapbook

alchemy NOUN = **magic**, witchcraft, wizardry, sorcery, makutu (*N.Z.*)

alcohol NOUN **1** *No alcohol is allowed on the premises.* = **drink**, spirits, liquor, intoxicant, juice (*informal*), booze (*informal*), the bottle (*informal*), grog (*informal, chiefly Austral. & N.Z.*), the hard stuff (*informal*), strong drink, Dutch courage (*informal*), firewater, John Barleycorn, hooch or hootch (*informal, chiefly U.S. & Canad.*) **2** *Products for dry skin have little or no alcohol.* = **ethanol**, ethyl alcohol ■ **RELATED WORD:** *mania* dipsomania

alcoholic NOUN *He admitted publicly that he was an alcoholic.* = **drinker**, drunkard, drunk,

boozer (*informal*), toper, soak (*slang*), lush (*slang*), sponge (*informal*), carouser, sot, tippler, wino (*informal*), inebriate, dipsomaniac, hard drinker ▶ ADJECTIVE *tea, coffee, and alcoholic beverages* = **intoxicating**, hard, strong, stiff, brewed, fermented, distilled, vinous, inebriating, spirituous, inebriant

alcove NOUN = **recess**, corner, bay, niche, bower, compartment, cubicle, nook, cubbyhole

alert ADJECTIVE **1** *He had been spotted by an alert neighbour.* = **attentive**, careful, awake, wary, vigilant, perceptive, watchful, ready, on the lookout, circumspect, observant, on guard, wide-awake, on your toes, on the watch, keeping a weather eye on, heedful ■ **OPPOSITE:** careless **2** *His grandfather is still alert at 93.* = **quick-witted**, spirited, quick, bright (*informal*), sharp, active, lively, brisk, on the ball (*informal*), nimble, agile, sprightly, bright-eyed and bushy-tailed (*informal*) ▶ NOUN *Due to a security alert, the train did not stop at our station.* = **warning**, signal, alarm, siren ■ **OPPOSITE:** all clear ▶ VERB *I was hoping he'd alert the police.* = **warn**, signal, inform, alarm, notify, tip off, forewarn ■ **OPPOSITE:** lull

alertness NOUN = **watchfulness**, vigilance, agility, wariness, quickness, liveliness, readiness, circumspection, attentiveness, spiritedness, briskness, nimbleness, perceptiveness, carefulness, sprightliness, promptitude, activeness, heedfulness

alias NOUN *He had rented a house using an alias.* = **pseudonym**, pen name, assumed name, stage name, nom de guerre, nom de plume, sock puppet (*Computing*) ▶ ADVERB *Richard Thorp, alias Alan Turner* = **also known as**, otherwise, also called, otherwise known as, a.k.a. (*informal*)

alibi NOUN = **excuse**, reason, defence, explanation, plea, justification, pretext

alien NOUN *I never took citizenship so was a resident alien.* = **foreigner**, incomer, immigrant, stranger, outsider, newcomer, asylum seeker, outlander ■ **OPPOSITE:** citizen ▶ ADJECTIVE **1** *They were afraid of the presence of alien troops in the region.* = **foreign**, outside, strange, imported, overseas, unknown, exotic, unfamiliar, not native, not naturalized **2** *His work offers an insight into an alien culture.* = **strange**, new, foreign, novel, remote, unknown, exotic, unfamiliar, estranged, outlandish, untried, unexplored ■ **OPPOSITE:** similar ∙ **alien to** *Such an attitude is alien to most entrepreneurs.* = **unfamiliar to**, opposed to, contrary to, separated from, conflicting with, incompatible with, inappropriate to, repugnant to, adverse to

alienate VERB *The government cannot afford to alienate either group.* = **antagonize**, anger, annoy, offend, irritate, hassle (*informal*), gall, repel, estrange, lose the affection of, disaffect, hack off (*informal*)

alienation NOUN = **estrangement**, setting against, divorce, withdrawal, separation, turning away, indifference, breaking off, diversion, rupture, disaffection, remoteness

alight¹ VERB **1** *Two men alighted from the vehicle.* = **get off**, descend, get down, disembark, dismount **2** *A thrush alighted on a branch of the pine tree.* = **land**, light, settle, come down, descend, perch, touch down, come to rest ■ **OPPOSITE:** take off

alight² ADJECTIVE **1** *Her face was alight with happiness.* = **lit up**, bright, brilliant, shining, illuminated, fiery **2** *The rioters set several buildings alight.* = **on fire**, ignited, set ablaze, lit, burning, aflame, blazing, flaming, flaring

align VERB **1** *The prime minister is aligning himself with the liberals.* = **ally**, side, join, associate, affiliate, cooperate, sympathize **2** *A tripod would be useful to align and steady the camera.* = **line up**, even, order, range, sequence, regulate, straighten, coordinate, even up, make parallel, arrange in line

alignment NOUN **1** *Their alignment with the old administration cost them the election.* = **alliance**, union, association, agreement, sympathy, cooperation, affiliation **2** *a link between the alignment of the planets and events on earth* = **lining up**, line, order, ranging, arrangement, evening, sequence, regulating, adjustment, coordination, straightening up, evening up

alike ADJECTIVE *We are very alike.* = **similar**, close, the same, equal, equivalent, uniform, parallel, resembling, identical, corresponding, akin, duplicate, analogous, homogeneous, of a piece, cut from the same cloth, like two peas in a pod ■ **OPPOSITE:** different ▶ ADVERB *They even dressed alike.* = **similarly**, identically, equally, uniformly, correspondingly, analogously ■ **OPPOSITE:** differently

alive ADJECTIVE **1** *She does not know if he is alive or dead.* = **living**, breathing, animate, having life, subsisting, existing, functioning, alive and kicking, in the land of the living (*informal*) ■ **OPPOSITE:** dead **2** *Factories are trying to stay alive by cutting costs.* = **in existence**, existing, functioning, active, operative, in force, on-going, prevalent, existent, extant ■ **OPPOSITE:** inoperative

3 *I never expected to feel so alive in my life again.* = **lively**, spirited, active, vital, alert, eager, quick, awake, vigorous, cheerful, energetic, animated, brisk, agile, perky, chirpy (*informal*), sprightly, vivacious, full of life, spry, full of beans (*informal*), zestful ■ **OPPOSITE:** dull • **alive to** *You must be alive to opportunity!* = **aware of**, sensitive to, susceptible to, alert to, eager for, awake to, cognizant of, sensible of

all DETERMINER **1** *I'd spent all I had, every last penny.* = **the whole amount**, everything, the whole, the total, the sum, the total amount, the aggregate, the totality, the sum total, the entirety, the entire amount, the complete amount **2** *There is built-in storage space in all bedrooms.* = **every**, each, every single, every one of, each and every ▶ ADJECTIVE *In all fairness, she isn't dishonest.* = **complete**, greatest, full, total, perfect, entire, utter ▶ ADVERB = **completely**, totally, fully, entirely, absolutely, altogether, wholly, utterly ■ **RELATED WORDS:** *prefixes* pan-, panto-

allay VERB = **reduce**, quiet, relax, ease, calm, smooth, relieve, check, moderate, dull, diminish, compose, soften, blunt, soothe, subdue, lessen, alleviate, appease, quell, mitigate, assuage, pacify, mollify

allegation NOUN = **claim**, charge, statement, profession, declaration, plea, accusation, assertion, affirmation, deposition, avowal, asseveration (*formal*), averment

allege VERB = **claim**, hold, charge, challenge, state, maintain, advance, declare, assert, uphold, put forward, affirm, profess, depose, avow, aver, asseverate (*formal*) ■ **OPPOSITE:** deny

alleged ADJECTIVE = **claimed**, supposed, declared, assumed, so-called, apparent, rumoured, stated, described, asserted, designated, presumed, affirmed, professed, reputed, hypothetical, putative (*formal*), presupposed, averred, unproved

allegedly ADVERB = **supposedly**, apparently, reportedly, by all accounts, reputedly, purportedly

allegiance NOUN = **loyalty**, duty, obligation, devotion, fidelity, homage, obedience, adherence, constancy, faithfulness, troth (*archaic*), fealty ■ **OPPOSITE:** disloyalty

allegorical ADJECTIVE = **symbolic**, figurative, symbolizing, emblematic, parabolic

allegory NOUN = **symbol**, story, tale, myth, symbolism, emblem, fable, parable, apologue

a

allergic ADJECTIVE *I'm allergic to cats.*
= **sensitive**, affected, susceptible,
sensitized, hypersensitive • **allergic to**
He was allergic to risk. = **averse to**, opposed
to, hostile to, loath to, disinclined to,
antipathetic to

allergy NOUN **1** *Food allergies result in many
and varied symptoms.* = **sensitivity**, reaction,
susceptibility, antipathy, hypersensitivity,
sensitiveness **2** *I developed an allergy to the
company of couples.* = **dislike**, hatred,
hostility, aversion, loathing, disgust,
antipathy, animosity, displeasure,
antagonism, distaste, enmity, opposition,
repugnance, disinclination

alleviate VERB = **ease**, reduce, relieve,
moderate, smooth, dull, diminish, soften,
check, blunt, soothe, subdue, lessen,
lighten, quell, allay, mitigate, abate,
slacken, assuage, quench, mollify, slake,
palliate

alley NOUN = **passage**, walk, lane,
pathway, alleyway, passageway,
backstreet

alliance NOUN = **union**, league,
association, agreement, marriage,
connection, combination, coalition,
treaty, partnership, federation, pact,
compact, confederation, affinity,
affiliation, confederacy, concordat
■ **OPPOSITE:** division

allied ADJECTIVE **1** *forces from three allied
nations* = **united**, joined, linked, related,
married, joint, combined, bound,
integrated, unified, affiliated, leagued,
confederate, amalgamated, cooperating,
in league, hand in glove (*informal*), in
cahoots (*informal*) **2** *doctors and other allied
medical professionals* = **connected**, joined,
linked, tied, related, associated,
syndicated, affiliated, kindred

all-important ADJECTIVE = **essential**,
central, significant, key, necessary, vital,
critical, crucial (*informal*), pivotal,
momentous, consequential

allocate VERB = **assign**, grant, distribute,
designate, set aside, earmark, give out,
consign, allow, budget, allot, mete, share
out, apportion, appropriate

allocation NOUN **1** *During rationing we had a
sugar allocation.* = **allowance**, share,
measure, grant, portion, quota, lot, ration,
stint, stipend **2** *Town planning and land
allocation had to be co-ordinated.*
= **assignment**, allowance, rationing,
allotment, apportionment, appropriation

allot VERB = **assign**, allocate, designate, set
aside, earmark, mete, share out,
apportion, budget, appropriate

allotment NOUN **1** *She was just back from
working on her allotment.* = **plot**, patch, tract,
kitchen garden **2** *His meagre allotment of gas
had to be saved for emergencies.*
= **assignment**, share, measure, grant,
allowance, portion, quota, lot, ration,
allocation, stint, appropriation, stipend,
apportionment

allotted VERB = **assigned**, given, allocated,
designated, set aside, earmarked,
apportioned

all-out *or* **all out** ADJECTIVE *He launched an
all-out attack on his critics.* = **total**, full,
complete, determined, supreme,
maximum, outright, thorough, unlimited,
full-scale, optimum, exhaustive, resolute,
full-on (*informal*), unrestrained,
unremitting, thoroughgoing, unstinted
■ **OPPOSITE:** half-hearted ▶ ADVERB *We will
be going all out to make sure it doesn't happen
again.* = **energetically**, hard, strongly,
sharply, heavily, severely, fiercely,
vigorously, intensely, violently, powerfully,
forcibly, forcefully, with all your might, with
might and main

allow VERB **1** *Smoking will not be allowed.*
= **permit**, approve, enable, sanction,
endure, license, brook, endorse, warrant,
tolerate, put up with (*informal*), authorize,
stand, suffer, bear ■ **OPPOSITE:** prohibit
2 *Would you allow me to accompany you?* = **let**,
permit, sanction, entitle, authorize,
license, tolerate, consent to, countenance,
concede to, assent to, give leave to, give
the green light for, give a blank cheque to
■ **OPPOSITE:** forbid **3** *Please allow 28 days for
delivery.* = **give**, provide, grant, spare,
devote, assign, allocate, set aside, deduct,
earmark, remit, allot **4** *He allows that the
development may result in social inequality.*
= **acknowledge**, accept, admit, grant,
recognize, yield, concede, confess,
acquiesce • **allow for something** *You have
to allow for a certain amount of error.* = **take
into account**, consider, plan for,
accommodate, provide for, arrange for,
foresee, make provision for, make
allowances for, make concessions for, keep
in mind, set something aside for, take into
consideration

allowable ADJECTIVE = **permissible**, all
right, approved, appropriate, suitable,
acceptable, tolerable, admissible,
sufferable, sanctionable

allowance NOUN **1** *I weighed out my allowance
of sugar.* = **portion**, lot, share, amount,
measure, grant, pension, subsidy, quota,
allocation, stint, annuity, allotment,
remittance, stipend, apportionment

2 *The boy was given an allowance for his own needs.* = **pocket money**, grant, fee, payment, consideration, ration, handout, remittance **3** *those earning less than the basic tax allowance* = **concession**, discount, reduction, repayment, deduction, rebate

alloy NOUN *Bronze is an alloy of copper and tin.* = **mixture**, combination, compound, blend, hybrid, composite, amalgam, meld, admixture

all right ADJECTIVE **1** *'How was the school you attended?' 'It was all right.'* = **satisfactory**, O.K. or okay (*informal*), average, fair, sufficient, standard, acceptable, good enough, adequate, so-so (*informal*), up to scratch (*informal*), passable, up to standard, up to the mark, unobjectionable ■ **OPPOSITE:** unsatisfactory **2** *Are you all right now?* = **well**, O.K. or okay (*informal*), strong, whole (*archaic*), sound, fit, safe, healthy, hale (*old-fashioned*), unharmed, out of the woods, uninjured, unimpaired, up to par ■ **OPPOSITE:** ill ▶ ADVERB *Things have thankfully worked out all right.* = **satisfactorily**, O.K. or okay (*informal*), reasonably, well enough, adequately, suitably, acceptably, passably, unobjectionably

allude to VERB = **refer to**, suggest, mention, speak of, imply, intimate, hint at, remark on, insinuate, touch upon

allure NOUN *It's a game that has really lost its allure.* = **attractiveness**, appeal, charm, attraction, lure, temptation, glamour, persuasion, enchantment, enticement, seductiveness ▶ VERB *The dog was allured by the smell of roasting meat.* = **attract**, persuade, charm, win over, tempt, lure, seduce, entice, enchant, lead on, coax, captivate, beguile, cajole, decoy, inveigle

alluring ADJECTIVE = **attractive**, fascinating, enchanting, seductive, tempting, sexy, intriguing, fetching (*informal*), glamorous, captivating, beguiling, bewitching, come-hither, hot (*informal*) ■ **OPPOSITE:** unattractive

allusion NOUN = **reference**, mention, suggestion, hint, implication, innuendo, intimation, insinuation, casual remark, indirect reference

ally NOUN *She is a close ally of the Prime Minister.* = **partner**, friend, colleague, associate, mate (*informal*), blood *or* blud (*Brit. slang*), accessory, comrade, helper, collaborator, accomplice, confederate, co-worker, bedfellow, cobber (*Austral. & N.Z., old-fashioned, informal*), coadjutor, abettor, E hoa (*N.Z.*) ■ **OPPOSITE:** opponent
• **ally yourself with something** *or* **someone**

He will have to ally himself with the new movement. = **unite with**, join, associate with, connect with, unify, league with, affiliate with, collaborate with, join forces with, confederate, band together with

almighty ADJECTIVE **1** *strong belief in an almighty creator* = **all-powerful**, supreme, absolute, unlimited, invincible, omnipotent ■ **OPPOSITE:** powerless **2** *I had the most almighty row with my manager.* = **great**, terrible, enormous, desperate, severe, intense, awful, loud, excessive ■ **OPPOSITE:** slight

almost ADVERB = **nearly**, about, approaching, close to, virtually, practically, roughly, all but, just about, not quite, on the brink of, not far from, approximately, well-nigh, as good as

alms PLURAL NOUN = **donation**, relief, gift, charity, bounty, benefaction, koha (*N.Z.*)

aloft ADVERB **1** *Four of the nine balloons were still aloft the next day.* = **in the air**, up, higher, above, overhead, in the sky, on high, high up, up above **2** *He lifted the cup aloft.* = **upward**, skyward, heavenward

alone ADJECTIVE **1** *He was all alone in the middle of the hall.* = **solitary**, isolated, sole, separate, apart, abandoned, detached, by yourself, unattended, unaccompanied, out on a limb, unescorted, on your tod (*slang*) ■ **OPPOSITE:** accompanied **2** *Never in her life had she felt so alone.* = **lonely**, abandoned, deserted, isolated, solitary, estranged, desolate, forsaken, forlorn, destitute, lonesome (*chiefly U.S. & Canad.*), friendless ▶ ADVERB **1** *You alone should determine what is right for you.* = **solely**, only, individually, singly, exclusively, uniquely **2** *He was working alone, and did not have an accomplice.* = **by yourself**, independently, unaided, unaccompanied, without help, on your own, unassisted, without assistance, under your own steam ■ **OPPOSITE:** with help

aloof ADJECTIVE = **distant**, cold, reserved, cool, formal, remote, forbidding, detached, indifferent, chilly, unfriendly, unsympathetic, uninterested, haughty, unresponsive, supercilious, unapproachable, unsociable, standoffish ■ **OPPOSITE:** friendly

aloud ADVERB = **out loud**, clearly, plainly, distinctly, audibly, intelligibly

alphabet NOUN = **letters**, script, writing system, syllabary

already ADVERB = **before now**, before, previously, at present, by now, by then, even now, by this time, just now, by that time, heretofore, as of now

a

also ADVERB = **and**, too, further, plus, along with, in addition, as well, moreover, besides, furthermore, what's more, on top of that, to boot, additionally, into the bargain, as well as

alter VERB **1** *They have never altered their programmes.* = **modify**, change, reform, shift, vary, transform, adjust, adapt, revise, amend, diversify, remodel, tweak (*informal*), recast, reshape, metamorphose, transmute **2** *Little had altered in the village.* = **change**, turn, vary, transform, adjust, adapt, metamorphose

alteration NOUN **1** *Making some simple alterations to your diet will make you feel fitter.* = **change**, adjustment, shift, amendment, conversion, modification **2** *Her jacket and skirt were still awaiting alteration.* = **adjustment**, change, amendment, variation, conversion, transformation, adaptation, difference, revision, modification, remodelling, reformation, diversification, metamorphosis, variance, reshaping, transmutation

altercation NOUN = **argument**, row, clash, disagreement, dispute, controversy, contention, quarrel, squabble, wrangle, bickering, discord, dissension

alternate VERB **1** *Moments of beauty alternate with slapstick comedy.* = **interchange**, change, alter, fluctuate, intersperse, take turns, oscillate, chop and change, follow one another, follow in turn **2** *Now you just alternate layers of that mixture and eggplant.* = **intersperse**, interchange, exchange, swap, stagger, rotate ▶ ADJECTIVE **1** *They were streaked with alternate bands of colour.* = **alternating**, interchanging, every other, rotating, every second, sequential **2** *alternate forms of medical treatment* = **substitute**, alternative, other, different, replacement, complementary ▶ NOUN *In most jurisdictions, twelve jurors and two alternates are chosen.* = **substitute**, reserve, deputy, relief, replacement, stand-by, makeshift

alternating ADJECTIVE = **interchanging**, changing, shifting, swinging, rotating, fluctuating, occurring by turns, oscillating, vacillating, seesawing

alternative NOUN *New treatments may provide an alternative to painkillers.* = **substitute**, choice, other, option, preference, recourse ▶ ADJECTIVE *There are alternative methods of transport available.* = **different**, other, substitute, alternate

alternatively ADVERB = **or**, instead, otherwise, on the other hand, if not,

then again, as an alternative, by way of alternative, as another option

although CONJUNCTION = **though**, while, even if, even though, whilst, albeit, despite the fact that, notwithstanding, even supposing, tho'

altitude NOUN = **height**, summit, peak, elevation, loftiness

altogether ADVERB **1** *She wasn't altogether sorry to be leaving.* = **absolutely**, quite, completely, totally, perfectly, fully, thoroughly, wholly, utterly, downright, one hundred per cent (*informal*), undisputedly, lock, stock and barrel **2** *The choice of language is altogether different.* = **completely**, all, fully, entirely, comprehensively, thoroughly, wholly, every inch, one hundred per cent (*informal*), in every respect ■ OPPOSITE: partially **3** *Altogether, it was a delightful town garden.* = **on the whole**, generally, mostly, in general, collectively, all things considered, on average, for the most part, all in all, on balance, in toto (*Latin*), as a whole **4** *Altogether seven inmates escaped.* = **in total**, in all, all told, taken together, in sum, everything included, in toto (*Latin*)

> USAGE The single-word form *altogether* should not be used as an alternative to *all together* because the meanings are very distinct. *Altogether* is an adverb meaning 'absolutely' or, in a different sense, 'in total'. *All together*, however, means 'all at the same time' or 'all in the same place'. The distinction can be seen in the following example: *altogether there were six or seven families sharing the flat's facilities* means 'in total', while *there were six or seven families all together in one flat*, means 'all crowded in together'.

altruism NOUN = **selflessness**, charity, consideration, goodwill, generosity, self-sacrifice, philanthropy, benevolence, magnanimity, humanitarianism, unselfishness, beneficence, charitableness, greatheartedness, bigheartedness ■ OPPOSITE: self-interest

altruistic ADJECTIVE = **selfless**, generous, humanitarian, charitable, benevolent, considerate, self-sacrificing, philanthropic, unselfish, public-spirited ■ OPPOSITE: self-interested

always ADVERB **1** *Always lock your garage.* = **habitually**, regularly, every time, inevitably, consistently, invariably, aye (*Scot.*), perpetually, without exception, customarily, unfailingly, on every occasion, day in, day out ■ OPPOSITE: seldom **2** = **forever**, for keeps, eternally, for all time, evermore, till the cows come home (*informal*), till Doomsday **3** *She was always moving things around.* = **continually**, constantly, all the time, forever, repeatedly, aye (*Scot.*), endlessly, persistently, eternally, perpetually, incessantly, interminably, unceasingly, everlastingly, in perpetuum (*Latin*)

amalgam NOUN = **combination**, mixture, compound, blend, union, composite, fusion, alloy, amalgamation, meld, admixture

amalgamate VERB = **combine**, unite, ally, compound, blend, incorporate, integrate, merge, fuse, mingle, alloy, coalesce, meld, commingle, intermix ■ **OPPOSITE:** divide

amalgamation NOUN = **combination**, union, joining, mixing, alliance, coalition, merger, mixture, compound, blend, integration, composite, fusion, mingling, alloy, amalgamating, incorporation, amalgam, meld, admixture, commingling

amass VERB = **collect**, gather, assemble, compile, accumulate, aggregate, pile up, garner, hoard, scrape together, rake up, heap up

amateur NOUN = **nonprofessional**, outsider, layperson, layman *or* woman *or* person, dilettante, non-specialist, dabbler

amateurish ADJECTIVE = **unprofessional**, amateur, crude, bungling, clumsy, inexpert, unaccomplished, unskilful ■ **OPPOSITE:** professional

amaze VERB = **astonish**, surprise, shock, stun, alarm, stagger, startle, bewilder, astound, daze, confound, stupefy, flabbergast, bowl someone over (*informal*), boggle someone's mind, dumbfound

amazement NOUN = **astonishment**, surprise, wonder, shock, confusion, admiration, awe, marvel, bewilderment, wonderment, perplexity, stupefaction

amazing ADJECTIVE = **astonishing**, striking, surprising, brilliant, stunning, impressive, overwhelming, staggering, sensational (*informal*), bewildering, breathtaking, astounding, eye-opening, wondrous (*archaic*, *literary*), mind-boggling, jaw-dropping, stupefying

ambassador NOUN = **representative**, minister, agent, deputy, diplomat, envoy, consul, attaché, emissary, legate, plenipotentiary

ambience NOUN = **atmosphere**, feel, setting, air, quality, character, spirit, surroundings, tone, mood, impression, flavour, temper, tenor, aura, complexion, vibes (*slang*), vibrations (*slang*), milieu

ambiguity NOUN = **vagueness**, doubt, puzzle, uncertainty, obscurity, enigma, equivocation, inconclusiveness, indefiniteness, dubiety, dubiousness, tergiversation, indeterminateness, equivocality, doubtfulness, equivocacy

ambiguous ADJECTIVE = **unclear**, puzzling, uncertain, obscure, vague, doubtful, dubious, enigmatic, indefinite, inconclusive, cryptic, indeterminate, equivocal, Delphic, oracular, enigmatical, clear as mud (*informal*) ■ **OPPOSITE:** clear

ambition NOUN **1** *My ambition is to sail round the world.* = **goal**, end, hope, design, dream, target, aim, wish, purpose, desire, intention, objective, intent, aspiration, Holy Grail (*informal*) **2** *a mixture of ambition and ruthlessness* = **enterprise**, longing, drive, fire, spirit, desire, passion, enthusiasm, warmth, striving, initiative, aspiration, yearning, devotion, zeal, verve, zest, fervour, eagerness, gusto, hankering, get-up-and-go (*informal*), ardour, keenness, avidity, fervency

ambitious ADJECTIVE **1** *He's a very ambitious lad.* = **enterprising**, spirited, keen, active, daring, eager, intent, enthusiastic, hopeful, striving, vigorous, aspiring, energetic, adventurous, avid, zealous, intrepid, resourceful, purposeful, desirous ■ **OPPOSITE:** unambitious **2** *Their goal was extraordinarily ambitious.* = **demanding**, trying, hard, taxing, difficult, challenging, tough, severe, impressive, exhausting, exacting, bold, elaborate, formidable, energetic, strenuous, pretentious, arduous, grandiose, industrious ■ **OPPOSITE:** modest

ambivalence NOUN = **indecision**, doubt, opposition, conflict, uncertainty, contradiction, wavering, fluctuation, hesitancy, equivocation, vacillation, irresolution

ambivalent ADJECTIVE = **undecided**, mixed, conflicting, opposed, uncertain, doubtful, unsure, contradictory, wavering, unresolved, fluctuating, hesitant, inconclusive, debatable, equivocal, vacillating, warring, irresolute ■ **OPPOSITE:** definite

amble VERB = **stroll**, walk, wander, ramble, meander, saunter, dawdle, mosey (*informal*)

ambush VERB *Rebels ambushed and killed 10 patrolmen.* = **trap**, attack, surprise, deceive, dupe, ensnare, waylay, ambuscade, bushwhack (*U.S.*) ▶ NOUN *A police officer has been shot dead in an ambush.* = **trap**, snare, attack, lure, waylaying, ambuscade

ameliorate VERB = **improve**, better, benefit, reform, advance, promote, amend, elevate, raise, mend, mitigate, make better, assuage, meliorate

a

USAGE *Ameliorate* is sometimes confused with *alleviate* but the words are not synonymous. *Ameliorate* comes ultimately from the Latin for 'better', and means 'to improve'. The nouns it typically goes with are *condition* and *situation*. *Alleviate* means 'to lessen', and frequently occurs with *poverty*, *suffering*, *pain*, *symptoms*, and *effects*. Occasionally *ameliorate* is used with *effects* and *poverty* where the other verb may be more appropriate.

amenable ADJECTIVE = **receptive**, open, susceptible, responsive, agreeable, compliant, tractable, acquiescent, persuadable, able to be influenced ■ **OPPOSITE:** stubborn

amend VERB *The committee put forward proposals to amend the penal system.* = **change**, improve, reform, fix, correct, repair, edit, alter, enhance, update, revise, modify, remedy, rewrite, mend, rectify, tweak (*informal*), ameliorate, redraw

amendment NOUN **1** *an amendment to the defence bill* = **addition**, change, adjustment, attachment, adaptation, revision, modification, alteration, remodelling, reformation, clarification, adjunct, addendum **2** *We are making a few amendments to the document.* = **change**, improvement, repair, edit, remedy, correction, revision, modification, alteration, mending, enhancement, reform, betterment, rectification, amelioration, emendation

amends PLURAL NOUN *I want to make amends for my earlier mistake.* = **compensation**, apology, restoration, redress, reparation, indemnity, restitution, atonement, recompense, expiation, requital

amenity NOUN **1** *The hotel amenities include a health club and banqueting rooms.* = **facility**, service, advantage, comfort, convenience **2** *a man of little amenity* = **refinement**, politeness, affability, amiability, courtesy, mildness, pleasantness, suavity, agreeableness, complaisance ■ **OPPOSITE:** rudeness

American ADJECTIVE *the American ambassador at the UN* = **Yankee** or **Yank**, U.S. ► NOUN *The 1990 Nobel Prize for medicine was won by two Americans.* = **Yankee** or **Yank**, Yankee Doodle

amiable ADJECTIVE = **pleasant**, kind, kindly, pleasing, friendly, attractive, engaging, charming, obliging, delightful, cheerful, benign, winning, agreeable, good-humoured, lovable, sociable, genial, affable, congenial, winsome, good-natured, sweet-tempered, likable or likeable ■ **OPPOSITE:** unfriendly

amicable ADJECTIVE = **friendly**, kindly, brotherly, civil, neighbourly, peaceful, polite, harmonious, good-humoured, amiable, courteous, cordial, sociable, fraternal, peaceable ■ **OPPOSITE:** unfriendly

amid or **amidst** PREPOSITION **1** *She cancelled a foreign trip amid growing concerns of a domestic crisis.* = **during**, among, at a time of, in an atmosphere of **2** *a tiny bungalow amid clusters of trees* = **in the middle of**, among, surrounded by, amongst, in the midst of, in the thick of

amiss ADJECTIVE *Their instincts warned them something was amiss.* = **wrong**, mistaken, confused, false, inappropriate, rotten, incorrect, faulty, inaccurate, unsuitable, improper, defective, out of order, awry, erroneous, untoward, fallacious ■ **OPPOSITE:** right • **take something amiss** *He took it amiss when I asked to speak to someone else.* = **take as an insult**, take wrongly, take as offensive, take out of turn

ammunition NOUN = **munitions**, rounds, shot, shells, powder, explosives, cartridges, armaments, materiel, shot and shell

amnesty NOUN = **general pardon**, mercy, pardoning, immunity, forgiveness, reprieve, oblivion, remission, clemency, dispensation, absolution, condonation

amok or **amuck** ADVERB • **run amok** = **go wild**, turn violent, go berserk, lose control, go into a frenzy

among or **amongst** PREPOSITION **1** *They walked among the crowds in the large town square.* = **in the midst of**, with, together with, in the middle of, amid, surrounded by, amidst, in the thick of **2** *Among the speakers was the new Indian ambassador.* = **in the group of**, one of, part of, included in, in the company of, in the class of, in the number of **3** *Most of the furniture was distributed among friends.* = **between**, to **4** *The directors have been arguing amongst themselves.* = **with one another**, mutually, by all of, by the whole of, by the joint action of

amoral ADJECTIVE = **unethical**, nonmoral, unvirtuous

USAGE *Amoral* is sometimes confused with *immoral*. The *a-* at the beginning of the word means 'without' or 'lacking', so the word is properly used of people who have no moral code, or about places or situations where moral considerations do not apply: *the film was violent and amoral*. In contrast *immoral* should be used to talk about the breaking of moral rules, as in: *I think drug dealing is the most immoral and evil of all human activities.*

amorous ADJECTIVE = **loving**, in love, tender, passionate, fond, erotic, affectionate, ardent, impassioned, doting, enamoured, lustful, attached, lovesick, amatory ■ **OPPOSITE:** cold

amorphous ADJECTIVE = **shapeless**, vague, irregular, nondescript, indeterminate, unstructured, nebulous, formless, inchoate, characterless, unformed, unshaped, unshapen ■ **OPPOSITE:** definite

amount NOUN **1** *I still do a certain amount of work for them.* = **quantity**, lot, measure, size, supply, mass, volume, capacity, extent, bulk, number, magnitude, expanse **2** *If you always pay the full amount, this won't affect you.* = **total**, whole, mass, addition, sum, lot, extent, aggregate, entirety, totality, sum total • **amount to something 1** *The banks have what amounts to a monopoly.* = **add up to**, mean, total, equal, constitute, comprise, aggregate, purport, be equivalent to **2** *My music teacher said I'd never amount to anything.* = **come to**, become, grow to, develop into, advance to, progress to, mature into

> **USAGE** Although it is common to use a plural noun after *amount of*, for example in the *amount of people* and the *amount of goods*, this should be avoided. Preferred alternatives would be to use *quantity*, as in the *quantity of people*, or *number*, as in the *number of goods*.

amour NOUN = **love affair**, relationship, affair, romance, intrigue, liaison, affaire de coeur (*French*)

ample ADJECTIVE **1** *The design gave ample space for a good-sized kitchen.* = **plenty of**, great, rich, liberal, broad, generous, lavish, spacious, abounding, abundant, plentiful, expansive, copious, roomy, unrestricted, voluminous, capacious, profuse, commodious, plenteous ■ **OPPOSITE:** insufficient **2** *He was asleep with his arms crossed on his ample stomach.* = **large**, great, big, full, wide, broad, extensive, generous, abundant, voluminous, bountiful

amplification NOUN **1** *a voice that needed no amplification* = **increase**, boosting, stretching, strengthening, expansion, extension, widening, raising, heightening, deepening, lengthening, enlargement, intensification, magnification, dilation, augmentation **2** *They demanded amplification of the imprecise statement.* = **explanation**, development, expansion, supplementing, fleshing out, elaboration, rounding out, augmentation, expatiation

amplify VERB **1** *The music was amplified with microphones.* = **expand**, raise, extend, boost, stretch, strengthen, increase, widen, intensify, heighten, deepen, enlarge, lengthen, magnify, augment, dilate ■ **OPPOSITE:** reduce **2** *Intelligent guesswork must be used to amplify the facts.* = **go into detail**, develop, explain, expand, supplement, elaborate, augment, flesh out, round out, enlarge on, expatiate ■ **OPPOSITE:** simplify

amplitude NOUN **1** *The operatic amplitude of her voice suits the occasion.* = **extent**, reach, range, size, mass, sweep, dimension, bulk, scope, width, magnitude, compass, greatness, breadth, expanse, vastness, spaciousness, bigness, largeness, hugeness, capaciousness **2** *The character comes to imply an amplitude of meanings.* = **fullness**, abundance, richness, plethora, profusion, completeness, plenitude, copiousness, ampleness

amply ADVERB = **fully**, well, greatly, completely, richly, liberally, thoroughly, substantially, lavishly, extensively, generously, abundantly, profusely, copiously, plentifully, unstintingly, bountifully, without stinting, plenteously, capaciously ■ **OPPOSITE:** insufficiently

amputate VERB = **cut off**, remove, separate, sever, curtail, truncate, lop off

amuck *see* **amok**

amuse VERB **1** *The thought seemed to amuse her.* = **entertain**, please, delight, charm, cheer, tickle, gratify, beguile, enliven, regale, gladden ■ **OPPOSITE:** bore **2** *Put a selection of toys in his cot to amuse him if he wakes early.* = **occupy**, interest, involve, engage, entertain, absorb, divert, engross

amusement NOUN **1** *He watched with amusement to see the child so absorbed.* = **enjoyment**, delight, entertainment, cheer, laughter, mirth, hilarity, merriment, gladdening, beguilement, regalement ■ **OPPOSITE:** boredom **2** *It's unacceptable to keep animals confined for our amusement.* = **diversion**, interest, sport, pleasing, fun, pleasure, recreation, entertainment, gratification **3** *People had very few amusements to choose from in those days.* = **pastime**, game, sport, joke, entertainment, hobby, recreation, distraction, diversion, lark, prank

amusing ADJECTIVE = **funny**, humorous, gratifying, laughable, farcical, comical, droll, interesting, pleasing, charming, cheering, entertaining, comic, pleasant, lively, diverting, delightful, enjoyable, cheerful, witty, merry, gladdening, facetious, jocular, rib-tickling, waggish ■ **OPPOSITE:** boring

anaemic ADJECTIVE **1** *Losing a lot of blood makes you tired and anaemic.* = **pale**, weak, dull, frail, feeble, wan, sickly, bloodless, colourless, infirm, pallid, ashen, characterless, enervated, like death warmed up (*informal*) ■ **OPPOSITE:** rosy **2** *We will see some economic recovery, but it will be very anaemic.* = **weak**, feeble

anaesthetic NOUN *The operation is carried out under general anaesthetic.* = **painkiller**, narcotic, sedative, opiate, anodyne, analgesic, soporific, stupefacient, stupefactive ▶ ADJECTIVE *They are rendered unconscious by anaesthetic darts.* = **painkilling**, dulling, numbing, narcotic, sedative, opiate, deadening, anodyne, analgesic, soporific, sleep-inducing, stupefacient, stupefactive

analogous ADJECTIVE = **similar**, like, related, equivalent, parallel, resembling, alike, corresponding, comparable, akin, homologous ■ **OPPOSITE:** different

> **USAGE** The correct word to use after *analogous* is *to*, not *with*, for example: *swimming has no event that is analogous to the 100 metres in athletics* (not *analogous with the 100 metres in athletics*).

analogy NOUN = **similarity**, relation, comparison, parallel, correspondence, resemblance, correlation, likeness, equivalence, homology, similitude

analyse VERB **1** *This book teaches you to analyse causes of stress in your life.* = **examine**, test, study, research, judge, estimate, survey, investigate, interpret, evaluate, inspect, work over **2** *We haven't had time to analyse those samples yet.* = **break down**, consider, study, separate, divide, resolve, dissolve, dissect, think through, assay, anatomize

analysis NOUN **1** *We did an analysis of the way they have spent money in the past.* = **study**, reasoning, opinion, judgment, interpretation, evaluation, estimation, dissection **2** *They collect blood samples for analysis at the laboratory.* = **examination**, test, division, inquiry, investigation, resolution, interpretation, breakdown, scanning, separation, evaluation, scrutiny, sifting, anatomy, dissolution, dissection, assay, perusal, anatomization

analytic or **analytical** ADJECTIVE = **rational**, questioning, testing, detailed, searching, organized, exact, precise, logical, systematic, inquiring, diagnostic, investigative, dissecting, explanatory, discrete, inquisitive, interpretive, studious, interpretative, expository

anarchic ADJECTIVE = **lawless**, rioting, confused, disordered, revolutionary, chaotic, rebellious, riotous, disorganized, misruled, ungoverned, misgoverned ■ **OPPOSITE:** law-abiding

anarchist NOUN = **revolutionary**, rebel, terrorist, insurgent, nihilist

anarchy NOUN = **lawlessness**, revolution, riot, disorder, confusion, chaos, rebellion, misrule, disorganization, misgovernment ■ **OPPOSITE:** order

anathema NOUN = **abomination**, bête noire, enemy, pariah, bane, bugbear

anatomy NOUN **1** *He had worked extensively on the anatomy of living animals.* = **structure**, build, make-up, frame, framework, composition **2** *a troubling essay on the anatomy of nationhood* = **examination**, study, division, inquiry, investigation, analysis, dismemberment, dissection

ancestor NOUN = **forefather**, predecessor, precursor, forerunner, forebear, antecedent, progenitor, tupuna *or* tipuna (*N.Z.*) ■ **OPPOSITE:** descendant

ancestral ADJECTIVE = **inherited**, hereditary, patriarchal, antecedent, forefatherly, genealogical, lineal, ancestorial

ancestry NOUN = **origin**, house, family, line, race, stock, blood, ancestors, descent, pedigree, extraction, lineage, forebears, antecedents, parentage, forefathers, genealogy, derivation, progenitors

anchor NOUN *We lost our anchor, which caused the boat to drift.* = **mooring**, hook (*Nautical*), bower (*Nautical*), kedge, drogue, sheet anchor ▶ VERB **1** *The ship was anchored by the pier.* = **moor**, harbour, dock, tie up, kedge **2** *We anchored off the beach.* = **dock**, moor, harbour, drop anchor, kedge, cast anchor, drop the hook, let go the anchor, lay anchor, come to anchor **3** *The child's seatbelt was not properly anchored in the car.* = **secure**, tie, fix, bind, chain, attach, bolt, fasten, affix

anchorage NOUN = **berth**, haven, port, harbour, dock, quay, dockage, moorage, harbourage

ancient ADJECTIVE **1** *They believed ancient Greece and Rome were vital sources of learning.* = **classical**, old, former, past, bygone, primordial, primeval, olden **2** *ancient rites* = **very old**, early, aged, antique, obsolete, archaic, age-old, bygone, antiquated, hoary, olden, superannuated, antediluvian, timeworn, old as the hills **3** = **old-fashioned**, dated, outdated, obsolete, out of date, unfashionable, outmoded, passé ■ **OPPOSITE:** up-to-date

ancillary ADJECTIVE = **supplementary**, supporting, extra, additional, secondary, subsidiary, accessory, subordinate, auxiliary, contributory ■ **OPPOSITE:** major

and CONJUNCTION **1** *When he returned, she and her boyfriend had already gone.* = **also**, including, along with, together with, in addition to, as well as **2** *These airlines fly to isolated places. And business travellers use them.* = **moreover**, plus, furthermore

> **USAGE** The forms *try and do something* and *wait and do something* should only be used in informal or spoken English. In more formal writing, use *try to* and *wait to*, for example: *we must try to prevent this happening* (not *try and prevent*).

android NOUN = **robot**, automaton, humanoid, cyborg, mechanical man *or* woman, bionic man *or* woman

anecdote NOUN = **story**, tale, sketch, short story, yarn (*informal*), reminiscence, urban myth, urban legend

anew ADVERB = **again**, once again, once more, over again, from the beginning, from scratch, another time, afresh

angel NOUN **1** *a choir of angels* = **divine messenger**, spirit, cherub, archangel, seraph, guardian being, guardian spirit **2** *Thank you. You're an angel.* = **dear**, ideal, beauty, saint, treasure, darling, dream, jewel, gem, paragon

angelic ADJECTIVE **1** *an angelic little face* = **pure**, beautiful, lovely, innocent, entrancing, virtuous, saintly, adorable, beatific **2** *angelic choirs* = **heavenly**, celestial, ethereal, cherubic, seraphic ■ **OPPOSITE:** demonic

anger NOUN *He cried with anger and frustration.* = **rage**, passion, outrage, temper, fury, resentment, irritation, wrath, indignation, annoyance, agitation, ire, antagonism, displeasure, exasperation, irritability, spleen, pique, ill temper, vehemence, vexation, high dudgeon, ill humour, choler ■ **OPPOSITE:** calmness
▶ VERB *The decision to allow more construction angered the residents.* = **enrage**, provoke, outrage, annoy, offend, excite, irritate, infuriate, hassle (*informal*), aggravate (*informal*), incense, fret, gall, madden, exasperate, nettle, vex, affront, displease, rile, pique, get on someone's nerves (*informal*), antagonize, get someone's back up, put someone's back up, nark (*Brit., Austral. & N.Z. slang*), make someone's blood boil, get in someone's hair (*informal*), get someone's dander up (*informal*)
■ **OPPOSITE:** soothe

angle NOUN **1** *The boat was leaning at a 30-degree angle.* = **gradient**, bank, slope, incline, inclination **2** *brackets to adjust the steering wheel's angle* = **intersection**, point, edge, corner, knee, bend, elbow, crook, crotch, nook, cusp **3** *He was considering the idea from all angles.* = **point of view**, position, approach, direction, aspect, perspective, outlook, viewpoint, slant, standpoint, take (*informal*), side

angler NOUN = **fisherman** *or* **woman**, fisher, piscator *or* piscatrix

angry ADJECTIVE = **furious**, cross, heated, mad (*informal*), raging, provoked, outraged, annoyed, passionate, irritated, raving, hacked (off) (*U.S. slang*), choked, infuriated, hot, incensed, enraged, ranting, exasperated, irritable, resentful, nettled, snappy, indignant, irate, tumultuous, displeased, uptight (*informal*), riled, up in arms, incandescent, ill-tempered, irascible, antagonized, waspish, piqued, hot under the collar (*informal*), on the warpath, hopping mad (*informal*), foaming at the mouth, choleric, splenetic, wrathful, at daggers drawn, in high dudgeon, as black as thunder, ireful, tooshie (*Austral. slang*), off the air (*Austral. slang*), aerated
■ **OPPOSITE:** calm

> **USAGE** Some people feel it is more correct to talk about being *angry with* someone than being *angry at* them. In British English, *angry with* is still more common than *angry at*, but *angry at* is used more commonly in American English.

angst NOUN = **anxiety**, worry, distress, torment, unease, apprehension, agitation, malaise, perturbation, vexation, fretfulness, disquietude, inquietude (*formal*) ■ **OPPOSITE:** peace of mind

anguish NOUN = **suffering**, pain, torture, distress, grief, misery, agony, torment, sorrow, woe, heartache, heartbreak, pang, throe

anguished ADJECTIVE = **suffering**, wounded, tortured, distressed, tormented, afflicted, agonized, grief-stricken, wretched, brokenhearted

angular ADJECTIVE = **skinny**, spare, lean, gaunt, bony, lanky, scrawny, lank, rangy, rawboned, macilent (*rare*)

animal NOUN **1** *I was attacked by wild animals.* = **creature**, beast, brute **2** *Desperation can turn people into animals.* = **brute**, devil, monster, savage, beast, bastard (*informal, offensive*), villain, barbarian, swine (*informal*), wild person ▶ ADJECTIVE *the animal side of human nature* = **physical**, gross, fleshly, bodily, sensual, carnal, brutish, bestial, animalistic ■ **RELATED WORD:** prefix zoo-

animate ADJECTIVE *the study of animate and inanimate aspects of the natural world* = **living**, live, moving, alive, breathing, alive and kicking ▶ VERB *There was little about the game to animate the crowd.* = **enliven**, encourage, excite, urge, inspire, stir, spark, move, fire, spur, stimulate, revive, activate, rouse, prod, quicken, incite, instigate, kick-start (*informal*), impel, energize, kindle, embolden, liven up, breathe life into, invigorate, gladden, gee up, vitalize, vivify, inspirit ■ **OPPOSITE:** inhibit

animated ADJECTIVE = **lively**, spirited, quick, excited, active, vital, dynamic, enthusiastic, passionate, vivid, vigorous, energetic, vibrant, brisk, buoyant, ardent, airy, fervent, zealous, elated, ebullient, sparky, sprightly, vivacious, gay, alive and kicking, full of beans (*informal*), zestful ■ **OPPOSITE:** listless

animation NOUN = **liveliness**, life, action, activity, energy, spirit, passion, enthusiasm, excitement, pep, sparkle, vitality, vigour, zeal, verve, zest, fervour, high spirits, dynamism, buoyancy, elation, exhilaration, gaiety, ardour, vibrancy, brio, zing (*informal*), vivacity, ebullience, briskness, airiness, sprightliness, pizzazz or pizazz (*informal*)

animosity NOUN = **hostility**, hate, hatred, resentment, bitterness, malice, antagonism, antipathy, enmity, acrimony, rancour, bad blood, ill will, animus, malevolence, virulence, malignity ■ **OPPOSITE:** friendliness

animus NOUN = **ill will**, hate, hostility, hatred, resentment, bitterness, malice, animosity, antagonism, antipathy, enmity, acrimony, rancour, bad blood, malevolence, virulence, malignity

annals PLURAL NOUN = **records**, history, accounts, registers, journals, memorials, archives, chronicles

annex VERB **1** *Rome annexed the Nabatean kingdom in 106 AD.* = **seize**, take over, appropriate, acquire, occupy, conquer, expropriate (*formal*), arrogate **2** *A gate goes through to the annexed garden.* = **join**, unite, add, connect, attach, tack, adjoin, fasten, affix, append (*formal*), subjoin ■ **OPPOSITE:** detach

annexation NOUN = **seizure**, takeover, occupation, conquest, appropriation, annexing, expropriation (*formal*), arrogation

annexe NOUN **1** *They are planning to set up a museum in an annexe to the theatre.* = **extension**, wing, ell, supplementary building **2** *The annexe lists and discusses eight*

titles. = **appendix**, addition, supplement, attachment, adjunct, addendum, affixment

annihilate VERB = **destroy**, abolish, wipe out, erase, eradicate, extinguish, obliterate, liquidate, root out, exterminate, nullify, extirpate, wipe from the face of the earth, kennet (*Austral. slang*), jeff (*Austral. slang*)

annihilation NOUN = **destruction**, wiping out, abolition, extinction, extinguishing, liquidation, rooting out, extermination, eradication, erasure, obliteration, nullification, extirpation

anniversary NOUN = **jubilee**, remembrance, commemoration

annotate VERB = **make notes on**, explain, note, illustrate, comment on, interpret, gloss, footnote, commentate, elucidate, make observations on

annotation NOUN = **note**, comment, explanation, observation, interpretation, illustration, commentary, gloss, footnote, exegesis, explication, elucidation

announce VERB **1** *The couple were planning to announce their engagement.* = **make known**, tell, report, reveal, publish, declare, advertise, broadcast, disclose, post, tweet, intimate, proclaim, trumpet, make public, publicize, divulge, promulgate, propound, shout from the rooftops (*informal*) ■ **OPPOSITE:** keep secret **2** *The doorbell of the shop announced the arrival of a customer.* = **be a sign of**, signal, herald, warn of, signify, augur, harbinger, presage, foretell, portend, betoken

announcement NOUN **1** *There has been no formal announcement by either government.* = **statement**, communication, broadcast, explanation, publication, declaration, advertisement, testimony, disclosure, bulletin, communiqué, proclamation, utterance, intimation, promulgation, divulgence **2** *the announcement of their engagement* = **declaration**, report, reporting, publication, revelation, disclosure, proclamation, intimation, promulgation, divulgence

announcer NOUN = **presenter**, newscaster, reporter, commentator, broadcaster, newsreader, master or mistress of ceremonies, anchorman or woman or person, anchor

annoy VERB = **irritate**, trouble, bore, anger, harry, bother, disturb, provoke, get (*informal*), bug (*informal*), needle (*informal*), plague, tease, harass, hassle (*informal*), aggravate (*informal*), badger, gall, madden, ruffle, exasperate, nettle, molest, pester, vex, displease, irk, bedevil, rile, peeve, get under your skin (*informal*), get on your nerves (*informal*), nark (*Brit., Austral. & N.Z. slang*), get up your nose (*informal*), give someone grief (*Brit. & S. African*), make your blood boil, rub someone up the wrong way (*informal*), get your goat (*slang*), get in your hair (*informal*), get on your wick (*Brit. slang*), get your dander up (*informal*), get your back up, incommode (*formal*), put your back up, hack you off (*informal*) ■ **OPPOSITE:** soothe

annoyance NOUN 1 *To her annoyance the stranger did not go away.* = **irritation**, trouble, anger, bother, grief (*informal*), harassment, disturbance, hassle (*informal*), nuisance, provocation, displeasure, exasperation, aggravation (*informal*), vexation, pique, bedevilment 2 *Snoring can be more than an annoyance.* = **nuisance**, bother, pain (*informal*), bind (*informal*), bore, drag (*informal*), plague, tease, pest, gall, pain in the neck (*informal*)

annoyed ADJECTIVE = **irritated**, bothered, harassed, hassled (*informal*), aggravated (*informal*), maddened, ruffled, exasperated, nettled, vexed, miffed (*informal*), displeased, irked, riled, harried, peeved (*informal*), piqued, browned off (*informal*)

annoying ADJECTIVE = **irritating**, boring, disturbing, provoking, teasing, harassing, aggravating (*informal*), troublesome, galling, maddening, exasperating, displeasing, bedevilling, peeving (*informal*), irksome, bothersome, vexatious ■ **OPPOSITE:** delightful

annual ADJECTIVE 1 *the annual conference of the trade union movement* = **once a year**, yearly 2 *annual costs, £1,600* = **yearlong**, yearly

annually ADVERB 1 *Companies report to their shareholders annually.* = **once a year**, yearly, each year, every year, per year, by the year, every twelve months, per annum, year after year 2 *They hire 300 staff annually.* = **per year**, yearly, each year, every year, by the year, per annum

annul VERB = **invalidate**, reverse, cancel, abolish, void, repeal, recall, revoke, retract, negate, rescind, nullify, obviate, abrogate, countermand, declare or render null and void ■ **OPPOSITE:** restore

anodyne ADJECTIVE *Their quarterly meetings were anodyne affairs.* = **bland**, dull, boring, insipid, unexciting, uninspiring, uninteresting, mind-numbing (*informal*) ▶ NOUN *Leisure is a kind of anodyne.* = **painkiller**, narcotic, palliative, analgesic, pain reliever

anoint VERB 1 *He anointed my forehead with oil.* = **smear**, oil, rub, grease, spread over, daub, embrocate 2 *The Pope has anointed him as Archbishop.* = **consecrate**, bless, sanctify, hallow, anele (*archaic*)

anomalous ADJECTIVE = **unusual**, odd, rare, bizarre, exceptional, peculiar, eccentric, abnormal, irregular, inconsistent, off-the-wall (*slang*), incongruous, deviating, oddball (*informal*), atypical, aberrant, outré ■ **OPPOSITE:** normal

anomaly NOUN = **irregularity**, departure, exception, abnormality, rarity, inconsistency, deviation, eccentricity, oddity, aberration, peculiarity, incongruity

anon ADVERB = **soon**, presently, shortly, promptly, before long, forthwith, betimes (*archaic*), erelong (*archaic, poetic*), in a couple of shakes (*informal*)

anonymity NOUN 1 *Both mother and daughter have requested anonymity.* = **namelessness**, innominateness 2 *the anonymity of the rented room* = **unremarkability** or **unremarkableness**, characterlessness, unsingularity

anonymous ADJECTIVE 1 *You can remain anonymous if you wish.* = **unnamed**, unknown, unidentified, nameless, unacknowledged, incognito, unauthenticated, innominate ■ **OPPOSITE:** identified 2 *I heard that an anonymous note was actually being circulated.* = **unsigned**, uncredited, unattributed, unattested ■ **OPPOSITE:** signed 3 *It's nice to stay in a home rather than an anonymous holiday flat.* = **nondescript**, impersonal, faceless, colourless, undistinguished, unexceptional, characterless

answer VERB 1 *He paused before answering.* = **reply**, explain, respond, resolve, acknowledge, react, return, retort, rejoin, refute ■ **OPPOSITE:** ask 2 *We must ensure we answer real needs.* = **satisfy**, meet, serve, fit, fill, suit, solve, fulfil, suffice, measure up to ▶ NOUN 1 *Without waiting for an answer, he turned and went in.* = **reply**, response, reaction, resolution, explanation, plea, comeback, retort, report, return, defence, acknowledgement, riposte, counterattack, refutation, rejoinder ■ **OPPOSITE:** question 2 *Simply marking an answer wrong will not help the student.* = **solution**, resolution, explanation 3 *Prison is not the answer for most young offenders.* = **remedy**, solution, vindication • **answer to someone** *He answers to a boss he has met once in 18 months.* = **be responsible to**, obey, work under, be ruled by, be managed by, be subordinate to, be accountable to, be answerable to

a

answerable ADJECTIVE = **responsible for** or **to**, to blame for, liable for or to, accountable for or to, chargeable for, subject to

answer back VERB = **be impertinent**, argue, dispute, disagree, retort, contradict, rebut, talk back, be cheeky

antagonism NOUN = **hostility**, competition, opposition, conflict, rivalry, contention, friction, discord, antipathy, dissension ■ **OPPOSITE:** friendship

antagonist NOUN = **opponent**, rival, opposer, enemy, competitor, contender, foe (formal, literary), adversary

antagonistic ADJECTIVE = **hostile**, opposed, resistant, at odds, incompatible, set against, averse, unfriendly, at variance, inimical, antipathetic, ill-disposed

> **USAGE** A useful synonym for *antagonistic*, for example in *public opinion is antagonistic to nuclear energy*, is *averse*. However, this alternative should be used with care as a very common error is to confuse it with *adverse*. *Averse* is usually followed by *to* and is meant to convey a strong dislike or hostility towards something, normally expressed by a person or people. *Adverse* is wrong in this context and should be used in relation to conditions or results: *adverse road conditions*.

antagonize VERB = **annoy**, anger, insult, offend, irritate, alienate, hassle (informal), aggravate (informal), gall, repel, estrange, get under your skin (informal), get on your nerves (informal), nark (Brit., Austral. & N.Z. slang), get up your nose (informal), be on your back (slang), rub (someone) up the wrong way (informal), disaffect, get in your hair (informal), get on your wick (Brit. slang), hack you off (informal) ■ **OPPOSITE:** pacify

antecedent ADJECTIVE *They were allowed to take account of antecedent legislation.* = **preceding**, earlier, former, previous, prior, preliminary, foregoing, anterior, precursory ■ **OPPOSITE:** subsequent

anterior ADJECTIVE **1** *the left anterior descending artery* = **front**, forward, fore, frontward **2** *memories of our anterior existences* = **earlier**, former, previous, prior, preceding, introductory, foregoing, antecedent

anthem NOUN = **song of praise**, carol, chant, hymn, psalm, paean, chorale, canticle

anthology NOUN = **collection**, choice, selection, treasury, digest, compilation, garland, compendium, miscellany, analects

anticipate VERB **1** *We could not have anticipated the result of our campaigning.*

= **expect**, predict, forecast, prepare for, look for, hope for, envisage, foresee, bank on, apprehend, foretell, think likely, count upon **2** *We are all eagerly anticipating the next match.* = **await**, look forward to, count the hours until

anticipation NOUN = **expectancy**, hope, expectation, apprehension, foresight, premonition, preconception, foretaste, prescience, forethought, presentiment

anticlimax NOUN = **disappointment**, letdown, comedown (informal), bathos ■ **OPPOSITE:** climax

antics PLURAL NOUN = **clowning**, tricks, stunts, mischief, larks, capers, pranks, frolics, escapades, foolishness, silliness, playfulness, skylarking, horseplay, buffoonery, tomfoolery, monkey tricks

antidote NOUN = **remedy**, cure, preventive, corrective, neutralizer, nostrum, countermeasure, antitoxin, antivenin, counteragent

antipathy NOUN = **hostility**, opposition, disgust, dislike, hatred, loathing, distaste, animosity, aversion, antagonism, enmity, rancour, bad blood, incompatibility, ill will, animus, repulsion, abhorrence, repugnance, odium (formal), contrariety ■ **OPPOSITE:** affinity

antiquated ADJECTIVE = **obsolete**, old, aged, ancient, antique, old-fashioned, elderly, dated, past it (informal), out-of-date, archaic, outmoded, passé, old hat, hoary, superannuated, antediluvian, outworn, cobwebby, old as the hills ■ **OPPOSITE:** up-to-date

antique NOUN *a genuine antique* = **period piece**, relic, bygone, heirloom, collector's item, museum piece, object of virtu
▶ ADJECTIVE **1** *antique silver jewellery* = **vintage**, classic, antiquarian, olden **2** *Their aim is to break taboos and change antique laws.* = **old-fashioned**, old, aged, ancient, remote, elderly, primitive, outdated, obsolete, archaic, bygone, primordial, primeval, immemorial, superannuated

antiquity NOUN **1** *famous monuments of classical antiquity* = **distant past**, ancient times, time immemorial, olden days **2** *a town of great antiquity* = **old age**, age, oldness, ancientness, elderliness

antiseptic ADJECTIVE *These herbs have strong antiseptic qualities.* = **hygienic**, clean, pure, sterile, sanitary, uncontaminated, unpolluted, germ-free, aseptic ■ **OPPOSITE:** unhygienic ▶ NOUN *She bathed the cut with antiseptic.* = **disinfectant**, purifier, bactericide, germicide

antisocial ADJECTIVE **1** *a group of unhappy citizens who will become aggressive and antisocial* = **unsociable**, reserved, retiring, withdrawn, alienated, unfriendly, uncommunicative, misanthropic, asocial ■ **OPPOSITE:** sociable **2** *places blighted by vandalism and antisocial behaviour* = **disruptive**, disorderly, hostile, menacing, rebellious, belligerent, antagonistic, uncooperative

antithesis NOUN **1** *They are the antithesis of the typical married couple.* = **opposite**, contrast, reverse, contrary, converse, inverse, antipode **2** *the antithesis between instinct and reason* = **contrast**, opposition, contradiction, reversal, inversion, contrariety, contraposition

anxiety NOUN = **uneasiness**, concern, care, worry, doubt, tension, alarm, distress, suspicion, angst, unease, apprehension, misgiving, suspense, nervousness, disquiet, trepidation (*formal*), foreboding, restlessness, solicitude, perturbation, watchfulness, fretfulness, disquietude, apprehensiveness, dubiety ■ **OPPOSITE:** confidence

anxious ADJECTIVE **1** *I am anxious that there should be no delay.* = **eager**, keen, intent, yearning, impatient, itching, ardent, avid, expectant, desirous ■ **OPPOSITE:** reluctant **2** *She admitted she was still anxious about the situation.* = **uneasy**, concerned, worried, troubled, upset, careful, wired (*slang*), nervous, disturbed, distressed, uncomfortable, tense, fearful, unsettled, restless, agitated, taut, disquieted, apprehensive, edgy, watchful, jittery (*informal*), perturbed, on edge, ill at ease, twitchy (*informal*), solicitous, overwrought, fretful, on tenterhooks, in suspense, hot and bothered, unquiet (*chiefly literary*), like a fish out of water, antsy (*informal*), angsty, on pins and needles, discomposed ■ **OPPOSITE:** confident

apace ADVERB = **quickly**, rapidly, swiftly, speedily, without delay, at full speed, expeditiously, posthaste, with dispatch

apart ADVERB **1** *He took the clock apart to see what was wrong with it.* = **to pieces**, to bits, asunder (*literary*), into parts **2** *They live 25 miles apart.* = **away from each other**, distant from each other **3** *He saw her standing some distance apart.* = **aside**, away, alone, independently, separately, singly, excluded, isolated, cut off, to one side, to yourself, by itself, aloof, to itself, by yourself, out on a limb • **apart from** *The room was empty apart from one man seated beside the fire.* = **except for**, excepting, other than, excluding, besides, not including, aside from, but, save, bar, not counting

apartment NOUN **1** *She has her own apartment and her own car.* = **flat**, room, suite, compartment, penthouse, duplex (*U.S. & Canad.*), crib, bachelor apartment (*Canad.*) **2** *the private apartments of the Prince of Wales at St James's Palace* = **rooms**, quarters, chambers, accommodation, living quarters

apathetic ADJECTIVE = **uninterested**, passive, indifferent, sluggish, unmoved, stoic, stoical, unconcerned, listless, cold, cool, impassive, unresponsive, phlegmatic, unfeeling, unemotional, torpid, emotionless, insensible ■ **OPPOSITE:** interested

apathy NOUN = **lack of interest**, indifference, inertia, coolness, passivity, coldness, stoicism, nonchalance, torpor, phlegm, sluggishness, listlessness, unconcern, insensibility, unresponsiveness, impassivity, passiveness, impassibility, unfeelingness, emotionlessness, uninterestedness ■ **OPPOSITE:** interest

ape VERB = **imitate**, copy, mirror, echo, mock, parrot, mimic, parody, caricature, affect, counterfeit

aperture NOUN = **opening**, space, hole, crack, gap, rent, passage, breach, slot, vent, rift, slit, cleft, eye, chink, fissure, orifice, perforation, eyelet, interstice

apex NOUN **1** *At the apex of the party was the central committee.* = **culmination**, top, crown, height, climax, highest point, zenith, apogee, acme ■ **OPPOSITE:** depths **2** *She led me up a gloomy corridor to the apex of the pyramid.* = **highest point**, point, top, tip, summit, peak, crest, pinnacle, vertex ■ **OPPOSITE:** lowest point

aphorism NOUN = **saying**, maxim, gnome, adage, proverb, dictum, precept, axiom, apothegm, saw

aphrodisiac NOUN *Asparagus is reputed to be an aphrodisiac.* = **love potion**, philtre ▶ ADJECTIVE *plants with aphrodisiac qualities* = **erotic** *or* **erotical**, exciting, stimulating, arousing, venereal

apiece ADVERB = **each**, individually, separately, for each, to each, respectively, from each, severally ■ **OPPOSITE:** all together

aplenty ADJECTIVE *There were problems aplenty, and it was an uncomfortable evening.* = **in plenty**, to spare, galore, in abundance, in quantity, in profusion, à gogo (*informal*) ▶ ADVERB *Wickets continued to fall aplenty.* = **plentifully**, in abundance, abundantly, in quantity, in plenty, copiously, plenteously

aplomb NOUN = **self-possession**, confidence, stability, self-confidence, composure, poise, coolness, calmness, equanimity, balance, self-assurance, sang-froid, level-headedness ■ **OPPOSITE:** self-consciousness

apocalypse NOUN = **destruction**, holocaust, havoc, devastation, carnage, conflagration, cataclysm

apocryphal ADJECTIVE = **dubious**, legendary, doubtful, questionable, mythical, spurious, fictitious, unsubstantiated, equivocal, unverified, unauthenticated, uncanonical ■ **OPPOSITE:** factual

apogee NOUN = **highest point**, top, tip, crown, summit, height, peak, climax, crest, pinnacle, culmination, zenith, apex, acme, vertex

apologetic ADJECTIVE = **regretful**, sorry, rueful, contrite, remorseful, penitent

apologize VERB = **say sorry**, express regret, ask forgiveness, make an apology, beg pardon, say you are sorry

apology NOUN *We received a letter of apology.* = **regret**, explanation, excuse, confession, extenuation • **apology for something** or **someone** *What an apology for a leader!* = **mockery of**, excuse for, imitation of, caricature of, travesty of, poor substitute for

apostle NOUN **1** *the twelve apostles* = **evangelist**, herald, missionary, preacher, messenger, proselytizer **2** *They present themselves as apostles of free trade.* = **supporter**, champion, advocate, pioneer, proponent, propagandist, propagator

apotheosis NOUN = **deification**, elevation, exaltation, glorification, idealization, idolization

appal VERB = **horrify**, shock, alarm, frighten, scare, terrify, outrage, disgust, dishearten, revolt, intimidate, dismay, daunt, sicken, astound, harrow, unnerve, petrify, scandalize, make your hair stand on end (*informal*)

appalled ADJECTIVE = **horrified**, shocked, stunned, alarmed, frightened, scared, terrified, outraged, dismayed, daunted, astounded, unnerved, disquieted, petrified, disheartened

appalling ADJECTIVE **1** *They have been living under the most appalling conditions.* = **horrifying**, shocking (*informal*), terrible, alarming, frightening, scaring, awful, terrifying, horrible, grim, dreadful, intimidating, dismaying, horrific, fearful (*informal*), daunting, dire, astounding, ghastly, hideous, shameful, harrowing,

vile, unnerving, petrifying, horrid, unspeakable, frightful, nightmarish, abominable, disheartening, godawful (*slang*), hellacious (*U.S. slang*) ■ **OPPOSITE:** reassuring **2** *I've got the most appalling headache.* = **awful**, terrible, tremendous, distressing, horrible, dreadful, horrendous, ghastly, godawful (*slang*)

apparatus NOUN **1** *a massive bureaucratic apparatus* = **organization**, system, network, structure, bureaucracy, hierarchy, setup (*informal*), chain of command **2** *He was rescued by firefighters wearing breathing apparatus.* = **equipment**, machine, tackle, gear, means, materials, device, tools, implements, mechanism, outfit, machinery, appliance, utensils, contraption (*informal*)

apparel NOUN = **clothing**, dress, clothes, equipment, gear (*informal*), habit, outfit, costume, threads (*slang*), array (*poetic*), garments, robes, trappings, attire, garb, accoutrements, vestments, raiment (*archaic, poetic*), schmutter (*slang*), habiliments

apparent ADJECTIVE **1** *I was a bit depressed by our apparent lack of progress.* = **seeming**, supposed, alleged, outward, exterior, superficial, ostensible, specious ■ **OPPOSITE:** actual **2** *The presence of a star is already apparent in the early film.* = **obvious**, marked, clear, plain, visible, bold, patent, evident, distinct, open, understandable, manifest, noticeable, blatant, conspicuous, overt, unmistakable, palpable, undeniable, discernible, salient, self-evident, indisputable, much in evidence, undisguised, unconcealed, indubitable, staring you in the face (*informal*), plain as the nose on your face ■ **OPPOSITE:** unclear

apparently ADVERB = **seemingly**, outwardly, ostensibly, speciously

apparition NOUN = **ghost**, spirit, shade (*literary*), phantom, spectre, spook (*informal*), wraith, chimera, revenant, visitant, eidolon, atua (*N.Z.*), kehua (*N.Z.*)

appeal VERB *The UN has appealed for help from the international community.* = **plead**, call, ask, apply, refer, request, sue, lobby, pray, beg, petition, solicit, implore, beseech, entreat, importune, adjure, supplicate ■ **OPPOSITE:** refuse ▶ NOUN **1** *The government issued a last-minute appeal to him to return.* = **plea**, call, application, request, prayer, petition, overture, invocation, solicitation, entreaty, supplication (*formal*), suit, cry from the heart, adjuration ■ **OPPOSITE:** refusal **2** *It was meant to give the*

party greater public appeal. = **attraction**, charm, fascination, charisma, beauty, attractiveness, allure, magnetism, enchantment, seductiveness, interestingness, engagingness, pleasingness ■ **OPPOSITE:** repulsiveness
• **appeal to someone** *The idea appealed to him.* = **attract**, interest, draw (*informal*), please, invite, engage, charm, fascinate, tempt, lure, entice, enchant, captivate, allure, bewitch

appealing ADJECTIVE = **attractive**, inviting, engaging, charming, winning, desirable, endearing, alluring, winsome, prepossessing ■ **OPPOSITE:** repellent

appear VERB **1** *It appears that some missiles have been moved.* = **seem**, be clear, be obvious, be evident, look (like or as if), be apparent, be plain, be manifest, be patent **2** *She did her best to appear more confident than she felt.* = **look (like** or **as if)**, seem, occur, look to be, come across as, strike you as **3** *A woman appeared at the far end of the street.* = **come into view**, emerge, occur, attend, surface, come out, turn out, arise, turn up, be present, loom, show (*informal*), issue, develop, arrive, show up (*informal*), come to light, crop up (*informal*), materialize, come forth, come into sight, show your face ■ **OPPOSITE:** disappear **4** *a poem which appeared in his last collection of verse* = **come into being**, come out, be published, be developed, be created, be invented, become available, come into existence **5** *She appeared in several of his plays.* = **perform**, play, act, enter, come on, take part, play a part, be exhibited, come onstage

appearance NOUN **1** *He had the appearance of a college student.* = **look**, face, form, air, figure, image, looks, bearing, aspect, manner, expression, demeanour, mien (*literary*) **2** *The sudden appearance of the deer caught me by surprise.* = **arrival**, appearing, presence, turning up, introduction, showing up (*informal*), emergence, advent **3** *They gave the appearance of being on both sides.* = **impression**, air, front, image, illusion, guise, façade, pretence, veneer, semblance, outward show

appease VERB **1** *The offer has not appeased separatists.* = **pacify**, satisfy, calm, soothe, quiet, placate, mollify, conciliate ■ **OPPOSITE:** anger **2** *Cash is on hand to appease mounting frustration.* = **ease**, satisfy, calm, relieve, diminish, compose, quiet, blunt, soothe, subdue, lessen, alleviate, lull, quell, allay, mitigate, assuage, quench, tranquillize

appeasement NOUN **1** *He denies there is a policy of appeasement.* = **pacification**, compromise, accommodation, concession, conciliation, acceding, propitiation, mollification, placation **2** *the appeasement of terror* = **easing**, relieving, satisfaction, softening, blunting, soothing, quieting, lessening, lulling, quelling, solace, quenching, mitigation, abatement, alleviation, assuagement, tranquillization

appellation NOUN = **name**, term, style, title, address, description, designation, epithet, sobriquet

append VERB = **add**, attach, join, hang, adjoin, fasten, annex, tag on, affix, tack on, subjoin ■ **OPPOSITE:** detach

appendage NOUN = **attachment**, addition, supplement, accessory, appendix, auxiliary, affix, ancillary, adjunct, annexe, addendum, appurtenance

appendix NOUN = **supplement**, add-on, postscript, adjunct, appendage, addendum, addition, codicil

appetite NOUN **1** *a slight fever, headache and loss of appetite* = **hunger** **2** *our growing appetite for scandal* = **desire**, liking, longing, demand, taste, passion, stomach, hunger, willingness, relish, craving, yearning, inclination, zeal, zest, propensity, hankering, proclivity, appetence, appetency ■ **OPPOSITE:** distaste

appetizer NOUN = **hors d'oeuvre**, titbit, antipasto, canapé

applaud VERB **1** *The audience laughed and applauded.* = **clap**, encourage, praise, cheer, hail, acclaim, laud (*literary*), give (someone) a big hand ■ **OPPOSITE:** boo **2** *You should be applauded for your courage.* = **praise**, celebrate, approve, acclaim, compliment, salute, commend, extol, crack up (*informal*), big up (*slang*), eulogize ■ **OPPOSITE:** criticize

applause NOUN = **ovation**, praise, cheering, cheers, approval, acclaim, clapping, accolade, big hand, commendation, hand-clapping, approbation, acclamation, eulogizing, plaudit

appliance NOUN = **device**, machine, tool, instrument, implement, mechanism, apparatus, gadget, waldo

applicable ADJECTIVE = **appropriate**, fitting, fit, suited, useful, suitable, relevant, to the point, apt, pertinent, befitting, apposite, apropos, germane, to the purpose ■ **OPPOSITE:** inappropriate

applicant NOUN = **candidate**, entrant, claimant, suitor, petitioner, aspirant, inquirer, job-seeker, suppliant, postulant

application NOUN **1** *His application for membership was rejected.* = **request**, claim, demand, appeal, suit, inquiry, plea, petition, requisition, solicitation **2** *Students learned the practical application of the theory.* = **relevance**, use, value, practice, bearing, exercise, purpose, function, appropriateness, aptness, pertinence, appositeness, germaneness **3** *his immense talent and unremitting application* = **effort**, work, study, industry, labour, trouble, attention, struggle, pains, commitment, hard work, endeavour, dedication, toil, diligence, perseverance, travail (*literary*), attentiveness, assiduity, blood, sweat, and tears (*informal*) **4** = **program**, package, software, app (*informal*), killer application *or* killer app

apply VERB **1** *I am continuing to apply for jobs.* = **request**, seek, appeal, put in, petition, inquire, solicit, claim, sue, requisition, make application **2** *The rule applies where a person owns stock in a company.* = **be relevant**, concern, relate, refer, be fitting, be appropriate, be significant, fit, suit, pertain, be applicable, bear upon, appertain **3** *The government appears to be applying the same principle.* = **use**, exercise, carry out, employ, engage, implement, practise, execute, assign, administer, exert, enact, utilize, bring to bear, put to use, bring into play **4** *Applying the dye can be messy, particularly on long hair.* = **put on**, work in, cover with, lay on, paint on, anoint, spread on, rub in, smear on, shampoo in, bring into contact with • **apply yourself** *If you apply yourself, there's no reason why you shouldn't pass.* = **work hard**, concentrate, study, pay attention, try, commit yourself, buckle down (*informal*), be assiduous, devote yourself, be diligent, dedicate yourself, make an effort, address yourself, be industrious, persevere

appoint VERB **1** *It made sense to appoint a banker to this job.* = **assign**, name, choose, commission, select, elect, install, delegate, nominate ■ **OPPOSITE:** fire **2** *We met at the time appointed.* = **decide**, set, choose, establish, determine, settle, fix, arrange, specify, assign, designate, allot ■ **OPPOSITE:** cancel

appointed ADJECTIVE **1** *The appointed hour for the ceremony was drawing near.* = **decided**, set, chosen, established, determined, settled, fixed, arranged, assigned, designated, allotted **2** *The recently appointed captain led by example in the first game.* = **assigned**, named, chosen, commissioned, selected, elected, installed, delegated, nominated **3** *beautiful, well-appointed houses* = **equipped**, provided, supplied, furnished, fitted out

appointment NOUN **1** *his appointment as foreign minister in 1985* = **selection**, naming, election, choosing, choice, commissioning, delegation, nomination, installation, assignment, allotment, designation **2** *He is to take up an appointment as a researcher with the Society.* = **job**, office, position, post, situation, place, station, employment, assignment, berth (*informal*) **3** *She has an appointment with her accountant.* = **meeting**, interview, date, session, arrangement, consultation, engagement, fixture, rendezvous, tryst (*archaic*), assignation **4** *He is the new appointment at RSA.* = **appointee**, candidate, representative, delegate, nominee, office-holder

apportion VERB = **divide**, share, deal, distribute, assign, allocate, dispense, give out, allot, mete out, dole out, measure out, parcel out, ration out

apposite ADJECTIVE = **appropriate**, fitting, suited, suitable, relevant, proper, to the point, apt, applicable, pertinent, befitting, apropos, germane, to the purpose, appertaining ■ **OPPOSITE:** inappropriate

appraisal NOUN **1** *Self-appraisal is never easy.* = **assessment**, opinion, estimate, judgment, evaluation, estimation, sizing up (*informal*), recce (*slang*) **2** *He has resisted being drawn into the business of cost appraisal.* = **valuation**, pricing, rating, survey, reckoning, assay

appraise VERB = **assess**, judge, review, estimate, survey, price, rate, value, evaluate, inspect, gauge, size up (*informal*), eye up, assay, recce (*slang*)

> **USAGE** *Appraise* is sometimes used where *apprise* is meant: *both patients had been fully apprised* (not *appraised*) *of the situation*. This may well be due to the fact that *appraise* is considerably more common, and that people therefore tend to associate this meaning mistakenly with a word they know better.

appreciable ADJECTIVE = **significant**, marked, obvious, considerable, substantial, visible, evident, pronounced, definite, noticeable, clear-cut, discernible, measurable, material, recognizable, detectable, perceptible, distinguishable, ascertainable, perceivable ■ **OPPOSITE:** insignificant

appreciably ADVERB = **significantly**, obviously, definitely, considerably, substantially, evidently, visibly, markedly, noticeably, palpably, perceptively, measurably, recognizably, discernibly, detectably, distinguishably, perceivably, ascertainably

appreciate VERB **1** *Anyone can appreciate our music.* = **enjoy**, like, value, regard, respect, prize, admire, treasure, esteem, relish, cherish, savour, rate highly ■ **OPPOSITE:** scorn **2** *She never really appreciated the depth of the conflict.* = **be aware of**, know, understand, estimate, realize, acknowledge, recognize, perceive, comprehend, take account of, be sensitive to, be conscious of, sympathize with, be alive to, be cognizant of ■ **OPPOSITE:** be unaware of **3** *I'd appreciate it if you didn't mention that.* = **be grateful for**, be obliged for, be thankful for, give thanks for, be indebted for, be in debt for, be appreciative of ■ **OPPOSITE:** be ungrateful for **4** *There is little confidence that houses will appreciate in value.* = **increase**, rise, grow, gain, improve, mount, enhance, soar, inflate ■ **OPPOSITE:** fall

appreciation NOUN **1** *They cheered in appreciation.* = **admiration**, liking, respect, assessment, esteem, relish, valuation, enjoyment, appraisal, estimation, responsiveness **2** *the gifts presented to them in appreciation of their work* = **gratitude**, thanks, recognition, obligation, acknowledgment, indebtedness, thankfulness, gratefulness ■ **OPPOSITE:** ingratitude **3** *They have a strong appreciation of the importance of economic incentives.* = **awareness**, understanding, regard, knowledge, recognition, perception, sympathy, consciousness, sensitivity, realization, comprehension, familiarity, mindfulness, cognizance ■ **OPPOSITE:** ignorance **4** *You have to take capital appreciation of the property into account.* = **increase**, rise, gain, growth, inflation, improvement, escalation, enhancement ■ **OPPOSITE:** fall **5** *I had written an appreciation of his work for a magazine.* = **review**, report, notice, analysis, criticism, praise, assessment, recognition, tribute, evaluation, critique, acclamation

appreciative ADJECTIVE **1** *There is a murmur of appreciative laughter.* = **enthusiastic**, understanding, pleased, aware, sensitive, conscious, admiring, sympathetic, supportive, responsive, knowledgeable, respectful, mindful, perceptive, in the know (*informal*), cognizant, regardful **2** *We are very appreciative of their support.* = **grateful**, obliged, thankful, indebted, beholden

apprehend VERB **1** *Police have not apprehended her killer.* = **arrest**, catch, lift (*slang*), nick (*slang, chiefly Brit.*), capture, seize, run in (*slang*), take, nail (*informal*), bust (*informal*), collar (*informal*), pinch (*informal*), nab (*informal*), take prisoner, feel your collar (*slang*) ■ **OPPOSITE:** release **2** *Only now can I begin to apprehend the power of these forces.* = **understand**, know, think, believe, imagine, realize, recognize, appreciate, perceive, grasp, conceive, comprehend, get the message, get the picture ■ **OPPOSITE:** be unaware of

apprehension NOUN **1** *It reflects real anger and apprehension about the future.* = **anxiety**, concern, fear, worry, doubt, alarm, suspicion, dread, unease, mistrust, misgiving, disquiet, premonition, trepidation (*formal*), foreboding, uneasiness, pins and needles, apprehensiveness ■ **OPPOSITE:** confidence **2** *information leading to the apprehension of the alleged killer* = **arrest**, catching, capture, taking, seizure ■ **OPPOSITE:** release **3** *the sudden apprehension of something* = **awareness**, understanding, knowledge, intelligence, ken, perception, grasp, comprehension ■ **OPPOSITE:** incomprehension

apprehensive ADJECTIVE = **anxious**, concerned, worried, afraid, alarmed, nervous, suspicious, doubtful, uneasy, fearful, disquieted, foreboding, twitchy (*informal*), mistrustful, antsy (*informal*) ■ **OPPOSITE:** confident

apprentice NOUN = **trainee**, student, pupil, novice, beginner, learner, neophyte (*formal*), tyro, probationer ■ **OPPOSITE:** master

apprenticeship NOUN = **traineeship**, probation, studentship, novitiate *or* noviciate

apprise VERB = **make aware**, tell, warn, advise, inform, communicate, notify, enlighten, acquaint, give notice, make cognizant

approach VERB **1** *When I approached them they fell silent.* = **move towards**, come to, reach, near, advance, catch up, meet, come close, gain on, converge on, come near, push forward, draw near, creep up on **2** *When he approached me about the job, my first reaction was disbelief.* = **make a proposal to**, speak to, apply to, appeal to, proposition, solicit, sound out, make overtures to, make advances to, broach the matter with **3** *The bank has approached the issue in a practical way.* = **set about**, tackle, undertake, embark on, get down to, launch into, begin work on, commence on, make a start on, enter upon **4** *They race at speeds approaching 200mph.* = **approximate**, touch (*informal*), be like, compare with, resemble, come close to, border on, verge on, be comparable to, come near to ▶ NOUN **1** *At their approach the little boy ran away and hid.* = **advance**, coming, nearing, appearance, arrival, advent, drawing near **2** *The path serves as an approach to the boat house.* = **access**, way, drive, road, passage, entrance, avenue, passageway **3** (*often plural*) *There had already been approaches from interested buyers.* = **proposal**, offer, appeal, advance, application, invitation, proposition, overture **4** *We will be exploring different approaches to information-gathering.* = **way**, means, course, style, attitude, method, technique, manner, procedure, mode, modus operandi **5** *the nearest approach to an apology we have so far heard* = **approximation**, likeness, semblance

approachable ADJECTIVE **1** *We found him very approachable and easy to talk to.* = **friendly**, open, cordial, sociable, affable, congenial ■ **OPPOSITE:** unfriendly **2** *It is approachable on foot for only a few hours a day.* = **accessible**, attainable, reachable, get-at-able (*informal*), come-at-able (*informal*) ■ **OPPOSITE:** inaccessible

appropriate ADJECTIVE *It is appropriate that Irish names dominate the list.* = **suitable**, right, fitting, fit, suited, correct, belonging, relevant, proper, to the point, in keeping, apt, applicable, pertinent, befitting, well-suited, well-timed, apposite, apropos, opportune (*formal*), becoming, seemly, felicitous, germane, to the purpose, appurtenant, congruous ■ **OPPOSITE:** unsuitable ▶ VERB **1** *Several other newspapers have appropriated the idea.* = **seize**, take, claim, assume, take over, acquire, confiscate, annex, usurp, impound, pre-empt, commandeer, take possession of, expropriate (*formal*), arrogate ■ **OPPOSITE:** relinquish **2** *He is sceptical that Congress will appropriate more money for this.* = **allocate**, allow, budget, devote, assign, designate, set aside, earmark, allot, share out, apportion ■ **OPPOSITE:** withhold **3** *What do they think about your appropriating their music and culture?* = **steal**, take, nick (*slang, chiefly Brit.*), pocket, pinch (*informal*), pirate, poach, swipe (*slang*), lift (*informal*), heist (*U.S. slang*), embezzle, blag (*slang*), pilfer, misappropriate, snitch (*slang*), purloin, filch, plagiarize, thieve, peculate (*literary*)

appropriateness NOUN = **suitability**, fitness, relevance, correctness, felicity, rightness, applicability, timeliness, aptness, pertinence, fittingness, seemliness, appositeness, properness, germaneness, opportuneness, becomingness, congruousness, felicitousness, well-suitedness

appropriation NOUN **1** *The government raised defence appropriations by 12 per cent.* = **setting aside**, assignment, allocation, earmarking, allotment, apportionment **2** *fraud and illegal appropriation of land* = **seizure**, taking, takeover, assumption, annexation, confiscation, commandeering, expropriation (*formal*), pre-emption, usurpation, impoundment, arrogation

approval NOUN **1** *The proposed modifications met with widespread approval.* = **consent**, agreement, sanction, licence, blessing, permission, recommendation, concession, confirmation, mandate, endorsement, leave, compliance, the go-ahead (*informal*), countenance, ratification, the green light, assent, authorization, validation, acquiescence, imprimatur, concurrence, O.K. or okay (*informal*), endorsation (*Canad.*) **2** *an obsessive drive to win his father's approval* = **favour**, liking, regard, respect, praise, esteem, acclaim, appreciation, encouragement, admiration, applause, commendation, approbation, good opinion ■ **OPPOSITE:** disapproval

approve VERB *MPs approved the bill by a majority of 97.* = **agree to**, second, allow, pass, accept, confirm, recommend, permit, sanction, advocate, bless, endorse, uphold, mandate, authorize, ratify, go along with, subscribe to, consent to, buy into (*informal*), validate, countenance, rubber stamp, accede to, give the go-ahead to (*informal*), give the green light to, assent to, concur in, O.K. or okay (*informal*) ■ **OPPOSITE:** veto • **approve of something** or **someone** *Not everyone approves of the festival.* = **favour**, like, support, respect, praise, appreciate, agree with, admire, endorse, esteem, acclaim, applaud, commend, be pleased with, have a good opinion of, regard highly, think highly of

approving ADJECTIVE = **favourable**, admiring, applauding, respectful, appreciative, commendatory, acclamatory

approximate ADJECTIVE *The times are approximate only.* = **rough**, close, general, near, estimated, loose, vague, hazy, sketchy, amorphous, imprecise, inexact, almost exact, almost accurate ■ **OPPOSITE:** exact • **approximate to** *Something* *approximating to a just outcome will be ensured.* = **resemble**, reach, approach, touch, come close to, border on, come near, verge on

approximately ADVERB = **almost**, about, around, generally, nearly, close to, relatively, roughly, loosely, just about, more or less, in the region of, in the vicinity of, not far off, in the neighbourhood of

approximation NOUN **1** *That's a fair approximation of the way the next boss will be chosen.* = **likeness**, approach, correspondence, resemblance, semblance **2** *That's an approximation, but my guess is there'll be a reasonable balance.* = **guess**, estimate, conjecture, estimation, guesswork, rough idea, rough calculation, ballpark figure (*informal*), ballpark estimate (*informal*)

a priori ADJECTIVE = **deduced**, deductive, inferential

apron NOUN = **pinny**, overall, pinafore (*informal*)

apropos ADJECTIVE *It was not apropos to join the conversation now.* = **appropriate**, right, seemly, fitting, fit, related, correct, belonging, suitable, relevant, proper, to the point, apt, applicable, pertinent, befitting, apposite, opportune (*formal*), germane, to the purpose • **apropos of** *Apropos of the party, have you had any further thoughts on a venue?* = **concerning**, about, re, regarding, respecting, on the subject of, in respect of, as to, with reference to, in re, in the matter of, as regards, in *or* with regard to

apt ADJECTIVE **1** *The words of this report are as apt today as they were in 1929.* = **appropriate**, timely, right, seemly, fitting, fit, related, correct, belonging, suitable, relevant, proper, to the point, applicable, pertinent, befitting, apposite, apropos, opportune (*formal*), germane, to the purpose ■ **OPPOSITE:** inappropriate **2** *She was apt to raise her voice and wave her hands about.* = **inclined**, likely, ready, disposed, prone, liable, given, predisposed, of a mind **3** *She was never a very apt student.* = **gifted**, skilled, expert, quick, bright (*informal*), talented, sharp, capable, smart, prompt, clever, intelligent, accomplished, ingenious, skilful, astute, adroit, teachable

aptitude NOUN = **gift**, ability, talent, capacity, intelligence, leaning, bent, tendency, faculty, capability, flair, inclination, disposition, knack, propensity, proficiency, predilection, cleverness, proclivity (*formal*), quickness, giftedness, proneness, aptness

arable ADJECTIVE = **productive**, fertile, fruitful, fecund, cultivable, farmable, ploughable, tillable

arbiter NOUN **1** *the court's role as arbiter in the law-making process* = **judge**, referee, umpire, umpie (*Austral. slang*), arbitrator, adjudicator **2** *Sequins have often aroused the scorn of arbiters of taste.* = **authority**, expert, master, governor, ruler, dictator, controller, lord, pundit

arbitrary ADJECTIVE **1** *Arbitrary arrests were common.* = **random**, chance, optional, subjective, unreasonable, inconsistent, erratic, discretionary, personal, fanciful, wilful, whimsical, capricious ■ **OPPOSITE:** logical **2** *the virtually unlimited arbitrary power of the state* = **dictatorial**, absolute, unlimited, uncontrolled, autocratic, dogmatic, imperious, domineering, unrestrained, overbearing, tyrannical, summary, magisterial, despotic, high-handed, peremptory, tyrannous

arbitrate VERB = **decide**, judge, determine, settle, referee, umpire, mediate, adjudicate, adjudge, pass judgment, sit in judgment

arbitration NOUN = **decision**, settlement, judgment, determination, adjudication, arbitrament

arbitrator NOUN = **judge**, referee, umpire, umpie (*Austral. slang*), arbiter, adjudicator

arc NOUN = **curve**, bend, bow, arch, crescent, half-moon

arcade NOUN = **gallery**, mall, cloister, portico, colonnade, covered walk, peristyle

arcane ADJECTIVE = **mysterious**, secret, hidden, esoteric, occult, recondite, cabbalistic

arch¹ NOUN **1** *The theatre is located under old railway arches in the East End.* = **archway**, curve, dome, span, vault **2** *Train the cane supports to form an arch.* = **curve**, bend, bow, crook, arc, hunch, sweep, hump, curvature, semicircle ▸ VERB *the domed ceiling arching overhead* = **curve**, bridge, bend, bow, span, arc

arch² ADJECTIVE *a slightly amused, arch expression* = **playful**, joking, teasing, humorous, sly, mischievous, saucy, tongue-in-cheek, jesting, jokey, pert, good-natured, roguish, frolicsome, waggish

archaic ADJECTIVE **1** *archaic sculpture and porcelain* = **old**, ancient, antique, primitive, bygone, olden (*archaic*) ■ **OPPOSITE:** modern **2** *These archaic practices are advocated by people of limited outlook.* = **old-fashioned**, obsolete, out of date, antiquated, outmoded, passé, old hat, behind the times, superannuated ■ **OPPOSITE:** up-to-date

arched ADJECTIVE = **curved**, domed, vaulted

archer NOUN = **bowman** (*archaic*), toxophilite (*formal*)

a

archetypal or **archetypical** ADJECTIVE
= **typical**, standard, model, original,
normal, classic, ideal, exemplary,
paradigmatic, prototypal, prototypic or
prototypical

archetype NOUN = **prime example**,
standard, model, original, pattern, classic,
ideal, norm, form, prototype, paradigm,
exemplar

architect NOUN **1** *Employ an architect to make
sure the plans comply with regulations.*
= **designer**, planner, draughtsman or
woman or person, master builder **2** *the
country's chief architect of economic reform*
= **creator**, father, shaper, engineer, author,
maker, designer, founder, deviser, planner,
inventor, contriver, originator, prime
mover, instigator, initiator

architecture NOUN **1** *He studied architecture
and design at college.* = **design**, planning,
building, construction, architectonics
2 *a fine example of Moroccan architecture*
= **construction**, design, style **3** *the
architecture of muscle fibres* = **structure**,
design, shape, make-up, construction,
framework, layout, anatomy

archive NOUN *I decided I would go to the archive
and look up the issue.* = **record office**,
museum, registry, repository ▸ PLURAL
NOUN *the archives of the Imperial War Museum*
= **records**, papers, accounts, rolls,
documents, files, registers, deeds,
chronicles, annals

arctic ADJECTIVE = **freezing**, cold, frozen,
icy, chilly, frosty, glacial, frigid, gelid,
frost-bound, cold as ice

Arctic ADJECTIVE = **polar**, far-northern,
hyperborean

ardent ADJECTIVE **1** *an ardent opponent of the
war* = **enthusiastic**, keen, eager, avid,
zealous, keen as mustard ■ OPPOSITE:
indifferent **2** *an ardent lover* = **passionate**,
warm, spirited, intense, flaming, fierce,
fiery, hot, fervent, impassioned, emotional,
ablaze, lusty, vehement, amorous,
hot-blooded, warm-blooded, fervid
■ OPPOSITE: cold

ardour NOUN **1** *Their romantic ardour had
cooled.* = **passion**, feeling, fire, heat, spirit,
intensity, warmth, devotion, fervour,
vehemence, fierceness **2** *my ardour for
football* = **enthusiasm**, zeal, eagerness,
earnestness, keenness, avidity

arduous ADJECTIVE = **difficult**, trying, hard,
tough, tiring, severe, painful, exhausting,
punishing, harsh, taxing, heavy, steep,
formidable, fatiguing, rigorous,
troublesome, gruelling, strenuous,
onerous, laborious, burdensome,
backbreaking, toilsome (*literary*)
■ OPPOSITE: easy

area NOUN **1** *the large number of community
groups in the area* = **region**, land, quarter,
division, sector, district, stretch, territory,
zone, plot, province, patch,
neighbourhood, sphere, turf (*slang*), realm,
domain, tract, locality, neck of the woods
(*informal*) **2** *You will notice that your baby has
two soft areas on its head.* = **part**, section,
sector, portion **3** *Although large in area, the
flat did not have many rooms.* = **range**, reach,
size, sweep, extent, scope, sphere, domain,
width, compass, breadth, parameters
(*informal*), latitude, expanse, radius, ambit,
footprint **4** *She wanted to be involved in every
area of my life.* = **realm**, part, department
(*informal*), field, province, arena, sphere,
domain

arena NOUN **1** *the largest indoor sports arena in
the world* = **ring**, ground, stage, field,
theatre, bowl, pitch, stadium, enclosure,
park (*U.S. & Canad.*), coliseum,
amphitheatre **2** *He has no intention of
withdrawing from the political arena.* = **scene**
(*informal*), world, area, stage, field, theatre,
sector, territory, province, forum, scope,
sphere, realm, domain

arguably ADVERB = **possibly**, potentially,
conceivably, plausibly, feasibly,
questionably, debatably, deniably,
disputably, contestably, controvertibly,
dubitably, refutably

argue VERB **1** *They were still arguing. I could
hear them down the road.* = **quarrel**, fight,
row, clash, dispute, disagree, feud,
squabble, spar, wrangle, bicker, have an
argument, cross swords, be at sixes and
sevens, fight like cat and dog, go at it
hammer and tongs, bandy words, altercate
2 *The two of them were arguing this point.*
= **discuss**, debate, dispute, thrash out,
exchange views on, controvert **3** *His lawyers
are arguing that he is unfit to stand trial.*
= **claim**, question, reason, challenge, insist,
maintain, hold, allege, plead, assert,
contend, uphold, profess, remonstrate
(*formal*), expostulate **4** *I'd like to argue in a
framework that is less exaggerated.*
= **demonstrate**, show, suggest, display,
indicate, imply, exhibit, denote, evince
(*formal*)

argument NOUN **1** *There's a strong argument
for lowering the price.* = **reason**, case,
reasoning, ground(s), defence, excuse,
logic, justification, rationale, polemic,
dialectic, line of reasoning, argumentation
2 *The issue has caused heated political
argument.* = **debate**, questioning, claim,

row, discussion, dispute, issue, controversy, pleading, plea, contention, assertion, polemic, altercation, remonstrance, expostulation, remonstration **3** *She got into a heated argument with a stranger.* = **quarrel**, fight, row, clash, dispute, controversy, disagreement, misunderstanding, feud, barney (*informal*), squabble, wrangle, bickering, difference of opinion, tiff, altercation ■ **OPPOSITE:** agreement

argumentative ADJECTIVE = **quarrelsome**, contrary, contentious, belligerent, combative, opinionated, litigious, disputatious ■ **OPPOSITE:** easy-going

arid ADJECTIVE **1** *the arid zones of the country* = **dry**, desert, dried up, barren, sterile, torrid, parched, waterless, moistureless ■ **OPPOSITE:** lush **2** *It had given him the only joy his arid life had ever known.* = **boring**, dull, tedious, dreary, dry, tiresome, lifeless, colourless, uninteresting, flat, uninspired, vapid, spiritless, jejune (*old-fashioned*), as dry as dust ■ **OPPOSITE:** exciting

arise VERB **1** *if a problem arises later in pregnancy* = **happen**, start, begin, follow, issue, result, appear, develop, emerge, occur, spring, set in, stem, originate, ensue, come about, commence, come to light, emanate, crop up (*informal*), come into being, materialize **2** *I arose from the chair and left.* = **get to your feet**, get up, rise, stand up, spring up, leap up **3** *He arose at 6:30 a.m. as usual.* = **get up**, wake up, awaken, get out of bed **4** *the flat terrace, from which arises the volume of the house* = **ascend**, rise, lift, mount, climb, tower, soar, move upward

aristocracy NOUN = **upper class**, elite, nobility, gentry, peerage, ruling class, patricians, upper crust (*informal*), noblesse (*literary*), haut monde (*French*), patriciate, body of nobles ■ **OPPOSITE:** commoners

aristocrat NOUN = **noble**, lord, lady, peer, patrician, grandee, nobleman, noblewoman, aristo (*informal*), childe (*archaic*), peeress

aristocratic ADJECTIVE **1** *a wealthy, aristocratic family* = **upper-class**, lordly, titled, gentle (*archaic*), elite, gentlemanly, noble, patrician, blue-blooded, well-born, highborn (*old-fashioned*) ■ **OPPOSITE:** common **2** *He laughed it off with aristocratic indifference.* = **refined**, fine, polished, elegant, stylish, dignified, haughty, courtly, snobbish, well-bred ■ **OPPOSITE:** vulgar

arm¹ NOUN **1** *She stretched her arms out.* = **upper limb**, limb, appendage **2** *the research arm of Congress* = **branch**, part, office, department, division, section, wing, sector, extension, detachment, offshoot, subdivision, subsection **3** *Local people say the long arm of the law was too heavy-handed.* = **authority**, might, force, power, strength, command, sway, potency **4** = **inlet**, bay, passage, entrance, creek, cove, fjord, bight, ingress, sea loch (*Scot.*), firth or frith (*Scot.*)
• **an arm and a leg** = **a lot of money**, a bomb (*Brit. slang*), a fortune, a pile (*informal*), big money, a packet (*slang*), a bundle (*slang*), big bucks (*informal, chiefly U.S.*), a tidy sum (*informal*), a king's ransom, a pretty penny (*informal*) • **would give your right arm for something** = **would do anything for**, would kill for, would sell your own grandmother for (*informal*), would give your eye teeth for

arm² VERB **1** *She had armed herself with a loaded rifle.* = **equip**, provide, supply, outfit, rig, array, furnish, issue with, deck out, accoutre **2** *She armed herself with all the knowledge she could gather.* = **provide**, prime, prepare, protect, guard, strengthen, outfit, equip, brace, fortify, forearm, make ready, gird your loins, jack up (*N.Z.*) ▶ PLURAL NOUN *The organization has an extensive supply of arms.* = **weapons**, guns, firearms, weaponry, armaments, ordnance, munitions, instruments of war

armada NOUN = **fleet**, navy, squadron, flotilla

armaments PLURAL NOUN = **weapons**, arms, guns, ammunition, weaponry, ordnance, munitions, materiel

armed ADJECTIVE = **carrying weapons**, provided, prepared, supplied, ready, protected, guarded, strengthened, equipped, primed, arrayed, furnished, fortified, in arms, forearmed, fitted out, under arms, girded, rigged out, tooled up (*slang*), accoutred

armistice NOUN = **truce**, peace, ceasefire, suspension of hostilities

armour NOUN = **protection**, covering, shield, sheathing, armour plate, chain mail, protective covering

armoured ADJECTIVE = **protected**, mailed, reinforced, toughened, bulletproof, armour-plated, steel-plated, ironclad, bombproof

armoury *or* (*U.S.*) **armory** NOUN = **arsenal**, magazine, ammunition dump, arms depot, ordnance depot

army NOUN **1** *After returning from abroad, he joined the army.* = **soldiers**, military, troops, armed force, legions, infantry, military force, land forces, land force, soldiery **2** *data collected by an army of volunteers* = **vast number**, host, gang, mob, flock, array, legion, swarm, sea, pack, horde, multitude, throng

aroma NOUN = **scent**, smell, perfume, fragrance, bouquet, savour, odour, redolence

aromatic ADJECTIVE = **fragrant**, perfumed, spicy, savoury, pungent, balmy, redolent, sweet-smelling, sweet-scented, odoriferous ■ **OPPOSITE:** smelly

around PREPOSITION **1** *The journey was around eighty miles.* = **approximately**, about, nearly, close to, roughly, just about, in the region of, circa (*of a date*), in the vicinity of, not far off, in the neighbourhood of **2** *a prosperous suburb built around a new mosque* = **surrounding**, about, enclosing, encompassing, framing, encircling, on all sides of, on every side of, environing ▶ ADVERB **1** *What are you doing following me around?* = **everywhere**, about, throughout, all over, here and there, on all sides, in all directions, to and fro **2** *It's important to have lots of people around.* = **near**, close, nearby, handy, at hand, close by, close at hand ■ **RELATED WORD:** *prefix* circum-

> **USAGE** In American English, *around* is used more often than *round* as an adverb and preposition, except in a few fixed phrases such as *all year round*. In British English, *round* is more commonly used as an adverb than *around*.

arousal NOUN = **stimulation**, movement, response, reaction, excitement, animation, stirring up, provocation, inflammation, agitation, exhilaration, incitement, enlivenment

arouse VERB **1** *His work has aroused intense interest.* = **stimulate**, encourage, inspire, prompt, spark, spur, foster, provoke, rouse, stir up, inflame, incite, instigate, whip up, summon up, whet, kindle, foment, call forth ■ **OPPOSITE:** quell **2** *He apologized, saying this subject always aroused him.* = **inflame**, move, warm, excite, spur, provoke, animate, prod, stir up, agitate, quicken, enliven, goad, foment **3** *We were aroused from our sleep by a knocking at the door.* = **awaken**, wake up, rouse, waken

arraign VERB = **accuse**, charge, prosecute, denounce, indict, impeach, incriminate, call to account, take to task

arrange VERB **1** *She arranged an appointment for Friday afternoon.* = **plan**, agree, prepare, determine, schedule, organize, construct, devise, contrive, fix up, jack up (*N.Z. informal*) **2** *He started to arrange the books in piles.* = **put in order**, group, form, order, sort, class, position, range, file, rank, line up, organize, set out, sequence, exhibit, sort out (*informal*), array, classify, tidy, marshal, align, categorize, systematize,

jack up (*N.Z. informal*) ■ **OPPOSITE:** disorganize **3** *The songs were arranged by a well-known pianist.* = **adapt**, score, orchestrate, harmonize, instrument

arrangement NOUN **1** (*often plural*) *I am in charge of all the travel arrangements.* = **plan**, planning, provision, preparation **2** *The caves can be visited only by prior arrangement.* = **agreement**, contract, settlement, appointment, compromise, deal (*informal*), pact, compact, covenant **3** *an imaginative flower arrangement* = **display**, grouping, system, order, ordering, design, ranging, structure, rank, organization, exhibition, line-up, presentation, array, marshalling, classification, disposition (*archaic*), alignment, setup (*informal*) **4** *an arrangement of a well-known piece by Mozart* = **adaptation**, score, version, interpretation, instrumentation, orchestration, harmonization

array NOUN **1** *the markets with their wonderful arrays of fruit and vegetables* = **arrangement**, show, order, supply, display, collection, exhibition, line-up, mixture, parade, formation, presentation, spectacle, marshalling, muster, disposition (*archaic*) **2** *Bathed, dressed in his finest array, he was ready.* = **clothing**, dress, clothes, threads (*slang*), garments, apparel (*old-fashioned*), attire, garb, finery, regalia, raiment (*archaic, poetic*), schmutter (*slang*) ▶ VERB **1** *A number of cups and saucers were arrayed on a side table.* = **arrange**, show, group, order, present, range, display, line up, sequence, parade, exhibit, unveil, dispose, draw up, marshal, lay out, muster, align, form up, place in order, set in line (*Military*) **2** *a priest arrayed in white vestments* = **dress**, supply, clothe, wrap, deck, outfit, decorate, equip, robe, get ready, adorn, apparel (*archaic*), festoon, attire, fit out, garb, bedeck, caparison, accoutre

arrest VERB **1** *Seven people were arrested for minor offences.* = **capture**, catch, lift (*slang*), nick (*slang, chiefly Brit.*), seize, run in (*slang*), nail (*informal*), bust (*informal*), collar (*informal*), take, detain, pinch (*informal*), nab (*informal*), apprehend, take prisoner, take into custody, lay hold of ■ **OPPOSITE:** release **2** *The new rules could arrest the development of good research.* = **stop**, end, hold, limit, check, block, slow, delay, halt, stall, stay, interrupt, suppress, restrain, hamper, inhibit, hinder, obstruct, retard, impede ■ **OPPOSITE:** speed up **3** *As he reached the hall, he saw what had arrested her.* = **fascinate**, hold, involve, catch, occupy, engage, grip, absorb, entrance, intrigue, rivet, enthral, mesmerize, engross, spellbind ▶ NOUN 1 *information leading to the arrest of the bombers* = **capture**, bust (*informal*), detention, seizure, apprehension ■ **OPPOSITE:** release 2 *a cardiac arrest* = **stoppage**, halt, suppression, obstruction, inhibition, blockage, hindrance ■ **OPPOSITE:** acceleration

arresting ADJECTIVE = **striking**, surprising, engaging, dramatic, stunning (*informal*), impressive, extraordinary, outstanding, remarkable, noticeable, conspicuous, salient, jaw-dropping ■ **OPPOSITE:** unremarkable

arrival NOUN 1 *the day after his arrival* = **appearance**, coming, arriving, entrance, advent, materialization 2 *They celebrated the arrival of the New Year.* = **coming**, happening, taking place, dawn (*literary*), emergence, occurrence, materialization 3 *A high proportion of the new arrivals are skilled professionals.* = **newcomer**, arriver, incomer, visitor, caller, entrant, comer, visitant

arrive VERB 1 *Fresh groups of guests arrived.* = **come**, appear, enter, turn up, show up (*informal*), materialize, draw near ■ **OPPOSITE:** depart 2 *They needed to be much further forward before winter arrived.* = **occur**, happen, take place, ensue, transpire (*informal*), fall, befall 3 *These are cars which show you've arrived.* = **succeed**, make it (*informal*), triumph, do well, thrive, flourish, be successful, make good, prosper, cut it (*informal*), reach the top, become famous, make the grade (*informal*), get to the top, crack it (*informal*), hit the jackpot (*informal*), turn out well, make your mark (*informal*), achieve recognition, do all right for yourself (*informal*) • **arrive at something** *She arrived at the airport early this morning.* = **reach**, make, get to, enter, land at, get as far as

arrogance NOUN = **conceit**, pride, swagger, pretension, presumption, bluster, hubris, pomposity, insolence, hauteur, pretentiousness, high-handedness, haughtiness, loftiness, imperiousness, pompousness, superciliousness, lordliness, conceitedness, contemptuousness, scornfulness, uppishness (*Brit. informal*), disdainfulness, overweeningness ■ **OPPOSITE:** modesty

arrogant ADJECTIVE = **conceited**, lordly, assuming, proud, swaggering, pompous, pretentious, stuck up (*informal*), cocky, contemptuous, blustering, imperious, overbearing, haughty, scornful, puffed up, egotistical, disdainful, self-important, presumptuous, high-handed, insolent, supercilious, high and mighty (*informal*),

overweening, immodest, swollen-headed, bigheaded (*informal*), uppish (*Brit. informal*) ■ **OPPOSITE:** modest

arrow NOUN 1 *warriors armed with bows and arrows* = **dart**, flight, reed (*archaic*), bolt, shaft (*archaic*), quarrel 2 *A series of arrows point the way to his grave.* = **pointer**, indicator, marker

arsenal NOUN 1 = **store**, stock, supply, magazine, stockpile 2 *Terrorists had broken into the arsenal and stolen a range of weapons.* = **armoury**, storehouse, ammunition dump, arms depot, ordnance depot

art NOUN 1 *the first exhibition of such art in the West* = **artwork**, style of art, fine art, creativity 2 *the art of conversation* = **skill**, knowledge, method, facility, craft, profession, expertise, competence, accomplishment, mastery, knack, ingenuity, finesse, aptitude, artistry, artifice (*archaic*), virtuosity, dexterity, cleverness, adroitness

artful ADJECTIVE 1 *the smiles and artifices of a subtly artful person* = **cunning**, designing, scheming, sharp, smart, clever, subtle, intriguing, tricky, shrewd, sly, wily, politic, crafty, foxy, deceitful ■ **OPPOSITE:** straightforward 2 *There is also an artful contrast of shapes.* = **skilful**, masterly, smart, clever, subtle, ingenious, adept, resourceful, proficient, adroit, dexterous ■ **OPPOSITE:** clumsy

article NOUN 1 *a newspaper article* = **feature**, story, paper, piece, item, creation, essay, composition, discourse, treatise 2 *household articles* = **thing**, piece, unit, item, object, device, tool, implement, commodity, gadget, utensil 3 *article 50 of the UN charter* = **clause**, point, part, heading, head, matter, detail, piece, particular, division, section, item, passage, portion, paragraph, proviso

articulate ADJECTIVE *She is an articulate young woman.* = **expressive**, clear, effective, vocal, meaningful, understandable, coherent, persuasive, fluent, eloquent, lucid, comprehensible, communicative, intelligible ■ **OPPOSITE:** incoherent ▶ VERB 1 *He failed to articulate an overall vision.* = **express**, say, tell, state, word, speak, declare, phrase, communicate, assert, pronounce, utter, couch, put across, enunciate, put into words, verbalize, asseverate (*formal*) 2 *He articulated each syllable.* = **pronounce**, say, talk, speak, voice, utter, enunciate, vocalize, enounce

articulation NOUN 1 *an actor able to sustain clear articulation over long periods* = **expression**, delivery, pronunciation, saying, talking, voicing, speaking, utterance, diction, enunciation, vocalization, verbalization **2** *a way of restricting their articulation of grievances* = **voicing**, statement, expression, verbalization **3** *the articulation of different modes of production* = **joint**, coupling, jointing, connection, hinge, juncture

artifice NOUN **1** *the artifice and illusion of sleight-of-hand card tricks* = **cunning**, scheming, trick, device, craft, tactic, manoeuvre, deception, hoax, expedient, ruse, guile, trickery, duplicity, subterfuge, stratagem, contrivance, chicanery, wile, craftiness, artfulness, slyness, machination **2** *a combination of theatrical artifice and dazzling cinematic movement* = **cleverness**, skill, facility, invention, ingenuity, finesse, inventiveness, deftness, adroitness

artificial ADJECTIVE **1** *free from artificial additives and flavours* = **synthetic**, manufactured, plastic (*slang*), man-made, non-natural **2** *The voice was affected, the accent artificial.* = **insincere**, forced, affected, assumed, phoney *or* phony (*informal*), put on, false, pretended, hollow, contrived, unnatural, feigned, spurious, meretricious ■ OPPOSITE: genuine **3** *The sauce was glutinous and tasted artificial.* = **fake**, mock, imitation, bogus, simulated, phoney *or* phony (*informal*), sham, pseudo (*informal*), fabricated, counterfeit, spurious, ersatz, specious ■ OPPOSITE: authentic

artillery NOUN = **big guns**, battery, cannon, ordnance, gunnery, cannonry

artisan NOUN = **craftsman** *or* **woman** *or* **person**, technician, mechanic, journeyman, artificer, handicraftsman, skilled worker

artist NOUN = **creator**, master, maker, craftsman *or* woman *or* person, artisan (*obsolete*), fine artist, draughtsman *or* woman *or* person

artiste NOUN = **performer**, player, entertainer, Thespian, trouper, play-actor

artistic ADJECTIVE **1** *They encourage children to be sensitive and artistic.* = **creative**, cultured, original, sensitive, sophisticated, refined, imaginative, aesthetic, discerning, eloquent, arty (*informal*) ■ OPPOSITE: untalented **2** *an artistic arrangement* = **beautiful**, fine, pleasing, lovely, creative, elegant, stylish, cultivated, imaginative, decorative, aesthetic, exquisite, graceful, expressive, ornamental, tasteful ■ OPPOSITE: unattractive

artistry NOUN = **skill**, art, style, taste, talent, craft, genius, creativity, touch, flair, brilliance, sensibility, accomplishment, mastery, finesse, craftsmanship, proficiency, virtuosity, workmanship, artistic ability

artless ADJECTIVE **1** *his artless air and charming smile* = **natural**, simple, fair, frank, plain, pure, open, round, true, direct, genuine, humble, straightforward, sincere, honest, candid, unaffected, upfront (*informal*), unpretentious, unadorned, dinkum (*Austral. & N.Z. informal*), guileless, uncontrived, undesigning ■ OPPOSITE: artificial **2** *a spiritless and artless display of incompetence* = **unskilled**, awkward, crude, primitive, rude, bungling, incompetent, clumsy, inept, untalented, maladroit ■ OPPOSITE: artful

arty ADJECTIVE = **artistic**, arty-farty (*informal*), arty-crafty (*informal*)

as CONJUNCTION **1** *All eyes were on him as he continued.* = **when**, while, just as, at the time that, during the time that **2** *Behave towards them as you would like to be treated.* = **in the way that**, like, in the manner that **3** *This is important as it sets the mood for the day.* = **since**, because, seeing that, considering that, on account of the fact that ▶ PREPOSITION *I had natural ability as a footballer.* = **in the role of**, being, under the name of, in the character of • **as for** *or* **to** *As for giving them guns, I don't think that's a very good idea.* = **with regard to**, about, re, concerning, regarding, respecting, relating to, with respect to, on the subject of, with reference to, in reference to, in the matter of, apropos of, as regards, anent (*Scot.*) • **as it were** *I understood the words, but I didn't, as it were, understand the question.* = **in a way**, to some extent, so to speak, in a manner of speaking, so to say

ascend VERB **1** *I held her hand as we ascended the steps.* = **climb**, scale, mount, go up ■ OPPOSITE: go down **2** *A number of steps ascend from the cobbled street.* = **slope upwards**, come up, rise up ■ OPPOSITE: slope downwards **3** *Keep the drill centred as it ascends and descends in the hole.* = **move up**, rise, go up ■ OPPOSITE: move down **4** *They ascended 55,900 feet in their balloon.* = **float up**, rise, climb, tower, go up, take off, soar, lift off, fly up ■ OPPOSITE: descend

ascendancy *or* **ascendence** NOUN = **influence**, power, control, rule, authority, command, reign, sovereignty, sway, dominance, domination, superiority, supremacy, mastery, dominion, upper hand, hegemony, prevalence, pre-eminence, predominance, rangatiratanga (*N.Z.*) ■ OPPOSITE: inferiority

ascendant or **ascendent** ADJECTIVE
Radical reformers are once more ascendant.
= **influential**, controlling, ruling, powerful,
commanding, supreme, superior,
dominant, prevailing, authoritative,
predominant, uppermost, pre-eminent
• **in the ascendant** *Geography, drama, art
and English are in the ascendant.* = **rising**,
increasing, growing, powerful, mounting,
climbing, dominating, commanding,
supreme, dominant, influential, prevailing,
flourishing, ascending, up-and-coming, on
the rise, uppermost, on the way up

ascension NOUN **1** *the first hot-air balloon
ascension* = **rise**, rising, mounting, climb,
ascending, ascent, moving upwards
2 *fifteen years after his ascension to the throne*
= **succession**, taking over, assumption,
inheritance, elevation, entering upon

ascent NOUN **1** *He led the first ascent of K2.*
= **climbing**, scaling, mounting, climb,
clambering, ascending, ascension **2** *It was a
tough course over a gradual ascent.* = **upward
slope**, rise, incline, ramp, gradient, rising
ground, acclivity **3** *The elevator began its slow
ascent.* = **rise**, rising, climb, ascension,
upward movement

ascertain VERB = **find out**, learn, discover,
determine, confirm, settle, identify,
establish, fix, verify, make certain, suss
(out) (*slang*), ferret out

ascetic NOUN *He left the luxuries of court for a
life as an ascetic.* = **recluse**, monk, nun,
abstainer, hermit, anchorite, self-denier
■ **OPPOSITE:** hedonist ▶ ADJECTIVE *priests
practising an ascetic life* = **self-denying**,
severe, plain, harsh, stern, rigorous,
austere, Spartan, self-disciplined, celibate,
puritanical, frugal, abstemious, abstinent
■ **OPPOSITE:** self-indulgent

ascribe VERB = **attribute**, credit, refer,
charge, assign, put down, set down,
impute

> **USAGE** *Ascribe* is sometimes used where
> *subscribe* is meant: *I do not subscribe* (not
> *ascribe*) *to this view of music.*

ashamed ADJECTIVE **1** *She was ashamed that
she looked so shabby.* = **embarrassed**, sorry,
guilty, upset, distressed, shy, humbled,
humiliated, blushing, self-conscious,
red-faced, chagrined, flustered, mortified,
sheepish, bashful, prudish, crestfallen,
discomfited, remorseful, abashed,
shamefaced, conscience-stricken,
discountenanced ■ **OPPOSITE:** proud **2** *She
made up the story because she was ashamed to
tell her family she was jobless.* = **reluctant**,
afraid, embarrassed, scared, unwilling,
loath, disinclined

ashen ADJECTIVE = **pale**, white, grey, wan,
livid, pasty, leaden, colourless, pallid,
anaemic, ashy, like death warmed up
(*informal*) ■ **OPPOSITE:** rosy

ashore ADVERB = **on land**, on the beach, on
the shore, aground, to the shore, on dry
land, shorewards, landwards

aside ADVERB *She closed the book and laid it
aside.* = **to one side**, away, alone,
separately, apart, alongside, beside, out of
the way, on one side, to the side, in
isolation, in reserve, out of mind ▶ NOUN
She mutters an aside to the camera.
= **interpolation**, remark, parenthesis,
digression, interposition, confidential
remark

ask VERB **1** *'How is Frank?' he asked.* = **inquire**,
question, quiz, query, interrogate
■ **OPPOSITE:** answer **2** *We had to ask him to
leave.* = **request**, apply to, appeal to, plead
with, demand, urge, sue, pray, beg,
petition, crave (*informal*), solicit, implore,
enjoin, beseech, entreat, supplicate
3 *She asked me back to her house.* = **invite**,
bid, summon

askance ADVERB **1** *They have always looked
askance at the western notion of democracy.*
= **suspiciously**, doubtfully, dubiously,
sceptically, disapprovingly, distrustfully,
mistrustfully **2** *'Do you play chess?' he asked,
looking askance at me.* = **out of the corner of
your eye**, sideways, indirectly, awry,
obliquely, with a side glance

askew ADJECTIVE *She stood there, hat askew.*
= **crooked**, awry, oblique, lopsided,
off-centre, cockeyed (*informal*), skewwhiff
(*Brit. informal*) ■ **OPPOSITE:** straight
▶ ADVERB *Some of the doors hung askew.*
= **crookedly**, to one side, awry, obliquely,
off-centre, aslant ■ **OPPOSITE:** straight

asleep ADJECTIVE = **sleeping**, napping,
dormant, crashed out (*slang*), dozing,
slumbering, snoozing (*informal*), fast
asleep, sound asleep, out for the count,
dead to the world (*informal*), in a deep sleep

aspect NOUN **1** *Climate affects every aspect of
our lives.* = **feature**, point, side, factor,
angle, characteristic, facet **2** *The house
has a south-west aspect.* = **position**, view,
situation, scene, bearing, direction,
prospect, exposure, point of view, outlook
3 *The snowy tree assumed a dumb, lifeless
aspect.* = **appearance**, look, air, condition,
quality, bearing, attitude, cast, manner,
expression, countenance (*literary*),
demeanour, mien (*literary*)

aspirant NOUN *He is among the few aspirants
with administrative experience.* = **candidate**,
applicant, hopeful, aspirer, seeker, suitor,

postulant ▶ ADJECTIVE *aspirant politicians* = **hopeful**, longing, ambitious, eager, striving, aspiring, endeavouring, wishful

aspiration NOUN = **aim**, longing, end, plan, hope, goal, design, dream, wish, desire, object, intention, objective, ambition, craving, endeavour, yearning, eagerness, Holy Grail (*informal*), hankering

aspire to VERB = **aim for**, desire, pursue, hope for, long for, crave, seek out, wish for, dream about, yearn for, hunger for, hanker after, be eager for, set your heart on, set your sights on, be ambitious for

aspiring ADJECTIVE = **hopeful**, longing, would-be, ambitious, eager, striving, endeavouring, wannabe (*informal*), wishful, aspirant

ass NOUN **1** *She was led up to the sanctuary on an ass.* = **donkey**, moke (*slang*), jennet **2** *He was regarded as a pompous ass.* = **fool**, jerk (*slang, chiefly U.S. & Canad.*), idiot, plank (*Brit. slang*), berk (*Brit. slang*), wally (*slang*), prat (*slang*), charlie (*Brit. informal*), plonker (*slang*), coot, twit (*informal, chiefly Brit.*), oaf, jackass, dipstick (*Brit. slang*), schmuck (*U.S. slang*), dork (*slang*), nitwit (*informal*), dolt, blockhead, ninny, divvy (*Brit. slang*), pillock (*Brit. slang*), nincompoop, dweeb (*U.S. slang*), putz (*U.S. slang*), weenie (*U.S. informal*), eejit (*Scot. & Irish*), numpty (*Scot. informal*), doofus (*slang, chiefly U.S.*), daftie (*informal*), twerp or twirp (*informal*), dorba or dorb (*Austral. slang*) ■ RELATED WORDS: *adjective* asinine; *name of male jack; name of female* jenny

assail VERB **1** *These newspapers assail the government each day.* = **criticize**, abuse, blast, put down, malign, berate, revile, vilify, tear into (*informal*), diss (*slang*), impugn, go for the jugular, lambast(e) **2** *He was assailed by a young man with a knife.* = **attack**, charge, assault, invade, set about, beset, fall upon, set upon, lay into (*informal*), maltreat, belabour

assailant NOUN = **attacker**, assaulter, invader, aggressor, assailer

assassin NOUN = **murderer**, killer, slayer, liquidator, executioner, hitman *or* woman (*slang*), eliminator (*slang*), hatchet man *or* woman *or* person (*slang*)

assassinate VERB = **murder**, kill, eliminate (*slang*), take out (*slang*), terminate, hit (*slang*), slay, blow away (*slang, chiefly U.S.*), liquidate

assassination NOUN = **murder**, killing, slaughter, purge, hit (*slang*), removal, elimination (*slang*), slaying, homicide, liquidation

assault NOUN *The rebels are poised for a new assault.* = **attack**, campaign, strike, rush, storm, storming, raid, invasion, charge, offensive, onset, onslaught, foray, incursion, act of aggression, inroad ■ OPPOSITE: defence ▶ VERB *The gang assaulted him with iron bars.* = **strike**, attack, beat, knock, punch, belt (*informal*), bang, batter, clip (*informal*), slap, bash (*informal*), deck (*slang*), sock (*slang*), chin (*slang*), smack, thump, set about, lay one on (*slang*), clout (*informal*), cuff, flog, whack, lob, beset, clobber (*slang*), smite (*archaic*), wallop (*informal*), swat, fall upon, set upon, lay into (*informal*), tonk (*slang*), lambast(e), belabour, beat *or* knock seven bells out of (*informal*)

assay VERB = **analyse**, examine, investigate, assess, weigh, evaluate, inspect, try, appraise

assemblage NOUN = **group**, company, meeting, body, crowd, collection, mass, gathering, rally, assembly, flock, congregation, accumulation, multitude, throng, hui (*N.Z.*), conclave, aggregation, convocation (*formal*), runanga (*N.Z.*)

assemble VERB **1** *There was nowhere for students to assemble before classes.* = **gather**, meet, collect, rally, flock, accumulate, come together, muster, convene, congregate, foregather ■ OPPOSITE: scatter **2** *The assembled multitude cheered as the leaders arrived.* = **bring together**, collect, gather, rally, summon, accumulate, round up, marshal, come together, muster, convene, amass, congregate, call together, foregather, convoke (*formal*) **3** *She was trying to assemble the bomb when it went off.* = **put together**, make, join, set up, manufacture, build up, connect, construct, erect, piece together, fabricate, fit together ■ OPPOSITE: take apart

assembly NOUN **1** *She waited until quiet settled on the assembly.* = **gathering**, group, meeting, body, council, conference, crowd, congress, audience, collection, mass, diet, rally, convention, flock, company, house, congregation, accumulation, multitude, throng, synod, hui (*N.Z.*), assemblage, conclave, aggregation, convocation (*formal*), jamaat, runanga (*N.Z.*) **2** *They are famous for their self assembly furniture range.* = **putting together**, joining, setting up, manufacture, construction, building up, connecting, erection, piecing together, fabrication, fitting together

assent NOUN *He gave his assent to the proposed legislation.* = **agreement**, accord, sanction, approval, permission, acceptance, consent, compliance, accession, acquiescence, concurrence ■ OPPOSITE: refusal • **assent**

to something I assented to the publisher's request to write this book. = **agree to**, allow, accept, grant, approve, permit, sanction, O.K., comply with, go along with, subscribe to, consent to, say yes to, accede to, fall in with, acquiesce in, concur with, give the green light to

assert VERB **1** We assert that the bill violates the First Amendment. = **state**, argue, maintain, declare, allege, swear, pronounce, contend, affirm, profess, attest, predicate, postulate, avow, aver, asseverate (formal), avouch (archaic) ■ **OPPOSITE:** deny **2** The republics began asserting their right to govern themselves. = **insist upon**, stress, defend, uphold, put forward, vindicate, press, stand up for ■ **OPPOSITE:** retract • **assert yourself** She's speaking up and asserting herself much more now. = **be forceful**, put your foot down (informal), put yourself forward, make your presence felt, exert your influence

assertion NOUN **1** assertions that the recession is truly over = **statement**, claim, allegation, profession, declaration, contention, affirmation, pronouncement, avowal, attestation, predication, asseveration (formal) **2** They have made the assertion of ethnic identity possible. = **insistence**, defence, stressing, maintenance, vindication

assertive ADJECTIVE = **confident**, firm, demanding, decided, forward, can-do (informal), positive, aggressive, decisive, forceful, emphatic, insistent, feisty (informal), pushy (informal), in-your-face (Brit. slang), dogmatic, strong-willed, domineering, overbearing, self-assured ■ **OPPOSITE:** meek

assertiveness NOUN = **confidence**, insistence, aggressiveness, firmness, decisiveness, dogmatism, forcefulness, positiveness, pushiness (informal), forwardness, self-assuredness, decidedness, domineeringness ■ **OPPOSITE:** meekness

assess VERB **1** The test was to assess aptitude rather than academic achievement. = **judge**, determine, estimate, fix, analyse, evaluate, rate, value, check out, compute, gauge, weigh up, appraise, size up (informal), eye up **2** What is the assessed value of the property? = **evaluate**, rate, tax, value, demand, estimate, fix, impose, levy

assessment NOUN **1** He was referred to a specialist for further assessment. = **judgment**, analysis, determination, evaluation, valuation, appraisal, estimation, rating, opinion, estimate, computation

2 inflated assessments of mortgaged property = **evaluation**, rating, rate, charge, tax, demand, fee, duty, toll, levy, tariff, taxation, valuation, impost

asset NOUN = **benefit**, help, service, aid, advantage, strength, resource, attraction, blessing, boon, good point, strong point, ace in the hole, feather in your cap, ace up your sleeve ■ **OPPOSITE:** disadvantage

assiduous ADJECTIVE = **diligent**, constant, steady, hard-working, persistent, attentive, persevering, laborious, industrious, indefatigable, studious, unflagging, untiring, sedulous, unwearied ■ **OPPOSITE:** lazy

assign VERB **1** Later in the year, she'll assign them research papers. = **give**, set, grant, allocate, give out, consign, allot, apportion **2** He assigned her all his land. = **allocate**, give, determine, fix, appoint, distribute, earmark, mete **3** Did you choose this country or were you simply assigned here? = **select for**, post, commission, elect, appoint, delegate, nominate, name, designate, choose for, stipulate for **4** Assign the letters of the alphabet their numerical values. = **attribute**, credit, put down, set down, ascribe, accredit

assignment NOUN **1** The course involves written assignments and practical tests. = **task**, work, job, charge, position, post, commission, exercise, responsibility, duty, mission, appointment, undertaking, occupation, chore **2** I only ever take photos on assignment. = **selection**, choice, option, appointment, delegation, nomination, designation **3** The state prohibited the assignment of licences to competitors. = **giving**, issuing, grant, distribution, allocation, earmarking, allotment, designation, consignment, dealing out, assignation (Scots Law), apportionment

assimilate VERB **1** They had been assimilated into the nation's culture. = **adjust**, fit, adapt, accommodate, accustom, conform, mingle, blend in, become like, homogenize, acclimatize, intermix, become similar, acculturate **2** My mind could only assimilate one possibility at a time. = **learn**, absorb, take in, incorporate, digest, imbibe (literary), ingest

assist VERB **1** They decided to assist me with my chores. = **help**, back, support, further, benefit, aid, encourage, work with, work for, relieve, collaborate with, cooperate with, abet, expedite, succour, lend a hand to, lend a helping hand to, give a leg up to (informal) **2** a chemical that assists in the manufacture of proteins = **facilitate**, help,

a

further, serve, aid, forward, promote, boost, ease, sustain, reinforce, speed up, pave the way for, make easy, expedite, oil the wheels, smooth the path of, assist the progress of ■ **OPPOSITE:** hinder

assistance NOUN = **help**, backing, service, support, benefit, aid, relief, boost, promotion, cooperation, encouragement, collaboration, reinforcement, helping hand, sustenance, succour, furtherance, abetment ■ **OPPOSITE:** hindrance

assistant NOUN = **helper**, partner, ally, colleague, associate, supporter, deputy, subsidiary, aide, aider, second, accessory, attendant, backer, protagonist, collaborator, accomplice, confederate, auxiliary, henchman or woman or person, right-hand man or woman or person, adjutant, helpmate, coadjutor (rare), abettor, cooperator

associate VERB 1 We've got the idea of associating progress with the future. = **connect**, couple, league, link, mix, relate, pair, ally, identify, unite, join, combine, attach, affiliate, fasten, correlate, confederate, yoke, affix, lump together, cohere, mention in the same breath, conjoin, think of together ■ **OPPOSITE:** separate 2 They found out they'd been associating with a murderer. = **socialize**, mix, hang (informal, chiefly U.S.), accompany, hang out (informal), run around (informal), mingle, be friends, befriend, consort, hang about, hobnob, fraternize ■ **OPPOSITE:** avoid ▶ NOUN the restaurant owner's business associates = **partner**, friend, ally, colleague, mate (informal), companion, comrade, affiliate, collaborator, confederate, co-worker, workmate, main man (slang, chiefly U.S.), cobber (Austral. & N.Z., old-fashioned, informal), confrère, compeer, E hoa (N.Z.)

associated ADJECTIVE = **connected**, united, joined, leagued, linked, tied, related, allied, combined, involved, bound, syndicated, affiliated, correlated, confederated, yoked

association NOUN 1 the British Olympic Association = **group**, company, club, order, union, class, society, league, band, set, troop, pack, camp, collection, gathering, organization, circle, corporation, alliance, coalition, partnership, federation, bunch (informal), formation, faction, cluster, syndicate, congregation, batch, confederation, cooperative, fraternity (U.S. & Canad.), affiliation, posse (slang), clique, confederacy, assemblage, social network (Computing) 2 The association between the two companies stretches back 30 years. = **friendship**, relationship, link, tie,

relations, bond, connection, partnership, attachment, intimacy, liaison, fellowship, affinity, familiarity, affiliation, companionship, comradeship, fraternization 3 the association of the colour black with death = **connection**, union, joining, linking, tie, mixing, relation, bond, pairing, combination, mixture, blend, identification, correlation, linkage, yoking, juxtaposition, lumping together, concomitance

assorted ADJECTIVE = **various**, different, mixed, varied, diverse, diversified, miscellaneous, sundry, motley, variegated, manifold (formal), heterogeneous ■ **OPPOSITE:** similar

assortment NOUN = **variety**, choice, collection, selection, mixture, diversity, array, jumble, medley, mixed bag (informal), potpourri, mélange (French), miscellany, mishmash, farrago, hotchpotch, salmagundi, pick 'n' mix

assuage VERB 1 She was trying to assuage her guilt. = **relieve**, ease, calm, moderate, temper, soothe, lessen, alleviate, lighten, allay, mitigate, quench, palliate ■ **OPPOSITE:** increase 2 The meat they'd managed to procure assuaged their hunger. = **calm**, still, quiet, relax, satisfy, soften, soothe, appease, lull, pacify, mollify, tranquillize ■ **OPPOSITE:** provoke

assume VERB 1 It is a mistake to assume that the two are similar. = **presume**, think, believe, expect, accept, suppose, imagine, suspect, guess (informal, chiefly U.S. & Canad.), take it, fancy, take for granted, infer, conjecture, postulate (formal), surmise, presuppose ■ **OPPOSITE:** know 2 She will assume the role of Chief Executive. = **take on**, begin, accept, manage, bear, handle, shoulder, take over, don, acquire, put on, take up, embrace, undertake, set about, attend to, take responsibility for, embark upon, enter upon 3 He assumed an air of superiority. = **simulate**, affect, adopt, put on, imitate, mimic, sham, counterfeit, feign, impersonate 4 If there is no president, power will be assumed by extremist forces. = **take over**, take, appropriate, acquire, seize, hijack, confiscate, wrest, usurp, lay claim to, pre-empt, commandeer, requisition, expropriate (formal), arrogate ■ **OPPOSITE:** give up

assumed ADJECTIVE = **false**, affected, made-up, pretended, fake, imitation, bogus, simulated, sham, counterfeit, feigned, spurious, fictitious, make-believe, pseudonymous, phoney or phony (informal) ■ **OPPOSITE:** real

assumption NOUN **1** *They are wrong in their assumption that we are all alike.*
= **presumption**, theory, opinion, belief, guess, expectation, fancy, suspicion, premise, acceptance, hypothesis, anticipation, inference, conjecture, surmise, supposition, presupposition, premise, postulation **2** = **taking on**, managing, handling, shouldering, putting on, taking up, takeover, acquisition **3** *the government's assumption of power* = **seizure**, taking, takeover, acquisition, appropriation, wresting, confiscation, commandeering, expropriation (*formal*), pre-empting, usurpation, arrogation

assurance NOUN **1** *an assurance that other forces will not move into the territory* = **promise**, statement, guarantee, commitment, pledge, profession, vow, declaration, assertion, oath, affirmation, protestation (*formal*), word, word of honour ■ **OPPOSITE:** lie **2** *He led the orchestra with assurance.* = **confidence**, conviction, courage, certainty, self-confidence, poise, assertiveness, security, faith, coolness, nerve, aplomb, boldness, self-reliance, firmness, self-assurance, certitude, sureness, self-possession, positiveness, assuredness ■ **OPPOSITE:** self-doubt

assure VERB **1** *'Everything's going to be okay,' he assured me.* = **convince**, encourage, persuade, satisfy, comfort, prove to, reassure, soothe, hearten, embolden, win someone over, bring someone round **2** *Last night's victory has assured their promotion.* = **make certain**, ensure, confirm, guarantee, secure, make sure, complete, seal, clinch **3** *We can assure you of our best service at all times.* = **promise to**, pledge to, vow to, guarantee to, swear to, attest to, confirm to, certify to, affirm to, give your word to, declare confidently to

assured ADJECTIVE **1** *He was much more assured than in recent appearances.* = **confident**, certain, positive, bold, poised, assertive, complacent, fearless, audacious, pushy (*informal*), brazen, self-confident, self-assured, self-possessed, overconfident, dauntless, sure of yourself ■ **OPPOSITE:** self-conscious **2** *Our victory is assured; nothing can stop us.* = **certain**, sure, ensured, confirmed, settled, guaranteed, fixed, secure, sealed, clinched, made certain, sound, in the bag (*slang*), dependable, beyond doubt, irrefutable, unquestionable, indubitable, nailed-on (*slang*) ■ **OPPOSITE:** doubtful

astonish VERB = **amaze**, surprise, stun, stagger, bewilder, astound, daze, confound, stupefy, boggle the mind, dumbfound, flabbergast (*informal*)

astonished ADJECTIVE = **amazed**, surprised, staggered, bewildered, astounded, dazed, stunned, confounded, perplexed, gobsmacked (*informal*), dumbfounded, flabbergasted (*informal*), stupefied

astonishing ADJECTIVE = **amazing**, striking, surprising, brilliant, stunning, impressive, overwhelming, staggering, startling, sensational (*informal*), bewildering, breathtaking, astounding, eye-opening, wondrous (*archaic, literary*), jaw-dropping, stupefying

astonishment NOUN = **amazement**, surprise, wonder, confusion, awe, consternation, bewilderment, wonderment, stupefaction

astound VERB = **amaze**, surprise, overwhelm, astonish, stagger, bewilder, daze, confound, stupefy, stun, take your breath away, boggle the mind, dumbfound, flabbergast (*informal*)

astounding ADJECTIVE = **amazing**, striking, surprising, brilliant, impressive, astonishing, staggering, sensational (*informal*), bewildering, stunning, breathtaking, wondrous (*archaic, literary*), jaw-dropping, eye-popping (*informal*), stupefying

astray ADJECTIVE or ADVERB *Many items of mail being sent to her have gone astray.* = **off the right track**, adrift, off course, off the mark, amiss • **lead someone astray** *The judge thought he'd been led astray by others.* = **lead into sin**, lead into error, lead into bad ways, lead into wrong

astringent ADJECTIVE **1** *an astringent lotion* = **contractive**, contractile, styptic **2** *an astringent satire on Hollywood* = **severe**, strict, exacting, harsh, grim, stern, hard, rigid, rigorous, stringent, austere, caustic, acerbic

astrology NOUN = **stargazing**, astromancy, horoscopy

astronaut NOUN = **space traveller**, cosmonaut, spaceman, spacewoman, space pilot

astronomical or **astronomic** ADJECTIVE = **huge**, great, giant, massive, vast, enormous, immense, titanic, infinite, gigantic, monumental (*informal*), colossal, boundless, galactic, Gargantuan, immeasurable

astute ADJECTIVE = **intelligent**, politic, bright (*informal*), sharp, keen, calculating, clever, subtle, penetrating, knowing, shrewd, cunning, discerning, sly, on the ball

a

(*informal*), canny, perceptive, wily, crafty, artful, insightful, foxy, adroit, sagacious (*formal*)

asunder ADVERB or ADJECTIVE (*literary*) = **to pieces**, apart, torn, rent, to bits, to shreds, in pieces, into pieces

asylum NOUN **1** *They applied for asylum after fleeing their home country.* = **refuge**, security, haven, safety, protection, preserve, shelter, retreat, harbour, sanctuary **2** *He spent the rest of his life in an asylum.* = **psychiatric hospital**, hospital, mental hospital, institution

atheism NOUN = **nonbelief**, disbelief, scepticism, infidelity, paganism, unbelief, freethinking, godlessness, irreligion, heathenism

atheist NOUN = **nonbeliever**, pagan, sceptic, disbeliever, heathen (*old-fashioned*), infidel, unbeliever, freethinker, irreligionist

athlete NOUN = **sportsperson**, player, runner, competitor, contender, sportsman, contestant, gymnast, games player, sportswoman

athletic ADJECTIVE *She was tall, with an athletic build.* = **fit**, strong, powerful, healthy, active, trim, strapping, robust, vigorous, energetic, muscular, swole (*slang*), hench (*informal*), two-fisted, sturdy, husky (*informal*), lusty, herculean, sinewy, brawny, able-bodied, well-proportioned ■ **OPPOSITE:** feeble

athletics PLURAL NOUN *intercollegiate athletics* = **sports**, games, races, exercises, contests, sporting events, gymnastics, track and field events, games of strength

atmosphere NOUN **1** *These gases pollute the atmosphere of towns and cities.* = **air**, sky, heavens, aerosphere **2** *The muted decor adds to the relaxed atmosphere.* = **feeling**, feel, air, quality, character, environment, spirit, surroundings, tone, mood, climate, flavour, aura, ambience, vibes (*slang*)

atom NOUN = **particle**, bit, spot, trace, scrap, molecule, grain, dot, fragment, fraction, shred, crumb, mite, jot, speck, morsel, mote, whit, tittle, iota, scintilla (*rare*)

atone VERB = **make amends**, pay, do penance, make reparation, make redress

atonement NOUN = **amends**, payment, compensation, satisfaction, redress, reparation, restitution, penance, recompense, expiation (*formal*), propitiation

atrocious ADJECTIVE **1** *The food here is atrocious.* = **shocking**, terrible (*informal*), appalling, horrible, godawful (*slang*), hellacious (*U.S. slang*), execrable,

detestable ■ **OPPOSITE:** fine **2** *The treatment of the prisoners was atrocious.* = **cruel**, savage, brutal, vicious, ruthless, infamous, monstrous, wicked, barbaric, inhuman, diabolical, heinous, flagrant, infernal, fiendish, villainous, nefarious, horrifying, grievous ■ **OPPOSITE:** kind

atrocity NOUN **1** *Those who committed this atrocity should be punished.* = **act of cruelty**, wrong, crime, horror, offence, evil, outrage, cruelty, brutality, obscenity, wrongdoing, enormity, monstrosity, transgression, abomination, barbarity, villainy **2** *stomach-churning tales of atrocity and massacre* = **cruelty**, wrong, horror, brutality, wrongdoing, enormity, savagery, ruthlessness, wickedness, inhumanity, infamy, transgression, barbarity, viciousness, villainy, baseness, monstrousness, heinousness, nefariousness, shockingness, atrociousness, fiendishness, barbarousness, grievousness, villainousness

atrophy VERB **1** *His muscle atrophied, and he had difficulty walking.* = **waste away**, waste, shrink, diminish, deteriorate, decay, dwindle, wither, wilt, degenerate, shrivel **2** *If you let your mind stagnate, this talent will atrophy.* = **decline**, waste, fade, shrink, diminish, deteriorate, dwindle, wither, wilt, degenerate, shrivel, waste away
▶ NOUN **1** *exercises to avoid atrophy of cartilage* = **wasting away**, decline, wasting, decay, decaying, withering, deterioration, meltdown (*informal*), shrivelling, degeneration, diminution **2** *levels of consciousness which are in danger of atrophy* = **wasting**, decline, decay, decaying, withering, deterioration, meltdown (*informal*), shrivelling, degeneration, diminution, wasting away

attach VERB **1** *Attach labels to things before you file them away.* = **affix**, stick, secure, bind, unite, add, join, couple, link, tie, fix, connect, lash, glue, adhere, fasten, annex, truss, yoke, append (*formal*), make fast, cohere, subjoin, bootstrap to ■ **OPPOSITE:** detach **2** *They have attached much significance to your visit.* = **ascribe**, connect, attribute, assign, place, associate, lay on, accredit, invest with, impute, reattribute • **attach yourself to** or **be attached to something** *He attached himself to a group of poets known as the Martians.* = **join**, accompany, associate with, combine with, join forces with, latch on to, unite with, sign up with, become associated with, sign on with, affiliate yourself with

a

attached ADJECTIVE I *wondered if he was attached.* = **spoken for**, married, partnered, engaged, accompanied • **attached to** *She is very attached to her family and friends.* = **fond of**, devoted to, affectionate towards, full of regard for

attachment NOUN **1** *I feel a strong attachment to my home town.* = **fondness**, liking, feeling, love, relationship, regard, bond, friendship, attraction, loyalty, affection, devotion, fidelity, affinity, tenderness, reverence, predilection, possessiveness, partiality, aroha (N.Z.) ■ OPPOSITE: aversion **2** *Some models come with attachments for dusting.* = **accessory**, fitting, extra, addition, component, extension, supplement, fixture, auxiliary, adaptor or adapter, supplementary part, add-on, adjunct, appendage, accoutrement, appurtenance

attack VERB **1** *The duo are believed to have attacked several people in South London.* = **assault**, strike (at), mug (*informal*), set about, ambush, assail, tear into, fall upon, set upon, lay into (*informal*) ■ OPPOSITE: defend **2** *The infantry's aim was to slow attacking forces.* = **invade**, occupy, raid, infringe, charge, rush, storm, encroach **3** *He publicly attacked the people who've been calling for a secret ballot.* = **criticize**, blame, abuse, blast, pan (*informal*), condemn, knock (*informal*), slam (*slang*), put down, slate (*informal*), have a go (at) (*informal*), censure, malign, berate, disparage, revile, vilify, tear into (*informal*), slag off (*Brit. slang*), throw shade (at) (*slang*), diss (*slang*), find fault with, impugn (*formal*), go for the jugular, lambast(e), pick holes in, excoriate, bite someone's head off, snap someone's head off, pick to pieces ▶ NOUN **1** *a campaign of air attacks on strategic targets* = **assault**, charge, campaign, strike, rush, raid, invasion, offensive, aggression, blitz, onset, onslaught, foray, incursion, inroad ■ OPPOSITE: defence **2** *He launched an attack on businesses for failing to invest.* = **criticism**, panning (*informal*), slating (*informal*), censure, disapproval, slagging (*slang*), abuse, knocking (*informal*), bad press, vilification, denigration, calumny, character assassination, disparagement, impugnment **3** *It brought on an attack of asthma.* = **bout**, fit, access, spell, stroke, seizure, spasm, convulsion, paroxysm

attacker NOUN = **assailant**, assaulter, raider, intruder, invader, aggressor, mugger

attain VERB **1** *He's halfway to attaining his pilot's licence.* = **obtain**, get, win, reach, effect, land (*informal*), score (*slang*), complete, gain, achieve, earn, secure, realize, acquire, fulfil, accomplish, grasp, reap, procure **2** *attaining a state of calmness and confidence* = **reach**, achieve, realize, acquire, arrive at, accomplish

attainable ADJECTIVE = **achievable**, possible, likely, potential, accessible, probable, at hand, feasible, within reach, practicable, obtainable, reachable, realizable, graspable, gettable, procurable, accomplishable ■ OPPOSITE: unattainable

attainment NOUN **1** *the attainment of independence* = **achievement**, getting, winning, reaching, gaining, obtaining, acquisition, feat, completion, reaping, accomplishment, realization, fulfilment, arrival at, procurement, acquirement **2** *their educational attainments* = **skill**, art, ability, talent, gift, achievement, capability, competence, accomplishment, mastery, proficiency

attempt VERB *We attempted to do something like that here.* = **try**, seek, aim, struggle, tackle, take on, experiment, venture, undertake, essay (*formal*), strive, endeavour, have a go at (*informal*), make an effort, make an attempt, have a crack at, have a shot at (*informal*), try your hand at, do your best to, jump through hoops (*informal*), have a stab at (*informal*), take the bit between your teeth ▶ NOUN **1** *a deliberate attempt to destabilize defence* = **try**, go (*informal*), shot (*informal*), effort, trial, bid, experiment, crack (*informal*), venture, undertaking, essay (*formal*), stab (*informal*), endeavour **2** *an attempt on the life of the Prime Minister* = **attack**, assault

attempted ADJECTIVE = **tried**, ventured, undertaken, endeavoured, assayed

attend VERB **1** *Thousands of people attended the funeral.* = **be present**, go to, visit, be at, be there, be here, frequent, haunt, appear at, turn up at, patronize, show up at (*informal*), show yourself, put in an appearance at, present yourself at ■ OPPOSITE: be absent **2** *I'm not sure what he said – I wasn't attending.* = **pay attention**, listen, follow, hear, mark, mind, watch, note, regard, notice, observe, look on, heed, take to heart, pay heed, hearken (*archaic*) ■ OPPOSITE: ignore **3** *horse-drawn coaches attended by liveried footmen* = **escort**, conduct, guard, shadow, accompany, companion, shepherd, convoy, usher, squire (*old-fashioned*), chaperon • **attend to someone** *The main thing is to attend to the injured.* = **look after**, help, mind, aid, tend, nurse, care for, take care of, minister to, administer to • **attend to something**

You had better attend to the matter in hand.
= **apply yourself to**, concentrate on, look after, take care of, see to, get to work on, devote yourself to, occupy yourself with

attendance NOUN **1** *Her attendance at school was sporadic.* = **presence**, being there, attending, appearance **2** *Some estimates put attendance at 60,000.* = **turnout**, audience, gate, congregation, house, crowd, throng, number present

attendant NOUN *He was working as a car-park attendant.* = **assistant**, guide, guard, servant, companion, aide, escort, follower, steward, waiter, usher, warden, helper, auxiliary, custodian, page, menial, concierge, underling (*derogatory*), lackey, chaperon, flunky ▶ ADJECTIVE *His victory, and all the attendant publicity, were deserved.* = **accompanying**, related, associated, accessory, consequent, resultant, concomitant

attention NOUN **1** *He turned his attention to the desperate state of housing in the province.* = **thinking**, thought, mind, notice, consideration, concentration, observation, scrutiny, heed, deliberation, contemplation, thoughtfulness, attentiveness, intentness, heedfulness **2** *a demanding baby who wants attention 24 hours a day* = **care**, support, concern, treatment, looking after, succour, ministration **3** *Let me draw your attention to some important issues.* = **awareness**, regard, notice, recognition, consideration, observation, consciousness ■ **OPPOSITE:** inattention ▶ PLURAL NOUN *He discovered that she had attracted the attentions of two other men.* = **courtesy**, compliments, regard, respect, care, consideration, deference, politeness, civility, gallantry, mindfulness, assiduities ■ **OPPOSITE:** discourtesy

attentive ADJECTIVE **1** *I wish you would be more attentive to detail.* = **intent**, listening, concentrating, careful, alert, awake, mindful, watchful, observant, studious, on your toes, heedful, regardful ■ **OPPOSITE:** heedless **2** *At parties he is always attentive to his wife.* = **considerate**, kind, civil, devoted, helpful, obliging, accommodating, polite, thoughtful, gracious, conscientious, respectful, courteous, gallant ■ **OPPOSITE:** neglectful

attenuate VERB = **weaken**, reduce, contract, lower, diminish, decrease, dilute, lessen, sap, water down, adulterate, enfeeble, enervate, devaluate

attenuated ADJECTIVE **1** *rounded arches and attenuated columns* = **slender**, extended, thinned, slimmed, refined, stretched out, lengthened, drawn out, spun out, elongated, rarefied **2** *The vaccination contains attenuated strains of the target virus.* = **weakened**, reduced, contracted, lowered, diminished, decreased, dilute, diluted, lessened, devalued, sapped, watered down, adulterated, enfeebled, enervated

attest VERB = **testify**, show, prove, confirm, display, declare, witness, demonstrate, seal, swear, exhibit, warrant, assert, manifest, give evidence, invoke, ratify, affirm, certify, verify, bear out, substantiate, corroborate, bear witness, authenticate, vouch for, evince (*formal*), aver, adjure ■ **OPPOSITE:** disprove

attic NOUN = **loft**, garret, roof space

attire NOUN = **clothes**, wear, dress, clothing, gear (*informal*), habit, uniform, outfit, costume, threads (*slang*), array (*poetic*), garments, robes, apparel (*old-fashioned*), garb, accoutrements, raiment (*archaic, poetic*), vestment, schmutter (*slang*), habiliments

attitude NOUN **1** *the general change in attitude towards them* = **opinion**, thinking, feeling, thought, view, position, approach, belief, mood, perspective, point of view, stance, outlook, viewpoint, slant, frame of mind **2** *He has a gentle attitude.* = **manner**, air, condition, bearing, aspect, carriage, disposition, demeanour, mien (*literary*) **3** *scenes of the king in various attitudes of worshipping* = **position**, bearing, pose, stance, carriage, posture

attorney NOUN = **lawyer**, solicitor, counsel, advocate, barrister, counsellor, legal adviser

attract VERB **1** *Summer attracts visitors to the countryside.* = **allure**, interest, draw, invite, persuade, engage, charm, appeal to, fascinate, win over, tempt, lure (*informal*), induce, incline, seduce, entice, enchant, endear, lead on, coax, captivate, beguile, cajole, bewitch, decoy, inveigle, pull, catch (someone's) eye ■ **OPPOSITE:** repel **2** *Anything with strong gravity attracts other things to it.* = **pull** (*informal*), draw, magnetize

attraction NOUN **1** *It was never a physical attraction, just a meeting of minds.* = **appeal**, interest, draw, pull (*informal*), come-on (*informal*), charm, incentive, invitation, lure, bait, temptation, fascination, attractiveness, allure, inducement, magnetism, enchantment, endearment, enticement, captivation, temptingness, pleasingness **2** *the gravitational attraction of the Sun* = **pull**, draw (*informal*), magnetism

attractive ADJECTIVE **1** *He was always very attractive to others.* = **seductive**, charming, tempting, interesting, pleasing, pretty, fair, beautiful, inviting, engaging, likable or likeable, lovely, winning, sexy (*informal*), pleasant, handsome, fetching (*informal*), good-looking, glamorous, gorgeous (*informal*), magnetic, cute, irresistible, enticing, provocative, captivating, beguiling, alluring, bonny (*Scot. & Northern English, dialect*), winsome, comely (*old-fashioned*), prepossessing, hot (*informal*), fit (*Brit. informal*), lush (*slang*) ■ **OPPOSITE:** unattractive **2** *Co-operation was more than just an attractive option.* = **appealing**, pleasing, inviting, fascinating, tempting, enticing, agreeable, irresistible ■ **OPPOSITE:** unappealing

attributable ADJECTIVE = **ascribable**, accountable, applicable, traceable, explicable, assignable, imputable, blamable or blameable, placeable, referable or referrable

attribute VERB *They attribute their success to external causes such as luck.* = **ascribe**, apply, credit, blame, refer, trace, assign, charge, allocate, put down, set down, allot, impute ▶ NOUN *He has every attribute a footballer could want.* = **quality**, point, mark, sign, note, feature, property, character, element, aspect, symbol, characteristic, indication, distinction, virtue, trait, hallmark (*Brit.*), facet, quirk, peculiarity, idiosyncrasy

attribution NOUN = **ascription**, charge, credit, blame, assignment, attachment, placement, referral, assignation, imputation

attrition NOUN = **wearing down**, harrying, weakening, harassment, thinning out, attenuation, debilitation

attuned ADJECTIVE = **accustomed**, adjusted, coordinated, in tune, in harmony, in accord, harmonized, familiarized, acclimatized

atypical ADJECTIVE = **unusual**, exceptional, uncommon, singular, deviant, unconventional, unique, unorthodox, uncharacteristic, out of the ordinary, unrepresentative, out of keeping, uncustomary, nonconforming, unconforming ■ **OPPOSITE:** normal

auburn ADJECTIVE = **reddish-brown**, tawny, russet, henna, rust-coloured, copper-coloured, chestnut-coloured, Titian red, nutbrown

audacious ADJECTIVE **1** *an audacious plan to win the presidency* = **daring**, enterprising, brave, bold, risky, rash, adventurous, reckless, courageous, fearless, intrepid, valiant, daredevil, death-defying, dauntless, venturesome ■ **OPPOSITE:** timid **2** *Audacious thieves stole her car from under her nose.* = **cheeky**, presumptuous, impertinent, insolent, impudent, forward, fresh (*informal*), assuming, rude, defiant, brazen, in-your-face (*Brit. slang*), shameless, sassy (*U.S. informal*), pert, disrespectful ■ **OPPOSITE:** tactful

audacity NOUN **1** *I was shocked at the audacity of the gangsters.* = **daring**, nerve, courage, guts (*informal*), bravery, boldness, recklessness, face (*informal*), front, enterprise, valour, fearlessness, rashness, adventurousness, intrepidity, audaciousness, dauntlessness, venturesomeness **2** *He had the audacity to look at his watch while I was talking.* = **cheek** (*informal*), nerve (*informal*), defiance, gall (*informal*), presumption, rudeness, chutzpah (*U.S. & Canad. informal*), insolence, impertinence, neck (*informal*), impudence, effrontery, brass neck (*Brit. informal*), shamelessness, sassiness (*U.S. informal*), forwardness, pertness, audaciousness, disrespectfulness

audible ADJECTIVE = **clear**, distinct, discernible, detectable, perceptible, hearable ■ **OPPOSITE:** inaudible

audience NOUN **1** *The entire audience broke into loud applause.* = **spectators**, company, house, crowd, gathering, gallery, assembly, viewers, listeners, patrons, congregation, turnout, onlookers, throng, assemblage **2** *She began to find a receptive audience for her work.* = **public**, market, following, fans, devotees, fanbase, aficionados **3** *The Prime Minister will seek an audience with the Queen today.* = **interview**, meeting, hearing, exchange, reception, consultation

audit VERB *Each year they audit our accounts and certify them as true and fair.* = **inspect**, check, review, balance, survey, examine, investigate, go through, assess, go over, evaluate, vet, verify, appraise, scrutinize, inquire into ▶ NOUN *The bank is carrying out an internal audit.* = **inspection**, check, checking, review, balancing, search, survey, investigation, examination, scan, scrutiny, supervision, surveillance, look-over, verification, once-over (*informal*), checkup, superintendence

augment VERB = **increase**, grow, raise, extend, boost, expand, add to, build up, strengthen, enhance, reinforce, swell, intensify, heighten, enlarge, multiply, inflate, magnify, amplify, dilate ■ **OPPOSITE:** diminish

a

augur VERB = **bode**, promise, predict, herald, signify, foreshadow, prophesy, harbinger, presage, prefigure, portend, betoken, be an omen of

august ADJECTIVE = **noble**, great, kingly, grand, excellent, imposing, impressive, superb, distinguished, magnificent, glorious, splendid, elevated, eminent, majestic, dignified, regal, stately, high-ranking, monumental, solemn, lofty, exalted

aura NOUN = **air**, feeling, feel, quality, atmosphere, tone, suggestion, mood, scent, aroma, odour, ambience, vibes (*slang*), vibrations (*slang*), emanation

auspices PLURAL NOUN = **support**, backing, control, charge, care, authority, championship, influence, protection, guidance, sponsorship, supervision, patronage, advocacy, countenance, aegis

auspicious ADJECTIVE = **favourable**, timely, happy, promising, encouraging, bright, lucky, hopeful, fortunate, prosperous, rosy, opportune (*formal*), propitious, felicitous ■ **OPPOSITE:** unpromising

austere ADJECTIVE 1 *an austere, distant, cold person* = **stern**, hard, serious, cold, severe, formal, grave, strict, exacting, harsh, stiff, forbidding, grim, rigorous, solemn, stringent, inflexible, unrelenting, unfeeling ■ **OPPOSITE:** kindly 2 *The church was austere and simple.* = **plain**, simple, severe, spare, harsh, stark, bleak, subdued, economical, Spartan, unadorned, unornamented, bare-bones ■ **OPPOSITE:** luxurious 3 *The life of the troops was comparatively austere.* = **ascetic**, strict, continent, exacting, rigid, sober, economical, solemn, Spartan, unrelenting, self-disciplined, puritanical, chaste, strait-laced, abstemious, self-denying, abstinent ■ **OPPOSITE:** abandoned

austerity NOUN 1 *abandoned buildings with a classical austerity* = **plainness**, economy, simplicity, severity, starkness, spareness, Spartanism 2 *the years of austerity which followed the war* = **asceticism**, economy, rigidity, abstinence, self-discipline, chastity, sobriety, continence, puritanism, solemnity, self-denial, strictness, abstemiousness, chasteness, exactingness, Spartanism

authentic ADJECTIVE 1 *patterns for making authentic border-style clothing* = **real**, true, original, actual, pure, genuine, valid, faithful, undisputed, veritable, lawful, on the level (*informal*), bona fide, dinkum (*Austral. & N.Z. informal*), pukka, the real McCoy, true-to-life, live (*of data*)

■ **OPPOSITE:** fake 2 *authentic details about the birth of the organization* = **accurate**, true, certain, reliable, legitimate, authoritative, factual, truthful, dependable, trustworthy, veracious ■ **OPPOSITE:** fictitious

authenticate VERB 1 *All the antiques have been authenticated.* = **verify**, guarantee, warrant, authorize, certify, avouch ■ **OPPOSITE:** invalidate 2 *He authenticated the accuracy of various details.* = **vouch for**, confirm, endorse, validate, attest

authenticity NOUN 1 *Some factors have cast doubt on the statue's authenticity.* = **genuineness**, purity, realness, veritableness 2 *The film's authenticity of detail has impressed critics.* = **accuracy**, truth, certainty, validity, reliability, legitimacy, verity, actuality, faithfulness, truthfulness, dependability, trustworthiness, authoritativeness, factualness

author NOUN 1 *She's the author of the book 'Give your Child Music'.* = **writer**, composer, novelist, hack, creator, columnist, scribbler, scribe, essayist, wordsmith, penpusher, littérateur, man or woman of letters 2 *the authors of the plan* = **creator**, father, mother, parent, maker, producer, framer, designer, founder, architect, planner, inventor, mover, originator, prime mover, doer, initiator, begetter, fabricator

authoritarian ADJECTIVE *There was a coup to restore authoritarian rule.* = **strict**, severe, absolute, harsh, rigid, autocratic, dictatorial, dogmatic, imperious, domineering, unyielding, tyrannical, disciplinarian, despotic, doctrinaire ■ **OPPOSITE:** lenient ▶ NOUN *He became an overly strict authoritarian.* = **disciplinarian**, dictator, tyrant, despot, autocrat, absolutist

authoritative ADJECTIVE 1 *She has an authoritative manner.* = **commanding**, lordly, masterly, imposing, dominating, confident, decisive, imperative, assertive, autocratic, dictatorial, dogmatic, imperious, self-assured, peremptory ■ **OPPOSITE:** timid 2 *The first authoritative study was published in 1840.* = **official**, approved, sanctioned, legitimate, sovereign, authorized, commanding ■ **OPPOSITE:** unofficial 3 *The evidence she uses is highly authoritative.* = **reliable**, learned, sound, true, accurate, valid, scholarly, faithful, authentic, definitive, factual, truthful, veritable, dependable, trustworthy ■ **OPPOSITE:** unreliable

authority NOUN 1 (*usually plural*) *This was a pretext for the authorities to cancel the elections.* = **powers that be**, government, police, officials, the state, management, administration, the system, the Establishment, Big Brother (*informal*), officialdom **2** *The judge has no authority to order a second trial.* = **prerogative**, right, influence, might, force, power, control, charge, rule, government, weight, strength, direction, command, licence, privilege, warrant, say-so, sway, domination, jurisdiction, supremacy, dominion, ascendancy, mana (*N.Z.*) **3** *Professor Ahmed is an authority on Russian affairs.* = **expert**, specialist, professional, master, ace (*informal*), scholar, guru, buff (*informal*), wizard, whizz (*informal*), virtuoso, connoisseur, arbiter, hotshot (*informal*), fundi (*S. African*) **4** *He has no natural authority.* = **command**, power, control, rule, management, direction, grasp, sway, domination, mastery, dominion **5** *She must first be given authority by her board.* = **permission**, leave, permit, sanction, licence, approval, go-ahead (*informal*), liberty, consent, warrant, say-so (*informal*), tolerance, justification, green light, assent, authorization, dispensation, carte blanche, a blank cheque, sufferance

authorization NOUN = **permission**, right, leave, power, authority, ability, strength, permit, sanction, licence, approval, warrant, say-so (*informal*), credentials, a blank cheque

authorize VERB **1** *They authorized him to use force if necessary.* = **empower**, commission, enable, entitle, mandate, accredit, give authority to **2** *We are willing to authorize a police raid.* = **permit**, allow, suffer, grant, confirm, agree to, approve, sanction, endure, license, endorse, warrant, tolerate, ratify, consent to, countenance, accredit, vouch for, give leave, give the green light for, give a blank cheque to, give authority for ■ **OPPOSITE:** forbid

authorized ADJECTIVE = **official**, commissioned, approved, licensed, ratified, signed and sealed

autobiography NOUN = **life story**, record, history, résumé, memoirs

autocracy NOUN = **dictatorship**, tyranny, despotism, absolutism

autocrat NOUN = **dictator**, tyrant, despot, absolutist

autocratic ADJECTIVE = **dictatorial**, absolute, unlimited, all-powerful, imperious, domineering, tyrannical, despotic, tyrannous

automatic ADJECTIVE **1** *Modern trains have automatic doors.* = **mechanical**, robot, automated, mechanized, push-button,

self-regulating, self-propelling, self-activating, self-moving, self-acting, hands-off ■ **OPPOSITE:** done by hand **2** *the automatic body functions, such as breathing* = **involuntary**, natural, unconscious, mechanical, spontaneous, reflex, instinctive, instinctual, unwilled ■ **OPPOSITE:** conscious **3** *They should face an automatic charge of manslaughter.* = **inevitable**, certain, necessary, assured, routine, unavoidable, inescapable

autonomous ADJECTIVE = **self-ruling**, free, independent, sovereign, self-sufficient, self-governing, self-determining

autonomy NOUN = **independence**, freedom, sovereignty, self-determination, self-government, self-rule, self-sufficiency, home rule, rangatiratanga (*N.Z.*) ■ **OPPOSITE:** dependency

autopsy NOUN = **postmortem**, dissection, postmortem examination, necropsy

auxiliary ADJECTIVE **1** *auxiliary fuel tanks* = **supplementary**, reserve, emergency, substitute, secondary, back-up, subsidiary, fall-back **2** *the army and auxiliary forces* = **supporting**, helping, aiding, assisting, accessory, ancillary ■ **OPPOSITE:** primary ▶ NOUN *a nursing auxiliary* = **helper**, partner, ally, associate, supporter, assistant, companion, accessory, subordinate, protagonist, accomplice, confederate, henchman *or* woman *or* person

avail NOUN *His efforts were to no avail.* = **benefit**, use, help, good, service, aid, profit, advantage, purpose, assistance, utility, effectiveness, mileage (*informal*), usefulness, efficacy • **avail yourself of something** *Guests should feel at liberty to avail themselves of your facilities.* = **make use of**, use, employ, exploit, take advantage of, profit from, make the most of, utilize, have recourse to, turn to account

availability NOUN = **accessibility**, readiness, handiness, attainability, obtainability

available ADJECTIVE = **accessible**, ready, to hand, convenient, handy, vacant, on hand, at hand, free, applicable, to be had, achievable, obtainable, on tap (*informal*), attainable, at your fingertips, at your disposal, ready for use ■ **OPPOSITE:** in use

avalanche NOUN **1** *Four people died when an avalanche buried them alive last week.* = **snow-slide**, landslide, landslip, snow-slip **2** *He was greeted with an avalanche of publicity.* = **large amount**, barrage, torrent, deluge, inundation

a

avant-garde ADJECTIVE = **progressive**, pioneering, way-out (*informal*), experimental, innovative, unconventional, far-out (*slang*), ground-breaking, innovatory ■ **OPPOSITE:** conservative

avarice NOUN = **greed**, meanness, penny-pinching, parsimony (*formal*), acquisitiveness, rapacity, cupidity (*formal*), stinginess, covetousness, miserliness, greediness, niggardliness, graspingness, close-fistedness, penuriousness ■ **OPPOSITE:** liberality

avenge VERB = **get revenge for**, revenge, repay, retaliate for, take revenge for, hit back for, requite, pay (someone) back for, get even for (*informal*), even the score for, get your own back for, take vengeance for, take satisfaction for, pay (someone) back in their own coin for

> USAGE In the past it was considered incorrect to use *avenge* with *yourself*, but this use is now acceptable and relatively common: *she was determined to avenge herself upon this monster*.

avenue NOUN = **street**, way, course, drive, road, pass, approach, channel, access, entry, route, path, passage, entrance, alley, pathway, boulevard, driveway, thoroughfare

average NOUN *The pay is about the average for a service industry.* = **standard**, normal, usual, par, mode, mean, rule, medium, norm, run of the mill, midpoint ▶ ADJECTIVE **1** *The average man burns over 2000 calories a day.* = **usual**, common, standard, general, normal, regular, ordinary, typical, commonplace, unexceptional ■ **OPPOSITE:** unusual **2** *The average age of the group was 23.* = **mean**, middle, medium, intermediate, median **3** *I was only average academically.* = **mediocre**, fair, ordinary, moderate, pedestrian, indifferent, not bad, middling, insignificant, so-so (*informal*), banal, second-rate, middle-of-the-road, tolerable (*informal*), run-of-the-mill, passable, undistinguished, uninspired, unexceptional, bog-standard (*Brit. & Irish slang*), no great shakes (*informal*), fair to middling (*informal*) ▶ VERB *pay increases averaging 9.75%* = **make on average**, be on average, even out to, do on average, balance out to • **on average** *On average we would be spending $200 a day.* = **usually**, generally, normally, typically, for the most part, as a rule

averse ADJECTIVE = **opposed**, reluctant, hostile, unwilling, backward, unfavourable, loath, disinclined, inimical, indisposed, antipathetic, ill-disposed ■ **OPPOSITE:** favourable

aversion NOUN = **hatred**, hate, horror, disgust, hostility, opposition, dislike, reluctance, loathing, distaste, animosity, revulsion, antipathy, repulsion, abhorrence, disinclination, repugnance, odium (*formal*), detestation, indisposition ■ **OPPOSITE:** love

avert VERB **1** *A fresh tragedy was narrowly averted yesterday.* = **ward off**, avoid, prevent, frustrate, fend off, preclude, stave off, forestall, deflect **2** *He kept his eyes averted.* = **turn away**, turn, turn aside

aviation NOUN = **flying**, flight, aeronautics, powered flight

aviator NOUN = **pilot**, flyer (*old-fashioned*), airman, airwoman, aeronaut

avid ADJECTIVE **1** *an avid collector of art* = **enthusiastic**, keen, devoted, intense, eager, passionate, ardent, fanatical, fervent, zealous, keen as mustard ■ **OPPOSITE:** indifferent **2** *He was avid for wealth.* = **insatiable**, hungry, greedy, thirsty, grasping, voracious, acquisitive, ravenous, rapacious, avaricious, covetous, athirst

avoid VERB **1** *She had to take emergency action to avoid a disaster.* = **prevent**, stop, frustrate, hamper, foil, inhibit, head off, avert, thwart, intercept, hinder, obstruct, impede, ward off, stave off, forestall, defend against **2** *He managed to avoid giving them an idea of what he was up to.* = **refrain from**, bypass, dodge, eschew, escape, duck (out of) (*informal*), fight shy of, shirk from **3** *He had ample time to swerve and avoid the woman.* = **keep away from**, dodge, shun, evade, steer clear of, sidestep, circumvent (*formal*), bypass, slip through the net, body-swerve, give a wide berth to

avoidable ADJECTIVE **1** *The tragedy was entirely avoidable.* = **preventable**, stoppable, avertible or avertable ■ **OPPOSITE:** unpreventable **2** *Smoking is an avoidable cause of disease and death.* = **escapable**, evadable ■ **OPPOSITE:** inevitable

avoidance NOUN **1** *tax avoidance* = **refraining**, dodging, shirking, eschewal **2** *Improve your health by stress avoidance.* = **prevention**, safeguard, precaution, anticipation, thwarting, elimination, deterrence, forestalling, prophylaxis, preclusion, obviation

avow VERB = **state**, maintain, declare, allege, recognize, swear, assert, proclaim, affirm, profess, aver, asseverate

avowed ADJECTIVE = **declared**, open, admitted, acknowledged, confessed, sworn, professed, self-proclaimed

await VERB **1** *Little was said as we awaited the arrival of the chairman.* = **wait for**, expect, look for, look forward to, anticipate, stay for **2** *A nasty surprise awaited them.* = **be in store for**, wait for, be ready for, lie in wait for, be in readiness for

awake VERB **1** *I awoke to the sound of the wind in the trees.* = **wake up**, come to, wake, stir, awaken, rouse **2** *He had awoken interest in the sport again.* = **alert**, excite, stimulate, provoke, revive, arouse, activate, awaken, fan, animate, stir up, incite, kick-start (*informal*), enliven, kindle, breathe life into, call forth, vivify **3** *The aim was to awaken an interest in foreign cultures.* = **stimulate**, excite, provoke, activate, alert, animate, fan, stir up, incite, kick-start (*informal*), enliven, kindle, breathe life into, call forth, vivify ▶ ADJECTIVE **1** *I don't stay awake at night worrying about that.* = **not sleeping**, sleepless, wide-awake, aware, waking, conscious, aroused, awakened, restless, restive, wakeful, bright-eyed and bushy-tailed ■ OPPOSITE: asleep **2** *They are awake to the challenge of stemming the exodus.* = **alert**, aware, on the lookout, alive, attentive, on the alert, observant, watchful, on guard, on your toes, heedful, vigilant

award VERB **1** *She was awarded the prize for both films.* = **present with**, give, grant, gift, distribute, render, assign, decree, hand out, confer, endow, bestow, allot, apportion, adjudge **2** *The contract has been awarded to a British shipyard.* = **grant**, give, render, assign, decree, accord, confer, adjudge ▶ NOUN **1** *this year's annual pay award* = **grant**, subsidy, scholarship, hand-out, endowment, stipend **2** *She presented a bravery award to the schoolgirl.* = **prize**, gift, trophy, decoration, grant, bonsela (*S. African*), koha (*N.Z.*) **3** *worker's compensation awards* = **settlement**, payment, compensation

aware ADJECTIVE *They are politically very aware.* = **informed**, enlightened, knowledgeable, learned, expert, versed, up to date, in the picture, in the know (*informal*), erudite, well-read, au fait (*French*), in the loop, well-briefed, au courant (*French*), clued-up (*informal*) ■ OPPOSITE: ignorant • **aware of** *They are well aware of the dangers.* = **knowing about**, familiar with, conscious of, wise to (*slang*), alert to, mindful of, acquainted with, alive to, awake to, privy to, hip to (*slang*), appreciative of, attentive to, conversant with, apprised of, cognizant of, sensible of

awareness NOUN • **awareness of** = **knowledge of**, understanding of, appreciation of, recognition of, attention to, perception of, consciousness of, acquaintance with, enlightenment with, sensibility to, realization of, familiarity with, mindfulness of, cognizance of, sentience of

away ADJECTIVE *She was away on a business trip.* = **absent**, out, gone, elsewhere, abroad, not there, not here, not present, on vacation, not at home ▶ ADVERB **1** *She drove away before he could speak again.* = **off**, elsewhere, abroad, hence, from here **2** *I put my journal away and prepared for bed.* = **aside**, out of the way, to one side **3** *They live thirty miles away from town.* = **at a distance**, far, apart, remote, isolated **4** *He would work away on his computer well into the night.* = **continuously**, repeatedly, relentlessly, incessantly, interminably, unremittingly, uninterruptedly

awe NOUN *She gazed in awe at the great stones.* = **wonder**, fear, respect, reverence, horror, terror, dread, admiration, amazement, astonishment, veneration ■ OPPOSITE: contempt ▶ VERB *I am still awed by his courage.* = **impress**, amaze, stun, frighten, terrify, cow, astonish, horrify, intimidate, daunt

awed ADJECTIVE = **impressed**, shocked, amazed, afraid, stunned, frightened, terrified, cowed, astonished, horrified, intimidated, fearful, daunted, dumbfounded, wonder-struck

awe-inspiring ADJECTIVE = **impressive**, striking, wonderful, amazing, stunning (*informal*), magnificent, astonishing, intimidating, awesome, daunting, breathtaking, eye-popping (*informal*), fearsome, wondrous (*archaic, literary*), jaw-dropping ■ OPPOSITE: unimpressive

awesome ADJECTIVE = **awe-inspiring**, striking, shocking, imposing, terrible, amazing, stunning (*informal*), wonderful, alarming, impressive, frightening, awful (*obsolete*), overwhelming, terrifying, magnificent, astonishing, horrible, dreadful, formidable, horrifying, intimidating, fearful (*informal*), daunting, breathtaking, majestic, solemn, fearsome, wondrous (*archaic, literary*), redoubtable, jaw-dropping, stupefying

awestruck or **awe-stricken** ADJECTIVE = **impressed**, shocked, amazed, stunned, afraid, frightened, terrified, cowed, astonished, horrified, intimidated, fearful, awed, daunted, awe-inspired, dumbfounded, struck dumb, wonder-struck

a

awful ADJECTIVE **1** *an awful smell of paint*
= **disgusting**, terrible, tremendous,
offensive, gross, nasty, foul, horrible,
dreadful, unpleasant, revolting, stinking
(*informal*), sickening, hideous, vulgar, vile,
distasteful, horrid (*informal*), frightful,
nauseating, odious, repugnant, loathsome,
abominable, nauseous, detestable,
godawful (*slang*), hellacious (*U.S. slang*),
festy (*Austral. slang*), yucko (*Austral. slang*)
2 *Even if the weather's awful there's still lots to
do.* = **bad**, poor, terrible (*informal*),
appalling, foul, rubbish (*slang*), dreadful,
unpleasant, dire, horrendous, ghastly, from
hell (*informal*), atrocious, deplorable,
abysmal, frightful, hellacious (*U.S. slang*)
■ **OPPOSITE:** wonderful **3** *The destruction was
massive; it was awful.* = **shocking**, serious,
alarming, distressing, dreadful, horrifying,
horrific, hideous, harrowing, gruesome
4 *I looked awful and felt quite sleepy.* = **unwell**,
poorly (*informal*), ill, terrible, sick, ugly,
crook (*Austral. & N.Z. informal*), unhealthy,
unsightly, queasy, out of sorts (*informal*),
off-colour, under the weather (*informal*),
green about the gills

awfully ADVERB **1** *That caramel looks awfully
good.* = **very**, extremely, terribly,
exceptionally, quite, very much, seriously
(*informal*), greatly, immensely, exceedingly,
excessively, dreadfully **2** *I played awfully, and
there are no excuses.* = **badly**, woefully,
dreadfully, inadequately, disgracefully,
wretchedly, unforgivably, shoddily,
reprehensibly, disreputably

awhile ADVERB = **for a while**, briefly, for a
moment, for a short time, for a little while
> USAGE *Awhile*, written as a single word,
> is an adverb meaning 'for a period of
> time'. It can only be used with a verb, for
> example: *he stood awhile in thought*. It is
> quite commonly written by mistake
> instead of the noun *a while*, meaning
> 'a period of time', so take care not to
> confuse the two parts of speech: *I
> thought about that for a while* (not *awhile*).

awkward ADJECTIVE **1** *There was an awkward
moment when people had to decide where to
stand.* = **embarrassing**, difficult,
compromising, sensitive, embarrassed,
painful, distressing, delicate,
uncomfortable, tricky, trying, humiliating,
unpleasant, sticky (*informal*), troublesome,
perplexing, disconcerting, inconvenient,
thorny, untimely, ill at ease, discomfiting,
ticklish, inopportune, toe-curling (*slang*),
barro (*Austral. slang*), cringeworthy (*Brit.
informal*) ■ **OPPOSITE:** comfortable **2** *It was
heavy enough to make it awkward to carry.*

= **inconvenient**, difficult, troublesome,
cumbersome, unwieldy, unmanageable,
clunky (*informal*), unhandy ■ **OPPOSITE:**
convenient **3** *She made an awkward gesture
with her hands.* = **clumsy**, stiff, rude,
blundering, coarse, bungling, lumbering,
inept, unskilled, bumbling, unwieldy,
ponderous, ungainly, gauche, gawky,
uncouth, unrefined, artless, inelegant,
uncoordinated, graceless, cack-handed
(*informal*), unpolished, clownish, oafish,
inexpert, maladroit, ill-bred, all thumbs,
ungraceful, skill-less, unskilful,
butterfingered (*informal*), unhandy,
ham-fisted or ham-handed (*informal*),
unco (*Austral. slang*) ■ **OPPOSITE:** graceful
4 *She's got to an age where she's being awkward.*
= **uncooperative**, trying, difficult,
annoying, unpredictable, unreasonable,
stubborn, troublesome, perverse, prickly,
exasperating, irritable, intractable, vexing,
unhelpful, touchy, obstinate, obstructive,
bloody-minded (*Brit. informal*), chippy
(*informal*), vexatious, hard to handle,
disobliging

awkwardness NOUN **1** *He displayed all the
awkwardness of adolescence.* = **clumsiness**,
stiffness, rudeness, coarseness, ineptness,
ill-breeding, artlessness, gaucheness,
inelegance, gaucherie, gracelessness,
oafishness, gawkiness, uncouthness,
maladroitness, ungainliness, clownishness,
inexpertness, uncoordination,
unskilfulness, unskilledness **2** *It was a
moment of some awkwardness in our
relationship.* = **embarrassment**, difficulty,
discomfort, delicacy, unpleasantness,
inconvenience, stickiness (*informal*),
painfulness, ticklishness, uphill (*S. African*),
thorniness, inopportuneness,
perplexingness, untimeliness

awry ADVERB *He was concerned that his hair
might go awry.* = **askew**, to one side, off
course, out of line, obliquely, unevenly,
off-centre, cockeyed (*informal*), out of true,
crookedly, skew-whiff (*informal*)
▶ ADJECTIVE *His dark hair was all awry.*
= **askew**, twisted, crooked, to one side,
uneven, off course, out of line,
asymmetrical, off-centre, cockeyed
(*informal*), misaligned, out of true,
skew-whiff (*informal*) ▶ ADVERB or
ADJECTIVE *a plan that had gone awry* = **wrong**,
amiss

axe NOUN *She took an axe and wrecked the car.*
= **hatchet**, chopper, tomahawk, cleaver,
adze ▶ VERB **1** *Community projects are being
axed by the government.* = **abandon**, end,
pull, eliminate, cancel, scrap, wind up, turn

off (*informal*), relegate, cut back, terminate, dispense with, discontinue, pull the plug on **2** *She was axed by the Edinburgh club in October after her comments about a referee.* = **dismiss**, fire (*informal*), sack (*informal*), remove, get rid of, discharge, throw out, oust, give (someone) their marching orders, give the boot to (*slang*), give the bullet to (*Brit. slang*), give the push to, kennet (*Austral. slang*), jeff (*Austral. slang*) • **an axe to grind** *I've got no axe to grind with him.* = **pet subject**, grievance, ulterior motive, private purpose, personal consideration, private ends • **the axe** *one of the four doctors facing the axe* = **the sack** (*informal*), dismissal, discharge, wind-up, the boot (*slang*), cancellation, cutback, termination, the chop (*slang*), the (old) heave-ho (*informal*), the order of the boot (*slang*)

axiom NOUN = **principle**, fundamental, maxim, gnome, adage, postulate, dictum, precept, aphorism, truism, apophthegm

axis NOUN = **pivot**, shaft, axle, spindle, centre line

axle NOUN = **shaft**, pin, rod, axis, pivot, spindle, arbor, mandrel

azure ADJECTIVE = **sky blue**, blue, clear blue, ultramarine, cerulean, sky-coloured

a

Bb

babble VERB **1** *They all babbled simultaneously.*
= **gabble**, chatter, gush, spout, waffle
(*informal, chiefly Brit.*), splutter, gaggle,
burble, prattle, gibber, rabbit on (*Brit.
informal*), jabber, prate, earbash (*Austral. &
N.Z. slang*) **2** *a brook babbling only yards from
the door* = **gurgle**, lap, bubble, splash,
murmur, ripple, burble, plash ▶ NOUN **1** *He
couldn't make himself heard above the babble.*
= **gabble**, chatter, burble, prattle, blabber
2 *lots of babble about strategies and tactics*
= **gibberish**, waffle (*informal, chiefly Brit.*),
drivel, twaddle
babe NOUN = **baby**, child, innocent, infant,
bairn (*Scot. & Northern English*), tacker
(*Austral. slang*), suckling, newborn child,
babe in arms, nursling
baby NOUN *My wife has just had a baby.*
= **child**, infant, babe, wean (*Scot.*), little
one, bairn (*Scot. & Northern English*),
suckling, newborn child, babe in arms,
sprog (*slang*), neonate, rug rat (*U.S. &
Canad. informal*), ankle biter (*Austral. slang*),
tacker (*Austral. slang*) ▶ ADJECTIVE *Serve with
baby new potatoes.* = **small**, little, minute,
tiny, mini, wee, miniature, dwarf,
diminutive, petite, midget, teeny (*informal*),
pocket-sized, undersized, teeny-weeny
(*informal*), Lilliputian, teensy-weensy
(*informal*), pygmy or pigmy ▶ VERB *My
parents never babied me.* = **spoil**, pamper,
cosset, coddle, pet, humour, indulge,
spoon-feed, mollycoddle, overindulge,
wrap up in cotton wool (*informal*)
back NOUN **1** *The treatment involved tiny
injections in the back.* = **spine**, backbone,
vertebrae, spinal column, vertebral column
2 *a room at the back of the shop* = **rear**, other
side, back end, rear side ■ OPPOSITE: front
3 = **end**, tail end **4** *She had written a poem on
the back of a postcard.* = **reverse**, rear, other
side, wrong side, underside, flip side, verso
▶ ADJECTIVE **1** *a path leading to the back garden*
= **rear** ■ OPPOSITE: front **2** *She could
remember sitting in the back seat of their car.*
= **rearmost**, hind, hindmost **3** *A handful of
back copies will give an indication of property
prices.* = **previous**, earlier, former, past,
elapsed ■ OPPOSITE: future **4** *They had*
transmitters taped to their back feathers. = **tail**,
end, rear, posterior ▶ VERB **1** *He is backed by
the civic movement.* = **support**, help, second,
aid, champion, encourage, favour, defend,
promote, sanction, sustain, assist,
advocate, endorse, side with, stand up for,
espouse, stand behind, countenance, abet,
stick up for (*informal*), take up the cudgels
for ■ OPPOSITE: oppose **2** *Murjani backed
him to start the new company.* = **subsidize**,
help, support, finance, sponsor, assist,
underwrite • **back down** *It's too late now to
back down.* = **give in**, collapse, withdraw,
yield, concede, submit, surrender, comply,
cave in (*informal*), capitulate, accede, admit
defeat, back-pedal • **back out** *I've already
promised I'll go – I can't back out now.*
= **withdraw**, retire, give up, pull out,
retreat, drop out, renege, cop out (*slang*),
chicken out (*informal*), detach yourself
• **back someone up** *The girl denied being
there, and the men backed her up.* = **support**,
second, aid, assist, stand by, bolster
• **behind someone's back** *You enjoy her
hospitality, and then criticize her behind her
back.* = **secretly**, covertly, surreptitiously,
furtively, conspiratorially, sneakily,
deceitfully ■ RELATED WORD: *adjective*
dorsal
backbone NOUN **1** *He was so thin that his
backbone was visible.* = **spinal column**,
spine, vertebrae, vertebral column
2 *the economic backbone of the nation*
= **foundation**, support, base, basis,
mainstay, bedrock **3** *You might be taking
drastic measures and you've got to have the
backbone to do that.* = **strength of
character**, will, character, bottle (*Brit.
slang*), resolution, resolve, nerve, daring,
courage, determination, guts, pluck,
stamina, grit, bravery, fortitude,
toughness, tenacity, willpower, mettle,
boldness, firmness, spunk (*informal*),
fearlessness, steadfastness, moral fibre,
hardihood, dauntlessness
backer NOUN **1** *I was looking for a backer to
assist me in the attempted buy-out.*
= **supporter**, second, ally, angel (*informal*),
patron, promoter, subscriber, underwriter,
helper, benefactor **2** *He became a backer of
reform at the height of the crisis.* = **advocate**,
supporter, patron, sponsor, promoter,
protagonist
backfire VERB = **fail**, founder, flop (*informal*),
rebound, fall through, fall flat, boomerang,
miscarry, misfire, go belly-up (*slang*), turn
out badly, meet with disaster
background NOUN **1** *Moulded by his
background, he could not escape traditional*

values. = **upbringing**, history, culture, environment, tradition, circumstances, breeding, milieu **2** *His background was in engineering.* = **experience**, grounding, education, preparation, qualifications, credentials **3** *The meeting takes place against a background of political violence.* = **circumstances**, history, conditions, situation, atmosphere, environment, framework, ambience, milieu, frame of reference

backing NOUN **1** *He said the president had the full backing of his government.* = **support**, seconding, championing, promotion, sanction, approval, blessing, encouragement, endorsement, patronage, accompaniment, advocacy, moral support, espousal **2** *She brought her action with the financial backing of the BBC.* = **assistance**, support, help, funds, aid, grant, subsidy, sponsorship, patronage

backlash NOUN = **reaction**, response, resistance, resentment, retaliation, repercussion, counterblast, counteraction, retroaction

backlog NOUN = **build-up**, stock, excess, accumulation, accretion

backside NOUN = **buttocks**, behind (*informal*), seat, bottom (*informal*), rear (*informal*), tail (*informal*), cheeks (*informal*), butt (*U.S. & Canad. informal*), bum (*Brit. slang*), buns (*U.S. slang*), rump, rear end, posterior, haunches, hindquarters, derrière (*euphemistic*), tush, fundament, gluteus maximus (*Anatomy*), coit (*Austral. slang*), nates (*Technical*), jacksy (*Brit. slang*), keister or keester (*slang, chiefly U.S.*)

backtrack VERB **1** (*often with* on) *The finance minister backtracked on the decision.* = **retract**, withdraw, retreat, draw back, recant **2** *We had to backtrack to the corner and cross the street.* = **retrace your steps**, go back, reverse, retreat, move back, back-pedal

backup NOUN **1** *There's no emergency backup immediately available if something goes wrong.* = **support**, backing, help, aid, reserves, assistance, reinforcement, auxiliaries **2** *She was added to the squad as a backup.* = **substitute**, reserve, relief, stand-in, replacement, stand-by, understudy, second string, locum

backward ADJECTIVE **1** *She did a backward flip.* = **reverse**, inverted, inverse, back to front, rearward ■ OPPOSITE: forward **2** *We need to accelerate the pace of change in our backward country.* = **underdeveloped**, undeveloped

backwardness NOUN *I was astonished at the backwardness of our country at the time.* = **lack of development**, underdevelopment

backwards *or* **backward** ADVERB = **towards the rear**, behind you, in reverse, rearwards

backwoods PLURAL NOUN = **sticks** (*informal*), outback, back country (*U.S.*), back of beyond, backlands (*U.S.*)

bacteria PLURAL NOUN = **microorganisms**, viruses, bugs (*slang*), germs, microbes, pathogens, bacilli

> USAGE *Bacteria* is a plural noun. It is therefore incorrect to talk about *a bacteria*, even though this is quite commonly heard, especially in the media. The correct singular is *a bacterium.*

bad ADJECTIVE **1** *Eating too much of any food can be bad for you.* = **harmful**, damaging, dangerous, disastrous, destructive, unhealthy, detrimental, hurtful, ruinous, deleterious (*formal*), injurious, disadvantageous ■ OPPOSITE: beneficial **2** *The pain is often so bad she wants to scream.* = **severe**, serious, terrible, acute, extreme, intense, painful, distressing, fierce, harsh **3** *The closure of the project is bad news for her staff.* = **unfavourable**, troubling, distressing, unfortunate, grim, discouraging, unpleasant, gloomy, adverse **4** *Many old people are living in bad housing.* = **inferior**, poor, inadequate, pathetic, faulty, duff (*Brit. informal*), unsatisfactory, mediocre, defective, second-class, deficient, imperfect, second-rate, shoddy, low-grade, erroneous, substandard, low-rent (*informal, chiefly U.S.*), two-bit (*U.S. & Canad. slang*), crappy (*slang*), end-of-the-pier (*Brit. informal*), poxy (*slang*), dime-a-dozen (*informal*), bush-league (*Austral. & N.Z. informal*), tinhorn (*U.S. slang*), half-pie (*N.Z. informal*), bodger or bodgie (*Austral. slang*), strictly for the birds (*informal*) ■ OPPOSITE: satisfactory **5** *He was a bad driver.* = **incompetent**, poor, useless (*informal*), incapable, unfit, inexpert **6** *Being scared of heights doesn't seem as bad as being scared of the dark.* = **grim**, severe, hard, tough **7** *I felt that I was a selfish, ungrateful, and generally bad person.* = **wicked**, criminal, evil, corrupt, worthless, base, vile, immoral, delinquent, sinful, depraved, debased, amoral, egregious, villainous, unprincipled, iniquitous, nefarious, dissolute, maleficent ■ OPPOSITE: virtuous **8** *You are a bad boy for repeating what I told you.* = **naughty**, defiant, perverse, wayward, mischievous, wicked, unruly, impish, undisciplined, roguish, disobedient ■ OPPOSITE: well-behaved **9** *You don't have to feel bad about relaxing.* = **guilty**, sorry, ashamed, apologetic, rueful, sheepish, contrite, remorseful, regretful, shamefaced, conscience-stricken **10** *They bought so much beef that some went bad.* = **rotten**, off, rank, sour, rancid, mouldy, fetid, putrid, festy (*Austral. slang*) • **not bad** *These are not bad for cheap shoes.* = **O.K.** *or* **okay**, fine, middling, average, fair, all right, acceptable, moderate, adequate, respectable, satisfactory, so-so, tolerable (*informal*), passable, fair to middling (*informal*)

baddie *or* **baddy** (*informal*) NOUN = **villain**, criminal, rogue, bad guy, scoundrel (*old-fashioned*), miscreant, antihero, evildoer, wrong 'un (*slang*) ■ **OPPOSITE:** goodie *or* goody

badge NOUN **1** *a badge depicting a party leader* = **image**, brand, stamp, identification, crest, emblem, insignia **2** *Urbanization became both a goal and a badge of progress.* = **mark**, sign, token

badger VERB = **pester**, worry, harry, bother, bug (*informal*), bully, plague, hound, get at, harass, nag, hassle (*informal*), chivvy, importune (*formal*), bend someone's ear (*informal*), be on someone's back (*slang*)

badly ADVERB **1** *I was angry because I played so badly.* = **poorly**, incorrectly, carelessly, inadequately, erroneously, imperfectly, ineptly, shoddily, defectively, faultily ■ **OPPOSITE:** well **2** *It was a gamble that went badly wrong.* = **severely**, greatly, deeply, seriously, gravely, desperately, sorely, dangerously, intensely, painfully, acutely, exceedingly **3** *All involved in the story came out badly.* = **unfavourably**, unsuccessfully

badness NOUN = **wickedness**, wrong, evil, corruption, sin, impropriety, immorality, villainy, naughtiness, sinfulness, foulness, baseness, rottenness, vileness, shamefulness ■ **OPPOSITE:** virtue

bad-tempered ADJECTIVE = **irritable**, cross, angry, tense, crabbed, fiery, grumbling, snarling, prickly, exasperated, edgy, snappy, sullen, touchy, surly, petulant, sulky, ill-tempered, irascible, cantankerous, tetchy, ratty (*Brit. & N.Z. informal*), tooshie (*Austral. slang*), testy, chippy (*informal*), fretful, grouchy (*informal*), querulous, peevish, crabby, huffy, dyspeptic, choleric, splenetic, crotchety (*informal*), oversensitive, snappish, ill-humoured, liverish, narky (*Brit. slang*), out of humour ■ **OPPOSITE:** good-tempered

baffle VERB = **puzzle**, beat (*slang*), amaze, confuse, stump, bewilder, astound, elude, confound, perplex, disconcert, mystify, flummox, boggle the mind of, dumbfound ■ **OPPOSITE:** explain

baffling ADJECTIVE = **puzzling**, strange, confusing, weird, mysterious, unclear, bewildering, elusive, enigmatic, perplexing, incomprehensible, mystifying, inexplicable, unaccountable, unfathomable ■ **OPPOSITE:** understandable

bag NOUN *She left the hotel carrying a shopping bag.* = **sack**, container, poke (*Scot.*), sac, receptacle ▶ VERB **1** *The smart ones will have already bagged their seats.* = **get**, take, land (*informal*), score (*slang*), gain, pick up, capture, acquire, get hold of, come by, procure, make sure of, win possession of **2** *Bag a rabbit for supper.* = **catch**, get, kill, shoot, capture, acquire, trap

baggage NOUN = **luggage**, things, cases, bags, equipment, gear, trunks, suitcases, belongings, paraphernalia, accoutrements, impedimenta

baggy ADJECTIVE = **loose**, hanging, slack, loosened, bulging, not fitting, sagging, sloppy, floppy, billowing, roomy, slackened, ill-fitting, droopy, oversize, not tight ■ **OPPOSITE:** tight

bail¹ NOUN *He was freed on bail pending an appeal.* = **security**, bond, guarantee, pledge, warranty, surety, guaranty • **bail out** *The pilot bailed out safely.* = **escape**, withdraw, get away, retreat, make your getaway, break free *or* out, make *or* effect your escape • **bail something** *or* **someone out** *They will discuss how to bail the economy out of its slump.* = **save**, help, free, release, aid, deliver, recover, rescue, get out, relieve, liberate, salvage, set free, save the life of, extricate, save (someone's) bacon (*Brit. informal*)

bail² *or* **bale** VERB *We kept her afloat for a couple of hours by bailing frantically.* = **scoop**, empty, dip, ladle, drain off

bait NOUN *bait to attract audiences for advertisements* = **lure**, attraction, incentive, carrot (*informal*), temptation, bribe, magnet, snare, inducement, decoy, carrot and stick, enticement, allurement ▶ VERB *He delighted in baiting his friends.* = **tease**, provoke, annoy, irritate, guy (*informal*), bother, needle (*informal*), plague (*informal*), mock, rag, rib (*informal*), wind up (*Brit. slang*), hound, torment, harass, ridicule, taunt, hassle (*informal*), aggravate (*informal*), badger, gall, persecute, pester, goad, irk, bedevil, take the mickey out of (*informal*), chaff, gibe, get on the nerves of (*informal*), nark (*Brit., Austral. & N.Z. slang*), be on the back of (*slang*), get in the hair of (*informal*), get *or* take a rise out of, hack you off (*informal*)

baked ADJECTIVE = **dry**, desert, seared, dried up, scorched, barren, sterile, arid, torrid, desiccated, sun-baked, waterless, moistureless

bakkie NOUN (S. African) = **truck**, pick-up, van, lorry, pick-up truck

balance VERB **1** He balanced a football on his head. = **stabilize**, level, steady ■ **OPPOSITE:** overbalance **2** Balance spicy dishes with mild ones. = **offset**, match, square, make up for, compensate for, counteract, neutralize, counterbalance, even up, equalize, counterpoise **3** She carefully tried to balance religious sensitivities against democratic freedom. = **weigh**, consider, compare, estimate, contrast, assess, evaluate, set against, juxtapose **4** He balanced his budget by rigid control over public expenditure. = **calculate**, rate, judge, total, determine, estimate, settle, count, square, reckon, work out, compute, gauge, tally ▶ NOUN **1** The medicines you are currently taking could be affecting your balance. = **equilibrium**, stability, steadiness, evenness, equipoise, counterpoise ■ **OPPOSITE:** instability **2** the ecological balance of the forest = **stability**, equanimity, constancy, steadiness **3** her ability to maintain the political balance = **parity**, equity, fairness, impartiality, equality, correspondence, equivalence **4** They were due to pay the balance on delivery. = **remainder**, rest, difference, surplus, residue **5** a balance of mind = **composure**, stability, restraint, self-control, poise, self-discipline, coolness, calmness, equanimity, self-restraint, steadiness, self-possession, self-mastery, strength of mind or will

balance sheet NOUN = **statement**, report, account, budget, ledger, financial statement, credits and debits sheet

balcony NOUN **1** He appeared on a second floor balcony to appeal to the crowd to be calm. = **terrace**, veranda **2** We took our seats in the balcony. = **upper circle**, gods, gallery

bald ADJECTIVE **1** The man's bald head was beaded with sweat. = **hairless**, bare, shorn, clean-shaven, tonsured, depilated, glabrous (Biology), baldheaded, baldpated **2** The bald truth is that he's just not happy. = **plain**, direct, simple, straight, frank, severe, bare, straightforward, blunt, rude, outright, downright, forthright, unadorned, unvarnished, straight from the shoulder

balding ADJECTIVE = **losing your hair**, receding, thin on top, becoming bald

baldness NOUN = **hairlessness**, alopecia (Pathology), baldheadedness, baldpatedness, glabrousness (Biology)

bale see **bail**

baleful ADJECTIVE = **menacing**, threatening, dangerous, frightening, evil, deadly, forbidding, intimidating, harmful, sinister, ominous, malignant, hurtful, vindictive, pernicious (formal), malevolent, noxious, venomous, ruinous, intimidatory, minatory, maleficent, bodeful, louring or lowering, minacious ■ **OPPOSITE:** friendly

balk or **baulk** VERB (usually with **at**) = **recoil**, resist, hesitate, dodge, falter, evade, shy away, flinch, quail, shirk, shrink, draw back, jib ■ **OPPOSITE:** accept

ball NOUN **1** a golf ball = **sphere**, drop, globe, pellet, orb, globule, spheroid **2** A cannon ball struck the ship. = **projectile**, shot, missile, bullet, ammunition, slug, pellet, grapeshot

ballast NOUN = **counterbalance**, balance, weight, stability, equilibrium, sandbag, counterweight, stabilizer

balloon VERB = **expand**, rise, increase, extend, swell, blow up, enlarge, inflate, bulge, billow, dilate, be inflated, puff out, become larger, distend, bloat, grow rapidly

ballot NOUN = **vote**, election, voting, poll, polling, referendum, show of hands

balm NOUN **1** The balm is very soothing. = **ointment**, cream, lotion, salve, emollient, balsam, liniment, embrocation, unguent **2** This place is a balm to the soul. = **comfort**, support, relief, cheer, consolation, solace, palliative, anodyne, succour, restorative, curative

balmy ADJECTIVE a balmy summer's evening = **mild**, warm, calm, moderate, pleasant, clement, tranquil, temperate, summery ■ **OPPOSITE:** rough

bamboozle VERB **1** He was bamboozled by conmen. = **cheat**, do (informal), kid (informal), skin (slang), trick, fool, take in (informal), con (informal), stiff, sting (informal), mislead, rip off (slang), thwart, deceive, fleece, hoax, defraud, dupe, beguile, gull (archaic), delude, swindle, stitch up (slang), victimize, hoodwink, double-cross (informal), diddle (informal), take for a ride (informal), do the dirty on (Brit. informal), bilk, pull a fast one on (informal), cozen **2** He bamboozled Mercer into defeat. = **puzzle**, confuse, stump, baffle, bewilder, confound, perplex, mystify, befuddle, flummox, nonplus

ban VERB **1** Last year arms sales were banned. = **prohibit**, black, bar, block, restrict, veto, forbid, boycott, suppress, outlaw, banish, disallow, proscribe, debar, blackball, interdict ■ **OPPOSITE:** permit **2** He was banned from driving for three years. = **bar**, prohibit, exclude, forbid, disqualify,

preclude, debar, declare ineligible ▶ NOUN
The General also lifted a ban on political parties.
= **prohibition**, block, restriction, veto,
boycott, embargo, injunction, censorship,
taboo, suppression, stoppage,
disqualification, interdiction, interdict,
proscription, disallowance, rahui (*N.Z.*),
restraining order (*U.S. Law*)
■ **OPPOSITE:** permission

banal ADJECTIVE = **unoriginal**, stock,
ordinary, boring, tired, routine, dull,
everyday, stereotypical, pedestrian,
commonplace, mundane, tedious, vanilla
(*slang*), dreary, stale, tiresome,
monotonous, humdrum, threadbare, trite,
unimaginative, uneventful, uninteresting,
clichéd, old hat, mind-numbing, hackneyed,
ho-hum (*informal*), vapid, repetitious,
wearisome, platitudinous, cliché-ridden,
unvaried ■ **OPPOSITE:** original

banality NOUN 1 *the banality of life*
= **unoriginality**, triviality, vapidity, triteness
2 *His ability to utter banalities never ceased to
amaze me.* = **cliché**, commonplace, platitude,
truism, bromide (*informal*), trite phrase

band¹ NOUN 1 *Local bands provide music for
dancing.* = **ensemble**, group, orchestra,
combo 2 *bands of government soldiers* = **gang**,
company, group, set, party, team, lot, club,
body, association, crowd, troop, pack,
camp, squad, crew (*informal*), assembly,
mob, horde, troupe, posse (*informal*),
clique, coterie, bevy • **band together**
*People living in a foreign city band together for
company.* = **unite**, group, join, league, ally,
associate, gather, pool, merge,
consolidate, affiliate, collaborate, join
forces, cooperate, confederate, pull
together, join together, federate, close
ranks, club together

band² NOUN 1 *She was wearing a trouser suit
and a band around her forehead.* = **headband**,
tie, strip, ribbon, fillet 2 *He placed a metal
band around the injured kneecap.* = **bandage**,
tie, binding, strip, belt, strap, cord, swathe,
fetter

bandage NOUN *His chest was swathed in
bandages.* = **dressing**, plaster, compress,
gauze ▶ VERB *Apply a dressing to the wound
and bandage it.* = **dress**, cover, bind, swathe

bandit NOUN = **robber**, gunman *or* woman,
crook (*informal*), outlaw, pirate, raider,
gangster, plunderer, mugger (*informal*),
hijacker, looter, highwayman *or* woman,
racketeer, desperado, marauder, brigand,
freebooter, footpad

bandy VERB = **exchange**, trade, pass,
throw, truck, swap, toss, shuffle,
commute, interchange, barter, reciprocate

bane NOUN = **plague** (*informal*), bête noire,
trial, disaster, evil, ruin, burden,
destruction, despair, misery, curse, pest,
torment, woe, nuisance, downfall,
calamity, scourge, affliction ■ **OPPOSITE:**
blessing

bang NOUN 1 *I heard four or five loud bangs.*
= **explosion**, report, shot, pop, clash,
crack, blast, burst, boom, slam, discharge,
thump, clap, thud, clang, peal, detonation
2 *a nasty bang on the head* = **blow**, hit, box,
knock, stroke, punch, belt (*informal*), rap,
bump, bash (*informal*), sock (*slang*), smack,
thump, buffet, clout (*informal*), cuff, clump
(*slang*), whack, wallop (*informal*), slosh (*Brit.
slang*), tonk (*informal*), clomp (*slang*) ▶ VERB
1 *The engine spat and banged.* = **resound**,
beat, crash, burst, boom, echo, drum,
explode, thunder, thump, throb, thud,
clang 2 *I didn't mean to bang into you.*
= **bump**, knock, elbow, jostle 3 (*often with
on*) *We could bang on the desks and shout until
they let us out.* = **hit**, pound, beat, strike,
crash, knock, belt (*informal*), hammer, slam,
rap, bump, bash (*informal*), thump, clatter,
pummel, tonk (*informal*), beat *or* knock
seven bells out of (*informal*) ▶ ADVERB *bang
in the middle of the track* = **exactly**, just,
straight, square, squarely, precisely, slap,
smack (*informal*), plumb (*informal*)

banish VERB 1 *I was banished from the small
bedroom upstairs.* = **exclude**, bar, ban,
dismiss, expel, throw out, oust, drive away,
eject, evict, shut out, ostracize 2 *He was
banished from England.* = **expel**, transport,
exile, outlaw, deport, drive away,
expatriate, excommunicate ■ **OPPOSITE:**
admit 3 *a public investment programme
intended to banish the recession* = **get rid of**,
remove, eliminate, eradicate, shake off,
dislodge, see the back of

banishment NOUN = **expulsion**, exile,
dismissal, removal, discharge,
transportation, exclusion, deportation,
eviction, ejection, extrusion, proscription,
expatriation, debarment

banisters PLURAL NOUN = **railing**, rail,
balustrade, handrail, balusters

bank¹ NOUN 1 *I had money in the bank.*
= **financial institution**, repository,
depository 2 *one of the largest data banks in
the world* = **store**, fund, stock, source,
supply, reserve, pool, reservoir,
accumulation, stockpile, hoard, storehouse
▶ VERB *Early bookings allow the operators to
bank the customers' deposits.* = **deposit**, keep,
save • **bank on something** *She is clearly
banking on her past to be the meal ticket for her
future.* = **rely on**, trust (in), depend on, look

to, believe in, count on, be sure of, lean on, be confident of, have confidence in, swear by, reckon on, repose (*formal*), trust in

bank² NOUN **1** *an old warehouse on the banks of the canal* = **side**, edge, margin, shore, brink, lakeside, waterside **2** *resting indolently upon a grassy bank* = **mound**, banking, rise, hill, mass, pile, heap, ridge, dune, embankment, knoll, hillock, kopje *or* koppie (*S. African*) ▸ VERB *A single-engine plane took off and banked above the highway.* = **tilt**, tip, pitch, heel, slope, incline, slant, cant, camber

bank³ NOUN *The typical labourer now sits in front of a bank of dials.* = **row**, group, line, train, range, series, file, rank, arrangement, sequence, succession, array, tier

bankrupt ADJECTIVE = **insolvent**, broke (*informal*), spent, ruined, wiped out (*informal*), impoverished, beggared, in the red, on the rocks, destitute, gone bust (*informal*), in receivership, gone to the wall, in the hands of the receivers, on your uppers, in queer street (*informal*)
■ **OPPOSITE:** solvent

bankruptcy NOUN = **insolvency**, failure, crash, disaster, ruin, liquidation, indebtedness

banner NOUN **1** = **flag**, standard, colours, jack, pennant, ensign, streamer, pennon **2** = **placard**

banquet NOUN = **feast**, spread (*informal*), dinner, meal, entertainment, revel, blowout (*slang*), repast, slap-up meal (*Brit. informal*), hakari (*N.Z.*)

banter NOUN *She heard them exchanging good-natured banter.* = **joking**, kidding (*informal*), ribbing (*informal*), teasing, jeering, mockery, derision, jesting, chaff, pleasantry, repartee, wordplay, badinage, chaffing, raillery, persiflage ▸ VERB *They shared a cocktail and bantered easily.* = **joke**, kid (*informal*), rib (*informal*), tease, taunt, jeer, josh (*slang, chiefly U.S. & Canad.*), jest, take the mickey (*informal*), chaff

baptism NOUN **1** *We are at a site of baptism, a place of worship.* = **christening**, sprinkling, purification, immersion **2** *The new boys face a tough baptism against Leeds.* = **initiation**, beginning, debut, introduction, admission, dedication, inauguration, induction, inception, rite of passage, commencement, investiture, baptism of fire, instatement

baptize VERB **1** *I think your mother was baptized a Catholic.* = **christen**, cleanse, immerse, purify, besprinkle **2** *baptized into the Church of England* = **initiate**, admit, introduce, invest, recruit, enrol, induct, indoctrinate, instate

bar NOUN **1** *the city's most popular country and western bar* = **public house**, pub (*informal, chiefly Brit.*), counter, inn, local (*Brit. informal*), lounge, saloon, tavern, canteen, watering hole (*facetious slang*), boozer (*Brit., Austral. & N.Z. informal*), beer parlour (*Canad.*), roadhouse, hostelry (*archaic, facetious*), alehouse (*archaic*), taproom **2** *a crowd throwing stones and iron bars* = **rod**, staff, stick, stake, rail, pole, paling, shaft, baton, mace, batten, palisade, crosspiece **3** *one of the fundamental bars to communication* = **obstacle**, block, barrier, hurdle, hitch, barricade, snag, deterrent, obstruction, stumbling block, impediment, hindrance, interdict ■ **OPPOSITE:** aid ▸ VERB **1** *For added safety, bar the door to the kitchen.* = **lock**, block, secure, chain, attach, anchor, bolt, blockade, barricade, fortify, fasten, latch, obstruct, make firm, make fast **2** *He stepped in front of her, barring her way.* = **block**, restrict, hold up, restrain, hamper, thwart, hinder, obstruct, impede, shut off **3** *They have been barred from playing in several countries.* = **exclude**, ban, forbid, prohibit, keep out of, disallow, shut out of, ostracize, debar, blackball, interdict, black
■ **OPPOSITE:** admit

barb NOUN **1** *Apply gentle pressure on the barb with the point of the pliers.* = **point**, spur, spike, thorn, bristle, quill, prickle, tine, prong **2** *The barb stung her exactly the way he hoped it would.* = **dig**, abuse, slight, insult, put-down, snub, sneer, scoff, rebuff, affront, slap in the face (*informal*), gibe, aspersion

barbarian NOUN **1** *Our maths teacher was a bully and a complete barbarian.* = **savage**, monster, beast, brute, yahoo, swine, ogre, sadist **2** *The visitors looked upon us all as barbarians.* = **lout**, hooligan, illiterate, vandal, yahoo, bigot, philistine, ned (*Scot. slang*), hoon (*Austral. & N.Z.*), cougan (*Austral. slang*), scozza (*Austral. slang*), bogan (*Austral. slang*), ruffian, ignoramus, boor, lowbrow, vulgarian ▸ ADJECTIVE *rude and barbarian people* = **uncivilized**, wild, rough, savage, crude, primitive, vulgar, illiterate, barbaric, philistine, uneducated, unsophisticated, barbarous, boorish, uncouth, uncultivated, lowbrow, uncultured, unmannered ■ **OPPOSITE:** civilized

barbaric ADJECTIVE **1** *a particularly barbaric act of violence* = **brutal**, fierce, cruel, savage, crude, vicious, ruthless, coarse, vulgar, heartless, inhuman, merciless, bloodthirsty, remorseless, barbarous, pitiless, uncouth **2** *a prehistoric and barbaric world* = **uncivilized**, wild, savage, primitive,

b

rude, barbarian, barbarous ■ **OPPOSITE:** civilized

barbarism NOUN = **cruelty**, outrage, atrocity, brutality, savagery, ruthlessness, wickedness, inhumanity, barbarity, viciousness, coarseness, crudity, monstrousness, heinousness, fiendishness, barbarousness

barbarity NOUN **1** = **viciousness**, horror, cruelty, brutality, ferocity, savagery, ruthlessness, inhumanity **2** *the barbarities committed by the invading army* = **atrocity**, cruelty, horror, inhumanity

barbarous ADJECTIVE **1** *He thought the poetry of Whitman barbarous.* = **uncivilized**, wild, rough, gross, savage, primitive, rude, coarse, vulgar, barbarian, philistine, uneducated, brutish, unsophisticated, uncouth, uncultivated, unpolished, uncultured, unmannered **2** *It was a barbarous attack on a purely civilian train.* = **brutal**, cruel, savage, vicious, ruthless, ferocious, monstrous, barbaric, heartless, inhuman, merciless, remorseless, pitiless

barbed ADJECTIVE **1** *barbed comments* = **cutting**, pointed, biting, critical, acid, hostile, nasty, harsh, savage, brutal, searing, withering, scathing, unkind, hurtful, belittling, sarcastic, caustic, scornful, vitriolic, trenchant, acrid, catty (*informal*), mordant, mordacious **2** *The factory was surrounded by barbed wire.* = **spiked**, pointed, toothed, hooked, notched, prickly, jagged, thorny, pronged, spiny, snaggy

bard NOUN = **poet**, singer, rhymer, minstrel, lyricist, troubadour

bare ADJECTIVE **1** *She seemed unaware that she was bare.* = **naked**, nude, stripped, exposed, uncovered, shorn, undressed, divested, denuded, in the raw (*informal*), disrobed, unclothed, buck naked (*slang*), unclad, scuddy (*slang*), without a stitch on (*informal*), in the bare scud (*Scot. slang*), naked as the day you were born (*informal*) ■ **OPPOSITE:** dressed **2** *bare wooden floors* = **simple**, basic, severe, spare, stark, austere, spartan, unadorned, unfussy, unvarnished, unembellished, unornamented, unpatterned, bare-bones ■ **OPPOSITE:** adorned **3** *a bare, draughty interviewing room* = **empty**, wanting, mean, lacking, deserted, vacant, void, scarce, barren, uninhabited, unoccupied, scanty, unfurnished ■ **OPPOSITE:** full **4** *Reporters were given nothing but the bare facts.* = **plain**, hard, simple, cold, basic, essential, obvious, sheer, patent, evident, stark, manifest, bald, literal, overt, unembellished

barely ADVERB = **only just**, just, hardly, scarcely, at a push, almost not ■ **OPPOSITE:** completely

bargain NOUN **1** *At this price the wine is a bargain.* = **good buy**, discount purchase, good deal, good value, steal (*informal*), snip (*informal*), giveaway, cheap purchase **2** *The treaty was based on a bargain between the governments.* = **agreement**, deal (*informal*), understanding, promise, contract, negotiation, arrangement, settlement, treaty, pledge, convention, transaction, engagement, pact, compact, covenant, stipulation ▶ VERB **1** *Shop in small local markets and don't be afraid to bargain.* = **haggle**, deal, sell, trade, traffic, barter, drive a hard bargain **2** *They prefer to bargain with individual clients, for cash.* = **negotiate**, deal, contract, mediate, covenant, stipulate, arbitrate, transact, cut a deal • **bargain for** or **on something** *The effects of this policy were more than they had bargained for.* = **anticipate**, expect, look for, imagine, predict, plan for, forecast, hope for, contemplate, be prepared for, foresee, foretell, count upon

barge NOUN *He lives on a barge and only works when he has to.* = **canal boat**, lighter, narrow boat, scow, flatboat • **barge in (on something** or **someone)** *Sorry to barge in like this, but I need your advice.* = **interrupt**, break in (on), muscle in (on) (*informal*), intrude (on), infringe (on), burst in (on), butt in (on), impose yourself (on), force your way in (on), elbow your way in (on) • **barge into someone** *He would barge into them and kick them in the shins.* = **bump into**, drive into, press, push against, shoulder, thrust, elbow into, shove into, collide with, jostle with, cannon into

bark¹ VERB **1** *Don't let the dogs bark.* = **yap**, bay, howl, snarl, growl, yelp, woof **2** *I didn't mean to bark at you.* = **shout**, snap, yell, snarl, growl, berate, bawl, bluster, raise your voice ▶ NOUN *The Doberman let out a string of roaring barks.* = **yap**, bay, howl, snarl, growl, yelp, woof

bark² NOUN *The spice comes from the inner bark of the tree.* = **covering**, casing, cover, skin, protection, layer, crust, housing, cortex (*Anatomy & Botany*), rind, husk ▶ VERB *She barked her shin off the edge of the drawer.* = **scrape**, skin, strip, rub, scratch, shave, graze, scuff, flay, abrade

barmy or **balmy** (*slang*) ADJECTIVE *This policy is absolutely barmy.* = **stupid**, bizarre, foolish, silly, daft (*informal*), irresponsible, irrational, senseless, preposterous, impractical, idiotic, inane, fatuous, dumb-ass (*slang*)

baroque ADJECTIVE = **ornate**, fancy, bizarre, elegant, decorated, elaborate, extravagant, flamboyant, grotesque, convoluted, flowery, rococo, florid, bedecked, overelaborate, overdecorated

barrack VERB = **heckle**, abuse, mock, bait, criticize, boo, taunt, jeer, shout down, diss (*slang*)

barracks PLURAL NOUN = **camp**, quarters, garrison, encampment, billet, cantonment, casern

barrage NOUN **1** *a barrage of anti-aircraft fire* = **bombardment**, attack, bombing, assault, shelling, battery, volley, blitz, salvo, strafe, fusillade, cannonade, curtain of fire **2** *a barrage of angry questions from the floor* = **torrent**, attack, mass, storm, assault, burst, stream, hail, outburst, rain, spate, onslaught, deluge, plethora, profusion

barren ADJECTIVE **1** *the Tibetan landscape of the high barren mountains* = **desolate**, empty, desert, waste **2** *He also wants to use water to irrigate barren desert land.* = **unproductive**, dry, useless, fruitless, arid, unprofitable, unfruitful ■ OPPOSITE: fertile **3** *My life has become barren.* = **dull**, boring, commonplace, tedious, dreary, stale, lacklustre, monotonous, uninspiring, humdrum, uninteresting, vapid, unrewarding, as dry as dust ■ OPPOSITE: interesting **4** *a three-year-old barren mare* = **infertile**, sterile, unproductive, nonproductive, infecund, unprolific

barricade NOUN *Large areas of the city have been closed off by barricades.* = **barrier**, wall, railing, fence, blockade, obstruction, rampart, fortification, bulwark, palisade, stockade ▶ VERB *The doors had been barricaded.* = **bar**, block, defend, secure, lock, bolt, blockade, fortify, fasten, latch, obstruct

barrier NOUN = **barricade**, wall, bar, block, railing, fence, pale, boundary, obstacle, ditch, blockade, obstruction, rampart, bulwark, palisade, stockade

barter VERB = **trade**, sell, exchange, switch, traffic, bargain, swap, haggle, drive a hard bargain

base¹ NOUN **1** *Line the base and sides of a 20cm deep round cake tin with paper.* = **bottom**, floor, lowest part, deepest part ■ OPPOSITE: top **2** *The mattress is best on a solid bed base.* = **support**, stand, foot, rest, bed, bottom, foundation, pedestal, groundwork **3** *The family base was crucial to my development.* = **foundation**, institution, organization, establishment, starting point **4** *Gunfire was heard at an army base close to the airport.* = **centre**, post, station, camp, settlement, headquarters **5** *For most of the spring and early summer her base was in Scotland.* = **home**, house, territory, pad (*slang*), residence, home ground, abode, stamping ground, dwelling place **6** *Oils may be mixed with a base and massaged into the skin.* = **essence**, source, basis, concentrate, root, core, extract ▶ VERB **1** *He based his conclusions on the evidence given by the prisoners.* = **ground**, found, build, rest, establish, depend, root, construct, derive, hinge **2** *We will base ourselves in the town.* = **place**, set, post, station, establish, fix, locate, install, garrison

base² ADJECTIVE *Love has the power to overcome the baser emotions.* = **dishonourable**, evil, corrupt, infamous, disgraceful, vulgar, shameful, vile, immoral, scandalous, wicked, sordid, abject, despicable, depraved, ignominious, disreputable, contemptible, villainous, ignoble, discreditable, scungy (*Austral. & N.Z.*) ■ OPPOSITE: honourable

baseless ADJECTIVE = **unfounded**, false, fabricated, unconfirmed, spurious, unjustified, unproven, unsubstantiated, groundless, unsupported, trumped up, without foundation, unjustifiable, uncorroborated, ungrounded, without basis ■ OPPOSITE: well-founded

bash VERB *My mother bashed her shin with a suitcase.* = **hit**, break, beat, strike, knock, smash, punch, belt (*informal*), crush, deck (*slang*), batter, slap, sock (*slang*), chin (*slang*), smack, thump, clout (*informal*), whack (*informal*), biff (*slang*), clobber (*slang*), wallop (*informal*), slosh (*Brit. slang*), tonk (*informal*), lay one on (*slang*), beat or knock seven bells out of (*informal*)

bashful ADJECTIVE = **shy**, reserved, retiring, nervous, modest, shrinking, blushing, constrained, timid, self-conscious, coy, reticent, self-effacing, aw-shucks (*slang, chiefly U.S.*), diffident, sheepish, mousy, timorous (*literary*), abashed, shamefaced, easily embarrassed, overmodest ■ OPPOSITE: forward

basic ADJECTIVE **1** *Access to justice is a basic right.* = **fundamental**, main, key, essential, primary, vital, principal, constitutional, cardinal, inherent, elementary, indispensable, innate, intrinsic, elemental, immanent **2** *shortages of even the most basic foodstuffs* = **vital**, needed, important, key, necessary, essential, primary, crucial (*informal*), fundamental, elementary, indispensable, requisite **3** *There are certain ethical principles that are basic to all the great religions.* = **essential**, central, key, vital, fundamental, underlying, indispensable ■ **OPPOSITE:** secondary **4** *There are three basic types of tea.* = **main**, key, essential, primary **5** *the extremely basic hotel room* = **plain**, simple, classic, severe, straightforward, Spartan, uncluttered, unadorned, unfussy, bog-standard (*informal*), unembellished, bare-bones, lo-fi ▶ **PLURAL NOUN** *Let's get down to basics and stop horsing around.* = **essentials**, facts, principles, fundamentals, practicalities, requisites, nuts and bolts (*informal*), hard facts, nitty-gritty (*informal*), rudiments, brass tacks (*informal*), necessaries

basically ADVERB = **essentially**, firstly, mainly, mostly, principally, fundamentally, primarily, at heart, inherently, intrinsically, at bottom, in substance, au fond (*French*)

basis NOUN **1** *We're going to be meeting there on a regular basis.* = **arrangement**, way, system, footing, agreement **2** *The UN plan is a possible basis for negotiation.* = **foundation**, support, base, ground, footing, theory, bottom, principle, premise, groundwork, principal element, chief ingredient

bask VERB *Crocodiles bask on the small sandy beaches.* = **lie**, relax, lounge, sprawl, loaf, lie about, swim in, sunbathe, recline, loll, laze, outspan (*S. African*), warm yourself, toast yourself • **bask in** *He smiled and basked in her approval.* = **enjoy**, relish, delight in, savour, revel in, wallow in, rejoice in, luxuriate in, indulge yourself in, take joy in, take pleasure in or from

bass ADJECTIVE = **deep**, low, resonant, sonorous, low-pitched, deep-toned

bastion NOUN = **stronghold**, support, defence, rock, prop, refuge, fortress, mainstay, citadel, bulwark, tower of strength, fastness

batch NOUN = **group**, set, lot, crowd, pack, collection, quantity, bunch, accumulation, assortment, consignment, assemblage, aggregation

bath NOUN *Have a bath every morning.* = **wash**, cleaning, washing, soaping, shower, soak, cleansing, scrub, scrubbing, bathe, shampoo, sponging, douse, douche, ablution ▶ VERB *Don't feel you have to bath your child every day.* = **clean**, wash, soap, shower, soak, cleanse, scrub, bathe, tub, sponge, rinse, douse, scrub down, lave (*archaic*)

bathe VERB **1** *small ponds for the birds to bathe in* = **swim 2** *Back home, he plays with, feeds and bathes the baby.* = **wash**, clean, bath, soap, shower, soak, cleanse, scrub, tub, sponge, rinse, scrub down, lave (*archaic*)

3 *She paused long enough to bathe her blistered feet.* = **cleanse**, clean, wash, soak, rinse **4** *The arena was bathed in warm sunshine.* = **cover**, flood, steep, engulf, immerse, overrun, suffuse, wash over ▶ NOUN *an early-morning bathe* = **swim**, dip, dook (*Scot.*)

bathroom NOUN = **lavatory**, toilet, loo (*Brit. informal*), washroom, can (*U.S. & Canad. slang*), john (*slang, chiefly U.S. & Canad.*), head(s) (*Nautical slang*), shower, convenience (*chiefly Brit.*), bog (*slang*), bogger (*Austral. slang*), brasco (*Austral. slang*), privy, cloakroom (*Brit.*), latrine, rest room, powder room, dunny (*Austral. & N.Z., old-fashioned*), water closet, khazi (*slang*), comfort station (*U.S.*), pissoir (*French*), Gents or Ladies, little boy's room or little girl's room (*informal*), (public) convenience, W.C.

baton NOUN = **stick**, club, staff, stake, pole, rod, crook, cane, mace, wand, truncheon (*Brit.*), sceptre, mere (*N.Z.*), patu (*N.Z.*)

battalion NOUN = **company**, army, force, team, host, division, troop, brigade, regiment, legion, contingent, squadron, military force, horde, multitude, throng

batten VERB (*usually with* **down**) *The roof was never securely battened down.* = **fasten**, unite, fix, secure, lock, bind, chain, connect, attach, seal, tighten, anchor, bolt, clamp down, affix, nail down, make firm, make fast, fasten down

batter VERB **1** *He battered his victim around the head.* = **beat**, hit, strike, knock, assault, smash, punch, belt (*informal*), deck (*slang*), bang, bash (*informal*), lash, thrash, pound, lick (*informal*), buffet, flog, maul, pelt, clobber (*slang*), smite, wallop (*informal*), pummel, tonk (*informal*), cudgel, thwack, lambast(e), belabour, dash against, beat the living daylights out of, lay one on (*slang*), drub, beat or knock seven bells out of (*informal*) **2** *a storm that's been battering the Northeast coastline* = **damage**, destroy, hurt, injure, harm, ruin, crush, mar, wreck, total (*slang*), shatter, weaken, bruise, demolish, shiver, trash (*slang*), maul, mutilate, mangle, mangulate (*Austral. slang*), disfigure, deface, play (merry) hell with (*informal*)

battered ADJECTIVE **1** *The assault left him battered and bruised.* = **beaten**, injured, harmed, crushed, bruised, squashed, beat-up (*informal*), oppressed, manhandled, black-and-blue, ill-treated, maltreated **2** *a battered leather suitcase* = **damaged**, broken-down, wrecked, beat-up (*informal*), ramshackle, dilapidated

battery NOUN **1** *They stopped beside a battery of abandoned guns.* = **artillery**, ordnance,

gunnery, gun emplacement, cannonry
2 *We give a battery of tests to each patient.*
= **series**, set, course, chain, string,
sequence, suite, succession **3** *He has served
three years for assault and battery.* = **beating**,
attack, assault, aggression, thumping,
onslaught, physical violence

battle NOUN **1** *a gun battle between police and
drug traffickers* = **fight**, war, attack, action,
struggle, conflict, clash, set-to (*informal*),
encounter, combat, scrap (*informal*), biffo
(*Austral. slang*), engagement, warfare, fray,
duel, skirmish, head-to-head, tussle,
scuffle, fracas, scrimmage, sparring match,
bagarre (*French*), melee or mêlée, boilover
(*Austral.*) ■ **OPPOSITE:** peace **2** *a renewed
political battle over their attitude to Europe*
= **conflict**, campaign, struggle, debate,
clash, dispute, contest, controversy,
disagreement, crusade, strife, head-to-
head, agitation **3** *the battle against crime*
= **campaign**, drive, movement, push
(*informal*), struggle ▶ VERB **1** *Many people
battled with police.* = **wrestle**, war, fight,
argue, dispute, contest, combat, contend,
feud, grapple, agitate, clamour, scuffle,
lock horns **2** *Doctors battled throughout the
night to save her life.* = **struggle**, work,
labour, strain, strive, go for it (*informal*), toil,
make every effort, go all out (*informal*),
bend over backwards (*informal*), go for
broke (*slang*), bust a gut (*informal*), give it
your best shot (*informal*), break your neck
(*informal*), exert yourself, make an all-out
effort, work like a Trojan, knock
yourself out (*informal*), do your damnedest
(*informal*), give it your all (*informal*), rupture
yourself (*informal*)

battle cry NOUN **1** *the ideological battle cry of
Hong Kong* = **slogan**, motto, watchword,
catch phrase, tag-line, catchword, catchcry
(*Austral.*) **2** *He screamed out a battle cry and
charged.* = **war cry**, rallying cry, war whoop

battlefield NOUN = **battleground**, front,
field, combat zone, field of battle

battleship NOUN = **warship**, gunboat,
man-of-war, ship of the line, capital ship

batty ADJECTIVE *He struck me as a game sort, if
ever so slightly batty.* = **eccentric**, odd, bats
(*slang*), peculiar, barmy (*slang*), off-the-wall
(*slang*), potty (*Brit. informal*), oddball
(*informal*), bonkers (*slang, chiefly Brit.*), dotty
(*slang, chiefly Brit.*), loopy (*informal*), outré,
gonzo (*slang*), as daft as a brush (*informal,
chiefly Brit.*)

bauble NOUN = **trinket**, ornament, trifle,
toy, plaything, bagatelle, gimcrack,
gewgaw, knick-knack, bibelot, kickshaw

bawdy ADJECTIVE = **rude**, blue, dirty, gross,

crude, erotic, obscene, coarse, filthy,
indecent, vulgar, improper, steamy
(*informal*), pornographic, raunchy
(*informal*), suggestive, racy, lewd, risqué,
X-rated (*informal*), salacious, prurient,
lascivious, smutty, lustful, lecherous,
ribald, libidinous, licentious, indelicate,
near the knuckle (*informal*), indecorous
■ **OPPOSITE:** clean

bawl VERB **1** *They were shouting and bawling at
each other.* = **shout**, call, scream, roar, yell,
howl, bellow, bay, clamour, holler
(*informal*), raise your voice, halloo, hollo,
vociferate **2** *One of the toddlers was bawling,
and another had a runny nose.* = **cry**, weep,
sob, wail, whine, whimper, whinge
(*informal*), keen, greet (*Scot., archaic*), squall,
blubber, snivel, shed tears, yowl, mewl,
howl your eyes out

bay[1] NOUN *a short ferry ride across the bay*
= **inlet**, sound, gulf, entrance, creek, cove,
fjord, arm (of the sea), bight, ingress,
natural harbour, sea loch (*Scot.*), firth or
frith (*Scot.*)

bay[2] NOUN *Hundreds of rolls of fabric were
stacked in the loading bay.* = **recess**, opening,
corner, niche, compartment, nook, alcove,
embrasure

bay[3] VERB *A dog suddenly howled, baying at the
moon.* = **howl**, cry, roar (*a hound*), bark,
lament, cry out, wail, growl, bellow, quest,
bell, clamour, yelp ▶ NOUN *She trembled at
the bay of the dogs.* = **cry**, bell, roar (*a hound*),
quest, bark, lament, howl, wail, growl,
bellow, clamour, yelp • **at bay** *Eating
oranges keeps colds at bay.* = **away**, off, at
arm's length

bayonet VERB = **stab**, cut, wound, knife,
slash, pierce, run through, spear, transfix,
impale, lacerate, stick

bazaar NOUN **1** *He was a vendor in Egypt's
open-air bazaar.* = **market**, exchange, fair,
marketplace, mart **2** *a church bazaar* = **fair**,
fête, gala, festival, garden party,
bring-and-buy

be VERB **1** *It hurt so badly he wished to cease to
be.* = **be alive**, live, exist, survive, breathe,
last, be present, continue, endure, be
living, be extant, happen **2** *The film's
premiere is next week.* = **take place**, happen,
occur, arise, come about, transpire
(*informal*), befall, come to pass

beach NOUN = **shore**, coast, sands, margin,
strand, seaside, shingle, lakeside, water's
edge, lido, foreshore, seashore, plage,
littoral, sea (*chiefly U.S.*)

beached ADJECTIVE = **stranded**, grounded,
abandoned, deserted, wrecked, ashore,
marooned, aground, high and dry

beacon NOUN 1 = **signal**, sign, rocket, beam, flare, bonfire, smoke signal, signal fire 2 = **lighthouse**, pharos, watchtower

bead NOUN *beads of blood* = **drop**, tear, bubble, pearl, dot, drip, blob, droplet, globule, driblet ▶ PLURAL NOUN *baubles, bangles and beads* = **necklace**, pearls, pendant, choker, necklace, chaplet

beady ADJECTIVE = **bright**, powerful, concentrated, sharp, intense, shining, glittering, gleaming, glinting

beak NOUN 1 *a black bird with a yellow beak* = **bill**, nib, neb (*archaic*, *dialect*), mandible 2 *his sharp, aristocratic beak* = **nose**, snout, hooter (*slang*), snitch (*slang*), conk (*slang*), neb (*archaic*, *dialect*), proboscis, schnozzle (*slang*, *chiefly U.S.*)

beam VERB 1 *She beamed at her friend with undisguised admiration.* = **smile**, grin 2 *The interview was beamed live across America.* = **transmit**, show, air, broadcast, cable, send out, relay, televise, stream, radio, emit, put on the air 3 *A sharp white spotlight beamed down on a small stage.* = **radiate**, flash, shine, glow, glitter, glare, gleam, emit light, give off light ▶ NOUN 1 *a beam of light* = **ray**, bar, flash, stream, glow, radiation, streak, emission, shaft, gleam, glint, glimmer 2 *The ceilings are supported by oak beams.* = **rafter**, support, timber, spar, plank, girder, joist 3 *She knew he had news, because of the beam on his face.* = **smile**, grin

beaming ADJECTIVE 1 *his mother's beaming face* = **smiling**, happy, grinning, pleasant, sunny, cheerful, cheery, joyful, chirpy (*informal*), light-hearted 2 *A beaming sun rose out of the sea.* = **radiating**, bright, brilliant, flashing, shining, glowing, sparkling, glittering, gleaming, glimmering, radiant, glistening, scintillating, burnished, lustrous

bear VERB 1 *a surveyor and his assistant bearing a torch* = **carry**, take, move, bring, lift, transfer, conduct, transport, haul, transmit, convey, relay, tote (*informal*), hump (*Brit. slang*), lug ■ OPPOSITE: put down 2 *The ice was not thick enough to bear the weight of marching men.* = **support**, shoulder, sustain, endure, uphold, withstand, bear up under ■ OPPOSITE: give up 3 *notepaper bearing the President's seal* = **display**, have, show, hold, carry, possess, exhibit 4 *She bore her sufferings bravely.* = **suffer**, feel, experience, go through, sustain, stomach, endure, undergo, admit, brook, hack (*slang*), abide, put up with (*informal*) 5 *He can't bear to talk about it, even to me.* = **bring yourself to**, allow, accept, permit, endure, tolerate, hack (*informal*),

countenance 6 *The plants grow and start to bear fruit.* = **produce**, develop, generate, yield, bring forth 7 *She bore a son called Karl.* = **give birth to**, produce, deliver, breed, bring forth, beget (*old-fashioned*) 8 *She bore no ill will. If they didn't like her, too bad.* = **exhibit**, hold, maintain, entertain, harbour, cherish 9 *There was elegance and simple dignity in the way he bore himself.* = **conduct**, carry, move, deport • **bear down on someone or something** *The storm is expected to bear down on the area in the early hours.* = **advance on**, attack, approach, move towards, close in on, converge on, move in on, come near to, draw near to • **bear down on something** or **someone** *She felt as if a great weight was bearing down on her shoulders.* = **press down**, push, strain, crush, compress, weigh down, encumber • **bear on something** *The remaining 32 examples do not bear on our problem.* = **be relevant to**, involve, concern, affect, regard, refer to, be part of, relate to, belong to, apply to, be appropriate, befit, pertain to, touch upon, appertain to • **bear something out** *His photographs do not quite bear this out.* = **support**, prove, confirm, justify, endorse, uphold, vindicate, validate, substantiate, corroborate, legitimize • **bear with someone** *If you'll bear with me, Frank, I can explain everything.* = **be patient with**, suffer, wait for, hold on (*informal*), stand by, tolerate, put up with (*informal*), make allowances for, hang fire

bearable ADJECTIVE = **tolerable**, acceptable, sustainable, manageable, passable, admissible, supportable, endurable, sufferable ■ OPPOSITE: intolerable

beard NOUN = **whiskers**, bristles, stubble, five-o'clock shadow

bearded ADJECTIVE = **unshaven**, hairy, whiskered, stubbly, bushy, shaggy, hirsute (*formal*), bristly, bewhiskered

bearer NOUN 1 *I hate to be the bearer of bad news.* = **agent**, carrier, courier, herald, envoy, messenger, conveyor, emissary, harbinger (*literary*) 2 *a flag bearer* = **carrier**, runner, servant, porter 3 *This voucher entitles the bearer to one free meal.* = **payee**, beneficiary, consignee

bearing NOUN 1 (*usually with on or upon*) *My father's achievements don't have any bearing on what I do.* = **relevance**, relation, application, connection, import, reference, significance, pertinence, appurtenance ■ OPPOSITE: irrelevance 2 *She later wrote warmly of his bearing and behaviour.* = **manner**, attitude, conduct, appearance,

aspect, presence, behaviour, tone, carriage, posture, demeanour, deportment, mien (*literary*), air, comportment **3** *I'm flying on a bearing of ninety-three degrees.* = **position**, course, direction, point of compass
▶ PLURAL NOUN *I lost my bearings and was just aware of cars roaring past.* = **way**, course, position, situation, track, aim, direction, location, orientation, whereabouts

bearish ADJECTIVE = **falling**, declining, slumping

beast NOUN **1** *the threats our ancestors faced from wild beasts* = **animal**, creature, brute **2** *He is an absolute beast in terms of his will to win.* = **brute**, monster, savage, barbarian, fiend, swine, ogre, ghoul, sadist

beastly ADJECTIVE **1** *The weather was beastly.* = **unpleasant**, mean, terrible (*informal*), awful, nasty, foul, rotten (*informal*), horrid (*informal*), disagreeable, irksome
■ **OPPOSITE:** pleasant **2** *He must be wondering why everyone is being so beastly to him.* = **cruel**, mean (*informal*), nasty, harsh, savage, brutal, coarse, monstrous, malicious, insensitive, sadistic, unfriendly, unsympathetic, uncaring, spiteful, thoughtless, brutish, barbarous, unfeeling, inconsiderate, bestial, uncharitable, unchristian, hardhearted ■ **OPPOSITE:** humane

beat VERB **1** *They were beaten with baseball bats.* = **batter**, break, hit, strike, knock, punch, belt (*informal*), whip, deck (*slang*), bruise, bash (*informal*), sock (*slang*), lash, chin (*slang*), pound, smack, thrash, cane, thump, lick (*informal*), buffet, clout (*informal*), flog, whack (*informal*), maul, clobber (*slang*), wallop (*informal*), tonk (*informal*), cudgel, thwack (*informal*), lambast(e), lay one on (*slang*), drub, beat or knock seven bells out of (*informal*) **2** *The rain was beating on the window panes.* = **pound**, strike, hammer (*informal*), batter, thrash, pelt **3** *I felt my heart beat faster.* = **throb**, pulse, tick, thump, tremble, pound, quake, quiver, vibrate, pulsate, palpitate **4** *When you beat the drum, you feel good.* = **hit**, strike, bang **5** *Its wings beat slowly.* = **flap**, thrash, flutter, agitate, wag, swish **6** *She was easily beaten into third place.* = **defeat**, outdo, trounce, overcome, stuff (*slang*), master, tank (*slang*), crush, overwhelm, conquer, lick (*informal*), undo, subdue, excel, surpass, overpower, outstrip, clobber (*slang*), vanquish, outrun, subjugate, run rings around (*informal*), wipe the floor with (*informal*), knock spots off (*informal*), make mincemeat of (*informal*), pip at the post, outplay, blow out of the water (*slang*), put

in the shade (*informal*), bring to their knees
▶ NOUN **1** *He could hear the beat of his heart.* = **throb**, pounding, pulse, thumping, vibration, pulsating, palpitation, pulsation **2** *I was a relatively new PC on the beat, stationed in Hendon.* = **route**, way, course, rounds, path, circuit • **beat it** *Beat it before it's too late.* = **go away**, leave, depart, get lost (*informal*), shoo, exit, go to hell (*informal*), hook it (*slang*), scarper (*Brit. slang*), pack your bags (*informal*), make tracks, hop it (*slang*), scram (*informal*), get on your bike (*Brit. slang*), skedaddle (*informal*), sling your hook (*Brit. slang*), vamoose (*slang, chiefly U.S.*), voetsek (*S. African, offensive*), rack off (*Austral. & N.Z. slang*) • **beat someone up** *Then they actually beat me up as well.* = **assault**, attack, batter, thrash, set about, do over (*Brit., Austral. & N.Z. slang*), work over (*slang*), clobber (*slang*), assail, set upon, lay into (*informal*), put the boot in (*slang*), lambast(e), duff up (*Brit. slang*), beat the living daylights out of (*informal*), knock about or around, fill in (*Brit. slang*), beat or knock seven bells out of (*informal*)

beaten ADJECTIVE **1** *Before you is a well-worn path of beaten earth.* = **well-trodden**, worn, trodden, trampled, well-used, much travelled **2** *Cool a little and slowly add the beaten eggs.* = **stirred**, mixed, whipped, blended, whisked, frothy, foamy **3** *brightly painted beaten metal* = **shaped**, worked, formed, stamped, hammered, forged **4** *They had looked a beaten side with just seven minutes left.* = **defeated**, overcome, frustrated, overwhelmed, cowed, thwarted, vanquished, disheartened

beating NOUN **1** *the savage beating of a prisoner* = **thrashing**, hiding (*informal*), belting (*informal*), whipping (*slang*), slapping, tanning, lashing, smacking, caning, pasting (*slang*), flogging, drubbing, corporal punishment, chastisement **2** *A beating at Wembley would be too much of a trauma for them.* = **defeat**, ruin, overthrow, pasting (*slang*), conquest, rout, downfall

beau NOUN (*old-fashioned*) = **boyfriend**, man, guy (*informal*), date, lover, young man, steady, escort, admirer, fiancé, sweetheart, suitor, swain (*archaic*), toy boy, leman (*archaic*), fancy man (*slang*), bae (*U.S. informal*)

beautiful ADJECTIVE = **attractive**, pretty, lovely, stunning (*informal*), charming, tempting, pleasant, handsome, fetching (*informal*), good-looking, gorgeous (*informal*), fine, pleasing, fair, magnetic, delightful, cute, exquisite, enticing, seductive, graceful, captivating, appealing,

b

radiant, alluring, drop-dead (*slang*), ravishing, bonny (*Scot. & Northern English, dialect*), winsome, comely (*old-fashioned*), prepossessing, hot (*informal*), fit (*Brit. informal*) ■ **OPPOSITE:** ugly

beautify VERB = **make beautiful**, enhance, decorate, enrich, adorn, garnish, ornament, gild, embellish, grace, festoon, bedeck, glamorize

beauty NOUN **1** *an area of outstanding natural beauty* = **attractiveness**, charm, grace, bloom, glamour, fairness, elegance, symmetry (*formal, literary*), allure, loveliness, handsomeness, pulchritude, comeliness, exquisiteness, seemliness ■ **OPPOSITE:** ugliness **2** *She is known as a great beauty.* = **good-looker**, looker (*informal*), lovely (*slang*), sensation, dazzler, belle, goddess, Venus, peach (*informal*), cracker (*slang*), wow (*slang, chiefly U.S.*), dolly (*slang*), knockout (*informal*), heart-throb, stunner (*informal*), charmer, smasher (*informal*), humdinger (*slang*), glamour puss, beaut (*Austral. & N.Z. slang*) **3** *the beauty of such water-based minerals* = **advantage**, good, use, benefit, profit, gain, asset, attraction, blessing, good thing, utility, excellence, boon ■ **OPPOSITE:** disadvantage

becalmed ADJECTIVE = **still**, stuck, settled, stranded, motionless

because CONJUNCTION *They could not obey the command because they had no ammunition.* = **since**, as, in that • **because of** *He failed because of a lack of money.* = **as a result of**, on account of, by reason of, thanks to, owing to

> **USAGE** The phrase *on account of* can provide a useful alternative to *because of* in writing. It occurs relatively infrequently in spoken language, where it is sometimes followed by a clause, as in *on account of I don't do drugs*. However, this use is considered nonstandard.

beckon VERB **1** *He beckoned to the waiter.* = **gesture**, sign, wave, indicate, signal, nod, motion, summon, gesticulate **2** *All the attractions of the peninsula beckon.* = **lure**, call, draw, pull (*informal*), attract, invite, tempt, entice, coax, allure

become VERB **1** *After leaving school, he became a professional footballer.* = **come to be**, develop into, be transformed into, grow into, change into, evolve into, alter to, mature into, metamorphose into, ripen into **2** *Does khaki become you?* = **suit**, fit, enhance, flatter, ornament, embellish, grace, harmonize with, set off • **become of something** or **someone** *What will become of him?* = **happen to**, befall (*archaic, literary*), betide

becoming ADJECTIVE **1** *Softer fabrics are much more becoming than stiffer ones.* = **flattering**, pretty, attractive, enhancing, neat, graceful, tasteful, well-chosen, comely (*old-fashioned*) ■ **OPPOSITE:** unflattering **2** *This behaviour is not becoming among our politicians.* = **appropriate**, right, seemly, fitting, fit, correct, suitable, decent, proper, worthy, in keeping, compatible, befitting, decorous, comme il faut (*French*), congruous, meet (*archaic*) ■ **OPPOSITE:** inappropriate

bed NOUN **1** *She went in to her bedroom and lay down on the bed.* = **bedstead**, couch, berth, cot, pallet, divan **2** *beds of strawberries and rhubarb* = **plot**, area, row, strip, patch, ground, land, garden, border **3** *the bare bed of a dry stream* = **bottom**, ground, floor **4** *a sandstone bed* = **base**, footing, basis, bottom, foundation, underpinning, groundwork, bedrock, substructure, substratum ▸ VERB *The slabs can then be bedded on mortar to give rigid paving.* = **fix**, set, found, base, plant, establish, settle, root, sink, insert, implant, embed • **bed down** *They bedded down in the fields.* = **sleep**, lie down, retire, turn in (*informal*), settle down, kip (*Brit. slang*), hit the hay (*slang*)

bedclothes PLURAL NOUN = **bedding**, covers, sheets, blankets, linen, pillow, quilt, duvet, pillowcase, bed linen, coverlet, eiderdown

bedding NOUN = **bedclothes**, covers, sheets, blankets, linen, pillow, quilt, duvet, pillowcase, bed linen, coverlet, eiderdown

bedeck VERB = **decorate**, grace, trim, array, enrich, adorn, garnish, ornament, embellish, festoon, beautify, bedight (*archaic*), bedizen (*archaic*), engarland

bedevil VERB = **plague**, worry, trouble, frustrate, torture, irritate, torment, harass, hassle (*informal*), aggravate (*informal*), afflict, pester, vex, irk

bedlam NOUN = **pandemonium**, noise, confusion, chaos, turmoil, clamour, furore, uproar, commotion, rumpus, babel, tumult, hubbub, ruction (*informal*), hullabaloo, hue and cry, ruckus (*informal*)

bedraggled ADJECTIVE = **messy**, soiled, dirty, disordered, stained, dripping, muddied, muddy, drenched, ruffled, untidy, sodden, sullied, dishevelled, rumpled, unkempt, tousled, disarranged, disarrayed, daggy (*Austral. & N.Z. informal*)

bedridden ADJECTIVE = **confined to bed**, confined, incapacitated, laid up (*informal*), flat on your back

bedrock NOUN **1** *Mutual trust is the bedrock of a relationship.* = **first principle**, rule, basis, basics, principle, essentials, roots, core, fundamentals, cornerstone, nuts and bolts (*informal*), sine qua non (*Latin*), rudiment **2** *It took five years to drill down to bedrock.* = **bottom**, bed, foundation, underpinning, rock bottom, substructure, substratum

bee NOUN ■ **RELATED WORDS:** *adjective* apian; *collective nouns* swarm, grist; *name of home* hive, apiary

beef NOUN = **complaint**, dispute, grievance, problem, grumble, criticism, objection, dissatisfaction, annoyance, grouse, gripe (*informal*), protestation, grouch (*informal*), remonstrance

beefy ADJECTIVE = **brawny**, strong, powerful, athletic, strapping, robust, hefty (*informal*), muscular, swole (*slang*), hench (*informal*), sturdy, stalwart, bulky, burly, stocky, hulking, well-built, herculean, sinewy, thickset ■ **OPPOSITE:** scrawny

beehive NOUN = **hive**, colony, comb, swarm, honeycomb, apiary

beer NOUN = **ale**, brew, swipes (*Brit. slang*), wallop (*Brit. slang*), hop juice, amber fluid *or* nectar (*Austral. informal*), tinnie *or* tinny (*Austral. slang*)

beer parlour NOUN (*Canad.*) = **tavern**, inn, bar, pub (*informal, chiefly Brit.*), public house, watering hole (*facetious slang*), boozer (*Brit., Austral. & N.Z. informal*), beverage room (*Canad.*), hostelry

befall VERB = **happen to**, fall upon, occur in, take place in, ensue in, transpire in (*informal*), materialize in, come to pass in

befit VERB = **be appropriate for**, become, suit, be fitting for, be suitable for, be seemly for, behove (*U.S.*)

befitting ADJECTIVE = **appropriate to**, right for, suitable for, fitting for, fit for, becoming to, seemly for, proper for, apposite to, meet (*archaic*) ■ **OPPOSITE:** unsuitable for

before PREPOSITION **1** *Annie was born a few weeks before Christmas.* = **earlier than**, ahead of, prior to, in advance of ■ **OPPOSITE:** after **2** *They stopped before a large white villa.* = **in front of**, ahead of, in advance of, to the fore of **3** *The Government will appear before the committee.* = **in the presence of**, in front of **4** *I saw before me an idyllic life.* = **ahead of**, in front of, in advance of ▶ ADVERB **1** *The war had ended only a month or so before.* = **previously**, earlier, sooner, in advance, formerly ■ **OPPOSITE:** after **2** *I've been here before.* = **in the past**, earlier, once, previously, formerly, at one time, hitherto (*formal*), beforehand, a while ago, heretofore, in days *or* years gone by
■ **RELATED WORDS:** *prefixes* ante-, fore-, pre-

beforehand ADVERB = **in advance**, before, earlier, already, sooner, ahead, previously, in anticipation, before now, ahead of time

befriend VERB = **make friends with**, back, help, support, benefit, aid, encourage, welcome, favour, advise, sustain, assist, stand by, uphold, side with, patronize, succour

befuddle VERB = **confuse**, puzzle, baffle, bewilder, muddle, daze, perplex, mystify, disorient, faze, stupefy, flummox, bemuse, intoxicate ■ **OPPOSITE:** make clear

befuddled ADJECTIVE = **confused**, upset, puzzled, baffled, at sea, bewildered, muddled, dazed, perplexed, taken aback, intoxicated, disorientated, disorganized, muzzy (*U.S. informal*), groggy (*informal*), flummoxed, woozy (*informal*), at sixes and sevens, fuddled, inebriated, thrown off balance, discombobulated (*informal, chiefly U.S. & Canad.*), not with it (*informal*), not knowing if you are coming or going

beg VERB **1** *I begged him to come back to England with me.* = **implore**, plead with, beseech, desire (*formal*), request, pray, petition, conjure (*formal*), crave (*informal*), solicit, entreat, importune (*formal*), supplicate, go on bended knee to **2** *I was surrounded by people begging for food.* = **scrounge** (*informal*), bum (*informal*), blag (*slang*), touch (someone) for (*slang*), mooch (*slang*), cadge, forage for, hunt around (for), sponge on (someone) for, freeload (*slang*), seek charity, call for alms, solicit charity
■ **OPPOSITE:** give **3** *The research begs a number of questions.* = **dodge**, avoid, get out of, duck (*informal*), hedge, parry, shun, evade, elude, fudge, fend off, eschew, flannel (*Brit. informal*), sidestep, shirk, equivocate, body-swerve

beget VERB **1** *Poverty begets debt.* = **cause**, bring, produce, create, effect, lead to, occasion (*formal*), result in, generate, provoke, induce, bring about, give rise to, precipitate, incite, engender **2** *He wanted to beget an heir.* = **father**, breed, generate, sire, get, propagate, procreate (*formal*)

beggar NOUN *Now I am a beggar, having lost everything except life.* = **vagrant**, tramp, bankrupt, bum (*informal*), derelict, drifter, down-and-out, pauper, hobo (*chiefly U.S.*), vagabond, bag lady (*chiefly U.S.*), dosser (*Brit. slang*), derro (*Austral. slang*), starveling ▶ VERB *The statistics beggar belief.* = **defy**, challenge, defeat, frustrate, foil, baffle, thwart, withstand, surpass, elude, repel

begin VERB **1** *He stood up and began to walk around the room.* = **start**, commence, proceed ■ **OPPOSITE:** stop **2** *The US wants to begin talks immediately.* = **commence**, start,

b

initiate, embark on, set about, instigate, inaugurate, institute, make a beginning, set on foot **3** *He didn't know how to begin.* = **start talking**, start, initiate, commence, begin business, get or start the ball rolling **4** *It began as a local festival.* = **come into existence**, start, appear, emerge, spring, be born, arise, dawn, be developed, be created, originate, commence, be invented, become available, crop up (*informal*), come into being **5** *The fate line begins close to the wrist.* = **emerge**, start, spring, stem, derive, issue, originate
■ **OPPOSITE:** end

beginner NOUN = **novice**, student, pupil, convert, recruit, amateur, initiate, newcomer, starter, trainee, apprentice, cub, fledgling, learner, freshman, neophyte (*formal*), tyro, probationer, greenhorn (*informal*), novitiate, tenderfoot, proselyte
■ **OPPOSITE:** expert

beginning NOUN **1** *Think of this as a new beginning.* = **start**, opening, break (*informal*), chance, source, opportunity, birth, origin, introduction, outset, starting point, onset, overture, initiation, inauguration, inception, commencement, opening move
■ **OPPOSITE:** end **2** *The question was raised at the beginning of this chapter.* = **outset**, start, opening, birth, onset, prelude, preface, commencement, kickoff (*informal*) **3** *His views come from his own humble beginnings.* = **origins**, family, beginnings, stock, birth, roots, heritage, descent, pedigree, extraction, ancestry, lineage, parentage, stirps

begrudge VERB **1** *I certainly don't begrudge him the Nobel Prize.* = **resent**, envy, grudge, be jealous of **2** *She spends £2,000 a year on it and she doesn't begrudge a penny.* = **be bitter about**, object to, be angry about, give reluctantly, bear a grudge about, be in a huff about, give stingily, have hard feelings about

beguile VERB **1** *Her paintings beguiled the critics.* = **charm**, please, attract, delight, occupy, cheer, fascinate, entertain, absorb, entrance, win over, amuse, divert, distract, enchant, captivate, solace, allure, bewitch, mesmerize, engross, enrapture, tickle the fancy of **2** *He used his newspapers to beguile his readers.* = **fool**, trick, take in, cheat, con (*informal*), mislead, impose on, deceive, dupe, gull (*archaic*), delude, bamboozle, hoodwink, take for a ride (*informal*), befool
■ **OPPOSITE:** enlighten

beguiling ADJECTIVE = **charming**, interesting, pleasing, attractive, engaging, lovely, entertaining, pleasant, intriguing, diverting, delightful, irresistible,

enchanting, seductive, captivating, enthralling, winning, eye-catching, alluring, bewitching, delectable, winsome, likable or likeable

behalf NOUN • **on behalf of something** or **someone** or **on something** or **someone's behalf 1** *She made an emotional public appeal on her son's behalf.* = **as a representative of**, representing, in the name of, as a spokesperson for **2** *The honour recognizes work done on behalf of classical theatre.* = **for the benefit of**, for the sake of, in support of, on the side of, in the interests of, on account of, for the good of, in defence of, to the advantage of, for the profit of

> USAGE *On behalf of* is sometimes wrongly used as an alternative to *on the part of*. The distinction is that *on behalf of someone* means 'for someone's benefit' or 'representing someone', while *on the part of someone* can be roughly paraphrased as 'by someone'.

behave VERB **1** *He'd behaved badly.* = **act**, react, conduct yourself, acquit yourself, comport yourself **2** (*often reflexive*) *You have to behave.* = **be well-behaved**, be good, be polite, mind your manners, keep your nose clean, act correctly, act politely, conduct yourself properly ■ **OPPOSITE:** misbehave

behaviour NOUN **1** *He was asked to explain his extraordinary behaviour.* = **conduct**, ways, actions, bearing, attitude, manner, manners, carriage, demeanour, deportment, mien (*literary*), comportment **2** *This process modifies the cell's behaviour.* = **action**, working, running, performance, operation, practice, conduct, functioning

behead VERB = **decapitate**, execute, guillotine

behest NOUN • **at someone's behest** = **at someone's command**, by someone's order, at someone's demand, at someone's wish, by someone's decree, at someone's bidding, at someone's instruction, by someone's mandate, at someone's dictate, at someone's commandment

behind PREPOSITION **1** *They were parked behind the truck.* = **at the rear of**, at the back of, at the heels of **2** *I wandered along behind him.* = **after**, following **3** *He had the state's judicial power behind him.* = **supporting**, for, backing, on the side of, in agreement with **4** *I'd like to know who was behind this plot.* = **causing**, responsible for, the cause of, initiating, at the bottom of, to blame for, instigating **5** *The work is 22 weeks behind schedule.* = **later than**, after ▶ ADVERB **1** *They were grabbed from behind.* = **the back**, the rear **2** *The troopers followed behind.* = **after**, next, following, afterwards, subsequently, in the wake (of) ■ **OPPOSITE:** in advance of **3** *The accounts are more than three months behind.* = **overdue**, in debt, in arrears, behindhand **4** *They were falling behind with their mortgage payments.* = **overdue**, in debt, in arrears, behindhand ▶ NOUN *jeans that actually flatter your behind* = **bottom** (*informal*), seat, bum (*Brit. slang*), butt (*U.S. & Canad. informal*), buns (*U.S. slang*), buttocks, rump, posterior, tail (*informal*), derrière (*euphemistic*), tush (*U.S. slang*), jacksy (*Brit. slang*)

behold VERB = **look at**, see, view, eye, consider, study, watch, check, regard, survey, witness, clock (*Brit. slang*), examine, observe, perceive, gaze, scan, contemplate, check out (*informal*), inspect, discern, eyeball (*slang*), scrutinize, recce (*slang*), get a load of (*informal*), take a gander at (*informal*), take a dekko at (*Brit. slang*), feast your eyes upon

beholden ADJECTIVE = **indebted**, bound, owing, grateful, obliged, in debt, obligated, under obligation

beige NOUN or ADJECTIVE = **fawn**, coffee, cream, sand, neutral, mushroom, tan, biscuit, camel, buff, cinnamon, khaki, oatmeal, ecru, café au lait (*French*)

being NOUN **1** *beings from outer space* = **individual**, thing, body (*informal*), animal, creature, human being, beast, mortal, living thing **2** *the complex process by which the novel is brought into being* = **life**, living, reality, animation, actuality ■ **OPPOSITE:** nonexistence **3** *The music seemed to touch his very being.* = **soul**, spirit, presence, substance, creature, essence, organism, entity

belated ADJECTIVE = **late**, delayed, overdue, late in the day, tardy, behind time, unpunctual, behindhand

belch VERB **1** *He covered his mouth with his hand and belched discreetly.* = **burp**, eructate, eruct **2** *Tired old trucks belched black smoke.* = **emit**, discharge, erupt, send out, throw out, vent, vomit, issue, give out, gush, eject, diffuse, emanate, exude, give off, exhale, cast out, disgorge, give vent to, send forth, spew forth, breathe forth

beleaguered ADJECTIVE **1** *There have been seven attempts against the beleaguered government.* = **harassed**, troubled, plagued, tormented, hassled (*informal*), aggravated (*informal*), badgered, persecuted, pestered, vexed, put upon **2** *The rebels continue to push their way towards the beleaguered capital.* = **besieged**, surrounded, blockaded, encompassed, beset, encircled, assailed, hemmed in, hedged in, environed

belie VERB **1** *Her expression belies her good humour.* = **misrepresent**, disguise, conceal, distort, misinterpret, falsify, gloss over **2** *The facts of the situation belie his testimony.* = **disprove**, deny, expose, discredit, contradict, refute, repudiate, negate, invalidate, rebut, give the lie to, make a nonsense of, gainsay (*archaic, literary*), prove false, blow out of the water (*slang*), controvert, confute

belief NOUN **1** *a belief in personal liberty* = **trust**, confidence, conviction, reliance ■ **OPPOSITE:** disbelief **2** *He refuses to compete on Sundays because of his religious beliefs.* = **faith**, principles, doctrine, ideology, creed, dogma, tenet, credence, credo **3** *It is my belief that a common ground can be found.* = **opinion**, feeling, idea, view, theory, impression, assessment, notion, judgment, point of view, sentiment, persuasion, presumption

believable ADJECTIVE = **credible**, possible, likely, acceptable, reliable, authentic, probable, plausible, imaginable, trustworthy, creditable ■ **OPPOSITE:** unbelievable

believe VERB **1** *I believe you have something of mine.* = **think**, consider, judge, suppose, maintain, estimate, imagine, assume, gather, guess (*informal, chiefly U.S. & Canad.*), reckon, conclude, deem, speculate, presume, conjecture, postulate (*formal*), surmise **2** *Don't believe what you read in the papers.* = **accept**, hold, buy (*slang*), trust, credit, depend on, rely on, swallow (*informal*), count on, buy into (*slang*), have faith in, swear by, be certain of, be convinced of, place confidence in, presume true, take as gospel, take on (*U.S.*) ■ **OPPOSITE:** disbelieve • **believe in something** *He believed in marital fidelity.* = **advocate**, champion, approve of, swear by

believer NOUN = **follower**, supporter, convert, disciple, protagonist, devotee, worshipper, apostle, adherent, zealot, upholder, proselyte ■ **OPPOSITE:** sceptic

belittle VERB = **run down**, dismiss, diminish, put down, underestimate, discredit, ridicule, scorn, rubbish (*informal*), degrade, minimize, downgrade, undervalue, knock (*informal*), deride, malign, detract from, denigrate, scoff at, disparage, decry, sneer at, underrate, deprecate, depreciate, defame, derogate ■ **OPPOSITE:** praise

belle NOUN = **beauty**, looker (*informal*), lovely, good-looker, goddess, Venus, peach (*informal*), cracker (*informal*), stunner (*informal*), charmer

bellicose ADJECTIVE = **aggressive**, offensive, hostile, destructive, defiant, provocative, belligerent, combative, antagonistic, pugnacious, hawkish, warlike, quarrelsome, militaristic, sabre-rattling, jingoistic, warmongering

belligerence NOUN = **aggressiveness**, hostility, animosity, antagonism, destructiveness, pugnacity, combativeness, offensiveness, unfriendliness

belligerent ADJECTIVE *He was almost back to his belligerent mood of twelve months ago.* = **aggressive**, hostile, contentious, combative, unfriendly, antagonistic, pugnacious, argumentative, bellicose, quarrelsome, aggro (*Austral. & N.Z.*), aggers (*Austral. slang*), biffo (*Austral. slang*), litigious ■ **OPPOSITE:** friendly ▶ NOUN *The belligerents were due to settle their differences.* = **fighter**, battler, militant, contender, contestant, combatant, antagonist, warring nation, disputant

bellow VERB *He bellowed the information into the telephone.* = **shout**, call, cry (out), scream, roar, yell, howl, shriek, clamour, bawl, holler (*informal*) ▶ NOUN *a bellow of tearful rage* = **shout**, call, cry, scream, roar, yell, howl, shriek, bell, clamour, bawl

belly NOUN = **stomach**, insides (*informal*), gut, abdomen, tummy (*informal*), paunch, vitals, breadbasket (*slang*), potbelly, corporation (*informal*), puku (*N.Z.*)

belong VERB = **go with**, fit into, be part of, relate to, attach to, be connected with, pertain to, have as a proper place

belonging NOUN = **fellowship**, relationship, association, loyalty, acceptance, attachment, inclusion, affinity, rapport, affiliation, kinship

belongings PLURAL NOUN = **possessions**, goods, things, effects, property, stuff, gear, paraphernalia, personal property, accoutrements, chattels, goods and chattels

beloved ADJECTIVE = **dear**, loved, valued, prized, dearest, sweet (*archaic*), admired, treasured, precious, darling, worshipped, adored, cherished, revered

below PREPOSITION **1** *The boat dipped below the surface of the water.* = **under**, underneath, lower than **2** *Night temperatures can drop below 15 degrees Celsius.* = **less than**, lower than **3** *white-collar staff below chief officer level* = **subordinate to**, subject to, inferior to, lesser than ▶ ADVERB **1** *Spread out below was a huge crowd.* = **lower**, down, under, beneath, underneath **2** *Please write to me at the address below.* = **beneath**, following,

at the end, underneath, at the bottom, further on

belt NOUN **1** *He wore a belt with a large brass buckle.* = **waistband**, band, sash, girdle, girth, cummerbund, cincture **2** *The turning disc is connected by a drive belt to an electric motor.* = **conveyor belt**, band, loop, fan belt, drive belt **3** *a belt of trees* = **zone**, area, region, section, sector, district, stretch, strip, layer, patch, portion, tract • **below the belt** *Do you think it's a bit below the belt, what they're doing?* = **unfair**, foul, crooked (*informal*), cowardly, sly, fraudulent, unjust, dishonest, deceptive, unscrupulous, devious, unethical, sneaky, furtive, deceitful, surreptitious, dishonourable, unsporting, unsportsmanlike, underhanded, not playing the game (*informal*)

bemoan VERB = **lament**, regret, complain about, rue (*literary*), deplore, grieve for, weep for, bewail, cry over spilt milk, express sorrow about, moan over

bemused ADJECTIVE = **puzzled**, stunned, confused, stumped, baffled, at sea, bewildered, muddled, preoccupied, dazed, perplexed, mystified, engrossed, clueless, stupefied, nonplussed, absent-minded, flummoxed, half-drunk, fuddled

bench NOUN **1** *We sat down on a park bench.* = **seat**, stall, pew **2** *the laboratory bench* = **worktable**, stand, table, counter, slab, trestle table, workbench • **the bench** *It shows how seriously the bench viewed these offences.* = **court**, judge, judges, magistrate, magistrates, tribunal, judiciary, courtroom

benchmark NOUN = **reference point**, gauge, yardstick, measure, level, example, standard, model, reference, par, criterion, norm, touchstone

bend VERB **1** *Bend the bar into a horseshoe.* = **twist**, turn, wind, lean, hook, bow, curve, arch, incline, arc, deflect, warp, buckle, coil, flex, stoop, veer, swerve, diverge, contort, inflect, incurvate **2** *Congress has to bend to his will.* = **submit**, yield, bow, surrender, give in, give way, cede, capitulate, resign yourself **3** *He's very decisive. You cannot bend him.* = **force**, direct, influence, shape, persuade, compel, mould, sway ▶ NOUN *The crash occurred on a sharp bend.* = **curve**, turn, corner, hook, twist, angle, bow, loop, arc, zigzag, camber

beneath PREPOSITION **1** *She found pleasure in sitting beneath the trees.* = **under**, below, underneath, lower than ■ **OPPOSITE:** over **2** *She decided he was beneath her.* = **inferior to**, below **3** *Many find themselves having to take jobs far beneath them.* = **unworthy of**, unfitting for, unsuitable for, inappropriate for, unbefitting ▶ ADVERB *On a shelf beneath he spotted a photo album.* = **underneath**, below, in a lower place ■ **RELATED WORD:** prefix sub-

benefactor NOUN = **supporter**, friend, champion, defender, sponsor, angel (*informal*), patron, promoter, contributor, backer, helper, subsidizer, philanthropist, upholder, well-wisher

beneficial ADJECTIVE = **favourable**, useful, valuable, helpful, profitable, benign, wholesome, advantageous, expedient, salutary, healthful, serviceable, salubrious, gainful ■ **OPPOSITE:** harmful

beneficiary NOUN **1** *The main beneficiaries of pension equality so far have been men.* = **recipient**, receiver, payee, assignee, legatee **2** *a sole beneficiary of a will* = **heir**, inheritor

benefit NOUN **1** *I'm a great believer in the benefits of this form of therapy.* = **good**, use, help, profit, gain, favour, utility, boon, mileage (*informal*), avail ■ **OPPOSITE:** harm **2** *This could now work to his benefit.* = **advantage**, interest, aid, gain, favour, assistance, betterment ▶ VERB **1** *Both sides have benefited from the talks.* = **profit from**, make the most of, gain from, do well out of, reap benefits from, turn to your advantage **2** *a variety of government schemes benefiting children* = **help**, serve, aid, profit, improve, advance, advantage, enhance, assist, avail ■ **OPPOSITE:** harm

benevolence NOUN = **kindness**, understanding, charity, grace, sympathy, humanity, tolerance, goodness, goodwill, compassion, generosity, indulgence, decency, altruism, clemency, gentleness, philanthropy, magnanimity, fellow feeling, beneficence, kindliness, kind-heartedness, aroha (*N.Z.*) ■ **OPPOSITE:** ill will

benevolent ADJECTIVE = **kind**, good, kindly, understanding, caring, liberal, generous, obliging, sympathetic, humanitarian, charitable, benign, humane, compassionate, gracious, indulgent, amiable, amicable, lenient, cordial, considerate, affable, congenial, altruistic, philanthropic, bountiful, beneficent, well-disposed, kind-hearted, warm-hearted, bounteous, tender-hearted

benighted ADJECTIVE = **uncivilized**, crude, primitive, backward, uncultivated, unenlightened

benign ADJECTIVE **1** *Critics of the scheme take a less benign view.* = **benevolent**, kind, kindly, warm, liberal, friendly, generous, obliging, sympathetic, favourable, compassionate, gracious, amiable, genial, affable, complaisant ■ **OPPOSITE:** unkind **2** *It wasn't cancer, only a benign tumour.* = **harmless**, innocent, superficial, innocuous, curable, inoffensive, not dangerous, remediable ■ **OPPOSITE:** malignant **3** *relatively benign economic conditions* = **favourable**, good, encouraging, warm, moderate, beneficial, clement, advantageous, salutary, auspicious, propitious ■ **OPPOSITE:** unfavourable

bent ADJECTIVE **1** *The trees were all bent and twisted from the wind.* = **misshapen**, twisted, angled, bowed, curved, arched, crooked, distorted, warped, deformed, tortuous, disfigured, out of shape ■ **OPPOSITE:** straight **2** *a bent, frail, old man* = **stooped**, bowed, arched, hunched ▶ NOUN *a bent for natural history* = **inclination**, ability, taste, facility, talent, leaning, tendency, preference, faculty, forte, flair, knack, penchant, bag (*slang*), propensity, aptitude, predisposition, predilection, proclivity (*formal*), turn of mind • **bent on** *They are bent on revenge.* = **intent on**, set on, fixed on, predisposed to, resolved on, insistent on

bequeath VERB **1** *He bequeathed all his silver to his children.* = **leave**, will, give, grant, commit, transmit, hand down, endow, bestow, entrust, leave to by will **2** *She bequeaths her successor an economy that is doing quite well.* = **give**, offer, accord, grant, afford, contribute, yield, lend, pass on, transmit, confer, bestow, impart

bequest NOUN = **legacy**, gift, settlement, heritage, trust, endowment, estate, inheritance, dower, bestowal, koha (*N.Z.*)

berate VERB = **scold**, rebuke, reprimand, reproach, blast, carpet (*informal*), put down, criticize, slate (*informal, chiefly Brit.*), censure, castigate, revile, chide, harangue, tear into (*informal*), tell off (*informal*), rail at, read the riot act to, reprove, upbraid, slap on the wrist, lambast(e), bawl out (*informal*), excoriate, rap over the knuckles, chew out (*U.S. & Canad. informal*), tear (someone) off a strip (*Brit. informal*), give a rocket (*Brit. & N.Z. informal*), vituperate ■ **OPPOSITE:** praise

bereavement NOUN = **loss**, death, misfortune, deprivation, affliction, tribulation

bereft ADJECTIVE • **bereft of** = **deprived of**, without, minus, lacking in, devoid of, cut off from, parted from, sans (*archaic*), robbed of, empty of, denuded of

berg NOUN (*S. African*) = **mountain**, peak, mount, height, ben (*Scot.*), horn, ridge, fell (*Brit.*), alp, pinnacle, elevation, eminence

b

berserk ADJECTIVE = **crazy**, wild, mad
(*informal*), frantic, ape (*slang*), barro
(*Austral. slang*), off the air (*Austral. slang*),
porangi (*N.Z.*)

berth NOUN **1** *Golding booked a berth on the first
boat he could.* = **bunk**, bed, cot (*Nautical*),
hammock, billet **2** *A ship has applied to leave
its berth.* = **anchorage**, haven, slip, port,
harbour, dock, pier, wharf, quay ▸ VERB
The ship berthed in New York. = **anchor**, land,
dock, moor, tie up, drop anchor

beseech VERB = **beg**, ask, petition, call
upon, plead with, solicit, implore, entreat,
importune (*formal*), adjure, supplicate

beset VERB = **plague**, trouble, embarrass,
torture, haunt, torment, harass, afflict,
badger, perplex, pester, vex, entangle,
bedevil

besetting ADJECTIVE = **chronic**, persistent,
long-standing, prevalent, habitual,
ingrained, deep-seated, incurable,
deep-rooted, inveterate, incorrigible,
ineradicable

beside PREPOSITION *On the table beside an
empty plate was a pile of books.* = **next to**,
near, close to, neighbouring, alongside,
overlooking, next door to, adjacent to, at
the side of, abreast of, cheek by jowl with
• **beside yourself** *He was beside himself with
anxiety.* = **distraught**, desperate, mad,
distressed, frantic, frenzied, hysterical,
unbalanced, uncontrolled, deranged,
berserk, delirious, unhinged, very anxious,
overwrought, apoplectic, at the end of your
tether

> **USAGE** People occasionally confuse
> *beside* and *besides*. *Besides* is used for
> mentioning something that adds to
> what you have already said, for
> example: *I didn't feel like going and besides,
> I had nothing to wear.* *Beside* usually
> means *next to* or *at the side of something or
> someone*, for example: *he was standing
> beside me* (not *besides me*).

besides PREPOSITION *I asked him where he had
been in South America besides Peru.* = **apart
from**, barring, excepting, other than,
excluding, as well (as), in addition to, over
and above ▸ ADVERB *It doesn't fit you, and
besides it's dreadful!* = **also**, too, further,
otherwise, in addition, as well, moreover,
furthermore, what's more, into the bargain

besiege VERB **1** *She was besieged by the press
and the public.* = **harass**, worry, trouble,
harry, bother, disturb, plague, hound,
hassle (*informal*), badger, pester, importune
(*formal*), bend someone's ear (*informal*), give
someone grief (*Brit. &S. African*), beleaguer
2 *The main part of the army moved to besiege the*

town. = **surround**, confine, enclose,
blockade, encompass, beset, encircle, close
in on, hem in, shut in, lay siege to, hedge in,
environ, beleaguer, invest (*rare*)

besotted ADJECTIVE = **infatuated**,
charmed, captivated, beguiled, doting,
smitten, bewitched, bowled over (*informal*),
spellbound, enamoured, hypnotized,
swept off your feet

best ADJECTIVE **1** *He was the best player in the
world for most of the 1950s.* = **finest**, leading,
chief, supreme, principal, first, foremost,
superlative, pre-eminent, unsurpassed,
most accomplished, most skilful, most
excellent **2** *the best way to end the long-
running war* = **most fitting**, right, most
desirable, most apt, most advantageous,
most correct ▸ NOUN *You must do your best to
protect yourselves.* = **utmost**, most, greatest,
hardest, highest endeavour ▸ ADVERB *The
thing I liked best about the show was the music.*
= **most highly**, most fully, most deeply
• **the best** *We only offer the best to our clients.*
= **the finest**, the pick, the choice, the
flower, the cream, the elite, the crème de la
crème

bestow VERB = **present**, give, accord,
award, grant, commit, hand out, lavish,
confer, endow, entrust, impart, allot,
honour with, apportion ■ OPPOSITE:
obtain

bestseller NOUN = **success**, hit (*informal*),
winner, smash (*informal*), belter (*slang*),
sensation, blockbuster (*informal*), wow
(*slang*), market leader, smash hit (*informal*),
chart-topper (*informal*), runaway success,
number one ■ OPPOSITE: failure

bestselling ADJECTIVE = **successful**, top, hit
(*informal*), smash (*informal*), flourishing,
lucrative, smash-hit (*informal*), chart-
topping (*informal*), moneymaking, number
one, highly successful

bet VERB *I bet on a horse called Premonition.*
= **gamble**, chance, stake, venture, hazard,
speculate, punt (*chiefly Brit.*), wager, put
money, risk money, pledge money, put your
shirt on ▸ NOUN *He made a 30 mile trip to the
casino to place a bet.* = **gamble**, risk, stake,
venture, pledge, speculation, hazard,
flutter (*informal*), ante, punt (*chiefly Brit.*),
wager, long shot

betray VERB **1** *He might be seen as having
betrayed his mother.* = **be disloyal to**, break
with, grass on (*Brit. slang*), dob in (*Austral.
slang*), double-cross (*informal*), stab in the
back, be unfaithful to, sell down the river
(*informal*), grass up (*slang*), shop (*slang,
chiefly Brit.*), put the finger on (*informal*),
inform on or against **2** *She studied his face, but*

it betrayed nothing. = **give away**, tell, show, reveal, expose, disclose, uncover, manifest, divulge, blurt out, unmask, lay bare, tell on, let slip, evince (*formal*)

betrayal NOUN = **disloyalty**, sell-out (*informal*), deception, treason, treachery, trickery, duplicity, double-cross (*informal*), double-dealing, breach of trust, perfidy (*literary*), unfaithfulness, falseness, inconstancy ■ **OPPOSITE:** loyalty

better ADVERB **1** *I like your interpretation better than the one I was taught.* = **to a greater degree**, more completely, more thoroughly **2** *If we had played better, we might have won.* = **in a more excellent manner**, more effectively, more attractively, more advantageously, more competently, in a superior way ■ **OPPOSITE:** worse
▶ ADJECTIVE **1** *He is better now.* = **well**, stronger, improving, progressing, recovering, healthier, cured, mending, fitter, fully recovered, on the mend (*informal*), more healthy, less ill ■ **OPPOSITE:** worse **2** *I've been able to have a better car than I otherwise could have.* = **superior**, finer, worthier, higher-quality, surpassing, preferable, more appropriate, more useful, more valuable, more suitable, more desirable, streets ahead, more fitting, more expert ■ **OPPOSITE:** inferior ▶ VERB **1** *He bettered the old record of 4 minutes 24.* = **beat**, top, exceed, excel, surpass, outstrip, outdo, improve on or upon, cap (*informal*) **2** *Our parents came here with the hope of bettering themselves.* = **improve**, forward, reform, advance, promote, correct, amend, mend, rectify, augment, ameliorate, meliorate
• **get the better of someone** *He usually gets the better of them.* = **defeat**, beat, surpass, triumph over, outdo, trounce, outwit, best, subjugate, prevail over, outsmart, get the upper hand, score off, run rings around (*informal*), wipe the floor with (*informal*), make mincemeat of (*informal*), blow out of the water (*slang*)

betterment NOUN = **improvement**, gain, advancement, enhancement, edification, amelioration, melioration

between PREPOSITION = **amidst**, among, mid, in the middle of, betwixt ■ **RELATED WORD:** *prefix* inter-

▎ USAGE After *distribute* and words with a similar meaning, *among* should be used rather than *between*: *share out the sweets among the children* (not *between the children*, unless there are only two children).

beverage NOUN = **drink**, liquid, liquor, refreshment, draught, bevvy (*dialect*),

libation (*facetious*), thirst quencher, potable, potation

beverage room NOUN (*Canad.*) = **tavern**, inn, bar, pub (*informal, chiefly Brit.*), public house, watering hole (*facetious slang*), boozer (*Brit., Austral. & N.Z. informal*), beer parlour (*Canad.*), hostelry

bevy NOUN = **group**, company, set, party, band, crowd, troop, pack, collection, gathering, gang, bunch (*informal*), cluster, congregation, clump, troupe, posse (*slang*), clique, coterie, assemblage

beware VERB **1** *Beware, this recipe is not for slimmers.* = **be careful**, look out, watch out, be wary, be cautious, take heed, guard against something **2** *We should beware declaring victory too soon.* = **avoid**, mind, shun, refrain from, steer clear of, guard against

bewilder VERB = **confound**, surprise, stun, confuse, puzzle, baffle, mix up, daze, perplex, mystify, stupefy, befuddle, flummox, bemuse, dumbfound, nonplus, flabbergast (*informal*)

bewildered ADJECTIVE = **confused**, surprised, stunned, puzzled, uncertain, startled, baffled, at sea, awed, muddled, dizzy, dazed, perplexed, disconcerted, at a loss, mystified, taken aback, speechless, giddy, disorientated, bamboozled (*informal*), nonplussed, flummoxed, at sixes and sevens, thrown off balance, discombobulated (*informal, chiefly U.S. & Canad.*)

bewildering ADJECTIVE = **confusing**, surprising, amazing, stunning, puzzling, astonishing, staggering, eye-popping (*informal*), baffling, astounding, perplexing, mystifying, stupefying

bewitch VERB = **enchant**, attract, charm, fascinate, absorb, entrance, enthral, captivate, beguile, allure, ravish, mesmerize, hypnotize, cast a spell on, enrapture, spellbind ■ **OPPOSITE:** repulse

bewitched ADJECTIVE = **enchanted**, charmed, transformed, fascinated, entranced, possessed, captivated, enthralled, beguiled, ravished, spellbound, mesmerized, enamoured, hypnotized, enraptured, under a spell

beyond PREPOSITION **1** *They heard footsteps in the main room, beyond a door.* = **on the other side of**, outwith (*Scot.*) **2** *Few jockeys continue riding beyond the age of forty.* = **after**, over, past, above **3** *His interests extended beyond the fine arts.* = **past**, outwith (*Scot.*) **4** *I knew nothing beyond a few random facts.* = **except for**, but, save, apart from, other than, excluding, besides, aside from

b

5 *What he had done was beyond my comprehension.* = **exceeding**, surpassing, superior to, out of reach of 6 *The situation was beyond her control.* = **outside**, over, above, outwith (*Scot.*)

bias NOUN 1 *There were fierce attacks on the BBC for alleged political bias.* = **prejudice**, leaning, bent, tendency, inclination, penchant, intolerance, bigotry, propensity, favouritism, predisposition, nepotism, unfairness, predilection, proclivity (*formal*), partiality, narrow-mindedness, proneness, one-sidedness ■ **OPPOSITE:** impartiality 2 *The fabric, cut on the bias, hangs as light as a cobweb.* = **slant**, cross, angle, diagonal line ▶ VERB *We mustn't allow it to bias our teaching.* = **influence**, colour, weight, prejudice, distort, sway, warp, slant, predispose

biased ADJECTIVE = **prejudiced**, weighted, one-sided, partial, distorted, swayed, warped, slanted, embittered, predisposed, jaundiced

bicker VERB = **quarrel**, fight, argue, row (*informal*), clash, dispute, scrap (*informal*), disagree, fall out (*informal*), squabble, spar, wrangle, cross swords, fight like cat and dog, go at it hammer and tongs, altercate ■ **OPPOSITE:** agree

bid NOUN 1 *a bid to silence its critics* = **attempt**, try, effort, venture, undertaking, go (*informal*), shot (*informal*), stab (*informal*), crack (*informal*), endeavour 2 *He made an agreed takeover bid of £351 million.* = **offer**, price, attempt, amount, advance, proposal, sum, tender, proposition, submission ▶ VERB 1 *She wanted to bid for it.* = **make an offer**, offer, propose, submit, tender, proffer 2 *I bade her goodnight.* = **wish**, say, call, tell, greet 3 *I dare say he did as he was bidden.* = **tell**, call, ask, order, charge (*formal*), require, direct, desire (*formal*), invite, command, summon, instruct, solicit, enjoin

bidding NOUN 1 *the bidding of his backbenchers* = **order**, call, charge, demand, request, command, instruction, invitation, canon, beck, injunction, summons, behest, beck and call 2 *The bidding starts at £2 million.* = **offer**, proposal, auction, tender

big ADJECTIVE 1 *Australia's a big country.* = **large**, great, huge, giant, massive, vast, enormous, considerable, substantial, extensive, immense, spacious, gigantic, monumental (*informal*), mammoth, bulky, burly, colossal, stellar (*informal*), prodigious, hulking, ponderous, voluminous, elephantine, ginormous (*informal*), humongous *or* humungous (*informal*), sizable *or* sizeable, supersize

■ **OPPOSITE:** small 2 *Her problem was just too big for her to tackle on her own.* = **important**, serious, significant, grave, urgent, paramount, big-time (*informal*), far-reaching, momentous, major league (*informal*), weighty ■ **OPPOSITE:** unimportant 3 *Their father was very big in the army.* = **powerful**, important, prime, principal, prominent, dominant, influential, paramount, eminent, puissant, skookum (*Canad.*) 4 *He's a big boy now.* = **grown-up**, adult, grown, mature, elder, full-grown ■ **OPPOSITE:** young 5 *They describe him as an idealist with a big heart.* = **generous**, good, princely, noble, heroic, gracious, benevolent, disinterested, altruistic, unselfish, magnanimous, big-hearted

bighead NOUN = **boaster**, know-all (*informal*), swaggerer, self-seeker, egomaniac, egotist, braggart, braggadocio, narcissist, swell-head (*informal*), blowhard (*informal*), self-admirer, figjam (*Austral. slang*)

bigheaded ADJECTIVE = **boastful**, arrogant, swaggering, bragging, cocky, vaunting, conceited, puffed-up, bumptious, immodest, crowing, overconfident, vainglorious, swollen-headed, egotistic, full of yourself, too big for your boots *or* breeches

bigot NOUN = **fanatic**, racist, extremist, sectarian, maniac, fiend (*informal*), zealot, persecutor, dogmatist

bigoted ADJECTIVE = **intolerant**, twisted, prejudiced, biased, warped, sectarian, dogmatic, opinionated, narrow-minded, obstinate, illiberal ■ **OPPOSITE:** tolerant

bigotry NOUN = **intolerance**, discrimination, racism, prejudice, bias, ignorance, injustice, sexism, unfairness, fanaticism, sectarianism, racialism, dogmatism, faith hate, provincialism, narrow-mindedness, mindlessness, pig-ignorance (*slang*) ■ **OPPOSITE:** tolerance

bigwig NOUN = **important person**, somebody, celebrity, heavyweight (*informal*), notable, big name, mogul, big gun (*informal*), dignitary, celeb (*informal*), big shot (*informal*), personage, nob (*slang*), big cheese (*old-fashioned slang*), big noise (*informal*), big hitter (*informal*), heavy hitter (*informal*), panjandrum, notability, V.I.P. ■ **OPPOSITE:** nonentity

bile NOUN = **bitterness**, anger, hostility, resentment, animosity, venom, irritability, spleen, acrimony, pique, nastiness, rancour, virulence, asperity, ill humour, irascibility, peevishness, churlishness

bill¹ NOUN **1** *They couldn't afford to pay the bills.*
= **charges**, rate, costs, score, account,
damage (*informal*), statement, reckoning,
expense, tally, invoice, note of charge
2 *The bill was opposed by a large majority.*
= **act of parliament**, measure, proposal,
piece of legislation, projected law **3** *He is
topping the bill at a dusk-to-dawn party.* = **list**,
listing, programme, card, schedule,
agenda, catalogue, inventory, roster,
syllabus **4** *A sign forbids the posting of bills.*
= **advertisement**, notice, poster, leaflet,
bulletin, circular, handout, placard,
handbill, playbill ▶ VERB **1** *Are you going to bill
me for this?* = **charge**, debit, invoice, send a
statement to, send an invoice to **2** *They bill
it as Britain's most exciting museum.*
= **advertise**, post, announce, push
(*informal*), declare, promote, plug (*informal*),
proclaim, tout, flaunt, publicize, crack up
(*informal*), give advance notice of

bill² NOUN *Its legs and feet are grey, its bill
brownish-yellow.* = **beak**, nib, neb (*archaic,
dialect*), mandible

billet VERB *The soldiers were billeted in private
homes.* = **quarter**, post, station, locate,
install, accommodate, berth, garrison
▶ NOUN *We hid the radio in Hut 10, which was
our billet.* = **quarters**, accommodation,
lodging, barracks

billow VERB *the billowing sails* = **surge**, roll,
expand, swell, balloon, belly, bulge, dilate,
puff up, bloat ▶ NOUN *billows of almost solid
black smoke* = **surge**, wave, flow, rush, flood,
cloud, gush, deluge, upsurge, outpouring,
uprush

bind VERB **1** *The treaty binds them to respect
their neighbour's independence.* = **oblige**,
make, force, require, engage, compel,
prescribe, constrain, necessitate, impel,
obligate **2** *Bind the ends of the card together
with thread.* = **tie**, unite, join, stick, secure,
attach, wrap, rope, knot, strap, lash, glue,
tie up, hitch, paste, fasten, truss, make fast
■ **OPPOSITE:** untie **3** *All are bound by the same
strict etiquette.* = **restrict**, limit, handicap,
confine, detain, restrain, hamper, inhibit,
hinder, impede, hem in, keep within
bounds or limits **4** *These compounds bind with
genetic material in the liver.* = **fuse**, join, stick,
bond, cement, adhere **5** *Her mother bound
the wound with a rag soaked in iodine.*
= **bandage**, cover, dress, wrap, swathe,
encase ▶ NOUN *It is expensive to buy and a bind
to carry home.* = **nuisance**, inconvenience,
hassle (*informal*), drag (*informal*), spot
(*informal*), difficulty, bore, dilemma, pest,
hot water (*informal*), uphill (*S. African*),
predicament, annoyance, quandary, pain in

the neck (*informal*), pain in the backside
(*informal*), pain in the butt (*informal*)

binding ADJECTIVE = **compulsory**,
necessary, mandatory, imperative,
obligatory, conclusive, irrevocable,
unalterable, indissoluble ■ **OPPOSITE:**
optional

binge NOUN (*informal*) = **bout**, session
(*informal*), spell, fling, feast, stint, spree,
orgy, bender (*informal*), jag (*slang*), beano
(*Brit. slang*), blind (*slang*)

biography NOUN = **life story**, life, record,
account, profile, memoir, CV, life history,
curriculum vitae

bird NOUN = **feathered friend**, fowl,
songbird ■ **RELATED WORDS:** *adjective* avian;
name of male cock; *name of female* hen; *name
of young* chick, fledgeling, fledgling,
nestling; *collective nouns* flock, flight; *name of
home* nest

bird of prey NOUN ■ **RELATED WORD:**
adjective raptorial

birth NOUN **1** *She weighed 5lb 7oz at birth.*
= **childbirth**, delivery, nativity, parturition
■ **OPPOSITE:** death **2** *the birth of popular
democracy* = **beginning**, start, rise, source,
origin, emergence, outset, genesis,
initiation, inauguration, inception,
commencement, fountainhead **3** *people
of low birth* = **ancestry**, line, race, stock,
blood, background, breeding, strain,
descent, pedigree, extraction, lineage,
forebears, parentage, genealogy,
derivation ■ **RELATED WORD:** *adjective* natal

bisect VERB = **cut in two**, cross, separate,
split, halve, cut across, intersect, cut in half,
split down the middle, divide in two,
bifurcate

bit¹ NOUN **1** *a bit of cake* = **slice**, segment,
fragment, crumb, mouthful, small piece,
morsel **2** *crumpled bits of paper* = **piece**,
scrap, small piece **3** *All it required was a bit of
work.* = **jot**, whit, tittle, iota **4** *The best bit
was the car chase.* = **part**, moment, period
5 *Let's wait a bit.* = **little while**, time,
second, minute, moment, spell, instant,
tick (*Brit. informal*), jiffy (*informal*)

bit² NOUN *The horse can be controlled by a snaffle
bit and reins.* = **curb**, check, brake, restraint,
snaffle

bitchy ADJECTIVE = **spiteful**, mean, nasty,
cruel, vicious, malicious, barbed, vindictive,
malevolent, venomous, snide, rancorous,
catty (*informal*), backbiting, shrewish,
ill-natured, vixenish, snarky (*informal*)
■ **OPPOSITE:** nice

bite VERB **1** *Llamas won't bite or kick.* = **nip**, cut,
tear, wound, grip, snap, crush, rend
(*literary*), pierce, champ, pinch, chew,

crunch, clamp, nibble, gnaw, masticate
2 *nylon biting into the flesh* = **eat**, burn,
smart, sting, erode, tingle, eat away,
corrode, wear away ▶ NOUN **1** *a bite to eat*
= **snack**, food, piece, taste, refreshment,
mouthful, morsel, titbit, light meal **2** *The
boy had suffered a snake bite but he made a quick
recovery.* = **wound**, sting, pinch, nip, prick
3 *The novel seems to lack bite and tension.*
= **edge**, interest, force, punch (*informal*),
sting, zest, sharpness, keenness, pungency,
incisiveness, acuteness **4** *I'd have preferred a
bit more bite and not so much sugar.* = **kick**
(*informal*), edge, punch (*informal*), spice,
relish, zest, tang, sharpness, piquancy,
pungency, spiciness

biting ADJECTIVE **1** *a raw, biting northerly wind*
= **piercing**, cutting, cold, sharp, freezing,
frozen, bitter, raw, chill, harsh, penetrating,
arctic (*informal*), nipping, icy, blighting,
chilly, wintry, gelid, cold as ice **2** *This was the
most biting criticism made against her.*
= **sarcastic**, cutting, sharp, severe,
stinging, withering, scathing, acrimonious,
incisive, virulent, caustic, vitriolic,
trenchant, mordant, mordacious

bitter ADJECTIVE **1** *the scene of bitter fighting*
= **grievous**, hard, severe, distressing,
fierce, harsh, cruel, savage, ruthless, dire,
relentless, poignant, ferocious, galling,
unrelenting, merciless, remorseless,
gut-wrenching, vexatious, hard-hearted
■ OPPOSITE: pleasant **2** *She is said to be very
bitter about the way she was sacked.*
= **resentful**, hurt, wounded, angry,
offended, sour, put out, sore, choked,
crabbed, acrimonious, aggrieved, sullen,
miffed (*informal*), embittered, begrudging,
peeved (*informal*), piqued, rancorous
■ OPPOSITE: happy **3** *a night in the bitter cold*
= **freezing**, biting, severe, intense, raw,
fierce, chill, stinging, penetrating, arctic
(*informal*), icy, polar, Siberian, glacial,
wintry ■ OPPOSITE: mild **4** *The leaves taste
rather bitter.* = **sour**, biting, sharp, acid,
harsh, unpleasant, tart, astringent, acrid,
unsweetened, vinegary, acidulated, acerb
■ OPPOSITE: sweet

bitterly ADVERB **1** *They bitterly resented their
loss of power.* = **resentfully**, sourly, sorely,
tartly, grudgingly, sullenly, testily,
acrimoniously, caustically, mordantly,
irascibly **2** *It's been bitterly cold here in
Moscow.* = **intensely**, freezing, severely,
fiercely, icy, bitingly

bitterness NOUN **1** *I still feel bitterness and
anger.* = **resentment**, hurt, anger, hostility,
indignation, animosity, venom, acrimony,
pique, rancour, ill feeling, bad blood, ill will,

umbrage, vexation, asperity **2** *the strength
and bitterness of the drink* = **sourness**, acidity,
sharpness, tartness, acerbity, vinegariness

bizarre ADJECTIVE = **strange**, odd, unusual,
extraordinary, fantastic, curious, weird,
way-out (*informal*), peculiar, eccentric,
abnormal, ludicrous, queer (*informal*),
irregular, rum (*Brit. slang*), uncommon,
singular, grotesque, perplexing, uncanny,
mystifying, off-the-wall (*slang*), outlandish,
comical, oddball (*informal*), off the rails,
zany, unaccountable, off-beat, left-field
(*informal*), freakish, wacky (*informal*), outré,
cockamamie (*slang, chiefly U.S.*), daggy
(*Austral. & N.Z. informal*) ■ OPPOSITE: normal

black ADJECTIVE **1** *He had thick black hair.*
= **dark**, raven, ebony, sable, jet, dusky,
pitch-black, inky, swarthy, stygian,
coal-black, pitchy, murky ■ OPPOSITE: light
2 *After the tragic death of her son, she fell into a
black depression.* = **gloomy**, sad, depressing,
distressing, horrible, grim, bleak, hopeless,
dismal, ominous, sombre, morbid,
mournful, morose, lugubrious, joyless,
funereal, doleful, cheerless ■ OPPOSITE:
happy **3** *He had just undergone one of the
blackest days of his political career.* = **terrible**
(*informal*), bad, devastating, tragic, fatal,
unfortunate, dreadful, destructive,
unlucky, harmful, adverse, dire,
catastrophic, hapless, detrimental,
untoward, ruinous, calamitous,
cataclysmic, ill-starred, unpropitious,
ill-fated, cataclysmal **4** *the blackest laws in
the country's history* = **wicked**, bad, evil,
corrupt, vicious, immoral, depraved,
debased, amoral, villainous, unprincipled,
nefarious, dissolute, iniquitous, irreligious,
impious, unrighteous ■ OPPOSITE: good
5 = **cynical**, weird, ironic, pessimistic,
morbid, misanthropic, mordacious **6** *a
black look on your face* = **angry**, cross, furious,
hostile, sour, menacing, moody, resentful,
glowering, sulky, baleful, louring *or*
lowering ■ OPPOSITE: happy **7** *The whole
front of him was black with dirt.* = **dirty**, soiled,
stained, filthy, muddy, blackened, grubby,
dingy, grimy, sooty, mucky, scuzzy (*slang,
chiefly U.S.*), begrimed, festy (*Austral. slang*),
mud-encrusted, miry ■ OPPOSITE: clean
• **black out** *He felt so ill that he blacked out.*
= **pass out**, drop, collapse, faint, swoon,
lose consciousness, keel over (*informal*),
flake out (*informal*), become unconscious
• **black something out** *The whole city is
blacked out at night.* = **darken**, cover, shade,
conceal, obscure, eclipse, dim, blacken,
obfuscate (*formal*), make dark, make
darker, make dim • **in the black** *We*

certainly can't get married until we're in the black. = **in credit**, solid, solvent, in funds, financially sound, without debt, unindebted

black and white ADJECTIVE = **monochrome**, grey-scale • **in black and white** 1 She saw things in black and white. = in absolute terms, unconditionally, naively, unambiguously, uncompromisingly, simplistically, in oversimplified terms 2 He'd seen the proof in black and white. = in print, documented, on paper, written down, on record

blacken VERB 1 He watched the blackening clouds move in. = **darken**, deepen, grow black 2 The smoke blackened the sky like the apocalypse. = **make dark**, shadow, shade, obscure, overshadow, make darker, make dim 3 They're trying to blacken our name. = **discredit**, stain, disgrace, smear, knock (informal), degrade, rubbish (informal), taint, tarnish, censure, slur, slag (off) (slang), malign, reproach, denigrate, disparage, decry, vilify, slander, sully, dishonour, defile, defame, bad-mouth (slang), traduce, bring into disrepute, smirch, calumniate

blacklist VERB = **exclude**, bar, ban, reject, rule out, veto, boycott, embargo, expel, vote against, preclude, disallow, repudiate, proscribe, ostracize, debar, blackball

black magic NOUN = **witchcraft**, magic, witching, voodoo, the occult, wizardry, enchantment, sorcery, occultism, incantation, black art, witchery, necromancy, diabolism, sortilege, makutu (N.Z.)

blackmail NOUN It looks like the pictures were being used for blackmail. = **threat**, intimidation, ransom, compulsion, protection (informal), coercion, extortion, pay-off (informal), shakedown, hush money (slang), exaction ▶ VERB I thought he was trying to blackmail me into saying whatever he wanted. = **threaten**, force, squeeze, compel, exact, intimidate, wring, coerce, milk, wrest, dragoon, extort, bleed (informal), press-gang, hold to ransom

blackness NOUN = **darkness**, shade, gloom, dusk (poetic), obscurity, nightfall, murk, dimness, murkiness, duskiness, shadiness, melanism (technical), inkiness, nigrescence (rare) ■ OPPOSITE: light

blackout NOUN 1 a media blackout = **noncommunication**, secrecy, censorship, suppression, radio silence 2 an electricity blackout = **power cut**, power failure 3 I suffered a blackout which lasted for several minutes. = **unconsciousness**, collapse, faint, oblivion, swoon (literary), loss of consciousness, syncope (Pathology)

black sheep NOUN = **disgrace**, rebel, maverick, outcast, renegade, dropout, prodigal, individualist, nonconformist, ne'er-do-well, reprobate, wastrel, bad egg (old-fashioned, informal)

blame VERB 1 They blamed the army for most of the atrocities. = **hold responsible**, accuse, denounce, indict, impeach, incriminate, impute, recriminate, point a or the finger at ■ OPPOSITE: absolve 2 The police blamed the accident on black ice. = **attribute to**, credit to, assign to, put down to, impute to 3 (used in negative constructions) I do not blame them for trying to make some money. = **criticize**, charge, tax, blast, condemn, put down, disapprove of, censure, reproach, chide, admonish, tear into (informal), find fault with, reprove, upbraid, lambast(e), reprehend, express disapprobation of ■ OPPOSITE: praise ▶ NOUN I could not let an innocent man take the blame for this. = **responsibility**, liability, rap (slang), accountability, onus, culpability, answerability ■ OPPOSITE: praise

blameless ADJECTIVE = **innocent**, clear, clean, upright, stainless, honest, immaculate, impeccable, virtuous, faultless, squeaky-clean, unblemished, unsullied, uninvolved, unimpeachable, untarnished, above suspicion, irreproachable, guiltless, unspotted, unoffending ■ OPPOSITE: guilty

blanch VERB = **turn pale**, fade, pale, drain, bleach, wan, whiten, go white, become pallid, become or grow white

bland ADJECTIVE 1 It's easy on the ear but bland and forgettable. = **dull**, boring, weak, plain, flat, commonplace, tedious, vanilla (informal), dreary, tiresome, monotonous, run-of-the-mill, uninspiring, humdrum, unimaginative, uninteresting, insipid, unexciting, ho-hum (informal), vapid, unstimulating, undistinctive ■ OPPOSITE: exciting 2 It tasted bland and insipid, like warmed card. = **tasteless**, weak, watered-down, insipid, flavourless, thin, unstimulating, undistinctive

blank ADJECTIVE 1 He tore a blank page from his notebook. = **unmarked**, white, clear, clean, empty, plain, bare, void, spotless, unfilled, uncompleted ■ OPPOSITE: marked 2 He gave him a blank look. = **expressionless**, empty, dull, vague, hollow, vacant, lifeless, deadpan, straight-faced, vacuous, impassive, inscrutable, inane, wooden, poker-faced (informal) ■ OPPOSITE: expressive 3 Abbot looked blank. 'I don't follow, sir.' = **puzzled**, lost, confused, stumped, doubtful, baffled, stuck (informal), at sea, bewildered, muddled, mixed up, confounded, perplexed, disconcerted, at a loss, mystified, clueless, dumbfounded, nonplussed, uncomprehending, flummoxed **4** *a blank refusal to attend* = **absolute**, complete, total, utter, outright, thorough, downright, consummate, unqualified, out and out, unmitigated, unmixed ▸ NOUN **1** *Put a word in each blank to complete the sentence.* = **empty space**, space, gap **2** *Everything was a complete blank.* = **void**, vacuum, vacancy, emptiness, nothingness, vacuity, tabula rasa

blanket NOUN **1** *There was an old blanket in the trunk of my car.* = **cover**, rug, coverlet, afghan **2** *The mud disappeared under a blanket of snow.* = **covering**, cover, bed, sheet, coating, coat, layer, film, carpet, cloak, mantle, thickness ▸ VERB *More than a foot of snow blanketed parts of Michigan.* = **coat**, cover, hide, surround, cloud, mask, conceal, obscure, eclipse, cloak ▸ ADJECTIVE *the blanket coverage of the Olympics* = **comprehensive**, full, complete, wide, sweeping, broad, extensive, wide-ranging, thorough, inclusive, exhaustive, all-inclusive, all-embracing

blare VERB = **blast**, scream, boom, roar, thunder, trumpet, resound, hoot, toot, reverberate, sound out, honk, clang, peal

blarney NOUN = **flattery**, coaxing, exaggeration, fawning, adulation, wheedling, spiel, sweet talk (*informal*), flannel (*Brit. informal*), soft soap (*informal*), sycophancy, servility, obsequiousness, cajolery, blandishment, fulsomeness, toadyism, overpraise, false praise, honeyed words

blasé ADJECTIVE = **nonchalant**, cool, bored, distant, regardless, detached, weary, indifferent, careless, lukewarm, glutted, jaded, unmoved, unconcerned, impervious, uncaring, uninterested, apathetic, offhand, world-weary, heedless, satiated, unexcited, surfeited, cloyed ■ OPPOSITE: interested

blasphemous ADJECTIVE = **irreverent**, cheeky (*informal*), contemptuous, profane, disrespectful, godless, ungodly, sacrilegious, irreligious, impious
■ OPPOSITE: reverent

blasphemy NOUN = **irreverence**, swearing, cursing, indignity (*to God*), desecration, sacrilege, profanity, impiety, profanation, execration, profaneness, impiousness

blast NOUN **1** *250 people were killed in the blast.* = **explosion**, crash, burst, discharge, blow-up, eruption, detonation **2** *Blasts of cold air swept down from the mountains.* = **gust**, rush, storm, breeze, puff, gale,

flurry, tempest (*literary*), squall, strong breeze **3** *The buzzer suddenly responded in a long blast of sound.* = **blare**, blow, scream, trumpet, wail, resound, clamour, hoot, toot, honk, clang, peal ▸ VERB **1** *The explosion blasted out the external supporting wall.* = **blow up**, bomb, destroy, burst, ruin, break up, explode, shatter, demolish, rupture, dynamite, put paid to, blow sky-high **2** *They have blasted the report.* = **criticize**, attack, put down, censure, berate, castigate, tear into (*informal*), flay, rail at, lambast(e), chew out (*U.S. & Canad. informal*), throw shade (at) (*slang*)

blasted ADJECTIVE = **damned** (*slang*), confounded, hateful, infernal (*informal*), detestable

blastoff NOUN = **launch**, launching, take off, discharge, projection, lift-off, propelling, sendoff

blatant ADJECTIVE = **obvious**, open, clear, plain, naked, sheer, patent, evident, pronounced, straightforward, outright, glaring, manifest, bald, transparent, noticeable, conspicuous, overt, unmistakable, flaunting, palpable, undeniable, brazen, flagrant, indisputable, ostentatious, unmitigated, cut-and-dried (*informal*), undisguised, obtrusive, unsubtle, unconcealed ■ OPPOSITE: subtle

blaze VERB **1** *The log fire was blazing merrily.* = **burn**, glow, flare, flicker, be on fire, go up in flames, be ablaze, fire, flash, flame **2** *The gardens blazed with colour.* = **shine**, flash, beam, glow, flare, glare, gleam, shimmer, radiate **3** *His dark eyes were blazing with anger.* = **flare up**, rage, boil, explode, fume, seethe, be livid, be incandescent ▸ NOUN **1** *Two firefighters were hurt in a blaze which swept through a tower block.* = **inferno**, fire, flames, bonfire, combustion, conflagration **2** *I wanted the front garden to be a blaze of colour.* = **flash**, glow, glitter, flare, glare, gleam, brilliance, radiance

bleach VERB = **lighten**, wash out, blanch, peroxide, whiten, blench, etiolate

bleak ADJECTIVE **1** *The immediate outlook remains bleak.* = **dismal**, black, dark, depressing, grim, discouraging, gloomy, hopeless, dreary, sombre, unpromising, disheartening, joyless, cheerless, comfortless ■ OPPOSITE: cheerful **2** *The island's pretty bleak.* = **exposed**, open, empty, raw, bare, stark, barren, desolate, gaunt, windswept, weather-beaten, unsheltered ■ OPPOSITE: sheltered **3** *The weather can be quite bleak on the coast.* = **stormy**, cold, severe, bitter, rough, harsh, chilly, windy, tempestuous, intemperate

bleary ADJECTIVE = **dim**, blurred, fogged, murky, fuzzy, watery, misty, hazy, foggy, blurry, ill-defined, indistinct, rheumy

bleed VERB **1** *The wound was bleeding profusely.* = **lose blood**, flow, weep, trickle, gush, exude, spurt, shed blood **2** *The two colours will bleed into each other.* = **blend**, run, meet, unite, mix, combine, flow, fuse, mingle, converge, ooze, seep, amalgamate, meld, intermix **3** *They mean to bleed the common people dry.* = **extort**, milk, squeeze, drain, exhaust, fleece

blemish NOUN **1** *the blemish on his face* = **mark**, line, spot, scratch, bruise, scar, blur, defect, flaw, blot, smudge, imperfection, speck, blotch, disfigurement, pock, smirch ■ **OPPOSITE:** perfection **2** *the one blemish on an otherwise resounding success* = **defect**, fault, weakness, stain, disgrace, deficiency, shortcoming, taint, inadequacy, dishonour, demerit ▸ VERB *He wasn't about to blemish that pristine record.* = **dishonour**, mark, damage, spot, injure, ruin, mar, spoil, stain, blur, disgrace, impair, taint, tarnish, blot, smudge, disfigure, sully, deface, blotch, besmirch, smirch ■ **OPPOSITE:** enhance

blend VERB **1** *Blend the ingredients until you have a smooth cream.* = **mix**, join, combine, compound, incorporate, merge, put together, fuse, unite, mingle, alloy, synthesize, amalgamate, interweave, coalesce, intermingle, meld, intermix, commingle, commix **2** *Make sure all the patches blend together* = **go well**, match, fit, suit, go with, correspond, complement, coordinate, tone in, harmonize, cohere **3** *a band that blended jazz, folk and classical music* = **combine**, mix, link, integrate, merge, put together, fuse, unite, synthesize, marry, amalgamate ▸ NOUN *He makes up his own blends of flour.* = **mixture**, cross, mix, combination, compound, brew, composite, union, fusion, synthesis, alloy, medley, concoction, amalgam, amalgamation, meld, mélange (*French*), conglomeration, admixture

bless VERB **1** *Bless this couple and their loving commitment to one another.* = **sanctify**, dedicate, ordain, exalt, anoint, consecrate, hallow, invoke happiness on ■ **OPPOSITE:** curse **2** *If you have been blessed with this gift, you should use it.* = **endow**, give to, provide for, grant, favour, grace, bestow to ■ **OPPOSITE:** afflict **3** *Let us bless God for so uniting our hearts.* = **praise**, thank, worship, glorify, magnify, exalt, extol, pay homage to, give thanks to

blessed ADJECTIVE **1** *He's the son of a doctor, and well blessed with money.* = **endowed**,

supplied, granted, favoured, lucky, fortunate, furnished, bestowed, jammy (*Brit. slang*) **2** *The birth of a healthy baby is a truly blessed event.* = **happy**, contented, glad (*archaic*), merry, heartening, joyous, joyful, blissful **3** *After the ceremony, they were declared 'blessed'.* = **holy**, sacred, divine, adored, revered, hallowed, sanctified, beatified

blessing NOUN **1** *the blessings of prosperity* = **benefit**, help, service, profit, gain, advantage, favour, gift, windfall, kindness, boon, good fortune, bounty, godsend, manna from heaven ■ **OPPOSITE:** disadvantage **2** *They gave their formal blessing to the idea.* = **approval**, backing, support, agreement, regard, favour, sanction, go-ahead (*informal*), permission, leave, consent, mandate, endorsement, green light, ratification, assent, authorization, good wishes, acquiescence, approbation, concurrence, O.K. or okay (*informal*) ■ **OPPOSITE:** disapproval **3** *He said the blessing after taking the bread.* = **benediction**, grace, dedication, thanksgiving, invocation, commendation, consecration, benison ■ **OPPOSITE:** curse

blight NOUN **1** *urban blight and unacceptable poverty* = **curse**, suffering, evil, depression, corruption, distress, pollution, misery, plague (*informal*), hardship, woe, misfortune, contamination, adversity, scourge, affliction, bane, wretchedness ■ **OPPOSITE:** blessing **2** *the worst year of the potato blight* = **disease**, plague, pest, fungus, contamination, mildew, contagion, infestation, pestilence, canker, cancer ▸ VERB *families whose lives were blighted by unemployment* = **frustrate**, destroy, ruin, crush, mar, dash, wreck, spoil, crool or cruel (*Austral. slang*), scar, undo, mess up, annihilate, nullify, put a damper on

blind ADJECTIVE **1** *How would you describe colour to a blind person?* = **sightless**, unsighted, unseeing, visually impaired, visionless ■ **OPPOSITE:** sighted **2** (*usually followed by* **to**) *All the time I was blind to your suffering.* = **unaware of**, unconscious of, deaf to, ignorant of, indifferent to, insensitive to, oblivious of, unconcerned about, inconsiderate of, neglectful of, heedless of, insensible of, unmindful of, disregardful of ■ **OPPOSITE:** aware **3** *her blind faith in the wisdom of her elders* = **unquestioning**, prejudiced, wholesale, indiscriminate, uncritical, unreasoning, undiscriminating **4** *a blind corner* = **hidden**, concealed, obscured, dim, unseen, tucked away ■ **OPPOSITE:** open **5** *a dusty hotel room*

b

overlooking a blind alley = **dead-end**, closed, dark, obstructed, leading nowhere, without exit **6** *I went into a blind panic.* = **unthinking**, wild, violent, rash, reckless, irrational, hasty, senseless, mindless, uncontrollable, uncontrolled, unchecked, impetuous, intemperate, unconstrained

blinding ADJECTIVE **1** *the blinding lights of the delivery room* = **bright**, brilliant, intense, shining, glowing, blazing, dazzling, vivid, glaring, gleaming, beaming, effulgent, bedazzling **2** *waiting for a blinding revelation that never came* = **amazing**, striking, surprising, stunning (*informal*), impressive, astonishing, eye-popping (*informal*), staggering, sensational (*informal*), breathtaking, wondrous (*archaic, literary*), jaw-dropping, gee-whizz (*slang*)

blindly ADVERB **1** *Don't just blindly follow what the banker says.* = **thoughtlessly**, carelessly, recklessly, indiscriminately, unreasonably, impulsively, senselessly, heedlessly, regardlessly **2** *Panicking blindly they stumbled towards the exit.* = **wildly**, aimlessly, madly, frantically, confusedly

blink VERB **1** *She was blinking her eyes rapidly.* = **flutter**, wink, bat **2** *Green and yellow lights blinked on the surface of the harbour.* = **flash**, flicker, sparkle, wink, shimmer, twinkle, glimmer, scintillate • **on the blink** *an old TV that's on the blink* = **not working (properly)**, faulty, defective, playing up, out of action, malfunctioning, out of order, on the fritz (*U.S. slang*)

blinkered ADJECTIVE = **narrow-minded**, narrow, one-sided, prejudiced, biased, partial, discriminatory, parochial, constricted, insular, hidebound, one-eyed, lopsided ■ **OPPOSITE:** broad-minded

bliss NOUN **1** *It was a scene of such domestic bliss.* = **joy**, ecstasy, euphoria, rapture, nirvana, felicity, gladness, blissfulness, delight, pleasure, heaven (*informal*), satisfaction, happiness, paradise ■ **OPPOSITE:** misery **2** *the bliss beyond the now* = **beatitude**, ecstasy, exaltation, blessedness, felicity, holy joy

blissful ADJECTIVE **1** *There's nothing more blissful than lying by that pool.* = **delightful**, pleasing, satisfying, heavenly (*informal*), enjoyable, gratifying, pleasurable **2** *a blissful smile* = **happy**, joyful, satisfied, ecstatic, joyous, euphoric, rapturous

blister NOUN = **sore**, boil, swelling, cyst, pimple, wen, blain, carbuncle, pustule, bleb, furuncle (*Pathology*)

blitz NOUN = **attack**, strike, assault, raid, offensive, onslaught, bombardment, bombing campaign, blitzkrieg

blizzard NOUN = **snowstorm**, storm, tempest

bloated ADJECTIVE = **too full**, swollen up

blob NOUN = **drop**, ball, mass, pearl, lump, bead, dab, droplet, globule, glob, dewdrop

bloc NOUN = **group**, union, league, ring, alliance, coalition, axis, combine

block NOUN **1** *a block of ice* = **piece**, bar, square, mass, cake, brick, lump, chunk, cube, hunk, nugget, ingot **2** *a block to peace* = **obstruction**, bar, barrier, obstacle, impediment, hindrance ▸ VERB **1** *When the shrimp farm is built it will block the stream.* = **obstruct**, close, stop, cut off, plug, choke, clog, shut off, stop up, bung up (*informal*) ■ **OPPOSITE:** clear **2** *a row of spruce trees that blocked his view* = **obscure**, bar, cut off, interrupt, obstruct, get in the way of, shut off **3** *The police officer blocked his path.* = **shut off**, stop, bar, cut off, head off, hamper, obstruct, get in the way of

blockade NOUN = **stoppage**, block, barrier, restriction, obstacle, barricade, obstruction, impediment, hindrance, encirclement

blockage NOUN = **obstruction**, block, blocking, stoppage, impediment, occlusion

blog NOUN = **weblog**, microblog, vlog, blook, website, forum, chatroom, column, newsletter, podcast, profile (*on a social networking site*), webcast, vodcast

bloke NOUN = **man**, person, individual, customer (*informal*), character (*informal*), guy (*informal*), fellow, punter (*informal*), chap, boy, bod (*informal*)

blonde *or* **blond** ADJECTIVE **1** *The baby had blonde curls.* = **fair**, light, light-coloured, flaxen **2** *She was tall, blonde and attractive.* = **fair-haired**, golden-haired, tow-headed

blood NOUN **1** *an inherited defect in the blood* = **lifeblood**, gore, vital fluid **2** *He was of noble blood, and an officer.* = **family**, relations, birth, descent, extraction, ancestry, lineage, kinship, kindred • **bad blood** *There is, it seems, some bad blood between them.* = **hostility**, anger, offence, resentment, bitterness, animosity, antagonism, enmity, bad feeling, rancour, hard feelings, ill will, animus, dudgeon (*archaic*), disgruntlement, chip on your shoulder • **in cold blood** = **without emotion**, cruelly, ruthlessly, mercilessly, callously, indifferently, unmercifully

bloodless ADJECTIVE = **pale**, white, wan, sickly, pasty, colourless, pallid, anaemic, ashen, chalky, sallow, ashy, like death warmed up (*informal*)

bloodshed NOUN = **killing**, murder, massacre, slaughter, slaying, carnage, butchery, blood-letting, blood bath

bloodthirsty ADJECTIVE = **cruel**, savage, brutal, vicious, ruthless, ferocious, murderous, heartless, inhuman, merciless, cut-throat, remorseless, warlike, barbarous, pitiless

bloody ADJECTIVE **1** *Forty-three demonstrators were killed in bloody chaos.* = **cruel**, fierce, savage, brutal, vicious, ferocious, cut-throat, warlike, barbarous, sanguinary (*formal*) **2** *His fingers were bloody and cracked.* = **bloodstained**, raw, bleeding, blood-soaked, blood-spattered

bloody-minded ADJECTIVE = **difficult**, contrary, annoying, awkward, unreasonable, stubborn, perverse, exasperating, intractable, unhelpful, obstructive, cussed (*informal*), uncooperative, disobliging ■ **OPPOSITE:** helpful

bloom NOUN **1** *Harry carefully plucked the bloom.* = **flower**, bud, blossom **2** *in the full bloom of youth* = **prime**, flower, beauty, height, peak, flourishing, maturity, perfection, best days, heyday, zenith, full flowering **3** *The skin loses its youthful bloom.* = **glow**, flush, blush, freshness, lustre, radiance, rosiness ■ **OPPOSITE:** pallor
▶ VERB **1** *This plant blooms between May and June.* = **flower**, blossom, open, bud ■ **OPPOSITE:** wither **2** *Our relationship didn't bloom into a close friendship.* = **grow**, develop, wax **3** *Not many economies bloomed in 1990.* = **succeed**, flourish, thrive, prosper, fare well ■ **OPPOSITE:** fail

blossom NOUN *the blossoms of plants, shrubs and trees* = **flower**, bloom, bud, efflorescence, floret ▶ VERB **1** *Why do some people take longer than others to blossom?* = **develop**, bloom, grow, mature **2** *His musical career blossomed.* = **succeed**, progress, thrive, flourish, prosper **3** *Rain begins to fall and peach trees blossom.* = **flower**, bloom, bud

blot NOUN **1** *a blot on the reputation of the architectural profession* = **disgrace**, spot, fault, stain, scar, defect, flaw, taint, blemish, demerit, smirch, blot on your escutcheon **2** *an ink blot* = **spot**, mark, patch, smear, smudge, speck, blotch, splodge, stain ▶ VERB *Blot any excess oils with a tissue.* = **soak up**, take up, absorb, dry up
• **blot something out 1** *The victim's face was blotted out by a camera blur.* = **obliterate**, hide, shadow, disguise, obscure, blur, eclipse, block out, efface, obfuscate (*formal*) **2** *He is blotting certain memories out.* = **erase**, cancel, excise, obliterate, expunge (*formal*)

blotch NOUN = **mark**, spot, patch, splash, stain, blot, smudge, blemish, splodge, smirch, smutch

blow¹ VERB **1** *The wind blew her hair back from her forehead.* = **move**, carry, drive, bear, sweep, fling, whisk, buffet, whirl, waft **2** *Leaves were blowing around in the wind.* = **be carried**, hover, flutter, flit, flitter **3** *Take a deep breath and blow.* = **exhale**, breathe, pant, puff, breathe out, expel air **4** *South African football fans love to blow a horn called the vuvuzela.* = **play**, sound, pipe, trumpet, blare, toot • **blow over** *Wait, and it'll blow over.* = **die down**, end, pass, finish, cease, be forgotten, subside • **blow someone away 1** *She just totally blew me away with her singing.* = **bowl over**, amaze, stun, stagger, astound, electrify (*informal*), stupefy, flabbergast **2** *He'd like to get hold of a gun and blow the criminals away.* = **open fire on**, kill, blast (*slang*), bring down, zap (*slang*), pick off, pump full of lead (*slang*) • **blow something out** *I blew out the candle.* = **put out**, extinguish, snuff out • **blow something up 1** *He was jailed for forty-five years for trying to blow up a plane.* = **explode**, bomb, blast, dynamite, detonate, blow sky-high **2** *Other than blowing up a tyre I haven't done any car maintenance.* = **inflate**, pump up, fill, expand, swell, enlarge, puff up, distend **3** *Newspapers blew up the story.* = **exaggerate**, heighten, enlarge on, inflate, embroider, magnify, amplify, overstate, embellish, blow out of (all) proportion, make a mountain out of a molehill, make a production out of, make a federal case of (*U.S. informal*), hyperbolize **4** *The image is blown up on a large screen.* = **magnify**, increase, extend, stretch, expand, widen, broaden, lengthen, amplify, elongate, dilate, make larger • **blow up 1** *The bomb blew up as they slept.* = **explode**, burst, go off, shatter, erupt, detonate **2** (*informal*) *I'm sorry I blew up at you.* = **lose your temper**, rage, erupt, lose it (*informal*), crack up (*informal*), see red (*informal*), lose the plot (*informal*), become angry, go ballistic (*slang*), hit the roof (*informal*), blow a fuse (*slang, chiefly U.S.*), fly off the handle (*informal*), become enraged, go off the deep end (*informal*), wig out (*slang*), go up the wall (*slang*), go crook (*Austral. & N.Z. slang*), flip your lid (*slang*), blow your top **3** *The scandal blew up into a major political furore.* = **flare up**, widen, heighten, enlarge, broaden, magnify • **blow your top** *I just asked him why he was late and he blew his top.* = **lose your temper**, explode, blow up (*informal*), lose it (*informal*), see red (*informal*), lose the plot (*informal*), have a fit (*informal*), throw a tantrum, fly off the handle (*informal*), go spare (*Brit. slang*), fly into a temper, flip your lid (*slang*), do your nut (*Brit. slang*)

blow² NOUN **1** *He went off to hospital after a blow to the face.* = **knock**, stroke, punch, belt (*informal*), bang, rap, bash (*informal*), sock (*slang*), smack, thump, buffet, clout (*informal*), whack (*informal*), wallop (*informal*), slosh (*Brit. slang*), tonk (*informal*), clump (*slang*), clomp (*slang*) **2** *The ruling comes as a blow to environmentalists.* = **setback**, shock, upset, disaster, reverse, disappointment, catastrophe, misfortune, jolt, bombshell, calamity, affliction, whammy (*informal*), choker (*informal*), sucker punch, bummer (*slang*), bolt from the blue, comedown (*informal*)

blowout NOUN **1** *Once in a while we had a major blow-out.* = **binge** (*informal*), party, feast, rave (*Brit. slang*), spree, beano (*Brit. slang*), rave-up (*Brit. slang*), carousal, carouse, hooley *or* hoolie (*chiefly Irish & N.Z.*) **2** *A lorry travelling south had a blow-out and crashed.* = **puncture**, burst, flat, flat tyre, flattie (*N.Z.*)

bludge VERB = **slack**, skive (*Brit. informal*), idle, shirk, gold-brick (*U.S. slang*), bob off (*Brit. slang*), scrimshank (*Brit. Military slang*)

bludgeon VERB **1** *A wealthy businessman has been found bludgeoned to death.* = **club**, batter, beat, strike, belt (*informal*), clobber (*slang*), pound, cosh (*Brit.*), cudgel, beat *or* knock seven bells out of (*informal*) **2** *His relentless aggression bludgeons you into seeing his point.* = **bully**, force, cow, intimidate, railroad (*informal*), hector, coerce, bulldoze (*informal*), dragoon, steamroller, browbeat, tyrannize ▶ NOUN *The thieves beat him with their bludgeons.* = **club**, stick, baton, truncheon (*Brit.*), cosh (*Brit.*), cudgel, shillelagh, bastinado, mere (*N.Z.*), patu (*N.Z.*)

blue ADJECTIVE **1** *There's no earthly reason for me to feel so blue.* = **depressed**, low, sad, unhappy, fed up, gloomy, dismal, melancholy, glum, dejected, despondent, downcast, down in the dumps (*informal*), down in the mouth, low-spirited, down-hearted ■ **OPPOSITE:** happy **2** *blue movies* = **smutty**, dirty, naughty, obscene, indecent, vulgar, lewd, risqué, X-rated (*informal*), bawdy, near the knuckle (*informal*) ■ **OPPOSITE:** respectable ▶ PLURAL NOUN *Interfering in-laws are the prime sources of the blues.* = **depression**, gloom, melancholy, unhappiness, despondency, the hump (*Brit. informal*), dejection, moodiness, low spirits, the dumps (*informal*), the doldrums, gloominess, glumness

blue-collar ADJECTIVE *The plant employed more than a thousand blue-collar workers.* = **manual**, industrial, physical, manufacturing, labouring

blueprint NOUN **1** *the blueprint of a new plan of economic reform* = **scheme**, plan, design, system, idea, programme, proposal, strategy, pattern, suggestion, procedure, plot, draft, outline, sketch, proposition, prototype, layout, pilot scheme **2** *The documents contain a blueprint for a nuclear device.* = **plan**, scheme, project, pattern, draft, outline, sketch, layout

bluff¹ NOUN *The letter was a bluff.* = **deception**, show, lie, fraud, fake, sham, pretence, deceit, bravado, bluster, humbug, subterfuge, feint, mere show ▶ VERB *She tried to bluff her way through the test.* = **deceive**, lie, trick, fool, pretend, cheat, con, fake, mislead, sham, dupe, feign, delude, humbug, bamboozle (*informal*), hoodwink, double-cross (*informal*), pull the wool over someone's eyes

bluff² NOUN *a high bluff over the Congaree River* = **precipice**, bank, peak, cliff, ridge, crag, escarpment, promontory, scarp ▶ ADJECTIVE *a man with a bluff exterior* = **hearty**, open, frank, blunt, sincere, outspoken, honest, downright, cordial, genial, affable, ebullient, jovial, plain-spoken, good-natured, unreserved, back-slapping ■ **OPPOSITE:** tactful

blunder NOUN *I think we have made a tactical blunder.* = **mistake**, slip, fault, error, boob (*Brit. slang*), oversight, gaffe, slip-up (*informal*), indiscretion, impropriety, howler (*informal*), bloomer (*Brit. informal*), clanger (*informal*), faux pas, boo-boo (*informal*), gaucherie, barry *or* Barry Crocker (*Austral. slang*) ■ **OPPOSITE:** correctness ▶ VERB **1** *No doubt I had blundered again.* = **make a mistake**, blow it (*slang*), err, slip up (*informal*), cock up (*Brit. slang*), miscalculate, foul up, drop a clanger (*informal*), put your foot in it (*informal*), drop a brick (*Brit. informal*), screw up (*informal*) ■ **OPPOSITE:** be correct **2** *He had blundered into the table, upsetting the flowers.* = **stumble**, fall, reel, stagger, flounder, lurch, lose your balance

blunt ADJECTIVE **1** *She is blunt about her personal life.* = **frank**, forthright, straightforward, explicit, rude, outspoken, bluff, downright, upfront (*informal*), trenchant, brusque, plain-spoken, tactless, impolite, discourteous, unpolished, uncivil, straight from the shoulder ■ **OPPOSITE:** tactful **2** *a blunt object* = **dull**, rounded, dulled, edgeless, unsharpened

■ **OPPOSITE:** sharp ▶ VERB *Our appetite was blunted by the snacks.* = **dull**, weaken, soften, numb, dampen, water down, deaden, take the edge off ■ **OPPOSITE:** stimulate

blur NOUN *Her face is a blur.* = **haze**, confusion, fog, obscurity, dimness, cloudiness, blear, blurredness, indistinctness ▶ VERB **1** *If you move your eyes and your head, the picture will blur.* = **become indistinct**, soften, become vague, become hazy, become fuzzy **2** *Scientists are trying to blur the distinction between these questions.* = **obscure**, make indistinct, mask, soften, muddy, obfuscate (*formal*), make vague, befog, make hazy

blurred ADJECTIVE = **indistinct**, faint, vague, unclear, dim, fuzzy, misty, hazy, foggy, blurry, out of focus, ill-defined, lacking definition

blush VERB *I blushed scarlet at my stupidity.* = **turn red**, colour, burn, flame, glow, flush, crimson, redden, go red (*as a beetroot*), turn scarlet ■ **OPPOSITE:** turn pale ▶ NOUN *A blush spread over Brenda's cheeks.* = **reddening**, colour, glow, flush, pink tinge, rosiness, ruddiness, rosy tint

bluster VERB *He was still blustering, but there was panic in his eyes.* = **boast**, swagger, talk big (*slang*) ▶ NOUN *the bluster of their campaign* = **hot air**, boasting, bluff, swagger, swaggering (*informal*), swag (*slang*), bravado, bombast

blustery ADJECTIVE = **gusty**, wild, violent, stormy, windy, tempestuous, inclement, squally, blusterous

board NOUN **1** *The floor was draughty bare boards.* = **plank**, panel, timber, slat, piece of timber **2** *the US National Transportation Safety Board* = **council**, directors, committee, congress, ministry, advisers, panel, assembly, chamber, trustees, governing body, synod, directorate, quango, advisory group, conclave **3** *Free room and board are provided for all hotel staff.* = **meals**, provisions, victuals, daily meals ▶ VERB *I boarded the plane bound for England.* = **get on**, enter, mount, embark, entrain, embus, enplane ■ **OPPOSITE:** get off

boast VERB **1** *She boasted about her achievements.* = **brag**, crow, vaunt, bluster, talk big (*slang*), blow your own trumpet, show off, be proud of, flaunt, congratulate yourself on, flatter yourself, pride yourself on, skite (*Austral. & N.Z. informal*) ■ **OPPOSITE:** cover up **2** *The houses boast the latest energy-saving technology.* = **possess**, offer, present, exhibit ▶ NOUN *He was asked about earlier boasts of a quick victory.* = **bragging**, vaunting, rodomontade

(*literary*), gasconade (*rare*) ■ **OPPOSITE:** disclaimer

boat NOUN *One of the best ways to see the area is in a small boat.* = **vessel**, ship, craft, barge (*informal*), barque (*poetic*) • **in the same boat** *The police and I were in the same boat.* = **in the same situation**, alike, even, together, equal, on a par, on equal or even terms, on the same or equal footing • **miss the boat** *Big name companies have missed the boat.* = **miss your chance** or **opportunity**, miss out, be too late, lose out, blow your chance (*informal*) • **rock the boat** *I said I didn't want to rock the boat in any way.* = **cause trouble**, protest, object, dissent, make waves (*informal*), throw a spanner in the works, upset the apple cart

bob VERB *Balloons bobbed about in the sky.* = **bounce**, duck, leap, hop, weave, skip, jerk, wobble, quiver, oscillate, waggle • **bob up** *They will bob up like corks as they cook.* = **spring up**, rise, appear, emerge, surface, pop up, jump up, bounce up

bode VERB = **augur**, portend, threaten, predict, signify, foreshadow, presage, betoken, be an omen, forebode

bodily ADJECTIVE = **physical**, material, actual, substantial (*formal*), fleshly, tangible, corporal, carnal, corporeal

body NOUN **1** *The largest organ in the body is the liver.* = **physique**, build, form, figure, shape, make-up, frame, constitution **2** *Cross your upper leg over your body.* = **torso**, trunk **3** *His body lay in state.* = **corpse**, dead body, remains, stiff (*slang*), relics, carcass, cadaver **4** *the police representative body* = **organization**, company, group, society, league, association, band, congress, institution, corporation, federation, outfit (*informal*), syndicate, bloc, confederation **5** *the preface, followed by the main body of the article* = **main part**, matter, material, mass, substance, bulk, essence **6** *It is probably the most polluted body of water in the world.* = **expanse**, mass, sweep **7** *The great body of people moved slowly forward.* = **mass**, company, press, army, host, crowd, majority, assembly, mob, herd, swarm, horde, multitude, throng, bevy **8** *a dry wine, with good body* = **consistency**, substance, texture, density, richness, firmness, solidity, viscosity ■ **RELATED WORDS:** *adjectives* corporal, physical

boffin NOUN = **expert**, authority, brain(s) (*informal*), intellectual, genius, guru, inventor, thinker, wizard, mastermind, intellect (*informal*), egghead, wonk (*informal*), brainbox, bluestocking (*usually derogatory*), maven (*U.S.*), fundi (*S. African*)

b

bog NOUN *We walked steadily across moor and bog.* = **marsh**, moss (*Scot. & Northern English, dialect*), swamp, slough, wetlands, fen, mire, quagmire, morass, marshland, peat bog, pakihi (*N.Z.*), muskeg (*Canad.*) • **bog something** or **someone down** *The talks have become bogged down with the issue of military reform.* = **hold up**, stick, delay, halt, stall, slow down, impede, slow up

bogey NOUN **1** *Age is another bogey for those in the acting profession.* = **bugbear**, bête noire, horror, nightmare, bugaboo **2** *It was no bogey, no demon.* = **spirit**, ghost, phantom, spectre, spook (*informal*), apparition, imp, sprite, goblin, bogeyman, hobgoblin, eidolon, atua (*N.Z.*), kehua (*N.Z.*)

boggle VERB = **confuse**, surprise, shock, amaze, stun, stagger, bewilder, astound, daze, confound, stupefy, dumbfound

bogus ADJECTIVE = **fake**, false, artificial, forged, dummy, imitation, sham, fraudulent, pseudo (*informal*), counterfeit, spurious, ersatz, phoney or phony (*informal*), assumed ■ **OPPOSITE:** genuine

bohemian ADJECTIVE (*sometimes cap.*) *bohemian pre-war poets* = **unconventional**, alternative, artistic, exotic, way-out (*informal*), eccentric, avant-garde, off-the-wall (*slang*), unorthodox, arty (*informal*), oddball (*informal*), offbeat, left bank, nonconformist, outré ■ **OPPOSITE:** conventional ▶ NOUN (*sometimes cap.*) *I am a bohemian. I have no roots.* = **nonconformist**, rebel, radical, eccentric, maverick, hippy, dropout, individualist, beatnik, iconoclast

boil¹ VERB **1** *I stood in the kitchen, waiting for the water to boil.* = **simmer**, bubble, foam, churn, seethe, fizz, froth, effervesce **2** *She was boiling with anger.* = **be furious**, storm, rage, rave, fume, be angry, crack up (*informal*), see red (*informal*), go ballistic (*slang*), be indignant, fulminate, foam at the mouth (*informal*), blow a fuse (*slang, chiefly U.S.*), fly off the handle (*informal*), go off the deep end (*informal*), wig out (*slang*), go up the wall (*slang*) • **boil something down** *He boils down red wine and uses what's left.* = **reduce**, concentrate, precipitate (*Chemistry*), thicken, condense, decoct

boil² NOUN *a boil on his nose* = **pustule**, gathering (*informal*), swelling, blister, blain, carbuncle, furuncle (*Pathology*)

boisterous ADJECTIVE **1** *a boisterous but good-natured crowd* = **unruly**, wild, disorderly, loud, noisy, wayward, rowdy, wilful, riotous, unrestrained, rollicking, impetuous, rumbustious, uproarious, obstreperous, clamorous ■ **OPPOSITE:** self-controlled **2** *The boisterous wind had been*

making the sea increasingly choppy. = **stormy**, rough, raging, turbulent, tumultuous, tempestuous, blustery, gusty, squally ■ **OPPOSITE:** calm

bold ADJECTIVE **1** *She becomes a bold, daring rebel.* = **fearless**, enterprising, brave, daring, heroic, adventurous, courageous, gritty, gallant, gutsy (*slang*), audacious, intrepid, valiant, plucky, undaunted, unafraid, unflinching, dauntless, lion-hearted, valorous ■ **OPPOSITE:** timid **2** *Some young people may seem bold and confident, but inside they are very fragile.* = **impudent**, forward, fresh (*informal*), confident, rude, cheeky, brash, feisty (*informal*), saucy, pushy (*informal*), brazen, in-your-face (*Brit. slang*), shameless, sassy (*U.S. informal*), unabashed, pert, insolent, barefaced, spirited, forceful ■ **OPPOSITE:** shy **3** *bold, dramatic colours* = **bright**, conspicuous, strong, striking, loud, prominent, lively, pronounced, colourful, vivid, flashy, eye-catching, salient, showy ■ **OPPOSITE:** soft

bolster VERB = **support**, help, aid, maintain, boost, strengthen, assist, prop, reinforce, hold up, cushion, brace, shore up, augment, buttress, buoy up, give a leg up to (*informal*)

bolt NOUN **1** *details right down to the dimensions of nuts and bolts* = **pin**, rod, peg, rivet **2** *I heard him slide the bolt across the door.* = **bar**, catch, lock, latch, fastener, sliding bar **3** *He pulled the crossbow bolt from his head.* = **arrow**, missile, shaft, dart, projectile **4** *a bolt for freedom* = **dash**, race, flight, spring, rush, rush, bound, sprint, dart, spurt ▶ VERB **1** *He reminded her to lock and bolt the kitchen door behind her.* = **lock**, close, bar, secure, fasten, latch **2** *I made some excuse and bolted towards the exit.* = **dash**, run, fly, spring, jump, rush, bound, leap, sprint, hurtle **3** *Don't bolt your food.* = **gobble**, stuff, wolf, cram, gorge, devour, gulp, guzzle, swallow whole

bomb NOUN *There were two bomb explosions in the city overnight.* = **explosive**, charge, mine, shell, missile, device, rocket, grenade, torpedo, bombshell, projectile ▶ VERB *Airforce jets bombed the city at night.* = **blow up**, attack, destroy, assault, shell, blast, blitz, bombard, torpedo, open fire on, strafe, fire upon, blow sky-high

bombard VERB **1** *The media bombards us with images of celebrity culture.* = **attack**, assault, batter, barrage, besiege, beset, assail **2** *Rebel artillery units have regularly bombarded the airport.* = **bomb**, shell, blast, blitz, open fire, strafe, fire upon

bombardment NOUN = **bombing**, attack, fire, assault, shelling, blitz, barrage, flak, strafe, fusillade, cannonade

b

bombast NOUN = **pomposity**, ranting, bragging, hot air (*informal*), bluster, grandiosity, braggadocio, grandiloquence, rodomontade (*literary*), gasconade (*rare*), extravagant boasting, magniloquence

bombastic ADJECTIVE = **grandiloquent**, inflated, ranting, windy, high-flown, pompous, grandiose, histrionic, wordy, verbose, declamatory, fustian, magniloquent

bona fide ADJECTIVE = **genuine**, real, true, legal, actual, legitimate, authentic, honest, veritable, lawful, on the level (*informal*), kosher (*informal*), dinkum (*Austral. & N.Z. informal*), the real McCoy ■ **OPPOSITE:** bogus

bond NOUN **1** *the bond that linked them* = **tie**, union, coupling, link, association, relation, connection, alliance, attachment, affinity, affiliation **2** *He managed to break free of his bonds.* = **fastening**, band, tie, binding, chain, cord, shackle, fetter, manacle **3** *I'm not about to betray my bond with my brother.* = **agreement**, word, promise, contract, guarantee, pledge, obligation, compact, covenant ▶ VERB **1** *They all bonded while working together.* = **form friendships**, connect **2** *Strips of wood are bonded together and moulded by machine.* = **fix**, hold, bind, connect, glue, gum, fuse, stick, paste, fasten

bondage NOUN = **slavery**, imprisonment, captivity, confinement, yoke, duress, servitude, enslavement, subjugation, serfdom, subjection, vassalage, thraldom, enthralment

bonny ADJECTIVE = **beautiful**, pretty, fair, sweet, appealing, attractive, lovely, charming, handsome, good-looking, gorgeous (*informal*), radiant, alluring, comely (*old-fashioned*), fit (*Brit. informal*)

bonus NOUN **1** *a special end-of-year bonus* = **extra**, benefit, commission, prize, gift, reward, premium, dividend, hand-out, perk (*Brit. informal*), bounty, gratuity, honorarium **2** *Anything else would be a bonus.* = **advantage**, benefit, gain, extra, plus (*informal*), asset, perk (*Brit. informal*), icing on the cake

bony ADJECTIVE = **thin**, lean, skinny, angular, gaunt, skeletal, haggard, emaciated, scrawny, undernourished, cadaverous, rawboned, macilent (*rare*)

book NOUN **1** *a book about witches* = **work**, title, volume, publication, manual, paperback, textbook, tract, hardback, tome, e-book or ebook, blook **2** *I had several names in my little black book that I called regularly.* = **notebook**, album, journal, diary,

pad, record book, Filofax®, notepad, exercise book, jotter, memorandum book, e-book or ebook, blook ▶ VERB *She booked herself a flight home last night.* = **reserve**, schedule, engage, line up, organize, charter, arrange for, procure, make reservations, e-book or ebook • **book in** *We were happy to book in at the Royal Pavilion Hotel.* = **register**, enter, enrol

booking NOUN = **reservation**, date, appointment

bookish ADJECTIVE = **studious**, learned, academic, intellectual, literary, scholarly, erudite, pedantic, well-read, donnish

booklet NOUN = **brochure**, leaflet, hand-out, pamphlet, folder, mailshot, handbill

boom NOUN **1** *an economic boom* = **expansion**, increase, development, growth, advance, jump, boost, improvement, spurt, upsurge, upturn, upswing ■ **OPPOSITE:** decline **2** *The stillness of the night was broken by the boom of a cannon.* = **bang**, report, shot, crash, clash, blast, burst, explosion, roar, thunder, rumble, clap, peal, detonation ▶ VERB **1** *Lipstick sales have boomed even more.* = **increase**, flourish, grow, develop, succeed, expand, strengthen, do well, swell, thrive, intensify, prosper, burgeon, spurt ■ **OPPOSITE:** fall **2** *Thunder boomed like battlefield cannons over Crooked Mountain.* = **bang**, roll, crash, blast, echo, drum, explode, roar, thunder, rumble, resound, reverberate, peal

boomerang VERB = **rebound**, backfire, come home to roost

boon NOUN **1** *This battery booster is a boon for photographers.* = **benefit**, advantage, blessing, godsend, gift **2** *She begged him to grant her one boon.* = **gift**, present, grant, favour, donation, hand-out, gratuity, benefaction

boorish ADJECTIVE = **loutish**, gross, crude, rude, hick (*informal, chiefly U.S. & Canad.*), coarse, vulgar, rustic, barbaric, churlish, uneducated, bearish, uncouth, unrefined, uncivilized, clownish, oafish, ill-bred, lubberly ■ **OPPOSITE:** refined

boost VERB *They need to take action to boost sales.* = **increase**, develop, raise, expand, add to, build up, heighten, enlarge, inflate, magnify, amplify, augment, jack up ■ **OPPOSITE:** decrease ▶ NOUN **1** *The paper is enjoying a boost in circulation.* = **rise**, increase, advance, jump, addition, improvement, expansion, upsurge, upturn, increment, upswing, upward turn ■ **OPPOSITE:** fall **2** *It did give me a boost to win such an event.* = **encouragement**, help

boot VERB *One guy booted the door down.*
= **kick**, punt, put the boot in(to) (*slang*),
drop-kick • **boot someone out** *Members
may be booted out if they don't attend meetings.*
= **dismiss**, sack (*informal*), expel, throw out,
oust, relegate, kick out, eject, kiss off
(*slang, chiefly U.S. & Canad.*), show someone
the door, give someone the boot (*slang*),
give someone their marching orders, give
someone the bullet (*Brit. slang*), give
someone the bum's rush (*slang*), throw out
on your ear (*informal*), give someone the
heave or push (*informal*)

bootleg ADJECTIVE = **illicit**, illegal, outlawed,
pirate, unofficial, black-market, unlicensed,
under-the-table, unauthorized, contraband,
hooky (*slang*), under-the-counter
■ **OPPOSITE:** official

booty NOUN = **plunder**, winnings, gains,
haul, spoils, prey, loot, takings, pillage,
swag (*slang*), boodle (*slang, chiefly U.S.*)

booze VERB *a load of drunken people who had
been boozing all afternoon* = **drink**, indulge,
get drunk, tipple, imbibe (*formal*), tope,
carouse, bevvy (*dialect*), get plastered, drink
like a fish, get soused, get tanked up
(*informal*), go on a binge or bender
(*informal*), hit the booze or bottle (*informal*)

boozer NOUN **1** *I just popped into the boozer for
a drink.* = **pub**, local (*Brit. informal*), bar
(*informal, chiefly Brit.*), inn, tavern, beer
parlour (*Canad.*), beverage room (*Canad.*),
public house, watering hole (*facetious
slang*), roadhouse, hostelry, alehouse
(*archaic*), taproom **2** *We always thought he
was a bit of a boozer.* = **drinker**, toper, drunk,
soak (*slang*), alcoholic, lush (*slang*),
drunkard, sot, tippler, wino (*informal*),
alko or alco (*Austral. slang*), inebriate

border NOUN **1** *Clifford is enjoying life north of
the border.* = **frontier**, line, marches, limit,
bounds, boundary, perimeter, borderline,
borderland **2** *pillowcases trimmed with a
hand-crocheted border* = **edge**, lip, margin, skirt,
verge (*Brit.*), rim, hem, brim, flange ▸ VERB
*white sand bordered by palm trees and tropical
flowers* = **edge**, bound, decorate, trim,
fringe, rim, hem • **border on something**
The atmosphere borders on the surreal. = **come
close to**, approach, be like, resemble, be
similar to, approximate, come near

borderline ADJECTIVE = **marginal**,
bordering, doubtful, peripheral, indefinite,
indeterminate, equivocal, inexact,
unclassifiable

bore¹ VERB *Get the special drill bit to bore the
correct-size hole.* = **drill**, mine, sink, tunnel,
pierce, penetrate, burrow, puncture,
perforate, gouge out

bore² VERB *Dickie bored him all through the meal
with stories of the Navy.* = **tire**, exhaust,
annoy, fatigue, weary, wear out, jade, wear
down, be tedious, pall on, send to sleep
■ **OPPOSITE:** excite ▸ NOUN *He's a bore and a
fool.* = **nuisance**, pain (*informal*), drag
(*informal*), headache (*informal*), yawn
(*informal*), anorak (*informal*), pain in the
neck (*informal*), dullard, dull person,
tiresome person, wearisome talker

bored ADJECTIVE = **fed up**, tired, hacked (off)
(*U.S. slang*), wearied, weary, uninterested,
sick and tired (*informal*), listless, browned-
off (*informal*), brassed off (*Brit. slang*),
ennuied, hoha (*N.Z.*)

boredom NOUN = **tedium**, apathy,
doldrums, weariness, monotony, dullness,
sameness, ennui (*literary*), flatness,
world-weariness, tediousness,
irksomeness ■ **OPPOSITE:** excitement

boring ADJECTIVE = **uninteresting**, dull,
tedious, stale, tiresome, monotonous, old,
dead, flat, routine, humdrum, insipid,
mind-numbing, unexciting, ho-hum
(*informal*), repetitious, wearisome,
unvaried, yawnsome

born VERB *She was born in London on April 29,
1923.* = **brought into this world**, delivered

> **USAGE** This word is spelled without an
> *e*: *a new baby was born.* The word *borne*,
> spelled with an *e*, is the past participle of
> the verb *bear*: *he had borne his ordeal with
> great courage*, not *he had born his ordeal
> with great courage*.

borrow VERB **1** *Can I borrow a pen please?*
= **take on loan**, touch (someone) for
(*slang*), scrounge (*informal*), blag (*slang*),
mooch (*slang*), cadge, use temporarily, take
and return ■ **OPPOSITE:** lend **2** *I borrowed his
words for my book's title.* = **steal**, take, use,
copy, adopt, appropriate, acquire, pinch
(*informal*), pirate, poach, pilfer, filch,
plagiarize

bosom NOUN **1** *a flattering style accentuating
the bosom* = **breast**, chest, front, bust, teats,
thorax **2** *He went back to the snug bosom of his
family.* = **midst**, centre, heart, protection,
circle, shelter **3** *Something gentle seemed to
move in her bosom.* = **heart**, feelings, spirit,
soul, emotions, sympathies, sentiments,
affections ▸ ADJECTIVE *They were bosom
friends.* = **intimate**, close, warm, dear,
friendly, confidential, cherished, boon,
very dear

boss NOUN *He cannot stand his boss.*
= **manager**, head, leader, director, chief,
executive, owner, master, governor
(*informal*), employer, administrator,
supervisor, superintendent, gaffer

(informal, chiefly Brit.), foreman or woman or person, overseer, kingpin, big cheese (old-fashioned slang), numero uno (informal), Mister Big (slang, chiefly U.S.), sherang (Austral. & N.Z.) ▸ **boss someone around** He started bossing people around and I didn't like it. = **order around**, dominate, bully, intimidate, oppress, dictate to, terrorize, put upon, push around (slang), browbeat, ride roughshod over, tyrannize, rule with an iron hand

bossy ADJECTIVE = **domineering**, lordly, arrogant, authoritarian, oppressive, hectoring, autocratic, dictatorial, coercive, imperious, overbearing, tyrannical, despotic, high-handed

botch VERB It's a silly idea, and he has botched it. = **spoil**, mar, bungle, fumble, screw up (informal), mess up, cock up (Brit. slang), mismanage, muff, make a nonsense of (informal), bodge (informal), make a pig's ear of (informal), flub (U.S. slang), crool or cruel (Austral. slang) ▸ NOUN I rather made a botch of that whole thing. = **mess**, failure, blunder, miscarriage, bungle, bungling, fumble, hash, cock-up (Brit. slang), pig's ear (informal), pig's breakfast (informal)

bother VERB 1 That kind of jealousy doesn't bother me. = **trouble**, concern, worry, upset, alarm, disturb, distress, annoy, dismay, gall, disconcert, vex, perturb, faze, put or get someone's back up 2 I don't know why he bothers me with this kind of rubbish. = **pester**, plague, irritate, put out, harass, nag, hassle (informal), inconvenience, molest, breathe down someone's neck, get on your nerves (informal), nark (Brit., Austral. & N.Z. slang), bend someone's ear (informal), give someone grief (Brit. & S. African), get on your wick (Brit. slang) ■ **OPPOSITE:** help ▸ NOUN Most men hate the bother of shaving. = **trouble**, problem, worry, difficulty, strain, grief (Brit. & S. African), fuss, pest, irritation, hassle (informal), nuisance, flurry, uphill (S. African), inconvenience, annoyance, aggravation (informal), vexation ■ **OPPOSITE:** help

bottleneck NOUN = **block**, hold-up, obstacle, congestion, obstruction, impediment, blockage, snarl-up (informal, chiefly Brit.), (traffic) jam

bottle shop NOUN (Austral. & N.Z.) = **off-licence** (Brit.), liquor store (U.S. & Canad.), bottle store (S. African), package store (U.S. & Canad.), offie or offy (Brit. informal)

bottle store NOUN (S. African) = **off-licence** (Brit.), liquor store (U.S. & Canad.), bottle shop (Austral. & N.Z.), package store (U.S. & Canad.), offie or offy (Brit. informal)

bottom NOUN 1 He sat at the bottom of the stairs. = **lowest part**, base, foot, bed, floor, basis, foundation, depths, support, pedestal, deepest part ■ **OPPOSITE:** top 2 the bottom of their shoes = **underside**, sole, underneath, lower side 3 She moved her large bottom on the window-seat. = **buttocks**, behind (informal), rear, butt (U.S. & Canad. informal), bum (Brit. slang), buns (U.S. slang), backside, rump, seat, tail (informal), rear end (informal), posterior, derrière (euphemistic), tush (U.S. slang), fundament (euphemistic), jacksy (Brit. slang) ▸ ADJECTIVE the bottom drawer of the cupboard = **lowest**, last, base, ground, basement, undermost ■ **OPPOSITE:** higher

bottomless ADJECTIVE 1 She does not have a bottomless purse. = **unlimited**, endless, infinite, limitless, boundless, inexhaustible, immeasurable, unbounded, illimitable 2 His eyes were like bottomless brown pools. = **deep**, profound, yawning, boundless, unfathomable, immeasurable, fathomless, abyssal

bounce VERB 1 The ball bounced past the right-hand post. = **rebound**, return, thump, recoil, ricochet, spring back, resile 2 Moira bounced into the office. = **bound**, spring, jump, leap, skip, caper, prance, gambol, jounce 3 He was bounced from two programmes for unbecoming conduct. = **throw out**, fire (informal), turn out, expel, oust, relegate, kick out (informal), drive out, eject, evict, boot out (informal), show someone the door, give someone the bum's rush (slang), throw out on your ear (informal) ▸ NOUN 1 the pace and steep bounce of the pitch = **springiness**, give, spring, bound, rebound, resilience, elasticity, recoil 2 the natural bounce of youth = **life**, go (informal), energy, pep, sparkle, zip (informal), vitality, animation, vigour, exuberance, dynamism, brio, vivacity, liveliness, vim, lustiness, vivaciousness

bouncing ADJECTIVE = **lively**, healthy, thriving, blooming, robust, vigorous, energetic, perky, sprightly, alive and kicking, fighting fit, full of beans (informal), fit as a fiddle (informal), bright-eyed and bushy-tailed

bouncy ADJECTIVE 1 She was bouncy and full of energy. = **lively**, active, enthusiastic, energetic, bubbly, exuberant, irrepressible, ebullient, perky, chirpy (informal), sprightly, vivacious, effervescent, chipper (informal), full of beans (informal), zestful, full of pep (informal), bright-eyed and bushy-tailed ■ **OPPOSITE:** listless 2 a bouncy chair = **springy**, flexible, elastic, resilient, rubbery, spongy ■ **OPPOSITE:** flat

b

b

bound¹ ADJECTIVE **1** *All members are bound by an oath of secrecy.* = **compelled**, obliged, forced, committed, pledged, constrained, obligated, beholden, duty-bound **2** *Her arms were bound to her sides.* = **tied**, fixed, secured, attached, lashed, tied up, fastened, trussed, pinioned, made fast **3** *There are bound to be price increases next year.* = **certain**, sure, fated, doomed, destined

bound² VERB *He bounded up the steps and pushed the bell of the door.* = **leap**, bob, spring, jump, bounce, skip, vault, pounce ▸ NOUN *With one bound Jack was free.* = **leap**, bob, spring, jump, bounce, hurdle, skip, vault, pounce, caper, prance, lope, frisk, gambol

bound³ VERB **1** *the trees that bounded the car park* = **surround**, confine, enclose, terminate, encircle, circumscribe, hem in, demarcate, delimit **2** *Our lives are bounded by work, family and television.* = **limit**, fix, define, restrict, confine, restrain, circumscribe, demarcate, delimit

boundary NOUN **1** *Drug traffickers operate across national boundaries.* = **frontier**, edge, border, march, barrier, margin, brink **2** *the western boundary of the wood* = **edges**, limits, bounds, pale, confines, fringes, verges, precinct, extremities **3** *the boundary between childhood and adulthood* = **dividing line**, borderline

boundless ADJECTIVE = **unlimited**, vast, endless, immense, infinite, untold, limitless, unending, inexhaustible, incalculable, immeasurable, unbounded, unconfined, measureless, illimitable
■ **OPPOSITE:** limited

bounds PLURAL NOUN *The bounds of the empire continued to expand.* = **boundary**, line, limit, edge, border, march, margin, pale, confines, fringe, verge, rim, perimeter, periphery

bountiful ADJECTIVE **1** *The land is bountiful and no one starves.* = **plentiful**, generous, lavish, ample, prolific, abundant, exuberant, copious, luxuriant, bounteous, plenteous **2** *Their bountiful host was bringing brandy, whisky and liqueurs.* = **generous**, kind, princely, liberal, charitable, hospitable, prodigal, open-handed, unstinting, beneficent, bounteous, munificent, ungrudging

bounty NOUN **1** *The aid organization would not allow such bounty.* = **generosity**, charity, assistance, kindness, philanthropy, benevolence, beneficence, liberality, almsgiving, open-handedness, largesse or largess **2** *autumn's bounty of fruits, seeds and berries* = **abundance**, plenty, exuberance, profusion, affluence, plenitude,

copiousness, plenteousness **3** *They paid bounties for people to give up their weapons.* = **reward**, present, grant, prize, payment, gift, compensation, bonus, premium, donation, recompense, gratuity, meed (*archaic*), largesse or largess, koha (*N.Z.*)

bouquet NOUN **1** *a bouquet of dried violets* = **bunch of flowers**, spray, garland, wreath, posy, buttonhole, corsage, nosegay, boutonniere **2** *a Sicilian wine with a light red colour and a bouquet of cloves* = **aroma**, smell, scent, perfume, fragrance, savour, odour, redolence

bourgeois ADJECTIVE = **middle-class**, traditional, conventional, materialistic, hidebound, Pooterish

bout NOUN **1** *I was suffering with a bout of nerves.* = **period**, time, term, fit, session, stretch, spell, turn, patch, interval, stint **2** *The latest bout of violence has claimed ten lives.* = **round**, run, course, series, session, cycle, sequence, stint, spree **3** *This will be his eighth title bout in 19 months.* = **fight**, match, battle, competition, struggle, contest, set-to (*informal*), encounter, engagement, head-to-head, boxing match

bovine ADJECTIVE = **dull**, heavy, slow, thick, stupid, dense, sluggish, lifeless, inactive, inert, lethargic, dozy (*Brit. informal*), listless, unresponsive, stolid, torpid, slothful (*formal*)

bow¹ VERB *He bowed slightly before taking her bag.* = **bend**, bob, nod, incline, stoop, droop, genuflect, make obeisance ▸ NOUN *I gave a theatrical bow and waved.* = **bending**, bob, nod, inclination, salaam, obeisance, kowtow, genuflection • **bow out** *He bowed out gracefully when his successor was appointed.* = **give up**, retire, withdraw, get out, resign, quit, pull out, step down (*informal*), back out, throw in the towel, cop out (*slang*), throw in the sponge, call it a day or night • **bow to something** *or* **someone** *She is having to bow to their terms.* = **give in to**, accept, comply with, succumb to, submit to, surrender to, yield to, defer to, concede to, acquiesce to, kowtow to

bow³ NOUN *spray from the ship's bow* = **prow**, head, stem, fore, beak

bowels PLURAL NOUN **1** *I had a relentless pain in my bowels.* = **guts**, insides (*informal*), intestines, innards (*informal*), entrails, viscera, vitals **2** *deep in the bowels of the earth* = **depths**, hold, middle, inside (*informal*), deep, interior, core, belly, midst, remotest part, deepest part, furthest part, innermost part

bower NOUN = **arbour**, grotto, alcove, summerhouse, shady recess, leafy shelter

bowl¹ NOUN *Put all the ingredients into a large bowl.* = **basin**, plate, dish, vessel

bowl² VERB **1** *He bowled each ball so well that we won two matches.* = **throw**, hurl, launch, cast, pitch, toss, fling, chuck (*informal*), lob (*informal*) **2** (*often with* **along**) *It felt just like old times, to bowl down to Knightsbridge.* = **drive**, shoot, speed, tear, barrel (along) (*informal, chiefly U.S. & Canad.*), trundle
• **bowl someone over 1** *People clung to trees as the flash flood bowled them over.* = **knock down**, fell, floor, deck (*slang*), overturn, overthrow, bring down **2** (*informal*) *I was bowled over by India.* = **surprise**, amaze, stun, overwhelm, astonish, stagger, startle, astound, take (someone) aback, stupefy, strike (someone) dumb, throw off balance, sweep off your feet, dumbfound

box¹ NOUN *They sat on wooden boxes.* = **container**, case, chest, trunk, pack, package, carton, casket, receptacle, ark (*dialect*), portmanteau, coffret, kist (*Scot. & Northern English, dialect*) ▶ VERB *He boxed the test pieces and shipped them back to Berlin.* = **pack**, package, wrap, encase, bundle up
• **box something** or **someone in** *He was boxed in with 300 metres to go.* = **confine**, contain, surround, trap, restrict, isolate, cage, enclose, restrain, imprison, shut up, incarcerate, hem in, shut in, coop up

box² VERB **1** *At school I boxed and played rugby.* = **fight**, spar, exchange blows **2** *They slapped my face and boxed my ears.* = **punch**, hit, strike, belt (*informal*), deck (*slang*), slap, sock (*slang*), buffet, clout (*informal*), cuff, whack (*informal*), wallop (*informal*), chin (*slang*), tonk (*informal*), thwack (*informal*), lay one on (*slang*)

boxer NOUN = **fighter**, pugilist, prizefighter, sparrer

boxing NOUN = **prizefighting**, the ring, sparring, fisticuffs, the fight game (*informal*), pugilism

boy NOUN = **lad**, kid (*informal*), youth, fellow (*old-fashioned*), youngster, chap (*informal*), schoolboy, junior, laddie (*Scot.*), stripling

boycott VERB = **embargo**, reject, snub, refrain from, spurn, blacklist, black, cold-shoulder, ostracize, blackball
■ **OPPOSITE:** support

boyfriend NOUN = **sweetheart**, man, lover, young man, steady, beloved, valentine, admirer, suitor, beau (*old-fashioned*), date, swain (*archaic*), toy boy, truelove, leman (*archaic*), inamorato, BF or bf (*informal*), bae (*U.S. informal*)

boyish ADJECTIVE = **youthful**, young, innocent, adolescent, juvenile, childish, immature

brace VERB **1** *He braced his back against the wall.* = **steady**, support, balance, secure, stabilize **2** *The lights showed the old timbers, used to brace the roof.* = **support**, strengthen, steady, prop, reinforce, hold up, tighten, shove, bolster, fortify, buttress, shove up
▶ NOUN *She wears a neck brace.* = **support**, stay, prop, bracer, bolster, bracket, reinforcement, strut, truss, buttress, stanchion

bracing ADJECTIVE = **refreshing**, fresh, cool, stimulating, reviving, lively, crisp, vigorous, rousing, brisk, uplifting, exhilarating, fortifying, chilly, rejuvenating, invigorating, energizing, healthful, restorative, tonic, rejuvenative ■ **OPPOSITE:** tiring

brag VERB = **boast**, crow, swagger, vaunt, bluster, talk big (*slang*), blow your own trumpet, blow your own horn (*U.S. & Canad.*)

braid VERB = **interweave**, weave, lace, intertwine, plait, entwine, twine, ravel, interlace

brain NOUN **1** *The eye grows independently of the brain.* = **cerebrum**, mind, grey matter (*informal*) **2** *I've never been much of a brain myself.* = **intellectual**, genius, scholar, sage, pundit, mastermind, intellect (*informal*), prodigy, highbrow, egghead (*informal*), brainbox, bluestocking (*usually derogatory*)
▶ PLURAL NOUN *They were not the only ones to have brains and ambition.* = **intelligence**, mind, reason, understanding, sense, capacity, smarts (*slang, chiefly U.S.*), wit, intellect, savvy (*slang*), nous (*Brit. slang*), suss (*slang*), shrewdness, sagacity
■ **RELATED WORD:** *adjective* cerebral

brainwashing NOUN = **indoctrination**, conditioning, persuasion, re-education

brainwave NOUN = **idea**, thought, bright idea, stroke of genius

brainy ADJECTIVE = **intelligent**, quick, bright (*informal*), sharp, brilliant, acute, smart, alert, clever, rational, knowing, quick-witted

brake NOUN *Illness had put a brake on his progress.* = **control**, check, curb, restraint, constraint, rein ▶ VERB *She braked to a halt and switched off.* = **slow**, decelerate, reduce speed

branch NOUN **1** *the low, overhanging branches of a giant pine tree* = **bough**, shoot, arm, spray, limb, sprig, offshoot, prong, ramification **2** *The local branch is handling the accounts.* = **office**, department, unit, wing, chapter, bureau, local office **3** *He had a fascination for submarines and joined this branch of the service.* = **division**, part, section, subdivision, subsection **4** *an experimental*

b

branch of naturopathic medicine = **discipline**, section, subdivision • **branch out** I continued studying moths, and branched out to other insects. = **expand**, diversify

brand NOUN **1** a supermarket's own brand = **trademark 2** The brand on the barrel stood for Elbert Anderson and Uncle Sam. = **label**, mark, sign, stamp, symbol, logo, trademark, marker, hallmark (Brit.), emblem **3** the brand of shame = **stigma**, mark, stain, disgrace, taint, slur, blot, infamy, smirch ▸ VERB **1** I was instantly branded as a rebel. = **stigmatize**, mark, label, expose, denounce, disgrace, discredit, censure, pillory, defame **2** The owner couldn't be bothered to brand the cattle. = **mark**, burn, label, stamp, scar

brandish VERB = **wave**, raise, display, shake, swing, exhibit, flourish, wield, flaunt

brash ADJECTIVE = **bold**, forward, rude, arrogant, cocky, pushy (informal), brazen, presumptuous, impertinent, insolent, impudent, bumptious, cocksure, overconfident, hubristic, full of yourself ■ **OPPOSITE:** timid

brassy ADJECTIVE **1** Musicians blast their brassy jazz from street corners. = **strident**, loud, harsh, piercing, jarring, noisy, grating, raucous, blaring, shrill, jangling, dissonant, cacophonous **2** brash and brassy advertising campaigns = **brazen**, forward, bold, brash, saucy, pushy (informal), pert, insolent, impudent, loud-mouthed, barefaced **3** a woman with big brassy ear-rings = **flashy**, loud, blatant, vulgar, gaudy, garish, jazzy (informal), showy, obtrusive ■ **OPPOSITE:** discreet

brat NOUN = **youngster**, kid (informal), urchin, imp, rascal, spoilt child, devil, puppy (informal), cub, scallywag (informal), whippersnapper, guttersnipe

bravado NOUN = **swagger**, boast, boasting, swaggering, vaunting, bluster, swashbuckling, bombast, braggadocio, boastfulness, fanfaronade (rare)

brave ADJECTIVE brave people who dare to challenge the tyrannical regimes = **courageous**, daring, bold, heroic, adventurous, gritty, fearless, resolute, gallant, gutsy (slang), audacious, intrepid, valiant, plucky, undaunted, unafraid, unflinching, dauntless, lion-hearted, valorous ■ **OPPOSITE:** timid ▸ VERB She had to brave his anger and confess. = **confront**, face, suffer, challenge, bear, tackle, dare, endure, defy, withstand, stand up to ■ **OPPOSITE:** give in to

bravery NOUN = **courage**, nerve, daring, pluck, spirit, bottle (Brit. slang), guts (informal), grit, fortitude, heroism, mettle, boldness, bravura, gallantry, valour, spunk (informal), hardiness, fearlessness, intrepidity, indomitability, hardihood, dauntlessness, doughtiness, pluckiness, lion-heartedness ■ **OPPOSITE:** cowardice

bravo INTERJECTION = **congratulations**, well done

bravura NOUN = **brilliance**, energy, spirit, display, punch (informal), dash, animation, vigour, verve, panache, boldness, virtuosity, élan, exhibitionism, brio, ostentation

brawl NOUN He had been in a drunken street brawl. = **fight**, battle, row (informal), clash, disorder, scrap (informal), fray, squabble, wrangle, skirmish, scuffle, punch-up (Brit. informal), free-for-all (informal), fracas, altercation, rumpus, broil, tumult, affray (Law), shindig (informal), donnybrook, ruckus (informal), scrimmage, shindy (informal), biffo (Austral. slang), bagarre (French), melee or mêlée ▸ VERB Gangs of youths brawled in the street. = **fight**, battle, scrap (informal), wrestle, wrangle, tussle, scuffle, go at it hammer and tongs, fight like Kilkenny cats, altercate

brawn NOUN = **muscle**, might, power, strength, muscles, beef (informal), flesh, vigour, robustness, muscularity, beefiness (informal), brawniness

bray VERB **1** The donkey brayed and tried to bolt. = **neigh**, bellow, screech, heehaw **2** Pavel brayed with angry laughter. = **roar**, trumpet, bellow, hoot ▸ NOUN **1** It was a strange laugh, like the bray of a donkey. = **neigh**, bellow, screech, heehaw **2** She cut him off with a bray of laughter. = **roar**, cry, shout, bellow, screech, hoot, bawl, harsh sound

brazen ADJECTIVE a brazen dive to win a free-kick = **bold**, forward, defiant, brash, saucy, audacious, pushy (informal), shameless, unabashed, pert, unashamed, insolent, impudent, immodest, barefaced, brassy (informal) ■ **OPPOSITE:** shy • **brazen it out** As for the scandal, he is as determined as ever to brazen it out. = **be unashamed**, persevere, be defiant, confront something, be impenitent, outface, outstare

breach NOUN **1** The congressman was accused of a breach of secrecy laws. = **nonobservance**, abuse, violation, infringement, trespass, disobedience, transgression, contravention, infraction, noncompliance ■ **OPPOSITE:** compliance **2** the breach between Tito and Stalin = **disagreement**, difference, division, separation, falling-out (informal), quarrel, alienation, variance, severance, disaffection, schism, parting of the ways, estrangement, dissension **3** *A large battering ram hammered a breach in the wall.* = **opening**, crack, break, hole, split, gap, rent, rift, rupture, aperture, chasm, cleft, fissure

bread NOUN **1** *I go to work, I put bread on the table, I pay the mortgage.* = **food**, provisions, fare, necessities, subsistence, kai (*N.Z. informal*), nourishment, sustenance, victuals, nutriment, viands, aliment **2** *a period in which you could earn your bread by the sweat of your brow* = **money**, funds, cash, finance, necessary (*informal*), silver, tin (*slang*), brass (*Northern English, dialect*), dough (*slang*), dosh (*Brit. & Austral. slang*), needful (*informal*), shekels (*informal*), dibs (*slang*), ackers (*slang*), spondulicks (*slang*), rhino (*Brit. slang*)

breadth NOUN **1** *The breadth of the whole camp was 400 metres.* = **width**, spread, beam, span, latitude, broadness, wideness **2** *The breadth of his knowledge filled me with admiration.* = **extent**, area, reach, range, measure, size, scale, spread, sweep, scope, magnitude, compass, expanse, vastness, amplitude, comprehensiveness, extensiveness

break VERB **1** *He fell through the window, breaking the glass.* = **shatter**, separate, destroy, split, divide, crack, snap, smash, crush, fragment, demolish, sever, trash (*slang*), disintegrate, splinter, smash to smithereens, shiver ■ **OPPOSITE:** repair **2** *She broke her leg in a skiing accident.* = **fracture**, crack, smash **3** *The bandage must be put on when the blister breaks.* = **burst**, tear, split **4** *We didn't know we were breaking the law.* = **disobey**, breach, defy, violate, disregard, flout, infringe, contravene (*formal*), transgress, go counter to, infract (*Law*) ■ **OPPOSITE:** obey **5** *He aims to break the vicious cycle.* = **stop**, cut, check, suspend, interrupt, cut short, discontinue **6** *The noise broke my concentration.* = **disturb**, interrupt **7** *They have yet to break the link with the trade unions.* = **end**, stop, cut, drop, give up, abandon, suspend, interrupt, terminate, put an end to, discontinue, pull the plug on **8** *He never let his jailers break him.* = **weaken**, undermine, cow, tame, subdue, demoralize, dispirit **9** *The newspapers can make or break you.* = **ruin**, destroy, crush, humiliate, bring down, bankrupt, degrade, impoverish, demote, make bankrupt, bring to ruin **10** *They broke for lunch.* = **pause**, stop briefly, stop, rest, halt, cease, take a break, have a breather (*informal*) **11** *We broke our journey at a small country hotel.* = **interrupt**, stop, suspend **12** *She was saved by bushes which broke her fall.* = **cushion**, reduce, ease, moderate, diminish, temper, soften, lessen, alleviate, lighten **13** *He resigned his post as Bishop when the scandal broke.* = **be revealed**, come out, be reported, be published, be announced, be made public, be proclaimed, be let out, be imparted, be divulged, come out in the wash **14** *I worried for ages and decided I had better break the news.* = **reveal**, tell, announce, declare, disclose, proclaim, divulge, make known **15** *The film has broken all box office records.* = **beat**, top, better, exceed, go beyond, excel, surpass, outstrip, outdo, cap (*informal*) **16** *(of dawn) They continued their search as dawn broke.* = **happen**, appear, emerge, occur, erupt, burst out, come forth suddenly ▶ NOUN **1** *a break in the earth's surface* = **fracture**, opening, tear, hole, split, crack, gap, rent, breach, rift, rupture, gash, cleft, fissure **2** *They always play that music during the break.* = **interval**, pause, recess, interlude, intermission, entr'acte **3** *They are currently taking a short break in Spain.* = **holiday**, leave, vacation, time off, recess, awayday, schoolie (*Austral.*), accumulated day off or ADO (*Austral.*) **4** *(informal) The rain was a lucky break for the American.* = **stroke of luck**, chance, opportunity, advantage, fortune, opening **5** *There is some threat of a break in relations between them.* = **breach**, split, dispute, separation, rift, rupture, alienation, disaffection, schism, estrangement • **break away** *I broke away from him and rushed out into the hall.* = **get away**, escape, flee, run away, break free, break loose, make your escape • **break down 1** *Their car broke down.* = **stop working**, stop, seize up, conk out (*informal*), go kaput (*informal*), go phut, cark it (*Austral. & N.Z. slang*) **2** *Paola's marriage broke down.* = **fail**, collapse, fall through, be unsuccessful, come unstuck, run aground, come to grief, come a cropper (*informal*), turn out badly **3** *The young woman broke down and cried.* = **be overcome**, crack up (*informal*), go to pieces • **break in 1** *The thief had broken in through a first-floor window.* = **break and enter**, enter, gain access **2** *Suddenly, O'Leary broke in with a suggestion.* = **interrupt**, intervene, interfere, intrude, burst in, interject, butt in, barge in, interpose, put your oar in, put your two cents in (*U.S. slang*) • **break off** *He broke off in mid-sentence.* = **stop talking**, pause, stumble, falter, fumble, hem and haw or hum and haw • **break out 1** *He was 29 when war broke out.* = **begin**, start, happen, occur, arise, set in, commence, spring up **2** *The two* *men broke out and cut through a perimeter fence.* = **escape**, flee, bolt, burst out, get free, break loose, abscond, do a bunk (*Brit. slang*), do a Skase (*Austral. informal*) **3** *A line of sweat broke out on her forehead.* = **erupt**, gush, flare up, burst out, burst forth, pour forth • **break someone in** *The band are breaking in a new backing vocalist.* = **initiate**, train, accustom, habituate • **break something in** *I'm breaking in these new boots.* = **prepare**, condition, tame • **break something off** *I broke off a large piece of the clay.* = **detach**, separate, divide, cut off, pull off, sever, part, remove, splinter, tear off, snap off • **break something up** *Police used tear gas to break up a demonstration.* = **stop**, end, suspend, disrupt, dismantle, disperse, terminate, disband, diffuse • **break through** *There is still scope for new writers to break through.* = **succeed**, make it (*informal*), achieve, do well, flourish, cut it (*informal*), get to the top, crack it (*informal*), make your mark (*informal*), shine forth • **break through something** *Protesters tried to break through a police cordon.* = **penetrate**, go through, get past, burst through • **break up 1** *The meeting broke up half an hour later.* = **finish**, be suspended, adjourn, recess **2** *My girlfriend and I have broken up.* = **split up**, separate, part, divorce, end a relationship **3** *The crowd broke up reluctantly.* = **scatter**, separate, divide, dissolve • **break with something** *or* **someone** *It was a tough decision for him to break with Leeds.* = **separate from**, drop (*informal*), reject, ditch (*slang*), renounce, depart from, break away from, part company with, repudiate, jilt

breakage NOUN = **break**, cut, tear, crack, rent, breach, fracture, rift, rupture, cleft, fissure

breakaway ADJECTIVE = **rebel**, revolutionary, rebellious, dissenting, insurgent, seceding, secessionist, heretical, mutinous, insubordinate, insurrectionary, schismatic

breakdown NOUN **1** *They often seem depressed and close to breakdown.* = **collapse**, crackup (*informal*) **2** *The organisers were given a breakdown of the costs.* = **analysis**, classification, dissection, categorization, detailed list, itemization

breaker NOUN = **wave**, roller, comber, billow, white horse, whitecap

break-in NOUN = **burglary**, robbery, breaking and entering, home invasion (*Austral. & N.Z.*)

breakneck ADJECTIVE = **dangerous**, rapid, excessive, rash, reckless, precipitate, headlong, express

breakthrough NOUN = **development**, advance, progress, improvement, discovery, find, finding, invention, step forward, leap forwards, turn of events, quantum leap

break-up NOUN **1** *a marital break-up* = **separation**, split, divorce, breakdown, ending, parting, breaking, splitting, wind-up, rift, disintegration, dissolution, termination **2** *the break-up of the Soviet Union* = **dissolution**, division, splitting, disintegration

breakwater NOUN = **sea wall**, spur, mole, jetty, groyne

breast NOUN **1** *Happiness flowered in her breast.* = **heart**, feelings, thoughts, soul, being, emotions, core, sentiments, seat of the affections **2** *A sports bra provides support for the breasts.* = **bosom**, mammary gland
■ RELATED WORD: *adjective* mammary

breath NOUN **1** *He took a deep breath and began to climb the stairs.* = **inhalation**, breathing, pant, gasp, gulp, wheeze, exhalation, respiration **2** *Not even a breath of wind stirred the pine branches.* = **gust**, sigh, puff, flutter, flurry, whiff, draught, waft, zephyr, slight movement, faint breeze **3** *It was left to her to add a breath of common sense.* = **trace**, suggestion, hint, whisper, suspicion, murmur, undertone, intimation **4** *He had to stop for breath.* = **rest**, breather (*informal*) **5** *Here is no light, no breath, no warm flesh.* = **life**, energy, existence, vitality, animation, life force, lifeblood, mauri (*N.Z.*)

breathe VERB **1** *Always breathe through your nose.* = **inhale and exhale**, pant, gasp, puff, gulp, wheeze, respire, draw in breath **2** *He never breathed a word about our conversation.* = **whisper**, say, voice, express, sigh, utter, articulate, murmur **3** *It is the readers who breathe life into a newspaper.* = **instil**, inspire, pass on, inject, impart, infuse, imbue

breather NOUN = **rest**, break, halt, pause, recess, breathing space, breath of air

breathless ADJECTIVE **1** *I was a little breathless and my heartbeat was fast.* = **out of breath**, winded, exhausted, panting, gasping, choking, gulping, wheezing, out of whack (*informal*), short-winded **2** *We were breathless with anticipation.* = **excited**, anxious, curious, eager, enthusiastic, impatient, agog, on tenterhooks, in suspense

breathtaking ADJECTIVE = **amazing**, striking, exciting, brilliant, dramatic, stunning (*informal*), impressive, thrilling, overwhelming, magnificent, astonishing, sensational, eye-popping (*informal*), awesome, wondrous (*archaic, literary*), awe-inspiring, jaw-dropping, heart-stirring

breed NOUN **1** *rare breeds of cattle* = **variety**, race, stock, type, species, strain, pedigree **2** *the new breed of walking holidays* = **kind**, sort, type, variety, brand, stamp ▶ VERB **1** *He lived alone, breeding horses and dogs.* = **rear**, tend, keep, raise, maintain, farm, look after, care for, bring up, nurture, nourish **2** *Frogs will usually breed in any convenient pond.* = **reproduce**, multiply, propagate, procreate (*formal*), produce offspring, bear young, bring forth young, generate offspring, beget offspring, develop **3** *If they are overlooked, it's bound to breed resentment.* = **produce**, cause, create, occasion (*formal*), generate, bring about, arouse, originate, give rise to, stir up

breeding NOUN = **refinement**, style, culture, taste, manners, polish, grace, courtesy, elegance, sophistication, delicacy, cultivation, politeness, civility, gentility, graciousness, urbanity, politesse

breeze NOUN *a cool summer breeze* = **light wind**, air, whiff, draught, gust, waft, zephyr, breath of wind, current of air, puff of air, capful of wind ▶ VERB *Lopez breezed into the room.* = **sweep**, move briskly, pass, trip, sail, hurry, sally, glide, flit

breezy ADJECTIVE **1** *his bright and breezy personality* = **carefree**, casual, lively, sparkling, sunny, informal, cheerful, animated, upbeat (*informal*), buoyant, airy, easy-going, genial, jaunty, chirpy (*informal*), sparky, sprightly, vivacious, debonair, blithe, free and easy, full of beans (*informal*), light, light-hearted ■ OPPOSITE: serious **2** *The day was breezy and warm.* = **windy**, fresh, airy, blustery, blowing, gusty, squally, blowy, blusterous ■ OPPOSITE: calm

brevity NOUN **1** *The bonus of this homely soup is the brevity of its cooking time.* = **shortness**, transience, impermanence, ephemerality, briefness, transitoriness **2** *The brevity of the letter concerned me.* = **conciseness**, economy, crispness, concision, terseness, succinctness, curtness, pithiness ■ OPPOSITE: wordiness

brew VERB **1** *He brewed a pot of coffee.* = **boil**, make, soak, steep, stew, infuse (*tea*) **2** *I brew my own beer.* = **make**, ferment, prepare by fermentation **3** *At home a crisis was brewing.* = **start**, develop, gather, foment **4** *We'd seen the storm brewing when we were out on the boat.* = **develop**, form, gather, foment ▶ NOUN *a mild herbal brew* = **drink**, preparation, mixture, blend, liquor, beverage, infusion, concoction, fermentation, distillation

bribe NOUN *He was being investigated for receiving bribes.* = **inducement**, incentive, pay-off (*informal*), graft (*informal*), sweetener (*slang*), kickback (*U.S.*), sop, backhander (*slang*), enticement, hush money (*slang*), payola (*informal*), allurement, corrupting gift, reward for treachery ▶ VERB *The company bribed the workers to be quiet.* = **buy off**, reward, pay off (*informal*), lure, corrupt, get at, square, suborn, grease the palm or hand of (*slang*), influence by gifts, oil the palm of (*informal*)

bribery NOUN = **corruption**, graft (*informal*), inducement, buying off, payola (*informal*), crookedness (*informal*), palm-greasing (*slang*), subornation

bric-a-brac NOUN = **knick-knacks**, ornaments, trinkets, baubles, curios, objets d'art (*French*), gewgaws, bibelots, kickshaws, objects of virtu

bridal ADJECTIVE = **matrimonial**, marriage, wedding, marital, bride's, nuptial, conjugal, spousal, connubial (*formal*), hymeneal

bride NOUN = **wife**, newly-wed, marriage partner, wifey (*informal*)

bridegroom NOUN = **husband**, groom, newly-wed, marriage partner

bridge NOUN **1** *He walked over the railway bridge.* = **arch**, span, viaduct, flyover, overpass, fixed link (*Canad.*) **2** *They saw themselves as a bridge to peace.* = **link**, tie, bond, connection ▶ VERB **1** *a tree used to bridge the river* = **span**, cross, go over, cross over, traverse, reach across, extend across, arch over **2** *She bridged the gap between pop music and opera.* = **reconcile**, unite, resolve

bridle NOUN *She dismounted and took her horse's bridle.* = **rein**, curb, control, check, restraint, trammels ▶ VERB **1** *He bridled at the shortness of her tone.* = **get angry**, draw (yourself) up, bristle, seethe, see red, be infuriated, rear up, be indignant, be maddened, raise your hackles, get your dander up (*slang*), get your back up **2** *I must learn to bridle my tongue.* = **curb**, control, master, govern, moderate, restrain, rein, subdue, repress, constrain, keep in check, check, keep a tight rein on, keep on a string

brief ADJECTIVE **1** *This time their visit is brief.* = **short**, fast, quick, temporary, fleeting, swift, short-lived, little, hasty, momentary, ephemeral, quickie (*informal*), transitory ■ OPPOSITE: long **2** *Write a very brief description of a typical problem.* = **concise**, short, limited, to the point, crisp, compressed, terse, curt, laconic, succinct, clipped, pithy, thumbnail, monosyllabic ■ OPPOSITE: long **3** *He was brief, rapid, decisive.* = **curt**, short, sharp, blunt, abrupt, brusque ▶ VERB *A spokesperson briefed reporters.* = **inform**, prime, prepare, advise, fill in (*informal*), instruct, clue in (*informal*), gen up (*Brit. informal*), put in the picture (*informal*), give a rundown, keep (someone) posted, give the gen (*Brit. informal*) ▶ NOUN **1** *He gives me my first brief of the situation.* = **summary**, résumé, outline, sketch, abstract, summing-up, digest, epitome, rundown, synopsis, précis, recapitulation, abridgment **2** *a lawyer's brief* = **case**, defence, argument, data, contention

briefing NOUN **1** *They're holding a press briefing tomorrow.* = **conference**, meeting, priming **2** *The Chancellor gives a twenty-minute briefing to his backbenchers.* = **instructions**, information, priming, directions, instruction, preparation, guidance, preamble, rundown

briefly ADVERB **1** *He smiled briefly.* = **quickly**, shortly, precisely, casually, temporarily, abruptly, hastily, briskly, momentarily, hurriedly, curtly, summarily, fleetingly, cursorily **2** *There are four alternatives; they are described briefly below.* = **in outline**, in brief, in passing, in a nutshell, concisely, in a few words

brigade NOUN **1** *the men of the Seventh Armoured Brigade* = **corps**, company, force, unit, division, troop, squad, crew, team, outfit (*informal*), regiment, contingent, squadron, detachment **2** *the healthy-eating brigade* = **group**, party, body, band, camp, squad, organization, crew (*informal*), bunch (*informal*)

bright ADJECTIVE **1** *a bright red dress* = **vivid**, rich, brilliant, intense, glowing, colourful, highly-coloured **2** *Newborns hate bright lights and loud noises.* = **shining**, flashing, beaming, glowing, blazing, sparkling, glittering, dazzling, illuminated, gleaming, shimmering, twinkling, radiant, luminous, glistening, resplendent, scintillating, lustrous, lambent, effulgent **3** *I was convinced that he was brighter than average.* = **intelligent**, smart, clever, knowing, thinking, quick, aware, sharp, keen, acute, alert, rational, penetrating, enlightened, apt, astute, brainy (*informal*), wide-awake, clear-headed, perspicacious (*formal*), quick-witted **4** *There are lots of books crammed with bright ideas.* = **clever**, brilliant, smart, sensible, cunning, ingenious, inventive, canny **5** *The boy was so bright and animated.* = **cheerful**, happy, glad (*archaic*), lively, jolly, merry, upbeat (*informal*), joyous, joyful, genial, chirpy (*informal*), sparky, vivacious, full of beans (*informal*), gay, light-hearted **6** *Both had successful careers and the future looked bright.* = **promising**, good, encouraging, excellent, golden,

optimistic, hopeful, favourable, prosperous, rosy, auspicious, propitious, palmy **7** *the bright winter sky* = **sunny**, clear, fair, pleasant, clement, lucid, cloudless, unclouded, sunlit ■ **OPPOSITE:** cloudy

brighten VERB **1** *Seeing him, she seemed to brighten a little.* = **cheer up**, rally, take heart, perk up, buck up (*informal*), become cheerful ■ **OPPOSITE:** become gloomy **2** *Her tearful eyes brightened with interest.* = **light up**, shine, glow, gleam, clear up, lighten, enliven ■ **OPPOSITE:** dim **3** *Planted tubs brightened the area outside the door.* = **enliven**, animate, make brighter, vitalize **4** *The sky above the ridge of the mountains brightened.* = **become brighter**, light up, glow, gleam, clear up

brightness NOUN **1** *You'll be impressed with the brightness of the colours.* = **vividness**, intensity, brilliance, splendour, resplendence **2** *Her brightness seemed quite intimidating to me.* = **intelligence**, intellect, brains (*informal*), awareness, sharpness, alertness, cleverness, quickness, acuity, brain power, smarts (*slang, chiefly U.S.*), smartness

brilliance *or* **brilliancy** NOUN **1** *His brilliance and genius will always remain.* = **cleverness**, talent, wisdom, distinction, genius, excellence, greatness, aptitude, inventiveness, acuity, giftedness, braininess ■ **OPPOSITE:** stupidity **2** *the brilliance of the sun on the water* = **brightness**, blaze, intensity, sparkle, glitter, dazzle, gleam, sheen, lustre, radiance, luminosity, vividness, resplendence, effulgence, refulgence ■ **OPPOSITE:** darkness **3** *The opera house was perfection, all brilliance and glamour.* = **splendour**, glamour, grandeur, magnificence, éclat, gorgeousness, illustriousness, pizzazz or pizazz (*informal*), gilt

brilliant ADJECTIVE **1** *She had a brilliant mind.* = **intelligent**, sharp, intellectual, alert, clever, quick, acute, profound, rational, penetrating, discerning, inventive, astute, brainy (*informal*), perspicacious (*formal*), quick-witted **2** *a brilliant pianist* = **expert**, masterly, talented, gifted, accomplished ■ **OPPOSITE:** untalented **3** *a brilliant success* = **splendid**, grand, famous, celebrated, rare, supreme, outstanding, remarkable, superb, magnificent, sterling, glorious, exceptional, notable, renowned, heroic, admirable, eminent, sublime, illustrious **4** *The event was held in brilliant sunshine.* = **bright**, shining, intense, sparkling, glittering, dazzling, vivid, radiant, luminous, ablaze, resplendent,

scintillating, lustrous, coruscating, refulgent (*literary*), lambent
■ **OPPOSITE:** dark

brim NOUN *He filled her glass right up to the brim.* = **rim**, edge, border, lip, margin, verge (*Brit.*), brink, flange ▶ VERB **1** *They are brimming with confidence.* = **be full**, spill, well over, run over, overflow, spill over, brim over **2** *Michael looked at him imploringly, his eyes brimming with tears.* = **fill**, well over, fill up, overflow

brine NOUN = **salt water**, saline solution, pickling solution

bring VERB **1** *My father brought home a book for me.* = **fetch**, take, carry, bear, transfer, deliver, transport, import, convey **2** *I brought him inside and dried him off.* = **take**, guide, conduct, accompany, escort, usher **3** *The revolution brought more trouble than it was worth.* = **cause**, produce, create, effect, occasion (*formal*), result in, contribute to, inflict, wreak, engender **4** *I could not even bring myself to enter the house.* = **make**, force, influence, convince, persuade, prompt, compel, induce, move, dispose, sway, prevail on or upon • **bring someone up** *She brought up four children.* = **rear**, raise, support, train, develop, teach, nurse, breed, foster, educate, care for, nurture • **bring something about** *The two sides are attempting to bring about fundamental changes.* = **cause**, produce, create, effect, manage, achieve, occasion (*formal*), realize, generate, accomplish, give rise to, make happen, effectuate, bring to pass • **bring something down 1** *They were threatening to bring down the government.* = **overturn**, reduce, undermine, overthrow, abase **2** *The air fares war will bring down prices.* = **reduce**, cut, drop, lower, slash, decrease **3** *The lumberjacks brought the tree down.* = **cut down**, level, fell, hew, lop, raze **4** *Such forces would normally bring the building down.* = **demolish**, level, destroy, dismantle, flatten, knock down, pull down, tear down, bulldoze, raze, kennet (*Austral. slang*), jeff (*Austral. slang*) • **bring something in 1** *They brought in a controversial law.* = **introduce**, start, found, launch, establish, set up, institute, organize, pioneer, initiate, usher in, inaugurate **2** *The business brings in about £60,000 a year.* = **produce**, return, net, realize, generate, be worth, yield, gross, fetch, accrue • **bring something off** *They were about to bring off an even bigger coup.* = **accomplish**, achieve, perform, carry out, succeed, execute, discharge, pull off, carry off, bring to pass • **bring something up** *Why are you bringing that up now?* = **mention**,

raise, introduce, point out, refer to, allude to, broach, call attention to, speak about or of

brink NOUN = **edge**, point, limit, border, lip, margin, boundary, skirt, frontier, fringe, verge (*Brit.*), threshold, rim, brim

brio NOUN = **energy**, spirit, enthusiasm, dash, pep, zip (*informal*), animation, vigour, verve, zest, panache, gusto, get-up-and-go (*informal*), élan, vivacity, liveliness

brisk ADJECTIVE **1** *The horse broke into a brisk trot.* = **quick**, lively, energetic, active, vigorous, animated, bustling, speedy, nimble, agile, sprightly, vivacious, spry
■ **OPPOSITE:** slow **2** *She attempted to reason with him in a rather brisk fashion.* = **short**, sharp, brief, blunt, rude, tart, abrupt, no-nonsense, terse, gruff, pithy, brusque, offhand, monosyllabic, ungracious, uncivil, snappish **3** *The breeze was cool, brisk and invigorating.* = **invigorating**, fresh, biting, sharp, keen, stimulating, crisp, bracing, refreshing, exhilarating, nippy
■ **OPPOSITE:** tiring

briskly ADVERB **1** *Eve walked briskly down the corridor.* = **quickly**, smartly, promptly, rapidly, readily, actively, efficiently, vigorously, energetically, pronto (*informal*), nimbly, posthaste **2** *A trader said gold was selling briskly on the local market.* = **rapidly**, quickly, apace (*literary*), pdq (*slang*) **3** *'Anyhow,' she added briskly, 'it's none of my business.'* = **brusquely**, firmly, decisively, incisively

bristle NOUN *two days' growth of bristles* = **hair**, spine, thorn, whisker, barb, stubble, prickle ▶ VERB **1** *It makes the hair on the nape of my neck bristle.* = **stand up**, rise, prickle, stand on end, horripilate **2** *He bristled with indignation.* = **be angry**, rage, seethe, flare up, bridle, see red, be infuriated, spit (*informal*), go ballistic (*slang*), be maddened, wig out (*slang*), get your dander up (*slang*) **3** *The country bristles with armed groups.* = **abound**, crawl, be alive, hum, swarm, teem, be thick

Briton NOUN = **Brit** (*informal*), limey (*U.S. & Canad. slang*), Britisher, pommy or pom (*Austral. & N.Z. slang*), Anglo-Saxon

brittle ADJECTIVE **1** *Pine is brittle and breaks easily.* = **fragile**, delicate, crisp, crumbling, frail, crumbly, breakable, shivery, friable, frangible, shatterable ■ **OPPOSITE:** tough **2** *a brittle man* = **tense**, nervous, edgy, stiff, wired (*slang*), irritable, curt

broach VERB **1** *Eventually I broached the subject of her early life.* = **bring up**, approach, introduce, mention, speak of, talk of, open up, hint at, touch on, raise the subject of

2 *He would ask the landlord to broach a new barrel of wine.* = **open**, crack, pierce, puncture, uncork

broad ADJECTIVE **1** *His shoulders were broad and his waist narrow.* = **wide**, large, ample, generous, expansive **2** *a broad expanse of lawn* = **large**, huge, comfortable, vast, extensive, ample, spacious, expansive, roomy, voluminous, capacious, uncrowded, commodious, beamy *(of a ship)*, sizable *or* sizeable ■ OPPOSITE: narrow **3** *A broad range of issues was discussed.* = **full**, general, comprehensive, complete, wide, global, catholic, sweeping, extensive, wide-ranging, umbrella, thorough, unlimited, inclusive, far-reaching, exhaustive, all-inclusive, all-embracing, overarching, encyclopedic **4** *a film with broad appeal* = **universal**, general, common, wide, sweeping, worldwide, widespread, wide-ranging, far-reaching **5** *a broad outline of the Society's development* = **general**, loose, vague, approximate, indefinite, ill-defined, inexact, nonspecific, unspecific, undetailed **6** *I was robbed in broad daylight.* = **clear**, open, full, plain **7** *Use wit rather than broad humour.* = **vulgar**, blue, dirty, gross, crude, rude, naughty, coarse, indecent, improper, suggestive, risqué, boorish, uncouth, unrefined, ribald, indelicate, near the knuckle *(informal)*, indecorous, unmannerly

broadcast NOUN *a broadcast on the national radio* = **transmission**, show, programme, telecast, podcast, webcast, vodcast, mobcast ▶ VERB **1** *CNN also broadcasts programmes in Europe.* = **transmit**, show, send, air, radio, cable, beam, send out, relay, televise, disseminate, put on the air, stream *(videos)*, podcast, open-line *(Canad.)* **2** *Don't broadcast your business outside the family.* = **make public**, report, announce, publish, spread, advertise, proclaim, circulate, disseminate, promulgate, shout from the rooftops *(informal)*

broaden VERB = **expand**, increase, develop, spread, extend, stretch, open up, swell, supplement, widen, enlarge, augment ■ OPPOSITE: restrict

broadly ADVERB **1** *He broadly got what he wanted out of his meeting.* = **in general**, largely, generally, mainly, widely, mostly, on the whole, predominantly, in the main, for the most part **2** *Charles grinned broadly.* = **widely**, greatly, hugely, vastly, extensively, expansively **3** *This gives children a more broadly based education.* = **generally**, commonly, widely, universally, popularly ■ OPPOSITE: narrowly

broadside NOUN = **attack**, criticism, censure, swipe, denunciation, diatribe, philippic

brochure NOUN = **booklet**, advertisement, leaflet, hand-out, circular, pamphlet, folder, mailshot, handbill

broekies PLURAL NOUN = **underpants**, pants *(Brit.)*, briefs, drawers, knickers, panties, boxer shorts, Y-fronts®, underdaks *(Austral. slang)*

broke ADJECTIVE = **penniless**, short, ruined, bust *(informal)*, bankrupt, impoverished, in the red, cleaned out *(slang)*, insolvent, down and out, skint *(Brit. slang)*, strapped for cash *(informal)*, dirt-poor *(informal)*, flat broke *(informal)*, penurious, on your uppers, stony-broke *(Brit. slang)*, in queer street *(informal)*, without two pennies to rub together *(informal)*, without a penny to your name ■ OPPOSITE: rich

broken ADJECTIVE **1** *nights of broken sleep* = **interrupted**, disturbed, incomplete, erratic, disconnected, intermittent, fragmentary, spasmodic, discontinuous **2** *Eric could only respond in broken English.* = **imperfect**, halting, hesitating, stammering, disjointed **3** *Damp air came through the broken window.* = **smashed**, destroyed, burst, shattered, fragmented, fractured, demolished, severed, ruptured, rent, separated, shivered **4** *a broken guitar and a rusty snare drum* = **defective**, not working, ruined, imperfect, out of order, not functioning, on the blink *(slang)*, on its last legs, kaput *(informal)* **5** *History is made up of broken promises.* = **violated**, forgotten, ignored, disregarded, not kept, infringed, retracted, disobeyed, dishonoured, transgressed, traduced **6** *He looked a broken man.* = **defeated**, beaten, crushed, humbled, tamed, subdued, oppressed, overpowered, vanquished, demoralized, browbeaten

broken-down ADJECTIVE = **not in working order**, old, worn out, out of order, dilapidated, not functioning, out of commission, on the blink *(slang)*, inoperative, kaput *(informal)*, in disrepair, on the fritz *(U.S. slang)*

brokenhearted ADJECTIVE = **heartbroken**, devastated, disappointed, despairing, miserable, choked, desolate, mournful, prostrated, grief-stricken, sorrowful, wretched, disconsolate, inconsolable, crestfallen, down in the dumps *(informal)*, heart-sick

broker NOUN = **dealer**, marketer, agent, trader, supplier, merchant, entrepreneur, negotiator, chandler, mediator, intermediary, wholesaler, middleman, factor (*Scot.*), purveyor, tradesperson, go-between, merchandiser

bronze ADJECTIVE = **reddish-brown**, copper, tan, rust, chestnut, brownish, copper-coloured, yellowish-brown, reddish-tan, metallic brown

brood NOUN **1** *The last brood of the pair was hatched.* = **offspring**, young, issue, breed, infants, clutch, hatch, litter, chicks, progeny **2** *She flew to the defence of her brood.* = **children**, family, offspring, progeny, nearest and dearest, flesh and blood, ainga (*N.Z.*) ▶ VERB *She constantly broods about her family.* = **think**, obsess, muse, ponder, fret, meditate, agonize, mull over, mope, ruminate, eat your heart out, dwell upon, repine

brook¹ NOUN *He threw the hatchet in the brook.* = **stream**, burn (*Scot. & Northern English*), rivulet, gill (*dialect*), beck, watercourse, rill, streamlet, runnel (*literary*)

brook² VERB *The army will brook no weakening of its power.* = **tolerate**, stand, allow, suffer, accept, bear, stomach, endure, swallow, hack (*slang*), abide, put up with (*informal*), withstand, countenance, support, thole (*dialect*)

brother NOUN **1** *Have you got any brothers and sisters?* = **male sibling 2** *their freedom-loving brothers* = **comrade**, partner, colleague, associate, mate (*informal*), pal (*informal*), companion, cock (*Brit. informal*), chum (*informal*), fellow member, confrère, compeer **3** *priests and religious brothers* = **monk**, cleric, friar, monastic, religious, regular ■ RELATED WORD: *adjective* fraternal

brotherhood NOUN **1** *He believed in the brotherhood of all peoples.* = **fellowship**, kinship, companionship, comradeship, friendliness, camaraderie, brotherliness **2** *a secret international brotherhood* = **association**, order, union, community, society, league, alliance, clan, guild, fraternity (*U.S. & Canad.*), clique, coterie

brotherly ADJECTIVE = **fraternal**, friendly, neighbourly, sympathetic, affectionate, benevolent, kind, amicable, altruistic, philanthropic

brow NOUN **1** *She wrinkled her brow inquisitively.* = **forehead**, temple **2** *He climbed to the brow of the hill.* = **top**, summit, peak, edge, tip, crown, verge, brink, rim, crest, brim

brown ADJECTIVE **1** *her deep brown eyes* = **brunette**, dark, bay, coffee, chocolate, brick, toasted, ginger, rust, chestnut, hazel, dun, auburn, tawny, umber, donkey brown, fuscous **2** *rows of bodies slowly going brown in*

the sun = **tanned**, browned, bronze, bronzed, tan, dusky, sunburnt ▶ VERB *He browned the chicken in a frying pan.* = **fry**, cook, grill, sear, sauté

browse VERB **1** *There are plenty of biographies for him to browse.* = **skim**, scan, glance at, survey, look through, look round, dip into, leaf through, peruse, flip through, examine cursorily **2** *three red deer stags browsing 50 yards from my lodge* = **graze**, eat, feed, crop, pasture, nibble

bruise NOUN *How did you get that bruise on your cheek?* = **discoloration**, mark, injury, trauma (*Pathology*), blemish, black mark, contusion (*formal*), black-and-blue mark ▶ VERB **1** *I had only bruised my knee.* = **hurt**, injure, mark, blacken **2** *Be sure to store them carefully or they'll get bruised.* = **damage**, mark, mar, blemish, discolour **3** *My ego is easily bruised.* = **injure**, hurt, pain, wound, slight, insult, sting, offend, grieve, displease, rile, pique

bruiser NOUN = **tough**, heavy (*slang*), rough (*informal*), bully, thug, gorilla (*informal*), hard man, rowdy, tough guy, hoodlum (*informal*), bully boy, ruffian, roughneck (*slang*)

brunt NOUN = **full force**, force, pressure, violence, shock, stress, impact, strain, burden, thrust

brush¹ NOUN **1** *Scrub lightly with a brush, then rinse.* = **broom**, sweeper, besom **2** *It is his third brush with the law in less than a year.* = **conflict**, fight, clash, set-to (*informal*), scrap (*informal*), confrontation, skirmish, tussle, fracas, spot of bother (*informal*), slight engagement **3** *the trauma of a brush with death* = **encounter**, meeting, confrontation, rendezvous ▶ VERB **1** *Have you brushed your teeth?* = **clean**, wash, polish, buff **2** *I felt her hair brushing the back of my shoulder.* = **touch**, come into contact with, sweep, kiss, stroke, glance, flick, scrape, graze, caress • **brush someone off** *She just brushed me off.* = **ignore**, cut (*informal*), reject, dismiss, slight, blank (*slang*), put down, snub, disregard, scorn, disdain, spurn, rebuff, repudiate, disown, cold-shoulder, kiss off (*slang, chiefly U.S. & Canad.*), send to Coventry • **brush something aside** *He brushed aside my views on politics.* = **dismiss**, ignore, discount, override, disregard, sweep aside, have no time for, kiss off (*slang, chiefly U.S. & Canad.*) • **brush something up** *or* **brush up on something** *I had hoped to brush up my Spanish.* = **revise**, study, go over, cram, polish up, read up on, relearn, bone up on (*informal*), refresh your memory

brush² NOUN *a meadow of low brush and grass* = **shrubs**, bushes, scrub, underwood, undergrowth, thicket, copse, brushwood

brusque ADJECTIVE = **curt**, short, sharp, blunt, tart, abrupt, hasty, terse, surly, gruff, impolite, monosyllabic, discourteous, unmannerly ■ **OPPOSITE:** polite

brutal ADJECTIVE **1** *He was the victim of a very brutal murder.* = **cruel**, harsh, savage, grim, vicious, ruthless, ferocious, callous, sadistic, heartless, atrocious, inhuman, merciless, cold-blooded, inhumane, brutish, bloodthirsty, remorseless, barbarous, pitiless, uncivilized, hard-hearted ■ **OPPOSITE:** kind **2** *She spoke with a brutal honesty.* = **harsh**, tough, severe, rough, rude, indifferent, insensitive, callous, merciless, unconcerned, uncaring, gruff, bearish, tactless, unfeeling, impolite, uncivil, unmannerly ■ **OPPOSITE:** sensitive

brutality NOUN = **cruelty**, atrocity, ferocity, savagery, ruthlessness, barbarism, inhumanity, barbarity, viciousness, brutishness, bloodthirstiness, savageness

brutally ADVERB = **cruelly**, fiercely, savagely, ruthlessly, viciously, mercilessly, ferociously, remorselessly, in cold blood, callously, murderously, pitilessly, heartlessly, inhumanly, barbarously, brutishly, barbarically, hardheartedly

brute NOUN **1** *a drunken brute* = **savage**, devil, monster, beast, barbarian, fiend, swine, ogre, ghoul, sadist **2** *a big brute of a dog* = **beast**, animal, creature, wild animal ▸ ADJECTIVE *He used brute force to take control.* = **physical**, bodily, mindless, instinctive, senseless, unthinking

brutish ADJECTIVE = **coarse**, stupid, gross, cruel, savage, crude, vulgar, barbarian, crass, boorish, uncouth, loutish, subhuman, swinish

bubble NOUN *a bubble of gas trapped under the surface* = **air ball**, drop, bead, blister, blob, droplet, globule, vesicle ▸ VERB **1** *Heat the seasoned stock until it is bubbling.* = **boil**, seethe **2** *The fermenting wine bubbled over the top.* = **foam**, fizz, froth, churn, agitate, percolate, effervesce **3** *He looked at the stream bubbling through the trees nearby.* = **gurgle**, splash, murmur, trickle, ripple, babble, trill, burble, lap, purl, plash

bubbly ADJECTIVE **1** *a bubbly girl who likes to laugh* = **lively**, happy, excited, animated, merry, bouncy, elated, sparky, alive and kicking, full of beans (*informal*) **2** *a nice hot bubbly bath* = **frothy**, sparkling, fizzy, effervescent, carbonated, foamy, sudsy, lathery

buccaneer NOUN = **pirate**, privateer, corsair, freebooter, sea-rover

buckle NOUN *He wore a belt with a large brass buckle.* = **fastener**, catch, clip, clasp, hasp ▸ VERB **1** *A man came out buckling his belt.* = **fasten**, close, secure, hook, clasp **2** *A freak wave had buckled the deck.* = **distort**, bend, warp, crumple, contort **3** *My right leg buckled under me.* = **collapse**, bend, twist, fold, give way, subside, cave in, crumple
• **buckle down** *I just buckled down and got on with playing.* = **apply yourself**, set to, fall to, pitch in, get busy, get cracking (*informal*), exert yourself, put your shoulder to the wheel

bud NOUN *The first buds appeared on the trees.* = **shoot**, branch, sprout, twig, sprig, offshoot, scion ▸ VERB *The leaves were budding on the trees now.* = **develop**, grow, shoot, sprout, burgeon, burst forth, pullulate

budding ADJECTIVE = **developing**, beginning, growing, promising, potential, burgeoning, fledgling, embryonic

buddy NOUN = **friend**, mate (*informal*), pal, companion, comrade, chum (*informal*), crony, blood or blud (*Brit. slang*), main man (*slang, chiefly U.S.*), homeboy (*slang, chiefly U.S.*), cobber (*Austral. & N.Z., old-fashioned, informal*), E hoa (*N.Z.*)

budge VERB **1** *Both sides say they will not budge.* = **yield**, change, bend, concede, surrender, comply, give way, capitulate **2** *The Prime Minister was not to be budged by the verbal assault.* = **persuade**, influence, convince, sway **3** *The snake still refused to budge.* = **move**, roll, slide, stir, give way, change position **4** *I pulled and pulled but I couldn't budge it.* = **dislodge**, move, push, roll, remove, transfer, shift, slide, stir, propel

budget NOUN *A designer would be beyond their budget.* = **allowance**, means, funds, income, finances, resources, allocation ▸ VERB *I'm learning how to budget my finances.* = **plan**, estimate, allocate, cost, ration, apportion, cost out

buff¹ ADJECTIVE *a buff envelope* = **fawn**, cream, tan, beige, yellowish, ecru, straw-coloured, sand-coloured, yellowish-brown, biscuit-coloured, camel-coloured, oatmeal-coloured ▸ VERB *He was already buffing the car's hubs.* = **polish**, clean, smooth, brush, shine, rub, wax, brighten, burnish • **in the buff** *My character had to appear in the buff for some scenes.* = **naked**, bare, nude, in the raw (*informal*), unclothed, in the altogether (*informal*), buck naked (*slang*), unclad, in your birthday suit (*informal*), scuddy (*slang*), without a stitch on (*informal*), with bare skin, in the bare scud (*Scot. slang*)

buff² NOUN *She is a real film buff.* = **expert**, fan, addict, enthusiast, freak (*informal*), admirer, whizz (*informal*), devotee, connoisseur, fiend (*informal*), grandmaster, hotshot (*informal*), aficionado, wonk (*informal*), maven (*U.S.*), fundi (*S. African*)

buffer NOUN = **safeguard**, screen, shield, cushion, intermediary, bulwark

buffet¹ NOUN **1** *A cold buffet had been laid out in the dining room.* = **smorgasbord**, counter, cold table **2** *We sat in the station buffet sipping tea.* = **snack bar**, café, cafeteria, brasserie, salad bar, refreshment counter

buffet² VERB *Their plane had been severely buffeted by storms.* = **knock**, push, bang, rap, slap, bump, smack, shove, thump, cuff, jolt, wallop (*informal*), box

buffoon NOUN = **clown**, fool, comic, comedian, wag, joker, jester, dag (*N.Z. informal*), harlequin, droll, silly billy (*informal*), joculator or (*fem.*) joculatrix

bug NOUN **1** *I think I've got a bit of a stomach bug.* = **illness**, disease, complaint, virus, infection, disorder, sickness, ailment, malaise, affliction, malady, lurgy (*informal*) **2** *There is a bug in the software.* = **fault**, failing, virus, error, defect, flaw, blemish, imperfection, glitch, gremlin, malware **3** *I've definitely been bitten by the gardening bug.* = **mania**, passion, rage, obsession, craze, fad, thing (*informal*) ▸ VERB **1** *He heard they were planning to bug his office.* = **tap**, eavesdrop, listen in on, wiretap **2** *I only did it to bug my parents.* = **annoy**, bother, disturb, needle (*informal*), plague, irritate, harass, hassle (*informal*), aggravate (*informal*), badger, gall, nettle, pester, vex, irk, get under your skin (*informal*), get on your nerves (*informal*), nark (*Brit., Austral. & N.Z. slang*), get up your nose (*informal*), be on your back (*slang*), get in your hair (*informal*), get on your wick (*Brit. slang*), hack you off (*informal*)

build VERB **1** *Developers are now proposing to build a hotel on the site.* = **construct**, make, raise, put up, assemble, erect, fabricate, form ■ **OPPOSITE:** demolish **2** *I wanted to build a relationship with my team.* = **establish**, start, begin, found, base, set up, institute, constitute, initiate, originate, formulate, inaugurate ■ **OPPOSITE:** finish **3** *Diplomats hope the meetings will build mutual trust.* = **develop**, increase, improve, extend, strengthen, intensify, enlarge, amplify, augment ■ **OPPOSITE:** decrease ▸ NOUN *the smallness of his build* = **physique**, form, body, figure, shape, structure, frame • **build**

something up *We can build up speed gradually and safely.* = **increase**, develop, improve, extend, expand, add to, strengthen, enhance, reinforce, intensify, heighten, fortify, amplify, augment

building NOUN = **structure**, house, construction, dwelling (*formal, literary*), erection, edifice, domicile, pile

build-up NOUN **1** *a build-up of troops* = **increase**, development, growth, expansion, accumulation, enlargement, escalation, upsurge, intensification, augmentation **2** *a build-up of gases in the city's sewers* = **accumulation**, accretion **3** *the build-up for the film* = **hype**, promotion, publicity, plug (*informal*), puff, razzmatazz (*slang*), brouhaha, ballyhoo (*informal*)

built-in ADJECTIVE = **essential**, integral, included, incorporated, inherent, implicit, in-built, intrinsic, inseparable, immanent

bulbous ADJECTIVE = **bulging**, rounded, swelling, swollen, bloated, convex

bulge VERB **1** *He bulges out of his black T-shirt.* = **swell out**, project, expand, swell, stand out, stick out, protrude, puff out, distend, bag **2** *Her eyes seemed to bulge like those of a toad.* = **stick out**, stand out, protrude ▸ NOUN **1** *Why won't those bulges on your hips and thighs go?* = **lump**, swelling, bump, projection, hump, protuberance, protrusion ■ **OPPOSITE:** hollow **2** *a bulge in aircraft sales* = **increase**, rise, boost, surge, intensification

bulk NOUN **1** *the shadowy bulk of an ancient barn* = **size**, volume, dimensions, magnitude, substance, vastness, amplitude, immensity, bigness, largeness, massiveness **2** *Despite his bulk he moved lightly on his feet.* = **weight**, size, mass, heaviness, poundage, portliness **3** *The vast bulk of imports and exports is carried by sea.* = **majority**, mass, most, body, quantity, best part, major part, lion's share, better part, generality, preponderance, main part, plurality, nearly all, greater number • **bulk large** *Propaganda bulks large in their plans.* = **be important**, dominate, loom, stand out, loom large, carry weight, preponderate, threaten

> **USAGE** The use of a plural noun after *bulk*, when it has the meaning 'majority', although common, is considered by some to be incorrect and should be avoided. This usage is most commonly encountered, according to the Bank of English, when referring to *funds* and *profits*: *the bulk of our profits stem from the sale of beer.* The synonyms *majority* and *most* would work better in this context.

b

bulky ADJECTIVE = **large**, big, huge, heavy, massive, enormous, substantial, immense, mega (*slang*), very large, mammoth, colossal, cumbersome, weighty, hulking, unwieldy, ponderous, voluminous, unmanageable, elephantine, massy, ginormous (*informal*), humongous or humungous (*informal*) ■ **OPPOSITE:** small

bulldoze VERB **1** *She defeated developers who wanted to bulldoze her home.* = **demolish**, level, destroy, flatten, knock down, tear down, raze, kennet (*Austral. slang*), jeff (*Austral. slang*) **2** *He bulldozed through the Tigers' defence.* = **push**, force, drive, thrust, shove, propel **3** *My parents tried to bulldoze me into going to college.* = **force**, bully, intimidate, railroad (*informal*), cow, hector, coerce, dragoon, browbeat, put the screws on

bullet NOUN = **projectile**, ball, shot, missile, slug, pellet

bulletin NOUN = **report**, account, statement, message, communication, announcement, dispatch, communiqué, notification, news flash

bully NOUN *I fell victim to the office bully.* = **persecutor**, tough, oppressor, tormentor, bully boy, browbeater, coercer, ruffian, intimidator ▶ VERB **1** *I wasn't going to let him bully me.* = **persecute**, intimidate, torment, hound, oppress, pick on, victimize, terrorize, push around (*slang*), ill-treat, ride roughshod over, maltreat, tyrannize, overbear **2** *She used to bully me into doing my schoolwork.* = **force**, coerce, railroad (*informal*), bulldoze (*informal*), dragoon, pressurize, browbeat, cow, hector, press-gang, domineer, bullyrag

bulwark NOUN **1** *a bulwark against the English* = **fortification**, defence, bastion, buttress, rampart, redoubt, outwork **2** *a bulwark of democracy* = **defence**, support, safeguard, security, guard, buffer, mainstay

bumbling ADJECTIVE = **clumsy**, awkward, blundering, bungling, incompetent, inefficient, lumbering, inept, maladroit, unco (*Austral. slang*) ■ **OPPOSITE:** efficient

bump VERB **1** *He bumped his head on the low beam.* = **knock**, hit, strike, crash, smash, slam, bang **2** *We left the road again and bumped over the mountainside.* = **jerk**, shake, bounce, rattle, jar, jog, lurch, jolt, jostle, jounce ▶ NOUN **1** *Small children often cry after a minor bump.* = **knock**, hit, blow, shock, impact, rap, collision, thump **2** *I felt a little bump and knew instinctively what had happened.* = **thud**, crash, knock, smash, bang, smack, thump, clump, wallop (*informal*), clunk, clonk **3** *She got a large bump*

on her forehead. = **lump**, swelling, bulge, hump, node, nodule, protuberance, contusion (*formal*) • **bump into someone** *I happened to bump into Federico in the hallway.* = **meet**, encounter, come across, run into, run across, meet up with, chance upon, happen upon, light upon • **bump someone off** *They will probably bump you off anyway.* = **murder**, kill, assassinate, remove, do in (*slang*), eliminate, take out (*slang*), wipe out (*informal*), dispatch, finish off, do away with, blow away (*slang, chiefly U.S.*), knock off (*slang*), liquidate, rub out (*U.S. slang*)

bumper ADJECTIVE = **exceptional**, excellent, exo (*Austral. slang*), massive, unusual, mega (*slang*), jumbo (*informal*), abundant, whacking (*informal, chiefly Brit.*), spanking (*informal*), whopping (*informal*), bountiful

bumpy ADJECTIVE **1** *bumpy cobbled streets* = **uneven**, rough, pitted, irregular, rutted, lumpy, potholed, knobby **2** *a hot and bumpy journey across the desert* = **jolting**, jarring, bouncy, choppy, jerky, bone-breaking, jolty

bunch NOUN **1** (*informal*) *The players were a great bunch.* = **group**, band, crowd, party, team, troop, gathering, crew (*informal*), gang, knot, mob, flock, swarm, multitude, posse (*informal*), bevy **2** *He had left a huge bunch of flowers in her hotel room.* = **bouquet**, spray, sheaf **3** *She had fallen asleep clutching a fat bunch of grapes.* = **cluster**, clump • **bunch together** or **up** *People bunched up at all the exits.* = **group**, crowd, mass, collect, assemble, cluster, flock, herd, huddle, congregate

bundle NOUN *He gathered the bundles of clothing into his arms.* = **bunch**, group, collection, mass, pile, quantity, stack, heap, rick, batch, accumulation, assortment ▶ VERB *They bundled him into a taxi.* = **push**, thrust, shove, throw, rush, hurry, hasten, jostle, hustle • **bundle someone up** *Harry greeted them bundled up in a long coat and a fur hat.* = **wrap up**, swathe, muffle up, clothe warmly • **bundle something up** *possessions bundled up and carried in weary arms* = **package**, tie, pack, bind, wrap, tie up, bale, fasten, truss, tie together, palletize

bungle VERB = **mess up**, blow (*slang*), ruin, spoil, blunder, fudge, screw up (*informal*), botch, cock up (*Brit. slang*), miscalculate, make a mess of, mismanage, muff, foul up, make a nonsense of (*informal*), bodge (*informal*), make a pig's ear of (*informal*), flub (*U.S. slang*), crool or cruel (*Austral. slang*), louse up (*slang*) ■ **OPPOSITE:** accomplish

bungling ADJECTIVE = **incompetent**, blundering, awkward, clumsy, inept, botching, cack-handed (informal), maladroit, ham-handed (informal), unskilful, ham-fisted (informal), unco (Austral. slang)

bunk² or **bunkum** NOUN Henry Ford's opinion was that 'history is bunk'. = **nonsense**, rubbish, rot, crap (slang), garbage (informal), trash, hot air (informal), tosh (slang, chiefly Brit.), bilge (informal), twaddle, tripe (informal), guff (slang), havers (Scot.), moonshine, malarkey, baloney (informal), hogwash, bizzo (Austral. slang), bull's wool (Austral. & N.Z. slang), hokum (slang, chiefly U.S. & Canad.), piffle (informal), tomfoolery, poppycock (informal), balderdash, bosh (informal), eyewash (informal), kak (S. African vulgar slang), stuff and nonsense, hooey (slang), tommyrot, horsefeathers (U.S. slang), tarradiddle

bunk³ NOUN • **do a bunk** The castle gatekeeper had done a bunk, but the caretaker let us in. = **run away**, flee, bolt, clear out (informal), beat it (slang), abscond, decamp, do a runner (slang), run for it (informal), cut and run (informal), scram (informal), fly the coop (U.S. & Canad. informal), skedaddle (informal), take a powder (U.S. & Canad. slang), take it on the lam (U.S. & Canad. slang), do a Skase (Austral. informal)

buoy NOUN We released the buoy and drifted back on the tide. = **float**, guide, signal, marker, beacon • **buoy someone up** They are buoyed up by a sense of hope. = **encourage**, support, boost, cheer, sustain, hearten, cheer up, keep afloat, gee up

buoyancy NOUN **1** Air can be pumped into the diving suit to increase buoyancy. = **floatability**, lightness, weightlessness **2** a mood of buoyancy and optimism = **cheerfulness**, bounce (informal), pep, animation, good humour, high spirits, zing (informal), liveliness, spiritedness, cheeriness, sunniness

buoyant ADJECTIVE **1** She was in a buoyant mood. = **cheerful**, happy, bright, lively, sunny, animated, upbeat (informal), joyful, carefree, bouncy, breezy, genial, jaunty, chirpy (informal), sparky, vivacious, debonair, blithe, full of beans (informal), peppy (informal), light-hearted ■ OPPOSITE: gloomy **2** a small and buoyant boat = **floating**, light, floatable

burden NOUN **1** Her illness will be an impossible burden on him. = **trouble**, care, worry, trial, weight, responsibility, stress, strain, anxiety, sorrow, grievance, affliction, onus, albatross, millstone, encumbrance **2** She heaved her burden into the back. = **load**, weight, cargo, freight, bale, consignment, encumbrance ▸ VERB We decided not to burden him with the news. = **weigh down**, worry, load, tax, strain, bother, overwhelm, handicap, oppress, inconvenience, overload, saddle with, encumber, trammel, incommode ■ RELATED WORD: adjective onerous

burdensome ADJECTIVE = **troublesome**, trying, taxing, difficult, heavy, crushing, exacting, oppressive, weighty, onerous, irksome

bureau NOUN **1** the foreign employment bureau = **agency** **2** the paper's Washington bureau = **office**, department, section, branch, station, unit, division, subdivision **3** A simple writing bureau sat in front of the window. = **desk**, writing desk

bureaucracy NOUN **1** State bureaucracies tend to stifle enterprise and initiative. = **government**, officials, authorities, administration, ministry, the system, civil service, directorate, officialdom, corridors of power **2** People complain about having to deal with too much bureaucracy. = **red tape**, regulations, officialdom, officialese, bumbledom

bureaucrat NOUN = **official**, minister, officer, administrator, civil servant, public servant, functionary, apparatchik, office-holder, mandarin

burglar NOUN = **housebreaker**, thief, robber, pilferer, filcher, cat burglar, sneak thief, picklock

burglary NOUN = **breaking and entering**, housebreaking, break-in, home invasion (Austral. & N.Z.)

burial NOUN = **funeral**, interment, burying, obsequies, entombment, inhumation, exequies, sepulture

burial ground NOUN = **graveyard**, cemetery, churchyard, necropolis, God's acre

burlesque NOUN The book read like a black comic burlesque. = **parody**, mockery, satire, caricature, send-up (Brit. informal), spoof (informal), travesty, takeoff (informal) ▸ ADJECTIVE a trio of burlesque stereotypes = **satirical**, comic, mocking, mock, farcical, travestying, ironical, parodic, mock-heroic, caricatural, hudibrastic

burly ADJECTIVE = **brawny**, strong, powerful, big, strapping, hefty, muscular, swole (slang), hench (informal), sturdy, stout, bulky, stocky, hulking, beefy (informal), well-built, thickset ■ OPPOSITE: scrawny

burn VERB **1** I suddenly realized the blanket was burning. = **be on fire**, blaze, be ablaze, smoke, flame, glow, flare, flicker, go up in flames **2** *He found out he'd won the Lottery, but he'd burnt the ticket.* = **set on fire**, light, ignite, kindle, incinerate, reduce to ashes **3** *I burnt the toast.* = **scorch**, toast, sear, char, singe, brand **4** *smoke that burns and stings your eyes* = **sting**, hurt, smart, tingle, bite, pain **5** *She was burning with a fierce ambition.* = **be passionate**, blaze, be excited, be aroused, be inflamed **6** *He was burning with rage.* = **seethe**, fume, be angry, simmer, smoulder

burning ADJECTIVE **1** *I had a burning ambition to become a journalist.* = **intense**, passionate, earnest, eager, frantic, frenzied, ardent, fervent, impassioned, zealous, vehement, all-consuming, fervid ■ **OPPOSITE:** mild **2** *a burning question* = **crucial** (*informal*), important, pressing, significant, essential, vital, critical, acute, compelling, urgent

burnish VERB = **polish**, shine, buff, brighten, rub up, furbish (*formal*)
■ **OPPOSITE:** scuff

burrow NOUN *a rabbit's burrow* = **hole**, shelter, tunnel, den, lair, retreat ▶ VERB **1** *The larvae burrow into cracks in the floor.* = **dig**, tunnel, excavate **2** *He burrowed into the pile of charts.* = **delve**, search, dig, probe, ferret, rummage, forage, fossick (*Austral. & N.Z.*)

burst VERB **1** *The driver lost control when a tyre burst.* = **explode**, blow up, break, split, crack, shatter, fragment, shiver, disintegrate, puncture, rupture, rend asunder **2** *Water burst through the dam and flooded their villages.* = **rush**, run, break, break out, erupt, spout, gush forth **3** *Gunmen burst into his home and opened fire.* = **barge**, charge, rush, shove ▶ NOUN **1** *short bursts of activity* = **rush**, surge, fit, outbreak, outburst, spate, gush, torrent, eruption, spurt, outpouring **2** *a burst of machine-gun fire* = **explosion**, crack, blast, blasting, bang, discharge

bury VERB **1** *soldiers who helped to bury the dead* = **inter**, lay to rest, entomb, sepulchre, consign to the grave, inearth, inhume, inurn ■ **OPPOSITE:** dig up **2** *She buried it under some leaves.* = **hide**, cover, conceal, stash (*informal*), secrete, cache, stow away ■ **OPPOSITE:** uncover **3** *She buried her face in the pillows.* = **sink**, embed, immerse, enfold **4** *It is time to bury our past misunderstandings.* = **forget**, draw a veil over, think no more of, put in the past, not give another thought to **5** *His reaction was to withdraw, to bury himself in work.* = **engross**, involve, occupy, interest, busy, engage, absorb, preoccupy, immerse

bush NOUN *Trees and bushes grow down to the water's edge.* = **shrub**, plant, hedge, thicket, shrubbery • **the bush** *He caught sunstroke while travelling in the bush.* = **the wilds**, brush, scrub, woodland, backwoods, back country (*U.S.*), scrubland, backlands (*U.S.*)

bushy ADJECTIVE = **thick**, bristling, spreading, rough, stiff, fuzzy, fluffy, unruly, shaggy, wiry, luxuriant, bristly

busily ADVERB = **actively**, briskly, intently, earnestly, strenuously, speedily, purposefully, diligently, energetically, assiduously, industriously

business NOUN **1** *young people seeking a career in business* = **trade**, selling, trading, industry, manufacturing, commerce, dealings, merchandising **2** *The company was a family business.* = **establishment**, company, firm, concern, organization, corporation, venture, enterprise **3** *May I ask what business you are in?* = **profession**, work, calling, job, line, trade, career, function, employment, craft, occupation, pursuit, vocation, métier **4** *Parenting can be a stressful business.* = **matter**, issue, subject, point, problem, question, responsibility, task, duty, function, topic, assignment **5** *How much I earn is my own business.* = **concern**, affair

businesslike ADJECTIVE = **efficient**, professional, practical, regular, correct, organized, routine, thorough, systematic, orderly, matter-of-fact, methodical, well-ordered, workaday ■ **OPPOSITE:** inefficient

businessman *or* **businesswoman** *or* **businessperson** NOUN = **executive**, director, manager, merchant, capitalist, administrator, entrepreneur, tycoon, industrialist, financier, tradesperson, homme *or* femme d'affaires (*French*)

bust¹ NOUN *Her bust measurement is 38.* = **bosom**, breasts, chest, front

bust² (*informal*) VERB **1** *They will have to bust the door to get him out.* = **break**, smash, split, burst, shatter, fracture, rupture, break into fragments **2** *They were busted for possession of cannabis.* = **arrest**, catch, lift (*slang*), raid, cop (*slang*), nail (*informal*), collar (*informal*), nab (*informal*), feel your collar (*slang*)
▶ NOUN *He was imprisoned after a drug bust.* = **arrest**, capture, raid, cop (*slang*) • **go bust** *Hundreds of restaurants went bust last year.* = **go bankrupt**, fail, break, be ruined, become insolvent

bustle VERB *My parents bustled around the kitchen.* = **hurry**, tear, rush, dash, scramble, fuss, flutter, beetle, hasten, scuttle, scurry, scamper ■ **OPPOSITE:** idle ▶ NOUN *the hustle and bustle of modern life* = **activity**, to-do, stir, excitement, hurry, fuss, flurry, haste, agitation, commotion, ado, tumult, hurly-burly, pother (*literary*) ■ **OPPOSITE:** inactivity

bustling ADJECTIVE = **busy**, full, crowded, rushing, active, stirring, lively, buzzing, energetic, humming, swarming, thronged, hustling, teeming, astir

busy ADJECTIVE **1** *He's a very busy man.* = **active**, brisk, diligent, industrious, assiduous, rushed off your feet ■ **OPPOSITE:** idle **2** *Life is what happens to you while you're busy making other plans.* = **occupied with**, working, engaged in, on duty, employed in, hard at work, engrossed in, in harness, on active service ■ **OPPOSITE:** unoccupied **3** *I'd had a busy day and was rather tired.* = **hectic**, full, active, tiring, exacting, energetic, strenuous, on the go (*informal*) • **busy yourself** *He busied himself with the camera.* = **occupy yourself**, be engrossed, immerse yourself, involve yourself, amuse yourself, absorb yourself, employ yourself, engage yourself, keep busy or occupied

but CONJUNCTION *'But,' he added, 'the vast majority must accept a common future.'* = **however**, still, yet, nevertheless ▶ PREPOSITION *He was forced to wind up everything but the hotel business.* = **except (for)**, save, bar, barring, excepting, excluding, with the exception of ▶ ADVERB *St Anton is but a snowball's throw away from Lech.* = **only**, just, simply, merely

butcher NOUN *This bunch are mere brutes and butchers.* = **murderer**, killer, slaughterer, slayer, destroyer, liquidator, executioner, cut-throat, exterminator ▶ VERB **1** *Flint was used for butchering meat in the Stone Age.* = **slaughter**, prepare, carve, cut up, dress, cut, clean, joint **2** *Our people are being butchered in their own homes.* = **kill**, slaughter, massacre, destroy, cut down, assassinate, slay (*archaic, literary*), liquidate, exterminate, put to the sword **3** *I am not in Cannes because they butchered my film.* = **mess up**, destroy, ruin, wreck, spoil, mutilate, botch, bodge (*informal*)

butchery NOUN = **slaughter**, killing, murder, massacre, bloodshed, carnage, mass murder, blood-letting, blood bath

butt¹ NOUN **1** *Troops used tear gas and rifle butts to break up the protests.* = **end**, handle, shaft, stock, shank, hilt, haft **2** *He paused to stub out the butt of his cigar.* = **stub**, end, base, foot, tip, tail, leftover, fag end (*informal*)

butt² NOUN *He is still the butt of cruel jokes about his humble origins.* = **target**, victim, object, point, mark, subject, dupe, laughing stock, Aunt Sally

butt³ VERB *The male butted me.* = **knock**, push, bump, punch, buck, thrust, ram, shove, poke, buffet, prod, jab, bunt • **butt in 1** *Nobody asked you to butt in.* = **interfere**, meddle, intrude, heckle, barge in (*informal*), stick your nose in, put your oar in **2** *Could I just butt in here and say something?* = **interrupt**, cut in, break in, chip in (*informal*), put your two cents in (*U.S. slang*)

butt⁴ NOUN *The hose is great for watering your garden from your water butt.* = **cask**, drum, barrel, cylinder

butter VERB • **butter someone up** = **flatter**, coax, cajole, pander to, blarney, wheedle, suck up to (*informal*), soft-soap, fawn on or upon

butterfly NOUN ■ **RELATED WORDS:** *name of young* caterpillar, chrysalis, chrysalid; *enthusiast* lepidopterist

buttocks NOUN = **bottom** (*informal*), behind (*informal*), bum (*Brit. slang*), backside (*informal*), seat, rear (*informal*), tail (*informal*), butt (*U.S. & Canad. informal*), buns (*U.S. slang*), rump, posterior, haunches, hindquarters, derrière (*euphemistic*), tush (*U.S. slang*), fundament (*euphemistic*), gluteus maximus (*Anatomy*), jacksy (*Brit. slang*)

buttonhole VERB = **detain**, catch, grab, intercept, accost, waylay, take aside

buttress NOUN *a buttress of rock* = **support**, shore, prop, brace, pier, reinforcement, strut, mainstay, stanchion, stay, abutment ▶ VERB *His tough line is buttressed by a democratic mandate.* = **support**, sustain, strengthen, shore, prop, reinforce, back up, brace, uphold, bolster, prop up, shore up, augment

buxom ADJECTIVE = **plump**, ample, voluptuous, busty, well-rounded, curvaceous (*informal*), comely (*old-fashioned*), bosomy, full-bosomed ■ **OPPOSITE:** slender

buy VERB *He could not afford to buy a house.* = **purchase**, get, score (*slang*), secure, pay for, obtain, acquire, invest in, shop for, procure ■ **OPPOSITE:** sell ▶ NOUN *a good buy* = **purchase**, deal (*informal*), bargain, acquisition, steal (*informal*), snip (*informal*), giveaway • **buy someone off** *policies designed to buy off reluctant voters* = **bribe**, square, fix (*informal*), pay off (*informal*), lure, corrupt, get at, suborn, grease someone's palm (*slang*), influence by gifts, oil the palm of (*informal*)

buzz VERB *Attack helicopters buzzed across the city.* = **hum**, whizz, drone, whir ▶ NOUN **1** *the irritating buzz of an insect* = **hum**, buzzing, murmur, drone, whir, bombilation or bombination (*literary*) **2** *The buzz is that she knows something.* = **gossip**, news, report, latest (*informal*), word, scandal, rumour, whisper (*informal*), dirt (*slang*), gen (*Brit. informal*), hearsay, scuttlebutt (*U.S. slang*), goss (*informal*)

by PREPOSITION **1** *The feast was served by smart waiters in black shirts.* = **through**, under the aegis of, through the agency of **2** *The train passes by Oxford.* = **via**, over, by way of **3** *She was sitting in a rocking chair by the window.* = **near**, past, along, close to, closest to, neighbouring, next to, beside, nearest to, adjoining, adjacent to ▸ ADVERB *Large numbers of security police stood by.* = **nearby**, close, handy, at hand, within reach • **by and by** *By and by the light gradually grew fainter.* = **presently**, shortly, soon, eventually, one day, before long, in a while, anon (*archaic, literary*), in the course of time, erelong (*archaic, poetic*)

bygone ADJECTIVE = **past**, former, previous, lost, forgotten, ancient, of old, one-time, departed, extinct, gone by, past recall, sunk in oblivion
■ **OPPOSITE:** future

bypass VERB **1** *Regulators worry that controls could easily be bypassed.* = **get round**, avoid, evade, circumvent (*formal*), outmanoeuvre, body-swerve **2** *Money for new roads to bypass cities.* = **go round**, skirt, circumvent, depart from, deviate from, pass round, detour round ■ **OPPOSITE:** cross

bystander NOUN = **onlooker**, passer-by, spectator, witness, observer, viewer, looker-on, watcher, eyewitness
■ **OPPOSITE:** participant

byword NOUN = **saying**, slogan, motto, maxim, gnome, adage, proverb, epithet, dictum, precept, aphorism, saw (*old-fashioned*), apophthegm

Cc

cab NOUN = **taxi**, minicab, taxicab, hackney, hackney carriage

cabal NOUN 1 *He had been chosen by a cabal of fellow senators.* = **clique**, set, party, league, camp, coalition, faction, caucus, junta, coterie, schism, confederacy, conclave 2 *The left saw it as a bourgeois cabal.* = **plot**, scheme, intrigue, conspiracy, machination

cabin NOUN 1 *The steward showed her to a small cabin.* = **room**, berth, quarters, compartment, deckhouse 2 *a log cabin in the woods* = **hut**, shed, cottage, lodge, cot (*archaic*), shack, chalet, shanty, hovel, bothy, whare (*N.Z.*)

cabinet NOUN 1 = **cupboard**, case, locker, dresser, closet (*U.S.*), press, chiffonier 2 (*often cap.*) = **council**, committee, administration, ministry, assembly, board

cache NOUN = **store**, fund, supply, reserve, treasury, accumulation, stockpile, hoard, stash (*informal*)

cackle VERB *The woman cackled with glee.* = **laugh**, giggle, chuckle ▸ NOUN *He let out a brief cackle of triumph.* = **laugh**, giggle, chuckle

cacophony NOUN = **discord**, racket, din, dissonance, disharmony, stridency

cad NOUN = **scoundrel** (*slang*), rat (*informal*), bounder (*Brit., old-fashioned slang*), cur, knave (*archaic*), rotter (*slang, chiefly Brit.*), heel, scumbag (*slang*), churl, dastard (*archaic*), wrong 'un (*slang*)

cadence NOUN 1 *He recognised the Polish cadences in her voice.* = **intonation**, accent, inflection, modulation 2 *There was a sudden shift in the cadence of the music.* = **rhythm**, beat, measure (*Prosody*), metre, pulse, throb, tempo, swing, lilt

café NOUN = **snack bar**, restaurant, cafeteria, coffee shop, brasserie, coffee bar, tearoom, lunchroom, eatery or eaterie

cage NOUN *I hate to see animals being kept in cages.* = **enclosure**, pen, coop, hutch, pound, corral (*U.S.*) ▸ VERB *Don't you think it's cruel to cage wild creatures?* = **shut up**, confine, restrain, imprison, lock up, mew, incarcerate, fence in, impound, coop up, immure (*archaic*), pound

cagey or **cagy** ADJECTIVE = **guarded**, reserved, careful, cautious, restrained, wary, discreet, shrewd, wily, reticent, noncommittal, chary ■ OPPOSITE: careless

cajole VERB = **persuade**, tempt, lure, flatter, manoeuvre, seduce, entice, coax, beguile, wheedle, sweet-talk (*informal*), inveigle

cake NOUN *He bought a cake of soap.* = **block**, bar, slab, lump, cube, loaf, mass ▸ VERB *The blood had begun to cake and turn brown.* = **solidify**, dry, consolidate, harden, thicken, congeal, coagulate, ossify, encrust

calamitous ADJECTIVE = **disastrous**, terrible, devastating, tragic, fatal, deadly, dreadful, dire, catastrophic, woeful, ruinous, cataclysmic ■ OPPOSITE: fortunate

calamity NOUN = **disaster**, tragedy, ruin, distress, reversal of fortune, hardship, catastrophe, woe, misfortune, downfall, adversity, scourge, mishap, affliction, trial, tribulation, misadventure, cataclysm, wretchedness, mischance ■ OPPOSITE: benefit

calculate VERB 1 *From this we can calculate the total mass in the galaxy.* = **work out**, value, judge, determine, estimate, count, reckon, weigh, consider, compute, rate, gauge, enumerate, figure 2 *Its twin engines were calculated to give additional safety.* = **plan**, design, aim, intend, frame, arrange, formulate, contrive

calculated ADJECTIVE = **deliberate**, planned, considered, studied, intended, intentional, designed, aimed, purposeful, premeditated ■ OPPOSITE: unplanned

calculating ADJECTIVE = **scheming**, designing, sharp, shrewd, cunning, contriving, sly, canny, devious, manipulative, crafty, Machiavellian ■ OPPOSITE: direct

calculation NOUN 1 *He made a quick calculation on a scrap of paper.* = **computation**, working out, reckoning, figuring, estimate, forecast, judgment, estimation, result, answer 2 *an act of cold, unspeakably cruel calculation* = **planning**, intention, deliberation, foresight, contrivance, forethought, circumspection, premeditation

calibrate VERB = **measure**, gauge

calibre or (*U.S.*) **caliber** NOUN 1 *I was impressed by the high calibre of the candidates.* = **worth**, quality, ability, talent, gifts, capacity, merit, distinction, faculty, endowment, stature 2 = **standard**, level, quality, grade 3 *Next morning she was arrested and a .44 calibre revolver was found in her possession.* = **diameter**, bore, gauge, measure

C

call VERB **1** *They called their daughter Mischa.*
= **name**, entitle, dub, designate, term,
style, label, describe as, christen,
denominate **2** *His own party called him a
traitor.* = **consider**, think, judge, estimate,
describe as, refer to as, regard as **3** *'Boys!' he
called, 'Dinner's ready!'* = **cry**, announce,
shout, scream, proclaim, yell, cry out,
whoop ■ **OPPOSITE:** whisper **4** *Will you call
me as soon as you hear anything?* = **phone**,
contact, telephone, ring (up) (*informal*,
chiefly Brit.), give (someone) a bell (*Brit.
slang*), Skype®, video call **5** *He called me over
the tannoy.* = **hail**, address, summon,
contact, halloo **6** *The group promised to call a
meeting of shareholders.* = **summon**, gather,
invite, rally, assemble, muster, convene,
convoke, collect ■ **OPPOSITE:** dismiss **7** *I'm
late for work! Why didn't you call me earlier?*
= **waken**, wake, wake up, arouse, awaken,
rouse ▶ NOUN **1** = **telephone call**, bell
(*informal*), phone call, buzz (*informal*), ring
(*informal*), video call, Skype® **2** *I decided to
pay a call on Faraz.* = **visit 3** *There was a call by
the trade unions for members to stay home for
the duration of the strike.* = **request**, order,
demand, appeal, notice, command,
announcement, invitation, plea, summons,
supplication (*formal*) **4** (*used in negative
constructions*) *There was no call for him to talk
to you like he did.* = **need**, cause, reason,
grounds, occasion, excuse, justification,
claim **5** *a sailor who could not resist the call of
the sea* = **attraction**, draw (*informal*), pull
(*informal*), appeal, lure, attractiveness,
allure, magnetism **6** *He heard calls coming
from the cellar.* = **cry**, shout, scream, yell,
whoop ■ **OPPOSITE:** whisper • **call for
someone** *I shall call for you at 7 o'clock.*
= **fetch**, pick up, collect, uplift (*Scot.*) • **call
for something 1** *They angrily called for his
resignation.* = **demand**, order, request, insist
on, cry out for **2** *It's a situation that calls for a
blend of delicacy and force.* = **require**, need,
involve, demand, occasion, entail,
necessitate • **call on someone 1** *He was
frequently called on to resolve conflicts.*
= **request**, ask, bid, invite, appeal to,
summon, invoke, call upon, entreat,
supplicate **2** *I'm leaving early tomorrow to call
on a friend.* = **visit**, look up, drop in on, look
in on, see • **call someone up 1** *She called me
up to ask how I was.* = **telephone**, phone,
ring (*chiefly Brit.*), buzz (*informal*), dial, call
up, give (someone) a ring (*informal, chiefly
Brit.*), put a call through to, give (someone)
a call, give (someone) a buzz (*informal*), give
(someone) a bell (*Brit. slang*), give
(someone) a tinkle (*Brit. informal*), get on

the blower to (*informal*) **2** *The United States
has called up some 150,000 military reservists.*
= **enlist**, draft, recruit, muster
calling NOUN = **profession**, work, business,
line, trade, career, mission, employment,
province, occupation, pursuit, vocation,
walk of life, life's work, métier
callous ADJECTIVE = **heartless**, cold, harsh,
hardened, indifferent, insensitive,
hard-boiled (*informal*), unsympathetic,
uncaring, soulless, hard-bitten, unfeeling,
obdurate, case-hardened, hardhearted
■ **OPPOSITE:** compassionate
callousness NOUN = **heartlessness**,
insensitivity, hardness, coldness,
harshness, obduracy, soullessness,
hardheartedness, obdurateness
callow ADJECTIVE = **inexperienced**,
juvenile, naïve, immature, raw, untried,
green, unsophisticated, puerile, guileless,
jejune (*formal*), unfledged
calm ADJECTIVE **1** *Try to keep calm and just tell
me what happened.* = **cool**, relaxed,
composed, sedate, undisturbed, collected,
unmoved, dispassionate, unfazed
(*informal*), impassive, unflappable
(*informal*), unruffled, unemotional,
self-possessed, imperturbable, equable,
keeping your cool, unexcited, ~~unexcitable~~,
as cool as a cucumber, chilled (*informal*)
■ **OPPOSITE:** excited **2** *The normally calm
waters of Mururoa lagoon heaved and frothed.*
= **still**, quiet, smooth, peaceful, mild,
serene, tranquil, placid, halcyon, balmy,
restful, windless, pacific ■ **OPPOSITE:** rough
▶ NOUN **1** *He felt a sudden sense of calm and
contentment.* = **peacefulness**, peace,
serenity, calmness **2** *the rural calm of Grand
Rapids, Michigan* = **stillness**, peace, quiet,
hush, serenity, tranquillity, repose,
calmness, peacefulness **3** *Church leaders
have appealed for calm.* = **peace**, calmness
■ **OPPOSITE:** disturbance ▶ VERB **1** *She had a
drink to calm her nerves.* = **soothe**, settle,
quiet, relax, appease, still, allay, assuage,
quieten ■ **OPPOSITE:** excite **2** *Officials hoped
this action would calm the situation.* = **placate**,
hush, pacify, mollify ■ **OPPOSITE:** aggravate
calmly ADVERB = **coolly**, casually, sedately,
serenely, nonchalantly, impassively,
dispassionately, placidly, unflinchingly,
equably, imperturbably, tranquilly,
composedly, collectedly, self-possessedly
camaraderie NOUN = **comradeship**,
fellowship, brotherhood, companionship,
togetherness, esprit de corps, good-
fellowship, companionship
camouflage NOUN **1** *Many animals employ
camouflage to hide from predators.*

= **protective colouring**, mimicry, false appearance, deceptive markings **2** *Her merrymaking was only a camouflage to disguise her grief.* = **disguise**, front (*informal*), cover, screen, blind, mask, cloak, guise, masquerade, subterfuge, concealment ▶ VERB *This is another clever attempt to camouflage reality.* = **disguise**, cover, screen, hide, mask, conceal, obscure, veil, cloak, obfuscate (*formal*) ■ **OPPOSITE:** reveal

camp¹ NOUN **1** *The camp was in a densely-forested area.* = **camp site**, tents, encampment, camping ground **2** *He was held in a military camp for three days.* = **bivouac**, cantonment (*Military*)

camp² ADJECTIVE *All the characters are either too camp or too dull.* = **affected**, mannered, artificial, posturing, ostentatious, campy (*informal*), camped up (*informal*)

campaign NOUN **1** *A new campaign has begun to encourage more people to become blood donors.* = **drive**, appeal, movement, push (*informal*), offensive, crusade **2** *The General's campaign against the militia has so far failed.* = **operation**, drive, attack, movement, push, offensive, expedition, crusade

campaigner NOUN = **demonstrator**, champion, advocate, activist, reformer, crusader

canal NOUN = **waterway**, channel, passage, conduit, duct, watercourse

cancel VERB **1** *The foreign minister has cancelled his visit to Washington.* = **call off**, drop, abandon, forget about **2** *Her insurance had been cancelled by the company.* = **annul**, abolish, repeal, abort, quash, do away with, revoke, repudiate, rescind, obviate, abrogate, countermand, eliminate • **cancel something out** *These two opposing factors tend to cancel each other out.* = **counterbalance**, offset, make up for, compensate for, redeem, neutralize, nullify, obviate, balance out

cancellation NOUN **1** *No reason has been given for the cancellation of the event.* = **abandonment**, abandoning **2** *a march calling for the cancellation of debt* = **annulment**, abolition, repeal, elimination, quashing, revocation

cancer NOUN **1** *Researchers claim that lifestyle changes can be a real help in preventing cancer.* = **growth**, tumour, carcinoma (*Pathology*), malignancy **2** *There's a cancer in the system.* = **evil**, corruption, rot, sickness, blight, pestilence, canker ■ **RELATED WORD:** *prefix* carcino-

candid ADJECTIVE **1** *a candid account of her life in the limelight* = **honest**, just, open, truthful, fair, plain, straightforward, blunt, sincere, outspoken, downright, impartial, forthright, upfront (*informal*), unequivocal, unbiased, guileless, unprejudiced, free, round, frank ■ **OPPOSITE:** diplomatic **2** *There are also some candid pictures taken when he was young.* = **informal**, impromptu, uncontrived, unposed

candidate NOUN = **contender**, competitor, applicant, nominee, entrant, claimant, contestant, suitor, aspirant, possibility, runner

candour NOUN = **honesty**, simplicity, fairness, sincerity, impartiality, frankness, directness, truthfulness, outspokenness, forthrightness, straightforwardness, ingenuousness, artlessness, guilelessness, openness, unequivocalness, naïveté ■ **OPPOSITE:** dishonesty

cannabis NOUN = **marijuana**, pot (*slang*), dope (*slang*), hash (*slang*), blow (*slang*), smoke (*informal*), stuff (*slang*), leaf (*slang*), tea (*U.S. slang*), grass (*slang*), chronic (*U.S. slang*), weed (*slang*), hemp, gage (*U.S., obsolete slang*), hashish, mary jane (*U.S. slang*), ganja, bhang, kif, sinsemilla, dagga (*S. African*), charas

cannon NOUN = **gun**, big gun, artillery piece, field gun, mortar

canny ADJECTIVE = **shrewd**, knowing, sharp, acute, careful, wise, clever, subtle, cautious, prudent, astute, on the ball (*informal*), artful, judicious, circumspect, perspicacious (*formal*), sagacious (*formal*), worldly-wise ■ **OPPOSITE:** inept

canon NOUN **1** *These measures offended all the accepted canons of political economy.* = **rule**, standard, principle, regulation, formula, criterion, dictate, statute, yardstick, precept **2** *the body of work which constitutes the canon of English literature as taught in schools* = **list**, index, catalogue, syllabus, roll

canopy NOUN = **awning**, covering, shade, shelter, sunshade

cant¹ NOUN **1** *Politicians are holding forth with their usual hypocritical cant.* = **hypocrisy**, pretence, lip service, humbug, insincerity, pretentiousness, sanctimoniousness, pious platitudes, affected piety, sham holiness **2** *He resorted to a lot of pseudo-psychological cant to confuse me.* = **jargon**, slang, vernacular, patter, lingo (*informal*), argot

cant² VERB *The helicopter canted inward towards the landing area.* = **tilt**, angle, slope, incline, slant, bevel, rise

cantankerous ADJECTIVE = **bad-tempered**, contrary, perverse, irritable, crusty, grumpy, disagreeable, cranky (*U.S., Canad. & Irish informal*), irascible, tetchy, ratty (*Brit. & N.Z. informal*), testy, quarrelsome, waspish, grouchy (*informal*), peevish, crabby, choleric, crotchety (*informal*), ill-humoured, captious, difficult ■ **OPPOSITE:** cheerful

canter VERB *The competitors cantered into the arena.* = **jog**, lope ▸ NOUN *He set off at a canter.* = **jog**, lope, easy gait, dogtrot

canvass VERB **1** *I'm canvassing for the Labour Party.* = **campaign**, solicit votes, electioneer **2** *The survey canvassed the views of almost 80 economists.* = **poll**, study, examine, investigate, analyse, scan, inspect, sift, scrutinize

canyon NOUN = **gorge**, pass, gulf, valley, clough (*dialect*), gully, ravine, defile, gulch (*U.S. & Canad.*), coulee (*U.S.*)

cap VERB **1** *He always has to cap everyone else's achievements.* = **beat**, top, better, exceed, eclipse, lick (*informal*), surpass, transcend, outstrip, outdo, run rings around (*informal*), put in the shade, overtop **2** *home-made scones capped with cream* = **top**, cover, crown **3** = **complete**, crown

capability NOUN = **ability**, means, power, potential, facility, capacity, qualification(s), faculty, competence, proficiency, wherewithal, potentiality ■ **OPPOSITE:** inability

capable ADJECTIVE **1** *Such a weapon would be capable of firing conventional or nuclear shells.* = **able**, fitted, suited, adapted, adequate ■ **OPPOSITE:** incapable **2** *She's a very capable administrator.* = **accomplished**, experienced, masterly, qualified, talented, gifted, efficient, clever, intelligent, competent, apt, skilful, adept, proficient ■ **OPPOSITE:** incompetent

capacious ADJECTIVE = **spacious**, wide, broad, vast, substantial, comprehensive, extensive, generous, ample, expansive, roomy, voluminous, commodious, sizable or sizeable ■ **OPPOSITE:** limited

capacity NOUN **1** *Our capacity for giving care, love and attention is limited.* = **ability**, power, strength, facility, gift, intelligence, efficiency, genius, faculty, capability, forte, readiness, aptitude, aptness, competence or competency **2** *an aircraft with a bomb-carrying capacity of 454 kg* = **size**, room, range, space, volume, extent, dimensions, scope, magnitude, compass, amplitude **3** *She was visiting in her official capacity as co-chairperson.* = **function**, position, role, post, appointment, province, sphere, service, office

cape NOUN = **headland**, point, head, peninsula, ness (*archaic*), promontory

caper VERB *The children were capering about, shouting and laughing.* = **dance**, trip, spring, jump, bound, leap, bounce, hop, skip, romp, frolic, cavort, frisk, gambol ▸ NOUN *Jack would have nothing to do with such childish capers.* = **escapade**, sport, stunt, mischief, lark (*informal*), prank, jest, practical joke, high jinks, antic, jape, shenanigan (*informal*)

capital NOUN *The company is having difficulties in raising capital.* = **money**, funds, stock, investment(s), property, cash, finance, finances, financing, resources, assets, wealth, principal, means, wherewithal ▸ ADJECTIVE *They had a capital time in London.* = **first-rate**, fine, excellent, superb, sterling, splendid, world-class

capitalism NOUN = **private enterprise**, free enterprise, private ownership, laissez faire or laisser faire

capitalize VERB *The company will be capitalized at £50 million.* = **sell**, put up for sale, trade, dispose of • **capitalize on something** *The rebels seemed to be trying to capitalize on the public's discontent.* = **take advantage of**, exploit, benefit from, profit from, make the most of, gain from, cash in on (*informal*)

capitulate VERB = **give in**, yield, concede, submit, surrender, comply, give up, come to terms, succumb, cave in (*informal*), relent ■ **OPPOSITE:** resist

capitulation NOUN = **surrender**, yielding, submission, cave-in (*informal*)

caprice NOUN = **whim**, notion, impulse, freak, fad, quirk, vagary, whimsy, humour, fancy, fickleness, inconstancy, fitfulness, changeableness

capricious ADJECTIVE = **unpredictable**, variable, unstable, inconsistent, erratic, quirky, fickle, impulsive, mercurial, freakish, fitful, inconstant ■ **OPPOSITE:** consistent

capsize VERB = **overturn**, turn over, invert, tip over, keel over, turn turtle, upset

capsule NOUN **1** *You can also take red ginseng in convenient capsule form.* = **pill**, tablet, lozenge, bolus **2** *Each flower is globular, with an egg-shaped capsule.* = **pod**, case, shell, vessel, sheath, receptacle, seed case

captain NOUN **1** *He is a former English cricket captain.* = **leader**, boss, master, skipper, chieftain, head, number one (*informal*), chief **2** *a German sea captain* = **commander**, officer, skipper, (senior) pilot

captivate VERB = **charm**, attract, fascinate, absorb, entrance, dazzle, seduce, enchant, enthral, beguile, allure, bewitch, ravish, enslave, mesmerize, ensnare, hypnotize, enrapture, sweep off your feet, enamour, infatuate ■ **OPPOSITE:** repel

captive ADJECTIVE *Her heart had begun to pound inside her chest like a captive animal.*
= **confined**, caged, imprisoned, locked up, enslaved, incarcerated, ensnared, subjugated, penned, restricted ▶ NOUN *He described the difficulties of surviving for four months as a captive.* = **prisoner**, hostage, convict, prisoner of war, detainee, internee

captivity NOUN = **confinement**, custody, detention, imprisonment, incarceration, internment, durance (*archaic*), restraint

captor NOUN = **jailer** *or* **gaoler**, guard, keeper, custodian

capture VERB *The police gave chase and captured him as he was trying to escape.*
= **catch**, arrest, take, bag, secure, seize, nail (*informal*), collar (*informal*), nab (*informal*), apprehend, lift (*slang*), take prisoner, take into custody, feel your collar (*slang*) ■ OPPOSITE: release ▶ NOUN *The shooting happened while the man was trying to evade capture.* = **arrest**, catching, trapping, imprisonment, seizure, apprehension, taking, taking captive

car NOUN **1** *They arrived by car.* = **vehicle**, motor, wheels (*informal*), auto (*U.S.*), automobile, jalopy (*informal*), motor car, machine **2** (*U.S. & Canad.*) *Tour buses have replaced railway cars.* = **(railway) carriage**, coach, cable car, dining car, sleeping car, buffet car, van

carcass NOUN **1** *A cluster of vultures crouched on the carcass of a dead buffalo.* = **body**, remains, corpse, skeleton, dead body, cadaver (*Medical*) **2** *At one end of the camp lies the carcass of an aircraft which crashed in the mountains.* = **remains**, shell, framework, debris, remnants, hulk

cardinal ADJECTIVE = **principal**, first, highest, greatest, leading, important, chief, main, prime, central, key, essential, primary, fundamental, paramount, foremost, pre-eminent ■ OPPOSITE: secondary

care VERB *a company that cares about the environment* = **be concerned**, mind, bother, be interested, be bothered, give a damn, concern yourself ▶ NOUN **1** *the orphans who were in her care* = **custody**, keeping, control, charge, management, protection, supervision, guardianship, safekeeping, ministration **2** *I chose my words with care.*
= **caution**, attention, regard, pains, consideration, heed, prudence, vigilance, forethought, circumspection, watchfulness, meticulousness, carefulness ■ OPPOSITE: carelessness **3** *He never seemed to have a care in the world.* = **worry**, concern, pressure, trouble, responsibility, stress,

burden, anxiety, hardship, woe, disquiet, affliction, tribulation, perplexity, vexation ■ OPPOSITE: pleasure • **care for someone 1** *They hired a nurse to care for her.* = **look after**, mind, tend, attend, nurse, minister to, watch over **2** *He wanted me to know that he still cared for me.* = **love**, desire, be fond of, want, prize, find congenial • **care for something** *or* **someone** *I don't care for seafood very much.* = **like**, enjoy, take to, relish, be fond of, be keen on, be partial to • **take care of something** *or* **someone 1** = **look after**, mind, watch, protect, tend, nurse, care for, provide for **2** = **deal with**, manage, cope with, see to, handle

career NOUN **1** *She is now concentrating on a career as a fashion designer.* = **occupation**, calling, employment, pursuit, vocation, livelihood, life's work **2** *The club has had an interesting, if chequered, career.* = **progress**, course, path, procedure, passage ▶ VERB *The car went careering off down the track.*
= **rush**, race, speed, tear, dash, barrel (along) (*informal, chiefly U.S. & Canad.*), bolt, hurtle, burn rubber (*informal*)

carefree ADJECTIVE = **untroubled**, happy, cheerful, careless, buoyant, airy, radiant, easy-going, cheery, breezy, halcyon, sunny, jaunty, chirpy (*informal*), happy-go-lucky, blithe, insouciant, light-hearted
■ OPPOSITE: unhappy

careful ADJECTIVE **1** *One has to be extremely careful when dealing with these people.*
= **cautious**, painstaking, scrupulous, fastidious, circumspect, punctilious (*formal*), chary, heedful, thoughtful, discreet ■ OPPOSITE: careless **2** *He decided to prosecute her after careful consideration of all the facts.* = **thorough**, full, particular, accurate, precise, intensive, in-depth, meticulous, conscientious, attentive, exhaustive, painstaking, scrupulous, assiduous ■ OPPOSITE: casual **3** *Train your children to be careful with their pocket-money.*
= **prudent**, sparing, economical, canny, provident, frugal, thrifty

careless ADJECTIVE **1** *He pleaded guilty to careless driving.* = **slapdash**, irresponsible, sloppy (*informal*), cavalier, offhand, neglectful, slipshod, lackadaisical, inattentive ■ OPPOSITE: careful **2** *She's careless about her personal hygiene.*
= **negligent**, hasty, unconcerned, cursory, perfunctory, thoughtless, indiscreet, unthinking, forgetful, absent-minded, inconsiderate, heedless, remiss (*formal*), incautious, unmindful ■ OPPOSITE: careful **3** *With a careless flip of his wrists, he sent the ball on its way.* = **nonchalant**, casual,

offhand, artless, unstudied ■ **OPPOSITE:** careful

carelessness NOUN = **negligence**, neglect, omission, indiscretion, inaccuracy, irresponsibility, slackness, inattention, sloppiness (*informal*), laxity, thoughtlessness, laxness, remissness

caress NOUN *Margaret held my arm in a gentle caress.* = **stroke**, pat, kiss, embrace, hug, cuddle, fondling ▶ VERB *They kissed and caressed one another.* = **stroke**, cuddle, fondle, pet, embrace, hug, nuzzle, neck (*informal*), kiss

caretaker NOUN *The caretaker sleeps in the building all night.* = **warden**, keeper, porter (*Brit.*), superintendent (*U.S.*), curator, custodian, watchman, janitor, concierge ▶ ADJECTIVE *The administration intends to hand over power to a caretaker government.* = **temporary**, holding, short-term, interim

cargo NOUN = **load**, goods, contents, shipment, freight, merchandise, baggage, ware, consignment, tonnage, lading

caricature NOUN *a chalk-drawn caricature of a pop-eyed judge brandishing a gavel* = **parody**, cartoon, distortion, satire, send-up (*Brit. informal*), travesty, takeoff (*informal*), lampoon, burlesque, mimicry, farce ▶ VERB *Her political career has been caricatured in the newspapers.* = **parody**, take off (*informal*), mock, distort, ridicule, mimic, send up (*Brit. informal*), lampoon, burlesque, satirize

caring ADJECTIVE = **compassionate**, loving, kindly, warm, soft, sensitive, tender, sympathetic, responsive, receptive, considerate, warmhearted, tenderhearted, softhearted, touchy-feely (*informal*)

carnage NOUN = **slaughter**, murder, massacre, holocaust, havoc, bloodshed, shambles, mass murder, butchery, blood bath

carnal ADJECTIVE = **sexual**, animal, sexy (*informal*), fleshly, erotic, sensual, randy (*informal, chiefly Brit.*), steamy (*informal*), raunchy (*informal*), sensuous, voluptuous, lewd, wanton, amorous, salacious, prurient, impure, lascivious, lustful, lecherous, libidinous, licentious, unchaste

carnival NOUN = **festival**, fair, fête, celebration, gala, jubilee, jamboree, Mardi Gras, revelry, merrymaking, fiesta, holiday

carol NOUN = **song**, noel, hymn, Christmas song, canticle

carouse VERB = **drink**, booze (*informal*), revel, imbibe (*formal*), quaff, pub-crawl (*informal, chiefly Brit.*), bevvy (*dialect*), make merry, bend the elbow (*informal*), roister

carp VERB = **find fault**, complain, beef (*slang*), criticize, nag, censure, reproach,

quibble, cavil, pick holes, kvetch (*U.S. slang*), nit-pick (*informal*) ■ **OPPOSITE:** praise

carpenter NOUN = **joiner**, cabinet-maker, woodworker

carping ADJECTIVE = **fault-finding**, critical, nagging, picky (*informal*), nit-picking (*informal*), hard to please, cavilling, captious, nit-picky (*informal*)

carriage NOUN 1 *He followed in an open carriage drawn by six grey horses.* = **vehicle**, coach, trap, gig, cab, wagon, hackney, conveyance (*old-fashioned*) 2 *It costs £10.86 for one litre, including carriage.* = **transportation**, transport, delivery, conveying, freight, conveyance, carrying 3 *Her voice is cultured and her carriage is regal.* = **bearing**, posture, gait, deportment, air

carry VERB 1 *He carried the plate through to the dining room.* = **convey**, take, move, bring, bear, lift, transfer, conduct, transport, haul, transmit, fetch, relay, cart, tote (*informal*), hump (*Brit. slang*), lug 2 *The ship can carry seventy passengers.* = **transport**, take, transfer, transmit 3 *This horse can't carry your weight.* = **support**, stand, bear, maintain, shoulder, sustain, hold up, suffer, uphold, bolster, underpin 4 *Frogs eat pests which carry diseases.* = **transmit**, transfer, spread, pass on 5 *Several magazines carried the story.* = **publish**, include, release, display, print, broadcast, communicate, disseminate, give 6 *It was this point of view that carried the day.* = **win**, gain, secure, capture, accomplish • **carry on** 1 *Her bravery has given him the will to carry on.* = **continue**, last, endure, persist, keep going, persevere, crack on (*informal*) 2 *They were yelling and laughing and carrying on.* = **make a fuss**, act up (*informal*), misbehave, create (*slang*), raise Cain • **carry something on** *The consulate will carry on a political dialogue.* = **engage in**, conduct, carry out, undertake, embark on, enter into • **carry something out** *Commitments have been made with very little intention of carrying them out.* = **perform**, effect, achieve, realize, implement, fulfil, accomplish, execute, discharge, consummate, carry through

carry-on NOUN = **fuss**, disturbance, racket, fracas, commotion, rumpus, tumult, hubbub, shindy (*informal*)

carton NOUN = **box**, case, pack, package, container

cartoon NOUN 1 *The newspaper printed a cartoon depicting the president as a used car salesman.* = **drawing**, parody, satire, caricature, comic strip, takeoff (*informal*), lampoon, sketch 2 *We read the papers while* the kids watched cartoons. = **animation**, animated film, animated cartoon

cartridge NOUN **1** *Gun and cartridge manufacturers will lose money if the game laws are amended.* = **shell**, round, charge **2** *Change the filter cartridge as often as instructed by the manufacturer.* = **container**, case, magazine, cassette, cylinder, capsule

carve VERB **1** *One of the prisoners has carved a beautiful chess set.* = **sculpt**, form, cut, chip, sculpture, whittle, chisel, hew (*old-fashioned*), fashion **2** *He carved his name on his desk.* = **etch**, engrave, inscribe, fashion, slash

carving NOUN = **sculpture**

cascade NOUN *She stood still for a moment under the cascade of water.* = **waterfall**, falls, torrent, flood, shower, fountain, avalanche, deluge, downpour, outpouring, cataract ▶ VERB *A waterfall cascades down the cliff from the hills.* = **flow**, fall, flood, pour, plunge, surge, spill, tumble, descend, overflow, gush, teem, pitch

case¹ NOUN **1** *In extreme cases, insurance companies can prosecute for fraud.* = **situation**, event, circumstance(s), state, position, condition, context, dilemma, plight, contingency, predicament **2** *Some cases of arthritis respond to a gluten-free diet.* = **instance**, example, occasion, specimen, occurrence **3** *He lost his case at the European Court of Human Rights.* = **lawsuit**, process, trial, suit, proceedings, dispute, cause, action

case² NOUN **1** *There was a ten-foot long stuffed alligator in a glass case.* = **cabinet**, box, chest, holder **2** *She held up a blue spectacle case.* = **container**, compact, capsule, carton, cartridge, canister, casket, receptacle **3** *The porter brought my cases down and called for a taxi.* = **suitcase**, bag, grip, trunk, holdall, portmanteau, valise **4** *The winner will receive a case of champagne.* = **crate**, box **5** *Vanilla is the seed case of a South American orchid.* = **covering**, casing, cover, shell, wrapping, jacket, envelope, capsule, folder, sheath, wrapper, integument

cash NOUN = **money**, change, funds, notes, ready (*informal*), the necessary (*informal*), resources, currency, silver, bread (*slang*), coin, tin (*slang*), brass (*Northern English, dialect*), dough (*slang*), rhino (*Brit. slang*), banknotes, bullion, dosh (*Brit. & Austral. slang*), wherewithal, coinage, needful (*informal*), specie, shekels (*informal*), dibs (*slang*), ready money, ackers (*slang*), spondulicks (*slang*)

cashier¹ NOUN *The cashier said that he would fetch the manager.* = **teller**, accountant, clerk, treasurer, bank clerk, purser, bursar, banker

cashier² VERB *Many officers were cashiered on political grounds.* = **dismiss**, discharge, expel, cast off, drum out, give the boot to (*slang*)

casing NOUN = **covering**, case, cover, shell, container, integument

cask NOUN = **barrel**, drum, cylinder, keg

casket NOUN = **box**, case, chest, coffer, ark (*dialect*), jewel box, kist (*Scot. & Northern English, dialect*)

cast NOUN **1** *The show is very amusing and the cast are excellent.* = **actors**, company, players, characters, troupe, dramatis personae **2** *Hers was an essentially optimistic cast of mind.* = **type**, turn, sort, kind, style, stamp ▶ VERB **1** *She has been cast in the lead role.* = **choose**, name, pick, select, appoint, assign, allot **2** *He cast a stern glance at the two men.* = **bestow**, give, level, accord, direct, confer **3** *The moon cast a bright light over the yard.* = **give out**, spread, deposit, shed, distribute, scatter, emit, radiate, bestow, diffuse **4** *She took a pebble and cast it into the water.* = **throw**, project, launch, pitch, shed, shy, toss, thrust, hurl, fling, chuck (*informal*), sling, lob, impel, drive, drop **5** *This statue of Neptune is cast in bronze.* = **mould**, set, found, form, model, shape • **cast someone down** *I am not too easily cast down by changes of fortune.* = **discourage**, depress, desolate, dishearten, dispirit, deject

caste NOUN = **class**, order, race, station, rank, status, stratum, social order, lineage

castigate VERB = **reprimand**, blast, carpet (*informal*), put down, criticize, lash, slate (*informal, chiefly Brit.*), censure, rebuke, scold, berate, dress down (*informal*), chastise, chasten, tear into (*informal*), diss (*slang*), read the riot act, slap on the wrist, lambast(e), bawl out (*informal*), excoriate, rap over the knuckles, haul over the coals (*informal*), chew out (*U.S. & Canad. informal*), tear (someone) off a strip (*Brit. informal*), give a rocket (*Brit. & N.Z. informal*)

cast-iron ADJECTIVE = **certain**, established, settled, guaranteed, fixed, definite, copper-bottomed, idiot-proof, nailed-on (*slang*)

castle NOUN = **fortress**, keep, palace, tower, peel, chateau, stronghold, citadel, fastness

castrate VERB = **neuter**, emasculate, geld

casual ADJECTIVE **1** *an easy-going young man with a casual approach to life* = **careless**, relaxed, informal, indifferent, unconcerned, apathetic, blasé, offhand, nonchalant, insouciant, lackadaisical ■ **OPPOSITE:** serious **2** *It was just a casual meeting.* = **chance**, unexpected, random, accidental, incidental, unforeseen, unintentional, fortuitous (*informal*), serendipitous, unpremeditated ■ **OPPOSITE:** planned **3** *I bought casual clothes for the weekend.* = **informal**, leisure, sporty, non-dressy ■ **OPPOSITE:** formal

casualty NOUN **1** *Troops fired on the demonstrators, causing many casualties.* = **fatality**, death, loss, wounded **2** *The company has been one of the greatest casualties of the recession.* = **victim**, sufferer

cat NOUN = **feline**, pussy (*informal*), moggy (*slang*), puss (*informal*), ballarat (*Austral. informal*), tabby ■ **RELATED WORDS:** adjective feline; *name of male* tom; *name of female* queen; *name of young* kitten

cataclysm NOUN = **disaster**, collapse, catastrophe, upheaval, debacle, devastation, calamity

cataclysmic ADJECTIVE = **disastrous**, devastating, catastrophic, calamitous

catalogue *or* (*U.S.*) **catalog** NOUN *One of the authors of the catalogue is the Professor of Art History.* = **list**, record, schedule, index, register, directory, inventory, gazetteer ▶ VERB *The Royal Greenwich Observatory was founded to observe and catalogue the stars.* = **list**, file, index, register, classify, inventory, tabulate, alphabetize

catapult NOUN *They were hit twice by missiles fired from a catapult.* = **sling**, slingshot (*U.S.*), trebuchet, ballista ▶ VERB *He was catapulted into the side of the van.* = **shoot**, pitch, plunge, toss, hurl, propel, hurtle, heave

cataract NOUN **1** *a battle with blindness caused by cataracts* = **opacity** (*of the eye*) **2** *There was an impressive cataract at the end of the glen.* = **waterfall**, falls, rapids, cascade, torrent, deluge, downpour, Niagara

catastrophe NOUN = **disaster**, tragedy, calamity, meltdown (*informal*), cataclysm, trouble, trial, blow, failure, reverse, misfortune, devastation, adversity, mishap, affliction, whammy (*informal*), bummer (*slang*), mischance, fiasco

catastrophic ADJECTIVE = **disastrous**, devastating, tragic, calamitous, cataclysmic

catch VERB **1** *Police say they are confident of catching the killer.* = **capture**, arrest, trap, seize, nail (*informal*), nab (*informal*), snare, lift (*slang*), apprehend, ensnare, entrap, feel your collar (*slang*) ■ **OPPOSITE:** free **2** *The locals were encouraged to catch and kill the birds.* = **trap**, capture, snare, entangle, ensnare, entrap **3** *I jumped up to catch the ball and fell over.* = **seize**, get, grab, snatch **4** *He knelt beside her and caught her hand in both of his.* = **grab**, take, grip, seize, grasp, clutch,

lay hold of ■ **OPPOSITE:** release **5** *He caught a youth breaking into his car.* = **discover**, surprise, find out, expose, detect, catch in the act, take unawares **6** *The more stress you are under, the more likely you are to catch a cold.* = **contract**, get, develop, suffer from, incur, succumb to, go down with ■ **OPPOSITE:** escape ▶ NOUN **1** *Always fit windows with safety locks or catches.* = **fastener**, hook, clip, bolt, latch, clasp, hasp, hook and eye, snib (*Scot.*), sneck (*dialect, chiefly Scot. & Northern English*) **2** (*informal*) *It sounds too good to be true – what's the catch?* = **drawback**, trick, trap, disadvantage, hitch, snag, stumbling block, fly in the ointment ■ **OPPOSITE:** advantage • **catch on 1** (*informal*) *He tried to explain it to me, but it took me a while to catch on.* = **understand**, see, find out, grasp, see through, comprehend, twig (*Brit. informal*), get the picture, see the light of day **2** *The idea has been around for ages without catching on.* = **become popular**, take off, become trendy, come into fashion

catchcry NOUN = **catch phrase**, slogan, saying, quotation, motto

catching ADJECTIVE = **infectious**, contagious, transferable, communicable, infective, transmittable ■ **OPPOSITE:** non-infectious

catch phrase NOUN = **slogan**, saying, quotation, motto, catchword, catchcry (*Austral.*)

catchy ADJECTIVE = **memorable**, haunting, unforgettable, captivating

categorical ADJECTIVE = **absolute**, direct, express, positive, explicit, unconditional, emphatic, downright, unequivocal, unqualified, unambiguous, unreserved ■ **OPPOSITE:** vague

category NOUN = **class**, grouping, heading, head, order, sort, list, department, type, division, section, rank, grade, classification, genre

cater VERB • **cater for something** *or* **someone 1** *Thirty restaurants and hotels catered for the event.* = **provide for**, supply, provision, purvey, victual **2** *We have to cater for the demands of the marketplace.* = **take into account**, consider, bear in mind, make allowance for, have regard for • **cater to something** *or* **someone** *His parents spoil him and cater to his every whim.* = **indulge**, spoil, minister to, pamper, gratify, pander to, coddle, mollycoddle

catharsis NOUN = **release**, cleansing, purging, purification

catholic ADJECTIVE = **wide**, general, liberal, global, varied, comprehensive, universal, world-wide, tolerant, eclectic, all-inclusive, ecumenical, all-embracing, broad-minded, unbigoted, unsectarian, multicultural, multiculti (*informal*) ■ **OPPOSITE:** limited

cattle PLURAL NOUN = **cows**, stock, beasts, livestock, bovines ■ **RELATED WORDS:** *adjective* bovine; *collective nouns* drove, herd

caucus NOUN = **group**, division, section, camp, sector, lobby, bloc, contingent, pressure group, junta, public-interest group (*U.S. & Canad.*)

cause NOUN **1** *The article lists the major causes of panic attacks.* = **origin**, source, agency, spring, agent, maker, producer, root, beginning, creator, genesis, originator, prime mover, mainspring ■ **OPPOSITE:** result **2** *There is obvious cause for concern.* = **reason**, call, need, grounds, basis, incentive, motive, motivation, justification, inducement **3** *His comments have done nothing to help the cause of peace.* = **aim**, movement, purpose, principle, object, ideal, enterprise, end ▶ VERB *I don't want to cause any trouble.* = **produce**, begin, create, effect, lead to, occasion (*formal*), result in, generate, provoke, compel, motivate, induce, bring about, give rise to, precipitate, incite, engender ■ **OPPOSITE:** prevent

caustic ADJECTIVE **1** *This substance is caustic; use gloves when handling it.* = **burning**, corrosive, corroding, astringent, vitriolic, acrid **2** *He was well known for his abrasive wit and caustic comments.* = **sarcastic**, biting, keen, cutting, severe, stinging, scathing, acrimonious, pungent, vitriolic, trenchant, mordant ■ **OPPOSITE:** kind

caution NOUN **1** *Drivers are urged to exercise extreme caution in icy weather.* = **care**, discretion, heed, prudence, vigilance, alertness, forethought, circumspection, watchfulness, belt and braces, carefulness, heedfulness ■ **OPPOSITE:** carelessness **2** *The others got off with a caution but I was fined.* = **reprimand**, warning, injunction, admonition ▶ VERB **1** *He cautioned against having unrealistic expectations.* = **warn**, urge, advise, alert, tip off, forewarn, put you on your guard **2** *The two men were cautioned but the police say they will not be charged.* = **reprimand**, warn, admonish, give an injunction to

cautious ADJECTIVE = **careful**, guarded, alert, wary, discreet, tentative, prudent, vigilant, watchful, judicious, circumspect, cagey (*informal*), on your toes, chary, belt-and-braces, keeping a weather eye on ■ **OPPOSITE:** careless

cautiously ADVERB = **carefully**, alertly, discreetly, tentatively, warily, prudently,

judiciously, guardedly, circumspectly, watchfully, vigilantly, cagily (*informal*), mindfully

cavalcade NOUN = **parade**, train, procession, march-past

cavalier ADJECTIVE = **offhand**, lordly, arrogant, lofty, curt, condescending, haughty, scornful, disdainful, insolent, supercilious

cavalry NOUN = **horsemen**, horse, mounted troops ■ **OPPOSITE:** infantrymen

cave NOUN = **hollow**, cavern, grotto, den, cavity

caveat NOUN = **warning**, caution, admonition, qualification, proviso, reservation, condition

cavern NOUN = **cave**, hollow, grotto, underground chamber

cavernous ADJECTIVE = **vast**, wide, huge, enormous, extensive, immense, spacious, expansive, capacious, commodious

cavity NOUN = **hollow**, hole, gap, pit, dent, crater

cavort VERB = **frolic**, sport, romp, caper, prance, frisk, gambol

cease VERB **1** *Almost miraculously, the noise ceased.* = **stop**, end, finish, be over, come to an end, peter out, die away ■ **OPPOSITE:** start **2** *A small number of firms have ceased trading.* = **discontinue**, end, stop, fail, finish, give up, conclude, suspend, halt, terminate, break off, refrain, leave off, give over (*informal*), bring to an end, desist, belay (*Nautical*) ■ **OPPOSITE:** begin

ceaseless ADJECTIVE = **continual**, constant, endless, continuous, eternal, perennial, perpetual, never-ending, interminable, incessant, everlasting, unending, unremitting, nonstop, untiring ■ **OPPOSITE:** occasional

cede VERB = **surrender**, grant, transfer, abandon, yield, concede, hand over, relinquish, renounce, make over, abdicate

celebrate VERB **1** *I was in a mood to celebrate.* = **rejoice**, party, enjoy yourself, carouse, live it up (*informal*), whoop it up (*informal*), make merry, paint the town red (*informal*), go on a spree, put the flags out, roister, kill the fatted calf **2** *Tom celebrated his birthday two days ago.* = **commemorate**, honour, observe, toast, drink to, keep **3** *Pope John Paul celebrated mass today in a city in central Poland.* = **perform**, observe, preside over, officiate at, solemnize **4** *a festival to celebrate the life and work of this great composer* = **praise**, honour, commend (*informal*), glorify, publicize, exalt, laud (*literary*), extol, eulogize

celebrated ADJECTIVE = **renowned**, popular, famous, outstanding, distinguished, well-known, prominent, glorious, acclaimed, notable, eminent, revered, famed, illustrious, pre-eminent, lionized ■ **OPPOSITE:** unknown

celebration NOUN **1** *There was a celebration in our house that night.* = **party**, festival, gala, jubilee, festivity, rave (*Brit. slang*), beano (*Brit. slang*), revelry, red-letter day, rave-up (*Brit. slang*), merrymaking, carousal, -fest (*in combination*), hooley *or* hoolie (*chiefly Irish & N.Z.*) **2** *This was not a memorial service but a celebration of his life.* = **commemoration**, honouring, remembrance **3** *the celebration of Mass in Latin* = **performance**, observance, solemnization

celebrity NOUN **1** *At the age of twelve, he was already a celebrity.* = **personality**, name, star, superstar, big name, dignitary, luminary, bigwig (*informal*), celeb (*informal*), face (*informal*), big shot (*informal*), personage, megastar (*informal*), V.I.P. ■ **OPPOSITE:** nobody **2** *She has finally achieved celebrity after 25 years as a performer.* = **fame**, reputation, honour, glory, popularity, distinction, prestige, prominence, stardom, renown, pre-eminence, repute, éclat, notability ■ **OPPOSITE:** obscurity

celestial ADJECTIVE **1** *the clusters of celestial bodies in the ever-expanding universe* = **astronomical**, planetary, stellar, astral, extraterrestrial **2** *gods and other celestial beings* = **heavenly**, spiritual, divine, eternal, sublime, immortal, supernatural, astral, ethereal, angelic, godlike, seraphic

celibacy NOUN = **chastity**, purity, virginity, continence, singleness

celibate ADJECTIVE = **chaste**, single, unmarried, pure, virgin, continent

cell NOUN **1** *They took her back to the cell, and just left her there to die.* = **room**, chamber, lock-up, compartment, cavity, cubicle, dungeon, stall **2** *a spy cell comprising several people* = **unit**, group, section, core, nucleus, caucus, coterie

cement NOUN **1** *The stone work has all been pointed with cement.* = **mortar**, plaster, paste **2** *Stick the pieces on with tile cement.* = **sealant**, glue, gum, adhesive, binder ▶ VERB *Most artificial joints are cemented into place.* = **stick**, join, bond, attach, seal, glue, plaster, gum, weld, solder

cemetery NOUN = **graveyard**, churchyard, burial ground, necropolis, God's acre

censor VERB = **expurgate**, cut, blue-pencil, bowdlerize

censorship NOUN = **expurgation**, blue pencil, purgation, bowdlerization *or* bowdlerisation, sanitization *or* sanitisation

censure VERB *I would not presume to censure him for his views.* = **criticize**, blame, abuse, condemn, carpet (*informal*), denounce, put down, slate (*informal, chiefly U.S.*), rebuke, reprimand, reproach, scold, berate, castigate, chide, tear into (*informal*), diss (*slang*), blast, read the riot act, reprove, upbraid, slap on the wrist, damn, lambast(e), bawl out (*informal*), excoriate, rap over the knuckles, chew out (*U.S. & Canad. informal*), tear (someone) off a strip (*Brit. informal*), give (someone) a rocket (*Brit. & N.Z. informal*), reprehend ■ **OPPOSITE:** applaud ▶ NOUN *It is a controversial policy which has attracted international censure.* = **disapproval**, criticism, blame, condemnation, rebuke, reprimand, reproach, dressing down (*informal*), stick (*slang*), stricture, reproof, castigation, obloquy, remonstrance ■ **OPPOSITE:** approval

central ADJECTIVE **1** *She had a house in central London.* = **inner**, middle, mid, interior ■ **OPPOSITE:** outer **2** *a central part of government policy* = **main**, central, chief, key, essential, primary, principal, fundamental, focal ■ **OPPOSITE:** minor

centralize VERB = **unify**, concentrate, incorporate, compact, streamline, converge, condense, amalgamate, rationalize

centre NOUN *A large wooden table dominates the centre of the room.* = **middle**, heart, focus, core, nucleus, hub, pivot, kernel, crux, bull's-eye, midpoint ■ **OPPOSITE:** edge
• **centre on something** *or* **someone** *Our efforts centre on helping patients to overcome illness; All his thoughts are centred on himself.* = **focus**, concentrate, cluster, revolve, converge

centrepiece NOUN = **focus**, highlight, hub, star

ceremonial ADJECTIVE *He represented the nation on ceremonial occasions.* = **formal**, public, official, ritual, stately, solemn, liturgical, courtly, ritualistic ■ **OPPOSITE:** informal ▶ NOUN *It is difficult to imagine a more impressive ceremonial.* = **ritual**, ceremony, rite, formality, solemnity

ceremony NOUN **1** *The flag was blessed in a ceremony in the local cathedral.* = **ritual**, service, rite, observance, commemoration, solemnities **2** *He was crowned with great ceremony.* = **formality**, ceremonial, propriety, decorum, formal courtesy

certain ADJECTIVE **1** *She's absolutely certain she's going to make it as a singer.* = **sure**, convinced, positive, confident, satisfied, assured, free from doubt ■ **OPPOSITE:** unsure **2** *They say he's certain to get a nomination for best supporting actor.* = **bound**, sure, fated, destined ■ **OPPOSITE:** unlikely **3** *They intervened to save him from certain death.* = **inevitable**, unavoidable, inescapable, inexorable, ineluctable **4** *One thing is certain – they have the utmost respect for each other.* = **known**, true, positive, plain, ascertained, unmistakable, conclusive, undoubted, unequivocal, undeniable, irrefutable, unquestionable, incontrovertible, indubitable, nailed-on (*slang*) ■ **OPPOSITE:** doubtful **5** *He has to pay a certain sum in child support every month.* = **fixed**, decided, established, settled, definite ■ **OPPOSITE:** indefinite **6** *A certain person has been looking for you.* = **particular**, special, individual, specific

certainly ADVERB = **definitely**, surely, truly, absolutely, undoubtedly, positively, decidedly, without doubt, unquestionably, undeniably, without question, unequivocally, indisputably, assuredly, indubitably, doubtlessly, come hell or high water, irrefutably

certainty NOUN **1** *I have said with absolute certainty that there will be no change of policy.* = **confidence**, trust, faith, conviction, assurance, certitude, sureness, positiveness ■ **OPPOSITE:** doubt **2** *There is too little certainty about the outcome yet.* = **inevitability** ■ **OPPOSITE:** uncertainty **3** *A general election became a certainty three weeks ago.* = **fact**, truth, reality, sure thing (*informal*), surety, banker

certificate NOUN = **document**, licence, warrant, voucher, diploma, testimonial, authorization, credential(s)

certify VERB = **confirm**, show, declare, guarantee, witness, assure, endorse, testify, notify, verify, ascertain, validate, attest, corroborate, avow, authenticate, vouch for, aver

cessation NOUN = **ceasing**, ending, break, halt, halting, pause, suspension, interruption, respite, standstill, stoppage, termination, let-up (*informal*), remission, abeyance, discontinuance, stay

chafe VERB **1** *The shorts were chafing my thighs.* = **rub**, scratch, scrape, rasp, abrade **2** *He chafed at having to take orders from someone else.* = **be annoyed**, rage, fume, be angry, fret, be offended, be irritated, be incensed, be impatient, be exasperated, be inflamed, be ruffled, be vexed, be narked (*Brit., Austral. & N.Z. slang*)

chaff NOUN = **husks**, remains, refuse,

waste, hulls, rubbish, trash (*U.S. & Canad.*), dregs

chagrin NOUN *Much to his chagrin, she didn't remember him at all.* = **annoyance**, embarrassment, humiliation, dissatisfaction, disquiet, displeasure, mortification, discomfiture, vexation, discomposure ▶ VERB *He was chagrined at missing such an easy goal.* = **annoy**, embarrass, humiliate, disquiet, vex, displease, mortify, discomfit, dissatisfy, discompose

chain NOUN **1** *The dogs were growling and pulling at their chains.* = **tether**, coupling, link, bond, shackle, fetter, manacle **2** *a horrific chain of events* = **series**, set, train, string, sequence, succession, progression, concatenation ▶ VERB *We were kept in a cell, chained to the wall.* = **bind**, confine, restrain, handcuff, shackle, tether, fetter, manacle

chairman or **chairwoman** or **chairperson** NOUN **1** *I had done business with the company's chairwoman.* = **director**, president, chief, executive, chairperson, chair **2** *The chairman declared the meeting open.* = **master** or **mistress of ceremonies**, spokesperson, chair, speaker, MC

> **USAGE** The general trend of nonsexist language is to find a term which can apply to both sexes equally, as in the use of *actor* to refer to both men and women. *Chairman* can seem inappropriate when applied to a woman, while *chairwoman* specifies gender, therefore the terms *chair* and *chairperson* are often preferred as alternatives.

chalk up VERB **1** *The team chalked up one win after another.* = **score**, win, gain, achieve, accumulate, attain **2** *I just chalked his odd behaviour up to midlife crisis.* = **record**, mark, enter, credit, register, log, tally

challenge NOUN **1** *I like a challenge, and they don't come much bigger than this.* = **dare**, provocation, summons to contest, wero (*N.Z.*) **2** *In December, she saw off the first challenge to her leadership.* = **test**, trial, opposition, confrontation, defiance, ultimatum, face-off (*slang*) ▶ VERB **1** *The move was immediately challenged by the opposition.* = **dispute**, question, tackle, confront, defy, object to, disagree with, take issue with, impugn (*formal*), throw down (*U.S. slang*) **2** *He left a note at the crime scene, challenging detectives to catch him.* = **dare**, invite, provoke, defy, summon, call out, throw down the gauntlet **3** *a task that would challenge his courage* = **test**, try, tax **4** *The men opened fire after they were challenged by the guard.* = **question**, interrogate, accost

chamber NOUN 1 *We are going to be in the council chamber when he speaks.* = **hall**, room 2 *the main political chamber of the Slovenian parliament* = **council**, assembly, legislature, legislative body 3 *We shall dine together in my chamber.* = **room**, bedroom, enclosure, cubicle 4 *The incinerator works by focusing the sun's rays onto a cylindrical glass chamber.* = **compartment**, hollow, cavity

champion NOUN 1 *Kasparov became a world chess champion.* = **winner**, hero, victor, conqueror, title holder, warrior 2 *He received acclaim as a champion of the oppressed.* = **defender**, guardian, patron, backer, protector, upholder, vindicator ▶ VERB *He passionately championed the poor.* = **support**, back, defend, promote, advocate, fight for, uphold, espouse, stick up for (*informal*)

chance NOUN 1 *This partnership has a good chance of success.* = **probability**, odds, possibility, prospect, liability, likelihood ■ OPPOSITE: certainty 2 *All eligible people will get a chance to vote.* = **opportunity**, opening, occasion, time, scope, window 3 *I met him quite by chance.* = **accident**, fortune, luck, fate, destiny, coincidence, misfortune, providence ■ OPPOSITE: design 4 *I certainly think it's worth taking a chance.* = **risk**, speculation, gamble, hazard ▶ ADJECTIVE *He describes their chance meeting as intense.* = **accidental**, random, casual, incidental, unforeseen, unintentional, fortuitous, inadvertent, serendipitous, unforeseeable, unlooked-for ■ OPPOSITE: planned ▶ VERB 1 *A man I chanced to meet proved to be a most unusual character.* = **happen** 2 *No sniper would chance a shot from amongst that crowd.* = **risk**, try, stake, venture, gamble, hazard, wager
■ RELATED WORD: *adjective* fortuitous

change NOUN 1 *They are going to have to make some drastic changes.* = **alteration**, innovation, transformation, modification, mutation, metamorphosis, permutation, transmutation, difference, revolution, transition 2 *It makes a nice change to see you in a good mood for once.* = **variety**, break (*informal*), departure, variation, novelty, diversion (*Brit.*), whole new ball game (*informal*) ■ OPPOSITE: monotony 3 *He stuffed a bag with a few changes of clothing.* = **exchange**, trade, conversion, swap, substitution, interchange ▶ VERB 1 *They should change the law to make it illegal to own replica weapons.* = **alter**, reform, transform, adjust, moderate, revise, modify, remodel, reorganize, restyle, convert ■ OPPOSITE: keep 2 *We are trying to detect and understand how the climate changes.* = **shift**, vary,

transform, alter, modify, diversify, fluctuate, mutate, metamorphose, transmute ■ OPPOSITE: stay 3 *Can we change it for another if it doesn't work properly?* = **exchange**, trade, replace, substitute, swap, interchange

changeable ADJECTIVE = **variable**, shifting, mobile, uncertain, volatile, unsettled, unpredictable, versatile, unstable, irregular, erratic, wavering, uneven, unreliable, fickle, temperamental, whimsical, mercurial, capricious, unsteady, protean, vacillating, fitful, mutable, inconstant ■ OPPOSITE: constant

channel NOUN 1 *We'll be lodging a complaint through the official channels.* = **means**, way, course, approach, medium, route, path, avenue 2 *Oil spilled into the channel following a collision between a tanker and a trawler.* = **strait**, sound, route, passage, canal, waterway, main 3 *Keep the drainage channel clear.* = **duct**, chamber, artery, groove, gutter, furrow, conduit ▶ VERB *Stefan is channelling all his energies into his novel.* = **direct**, guide, conduct, transmit, convey

chant NOUN *We were listening to a sublime Gregorian chant.* = **song**, carol, chorus, melody, psalm ▶ VERB *Flowers were strewn on the ground as monks chanted and prayed.* = **sing**, chorus, recite, intone, carol

chaos NOUN = **disorder**, confusion, mayhem, havoc (*informal*), anarchy, lawlessness, pandemonium, entropy, bedlam, tumult, disorganization ■ OPPOSITE: orderliness

chaotic ADJECTIVE = **disordered**, confused, uncontrolled, anarchic, tumultuous, lawless, riotous, topsy-turvy, disorganized, purposeless

chap NOUN = **fellow** (*old-fashioned*), man, person, individual, type, sort, customer (*informal*), character, guy (*informal*), bloke (*Brit. informal*), cove (*slang*), dude (*U.S. & Canad. informal*), boykie (*S. African informal*)

chapter NOUN 1 *I took the title of this chapter from one of my favorite songs.* = **section**, part, stage, division, episode, topic, segment, instalment 2 *It was one of the most dramatic chapters of recent British politics.* = **period**, time, stage, phase

char VERB = **scorch**, sear, singe

character NOUN 1 *There is a side to his character which you haven't seen yet.* = **personality**, nature, make-up, cast, constitution, bent, attributes, temper, temperament, complexion, disposition, individuality, marked traits 2 *Moscow's reforms were socialist in character.* = **nature**, kind, quality, constitution, calibre 3 *What* an unpleasant character he is! = **person**, sort, individual, type, guy (informal), fellow **4** He's begun a series of attacks on my character. = **reputation**, honour, integrity, good name, rectitude **5** He plays the film's central character. = **role**, part, persona **6** He'll be sadly missed. He was a real character. = **eccentric**, card (informal), original, nut (slang), flake (slang, chiefly U.S.), oddity, oddball (informal), odd bod (informal), queer fish (Brit. informal) **7** Chinese characters inscribed on a plaque = **symbol**, mark, sign, letter, figure, type, device, logo, emblem, rune, cipher, hieroglyph

characteristic NOUN Genes determine the characteristics of every living thing. = **feature**, mark, quality, property, attribute, faculty, trait, quirk, peculiarity, idiosyncrasy ▶ ADJECTIVE Windmills are a characteristic feature of the landscape. = **typical**, special, individual, specific, representative, distinguishing, distinctive, peculiar, singular, idiosyncratic, symptomatic ■ **OPPOSITE:** rare

characterize VERB = **distinguish**, mark, identify, brand, inform, stamp, typify

charade NOUN = **pretence**, farce, parody, pantomime, fake

charge VERB **1** They have all the evidence required to charge him. = **accuse**, indict, impeach, incriminate, arraign ■ **OPPOSITE:** acquit **2** Our general ordered us to charge the enemy. = **attack**, assault, assail ■ **OPPOSITE:** retreat **3** He charged into the room. = **rush**, storm, stampede **4** a performance that was charged with energy = **fill**, load, instil, suffuse, lade ▶ NOUN **1** We can arrange this for a small charge. = **price**, rate, cost, amount, payment, expense, toll, expenditure, outlay, damage (informal) **2** They appeared at court to deny charges of murder. = **accusation**, allegation, indictment, imputation ■ **OPPOSITE:** acquittal **3** I have been given charge of this class. = **care**, trust, responsibility, custody, safekeeping **4** I did not consider it any part of my charge to come up with marketing ideas. = **duty**, office, concern, responsibility, remit **5** The coach tried to get his charges motivated. = **ward**, pupil, protégé, dependant **6** He led the bayonet charge from the front. = **attack**, rush, assault, onset, onslaught, stampede, sortie ■ **OPPOSITE:** retreat

charisma NOUN = **charm**, appeal, personality, attraction, lure, allure, magnetism, force of personality, mojo (slang)

charismatic ADJECTIVE = **charming**, appealing, attractive, influential, magnetic, enticing, alluring

charitable ADJECTIVE **1** He made large donations to numerous charitable organizations. = **benevolent**, liberal, generous, lavish, philanthropic, bountiful, beneficent ■ **OPPOSITE:** mean **2** Some people take a less charitable view of his behaviour. = **kind**, understanding, forgiving, sympathetic, favourable, tolerant, indulgent, lenient, considerate, magnanimous, broad-minded ■ **OPPOSITE:** unkind

charity NOUN **1** The National Trust is a registered charity. = **charitable organization**, fund, movement, trust, endowment **2** My mum was very proud. She wouldn't accept charity. = **donations**, help, relief, gift, contributions, assistance, hand-out, philanthropy, alms-giving, benefaction, largesse or largess, koha (N.Z.) ■ **OPPOSITE:** meanness **3** He had no sense of right and wrong, no charity, no humanity. = **kindness**, love, pity, humanity, affection, goodness, goodwill, compassion, generosity, indulgence, bounty, altruism, benevolence, fellow feeling, bountifulness, tenderheartedness, aroha (N.Z.) ■ **OPPOSITE:** ill will

charlatan NOUN = **fraud** (informal), cheat, fake, sham, pretender, quack, conman or woman (informal), con artist (informal), impostor, fraudster, swindler, mountebank, grifter (slang, chiefly U.S. & Canad.), phoney or phony (informal), rorter (Austral. slang), rogue trader

charm NOUN **1** He was a man of great distinction and charm. = **attraction**, appeal, fascination, allure, magnetism, desirability, allurement ■ **OPPOSITE:** repulsiveness **2** She wore a silver bracelet hung with charms. = **trinket 3** He carried a rabbit's foot as a good luck charm. = **talisman**, amulet, lucky piece, good-luck piece, fetish **4** They cross their fingers and spit over their shoulders as a charm against the evil eye. = **spell**, magic, enchantment, sorcery, makutu (N.Z.) ▶ VERB **1** My brother charms everyone he meets. = **attract**, win, please, delight, fascinate, absorb, entrance, win over, enchant, captivate, beguile, allure, bewitch, ravish, mesmerize, enrapture, enamour ■ **OPPOSITE:** repel **2** I'm sure you'll be able to charm him into taking you. = **persuade**, seduce, coax, beguile, cajole, sweet-talk (informal)

charming ADJECTIVE = **attractive**, pleasing, appealing, engaging, lovely, winning, pleasant, fetching (informal), delightful, cute, irresistible, seductive, captivating, eye-catching, bewitching, delectable, winsome, likable or likeable ■ **OPPOSITE:** unpleasant

chart | 132

chart NOUN *The chart below shows the results of our survey.* = **table**, diagram, blueprint, graph, tabulation, plan, map ▶ VERB **1** *These seas have been well charted.* = **plot**, map out, delineate, sketch, draft, graph, tabulate **2** *Bulletin boards charted each executive's progress.* = **monitor**, follow, record, note, document, register, trace, outline, log, graph, tabulate

charter NOUN **1** *In Britain, city status is granted by royal charter.* = **document**, right, contract, bond, permit, licence, concession, privilege, franchise, deed, prerogative, indenture **2** *The Prime Minister also attacked the social charter.* = **constitution**, laws, rules, code ▶ VERB **1** *He chartered a jet to fly her home.* = **hire**, commission, employ, rent, lease **2** *The council is chartered to promote the understanding of British culture throughout the world.* = **authorize**, permit, sanction, entitle, license, empower, give authority

chase VERB **1** *She chased the thief for 100 yards.* = **pursue**, follow, track, hunt, run after, course **2** *Some farmers chase you off their land quite aggressively.* = **drive away**, drive, expel, hound, send away, send packing, put to flight **3** *They chased down the stairs into the alley.* = **rush**, run, race, shoot, fly, speed, dash, sprint, bolt, dart, hotfoot ▶ NOUN *He was arrested after a car chase.* = **pursuit**, race, hunt, hunting

chasm NOUN **1** *The chasm was deep and its sides almost vertical.* = **gulf**, opening, crack, gap, rent, hollow, void, gorge, crater, cavity, abyss, ravine, cleft, fissure, crevasse **2** *the chasm that separates the rich from the poor* = **gap**, division, gulf, split, breach, rift, alienation, hiatus

chassis NOUN = **frame**, framework, fuselage, bodywork, substructure

chaste ADJECTIVE **1** *The character was pure, with chaste thoughts.* = **pure**, moral, decent, innocent, immaculate, wholesome, virtuous, virginal, unsullied, uncontaminated, undefiled, incorrupt, celibate ■ OPPOSITE: promiscuous **2** *Beyond them she could see the dim, chaste interior of the room.* = **simple**, quiet, elegant, modest, refined, restrained, austere, unaffected, decorous

chasten VERB = **subdue**, discipline, cow, curb, humble, soften, humiliate, tame, afflict, repress, put in your place

chastise VERB = **scold**, blame, correct, discipline, lecture, carpet (*informal*), censure, rebuke, reprimand, reproach, berate, tick off (*informal*), castigate, chide, tell off (*informal*), find fault with,

remonstrate with, bring (someone) to book, take (someone) to task, reprove, upbraid, bawl out (*informal*), give (someone) a talking-to (*informal*), haul (someone) over the coals (*informal*), chew (someone) out (*U.S. & Canad. informal*), give (someone) a dressing-down, give (someone) a rocket (*Brit. & N.Z. informal*), give (someone) a row ■ OPPOSITE: praise

chastity NOUN = **purity**, virtue, innocence, modesty, virginity, celibacy, continence, maidenhood ■ OPPOSITE: promiscuity

chat VERB *I was just chatting to him the other day.* = **talk**, gossip, jaw (*slang*), natter, blather, schmooze (*slang*), blether (*Scot.*), shoot the breeze (*U.S. slang*), chew the rag or fat (*slang*) ▶ NOUN *She asked me into her office for a chat.* = **talk**, tête-à-tête, conversation, gossip, heart-to-heart, natter, blather, schmooze (*slang*), blether (*Scot.*), chinwag (*Brit. informal*), confab (*informal*), craic (*Irish informal*), korero (*N.Z.*)

chatter VERB *Everyone was chattering away in different languages.* = **prattle**, chat, rabbit on (*Brit. informal*), babble, gab (*informal*), natter, tattle, jabber, blather, schmooze (*slang*), blether (*Scot.*), run off at the mouth (*U.S. slang*), prate, gossip ▶ NOUN *She kept up a steady stream of chatter the whole time.* = **prattle**, chat, rabbit (*Brit. informal*), gossip, babble, twaddle, gab (*informal*), natter, tattle, jabber, blather, blether (*Scot.*)

chatty ADJECTIVE = **talkative**, informal, effusive, garrulous, gabby (*informal*), gossipy, newsy (*informal*) ■ OPPOSITE: quiet

cheap ADJECTIVE **1** *Smoke detectors are cheap and easy to put up.* = **inexpensive**, sale, economy, reduced, keen, reasonable, bargain, low-priced, low-cost, cut-price, economical, cheapo (*informal*) ■ OPPOSITE: expensive **2** *Don't resort to cheap copies; save up for the real thing.* = **inferior**, poor, worthless, second-rate, shoddy, tawdry, tatty (*Brit.*), trashy, substandard, low-rent (*informal, chiefly U.S.*), two-bit (*U.S. & Canad. slang*), crappy (*slang*), two a penny, rubbishy, dime-a-dozen (*informal*), tinhorn (*U.S. slang*), bodger or bodgie (*Austral. slang*) ■ OPPOSITE: good **3** *That was a cheap trick to play on anyone.* = **despicable**, mean, low, base, vulgar, sordid, contemptible, scurvy (*old-fashioned*), scungy (*Austral. & N.Z.*) ■ OPPOSITE: decent

cheapen VERB = **degrade**, lower, discredit, devalue, demean, belittle, depreciate, debase, derogate

cheat VERB **1** *He cheated people out of their life savings.* = **deceive**, skin (*slang*), trick, fool, take in (*informal*), con (*informal*), stiff (*slang*), sting (*informal*), mislead, rip off (*slang*), fleece, hoax, defraud, dupe, beguile, gull (*archaic*), do (*informal*), swindle, stitch up (*slang*), victimize, bamboozle (*informal*), hoodwink, double-cross (*informal*), diddle (*informal*), take for a ride (*informal*), bilk, pull a fast one on (*informal*), screw (*informal*), finagle (*informal*), scam (*slang*) **2** *He cheated death when he was rescued from the blazing cottage.* = **foil**, check, defeat, prevent, frustrate, deprive, baffle, thwart ▶ NOUN *He's nothing but a rotten cheat.* = **deceiver**, sharper, cheater, shark, charlatan, trickster, conman or woman (*informal*), con artist (*informal*), impostor, fraudster, double-crosser (*informal*), swindler, grifter (*slang, chiefly U.S. & Canad.*), rorter (*Austral. slang*), chiseller (*informal*), rogue trader

check VERB **1** (*often with* **out**) *Check the accuracy of every detail in your CV.* = **examine**, test, study, look at, research, note, confirm, investigate, monitor, probe, tick, vet, inspect, look over, verify, work over, scrutinize, make sure of, inquire into, take a dekko at (*Brit. slang*), parse (*computer code*) ■ **OPPOSITE:** overlook **2** *Today's meeting must focus on checking the spread of violence.* = **stop**, control, limit, arrest, delay, halt, curb, bar, restrain, inhibit, rein, thwart, hinder, repress, obstruct, retard, impede, bridle, stem the flow of, nip in the bud, put a spoke in someone's wheel ■ **OPPOSITE:** further ▶ NOUN **1** *He is being constantly monitored with regular checks on his blood pressure.* = **examination**, test, research, investigation, inspection, scrutiny, once-over (*informal*) **2** *There is a check on the number of people allowed in the venue.* = **control**, limitation, restraint, constraint, rein, obstacle, curb, obstruction, stoppage, inhibition, impediment, hindrance, damper

cheek NOUN = **impudence**, face (*informal*), front, nerve (*informal*), sauce (*informal*), gall (*informal*), disrespect, audacity, neck (*informal*), lip (*slang*), temerity, chutzpah (*U.S. & Canad. informal*), insolence, impertinence, effrontery, brass neck (*Brit. informal*), brazenness, sassiness (*U.S. informal*)

cheeky ADJECTIVE = **impudent**, rude, forward, fresh (*informal*), insulting, saucy, audacious, sassy (*U.S. informal*), pert, disrespectful, impertinent, insolent, lippy (*U.S. & Canad. slang*) ■ **OPPOSITE:** respectful

cheer VERB **1** *Cheering crowds lined the route.* = **applaud**, hail, acclaim, clap, hurrah ■ **OPPOSITE:** boo **2** *The people around him were cheered by his presence.* = **hearten**, encourage, warm, comfort, elevate, animate, console, uplift, brighten,

exhilarate, solace, enliven, cheer up, buoy up, gladden, elate, inspirit ■ **OPPOSITE:** dishearten ▶ NOUN **1** *The colonel was rewarded by a resounding cheer from his men.* = **applause**, ovation **2** *This news did not bring them much cheer.* = **cheerfulness**, comfort, joy, optimism, animation, glee, solace, buoyancy, mirth, gaiety, merriment, liveliness, gladness, hopefulness, merry-making • **cheer someone up** *She chatted away brightly, trying to cheer him up.* = **comfort**, encourage, brighten, hearten, enliven, gladden, gee up, jolly along (*informal*) • **cheer up** *Cheer up, things could be a lot worse.* = **take heart**, rally, perk up, buck up (*informal*)

cheerful ADJECTIVE **1** *They are both very cheerful in spite of their circumstances.* = **happy**, bright, contented, glad, optimistic, bucked (*informal*), enthusiastic, sparkling, gay, sunny, perky, jolly, animated, merry, upbeat (*informal*), buoyant, hearty, cheery, joyful, jovial, genial, jaunty, chirpy (*informal*), sprightly, blithe, light-hearted ■ **OPPOSITE:** sad **2** *The room is bright and cheerful.* = **pleasant**, bright, sunny, gay, enlivening ■ **OPPOSITE:** gloomy

cheerfulness NOUN = **happiness**, good humour, exuberance, high spirits, buoyancy, gaiety, good cheer, gladness, geniality, light-heartedness, jauntiness, joyousness

cheery ADJECTIVE = **cheerful**, happy, pleasant, lively, sunny, upbeat (*informal*), good-humoured, carefree, breezy, genial, chirpy (*informal*), jovial, full of beans (*informal*)

chemical NOUN = **compound**, drug, substance, synthetic substance, potion

chemist NOUN = **pharmacist**, apothecary (*obsolete*), pharmacologist, dispenser

cherish VERB **1** *I will cherish the memory of that visit for many years to come.* = **cling to**, prize, treasure, hold dear, cleave to ■ **OPPOSITE:** despise **2** *He genuinely loved and cherished his children.* = **care for**, love, support, comfort, look after, shelter, treasure, nurture, cosset, hold dear ■ **OPPOSITE:** neglect **3** *She cherished an ambition to be an actor.* = **harbour**, nurse, sustain, foster, entertain

chest NOUN **1** *I crossed my arms over my chest.* = **breast**, front **2** *At the very bottom of the chest were some carving tools.* = **box**, case, trunk, crate, coffer, ark (*dialect*), casket, strongbox ■ **RELATED WORD:** adjective pectoral

chew VERB *Be careful to eat slowly and chew your food well.* = **munch**, bite, grind, champ, crunch, gnaw, chomp, masticate • **chew something over** *You might want to sit back and chew things over for a while.* = **consider**, weigh up, ponder, mull (over), meditate on, reflect upon, muse on, ruminate, deliberate upon

chewy ADJECTIVE = **tough**, fibrous, leathery, as tough as old boots

chic ADJECTIVE = **stylish**, smart, elegant, fashionable, trendy (*Brit. informal*), up-to-date, modish, à la mode, voguish (*informal*), schmick (*Austral. informal*) ■ **OPPOSITE:** unfashionable

chide VERB = **scold**, blame, lecture, carpet (*informal*), put down, criticize, slate (*informal, chiefly Brit.*), censure, rebuke, reprimand, reproach, berate, tick off (*informal*), admonish, tear into (*informal*), blast, tell off (*informal*), find fault, diss (*slang*), read the riot act, reprove, upbraid, slap on the wrist, lambast(e), bawl out (*informal*), rap over the knuckles, chew out (*U.S. & Canad. informal*), tear (someone) off a strip (*Brit. informal*), give (someone) a rocket (*Brit. & N.Z. informal*), reprehend, give (someone) a row (*Scot. informal*)

chief NOUN *The new leader is the deputy chief of the territory's defence force.* = **head**, leader, director, manager, lord, boss (*informal*), captain, master, governor, commander, principal, superior, ruler, superintendent, chieftain, ringleader, ariki (*N.Z.*), sherang (*Austral. & N.Z.*) ■ **OPPOSITE:** subordinate ▶ ADJECTIVE *Financial stress is acknowledged as a chief reason for divorce.* = **primary**, highest, leading, main, prime, capital, central, key, essential, premier, supreme, most important, outstanding, principal, prevailing, cardinal, paramount, big-time (*informal*), foremost, major league (*informal*), predominant, uppermost, pre-eminent, especial ■ **OPPOSITE:** minor

chiefly ADVERB **1** *We are chiefly concerned with the welfare of the children.* = **especially**, essentially, principally, primarily, above all **2** *a committee composed chiefly of the leaders of rival factions* = **mainly**, largely, usually, mostly, in general, on the whole, predominantly, in the main

child NOUN **1** *This film is not suitable for children.* = **youngster**, baby, kid (*informal*), minor, infant, babe, juvenile, toddler, tot, wean (*Scot.*), little one, brat, bairn (*Scot. & Northern English*), suckling, nipper (*informal*), chit, babe in arms, sprog (*slang*), munchkin (*informal, chiefly U.S.*), rug rat (*slang*), nursling, littlie (*Austral. informal*), ankle-biter (*Austral. & U.S. slang*), tacker (*Austral. slang*) **2** *How many children do*

you have? = **offspring**, issue, descendant, progeny ■ **RELATED WORDS:** *adjective* filial; *prefix* paedo-

childbirth NOUN = **child-bearing**, labour, delivery, lying-in, confinement, parturition ■ **RELATED WORDS:** *adjectives* natal, obstetric

childhood NOUN = **youth**, minority, infancy, schooldays, immaturity, boyhood *or* girlhood

childish ADJECTIVE **1** *One of his most appealing qualities is his childish enthusiasm.* = **youthful**, young, boyish *or* girlish **2** *I've never seen such selfish and childish behaviour.* = **immature**, silly, juvenile, foolish, trifling, frivolous, infantile, puerile ■ **OPPOSITE:** mature

childlike ADJECTIVE = **innocent**, trusting, simple, naive, credulous, artless, ingenuous, guileless, unfeigned, trustful

chill VERB **1** *Chill the fruit salad until serving time.* = **cool**, refrigerate, freeze **2** *There was a coldness in her voice which chilled him.* = **dishearten**, depress, discourage, dismay, dampen, deject ▶ NOUN **1** *September is here, bringing with it a chill in the mornings.* = **coldness**, bite, nip, sharpness, coolness, rawness, crispness, frigidity **2** *He smiled an odd smile that sent a chill through me.* = **shiver**, frisson, goose pimples, goose flesh ▶ ADJECTIVE *A chill wind was blowing.* = **chilly**, biting, sharp, freezing, raw, bleak, wintry, frigid, parky (*Brit. informal*)

chilly ADJECTIVE **1** *It was a chilly afternoon.* = **cool**, fresh, sharp, crisp, penetrating, brisk, breezy, draughty, nippy, parky (*Brit. informal*), blowy ■ **OPPOSITE:** warm **2** *I was slightly afraid of his chilly, distant politeness.* = **unfriendly**, hostile, unsympathetic, frigid, unresponsive, unwelcoming, cold as ice ■ **OPPOSITE:** friendly

chime VERB *The station clock chimed three o'clock.* = **ring** ▶ NOUN *the chime of the station clock* = **sound**, boom, toll, jingle, dong, tinkle, clang, peal

chimera NOUN = **illusion**, dream, fantasy, delusion, spectre, snare, hallucination, figment, ignis fatuus, will-o'-the-wisp

china¹ NOUN *I collect blue and white china.* = **pottery**, ceramics, ware, porcelain, crockery, tableware, service

china² NOUN *How are you, my old china?* = **friend**, pal (*informal*), mate (*informal*), buddy (*informal*), companion, best friend, intimate, cock (*Brit. informal*), close friend, comrade, chum (*informal*), crony, main man (*slang, chiefly U.S.*), soul mate, homeboy (*slang, chiefly U.S.*), cobber (*Austral. & N.Z., old-fashioned, informal*), bosom friend, boon companion, E hoa (*N.Z.*)

Chinese ADJECTIVE ■ **RELATED WORD:** *prefix* Sino-

chink NOUN = **opening**, crack, gap, rift, aperture, cleft, crevice, fissure, cranny

chip NOUN **1** *His eyes gleamed like chips of blue glass.* = **fragment**, scrap, shaving, flake, paring, wafer, sliver, shard **2** *The washbasin had a small chip in it.* = **scratch**, nick, flaw, notch, dent **3** *He gambled all his chips on one number.* = **counter**, disc, token ▶ VERB **1** *The blow chipped the woman's tooth.* = **nick**, damage, gash **2** *a sculptor chipping at a block of marble* = **chisel**, whittle • **chip in 1** *We'll all chip in for the petrol and food.* = **contribute**, pay, donate, subscribe, go Dutch (*informal*) **2** *He chipped in, 'That's right,' before she could answer.* = **interpose**, put in, interrupt, interject, butt in, put your oar in

chirp VERB = **chirrup**, pipe, peep, warble, twitter, cheep, tweet

chirpy ADJECTIVE = **cheerful**, happy, bright, enthusiastic, lively, sparkling, sunny, jolly, animated, buoyant, radiant, jaunty, sprightly, in high spirits, blithe, full of beans (*informal*), light-hearted

chivalry NOUN **1** *He always treated women with old-fashioned chivalry.* = **courtesy**, politeness, gallantry, courtliness, gentlemanliness **2** *Our story is set in England, in the age of chivalry.* = **knight-errantry**, knighthood, gallantry, courtliness

choice NOUN **1** *It's available in a choice of colours.* = **range**, variety, selection, assortment **2** *His choice of words made Rajiv angry.* = **selection**, preference, election, pick **3** *If I had any choice in the matter, I wouldn't have gone.* = **option**, say, alternative ▶ ADJECTIVE *The finest array of choicest foods is to be found within their Food Hall.* = **best**, bad (*slang*), special, prime, nice, prize, select, excellent, elect, crucial (*slang*), exclusive, elite, superior, exquisite, def (*slang*), sick (*slang*), booshit (*Austral. slang*), exo (*Austral. slang*), sik (*Austral. slang*), hand-picked, dainty, rad (*informal*), phat (*slang*), schmick (*Austral. informal*)

choke VERB **1** *Dense smoke swirled and billowed, its fumes choking her.* = **suffocate**, stifle, smother, overpower, asphyxiate **2** *They choked him with his tie.* = **strangle**, throttle, asphyxiate **3** *The village roads are choked with traffic.* = **block**, dam, clog, obstruct, bung, constrict, occlude (*formal*), congest, close, stop, bar

choose VERB **1** *I chose him to accompany me on my trip.* = **pick**, take, prefer, select, elect, adopt, opt for, designate, single out, espouse, settle on, fix on, cherry-pick, settle upon, predestine ■ **OPPOSITE:** reject

2 *You can just take out the interest every year, if you choose.* = **wish**, want, desire, see fit

choosy ADJECTIVE = **fussy**, particular, exacting, discriminating, selective, fastidious, picky (*informal*), finicky, faddy, nit-picky (*informal*) ■ **OPPOSITE:** indiscriminating

chop VERB *We were set to work chopping wood.* = **cut**, fell, axe, slash, hack, sever, shear, cleave, hew, lop, truncate • **chop something up** *Chop up three firm tomatoes.* = **cut up**, divide, fragment, cube, dice, mince • **the chop** *I was amazed when I got the chop from the team.* = **the sack**, sacking (*informal*), dismissal, the boot (*slang*), your cards (*informal*), the axe (*informal*), termination, the (old) heave-ho (*informal*), the order of the boot (*slang*)

choppy ADJECTIVE = **rough**, broken, ruffled, tempestuous, blustery, squally ■ **OPPOSITE:** calm

chore NOUN = **task**, job, duty, burden, hassle (*informal*), fag (*informal*), errand, no picnic

chortle VERB *He began chortling heartily.* = **chuckle**, laugh, cackle, guffaw ▶ NOUN *The man broke into a wheezy chortle of amusement.* = **chuckle**, laugh, cackle, guffaw

chorus NOUN **1** *Everyone joined in the chorus.* = **refrain**, response, strain, burden **2** *The chorus was singing 'The Ode to Joy'.* = **choir**, singers, ensemble, vocalists, choristers • **in chorus** *'Let us in,' they all wailed in chorus.* = **in unison**, as one, all together, in concert, in harmony, in accord, with one voice

christen VERB **1** *She was born in March and christened in June.* = **baptize**, name **2** *a boat which he christened 'the Stray Cat'* = **name**, call, term, style, title, dub, designate

Christmas NOUN = **the festive season**, Noël, Xmas (*informal*), Yule (*archaic*), Yuletide (*archaic*)

chronic ADJECTIVE **1** *He has to live with chronic back pain.* = **persistent**, constant, continual, deep-seated, incurable, deep-rooted, ineradicable **2** *The programme was chronic, all banal dialogue and canned laughter.* = **dreadful**, awful, appalling, atrocious (*informal*), abysmal

chronicle VERB *The rise of collectivism in Britain has been chronicled by several historians.* = **record**, tell, report, enter, relate, register, recount, set down, narrate, put on record, log, blog ▶ NOUN *this vast chronicle of Napoleonic times* = **record**, story, history, account, register, journal, diary, narrative, annals, log, blog

chronicler NOUN = **recorder**, reporter, historian, narrator, scribe, diarist, annalist

chronological ADJECTIVE = **sequential**, ordered, historical, progressive, consecutive, in sequence ■ **OPPOSITE:** random

chubby ADJECTIVE = **plump**, stout, fleshy, tubby, flabby, portly, buxom, roly-poly, rotund, round, podgy ■ **OPPOSITE:** skinny

chuck VERB **1** *Someone chucked a bottle and it caught me on the side of the head.* = **throw**, cast, pitch, shy, toss, hurl, fling, sling (*informal*), heave **2** (*often with* **away** *or* **out**) *I chucked a whole lot of old magazines and papers.* = **throw out**, dump (*informal*), scrap, get rid of, bin (*informal*), ditch (*slang*), junk (*informal*), discard, dispose of, dispense with, jettison **3** *Last summer, he chucked his job and went on the road.* = **give up** *or* **over**, leave, stop, abandon, cease, resign from, pack in, jack in (*informal*) **4** *It smelt so bad I thought I was going to chuck.* = **vomit**, throw up (*informal*), spew, heave (*slang*), puke (*slang*), barf (*U.S. slang*), chunder (*slang, chiefly Austral.*), upchuck (*U.S. slang*), do a technicolour yawn (*slang*), toss your cookies (*U.S. slang*)

chuckle VERB *He chuckled appreciatively at her riposte.* = **laugh**, giggle, snigger, chortle, titter ▸ NOUN *She gave a soft chuckle and said, 'No chance'.* = **laugh**, giggle, snigger, chortle, titter

chum NOUN = **friend**, mate (*informal*), pal (*informal*), companion, cock (*Brit. informal*), comrade, crony, blood *or* blud (*Brit. slang*), main man (*slang, chiefly U.S.*), cobber (*Austral. & N.Z., old-fashioned, informal*), E hoa (*N.Z.*)

chummy ADJECTIVE = **friendly**, close, thick (*informal*), pally (*informal*), intimate, affectionate, buddy-buddy (*slang, chiefly U.S. & Canad.*), palsy-walsy (*informal*), matey *or* maty (*Brit. informal*)

chunk NOUN = **piece**, block, mass, portion, lump, slab, hunk, nugget, wad, dollop (*informal*), wodge (*Brit. informal*)

chunky ADJECTIVE *The sergeant was a chunky man in his late twenties.* = **thickset**, stocky, beefy (*informal*), stubby, dumpy

church NOUN = **chapel**, temple, cathedral, kirk (*Scot.*), minster, tabernacle, place of worship, house of God, megachurch (*U.S.*)
■ **RELATED WORD:** *adjective* ecclesiastical

churlish ADJECTIVE = **rude**, harsh, vulgar, sullen, surly, morose, brusque, ill-tempered, boorish, uncouth, impolite, loutish, oafish, uncivil, unmannerly ■ **OPPOSITE:** polite

churn VERB **1** *The powerful thrust of the boat's engine churned the water.* = **stir up**, beat, disturb, swirl, agitate **2** *Churning seas smash against the steep cliffs.* = **swirl**, boil, toss, foam, seethe, froth

cigarette NOUN = **fag** (*Brit. slang*), smoke, gasper (*slang*), ciggy (*informal*), coffin nail (*slang*), cancer stick (*slang*)

cinema NOUN **1** *They decided to spend an evening at the cinema.* = **pictures**, movies, picture-house, flicks (*slang*) **2** *Contemporary African cinema has much to offer in its vitality and freshness.* = **films**, pictures, movies, the big screen (*informal*), motion pictures, the silver screen

cipher NOUN **1** *The codebreakers cracked the cipher.* = **code**, coded message, cryptogram **2** *They were little more than ciphers who faithfully carried out their master's commands.* = **nobody**, nonentity

circa PREPOSITION = **approximately**, about, around, roughly, in the region of, round about

circle NOUN **1** *The flag was red with a large white circle.* = **ring**, round, band, disc, loop, hoop, cordon, perimeter, halo **2** *a small circle of friends* = **group**, company, set, school, club, order, class, society, crowd, assembly, fellowship, fraternity, clique, coterie **3** *She moved only in the most exalted circles.* = **sphere**, world, area, range, field, scene (*informal*), orbit, realm, milieu ▸ VERB **1** *This is the ring road that circles the city.* = **go round**, ring, surround, belt, curve, enclose, encompass, compass, envelop, encircle, circumscribe, hem in, gird, circumnavigate, enwreath **2** *There were two helicopters circling around.* = **wheel**, spiral, revolve, rotate, whirl, pivot

circuit NOUN **1** *I get asked this question a lot when I'm on the lecture circuit.* = **course**, round, tour, track, route, journey **2** *the historic racing circuit at Monza* = **racetrack**, course, track, racecourse **3** *She made a slow circuit of the room.* = **lap**, round, tour, revolution, orbit, perambulation

circuitous ADJECTIVE **1** *They were taken on a circuitous route home.* = **indirect**, winding, rambling, roundabout, meandering, tortuous, labyrinthine ■ **OPPOSITE:** direct **2** *He has a pedantic and circuitous writing style.* = **oblique**, indirect

circular ADJECTIVE **1** *The car turned into a spacious, circular courtyard.* = **round**, ring-shaped, discoid **2** *Both sides of the river can be explored on this circular walk.* = **circuitous**, cyclical, orbital ▸ NOUN *A circular has been sent to 1,800 newspapers.* = **advertisement**, notice, ad (*informal*), announcement, advert (*Brit.*), press release

circulate VERB **1** *Public employees are circulating a petition calling for his reinstatement.* = **spread**, issue, publish, broadcast, distribute, diffuse, publicize, propagate, disseminate, promulgate, make known **2** *Cooking odours can circulate throughout the entire house.* = **flow**, revolve, rotate, radiate

circulation NOUN **1** *The paper once had the highest circulation of any daily in the country.* = **distribution**, currency, readership **2** *Anyone with circulation problems should seek medical advice before flying.* = **bloodstream**, blood flow **3** *Fit a ventilated lid to allow circulation of air.* = **flow**, circling, motion, rotation **4** *measures inhibiting the circulation of useful information* = **spread**, distribution, transmission, dissemination

circumference NOUN = **edge**, limits, border, bounds, outline, boundary, fringe, verge (*Brit.*), rim, perimeter, periphery, extremity

circumscribe VERB = **restrict**, limit, define, confine, restrain, delineate, hem in, demarcate, delimit, straiten

circumspect ADJECTIVE = **cautious**, politic, guarded, careful, wary, discriminating, discreet, sage, prudent, canny, attentive, vigilant, watchful, judicious, observant, sagacious (*formal*), heedful ■ **OPPOSITE:** rash

circumstance NOUN **1** (*usually plural*) *They say they will never, under any circumstances, be the first to use force.* = **condition**, situation, scenario, contingency, state of affairs, lie of the land **2** (*usually plural*) *I'm making inquiries about the circumstances of her disappearance.* = **detail**, fact, event, particular, respect, factor **3** (*usually plural*) *I'm not sure how impressed Dad was by this change in my circumstances.* = **situation**, state, means, position, station, resources, status, lifestyle **4** *These people are innocent victims of circumstance.* = **chance**, the times, accident, fortune, luck, fate, destiny, misfortune, providence

circumstantial ADJECTIVE **1** *He was convicted on purely circumstantial evidence.* = **indirect**, contingent, incidental, inferential, presumptive, conjectural, founded on circumstances **2** *The reasons for the project collapsing were circumstantial.* = **detailed**, particular, specific

circumvent VERB **1** *Military rulers tried to circumvent the treaty.* = **evade**, bypass, elude, steer clear of, sidestep **2** = **outwit**, trick, mislead, thwart, deceive, dupe, beguile, outflank, hoodwink

cistern NOUN = **tank**, vat, basin, reservoir, sink

citadel NOUN = **fortress**, keep, tower, stronghold, bastion, fortification, fastness

citation NOUN **1** *His citation says he showed outstanding and exemplary courage.* = **commendation**, award, mention **2** *The text is full of Biblical citations.* = **quotation**, quote (*informal*), reference, passage, illustration, excerpt

cite VERB **1** *She cites a favourite poem by Pablo Neruda.* = **quote**, name, evidence, advance, mention, extract, specify, allude to, enumerate, adduce **2** *The judge ruled a mistrial and cited the prosecutors for gross misconduct.* = **summon**, call, subpoena

citizen NOUN = **inhabitant**, resident, dweller, ratepayer, denizen, subject, freeman *or* woman, burgher, townsman *or* woman *or* person ■ **RELATED WORD:** *adjective* civil

city NOUN = **town**, metropolis, municipality, conurbation, megalopolis ■ **RELATED WORD:** *adjective* civic

civic ADJECTIVE = **public**, community, borough, municipal, communal, urban, local

civil ADJECTIVE **1** *This civil unrest threatens the economy.* = **civic**, home, political, domestic, interior, municipal ■ **OPPOSITE:** state **2** *He couldn't even bring himself to be civil to Pauline.* = **polite**, obliging, accommodating, civilized, courteous, considerate, affable, courtly, well-bred, complaisant, well-mannered ■ **OPPOSITE:** rude

civility NOUN = **politeness**, consideration, courtesy, tact, good manners, graciousness, cordiality, affability, amiability, complaisance, courteousness

civilization NOUN **1** *He believed Western civilization was in grave economic and cultural danger.* = **society**, people, community, nation, polity **2** *a race with an advanced state of civilization* = **culture**, development, education, progress, enlightenment, sophistication, advancement, cultivation, refinement

civilize VERB = **cultivate**, improve, polish, educate, refine, tame, enlighten, humanize, sophisticate

civilized ADJECTIVE **1** *All truly civilized countries must deplore torture.* = **cultured**, educated, sophisticated, enlightened, humane ■ **OPPOSITE:** primitive **2** *Our divorce was conducted in a very civilized manner.* = **polite**, mannerly, tolerant, gracious, courteous, affable, well-behaved, well-mannered

clad ADJECTIVE = **dressed**, clothed, arrayed, draped, fitted out, decked out, attired, rigged out (*informal*), covered

claim VERB **1** *He claimed that it was a conspiracy against him.* = **assert**, insist, maintain, allege, uphold, profess, hold **2** *Now they are* returning to claim what is theirs. = **take**, receive, pick up, collect, lay claim to **3** They intend to claim for damages against the three doctors. = **demand**, call for, ask for, insist on ▸ NOUN **1** There is no evidence to support her claim that her son was injured. = **assertion**, statement, allegation, declaration, contention, pretension, affirmation, protestation (formal) **2** The office has been dealing with their claim for benefits. = **demand**, application, request, petition, call **3** The Tudors had a tenuous claim to the monarchy. = **right**, title, entitlement

claimant NOUN = **applicant**, pretender, petitioner, supplicant (formal), suppliant

clairvoyant ADJECTIVE a fortune-teller who claims to have clairvoyant powers = **psychic**, visionary, prophetic, prescient, telepathic, fey, second-sighted, extrasensory, oracular, sibylline ▸ NOUN You don't need to be a clairvoyant to see how this is going to turn out. = **psychic**, diviner, prophet, visionary, oracle, seer, augur, fortune-teller, soothsayer, sibyl, prophetess, telepath

clamber VERB = **climb**, scale, scramble, claw, shin, scrabble

clammy ADJECTIVE **1** My shirt was clammy with sweat. = **moist**, sweating, damp, sticky, sweaty, slimy **2** As you peer down into this pit, the clammy atmosphere rises to meet your skin. = **damp**, humid, dank, muggy, close

clamour NOUN = **noise**, shouting, racket, outcry, din, uproar, agitation, blare, commotion, babel, hubbub, brouhaha, hullabaloo, shout

clamp NOUN This clamp is ideal for holding frames and other items. = **vice**, press, grip, bracket, fastener ▸ VERB U-bolts are used to clamp the microphones to the pole. = **fasten**, fix, secure, clinch, brace, make fast

clan NOUN **1** A clash had taken place between rival clans. = **family**, house, group, order, race, society, band, tribe, sept, fraternity (U.S. & Canad.), brotherhood, sodality, ainga (N.Z.), ngai or ngati (N.Z.) **2** a powerful clan of industrialists from Monterrey = **group**, set, crowd, circle, crew (informal), gang, faction, coterie, schism, cabal

clandestine ADJECTIVE = **secret**, private, hidden, underground, concealed, closet, covert, sly, furtive, underhand, surreptitious, stealthy, cloak-and-dagger, under-the-counter

clang VERB A little later the church bell clanged. = **ring**, toll, resound, chime, reverberate, jangle, clank, bong, clash ▸ NOUN He pulled the gates shut with a clang. = **ringing**, clash, jangle, knell, clank, reverberation, ding-dong, clangour

clap VERB **1** The men danced and the women clapped. = **applaud**, cheer, acclaim, give (someone) a big hand ■ OPPOSITE: boo **2** He clapped me on the back and boomed, 'Well done.' = **strike**, pat, punch, bang, thrust, slap, whack, wallop (informal), thwack

clarification NOUN = **explanation**, interpretation, exposition, illumination, simplification, elucidation

clarify VERB **1** A bank spokesman was unable to clarify the situation. = **explain**, resolve, interpret, illuminate, clear up, simplify, make plain, elucidate, explicate (formal), clear the air about, throw or shed light on **2** Clarify the butter by bringing it to a simmer in a small pan. = **refine**, cleanse, purify

clarity NOUN **1** the clarity with which the author explains this technical subject = **clearness**, precision, simplicity, transparency, lucidity, explicitness, intelligibility, obviousness, straightforwardness, comprehensibility ■ OPPOSITE: obscurity **2** The first thing to strike me was the incredible clarity of the water. = **transparency**, clearness ■ OPPOSITE: cloudiness

clash VERB **1** A group of 400 demonstrators clashed with police. = **conflict**, grapple, wrangle, lock horns, cross swords, war, feud, quarrel **2** Don't make policy decisions which clash with company thinking. = **disagree**, conflict, vary, counter, differ, depart, contradict, diverge, deviate, run counter to, be dissimilar, be discordant **3** The red door clashed with the pink walls. = **not go**, jar, not match, be discordant **4** The golden bangles on her arms clashed and jangled. = **crash**, bang, rattle, jar, clatter, jangle, clang, clank ▸ NOUN **1** There are reports of clashes between militants and the security forces in the city. = **conflict**, fight, brush, confrontation, collision, showdown (informal), boilover (Austral.) **2** Inside government, there was a clash of views. = **disagreement**, difference, division, argument, dispute, dissent, difference of opinion

clasp VERB Mary clasped the children to her desperately. = **grasp**, hold, press, grip, seize, squeeze, embrace, clutch, hug, enfold ▸ NOUN **1** He gripped my hand in a strong clasp. = **grasp**, hold, grip, embrace, hug **2** She undid the clasp of the hooded cloak she was wearing. = **fastening**, catch, grip, hook, snap, pin, clip, buckle, brooch, fastener, hasp, press stud

class NOUN **1** the relationship between different social classes = **group**, grouping, set, order, league, division, rank, caste, status, sphere **2** a new class of personal computer = **type**, set, sort, kind, collection, species, grade, category, stamp, genre, classification, denomination, genus ▶ VERB *I would class my garden as being medium in size.* = **classify**, group, rate, rank, brand, label, grade, designate, categorize, codify

classic ADJECTIVE **1** *This is a classic example of media hype.* = **typical**, standard, model, regular, usual, ideal, characteristic, definitive, archetypal, exemplary, quintessential, time-honoured, paradigmatic, dinki-di (*Austral. informal*) **2** *Aldous Huxley's classic work, The Perennial Philosophy* = **masterly**, best, finest, master, world-class, consummate, first-rate ■ OPPOSITE: second-rate **3** *These are classic designs which will fit in well anywhere.* = **lasting**, enduring, abiding, immortal, undying, ageless, deathless ▶ NOUN *The album is one of the classics of modern popular music.* = **standard**, masterpiece, prototype, paradigm, exemplar, masterwork, model

classification NOUN **1** *the accepted classification of the animal and plant kingdoms* = **categorization**, grading, cataloguing, taxonomy, codification, sorting, analysis, arrangement, profiling **2** *several different classifications of vehicles* = **class**, grouping, heading, head, order, sort, list, department, type, division, section, rank, grade

classify VERB = **categorize**, sort, file, rank, arrange, grade, catalogue, codify, pigeonhole, tabulate, systematize

classy ADJECTIVE = **high-class**, select, exclusive, superior, elegant, stylish, posh (*informal, chiefly Brit.*), swish (*informal, chiefly Brit.*), up-market, urbane, swanky (*informal*), top-drawer, ritzy (*slang*), high-toned, schmick (*Austral. informal*)

clause NOUN = **section**, condition, article, item, chapter, rider, provision, passage, point, part, heading, paragraph, specification, proviso, stipulation

claw NOUN **1** *The cat's claws got caught in my clothes.* = **nail**, talon **2** *The lobster has two large claws.* = **pincer**, nipper ▶ VERB *The wolf clawed at the tree and howled the whole night.* = **scratch**, tear, dig, rip, scrape, graze, maul, scrabble, mangle, mangulate (*Austral. slang*), lacerate

clean ADJECTIVE **1** *Disease is not a problem because clean water is available.* = **hygienic**, natural, fresh, sterile, pure, purified, antiseptic, sterilized, unadulterated, uncontaminated, unpolluted, decontaminated ■ OPPOSITE: contaminated **2** *He wore his cleanest slacks and a navy blazer.* = **spotless**, fresh, washed,

immaculate, laundered, impeccable, flawless, sanitary, faultless, squeaky-clean, hygienic, unblemished, unsullied, unstained, unsoiled, unspotted ■ OPPOSITE: dirty **3** *He became a model of clean living.* = **moral**, good, pure, decent, innocent, respectable, upright, honourable, impeccable, exemplary, virtuous, chaste, undefiled ■ OPPOSITE: immoral **4** *It is time for a clean break with the past.* = **complete**, final, whole, total, perfect, entire, decisive, thorough, conclusive, unimpaired **5** *I admire the clean lines of Shaker furniture.* = **neat**, simple, elegant, trim, delicate, tidy, graceful, uncluttered ■ OPPOSITE: untidy ▶ VERB *Her father cleaned his glasses with a paper napkin.* = **cleanse**, wash, bath, sweep, dust, wipe, vacuum, scrub, sponge, rinse, mop, launder, scour, purify, do up, swab, disinfect, deodorize, sanitize, deep clean ■ OPPOSITE: dirty

clean-cut ADJECTIVE = **neat**, trim, tidy, chiselled

cleanliness NOUN = **cleanness**, purity, freshness, whiteness, sterility, spotlessness

cleanse VERB **1** *Your body is beginning to cleanse itself of toxins.* = **purify**, clear, purge **2** *Confession cleanses the soul.* = **absolve**, clear, purge, purify **3** *She demonstrated the proper way to cleanse the face.* = **clean**, wash, scrub, rinse, scour

cleanser NOUN = **detergent**, soap, solvent, disinfectant, soap powder, purifier, scourer, wash

clear ADJECTIVE **1** *The book is clear, readable and amply illustrated.* = **comprehensible**, explicit, articulate, understandable, coherent, lucid, user-friendly, intelligible ■ OPPOSITE: confused **2** *He repeated his answer in a clear, firm voice.* = **distinct**, audible, perceptible ■ OPPOSITE: indistinct **3** *It was a clear case of mistaken identity.* = **obvious**, plain, apparent, bold, patent, evident, distinct, pronounced, definite, manifest, blatant, conspicuous, unmistakable, express, palpable, unequivocal, recognizable, unambiguous, unquestionable, cut-and-dried (*informal*), incontrovertible ■ OPPOSITE: ambiguous **4** *It is important to be clear on what the author is saying here.* = **certain**, sure, convinced, positive, satisfied, resolved, explicit, definite, decided ■ OPPOSITE: confused **5** *The water is clear and plenty of fish are visible.* = **transparent**, see-through, translucent, crystalline, glassy, limpid, pellucid ■ OPPOSITE: opaque **6** *All exits must be kept clear in case of fire or a bomb scare.*

= **unobstructed**, open, free, empty, unhindered, unimpeded, unhampered ■ OPPOSITE: blocked **7** *Most places will be dry with clear skies.* = **bright**, fine, fair, shining, sunny, luminous, halcyon, cloudless, undimmed, light, unclouded ■ OPPOSITE: cloudy **8** *I can look back on things with a clear conscience.* = **untroubled**, clean, pure, innocent, stainless, immaculate, unblemished, untarnished, guiltless, sinless, undefiled ▶ VERB **1** *We called in a plumber to clear our blocked sink.* = **unblock**, unclog, free, loosen, extricate, disengage, open, disentangle **2** *Firefighters were still clearing rubble from the scene.* = **remove**, clean, wipe, cleanse, tidy (up), sweep away **3** *As the weather cleared, helicopters began to ferry the injured to hospital.* = **brighten**, break up, lighten **4** *The horse cleared the fence by several inches.* = **pass over**, jump, leap, vault, miss **5** *In a final effort to clear her name, she is writing a book.* = **absolve**, acquit, vindicate, exonerate ■ OPPOSITE: blame • **clear out** *'Clear out!' he bawled, 'This is private property.'* = **go away**, leave, retire, withdraw, depart, beat it (*slang*), decamp, hook it (*slang*), slope off, pack your bags (*informal*), make tracks, take yourself off, make yourself scarce, rack off (*Austral. & N.Z. slang*) • **clear something out 1** *I took the precaution of clearing out my desk before I left.* = **empty**, sort, tidy up **2** *It'll take you a month just to clear out all this rubbish.* = **get rid of**, remove, dump, dispose of, throw away or out • **clear something up 1** *I told you to clear up your room.* = **tidy (up)**, order, straighten, rearrange, put in order **2** *During dinner the confusion was cleared up.* = **solve**, explain, resolve, clarify, unravel, straighten out, elucidate

clearance NOUN **1** *By the late fifties, slum clearance was the watchword in town planning.* = **evacuation**, emptying, withdrawal, removal, eviction, depopulation **2** *He has a security clearance that allows him access to classified information.* = **permission**, consent, endorsement, green light, authorization, blank cheque, go-ahead (*informal*), leave, sanction, O.K. or okay (*informal*) **3** *The lowest fixed bridge has 12.8m clearance.* = **space**, gap, margin, allowance, headroom

clear-cut ADJECTIVE = **straightforward**, specific, plain, precise, black-and-white, explicit, definite, unequivocal, unambiguous, cut-and-dried (*informal*)

clearing NOUN = **glade**, space, dell

clearly ADVERB **1** *He clearly believes that he is in the right.* = **obviously**, undoubtedly,

evidently, distinctly, markedly, overtly, undeniably, beyond doubt, incontrovertibly, incontestably, openly **2** *Write your address clearly on the back of the envelope.* = **legibly**, distinctly **3** *Please speak clearly after the tone.* = **audibly**, distinctly, intelligibly, comprehensibly

cleave[1] VERB *a tool for cleaving watermelons* = **split**, open, divide, crack, slice, rend (*literary*), sever, part, hew, tear asunder, sunder

cleave[2] VERB • **cleave to** = **stick to**, stand by, cling to, hold to, be devoted to, adhere to, be attached to, abide by, be true to

cleft NOUN = **opening**, break, crack, gap, rent, breach, fracture, rift, chink, crevice, fissure, cranny

clemency NOUN = **mercy**, pity, humanity, compassion, kindness, forgiveness, indulgence, leniency, forbearance, quarter

clement ADJECTIVE = **mild**, fine, fair, calm, temperate, balmy

clergy NOUN = **priesthood**, ministry, clerics, clergymen or women, churchmen or women, the cloth, holy orders, ecclesiastics ■ RELATED WORDS: *adjectives* clerical, pastoral

clergyman or **clergywoman** NOUN = **minister**, member of the clergy, priest, vicar, parson, reverend (*informal*), rabbi, pastor, chaplain, cleric, rector, curate, father, churchman or woman, padre, man or woman or person of God, man or woman or person of the cloth, divine

clerical ADJECTIVE **1** *The hospital blamed the mix-up on a clerical error.* = **administrative**, office, bureaucratic, secretarial, book-keeping, stenographic **2** *a clergyman who had failed to carry out his clerical duties* = **ecclesiastical**, priestly, pastoral, sacerdotal

clever ADJECTIVE **1** *My sister has always been the clever one in our family.* = **intelligent**, quick, bright (*informal*), talented, gifted, keen, capable, smart, sensible, rational, witty, apt, discerning, knowledgeable, astute, brainy (*informal*), quick-witted, sagacious (*formal*), knowing, deep, expert **2** *It's a very clever idea.* = **shrewd**, bright (*informal*), cunning, ingenious, inventive, astute, resourceful, canny ■ OPPOSITE: unimaginative **3** *My father was very clever with his hands.* = **skilful**, able, talented, gifted, capable, inventive, adroit, dexterous ■ OPPOSITE: inept

cleverness NOUN **1** *He congratulated himself on his cleverness.* = **intelligence**, sense, brains, wit, brightness (*informal*), nous (*Brit. slang*), suss (*slang*), quickness, gumption

(*Brit. informal*), sagacity, smartness, astuteness, quick wits, smarts (*slang, chiefly U.S.*) **2** *a policy almost Machiavellian in its cleverness* = **shrewdness**, sharpness, resourcefulness, canniness **3** *The artist demonstrates a cleverness with colours and textures.* = **dexterity**, ability, talent, gift, flair, ingenuity, adroitness

cliché NOUN = **platitude**, stereotype, commonplace, banality, truism, bromide, old saw, hackneyed phrase, chestnut (*informal*)

click NOUN *I heard a click and then the telephone message started to play.* = **snap**, beat, tick, clack ▸ VERB **1** *Camera shutters clicked all around me.* = **snap**, beat, tick, clack **2** *When I saw the TV report, it all suddenly clicked.* = **become clear**, come home (to), make sense, fall into place **3** *They clicked immediately; they liked all the same things.* = **get on**, be compatible, hit it off (*informal*), be on the same wavelength, get on like a house on fire (*informal*), take to each other, feel a rapport

client NOUN = **customer**, consumer, buyer, patron, shopper, habitué, patient

clientele NOUN = **customers**, market, business, following, trade, regulars, clients, patronage

cliff NOUN = **rock face**, overhang, crag, precipice, escarpment, face, scar, bluff

climactic ADJECTIVE = **crucial**, central, critical, peak, decisive, paramount, pivotal

> **USAGE** Climatic is sometimes wrongly used where *climactic* is meant. *Climatic* should be used to talk about things relating to climate; *climactic* is used to describe something which forms a climax: *the climactic moment of the Revolution*.

climate NOUN **1** *the hot and humid climate of Cyprus* = **weather**, country, region, temperature, clime **2** *A major change of political climate is unlikely.* = **atmosphere**, environment, spirit, surroundings, tone, mood, trend, flavour, feeling, tendency, temper, ambience, vibes (*slang*)

climax NOUN *Reaching the Olympics was the climax of her career.* = **culmination**, head, top, summit, height, highlight, peak, pay-off (*informal*), crest, high point, zenith, apogee, high spot (*informal*), acme, ne plus ultra (*Latin*) ▸ VERB *They did a series of charity events climaxing in a midsummer concert.* = **culminate**, end, finish, conclude, peak, come to a head

climb VERB **1** *Climbing the first hill took half an hour.* = **ascend**, scale, mount, go up, clamber, shin up **2** *He climbed down from the cab.*

= **clamber**, descend, scramble, dismount **3** *My Tokyo-bound plane climbed above the city.* = **rise**, go up, soar, ascend, fly up • **climb down** *He has climbed down on pledges to reduce capital gains tax.* = **back down**, withdraw, yield, concede, retreat, surrender, give in, cave in (*informal*), retract, admit defeat, back-pedal, eat your words, eat crow (*U.S. informal*)

clinch VERB **1** *We are about to clinch a deal with an American manufacturer.* = **secure**, close, confirm, conclude, seal, verify, sew up (*informal*), close out, set the seal on **2** *Evidently this information clinched the matter.* = **settle**, decide, determine, tip the balance

cling VERB **1** *She had to cling onto the door handle until the pain passed.* = **clutch**, grip, embrace, grasp, hug, hold on to, clasp **2** *His sodden trousers were clinging to his shins.* = **stick to**, attach to, adhere to, fasten to, twine round • **cling to something** *They still cling to their beliefs.* = **adhere to**, maintain, stand by, cherish, abide by, be true to, be loyal to, be faithful to, cleave to

clinical ADJECTIVE = **unemotional**, cold, scientific, objective, detached, analytic, impersonal, antiseptic, disinterested, dispassionate, emotionless

clip¹ VERB **1** *I saw an old man out clipping his hedge.* = **trim**, cut, crop, dock, prune, shorten, shear, cut short, snip, pare **2** *I'd have clipped his ear for him if he'd been my kid.* = **smack**, strike, box, knock, punch, belt (*informal*), thump, clout (*informal*), cuff, whack, wallop (*informal*), skelp (*dialect*) ▸ NOUN **1** *The boy was later given a clip round the ear by his father.* = **smack**, strike, box, knock, punch, belt (*informal*), thump, clout (*informal*), cuff, whack, wallop (*informal*), skelp (*dialect*) **2** *They trotted along at a brisk clip.* = **speed**, rate, pace, gallop, lick (*informal*), velocity

clip² VERB *He clipped his flashlight to his belt.* = **attach**, fix, secure, connect, pin, staple, fasten, affix, hold

clipping NOUN = **cutting**, passage, extract, excerpt, piece, article

clique NOUN = **group**, set, crowd, pack, circle, crew (*informal*), gang, faction, mob, clan, posse (*informal*), coterie, schism, cabal

cloak NOUN **1** *She set out, wrapping her cloak about her.* = **cape**, coat, wrap, mantle (*archaic*) **2** *Today most of England will be under a cloak of thick mist.* = **covering**, layer, blanket, shroud **3** *Individualism is sometimes used as a cloak for self-interest.* = **disguise**, front (*informal*), cover, screen, blind, mask, shield, cover-up, façade, pretext, smoke screen ▸ VERB **1** *The coastline was cloaked in fog.*

= **cover**, coat, wrap, blanket, shroud, envelop **2** *He uses jargon to cloak his inefficiency.* = **hide**, cover, screen, mask, disguise, conceal, obscure, veil, camouflage

clobber¹ VERB *She clobbered him with a vase.* = **batter**, beat, assault, smash, bash (*informal*), lash, thrash, pound, beat up (*informal*), wallop (*informal*), pummel, rough up (*informal*), lambast(e), belabour, duff up (*informal*), beat or knock seven bells out of (*informal*)

clobber² NOUN *His house is filled with a load of old clobber.* = **belongings**, things, effects, property, stuff, gear, possessions, paraphernalia, accoutrements, chattels

clog VERB = **obstruct**, block, jam, hamper, hinder, impede, bung, stop up, dam up, occlude (*formal*), congest

cloistered ADJECTIVE = **sheltered**, protected, restricted, shielded, confined, insulated, secluded, reclusive, shut off, sequestered, withdrawn, cloistral
■ **OPPOSITE:** public

close¹ ADJECTIVE **1** *The hotel is close to Sydney airport.* = **near**, neighbouring, nearby, handy, adjacent, adjoining, hard by, just round the corner, within striking distance (*informal*), cheek by jowl, proximate, within spitting distance (*informal*), within sniffing distance, a hop, skip and a jump away
■ **OPPOSITE:** far **2** *She and Linda became very close.* = **intimate**, loving, friendly, familiar, thick (*informal*), attached, devoted, confidential, inseparable, dear ■ **OPPOSITE:** distant **3** *There is a close resemblance between them.* = **noticeable**, marked, strong, distinct, pronounced **4** *His recent actions have been the subject of close scrutiny.* = **careful**, detailed, searching, concentrated, keen, intense, minute, alert, intent, thorough, rigorous, attentive, painstaking, assiduous **5** *It is still a close contest between the two leading parties.* = **even**, level, neck and neck, fifty-fifty (*informal*), evenly matched, equally balanced **6** *A White House official said an agreement is close.* = **imminent**, near, approaching, impending, at hand, upcoming, nigh, just round the corner
■ **OPPOSITE:** far away **7** *They sat in that hot, close room for two hours.* = **stifling**, confined, oppressive, stale, suffocating, stuffy, humid, sweltering, airless, muggy, unventilated, heavy, thick ■ **OPPOSITE:** airy **8** *The poem is a close translation from the original Latin.* = **accurate**, strict, exact, precise, faithful, literal, conscientious

close² VERB **1** *If you are cold, close the window.*

= **shut**, lock, push to, fasten, secure
■ **OPPOSITE:** open **2** *Many enterprises will be forced to close because of the recession.* = **shut down**, finish, cease, discontinue **3** *There are rumours of plans to close the local college.*
= **wind up**, finish, axe (*informal*), shut down, terminate, discontinue, mothball **4** *The government has closed the border crossing.*
= **block up**, bar, seal, shut up ■ **OPPOSITE:** open **5** *He closed the meeting with his customary address.* = **end**, finish, complete, conclude, wind up, culminate, terminate
■ **OPPOSITE:** begin **6** *I need another $30,000 to close the deal.* = **clinch**, confirm, secure, conclude, seal, verify, sew up (*informal*), close out, set the seal on **7** *His fingers closed around her wrist.* = **come together**, join, connect ■ **OPPOSITE:** separate ▶ NOUN *Her retirement brings to a close a successful chapter in the school's history.* = **end**, ending, finish, conclusion, completion, finale, culmination, denouement

closed ADJECTIVE **1** *Her bedroom door was closed.* = **shut**, locked, sealed, fastened
■ **OPPOSITE:** open **2** *The airport shop was closed.* = **shut down**, out of business, out of service **3** *No-one was admitted to this closed circle of elite students.* = **exclusive**, select, restricted **4** *I now consider the matter closed.*
= **finished**, over, ended, decided, settled, concluded, resolved, terminated

closet NOUN *Perhaps there's room in the broom closet.* = **cupboard**, cabinet, recess, cubicle, cubbyhole ▶ ADJECTIVE *He is a closet folk enthusiast.* = **secret**, private, hidden, unknown, concealed, covert, unrevealed

closure NOUN = **closing**, end, finish, conclusion, stoppage, termination, cessation

clot VERB *The patient's blood refused to clot.* = **congeal**, thicken, curdle, coalesce, jell, coagulate

cloth NOUN = **fabric**, material, textiles, dry goods, stuff

clothe VERB = **dress**, outfit, rig, array, robe, drape, get ready, swathe, apparel, attire, fit out, garb, doll up (*slang*), accoutre, cover, deck ■ **OPPOSITE:** undress

clothes PLURAL NOUN = **clothing**, wear, dress, gear (*informal*), habits, get-up (*informal*), outfit, costume, threads (*slang*), wardrobe, ensemble, garments, duds (*informal*), apparel, clobber (*Brit. slang*), attire, garb, togs (*informal*), vestments, glad rags (*informal*), raiment (*archaic, poetic*), rigout (*informal*)

clothing NOUN = **clothes**, wear, dress, gear (*informal*), habits, get-up (*informal*), outfit, costume, threads (*slang*), wardrobe, ensemble, garments, duds (*informal*), apparel, clobber (*Brit. slang*), attire, garb, togs (*informal*), vestments, glad rags (*informal*), raiment (*archaic, poetic*), rigout (*informal*)

cloud NOUN **1** *The sun was almost entirely obscured by cloud.* = **mist**, fog, haze, obscurity, vapour, nebula, murk, darkness, gloom **2** *The hens darted away on all sides, raising a cloud of dust.* = **billow**, mass, shower, puff ▶ VERB **1** *Perhaps anger has clouded his vision.* = **confuse**, obscure, distort, impair, muddle, disorient **2** *The sky clouded and a light rain began to fall.* = **darken**, dim, be overshadowed, be overcast

cloudy ADJECTIVE **1** *It was a cloudy, windy day.* = **dull**, dark, dim, gloomy, dismal, sombre, overcast, leaden, sunless, louring or lowering ■ OPPOSITE: clear **2** *She could just barely see him through the cloudy water.* = **opaque**, muddy, murky **3** *The legal position on this issue is very cloudy.* = **vague**, confused, obscure, blurred, unclear, hazy, indistinct ■ OPPOSITE: plain

clout (*informal*) VERB *The officer clouted him on the head.* = **hit**, strike, punch, deck (*slang*), slap, sock (*slang*), chin (*slang*), smack, thump, cuff, clobber (*slang*), wallop (*informal*), box, wham, lay one on (*slang*), skelp (*dialect*) ▶ NOUN **1** *I was half tempted to give them a clout myself.* = **thump**, blow, crack (*informal*), punch, slap, sock (*slang*), cuff, wallop (*informal*), skelp (*dialect*) **2** *The two firms wield enormous clout in financial markets.* = **influence**, power, standing, authority, pull (*informal*), weight, bottom, prestige, mana (*N.Z.*)

cloven ADJECTIVE = **split**, divided, cleft, bisected

clown NOUN **1** *a classic circus clown with a big red nose and baggy suit* = **comedian**, fool, harlequin, jester, buffoon, pierrot, dolt **2** *He gained a reputation as the class clown.* = **joker**, comic, prankster **3** *I could do a better job than those clowns in Washington.* = **fool**, dope (*informal*), jerk (*slang, chiefly U.S. & Canad.*), idiot, ass, berk (*Brit. slang*), prat (*slang*), moron, twit (*informal, chiefly Brit.*), imbecile (*informal*), ignoramus, jackass, dolt, blockhead, ninny, putz (*U.S. slang*), eejit (*Scot. & Irish*), doofus (*slang, chiefly U.S.*), dorba or dorb (*Austral. slang*), bogan (*Austral. slang*), lamebrain (*informal*), numbskull or numskull ▶ VERB (*usually with* **around**) *He clowned a lot and antagonized his workmates.* = **play the fool**, mess about, jest, act the fool, act the goat, play the goat

cloying ADJECTIVE **1** *Her cheap, cloying scent enveloped him.* = **sickly**, nauseating, icky (*informal*), treacly, oversweet, excessive **2** *The film is sentimental but rarely cloying.* = **over-sentimental**, sickly, nauseating, mushy (*informal*), twee, slushy, mawkish, icky (*informal*), treacly, oversweet

club NOUN **1** *He was a member of the local youth club.* = **association**, company, group, union, society, circle, lodge, guild, fraternity (*U.S. & Canad.*), set, order, sodality **2** *Men armed with knives and clubs attacked his home.* = **stick**, bat, bludgeon, truncheon (*Brit.*), cosh (*Brit.*), cudgel ▶ VERB *Two thugs clubbed him with baseball bats.* = **beat**, strike, hammer (*informal*), batter, bash, clout (*informal*), bludgeon, clobber (*slang*), pummel, cosh (*Brit.*), beat or knock seven bells out of (*informal*)

clue NOUN = **indication**, lead, sign, evidence, tip, suggestion, trace, hint, suspicion, pointer, tip-off, inkling, intimation

clueless ADJECTIVE = **stupid**, thick, dull, naive, dim (*informal*), dense, dumb (*informal*), simple-minded, dozy (*Brit. informal*), simple, slow, witless, dopey (*informal*), unintelligent, half-witted, slow on the uptake (*informal*)

clump NOUN *There was a clump of trees bordering the side of the road.* = **cluster**, group, bunch, bundle, shock ▶ VERB *They went clumping up the stairs to bed.* = **stomp**, stamp, stump, thump, lumber, tramp, plod, thud, clomp

clumsiness NOUN **1** *I was embarrassed by my clumsiness on the dance-floor.* = **awkwardness**, ineptitude, heaviness, ineptness, inelegance, ponderousness, gracelessness, gawkiness, maladroitness, ungainliness **2** *He cursed himself for his clumsiness and insensitivity.* = **insensitivity**, heavy-handedness, tactlessness, gaucheness, lack of tact, uncouthness

clumsy ADJECTIVE **1** *I'd never seen a clumsier, less coordinated boxer.* = **awkward**, blundering, bungling, lumbering, inept, bumbling, ponderous, ungainly, gauche, accident-prone, gawky, heavy, uncoordinated, cack-handed (*informal*), inexpert, maladroit, ham-handed (*informal*), like a bull in a china shop, klutzy (*U.S. & Canad. slang*), unskilful, butterfingered (*informal*), ham-fisted (*informal*), unco (*Austral. slang*) ■ OPPOSITE: skilful **2** *The keyboard is a large and clumsy instrument.* = **unwieldy**, ill-shaped, unhandy, clunky (*informal*)

cluster NOUN *A cluster of men blocked the doorway.* = **gathering**, group, collection, bunch (*informal*), knot, clump, assemblage, aggregate ▶ VERB *The passengers clustered together in small groups.* = **gather**, group, collect, bunch, assemble, flock, huddle

clutch VERB **1** *She was clutching a photograph in her hand.* = **hold**, grip, embrace, grasp, cling to, clasp **2** *I staggered and had to clutch at a chair for support.* = **seize**, catch, grab, grasp, snatch ▶ PLURAL NOUN *He escaped his captors' clutches by jumping from a moving vehicle.* = **power**, hands, control, grip, possession, grasp, custody, sway, keeping, claws

clutter NOUN *She preferred her work area to be free of clutter.* = **untidiness**, mess, disorder, confusion, litter, muddle, disarray, jumble, hotchpotch ■ OPPOSITE: order ▶ VERB *I don't want to clutter the room up with too much junk.* = **litter**, scatter, strew, mess up ■ OPPOSITE: tidy

cluttered ADJECTIVE = **untidy**, confused, disordered, littered, messy, muddled, jumbled, disarrayed

coach NOUN **1** *He has joined the team as a coach.* = **instructor**, teacher, trainer, tutor, handler **2** *I hate travelling by coach.* = **bus**, charabanc ▶ VERB *He coached me for my French exam.* = **instruct**, train, prepare, exercise, drill, tutor, cram

coalesce VERB = **blend**, unite, mix, combine, incorporate, integrate, merge, consolidate, come together, fuse, amalgamate, meld, cohere

coalition NOUN = **alliance**, union, league, association, combination, merger, integration, compact, conjunction, bloc, confederation, fusion, affiliation, amalgam, amalgamation, confederacy

coarse ADJECTIVE **1** *He wore a shepherd's tunic of coarse cloth.* = **rough**, crude, unfinished, homespun, impure, unrefined, rough-hewn, unprocessed, unpolished, coarse-grained, unpurified ■ OPPOSITE: smooth **2** *He has a very coarse sense of humour.* = **vulgar**, offensive, rude, indecent, improper, raunchy (*informal*), earthy, foul-mouthed, bawdy, impure, smutty, impolite, ribald, immodest, indelicate **3** *They don't know how to behave, and are coarse and insulting.* = **loutish**, rough, brutish, boorish, uncivil ■ OPPOSITE: well-mannered

coast NOUN *Camp sites are usually situated along the coast.* = **shore**, border, beach, strand, seaside, coastline, seaboard ▶ VERB *I slipped into neutral gear and coasted down the slope.* = **cruise**, sail, drift, taxi, glide, freewheel ■ RELATED WORD: *adjective* littoral

coat NOUN **1** *Vitamin B6 is great for improving the condition of dogs' and horses' coats.* = **fur**, hair, skin, hide, wool, fleece, pelt **2** *The front door needs a new coat of paint.* = **layer**, covering, coating, overlay ▶ VERB *Coat the fish with seasoned flour.* = **cover**, spread, plaster, smear

coating NOUN = **layer**, covering, finish, skin, sheet, coat, dusting, blanket, membrane, glaze, film, varnish, veneer, patina, lamination

coat of arms NOUN = **heraldry**, crest, insignia, escutcheon, blazonry

coax VERB = **persuade**, cajole, talk into, wheedle, sweet-talk (*informal*), prevail upon, inveigle, soft-soap (*informal*), twist (someone's) arm, flatter, entice, beguile, allure ■ OPPOSITE: bully

cobber NOUN = **friend**, pal (*informal*), mate (*informal*), buddy (*informal*), china (*Brit. & S. African informal*), best friend, intimate, cock (*Brit. informal*), close friend, comrade, chum (*informal*), crony, alter ego, main man (*slang, chiefly U.S.*), soul mate, homeboy (*slang, chiefly U.S.*), bosom friend, boon companion, E hoa (*N.Z.*)

cock NOUN *We heard the sound of a cock crowing in the yard.* = **cockerel**, rooster, chanticleer ▶ VERB *He suddenly cocked an ear and listened.* = **raise**, prick up, perk up

cocktail NOUN = **mixture**, combination, compound, blend, concoction, mix, amalgamation, admixture

cocky[1] ADJECTIVE *He was a little cocky because he was winning all the time.* = **overconfident**, arrogant, brash, swaggering, conceited, egotistical, cocksure, swollen-headed, vain, full of yourself ■ OPPOSITE: modest

cocky[2] *or* **cockie** (*Austral. & N.Z. informal*) NOUN *He got some casual work with the cane cockies on Maroochy River.* = **farmer**, smallholder, crofter (*Scot.*), grazier, agriculturalist, rancher, husbandman

cocoon VERB **1** *She lay on the sofa, cocooned in blankets.* = **wrap**, swathe, envelop, swaddle, pad **2** *I was cocooned in my own safe little world.* = **protect**, shelter, cushion, insulate, screen

coddle VERB = **pamper**, spoil, indulge, cosset, baby, nurse, pet, wet-nurse (*informal*), mollycoddle

code NOUN **1** *All employees are expected to observe our code of conduct.* = **principles**, rules, manners, custom, convention, ethics, maxim, etiquette, system, kawa (*N.Z.*), tikanga (*N.Z.*) **2** *They used elaborate secret codes.* = **cipher**, cryptograph

codify VERB = **systematize**, catalogue, classify, summarize, tabulate, collect, organize

coerce VERB = **force**, compel, bully, intimidate, railroad (*informal*), constrain, bulldoze (*informal*), dragoon, pressurize, browbeat, press-gang, twist (someone's) arm (*informal*), drive

coercion NOUN = **force**, pressure, threats, bullying, constraint, intimidation, compulsion, duress, browbeating, strong-arm tactics (*informal*)

cogent ADJECTIVE = **convincing**, strong, powerful, effective, compelling, urgent, influential, potent, irresistible, compulsive, forceful, conclusive, weighty, forcible

cognition NOUN = **perception**, reasoning, understanding, intelligence, awareness, insight, comprehension, apprehension, discernment

coherence NOUN = **consistency**, rationality, concordance, consonance, congruity, union, agreement, connection, unity, correspondence

coherent ADJECTIVE **1** *He has failed to work out a coherent strategy for modernising the service.* = **consistent**, reasoned, organized, rational, logical, meaningful, systematic, orderly ■ OPPOSITE: inconsistent **2** *She's so calm when she speaks in public. I wish I could be that coherent.* = **articulate**, lucid, comprehensible, intelligible ■ OPPOSITE: unintelligible

cohort NOUN *We now have results for the first cohort of pupils to be assessed.* = **group**, set, band, contingent, batch

coil VERB **1** *I turned off the water and began to coil the hose.* = **wind**, twist, curl, loop, spiral, twine **2** *A python had coiled itself around the branch of the tree.* = **curl**, wind, twist, snake, loop, entwine, twine, wreathe, convolute

coin NOUN *My pocket was full of coins.* = **money**, change, cash, silver, copper, dosh (*Brit. & Austral. slang*), specie, kembla (*Austral. slang*) ▶ VERB *The phrase 'cosmic ray' was coined by R. A. Millikan in 1925.* = **invent**, create, make up, frame, forge, conceive, originate, formulate, fabricate, think up ■ RELATED WORD: enthusiast numismatist

coincide VERB **1** *The exhibition coincides with the 50th anniversary of Potter's death.* = **occur simultaneously**, coexist, synchronize, be concurrent **2** *a case in which public and private interests coincide* = **agree**, match, accord, square, correspond, tally, concur, harmonize ■ OPPOSITE: disagree

coincidence NOUN = **chance**, accident, luck, fluke, eventuality, stroke of luck, happy accident, fortuity

coincidental ADJECTIVE = **accidental**, unintentional, unintended, unplanned, fortuitous, fluky (*informal*), chance, casual ■ OPPOSITE: deliberate

cold ADJECTIVE **1** *It was bitterly cold outside.* = **chilly**, biting, freezing, bitter, raw, chill, harsh, bleak, arctic (*informal*), icy, frosty, wintry, frigid, inclement, parky (*Brit. informal*), cool ■ OPPOSITE: hot **2** *I'm hungry, I'm cold and I have nowhere to sleep.* = **freezing**, frozen, chilled, numb, chilly, shivery, benumbed, frozen to the marrow **3** *She is a cold, unfeeling woman.* = **distant**, reserved, indifferent, aloof, glacial, cold-blooded, apathetic, frigid, unresponsive, unfeeling, passionless, undemonstrative, standoffish ■ OPPOSITE: emotional **4** *The president is likely to receive a cold reception when he speaks today.* = **unfriendly**, indifferent, stony, lukewarm, glacial, unmoved, unsympathetic, apathetic, frigid, inhospitable, unresponsive ■ OPPOSITE: friendly ▶ NOUN *He must have come inside to get out of the cold.* = **coldness**, chill, frigidity, chilliness, frostiness, iciness

cold-blooded ADJECTIVE = **callous**, cruel, savage, brutal, ruthless, steely, heartless, inhuman, merciless, unmoved, dispassionate, barbarous, pitiless, unfeeling, unemotional, stony-hearted ■ OPPOSITE: caring

collaborate VERB **1** *The two writers collaborated on a new show.* = **work together**, team up, join forces, cooperate, play ball (*informal*), participate **2** *He was accused of having collaborated with the secret police.* = **conspire**, cooperate, collude, fraternize

collaboration NOUN **1** *There is substantial collaboration with neighbouring departments.* = **teamwork**, partnership, cooperation, association, alliance, concert **2** *rumours of his collaboration with the occupying forces during the war* = **conspiring**, cooperation, collusion, fraternization

collaborator NOUN **1** *She was an important collaborator on that novel.* = **co-worker**, partner, colleague, associate, team-mate, confederate **2** *Two alleged collaborators were shot dead by masked activists.* = **traitor**, turncoat, quisling, collaborationist, fraternizer

collapse VERB **1** *A section of the Bay Bridge had collapsed.* = **fall down**, fall, give way, subside, cave in, crumple, fall apart at the seams **2** *His business empire collapsed under a massive burden of debt.* = **fail**, fold, founder, break down, fall through, come to nothing, go belly-up (*informal*) **3** *There were people in the streets collapsing from hunger.* = **faint**, break down, pass out, black out, swoon (*literary*), crack up (*informal*), keel over (*informal*), flake out (*informal*) ▶ NOUN **1** *Floods and a collapse of the tunnel roof were a constant risk.* = **falling down**, ruin, falling apart, cave-in, disintegration, subsidence **2** *Their economy is teetering on the edge of collapse.* = **failure**, slump, breakdown, flop (*informal*), downfall **3** *A few days after his collapse he was sitting up in bed.* = **faint**, breakdown, blackout, prostration

collar VERB = **seize**, catch, arrest, appropriate, grab, capture, nail (*informal*), nab (*informal*), apprehend, lay hands on

collate VERB = **collect**, gather, organize, assemble, compose, adduce, systematize

collateral NOUN = **security**, guarantee, deposit, assurance, surety, pledge

colleague NOUN = **fellow worker**, partner, ally, associate, assistant, team-mate, companion, comrade, helper, collaborator, confederate, auxiliary, workmate, co-worker, confrère

collect VERB **1** *Two young girls were collecting firewood.* = **gather**, save, assemble, heap, accumulate, aggregate, amass, stockpile, hoard ■ **OPPOSITE:** scatter **2** *They collected donations for a fund to help the earthquake victims.* = **raise**, secure, gather, obtain, acquire, muster, solicit **3** *A crowd collected outside.* = **assemble**, meet, rally, cluster, come together, convene, converge, congregate, flock together ■ **OPPOSITE:** disperse

collected ADJECTIVE = **calm**, together (*slang*), cool, confident, composed, poised, serene, sedate, self-controlled, unfazed (*informal*), unperturbed, unruffled, self-possessed, keeping your cool, unperturbable, as cool as a cucumber, chilled (*informal*) ■ **OPPOSITE:** nervous

collection NOUN **1** *He has gathered a large collection of prints and paintings over the years.* = **accumulation**, set, store, mass, pile, heap, stockpile, hoard, aggregate, congeries **2** *Two years ago he published a collection of short stories.* = **compilation**, accumulation, anthology **3** *A collection of people of all ages assembled to pay their respects.* = **group**, company, crowd, gathering, assembly, cluster, congregation, assortment, assemblage **4** *computer systems designed to speed up the collection of information* = **gathering**, acquisition, accumulation **5** *I asked if we could arrange a collection for the refugees.* = **contribution**, donation, alms **6** *I put a five-pound note in the church collection.* = **offering**, offertory

collective ADJECTIVE **1** *It was a collective decision taken by the full board.* = **joint**, united, shared, common, combined, corporate, concerted, unified, cooperative ■ **OPPOSITE:** individual **2** *Their collective volume wasn't very large.* = **combined**,

aggregate, composite, cumulative ■ **OPPOSITE:** separate

collide VERB **1** *Two trains collided head-on early this morning.* = **crash**, clash, meet head-on, come into collision **2** *It is likely that their interests will collide.* = **conflict**, clash, be incompatible, be at variance

collision NOUN **1** *Their van was involved in a collision with a car.* = **crash**, impact, accident, smash, bump, pile-up (*informal*), prang (*informal*) **2** *a collision between two strong personalities* = **conflict**, opposition, clash, clashing, encounter, disagreement, incompatibility

colloquial ADJECTIVE = **informal**, familiar, everyday, vernacular, conversational, demotic, idiomatic

collude VERB = **conspire**, scheme, plot, intrigue, collaborate, contrive, abet, connive, be in cahoots (*informal*), machinate

collusion NOUN = **conspiracy**, intrigue, deceit, complicity, connivance, secret understanding

colonist NOUN = **settler**, immigrant, pioneer, colonial, homesteader (*U.S.*), colonizer, frontiersman

colonize VERB = **settle**, populate, put down roots in, people, pioneer, open up

colonnade NOUN = **cloisters**, arcade, portico, covered walk

colony NOUN = **settlement**, territory, province, possession, dependency, outpost, dominion, satellite state, community

colossal ADJECTIVE = **huge**, massive, vast, enormous, immense, titanic, gigantic, monumental (*informal*), monstrous, mammoth, mountainous, stellar (*informal*), prodigious, gargantuan, herculean, elephantine, humongous or humungous (*informal*), supersize ■ **OPPOSITE:** tiny

colour or (*U.S.*) **color** NOUN **1** *The badges come in twenty different colours and shapes.* = **hue**, tone, shade, tint, tinge, tincture, colourway **2** *the latest range of lip and eye colours* = **paint**, stain, dye, tint, pigment, tincture, coloration, colourwash, colorant **3** *The ceremony brought a touch of colour to the normally drab proceedings.* = **liveliness**, life, interest, excitement, animation, zest ▶ PLURAL NOUN **1** *Troops raised the country's colours in a special ceremony.* = **flag**, standard, banner, emblem, ensign **2** *After we were married, he showed his true colours.* = **nature**, quality, character, aspect, personality, stamp, traits, temperament ▶ VERB **1** *He couldn't help noticing that she coloured slightly.* = **blush**, flush, crimson, redden, go crimson, burn, go as red as a beetroot **2** *The attitude of parents colours the way their children behave.* = **influence**, affect, prejudice, distort, pervert, taint, slant **3** *He wrote a highly coloured account of his childhood.* = **exaggerate**, disguise, embroider, misrepresent, falsify, gloss over

colourful ADJECTIVE **1** *Everyone was dressed in colourful clothes.* = **bright**, rich, brilliant, intense, vivid, vibrant, psychedelic, motley, variegated, jazzy (*informal*), multicoloured, Day-glo®, kaleidoscopic ■ **OPPOSITE:** drab **2** *an irreverent and colourful tale of Restoration England* = **interesting**, rich, unusual, stimulating, graphic, lively, distinctive, vivid, picturesque, characterful
■ **OPPOSITE:** boring

colourless ADJECTIVE **1** *a colourless, almost odourless liquid* = **uncoloured**, faded, neutral, bleached, washed out, achromatic **2** *Her face was colourless, and she was shaking.* = **ashen**, washed out, wan, sickly, anaemic ■ **OPPOSITE:** radiant **3** *He is a drab, colourless little man.* = **uninteresting**, dull, tame, dreary, drab, lacklustre, vacuous, insipid, vapid, characterless, unmemorable
■ **OPPOSITE:** interesting

column NOUN **1** *Great stone steps led past Greek columns to the main building.* = **pillar**, support, post, shaft, upright, obelisk **2** *There were reports of columns of military vehicles appearing on the streets.* = **line**, train, row, file, rank, string, queue, procession, cavalcade

columnist NOUN = **journalist**, correspondent, editor, reporter, critic, reviewer, gossip columnist, journo (*slang*)

coma NOUN = **unconsciousness**, trance, oblivion, lethargy, stupor, torpor, insensibility

comatose ADJECTIVE **1** *The right side of my brain had been so severely bruised that I was comatose for a month.* = **unconscious**, in a coma, out cold, insensible **2** *Granpa lies comatose on the sofa.* = **inert**, stupefied, out cold, somnolent, torpid, insensible, dead to the world (*informal*), drugged

comb VERB **1** *Her reddish hair was cut short and neatly combed.* = **untangle**, arrange, groom, dress **2** *Officers combed the woods for the murder weapon.* = **search**, hunt through, sweep, rake, sift, scour, rummage, ransack, forage, fossick (*Austral. & N.Z.*), go through with a fine-tooth comb

combat NOUN *Over 16 million men died in combat during the war.* = **fight**, war, action, battle, conflict, engagement, warfare, skirmish ■ **OPPOSITE:** peace ▶ VERB *new government measures to combat crime* = **fight**,

battle against, oppose, contest, engage, cope with, resist, defy, withstand, struggle against, contend with, do battle with, strive against ■ **OPPOSITE:** support

combatant NOUN *His grandfather was a Boer war combatant.* = **fighter**, soldier, warrior, contender, gladiator, belligerent, antagonist, fighting man, serviceman or servicewoman ▶ ADJECTIVE *the monitoring of ceasefires between combatant states* = **fighting**, warring, battling, conflicting, opposing, contending, belligerent, combative

combative ADJECTIVE = **aggressive**, militant, contentious, belligerent, antagonistic, pugnacious, warlike, bellicose, truculent, quarrelsome ■ **OPPOSITE:** nonaggressive

combination NOUN **1** *A combination of factors are to blame.* = **mixture**, mix, compound, blend, composite, amalgam, amalgamation, meld, coalescence **2** *The company's chief executive has proposed a merger or other business combination.* = **association**, union, alliance, coalition, merger, federation, consortium, unification, syndicate, confederation, cartel, confederacy, cabal

combine VERB **1** *Combine the flour with water to make a paste.* = **amalgamate**, marry, mix, bond, bind, compound, blend, incorporate, integrate, merge, put together, fuse, synthesize ■ **OPPOSITE:** separate **2** *Disease and starvation are combining to kill thousands.* = **join together**, link, connect, integrate, merge, fuse, amalgamate, meld **3** *Different states or groups can combine to enlarge their markets.* = **unite**, associate, team up, unify, get together, collaborate, join forces, cooperate, join together, pool resources ■ **OPPOSITE:** split up

combustible ADJECTIVE = **flammable**, explosive, incendiary, inflammable

come VERB **1** *We heard the train coming.* = **approach**, near, advance, move towards, draw near **2** *Two police officers came into the hall.* = **arrive**, move, appear, enter, turn up (*informal*), show up (*informal*), materialize **3** *The water came to his chest.* = **reach**, extend **4** *Saturday's incident came without warning.* = **happen**, fall, occur, take place, come about, come to pass **5** *The wallpaper comes in black and white only.* = **be available**, be made, be offered, be produced, be on offer

• **come about** *A lasting solution to this problem can only come about through dialogue.* = **happen**, result, occur, take place, arise, transpire (*informal*), befall, come to pass

• **come across as something** *or* **someone**

= **seem**, look, seem to be, appear to be, give the impression of being • **come across someone** *I recently came across a college friend in New York.* = **meet**, encounter, run into, bump into *(informal)* • **come across something** *He came across the jawbone of a 4.5 million-year-old marsupial.* = **find**, discover, notice, unearth, stumble upon, hit upon, chance upon, happen upon, light upon • **come at someone** *A man came at him with an axe.* = **attack**, charge, rush, go for, assault, fly at, assail, fall upon, rush at • **come back** *She came back half an hour later.* = **return**, reappear, re-enter • **come between people** *It's difficult to imagine anything coming between them.* = **separate**, part, divide, alienate, estrange, set at odds • **come by something** *How did you come by that cheque?* = **get**, win, land *(informal)*, score *(slang)*, secure, obtain, acquire, get hold of, procure, take possession of • **come down** 1 *Interest rates are coming down.* = **decrease**, fall, drop, reduce, go down, diminish, lessen, become lower 2 *The rain began to come down.* = **fall**, descend • **come down on someone** *If she came down too hard on him, he would rebel.* = **reprimand**, blast, carpet *(informal)*, put down, criticize, jump on *(informal)*, rebuke, dress down *(informal)*, tear into *(informal)*, diss *(slang)*, read the riot act, lambast(e), bawl out *(informal)*, rap over the knuckles, chew out *(U.S. & Canad. informal)*, tear (someone) off a strip *(Brit. informal)*, give (someone) a rocket *(Brit. & N.Z. informal)* • **come down on something** *(one or other side of an argument) He clearly came down on the side of the President.* = **decide on**, choose, favour • **come down to something** *In the end it all comes down to a matter of personal preference.* = **amount to**, boil down to • **come down with something** *(an illness) He came down with chickenpox.* = **catch**, get, take, contract, fall victim to, fall ill, be stricken with, take sick, sicken with • **come forward** *A witness came forward to say that she had seen him that night.* = **volunteer**, step forward, present yourself, offer your services • **come from something** 1 *Nearly half the students come from France.* = **be from**, originate, hail from, be a native of 2 *Chocolate comes from the cacao tree.* = **be obtained**, be from, issue, emerge, flow, arise, originate, emanate • **come in** 1 *They were scared when they first came in.* = **arrive**, enter, appear, show up *(informal)*, cross the threshold 2 *My horse came in third in the second race.* = **finish** • **come in for something** *(criticism or blame) The plans have already come in for fierce criticism.* = **receive**, get, suffer, endure, be subjected to, bear the brunt of, be the object of • **come into something** *(money or property) My father has just come into a fortune.* = **inherit**, be left, acquire, succeed to, be bequeathed, fall heir to • **come off** *It was a good try but it didn't quite come off.* = **succeed**, work out, be successful, pan out *(informal)*, turn out well • **come on** 1 *He is coming on very well at the violin.* = **progress**, develop, improve, advance, proceed, make headway 2 *Winter is coming on.* = **begin**, appear, take place • **come out** 1 *The book comes out this week.* = **be published**, appear, be released, be issued, be launched 2 *The truth is beginning to come out now.* = **be revealed**, emerge, be reported, be announced, become apparent, come to light, be divulged 3 *I'm sure it will come out all right in the end.* = **turn out**, result, end up, work out, pan out *(informal)* • **come out with something** *Everyone burst out laughing when he came out with this remark.* = **say**, speak, utter, let out • **come round** or **around** 1 *Beryl came round last night to apologize.* = **call**, visit, drop in, stop by, pop in 2 *It looks like they're coming around to our way of thinking.* = **change your opinion**, yield, concede, mellow, relent, accede, acquiesce 3 *When I came round I was on the kitchen floor.* = **regain consciousness**, come to, recover, rally, revive • **come through** *He's putting his job at risk if he doesn't come through.* = **succeed**, triumph, prevail, make the grade *(informal)* • **come through something** *(a negative or bad experience) We've come through some rough times.* = **survive**, overcome, endure, withstand, weather, pull through • **come to** *When he came to and raised his head he saw Barney.* = **revive**, recover, rally, come round, regain consciousness • **come to something** *The bill came to over a hundred pounds.* = **amount to**, total, add up to • **come up** *Sorry I'm late – something came up at home.* = **happen**, occur, arise, turn up, spring up, crop up • **come up to something** *Her work did not come up to his exacting standards.* = **measure up to**, meet, match, approach, rival, equal, compare with, resemble, admit of comparison with, stand or bear comparison with • **come up with something** *Several members have come up with suggestions of their own.* = **produce**, offer, provide, present, suggest, advance, propose, submit, furnish

comeback NOUN 1 *(informal) The former world champion is making a comeback.* = **return**, revival, rebound, resurgence, rally, recovery, triumph **2** *I tried to think of a witty comeback.* = **response**, reply, retort, retaliation, riposte, rejoinder

comedian NOUN = **comic**, laugh (*informal*), wit, clown, funny man or woman, humorist, wag, joker, jester, dag (*N.Z. informal*), card (*informal*)

comedy NOUN **1** *a comedy set in 18th-century Ireland* = **light entertainment**, sitcom (*informal*), soap opera (*slang*), soapie or soapy (*Austral.*) ■ **OPPOSITE:** tragedy **2** *He and I provided the comedy with songs and monologues.* = **humour**, fun, joking, farce, jesting, slapstick, wisecracking, hilarity, witticisms, facetiousness, chaffing ■ **OPPOSITE:** seriousness

comfort NOUN **1** *She had enough money to live in comfort for the rest of her life.* = **ease**, luxury, wellbeing, opulence **2** *I tried to find some words of comfort to offer her.* = **consolation**, cheer, encouragement, succour, help, support, aid, relief, ease, compensation, alleviation ■ **OPPOSITE:** annoyance ▶ VERB *He put his arm round her, trying to comfort her.* = **console**, encourage, ease, cheer, strengthen, relieve, reassure, soothe, hearten, solace, assuage, gladden, commiserate with ■ **OPPOSITE:** distress

comfortable ADJECTIVE **1** *Dress in loose comfortable clothes that do not make you feel restricted.* = **loose-fitting**, loose, adequate, ample, snug, roomy, commodious ■ **OPPOSITE:** tight-fitting **2** *A home should be comfortable and friendly.* = **pleasant**, homely, easy, relaxing, delightful, enjoyable, cosy, agreeable, restful ■ **OPPOSITE:** unpleasant **3** *Lie down on your bed and make yourself comfortable.* = **at ease**, happy, at home, contented, relaxed, serene ■ **OPPOSITE:** uncomfortable **4** *She came from a stable, comfortable, middle-class family.* = **well-off**, prosperous, affluent, well-to-do, comfortably-off, in clover (*informal*)

comforting ADJECTIVE = **consoling**, encouraging, cheering, reassuring, soothing, heart-warming, inspiriting ■ **OPPOSITE:** upsetting

comic ADJECTIVE *The novel is both comic and tragic.* = **funny**, amusing, witty, humorous, farcical, comical, light, joking, droll, facetious, jocular, waggish ■ **OPPOSITE:** sad ▶ NOUN *At that time he was still a penniless, unknown comic.* = **comedian**, funny man or woman, humorist, wit, clown, wag, jester, dag (*N.Z. informal*), buffoon

comical ADJECTIVE = **funny**, entertaining, comic, silly, amusing, ridiculous, diverting, absurd, hilarious, ludicrous, humorous, priceless (*informal*), laughable, farcical, whimsical, zany, droll, risible (*formal*), side-splitting

coming ADJECTIVE **1** *This obviously depends on the weather in the coming months.* = **approaching**, next, future, near, due, forthcoming, imminent, in store, impending, at hand, upcoming, on the cards, in the wind, nigh, just round the corner **2** *He is widely regarded as the coming man of Scottish rugby.* = **up-and-coming**, future, promising, aspiring ▶ NOUN *Most of us welcome the coming of summer.* = **arrival**, approach, advent, accession

command VERB **1** *He commanded his troops to attack.* = **order**, tell, charge (*formal*), demand, require, direct, bid, compel, enjoin ■ **OPPOSITE:** beg **2** *the French general who commands the UN troops in the region* = **have authority over**, lead, head, control, rule, manage, handle, dominate, govern, administer, supervise, be in charge of, reign over ■ **OPPOSITE:** be subordinate to ▶ NOUN **1** *The tanker failed to respond to a command to stop.* = **order**, demand, direction, instruction, dictate, requirement, decree, bidding, mandate, canon, directive, injunction, fiat, ultimatum, commandment, edict, behest, precept **2** *the struggle for command of the air* = **domination**, control, rule, grasp, sway, mastery, dominion, upper hand, power, government **3** *In 1942 he took command of 108 Squadron.* = **management**, power, control, charge, authority, direction, supervision

commandeer VERB = **seize**, appropriate, hijack, confiscate, requisition, sequester, expropriate (*formal*), sequestrate

commander NOUN = **leader**, director, chief, officer, boss, head, captain, ruler, commander-in-chief, commanding officer, C in C, C.O., sherang (*Austral. & N.Z.*)

commanding ADJECTIVE **1** *Right now you're in a very commanding position.* = **dominant**, controlling, dominating, superior, decisive, advantageous **2** *The voice at the other end of the line was serious and commanding.* = **authoritative**, imposing, impressive, compelling, assertive, forceful, autocratic, peremptory ■ **OPPOSITE:** unassertive

commemorate VERB = **celebrate**, remember, honour, recognize, salute, pay tribute to, immortalize, memorialize ■ **OPPOSITE:** ignore

commemoration NOUN **1** *A special commemoration for her will be held next week.* = **ceremony**, tribute, memorial service, testimonial **2** *a march in commemoration of the victims* = **remembrance**, honour, tribute

C

commemorative ADJECTIVE = **memorial**, celebratory

commence VERB 1 *They commenced a systematic search of the area.* = **embark on**, start, open, begin, initiate, originate, instigate, inaugurate, enter upon ■ **OPPOSITE:** stop 2 *The academic year commences at the beginning of October.* = **start**, open, begin, go ahead ■ **OPPOSITE:** end

commencement NOUN = **beginning**, start, opening, launch, birth, origin, dawn (*literary*), outset, onset, initiation, inauguration, inception, embarkation

commend VERB 1 *She was highly commended for her bravery.* = **praise**, acclaim, applaud, compliment, extol, approve, big up (*slang*), eulogize, speak highly of ■ **OPPOSITE:** criticize 2 *I can commend it to you as a sensible course of action.* = **recommend**, suggest, approve, advocate, endorse, vouch for, put in a good word for

commendable ADJECTIVE = **praiseworthy**, deserving, worthy, admirable, exemplary, creditable, laudable, meritorious, estimable

commendation NOUN = **praise**, credit, approval, acclaim, encouragement, Brownie points, approbation, acclamation, good opinion, panegyric, encomium

commensurate ADJECTIVE 1 *Employees are paid salaries commensurate with those of teachers.* = **equivalent**, consistent, corresponding, comparable, compatible, in accord, proportionate, coextensive 2 *The resources available are in no way commensurate to the need.* = **appropriate**, fitting, fit, due, sufficient, adequate

comment VERB 1 *Stuart commented that this was very true.* = **remark**, say, note, mention, point out, observe, utter, opine, interpose 2 (*usually with* **on**) *So far Mr Aziz has not commented on these reports.* = **remark on**, explain, talk about, discuss, speak about, say something about, allude to, elucidate, make a comment on ▶ NOUN 1 *He made these comments at a news conference.* = **remark**, statement, observation 2 *He had added a few comments in the margin.* = **note**, criticism, explanation, illustration, commentary, exposition, annotation, elucidation

commentary NOUN 1 *He gave the listening crowd a running commentary on the game.* = **narration**, report, review, explanation, description, voice-over 2 *He will be writing a twice-weekly commentary on American society and culture.* = **analysis**, notes, review, critique, treatise

commentator NOUN 1 *a sports commentator* = **reporter**, special correspondent, sportscaster, commenter 2 *He is a commentator on African affairs.* = **critic**, interpreter, annotator

commercial ADJECTIVE 1 *In its heyday it was a major centre of commercial activity.* = **mercantile**, business, trade, trading, sales 2 *Whether the project will be a commercial success is still uncertain.* = **profitable**, popular, in demand, marketable, saleable 3 *There's a feeling among a lot of people that music has become too commercial.* = **materialistic**, mercenary, profit-making, venal, monetary, exploited, pecuniary

commiserate VERB (*often with* **with**) = **sympathize**, pity, feel for, console, condole

commission VERB *You can commission them to paint something especially for you.* = **appoint**, order, contract, select, engage, delegate, nominate, authorize, empower, depute ▶ NOUN 1 *She approached me with a commission to write the screen play for the film.* = **duty**, authority, trust, charge, task, function, mission, employment, appointment, warrant, mandate, errand 2 *He got a commission for bringing in new clients.* = **fee**, cut (*informal*), compensation, percentage, allowance, royalties, brokerage, rake-off (*slang*) 3 *The authorities have been asked to set up a commission to investigate the murders.* = **committee**, board, representatives, commissioners, delegation, deputation, body of commissioners

commit VERB 1 *I have never committed any crime.* = **do**, perform, carry out, execute, enact, perpetrate 2 *The government have committed billions of pounds to the programme.* = **give**, deliver, engage, deposit, hand over, commend (*formal*), entrust, consign ■ **OPPOSITE:** withhold 3 *Offenders would be committed to these prisons by local courts.* = **put in custody**, confine, imprison, consign ■ **OPPOSITE:** release • **commit yourself to something** *She didn't want to commit herself to working at weekends.* = **pledge to**, promise to, bind yourself to, make yourself liable for, obligate yourself to

commitment NOUN 1 *a commitment to the ideals of Bolshevism* = **dedication**, loyalty, devotion, adherence ■ **OPPOSITE:** indecisiveness 2 *I've got too many commitments to take on anything more right now.* = **responsibility**, tie, duty, obligation, liability, engagement 3 *We made a commitment to keep working together.* = **pledge**, promise, guarantee, undertaking, vow, assurance, word ■ **OPPOSITE:** disavowal

committee NOUN = **group**, commission, panel, delegation, subcommittee, deputation

commodity NOUN (*usually plural*) = **goods**, produce, stock, products, merchandise, wares

common ADJECTIVE **1** *Earthquakes are fairly common in this part of the world.* = **usual**, standard, daily, regular, ordinary, familiar, plain, conventional, routine, frequent, everyday, customary, commonplace, vanilla (*slang*), habitual, run-of-the-mill, humdrum, stock, workaday, bog-standard (*Brit. & Irish slang*), a dime a dozen ■ **OPPOSITE:** rare **2** *It is common practice to invest in holiday homes in the area.* = **popular**, general, accepted, standard, routine, widespread, universal, prevailing, prevalent **3** *They share a common language.* = **shared**, collective **4** *He proclaims himself to be the voice of the common man.* = **ordinary**, average, simple, typical, undistinguished, dinki-di (*Austral. informal*) ■ **OPPOSITE:** important **5** *She might be a little common at times, but she was certainly not boring.* = **vulgar**, low, inferior, coarse, plebeian ■ **OPPOSITE:** refined **6** *social policies which promote the common good* = **collective**, public, community, social, communal ■ **OPPOSITE:** personal

commonplace ADJECTIVE *The practice was virtually unheard of twenty years ago, but has now become commonplace.* = **everyday**, common, ordinary, widespread, pedestrian, customary, mundane, vanilla (*slang*), banal, run-of-the-mill, humdrum, dime-a-dozen (*informal*) ■ **OPPOSITE:** rare ▸ NOUN *It is a commonplace to say that the poetry of the first world war was greater than that of the second.* = **cliché**, platitude, banality, truism

common sense NOUN = **good sense**, sound judgment, level-headedness, practicality, prudence, nous (*Brit. slang*), soundness, reasonableness, gumption (*Brit. informal*), horse sense, native intelligence, mother wit, smarts (*slang, chiefly U.S.*), wit

common-sense ADJECTIVE = **sensible**, sound, practical, reasonable, realistic, shrewd, down-to-earth, matter-of-fact, sane, astute, judicious, level-headed, hard-headed, grounded ■ **OPPOSITE:** foolish

commotion NOUN = **disturbance**, to-do, riot, disorder, excitement, fuss, turmoil, racket, upheaval, bustle, furore, outcry, uproar, ferment, agitation, ado, rumpus, tumult, hubbub, hurly-burly, brouhaha, hullabaloo, hue and cry

communal ADJECTIVE **1** *Communal violence broke out in different parts of the country.* = **community**, neighbourhood **2** *The inmates ate in a communal dining room.* = **public**, shared, general, joint, collective, communistic ■ **OPPOSITE:** private

commune NOUN = **community**, collective, cooperative, kibbutz

commune with VERB **1** *He set off from the lodge to commune with nature.* = **contemplate**, ponder, reflect on, muse on, meditate on **2** *We were encouraged to commune with grown-ups as equals.* = **talk to**, communicate with, discuss with, confer with, converse with, discourse with, parley with, korero (*N.Z.*)

communicable ADJECTIVE = **infectious**, catching, contagious, transferable, transmittable

communicate VERB **1** *My natural mother has never communicated with me.* = **contact**, talk, speak, phone, correspond, make contact, be in touch, ring up (*informal, chiefly Brit.*), be in contact, get in contact, email or e-mail, text, message **2** *The result will be communicated to parents.* = **make known**, report, announce, reveal, publish, declare, spread, disclose, pass on, proclaim, transmit, convey, impart, divulge, disseminate ■ **OPPOSITE:** keep secret **3** *typhus, a disease communicated by body lice* = **pass on**, transfer, spread, transmit

communication NOUN **1** *The problem is a lack of real communication between you.* = **contact**, conversation, correspondence, intercourse, link, relations, connection **2** *Treatment involves the communication of information.* = **passing on**, spread, circulation, transmission, disclosure, imparting, dissemination, conveyance **3** *The ambassador has brought a communication from the President.* = **message**, news, report, word, information, statement, intelligence, announcement, disclosure, dispatch, email or e-mail, text ▸ PLURAL NOUN *Violent rain has caused flooding and cut communications between neighbouring towns.* = **connections**, travel, links, transport, routes

communicative ADJECTIVE = **talkative**, open, frank, forthcoming, outgoing, informative, candid, expansive, chatty, voluble, loquacious, unreserved ■ **OPPOSITE:** reserved

communion NOUN = **affinity**, accord, agreement, unity, sympathy, harmony, intercourse, fellowship, communing, closeness, rapport, converse, togetherness, concord

Communion NOUN = **Eucharist**, Mass, Sacrament, Lord's Supper

communiqué NOUN = **announcement**, report, bulletin, dispatch, news flash, official communication

communism NOUN (usually cap.) = **socialism**, Marxism, Stalinism, collectivism, Bolshevism, Marxism-Leninism, state socialism, Maoism, Trotskyism, Eurocommunism, Titoism

communist NOUN (often cap.) = **socialist**, Red (informal), Marxist, Bolshevik, collectivist

community NOUN 1 He's well liked by the local community. = **society**, people, public, association, population, residents, commonwealth, general public, populace, body politic, state, company 2 a township on the outskirts of the mining community = **district**, area, quarter, region, sector, parish, neighbourhood, vicinity, locality, locality, locale, neck of the woods (informal)

commute VERB 1 He commutes to London every day. = **travel** 2 His death sentence was commuted to life imprisonment. = **reduce**, cut, modify, shorten, alleviate, curtail, remit, mitigate

commuter NOUN = **daily traveller**, passenger, suburbanite

compact¹ ADJECTIVE 1 a thick, bare trunk crowned by a compact mass of dark-green leaves = **closely packed**, firm, solid, thick, dense, compressed, condensed, impenetrable, impermeable, pressed together ■ **OPPOSITE:** loose 2 The strength of the series is in its concise, compact short-story quality. = **concise**, brief, to the point, succinct, terse, laconic, pithy, epigrammatic, pointed ■ **OPPOSITE:** lengthy ▶ VERB The soil settles and is compacted by the winter rain. = **pack closely**, stuff, cram, compress, condense, tamp ■ **OPPOSITE:** loosen

compact² NOUN The Pilgrims signed a democratic compact aboard the Mayflower. = **agreement**, deal (informal), understanding, contract, bond, arrangement, alliance, treaty, bargain, pact, covenant, entente, concordat

companion NOUN 1 He has been her constant companion for the last six years. = **friend**, partner, ally, colleague, associate, mate (informal), gossip (archaic), buddy (informal), comrade, accomplice, crony, confederate, plus-one (informal), consort, main man (slang, chiefly U.S.), homeboy (slang, chiefly U.S.), cobber (Austral. & N.Z., old-fashioned, informal) 2 She was employed as companion to a wealthy old woman. = **assistant**, aide, escort, attendant 3 The book was written as the companion to a trilogy of television

documentaries. = **complement**, match, fellow, mate, twin, counterpart

companionship NOUN = **fellowship**, company, friendship, fraternity, rapport, camaraderie, togetherness, comradeship, amity (formal), esprit de corps, conviviality

company NOUN 1 She worked in an insurance company. = **business**, firm, association, corporation, partnership, establishment, syndicate, house, concern 2 He was a notable young actor in a company of rising stars. = **group**, troupe, set, community, league, band, crowd, camp, collection, gathering, circle, crew (informal), assembly, convention, ensemble, throng, coterie, bevy, assemblage, party, body 3 The division consists of two tank companies and one infantry company. = **troop**, unit, squad, team 4 I would be grateful for your company on the drive back. = **companionship**, society (old-fashioned), presence, fellowship 5 Oh, I'm sorry, I didn't realise you had company. = **guests**, party, visitors, callers

comparable ADJECTIVE 1 They should be paid the same wages for work of comparable value. = **equal**, equivalent, on a par, tantamount, a match, proportionate, commensurate, as good ■ **OPPOSITE:** unequal 2 The scoring systems used in the two studies are not directly comparable. = **similar**, related, alike, corresponding, akin, analogous, of a piece, cognate, cut from the same cloth

comparative ADJECTIVE = **relative**, qualified, by comparison, approximate

compare VERB Compare the two illustrations in Fig 60. = **contrast**, balance, weigh, set against, collate, juxtapose • **compare to something** Commentators compared his work to that of James Joyce. = **liken to**, parallel, identify with, equate to, correlate to, mention in the same breath as • **compare with something** The flowers here do not compare with those at home. = **be as good as**, match, approach, equal, compete with, come up to, vie, be on a par with, be the equal of, approximate to, hold a candle to, bear comparison, be in the same class as

comparison NOUN 1 There are no previous statistics for comparison. = **contrast**, distinction, differentiation, juxtaposition, collation 2 There is no comparison between the picture quality of the two formats. = **similarity**, analogy, resemblance, correlation, likeness, comparability

compartment NOUN 1 We shared our compartment with a group of students. = **section**, carriage, berth 2 I put the ice cream in the freezer compartment of the fridge. = **bay**, chamber, booth, locker, niche, cubicle, alcove, pigeonhole, cubbyhole, cell **3** *We usually put the mind, the body and the spirit into three separate compartments.* = **category**, area, department, division, section, subdivision

compass NOUN *Within the compass of a book of this size, such a comprehensive survey is not practicable.* = **range**, field, area, reach, scope, sphere, limit, stretch, bound, extent, zone, boundary, realm

compassion NOUN = **sympathy**, understanding, charity, pity, humanity, mercy, heart, quarter, sorrow, kindness, tenderness, condolence, clemency, commiseration, fellow feeling, soft-heartedness, tender-heartedness, aroha (*N.Z.*) ■ OPPOSITE: indifference

compassionate ADJECTIVE = **sympathetic**, kindly, understanding, tender, pitying, humanitarian, charitable, humane, indulgent, benevolent, lenient, merciful, kind-hearted, tender-hearted ■ OPPOSITE: uncaring

compatibility NOUN **1** *The committee will consider the bill's compatibility with human rights law.* = **agreement**, consistency, accordance, affinity, conformity, concord, congruity, accord **2** *Dating allows people to check out their compatibility before making a commitment to one another.* = **like-mindedness**, harmony, empathy, rapport, single-mindedness, amity (*formal*), sympathy, congeniality

compatible ADJECTIVE **1** *Free enterprise, he argued, was compatible with Russian values and traditions.* = **consistent**, in keeping, consonant, congenial, congruent, reconcilable, congruous, accordant, agreeable ■ OPPOSITE: inappropriate **2** *She and I are very compatible – we're interested in all the same things.* = **like-minded**, harmonious, in harmony, in accord, of one mind, of the same mind, en rapport (*French*) ■ OPPOSITE: incompatible

compatriot NOUN = **fellow countryman**, countryman, fellow citizen

compel VERB = **force**, make, urge, enforce, railroad (*informal*), drive, oblige, constrain, hustle (*slang*), necessitate, coerce, bulldoze (*informal*), impel, dragoon

compelling ADJECTIVE **1** *He puts forward a compelling argument against the government's policy.* = **convincing**, telling, powerful, forceful, conclusive, weighty, cogent, irrefutable **2** *Her eyes were her best feature, wide-set and compelling.* = **fascinating**, gripping, irresistible, enchanting, enthralling, hypnotic, spellbinding, mesmeric ■ OPPOSITE: boring

compendium NOUN = **collection**, summary, abstract, digest, compilation, epitome, synopsis, précis

compensate VERB **1** *To ease financial difficulties, farmers could be compensated for their loss of subsidies.* = **recompense**, repay, refund, reimburse, indemnify, make restitution, requite, remunerate (*formal*), satisfy, make good **2** *She compensated for her burst of anger by doing even more for her colleagues.* = **make amends for**, make up for, atone for, pay for, do penance for, cancel out, make reparation for, make redress for **3** *The rewards more than compensated for the inconveniences involved in making the trip.* = **balance**, cancel (out), offset, make up for, redress, counteract, neutralize, counterbalance

compensation NOUN **1** *He received one year's salary as compensation for loss of office.* = **reparation**, damages, payment, recompense, indemnification, offset, remuneration, indemnity, restitution, reimbursement, requital **2** *The present she left him was no compensation for her absence.* = **recompense**, amends, reparation, restitution, atonement

compete VERB **1** *The stores will inevitably end up competing with each other for increased market shares.* = **contend**, fight, rival, vie, challenge, struggle, contest, strive, pit yourself against **2** *He has competed twice in the Berlin marathon.* = **take part**, participate, be in the running, be a competitor, be a contestant, play

competence NOUN **1** *I regard him as a man of integrity and high professional competence.* = **ability**, skill, talent, capacity, expertise, proficiency, competency, capability ■ OPPOSITE: incompetence **2** *They questioned her competence as a mother.* = **fitness**, suitability, adequacy, appropriateness ■ OPPOSITE: inadequacy

competent ADJECTIVE **1** *He was a loyal and very competent civil servant.* = **able**, skilled, capable, clever, endowed, proficient ■ OPPOSITE: incompetent **2** *I don't feel competent to deal with a medical emergency.* = **fit**, qualified, equal, appropriate, suitable, sufficient, adequate ■ OPPOSITE: unqualified

competition NOUN **1** *There's been some fierce competition for the title.* = **rivalry**, opposition, struggle, contest, contention, strife, one-upmanship (*informal*) **2** *In this business you have to stay one step ahead of the competition.* = **opposition**, field, rivals, challengers **3** *He will be banned from international competitions for four years.*

= **contest**, event, championship, tournament, head-to-head

competitive ADJECTIVE **1** *Modelling is a tough, competitive world.* = **cut-throat**, aggressive, fierce, ruthless, relentless, antagonistic, dog-eat-dog **2** *He has always been a fiercely competitive player.* = **ambitious**, pushing, opposing, aggressive, two-fisted, vying, contentious, combative

competitor NOUN **1** *The bank isn't performing as well as some of its competitors.* = **rival**, competition, opposition, adversary, antagonist **2** *One of the oldest competitors in the race won the silver medal.* = **contestant**, participant, contender, challenger, entrant, player, opponent

compilation NOUN = **collection**, treasury, accumulation, anthology, assortment, assemblage

compile VERB = **put together**, collect, gather, organize, accumulate, marshal, garner, amass, cull, anthologize

complacency NOUN = **smugness**, satisfaction, gratification, contentment, self-congratulation, self-satisfaction

complacent ADJECTIVE = **smug**, self-satisfied, pleased with yourself, resting on your laurels, pleased, contented, satisfied, gratified, serene, unconcerned, self-righteous, self-assured, self-contented ■ **OPPOSITE:** insecure

complain VERB = **find fault**, moan (*informal*), grumble, whinge (*informal*), beef (*slang*), carp, fuss, bitch (*slang*), groan, grieve, lament, whine, growl, deplore, grouse, gripe (*informal*), bemoan, bleat, put the boot in (*slang*), bewail, kick up a fuss (*informal*), grouch (*informal*), bellyache (*slang*), kvetch (*U.S. slang*), nit-pick (*informal*)

complaint NOUN **1** *There have been a number of complaints about the standard of service.* = **protest**, accusation, objection, grievance, remonstrance (*formal*), charge **2** *I don't have any complaints about the way I've been treated.* = **grumble**, criticism, beef (*slang*), moan, bitch (*slang*), lament, grievance, wail, dissatisfaction, annoyance, grouse, gripe (*informal*), grouch (*informal*), plaint, fault-finding **3** *Eczema is a common skin complaint.* = **disorder**, problem, trouble, disease, upset, illness, sickness, ailment, affliction, malady, indisposition

complement VERB *Nutmeg complements the flavour of these beans perfectly.* = **enhance**, complete, improve, boost, crown, add to, set off, heighten, augment, round off ▶ NOUN **1** *The green wallpaper is the perfect complement to the old pine of the dresser.*

= **accompaniment**, companion, accessory, completion, finishing touch, rounding-off, adjunct, supplement **2** *Each ship had a complement of around a dozen officers and 250 men.* = **total**, capacity, quota, aggregate, contingent, entirety

> **USAGE** This is sometimes confused with *compliment* but the two words have very different meanings. As the synonyms show, the verb form of *complement* means 'to enhance' and 'to complete' something. In contrast, common synonyms of *compliment* as a verb are *praise*, *commend*, and *flatter*.

complementary ADJECTIVE = **matching**, companion, corresponding, compatible, reciprocal, interrelating, interdependent, harmonizing ■ **OPPOSITE:** incompatible

complete ADJECTIVE **1** *He made me look like a complete idiot.* = **total**, perfect, absolute, utter, outright, thorough, consummate, out-and-out, unmitigated, dyed-in-the-wool, thoroughgoing, deep-dyed **2** *A complete tenement block was burnt to the ground.* = **whole**, full, entire ■ **OPPOSITE:** partial **3** *Scientists have found the oldest complete skeleton of an ape-like man.* = **entire**, full, whole, intact, unbroken, faultless, undivided, unimpaired ■ **OPPOSITE:** incomplete **4** *the complete works of Shakespeare* = **unabridged**, full, entire **5** *The work of restoring the farmhouse is complete.* = **finished**, done, ended, completed, achieved, concluded, fulfilled, accomplished ■ **OPPOSITE:** unfinished ▶ VERB **1** *the stickers needed to complete the collection* = **perfect**, accomplish, finish off, round off, crown, cap ■ **OPPOSITE:** spoil **2** *He had just completed his first novel.* = **finish**, conclude, fulfil, accomplish, do, end, close, achieve, perform, settle, realize, execute, discharge, wrap up (*informal*), terminate, finalize ■ **OPPOSITE:** start

completely ADVERB = **totally**, entirely, wholly, utterly, quite, perfectly, fully, solidly, absolutely, altogether, thoroughly, in full, every inch, en masse, heart and soul, a hundred per cent, one hundred per cent, from beginning to end, down to the ground, root and branch, in toto (*Latin*), from A to Z, hook, line and sinker, lock, stock and barrel

completion NOUN = **finishing**, end, close, conclusion, accomplishment, realization, fulfilment, culmination, attainment, fruition, consummation, finalization

complex ADJECTIVE **1** *His complex compositions are built up of many overlapping layers.* = **compound**, compounded, multiple, composite, manifold (*formal*), heterogeneous, multifarious **2** *in-depth coverage of today's complex issues* = **complicated**, difficult, involved, mixed, elaborate, tangled, mingled, intricate, tortuous, convoluted, knotty, labyrinthine, circuitous ■ OPPOSITE: simple ▶ NOUN **1** *Our philosophy is a complex of many tightly interrelated ideas.* = **structure**, system, scheme, network, organization, aggregate, composite, synthesis **2** *I have never had a complex about my weight.* = **obsession**, preoccupation, phobia, fixation, fixed idea, idée fixe (*French*)

> USAGE Although *complex* and *complicated* are close in meaning, care should be taken when using one as a synonym of the other. *Complex* should be used to say that something consists of several parts rather than that it is difficult to understand, analyse, or deal with, which is what *complicated* inherently means. In the following real example a clear distinction is made between the two words: *the British benefits system is phenomenally complex and is administered by a complicated range of agencies*.

complexion NOUN **1** *She had short brown hair and a pale complexion.* = **skin**, colour, colouring, hue, skin tone, pigmentation **2** *The political complexion of the government has changed.* = **nature**, character, make-up, cast, stamp, disposition

complexity NOUN = **complication**, involvement, intricacy, entanglement, convolution

compliance NOUN **1** *The company says it is in full compliance with US labor laws.* = **conformity**, agreement, obedience, assent, observance, concurrence ■ OPPOSITE: disobedience **2** *We seem to have reached unprecedented depths of compliance and timidity.* = **submissiveness**, yielding, submission, obedience, deference, passivity, acquiescence, complaisance, consent ■ OPPOSITE: defiance

compliant ADJECTIVE = **obedient**, willing, accepting, yielding, obliging, accommodating, passive, cooperative, agreeable, submissive, conformist, deferential, acquiescent, complaisant, conformable

complicate VERB = **make difficult**, confuse, muddle, embroil, entangle, make intricate, involve ■ OPPOSITE: simplify

complicated ADJECTIVE **1** *The political situation in this region is very complicated.*

= **involved**, difficult, puzzling, troublesome, problematic, perplexing ■ OPPOSITE: simple **2** *a complicated voting system* = **complex**, involved, elaborate, intricate, Byzantine ■ OPPOSITE: understandable

complication NOUN **1** *The age difference was a complication to the relationship.* = **problem**, difficulty, obstacle, drawback, snag, uphill (*S. African*), stumbling block, aggravation **2** *His poetry was characterised by a complication of imagery and ideas.* = **complexity**, combination, mixture, web, confusion, intricacy, entanglement

complicity NOUN = **collusion**, conspiracy, collaboration, connivance, abetment

compliment NOUN *She accepted the compliment with good grace.* = **praise**, honour, tribute, courtesy, admiration, bouquet, flattery, eulogy ■ OPPOSITE: criticism ▶ PLURAL NOUN **1** *Give my compliments to all your colleagues.* = **greetings**, regards, respects, good wishes, salutation ■ OPPOSITE: insult **2** *That was an excellent meal – my compliments to the chef.* = **congratulations**, praise, commendation ▶ VERB *They complimented me on my performance.* = **praise**, flatter, salute, congratulate, pay tribute to, commend, laud, extol, crack up (*informal*), pat on the back, sing the praises of, wax lyrical about, big up (*slang*), speak highly of ■ OPPOSITE: criticize

> USAGE *Compliment* is sometimes confused with *complement*.

complimentary ADJECTIVE **1** *We often get complimentary remarks regarding the quality of our service.* = **flattering**, approving, appreciative, congratulatory, eulogistic, commendatory ■ OPPOSITE: critical **2** *He had complimentary tickets for the show.* = **free**, donated, courtesy, honorary, free of charge, on the house, gratuitous, gratis

comply VERB = **obey**, follow, respect, agree to, satisfy, observe, fulfil, submit to, conform to, adhere to, abide by, consent to, yield to, defer to, accede to, act in accordance with, perform, acquiesce with ■ OPPOSITE: defy

component NOUN *Enriched uranium is a key component of nuclear weapons.* = **part**, piece, unit, item, element, ingredient, constituent ▶ ADJECTIVE *Polish factories will be making component parts for the aircraft.* = **constituent**, composing, inherent, intrinsic

compose VERB **1** *They agreed to form a council composed of leaders of the rival factions.* = **put together**, make up, constitute, comprise, make, build, form, fashion, construct, compound ■ **OPPOSITE:** destroy **2** *He started at once to compose a reply to her letter.* = **create**, write, produce, imagine, frame, invent, devise, contrive **3** *The drawing is beautifully composed.* = **arrange**, make up, construct, put together, order, organize • **compose yourself** *She quickly composed herself before she entered the room.* = **calm yourself**, be still, control yourself, settle yourself, collect yourself, pull yourself together

composed ADJECTIVE = **calm**, together (*slang*), cool, collected, relaxed, confident, poised, at ease, laid-back (*informal*), serene, tranquil, sedate, self-controlled, level-headed, unfazed (*informal*), unflappable, unruffled, self-possessed, imperturbable, unworried, keeping your cool, as cool as a cucumber, chilled (*informal*), grounded ■ **OPPOSITE:** agitated

composite ADJECTIVE *The chassis is made of a complex composite structure incorporating carbon fibre.* = **compound**, mixed, combined, complex, blended, conglomerate, synthesized ▶ NOUN *Spain is a composite of diverse traditions and people.* = **compound**, blend, conglomerate, fusion, synthesis, amalgam, meld

composition NOUN **1** *Materials of different composition absorb and reflect light differently.* = **design**, form, structure, make-up, organization, arrangement, constitution, formation, layout, configuration **2** *Bach's compositions are undoubtedly among the greatest ever written.* = **creation**, work, piece, production, opus, masterpiece, chef-d'oeuvre (*French*) **3** *Write a composition on the subject 'What I Did on My Holidays'.* = **essay**, writing, study, exercise, treatise, literary work **4** *Let us study the composition of this painting.* = **arrangement**, balance, proportion, harmony, symmetry, concord, consonance (*formal*), placing **5** *These plays are arranged in order of their composition.* = **production**, creation, making, fashioning, formation, putting together, invention, compilation, formulation

compost NOUN = **fertilizer**, mulch, humus

composure NOUN = **calmness**, calm, poise, self-possession, cool (*slang*), ease, dignity, serenity, tranquillity, coolness, aplomb, equanimity, self-assurance, sang-froid, placidity, sedateness ■ **OPPOSITE:** agitation

compound NOUN *Organic compounds contain carbon in their molecules.* = **combination**, mixture, blend, composite, conglomerate,

fusion, synthesis, alloy, medley, amalgam, meld, composition ■ **OPPOSITE:** element ▶ ADJECTIVE *a tall shrub with shiny compound leaves* = **complex**, multiple, composite, conglomerate, intricate, not simple ■ **OPPOSITE:** simple ▶ VERB **1** *Additional bloodshed will only compound the misery.* = **intensify**, add to, complicate, worsen, heighten, exacerbate, aggravate, magnify, augment, add insult to injury ■ **OPPOSITE:** lessen **2** *An emotion oddly compounded of pleasure and bitterness flooded over me.* = **combine**, unite, mix, blend, fuse, mingle, synthesize, concoct, amalgamate, coalesce, intermingle, meld ■ **OPPOSITE:** divide

comprehend VERB = **understand**, see, take in, perceive, grasp, conceive, make out, discern, assimilate, see the light, fathom, apprehend, get the hang of (*informal*), get the picture, know ■ **OPPOSITE:** misunderstand

comprehensible ADJECTIVE = **understandable**, clear, plain, explicit, coherent, user-friendly, intelligible

comprehension NOUN = **understanding**, grasp, conception, realization, sense, knowledge, intelligence, judgment, perception, discernment ■ **OPPOSITE:** incomprehension

comprehensive ADJECTIVE = **broad**, full, complete, wide, catholic, sweeping, extensive, blanket, umbrella, thorough, inclusive, exhaustive, all-inclusive, all-embracing, overarching, encyclopedic ■ **OPPOSITE:** limited

compress VERB **1** *Poor posture can compress the body's organs.* = **squeeze**, crush, squash, constrict, press, crowd, wedge, cram **2** *Textbooks compressed six millennia of Egyptian history into a few pages.* = **condense**, contract, concentrate, compact, shorten, summarize, abbreviate, zip (*data*)

compressed ADJECTIVE **1** *a biodegradable product made from compressed peat and cellulose* = **squeezed**, concentrated, compact, compacted, consolidated, squashed, flattened, constricted **2** *All those three books are compressed into one volume.* = **reduced**, compacted, shortened, abridged

compression NOUN = **squeezing**, pressing, crushing, consolidation, condensation, constriction

comprise VERB **1** *The exhibition comprises 50 oils and watercolours.* = **be composed of**, include, contain, consist of, take in, embrace, encompass, comprehend **2** *Women comprise 44% of hospital medical staff.* = **make up**, form, constitute, compose

USAGE The use of *of* after *comprise* should be avoided: *the library comprises* (not *comprises of*) *6,500,000 books and manuscripts*. *Consist*, however, should be followed by *of* when used in this way: *Her crew consisted of children from Devon and Cornwall*.

compromise NOUN *Be willing to make compromises between what your partner wants and what you want.* = **give-and-take**, agreement, settlement, accommodation, concession, adjustment, trade-off, middle ground, half measures ■ **OPPOSITE:** disagreement ▶ VERB **1** *I don't think we can compromise on fundamental principles.* = **meet halfway**, concede, make concessions, give and take, strike a balance, strike a happy medium, go fifty-fifty (*informal*) ■ **OPPOSITE:** disagree **2** *He had compromised himself by accepting the money.* = **undermine**, expose, embarrass, weaken, prejudice, endanger, discredit, implicate, jeopardize, dishonour, imperil ■ **OPPOSITE:** support

compulsion NOUN **1** *He felt a compulsion to talk about his ex-wife all the time.* = **urge**, need, obsession, necessity, preoccupation, drive **2** *Students learn more when they are in classes out of choice rather than compulsion.* = **force**, pressure, obligation, constraint, urgency, coercion, duress, demand

compulsive ADJECTIVE **1** *He is a compulsive liar.* = **obsessive**, confirmed, chronic, persistent, addictive, uncontrollable, incurable, inveterate, incorrigible **2** *This really is compulsive reading.* = **fascinating**, gripping, absorbing, compelling, captivating, enthralling, hypnotic, engrossing, spellbinding **3** *an almost compulsive desire to play tricks* = **irresistible**, overwhelming, compelling, urgent, besetting, uncontrollable, driving

compulsory ADJECTIVE = **obligatory**, forced, required, binding, mandatory, imperative, requisite, de rigueur (*French*) ■ **OPPOSITE:** voluntary

compute VERB = **calculate**, rate, figure, total, measure, estimate, count, reckon, sum, figure out, add up, tally, enumerate

comrade NOUN = **companion**, friend, partner, ally, colleague, associate, fellow, mate (*informal*), pal (*informal*), buddy (*informal*), compatriot, crony, confederate, co-worker, main man (*slang, chiefly U.S.*), blood (*Brit. slang*), homeboy (*slang, chiefly U.S.*), cobber (*Austral. & N.Z., old-fashioned, informal*), compeer

comradeship NOUN = **fellowship**, solidarity, fraternity, brotherhood, sisterhood, companionship, camaraderie

con (*informal*) VERB *She claimed that a fraudster had conned her out of her life savings.* = **swindle**, trick, cheat, rip off (*slang*), kid (*informal*), skin (*slang*), stiff (*slang*), mislead, deceive, hoax, defraud, dupe, gull (*archaic*), rook (*slang*), humbug, bamboozle (*informal*), hoodwink, double-cross (*informal*), diddle (*informal*), take for a ride (*informal*), inveigle, do the dirty on (*Brit. informal*), bilk, sell a pup, pull a fast one on (*informal*), scam (*slang*) ▶ NOUN *I am afraid you have been the victim of a con.* = **swindle**, trick, fraud, deception, scam (*slang*), sting (*informal*), bluff, fastie (*Austral. slang*)

concave ADJECTIVE = **hollow**, cupped, depressed, scooped, hollowed, excavated, sunken, indented ■ **OPPOSITE:** convex

conceal VERB **1** *The device, concealed in a dustbin, was defused by police.* = **hide**, bury, stash (*informal*), secrete, cover, screen, disguise, obscure, camouflage ■ **OPPOSITE:** reveal **2** *Robert could not conceal his relief.* = **keep secret**, hide, disguise, mask, suppress, veil, dissemble, draw a veil over, keep dark, keep under your hat ■ **OPPOSITE:** show

concealed ADJECTIVE = **hidden**, covered, secret, screened, masked, obscured, covert, unseen, tucked away, secreted, under wraps, inconspicuous

concealment NOUN **1** *The criminals vainly sought concealment from the searchlight.* = **cover**, hiding, camouflage, hiding place **2** *His concealment of his true motives was masterly.* = **cover-up**, disguise, keeping secret ■ **OPPOSITE:** disclosure

concede VERB **1** *She finally conceded that he was right.* = **admit**, allow, accept, acknowledge, own, grant, confess ■ **OPPOSITE:** deny **2** *The government has never conceded that territory to the rebels.* = **give up**, yield, hand over, surrender, relinquish, cede ■ **OPPOSITE:** conquer

conceit NOUN **1** *He knew, without conceit, that he was considered a genius.* = **self-importance**, vanity, arrogance, complacency, pride, swagger, narcissism, egotism, self-love, amour-propre, vainglory **2** *Critics may complain that the novel's central conceit is rather simplistic.* = **image**, idea, concept, metaphor, imagery, figure of speech, trope

conceited ADJECTIVE = **self-important**, vain, arrogant, stuck up (*informal*), cocky, narcissistic, puffed up, egotistical, overweening, immodest, vainglorious, swollen-headed, bigheaded (*informal*), full of yourself, too big for your boots *or* breeches ■ **OPPOSITE:** modest

conceivable ADJECTIVE = **imaginable**, possible, credible, believable, thinkable ■ OPPOSITE: inconceivable

conceive VERB **1** *We now cannot conceive of a world without electricity.* = **imagine**, envisage, comprehend, visualize, think, believe, suppose, fancy, appreciate, grasp, apprehend **2** *I began to conceive a plan of attack.* = **think up**, form, produce, create, develop, design, project, purpose, devise, formulate, contrive **3** *women who plan to conceive when they are older* = **become pregnant**, get pregnant, become impregnated

concentrate VERB **1** *Try to concentrate on what you're doing.* = **focus your attention**, focus, pay attention, be engrossed, apply yourself ■ OPPOSITE: pay no attention **2** *We should concentrate our efforts on tackling crime in the inner cities.* = **focus**, centre, converge, bring to bear **3** *Most poor people are concentrated in this area.* = **gather**, collect, cluster, accumulate, congregate ■ OPPOSITE: scatter

concentrated ADJECTIVE **1** *Sweeten dishes with honey or concentrated apple juice.* = **condensed**, rich, undiluted, reduced, evaporated, thickened, boiled down **2** *She makes a concentrated effort to keep her feet on the ground.* = **intense**, hard, deep, intensive, all-out (*informal*)

concentration NOUN **1** *His talking kept breaking my concentration.* = **attention**, application, absorption, single-mindedness, intentness ■ OPPOSITE: inattention **2** *This concentration of effort and resources should not be to the exclusion of everything else.* = **focusing**, centring, consolidation, convergence, bringing to bear, intensification, centralization **3** *The area has one of the world's greatest concentrations of wildlife.* = **convergence**, collection, mass, cluster, accumulation, aggregation ■ OPPOSITE: scattering

concept NOUN = **idea**, view, image, theory, impression, notion, conception, hypothesis, abstraction, conceptualization

conception NOUN **1** *He doesn't have the slightest conception of teamwork.* = **understanding**, idea, picture, impression, perception, clue, appreciation, comprehension, inkling **2** *The symphony is admirable in its conception.* = **idea**, plan, design, image, concept, notion **3** *Six weeks after conception your baby is the size of your little fingernail.* = **impregnation**, insemination, fertilization, germination **4** *It is six years since the project's conception.* = **origin**, beginning, launching, birth, formation, invention, outset, initiation, inception

concern NOUN **1** *The move follows growing public concern over the spread of the disease.* = **anxiety**, fear, worry, distress, unease, apprehension, misgiving, disquiet **2** *His concern was that people would know that he was responsible.* = **worry**, care, anxiety **3** *Politicians cannot ignore the concerns of young people.* = **affair**, issue, matter, consideration **4** *He had only gone along out of concern for his two grandsons.* = **care**, interest, regard, consideration, solicitude, attentiveness **5** *The technical aspects are not my concern.* = **business**, job, charge, matter, department, field, affair, responsibility, task, mission, pigeon (*informal*) **6** *If not a large concern, his business was at least a successful one.* = **company**, house, business, firm, organization, corporation, enterprise, establishment **7** *The survey's findings are a matter of great concern.* = **importance**, interest, bearing, relevance ▸ VERB **1** *It concerned her that Bess was developing a crush on Max.* = **worry**, trouble, bother, disturb, distress, disquiet, perturb, make uneasy, make anxious **2** *The bulk of the book concerns the author's childhood.* = **be about**, cover, deal with, go into, relate to, have to do with **3** *This matter doesn't concern you, so stay out of it.* = **be relevant to**, involve, affect, regard, apply to, bear on, have something to do with, pertain to, interest, touch

concerned ADJECTIVE **1** *I believe he was concerned in all those matters you mention.* = **involved**, interested, active, mixed up, implicated, privy to **2** *I've been very concerned about the situation.* = **worried**, troubled, upset, bothered, disturbed, anxious, distressed, uneasy ■ OPPOSITE: indifferent **3** *A concerned friend put a comforting arm around her shoulder.* = **caring**, attentive, solicitous

concerning PREPOSITION = **regarding**, about, re, touching, respecting, relating to, on the subject of, as to, with reference to, in the matter of, apropos of, as regards

concert • **in concert** = **together**, jointly, unanimously, in unison, in league, in collaboration, shoulder to shoulder, concertedly

concerted ADJECTIVE = **coordinated**, united, joint, combined, collaborative ■ OPPOSITE: separate

concession NOUN **1** *We had to make sweeping concessions in order to reach a settlement.* = **compromise**, agreement, settlement, accommodation, adjustment, trade-off, give-and-take, half measures **2** *The government has granted concessions to three* *private companies.* = **privilege**, right, permit, licence, franchise, entitlement, indulgence, prerogative **3** *We don't know how long the government will allow these tax concessions to continue.* = **reduction**, saving, grant, discount, allowance **4** *He said there'd be no concession of territory.* = **surrender**, yielding, conceding, renunciation, relinquishment

conciliation NOUN = **pacification**, reconciliation, disarming, appeasement, propitiation, mollification, soothing, placation

conciliatory ADJECTIVE = **pacifying**, pacific, disarming, appeasing, mollifying, peaceable, placatory, soothing

concise ADJECTIVE = **brief**, short, to the point, compact, summary, compressed, condensed, terse, laconic, succinct, pithy, synoptic, epigrammatic, compendious ■ **OPPOSITE:** rambling

conclave NOUN = **secret** *or* **private meeting**, council, conference, congress, session, cabinet, assembly, parley, runanga (*N.Z.*)

conclude VERB **1** *We concluded that he was telling the truth.* = **decide**, judge, establish, suppose, determine, assume, gather, reckon (*informal*), work out, infer, deduce, surmise **2** *The evening concluded with dinner and speeches.* = **come to an end**, end, close, finish, wind up, draw to a close ■ **OPPOSITE:** begin **3** *They concluded their annual summit meeting today.* = **bring to an end**, end, close, finish, complete, wind up, terminate, round off ■ **OPPOSITE:** begin **4** *If the clubs cannot conclude a deal, an independent tribunal will decide.* = **accomplish**, effect, settle, bring about, fix, carry out, resolve, clinch, pull off, bring off (*informal*)

conclusion NOUN **1** *We came to the conclusion that it was too difficult to combine the two techniques.* = **decision**, agreement, opinion, settlement, resolution, conviction, verdict, judgment, deduction, inference **2** *At the conclusion of the programme, viewers were invited to phone in.* = **end**, ending, close, finish, completion, finale, termination, bitter end, result **3** *Executives said it was the logical conclusion of the process.* = **outcome**, result, upshot, consequence, sequel, culmination, end result, issue • **in conclusion** *In conclusion, walking is a cheap, safe form of exercise.* = **finally**, lastly, in closing, to sum up

conclusive ADJECTIVE = **decisive**, final, convincing, clinching, definite, definitive, irrefutable, unanswerable, unarguable, ultimate ■ **OPPOSITE:** inconclusive

concoct VERB = **make up**, design, prepare, manufacture, plot, invent, devise, brew, hatch, formulate, contrive, fabricate, think up, cook up (*informal*), trump up, project

concoction NOUN = **mixture**, preparation, compound, brew, combination, creation, blend

concord NOUN = **treaty**, agreement, convention, compact, protocol, entente, concordat

concourse NOUN = **crowd**, collection, gathering, assembly, crush, multitude, throng, convergence, hui (*N.Z.*), assemblage, meeting, runanga (*N.Z.*)

concrete NOUN *The posts have to be set in concrete.* = **cement** (*not in technical usage*)
▶ ADJECTIVE **1** *He had no concrete evidence.* = **specific**, precise, explicit, definite, clear-cut, unequivocal, unambiguous ■ **OPPOSITE:** vague **2** *using concrete objects to teach addition and subtraction* = **real**, material, actual, substantial (*formal*), sensible, tangible, factual ■ **OPPOSITE:** abstract

concubine NOUN = **mistress**, courtesan, kept woman

concur VERB = **agree**, accord, approve, assent, accede, acquiesce

concurrent ADJECTIVE = **simultaneous**, coexisting, concomitant, contemporaneous, coincident, synchronous, concerted

concussion NOUN **1** *She fell off a horse and suffered a concussion.* = **shock**, brain injury **2** *I was blown off the deck by the concussion of the torpedoes.* = **impact**, crash, shaking, clash, jarring, collision, jolt, jolting

condemn VERB **1** *Political leaders united yesterday to condemn the latest wave of violence.* = **denounce**, damn, criticize, disapprove, censure, reprove, upbraid, excoriate (*literary*), reprehend, blame ■ **OPPOSITE:** approve **2** *He was condemned to life imprisonment.* = **sentence**, convict, damn, doom, pass sentence on ■ **OPPOSITE:** acquit

condemnation NOUN = **denunciation**, blame, censure, disapproval, reproach, stricture, reproof, denouncement

condensation NOUN **1** *The surface refrigeration allows the condensation of water.* = **distillation**, precipitation, liquefaction **2** *a condensation of a book that offers ten ways to be a better manager* = **abridgment**, summary, abstract, digest, contraction, synopsis, précis, encapsulation

condense VERB **1** *The English translation has been condensed into a single more readable book.* = **abridge**, contract, concentrate, compact, shorten, summarize, compress,

encapsulate, abbreviate, epitomize, précis
■ **OPPOSITE:** expand **2** *The compressed gas is cooled and condenses into a liquid.*
= **concentrate**, reduce, precipitate (*Chemistry*), thicken, boil down, solidify, coagulate ■ **OPPOSITE:** dilute

condensed ADJECTIVE **1** *I also produced a condensed version of the paper.* = **abridged**, concentrated, compressed, potted, shortened, summarized, slimmed-down, encapsulated **2** *condensed milk*
= **concentrated**, reduced, thickened, boiled down, precipitated (*Chemistry*)

condescend VERB **1** *a writer who does not condescend to his readers* = **patronize**, talk down to, treat like a child, treat as inferior, treat condescendingly **2** *He never condescended to notice me.* = **deign**, see fit, lower yourself, be courteous enough, bend, submit, stoop, unbend (*informal*), vouchsafe, come down off your high horse (*informal*), humble or demean yourself

condescending ADJECTIVE = **patronizing**, lordly, superior, lofty, snooty (*informal*), snobbish, disdainful, supercilious, toffee-nosed (*slang, chiefly Brit.*), on your high horse (*informal*)

condescension NOUN = **patronizing attitude**, superiority, disdain, haughtiness, loftiness, superciliousness, lordliness, airs

condition NOUN **1** *The two-bedroom chalet is in good condition.* = **state**, order, shape, nick (*Brit. informal*), trim **2** *The government has to encourage people to better their condition.*
= **situation**, state, position, status, circumstances, plight, status quo (*Latin*), case, predicament **3** *She had agreed to a summit subject to certain conditions.*
= **requirement**, terms, rider, provision, restriction, qualification, limitation, modification, requisite, prerequisite, proviso, stipulation, rule, demand **4** *She was in fine condition for a woman of her age.*
= **health**, shape, fitness, trim, form, kilter, state of health, fettle, order **5** *Doctors suspect he may have a heart condition.* = **ailment**, problem, complaint, weakness, malady, infirmity ▶ PLURAL NOUN *The conditions in the camp are just awful.* = **circumstances**, situation, environment, surroundings, way of life, milieu ▶ VERB *We have been conditioned to believe that it is weak to be scared.* = **train**, teach, educate, adapt, accustom, inure, habituate

conditional ADJECTIVE = **dependent**, limited, qualified, contingent, provisional, with reservations ■ **OPPOSITE:** unconditional

conditioning NOUN = **training**, education, teaching, accustoming, habituation

condom NOUN = **sheath**, prophylactic, safe (*U.S. & Canad. slang*), rubber (*slang*), scumbag (*U.S. slang*), French letter (*slang*), jimmy hat (*slang*), French tickler (*slang*)

condone VERB = **overlook**, excuse, forgive, pardon, disregard, turn a blind eye to, wink at, look the other way, make allowance for, let pass ■ **OPPOSITE:** condemn

conducive ADJECTIVE = **favourable**, helpful, productive, contributory, calculated to produce, leading, tending

conduct VERB **1** *I decided to conduct an experiment.* = **carry out**, run, control, manage, direct, handle, organize, govern, regulate, administer, supervise, preside over **2** *He asked if he might conduct us to the ball.* = **accompany**, lead, escort, guide, attend, steer, convey, usher, pilot ▶ NOUN **1** *Also up for discussion will be the conduct of free and fair elections.* = **management**, running, control, handling, administration, direction, leadership, organization, guidance, supervision **2** *Other people judge you by your conduct.* = **behaviour**, ways, bearing, attitude, manners, carriage, demeanour, deportment, mien (*literary*), comportment • **conduct yourself** *The way he conducts himself reflects on the party.*
= **behave yourself**, act, carry yourself, acquit yourself, deport yourself, comport yourself

conduit NOUN = **passage**, channel, tube, pipe, canal, duct, main

confederacy NOUN = **union**, league, alliance, coalition, federation, compact, confederation, covenant, bund

confederate NOUN *The conspirators were joined by their confederates.* = **associate**, partner, ally, colleague, accessory, accomplice, abettor ▶ ADJECTIVE *They wanted to establish a confederate Europe.*
= **allied**, federal, associated, combined, federated, in alliance

confer VERB **1** *He conferred with Hill and the others in his office.* = **discuss**, talk, consult, deliberate, discourse, converse, parley **2** *An honorary degree was conferred on him by the University of Vienna.* = **grant**, give, present, accord, award, hand out, bestow, vouchsafe (*old-fashioned*)

conference NOUN = **meeting**, congress, discussion, convention, forum, consultation, seminar, symposium, hui (*N.Z.*), convocation, colloquium

confess VERB **1** *He has confessed to seventeen murders.* = **admit**, acknowledge, disclose, confide, own up, come clean (*informal*), divulge, blurt out, come out of the closet, make a clean breast of, get (something) off

your chest (*informal*), spill your guts (*slang*), fess up (*U.S.*), sing (*slang, chiefly U.S.*)
■ **OPPOSITE:** cover up **2** *I must confess I'm not a great sports enthusiast.* = **declare**, own up, allow, prove, reveal, grant, confirm, concede, assert, manifest, affirm, profess, attest, evince (*formal*), aver

confession NOUN = **admission**, revelation, disclosure, acknowledgement, avowal, divulgence, exposure, unbosoming

confidant *or* **confidante** NOUN = **close friend**, familiar, intimate, crony, alter ego, bosom friend

confide VERB = **tell**, admit, reveal, confess, whisper, disclose, impart, divulge, breathe

confidence NOUN **1** *I have every confidence in you.* = **trust**, belief, faith, dependence, reliance, credence ■ **OPPOSITE:** distrust **2** *She always thinks the worst of herself and has no confidence whatsoever.* = **self-assurance**, courage, assurance, aplomb, boldness, self-reliance, self-possession, nerve ■ **OPPOSITE:** shyness **3** *I'm not in the habit of exchanging confidences with her.* = **secret** • **in confidence** *I'm telling you all these things in confidence.* = **in secrecy**, privately, confidentially, between you and me (and the gatepost), (just) between ourselves

confident ADJECTIVE **1** *I am confident that everything will come out right in time.* = **certain**, sure, convinced, positive, secure, satisfied, counting on ■ **OPPOSITE:** unsure **2** *In time he became more confident and relaxed.* = **self-assured**, positive, assured, bold, assertive, self-confident, self-reliant, self-possessed, sure of yourself, can-do (*informal*) ■ **OPPOSITE:** insecure

confidential ADJECTIVE **1** *She accused them of leaking confidential information.* = **secret**, private, intimate, classified, privy (*archaic*), off the record, hush-hush (*informal*), closed or closed source (*Computing*), protected (*Computing*) **2** *He adopted a confidential tone of voice.* = **secretive**, low, soft, hushed

confidentially ADVERB = **in secret**, privately, personally, behind closed doors, in confidence, in camera, between ourselves, sub rosa (*literary*)

configuration NOUN = **arrangement**, form, shape, cast, outline, contour, conformation, figure

confine VERB **1** *He has been confined to his barracks.* = **imprison**, enclose, shut up, intern, incarcerate, circumscribe, hem in, immure (*archaic*), keep, cage **2** *She had largely confined her activities to the world of big business.* = **restrict**, limit ► PLURAL NOUN *The movie is set entirely within the confines of the abandoned factory.* = **limits**, bounds,

boundaries, compass, precincts, circumference, edge, pale

confined ADJECTIVE = **restricted**, small, limited, narrow, enclosed, cramped

confinement NOUN **1** *She had been held in solitary confinement for four months.* = **imprisonment**, custody, detention, incarceration, internment, porridge (*slang*) **2** *His pregnant wife is near her confinement.* = **childbirth**, labour, travail, childbed, accouchement (*French*), time

confirm VERB **1** *This confirms what I suspected all along.* = **prove**, support, establish, back up, verify, validate, bear out, substantiate, corroborate, authenticate **2** *Mrs Suarez is due to be confirmed as President on Friday.* = **ratify**, establish, approve, sanction, endorse, authorize, certify, validate, authenticate **3** *He has confirmed his position as the world's number one snooker player.* = **strengthen**, establish, settle, fix, secure, assure, reinforce, clinch, verify, fortify

confirmation NOUN **1** *He took her resignation as confirmation of their suspicions.* = **proof**, evidence, testimony, verification, ratification, validation, corroboration, authentication ■ **OPPOSITE:** repudiation **2** *She glanced over at James for confirmation of what she'd said.* = **affirmation**, approval, acceptance, endorsement, ratification, assent, agreement ■ **OPPOSITE:** disapproval

confirmed ADJECTIVE = **long-established**, seasoned, rooted, chronic, hardened, habitual, ingrained, inveterate, inured, dyed-in-the-wool

confiscate VERB = **seize**, appropriate, impound, commandeer, sequester, expropriate (*formal*) ■ **OPPOSITE:** give back

confiscation NOUN = **seizure**, appropriation, impounding, forfeiture, expropriation (*formal*), sequestration, takeover

conflagration NOUN = **fire**, blaze, holocaust, inferno, wildfire

conflict NOUN **1** *Try to keep any conflict between you and your ex-partner to a minimum.* = **dispute**, difference, opposition, hostility, disagreement, friction, strife, fighting, antagonism, variance, discord, bad blood, dissension, divided loyalties, cyberwar ■ **OPPOSITE:** agreement **2** *the anguish of his own inner conflict* = **struggle**, battle, clash, strife **3** *The National Security Council has met to discuss ways of preventing a military conflict.* = **battle**, war, fight, clash, contest, set-to (*informal*), encounter, combat, engagement, warfare, collision, contention, strife, head-to-head, fracas,

boilover (*Austral.*) ■ **OPPOSITE:** peace
▶ VERB *He held firm opinions which sometimes conflicted with my own.* = **be incompatible**, clash, differ, disagree, contend, strive, collide, be at variance ■ **OPPOSITE:** agree

conflicting ADJECTIVE = **incompatible**, opposed, opposing, clashing, contrary, adverse, contradictory, inconsistent, paradoxical, discordant ■ **OPPOSITE:** agreeing

conform VERB **1** *Children who can't or won't conform are often bullied.* = **fit in**, follow, yield, adjust, adapt, comply, obey, fall in, toe the line, follow the crowd, run with the pack, follow convention **2** (*with* **with**) *These activities do not conform with diplomatic rules and regulations.* = **fulfil**, meet, match, suit, satisfy, agree with, obey, abide by, accord with, square with, correspond with, tally with, harmonize with

conformation NOUN = **shape**, build, form, structure, arrangement, outline, framework, anatomy, configuration

conformist NOUN = **traditionalist**, conservative, reactionary, Babbitt (*U.S.*), stickler, yes man, stick-in-the-mud (*informal*), conventionalist

conformity NOUN **1** *The prime minister is, in conformity with the constitution, chosen by the president.* = **compliance**, agreement, accordance, observance, conformance, obedience **2** *Excessive conformity is usually caused by fear of disapproval.* = **conventionality**, compliance, allegiance, orthodoxy, observance, traditionalism, Babbittry (*U.S.*)

confound VERB **1** *For many years medical scientists were confounded by these seemingly contradictory facts.* = **bewilder**, baffle, amaze, confuse, astonish, startle, mix up, astound, perplex, surprise, mystify, flummox, boggle the mind, be all Greek to (*informal*), dumbfound, nonplus, flabbergast (*informal*) **2** *The findings confound all the government's predictions.* = **disprove**, contradict, refute, negate, destroy, ruin, overwhelm, explode, overthrow, demolish, annihilate, give the lie to, make a nonsense of, prove false, blow out of the water (*slang*), controvert, confute

confront VERB **1** *We are learning how to confront death.* = **tackle**, deal with, cope with, brave, beard, face up to, meet head-on **2** *the environmental crisis which confronts us all* = **trouble**, face, afflict, perplex, perturb, bedevil **3** *She pushed her way through the mob and confronted him face to face.* = **challenge**, face, oppose, tackle, encounter, defy, call out, stand up to, come

face to face with, accost, face off (*slang*) ■ **OPPOSITE:** evade

confrontation NOUN = **conflict**, fight, crisis, contest, set-to (*informal*), encounter, showdown (*informal*), head-to-head, face-off (*slang*), boilover (*Austral.*)

confuse VERB **1** *I can't see how anyone could confuse you two with each other.* = **mix up with**, take for, mistake for, muddle with **2** *Politics just confuses me.* = **bewilder**, puzzle, baffle, perplex, mystify, fluster, faze, flummox, bemuse, be all Greek to (*informal*), nonplus **3** *His critics accused him of trying to confuse the issue.* = **obscure**, cloud, complicate, muddle, darken, make more difficult, muddy the waters

confused ADJECTIVE **1** *People are confused about what they should eat to stay healthy.* = **bewildered**, puzzled, baffled, at sea, muddled, dazed, perplexed, at a loss, taken aback, disorientated, muzzy (*U.S. informal*), nonplussed, flummoxed, at sixes and sevens, thrown off balance, discombobulated (*informal, chiefly U.S. & Canad.*), not with it (*informal*), not knowing if you are coming or going ■ **OPPOSITE:** enlightened **2** *The situation remains confused as both sides claim victory.* = **disorderly**, disordered, chaotic, mixed up, jumbled, untidy, out of order, in disarray, topsy-turvy, disorganized, higgledy-piggledy (*informal*), at sixes and sevens, disarranged, disarrayed ■ **OPPOSITE:** tidy

confusing ADJECTIVE = **bewildering**, complicated, puzzling, misleading, unclear, baffling, muddling, contradictory, ambiguous, inconsistent, perplexing, clear as mud (*informal*) ■ **OPPOSITE:** clear

confusion NOUN **1** *Omissions in my recent article may have caused some confusion.* = **bewilderment**, doubt, uncertainty, puzzlement, perplexity, mystification, bafflement, perturbation ■ **OPPOSITE:** enlightenment **2** *The rebel leader seems to have escaped in the confusion.* = **disorder**, chaos, turmoil, upheaval, muddle, bustle, shambles, disarray, commotion, disorganization, disarrangement ■ **OPPOSITE:** order **3** *I left his office in a state of confusion.* = **puzzlement**, bewilderment, perplexity, bafflement, mystification, perturbation

congeal VERB = **thicken**, set, freeze, harden, clot, stiffen, condense, solidify, curdle, jell, coagulate

congenial ADJECTIVE = **pleasant**, kindly, pleasing, friendly, agreeable, cordial, sociable, genial, affable, convivial, companionable, favourable, complaisant

congenital ADJECTIVE **1** *He has a congenital heart disease.* = **inborn**, innate, inherent, hereditary, natural, constitutional, inherited, inbred **2** *He is a congenital liar.* = **complete**, confirmed, chronic, utter, hardened, thorough, habitual, incurable, inveterate, incorrigible, deep-dyed

congested ADJECTIVE **1** *Some areas are congested with both cars and people.* = **packed (out)**, crowded, overcrowded, teeming **2** *Without treatment, the arteries can become dangerously congested.* = **clogged**, jammed, blocked-up, overfilled, stuffed, packed, crammed, overflowing, stuffed-up
■ **OPPOSITE:** clear

congestion NOUN = **overcrowding**, crowding, mass, jam, clogging, bottleneck, snarl-up (*informal, chiefly Brit.*)

conglomerate NOUN = **corporation**, multinational, corporate body, business, association, consortium, aggregate, agglomerate

congratulate VERB = **compliment**, pat on the back, wish joy to

congratulations PLURAL NOUN *I offer you my congratulations on your appointment as chief executive.* = **good wishes**, greetings, compliments, best wishes, pat on the back, felicitations ▶ INTERJECTION *Congratulations! You have a healthy baby boy.* = **good wishes**, greetings, compliments, best wishes, felicitations

congregate VERB = **come together**, meet, mass, collect, gather, concentrate, rally, assemble, flock, muster, convene, converge, throng, rendezvous, foregather, convoke (*formal*) ■ **OPPOSITE:** disperse

congregation NOUN = **parishioners**, host, brethren, crowd, assembly, parish, flock, fellowship, multitude, throng, laity

congress NOUN **1** *A lot has changed since the party congress.* = **meeting**, council, conference, diet, assembly, convention, conclave, legislative assembly, convocation (*formal*), hui (N.Z.), runanga (N.Z.) **2** *It's far from certain that the congress will approve them.* = **legislature**, house, council, parliament, representatives, delegates, quango, legislative assembly, chamber of deputies, House of Representatives (N.Z.)

conical *or* **conic** ADJECTIVE = **cone-shaped**, pointed, tapered, tapering, pyramidal, funnel-shaped

conjecture NOUN *Your assertion is merely a conjecture, not a fact.* = **guess**, theory, fancy, notion, speculation, assumption, hypothesis, inference, presumption, surmise, theorizing, guesswork, supposition, shot in the dark, guesstimate (*informal*) ▶ VERB *This may or may not be true; we are all conjecturing here.* = **guess**, speculate, surmise, theorize, suppose, imagine, assume, fancy, infer, hypothesize

conjunction NOUN = **combination**, union, joining, association, coincidence, juxtaposition, concurrence

conjure VERB **1** *They managed to conjure an impressive victory.* = **produce**, generate, bring about, give rise to, make, create, effect, produce as if by magic **2** (*often with* **up**) *The ouija board is used to conjure up spirits and communicate with them.* = **summon up**, raise, invoke, rouse, call upon • **conjure something up** *When he closed his eyes, he could conjure up almost every event of his life.* = **bring to mind**, recall, evoke, recreate, recollect, produce as if by magic

conjuring NOUN = **magic**, juggling, trickery, sleight of hand

connect VERB **1** *You can connect the machine to your hi-fi.* = **link**, join, couple, attach, fasten, affix, unite ■ **OPPOSITE:** separate **2** *There is no evidence to connect him to the robberies.* = **associate**, unite, join, couple, league, link, mix, relate, pair, ally, identify, combine, affiliate, correlate, confederate, lump together, mention in the same breath, think of together

connected ADJECTIVE = **linked**, united, joined, coupled, related, allied, associated, combined, bracketed, affiliated, akin, banded together

connection NOUN **1** *There is no evidence of any connection between the two events.* = **association**, relationship, link, relation, bond, correspondence, relevance, tie-in, correlation, interrelation **2** *I no longer have any connection with my ex-husband's family.* = **communication**, alliance, commerce (*literary*), attachment, intercourse, liaison, affinity, affiliation, union **3** *Check radiators for small leaks, especially round pipework connections.* = **link**, coupling, junction, fastening, tie, portal (*Computing*), USB port **4** *She used her connections to full advantage.* = **contact**, friend, relation, ally, associate, relative, acquaintance, kin, kindred, kinsman *or* woman *or* person, kith **5** *13 men have been questioned in connection with the murder.* = **context**, relation, reference, frame of reference

connivance NOUN = **collusion**, intrigue, conspiring, complicity, abetting, tacit consent, abetment

connive VERB *Senior politicians connived to ensure that he was not released.* = **conspire**, scheme, plot, intrigue, collude

connoisseur NOUN = **expert**, authority, judge, specialist, buff (*informal*), devotee, whiz (*informal*), arbiter, aficionado, savant, maven (*U.S.*), appreciator, cognoscente, fundi (*S. African*)

connotation NOUN = **implication**, colouring, association, suggestion, significance, nuance, undertone

connote VERB = **imply**, suggest, indicate, intimate, signify, hint at, betoken, involve

conquer VERB 1 *Early in the eleventh century the whole of England was again conquered by the Vikings.* = **seize**, obtain, acquire, occupy, overrun, annex, win 2 *a Navajo myth about a great warrior who conquers the spiritual enemies of his people* = **defeat**, overcome, overthrow, beat, stuff (*slang*), master, tank (*slang*), triumph, crush, humble, lick (*informal*), undo, subdue, rout, overpower, quell, get the better of, clobber (*slang*), vanquish, subjugate, prevail over, checkmate, run rings around (*informal*), wipe the floor with (*informal*), make mincemeat of (*informal*), put in their place, blow out of the water (*slang*), bring to their knees ■ **OPPOSITE:** lose to 3 *I had learned to conquer my fear of spiders.* = **overcome**, beat, defeat, master, rise above, overpower, get the better of, surmount, best

conqueror NOUN = **winner**, champion, master, victor, conquistador, lord

conquest NOUN 1 *He had led the conquest of southern Poland in 1939.* = **takeover**, coup, acquisition, invasion, occupation, appropriation, annexation, subjugation, subjection 2 *This hidden treasure charts the brutal Spanish conquest of the Aztecs.* = **defeat**, victory, triumph, overthrow, pasting (*slang*), rout, mastery, vanquishment 3 *people who boast about their sexual conquests* = **seduction** 4 *She threw a party at her home to show off her latest conquest.* = **catch**, prize, supporter, acquisition, follower, admirer, worshipper, adherent, fan, feather in your cap

conscience NOUN 1 *I have battled with my conscience over whether I should speak up or not.* = **principles**, scruples, moral sense, sense of right and wrong, still small voice 2 *She was suffering terrible pangs of conscience about what she had done.* = **guilt**, shame, regret, remorse, contrition, self-reproach, self-condemnation • **in all conscience** *She could not, in all conscience, back out on her deal with him.* = **in fairness**, rightly, certainly, fairly, truly, honestly, in truth, assuredly

conscientious ADJECTIVE = **thorough**, particular, careful, exact, faithful, meticulous, painstaking, diligent, punctilious (*formal*) ■ **OPPOSITE:** careless

conscious ADJECTIVE 1 (*often with* **of**) *She was very conscious of Max studying her.* = **aware of**, wise to (*slang*), alert to, responsive to, cognizant of, sensible of, clued-up on (*informal*), percipient of ■ **OPPOSITE:** unaware 2 *Make a conscious effort to relax your muscles.* = **deliberate**, knowing, reasoning, studied, responsible, calculated, rational, reflective, self-conscious, intentional, wilful, premeditated ■ **OPPOSITE:** unintentional 3 *She was fully conscious throughout the operation.* = **awake**, wide-awake, sentient, alive ■ **OPPOSITE:** asleep

consciousness NOUN = **awareness**, understanding, knowledge, recognition, enlightenment, sensibility, realization, apprehension

consecrate VERB = **sanctify**, dedicate, ordain, exalt, venerate, set apart, hallow, devote

consecutive ADJECTIVE = **successive**, running, following, succeeding, in turn, uninterrupted, chronological, sequential, in sequence, seriatim

consensus NOUN = **agreement**, general agreement, unanimity, common consent, unity, harmony, assent, concord, concurrence, kotahitanga (*N.Z.*)

> **USAGE** The original meaning of the word *consensus* is a *collective opinion*. Because the concept of 'opinion' is contained within this word, a few people argue that the phrase *a consensus of opinion* is incorrect and should be avoided. However, this common use of the word is unlikely to jar with the majority of speakers.

consent NOUN *Can my child be medically examined without my consent?* = **agreement**, sanction, approval, go-ahead (*informal*), permission, compliance, green light, assent, acquiescence, concurrence, O.K. or okay (*informal*) ■ **OPPOSITE:** refusal ▶ VERB *I was a little surprised when she consented to my proposal.* = **agree**, approve, yield, permit, comply, concur, assent, accede, acquiesce, play ball (*informal*) ■ **OPPOSITE:** refuse

consequence NOUN 1 *Her lawyers said she understood the consequences of her actions.* = **result**, effect, outcome, repercussion, end, issue, event, sequel, end result, upshot 2 *This question is of little consequence.* = **importance**, interest, concern, moment, value, account, note, weight, import (*formal*), significance, portent 3 *He was a sad little man of no consequence.* = **status**, standing, bottom, rank, distinction,

eminence, repute, notability • **in consequence** *His death was totally unexpected and, in consequence, no plans had been made for his replacement.*
= **consequently**, as a result, so, then, thus, therefore, hence, accordingly, for that reason, thence, ergo

consequent ADJECTIVE = **following**, resulting, subsequent, successive, ensuing, resultant, sequential

consequential ADJECTIVE **1** *The company disclaims any liability for incidental or consequential damages.* = **resulting**, subsequent, successive, ensuing, indirect, consequent, resultant, sequential, following **2** *From a medical standpoint, a week is usually not a consequential delay.*
= **important**, serious, significant, grave, far-reaching, momentous, weighty, eventful

consequently ADVERB = **as a result**, thus, therefore, necessarily, hence, subsequently, accordingly, for that reason, thence, ergo

conservation NOUN **1** *Attention must be paid to the conservation of the environment.*
= **preservation**, saving, protection, maintenance, custody, safeguarding, upkeep, guardianship, safekeeping **2** *projects aimed at energy conservation*
= **economy**, saving, thrift, husbandry, careful management, thriftiness

conservative ADJECTIVE *People tend to be more adventurous when they're young and more conservative as they get older.* = **traditional**, guarded, quiet, conventional, moderate, cautious, sober, reactionary, die-hard, middle-of-the-road, hidebound
■ **OPPOSITE:** radical ▶ NOUN *The new judge is regarded as a conservative.* = **traditionalist**, moderate, reactionary, die-hard, middle-of-the-roader, stick-in-the-mud (*informal*)
■ **OPPOSITE:** radical

conservatory NOUN = **greenhouse**, hothouse, glasshouse

conserve VERB **1** *The factory has closed over the weekend to conserve energy.* = **save**, husband, take care of, hoard, store up, go easy on, use sparingly ■ **OPPOSITE:** waste **2** *an increase in US aid to help developing countries conserve their forests* = **protect**, keep, save, preserve

consider VERB **1** *I had always considered myself a strong, competent woman.* = **think**, see, believe, rate, judge, suppose, deem, view as, look upon, regard as, hold to be, adjudge **2** *Consider how much you can afford to pay.* = **think about**, study, reflect on, examine, weigh, contemplate, deliberate, muse, ponder, revolve, meditate, work

over, mull over, eye up, ruminate, chew over, cogitate, turn over in your mind **3** *You have to consider the feelings of those around you.*
= **bear in mind**, remember, regard, respect, think about, care for, take into account, reckon with, take into consideration, make allowance for, keep in view

considerable ADJECTIVE *We have already spent a considerable amount of money on repairs.*
= **large**, goodly, much, great, marked, comfortable, substantial, reasonable, tidy (*informal*), lavish, ample, noticeable, abundant, plentiful, tolerable, appreciable, sizable *or* sizeable ■ **OPPOSITE:** small

considerably ADVERB = **greatly**, very much, seriously (*informal*), significantly, remarkably, substantially, markedly, noticeably, appreciably

considerate ADJECTIVE = **thoughtful**, kind, kindly, concerned, obliging, attentive, mindful, unselfish, solicitous ■ **OPPOSITE:** inconsiderate

consideration NOUN **1** *He said there should be careful consideration of the company's future role.* = **thought**, study, review, attention, regard, analysis, examination, reflection, scrutiny, deliberation, contemplation, perusal, cogitation **2** *Show consideration for other rail travellers.* = **thoughtfulness**, concern, respect, kindness, friendliness, tact, solicitude, kindliness, considerateness **3** *Price was a major consideration in our choice of house.* = **factor**, point, issue, concern, element, aspect, determinant **4** *He does odd jobs for a consideration.* = **payment**, fee, reward, remuneration, recompense, perquisite, tip • **take something into consideration** *Other factors must also be taken into consideration.* = **bear in mind**, consider, remember, think about, weigh, take into account, make allowance for, keep in view

considering PREPOSITION *The former hostage is in remarkably good shape considering his ordeal.* = **taking into account**, in the light of, bearing in mind, in view of, keeping in mind, taking into consideration ▶ ADVERB *I think you've got off very lightly, considering.*
= **all things considered**, all in all, taking everything into consideration, taking everything into account

consign VERB **1** *For decades, many of his works were consigned to the basements of museums.*
= **put away**, commit, deposit, relegate **2** *He had managed to obtain arms in France and have them safely consigned to America.*
= **deliver**, ship, transfer, transmit, convey

consignment NOUN = **shipment**, delivery, batch, goods

consist VERB • **consist in something** His work as a consultant consists in advising foreign companies. = **lie in**, involve, reside in, be expressed by, subsist in, be found or contained in • **consist of something** My diet consisted almost exclusively of fruit. = **be made up of**, include, contain, incorporate, amount to, comprise, be composed of

consistency NOUN **1** There's always a lack of consistency in matters of foreign policy. = **agreement**, harmony, correspondence, accordance, regularity, coherence, compatibility, uniformity, constancy, steadiness, steadfastness, evenness, congruity **2** I added a little milk to mix the dough to the right consistency. = **texture**, density, thickness, firmness, viscosity, compactness

consistent ADJECTIVE **1** He has never been the most consistent of players. = **steady**, even, regular, stable, constant, persistent, dependable, unchanging, true to type, undeviating ■ **OPPOSITE:** erratic **2** These new goals are not consistent with the existing policies. = **compatible**, agreeing, in keeping, harmonious, in harmony, consonant, in accord, congruent, congruous, accordant ■ **OPPOSITE:** incompatible **3** A theory should be internally consistent. = **coherent**, logical, compatible, harmonious, consonant, all of a piece ■ **OPPOSITE:** contradictory

consolation NOUN = **comfort**, help, support, relief, ease, cheer, encouragement, solace, succour, alleviation, assuagement

console VERB = **comfort**, cheer, relieve, soothe, support, encourage, calm, solace, assuage, succour, express sympathy for ■ **OPPOSITE:** distress

consolidate VERB **1** The Prime Minister hopes to consolidate existing trade ties between the two countries. = **strengthen**, secure, reinforce, cement, fortify, stabilize **2** The state's four higher education boards are to be consolidated. = **combine**, unite, join, marry, merge, unify, amalgamate, federate, conjoin

consolidation NOUN **1** Change brought about the growth and consolidation of the working class. = **strengthening**, reinforcement, fortification, stabilization **2** Further consolidations in the industry may follow. = **combination**, union, association, alliance, merger, federation, amalgamation

consort VERB He regularly consorted with criminals. = **associate with**, mix with, mingle with, hang with (informal, chiefly U.S.), go around with, keep company with, fraternize with, hang about, around or out with ▶ NOUN Queen Victoria's consort,

Prince Albert = **spouse**, wife, husband, partner, associate, fellow, companion, significant other (informal, chiefly U.S.), wahine (N.Z.), wifey (informal), hubby (informal)

conspicuous ADJECTIVE = **obvious**, clear, apparent, visible, patent, evident, manifest, noticeable, blatant, discernible, salient, perceptible, easily seen ■ **OPPOSITE:** inconspicuous

conspiracy NOUN = **plot**, scheme, intrigue, collusion, confederacy, cabal, frame-up (slang), machination, league, golden circle

conspirator NOUN = **plotter**, intriguer, conspirer, traitor, schemer

conspire VERB **1** I had a persecution complex and thought people were conspiring against me. = **plot**, scheme, intrigue, devise, manoeuvre, contrive, machinate, plan, hatch treason **2** History and geography have conspired to bring the country to a moment of decision. = **work together**, combine, contribute, cooperate, concur, tend, conduce

constancy NOUN **1** Climate reflects a basic struggle between constancy and change. = **steadiness**, stability, regularity, uniformity, perseverance, firmness, permanence **2** Even before they were married, she had worried about her partner's constancy. = **faithfulness**, loyalty, devotion, fidelity, dependability, trustworthiness, steadfastness

constant ADJECTIVE **1** The frontier was a constant source of conflict. = **continuous**, sustained, endless, persistent, eternal, relentless, perpetual, continual, never-ending, habitual, uninterrupted, interminable, unrelenting, incessant, everlasting, ceaseless, unremitting, nonstop ■ **OPPOSITE:** occasional **2** The temperature should be kept more or less constant. = **unchanging**, even, fixed, regular, permanent, stable, steady, uniform, continual, unbroken, immutable, immovable, invariable, unalterable, unvarying, firm ■ **OPPOSITE:** changing **3** She couldn't bear the thought of losing her constant companion. = **faithful**, true, devoted, loyal, stalwart, staunch, dependable, trustworthy, trusty, steadfast, unfailing, tried-and-true ■ **OPPOSITE:** undependable

constantly ADVERB = **continuously**, always, all the time, invariably, continually, aye (Scot.), endlessly, relentlessly, persistently, perpetually, night and day, incessantly, nonstop, interminably, everlastingly, morning, noon and night ■ **OPPOSITE:** occasionally

consternation NOUN = **dismay**, shock, alarm, horror, panic, anxiety, distress, confusion, terror, dread, fright, amazement, fear, bewilderment, trepidation (*formal*)

constituent NOUN **1** *They plan to consult their constituents before taking action.* = **voter**, elector, member of the electorate **2** *Caffeine is the active constituent of drinks such as tea and coffee.* = **component**, element, ingredient, part, unit, factor, principle ▶ ADJECTIVE *The fuel is dissolved in nitric acid and separated into its constituent parts.* = **component**, basic, essential, integral, elemental

constitute VERB **1** *The result of the vote hardly constitutes a victory.* = **represent**, be, consist of, embody, exemplify, be equivalent to **2** *The country's ethnic minorities constitute 7 per cent of its total population.* = **make up**, make, form, compose, comprise **3** *On 6 July a People's Revolutionary Government was constituted.* = **set up**, found, name, create, commission, establish, appoint, delegate, nominate, enact, authorize, empower, ordain, depute

constitution NOUN **1** *He must have an extremely strong constitution.* = **state of health**, build, body, make-up, frame, physique, physical condition **2** *a small research team looking into the chemical constitution of coal* = **structure**, form, nature, make-up, organization, establishment, formation, composition, character, temper, temperament, disposition

constitutional ADJECTIVE = **legitimate**, official, legal, chartered, statutory, vested

constrain VERB **1** *I was constrained by family commitments.* = **restrict**, confine, curb, restrain, rein, constrict, hem in, straiten, check, chain **2** *Individuals will be constrained to make many sacrifices for the greater good.* = **force**, pressure, urge, bind, compel, oblige, necessitate, coerce, impel, pressurize, drive

constraint NOUN **1** *Their decision to abandon the trip was made because of financial constraints.* = **restriction**, limitation, curb, rein, deterrent, hindrance, damper, check **2** *People are not morally responsible for that which they do under constraint or compulsion.* = **force**, pressure, necessity, restraint, compulsion, coercion **3** *She feels no constraint in discussing private matters.* = **repression**, reservation, embarrassment, restraint, inhibition, timidity, diffidence, bashfulness

constrict VERB **1** *Severe migraine can be treated with a drug which constricts the blood vessels.* = **squeeze**, contract, narrow, restrict, shrink, tighten, pinch, choke, cramp, strangle, compress, strangulate **2** *Senators crafting the bill were frequently constricted by budget limits.* = **limit**, restrict, confine, curb, inhibit, delimit, straiten

constriction NOUN = **tightness**, pressure, narrowing, reduction, squeezing, restriction, constraint, cramp, compression, blockage, limitation, impediment, stricture

construct VERB **1** *The boxes should be constructed from rough-sawn timber.* = **build**, make, form, create, design, raise, establish, set up, fashion, shape, engineer, frame, manufacture, put up, assemble, put together, erect, fabricate ■ **OPPOSITE:** demolish **2** *You will find it difficult to construct a spending plan without first recording your outgoings.* = **create**, make, form, set up, organize, compose, put together, formulate

construction NOUN **1** *With the exception of teak, this is the finest wood for boat construction.* = **building**, assembly, creation, formation, composition, erection, fabrication **2** *The British pavilion is an impressive steel and glass construction.* = **structure**, building, edifice, form, figure, shape **3** *He put the wrong construction on what he saw.* = **interpretation**, meaning, reading, sense, explanation, rendering, take (*informal*), inference

constructive ADJECTIVE = **helpful**, positive, useful, practical, valuable, productive ■ **OPPOSITE:** unproductive

construe VERB = **interpret**, take, read, explain

consult VERB **1** *Consult your doctor before undertaking a strenuous exercise programme.* = **ask**, refer to, turn to, interrogate, take counsel, ask advice of, pick (someone's) brains, question **2** *The umpires consulted quickly.* = **confer**, talk, debate, deliberate, commune, compare notes, consider **3** *He had to consult a pocket dictionary.* = **refer to**, check in, look in

consultant NOUN = **specialist**, adviser, counsellor, authority

consultation NOUN **1** *Next week she'll be in Florida for consultations with her Mexican counterpart.* = **discussion**, talk, council, conference, dialogue **2** *A personal diet plan is devised after a consultation with a nutritionist.* = **meeting**, interview, session, appointment, examination, deliberation, hearing

consume VERB **1** *Andrew would consume nearly two pounds of cheese per day.* = **eat**, swallow, devour, put away, gobble (up), eat up, guzzle, polish off (informal) **2** Some refrigerators consume 70 per cent less electricity than the least efficient models. = **use up**, use, spend, waste, employ, absorb, drain, exhaust, deplete, squander, utilize, dissipate, expend, eat up, fritter away **3** Fire consumed the building. = **destroy**, devastate, demolish (facetious), ravage, annihilate, lay waste **4** (often passive) I was consumed by fear. = **obsess**, dominate, absorb, preoccupy, devour, eat up, monopolize, engross

consumer NOUN = **buyer**, customer, user, shopper, purchaser

consuming ADJECTIVE = **overwhelming**, gripping, absorbing, compelling, devouring, engrossing, immoderate

consummate ADJECTIVE **1** He acted the part with consummate skill. = **skilled**, perfect, supreme, polished, superb, practised, accomplished, matchless **2** He was a consummate liar and exaggerator. = **complete**, total, supreme, extreme, ultimate, absolute, utter, conspicuous, unqualified, deep-dyed ▶ VERB No one has yet been able to consummate a deal. = **complete**, finish, achieve, conclude, perform, perfect, carry out, crown, fulfil, end, accomplish, effectuate, put the tin lid on ■ **OPPOSITE:** initiate

consummation NOUN = **completion**, end, achievement, perfection, realization, fulfilment, culmination

consumption NOUN **1** The laws have led to a reduction in fuel consumption. = **using up**, use, loss, waste, drain, consuming, expenditure, exhaustion, depletion, utilization, dissipation **2** an opera about a poet dying of consumption in a garret = **tuberculosis**, atrophy, T.B., emaciation

contact NOUN **1** Opposition leaders are denying any contact with the government. = **communication**, link, association, connection, correspondence, intercourse **2** Hepatitis B virus is spread by contact with infected blood. = **touch**, contiguity **3** Her business contacts described her as 'a very determined woman'. = **connection**, colleague, associate, liaison, acquaintance, confederate ▶ VERB When she first contacted me, she was upset. = **get** or **be in touch with**, call, reach, approach, phone, ring (up) (informal, chiefly Brit.), write to, speak to, communicate with, get hold of, touch base with (U.S. & Canad. informal), reach out to, email or e-mail, text, message

contagion NOUN = **spread**, spreading, communication, passage, proliferation, diffusion, transference, dissemination, dispersal, transmittal

contagious ADJECTIVE = **infectious**, catching, spreading, epidemic, communicable, transmissible

contain VERB **1** Factory shops contain a wide range of cheap furnishings. = **hold**, incorporate, accommodate, enclose, have capacity for **2** The committee contains 11 Democrats and nine Republicans. = **include**, consist of, embrace, comprise, embody, comprehend **3** The city authorities said the curfew had contained the violence. = **restrain**, control, hold in, curb, suppress, hold back, stifle, repress, keep a tight rein on

container NOUN = **holder**, vessel, repository, receptacle

contaminate VERB = **pollute**, infect, stain, corrupt, taint, sully, defile, adulterate, befoul, soil ■ **OPPOSITE:** purify

contaminated ADJECTIVE = **polluted**, dirtied, poisoned, infected, stained, corrupted, tainted, sullied, defiled, soiled, adulterated

contamination NOUN = **pollution**, dirtying, infection, corruption, poisoning, decay, taint, filth, impurity, contagion, adulteration, foulness, defilement

contemplate VERB **1** He contemplated a career as an army medical doctor. = **consider**, plan, think of, propose, intend, envisage, foresee, have in view or in mind **2** He lay in his hospital bed and cried as he contemplated his future. = **think about**, consider, ponder, mull over, reflect upon, ruminate (upon), meditate on, brood over, muse over, deliberate over, revolve or turn over in your mind **3** She contemplated her hands thoughtfully. = **look at**, examine, observe, check out (informal), inspect, gaze at, behold (archaic, literary), eye up, view, study, regard, survey, stare at, scrutinize, eye

contemplation NOUN **1** The garden is a place of quiet contemplation. = **thought**, consideration, reflection, musing, meditation, pondering, deliberation, reverie, rumination, cogitation **2** I was lost in contemplation of the landscape. = **observation**, viewing, looking at, survey, examination, inspection, scrutiny, gazing at

contemplative ADJECTIVE = **thoughtful**, reflective, introspective, rapt, meditative, pensive, ruminative, in a brown study, intent, musing, deep or lost in thought

contemporary ADJECTIVE **1** The gallery holds regular exhibitions of contemporary art, sculpture and photography. = **modern**, latest, recent, current, with it (old-fashioned, informal), trendy (Brit. informal), up-to-date, present-day, in fashion, up-to-the-minute, à la mode, newfangled, happening (*informal*), present, ultramodern ■ **OPPOSITE:** old-fashioned **2** *The book draws upon official records and the reports of contemporary witnesses.* = **coexisting**, concurrent, contemporaneous, synchronous, coexistent ▶ NOUN *a glossary of terms used by Shakespeare and his contemporaries* = **peer**, fellow, equal

> **USAGE** Since *contemporary* can mean either 'of the present period' or 'of the same period', it is best to avoid it where ambiguity might arise, as in *a production of Othello in contemporary dress*. A synonym such as *modern* or *present-day* would clarify if the sense 'of the present period' were being used, while a specific term, such as *Elizabethan*, would be appropriate if the sense 'of the same period' were being used.

contempt NOUN = **scorn**, disdain, mockery, derision, disrespect, disregard ■ **OPPOSITE:** respect

contemptible ADJECTIVE = **despicable**, mean, low, base, cheap (*informal*), worthless, shameful, shabby, vile, degenerate, low-down (*informal*), paltry, pitiful, abject, ignominious, measly (*informal*), scurvy (*old-fashioned*), detestable, odious ■ **OPPOSITE:** admirable

contemptuous ADJECTIVE = **scornful**, insulting, arrogant, withering, sneering, cavalier, condescending, haughty, disdainful, insolent, derisive, supercilious, high and mighty, on your high horse (*informal*) ■ **OPPOSITE:** respectful

contend VERB **1** *The government contends that he is a fundamentalist.* = **argue**, hold, maintain, allege, assert, affirm, avow, aver **2** *The two main groups contended for power.* = **compete**, fight, struggle, clash, contest, strive, vie, grapple, jostle, skirmish

contender NOUN = **competitor**, rival, candidate, applicant, hopeful, contestant, aspirant

content[1] NOUN **1** *She is reluctant to discuss the content of the play.* = **subject matter**, ideas, matter, material, theme, text, substance, essence, gist **2** *Sunflower margarine has the same fat content as butter.* = **amount**, measure, size, load, volume, capacity ▶ PLURAL NOUN **1** *Empty the contents of the pan into the sieve.* = **constituents**, elements, load, ingredients **2** *There is no initial list of contents at the start of the book.* = **subjects**, chapters, themes, topics, subject matter, divisions

content[2] ADJECTIVE *I'm perfectly content with the way the campaign has gone.* = **satisfied**, happy, pleased, contented, comfortable, fulfilled, at ease, gratified, agreeable, willing to accept ▶ NOUN *Once he'd retired, he could potter about the garden to his heart's content.* = **satisfaction**, peace, ease, pleasure, comfort, peace of mind, gratification, contentment • **content yourself with something** *She had to content herself with the knowledge that she had been right.* = **satisfy yourself with**, be happy with, be satisfied with, be content with

contented ADJECTIVE = **satisfied**, happy, pleased, content, comfortable, glad, cheerful, at ease, thankful, gratified, serene, at peace ■ **OPPOSITE:** discontented

contention NOUN **1** *Sufficient research evidence exists to support this contention.* = **assertion**, claim, stand, idea, view, position, opinion, argument, belief, allegation, profession, declaration, thesis, affirmation **2** *They generally tried to avoid subjects of contention between them.* = **dispute**, hostility, disagreement, feuding, strife, wrangling, discord, enmity, dissension

contentious ADJECTIVE = **argumentative**, wrangling, perverse, bickering, combative, pugnacious, quarrelsome, litigious, querulous, cavilling, disputatious, factious, captious

contentment NOUN = **satisfaction**, peace, content, ease, pleasure, comfort, happiness, fulfilment, gratification, serenity, equanimity, gladness, repletion, contentedness ■ **OPPOSITE:** discontent

contest NOUN **1** *Few contests in the recent history of British boxing have been as thrilling.* = **competition**, game, match, trial, tournament, head-to-head **2** *a bitter contest over who should control the state's future* = **struggle**, fight, battle, debate, conflict, dispute, encounter, controversy, combat, discord ▶ VERB **1** *He quickly won his party's nomination to contest the elections.* = **compete in**, take part in, fight in, go in for, contend for, vie in **2** *Your former employer has to reply within 14 days in order to contest the case.* = **oppose**, question, challenge, argue, debate, dispute, object to, litigate, call in or into question

contestant NOUN = **competitor**, candidate, participant, contender, entrant, player, aspirant

context NOUN **1** *the historical context in which Chaucer wrote* = **circumstances**, times, conditions, situation, ambience **2** *Without a context, I would have to assume it was written by a man.* = **frame of reference**, background, framework, relation, connection

contingency NOUN = **possibility**, happening, chance, event, incident, accident, emergency, uncertainty, eventuality, juncture

contingent NOUN *There were contingents from the navies of virtually all UN countries.* = **group**, detachment, deputation, set, body, section, bunch (*informal*), quota, batch ▸ ADJECTIVE *The secular nature of the country's democracy is not a contingent fact; it has been intrinsic to democratic success.* = **chance**, random, casual, uncertain, accidental, haphazard, fortuitous

• **contingent on** *Growth is contingent on improved incomes.* = **dependent on**, subject to, controlled by, conditional on

continual ADJECTIVE **1** *Despite continual pain, he refused all drugs.* = **constant**, endless, continuous, eternal, perpetual, uninterrupted, interminable, incessant, everlasting, unremitting, unceasing ■ OPPOSITE: erratic **2** *She suffered continual police harassment.* = **frequent**, regular, repeated, repetitive, recurrent, oft-repeated ■ OPPOSITE: occasional

continually ADVERB **1** *The large rotating fans whirred continually.* = **constantly**, always, all the time, forever, aye (*Scot.*), endlessly, eternally, incessantly, nonstop, interminably, everlastingly **2** *He continually changed his mind.* = **repeatedly**, often, frequently, many times, over and over, again and again, time and (time) again, persistently, time after time, many a time and oft (*archaic, poetic*)

continuance NOUN = **perpetuation**, lasting, carrying on, keeping up, endurance, continuation, prolongation

continuation NOUN **1** *What we'll see in the future is a continuation of this trend.* = **continuing**, lasting, carrying on, maintenance, keeping up, endurance, perpetuation, prolongation **2** *This chapter is a continuation of Chapter 8.* = **addition**, extension, supplement, sequel, resumption, postscript

continue VERB **1** *Outside the hall, people continued their vigil.* = **keep on**, go on, maintain, pursue, sustain, carry on, stick to, keep up, prolong, persist in, keep at, persevere, stick at, press on with ■ OPPOSITE: stop **2** *As the investigation continued, the plot began to thicken.* = **go on**, advance, progress, proceed, carry on, keep going, crack on (*informal*) **3** *She looked up for a moment, then continued drawing.* = **resume**, return to, take up again, proceed, carry on, recommence, pick up where you left off ■ OPPOSITE: stop **4** *For ten days I continued in*

this state. = **remain**, last, stay, rest, survive, carry on, live on, endure, stay on, persist, abide ■ OPPOSITE: quit

continuing ADJECTIVE = **lasting**, sustained, enduring, ongoing, in progress

continuity NOUN = **cohesion**, flow, connection, sequence, succession, progression, wholeness, interrelationship

continuous ADJECTIVE = **constant**, continued, extended, prolonged, unbroken, uninterrupted, unceasing ■ OPPOSITE: occasional

contort VERB = **twist**, knot, distort, warp, deform, misshape

contortion NOUN = **twist**, distortion, deformity, convolution, bend, knot, warp

contour NOUN = **outline**, profile, lines, form, figure, shape, relief, curve, silhouette

contraband ADJECTIVE = **smuggled**, illegal, illicit, black-market, hot (*informal*), banned, forbidden, prohibited, unlawful, bootleg, bootlegged, interdicted

contract NOUN *The company won a prestigious contract for work on the building.* = **agreement**, deal (*informal*), commission, commitment, arrangement, understanding, settlement, treaty, bargain, convention, engagement, pact, compact, covenant, bond, stipulation, concordat ▸ VERB **1** *He has contracted to lease part of the collection to a museum in Japan.* = **agree**, arrange, negotiate, engage, pledge, bargain, undertake, come to terms, shake hands, covenant, make a deal, commit yourself, enter into an agreement ■ OPPOSITE: refuse **2** *New research shows that an excess of meat and salt can contract muscles.* = **constrict**, confine, tighten, shorten, wither, compress, condense, shrivel **3** *As we move our bodies, our muscles contract and relax.* = **tighten**, narrow, knit, purse, shorten, pucker ■ OPPOSITE: stretch **4** *Output fell last year and is expected to contract further this year.* = **lessen**, reduce, shrink, diminish, decrease, dwindle ■ OPPOSITE: increase **5** *Norton had contracted tuberculosis and been sent off to a sanatorium.* = **catch**, get, develop, acquire, incur, be infected with, go down with, be afflicted with ■ OPPOSITE: avoid

contraction NOUN **1** *Cramp is caused by contraction of the muscles.* = **tightening**, narrowing, tensing, shortening, drawing in, constricting, shrinkage **2** *'It's' is a contraction of 'it is'.* = **abbreviation**, reduction, shortening, compression, diminution, constriction, elision

contradict VERB **1** *We knew she was wrong, but nobody liked to contradict her.* = **dispute**, deny, challenge, belie, fly in the face of, make a nonsense of, be at variance with **2** *The result appears to contradict a major study carried out last December.* = **negate**, deny, oppose, counter, contravene, rebut, impugn, controvert ■ **OPPOSITE:** confirm

contradiction NOUN **1** *Dee saw no contradiction between his religion and his philosophy.* = **conflict**, inconsistency, contravention, incongruity, confutation **2** *What he does is a contradiction of what he says.* = **negation**, opposite, denial, antithesis

contradictory ADJECTIVE = **inconsistent**, conflicting, opposed, opposite, contrary, incompatible, paradoxical, irreconcilable, antithetical, discrepant

contraption NOUN = **device**, instrument, mechanism, apparatus, gadget, contrivance, rig

contrary ADJECTIVE **1** *His sister was of the contrary opinion to his.* = **opposite**, different, opposed, clashing, counter, reverse, differing, adverse, contradictory, inconsistent, diametrically opposed, antithetical ■ **OPPOSITE:** in agreement **2** *Why must you always be so contrary?* = **perverse**, difficult, awkward, wayward, intractable, wilful, obstinate, cussed (*informal*), stroppy (*Brit. slang*), cantankerous, disobliging, unaccommodating, thrawn (*Scot. & Northern English, dialect*) ■ **OPPOSITE:** cooperative ▶ NOUN *Let me assure you that the contrary is, in fact, the case.* = **opposite**, reverse, converse, antithesis • **on the contrary** *The government must, on the contrary, re-establish its authority.* = **quite the opposite** *or* **reverse**, on the other hand, in contrast, conversely

contrast NOUN *The two women provided a startling contrast in appearance.* = **difference**, opposition, comparison, distinction, foil, disparity, differentiation, divergence, dissimilarity, contrariety ▶ VERB **1** *She contrasted the situation then with the present crisis.* = **differentiate**, compare, oppose, distinguish, set in opposition **2** *Johnstone's easy charm contrasted with the prickliness of his boss.* = **differ**, be contrary, be distinct, be at variance, be dissimilar

contravene VERB **1** *He said the article did not contravene the industry's code of conduct.* = **break**, violate, go against, infringe, disobey, transgress **2** *This deportation order contravenes basic human rights.* = **conflict with**, cross, oppose, interfere with, thwart, contradict, hinder, go against, refute, counteract

contravention NOUN **1** *They are in direct contravention of the law.* = **breach**, violation, infringement, trespass, disobedience, transgression, infraction **2** *He denied that the new laws were a contravention of fundamental rights.* = **conflict**, interference, contradiction, hindrance, rebuttal, refutation, disputation, counteraction

contribute VERB *They say they would like to contribute more to charity.* = **give**, provide, supply, donate, furnish, subscribe, chip in (*informal*), bestow • **contribute to something** *Design faults in the boat contributed to the tragedy.* = **be partly responsible for**, lead to, be instrumental in, be conducive to, conduce to, help

contribution NOUN = **gift**, offering, grant, donation, input, subscription, bestowal, koha (*N.Z.*)

contributor NOUN **1** *He is the institute's leading financial contributor and is active in fund-raising.* = **donor**, supporter, patron, subscriber, backer, bestower, giver **2** *All of the pieces by the magazine's contributors appear anonymously.* = **writer**, correspondent, reporter, journalist, freelance, freelancer, journo (*slang*)

contrite ADJECTIVE = **sorry**, humble, chastened, sorrowful, repentant, remorseful, regretful, penitent, conscience-stricken, in sackcloth and ashes

contrition NOUN = **regret**, sorrow, remorse, repentance, compunction, penitence, self-reproach

contrivance NOUN **1** *They wear simple clothes and shun modern contrivances.* = **device**, machine, equipment, gear, instrument, implement, mechanism, invention, appliance, apparatus, gadget, contraption (*informal*) **2** *It is nothing more than a contrivance to raise prices.* = **stratagem**, plan, design, measure, scheme, trick, plot, dodge, expedient, ruse, artifice, machination

contrive VERB **1** *The oil companies were accused of contriving a shortage of gasoline to justify price increases.* = **devise**, plan, fabricate, create, design, scheme, engineer, frame, manufacture, plot, construct, invent, improvise, concoct, wangle (*informal*) **2** *Somehow he contrived to pass her a note without the teacher seeing it.* = **manage**, succeed, arrange, manoeuvre

contrived ADJECTIVE = **forced**, planned, laboured, strained, artificial, elaborate, unnatural, overdone, recherché ■ **OPPOSITE:** natural

control NOUN **1** *The first aim of his government would be to establish control over the republic's* territory. = **power**, government, rule, authority, management, direction, command, discipline, guidance, supervision, jurisdiction, supremacy, mastery, superintendence, charge **2** *There are to be tighter controls on land speculation.* = **restraint**, check, regulation, brake, limitation, curb **3** *He had a terrible temper, and sometimes lost control completely.* = **self-discipline**, cool (*slang*), calmness, self-restraint, restraint, coolness, self-mastery, self-command **4** *She adjusted the temperature control.* = **switch**, instrument, button, dial, lever, knob ▶ PLURAL NOUN *She would rather be at the controls of a plane than in the passenger section.* = **instruments**, dash, dials, console, dashboard, control panel ▶ VERB **1** *He now controls the largest retail development empire in southern California.* = **have power over**, lead, rule, manage, boss (*informal*), direct, handle, conduct, dominate, command, pilot, govern, steer, administer, oversee, supervise, manipulate, call the shots, call the tune, reign over, keep a tight rein on, have charge of, superintend, have (someone) in your pocket, keep on a string **2** *The government tried to control rising health-care costs.* = **limit**, restrict, curb, delimit **3** *Try to control that temper of yours.* = **restrain**, limit, check, contain, master, curb, hold back, subdue, repress, constrain, bridle, rein in

controversial ADJECTIVE = **disputed**, contended, contentious, at issue, debatable, polemic, under discussion, open to question, disputable

controversy NOUN = **argument**, debate, row, discussion, dispute, contention, quarrel, squabble, strife, wrangle, wrangling, polemic, altercation, dissension

conundrum NOUN = **puzzle**, problem, riddle, enigma, teaser, poser, brain-teaser (*informal*)

convalesce VERB = **recover**, rest, rally, rehabilitate, recuperate, improve

convalescence NOUN = **recovery**, rehabilitation, recuperation, return to health, improvement

convalescent ADJECTIVE = **recovering**, getting better, recuperating, on the mend, improving, mending

convene VERB **1** *He convened a meeting of all the managers.* = **call**, gather, assemble, summon, bring together, muster, convoke (*formal*) **2** *Senior officials convened in Dakar for an emergency meeting.* = **meet**, gather, rally, assemble, come together, muster, congregate

convenience NOUN **1** *He was happy to make a detour for her convenience.* = **benefit**, good, interest, advantage **2** *She was delighted with the convenience of this arrangement.* = **suitability**, fitness, appropriateness, opportuneness **3** *the convenience of mobile phones* = **usefulness**, utility, serviceability, handiness ■ OPPOSITE: uselessness **4** *They miss the convenience of London's tubes and buses.* = **accessibility**, availability, nearness, handiness **5** *The chalets have all the modern conveniences.* = **appliance**, facility, comfort, amenity, labour-saving device, help • **at your convenience** *Please call me to set up an appointment at your convenience.* = **at a suitable time**, at your leisure, in your own time, whenever you like, in your spare time, in a spare moment

convenient ADJECTIVE **1** *The family found it more convenient to eat in the kitchen.* = **suitable**, fitting, fit, handy, satisfactory **2** *Pre-prepared foods are a tempting and convenient option.* = **useful**, practical, handy, serviceable, labour-saving ■ OPPOSITE: useless **3** *The location is convenient for the airport.* = **nearby**, available, accessible, handy, at hand, within reach, close at hand, just round the corner ■ OPPOSITE: inaccessible **4** *She will try to arrange a mutually convenient time for an interview.* = **appropriate**, timely, suited, suitable, beneficial, well-timed, opportune (*formal*), seasonable, helpful

convent NOUN = **nunnery**, religious community, religious house

convention NOUN **1** *It's just a social convention that men don't wear skirts.* = **custom**, practice, tradition, code, usage, protocol, formality, etiquette, propriety, kawa (*N.Z.*), tikanga (*N.Z.*), rule **2** *the importance of observing the Geneva convention on human rights* = **agreement**, contract, treaty, bargain, pact, compact, protocol, stipulation, concordat **3** *I flew to Boston to attend the annual convention of the Parapsychological Association.* = **assembly**, meeting, council, conference, congress, convocation (*formal*), hui (*N.Z.*), runanga (*N.Z.*)

conventional ADJECTIVE **1** *a respectable married woman with conventional opinions* = **proper**, conservative, correct, formal, respectable, bourgeois, genteel, staid, conformist, decorous, Pooterish **2** *the cost of fuel and electricity used by a conventional system* = **ordinary**, standard, normal, regular, usual, vanilla (*slang*), habitual, bog-standard (*Brit. & Irish slang*), common **3** *The conventional wisdom on these matters is*

being challenged. = **traditional**, accepted, prevailing, orthodox, customary, prevalent, hidebound, wonted **4** *This is a rather conventional work by a mediocre author.* = **unoriginal**, routine, stereotyped, pedestrian, commonplace, banal, prosaic, run-of-the-mill, hackneyed, vanilla (*slang*)
■ **OPPOSITE:** unconventional

converge VERB *As they flow south, the five rivers converge.* = **come together**, meet, join, combine, gather, merge, coincide, mingle, intersect • **converge on something** *Hundreds of coaches will converge on the capital.* = **close in on**, arrive at, move towards, home in on, come together at

convergence NOUN = **meeting**, junction, intersection, confluence, concentration, blending, merging, coincidence, conjunction, mingling, concurrence, conflux

conversation NOUN = **talk**, exchange, discussion, dialogue, tête-à-tête, conference, communication, chat, gossip, intercourse, discourse, communion, converse, powwow, colloquy (*formal*), chinwag (*Brit. informal*), confabulation, confab (*informal*), craic (*Irish informal*), korero (*N.Z.*) ■ **RELATED WORD:** *adjective* colloquial

conversational ADJECTIVE = **chatty**, informal, communicative, colloquial

converse¹ VERB *They were conversing in German, their only common language.* = **talk**, speak, chat, communicate, discourse, confer, commune, exchange views, shoot the breeze (*slang, chiefly U.S. & Canad.*), korero (*N.Z.*)

converse² NOUN *If that is true, the converse is equally so.* = **opposite**, reverse, contrary, other side of the coin, obverse, antithesis
▶ ADJECTIVE *Stress reduction techniques have the converse effect on the immune system.* = **opposite**, counter, reverse, contrary

conversion NOUN **1** *the conversion of disused rail lines into cycle routes* = **change**, transformation, metamorphosis, transfiguration, transmutation, transmogrification (*humorous*) **2** *A loft conversion can add considerably to the value of a house.* = **adaptation**, reconstruction, modification, alteration, remodelling, reorganization **3** *his conversion to Christianity* = **reformation**, rebirth, change of heart, proselytization

convert VERB **1** *a handy table which converts into an ironing board* = **change**, turn, transform, alter, metamorphose, transpose, transmute, transmogrify (*humorous*) **2** *By converting the loft, they were*

able to have two extra bedrooms. = **adapt**, modify, remodel, reorganize, customize, restyle **3** *religious people who try to convert others* = **reform**, save, convince, proselytize, bring to God ▶ NOUN *She was a recent convert to Roman Catholicism.* = **neophyte** (*formal*), disciple, proselyte, catechumen

convertible ADJECTIVE = **changeable**, interchangeable, exchangeable, adjustable, adaptable

convex ADJECTIVE = **rounded**, bulging, protuberant, gibbous, outcurved
■ **OPPOSITE:** concave

convey VERB **1** *I tried to convey the wonder of the experience to my husband.* = **communicate**, impart, reveal, relate, disclose, make known, tell **2** *They borrowed our boats to convey themselves across the river.* = **carry**, transport, move, bring, support, bear, conduct, transmit, fetch

conveyance NOUN **1** *He had never travelled in such a strange conveyance before.* = **vehicle**, transport **2** *the conveyance of bicycles on local trains* = **transportation**, movement, transfer, transport, transmission, carriage, transference

convict VERB *There was sufficient evidence to convict him.* = **find guilty**, sentence, condemn, imprison, pronounce guilty
▶ NOUN *The prison houses only lifers and convicts on death row.* = **prisoner**, criminal, con (*slang*), lag (*slang*), villain, felon, jailbird, malefactor

conviction NOUN **1** *Their religious convictions prevented them from taking up arms.* = **belief**, view, opinion, principle, faith, persuasion, creed, tenet, kaupapa (*N.Z.*) **2** *He preaches with conviction.* = **certainty**, confidence, assurance, fervour, firmness, earnestness, certitude

convince VERB **1** *I soon convinced him of my innocence.* = **assure**, persuade, satisfy, prove to, reassure **2** *He convinced her to go ahead and marry Bud.* = **persuade**, induce, coax, talk into, prevail upon, inveigle, twist (someone's) arm, bring round to the idea of

┃ **USAGE** The use of *convince* to talk about
┃ persuading someone to do something is
┃ considered by many British speakers to
┃ be wrong or unacceptable. It would be
┃ preferable to use an alternative such as
┃ *persuade* or *talk into*.

convincing ADJECTIVE = **persuasive**, credible, conclusive, incontrovertible, telling, likely, powerful, impressive, probable, plausible, cogent ■ **OPPOSITE:** unconvincing

convivial ADJECTIVE = **sociable**, friendly, lively, cheerful, jolly, merry, festive, hearty, genial, fun-loving, jovial, back-slapping, gay, partyish (*informal*)

convocation NOUN = **meeting**, congress, convention, synod, diet, assembly, concourse, council, assemblage, conclave, hui (*N.Z.*), runanga (*N.Z.*)

convoy VERB = **escort**, conduct, accompany, shepherd, protect, attend, guard, pilot, usher

convulse VERB 1 *He let out a cry that convulsed his whole body.* = **shake**, twist, agitate, contort 2 *Olivia's face convulsed in a series of spasms.* = **twist**, contort, work

convulsion NOUN 1 *He fell to the floor in the grip of an epileptic convulsion.* = **spasm**, fit, shaking, seizure, contraction, tremor, cramp, contortion, paroxysm 2 *It was a decade that saw many great social, economic and political convulsions.* = **upheaval**, disturbance, furore, turbulence, agitation, commotion, tumult

cool ADJECTIVE 1 *I felt a current of cool air.* = **cold**, chilled, chilling, refreshing, chilly, nippy ■ OPPOSITE: warm 2 *He was marvellously cool, smiling as if nothing had happened.* = **calm**, together (*slang*), collected, relaxed, cómposed, laid-back (*informal*), serene, sedate, self-controlled, placid, level-headed, dispassionate, unfazed (*informal*), unruffled, unemotional, self-possessed, imperturbable, unexcited, chilled (*informal*) ■ OPPOSITE: agitated 3 *People found her too cool, aloof and arrogant.* = **unfriendly**, reserved, distant, indifferent, aloof, lukewarm, unconcerned, uninterested, frigid, unresponsive, offhand, unenthusiastic, uncommunicative, unwelcoming, standoffish ■ OPPOSITE: friendly 4 *The idea met with a cool response.* = **unenthusiastic**, indifferent, lukewarm, uninterested, apathetic, unresponsive, unwelcoming 5 *He was trying to be really cool and trendy.* = **fashionable**, with it (*old-fashioned, informal*), hip (*slang*), stylish, trendy (*Brit. informal*), on trend, chic, up-to-date, urbane, up-to-the-minute, voguish (*informal*), trendsetting, nang (*Brit. slang*), schmick (*Austral. informal*) 6 *She displayed a cool disregard for the rules.* = **impudent**, bold, cheeky, audacious, brazen, shameless, presumptuous, impertinent ▸ VERB 1 *Drain the meat and allow it to cool.* = **lose heat**, cool off ■ OPPOSITE: warm (up) 2 *Huge fans are used to cool the factory.* = **make cool**, freeze, chill, refrigerate, cool off ■ OPPOSITE: warm (up) 3 *Within a few minutes their tempers had cooled.* = **calm (down)**, lessen, abate 4 *The problems in the project cooled her enthusiasm.*

= **lessen**, calm (down), quiet, moderate, temper, dampen, allay, abate, assuage ▸ NOUN 1 *She walked into the cool of the hallway.* = **coldness**, chill, coolness 2 (*slang*) *She kept her cool and managed to get herself out of the situation.* = **calmness**, control, temper, composure, self-control, poise, self-discipline, self-possession

coolness NOUN 1 *He felt the coolness of the tiled floor.* = **coldness**, freshness, chilliness, nippiness ■ OPPOSITE: warmness 2 *They praised him for his coolness under pressure.* = **calmness**, control, composure, self-control, self-discipline, self-possession, level-headedness, imperturbability, sedateness, placidness ■ OPPOSITE: agitation 3 *She seemed quite unaware of the sudden coolness of her friend's manner.* = **unfriendliness**, reserve, distance, indifference, apathy, remoteness, aloofness, frigidity, unconcern, unresponsiveness, frostiness, offhandedness ■ OPPOSITE: friendliness 4 *The coolness of his suggestion took her breath away.* = **impudence**, audacity, boldness, insolence, impertinence, shamelessness, cheekiness, brazenness, presumptuousness, audaciousness

coop NOUN *Behind the house, the pair set up a chicken coop.* = **pen**, pound, box, cage, enclosure, hutch, corral (*chiefly U.S. & Canad.*) • **coop someone up** *He was cooped up in a cell with ten other inmates.* = **confine**, imprison, shut up, impound, pound, pen, cage, immure (*archaic*)

cooperate VERB 1 *The two parties are cooperating more than they have done in years.* = **work together**, collaborate, coordinate, join forces, conspire, concur, pull together, pool resources, combine your efforts ■ OPPOSITE: conflict 2 *He agreed to cooperate with the police investigation.* = **help**, contribute to, assist, go along with, aid, pitch in, abet, play ball (*informal*), lend a helping hand ■ OPPOSITE: oppose

cooperation NOUN 1 *A deal with Japan could open the door to economic cooperation with East Asia.* = **teamwork**, concert, unity, collaboration, give-and-take, combined effort, esprit de corps, concurrence, kotahitanga (*N.Z.*) ■ OPPOSITE: opposition 2 *The police asked for the public's cooperation in their hunt for the missing child.* = **help**, assistance, participation, responsiveness, helpfulness ■ OPPOSITE: hindrance

cooperative ADJECTIVE 1 *The visit was intended to develop cooperative relations between the countries.* = **shared**, united, joint, combined, concerted, collective, unified, coordinated, collaborative **2** *I made every effort to be cooperative.* = **helpful**, obliging, accommodating, supportive, responsive, onside (*informal*)

coordinate VERB **1** *Officials visited the earthquake zone to coordinate the relief effort.* = **organize**, synchronize, integrate, bring together, mesh, correlate, systematize **2** *I'll show you how to coordinate pattern and colours.* = **match**, blend, harmonize • **coordinate with** *Choose a fabric that coordinates with your colour scheme.* = **go with**, match, blend with, harmonize with

cope VERB *It was amazing how my mother coped after my father died.* = **manage**, get by (*informal*), struggle through, rise to the occasion, survive, carry on, make out (*informal*), make the grade, hold your own • **cope with something** *She has had to cope with losing all her previous status and money.* = **deal with**, handle, struggle with, grapple with, wrestle with, contend with, tangle with, tussle with, weather

copious ADJECTIVE = **abundant**, liberal, generous, lavish, full, rich, extensive, ample, overflowing, plentiful, exuberant, bountiful, luxuriant, profuse, bounteous, superabundant, plenteous

cop out VERB = **avoid**, dodge, abandon, withdraw from, desert, quit, skip, renounce, revoke, renege, skive (*Brit. slang*), bludge (*Austral. & N.Z. informal*)

cop-out NOUN = **pretence**, dodge, pretext, fraud, alibi

copulate VERB = **have intercourse**, have sex

copy NOUN *Always keep a copy of everything in your own files.* = **reproduction**, duplicate, photocopy, carbon copy, image, print, fax, representation, fake, replica, imitation, forgery, counterfeit, Xerox®, transcription, likeness, replication, facsimile, Photostat® ■ **OPPOSITE:** original ▶ VERB **1** *She never participated in copying classified documents for anyone.* = **reproduce**, replicate, duplicate, photocopy, transcribe, counterfeit, Xerox®, Photostat® ■ **OPPOSITE:** create **2** *We all tend to copy people we admire.* = **imitate**, act like, emulate, behave like, follow, repeat, mirror, echo, parrot, ape, mimic, simulate, follow suit, follow the example of

cord NOUN = **rope**, line, string, twine

cordial ADJECTIVE **1** *I had never known him to be so chatty and cordial.* = **warm**, welcoming, friendly, cheerful, affectionate, hearty, agreeable, sociable, genial, affable, congenial, warm-hearted ■ **OPPOSITE:** unfriendly **2** *She didn't bother to hide her cordial dislike of him.* = **wholehearted**, earnest, sincere, heartfelt

cordon NOUN *Police formed a cordon between the two crowds.* = **chain**, line, ring, barrier, picket line • **cordon something off** *The police cordoned the area off.* = **surround**, isolate, close off, fence off, separate, enclose, picket, encircle

core NOUN **1** *Lava is molten rock from the earth's core* = **centre 2** *He has the ability to get straight to the core of a problem.* = **heart**, essence, nucleus, kernel, crux, gist, nub, pith

corner NOUN **1** *the corner of a door* = **angle**, joint, crook **2** *He waited until the man had turned the corner.* = **bend**, curve **3** *She hid it away in a corner of her room.* = **space**, hole, niche, recess, cavity, hideaway, nook, cranny, hide-out, hidey-hole (*informal*) **4** *He appears to have got himself into a tight corner.* = **tight spot**, predicament, tricky situation, spot (*informal*), hole (*informal*), hot water (*informal*), pickle (*informal*) ▶ VERB **1** *The police moved in with tear gas and cornered him.* = **trap**, catch, run to earth, bring to bay **2** (*a market*) *This restaurant has cornered the market for specialist paellas.* = **monopolize**, take over, dominate, control, hog (*slang*), engross, exercise or have a monopoly of

cornerstone NOUN = **basis**, key, premise, starting point, bedrock

corny ADJECTIVE **1** *I know it sounds corny, but I'm not motivated by money.* = **unoriginal**, banal, trite, hackneyed, dull, old-fashioned, stereotyped, commonplace, feeble, stale, old hat **2** *a corny old love song* = **sentimental**, mushy (*informal*), maudlin, slushy (*informal*), mawkish, schmaltzy (*slang*)

corollary NOUN = **consequence**, result, effect, outcome, sequel, end result, upshot

corporal ADJECTIVE = **bodily**, physical, fleshly, anatomical, carnal, corporeal (*archaic*), material

corporate ADJECTIVE = **collective**, collaborative, united, shared, allied, joint, combined, pooled, merged, communal

corporation NOUN **1** *chairman of a huge multi-national corporation* = **business**, company, concern, firm, society, association, organization, enterprise, establishment, corporate body **2** *The local corporation has given permission for the work to proceed.* = **town council**, council, municipal authorities, civic authorities

corps NOUN = **team**, unit, regiment, detachment, company, body, band, division, troop, squad, crew, contingent, squadron

corpse NOUN = **body**, remains, carcass, cadaver, stiff (*slang*)

corpus NOUN = **collection**, body, whole, compilation, entirety, oeuvre (*French*), complete works

corral VERB *They were corralled into a hastily constructed shelter.* = **enclose**, confine, cage, fence in, impound, pen in, coop up

correct ADJECTIVE **1** *The information was correct at the time of going to press.* = **accurate**, right, true, exact, precise, flawless, faultless, on the right lines, O.K. or okay (*informal*) ■ **OPPOSITE:** inaccurate **2** *The use of the correct procedure is vital.* = **right**, standard, regular, appropriate, acceptable, strict, proper, precise **3** *They refuse to adopt the rules of correct behaviour.* = **proper**, seemly, standard, fitting, diplomatic, kosher (*informal*) ■ **OPPOSITE:** inappropriate ▶ VERB **1** *You may need surgery to correct the problem.* = **rectify**, remedy, redress, right, improve, reform, cure, adjust, regulate, amend, set the record straight, emend ■ **OPPOSITE:** spoil **2** *He gently corrected me for using the wrong word.* = **rebuke**, discipline, reprimand, chide, admonish, chastise, chasten, reprove, punish ■ **OPPOSITE:** praise

correction NOUN **1** *They have made several corrections and additions to the document.* = **rectification**, improvement, amendment, adjustment, modification, alteration, emendation **2** *jails and other places of correction* = **punishment**, discipline, reformation, admonition, chastisement, reproof, castigation

corrective ADJECTIVE **1** *She has received extensive corrective surgery to her skull.* = **remedial**, therapeutic, palliative, restorative, rehabilitative **2** *He was placed in a corrective institution for children.* = **disciplinary**, punitive, penal, reformatory

correctly ADVERB = **rightly**, right, perfectly, properly, precisely, accurately, aright

correctness NOUN **1** *Please check the correctness of the details on this form.* = **truth**, accuracy, precision, exactitude, exactness, faultlessness **2** *He conducted himself with formal correctness at all times.* = **decorum**, propriety, good manners, civility, good breeding, bon ton (*French*)

correlate VERB **1** *Obesity correlates with increased risk of heart disease and stroke.* = **correspond**, parallel, be connected, equate, tie in, match **2** *attempts to correlate specific language functions with particular parts of the brain* = **connect**, compare, associate, tie in, coordinate, match

correlation NOUN = **correspondence**, link, relation, connection, equivalence

correspond VERB **1** *The two maps of London correspond closely.* = **be consistent**, match, agree, accord, fit, square, coincide, complement, be related, tally, conform, correlate, dovetail, harmonize ■ **OPPOSITE:** differ **2** *We corresponded regularly for years.* = **communicate**, write, keep in touch, exchange letters, email or e-mail, text

correspondence NOUN **1** *The judges' decision is final and no correspondence will be entered into.* = **communication**, writing, contact **2** *He always replied to his correspondence promptly.* = **letters**, post, mail **3** *correspondences between Eastern religions and Christianity* = **relation**, match, agreement, fitness, comparison, harmony, coincidence, similarity, analogy, correlation, conformity, comparability, concurrence, congruity

correspondent NOUN **1** *Here is a special report from our Europe correspondent.* = **reporter**, journalist, contributor, special correspondent, journo (*slang*), hack **2** *He wasn't a good correspondent and only wrote to me once a year.* = **letter writer**, pen friend or pen pal

corresponding ADJECTIVE = **equivalent**, matching, similar, related, correspondent, identical, complementary, synonymous, reciprocal, analogous, interrelated, correlative

corridor NOUN = **passage**, alley, aisle, hallway, passageway

corroborate VERB = **support**, establish, confirm, document, sustain, back up, endorse, ratify, validate, bear out, substantiate, authenticate ■ **OPPOSITE:** contradict

corrode VERB = **eat away**, waste, consume, corrupt, deteriorate, erode, rust, gnaw, oxidize

corrosive ADJECTIVE *Sodium and sulphur are highly corrosive elements.* = **corroding**, wasting, caustic, vitriolic, acrid, erosive

corrugated ADJECTIVE = **furrowed**, channelled, ridged, grooved, wrinkled, creased, fluted, rumpled, puckered, crinkled

corrupt ADJECTIVE **1** *corrupt politicians who took bribes* = **dishonest**, bent (*slang*), crooked (*informal*), rotten, shady (*informal*), fraudulent, unscrupulous, unethical, venal, unprincipled ■ **OPPOSITE:** honest **2** *the flamboyant and morally corrupt court of Charles the Second* = **depraved**, abandoned, vicious, degenerate, debased, demoralized, profligate, dishonoured, defiled, dissolute **3** *a corrupt text of a poem by Milton* = **distorted**, doctored, altered, falsified ▶ VERB **1** *The ability to corrupt judges was fundamental to their operations.* = **bribe**, square, fix (*informal*), buy off, suborn, grease (someone's) palm (*slang*) **2** *Cruelty*

depraves and corrupts. = **deprave**, pervert, subvert, debase, demoralize, debauch
■ **OPPOSITE:** reform **3** Computer hackers often break into important sites to corrupt files. = **distort**, doctor, tamper with

corruption NOUN **1** He faces 54 charges of corruption and tax evasion. = **dishonesty**, fraud, fiddling (informal), graft (informal), bribery, extortion, profiteering, breach of trust, venality, shady dealings (informal), shadiness **2** It was a society sinking into corruption and vice. = **depravity**, vice, evil, degradation, perversion, decadence, impurity, wickedness, degeneration, immorality, iniquity, profligacy, viciousness, sinfulness, turpitude (formal), baseness **3** The name 'Santa Claus' is a corruption of 'Saint Nicholas'. = **distortion**, doctoring, falsification

corset NOUN = **girdle**, bodice, foundation garment, panty girdle, stays (rare)

cortege NOUN = **procession**, train, entourage, cavalcade, retinue, suite

cosmetic ADJECTIVE = **superficial**, surface, touching-up, nonessential

cosmic ADJECTIVE **1** Inside the heliosphere we are screened from cosmic rays. = **extraterrestrial**, stellar **2** There are cosmic laws governing our world. = **universal**, general, omnipresent, all-embracing, overarching **3** It was an understatement of cosmic proportions. = **vast**, huge, immense, infinite, grandiose, limitless, measureless

cosmonaut NOUN = **astronaut**, spaceman, spacewoman, space pilot, space cadet

cosmopolitan ADJECTIVE = **sophisticated**, worldly, cultured, refined, cultivated, urbane, well-travelled, worldly-wise
■ **OPPOSITE:** unsophisticated

cosmos NOUN = **universe**, world, creation, macrocosm

cosset VERB = **pamper**, baby, pet, coddle, mollycoddle, wrap up in cotton wool (informal)

cost NOUN **1** The cost of a loaf of bread has increased five-fold. = **price**, worth, expense, rate, charge, figure, damage (informal), amount, payment, expenditure, outlay **2** a man who always looks after 'number one', whatever the cost to others = **loss**, suffering, damage, injury, penalty, hurt, expense, harm, sacrifice, deprivation, detriment
▶ PLURAL NOUN The company admits its costs are still too high. = **expenses**, spending, expenditure, overheads, outgoings, outlay, budget ▶ VERB **1** The course is limited to 12 people and costs £50. = **sell at**, come to, set (someone) back (informal), be priced at, command a price of **2** The operation saved his

life, but cost him his sight. = **lose**, deprive of, cheat of • **at all costs** We must avoid any further delay at all costs. = **no matter what**, regardless, whatever happens, at any price, come what may, without fail

costly ADJECTIVE **1** Having curtains professionally made can be costly. = **expensive**, dear, stiff, excessive, steep (informal), highly-priced, exorbitant, extortionate
■ **OPPOSITE:** inexpensive **2** the exceptionally beautiful and costly cloths made in northern Italy = **splendid**, rich, valuable, precious, gorgeous, lavish, luxurious, sumptuous, priceless, opulent **3** If you follow the procedures correctly you will avoid costly mistakes. = **damaging**, disastrous, harmful, catastrophic, loss-making, ruinous, deleterious (formal)

costume NOUN = **outfit**, dress, clothing, get-up (informal), uniform, ensemble, robes, livery, apparel (old-fashioned), attire, garb, national dress

cosy ADJECTIVE **1** Guests can relax in the cosy bar before dinner. = **comfortable**, homely, warm, intimate, snug, comfy (informal), sheltered **2** I was lying cosy in bed with the Sunday papers. = **snug**, warm, secure, comfortable, sheltered, comfy (informal), tucked up, cuddled up, snuggled down **3** a cosy chat between friends = **intimate**, friendly, informal

coterie NOUN = **clique**, group, set, camp, circle, gang, outfit (informal), posse (informal), cabal

cottage NOUN = **cabin**, lodge, hut, shack, chalet, but-and-ben (Scot.), cot, whare (N.Z.)

couch NOUN He lay down on the couch. = **sofa**, bed, chesterfield, ottoman, settee, divan, chaise longue, day bed ▶ VERB This time the proposal was couched as an ultimatum. = **express**, word, frame, phrase, utter, set forth

cough VERB She began to cough violently. = **clear your throat**, bark, hawk, hack (informal), hem ▶ NOUN He put a hand over his mouth to cover a cough. = **frog** or **tickle in your throat**, bark, hack (informal) • **cough up** I'll have to cough up $10,000 for repairs. = **fork out**, deliver, hand over, surrender, come across (informal), shell out (informal), ante up (informal, chiefly U.S.)

council NOUN **1** The city council has voted almost unanimously in favour of the proposal. = **committee**, governing body, board, panel, quango, jamáat **2** The powers of the King had been handed over temporarily to a council of ministers. = **governing body**, house, parliament, congress, cabinet, ministry, diet, panel, assembly, chamber, convention, synod, conclave, convocation (formal), conference, runanga (N.Z.)

counsel NOUN **1** He had always been able to count on her wise counsel. = **advice**, information, warning, direction, suggestion, recommendation, caution, guidance, admonition **2** The defence counsel warned that the judge should stop the trial. = **legal adviser**, lawyer, attorney, solicitor, advocate, barrister ▶ VERB My advisors counselled me to do nothing. = **advise**, recommend, advocate, prescribe, warn, urge, caution, instruct, exhort (formal), admonish

count VERB **1** (often with **up**) I counted the money. It came to more than five hundred pounds. = **add (up)**, total, reckon (up), tot up, score, check, estimate, calculate, compute, tally, number, enumerate, cast up **2** It's as if your opinions just don't count. = **matter**, be important, cut any ice (informal), carry weight, tell, rate, weigh, signify (informal), enter into consideration **3** I count him as one of my best friends. = **consider**, judge, regard, deem, think of, rate, esteem (formal), look upon, impute **4** The years before their arrival in prison are not counted as part of their sentence. = **include**, number among, take into account or consideration ▶ NOUN At the last count the police had 247 people in custody. = **calculation**, poll, reckoning, sum, tally, numbering, computation, enumeration • **count on or upon something** or **someone** I'm counting on your support. = **depend on**, trust, rely on, bank on, take for granted, lean on, reckon on, take on trust, believe in, pin your faith on • **count someone out** If it means working extra hours, you can count me out. = **leave out**, except, exclude, disregard, pass over, leave out of account

countenance NOUN He met each inquiry with an impassive countenance. = **face**, features, expression, look, appearance, aspect, visage, mien (literary), physiognomy ▶ VERB The planners will not countenance any changes to the exterior of the barn. = **tolerate**, sanction, endorse, condone, support, encourage, approve, endure, brook, stand for (informal), hack (slang), put up with (informal)

counter VERB **1** They discussed a plan to counter the effects of such a blockade. = **oppose**, meet, block, resist, offset, parry, deflect, repel, rebuff, fend off, counteract, ward off, stave off, repulse, obviate (formal), hold at bay **2** The union countered with letters rebutting the company's claim. = **retaliate**, return, answer, reply, respond, come back, retort, hit back,

refute, rejoin, strike back ■ **OPPOSITE:** yield ▶ ADVERB Their findings ran counter to all expectations. = **opposite to**, against, versus, conversely, in defiance of, at variance with, contrarily, contrariwise ■ **OPPOSITE:** in accordance with ▶ ADJECTIVE These charges and counter charges are being exchanged at an important time. = **opposing**, conflicting, opposed, contrasting, opposite, contrary, adverse, contradictory, obverse, against ■ **OPPOSITE:** similar

counteract VERB **1** Many countries within the region are planning measures to counteract a missile attack. = **act against**, check, defeat, prevent, oppose, resist, frustrate, foil, thwart, hinder, cross **2** pills to counteract high blood pressure = **offset**, negate, neutralize, invalidate, counterbalance, annul, obviate (formal), countervail

counterbalance VERB = **offset**, balance out, compensate for, make up for, counterpoise, countervail

counterfeit ADJECTIVE He admitted possessing and delivering counterfeit currency. = **fake**, copied, false, forged, imitation, bogus, simulated, sham, fraudulent, feigned, spurious, ersatz, phoney or phony (informal), pseud or pseudo (informal) ■ **OPPOSITE:** genuine ▶ NOUN Counterfeits of the company's goods are flooding Europe. = **fake**, copy, reproduction, imitation, sham, forgery, phoney or phony (informal), fraud, warez (Computing) ■ **OPPOSITE:** the real thing ▶ VERB He financed a plot to counterfeit gold coins. = **fake**, copy, forge, imitate, simulate, sham, fabricate, feign

counterpart NOUN = **opposite number**, equal, twin, equivalent, peer, match, fellow, mate

countless ADJECTIVE = **innumerable**, legion, infinite, myriad, untold, limitless, incalculable, immeasurable, numberless, uncounted, multitudinous, endless, measureless ■ **OPPOSITE:** limited

country NOUN **1** the disputed boundary between the two countries = **nation**, state, land, commonwealth, kingdom, realm, sovereign state, people **2** Seventy per cent of this country is opposed to blood sports. = **people**, community, nation, society, citizens, voters, inhabitants, grass roots, electors, populace, citizenry, public **3** They live somewhere way out in the country. = **countryside**, rural areas, provinces, outdoors, sticks (informal), farmland, outback (Austral. & N.Z.), the middle of nowhere, green belt, wide open spaces (informal), backwoods, back country (U.S.), the back of beyond, bush (N.Z. & S. African),

backlands (*U.S.*), boondocks (*U.S. slang*)
■ **OPPOSITE:** town **4** *This is some of the best walking country in the district.* = **territory**, part, land, region, terrain **5** *I am willing to serve my country.* = **native land**, nationality, homeland, motherland, fatherland, patria (*Latin*), Hawaiki (*N.Z.*), Godzone (*Austral. informal*) ▶ ADJECTIVE *I want to live a simple country life.* = **rural**, pastoral, rustic, agrarian, bucolic, Arcadian ■ **OPPOSITE:** urban ■ **RELATED WORDS:** *adjectives* pastoral, rural

countryman *or* **countrywoman** *or* **countryperson** NOUN **1** *He beat his fellow countryman in the final.* = **compatriot**, fellow citizen **2** *With her horses, dogs and tweeds she is above all a countrywoman.* = **yokel**, farmer, peasant, provincial, hick (*informal, chiefly U.S. & Canad.*), rustic, swain (*archaic*), hillbilly, bucolic, country dweller, hayseed (*U.S. & Canad. informal*), clodhopper (*informal*), cockie (*N.Z.*), (country) bumpkin

countryside NOUN = **country**, rural areas, outdoors, farmland, outback (*Austral. & N.Z.*), green belt, wide open spaces (*informal*), sticks (*informal*)

county NOUN *He is living now in his mother's home county of Oxfordshire.* = **province**, district, shire ▶ ADJECTIVE (*informal*) *They were all upper-crust ladies, pillars of the county set.* = **upper-class**, upper-crust (*informal*), tweedy, plummy (*informal*), green-wellie, huntin', shootin', and fishin' (*informal*)

coup NOUN = **masterstroke**, feat, stunt, action, stroke, exploit, manoeuvre, deed, accomplishment, tour de force (*French*), stratagem, stroke of genius

coup d'état NOUN = **overthrow**, takeover, coup, rebellion, putsch, seizure of power, palace revolution

couple NOUN *There are a couple of police officers standing guard.* = **pair**, two, brace, span (*of horses or oxen*), duo, twain (*archaic*), twosome • **couple something to something** *The engine is coupled to a semiautomatic gearbox.* = **link to**, connect to, pair with, unite with, join to, hitch to, buckle to, clasp to, yoke to, conjoin to

coupon NOUN = **slip**, ticket, certificate, token, voucher, card, detachable portion

courage NOUN = **bravery**, nerve, fortitude, boldness, balls (*vulgar slang*), bottle (*Brit. slang*), resolution, daring, guts (*informal*), pluck, grit, heroism, mettle, firmness, gallantry, valour, spunk (*informal*), fearlessness, intrepidity ■ **OPPOSITE:** cowardice

courageous ADJECTIVE = **brave**, daring, bold, plucky, hardy, heroic, gritty, stalwart, fearless, resolute, gallant, audacious, intrepid, valiant, indomitable, dauntless, ballsy (*slang*), lion-hearted, valorous, stouthearted ■ **OPPOSITE:** cowardly

courier NOUN **1** *The documents were delivered by a private courier.* = **messenger**, runner, carrier, bearer, herald, envoy, emissary **2** *He was a travel courier.* = **guide**, representative, escort, conductor, chaperon, cicerone (*literary*), dragoman

course NOUN **1** *For nearly four hours we maintained our course northwards.* = **route**, way, line, road, track, channel, direction, path, passage, trail, orbit, tack, trajectory **2** *Resignation is the only course left open to him.* = **procedure**, plan, policy, programme, method, conduct, behaviour, manner, mode, regimen **3** *a series of naval battles which altered the course of history* = **progression**, order, unfolding, development, movement, advance, progress, flow, sequence, succession, continuity, advancement, furtherance, march **4** *I'll shortly be beginning a course on the modern novel.* = **classes**, course of study, programme, schedule, lectures, curriculum, studies **5** *On the Tour de France, 200 cyclists cover a course of 2,000 miles.* = **racecourse**, race, circuit, cinder track, lap **6** *In the course of the 1930s, steel production in Britain approximately doubled.* = **period**, time, duration, term, passing, sweep, passage, lapse ▶ VERB **1** *The tears coursed down his cheeks.* = **run**, flow, stream, gush, race, speed, surge, dash, tumble, scud, move apace **2** *a ban on dogs coursing hares* = **hunt**, follow, chase, pursue • **in due course** *I hope that it will be possible in due course.* = **in time**, finally, eventually, in the end, sooner or later, in the course of time • **of course** *There'll be the usual inquiry, of course.* = **naturally**, certainly, obviously, definitely, undoubtedly, needless to say, without a doubt, indubitably

court NOUN **1** *At this rate, you could find yourself in court for assault.* = **law court**, bar, bench, tribunal, court of justice, seat of judgment **2** *She came to visit England, where she was presented at the court of James I.* = **palace**, hall, castle, manor **3** *tales of King Arthur and his court* = **royal household**, train, suite, attendants, entourage, retinue, cortege ▶ VERB **1** *The pledge to protect pensions was designed to court elderly voters.* = **cultivate**, seek, flatter, solicit, pander to, curry favour with, fawn upon **2** *If he thinks he can remain in power by force he is courting disaster.* = **invite**, seek, attract, prompt, provoke, bring about, incite

3 *I was courting him at 19 and married him when I was 21.* = **woo**, go (out) with, go steady with (*informal*), date, chase, pursue, take out, make love to, run after, walk out with, keep company with, pay court to, set your cap at, pay your addresses to, step out with (*informal*)

courteous ADJECTIVE = **polite**, civil, respectful, mannerly, polished, refined, gracious, gallant, affable, urbane, courtly, well-bred, well-mannered ■ **OPPOSITE:** discourteous

courtesy NOUN **1** *He always treats everyone with the utmost courtesy.* = **politeness**, grace, good manners, civility, gallantry, good breeding, graciousness, affability, urbanity, courtliness **2** *If you're not coming, at least do me the courtesy of letting me know.* = **favour**, consideration, generosity, kindness, indulgence, benevolence

courtier NOUN = **attendant**, follower, squire, train-bearer

courtly ADJECTIVE = **ceremonious**, civil, formal, obliging, refined, polite, dignified, stately, aristocratic, gallant, affable, urbane, decorous, chivalrous, highbred

courtship NOUN = **wooing**, courting, suit, romance, engagement, keeping company

courtyard NOUN = **yard**, square, piazza, quadrangle, area, plaza, enclosure, cloister, quad (*informal*), peristyle

cove NOUN = **bay**, sound, creek, inlet, bayou, firth or frith (*Scot.*), anchorage

covenant NOUN **1** *the United Nations covenant on civil and political rights* = **promise**, contract, agreement, commitment, arrangement, treaty, pledge, bargain, convention, pact, compact, concordat, trust **2** *If you make regular gifts through a covenant we can reclaim the income tax.* = **deed**, contract, bond

cover VERB **1** *the black patch which covered his left eye* = **conceal**, cover up, screen, hide, shade, curtain, mask, disguise, obscure, hood, veil, cloak, shroud, camouflage, enshroud ■ **OPPOSITE:** reveal **2** *He covered his head with a turban.* = **clothe**, invest, dress, wrap, envelop ■ **OPPOSITE:** uncover **3** *The clouds had spread and nearly covered the entire sky.* = **overlay**, blanket, eclipse, mantle, canopy, overspread, layer **4** *She was soaking wet and covered with mud.* = **coat**, cake, plaster, smear, envelop, spread, encase, daub, overspread **5** *Nearly a foot of water covered the streets.* = **submerge**, flood, engulf, overrun, wash over **6** *It would not be easy to cover ten miles on that amount of petrol.* = **travel over**, cross, traverse, pass through or over, range **7** *You make a run for it and I'll*

cover you. = **protect**, guard, defend, shelter, shield, watch over **8** *These items are not covered by your medical insurance.* = **insure**, compensate, provide for, offset, balance, make good, make up for, take account of, counterbalance **9** *The law covers four categories of experiments.* = **deal with**, refer to, provide for, take account of, include, involve, contain, embrace, incorporate, comprise, embody, encompass, comprehend ■ **OPPOSITE:** exclude **10** *In this lecture, I aim to cover several topics.* = **consider**, deal with, examine, investigate, detail, describe, survey, refer to, tell of, recount **11** *He was sent to Italy to cover the World Cup.* = **report on**, write about, commentate on, give an account of, relate, tell of, narrate, write up **12** *She took out another loan to cover her debts.* = **pay for**, fund, provide for, offset, be enough for ▶ NOUN **1** *There were barren wastes of field with no trees and no cover.* = **protection**, shelter, shield, refuge, defence, woods, guard, sanctuary, camouflage, hiding place, undergrowth, concealment **2** *Make sure that the firm's accident cover is adequate.* = **insurance**, payment, protection, compensation, indemnity, reimbursement **3** *Put a polythene cover over it to protect it from dust.* = **covering**, case, top, cap, coating, envelope, lid, canopy, sheath, wrapper, awning **4** *He groaned and slid farther under the covers.* = **bedclothes**, bedding, sheet, blanket, quilt, duvet, eiderdown **5** *a small book with a green cover* = **jacket**, case, binding, wrapper **6** *The grocery store was just a cover for their betting shop.* = **disguise**, front (*informal*), screen, mask, cover-up, veil, cloak, façade, pretence, pretext, window-dressing, smoke screen • **cover for someone** *She did not have enough nurses to cover for those who were off sick.* = **stand in for**, take over, substitute, relieve, double for, fill in for, hold the fort for (*informal*) • **cover something up** *They knew they had done something wrong and lied to cover it up.* = **conceal**, hide, suppress, repress, keep secret, whitewash (*informal*), hush up, sweep under the carpet, draw a veil over, keep silent about, cover your tracks, keep dark, feign ignorance about, keep under your hat (*informal*)

coverage NOUN = **reporting**, treatment, analysis, description, reportage

covering NOUN *Sawdust was used as a hygienic floor covering.* = **cover**, coating, casing, wrapping, layer, blanket ▶ ADJECTIVE *Include a covering letter with your CV.* = **explanatory**, accompanying, introductory, descriptive

covert ADJECTIVE = **secret**, private, hidden, disguised, concealed, veiled, sly, clandestine, underhand, unsuspected, surreptitious, stealthy

cover-up NOUN = **concealment**, conspiracy, whitewash (*informal*), complicity, front (*informal*), smoke screen

covet VERB = **long for**, desire, fancy (*informal*), envy, crave, aspire to, yearn for, thirst for, begrudge, hanker after, lust after, set your heart on, have your eye on, would give your eyeteeth for

cow VERB = **intimidate**, daunt, frighten, scare, bully, dismay, awe, subdue, unnerve, overawe, terrorize, browbeat, psych out (*informal*), dishearten

coward NOUN = **wimp** (*informal*), chicken (*slang*), scaredy-cat (*informal*), sneak, pussy (*slang, chiefly U.S.*), yellow-belly (*slang*)

cowardice NOUN = **faint-heartedness**, weakness, softness, fearfulness, pusillanimity, spinelessness, timorousness

cowardly ADJECTIVE = **faint-hearted**, scared, spineless, gutless (*informal*), base, soft, yellow (*informal*), weak, chicken (*slang*), shrinking, fearful, craven, abject, dastardly (*old-fashioned*), timorous (*literary*), weak-kneed (*informal*), pusillanimous, chicken-hearted, lily-livered (*old-fashioned*), white-livered, sookie (*N.Z.*) ■ OPPOSITE: brave

cowboy NOUN = **cowhand**, drover, herder, rancher, stockman, cattleman, herdsman or woman (*Brit.*), gaucho, buckaroo (*U.S.*), ranchero (*U.S.*), cowpuncher (*U.S. informal*), broncobuster (*U.S.*), wrangler (*U.S.*)

cower VERB = **cringe**, shrink, tremble, crouch, flinch, quail, draw back, grovel

coy ADJECTIVE **1** *They are demure without being coy*. = **modest**, retiring, shy, shrinking, arch, timid, self-effacing, demure, flirtatious, bashful, prudish, aw-shucks, skittish, coquettish, kittenish, overmodest ■ OPPOSITE: bold **2** *The hotel are understandably coy about the incident.* = **uncommunicative**, mum, secretive, reserved, quiet, silent, evasive, taciturn, unforthcoming, tight-lipped, close-lipped

crack VERB **1** *A gas main had cracked under my neighbour's garage.* = **break**, split, burst, snap, fracture, splinter, craze, rive **2** *Thunder cracked in the sky.* = **snap**, ring, crash, burst, explode, crackle, pop, detonate **3** *She drew back her fist and cracked him on the jaw.* = **hit**, clip (*informal*), slap, smack, thump, buffet, clout (*informal*), cuff, whack, wallop (*informal*), chop **4** *Crack the eggs into a bowl.* = **cleave**, break **5** *He has finally cracked the code after years of painstaking*

research. = **solve**, work out, resolve, interpret, clarify, clear up, fathom, decipher, suss (out) (*slang*), get to the bottom of, disentangle, elucidate, get the answer to **6** *She's calm and strong, and will not crack under pressure.* = **break down**, collapse, yield, give in, give way, succumb, lose control, be overcome, go to pieces ▶ NOUN **1** *She watched him though a crack in the curtains.* = **break**, chink, gap, breach, fracture, rift, cleft, crevice, fissure, cranny, interstice **2** *The plate had a crack in it.* = **split**, break, chip, breach, fracture, rupture, cleft **3** *Suddenly there was a loud crack and glass flew into the air.* = **snap**, pop, crash, burst, explosion, clap, report **4** *He took a crack on the head during the game.* = **blow**, slap, smack, thump, buffet, clout (*informal*), cuff, whack, wallop (*informal*), clip (*informal*) **5** *I'd love to have a crack at the title next year.* = **attempt**, go (*informal*), try, shot (*informal*), opportunity, stab (*informal*) **6** *He made a nasty crack about her weight.* = **joke**, dig, insult, gag (*informal*), quip, jibe, wisecrack, witticism, funny remark, smart-alecky remark ▶ ADJECTIVE *He is said to be a crack shot.* = **first-class**, choice, excellent, ace (*informal*), elite, superior, world-class, first-rate, hand-picked • **crack up 1** *He's going to crack up if he doesn't take a break soon.* = **have a breakdown**, collapse, break down, go to pieces, come apart at the seams (*informal*), go out of your mind **2** *We all just cracked up when he told us.* = **burst out laughing**, laugh, fall about (laughing), guffaw, roar with laughter, be in stitches, split your sides

crackdown NOUN = **clampdown**, crushing, repression, suppression

cracked ADJECTIVE *a cracked mirror* = **broken**, damaged, split, chipped, flawed, faulty, crazed, defective, imperfect, fissured

cradle NOUN **1** *The baby sleeps in the cradle upstairs.* = **crib**, cot, Moses basket, bassinet **2** *the cradle of capitalism* = **birthplace**, beginning, source, spring, origin, fount, fountainhead, wellspring ▶ VERB *I cradled her in my arms.* = **hold**, support, rock, nurse, nestle

craft NOUN **1** *We sighted a small craft on the horizon.* = **vessel**, boat, ship, plane, aircraft, spacecraft, barque **2** *All kinds of traditional crafts are preserved here.* = **occupation**, work, calling, business, line, trade, employment, pursuit, vocation, handiwork, handicraft **3** *Lilyanne learned the craft of cooking from her grandmother.* = **skill**, art, ability, technique, know-how (*informal*), expertise, knack, aptitude, artistry, dexterity, workmanship

4 *They defeated their enemies through craft and cunning.* = **cunning**, ingenuity, guile, cleverness, scheme, subtlety, deceit, ruse, artifice, trickery, wiles, duplicity, subterfuge, contrivance, shrewdness, artfulness

craftsman or **craftswoman** or **craftsperson** NOUN = **skilled worker**, artisan, master, maker, wright, technician, artificer, smith, crafter

craftsmanship NOUN = **workmanship**, technique, expertise, mastery, artistry

crafty ADJECTIVE = **cunning**, scheming, sly, devious, knowing, designing, sharp, calculating, subtle, tricky, shrewd, astute, fraudulent, canny, wily, insidious, artful, foxy, deceitful, duplicitous, tricksy, guileful ■ **OPPOSITE:** open

crag NOUN = **rock**, peak, bluff, pinnacle, tor, aiguille

craggy ADJECTIVE = **rocky**, broken, rough, rugged, uneven, jagged, stony, precipitous, jaggy (*Scot.*)

cram VERB **1** *She pulled off her school hat and crammed it into a wastebasket.* = **stuff**, force, jam, ram, shove, compress, compact **2** *She crammed her mouth with nuts.* = **pack**, fill, stuff **3** *We crammed into my car and set off.* = **squeeze**, press, crowd, pack, crush, pack in, fill to overflowing, overfill, overcrowd **4** *She was cramming hard for her exam.* = **study**, revise, swot (*informal*), bone up (*informal*), grind, swot up, mug up (*slang*)

cramp¹ NOUN *She started getting stomach cramps this morning.* = **spasm**, pain, ache, contraction, pang, stiffness, stitch, convulsion, twinge, crick, shooting pain

cramp² VERB *Like more and more women, she believes wedlock would cramp her style.* = **restrict**, hamper, inhibit, hinder, check, handicap, confine, hamstring, constrain, obstruct, impede, shackle, circumscribe, encumber

cramped ADJECTIVE = **restricted**, confined, overcrowded, crowded, packed, narrow, squeezed, uncomfortable, awkward, closed in, congested, circumscribed, jammed in, hemmed in ■ **OPPOSITE:** spacious

crank NOUN = **eccentric**, freak (*informal*), oddball (*informal*), weirdo or weirdie (*informal*), case (*informal*), character (*informal*), nut (*slang*), flake (*slang, chiefly U.S.*), screwball (*slang, chiefly U.S. & Canad.*), odd fish (*informal*), kook (*U.S. & Canad. informal*), queer fish (*Brit. informal*), rum customer (*Brit. slang*)

cranky ADJECTIVE = **eccentric**, wacky (*informal*), oddball (*informal*), freakish, odd,

strange, funny (*informal*), bizarre, peculiar, queer (*informal*), rum (*Brit. slang*), quirky, idiosyncratic, off-the-wall (*slang*), freaky (*slang*), outré, daggy (*Austral. & N.Z. informal*)

cranny NOUN = **crevice**, opening, hole, crack, gap, breach, rift, nook, cleft, chink, fissure, interstice

crash NOUN **1** *His elder son was killed in a car crash a few years ago.* = **collision**, accident, smash, wreck, prang (*informal*), bump, pile-up (*informal*), smash-up **2** *Two people in the flat recalled hearing a loud crash about 1.30am.* = **smash**, clash, boom, smashing, bang, thunder, thump, racket, din, clatter, clattering, thud, clang **3** *He predicted correctly that there was going to be a stock market crash.* = **collapse**, failure, depression, ruin, bankruptcy, downfall ▶ VERB **1** *He lost his balance and crashed to the floor.* = **fall**, pitch, plunge, sprawl, topple, lurch, hurtle, come a cropper (*informal*), overbalance, fall headlong **2** *We heard the sound of an animal crashing through the undergrowth.* = **plunge**, hurtle, precipitate yourself **3** *Her glass fell on the floor and crashed into a thousand pieces.* = **smash**, break, break up, shatter, fragment, fracture, shiver, disintegrate, splinter, dash to pieces **4** *When the market crashed they assumed the deal would be cancelled.* = **collapse**, fail, go under, be ruined, go bust (*informal*), fold up, go broke (*informal*), go to the wall, go belly up (*informal*), smash, fold ▶ ADJECTIVE *I might take a crash course in typing.* = **intensive**, concentrated, immediate, urgent, round-the-clock, emergency • **crash into** *His car crashed into the rear of a van.* = **collide with**, hit, bump into, bang into, run into, drive into, plough into, hurtle into

crass ADJECTIVE = **insensitive**, stupid, gross, blundering, dense, coarse, witless, boorish, obtuse, unrefined, asinine, indelicate, oafish, lumpish, doltish ■ **OPPOSITE:** sensitive

crate NOUN *A crane was already unloading crates and pallets.* = **container**, case, box, packing case, tea chest ▶ VERB *The plane had been dismantled, crated, and shipped to London.* = **box**, pack, enclose, pack up, encase, case

crater NOUN = **hollow**, hole, depression, dip, cavity, shell hole

crave VERB **1** *There may be certain times of day when smokers crave a cigarette.* = **long for**, yearn for, hanker after, be dying for, want, need, require, desire, fancy (*informal*), hope for, cry out for (*informal*), thirst for, pine for, covet, lust after, pant for, sigh for, set your

heart on, hunger after, eat your heart out
over, would give your eyeteeth for **2** *If I may
crave your lordship's indulgence, I would like to
consult my client.* = **beg**, ask for, seek,
petition, pray for, plead for, solicit, implore,
beseech, entreat, supplicate

craven ADJECTIVE = **cowardly**, weak,
scared, fearful, abject, dastardly (*old-
fashioned*), mean-spirited, timorous
(*literary*), pusillanimous (*formal*), chicken-
hearted, yellow (*informal*), lily-livered

craving NOUN = **longing**, hope, desire,
urge, yen (*informal*), hunger, appetite, ache,
lust, yearning, thirst, hankering

crawl VERB **1** *I began to crawl on my hands and
knees towards the door.* = **creep**, slither, go on
all fours, move on hands and knees, inch,
drag, wriggle, writhe, move at a snail's
pace, worm your way, advance slowly, pull
or drag yourself along ■ **OPPOSITE:** run **2** *I'll
apologize to him, but I won't crawl.* = **grovel**,
creep, cringe, humble yourself, abase
yourself • **be crawling with something**
This place is crawling with police. = **be full of**,
teem with, be alive with, swarm with, be
overrun with (*slang*), be lousy with • **crawl
to someone** *I'd have to crawl to her to keep my
job.* = **fawn on**, pander to, suck up to
(*slang*), toady to, truckle to, lick someone's
boots (*slang*)

craze NOUN = **fad**, thing (*informal*), fashion,
trend, passion, rage, enthusiasm, mode,
vogue, novelty, preoccupation, mania,
infatuation, the latest thing (*informal*)

crazed ADJECTIVE *the manager's crazed antics
on the touchline* = **mad**, crazy, raving,
unbalanced, deranged, berserk, unhinged,
berko (*Austral. slang*), off the air (*Austral.
slang*), porangi (*N.Z.*)

crazy ADJECTIVE **1** *The story lurches from one
crazy situation to another.* = **strange**, odd,
bizarre, fantastic, silly, weird, ridiculous,
outrageous, peculiar, eccentric, rum (*Brit.
slang*), oddball (*informal*), cray cray (*slang*),
cockamamie (*slang, chiefly U.S.*), off the air
(*Austral. slang*), porangi (*N.Z.*), daggy
(*Austral. & N.Z. informal*) ■ **OPPOSITE:**
normal **2** *I know it sounds a crazy idea,
but hear me out.* = **ridiculous**, wild,
absurd, inappropriate, foolish, ludicrous,
irresponsible, unrealistic, unwise, senseless,
preposterous, potty (*Brit. informal*),
short-sighted, unworkable, foolhardy,
idiotic, nonsensical, half-baked (*informal*),
inane, fatuous, ill-conceived, quixotic,
imprudent, impracticable, cockeyed
(*informal*), cockamamie (*slang, chiefly U.S.*),
porangi (*N.Z.*) ■ **OPPOSITE:** sensible
3 *He's crazy about football.* = **fanatical**, wild

(*informal*), mad, devoted, enthusiastic,
passionate, hysterical, ardent, very keen,
zealous, smitten, infatuated, enamoured
■ **OPPOSITE:** uninterested

creak VERB = **squeak**, grind, scrape, groan,
grate, screech, squeal, scratch, rasp

creaky ADJECTIVE *She pushed open the creaky
door.* = **squeaky**, creaking, squeaking,
unoiled, grating, rusty, rasping, raspy

cream NOUN **1** *Gently apply the cream to the
affected areas.* = **lotion**, ointment, oil,
essence, cosmetic, paste, emulsion, salve,
liniment, unguent **2** *The event was attended
by the cream of Hollywood society.* = **best**, elite,
prime, pick, flower, the crème de la crème
▶ ADJECTIVE *cream silk stockings* = **off-white**,
ivory, yellowish-white

creamy ADJECTIVE **1** *creamy mashed potato*
= **milky**, buttery **2** *Whisk the mixture until it is
smooth and creamy.* = **smooth**, soft,
creamed, lush, oily, velvety, rich

crease NOUN **1** *She frowned at the creases in
her silk dress.* = **fold**, ruck, line, tuck, ridge,
groove, pucker, corrugation **2** *There were
tiny creases at the corner of his eyes.* = **wrinkle**,
line, crow's-foot ▶ VERB **1** *Most outfits crease
a bit when you're travelling.* = **crumple**,
rumple, pucker, crinkle, fold, ridge, double
up, crimp, ruck up, corrugate **2** *His face
creased with mirth.* = **wrinkle**, crumple,
screw up

create VERB **1** *Criticism will only create feelings
of failure.* = **cause**, lead to, occasion (*formal*),
beget (*old-fashioned*), bring about **2** *He's
creating a whole new language of painting.*
= **make**, form, produce, develop, design,
generate, invent, coin, compose, devise,
initiate, hatch, originate, formulate, give
birth to, spawn, dream up (*informal*),
concoct, beget, give life to, bring into
being or existence ■ **OPPOSITE:** destroy
3 *They are about to create a scholarship fund for
disadvantaged students.* = **appoint**, make,
found, establish, set up, invest, install,
constitute

creation NOUN **1** *the origin of all creation*
= **universe**, world, life, nature, cosmos,
natural world, living world, all living things
2 *The bathroom is entirely my own creation.*
= **invention**, production, concept,
achievement, brainchild (*informal*),
concoction, handiwork, pièce de résistance
(*French*), magnum opus, chef-d'oeuvre
(*French*) **3** *the time and effort involved in the
creation of a work of art* = **making**,
generation, formation, conception, genesis
4 *He said all sides were committed to the
creation of a democratic state.* = **setting up**,
development, production, institution,

foundation, constitution, establishment, formation, laying down, inception, origination

creative ADJECTIVE = **imaginative**, gifted, artistic, inventive, original, inspired, clever, productive, fertile, ingenious, visionary

creativity NOUN = **imagination**, talent, inspiration, productivity, fertility, ingenuity, originality, inventiveness, cleverness, fecundity

creator NOUN 1 *George Lucas, the creator of the Star Wars films* = **maker**, father, mother, parent, author, framer, designer, architect, inventor, originator, initiator, begetter 2 *(usually cap.) This was the first object placed in the heavens by the Creator.* = **God**, Maker

creature NOUN 1 *Many cultures believe that every living creature possesses a spirit.* = **living thing**, being, animal, beast, brute, critter (*U.S., dialect*), quadruped, dumb animal, lower animal 2 *He is one of the most amiable creatures in existence.* = **person**, man, woman, individual, character (*informal*), fellow (*old-fashioned*), soul, human being, mortal, body (*informal*) 3 *We are not merely creatures of our employers.* = **minion**, tool, instrument (*informal*), puppet, cohort (*chiefly U.S.*), dependant, retainer, hanger-on, lackey

credence NOUN 1 *Further studies are needed to lend credence to this notion.* = **credibility**, credit, plausibility, believability 2 *Seismologists give this idea little credence.* = **belief**, trust, confidence, faith, acceptance, assurance, certainty, dependence, reliance

credentials PLURAL NOUN 1 *He has the right credentials for the job.* = **qualifications**, ability, skill, capacity, fitness, attribute, capability, endowment(s), accomplishment, eligibility, aptitude, suitability 2 *He called at Government House to present his credentials.* = **certification**, document, reference(s), papers, title, card, licence, recommendation, passport, warrant, voucher, deed, testament, diploma, testimonial, authorization, missive, letters of credence, attestation, letter of recommendation *or* introduction

credibility NOUN = **believability**, reliability, plausibility, trustworthiness, tenability

credible ADJECTIVE 1 *This claim seems perfectly credible to me.* = **believable**, possible, likely, reasonable, probable, plausible, conceivable, imaginable, tenable, verisimilar ■ **OPPOSITE:** unbelievable 2 *the evidence of credible witnesses* = **reliable**, honest, dependable, trustworthy, sincere, trusty ■ **OPPOSITE:** unreliable

credit NOUN 1 *It would be wrong of us to take all the credit for this result.* = **praise**, honour, recognition, glory, thanks, approval, fame, tribute, merit, acclaim, acknowledgment, kudos, commendation, Brownie points 2 *He is a credit to his family.* = **source of satisfaction** *or* **pride**, asset, honour, feather in your cap 3 *His remarks lost him credit with many people.* = **prestige**, reputation, standing, position, character, influence, regard, status, esteem, clout (*informal*), good name, estimation, repute 4 *At first this theory met with little credit.* = **belief**, trust, confidence, faith, reliance, credence ▸ VERB *You can't credit anything he says.* = **believe**, rely on, have faith in, trust, buy (*slang*), accept, depend on, swallow (*informal*), fall for, bank on • **credit someone with something** *You don't credit me with any intelligence at all, do you?* = **attribute to**, assign to, ascribe to, accredit to, impute to, chalk up to (*informal*) • **credit something to someone** *Although the song is usually credited to Lennon and McCartney, it was written by McCartney alone.* = **attribute to**, ascribe to, accredit to, impute to, chalk up to (*informal*) • **on credit** *They bought most of their furniture on credit.* = **on account**, by instalments, on tick (*informal*), on hire-purchase, on the slate (*informal*), by deferred payment, on (the) H.P.

creditable ADJECTIVE = **praiseworthy**, worthy, respectable, admirable, honourable, exemplary, reputable, commendable, laudable, meritorious, estimable

credulity NOUN = **gullibility**, naïveté *or* naivety, blind faith, credulousness

creed NOUN = **belief**, principles, profession (*of faith*), doctrine, canon, persuasion, dogma, tenet, credo, catechism, articles of faith

creek NOUN 1 *The offshore fishermen took shelter from the storm in a creek.* = **inlet**, bay, cove, bight, firth *or* frith (*Scot.*) 2 *Follow Austin Creek for a few miles.* = **stream**, brook, tributary, bayou, rivulet, watercourse, streamlet, runnel

creep VERB 1 *The rabbit crept off and hid in a hole.* = **crawl**, worm, wriggle, squirm, slither, writhe, drag yourself, edge, inch, crawl on all fours 2 *I went back to the hotel and crept up to my room.* = **sneak**, steal, tiptoe, slink, skulk, approach unnoticed ▸ NOUN *He's a smug, sanctimonious little creep.* = **bootlicker** (*informal*), sneak, sycophant, crawler (*slang*), toady • **give someone the creeps** = **disgust**, frighten, scare, repel, repulse, make your hair stand on end, make you squirm

creeper NOUN = **climbing plant**, runner, vine (*chiefly U.S.*), climber, rambler, trailing plant

creepy ADJECTIVE = **disturbing**, threatening, frightening, terrifying, weird, forbidding, horrible, menacing, unpleasant, scary (*informal*), sinister, ominous, eerie, macabre, nightmarish, hair-raising, awful

crescent NOUN *a flag with a white crescent on a red ground* = **meniscus**, sickle, new moon, half-moon, old moon, sickle-shape

crest NOUN **1** *He reached the crest of the hill.* = **top**, summit, peak, ridge, highest point, pinnacle, apex, head, crown, height **2** *Both birds had a dark blue crest.* = **tuft**, crown, comb, plume, mane, tassel, topknot, cockscomb **3** *On the wall is the family crest.* = **emblem**, badge, symbol, insignia, charge, bearings, device

crestfallen ADJECTIVE = **disappointed**, depressed, discouraged, dejected, despondent, downcast, disheartened, disconsolate, downhearted, sick as a parrot (*informal*), choked ■ OPPOSITE: elated

crevice NOUN = **gap**, opening, hole, split, crack, rent, fracture, rift, slit, cleft, chink, fissure, cranny, interstice

crew NOUN **1** *These vessels carry small crews of around twenty people.* = **(ship's) company**, hands, (ship's) complement **2** *The film crew spent nearly twelve weeks shooting in Thailand.* = **team**, company, party, squad, gang, corps, working party, posse **3** *a motley crew of college friends* = **crowd**, set, lot, bunch (*informal*), band, troop, pack, camp, gang, mob, herd, swarm, company, horde, posse (*informal*), assemblage

crib NOUN **1** *She placed the baby back in its crib.* = **cradle**, bed, cot, bassinet, Moses basket **2** *Only desperate students take cribs into the exam with them.* = **translation**, notes, key, trot (*U.S. slang*) **3** *Each calf in the dairy has its own little crib.* = **manger**, box, stall, rack, bunker ▶ VERB *He had been caught cribbing in an exam.* = **copy**, cheat, pirate, pilfer, purloin (*formal*), plagiarize, pass off as your own work

crick NOUN *I've got a crick in my neck from looking up at the screen.* = **spasm**, cramp, convulsion, twinge ▶ VERB *I cricked my back from sitting in the same position for too long.* = **rick**, jar, wrench

crime NOUN **1** *He has committed no crime and poses no danger to the public.* = **offence**, job (*informal*), wrong, fault, outrage, atrocity,

violation, trespass, felony, misdemeanour, misdeed, transgression, unlawful act **2** *Much of the city's crime revolves around protection rackets.* = **lawbreaking**, corruption, delinquency, illegality, wrong, vice, sin, guilt, misconduct, wrongdoing, wickedness, iniquity, villainy, unrighteousness, malefaction, e-crime or ecrime, cybercrime

criminal NOUN *He was put in a cell with several hardened criminals.* = **lawbreaker**, convict, con (*slang*), offender, crook (*informal*), lag (*slang*), villain, culprit, sinner, delinquent, felon, conman or woman (*informal*), con artist (*informal*), rorter (*Austral. slang*), jailbird, malefactor, evildoer, transgressor, skelm (*S. African*), rogue trader, perp (*U.S. & Canad. informal*) ▶ ADJECTIVE **1** *The entire party cannot be blamed for the criminal actions of a few members.* = **unlawful**, illicit, lawless, wrong, illegal, corrupt, crooked (*informal*), vicious, immoral, wicked, culpable, under-the-table, villainous, nefarious, iniquitous, indictable, felonious, bent (*slang*) ■ OPPOSITE: lawful **2** *This project is a criminal waste of time and resources.* = **disgraceful**, ridiculous, foolish, senseless, scandalous, preposterous, deplorable

criminality NOUN = **illegality**, crime, corruption, delinquency, wrongdoing, lawlessness, wickedness, depravity, culpability, villainy, turpitude (*formal*)

cringe VERB **1** *I cringed in horror.* = **shrink**, flinch, quail, recoil, start, shy, tremble, quiver, cower, draw back, blench **2** *The idea makes me cringe.* = **wince**, squirm, writhe

crinkle NOUN *The fabric was smooth, without a crinkle.* = **crease**, wrinkle, crumple, ruffle, twist, fold, curl, rumple, pucker, crimp

cripple VERB *A total cut-off of supplies would cripple the country's economy.* = **damage**, destroy, ruin, bring to a standstill, halt, spoil, cramp, impair, put paid to, vitiate, put out of action ■ OPPOSITE: help

crippled ADJECTIVE **1** *a crippled horse* = **disabled**, paralysed, incapacitated, enfeebled **2** *a crippled economy* = **damaged**, destroyed, ruined, spoiled, weakened, impaired, incapacitated

crisis NOUN **1** *Strikes worsened the country's economic crisis.* = **emergency**, plight, catastrophe, predicament, pass, trouble, disaster, mess, dilemma, strait, deep water, meltdown (*informal*), extremity, quandary, dire straits, exigency, critical situation **2** *The anxiety that had been building within him reached a crisis.* = **critical point**, climax, point of no return, height, confrontation, crunch (*informal*), turning point, culmination, crux, moment of truth, climacteric, tipping point

crisp ADJECTIVE **1** *Bake the potatoes till they're nice and crisp.* = **firm**, crunchy, crispy, crumbly, fresh, brittle, unwilted ■ **OPPOSITE:** soft **2** *a crisp autumn day* = **bracing**, fresh, refreshing, brisk, invigorating ■ **OPPOSITE:** warm **3** *He wore a panama hat and a crisp white suit.* = **clean**, smart, trim, neat, tidy, orderly, spruce, snappy, clean-cut, well-groomed, well-pressed **4** *In a clear, crisp voice, he began his speech.* = **brief**, clear, short, tart, incisive, terse, succinct, pithy, brusque

criterion NOUN = **standard**, test, rule, measure, principle, proof, par, norm, canon, gauge, yardstick, touchstone, bench mark

> **USAGE** The word *criteria* is the plural of *criterion* and it is incorrect to use it as an alternative singular form; *these criteria are not valid* is correct, and so is *this criterion is not valid*, but not *this criteria is not valid*.

critic NOUN **1** *The New York critics had praised her performance.* = **judge**, authority, expert, analyst, commentator, pundit, reviewer, connoisseur, arbiter, expositor **2** *He became a fierce critic of the tobacco industry.* = **fault-finder**, attacker, detractor, knocker (*informal*)

critical ADJECTIVE **1** *The incident happened at a critical point in the campaign.* = **crucial**, decisive, momentous, deciding, pressing, serious, vital, psychological, urgent, all-important, pivotal, high-priority, now or never ■ **OPPOSITE:** unimportant **2** *Ten of the injured are said to be in a critical condition.* = **grave**, serious, dangerous, acute, risky, hairy (*slang*), precarious, perilous ■ **OPPOSITE:** safe **3** *He has apologized for critical remarks he made about the referee.* = **disparaging**, disapproving, scathing, derogatory, nit-picking (*informal*), censorious, cavilling, fault-finding, captious, carping, niggling, nit-picky (*informal*) ■ **OPPOSITE:** complimentary **4** *What is needed is a critical analysis of the evidence.* = **analytical**, penetrating, discriminating, discerning, diagnostic, perceptive, judicious, accurate, precise ■ **OPPOSITE:** undiscriminating

criticism NOUN **1** *The policy had repeatedly come under strong criticism.* = **fault-finding**, censure, disapproval, disparagement, stick (*slang*), knocking (*informal*), panning (*informal*), slamming (*slang*), slating (*informal*), flak (*informal*), slagging (*slang*),

strictures, bad press, denigration, brickbats (*informal*), character assassination, critical remarks, animadversion **2** *Her work includes novels, poetry and literary criticism.* = **analysis**, review, notice, assessment, judgment, commentary, evaluation, appreciation, appraisal, critique, elucidation

criticize VERB = **find fault with**, censure, disapprove of, knock (*informal*), blast, pan (*informal*), condemn, slam (*slang*), carp, put down, slate (*informal*), have a go (at) (*informal*), throw shade (at) (*slang*), disparage, tear into (*informal*), diss (*slang*), nag at, lambast(e), pick holes in, pick to pieces, give (someone or something) a bad press, pass strictures upon, nit-pick (*informal*) ■ **OPPOSITE:** praise

critique NOUN = **essay**, review, analysis, assessment, examination, commentary, appraisal, treatise

croak VERB **1** *Frogs croaked in the reeds.* = **grunt**, squawk, caw **2** *Daniel managed to croak, 'Help me.'* = **rasp**, gasp, grunt, wheeze, utter or speak harshly, utter or speak huskily, utter or speak throatily **3** *I've nearly croaked twice and am grateful to be alive.* = **die**, expire, pass away, perish, buy it (*U.S. slang*), check out (*U.S. slang*), kick it (*slang*), go belly-up (*slang*), peg out (*informal*), kick the bucket (*informal*), buy the farm (*U.S. slang*), peg it (*informal*), cark it (*Austral. & N.Z. slang*), pop your clogs (*informal*), hop the twig (*informal*)

crone NOUN = **old woman**, witch, hag, old bag (*derogatory slang*), old bat (*derogatory slang*), kuia (*N.Z.*)

crony NOUN = **friend**, china (*Brit. slang*), colleague, associate, mate (*informal*), pal (*informal*), companion, cock (*Brit. informal*), buddy (*informal*), comrade, chum (*informal*), accomplice, ally, sidekick (*slang*), blood or blud (*Brit. slang*), main man (*slang, chiefly U.S.*), homeboy (*slang, chiefly U.S.*), cobber (*Austral. & N.Z., old-fashioned, informal*)

crook NOUN *The man is a crook and a liar.* = **criminal**, rogue, cheat, thief, shark, lag (*slang*), villain, robber, racketeer, fraudster, swindler, knave (*archaic*), grifter (*slang, chiefly U.S. & Canad.*), chiseller (*informal*), skelm (*S. African*) ▶ VERB *He crooked his finger and said, 'Come here.'* = **bend**, hook, angle, bow, curve, curl, cock, flex ▶ ADJECTIVE *He admitted to feeling a bit crook.* = **ill**, sick, poorly (*informal*), funny (*informal*), weak, ailing, queer, frail, feeble, unhealthy, seedy (*informal*), sickly, unwell, laid up (*informal*), queasy, infirm, out of sorts (*informal*), dicky (*Brit. informal*), nauseous, off-colour, under the weather (*informal*), at death's door, indisposed, peaky, on the sick list (*informal*), green about the gills • **go (off) crook** *She went crook when I confessed.* = **lose your temper**, be furious, rage, go mad, lose it (*informal*), seethe, crack up (*informal*), see red (*informal*), lose the plot (*informal*), go ballistic (*slang*), blow a fuse (*slang, chiefly U.S.*), fly off the handle (*informal*), be incandescent, go off the deep end (*informal*), throw a fit (*informal*), wig out (*slang*), go up the wall (*slang*), blow your top, lose your rag (*slang*), be beside yourself, flip your lid (*slang*)

crooked ADJECTIVE **1** *the crooked line of his broken nose* = **bent**, twisted, bowed, curved, irregular, warped, deviating, out of shape, misshapen ■ **OPPOSITE:** straight **2** *He gave her a crooked grin.* = **at an angle**, angled, tilted, to one side, uneven, slanted, slanting, squint, awry, lopsided, askew, asymmetric, off-centre, skewwhiff (*Brit. informal*), unsymmetrical **3** *She might expose his crooked business deals to the authorities.* = **dishonest**, criminal, illegal, corrupt, dubious, questionable, unlawful, shady (*informal*), fraudulent, unscrupulous, under-the-table, bent (*slang*), shifty, deceitful, underhand, unprincipled, dishonourable, nefarious, knavish (*archaic*) ■ **OPPOSITE:** honest

croon VERB **1** *a nightclub singer who crooned romantic songs* = **sing**, warble **2** *The man was crooning soft words of encouragement.* = **say softly**, breathe, hum, purr

crop NOUN *a fine crop of apples* = **yield**, produce, gathering, fruits, harvest, vintage, reaping, season's growth ▶ VERB **1** *I started cropping my beans in July.* = **harvest**, pick, collect, gather, bring in, reap, bring home, garner, mow **2** *I let the horse drop his head to crop the grass.* = **graze**, eat, browse, feed on, nibble **3** *She cropped her hair and dyed it blonde.* = **cut**, reduce, trim, clip, dock, prune, shorten, shear, snip, pare, lop • **crop up** *As we get older health problems often crop up.* = **happen**, appear, emerge, occur, arise, turn up, spring up

cross VERB **1** *She was partly to blame for failing to look as she crossed the road.* = **go across**, pass over, traverse, cut across, move across, travel across **2** *A bridge crosses the river about half a mile outside the village.* = **span**, bridge, ford, go across, extend over **3** *The two roads cross at this junction.* = **intersect**, meet, intertwine, crisscross **4** *He was not a man to cross.* = **oppose**, interfere with, hinder, obstruct, deny, block, resist, frustrate, foil, thwart, impede **5** *These small flowers were later crossed with a*

white flowering species. = **interbreed**, mix, blend, cross-pollinate, crossbreed, hybridize, cross-fertilize, intercross ▶ NOUN **1** *She wore a cross on a silver chain.* = **crucifix** **2** *Being labelled a cheat is a cross I have to bear.* = **trouble**, worry, trial, load, burden, grief, misery, woe, misfortune, affliction, tribulation **3** *The noise that came out was a cross between a laugh and a bark.* = **mixture**, combination, blend, amalgam, amalgamation **4** *a cross between a collie and a poodle* = **crossbreed**, hybrid ▶ ADJECTIVE *Everyone was getting bored and cross.* = **angry**, impatient, irritable, annoyed, put out, hacked (off) (*informal*), crusty, snappy, grumpy, vexed, sullen, surly, fractious, petulant, disagreeable, short, churlish, peeved (*informal*), ill-tempered, irascible, cantankerous, tetchy, ratty (*Brit. & N.Z. informal*), tooshie (*Austral. slang*), testy, fretful, waspish, in a bad mood, grouchy (*informal*), querulous, shirty (*slang, chiefly Brit.*), peevish, splenetic, crotchety (*informal*), snappish, ill-humoured, captious, pettish, out of humour, hoha (*N.Z.*) ■ **OPPOSITE:** good-humoured • **cross something out** or **off** *He crossed her name off the list.* = **strike off** or **out**, eliminate, cancel, delete, blue-pencil, score off or out

cross-examine VERB = **question**, grill (*informal*), quiz, interrogate, catechize, pump

crotch NOUN = **groin**, lap, crutch

crouch VERB = **bend down**, kneel, squat, stoop, bow, duck, hunch

crow VERB = **gloat**, triumph, boast, swagger, brag, vaunt, bluster, exult, blow your own trumpet

crowd NOUN **1** *It took some two hours before the crowd was fully dispersed.* = **multitude**, mass, assembly, throng, company, press, army, host, pack, mob, flock, herd, swarm, horde, rabble, concourse, bevy **2** *All the old crowd from my university days were there.* = **group**, set, lot, circle, gang, bunch (*informal*), clique **3** *When the song finished, the crowd went wild.* = **audience**, spectators, house, gate, attendance ▶ VERB **1** *A throng of fashionable young people crowded around the stage.* = **flock**, press, push, mass, collect, gather, stream, surge, cluster, muster, huddle, swarm, throng, congregate, foregather **2** *A group of journalists were crowded into a minibus.* = **squeeze**, pack, pile, bundle, cram **3** *Demonstrators crowded the streets shouting slogans.* = **congest**, pack, cram **4** *It had been a tense, restless day with people crowding her all the time.* = **jostle**, batter, butt, push, elbow, shove • **the crowd** *You can learn to stand out from the crowd.*

= **the masses**, the people, the public, the mob, the rank and file, the populace, the rabble, the proletariat, the hoi polloi, the riffraff, the vulgar herd

crowded ADJECTIVE = **packed**, full, busy, mobbed, cramped, swarming, overflowing, thronged, teeming, congested, populous, jam-packed, crushed

crown NOUN 1 *a beautiful woman wearing a golden crown* = **coronet**, tiara, diadem (*old-fashioned*), circlet, coronal (*poetic*), chaplet 2 *He won the middleweight crown in 1947.* = **laurel wreath**, trophy, distinction, prize, honour, garland, laurels, wreath, kudos 3 *We stood on the crown of the hill.* = **high point**, head, top, tip, summit, crest, pinnacle, apex ▶ VERB 1 *He had himself crowned as Emperor.* = **install**, invest, honour, dignify, ordain, inaugurate 2 *A rugged castle crowns the cliffs.* = **top**, cap, be on top of, surmount (*formal*) 3 *The summit was crowned by the signing of the historical treaty.* = **cap**, finish, complete, perfect, fulfil, consummate, round off, put the finishing touch to, put the tin lid on, be the climax or culmination of 4 *I felt like crowning him with the frying pan.* = **strike**, belt (*informal*), bash, hit over the head, box, punch, cuff, biff (*slang*), wallop • **the Crown** 1 *loyal subjects of the Crown* = **monarch**, ruler, sovereign, rex or regina (*Latin*), emperor or empress, king or queen 2 *All treasure trove is the property of the Crown.* = **monarchy**, sovereignty, royalty

crucial ADJECTIVE 1 (*informal*) *the most crucial election campaign in years* = **vital**, important, pressing, essential, urgent, momentous, high-priority 2 *At the crucial moment, his nerve failed.* = **critical**, central, key, psychological, decisive, pivotal, now or never

crucify VERB 1 *the day that Christ was crucified* = **execute**, put to death, nail to a cross 2 *She was crucified by the critics for her performance.* = **pan** (*informal*), rubbish (*informal*), ridicule, slag (off) (*slang*), lampoon, wipe the floor with (*informal*), tear to pieces 3 *He had been crucified by guilt ever since his child's death.* = **torture**, rack, torment, harrow

crude ADJECTIVE 1 *a crude way of assessing the risk of heart disease* = **rough**, undeveloped, basic, outline, unfinished, makeshift, sketchy, unformed 2 *crude wooden carvings* = **simple**, rudimentary, basic, primitive, coarse, clumsy, rough-and-ready, rough-hewn 3 *a crude sense of humour* = **vulgar**, dirty, rude, obscene, coarse, indecent, crass, tasteless, lewd, X-rated

(*informal*), boorish, smutty, uncouth, gross ■ **OPPOSITE:** tasteful 4 *8.5 million tonnes of crude steel* = **unrefined**, natural, raw, unprocessed, unpolished, unprepared ■ **OPPOSITE:** processed

crudely ADVERB 1 *The donors can be split – a little crudely – into two groups.* = **roughly**, basically, sketchily 2 *a crudely carved wooden form* = **simply**, roughly, basically, coarsely, clumsily 3 *She spoke crudely to the assembled journalists.* = **vulgarly**, rudely, coarsely, crassly, indecently, obscenely, lewdly, impolitely, tastelessly

cruel ADJECTIVE 1 *They should spend a long time in jail to reflect on their cruel acts.* = **brutal**, ruthless, callous, sadistic, inhumane, hard, fell (*archaic*), severe, harsh, savage, grim, vicious, relentless, murderous, monstrous, unnatural, unkind, heartless, atrocious, inhuman, merciless, cold-blooded, malevolent, hellish (*informal*), depraved, spiteful, brutish, bloodthirsty, remorseless, barbarous, pitiless, unfeeling, hard-hearted, stony-hearted ■ **OPPOSITE:** kind 2 *Fate dealt him a cruel blow.* = **bitter**, severe, painful, ruthless, traumatic, grievous, unrelenting, merciless, pitiless

cruelly ADVERB 1 *Douglas was often treated cruelly by his fellow-pupils.* = **brutally**, severely, savagely, viciously, mercilessly, in cold blood, callously, monstrously, unmercifully, sadistically, pitilessly, spitefully, heartlessly, barbarously 2 *His life has been cruelly shattered by an event not of his own making.* = **bitterly**, deeply, severely, mortally, painfully, ruthlessly, mercilessly, grievously, pitilessly, traumatically

cruelty NOUN = **brutality**, spite, severity, savagery, ruthlessness, sadism, depravity, harshness, inhumanity, barbarity, callousness, viciousness, bestiality, heartlessness, spitefulness, bloodthirstiness, mercilessness, fiendishness, hardheartedness

cruise NOUN *He and his wife were planning to go on a world cruise.* = **sail**, voyage, boat trip, sea trip ▶ VERB 1 *She wants to cruise the canals of France in a barge.* = **sail**, coast, voyage 2 *A black and white police car cruised past.* = **travel along**, coast, drift, keep a steady pace

crumb NOUN 1 *I stood up, brushing crumbs from my trousers.* = **bit**, grain, particle, fragment, shred, speck, sliver, morsel 2 *There is one crumb of comfort – at least we've still got each other.* = **morsel**, scrap, atom, shred, mite, snippet, sliver, soupçon (*French*)

crumble VERB 1 *Under the pressure, the flint crumbled into fragments.* = **disintegrate**, collapse, break up, deteriorate, decay, fall apart, perish, degenerate, decompose, tumble down, moulder, go to pieces **2** *Roughly crumble the cheese into a bowl.* = **crush**, fragment, crumb, pulverize, pound, grind, powder, granulate **3** *Their economy crumbled under the weight of United Nations sanctions.* = **collapse**, break down, deteriorate, decay, fall apart, degenerate, go to pieces, go to rack and ruin

crummy ADJECTIVE = **second-rate**, cheap, inferior, substandard, poor, pants (*informal*), miserable, rotten (*informal*), duff (*Brit. informal*), lousy (*slang*), shoddy, trashy, low-rent (*informal, chiefly U.S.*), for the birds (*informal*), third-rate, contemptible, two-bit (*U.S. & Canad. slang*), crappy (*slang*), rubbishy, poxy (*slang*), dime-a-dozen (*informal*), bodger or bodgie (*Austral. slang*), bush-league (*Austral. & N.Z. informal*), tinhorn (*U.S. slang*), of a sort or of sorts, strictly for the birds (*informal*)

crumple VERB **1** *She crumpled the paper in her hand.* = **crush**, squash, screw up, scrumple **2** *She sat down carefully, so as not to crumple her skirt.* = **crease**, wrinkle, rumple, ruffle, pucker **3** *He crumpled to the floor in agony.* = **collapse**, sink, go down, fall **4** *Sometimes we just crumpled under our grief.* = **break down**, fall, collapse, give way, cave in, go to pieces **5** *She faltered, and then her face crumpled once more.* = **screw up**, pucker

crunch VERB = **chomp**, champ, munch, masticate, chew noisily, grind • **the crunch** *He can rely on my support when the crunch comes.* = **critical point**, test, crisis, emergency, crux, moment of truth, hour of decision

crusade NOUN *a crusade against racism* = **campaign**, drive, movement, cause, push (*informal*) ▶ VERB *a newspaper that has crusaded against drug traffickers* = **campaign**, fight, push, struggle, lobby, agitate, work

crusader NOUN = **campaigner**, champion, advocate, activist, reformer

crush VERB **1** *Their vehicle was crushed by an army tank.* = **squash**, pound, break, smash, squeeze, crumble, crunch, mash, compress, press, crumple, pulverize **2** *I don't want to crush my skirt.* = **crease**, wrinkle, crumple, rumple, scrumple, ruffle **3** *The military operation was the first step in a plan to crush the uprising.* = **overcome**, overwhelm, put down, subdue, overpower, quash, quell, extinguish, stamp out, vanquish (*literary*), conquer **4** *Listen to criticism but don't be crushed by it.* = **demoralize**, depress, devastate, discourage, humble, put down (*slang*), humiliate, squash, flatten (*informal*),

deflate, mortify, psych out (*informal*), dishearten, dispirit, deject **5** *He crushed her in his arms.* = **squeeze**, press, embrace, hug, enfold ▶ NOUN *They got separated from each other in the crush.* = **crowd**, mob, horde, throng, press, pack, mass, jam, herd, huddle, swarm, multitude, rabble

crust NOUN = **layer**, covering, coating, incrustation, film, outside, skin, surface, shell, coat, caking, scab, concretion

crusty ADJECTIVE **1** *crusty french loaves* = **crispy**, well-baked, crisp, well-done, brittle, friable, hard, short **2** *a crusty old colonel with a gruff manner* = **irritable**, short, cross, prickly, touchy, curt, surly, gruff, brusque, cantankerous, tetchy, ratty (*Brit. & N.Z. informal*), testy, chippy (*informal*), short-tempered, peevish, crabby, choleric, splenetic, ill-humoured, captious, snappish or snappy

crux NOUN = **crucial point**, heart, core, essence, nub, decisive point

cry VERB **1** *I hung up the phone and started to cry.* = **weep**, sob, bawl, shed tears, keen, greet (*Scot., archaic*), wail, whine, whimper, whinge (*informal*), blubber, snivel, yowl, howl your eyes out ■ OPPOSITE: laugh **2** *'You're under arrest!' he cried.* = **shout**, call, scream, roar, hail, yell, howl, call out, exclaim, shriek, bellow, whoop, screech, bawl, holler (*informal*), ejaculate, sing out, halloo, vociferate ■ OPPOSITE: whisper **3** *In the street below, a peddler was crying his wares.* = **announce**, hawk, advertise, proclaim, bark (*informal*), trumpet, shout from the rooftops (*informal*) ▶ NOUN **1** *Have a good cry if you want to.* = **weep**, greet (*Scot., archaic*), sob, howl, bawl, blubber, snivel **2** *Her brother gave a cry of recognition.* = **shout**, call, scream, roar, yell, howl, shriek, bellow, whoop, screech, hoot, ejaculation (*literary*), bawl, holler (*informal*), exclamation, squawk, yelp, yoo-hoo **3** = **weeping**, sobbing, blubbering, snivelling • **cry off** *She caught flu and had to cry off at the last minute.* = **back out**, withdraw, quit, cop out (*slang*), beg off, excuse yourself

crypt NOUN = **vault**, tomb, catacomb

cryptic ADJECTIVE = **mysterious**, dark, coded, puzzling, obscure, vague, veiled, ambiguous, enigmatic, perplexing, arcane, equivocal, abstruse, Delphic, oracular

crystallize VERB = **harden**, solidify, coalesce, form crystals

cub NOUN = **young**, baby, offspring, whelp ■ RELATED WORD: *collective noun* litter

cuddle VERB **1** *He cuddled their newborn baby.* = **hug**, embrace, clasp, fondle, cosset **2** *They used to kiss and cuddle in front of everyone.*

c

= **pet** (*informal*), hug, canoodle (*slang*), bill and coo • **cuddle up** *My cat cuddled up to me.* = **snuggle**, nestle

cuddly ADJECTIVE = **soft**, plump, buxom, curvaceous (*informal*), warm

cue NOUN = **signal**, sign, nod, hint, prompt, reminder, suggestion

cuff[1] NOUN • **off the cuff 1** *I didn't mean any offence. It was just an off-the-cuff remark.* = **impromptu**, spontaneous, improvised, offhand, unrehearsed, extempore **2** *He was speaking off the cuff when he made this suggestion.* = **without preparation**, spontaneously, impromptu, offhand, on the spur of the moment, ad lib, extempore, off the top of your head

cuff[2] NOUN *He gave Billy a cuff.* = **smack**, blow, knock, punch, thump, box, belt (*informal*), rap, slap, clout (*informal*), whack, biff (*slang*)

cul-de-sac NOUN = **dead end**, blind alley

cull VERB = **select**, collect, gather, amass, choose, pick, pick up, pluck, glean, cherry-pick

culminate VERB = **end up**, end, close, finish, conclude, wind up, climax, terminate, come to a head, come to a climax, rise to a crescendo

culmination NOUN = **climax**, conclusion, completion, finale, consummation

culpability NOUN = **fault**, blame, responsibility, liability, accountability

culpable ADJECTIVE = **blameworthy**, wrong, guilty, to blame, liable, in the wrong, at fault, sinful, answerable, found wanting, reprehensible ■ **OPPOSITE:** blameless

culprit NOUN = **offender**, criminal, villain, sinner, delinquent, felon, person responsible, guilty party, wrongdoer, miscreant, evildoer, transgressor, perp (*U.S. & Canad. informal*)

cult NOUN **1** *He is believed to have joined a religious cult.* = **sect**, following, body, faction, party, school, church, faith, religion, denomination, clique, hauhau (*N.Z.*) **2** *The programme has become something of a cult among thirty-somethings.* = **craze**, fashion, trend, fad **3** *The cult of personality surrounding pop stars leaves me cold.* = **obsession**, worship, admiration, devotion, reverence, veneration, idolization

cultivate VERB **1** *She cultivated a small garden of her own.* = **farm**, work, plant, tend, till, harvest, plough, bring under cultivation **2** *Try to cultivate a positive mental attitude.* = **develop**, establish, acquire, foster, devote yourself to, pursue **3** *He only cultivates people who may be of use to him.*

= **court**, associate with, seek out, run after, consort with, butter up, dance attendance upon, seek someone's company or friendship, take trouble or pains with **4** *She went out of her way to cultivate his friendship.* = **foster**, further, forward, encourage **5** *My father encouraged me to cultivate my mind.* = **improve**, better, train, discipline, polish, refine, elevate, enrich, civilize

cultivated ADJECTIVE = **refined**, cultured, advanced, polished, educated, sophisticated, accomplished, discriminating, enlightened, discerning, civilized, genteel, well-educated, urbane, erudite, well-bred

cultivation NOUN **1** *environments where aridity makes cultivation of the land difficult* = **farming**, working, gardening, tilling, ploughing, husbandry, agronomy **2** *groups that want a ban on the cultivation of GM crops* = **growing**, planting, production, farming **3** *the cultivation of a positive approach to life and health* = **development**, fostering, pursuit, devotion to **4** *those who devote themselves to the cultivation of the arts* = **promotion**, support, encouragement, nurture, patronage, advancement, advocacy, enhancement, furtherance **5** *He was a man of cultivation and scholarship.* = **refinement**, letters, learning, education, culture, taste, breeding, manners, polish, discrimination, civilization, enlightenment, sophistication, good taste, civility, gentility, discernment

cultural ADJECTIVE **1** *a deep sense of honour which was part of his cultural heritage* = **ethnic**, national, native, folk, racial **2** *This holiday was a rich cultural experience.* = **artistic**, educational, elevating, aesthetic, enriching, broadening, enlightening, developmental, civilizing, edifying, educative

culture NOUN **1** *France's Minister of Culture and Education* = **the arts 2** *people of different cultures* = **civilization**, society, customs, way of life **3** *Social workers say this has created a culture of dependency.* = **lifestyle**, habit, way of life, mores **4** *He was a well-travelled man of culture and breeding.* = **refinement**, education, breeding, polish, enlightenment, accomplishment, sophistication, good taste, erudition, gentility, urbanity

cultured ADJECTIVE = **refined**, advanced, polished, intellectual, educated, sophisticated, accomplished, scholarly, enlightened, knowledgeable, well-informed, genteel, urbane, erudite, highbrow, well-bred, well-read ■ **OPPOSITE:** uneducated

culvert NOUN = **drain**, channel, gutter, conduit, watercourse

cumbersome ADJECTIVE **1** *Although the machine looks cumbersome, it is easy to use.* = **awkward**, heavy, hefty (*informal*), clumsy, bulky, weighty, impractical, inconvenient, burdensome, unmanageable, clunky (*informal*) ■ **OPPOSITE:** easy to use **2** *an old and cumbersome computer system* = **inefficient**, unwieldy, badly organized ■ **OPPOSITE:** efficient

cumulative ADJECTIVE = **collective**, increasing, aggregate, amassed, accruing, snowballing, accumulative

cunning ADJECTIVE **1** *He's a cunning, devious, good-for-nothing so-and-so.* = **crafty**, sly, devious, artful, sharp, subtle, tricky, shrewd, astute, canny, wily, Machiavellian, shifty (*informal*), foxy, guileful ■ **OPPOSITE:** frank **2** *I came up with a cunning plan.* = **ingenious**, subtle, imaginative, shrewd, sly, astute, devious, artful, Machiavellian **3** *The artist's cunning use of light and shadow creates perspective.* = **skilful**, clever, deft, adroit, dexterous ■ **OPPOSITE:** clumsy ▶ NOUN **1** *an example of the cunning of modern art thieves* = **craftiness**, guile, trickery, shrewdness, deviousness, artfulness, slyness, wiliness ■ **OPPOSITE:** candour **2** *He tackled the problem with skill and cunning.* = **skill**, art, ability, craft, subtlety, ingenuity, finesse, artifice, dexterity, cleverness, deftness, astuteness, adroitness ■ **OPPOSITE:** clumsiness

cup NOUN **1** *a set of matching cups and saucers* = **mug**, goblet, chalice, teacup, beaker, demitasse, bowl **2** *First prize is a silver cup and a scroll.* = **trophy**

cupboard NOUN = **cabinet**, closet (*U.S.*), locker, press

curative ADJECTIVE = **restorative**, healing, therapeutic, tonic, corrective, medicinal, remedial, salutary, healthful, health-giving

curb VERB *He must learn to curb that temper of his.* = **restrain**, control, check, contain, restrict, moderate, suppress, inhibit, subdue, hinder, repress, constrain, retard, impede, stem the flow of, keep a tight rein on ▶ NOUN *He called for much stricter curbs on spending.* = **restraint**, control, check, brake, limitation, rein, deterrent, bridle

curdle VERB = **congeal**, clot, thicken, condense, turn sour, solidify, coagulate ■ **OPPOSITE:** dissolve

cure VERB **1** *An operation finally cured his shin injury.* = **make better**, correct, heal, relieve, remedy, mend, rehabilitate, help, ease **2** *I was cured almost overnight.* = **restore to health**, restore, heal **3** *Legs of pork were cured and smoked over the fire.* = **preserve**, smoke, dry, salt, pickle, kipper ▶ NOUN *There is still no cure for the common cold.* = **remedy**, treatment, medicine, healing, antidote, corrective, panacea, restorative, nostrum

cure-all NOUN = **panacea**, elixir, nostrum, elixir vitae (*Latin*)

curio NOUN = **collector's item**, antique, trinket, knick-knack, bibelot

curiosity NOUN **1** *Mr Lim was a constant source of curiosity to his neighbours.* = **inquisitiveness**, interest, prying, snooping (*informal*), nosiness (*informal*), infomania **2** *The company is a curiosity in the world of publishing.* = **oddity**, wonder, sight, phenomenon, spectacle, freak, marvel, novelty, rarity **3** *The mantelpieces and windowsills are adorned with curiosities.* = **collector's item**, trinket, curio, knick-knack, objet d'art (*French*), bibelot

curious ADJECTIVE **1** *He was intensely curious about the world around him.* = **inquisitive**, interested, questioning, searching, inquiring, peering, puzzled, peeping, meddling, prying, snoopy (*informal*), nosy (*informal*) ■ **OPPOSITE:** uninterested **2** *A lot of curious things have happened here in the past few weeks.* = **strange**, unusual, bizarre, odd, novel, wonderful, rare, unique, extraordinary, puzzling, unexpected, exotic, mysterious, marvellous, peculiar, queer (*informal*), rum (*Brit. slang*), singular, unconventional, quaint, unorthodox ■ **OPPOSITE:** ordinary

curl NOUN **1** *a little girl with blonde curls* = **ringlet**, lock **2** *A thick curl of smoke rose from the rusty stove.* = **twist**, spiral, coil, kink, whorl, curlicue ▶ VERB **1** *She had curled her hair for the event.* = **crimp**, wave, perm, frizz **2** *Smoke was curling up the chimney.* = **twirl**, turn, bend, twist, curve, loop, spiral, coil, meander, writhe, corkscrew, wreathe **3** *She curled her fingers round his wrist.* = **wind**, entwine, twine

curly ADJECTIVE = **wavy**, waved, curled, curling, fuzzy, kinky, permed, corkscrew, crimped, frizzy

currency NOUN **1** *The country's central bank has introduced a new currency.* = **money**, coinage, legal tender, medium of exchange, bills, notes, coins **2** *His theory has gained wide currency in America.* = **acceptance**, exposure, popularity, circulation, vogue, prevalence

current NOUN **1** *The swimmers were swept away by the strong current.* = **flow**, course, undertow, jet, stream, tide, progression, river, tideway **2** *I felt a current of cool air blowing in my face.* = **draught**, flow, breeze,

C

puff **3** *A strong current of nationalism is running through the country.* = **mood**, feeling, spirit, atmosphere, trend, tendency, drift, inclination, vibe (*slang*), undercurrent
▶ ADJECTIVE **1** *current trends in the music scene* = **present**, fashionable, ongoing, up-to-date, in, now (*informal*), happening (*informal*), contemporary, in the news, sexy (*informal*), trendy (*Brit. informal*), topical, present-day, in fashion, on trend, in vogue, up-to-the-minute, live (*data*) ■ OPPOSITE: out-of-date **2** *the prevailing tide of current opinion* = **prevalent**, general, common, accepted, popular, widespread, in the air, prevailing, circulating, going around, customary, rife, in circulation

curse VERB **1** *He cursed continuously at passers-by.* = **swear**, cuss (*informal*), blaspheme, use bad language, turn the air blue (*informal*), be foul-mouthed, take the Lord's name in vain **2** *He cursed her for having been so careless.* = **abuse**, damn, scold, swear at, revile, vilify, fulminate, execrate, vituperate, imprecate **3** *I began to think that I was cursed.* = **put a curse on**, damn, doom, jinx, excommunicate, execrate, put a jinx on, accurse, imprecate, anathematize **4** *I am cursed with a bad memory.* = **afflict**, trouble, burden ▶ NOUN **1** *She shot him an angry look and a curse.* = **oath**, obscenity, blasphemy, expletive, profanity, imprecation, swearword **2** *He believes someone has put a curse on him.* = **malediction**, jinx, anathema, hoodoo (*informal*), evil eye, excommunication, imprecation, execration **3** *Small acts of kindness can lift the curse of loneliness.* = **affliction**, evil, plague (*informal*), scourge, cross, trouble, disaster, burden, ordeal, torment, hardship, misfortune, calamity, tribulation, bane, vexation

cursed ADJECTIVE = **under a curse**, damned, doomed, jinxed, bedevilled, fey (*Scot.*), star-crossed, accursed, ill-fated

cursory ADJECTIVE = **brief**, passing, rapid, casual, summary, slight, hurried, careless, superficial, hasty, perfunctory, desultory, offhand, slapdash

curt ADJECTIVE = **terse**, short, brief, sharp, summary, blunt, rude, tart, abrupt, gruff, brusque, offhand, ungracious, uncivil, unceremonious, snappish

curtail VERB = **reduce**, cut, diminish, decrease, dock, cut back, shorten, lessen, cut short, pare down, retrench

curtain NOUN *Her bedroom curtains were drawn.* = **hanging**, drape (*chiefly U.S.*), portière • **curtain something off** *The bed was a massive four-poster, curtained off by*

ragged draperies. = **conceal**, screen, hide, veil, drape, shroud, shut off

curvaceous ADJECTIVE = **shapely**, voluptuous, curvy, busty, well-rounded, buxom, full-figured, bosomy, Rubenesque

curvature NOUN = **curving**, bend, curve, arching, arc

curve NOUN *a curve in the road* = **bend**, turn, loop, arc, curvature, camber ▶ VERB *The track curved away below him.* = **bend**, turn, wind, twist, bow, arch, snake, arc, coil, swerve ■ RELATED WORD: *adjective* sinuous

curved ADJECTIVE = **bent**, rounded, sweeping, twisted, bowed, arched, arced, humped, serpentine, sinuous, twisty

cushion NOUN *Her leg was propped up on two cushions.* = **pillow**, pad, bolster, headrest, beanbag, scatter cushion, hassock ▶ VERB **1** *The suspension is designed to cushion passengers from the effects of riding over rough roads.* = **protect**, support, bolster, cradle, buttress **2** *He spoke gently, trying to cushion the blow of rejection.* = **soften**, dampen, muffle, mitigate, deaden, suppress, stifle

cushy ADJECTIVE = **easy**, soft (*informal*), comfortable, undemanding, jammy (*Brit. slang*)

custodian NOUN = **keeper**, guardian, superintendent (*U.S.*), warden, caretaker, curator, protector, warder, watchman, overseer

custody NOUN **1** *I'm taking him to court to get custody of the children.* = **care**, charge, protection, supervision, preservation, auspices, aegis, tutelage (*formal*), guardianship, safekeeping, keeping, trusteeship, custodianship **2** *Three people appeared in court and two of them were remanded in custody.* = **imprisonment**, detention, confinement, incarceration

custom NOUN **1** *The custom of lighting the Olympic flame goes back centuries.* = **tradition**, practice, convention, ritual, form, policy, rule, style, fashion, usage, formality, etiquette, observance, praxis, unwritten law, kaupapa (*N.Z.*) **2** *It was his custom to approach every problem cautiously.* = **habit**, way, practice, manner, procedure, routine, mode, wont **3** *Providing discounts is not the only way to win custom.* = **customers**, business, trade, patronage

customarily ADVERB = **usually**, generally, commonly, regularly, normally, traditionally, ordinarily, habitually, in the ordinary way, as a rule

customary ADJECTIVE **1** *It is customary to offer a drink or a snack to guests.* = **usual**, general, common, accepted, established, traditional, normal, ordinary, familiar, acknowledged, conventional, routine, everyday ■ **OPPOSITE:** unusual **2** *She took her customary seat behind her desk.* = **accustomed**, regular, usual, habitual, wonted

customer NOUN = **client**, consumer, regular (*informal*), buyer, patron, shopper, purchaser, habitué

customs PLURAL NOUN = **import charges**, tax, duty, toll, tariff

cut VERB **1** *Thieves cut a hole in the fence.* = **slit**, saw, score, nick, slice, slash, pierce, hack, penetrate, notch **2** *Cut the tomatoes into small pieces.* = **chop**, split, divide, slice, segment, dissect, cleave, part **3** *Mr Long was cutting himself a piece of the cake.* = **carve**, slice **4** *I cut the rope with scissors.* = **sever**, cut in two, sunder **5** *Geometric motifs are cut into the stone walls.* = **shape**, carve, engrave, chisel, form, score, fashion, chip, sculpture, whittle, sculpt, inscribe, hew (*old-fashioned*) **6** *I cut myself shaving.* = **slash**, nick, wound, lance, gash, lacerate, incise **7** *The previous tenants hadn't even cut the grass.* = **clip**, mow, trim, dock, prune, snip, pare, lop **8** *She cut his ragged hair and shaved off his beard.* = **trim**, shave, hack, snip **9** *The first priority is to cut costs.* = **reduce**, lower, slim (down), diminish, slash, decrease, cut back, rationalize, ease up on, downsize, kennet (*Austral. slang*), jeff (*Austral. slang*) ■ **OPPOSITE:** increase **10** *He has cut the play judiciously.* = **abridge**, edit, shorten, curtail, condense, abbreviate, précis ■ **OPPOSITE:** extend **11** = **delete**, take out, expurgate **12** *The personal criticism has cut him deeply.* = **hurt**, wound, upset, sting, grieve, pain, hurt someone's feelings **13** *She just cut me in the street.* = **ignore**, avoid, slight, blank (*slang*), snub, spurn, freeze (someone) out (*informal*), cold-shoulder, turn your back on, send to Coventry, look straight through (someone) ■ **OPPOSITE:** greet **14** *a straight line that cuts the vertical axis* = **cross**, interrupt, intersect, bisect ► NOUN **1** *The operation involves making several cuts in the cornea.* = **incision**, nick, rent, stroke, rip, slash, groove, slit, snip **2** *He had sustained a cut on his left eyebrow.* = **gash**, nick, wound, slash, graze, laceration **3** *The economy needs an immediate two per cent cut in interest rates.* = **reduction**, fall, lowering, slash, decrease, cutback, diminution **4** *The lawyers, of course, will take their cut of the profits.* = **share**, piece, slice, percentage, portion, kickback (*chiefly U.S.*), rake-off (*slang*) **5** *The cut of her clothes made her look slimmer and taller.* = **style**, look, form, fashion, shape, mode, configuration • **a cut above something** or **someone** *He's a cut above the usual boys she goes out with.* = **superior to**, better than, more efficient than, more reliable than, streets ahead of, more useful than, more capable than, more competent than • **be cut out for something** *He wasn't cut out for politics.* = **be suited for**, be designed for, be fitted for, be suitable for, be adapted for, be equipped for, be adequate for, be eligible for, be competent for, be qualified for • **cut in** *'That's not true,' the duchess cut in suddenly.* = **interrupt**, break in, butt in, interpose • **cut someone down to size** *It's high time someone cut that arrogant little creep down to size.* = **make (someone) look small**, humble, humiliate, bring (someone) low, take (someone) down a peg (*informal*), abash, crush, put (someone) in their place, take the wind out of (someone's) sails • **cut someone off 1** *The exiles had been cut off from all contact with their homeland.* = **separate**, isolate, sever, keep apart **2** *'But sir, I'm under orders to -' Clark cut him off. 'Don't argue with me.'* = **interrupt**, stop, break in, butt in, interpose **3** *His father cut him off without a penny.* = **disinherit**, renounce, disown • **cut someone out** *He felt that he was being cut out of the decision-making process completely.* = **exclude**, eliminate, oust, displace, supersede, supplant • **cut someone up** *They threatened to cut me up and leave me to die.* = **slash**, injure, wound, knife, lacerate • **cut something back 1** *The government has cut back on defence spending.* = **reduce**, check, lower, slash, decrease, curb, lessen, economize, downsize, retrench, draw or pull in your horns (*informal*), kennet (*Austral. slang*), jeff (*Austral. slang*) **2** *Cut back the root of the bulb to within half an inch of the base.* = **trim**, prune, shorten • **cut something down 1** *Car owners were asked to cut down their travel.* = **reduce**, moderate, decrease, lessen, lower **2** *A vandal with a chainsaw cut down several trees in the park.* = **fell**, level, hew, lop • **cut something off** *The rebels have cut off the electricity supply from the capital.* = **discontinue**, disconnect, suspend, halt, obstruct, bring to an end • **cut something out 1** *All the violent scenes had been cut out of the film.* = **remove**, extract, censor, delete, edit out **2** *You can cut that behaviour out right now.* = **stop**, cease, refrain from, pack in, kick (*informal*), give up, sever • **be cut up** *Terry was very cut up by Jim's death.* = **be upset**, be disturbed, be distressed, be stricken, be agitated, be heartbroken, be desolated, be dejected, be wretched • **cut something up** *Cut the sausages up and cook them over a medium heat.*

= **chop**, divide, slice, carve, dice, mince

cutback NOUN = **reduction**, cut, retrenchment, economy, decrease, lessening

cute ADJECTIVE = **appealing**, sweet, attractive, engaging, charming, delightful, lovable, winsome, winning, cutesy (*informal*)

cut-price ADJECTIVE = **cheap**, sale, reduced, bargain, cut-rate (*chiefly U.S.*), cheapo (*informal*)

cut-throat ADJECTIVE **1** *the cut-throat world of international finance* = **competitive**, fierce, ruthless, relentless, unprincipled, dog-eat-dog **2** *Captain Hook and his band of cut-throat pirates* = **murderous**, violent, bloody, cruel, savage, ferocious, bloodthirsty, barbarous, homicidal, thuggish, death-dealing

cutting ADJECTIVE **1** *People make cutting remarks to help themselves feel superior to others.* = **hurtful**, wounding, severe, acid, bitter, malicious, scathing, acrimonious, barbed, sarcastic, sardonic, caustic, vitriolic, trenchant, pointed ■ OPPOSITE: kind **2** *a cutting wind* = **piercing**, biting, sharp, keen, bitter, raw, chilling, stinging, penetrating, numbing ■ OPPOSITE: pleasant

cycle NOUN = **series of events**, round, circle, revolution, rotation

cyclone NOUN = **typhoon**, hurricane, tornado, whirlwind, tempest (*literary*), twister (*U.S. informal*), storm

cynic NOUN = **sceptic**, doubter, pessimist, misanthrope, misanthropist, scoffer

cynical ADJECTIVE **1** *He has a very cynical view of the world.* = **sceptical**, mocking, ironic, sneering, pessimistic, scoffing, contemptuous, sarcastic, sardonic, scornful, distrustful, derisive, misanthropic ■ OPPOSITE: trusting **2** *My experiences have made me cynical about relationships.* = **unbelieving**, sceptical, disillusioned, pessimistic, disbelieving, mistrustful ■ OPPOSITE: optimistic

cynicism NOUN **1** *I found Ben's cynicism wearing at times.* = **scepticism**, pessimism, sarcasm, misanthropy, sardonicism **2** *This talk betrays a certain cynicism about free trade.* = **disbelief**, doubt, scepticism, mistrust

cyst NOUN = **sac**, growth, blister, wen, vesicle

Dd

dab VERB **1** *dabbing her eyes with a tissue* = **pat**, touch, tap, wipe, blot, swab **2** *She dabbed iodine on the cuts.* = **apply**, daub, stipple ▸ NOUN **1** *a dab of glue* = **spot** (*Brit.*), bit, drop, pat, fleck, smudge, speck, dollop (*informal*), smidgen *or* smidgin (*informal, chiefly U.S. & Canad.*) **2** *just one dab of the right fragrance* = **touch**, stroke, flick, smudge

dabble VERB (*usually with* **in** *or* **with**) = **play (at** *or* **with)**, potter, tinker (with), trifle (with), dip into, dally (with)

daft (*chiefly Brit. informal*) ADJECTIVE *I wasn't so daft as to believe him.* = **stupid**, crazy (*informal*), silly, foolish, giddy, goofy, idiotic, inane, loopy (*informal*), witless, dopey (*informal*), scatty (*Brit. informal*), asinine • **daft about** *He's just daft about her.* = **enthusiastic about**, mad about, crazy about (*informal*), doting on, besotted with, sweet on, nuts about (*slang*), potty about (*Brit. informal*), infatuated by, dotty about (*slang, chiefly Brit.*), nutty about (*informal*)

dag NOUN *He does all these great impersonations – he's such a dag.* = **joker**, comic, wag, wit, comedian, clown, kidder (*informal*), jester, humorist, prankster • **rattle your dags** *You'd better rattle your dags and get on with this before the boss gets back.* = **hurry up**, get a move on, step on it (*informal*), get your skates on (*informal*), make haste

dagga (*S. African*) NOUN = **cannabis**, marijuana, pot (*slang*), dope (*slang*), hash (*slang*), black (*slang*), blow (*slang*), smoke (*informal*), stuff (*slang*), leaf (*slang*), tea (*U.S. slang*), grass (*slang*), chronic (*U.S. slang*), weed (*slang*), hemp, gage (*U.S., obsolete slang*), hashish, mary jane (*U.S. slang*), ganja, bhang, kif, wacky baccy (*slang*), sinsemilla, charas

dagger NOUN *The collection includes a jewelled dagger from Cambodia.* = **knife**, bayonet, dirk, stiletto, poniard, skean • **at daggers drawn** *She and her mother were at daggers drawn.* = **on bad terms**, at odds, at war, at loggerheads, up in arms, at enmity • **look daggers at someone** *The girls looked daggers at me.* = **glare**, frown, scowl, glower, look black, lour *or* lower

daggy ADJECTIVE **1** = **untidy**, unkempt, dishevelled, tousled, disordered, messy, ruffled, scruffy, rumpled, bedraggled, ratty (*informal*), straggly, windblown, disarranged, mussed up (*informal*) **2** = **eccentric**, odd, strange, bizarre, weird, peculiar, abnormal, queer (*informal*), irregular, uncommon, quirky, singular, unconventional, idiosyncratic, off-the-wall (*slang*), outlandish, whimsical, rum (*Brit. slang*), capricious, anomalous, freakish, aberrant, outré

daily ADJECTIVE **1** *the company's daily turnover* = **everyday**, regular, circadian (*Biology*), diurnal, quotidian **2** *factors which deeply influence daily life* = **day-to-day**, common, ordinary, routine, everyday, commonplace, quotidian ▸ ADVERB *The shop is open daily.* = **every day**, day by day, day after day, once a day, per diem

dainty ADJECTIVE **1** *a pair of the daintiest little kid slippers* = **delicate**, pretty, charming, fine, elegant, neat, exquisite, graceful, petite ■ OPPOSITE: clumsy **2** *a dainty morsel* = **delectable**, choice, delicious, tender, tasty, savoury, palatable, toothsome **3** *They cater for a range of tastes, from the dainty to the extravagant.* = **particular**, nice, refined, fussy, scrupulous, fastidious, choosy (*informal*), picky (*informal*), finicky, finical

dais NOUN = **platform**, stage, podium, rostrum, estrade (*rare*)

dale NOUN = **valley**, glen, vale, dell, dingle, strath (*Scot.*), coomb

dalliance NOUN = **dabbling**, playing, toying, trifling

dally VERB *He did not dally long over his meal.* = **waste time**, delay, fool (about *or* around), linger, hang about, loiter, while away, dawdle, fritter away, procrastinate, tarry, dilly-dally (*informal*), drag your feet *or* heels ■ OPPOSITE: hurry (up) • **dally with someone** *He undermined his managerial position by dallying with junior associates.* = **flirt with**, tease, lead on, toy with, play around with, fool (about *or* around) with, trifle with, play fast and loose with (*informal*), frivol with (*informal*)

dam NOUN *They went ahead with plans to build a dam across the river.* = **barrier**, wall, barrage, obstruction, embankment, hindrance ▸ VERB *The reservoir was formed by damming the River Blith.* = **block up**, block, hold in, restrict, check, confine, choke, hold back, barricade, obstruct

damage NOUN **1** *There have been many reports of minor damage to buildings.* = **destruction**, harm, loss, injury, suffering, hurt, ruin, crushing, wrecking, shattering, devastation, detriment, mutilation, impairment, annihilation, ruination ■ **OPPOSITE:** improvement **2** *The administration wants to limit the damage done to international relations.* = **harm**, loss, injury, abuse, ill, impairment **3** *What's the damage for these tickets?* = **cost**, price, charge, rate, bill, figure, amount, total, payment, expense, outlay ▶ VERB *He damaged the car with a baseball bat.* = **spoil**, hurt, injure, smash, harm, ruin, crush, devastate, mar, wreck, shatter, weaken, gut, demolish, undo, trash (*slang*), total (*slang*), impair, ravage, mutilate, annihilate, incapacitate, raze, deface, play (merry) hell with (*informal*) ■ **OPPOSITE:** fix ▶ PLURAL NOUN *He was vindicated in court and damages were awarded.* = **compensation**, fine, payment, satisfaction, amends, reparation, indemnity, restitution, reimbursement, atonement, recompense, indemnification, meed (*archaic*), requital

damaging ADJECTIVE = **harmful**, detrimental, hurtful, ruinous, toxic, prejudicial, deleterious (*formal*), injurious, disadvantageous ■ **OPPOSITE:** helpful

dame NOUN *(with cap.) a Dame of the British Empire* = **lady**, baroness, dowager, grande dame (*French*), noblewoman, peeress

damn VERB **1** *You can't damn him for his beliefs.* = **criticize**, condemn, blast, pan (*informal*), slam (*slang*), denounce, put down, slate (*informal*), censure, castigate, tear into (*informal*), diss (*slang*), inveigh against, lambast(e), excoriate, denunciate **2** *damning and cursing* = **curse**, abuse, swear, revile, blaspheme, execrate, imprecate, anathematize ■ **OPPOSITES:** bless, adore, magnify (*archaic*), glorify, exalt, pay homage to **3** *damned to a life of poverty* = **sentence**, condemn, doom ■ **OPPOSITE:** praise • **not give a damn** *Frankly, my dear, I don't give a damn.* = **not care**, not mind, be indifferent, not give a hoot, not care a jot, not give two hoots, not care a whit, not care a brass farthing, not give a monkey's (*slang*)

damnation NOUN = **condemnation**, damning, sending to hell, consigning to perdition

damned ADJECTIVE = **infernal**, accursed, detestable, revolting, infamous, confounded, despicable, abhorred, hateful, loathsome, abominable, freaking (*slang, chiefly U.S.*)

damning ADJECTIVE = **incriminating**, implicating, condemnatory, dooming, accusatorial, damnatory, implicative

damp ADJECTIVE *She wiped the table with a damp cloth.* = **moist**, wet, dripping, soggy, humid, sodden, dank, sopping, clammy, dewy, muggy, drizzly, vaporous ■ **OPPOSITE:** dry ▶ NOUN *There was damp everywhere in the house.* = **moisture**, liquid, humidity, drizzle, dew, dampness, wetness, dankness, clamminess, mugginess ■ **OPPOSITE:** dryness ▶ VERB *She damped a hand towel and laid it across her head.* = **moisten**, wet, soak, dampen, lick, moisturize, humidify • **damp something down** *He tried to damp down his panic.* = **curb**, reduce, check, cool, moderate, dash, chill, dull, diminish, discourage, restrain, inhibit, stifle, allay, deaden, pour cold water on

dampen VERB **1** *Nothing seemed to dampen his enthusiasm.* = **reduce**, check, moderate, dash, dull, restrain, deter, stifle, lessen, smother, muffle, deaden **2** *She took the time to dampen a cloth and wash her face.* = **moisten**, wet, spray, make damp, bedew, besprinkle

damper NOUN = **discouragement**, cloud, chill, curb, restraint, gloom, cold water (*informal*), pall

dampness NOUN = **moistness**, damp, moisture, humidity, wetness, sogginess, dankness, clamminess, mugginess ■ **OPPOSITE:** dryness

dance VERB **1** *They like to dance to the music on the radio.* = **prance**, rock, trip, swing, spin, hop, skip, sway, whirl, caper, jig, frolic, cavort, gambol, bob up and down, cut a rug (*informal*) **2** *He danced off down the road.* = **caper**, trip, spring, jump, bound, leap, bounce, hop, skip, romp, frolic, cavort, gambol ▶ NOUN *She often went to dances and parties in the village.* = **ball**, social, hop (*informal*), disco, knees-up (*Brit. informal*), discotheque, dancing party, B and S (*Austral. informal*)

dancer NOUN = **ballerina**, hoofer (*slang*), Terpsichorean

dandy NOUN *a handsome young dandy* = **fop**, beau, swell (*informal*), blood (*rare*), buck (*archaic*), blade (*archaic*), peacock, dude (*U.S. & Canad. informal*), toff (*Brit. slang*), macaroni (*obsolete*), man about town, popinjay, coxcomb ▶ ADJECTIVE *Everything's fine and dandy.* = **excellent**, great (*informal*), fine, capital (*old-fashioned*), splendid, first-rate

danger NOUN **1** *Your life is in danger.* = **jeopardy**, vulnerability, insecurity, precariousness, endangerment **2** *These roads are a danger to cyclists.* = **hazard**, risk, threat, menace, peril, pitfall

dangerous ADJECTIVE = **perilous**, threatening, risky, hazardous, exposed, alarming, vulnerable, nasty, ugly, menacing, insecure, hairy (*slang*), unsafe,

precarious, treacherous, breakneck, parlous (*archaic*), fraught with danger, chancy (*informal*), unchancy (*Scot.*)
■ **OPPOSITE:** safe

dangerously ADVERB *She rushed downstairs dangerously fast.* = **perilously**, alarmingly, carelessly, precariously, recklessly, daringly, riskily, harmfully, hazardously, unsafely, unsecurely

dangle VERB **1** *A gold bracelet dangled from her left wrist.* = **hang**, swing, trail, sway, flap, hang down, depend **2** *They dangled rich rewards before me.* = **offer**, flourish, brandish, flaunt, tempt someone with, lure someone with, entice someone with, tantalize someone with

dangling ADJECTIVE = **hanging**, swinging, loose, trailing, swaying, disconnected, drooping, unconnected

dank ADJECTIVE = **damp**, dripping, moist, soggy, clammy, dewy

dapper ADJECTIVE (*of a man*) = **neat**, nice, smart, trim, stylish, spruce, dainty, natty (*informal*), well-groomed, well turned out, trig (*archaic, dialect*), soigné ■ **OPPOSITE:** untidy

dappled ADJECTIVE = **mottled**, spotted, speckled, pied, flecked, variegated, checkered, freckled, stippled, piebald, brindled

dare VERB **1** *I didn't dare to tell my uncle what had happened.* = **risk doing**, venture, presume, make bold (*archaic*), hazard doing, brave doing **2** *She dared me to ask him out.* = **challenge**, provoke, defy, taunt, goad, throw down the gauntlet

daredevil NOUN *a tragic ending for a daredevil whose luck ran out* = **adventurer**, show-off (*informal*), madcap, desperado, exhibitionist, stuntman *or* woman *or* person, hot dog (*chiefly U.S.*), adrenalin junky (*slang*) ▶ ADJECTIVE *He gets his kicks from daredevil car-racing.* = **daring**, bold, adventurous, reckless, audacious, madcap, death-defying

daring ADJECTIVE *a daring rescue attempt* = **brave**, bold, adventurous, rash, have-a-go (*informal*), reckless, fearless, audacious, intrepid, impulsive, valiant, plucky, game (*informal*), daredevil, venturesome, (as) game as Ned Kelly (*Austral. slang*) ■ **OPPOSITE:** timid ▶ NOUN *His daring may have cost him his life.* = **bravery**, nerve (*informal*), courage, face (*informal*), spirit, bottle (*Brit. slang*), guts (*informal*), pluck, grit, audacity, boldness, temerity, derring-do (*archaic*), spunk (*informal*), fearlessness, rashness, intrepidity
■ **OPPOSITE:** timidity

dark ADJECTIVE **1** *It was a dark and stormy night.* = **dim**, murky, shady, shadowy, grey, cloudy, dingy, overcast, dusky, unlit, pitch-black, indistinct, poorly lit, sunless, tenebrous, darksome (*literary*), pitchy, unilluminated **2** *magicians who harnessed dark powers* = **evil**, foul, horrible, sinister, infamous, vile, satanic, wicked, atrocious, sinful, hellish (*informal*), infernal (*informal*), nefarious, damnable (*informal*) **3** *the dark recesses of the mind* = **secret**, deep, hidden, mysterious, concealed, obscure, mystic, enigmatic, puzzling, occult, arcane, cryptic, abstruse, recondite, Delphic **4** *His endless chatter kept me from thinking dark thoughts.* = **gloomy**, sad, grim, miserable, low, bleak, moody, dismal, pessimistic, melancholy, sombre, morbid, glum, mournful, morose, joyless, doleful, cheerless ■ **OPPOSITE:** cheerful **5** *He shot her a dark glance.* = **angry**, threatening, forbidding, frowning, ominous, dour, scowling, sullen, glum, glowering, sulky ▶ NOUN **1** *I've always been afraid of the dark.* = **darkness**, shadows, gloom, dusk (*poetic*), obscurity, murk, dimness, semi-darkness, murkiness **2** *after dark* = **night**, twilight, evening, evo (*Austral. slang*), dusk, night-time, nightfall

darken VERB **1** *A storm darkened the sky.* = **cloud**, shadow, shade, obscure, eclipse, dim, deepen, overshadow, blacken, becloud ■ **OPPOSITE:** brighten **2** *She darkened her eyebrows with mascara.* = **make dark**, shade, blacken, make darker, deepen **3** *His face suddenly darkened.* = **become gloomy**, blacken, become angry, look black, go crook (*Austral. & N.Z. slang*), grow troubled ■ **OPPOSITE:** become cheerful **4** *Nothing was going to darken his mood today.* = **sadden**, upset, cloud, blacken, cast a pall over, cast a gloom upon

darkness NOUN = **dark**, shadows, shade, gloom, obscurity, blackness, murk, dimness, murkiness, duskiness, shadiness

darling NOUN **1** *Hello, darling!* = **beloved**, love, dear, dearest, angel (*informal*), treasure, precious, loved one, sweetheart, sweetie, truelove, dear one **2** *He was the darling of the family.* = **favourite**, pet, spoilt child, apple of your eye, blue-eyed boy, fair-haired boy (*U.S.*) ▶ ADJECTIVE **1** *my darling baby boy* = **beloved**, dear, dearest, sweet (*archaic*), treasured, precious, adored, cherished, revered **2** *a perfectly darling little house* = **adorable**, sweet, attractive, lovely, charming, cute, enchanting, captivating

darn VERB *His aunt darned his old socks.* = **mend**, repair, patch, stitch, sew up, cobble up ▶ NOUN *blue woollen stockings with untidy darns* = **mend**, patch, reinforcement, invisible repair

dart VERB *She darted away through the trees.* = **dash**, run, race, shoot, fly, speed, spring, tear, rush, bound, flash, hurry, sprint, bolt, hasten, whizz, haste, flit, scoot

dash VERB **1** *Suddenly she dashed out into the garden.* = **rush**, run, race, shoot, fly, career, speed, spring, tear, bound, hurry, barrel (along) (*informal, chiefly U.S. & Canad.*), sprint, bolt, dart, hasten, scurry, haste, stampede, burn rubber (*informal*), make haste, hotfoot ■ **OPPOSITE:** dawdle **2** *She dashed the doll against the stone wall.* = **throw**, cast, pitch, slam, toss, hurl, fling, chuck (*informal*), propel, project, sling (*informal*), lob (*informal*) **3** *The waves dashed against the side of the ship.* = **crash**, break, smash, shatter, shiver, splinter **4** *They had their hopes raised and then dashed.* = **disappoint**, ruin, frustrate, spoil, foil, undo, thwart, dampen, confound, crool or cruel (*Austral. slang*) ▶ NOUN **1** *a 160-mile dash to hospital* = **rush**, run, race, sprint, bolt, dart, spurt, sortie **2** *Add a dash of balsamic vinegar.* = **drop**, little, bit, shot (*informal*), touch, spot (*Brit.*), suggestion, trace, hint, pinch, sprinkling, tot, trickle, nip, tinge, soupçon (*French*) ■ **OPPOSITE:** lot **3** *He played with great fire and dash.* = **style**, spirit, flair (*informal*), flourish, vigour, verve, panache, élan, brio, vivacity

dashing ADJECTIVE = **stylish**, smart, elegant, dazzling, flamboyant, sporty, swish (*informal, chiefly Brit.*), urbane, jaunty, dapper, showy

dastardly ADJECTIVE = **despicable**, mean, low, base, sneaking, cowardly, craven, vile, abject, sneaky, contemptible, underhand, weak-kneed (*informal*), faint-hearted, spiritless, recreant (*archaic*), caitiff (*archaic*), niddering (*archaic*)

data NOUN **1** = **details**, facts, figures, materials, documents, intelligence, statistics, gen (*Brit. informal*), dope (*informal*), info (*informal*) **2** = **information**, input

> **USAGE** From a historical point of view only, the word *data* is a plural. In fact, in many cases it is not clear from context if it is being used as a singular or plural, so there is no issue: *when next needed the data can be accessed very quickly.* When it is necessary to specify, the preferred usage nowadays in general language is to treat it as singular, as in: *this data is useful to the government in the planning of housing services.* There are rather more examples

> in the Bank of English of *these data* than *this data*, with a marked preference for the plural in academic and scientific writing. As regards *data is* versus *data are*, the preference for the plural form overall is even more marked in that kind of writing. When speaking, however, it is best to opt for treating the word as singular, except in precise scientific contexts. The singular form *datum* is comparatively rare in the sense of a single item of data.

date NOUN **1** *An inquest will be held at a later date.* = **time**, stage, period **2** *We made a date to view the exhibition.* = **appointment**, meeting, meet-up, arrangement, commitment, engagement, rendezvous, tryst, assignation **3** *I was his date for the dance.* = **partner**, escort, friend, steady (*informal*), plus-one (*informal*) ▶ VERB **1** *It is difficult to date the relic.* = **put a date on**, determine the date of, assign a date to, fix the period of **2** *It always looks smart and will never date.* = **become dated**, become old-fashioned, obsolesce • **date from** or **date back to** (*a time or date*) *The palace dates back to the 16th century.* = **come from**, belong to, originate in, exist from, bear a date of • **to date** *This is her finest novel to date.* = **up to now**, yet, so far, until now, now, as yet, thus far, up to this point, up to the present

dated ADJECTIVE = **old-fashioned**, outdated, out of date, obsolete, archaic, unfashionable, antiquated, outmoded, passé, out, old hat, untrendy (*Brit. informal*), démodé (*French*), out of the ark (*informal*) ■ **OPPOSITE:** modern

daub VERB *They daubed his home with slogans.* = **smear**, dirty, splatter, stain, spatter, sully, deface, smirch, begrime, besmear, bedaub, paint, coat, stain, plaster, slap on (*informal*) ▶ NOUN *Apply an extra daub of colour.* = **smear**, spot, stain, blot, blotch, splodge, splotch, smirch

daughter NOUN **1** = **female child**, girl **2** = **descendant**, girl ■ **RELATED WORD:** *adjective* filial

daunt VERB = **discourage**, alarm, shake, frighten, scare, terrify, cow, intimidate, deter, dismay, put off, subdue, overawe, frighten off, dishearten, dispirit ■ **OPPOSITE:** reassure

daunted ADJECTIVE = **intimidated**, alarmed, shaken, frightened, overcome, cowed, discouraged, deterred, dismayed, put off, disillusioned, unnerved, demoralized, dispirited, downcast

daunting ADJECTIVE = **intimidating**, alarming, frightening, discouraging, awesome, unnerving, disconcerting, demoralizing, off-putting (*Brit. informal*), disheartening ■ **OPPOSITE:** reassuring

dawdle VERB **1** *They dawdled arm in arm past the shopfronts.* = **waste time**, potter, trail, lag, idle, loaf, hang about, dally, loiter, dilly-dally (*informal*), drag your feet *or* heels ■ **OPPOSITE:** hurry **2** *I dawdled over a beer.* = **linger**, idle, dally, take your time, procrastinate, drag your feet *or* heels

dawn NOUN **1** *She woke at dawn.* = **daybreak**, morning, sunrise, dawning, daylight, aurora (*poetic*), crack of dawn, sunup, cockcrow, dayspring (*poetic*) **2** *the dawn of the radio age* = **beginning**, start, birth, rise, origin, dawning, unfolding, emergence, outset, onset, advent, genesis, inception ▶ VERB **1** *A new era seemed about to dawn.* = **begin**, start, open, rise, develop, emerge, unfold, originate **2** *The next day dawned.* = **grow light**, break, brighten, lighten • **dawn on** *or* **upon someone** *Then the chilling truth dawned on me.* = **hit**, strike, occur to, register (*informal*), become apparent, come to mind, cross your mind, come into your head, flash across your mind

day NOUN **1** *The conference is on for three days.* = **twenty-four hours**, working day **2** *They sleep during the day.* = **daytime**, daylight, daylight hours **3** *What day are you leaving?* = **date**, particular day **4** *In my day we treated our elders with more respect.* = **time**, age, era, prime, period, generation, heyday, epoch • **call it a day** *Faced with such opposition, he had no choice but to call it a day.* = **stop**, finish, cease, pack up (*informal*), leave off, knock off (*informal*), desist, pack it in (*slang*), shut up shop, jack it in, chuck it in (*informal*), give up *or* over • **day after day** *In this job I just do the same thing day after day.* = **continually**, regularly, relentlessly, persistently, incessantly, nonstop, unremittingly, monotonously, unfalteringly • **day by day** *Day by day, he got weaker.* = **gradually**, slowly, progressively, daily, steadily, bit by bit, little by little, by degrees ■ **RELATED WORD:** *adjective* diurnal

daybreak NOUN = **dawn**, morning, sunrise, first light, crack of dawn, break of day, sunup, cockcrow, dayspring (*poetic*)

daydream NOUN *She perpetually drifted off into daydreams and made up fantasy stories in her head.* = **fantasy**, dream, imagining, fancy, reverie, figment of the imagination, wish, pipe dream, fond hope, castle in the air *or* in Spain ▶ VERB *He daydreams of being a famous journalist.* = **fantasize**, dream, imagine, envision, stargaze

daylight NOUN **1** *Lack of daylight can make people feel depressed.* = **sunlight**, sunshine, light of day **2** *It was still daylight but many cars had their headlamps on.* = **daytime**, broad daylight, daylight hours

day-to-day ADJECTIVE = **everyday**, regular, usual, routine, accustomed, customary, habitual, run-of-the-mill, wonted

daze VERB **1** *The blow caught me on the temple and dazed me.* = **stun**, shock, paralyse, numb, stupefy, benumb **2** *We were dazed by the sheer size of the spectacle.* = **confuse**, surprise, amaze, blind, astonish, stagger, startle, dazzle, bewilder, astound, perplex, flummox, dumbfound, nonplus, flabbergast (*informal*), befog ▶ NOUN *I was walking around in a daze.* = **shock**, confusion, distraction, trance, bewilderment, stupor, trancelike state

dazed ADJECTIVE = **shocked**, stunned, confused, staggered, baffled, at sea, bewildered, muddled, numbed, dizzy, bemused, perplexed, disorientated, flabbergasted (*informal*), dopey (*slang*), groggy (*informal*), stupefied, nonplussed, light-headed, flummoxed, punch-drunk, woozy (*informal*), fuddled

dazzle VERB **1** *He dazzled them with his knowledge of the world.* = **impress**, amaze, fascinate, overwhelm, astonish, awe, overpower, bowl over (*informal*), overawe, hypnotize, stupefy, take your breath away, strike dumb **2** *She was dazzled by the lights.* = **blind**, confuse, daze, bedazzle ▶ NOUN *The dazzle of stardom and status attracts them.* = **splendour**, sparkle, glitter, flash, brilliance, magnificence, razzmatazz (*slang*), razzle-dazzle (*slang*), éclat

dazzling ADJECTIVE = **splendid**, brilliant, stunning (*informal*), superb, divine (*informal*), glorious, sparkling, glittering, sensational (*informal*), sublime, virtuoso, drop-dead (*slang*), ravishing, scintillating ■ **OPPOSITE:** ordinary

dead ADJECTIVE **1** *My husband's been dead for a year now.* = **deceased**, gone, departed (*euphemistic*), late, perished, extinct, defunct, passed away, pushing up (the) daisies ■ **OPPOSITE:** alive **2** *The polluted and stagnant water seems dead.* = **inanimate**, still, barren (*old-fashioned*), sterile, lifeless, inert, uninhabited **3** *It was a horrible, dead little town.* = **boring**, dull, dreary, flat, plain, stale, tasteless, humdrum, uninteresting, insipid, ho-hum (*informal*), vapid, dead-and-alive **4** *This battery's dead.* = **not working**, useless, inactive, inoperative ■ **OPPOSITE:** working **5** *dead languages* = **obsolete**, old, antique, discarded, extinct, archaic, disused **6** *He watched the procedure with cold, dead eyes.* = **spiritless**, cold, dull, wooden, glazed, indifferent, callous, lukewarm, inhuman, unsympathetic, apathetic, frigid, glassy, unresponsive, unfeeling, torpid ■ **OPPOSITE:** lively **7** *My arm had gone dead.* = **numb**, frozen, paralysed, insensitive, inert, deadened, immobilized, unfeeling, torpid, insensible, benumbed **8** *(of a centre, silence, or stop) They hurried about in dead silence.* = **total**, complete, perfect, entire, absolute, utter, outright, thorough, downright, unqualified **9** *I must get some sleep – I'm absolutely dead.* = **exhausted**, tired, worn out, spent, wasted, done in *(informal)*, all in *(slang)*, drained, wiped out *(informal)*, sapped, knackered *(slang)*, prostrated, clapped out *(Brit., Austral. & N.Z. informal)*, tired out, ready to drop, dog-tired *(informal)*, zonked *(slang)*, dead tired, dead beat *(informal)*, shagged out *(Brit. slang)*, worn to a frazzle *(informal)*, on your last legs *(informal)*, creamcrackered *(Brit. slang)* ▸ NOUN *in the dead of night* = **middle**, heart, depth, thick, midst ▸ ADVERB *You're dead right.* = **exactly**, quite, completely, totally, directly, perfectly, fully, entirely, absolutely, thoroughly, wholly, utterly, consummately, wholeheartedly, unconditionally, to the hilt, one hundred per cent, unmitigatedly

deadbeat NOUN = **layabout**, bum *(informal)*, waster, lounger, piker *(Austral. & N.Z. slang)*, sponge *(informal)*, parasite, drone, loafer, slacker *(informal)*, scrounger *(informal)*, skiver *(Brit. slang)*, idler, freeloader *(slang)*, good-for-nothing, sponger *(informal)*, wastrel, bludger *(Austral. & N.Z. informal)*, cadger, quandong *(Austral. slang)*

deaden VERB **1** *He needs morphine to deaden the pain in his chest.* = **reduce**, dull, diminish, check, weaken, cushion, damp, suppress, blunt, paralyse, impair, numb, lessen, alleviate, smother, dampen, anaesthetize, benumb **2** *They managed to deaden the sound.* = **suppress**, reduce, dull, diminish, cushion, damp, mute, stifle, hush, lessen, smother, dampen, muffle, quieten

deadline NOUN = **time limit**, cutoff point, target date or time, limit

deadlock NOUN **1** *Peace talks ended in a deadlock last month.* = **impasse**, stalemate, standstill, halt, cessation, gridlock, standoff, full stop **2** *Dembele broke the deadlock with a late goal.* = **tie**, draw, stalemate, impasse, standstill, gridlock, standoff, dead heat

deadly ADJECTIVE **1** *a deadly disease currently affecting dolphins* = **lethal**, fatal, deathly, dangerous, devastating, destructive, mortal, murderous, poisonous, toxic, malignant, virulent, pernicious *(formal)*, noxious, venomous, baleful, death-dealing, baneful **2** *She found the party deadly.* = **boring**, dull, tedious, flat, monotonous, uninteresting, mind-numbing, unexciting, ho-hum *(informal)*, wearisome, as dry as dust **3** *The deadly pallor of her skin.* = **deathly**, white, pale, ghostly, ghastly, wan, pasty, colourless, pallid, anaemic, ashen, sallow, whitish, cadaverous, waxen, ashy, deathlike, wheyfaced

deadpan ADJECTIVE = **expressionless**, empty, blank, wooden, straight-faced, vacuous, impassive, inscrutable, poker-faced, inexpressive

deaf ADJECTIVE **1** *She is now profoundly deaf.* = **hard of hearing**, without hearing, stone deaf **2** *The assembly were deaf to all pleas for financial help.* = **oblivious**, indifferent, unmoved, unconcerned, unsympathetic, impervious, unresponsive, heedless, unhearing

deafen VERB = **make deaf**, split or burst the eardrums

deafening ADJECTIVE = **ear-splitting**, intense, piercing, ringing, booming, overpowering, resounding, dinning, thunderous, ear-piercing

deal NOUN **1** *(informal) Japan has done a deal with America on rice exports.* = **agreement**, understanding, contract, business, negotiation, arrangement, bargain, transaction, pact **2** *a great deal of money* = **amount**, quantity, measure, degree, mass, volume, share, portion, bulk • **deal in something** *The company deals in antiques.* = **sell**, trade in, stock, traffic in, buy and sell • **deal something out** *a failure to deal out effective punishments to offenders* = **distribute**, give, administer, share, divide, assign, allocate, dispense, bestow, allot, mete out, dole out, apportion • **deal with something** *the parts of the book which deal with events in Florence* = **be concerned with**, involve, concern, touch, regard, apply to, bear on, pertain to, be relevant to, treat of • **deal with something** or **someone 1** *the way in which the company deals with complaints* = **handle**, manage, treat, cope with, take care of, see to, attend to, get to grips with, come to grips with **2** *He's a hard man to deal with.* = **behave towards**, act towards, conduct yourself towards

dealer NOUN = **trader**, marketer, merchant, supplier, wholesaler, purveyor, tradesperson, merchandiser

dealings PLURAL NOUN = **business**, selling, trading, trade, traffic, truck, bargaining, commerce, transactions, business relations

dear ADJECTIVE **1** *Mrs Cavendish is a dear friend of mine.* = **beloved**, close, valued, favourite, respected, prized, dearest, sweet (*archaic*), treasured, precious, darling, intimate, esteemed, cherished, revered ■ **OPPOSITE:** hated **2** *Don't buy that one – it's too dear.* = **expensive**, costly, high-priced, excessive, pricey (*informal*), at a premium, overpriced, exorbitant ■ **OPPOSITE:** cheap ▶ NOUN *Yes, my dear.* = **darling**, love, dearest, sweet, angel (*informal*), treasure, precious, beloved, loved one, sweetheart, truelove

dearly ADVERB **1** *She would dearly love to marry.* = **very much**, greatly, extremely, profoundly **2** *He is paying dearly for his folly.* = **at great cost**, dear, at a high price, at a heavy cost

dearth NOUN = **lack**, want, need, absence, poverty, shortage, deficiency, famine, inadequacy, scarcity, paucity (*formal*), insufficiency, sparsity, scantiness, exiguousness

death NOUN **1** *There had been a death in the family.* = **dying**, demise (*euphemistic*), bereavement, end, passing, release, loss, departure, curtains (*informal*), cessation, expiration, decease, quietus ■ **OPPOSITE:** birth **2** *the death of everything he had ever hoped for* = **destruction**, ending, finish, ruin, wiping out, undoing, extinction, elimination, downfall, extermination, annihilation, obliteration, ruination ■ **OPPOSITE:** beginning **3** (*usually cap.*) *Carrying a long scythe is the hooded figure of Death.* = **the Grim Reaper**, the Dark Angel ■ **RELATED WORDS:** *adjectives* fatal, lethal, mortal

deathly ADJECTIVE **1** *the deathly pallor of her cheeks* = **deathlike**, white, pale, ghastly, wan, gaunt, haggard, bloodless, pallid, ashen, sallow, cadaverous, ashy, like death warmed up (*informal*) **2** *a deathly illness* = **fatal**, terminal, deadly, terrible, destructive, lethal, mortal, malignant, incurable, pernicious (*formal*)

debacle *or* **débâcle** NOUN = **disaster**, catastrophe, fiasco

debar VERB = **bar**, exclude, prohibit, black, stop, keep out, preclude, shut out, blackball, interdict, refuse admission to

debase VERB **1** *He claims that advertising debases the English language.* = **corrupt**, contaminate, devalue, pollute, impair, taint, depreciate, defile, adulterate, vitiate, bastardize ■ **OPPOSITE:** purify **2** *I won't debase myself by answering that question.* = **degrade**, reduce, lower, shame, humble,

disgrace, humiliate, demean, drag down, dishonour, cheapen, abase ■ **OPPOSITE:** exalt

debased ADJECTIVE **1** *a debased form of worship* = **corrupt**, devalued, reduced, lowered, mixed, contaminated, polluted, depreciated, impure, adulterated **2** *a dysfunctional and morally debased organization* = **degraded**, corrupt, fallen, low, base, abandoned, perverted, vile, sordid, depraved, debauched, scungy (*Austral. & N.Z.*) ■ **OPPOSITE:** virtuous

debatable ADJECTIVE = **doubtful**, uncertain, dubious, controversial, unsettled, questionable, undecided, borderline, in dispute, moot, arguable, iffy (*informal*), open to question, disputable

debate NOUN *There has been a lot of debate about this point.* = **discussion**, talk, argument, dispute, analysis, conversation, consideration, controversy, dialogue, contention, deliberation, polemic, altercation, disputation ▶ VERB **1** *The causes of depression are much debated.* = **discuss**, question, talk about, argue about, dispute, examine, contest, deliberate, contend, wrangle, thrash out, controvert **2** *He debated whether to have a dessert.* = **consider**, reflect, think about, weigh, contemplate, deliberate, ponder, revolve, mull over, ruminate, give thought to, cogitate, meditate upon

debauched ADJECTIVE = **corrupt**, abandoned, perverted, degraded, degenerate, immoral, dissipated, sleazy, depraved, wanton, debased, profligate, dissolute, licentious, pervy (*slang*)

debauchery NOUN = **depravity**, excess, lust, revel, indulgence, orgy, incontinence, gluttony, dissipation, licentiousness, intemperance, overindulgence, lewdness, dissoluteness, carousal

debilitate VERB = **weaken**, exhaust, wear out, sap, incapacitate, prostrate, enfeeble, enervate, devitalize ■ **OPPOSITE:** invigorate

debilitating ADJECTIVE = **weakening**, tiring, exhausting, draining, fatiguing, wearing, sapping, incapacitating, enervating, enfeebling, devitalizing ■ **OPPOSITE:** invigorating

debonair ADJECTIVE = **elegant**, charming, dashing (*old-fashioned*), smooth, refined, courteous, affable, suave, urbane, well-bred

debrief VERB = **interrogate**, question, examine, probe, quiz, cross-examine

debris NOUN = **remains**, bits, pieces, waste, ruins, wreck, rubbish, fragments, litter, rubble, wreckage, brash, detritus, dross

debt NOUN *He is still paying off his debts.*
= **debit**, bill, score, due, duty, commitment,
obligation, liability, arrears • **in debt** *You
shouldn't borrow more money if you're already in
debt.* = **owing**, liable, accountable, in the
red (*informal*), in arrears, beholden, in hock
(*informal, chiefly U.S.*)

debtor NOUN = **borrower**, mortgagor

debunk VERB = **expose**, show up, mock,
ridicule, puncture, deflate, disparage,
lampoon, cut down to size

debut NOUN **1** = **entrance**, beginning,
launch, launching, introduction, first
appearance, inauguration
2 = **presentation**, coming out,
introduction, first appearance, launching,
initiation

decadence NOUN = **degeneration**, decline,
corruption, fall, decay, deterioration,
dissolution, perversion, dissipation,
debasement, retrogression

decadent ADJECTIVE = **degenerate**,
abandoned, corrupt, degraded, immoral,
self-indulgent, depraved, debased,
debauched, dissolute ■ **OPPOSITE:** moral

decamp VERB = **make off**, fly, escape,
desert, flee, bolt, run away, flit (*informal*),
abscond, hook it (*slang*), sneak off, do a
runner (*slang*), scarper (*Brit. slang*), steal
away, do a bunk (*Brit. slang*), fly the coop
(*U.S. & Canad. informal*), skedaddle
(*informal*), hightail it (*informal, chiefly U.S.*),
take a powder (*U.S. & Canad. slang*), take it
on the lam (*U.S. & Canad. slang*), do a Skase
(*Austral. informal*)

decant VERB = **transfer**, tap, drain, pour
out, draw off, let flow

decapitate VERB = **behead**, execute,
guillotine

decay VERB **1** *The dead leaves slowly decayed.*
= **rot**, break down, disintegrate, spoil,
crumble, deteriorate, perish, degenerate,
fester, decompose, mortify, moulder, go
bad, putrefy (*formal*) **2** *The work ethic in this
country has decayed over the past 30 years.*
= **decline**, sink, break down, diminish,
dissolve, crumble, deteriorate, fall off,
dwindle, lessen, wane, disintegrate,
degenerate ■ **OPPOSITE:** grow ▶ NOUN
1 *Plaque causes tooth decay and gum disease.*
= **rot**, rotting, deterioration, corruption,
mould, blight, perishing, disintegration,
corrosion, decomposition, gangrene,
mortification, canker, caries, putrefaction,
putrescence, cariosity, putridity **2** *problems
of urban decay and gang violence* = **decline**,
collapse, deterioration, failing, fading,
decadence, degeneration, degeneracy
■ **OPPOSITE:** growth

decayed ADJECTIVE = **rotten**, bad, decaying,
wasted, spoiled, perished, festering,
decomposed, corroded, unsound, putrid,
putrefied, putrescent, carrion, carious

decaying ADJECTIVE = **rotting**,
deteriorating, disintegrating, crumbling,
perishing, wasting away, wearing away,
gangrenous, putrefacient

deceased ADJECTIVE = **dead**, late, departed
(*euphemistic*), lost, gone, expired, defunct,
lifeless, pushing up daisies (*informal*)

deceit NOUN = **lying**, fraud, cheating,
deception, hypocrisy, cunning, pretence,
treachery, dishonesty, guile, artifice,
trickery, misrepresentation, duplicity,
subterfuge, feint, double-dealing,
chicanery, wile, dissimulation, craftiness,
imposture, fraudulence, slyness,
deceitfulness, underhandedness
■ **OPPOSITE:** honesty

deceitful ADJECTIVE = **dishonest**, false,
deceiving, fraudulent, treacherous,
deceptive, hypocritical, counterfeit, crafty,
sneaky, illusory, two-faced, disingenuous,
untrustworthy, underhand, insincere,
double-dealing, duplicitous, fallacious,
guileful, knavish (*archaic*)

deceive VERB *He has deceived and disillusioned
us all.* = **take in**, trick, fool (*informal*), cheat,
con (*informal*), kid (*informal*), stiff (*slang*),
sting (*informal*), mislead, betray, lead
(someone) on (*informal*), hoax, dupe,
beguile, delude, swindle, outwit, ensnare,
bamboozle (*informal*), hoodwink, entrap,
double-cross (*informal*), take for a ride
(*informal*), pull a fast one on (*slang*), cozen,
scam (*slang*), pull the wool over
(someone's) eyes

decency NOUN **1** *His sense of decency forced
him to resign.* = **propriety**, correctness,
decorum, fitness, good form, respectability,
etiquette, appropriateness, seemliness
2 *He did not have the decency to inform me of his
plans.* = **courtesy**, grace, politeness, good
manners, civility, good breeding,
graciousness, urbanity, courteousness,
gallantness

decent ADJECTIVE **1** *Nearby there is a village
with a decent pub.* = **satisfactory**, average,
fair, all right, reasonable, suitable,
sufficient, acceptable, good enough,
adequate, competent, ample, tolerable
(*informal*), up to scratch, passable, up to
standard, up to the mark ■ **OPPOSITE:**
unsatisfactory **2** *They married after a decent
interval.* = **proper**, becoming, seemly,
fitting, fit, appropriate, suitable,
respectable, befitting, decorous, comme
il faut (*French*) ■ **OPPOSITE:** improper

3 *Most people around here are decent folk.*
= **good**, kind, friendly, neighbourly,
generous, helpful, obliging, accommodating,
sympathetic, comradely, benign, gracious,
benevolent, courteous, amiable, amicable,
sociable, genial, peaceable, companionable,
well-disposed **4** *The character is portrayed as*
noble and decent. = **respectable**, nice, pure,
proper, modest, polite, chaste, presentable,
decorous

deception NOUN **1** *He admitted conspiring*
to obtain property by deception. = **trickery**,
fraud, deceit, hypocrisy, cunning,
treachery, guile, duplicity, insincerity,
legerdemain, dissimulation, craftiness,
fraudulence, deceitfulness, deceptiveness
■ **OPPOSITE:** honesty **2** *You've been the victim*
of a rather cruel deception. = **trick**, lie, fraud,
cheat, bluff, sham, snare, hoax, decoy,
ruse, artifice, subterfuge, canard, feint,
stratagem, porky (*Brit. slang*), pork pie
(*Brit. slang*), wile, hokum (*slang, chiefly*
U.S. & Canad.), leg-pull (*Brit. informal*),
imposture, snow job (*slang, chiefly U.S.*
& Canad.), fastie (*Austral. slang*)

deceptive ADJECTIVE **1** *Appearances can be*
deceptive. = **misleading**, false, fake, mock,
ambiguous, unreliable, spurious, illusory,
specious, fallacious, delusive **2** *Her worst*
fault is a strongly deceptive streak.
= **dishonest**, deceiving, fraudulent,
treacherous, hypocritical, crafty, sneaky,
two-faced, disingenuous, deceitful,
untrustworthy, underhand, insincere,
duplicitous, guileful

decide VERB **1** *I can't decide what to do.*
= **make a decision**, make up your mind,
reach *or* come to a decision, end, choose,
determine, purpose, elect, conclude,
commit yourself, come to a conclusion
■ **OPPOSITE:** hesitate **2** *This is a question that*
should be decided by government. = **resolve**,
answer, determine, settle, conclude,
decree, clear up, ordain, adjudicate,
adjudge, arbitrate **3** *The goal that decided the*
match came just before half-time. = **settle**,
determine, conclude, resolve

decided ADJECTIVE **1** *We were at a decided*
disadvantage. = **definite**, certain, positive,
absolute, distinct, pronounced, clear-cut,
undisputed, unequivocal, undeniable,
unambiguous, indisputable, categorical,
unquestionable ■ **OPPOSITE:** doubtful **2** *a*
man of very decided opinions = **determined**,
firm, decisive, assertive, emphatic,
resolute, strong-willed, unhesitating,
unfaltering ■ **OPPOSITE:** irresolute

decidedly ADVERB = **definitely**, clearly,
certainly, absolutely, positively, distinctly,

downright, decisively, unequivocally,
unmistakably

deciding ADJECTIVE = **determining**, chief,
prime, significant, critical, crucial,
principal, influential, decisive, conclusive

decimate VERB = **destroy**, devastate, wipe
out, ravage, eradicate, annihilate, put paid
to, lay waste, wreak havoc on

> **USAGE** This word, which comes
> from Latin, originally referred to the
> slaughtering of one in ten soldiers, a
> practice of the army of Ancient Rome.
> In current language, however, the
> meaning of the word has broadened and
> it is now used not only to describe the
> destruction of people and animals, but
> also of institutions: *overseas visitors will*
> *stay away in droves, decimating the tourist*
> *industry.* Synonyms such as *destroy*
> (for people and animals) and *reduce*
> (for institutions) are appropriate
> alternatives.

decipher VERB **1** *I'm still no closer to*
deciphering the code. = **decode**, crack, solve,
understand, explain, reveal, figure out
(*informal*), unravel, suss (out) (*slang*) **2** *I can't*
decipher these notes. = **figure out**, read,
understand, interpret (*informal*), make out,
unravel, deduce, construe, suss (out) (*slang*)

decision NOUN **1** *The judge's decision was*
greeted with dismay. = **judgment**, finding,
ruling, order, result, sentence, settlement,
resolution, conclusion, outcome, verdict,
decree, arbitration **2** *He is very much a man of*
decision and action. = **decisiveness**, purpose,
resolution, resolve, determination,
firmness, forcefulness, purposefulness,
resoluteness, strength of mind *or* will

decisive ADJECTIVE **1** *a decisive victory in the*
elections = **crucial**, significant, critical, final,
positive, absolute, influential, definite,
definitive, momentous, conclusive, fateful
■ **OPPOSITE:** uncertain **2** *Firm decisive action*
will be taken to end the incident. = **resolute**,
decided, firm, determined, forceful,
uncompromising, incisive, trenchant,
strong-minded ■ **OPPOSITE:** indecisive

deck VERB *The house was decked with flowers.*
= **decorate**, dress, trim, clothe, grace,
array, garland, adorn, ornament,
embellish, apparel (*archaic*), festoon, attire,
bedeck, beautify, bedight (*archaic*), bedizen
(*archaic*), engarland • **deck someone** *or*
something out *She had decked him out in*
expensive clothes. = **dress up**, doll up (*slang*),
prettify, trick out, rig out, pretty up, prink,
tog up *or* out

declaim VERB *He used to declaim verse to us*
with immense energy. = **speak**, lecture,

proclaim, recite, rant, harangue, hold forth, spiel (*informal*), orate, perorate
• **declaim against something** or **someone** *He declaimed against the injustice of his treatment.* = **protest against**, attack, rail at or against, denounce, decry, inveigh against (*formal*)

declaration NOUN **1** *The two countries will sign the declaration of peace tomorrow.* = **announcement**, proclamation, decree, notice, manifesto, notification, edict, pronouncement, promulgation, pronunciamento **2** *declarations of undying love* = **affirmation**, profession, assertion, revelation, disclosure, acknowledgement, protestation (*formal*), avowal, averment **3** *I signed a declaration allowing my doctor to disclose my medical details.* = **statement**, testimony, deposition, attestation

declare VERB **1** *He declared his intention to become the best golfer in the world.* = **state**, claim, announce, voice, express, maintain, confirm, assert, proclaim, pronounce, utter, notify, affirm, profess, avow, aver, asseverate (*formal*) **2** *They declare that there is no lawful impediment to the marriage.* = **testify**, state, witness, swear, assert, affirm, certify, attest, bear witness, vouch, give testimony, asseverate **3** *Anyone carrying money into or out of the country must declare it.* = **make known**, tell, reveal, show, broadcast, confess, communicate, disclose, convey, manifest, make public

decline VERB **1** *a declining birth rate* = **fall**, fail, drop, contract, lower, sink, flag, fade, shrink, diminish, decrease, slow down, fall off, dwindle, lessen, wane, ebb, slacken ■ **OPPOSITE:** rise **2** *Her father's health has declined significantly in recent months.* = **deteriorate**, fade, weaken, pine, decay, worsen, lapse, languish, degenerate, droop ■ **OPPOSITE:** improve **3** *He declined their invitation.* = **refuse**, reject, turn down, avoid, deny, spurn, abstain, forgo, send your regrets, say 'no' ■ **OPPOSITE:** accept ▶ NOUN **1** *The first signs of economic decline became visible.* = **depression**, recession, slump, falling off, downturn, dwindling, lessening, diminution, abatement ■ **OPPOSITE:** rise **2** *Rome's decline in the fifth century.* = **deterioration**, fall, failing, slump, weakening, decay, worsening, descent, downturn, disintegration, degeneration, atrophy, decrepitude, retrogression, enfeeblement ■ **OPPOSITE:** improvement

decode VERB **1** *The secret documents were intercepted and decoded.* = **decipher**, crack, work out, solve, interpret, unscramble, decrypt, descramble ■ **OPPOSITE:** encode

2 *You don't need to be a genius to decode his work.* = **understand**, explain, interpret, make sense of, construe, decipher, elucidate, throw light on, explicate (*formal*)

decompose VERB **1** *foods which decompose and rot* = **rot**, spoil, corrupt, crumble, decay, perish, fester, corrode, moulder, go bad, putrefy (*formal*) **2** *Plastics take years to decompose.* = **break down**, break up, crumble, deteriorate, fall apart, disintegrate, degenerate

decomposition NOUN *The bodies were in an advanced state of decomposition.* = **rot**, corruption, decay, rotting, perishing, mortification, putrefaction, putrescence, putridity

decor or **décor** NOUN = **decoration**, colour scheme, ornamentation, furnishing style

decorate VERB **1** *He decorated the box with glitter and ribbons.* = **adorn**, deck, trim, embroider, garnish, ornament, embellish, festoon, bedeck, beautify, grace, engarland **2** *a small, badly decorated office* = **do up**, paper, paint, wallpaper, renovate (*informal*), furbish **3** *She was decorated for her services to the nation.* = **pin a medal on**, cite, confer an honour on or upon

decoration NOUN **1** *He played a part in the decoration of the tree.* = **adornment**, trimming, garnishing, enhancement, elaboration, embellishment, ornamentation, beautification **2** *We were putting the Christmas decorations up.* = **ornament**, trimmings, garnish, frill, scroll, spangle, festoon, trinket, bauble, flounce, arabesque, curlicue, furbelow, falderal, cartouch(e) **3** *He was awarded several military decorations.* = **medal**, award, order, star, colours, ribbon, badge, emblem, garter

decorative ADJECTIVE = **ornamental**, fancy, pretty, attractive, enhancing, adorning, for show, embellishing, showy, beautifying, nonfunctional, arty-crafty

decorum NOUN = **propriety**, decency, etiquette, breeding, protocol, respectability, politeness, good manners, good grace, gentility, deportment, courtliness, politesse, punctilio, seemliness ■ **OPPOSITE:** impropriety

decoy NOUN = **lure**, attraction, bait, trap, inducement, enticement, ensnarement

decrease VERB **1** *Population growth is decreasing each year.* = **drop**, decline, lessen, contract, lower, ease, shrink, diminish, fall off, dwindle, wane, subside, abate, peter out, slacken **2** *The drug is said to decrease the risk of heart attack.* = **reduce**, cut, lower, contract, depress, moderate, weaken, diminish, turn down, slow down, cut down, shorten, dilute, impair, lessen, curtail, wind down, abate, tone down, truncate, abridge, downsize ■ **OPPOSITE:** increase ▶ NOUN *There has been a decrease in the number of young unemployed people.* = **lessening**, decline, reduction, loss, falling off, downturn, dwindling, contraction, ebb, cutback, subsidence, curtailment, shrinkage, diminution, abatement ■ **OPPOSITE:** growth

decree NOUN 1 *He issued a decree ordering all unofficial armed groups to disband.* = **law**, order, ruling, act, demand, command, regulation, mandate, canon, statute, covenant, ordinance, proclamation, enactment, edict, dictum, precept 2 *court decrees relating to marital property* = **judgment**, finding, order, result, ruling, decision, award, conclusion, verdict, arbitration ▶ VERB *He got the two men off the hook by decreeing a general amnesty.* = **order**, rule, command, decide, demand, establish, determine, proclaim, dictate, prescribe, pronounce, lay down, enact, ordain (*formal*)

decrepit ADJECTIVE *The film was shot in a decrepit police station.* = **ruined**, broken-down, battered, crumbling, rundown, deteriorated, decaying, beat-up (*informal*), shabby, worn-out, ramshackle, dilapidated, antiquated, rickety, weather-beaten, tumbledown

decry VERB = **condemn**, blame, abuse, blast, denounce, put down, criticize, run down, discredit, censure, detract, denigrate, belittle, disparage, rail against, depreciate, tear into (*informal*), diss (*slang*), lambast(e), traduce (*formal*), excoriate, derogate, cry down, asperse

dedicate VERB 1 *He dedicated himself to politics.* = **devote**, give, apply, commit, concern, occupy, pledge, surrender, give over to 2 *This book is dedicated to the memory of my sister.* = **offer**, address, assign, inscribe 3 *The church is dedicated to a saint.* = **consecrate**, bless, sanctify, set apart, hallow

dedicated ADJECTIVE = **committed**, devoted, sworn, enthusiastic, single-minded, zealous, purposeful, given over to, wholehearted ■ **OPPOSITE:** indifferent

dedication NOUN 1 *To be successful takes hard work and dedication.* = **commitment**, loyalty, devotion, allegiance, adherence, single-mindedness, faithfulness, wholeheartedness ■ **OPPOSITE:** indifference 2 *His book contains a dedication to his parents.* = **inscription**, message, address

deduce VERB = **work out**, reason, understand, gather, conclude, derive, infer, glean

deduct VERB = **subtract**, remove, take off, withdraw, take out, take from, take away, reduce by, knock off (*informal*), decrease by ■ **OPPOSITE:** add

deduction NOUN 1 *It was a pretty astute deduction.* = **conclusion**, finding, verdict, judgment, assumption, inference, corollary 2 *'How did you guess?' 'Deduction,' he replied.* = **reasoning**, thinking, thought, reason, analysis, logic, cogitation, ratiocination 3 *your gross income, before tax and insurance deductions* = **discount**, reduction, cut, concession, allowance, decrease, rebate, diminution 4 *the deduction of tax at 20%* = **subtraction**, reduction, allowance, concession

deed NOUN 1 *His heroic deeds were celebrated in every corner of the country.* = **action**, act, performance, achievement, exploit, feat 2 *He asked if I had the deeds to his father's property.* = **document**, title, contract, title deed, indenture

deem VERB = **consider**, think, believe, hold, account, judge, suppose, regard, estimate, imagine, reckon, esteem (*formal*), conceive

deep ADJECTIVE 1 *The workers had dug a deep hole in the centre of the garden.* = **big**, wide, broad, profound, yawning, cavernous, bottomless, unfathomable, fathomless, abyssal ■ **OPPOSITE:** shallow 2 *a period of deep personal crisis* = **intense**, great, serious (*informal*), acute, extreme, grave, profound, heartfelt, unqualified, abject, deeply felt, heartrending ■ **OPPOSITE:** superficial 3 *He fell into a deep sleep.* = **sound**, peaceful, profound, unbroken, undisturbed, untroubled 4 (*with* **in**) *Before long we were deep in conversation.* = **absorbed in**, lost in, gripped by, intent on, preoccupied with, carried away by, immersed in, engrossed in, rapt by 5 *She gave him a long deep look.* = **wise**, learned, searching, keen, critical, acute, profound, penetrating, discriminating, shrewd, discerning, astute, perceptive, incisive, perspicacious, sagacious ■ **OPPOSITE:** simple 6 *rich, deep colours* = **dark**, strong, rich, warm, intense, vivid ■ **OPPOSITE:** light 7 *His voice was deep and mellow.* = **low**, booming, bass, full, mellow, resonant, sonorous, mellifluous, dulcet, low-pitched, full-toned ■ **OPPOSITE:** high 8 *a very deep individual* = **astute**, knowing, clever, designing, scheming, sharp, smart, intelligent, discriminating, shrewd, cunning, discerning, canny, devious, perceptive, insidious, artful, far-sighted, far-seeing, perspicacious, sagacious (formal) ■ **OPPOSITE:** simple **9** *a deep, dark secret* = **secret**, hidden, unknown, mysterious, concealed, obscure, abstract, veiled, esoteric, mystifying, impenetrable, arcane, abstruse, recondite ▶ NOUN *in the deep of night* = **middle**, heart, midst, dead, thick, culmination ▶ ADVERB **1** *They travelled deep into the forest.* = **far**, a long way, a good way, miles, deeply, far down, a great distance **2** *We talked deep into the night.* = **late**, far • *the deep whales and other creatures of the deep* = **the ocean**, the sea, the waves, the main, the drink (informal), the high seas, the briny (informal)

deepen VERB **1** *Sloane's uneasiness deepened.* = **intensify**, increase, grow, strengthen, reinforce, escalate, magnify, augment **2** *The tunnels have been widened and deepened.* = **dig out**, excavate, scoop out, hollow out, scrape out

deeply ADVERB = **thoroughly**, completely, seriously, sadly, severely, gravely, profoundly, intensely, to the heart, passionately, acutely, to the core, feelingly, movingly, distressingly, to the quick, affecting

deep-rooted or **deep-seated** ADJECTIVE = **fixed**, confirmed, rooted, settled, entrenched, ingrained, inveterate, dyed-in-the-wool, ineradicable
■ **OPPOSITE:** superficial

deface VERB = **vandalize**, damage, destroy, total (slang), injure, mar, spoil, trash (slang), impair, tarnish, obliterate, mutilate, deform, blemish, disfigure, sully

de facto ADVERB *Tighter regulation has de facto already begun.* = **in fact**, really, actually, in effect, in reality ▶ ADJECTIVE *a de facto recognition of the republic's independence* = **actual**, real, existing

defamation NOUN = **slander**, smear, libel, scandal, slur, vilification, opprobrium, denigration, calumny, character assassination, disparagement, obloquy, aspersion, traducement

defamatory ADJECTIVE = **slanderous**, insulting, abusive, denigrating, disparaging, vilifying, derogatory, injurious, libellous, vituperative, calumnious, contumelious

defame VERB = **slander**, smear, libel, discredit, knock (informal), rubbish (informal), disgrace, blacken, slag (off) (slang), detract, malign, denigrate, disparage, vilify, dishonour, stigmatize, bad-mouth (slang), besmirch, traduce (formal), cast aspersions on, speak evil of, cast a slur on, calumniate, vituperate, asperse

default NOUN **1** *The other team failed to turn up so we won by default.* = **failure**, want, lack, fault, absence, neglect, defect, deficiency, lapse, omission, dereliction **2** *The country can't pay its foreign debts and default is inevitable.* = **nonpayment**, evasion ▶ VERB *Many borrowers are defaulting on loans.* = **fail to pay**, dodge, evade, rat (informal), neglect, levant (Brit.), welch or welsh (slang)

defeat VERB **1** *His guerrillas defeated the colonial army.* = **beat**, crush, overwhelm, conquer, stuff (slang), master, worst, tank (slang), overthrow, lick (informal), undo, subdue, rout, overpower, quell, trounce, clobber (slang), vanquish, repulse, subjugate, run rings around (informal), wipe the floor with (informal), make mincemeat of (informal), pip at the post, outplay, blow out of the water (slang) ■ **OPPOSITE:** surrender **2** *The challenges of constructing such a huge novel almost defeated her.* = **frustrate**, foil, thwart, ruin, baffle, confound, balk, get the better of, forestall, stymie ▶ NOUN **1** *The vote was seen as something of a defeat for the lobbyists.* = **conquest**, beating, overthrow, pasting (slang), rout, debacle, trouncing, repulse, vanquishment ■ **OPPOSITE:** victory **2** *the final defeat of all his hopes* = **frustration**, failure, reverse, disappointment, setback, thwarting

defeated ADJECTIVE = **beaten**, crushed, conquered, worsted, routed, overcome, overwhelmed, thrashed, licked (informal), thwarted, overpowered, balked, trounced, vanquished, checkmated, bested
■ **OPPOSITE:** victorious

defeatist NOUN *a defeatist might give up at this point* = **pessimist**, sceptic, scoffer, doubter, quitter, prophet of doom, yielder ▶ ADJECTIVE *Don't go out there with a defeatist attitude.* = **pessimistic**, resigned, despairing, hopeless, foreboding, despondent, fatalistic

defecate VERB = **excrete**, eliminate, discharge, evacuate (Physiology), dump (slang, chiefly U.S.), pass a motion, move the bowels, empty the bowels, open the bowels, egest, void excrement

defect NOUN *The report pointed out the defects in the present system.* = **deficiency**, want, failing, lack, mistake, fault, error, absence, weakness, flaw, shortcoming, inadequacy, imperfection, frailty, foible ▶ VERB *She insisted that customers who had defected to cheaper coffee shops would return eventually.* = **desert**, rebel, quit, revolt, change sides, apostatize, tergiversate

defection NOUN = **desertion**, revolt, rebellion, abandonment, dereliction, backsliding, apostasy

defective ADJECTIVE **1** *Retailers can return defective merchandise.* = **faulty**, broken, not working, flawed, imperfect, out of order, on the blink (*slang*), buggy (*Computing*) ■ **OPPOSITE:** perfect **2** *food which is defective in nutritional quality* = **deficient**, lacking, short, inadequate, insufficient, incomplete, scant ■ **OPPOSITE:** adequate

defector NOUN = **deserter**, renegade, turncoat, apostate, recreant (*archaic*), runagate (*archaic*), tergiversator

defence or (U.S.) **defense** NOUN **1** *The land was flat, giving no scope for defence.* = **protection**, cover, security, guard, shelter, refuge, resistance, safeguard, immunity **2** *Twenty-eight per cent of the national budget is spent on defence.* = **armaments**, weapons **3** *a spirited defence of the government's economic progress* = **argument**, explanation, excuse, plea, apology, justification, vindication, rationalization, apologia, exoneration, exculpation, extenuation **4** *His defence was that records were fabricated by the police.* = **plea** (*Law*), case, claim, pleading, declaration, testimony, denial, alibi, vindication, rebuttal ▶ PLURAL NOUN *Soldiers are beginning to strengthen the city's defences.* = **shield**, barricade, fortification, bastion, buttress, rampart, bulwark, fastness, fortified pa (*N.Z.*)

defenceless or (U.S.) **defenseless** ADJECTIVE = **helpless**, exposed, vulnerable, naked, endangered, powerless, wide open, unarmed, unprotected, unguarded ■ **OPPOSITE:** safe

defend VERB **1** *They defended themselves against some thugs.* = **protect**, cover, guard, screen, secure, preserve, look after, shelter, shield, harbour, safeguard, fortify, ward off, watch over, stick up for (*informal*), keep safe, give sanctuary **2** *The committee strongly defended its decision.* = **support**, champion, justify, maintain, sustain, plead for, endorse, assert, stand by, uphold, vindicate, stand up for, espouse, speak up for, stick up for (*informal*)

defendant NOUN = **accused**, respondent, appellant, litigant, prisoner at the bar

defender NOUN **1** *a strong defender of human rights* = **supporter**, champion, advocate, sponsor, follower, patron, apologist, upholder, vindicator **2** *He proclaims himself a defender of the environment.* = **protector**, guard, guardian, escort, bodyguard, guardian angel

defensible ADJECTIVE *Her reasons for action are morally defensible.* = **justifiable**, right, sound, reasonable, acceptable, sensible, valid, legitimate, plausible, permissible, well-founded, tenable, excusable, pardonable, vindicable ■ **OPPOSITE:** unjustifiable

defensive ADJECTIVE **1** *hastily organized defensive measures* = **protective**, defending, opposing, safeguarding, watchful, on the defensive, on guard **2** *She heard the blustering, defensive note in his voice.* = **oversensitive**, uptight (*informal*)

defensively ADVERB = **in self-defence**, in defence, suspiciously, on the defensive

defer¹ VERB = **postpone**, delay, put off, suspend, shelve, set aside, adjourn, hold over, procrastinate, put on ice (*informal*), put on the back burner (*informal*), protract, take a rain check on (*U.S. & Canad. informal*), prorogue

defer² VERB (*with* **to**) = **comply with**, give way to, submit to, bow to, give in to, yield to, accede to, capitulate to

deference NOUN **1** *Out of deference to his feelings, I refrained from commenting.* = **respect**, regard, consideration, attention, honour, esteem, courtesy, homage, reverence, politeness, civility, veneration, thoughtfulness ■ **OPPOSITE:** disrespect **2** *a chain of social command linked by deference to authority* = **obedience**, yielding, submission, compliance, capitulation, acquiescence, obeisance, complaisance ■ **OPPOSITE:** disobedience

deferential ADJECTIVE = **respectful**, civil, polite, courteous, considerate, obedient, submissive, dutiful, ingratiating, reverential, obsequious, complaisant, obeisant, regardful

defiance NOUN = **resistance**, challenge, opposition, confrontation, contempt, disregard, provocation, disobedience, insolence, insubordination, rebelliousness, recalcitrance, contumacy (*literary*) ■ **OPPOSITE:** obedience

defiant ADJECTIVE = **resisting**, challenging, rebellious, daring, aggressive, bold, provocative, audacious, recalcitrant, antagonistic, insolent, mutinous, disobedient, refractory, insubordinate, contumacious (*literary*) ■ **OPPOSITE:** obedient

deficiency NOUN **1** *They did tests for signs of vitamin deficiency.* = **lack**, want, deficit, absence, shortage, deprivation, inadequacy, scarcity, dearth, privation (*formal*), insufficiency, scantiness ■ **OPPOSITE:** sufficiency **2** *the most serious deficiency in their air defence* = **failing**, fault, weakness, defect, flaw, drawback, shortcoming, imperfection, frailty, demerit

deficient ADJECTIVE **1** *a diet deficient in vitamins* = **lacking**, wanting, needing, short, inadequate, insufficient, scarce, scant, meagre, skimpy, scanty, exiguous (*formal*) **2** *deficient landing systems* = **unsatisfactory**, weak, flawed, inferior, impaired, faulty, incomplete, defective, imperfect

deficit NOUN = **shortfall**, shortage, deficiency, loss, default, arrears

defile VERB **1** *He felt his father's memory had been defiled by the article.* = **degrade**, stain, disgrace, sully, debase, dishonour, besmirch, smirch **2** *Who gave you permission to defile this sacred place?* = **desecrate**, violate, contaminate, abuse, pollute, profane, dishonour, despoil, treat sacrilegiously **3** *piles of old clothes defiled with excrement* = **dirty**, soil, contaminate, smear, pollute, taint, tarnish, make foul, smirch, befoul

define VERB **1** *Armed forces were deployed to define military zones.* = **mark out**, outline, limit, bound, delineate, circumscribe, demarcate, delimit **2** *How exactly do you define reasonable behaviour?* = **describe**, interpret, characterize, explain, spell out, expound **3** *The Court must define the limits of its authority.* = **establish**, detail, determine, specify, designate

definite ADJECTIVE **1** *It's too soon to give a definite answer.* = **specific**, exact, precise, clear, particular, express, determined, fixed, black-and-white, explicit, clear-cut, cut-and-dried (*informal*), clearly defined ■ **OPPOSITE:** vague **2** *We didn't have any definite proof.* = **clear**, explicit, black-and-white, clear-cut, unequivocal, unambiguous, guaranteed, cut-and-dried (*informal*) **3** *There has been a definite improvement.* = **noticeable**, marked, clear, decided, striking, noted, particular, obvious, dramatic, considerable, remarkable, apparent, evident, distinct, notable, manifest, conspicuous **4** *She is very definite about her feelings.* = **certain**, decided, sure, settled, convinced, positive, confident, assured ■ **OPPOSITE:** uncertain

> USAGE *Definite* and *definitive* should be carefully distinguished. *Definite* indicates precision and firmness, as in *a definite decision. Definitive* includes these senses but also indicates conclusiveness. *A definite answer* indicates a clear and firm answer to a particular question; *a definitive answer* implies an authoritative resolution of a complex question.

definitely ADVERB = **certainly**, clearly, obviously, surely, easily, plainly, absolutely, positively, decidedly, needless to say, without doubt, unquestionably, undeniably, categorically, without question, unequivocally, unmistakably, far and away, without fail, beyond any doubt, indubitably, come hell or high water (*informal*)

definition NOUN **1** *There is no general agreement on a standard definition of sanity.* = **description**, interpretation, explanation, clarification, exposition, explication, elucidation, statement of meaning **2** *This printer has excellent definition.* = **sharpness**, focus, clarity, contrast, precision, distinctness

definitive ADJECTIVE **1** *No one has come up with a definitive answer to that question.* = **final**, convincing, absolute, clinching, decisive, definite, conclusive, irrefutable **2** *It is still the definitive book on the islands.* = **authoritative**, greatest, ultimate, reliable, most significant, exhaustive, superlative, mother of all (*informal*)

deflate VERB **1** *Her comments deflated him a bit.* = **humiliate**, humble, squash, put down (*slang*), disconcert, chasten, mortify, dispirit **2** *The vandals had deflated his car's tyres.* = **puncture**, flatten, empty ■ **OPPOSITE:** inflate **3** *The balloon began to deflate.* = **collapse**, go down, contract, empty, shrink, void, flatten ■ **OPPOSITE:** expand **4** *artificially deflated prices* = **reduce**, depress, decrease, diminish, devalue, depreciate

deflect VERB = **turn aside**, turn, avert, bend, twist, sidetrack

deflection NOUN = **deviation**, bending, veering, swerving, divergence, turning aside, refraction, declination

deform VERB **1** *Severe rheumatoid arthritis deforms limbs.* = **disfigure**, twist, injure, cripple, ruin, mar, spoil, mutilate, maim, deface **2** *Plastic deforms when subjected to heat.* = **distort**, twist, warp, buckle, mangle, contort, gnarl, misshape, malform

deformation NOUN = **distortion**, warping, contortion, malformation, disfiguration, misshapenness

deformed ADJECTIVE = **distorted**, bent, twisted, crooked, warped, maimed, marred, mangled, disfigured, misshapen, malformed, misbegotten

deformity NOUN **1** *physical deformities* = **abnormality**, defect, malformation, disfigurement **2** *Bones grind against each other, leading to pain and deformity.* = **distortion**, irregularity, misshapenness, misproportion

defraud VERB = **cheat**, rob, con (*informal*), do (*slang*), skin (*slang*), stiff (*slang*), rip off (slang), fleece, swindle, stitch up (slang), rook (slang), diddle (informal), bilk, gyp (slang), pull a fast one on (informal), cozen, scam (slang)

defray VERB (costs or expenses) = **pay**, meet, cover, clear, settle, discharge

deft ADJECTIVE = **skilful**, able, expert, clever, neat, handy, adept, nimble, proficient, agile, adroit, dexterous ■ **OPPOSITE:** clumsy

defunct ADJECTIVE 1 the leader of the now defunct Social Democratic Party = **dead**, extinct, gone, departed (euphemistic), expired, deceased, bygone, nonexistent 2 He looked at the defunct apparatus and diagnosed the problem. = **not functioning**, obsolete, out of commission, inoperative

defuse VERB 1 Officials will hold talks aimed at defusing tensions over trade. = **calm**, settle, cool, contain, smooth, stabilize, damp down, take the heat or sting out of ■ **OPPOSITE:** aggravate 2 Police have defused a bomb. = **deactivate**, disable, disarm, make safe ■ **OPPOSITE:** activate

defy VERB 1 This was the first time that I had dared to defy her. = **resist**, oppose, confront, face, brave, beard, disregard, stand up to, spurn, flout, disobey, hold out against, put up a fight (against), hurl defiance at, contemn 2 He defied me to come up with a better idea. = **challenge**, dare, provoke 3 a fragrance that defies description = **foil**, defeat, escape, frustrate, be beyond, baffle, thwart, elude, confound

degenerate VERB He degenerated into drug and alcohol abuse. = **decline**, slip, sink, decrease, deteriorate, worsen, rot, decay, lapse, fall off, regress, go to pot, retrogress ▶ ADJECTIVE the degenerate attitudes he found among some of his fellow officers = **depraved**, base, corrupt, fallen, low, perverted, degraded, degenerated, immoral, decadent, debased, debauched, dissolute, pervy (slang)

degeneration NOUN = **deterioration**, decline, dissolution, descent, regression, dissipation, degeneracy, debasement

degradation NOUN 1 scenes of misery and degradation = **disgrace**, shame, humiliation, discredit, ignominy, dishonour, mortification 2 the progressive degradation of the state = **deterioration**, decline, decadence, degeneration, perversion, degeneracy, debasement, abasement

degrade VERB 1 No-one should feel degraded at their place of work. = **demean**, disgrace, humiliate, injure, shame, corrupt, humble, discredit, pervert, debase, dishonour, cheapen ■ **OPPOSITE:** ennoble 2 He was degraded to a lower rank. = **demote**, reduce,

lower, downgrade, depose, cashier ■ **OPPOSITE:** promote

degraded ADJECTIVE 1 I felt cheap and degraded by his actions. = **humiliated**, embarrassed, shamed, mortified, debased, discomfited, abased 2 morally degraded individuals = **corrupt**, low, base, abandoned, vicious, vile, sordid, decadent, despicable, depraved, debased, profligate, disreputable, debauched, dissolute, scungy (Austral. & N.Z.)

degrading ADJECTIVE = **demeaning**, lowering, humiliating, disgraceful, shameful, unworthy, debasing, undignified, contemptible, cheapening, dishonourable, infra dig (informal)

degree NOUN 1 They achieved varying degrees of success. = **amount**, measure, rate, stage, extent, grade, proportion, gradation 2 the fall of a man of high degree and noble character = **rank**, order, standing, level, class, position, station, status, grade, caste, nobility, echelon • **by degrees** The crowd was thinning, but only by degrees. = **little by little**, slowly, gradually, moderately, gently, piecemeal, bit by bit, imperceptibly, inch by inch, unhurriedly

dehydrate VERB = **dry**, evaporate, parch, desiccate, exsiccate

deign VERB = **condescend**, consent, stoop, see fit, think fit, lower yourself, deem it worthy

deity NOUN = **god**, goddess, immortal, divinity, godhead, divine being, supreme being, celestial being, atua (N.Z.)

dejected ADJECTIVE = **downhearted**, down, low, blue, sad, depressed, miserable, gloomy, dismal, melancholy, glum, despondent, downcast, morose, disheartened, wretched, disconsolate, crestfallen, doleful, down in the dumps (informal), cast down, sick as a parrot (informal), woebegone, low-spirited ■ **OPPOSITE:** cheerful

delay VERB 1 I delayed my departure until she could join me. = **put off**, suspend, postpone, stall, shelve, prolong, defer, hold over, temporize, put on the back burner (informal), protract, take a rain check on (U.S. & Canad. informal) 2 The passengers were delayed by bad weather. = **hold up**, detain, hold back, stop, arrest, halt, hinder, obstruct, retard, impede, bog down, set back, slow up ■ **OPPOSITE:** speed (up) 3 If he delayed any longer, the sun would be up. = **linger**, lag, loiter, dawdle, tarry, dilly-dally (informal), drag your feet or heels (informal) ▶ NOUN 1 Air restrictions might mean delays for Easter holidaymakers. = **hold-up**, wait, check, setback, interruption, obstruction, stoppage, impediment, hindrance **2** *We'll send you a quote without delay.* = **dawdling**, lingering, loitering, procrastination, tarrying, dilly-dallying (*informal*)

delectable ADJECTIVE **1** *a delectable dessert* = **delicious**, tasty, luscious, inviting, satisfying, pleasant, delightful, enjoyable, lush, enticing, gratifying, dainty, yummy (*slang*), scrumptious (*informal*), appetizing, toothsome, lekker (*S. African slang*), yummo (*Austral. slang*) ■ **OPPOSITE:** disgusting **2** *The Great Lake, built in the 1790s, is a delectable sight.* = **charming**, pleasant, delightful, agreeable, adorable

delegate NOUN *The rebels' chief delegate repeated their demands.* = **representative**, agent, deputy, ambassador, commissioner, envoy, proxy, depute (*Scot.*), legate, spokesman *or* woman *or* person ▶ VERB **1** *Many employers find it hard to delegate duties.* = **entrust**, transfer, hand over, give, pass on, assign, relegate, consign, devolve **2** *Officials have been delegated to start work on a settlement.* = **appoint**, commission, select, contract, engage, nominate, designate, mandate, authorize, empower, accredit, depute

delegation NOUN **1** *They sent a delegation to the talks.* = **deputation**, envoys, contingent, commission, embassy, legation **2** *the delegation of his responsibilities to his assistant* = **commissioning**, relegation, assignment, devolution, committal, deputizing, entrustment

delete VERB = **remove**, cancel, cut out, erase, edit, excise, strike out, obliterate, efface, blot out, cross out, expunge (*formal*), dele, rub out, edit out, blue-pencil

deliberate ADJECTIVE **1** *The attack was deliberate and unprovoked.* = **intentional**, meant, planned, considered, studied, designed, intended, conscious, calculated, thoughtful, wilful, purposeful, premeditated, prearranged, done on purpose ■ **OPPOSITE:** accidental **2** *His movements were gentle and deliberate.* = **careful**, measured, slow, cautious, wary, thoughtful, prudent, circumspect, methodical, unhurried, heedful ■ **OPPOSITE:** hurried ▶ VERB *The jury deliberated for two hours before returning with the verdict.* = **consider**, think, ponder, discuss, debate, reflect, consult, weigh, meditate, mull over, ruminate, cogitate

deliberately ADVERB = **intentionally**, on purpose, consciously, emphatically, knowingly, resolutely, pointedly, determinedly, wilfully, by design, studiously, in cold blood, wittingly, calculatingly

deliberation NOUN **1** *His decision was the result of great deliberation.* = **consideration**, thought, reflection, study, speculation, calculation, meditation, forethought, circumspection, cogitation **2** (*usually plural*) *The outcome of the deliberations was inconclusive.* = **discussion**, talk, conference, exchange, debate, analysis, conversation, dialogue, consultation, seminar, symposium, colloquy (*formal*), confabulation

delicacy NOUN **1** *the delicacy of the crystal glasses* = **fragility**, frailty, brittleness, flimsiness, frailness, frangibility **2** *The dancers were the epitome of delicacy and grace.* = **daintiness**, charm, grace, elegance, neatness, prettiness, slenderness, exquisiteness **3** *the delicacy of the political situation* = **difficulty**, sensitivity, stickiness (*informal*), precariousness, critical nature, touchiness, ticklishness **4** *He's shown considerable delicacy and tact.* = **sensitivity**, understanding, consideration, judgment, perception, diplomacy, discretion, skill, finesse, tact, thoughtfulness, savoir-faire, adroitness, sensitiveness **5** *course after course of mouthwatering delicacies* = **treat**, luxury, goody, savoury, dainty, morsel, titbit, choice item, juicy bit, bonne bouche (*French*) **6** *He played with a superb delicacy of touch.* = **lightness**, accuracy, precision, elegance, sensibility, purity, subtlety, refinement, finesse, nicety, fineness, exquisiteness

delicate ADJECTIVE **1** *china with a delicate design* = **fine**, detailed, elegant, exquisite, graceful **2** *The colours are delicate and tasteful.* = **subtle**, fine, nice, soft, delicious, faint, refined, muted, subdued, pastel, understated, dainty **3** *Although the material looks tough, it is very delicate.* = **fragile**, weak, frail, brittle, tender, flimsy, dainty, breakable, frangible **4** *the delicate issue of adoption* = **difficult**, critical, sensitive, complicated, sticky (*informal*), problematic, precarious, thorny, touchy, knotty, ticklish **5** *A cosmetic surgeon performed the delicate operation.* = **skilled**, accurate, precise, deft **6** *He didn't want to offend my delicate sensibilities.* = **fastidious**, nice, critical, pure, Victorian, proper, refined, discriminating, stuffy, scrupulous, prim, puritanical, squeamish, prudish, prissy (*informal*), strait-laced ■ **OPPOSITE:** crude **7** *a situation which requires delicate handling* = **diplomatic**, sensitive, careful, subtle, thoughtful, discreet, prudent, considerate, judicious, tactful ■ **OPPOSITE:** insensitive

delicately ADVERB **1** *soup delicately flavoured with nutmeg* = **finely**, lightly, subtly, softly, carefully, precisely, elegantly, gracefully, deftly, exquisitely, skilfully, daintily **2** *a delicately-worded memo* = **tactfully**, carefully, subtly, discreetly, thoughtfully, diplomatically, sensitively, prudently, judiciously, considerately

delicious ADJECTIVE **1** *a wide selection of delicious meals to choose from* = **delectable**, tasty, luscious, choice, savoury, palatable, dainty, mouthwatering, yummy (*slang*), scrumptious (*informal*), appetizing, toothsome, ambrosial, lekker (*S. African slang*), nectareous, yummo (*Austral. slang*) ■ **OPPOSITE:** unpleasant **2** *a delicious feeling of anticipation* = **delightful**, pleasing, charming, heavenly (*informal*), thrilling, entertaining, pleasant, enjoyable, exquisite, captivating, agreeable, pleasurable, rapturous, delectable ■ **OPPOSITE:** unpleasant

delight VERB *The report has delighted environmentalists.* = **please**, satisfy, content, thrill, charm, cheer, amuse, divert, enchant, rejoice, gratify, ravish, gladden, give pleasure to, tickle pink (*informal*) ■ **OPPOSITE:** displease ▶ NOUN *To my delight, the plan worked perfectly.* = **pleasure**, joy, satisfaction, comfort, happiness, ecstasy, enjoyment, bliss, felicity, glee, gratification, rapture, gladness ■ **OPPOSITE:** displeasure • **delight in** *or* **take a delight in something** *or* **someone** *He delighted in sharing his news.* = **like**, love, enjoy, appreciate, relish, indulge in, savour, revel in, take pleasure in, glory in, luxuriate in

delighted ADJECTIVE = **pleased**, happy, charmed, thrilled, enchanted, ecstatic, captivated, jubilant, joyous, elated, over the moon (*informal*), overjoyed, rapt, gladdened, cock-a-hoop, blissed out, in seventh heaven, sent, stoked (*Austral. & N.Z. informal*)

delightful ADJECTIVE = **pleasant**, pleasing, charming, engaging, heavenly (*informal*), thrilling, fascinating, entertaining, amusing, enjoyable, enchanting, captivating, gratifying, agreeable, pleasurable, ravishing, rapturous ■ **OPPOSITE:** unpleasant

delineate VERB *The relationship between Church and State was delineated in a formal agreement.* = **outline**, describe, draw, picture, paint, chart, trace, portray, sketch, render, depict, characterize, map out

delinquency NOUN = **crime**, misconduct, wrongdoing, fault, offence, misdemeanour, misdeed, misbehaviour, villainy, lawbreaking

delinquent NOUN = **criminal**, offender, villain, culprit, young offender, wrongdoer, juvenile delinquent, miscreant, malefactor, lawbreaker

delirious ADJECTIVE *He was delirious with joy.* = **ecstatic**, wild, excited, frantic, frenzied, hysterical, carried away, blissed out, beside yourself, sent, Corybantic ■ **OPPOSITE:** calm

delirium NOUN *She was in a delirium of panic.* = **frenzy**, passion, rage, fever, fury, ecstasy, hysteria

deliver VERB **1** *The pizza will be delivered in 20 minutes.* = **bring**, carry, bear, transport, distribute, convey, cart **2** (*sometimes with* **over** *or* **up**) *He was led in handcuffs and delivered over to me.* = **hand over**, present, commit, give up, yield, surrender, turn over, relinquish, make over **3** *He will deliver a speech about schools.* = **give**, read, present, announce, publish, declare, proclaim, pronounce, utter, give forth **4** *A single blow had been delivered to the head.* = **strike**, give, deal, launch, throw, direct, aim, administer, inflict **5** *Mercifully, I was delivered from that pain.* = **release**, free, save, rescue, loose, discharge, liberate, acquit, redeem, ransom, emancipate

deliverance NOUN = **release**, rescue, liberation, salvation, redemption, ransom, emancipation

delivery NOUN **1** *the delivery of goods and resources* = **handing over**, transfer, distribution, transmission, dispatch, consignment, conveyance, transmittal **2** *a delivery of fresh eggs* = **consignment**, goods, shipment, batch **3** *His speeches were magnificent but his delivery was hopeless.* = **speech**, speaking, expression, pronunciation, utterance, articulation, intonation, diction, elocution, enunciation, vocalization **4** *She had an easy delivery.* = **childbirth**, labour, confinement, parturition

delude VERB = **deceive**, kid (*informal*), fool, trick, take in (*informal*), cheat, con (*informal*), mislead, impose on, hoax, dupe, beguile, gull (*archaic*), bamboozle (*informal*), hoodwink, take for a ride (*informal*), pull the wool over someone's eyes, lead up the garden path (*informal*), cozen, misguide, scam (*slang*)

deluge NOUN **1** *a deluge of criticism* = **rush**, flood, avalanche, barrage, spate, torrent **2** *A dozen homes were damaged in the deluge.* = **flood**, spate, overflowing, torrent, downpour, cataclysm, inundation ▶ VERB **1** *The office was deluged with complaints.* = **overwhelm**, swamp, engulf, overload, overrun, inundate **2** *Torrential rain deluged the capital.* = **flood**, drown, swamp, submerge, soak, drench, inundate, douse

delusion NOUN = **misconception**, mistaken idea, misapprehension, fancy, illusion, deception, hallucination, fallacy, self-deception, false impression, phantasm, misbelief

deluxe *or* **de luxe** ADJECTIVE = **luxurious**, grand, select, special, expensive, rich, exclusive, superior, elegant, costly, splendid, gorgeous, sumptuous, plush (*informal*), opulent, palatial, splendiferous (*facetious*)

delve VERB **1** *She delved into her mother's past.* = **research**, investigate, explore, examine, probe, look into, burrow into, dig into **2** *He delved into his rucksack and pulled out a folder.* = **rummage**, search, look, burrow, ransack, forage, dig, fossick (*Austral. & N.Z.*)

demagogue NOUN = **agitator**, firebrand, haranguer, rabble-rouser, soapbox orator

demand VERB **1** *She demanded an immediate apology.* = **request**, ask (for), order, expect, claim, seek, call for, insist on, exact, appeal for, solicit **2** *'What do you expect me to do about it?' she demanded.* = **challenge**, ask, question, inquire **3** *The task demands much patience and hard work.* = **require**, take, want, need, involve, call for, entail, necessitate, cry out for ■ OPPOSITE: provide ▶ NOUN **1** *He grew ever more fierce in his demands.* = **request**, order, charge, bidding **2** *The demand for coal is down.* = **need**, want, call, market, claim, requirement, necessity • **in demand** *He was much in demand as a lecturer.* = **sought after**, needed, popular, favoured, requested, in favour, fashionable, well-liked, in vogue, like gold dust

demanding ADJECTIVE *It is a demanding job.* = **difficult**, trying, hard, taxing, wearing, challenging, tough, exhausting, exacting, exigent ■ OPPOSITE: easy

demarcation NOUN **1** *the demarcation of the border between the two countries* = **limit**, bound, margin, boundary, confine, enclosure, pale **2** *The demarcation of duties became more blurred.* = **delimitation**, division, distinction, separation, differentiation

demean VERB *All this talk of money just demeans us.* = **degrade**, lower, debase, humble, abase • **demean yourself** *I wasn't going to demean myself by answering him.* = **lower yourself**, humiliate yourself, humble yourself, debase yourself, downgrade yourself, abase yourself, belittle yourself, degrade yourself

demeanour *or* (*U.S.*) **demeanor** NOUN **1** = **behaviour**, conduct, manner **2** = **bearing**, air, manner, carriage, deportment, mien (*literary*), comportment

demented ADJECTIVE *Sid broke into demented laughter.* = **mad**, crazy, frenzied, manic, crazed, deranged, maniacal

demise NOUN **1** *the demise of the reform movement* = **failure**, end, fall, defeat, collapse, ruin, breakdown, overthrow, downfall, dissolution, termination **2** *Smoking was the cause of his early demise.* = **death**, end, dying, passing, departure, expiration, decease

democracy NOUN = **self-government**, republic, commonwealth, representative government, government by the people

democratic ADJECTIVE = **self-governing**, popular, republican, representative, autonomous, populist, egalitarian

demolish VERB **1** *The building is being demolished to make way for a motorway.* = **knock down**, level, destroy, ruin, overthrow, dismantle, flatten, trash (*slang*), total (*slang*), tear down, bulldoze, raze, pulverize ■ OPPOSITE: build **2** *Their intention was to demolish his reputation.* = **destroy**, wreck, overturn, overthrow, undo, blow out of the water (*slang*) **3** *We demolished a six-pack of beer.* = **devour**, eat, consume, swallow, bolt, gorge, put away, gobble up, guzzle, polish off (*informal*), gulp down, wolf down, pig out on (*slang*)

demolition NOUN = **knocking down**, levelling, destruction, explosion, wrecking, tearing down, bulldozing, razing

demon NOUN **1** *They believed he was possessed by evil demons.* = **evil spirit**, devil, fiend, goblin, ghoul, malignant spirit, atua (*N.Z.*), wairua (*N.Z.*) **2** *He is a demon for discipline.* = **wizard**, master, ace (*informal*), addict, fanatic, fiend (*informal*) **3** *He was a dictator and a demon.* = **monster**, beast, villain, rogue, barbarian, brute, ogre

demonic, demoniac *or* **demoniacal** ADJECTIVE **1** *demonic forces* = **devilish**, satanic, diabolical, hellish, infernal (*informal*), fiendish, diabolic **2** *a demonic drive to succeed* = **frenzied**, mad, furious, frantic, hectic, manic, crazed, frenetic, maniacal, like one possessed

demonstrable ADJECTIVE = **provable**, obvious, evident, certain, positive, unmistakable, palpable, undeniable, self-evident, verifiable, irrefutable, incontrovertible, axiomatic, indubitable, attestable, evincible

demonstrate VERB **1** *You have to demonstrate that you are reliable.* = **prove**, show, establish, indicate, make clear, manifest, evidence, testify to, evince (*formal*), show clearly, flag up **2** *Have they demonstrated a commitment to democracy?* = **show**, evidence, express, display, indicate, exhibit, manifest, make clear or plain, flag up **3** *Vast crowds have been demonstrating against the reforms.* = **march**, protest, rally, object, parade, picket, say no to, remonstrate (*formal*), take up the cudgels, express disapproval, hikoi (*N.Z.*) **4** *He demonstrated how to peel and chop garlic.* = **describe**, show, explain, teach, illustrate

demonstration NOUN **1** *Riot police broke up the demonstration.* = **march**, protest, rally, sit-in, parade, procession, demo (*informal*), picket, mass lobby, hikoi (*N.Z.*) **2** *a cookery demonstration* = **display**, show, performance, explanation, description, presentation, demo (*informal*), exposition **3** *an unprecedented demonstration of people power* = **indication**, proof, testimony, confirmation, affirmation, validation, substantiation, attestation **4** *physical demonstrations of affection* = **exhibition**, display, expression, illustration

demoralize VERB = **dishearten**, undermine, discourage, shake, depress, weaken, rattle (*informal*), daunt, unnerve, disconcert, psych out (*informal*), dispirit, deject ■ **OPPOSITE:** encourage

demoralized ADJECTIVE = **disheartened**, undermined, discouraged, broken, depressed, crushed, weakened, subdued, unnerved, unmanned, dispirited, downcast, sick as a parrot (*informal*)

demoralizing ADJECTIVE = **disheartening**, discouraging, depressing, crushing, disappointing, daunting, dampening, dispiriting ■ **OPPOSITE:** encouraging

demote VERB = **downgrade**, relegate, degrade, kick downstairs (*slang*), declass, disrate (*Naval*), lower in rank ■ **OPPOSITE:** promote

demur VERB *At first I demurred when he asked me to do it.* = **object**, refuse, protest, doubt, dispute, pause, disagree, hesitate, waver, balk, take exception, cavil ▶ NOUN *She entered without demur.* = **objection**, protest, dissent, hesitation, misgiving, qualm, scruple, compunction, demurral, demurrer

demure ADJECTIVE = **shy**, reserved, modest, retiring, reticent, unassuming, diffident, decorous ■ **OPPOSITE:** brazen

den NOUN **1** *The skunk makes its den in burrows and hollow logs.* = **lair**, hole, shelter, cave, haunt, cavern, hide-out **2** *The walls of his den were covered in posters.* = **study**, retreat, sanctuary, hideaway, cloister, sanctum, cubbyhole, snuggery

denial NOUN **1** *their previous denial that chemical weapons were being used* = **negation**, dismissal, contradiction, dissent, disclaimer, retraction, repudiation, disavowal, adjuration ■ **OPPOSITE:** admission **2** *the denial of visas to international workers* = **refusal**, veto, rejection, prohibition, rebuff, repulse

denigrate VERB = **disparage**, run down, slag (off) (*slang*), knock (*informal*), rubbish (*informal*), blacken, malign, belittle, decry, revile, vilify, slander, defame, bad-mouth (*slang*), besmirch, impugn, calumniate, asperse ■ **OPPOSITE:** praise

denizen NOUN = **inhabitant**, resident, citizen, occupant, dweller

denomination NOUN **1** *Acceptance of women preachers varies from one denomination to another.* = **religious group**, belief, sect, persuasion, creed, school, hauhau (*N.Z.*) **2** *a pile of bank notes, mostly in small denominations* = **unit**, value, size, grade

denote VERB = **indicate**, show, mean, mark, express, import, imply, designate, signify, typify, betoken

denouement *or* **dénouement** NOUN = **outcome**, end, result, consequence, resolution, conclusion, end result, upshot

denounce VERB **1** *The leaders took the opportunity to denounce the attacks.* = **condemn**, attack, censure, decry, castigate, revile, damn, vilify, proscribe, stigmatize, impugn, excoriate, declaim against **2** *Informers might at any moment denounce them to the authorities.* = **report**, dob in (*Austral. slang*)

dense ADJECTIVE **1** *a large, dense forest* = **thick**, close, heavy, solid, substantial, compact, compressed, condensed, impenetrable, close-knit, thickset ■ **OPPOSITE:** thin **2** *a dense column of smoke* = **heavy**, thick, substantial, opaque, impenetrable **3** *You can be a bit dense sometimes.* = **stupid** (*informal*), slow, thick, dull, dumb (*informal*), crass, dozy (*Brit. informal*), dozy (*Brit. informal*), stolid, dopey (*informal*), moronic, obtuse, brainless, blockheaded, braindead (*informal*), dumb-ass (*informal*), dead from the neck up (*informal*), thickheaded, blockish, dim-witted (*informal*), slow-witted, thick-witted ■ **OPPOSITE:** bright

density NOUN **1** *The region has a high population density.* = **tightness**, closeness, thickness, compactness, impenetrability, denseness, crowdedness **2** *Jupiter's moon Io has a density of 3.5 grams per cubic centimetre.* = **mass**, body, bulk, consistency, solidity

dent NOUN *There was a dent in the bonnet of the car.* = **hollow**, chip, indentation, depression, impression, pit, dip, crater, ding (*Austral. & N.Z.*, *obsolete*, *informal*), dimple, concavity ▶ VERB *The table's brass feet dented the carpet's thick pile.* = **make a dent in**, press in, gouge, depress, hollow, imprint, push in, dint, make concave

denude VERB = **strip**, expose, bare, uncover, divest, lay bare

denunciation NOUN 1 *a stinging denunciation of his critics* = **condemnation**, criticism, accusation, censure, stick (*slang*), invective, character assassination, stigmatization, castigation, obloquy, denouncement, fulmination 2 *Denunciation by family, friends and colleagues inevitably sowed distrust.* = **implication**, accusation, indictment, incrimination, denouncement, inculpation

deny VERB 1 *She denied the accusations.* = **contradict**, oppose, counter, disagree with, rebuff, negate, rebut, refute, gainsay (*archaic, literary*) ■ **OPPOSITE:** admit 2 *I denied my parents because I wanted to become someone else.* = **renounce**, reject, discard, revoke, retract, repudiate, renege, disown, rebut, disavow, recant, disclaim, abjure, abnegate, refuse to acknowledge *or* recognize 3 *His ex-wife denies him access to his children.* = **refuse**, decline, forbid, reject, rule out, veto, turn down, prohibit, withhold, preclude, disallow, negate, begrudge, interdict ■ **OPPOSITE:** permit

deodorant NOUN 1 *He took a can of deodorant and sprayed his armpits.* = **antiperspirant**, deodorizer 2 *She didn't like the smell of the carpet deodorant in the limousine.* = **deodorizer**, disinfectant, air freshener, fumigant

depart VERB 1 *In the morning Mr McDonald departed for Sydney.* = **leave**, go, withdraw, retire, disappear, quit, retreat, exit, go away, vanish, absent (yourself), start out, migrate, set forth, take (your) leave, decamp, hook it (*slang*), slope off, pack your bags (*informal*), make tracks, rack off (*Austral. & N.Z. slang*) ■ **OPPOSITE:** arrive 2 *It takes a brave cook to depart radically from the traditional menu.* = **deviate**, vary, differ, stray, veer, swerve, diverge, digress, turn aside 3 *A number of staff departed during her reign as manager.* = **resign**, leave, quit, step down (*informal*), give in your notice, call it a day *or* night, vacate your post

departed ADJECTIVE = **dead**, late, deceased, expired, perished

department NOUN 1 *He worked in the sales department.* = **section**, office, unit, station, division, branch, bureau, subdivision 2 *Sorry, I don't know – that's not my department.* = **area**, line, responsibility, function, province, sphere, realm, domain, speciality

departure NOUN 1 *The airline has more than 90 scheduled departures from here each day.* = **leaving**, going, retirement, withdrawal, exit, going away, removal, exodus, leave-taking ■ **OPPOSITE:** arrival 2 *This would inevitably involve his departure from the post.* = **retirement**, going, withdrawal, exit, going away, removal 3 *This album is a considerable departure from her previous work.* = **shift**, change, difference, variation, innovation, novelty, veering, deviation, branching out, divergence, digression

dependable ADJECTIVE = **reliable**, sure, responsible, steady, faithful, staunch, reputable, trustworthy, trusty, go-to, unfailing ■ **OPPOSITE:** undependable

dependant NOUN = **relative**, rellie (*Austral. slang*), child, minor, subordinate, cohort (*chiefly U.S.*), protégé, henchman *or* woman *or* person, retainer, hanger-on, minion, vassal

dependence *or* (*sometimes U.S.*) **dependance** NOUN *the city's traditional dependence on tourism* = **reliance**, trust, hope, confidence, belief, faith, expectation, assurance

dependency *or* (*sometimes U.S.*) **dependancy** NOUN 1 *I am concerned by his dependency on his mother.* = **overreliance**, attachment 2 *He began to show signs of alcohol and drug dependency.* = **addiction**, dependence, craving, need, habit, obsession, enslavement, overreliance

dependent *or* (*sometimes U.S.*) **dependant** ADJECTIVE 1 *I refuse to be dependent, despite having a baby to care for.* = **reliant**, vulnerable, helpless, powerless, weak, defenceless ■ **OPPOSITE:** independent 2 *companies whose earnings are largely dependent on foreign economies* = **determined by**, depending on, subject to, influenced by, relative to, liable to, conditional on, contingent on • **dependent on** *or* **upon** *He was dependent on his parents for everything.* = **reliant on**, relying on, counting on

depend on VERB 1 *What happened later would depend on his talk with her.* = **be determined by**, be based on, be subject to, hang on, rest on, revolve around, hinge on, be subordinate to, be contingent on 2 *She assured him that he could depend on her.* = **count on**, turn to, trust in, bank on, lean on, rely upon, confide in, build upon, calculate on, reckon on

depict VERB 1 *a gallery of pictures depicting famous battles* = **illustrate**, portray, picture, paint, outline, draw, sketch, render, reproduce, sculpt, delineate, limn 2 *Children's books often depict animals as gentle* *creatures.* = **describe**, present, represent, detail, outline, sketch, characterize

depiction NOUN **1** *The vase has a depiction of a man playing a lyre.* = **picture**, drawing, image, outline, illustration, sketch, likeness, delineation **2** *the depiction of politicians in the mainstream media* = **representation**, description, portrait, illustration, sketch, portrayal

deplete VERB = **use up**, reduce, drain, exhaust, consume, empty, decrease, evacuate, lessen, impoverish, expend ■ **OPPOSITE:** increase

depleted ADJECTIVE = **used (up)**, drained, exhausted, consumed, spent, reduced, emptied, weakened, decreased, lessened, worn out, depreciated

depletion NOUN = **using up**, reduction, drain, consumption, lowering, decrease, expenditure, deficiency, dwindling, lessening, exhaustion, diminution

deplorable ADJECTIVE **1** *Many of them work under deplorable conditions.* = **terrible** (*informal*), distressing, dreadful, sad, unfortunate, disastrous, miserable, dire, melancholy, heartbreaking, grievous, regrettable, lamentable, calamitous, wretched, pitiable ■ **OPPOSITE:** excellent **2** *Sexual harassment is deplorable.* = **disgraceful**, shameful, scandalous, reprehensible, disreputable, dishonourable, execrable, blameworthy, opprobrious ■ **OPPOSITE:** admirable

deplore VERB **1** *He says he deplores violence.* = **disapprove of**, condemn, object to, denounce, censure, abhor, deprecate, take a dim view of, excoriate (*literary*) **2** *They deplored the heavy loss of life in the earthquake.* = **lament**, regret, mourn, rue (*literary*), bemoan, grieve for, bewail, sorrow over

deploy VERB (*troops or military resources*) = **use**, station, set up, position, arrange, set out, dispose, utilize, spread out, distribute

deployment NOUN (*of troops or military resources*) = **use**, stationing, spread, organization, arrangement, positioning, disposition (*archaic*), setup (*informal*), utilization

deport VERB = **expel**, exile, throw out, oust, banish, expatriate, extradite, evict, send packing, show you the door

deportation NOUN = **expulsion**, exile, removal, transportation, exclusion, extradition, eviction, ejection, banishment, expatriation, debarment

depose VERB = **oust**, dismiss, displace, degrade, downgrade, cashier, demote, dethrone, remove from office

deposit VERB **1** *The barman deposited a glass*

and two bottles of beer in front of him. = **put**, place, lay, drop, settle **2** *You are advised to deposit valuables in the hotel safe.* = **store**, keep, put, bank, save, lodge, entrust, consign, hoard, stash (*informal*), lock away, put in storage ▶ NOUN **1** *A deposit of £20 is required when ordering.* = **down payment**, security, stake, pledge, warranty, instalment, retainer, part payment **2** *underground deposits of gold and diamonds* = **accumulation**, growth, mass, build-up, layer **3** *A powdery deposit had settled at the bottom of the glass.* = **sediment**, grounds, residue, lees, precipitate, deposition, silt, dregs, alluvium, settlings

deposition NOUN **1** *The material would be checked against depositions from other witnesses.* = **sworn statement** (*Law*), evidence, testimony, declaration, affidavit **2** *It was this issue which led to the deposition of the leader.* = **removal**, dismissal, ousting, toppling, expulsion, displacement, unseating, dethronement

depository NOUN = **storehouse**, store, warehouse, depot, repository, safe-deposit box

depot NOUN **1** *a government arms depot* = **arsenal**, warehouse, storehouse, repository, depository, dump **2** *She was reunited with her boyfriend in the bus depot.* = **bus station**, station, garage, terminus

deprave VERB = **corrupt**, pervert, degrade, seduce, subvert, debase, demoralize, debauch, brutalize, lead astray, vitiate

depraved ADJECTIVE = **corrupt**, abandoned, perverted, evil, vicious, degraded, vile, degenerate, immoral, wicked, shameless, sinful, lewd, debased, profligate, debauched, lascivious, dissolute, licentious, pervy (*slang*) ■ **OPPOSITE:** moral

depravity NOUN = **corruption**, vice, evil, criminality, wickedness, immorality, iniquity, profligacy, debauchery, viciousness, degeneracy, sinfulness, debasement, turpitude (*formal*), baseness, depravation, vitiation

deprecate VERB *They deprecate him and refer to him as 'a bit of a red'.* = **disparage**, criticize, run down, discredit, scorn, deride, detract, malign, denigrate, belittle, vilify, knock (*informal*), diss (*slang*), throw shade (at) (*slang*), bad-mouth (*slang*), lambast(e)

depreciate VERB **1** *The demand for foreign currency depreciates the real value of local currencies.* = **decrease**, reduce, lessen, devalue, deflate, lower in value, devaluate ■ **OPPOSITE:** augment **2** *The euro is depreciating against the dollar.* = **lose value**, devalue, devaluate ■ **OPPOSITE:** appreciate

d

> **USAGE** The word *depreciate* is not synonymous with *deprecate*. *Depreciate* means 'to reduce or decline in value or price' while *deprecate* means 'to express disapproval of'.

depreciation NOUN = **devaluation**, fall, drop, depression, slump, deflation

depress VERB **1** *The state of the country depresses me.* = **sadden**, upset, distress, chill, discourage, grieve, daunt, oppress, desolate, weigh down, cast down, bring tears to your eyes, make sad, dishearten, dispirit, make your heart bleed, aggrieve, deject, make despondent, cast a gloom upon, harsh someone's mellow *or* buzz (*slang*) ■ **OPPOSITE:** cheer **2** *The stronger currency depressed sales.* = **lower**, cut, reduce, diminish, decrease, impair, lessen ■ **OPPOSITE:** raise **3** *A dearth of buyers has depressed prices.* = **devalue**, depreciate, cheapen, devaluate **4** *He depressed the pedal that lowered the chair.* = **press down**, push, squeeze, lower, flatten, compress, push down, bear down on

depressed ADJECTIVE **1** *He seemed somewhat depressed.* = **sad**, down, low, blue, unhappy, discouraged, fed up, moody, gloomy, pessimistic, melancholy, sombre, glum, mournful, dejected, despondent, dispirited, downcast, morose, disconsolate, crestfallen, doleful, downhearted, heavy-hearted, down in the dumps (*informal*), cheerless, woebegone, down in the mouth (*informal*), low-spirited **2** *attempts to encourage investment in depressed areas* = **poverty-stricken**, poor, deprived, distressed, disadvantaged, rundown, impoverished, needy, destitute, down at heel **3** *We need to prevent further falls in already depressed prices.* = **lowered**, devalued, weakened, impaired, depreciated, cheapened **4** *Manual pressure is applied to a depressed point on the body.* = **sunken**, hollow, recessed, set back, indented, concave

depressing ADJECTIVE = **bleak**, black, sad, distressing, discouraging, gloomy, daunting, hopeless, dismal, melancholy, dreary, harrowing, saddening, sombre, heartbreaking, dispiriting, disheartening, funereal, dejecting

depression NOUN **1** *I slid into a depression and became morbidly fascinated with death.* = **despair**, misery, sadness, the dumps (*informal*), the blues, melancholy, unhappiness, hopelessness, despondency, the hump (*Brit. informal*), bleakness, melancholia, dejection, wretchedness, low spirits, gloominess, dolefulness, cheerlessness, downheartedness **2** *He never forgot the hardships he witnessed during the depression.* = **recession**, slump, economic decline, credit crunch, stagnation, inactivity, hard *or* bad times **3** *an area pockmarked by rainfilled depressions* = **hollow**, pit, dip, bowl, valley, sink, impression, dent, sag, cavity, excavation, indentation, dimple, concavity

deprivation NOUN **1** *Millions suffer from sleep deprivation caused by long work hours.* = **lack**, denial, withdrawal, removal, expropriation, divestment, dispossession, deprival **2** *Single women with children are likely to suffer financial deprivation.* = **want**, need, hardship, suffering, distress, disadvantage, oppression, detriment, privation (*formal*), destitution

deprive VERB = **dispossess**, rob, strip, divest, expropriate, despoil (*formal*), bereave

deprived ADJECTIVE = **poor**, disadvantaged, needy, in need, lacking, bereft, destitute, in want, denuded, down at heel, necessitous (*literary*) ■ **OPPOSITE:** prosperous

depth NOUN **1** *The fish were detected at depths of more than a kilometre.* = **deepness**, drop, measure, extent, profundity, profoundness **2** *I am well aware of the depth of feeling that exists in the town.* = **strength**, intensity, seriousness, severity, extremity, keenness, intenseness **3** *His writing has a depth that will outlast him.* = **insight**, intelligence, wisdom, penetration, profundity, acuity, discernment, perspicacity (*formal*), sagacity, astuteness, profoundness, perspicuity ■ **OPPOSITE:** superficiality **4** *We were impressed with the depth of her knowledge.* = **breadth**, degree, magnitude, amplitude **5** *The blue base gives the red paint more depth.* = **intensity**, strength, warmth, richness, brightness, vibrancy, vividness **6** *His music lacks depth.* = **complexity**, intricacy, elaboration, obscurity, abstruseness, reconditeness ▶ PLURAL NOUN **1** *A sound came from the depths of the forest.* = **deepest part**, middle, midst, remotest part, furthest part, innermost part **2** *a man who had plumbed the depths of despair* = **most intense part**, pit, void, abyss, chasm, deepest part, furthest part, bottomless depth

deputy NOUN *France's minister for culture and his deputy attended the meeting.* = **substitute**, representative, ambassador, agent, commissioner, delegate, lieutenant, proxy, surrogate, second-in-command, nuncio, legate, vicegerent, number two ▶ MODIFIER *the academy's deputy director* = **assistant**, subordinate, depute (*Scot.*)

deranged ADJECTIVE *a deranged and motiveless rampage* = **mad**, crazy, distracted, frantic, frenzied, irrational, maddened, crazed, demented, berserk, delirious

derelict ADJECTIVE **1** *The haul was found dumped in a derelict warehouse.* = **abandoned**, deserted, ruined, neglected, discarded, forsaken, dilapidated **2** *They would be derelict in their duty not to pursue it.* = **negligent**, slack, irresponsible, careless, lax, remiss (*formal*) ▶ NOUN *A confused and wizened derelict wandered in off the street.* = **vagrant**, tramp, bum (*informal*), outcast, drifter, down-and-out, hobo (*chiefly U.S.*), vagabond, bag lady, dosser (*Brit. slang*), derro (*Austral. slang*)

dereliction NOUN **1** *The previous owners had rescued the building from dereliction.* = **abandonment**, desertion, renunciation, relinquishment **2** *(of duty) He pleaded guilty to wilful dereliction of duty.* = **negligence**, failure, neglect, evasion, delinquency, abdication, faithlessness, nonperformance, remissness

deride VERB = **mock**, ridicule, scorn, knock (*informal*), insult, taunt, sneer, jeer, disdain, scoff, detract, flout, disparage, chaff, gibe, pooh-pooh, contemn

derision NOUN = **mockery**, laughter, contempt, ridicule, scorn, insult, sneering, disdain, scoffing, disrespect, denigration, disparagement, contumely (*literary*), raillery

derisory ADJECTIVE = **ridiculous**, insulting, outrageous, ludicrous, preposterous, laughable, contemptible

derivation NOUN = **origin**, source, basis, beginning, root, foundation, descent, ancestry, genealogy, etymology

derivative ADJECTIVE *their dull, derivative debut album* = **unoriginal**, copied, second-hand, rehashed, imitative, plagiarized, uninventive, plagiaristic ■ OPPOSITE: original ▶ NOUN *a synthetic derivative of vitamin A* = **by-product**, spin-off, offshoot, descendant, derivation, outgrowth

derive VERB *He is one of those people who derives pleasure from helping others.* = **obtain**, get, receive, draw, gain, collect, gather, extract, elicit, glean, procure • **derive from something** *The word Druid may derive from 'drus', meaning 'oak tree'.* = **come from**, stem from, arise from, flow from, spring from, emanate from, proceed from, descend from, issue from, originate from

derogatory ADJECTIVE = **disparaging**, damaging, offensive, slighting, detracting, belittling, unfavourable, unflattering, dishonouring, defamatory, injurious, discreditable, uncomplimentary, depreciative ■ OPPOSITE: complimentary

descend VERB **1** *Disaster struck as the plane descended through the mist.* = **fall**, drop, sink, go down, plunge, dive, tumble, plummet, subside, move down ■ OPPOSITE: rise **2** = **get off 3** *Things are cooler and more damp as we descend to the cellar.* = **go down**, come down, walk down, move down, climb down **4** *The path descended steeply to the rushing river.* = **slope**, dip, incline, slant, gravitate • **be descended from** *He was proud to be descended from tradesmen.* = **originate from**, derive from, spring from, proceed from, issue from • **descend on something** or **someone** *Drunken mobs descended on their homes.* = **attack**, assault, raid, invade, swoop, pounce, assail, arrive, come in force • **descend to something** *She's got too much dignity to descend to writing anonymous letters.* = **lower yourself to**, stoop to, condescend to, abase yourself by

descendant NOUN = **successor**, child, issue, son, daughter, heir, offspring, progeny, scion, inheritor ■ OPPOSITE: ancestor

descent NOUN **1** *The airplane crashed on its descent into the airport.* = **fall**, drop, plunge, coming down, swoop **2** *On the descents, cyclists freewheel past cars.* = **slope**, drop, dip, incline, slant, declination, declivity **3** *his swift descent from respected academic to homeless derelict* = **decline**, deterioration, degradation, decadence, degeneration, debasement **4** *All the contributors were of foreign descent.* = **origin**, extraction, ancestry, lineage, family tree, parentage, heredity, genealogy, derivation

describe VERB **1** *We asked her to describe what she had seen.* = **relate**, tell, report, present, detail, explain, express, illustrate, specify, chronicle, recount, recite, impart, narrate, set forth, give an account of **2** *Even his allies describe him as forceful, aggressive and determined.* = **portray**, depict, characterize, define, sketch **3** *The ball described a perfect arc across the field.* = **trace**, draw, outline, mark out, delineate

description NOUN **1** *He gave a description of the surgery he was about to perform.* = **account**, report, explanation, representation, sketch, narrative, portrayal, depiction, narration, characterization, delineation **2** *his description of the country as a 'police state'* = **calling**, naming, branding, labelling, dubbing, designation **3** *Events of this description occurred daily.* = **kind**, sort, type, order, class, variety, brand, species, breed, category, kidney, genre, genus, ilk

descriptive ADJECTIVE = **graphic**, vivid, expressive, picturesque, detailed, explanatory, pictorial, illustrative, depictive

d

desecrate VERB = **profane**, dishonour, defile, violate, contaminate, pollute, pervert, despoil, blaspheme, commit sacrilege ■ **OPPOSITE:** revere

desert¹ NOUN *The vehicles have been modified to suit conditions in the desert.* = **wilderness**, waste, wilds, wasteland ▶ ADJECTIVE *the desert wastes of Mexico* = **barren**, dry, waste, wild, empty, bare, lonely, solitary, desolate, arid, unproductive, infertile, uninhabited, uncultivated, unfruitful, untilled

desert² VERB **1** *Poor farmers are deserting their fields and looking for jobs.* = **abandon**, leave, give up, quit (*informal*), withdraw from, move out of, relinquish, renounce, vacate, forsake, go away from, leave empty, relinquish possession of **2** *Her husband deserted her years ago.* = **leave**, abandon, strand, betray, maroon, walk out on (*informal*), forsake, jilt, run out on (*informal*), throw over, leave stranded, leave high and dry, leave (someone) in the lurch ■ **OPPOSITE:** take care of **3** *He deserted from the army last month.* = **abscond**, defect, decamp, go over the hill (*Military slang*)

desert³ NOUN • **just deserts** = **due**, payment, reward, punishment, right, return, retribution, recompense, comeuppance (*slang*), meed (*archaic*), requital, guerdon (*poetic*)

deserted ADJECTIVE **1** *a deserted town* = **empty**, abandoned, desolate, neglected, lonely, vacant, derelict, bereft, unoccupied, godforsaken **2** *a support group for deserted spouses* = **abandoned**, neglected, forsaken, lonely, forlorn, cast off, left stranded, left in the lurch, unfriended

deserter NOUN = **defector**, runaway, fugitive, traitor, renegade, truant, escapee, absconder, apostate

desertion NOUN **1** *It was a long time since she'd referred to her father's desertion of them.* = **abandonment**, betrayal, forsaking, dereliction, relinquishment **2** *mass desertion by the electorate* = **defection**, apostasy **3** *The high rate of desertion has added to the army's woes.* = **absconding**, flight, escape (*informal*), evasion, truancy

deserve VERB = **merit**, warrant, be entitled to, have a right to, win, rate, earn, justify, be worthy of, have a claim to

deserved ADJECTIVE = **well-earned**, just, right, meet (*archaic*), fitting, due, fair, earned, appropriate, justified, suitable, merited, proper, warranted, rightful, justifiable, condign

deservedly ADVERB = **rightly**, fittingly, fairly, appropriately, properly, duly, justifiably, justly, by rights, rightfully,

according to your due, condignly ■ **OPPOSITE:** undeservedly

deserving ADJECTIVE = **worthy**, righteous, commendable, laudable, praiseworthy, meritorious, estimable ■ **OPPOSITE:** undeserving

desiccate VERB = **dry**, drain, evaporate, dehydrate, parch, exsiccate

design VERB **1** *They have designed a machine that is both attractive and practical.* = **plan**, describe, draw, draft, trace, outline, invent, devise, sketch, formulate, contrive, think out, delineate **2** *We may be able to design a course to suit your particular needs.* = **create**, make, plan, project, fashion, scheme, propose, invent, devise, tailor, draw up, conceive, originate, contrive, fabricate, think up **3** *a compromise designed to please everyone* = **intend**, mean, plan, aim, purpose ▶ NOUN **1** *The pictures are based on simple geometric designs.* = **pattern**, form, figure, style, shape, organization, arrangement, construction, motif, configuration **2** *They drew up the design in a week.* = **plan**, drawing, model, scheme, draft, outline, sketch, blueprint, delineation **3** *Is there some design in having him here?* = **intention**, end, point, aim, goal, target, purpose, object, objective, intent

designate VERB **1** *one man interviewed in our study, whom we shall designate as 'Mr E'* = **name**, call, term, style, label, entitle, dub, nominate, christen **2** *I live in Exmoor, which is designated as a national park.* = **specify**, describe, indicate, define, characterize, stipulate, denote **3** = **choose**, reserve, select, label, flag, assign, allocate, set aside **4** *We need to designate someone as our spokesperson.* = **appoint**, name, choose, commission, select, elect, delegate, nominate, assign, depute

designation NOUN **1** *Level 4 alert is a designation reserved for very serious incidents.* = **name**, title, label, description, denomination, epithet **2** *the designation of the city as a centre of culture* = **appointment**, specification, classification **3** *the designation of Ali as Prophet Muhammad's successor* = **election**, choice, selection, appointment, nomination

designer NOUN **1** *She is a fashion designer.* = **couturier**, stylist **2** *Paxton was a brilliant designer of cast-iron structures.* = **producer**, architect, deviser, creator, planner, inventor, artificer, originator

designing ADJECTIVE = **scheming**, plotting, intriguing, crooked (*informal*), shrewd, conspiring, cunning, sly, astute, treacherous, unscrupulous, devious, wily, crafty, artful, conniving, Machiavellian, deceitful

desirability NOUN = **worth**, value, benefit, profit, advantage, merit, usefulness

desirable ADJECTIVE 1 *Prolonged negotiation was not desirable.* = **advantageous**, useful, valuable, helpful, profitable, of service, convenient, worthwhile, beneficial, preferable, advisable ■ **OPPOSITE:** disadvantageous 2 = **popular** ■ **OPPOSITE:** unpopular 3 *the young women whom his classmates thought most desirable* = **attractive**, appealing, beautiful, winning, interesting, pleasing, pretty, fair, inviting, engaging, lovely, charming, fascinating, sexy (*informal*), handsome, fetching (*informal*), good-looking, eligible, glamorous, gorgeous (*informal*), magnetic, cute, lush (*slang*), enticing, seductive, captivating, alluring, adorable, bonny (*Scot. & Northern English, dialect*), winsome, comely (*old-fashioned*), prepossessing ■ **OPPOSITE:** unattractive

desire VERB 1 *He was bored and desired change in his life.* = **want**, long for, crave, fancy (*informal*), hope for, ache for, covet, aspire to, wish for, yearn for, thirst for, hanker after, set your heart on, desiderate 2 *His Majesty desires me to make his wishes known to you.* = **request**, ask, petition, solicit, entreat, importune (*formal*) ▶ NOUN 1 *I had a strong desire to help and care for people.* = **wish**, want, longing, need, hope, urge, yen (*informal*), hunger, appetite, aspiration, ache, craving, yearning, inclination, thirst, hankering 2 *Aaron was suddenly overwhelmed by desire.* = **lust**, passion, libido, appetite, lechery, carnality, lasciviousness, concupiscence, randiness (*informal, chiefly Brit.*), lustfulness

desired ADJECTIVE = **required**, necessary, correct, appropriate, right, expected, fitting, particular, express, accurate, proper, exact

desist VERB = **stop**, cease, refrain from, end, kick (*informal*), give up, suspend, break off, abstain, discontinue, leave off, have done with, give over (*informal*), forbear, belay (*Nautical*)

desolate ADJECTIVE 1 *a desolate, godforsaken place* = **uninhabited**, deserted, bare, waste, wild, ruined, bleak, solitary, barren, dreary, godforsaken, unfrequented ■ **OPPOSITE:** inhabited 2 *He was desolate without her.* = **miserable**, depressed, lonely, lonesome (*chiefly U.S. & Canad.*), gloomy, dismal, melancholy, forlorn, bereft, dejected, despondent, downcast, wretched, disconsolate, down in the

dumps (*informal*), cheerless, comfortless, companionless ■ **OPPOSITE:** happy ▶ VERB 1 *I was desolated by the news.* = **deject**, depress, distress, discourage, dismay, grieve, daunt, dishearten ■ **OPPOSITE:** cheer 2 *A great famine desolated the country.* = **destroy**, ruin, devastate, ravage, lay low, lay waste, despoil (*formal*), depopulate

desolation NOUN 1 *He expresses his sense of desolation without self-pity.* = **misery**, distress, despair, gloom, sadness, woe, anguish, melancholy, unhappiness, dejection, wretchedness, gloominess 2 *We looked out upon a scene of utter desolation.* = **bleakness**, isolation, loneliness, solitude, wildness, barrenness, solitariness, forlornness, desolateness 3 *The army left a trail of desolation and death in its wake.* = **ruin**, destruction, havoc, devastation, ruination

despair VERB *He despairs at much of the press criticism.* = **lose hope**, give up, lose heart, be despondent, be dejected ▶ NOUN *She shook her head in despair at the futility of it all.* = **despondency**, depression, misery, gloom, desperation, anguish, melancholy, hopelessness, dejection, wretchedness, disheartenment

despairing ADJECTIVE = **hopeless**, desperate, depressed, anxious, miserable, frantic, dismal, suicidal, melancholy, dejected, broken-hearted, despondent, downcast, grief-stricken, wretched, disconsolate, inconsolable, down in the dumps (*informal*), at the end of your tether

despatch *see* **dispatch**

desperado NOUN = **criminal**, thug, outlaw, villain, gangster, gunman or woman, bandit, mugger (*informal*), cut-throat, hoodlum (*chiefly U.S.*), ruffian, heavy (*slang*), lawbreaker, skelm (*S. African*)

desperate ADJECTIVE 1 *Her people were poor, desperate and starving.* = **hopeless**, despairing, in despair, forlorn, abject, dejected, despondent, demoralized, wretched, disconsolate, inconsolable, downhearted, at the end of your tether 2 *Troops are needed to get food to people in desperate need.* = **grave**, great, pressing, serious, critical, acute, severe, extreme, urgent, dire, drastic, very grave 3 *a desperate rescue attempt* = **last-ditch**, dangerous, daring, determined, wild, violent, furious, risky, frantic, rash, hazardous, precipitate, hasty, audacious, madcap, foolhardy, headstrong, impetuous, death-defying

desperately ADVERB = **gravely**, badly, seriously, severely, dangerously, perilously

desperation NOUN 1 *this feeling of desperation and helplessness* = **misery**, worry, trouble, pain, anxiety, torture, despair, agony, sorrow, distraction, anguish, unhappiness, heartache, hopelessness, despondency **2** *It was an act of sheer desperation.* = **recklessness**, madness (*informal*), defiance, frenzy, impetuosity, rashness, foolhardiness, heedlessness

despicable ADJECTIVE = **contemptible**, mean, low, base, cheap (*informal*), infamous, degrading, worthless, disgraceful, shameful, vile, sordid, pitiful, abject, hateful, reprehensible, ignominious, disreputable, wretched, scurvy (*old-fashioned*), detestable, scungy (*Austral. & N.Z.*), beyond contempt ■ **OPPOSITE:** admirable

despise VERB = **look down on**, loathe, scorn, disdain, spurn, undervalue, deride, detest, revile, abhor, have a down on (*informal*), contemn ■ **OPPOSITE:** admire

despite PREPOSITION = **in spite of**, in the face of, regardless of, even with, notwithstanding, in defiance of, in the teeth of, undeterred by, in contempt of

despondency NOUN = **dejection**, depression, despair, misery, gloom, sadness, desperation, melancholy, hopelessness, the hump (*Brit. informal*), discouragement, wretchedness, low spirits, disconsolateness, dispiritedness, downheartedness

despondent ADJECTIVE = **dejected**, sad, depressed, down, low, blue, despairing, discouraged, miserable, gloomy, hopeless, dismal, melancholy, in despair, glum, dispirited, downcast, morose, disheartened, sorrowful, wretched, disconsolate, doleful, downhearted, down in the dumps (*informal*), sick as a parrot (*informal*), woebegone, low-spirited ■ **OPPOSITE:** cheerful

despot NOUN = **tyrant**, dictator, oppressor, autocrat, monocrat

despotic ADJECTIVE = **tyrannical**, authoritarian, dictatorial, absolute, arrogant, oppressive, autocratic, imperious, domineering, monocratic

despotism NOUN = **tyranny**, dictatorship, oppression, totalitarianism, autocracy, absolutism, autarchy, monocracy

dessert NOUN = **pudding**, sweet (*informal*), afters (*Brit. informal*), second course, last course, sweet course

destination NOUN = **stop**, station, haven, harbour, resting-place, terminus, journey's end, landing-place

destined ADJECTIVE *He feels that he was destined to become a musician.* = **fated**, meant, intended, designed, certain, bound, doomed,
ordained, predestined, foreordained
• **destined for** *products destined for the south* = **bound for**, booked for, directed towards, scheduled for, routed for, heading for, assigned to, en route to, on the road to

destiny NOUN **1** *We are masters of our own destiny.* = **fate**, fortune, lot, portion, doom, nemesis, divine decree **2** (*usually cap.*) *Is it Destiny or accident that brings people together?* = **fortune**, chance, karma, providence, kismet, predestination, divine will

destitute ADJECTIVE *destitute children who live on the streets* = **penniless**, poor, impoverished, distressed, needy, on the rocks, insolvent, poverty-stricken, down and out, indigent (*formal*), impecunious, dirt-poor (*informal*), on the breadline (*informal*), flat broke (*informal*), short, penurious, on your uppers, necessitous (*literary*), in queer street (*informal*), moneyless, without two pennies to rub together (*informal*) • **destitute of** *a country destitute of natural resources* = **lacking**, wanting, without, in need of, deprived of, devoid of, bereft of, empty of, drained of, deficient in, depleted in

destroy VERB **1** *The building was completely destroyed.* = **ruin**, smash, crush, waste, devastate, break down, wreck, shatter, gut, wipe out, dispatch, dismantle, demolish, trash (*slang*), total (*slang*), ravage, slay (*archaic, literary*), eradicate, torpedo, extinguish, desolate, annihilate, put paid to, raze, blow to bits, extirpate, blow sky-high **2** *The horse had to be destroyed.* = **slaughter**, kill, exterminate

destruction NOUN **1** *the extensive destruction caused by the rioters* = **ruin**, havoc, wreckage, crushing, wrecking, shattering, undoing, demolition, devastation, annihilation, ruination **2** *Our objective was the destruction of the enemy forces.* = **massacre**, slaughter, overwhelming, overthrow, extinction, end, downfall, liquidation, obliteration, extermination, eradication **3** *the destruction of animals infected with foot-and-mouth disease* = **slaughter**

destructive ADJECTIVE **1** *the awesome destructive power of nuclear weapons* = **devastating**, fatal, deadly, lethal, harmful, damaging, catastrophic, detrimental, hurtful, pernicious (*formal*), noxious, ruinous, calamitous, cataclysmic, baleful, deleterious (*formal*), injurious, baneful, maleficent **2** *Try to give constructive rather than destructive criticism.* = **negative**, hostile, discouraging, undermining, contrary, vicious, adverse, discrediting, disparaging, antagonistic, derogatory

desultory ADJECTIVE = **random**, vague, irregular, loose, rambling, inconsistent, erratic, disconnected, haphazard, cursory, aimless, off and on, fitful, spasmodic, discursive, unsystematic, inconstant, maundering, unmethodical

detach VERB **1** *Detach the bottom part from the form and keep it for reference.* = **separate**, free, remove, divide, isolate, cut off, sever, loosen, segregate, disconnect, tear off, disengage, disentangle, unfasten, disunite, uncouple, unhitch, disjoin, unbridle ■ **OPPOSITE:** attach **2** *Gerda gently detached her wrists from her friend's fingers.* = **free**, remove, separate, isolate, cut off, segregate, disengage

detached ADJECTIVE **1** *The piece is written in a detached, precise style.* = **objective**, neutral, impartial, reserved, aloof, impersonal, disinterested, unbiased, dispassionate, uncommitted, uninvolved, unprejudiced ■ **OPPOSITE:** subjective **2** *He lost his sight because of a detached retina.* = **separate**, free, severed, disconnected, loosened, discrete, unconnected, undivided, disjoined

detachment NOUN **1** *her professional detachment* = **indifference**, fairness, neutrality, objectivity, impartiality, coolness, remoteness, nonchalance, aloofness, unconcern, disinterestedness, nonpartisanship **2** *a detachment of marines* = **unit**, party, force, body, detail, squad, patrol, task force

detail NOUN **1** *I recall every detail of the party.* = **point**, fact, feature, particular, respect, factor, count, item, instance, element, aspect, specific, component, facet, technicality **2** *Only minor details now remain to be settled.* = **fine point**, part, particular, nicety, minutiae, triviality **3** *His personal detail totalled sixty men.* = **party**, force, body, duty, squad, assignment, fatigue, detachment ▶ VERB **1** *The report detailed the human rights abuses committed.* = **list**, describe, relate, catalogue, portray, specify, depict, recount, rehearse, recite, narrate, delineate, enumerate, itemize, tabulate, particularize **2** *He detailed someone to take it to the Incident Room.* = **appoint**, name, choose, commission, select, elect, delegate, nominate, assign, allocate, charge • **in detail** *Examine the wording in detail before deciding on the final text.* = **comprehensively**, completely, fully, thoroughly, extensively, inside out, exhaustively, point by point, item by item

detailed ADJECTIVE **1** *a detailed account of the discussions* = **comprehensive**, full, complete, minute, particular, specific, extensive, exact, thorough, meticulous, exhaustive, all-embracing, itemized, encyclopedic, blow-by-blow, particularized ■ **OPPOSITE:** brief **2** *detailed line drawings* = **complicated**, involved, complex, fancy, elaborate, intricate, meticulous, convoluted

detain VERB **1** *He was arrested and detained for questioning.* = **hold**, arrest, confine, restrain, imprison, intern, take prisoner, take into custody, hold in custody **2** *We won't detain you any further.* = **delay**, keep, stop, hold up, hamper, hinder, retard, impede, keep back, slow up or down

detect VERB **1** *equipment used to detect radiation* = **discover**, find, reveal, catch, expose, disclose, uncover, track down, unmask **2** *He could detect a certain sadness in her face.* = **notice**, see, spot, catch, note, identify, observe, remark, recognize, distinguish, perceive, scent, discern, ascertain, descry

detection NOUN = **discovery**, exposure, uncovering, tracking down, unearthing, unmasking, ferreting out

detective NOUN = **investigator**, cop (*slang*), copper (*slang*), dick (*slang, chiefly U.S.*), constable, tec (*slang*), private eye, sleuth (*informal*), private investigator, gumshoe (*U.S. slang*), bizzy (*slang*), C.I.D. man

detention NOUN = **imprisonment**, custody, restraint, keeping in, quarantine, confinement, porridge (*slang*), incarceration ■ **OPPOSITE:** release

deter VERB **1** *Jail sentences have done nothing to deter the offenders.* = **discourage**, inhibit, put off, frighten, intimidate, daunt, hinder, dissuade, talk out of **2** *Tuition fees can deter some people from going to university.* = **prevent**, stop, check, curb, damp, restrain, prohibit, hinder, debar

detergent NOUN *He squeezed some detergent over the dishes.* = **cleaner**, cleanser ▶ ADJECTIVE *low-lather detergent powders* = **cleansing**, cleaning, purifying, abstergent, detersive

deteriorate VERB **1** *There are fears that the situation may deteriorate.* = **decline**, worsen, degenerate, slump, degrade, depreciate, go downhill, go to the dogs (*informal*), go to pot ■ **OPPOSITE:** improve **2** *X-rays are used to prevent fresh food from deteriorating.* = **disintegrate**, decay, spoil, fade, break down, weaken, crumble, fall apart, ebb, decompose, wear away, retrogress

deterioration NOUN **1** *the rapid deterioration in relations between the two countries* = **decline**, fall, drop, slump, worsening,

d

downturn, depreciation, degradation, degeneration, debasement, retrogression, vitiation, dégringolade (*French*) **2** *enzymes that cause the deterioration of food* = **disintegration**, corrosion, atrophy

determination NOUN **1** *They acted with great courage and determination*. = **resolution**, purpose, resolve, drive, energy, conviction, courage, dedication, backbone, fortitude, persistence, tenacity, perseverance, willpower, boldness, firmness, staying power, stubbornness, constancy, single-mindedness, earnestness, obstinacy, steadfastness, doggedness, relentlessness, resoluteness, indomitability, staunchness ■ **OPPOSITE:** indecision **2** *A determination will be made as to the future of the treaty*. = **decision**, ruling, settlement, resolution, resolve, conclusion, verdict, judgment

determine VERB **1** *What determines whether you are a success or a failure?* = **affect**, control, decide, rule, condition, direct, influence, shape, govern, regulate, ordain (*formal*) **2** *The investigation will determine what really happened*. = **settle**, learn, establish, discover, check, find out, work out, detect, certify, verify, ascertain **3** *The people have a right to determine their own future*. = **decide on**, choose, establish, purpose, fix, elect, resolve **4** *I determined that I would ask him outright*. = **decide**, purpose, conclude, resolve, make up your mind

determined ADJECTIVE *He is making a determined effort to regain lost ground*. = **resolute**, firm, dogged, fixed, constant, bold, intent, persistent, relentless, stalwart, persevering, single-minded, purposeful, tenacious, undaunted, strong-willed, steadfast, unwavering, immovable, unflinching, strong-minded

determining ADJECTIVE = **deciding**, important, settling, essential, critical, crucial (*informal*), decisive, final, definitive, conclusive

deterrent NOUN = **discouragement**, obstacle, curb, restraint, impediment, check, hindrance, disincentive, defensive measures, determent ■ **OPPOSITE:** incentive

detest VERB = **hate**, loathe, despise, abhor, be hostile to, recoil from, be repelled by, have an aversion to, abominate, dislike intensely, execrate, feel aversion towards, feel disgust towards, feel hostility towards, feel repugnance towards ■ **OPPOSITE:** love

dethrone VERB = **depose**, overthrow, oust, unseat, uncrown

detonate VERB *The terrorists planted and*

detonated the bomb. = **set off**, trigger, explode, discharge, blow up, touch off

detonation NOUN = **explosion**, blast, bang, report, boom, discharge, fulmination

detour NOUN = **diversion** (*Brit*.), bypass, deviation, circuitous route, roundabout way, indirect course

detract from VERB **1** *Her faults did not seem to detract from her appeal*. = **lessen**, reduce, diminish, lower, take away from, derogate, devaluate ■ **OPPOSITE:** enhance **2** *They can only detract attention from the serious issues*. = **divert**, shift, distract, deflect, draw or lead away from

> ▌ **USAGE** *Detract* is sometimes wrongly used where *distract* is meant: *a noise distracted* (not *detracted*) *my attention*.

detractor NOUN = **slanderer**, belittler, disparager, defamer, traducer, muckraker, scandalmonger, denigrator, backbiter, derogator (*rare*)

detriment NOUN = **damage**, loss, harm, injury, hurt, prejudice, disadvantage, impairment, disservice

detrimental ADJECTIVE = **damaging**, destructive, harmful, adverse, pernicious (*formal*), unfavourable, prejudicial, baleful, deleterious (*formal*), injurious, inimical, disadvantageous ■ **OPPOSITE:** beneficial

devastate VERB **1** *A fire devastated large parts of the castle*. = **destroy**, waste, ruin, sack, wreck, spoil, demolish, trash (*slang*), level, total (*slang*), ravage, plunder, desolate, pillage, raze, lay waste, despoil (*formal*) **2** *If word of this gets out, it will devastate his family*. = **shatter**, overwhelm, confound, floor (*informal*)

devastating ADJECTIVE **1** *the devastating force of the floods* = **destructive**, damaging, catastrophic, harmful, detrimental, pernicious (*formal*), ruinous, calamitous, cataclysmic, deleterious (*formal*), injurious, maleficent **2** *The diagnosis was devastating. She had cancer*. = **traumatic**, shocking, upsetting, disturbing, painful, scarring **3** *his devastating criticism of the Prime Minister* = **savage**, cutting, overwhelming, withering, overpowering, satirical, incisive, sardonic, caustic, vitriolic, trenchant, mordant

devastation NOUN = **destruction**, ruin, havoc, ravages, demolition, plunder, pillage, desolation, depredation, ruination, spoliation

develop VERB **1** *Children develop at different rates*. = **grow**, advance, progress, mature, evolve, flourish, blossom, ripen **2** *a problem which developed from a leg injury* = **result**, follow, arise, issue, happen, spring, stem, derive, break out, ensue, come about, be a direct result of **3** *her dreams of developing her own business* = **establish**, set up, promote, generate, undertake, initiate, embark on, cultivate, instigate, inaugurate, set in motion **4** *She developed a taste for expensive nightclubs.* = **form**, start, begin, contract, establish, pick up, breed, acquire, generate, foster, originate **5** *They allowed me to develop their original idea.* = **expand**, extend, work out, elaborate, unfold, enlarge, broaden, amplify, augment, dilate upon

development NOUN **1** *the development of the embryo* = **growth**, increase, growing, advance, progress, spread, expansion, extension, evolution, widening, maturing, unfolding, unravelling, advancement, progression, thickening, enlargement **2** *the development of new and innovative services* = **establishment**, forming, generation, institution, invention, initiation, inauguration, instigation, origination **3** *There has been a significant development in the case.* = **event**, change, happening, issue, result, situation, incident, circumstance, improvement, outcome, phenomenon, evolution, unfolding, occurrence, upshot, turn of events, evolvement

deviant ADJECTIVE *social reactions to deviant and criminal behaviour* = **perverted**, sick (*informal*), twisted, bent (*slang*), abnormal, warped, perverse, wayward, devious, deviate, freaky (*slang*), aberrant, pervy (*slang*), sicko (*informal*) ■ **OPPOSITE:** normal ▶ NOUN *a dangerous deviant who caused trouble* = **pervert**, freak, misfit, sicko (*informal*), odd type

deviate VERB = **differ**, vary, depart, part, turn, bend, drift, wander, stray, veer, swerve, meander, diverge, digress, turn aside

deviation NOUN = **departure**, change, variation, shift, alteration, discrepancy, inconsistency, disparity, aberration, variance, divergence, fluctuation, irregularity, digression

device NOUN **1** *This device can measure minute quantities of matter.* = **gadget**, machine, tool, instrument, implement, invention, appliance, apparatus, gimmick, utensil, contraption (*informal*), contrivance, waldo, gizmo or gismo (*slang*) **2** *You can use the same login across all your devices.* = **smartphone**, tablet, laptop, iPad®, iPhone®, Kindle®, BlackBerry® **3** *His actions are obviously a device to buy time.* = **ploy**, scheme, strategy, plan, design, project, shift, trick, manoeuvre, stunt, dodge, expedient, ruse, artifice, gambit, stratagem, wile

devil NOUN **1** *the image of devils with horns and cloven hoofs* = **evil spirit**, demon, fiend, ghoul, hellhound, atua (*N.Z.*), wairua (*N.Z.*) **2** *the savage devils who mugged my friend* = **brute**, monster, savage, beast, villain, rogue, barbarian, fiend, terror, swine, ogre **3** *I feel sorry for the poor devil who marries you.* = **person**, individual, soul, creature, thing, human being, beggar **4** *You cheeky little devil!* = **scamp**, monkey (*informal*), rogue, imp, rascal, tyke (*informal*), scoundrel, scallywag (*informal*), mischief-maker, whippersnapper, toerag (*slang*), pickle (*Brit. informal*), nointer (*Austral. slang*) • **the Devil** *the eternal conflict between God and the Devil* = **Satan**, Lucifer, Prince of Darkness, Old One, Deuce, Old Gentleman (*informal*), Lord of the Flies, Old Harry (*informal*), Mephistopheles, Evil One, Beelzebub, Old Nick (*informal*), Mephisto, Belial, Clootie (*Scot.*), deil (*Scot.*), Apollyon, Old Scratch (*informal*), Foul Fiend, Wicked One, archfiend, Old Hornie (*informal*), Abbadon

devilish ADJECTIVE **1** *devilish instruments of torture* = **fiendish**, diabolical, wicked, satanic, atrocious, hellish, infernal (*informal*), accursed, execrable, detestable, damnable (*informal*), diabolic **2** *It was a devilish puzzle to solve.* = **difficult**, involved, complex, complicated, baffling, intricate, perplexing, thorny, knotty, problematical, ticklish

devious ADJECTIVE **1** *She tracked down the other woman by devious means.* = **sly**, scheming, calculating, tricky, crooked (*informal*), indirect, treacherous, dishonest, wily, insidious, evasive, deceitful, underhand, insincere, surreptitious, double-dealing, not straightforward ■ **OPPOSITE:** straightforward **2** *He followed a devious route.* = **indirect**, roundabout, wandering, crooked, rambling, tortuous, deviating, circuitous, excursive ■ **OPPOSITE:** direct

devise VERB = **work out**, plan, form, design, imagine, frame, arrange, plot, construct, invent, conceive, formulate, contrive, dream up, concoct, think up

devoid ADJECTIVE (*with* **of**) = **lacking in**, without, free from, wanting in, sans (*archaic*), bereft of, empty of, deficient in, denuded of, barren of

devolution NOUN = **transfer of power**, decentralization, distribution of power, surrender of power, relinquishment of power

devolve VERB (*with* **on**, **upon**, **to**, *etc*) = **transfer**, entrust, consign, depute

devote VERB = **dedicate**, give, commit, apply, reserve, pledge, surrender, assign, allot, give over, consecrate, set apart

devoted ADJECTIVE = **dedicated**, loving, committed, concerned, caring, true, constant, loyal, faithful, fond, ardent, staunch, devout, steadfast ■ **OPPOSITE:** disloyal

devotee NOUN 1 *She is a devotee of Bach's music.* = **enthusiast**, fan, supporter, follower, addict, admirer, buff (*informal*), fanatic, adherent, aficionado, fanboy (*informal*), fangirl (*informal*) 2 *devotees of the Hare Krishna movement* = **follower**, student, supporter, pupil, convert, believer, partisan, disciple, learner, apostle, adherent, votary, proselyte, catechumen

devotion NOUN 1 *I was impressed by his devotion to his family.* = **love**, passion, affection, intensity, attachment, zeal, fondness, fervour, adoration, ardour, earnestness 2 *devotion to the cause* = **dedication**, commitment, loyalty, allegiance, fidelity, adherence, constancy, faithfulness ■ **OPPOSITE:** indifference 3 *He was kneeling by his bed in an attitude of devotion.* = **worship**, reverence, spirituality, holiness, piety, sanctity, adoration, godliness, religiousness, devoutness ■ **OPPOSITE:** irreverence ▶ PLURAL NOUN *He performs his devotions twice a day.* = **prayers**, religious observance, church service, divine office

devotional ADJECTIVE = **religious**, spiritual, holy, sacred, devout, pious, reverential

devour VERB 1 *She devoured half an apple pie.* = **eat**, consume, swallow, bolt, dispatch, cram, stuff, wolf, gorge, gulp, gobble, guzzle, polish off (*informal*), pig out on (*slang*) 2 *He devoured 17 novels during his tour of India.* = **enjoy**, go through, absorb, appreciate, take in, relish, drink in, delight in, revel in, be preoccupied with, feast on, be engrossed in, read compulsively *or* voraciously

devouring ADJECTIVE = **overwhelming**, powerful, intense, flaming, consuming, excessive, passionate, insatiable

devout ADJECTIVE 1 *She was a devout Christian.* = **religious**, godly, pious, pure, holy, orthodox, saintly, reverent, prayerful ■ **OPPOSITE:** irreverent 2 *a devout belief in human kindness* = **sincere**, serious, deep, earnest, genuine, devoted, intense, passionate, profound, ardent, fervent, heartfelt, zealous, dinkum (*Austral. & N.Z. informal*) ■ **OPPOSITE:** indifferent

dexterity NOUN 1 *He showed great dexterity on the guitar.* = **skill**, expertise, mastery, touch, facility, craft, knack, finesse, artistry, proficiency, smoothness, neatness, deftness, nimbleness, adroitness, effortlessness, handiness ■ **OPPOSITE:** incompetence 2 *the wit and verbal dexterity of the script* = **cleverness**, art, ability, ingenuity, readiness, aptitude, adroitness, aptness, expertness, skilfulness

diabolical ADJECTIVE 1 *the diabolical treatment of their prisoners* = **dreadful**, shocking (*informal*), terrible, appalling, nasty, tricky, unpleasant, outrageous, vile, excruciating, atrocious (*informal*), abysmal, damnable 2 *sins committed in a spirit of diabolical enjoyment* = **wicked**, cruel, savage, monstrous, malicious, satanic, from hell (*informal*), malignant, unspeakable, inhuman, implacable, malevolent, hellish, devilish, infernal (*informal*), fiendish, ungodly, black-hearted, demoniac, hellacious (*U.S. slang*)

diagnose VERB = **identify**, determine, recognize, distinguish, interpret, pronounce, pinpoint

diagnosis NOUN 1 *Diagnosis of this disease can be very difficult.* = **identification**, discovery, recognition, detection 2 *She needs to have a second test to confirm the diagnosis.* = **opinion**, conclusion, interpretation, pronouncement

diagnostic ADJECTIVE = **symptomatic**, particular, distinguishing, distinctive, peculiar, indicative, idiosyncratic, recognizable, demonstrative

diagonal ADJECTIVE = **slanting**, angled, oblique, cross, crosswise, crossways, cater-cornered (*U.S. informal*), cornerways

diagonally ADVERB = **aslant**, obliquely, on the cross, at an angle, crosswise, on the bias, cornerwise

diagram NOUN = **plan**, figure, drawing, chart, outline, representation, sketch, layout, graph

dialect NOUN = **language**, speech, tongue, jargon, idiom, vernacular, brogue, lingo (*informal*), patois, provincialism, localism

dialectic NOUN = **debate**, reasoning, discussion, logic, contention, polemics, disputation, argumentation, ratiocination

dialogue NOUN 1 *He wants to open a dialogue with the protesters.* = **discussion**, conference, exchange, debate, confabulation (*formal*) 2 *Those who witnessed their dialogue spoke of high emotion.* = **conversation**, discussion, communication, discourse, converse, colloquy, confabulation, duologue, interlocution 3 *The play's dialogue is sharp and witty.* = **script**, conversation, lines, spoken part

diametrically ADVERB = **completely**, totally, entirely, absolutely, utterly

diarrhoea or (U.S.) **diarrhea** NOUN
= **the runs**, the trots (informal),
dysentery, looseness, the skits (informal),
Montezuma's revenge (informal), gippy
tummy, holiday tummy, Spanish tummy,
the skitters (informal)

diary NOUN **1** the most famous descriptive
passage in his diary = **journal**, chronicle,
day-to-day account, blog (informal) **2** My
diary is pretty full next week. = **engagement
book**, Filofax®, appointment book

diatribe NOUN = **tirade**, abuse, criticism,
denunciation, reviling, stricture, harangue,
invective, vituperation, stream of abuse,
verbal onslaught, philippic

dicey ADJECTIVE = **dangerous**, difficult, tricky,
risky, hairy (slang), ticklish, chancy (informal)

dichotomy NOUN = **division**, split,
separation, disjunction

dicky ADJECTIVE = **weak**, queer (informal),
shaky, unreliable, unsteady, unsound,
fluttery

dictate VERB He dictates his novels to his
secretary. = **speak**, say, utter, read out
▶ NOUN **1** They must abide by the dictates of the
new government. = **command**, order, decree,
word, demand, direction, requirement,
bidding, mandate, injunction, statute, fiat,
ultimatum, ordinance, edict, behest **2** We
have followed the dictates of our consciences.
= **principle**, law, rule, standard, code,
criterion, ethic, canon, maxim, dictum,
precept, axiom, moral law • **dictate to
someone** What gives them the right to dictate
to us? = **order (about)**, direct, lay down the
law, pronounce to

dictator NOUN = **absolute ruler**, tyrant,
despot, oppressor, autocrat, absolutist,
martinet

dictatorial ADJECTIVE **1** He suspended the
constitution and assumed dictatorial powers.
= **absolute**, unlimited, totalitarian,
autocratic, unrestricted, tyrannical,
despotic ■ **OPPOSITE**: democratic **2** a
dictatorial management style = **domineering**,
authoritarian, oppressive, bossy (informal),
imperious, overbearing, magisterial,
iron-handed, dogmatical ■ **OPPOSITE**:
servile

dictatorship NOUN = **absolute rule**,
tyranny, totalitarianism, authoritarianism,
reign of terror, despotism, autocracy,
absolutism

diction NOUN = **pronunciation**, speech,
articulation, delivery, fluency, inflection,
intonation, elocution, enunciation

dictionary NOUN = **wordbook**,
vocabulary, glossary, encyclopedia,
lexicon, concordance

dictum NOUN **1** the dictum that it is preferable
to be roughly right than precisely wrong
= **saying**, saw (old-fashioned), maxim,
adage, proverb, precept, axiom, gnome
2 his dictum that the priority of the government
must be the health of the people = **decree**,
order, demand, statement, command,
dictate, canon, fiat, edict, pronouncement

didactic ADJECTIVE **1** In totalitarian societies,
art exists solely for didactic purposes.
= **instructive**, educational, enlightening,
moral, edifying, homiletic, preceptive **2** He
adopts a lofty, didactic tone when addressing
people. = **pedantic**, academic, formal,
pompous, schoolmasterly, erudite,
bookish, abstruse, moralizing, priggish,
pedagogic

die VERB **1** His mother died when he was a child.
= **pass away**, depart, expire, perish, buy it
(U.S. slang), check out (U.S. slang), kick it
(slang), croak (slang), give up the ghost, go
belly-up (slang), snuff it (slang), peg out
(informal), kick the bucket (slang), buy the
farm (U.S. slang), peg it (informal), decease,
cark it (Austral. & N.Z. slang), pop your clogs
(informal), breathe your last, hop the twig
(slang) ■ **OPPOSITE**: live **2** The engine coughed,
spluttered, and died. = **stop**, fail, halt, break
down, run down, stop working, peter out,
fizzle out, lose power, seize up, conk out
(informal), go kaput (informal), go phut, fade
out or away **3** My love for you will never die.
= **dwindle**, end, decline, pass, disappear,
sink, fade, weaken, diminish, vanish,
decrease, decay, lapse, wither, wilt, lessen,
wane, subside, ebb, die down, die out,
abate, peter out, die away, grow less
■ **OPPOSITE**: increase • **be dying for
something** I'm dying for a cigarette. = **long
for**, want, desire, crave, yearn for, hunger
for, pine for, hanker after, be eager for, ache
for, swoon over, languish for, set your heart
on • **be dying of something** I'm dying of
thirst. = **be overcome with**, succumb to,
collapse with

die-hard or **diehard** NOUN Fanatical diehards
are hellbent on derailing the peace process.
= **reactionary**, fanatic, zealot,
intransigent, stick-in-the-mud (informal),
old fogey, ultraconservative

diet¹ NOUN Watch your diet – you need plenty
of fruit and vegetables. = **food**, provisions,
fare, rations, subsistence, kai (N.Z.
informal), nourishment, sustenance,
victuals, commons, edibles, comestibles,
nutriment, viands, aliment **2** Have you been
on a diet? You've lost a lot of weight. = **fast**,
regime, abstinence, regimen, dietary
regime ▶ VERB Most of us have dieted at some

d

time in our lives. = **slim**, fast, lose weight, abstain, eat sparingly ■ **OPPOSITE:** overindulge

diet² NOUN (*often cap.*) *The Diet has time to discuss the bill only until the 10th November.* = **council**, meeting, parliament, sitting, congress, chamber, convention, legislature, legislative assembly

dieter NOUN = **slimmer**, weight watcher, calorie counter, faster, reducer

differ VERB **1** *His story differed from his mother's in several respects.* = **be dissimilar**, contradict, contrast with, vary, counter, belie, depart from, diverge, negate, fly in the face of, run counter to, be distinct, stand apart, make a nonsense of, be at variance with ■ **OPPOSITE:** accord **2** *The two leaders have differed on the issue of sanctions.* = **disagree**, clash, dispute, dissent ■ **OPPOSITE:** agree

difference NOUN **1** *the vast difference in size* = **dissimilarity**, contrast, variation, change, variety, exception, distinction, diversity, alteration, discrepancy, disparity, deviation, differentiation, peculiarity, divergence, singularity, particularity, distinctness, unlikeness ■ **OPPOSITE:** similarity **2** *They pledge to refund the difference within 48 hours.* = **remainder**, rest, balance, remains, excess **3** *They are learning how to resolve their differences.* = **disagreement**, conflict, argument, row, clash, dispute, set-to (*informal*), controversy, contention, quarrel, strife, wrangle, tiff, contretemps, discordance, contrariety ■ **OPPOSITE:** agreement

different ADJECTIVE **1** *We have totally different views.* = **dissimilar**, opposed, contrasting, changed, clashing, unlike, altered, diverse, at odds, inconsistent, disparate, deviating, divergent, at variance, discrepant, streets apart **2** *Different countries specialise in different products.* = **various**, some, many, several, varied, numerous, diverse, divers (*archaic*), assorted, miscellaneous, sundry, manifold (*formal*), multifarious **3** *Try to think of a menu that is interesting and different.* = **unusual**, unique, special, strange, rare, extraordinary, bizarre, distinctive, something else, peculiar, uncommon, singular, unconventional, out of the ordinary, left-field (*informal*), atypical **4** *What you do in the privacy of your own home is a different matter.* = **other**, another, separate, individual, distinct, discrete

> **USAGE** On the whole, *different from* is preferable to *different to* and *different than*, both of which are considered unacceptable by some people. *Different*

to is often heard in British English, but is thought by some people to be incorrect; and *different than*, though acceptable in American English, is often regarded as unacceptable in British English. This makes *different from* the safest option: *this result is only slightly different from that obtained in the US* – or you can rephrase the sentence: *this result differs only slightly from that obtained in the US.*

differential ADJECTIVE *They may be forced to eliminate differential voting rights.* = **distinctive**, distinguishing, discriminative, diacritical ▶ NOUN *Industrial wage differentials widened.* = **difference**, discrepancy, disparity, amount of difference

differentiate VERB **1** *He cannot differentiate between his imagination and the real world.* = **distinguish**, separate, discriminate, contrast, discern, mark off, make a distinction, tell apart, set off *or* apart **2** *distinctive policies that differentiate them from the other parties* = **make different**, separate, distinguish, characterize, single out, segregate, individualize, mark off, set apart, set off **3** *These ectodermal cells differentiate into two cell types.* = **become different**, change, convert, transform, alter, adapt, modify

differently ADVERB = **dissimilarly**, otherwise, in another way, in contrary fashion ■ **OPPOSITE:** similarly

difficult ADJECTIVE **1** *It is difficult for some people to get jobs.* = **hard**, tough, taxing, demanding, challenging, painful, exacting, formidable, uphill, strenuous, problematic, arduous, onerous, laborious, burdensome, wearisome, no picnic (*informal*), toilsome, like getting blood out of a stone ■ **OPPOSITE:** easy **2** *It was a very difficult decision to make.* = **problematical**, involved, complex, complicated, delicate, obscure, abstract, baffling, intricate, perplexing, thorny, knotty, abstruse, ticklish, enigmatical ■ **OPPOSITE:** simple **3** *I had a feeling you were going to be difficult about this.* = **troublesome**, trying, awkward, demanding, rigid, stubborn, perverse, fussy, tiresome, intractable, fastidious, fractious, unyielding, obstinate, intransigent, unmanageable, unbending, uncooperative, hard to please, refractory, obstreperous, pig-headed, bull-headed, unaccommodating, unamenable ■ **OPPOSITE:** cooperative **4** *These are difficult times.* = **tough**, trying, hard, dark, grim, straitened, full of hardship ■ **OPPOSITE:** easy

difficulty NOUN **1** *The main difficulty has been getting enough students to try out the scheme.*

= **problem**, trouble, obstacle, hurdle, dilemma, hazard, complication, hassle (*informal*), snag, uphill (*S. African*), predicament, pitfall, stumbling block, impediment, hindrance, tribulation, quandary, can of worms (*informal*), point at issue, disputed point **2** *The injured man mounted his horse with difficulty.* = **hardship**, labour, pain, strain, awkwardness, painfulness, strenuousness, arduousness, laboriousness

diffident ADJECTIVE = **shy**, reserved, withdrawn, reluctant, modest, shrinking, doubtful, backward, unsure, insecure, constrained, timid, self-conscious, hesitant, meek, unassuming, unobtrusive, self-effacing, sheepish, aw-shucks, bashful, timorous (*literary*), unassertive

diffuse VERB *Our aim is to diffuse new ideas obtained from elsewhere.* = **spread**, distribute, scatter, circulate, disperse, dispense, dispel, dissipate, propagate, disseminate ▶ ADJECTIVE **1** *a diffuse community* = **spread-out**, scattered, dispersed, unconcentrated ■ OPPOSITE: concentrated **2** *His writing is so diffuse that it is almost impossible to understand.* = **rambling**, loose, vague, meandering, waffling (*informal*), long-winded, wordy, discursive, verbose, prolix, maundering, digressive, diffusive, circumlocutory

■ OPPOSITE: concise

> USAGE This word is quite commonly misused instead of *defuse*, when talking about calming down a situation. However, the words are very different in meaning and should never be used as alternatives to each other.

diffusion NOUN = **spreading**, distribution, scattering, circulation, expansion, propagation, dissemination, dispersal, dispersion, dissipation

dig VERB **1** *Dig a large hole and bang the stake in.* = **hollow out**, mine, pierce, quarry, excavate, gouge, scoop out **2** *I changed into clothes more suited to digging.* = **delve**, tunnel, burrow, grub **3** *He was outside digging the garden.* = **turn over**, till, break up, hoe **4** *He dug around in his pocket for his keys.* = **search**, hunt, root, delve, forage, dig down, fossick (*Austral. & N.Z.*) **5** *She dug her nails into his flesh.* = **poke**, drive, push, stick, punch, stab, thrust, shove, prod, jab **6** *I really dig this band's energy.* = **like**, enjoy, go for, appreciate, groove (*obsolete slang*), delight in, be fond of, be keen on, be partial to **7** *Can you dig what I'm trying to say?* = **understand**, follow ▶ NOUN **1** *She couldn't resist a dig at him after his unfortunate performance.* = **cutting remark**, crack

(*slang*), insult, taunt, sneer, jeer, quip, barb, wisecrack (*informal*), gibe **2** *She silenced him with a sharp dig in the small of the back.* = **poke**, thrust, butt, nudge, prod, jab, punch • **dig in** *Pull up a chair and dig in.* = **begin** *or* **start eating**, tuck in (*informal*)

digest VERB **1** *She couldn't digest food properly.* = **ingest**, absorb, incorporate, dissolve, assimilate **2** *She read everything, digesting every fragment of news.* = **take in**, master, absorb, grasp, drink in, soak up, devour, assimilate ▶ NOUN *a regular digest of environmental statistics* = **summary**, résumé, abstract, epitome, condensation, compendium, synopsis, précis, abridgment

digestion NOUN = **ingestion**, absorption, incorporation, assimilation ■ RELATED WORD: *adjective* peptic

digit NOUN = **finger**, toe

dignified ADJECTIVE = **distinguished**, august, reserved, imposing, formal, grave, noble, upright, stately, solemn, lofty, exalted, decorous ■ OPPOSITE: undignified

dignify VERB = **distinguish**, honour, grace, raise, advance, promote, elevate, glorify, exalt, ennoble, aggrandize

dignitary NOUN = **public figure**, worthy, notable, high-up (*informal*), bigwig (*informal*), celeb (*informal*), personage, pillar of society, pillar of the church, notability, pillar of the state, V.I.P.

dignity NOUN **1** *Everyone admired her extraordinary dignity and composure.* = **decorum**, breeding, gravity, majesty, grandeur, respectability, nobility, propriety, solemnity, gentility, courtliness, loftiness, stateliness **2** *Admit that you were wrong. You won't lose dignity.* = **self-importance**, pride, self-esteem, self-respect, self-regard, self-possession, amour-propre (*French*)

digress VERB = **wander**, drift, stray, depart, ramble, meander, diverge, deviate, turn aside, be diffuse, expatiate, go off at a tangent, get off the point *or* subject

dilapidated ADJECTIVE = **ruined**, fallen in, broken-down, battered, neglected, crumbling, rundown, decayed, decaying, falling apart, beat-up (*informal*), shaky, shabby, worn-out, ramshackle, in ruins, rickety, decrepit, tumbledown, uncared for, gone to rack and ruin

dilate VERB = **enlarge**, extend, stretch, expand, swell, widen, broaden, puff out, distend ■ OPPOSITE: contract

dilemma NOUN = **predicament**, problem, difficulty, spot (*informal*), fix (*informal*), mess, puzzle, jam (*informal*), embarrassment, plight, strait, pickle (*informal*), how-do-you-do (*informal*),

quandary, perplexity, tight corner or spot
• **on the horns of a dilemma** *I found myself on the horns of a dilemma – whatever I did, it would be wrong.* = **between the devil and the deep blue sea**, between a rock and a hard place (*informal*), between Scylla and Charybdis

> **USAGE** The use of *dilemma* to refer to a problem that seems incapable of solution is considered by some people to be incorrect. To avoid this misuse of the word, an appropriate alternative such as *predicament* could be used.

dilettante NOUN = **amateur**, aesthete, dabbler, trifler, nonprofessional

diligence NOUN = **application**, industry, care, activity, attention, perseverance, earnestness, attentiveness, assiduity, intentness, assiduousness, laboriousness, heedfulness, sedulousness

diligent ADJECTIVE = **hard-working**, careful, conscientious, earnest, active, busy, persistent, attentive, persevering, tireless, painstaking, laborious, industrious, indefatigable, studious, assiduous, sedulous ■ **OPPOSITE:** indifferent

dilute VERB **1** *Dilute the syrup well with cooled, boiled water.* = **water down**, thin (out), weaken, adulterate, make thinner, cut (*informal*) ■ **OPPOSITE:** condense **2** *It was a clear attempt to dilute the power of the protest.* = **reduce**, weaken, diminish, temper, decrease, lessen, diffuse, mitigate, attenuate ■ **OPPOSITE:** intensify

diluted ADJECTIVE = **watered down**, thinned, weak, weakened, dilute, watery, adulterated, cut (*informal*), wishy-washy (*informal*)

dim ADJECTIVE **1** *She stood waiting in the dim light.* = **dull**, weak, pale, muted, subdued, feeble, murky, opaque, dingy, subfusc **2** *The room was dim and cool and quiet.* = **poorly lit**, dark, gloomy, murky, shady, shadowy, dusky, crepuscular, darkish, tenebrous, unilluminated, caliginous (*archaic*) **3** *a dim February day* = **cloudy**, grey, gloomy, dismal, overcast, leaden ■ **OPPOSITE:** bright **4** *His torch picked out the dim figures.* = **unclear**, obscured, faint, blurred, fuzzy, shadowy, hazy, indistinguishable, bleary, undefined, out of focus, ill-defined, indistinct, indiscernible ■ **OPPOSITE:** distinct **5** *The era of social activism is all but a dim memory.* = **obscure**, remote, vague, confused, shadowy, imperfect, hazy, intangible, indistinct **6** *The prospects for a peaceful solution are dim.* = **unfavourable**, bad, black, depressing, discouraging,

gloomy, dismal, sombre, unpromising, dispiriting, disheartening ▶ VERB **1** *Dim the overhead lights.* = **turn down**, lower, fade, dull, bedim **2** *The houselights dimmed.* = **grow** or **become faint**, fade, dull, grow or become dim **3** *The dusk sky dims to a chilly indigo.* = **darken**, dull, cloud over

dimension NOUN **1** *This adds a new dimension to our work.* = **aspect**, side, feature, angle, facet **2** *She did not understand the dimension of her plight.* = **extent**, size, magnitude, importance, scope, greatness, amplitude, largeness ▶ PLURAL NOUN *the grandiose dimensions of the room* = **proportions**, range, size, scale, measure, volume, capacity, bulk, measurement, amplitude, bigness

diminish VERB **1** *The threat of war has diminished.* = **decrease**, decline, lessen, contract, weaken, shrink, dwindle, wane, recede, subside, ebb, taper, die out, fade away, abate, peter out ■ **OPPOSITE:** grow **2** *Federalism is intended to diminish the power of the central state.* = **reduce**, cut, decrease, lessen, contract, lower, weaken, curtail, abate, retrench ■ **OPPOSITE:** increase **3** *We never diminish each other, even when we're angry.* = **belittle**, scorn, devalue, undervalue, deride, demean, denigrate, scoff at, disparage, decry, sneer at, underrate, deprecate, depreciate, cheapen, derogate

diminution NOUN **1** *a slight diminution in asset value* = **decrease**, decline, lessening, weakening, decay, contraction, abatement **2** *The president has accepted a diminution of his original powers.* = **reduction**, cut, decrease, weakening, deduction, contraction, lessening, cutback, retrenchment, abatement, curtailment

diminutive ADJECTIVE = **small**, little, tiny, minute, pocket(-sized), mini, wee, miniature, petite, midget, undersized, teeny-weeny, Lilliputian, bantam, teensy-weensy, pygmy or pigmy ■ **OPPOSITE:** giant

din NOUN = **noise**, row, racket, crash, clash, shout, outcry, clamour, clatter, uproar, commotion, pandemonium, babel, hubbub, hullabaloo, clangour ■ **OPPOSITE:** silence

dine VERB *He dines alone most nights.* = **eat**, lunch, feast, sup, chow down (*slang*) • **dine on** or **off something** *I could dine on caviar and champagne for the rest of my life.* = **eat**, consume, feed on

dingy ADJECTIVE = **discoloured**, soiled, dirty, shabby, faded, seedy, grimy

dinkum ADJECTIVE = **genuine**, honest, natural, frank, sincere, candid, upfront (*informal*), artless, guileless

dinky ADJECTIVE = **cute**, small, neat, mini, trim, miniature, petite, dainty, natty (informal), cutesy (informal)

dinner NOUN **1** Would you like to stay and have dinner? = **meal**, main meal, spread (informal), repast, blowout (slang), collation, refection **2** The annual dinner was held in the spring. = **banquet**, feast, blowout (slang), repast, beanfeast (Brit. informal), carousal, hakari (N.Z.)

dinosaur NOUN = **fuddy-duddy** (informal), anachronism, dodo (informal), stick-in-the-mud (informal), antique (informal), fossil (informal), relic (informal), back number (informal)

dint NOUN • **by dint of** = **by means of**, using, by virtue of, by force of

diocese NOUN = **bishopric**, see

dip VERB **1** Dip the food into the sauce. = **plunge**, immerse, bathe, duck, rinse, douse, dunk, souse **2** The sun dipped below the horizon. = **drop (down)**, set, fall, lower, disappear, sink, fade, slump, descend, tilt, subside, sag, droop **3** a path which suddenly dips down into a tunnel = **slope**, drop (down), descend, fall, decline, pitch, sink, incline, drop away ▸ NOUN **1** Freshen the salad leaves with a quick dip into cold water. = **plunge**, ducking, soaking, drenching, immersion, douche, submersion **2** She acknowledged me with a slight dip of the head. = **nod**, drop, lowering, slump, sag **3** Turn right where the road makes a dip. = **hollow**, hole, depression, pit, basin, dent, trough, indentation, concavity **4** sheep dip = **mixture**, solution, preparation, suspension, infusion, concoction, dilution • **dip into something 1** a chance to dip into a wide selection of books = **sample**, try, skim, play at, glance at, run over, browse, dabble, peruse, surf (Computing) **2** She was forced to dip into her savings. = **draw upon**, use, employ, extract, take from, make use of, fall back on, reach into, have recourse to

diplomacy NOUN **1** Today's resolution is significant for American diplomacy. = **statesmanship**, statecraft, international negotiation **2** It took all his powers of diplomacy to get her to return. = **tact**, skill, sensitivity, craft, discretion, subtlety, delicacy, finesse, savoir-faire, artfulness ■ OPPOSITE: tactlessness

diplomat NOUN = **official**, ambassador, envoy, statesperson, consul, attaché, emissary, chargé d'affaires

diplomatic ADJECTIVE **1** The two countries have resumed full diplomatic relations. = **consular**, official, foreign-office, ambassadorial, foreign-politic **2** She is very

direct. I tend to be more diplomatic. = **tactful**, politic, sensitive, subtle, delicate, polite, discreet, prudent, adept, judicious, treating with kid gloves ■ OPPOSITE: tactless

dire ADJECTIVE = **desperate**, pressing, crying, critical, terrible, crucial, alarming, extreme, awful, appalling, urgent, cruel, horrible, disastrous, grim, dreadful, gloomy, fearful (informal), dismal, drastic, catastrophic, ominous, horrid (informal), woeful, ruinous, calamitous, cataclysmic, portentous, godawful (slang), exigent, bodeful

direct VERB **1** He directed the tiny beam of light at the roof. = **aim**, point, turn, level, train, focus, fix, cast **2** A guard directed them to the right. = **guide**, show, lead, point the way, point in the direction of **3** She will direct day-to-day operations. = **control**, run, manage, lead, rule, guide, handle, conduct, advise, govern, regulate, administer, oversee, supervise, dispose, preside over, mastermind, call the shots, call the tune, superintend **4** They have been directed to give special attention to poverty. = **order**, command, instruct, charge (formal), demand, require, bid, enjoin, adjure **5** Please direct your replies to the editor. = **address**, send, mail, route, label, superscribe ▸ ADJECTIVE **1** They took the direct route. = **quickest**, shortest **2** a direct flight from Glasgow = **straight**, through ■ OPPOSITE: circuitous **3** He has direct experience of the process. = **first-hand**, personal, immediate ■ OPPOSITE: indirect **4** We deny there is any direct connection between the two cases. = **clear**, specific, plain, absolute, distinct, definite, explicit, downright, point-blank, unequivocal, unqualified, unambiguous, categorical ■ OPPOSITE: ambiguous **5** She avoided giving a direct answer. = **straightforward**, open, straight, frank, blunt, sincere, outspoken, honest, matter-of-fact, downright, candid, forthright, truthful, upfront (informal), man-to-man, plain-spoken ■ OPPOSITE: indirect **6** It was a direct quotation from his earlier speech. = **verbatim**, exact, word-for-word, strict, accurate, faithful, letter-for-letter ▸ ADVERB You can fly there direct from Glasgow. = **non-stop**, straight

direction NOUN **1** We drove ten miles in the opposite direction. = **way**, course, line, road, track, bearing, route, path **2** They threatened a mass walk-out if the party did not change direction. = **tendency**, bent, current, trend, leaning, drift, bias, orientation, tack, tenor, proclivity (formal) **3** The house was built under the direction of his partner. = **management**, government, control, charge, administration, leadership, command, guidance, supervision, governance, oversight, superintendence

directions PLURAL NOUN Don't throw away the directions until we've finished cooking. = **instructions**, rules, information, plan, briefing, regulations, recommendations, indication, guidelines, guidance

directive NOUN = **order**, ruling, regulation, charge, notice, command, instruction, dictate, decree, mandate, canon, injunction, imperative, fiat, ordinance, edict

directly ADVERB 1 The plane will fly the hostages directly back home. = **straight**, unswervingly, without deviation, by the shortest route, in a beeline 2 Directly after the meeting, an official appealed on television. = **immediately**, promptly, instantly, right away, straightaway, speedily, instantaneously, pronto (informal), pdq (slang) 3 He'll be there directly. = **at once**, presently, soon, quickly, as soon as possible, in a second, straightaway, forthwith, posthaste 4 She explained simply and directly what she hoped to achieve. = **honestly**, openly, frankly, plainly, face-to-face, overtly, point-blank, unequivocally, truthfully, candidly, unreservedly, straightforwardly, straight from the shoulder (informal), without prevarication

directness NOUN = **honesty**, candour, frankness, sincerity, plain speaking, bluntness, outspokenness, forthrightness, straightforwardness

director NOUN = **controller**, head, leader, manager, chief, executive, chairperson, boss (informal), producer, governor, principal, administrator, supervisor, organizer, helmer, sherang (Austral. & N.Z.)

dirge NOUN = **lament**, requiem, elegy, death march, threnody (formal), dead march, funeral song, coronach (Scot. & Irish)

dirt NOUN 1 I started to scrub off the dirt. = **filth**, muck, grime, dust, mud, stain, crap (slang), tarnish, smudge, mire, impurity, slob (Irish), crud (slang), kak (S. African vulgar slang), grot (slang) 2 They all sit on the dirt in the shade of a tree. = **soil**, ground, earth, clay, turf, clod, loam, loam

dirty ADJECTIVE 1 The woman had matted hair and dirty fingernails. = **filthy**, soiled, grubby, nasty, foul, muddy, polluted, messy, sullied, grimy, unclean, mucky, grotty (slang), grungy (slang, chiefly U.S. & Canad.), scuzzy (slang, chiefly U.S.), begrimed, festy (Austral.

slang) ■ OPPOSITE: clean 2 Their opponents used dirty tactics. = **dishonest**, illegal, unfair, cheating, corrupt, crooked (informal), deceiving, fraudulent, treacherous, deceptive, unscrupulous, crafty, deceitful, double-dealing, unsporting, knavish (archaic) ■ OPPOSITE: honest 3 He laughed at their dirty jokes. = **obscene**, rude, coarse, indecent, blue, offensive, gross, filthy, vulgar, pornographic, sleazy, suggestive, lewd, risqué, X-rated (informal), bawdy, salacious, smutty, off-colour, unwholesome ■ OPPOSITE: decent 4 That was a dirty trick to play. = **despicable**, mean, low, base, cheap (informal), nasty, cowardly, beggarly, worthless, shameful, shabby, vile, sordid, low-down (informal), abject, squalid, ignominious, contemptible, wretched, scurvy (old-fashioned), detestable, scungy (Austral. & N.Z.) ▶ VERB He was afraid the dog's hairs might dirty the seats. = **soil**, foul, stain, spoil, smear, muddy, pollute, blacken, mess up, smudge, sully, defile, smirch, begrime ■ OPPOSITE: clean

disability NOUN = **condition**, disorder, infirmity, handicap (old-fashioned, offensive)

disabled ADJECTIVE = **with a disability**, paralysed, handicapped (old-fashioned, offensive)

> **USAGE** Referring to people with disabilities as the disabled can cause offence and should be avoided. Instead, use people with disabilities or disabled people.

disabuse VERB (someone of an idea or notion) = **enlighten**, correct, set right, open the eyes of, set straight, shatter (someone's) illusions, free from error, undeceive

disadvantage NOUN 1 They suffer the disadvantage of having been political exiles. = **drawback**, trouble, burden, weakness, handicap, liability, minus (informal), flaw, hardship, nuisance, snag, inconvenience, downside, impediment, hindrance, privation, weak point, fly in the ointment (informal) ■ OPPOSITE: advantage 2 An attempt to prevent an election would be to their disadvantage. = **harm**, loss, damage, injury, hurt, prejudice, detriment, disservice ■ OPPOSITE: benefit • **at a disadvantage** Children from poor families were at a distinct disadvantage. = **exposed**, vulnerable, wide open, unprotected, defenceless, open to attack, assailable

disadvantaged ADJECTIVE = **deprived**, struggling, impoverished, discriminated against, underprivileged

disaffected ADJECTIVE = **alienated**, resentful, discontented, hostile, estranged, dissatisfied, rebellious, antagonistic, disloyal, seditious, mutinous, uncompliant, unsubmissive

disaffection NOUN = **alienation**, resentment, discontent, hostility, dislike, disagreement, dissatisfaction, animosity, aversion, antagonism, antipathy, disloyalty, estrangement, ill will, repugnance, unfriendliness

disagree VERB **1** *The two men disagreed about what to do next.* = **differ (in opinion)**, argue, debate, clash, dispute, contest, fall out (*informal*), contend, dissent, quarrel, wrangle, bicker, take issue with, have words (*informal*), cross swords, be at sixes and sevens ■ **OPPOSITE:** agree **2** *Orange juice seems to disagree with some babies.* = **make ill**, upset, sicken, trouble, hurt, bother, distress, discomfort, nauseate, be injurious • **disagree with something** *or* **someone** *I disagree with all laws in principle.* = **oppose**, object to, dissent from

disagreeable ADJECTIVE **1** *a disagreeable odour* = **nasty**, offensive, disgusting, unpleasant, distasteful, horrid (*informal*), repellent, unsavoury, obnoxious, unpalatable, displeasing, repulsive, objectionable, repugnant, uninviting, yucky *or* yukky (*slang*), yucko (*Austral. slang*) ■ **OPPOSITE:** pleasant **2** *He's a shallow, disagreeable man.* = **ill-natured**, difficult, nasty, cross, contrary, unpleasant, rude, irritable, unfriendly, bad-tempered, surly, churlish, brusque, tetchy, ratty (*Brit. & N.Z. informal*), peevish, ungracious, disobliging, unlikable *or* unlikeable ■ **OPPOSITE:** good-natured

disagreement NOUN *My instructor and I had a brief disagreement.* = **argument**, row, difference, division, debate, conflict, clash, dispute, falling out, misunderstanding, dissent, quarrel, squabble, strife, wrangle, discord, tiff, altercation ■ **OPPOSITE:** agreement

disallow VERB = **reject**, refuse, ban, dismiss, cancel, veto, forbid, embargo, prohibit, rebuff, repudiate, disown, proscribe, disavow, disclaim, abjure

disappear VERB **1** *The car drove off and disappeared from sight.* = **vanish**, recede, drop out of sight, vanish off the face of the earth, evanesce (*formal*), be lost to view *or* sight ■ **OPPOSITE:** appear **2** *The problem should disappear altogether by the age of five.* = **pass**, wane, ebb, fade away **3** *The prisoner disappeared after being released on bail.* = **flee**, bolt, run away, fly, escape, split (*slang*), retire, withdraw, take off (*informal*), get away, vanish, depart, go, make off,

abscond, take flight, do a runner (*slang*), scarper (*Brit. slang*), slope off, cut and run (*informal*), beat a hasty retreat, make your escape, make your getaway **4** *My wallet seems to have disappeared.* = **be lost**, be taken, be stolen, go missing, be mislaid **5** *The immediate threat has disappeared.* = **cease**, end, fade, vanish, dissolve, expire, evaporate, perish, die out, pass away, cease to exist, melt away, leave no trace, cease to be known

disappearance NOUN **1** *the gradual disappearance of the pain* = **vanishing**, going, passing, disappearing, fading, melting, eclipse, evaporation, evanescence **2** *his disappearance while out on bail* = **flight**, departure, desertion, disappearing trick **3** *Police are investigating the disappearance of confidential files.* = **loss**, losing, mislaying

disappoint VERB **1** *He said that he was surprised and disappointed by the decision.* = **let down**, dismay, fail, dash, disillusion, sadden, vex, chagrin, dishearten, disenchant, dissatisfy, disgruntle **2** *My hopes have been disappointed many times before.* = **frustrate**, foil, thwart, defeat, baffle, balk

disappointed ADJECTIVE = **let down**, upset, distressed, discouraged, depressed, choked, disillusioned, discontented, dejected, disheartened, disgruntled, dissatisfied, downcast, saddened, disenchanted, despondent, downhearted, cast down ■ **OPPOSITE:** satisfied

disappointing ADJECTIVE = **unsatisfactory**, inadequate, discouraging, sorry, upsetting, sad, depressing, unhappy, unexpected, pathetic, inferior, insufficient, lame, disconcerting, second-rate, unworthy, not much cop (*Brit. slang*)

disappointment NOUN **1** *They expressed their disappointment at what had happened.* = **regret**, distress, discontent, dissatisfaction, disillusionment, displeasure, chagrin, disenchantment, dejection, despondency, discouragement, mortification, unfulfilment **2** *The defeat was a bitter disappointment.* = **letdown**, blow, disaster, failure, setback, fiasco, misfortune, calamity, whammy (*informal*), choker (*informal*), washout (*informal*) **3** *There was resentment among the people at the disappointment of their hopes.* = **frustration**, failure, ill-success

disapproval NOUN = **displeasure**, criticism, objection, condemnation, dissatisfaction, censure, reproach, denunciation, deprecation, disapprobation, stick (*slang*)

d

disapprove VERB **1** *My mother disapproved of my working in a pub.* = **condemn**, object to, dislike, censure, deplore, deprecate, frown on, take exception to, take a dim view of, find unacceptable, have a down on (*informal*), discountenance, look down your nose at (*informal*), raise an *or* your eyebrow ■ **OPPOSITE:** approve **2** *The judge disapproved the adoption because of my criminal record.* = **turn down**, reject, veto, set aside, spurn, disallow ■ **OPPOSITE:** endorse

disapproving ADJECTIVE = **critical**, discouraging, frowning, disparaging, censorious, reproachful, deprecatory, condemnatory, denunciatory, disapprobatory, boot-faced (*informal*) ■ **OPPOSITE:** approving

disarm VERB **1** *The forces in the territory should disarm.* = **demilitarize**, disband, demobilize, deactivate **2** *She did her best to disarm her critics.* = **win over**, persuade

disarmament NOUN = **arms reduction**, demobilization, arms limitation, demilitarization, de-escalation

disarming ADJECTIVE = **charming**, winning, irresistible, persuasive, likable *or* likeable

disarray NOUN **1** *The feud has plunged the country into political disarray.* = **confusion**, upset, disorder, indiscipline, disunity, disharmony, disorganization, unruliness, discomposure, disorderliness ■ **OPPOSITE:** order **2** *He found the room in disarray.* = **untidiness**, state, mess, chaos, tangle, mix-up, muddle, clutter, shambles, jumble, hotchpotch, hodgepodge (*U.S.*), dishevelment, pig's breakfast (*informal*) ■ **OPPOSITE:** tidiness

disaster NOUN **1** *the second air disaster in less than two months* = **catastrophe**, trouble, blow, accident, stroke, reverse, tragedy, ruin, misfortune, adversity, calamity, mishap, whammy (*informal*), misadventure, car crash (*informal*), train wreck (*informal*), cataclysm, act of God, bummer (*slang*), ruination, mischance **2** *The whole production was a disaster.* = **failure**, mess, flop (*informal*), catastrophe, rout, debacle, cock-up (*Brit. slang*), washout (*informal*)

disastrous ADJECTIVE **1** *the recent, disastrous earthquake* = **terrible**, devastating, tragic, fatal, unfortunate, dreadful, destructive, unlucky, harmful, adverse, dire, catastrophic, detrimental, untoward, ruinous, calamitous, cataclysmic, ill-starred, unpropitious, ill-fated, cataclysmal **2** *The team has had another disastrous day.* = **unsuccessful**, devastating, tragic, calamitous, cataclysmic

disavow VERB = **deny**, reject, contradict, retract, repudiate, disown, rebut, disclaim, forswear, gainsay (*archaic, literary*), abjure

disband VERB **1** *All the armed groups will be disbanded.* = **dismiss**, separate, break up, scatter, dissolve, let go, disperse, send home, demobilize **2** *The rebels have agreed to disband by the end of the month.* = **break up**, separate, scatter, disperse, part company, go (their) separate ways

disbelief NOUN = **scepticism**, doubt, distrust, mistrust, incredulity, unbelief, dubiety ■ **OPPOSITE:** belief

disbelieve VERB = **doubt**, reject, discount, suspect, discredit, not accept, mistrust, not buy (*slang*), repudiate, scoff at, not credit, not swallow (*informal*), give no credence to

disburse VERB = **pay out**, spend, lay out, fork out (*slang*), expend, shell out (*informal*)

> **USAGE** *Disburse* is sometimes wrongly used where *disperse* is meant: *the police used water cannons to disperse* (not *disburse*) *the crowd.*

disbursement NOUN = **payment**, spending, expenditure, disposal, outlay

disc NOUN **1** *a revolving disc with replaceable blades* = **circle**, plate, saucer, discus **2** *This disc includes the piano sonata in C minor.* = **record**, vinyl, gramophone record, phonograph record (*U.S. & Canad.*), platter (*U.S. slang*)

> **USAGE** In British English, the spelling *disc* is generally preferred, except when using the word in its computer senses, where *disk* is preferred. In US English, the spelling *disk* is used for all senses.

discard VERB = **get rid of**, drop, remove, throw away *or* out, reject, abandon, dump (*informal*), shed, scrap, axe (*informal*), ditch (*slang*), junk (*informal*), chuck (*informal*), dispose of, relinquish, dispense with, jettison, repudiate, cast aside ■ **OPPOSITE:** keep

discern VERB = **see**, perceive, make out, notice, observe, recognize, behold (*archaic, literary*), catch sight of, suss (out) (*slang*), espy, descry

discernible ADJECTIVE = **clear**, obvious, apparent, plain, visible, distinct, noticeable, recognizable, detectable, observable, perceptible, distinguishable, appreciable, discoverable

discerning ADJECTIVE = **discriminating**, knowing, sharp, critical, acute, sensitive, wise, intelligent, subtle, piercing, penetrating, shrewd, ingenious, astute, perceptive, judicious, clear-sighted, percipient, perspicacious (*formal*), sagacious (*formal*)

discharge VERB 1 *You are being discharged on medical grounds.* = **release**, free, clear, liberate, pardon, let go, acquit, allow to go, set free, exonerate, absolve 2 *He was dishonourably discharged from the army.* = **dismiss**, sack (*informal*), fire (*informal*), remove, expel, discard, oust, eject, cashier, give (someone) the boot (*slang*), give (someone) the sack (*informal*), kennet (*Austral. slang*), jeff (*Austral. slang*) 3 *the quiet competence with which he discharged his many duties* = **carry out**, perform, fulfil, accomplish, do, effect, realize, observe, implement, execute, carry through 4 *The goods will be sold in order to discharge the debt.* = **pay**, meet, clear, settle, square (up), honour, satisfy, relieve, liquidate 5 *The resulting salty water will be discharged at sea.* = **pour forth**, release, empty, leak, emit, dispense, void, gush, ooze, exude, give off, excrete, disembogue 6 *He was tried for unlawfully and dangerously discharging a weapon.* = **fire**, shoot, set off, explode, let off, detonate, let loose (*informal*) ▶ NOUN 1 *The doctors began to discuss his discharge from hospital.* = **release**, liberation, clearance, pardon, acquittal, remittance, exoneration 2 *They face receiving a dishonourable discharge from the Army.* = **dismissal**, notice (*Brit.*), removal, the boot (*slang*), expulsion, the sack (*informal*), the push (*slang*), marching orders (*informal*), ejection, demobilization, kiss-off (*slang, chiefly U.S. & Canad.*), the bum's rush (*slang*), the (old) heave-ho (*informal*), the order of the boot (*slang*), congé, your books or cards (*informal*) 3 *They develop a fever and a watery discharge from the eyes.* = **emission**, flow, ooze, secretion, excretion, pus, seepage, suppuration 4 *Where firearms are kept at home, the risk of accidental discharge is high.* = **firing**, report, shot, blast, burst, explosion, discharging, volley, salvo, detonation, fusillade 5 *free of any influence which might affect the discharge of his duties* = **carrying out**, performance, achievement, execution, accomplishment, fulfilment, observance

disciple NOUN 1 *Jesus and his disciples* = **apostle** 2 *a major intellectual figure with disciples throughout Europe* = **follower**, student, supporter, pupil, convert, believer, partisan, devotee, apostle, adherent, proselyte, votary, catechumen
■ **OPPOSITE:** teacher

disciplinarian NOUN = **authoritarian**, tyrant, despot, stickler, taskmaster, martinet, drill sergeant, strict teacher, hard master

discipline NOUN 1 *the need for strict discipline in military units* = **control**, rule, authority, direction, regulation, supervision, orderliness, strictness 2 *His image of calm, control and discipline that appealed to voters.* = **self-control**, control, restraint, self-discipline, coolness, cool (*slang*), willpower, calmness, self-restraint, orderliness, self-mastery, strength of mind or will 3 *inner disciplines like transcendental meditation* = **training**, practice, exercise, method, regulation, drill, regimen 4 *appropriate topics for the new discipline of political science* = **field of study**, area, subject, theme, topic, course, curriculum, speciality, subject matter, branch of knowledge, field of inquiry or reference
▶ VERB 1 *He was disciplined by his company, but not dismissed.* = **punish**, correct, reprimand, castigate, chastise, chasten, penalize, bring to book, reprove 2 *I'm very good at disciplining myself.* = **train**, control, govern, check, educate, regulate, instruct, restrain

disclaim VERB 1 *She disclaims any knowledge of her husband's business activities.* = **deny**, decline, reject, disallow, retract, repudiate, renege, rebut, disavow, abnegate, disaffirm 2 *the legislation which enabled him to disclaim his title* = **renounce**, reject, abandon, relinquish, disown, abdicate, forswear, abjure

disclaimer NOUN = **denial**, rejection, renunciation, retraction, repudiation, disavowal, abjuration

disclose VERB 1 *Neither side would disclose details of the transaction.* = **make known**, tell, reveal, publish, relate, broadcast, leak, confess, communicate, unveil, utter, make public, impart, divulge, out (*informal*), let slip, spill the beans about (*informal*), blow wide open (*slang*), get off your chest (*informal*), spill your guts about (*slang*)
■ **OPPOSITE:** keep secret 2 *clapboard façades that revolve to disclose snug interiors* = **show**, reveal, expose, discover, exhibit, unveil, uncover, lay bare, bring to light, take the wraps off ■ **OPPOSITE:** hide

disclosure NOUN 1 *unauthorised newspaper disclosures* = **revelation**, exposé, announcement, publication, leak, admission, declaration, confession, acknowledgment 2 *The disclosure of his marriage proposal was badly-timed.* = **uncovering**, publication, exposure, revelation, divulgence

discolour or (*U.S.*) **discolor** VERB 1 *Test first as this cleaner may discolour the fabric.* = **mark**, soil, mar, fade, stain, streak, tinge 2 *A tooth which has been hit hard may discolour.* = **stain**, fade, streak, rust, tarnish

discoloured or (U.S.) **discolored** ADJECTIVE = **stained**, tainted, tarnished, faded, pale, washed out, wan, blotched, besmirched, foxed, etiolated (formal)

discomfort NOUN **1** She suffered some discomfort, but no real pain. = **pain**, suffering, hurt, smarting, ache, throbbing, irritation, tenderness, pang, malaise, twinge, soreness ■ OPPOSITE: comfort **2** She heard the discomfort in his voice as he reluctantly agreed. = **uneasiness**, worry, anxiety, doubt, alarm, distress, suspicion, apprehension, misgiving, nervousness, disquiet, agitation, qualms, trepidation (formal), perturbation, apprehensiveness, dubiety, inquietude ■ OPPOSITE: reassurance **3** the hazards and discomforts of primitive continental travel = **inconvenience**, trouble, difficulty, bother, hardship, irritation, hassle (informal), nuisance, uphill (S. African), annoyance, awkwardness, unpleasantness, vexation ▸ VERB World leaders will have been greatly discomforted by these events. = **make uncomfortable**, worry, trouble, shake, alarm, disturb, distress, unsettle, ruffle, unnerve, disquiet, perturb, discomfit, discompose ■ OPPOSITE: reassure

disconcert VERB = **disturb**, worry, trouble, upset, confuse, rattle (informal), baffle, put off, unsettle, bewilder, shake up (informal), undo, flurry, agitate, ruffle, perplex, unnerve, unbalance, take aback, fluster, perturb, faze, flummox, throw off balance, nonplus, abash, discompose, put out of countenance

disconcerted ADJECTIVE = **disturbed**, worried, troubled, thrown (informal), upset, confused, embarrassed, annoyed, rattled (informal), distracted, at sea, unsettled, bewildered, shook up (informal), flurried, ruffled, taken aback, flustered, perturbed, fazed, nonplussed, flummoxed, caught off balance, out of countenance

disconcerting ADJECTIVE = **disturbing**, upsetting, alarming, confusing, embarrassing, awkward, distracting, dismaying, baffling, bewildering, perplexing, off-putting (Brit. informal), bothersome

disconnect VERB **1** The company has disconnected our electricity for non-payment. = **cut off 2** He disconnected the bottle from the overhead hook. = **detach**, separate, part, divide, sever, disengage, take apart, uncouple

disconnected ADJECTIVE **1** a sequence of utterly disconnected events = **unrelated 2** a meaningless jumble of disconnected words

= **confused**, mixed-up, rambling, irrational, jumbled, unintelligible, illogical, incoherent, disjointed, garbled, uncoordinated

disconsolate ADJECTIVE **1** I was disconsolate when the relationship ended. = **inconsolable**, crushed, despairing, miserable, hopeless, heartbroken, desolate, forlorn, woeful, grief-stricken, wretched **2** He was looking increasingly disconsolate. = **sad**, low, unhappy, miserable, gloomy, dismal, melancholy, forlorn, woeful; dejected, wretched, down in the dumps (informal)

discontent NOUN = **dissatisfaction**, unhappiness, displeasure, regret, envy, restlessness, uneasiness, vexation, discontentment, fretfulness

discontented ADJECTIVE = **dissatisfied**, complaining, unhappy, miserable, fed up, disgruntled, disaffected, vexed, displeased, fretful, cheesed off (Brit. slang), brassed off (Brit. slang), with a chip on your shoulder (informal) ■ OPPOSITE: satisfied

discontinue VERB = **stop**, end, finish, drop, kick (informal), give up, abandon, suspend, quit, halt, pause, cease, axe (informal), interrupt, terminate, break off, put an end to, refrain from, leave off, pull the plug on, belay (Nautical)

discontinued ADJECTIVE = **stopped**, ended, finished, abandoned, halted, terminated, no longer made, given up or over

discontinuity NOUN = **lack of unity**, disconnection, incoherence, disunion, lack of coherence, disjointedness, disconnectedness

discord NOUN = **disagreement**, division, conflict, difference, opposition, row, clashing, dispute, contention, friction, strife, wrangling, variance, disunity, dissension, incompatibility, discordance, lack of concord ■ OPPOSITE: agreement

discordant ADJECTIVE **1** He displays attitudes and conduct discordant with his culture. = **disagreeing**, conflicting, clashing, different, opposite, contrary, at odds, contradictory, inconsistent, incompatible, incongruous, divergent **2** They produced a discordant sound. = **harsh**, jarring, grating, strident, shrill, jangling, dissonant, cacophonous, inharmonious, unmelodious

discount VERB **1** Tour prices are being discounted. = **mark down**, reduce, lower **2** His theory was discounted immediately. = **disregard**, reject, ignore, overlook, discard, set aside, dispel, pass over, repudiate, disbelieve, brush off (slang), lay aside, pooh-pooh ▸ NOUN You often get a discount on discontinued goods. = **deduction**, cut, reduction, concession, allowance, rebate, cut price

discourage VERB **1** *Don't let this setback discourage you.* = **dishearten**, daunt, deter, crush, put off, depress, cow, dash, intimidate, dismay, unnerve, unman, overawe, demoralize, cast down, put a damper on, psych out (*informal*), dispirit, deject ■ **OPPOSITE:** hearten **2** *a campaign to discourage children from smoking* = **put off**, deter, prevent, dissuade, talk out of, discountenance ■ **OPPOSITE:** encourage

discouraged ADJECTIVE = **put off**, deterred, daunted, dashed, dismayed, pessimistic, dispirited, downcast, disheartened, crestfallen, sick as a parrot (*informal*)

discouragement NOUN **1** *Uncertainty is one of the major discouragements to investment.* = **deterrent**, opposition, obstacle, curb, check, setback, restraint, constraint, impediment, hindrance, damper, disincentive **2** *There's a sense of discouragement creeping into the workforce.* = **depression**, disappointment, despair, pessimism, hopelessness, despondency, loss of confidence, dejection, discomfiture, low spirits, downheartedness

discouraging ADJECTIVE = **disheartening**, disappointing, depressing, daunting, dampening, unfavourable, off-putting (*Brit. informal*), dispiriting, unpropitious

discourse NOUN **1** *a tradition of political discourse* = **conversation**, talk, discussion, speech, communication, chat, dialogue, converse **2** *He responds with a lengthy discourse on deployment strategy.* = **speech**, talk, address, essay, lecture, sermon, treatise, dissertation, homily, oration, disquisition, whaikorero (*N.Z.*)

discover VERB **1** *As he discovered, she had a brilliant mind.* = **find out**, see, learn, reveal, spot, determine, notice, realize, recognize, perceive, detect, disclose, uncover, discern, ascertain, suss (out) (*slang*), get wise to (*informal*) **2** *The suitcase was discovered on a roadside outside the city.* = **find**, come across, uncover, unearth, turn up, dig up, come upon, bring to light, light upon **3** *Scientists discovered a way of forming the image in a thin layer on the surface.* = **invent**, design, pioneer, devise, originate, contrive, conceive of

discoverer NOUN **1** *the myth of the heroic discoverer* = **explorer**, pioneer **2** *the discoverer of carbon-dioxide lasers* = **inventor**, author, originator, initiator

discovery NOUN **1** *The discovery that I already had a brother was a huge bombshell.* = **finding out**, news, announcement, revelation, disclosure, realization **2** *the discovery of new forensic techniques* = **invention**, launch, institution, introduction, pioneering, innovation, initiation, inauguration, induction, coinage, origination **3** *In that year, two momentous discoveries were made.* = **breakthrough**, find, finding, development, advance, leap, coup, invention, step forward, godsend, quantum leap **4** *the discovery of a cache of letters written from South America* = **finding**, turning up, locating, revelation, uncovering, disclosure, detection, espial

discredit VERB **1** *He says his accusers are trying to discredit him.* = **disgrace**, blame, shame, smear, stain, humiliate, degrade, taint, slur, detract from, disparage, vilify, slander, sully, dishonour, stigmatize, defame, bring into disrepute, bring shame upon ■ **OPPOSITE:** honour **2** *They realized there would be problems in discrediting the evidence.* = **dispute**, question, challenge, deny, reject, discount, distrust, mistrust, repudiate, cast doubt on or upon, disbelieve, pooh-pooh ▸ NOUN *His actions have brought discredit on the whole regiment.* = **disgrace**, scandal, shame, disrepute, smear, stigma, censure, slur, ignominy, dishonour, imputation, odium (*formal*), ill-repute, aspersion ■ **OPPOSITE:** honour

discredited ADJECTIVE = **rejected**, exposed, exploded, discarded, obsolete, refuted, debunked, outworn

discreet ADJECTIVE *He followed at a discreet distance.* = **tactful**, diplomatic, politic, reserved, guarded, careful, sensible, cautious, wary, discerning, prudent, considerate, judicious, circumspect, sagacious ■ **OPPOSITE:** tactless

discrepancy NOUN = **disagreement**, difference, variation, conflict, contradiction, inconsistency, disparity, variance, divergence, dissonance, incongruity, dissimilarity, discordance, contrariety

discrete ADJECTIVE = **separate**, individual, distinct, detached, disconnected, unattached, discontinuous

> **USAGE** This word is quite often used by mistake where *discreet* is intended: *reading is a set of discrete skills; she was discreet* (not *discrete*) *about the affair.*

discretion NOUN **1** *He conducted the whole affair with the utmost discretion.* = **tact**, care, consideration, judgment, caution, diplomacy, good sense, prudence, acumen, wariness, discernment, circumspection, sagacity, carefulness, judiciousness, heedfulness ■ **OPPOSITE:** tactlessness

2 *She was given the money to use at her own discretion.* = **choice**, will, wish, liking, mind, option, pleasure, preference, inclination, disposition, predilection, volition

discretionary ADJECTIVE = **optional**, arbitrary (*Law*), unrestricted, elective, open to choice, nonmandatory

discriminate VERB *He is incapable of discriminating between a good idea and a bad one.* = **differentiate**, distinguish, discern, separate, assess, evaluate, tell the difference, draw a distinction
 • **discriminate against someone** *They believe the law discriminates against women.* = **treat differently**, single out, victimize, disfavour, treat as inferior, show bias against, show prejudice against

discriminating ADJECTIVE = **discerning**, particular, keen, critical, acute, sensitive, refined, cultivated, selective, astute, tasteful, fastidious ■ OPPOSITE: undiscriminating

discrimination NOUN **1** *measures to counteract racial discrimination* = **prejudice**, bias, injustice, intolerance, bigotry, favouritism, unfairness, inequity **2** *He praised our taste and discrimination.* = **discernment**, taste, judgment, perception, insight, penetration, subtlety, refinement, acumen, keenness, sagacity, acuteness, clearness

discriminatory ADJECTIVE = **prejudiced**, biased, partial, weighted, favouring, one-sided, partisan, unjust, preferential, prejudicial, inequitable

discuss VERB = **talk about**, consider, debate, review, go into, examine, argue about, thrash out, ventilate, reason about, exchange views on, deliberate about, weigh up the pros and cons of, converse about, confer about

discussion NOUN **1** *There was a discussion about the wording of the report.* = **talk**, debate, argument, conference, exchange, review, conversation, consideration, dialogue, consultation, seminar, discourse, deliberation, symposium, colloquy (*formal*), confabulation, korero (*N.Z.*) **2** *For a discussion of nineteenth-century Russian politics, see chapter 4.* = **examination**, investigation, analysis, scrutiny, dissection

disdain NOUN *She looked at him with disdain.* = **contempt**, dislike, scorn, arrogance, indifference, sneering, derision, hauteur, snobbishness, contumely (*literary*), haughtiness, superciliousness ▶ VERB *a political leader who disdained the compromises of politics* = **scorn**, reject, despise, slight, disregard, spurn, undervalue, deride, look down on, belittle, sneer at, pooh-pooh,

contemn, look down your nose at (*informal*), misprize

disdainful ADJECTIVE = **contemptuous**, scornful, arrogant, superior, proud, sneering, aloof, haughty, derisive, supercilious, high and mighty (*informal*), hoity-toity (*informal*), turning up your nose (at), on your high horse (*informal*), looking down your nose (at)

disease NOUN **1** *illnesses such as heart disease* = **illness**, condition, complaint, upset, infection, disorder, sickness, ailment, affliction, malady, infirmity, indisposition, lurgy (*informal*) **2** *the disease of materialism at the core of our society* = **evil**, disorder, plague (*informal*), curse, cancer, blight, contamination, scourge, affliction, bane, contagion, malady, canker

diseased ADJECTIVE = **unhealthy**, sick, infected, rotten (*informal*), ailing, tainted, sickly, unwell, crook (*Austral. & N.Z. informal*), unsound, unwholesome

disembark VERB = **land**, get off, alight, arrive, step out, go ashore

disembodied ADJECTIVE = **ghostly**, phantom, spectral

disenchanted ADJECTIVE = **disillusioned**, disappointed, soured, cynical, indifferent, sick, let down, blasé, jaundiced, undeceived

disenchantment NOUN = **disillusionment**, disappointment, disillusion, rude awakening

disengage VERB **1** *He gently disengaged himself from his sister's tearful embrace.* = **release**, free, separate, ease, liberate, loosen, set free, extricate, untie, disentangle, unloose, unbridle **2** *More vigorous action is needed to force the army to disengage.* = **detach**, withdraw

disengaged ADJECTIVE = **unconnected**, separate, apart, detached, unattached

disengagement NOUN = **disconnection**, withdrawal, separation, detachment, disentanglement

disentangle VERB **1** *The author brilliantly disentangles complex debates.* = **resolve**, clear (up), work out, sort out, clarify, simplify **2** *They are looking at ways to disentangle him from this situation.* = **free**, separate, loose, detach, sever, disconnect, extricate, disengage **3** *The rope could not be disentangled and had to be cut.* = **untangle**, unravel, untwist, unsnarl

disfigure VERB **1** *These items could be used to injure or disfigure someone.* = **damage**, scar, mutilate, maim, injure, wound, deform **2** *ugly new houses which disfigure the countryside* = **mar**, distort, blemish, deface, make ugly, disfeature

disgorge VERB = **emit**, discharge, send out, expel, throw out, vent, throw up, eject, spout, spew, belch, send forth

disgrace NOUN **1** *I have brought disgrace upon my family.* = **shame**, contempt, discredit, degradation, disrepute, ignominy, dishonour, infamy, opprobrium, odium (*formal*), disfavour, obloquy, disesteem ■ **OPPOSITE:** honour **2** *the disgrace of having claimed a prize I didn't deserve* = **scandal**, stain, stigma, blot, blemish ▶ VERB *These soldiers have disgraced their regiment.* = **shame**, stain, humiliate, discredit, degrade, taint, sully, dishonour, stigmatize, defame, abase, bring shame upon ■ **OPPOSITE:** honour

disgraced ADJECTIVE = **shamed**, humiliated, discredited, branded, degraded, mortified, in disgrace, dishonoured, stigmatized, under a cloud, in the doghouse (*informal*)

disgraceful ADJECTIVE = **shameful**, shocking, scandalous, mean, low, infamous, degrading, unworthy, ignominious, disreputable, contemptible, dishonourable, detestable, discreditable, blameworthy, opprobrious

disgruntled ADJECTIVE = **discontented**, dissatisfied, annoyed, irritated, put out, hacked (off) (*U.S. slang*), grumpy, vexed, sullen, displeased, petulant, sulky, peeved, malcontent, testy, peevish, huffy, cheesed off (*Brit. slang*), hoha (*N.Z.*)

disguise VERB *She made no attempt to disguise her contempt.* = **hide**, cover, conceal, screen, mask, suppress, withhold, veil, cloak, shroud, camouflage, keep secret, hush up, draw a veil over, keep dark, keep under your hat ▶ NOUN *a ridiculous disguise* = **costume**, get-up (*informal*), mask, camouflage, false appearance

disguised ADJECTIVE **1** *a disguised bank robber* = **in disguise**, masked, camouflaged, undercover, incognito, unrecognizable **2** *Their HQ used to be a disguised builders' yard.* = **false**, assumed, pretend, artificial, forged, fake, mock, imitation, sham, pseudo (*informal*), counterfeit, feigned, phoney *or* phony (*informal*)

disgust VERB *He disgusted everyone with his boorish behaviour.* = **sicken**, outrage, offend, revolt, put off, repel, nauseate, gross out (*U.S. slang*), turn your stomach, fill with loathing, cause aversion ■ **OPPOSITE:** delight ▶ NOUN *Colleagues last night spoke of their disgust at the decision.* = **outrage**, shock, anger, hurt, fury, resentment, wrath, indignation

disgusted ADJECTIVE **1** *I'm disgusted with the way that he was treated.* = **outraged**,

appalled, offended, sickened, scandalized **2** *She was disgusted by the smell of the cheese.* = **sickened**, repelled, repulsed, nauseated

disgusting ADJECTIVE **1** = **sickening**, foul, revolting, gross, repellent, nauseating, repugnant, loathsome, festy (*Austral. slang*), yucko (*Austral. slang*) **2** = **appalling**, shocking, awful, offensive, dreadful, horrifying

dish NOUN **1** *Pile the potatoes into a warm serving dish.* = **bowl**, plate, platter, salver **2** *There are plenty of vegetarian dishes to choose from.* = **food**, fare, recipe • **dish something out** *The council wants to dish the money out to specific projects.* = **distribute**, assign, allocate, designate, set aside, hand out, earmark, inflict, mete out, dole out, share out, apportion • **dish something up** *They dished up the next course.* = **serve up**, serve, produce, present, hand out, ladle out, spoon out

disharmony NOUN = **discord**, conflict, clash, friction, discordance, disaccord, inharmoniousness

disheartened ADJECTIVE = **discouraged**, depressed, crushed, dismayed, choked, daunted, dejected, dispirited, downcast, crestfallen, downhearted, sick as a parrot (*informal*)

dishevelled *or* (*U.S.*) **disheveled** ADJECTIVE = **untidy**, disordered, messy, ruffled, rumpled, bedraggled, unkempt, tousled, hanging loose, blowsy, uncombed, disarranged, disarrayed, frowzy, daggy (*Austral. & N.Z. informal*) ■ **OPPOSITE:** tidy

dishonest ADJECTIVE = **deceitful**, corrupt, crooked (*informal*), designing, lying, bent (*slang*), false, unfair, cheating, deceiving, shady (*informal*), fraudulent, treacherous, deceptive, unscrupulous, crafty, swindling, disreputable, untrustworthy, double-dealing, unprincipled, mendacious, perfidious (*literary*), untruthful, guileful, knavish (*archaic*) ■ **OPPOSITE:** honest

dishonesty NOUN = **deceit**, fraud, corruption, cheating, graft (*informal*), treachery, trickery, criminality, duplicity, falsehood, chicanery, falsity, sharp practice, perfidy (*literary*), mendacity, fraudulence, crookedness, wiliness, unscrupulousness, improbity

dishonour *or* (*U.S.*) **dishonor** VERB *I don't want to dishonour the men and women who risk their lives to keep us safe.* = **disgrace**, shame, discredit, corrupt, degrade, blacken, sully, debase, debauch, defame, abase ■ **OPPOSITE:** respect ▶ NOUN *You have brought dishonour on a fine and venerable institution.* = **disgrace**, scandal, shame, discredit, degradation, disrepute, reproach, ignominy, infamy, opprobrium, odium (*formal*), disfavour, abasement, obloquy ■ **OPPOSITE:** honour

disillusion VERB = **shatter the illusions of**, disabuse, bring down to earth, open the eyes of, disenchant, undeceive

disillusioned ADJECTIVE = **disenchanted**, disappointed, enlightened, indifferent, disabused, sadder and wiser, undeceived

disillusionment NOUN = **disenchantment**, disappointment, disillusion, enlightenment, rude awakening, lost innocence

disincentive NOUN = **discouragement**, deterrent, impediment, damper, dissuasion, determent

disinclined ADJECTIVE = **reluctant**, unwilling, averse, opposed, resistant, hesitant, balking, loath, not in the mood, indisposed, antipathetic

disinfect VERB = **sterilize**, purify, decontaminate, clean, cleanse, fumigate, deodorize, sanitize ■ **OPPOSITE:** contaminate

disinfectant NOUN = **antiseptic**, sterilizer, germicide, sanitizer

disintegrate VERB = **break up**, crumble, fall apart, separate, shatter, splinter, break apart, fall to pieces, go to pieces, disunite

disinterest NOUN = **indifference**, apathy, lack of interest, disregard, detachment, absence of feeling

disinterested ADJECTIVE 1 *Scientists are expected to be impartial and disinterested.* = **impartial**, objective, neutral, detached, equitable, impersonal, unbiased, even-handed, unselfish, uninvolved, unprejudiced, free from self-interest ■ **OPPOSITE:** biased 2 *We had become jaded, disinterested and disillusioned.* = **indifferent**, apathetic, uninterested

> **USAGE** *Disinterested* is now so commonly used to mean 'not interested' that to avoid ambiguity it is often advisable to replace it by a synonym when the meaning intended is 'impartial, unbiased'. In the Bank of English about 10% of the examples of the word occur followed by *in*, and overall about a third of examples are of this usage.

disjointed ADJECTIVE 1 *his disjointed drunken ramblings* = **incoherent**, confused, disordered, rambling, disconnected, unconnected, loose, aimless, fitful, spasmodic 2 *our increasingly fragmented and disjointed society* = **disconnected**, separated, divided, split, displaced, dislocated, disunited

dislike VERB *We don't serve liver often because so many people dislike it.* = **hate**, object to, loathe, despise, shun, scorn, disapprove of, detest, abhor, recoil from, take a dim view of, be repelled by, be averse to, disfavour, have an aversion to, abominate, have a down on (*informal*), disrelish, have no taste or stomach for, not be able to bear or abide or stand ■ **OPPOSITE:** like ▶ NOUN *The two women viewed each other with dislike and suspicion.* = **hatred**, disgust, hostility, loathing, disapproval, distaste, animosity, aversion, antagonism, displeasure, antipathy, enmity, animus, disinclination, repugnance, odium (*formal*), detestation, disapprobation ■ **OPPOSITE:** liking

dislocate VERB 1 *She had dislocated her shoulder in the fall.* = **put out of joint**, disconnect, disengage, unhinge, disunite, disjoint, disarticulate 2 *The strike was designed to dislocate the economy.* = **disrupt**, disturb, disorder

dislocation NOUN 1 *The refugees have suffered a total dislocation of their lives.* = **disruption**, disorder, disturbance, disarray, disorganization 2 *He suffered a double dislocation of his left ankle.* = **putting out of joint**, unhinging, disengagement, disconnection, disarticulation

dislodge VERB 1 *Use a hoof pick to dislodge stones and dirt from your horse's feet.* = **displace**, remove, disturb, dig out, uproot, extricate, disentangle, knock loose 2 *The leader cannot dislodge her this time.* = **oust**, remove, expel, throw out, displace, topple, force out, eject, depose, unseat

disloyal ADJECTIVE = **treacherous**, false, unfaithful, subversive, two-faced, faithless, untrustworthy, perfidious (*literary*), apostate, traitorous ■ **OPPOSITE:** loyal

disloyalty NOUN = **treachery**, infidelity, breach of trust, double-dealing, falsity, perfidy (*literary*), unfaithfulness, falseness, betrayal of trust, inconstancy, deceitfulness, breaking of faith, Punic faith

dismal ADJECTIVE 1 *the country's dismal record in the Olympics* = **bad**, awful, dreadful, rotten (*informal*), terrible, poor, dire, duff (*Brit. informal*), abysmal, frightful, godawful (*slang*) 2 *You can't occupy yourself with dismal thoughts all the time.* = **sad**, gloomy, melancholy, black, dark, depressing, discouraging, bleak, dreary, sombre, forlorn, despondent, lugubrious, sorrowful, wretched, funereal, cheerless, dolorous ■ **OPPOSITE:** happy 3 *The main part of the hospital is pretty dismal.* = **gloomy**, depressing, dull, dreary, lugubrious, cheerless ■ **OPPOSITE:** cheerful

dismantle VERB = **take apart**, strip, demolish, raze, disassemble, unrig, take to pieces *or* bits

dismay VERB **1** *The committee was dismayed by what it had been told.* = **alarm**, frighten, scare, panic, distress, terrify, appal, startle, horrify, paralyse, unnerve, put the wind up (someone) (*informal*), give (someone) a turn (*informal*), affright, fill with consternation **2** *He was dismayed to learn that she was already married.* = **disappoint**, upset, sadden, dash, discourage, put off, daunt, disillusion, let down, vex, chagrin, dishearten, dispirit, disenchant, disgruntle ► NOUN **1** *They reacted to the news with dismay.* = **alarm**, fear, horror, panic, anxiety, distress, terror, dread, fright, unease, apprehension, nervousness, agitation, consternation, trepidation (*formal*), uneasiness **2** *Much to her dismay, he did not call.* = **disappointment**, upset, distress, frustration, dissatisfaction, disillusionment, chagrin, disenchantment, discouragement, mortification

dismember VERB = **cut into pieces**, divide, rend (*literary*), sever, mutilate, dissect, dislocate, amputate, disjoint, anatomize, dislimb

dismiss VERB **1** *She dismissed the reports as mere speculation.* = **reject**, disregard, spurn, repudiate, pooh-pooh **2** *I dismissed the thought from my mind.* = **banish**, drop, dispel, shelve, discard, set aside, eradicate, cast out, lay aside, put out of your mind **3** *the power to dismiss civil servants who refuse to work* = **sack** (*informal*), fire (*informal*), remove (*informal*), axe (*informal*), expel, discharge, oust, lay off, kick out (*informal*), cashier, send packing (*informal*), give (someone) notice, kiss off (*slang, chiefly U.S. & Canad.*), give (someone) their marching orders, give (someone) the push (*informal*), give (someone) the elbow, give (someone) the boot (*slang*), give (someone) the bullet (*Brit. slang*), kennet (*Austral. slang*), jeff (*Austral. slang*) **4** *Two more witnesses were called, heard and dismissed.* = **let go**, free, release, discharge, dissolve, liberate, disperse, disband, send away

dismissal NOUN = **the sack** (*informal*), removal, discharge, notice (*Brit.*), the boot (*slang*), expulsion (*slang*), the push (*slang*), marching orders (*informal*), kiss-off (*slang, chiefly U.S. & Canad.*), the bum's rush (*slang*), the (old) heave-ho (*informal*), the order of the boot (*slang*), your books *or* cards (*informal*)

dismount VERB = **get off**, descend, get down, alight, light

disobedience NOUN = **defiance**, mutiny, indiscipline, revolt, insubordination, waywardness, infraction, recalcitrance, noncompliance, unruliness, nonobservance

disobey VERB **1** *a naughty boy who often disobeyed his mother* = **defy**, ignore, rebel, resist, disregard, refuse to obey, dig your heels in (*informal*), go counter to **2** *He was forever disobeying the rules.* = **infringe**, defy, refuse to obey, flout, violate, contravene (*formal*), overstep, transgress, go counter to

disorder NOUN **1** *a rare nerve disorder that can cause paralysis of the arms* = **illness**, disease, complaint, condition, sickness, ailment, affliction, malady, infirmity, indisposition **2** *The emergency room was in disorder.* = **untidiness**, mess, confusion, chaos, havoc (*informal*), muddle, state, clutter, shambles, disarray, jumble, irregularity, disorganization, hotchpotch, derangement, hodgepodge (*U.S.*), pig's breakfast (*informal*), disorderliness **3** *He called on the authorities to stop public disorder.* = **disturbance**, fight, riot, turmoil, unrest, quarrel, upheaval, brawl, clamour, uproar, turbulence, fracas, commotion, rumpus, tumult, hubbub, shindig (*informal*), hullabaloo, scrimmage, unruliness, shindy (*informal*), bagarre (*French*), biffo (*Austral. slang*)

disorderly ADJECTIVE **1** *The desk was covered in a disorderly jumble of old papers.* = **untidy**, confused, chaotic, messy, irregular, jumbled, indiscriminate, shambolic (*informal*), disorganized, higgledy-piggledy (*informal*), unsystematic ■ OPPOSITE: tidy **2** *disorderly conduct* = **unruly**, disruptive, rowdy, turbulent, unlawful, stormy, rebellious, boisterous, tumultuous, lawless, riotous, unmanageable, ungovernable, refractory, obstreperous, indisciplined

disorganized ADJECTIVE = **muddled**, confused, disordered, shuffled, chaotic, jumbled, haphazard, unorganized, unsystematic, unmethodical

disorientate *or* **disorient** VERB = **confuse**, upset, perplex, dislocate, cause to lose your bearings

disorientated *or* **disoriented** ADJECTIVE = **confused**, lost, unsettled, bewildered, mixed up, perplexed, all at sea

disown VERB = **deny**, reject, abandon, renounce, disallow, retract, repudiate, cast off, rebut, disavow, disclaim, abnegate, refuse to acknowledge *or* recognize

disparage VERB = **run down**, dismiss, put down, criticize, underestimate, discredit, ridicule, scorn, minimize, disdain, undervalue, deride, slag (off) (*slang*), knock (*informal*), blast, rubbish (*informal*), malign, detract from, denigrate, belittle, decry, underrate, vilify, slander, deprecate, tear into (*informal*), diss (*slang*), throw shade (at) (*slang*), defame, bad-mouth (*slang*), lambast(e), traduce (*formal*), derogate, asperse

disparaging ADJECTIVE = **contemptuous**, damaging, critical, slighting, offensive, insulting, abusive, scathing, dismissive, belittling, unfavourable, derogatory, unflattering, scornful, disdainful, defamatory, derisive, libellous, slanderous, deprecatory, uncomplimentary, fault-finding, contumelious (*literary*) ■ **OPPOSITE:** complimentary

disparate ADJECTIVE = **different**, contrasting, unlike, contrary, distinct, diverse, at odds, dissimilar, discordant, at variance, discrepant

disparity NOUN = **difference**, gap, inequality, distinction, imbalance, discrepancy, incongruity, unevenness, dissimilarity, disproportion, unlikeness, dissimilitude

dispassionate ADJECTIVE 1 *He spoke in a flat dispassionate tone.* = **unemotional**, cool, collected, calm, moderate, composed, sober, serene, unmoved, temperate, unfazed (*informal*), unruffled, imperturbable, unexcited, unexcitable ■ **OPPOSITE:** emotional 2 *We try to be dispassionate about the cases we bring.* = **objective**, fair, neutral, detached, indifferent, impartial, impersonal, disinterested, unbiased, uninvolved, unprejudiced ■ **OPPOSITE:** biased

dispatch or **despatch** VERB 1 *He dispatched a text message to Harper.* = **send**, transmit, forward, express, communicate, consign, remit 2 *They may catch him and dispatch him immediately.* = **kill**, murder, destroy, do in (*slang*), eliminate (*slang*), take out (*slang*), execute, butcher, slaughter, assassinate, slay (*archaic, literary*), finish off, put an end to, do away with, blow away (*slang, chiefly U.S.*), liquidate, annihilate, exterminate, take (someone's) life, bump off (*slang*) 3 *He dispatched his business.* = **carry out**, perform, fulfil, effect, finish, achieve, settle, dismiss, conclude, accomplish, execute, discharge, dispose of, expedite, make short work of (*informal*) ▶ NOUN 1 *this dispatch from our West Africa correspondent* = **message**, news, report, story, letter, account, piece, item, document, communication, instruction, bulletin, communiqué, missive 2 *He feels we should act with despatch.* = **speed**, haste, promptness, alacrity, rapidity, quickness,

swiftness, briskness, expedition, celerity, promptitude, precipitateness

dispel VERB = **drive away**, dismiss, eliminate, resolve, scatter, expel, disperse, banish, rout, allay, dissipate, chase away

dispensation NOUN 1 *The committee were not prepared to grant special dispensation.* = **exemption**, licence, exception, permission, privilege, relaxation, immunity, relief, indulgence, reprieve, remission 2 *the dispensation of justice* = **distribution**, supplying, dealing out, appointment, endowment, allotment, consignment, disbursement, apportionment, bestowal, conferment

dispense VERB 1 *They had already dispensed £40,000 in grants.* = **distribute**, assign, allocate, allot, mete out, dole out, share out, apportion, deal out, disburse 2 *a store licensed to dispense prescriptions* = **prepare**, measure, supply, mix 3 *High Court judges dispensing justice round the country* = **administer**, direct, operate, carry out, implement, undertake, enforce, execute, apply, discharge 4 *No-one is dispensed from collaborating in this task.* = **exempt**, except, excuse, release, relieve, reprieve, let off (*informal*), exonerate • **dispense with something** or **someone** 1 *We'll dispense with formalities.* = **do away with**, ignore, give up, cancel, abolish, omit, disregard, pass over, brush aside, forgo, relinquish, render needless 2 *Up at the lectern he dispensed with his notes.* = **do without**, get rid of, dispose of, shake off

dispersal NOUN 1 *the plants' mechanisms of dispersal of their spores* = **scattering**, spread, distribution, dissemination, dissipation 2 *the dispersal of this negative attitude* = **spread**, broadcast, circulation, diffusion, dissemination

disperse VERB 1 *The rest of our equipment was now dispersed over the lake.* = **scatter**, spread, distribute, circulate, strew, diffuse, dissipate, disseminate, throw about 2 *The crowd dispersed peacefully.* = **break up**, separate, dismiss, disappear, send off, vanish, scatter, dissolve, rout, dispel, disband, part company, demobilize, go (their) separate ways ■ **OPPOSITE:** gather 3 *The fog dispersed and I became aware of the sun.* = **dissolve**, disappear, vanish, evaporate, break up, dissipate, melt away, evanesce (*formal*)

dispirited ADJECTIVE = **disheartened**, depressed, discouraged, down, low, sad, gloomy, glum, dejected, in the doldrums, despondent, downcast, morose, crestfallen, sick as a parrot (*informal*)

dispiriting ADJECTIVE = **disheartening**, disappointing, depressing, crushing, discouraging, daunting, sickening, saddening, demoralizing ■ **OPPOSITE:** reassuring

displace VERB 1 *These factories have displaced tourism.* = **replace**, succeed, take over from, supersede, oust, usurp, supplant, take the place of, crowd out, fill or step into (someone's) boots 2 *In Europe alone, 30 million people were displaced.* = **force out**, turn out, expel, throw out, oust, unsettle, kick out (*informal*), eject, evict, dislodge, boot out (*informal*), dispossess, turf out (*informal*) 3 *A strong wind is all it would take to displace the stones.* = **move**, shift, disturb, budge, misplace, disarrange, derange 4 *They displaced him in a coup.* = **remove**, fire (*informal*), dismiss, sack (*informal*), discharge, oust, depose, cashier, dethrone, remove from office

display VERB 1 *The cabinets display seventeenth-century porcelain.* = **show**, present, exhibit, unveil, open to view, take the wraps off, put on view ■ **OPPOSITE:** conceal 2 *She displayed her wound.* = **expose**, show, reveal, bare, exhibit, uncover, lay bare, expose to view 3 *It was unlike him to display his feelings.* = **demonstrate**, show, reveal, register, expose, disclose, betray, manifest, divulge, make known, evidence, evince (*formal*) 4 *She does not have to display her charms.* = **show off**, parade, exhibit, sport (*informal*), flash (*informal*), boast, flourish, brandish, flaunt, vaunt, make a (great) show of, disport, make an exhibition of ▶ NOUN 1 *an outward display of affection* = **proof**, exhibition, demonstration, evidence, expression, exposure, illustration, revelation, testimony, confirmation, manifestation, affirmation, substantiation 2 *a display of your work* = **exhibition**, show, demonstration, presentation, showing, array, expo (*informal*), exposition 3 *He embraced it with such confidence and display.* = **ostentation**, show, dash, flourish, fanfare, pomp 4 *a dazzling dance display* = **show**, exhibition, demonstration, parade, spectacle, pageant, pageantry

displease VERB = **annoy**, upset, anger, provoke, offend, irritate, put out, hassle (*informal*), aggravate (*informal*), incense, gall, exasperate, nettle, vex, irk, rile, pique, nark (*Brit., Austral. & N.Z. slang*), dissatisfy, put your back up, hack you off (*informal*)

displeasure NOUN = **annoyance**, anger, resentment, irritation, offence, dislike, wrath, dissatisfaction, disapproval, indignation, distaste, pique, vexation,

disgruntlement, disfavour, disapprobation ■ **OPPOSITE:** satisfaction

disposable ADJECTIVE 1 *disposable nappies for babies up to 8lb* = **throwaway**, paper, nonreturnable 2 *He had little disposable income.* = **available**, expendable, free for use, consumable, spendable, at your service

disposal NOUN *the disposal of radioactive waste* = **throwing away**, dumping (*informal*), scrapping, removal, discarding, clearance, jettisoning, ejection, riddance, relinquishment • **at your disposal** *Do you have this information at your disposal?* = **available**, ready, to hand, accessible, convenient, handy, on hand, at hand, obtainable, on tap (*informal*), expendable, at your fingertips, at your service, free for use, ready for use, consumable, spendable

dispose VERB 1 *He was preparing to dispose his effects about the room.* = **arrange**, put, place, group, set, order, stand, range, settle, fix, rank, distribute, array 2 *theologies which dispose their adherents to fanaticism* = **lead**, move, condition, influence, prompt, tempt, adapt, motivate, bias, induce, incline, predispose, actuate • **dispose of someone** *They had hired an assassin to dispose of him.* = **kill**, murder, destroy, do in (*slang*), take out (*slang*), execute, slaughter, dispatch, assassinate, slay, do away with, knock off (*slang*), liquidate, neutralize, exterminate, take (someone's) life, bump off (*slang*), wipe (someone) from the face of the earth (*informal*) • **dispose of something** 1 *Fold up the nappy and dispose of it.* = **get rid of**, destroy, dump (*informal*), scrap, bin (*informal*), junk (*informal*), chuck (*informal*), discard, unload, dispense with, jettison, get shot of, throw out or away 2 *the manner in which you disposed of that problem* = **deal with**, manage, treat, handle, settle, cope with, take care of, see to, finish with, attend to, get to grips with 3 *He managed to dispose of more money and goods.* = **give**, give up, part with, bestow, transfer, make over

disposed ADJECTIVE = **inclined**, given, likely, subject, ready, prone, liable, apt, predisposed, tending towards, of a mind to

disposition NOUN 1 *his friendly and cheerful disposition* = **character**, nature, spirit, make-up, constitution, temper, temperament 2 *They show no disposition to take risks.* = **tendency**, inclination, propensity, habit, leaning, bent, bias, readiness, predisposition, proclivity (*formal*), proneness 3 *the disposition of walls and entrances* = **arrangement**, grouping, ordering, organization, distribution, disposal, placement

d

dispossess VERB = **strip**, deprive

dispossessed ADJECTIVE = **destitute**, landless

disproportionate ADJECTIVE = **excessive**, too much, unreasonable, uneven, unequal, unbalanced, out of proportion, inordinate, incommensurate

disprove VERB = **prove false**, discredit, refute, contradict, negate, invalidate, rebut, give the lie to, make a nonsense of, blow out of the water (*slang*), controvert, confute ■ **OPPOSITE:** prove

dispute VERB **1** *He disputed the allegations.* = **contest**, question, challenge, deny, doubt, oppose, object to, contradict, rebut, impugn (*formal*), controvert, call in *or* into question **2** *Whole towns disputed with neighboring villages over boundaries.* = **argue**, fight, clash, row, disagree, fall out (*informal*), contend, feud, quarrel, brawl, squabble, spar, wrangle, bicker, have an argument, cross swords, be at sixes and sevens, fight like cat and dog, go at it hammer and tongs, altercate ▶ NOUN **1** *There has been much dispute over the ownership of the lease.* = **disagreement**, conflict, argument, falling out, dissent, friction, strife, discord, altercation **2** *The dispute between them is settled.* = **argument**, row, clash, controversy, disturbance, contention, feud, quarrel, brawl, squabble, wrangle, difference of opinion, tiff, dissension, shindig (*informal*), shindy (*informal*), bagarre (*French*)

disqualification NOUN = **ban**, exclusion, elimination, rejection, ineligibility, debarment, disenablement, disentitlement

disqualified ADJECTIVE = **eliminated**, knocked out, out of the running, debarred, ineligible

disqualify VERB = **ban**, rule out, prohibit, preclude, debar, declare ineligible, disentitle

disquiet NOUN *There is growing public disquiet.* = **uneasiness**, concern, fear, worry, alarm, anxiety, distress, unrest, angst, nervousness, trepidation (*formal*), foreboding, restlessness, fretfulness, disquietude ▶ VERB *She was obviously disquieted by the experience.* = **make uneasy**, concern, worry, trouble, upset, bother, disturb, distress, annoy, plague, unsettle, harass, hassle (*informal*), agitate, vex, perturb, discompose, incommode

disquieting ADJECTIVE = **worrying**, troubling, upsetting, disturbing, distressing, annoying, irritating, unsettling, harrowing, unnerving, disconcerting, vexing, perturbing, bothersome

disregard VERB *He disregarded the advice of his executives.* = **ignore**, discount, take no notice of, overlook, neglect, pass over, turn a blind eye to, disobey, laugh off, make light of, pay no attention to, pay no heed to, leave out of account, brush aside *or* away ■ **OPPOSITE:** pay attention to ▶ NOUN *a callous disregard for human life* = **ignoring**, neglect, contempt, indifference, negligence, disdain, disrespect, heedlessness

disrepair NOUN *The house was in a bad state of disrepair.* = **dilapidation**, collapse, decay, deterioration, ruination • **in disrepair** *Everything was in disrepair.* = **out of order**, broken, decayed, worn-out, decrepit, not functioning, out of commission, on the blink (*slang*), bust (*informal*), kaput (*informal*)

disreputable ADJECTIVE = **discreditable**, mean, low, base, shocking, disorderly, notorious, vicious, infamous, disgraceful, shameful, vile, shady (*informal*), scandalous, ignominious, contemptible, louche, unprincipled, dishonourable, opprobrious ■ **OPPOSITE:** respectable

disrepute NOUN = **discredit**, shame, disgrace, unpopularity, ignominy, dishonour, infamy, disfavour, ill repute, obloquy, ill favour, disesteem

disrespect NOUN = **contempt**, cheek (*informal*), disregard, rudeness, lack of respect, irreverence, insolence, impertinence, impudence, discourtesy, incivility, impoliteness, lese-majesty, unmannerliness ■ **OPPOSITE:** respect

disrespectful ADJECTIVE = **contemptuous**, insulting, rude, cheeky, irreverent, bad-mannered, impertinent, insolent, impolite, impudent, discourteous, uncivil, inconsiderate

disrupt VERB **1** *Anti-war protests disrupted the debate.* = **interrupt**, stop, upset, hold up, interfere with, unsettle, obstruct, cut short, intrude on, break up *or* into **2** *The drought has disrupted agricultural production.* = **disturb**, upset, confuse, disorder, spoil, unsettle, agitate, disorganize, disarrange, derange, throw into disorder

disruption NOUN = **disturbance**, disorder, confusion, interference, disarray, interruption, stoppage, disorderliness

disruptive ADJECTIVE = **disturbing**, upsetting, disorderly, unsettling, troublesome, unruly, obstreperous, troublemaking ■ **OPPOSITE:** well-behaved

dissatisfaction NOUN = **discontent**, frustration, resentment, regret, distress, disappointment, dismay, irritation, unhappiness, annoyance, displeasure, exasperation, chagrin

dissatisfied ADJECTIVE = **discontented**, frustrated, unhappy, disappointed, fed up, disgruntled, not satisfied, unfulfilled, displeased, unsatisfied, ungratified ■ **OPPOSITE:** satisfied

dissect VERB 1 *We dissected a frog in biology.* = **cut up** or **apart**, dismember, lay open, anatomize 2 *People want to dissect his work.* = **analyse**, study, investigate, research, explore, break down, inspect, scrutinize

dissection NOUN 1 *a growing supply of corpses for dissection* = **cutting up**, anatomy, autopsy, dismemberment, postmortem (examination), necropsy, anatomization 2 *the dissection of my proposals* = **analysis**, examination, breakdown, research, investigation, inspection, scrutiny

disseminate VERB = **spread**, publish, broadcast, distribute, scatter, proclaim, circulate, sow, disperse, diffuse, publicize, dissipate, propagate, promulgate

dissemination NOUN = **spread**, publishing, broadcasting, publication, distribution, circulation, diffusion, propagation, promulgation

dissension NOUN = **disagreement**, conflict, dissent, dispute, contention, quarreling, friction, strife, discord, discordance, conflict of opinion

dissent NOUN *He has responded harshly to any dissent.* = **disagreement**, opposition, protest, resistance, refusal, objection, discord, demur, dissension, dissidence, nonconformity, remonstrance ■ **OPPOSITE:** assent • **dissent from something** *No one dissents from the decision to unify.* = **disagree with**, object to, protest against, refuse to accept

dissenter NOUN = **objector**, dissident, nonconformist, protestant, disputant

dissenting ADJECTIVE = **disagreeing**, protesting, opposing, conflicting, differing, dissident

dissertation NOUN = **thesis**, essay, discourse, critique, exposition, treatise, disquisition

disservice NOUN = **wrong**, injury, harm, injustice, disfavour, unkindness, bad turn, ill turn ■ **OPPOSITE:** good turn

dissident ADJECTIVE *links with a dissident group* = **dissenting**, disagreeing, nonconformist, heterodox, schismatic, dissentient ▶ NOUN *political dissidents* = **protester**, rebel, dissenter, demonstrator, agitator, recusant, protest marcher

dissimilar ADJECTIVE = **different**, unlike, various, varied, diverse, assorted, unrelated, disparate, miscellaneous, sundry, divergent, manifold (*formal*), heterogeneous, mismatched, multifarious, not similar, not alike, not capable of comparison ■ **OPPOSITE:** alike

dissipate VERB 1 *The tension in the room had dissipated.* = **disappear**, fade, vanish, dissolve, disperse, evaporate, diffuse, melt away, evanesce (*formal*) 2 = **squander**, spend, waste, consume, run through, deplete, expend, fritter away, misspend, exhaust, consume, scatter

dissipated ADJECTIVE *He was still handsome though dissipated.* = **debauched**, abandoned, self-indulgent, profligate, intemperate, dissolute, rakish

dissociate or **disassociate** VERB *how to dissociate emotion from reason* = **separate**, distance, divorce, isolate, detach, segregate, disconnect, set apart • **dissociate yourself from something** or **someone** *He dissociated himself from his former friends.* = **break away from**, part company with, break off relations with

dissociation NOUN = **separation**, break, division, distancing, divorce, isolation, segregation, detachment, severance, disengagement, disconnection, disunion

dissolution NOUN 1 *He stayed on until the dissolution of the firm.* = **ending**, end, finish, conclusion, suspension, dismissal, termination, adjournment, disbandment, discontinuation ■ **OPPOSITE:** union 2 *the dissolution of a marriage* = **breaking up**, parting, divorce, separation, disintegration

dissolve VERB 1 *Heat gently until the sugar dissolves.* = **melt**, soften, thaw, flux, liquefy, deliquesce 2 *The King agreed to dissolve the present commission.* = **end**, dismiss, suspend, axe (*informal*), break up, wind up, overthrow, terminate, discontinue, dismantle, disband, disunite 3 *His new-found optimism dissolved.* = **disappear**, fade, vanish, break down, crumble, disperse, dwindle, evaporate, disintegrate, perish, diffuse, dissipate, decompose, melt away, waste away, evanesce • **dissolve into** or **in something** (*tears or laughter*) *She dissolved into tears.* = **break into**, burst into, give way to, launch into

dissonance or **dissonancy** NOUN = **discordance**, discord, jangle, cacophony, jarring, harshness, lack of harmony, unmelodiousness

distance NOUN 1 *They measured the distance between the island and the shore.* = **space**, length, extent, range, stretch, gap, interval, separation, span, width 2 *The distance wouldn't be a problem.* = **remoteness** 3 *There were periods of distance, of coldness.*

= **aloofness**, reserve, detachment, restraint, indifference, stiffness, coolness, coldness, remoteness, frigidity, uninvolvement, standoffishness • **go the distance** *Riders are determined to go the distance.* = **finish**, stay the course, complete, see through, bring to an end • **in the distance** *We suddenly saw her in the distance.* = **far off**, far away, on the horizon, afar, yonder

distant ADJECTIVE **1** *the war in that distant land* = **far-off**, far, remote, removed, abroad, out-of-the-way, far-flung, faraway, outlying, afar ■ **OPPOSITE:** close **2** *He's a distant relative.* = **remote**, slight **3** *He's direct and courteous, but distant.* = **reserved**, cold, withdrawn, cool, formal, remote, stiff, restrained, detached, indifferent, aloof, unfriendly, reticent, haughty, unapproachable, standoffish ■ **OPPOSITE:** friendly **4** *There was a distant look in her eyes.* = **faraway**, blank, abstracted, vague, absorbed, distracted, unaware, musing, vacant, preoccupied, bemused, oblivious, dreamy, daydreaming, absent-minded, inattentive

distaste NOUN = **dislike**, horror, disgust, loathing, aversion, revulsion, displeasure, antipathy, abhorrence, disinclination, repugnance, odium (*formal*), disfavour, detestation, disrelish

distasteful ADJECTIVE = **unpleasant**, offensive, obscene, undesirable, unsavoury, obnoxious, unpalatable, displeasing, repulsive, objectionable, disagreeable, repugnant, loathsome, abhorrent, nauseous, uninviting ■ **OPPOSITE:** enjoyable

distil VERB **1** *When water is used it must be distilled.* = **purify**, refine, evaporate, condense, sublimate, vaporize **2** *The oil is distilled from the berries.* = **extract**, express, squeeze, obtain, take out, draw out, separate out, press out

distillation NOUN = **essence**, extract, elixir, spirit, quintessence

distinct ADJECTIVE **1** *The book is divided into two distinct parts.* = **different**, individual, separate, disconnected, discrete, dissimilar, unconnected, unattached ■ **OPPOSITE:** similar **2** *to impart a distinct flavour with a minimum of cooking fat* = **striking**, sharp, dramatic, stunning (*informal*), outstanding, bold, noticeable, well-defined **3** *There was a distinct change in her attitude.* = **definite**, marked, clear, decided, obvious, sharp, plain, apparent, patent, evident, black-and-white, manifest, noticeable, conspicuous,

clear-cut, unmistakable, palpable, recognizable, unambiguous, observable, perceptible, appreciable ■ **OPPOSITE:** vague

distinction NOUN **1** *There were obvious distinctions between the two.* = **difference**, contrast, variation, differential, discrepancy, disparity, deviation, differentiation, fine line, distinctness, dissimilarity **2** *He is a composer of distinction and sensitivity.* = **excellence**, note, quality, worth, account, rank, reputation, importance, consequence, fame, celebrity, merit, superiority, prominence, greatness, eminence, renown, repute **3** *He has the distinction of being their greatest living writer.* = **feature**, quality, characteristic, name, mark, individuality, peculiarity, singularity, distinctiveness, particularity **4** *She had served her country with distinction and strength.* = **merit**, credit, honour, integrity, excellence, righteousness, rectitude, uprightness

distinctive ADJECTIVE = **characteristic**, special, individual, specific, unique, typical, extraordinary, distinguishing, peculiar, singular, idiosyncratic ■ **OPPOSITE:** ordinary

distinctly ADVERB **1** *two distinctly different sectors* = **definitely**, clearly, obviously, sharply, plainly, patently, manifestly, decidedly, markedly, noticeably, unmistakably, palpably **2** *'If I may speak, gentlemen,' he said distinctly.* = **clearly**, plainly, precisely

distinguish VERB **1** *Could he distinguish right from wrong?* = **differentiate**, determine, separate, discriminate, decide, judge, discern, ascertain, tell the difference, make a distinction, tell apart, tell between **2** *one of the things that distinguishes artists from other people* = **characterize**, mark, separate, single out, individualize, set apart **3** *He could distinguish voices.* = **make out**, recognize, perceive, know, see, tell, pick out, discern

distinguishable ADJECTIVE **1** *This port is distinguishable by its colour.* = **recognizable**, noticeable, conspicuous, discernible, obvious, evident, manifest, perceptible, well-marked **2** *Already shapes were more distinguishable.* = **conspicuous**, clear, strong, bright, plain, bold, pronounced, colourful, vivid, eye-catching, salient

distinguished ADJECTIVE = **eminent**, great, important, noted, famous, celebrated, well-known, prominent, esteemed, acclaimed, notable, renowned, prestigious, elevated, big-time (*informal*), famed, conspicuous, illustrious, major league (*informal*) ■ **OPPOSITE:** unknown

distinguishing ADJECTIVE
= **characteristic**, marked, distinctive, typical, peculiar, differentiating, individualistic

distort VERB **1** *The media distorts reality.*
= **misrepresent**, twist, bias, disguise, pervert, slant, colour, misinterpret, falsify, garble **2** *Make sure the image isn't distorted by lumps and bumps.* = **deform**, bend, twist, warp, buckle, mangle, mangulate (*Austral. slang*), disfigure, contort, gnarl, misshape, malform

distorted ADJECTIVE = **deformed**, bent, twisted, crooked, irregular, warped, buckled, disfigured, contorted, misshapen

distortion NOUN **1** *He accused reporters of wilful distortion.* = **misrepresentation**, bias, slant, perversion, falsification, colouring **2** *the gargoyle-like distortion of the statue's face* = **deformity**, bend, twist, warp, buckle, contortion, malformation, crookedness, twistedness

distract VERB **1** *Video games sometimes distract him from his homework.* = **divert**, sidetrack, draw away, turn aside, lead astray, draw or lead away from **2** *I took out a book and tried to distract myself.* = **amuse**, occupy, entertain, beguile, engross **3** *Another story of hers distracts me.* = **agitate**, trouble, disturb, confuse, puzzle, torment, bewilder, madden, confound, perplex, disconcert, derange, discompose

distracted ADJECTIVE *At work, he thought about the problem all day. He was distracted.*
= **agitated**, troubled, confused, puzzled, at sea, bewildered, bemused, confounded, perplexed, flustered, in a flap (*informal*)

distraction NOUN **1** *Total concentration is required with no distractions.* = **disturbance**, interference, diversion, interruption **2** *every conceivable distraction from shows to bouncy castles* = **entertainment**, recreation, amusement, diversion, pastime, divertissement, beguilement

distraught ADJECTIVE = **frantic**, wild, desperate, mad, anxious, distressed, raving, distracted, hysterical, worked-up, agitated, crazed, overwrought, out of your mind, at the end of your tether, wrought-up, beside yourself

distress VERB *I did not want to frighten or distress her.* = **upset**, worry, trouble, pain, wound, bother, disturb, dismay, grieve, torment, harass, afflict, harrow, agitate, sadden, perplex, disconcert, agonize, fluster, perturb, faze, throw (someone) off balance ▶ NOUN **1** *Her mouth grew stiff with pain and distress.* = **suffering**, pain, worry, anxiety, torture, grief, misery, agony, sadness, discomfort, torment, sorrow, woe, anguish, heartache, affliction, desolation, wretchedness **2** *There was little support to help them in their distress.* = **need**, suffering, trouble, trial, difficulties, poverty, misery, hard times, hardship, straits, misfortune, adversity, calamity, affliction, privation (*formal*), destitution, ill-fortune, ill-luck, indigence

distressed ADJECTIVE **1** *I felt distressed about my problem.* = **upset**, worried, troubled, anxious, distracted, tormented, distraught, afflicted, agitated, saddened, wretched **2** *investment in the nation's distressed areas* = **poverty-stricken**, poor, impoverished, needy, destitute, indigent (*formal*), down at heel, straitened, penurious

distressing ADJECTIVE = **upsetting**, worrying, disturbing, painful, affecting, sad, afflicting, harrowing, grievous, hurtful, lamentable, heart-breaking, nerve-racking, gut-wrenching, distressful (*literary*)

distribute VERB **1** *Students shouted slogans and distributed leaflets.* = **hand out**, dispense, give out, dish out (*informal*), disseminate, deal out, disburse, pass round **2** *to distribute a national newspaper* = **circulate**, deliver, convey **3** *He began to distribute jobs among his friends.* = **share**, give, deal, divide, assign, administer, allocate, dispose, dispense, allot, mete out, dole out, apportion, measure out **4** *Break the exhibition up and distribute it around existing museums.* = **spread**, scatter, disperse, diffuse, disseminate, strew

distribution NOUN **1** *He admitted there had been problems with distribution.* = **delivery**, mailing, transport, transportation, handling **2** *a more equitable distribution of wealth* = **sharing**, division, assignment, rationing, allocation, partition, allotment, dispensation, apportionment **3** *There will be a widespread distribution of leaflets.* = **spreading**, circulation, diffusion, scattering, propagation, dissemination, dispersal, dispersion **4** *those who control the distribution of jobs* = **spread**, organization, arrangement, location, placement, disposition (*archaic*)

district NOUN = **area**, community, region, sector, quarter, ward, parish, neighbourhood, vicinity, locality, locale, neck of the woods (*informal*)

distrust VERB *I don't have any reason to distrust them.* = **suspect**, doubt, discredit, be wary of, wonder about, mistrust, disbelieve, be suspicious of, be sceptical of, misbelieve
■ **OPPOSITE:** trust ▶ NOUN *an atmosphere of*

distrust = **suspicion**, question, doubt, disbelief, scepticism, mistrust, misgiving, qualm, wariness, lack of faith, dubiety ■ **OPPOSITE:** trust

distrustful ADJECTIVE = **suspicious**, doubting, wary, cynical, doubtful, sceptical, uneasy, dubious, distrusting, disbelieving, leery (*slang*), mistrustful, chary

disturb VERB **1** *I didn't want to disturb you.* = **interrupt**, trouble, bother, startle, plague, disrupt, put out, interfere with, rouse, hassle, inconvenience, pester, intrude on, butt in on **2** *He had been disturbed by the news of the attack.* = **upset**, concern, worry, trouble, shake, excite, alarm, confuse, distress, distract, dismay, unsettle, agitate, ruffle, confound, unnerve, vex, fluster, perturb, derange, discompose ■ **OPPOSITE:** calm **3** *His notes had not been disturbed.* = **muddle**, disorder, mix up, mess up, disorganize, jumble up, disarrange, muss (*U.S. & Canad.*)

disturbance NOUN **1** *During the disturbance, three men were hurt.* = **disorder**, bother (*informal*), turmoil, riot, upheaval, fray, brawl, uproar, agitation, fracas, commotion, rumpus, tumult, hubbub, shindig (*informal*), ruction (*informal*), ruckus (*informal*), shindy (*informal*) **2** *The home would cause less disturbance than a school.* = **upset**, bother, disorder, confusion, distraction, intrusion, interruption, annoyance, agitation, hindrance, perturbation, derangement **3** *Poor educational performance is linked to emotional disturbances.* = **problem**, disorder, upset, trouble

disturbed ADJECTIVE = **worried**, concerned, troubled, upset, bothered, nervous, anxious, uneasy ■ **OPPOSITE:** calm

disturbing ADJECTIVE = **worrying**, troubling, upsetting, alarming, frightening, distressing, startling, discouraging, dismaying, unsettling, harrowing, agitating, disconcerting, disquieting, perturbing

ditch NOUN *The car went out of control and ended up in a ditch.* = **channel**, drain, trench, dyke, furrow, gully, moat, watercourse ▶ VERB **1** = **get rid of**, dump (*informal*), scrap, discard, dispose of, dispense with, jettison, throw out *or* overboard **2** *I can't bring myself to ditch him.* = **leave**, drop, abandon, dump (*informal*), axe (*informal*), get rid of, bin (*informal*), chuck (*informal*), forsake, jilt

dither VERB *We're still dithering over whether to get married.* = **vacillate**, hesitate, waver,

haver, falter, hum and haw, faff about (*Brit. informal*), shillyshally (*informal*), swither (*Scot.*) ■ **OPPOSITE:** decide ▶ NOUN *I am in such a dither I forget to put the water in.* = **flutter**, flap (*informal*), fluster, bother, stew (*informal*), twitter (*informal*), tizzy (*informal*), pother, tiz-woz (*informal*)

diva NOUN = **singer**, opera singer, prima donna

dive VERB **1** *He tried to escape by diving into a river.* = **plunge**, drop, jump, pitch, leap, duck, dip, descend, plummet **2** *They are diving to collect marine organisms.* = **go underwater**, submerge **3** *His monoplane stalled and dived into the ground.* = **nose-dive**, fall, plunge, crash, pitch, swoop, plummet ▶ NOUN **1** *He made a sudden dive towards the man's legs.* = **plunge**, spring, jump, leap, dash, header (*informal*), swoop, lunge, nose dive **2** *We've played in all the dives about here.* = **sleazy bar**, joint (*slang*), honky-tonk (*U.S. slang*)

diverge VERB **1** *The aims of the partners began to diverge.* = **separate**, part, split, branch, divide, fork, divaricate **2** *Theory and practice sometimes diverged.* = **conflict**, differ, disagree, dissent, be at odds, be at variance **3** *a course that diverged from the coastline* = **deviate**, depart, stray, wander, meander, turn aside

divergence NOUN = **difference**, varying, departure, disparity, deviation, separation

divergent ADJECTIVE = **different**, conflicting, differing, disagreeing, diverse, separate, varying, variant, diverging, dissimilar, deviating

> **USAGE** Some people dislike the use of *divergent* in this sense, preferring synonyms such as *different* or *differing*.

diverse ADJECTIVE **1** *shops selling a diverse range of gifts* = **various**, mixed, varied, diversified, assorted, miscellaneous, several, sundry, motley, manifold (*formal*), heterogeneous, of every description **2** *Their attitudes were refreshingly diverse.* = **different**, contrasting, unlike, varying, differing, separate, distinct, disparate, discrete, dissimilar, divergent, discrepant

diversify VERB = **vary**, change, expand, transform, alter, spread out, branch out

diversion NOUN **1** *The whole argument is a diversion.* = **distraction**, deviation, deflection, digression **2** *Finger-painting is an excellent diversion.* = **pastime**, play, game, sport, delight, pleasure, entertainment, hobby, relaxation, recreation, enjoyment, distraction, amusement, gratification, divertissement, beguilement **3** *They turned back because of traffic diversions.* = **detour**, deviation, circuitous route, roundabout way, indirect course **4** = **deviation**, departure, straying, divergence, digression

diversity NOUN **1** *the cultural diversity of British society* = **difference**, diversification, variety, divergence, multiplicity, heterogeneity, variegation, diverseness **2** = **range**, variety, scope, sphere

divert VERB **1** *A new bypass will divert traffic from the A13.* = **redirect**, switch, avert, deflect, deviate, sidetrack, turn aside **2** *They want to divert the attention of the people from the real issues.* = **distract**, shift, deflect, detract, sidetrack, lead astray, draw or lead away from **3** *diverting her with jokes and fiery arguments* = **entertain**, delight, amuse, please, charm, gratify, beguile, regale

diverting ADJECTIVE = **entertaining**, amusing, enjoyable, fun, pleasant, humorous, beguiling

divest VERB **1** *They were divested of all their personal possessions.* = **deprive**, strip, dispossess, despoil (*formal*) **2** *the formalities of divesting her of her coat* = **strip**, remove, take off, undress, denude, disrobe, unclothe

divide VERB **1** *the artificial line that divided the city* = **separate**, part, split, cut (up), sever, shear, segregate, cleave, subdivide, bisect, sunder ■ OPPOSITE: join **2** *Divide the soup among four bowls.* = **share**, distribute, allocate, portion, dispense, allot, mete, dole out, apportion, deal out, measure out, divvy (up) (*informal*) **3** *She has done more to divide the group than anyone else.* = **split**, break up, alienate, embroil, come between, disunite, estrange, sow dissension, cause to disagree, set at variance or odds, set or pit against one another • **divide something up** *The idea is to divide up the country into four sectors.* = **group**, sort, separate, arrange, grade, classify, categorize

dividend NOUN = **bonus**, share, cut (*informal*), gain, extra, plus, portion, divvy (*informal*)

divination NOUN = **prediction**, divining, prophecy, presage, foretelling, clairvoyance, fortune-telling, prognostication, augury, soothsaying, sortilege

divine ADJECTIVE **1** *a gift from divine beings* = **heavenly**, spiritual, holy, immortal, supernatural, celestial, angelic, superhuman, godlike, cherubic, seraphic, supernal (*literary*), paradisaical **2** *the message of the Divine Book* = **sacred**, religious, holy, spiritual, blessed, revered, venerable, hallowed, consecrated, sanctified **3** *You look simply divine.* = **wonderful**, perfect, beautiful, excellent, lovely, stunning (*informal*), glorious, marvellous, splendid, gorgeous, delightful, exquisite, radiant, superlative, ravishing ▶ NOUN *He had the air of a divine.* = **priest**, minister, vicar, reverend, pastor, cleric, clergyman *or* woman, curate, churchman *or* woman, padre (*informal*), holy man *or* woman *or* person, man *or* woman *or* person of God, man *or* woman *or* person of the cloth, ecclesiastic ▶ VERB **1** *He had tried to divine her intentions.* = **guess**, understand, suppose, suspect, perceive, discern, infer, deduce, apprehend, conjecture, surmise, foretell, intuit, prognosticate **2** *I was divining for water.* = **dowse** (*for water or minerals*)

divinity NOUN **1** *He entered university to study arts and divinity.* = **theology**, religion, religious studies **2** *a lasting faith in the divinity of Christ's word* = **godliness**, holiness, sanctity, godhead, divine nature, godhood **3** *The three statues are Roman divinities.* = **deity**, spirit, genius, guardian spirit, daemon, god *or* goddess, atua (*N.Z.*)

division NOUN **1** *a division into two independent factions* = **separation**, dividing, splitting up, detaching, partition, cutting up, bisection **2** *the division of labour between workers and management* = **sharing**, distribution, assignment, rationing, allocation, allotment, apportionment **3** *the division between the prosperous west and the impoverished east* = **disagreement**, split, breach, feud, rift, rupture, abyss, chasm, variance, discord, difference of opinion, estrangement, disunion ■ OPPOSITE: unity **4** *the division between North and South Korea* = **dividing line**, border, boundary, divide, partition, demarcation, divider **5** *the sales division* = **department**, group, head, sector, branch, subdivision **6** *Each was divided into several divisions.* = **part**, bit, piece, section, sector, class, category, segment, portion, fraction, compartment

divisive ADJECTIVE = **disruptive**, unsettling, alienating, troublesome, controversial, contentious

divorce NOUN **1** *Numerous marriages now end in divorce.* = **separation**, split, break-up, parting, split-up, rift, dissolution, severance, estrangement, annulment, decree nisi, disunion **2** *a divorce between the government and trade unions* = **breach**, break, split, falling-out (*informal*), disagreement, feud, rift, bust-up (*informal*), rupture, abyss, chasm, schism, estrangement ▶ VERB **1** *My parents divorced when I was young.* = **split up**, separate, part company, annul your marriage, dissolve your marriage

2 *Most of our investors are able to divorce themselves from the emotional side of business.* = **separate**, divide, isolate, detach, distance, sever, disconnect, dissociate, set apart, disunite, sunder

divulge VERB = **make known**, tell, reveal, publish, declare, expose, leak, confess, exhibit, communicate, spill (*informal*), disclose, proclaim, betray, uncover, impart, promulgate, let slip, blow wide open (*slang*), get off your chest (*informal*), cough (*slang*), out (*informal*), spill your guts about (*slang*) ■ **OPPOSITE:** keep secret

dizzy ADJECTIVE **1** *She felt slightly dizzy.* = **giddy**, faint, light-headed, swimming, reeling, staggering, shaky, wobbly, off balance, unsteady, vertiginous, woozy (*informal*), weak at the knees **2** *Her wonderful dark good looks and wit made me dizzy.* = **confused**, dazzled, at sea, bewildered, muddled, bemused, dazed, disorientated, befuddled, light-headed, punch-drunk, fuddled **3** *a charmingly dizzy grandmother* = **scatterbrained**, silly, foolish, frivolous, giddy, capricious, forgetful, flighty, light-headed, scatty (*Brit. informal*), empty-headed, bird-brained (*informal*), featherbrained, ditzy or ditsy (*slang*) **4** *The gannets plunged from a dizzy height into the water.* = **steep**, towering, soaring, lofty, sky-high, vertiginous

do VERB **1** *I was trying to do some work.* = **perform**, work, achieve, carry out, produce, effect, complete, conclude, undertake, accomplish, execute, discharge, pull off, transact **2** *I go where I will and I do as I please.* = **behave**, act, conduct yourself, deport yourself, bear yourself, acquit yourself **3** *I'll do the dinner, you can help.* = **make**, prepare, fix, arrange, look after, organize, be responsible for, see to, get ready, make ready **4** *I could have done the crossword.* = **solve**, work out, resolve, figure out, decode, decipher, puzzle out **5** *She did well at school.* = **get on**, manage, fare, proceed, make out, prosper, get along **6** *I've always wanted to do a show on his life.* = **present**, give, show, act, produce, stage, perform, mount, put on **7** *A plain old 'I love you' won't do.* = **be adequate**, be enough, be sufficient, answer, serve, suit, content, satisfy, suffice, be of use, pass muster, cut the mustard, fill the bill (*informal*), meet requirements **8** *I'll tell you how they did me.* = **cheat**, trick, con (*informal*), skin (*slang*), stiff (*slang*), deceive, fleece, hoax, defraud, dupe, swindle, diddle (*informal*), take (someone) for a ride (*informal*), pull a fast one on (*informal*), cozen, scam (*slang*)

9 = **produce**, make, create, develop, manufacture, construct, invent, fabricate **10** *Families doing Europe can hire one of these motor-homes.* = **visit**, tour in or around, look at, cover, explore, take in (*informal*), stop in, journey through or around, travel in or around ▸ NOUN *They always have all-night dos there.* = **party**, gathering, function, social, event, affair, at-home, occasion, celebration, reception, bash (*informal*), rave (*Brit. slang*), get-together (*informal*), festivity, knees-up (*Brit. informal*), beano (*Brit. slang*), social gathering, shindig (*informal*), soirée, rave-up (*Brit. slang*), hooley or hoolie (*chiefly Irish & N.Z.*) • **do away with someone** *He tried to do away with her.* = **kill**, murder, do in (*slang*), destroy, take out (*slang*), dispatch, slay (*archaic, literary*), blow away (*slang, chiefly U.S.*), knock off (*slang*), liquidate, exterminate, take (someone's) life, bump off (*slang*) • **do away with something** *They must do away with nuclear weapons altogether.* = **get rid of**, remove, eliminate, axe (*informal*), abolish, junk (*informal*), pull, chuck (*informal*), discard, put an end to, dispense with, discontinue, put paid to, pull the plug on • **do's and don'ts** *Please advise me on the do's and dont's.* = **rules**, code, regulations, standards, instructions, customs, convention, usage, protocol, formalities, etiquette, p's and q's, good or proper behaviour • **do someone in 1** *Whoever did him in removed a brave man.* = **kill**, murder, destroy, eliminate (*slang*), take out (*slang*), execute, butcher, slaughter, dispatch, assassinate, slay (*archaic, literary*), do away with, blow away (*slang, chiefly U.S.*), knock off (*slang*), liquidate, annihilate, neutralize, take (someone's) life, bump off (*slang*) **2** *The Christmas thing kind of did me in.* = **exhaust**, tire, drain, shatter (*informal*), weaken, fatigue, weary, fag (*informal*), sap, wear out, tire out, knacker (*slang*) • **do without something** *or* **someone** *This is something we cannot do without.* = **manage without**, give up, dispense with, forgo, kick (*informal*), sacrifice, abstain from, get along without

docile ADJECTIVE = **obedient**, manageable, compliant, amenable, submissive, pliant, tractable, biddable, ductile, teachable (*rare*) ■ **OPPOSITE:** difficult

dock¹ NOUN *He brought his boat right into the dock at Southampton.* = **port**, haven, harbour, pier, wharf, quay, waterfront, anchorage ▸ VERB **1** *The vessel is about to dock in Singapore.* = **moor**, land, anchor, put in, tie up, berth, drop anchor **2** *(a spacecraft)*

The rocket has docked with the International Space Station. = **link up**, unite, join, couple, rendezvous, hook up

dock² VERB **1** *He threatened to dock her fee.* = **cut**, reduce, decrease, diminish, lessen ■ **OPPOSITE:** increase **2** *He had a point docked for insulting his opponent.* = **deduct**, subtract **3** *It is an offence for an unqualified person to dock a dog's tail.* = **cut off**, crop, clip, shorten, curtail, cut short

docket NOUN **1** *The clerk asked me to sign the docket.* = **label**, bill, ticket, certificate, tag, voucher, tab, receipt, tally, chit, chitty, counterfoil **2** *The Court has 1,400 appeals on its docket.* = **file**, index, register

doctor NOUN *Do not stop the treatment without consulting your doctor.* = **physician**, medic (*informal*), general practitioner, medical practitioner, G.P. ▶ VERB **1** *They doctored the photograph.* = **change**, alter, interfere with, disguise, pervert, fudge, tamper with, tinker with, misrepresent, falsify, meddle with, mess about with **2** *He doctored the dog food to administer the medicine.* = **add to**, spike, cut, mix something with something, dilute, water down, adulterate

doctrinaire ADJECTIVE **1** *forty-five years of doctrinaire Stalinism.* = **dogmatic**, rigid, fanatical, inflexible **2** *It is a doctrinaire scheme.* = **impractical**, theoretical, speculative, ideological, unrealistic, hypothetical, unpragmatic

doctrine NOUN = **teaching**, principle, belief, opinion, article, concept, conviction, canon, creed, dogma, tenet, precept, article of faith, kaupapa (*N.Z.*)

document NOUN *The foreign minister signed the document today.* = **paper**, form, certificate, report, record, testimonial, authorization, legal form ▶ VERB *The effects of smoking have been well documented.* = **support**, back up, certify, verify, detail, instance, validate, substantiate, corroborate, authenticate, give weight to, particularize

doddle NOUN = **piece of cake**, picnic (*informal*), child's play (*informal*), pushover (*slang, informal*), no sweat (*slang*), cinch (*slang*), cakewalk (*informal*), money for old rope, bludge (*Austral. & N.Z. informal*)

dodge VERB **1** *We dodged behind a pillar.* = **duck** (*informal*), dart, swerve, sidestep, shoot, shift, turn aside, body-swerve **2** *Thieves dodged the security system in the shop.* = **evade**, avoid, escape, get away from, elude, body-swerve, slip through the net of **3** *He has repeatedly dodged the question.* = **avoid**, hedge, parry, get out of, evade, shirk ▶ NOUN *It was probably just a dodge to*

stop you going away. = **trick**, scheme, ploy, trap, device, fraud, con (*slang*), manoeuvre, deception, scam (*slang*), gimmick, hoax, wheeze (*Brit. slang*), deceit, ruse, artifice, subterfuge, canard, feint, stratagem, contrivance, machination, fastie (*Austral. slang*)

dodgy ADJECTIVE **1** *He was a bit of a dodgy character.* = **nasty**, offensive, unpleasant, revolting, distasteful, repellent, unsavoury, obnoxious, repulsive, objectionable, repugnant, shonky (*Austral. & N.Z. informal*) **2** *Predicting voting trends is a dodgy business.* = **risky**, difficult, tricky, dangerous, delicate, uncertain, problematic(al), unreliable, dicky (*Brit. informal*), dicey (*informal, chiefly Brit.*), ticklish, chancy (*informal*), shonky (*Austral. & N.Z. informal*)

doer NOUN = **achiever**, organizer, powerhouse (*slang*), dynamo, live wire (*slang*), go-getter (*informal*), active person, wheeler-dealer (*informal*)

doff VERB **1** *The peasants doffed their hats.* = **tip**, raise, remove, lift, take off **2** *He doffed his shirt and jeans.* = **take off**, remove, shed, discard, throw off, cast off, slip out of, slip off

dog NOUN **1** *Outside a dog was barking.* = **hound**, canine, bitch, puppy, pup, mongrel, tyke, mutt (*slang*), pooch (*slang*), cur, man's best friend, kuri or goorie (*N.Z.*), brak (*S. African*) **2** *Out of my sight, you dog!* = **scoundrel** (*old-fashioned*), villain, cur, heel (*slang*), knave (*archaic*), blackguard ▶ VERB **1** *His career has been dogged by bad luck.* = **plague**, follow, trouble, haunt, hound, torment, afflict **2** *The three creatures had dogged him from hut to hut.* = **pursue**, follow, track, chase, shadow, harry, tail (*informal*), trail, hound, stalk, go after, give chase to • **dog-eat-dog** *TV is a dog-eat-dog business.* = **ruthless**, fierce, vicious, ferocious, cut-throat, with no holds barred ■ **RELATED WORDS:** *adjective* canine; *name of female* bitch; *name of young* pup, puppy

dogged ADJECTIVE = **determined**, steady, persistent, stubborn, firm, staunch, persevering, resolute, single-minded, tenacious, steadfast, unyielding, obstinate, indefatigable, immovable, stiff-necked, unshakable, unflagging, pertinacious ■ **OPPOSITE:** irresolute

dogma NOUN = **doctrine**, teachings, principle, opinion, article, belief, creed, tenet, precept, credo, article of faith, kaupapa (*N.Z.*)

dogmatic ADJECTIVE **1** *His dogmatic style deflects opposition.* = **opinionated**, arrogant, assertive, arbitrary, emphatic, downright, dictatorial, imperious, overbearing, categorical, magisterial, doctrinaire, obdurate, peremptory **2** *Dogmatic socialism does not offer a magic formula.* = **doctrinal**, authoritative, categorical, canonical, oracular, ex cathedra

doing NOUN **1** *Nothing deflates impossibility like the doing of it.* = **carrying out** or **through**, performance, execution, implementation **2** *It was all her doing.* = **handiwork**, act, action, achievement, exploit, deed

doings PLURAL NOUN *the everyday doings of a group of schoolchildren* = **deeds**, actions, exploits, concerns, events, affairs, happenings, proceedings, transactions, dealings, goings-on (*informal*)

doldrums PLURAL NOUN • **the doldrums** *He had been through the doldrums.* = **blues**, depression, dumps (*informal*), gloom, boredom, apathy, inertia, stagnation, inactivity, tedium, dullness, the hump (*Brit. informal*), ennui, torpor, lassitude, listlessness

dole NOUN *They hold out fragile arms for a dole of food.* = **share**, grant, gift, allowance, portion, donation, quota, parcel, handout, modicum, pittance, alms, gratuity, koha (*N.Z.*) • **dole something out** *I began to dole out the money.* = **give out**, share, deal out, distribute, divide, assign, administer, allocate, hand out, dispense, allot, mete, apportion

dollop NOUN **1** = **lump**, blob **2** = **helping**, serving, portion, scoop, gob

dolphin NOUN ■ **RELATED WORD:** *collective noun* school

domain NOUN *the great experimenters in the domain of art* = **area**, field, department (*informal*), discipline, sphere, realm, speciality

domestic ADJECTIVE **1** *sales in the domestic market* = **home**, internal, native, indigenous, not foreign **2** *a plan for sharing domestic chores* = **household**, home, family, private, domiciliary **3** *She was kind and domestic.* = **home-loving**, homely, stay-at-home, domesticated **4** *a domestic cat* = **domesticated**, trained, tame, house, pet, house-trained ▸ NOUN *She worked for 10 or 15 years as a domestic.* = **servant**, help, maid, woman (*informal*), daily, char (*informal*), charwoman, daily help

domesticate or (*sometimes U.S.*) **domesticize** VERB **1** *We domesticated the dog.* = **tame**, break, train, house-train, gentle **2** *New World peoples domesticated a cornucopia of plants.* = **naturalize**, accustom, familiarize, habituate, acclimatize

domesticated ADJECTIVE **1** *our domesticated animals and plants* = **tame**, broken (in), tamed ■ **OPPOSITE:** wild **2** *I have never been very domesticated.* = **home-loving**, homely, domestic, house-trained (*humorous*)

domesticity NOUN = **home life**, housekeeping, domestication, homemaking, housewifery, home-lovingness

dominance NOUN = **control**, government, power, rule, authority, command, sway, domination, supremacy, mastery, ascendancy, paramountcy

dominant ADJECTIVE **1** *She was a dominant figure in the film industry.* = **main**, chief, primary, outstanding, principal, prominent, influential, prevailing, paramount, prevalent, predominant, pre-eminent ■ **OPPOSITE:** minor **2** *controlled by the dominant class* = **controlling**, leading, ruling, commanding, supreme, governing, superior, presiding, authoritative, ascendant

dominate VERB **1** *No company should be permitted to dominate the market.* = **control**, lead, rule, direct, master, govern, monopolize, tyrannize, have the upper hand over, lead by the nose (*informal*), overbear, have the whip hand over, domineer, keep under your thumb **2** *The building dominates this whole place.* = **tower above**, overlook, survey, stand over, loom over, stand head and shoulders above, bestride

domination NOUN = **control**, power, rule, authority, influence, command, sway, dictatorship, repression, oppression, suppression, supremacy, mastery, tyranny, ascendancy, subordination, despotism, subjection

domineering ADJECTIVE = **overbearing**, arrogant, authoritarian, oppressive, autocratic, masterful, dictatorial, coercive, bossy (*informal*), imperious, tyrannical, magisterial, despotic, high-handed, iron-handed ■ **OPPOSITE:** submissive

dominion NOUN **1** *They believe they have dominion over us.* = **control**, government, power, rule, authority, command, sovereignty, sway, domination, jurisdiction, supremacy, mastery, ascendancy, mana (*N.Z.*) **2** *The Republic is a dominion of the Brazilian people.* = **kingdom**, territory, province, country, region, empire, patch, turf (*slang*), realm, domain

don VERB = **put on**, get into, dress in, pull on, change into, get dressed in, clothe yourself in, slip on or into

donate VERB = **give**, present, contribute,

grant, commit, gift, hand out, subscribe, endow, chip in (*informal*), bestow, entrust, impart, bequeath, make a gift of

donation NOUN = **contribution**, gift, subscription, offering, present, grant, hand-out, boon (*archaic*), alms, stipend, gratuity, benefaction, largesse *or* largess, koha (*N.Z.*)

done INTERJECTION '*You lead and we'll look for it.' – 'Done.*' = **agreed**, you're on (*informal*), O.K. *or* okay (*informal*), it's a bargain, it's a deal, ka pai (*N.Z.*) ▶ ADJECTIVE **1** *By evening the work is done, and just in time.* = **finished**, completed, accomplished, over, through, ended, perfected, realized, concluded, executed, terminated, consummated, in the can (*informal*) **2** *When the cake is done, remove it from the oven.* = **cooked**, ready, cooked enough, cooked to a turn, cooked sufficiently **3** *It simply isn't done.* = **acceptable**, proper, conventional, protocol, de rigueur (*French*) • **done for** *I thought we were all done for.* = **finished** (*informal*), lost, beaten, defeated, destroyed, ruined, broken, dashed, wrecked, doomed, foiled, undone • **done in** *or* **up** *You must be really done in.* = **exhausted**, bushed (*informal*), all in (*slang*), worn out, dead (*informal*), knackered (*slang*), clapped out (*Austral. & N.Z. informal*), tired out, ready to drop, dog-tired (*informal*), zonked (*slang*), dead beat (*informal*), fagged out (*informal*), worn to a frazzle (*informal*), on your last legs, creamcrackered (*Brit. slang*) • **have** *or* **be done with something** *or* **someone** *Let us have done with him.* = **be through with**, give up, be finished with, throw over, wash your hands of, end relations with

donor NOUN = **giver**, contributor, benefactor, philanthropist, grantor (*Law*), donator, almsgiver ■ **OPPOSITE:** recipient

doom NOUN *his warnings of impending doom* = **destruction**, ruin, catastrophe, death, downfall ▶ VERB *Some suggest the leisure park is doomed to failure.* = **condemn**, sentence, consign, foreordain, destine, predestine, preordain

doomed ADJECTIVE = **hopeless**, condemned, ill-fated, fated, unhappy, unfortunate, cursed, unlucky, blighted, hapless, bedevilled, luckless, ill-starred, star-crossed, ill-omened

door NOUN *I was knocking at the front door.* = **opening**, entry, entrance, exit, doorway, ingress, egress (*formal*) • **out of doors** *The weather was fine for working out of doors.* = **in the open air**, outside, outdoors, out,

alfresco • **show someone the door** *Would they forgive him or show him the door?* = **throw out**, remove, eject, evict, turn out, bounce (*slang*), oust, drive out, boot out (*informal*), ask to leave, show out, throw out on your ear (*informal*)

do-or-die ADJECTIVE = **desperate**, risky, hazardous, going for broke, win-or-bust, death-or-glory, kill-or-cure

dope NOUN **1** *A man asked them if they wanted to buy some dope.* = **drugs**, narcotics, opiates, dadah (*Austral. slang*) **2** *I don't feel I'm such a dope.* = **idiot**, fool, jerk (*slang, chiefly U.S. & Canad.*), plank (*Brit. slang*), charlie (*Brit. informal*), berk (*Brit. slang*), wally (*slang*), prat (*slang*), plonker (*slang*), coot, twit (*informal, chiefly Brit.*), dunce, nitwit (*informal*), dolt, blockhead, divvy (*Brit. slang*), pillock (*Brit. slang*), eejit (*Scot. & Irish*), dumb-ass (*slang*), numpty (*Scot. informal*), lamebrain (*informal*), numbskull *or* numskull, dorba *or* dorb (*Austral. slang*), mampara (*S. African informal*) **3** *They had plenty of dope on him.* = **information**, facts, details, material, news, intelligence, gen (*Brit. informal*), info (*informal*), inside information, lowdown (*informal*) ▶ VERB *The horse had been doped with sedatives.* = **drug**, doctor, knock out, inject, sedate, stupefy, anaesthetize, narcotize

dopey *or* **dopy** ADJECTIVE **1** *The medicine always made him feel dopey.* = **drowsy**, dazed, groggy (*informal*), drugged, muzzy, stupefied, half-asleep, woozy (*informal*) **2** *I was so dopey I believed him.* = **stupid**, simple, slow, thick, silly, foolish, dense, dumb (*informal*), senseless, goofy (*informal*), idiotic, dozy (*Brit. informal*), asinine, dumb-ass (*slang*)

dormant ADJECTIVE = **latent**, inactive, lurking, quiescent, unrealized, unexpressed, inoperative

dorp NOUN (*S. African*) = **town**, village, settlement, municipality, kainga *or* kaika (*N.Z.*)

dose NOUN **1** *A dose of penicillin can wipe out infection.* = **measure**, amount, allowance, portion, prescription, ration, draught, dosage, potion **2** = **quantity**, measure, supply, portion

dot NOUN *a small black dot in the middle* = **spot**, point, mark, circle, atom, dab, mite, fleck, jot, speck, full stop, speckle, mote, iota ▶ VERB *Small coastal towns dotted the area.* = **spot**, stud, fleck, speckle • **on the dot** *At nine o'clock on the dot, they arrived.* = **on time**, promptly, precisely, exactly (*informal*), to the minute, on the button (*informal*), punctually

d

dote (with **on** or **upon**) VERB = **adore**, prize, treasure, admire, hold dear, idolize, lavish affection on

doting ADJECTIVE = **adoring**, devoted, fond, foolish, indulgent, lovesick

dotty ADJECTIVE an inventive and dotty comedy show = **crazy**, wacky, peculiar, eccentric, batty (slang), off-the-wall (slang), potty (Brit. informal), oddball (informal), loopy (informal), crackpot (informal), outré, doolally (slang), off the air (Austral. slang), porangi (N.Z.), daggy (Austral. & N.Z. informal)

double ADJECTIVE **1** a pair of double doors into the room = **matching**, coupled, doubled, paired, twin, duplicate, in pairs, binate (Botany) **2** a woman who had lived a double life = **deceitful**, false, fraudulent, deceiving, treacherous, dishonest, deceptive, hypocritical, counterfeit, two-faced, disingenuous, insincere, double-dealing, duplicitous, perfidious (literary), knavish (archaic), Janus-faced **3** The book has a double meaning. = **dual**, enigmatic, cryptic, twofold, Delphic, enigmatical ▶ NOUN Your mother sees you as her double. = **twin**, lookalike, spitting image, copy, fellow, mate, counterpart, clone, replica, ringer (slang), impersonator (informal), dead ringer (slang), Doppelgänger, duplicate ▶ VERB **1** They need to double the number of managers. = **multiply by two**, duplicate, increase twofold, repeat, enlarge, magnify **2** He doubled the sheet back upon itself. = **fold up** or **over 3** (with **as**) The military greatcoat doubled as a bedroll. = **function as**, serve as **• at** or **on the double** Come to my office, please, on the double. = **at once**, now, immediately, directly, quickly, promptly, right now, straight away, right away, briskly, without delay, pronto (informal), at full speed, in double-quick time, this instant, this very minute, pdq (slang), posthaste, tout de suite (French)

double-cross VERB = **betray**, trick, cheat, mislead, two-time (informal), defraud, swindle, hoodwink, sell down the river (informal), cozen

doubly ADVERB = **twice as**, in two ways, twofold, as much again, in double measure

doubt NOUN **1** They were troubled and full of doubt. = **uncertainty**, confusion, hesitation, dilemma, scepticism, misgiving, suspense, indecision, bewilderment, lack of confidence, hesitancy, perplexity, vacillation, lack of conviction, irresolution, dubiety ■ OPPOSITE: certainty **2** Where there is doubt, may we bring faith. = **suspicion**, scepticism,

distrust, fear, apprehension, mistrust, misgivings, disquiet, qualms, incredulity, lack of faith ■ OPPOSITE: belief ▶ VERB **1** They doubted whether that could happen. = **be uncertain**, be sceptical, be dubious **2** Stop doubting and start loving. = **waver**, hesitate, vacillate, sway, fluctuate, dither (chiefly Brit.), haver, oscillate, chop and change, blow hot and cold (informal), keep changing your mind, shillyshally (informal), be irresolute or indecisive, swither (Scot.) **3** I have no reason to doubt his word. = **disbelieve**, question, suspect, query, distrust, mistrust, lack confidence in, misgive ■ OPPOSITE: believe **• no doubt** No doubt I'm biased. = **certainly**, surely, probably, admittedly, doubtless, assuredly, doubtlessly

> USAGE In affirmative sentences, whether was in the past the only word considered acceptable for linking the verb doubt to a following clause, for example I doubt whether he will come. Nowadays, doubt if and doubt that are both considered acceptable alternatives to doubt whether. In negative sentences, use that after doubt, for example I don't doubt that he is telling the truth. The old-fashioned form not doubt but that, as in I do not doubt but that he is telling the truth, is now rarely used and sounds very stiff and formal.

doubter NOUN = **sceptic**, questioner, disbeliever, agnostic, unbeliever, doubting Thomas

doubtful ADJECTIVE **1** It seemed doubtful that he would move at all. = **unlikely**, unclear, dubious, unsettled, dodgy (Brit., Austral. & N.Z. informal), questionable, ambiguous, improbable, indefinite, unconfirmed, inconclusive, debatable, indeterminate, iffy (informal), equivocal, inexact ■ OPPOSITE: certain **2** Why did he sound so doubtful? = **unsure**, uncertain, hesitant, suspicious, hesitating, sceptical, unsettled, tentative, wavering, unresolved, perplexed, undecided, unconvinced, vacillating, leery (slang), distrustful, in two minds (informal), irresolute ■ OPPOSITE: certain **3** They all seemed of very doubtful character. = **questionable**, suspect, suspicious, crooked (informal), dubious, dodgy (Brit., Austral. & N.Z. informal), slippery, shady (informal), unscrupulous, fishy (informal), shifty, disreputable, untrustworthy, shonky (Austral. & N.Z. informal)

> USAGE In the past, whether was the only word considered acceptable for linking the adjective doubtful in the sense of

'improbable' to a following clause, for example *it is doubtful whether he will come.* Nowadays, however, *doubtful if* and *doubtful that* are also considered acceptable.

doubtless ADVERB = **probably**, presumably, most likely

doughty ADJECTIVE = **intrepid**, brave, daring, bold, hardy, heroic, courageous, gritty, fearless, resolute, gallant, valiant, redoubtable, dauntless, valorous, stouthearted (*old-fashioned*)

dour ADJECTIVE = **gloomy**, forbidding, grim, sour, dismal, dreary, sullen, unfriendly, morose ■ **OPPOSITE:** cheery

douse or **dowse** VERB 1 *The crew began to douse the fire.* = **put out**, smother, blow out, extinguish, snuff (out) 2 *They doused him in petrol.* = **drench**, soak, steep, saturate, duck, submerge, immerse, dunk, souse, plunge into water

dovetail VERB = **correspond**, match, agree, accord, coincide, tally, conform, harmonize

dowdy ADJECTIVE = **frumpy**, old-fashioned, shabby, drab, tacky (*U.S. informal*), unfashionable, dingy, frumpish, ill-dressed, frowzy ■ **OPPOSITE:** chic

down ADJECTIVE *The old man sounded really down.* = **depressed**, low, sad, blue, unhappy, discouraged, miserable, fed up, dismal, pessimistic, melancholy, glum, dejected, despondent, dispirited, downcast, morose, disheartened, crestfallen, downhearted, down in the dumps (*informal*), sick as a parrot (*informal*), low-spirited ▶ VERB 1 *We downed several bottles of local wine.* = **swallow**, drink (down), drain, gulp (down), put away (*informal*), toss off 2 *A bank guard shot him and downed him.* = **bring down**, fell, knock down, throw, trip, floor, tackle, deck (*slang*), overthrow, prostrate

down-and-out ADJECTIVE *He looked unshaven, shabby and down-and-out.* = **destitute**, ruined, impoverished, derelict, penniless, dirt-poor (*informal*), flat broke (*informal*), on your uppers (*informal*), without two pennies to rub together (*informal*) ▶ NOUN *some poor down-and-out in need of a meal* = **vagrant**, tramp, bum (*informal*), beggar, derelict, outcast, pauper, vagabond, bag lady, dosser (*Brit. slang*), derro (*Austral. slang*)

downbeat ADJECTIVE 1 *The headlines were suitably downbeat.* = **low-key**, muted, subdued, sober, sombre 2 *They found him in gloomy, downbeat mood.* = **gloomy**, negative, depressed, pessimistic, unfavourable ■ **OPPOSITE:** cheerful

downcast ADJECTIVE = **dejected**, sad, depressed, unhappy, disappointed, discouraged, miserable, dismayed, choked, daunted, dismal, despondent, dispirited, disheartened, disconsolate, crestfallen, down in the dumps (*informal*), cheerless, sick as a parrot (*informal*) ■ **OPPOSITE:** cheerful

downfall NOUN = **ruin**, fall, destruction, collapse, breakdown, disgrace, overthrow, descent, undoing, comeuppance (*slang*), comedown

downgrade VERB 1 *His superiors downgraded him.* = **demote**, degrade, take down a peg (*informal*), lower or reduce in rank ■ **OPPOSITE:** promote 2 *He was never one to downgrade his talents.* = **run down**, denigrate, disparage, detract from, decry

down-market ADJECTIVE = **second-rate**, cheap, inferior, tacky (*informal*), shoddy, low-grade, tawdry, low-quality, down scale, two-bit (*U.S. & Canad. slang*), cheap and nasty (*informal*), lowbrow, bush-league (*Austral. & N.Z. informal*), bodger or bodgie (*Austral. slang*) ■ **OPPOSITE:** first-rate

downpour NOUN = **rainstorm**, flood, deluge, torrential rain, cloudburst, inundation

downright ADJECTIVE = **complete**, absolute, utter, total, positive (*informal*), clear, plain, simple, explicit, outright, blatant, unequivocal, unqualified, out-and-out, categorical, undisguised, thoroughgoing, arrant, deep-dyed

downside NOUN = **drawback**, disadvantage, snag, problem, trouble, minus (*informal*), flip side, other side of the coin (*informal*), bad or weak point ■ **OPPOSITE:** benefit

down-to-earth ADJECTIVE = **sensible**, practical, realistic, common-sense, matter-of-fact, sane, no-nonsense, hard-headed, unsentimental, plain-spoken, grounded

downtrodden ADJECTIVE = **oppressed**, abused, exploited, subservient, subjugated, tyrannized

downward ADJECTIVE = **descending**, declining, heading down, earthward

doze VERB *For a while she dozed fitfully.* = **nap**, sleep, slumber, nod, kip (*Brit. slang*), snooze (*informal*), catnap, drowse, sleep lightly, zizz (*Brit. informal*) ▶ NOUN *After lunch I had a doze.* = **nap**, kip (*Brit. slang*), snooze (*informal*), siesta, little sleep, catnap, forty winks (*informal*), shuteye (*slang*), zizz (*Brit. informal*)

drab ADJECTIVE = **dull**, grey, gloomy, dismal, dreary, shabby, sombre, lacklustre, flat, dingy, colourless, uninspired, vapid, cheerless ■ **OPPOSITE:** bright

draconian ADJECTIVE (*sometimes cap.*) = **severe**, hard, harsh, stern, drastic, stringent, punitive, austere, pitiless

draft NOUN **1** *I rewrote his first draft.* = **outline**, plan, sketch, version, rough, abstract, delineation, preliminary form **2** *The money was payable by a draft.* = **money order**, bill (of exchange), cheque, postal order ▸ VERB *He drafted a standard letter.* = **outline**, write, plan, produce, create, design, draw, frame, compose, devise, sketch, draw up, formulate, contrive, delineate

drag VERB **1** *He got up and dragged his chair towards the table.* = **pull**, draw, haul, trail, tow, tug, jerk, yank, hale, lug **2** *I was dragging behind* = **lag**, trail, linger, loiter, straggle, dawdle, hang back, tarry, draggle **3** *The minutes dragged past.* = **go slowly**, inch, creep, crawl, advance slowly ▸ NOUN *Shopping for clothes is a drag.* = **nuisance**, pain (*informal*), bore, bother, pest, hassle (*informal*), inconvenience, annoyance, pain in the neck, pain in the backside (*informal*), pain in the butt (*informal*) • **drag on** *The conflict has dragged on for two years.* = **last**, continue, carry on, remain, endure, persist, linger, abide • **drag yourself** *I managed to drag myself to the surgery.* = **go slowly**, creep, crawl, inch, shuffle, shamble, limp along, move at a snail's pace, advance slowly

dragoon VERB = **force**, drive, compel, bully, intimidate, railroad (*informal*), constrain, coerce, impel, strong-arm (*informal*), browbeat

drain NOUN **1** *He built his own house and laid his own drains.* = **sewer**, channel, pipe, sink, outlet, ditch, trench, conduit, duct, culvert, watercourse **2** *This has been a big drain on resources.* = **reduction**, strain, drag, expenditure, exhaustion, sapping, depletion ▸ VERB **1** *machines to drain water out of the mines* = **remove**, draw, empty, withdraw, milk, tap, pump, bleed (*informal*), evacuate **2** *I didn't know what we would find when we drained the pool.* = **empty 3** *The water drained away.* = **flow out**, leak, discharge, trickle, ooze, seep, exude, well out, effuse **4** *She drained the contents of her glass and refilled it.* = **drink up**, swallow, finish, neck, put away (*informal*), quaff, gulp down **5** *My emotional turmoil has drained me.* = **exhaust**, tire, wear out, strain, weaken, fatigue, weary, debilitate, prostrate, tax, tire out, enfeeble, enervate **6** *Deficits drain resources from the pool of national savings.* = **consume**, waste, exhaust, empty, deplete, use up, sap, dissipate, swallow up

• **down the drain** *His public image is down the drain.* = **gone**, lost, wasted, ruined, gone for good

drainage NOUN = **sewerage**, waste, sewage

dram NOUN = **measure**, shot (*informal*), drop, glass, tot, slug, snort (*slang*), snifter (*informal*)

drama NOUN **1** *He acted in radio dramas.* = **play**, show, stage show, stage play, dramatization, theatrical piece **2** *He knew nothing of Greek drama.* = **theatre**, acting, dramatic art, stagecraft, dramaturgy, Thespian art **3** *the drama of a hostage release* = **excitement**, crisis, dramatics, spectacle, turmoil, histrionics, theatrics

dramatic ADJECTIVE **1** *He witnessed many dramatic escapes.* = **exciting**, emotional, thrilling, tense, startling, sensational, breathtaking, electrifying, melodramatic, climactic, high-octane (*informal*), shock-horror (*facetious*), suspenseful **2** *a dramatic arts major in college* = **theatrical**, Thespian, dramaturgical, dramaturgic **3** *She lifted her hands in a dramatic gesture.* = **expressive 4** *the film's dramatic special effects* = **powerful**, striking, stunning (*informal*), impressive, effective, vivid, jaw-dropping ■ **OPPOSITE:** ordinary

dramatist NOUN = **playwright**, screenwriter, scriptwriter, dramaturge

dramatize VERB = **exaggerate**, overdo, overstate, lay it on (thick) (*slang*), play-act, play to the gallery, make a performance of

drape VERB **1** *He draped himself in the flag.* = **cover**, wrap, fold, array, adorn, swathe **2** *She draped her arm over the back of the couch.* = **hang**, drop, dangle, suspend, lean, droop, let fall

drastic ADJECTIVE = **extreme**, strong, radical, desperate, severe, harsh, dire, forceful

draught or (*U.S.*) **draft** NOUN **1** *Block draughts around doors and windows.* = **breeze**, current, movement, flow, puff, influx, gust, current of air **2** *He took a draught of beer.* = **drink**

draw VERB **1** *Draw a rough design for a logo.* = **sketch**, design, outline, trace, portray, paint, depict, mark out, map out, delineate **2** *He drew his chair nearer the fire.* = **pull**, drag, haul, tow, tug **3** *He paused, drawing a deep breath.* = **inhale**, breathe in, pull, inspire, suck, respire **4** *They still have to draw their water from wells.* = **extract**, take, remove, drain **5** *We drew the winning name.* = **choose**, pick, select, take, single out **6** *He draws two conclusions from this.* = **deduce**, make, get, take, derive, infer **7** *He wanted to draw*

attention to their plight. = **attract**, engage
8 *The game is currently drawing huge crowds*
= **entice**, bring in ▶ NOUN **1** *The game ended
in a draw.* = **tie**, deadlock, stalemate,
impasse, dead heat **2** *The draw of India lies in
its beauty.* = **appeal**, interest, pull (*informal*),
charm, attraction, lure, temptation,
fascination, attractiveness, allure,
magnetism, enchantment, enticement,
captivation, temptingness • **draw back**
I drew back with a horrified scream. = **recoil**,
withdraw, retreat, shrink, falter, back off,
shy away, flinch, retract, quail, start back
• **draw on** or **upon something** *He drew on
his experience as a yachtsman.* = **make use of**,
use, employ, rely on, exploit, extract, take
from, fall back on, have recourse to
• **draw something out** *She drew the speech
out interminably.* = **stretch out**, extend,
lengthen, elongate, attenuate • **draw
something up** *They drew up a formal
agreement.* = **draft**, write, produce,
create, prepare, frame, compose, devise,
formulate, contrive • **draw up** *A police car
drew up at the gate.* = **halt**, stop, pull up,
stop short, come to a stop

drawback NOUN = **disadvantage**, trouble,
difficulty, fault, handicap, obstacle, defect,
deficiency, flaw, hitch, nuisance, snag,
downside, stumbling block, impediment,
detriment, imperfection, hindrance, fly in
the ointment (*informal*) ■ **OPPOSITE:**
advantage

drawing NOUN = **picture**, illustration,
representation, cartoon, sketch, portrayal,
depiction, study, outline, delineation

drawl VERB = **speak** or **say slowly**

drawn ADJECTIVE = **tense**, worn, strained,
stressed, tired, pinched, fatigued,
harassed, fraught, sapped, harrowed,
haggard

dread VERB *I'm dreading Christmas this year.*
= **fear**, shrink from, cringe at the thought
of, quail from, shudder to think about, have
cold feet about (*informal*), anticipate with
horror, tremble to think about ▶ NOUN *She
thought with dread of the cold winters to come.*
= **fear**, alarm, horror, terror, dismay, fright,
apprehension, consternation, trepidation
(*formal*), apprehensiveness, affright

dreadful ADJECTIVE **1** *They told us the dreadful
news.* = **terrible**, shocking (*informal*), awful,
alarming, distressing, appalling, tragic,
horrible, formidable, fearful (*informal*), dire,
horrendous, hideous, monstrous, from hell
(*informal*), grievous, atrocious (*informal*),
frightful, godawful (*slang*), hellacious
(*U.S. slang*) **2** *We've made a dreadful mistake.*
= **serious**, terrible, awful, appalling,

horrendous, monstrous, unspeakable,
abysmal **3** = **awful**, terrible (*informal*),
horrendous, frightful

dream NOUN **1** *I had a dream that I was in an
old house.* = **vision**, illusion, delusion,
hallucination, reverie **2** *My dream is to have
a house in the country.* = **ambition**, wish,
fantasy, desire, Holy Grail (*informal*), pipe
dream **3** *I wandered around in a kind of dream.*
= **daydream 4** *This car really is a dream to
drive.* = **delight**, pleasure, joy, beauty,
treasure, gem, marvel, pearler (*Austral.
slang*), beaut (*Austral. & N.Z. slang*) ▶ VERB
1 *She dreamt about her baby.* = **have dreams**,
hallucinate **2** *She spent most of her time
looking out of the window and dreaming.*
= **daydream**, stargaze, build castles in the
air or in Spain ▶ ADJECTIVE • **dream of
something** or **someone** *She dreamed of
going to work overseas.* = **daydream about**,
fantasize about • **dream something up**
I dreamed up a plan. = **invent**, create,
imagine, devise, hatch, contrive, concoct,
think up, cook up (*informal*), spin

dreamer NOUN = **idealist**, visionary,
daydreamer, utopian, theorizer, fantasizer,
romancer, Don Quixote, escapist, Walter
Mitty, fantasist, fantast

dreamy ADJECTIVE **1** *His face assumed a dreamy
expression.* = **vague**, abstracted, absent,
musing, preoccupied, daydreaming,
faraway, pensive, in a reverie, with your
head in the clouds **2** *a dreamy, delicate song*
= **relaxing**, calming, romantic, gentle,
soothing, lulling **3** *full of dreamy ideals*
= **impractical**, vague, imaginary,
speculative, visionary, fanciful, quixotic,
dreamlike, airy-fairy ■ **OPPOSITE:** realistic

dreary ADJECTIVE **1** *They live such dreary lives.*
= **dull**, boring, tedious, routine, drab,
tiresome, lifeless, monotonous, humdrum,
colourless, uneventful, uninteresting,
mind-numbing, ho-hum (*informal*),
wearisome, as dry as dust ■ **OPPOSITE:**
exciting **2** *a dreary little town in the Midwest*
= **dismal**, depressing, bleak, sad, lonely,
gloomy, solitary, melancholy, sombre,
forlorn, glum, mournful, lonesome (*chiefly
U.S. & Canad.*), downcast, sorrowful,
wretched, joyless, funereal, doleful,
cheerless, drear, comfortless

dredge up VERB = **dig up**, raise, rake up,
discover, uncover, draw up, unearth, drag
up, fish up

dregs PLURAL NOUN = **sediment**, grounds,
lees, waste, deposit, trash, residue, scum,
dross, residuum, scourings, draff • **the
dregs** *the dregs of society* = **scum**, outcasts,
rabble (*derogatory*), down-and-outs,

d

good-for-nothings, riffraff, canaille (French), ragtag and bobtail

drench VERB = **soak**, flood, wet, duck, drown, steep, swamp, saturate, inundate, souse, imbrue

dress NOUN **1** *She was wearing a black dress.* = **frock**, gown, garment, robe **2** *a well-groomed gent in smart dress and specs* = **clothing**, clothes, gear (informal), costume, threads (slang), garments, apparel (old-fashioned), attire, garb, togs, raiment (archaic, poetic), vestment, schmutter (slang), habiliment ▸ VERB **1** *He told her to wait while he dressed.* = **put on clothes**, don clothes, slip on or into something ■ **OPPOSITE**: undress **2** *We dressed the baby in a warm outfit.* = **clothe 3** *I dressed her wounds.* = **bandage**, treat, plaster, bind up **4** *advice on how to dress a Christmas tree* = **decorate**, deck, adorn, trim, array, drape, ornament, embellish, festoon, bedeck, furbish, rig out **5** *He's so careless about dressing his hair.* = **arrange**, do (up), groom, set, prepare, comb (out), get ready • **dress someone down** *He dressed them down in public.* = **reprimand**, rebuke, scold, berate, castigate, tear into (informal), tell off (informal), read the riot act, reprove, upbraid, slap on the wrist, carpet (informal), bawl out (informal), rap over the knuckles, haul over the coals, chew out (U.S. & Canad. informal), tear (someone) off a strip (Brit. informal), give a rocket (Brit. & N.Z. informal) • **dress up 1** *She dressed up as a witch.* = **put on fancy dress**, wear a costume, disguise yourself **2** *She did not feel obliged to dress up for the cameras.* = **dress formally**, dress for dinner, doll yourself up (slang), put on your best bib and tucker (informal), put on your glad rags (informal)

dressmaker NOUN = **seamstress**, tailor, couturier, modiste

dribble VERB **1** *Sweat dribbled down his face.* = **run**, drip, trickle, drop, leak, ooze, seep, fall in drops **2** *She's dribbling on her collar.* = **drool**, drivel, slaver, slobber, drip saliva

drift VERB **1** *We proceeded to drift along the river.* = **float**, go (aimlessly), bob, coast, slip, sail, slide, glide, meander, waft, be carried along, move gently **2** *People drifted around the room.* = **wander**, stroll, stray, roam, meander, rove, range, straggle, traipse (informal), stravaig (Scot. & Northern English, dialect), peregrinate **3** *I let my attention drift.* = **stray**, wander, roam, meander, digress, get sidetracked, go off at a tangent, get off the point **4** *The snow, except where it drifted, was only calf-deep.* = **pile up**, gather, accumulate, amass, bank up ▸ NOUN

1 *A boy was trapped in a snow drift.* = **pile**, bank, mass, heap, mound, accumulation **2** *She was beginning to get his drift.* = **meaning**, point, gist, aim, direction, object, import, intention, implication, tendency, significance, thrust, tenor, purport

drifter NOUN = **wanderer**, bum (informal), tramp, itinerant, vagrant, hobo (U.S.), vagabond, rolling stone, bag lady (chiefly U.S.), derro (Austral. slang)

drill NOUN **1** *pneumatic drills* = **bit**, borer, gimlet, rotary tool, boring tool **2** *A local army base teaches them military drill.* = **training**, exercise, discipline, instruction, preparation, repetition **3** *a fire drill* = **practice** ▸ VERB **1** *I drilled five holes at equal distance.* = **bore**, pierce, penetrate, sink in, puncture, perforate **2** *He drills the choir to a high standard.* = **train**, coach, teach, exercise, discipline, practise, instruct, rehearse

drink VERB **1** *He drank his cup of tea.* = **swallow**, drain, sip, suck, gulp, sup, swig (informal), swill, guzzle, imbibe (formal), quaff, partake of, toss off **2** *He was smoking and drinking too much.* = **booze** (informal), tipple, tope, hit the bottle (informal), bevvy (dialect), bend the elbow (informal), go on a binge or bender (informal) ▸ NOUN **1** *a drink of water.* = **glass**, cup, swallow, sip, draught, gulp, swig (informal), taste, tipple, snifter (informal), noggin **2** *Can I offer you a drink?* = **beverage**, refreshment, potion, liquid, thirst quencher **3** *Too much drink is bad for your health.* = **alcohol**, booze (informal), liquor, spirits, the bottle (informal), Dutch courage, hooch or hootch (informal, chiefly U.S. & Canad.) • **drink something in** *She stood drinking in the view.* = **absorb**, take in, digest, pay attention to, soak up, devour, assimilate, be fascinated by, imbibe • **drink to something** *Let's drink to his memory.* = **toast**, salute, pledge the health of • **the drink** *His plane went down in the drink.* = **the sea**, the main, the deep, the ocean, the briny (informal)

drinker NOUN = **alcoholic**, drunk, boozer (informal), soak (slang), lush (slang), toper, sponge (informal), guzzler, drunkard, sot, tippler, wino (informal), inebriate, dipsomaniac, bibber, caner (slang)

drip VERB *a cloth that dripped pink drops upon the floor* = **drop**, splash, sprinkle, trickle, dribble, exude, drizzle, plop ▸ NOUN **1** *Drips of water rolled down his uniform.* = **drop**, bead, trickle, dribble, droplet, globule, pearl, driblet **2** *The kid is a drip!* = **weakling**, wet (Brit. informal), weed (informal), softie (informal), mummy's boy (informal), namby-pamby, ninny, milksop

drive VERB **1** I drove into town and went for dinner. = **go (by car)**, ride (by car), motor, travel by car **2** Don't expect to be able to drive a car or operate machinery. = **operate**, manage, direct, guide, handle, steer **3** pistons that drive the wheels = **push**, propel **4** I used the sledgehammer to drive the pegs in. = **thrust**, push, sink, dig, hammer, plunge, stab, ram **5** The shepherds drove the sheep up to pasture. = **herd**, urge, impel **6** Curiosity drove me to probe into what they worked on together. = **force**, press, prompt, spur, compel, motivate, oblige, railroad (informal), prod, constrain, prick, coerce, goad, impel, dragoon, actuate **7** For the next six years he drove himself mercilessly. = **work**, overwork, overburden ▶ NOUN **1** We might go for a drive on Sunday. = **run**, ride, trip, journey, spin (informal), hurl (Scot.), outing, excursion, jaunt **2** He is best remembered for his drive and enthusiasm. = **initiative**, push (informal), energy, enterprise, ambition, pep, motivation, zip (informal), vigour, get-up-and-go (informal) **3** the drive towards democracy = **campaign**, push (informal), crusade, action, effort, appeal, advance, surge **4** (Computing) = **storage device**, flash drive, key drive, keyring drive, microdrive, pen drive, thumb drive, USB drive, USB key • **drive at something** He wasn't sure what she was driving at. = **mean**, suggest, intend, refer to, imply, intimate, get at, hint at, have in mind, allude to, insinuate

drivel VERB I drivelled on about the big race that day. = **babble**, ramble, waffle (informal, chiefly Brit.), gab (informal), gas (informal), maunder, blether, prate ▶ NOUN What absolute drivel! = **nonsense**, rubbish, garbage, malarkey (informal), rot, crap (slang), trash, bunk (informal), blah (slang), hot air (informal), tosh (slang, chiefly Brit.), waffle (informal, chiefly Brit.), prating, pap, bilge (informal), twaddle, tripe (informal), dross, gibberish, guff (slang), moonshine, hogwash (informal), hokum (slang, chiefly U.S. & Canad.), piffle (informal), poppycock (informal), balderdash, bosh (informal), eyewash (informal), tommyrot, horsefeathers (U.S. slang), bunkum or buncombe (U.S. slang), bizzo (Austral. slang), bull's wool (Austral. & N.Z. slang)

drizzle NOUN The drizzle had stopped and the sun was breaking through. = **fine rain**, Scotch mist, smir (Scot.) ▶ VERB It was starting to drizzle. = **rain**, shower, spit, spray, sprinkle, mizzle (dialect), spot or spit with rain

droll ADJECTIVE = **amusing**, odd, funny, entertaining, comic, ridiculous, diverting, eccentric, ludicrous, humorous, quaint, off-the-wall (slang), laughable, farcical, whimsical, comical, oddball (informal), risible, jocular, clownish, waggish

drone[1] NOUN = **parasite**, skiver (Brit. slang), idler, lounger, leech, loafer, couch potato (slang), scrounger (informal), sponger (informal), sluggard, bludger (Austral. & N.Z. informal), quandong (Austral. slang)

drone[2] VERB **1** An invisible plane drones through the night sky. = **hum**, buzz, vibrate, purr, whirr, thrum **2** (often with **on**) Her voice droned on. = **speak monotonously**, drawl, chant, spout, intone, talk interminably ▶ NOUN the constant drone of the motorway = **hum**, buzz, purr, vibration, whirr, whirring, thrum

droning ADJECTIVE = **monotonous**, boring, tedious, drawling, soporific

drool VERB **1** The dog was drooling on my shoulder. = **dribble**, dribble, salivate, slaver, slobber, water at the mouth **2** (often with **over**) Fashion editors drooled over every item. = **gloat over**, pet, gush, make much of, rave about (informal), dote on, slobber over

droop VERB a young man with a drooping moustache = **sag**, drop, hang (down), sink, bend, dangle, fall down

droopy ADJECTIVE = **sagging**, limp, wilting, stooped, floppy, drooping, languid, flabby, languorous, pendulous (literary), lassitudinous

drop VERB **1** Temperatures can drop to freezing at night. = **fall**, lower, decline, diminish **2** (often with **away**) The ground dropped away steeply. = **decline**, fall, sink **3** Part of an aeroplane had dropped out of the sky and hit me. = **plunge**, fall, dive, tumble, descend, plummet **4** He felt hot tears dropping onto his fingers. = **drip**, trickle, dribble, fall in drops **5** She let her head drop. = **sink**, fall, descend, droop **6** He dropped me outside the hotel. = **set down**, leave, deposit, unload, let off **7** I was told to drop the idea. = **quit**, give up, abandon, cease, axe (informal), kick (informal), terminate, relinquish, remit, discontinue, forsake **8** She has dropped those friends who used to drink with her. = **abandon**, desert, forsake, repudiate, leave, jilt, throw over ▶ NOUN **1** He was prepared to take a drop in wages. = **decrease**, fall, cut, lowering, decline, reduction, slump, fall-off, downturn, deterioration, cutback, diminution, decrement **2** a drop of blue ink = **droplet**, bead, globule, bubble, pearl, drip, driblet **3** I'll have a drop of that milk. = **dash**, shot (informal), spot, taste, trace, pinch, sip, tot, trickle, nip, dab, mouthful **4** *There was a sheer drop just outside my window.* = **fall**, plunge, descent, abyss, chasm, precipice • **drop in** *I'll drop in on my way home.* = **visit**, call, stop, turn up, look up, call in, look in, pop in (*informal*), swing by (*informal*) • **drop off 1** *I was just dropping off.* = **fall asleep**, nod (off), doze (off), snooze (*informal*), catnap, drowse, have forty winks (*informal*) **2** *The toll of casualties has dropped off sharply.* = **decrease**, lower, decline, shrink, diminish, fall off, dwindle, lessen, wane, subside, slacken • **drop out** *He went to university, but dropped out after a year.* = **leave**, stop, give up, withdraw, quit, pull out, back out, renege, throw in the towel, cop out (*slang*), fall by the wayside • **drop out of something** *She had a troubled childhood and dropped out of high school.* = **discontinue**, give up, abandon, quit, cease, terminate, forsake • **drop someone off** *I'm going to drop you off and pick you up myself.* = **set down**, leave, deliver, let off, allow to alight

droppings PLURAL NOUN = **excrement**, stool, manure, dung, faeces, guano, excreta, doo-doo (*informal*), ordure, kak (*S. African vulgar slang*)

dross NOUN **1** = rubbish, remains, refuse, lees, waste, debris, dregs **2** *Why are you wasting your time reading that dross?* = **nonsense**, garbage (*chiefly U.S.*), drivel, twaddle, pants (*slang*), rot, crap (*slang*), trash, hot air (*informal*), tosh (*slang, chiefly Brit.*), pap, bilge (*informal*), tripe (*informal*), gibberish, guff (*slang*), havers (*Scot.*), moonshine, claptrap (*informal*), hogwash, hokum (*slang, chiefly U.S. & Canad.*), codswallop (*Brit. slang*), piffle (*informal*), poppycock (*informal*), balderdash, bosh (*informal*), wack (*U.S. slang*), eyewash (*informal*), stuff and nonsense, flapdoodle (*slang*), tommyrot, horsefeathers (*U.S. slang*), bunkum or buncombe, bizzo (*Austral. slang*), bull's wool (*Austral. & N.Z. slang*)

drought NOUN **1** *Drought and famines have killed up to two million people.* = **water shortage**, dryness, dry weather, dry spell, aridity, drouth (*Scot.*), parchedness ■ OPPOSITE: flood **2** *The Western world was suffering through the oil drought.* = **shortage**, lack, deficit, deficiency, want, need, shortfall, scarcity, dearth, insufficiency ■ OPPOSITE: abundance

drove NOUN (*often plural*) = **herd**, company, crowds, collection, gathering, mob, flocks, swarm, horde, multitude, throng

drown VERB **1** *He drowned during a storm.*

= **go down**, go under **2** *The country would be drowned in blood.* = **drench**, flood, soak, steep, swamp, saturate, engulf, submerge, immerse, inundate, deluge **3** (*often with out*) *His words were soon drowned by amplified police sirens.* = **overwhelm**, overcome, wipe out, overpower, obliterate, swallow up

drowsiness NOUN = **sleepiness**, tiredness, lethargy, torpor, sluggishness, languor (*literary*), somnolence, heavy eyelids, doziness, torpidity ■ OPPOSITE: wakefulness

drowsy ADJECTIVE **1** *He felt pleasantly drowsy.* = **sleepy**, tired, lethargic, heavy, nodding, dazed, dozy, comatose, dopey (*slang*), half asleep, somnolent, torpid ■ OPPOSITE: awake **2** *The drowsy air hummed with bees.* = **peaceful**, quiet, sleepy, soothing, lulling, dreamy, restful, soporific

drubbing NOUN = **beating**, defeat, hammering (*informal*), pounding, whipping, thrashing, licking (*informal*), pasting (*slang*), flogging, trouncing, clobbering (*slang*), walloping (*informal*), pummelling

drudge NOUN = **menial**, worker, servant, slave, toiler, dogsbody (*informal*), plodder, factotum, scullion (*archaic*), skivvy (*chiefly Brit.*), maid or man of all work

drudgery NOUN = **labour**, grind (*informal*), sweat (*informal*), hard work, slavery, chore, fag (*informal*), toil, slog, donkey-work, sweated labour, menial labour, skivvying (*Brit.*)

drug NOUN **1** *The drug will treat those infected.* = **medication**, medicine, remedy, physic, medicament **2** *the problem of drug abuse* = **narcotic** (*slang*), stimulant, opiate ▶ VERB *They drugged the guard dog.* = **knock out**, dope (*slang*), numb, deaden, stupefy, anaesthetize ■ RELATED WORD: combining form pharmaco-

drug addict NOUN = **user**, abuser, junkie (*informal*), tripper (*informal*), druggie (*informal*), acid head (*slang*), dope-fiend (*slang*)

drugged ADJECTIVE = **stoned**, high (*informal*), flying (*slang*), bombed (*slang*), tripping (*informal slang*), wasted (*slang*), smashed (*slang*), wrecked (*slang*), out of it (*slang*), doped (*slang*), under the influence (*informal*), on a trip (*informal*), spaced out (*slang*), comatose, stupefied, out of your mind (*slang*), zonked (*slang*), out to it (*Austral. & N.Z. slang*)

drum VERB *Rain drummed on the roof of the car.* = **pound**, beat, tap, rap, lash, thrash, tattoo, throb, pulsate, reverberate • **drum something into someone** *Examples were* *drummed into students' heads.* = **drive**, hammer, instil, din, harp on about • **drum something up** *drumming up business* = **seek**, attract, request, ask for, obtain, bid for, petition, round up, solicit, canvass

drunk ADJECTIVE *I got drunk and had to be carried home.* = **intoxicated**, loaded (*slang, chiefly U.S. & Canad.*), tight (*informal*), canned (*slang*), flying (*slang*), bombed (*slang*), stoned (*slang*), wasted (*slang*), smashed (*slang*), steaming (*slang*), wrecked (*slang*), soaked (*informal*), out of it (*slang*), plastered (*slang*), drunken, blitzed (*slang*), lit up (*slang*), merry (*Brit. informal*), stewed (*slang*), pickled (*informal*), bladdered (*slang*), under the influence (*informal*), sloshed (*slang*), tipsy, maudlin, well-oiled (*slang*), legless (*informal*), paralytic (*informal*), tired and emotional (*euphemistic*), steamboats (*Scot. slang*), tiddly (*slang, chiefly Brit.*), zonked (*slang*), blotto (*slang*), fuddled, inebriated, out to it (*Austral. & N.Z. slang*), sottish, tanked up (*slang*), bacchic, half seas over (*informal*), bevvied (*dialect*), babalas (*S. African*), fu' (*Scot.*), pie-eyed (*slang*) ▶ NOUN *A drunk lay in the alley.* = **drunkard**, alcoholic, lush (*slang*), boozer (*informal*), toper, sot, soak (*slang*), wino (*informal*), inebriate

drunkard NOUN = **drunk**, alcoholic, soak (*slang*), drinker, lush (*slang*), carouser, caner (*slang*), sot, tippler, toper, wino (*informal*), dipsomaniac, alko or alco (*Austral. slang*)

drunken ADJECTIVE **1** *Drunken yobs smashed shop windows.* = **intoxicated**, smashed (*slang*), drunk, flying (*slang*), bombed (*slang*), wasted (*slang*), steaming (*slang*), wrecked (*slang*), out of it (*slang*), boozing (*informal*), blitzed (*slang*), lit up (*slang*), bladdered (*slang*), under the influence (*informal*), tippling, toping, red-nosed, legless (*informal*), paralytic (*informal*), steamboats (*Scot. slang*), zonked (*slang*), bibulous, blotto (*slang*), inebriate, out to it (*Austral. & N.Z. slang*), sottish, bevvied (*dialect*), (gin-)sodden **2** *A loud, drunken party was raging nearby.* = **boozy**, dissipated (*informal*), riotous, debauched, dionysian, orgiastic, bacchanalian, bacchic, saturnalian

drunkenness NOUN = **intoxication**, alcoholism, intemperance, inebriation, dipsomania, tipsiness, insobriety, bibulousness, sottishness

dry ADJECTIVE **1** *a hard, dry desert landscape* = **dehydrated**, dried-up, arid, torrid, parched, desiccated, waterless, juiceless, sapless, moistureless ■ OPPOSITE: wet **2** *She heard the rustle of dry leaves.* = **dried**,

crisp, withered, brittle, shrivelled, crispy, parched, desiccated, sun-baked **3** *She was suddenly dry.* = **thirsty**, parched **4** *He is renowned for his dry wit.* = **sarcastic**, cutting, sharp, keen, cynical, low-key, sly, sardonic, deadpan, droll, ironical, quietly humorous **5** *The work was very dry and dull.* = **dull**, boring, tedious, commonplace, dreary, tiresome, monotonous, run-of-the-mill, humdrum, unimaginative, uninteresting, mind-numbing, ho-hum (*informal*) ■ OPPOSITE: interesting **6** *an infuriating list of dry facts and dates* = **plain**, simple, bare, basic, pure, stark, unembellished ▶ VERB **1** *Wash and dry the lettuce.* = **drain**, make dry **2** (*often with* **out**) *They bought a machine to dry the wood and cut costs.* = **dehydrate**, make dry, desiccate, sear, parch, dehumidify ■ OPPOSITE: wet • **dry out** *or* **up** *The pollen dries up and becomes hard.* = **become dry**, harden, wither, mummify, shrivel up, wizen

dryness NOUN **1** *the parched dryness of the air* = **aridity**, drought, dehydration, aridness, dehumidification, waterlessness, moisturelessness, parchedness **2** *Symptoms include dryness of the mouth.* = **thirstiness**, thirst, parchedness

dual ADJECTIVE = **twofold**, double, twin, matched, coupled, paired, duplicate, binary, duplex

duality NOUN = **dualism**, dichotomy, polarity, doubleness, biformity, duplexity

dub VERB = **name**, call, term, style, label, nickname, designate, christen, denominate

dubious ADJECTIVE **1** *dubious business dealings* = **suspect**, suspicious, crooked (*informal*), dodgy (*Brit., Austral. & N.Z. informal*), questionable, unreliable, shady (*informal*), unscrupulous, fishy (*informal*), disreputable, untrustworthy, undependable ■ OPPOSITE: trustworthy **2** *My parents were a bit dubious about it all.* = **unsure**, uncertain, suspicious, hesitating, doubtful, sceptical, tentative, wavering, hesitant, undecided, unconvinced, iffy (*informal*), leery (*slang*), distrustful, in two minds (*informal*) ■ OPPOSITE: sure **3** *This is a very dubious honour.* = **doubtful**, questionable, ambiguous, debatable, moot, arguable, equivocal, open to question, disputable

duck VERB **1** *He ducked in time to save his head from the blow.* = **bob**, drop, lower, bend, bow, dodge, crouch, stoop **2** *He had ducked the confrontation.* = **dodge**, avoid, escape, evade, elude, sidestep, circumvent (*formal*), shirk, body-swerve **3** *She splashed around in the pool trying to duck him.* = **dunk**, wet, plunge, dip, submerge, immerse, douse, souse

duct NOUN = **pipe**, channel, passage, tube, canal, funnel, conduit

dud ADJECTIVE *He replaced a dud valve.* = **faulty**, broken, failed, damaged, bust (*informal*), not working, useless, flawed, impaired, duff (*Brit. informal*), worthless, defective, imperfect, malfunctioning, out of order, unsound, not functioning, valueless, on the blink, inoperative, kaput (*informal*)

due ADJECTIVE **1** *The results are due at the end of the month.* = **expected**, scheduled, expected to arrive **2** *Treat them with due attention.* = **fitting**, deserved, appropriate, just, right, becoming, fit, justified, suitable, merited, proper, obligatory, rightful, requisite, well-earned, bounden **3** *I've got a tax rebate due.* = **payable**, outstanding, owed, owing, unpaid, in arrears ▶ NOUN *No doubt he felt it was his due.* = **right(s)**, privilege, deserts, merits, prerogative, comeuppance (*informal*) ▶ ADVERB *They headed due north.* = **directly**, dead, straight, exactly, undeviatingly

duel NOUN **1** *He killed a man in a duel.* = **single combat**, affair of honour **2** *sporadic artillery duels* = **contest**, fight, competition, clash, encounter, engagement, rivalry ▶ VERB *We duelled for two years.* = **fight**, struggle, clash, compete, contest, contend, vie with, lock horns

dues PLURAL NOUN = **membership fee**, charges, fee, contribution, levy

duff ADJECTIVE = **bad**, poor, useless, pathetic, inferior, worthless, unsatisfactory, defective, deficient, imperfect, substandard, low-rent (*informal, chiefly U.S.*), poxy (*slang*), pants (*informal*), bodger or bodgie (*Austral. slang*)

duffer NOUN = **clot**, blunderer (*Brit. informal*), booby, clod, oaf, bungler, galoot (*slang, chiefly U.S.*), lubber, lummox (*informal*)

dulcet ADJECTIVE = **sweet**, pleasing, musical, charming, pleasant, honeyed, delightful, soothing, agreeable, harmonious, melodious, mellifluous, euphonious, mellifluent

dull ADJECTIVE **1** *They can both be rather dull.* = **boring**, tedious, dreary, flat, dry, plain, commonplace, tiresome, monotonous, prosaic, run-of-the-mill, humdrum, unimaginative, dozy, uninteresting, mind-numbing, ho-hum (*informal*), vapid, as dry as dust ■ OPPOSITE: exciting **2** *We all feel dull and sleepy between 1 and 3pm.* = **lifeless**, dead, heavy, slow, indifferent, sluggish, insensitive, apathetic, listless, unresponsive, passionless, insensible

■ OPPOSITE: lively **3** *The stamp was a dull blue colour.* = **drab**, faded, muted, subdued, feeble, murky, sombre, toned-down, subfusc **4** *It's always dull and raining.* = **cloudy**, dim, gloomy, dismal, overcast, leaden, turbid ■ OPPOSITE: bright **5** *The box closed with a dull thud.* = **muted**, faint, suppressed, subdued, stifled, indistinct **6** *using the dull edge of her knife* = **blunt**, dulled, blunted, not keen, not sharp, edgeless, unsharpened ■ OPPOSITE: sharp ▶ VERB **1** *They gave him morphine to dull the pain.* = **relieve**, blunt, lessen, moderate, soften, alleviate, allay, mitigate, assuage, take the edge off, palliate **2** *Her eyes dulled and she gazed blankly.* = **cloud over**, darken, grow dim, become cloudy **3** *Her illness failed to dull her optimism.* = **dampen**, reduce, check, depress, moderate, discourage, stifle, lessen, smother, sadden, dishearten, dispirit, deject

dullness NOUN **1** *the dullness of their routine life* = **tediousness**, monotony, banality, flatness, dreariness, vapidity, insipidity ■ OPPOSITE: interest **2** *his dullness of mind* = **stupidity**, thickness, slowness, dimness, obtuseness, doziness (*Brit. informal*), dim-wittedness, dopiness (*slang*) ■ OPPOSITE: intelligence **3** *the dullness of an old painting* = **drabness**, greyness, dimness, gloominess, dinginess, colourlessness ■ OPPOSITE: brilliance

duly ADVERB **1** *He duly apologized for his behaviour.* = **properly**, fittingly, correctly, appropriately, accordingly, suitably, deservedly, rightfully, decorously, befittingly **2** *The engineer duly arrived, expecting to have to repair the boiler.* = **on time**, promptly, in good time, punctually, at the proper time

dumb ADJECTIVE **1** *We were all struck dumb for a minute.* = **silent**, mute, speechless, inarticulate, tongue-tied, wordless, voiceless, soundless, at a loss for words, mum **2** *I came up with this dumb idea.* = **stupid**, thick, dull, foolish, dense, dozy (*Brit. informal*), dim, obtuse, unintelligent, asinine, dim-witted (*informal*) ■ OPPOSITE: clever

dumbfounded ADJECTIVE = **amazed**, stunned, astonished, confused, overcome, overwhelmed, staggered, thrown, startled, at sea, dumb, bewildered, astounded, breathless, confounded, taken aback, speechless, bowled over (*informal*), gobsmacked (*Brit. slang*), flabbergasted (*informal*), nonplussed, lost for words, flummoxed, thunderstruck, knocked sideways (*informal*), knocked for six (*informal*)

dummy NOUN **1** *a shop-window dummy* = **model**, figure, mannequin, form, manikin, lay figure **2** *The police video camera was a dummy.* = **imitation**, copy, duplicate, sham, counterfeit, replica **3** *He's no dummy, this guy.* = **fool**, idiot, charlie (*Brit. informal*), dunce, schmuck (*U.S. slang*), nitwit (*informal*), dolt, blockhead, divvy (*Brit. slang*), fathead (*informal*), eejit (*Scot. & Irish*), dumb-ass (*slang*), numpty (*Scot. informal*), doofus (*slang, chiefly U.S.*), lamebrain (*informal*), numbskull or numskull, dorba or dorb (*Austral. slang*), mampara (*S. African informal*) ▸ ADJECTIVE *Soldiers were still using dummy guns.* = **imitation**, false, fake, artificial, mock, bogus, simulated, sham, phoney or phony (*informal*)

dummy run NOUN *They do a dummy run with the brakes.* = **practice**, trial, dry run

dump VERB **1** *We dumped our bags on the table.* = **drop**, deposit, throw down, let fall, fling down **2** *Untreated sewage is dumped into the sea.* = **get rid of**, tip, discharge, dispose of, unload, jettison, empty out, coup (*Scot.*), throw away or out **3** *Ministers believed it was vital to dump the tax.* = **scrap**, axe (*informal*), get rid of, abolish, junk (*informal*), put an end to, discontinue, jettison, put paid to ▸ NOUN **1** *The walled garden was used as a dump.* = **rubbish tip**, tip (*Brit.*), junkyard, rubbish heap, refuse heap **2** *'What a dump!' she said.* = **pigsty**, hole (*informal*), joint (*slang*), slum, shack, shanty, hovel

dumps PLURAL NOUN • **down in the dumps** = **down**, low, blue, sad, unhappy, low-spirited, discouraged, fed up, moody, pessimistic, melancholy, glum, dejected, despondent, dispirited, downcast, morose, crestfallen, downhearted

dumpy ADJECTIVE = **podgy**, homely, short, plump, squat, stout, chunky, chubby, tubby, roly-poly, pudgy, squab, fubsy (*archaic, dialect*)

dunce NOUN = **simpleton**, duffer (*informal*), bonehead (*slang*), loon (*informal*), goose (*informal*), ass, donkey, oaf, dullard (*old-fashioned*), dimwit (*informal*), ignoramus, nitwit (*informal*), dolt, blockhead, halfwit, nincompoop, fathead (*informal*), dunderhead, lamebrain (*informal*), thickhead, numbskull or numskull

dungeon NOUN = **prison**, cell, cage, vault, lockup, oubliette, calaboose (*U.S. informal*), donjon, boob (*Austral. slang*)

dunny NOUN = **toilet**, lavatory, bathroom, loo (*Brit. informal*), W.C., bog (*slang*), Gents or Ladies, can (*U.S. & Canad. slang*), john (*slang, chiefly U.S. & Canad.*), head(s)

(*Nautical slang*), throne (*informal*), closet, privy (*obsolete*), cloakroom (*Brit.*), urinal, latrine, washroom, powder room, crapper (*vulgar slang*), water closet, khazi (*slang*), pissoir (*French*), little boy's room or little girl's room (*informal*), (public) convenience, bogger (*Austral. slang*), brasco (*Austral. slang*)

dupe NOUN *an innocent dupe in a political scandal* = **victim**, mug (*Brit. slang*), sucker (*slang*), pigeon (*slang*), sap (*slang*), gull, pushover (*slang*), fall guy (*informal*), simpleton ▸ VERB *Some of the offenders duped the psychologists.* = **deceive**, trick, cheat, con (*informal*), kid (*informal*), rip off (*slang*), hoax, defraud, beguile, gull (*archaic*), delude, swindle, outwit, bamboozle (*informal*), hoodwink, take for a ride (*informal*), pull a fast one on (*informal*), cozen, scam (*slang*)

duplicate ADJECTIVE *a duplicate copy* = **identical**, matched, matching, twin, corresponding, twofold ▸ NOUN **1** *I've lost my card and have to get a duplicate.* = **copy**, facsimile **2** *Enclosed is a duplicate of the invoice we sent you last month.* = **photocopy**, copy, reproduction, replica, Xerox®, carbon copy, Photostat® ▸ VERB **1** *Scientists hope the work done can be duplicated elsewhere.* = **repeat**, reproduce, echo, copy, clone, replicate **2** *He was duplicating some articles.* = **copy**, photocopy, Xerox®, Photostat®

duplicity NOUN = **deceit**, fraud, deception, hypocrisy, dishonesty, guile, artifice, falsehood, double-dealing, chicanery, perfidy (*literary*), dissimulation ■ OPPOSITE: honesty

durable ADJECTIVE **1** *Fine bone china is strong and durable.* = **hard-wearing**, strong, tough, sound, substantial, reliable, resistant, sturdy, long-lasting ■ OPPOSITE: fragile **2** *We were unable to establish any durable agreement.* = **enduring**, lasting, permanent, continuing, firm, fast, fixed, constant, abiding, dependable, unwavering, unfaltering

duration NOUN = **length**, time, period, term, stretch, extent, spell, span, time frame, timeline

duress NOUN = **pressure**, threat, constraint, compulsion, coercion

dusk NOUN **1** *We arrived home at dusk.* = **twilight**, evening, evo (*Austral. slang*), nightfall, sunset, dark, sundown, eventide, gloaming (*Scot., poetic*) ■ OPPOSITE: dawn **2** *She turned and disappeared into the dusk.* = **shade**, darkness, gloom, obscurity, murk, shadowiness

dusky ADJECTIVE *He was walking down the road one dusky evening.* = **dim**, twilight, shady, shadowy, gloomy, murky, cloudy, overcast, crepuscular, darkish, twilit, tenebrous, caliginous (*archaic*)

dust NOUN **1** *I could see a thick layer of dust on the stairs.* = **grime**, grit, powdery dirt **2** *Your trousers will get dirty if you sit down in the dust.* = **earth**, ground, soil, dirt **3** *The air was black with coal dust.* = **particles**, powder, fine fragments ▸ VERB *Lightly dust the fish with flour.* = **sprinkle**, cover, powder, spread, spray, scatter, sift, dredge

dusty ADJECTIVE **1** *The books looked dusty and unused.* = **dirty**, grubby, unclean, unswept, undusted **2** *Inside the box was only a dusty substance.* = **powdery**, sandy, chalky, crumbly, granular, friable

dutiful ADJECTIVE = **conscientious**, devoted, obedient, respectful, compliant, submissive, docile, deferential, reverential, filial, punctilious, duteous (*archaic*) ■ OPPOSITE: disrespectful

duty NOUN **1** *My duty is to look after the animals.* = **responsibility**, job, task, work, calling, business, service, office, charge, role, function, mission, province, obligation, assignment, pigeon (*informal*), onus **2** *Duty on imports would also be reduced.* = **tax**, customs, toll, levy, tariff, excise, due, impost • **off duty** *I'm off duty.* = **off work**, off, free, on holiday, at leisure • **on duty** *Extra staff had been put on duty.* = **at work**, busy, engaged, on active service

dwarf NOUN *With the aid of magic the dwarfs created a wonderful rope.* = **gnome**, midget, Lilliputian, Tom Thumb, munchkin (*informal, chiefly U.S.*), homunculus, manikin, hop-o'-my-thumb, pygmy *or* pigmy ▸ ADJECTIVE *dwarf shrubs* = **miniature**, small, baby, tiny, pocket, dwarfed, diminutive, petite, bonsai, pint-sized (*informal*), undersized, teeny-weeny, Lilliputian, teensy-weensy ▸ VERB **1** *The huge sign dwarfed his figure.* = **tower above** *or* **over**, dominate, overlook, stand over, loom over, stand head and shoulders above **2** *completely dwarfing the achievements of others* = **eclipse**, tower above or over, put in the shade, diminish

dwell VERB = **live**, stay, reside (*formal*), rest, quarter, settle, lodge, abide, hang out (*informal*), sojourn, establish yourself • **dwell on** *or* **upon something** *I'd rather not dwell on the past.* = **go on about**, emphasize (*informal*), elaborate on, linger over, harp on about, be engrossed in, expatiate on, continue to think about, tarry over

dwelling NOUN = **home**, house, residence, abode, quarters, establishment, lodging, pad (*slang*), habitation, domicile, dwelling house, whare (*N.Z.*)

dwindle VERB = **lessen**, fall, decline, contract, sink, fade, weaken, shrink, diminish, decrease, decay, wither, wane, subside, ebb, die down, die out, abate, shrivel, peter out, die away, waste away, taper off, grow less ■ OPPOSITE: increase

dye NOUN *bottles of hair dye* = **colouring**, colour, pigment, stain, tint, tinge, colorant ▸ VERB *The woman spun and dyed the wool.* = **colour**, stain, tint, tinge, pigment, tincture

dying ADJECTIVE **1** *He is a dying man.* = **near death**, going, failing, fading, doomed, expiring, ebbing, near the end, moribund, fading fast, in extremis (*Latin*), at death's door, not long for this world, on your deathbed, breathing your last **2** *the dying wishes of her mother* = **final**, last, parting, departing **3** *Shipbuilding is a dying business.* = **failing**, declining, sinking, foundering, diminishing, decreasing, dwindling, subsiding

dynamic ADJECTIVE = **energetic**, spirited, powerful, active, vital, driving, electric, go-ahead, lively, magnetic, vigorous, animated, high-powered, forceful, go-getting (*informal*), tireless, indefatigable, high-octane (*informal*), zippy (*informal*), full of beans (*informal*) ■ OPPOSITE: apathetic

dynamism NOUN = **energy**, go (*informal*), drive, push (*informal*), initiative, enterprise, pep, zip (*informal*), vigour, zap (*slang*), get-up-and-go (*informal*), brio, liveliness, forcefulness

dynasty NOUN = **empire**, house, rule, regime, sovereignty

Ee

each ADJECTIVE *Each book is beautifully illustrated.* = **every**, every single ▶ PRONOUN *Three doctors each had a different diagnosis.* = **every one**, all, each one, each and every one, one and all ▶ ADVERB *The children were given one each.* = **apiece**, individually, singly, for each, to each, respectively, per person, from each, per head, per capita

> USAGE *Each* is a singular pronoun and should be used with a singular verb – for example, *each of the candidates was interviewed separately* (not *were interviewed separately*).

eager ADJECTIVE 1 (*often with* **to** *or* **for**) *Robert was eager to talk about life in the Army.* = **anxious**, keen, raring, hungry, intent, yearning, impatient, itching, thirsty, zealous ■ OPPOSITE: unenthusiastic 2 *He looked at the crowd of eager faces around him.* = **keen**, interested, earnest, intense, enthusiastic, passionate, ardent, avid, fervent, zealous, fervid, keen as mustard, bright-eyed and bushy-tailed (*informal*) ■ OPPOSITE: uninterested

eagerness NOUN 1 *an eagerness to learn* = **longing**, anxiety, hunger, yearning, zeal, impatience, impetuosity, avidity 2 *the voice of a woman speaking with breathless eagerness* = **passion**, interest, enthusiasm, intensity, fervour, ardour, earnestness, keenness, heartiness, thirst, intentness

ear NOUN 1 *He has a fine ear for music.* = **sensitivity**, taste, discrimination, appreciation, musical perception 2 *The lobbyists have the ear of influential western leaders.* = **attention**, hearing, regard, notice, consideration, observation, awareness, heed • **lend an ear** *Please lend an ear for a moment or two.* = **listen**, pay attention, heed, take notice, pay heed, hearken (*archaic*), give ear • **turn a deaf ear to something** = **ignore**, reject, overlook, neglect, disregard, pass over, take no notice of, be oblivious to, pay no attention to, give the cold shoulder to ■ RELATED WORD: *adjective* aural

early ADVERB 1 *She arrived early to get a good seat.* = **in good time**, beforehand, ahead of schedule, in advance, with time to spare, betimes (*archaic*) ■ OPPOSITE: late 2 *The snow came early that year.* = **too soon**, before the usual time, prematurely, ahead of time ■ OPPOSITE: late ▶ ADJECTIVE 1 *the book's early chapters* = **first**, opening, earliest, initial, introductory 2 *I decided to take early retirement.* = **premature**, forward, advanced, untimely, unseasonable ■ OPPOSITE: belated 3 *early man's cultural development* = **primitive**, first, earliest, young, original, undeveloped, primordial, primeval ■ OPPOSITE: developed

earmark VERB 1 *Extra money has been earmarked for the new projects.* = **set aside**, reserve, label, flag, tag, allocate, designate, mark out, keep back 2 *The factory was one of several earmarked for closure.* = **mark out**, identify, designate

earn VERB 1 *The dancers can earn up to £130 for each session.* = **be paid**, make, get, receive, draw, gain, net, collect, bring in, gross, procure, clear, get paid, take home 2 *Companies must earn a reputation for honesty.* = **deserve**, win, gain, attain, justify, merit, warrant, be entitled to, reap, be worthy of

earnest ADJECTIVE 1 *Ella was a pious, earnest young woman.* = **serious**, keen, grave, intense, steady, dedicated, eager, enthusiastic, passionate, sincere, thoughtful, solemn, ardent, fervent, impassioned, zealous, staid, keen as mustard ■ OPPOSITE: frivolous 2 *Despite their earnest efforts, they failed to win support.* = **determined**, firm, dogged, constant, urgent, intent, persistent, ardent, persevering, resolute, heartfelt, zealous, vehement, wholehearted ■ OPPOSITE: half-hearted

earnestness NOUN 1 *He spoke with intense earnestness.* = **seriousness**, resolution, passion, enthusiasm, warmth, gravity, urgency, zeal, sincerity, fervour, eagerness, ardour, keenness 2 *the earnestness of their struggle for freedom* = **determination**, resolve, urgency, zeal, ardour, vehemence

earnings PLURAL NOUN = **income**, pay, wages, revenue, reward, proceeds, salary, receipts, return, remuneration, takings, stipend, take-home pay, emolument, gross pay, net pay

earth NOUN 1 *The space shuttle returned safely to earth today.* = **world**, planet, globe, sphere, orb, earthly sphere, terrestrial sphere 2 *The earth shook under our feet.* = **ground**, land, dry land, terra firma 3 *The road winds through parched earth, scrub and cactus.* = **soil**, ground, land, dust, mould, clay, dirt, turf, sod, silt, topsoil, clod, loam ■ RELATED WORD: *adjective* terrestrial

earthenware NOUN = **crockery**, pots, ceramics, pottery, terracotta, crocks, faience, maiolica

earthly ADJECTIVE **1** *They lived in an earthly paradise.* = **worldly**, material, physical, secular, mortal, mundane, terrestrial, temporal, human, materialistic, profane, telluric, sublunary, non-spiritual, tellurian, terrene ■ OPPOSITE: spiritual **2** *He has forsworn all earthly pleasures for the duration of a season.* = **sensual**, worldly, base, physical, gross, low, fleshly, bodily, vile, sordid, carnal **3** *What earthly reason would they have for lying?* = **possible**, likely, practical, feasible, conceivable, imaginable

earthy ADJECTIVE **1** *his extremely earthy brand of humour* = **crude**, coarse, raunchy (*informal*), lusty, bawdy, ribald **2** *Strong, earthy colours add to the effect.* = **claylike**, soil-like

ease NOUN **1** *For ease of reference, only the relevant extracts of the regulations are included.* = **straightforwardness**, simplicity, readiness **2** *She lived a life of ease.* = **comfort**, luxury, leisure, relaxation, prosperity, affluence, rest, repose, restfulness ■ OPPOSITE: hardship **3** *Qigong exercises promote ease of mind and body.* = **peace of mind**, peace, content, quiet, comfort, happiness, enjoyment, serenity, tranquillity, contentment, calmness, quietude ■ OPPOSITE: agitation **4** *Co-stars particularly appreciate his ease on the set.* = **naturalness**, informality, freedom, liberty, unaffectedness, unconstraint, unreservedness, relaxedness ■ OPPOSITE: awkwardness ▶ VERB **1** *I gave him some brandy to ease the pain.* = **relieve**, calm, moderate, soothe, lessen, alleviate, appease, lighten, lower, allay, relax, still, mitigate, assuage, pacify, mollify, tranquillize, palliate ■ OPPOSITE: aggravate **2** *(often with* **off** *or* **up***) The heavy snow had eased a little.* = **reduce**, moderate, weaken, diminish, decrease, slow down, dwindle, lessen, die down, abate, slacken, grow less, de-escalate **3** *I eased my way towards the door.* = **move carefully**, edge, guide, slip, inch, slide, creep, squeeze, steer, manoeuvre **4** *The information pack is designed to ease the process of making a will.* = **facilitate**, further, aid, forward, smooth, assist, speed up, simplify, make easier, expedite, lessen the labour of ■ OPPOSITE: hinder

easily ADVERB **1** *It could easily be another year before we see any change.* = **without a doubt**, clearly, surely, certainly, obviously, definitely, plainly, absolutely, undoubtedly, unquestionably, undeniably, unequivocally, far and away, indisputably, beyond question, indubitably, doubtlessly **2** *Wear clothes you can remove easily.* = **without difficulty**, smoothly, readily, comfortably, effortlessly, simply, with ease, straightforwardly, without trouble, standing on your head, with your eyes closed *or* shut

easy ADJECTIVE **1** *This is not an easy task.* = **simple**, straightforward, no trouble, not difficult, effortless, painless, clear, light, uncomplicated, child's play (*informal*), plain sailing, undemanding, a pushover (*slang*), a piece of cake (*informal*), no bother, a bed of roses, easy-peasy (*slang*) ■ OPPOSITE: hard **2** *I was not altogether easy in my mind about this decision.* = **untroubled**, contented, relaxed, satisfied, calm, peaceful, serene, tranquil, quiet, undisturbed, unworried **3** *She laughed and joked and made easy conversation with everyone.* = **relaxed**, friendly, open, natural, pleasant, casual, informal, laid-back (*informal*), graceful, gracious, unaffected, easy-going, affable, unpretentious, unforced, undemanding, unconstrained, unceremonious ■ OPPOSITE: stiff **4** = **carefree**, comfortable, leisurely, trouble-free, untroubled, cushy (*informal*) ■ OPPOSITE: difficult **5** *I guess we've always been too easy with our children.* = **tolerant**, light, liberal, soft, flexible, mild, laid-back (*informal*), indulgent, easy-going, lenient, permissive, unoppressive ■ OPPOSITE: strict **6** *'Your father was not an easy child,' she told me.* = **accommodating**, yielding, manageable, easy-going, compliant, amenable, submissive, docile, pliant, tractable, biddable ■ OPPOSITE: difficult **7** *They were easy targets for conmen.* = **vulnerable**, soft (*informal*), naive, susceptible, gullible, exploitable **8** *the easy pace set by pilgrims heading to Canterbury* = **leisurely**, relaxed, comfortable, moderate, unhurried, undemanding

easy-going ADJECTIVE = **relaxed**, easy, liberal, calm, flexible, mild, casual, tolerant, laid-back (*informal*), indulgent, serene, lenient, carefree, placid, unconcerned, amenable, permissive, happy-go-lucky, unhurried, nonchalant, insouciant, even-tempered, easy-peasy (*slang*), chilled (*informal*) ■ OPPOSITE: tense

eat VERB **1** *She was eating a sandwich.* = **consume**, swallow, chew, scoff (*slang*), devour, munch, tuck into (*informal*), put away, gobble, polish off (*informal*), wolf down **2** *Let's go out to eat.* = **have a meal**, lunch, breakfast, dine, snack, feed, graze (*informal*), have lunch, have dinner, have breakfast, nosh (slang), take food, have supper, break bread, chow down (slang), take nourishment

eavesdrop VERB = **listen in**, spy, overhear, bug (informal), pry, tap in, snoop (informal), earwig (informal)

ebb VERB 1 We hopped from rock to rock as the tide ebbed from the causeway. = **flow back**, go out, withdraw, sink, retreat, fall back, wane, recede, fall away 2 There were occasions when my enthusiasm ebbed. = **decline**, drop, sink, flag, weaken, shrink, diminish, decrease, deteriorate, decay, dwindle, lessen, subside, degenerate, fall away, fade away, abate, peter out, slacken ▶ NOUN We decided to leave on the ebb at six o'clock next morning. = **flowing back**, going out, withdrawal, retreat, wane, waning, regression, low water, low tide, ebb tide, outgoing tide, falling tide, receding tide

ebony ADJECTIVE = **black**, dark, jet, raven, sable, pitch-black, jet-black, inky, coal-black

e-book or **ebook** NOUN = **electronic book**, iBook®, book ▶ VERB = **reserve**, book, schedule, engage, organize, arrange (for), procure, e-procure

ebullient ADJECTIVE = **exuberant**, excited, enthusiastic, buoyant, exhilarated, elated, irrepressible, vivacious, effervescent, effusive, in high spirits, zestful

eccentric ADJECTIVE an eccentric character who wears a beret and sunglasses = **odd**, strange, bizarre, weird, peculiar, abnormal, queer (informal), irregular, uncommon, quirky, singular, unconventional, idiosyncratic, off-the-wall (slang), outlandish, whimsical, rum (Brit. slang), capricious, anomalous, freakish, aberrant, outré, daggy (Austral. & N.Z. informal) ■ OPPOSITE: normal ▶ NOUN My other friend was a real English eccentric. = **crank** (informal), character (informal), nut (slang), freak (informal), flake (slang, chiefly U.S.), oddity, oddball (informal), loose cannon, nonconformist, case (informal), screwball (slang, chiefly U.S. & Canad.), card (informal), odd fish (informal), kook (U.S. & Canad. informal), queer fish (Brit. informal), rum customer (Brit. slang)

eccentricity NOUN 1 She is unusual to the point of eccentricity. = **oddity**, peculiarity, strangeness, irregularity, weirdness, singularity, oddness, waywardness, nonconformity, capriciousness, unconventionality, queerness (informal), bizarreness, whimsicality, freakishness, outlandishness 2 We all have our little eccentricities. = **foible**, anomaly, abnormality, quirk, oddity, aberration, peculiarity, idiosyncrasy

ecclesiastical ADJECTIVE = **clerical**, religious, church, churchly, priestly, spiritual, holy, divine, pastoral, sacerdotal

echelon NOUN = **level**, place, office, position, step, degree (archaic), rank, grade, tier, rung

echo NOUN 1 I heard nothing but the echoes of my own voice in the cave. = **reverberation**, ringing, repetition, answer, resonance, resounding 2 Their cover version is just a pale echo of the real thing. = **copy**, reflection, clone, reproduction, imitation, duplicate, double, reiteration 3 The accident has echoes of past disasters. = **reminder**, suggestion, trace, hint, recollection, vestige, evocation, intimation ▶ VERB 1 The distant crash of bombs echoes through the whole city. = **reverberate**, repeat, resound, ring, resonate 2 Many phrases in the last chapter echo earlier passages. = **recall**, reflect, copy, mirror, resemble, reproduce, parrot, imitate, reiterate, ape

eclectic ADJECTIVE = **diverse**, general, broad, varied, comprehensive, extensive, wide-ranging, selective, diversified, manifold (formal), heterogeneous, catholic, all-embracing, liberal, many-sided, multifarious, dilettantish

eclipse NOUN 1 a total eclipse of the sun = **obscuring**, covering, blocking, shading, dimming, extinction, darkening, blotting out, occultation 2 the eclipse of the influence of the Republican party in West Germany = **decline**, fall, loss, failure, weakening, deterioration, degeneration, diminution ▶ VERB 1 The gramophone was eclipsed by the compact disc. = **surpass**, exceed, overshadow, excel, transcend, outdo, outclass, outshine, leave or put in the shade (informal) 2 The sun was eclipsed by the moon. = **obscure**, cover, block, cloud, conceal, dim, veil, darken, shroud, extinguish, blot out

economic ADJECTIVE 1 The pace of economic growth is picking up. = **financial**, business, trade, industrial, commercial, mercantile 2 Their country faces an economic crisis. = **monetary**, financial, material, fiscal, budgetary, bread-and-butter (informal), pecuniary 3 Solar power can be an economic proposition. = **profitable**, successful, commercial, rewarding, productive, lucrative, worthwhile, viable, solvent, cost-effective, money-making, profit-making, remunerative 4 The new process is more economic but less environmentally friendly. = **economical**, fair, cheap, reasonable, modest, low-priced, inexpensive

economical ADJECTIVE 1 It is more economical to wash a full load. = **economic** (informal), fair, cheap, reasonable, modest, low-priced, inexpensive ■ **OPPOSITE:** expensive **2** As taxpayers we should be able to assume that the government is economical with our money. = **thrifty**, sparing, careful, prudent, provident, frugal, parsimonious, scrimping, economizing ■ **OPPOSITE:** extravagant **3** the practical, economical virtues of a small hatchback = **efficient**, sparing, cost-effective, money-saving, time-saving, work-saving, unwasteful ■ **OPPOSITE:** wasteful

economics NOUN = **finance**, commerce, the dismal science

economy NOUN **1** central bankers from leading economies = **financial system**, financial state **2** They have achieved quite remarkable effects with great economy of means. = **thrift**, saving, restraint, prudence, providence, husbandry, retrenchment, frugality, parsimony, thriftiness, sparingness

ecstasy NOUN = **rapture**, delight, joy, enthusiasm, frenzy, bliss, trance, euphoria, fervour, elation, rhapsody, exaltation, transport, ravishment ■ **OPPOSITE:** agony

ecstatic ADJECTIVE = **rapturous**, entranced, enthusiastic, frenzied, joyous, fervent, joyful, elated, over the moon (informal), overjoyed, blissful, delirious, euphoric, enraptured, on cloud nine (informal), cock-a-hoop, blissed out, transported, rhapsodic, sent, walking on air, in seventh heaven, floating on air, in exaltation, in transports of delight, stoked (Austral. & N.Z. informal)

ecumenical, oecumenical, ecumenic or **oecumenic** ADJECTIVE = **unifying**, universal, non-denominational, non-sectarian, general

eddy NOUN the swirling eddies of the fast-flowing river = **swirl**, whirlpool, vortex, undertow, tideway, counter-current, counterflow ▶ VERB The dust whirled and eddied in the sunlight. = **swirl**, turn, roll, spin, twist, surge, revolve, whirl, billow

edge NOUN **1** She was standing at the water's edge. = **border**, side, line, limit, bound, lip, margin, outline, boundary, fringe, verge, brink, threshold, rim, brim, perimeter, contour, periphery, flange **2** They have driven the rhino to the edge of extinction. = **verge**, point, brink, threshold **3** This could give them the edge over their oppponents. = **advantage**, lead, dominance, superiority, upper hand, head start, ascendancy, whip hand **4** Featuring new bands gives the show an edge. = **power**, interest, force, bite, effectiveness, animation, zest, incisiveness, powerful quality **5** There was an unpleasant edge to her voice. = **sharpness**, point, sting, urgency,

bitterness, keenness, pungency, acuteness ▶ VERB **1** He edged closer to the door. = **inch**, ease, creep, worm, slink, steal, sidle, work, move slowly **2** a chocolate brown jacket edged with yellow = **border**, shape, bind, trim, fringe, rim, hem, pipe • **on edge** Ever since their arrival she had felt on edge. = **tense**, excited, wired (slang), nervous, eager, impatient, irritable, apprehensive, edgy, uptight (informal), ill at ease, twitchy (informal), tetchy, on tenterhooks, keyed up, antsy (informal), adrenalized

edgy ADJECTIVE = **nervous**, wired (slang), anxious, tense, irritable, touchy, uptight (informal), on edge, nervy (Brit. informal), ill at ease, restive, twitchy (informal), irascible, tetchy, chippy (informal), on tenterhooks, keyed up, antsy (informal), on pins and needles, adrenalized

edible ADJECTIVE = **safe to eat**, harmless, wholesome, palatable, digestible, eatable, comestible (rare), fit to eat, good ■ **OPPOSITE:** inedible

edict NOUN = **decree**, law, act, order, ruling, demand, command, regulation, dictate, mandate, canon, manifesto, injunction, statute, fiat, ordinance, proclamation, enactment, dictum, pronouncement, ukase (rare), pronunciamento

edifice NOUN = **building**, house, structure, construction, pile, erection, habitation (formal)

edify VERB = **instruct**, school, teach, inform, guide, improve, educate, nurture, elevate, enlighten, uplift

edifying ADJECTIVE = **instructive**, improving, inspiring, elevating, enlightening, uplifting, instructional

edit VERB **1** The publisher has the right to edit the book once it has been written. = **revise**, check, improve, correct, polish, adapt, rewrite, censor, condense, annotate, rephrase, redraft, copy-edit, emend, prepare for publication, redact **2** She has edited a collection of essays. = **put together**, select, arrange, organize, assemble, compose, rearrange, reorder **3** I used to edit the college paper in the old days. = **be in charge of**, control, direct, be responsible for, be the editor of

edition NOUN **1** a rare first edition of a Dickens novel = **printing**, publication **2** The Christmas edition of the catalogue is out now. = **copy**, impression, number **3** = **version**, volume, issue **4** We'll be back in our next edition in a week's time. = **programme** (TV & Radio)

educate VERB = **teach**, school, train, coach, develop, improve, exercise, inform, discipline, rear, foster, mature, drill, tutor, instruct, cultivate, enlighten, civilize, edify, indoctrinate

educated ADJECTIVE **1** *He is an educated, amiable and decent man.* = **cultured**, lettered, intellectual, learned, informed, experienced, polished, literary, sophisticated, refined, cultivated, enlightened, knowledgeable, civilized, tasteful, urbane, erudite ■ **OPPOSITE:** uncultured **2** *The country's workforce is well educated and diligent.* = **taught**, schooled, coached, informed, tutored, instructed, nurtured, well-informed, well-read, well-taught ■ **OPPOSITE:** uneducated

education NOUN **1** *institutions for the care and education of children* = **teaching**, schooling, training, development, coaching, improvement, discipline, instruction, drilling, tutoring, nurture, tuition, enlightenment, erudition, indoctrination, edification, e-learning *or* elearning **2** = **learning**, schooling, culture, scholarship, civilization, cultivation, refinement

educational ADJECTIVE **1** *the British educational system* = **academic**, school, learning, teaching, scholastic, pedagogical, pedagogic **2** *The kids had an enjoyable and educational day.* = **instructive**, useful, cultural, illuminating, enlightening, informative, instructional, didactic, edifying, educative, heuristic

educator NOUN = **teacher**, professor, lecturer, don, coach, guide, fellow, trainer, tutor, instructor, mentor, schoolteacher, pedagogue, edifier, educationalist *or* educationist, schoolmaster *or* schoolmistress, master *or* mistress

eerie ADJECTIVE = **uncanny**, strange, frightening, ghostly, weird, mysterious, scary (*informal*), sinister, uneasy, fearful, awesome, unearthly, supernatural, unnatural, spooky (*informal*), creepy (*informal*), spectral, eldritch (*poetic*), preternatural

efface VERB = **obliterate**, remove, destroy, cancel, wipe out, erase, eradicate, excise, delete, annihilate, raze, blot out, cross out, expunge (*formal*), rub out, extirpate

effect NOUN **1** *the psychological effects of head injuries* = **result**, consequence, conclusion, outcome, event, issue, aftermath, fruit, end result, upshot **2** *The whole effect is cool, light and airy* = **impression**, feeling, impact, influence **3** *He told me to get lost, or words to that effect.* = **purpose**, meaning, impression, sense, import, drift, intent, essence, thread, tenor, purport **4** *We are now resuming diplomatic relations with*

immediate effect. = **implementation**, force, action, performance, operation, enforcement, execution ▶ VERB *Prospects for effecting real political change have taken a step backward.* = **bring about**, make, cause, produce, create, complete, achieve, perform, carry out, fulfil, accomplish, execute, initiate, give rise to, consummate, actuate, effectuate • **in effect** *The deal would create, in effect, the world's biggest airline.* = **in fact**, really, actually, essentially, virtually, effectively, in reality, in truth, as good as, in actual fact, to all intents and purposes, in all but name, in actuality, for practical purposes • **put, bring** *or* **carry into effect** *a decree bringing these political reforms into effect* = **implement**, perform, carry out, fulfil, enforce, execute, bring about, put into action, put into operation, bring into force • **take effect** *The ban takes effect from July.* = **produce results**, work, begin, come into force, become operative

> **USAGE** It is quite common for the verb *effect* to be mistakenly used where *affect* is intended. *Effect* is relatively uncommon and rather formal, and is a synonym of 'bring about'. Conversely, the noun *effect* is quite often mistakenly written with an initial *a*. The following are correct: *the group is still recovering from the effects of the recession; they really are powerless to effect any change.* The next two examples are incorrect: *the full affects of the shutdown won't be felt for several more days; men whose lack of hair doesn't effect their self-esteem.*

effective ADJECTIVE **1** *Antibiotics are effective against this organism.* = **efficient**, successful, useful, active, capable, valuable, helpful, adequate, productive, operative, competent, serviceable, efficacious, effectual ■ **OPPOSITE:** ineffective **2** *You can't make an effective argument if all you do is stridently voice your opinion.* = **powerful**, strong, convincing, persuasive, telling, impressive, compelling, potent, forceful, striking, emphatic, weighty, forcible, cogent ■ **OPPOSITE:** weak **3** *They have had effective control of the area.* = **virtual**, essential, practical, implied, implicit, tacit, unacknowledged **4** *The new rules will become effective in the next few days.* = **in operation**, official, current, legal, real, active, actual, in effect, valid, operative, in force, in execution ■ **OPPOSITE:** inoperative

effectiveness NOUN = **power**, effect, efficiency, success, strength, capability, use, validity, usefulness, potency, efficacy, fruitfulness, productiveness

effects PLURAL NOUN *His daughters came to collect his effects.* = **belongings**, goods, things, property, stuff, gear, furniture, possessions, trappings, paraphernalia, personal property, accoutrements, chattels, movables

effeminate ADJECTIVE = **womanly**, soft, feminine, unmanly, effete, foppish, womanish, womanlike

effervescent ADJECTIVE **1** *an effervescent mineral water* = **fizzy**, bubbling, sparkling, bubbly, foaming, fizzing, fermenting, frothing, frothy, aerated, carbonated, foamy, gassy ■ OPPOSITE: still **2** *one of Broadway's most effervescent stars* = **lively**, excited, dynamic, enthusiastic, sparkling, energetic, animated, merry, buoyant, exhilarated, bubbly, exuberant, high-spirited, irrepressible, ebullient, chirpy (*informal*), vital, scintillating, vivacious, zingy (*informal*) ■ OPPOSITE: dull

effete ADJECTIVE = **weak**, cowardly, feeble, ineffectual, decrepit, spineless, enfeebled, weak-kneed (*informal*), enervated, overrefined, chicken-hearted, wimpish *or* wimpy (*informal*)

efficacy NOUN = **effectiveness**, efficiency, power, value, success, strength, virtue, vigour, use, usefulness, potency, fruitfulness, productiveness, efficaciousness

efficiency NOUN **1** *ways to increase agricultural efficiency* = **effectiveness**, power, economy, productivity, organization, efficacy, cost-effectiveness, orderliness **2** *her efficiency as a manager* = **competence**, ability, skill, expertise, capability, readiness, professionalism, proficiency, adeptness, skilfulness

efficient ADJECTIVE **1** *a relatively cheap and efficient form of communication* = **effective**, successful, structured, productive, powerful, systematic, streamlined, cost-effective, methodical, well-organized, well-planned, labour-saving, effectual ■ OPPOSITE: inefficient **2** *a highly efficient worker* = **competent**, able, professional, capable, organized, productive, skilful, adept, ready, proficient, businesslike, well-organized, workmanlike ■ OPPOSITE: incompetent

effigy NOUN = **likeness**, figure, image, model, guy, carving, representation, statue, icon, idol, dummy, statuette

effluent NOUN = **waste**, discharge, flow, emission, sewage, pollutant, outpouring, outflow, exhalation, issue, emanation, liquid waste, efflux, effluvium, effluence

effort NOUN **1** *He made no effort to hide.* = **attempt**, try, endeavour, shot (*informal*), bid, essay (*formal*), go (*informal*), stab (*informal*) **2** *A great deal of effort had been put into the planning.* = **exertion**, work, labour, trouble, force, energy, struggle, stress, application, strain, striving, graft, toil, hard graft, travail (*literary*), elbow grease (*facetious*), blood, sweat, and tears (*informal*) *The gallery is showcasing her latest efforts.* = **achievement**, act, performance, product, job, production, creation, feat, deed, accomplishment, attainment

effortless ADJECTIVE **1** *In a single effortless motion, he scooped Frannie into his arms.* = **easy**, simple, flowing, smooth, graceful, painless, uncomplicated, trouble-free, facile, undemanding, easy-peasy (*slang*), untroublesome, unexacting ■ OPPOSITE: difficult **2** *He was known above all for his effortless charm.* = **natural**, simple, spontaneous, instinctive, intuitive

effusive ADJECTIVE = **demonstrative**, enthusiastic, lavish, extravagant, overflowing, gushing, exuberant, expansive, ebullient, free-flowing, unrestrained, talkative, fulsome, profuse, unreserved

egg NOUN *a baby bird hatching from its egg* = **ovum**, gamete, germ cell • **egg someone on** *She was egging him on to fight.* = **incite**, push, encourage, urge, prompt, spur, provoke, prod, goad, exhort (*formal*)

egocentric ADJECTIVE = **self-centred**, vain, selfish, narcissistic, self-absorbed, egotistical, inward looking, self-important, self-obsessed, self-seeking, egoistic, egoistical

egotism *or* **egoism** NOUN = **self-centredness**, self-esteem, vanity, superiority, self-interest, selfishness, narcissism, self-importance, self-regard, self-love, self-seeking, self-absorption, self-obsession, egocentricity, egomania, self-praise, vainglory, self-conceit, self-admiration, conceitedness

ejaculate VERB **1** *a tendency to ejaculate too quickly* = **have an orgasm**, come (*taboo slang*), climax **2** *'Good God!' Liz ejaculated.* = **exclaim**, declare, shout, call out, cry out, burst out, blurt out

ejaculation NOUN = **discharge**, release, emission, ejection

eject VERB **1** *They were forcibly ejected from the restaurant.* = **throw out**, remove, turn out, expel, exile, oust, banish, deport, drive out, evict, boot out (*informal*), force to leave, chuck out (*informal*), bounce, turf out (*informal*), give the bum's rush (*slang*), show someone the door, throw someone out on their ear (*informal*) **2** *She was ejected from her first job for persistent latecoming.* = **dismiss**, sack (*informal*), fire (*informal*), remove, get rid of, discharge, expel, throw out, oust, kick out (*informal*), kennet (*Austral. slang*), jeff (*Austral. slang*) **3** *He fired a single shot, then ejected the spent cartridge.* = **discharge**, expel, emit, give off **4** *The pilot ejected from the plane and escaped injury.* = **bail out**, escape, get out

ejection NOUN **1** *the ejection of hecklers at the meeting* = **expulsion**, removal, ouster (*Law*), deportation, eviction, banishment, exile **2** *These actions led to his ejection from office.* = **dismissal**, sacking (*informal*), firing (*informal*), removal, discharge, the boot (*slang*), expulsion, the sack (*informal*), dislodgement **3** *the ejection of an electron by an atomic nucleus* = **emission**, throwing out, expulsion, spouting, casting out, disgorgement

eke out VERB *I had to eke out my redundancy money for about ten weeks.* = **be sparing with**, stretch out, be economical with, economize on, husband, be frugal with
• **eke out a living** *people trying to eke out a living in forest areas* = **support yourself**, survive, get by, make ends meet, scrimp, save, scrimp and save

elaborate ADJECTIVE **1** *an elaborate research project* = **complicated**, detailed, studied, laboured, perfected, complex, careful, exact, precise, thorough, intricate, skilful, painstaking **2** *a designer known for his elaborate costumes* = **ornate**, detailed, involved, complex, fancy, complicated, decorated, extravagant, intricate, baroque, ornamented, fussy, embellished, showy, ostentatious, florid ■ **OPPOSITE:** plain
▶ VERB **1** *The plan was elaborated by five members of the council.* = **develop**, improve, enhance, polish, complicate, decorate, refine, garnish, ornament, flesh out **2** (*usually with on or upon*) *The spokesperson declined to elaborate on the statement.* = **expand upon**, extend upon, enlarge on, amplify upon, embellish, flesh out, add detail to ■ **OPPOSITE:** simplify

élan NOUN = **style**, spirit, dash, flair (*informal*), animation, vigour, verve, zest, panache, esprit, brio, vivacity, impetuosity

elapse VERB = **pass**, go, go by, lapse, pass by, slip away, roll on, slip by, roll by, glide by

elastic ADJECTIVE **1** *Work the dough until it is slightly elastic.* = **flexible**, yielding, supple, rubbery, pliable, plastic, springy, pliant, tensile, stretchy, ductile, stretchable
■ **OPPOSITE:** rigid **2** *an elastic interpretation of the rules* = **adaptable**, yielding, variable,

flexible, accommodating, tolerant, adjustable, supple, complaisant
■ **OPPOSITE:** inflexible

elasticity NOUN **1** *Daily facial exercises help to retain the skin's elasticity.* = **flexibility**, suppleness, plasticity, give (*informal*), pliability, ductility, springiness, pliancy, stretchiness, rubberiness **2** *the elasticity of demand for this commodity* = **adaptability**, accommodation, flexibility, tolerance, variability, suppleness, complaisance, adjustability, compliantness

elated ADJECTIVE = **joyful**, excited, delighted, proud, cheered, thrilled, elevated, animated, roused, exhilarated, ecstatic, jubilant, joyous, over the moon (*informal*), overjoyed, blissful, euphoric, rapt, gleeful, sent, puffed up, exultant, in high spirits, on cloud nine (*informal*), cock-a-hoop, blissed out, in seventh heaven, floating *or* walking on air, stoked (*Austral. & N.Z. informal*)
■ **OPPOSITE:** dejected

elation NOUN = **joy**, delight, thrill, excitement, ecstasy, bliss, euphoria, glee, rapture, high spirits, exhilaration, jubilation, exaltation, exultation, joyfulness, joyousness

elbow NOUN *The boat was moored at the elbow of the river.* = **joint**, turn, corner, bend, angle, curve ▶ VERB *They elbowed me out of the way.* = **push**, force, crowd (*informal*), shoulder, knock, bump, shove, nudge, jostle, hustle
• **at your elbow** *Her eye fell on a paragraph in the paper which lay at her elbow.* = **within reach**, near, to hand, handy, at hand, close by

elder ADJECTIVE *the elder of her two daughters* = **older**, first, senior, first-born, earlier born
▶ NOUN **1** *I was raised to always show respect to my elders.* = **older person**, senior **2** *He is now an elder of the village church.* = **church official**, leader, office bearer, presbyter

elect VERB **1** *The people have voted to elect a new president.* = **vote for**, choose, pick, determine, select, appoint, opt for, designate, pick out, settle on, decide upon **2** *Those electing to smoke will be seated at the rear.* = **choose**, decide, prefer, select, opt
▶ ADJECTIVE **1** *one of the elect few permitted to enter* = **selected**, chosen, picked, choice, preferred, select, elite, hand-picked **2** *the date when the president-elect takes office* = **future**, to-be, coming, next, appointed, designate, prospective

election NOUN **1** *Poland's first fully free elections for more than fifty years* = **vote**, poll, ballot, determination, referendum, franchise, plebiscite, show of hands **2** *the election of the Labour government in 1964*

= **appointment**, choosing, picking, choice, selection

elector NOUN = **voter**, chooser, selector, constituent, member of the electorate, member of a constituency, enfranchised person

electric ADJECTIVE **1** *her electric guitar* = **electric-powered**, powered, cordless, battery-operated, electrically-charged, mains-operated **2** *The atmosphere in the hall was electric.* = **charged**, exciting, stirring, thrilling, stimulating, dynamic, tense, rousing, electrifying, adrenalized

electrify VERB **1** *The spectators were electrified by his courage.* = **thrill**, shock, excite, amaze, stir, stimulate, astonish, startle, arouse, animate, rouse, astound, jolt, fire, galvanize, take your breath away ■ **OPPOSITE:** bore **2** *The west-coast line was electrified as long ago as 1974.* = **wire up**, wire, supply electricity to, convert to electricity

elegance NOUN = **style**, taste, beauty, grace, dignity, sophistication, grandeur, refinement, polish, gentility, sumptuousness, courtliness, gracefulness, tastefulness, exquisiteness

elegant ADJECTIVE **1** *Patricia looked as beautiful and elegant as always.* = **stylish**, fine, beautiful, sophisticated, delicate, artistic, handsome, fashionable, refined, cultivated, chic, luxurious, exquisite, nice, discerning, graceful, polished, sumptuous, genteel, choice, tasteful, urbane, courtly, modish, comely (*old-fashioned*), à la mode, schmick (*Austral. informal*) ■ **OPPOSITE:** inelegant **2** *The poem impressed me with its elegant simplicity.* = **ingenious**, simple, effective, appropriate, clever, neat, apt

elegiac ADJECTIVE = **lamenting**, sad, melancholy, nostalgic, mournful, plaintive, melancholic, sorrowful, funereal, valedictory, keening, dirgeful, threnodial, threnodic

elegy NOUN = **lament**, requiem, dirge, plaint (*archaic*), threnody, keen, funeral song, coronach (*Scot. & Irish*), funeral poem

element NOUN **1** *one of the key elements of the UN's peace plan* = **component**, part, feature, unit, section, factor, principle, aspect, detail, foundation, ingredient, constituent, subdivision **2** *The government must weed out criminal elements from the security forces.* = **group**, faction, clique, set, party, circle **3** *There is an element of truth in his accusation.* = **trace**, suggestion, hint, dash, suspicion, tinge, smattering, soupçon ▶ PLURAL NOUN *The area is exposed to the elements.* = **weather conditions**, climate, the weather, wind and rain, atmospheric

conditions, powers of nature, atmospheric forces • **in your element** *My stepmother was in her element, organizing everyone.* = **in a situation you enjoy**, in your natural environment, in familiar surroundings

elemental ADJECTIVE **1** *the elemental powers of the universe* = **primal**, original, primitive, primordial **2** *the elemental forces that shaped this rugged Atlantic coast* = **atmospheric**, natural, meteorological

elementary ADJECTIVE **1** *Literacy now includes elementary computer skills.* = **basic**, essential, primary, initial, fundamental, introductory, preparatory, rudimentary, elemental, bog-standard (*informal*) ■ **OPPOSITE:** advanced **2** *elementary questions designed to test numeracy* = **simple**, clear, easy, plain, straightforward, rudimentary, uncomplicated, facile, undemanding, unexacting ■ **OPPOSITE:** complicated

elevate VERB **1** *He was elevated to the post of Prime Minister.* = **promote**, raise, advance, upgrade, exalt, kick upstairs (*informal*), aggrandize, give advancement to **2** *Emotional stress can elevate blood pressure.* = **increase**, lift, raise, step up, intensify, move up, hoist, raise high **3** *She elevated the gun at the sky.* = **raise**, lift, heighten, uplift, hoist, lift up, raise up, hike up, upraise **4** *She bought some new clothes, but they failed to elevate her spirits.* = **cheer**, raise, excite, boost, animate, rouse, uplift, brighten, exhilarate, hearten, lift up, perk up, buoy up, gladden, elate

elevated ADJECTIVE **1** *His new job has given him a certain elevated status.* = **exalted**, high, important, august, grand, superior, noble, dignified, high-ranking, lofty **2** *the magazine's elevated tone* = **high-minded**, high, fine, grand, noble, inflated, dignified, sublime, lofty, high-flown, pompous, exalted, bombastic ■ **OPPOSITE:** humble **3** *an elevated platform on the stage* = **raised**, high, lifted up, upraised

elevation NOUN **1** *the addition of a two-storey wing on the north elevation* = **side**, back, face, front, aspect **2** *We're at an elevation of about 13,000 feet above sea level.* = **altitude**, height **3** *celebrating his elevation to the rank of Prime Minister* = **promotion**, upgrading, advancement, exaltation, preferment, aggrandizement **4** *The resort is built on an elevation overlooking the sea.* = **rise**, hill, mountain, height, mound, berg (*S. African*), high ground, higher ground, eminence, hillock, rising ground, acclivity

elicit VERB **1** *He was hopeful that his request would elicit a positive response.* = **bring about**, cause, derive, bring out, evoke, give rise to, draw out, bring forth, bring to light, call forth **2** *the attempts of the interrogator to elicit a confession* = **obtain**, extract, exact, evoke, wrest, draw out, extort, educe

eligible ADJECTIVE **1** *You could be eligible for a university scholarship.* = **entitled**, fit, qualified, suited, suitable ■ **OPPOSITE:** ineligible **2** *Britain's most eligible bachelor* = **available**, free, single, unmarried, unattached

eliminate VERB **1** *The Act has not eliminated discrimination in employment.* = **remove**, end, stop, withdraw, get rid of, abolish, cut out, dispose of, terminate, banish, eradicate, put an end to, do away with, dispense with, stamp out, exterminate, get shot of, wipe from the face of the earth **2** *I was eliminated from the 400 metres in the semifinals.* = **knock out**, drop, reject, exclude, axe (*informal*), get rid of, expel, leave out, throw out, omit, put out, eject **3** *They claimed that 87,000 'reactionaries' had been eliminated.* = **murder**, kill, do in (*slang*), take out (*slang*), terminate, slay, blow away (*slang, chiefly U.S.*), liquidate, annihilate, exterminate, bump off (*slang*), rub out (*U.S. slang*), waste (*informal*)

elite NOUN *a government comprised mainly of the elite* = **aristocracy**, best, pick, elect, cream, upper class, nobility, gentry, high society, the crème de la crème, flower, nonpareil ■ **OPPOSITE:** rabble ▶ ADJECTIVE *the elite troops of the President's bodyguard* = **leading**, best, finest, pick, choice, selected, elect, crack (*slang*), supreme, exclusive, privileged, first-class, foremost, first-rate, pre-eminent, most excellent

elitist ADJECTIVE *He described skiing as an elitist sport.* = **snobbish**, exclusive, superior, arrogant, selective, pretentious, stuck-up (*informal*), patronizing, condescending, snooty (*informal*), uppity, high and mighty (*informal*), hoity-toity (*informal*), high-hat (*informal, chiefly U.S.*), uppish (*Brit. informal*)

elixir NOUN **1** *a magical elixir of eternal youth* = **panacea**, cure-all, nostrum, sovereign remedy **2** *For severe teething pains, try an infant paracetamol elixir.* = **syrup**, essence, solution, concentrate, mixture, extract, potion, distillation, tincture, distillate

elliptical ADJECTIVE = **oblique**, concentrated, obscure, compact, indirect, ambiguous, concise, condensed, terse, cryptic, laconic, abstruse, recondite

elongate VERB = **lengthen**, extend, stretch (out), make longer

elongated ADJECTIVE = **extended**, long, stretched

elope VERB = **run away**, leave, escape, disappear, bolt, run off, slip away, abscond,

decamp, sneak off, steal away, do a bunk (*informal*)

eloquence NOUN **1** *the eloquence with which he delivered his message* = **fluency**, effectiveness, oratory, expressiveness, persuasiveness, forcefulness, gracefulness, powerfulness, whaikorero (*N.Z.*) **2** *the eloquence of her gestures* = **expressiveness**, significance, meaningfulness, pointedness

eloquent ADJECTIVE **1** *She made a very eloquent speech at the dinner.* = **silver-tongued**, moving, powerful, effective, stirring, articulate, persuasive, graceful, forceful, fluent, expressive, well-expressed ■ **OPPOSITE:** inarticulate **2** *Her only reply was an eloquent glance at the clock.* = **expressive**, telling, pointed, revealing, significant, pregnant, vivid, meaningful, indicative, suggestive

elsewhere ADVERB = **in** *or* **to another place**, away, abroad, hence (*archaic*), somewhere else, not here, in other places, in *or* to a different place

elucidate VERB = **clarify**, explain, illustrate, interpret, make clear, unfold, illuminate, spell out, clear up, gloss, expound, make plain, annotate, explicate (*formal*), shed *or* throw light upon

elude VERB **1** *The thieves managed to elude the police for months.* = **evade**, escape, lose, avoid, flee, duck (*informal*), dodge, get away from, shake off, run away from, circumvent (*formal*), outrun, body-swerve **2** *The appropriate word eluded him.* = **escape**, baffle, frustrate, puzzle, stump, be beyond (*someone*), confound

> **USAGE** *Elude* is sometimes wrongly used where *allude* is meant: *he was alluding* (not *eluding*) *to his previous visit to the city.*

elusive ADJECTIVE **1** *I had no luck in tracking down this elusive man.* = **difficult to catch**, tricky, slippery, difficult to find, evasive, shifty (*informal*) **2** *an attempt to recapture an elusive memory* = **indefinable**, puzzling, fleeting, subtle, baffling, indefinite, transient, intangible, indescribable, transitory, indistinct

> **USAGE** The spelling of *elusive*, as in *a shy, elusive character*, should be noted. This adjective derives from the verb *elude*, and should not be confused with the rare word *illusive* meaning 'not real' or 'based on illusion'.

emaciated ADJECTIVE = **skeletal**, thin, weak, lean, pinched, skinny, wasted, gaunt, bony, haggard, atrophied, scrawny, attenuate, attenuated, undernourished, scraggy, half-starved, cadaverous, macilent (*rare*)

email or **e-mail** NOUN = **mail**, electronic mail, webmail

emanate VERB **1** *He emanated sympathy.* = **give out**, send out, emit, radiate, exude, issue, give off, exhale, send forth **2** (often with **from**) *The aroma of burning wood emanated from the stove.* = **flow**, emerge, spring, proceed, arise, stem, derive, originate, issue, come forth

emancipate VERB = **free**, release, liberate, set free, deliver, discharge, let out, let loose, untie, unchain, enfranchise, unshackle, disencumber, unfetter, unbridle, disenthral, manumit ■ **OPPOSITE:** enslave

emancipation NOUN = **liberation**, freedom, freeing, release, liberty, discharge, liberating, setting free, letting loose, untying, deliverance, unchaining, manumission, enfranchisement, unshackling, unfettering ■ **OPPOSITE:** slavery

emasculate VERB = **weaken**, soften, cripple, impoverish, debilitate, reduce the power of, enfeeble, make feeble, enervate, deprive of force

embalm VERB = **preserve**, lay out, mummify

embargo NOUN *The UN has imposed an arms embargo against the country.* = **ban**, bar, block, barrier, restriction, boycott, restraint, check, prohibition, moratorium, stoppage, impediment, blockage, hindrance, interdiction, interdict, proscription, rahui (N.Z.) ▶ VERB *They embargoed oil shipments to the US.* = **block**, stop, bar, ban, restrict, boycott, check, prohibit, impede, blacklist, proscribe, ostracize, debar, interdict

embark VERB *They embarked on the battle cruiser HMS Renown.* = **go aboard**, climb aboard, board ship, step aboard, go on board, take ship ■ **OPPOSITE:** get off
• **embark on something** *He is embarking on a new career as a writer.* = **begin**, start, launch, enter, engage, take up, set out, undertake, initiate, set about, plunge into, commence, broach

embarrass VERB = **shame**, distress, show up (informal), humiliate, disconcert, chagrin, fluster, mortify, faze, discomfit, make uncomfortable, make awkward, discountenance, nonplus, abash, discompose, make ashamed, put out of countenance

embarrassed ADJECTIVE = **ashamed**, upset, shamed, uncomfortable, shown-up, awkward, abashed, humiliated, uneasy, unsettled, self-conscious, thrown, disconcerted, red-faced, chagrined, flustered, mortified, sheepish, discomfited, discountenanced, caught with egg on your face, not know where to put yourself, put out of countenance

embarrassing ADJECTIVE = **humiliating**, upsetting, compromising, shaming, distressing, delicate, uncomfortable, awkward, tricky, sensitive, troublesome, shameful, disconcerting, touchy, mortifying, discomfiting, toe-curling (slang), cringe-making (Brit. informal), cringeworthy (Brit. informal), barro (Austral. slang)

embarrassment NOUN **1** *We apologize for any embarrassment this statement may have caused.* = **shame**, distress, showing up (informal), humiliation, discomfort, unease, chagrin, self-consciousness, awkwardness, mortification, discomfiture, bashfulness, discomposure **2** *The poverty figures were an embarrassment to the president.* = **problem**, difficulty, nuisance, source of trouble, thorn in your flesh **3** *He is in a state of temporary financial embarrassment.* = **predicament**, problem, difficulty, mess (informal), jam (informal), plight, scrape (informal), pickle (informal)

embed or **imbed** VERB (often with **in**) = **fix**, set, plant, root, sink, lodge, insert, implant, drive in, dig in, hammer in, ram in

embellish VERB **1** *The boat was embellished with red and blue carvings.* = **decorate**, enhance, adorn, dress, grace, deck, trim, dress up, enrich, garnish, ornament, gild, festoon, bedeck, tart up (slang), beautify **2** *He embellished the story with invented dialogue and extra details.* = **elaborate**, colour, exaggerate, dress up, embroider, varnish

embellishment NOUN **1** *Florence is full of buildings with bits of decoration and embellishment.* = **decoration**, garnishing, ornament, gilding, enhancement, enrichment, adornment, ornamentation, trimming, beautification **2** *I lack the story-teller's gift of embellishment.* = **elaboration**, exaggeration, embroidery

ember NOUN (usually plural) = **cinders**, ashes, residue, live coals

embezzle VERB = **misappropriate**, steal, appropriate, rob, pocket, nick (slang, chiefly Brit.), pinch (informal), rip off (slang), siphon off, pilfer, purloin (formal), filch, help yourself to, thieve, defalcate (Law), peculate

embezzlement NOUN = **misappropriation**, stealing, robbing, fraud, pocketing, theft, robbery, nicking (slang, chiefly Brit.), pinching (informal), appropriation, siphoning off, thieving, pilfering, larceny, purloining, filching, pilferage, peculation, defalcation (Law)

embittered ADJECTIVE = **resentful**, angry, acid, bitter, sour, soured, alienated, disillusioned, disaffected, venomous, rancorous, at daggers drawn (*informal*), nursing a grudge, with a chip on your shoulder (*informal*)

emblazon VERB = **decorate**, show, display, present, colour, paint, illuminate, adorn, ornament, embellish, blazon

emblem NOUN **1** *the emblem of the Red Cross* = **crest**, mark, design, image, figure, seal, shield, badge, insignia, coat of arms, heraldic device, sigil (*rare*) **2** *The eagle was an emblem of strength and courage.* = **representation**, symbol, mark, sign, type, token

emblematic or **emblematical** ADJECTIVE **1** *Dogs are emblematic of faithfulness.* = **symbolic**, significant, figurative, allegorical **2** *This comment is emblematic of his no-nonsense approach to life.* = **characteristic**, representative, typical, symptomatic

embodiment NOUN = **personification**, example, model, type, ideal, expression, symbol, representation, manifestation, realization, incarnation, paradigm, epitome, incorporation, paragon, perfect example, exemplar, quintessence, actualization, exemplification, reification, avatar

embody VERB **1** *Jack Kennedy embodied all the hopes of the 1960s.* = **personify**, represent, express, realize, incorporate, stand for, manifest, exemplify, symbolize, typify, incarnate, actualize, reify, concretize **2** (*often with* **in**) *The proposal has been embodied in a draft resolution.* = **incorporate**, include, contain, combine, collect, concentrate, organize, take in, integrate, consolidate, bring together, encompass, comprehend, codify, systematize

embolden VERB = **encourage**, cheer, stir, strengthen, nerve, stimulate, reassure, fire, animate, rouse, inflame, hearten, invigorate, gee up, make brave, give courage, vitalize, inspirit

embrace VERB **1** *Penelope came forward and embraced her sister.* = **hug**, hold, cuddle, seize, squeeze, grasp, clasp, envelop, encircle, enfold, canoodle (*slang*), take or hold in your arms **2** *He embraces the new information age.* = **accept**, support, receive, welcome, adopt, grab, take up, seize, make use of, espouse, take on board, welcome with open arms, avail yourself of, receive enthusiastically **3** *a theory that would embrace the whole field of human endeavour* = **include**, involve, cover, deal with, contain, take in, incorporate, comprise, enclose, provide for, take into account, embody, encompass, comprehend, subsume ▸ NOUN *a young couple locked in a passionate embrace* = **hug**, hold, cuddle, squeeze, clinch (*slang*), clasp, canoodle (*slang*)

embroil VERB = **involve**, complicate, mix up, implicate, entangle, mire, ensnare, encumber, enmesh

embryo NOUN **1** *The embryo lives in the amniotic cavity.* = **fetus**, unborn child, fertilized egg **2** *The League of Nations was the embryo of the UN.* = **germ**, beginning, source, root, seed, nucleus, rudiment

embryonic or **embryonal** ADJECTIVE = **rudimentary**, early, beginning, primary, budding, fledgling, immature, seminal, nascent, undeveloped, incipient, inchoate, unformed, germinal ■ OPPOSITE: advanced

emerge VERB **1** *He was waiting outside as she emerged from the building.* = **come out**, appear, come up, surface, rise, proceed, arise, turn up, spring up, emanate, materialize, issue, come into view, come forth, become visible, manifest yourself ■ OPPOSITE: withdraw **2** *Several interesting facts emerged from his story.* = **become apparent**, develop, come out, turn up, become known, come to light, crop up, transpire, materialize, become evident, come out in the wash

emergence NOUN **1** *the emergence of new democracies in Central Europe* = **coming**, development, arrival, surfacing, rise, appearance, arising, turning up, issue, dawn (*literary*), advent, emanation, materialization **2** *Following the emergence of new facts, the conviction was quashed.* = **disclosure**, publishing, broadcasting, broadcast, publication, declaration, revelation, becoming known, becoming apparent, coming to light, becoming evident

emergency NOUN *He has the ability to deal with emergencies quickly.* = **crisis**, danger, difficulty, accident, disaster, necessity, pinch, plight, scrape (*informal*), strait, catastrophe, predicament, calamity, extremity, quandary, exigency, critical situation, urgent situation ▸ ADJECTIVE **1** *She made an emergency appointment.* = **urgent**, crisis, immediate **2** *The plane is carrying emergency supplies.* = **alternative**, extra, additional, substitute, replacement, temporary, makeshift, stopgap

emergent ADJECTIVE = **developing**, coming, beginning, rising, appearing, budding, burgeoning, fledgling, nascent, incipient

emigrate VERB = **move abroad**, move, relocate, migrate, remove, resettle, leave your country

emigration NOUN = **departure**, removal, migration, exodus, relocation, resettlement

eminence NOUN **1** *pilots who achieved eminence in the aeronautical world* = **prominence**, reputation, importance, fame, celebrity, distinction, note, esteem, rank, dignity, prestige, superiority, greatness, renown, pre-eminence, repute, notability, illustriousness **2** *The house is built on an eminence, and has a pleasing prospect.* = **high ground**, bank, rise, hill, summit, height, mound, elevation, knoll, hillock, kopje *or* koppie (*S. African*)

eminent ADJECTIVE = **prominent**, high, great, important, noted, respected, grand, famous, celebrated, outstanding, distinguished, well-known, superior, esteemed, notable, renowned, prestigious, elevated, paramount, big-time (*informal*), foremost, high-ranking, conspicuous, illustrious, major league (*informal*), exalted, noteworthy, pre-eminent ■ **OPPOSITE:** unknown

emissary NOUN = **envoy**, agent, deputy, representative, ambassador, diplomat, delegate, courier, herald, messenger, consul, attaché, go-between, legate

emission NOUN = **giving off** *or* **out**, release, shedding, leak, radiation, discharge, transmission, venting, issue, diffusion, utterance, ejaculation, outflow, issuance, ejection, exhalation, emanation, exudation

emit VERB **1** *The stove emitted a cloud of evil-smelling smoke.* = **give off**, release, shed, leak, transmit, discharge, send out, throw out, vent, issue, give out, radiate, eject, pour out, diffuse, emanate, exude, exhale, breathe out, cast out, give vent to, send forth ■ **OPPOSITE:** absorb **2** *Polly blinked and emitted a small cry.* = **utter**, produce, voice, give out, let out

emotion NOUN **1** *Her voice trembled with emotion.* = **feeling**, spirit, soul, passion, excitement, sensation, sentiment, agitation, fervour, ardour, vehemence, perturbation **2** *the split between reason and emotion* = **instinct**, sentiment, sensibility, intuition, tenderness, gut feeling, soft-heartedness

emotional ADJECTIVE **1** *Victims are left with emotional problems that can last for life.* = **psychological**, private, personal, hidden, spiritual, inner **2** *It was a very emotional moment.* = **moving**, touching, affecting, exciting, stirring, thrilling, sentimental,

poignant, emotive, heart-rending, heart-warming, tear-jerking (*informal*) **3** *I wondered why the campaign for proper spelling had become such an emotional issue.* = **emotive**, sensitive, controversial, delicate, contentious, heated, inflammatory, touchy **4** *I don't get as emotional as I once did.* = **passionate**, enthusiastic, sentimental, fiery, feeling, susceptible, responsive, ardent, fervent, zealous, temperamental, excitable, demonstrative, hot-blooded, fervid, touchy-feely (*informal*) ■ **OPPOSITE:** dispassionate

> **USAGE** Although *emotive* can be used as a synonym of *emotional*, there are differences in meaning that should first be understood. *Emotional* is the more general and neutral word for referring to anything to do with the emotions and emotional states. *Emotive* has the more restricted meaning of 'tending to arouse emotion', and is often associated with issues, subjects, language, and words. However, since *emotional* can also mean 'arousing emotion', with certain nouns it is possible to use either word, depending on the slant one wishes to give: *an emotive/emotional appeal on behalf of the disadvantaged young.*

emotive ADJECTIVE **1** *Such a complex and emotive subject deserves deeper analysis.* = **sensitive**, controversial, delicate, contentious, inflammatory, touchy **2** *He made an emotive speech to his fans.* = **moving**, touching, affecting, emotional, exciting, stirring, thrilling, sentimental, poignant, heart-rending, heart-warming, tear-jerking (*informal*)

empathize VERB • **empathize with** = **identify with**, understand, relate to, feel for, sympathize with, have a rapport with, feel at one with, be on the same wavelength as

emphasis NOUN **1** *Too much emphasis is placed on research.* = **importance**, attention, weight, significance, stress, strength, priority, moment, intensity, insistence, prominence, underscoring, pre-eminence **2** *The emphasis is on the first syllable of the word.* = **stress**, accent, accentuation, force, weight

emphasize VERB **1** *I should emphasize that nothing has been finally decided as yet.* = **highlight**, stress, insist, underline, draw attention to, flag up, dwell on, underscore, weight, play up, make a point of, give priority to, press home, give prominence to, prioritize ■ **OPPOSITE:** minimize

2 *'That's up to you,' I said, emphasizing the 'you'.*
= **stress**, accent, accentuate, lay stress on,
put the accent on

emphatic ADJECTIVE **1** *His response was
immediate and emphatic.* = **forceful**, decided,
certain, direct, earnest, positive, absolute,
distinct, definite, vigorous, energetic,
unmistakable, insistent, unequivocal,
vehement, forcible, categorical
■ **OPPOSITE:** hesitant **2** *Yesterday's emphatic
victory was their fifth in succession.*
= **significant**, marked, strong, striking,
powerful, telling, storming (*informal*),
impressive, pronounced, decisive,
resounding, momentous, conclusive
■ **OPPOSITE:** insignificant

empire NOUN **1** *the fall of the Roman empire*
= **kingdom**, territory, province, federation,
commonwealth, realm, domain, imperium
(*rare*) **2** *control of a huge publishing empire*
= **organization**, company, business, firm,
concern, corporation, consortium,
syndicate, multinational, conglomeration
■ **RELATED WORD:** *adjective* imperial

empirical ADJECTIVE = **first-hand**, direct,
observed, practical, actual, experimental,
pragmatic, factual, experiential
■ **OPPOSITE:** hypothetical

employ VERB **1** *The company employs 18 staff.*
= **hire**, commission, appoint, take on,
retain, engage, recruit, sign up, enlist,
enrol, have on the payroll **2** *the approaches
and methods we employed in this study* = **use**,
apply, exercise, exert, make use of, utilize,
ply, bring to bear, put to use, bring into
play, avail yourself of **3** *Your time could be
usefully employed in attending to business
matters.* = **spend**, fill, occupy, involve,
engage, take up, make use of, use up

employed ADJECTIVE **1** *He was employed on a
part-time basis.* = **working**, in work, having a
job, in employment, in a job, earning your
living ■ **OPPOSITE:** out of work **2** *You have
enough work to keep you fully employed.* = **busy**,
active, occupied, engaged, hard at work, in
harness, rushed off your feet ■ **OPPOSITE:** idle

employee or (*sometimes U.S.*) **employe**
NOUN = **worker**, labourer, workman or
woman or person, staff member, member
of staff, hand, wage-earner, white-collar
worker, blue-collar worker, hired hand,
job-holder, member of the workforce

employer NOUN **1** *It is a privilege to work for
such an excellent employer.* = **boss** (*informal*),
manager, head, leader, director, chief,
executive, owner, master, chief executive,
governor (*informal*), skipper, managing
director, administrator, patron, supervisor,
superintendent, gaffer (*informal, chiefly

Brit.), foreman or woman or person,
proprietor, overseer, kingpin, honcho
(*informal*), big cheese (*slang, old-fashioned*),
numero uno (*informal*), Mister Big (*slang,
chiefly U.S.*), sherang (*Austral. & N.Z.*)
2 *Shorts is Ulster's biggest private-sector
employer.* = **company**, business, firm,
organization, establishment, outfit
(*informal*)

employment NOUN **1** *She was unable to
find employment in the area.* = **job**, work,
business, position, trade, post, situation,
employ, calling, profession, occupation,
pursuit, vocation, métier **2** *a ban on the
employment of children under the age of nine*
= **taking on**, commissioning, appointing,
hire, hiring, retaining, engaging,
appointment, recruiting, engagement,
recruitment, enlisting, enrolling,
enlistment, enrolment **3** *the employment of
the safety car* = **use**, application, exertion,
exercise, utilization

emporium NOUN = **shop**, market, store,
supermarket, outlet, warehouse,
department store, mart, boutique, bazaar,
retail outlet, superstore, hypermarket

empower VERB **1** *The trustees of the museum
are empowered to sell items from its collection.*
= **authorize**, allow, commission, qualify,
permit, sanction, entitle, delegate, license,
warrant, give power to, give authority to,
invest with power **2** *empowering the
underprivileged by means of education*
= **enable**, equip, emancipate, give means
to, enfranchise

emptiness NOUN **1** *suffering from feelings
of emptiness and depression* = **futility**,
banality, worthlessness, hollowness,
pointlessness, meaninglessness,
barrenness, senselessness, aimlessness,
purposelessness, unsatisfactoriness,
valuelessness **2** *the unsoundness and
emptiness of his beliefs* = **meaninglessness**,
vanity, banality, frivolity, idleness, unreality,
silliness, triviality, ineffectiveness,
cheapness, insincerity, worthlessness,
hollowness, inanity, unsubstantiality,
trivialness, vainness **3** *She wanted a man
to fill the emptiness in her life.* = **void**, gap,
vacuum, empty space, nothingness, blank
space, free space, vacuity **4** *the emptiness of
the desert* = **bareness**, waste, desolation,
destitution, blankness, barrenness,
desertedness, vacantness **5** *There was
an emptiness about her eyes, as if she were
in a state of shock.* = **blankness**, vacancy,
vacuity, impassivity, vacuousness,
expressionlessness, stoniness,
unintelligence, absentness, vacantness

e

empty ADJECTIVE **1** *The room was bare and empty.* = **bare**, clear, abandoned, deserted, vacant, free, void (*old-fashioned*), desolate, destitute, uninhabited, unoccupied, waste, unfurnished, untenanted, without contents ■ **OPPOSITE:** full **2** *The gang said they were going to beat him, but he knew it was an empty threat.* = **meaningless**, cheap, hollow, vain, idle, trivial, ineffective, futile, insubstantial, insincere **3** *My life was hectic but empty before I met him.* = **worthless**, meaningless, hollow, pointless, unsatisfactory, futile, unreal, senseless, frivolous, fruitless, aimless, inane, valueless, purposeless, otiose, bootless (*old-fashioned*) ■ **OPPOSITE:** meaningful **4** *She saw the empty look in his eyes as she left.* = **blank**, absent, vacant, stony, deadpan, vacuous, impassive, expressionless, unintelligent ▸ VERB **1** *I emptied the ashtray.* = **clear**, drain, gut, void, unload, pour out, unpack, unburden, remove the contents of ■ **OPPOSITE:** fill **2** *Cross emptied his glass with one swallow.* = **exhaust**, consume the contents of, void, deplete, use up ■ **OPPOSITE:** replenish **3** *a bore who could empty a room in two minutes just by talking about himself* = **evacuate**, clear, vacate

emulate VERB = **imitate**, follow, copy, mirror, echo, mimic, take after, follow in the footsteps of, follow the example of, take a leaf out of someone's book, model yourself on

emulation NOUN = **imitation**, following, copying, mirroring, reproduction, mimicry

enable VERB **1** *The new test should enable doctors to detect the disease early.* = **allow**, permit, facilitate, empower, give someone the opportunity, give someone the means ■ **OPPOSITE:** prevent **2** *The authorities have refused visas to enable them to enter the country.* = **authorize**, allow, commission, permit, qualify, sanction, entitle, license, warrant, empower, give someone the right ■ **OPPOSITE:** stop

enact VERB **1** *The bill would be submitted for discussion before being enacted as law.* = **establish**, order, pass, command, approve, sanction, proclaim, decree, authorize, ratify, ordain (*formal*), validate, legislate, make law **2** *She enacted the stories told to her by her father.* = **perform**, play, act, present, stage, represent, put on, portray, depict, act out, play the part of, appear as or in, personate

enactment or **enaction** NOUN **1** *the enactment of a Bill of Rights* = **passing**, legislation, sanction, approval, establishment, proclamation, ratification, authorization, validation, making law **2** *enactments which empowered the court to require security to be given* = **decree**, order, law, act, ruling, bill, measure, command, legislation, regulation, resolution, dictate, canon, statute, ordinance, commandment, edict, bylaw **3** *The building was also used for the enactment of plays.* = **portrayal**, staging, performance, playing, acting, performing, representation, depiction, play-acting, personation

enamoured ADJECTIVE • **enamoured with** or **of** = **in love with**, taken with, charmed by, fascinated by, entranced by, fond of, enchanted by, captivated by, enthralled by, smitten with, besotted with, bewitched by, crazy about (*informal*), infatuated with, enraptured by, wild about (*informal*), swept off your feet by, nuts on or about (*slang*)

encampment NOUN = **camp**, base, post, station, quarters, campsite, bivouac, camping ground, cantonment

encapsulate or **incapsulate** VERB = **sum up**, digest, summarize, compress, condense, abbreviate, epitomize, abridge, précis

enchant VERB = **fascinate**, delight, charm, entrance, dazzle, captivate, enthral, beguile, bewitch, ravish, mesmerize, hypnotize, cast a spell on, enrapture, enamour, spellbind

enchanting ADJECTIVE = **delightful**, fascinating, appealing, attractive, lovely, charming, entrancing, pleasant, endearing, captivating, alluring, bewitching, ravishing, winsome, Orphean

enchantment NOUN **1** *The campsite had its own peculiar enchantment.* = **charm**, fascination, delight, beauty, joy, attraction, bliss, allure, transport, rapture, mesmerism, ravishment, captivation, beguilement, allurement **2** *an effective countercharm against enchantment by the faerie folk* = **spell**, magic, charm, witchcraft, voodoo, wizardry, sorcery, occultism, incantation, necromancy, conjuration, makutu (*N.Z.*)

encircle VERB = **surround**, ring, circle, enclose, encompass, compass, envelop, girdle, circumscribe, hem in, enfold, environ, gird in, begird (*poetic*), enwreath

enclose or **inclose** VERB **1** *The land was enclosed by an eight-foot wire fence.* = **surround**, cover, circle, bound, wrap, fence, pound, pen, hedge, confine, close in, encompass, wall in, encircle, encase, fence in, impound, circumscribe, hem in, shut in, environ **2** *Please enclose a copy of your CV.* = **send with**, include, put in, insert

encompass VERB **1** *His repertoire encompassed everything from Bach to Scott Joplin.* = **include**, hold, involve, cover, admit, deal with, contain, take in, embrace, incorporate, comprise, embody, comprehend, subsume **2** *Egypt is encompassed by the Mediterranean, Sudan, the Red Sea and Libya.* = **surround**, circle, enclose, close in, envelop, encircle, fence in, ring, girdle, circumscribe, hem in, shut in, environ, enwreath

encounter VERB **1** *Every day we encounter stresses of one kind or another.* = **experience**, meet, face, suffer, have, go through, sustain, endure, undergo, run into, live through **2** *Did you encounter anyone on your walk?* = **meet**, confront, come across, run into (*informal*), bump into (*informal*), run across, come upon, chance upon, meet by chance, happen on or upon **3** *They were about to cross the border and encounter Iraqi troops.* = **battle with**, attack, fight, oppose, engage with, confront, combat, clash with, contend with, strive against, struggle with, grapple with, face off (*slang*), do battle with, cross swords with, come into conflict with, meet head on ▸ NOUN **1** *an encounter with a remarkable man* = **meeting**, brush, confrontation, rendezvous, chance meeting **2** *They were killed in an encounter with security forces near the border.* = **battle**, fight, action, conflict, clash, dispute, contest, set to (*informal*), run-in (*informal*), combat, confrontation, engagement, collision, skirmish, head-to-head, face-off (*slang*)

encourage VERB **1** *When things aren't going well, he always encourages me.* = **inspire**, comfort, rally, cheer, stimulate, reassure, animate, console, rouse, hearten, cheer up, embolden, buoy up, pep up, boost someone's morale, give hope to, buck up (*informal*), gee up, lift the spirits of, give confidence to, inspirit ■ OPPOSITE: discourage **2** *He encouraged her to quit her job.* = **urge**, persuade, prompt, spur, coax, incite, egg on, abet ■ OPPOSITE: dissuade **3** *Their task is to encourage private investment in Russia.* = **promote**, back, help, support, increase, further, aid, forward, advance, favour, boost, strengthen, foster, advocate, stimulate, endorse, commend, succour ■ OPPOSITE: prevent

encouragement NOUN **1** *Thanks for all your advice and encouragement.* = **inspiration**, help, support, aid, favour, comfort, comforting, cheer, cheering, consolation, reassurance, morale boosting, succour **2** *She had needed no encouragement to accept his invitation.* = **urging**, prompting, stimulus, persuasion, coaxing, egging on, incitement **3** *The encouragement of trade will benefit the process of economic reform.* = **promotion**, backing, support, boost, endorsement, stimulation, advocacy, furtherance

encouraging ADJECTIVE = **promising**, good, bright, comforting, cheering, stimulating, reassuring, hopeful, satisfactory, cheerful, favourable, rosy, heartening, auspicious, propitious ■ OPPOSITE: discouraging

encroach VERB (*often with* **on** *or* **upon**) = **intrude**, invade, trespass, infringe, usurp, impinge, trench, overstep, make inroads, impose yourself

encroachment NOUN = **intrusion**, invasion, violation, infringement, trespass, incursion, usurpation, inroad, impingement

encumber VERB **1** *The company is still labouring under the debt burden that it was encumbered with ten years ago.* = **burden**, load, embarrass, saddle, oppress, obstruct, retard, weigh down **2** *fishermen encumbered with bulky clothing and boots* = **hamper**, restrict, handicap, slow down, cramp, inhibit, clog, hinder, inconvenience, overload, impede, weigh down, trammel, incommode (*formal*)

encyclopedic *or* **encyclopaedic** ADJECTIVE = **comprehensive**, full, complete, vast, universal, wide-ranging, thorough, in-depth, exhaustive, all-inclusive, all-embracing, all-encompassing, thoroughgoing

end NOUN **1** *The report is expected by the end of the year.* = **close**, ending, finish, expiry, expiration ■ OPPOSITE: beginning **2** *His big scene comes towards the end of the film.* = **conclusion**, ending, climax, completion, finale, culmination, denouement, consummation ■ OPPOSITE: start **3** *She brought the interview to an abrupt end.* = **finish**, close, stop, resolution, conclusion, closure, wind-up, completion, termination, cessation **4** *Surveillance equipment is placed at both ends of the tunnel.* = **extremity**, limit, edge, border, bound, extent, extreme, margin, boundary, terminus **5** *He tapped the ends of his fingers together.* = **tip**, point, head, peak, extremity **6** *another policy designed to achieve the same end* = **purpose**, point, reason, goal, design, target, aim, object, mission, intention, objective, drift, intent, aspiration **7** *The end justifies the means.* = **outcome**, result, consequence, resolution, conclusion, completion, issue, sequel, end result, attainment, upshot, consummation **8** *Soon after we spoke to him,* he met a violent end. = **death**, dying, ruin, destruction, passing on, doom, demise (*euphemistic*), extinction, dissolution, passing away, extermination, annihilation, expiration, ruination **9** an ashtray overflowing with cigarette ends = **remnant**, butt, bit, stub, scrap, fragment, stump, remainder, leftover, tail end, oddment, tag end ▶ VERB **1** Talks have resumed to try to end the fighting. = **stop**, finish, complete, resolve, halt, cease, axe (*informal*), dissolve, wind up, terminate, call off, discontinue, put paid to, bring to an end, pull the plug on, call a halt to, nip in the bud, belay (*Nautical*) ■ OPPOSITE: start **2** The book ends on a lengthy description of Hawaii. = **finish**, close, conclude, wind up, culminate, terminate, come to an end, draw to a close ■ OPPOSITE: begin **3** I believe you should be free to end your own life. = **destroy**, take, kill, abolish, put an end to, do away with, extinguish, annihilate, exterminate, put to death • **end up 1** The car ended up at the bottom of the river. = **finish up**, stop, wind up, come to a halt, fetch up (*informal*) **2** We could end up as millionaires. = **turn out to be**, finish as, finish up, pan out (*informal*), become eventually ■ RELATED WORDS: adjectives final, terminal, ultimate

endanger VERB = **put at risk**, risk, threaten, compromise, hazard, jeopardize, imperil, put in danger, expose to danger ■ OPPOSITE: save

endear VERB = **attract**, draw, bind, engage, charm, attach, win, incline, captivate

endearing ADJECTIVE = **attractive**, winning, pleasing, appealing, sweet, engaging, charming, pleasant, cute, enticing, captivating, lovable, alluring, adorable, winsome, cutesy (*informal*)

endeavour (*formal*) VERB I will endeavour to rectify the situation. = **try**, labour, attempt, aim, struggle, venture, undertake, essay (*formal*), strive, aspire, have a go, go for it (*informal*), make an effort, have a shot (*informal*), have a crack (*informal*), take pains, bend over backwards (*informal*), do your best, go for broke (*slang*), bust a gut (*informal*), give it your best shot (*informal*), jump through hoops (*informal*), have a stab (*informal*), break your neck (*informal*), make an all-out effort (*informal*), knock yourself out (*informal*), do your damnedest (*informal*), give it your all (*informal*), rupture yourself (*informal*) ▶ NOUN His first endeavours in the field were wedding films. = **attempt**, try, shot (*informal*), effort, trial, go (*informal*), aim, bid, crack (*informal*), venture, enterprise, undertaking, essay (*formal*), stab (*informal*)

ended ADJECTIVE = **finished**, done, over, through, closed, past, complete, done with, settled, all over (bar the shouting), no more, concluded, accomplished, wrapped-up (*informal*), at an end, finis

ending NOUN = **finish**, end, close, resolution, conclusion, summing up, wind-up, completion, finale, termination, culmination, cessation, denouement, last part, consummation ■ OPPOSITE: start

endless ADJECTIVE **1** causing over 25,000 deaths in a seemingly endless war = **eternal**, constant, infinite, perpetual, continual, immortal, unbroken, unlimited, uninterrupted, limitless, interminable, incessant, boundless, everlasting, unending, ceaseless, inexhaustible, undying, unceasing, unbounded, measureless, unfading ■ OPPOSITE: temporary **2** I am sick to death of your endless complaints. = **interminable**, constant, persistent, perpetual, never-ending, incessant, monotonous, overlong **3** an endless conveyor belt = **continuous**, unbroken, uninterrupted, undivided, without end

endorse or **indorse** VERB **1** I can endorse this statement wholeheartedly. = **approve**, back, support, champion, favour, promote, recommend, sanction, sustain, advocate, warrant, prescribe, uphold, authorize, ratify, affirm, approve of, subscribe to, espouse, vouch for, throw your weight behind **2** The payee must endorse the cheque. = **sign**, initial, countersign, sign on the back of, superscribe, undersign

endorsement or **indorsement** NOUN = **approval**, backing, support, championing, favour, promotion, sanction, recommendation, acceptance, agreement, warrant, confirmation, upholding, subscription, fiat, advocacy, affirmation, ratification, authorization, seal of approval, approbation, espousal, O.K. or okay (*informal*)

endow VERB **1** The ambassador has endowed a public-service fellowship programme. = **finance**, fund, pay for, award, grant, invest in, confer, settle on, bestow, make over, bequeath, purvey, donate money to **2** Herbs have been used for centuries to endow a whole range of foods with subtle flavours. = **imbue**, steep, bathe, saturate, pervade, instil, infuse, permeate, impregnate, inculcate

endowed ADJECTIVE (*usually with* **with**) = **provided**, favoured, graced, blessed, supplied, furnished, enriched

endowment NOUN **1** The company gave the Oxford Union a generous £1m endowment.

= **provision**, fund, funding, award, income, grant, gift, contribution, revenue, subsidy, presentation, donation, legacy, hand-out, boon (*archaic*), bequest, stipend, bestowal, benefaction, largesse *or* largess, koha (*N.Z.*) **2** (*usually plural*) *individuals with higher-than-average intellectual endowments* = **talent**, power, feature, quality, ability, gift, capacity, characteristic, attribute, qualification, genius, faculty, capability, flair, aptitude

endurance NOUN **1** *a test of endurance* = **staying power**, strength, resolution, resignation, determination, patience, submission, stamina, fortitude, persistence, tenacity, perseverance, toleration, sufferance, doggedness, stickability (*informal*), pertinacity **2** *The book is about the endurance of the class system in Britain.* = **permanence**, stability, continuity, duration, continuation, longevity, durability, continuance, immutability, lastingness

endure VERB **1** *He'd endured years of pain and sleepless nights because of arthritis.* = **experience**, suffer, bear, weather, meet, go through, encounter, cope with, sustain, brave, undergo, withstand, live through, thole (*Scot.*) **2** *I simply can't endure another moment of her company.* = **put up with**, stand, suffer, bear, allow, accept, stick (*slang*), take (*informal*), permit, stomach, swallow, brook, tolerate, hack (*slang*), abide, submit to, countenance, stick out (*informal*), take patiently **3** *Somehow the language endures and continues to survive to this day.* = **last**, live, continue, remain, stay, hold, stand, go on, survive, live on, prevail, persist, abide, be durable, wear well

enduring ADJECTIVE = **long-lasting**, lasting, living, continuing, remaining, firm, surviving, permanent, constant, steady, prevailing, persisting, abiding, perennial, durable, immortal, steadfast, unwavering, immovable, imperishable, unfaltering ■ OPPOSITE: brief

enemy NOUN = **foe** (*formal*, *literary*), rival, opponent, the opposition, competitor, the other side, adversary, antagonist ■ OPPOSITE: friend ■ RELATED WORD: *adjective* inimical

energetic ADJECTIVE **1** *an energetic public-relations campaign* = **forceful**, strong, determined, powerful, storming (*informal*), active, aggressive, dynamic, vigorous, potent, hard-hitting, high-powered, strenuous, punchy (*informal*), forcible, high-octane (*informal*) **2** *Two-year-olds can be incredibly energetic.* = **lively**, spirited, active, dynamic, vigorous, animated, brisk, tireless, bouncy, indefatigable, alive and kicking, zippy (*informal*), full of beans (*informal*), bright-eyed and bushy-tailed (*informal*) ■ OPPOSITE: lethargic **3** *an energetic exercise routine* = **strenuous**, hard, taxing, demanding, tough, exhausting, vigorous, arduous

energize VERB **1** *their ability to energize their followers* = **stimulate**, drive, stir, motivate, activate, animate, enthuse, quicken, enliven, galvanize, liven up, pep up, invigorate, vitalize, inspirit **2** *When energized, the coil creates an electromagnetic force.* = **stimulate**, operate, trigger, turn on, start up, activate, switch on, kick-start, electrify, actuate

energy NOUN **1** *He was saving his energy for the big race in Belgium.* = **strength**, might, force, power, activity, intensity, stamina, exertion, forcefulness **2** *At 65 years old, her energy and looks are wonderful.* = **liveliness**, life, drive, fire, spirit, determination, pep, go (*informal*), zip (*informal*), vitality, animation, vigour, verve, zest, resilience, get-up-and-go (*informal*), élan, brio, vivacity, vim **3** *Oil shortages have brought an energy crisis.* = **power**

enfold *or* **infold** VERB **1** *Wood was comfortably enfolded in a woolly dressing-gown.* = **wrap**, surround, enclose, wrap up, encompass, shroud, immerse, swathe, envelop, sheathe, enwrap **2** *He enfolded her gently in his arms.* = **embrace**, hold, fold, hug, cuddle, clasp

enforce VERB **1** *The measures are being enforced by Interior Ministry troops.* = **carry out**, apply, implement, fulfil, execute, administer, put into effect, put into action, put into operation, put in force **2** *They tried to limit the cost by enforcing a low-tech specification.* = **impose**, force, require, urge, insist on, compel, exact, oblige, constrain, coerce

enforced ADJECTIVE = **imposed**, required, necessary, compelled, dictated, prescribed, compulsory, mandatory, constrained, ordained, obligatory, unavoidable, involuntary

enforcement NOUN **1** *the adequate enforcement of the law* = **administration**, carrying out, application, prosecution, execution, implementation, reinforcement, fulfilment **2** *the stricter enforcement of speed limits for vehicles* = **imposition**, requirement, obligation, insistence, exaction (*formal*)

engage VERB **1** *They continue to engage in terrorist activities.* = **participate in**, join in, take part in, undertake, practise, embark on, enter into, become involved in, set about, partake of **2** *He engaged us with tales of his adventures.* = **captivate**, win, draw, catch, arrest, fix, attract, capture, charm, attach, fascinate, enchant, allure, enamour **3** *She tried to engage me in conversation.* = **occupy**, involve, draw, busy, grip, absorb, tie up, preoccupy, immerse, engross **4** *We have been able to engage some staff.* = **employ**, commission, appoint, take on, hire, retain, recruit, enlist, enrol, put on the payroll ■ **OPPOSITE:** dismiss **5** *I managed to engage a room for the night.* = **book**, reserve, secure, hire, rent, charter, lease, prearrange **6** *Press the lever until you hear the catch engage.* = **interlock**, join, interact, mesh, interconnect, dovetail **7** *Show me how to engage the four-wheel drive.* = **set going**, apply, trigger, activate, switch on, energize, bring into operation **8** *They could engage the enemy beyond the range of the torpedoes.* = **begin battle with**, attack, take on, encounter, combat, fall on, battle with, meet, fight with, assail, face off (*slang*), wage war on, join battle with, give battle to, come to close quarters with

engaged ADJECTIVE **1** *the various projects he was engaged on* = **occupied**, working, involved, committed, employed, busy, absorbed, tied up, preoccupied, engrossed **2** *He was engaged to Miss Julia Boardman.* = **betrothed** (*old-fashioned*), promised, pledged, affianced (*old-fashioned*), promised in marriage ■ **OPPOSITE:** unattached **3** *We tried to phone you back but the line was engaged.* = **in use**, busy, tied up, unavailable ■ **OPPOSITE:** free

engagement NOUN **1** *He had an engagement at a restaurant in Greek Street at eight.* = **appointment**, meeting, interview, date, commitment, arrangement, rendezvous **2** *I've broken off my engagement to Arthur.* = **betrothal** (*old-fashioned*), marriage contract, troth (*archaic*), agreement to marry **3** *The constitution prevents them from military engagement on foreign soil.* = **battle**, fight, conflict, action, struggle, clash, contest, encounter, combat, confrontation, skirmish, face-off (*slang*) **4** *his proactive engagement in the peace process* = **participation**, joining, taking part, involvement **5** *her first official engagement as foreign minister* = **job**, work, post, situation, commission, employment, appointment, gig (*informal*), stint

engaging ADJECTIVE = **charming**, interesting, pleasing, appealing, attractive, lovely, fascinating, entertaining, winning, pleasant, fetching (*informal*), delightful, cute, enchanting, captivating, agreeable,

lovable, winsome, cutesy (*informal*), likable or likeable ■ **OPPOSITE:** unpleasant

engender VERB *Insults engender hatred against those who indulge in them.* = **produce**, make, cause, create, lead to, occasion (*formal*), excite, result in, breed, generate, provoke, induce, bring about, arouse, give rise to, precipitate, incite, instigate, foment, beget (*old-fashioned*)

engine NOUN = **machine**, motor, mechanism, generator, dynamo

engineer NOUN **1** *a fully qualified civil engineer* = **designer**, producer, architect, developer, deviser, creator, planner, inventor, stylist, artificer, originator, couturier **2** *They sent a service engineer to repair the disk drive.* = **worker**, specialist, operator, practitioner, operative, driver, conductor, technician, handler, skilled employee ▶ VERB **1** *The canals were both engineered by a farmer's son.* = **design**, plan, create, construct, devise, originate **2** *a short-lived coup engineered by the army* = **bring about**, plan, control, cause, effect, manage, set up (*informal*), scheme, arrange, plot, manoeuvre, encompass, mastermind, orchestrate, contrive, concoct, wangle (*informal*), finagle (*informal*)

engrave VERB = **carve**, cut, etch, inscribe, chisel, incise, chase, enchase (*rare*), grave (*archaic*)

engraved ADJECTIVE = **fixed**, set, printed, impressed, lodged, embedded, imprinted, etched, ingrained, infixed

engraving NOUN **1** *the engraving of Shakespeare at the front of the book* = **print**, block, impression, carving, etching, inscription, plate, woodcut, dry point **2** *Glass engraving has increased in popularity over recent years.* = **cutting**, carving, etching, inscribing, chiselling, inscription, chasing, dry point, enchasing (*rare*)

engrossed ADJECTIVE = **absorbed**, lost, involved, occupied, deep, engaged, gripped, fascinated, caught up, intrigued, intent, preoccupied, immersed, riveted, captivated, enthralled, rapt

engrossing ADJECTIVE = **absorbing**, interesting, arresting, engaging, gripping, fascinating, compelling, intriguing, riveting, captivating, enthralling

engulf or **ingulf** VERB **1** *The flat was engulfed in flames.* = **immerse**, bury, flood (out), plunge, consume, drown, swamp, encompass, submerge, overrun, inundate, deluge, envelop, swallow up **2** *He was engulfed by a feeling of emptiness.* = **overwhelm**, overcome, crush, absorb, swamp, engross

enhance VERB = **improve**, better, increase, raise, lift, boost, add to, strengthen, reinforce, swell, intensify, heighten, elevate, magnify, augment, exalt, embellish, ameliorate ■ OPPOSITE: reduce

enhancement NOUN = **improvement**, strengthening, heightening, enrichment, increment, embellishment, boost, betterment, augmentation, amelioration

enigma NOUN = **mystery**, problem, puzzle, riddle, paradox, conundrum, teaser

enigmatic or **enigmatical** ADJECTIVE = **mysterious**, puzzling, obscure, baffling, ambiguous, perplexing, incomprehensible, mystifying, inexplicable, unintelligible, paradoxical, cryptic, inscrutable, unfathomable, indecipherable, recondite, Delphic, oracular, sphinxlike ■ OPPOSITE: straightforward

enjoin VERB **1** *She enjoined me strictly not to tell anyone else.* = **order**, charge (*formal*), warn, urge, require, direct, bid, command, advise, counsel, prescribe, instruct, call upon **2** *the government's attempt to enjoin the publication of the book* = **prohibit**, bar, ban, forbid, restrain, preclude, disallow, proscribe, interdict, place an injunction on

enjoy VERB **1** *He enjoys playing cricket.* = **take pleasure in** or **from**, like, love, appreciate, relish, delight in, revel in, be pleased with, be fond of, be keen on, rejoice in, be entertained by, find pleasure in, find satisfaction in, take joy in ■ OPPOSITE: hate **2** *The average German will enjoy 40 days' paid holiday this year.* = **have**, use, own, experience, possess, have the benefit of, reap the benefits of, have the use of, be blessed or favoured with • **enjoy yourself** *He's too busy enjoying himself to get much work done.* = **have a good time**, be happy, have fun, have a field day (*informal*), have a ball (*informal*), live life to the full, make merry, let your hair down

enjoyable ADJECTIVE = **pleasurable**, good, great, fine, pleasing, nice, satisfying, lovely, entertaining, pleasant, amusing, delicious, delightful, gratifying, agreeable, delectable, to your liking ■ OPPOSITE: unpleasant

enjoyment NOUN **1** *She ate with great enjoyment.* = **pleasure**, liking, fun, delight, entertainment, joy, satisfaction, happiness, relish, recreation, amusement, indulgence, diversion, zest, gratification, gusto, gladness, delectation (*formal*), beer and skittles (*informal*) **2** *the enjoyment of equal freedom by all* = **benefit**, use, advantage, favour, possession, blessing

enlarge VERB **1** *plans to enlarge the park into a 30,000 all-seater stadium* = **expand**, increase, extend, add to, build up, widen, intensify, blow up (*informal*), heighten, broaden, inflate, lengthen, magnify, amplify, augment, make bigger, elongate, make larger ■ OPPOSITE: reduce **2** *The glands in the neck may enlarge.* = **grow**, increase, extend, stretch, expand, swell, wax, multiply, inflate, lengthen, diffuse, elongate, dilate, become bigger, puff up, grow larger, grow bigger, become larger, distend, bloat • **enlarge on something** *I wish to enlarge on the statement I made yesterday.* = **expand on**, develop, add to, fill out, elaborate on, flesh out, expatiate on, give further details about

enlighten VERB = **inform**, tell, teach, advise, counsel, educate, instruct, illuminate, make aware, edify, apprise, let know, cause to understand

enlightened ADJECTIVE = **informed**, aware, liberal, reasonable, educated, sophisticated, refined, cultivated, open-minded, knowledgeable, literate, broad-minded ■ OPPOSITE: ignorant

enlightenment NOUN = **understanding**, information, learning, education, teaching, knowledge, instruction, awareness, wisdom, insight, literacy, sophistication, comprehension, cultivation, refinement, open-mindedness, edification, broad-mindedness

enlist VERB **1** *He enlisted as a private in the Mexican War.* = **join up**, join, enter (into), register, volunteer, sign up, enrol **2** *I had to enlist the help of several neighbours to clear the mess.* = **obtain**, get, gain, secure, engage, procure

enliven VERB = **cheer up**, excite, inspire, cheer, spark, enhance, stimulate, wake up, animate, fire, rouse, brighten, exhilarate, quicken, hearten, perk up, liven up, buoy up, pep up, invigorate, gladden, vitalize, vivify, inspirit, make more exciting, make more lively ■ OPPOSITE: subdue

en masse ADVERB = **all together**, together, as one, as a whole, ensemble, as a group, in a group, all at once, in a mass, as a body, in a body

enmity NOUN = **hostility**, hate, spite, hatred, bitterness, friction, malice, animosity, aversion, venom, antagonism, antipathy, acrimony, rancour, bad blood, ill will, animus, malevolence, malignity ■ OPPOSITE: friendship

ennoble VERB **1** *the sciences and arts, which ennoble and embellish human life* = **dignify**, honour, enhance, elevate, magnify, raise, glorify, exalt, aggrandize **2** *He had been ennobled for arranging a government loan in 1836.*

= **raise to the peerage**, kick upstairs (*informal*), make noble

ennui NOUN = **boredom**, dissatisfaction, tiredness, the doldrums, lethargy, tedium, lassitude, listlessness

enormity NOUN **1** *I was appalled by the enormity of the task ahead of us.* = **hugeness**, extent, magnitude, greatness, vastness, immensity, massiveness, enormousness, extensiveness **2** *the enormity of the crime they had committed* = **wickedness**, disgrace, atrocity, depravity, viciousness, villainy, turpitude (*formal*), outrageousness, baseness, vileness, evilness, monstrousness, heinousness, nefariousness, atrociousness **3** *the horrific enormities perpetrated on the islanders* = **atrocity**, crime, horror, evil, outrage, disgrace, monstrosity, abomination, barbarity, villainy

enormous ADJECTIVE = **huge**, massive, vast, extensive, tremendous, gross, excessive, immense, titanic, jumbo (*informal*), gigantic, monstrous, mammoth, colossal, mountainous, stellar (*informal*), prodigious, gargantuan, elephantine, astronomic, ginormous (*informal*), Brobdingnagian, humongous *or* humungous (*informal*), supersize ■ OPPOSITE: tiny

enough ADJECTIVE *They had enough money for a one-way ticket.* = **sufficient**, adequate, ample, abundant, as much as you need, as much as is necessary ▶ PRONOUN *I hope you brought enough for everyone.* = **sufficiency**, plenty, sufficient, abundance, adequacy, right amount, ample supply ▶ ADVERB *Do you think sentences for criminals are tough enough already?* = **sufficiently**, amply, fairly, moderately, reasonably, adequately, satisfactorily, abundantly, tolerably, passably

enquire *see* **inquire**

enquiry *see* **inquiry**

enrage VERB = **anger**, provoke, irritate, infuriate, aggravate (*informal*), incense, gall, madden, inflame, exasperate, incite, antagonize, make you angry, nark (*Brit.*, *Austral. & N.Z. slang*), make your blood boil, get your back up, make you see red (*informal*), put your back up ■ OPPOSITE: calm

enraged ADJECTIVE = **furious**, cross, wild, angry, angered, mad (*informal*), raging, irritated, fuming, choked, infuriated, aggravated (*informal*), incensed, inflamed, exasperated, very angry, irate, livid (*informal*), incandescent, on the warpath, fit to be tied (*slang*), boiling mad, raging

mad, tooshie (*Austral. slang*), off the air (*Austral. slang*)

enraptured ADJECTIVE = **enchanted**, delighted, charmed, fascinated, absorbed, entranced, captivated, transported, enthralled, beguiled, bewitched, ravished, spellbound, enamoured

enrich VERB **1** *A good book can enrich someone's life for ever.* = **enhance**, develop, improve, boost, supplement, refine, cultivate, heighten, endow, augment, ameliorate, aggrandize **2** *He enriched himself at the expense of others.* = **make rich**, make wealthy, make affluent, make prosperous, make well-off

enrol *or* (*U.S.*) **enroll** VERB **1** *To enrol for the conference, fill in the attached form.* = **enlist**, register, be accepted, be admitted, join up, matriculate, put your name down for, sign up *or* on **2** *I thought I'd enrol you with an art group at the school.* = **recruit**, take on, engage, enlist

enrolment *or* (*U.S.*) **enrollment** NOUN = **enlistment**, admission, acceptance, engagement, registration, recruitment, matriculation, signing on *or* up

en route ADVERB = **on** *or* **along the way**, travelling, on the road, in transit, on the journey

ensemble NOUN **1** *an ensemble of young musicians* = **group**, company, band, troupe, cast, orchestra, chorus, supporting cast **2** *The state is an ensemble of political and social structures.* = **collection**, set, body, whole, total, sum, combination, entity, aggregate, entirety, totality, assemblage, conglomeration **3** *a dashing ensemble in navy and white* = **outfit**, suit, get-up (*informal*), costume

enshrine VERB = **preserve**, protect, treasure, cherish, revere, exalt, consecrate, embalm, sanctify, hallow, apotheosize

ensign NOUN = **flag**, standard, colours, banner, badge, pennant, streamer, jack, pennon

enslave VERB = **subjugate**, bind, dominate, trap, suppress, enthral, yoke, tyrannize, sell into slavery, reduce to slavery, enchain

ensnare VERB = **trap**, catch, capture, seize, snarl, embroil, net, snare, entangle, entrap, enmesh

ensue VERB = **follow**, result, develop, succeed, proceed, arise, stem, derive, come after, issue, befall, flow, come next, come to pass (*archaic*), supervene, be consequent on, turn out *or* up ■ OPPOSITE: come first

ensure *or* (*esp. U.S.*) **insure** VERB **1** *Steps must be taken to ensure this never happens again.* = **make certain**, guarantee, secure, make sure, confirm, warrant, certify **2** *The plan is aimed at ensuring the future of freshwater fish species.* = **protect**, defend, secure, safeguard, guard, make safe

entail VERB = **involve**, require, cause, produce, demand, lead to, call for, occasion (*formal*), need, impose, result in, bring about, give rise to, encompass, necessitate

entangle VERB **1** *The door handle had entangled itself with the strap of her bag.* = **tangle**, catch, trap, twist, knot, mat, mix up, snag, snarl, snare, jumble, ravel, trammel, enmesh ■ **OPPOSITE:** disentangle **2** *Bureaucracy can entangle ventures for months.* = **embroil**, involve, complicate, mix up, muddle, implicate, bog down, enmesh

entanglement NOUN = **becoming entangled**, mix-up, becoming enmeshed, becoming ensnared, becoming jumbled, entrapment, snarl-up (*informal, chiefly Brit.*), ensnarement

enter VERB **1** *He entered and stood near the door.* = **come** or **go in** or **into**, arrive, set foot in somewhere, cross the threshold of somewhere, make an entrance ■ **OPPOSITE:** exit **2** *The bullet entered his right eye.* = **penetrate**, get in, insert into, pierce, pass into, perforate **3** *She entered the company as a junior trainee.* = **join**, start work at, begin work at, sign up for, enrol in, become a member of, enlist in, commit yourself to ■ **OPPOSITE:** leave **4** *A million young people enter the labour market each year.* = **participate in**, join (in), be involved in, get involved in, play a part in, partake in, associate yourself with, start to be in **5** *I have entered a new phase in my life.* = **begin**, start, take up, move into, set about, commence, set out on, embark upon **6** *As a boy he entered many music competitions.* = **compete in**, contest, take part in, join in, fight, sign up for, go in for **7** *Prue entered the passage in her notebook, then read it aloud again.* = **record**, note, register, log, list, write down, take down, inscribe, set down, put in writing **8** *I entered a plea of guilty to the charges.* = **submit**, offer, present, table (*Brit.*), register, lodge, tender, put forward, proffer

enterprise NOUN **1** *There are plenty of small industrial enterprises.* = **firm**, company, business, concern, operation, organization, establishment, commercial undertaking **2** *Horse breeding is a risky enterprise.* = **venture**, operation, project, adventure, undertaking, programme, pursuit, endeavour **3** *His trouble is that he lacks enterprise.* = **initiative**, energy, spirit, resource, daring, enthusiasm, push

(*informal*), imagination, drive, pep, readiness, vigour, zeal, ingenuity, originality, eagerness, audacity, boldness, get-up-and-go (*informal*), alertness, resourcefulness, gumption (*informal*), adventurousness, imaginativeness

enterprising ADJECTIVE = **resourceful**, original, spirited, keen, active, daring, alert, eager, bold, enthusiastic, vigorous, imaginative, energetic, adventurous, ingenious, up-and-coming, audacious, zealous, intrepid, venturesome

entertain VERB **1** *He entertained us with anecdotes about his job.* = **amuse**, interest, please, delight, occupy, charm, enthral, cheer, divert, recreate (*rare*), regale, give pleasure to **2** *I don't really like to entertain guests any more.* = **show hospitality to**, receive, accommodate, treat, put up, lodge, be host to, have company of, invite round, ask round, invite to a meal, ask for a meal **3** *I wouldn't entertain the idea of doing such a job.* = **consider**, support, maintain, imagine, think about, hold, foster, harbour, contemplate, conceive of, ponder, cherish, bear in mind, keep in mind, think over, muse over, give thought to, cogitate on, allow yourself to consider

entertaining ADJECTIVE = **enjoyable**, interesting, pleasing, funny, charming, cheering, pleasant, amusing, diverting, delightful, witty, humorous, pleasurable, recreative (*rare*)

entertainment NOUN **1** *I play the piano purely for my own entertainment.* = **enjoyment**, fun, pleasure, leisure, satisfaction, relaxation, recreation, distraction, amusement, diversion **2** *He organized entertainments and events for elderly people.* = **pastime**, show, sport, performance, play, treat, presentation, leisure activity, beer and skittles

enthral or (*U.S.*) **enthrall** VERB = **engross**, charm, grip, fascinate, absorb, entrance, bewitch, intrigue, enchant, rivet, captivate, beguile, ravish, mesmerize, hypnotize, enrapture, hold spellbound, spellbind

enthralling ADJECTIVE = **engrossing**, charming, gripping, fascinating, entrancing, compelling, intriguing, compulsive, enchanting, riveting, captivating, beguiling, mesmerizing, hypnotizing, spellbinding

enthusiasm NOUN **1** *Her lack of enthusiasm filled me with disappointment.* = **keenness**, interest, passion, excitement, warmth, motivation, relish, devotion, zeal, zest, fervour, eagerness, ardour, vehemence, earnestness, zing (*informal*), avidity

2 *the current enthusiasm for skateboarding*
= **interest**, passion, rage, hobby, obsession, craze, fad (*informal*), mania, hobbyhorse

enthusiast NOUN = **fan**, supporter, lover, follower, addict, freak (*informal*), admirer, buff (*informal*), fanatic, devotee, fiend (*informal*), adherent, zealot, aficionado, groupie (*slang*)

enthusiastic ADJECTIVE = **keen**, earnest, spirited, committed, excited, devoted, warm, eager, lively, passionate, vigorous, ardent, hearty, exuberant, avid, fervent, zealous, ebullient, vehement, wholehearted, full of beans (*informal*), fervid, keen as mustard, bright-eyed and bushy-tailed (*informal*)
■ **OPPOSITE:** apathetic

entice VERB = **lure**, attract, invite, persuade, draw, tempt, induce, seduce, lead on, coax, beguile, allure, cajole, decoy, wheedle, prevail on, inveigle, dangle a carrot in front of

enticing ADJECTIVE = **attractive**, appealing, inviting, charming, fascinating, tempting, intriguing, irresistible, persuasive, seductive, captivating, beguiling, alluring
■ **OPPOSITE:** unattractive

entire ADJECTIVE **1** *He had spent his entire life in China as a doctor.* = **continuous**, unified, unbroken, uninterrupted, undivided
2 *Treatment is more effective if the entire family is involved.* = **whole**, full, complete, total
3 *He assured me of his entire confidence in me.*
= **absolute**, full, total, utter, outright, thorough, unqualified, unrestricted, undiminished, unmitigated, unreserved
4 *No document is entire, and it is often unclear in what order the pieces fit together.* = **intact**, whole, perfect, unmarked, unbroken, sound, unharmed, undamaged, without a scratch, unmarred

entirely ADVERB **1** *The two cases are entirely different.* = **completely**, totally, perfectly, absolutely, fully, altogether, thoroughly, wholly, utterly, every inch, without exception, unreservedly, in every respect, without reservation, lock, stock and barrel
■ **OPPOSITE:** partly **2** *The whole episode was entirely my fault.* = **only**, exclusively, solely

entirety NOUN = **whole**, total, sum, unity, aggregate, totality

entitle VERB **1** *Your contract entitles you to a full refund.* = **give the right to**, allow, enable, permit, sanction, license, qualify for, warrant, authorize, empower, enfranchise, make eligible **2** *an instrumental piece entitled 'Changing States'* = **call**, name, title, term, style, label, dub, designate, characterize, christen, give the title of, denominate

entity NOUN **1** *the concept of the earth as a living entity* = **thing**, being, body (*informal*), individual, object, presence, existence, substance, quantity, creature, organism **2** *key periods of national or cultural entity and development* = **essential nature**, being, existence, essence, quintessence, real nature, quiddity (*Philosophy*)

entomb VERB = **bury**, inter, lay to rest, sepulchre, place in a tomb, inhume, inurn

entourage NOUN = **retinue**, company, following, staff, court, train, suite, escort, cortege

entrails PLURAL NOUN = **intestines**, insides (*informal*), guts, bowels, offal, internal organs, innards (*informal*), vital organs, viscera

entrance¹ NOUN **1** *He drove in through a side entrance.* = **way in**, opening, door, approach, access, entry, gate, passage, avenue, doorway, portal (*literary*), inlet, ingress, means of access ■ **OPPOSITE:** exit **2** *The audience chanted his name as he made his entrance.* = **appearance**, coming in, entry, arrival, introduction, ingress ■ **OPPOSITE:** exit **3** *Hewitt gained entrance to the house by pretending to be a heating engineer.*
= **admission**, access, entry, entrée, admittance, permission to enter, ingress, right of entry

entrance² VERB **1** *She entranced the audience with her classical Indian singing.* = **enchant**, delight, charm, absorb, fascinate, dazzle, captivate, transport, enthral, beguile, bewitch, ravish, gladden, enrapture, spellbind ■ **OPPOSITE:** bore **2** *The sailors were entranced by the voices of the sirens.*
= **mesmerize**, bewitch, hypnotize, put a spell on, cast a spell on, put in a trance

entrant NOUN **1** *the newest entrant to the political scene* = **newcomer**, novice, initiate, beginner, trainee, apprentice, convert, new member, fresher, neophyte (*formal*), tyro, probationer **2** *All items submitted for the competition must be the entrant's own work.*
= **competitor**, player, candidate, entry, participant, applicant, contender, contestant

entrap VERB **1** *They tried to entrap us into breaking the law.* = **trick**, lure, seduce, entice, deceive, implicate, lead on, embroil, beguile, allure, entangle, ensnare, inveigle, set a trap for, enmesh **2** *The whale's mouth contains filters which entrap plankton.* = **catch**, net, capture, trap, snare, entangle, ensnare

entreaty NOUN = **plea**, appeal, suit, request, prayer, petition, exhortation (*formal*), solicitation, supplication (*formal*), importunity, earnest request

entrench or **intrench** VERB = **fix**, set, establish, plant, seat, settle, root, install, lodge, anchor, implant, embed, dig in, ensconce, ingrain

entrenched or **intrenched** ADJECTIVE = **fixed**, set, firm, rooted, well-established, ingrained, deep-seated, deep-rooted, indelible, unshakeable or unshakable, ineradicable

entrepreneur NOUN = **businessperson**, tycoon, director, executive, contractor, industrialist, financier, speculator, magnate, impresario, business executive

entrust or **intrust** VERB **1** *her reluctance to entrust her children to the care of someone else* = **give custody of**, trust, deliver, commit, delegate, hand over, turn over, confide (*formal*), commend (*formal*), consign **2** (*usually with* **with**) *They are prepared to entrust him with the leadership of the party.* = **assign**, charge (*formal*), trust, invest, authorize

entry NOUN **1** *Entry to the museum is free.* = **admission**, access, entrance, admittance, entrée, permission to enter, right of entry **2** *He made his triumphal entry into Mexico.* = **coming in**, entering, appearance, arrival, entrance ■ **OPPOSITE:** exit **3** *rites of passage which mark entry into adult life* = **introduction**, presentation, initiation, inauguration, induction, debut, investiture **4** *Her diary entry for that day records his visit.* = **record**, listing, account, note, minute, statement, item, registration, memo, memorandum, jotting **5** *The winner was selected from hundreds of entries.* = **competitor**, player, attempt, effort, candidate, participant, challenger, submission, entrant, contestant **6** *A lorry blocked the entry to the school.* = **way in**, opening, door, approach, access, gate, passage, entrance, avenue, doorway, portal (*literary*), inlet, passageway, ingress, means of access

entwine or **intwine** VERB = **twist**, surround, embrace, weave, knit, braid, encircle, wind, intertwine, interweave, plait, twine, ravel, interlace, entwist (*archaic*) ■ **OPPOSITE:** disentangle

enumerate VERB **1** *She enumerated all the reasons why she wanted to leave him.* = **list**, tell, name, detail, relate, mention, quote, cite, specify, spell out, recount, recite, itemize, recapitulate **2** *They enumerated the casualties.* = **count**, calculate, sum up, total, reckon, compute, add up, tally, number

enunciate VERB **1** *She enunciated each word slowly and carefully.* = **pronounce**, say, speak, voice, sound, utter, articulate, vocalize, enounce (*formal*) **2** *He was always ready to enunciate his views to anyone who would listen.* = **state**, declare, proclaim, pronounce, publish, promulgate, propound

envelop VERB = **enclose**, cover, hide, surround, wrap around, embrace, blanket, conceal, obscure, veil, encompass, engulf, cloak, shroud, swathe, encircle, encase, swaddle, sheathe, enfold, enwrap

envelope NOUN = **wrapping**, casing, case, covering, cover, skin, shell, coating, jacket, sleeve, sheath, wrapper

enviable ADJECTIVE = **desirable**, favoured, privileged, fortunate, lucky, blessed, advantageous, to die for (*informal*), much to be desired, covetable
■ **OPPOSITE:** undesirable

envious ADJECTIVE = **covetous**, jealous, grudging, malicious, resentful, green-eyed, begrudging, spiteful, jaundiced, green with envy

environment NOUN **1** *The children were brought up in completely different environments.* = **surroundings**, setting, conditions, situation, medium, scene (*informal*), circumstances, territory, background, atmosphere, context, habitat, domain, milieu, locale **2** *the maintenance of a safe environment for marine mammals* = **habitat**, home, surroundings, territory, terrain, locality, natural home

environmental ADJECTIVE = **ecological**, green, eco-friendly

environmentalist NOUN = **conservationist**, ecologist, green, friend of the earth

environs PLURAL NOUN = **surrounding area**, surroundings, district, suburbs, neighbourhood, outskirts, precincts, vicinity, locality, purlieus

envisage VERB **1** *I can't envisage being married to someone like him.* = **imagine**, contemplate, conceive (of), visualize, picture, fancy, think up, conceptualize **2** *Scientists envisage a major breakthrough in the next few years.* = **foresee**, see, expect, predict, anticipate, envision

envision VERB = **conceive of**, expect, imagine, predict, anticipate, see, contemplate, envisage, foresee, visualize

envoy NOUN **1** *A French envoy arrived in Beirut on Sunday.* = **ambassador**, minister, diplomat, emissary, legate, plenipotentiary **2** *the Secretary General's personal envoy* = **messenger**, agent, deputy, representative, delegate, courier, intermediary, emissary

envy NOUN *He admitted his feelings of envy towards his brother.* = **covetousness**, spite, hatred, resentment, jealousy, bitterness, malice, ill will, malignity, resentfulness, enviousness (*informal*) ▶ VERB **1** *I have a famous brother and a lot of people envy me for that.* = **be jealous (of)**, resent, begrudge, be envious (of) **2** *He envied her peace of mind.* = **covet**, desire, crave, aspire to, yearn for, hanker after

ephemeral ADJECTIVE = **transient**, short, passing, brief, temporary, fleeting, short-lived, fugitive, flitting, momentary, transitory, evanescent (*formal*), impermanent, fugacious ■ **OPPOSITE:** eternal

epidemic ADJECTIVE *The crisis was reaching epidemic proportions.* = **widespread**, wide-ranging, general, sweeping, prevailing, rampant, prevalent, rife, pandemic ▶ NOUN **1** *A flu epidemic is sweeping through Britain.* = **outbreak**, plague, growth, spread, scourge, contagion **2** *an epidemic of crimes* = **spate**, plague, outbreak, wave, rash, eruption, upsurge

epilogue NOUN = **conclusion**, postscript, coda, afterword, concluding speech ■ **OPPOSITE:** prologue

episode NOUN **1** *an unhappy episode in my life* = **event**, experience, happening, matter, affair, incident, circumstance, adventure, business, occurrence, escapade **2** *The final episode will be shown next Saturday.* = **instalment**, part, act, scene, section, chapter, passage, webisode

episodic *or* **episodical** ADJECTIVE **1** *episodic attacks of fever* = **irregular**, occasional, sporadic, intermittent **2** *an episodic narrative of unrelated characters* = **disconnected**, irregular, rambling, anecdotal, disjointed, wandering, discursive, digressive

epistle NOUN = **letter**, note, message, communication, missive

epitaph NOUN **1** *a fitting epitaph for a great man* = **commemoration**, elegy, obituary **2** *His words are carved as his epitaph on the headstone of his grave.* = **inscription**, engraving

epithet NOUN **1** *players who fitted their manager's epithet of 'headless chickens'* = **name**, title, description, tag, nickname, designation, appellation (*formal*), sobriquet, moniker *or* monicker (*slang*) **2** *a stream of obscene epithets* = **curse**, obscenity, blasphemy, swear word, imprecation (*formal*)

epitome NOUN = **personification**, essence, embodiment, type, representation, norm, archetype, exemplar, typical example, quintessence

epitomize VERB = **typify**, represent, illustrate, embody, exemplify, symbolize, personify, incarnate

epoch NOUN = **era**, time, age, period, date, aeon

equal ADJECTIVE **1** (*often with* **to** *or* **with**) *a population having equal numbers of men and women* = **identical**, the same, matched, matching, like, equivalent, uniform, alike, corresponding, tantamount, one and the same, proportionate, commensurate ■ **OPPOSITE:** unequal **2** *Women demand equal rights with men.* = **fair**, just, impartial, egalitarian, unbiased, even-handed, equable ■ **OPPOSITE:** unfair **3** *an equal contest* = **even**, balanced, fifty-fifty (*informal*), evenly matched, evenly balanced, evenly proportioned ■ **OPPOSITE:** uneven **4** (*with* **to**) *She wanted to show she was equal to any test they gave her.* = **capable of**, adequate for ▶ NOUN *She was one of the boys, their equal.* = **match**, equivalent, fellow, twin, mate, peer, parallel, counterpart, compeer ▶ VERB **1** *The average pay rise equalled 1.41 times inflation.* = **amount to**, make, come to, total, balance, agree with, level, parallel, tie with, equate, correspond to, be equal to, square with, be tantamount to, equalize, tally with, be level with, be even with ■ **OPPOSITE:** be unequal to **2** *The victory equalled Scotland's best in history.* = **be equal to**, match, reach, rival, come up to, be level with, be even with **3** *No amount of money can equal memories like that.* = **be as good as**, match, compare with, equate with, measure up to, be as great as

equality NOUN **1** *the principle of racial equality* = **fairness**, equal opportunity, equal treatment, egalitarianism, fair treatment, justness ■ **OPPOSITE:** inequality **2** *They advocate the unconditional equality of incomes.* = **sameness**, balance, identity, similarity, correspondence, parity, likeness, uniformity, equivalence, evenness, coequality, equatability ■ **OPPOSITE:** disparity

equalize VERB **1** *Such measures are needed to equalize wage rates between countries.* = **make equal**, match, level, balance, square, equal, smooth, equate, standardize, even out, even up, regularize, make level **2** *Brazil equalized with only 16 minutes remaining.* = **draw level**, level the score, square the score, make the score level

equanimity NOUN = **composure**, peace, calm, poise, serenity, tranquillity, coolness, aplomb, calmness, phlegm, steadiness, presence of mind, sang-froid, self-possession, placidity, level-headedness, imperturbability

equate VERB **1** *I equate suits with power and authority.* = **identify**, associate, connect, compare, relate, mention in the same breath, think of in connection with, think of together **2** *relying on arbitrage to equate prices between the various stock exchanges* = **make equal**, match, balance, square, even up, equalize

equation NOUN = **equating**, match, agreement, balancing, pairing, comparison, parallel, equality, correspondence, likeness, equivalence, equalization

equestrian ADJECTIVE = **riding**, mounted, horse riding

equilibrium NOUN **1** *For the economy to be in equilibrium, income must equal expenditure.* = **stability**, balance, symmetry, steadiness, evenness, equipoise, counterpoise **2** *I paused and took deep breaths to restore my equilibrium.* = **composure**, calm, stability, poise, serenity, coolness, calmness, equanimity, steadiness, self-possession, collectedness

equip VERB **1** *The country did not have the funds to equip the reserve army properly.* = **supply**, provide, stock, dress, outfit, arm, rig, array, furnish, endow, attire, fit out, deck out, kit out, fit up, accoutre **2** *Our aim is to provide courses which equip students for future employment.* = **prepare**, qualify, educate, get ready, endow

equipment NOUN = **apparatus**, stock, supplies, material, stuff, tackle, gear, tools, provisions, kit, rig, baggage, paraphernalia, accoutrements, appurtenances, equipage

equitable ADJECTIVE = **even-handed**, just, right, fair, due, reasonable, proper, honest, impartial, rightful, unbiased, dispassionate, proportionate, unprejudiced, nondiscriminatory

equity NOUN = **fairness**, justice, integrity, honesty, fair play, righteousness, impartiality, rectitude, reasonableness, even-handedness, fair-mindedness, uprightness, equitableness
■ **OPPOSITE:** unfairness

equivalence or **equivalency** NOUN = **equality**, correspondence, agreement, similarity, identity, parallel, match, parity, conformity, likeness, sameness, parallelism, evenness, synonymy, alikeness, interchangeableness

equivalent ADJECTIVE *One hand is equivalent to four inches.* = **equal**, even, same, comparable, parallel, identical, alike, corresponding, correspondent, synonymous, of a kind, tantamount, interchangeable, of a piece with, commensurate, homologous
■ **OPPOSITE:** different ▶ NOUN RTE,

the Irish equivalent of the BBC = **equal**, counterpart, correspondent, twin, peer, parallel, match, opposite number

equivocal ADJECTIVE = **ambiguous**, uncertain, misleading, obscure, suspicious, vague, doubtful, dubious, questionable, ambivalent, indefinite, evasive, oblique, indeterminate, prevaricating, oracular
■ **OPPOSITE:** clear

era NOUN = **age**, time, period, stage, date, generation, cycle, epoch, aeon, day *or* days

eradicate VERB = **wipe out**, eliminate, remove, destroy, get rid of, abolish, erase, excise, extinguish, stamp out, obliterate, uproot, weed out, annihilate, put paid to, root out, efface, exterminate, expunge (*formal*), extirpate, wipe from the face of the earth

eradication NOUN = **wiping out**, abolition, destruction, elimination, removal, extinction, extermination, annihilation, erasure, obliteration, effacement, extirpation, expunction

erase VERB **1** *They are desperate to erase the memory of their defeat.* = **delete**, cancel out, wipe out, remove, eradicate, excise, obliterate, efface, blot out, expunge (*formal*) **2** *She erased the words from the blackboard.* = **rub out**, remove, wipe out, delete, scratch out

e-reader or **eReader** NOUN = **electronic book**, e-book or ebook, book

erect ADJECTIVE *Her head was erect and her back was straight.* = **upright**, raised, straight, standing, stiff, firm, rigid, vertical, elevated, perpendicular, pricked-up
■ **OPPOSITE:** bent ▶ VERB **1** *Demonstrators have erected barricades in the roads.* = **build**, raise, set up, lift, pitch, mount, stand up, rear, construct, put up, assemble, put together, elevate ■ **OPPOSITE:** demolish **2** *the edifice of free trade which has been erected since the war* = **found**, establish, form, create, set up, institute, organize, put up, initiate

erection NOUN *the erection of temporary fencing to protect hedges under repair* = **building**, setting-up, manufacture, construction, assembly, creation, establishment, elevation, fabrication

ergo CONJUNCTION = **therefore**, so, then, thus, hence, consequently, accordingly, for that reason, in consequence

erode VERB **1** *The beach had all but totally eroded.* = **disintegrate**, crumble, deteriorate, corrode, break up, grind down, waste away, wear down *or* away **2** *Once exposed, soil is quickly eroded by wind and rain.* = **destroy**, consume, spoil, crumble, eat away, corrode, break up, grind down, abrade, wear down or away **3** *His fumbling of the issue of reform has eroded his authority.* = **weaken**, destroy, undermine, diminish, impair, lessen, wear away

erosion NOUN **1** *erosion of the river valleys* = **disintegration**, deterioration, corrosion, corrasion, wearing down or away, grinding down **2** *an erosion of moral standards* = **deterioration**, wearing, undermining, destruction, consumption, weakening, spoiling, attrition, eating away, abrasion, grinding down, wearing down or away

erotic ADJECTIVE = **sexual**, sexy (*informal*), crude, explicit, rousing, sensual, seductive, vulgar, stimulating, steamy (*informal*), suggestive, aphrodisiac, carnal, titillating, bawdy, lustful, sexually arousing, erogenous, amatory

err VERB **1** *The contractors seriously erred in their original estimates.* = **make a mistake**, mistake, go wrong, blunder, slip up (*informal*), misjudge, be incorrect, be inaccurate, miscalculate, go astray, be in error, put your foot in it (*informal*), misapprehend, blot your copybook (*informal*), drop a brick or clanger (*informal*) **2** *If he errs again, he will be severely punished.* = **sin**, fall, offend, lapse, trespass, do wrong, deviate, misbehave, go astray, transgress, be out of order, blot your copybook (*informal*)

errand NOUN = **job**, charge, commission, message (*Scot.*), task, mission

errant ADJECTIVE = **sinning**, offending, straying, wayward, deviant, erring, aberrant

erratic ADJECTIVE = **unpredictable**, variable, unstable, irregular, shifting, eccentric, abnormal, inconsistent, uneven, unreliable, wayward, capricious, desultory, changeable, aberrant, fitful, inconstant ■ **OPPOSITE:** regular

erroneous ADJECTIVE = **incorrect**, wrong, mistaken, false, flawed, faulty, inaccurate, untrue, invalid, unfounded, spurious, amiss, unsound, wide of the mark, inexact, fallacious ■ **OPPOSITE:** correct

error NOUN = **mistake**, slip, fault, blunder, flaw, boob (*Brit. slang*), delusion, oversight, misconception, fallacy, inaccuracy, howler (*informal*), bloomer (*Brit. informal*), miscalculation, misapprehension, solecism (*formal*), erratum, barry or Barry Crocker (*Austral. slang*), boner (*slang, chiefly U.S.*)

ersatz ADJECTIVE = **artificial**, substitute, pretend, fake, imitation, synthetic, bogus, simulated, sham, counterfeit, spurious, phoney or phony (*informal*)

erstwhile ADJECTIVE = **former**, old, late, previous, once, past, ex (*informal*), one-time, sometime, bygone, quondam

erudite ADJECTIVE = **learned**, lettered, cultured, educated, scholarly, cultivated, knowledgeable, literate, well-educated, well-read ■ **OPPOSITE:** uneducated

erudition NOUN = **learning**, education, knowledge, scholarship, letters, lore, academic knowledge

erupt VERB **1** *The volcano erupted in 1980.* = **explode**, blow up, flare up, emit lava **2** *Lava erupted from the volcano and flowed over the ridge.* = **gush**, burst out, be ejected, burst forth, pour forth, belch forth, spew forth or out **3** *Heavy fighting erupted again two days after the cease-fire.* = **start**, break out, begin, explode, flare up, burst out, boil over **4** *My skin erupted in pimples.* = **break out**, appear, flare up

eruption NOUN **1** *the volcanic eruption of Tambora in 1815* = **explosion**, discharge, outburst, venting, ejection **2** *the sudden eruption of violence on the streets of the city* = **flare-up**, outbreak, sally **3** *an unpleasant eruption of boils* = **inflammation**, outbreak, rash, flare-up

escalate VERB **1** *Unions and management fear the dispute could escalate.* = **grow**, increase, extend, intensify, expand, surge, be increased, mount, heighten ■ **OPPOSITE:** decrease **2** *Defeat could cause one side or the other to escalate the conflict.* = **increase**, develop, extend, intensify, expand, build up, step up, heighten, enlarge, magnify, amplify ■ **OPPOSITE:** lessen

escalation NOUN = **increase**, rise, build-up, expansion, heightening, developing, acceleration, upsurge, intensification, amplification

escapade NOUN = **adventure**, fling, stunt, romp, trick, scrape (*informal*), spree, mischief, lark (*informal*), caper, prank, antic

escape VERB **1** *A prisoner has escaped from a jail in Northern England.* = **get away**, flee, take off, fly, bolt, skip, slip away, abscond, decamp, hook it (*slang*), do a runner (*slang*), do a bunk (*Brit. slang*), fly the coop (*U.S. & Canad. informal*), make a break for it, slip through your fingers, skedaddle (*informal*), take a powder (*U.S. & Canad. slang*), make your getaway, take it on the lam (*U.S. & Canad. slang*), break free or out, make or effect your escape, run away or off, do a Skase (*Austral. informal*) **2** *He was lucky to escape serious injury.* = **avoid**, miss, evade, dodge, shun, elude, duck (*informal*), steer clear of, circumvent (*formal*), body-swerve **3** *an actor whose name escapes me for the* moment = **be forgotten by**, be beyond (someone), baffle, elude, puzzle, stump **4** (usually with **from**) Leave a vent open to let some of the moist air escape. = **leak out**, flow out, drain away, discharge, gush out, emanate, seep out, exude, spurt out, spill out, pour forth ▶ NOUN **1** He made his escape from the country. = **getaway**, break, flight, break-out, bolt, decampment **2** his narrow escape from bankruptcy = **avoidance**, evasion, circumvention, elusion **3** For me television is an escape. = **relaxation**, relief, recreation, distraction, diversion, pastime **4** You should report any suspected gas escape immediately. = **leak**, emission, discharge, outpouring, gush, spurt, outflow, leakage, drain, seepage, issue, emanation, efflux, effluence, outpour

eschew VERB = **avoid**, give up, abandon, have nothing to do with, shun, elude, renounce, refrain from, forgo, abstain from, fight shy of, forswear, abjure, kick (informal), swear off, give a wide berth to, keep or steer clear of

escort NOUN **1** He arrived with a police escort. = **guard**, protection, safeguard, bodyguard, company, train, convoy, entourage, retinue, cortege **2** My sister needed an escort for a company dinner. = **companion**, partner, attendant, guide, squire (rare), protector, beau (old-fashioned), chaperon ▶ VERB I escorted him to the door. = **accompany**, lead, partner, conduct, guide, guard, shepherd, convoy, usher, squire (old-fashioned), hold (someone's) hand, chaperon

esoteric ADJECTIVE = **obscure**, private, secret, hidden, inner, mysterious, mystical, mystic, occult, arcane, hypermetric, cryptic, inscrutable, abstruse, recondite, cabbalistic

especially ADVERB **1** The group is said to be gaining support, especially in the rural areas. = **notably**, largely, chiefly, mainly, mostly, principally, strikingly, conspicuously, outstandingly **2** Giving up smoking can be especially difficult. = **very**, specially, particularly, signally, extremely, remarkably, unusually, exceptionally, extraordinarily, markedly, supremely, uncommonly **3** The system we design will be especially for you. = **particularly**, expressly, exclusively, precisely, specifically, uniquely, peculiarly, singularly

espionage NOUN = **spying**, intelligence, surveillance, counter-intelligence, undercover work

espouse VERB = **support**, back, champion, promote, maintain, defend, adopt, take up, advocate, embrace, uphold, stand up for

espy VERB = **catch sight of**, see, discover, spot, notice, sight, observe, spy, perceive, detect, glimpse, make out, discern, behold (archaic, literary), catch a glimpse of, descry

essay NOUN **1** He was asked to write an essay about his home town. = **composition**, study, paper, article, piece, assignment, discourse, tract, treatise, dissertation, disquisition **2** My first essay in running a company was a disaster. = **attempt**, go (informal), try, effort, shot (informal), trial, struggle, bid, test, experiment, crack (informal), venture, undertaking, stab (informal), endeavour, exertion ▶ VERB She essayed a smile, but it was a dismal failure. = **attempt**, try, test, take on, undertake, strive for, endeavour, have a go at, try out, have a shot at (informal), have a crack at (informal), have a bash at (informal)

essence NOUN **1** Some claim that Ireland's very essence is expressed through its language. = **fundamental nature**, nature, being, life, meaning, heart, spirit, principle, soul, core, substance, significance, entity, bottom line, essential part, kernel, crux, lifeblood, pith, quintessence, basic characteristic, quiddity **2** Add a few drops of vanilla essence. = **concentrate**, spirits, extract, elixir, tincture, distillate • **in essence** In essence, we share the same ideology. = **essentially**, materially, virtually, basically, fundamentally, in effect, substantially, in the main, to all intents and purposes, in substance • **of the essence** Time is of the essence with this project. = **vitally important**, essential, vital, critical, crucial (informal), key, indispensable, of the utmost importance

essential ADJECTIVE **1** It is absolutely essential that we find this man quickly. = **vital**, important, needed, necessary, critical, crucial (informal), key, indispensable, requisite, vitally important, must-have ■ OPPOSITE: unimportant **2** Two essential elements must be proven: motive and opportunity. = **fundamental**, main, basic, radical, key, principal, constitutional, cardinal, inherent, elementary, innate, hard-wired, intrinsic, elemental, immanent ■ OPPOSITE: secondary **3** essential oils used in aromatherapy = **concentrated**, extracted, refined, volatile, rectified, distilled ▶ NOUN the essentials of everyday life, such as food and water = **prerequisite**, principle, fundamental, necessity, must, basic, requisite, vital part, sine qua non (Latin), rudiment, must-have

establish VERB **1** They established the school in 1989. = **set up**, found, start, create, institute, organize, install, constitute, inaugurate **2** *An autopsy was being done to establish the cause of death.* = **prove**, show, confirm, demonstrate, ratify, certify, verify, validate, substantiate, corroborate, authenticate **3** *He has established himself as a pivotal figure in US politics.* = **secure**, form, base, ground, plant, settle, fix, root, implant, entrench, ensconce, put down roots

establishment NOUN **1** *discussions to explore the establishment of diplomatic relations* = **creation**, founding, setting up, foundation, institution, organization, formation, installation, inauguration, enactment **2** *Shops and other commercial establishments remained closed today.* = **organization**, company, business, firm, house, concern, operation, structure, institution, institute, corporation, enterprise, outfit (*informal*), premises, setup (*informal*) **3** *a scientific research establishment* = **office**, house, building, plant, quarters, factory

Establishment NOUN • **the Establishment** *the revolution against the Establishment* = **the authorities**, the system, the powers that be, the ruling class, the established order, institutionalized authority

estate NOUN **1** *a shooting party on his estate in Yorkshire* = **lands**, property, area, grounds, domain, manor, holdings, demesne, homestead (*U.S. & Canad.*) **2** *an industrial estate* = **area**, centre, park, development, site, zone, plot **3** *His estate was valued at £100,000.* = **property**, capital, assets, fortune, goods, effects, wealth, possessions, belongings

esteem VERB *a scholar whom he highly esteemed* = **respect**, admire, think highly of, like, love, value, prize, honour, treasure, cherish, revere, reverence, be fond of, venerate, regard highly, take off your hat to ▸ NOUN *He is held in high esteem by his colleagues.* = **respect**, regard, honour, consideration, admiration, reverence, estimation, veneration

estimate VERB **1** *His personal riches were estimated at over £80 million.* = **calculate roughly**, value, guess, judge, reckon, assess, evaluate, gauge, number, appraise **2** *Officials estimate it will be two days before electricity is restored to the island.* = **think**, believe, consider, rate, judge, hold, rank, guess, reckon (*informal*), assess, conjecture, surmise ▸ NOUN **1** *This figure is five times the original estimate.* = **approximate calculation**, guess, reckoning, assessment, judgment, evaluation,

valuation, appraisal, educated guess, guesstimate (*informal*), rough calculation, ballpark figure (*informal*), approximate cost, approximate price, appraisement **2** *I was wrong in my estimate of his capabilities.* = **assessment**, opinion, belief, appraisal, evaluation, conjecture, appraisement, judgment, estimation, surmise

estimation NOUN **1** *He has gone down considerably in my estimation.* = **opinion**, view, regard, belief, honour, credit, consideration, judgment, esteem, evaluation, admiration, reverence, veneration, good opinion, considered opinion **2** *estimations of pre-tax profits of £12.5 million* = **estimate**, reckoning, assessment, appreciation, valuation, appraisal, guesstimate (*informal*), ballpark figure (*informal*)

estrangement NOUN = **alienation**, parting, division, split, withdrawal, break-up, breach, hostility, separation, withholding, disaffection, disunity, dissociation, antagonization

estuary NOUN = **inlet**, mouth, creek, firth, fjord

et cetera *or* **etcetera** ADVERB = **and so on**, and so forth, etc.

> USAGE The literal meaning of the Latin phrase *et cetera* is 'and other things'. The use of *and* in a list ending with *et cetera*, as in *we bought bread, cheese, butter, and et cetera*, is therefore redundant. Nor is there ever any need to repeat the phrase *et cetera* for emphasis at the end of a list. Such repetition, as in *he bought paper, ink, notebooks, et cetera, et cetera* is very informal and should not be used in writing or formal speaking.

etch VERB **1** *a simple band of heavy gold etched with runes* = **engrave**, cut, impress, stamp, carve, imprint, inscribe, furrow, incise, ingrain **2** *The acid etched holes in the surface.* = **corrode**, eat into, burn into

etching NOUN = **print**, impression, carving, engraving, imprint, inscription

eternal ADJECTIVE **1** *the quest for eternal youth* = **everlasting**, lasting, permanent, enduring, endless, perennial, perpetual, timeless, immortal, unending, unchanging, immutable, indestructible, undying, without end, unceasing, imperishable, deathless, sempiternal (*literary*) ■ OPPOSITE: transitory **2** *In the background was that eternal humming noise.* = **interminable**, constant, endless, abiding, infinite, continual, immortal, never-ending, everlasting, ceaseless, unremitting, deathless ■ OPPOSITE: occasional

eternity NOUN **1** *I have always found the thought of eternity terrifying.* = **the afterlife**, heaven (*informal*), paradise, the next world, the hereafter **2** *the idea that our species will survive for all eternity* = **perpetuity**, immortality, infinity, timelessness, endlessness, infinitude, time without end **3** *The war went on for an eternity.* = **ages**, years, an age, centuries, for ever (*informal*), aeons, donkey's years (*informal*), yonks (*informal*), a month of Sundays (*informal*), a long time or while, an age or eternity

ethereal ADJECTIVE **1** *the ethereal world of romantic fiction* = **insubstantial**, light, fairy, aerial, airy, intangible, rarefied, impalpable (*formal*) **2** *the ethereal realm of the divine* = **spiritual**, heavenly (*informal*), unearthly, sublime, celestial, unworldly, empyreal

ethical ADJECTIVE **1** *the ethical dilemmas of genetic engineering* = **moral**, behavioural **2** *Would it be ethical to lie to save a person's life?* = **right**, morally right, morally acceptable, good, just, fitting, fair, responsible, principled, correct, decent, proper, upright, honourable, honest, righteous, virtuous
■ **OPPOSITE:** unethical

ethics PLURAL NOUN = **moral code**, standards, principles, morals, conscience, morality, moral values, moral principles, moral philosophy, rules of conduct, moral beliefs, tikanga (*N.Z.*)

ethnic *or* **ethnical** ADJECTIVE = **cultural**, national, traditional, native, folk, racial, genetic, indigenous

ethos NOUN = **spirit**, character, attitude, beliefs, ethic, tenor, disposition

etiquette NOUN = **good** *or* **proper behaviour**, manners, rules, code, customs, convention, courtesy, usage, protocol, formalities, propriety, politeness, good manners, decorum, civility, politesse, p's and q's, polite behaviour, kawa (*N.Z.*), tikanga (*N.Z.*)

eulogy NOUN = **praise**, tribute, acclaim, compliment, applause, accolade, paean (*literary*), commendation, exaltation, glorification, acclamation, panegyric, encomium, plaudit, laudation

euphoria NOUN = **elation**, joy, ecstasy, bliss, glee, rapture, high spirits, exhilaration, jubilation, intoxication, transport, exaltation, joyousness
■ **OPPOSITE:** despondency

euthanasia NOUN = **assisted suicide**, mercy killing

evacuate VERB **1** *18,000 people have been evacuated from the city.* = **remove**, clear, withdraw, expel, move out, send to a safe place **2** *The residents have evacuated the area.*
= **abandon**, leave, clear, desert, quit, depart (from), withdraw from, pull out of, move out of, relinquish, vacate, forsake, decamp from

evacuation NOUN **1** *an evacuation of the city's four million inhabitants* = **removal**, departure, withdrawal, clearance, flight, expulsion, exodus **2** *a huge blaze that led to a mass evacuation of staff and patients* = **abandonment**, withdrawal from, pulling out, moving out, clearance from, vacation from

evade VERB **1** *He managed to evade the police for six months.* = **avoid**, escape, dodge, get away from, shun, elude, eschew, steer clear of, sidestep, circumvent (*formal*), duck (*informal*), shirk, slip through the net of, escape the clutches of, body-swerve
■ **OPPOSITE:** face **2** *Mr Patel denied that he was evading the question.* = **avoid answering**, parry, circumvent, fend off, balk, cop out of (*slang*), fence, fudge, hedge, prevaricate, flannel (*Brit. informal*), beat about the bush about, equivocate

evaluate VERB = **assess**, rate, value, judge, estimate, rank, reckon, weigh, calculate, gauge, weigh up, appraise, size up (*informal*), assay

evaluation NOUN = **assessment**, rating, judgment, calculation, valuation, appraisal, estimation

evangelical ADJECTIVE = **crusading**, converting, missionary, zealous, revivalist, proselytizing, propagandizing

evaporate VERB **1** *Moisture is drawn to the surface of the fabric so that it evaporates.* = **disappear**, vaporize, dematerialize, evanesce (*formal*), melt, vanish, dissolve, disperse, dry up, dispel, dissipate, fade away, melt away **2** *The water is evaporated by the sun.* = **dry up**, dry, dehydrate, vaporize, desiccate **3** *My anger evaporated and I wanted to cry.* = **fade away**, disappear, fade, melt, vanish, dissolve, disperse, dissipate, melt away

evaporation NOUN **1** *The cooling effect is caused by the evaporation of sweat on the skin.* = **vaporization**, vanishing, disappearance, dispelling, dissolution, fading away, melting away, dispersal, dissipation, evanescence, dematerialization **2** *an increase in evaporation of both lake and ground water* = **drying up**, drying, dehydration, desiccation, vaporization

evasion NOUN **1** *an evasion of responsibility* = **avoidance**, escape, dodging, shirking, cop-out (*slang*), circumvention, elusion **2** *They face accusations from the Opposition Party of evasion and cover-up.* = **deception**, shuffling, cunning, fudging, pretext, ruse, artifice, trickery, subterfuge, equivocation, prevarication, sophistry, evasiveness, obliqueness, sophism

evasive ADJECTIVE **1** *He was evasive about the circumstances of their first meeting.*
= **deceptive**, misleading, indirect, cunning, slippery, tricky, shuffling, devious, oblique, shifty (*informal*), cagey (*informal*), deceitful, dissembling, prevaricating, equivocating, sophistical, casuistic, casuistical, elusive ■ **OPPOSITE:** straightforward **2** *Four high-flying warplanes had to take evasive action.*
= **avoiding**, escaping, circumventing

eve NOUN **1** *the eve of his 27th birthday* = **night before**, day before, vigil **2** *when Europe stood on the eve of war in 1914* = **brink**, point, edge, verge, threshold

even ADJECTIVE **1** *It is important to have an even temperature when you work.* = **regular**, stable, constant, steady, smooth, uniform, unbroken, uninterrupted, unwavering, unvarying, metrical ■ **OPPOSITE:** variable **2** *The tables are fitted with a glass top to provide an even surface.* = **level**, straight, flat, plane, smooth, true, steady, uniform, parallel, flush, horizontal, plumb ■ **OPPOSITE:** uneven **3** *Divide the dough into 12 even pieces.* = **equal**, like, the same, matching, similar, uniform, parallel, identical, comparable, commensurate, coequal ■ **OPPOSITE:** unequal **4** *It was an even game.* = **equally matched**, level, tied, drawn, on a par, neck and neck, fifty-fifty (*informal*), equalized, all square, equally balanced ■ **OPPOSITE:** ill-matched **5** *You don't owe me anything now. We're even.* = **square**, quits, on the same level, on an equal footing **6** *Normally Rosa had an even temper; she was rarely irritable.* = **calm**, stable, steady, composed, peaceful, serene, cool, tranquil, well-balanced, placid, undisturbed, unruffled, imperturbable, equable, even-tempered, unexcitable, equanimous ■ **OPPOSITE:** excitable **7** *We all have an even chance of winning.* = **fair**, just, balanced, equitable, impartial, disinterested, unbiased, dispassionate, fair and square, unprejudiced ■ **OPPOSITE:** unfair ▸ ADVERB **1** *He distrusted me even though I was trying to help him.* = **despite**, in spite of, disregarding, notwithstanding, in spite of the fact that, regardless of the fact that **2** *Stan was speaking even more slowly than usual.* = **all the more**, much, still, yet, to a greater extent, to a greater degree • **even as** *Even as she said this, she knew it was not quite true.* = **while**, just as, whilst, at the time that, at the same time as, exactly as, during the

time that • **even so** *The bus was half empty. Even so, he came and sat next to me.*
= **nevertheless**, still, however, yet, despite that, in spite of (that), nonetheless, all the same, notwithstanding, notwithstanding that, be that as it may • **even something out** *Rates of house price inflation have evened out between the North and South of the country.* = **make** or **become level**, align, level, square, smooth, steady, flatten, stabilize, balance out, regularize • **even something up** *These measures would help to even up the balance of power.* = **equalize**, match, balance, equal • **get even (with)** *I'm going to get even if it's the last thing I do.* = **pay back**, repay, reciprocate, even the score, requite, get your own back, settle the score, take vengeance, take an eye for an eye, be revenged or revenge yourself, give tit for tat, pay (someone) back in their own coin, return like for like

even-handed ADJECTIVE = **fair**, just, balanced, equitable, impartial, disinterested, unbiased, fair and square, unprejudiced

evening NOUN = **dusk** (*archaic*), night, sunset, twilight, sundown, eve, vesper (*archaic*), eventide (*archaic, poetic*), gloaming (*Scot., poetic*), e'en (*archaic, poetic*), close of day, crepuscule, even, evo (*Austral. slang*)

event NOUN **1** *in the wake of recent events in Europe* = **incident**, happening, experience, matter, affair, occasion, proceeding, fact, business, circumstance, episode, adventure, milestone, occurrence, escapade **2** *major sporting events* = **competition**, game, tournament, contest, bout • **in any event** or **at all events** *It is not going to be an easy decision, in any event.* = **whatever happens**, regardless, in any case, no matter what, at any rate, come what may • **in the event of** *The bank will make an immediate refund in the event of any error.* = **in the eventuality of**, in the situation of, in the likelihood of

eventful ADJECTIVE = **exciting**, active, busy, dramatic, remarkable, historic, full, lively, memorable, notable, momentous, fateful, noteworthy, consequential ■ **OPPOSITE:** dull

eventual ADJECTIVE = **final**, later, resulting, future, overall, concluding, ultimate, prospective, ensuing, consequent

eventuality NOUN = **possibility**, event, likelihood, probability, case, chance, contingency

eventually ADVERB = **in the end**, finally, one day, after all, some time, ultimately, at the end of the day, in the long run, sooner or later, some day, when all is said and done, in the fullness of time, in the course of time

ever ADVERB **1** *Don't you ever talk to me like that again!* = **at any time**, at all, in any case, at any point, by any chance, on any occasion, at any period **2** *Mother, ever the peacemaker, told us to stop fighting.* = **always**, for ever, at all times, relentlessly, eternally, evermore, unceasingly, to the end of time, everlastingly, unendingly, aye (*Scot.*) **3** *They grew ever further apart as time went on.* = **constantly**, continually, endlessly, perpetually, incessantly, unceasingly, unendingly

everlasting ADJECTIVE **1** *The icon embodies a potent symbol of everlasting life.* = **eternal**, endless, abiding, infinite, perpetual, timeless, immortal, never-ending, indestructible, undying, imperishable, deathless ■ **OPPOSITE:** transitory **2** *I'm tired of your everlasting bickering.* = **continual**, constant, endless, continuous, never-ending, interminable, incessant, ceaseless, unremitting, unceasing

every ADJECTIVE = **each**, each and every, every single

everybody PRONOUN = **everyone**, each one, the whole world, each person, every person, all and sundry, one and all

everyday ADJECTIVE **1** *opportunities for improving fitness in your everyday routine* = **daily**, day-to-day, diurnal, quotidian ■ **OPPOSITE:** occasional **2** *an exhilarating escape from the drudgery of everyday life* = **ordinary**, common, usual, familiar, conventional, routine, dull, stock, accustomed, customary, commonplace, mundane, vanilla (*slang*), banal, habitual, run-of-the-mill, unimaginative, workaday, unexceptional, bog-standard (*Brit. & Irish slang*), common or garden (*informal*), dime-a-dozen (*informal*), wonted ■ **OPPOSITE:** unusual

everyone PRONOUN = **everybody**, each one, the whole world, each person, every person, all and sundry, one and all

> **USAGE** *Everyone* and *everybody* are interchangeable, and can be used as synonyms of each other in any context. Care should be taken, however, to distinguish between *everyone* as a single word and *every one* as two words, the latter form correctly being used to refer to each individual person or thing in a particular group: *every one of them is wrong*.

everything PRONOUN = **all**, the whole, the total, the lot, the sum, the whole lot, the aggregate, the entirety, each thing, the whole caboodle (*informal*), the whole kit and caboodle (*informal*)

everywhere ADVERB **1** *I looked everywhere but I couldn't find him.* = **all over**, all around, the world over, high and low, in each place, in every nook and cranny, far and wide or near, to or in every place **2** *There were clothes scattered around everywhere.* = **all around**, all over, in each place, in every nook and cranny, ubiquitously, far and wide or near, to or in every place

evict VERB = **expel**, remove, turn out, put out, throw out, oust, kick out (*informal*), eject, dislodge, boot out (*informal*), force to leave, dispossess, chuck out (*informal*), show the door (to), turf out (*informal*), throw on to the streets

eviction NOUN = **expulsion**, removal, clearance, ouster (*Law*), ejection, dispossession, dislodgement

evidence NOUN **1** *There is no evidence to support this theory.* = **proof**, grounds, data, demonstration, confirmation, verification, corroboration, authentication, substantiation **2** *Police said there was no evidence of a struggle.* = **sign(s)**, mark, suggestion, trace, indication, token, manifestation **3** *Forensic scientists will be called to give evidence.* = **testimony**, statement, witness, declaration, submission, affirmation, deposition, avowal, attestation, averment ▶ VERB *He still has a lot to learn, as is evidenced by his recent behaviour.* = **show**, prove, reveal, display, indicate, witness, demonstrate, exhibit, manifest, signify, denote, testify to, evince (*formal*)

evident ADJECTIVE = **obvious**, clear, plain, apparent, visible, patent, manifest, tangible, noticeable, blatant, conspicuous, unmistakable, palpable, salient, indisputable, perceptible, incontrovertible, incontestable, plain as the nose on your face ■ **OPPOSITE:** hidden

evidently ADVERB **1** *She had evidently just woken up.* = **obviously**, clearly, plainly, patently, undoubtedly, manifestly, doubtless, without question, unmistakably, indisputably, doubtlessly, incontrovertibly, incontestably **2** *Ellis evidently wished to negotiate downwards, after Atkinson had set the guidelines.* = **apparently**, it seems, seemingly, outwardly, it would seem, ostensibly, so it seems, to all appearances

evil ADJECTIVE **1** *the country's most evil criminals* = **wicked**, bad, wrong, corrupt, vicious, vile, malicious, base, immoral, malignant, sinful, unholy, malevolent, heinous, depraved, villainous, nefarious, iniquitous, reprobate, maleficent **2** *Few people would not* condemn slavery as evil. = **harmful**, painful, disastrous, destructive, dire, catastrophic, mischievous, detrimental, hurtful, woeful, pernicious (formal), ruinous, sorrowful, deleterious (formal), injurious, baneful (archaic) **3** This place is said to be haunted by an evil spirit. = **demonic**, satanic, diabolical, hellish, devilish, infernal (informal), fiendish **4** There was an evil stench in the room. = **offensive**, nasty, foul, unpleasant, vile, noxious, disagreeable, putrid, pestilential, mephitic **5** people of honour who happen to have fallen upon evil times = **unfortunate**, unlucky, unfavourable, ruinous, calamitous, inauspicious ▶ NOUN **1** We are being attacked by the forces of evil. = **wickedness**, bad, wrong, vice, corruption, sin, wrongdoing, depravity, immorality, iniquity, badness, viciousness, villainy, sinfulness, turpitude (formal), baseness, malignity, heinousness, maleficence **2** those who see money as the root of all evil = **harm**, suffering, pain, hurt, misery, sorrow, woe **3** Racism is one of the greatest evils in the world. = **act of cruelty**, crime, ill, horror, outrage, cruelty, brutality, misfortune, mischief, affliction, monstrosity, abomination, barbarity, villainy

evince VERB = **show**, evidence, reveal, establish, express, display, indicate, demonstrate, exhibit, make clear, manifest, signify, attest, bespeak, betoken, make evident

evoke VERB **1** The programme has evoked a storm of protest. = **arouse**, cause, excite, stimulate, induce, awaken, give rise to, stir up, rekindle, summon up ■ **OPPOSITE:** suppress **2** Hearing these songs can still evoke strong memories and emotions. = **provoke**, produce, elicit, call to mind, call forth, educe (rare)

evolution NOUN **1** the evolution of plants and animals = **rise**, development, adaptation, natural selection, Darwinism, survival of the fittest, evolvement **2** a crucial period in the evolution of modern physics = **development**, growth, advance, progress, working out, expansion, extension, unfolding, progression, enlargement, maturation, unrolling

evolve VERB **1** Modern birds evolved from dinosaurs. = **develop**, metamorphose, adapt yourself **2** Popular music evolved from folk songs. = **grow**, develop, advance, progress, mature **3** He evolved a working method from which he has never departed. = **work out**, develop, progress, expand, elaborate, unfold, enlarge, unroll

exacerbate VERB = **irritate**, excite, provoke, infuriate, aggravate (informal), enrage, madden, inflame, exasperate, vex, embitter, add insult to injury, fan the flames of, envenom

exact ADJECTIVE **1** I can't remember the exact words he used. = **accurate**, very, correct, true, particular, right, express, specific, careful, precise, identical, authentic, faithful, explicit, definite, orderly, literal, unequivocal, faultless, on the money (informal), unerring, veracious ■ **OPPOSITE:** approximate **2** She is very punctual and very exact in her duties. = **meticulous**, severe, careful, strict, exacting, precise, rigorous, painstaking, scrupulous, methodical, punctilious (formal) ▶ VERB **1** He has exacted a high price for his co-operation. = **demand**, claim, require, call for, force, impose, command, squeeze, extract, compel, wring, wrest, insist upon, extort **2** I devised a perfect plan to exact my revenge. = **inflict**, apply, impose, administer, mete out, deal out

exacting ADJECTIVE **1** He was not well enough to carry out such an exacting task. = **demanding**, hard, taxing, difficult, tough, painstaking ■ **OPPOSITE:** easy **2** Our new manager has very exacting standards. = **strict**, severe, harsh, stern, rigid, rigorous, stringent, oppressive, imperious, unsparing

exactly ADVERB **1** Can you describe exactly what he looked like? = **accurately**, correctly, definitely, truly, precisely, strictly, literally, faithfully, explicitly, rigorously, unequivocally, scrupulously, truthfully, methodically, unerringly, faultlessly, veraciously **2** He arrived at exactly five o'clock. = **precisely**, just, expressly, prompt (informal), specifically, bang on (informal), to the letter, on the button (informal) ▶ SENTENCE SUBSTITUTE 'We don't know the answer to that.' – 'Exactly. So shut up and stop speculating.' = **precisely**, yes, quite, of course, certainly, indeed, truly, that's right, absolutely, spot-on (Brit. informal), just so, quite so, ya (S. African), as you say, you got it (informal), assuredly, yebo (S. African informal) • **not exactly** Sailing is not exactly a cheap hobby. = **not at all**, hardly, not really, not quite, certainly not, by no means, in no way, not by any means, in no manner

exaggerate VERB = **overstate**, emphasize, enlarge, inflate, embroider, magnify, overdo, amplify, exalt, embellish, overestimate, overemphasize, pile it on about (informal), blow up out of all proportion, lay it on thick about (informal), lay it on with a trowel about (informal), make a production (out) of (*informal*), make a federal case of (*U.S. informal*), hyperbolize

exaggerated ADJECTIVE = **overstated**, extreme, excessive, over the top (*informal*), inflated, extravagant, overdone, tall (*informal*), amplified, hyped, pretentious, exalted (*informal*), overestimated, overblown, fulsome, hyperbolic, highly coloured, O.T.T. (*slang*)

exaggeration NOUN = **overstatement**, inflation, emphasis, excess, enlargement, pretension, extravagance, hyperbole, magnification, amplification, embellishment, exaltation, pretentiousness, overemphasis, overestimation ■ **OPPOSITE:** understatement

exalt VERB 1 *This book exalts her as a genius.* = **praise**, acclaim, applaud, pay tribute to, bless, worship, magnify (*archaic*), glorify, reverence, laud (*literary*), extol, crack up (*informal*), pay homage to, idolize, apotheosize, set on a pedestal 2 *Great music exalts the human spirit.* = **uplift**, raise, lift, excite, delight, inspire, thrill, stimulate, arouse, heighten, elevate, animate, exhilarate, electrify, fire the imagination of, fill with joy, elate, inspirit

exaltation NOUN 1 *The city was swept up in the mood of exaltation.* = **elation**, delight, joy, excitement, inspiration, ecstasy, stimulation, bliss, transport, animation, elevation, rapture, exhilaration, jubilation, exultation, joyousness 2 *The poem is an exaltation of love.* = **praise**, tribute, worship, acclaim, applause, glory, blessing, homage, reverence, magnification, apotheosis, glorification, acclamation, panegyric, idolization, extolment, lionization, laudation

exalted ADJECTIVE 1 *I seldom move in such exalted circles.* = **high-ranking**, high, grand, honoured, intellectual, noble, prestigious, august, elevated, eminent, dignified, lofty 2 *I don't think of poetry as an exalted calling, as some poets do.* = **noble**, ideal, superior, elevated, intellectual, uplifting, sublime, lofty, high-minded 3 *She had the look of someone exalted by an excess of joy.* = **elated**, excited, inspired, stimulated, elevated, animated, uplifted, transported, exhilarated, ecstatic, jubilant, joyous, joyful, over the moon (*informal*), blissful, rapturous, exultant, in high spirits, on cloud nine (*informal*), cock-a-hoop, in seventh heaven, inspirited, stoked (*Austral. & N.Z. informal*)

examination NOUN 1 *a routine medical examination* = **checkup**, analysis, going-over (*informal*), exploration, health

check, check, medical, once-over (*informal*) 2 *accusations of cheating in school examinations* = **exam**, test, research, paper, investigation, practical, assessment, quiz, evaluation, oral, appraisal, catechism

examine VERB 1 *He examined her passport and stamped it.* = **inspect**, test, consider, study, check, research, review, survey, investigate, explore, probe, analyse, scan, vet, check out, ponder, look over, look at, sift through, work over, pore over, appraise, scrutinize, peruse, take stock of, assay, recce (*slang*), look at carefully, go over or through 2 *The doctor examined her, but could find nothing wrong.* = **check**, analyse, check over 3 *the pressures of being judged and examined by our teachers* = **test**, question, assess, quiz, evaluate, appraise, catechize 4 *I was called and examined as a witness.* = **question**, quiz, interrogate, cross-examine, grill (*informal*), give the third degree to (*informal*)

example NOUN 1 *examples of prejudice in society* = **instance**, specimen, case, sample, illustration, case in point, particular case, particular instance, typical case, exemplification, representative case 2 *This piece is a perfect example of symphonic construction.* = **illustration**, model, ideal, standard, norm, precedent, pattern, prototype, paradigm, archetype, paragon, exemplar 3 *We were punished as an example to others.* = **warning**, lesson, caution, deterrent, admonition • **for example** *You could, for example, walk instead of taking the car.* = **as an illustration**, like, such as, for instance, to illustrate, by way of illustration, exempli gratia (*Latin*), to cite an instance, e.g.

exasperate VERB = **irritate**, anger, provoke, annoy, rouse, infuriate, hassle (*informal*), exacerbate, aggravate (*informal*), incense, enrage, gall, madden, inflame, bug (*informal*), nettle, get to (*informal*), vex, embitter, irk, rile (*informal*), pique, rankle, peeve (*informal*), needle (*informal*), get on your nerves (*informal*), try the patience of, nark (*Brit., Austral. & N.Z. slang*), get in your hair (*informal*), get on your wick (*Brit. slang*), hack you off (*informal*) ■ **OPPOSITE:** calm

exasperating ADJECTIVE = **irritating**, provoking, annoying, infuriating, aggravating (*informal*), galling, maddening, vexing, irksome, enough to drive you up the wall (*informal*), enough to try the patience of a saint

exasperation NOUN = **irritation**, anger, rage, fury, wrath, provocation, passion, annoyance, ire (*literary*), pique, aggravation (*informal*), vexation, exacerbation

excavate VERB **1** *A team of archaeologists is excavating the site.* = **dig up**, mine, dig, tunnel, scoop, cut, hollow, trench, burrow, quarry, delve, gouge **2** *They have excavated the fossil remains of a prehistoric man.* = **unearth**, expose, uncover, dig out, exhume, lay bare, bring to light, bring to the surface, disinter

excavation NOUN = **hole**, mine, pit, ditch, shaft, cutting, cut, hollow, trench, burrow, quarry, dig, trough, cavity, dugout, diggings

exceed VERB **1** *His performance exceeded all expectations.* = **surpass**, better, pass, eclipse, beat, cap (*informal*), top, be over, be more than, overtake, go beyond, excel, transcend, be greater than, outstrip, outdo, outreach, be larger than, outshine, surmount, be superior to, outrun, run rings around (*informal*), outdistance, knock spots off (*informal*), put in the shade (*informal*) **2** *This programme exceeded the bounds of taste and decency.* = **go over the limit of**, go beyond, overstep, go beyond the bounds of

exceeding ADJECTIVE = **extraordinary**, great, huge, vast, enormous, superior, excessive, exceptional, surpassing, superlative, pre-eminent, streets ahead

exceedingly ADVERB = **extremely**, very, highly, greatly, especially, hugely, seriously (*informal*), vastly, unusually, enormously, exceptionally, extraordinarily, excessively, superlatively, inordinately, to a fault, to the nth degree, surpassingly

excel VERB *Few dancers have excelled her in virtuosity.* = **be superior**, better, pass, eclipse, beat, top, cap (*informal*), exceed, go beyond, surpass, transcend, outdo, outshine, surmount, run rings around (*informal*), put in the shade (*informal*), outrival • **excel in** or **at something** *She excelled at outdoor sports.* = **be good at**, be master of, predominate in, shine at, be proficient in, show talent in, be skilful at, have (something) down to a fine art, be talented at

excellence NOUN = **high quality**, worth, merit, distinction, virtue, goodness, perfection, superiority, purity, greatness, supremacy, eminence, virtuosity, transcendence, pre-eminence, fineness

excellent ADJECTIVE = **outstanding**, good, great (*informal*), fine, prime, capital, noted, choice, champion, cool (*informal*), select, brilliant, very good, cracking (*Brit. informal*), crucial (*slang*), mean (*slang*), superb, distinguished, fantastic (*informal*), magnificent, superior, sterling, worthy, first-class, marvellous, exceptional, terrific (*informal*), splendid, notable, mega (*slang*), topping (*Brit. slang*), sovereign, dope (*slang*), sick (*slang*), world-class, exquisite, admirable, exemplary, wicked (*slang*), first-rate, def (*slang*), superlative, top-notch (*informal*), brill (*informal*), nang (*Brit. slang*), pre-eminent, meritorious, estimable, tiptop, bodacious (*slang, chiefly U.S.*), boffo (*slang*), jim-dandy (*slang*), A1 or A-one (*informal*), bitchin' (*U.S. slang*), chillin' (*U.S. slang*), booshit (*Austral. slang*), exo (*Austral. slang*), sik (*Austral. slang*), rad (*informal*), phat (*slang*), schmick (*Austral. informal*), beaut (*informal*), barrie (*Scot. slang*), belting (*Brit. slang*), pearler (*Austral. slang*), bakgat (*S. African*)
■ **OPPOSITE:** terrible

except PREPOSITION (*often with* **for**) *I don't drink, except for the occasional glass of wine.* = **apart from**, but for, saving, bar, barring, excepting, other than, excluding, omitting, with the exception of, aside from, save (*archaic*), not counting, exclusive of ▶ VERB *Present company excepted, who is your favourite colleague?* = **exclude**, rule out, leave out, omit, disregard, pass over

exception NOUN *an exception to the usual rule* = **special case**, departure, freak, anomaly, inconsistency, deviation, quirk, oddity, peculiarity, irregularity • **take exception** (*usually with* **to**) *I take exception to being checked up on like this.* = **object to**, disagree with, take offence at, take umbrage at, be resentful of, be offended at, demur at, quibble at

exceptional ADJECTIVE **1** *His piano playing is exceptional.* = **remarkable**, special, excellent, extraordinary, outstanding, superior, first-class, marvellous, notable, phenomenal, first-rate, prodigious, unsurpassed, one in a million, bodacious (*slang, chiefly U.S.*), unexcelled ■ **OPPOSITE:** average **2** *The courts hold that this case is exceptional.* = **unusual**, special, odd, strange, rare, extraordinary, unprecedented, peculiar, abnormal, irregular, uncommon, inconsistent, singular, deviant, anomalous, atypical, aberrant ■ **OPPOSITE:** ordinary

excerpt NOUN *an excerpt from Tchaikovsky's 'Nutcracker'* = **extract**, part, piece, section, selection, passage, portion, fragment, quotation, citation, pericope ▶ VERB *The readings were excerpted from his autobiography.* = **extract**, take, select, quote, cite, pick out, cull

excess NOUN **1** *Avoid an excess of sugar in your diet.* = **surfeit**, surplus, overdose, overflow, overload, plethora, glut, overabundance,

superabundance, superfluity ■ **OPPOSITE:** shortage **2** *He had led a life of excess.* = **overindulgence**, extravagance, profligacy, debauchery, dissipation, intemperance, indulgence, prodigality, extreme behaviour, immoral behaviour, dissoluteness, immoderation, exorbitance, unrestraint ■ **OPPOSITE:** moderation
▶ ADJECTIVE *After cooking the fish, pour off any excess fat.* = **spare**, remaining, extra, additional, surplus, unwanted, redundant, residual, leftover, superfluous, unneeded

excessive ADJECTIVE **1** *The length of the prison sentence was excessive.* = **immoderate**, too much, enormous, extreme, exaggerated, over the top (*slang*), extravagant, needless, unreasonable, disproportionate, undue, uncontrolled, superfluous, prodigal, unrestrained, profligate, inordinate, fulsome, intemperate, unconscionable, overmuch, O.T.T. (*slang*) **2** *banks which cripple their customers with excessive charges* = **inordinate**, unfair, unreasonable, disproportionate, undue, unwarranted, exorbitant, over the odds, extortionate, immoderate

exchange VERB *We exchanged addresses.* = **interchange**, change, trade, switch, swap, truck, barter, reciprocate, bandy, give to each other, give to one another
▶ NOUN **1** *I had a brief exchange with him before I left.* = **conversation**, talk, word, discussion, chat, dialogue, natter, powwow **2** *a free exchange of information* = **interchange**, dealing, trade, switch, swap, traffic, trafficking, truck, swapping, substitution, barter, bartering, reciprocity, tit for tat, quid pro quo **3** *the Stock Exchange* = **market**, money market, Bourse

excise¹ NOUN *Smokers will be hit by increases in tax and excise.* = **tax**, duty, customs, toll, levy, tariff, surcharge, impost

excise² VERB **1** *a crusade to excise racist and sexist references in newspapers* = **delete**, cut, remove, erase, destroy, eradicate, strike out, exterminate, cross out, expunge (*formal*), extirpate, wipe from the face of the earth **2** *She has already had one skin cancer excised.* = **cut off** *or* **out** *or* **away**, remove, take out, extract

excitable ADJECTIVE = **nervous**, emotional, violent, sensitive, tense, passionate, volatile, hasty, edgy, temperamental, touchy, mercurial, uptight (*informal*), irascible, testy, hot-headed, chippy (*informal*), hot-tempered, quick-tempered, highly strung, adrenalized ■ **OPPOSITE:** calm

excite VERB **1** *I only take on work that excites me.* = **thrill**, inspire, stir, stimulate, provoke,

awaken, animate, move, fire, rouse, exhilarate, agitate, quicken, inflame, enliven, galvanize, foment **2** *The proposal failed to excite our interest.* = **arouse**, stimulate, provoke, evoke, rouse, stir up, fire, elicit, work up, incite, instigate, whet, kindle, waken

excited ADJECTIVE **1** *He was so excited he could hardly speak.* = **thrilled**, stirred, stimulated, enthusiastic, high (*informal*), moved, wild, aroused, awakened, animated, roused, tumultuous, aflame **2** *There's no need to get so excited.* = **agitated**, worried, stressed, alarmed, nervous, disturbed, tense, flurried, worked up, feverish, overwrought, hot and bothered (*informal*), discomposed, adrenalized

excitement NOUN **1** *The audience was in a state of great excitement.* = **exhilaration**, action, activity, passion, heat, thrill, adventure, enthusiasm, fever, warmth, flurry, animation, furore, ferment, agitation, commotion, elation, ado, tumult, perturbation, discomposure **2** *The game had its challenges, excitements and rewards.* = **pleasure**, thrill, sensation, stimulation, tingle, kick (*informal*)

exciting ADJECTIVE *the most exciting adventure of their lives* = **stimulating**, inspiring, dramatic, gripping, stirring, thrilling, moving, sensational, rousing, exhilarating, electrifying, intoxicating, rip-roaring (*informal*) ■ **OPPOSITE:** boring

exclaim VERB = **cry out**, call, declare, cry, shout, proclaim, yell, utter, call out, ejaculate (*literary*), vociferate

exclamation NOUN = **cry**, call, shout, yell, outcry, utterance, ejaculation (*literary*), expletive, interjection, vociferation

exclude VERB **1** *The orchestra excluded children under twelve.* = **keep out**, bar, ban, veto, refuse, forbid, boycott, embargo, prohibit, disallow, shut out, proscribe, black, refuse to admit, ostracize, debar, blackball, interdict, prevent from entering ■ **OPPOSITE:** let in **2** *Vegetarians exclude meat products from their diet.* = **omit**, reject, eliminate, rule out, miss out, leave out, preclude, repudiate ■ **OPPOSITE:** include **3** *We can't exclude the possibility of suicide.* = **eliminate**, reject, ignore, rule out, except, leave out, set aside, omit, pass over, not count, repudiate, count out

exclusion NOUN **1** *They demand the exclusion of persistent cheats.* = **ban**, bar, veto, refusal, boycott, embargo, prohibition, disqualification, interdict, proscription, debarment, preclusion, forbiddance, nonadmission **2** *the exclusion of dairy products* *from your diet* = **elimination**, exception, missing out, rejection, leaving out, omission, repudiation

exclusive ADJECTIVE **1** *He is a member of Britain's most exclusive club.* = **select**, fashionable, stylish, private, limited, choice, narrow, closed, restricted, elegant, posh (*informal, chiefly Brit.*), chic, selfish, classy (*slang*), restrictive, aristocratic, high-class, swish (*informal, chiefly Brit.*), up-market, snobbish, top-drawer, ritzy (*slang*), high-toned, clannish, discriminative, cliquish ■ **OPPOSITE:** unrestricted **2** *We have exclusive use of a 60-foot boat.* = **sole**, only, full, whole, single, private, complete, total, entire, unique, absolute, undivided, unshared ■ **OPPOSITE:** shared **3** *She wants her father's exclusive attention.* = **entire**, full, whole, complete, total, absolute, undivided **4** *Infatuations are not exclusive to the very young.* = **limited**, unique, restricted, confined, peculiar • **exclusive of** *All charges are exclusive of value added tax.* = **except for**, excepting, excluding, ruling out, not including, omitting, not counting, leaving aside, debarring

excommunicate VERB = **expel**, ban, remove, exclude, denounce, banish, eject, repudiate, proscribe, cast out, unchurch, anathematize

excrement NOUN = **faeces**, dung, stool, droppings, motion, mess (*of a domestic animal*), defecation, excreta, ordure, kak (*S. African vulgar slang*), night soil

excrete VERB = **defecate**, discharge, expel, evacuate, eliminate, void, eject, exude, egest

excruciating ADJECTIVE = **agonizing**, acute, severe, extreme, burning, violent, intense, piercing, racking, searing, tormenting, exquisite, harrowing, unbearable, insufferable, torturous, unendurable

excursion NOUN = **trip**, airing, tour, journey, outing, expedition, ramble, day trip, jaunt, pleasure trip

excuse VERB **1** *I know you're upset but that doesn't excuse your behaviour.* = **justify**, explain, defend, vindicate, condone, mitigate, apologize for, make excuses for ■ **OPPOSITE:** blame **2** *Please excuse me for my late arrival.* = **forgive**, pardon, overlook, tolerate, indulge, acquit, pass over, turn a blind eye to, exonerate, absolve, bear with, wink at, make allowances for, extenuate, exculpate **3** *She was excused from her duties for the day.* = **free**, relieve, liberate, exempt, release, spare, discharge, let off, absolve

■ **OPPOSITE:** convict ▶ NOUN **1** *There is no excuse for what he did.* = **justification**, reason, explanation, defence, grounds, plea, apology, pretext, vindication, mitigation, mitigating circumstances, extenuation ■ **OPPOSITE:** accusation **2** *It was just an excuse to get out of going to school.* = **pretext**, evasion, pretence, cover-up, expedient, get-out, cop-out (*slang*), subterfuge **3** *He is a pathetic excuse for a father.* = **poor substitute**, apology, mockery, travesty

execute VERB **1** *His father had been executed for treason.* = **put to death**, kill, shoot, hang, behead, decapitate, guillotine, electrocute **2** *We are going to execute our campaign plan to the letter.* = **carry out**, effect, finish, complete, achieve, realize, do, implement, fulfil, enforce, accomplish, render, discharge, administer, prosecute, enact, consummate, put into effect, bring off **3** *The landing was skilfully executed.* = **perform**, do, carry out, accomplish

execution NOUN **1** *He was sentenced to execution by lethal injection.* = **killing**, hanging, the death penalty, the rope, capital punishment, beheading, the electric chair, the guillotine, the noose, the scaffold, electrocution, decapitation, the firing squad, necktie party (*informal*) **2** *the unquestioning execution of his orders* = **carrying out**, performance, operation, administration, achievement, effect, prosecution, rendering, discharge, enforcement, implementation, completion, accomplishment, realization, enactment, bringing off, consummation **3** *his masterly execution of a difficult piece* = **performance**, style, delivery, manner, technique, mode, presentation, rendition

executioner NOUN = **hangman**, firing squad, headsman, public executioner, Jack Ketch

executive NOUN **1** *a senior bank executive* = **administrator**, official, director, manager, chairperson, managing director, controller, chief executive officer, senior manager **2** *the executive of the National Union of Students* = **administration**, government, directors, management, leadership, hierarchy, directorate ▶ ADJECTIVE *She sits on the executive committee of the company.* = **administrative**, controlling, directing, governing, regulating, decision-making, managerial

exemplar NOUN **1** *They viewed their new building as an exemplar of taste.* = **model**, example, standard, ideal, criterion, paradigm, epitome, paragon **2** *One of the* *wittiest exemplars of the technique was M.C. Escher.* = **example**, instance, illustration, type, specimen, prototype, typical example, representative example, exemplification

exemplary ADJECTIVE **1** *He showed outstanding and exemplary courage in the face of danger.* = **ideal**, good, fine, model, excellent, sterling, admirable, honourable, commendable, laudable, praiseworthy, meritorious, estimable, punctilious **2** *an exemplary case of how issues of this sort can be resolved* = **typical**, representative, characteristic, illustrative **3** *He demanded exemplary sentences for those behind the violence.* = **warning**, harsh, cautionary, admonitory, monitory

exemplify VERB = **show**, represent, display, demonstrate, instance, illustrate, exhibit, depict, manifest, evidence, embody, serve as an example of

exempt VERB *Companies with fewer than 55 employees would be exempted from these requirements.* = **grant immunity**, free, except, excuse, release, spare, relieve, discharge, liberate, let off, exonerate, absolve ▶ ADJECTIVE *Men in college were exempt from military service.* = **immune**, free, excepted, excused, released, spared, clear, discharged, liberated, not subject to, absolved, not liable to ■ **OPPOSITE:** liable

exemption NOUN = **immunity**, freedom, privilege, relief, exception, discharge, release, dispensation, absolution, exoneration

exercise VERB **1** *They are merely exercising their right to free speech.* = **put to use**, use, apply, employ, practise, exert, enjoy, wield, utilize, bring to bear, avail yourself of **2** *She exercises two or three times a week.* = **train**, work out, practise, drill, keep fit, inure, do exercises **3** *an issue that has long exercised the finest scientific minds* = **worry**, concern, occupy, try, trouble, pain, disturb, burden, distress, preoccupy, agitate, perplex, vex, perturb ▶ NOUN **1** *Leadership does not rest on the exercise of force alone.* = **use**, practice, application, operation, employment, discharge, implementation, enjoyment, accomplishment, fulfilment, exertion, utilization **2** *Lack of exercise can lead to feelings of depression and exhaustion.* = **exertion**, training, activity, action, work, labour, effort, movement, discipline, toil, physical activity **3** *a missile being used in a military exercise* = **manoeuvre**, campaign, operation, movement, deployment **4** *Try working through the opening exercises in this chapter.* = **task**, problem, lesson,

assignment, work, schooling, practice, schoolwork

exert VERB *He exerted all his considerable charm to get her to agree.* = **apply**, use, exercise, employ, wield, make use of, utilize, expend, bring to bear, put forth, bring into play
• **exert yourself** *He never exerts himself for other people.* = **make an effort**, work, labour, struggle, strain, strive, endeavour, go for it (*informal*), try hard, toil, bend over backwards (*informal*), do your best, go for broke (*slang*), bust a gut (*informal*), spare no effort, make a great effort, give it your best shot (*informal*), break your neck (*informal*), apply yourself, put yourself out, make an all-out effort (*informal*), get your finger out (*Brit. informal*), pull your finger out (*Brit. informal*), knock yourself out (*informal*), do your damnedest (*informal*), give it your all (*informal*), rupture yourself (*informal*)

exertion NOUN **1** *panting from the exertion of climbing the stairs* = **effort**, action, exercise, struggle, industry, labour, trial, pains, stretch, strain, endeavour, toil, travail (*literary*), elbow grease (*facetious*) **2** *the exertion of legislative power* = **use**, exercise, application, employment, bringing to bear, utilization

exhale VERB = **give off**, emit, steam, discharge, send out, evaporate, issue, eject, emanate

exhaust VERB **1** *The effort of speaking had exhausted him.* = **tire out**, tire, fatigue, drain, weaken, weary, sap, wear out, debilitate, prostrate, enfeeble, make tired, enervate **2** *We have exhausted almost all our food supplies.* = **use up**, spend, finish, consume, waste, go through, run through, deplete, squander, dissipate, expend

exhausted ADJECTIVE **1** *She was too exhausted even to think clearly.* = **worn out**, tired out, drained, spent, beat (*slang*), bushed (*informal*), dead (*informal*), wasted, done in (*informal*), weak, all in (*slang*), fatigued, wiped out (*informal*), sapped, debilitated, jaded, knackered (*slang*), prostrated, clapped out (*Brit., Austral. & N.Z. informal*), effete, enfeebled, enervated, ready to drop, dog-tired (*informal*), zonked (*slang*), dead tired, dead beat (*informal*), shagged out (*Brit. slang*), fagged out (*informal*), worn to a frazzle (*informal*), on your last legs (*informal*), creamcrackered (*Brit. slang*), out on your feet (*informal*) ■ **OPPOSITE:** invigorated **2** *Mining companies are shutting down operations as the coal supply is exhausted.* = **used up**, consumed, spent, finished, gone, depleted, dissipated, expended, at an end ■ **OPPOSITE:** replenished

exhausting ADJECTIVE = **tiring**, hard, testing, taxing, difficult, draining, punishing, crippling, fatiguing, wearying, gruelling, sapping, debilitating, strenuous, arduous, laborious, enervating, backbreaking

exhaustion NOUN 1 *He is suffering from nervous exhaustion.* = **tiredness**, fatigue, weariness, lassitude, feebleness, prostration, debilitation, enervation 2 *the exhaustion of the country's resources* = **depletion**, emptying, consumption, using up

exhaustive ADJECTIVE = **thorough**, detailed, complete, full, total, sweeping, comprehensive, extensive, intensive, full-scale, in-depth, far-reaching, all-inclusive, all-embracing, encyclopedic, thoroughgoing ■ **OPPOSITE:** superficial

exhibit VERB 1 *He has exhibited signs of anxiety and stress.* = **show**, reveal, display, demonstrate, air, evidence, express, indicate, disclose, manifest, evince (*formal*), make clear or plain 2 *Her work was exhibited in the best galleries in Europe.* = **display**, show, present, set out, parade, unveil, flaunt, put on view ▶ NOUN *He showed me round the exhibits in the museum.* = **object**, piece, model, article, illustration

exhibition NOUN 1 *an exhibition of expressionist art* = **show**, display, exhibit, showing, fair, representation, presentation, spectacle, showcase, expo (*informal*), exposition, ex (*Canad. informal*) 2 *He treated the fans to an exhibition of power and speed.* = **display**, show, performance, demonstration, airing, revelation, manifestation

exhilarate VERB = **excite**, delight, cheer, thrill, stimulate, animate, exalt, lift, enliven, invigorate, gladden, elate, inspirit, pep or perk up

exhilarating ADJECTIVE = **exciting**, thrilling, stimulating, breathtaking, cheering, exalting, enlivening, invigorating, gladdening, vitalizing, exhilarant

exhilaration NOUN = **excitement**, delight, joy, happiness, animation, high spirits, elation, mirth, gaiety, hilarity, exaltation, cheerfulness, vivacity, liveliness, gladness, joyfulness, sprightliness, gleefulness ■ **OPPOSITE:** depression

exhort VERB = **urge**, warn, encourage, advise, bid, persuade, prompt, spur, press, counsel, caution, call upon, incite, goad, admonish, enjoin, beseech, entreat

exhortation NOUN = **urging**, warning, advice, counsel, lecture, caution, bidding, encouragement, sermon, persuasion, goading, incitement, admonition, beseeching, entreaty, clarion call, enjoiner (*rare*)

exhume VERB = **dig up**, unearth, disinter, unbury, disentomb ■ **OPPOSITE:** bury

exile NOUN 1 *During his exile, he began writing books.* = **banishment**, expulsion, deportation, eviction, separation, ostracism, proscription, expatriation 2 *the release of all political prisoners and the return of exiles* = **expatriate**, refugee, outcast, émigré, deportee ▶ VERB *Dante was exiled from Florence in 1302 because of his political activities.* = **banish**, expel, throw out, deport, oust, drive out, eject, expatriate, proscribe, cast out, ostracize

exiled ADJECTIVE = **banished**, deported, expatriate, outcast, refugee, ostracized, expat

exist VERB 1 *Many people believe that the Loch Ness Monster does exist.* = **live**, be present, be living, last, survive, breathe, endure, be in existence, be, be extant, have breath 2 *the social climate which existed 20 years ago* = **occur**, happen, stand, remain, obtain (*formal*), be present, prevail, abide 3 *the problems of having to exist on unemployment benefit* = **survive**, stay alive, make ends meet, subsist, eke out a living, scrape by, scrimp and save, support yourself, keep your head above water, get along or by

> **USAGE** Although *be extant* is given as a synonym of *exist*, according to some, *extant* should properly be used only where there is a connotation of survival, often against all odds: *the oldest extant document dates from 1492*. Using *extant* where the phrase *in existence* can be substituted would in this view be incorrect: *in existence (not extant) for nearly 15 years, they have been consistently one of the finest rock bands on the planet*. In practice, however, the distinct meanings of the two phrases often overlap: *these beasts, the largest primates on the planet and the greatest of the great apes, are man's closest living relatives and the only extant primates with which we share close physical characteristics*.

existence NOUN 1 *Public worries about accidents are threatening the very existence of the nuclear power industry.* = **reality**, being, life, survival, duration, endurance, continuation, subsistence, actuality, continuance 2 *the man who rescued her from her wretched existence* = **life**, situation, way of life, lifestyle 3 *pondering the mysteries of existence* = **creation**, life, the world, reality, the human condition, this mortal coil

existent ADJECTIVE = **in existence**, living, existing, surviving, around, standing, remaining, present, current, alive, enduring, prevailing, abiding, to the fore (*Scot.*), extant

existing ADJECTIVE = **in existence**, living, present, surviving, remaining, available, alive, in operation, extant, alive and kicking ■ **OPPOSITE:** gone

exit NOUN **1** *We headed quickly for the fire exit.* = **way out**, door, gate, outlet, doorway, vent, gateway, escape route, passage out, egress (*formal*) ■ **OPPOSITE:** entry **2** *She made a dignified exit.* = **departure**, withdrawal, retreat, farewell, going, retirement, goodbye, exodus, evacuation, decamping, leave-taking, adieu ▸ VERB *He exited without saying goodbye.* = **depart**, leave, go out, withdraw, retire, quit, retreat, go away, say goodbye, bid farewell, make tracks, take your leave, go offstage (*Theatre*) ■ **OPPOSITE:** enter

exodus NOUN = **departure**, withdrawal, retreat, leaving, flight, retirement, exit, migration, evacuation

exonerate VERB = **acquit**, clear, excuse, pardon, justify, discharge, vindicate, absolve, exculpate

exorbitant ADJECTIVE = **excessive**, high, expensive, extreme, ridiculous, outrageous, extravagant, unreasonable, undue, preposterous, unwarranted, inordinate, extortionate, unconscionable, immoderate ■ **OPPOSITE:** reasonable

exorcism NOUN = **driving out**, cleansing, expulsion, purification, deliverance, casting out, adjuration

exorcize VERB **1** *He tried to exorcise the pain of his childhood trauma.* = **drive out**, expel, cast out, adjure **2** *They came to our house and exorcized me.* = **purify**, free, cleanse

exotic ADJECTIVE **1** *his striking and exotic appearance* = **unusual**, different, striking, strange, extraordinary, bizarre, fascinating, curious, mysterious, colourful, glamorous, peculiar, unfamiliar, outlandish ■ **OPPOSITE:** ordinary **2** *travelling around the globe to collect rare and exotic plant species* = **foreign**, alien, tropical, external, extraneous, naturalized, extrinsic, not native

expand VERB **1** *Water expands as it freezes.* = **get bigger**, increase, grow, extend, swell, widen, blow up, wax, heighten, enlarge, multiply, inflate, thicken, fill out, lengthen, fatten, dilate, become bigger, puff up, become larger, distend ■ **OPPOSITE:** contract **2** *We can expand the size of the image.* = **make bigger**, increase, develop, extend, widen, blow up, heighten, enlarge, multiply, broaden, inflate, thicken, fill out, lengthen, magnify, amplify, augment, dilate, make larger, distend, bloat, protract ■ **OPPOSITE:** reduce **3** *The flowers fully expand at night.* = **spread (out)**, open (out), stretch (out), unfold, unravel, diffuse, unfurl, unroll, outspread • **expand on something** *He expanded on some remarks he made in his last speech.* = **go into detail about**, embellish, elaborate on, develop, flesh out, expound on, enlarge on, expatiate on, add detail to

expanse NOUN = **area**, range, field, space, stretch, sweep, extent, plain, tract, breadth

expansion NOUN **1** *the rapid expansion of private health insurance* = **increase**, development, growth, spread, diffusion, magnification, multiplication, amplification, augmentation **2** *Slow breathing allows for full expansion of the lungs.* = **enlargement**, inflation, increase, growth, swelling, unfolding, expanse, unfurling, opening out, distension

expansive ADJECTIVE **1** *an expansive grassy play area* = **wide**, broad, extensive, spacious, sweeping **2** *the book's expansive coverage of this period* = **comprehensive**, extensive, broad, wide, widespread, wide-ranging, thorough, inclusive, far-reaching, voluminous, all-embracing **3** *He became more expansive as he began to relax.* = **talkative**, open, friendly, outgoing, free, easy, warm, sociable, genial, affable, communicative, effusive, garrulous, loquacious, unreserved

expatriate ADJECTIVE *The military is preparing to evacuate women and children of expatriate families.* = **exiled**, refugee, banished, emigrant, émigré, expat ▸ NOUN *British expatriates in Spain* = **exile**, refugee, emigrant, émigré

expect VERB **1** *We expect the talks will continue until tomorrow.* = **think**, believe, suppose, assume, trust, imagine, reckon (*informal*), forecast, calculate, presume, foresee, conjecture, surmise, think likely **2** *I wasn't expecting to see you today.* = **anticipate**, look forward to, predict, envisage, await, hope for, contemplate, bargain for, look ahead to **3** *He expects total obedience and blind loyalty from his staff.* = **require**, demand, want, wish, look for, call for, ask for, hope for, insist on, count on, rely upon

expectancy NOUN **1** *the average life expectancy of the British male* = **likelihood**, prospect, tendency, outlook, probability **2** *The atmosphere here at the stadium is one of expectancy.* = **expectation**, hope, anticipation, waiting, belief, looking forward, assumption, prediction, probability, suspense, presumption, conjecture, surmise, supposition

expectant ADJECTIVE **1** *She turned to me with an expectant look on her face.* = **expecting**, excited, anticipating, anxious, ready, awaiting, eager, hopeful, apprehensive, watchful, in suspense **2** *antenatal classes for expectant mothers* = **pregnant**, expecting (*informal*), gravid, enceinte

expectation NOUN **1** (*usually plural*) *Sales of the car have far exceeded expectations.* = **projection**, supposition, assumption, calculation, belief, forecast, assurance, likelihood, probability, presumption, conjecture, surmise, presupposition **2** *His nerves tingled with expectation.* = **anticipation**, hope, possibility, prospect, chance, fear, promise, looking forward, excitement, prediction, outlook, expectancy, apprehension, suspense **3** (*usually plural*) *Sometimes people have unreasonable expectations of the medical profession.* = **requirement**, demand, want, wish, insistence, reliance

expected ADJECTIVE = **anticipated**, wanted, promised, looked-for, predicted, forecast, awaited, hoped-for, counted on, long-awaited

expecting ADJECTIVE = **pregnant**, with child, expectant, in the club (*Brit. slang*), in the family way (*informal*), gravid, enceinte

expediency *or* **expedience** NOUN = **suitability**, benefit, fitness, utility, effectiveness, convenience, profitability, practicality, usefulness, prudence, pragmatism, propriety, desirability, appropriateness, utilitarianism, helpfulness, advisability, aptness, judiciousness, properness, meetness, advantageousness

expedient ADJECTIVE *It might be expedient to keep this information to yourself.* = **advantageous**, effective, useful, profitable, fit, politic, appropriate, practical, suitable, helpful, proper, convenient, desirable, worthwhile, beneficial, pragmatic, prudent, advisable, utilitarian, judicious, opportune (*formal*) ■ **OPPOSITE:** unwise ▶ NOUN *I reduced my spending by the simple expedient of destroying my credit cards.* = **means**, measure, scheme, method, resource, resort, device, manoeuvre, expediency, stratagem, contrivance, stopgap, backstop

expedite VERB = **speed (up)**, forward, promote, advance, press, urge, rush, assist, hurry, accelerate, dispatch, facilitate, hasten, precipitate, quicken ■ **OPPOSITE:** hold up

expedition NOUN **1** *Byrd's 1928 expedition to Antarctica* = **journey**, exploration, mission, voyage, tour, enterprise, undertaking, quest, trek **2** *Forty-three members of the expedition were killed.* = **team**, crew, party, group, company, travellers, explorers, voyagers, wayfarers **3** *We went on a shopping expedition.* = **trip**, tour, outing, excursion, jaunt

expel VERB **1** *secondary school students expelled for cheating in exams* = **throw out**, exclude, ban, bar, dismiss, discharge, relegate, kick out (*informal*), ask to leave, send packing, turf out (*informal*), black, debar, drum out, blackball, give the bum's rush (*slang*), show you the door, throw out on your ear (*informal*) ■ **OPPOSITE:** let in **2** *An American academic was expelled from the country yesterday.* = **banish**, exile, oust, deport, expatriate, evict, force to leave, proscribe ■ **OPPOSITE:** take in **3** *Poisonous gas is expelled into the atmosphere.* = **drive out**, discharge, throw out, force out, let out, eject, issue, dislodge, spew, belch, cast out

expend VERB **1** *the number of calories you expend through exercise* = **use (up)**, employ, go through (*informal*), exhaust, consume, dissipate **2** *the amount of money expended on this project so far* = **spend**, pay out, lay out (*informal*), fork out (*slang*), shell out, disburse

expendable ADJECTIVE = **dispensable**, unnecessary, unimportant, replaceable, nonessential, inessential ■ **OPPOSITE:** indispensable

expenditure NOUN **1** *The government should reduce their expenditure on defence.* = **spending**, payment, expense, outgoings, cost, charge, outlay, disbursement **2** *The rewards justified the expenditure of effort.* = **consumption**, use, using, application, output

expense NOUN *She has refurbished the whole place at vast expense.* = **cost**, charge, expenditure, payment, spending, output, toll, consumption, outlay, disbursement • **at the expense of** *The company has increased productivity at the expense of safety.* = **with the sacrifice of**, with the loss of, at the cost of, at the price of

expensive ADJECTIVE = **costly**, high-priced, lavish, extravagant, rich, dear, stiff, excessive, steep (*informal*), pricey, overpriced, exorbitant ■ **OPPOSITE:** cheap

experience NOUN **1** *He lacks experience of international rugby.* = **knowledge**, understanding, practice, skill, evidence, trial, contact, expertise, know-how (*informal*), proof, involvement, exposure, observation, participation, familiarity, practical knowledge **2** *It was an experience I would not like to go through again.* = **event**, affair, incident, happening, test, trial, encounter, episode, adventure, ordeal, occurrence ▶ VERB *couples who have experienced the trauma of divorce* = **undergo**, have, know, feel, try, meet, face, suffer, taste, go through, observe, sample, encounter, sustain, perceive, endure, participate in, run into, live through, behold (*archaic, literary*), come up against, apprehend, become familiar with

experienced ADJECTIVE **1** *a team made up of experienced professionals* = **knowledgeable**, trained, professional, skilled, tried, tested, seasoned, expert, master, qualified, familiar, capable, veteran, practised, accomplished, competent, skilful, adept, well-versed ■ **OPPOSITE:** inexperienced **2** *Perhaps I'm a bit more experienced about life than you are.* = **worldly-wise**, knowing, worldly, wise, mature, sophisticated

experiment NOUN **1** *a proposed new law banning animal experiments* = **test**, trial, investigation, examination, venture, procedure, demonstration, observation, try-out, assay, trial run, scientific test, dummy run **2** *The only way to find out is by experiment.* = **research**, investigation, analysis, observation, research and development, experimentation, trial and error ▶ VERB *Scientists have been experimenting with a new drug.* = **test**, investigate, trial, research, try, examine, pilot, sample, verify, put to the test, assay

experimental ADJECTIVE **1** *The technique is still in the experimental stages.* = **test**, trial, pilot, preliminary, provisional, tentative, speculative, empirical, exploratory, trial-and-error, fact-finding, probationary **2** *He writes bizarre and highly experimental music.* = **innovative**, new, original, radical, creative, ingenious, avant-garde, inventive, ground-breaking

expert NOUN *an expert in computer graphics* = **specialist**, authority, professional, master, pro (*informal*), ace (*informal*), genius, guru, pundit, buff (*informal*), wizard, adept, whizz (*informal*), maestro, virtuoso, connoisseur, hotshot (*informal*), past master, dab hand (*Brit. informal*), wonk (*informal*), maven (*U.S.*), fundi (*S. African*), geek (*informal*) ■ **OPPOSITE:** amateur ▶ ADJECTIVE *The faces of the waxworks are modelled by expert sculptors.* = **skilful**, trained, experienced, able, professional, skilled, master, masterly, qualified, talented, outstanding, clever, practised,

accomplished, handy, competent, apt, adept, knowledgeable, virtuoso, deft, proficient, facile, adroit, dexterous, leet (*Computing slang*) ■ **OPPOSITE:** unskilled

expertise NOUN = **skill**, knowledge, know-how (*informal*), facility, grip, craft, judgment, grasp, mastery, knack, proficiency, dexterity, cleverness, deftness, adroitness, aptness, expertness, knowing inside out, ableness, masterliness, skilfulness

expiration NOUN = **expiry**, end, finish, conclusion, close, termination, cessation

expire VERB **1** *He continued to live in the States after his visa had expired.* = **become invalid**, end, finish, conclude, close, stop, run out, cease, lapse, terminate, come to an end, be no longer valid **2** *He expired in excruciating agony.* = **die**, decease, depart, buy it (*U.S. slang*), check out (*U.S. slang*), perish, kick it (*slang*), croak (*slang*), go belly-up (*slang*), snuff it (*informal*), peg out (*informal*), kick the bucket (*informal*), peg it (*informal*), depart this life, meet your maker, cark it (*Austral. & N.Z. slang*), pop your clogs (*informal*), pass away or on

expiry NOUN = **expiration**, ending, end, conclusion, close, demise (*euphemistic*), lapsing, lapse, termination, cessation

explain VERB **1** *He explained the process to us in simple terms.* = **make clear** or **plain**, describe, demonstrate, illustrate, teach, define, solve, resolve, interpret, disclose, unfold, clarify, clear up, simplify, expound, elucidate, put into words, throw light on, explicate (*formal*), give the details of **2** *Can you explain why you didn't call me?* = **account for**, excuse, justify, give a reason for, give an explanation for

explanation NOUN **1** *The president has given no explanation for his behaviour.* = **reason**, meaning, cause, sense, answer, account, excuse, motive, justification, vindication, mitigation, the why and wherefore **2** *his lucid explanation of the mysteries of cricket* = **description**, report, definition, demonstration, teaching, resolution, interpretation, illustration, clarification, exposition, simplification, explication, elucidation

explanatory or **explanative** ADJECTIVE = **descriptive**, interpretive, illustrative, interpretative, demonstrative, justifying, expository, illuminative, elucidatory, explicative

explicit ADJECTIVE **1** *He left explicit instructions on how to set the alarm.* = **clear**, obvious, specific, direct, certain, express, plain, absolute, exact, precise, straightforward, definite, overt, unequivocal, unqualified, unambiguous, categorical ■ **OPPOSITE:** vague **2** *songs containing explicit references to sexual activity* = **frank**, direct, open, specific, positive, plain, patent, graphic, distinct, outspoken, upfront (*informal*), unambiguous, unrestricted, unrestrained, uncensored, unreserved ■ **OPPOSITE:** indirect

explode VERB **1** *They were clearing up when the second bomb exploded.* = **blow up**, erupt, burst, go off, shatter, shiver **2** *The first test atomic bomb was exploded in the New Mexico desert.* = **detonate**, set off, discharge, let off **3** *He exploded with rage at the accusation.* = **lose your temper**, rage, erupt, blow up (*informal*), lose it (*informal*), crack up (*informal*), see red (*informal*), lose the plot (*informal*), become angry, have a fit (*informal*), go ballistic (*slang*), hit the roof (*informal*), throw a tantrum, blow a fuse (*slang, chiefly U.S.*), go berserk (*slang*), go mad (*slang*), fly off the handle (*informal*), go spare (*Brit. slang*), become enraged, go off the deep end (*informal*), go up the wall (*slang*), blow your top (*informal*), go crook (*Austral. & N.Z. slang*), fly into a temper, flip your lid (*slang*), do your nut (*Brit. slang*) **4** *The population has exploded in the last twenty years.* = **increase**, grow, develop, extend, advance, shoot up, soar, boost, expand, build up, swell, step up (*informal*), escalate, multiply, proliferate, snowball, aggrandize **5** *She explodes the myth that supermodels are bubble-headed egomaniacs.* = **disprove**, discredit, refute, belie, demolish, repudiate, put paid to, invalidate, debunk, prove impossible, prove wrong, give the lie to, blow out of the water (*slang*)

exploit NOUN *His wartime exploits were made into a TV series.* = **feat**, act, achievement, enterprise, adventure, stunt, deed, accomplishment, attainment, escapade ▶ VERB **1** *Casual workers are being exploited for slave wages.* = **take advantage of**, abuse, use, manipulate, milk, misuse, dump on (*slang, chiefly U.S.*), ill-treat, play on or upon **2** *The opposition are exploiting the situation to their advantage.* = **make the best use of**, use, make use of, utilize, cash in on (*informal*), capitalize on, put to use, make capital out of, use to advantage, use to good advantage, live off the backs of, turn to account, profit by or from

exploitation NOUN **1** *the exploitation of working women* = **misuse**, abuse, manipulation, imposition, using, ill-treatment **2** *the exploitation of the famine by local politicians* = **capitalization**, utilization, using to good advantage, trading upon

exploration NOUN **1** *We devoted a week to the exploration of the Mayan sites of Copan.* = **expedition**, tour, trip, survey, travel, journey, reconnaissance, recce (*slang*) **2** *an exploration of Celtic mythology* = **investigation**, study, research, survey, search, inquiry, analysis, examination, probe, inspection, scrutiny, once-over (*informal*)

exploratory ADJECTIVE = **investigative**, trial, searching, probing, experimental, analytic, fact-finding

explore VERB **1** *We explored the old part of the town.* = **travel around**, tour, survey, scout, traverse, range over, recce (*slang*), reconnoitre, case (*slang*), have or take a look around **2** *The film explores the relationship between artist and instrument.* = **investigate**, consider, research, survey, search, prospect, examine, probe, analyse, look into, inspect, work over, scrutinize, inquire into

explosion NOUN **1** *Three people were killed in a bomb explosion today.* = **blast**, crack, burst, bang, discharge, report, blowing up, outburst, clap, detonation **2** *a population explosion* = **increase**, rise, development, growth, boost, expansion, enlargement, escalation, upturn **3** *His reaction was an explosion of anger.* = **outburst**, fit, storm, attack, surge, flare-up, eruption, paroxysm **4** *an explosion of violence in the country's capital* = **outbreak**, flare-up, eruption, upsurge

explosive ADJECTIVE **1** *Highly explosive gas is naturally found in coal mines.* = **unstable**, dangerous, volatile, hazardous, unsafe, perilous, combustible, inflammable **2** *a potentially explosive situation* = **dangerous**, worrying, strained, anxious, charged, ugly, tense, hazardous, stressful, perilous, nerve-racking, overwrought **3** *He inherited his father's explosive temper.* = **fiery**, violent, volatile, stormy, touchy, vehement, chippy (*informal*) ▶ NOUN *A large quantity of arms and explosives was seized.* = **bomb**, mine, shell, missile, rocket, grenade, charge, torpedo, incendiary

exponent NOUN **1** *a leading exponent of genetic engineering* = **advocate**, champion, supporter, defender, spokesman or woman or person, promoter, backer, spokesperson, proponent, propagandist, upholder **2** *the great exponent of Bach, Glenn Gould* = **performer**, player, interpreter, presenter, executant

expose VERB **1** *He pulled up his T-shirt, exposing his white belly.* = **uncover**, show, reveal, display, exhibit, present, unveil, manifest, lay bare, take the wraps off, put on view

■ **OPPOSITE:** hide **2** *After the scandal was exposed, he committed suicide.* = **reveal**, disclose, uncover, air, detect, betray, show up, denounce, unearth, let out, divulge, unmask, lay bare, make known, bring to light, out (*informal*), smoke out, blow wide open (*slang*) ■ **OPPOSITE:** keep secret **3** *people exposed to high levels of radiation* = **make vulnerable**, subject, leave open, lay open • **expose someone to something** *when women from these societies become exposed to Western culture* = **introduce to**, acquaint with, bring into contact with, familiarize with, make familiar with, make conversant with

exposé NOUN = **exposure**, revelation, uncovering, disclosure, divulgence

exposed ADJECTIVE **1** *Skin cancer is most likely to occur on exposed parts of the body.* = **unconcealed**, revealed, bare, exhibited, unveiled, shown, uncovered, on display, on show, on view, laid bare, made manifest **2** *This part of the coast is very exposed.* = **unsheltered**, open, unprotected, open to the elements **3** *The troops are exposed to attack by the enemy.* = **vulnerable**, open, subject, in danger, liable, susceptible, wide open, left open, laid bare, in peril, laid open

exposition NOUN **1** *Her speech was an exposition of her beliefs in freedom and justice.* = **explanation**, account, description, interpretation, illustration, presentation, commentary, critique, exegesis, explication, elucidation **2** *an art exposition* = **exhibition**, show, fair, display, demonstration, presentation, expo (*informal*)

exposure NOUN **1** *Exposure to lead is known to damage the brains of young children.* = **vulnerability**, subjection, susceptibility, laying open **2** *Two people died of exposure in Chicago overnight.* = **hypothermia**, frostbite, extreme cold, intense cold **3** *the exposure of Anthony Blunt as a former Soviet spy* = **revelation**, exposé, uncovering, disclosure, airing, manifestation, detection, divulging, denunciation, unmasking, divulgence **4** *The candidates have been getting a lot of exposure on TV.* = **publicity**, promotion, attention, advertising, plugging (*informal*), propaganda, hype, pushing, media hype **5** *exposure of the skin to sunlight* = **uncovering**, showing, display, exhibition, baring, revelation, presentation, unveiling, manifestation **6** *Repeated exposure to the music reveals its hidden depths.* = **contact**, experience, awareness, acquaintance, familiarity

expound VERB = **explain**, describe, illustrate, interpret, unfold, spell out, set forth, elucidate, explicate (*formal*)

express VERB **1** *He expressed grave concern at their attitude.* = **state**, communicate, convey, articulate, say, tell, put, word, speak, voice, declare, phrase, assert, pronounce, utter, couch, put across, enunciate, put into words, give voice to, verbalize, asseverate (*formal*) **2** *He expressed his anger in a destructive way.* = **show**, indicate, exhibit, demonstrate, reveal, disclose, intimate, convey, testify to, depict, designate, manifest, embody, signify, symbolize, denote, divulge, bespeak, make known, evince (*formal*)
▶ ADJECTIVE **1** *I was warned not to leave my post without express orders.* = **explicit**, clear, direct, precise, pointed, certain, plain, accurate, exact, distinct, definite, outright, unambiguous, categorical **2** *I bought the camera with the express purpose of taking nature photos.* = **specific**, exclusive, particular, sole, special, deliberate, singular, clear-cut, especial **3** *A special express service is available.* = **fast**, direct, quick, rapid, priority, prompt, swift, high-speed, speedy, quickie (*informal*), nonstop, expeditious

expression NOUN **1** *From Cairo came expressions of regret at the attack.* = **statement**, declaration, announcement, communication, mention, assertion, utterance, articulation, pronouncement, enunciation, verbalization, asseveration **2** *We attended as an expression of solidarity.* = **indication**, demonstration, exhibition, display, showing, show, sign, symbol, representation, token, manifestation, embodiment **3** *He sat there with a sad expression on his face.* = **look**, countenance (*literary*), face, air, appearance, aspect, mien (*literary*) **4** *She puts a lot of expression into her playing.* = **intonation**, style, delivery, phrasing, emphasis, execution, diction **5** *He uses some remarkably coarse expressions.* = **phrase**, saying, word, wording, term, language, speech, remark, maxim, idiom, adage, choice of words, turn of phrase, phraseology, locution, set phrase

expressionless ADJECTIVE = **blank**, empty, deadpan, straight-faced, wooden, dull, vacuous, inscrutable, poker-faced (*informal*)

expressive ADJECTIVE **1** *She had a small, expressive face.* = **vivid**, strong, striking, telling, moving, lively, sympathetic, energetic, poignant, emphatic, eloquent, forcible ■ **OPPOSITE:** impassive **2** (*with* **of**) *All his poems are expressive of his love for nature.* = **meaningful**, indicative, suggestive,

e

demonstrative, revealing, significant, allusive

expressly ADVERB **1** *They had expressly forbidden me to go out on my own.* = **explicitly**, clearly, plainly, absolutely, positively, definitely, outright, manifestly, distinctly, decidedly, categorically, pointedly, unequivocally, unmistakably, in no uncertain terms, unambiguously **2** *Bleasdale had written the role expressly for this actor.* = **specifically**, specially, especially, particularly, purposely, exclusively, precisely, solely, exactly, deliberately, intentionally, on purpose

expropriate VERB = **seize**, take, appropriate, confiscate, assume, take over, take away, commandeer, requisition, arrogate

expropriation NOUN = **seizure**, takeover, impounding, confiscation, commandeering, requisitioning, sequestration, disseisin (*Law*)

expulsion NOUN **1** *Her behaviour led to her expulsion from school.* = **ejection**, exclusion, dismissal, removal, exile, discharge, eviction, banishment, extrusion, proscription, expatriation, debarment, dislodgment **2** *the expulsion of waste products from the body* = **discharge**, emptying, emission, voiding, spewing, secretion, excretion, ejection, seepage, suppuration

expunge VERB = **erase**, remove, destroy, abolish, cancel, get rid of, wipe out, eradicate, excise, delete, extinguish, strike out, obliterate, annihilate, efface, exterminate, annul, raze, blot out, extirpate

exquisite ADJECTIVE **1** *She has exquisite manners.* = **beautiful**, elegant, graceful, pleasing, attractive, lovely, charming, comely (*old-fashioned*) ■ **OPPOSITE:** unattractive **2** *These panels of glazed tiles are exquisite works of art.* = **fine**, beautiful, lovely, elegant, precious, delicate, dainty **3** *His words gave her exquisite pain.* = **intense**, acute, severe, sharp, keen, extreme, piercing, poignant, excruciating **4** *The house was furnished with exquisite taste.* = **refined**, cultivated, discriminating, sensitive, polished, selective, discerning, impeccable, meticulous, consummate, appreciative, fastidious **5** *The hotel features friendly staff and exquisite cuisine.* = **excellent**, fine, outstanding, superb, choice, perfect, select, delicious, divine (*informal*), splendid, admirable, consummate, flawless, superlative, incomparable, peerless, matchless ■ **OPPOSITE:** imperfect

extant ADJECTIVE = **in existence**, existing, remaining, surviving, living, existent, subsisting, undestroyed

USAGE Used carefully, the word *extant* describes something that has survived, often against all odds. It therefore carries a slightly more specific meaning than *in existence*, and should not be considered as being automatically interchangeable with this phrase. For example, you might say *the oldest extant document dates from 1492*; but *in existence* (not *extant*) *for 15 years, they are still one of the most successful bands in the world.* In many contexts, however, these ideas overlap, leaving the writer to decide whether *extant* or *in existence* best expresses the intended meaning.

extend VERB **1** *The territory extends over one fifth of Canada's land mass.* = **spread out**, reach, stretch, continue, carry on **2** *Stand straight with your arms extended at your sides.* = **stretch**, stretch out, spread out, unfurl, straighten out, unroll **3** *His playing career extended from 1894 to 1920.* = **last**, continue, go on, stretch, carry on **4** *Allow about a quarter of an inch to extend beyond your palm.* = **protrude**, project, stand out, bulge, stick out, hang, overhang, jut out **5** *His possessiveness extends to people as well as property.* = **reach**, spread, go as far as **6** *They have added three new products to extend their range.* = **widen**, increase, develop, expand, spread, add to, enhance, supplement, enlarge, broaden, diversify, amplify, augment ■ **OPPOSITE:** reduce **7** *They have extended the deadline by 24 hours.* = **make longer**, prolong, lengthen, draw out, spin out, elongate, drag out, protract ■ **OPPOSITE:** shorten **8** *'I'm Chuck,' the man said, extending his hand.* = **offer**, give, hold out, present, grant, advance, yield, reach out, confer, stretch out, stick out, bestow, impart, proffer, put forth ■ **OPPOSITE:** withdraw

extended ADJECTIVE **1** *He and Naomi spent an extended period getting to know one another.* = **lengthened**, long, prolonged, protracted, stretched out, drawn-out, unfurled, elongated, unrolled **2** *a tribal society grouped in huge extended families* = **broad**, wide, expanded, extensive, widespread, comprehensive, large-scale, enlarged, far-reaching **3** *She found herself kissing the old woman's extended hand.* = **outstretched**, conferred, stretched out, proffered

extension NOUN **1** *the new extension to London's National Gallery* = **annexe**, wing, addition, supplement, branch, appendix, add-on, adjunct, appendage, ell, addendum **2** *He has been granted a six-month* *extension to his visa.* = **lengthening**, extra time, continuation, postponement, prolongation, additional period of time, protraction **3** *The agreement we have reached is a natural extension of our relationship.* = **development**, expansion, widening, increase, stretching, broadening, continuation, enlargement, diversification, amplification, elongation, augmentation

extensive ADJECTIVE **1** *This 18th-century manor house is set in extensive grounds.* = **large**, considerable, substantial, spacious, wide, sweeping, broad, expansive, capacious, commodious ■ **OPPOSITE:** confined **2** *The story generated extensive comment on social media.* = **comprehensive**, complete, thorough, lengthy, long, wide, wholesale, pervasive, protracted, all-inclusive ■ **OPPOSITE:** restricted **3** *The blast caused extensive damage.* = **great**, large, huge, extended, vast, widespread, comprehensive, universal, large-scale, far-reaching, prevalent, far-flung, all-inclusive, voluminous, humongous *or* humungous (*informal*) ■ **OPPOSITE:** limited

extent NOUN **1** *The full extent of the losses was revealed yesterday.* = **magnitude**, amount, degree, scale, level, measure, stretch, quantity, bulk, duration, expanse, amplitude **2** *an estate about seven or eight acres in extent* = **size**, area, range, length, reach, bounds, sweep, sphere, width, compass, breadth, ambit

exterior NOUN *The exterior of the building was a masterpiece of architecture.* = **outside**, face, surface, covering, finish, skin, appearance, aspect, shell, coating, façade, outside surface ▶ ADJECTIVE *The exterior walls were made of pre-formed concrete.* = **outer**, outside, external, surface, outward, superficial, outermost ■ **OPPOSITE:** inner

exterminate VERB = **destroy**, kill, eliminate, abolish, eradicate, annihilate, extirpate

extermination NOUN = **destruction**, murder, massacre, slaughter, killing, wiping out, genocide, elimination, mass murder, annihilation, eradication, extirpation

external ADJECTIVE **1** *the external surface of the wall* = **outer**, outside, surface, apparent, visible, outward, exterior, superficial, outermost ■ **OPPOSITE:** internal **2** *the commissioner for external affairs* = **foreign**, international, alien, exotic, exterior, extraneous, extrinsic ■ **OPPOSITE:** domestic **3** *The papers are checked by external examiners.* = **outside**, visiting, independent, extramural ■ **OPPOSITE:** inside

extinct ADJECTIVE **1** *It is 250 years since the wolf became extinct in Britain.* = **dead**, lost, gone, vanished, defunct ■ **OPPOSITE:** living **2** *The island's tallest volcano is long extinct.* = **inactive**, extinguished, doused, out, snuffed out, quenched

extinction NOUN = **dying out**, death, destruction, abolition, oblivion, extermination, annihilation, eradication, obliteration, excision, extirpation

extinguish VERB **1** *It took about 50 minutes to extinguish the fire.* = **put out**, stifle, smother, blow out, douse, snuff out, quench **2** *The message extinguished her hopes of Richard's return.* = **destroy**, end, kill (*informal*), remove, eliminate, obscure, abolish, suppress, wipe out, erase, eradicate, annihilate, put paid to, exterminate, expunge (*formal*), extirpate

extol VERB = **praise**, acclaim, applaud, pay tribute to, celebrate, commend, magnify (*archaic*), glorify, exalt, laud (*literary*), crack up (*informal*), sing the praises of, eulogize, cry up, panegyrize

extort VERB = **extract**, force, squeeze, exact, bully, bleed (*informal*), blackmail, wring, coerce, wrest

extortion NOUN = **blackmail**, force, oppression, compulsion, coercion, shakedown (*U.S. slang*), rapacity, exaction (*formal*)

extortionate ADJECTIVE *the extortionate price of designer clothes* = **exorbitant**, excessive, outrageous, unreasonable, inflated, extravagant, preposterous, sky-high, inordinate, immoderate ■ **OPPOSITE:** reasonable

extra ADJECTIVE **1** *Extra staff have been taken on to cover busy periods.* = **additional**, more, new, other, added, further, fresh, accessory, supplementary, auxiliary, add-on, supplemental, ancillary ■ **OPPOSITE:** vital **2** *This exercise will help you burn up any extra calories.* = **surplus**, excess, reserve, spare, unnecessary, redundant, needless, unused, leftover, superfluous, extraneous, unneeded, inessential, supernumerary, supererogatory ▶ NOUN *Optional extras including cooking tuition.* = **addition**, bonus, supplement, accessory, complement, add-on, affix, adjunct, appendage, addendum, supernumerary, appurtenance ■ **OPPOSITE:** necessity ▶ ADVERB **1** *You may be charged extra for this service.* = **in addition**, additionally, over and above **2** *Try extra hard to be nice to him.* = **exceptionally**, very, specially, especially, particularly, extremely, remarkably, unusually, extraordinarily, uncommonly

extract VERB **1** *Citric acid can be extracted from the juice of oranges.* = **obtain**, take out, distil, squeeze out, draw out, express, separate out, press out **2** *He extracted a small notebook from his pocket.* = **take out**, draw, pull, remove, withdraw, pull out, bring out **3** *She has to have a tooth extracted at 3 today.* = **pull out**, remove, take out, draw, uproot, pluck out, extirpate **4** *He tried to extract further information from the witness.* = **elicit**, get, obtain, force, draw, gather, derive, exact, bring out, evoke, reap, wring, glean, coerce, wrest **5** *material extracted from a range of texts* = **select**, quote, cite, abstract, choose, cut out, reproduce, cull, copy out ▶ NOUN **1** *He read us an extract from his latest novel.* = **passage**, selection, excerpt, cutting, clipping, abstract, quotation, citation **2** *fragrances taken from plant extracts* = **essence**, solution, concentrate, juice, distillation, decoction, distillate

> **USAGE** People sometimes use *extract* where *extricate* would be better. Although both words can refer to a physical act of removal from a place, *extract* has a more general sense than *extricate*. *Extricate* has additional overtones of 'difficulty', and is most commonly used with reference to getting a person – particularly *yourself* – out of a situation. So, for example, you might say *he will find it difficult to extricate himself* (not *extract himself*) *from this situation*.

extraction NOUN **1** *a young Brazilian of German extraction* = **origin**, family, ancestry, descent, race, stock, blood, birth, pedigree, lineage, parentage, derivation **2** *the extraction of wisdom teeth* = **taking out**, drawing, pulling, withdrawal, removal, uprooting, extirpation **3** *High temperatures are used during the extraction of cooking oils.* = **distillation**, separation, derivation

extraneous ADJECTIVE **1** *Just give me the basic facts, with no extraneous details.* = **nonessential**, unnecessary, extra, additional, redundant, needless, peripheral, supplementary, incidental, superfluous, unneeded, inessential, adventitious, unessential **2** *Let's not allow ourselves to be sidetracked by extraneous questions.* = **irrelevant**, inappropriate, unrelated, unconnected, immaterial, beside the point, impertinent, inadmissible, off the subject, inapplicable, inapt, inapposite

extraordinary ADJECTIVE **1** *He is an extraordinary musician.* = **remarkable**, special, wonderful, outstanding, rare, amazing, fantastic (*informal*), astonishing, marvellous, eye-popping (*informal*), exceptional, notable, serious (*informal*), phenomenal, singular, wondrous (*archaic*, *literary*), out of this world (*informal*), extremely good ■ OPPOSITE: unremarkable **2** *What an extraordinary thing to happen!* = **unusual**, surprising, odd, strange, unique, remarkable, bizarre, curious, weird, unprecedented, peculiar, unfamiliar, uncommon, unheard-of, unwonted ■ OPPOSITE: ordinary

extravagance NOUN **1** *He was accused of gross mismanagement and financial extravagance.* = **overspending**, squandering, profusion, profligacy, wastefulness, waste, lavishness, prodigality, improvidence **2** *Our only extravagance is two holidays a year.* = **luxury**, treat, indulgence, extra, frill, nonessential **3** *the ridiculous extravagance of his claims* = **excess**, folly, exaggeration, absurdity, recklessness, wildness, dissipation, outrageousness, unreasonableness, preposterousness, immoderation, exorbitance, unrestraint

extravagant ADJECTIVE **1** *his extravagant lifestyle* = **wasteful**, excessive, lavish, prodigal, profligate, spendthrift, imprudent, improvident ■ OPPOSITE: economical **2** *Her aunt gave her an uncharacteristically extravagant gift.* = **overpriced**, expensive, costly **3** *hotels charging extravagant prices* = **exorbitant**, excessive, steep (*informal*), unreasonable, inordinate, extortionate ■ OPPOSITE: reasonable **4** *He was extravagant in his admiration of Lillie.* = **excessive**, exaggerated, outrageous, wild, fantastic, absurd, foolish, over the top (*slang*), unreasonable, preposterous, fanciful, unrestrained, inordinate, outré, immoderate, O.T.T. (*slang*) ■ OPPOSITE: moderate **5** *The couple wed in extravagant style.* = **showy**, elaborate, flamboyant, impressive, fancy, flashy, ornate, pretentious, grandiose, gaudy, garish, ostentatious ■ OPPOSITE: restrained

extravaganza NOUN = **spectacular**, show, spectacle, display, pageant, flight of fancy

extreme ADJECTIVE **1** *people living in extreme poverty* = **great**, high, highest, greatest, worst, supreme, acute, severe, maximum, intense, ultimate, utmost, mother of all (*informal*), uttermost ■ OPPOSITE: mild **2** *The scheme was rejected as being too extreme.* = **severe**, radical, strict, harsh, stern, rigid, dire, drastic, uncompromising, unbending **3** *his extreme political views* = **radical**, unusual, excessive, exceptional, exaggerated, outrageous, over the top (slang), unreasonable, uncommon, unconventional, fanatical, zealous, out-and-out, inordinate, egregious, intemperate, immoderate, O.T.T. (slang), swivel-eyed (slang) ■ **OPPOSITE:** moderate **4** the room at the extreme end of the corridor = **farthest**, furthest, far, final, last, ultimate, remotest, terminal, utmost, far-off, faraway, outermost, most distant, uttermost ■ **OPPOSITE:** nearest ▶ NOUN a 'middle way' between the extremes of success and failure = **limit**, end, edge, opposite, pole, ultimate, boundary, antithesis, extremity, acme

extremely ADVERB = **very**, highly, greatly, particularly, severely, terribly, ultra, utterly, unusually, exceptionally, extraordinarily, intensely, tremendously, markedly, awfully (informal), acutely, exceedingly, excessively, inordinately, uncommonly, to a fault, to the nth degree, to or in the extreme

extremist NOUN Police believe the bombing was the work of extremists. = **radical**, activist, militant, enthusiast, fanatic, devotee, die-hard, bigot, zealot, energumen ▶ ADJECTIVE The riots were organized by extremist groups. = **extreme**, wild, mad, enthusiastic, passionate, frenzied, obsessive, fanatical, fervent, zealous, bigoted, rabid, immoderate, overenthusiastic, swivel-eyed (slang)

extremity NOUN **1** a small port on the north-western extremity of the island = **limit**, end, edge, border, top, tip, bound, minimum, extreme, maximum, pole, margin, boundary, terminal, frontier, verge (Brit.), brink, rim, brim, pinnacle, termination, nadir, zenith, apex, terminus, apogee, farthest point, furthest point, acme **2** his lack of restraint in the extremity of his grief = **depth**, height, excess, climax, consummation, acuteness **3** Even in extremity, she never lost her sense of humour. = **crisis**, trouble, emergency, disaster, setback, pinch, plight, hardship, adversity, dire straits, exigency, extreme suffering ▶ PLURAL NOUN Rheumatoid arthritis affects the extremities and limbs. = **hands and feet**, limbs, fingers and toes

extricate VERB **1** an attempt to extricate himself from his financial difficulties = **withdraw**, relieve, free, clear, deliver, liberate, wriggle out of, get (someone) off the hook (slang), disembarrass **2** Emergency workers tried to extricate the survivors from the wreckage. = **free**, clear, release, remove, rescue, get out, disengage, disentangle

extrovert or **extravert** NOUN He was a showman, an extrovert who revelled in controversy. = **outgoing person**, mingler, socializer, mixer, life and soul of the party ■ **OPPOSITE:** introvert ▶ ADJECTIVE His extrovert personality won him many friends. = **sociable**, social, lively, outgoing, hearty, exuberant, amiable, gregarious ■ **OPPOSITE:** introverted

exuberance NOUN **1** Her burst of exuberance overwhelmed me. = **high spirits**, energy, enthusiasm, vitality, life, spirit, excitement, pep, animation, vigour, zest, eagerness, buoyancy, exhilaration, cheerfulness, brio, vivacity, ebullience, liveliness, effervescence, sprightliness **2** the exuberance of plant life in the region = **luxuriance**, abundance, richness, profusion, plenitude, lushness, superabundance, lavishness, rankness, copiousness

exuberant ADJECTIVE **1** Our son was a highly active and exuberant little person. = **high-spirited**, spirited, enthusiastic, lively, excited, eager, sparkling, vigorous, cheerful, energetic, animated, upbeat (informal), buoyant, exhilarated, elated, ebullient, chirpy (informal), sprightly, vivacious, effervescent, full of life, full of beans (informal), zestful ■ **OPPOSITE:** subdued **2** hillsides ablaze with exuberant flowers and shrubs = **luxuriant**, rich, lavish, abundant, lush, overflowing, plentiful, teeming, copious, profuse, superabundant, plenteous **3** exuberant praise = **fulsome**, excessive, exaggerated, lavish, overdone, superfluous, prodigal, effusive

exude VERB **1** She exudes an air of confidence. = **radiate**, show, display, exhibit, manifest, emanate **2** Nearby was a factory which exuded a pungent smell. = **emit**, leak, discharge, ooze, emanate, issue, secrete, excrete **3** the fluid that exudes from the cane toad's back = **seep**, leak, sweat, bleed, weep, trickle, ooze, emanate, issue, filter through, well forth

exult VERB **1** He seemed calm, but inwardly he exulted. = **be joyful**, be delighted, rejoice, be overjoyed, celebrate, be elated, be jubilant, jump for joy, make merry, be in high spirits, jubilate **2** (often with **over**) She was still exulting over her victory. = **revel**, glory in, boast, crow, taunt, brag, vaunt, drool, gloat, take delight in

exultant ADJECTIVE = **joyful**, delighted, flushed, triumphant, revelling, rejoicing, jubilant, joyous, transported, elated, over the moon (informal), overjoyed, rapt, gleeful, exulting, cock-a-hoop, stoked (Austral. & N.Z. informal)

eye NOUN **1** *She is blind in one eye.* = **eyeball**, optic (*informal*), peeper (*slang*), orb (*poetic*), organ of vision, organ of sight **2** (*often plural*) *her sharp eyes and acute hearing* = **eyesight**, sight, vision, observation, perception, ability to see, range of vision, power of seeing **3** *He has an eye for talent.* = **appreciation**, taste, recognition, judgment, discrimination, perception, discernment **4** *He played under his grandmother's watchful eye.* = **observance**, observation, supervision, surveillance, attention, notice, inspection, heed, vigil, watch, lookout, vigilance, alertness, watchfulness **5** *the eye of the hurricane* = **centre**, heart, middle, mid, core, nucleus ▶ VERB *We eyed each other thoughtfully.* = **look at**, view, study, watch, check, regard, survey, clock (*Brit. slang*), observe, stare at, scan, contemplate, check out (*informal*), inspect, glance at, gaze at, behold (*archaic, literary*), eyeball (*slang*), scrutinize, peruse, get a load of (*informal*), take a dekko at (*Brit. slang*), have or take a look at • **an eye for an eye** *Their philosophy was an eye for an eye and a tooth for a tooth.* = **retaliation**, justice, revenge, vengeance, reprisal, retribution, requital, lex talionis • **turn a blind eye to** or **close your eyes to** *They just closed their eyes to what was going on.* = **ignore**, reject, overlook, disregard, pass over, take no notice of, be oblivious to, pay no attention to, turn your back on, turn a deaf ear to, bury your head in the sand • **eye something** or **someone up** *Some girls were eyeing him up from a nearby table.* = **ogle**, leer at, make eyes at, give (someone) the (glad)

eye • **in** or **to someone's eyes** = **in the opinion of**, in the mind of, from someone's viewpoint, in the judgment of, in someone's point of view, in the belief of • **see eye to eye (with)** *They saw eye to eye on almost every aspect of the production.* = **agree (with)**, accord (with), get on (with), fall in (with), coincide (with), go along (with), subscribe (to), be united (with), concur (with), harmonize (with), speak the same language (as), be on the same wavelength (as), be of the same mind (as), be in unison (with) • **set, clap** or **lay eyes on someone** *I haven't set eyes on him for years.* = **see**, meet, notice, observe, encounter, come across, run into, behold (*archaic, literary*) • **up to your eyes (in)** *I am up to my eyes in work just now.* = **very busy (with)**, overwhelmed (with), caught up (in), inundated (by), wrapped up (in), engaged (in), flooded out (by), fully occupied (with), up to here (with), up to your elbows (in) ■ **RELATED WORDS:** *adjectives* ocular, ophthalmic, optic

eye-catching ADJECTIVE = **striking**, arresting, attractive, dramatic, spectacular, captivating, showy

eyesight NOUN = **vision**, sight, observation, perception, ability to see, range of vision, power of seeing, power of sight

eyesore NOUN = **mess**, blight, blot, blemish, sight (*informal*), horror, disgrace, atrocity, ugliness, monstrosity, disfigurement

eyewitness NOUN = **observer**, witness, spectator, looker-on, viewer, passer-by, watcher, onlooker, bystander

Ff

fable NOUN **1** *Each tale has the timeless quality of fable.* = **legend**, myth, parable, allegory, story, tale, apologue **2** *Is reincarnation fact or fable?* = **fiction**, lie, fantasy, myth, romance, invention, yarn (*informal*), fabrication, falsehood, fib, figment, untruth, fairy story (*informal*), urban myth, white lie, tall story (*informal*), urban legend ■ **OPPOSITE:** fact

fabled ADJECTIVE = **legendary**, fictional, famed, mythical, storied, famous, fabulous

fabric NOUN **1** *small squares of red cotton fabric* = **cloth**, material, stuff, textile, web **2** *The fabric of society has been deeply damaged.* = **framework**, structure, make-up, organization, frame, foundations, construction, constitution, infrastructure **3** *Condensation will eventually cause the fabric of the building to rot away.* = **structure**, foundations, construction, framework, infrastructure

fabricate VERB **1** *All four claim that officers fabricated evidence against them.* = **make up**, invent, concoct, falsify, form, coin, devise, forge, fake, feign, trump up **2** *All the tools are fabricated from high-quality steel.* = **manufacture**, make, build, form, fashion, shape, frame, construct, assemble, erect

fabrication NOUN **1** *She described the interview with her as a 'complete fabrication'.* = **forgery**, lie, fiction, myth, fake, invention, fable, concoction, falsehood, figment, untruth, porky (*Brit. slang*), fairy story (*informal*), pork pie (*Brit. slang*), cock-and-bull story (*informal*) **2** *More than 200 improvements were made in the design and fabrication of the shuttle.* = **manufacture**, production, construction, assembly, erection, assemblage, building

fabulous ADJECTIVE **1** *The scenery and weather were fabulous.* = **wonderful**, excellent, brilliant, superb, spectacular, fantastic (*informal*), marvellous, sensational (*informal*), first-rate, brill (*informal*), magic (*informal*), out-of-this-world (*informal*) ■ **OPPOSITE:** ordinary **2** *You'll be entered in our free draw to win this fabulous prize.* = **astounding**, amazing, extraordinary, remarkable, incredible (*informal*), astonishing, eye-popping (*informal*), legendary, immense, unbelievable, breathtaking, phenomenal, inconceivable **3** *The chimaera of myth is a fabulous beast made up of the parts of other animals.* = **legendary**, imaginary, mythical, fictitious, made-up, fantastic, invented, unreal, mythological, apocryphal

façade NOUN **1** *the façade of the building* = **front**, face, exterior, frontage **2** *They hid the troubles plaguing their marriage behind a façade of family togetherness.* = **show**, front, appearance, mask, exterior, guise, pretence, veneer, semblance

face NOUN **1** *She had a beautiful face.* = **countenance**, features, kisser (*slang*), profile, dial (*Brit. slang*), mug (*slang*), visage, physiognomy, lineaments, phiz or phizog (*slang*) **2** *He was walking around with a sad face.* = **expression**, look, air, appearance, aspect, countenance (*literary*) **3** *We climbed 200 feet up the cliff face.* = **side**, front, cover, outside, surface, aspect, exterior, right side, elevation, facet, vertical surface **4** = **dial**, display **5** = **nature**, image, character, appearance, concept, conception, make-up **6** = **self-respect**, respect, reputation, dignity, standing, authority, image, regard, status, honour, esteem, prestige, self-image, mana (*N.Z.*) **7** *I haven't the face to ask her for money.* = **impudence**, front, confidence, audacity, nerve (*informal*), neck (*informal*), sauce (*informal*), cheek (*informal*), assurance, gall (*informal*), presumption, boldness, chutzpah (*U.S. & Canad. informal*), sass (*U.S. & Canad. informal*), effrontery, brass neck (*Brit. informal*), sassiness (*U.S. informal*) ▶ VERB **1** (*often with* **to**, **towards**, *or* **on**) *The garden faces south.* = **look onto**, overlook, be opposite, look out on, front onto, give towards or onto **2** *She looked relaxed and calm as she faced the press.* = **confront**, meet, encounter, deal with, oppose, tackle, cope with, experience, brave, defy, come up against, be confronted by, face off (*slang*) • **face someone down** = **intimidate**, defeat, confront, subdue, disconcert • **face up to** *You must face up to the truth that the relationship has ended.* = **accept**, deal with, tackle, acknowledge, cope with, confront, come to terms with, meet head-on, reconcile yourself to • **make** or **pull a face at someone** *She made a face at him behind his back.* = **scowl**, frown, pout, grimace, smirk, moue (*French*) • **on the face of it** *On the face of it, that seems to make sense.* = **to all appearances**, apparently, seemingly, outwardly, at first sight, at face value, to the eye • **show your face** I felt I ought to show my face at her father's funeral. = **turn up**, come, appear, be seen, show up (informal), put in or make an appearance, approach

faceless ADJECTIVE = **impersonal**, remote, unknown, unidentified, anonymous

face-lift NOUN **1** Nothing gives a room a faster face-lift than a coat of paint. = **renovation**, improvement, restoration, refurbishing, modernization, redecoration **2** A face-lift is just one example of cosmetic surgery. = **cosmetic surgery**, plastic surgery

facet NOUN The website documents every facet of the director's career. = **aspect**, part, face, side, phase, angle **2** The stones shone back at her, a thousand facets of light in their white-gold settings. = **face**, side, surface, plane, slant

facile ADJECTIVE **1** I hated him making facile suggestions when I knew the problem was extremely complex. = **superficial**, shallow, slick, glib, hasty, cursory **2** His facile win tells us he's in form. = **effortless**, easy, simple, quick, ready, smooth, skilful, adept, fluent, uncomplicated, proficient, adroit, dexterous, light ■ **OPPOSITE:** difficult

facilitate VERB = **further**, help, forward, promote, ease, speed up, pave the way for, make easy, expedite, oil the wheels of, smooth the path of, assist the progress of ■ **OPPOSITE:** hinder

facility NOUN **1** (often plural) What recreational facilities are now available? = **amenity**, means, aid, opportunity, advantage, resource, equipment, provision, convenience, appliance **2** The bank will not extend the borrowing facility. = **opportunity**, possibility, convenience **3** They shared a facility for languages. = **ability**, skill, talent, gift, craft, efficiency, knack, fluency, proficiency, dexterity, quickness, adroitness, expertness, skilfulness **4** He had always spoken with facility. = **ease**, readiness, fluency, smoothness, effortlessness ■ **OPPOSITE:** difficulty

facsimile NOUN = **copy**, print, carbon, reproduction, replica, transcript, duplicate, photocopy, Xerox®, carbon copy, Photostat®, fax

fact NOUN **1** How much was fact and how much fancy no one knew. = **truth**, reality, gospel (truth), certainty, verity, actuality, naked truth ■ **OPPOSITE:** fiction **2** The lorries always left in the dead of night when there were few witnesses around to record the fact. = **detail**, point, feature, particular, item, specific, circumstance **3** He was sure the gun was planted after the fact. = **event**, happening, act, performance, incident, deed, occurrence, fait accompli (French)

▶ PLURAL NOUN There is so much information you can find the facts for yourself. = **information**, details, data, the score (informal), gen (Brit. informal), info (informal), the whole story, ins and outs, the lowdown (informal) • **as a matter of fact** or **in fact** or **in point of fact** That sounds rather simple, but in fact it's very difficult. = **actually**, really, indeed, truly, in reality, in truth, to tell the truth, in actual fact

faction NOUN **1** A peace agreement will be signed by the leaders of the country's warring factions. = **group**, set, party, division, section, camp, sector, minority, combination, coalition, gang, lobby, bloc, contingent, pressure group, caucus, junta, clique, coterie, schism, confederacy, splinter group, cabal, ginger group, public-interest group (U.S. & Canad.) **2** Faction and self-interest appear to be the norm. = **dissension**, division, conflict, rebellion, disagreement, friction, strife, turbulence, variance, discord, infighting, disunity, sedition, tumult, disharmony, divisiveness ■ **OPPOSITE:** agreement

factor NOUN = **element**, thing, point, part, cause, influence, item, aspect, circumstance, characteristic, consideration, component, determinant

> **USAGE** In strict usage, factor should only be used to refer to something which contributes to a result. It should not be used to refer to a part of something, such as a plan or arrangement; more appropriate alternatives to factor in this sense are words such as component or element.

factory NOUN = **works**, plant, mill, workshop, assembly line, shop floor, manufactory (obsolete)

factual ADJECTIVE = **true**, objective, authentic, unbiased, close, real, sure, correct, genuine, accurate, exact, precise, faithful, credible, matter-of-fact, literal, veritable, circumstantial, unadorned, dinkum (Austral. & N.Z. informal), true-to-life ■ **OPPOSITE:** fictitious

faculty NOUN **1** A faculty for self-preservation is necessary when you have friends like hers. = **ability**, power, skill, facility, talent, gift, capacity, bent, capability, readiness, knack, propensity, aptitude, dexterity, cleverness, adroitness, turn ■ **OPPOSITE:** failing **2** the Faculty of Social and Political Sciences = **department**, school, discipline, profession, branch of learning **3** The faculty agreed on a change in the requirements. = **teaching staff**, staff, teachers, professors, lecturers (chiefly U.S.)

4 *He was drunk and not in control of his faculties.* = **power**, reason, sense, intelligence, mental ability, physical ability

fad NOUN = **craze**, fashion, trend, fancy, rage, mode, vogue, whim, mania, affectation

fade VERB **1** *All colour fades, especially under the impact of direct sunlight.* = **become pale**, dull, dim, bleach, wash out, blanch, discolour, blench, lose colour, lose lustre, decolour **2** *Even a soft light fades the carpets in a room.* = **make pale**, dull, dim, bleach, wash out, blanch, discolour, decolour **3** *The sound of the last bomber's engines faded into the distance.* = **grow dim**, dim, fade away, become less loud **4** (*usually with* **away** *or* **out**) *After that all her worries faded away.* = **dwindle**, disappear, vanish, melt away, fall, fail, decline, flag, dissolve, dim, disperse, wither, wilt, wane, perish, ebb, languish, die out, droop, shrivel, die away, waste away, vanish into thin air, become unimportant, evanesce (*formal*), etiolate

faded ADJECTIVE = **discoloured**, pale, bleached, washed out, dull, dim, indistinct, etiolated (*formal*), lustreless

fading ADJECTIVE = **declining**, dying, disappearing, vanishing, decreasing, on the decline

faeces *or* (*esp. U.S.*) **feces** PLURAL NOUN = **excrement**, stools, excreta, bodily waste, dung, droppings, ordure

fail VERB **1** *He was afraid the revolution they had started would fail.* = **be unsuccessful**, founder, fall flat, come to nothing, fall, miss, go down, break down, flop (*informal*), be defeated, fall short, fall through, fall short of, fizzle out (*informal*), come unstuck, run aground, miscarry, be in vain, misfire, fall by the wayside, go astray, come to grief, come a cropper (*informal*), bite the dust, go up in smoke, go belly-up (*slang*), come to naught, lay an egg (*slang, chiefly U.S. & Canad.*), go by the board, not make the grade (*informal*), go down like a lead balloon (*informal*), turn out badly, fall flat on your face, meet with disaster, be found lacking or wanting ■ OPPOSITE: succeed **2** *We waited twenty-one years; don't fail us now.* = **disappoint**, abandon, desert, neglect, omit, let down, forsake, turn your back on, be disloyal to, break your word, forget **3** *The lights mysteriously failed.* = **stop working**, stop, die, give up, break down, cease, stall, cut out, malfunction, conk out (*informal*), crash (*a computer*), go on the blink (*informal*), go phut **4** *In fact many food crops failed because of the drought.* = **wither**, perish, sag, droop, waste away, shrivel up **5** *So far this*

year, 104 banks have failed. = **go bankrupt**, crash, collapse, fold (*informal*), close down, go under, go bust (*informal*), go out of business, be wound up, go broke (*informal*), go to the wall, go into receivership, go into liquidation, become insolvent, smash **6** *He was 58 and his health was failing rapidly.* = **decline**, fade, weaken, deteriorate, dwindle, sicken, degenerate, fall apart at the seams, be on your last legs (*informal*) **7** *Here in the hills, the light failed more quickly.* = **give out**, disappear, fade, dim, dwindle, wane, gutter, languish, peter out, die away, grow dim, sink • **without fail** *He attended every meeting without fail.* = **without exception**, regularly, constantly, invariably, religiously, unfailingly, conscientiously, like clockwork, punctually, dependably

failing NOUN *He had invented an imaginary son, in order to make up for his real son's failings.* = **shortcoming**, failure, fault, error, weakness, defect, deficiency, lapse, flaw, miscarriage, drawback, misfortune, blemish, imperfection, frailty, foible, blind spot ■ OPPOSITE: strength ▶ PREPOSITION *Find someone who will let you talk things through, or failing that, write down your thoughts.* = **in the absence of**, lacking, in default of

failure NOUN **1** *The policy is doomed to failure.* = **lack of success**, defeat, collapse, abortion, wreck, frustration, breakdown, overthrow, miscarriage, fiasco, downfall ■ OPPOSITE: success **2** *I just felt I had been a failure in my personal life.* = **loser**, disappointment, no-good, flop (*informal*), write-off, incompetent, no-hoper (*chiefly Austral.*), dud (*informal*), clinker (*slang, chiefly U.S.*), black sheep, washout (*informal*), clunker (*informal*), dead duck (*slang*), ne'er-do-well, nonstarter **3** *They didn't prove his case of a failure of duty.* = **negligence**, neglect, deficiency, default, shortcoming, omission, oversight, dereliction, nonperformance, nonobservance, nonsuccess, remissness ■ OPPOSITE: observance **4** *There were also several accidents mainly caused by engine failures on take-off.* = **breakdown**, stalling, cutting out, malfunction, crash, disruption, stoppage, mishap, conking out (*informal*) **5** *He was being treated for kidney failure.* = **failing**, deterioration, decay, loss, decline **6** *Business failures rose 16% last month.* = **bankruptcy**, crash, collapse, ruin, folding (*informal*), closure, winding up, downfall, going under, liquidation, insolvency ■ OPPOSITE: prosperity

faint ADJECTIVE **1** *He became aware of the soft, faint sounds of water dripping.* = **dim**, low, light, soft, thin, faded, whispered, distant, dull, delicate, vague, unclear, muted, subdued, faltering, hushed, bleached, feeble, indefinite, muffled, hazy, ill-defined, indistinct ■ **OPPOSITE:** clear **2** *She made a faint attempt at a laugh.* = **slight**, weak, feeble, unenthusiastic, remote, slim, vague, slender **3** *He let his arm flail out in a faint attempt to grab the rope.* = **timid**, weak, feeble, lame, unconvincing, unenthusiastic, timorous (*literary*), faint-hearted, spiritless, half-hearted, lily-livered (*old-fashioned*) ■ **OPPOSITE:** brave **4** *Other signs of angina are nausea, feeling faint and shortness of breath.* = **dizzy**, giddy, light-headed, vertiginous, weak, exhausted, fatigued, faltering, wobbly, drooping, languid, lethargic, muzzy, woozy (*informal*), weak at the knees, enervated ■ **OPPOSITE:** energetic ▶ VERB *I thought he'd faint when I kissed him.* = **pass out**, black out, lose consciousness, keel over (*informal*), fail, go out, collapse, fade, weaken, languish, swoon (*literary*), flake out (*informal*) ▶ NOUN *She slumped on the ground in a faint.* = **blackout**, collapse, coma, swoon (*literary*), unconsciousness, syncope (*Pathology*)

faintly ADVERB **1** *She felt faintly ridiculous.* = **slightly**, rather, a little, somewhat, dimly **2** *The voice came faintly back to us across the water.* = **softly**, weakly, feebly, in a whisper, indistinctly, unclearly

fair¹ ADJECTIVE **1** *I wanted them to get a fair deal.* = **unbiased**, impartial, even-handed, unprejudiced, just, clean, square, equal, objective, reasonable, proper, legitimate, upright, honourable, honest, equitable, lawful, trustworthy, on the level (*informal*), disinterested, dispassionate, above board, according to the rules ■ **OPPOSITE:** unfair **2** *He had a fair command of English.* = **respectable**, middling, average, reasonable, decent, acceptable, moderate, adequate, satisfactory, not bad, mediocre, so-so (*informal*), tolerable, passable, O.K. or okay (*informal*), all right **3** *She had bright eyes and fair hair.* = **light**, golden, blonde, blond, yellowish, fair-haired, light-coloured, flaxen-haired, towheaded, tow-haired **4** *It's important to protect my fair skin from the sun.* = **light-complexioned**, white, pale **5** *Weather conditions were fair.* = **fine**, clear, dry, bright, pleasant, sunny, favourable, clement, cloudless, unclouded, sunshiny **6** *Faint heart never won fair lady.* = **beautiful**, pretty, attractive, lovely, handsome,

good-looking, bonny (*Scot. & Northern English, dialect*), comely (*old-fashioned*), beauteous, well-favoured, fit (*Brit. informal*) ■ **OPPOSITE:** ugly • **fair and square** *We were beaten fair and square.* = **honestly**, straight, legally, on the level (*informal*), by the book, lawfully, above board, according to the rules, without cheating

fair² NOUN **1** *I used to love going to the fair when I was young.* = **carnival**, fête, gala, bazaar **2** *The date for the book fair has been changed.* = **exhibition**, show, market, festival, mart, expo (*informal*), exposition

fairly ADVERB **1** *They solved their problems quickly and fairly.* = **equitably**, objectively, legitimately, honestly, justly, lawfully, without prejudice, dispassionately, impartially, even-handedly, without bias **2** *We did fairly well.* = **moderately**, rather, quite, somewhat, reasonably, adequately, pretty well, tolerably, passably **3** *He fairly flew across the room.* = **positively**, really, simply, absolutely, in a manner of speaking, veritably **4** *It can no doubt be fairly argued that he is entitled to every penny.* = **deservedly**, objectively, honestly, justifiably, justly, impartially, equitably, without fear or favour, properly

fair-minded ADJECTIVE = **impartial**, just, fair, reasonable, open-minded, disinterested, unbiased, even-handed, unprejudiced

fairness NOUN = **impartiality**, justice, equity, legitimacy, decency, disinterestedness, uprightness, rightfulness, equitableness

fairy NOUN = **sprite**, elf, brownie, hob, pixie, puck, imp, leprechaun, peri, Robin Goodfellow

fairy tale or **fairy story** NOUN **1** *She was like a princess in a fairy tale.* = **folk tale**, romance, traditional story **2** *Many of those who write books lie much more than those who tell fairy tales.* = **lie**, fantasy, fiction, invention, fabrication, untruth, porky (*Brit. slang*), pork pie (*Brit. slang*), urban myth, tall story, urban legend, cock-and-bull story (*informal*)

faith NOUN **1** *She had placed a great deal of faith in him.* = **confidence**, trust, credit, conviction, assurance, dependence, reliance, credence ■ **OPPOSITE:** distrust **2** *England shifted officially from a Catholic to a Protestant faith in the 16th century.* = **religion**, church, belief, persuasion, creed, communion, denomination, dogma ■ **OPPOSITE:** agnosticism

faithful ADJECTIVE **1** *Older Americans are among this country's most faithful voters.* = **loyal**, true, committed, constant, attached, devoted, dedicated, reliable, staunch, truthful, dependable, trusty, steadfast, unwavering, true-blue, immovable, unswerving ■ **OPPOSITE:** disloyal **2** *His screenplay is faithful to the novel.* = **accurate**, just, close, true, strict, exact, precise • **the faithful** *The faithful revered him then as a prophet.* = **believers**, brethren, followers, congregation, adherents, the elect, communicants

faithfulness NOUN = **loyalty**, devotion, fidelity, constancy, dependability, trustworthiness, fealty, adherence

faithless ADJECTIVE = **disloyal**, unreliable, unfaithful, untrustworthy, doubting, false, untrue, treacherous, dishonest, fickle, perfidious (*literary*), untruthful, traitorous, unbelieving, inconstant, false-hearted, recreant (*archaic*)

fake VERB **1** *Did they fake this evidence?* = **forge**, copy, reproduce, fabricate, counterfeit, falsify **2** *He faked nonchalance.* = **sham**, affect, assume, put on, pretend, simulate, feign, go through the motions of ▶ NOUN **1** *It is filled with famous works of art, and every one of them is a fake.* = **forgery**, copy, fraud (*informal*), reproduction, dummy, imitation, hoax, counterfeit **2** *She denied claims that she is a fake.* = **charlatan**, deceiver, sham, quack, mountebank, phoney *or* phony (*informal*) ▶ ADJECTIVE *The bank manager is said to have issued fake certificates.* = **artificial**, false, forged, counterfeit, affected, assumed, put-on, pretend (*informal*), mock, imitation, sham, pseudo (*informal*), feigned, pinchbeck, phoney *or* phony (*informal*) ■ **OPPOSITE:** genuine

fall VERB **1** *Her father fell into the sea after a massive heart attack.* = **drop**, plunge, tumble, plummet, trip, settle, crash, collapse, pitch, sink, go down, come down, dive, stumble, descend, topple, subside, cascade, trip over, drop down, nose-dive, come a cropper (*informal*), keel over, face-plant (*informal*), go head over heels ■ **OPPOSITE:** rise **2** *Her weight fell to under seven stone.* = **decrease**, drop, decline, go down, flag, slump, diminish, fall off, dwindle, lessen, subside, ebb, abate, depreciate, become lower ■ **OPPOSITE:** increase **3** *the days before Constantinople fell to the Ottomans* = **be overthrown**, be taken, surrender, succumb, yield, submit, give way, capitulate, be conquered, give in *or* up, pass into enemy hands ■ **OPPOSITE:** triumph **4** *Another wave of troops followed the first, running past those who had fallen.* = **be killed**, die, be lost, perish, be slain, be a casualty, meet your end ■ **OPPOSITE:** survive **5** *Easter*

falls in early April. = **occur**, happen, come about, chance, take place, fall out, befall, come to pass ▶ NOUN **1** *The helmets are designed to withstand impacts equivalent to a fall from a bicycle.* = **drop**, slip, plunge, dive, spill, tumble, descent, plummet, nose dive **2** *There was a sharp fall in the value of the pound.* = **decrease**, drop, lowering, decline, reduction, slump, dip, falling off, dwindling, lessening, diminution, cut **3** *the fall of Rome* = **collapse**, defeat, surrender, downfall, death, failure, ruin, resignation, destruction, overthrow, submission, capitulation **4** *a fall of 3.5 kilometres* = **slope**, incline, descent, downgrade, slant, declivity ▶ PLURAL NOUN *The falls have always been an insurmountable obstacle for salmon and sea trout.* = **waterfall**, rapids, cascade, cataract, linn (*Scot.*), force (*Northern English, dialect*) • **fall apart 1** *The work was never finished and bit by bit the building fell apart.* = **break up**, crumble, disintegrate, fall to bits, go to seed, come apart at the seams, break into pieces, go *or* come to pieces, shatter **2** *The national coalition fell apart five weeks ago.* = **break down**, dissolve, disperse, disband, lose cohesion **3** *I was falling apart.* = **go to pieces**, break down, crack up (*informal*), have a breakdown, crumble • **fall away 1** *On either side of the tracks the ground fell away sharply.* = **slope**, drop, go down, incline, incline downwards **2** *Demand began to fall away.* = **decrease**, drop, diminish, fall off, dwindle, lessen • **fall back** *The congregation fell back from them as they entered.* = **retreat**, retire, withdraw, move back, recede, pull back, back off, recoil, draw back • **fall back on something** *or* **someone** *When necessary, instinct is the most reliable resource you can fall back on.* = **resort to**, have recourse to, employ, turn to, make use of, call upon, press into service • **fall behind 1** *The horse fell behind on the final furlong.* = **lag**, trail, be left behind, drop back, get left behind, lose your place **2** *He faces losing his home after falling behind with the payments.* = **be in arrears**, be late, not keep up • **fall down** (*often with* **on**) *That is where his argument falls down.* = **fail**, disappoint, go wrong, fall short, fail to make the grade, prove unsuccessful • **fall for someone** *I just fell for him right away.* = **fall in love with**, become infatuated with, be smitten by, be swept off your feet by, desire, fancy (*Brit. informal*), succumb to the charms of, lose your head over • **fall for something** *It was just a line to get you out of here, and you fell for it!* = **be fooled by**, be deceived by, be taken in by, be duped by, buy (*slang*), accept, swallow (*informal*), take on board, give credence to • **fall in** *Part of my bedroom ceiling has fallen in.* = **collapse**, sink, cave in, crash in, fall to the ground, fall apart at the seams, come down about your ears • **fall in with someone** *At University he had fallen in with a small clique of literature students.* = **make friends with**, go around with, become friendly with, hang about with (*informal*) • **fall in with something** *Her reluctance to fall in with his plans led to trouble.* = **go along with**, support, accept, agree with, comply with, submit to, yield to, buy into (*informal*), cooperate with, assent, take on board, concur with • **fall off 1** *He fell off at the second fence.* = **tumble**, topple, plummet, be unseated, come a cropper or purler (*informal*), take a fall or tumble **2** *Unemployment is rising again and retail buying has fallen off.* = **decrease**, drop, reduce, decline, fade, slump, weaken, shrink, diminish, dwindle, lessen, wane, subside, fall away, peter out, slacken, tail off (*informal*), ebb away, go down or downhill • **fall on** or **upon something** or **someone** *They fell upon the enemy from the rear.* = **attack**, assault, snatch, assail, tear into (*informal*), lay into, descend upon, pitch into (*informal*), belabour, let fly at, set upon or about • **fall out** *She fell out with her husband.* = **argue**, fight, row, clash, differ, disagree, quarrel, squabble, have a row, have words, come to blows, cross swords, altercate • **fall short** (*often with of*) *His achievements are bound to fall short of his ambitions.* = **be lacking**, miss, fail, disappoint, be wanting, be inadequate, be deficient, fall down on (*informal*), prove inadequate, not come up to expectations or scratch (*informal*) • **fall through** *The deal fell through.* = **fail**, be unsuccessful, come to nothing, fizzle out (*informal*), miscarry, go awry, go by the board • **fall to someone** *It fell to me to get rid of them.* = **be the responsibility of**, be up to, come down to, devolve upon • **fall to something** *They fell to fighting among themselves.* = **begin**, start, set to, set about, commence, apply yourself to

fallacy NOUN = **error**, mistake, illusion, flaw, deception, delusion, inconsistency, misconception, deceit, falsehood, untruth, misapprehension, sophistry, casuistry, sophism, faultiness

fallen ADJECTIVE **1** *Mourners lined the streets to honour the fallen troops.* = **killed**, lost, dead, slaughtered, slain, perished **2** *The heroine is depicted as a fallen woman.* = **dishonoured**, lost, loose (*old-fashioned*), shamed, ruined, disgraced, immoral, sinful, unchaste

fallible ADJECTIVE = **imperfect**, weak, uncertain, ignorant, mortal, frail, erring, prone to error ■ **OPPOSITE:** infallible

fallow ADJECTIVE **1** *The fields lay fallow.* = **uncultivated**, unused, undeveloped, unplanted, untilled **2** *There followed something of a fallow period.* = **inactive**, resting, idle, dormant, inert

false ADJECTIVE **1** *This resulted in false information being entered.* = **incorrect**, wrong, mistaken, misleading, faulty, inaccurate, invalid, improper, unfounded, erroneous, inexact ■ **OPPOSITE:** correct **2** *You do not know whether what you are told is true or false.* = **untrue**, fraudulent, unreal, concocted, fictitious, trumped up, fallacious, untruthful, truthless ■ **OPPOSITE:** true **3** *He paid for a false passport.* = **artificial**, forged, fake, mock, reproduction, synthetic, replica, imitation, bogus, simulated, sham, pseudo (*informal*), counterfeit, feigned, spurious, ersatz, pretended ■ **OPPOSITE:** real **4** *She was a false friend, envious of her lifestyle and her successful career.* = **treacherous**, lying, deceiving, unreliable, two-timing (*informal*), dishonest, deceptive, hypocritical, unfaithful, two-faced, disloyal, unsound, deceitful, faithless, untrustworthy, insincere, double-dealing, dishonourable, duplicitous, mendacious, perfidious (*literary*), treasonable, traitorous, inconstant, delusive, false-hearted ■ **OPPOSITE:** loyal

falsehood NOUN **1** *She called the verdict a victory of truth over falsehood.* = **untruthfulness**, deception, deceit, dishonesty, prevarication, mendacity, dissimulation, perjury, inveracity (*rare*) **2** *He accused them of knowingly spreading falsehoods about him.* = **lie**, story (*informal*), fiction, fabrication, fib, untruth, porky (*Brit. slang*), pork pie (*Brit. slang*), misstatement

falsify VERB = **alter**, forge, fake, tamper with, doctor, cook (*slang*), distort, pervert, belie, counterfeit, misrepresent, garble, misstate

falter VERB **1** *I have not faltered in my quest for a new future.* = **hesitate**, delay, waver, vacillate, break ■ **OPPOSITE:** persevere **2** *As he neared the house, he faltered.* = **tumble**, shake, tremble, totter **3** *Her voice faltered and she had to stop a moment to control it.* = **stutter**, pause, stumble, hesitate, stammer, speak haltingly

faltering ADJECTIVE = **hesitant**, broken, weak, uncertain, stumbling, tentative, stammering, timid, irresolute

fame NOUN = **prominence**, glory, celebrity,

stardom, name, credit, reputation, honour, prestige, stature, eminence, renown, repute, public esteem, illustriousness ■ **OPPOSITE:** obscurity

famed ADJECTIVE = **renowned**, celebrated, recognized, well-known, acclaimed, widely-known

familiar ADJECTIVE **1** *They are already familiar faces on our TV screens.* = **well-known**, household, everyday, recognized, common, stock, domestic, repeated, ordinary, conventional, routine, frequent, accustomed, customary, mundane, recognizable, common or garden (*informal*) ■ **OPPOSITE:** unfamiliar **2** *the old familiar relationship* = **friendly**, close, dear, intimate, confidential, amicable, chummy (*informal*), buddy-buddy (*slang, chiefly U.S. & Canad.*), palsy-walsy (*informal*) ■ **OPPOSITE:** formal **3** *the comfortable, familiar atmosphere* = **relaxed**, open, easy, friendly, free, near, comfortable, intimate, casual, informal, amicable, cordial, free-and-easy, unreserved, unconstrained, unceremonious, hail-fellow-well-met **4** *The driver of that taxi-cab seemed to me familiar to the point of impertinence.* = **disrespectful**, forward, bold, presuming, intrusive, presumptuous, impudent, overfamiliar, overfree • **familiar with** *only too familiar with the problems* = **acquainted with**, aware of, introduced to, conscious of, at home with, no stranger to, informed about, abreast of, knowledgeable about, versed in, well up in, proficient in, conversant with, on speaking terms with, in the know about, *au courant* with, *au fait* with

familiarity NOUN **1** *The enemy would always have the advantage of familiarity with the rugged terrain.* = **acquaintance**, experience, understanding, knowledge, awareness, grasp, acquaintanceship ■ **OPPOSITE:** unfamiliarity **2** *Close personal familiarity between councillors and staff can prove embarrassing.* = **friendliness**, friendship, intimacy, closeness, freedom, ease, openness, fellowship, informality, sociability, naturalness, absence of reserve, unceremoniousness ■ **OPPOSITE:** formality **3** *He had behaved with undue and oily familiarity.* = **disrespect**, forwardness, overfamiliarity, liberties, liberty, cheek, presumption, boldness ■ **OPPOSITE:** respect

familiarize VERB = **accustom**, instruct, habituate, make used to, school, season, train, prime, coach, get to know (about), inure, bring into common use, make conversant

family NOUN **1** *His family are completely behind him, whatever he decides.* = **relations**, people, children, issue, relatives, household, folk (*informal*), offspring, descendants, brood, kin, nuclear family, progeny, kindred, next of kin, kinsmen, ménage, kith and kin, your nearest and dearest, kinsfolk, your own flesh and blood, ainga (*N.Z.*), cuzzies or cuzzie-bros (*N.Z.*), rellies (*Austral. slang*) **2** *Are you going to have a family?* = **children**, kids (*informal*), offspring, little ones, munchkins (*informal, chiefly U.S.*), littlies (*Austral. informal*) **3** *Her family came to Los Angeles at the turn of the century.* = **ancestors**, forebears, parentage, forefathers, house, line, race, blood, birth, strain, tribe, sept, clan, descent, dynasty, pedigree, extraction, ancestry, lineage, genealogy, line of descent, stemma, stirps **4** *foods in the cabbage family, such as Brussels sprouts* = **species**, group, class, system, order, kind, network, genre, classification, subdivision, subclass ■ **RELATED WORD:** *adjective* familial

USAGE Some careful writers insist that a singular verb should always be used with collective nouns such as *government, team, family, committee,* and *class,* for example: *the class is doing a project on Vikings; the company is mounting a big sales campaign.* In British usage, however, a plural verb is often used with a collective noun, especially where the emphasis is on a collection of individual objects or people rather than a group regarded as a unit: *the family are all on holiday.* The most important thing to remember is never to treat the same collective noun as both singular and plural in the same sentence: *the family is well and sends its best wishes* or *the family are well and send their best wishes,* but not *the family is well and send their best wishes.*

family tree NOUN = **lineage**, genealogy, line of descent, ancestral tree, line, descent, pedigree, extraction, ancestry, blood line, stemma, stirps, whakapapa (*N.Z.*)

famine NOUN = **hunger**, want, starvation, deprivation, scarcity, dearth, destitution

famous ADJECTIVE = **well-known**, celebrated, acclaimed, notable, noted, excellent, signal, honoured, remarkable, distinguished, prominent, glorious, legendary, renowned, eminent, conspicuous, illustrious, much-publicized, lionized, far-famed ■ **OPPOSITE:** unknown

fan¹ NOUN *He cools himself with an electric fan.* = **blower**, ventilator, air conditioner, vane, punkah (*in India*), blade, propeller ▶ VERB

1 *She fanned herself with a piece of cardboard.* = **blow**, cool, refresh, air-condition, ventilate, air-cool, winnow (*rare*) **2** *economic problems which often fan hatred* = **stimulate**, increase, excite, provoke, arouse, rouse, stir up, work up, agitate, whip up, add fuel to the flames, impassion, enkindle **3** (*often with* **out**) *The main body of troops fanned out to the west.* = **spread out**, spread, lay out, disperse, unfurl, open out, space out

fan² NOUN **1** *As a boy he was a Manchester United fan.* = **supporter**, lover, follower, enthusiast, admirer, fanboy (*informal*), fangirl (*informal*), groupie (*slang*), rooter (*U.S.*) **2** = **devotee**, addict, freak (*informal*), buff (*informal*), fiend (*informal*), adherent, zealot, aficionado, groupie (*slang*)

fanatic NOUN = **extremist**, activist, militant, addict, enthusiast, buff (*informal*), visionary, devotee, bigot, zealot, energumen

fanatical ADJECTIVE = **obsessive**, burning, wild, mad, extreme, enthusiastic, passionate, frenzied, visionary, fervent, zealous, bigoted, rabid, immoderate, overenthusiastic, swivel-eyed (*slang*)

fanaticism NOUN = **immoderation**, enthusiasm, madness, devotion, dedication, zeal, bigotry, extremism, infatuation, single-mindedness, zealotry, obsessiveness, monomania, overenthusiasm

fancier NOUN = **expert**, amateur, breeder, connoisseur, aficionado

fanciful ADJECTIVE = **unreal**, wild, ideal, romantic, fantastic, curious, fabulous, imaginative, imaginary, poetic, extravagant, visionary, fairy-tale, mythical, whimsical, capricious, chimerical
■ OPPOSITE: unimaginative

fancy ADJECTIVE **1** *It was packaged in a fancy plastic case with attractive graphics.* = **elaborate**, decorated, decorative, extravagant, intricate, baroque, ornamented, ornamental, ornate, elegant, fanciful, embellished ■ OPPOSITE: plain **2** *They sent me to a fancy private school.* = **expensive**, high-quality, classy (*informal*), flashy, swish (*informal*), showy, ostentatious ▶ NOUN **1** *His interest was just a passing fancy.* = **whim**, thought, idea, desire, urge, notion, humour, impulse, inclination, caprice **2** *His book is a bold surrealist mixture of fact and fancy.* = **delusion**, dream, vision, fantasy, nightmare, daydream, chimera, phantasm ▶ VERB **1** *I just fancied a drink.* = **wish for**, want, desire, would like, hope for, dream of, relish, long for, crave, be attracted to, yearn for, thirst for, hanker after, have a yen for **2** *I think he thinks I fancy him.* = **be attracted to**, find attractive, desire, lust after, like, prefer, favour, take to, go for, be captivated by, have an eye for, have a thing about (*informal*), have eyes for, take a liking to **3** *She fancied he was trying to hide a smile.* = **suppose**, think, believe, imagine, guess (*informal, chiefly U.S. & Canad.*), reckon, conceive, infer, conjecture, surmise, think likely, be inclined to think
• **fancy yourself** *She really fancies herself in that new outfit.* = **think you are God's gift**, have a high opinion of yourself, think you are the cat's whiskers • **take a fancy to something** or **someone** *Sylvia took quite a fancy to him.* = **start liking**, like, want, be fond of, hanker after, have a partiality for

fanfare NOUN = **trumpet call**, flourish, trump (*archaic*), tucket (*archaic*), fanfaronade

fang NOUN = **tooth**, tusk

fantasize VERB = **daydream**, imagine, invent, romance, envision, hallucinate, see visions, live in a dream world, build castles in the air, give free rein to the imagination

fantastic ADJECTIVE **1** *I have a fantastic social life.* = **wonderful**, great (*informal*), excellent, very good, mean (*slang*), topping (*Brit. slang*), cracking (*Brit. informal*), crucial (*slang*), smashing (*informal*), superb, tremendous (*informal*), magnificent, marvellous, terrific (*informal*), sensational (*informal*), mega (*slang*), awesome (*slang*), dope (*slang*), sick (*slang*), world-class, first-rate, def (*slang*), brill (*informal*), out of this world (*informal*), boffo (*slang*), jim-dandy (*slang*), bitchin' (*U.S. slang*), chillin' (*U.S. slang*), booshit (*Austral. slang*), exo (*Austral. slang*), sik (*Austral. slang*), rad (*informal*), phat (*slang*), schmick (*Austral. informal*), beaut (*informal*), barrie (*Scot. slang*), belting (*Brit. slang*), pearler (*Austral. slang*) ■ OPPOSITE: ordinary **2** *fantastic amounts of money* = **enormous**, great, huge, vast, severe, extreme, overwhelming, tremendous, immense **3** *outlandish and fantastic images* = **strange**, bizarre, weird, exotic, peculiar, imaginative, queer, grotesque, quaint, unreal, fanciful, outlandish, whimsical, freakish, chimerical, phantasmagorical **4** *He had cooked up some fantastic story about how the ring had come into his possession.* = **implausible**, unlikely, incredible, absurd, irrational, preposterous, capricious, cock-and-bull (*informal*), cockamamie (*slang, chiefly U.S.*), mad

fantasy or **phantasy** NOUN **1** *Everyone's had a fantasy about winning the lottery.* = **daydream**, dream, wish, fancy, delusion, reverie, flight of fancy, pipe dream **2** *a world of imagination and fantasy* = **imagination**, fancy (*old-fashioned*, *literary*), invention, creativity, originality

far ADVERB **1** *They came from far away.* = **a long way**, miles, deep, a good way, afar, a great distance **2** *He was a far better cook than Amy.* = **much**, greatly, very much, extremely, significantly, considerably, decidedly, markedly, incomparably • **by far** or **far and away** *by far the most successful* = **very much**, easily, immeasurably, by a long way, incomparably, to a great degree, by a long shot, by a long chalk (*informal*), by a great amount • **far and wide** *His fame spread far and wide.* = **extensively**, everywhere, worldwide, far and near, widely, broadly, in all places, in every nook and cranny, here, there and everywhere • **far from** *She is far from happy.* = **not at all**, not, by no means, absolutely not • **so far 1** *Their loyalty only went so far.* = **up to a point**, to a certain extent, to a limited extent **2** *So far, they have had no success.* = **up to now**, to date, until now, thus far, up to the present

faraway ADJECTIVE **1** *They had just returned from faraway places.* = **distant**, far, remote, far-off, far-removed, far-flung, outlying, beyond the horizon **2** *She smiled with a faraway look in her eyes.* = **dreamy**, lost, distant, abstracted, vague, absent

farce NOUN **1** *The plot often borders on farce.* = **comedy**, satire, slapstick, burlesque, buffoonery, broad comedy **2** *The election was a farce, as only 22% of voters cast their ballots.* = **mockery**, joke, nonsense, parody, shambles, sham, absurdity, malarkey, travesty, ridiculousness

farcical ADJECTIVE **1** *a farcical nine months' jail sentence* = **ludicrous**, ridiculous, absurd, preposterous, laughable, nonsensical, derisory, risible (*formal*) **2** *from farcical humour to deepest tragedy* = **comic**, funny, amusing, slapstick, droll, custard-pie, diverting

fare NOUN **1** *He could barely afford the railway fare.* = **charge**, price, ticket price, transport cost, ticket money, passage money **2** *traditional Portuguese fare* = **food**, meals, diet, provisions, board, commons, table (*formal*), feed, menu, rations, tack (*informal*), kai (*N.Z. informal*), nourishment, sustenance, victuals, nosebag (*slang*), nutriment, vittles (*obsolete*, *dialect*), eatables **3** *The taxi driver picked up a fare.* = **passenger**, customer, pick-up (*informal*), traveller ▶ VERB **1** *He was not faring well.* = **get on**, do, manage, make out, prosper, get along **2** (*used impersonally*) *The show*

fared quite well. = **happen**, go, turn out, proceed, pan out (*informal*)

farewell INTERJECTION *'Farewell, lad, and may we meet again soon.'* = **goodbye**, bye (*informal*), so long, see you, take care, good morning, bye-bye (*informal*), good day, all the best, good night, good evening, good afternoon, see you later, ciao (*Italian*), have a nice day (*U.S.*), adieu (*French*), au revoir (*French*), be seeing you, auf Wiedersehen (*German*), adios (*Spanish*), mind how you go, haere ra (*N.Z.*) ▶ NOUN *a touching farewell* = **goodbye**, parting, departure, leave-taking, adieu, valediction, sendoff (*informal*), adieux or adieus

far-fetched ADJECTIVE = **unconvincing**, unlikely, strained, fantastic, incredible, doubtful, unbelievable, dubious, unrealistic, improbable, unnatural, preposterous, implausible, hard to swallow (*informal*), cock-and-bull (*informal*)
■ OPPOSITE: believable

farm NOUN *We have a small farm.* = **smallholding**, holding, ranch (*chiefly U.S. & Canad.*), farmstead, land, station (*Austral. & N.Z.*), acres, vineyard, plantation, croft (*Scot.*), grange, homestead, acreage ▶ VERB *They had farmed the same land for generations.* = **cultivate**, work, plant, operate, till the soil, grow crops on, bring under cultivation, keep animals on, practise husbandry

farmer NOUN = **agriculturist**, yeoman, smallholder, crofter (*Scot.*), grazier, agriculturalist, rancher, agronomist, husbandman, cockie or cocky (*Austral. & N.Z. informal*)

farming NOUN = **agriculture**, cultivation, husbandry, land management, agronomy, tilling

far-out ADJECTIVE = **strange**, wild, unusual, bizarre, weird, avant-garde, unconventional, off-the-wall (*slang*), outlandish, outré, advanced

far-reaching ADJECTIVE = **extensive**, important, significant, sweeping, broad, widespread, pervasive, momentous

far-sighted ADJECTIVE = **prudent**, acute, wise, cautious, sage, shrewd, discerning, canny, provident, judicious, prescient, far-seeing, politic

fascinate VERB = **entrance**, delight, charm, absorb, intrigue, enchant, rivet, captivate, enthral, beguile, allure, bewitch, ravish, transfix, mesmerize, hypnotize, engross, enrapture, interest greatly, enamour, hold spellbound, spellbind, infatuate
■ OPPOSITE: bore

fascinated ADJECTIVE = **entranced**, charmed, absorbed, very interested, captivated, hooked on, enthralled, beguiled, smitten, bewitched, engrossed, spellbound, infatuated, hypnotized, under a spell

fascinating ADJECTIVE = **captivating**, engaging, gripping, compelling, intriguing, very interesting, irresistible, enticing, enchanting, seductive, riveting, alluring, bewitching, ravishing, engrossing ■ **OPPOSITE:** boring

fascination NOUN = **attraction**, pull, spell, magic, charm, lure, glamour, allure, magnetism, enchantment, sorcery

fascism NOUN (*sometimes cap.*) = **authoritarianism**, dictatorship, totalitarianism, despotism, autocracy, absolutism

fashion VERB **1** *The desk was fashioned out of oak.* = **make**, shape, cast, construct, work, form, create, design, manufacture, forge, mould, contrive, fabricate **2** *dresses fashioned to hide the bulges* = **fit**, adapt, tailor, suit, adjust, accommodate • **after a fashion** *He knew the way, after a fashion.* = **to some extent**, somehow, in a way, moderately, to a certain extent, to a degree, somehow or other, in a manner of speaking

fashionable ADJECTIVE = **popular**, in fashion, trendy (*Brit. informal*), cool (*slang*), in (*informal*), latest, happening (*informal*), current, modern, on trend, with it (*old-fashioned, informal*), usual, smart, hip (*slang*), prevailing, stylish, chic, up-to-date, customary, genteel, in vogue, all the rage, up-to-the-minute, modish, à la mode, designer, voguish (*informal*), trendsetting, all the go (*informal*), schmick (*Austral. informal*), funky ■ **OPPOSITE:** unfashionable

fast¹ ADJECTIVE **1** *She walked at a fast pace.* = **quick**, flying, winged, rapid, fleet, hurried, accelerated, swift, speedy, brisk, hasty, nimble, mercurial, sprightly, nippy (*Brit. informal*) ■ **OPPOSITE:** slow **2** *He held the gate fast.* = **fixed**, firm, sound, stuck, secure, tight, jammed, fortified, fastened, impregnable, immovable ■ **OPPOSITE:** unstable **3** *She has made headlines for her wealth and fast lifestyle.* = **dissipated**, wild, exciting, loose (*old-fashioned*), extravagant, reckless, immoral, promiscuous, giddy, self-indulgent, wanton, profligate, impure, intemperate, dissolute, rakish, licentious, gadabout (*informal*) **4** *The men had always been fast friends.* = **close**, lasting, firm, permanent, constant, devoted, loyal, faithful, stalwart, staunch, steadfast, unwavering ▶ ADVERB **1** *She drives terrifically fast.* = **quickly**, rapidly, swiftly, hastily,

hurriedly, speedily, presto, apace (*literary*), in haste, like a shot (*informal*), at full speed, hell for leather (*informal*), like lightning, hotfoot, like a flash, at a rate of knots, like the clappers (*Brit. informal*), like a bat out of hell (*slang*), pdq (*slang*), like nobody's business (*informal*), posthaste, like greased lightning (*informal*), with all haste ■ **OPPOSITE:** slowly **2** *We can only try to hold fast to our principles.* = **firmly**, staunchly, resolutely, steadfastly, determinedly, unwaveringly, unchangeably **3** *She held fast to the stair rail.* = **securely**, firmly, tightly, fixedly **4** *The tanker is stuck fast on the rocks.* = **fixedly**, firmly, soundly, deeply, securely, tightly **5** *He lived fast and died young.* = **recklessly**, wildly, loosely, extravagantly, promiscuously, rakishly, intemperately

fast² VERB *She had fasted to lose weight.* = **go hungry**, abstain, go without food, deny yourself, practise abstention, refrain from food or eating ▶ NOUN *The fast is broken, traditionally with dates and water.* = **fasting**, diet, abstinence

fasten VERB **1** *He fastened the door behind him.* = **secure**, close, lock, chain, seal, bolt, do up **2** *The dress fastens down the back.* = **tie**, bind, lace, tie up **3** *Use screws to fasten the shelf to the wall.* = **fix**, join, link, connect, grip, attach, anchor, affix, make firm, make fast **4** (*often with on or upon*) *Her thoughts fastened on one event.* = **concentrate**, focus, fix **5** *They fastened their gaze on the table and did not look up.* = **direct**, aim, focus, fix, concentrate, bend, rivet

fastening NOUN = **tie**, union, coupling, link, linking, bond, joint, binding, connection, attachment, junction, zip, fusion, clasp, concatenation (*formal*), ligature, affixation

fastidious ADJECTIVE = **particular**, meticulous, fussy, overdelicate, difficult, nice, critical, discriminating, dainty, squeamish, choosy (*informal*), picky (*informal*), hard to please, finicky, punctilious (*formal*), pernickety, hypercritical, overnice, nit-picky (*informal*) ■ **OPPOSITE:** careless

fat NOUN *ways of reducing body fat* = **fatness**, flesh (*informal*), bulk, obesity, cellulite, weight problem, flab, blubber, paunch, fatty tissue, adipose tissue, corpulence, beef (*informal*) ▶ ADJECTIVE **1** *I can eat what I like without getting fat.* = **overweight**, large, heavy, plump, gross, stout, obese, fleshy, beefy (*informal*), tubby, portly, roly-poly, rotund, podgy, corpulent, elephantine, broad in the beam (*informal*), solid ■ **OPPOSITE:** thin **2** *They are set to make a fat profit.* = **large**, rich, substantial, thriving, flourishing, profitable, productive, lucrative, fertile, lush, prosperous, affluent, fruitful; cushy (*slang*), jammy (*Brit. slang*), remunerative ■ **OPPOSITE:** scanty **3** *Most heart cases are the better for cutting out fat meat.* = **fatty**, greasy, lipid, adipose, oleaginous, suety, oily ■ **OPPOSITE:** lean • **a fat chance** *You've got a fat chance of getting there on time.* = **no chance**, (a) slim chance, very little chance, not much chance

fatal ADJECTIVE **1** *It dealt a fatal blow to his chances.* = **disastrous**, devastating, crippling, lethal, catastrophic, ruinous, calamitous, baleful, baneful ■ **OPPOSITE:** minor **2** *putting off that fatal moment* = **decisive**, final, determining, critical, crucial, fateful **3** *She had suffered a fatal heart attack.* = **lethal**, deadly, mortal, causing death, final, killing, terminal, destructive, malignant, incurable, pernicious (*formal*) ■ **OPPOSITE:** harmless

fatalism NOUN = **resignation**, acceptance, passivity, determinism, stoicism, necessitarianism, predestinarianism

fatality NOUN = **casualty**, death, loss, victim

fate NOUN **1** *I see no use quarrelling with fate.* = **destiny**, chance, fortune, luck, the stars, weird (*archaic*), providence, nemesis, kismet, predestination, divine will **2** *You cannot choose your fate.* = **fortune**, destiny, lot, portion, cup, horoscope **3** *What will be the fate of the elections?* = **outcome**, future, destiny, end, issue, upshot **4** *This new proposal seems doomed to the same fate.* = **downfall**, end, death, ruin, destruction, doom, demise

fated ADJECTIVE = **destined**, doomed, predestined, preordained, foreordained, pre-elected

fateful ADJECTIVE **1** *What changed for him in that fateful year?* = **crucial** (*informal*), important, significant, critical, decisive, momentous, portentous ■ **OPPOSITE:** unimportant **2** *He had sailed on his third and fateful voyage.* = **disastrous**, fatal, deadly, destructive, lethal, ominous, ruinous

father NOUN **1** *He was a good father to my children.* = **daddy** (*informal*), dad (*informal*), male parent, patriarch, pop (*U.S. informal*), governor (*informal*), old man (*Brit. informal*), pa (*informal*), old boy (*informal*), papa (*old-fashioned, informal*), sire, pater (*old-fashioned*), biological father, foster father, begetter, paterfamilias, birth father **2** *He was the father of modern photography.* = **founder**, author, maker, architect, creator, inventor, originator, prime mover, initiator **3** (*often plural*) *land of my fathers* = **forefather**, predecessor, ancestor,

forebear, progenitor, tupuna *or* tipuna (*N.Z.*) **4** (*usually plural*) *City fathers tried to revive the town's economy.* = **leader**, senator, elder, patron, patriarch, guiding light, city father, kaumatua (*N.Z.*) ▶ VERB **1** *He fathered at least three children.* = **sire**, parent, conceive, bring to life, beget, procreate (*formal*), bring into being, give life to, get **2** *He fathered the modern computer.* = **originate**, found, create, establish, author, institute, invent, engender ■ **RELATED WORD:** *adjective* paternal

Father NOUN *The prior, Father Alessandro, came over to talk to them.* = **priest**, minister, vicar, parson, pastor, cleric, churchman, padre (*informal*), confessor, abbé, curé, man of God

fatherland NOUN = **homeland**, motherland, old country, native land, land of your birth, land of your fathers, whenua (*N.Z.*), Godzone (*Austral. informal*)

fatherly ADJECTIVE = **paternal**, kind, kindly, tender, protective, supportive, benign, affectionate, indulgent, patriarchal, benevolent, forbearing

fathom VERB = **understand**, grasp, comprehend, interpret, get to the bottom of

fatigue NOUN *Those affected suffer extreme fatigue.* = **tiredness**, lethargy, weariness, ennui (*literary*), heaviness, debility, languor, listlessness, overtiredness ■ **OPPOSITE:** freshness ▶ VERB *It fatigues me to list them all.* = **tire**, exhaust, weaken, weary, drain, fag (out) (*informal*), whack (*Brit. informal*), wear out, jade, take it out of (*informal*), poop (*informal*), tire out, knacker (*slang*), drain of energy, overtire ■ **OPPOSITE:** refresh

fatigued ADJECTIVE = **tired**, exhausted, weary, tired out, bushed (*informal*), wasted, all in (*slang*), fagged (out) (*informal*), whacked (*Brit. informal*), jaded, knackered (*slang*), clapped out (*Austral. & N.Z. informal*), overtired, zonked (*slang*), dead beat (*informal*), jiggered (*informal*), on your last legs, creamcrackered (*Brit. informal*)

fatten VERB **1** *The creature continued to grow and fatten.* = **grow fat**, spread, expand, swell, thrive, broaden, thicken, put on weight, gain weight, coarsen, become fat, become fatter **2** *They fattened up ducks and geese.* = **feed up**, feed, stuff, build up, cram, nourish, distend, bloat, overfeed

fatty ADJECTIVE = **greasy**, fat, creamy, oily, adipose, oleaginous, suety, rich

fatuous ADJECTIVE = **foolish**, stupid, silly, dull, absurd, dense, ludicrous, mindless, idiotic, vacuous, inane, witless, puerile, brainless, asinine, weak-minded, dumb-ass (*slang*)

faucet NOUN = **tap**, spout, spigot, stopcock, valve

fault NOUN **1** *It was all my fault we quarrelled.* = **responsibility**, liability, guilt, accountability, culpability **2** *It was a genuine fault.* = **mistake**, slip, error, offence, blunder, lapse, negligence, omission, boob (*Brit. slang*), oversight, slip-up, indiscretion, inaccuracy, howler (*informal*), glitch (*informal*), error of judgment, boo-boo (*informal*), barry or Barry Crocker (*Austral. slang*) **3** *His manners always made her blind to his faults.* = **failing**, lack, weakness, defect, deficiency, flaw, drawback, shortcoming, snag, blemish, imperfection, Achilles heel, weak point, infirmity, demerit ■ **OPPOSITE:** strength ▶ VERB *You can't fault them for lack of invention.* = **criticize**, blame, complain, condemn, moan about, censure, hold (someone) responsible, hold (someone) accountable, find fault with, call to account, impugn (*formal*), find lacking, hold (someone) to blame • **at fault** *She didn't accept that she was at fault.* = **guilty**, responsible, to blame, accountable, in the wrong, culpable, answerable, blamable • **find fault with something** *or* **someone** *I do tend to find fault with everybody.* = **criticize**, complain about, whinge about (*informal*), whine about (*informal*), quibble, diss (*slang*), carp at, take to task, pick holes in, grouse about (*informal*), haul over the coals (*informal*), pull to pieces, nit-pick (*informal*) • **to a fault** *She was generous to a fault.* = **excessively**, overly (*U.S.*), unduly, ridiculously, in the extreme, needlessly, out of all proportion, preposterously, overmuch, immoderately

faultless ADJECTIVE = **flawless**, model, perfect, classic, correct, accurate, faithful, impeccable, exemplary, foolproof, unblemished

faulty ADJECTIVE **1** *They will repair the faulty equipment.* = **defective**, damaged, not working, malfunctioning, broken, bad, flawed, impaired, imperfect, blemished, out of order, on the blink, buggy (*a computer*) **2** *Their interpretation was faulty.* = **incorrect**, wrong, flawed, inaccurate, bad, weak, invalid, erroneous, unsound, imprecise, fallacious

faux pas NOUN = **gaffe**, blunder, indiscretion, impropriety, bloomer (*Brit. informal*), boob (*Brit. slang*), clanger (*informal*), solecism, breach of etiquette, gaucherie, barbecue stopper (*Austral. informal*)

favour *or* (*U.S.*) **favor** NOUN **1** *They viewed him with favour.* = **approval**, grace, esteem, goodwill, kindness, friendliness, commendation, partiality, approbation, kind regard ■ **OPPOSITE:** disapproval **2** *The referee was accused of showing favour to the home team.* = **favouritism**, preference, bias, nepotism, preferential treatment, partisanship, jobs for the boys (*informal*), partiality, one-sidedness **3** *She wanted to win the favour of the voters.* = **support**, backing, aid, championship, promotion, assistance, patronage, espousal, good opinion **4** *I've come to ask for a favour.* = **good turn**, service, benefit, courtesy, kindness, indulgence, boon (*archaic*), good deed, kind act, obligement (*Scot., archaic*) ■ **OPPOSITE:** wrong **5** *place cards and wedding favours* = **memento**, present, gift, token, souvenir, keepsake, love-token ▶ VERB **1** *She favours community activism over legislation.* = **prefer**, opt for, like better, incline towards, choose, pick, desire, select, elect, adopt, go for, fancy (*Brit. informal*), single out, plump for, be partial to ■ **OPPOSITE:** object to **2** *There was good reason for favouring him.* = **indulge**, reward, spoil, esteem, side with, pamper, befriend, be partial to, smile upon, pull strings for (*informal*), have in your good books, treat with partiality, value **3** *We favour greater protection of the environment.* = **support**, like, back, choose, champion, encourage, approve, fancy, advocate, opt for, subscribe to, commend, stand up for, espouse, be in favour of, countenance, patronize ■ **OPPOSITE:** oppose **4** *Circumstances favoured them.* = **help**, benefit, aid, advance, promote, assist, accommodate, facilitate, abet, succour, do a kindness to **5** *The beautiful girls would favour me with a look.* = **oblige**, please, honour, accommodate, benefit • **in favour of** *They were in favour of the decision.* = **for**, backing, supporting, behind, pro, all for (*informal*), on the side of, right behind

favourable *or* (*U.S.*) **favorable** ADJECTIVE **1** *He made favourable comments about her work.* = **positive**, kind, understanding, encouraging, welcoming, friendly, approving, praising, reassuring, enthusiastic, sympathetic, benign, commending, complimentary, agreeable, amicable, well-disposed, commendatory ■ **OPPOSITE:** disapproving **2** *I am expecting a favourable reply.* = **affirmative**, agreeing, confirming, positive, assenting, corroborative **3** *favourable weather conditions* = **advantageous**, timely, good, promising, fit, encouraging, fair, appropriate, suitable, helpful, hopeful, convenient, beneficial, auspicious, opportune (*formal*), propitious ■ **OPPOSITE:** disadvantageous

favourably *or* (U.S.) **favorably** ADVERB **1** *She responded favourably to my suggestions.* = **positively**, well, enthusiastically, helpfully, graciously, approvingly, agreeably, with approval, without prejudice, genially, with approbation, in a kindly manner, with cordiality **2** *They are far more favourably placed than their opponents.* = **advantageously**, well, fortunately, conveniently, profitably, to your advantage, auspiciously, opportunely

favourite *or* (U.S.) **favorite** ADJECTIVE *Her favourite writer is Charles Dickens.* = **preferred**, favoured, best-loved, most-liked, special, choice, dearest, pet, esteemed, fave (*informal*) ▸ NOUN *He was a favourite of the king.* = **darling**, pet, preference, blue-eyed boy (*informal*), pick, choice, dear, beloved, idol, fave (*informal*), teacher's pet, the apple of your eye

favouritism *or* (U.S.) **favoritism** NOUN = **bias**, preference, nepotism, preferential treatment, partisanship, jobs for the boys (*informal*), partiality, one-sidedness
■ **OPPOSITE:** impartiality

fawn¹ ADJECTIVE *She put on a light fawn coat.* = **beige**, neutral, buff, yellowish-brown, greyish-brown

fawn² VERB (*usually with* **on** *or* **upon**) *People fawn on you when you're famous.* = **ingratiate yourself**, court, flatter, pander to, creep, crawl, kneel, cringe, grovel, curry favour, toady, pay court, kowtow, bow and scrape, dance attendance, truckle, be obsequious, be servile, lick (someone's) boots

fawning ADJECTIVE = **obsequious**, crawling, flattering, cringing, abject, grovelling, prostrate, deferential, sycophantic, servile, slavish, bowing and scraping, bootlicking (*informal*)

fear NOUN **1** *I shivered with fear at the sound of gunfire.* = **dread**, horror, panic, terror, dismay, awe, fright, tremors, qualms, consternation, alarm, trepidation (*formal*), timidity, fearfulness, blue funk (*informal*), apprehensiveness, cravenness **2** *Flying was his greatest fear.* = **bugbear**, bête noire, horror, nightmare, anxiety, terror, dread, spectre, phobia, bogey, thing (*informal*) **3** *His fear might be groundless.* = **anxiety**, concern, worry, doubt, nerves (*informal*), distress, suspicion, willies (*informal*), creeps (*informal*), butterflies (*informal*), funk (*informal*), angst, unease, apprehension, misgiving(s), nervousness, agitation, foreboding(s), uneasiness, solicitude, blue funk (*informal*), heebie-jeebies (*informal*), collywobbles (*informal*), disquietude **4** *There is no fear of God before their eyes.* = **awe**, wonder, respect, worship, dread, reverence, veneration ▸ VERB **1** *If people fear you they respect you.* = **be afraid of**, dread, be scared of, be frightened of, shudder at, be fearful of, be apprehensive about, tremble at, be terrified by, have a horror of, take fright at, have a phobia about, have qualms about, live in dread of, be in a blue funk about (*informal*), have butterflies in your stomach about (*informal*), shake in your shoes about **2** *They feared God in a way which most modern men can hardly imagine.* = **revere**, respect, reverence, venerate, stand in awe of **3** *I fear that a land war now looks probable.* = **regret**, feel, suspect, have a feeling, have a hunch, have a sneaking suspicion, have a funny feeling • **fear for something** *or* **someone** *He fled, saying he feared for his life.* = **worry about**, be concerned about, be anxious about, tremble for, be distressed about, feel concern for, be disquieted over

fearful ADJECTIVE **1** *They were fearful that the fighting might spread.* = **scared**, afraid, alarmed, frightened, nervous, terrified, apprehensive, petrified, jittery (*informal*)
■ **OPPOSITE:** unafraid **2** *I had often been very fearful and isolated.* = **timid**, afraid, frightened, scared, alarmed, wired (*slang*), nervous, anxious, shrinking, tense, intimidated, uneasy, hesitant, apprehensive, jittery (*informal*), panicky, nervy (*Brit. informal*), diffident, jumpy, timorous (*literary*), pusillanimous (*formal*), faint-hearted ■ **OPPOSITE:** brave **3** *The earthquake was a fearful disaster.* = **frightful**, shocking (*informal*), terrible, awful, distressing, appalling, horrible, grim, dreadful, horrific, dire, horrendous, ghastly, hideous, monstrous, harrowing, gruesome, grievous, unspeakable, atrocious (*informal*), hair-raising, hellacious (*U.S. slang*)

fearfully ADVERB **1** *Softly, fearfully, he stole from the room.* = **nervously**, uneasily, timidly, apprehensively, diffidently, in fear and trembling, timorously, with bated breath, with many misgivings *or* forebodings, with your heart in your mouth **2** *This dress is fearfully expensive.* = **very**, terribly, horribly, tremendously, awfully (*informal*), exceedingly, excessively, dreadfully, frightfully

fearless ADJECTIVE = **intrepid**, confident, brave, daring, bold, heroic, courageous, gallant, gutsy (*slang*), valiant, plucky, game (*informal*), doughty, undaunted, indomitable, unabashed, unafraid, unflinching, dauntless, lion-hearted, valorous, (as) game as Ned Kelly (*Austral. slang*)

fearsome ADJECTIVE = **formidable**, alarming, frightening, awful (*obsolete*), terrifying, appalling, horrifying, menacing, dismaying, awesome, daunting, horrendous, unnerving, hair-raising, awe-inspiring, baleful, hellacious (*U.S. slang*)

feasibility NOUN = **possibility**, viability, usefulness, expediency, practicability, workability

feasible ADJECTIVE = **practicable**, possible, reasonable, viable, workable, achievable, attainable, realizable, likely ■ **OPPOSITE:** impracticable

feast NOUN **1** *Lunch was a feast of meat, vegetables, cheese, and wine.* = **banquet**, repast, spread (*informal*), dinner, entertainment, barbecue, revel, junket, beano (*Brit. slang*), blowout (*slang*), carouse, slap-up meal (*Brit. informal*), beanfeast (*Brit. informal*), jollification, carousal, festive board, treat, hakari (*N.Z.*) **2** *The feast of Passover began last night.* = **festival**, holiday, fête, celebration, holy day, red-letter day, religious festival, saint's day, -fest, gala day **3** *Chicago provides a feast for the ears of any music lover.* = **treat**, delight, pleasure, enjoyment, gratification, cornucopia ▶ VERB *We feasted on cakes and ice cream.* = **eat your fill**, wine and dine, overindulge, eat to your heart's content, stuff yourself, consume, indulge, gorge, devour, pig out (*slang*), stuff your face (*slang*), fare sumptuously, gormandize
• **feast your eyes on something** *She stood feasting her eyes on the view.* = **look at with delight**, gaze at, devour with your eyes

feat NOUN = **accomplishment**, act, performance, achievement, enterprise, undertaking, exploit, deed, attainment, feather in your cap

feather NOUN = **plume**

feathery ADJECTIVE = **downy**, soft, feathered, fluffy, plumed, wispy, plumy, plumate or plumose (*Botany & Zoology*), light

feature NOUN **1** *The gardens are a special feature of this property.* = **aspect**, quality, characteristic, attribute, point, mark, property, factor, trait, hallmark, facet, peculiarity **2** *a special feature on breast cancer research* = **article**, report, story, piece, comment, item, column **3** *the most striking feature of the whole garden* = **highlight**, draw, attraction, innovation, speciality, specialty, main item, crowd puller (*informal*), special attraction, special **4** *She arranged her features in a bland expression.* = **face**, countenance (*literary*), physiognomy, lineaments ▶ VERB **1** *This event features a stunning catwalk show.*

= **spotlight**, present, promote, set off, emphasize, play up, accentuate, foreground, call attention to, give prominence to, give the full works (*slang*) **2** *She featured in a Hollywood film.* = **star**, appear, headline, participate, play a part

febrile ADJECTIVE = **feverish**, hot, fevered, flushed, fiery, inflamed, delirious, pyretic (*Medical*)

feckless ADJECTIVE = **irresponsible**, useless (*informal*), hopeless (*informal*), incompetent, feeble, worthless, futile, ineffectual, aimless, good-for-nothing, shiftless, weak

federation NOUN = **union**, league, association, alliance, combination, coalition, partnership, consortium, syndicate, confederation, amalgamation, confederacy, entente, Bund (*German*), copartnership, federacy

fed up ADJECTIVE = **cheesed off**, down, depressed, bored, tired, annoyed, hacked (off) (*U.S. slang*), weary, gloomy, blue, dismal, discontented, dissatisfied, glum, sick and tired (*informal*), browned-off (*informal*), down in the mouth (*informal*), brassed off (*Brit. slang*), hoha (*N.Z.*)

fee NOUN = **charge**, pay, price, cost, bill, account, payment, wage, reward, hire, salary, compensation, toll, remuneration, recompense, emolument, honorarium, meed (*archaic*)

feeble ADJECTIVE **1** *He was old and feeble.* = **weak**, failing, exhausted, weakened, delicate, faint, powerless, frail, debilitated, sickly, languid, puny, weedy (*informal*), infirm, effete, enfeebled, doddering, enervated, etiolated, shilpit (*Scot.*) ■ **OPPOSITE:** strong **2** *He said the Government had been feeble.* = **inadequate**, weak, pathetic, insufficient, incompetent, ineffective, inefficient, lame, insignificant, ineffectual, indecisive **3** *This is a feeble argument.* = **unconvincing**, poor, thin, weak, slight, tame, pathetic, lame, flimsy, paltry, flat ■ **OPPOSITE:** effective

feed VERB **1** *Feeding a hungry family is expensive.* = **cater for**, provide for, nourish, provide with food, supply, sustain, nurture, cook for, wine and dine, victual, provision **2** *The cows stopped feeding.* = **graze**, eat, browse, pasture **3** *When a baby is thirsty, it feeds more often.* = **eat**, drink milk, take nourishment **4** *blood vessels that feed blood to the brain* = **supply**, take, send, carry, convey, impart **5** *He fed information to a rival company.* = **disclose**, give, tell, reveal, supply, communicate, pass on, impart, divulge, make known **6** *Wealth is feeding our obsession* *with house prices.* = **encourage**, boost, fuel, strengthen, foster, minister to, bolster, fortify, augment, make stronger ▶ NOUN **1** *a crop grown for animal feed* = **food**, fodder, forage, silage, provender, pasturage **2** *She's had a good feed.* = **meal**, spread (*informal*), dinner, lunch, tea, breakfast, feast, supper, tuck-in (*informal*), nosh (*slang*), repast, nosh-up (*Brit. slang*) • **feed on something** *The insects breed and feed on particular cacti.* = **live on**, depend on, devour, exist on, partake of, subsist on

feel VERB **1** *He was still feeling pain from a stomach injury.* = **experience**, suffer, bear, go through, endure, undergo, have a sensation of, have **2** *The doctor felt his head.* = **touch**, handle, manipulate, run your hands over, finger, stroke, paw, maul, caress, fondle **3** *He felt her leg brushing against his.* = **be aware of**, have a sensation of, be sensible of, enjoy **4** *She felt something was nearby.* = **perceive**, sense, detect, discern, know, experience, notice, observe **5** *I felt my way down the wooden staircase.* = **grope**, explore, fumble, sound **6** *I feel that he still misses her.* = **sense**, be aware, be convinced, have a feeling, have the impression, intuit, have a hunch, feel in your bones **7** *They felt that the police could not guarantee their safety.* = **believe**, consider, judge, deem, think, hold, be of the opinion that **8** *The air feels wet and cold on these evenings.* = **seem**, appear, strike you as **9** *The charity is still feeling the effects of revelations about its former president.* = **notice**, note, observe, perceive, detect, discern ▶ NOUN **1** *a crisp papery feel* = **texture**, finish, touch, surface, surface quality **2** *He wanted to get the feel of the place.* = **impression**, feeling, air, sense, quality, atmosphere, mood, aura, ambience, vibes (*slang*) • **feel for someone** *I really felt for her.* = **feel compassion for**, pity, feel sorry for, sympathize with, be moved by, be sorry for, empathize, commiserate with, bleed for, feel sympathy for, condole with • **feel like something** *I feel like a little exercise.* = **want**, desire, would like, fancy (*informal*), wish for, could do with, feel the need for, feel inclined, feel up to, have the inclination for

feeler • **put out feelers** = **approach**, probe, test of the waters, overture, trial, launch a trial balloon

feeling NOUN **1** *Strong feelings of pride welled up in me.* = **emotion**, sentiment **2** *She has strong feelings about the growth in violence.* = **opinion**, view, attitude, belief, point of view, instinct, inclination **3** *a voice that trembles with feeling* = **passion**, heat, emotion, intensity, warmth, sentimentality **4** *He never lost his feeling for her.* = **ardour**, love, care, affection, warmth, tenderness, fondness, fervour **5** *He felt a rush of feeling for the woman.* = **sympathy**, understanding, concern, pity, appreciation, sensitivity, compassion, sorrow, sensibility, empathy, fellow feeling **6** *Focus on the feeling of relaxation.* = **sensation**, sense, impression, awareness **7** *After the accident he had no feeling in his legs.* = **sense of touch**, sense, perception, sensation, feel, touch **8** *I have a feeling that everything will come right for us.* = **impression**, idea, sense, notion, suspicion, consciousness, hunch, apprehension, inkling, presentiment **9** *a feeling of opulence and grandeur* = **atmosphere**, mood, aura, ambience, feel, air, quality, vibes (*slang*) ▶ PLURAL NOUN *She was afraid of hurting my feelings.* = **emotions**, ego, self-esteem, sensibilities, susceptibilities, sensitivities • **bad feeling** *There's been some bad feeling between them.* = **hostility**, anger, dislike, resentment, bitterness, distrust, enmity, ill feeling, ill will, upset

feign VERB = **pretend**, affect, assume, put on, devise, forge, fake, imitate, simulate, sham, act, fabricate, counterfeit, give the appearance of, dissemble, make a show of

feigned ADJECTIVE = **pretended**, affected, assumed, false, artificial, fake, imitation, simulated, sham, pseudo (*informal*), fabricated, counterfeit, spurious, ersatz, insincere

feint NOUN = **bluff**, manoeuvre, dodge, mock attack, play, blind, distraction, pretence, expedient, ruse, artifice, gambit, subterfuge, stratagem, wile

feisty ADJECTIVE = **fiery**, spirited, bold, plucky, vivacious, (as) game as Ned Kelly (*Austral. slang*)

felicity NOUN **1** *a period of domestic felicity* = **happiness**, joy, ecstasy, bliss, delectation (*formal*), blessedness, blissfulness **2** *his felicity of word and phrase* = **aptness**, grace, effectiveness, suitability, propriety, appropriateness, applicability, becomingness, suitableness

feline ADJECTIVE **1** *a black, furry, feline creature* = **catlike**, leonine **2** *He moves with feline pace.* = **graceful**, flowing, smooth, elegant, sleek, slinky, sinuous, stealthy

fell VERB **1** *Badly infected trees should be felled.* = **cut down**, cut, level, demolish, flatten, knock down, hew, raze **2** *A blow on the head felled him.* = **knock down**, floor, flatten (*informal*), strike down, prostrate, deck (*slang*)

fellow NOUN **1** *He appeared to be a fine fellow.*
= **man**, boy, person, individual, customer
(*informal*), character, guy (*informal*), bloke
(*Brit. informal*), punter (*informal*), chap
(*informal*), boykie (*S. African informal*)
2 *He stood out from all his fellows at work.*
= **associate**, colleague, peer, co-worker,
member, friend, partner, equal,
companion, comrade, crony, compeer
▶ MODIFIER *My fellow inmates treated me with
kindness.* = **co-**, similar, related, allied,
associate, associated, affiliated, akin, like

fellowship NOUN **1** *the National Youth
Fellowship* = **society**, club, league,
association, organization, guild, fraternity
(*U.S. & Canad.*), brotherhood, sisterhood,
order, sodality **2** *a sense of community and
fellowship* = **camaraderie**, intimacy,
communion, familiarity, brotherhood,
companionship, sociability, amity (*formal*),
kindliness, fraternization,
companionability, intercourse

feminine ADJECTIVE *traditional expectations of
feminine behaviour* = **womanly**, girlie, girlish,
ladylike ■ **OPPOSITE:** masculine

femininity NOUN = **womanliness**,
womanhood, gentleness, girlishness,
feminineness, muliebrity

fen NOUN = **marsh**, moss (*Scot.*), swamp,
bog, slough, quagmire, holm (*dialect*),
morass, pakihi (*N.Z.*), muskeg (*Canad.*)

fence NOUN *They climbed over the fence into the
field.* = **barrier**, wall, defence, guard,
railings, paling, shield, hedge, barricade,
hedgerow, rampart, palisade, stockade,
barbed wire ▶ VERB (*with* **in** *or* **off**) *They
intend to fence in about 100 acres of land.*
= **enclose**, surround, bound, hedge, pound,
protect, separate, guard, defend, secure,
pen, restrict, confine, fortify, encircle, coop,
impound, circumscribe • **sit on the fence**
*He is sitting on the fence, refusing to commit
himself.* = **be uncommitted**, be uncertain,
be undecided, vacillate, be in two minds,
blow hot and cold (*informal*), be irresolute,
avoid committing yourself

fend VERB • **fend for yourself** *She was just
left to fend for herself.* = **look after yourself**,
support yourself, sustain yourself, take care
of yourself, provide for yourself, make do,
make provision for yourself, shift for
yourself • **fend something** *or* **someone
off 1** *She fended off questions from the Press.*
= **deflect**, resist, parry, avert, ward off,
stave off, turn aside, hold *or* keep at bay
2 *He raised his hand to fend off the blow.* = **beat
off**, resist, parry, avert, deflect, repel, drive
back, ward off, stave off, repulse, keep off,
turn aside, hold *or* keep at bay

feral ADJECTIVE **1** *There are many feral cats
roaming the area.* = **wild**, untamed,
uncultivated, undomesticated, unbroken
2 *the feral scowl of the street mugger* = **savage**,
fierce, brutal, ferocious, fell, wild, vicious,
bestial

ferment NOUN *The country is in a state of
political ferment.* = **commotion**, turmoil,
unrest, turbulence, trouble, heat,
excitement, glow, fever, disruption, frenzy,
stew, furore, uproar, agitation, tumult,
hubbub, brouhaha, imbroglio, state of
unrest ■ **OPPOSITE:** tranquillity ▶ VERB
1 *red wine made from grapes left to ferment for
three weeks* = **brew**, froth, concoct,
effervesce, work, rise, heat, boil, bubble,
foam, seethe, leaven **2** *They tried to ferment
political unrest.* = **stir up**, excite, provoke,
rouse, agitate, inflame, incite

ferocious ADJECTIVE **1** *By its nature a lion is
ferocious.* = **fierce**, violent, savage, ravening,
predatory, feral, rapacious, wild
■ **OPPOSITE:** gentle **2** *Fighting has been
ferocious.* = **cruel**, bitter, brutal, vicious,
ruthless, relentless, barbaric, merciless,
brutish, bloodthirsty, barbarous, pitiless,
tigerish

ferocity NOUN = **savagery**, violence,
cruelty, brutality, ruthlessness, inhumanity,
wildness, barbarity, viciousness, fierceness,
rapacity, bloodthirstiness, savageness,
ferociousness

ferry NOUN *They crossed the river by ferry.*
= **ferry boat**, boat, ship, passenger boat,
packet boat, packet ▶ VERB *They ferried in
more soldiers to help with the search.*
= **transport**, bring, carry, ship, take, run,
shuttle, convey, chauffeur

fertile ADJECTIVE = **productive**, rich,
flowering, lush, fat, yielding, prolific,
abundant, plentiful, fruitful, teeming,
luxuriant, generative, fecund, fruit-
bearing, flowing with milk and honey,
plenteous ■ **OPPOSITE:** barren

fertility NOUN = **fruitfulness**, abundance,
richness, fecundity, luxuriance,
productiveness

fertilization *or* **fertilisation** NOUN
= **insemination**, propagation, procreation,
implantation, pollination, impregnation

fertilize VERB **1** *sperm levels needed to fertilize
the egg* = **inseminate**, impregnate,
pollinate, make pregnant, fructify, make
fruitful, fecundate **2** *grown in recently
fertilized soil* = **enrich**, feed, compost, manure,
mulch, top-dress, dress, fertigate (*Austral.*)

fertilizer NOUN = **compost**, muck, manure,
dung, guano, marl, bone meal, dressing,
toad juice (*Austral.*)

fervent ADJECTIVE = **ardent**, earnest,
enthusiastic, fervid, passionate, warm,
excited, emotional, intense, flaming, eager,
animated, fiery, ecstatic, devout, heartfelt,
impassioned, zealous, vehement, perfervid
(*literary*) ■ **OPPOSITE:** apathetic

> USAGE Care should be taken when
> using *fervid* as an alternative to *fervent*.
> Although both come from the same root
> and share the meaning 'intense, ardent',
> *fervent* has largely positive connotations,
> and is associated with hopes, wishes,
> and beliefs, or admirers, supporters, and
> fans: *she inspired her pupils with a fervent
> desire to learn*. Apart from being used less
> often than *fervent*, *fervid* is chiefly
> negative: *in the fervid politics of
> New York city*.

fervour or (*U.S.*) **fervor** NOUN = **ardour**,
passion, enthusiasm, excitement,
intensity, warmth, animation, zeal,
eagerness, vehemence, earnestness,
fervency

fester VERB 1 *Resentments are starting to fester.*
= **intensify**, gall, smoulder, chafe, irk,
rankle, aggravate 2 *The wound is festering
and gangrene has set in.* = **putrefy**, decay,
become infected, become inflamed,
suppurate, ulcerate, maturate, gather

festering ADJECTIVE = **septic**, infected,
poisonous, inflamed, pussy, suppurating,
ulcerated, purulent, maturating,
gathering

festival NOUN 1 *The Festival will provide
spectacles like river pageants.* = **celebration**,
fair, carnival, gala, treat, fête,
entertainment, jubilee, fiesta, festivities,
jamboree, -fest, field day 2 *the Jewish festival
of the Passover* = **holy day**, holiday, feast,
commemoration, feast day, red-letter day,
saint's day, fiesta, fête, anniversary

festive ADJECTIVE = **celebratory**, happy,
holiday, carnival, jolly, merry, gala, hearty,
jubilant, cheery, joyous, joyful, jovial,
convivial, gleeful, back-slapping,
Christmassy, mirthful, sportive, light-
hearted, festal, gay ■ **OPPOSITE:** mournful

festivity NOUN 1 *There was a general air of
festivity and abandon.* = **merrymaking**, fun,
pleasure, amusement, mirth, gaiety,
merriment, revelry, conviviality, joviality,
joyfulness, jollification, sport 2 (*often plural*)
The festivities included a firework display.
= **celebration**, party, festival,
entertainment, rave (*Brit. slang*), beano
(*Brit. slang*), fun and games, rave-up (*Brit.
slang*), jollification, festive event, carousal,
festive proceedings, hooley or hoolie
(*chiefly Irish & N.Z.*)

festoon NOUN *festoons of laurel and magnolia*
= **decoration**, garland, swathe, wreath,
swag, lei, chaplet ▶ VERB *The temples are
festooned with lights.* = **decorate**, deck,
array, drape, garland, swathe, bedeck,
wreathe, beribbon, engarland, hang

fetch VERB 1 *She fetched a towel from the
bathroom.* = **bring**, pick up, collect, go and
get, get, carry, deliver, conduct, transport,
go for, obtain, escort, convey, retrieve
2 *The painting is expected to fetch two million
pounds.* = **sell for**, make, raise, earn, realize,
go for, yield, bring in • **fetch up** *We
eventually fetched up at their house.* = **end up**,
reach, arrive, turn up, come, stop, land,
halt, finish up

fetching ADJECTIVE = **attractive**, sweet,
charming, enchanting, fascinating,
intriguing, cute, enticing, captivating,
alluring, winsome

fête or **fete** NOUN *The Vicar is organizing a
church fete.* = **fair**, festival, gala, bazaar,
garden party, sale of work ▶ VERB *The
composer was fêted at a special dinner.*
= **entertain**, welcome, honour, make
much of, wine and dine, hold a reception
for (someone), lionize, bring out the red
carpet for (someone), kill the fatted calf for
(someone), treat

fetish NOUN 1 *I've got a bit of a shoe fetish.*
= **fixation**, obsession, mania, thing
(*informal*), idée fixe (*French*) 2 *Tribal elders
carried the sacred fetishes.* = **talisman**,
amulet, cult object

fetter PLURAL NOUN 1 *without the fetters of
restrictive rules* = **restraints**, checks, curbs,
constraints, captivity, obstructions,
bondage, hindrances 2 *He saw a boy in fetters
in the dungeon.* = **chains**, bonds, irons,
shackles, manacles, leg irons, gyves
(*archaic*), bilboes ▶ VERB 1 *He would not be
fettered by bureaucracy.* = **restrict**, bind,
confine, curb, restrain, hamstring, hamper,
encumber, clip someone's wings, trammel,
straiten 2 *My foes fettered me hand and foot.*
= **chain**, tie, tie up, shackle, hobble, hold
captive, manacle, gyve (*archaic*), put a
straitjacket on

feud NOUN *a long and bitter feud between
families* = **hostility**, row, conflict,
argument, faction, falling out,
disagreement, rivalry, contention,
quarrel, grudge, strife, bickering,
vendetta, discord, enmity, broil, bad blood,
estrangement, dissension ▶ VERB *He feuded
with his ex-wife.* = **quarrel**, row, clash,
dispute, fall out (*informal*), contend,
brawl, war, squabble, duel, bicker,
be at odds, be at daggers drawn

fever NOUN **1** *Symptoms of the disease include fever and weight loss.* = **ague**, high temperature, feverishness, pyrexia (*Medical*) **2** *I got married in a fever of excitement.* = **excitement**, heat, passion, intensity, flush, turmoil, ecstasy, frenzy, ferment, agitation, fervour, restlessness, delirium ■ **RELATED WORD:** *adjective* febrile

fevered ADJECTIVE = **frantic**, excited, desperate, distracted, frenzied, impatient, obsessive, restless, agitated, frenetic, overwrought

feverish *or* **fevorous** ADJECTIVE **1** *a state of feverish excitement* = **frantic**, excited, desperate, distracted, frenzied, impatient, obsessive, restless, agitated, frenetic, overwrought ■ **OPPOSITE:** calm **2** *She looked feverish; her eyes glistened.* = **hot**, burning, flaming, fevered, flushed, hectic, inflamed, febrile (*formal*), pyretic (*Medical*)

few ADJECTIVE *In some districts there are few survivors.* = **not many**, one or two, hardly any, scarcely any, rare, thin, scattered, insufficient, scarce, scant, meagre, negligible, sporadic, sparse, infrequent, scanty, inconsiderable ■ **OPPOSITE:** many ▶ PRONOUN *A strict diet is appropriate for only a few.* = **a small number**, a handful, a sprinkling, a scattering, some, scarcely any • **few and far between** *Successful women politicians were few and far between.* = **scarce**, rare, unusual, scattered, irregular, uncommon, in short supply, hard to come by, infrequent, thin on the ground, widely spaced, seldom met with

fiancé *or* **fiancée** NOUN = **husband-** *or* **wife-to-be**, intended (*informal*), betrothed, prospective spouse, future husband *or* wife

fiasco NOUN = **flop** (*informal*), failure, disaster, ruin, mess (*informal*), catastrophe, rout, debacle, cock-up (*Brit. slang*), washout (*informal*)

fib NOUN = **lie**, story (*informal*), fiction, untruth, whopper (*informal*), porky (*Brit. slang*), pork pie (*Brit. slang*), white lie, prevarication

fibre *or* (*U.S.*) **fiber** NOUN *a variety of coloured fibres* = **thread**, strand, filament, tendril, pile, texture, staple, wisp, fibril • **moral fibre** *They all lacked courage, backbone or moral fibre.* = **strength of character**, strength, resolution, resolve, stamina, backbone, toughness

fickle ADJECTIVE = **capricious**, variable, volatile, unpredictable, unstable, unfaithful, temperamental, mercurial, unsteady, faithless, changeable, quicksilver, vacillating, fitful, flighty, blowing hot and cold, mutable, irresolute, inconstant ■ **OPPOSITE:** constant

fiction NOUN **1** *She is a writer of historical fiction.* = **tale**, story, novel, legend, myth, romance, fable, storytelling, narration, creative writing, work of imagination **2** *a story of truth or fiction* = **imagination**, fancy (*old-fashioned*, *literary*), fantasy, creativity **3** *Total recycling is a fiction.* = **lie**, fancy, fantasy, invention, improvisation, fabrication, concoction, falsehood, untruth, porky (*Brit. slang*), pork pie (*Brit. slang*), urban myth, tall story, urban legend, cock and bull story (*informal*), figment of the imagination

fictional ADJECTIVE = **imaginary**, made-up, invented, legendary, unreal, nonexistent

fictitious ADJECTIVE **1** *a source of fictitious rumours* = **false**, made-up, bogus, untrue, non-existent, fabricated, counterfeit, feigned, spurious, apocryphal ■ **OPPOSITE:** true **2** *Persons portrayed in this production are fictitious.* = **imaginary**, imagined, made-up, assumed, invented, artificial, improvised, mythical, unreal, fanciful, make-believe

fiddle NOUN **1** *legitimate businesses that act as a cover for tax fiddles* = **fraud**, racket, scam (*slang*), piece of sharp practice, fix, sting (*informal*), graft (*informal*), swindle, wangle (*informal*) **2** *He played the fiddle at local dances.* = **violin** ▶ VERB **1** (*often with* **with**) *She fiddled with a pen on the desk.* = **fidget**, play, finger, toy, tamper, trifle, mess about *or* around **2** (*often with* **with**) *He fiddled with the radio dial.* = **tinker**, adjust, interfere, mess about *or* around **3** *Stop fiddling your expenses account.* = **cheat**, cook (*informal*), fix, manoeuvre (*informal*), graft (*informal*), diddle (*informal*), wangle (*informal*), gerrymander, finagle (*informal*)

fiddling ADJECTIVE = **trivial**, small, petty, trifling, insignificant, unimportant, pettifogging, futile

fidelity NOUN **1** *I had to promise fidelity to the Queen.* = **loyalty**, faith, integrity, devotion, allegiance, constancy, faithfulness, dependability, trustworthiness, troth (*archaic*), fealty, staunchness, devotedness, lealty (*archaic*), true-heartedness ■ **OPPOSITE:** disloyalty **2** *the fidelity of these early documents* = **accuracy**, precision, correspondence, closeness, adherence, faithfulness, exactitude, exactness, scrupulousness, preciseness ■ **OPPOSITE:** inaccuracy

fidget VERB = **move restlessly**, fiddle (*informal*), bustle, twitch, fret, squirm, chafe, jiggle, jitter (*informal*), be like a cat on hot bricks (*informal*), worry

field NOUN **1** *They went for walks together in the fields.* = **meadow**, land, green, lea (*poetic*), pasture, mead (*archaic*), greensward (*archaic, literary*) **2** *They are both experts in their field.* = **speciality**, line, area, department (*informal*), environment, territory, discipline, province, pale, confines, sphere, domain, specialty, sphere of influence, purview, metier, sphere of activity, bailiwick, sphere of interest, sphere of study **3** *Our field of vision is surprisingly wide.* = **line**, reach, range, limits, bounds, sweep, scope **4** *The two most experienced athletes led the field.* = **competitors**, competition, candidates, runners, applicants, entrants, contestants ▶ VERB **1** *He fielded questions from journalists.* = **deal with**, answer, handle, respond to, reply to, deflect, turn aside **2** *He fielded the ball and threw it at the wicket.* = **retrieve**, return, stop, catch, pick up

fiend NOUN **1** *a saint to his parents and a fiend to his children* = **brute**, monster, savage, beast, degenerate, barbarian, ogre, ghoul **2** *a strong-tea fiend* = **enthusiast**, fan, addict, freak (*informal*), fanatic, maniac, energumen **3** *She is a fiend incarnate, leading these people to eternal damnation.* = **demon**, devil, evil spirit, hellhound, atua (*N.Z.*)

fiendish ADJECTIVE **1** *It is a fiendish question without an easy answer.* = **difficult**, involved, complex, puzzling, baffling, intricate, thorny, knotty **2** *a fiendish act of wickedness* = **wicked**, cruel, savage, monstrous, malicious, satanic, malignant, unspeakable, atrocious, inhuman, diabolical, implacable, malevolent, hellish (*informal*), devilish, infernal (*informal*), accursed, ungodly, black-hearted, demoniac

fierce ADJECTIVE **1** *the teeth of some fierce animal* = **ferocious**, wild, dangerous, cruel, savage, brutal, aggressive, menacing, vicious, fiery, murderous, uncontrollable, feral, untamed, barbarous, fell (*archaic*), threatening, baleful, truculent, tigerish, aggers (*Austral. slang*), biffo (*Austral. slang*) ■ **OPPOSITE:** gentle **2** *He inspires fierce loyalty in his friends.* = **intense**, strong, keen, passionate, relentless, cut-throat **3** *Two climbers were trapped by a fierce storm.* = **stormy**, strong, powerful, violent, intense, raging, furious, howling, uncontrollable, boisterous, tumultuous, tempestuous, blustery, inclement ■ **OPPOSITE:** tranquil

fiercely ADVERB = **ferociously**, savagely, passionately, furiously, viciously, menacingly, tooth and nail, in a frenzy, like cat and dog, frenziedly, tigerishly, with no holds barred, tempestuously, with bared teeth, uncontrolledly

fiery ADJECTIVE **1** *People set up fiery barricades.* = **burning**, flaming, glowing, blazing, on fire, red-hot, ablaze, in flames, aflame, afire **2** *I see you have a fiery temper.* = **excitable**, violent, fierce, passionate, irritable, impetuous, irascible, peppery, hot-headed, choleric

fiesta NOUN = **carnival**, party, holiday, fair, fête, festival, celebration, feast, revel, jubilee, festivity, jamboree, Mardi Gras, revelry, Saturnalia, saint's day, merrymaking, carousal, bacchanal *or* bacchanalia, gala

fight VERB **1** *She devoted her life to fighting poverty.* = **oppose**, campaign against, dispute, contest, resist, defy, contend, withstand, stand up to, take issue with, make a stand against **2** *He had to fight hard for his place in the team.* = **strive**, battle, push, struggle, contend **3** *The Sioux fought other tribes for territorial rights.* = **battle**, assault, combat, war with; go to war, do battle, wage war, take up arms, bear arms against, engage in hostilities, carry on war, engage **4** *They fought a war against injustice.* = **engage in**, conduct, wage, pursue, carry on **5** *He fought in the war and was taken prisoner.* = **take the field**, cross swords, taste battle **6** *He was formally disciplined for fighting at work.* = **brawl**, clash, scrap (*informal*), exchange blows, struggle, row, tilt, wrestle, feud, grapple, tussle, joust, come to blows, lock horns, fight like Kilkenny cats **7** *I'd like to fight him for the title.* = **box**, spar with, exchange blows with ▶ NOUN **1** *I will continue the fight for justice.* = **battle**, campaign, movement, struggle **2** *They used to be allies in the fight against the old Communist regime.* = **conflict**, war, action, clash, contest, encounter, brush, combat, engagement, hostilities, skirmish, passage of arms **3** *He got a bloody nose in a fight.* = **brawl**, set-to (*informal*), riot, scrap (*informal*), confrontation, rumble (*U.S. & N.Z. slang*), fray, duel, skirmish, head-to-head, tussle, scuffle, free-for-all (*informal*), fracas, altercation, dogfight, joust, dissension, affray (*Law*), shindig (*informal*), scrimmage, sparring match, exchange of blows, shindy (*informal*), melee *or* mêlée, biffo (*Austral. slang*), boilover (*Austral.*) **4** *He had a big fight with his dad last night.* = **row**, argument, dispute, quarrel, squabble **5** *The referee stopped the fight in the second round.* = **match**, contest, bout, battle, competition, struggle, set-to, encounter, engagement, head-to-head, boxing match **6** *We had a lot of fight in us.* = **resistance**, spirit, pluck, militancy, mettle, belligerence, will to resist, gameness, pluckiness • **fight shy of something** *It's no use fighting shy of publicity.* = **avoid**, shun, steer clear of, duck out of (*informal*), keep at arm's length, hang back from, keep aloof from

fighter NOUN **1** *She's a real fighter and has always defied the odds.* = **combatant**, battler, militant, contender, contestant, belligerent, antagonist, disputant **2** *a tough little street fighter* = **boxer**, wrestler, bruiser (*informal*), pugilist, prize fighter **3** *The Spartans were the best fighters in Ancient Greece.* = **soldier**, warrior, fighting man or woman, man-at-arms

figment NOUN = **invention**, production, fancy, creation, fiction, fable, improvisation, fabrication, falsehood

figurative ADJECTIVE = **symbolical**, representative, abstract, allegorical, typical, tropical (*Rhetoric*), imaginative, ornate, descriptive, fanciful, pictorial, metaphorical, flowery, florid, poetical, emblematical ■ **OPPOSITE:** literal

figure NOUN **1** *Deduct the second figure from the first.* = **digit**, character, symbol, number, numeral, cipher **2** *A figure appeared in the doorway.* = **outline**, form, shape, shadow, profile, silhouette **3** *Take pride in your health and your figure.* = **shape**, build, body, frame, proportions, chassis (*slang*), torso, physique **4** *The movement is supported by key figures.* = **personage**, force, face (*informal*), leader, person, individual, character (*informal*), presence, somebody, personality, celebrity, worthy, notable, big name, dignitary, notability **5** *Figure 26 shows a small circular garden of herbs.* = **diagram**, drawing, picture, illustration, representation, sketch, emblem **6** *The impulsive singer had the figure cut into his shaven hair.* = **design**, shape, pattern, device, motif, depiction **7** *It's hard to put a figure on the damage.* = **price**, cost, value, amount, total, sum ▸ VERB **1** *When I finished, he said, 'Yeah. That figures'.* = **make sense**, follow, be expected, add up, go without saying, seem reasonable **2** (*usually with* **in**) *I didn't figure in his plans.* = **feature**, act, appear, contribute to, be included, be mentioned, play a part, be featured, have a place in, be conspicuous **3** *Figure the interest rate.* = **calculate**, work out, compute, tot up, add, total, count, reckon, sum, tally • **figure on something** *I never figured on that scenario.* = **plan on**, depend on, rely on, count on, bargain on • **figure something out** *I want to figure out how much it'll cost.* = **calculate**, reckon, work out, compute • **figure something or**

someone out *How do you figure that out?;* *I can't figure that guy out at all.* = **understand**, make out, fathom, make head or tail of (*informal*), see, solve, resolve, comprehend, make sense of, decipher, think through, suss (out) (*slang*)

figurehead NOUN = **nominal head**, leader in name only, titular head, frontman or woman or person, name, token, dummy, puppet, mouthpiece, cipher, nonentity, straw man (*chiefly U.S.*), man of straw

figure of speech NOUN = **expression**, image, turn of phrase, trope

filament NOUN = **strand**, string, wire, fibre, thread, staple, wisp, cilium (*Biology & Zoology*), fibril, pile

file¹ NOUN **1** *a file of insurance papers* = **folder**, case, portfolio, binder **2** *We have files on people's tax details.* = **dossier**, record, information, data, documents, case history, report, case **3** *A file of soldiers, marched past.* = **line**, row, chain, string, column, queue, procession ▸ VERB **1** *Papers are filed alphabetically.* = **arrange**, order, classify, put in place, slot in (*informal*), categorize, pigeonhole, put in order **2** *They have filed formal complaints.* = **register**, record, enter, log, put on record **3** *They filed into the room and sat down.* = **march**, troop, parade, walk in line, walk behind one another

file² VERB *shaping and filing nails* = **smooth**, shape, polish, rub, refine, scrape, rasp, burnish, rub down, abrade

filibuster NOUN *The Senator used a filibuster to stop the bill.* = **obstruction**, delay, postponement, hindrance, procrastination ▸ VERB *They threatened to filibuster until Senate adjourns.* = **obstruct**, prevent, delay, put off, hinder, play for time, procrastinate

filigree NOUN = **wirework**, lace, lattice, tracery, lacework

fill VERB **1** *While the bath was filling, he undressed.* = **top up**, fill up, make full, become full, brim over **2** *Your lungs fill with air.* = **swell**, expand, inflate, become bloated, extend, balloon, fatten **3** *Thousands of people filled the streets.* = **pack**, crowd, squeeze, cram, throng **4** *I fill the shelves in a supermarket until 12pm.* = **stock**, supply, store, pack, load, furnish, replenish **5** *Fill the holes with plaster.* = **plug**, close, stop, seal, cork, bung, block up, stop up **6** *The barn was filled with the smell of hay.* = **saturate**, charge, pervade, permeate, imbue, impregnate, suffuse, overspread **7** *a widowed father struggling to fill the role of both parents* = **fulfil**, hold, perform, carry out, occupy, take up, execute, discharge, officiate **8** (*often with* **up**) *They filled themselves with chocolate cake.* = **satisfy**, stuff, gorge, glut, satiate, sate • **fill in for someone** *relief employees who fill in for workers while on break* = **replace**, represent, substitute for, cover for, take over from, act for, stand in for, sub for, deputize for • **fill someone in** *I'll fill him in on the details.* = **inform**, acquaint, advise of, apprise of, bring up to date with, update with, put wise to (*slang*), give the facts or background of • **fill something in** *Fill in the coupon and send it to the above address.* = **complete**, answer, fill up, fill out (*U.S.*) • **your fill** *We have had our fill of disappointments.* = **sufficient**, enough, plenty, ample, all you want, a sufficiency

filling NOUN *Make the filling from down or feathers.* = **stuffing**, padding, filler, wadding, inside, insides, contents, innards (*informal*) ▶ ADJECTIVE *a well-spiced and filling meal* = **satisfying**, heavy, square, substantial, ample

fillip NOUN = **boost**, push, spur, spice, incentive, stimulus, prod, zest, goad

film NOUN **1** *He appeared in the star role of the film.* = **movie**, picture, flick (*slang*), motion picture, MPEG, MP4 **2** *She went on to a successful career in film and television.* = **cinema**, the movies **3** *The sea is coated with a film of sewage.* = **layer**, covering, cover, skin, coating, coat, dusting, tissue, membrane, scum, gauze, integument, pellicle **4** *There was a sort of film over my eyes.* = **haze**, cloud, blur, mist, veil, opacity, haziness, mistiness ▶ VERB **1** *We filmed the scene in one hour.* = **photograph**, record, shoot, video, videotape, take **2** *He filmed her life story.* = **adapt for the screen**, make into a film ■ **RELATED WORD:** *adjective* cinematic

filter NOUN *a paper coffee filter* = **sieve**, mesh, gauze, strainer, membrane, riddle, sifter ▶ VERB **1** *Water filtered through the peat.* = **trickle**, leach, seep, percolate, well, escape, leak, penetrate, ooze, dribble, exude **2** (*with* **through**) *The best prevention for cholera is to filter water.* = **purify**, treat, strain, refine, riddle, sift, sieve, winnow, filtrate, screen

filth NOUN **1** *tons of filth and sewage* = **dirt**, refuse, pollution, muck, garbage, sewage, contamination, dung, sludge, squalor, grime, faeces, slime, excrement, nastiness, carrion, excreta, crud (*slang*), foulness, putrefaction, ordure, defilement, kak (*S. African vulgar slang*), grot (*slang*), filthiness, uncleanness, putrescence, foul matter **2** *The dialogue was all filth and innuendo.* = **obscenity**, corruption, pornography, indecency, impurity, vulgarity, smut, vileness, dirty-mindedness

filthy ADJECTIVE **1** *The water looks stale and filthy.* = **dirty**, nasty, foul, polluted, vile, squalid, slimy, unclean, putrid, faecal, scummy, scuzzy (*slang, chiefly U.S.*), feculent, festy (*Austral. slang*) **2** *He always wore a filthy old jacket.* = **grimy**, black, muddy, smoky, blackened, grubby, sooty, unwashed, mucky, scuzzy (*slang, chiefly U.S.*), begrimed, mud-encrusted, miry, festy (*Austral. slang*) **3** *The play was full of filthy foul language.* = **obscene**, foul, corrupt, coarse, indecent, pornographic, suggestive, lewd, depraved, foul-mouthed, X-rated (*informal*), bawdy, impure, smutty, licentious **4** *'You filthy swine!' Penelope shouted.* = **despicable**, mean, low, base, offensive, vicious, vile, contemptible, scurvy (*old-fashioned*)

final ADJECTIVE **1** *the final book in the series* = **last**, latest, end, closing, finishing, concluding, ultimate, terminal, last-minute, eventual, terminating ■ **OPPOSITE:** first **2** *The judge's decision is final.* = **irrevocable**, absolute, decisive, definitive, decided, finished, settled, definite, conclusive, irrefutable, incontrovertible, unalterable, determinate, net-net (*informal*)

finale NOUN = **climax**, ending, close, conclusion, culmination, denouement, last part, epilogue, last act, crowning glory, finis ■ **OPPOSITE:** opening

finality NOUN = **conclusiveness**, resolution, decisiveness, certitude, definiteness, irrevocability, inevitableness, unavoidability, decidedness

finalize VERB = **complete**, settle, conclude, tie up, decide, agree, work out, clinch, wrap up (*informal*), shake hands, sew up (*informal*), complete the arrangements for

finally ADVERB **1** *The food finally arrived at the end of the week.* = **eventually**, at last, in the end, ultimately, at the last, at the end of the day, in the long run, at length, at the last moment, at long last, when all is said and done, in the fullness of time, after a long time **2** *Finally came the dessert trolley.* = **lastly**, in the end, ultimately **3** *Finally, a word or two of advice.* = **in conclusion**, lastly, in closing, to conclude, to sum up, in summary **4** *Finally they are drawing a line under the affair.* = **conclusively**, for good, permanently, for ever, completely, definitely, once and for all, decisively, convincingly, inexorably, irrevocably, for all time, inescapably, beyond the shadow of a doubt

finance NOUN *a major player in the world of high finance* = **economics**, business, money, banking, accounts, investment, commerce, financial affairs, money management

▶ PLURAL NOUN *I like to manage the day-to-day finances.* = **resources**, money, funds, capital, cash, affairs, budgeting, assets, cash flow, financial affairs, money management, wherewithal, financial condition ▶ VERB *new taxes to finance increased military expenditure* = **fund**, back, support, pay for, guarantee, float, invest in, underwrite, endow, subsidize, bankroll (*informal*), set up in business, provide security for, provide money for

financial ADJECTIVE = **economic**, business, money, budgeting, budgetary, commercial, monetary, fiscal, pecuniary, pocketbook

find VERB **1** *The police also found a pistol.* = **discover**, turn up, uncover, unearth, spot, expose, come up with, locate, detect, come across, track down, catch sight of, stumble upon, hit upon, espy, ferret out, chance upon, light upon, put your finger on, lay your hand on, run to ground, run to earth, descry ■ OPPOSITE: lose **2** *Luckily she found her bag.* = **regain**, recover, get back, retrieve, repossess **3** *Many people here cannot find work.* = **obtain**, get, come by, procure, win, gain, achieve, earn, acquire, attain **4** *They found her walking alone on the beach.* = **encounter**, meet, recognize **5** *The study found that heart disease can begin in childhood.* = **observe**, learn, note, discover, notice, realize, remark, come up with, arrive at, perceive, detect, become aware, experience, ascertain **6** *Could anyone find pleasure in killing this creature?* = **feel**, have, experience, sense, obtain, know **7** *Their parents can usually find the money for them.* = **provide**, supply, contribute, furnish, cough up (*informal*), purvey, be responsible for, bring ▶ NOUN *Another lucky find was a pair of candle-holders.* = **discovery**, catch, asset, bargain, acquisition, good buy • **find someone out** *I wondered for a moment if she'd found me out.* = **detect**, catch, unmask, rumble (*Brit. informal*), reveal, expose, disclose, uncover, suss (out) (*slang*), bring to light • **find something out** *It was such a relief to find out that I'd passed my exams.* = **learn**, discover, realize, observe, perceive, detect, become aware, come to know, note

finding NOUN = **judgment**, ruling, decision, award, conclusion, verdict, recommendation, decree, pronouncement

fine¹ ADJECTIVE **1** *This is a fine book.* = **excellent**, good, great (*informal*), striking, choice, beautiful, masterly, select, rare, very good, supreme, impressive, outstanding, magnificent, superior, accomplished, sterling, first-class, divine (*informal*), exceptional, splendid, world-

class, exquisite, admirable, skilful, ornate, first-rate, showy, bakgat (*S. African*) ■ OPPOSITE: poor **2** *It's fine to ask questions as we go along.* = **satisfactory**, good, all right, suitable, acceptable, convenient, agreeable, hunky-dory (*informal*), fair, O.K. or okay (*informal*) **3** *The heat scorched the fine hairs on her arms.* = **thin**, small, light, narrow, wispy **4** *Her suit was of a pale grey fine material.* = **delicate**, light, thin, sheer, lightweight, flimsy, wispy, gossamer, diaphanous, gauzy, chiffony ■ OPPOSITE: coarse **5** *We waited in our fine clothes.* = **stylish**, expensive, elegant, refined, tasteful, quality, schmick (*Austral. informal*) **6** *She wears fine jewellery wherever she goes.* = **exquisite**, delicate, fragile, dainty **7** *They are reserving judgement on the fine detail.* = **minute**, exact, precise, nice **8** *She has a fine eye for detail.* = **keen**, minute, nice, quick, sharp, critical, acute, sensitive, subtle, precise, refined, discriminating, tenuous, fastidious, hairsplitting **9** *He had a fine mind and excellent knowledge.* = **brilliant**, quick, keen, alert, clever, intelligent, penetrating, astute **10** *tapering to a fine point* = **sharp**, keen, polished, honed, razor-sharp, cutting **11** *You're a very fine woman.* = **good-looking**, striking, pretty, attractive, lovely, smart, handsome, stylish, bonny (*Scot. & Northern English, dialect*), well-favoured, fit (*Brit. informal*) **12** *I'll do the garden if the weather is fine.* = **sunny**, clear, fair, dry, bright, pleasant, clement, balmy, cloudless ■ OPPOSITE: cloudy **13** *a light, fine oil, high in vitamin content* = **pure**, clear, refined, unadulterated, unalloyed, unpolluted, solid, sterling

fine² NOUN *If convicted he faces a fine of one million dollars.* = **penalty**, damages, punishment, forfeit, financial penalty, amercement (*obsolete*) ▶ VERB *She was fined £300 and banned from driving.* = **penalize**, charge, punish

finery NOUN = **splendour**, trappings, frippery, glad rags (*informal*), gear (*informal*), decorations, ornaments, trinkets, Sunday best, gewgaws, showiness, best bib and tucker (*informal*), bling (*slang*)

finesse NOUN **1** = **skill**, style, know-how (*informal*), polish, craft, sophistication, cleverness, quickness, adroitness, adeptness **2** *handling diplomatic challenges with finesse* = **diplomacy**, discretion, subtlety, delicacy, tact, savoir-faire, artfulness, adeptness ▶ VERB *a typical politician trying to finesse a sticky situation* = **manoeuvre**, steer, manipulate, bluff

finger NOUN 1 = **digit**, thumb, forefinger, little finger, index finger, middle finger, ring finger, third finger, first finger, second finger, fourth finger 2 = **strip**, piece, band, sliver, bit ▶ VERB 1 *He fingered the few coins in his pocket.* = **touch**, feel, handle, play with, manipulate, paw (*informal*), maul, toy with, fiddle with (*informal*), meddle with, play about with 2 = **inform on**, shop (*slang, chiefly Brit.*), grass (*Brit. slang*), rat (*informal*), betray, notify, peach (*slang*), tip off, squeal (*slang*), leak to, incriminate, tell on (*informal*), blow the whistle on (*informal*), snitch (*slang*), blab, nark (*Brit., Austral. & N.Z. slang*), inculpate, dob in (*Austral. slang*) • **put your finger on something** *She couldn't quite put her finger on the reason.* = **identify**, place, remember, discover, indicate, recall, find out, locate, pin down, bring to mind, hit upon, hit the nail on the head ■ **RELATED WORD:** *adjective* digital

finish VERB 1 *He was cheered when he finished his speech.* = **stop**, close, complete, achieve, conclude, cease, accomplish, execute, discharge, culminate, wrap up (*informal*), terminate, round off, bring to a close *or* conclusion ■ **OPPOSITE:** start 2 *They've been working to finish a report this week.* = **get done**, complete, put the finishing touch(es) to, finalize, do, deal with, settle, conclude, fulfil, carry through, get out of the way, make short work of 3 *The teaching day finished at around 4pm.* = **end**, stop, conclude, wind up, terminate 4 *He finished his dinner and left.* = **consume**, dispose of, devour, polish off, drink, eat, drain, get through, dispatch, deplete 5 *Once you have finished all 21 pills, stop for seven days.* = **use up**, use, spend, empty, exhaust, expend 6 *The bowl is finished in a pearlized lustre.* = **coat**, polish, stain, texture, wax, varnish, gild, veneer, lacquer, smooth off, face 7 (*often with* **off**) *I played well but I didn't finish him off.* = **destroy**, defeat, overcome, bring down, best, worst, ruin, get rid of, dispose of, rout, put an end to, overpower, annihilate, put paid to, move in for the kill, drive to the wall, administer *or* give the coup de grâce 8 (*often with* **off**) *A further volley of bullets finished him off.* = **kill**, murder, destroy, do in (*slang*), take out (*slang*), massacre, butcher, slaughter, dispatch, slay (*archaic, literary*), eradicate, do away with, blow away (*slang, chiefly U.S.*), knock off (*slang*), annihilate, exterminate, take (someone's) life, bump off (*slang*) ▶ NOUN 1 *I intend to see the job through to the finish.* = **end**, ending, close, closing, conclusion, run-in, winding up (*informal*), wind-up,

completion, finale, termination, culmination, cessation, last stage(s), denouement, finalization ■ **OPPOSITE:** beginning 2 *The finish of the woodwork was excellent.* = **surface**, appearance, polish, shine, grain, glaze, veneer, lacquer, lustre, smoothness, patina

finished ADJECTIVE 1 *Finally, last spring, the film was finished.* = **over**, done, completed, achieved, through, ended, closed, full, final, complete, in the past, concluded, shut, accomplished, executed, tied up, wrapped up (*informal*), terminated, sewn up (*informal*), finalized, over and done with ■ **OPPOSITE:** begun 2 *'This business is finished,' he said sadly.* = **ruined**, done for (*informal*), doomed, bankrupt, through, lost, gone, defeated, devastated, wrecked, wiped out, undone, washed up (*informal*), wound up, liquidated

finite ADJECTIVE = **limited**, bounded, restricted, demarcated, conditioned, circumscribed, delimited, terminable, subject to limitations ■ **OPPOSITE:** infinite

fire NOUN 1 *A forest fire is sweeping across the country.* = **flames**, blaze, combustion, inferno, conflagration, holocaust 2 *His punishing schedule seemed to dim his fire at times.* = **passion**, force, light, energy, heat, spirit, enthusiasm, excitement, dash, intensity, sparkle, life, vitality, animation, vigour, zeal, splendour, verve, fervour, eagerness, dynamism, lustre, radiance, virtuosity, élan, ardour, brio, vivacity, impetuosity, burning passion, scintillation, fervency, pizzazz *or* pizazz (*informal*) 3 *His car was raked with fire from automatic weapons.* = **bombardment**, shooting, firing, shelling, hail, volley, barrage, gunfire, sniping, flak, salvo, fusillade, cannonade ▶ VERB 1 *a huge gun designed to fire nuclear or chemical shells* = **let off**, shoot, launch, shell, loose, set off, discharge, hurl, eject, detonate, let loose (*informal*), touch off 2 *Soldiers fired rubber bullets to disperse crowds.* = **shoot**, explode, discharge, detonate, pull the trigger 3 *She was fired from her job.* = **dismiss**, sack (*informal*), get rid of, discharge, lay off, make redundant, cashier, give notice, show the door, give the boot (*slang*), kiss off (*slang, chiefly U.S. & Canad.*), give the push, give the bullet (*Brit. slang*), give marching orders, give someone their cards, give the sack to (*informal*), kennet (*Austral. slang*), jeff (*Austral. slang*) 4 *They were fired with an enthusiasm for public speaking.* = **inspire**, excite, stir, stimulate, motivate, irritate, arouse, awaken, animate, rouse, stir up, quicken, inflame, incite, electrify, enliven,

spur on, galvanize, inspirit, impassion
5 *matches, turpentine and cotton, with which
they fired the houses* = **set fire to**, torch,
ignite, set on fire, kindle, set alight, set
ablaze, put a match to, set aflame,
enkindle, light • **on fire 1** *The captain radioed
that the ship was on fire.* = **burning**, flaming,
blazing, alight, ablaze, in flames, aflame,
fiery **2** *He was on fire, youthfully impatient.*
= **ardent**, excited, inspired, eager,
enthusiastic, passionate, fervent
■ **RELATED WORD:** *mania* pyromania

firearm NOUN = **gun**, weapon, handgun,
revolver, shooter (*slang*), piece (*slang*),
rod (*slang*), pistol, heater (*U.S. slang*)

firebrand NOUN = **rabble-rouser**, activist,
incendiary, fomenter, instigator, agitator,
demagogue, tub-thumper, soapbox orator

fireworks PLURAL NOUN **1** *The rally ended
with spectacular fireworks and band music.*
= **pyrotechnics**, illuminations, feux
d'artifice **2** *The big media companies will be
forced to compete, and we should see some
fireworks.* = **trouble**, row, storm, rage,
temper, wax (*informal, chiefly Brit.*),
uproar, hysterics, paroxysms, fit of rage

firm¹ ADJECTIVE **1** *Fruit should be firm and
excellent in condition.* = **hard**, solid, compact,
dense, set, concentrated, stiff, compacted,
rigid, compressed, inflexible, solidified,
unyielding, congealed, inelastic, jelled,
close-grained, jellified ■ **OPPOSITE:** soft
2 *Use a firm platform or a sturdy ladder.*
= **secure**, strong, fixed, secured, rooted,
stable, steady, anchored, braced, robust,
cemented, fast, sturdy, embedded,
fastened, riveted, taut, stationary,
motionless, immovable, unmoving,
unshakeable, unfluctuating ■ **OPPOSITE:**
unstable **3** *The quick handshake was firm
and cool.* = **strong**, close, tight, steady
4 *They needed the guiding hand of a firm
parent.* = **strict**, unwavering, unswerving,
unshakeable, constant, stalwart, resolute,
inflexible, steadfast, unyielding,
immovable, unflinching, unbending,
obdurate, unalterable, unfaltering
5 *He held a firm belief in the afterlife.*
= **determined**, true, settled, fixed,
resolved, strict, definite, set on, adamant,
stalwart, staunch, resolute, inflexible,
steadfast, unyielding, unwavering,
immovable, unflinching, unswerving,
unbending, obdurate, unshakeable,
unalterable, unshaken, unfaltering
■ **OPPOSITE:** wavering **6** *firm evidence*
= **definite**, hard, clear, confirmed,
settled, fixed, hard-and-fast,
cut-and-dried (*informal*)

firm² NOUN *The firm's employees were expecting
large bonuses.* = **company**, business,
concern, association, organization, house,
corporation, venture, enterprise,
partnership, establishment, undertaking,
outfit (*informal*), consortium, conglomerate

firmament NOUN = **sky**, skies, heaven,
heavens, the blue, vault, welkin (*archaic*),
empyrean (*poetic*), vault of heaven,
rangi (*N.Z.*)

firmly ADVERB **1** *The door is locked and the
windows are firmly shut.* = **securely**, safely,
tightly **2** *boards firmly fixed to metal posts in
the ground* = **immovably**, securely, steadily,
like a rock, unflinchingly, enduringly,
motionlessly, unshakeably **3** *She held me
firmly by the elbow.* = **steadily**, securely,
tightly, unflinchingly **4** *Political opinions are
firmly held.* = **resolutely**, strictly, staunchly,
steadfastly, determinedly, through thick
and thin, with decision, with a rod of iron,
definitely, unwaveringly, unchangeably

firmness NOUN **1** *the firmness of the ground*
= **hardness**, resistance, density, rigidity,
stiffness, solidity, inflexibility,
compactness, fixedness, inelasticity
2 *testing the firmness of the nearest stakes*
= **steadiness**, tension, stability, tightness,
soundness, tautness, tensile strength,
immovability **3** *He was surprised at the
firmness of her grip.* = **strength**, tightness,
steadiness **4** *There was no denying his
considerable firmness of purpose.* = **resolve**,
resolution, constancy, inflexibility,
steadfastness, obduracy, strictness,
strength of will, fixity, fixedness,
staunchness

first ADJECTIVE **1** *The first men of this race lived
like gods.* = **earliest**, initial, opening,
introductory, original, maiden, primitive,
primordial, primeval, pristine **2** *The first
prize is thirty-one thousand pounds.* = **top**,
best, winning, premier **3** *It is time to go back
to first principles.* = **elementary**, key, basic,
primary, fundamental, cardinal,
rudimentary, elemental **4** *The first priority
for development is to defeat inflation.*
= **foremost**, highest, greatest, leading,
head, ruling, chief, prime, supreme,
principal, paramount, overriding,
pre-eminent ▶ NOUN *It is a first for New York.*
= **novelty**, innovation, originality, new
experience ▶ ADVERB *I do not remember who
spoke first.* = **to begin with**, firstly, initially,
at the beginning, in the first place,
beforehand, to start with, at the outset,
before all else • **from the first** *You knew
about me from the first, didn't you?* = **from the
start**, from the beginning, from the outset,

from the very beginning, from the introduction, from the starting point, from the inception, from the commencement, from the word 'go' (*informal*)

first class *or* **first-class** ADJECTIVE = **excellent**, great (*informal*), very good, superb, topping (*Brit. slang*), top, tops (*slang*), bad (*slang*), prime, capital, choice, champion, cool (*informal*), brilliant, crack (*slang*), mean (*slang*), cracking (*Brit. informal*), crucial (*slang*), outstanding, premium, ace (*informal*), marvellous, exceptional, mega (*slang*), sovereign, dope (*slang*), world-class, blue-chip, top-flight, top-class, five-star, exemplary, wicked (*slang*), first-rate, def (*slang*), sick (*slang*), superlative, second to none, top-notch (*informal*), brill (*informal*), top-drawer, matchless, tiptop, boffo (*slang*), jim-dandy (*slang*), twenty-four carat, A1 *or* A-one (*informal*), bitchin' (*U.S. slang*), chillin' (*U.S. slang*), booshit (*Austral. slang*), exo (*Austral. slang*), sik (*Austral. slang*), rad (*informal*), phat (*slang*), schmick (*Austral. informal*), beaut (*informal*), barrie (*Scot. slang*), belting (*Brit. slang*), pearler (*Austral. slang*) ■ **OPPOSITE:** terrible

first-hand ADJECTIVE *He'll get a first-hand briefing on the emergency.* = **direct**, personal, immediate, face-to-face, straight from the horse's mouth • **at first hand** *I heard all about it first-hand.* = **directly**, personally, immediately, face-to-face, straight from the horse's mouth

first-rate ADJECTIVE = **excellent**, outstanding, first class, exceptional, mean (*slang*), topping (*Brit. slang*), top, tops (*slang*), prime, cool (*informal*), crack (*slang*), cracking (*Brit. informal*), crucial (*slang*), exclusive, superb, mega (*slang*), sovereign, dope (*slang*), sick (*slang*), world-class, admirable, wicked (*slang*), def (*slang*), superlative, second to none, top-notch (*informal*), brill (*informal*), tiptop, bodacious (*slang, chiefly U.S.*), boffo (*slang*), jim-dandy (*slang*), A1 *or* A-one (*informal*), bitchin' (*U.S. slang*), chillin' (*U.S. slang*), booshit (*Austral. slang*), exo (*Austral. slang*), sik (*Austral. slang*), rad (*informal*), phat (*slang*), schmick (*Austral. informal*)

fiscal ADJECTIVE = **financial**, money, economic, monetary, budgetary, pecuniary, tax

fish VERB **1** *He learnt to fish in the River Cam.* = **angle**, net, cast, trawl **2** *He fished in his pocket for the key.* = **look (for)**, search, delve, ferret, rummage, fossick (*Austral. & N.Z.*) • **fish for something** *She may be fishing for a compliment.* = **seek**, look for, angle for, try to

get, hope for, hunt for, hint at, elicit, solicit, invite, search for • **fish something out** *She fished out a pair of his socks.* = **pull out**, produce, take out, extract, bring out, extricate, haul out, find ■ **RELATED WORDS:** *adjectives* piscine, ichthyoid; *name of young fry*; *collective nouns* shoal

fishy ADJECTIVE **1** *It hasn't a very strong fishy flavour.* = **fishlike**, piscine, piscatorial, piscatory **2** *There seems to be something fishy going on.* = **suspicious**, odd, suspect, unlikely, funny (*informal*), doubtful, dubious, dodgy (*Brit., Austral. & N.Z. informal*), queer, rum (*Brit. slang*), questionable, improbable, implausible, cock-and-bull (*informal*), shonky (*Austral. & N.Z. informal*)

fission NOUN = **splitting**, parting, breaking, division, rending, rupture, cleavage, schism, scission

fissure NOUN = **crack**, opening, hole, split, gap, rent, fault, breach, break, fracture, rift, slit, rupture, cleavage, cleft, chink, crevice, cranny, interstice

fit¹ VERB **1** *She was having her wedding dress fitted.* = **adapt**, fashion, shape, arrange, alter, adjust, modify, tweak (*informal*), customize **2** *She fitted her key in the lock.* = **place**, position, insert **3** *Fit hinge bolts to give support to the door lock.* = **attach**, join, connect, interlock **4** *She doesn't fit the description of the suspect.* = **suit**, meet, match, belong to, agree with, go with, conform to, correspond to, accord with, be appropriate to, concur with, tally with, dovetail with, be consonant with **5** *The bombs were fitted with time devices.* = **equip**, provide, arm, prepare, outfit, accommodate, fit out, kit out, rig out, accoutre ▶ ADJECTIVE **1** *You're not fit to be in charge!* = **appropriate**, qualified, suitable, competent, right, becoming, meet (*archaic*), seemly, trained, able, prepared, fitting, fitted, ready, skilled, correct, deserving, capable, adapted, proper, equipped, good enough, adequate, worthy, convenient, apt, well-suited, expedient, apposite ■ **OPPOSITE:** inappropriate **2** *It will take a very fit person to beat me.* = **healthy**, strong, robust, sturdy, well, trim, strapping, hale (*old-fashioned*), in good shape, in good condition, in good health, toned up, as right as rain, in good trim, able-bodied ■ **OPPOSITE:** unfit

fit² NOUN **1** *Once a fit has started there's nothing you can do to stop it.* = **seizure**, attack, bout, spasm, convulsion, paroxysm **2** *I broke into a fit of giggles.* = **bout**, burst, outbreak, outburst, spell • **have a fit** *He'd have a fit if*

f

he knew what we were up to! = **go mad**, explode, blow up (*informal*), lose it (*informal*), see red (*informal*), lose the plot (*informal*), throw a tantrum, fly off the handle (*informal*), go spare (*Brit. slang*), blow your top (*informal*), fly into a temper, flip your lid (*slang*), do your nut (*Brit. slang*) • **in** or **by fits and starts** *Military technology advances by fits and starts.* = **spasmodically**, sporadically, erratically, fitfully, on and off, irregularly, intermittently, off and on, unsystematically

fitful ADJECTIVE = **irregular**, broken, disturbed, erratic, variable, flickering, unstable, uneven, fluctuating, sporadic, intermittent, impulsive, haphazard, desultory, spasmodic, inconstant
■ **OPPOSITE:** regular

fitfully ADVERB = **irregularly**, on and off, intermittently, sporadically, off and on, erratically, in fits and starts, spasmodically, in snatches, desultorily, by fits and starts, interruptedly

fitness NOUN **1** *There is a debate about his fitness for the job.* = **appropriateness**, qualifications, adaptation, competence, readiness, eligibility, suitability, propriety, preparedness, applicability, aptness, pertinence, seemliness **2** *Squash was thought to offer all-round fitness.* = **health**, strength, good health, vigour, good condition, wellness, robustness

fitted ADJECTIVE = **built-in**, permanent

fitting ADJECTIVE *The President's address was a fitting end to the campaign.* = **appropriate**, suitable, proper, apt, right, becoming, meet (*archaic*), seemly, correct, decent, desirable, apposite, decorous, comme il faut (*French*) ■ **OPPOSITE:** unsuitable
▶ NOUN *brass light fittings* = **accessory**, part, piece, unit, connection, component, attachment ▶ PLURAL NOUN *He has made fittings for antique cars.* = **furnishings**, extras, equipment, fixtures, appointments, furniture, trimmings, accessories, conveniences, accoutrements, bells and whistles, fitments, appurtenances

fix VERB **1** *Fix the photo to the card using double-sided tape* = **place**, join, stick (*informal*), attach, set, position, couple, plant, link, establish, tie, settle, secure, bind, root, connect, locate, pin, install, anchor, glue, cement, implant, embed, fasten, make fast **2** (*often with* **up**) *He's fixed a time when I can see him.* = **decide**, set, name, choose, limit, establish, determine, settle, appoint, arrange, define, conclude, resolve, arrive at, specify, agree on **3** (*often with* **up**) *I've fixed it for you to see them.*

= **arrange**, organize, sort out, see to, make arrangements for **4** *If something is broken, we fix it.* = **repair**, mend, service, sort, correct, restore, adjust, regulate, see to, overhaul, patch up, get working, put right, put to rights **5** *Attention is fixed on the stock market.* = **focus**, direct at, level at, fasten on, rivet on **6** *They offered players bribes to fix a league match.* = **rig**, set up (*informal*), influence, manipulate, bribe, manoeuvre, fiddle (*informal*), pull strings (*informal*) **7** *Egg yolk is used to fix the pigment.* = **stabilize**, set, consolidate, harden, thicken, stiffen, solidify, congeal, rigidify ▶ NOUN *The government has got itself in a fix.* = **mess**, spot (*informal*), corner, hole (*slang*), difficulty, jam (*informal*), dilemma, embarrassment, plight, hot water (*informal*), pickle (*informal*), uphill (*S. African*), predicament, difficult situation, quandary, tight spot, ticklish situation • **fix someone up** (*often with* **with**) *We'll fix him up with a job.* = **provide**, supply, accommodate, bring about, furnish, lay on, arrange for • **fix something up** *I fixed up an appointment to see her.* = **arrange**, plan, settle, fix, organize, sort out, agree on, make arrangements for

fixated ADJECTIVE = **obsessed**, fascinated, preoccupied, captivated, attached, devoted, absorbed, caught up in, single-minded, smitten, taken up with, besotted, wrapped up in, engrossed, spellbound, infatuated, mesmerized, hypnotized, hung up on (*slang*), monomaniacal, prepossessed
■ **OPPOSITE:** uninterested

fixation NOUN = **obsession**, complex (*informal*), addiction, hang-up (*informal*), preoccupation, mania, infatuation, idée fixe (*French*), thing (*informal*)

fixed ADJECTIVE **1** *people who have fixed ideas about things* = **inflexible**, set, steady, resolute, unwavering, unflinching, unblinking, unbending, undeviating
■ **OPPOSITE:** wavering **2** *The locking frame can secure bikes to any fixed object.* = **immovable**, set, established, secure, rooted, permanent, attached, anchored, rigid, made fast ■ **OPPOSITE:** mobile **3** *The deal was settled at a prearranged fixed price.* = **agreed**, set, planned, decided, established, settled, arranged, resolved, specified, definite **4** *Some races are fixed.* = **rigged**, framed, put-up, manipulated, packed

fizz VERB **1** *She was holding a tray of glasses that fizzed.* = **bubble**, froth, fizzle, effervesce, produce bubbles **2** *The engine fizzed and went dead.* = **sputter**, buzz, sparkle, hiss, crackle

fizzle VERB (*often with* **out**) = **die away**, fail, collapse, fold (*informal*), abort, fall through, peter out, come to nothing, miss the mark, end in disappointment

fizzy ADJECTIVE = **bubbly**, bubbling, sparkling, effervescent, carbonated, gassy

flab NOUN = **fat**, flesh, flabbiness, fleshiness, weight, beef (*informal*), heaviness, slackness, plumpness, loose flesh

flabbergasted ADJECTIVE = **astonished**, amazed, stunned, overcome, overwhelmed, staggered, astounded, dazed, confounded, disconcerted, speechless, bowled over (*informal*), gobsmacked (*Brit. slang*), dumbfounded, nonplussed, lost for words, struck dumb, abashed, rendered speechless

flabby ADJECTIVE 1 *bulging thighs and flabby stomach* = **limp**, hanging, loose, slack, unfit, sagging, sloppy, baggy, floppy, lax, drooping, flaccid, pendulous (*literary*), toneless, yielding ■ OPPOSITE: firm 2 *Many signs of flabby management remain.* = **weak**, ineffective, feeble, impotent, wasteful, ineffectual, disorganized, spineless, effete, boneless, nerveless, enervated, wussy (*slang*), wimpish or wimpy (*informal*)

flaccid ADJECTIVE = **limp**, soft, weak, loose, slack, lax, drooping, flabby, nerveless

flag¹ NOUN *They raised the white flag in surrender.* = **banner**, standard, colours, jack, pennant, ensign, streamer, pennon, banderole, gonfalon ▶ VERB 1 *I promise to flag these things more clearly.* = **mark**, identify, indicate, label, tab, pick out, note, docket 2 (*often with* **down**) *They flagged a car down.* = **hail**, stop, signal, salute, wave down

flag² VERB *His enthusiasm was in no way flagging.* = **weaken**, fall, die, fail, decline, sink, fade, slump, pine, faint, weary, fall off, succumb, falter, wilt, wane, ebb, sag, languish, abate, droop, peter out, taper off, feel the pace, lose your strength

flagging ADJECTIVE = **weakening**, failing, declining, waning, giving up, tiring, sinking, fading, decreasing, slowing down, deteriorating, wearying, faltering, wilting, ebbing

flagrant ADJECTIVE = **outrageous**, open, blatant, barefaced, shocking, crying, enormous, awful, bold, dreadful, notorious, glaring, infamous, scandalous, flaunting, atrocious, brazen, shameless, out-and-out, heinous, ostentatious, egregious, undisguised, immodest, arrant, flagitious ■ OPPOSITE: slight

flagstone NOUN = **paving stone**, flag, slab, block

flail VERB = **thrash**, beat, windmill, thresh

flair NOUN 1 *She has a flair for languages.* = **ability**, feel, talent, gift, genius, faculty, accomplishment, mastery, knack, aptitude 2 *the panache and flair you'd expect* = **style**, taste, dash, chic, elegance, panache, discernment, stylishness

flak NOUN = **criticism**, stick (*slang*), opposition, abuse, complaints, hostility, condemnation, censure, disapproval, bad press, denigration, brickbats (*informal*), disparagement, fault-finding, disapprobation

flake NOUN *flakes of paint* = **chip**, scale, layer, peeling, shaving, disk, wafer, sliver, lamina, squama (*Biology*) ▶ VERB *Some of the shell had flaked away.* = **chip**, scale (off), peel (off), blister, desquamate

flamboyance NOUN = **showiness**, show, style, dash, sparkle, chic, flair (*informal*), verve, swagger, swag (*slang*), extravagance, panache, pomp, glitz (*informal*), élan, bravura, swank (*informal*), theatricality, exhibitionism, brio, ostentation, stylishness, flashiness, flamboyancy, floridity, pizzazz or pizazz (*informal*) ■ OPPOSITE: restraint

flamboyant ADJECTIVE 1 *He was a flamboyant personality.* = **camp** (*informal*), dashing, theatrical 2 *flamboyant architectural paint effects* = **showy**, rich, elaborate, over the top (*informal*), extravagant, baroque, ornate, ostentatious, rococo 3 *He wears flamboyant clothes.* = **colourful**, striking, exciting, brilliant, glamorous, stylish, dazzling, glitzy (*slang*), showy, florid, bling (*slang*), swashbuckling

flame NOUN 1 *a huge ball of flame* = **fire**, light, spark, glow, blaze, brightness, inferno 2 *that burning flame of love* = **passion**, fire, enthusiasm, intensity, affection, warmth, fervour, ardour, keenness, fervency 3 *She kept inviting his old flame round to their house.* = **sweetheart**, partner, lover, girlfriend, boyfriend, beloved, heart-throb (*Brit.*), beau (*old-fashioned*), ladylove (*old-fashioned*) ▶ VERB *His dark eyes flamed with rage.* = **burn**, flash, shine, glow, blaze, flare, glare

flaming ADJECTIVE 1 *A group followed carrying flaming torches.* = **burning**, blazing, fiery, ignited, red, brilliant, raging, glowing, red-hot, ablaze, in flames, afire 2 *She had a flaming row with her lover.* = **intense**, angry, raging, impassioned, hot, aroused, vivid, frenzied, ardent, scintillating, vehement

flammable ADJECTIVE = **combustible**, incendiary, inflammable, ignitable

USAGE *Flammable* and *inflammable* are interchangeable when used of the properties of materials. *Flammable* is, however, often preferred for warning labels as there is less likelihood of misunderstanding (*inflammable* being sometimes taken to mean *not flammable*). *Inflammable* is preferred in figurative contexts: *this could prove to be an inflammable situation*.

flank NOUN **1** *He put his hand on the dog's flank.* = **side**, quarter, hip, thigh, loin, haunch, ham **2** *The assault element opened up from their right flank.* = **wing**, side, sector, aspect ▸ VERB *The altar was flanked by two Christmas trees.* = **border**, line, wall, screen, edge, circle, bound, skirt, fringe, book-end

flannel VERB *He flannelled and prevaricated.* = **prevaricate**, hedge, flatter, waffle (*informal, chiefly Brit.*), blarney, sweet-talk (*informal*), soft-soap (*informal*), equivocate, butter up, pull the wool over (someone's) eyes

flap VERB **1** *Sheets flapped on the clothes line.* = **flutter**, wave, swing, swish, flail **2** *The bird flapped its wings furiously.* = **beat**, wave, thrash, flutter, agitate, wag, vibrate, shake, thresh **3** *There's no point in you flapping around in the kitchen, making your guest feel uneasy.* = **panic**, fuss, dither (*chiefly Brit.*) ▸ NOUN **1** *He drew back the tent flap and strode out.* = **cover**, covering, tail, fold, skirt, tab, overlap, fly, apron, lapel, lappet **2** *the gunshot flap of a topsail* = **flutter**, beating, waving, shaking, swinging, bang, banging, swish **3** *Wherever he goes, there's always a flap.* = **panic**, state (*informal*), agitation, commotion, sweat (*informal*), stew (*informal*), dither (*chiefly Brit.*), fluster, twitter (*informal*), tizzy (*informal*)

flare VERB **1** *Camp fires flared like beacons in the dark.* = **blaze**, flame, dazzle, glare, flicker, flutter, waver, burn up **2** *a dress cut to flare from the hips* = **widen**, spread, broaden, spread out, dilate, splay ▸ NOUN *The flare of fires lights up the blacked-out streets.* = **flame**, burst, flash, blaze, dazzle, glare, flicker • **flare up** *The fire flared up again.* = **burn**, explode, blaze, be on fire, go up in flames, be alight, flame

flash NOUN **1** *a sudden flash of lightning* = **blaze**, ray, burst, spark, beam, sparkle, streak, flare, dazzle, shaft, glare, gleam, flicker, shimmer, twinkle, scintillation, coruscation **2** *The essay could do with a flash of wit.* = **burst**, show, sign, touch, display, rush, demonstration, surge, outbreak, outburst, manifestation ▸ VERB **1** *Lightning flashed among the distant dark clouds.* = **blaze**,

shine, beam, sparkle, glitter, flare, glare, gleam, light up, flicker, shimmer, twinkle, glint, glisten, scintillate, coruscate **2** *Cars flashed by every few minutes.* = **speed**, race, shoot, fly, tear, sweep, dash, barrel (along) (*informal, chiefly U.S. & Canad.*), whistle, sprint, bolt, streak, dart, zoom, burn rubber (*informal*) **3** *He flashed his official card.* = **show quickly**, display, expose, exhibit, flourish, show off, flaunt ▸ ADJECTIVE *flash jewellery and watches* = **ostentatious**, smart, glamorous, trendy, showy, cheap, bling (*slang*) • **in a flash** *The answer came to him in a flash.* = **in a moment**, in a second, in an instant, in a split second, in a trice, in a jiffy (*informal*), in the twinkling of an eye, in a twinkling, in two shakes of a lamb's tail (*informal*), in the bat of an eye (*informal*)

flashy ADJECTIVE = **showy**, loud, over the top (*informal*), flamboyant, brash, tacky (*informal*), flaunting, glitzy (*slang*), tasteless, naff (*Brit. slang*), gaudy, garish, jazzy (*informal*), tawdry, ostentatious, snazzy (*informal*), glittery, meretricious, cheap and nasty, in poor taste, tinselly, bling (*slang*) ■ **OPPOSITE:** plain

flat[1] ADJECTIVE **1** *Sit the cup on a flat surface while measuring.* = **even**, level, levelled, plane, smooth, uniform, horizontal, unbroken, planar ■ **OPPOSITE:** uneven **2** *Two men near him threw themselves flat.* = **horizontal**, prone, outstretched, reclining, prostrate, laid low, supine, recumbent, lying full length ■ **OPPOSITE:** upright **3** *It was impossible to ride with a flat tyre.* = **punctured**, collapsed, burst, blown out, deflated, empty **4** *The battery was flat.* = **used up**, finished, empty, drained, expired **5** *She is likely to give you a flat refusal.* = **absolute**, firm, direct, straight, positive, fixed, plain, final, explicit, definite, outright, unconditional, downright, unmistakable, unequivocal, unqualified, out-and-out, categorical, peremptory **6** *The past few days have been flat and empty.* = **dull**, dead, empty, boring, depressing, pointless, tedious, stale, lacklustre, tiresome, lifeless, monotonous, uninteresting, insipid, unexciting, spiritless ■ **OPPOSITE:** exciting **7** *I've been feeling flat at times.* = **without energy**, empty, weak, tired, depressed, drained, weary, worn out, dispirited, downhearted, tired out **8** *Her voice was flat, with no hope in it.* = **monotonous**, boring, uniform, dull, tedious, droning, tiresome, unchanging, colourless, toneless, samey (*informal*), uninflected, unvaried ▸ NOUN (*often plural*) *salt marshes and mud flats* = **plain**, strand, shallow, marsh, swamp, shoal, lowland, mud flat ▸ ADVERB *He had turned her down flat.* = **completely**, directly, absolutely, categorically, precisely, exactly, utterly, outright, point blank, unequivocally • **flat out** *Everyone is working flat out.* = **at full speed**, all out, to the full, hell for leather (*informal*), as hard as possible, at full tilt, at full gallop, posthaste, for all you are worth, under full steam

flat² NOUN *We used to live together in a flat.* = **apartment** (*chiefly U.S.*), rooms, quarters, digs, suite, penthouse, living quarters, duplex (*U.S. & Canad.*), bachelor apartment (*Canad.*)

flatly ADVERB = **absolutely**, completely, positively, categorically, unequivocally, unhesitatingly

flatten VERB **1** (*sometimes with* **out**) *How do you put enough pressure on to the metal to flatten it?* = **level**, roll, plaster, squash, compress, trample, iron out, even out, smooth off **2** (*sometimes with* **out**) *Bombing raids flattened much of the area.* = **destroy**, level, ruin, demolish, knock down, pull down, tear down, throw down, bulldoze, raze, remove, kennet (*Austral. slang*), jeff (*Austral. slang*) **3** *She could flatten me with one blow.* = **knock down**, fell, floor, deck (*slang*), bowl over, prostrate, knock off your feet **4** *The champion has run out of opponents to flatten.* = **crush**, beat, defeat, trounce, master, worst, overwhelm, conquer, lick (*informal*), undo, subdue, rout, overpower, quell, clobber (*slang*), vanquish, run rings around (*informal*), wipe the floor with (*informal*), make mincemeat of (*informal*), blow out of the water (*slang*)

flatter VERB **1** *I knew he was just flattering me.* = **praise**, compliment, pander to, sweet-talk (*informal*), court, humour, puff, flannel (*Brit. informal*), fawn, cajole, lay it on (thick) (*slang*), wheedle, inveigle, soft-soap (*informal*), butter up, blandish **2** *Orange flatters those with golden skin tones.* = **suit**, become, enhance, set off, embellish, do something for, show to advantage

flattering ADJECTIVE **1** *It wasn't a very flattering photograph.* = **becoming**, kind, effective, enhancing, well-chosen ■ OPPOSITE: unflattering **2** *The press was flattering.* = **ingratiating**, complimentary, gratifying, fawning, sugary, fulsome, laudatory, adulatory, honeyed, honey-tongued ■ OPPOSITE: uncomplimentary

flattery NOUN = **obsequiousness**, fawning, adulation, sweet-talk (*informal*), flannel (*Brit. informal*), blarney, soft-soap (*informal*), sycophancy, servility, cajolery,

blandishment, fulsomeness, toadyism, false praise, honeyed words

flatulence NOUN *Avoid any food that causes flatulence.* = **wind**, borborygmus (*Medical*), eructation

flaunt VERB = **show off**, display, boast, parade, exhibit, flourish, brandish, vaunt, make a (great) show of, sport (*informal*), disport, make an exhibition of, flash about

> USAGE *Flaunt* is sometimes wrongly used where *flout* is meant: *they must be prevented from flouting (not flaunting) the law.*

flavour or (*U.S.*) **flavor** NOUN **1** *The cheese has a strong flavour.* = **taste**, seasoning, flavouring, savour, extract, essence, relish, smack, aroma, odour, zest, tang, zing (*informal*), piquancy, tastiness ■ OPPOSITE: blandness **2** *clothes with a nostalgic Forties flavour* = **quality**, feeling, feel, style, property, touch, character, aspect, tone, suggestion, stamp, essence, tinge, soupçon (*French*) ▸ VERB *Flavour dishes with exotic herbs and spices.* = **season**, spice, add flavour to, enrich, infuse, imbue, pep up, leaven, ginger up, lace

flavouring or **flavoring** NOUN = **essence**, extract, zest, tincture, spirit

flaw NOUN **1** *The only flaw in his character is a short temper.* = **weakness**, failing, defect, weak spot, spot, fault, scar, blemish, imperfection, speck, disfigurement, chink in your armour **2** *a flaw in the rock wide enough for a foot* = **crack**, break, split, breach, tear, rent, fracture, rift, cleft, crevice, fissure, scission

flawed ADJECTIVE **1** *the unique beauty of a flawed object* = **damaged**, defective, imperfect, blemished, broken, cracked, chipped, faulty **2** *The tests were seriously flawed.* = **erroneous**, incorrect, inaccurate, invalid, wrong, mistaken, false, faulty, untrue, unfounded, spurious, amiss, unsound, wide of the mark, inexact, fallacious

flawless ADJECTIVE *She has a flawless complexion.* = **perfect**, impeccable, faultless, spotless, unblemished, unsullied

flay VERB **1** *His skin was flayed by barbed wire.* = **skin**, strip, peel, scrape, excoriate, remove the skin from **2** *The critics flayed him with accusations of misanthropy.* = **upbraid**, slam (*slang*), castigate, revile, tear into (*informal*), diss (*slang*), excoriate, tear a strip off, execrate, pull to pieces (*informal*), give a tongue-lashing, criticize severely

fleck NOUN *His hair is dark grey with flecks of ginger.* = **mark**, speck, streak, spot, dot, pinpoint, speckle ▸ VERB *patches of red paint* *which flecked her blouse* = **speckle**, mark, spot, dust, dot, streak, dapple, stipple, mottle, variegate, bespeckle, besprinkle

fledgling *or* **fledgeling** NOUN *It is against the law to disturb fledglings in nests.* = **chick**, nestling, young bird

flee VERB = **run away**, leave, escape, bolt, fly, avoid, split (*slang*), take off (*informal*), get away, vanish, depart, run off, shun, make off, abscond, decamp, take flight, hook it (*slang*), do a runner (*slang*), scarper (*Brit. slang*), slope off, cut and run (*informal*), make a run for it, beat a hasty retreat, turn tail, fly the coop (*U.S. & Canad. informal*), make a quick exit, skedaddle (*informal*), make yourself scarce (*informal*), take a powder (*U.S. & Canad. slang*), make your escape, make your getaway, take it on the lam (*U.S. & Canad. slang*), take to your heels

fleece NOUN *a blanket of lamb's fleece* = **wool**, hair, coat, fur, coat of wool ▶ VERB *She claims he fleeced her out of thousands of pounds.* = **cheat**, skin (*slang*), steal, rob, con (*informal*), rifle, stiff (*slang*), soak (*U.S. & Canad. slang*), bleed (*informal*), rip off (*slang*), plunder, defraud, overcharge, swindle, rook (*slang*), diddle (*informal*), take for a ride (*informal*), despoil, take to the cleaners (*slang*), sell a pup, cozen (*literary*), mulct, scam (*slang*)

fleet[1] NOUN *damage inflicted upon the British fleet* = **navy**, vessels, task force, squadron, warships, flotilla, armada, naval force, sea power, argosy

fleet[2] ADJECTIVE *He was fleet as a deer.* = **swift**, flying, fast, quick, winged, rapid, speedy, nimble, mercurial, meteoric, nimble-footed

fleeting ADJECTIVE = **momentary**, short, passing, flying, brief, temporary, short-lived, fugitive, transient, flitting, ephemeral, transitory, evanescent (*formal*), fugacious, here today, gone tomorrow ■ **OPPOSITE:** lasting

flesh NOUN **1** *Illness had wasted the flesh from her body.* = **fat**, muscle, beef (*informal*), tissue, body, brawn **2** (*informal*) *porcine wrinkles of flesh* = **fatness**, fat, adipose tissue, corpulence, weight **3** *the pale pink flesh of trout and salmon* = **meat**, food **4** *the sins of the flesh* = **physical nature**, sensuality, physicality, carnality, body, human nature, flesh and blood, animality, sinful nature **5** = mankind • **your own flesh and blood** *The kid was his own flesh and blood.* = **family**, blood, relations, relatives, kin, kindred, kith and kin, blood relations, kinsfolk, ainga (*N.Z.*), rellies (*Austral. slang*) ■ **RELATED WORD:** adjective **carnal**

fleshy ADJECTIVE = **plump**, fat, chubby, obese, hefty, overweight, ample, stout, chunky, meaty, beefy (*informal*), tubby, podgy, brawny, corpulent, well-padded

flex VERB = **bend**, contract, stretch, angle, curve, tighten, crook, move

flexibility NOUN **1** *The flexibility of the lens decreases with age.* = **elasticity**, pliability, springiness, pliancy, tensility, give (*informal*) **2** *the flexibility of distance learning* = **adaptability**, openness, versatility, adjustability **3** *They should be ready to show some flexibility.* = **complaisance**, accommodation, give and take, amenability

flexible ADJECTIVE **1** *brushes with long, flexible bristles* = **pliable**, plastic, yielding, elastic, supple, lithe, limber, springy, willowy, pliant, tensile, stretchy, whippy, lissom(e), ductile, bendable, mouldable ■ **OPPOSITE:** rigid **2** *flexible working hours* = **adaptable**, open, variable, adjustable, discretionary ■ **OPPOSITE:** inflexible **3** *Their boss was flexible and lenient.* = **compliant**, accommodating, manageable, amenable, docile, tractable, biddable, complaisant, responsive, gentle ■ **OPPOSITE:** unyielding

flick VERB **1** *The man flicked his gun up from beside his thigh.* = **jerk**, pull, tug, lurch, jolt **2** *She flicked a speck of fluff from her sleeve.* = **strike**, tap, jab, remove quickly, hit, touch, stroke, rap, flip, peck, whisk, dab, fillip ▶ NOUN *a flick of a paintbrush* = **tap**, touch, sweep, stroke, rap, flip, peck, whisk, jab • **flick through something** *She flicked through some magazines.* = **browse**, glance at, skim, leaf through, flip through, thumb through, skip through

flicker VERB **1** *Firelight flickered on the faded furnishings.* = **twinkle**, flash, sparkle, flare, shimmer, gutter, glimmer **2** *Her eyelids flickered then opened.* = **flutter**, waver, quiver, vibrate ▶ NOUN **1** *I saw the flicker of flames.* = **glimmer**, flash, spark, flare, gleam **2** *He felt a flicker of regret.* = **trace**, drop, breath, spark, atom, glimmer, vestige, iota

flier *see* **flyer**

flight[1] NOUN **1** *The flight will take four hours.* = **journey**, trip, voyage **2** *Supersonic flight could become a routine form of travel.* = **aviation**, flying, air transport, aeronautics, aerial navigation **3** *These hawks are magnificent in flight.* = **flying**, winging, mounting, soaring, ability to fly **4** *a flight of green parrots* = **flock**, group, unit, cloud, formation, squadron, swarm, flying group

flight[2] NOUN *his secret flight into exile* = **escape**, fleeing, departure, retreat, exit, running away, exodus, getaway, absconding • **put to flight** *We were put to* *flight by a herd of bullocks.* = **drive off**, scatter, disperse, rout, stampede, scare off, send packing, chase off • **take (to) flight** *He decided to take flight immediately.* = **run away** or **off**, flee, bolt, abscond, decamp, do a runner (*slang*), turn tail, do a bunk (*Brit. slang*), fly the coop (*U.S. & Canad. informal*), beat a retreat, light out (*informal*), skedaddle (*informal*), make a hasty retreat, take a powder (*U.S. & Canad. slang*), withdraw hastily, take it on the lam (*U.S. & Canad. slang*), do a Skase (*Austral. informal*)

flighty ADJECTIVE = **frivolous**, wild, volatile, unstable, irresponsible, dizzy (*informal*), fickle, unbalanced, impulsive, mercurial, giddy, capricious, unsteady, thoughtless, changeable, impetuous, skittish, light-headed, harebrained, scatterbrained, ditzy or ditsy (*slang*)

flimsy ADJECTIVE **1** *a flimsy wooden door* = **fragile**, weak, slight, delicate, shallow, shaky, frail, superficial, makeshift, rickety, insubstantial, gimcrack, unsubstantial ■ OPPOSITE: sturdy **2** *a flimsy pink chiffon nightgown* = **thin**, light, sheer, transparent, chiffon, gossamer, gauzy **3** *The charges were based on flimsy evidence.* = **unconvincing**, poor, thin, weak, inadequate, pathetic, transparent, trivial, feeble, unsatisfactory, frivolous, tenuous, implausible

flinch VERB **1** *The slightest pressure made her flinch.* = **wince**, start, duck, shrink, cringe, quail, recoil, cower, blench **2** (*often with* **from**) *He has never flinched from harsh decisions.* = **shy away**, shrink, withdraw, flee, retreat, back off, swerve, shirk, draw back, baulk

fling VERB *I flung the book on a table.* = **throw**, toss, hurl, chuck (*informal*), launch, cast, pitch, send, shy, jerk, propel, sling (*informal*), precipitate, lob (*informal*), catapult, heave, let fly ▶ NOUN **1** *the last fling before you take up a job* = **binge** (*informal*), good time, bash, bit of fun, party, rave (*Brit. slang*), spree, indulgence (*informal*), beano (*Brit. slang*), night on the town, rave-up (*Brit. slang*), hooley or hoolie (*chiefly Irish & N.Z.*) **2** *the England bowler's chance of a fling at South Africa in the second Test today* = **try**, go (*informal*), attempt, shot (*informal*), trial, crack (*informal*), venture, gamble, stab (*informal*), bash (*informal*), whirl (*informal*)

flip VERB **1** *He walked out, flipping off the lights.* = **flick**, switch, snap, click, jerk **2** *The plane flipped over and burst into flames.* = **spin**, turn, overturn, turn over, roll over, twist **3** *I flipped a cigarette butt out of the window.* = **toss**, throw, cast, pitch, flick, fling, sling (*informal*) ▶ NOUN *having gambled all on the*

flip of a coin = **toss**, throw, cast, pitch, spin, snap, twist, flick, jerk

flippant ADJECTIVE = **frivolous**, rude, cheeky, irreverent, flip (*informal*), superficial, saucy, glib, pert, disrespectful, offhand, impertinent, impudent ■ OPPOSITE: serious

flirt VERB **1** *He's flirting with all the women.* = **chat up**, lead on (*informal*), dally with, make advances at, make eyes at, coquet, philander, make sheep's eyes at **2** (*usually with* **with**) *My mother used to flirt with nationalism.* = **toy with**, consider, entertain, play with, dabble in, trifle with, give a thought to, expose yourself to ▶ NOUN *She's a born flirt.* = **tease**, philanderer, coquette, heart-breaker, wanton, trifler

flirtation NOUN = **teasing**, philandering, dalliance, coquetry, toying, intrigue, trifling

flirtatious ADJECTIVE = **teasing**, flirty, coquettish, amorous, come-on (*informal*), arch, enticing, provocative, coy, come-hither, sportive

flit VERB = **fly**, dash, dart, skim, pass, speed, wing, flash, fleet, whisk, flutter

float VERB **1** *barges floating quietly by the grassy river banks* = **glide**, sail, drift, move gently, bob, coast, slide, be carried, slip along **2** *Empty things float.* = **be buoyant**, stay afloat, be or lie on the surface, rest on water, hang, hover, poise, displace water ■ OPPOSITE: sink **3** *He floated his firm on the Stock Market.* = **launch**, offer, sell, set up, promote, get going, push off ■ OPPOSITE: dissolve

floating ADJECTIVE **1** *Floating voters appear to have deserted the party.* = **uncommitted**, wavering, undecided, indecisive, vacillating, sitting on the fence (*informal*), unaffiliated, independent **2** *a house I shared with a floating population of others* = **free**, wandering, variable, fluctuating, unattached, migratory, movable, unfixed

flock NOUN **1** *They kept a small flock of sheep.* = **herd**, group, flight, drove, colony, gaggle, skein **2** *his flock of advisors* = **crowd**, company, group, host, collection, mass, gathering, assembly, convoy, herd, congregation, horde, multitude, throng, bevy ▶ VERB **1** *The public have flocked to the show.* = **stream**, crowd, mass, swarm, throng **2** *The crowds flocked around her.* = **gather**, group, crowd, mass, collect, assemble, herd, huddle, converge, throng, congregate, troop

flog VERB = **beat**, whip, lash, thrash, whack, scourge, hit hard, trounce, castigate, chastise, flay, lambast(e), flagellate, punish severely, beat or knock seven bells out of (*informal*)

flogging NOUN = **beating**, hiding (*informal*),
whipping, lashing, thrashing, caning,
scourging, trouncing, flagellation,
horsewhipping

flood NOUN **1** *This is the sort of flood dreaded by
cavers.* = **deluge**, downpour, flash flood,
inundation, tide, overflow, torrent, spate,
freshet **2** *Each year brings a flood of new
university graduates.* = **torrent**, flow, rush,
stream, tide, abundance, multitude, glut,
outpouring, profusion **3** *He received a flood of
complaints.* = **series**, stream, avalanche,
barrage, spate, torrent **4** *She broke into a
flood of tears.* = **outpouring**, rush, stream,
surge, torrent ▶ VERB **1** *The house was
flooded.* = **immerse**, swamp, submerge,
inundate, deluge, drown, cover with water
2 *Many streams have flooded their banks.*
= **pour over**, swamp, run over, overflow,
inundate, brim over **3** *Large numbers of
tourists have flooded the city.* = **engulf**, flow
into, rush into, sweep into, overwhelm,
surge into, swarm into, pour into, gush
into **4** *a policy aimed at flooding Europe with
exports* = **saturate**, fill, choke, swamp, glut,
oversupply, overfill **5** *Enquiries flooded in from
all over the world.* = **stream**, flow, rush, pour,
surge ■ RELATED WORDS: *adjectives* fluvial,
diluvial

floor NOUN **1** *We were sitting on the floor
watching TV.* = **ground** **2** *It's on the fifth floor
of the hospital.* = **storey**, level, stage, tier
▶ VERB **1** *I was floored by the announcement.*
= **disconcert**, stump, baffle, confound,
beat, throw (*informal*), defeat, puzzle,
conquer, overthrow, bewilder, perplex,
bowl over (*informal*), faze, discomfit, bring
up short, dumbfound, nonplus **2** *He was
floored twice in the second round.* = **knock down**,
fell, knock over, prostrate, deck (*slang*)

flop VERB **1** *She flopped, exhausted, onto a sofa.*
= **slump**, fall, drop, collapse, sink, tumble,
topple **2** *His hair flopped over his left eye.*
= **hang down**, hang, dangle, sag, droop,
hang limply **3** *The film flopped badly at the box
office.* = **fail**, close, bomb (*U.S. & Canad.
slang*), fold (*informal*), founder, fall short, fall
flat, come to nothing, come unstuck,
misfire, go belly-up (*slang*), go down like a
lead balloon (*informal*) ■ OPPOSITE: succeed
▶ NOUN *The public decide whether a film is a hit
or a flop.* = **failure**, disaster, loser, fiasco,
debacle, washout (*informal*), cockup (*Brit.
slang*), nonstarter ■ OPPOSITE: success

floppy ADJECTIVE = **droopy**, soft, loose,
hanging, limp, flapping, sagging, baggy,
flip-flop, flaccid, pendulous (*literary*)

floral ADJECTIVE = **flowery**,
flower-patterned

florid ADJECTIVE **1** *a liking for florid writing*
= **flowery**, high-flown, figurative,
grandiloquent, euphuistic **2** *the cast-iron
fireplace and the florid ceiling* = **ornate**, busy,
flamboyant, baroque, fussy, embellished,
flowery, overelaborate ■ OPPOSITE: plain
3 *He was a stout, florid man.* = **flushed**, ruddy,
rubicund, high-coloured, high-
complexioned, blowsy ■ OPPOSITE: pale

flotsam NOUN **1** = **debris**, rubbish,
wreckage, detritus, jetsam **2** = **junk**,
debris, sweepings, rubbish, odds and ends

flounce VERB (*often with* **out**, **away**, **off**, *etc*)
= **bounce**, storm, stamp, go quickly, throw,
spring, toss, fling, jerk

flounder VERB **1** *The economy was floundering.*
= **falter**, struggle, stall, slow down, run
into trouble, come unstuck (*informal*), be in
difficulties, hit a bad patch **2** *The president is
floundering, trying to jump-start his campaign.*
= **dither**, struggle, blunder, be confused,
falter, be in the dark, be out of your depth
3 *men floundering about in the water*
= **struggle**, toss, thrash, plunge, stumble,
tumble, muddle, fumble, grope, wallow

> USAGE *Flounder* is sometimes wrongly
> used where *founder* is meant: *the project
> foundered* (not *floundered*) *because of lack
> of funds.*

flourish VERB **1** *Business soon flourished.*
= **thrive**, increase, develop, advance,
abound, progress, boom, bloom, blossom,
prosper, burgeon ■ OPPOSITE: fail **2** *On
graduation she flourished as a journalist.*
= **succeed**, do well, be successful, move
ahead, get ahead, go places (*informal*), go
great guns (*slang*), go up in the world **3** *The
plant is flourishing particularly well.* = **grow**,
thrive, develop, flower, succeed, get on,
bloom, blossom, prosper, bear fruit, be
vigorous, be in your prime **4** *He flourished his
glass to make the point.* = **wave**, brandish,
sweep, swish, display, shake, swing, wield,
flutter, wag, flaunt, vaunt, twirl ▶ NOUN
1 *with a flourish of the hand* = **wave**, sweep,
brandish, swish, shaking, swing, dash,
brandishing, twirling, twirl, showy gesture
2 *with a flourish of church bells* = **show**,
display, parade, fanfare **3** *She underlined her
name with a showy flourish.* = **curlicue**,
sweep, decoration, swirl, plume,
embellishment, ornamentation

flourishing ADJECTIVE = **thriving**, successful,
doing well, blooming, mushrooming,
prospering, rampant, burgeoning, on a roll,
going places, going strong, in the pink, in
top form, on the up and up (*informal*)

flout VERB = **defy**, scorn, spurn, scoff at,
outrage, insult, mock, scout (*archaic*),

ridicule, taunt, deride, sneer at, jeer at, laugh in the face of, show contempt for, gibe at, treat with disdain ■ **OPPOSITE:** respect

flow VERB 1 *A stream flowed down into the valley.* = **run**, course, rush, sweep, move, issue, pass, roll, flood, pour, slide, proceed, stream, run out, surge, spill, go along, circulate, swirl, glide, ripple, cascade, whirl, overflow, gush, inundate, deluge, spurt, teem, spew, squirt, purl, well forth 2 *Large numbers of refugees continue to flow into the country.* = **pour**, move, sweep, flood, stream, overflow 3 *Undesirable consequences flow from these misconceptions.* = **issue**, follow, result, emerge, spring, pour, proceed, arise, derive, ensue, emanate ▸ NOUN 1 *watching the quiet flow of the olive-green water* = **stream**, current, movement, motion, course, issue, flood, drift, tide, spate, gush, flux, outpouring, outflow, undertow, tideway 2 *the opportunity to control the flow of information* = **outpouring**, flood, stream, succession, train, plenty, abundance, deluge, plethora, outflow, effusion, emanation

flower NOUN 1 *Each individual flower is tiny.* = **bloom**, blossom, efflorescence 2 *the flower of American manhood* = **elite**, best, prime, finest, pick, choice, cream, height, the crème de la crème, choicest part 3 *You are hardly in the first flower of youth.* = **height**, prime, peak, vigour, freshness; greatest or finest point ▸ VERB 1 *Several of these plants will flower this year.* = **bloom**, open, mature, flourish, unfold, blossom, burgeon, effloresce 2 *Their relationship flowered.* = **blossom**, grow, develop, progress, mature, thrive, flourish, bloom, bud, prosper ■ **RELATED WORDS:** *adjective* floral; *prefix* antho-

flowering ADJECTIVE = **blooming**, in flower, in bloom, in blossom, out, open, ready, blossoming, florescent, abloom

flowery ADJECTIVE 1 *The baby was dressed in a flowery jumpsuit.* = **floral**, flower-patterned 2 *They were using uncommonly flowery language.* = **ornate**, fancy, rhetorical, high-flown, embellished, figurative, florid, overwrought, euphuistic, baroque ■ **OPPOSITE:** plain

flowing ADJECTIVE 1 *fragrance borne by the swiftly flowing stream* = **streaming**, rushing, gushing, teeming, falling, full, rolling, sweeping, flooded, fluid, prolific, abundant, overrun, brimming over 2 *a smooth flowing line against a cloudless sky* = **sleek**, smooth, fluid, unbroken, uninterrupted 3 *his own rhetoric and flowing style of delivery* = **fluent**,

easy, natural, continuous, effortless, uninterrupted, free-flowing, cursive, rich

fluctuate VERB 1 *Body temperatures can fluctuate when you are ill.* = **change**, swing, vary, alter, hesitate, alternate, waver, veer, rise and fall, go up and down, ebb and flow, seesaw 2 *the constantly fluctuating price of crude oil* = **shift**, undulate, oscillate, vacillate

fluctuation NOUN = **change**, shift, swing, variation, instability, alteration, wavering, oscillation, alternation, vacillation, unsteadiness, inconstancy

fluency NOUN = **ease**, control, facility, command, assurance, readiness, smoothness, slickness, glibness, volubility, articulateness

fluent ADJECTIVE = **effortless**, natural, articulate, well-versed, glib, facile, voluble, smooth-spoken

fluff NOUN *bits of fluff on the sleeve of her jumper* = **fuzz**, down, pile, dust, fibre, threads, nap, lint, oose (*Scot.*), dustball ▸ VERB *She fluffed her interview at Oxford.* = **mess up**, spoil, bungle, screw up (*informal, informal*), cock up (*Brit. slang*), foul up (*informal*), make a nonsense of, be unsuccessful in, make a mess off, muddle, crool or cruel (*Austral. slang*)

fluffy ADJECTIVE = **soft**, fuzzy, feathery, downy, fleecy, flossy

fluid NOUN *Make sure that you drink plenty of fluids.* = **liquid**, solution, juice, liquor, sap ▸ ADJECTIVE 1 *The situation is extremely fluid.* = **changeable**, mobile, flexible, volatile, unstable, adjustable, fluctuating, indefinite, shifting, floating, adaptable, mercurial, protean, mutable ■ **OPPOSITE:** fixed 2 *List the fluid and cellular components of blood.* = **liquid**, running, flowing, watery, molten, melted, runny, liquefied, in solution, aqueous ■ **OPPOSITE:** solid

fluke NOUN *The discovery was something of a fluke.* = **stroke of luck**, accident, coincidence, chance occurrence, chance, stroke, blessing, freak, windfall, quirk, lucky break, serendipity, quirk of fate, fortuity, break (*informal*)

flunk VERB = **fail**, screw up (*informal*), flop in (*informal*), plough (*Brit. slang*), be unsuccessful in, not make the grade at (*informal*), not come up to scratch in (*informal*), not come up to the mark in (*informal*)

flurry NOUN 1 *There was a flurry of excitement.* = **commotion**, stir, bustle, flutter, to-do, excitement, hurry, fuss, disturbance, flap (*informal*), whirl, furore, ferment, agitation, fluster, ado, tumult 2 *a flurry of diplomatic activity* = **burst**, spell, bout, outbreak, spurt

3 *A flurry of snowflakes was scudding by the window.* = **gust**, shower, gale, swirl, squall, storm

flush¹ VERB **1** *He turned away, his face flushing.* = **blush**, colour, burn, flame, glow, crimson, redden, suffuse, turn red, go red, colour up, go as red as a beetroot **2** *Flush the eye with clean cold water.* = **cleanse**, wash out, swab, rinse out, flood, drench, syringe, swill, hose down, douche **3** *Flush the contents down the lavatory.* = **expel**, drive, eject, dislodge ▶ NOUN **1** *There was a slight flush on his cheeks.* = **blush**, colour, glow, reddening, redness, rosiness **2** *the first flush of young love* = **bloom**, glow, vigour, freshness

flush² ADJECTIVE **1** *Make sure the tile is flush with the surrounding tiles.* = **level**, even, true, flat, square, plane **2** *Many developing countries were flush with dollars.* = **wealthy**, rich, rolling (*slang*), well-off, in the money (*informal*), in funds, well-heeled (*informal*), replete, moneyed, well-supplied, minted (*Brit. slang*) **3** *If we're feeling flush we'll give them champagne.* = **affluent**, liberal, generous, lavish, abundant, overflowing, plentiful, prodigal, full ▶ ADVERB *The edges fit flush with the walls.* = **level**, even, touching, squarely, in contact, hard (against)

flush³ VERB (*often with* **out**) *They flushed them out of their hiding places.* = **drive out**, force, dislodge, put to flight, start, discover, disturb, uncover, rouse

flushed ADJECTIVE **1** (*often with* **with**) *She was flushed with the success of the venture.* = **exhilarated**, excited, aroused, elated, high (*informal*), inspired, thrilled, animated, enthused, intoxicated, stoked (*Austral. & N.Z. informal*) **2** *People with flushed faces pass by.* = **blushing**, red, hot, burning, embarrassed, glowing, rosy, crimson, feverish, ruddy, rubicund (*old-fashioned*)

fluster VERB = **upset**, bother, disturb, ruffle, heat, excite, confuse, hurry, rattle (*informal*), bustle, hassle (*informal*), flurry, agitate, confound, unnerve, perturb, throw off balance, make nervous

fluted ADJECTIVE = **grooved**, channelled, furrowed, corrugated

flutter VERB **1** *a butterfly fluttering its wings* = **beat**, bat, flap, tremble, shiver, flicker, ripple, waver, fluctuate, agitate, ruffle, quiver, vibrate, palpitate **2** *The birds were fluttering among the trees.* = **flit**, hover, flitter ▶ NOUN **1** *She felt a flutter of trepidation in her stomach.* = **tremor**, tremble, shiver, shudder, palpitation **2** *loud twittering and a desperate flutter of wings* = **vibration**, twitching, quiver, quivering **3** *She was in*

a flutter. = **agitation**, state (*informal*), confusion, excitement, flap (*informal*), tremble, flurry, dither (*chiefly Brit.*), commotion, fluster, tumult, perturbation, state of nervous excitement

flux NOUN **1** *a period of economic flux* = **instability**, change, transition, unrest, modification, alteration, mutation, fluctuation, mutability **2** *the flux of cosmic rays* = **flow**, movement, motion, fluidity

fly¹ VERB **1** *The bird flew away.* = **take wing**, soar, glide, take to the air, wing, mount, sail, hover, flutter, flit **2** *He flew a small plane to Cuba.* = **pilot**, control, operate, steer, manoeuvre, navigate, be at the controls, aviate **3** *The relief supplies are being flown from Pisa.* = **airlift**, send by plane, take by plane, take in an aircraft **4** *A flag was flying on the new HQ.* = **flutter**, wave, float, flap **5** *He sailed in a ship flying a red flag.* = **display**, show, flourish, brandish **6** *I flew downstairs.* = **rush**, race, shoot, career, speed, tear, dash, hurry, barrel (along) (*informal, chiefly U.S. & Canad.*), sprint, bolt, dart, zoom, hare (*Brit. informal*), hasten, whizz (*informal*), scoot, scamper, burn rubber (*informal*), be off like a shot (*informal*) **7** *We walked and the time flew by.* = **pass swiftly**, pass, glide, slip away, roll on, flit, elapse, run its course, go quickly **8** *I'll have to fly.* = **leave**, disappear, get away, depart, run, escape, flee, take off, run from, shun, clear out (*informal*), light out (*informal*), abscond, decamp, take flight, do a runner (*slang*), run for it, cut and run (*informal*), fly the coop (*U.S. & Canad. informal*), beat a retreat, make a quick exit, make a getaway, show a clean pair of heels, skedaddle (*informal*), hightail (*informal, chiefly U.S.*), take a powder (*U.S. & Canad. slang*), hasten away, make your escape, take it on the lam (*U.S. & Canad. slang*), take to your heels • **fly in the ointment** = **problem**, difficulty, rub, flaw, hitch, drawback, snag, small problem • **let fly** *She let fly with a string of obscenities.* = **lose your temper**, lash out, burst forth, keep nothing back, give free rein, let (someone) • **let something fly** *The midfielder let fly a powerful shot.* = **throw**, launch, cast, hurl, shoot, fire, fling, chuck (*informal*), sling, lob (*informal*), hurtle, let off, heave

fly² ADJECTIVE *He is devious and very fly.* = **cunning**, knowing, sharp, smart, careful, shrewd, astute, on the ball (*informal*), canny, wide-awake, nobody's fool, not born yesterday

flyer *or* **flier** NOUN **1** *escape lines for shot-down allied flyers* = **pilot**, aeronaut, airman *or* airwoman, aviator *or* aviatrix **2** *regular* *business flyers* = **air traveller**, air passenger **3** *posters, newsletters and flyers* = **handbill**, bill, notice, leaf, release, literature (*informal*), leaflet, advert (*Brit.*), circular, booklet, pamphlet, handout, throwaway (*U.S.*), promotional material, publicity material **4** *At this point he took a flyer off the front.* = **jump**, spring, bound, leap, hurdle, vault, jeté, flying or running jump

flying ADJECTIVE **1** *a species of flying insect* = **airborne**, waving, winging, floating, streaming, soaring, in the air, hovering, flapping, gliding, fluttering, wind-borne, volitant **2** *He made a flying start to the final.* = **fast**, running, express, speedy, winged, mobile, rapid, fleet, mercurial **3** *I paid a flying visit to the capital.* = **hurried**, brief, rushed, fleeting, short-lived, hasty, transitory, fugacious

foam NOUN *The water curved round the rock in bursts of foam.* = **froth**, spray, bubbles, lather, suds, spume, head ▸ VERB *We watched the water foam and bubble.* = **bubble**, boil, fizz, froth, lather, effervesce

fob VERB • **fob someone off** *I've asked her but she fobs me off with excuses.* = **put off**, deceive, appease, flannel (*Brit. informal*), give (someone) the run-around (*informal*), stall, equivocate with • **fob something off on someone** *He likes to fob his work off on others.* = **pass off**, dump, get rid of, inflict, unload, foist, palm off

focus NOUN **1** *The children are the focus of her life.* = **centre**, focal point, central point, core, bull's eye, centre of attraction, centre of activity, cynosure (*literary*) **2** *the focus of the campaign for Black rights* = **focal point**, heart, target, headquarters, hub, meeting place ▸ VERB **1** (*often with* **on**) *The summit is expected to focus on arms control.* = **concentrate**, centre, spotlight, zero in on (*informal*), meet, join, direct, aim, pinpoint, converge, rivet, bring to bear, zoom in **2** *He focused the binoculars on the boat.* = **fix**, train, direct, aim

fodder NOUN = **feed**, food, rations, tack (*informal*), foodstuff, kai (*N.Z. informal*), forage, victuals, provender, vittles (*obsolete, dialect*)

foe NOUN = **enemy**, rival, opponent, adversary, antagonist, foeman (*archaic*) ■ OPPOSITE: friend

fog NOUN **1** *The crash happened in thick fog.* = **mist**, gloom, haze, smog, murk, miasma, murkiness, peasouper (*informal*) **2** *He was in a fog when he got up.* = **stupor**, confusion, trance, daze, haze, disorientation ▸ VERB **1** *The windows fogged immediately.* = **mist over** or **up**, cloud over, steam up, become

misty **2** *His mind was fogged with fatigue.* = **daze**, cloud, dim, muddle, blind, confuse, obscure, bewilder, darken, perplex, stupefy, befuddle, muddy the waters, obfuscate (*formal*), blear, becloud, bedim

foggy ADJECTIVE **1** *Conditions were damp and foggy this morning.* = **misty**, grey, murky, cloudy, obscure, blurred, dim, hazy, nebulous, indistinct, soupy, smoggy, vaporous, brumous (*rare*) ■ OPPOSITE: clear **2** *My foggy brain sifted through the possibilities.* = **unclear**, confused, clouded, stupid, obscure, vague, dim (*informal*), bewildered, muddled, dazed, cloudy, stupefied, indistinct, befuddled, dark ■ OPPOSITE: sharp

foible NOUN = **idiosyncrasy**, failing, fault, weakness, defect, quirk, imperfection, peculiarity, weak point, infirmity

foil¹ VERB *A brave police chief foiled an armed robbery.* = **thwart**, stop, check, defeat, disappoint, counter, frustrate, hamper, baffle, elude, balk, circumvent, outwit, nullify, checkmate, nip in the bud, put a spoke in (someone's) wheel (*Brit.*)

foil² NOUN *A cold beer is the perfect foil for a curry.* = **complement**, setting, relief, contrast, background, antithesis

foist VERB • **foist something on** or **upon someone** *I don't foist my beliefs on other people.* = **force**, impose

fold VERB **1** *He folded the paper carefully.* = **bend**, double, gather, tuck, overlap, crease, pleat, intertwine, double over, turn under **2** (*often with* **up**) *The company folded in 1990.* = **go bankrupt**, close, fail, crash, collapse, founder, shut down, go under, be ruined, go bust (*informal*), go to the wall, go belly-up (*slang*) **3** (*with* **in**) *He folded her in his arms.* = **wrap**, envelop, entwine, enfold **4** (*often with* **up** or **in**) *an object folded neatly in tissue-paper* = **wrap up**, wrap, enclose, envelop, do up, enfold ▸ NOUN *Make another fold and turn the ends together.* = **crease**, turn, gather, bend, layer, overlap, wrinkle, pleat, ruffle, furrow, knife-edge, double thickness, folded portion

folder NOUN = **file**, portfolio, envelope, dossier, binder

folk NOUN **1** *the innate reserve of country folk* = **people**, persons, humans, individuals, men and women, human beings, humanity, inhabitants, humankind, mankind, mortals **2** (*usually plural*) *I've been avoiding my folks lately.* = **family**, parents, relations, relatives, tribe, clan, kin, kindred, ainga (*N.Z.*), rellies (*Austral. slang*)

follow VERB **1** *Please follow me, madam.* = **accompany**, attend, escort, come after, go behind, tag along behind, bring up the rear, come behind, come or go with, tread on the heels of **2** *I think we're being followed.* = **pursue**, track, dog, hunt, chase, shadow, tail (*informal*), trail, hound, stalk, run after ■ **OPPOSITE:** avoid **3** *the rioting and looting that followed the verdict* = **come after**, go after, come next ■ **OPPOSITE:** precede **4** *If the explanation is right, two things will follow.* = **result**, issue, develop, spring, flow, proceed, arise, ensue, emanate, be consequent, supervene **5** *Take care to follow the instructions.* = **obey**, observe, comply with, adhere to, mind, watch, note, regard, stick to, heed, conform to, keep to, pay attention to, be guided by, toe the line, act according to, act in accordance with, give allegiance to ■ **OPPOSITE:** ignore **6** *I hope other women will follow my example.* = **copy**, imitate, emulate, mimic, model, adopt, live up to, take a leaf out of someone's book, take as an example, pattern yourself upon **7** *He followed his father and became a surgeon.* = **succeed**, replace, come after, take over from, come next, supersede, supplant, take the place of, step into the shoes of **8** *Can you follow the plot so far?* = **understand**, get, see, catch, realize, appreciate, take in, grasp, catch on (*informal*), keep up with, comprehend, fathom, get the hang of (*informal*), get the picture **9** *the millions of people who follow football* = **keep up with**, support, be interested in, cultivate, be devoted to, be a fan of, keep abreast of, be a devotee or supporter of • **follow something through** *They have been unwilling to follow through their ideas.* = **complete**, conclude, pursue, see through, consummate, bring to a conclusion

follower NOUN **1** *violent clashes between followers of the two organizations* = **supporter**, fan, representative, convert, believer, admirer, backer, partisan, disciple, protagonist, devotee, worshipper, apostle, pupil, cohort (*chiefly U.S.*), adherent, henchman or woman or person, groupie (*slang*), habitué, votary ■ **OPPOSITE:** leader **2** *the ringleader and his two thuggish followers* = **attendant**, assistant, companion, helper, sidekick (*slang*), henchman or woman or person, retainer (*History*), hanger-on, minion, lackey ■ **OPPOSITE:** opponent

following ADJECTIVE **1** *We went to dinner the following evening.* = **next**, subsequent, successive, ensuing, coming, later, succeeding, specified, consequent, consequential **2** *Write down the following*

information. = **coming**, about to be mentioned ▶ NOUN *Rugby League enjoys a huge following.* = **supporters**, backing, public, support, train, fans, audience, circle, suite, patronage, clientele, entourage, coterie, retinue

folly NOUN = **foolishness**, bêtise (*rare*), nonsense, madness, stupidity, absurdity, indiscretion, recklessness, silliness, idiocy, irrationality, imprudence, rashness, fatuity, preposterousness, daftness (*informal*), desipience ■ **OPPOSITE:** wisdom

foment VERB = **stir up**, raise, encourage, promote, excite, spur, foster, stimulate, provoke, brew, arouse, rouse, agitate, quicken, incite, instigate, whip up, goad, abet, sow the seeds of, fan the flames

> ▌ **USAGE** Both *foment* and *ferment* can be used to talk about stirring up trouble: *he was accused of fomenting/fermenting unrest.* Only *ferment* can be used intransitively or as a noun: *his anger continued to ferment* (not *foment*); *rural areas were unaffected by the ferment in the cities.*

fond ADJECTIVE **1** *She gave him a fond smile.* = **loving**, caring, warm, devoted, tender, adoring, affectionate, indulgent, doting, amorous ■ **OPPOSITE:** indifferent **2** *My fond hope is that we'll be ready on time.* = **unrealistic**, empty, naive, vain, foolish, deluded, indiscreet, credulous, overoptimistic, delusive, delusory, absurd ■ **OPPOSITE:** sensible • **fond of 1** *I am very fond of Michael.* = **attached to**, in love with, keen on, attracted to, having a soft spot for, enamoured of **2** *He was fond of marmalade.* = **keen on**, into (*informal*), hooked on, partial to, having a soft spot for, having a taste for, addicted to, having a liking for, predisposed towards, having a fancy for

fondle VERB = **caress**, pet, cuddle, touch gently, pat, stroke, dandle

fondly ADVERB **1** *Their eyes met fondly across the table.* = **lovingly**, tenderly, affectionately, amorously, dearly, possessively, with affection, indulgently, adoringly **2** *I fondly imagined my life could be better.* = **unrealistically**, stupidly, vainly, foolishly, naively, credulously

fondness NOUN **1** *a great fondness for children* = **devotion**, love, affection, warmth, attachment, kindness, tenderness, care, aroha (*N.Z.*) ■ **OPPOSITE:** dislike **2** *I've always had a fondness for jewels.* = **liking**, love, taste, fancy, attraction, weakness, preference, attachment, penchant, susceptibility, predisposition, soft spot, predilection, partiality

food NOUN = **nourishment**, cooking, provisions, fare, board, commons, table (*formal*), eats (*slang*), stores, feed, diet, meat, bread, menu, tuck (*informal*), tucker (*Austral. & N.Z. informal*), rations, nutrition, cuisine, tack (*informal*), refreshment, scoff (*slang*), nibbles, grub (*slang*), foodstuffs, subsistence, kai (*N.Z. informal*), larder, chow (*informal*), sustenance, nosh (*slang*), daily bread, victuals, edibles, comestibles, provender, nosebag (*slang*), pabulum (*rare*), nutriment, vittles (*obsolete, dialect*), viands, aliment, eatables (*slang*), survival rations ■ **RELATED WORDS:** *adjective* alimentary; *noun* gastronomy

fool NOUN **1** *She'd been a fool to get involved with him.* = **idiot**, mug (*Brit. slang*), berk (*Brit. slang*), silly, goose (*informal*), dope (*informal*), dummy (*slang*), clot (*Brit. informal*), sap (*slang*), wally (*slang*), plonker (*slang*), nit (*informal*), twit (*informal, chiefly Brit.*), bonehead (*slang*), chump (*informal*), dunce, clod, jackass, schmuck (*U.S. slang*), nitwit (*informal*), dolt, blockhead, ninny, divvy (*Brit. slang*), bird-brain (*informal*), pillock (*Brit. slang*), nincompoop, putz (*U.S. slang*), fathead (*informal*), eejit (*Scot. & Irish*), dumb-ass (*slang*), pea-brain (*slang*), dunderhead, numpty (*Scot. informal*), doofus (*slang, chiefly U.S.*), lamebrain (*informal*), numbskull or numskull, dorba or dorb (*Austral. slang*), mampara (*S. African informal*) ■ **OPPOSITE:** genius **2** *He feels she has made a fool of him.* = **dupe**, butt, mug (*Brit. slang*), sucker (*slang*), gull (*archaic*), stooge (*slang*), laughing stock, pushover (*informal*), fall guy (*informal*), chump (*informal*), greenhorn (*informal*), easy mark (*informal*) **3** *Every good court has its resident fool.* = **jester**, comic, clown, harlequin, motley, buffoon, pierrot, court jester, punchinello, joculator or (*fem.*) joculatrix, merry-andrew ▶ VERB *Art dealers fool a lot of people.* = **deceive**, cheat, mislead, delude, kid (*informal*), trick, take in, con (*informal*), stiff (*slang*), have (someone) on, bluff, hoax, dupe, beguile, gull (*archaic*), swindle, make a fool of, bamboozle, hoodwink, take for a ride (*informal*), put one over on (*informal*), play a trick on, pull a fast one on (*informal*), scam (*slang*) • **fool around with something** *He was fooling around with his cot, and he fell out of bed.* = **play around with**, play with, tamper with, toy with, mess around with, meddle with, trifle with, fiddle around with (*informal*), monkey around with

foolhardy ADJECTIVE = **rash**, risky, irresponsible, reckless, precipitate, unwise, impulsive, madcap, impetuous, hot-headed, imprudent, incautious, venturesome, venturous, temerarious ■ **OPPOSITE:** cautious

foolish ADJECTIVE **1** *It would be foolish to raise hopes unnecessarily.* = **unwise**, silly, absurd, rash, unreasonable, senseless, short-sighted, ill-advised, foolhardy, nonsensical, inane, indiscreet, ill-judged, ill-considered, imprudent, unintelligent, asinine, injudicious, incautious ■ **OPPOSITE:** sensible **2** *How foolish I was not to have seen my doctor earlier.* = **silly**, stupid, mad, daft (*informal*), crazy (*informal*), ridiculous, dumb (*informal*), ludicrous, senseless, barmy (*slang*), potty (*Brit. informal*), goofy (*informal*), idiotic, half-baked (*informal*), dotty (*slang*), inane, fatuous, loopy (*informal*), witless, brainless, harebrained, as daft as a brush (*informal, chiefly Brit.*), doltish

foolishly ADVERB = **unwisely**, stupidly, mistakenly, absurdly, like a fool, idiotically, incautiously, imprudently, ill-advisedly, indiscreetly, short-sightedly, injudiciously, without due consideration

foolishness NOUN **1** *the foolishness of dangerously squabbling politicians* = **stupidity**, irresponsibility, recklessness, idiocy, weakness, absurdity, indiscretion, silliness, inanity, imprudence, rashness, foolhardiness, folly, bêtise (*rare*) **2** *I don't have time to listen to this foolishness.* = **nonsense**, carrying-on (*informal, chiefly Brit.*), rubbish, trash, bunk (*informal*), malarkey (*informal*), claptrap (*informal*), rigmarole, foolery, bunkum or buncombe

foolproof ADJECTIVE = **infallible**, certain, safe, guaranteed, never-failing, unassailable, sure-fire (*informal*), unbreakable

foot PLURAL NOUN = **tootsies** (*informal*) ▶ NOUN **1** = **paw**, pad, trotter, hoof **2** = **bottom**, end, base, foundation, lowest part • **drag your feet** = **stall**, procrastinate, block, hold back, obstruct

foothold NOUN **1** = **basis**, standing, base, position, foundation **2** = **toehold**, hold, support, footing, grip

footing NOUN **1** *a sounder financial footing for the future* = **basis**, foundation, foothold, base position, ground, settlement, establishment, installation, groundwork **2** *They are trying to compete on an equal footing.* = **relationship**, terms, position, basis, state, standing, condition, relations, rank, status, grade **3** *He lost his footing and slid into the water.* = **foothold**, hold, grip, toehold, support

footpath NOUN = **pavement**, sidewalk (*U.S. & Canad.*)

footstep NOUN **1** *I heard footsteps outside.* = **step**, tread, footfall **2** *people's footsteps in the snow* = **footprint**, mark, track, trace, outline, imprint, indentation, footmark

footwear NOUN = **footgear**, boots, shoes, slippers, sandals

forage NOUN (*for cattle*) *forage needed to feed one cow and its calf* = **fodder**, food, feed, foodstuffs, provender ▶ VERB *They were forced to forage for clothes and fuel.* = **search**, hunt, scavenge, cast about, seek, explore, raid, scour, plunder, look round, rummage, ransack, scrounge (*informal*), fossick (*Austral. & N.Z.*)

foray NOUN = **raid**, sally, incursion, inroad, attack, assault, invasion, swoop, reconnaissance, sortie, irruption

forbearance NOUN **1** *a high degree of tolerance and forbearance* = **patience**, resignation, restraint, tolerance, indulgence, long-suffering, moderation, self-control, leniency, temperance, mildness, lenity, longanimity (*rare*) ■ OPPOSITE: impatience **2** *forbearance from military action* = **abstinence**, refraining, avoidance

forbid VERB = **prohibit**, ban, disallow, proscribe, exclude, rule out, veto, outlaw, inhibit, hinder, preclude, make illegal, debar, interdict ■ OPPOSITE: permit

> USAGE Traditionally, it has been considered more correct to talk about *forbidding someone to do something*, rather than *forbidding someone from doing something*. Recently, however, the *from* option has become generally more acceptable, so that *he was forbidden to come in* and *he was forbidden from coming in* may both now be considered correct.

forbidden ADJECTIVE = **prohibited**, banned, vetoed, outlawed, taboo, out of bounds, proscribed, verboten (*German*)

forbidding ADJECTIVE = **threatening**, severe, frightening, hostile, grim, menacing, sinister, daunting, ominous, unfriendly, foreboding, baleful, bodeful ■ OPPOSITE: inviting

force NOUN **1** *calls for the siege to be ended by force* = **compulsion**, pressure, violence, enforcement, constraint, oppression, coercion, duress, arm-twisting (*informal*) **2** *slamming the door behind her with all her force* = **power**, might, pressure, energy, stress, strength, impact, muscle, momentum, impulse, stimulus, vigour, potency, dynamism, life ■ OPPOSITE: weakness **3** *He changed our world through the force of his ideas.* = **influence**, power, effect, authority,

weight, strength, punch (*informal*), significance, effectiveness, validity, efficacy, soundness, persuasiveness, cogency, bite **4** *I took a step back from the force of his rage.* = **intensity**, vigour, vehemence, fierceness, drive, emphasis, persistence **5** *a pan-European peace-keeping force* = **army**, unit, division, corps, company, body, host, troop, squad, patrol, regiment, battalion, legion, squadron, detachment ▶ VERB **1** *They forced him to work for them at gun point.* = **compel**, make, drive, press, pressure, urge, overcome, oblige, railroad (*informal*), constrain, necessitate, coerce, impel, strong-arm (*informal*), dragoon, pressurize, press-gang, put the squeeze on (*informal*), obligate, twist (someone's) arm, put the screws on (*informal*), bring pressure to bear upon **2** *To force this agreement on the nation is wrong.* = **impose**, foist **3** *The extra weight of the crash helmet forced my head backwards.* = **push**, thrust, propel **4** *The police forced the door of the flat and arrested him.* = **break open**, blast, wrench, prise, wrest, use violence on **5** *using torture to force a confession out of a suspect* = **extort**, drag, exact, wring ■ OPPOSITE: coax • **in force 1** *The new tax is already in force.* = **valid**, working, current, effective, binding, operative, operational, in operation, on the statute book **2** *Voters turned out in force.* = **in great numbers**, all together, in full strength

forced ADJECTIVE **1** *a system of forced labour* = **compulsory**, enforced, slave, unwilling, mandatory, obligatory, involuntary, conscripted ■ OPPOSITE: voluntary **2** *a forced smile* = **false**, affected, strained, wooden, stiff, artificial, contrived, unnatural, insincere, laboured ■ OPPOSITE: natural

forceful ADJECTIVE **1** *He was a man of forceful character.* = **dynamic**, powerful, vigorous, potent, assertive ■ OPPOSITE: weak **2** *This is a forceful argument for joining them.* = **powerful**, strong, convincing, effective, compelling, persuasive, weighty, pithy, cogent, telling

forcible ADJECTIVE **1** *forcible resettlement of villagers* = **violent**, armed, aggressive, compulsory, drastic, coercive **2** *He is a forcible advocate for the arts.* = **compelling**, strong, powerful, effective, active, impressive, efficient, valid, mighty, potent, energetic, forceful, weighty, cogent

forcibly ADVERB = **by force**, compulsorily, under protest, against your will, under compulsion, by main force, willy-nilly

forebear or **forbear** NOUN = **ancestor**, father, predecessor, forerunner, forefather, progenitor, tupuna or tipuna (N.Z.)

foreboding NOUN 1 *an uneasy sense of foreboding* = **dread**, fear, anxiety, chill, unease, apprehension, misgiving, premonition, presentiment, apprehensiveness 2 *No one paid any attention to their gloomy forebodings.* = **omen**, warning, prediction, portent, sign, token, foreshadowing, presage, prognostication, augury, foretoken

forecast VERB *They forecast a defeat for the Prime Minister.* = **predict**, anticipate, foresee, foretell, call, plan, estimate, calculate, divine, prophesy, augur, forewarn, prognosticate, vaticinate (*rare*)
▶ NOUN *He delivered his election forecast.* = **prediction**, projection, anticipation, prognosis, planning, guess, outlook, prophecy, foresight, conjecture, forewarning, forethought

forefather NOUN = **ancestor**, father, predecessor, forerunner, forebear, progenitor, procreator, primogenitor, tupuna or tipuna (N.Z.)

forefront NOUN = **lead**, centre, front, fore, spearhead, prominence, vanguard, foreground, leading position, van

forego *see* **forgo**

foregoing ADJECTIVE = **preceding**, former, above, previous, prior, antecedent, anterior, just mentioned, previously stated

foreground NOUN 1 *the foreground of this boldly painted landscape* = **front**, focus, forefront 2 *This worry has come to the foreground in recent years.* = **prominence**, limelight, fore, forefront

foreign ADJECTIVE 1 *a foreign language* = **alien**, overseas, exotic, unknown, outside, strange, imported, borrowed, remote, distant, external, unfamiliar, far off, outlandish, beyond your ken
■ OPPOSITE: native 2 *Her body rejected the transplanted organ as a foreign object.* = **unassimilable**, external, extraneous, outside 3 *He fell into a gloomy mood that was usually so foreign to him.* = **uncharacteristic**, inappropriate, unrelated, incongruous, inapposite, irrelevant

foreigner NOUN = **alien**, incomer, immigrant, non-native, stranger, newcomer, settler, outlander
■ RELATED WORD: *phobia* xenophobia

foremost ADJECTIVE = **leading**, best, first, highest, front, chief, prime, primary, supreme, initial, most important, principal, paramount, inaugural, pre-eminent, headmost

forerunner NOUN 1 *Some respiratory symptoms can be the forerunners of asthma.* = **omen**, sign, indication, token, premonition, portent, augury, prognostic, foretoken, harbinger (*literary*) 2 *Quince jam was the forerunner of marmalade.* = **precursor**, predecessor, ancestor, prototype, forebear, progenitor, herald (*literary*)

foresee VERB = **predict**, forecast, anticipate, envisage, prophesy, foretell, forebode, vaticinate (*rare*), divine

foreshadow VERB = **predict**, suggest, promise, indicate, signal, imply, bode, prophesy, augur, presage, prefigure, portend, betoken, adumbrate, forebode

foresight NOUN = **forethought**, prudence, circumspection, far-sightedness, care, provision, caution, precaution, anticipation, preparedness, prescience (*formal*), premeditation, prevision (*rare*)
■ OPPOSITE: hindsight

forestall VERB = **prevent**, stop, frustrate, anticipate, head off, parry, thwart, intercept, hinder, preclude, balk, circumvent, obviate (*formal*), nip in the bud, provide against

forestry NOUN = **woodcraft**, silviculture, arboriculture, dendrology (*Botany*), woodmanship

foretaste NOUN = **sample**, example, indication, preview, trailer, prelude, whiff, foretoken, warning

foretell VERB = **predict**, forecast, prophesy, portend, call, signify, bode, foreshadow, augur, presage, forewarn, prognosticate, adumbrate, forebode, foreshow, soothsay, vaticinate (*rare*)

forever or **for ever** ADVERB 1 *We will live together forever.* = **evermore**, always, ever, for good, for keeps, for all time, in perpetuity, for good and all (*informal*), till the cows come home (*informal*), world without end, till the end of time, till Doomsday 2 *He was forever attempting to arrange deals.* = **constantly**, always, all the time, continually, endlessly, persistently, eternally, perpetually, incessantly, interminably, unremittingly, everlastingly
▌ USAGE *Forever* and *for ever* can both be used to say that something is without end. For all other meanings, *forever* is the preferred form.

forewarn VERB = **alert**, advise, caution, tip off, apprise, give fair warning, put on guard, put on the qui vive

foreword NOUN = **introduction**, preliminary, preface, preamble, prologue, prolegomenon

forfeit NOUN *That is the forfeit he must pay.*
= **penalty**, fine, damages, forfeiture, loss,
mulct, amercement (*obsolete*) ▶ VERB *He
was ordered to forfeit more than £1.5m in profits.*
= **relinquish**, lose, give up, surrender,
renounce, be deprived of, say goodbye to,
be stripped of

forfeiture NOUN = **loss**, giving up,
surrender, forfeiting, confiscation,
sequestration (*Law*), relinquishment

forge VERB **1** *They agreed to forge closer
economic ties.* = **form**, build, create,
establish, set up, fashion, shape,
frame, construct, invent, devise, mould,
contrive, fabricate, hammer out, make,
work **2** *They forged dollar notes.* = **fake**,
copy, reproduce, imitate, counterfeit,
feign, falsify, coin **3** *To forge a blade takes
great skill.* = **create**, make, work, found,
form, model, fashion, shape, cast,
turn out, construct, devise, mould,
contrive, fabricate, hammer out,
beat into shape

forged ADJECTIVE **1** *She was carrying a forged
American passport.* = **fake**, copy, false,
counterfeit, pretend, artificial, mock,
pirated, reproduction, synthetic, imitation,
bogus, simulated, duplicate, quasi, sham,
fraudulent, pseudo, fabricated, copycat
(*informal*), falsified, ersatz, unoriginal,
ungenuine, phony *or* phoney (*informal*)
■ **OPPOSITE:** genuine **2** *fifteen tons of forged
steel parts* = **formed**, worked, founded,
modelled, fashioned, shaped, cast, framed,
stamped, crafted, moulded, minted,
hammered out, beat out, beaten into
shape

forger NOUN = **counterfeiter**, copier,
copyist, falsifier, coiner

forgery NOUN **1** *He was found guilty of
forgery.* = **falsification**, faking, pirating,
counterfeiting, fraudulence, fraudulent
imitation, coining **2** *The letter was a forgery.*
= **fake**, imitation, sham, counterfeit,
falsification, phoney *or* phony (*informal*),
warez (*Computing*)

forget VERB **1** *She forgot where she left the car.*
= **fail to remember**, not remember, not
recollect, let slip from the memory, fail to
bring to mind ■ **OPPOSITE:** remember
2 *Don't forget that all dogs need a supply of
water.* = **neglect**, overlook, omit, not
remember, be remiss, fail to remember
3 *I forgot my passport.* = **leave behind**, lose,
lose sight of, mislay **4** *I can't forget what
happened today.* = **dismiss from your mind**,
ignore, overlook, stop thinking about, let
bygones be bygones, consign to oblivion,
put out of your mind

forgetful ADJECTIVE = **absent-minded**,
vague, careless, neglectful, oblivious, lax,
negligent, dreamy, slapdash, heedless,
slipshod, inattentive, unmindful, apt to
forget, having a memory like a sieve
■ **OPPOSITE:** mindful

forgetfulness NOUN = **absent-
mindedness**, oblivion, inattention,
carelessness, abstraction, laxity, laxness,
dreaminess, obliviousness, lapse of
memory, heedlessness, woolgathering

forgive VERB = **excuse**, pardon, bear no
malice towards, not hold something
against, understand, acquit, condone,
remit, let off (*informal*), turn a blind eye to,
exonerate, absolve, bury the hatchet, let
bygones be bygones, turn a deaf ear to,
accept (someone's) apology ■ **OPPOSITE:**
blame

forgiveness NOUN = **pardon**, mercy,
absolution, exoneration, overlooking,
amnesty, acquittal, remission,
condonation

forgiving ADJECTIVE = **lenient**, tolerant,
compassionate, clement, patient, mild,
humane, gracious, long-suffering, merciful,
magnanimous, forbearing, willing to
forgive, soft-hearted

forgo *or* **forego** VERB = **give up**, sacrifice,
surrender, do without, kick (*informal*),
abandon, resign, yield, relinquish,
renounce, waive, say goodbye to, cede,
abjure, leave alone *or* out

fork VERB = **branch**, part, separate, split,
divide, diverge, subdivide, branch off, go
separate ways, bifurcate

forked ADJECTIVE = **branching**, split,
branched, divided, angled, pronged,
zigzag, tined, Y-shaped, bifurcate(d)

forlorn ADJECTIVE **1** *He looked a forlorn figure as
he limped off.* = **miserable**, helpless,
pathetic, pitiful, lost, forgotten,
abandoned, unhappy, lonely, lonesome
(*chiefly U.S. & Canad.*), homeless, forsaken,
bereft, destitute, wretched, disconsolate,
friendless, down in the dumps (*informal*),
pitiable, cheerless, woebegone,
comfortless ■ **OPPOSITE:** cheerful **2** *The
once glorious palaces stood empty and forlorn.*
= **abandoned**, deserted, ruined, bleak,
dreary, desolate, godforsaken, waste
3 *a forlorn effort to keep from losing my mind*
= **hopeless**, useless, vain, pointless, futile,
no-win, unattainable, impracticable,
unachievable, impossible, not having a
prayer

form NOUN **1** *He contracted a rare form of
cancer.* = **type**, sort, kind, variety, way,
system, order, class, style, practice,

method, species, manner, stamp, description **2** *Valleys often take the form of deep canyons.* = **shape**, formation, configuration, construction, cut, model, fashion, structure, pattern, cast, appearance, stamp, mould **3** *the sustained narrative form of the novel* = **structure**, plan, order, organization, arrangement, construction, proportion, format, framework, harmony, symmetry, orderliness **4** *her petite form and delicate features* = **build**, being, body, figure, shape, frame, outline, anatomy, silhouette, physique, person **5** *He's now fighting his way back to top form.* = **condition**, health, shape, nick (*informal*), fitness, trim, good condition, good spirits, fettle **6** *You will be asked to fill in an application form.* = **document**, paper, sheet, questionnaire, application **7** *a frequent broadcaster on correct form and dress* = **procedure**, behaviour, manners, etiquette, use, rule, conduct, ceremony, custom, convention, ritual, done thing, usage, protocol, formality, wont, right practice, kawa (*N.Z.*), tikanga (*N.Z.*) **8** *I was going into the sixth form at school.* = **class**, year, set, rank, grade, stream **9** *The rejoicing took the form of exuberant masquerades.* = **mode**, character, shape, appearance, arrangement, manifestation, guise, semblance, design ▶ VERB **1** *He gave orders for the cadets to form into lines.* = **arrange**, combine, line up, organize, assemble, dispose, draw up **2** *The bowl was formed out of clay.* = **make**, produce, model, fashion, build, create, shape, manufacture, stamp, construct, assemble, forge, mould, fabricate **3** *Women formed the majority of the group's membership.* = **constitute**, make up, compose, comprise, serve as, make **4** *You may want to form a company to buy a joint freehold.* = **establish**, start, found, launch, set up, invent, devise, put together, bring about, contrive **5** *Stalactites and stalagmites began to form.* = **take shape**, grow, develop, materialize, rise, appear, settle, show up (*informal*), accumulate, come into being, crystallize, become visible **6** *She rapidly formed a plan.* = **draw up**, design, devise, formulate, plan, pattern, frame, organize, think up **7** *It is easier to form good habits than to break bad ones.* = **develop**, pick up, acquire, cultivate, contract, get into (*informal*) **8** *Anger at injustice formed his character.* = **train**, develop, shape, mould, school, teach, guide, discipline, rear, educate, bring up, instruct

formal ADJECTIVE **1** *He wrote a very formal letter of apology.* = **serious**, stiff, detached, aloof, official, reserved, correct, conventional, remote, exact, precise, starched, prim, unbending, punctilious (*formal*), ceremonious ■ **OPPOSITE:** informal **2** *No formal announcement has been made.* = **official**, express, explicit, authorized, set, legal, fixed, regular, approved, strict, endorsed, prescribed, rigid, certified, solemn, lawful, methodical, pro forma (*Latin*) **3** *They arranged a formal dinner after the play.* = **ceremonial**, traditional, solemn, ritualistic, dressy **4** *He didn't have any formal dance training.* = **conventional**, established, traditional

formality NOUN **1** *Her formality and seriousness amused him.* = **correctness**, seriousness, decorum, ceremoniousness, protocol, etiquette, politesse, p's and q's, punctilio **2** *The will was read, but it was a formality.* = **convention**, form, conventionality, matter of form, procedure, ceremony, custom, gesture, ritual, rite

format NOUN = **arrangement**, form, style, make-up, look, plan, design, type, appearance, construction, presentation, layout

formation NOUN **1** *the formation of a new government* = **establishment**, founding, forming, setting up, starting, production, generation, organization, manufacture, constitution **2** *The formation of my character and temperament.* = **development**, shaping, constitution, evolution, moulding, composition, compilation, accumulation, genesis, crystallization **3** *He was flying in formation with seven other jets.* = **arrangement**, grouping, figure, design, structure, pattern, rank, organization, array, disposition (*archaic*), configuration

formative ADJECTIVE **1** *She spent her formative years growing up in London.* = **developmental**, sensitive, susceptible, impressionable, malleable, pliant, mouldable **2** *a formative influence on his life* = **influential**, determinative, controlling, important, shaping, significant, moulding, decisive, developmental

former ADJECTIVE **1** *I learned from my former boss that it was fun to work.* = **previous**, one-time, erstwhile, ex-, late, earlier, prior, sometime, foregoing, antecedent, anterior, quondam, whilom (*archaic*), ci-devant (*French*) ■ **OPPOSITE:** current **2** *Remember him as he was in former years.* = **past**, earlier, long ago, bygone, old, ancient, departed, old-time, long gone, of yore ■ **OPPOSITE:** present **3** *Most people can be forgiven for choosing* *the former option.* = **aforementioned**, above, first mentioned, aforesaid, preceding, foregoing

formerly ADVERB = **previously**, earlier, in the past, at one time, before, lately, once, already, heretofore, aforetime (*archaic*)

formidable ADJECTIVE **1** *We have a formidable task ahead of us.* = **difficult**, taxing, challenging, overwhelming, staggering, daunting, mammoth, colossal, arduous, very great, onerous, toilsome (*literary*) ■ **OPPOSITE:** easy **2** *She looked every bit as formidable as her mother.* = **impressive**, great (*informal*), powerful, tremendous, mighty, terrific, awesome, invincible, indomitable, redoubtable, puissant **3** *a formidable, well-trained, well-equipped fighting force* = **intimidating**, threatening, dangerous, terrifying, appalling, horrible, dreadful, menacing, dismaying, fearful (*informal*), daunting, frightful, baleful, shocking (*informal*) ■ **OPPOSITE:** encouraging

formula NOUN **1** *The new peace formula means hostilities have ended.* = **method**, plan, policy, rule, principle, procedure, recipe, prescription, blueprint, precept, modus operandi, way **2** *He developed a mathematical formula.* = **form of words**, code, phrase, formulary, set expression **3** *bottles of formula* = **mixture**, preparation, compound, composition, concoction, tincture, medicine

formulate VERB **1** *He formulated his plan for escape.* = **devise**, plan, develop, prepare, work out, invent, evolve, coin, forge, draw up, originate, map out **2** *I was impressed by how he formulated his ideas.* = **express**, detail, frame, define, specify, articulate, set down, codify, put into words, systematize, particularize, give form to

forsake VERB **1** *I still love him and would never forsake him.* = **desert**, leave, abandon, quit, strand, jettison, repudiate, cast off, disown, jilt, throw over, leave in the lurch **2** *She forsook her notebook for new technology.* = **give up**, set aside, relinquish, forgo, kick (*informal*), yield, surrender, renounce, have done with, stop using, abdicate, stop having, turn your back on, forswear **3** *He has no plans to forsake the hills.* = **abandon**, leave, go away from, take your leave of

forsaken ADJECTIVE **1** *She felt forsaken and gave up any attempt at order.* = **abandoned**, ignored, lonely, lonesome (*chiefly U.S. & Canad.*), stranded, ditched, left behind, marooned, outcast, forlorn, cast off, jilted, friendless, left in the lurch **2** *a forsaken church and a derelict hotel* = **deserted**, abandoned, isolated, solitary, desolate, forlorn, destitute, disowned, godforsaken

fort NOUN *Soldiers inside the fort are under sustained attack.* = **fortress**, keep, station, camp, tower, castle, garrison, stronghold, citadel, fortification, redoubt, fastness, blockhouse, fortified pa (*N.Z.*) • **hold the fort** *His partner is holding the fort while he is away.* = **take responsibility**, cover, stand in, carry on, take over the reins, maintain the status quo, deputize, keep things moving, keep things on an even keel

forte NOUN = **speciality**, strength, talent, strong point, métier, long suit (*informal*), gift ■ **OPPOSITE:** weak point

forth ADVERB **1** *Go forth into the desert.* = **forward**, out, away, ahead, onward, outward **2** *She brought forth a small gold amulet.* = **out**, into the open, out of concealment

forthcoming ADJECTIVE **1** *his opponents in the forthcoming election* = **approaching**, coming, expected, future, imminent, prospective, impending, upcoming **2** *They promised that the money would be forthcoming.* = **available**, ready, accessible, at hand, in evidence, obtainable, on tap (*informal*) **3** *She was very forthcoming in court.* = **communicative**, open, free, informative, expansive, sociable, chatty, talkative, unreserved

forthright ADJECTIVE = **outspoken**, open, direct, frank, straightforward, blunt, downright, candid, upfront (*informal*), plain-spoken, straight from the shoulder (*informal*) ■ **OPPOSITE:** secretive

forthwith ADVERB = **immediately**, directly, instantly, at once, right away, straightaway, without delay, tout de suite (*French*), quickly

fortification NOUN **1** *Europe's fortification of its frontiers* = **reinforcement**, protecting, securing, protection, strengthening, reinforcing, embattlement **2** *troops stationed just behind the fortification* = **defence**, keep, protection, castle, fort, fortress, stronghold, bastion, citadel, bulwark, fastness, fortified pa (*N.Z.*) **3** *nutrient fortification of food* = **strengthening**, supplementing, reinforcement

fortify VERB **1** *British soldiers working to fortify an airbase* = **protect**, defend, secure, strengthen, reinforce, support, brace, garrison, shore up, augment, buttress, make stronger, embattle **2** *All sherry is made from wine fortified with brandy.* = **strengthen**, add alcohol to **3** *The volunteers were fortified by their patriotic belief.* = **sustain**, encourage, confirm, cheer, strengthen, reassure, brace, stiffen, hearten, embolden, invigorate ■ **OPPOSITE:** dishearten

fortitude NOUN = **courage**, strength, resolution, determination, guts (*informal*), patience, pluck, grit, endurance, bravery, backbone, perseverance, firmness, staying power, valour, fearlessness, strength of mind, intrepidity, hardihood, dauntlessness, stouteartedness

fortress NOUN = **castle**, fort, stronghold, citadel, redoubt, fastness, fortified pa (*N.Z.*)

fortuitous ADJECTIVE **1** *a fortuitous quirk of fate* = **chance**, lucky, random, casual, contingent, accidental, arbitrary, incidental, unforeseen **2** *It was a fortuitous discovery.* = **lucky**, happy, fortunate, serendipitous, providential, fluky (*informal*)

fortunate ADJECTIVE **1** *He has had a very fortunate life.* = **lucky**, happy, favoured, bright, golden, rosy, on a roll, jammy (*Brit. slang*), in luck, having a charmed life, born with a silver spoon in your mouth ■ **OPPOSITE:** unfortunate **2** *It was fortunate that the water was shallow.* = **providential**, auspicious, fortuitous, felicitous, timely, promising, encouraging, helpful, profitable, convenient, favourable, advantageous, expedient, opportune (*formal*), propitious

fortunately ADVERB = **luckily**, happily, as luck would have it, providentially, by good luck, by a happy chance

fortune NOUN **1** *Eating out all the time costs a fortune.* = **large sum of money**, bomb (*Brit. slang*), packet (*slang*), bundle (*slang*), big money, big bucks (*informal, chiefly U.S.*), megabucks (*U.S. & Canad. slang*), an arm and a leg (*informal*), king's ransom, pretty penny (*informal*), top whack (*informal*) **2** *He made his fortune in car sales.* = **wealth**, means, property, riches, resources, assets, pile (*informal*), possessions, treasure, prosperity, mint, gold mine, wad (*U.S. & Canad. slang*), affluence, opulence, tidy sum (*informal*) ■ **OPPOSITE:** poverty **3** *Such good fortune must be shared with my friends.* = **luck**, accident, fluke (*informal*), stroke of luck, serendipity, hap (*archaic*), twist of fate, run of luck **4** *He is certainly being smiled on by fortune.* = **chance**, fate, destiny, providence, the stars, Lady Luck, kismet, fortuity **5** (*often plural*) *She kept up with the fortunes of the family.* = **destiny**, life, lot, experiences, history, condition, success, means, circumstances, expectation, adventures

forum NOUN **1** *a forum where problems could be discussed* = **meeting**, conference, assembly, meeting place, court, body, council, parliament, congress, gathering, diet, senate, rally, convention, tribunal (*archaic, literary*), seminar, get-together (*informal*), congregation, caucus (*chiefly U.S. & Canad.*), synod, convergence, symposium, hui (*N.Z.*), moot, assemblage, conclave, convocation (*formal*), consistory (*in various Churches*), ecclesia (*in Church use*), colloquium, folkmoot (*in medieval England*), runanga (*N.Z.*) **2** *Generals appeared before the excited crowds in the Forum.* = **public square**, court, square, chamber, platform, arena, pulpit, meeting place, amphitheatre, stage, rostrum, agora (*in ancient Greece*)

forward ADJECTIVE **1** *to allow more troops to move to forward positions* = **leading**, first, head, front, advance, foremost, fore **2** *The University system requires more forward planning.* = **future**, early, advanced, progressive, premature, prospective, onward, forward-looking **3** *She is very forward and confident.* = **presumptuous**, confident, familiar, bold, fresh (*informal*), assuming, presuming, cheeky, brash, pushy (*informal*), brazen, shameless, sassy (*U.S. informal*), pert, impertinent, impudent, bare-faced, overweening, immodest, brass-necked (*Brit. informal*), overfamiliar, brazen-faced, overassertive ■ **OPPOSITE:** shy ► ADVERB *Over the years similar theories have been put forward.* = **into the open**, out, to light, to the front, to the surface, into consideration, into view, into prominence ► VERB **1** *He forwarded their cause with courage, skill and humour.* = **further**, back, help, support, aid, encourage, speed, advance, favour, promote, foster, assist, hurry, hasten, expedite ■ **OPPOSITE:** retard **2** *The document was forwarded to the President.* = **send on**, send, post, pass on, ship, route, transmit, dispatch, freight, redirect

forwards *or* **forward** ADVERB **1** *Duleep walked forward into the room.* = **forth** (*formal, old-fashioned*), on, ahead, onwards ■ **OPPOSITE:** backward(s) **2** *His work from that time forward was confined to portraits.* = **on**, onward, onwards

fossick VERB (*Austral. & N.Z.*) = **search**, hunt, explore, ferret, check, forage, rummage

foster VERB **1** *She has fostered more than 100 children.* = **bring up**, raise, parent, nurse, look after, rear, care for, take care of, nurture **2** *They are keen to foster trading links with the West.* = **develop**, support, further, encourage, feed, promote, stimulate, uphold, nurture, cultivate, foment ■ **OPPOSITE:** suppress **3** *She fostered a fierce ambition.* = **cherish**, sustain, entertain, harbour, accommodate, nourish

foul ADJECTIVE **1** *foul, polluted water* = **dirty**, rank, offensive, nasty, disgusting, unpleasant, revolting, contaminated, rotten, polluted, stinking, filthy, tainted, grubby, repellent, squalid, repulsive, sullied, grimy, nauseating, loathsome, unclean, impure, grotty (*slang*), fetid, grungy (*slang*, *chiefly U.S. & Canad.*), putrid, malodorous, noisome, scuzzy (*slang*, *chiefly U.S.*), mephitic, olid, yucky or yukky (*slang*), festy (*Austral. slang*), yucko (*Austral. slang*) ■ **OPPOSITE:** clean **2** *He was sent off for using foul language.* = **obscene**, crude, indecent, foul-mouthed, low, blue, dirty, gross, abusive, coarse, filthy, vulgar, lewd, profane, blasphemous, scurrilous, smutty, scatological **3** *The weather was foul, with heavy hail and snow.* = **stormy**, bad, wild, rough, wet, rainy, murky, foggy, disagreeable, blustery **4** *a foul tackle* = **unfair**, illegal, dirty, crooked (*informal*), shady (*informal*), fraudulent, unjust, dishonest, unscrupulous, underhand, inequitable, unsportsmanlike, unsporting **5** *He is accused of all manner of foul deeds.* = **offensive**, bad, base, wrong, evil, notorious, corrupt, vicious, infamous, disgraceful, shameful, vile, immoral, scandalous, wicked, sinful, despicable, heinous, hateful, abhorrent, egregious, abominable, dishonourable, nefarious, iniquitous, detestable ■ **OPPOSITE:** admirable ▶ VERB **1** *sea grass fouled with black tar* = **dirty**, soil, stain, contaminate, smear, pollute, taint, sully, defile, besmirch, smirch, begrime, besmear ■ **OPPOSITE:** clean **2** *The pipe was fouled with grain.* = **clog**, block, jam, choke **3** *The freighter fouled its propeller in fishing nets.* = **entangle**, catch, twist, snarl, ensnare, tangle up • **foul something up** *There are risks that laboratories may foul up these tests.* = **bungle**, spoil, botch, mess up, cock up (*Brit. slang*), make a mess of, mismanage, make a nonsense of, muck up (*slang*), bodge (*informal*), make a pig's ear of (*informal*), put a spanner in the works (*Brit. informal*), flub (*U.S. slang*), crool or cruel (*Austral. slang*)

foul play NOUN = **crime**, fraud, corruption, deception, treachery, criminal activity, duplicity, dirty work, double-dealing, skulduggery (*informal*), chicanery, villainy, sharp practice, perfidy (*literary*), roguery, dishonest behaviour

found VERB **1** *He founded the Centre for Journalism Studies.* = **establish**, start, set up, begin, create, institute, organize, construct, constitute, originate, endow, inaugurate, bring into being **2** *The town was founded in 1610.* = **erect**, build, construct, raise, settle

foundation NOUN **1** *Best friends are the foundation of my life.* = **basis**, heart, root, mainstay, beginning, support, ground, rest, key, principle, fundamental, premise, starting point, principal element **2** (*often plural*) *vertical or lateral support for building foundations* = **substructure**, underpinning, groundwork, bedrock, base, footing, bottom **3** *the foundation of the modern welfare state* = **setting up**, institution, instituting, organization, settlement, establishment, initiating, originating, starting, endowment, inauguration

founded ADJECTIVE • **founded on** = **based on**, built on, rooted in, grounded on, established on

founder¹ NOUN *She was the founder of the medical faculty.* = **initiator**, father, establisher, author, maker, framer, designer, architect, builder, creator, beginner, generator, inventor, organizer, patriarch, benefactor, originator, constructor, institutor

founder² VERB **1** *The talks have foundered.* = **fail**, collapse, break down, abort, fall through, be unsuccessful, come to nothing, come unstuck, miscarry, misfire, fall by the wayside, come to grief, bite the dust, go belly-up (*slang*), go down like a lead balloon (*informal*) **2** *Three ships foundered in heavy seas.* = **sink**, go down, be lost, submerge, capsize, go to the bottom

> **USAGE** *Founder* is sometimes wrongly used where *flounder* is meant: *this unexpected turn of events left him floundering* (not *foundering*).

fountain NOUN **1** *In the centre of the courtyard was a round fountain.* = **font**, spring, reservoir, spout, fount, water feature, well **2** *The volcano spewed a fountain of molten rock.* = **jet**, stream, spray, gush **3** *You are a fountain of ideas.* = **source**, fount, wellspring, wellhead, beginning, rise, cause, origin, genesis, commencement, derivation, fountainhead

fowl NOUN = **poultry** ■ **RELATED WORDS:** *name of male* cock; *name of female* hen

foxy ADJECTIVE = **crafty**, knowing, sharp, tricky, shrewd, cunning, sly, astute, canny, devious, wily, artful, guileful

foyer NOUN = **entrance hall**, lobby, reception area, vestibule, anteroom, antechamber

fracas NOUN = **brawl**, fight, trouble, row, riot, disturbance, quarrel, uproar, skirmish, scuffle, free-for-all (*informal*), rumpus, aggro (*slang*), affray (*Law*), shindig (*informal*), donnybrook, scrimmage, shindy (*informal*), bagarre (*French*), melee or mêlée, biffo (*Austral. slang*)

fraction NOUN **1** *I opened my eyes a fraction.* = **bit**, little bit, mite, jot, tiny amount, iota, scintilla **2** *only a small fraction of the cost* = **percentage**, share, cut (*informal*), division, section, proportion, slice, ratio, portion, quota, subdivision, moiety **3** *You will find only a fraction of the collection on display.* = **fragment**, part, piece, section, sector, selection, segment

fractious ADJECTIVE = **irritable**, cross, awkward, unruly, touchy, recalcitrant, petulant, tetchy, ratty (*Brit. & N.Z. informal*), testy, chippy (*informal*), fretful, grouchy (*informal*), querulous, peevish, refractory, crabby, captious, froward (*archaic*), pettish ■ **OPPOSITE:** affable

fracture NOUN **1** *a double fracture of the right arm* = **break**, split, crack **2** *large fractures in the crust creating the valleys* = **cleft**, opening, split, crack, gap, rent, breach, rift, rupture, crevice, fissure, schism ▸ VERB **1** *You've fractured a rib.* = **break**, crack **2** *a society that could fracture along class lines* = **split**, separate, divide, rend (*literary*), fragment, splinter, rupture

fragile ADJECTIVE **1** *The fragile government was on the brink of collapse.* = **unstable**, weak, vulnerable, delicate, uncertain, insecure, precarious, flimsy **2** *Coffee was served to them in cups of fragile china.* = **fine**, weak, delicate, frail, feeble, brittle, flimsy, dainty, easily broken, breakable, frangible ■ **OPPOSITE:** durable **3** *He felt irritated and strangely fragile.* = **unwell**, poorly (*informal*), weak, delicate, crook (*Austral. & N.Z. informal*), shaky, frail, feeble, sickly, unsteady, infirm

fragility NOUN = **weakness**, delicacy, frailty, infirmity, feebleness, brittleness, frangibility

fragment NOUN *She read everything, digesting every fragment of news.* = **piece**, part, bit, scrap, particle, portion, fraction, shiver, shred, remnant, speck, sliver, wisp, morsel, oddment, chip ▸ VERB **1** *It's an exploded fracture – the bones have fragmented.* = **break**, split, shatter, crumble, shiver, disintegrate, splinter, come apart, break into pieces, come to pieces ■ **OPPOSITE:** fuse **2** *Their country's government has fragmented into disarray.* = **break up**, divide, split up, disunite

fragmentary ADJECTIVE = **incomplete**, broken, scattered, partial, disconnected, discrete, sketchy, piecemeal, incoherent, scrappy, disjointed, bitty, unsystematic

fragrance or **fragrancy** NOUN **1** *a shrubby plant with a strong fragrance* = **scent**, smell, perfume, bouquet, aroma, balm, sweet smell, sweet odour, redolence, fragrancy

■ **OPPOSITE:** stink **2** *The advertisement is for a male fragrance.* = **perfume**, scent, cologne, eau de toilette, eau de Cologne, toilet water, Cologne water

fragrant ADJECTIVE = **aromatic**, perfumed, balmy, redolent, sweet-smelling, sweet-scented, odorous, ambrosial, odoriferous ■ **OPPOSITE:** stinking

frail ADJECTIVE **1** *She lay in bed looking particularly frail.* = **feeble**, weak, puny, decrepit, infirm ■ **OPPOSITE:** strong **2** *The frail craft rocked as he clambered in.* = **flimsy**, weak, vulnerable, delicate, fragile, brittle, unsound, wispy, insubstantial, breakable, frangible, slight

frailty NOUN **1** *a triumph of will over human frailty* = **weakness**, susceptibility, fallibility, peccability ■ **OPPOSITE:** strength **2** *She died after a long period of increasing frailty.* = **infirmity**, poor health, feebleness, puniness, frailness **3** *She is aware of his faults and frailties.* = **fault**, failing, vice, weakness, defect, deficiency, flaw, shortcoming, blemish, imperfection, foible, weak point, peccadillo, chink in your armour
■ **OPPOSITE:** strong point

frame NOUN **1** *She kept a picture of her mother in a silver frame.* = **mounting**, setting, surround, mount **2** *He supplied housebuilders with modern timber frames.* = **casing**, framework, structure, shell, system, form, construction, fabric, skeleton, chassis **3** *belts pulled tight against their bony frames* = **physique**, build, form, body, figure, skeleton, anatomy, carcass, morphology ▸ VERB **1** *The picture is now ready to be framed.* = **mount**, case, enclose **2** *The swimming pool is framed by tropical gardens.* = **surround**, ring, enclose, close in, encompass, envelop, encircle, fence in, hem in **3** *A convention was set up to frame a constitution.* = **devise**, plan, form, shape, institute, draft, compose, sketch, forge, put together, conceive, hatch, draw up, formulate, contrive, map out, concoct, cook up, block out • **frame of mind** *She was not in the right frame of mind to continue.* = **mood**, state, spirit, attitude, humour, temper, outlook, disposition, mind-set, fettle

framework NOUN **1** *within the framework of federal regulations* = **system**, plan, order, scheme, arrangement, fabric, schema, frame of reference, the bare bones **2** *wooden shelves on a steel framework* = **structure**, body, frame, foundation, shell, fabric, skeleton

franchise NOUN **1** *the franchise to build and operate the tunnel* = **authorization**, right, permit, licence, charter, privilege, prerogative **2** *the introduction of universal franchise* = **vote**, voting rights, suffrage

frank ADJECTIVE **1** *They had a frank discussion about the issue.* = **candid**, open, free, round, direct, plain, straightforward, blunt, outright, sincere, outspoken, honest, downright, truthful, forthright, upfront (*informal*), unrestricted, plain-spoken, unreserved, artless, ingenuous, straight from the shoulder (*informal*) ■ **OPPOSITE:** secretive **2** *with frank admiration on his face* = **unconcealed**, open, undisguised, dinkum (*Austral. & N.Z. informal*)

frankly ADVERB **1** *Quite frankly, I don't care.* = **honestly**, sincerely, in truth, candidly, to tell (you) the truth, to be frank (with you), to be honest **2** *The leaders have been speaking frankly about their problems.* = **openly**, freely, directly, straight, plainly, bluntly, overtly, candidly, without reserve, straight from the shoulder

frankness NOUN = **outspokenness**, openness, candour, truthfulness, plain speaking, bluntness, forthrightness, laying it on the line, ingenuousness, absence of reserve

frantic ADJECTIVE **1** *A bird had been locked in and was now quite frantic.* = **frenzied**, wild, mad (*informal*), raging, furious, raving, distracted, distraught, berserk, uptight (*informal*), overwrought, at the end of your tether, beside yourself, at your wits' end, berko (*Austral. slang*) ■ **OPPOSITE:** calm **2** *A busy night in the restaurant is frantic in the kitchen.* = **hectic**, desperate, frenzied, fraught (*informal*), frenetic

fraternity NOUN **1** *He needs the fraternity of others.* = **companionship**, fellowship, brotherhood, kinship, camaraderie, comradeship **2** *the spread of stolen guns among the criminal fraternity* = **circle**, company, set, order, clan, guild **3** *He joined a college fraternity.* = **brotherhood**, club, union, society, league, association, sodality

fraud NOUN **1** *He was jailed for two years for fraud.* = **deception**, deceit, treachery, swindling, guile, trickery, duplicity, double-dealing, chicanery, sharp practice, imposture, fraudulence, spuriousness ■ **OPPOSITE:** honesty **2** *a fraud involving pension and social security claims* = **scam**, craft, cheat, sting (*informal*), deception (*slang*), artifice, humbug, canard, stratagems, chicane **3** *He never wrote the letter; it was a fraud.* = **hoax**, trick, cheat, con (*informal*), deception, sham, spoof (*informal*), prank, swindle, ruse, practical joke, joke, fast one (*informal*), imposture, fastie (*Austral. slang*) **4** *He believes many*

psychics are frauds. = **impostor**, cheat, fake, bluffer, sham, hoax, hoaxer, forgery, counterfeit, pretender, charlatan, quack, fraudster, swindler, mountebank, grifter (*slang, chiefly U.S. & Canad.*), double-dealer, phoney or phony (*informal*)

fraudulent ADJECTIVE = **deceitful**, false, crooked (*informal*), untrue, sham, treacherous, dishonest, deceptive, counterfeit, spurious, crafty, swindling, double-dealing, duplicitous, knavish (*archaic*), phoney or phony (*informal*), criminal ■ **OPPOSITE:** genuine

fraught ADJECTIVE **1** *It has been a somewhat fraught day.* = **tense**, trying, difficult, distressing, tricky, emotionally charged **2** *She's depressed, fraught, and exhausted.* = **agitated**, wired (*slang*), anxious, distressed, tense, distracted, emotive, uptight (*informal*), emotionally charged, strung-up, on tenterhooks, hag-ridden, adrenalized • **fraught with** *The production has been fraught with problems.* = **filled with**, full of, charged with, accompanied by, attended by, stuffed with, laden with, heavy with, bristling with, replete with, abounding with

fray[1] NOUN *Today he entered the fray on the side of the moderates.* = **fight**, battle, row, conflict, clash, set-to (*informal*), riot, combat, disturbance, rumble (*U.S. & N.Z. slang*), quarrel, brawl, skirmish, scuffle, rumpus, broil, affray (*Law*), shindig (*informal*), donnybrook, battle royal, ruckus (*informal*), scrimmage, shindy (*informal*), bagarre (*French*), melee or mêlée, biffo (*Austral. slang*), boilover (*Austral.*)

fray[2] VERB *The stitching had begun to fray at the edges.* = **wear thin**, wear, rub, fret, wear out, chafe, wear away, become threadbare

frayed ADJECTIVE **1** *a shapeless and frayed jumper* = **worn**, ragged, worn out, tattered, threadbare, worn thin, out at elbows **2** *Nerves are frayed all round.* = **strained**, stressed, tense, edgy, uptight (*informal*), frazzled

freak MODIFIER *The ferry was hit by a freak wave off the coast.* = **abnormal**, chance, unusual, unexpected, exceptional, unpredictable, queer, erratic, unparalleled, unforeseen, fortuitous, unaccountable, atypical, aberrant, fluky (*informal*), odd, bizarre ▶ NOUN **1** *He's a self-confessed computer freak.* = **enthusiast**, fan, nut (*slang*), addict, buff (*informal*), fanatic, devotee, fiend (*informal*), aficionado **2** *The cast consisted of a bunch of freaks and social misfits.* = **eccentric**, oddity, case (*informal*), character (*informal*), flake (*slang, chiefly U.S.*), oddball (*informal*), nonconformist, screwball (*slang, chiefly U.S. & Canad.*), odd fish (*informal*), kook (*U.S. & Canad. informal*), queer fish (*Brit. informal*)

freakish ADJECTIVE *a freakish monstrous thing, something out of a dream* = **odd**, strange, fantastic, weird, abnormal, monstrous, grotesque, unnatural, unconventional, outlandish, freaky (*slang*), aberrant, outré, malformed, preternatural, teratoid (*Biology*)

freaky ADJECTIVE = **weird**, odd, wild, strange, crazy, bizarre, abnormal, queer, rum (*Brit. slang*), unconventional, far-out (*slang*), freakish

free ADJECTIVE **1** *The seminars are free, with lunch provided.* = **complimentary**, for free (*informal*), for nothing, unpaid, for love, free of charge, on the house, without charge, gratuitous, at no cost, gratis, buckshee (*Brit. slang*), open *or* open source (*Computing*) **2** *The government will be free to pursue its economic policies.* = **allowed**, permitted, unrestricted, unimpeded, open, clear, able, loose, unattached, unregulated, disengaged, untrammelled, unobstructed, unhampered, unengaged **3** *All the hostages are free.* = **at liberty**, loose, liberated, at large, off the hook (*slang*), on the loose ■ OPPOSITE: confined **4** *I was young, free and single at the time.* = **independent**, unfettered, unrestrained, uncommitted, footloose, unconstrained, unengaged, not tied down **5** *There's only one seat free on the train.* = **available**, extra, empty, spare, vacant, unused, uninhabited, unoccupied, untaken **6** (*often with of or with*) *They weren't always so free with their advice.* = **generous**, willing, liberal, eager, lavish, charitable, hospitable, prodigal, bountiful, open-handed, unstinting, unsparing, bounteous, munificent, big (*informal*) ■ OPPOSITE: mean **7** *We cannot survive as a free nation.* = **autonomous**, independent, democratic, sovereign, self-ruling, self-governing, emancipated, self-determining, autarchic **8** *a confidential but free manner* = **relaxed**, open, easy, forward, natural, frank, liberal, familiar, loose, casual, informal, spontaneous, laid-back (*informal*), easy-going (*informal*), lax, uninhibited, unforced, free and easy, unbidden, unconstrained, unceremonious ■ OPPOSITE: formal ▶ ADVERB *Two stubby legs swing free.* = **freely**, easily, loosely, smoothly, idly ▶ VERB **1** (*often with of or from*) *It will free us of a whole lot of debt.* = **clear**, deliver, disengage, cut loose, release, rescue, rid, relieve, exempt, undo,

redeem, ransom, extricate, unburden, unshackle **2** *They are going to free more prisoners.* = **release**, liberate, let out, set free, deliver, loose, discharge, unleash, let go, untie, emancipate, unchain, turn loose, uncage, set at liberty, unfetter, disenthrall, unbridle, manumit ■ OPPOSITE: confine **3** *It took firefighters two hours to free us.* = **disentangle**, extricate, disengage, detach, separate, loose, unfold, unravel, disconnect, untangle, untwist, unsnarl
• **free and easy** *She had a free and easy approach.* = **relaxed**, liberal, casual, informal, tolerant, laid-back (*informal*), easy-going, lax, lenient, uninhibited, unceremonious • **free of** *or* **from** *She retains her slim figure and is free of wrinkles.* = **unaffected by**, without, above, lacking (in), beyond, clear of, devoid of, exempt from, immune to, sans (*archaic*), safe from, untouched by, deficient in, unencumbered by, not liable to

freedom NOUN **1** *They want greater political freedom.* = **independence**, democracy, sovereignty, autonomy, self-determination, emancipation, self-government, home rule, autarchy, rangatiratanga (*N.Z.*) **2** *All hostages and detainees would gain their freedom.* = **liberty**, release, discharge, emancipation, deliverance, manumission ■ OPPOSITE: captivity **3** (*usually with from*) *freedom from government control* = **exemption**, release, relief, privilege, immunity, impunity **4** *freedom to buy and sell at the best price* = **licence**, latitude, a free hand, free rein, play, power, range, opportunity, ability, facility, scope, flexibility, discretion, leeway, carte blanche, blank cheque, elbowroom ■ OPPOSITE: restriction **5** *His freedom of manner ran contrary to the norm.* = **openness**, ease, directness, naturalness, abandon, familiarity, candour, frankness, informality, casualness, ingenuousness, lack of restraint *or* reserve, unconstraint ■ OPPOSITE: restraint

free-for-all NOUN = **fight**, row, riot, brawl, fracas, affray (*Law*), dust-up (*informal*), shindig (*informal*), donnybrook, scrimmage, shindy (*informal*), bagarre (*French*), melee *or* mêlée, biffo (*Austral. slang*)

freely ADVERB **1** *She was spending very freely.* = **abundantly**, liberally, lavishly, like water, extravagantly, copiously, unstintingly, with a free hand, bountifully, open-handedly, amply **2** *He had someone to whom he could talk freely.* = **openly**, frankly, plainly, candidly, unreservedly, straightforwardly, without reserve **3** *I freely admit that I live for racing.*

f

= **willingly**, readily, voluntarily, spontaneously, without prompting, of your own free will, of your own accord **4** *You must allow the clubhead to swing freely.* = **easily**, cleanly, loosely, smoothly, readily **5** *They cast their votes freely.* = **without restraint**, voluntarily, willingly, unchallenged, as you please, without being forced, without let or hindrance

freeway NOUN (*U.S. & Austral.*) = **motorway** (*Brit.*), autobahn (*German*), autoroute (*French*), autostrada (*Italian*)

freewheel VERB = **coast**, drift, glide, relax your efforts, rest on your oars, float

freeze VERB **1** *The ground froze solid.* = **ice over** *or* **up**, harden, stiffen, solidify, congeal, become solid, glaciate **2** *The cold morning froze my fingers.* = **chill**, benumb **3** *Wages have been frozen and workers laid off.* = **fix**, hold, limit, hold up, peg **4** *They have already frozen their aid programme.* = **suspend**, stop, shelve, curb, cut short, discontinue

freezing ADJECTIVE **1** *a freezing January afternoon* = **icy**, biting, bitter, raw, chill, chilled, penetrating, arctic (*informal*), numbing, polar, Siberian, frosty, glacial, wintry, parky (*Brit. informal*), cold as ice, frost-bound, cutting **2** *You must be freezing!* = **frozen**, chilled, numb, chilly, very cold, shivery, benumbed, frozen to the marrow

freight NOUN **1** *France derives 16% of revenue from air freight.* = **transportation**, traffic, delivery, carriage, shipment, haulage, conveyance, transport **2** *26 tonnes of freight* = **cargo**, goods, contents, load, lading, delivery, burden, haul, bulk, shipment, merchandise, bales, consignment, payload, tonnage

French ADJECTIVE *All the staff are French.* = **Gallic** ■ RELATED WORDS: *prefixes* Franco-, Gallo-

frenetic ADJECTIVE = **frantic**, wild, excited, crazy, frenzied, fanatical, unbalanced, overwrought, maniacal

frenzied ADJECTIVE = **uncontrolled**, wild, excited, mad, crazy, furious, frantic, distraught, hysterical, agitated, frenetic, feverish, rabid, maniacal

frenzy NOUN **1** *The country was gripped by a frenzy of nationalism.* = **fit**, burst, bout, outburst, spasm, convulsion, paroxysm **2** *Something like a frenzy enveloped them.* = **fury**, transport, passion, rage, madness, turmoil, distraction, seizure, hysteria, mania, agitation, aberration, delirium, paroxysm ■ OPPOSITE: calm

frequency NOUN = **recurrence**, repetition, constancy, periodicity, commonness, frequentness, prevalence

frequent ADJECTIVE *He is a frequent visitor to the house.* = **common**, repeated, usual, familiar, constant, everyday, persistent, reiterated, recurring, customary, continual, recurrent, habitual, incessant ■ OPPOSITE: infrequent ▶ VERB *I hear she frequents that restaurant.* = **visit**, attend, haunt, be found at, patronize, hang out at (*informal*), visit often, go to regularly, be a regular customer of ■ OPPOSITE: keep away

frequently ADVERB = **often**, commonly, repeatedly, many times, very often, oft (*archaic, poetic*), over and over again, habitually, customarily, oftentimes (*archaic*), not infrequently, many a time, much ■ OPPOSITE: infrequently

fresh ADJECTIVE **1** *He asked the police to make fresh enquiries.* = **additional**, more, new, other, added, further, extra, renewed, supplementary, auxiliary **2** *A meal with fresh ingredients doesn't take long to prepare.* = **natural**, raw, crude, unsalted, unprocessed, uncured, unpreserved, undried, green ■ OPPOSITE: preserved **3** *These designers are full of fresh ideas.* = **new**, original, novel, unusual, latest, different, recent, modern, up-to-date, this season's, unconventional, unorthodox, ground-breaking, left-field (*informal*), new-fangled, modernistic ■ OPPOSITE: old **4** *The air was fresh and she felt revived.* = **invigorating**, clear, clean, bright, sweet, pure, stiff, crisp, sparkling, bracing, refreshing, brisk, spanking, unpolluted ■ OPPOSITE: stale **5** *The breeze was fresh and from the north.* = **cool**, cold, refreshing, brisk, chilly, nippy **6** *a semi-circular mosaic, its colours still fresh* = **vivid**, bright, verdant (*literary*), undimmed, unfaded ■ OPPOSITE: old **7** *His fresh complexion made him look young.* = **rosy**, clear, fair, bright, healthy, glowing, hardy, blooming, wholesome, ruddy, florid, dewy, good ■ OPPOSITE: pallid **8** *I nearly always wake up fresh and rested.* = **lively**, rested, bright, keen, vital, restored, alert, bouncing, revived, refreshed, vigorous, energetic, sprightly, invigorated, spry, chipper (*informal*), full of beans (*informal*), like a new man *or* woman *or* person, full of vim and vigour, unwearied, bright-eyed and bushy-tailed (*informal*) ■ OPPOSITE: weary **9** *The soldiers were fresh recruits.* = **inexperienced**, new, young, green, natural, raw, youthful, unqualified, callow, untrained, untried, artless, uncultivated, wet behind the ears ■ OPPOSITE: experienced **10** *Don't get fresh with me.* = **cheeky** (*informal*), bold, brazen, impertinent, forward, familiar, flip (*informal*), saucy, audacious, sassy (*U.S. informal*), pert, disrespectful, presumptuous, insolent, impudent, smart-alecky (*informal*) ■ **OPPOSITE:** well-mannered

freshen VERB = **refresh**, restore, rouse, enliven, revitalize, spruce up, liven up, freshen up, titivate

freshness NOUN **1** *They have a freshness and individuality that others lack.* = **novelty**, creativity, originality, inventiveness, newness, innovativeness **2** *the freshness of early morning* = **cleanness**, shine, glow, bloom, sparkle, vigour, brightness, wholesomeness, clearness, dewiness

fret VERB **1** *I was constantly fretting about others' problems.* = **worry**, anguish, brood, agonize, obsess, lose sleep, upset yourself, distress yourself **2** *The quickening of time frets me.* = **annoy**, trouble, bother, disturb, distress, provoke, irritate, grieve, torment, harass, nag, gall, agitate, ruffle, nettle, vex, goad, chagrin, irk, rile, pique, peeve (*informal*), rankle with

friction NOUN **1** *There was friction between the children.* = **conflict**, opposition, hostility, resentment, disagreement, rivalry, discontent, wrangling, bickering, animosity, antagonism, discord, bad feeling, bad blood, dissension, incompatibility, disharmony, dispute **2** *The pistons are graphite-coated to prevent friction.* = **resistance**, rubbing, scraping, grating, irritation, erosion, fretting, attrition, rasping, chafing, abrasion, wearing away

friend NOUN **1** *I had a long talk with my best friend.* = **companion**, pal (*informal*), mate (*informal*), buddy (*informal*), partner, china (*Brit. & S. African informal*), familiar, best friend, intimate, close friend, comrade, chum (*informal*), crony, alter ego, confidant, playmate, confidante, blood (*Brit. slang*), main man (*slang, chiefly U.S.*), soul mate, homeboy (*slang, chiefly U.S.*), cobber (*Austral. & N.Z.*), cuzzie or cuzzie-bro (*N.Z.*), E hoa (*N.Z., old-fashioned, informal*), bosom friend, boon companion, Achates ■ **OPPOSITE:** foe **2** *the Friends of Birmingham Royal Ballet* = **supporter**, ally, associate, sponsor, advocate, patron, backer, partisan, protagonist, benefactor, adherent, well-wisher ▶ VERB (*Computing*) = **add**, follow ■ **OPPOSITES:** defriend, unfollow

friendliness NOUN = **amiability**, warmth, sociability, conviviality, neighbourliness, affability, geniality, kindliness, congeniality, companionability, mateyness or matiness (*Brit. informal*), open arms

friendly ADJECTIVE **1** *He has been friendly to me.* = **amiable**, kind, kindly, welcoming, warm, neighbourly, thick (*informal*), attached, pally (*informal*), helpful, sympathetic, fond, outgoing, comradely, confiding, affectionate, receptive, benevolent, attentive, sociable, genial, affable, fraternal, good, close, on good terms, chummy (*informal*), peaceable, companionable, clubby, well-disposed, buddy-buddy (*slang, chiefly U.S. & Canad.*), palsy-walsy (*informal*), matey or maty (*Brit. informal*), on visiting terms **2** *a friendly atmosphere* = **amicable**, warm, familiar, pleasant, intimate, informal, benign, conciliatory, cordial, congenial, convivial ■ **OPPOSITE:** unfriendly

friendship NOUN **1** *They struck up a close friendship.* = **attachment**, relationship, bond, alliance, link, association, tie, bromance (*informal*) **2** *a whole new world of friendship and adventure* = **friendliness**, affection, harmony, goodwill, intimacy, affinity, familiarity, closeness, rapport, fondness, companionship, concord, benevolence, comradeship, amity (*formal*), good-fellowship ■ **OPPOSITE:** unfriendliness **3** *He really values your friendship.* = **closeness**, love, regard, affection, intimacy, fondness, companionship, comradeship

fright NOUN **1** *To hide my fright I asked a question.* = **fear**, shock, alarm, horror, panic, terror, dread, dismay, quaking, apprehension, consternation, trepidation (*formal*), cold sweat, fear and trembling, (blue) funk (*informal*) ■ **OPPOSITE:** courage **2** *The snake gave everyone a fright.* = **scare**, start, turn (*informal*), surprise, shock, jolt, the creeps (*informal*), the shivers, the willies (*slang*), the heebie-jeebies (*slang*) **3** *She looked a fright in a long dark wig.* = **sight** (*informal*), mess (*informal*), eyesore, scarecrow

frighten VERB = **scare**, shock, alarm, terrify, cow, appal, startle, intimidate, dismay, daunt, unnerve, petrify, unman, terrorize, scare (someone) stiff, put the wind up (someone) (*informal*), scare the living daylights out of (someone) (*informal*), make your hair stand on end (*informal*), get the wind up, make your blood run cold, throw into a panic, affright (*archaic*), freeze your blood, make (someone) jump out of their skin (*informal*), throw into a fright ■ **OPPOSITE:** reassure

frightened ADJECTIVE = **afraid**, alarmed, scared, terrified, shocked, frozen, cowed, startled, dismayed, unnerved, petrified, flustered, panicky, terrorized, in a panic, scared stiff, in a cold sweat, abashed, terror-stricken, affrighted (*archaic*), in fear and trepidation, numb with fear

frightening ADJECTIVE = **terrifying**, shocking (*informal*), alarming, appalling, startling, dreadful, horrifying, menacing, intimidating, dismaying, scary (*informal*), fearful, daunting, fearsome, unnerving, spooky (*informal*), hair-raising, baleful, spine-chilling, bloodcurdling

frightful ADJECTIVE **1** *refugees trapped in frightful conditions* = **terrible**, shocking (*informal*), alarming, awful, appalling, horrible, grim, terrifying, dreadful, dread (*literary*), fearful (*informal*), traumatic, dire, horrendous, ghastly, hideous, harrowing, gruesome, unnerving, lurid, from hell (*informal*), grisly, macabre, petrifying, horrid, unspeakable, godawful (*slang*), hellacious (*U.S. slang*) ■ OPPOSITE: pleasant **2** *He got himself into a frightful muddle.* = **dreadful**, great, terrible, extreme, awful, annoying, unpleasant, disagreeable, insufferable ■ OPPOSITE: slight

frigid ADJECTIVE **1** *The water was too frigid to allow him to remain submerged.* = **freezing**, cold, frozen, icy, chill, arctic (*informal*), Siberian, frosty, cool, glacial, wintry, gelid, frost-bound, hyperboreal ■ OPPOSITE: hot **2** *She replied with a frigid smile.* = **chilly**, formal, stiff, forbidding, rigid, passive, icy, austere, aloof, lifeless, repellent, unresponsive, unfeeling, unbending, unapproachable, passionless, unloving, cold as ice, cold-hearted ■ OPPOSITE: warm

frill NOUN **1** *net curtains with frills* = **ruffle**, gathering, tuck, ruff, flounce, ruche, ruching, furbelow, purfle **2** (*often plural*) *The booklet restricts itself to facts without frills.* = **trimmings**, extras, additions, fuss, jazz (*slang*), dressing up, decoration(s), bits and pieces, icing on the cake, finery, embellishments, affectation(s), ornamentation, ostentation, frippery, bells and whistles, tomfoolery, gewgaws, superfluities, fanciness, frilliness, fandangles

frilly ADJECTIVE = **ruffled**, fancy, lacy, frothy, ruched, flouncy

fringe NOUN **1** *The jacket had leather fringes.* = **border**, edging, edge, binding, trimming, hem, frill, tassel, flounce **2** *They lived together on the fringe of the campus.* = **edge**, limits, border, margin, march, marches, outskirts, perimeter, periphery, borderline ▶ MODIFIER *numerous fringe meetings held during the conference* = **unofficial**, alternative, radical, innovative, avant-

garde, unconventional, unorthodox ▶ VERB *Swampy islands of vegetation fringe the coastline.* = **border**, edge, surround, bound, skirt, trim, enclose, flank

fringed ADJECTIVE **1** *She wore a fringed scarf.* = **bordered**, edged, befringed **2** *tiny islands fringed with golden sand* = **edged**, bordered, margined, outlined

frisk VERB **1** *He pushed him against the wall and frisked him.* = **search**, check, inspect, run over, shake down (*U.S. slang*), body-search **2** *creatures that grunted and frisked about* = **frolic**, play, sport, dance, trip, jump, bounce, hop, skip, romp, caper, prance, cavort, gambol, rollick, curvet

frisky ADJECTIVE = **lively**, spirited, romping, playful, bouncy, high-spirited, rollicking, in high spirits, full of beans (*informal*), coltish, kittenish, frolicsome, ludic (*literary*), sportive, full of joie de vivre ■ OPPOSITE: sedate

fritter VERB (*usually with* **away**) = **squander**, waste, run through, dissipate, misspend, idle away, fool away, spend like water

frivolous ADJECTIVE **1** *I was a bit too frivolous to be a doctor.* = **flippant**, foolish, dizzy (*informal*), superficial, silly, flip (*informal*), juvenile, idle, childish, giddy, puerile, flighty, ill-considered, empty-headed, light-hearted, nonserious, light-minded, ditzy or ditsy (*slang*) ■ OPPOSITE: serious **2** *wasting money on frivolous projects* = **trivial**, petty, trifling, unimportant, light, minor, shallow, pointless, extravagant, peripheral, niggling, paltry, impractical, nickel-and-dime (*U.S. slang*), footling (*informal*) ■ OPPOSITE: important

frivolousness *or* **frivolity** NOUN = **flippancy**, fun, nonsense, folly, trifling, lightness, jest, gaiety, silliness, triviality, superficiality, levity, shallowness, childishness, giddiness, flummery, light-heartedness, puerility, flightiness, frivolousness ■ OPPOSITE: seriousness

frizzy ADJECTIVE = **tight-curled**, crisp, corrugated, wiry, crimped, frizzed

frog NOUN ■ RELATED WORD: *name of young tadpole*

frolic NOUN *Their relationship is never short on fun and frolic.* = **merriment**, sport, fun, amusement, gaiety, fun and games, skylarking (*informal*), high jinks, drollery ▶ VERB *Tourists sunbathe and frolic in the ocean.* = **play**, romp, lark, caper, cavort, frisk, gambol, make merry, rollick, cut capers, sport

front NOUN **1** *Stand at the front of the line.* = **head**, start, lead, beginning, top, fore, forefront **2** *Attached to the front of the house* *was a veranda.* = **exterior**, facing, face, façade, frontage, anterior, obverse, forepart **3** *the front of the picture* = **foreground**, fore, forefront, nearest part **4** *Her husband is fighting at the front.* = **front line**, trenches, vanguard, firing line, van **5** *He kept up a brave front.* = **appearance**, show, face, air, bearing, aspect, manner, expression, exterior, countenance (*literary*), demeanour, mien (*literary*) **6** *a front for crime syndicates* = **disguise**, cover, blind, mask, cover-up, cloak, façade, pretext ▶ ADJECTIVE **1** *She is still missing her front teeth.* = **foremost**, at the front ■ OPPOSITE: back **2** *He is the front runner for the star role.* = **leading**, first, lead, head, foremost, topmost, headmost ▶ VERB (*often with* **on** *or* **onto**) *Victorian houses fronting onto the pavement* = **face onto**, overlook, look out on, have a view of, look over or onto

frontier NOUN = **border**, limit, edge, bound, boundary, confines, verge (*Brit.*), perimeter, borderline, dividing line, borderland, marches

frost NOUN = **hoarfrost**, freeze, freeze-up, Jack Frost, rime

frosty ADJECTIVE **1** *sharp, frosty nights* = **cold**, frozen, icy, chilly, wintry, parky (*Brit. informal*) **2** *a cat lifting its paws off the frosty stones* = **icy**, ice-capped, icicled, hoar (*rare*), rimy **3** *He may get a frosty reception.* = **unfriendly**, discouraging, icy, frigid, off-putting (*Brit. informal*), unenthusiastic, unwelcoming, standoffish, cold as ice

froth NOUN *the froth on the top of a glass of beer* = **foam**, head, bubbles, lather, suds, spume, effervescence, scum ▶ VERB *The sea froths over my feet.* = **fizz**, foam, come to a head, lather, bubble over, effervesce

frothy ADJECTIVE **1** *frothy milk shakes* = **foamy**, foaming, bubbly, effervescent, sudsy, spumous, spumescent, spumy **2** *the kind of frothy songs one hears* = **trivial**, light, empty, slight, unnecessary, vain, petty, trifling, frivolous, frilly, unsubstantial

frown VERB *He frowned at her anxiously.* = **scowl**, glare, glower, make a face, look daggers, knit your brows, give a dirty look, lour or lower ▶ NOUN *a deep frown on the boy's face* = **scowl**, glare, glower, dirty look • **frown on** *This practice is frowned upon as being wasteful.* = **disapprove of**, dislike, discourage, take a dim view of, look askance at, discountenance, view with disfavour, not take kindly to, show disapproval or displeasure

frozen ADJECTIVE **1** *the frozen bleakness of the Far North* = **icy**, hard, solid, frosted, arctic (*informal*), ice-covered, icebound **2** *frozen*

desserts like ice cream = **chilled**, cold, iced, refrigerated, ice-cold **3** *I'm frozen out here.* = **ice-cold**, freezing, numb, very cold, frigid, frozen stiff, chilled to the marrow **4** *She was frozen in horror.* = **motionless**, rooted, petrified, stock-still, turned to stone, stopped dead in your tracks **5** *Prices would be frozen and wages raised.* = **fixed**, held, stopped, limited, suspended, pegged (*of a price*)

frugal ADJECTIVE **1** *She lives a frugal life.* = **thrifty**, sparing, careful, prudent, provident, parsimonious, abstemious, penny-wise, saving, cheeseparing ■ OPPOSITE: wasteful **2** *Her diet was frugal.* = **meagre**, economical, niggardly

fruit NOUN **1** *The fruit has got a long storage life.* = **produce**, crop, yield, harvest **2** (*often plural*) *The findings are the fruit of more than three years' research.* = **result**, reward, outcome, end result, return, effect, benefit, profit, advantage, consequence

fruitful ADJECTIVE **1** *We had a long, fruitful relationship.* = **useful**, successful, effective, rewarding, profitable, productive, worthwhile, beneficial, advantageous, well-spent, gainful ■ OPPOSITE: useless **2** *a landscape that was fruitful and lush* = **fertile**, fecund, fructiferous ■ OPPOSITE: barren **3** *blossoms on a fruitful tree* = **productive**, prolific, abundant, plentiful, rich, flush, spawning, copious, profuse, plenteous

fruition NOUN = **fulfilment**, maturity, completion, perfection, enjoyment, realization, attainment, maturation, consummation, ripeness, actualization, materialization

fruitless ADJECTIVE = **useless**, vain, unsuccessful, in vain, pointless, futile, unproductive, abortive, to no avail, ineffectual, unprofitable, to no effect, unavailing, unfruitful, profitless, bootless ■ OPPOSITE: fruitful

fruity ADJECTIVE **1** *a lovely, fruity wine* = **rich**, full, mellow **2** *He had a solid, fruity laugh.* = **resonant**, full, deep, rich, vibrant, mellow **3** *a fruity joke* = **risqué**, indecent, suggestive, racy, blue, ripe, spicy (*informal*), vulgar, juicy, titillating, bawdy, salacious, smutty, indelicate, near the knuckle (*informal*)

frumpy *or* **frumpish** ADJECTIVE = **dowdy**, dated, dreary, out of date, drab, unfashionable, dingy, mumsy, badly-dressed

frustrate VERB **1** *These questions frustrated me.* = **discourage**, anger, depress, annoy, infuriate, exasperate, dishearten, dissatisfy ■ OPPOSITE: encourage **2** *The government*

has deliberately frustrated his efforts. = **thwart**, stop, check, block, defeat, disappoint, counter, confront, spoil, foil, baffle, inhibit, hobble, balk, circumvent, forestall, neutralize, stymie, nullify, render null and void, crool or cruel (Austral. slang)
■ **OPPOSITE:** further

frustrated ADJECTIVE = **disappointed**, discouraged, infuriated, discontented, exasperated, resentful, embittered, irked, disheartened, carrying a chip on your shoulder (informal)

frustration NOUN **1** a man fed up with the frustrations of everyday life = **annoyance**, disappointment, resentment, irritation, grievance, dissatisfaction, exasperation, vexation **2** the frustration of their plan = **obstruction**, blocking, curbing, foiling, failure, spoiling, thwarting, contravention, circumvention, nonfulfilment, nonsuccess

fudge VERB = **misrepresent**, avoid, dodge, evade, hedge, stall, fake, flannel (Brit. informal), patch up, falsify, equivocate

fuel NOUN **1** Babies and toddlers need fuel for growth. = **nourishment**, food, kai (N.Z. informal), sustenance **2** His comments are bound to add fuel to the debate. = **incitement**, encouragement, ammunition, provocation, food, material, incentive, fodder ▸ VERB The economic boom was fuelled by easy credit. = **inflame**, power, charge, fire, fan, encourage, feed, boost, sustain, stimulate, nourish, incite, whip up, stoke up

fugitive NOUN = **runaway**, refugee, deserter, outlaw, escapee, runagate (archaic)

fulfil or (U.S.) **fulfill** VERB **1** He is too ill to fulfil his duties. = **carry out**, perform, execute, discharge, keep, effect, finish, complete, achieve, conclude, accomplish, bring to completion ■ **OPPOSITE:** neglect **2** He decided to fulfil his dream and go to college. = **achieve**, realize, satisfy, attain, consummate, bring to fruition, perfect **3** After the war, nothing quite fulfilled her. = **satisfy**, please, content, cheer, refresh, gratify, make happy **4** All the necessary conditions were fulfilled. = **comply with**, meet, fill, satisfy, observe, obey, conform to, answer

fulfilment or (U.S.) **fulfillment** NOUN = **achievement**, effecting, implementation, carrying out or through, end, crowning, discharge, discharging, completion, perfection, accomplishment, realization, attainment, observance, consummation

full ADJECTIVE **1** Repeat the layers until the terrine is full. = **filled**, stocked, brimming, replete, complete, entire, loaded, sufficient, intact, gorged, saturated, bursting at the seams, brimful **2** The centre is full beyond capacity. = **crammed**, crowded, packed, crushed, jammed, in use, congested, chock-full, chock-a-block
■ **OPPOSITE:** empty **3** The cheap seats were all full. = **occupied**, taken, in use, unavailable **4** It's healthy to stop eating when I'm full. = **satiated**, satisfied, having had enough, replete, sated **5** Full details will be sent to you. = **extensive**, detailed, complete, broad, generous, adequate, ample, abundant, plentiful, copious, plenary, plenteous
■ **OPPOSITE:** incomplete **6** They can now publish a full list of candidates. = **comprehensive**, complete, thorough, exhaustive, all-inclusive, all-embracing, unabridged **7** Italian plum tomatoes have a full flavour. = **rounded**, strong, rich, powerful, intense, pungent **8** large sizes for customers with a fuller figure = **plump**, rounded, voluptuous, shapely, well-rounded, buxom, curvaceous (informal) **9** My wedding dress has a very full skirt. = **voluminous**, large, loose, baggy, billowing, puffy, capacious, loose-fitting, balloon-like ■ **OPPOSITE:** tight **10** She has a full voice; mine is a bit lighter. = **rich**, strong, deep, loud, distinct, resonant, sonorous, clear ■ **OPPOSITE:** thin • **in full** We will refund your money in full. = **completely**, fully, in total, without exception, in its entirety, in toto (Latin) • **to the full** She has a good mind which should be used to the full. = **thoroughly**, completely, fully, entirely, to the limit, without reservation, to the utmost

full-blooded ADJECTIVE = **wholehearted**, full, complete, sweeping, thorough, uncompromising, exhaustive, all-embracing

full-blown ADJECTIVE **1** You're talking this thing up into a full-blown conspiracy. = **fully developed**, total, full-scale, fully fledged, full, whole, developed, complete, advanced, entire, full-sized, fully grown, fully formed ■ **OPPOSITE:** undeveloped **2** the faded hues of full-blown roses = **in full bloom**, full, flowering, unfolded, blossoming, opened out

full-bodied ADJECTIVE = **rich**, strong, big, heavy, heady, mellow, fruity, redolent, full-flavoured, well-matured

fullness or (U.S.) **fulness** NOUN **1** High-fibre diets give the feeling of fullness. = **plenty**, glut, saturation, sufficiency, profusion, satiety, repletion, copiousness, ampleness, adequateness **2** She displayed the fullness of her cycling talent. = **completeness**, wealth, entirety, totality, wholeness, vastness, plenitude, comprehensiveness, broadness, extensiveness **3** *I accept my body with all its curves and fullness.* = **roundness**, voluptuousness, curvaceousness, swelling, enlargement, dilation, distension, tumescence **4** *with modest riffs and a fullness in sound* = **richness**, strength, resonance, loudness, clearness

full-scale ADJECTIVE = **major**, extensive, wide-ranging, all-out, sweeping, comprehensive, proper, thorough, in-depth, exhaustive, all-encompassing, thoroughgoing, full-dress

fully ADVERB **1** *She was fully aware of my thoughts.* = **completely**, totally, perfectly, entirely, absolutely, altogether, thoroughly, intimately, wholly, positively, utterly, every inch, heart and soul, to the hilt, one hundred per cent, in all respects, from first to last, lock, stock and barrel **2** *He had still not fully recovered.* = **in all respects**, completely, totally, entirely, altogether, thoroughly, wholly **3** *These debates are discussed fully later in the book.* = **adequately**, amply, comprehensively, sufficiently, enough, satisfactorily, abundantly, plentifully **4** *He set his sights and let fly from fully 35 yards.* = **at least**, quite, without (any) exaggeration, without a word of a lie (*informal*)

fully-fledged *or* **full-fledged** ADJECTIVE = **experienced**, trained, senior, professional, qualified, mature, proficient, time-served

fulsome ADJECTIVE = **extravagant**, excessive, over the top, sickening, overdone, fawning, nauseating, inordinate, ingratiating, cloying, insincere, saccharine, sycophantic, unctuous, smarmy (*Brit. informal*), immoderate, adulatory, gross

> USAGE In journalism, *fulsome* is often used simply to mean 'extremely complimentary' or 'full, rich, or abundant'. In other kinds of writing, however, this word should only be used if you intend to suggest negative overtones of excess or insincerity.

fumble VERB **1** (*often with* **for** *or* **with**) *She crept from the bed and fumbled for her dressing gown.* = **grope**, flounder, paw (*informal*), scrabble, feel around **2** *I'd hate to fumble a chance like this.* = **bungle**, spoil, botch, mess up, cock up (*Brit. slang*), mishandle, mismanage, muff, make a hash of (*informal*), make a nonsense of, bodge (*informal*), misfield, crool *or* cruel (*Austral. slang*)

fume VERB *I fumed when my proposal was rejected.* = **rage**, boil, seethe, see red (*informal*), storm, rave, rant, smoulder, crack up (*informal*), go ballistic (*slang*), champ at the bit (*informal*), blow a fuse (*slang, chiefly U.S.*), fly off the handle (*informal*), get hot under the collar (*informal*), go off the deep end (*informal*), wig out (*slang*), go up the wall (*slang*), get steamed up about (*slang*) ▶ NOUN **1** (*often plural*) *car exhaust fumes* = **smoke**, gas, exhaust, pollution, haze, vapour, smog, miasma, exhalation, effluvium **2** *stale alcohol fumes* = **stench**, stink, whiff (*Brit. slang*), reek, pong (*Brit. informal*), foul smell, niff (*Brit. slang*), malodour, mephitis, fetor, noisomeness

fuming ADJECTIVE = **furious**, angry, raging, choked, roused, incensed, enraged, seething, up in arms, incandescent, in a rage, on the warpath (*informal*), foaming at the mouth, at boiling point (*informal*), all steamed up (*slang*), tooshie (*Austral. slang*)

fun NOUN **1** *You still have time to join in the fun.* = **amusement**, sport, treat, pleasure, entertainment, cheer, good time, recreation, enjoyment, romp, distraction, diversion, frolic, junketing, merriment, whoopee (*informal*), high jinks, living it up, jollity, beer and skittles (*informal*), merrymaking, jollification **2** *There was lots of fun going on last night.* = **joking**, clowning, merriment, playfulness, play, game, sport, nonsense, teasing, jesting, skylarking (*informal*), horseplay, buffoonery, tomfoolery, jocularity, foolery **3** *She had a great sense of fun.* = **enjoyment**, pleasure, joy, cheer, mirth, gaiety ■ OPPOSITE: gloom ▶ MODIFIER *It was a fun evening.* = **enjoyable**, entertaining, pleasant, amusing, lively, diverting, witty, convivial • **for** *or* **in fun** *Don't say such things, even in fun.* = **for a joke**, tongue in cheek, jokingly, playfully, for a laugh, mischievously, in jest, teasingly, with a straight face, facetiously, light-heartedly, roguishly, with a gleam *or* twinkle in your eye • **make fun of something** *or* **someone** *Don't make fun of me!* = **mock**, tease, ridicule, poke fun at, take off, rag, rib (*informal*), laugh at, taunt, mimic, parody, deride, send up (*Brit. informal*), scoff at, sneer at, lampoon, make a fool of, pour scorn on, take the mickey out of (*Brit. informal*), satirize, pull someone's leg, hold up to ridicule, make a monkey of, make sport of, make the butt of, make game of

function NOUN **1** *The main function of merchant banks is to raise capital.* = **purpose**, business, job, concern, use, part, office, charge, role, post, operation, situation, activity, exercise, responsibility, task, duty, mission, employment, capacity, province, occupation, raison d'être (*French*) **2** *We were going down to a function in London.* = **reception**, party, affair, gathering, bash (*informal*), lig (*Brit. slang*), social occasion, soiree, do (*informal*) ▶ VERB **1** *The authorities say the prison is now functioning properly.* = **work**, run, operate, perform, be in business, be in running order, be in operation or action, go **2** (*with* **as**) *On weekdays, one third of the room functions as a workspace.* = **act**, serve, operate, perform, behave, officiate, act the part of, do duty, have the role of, be in commission, be in operation or action, serve your turn

functional ADJECTIVE **1** *The decor is functional.* = **practical**, utility, utilitarian, serviceable, hard-wearing, useful **2** *We have fully functional smoke alarms on all staircases.* = **working**, operative, operational, in working order, going, prepared, ready, viable, up and running, workable, usable

functionary NOUN = **officer**, official, dignitary, office holder, office bearer, employee

fund NOUN **1** *a scholarship fund for undergraduate students* = **reserve**, stock, supply, store, collection, pool, foundation, endowment, tontine **2** *He has an extraordinary fund of energy.* = **store**, stock, source, supply, mine, reserve, treasury, vein, reservoir, accumulation, hoard, repository ▶ VERB *The foundation has funded a variety of faculty programs.* = **finance**, back, support, pay for, promote, float, endow, subsidize, stake, capitalize, provide money for, put up the money for

fundamental ADJECTIVE **1** *the fundamental principles of democracy* = **central**, first, most important, prime, key, necessary, basic, essential, primary, vital, radical, principal, cardinal, integral, indispensable, intrinsic ■ OPPOSITE: incidental **2** *The two leaders have very fundamental differences.* = **basic**, essential, underlying, organic, profound, elementary, rudimentary

fundamentally ADVERB **1** *Fundamentally, women like him for his sensitivity.* = **basically**, at heart, at bottom **2** *He disagreed fundamentally with her judgment.* = **essentially**, radically, basically, primarily, profoundly, intrinsically

fundi NOUN (*S. African*) = **expert**, authority, specialist, professional, master, pro (*informal*), ace (*informal*), genius, guru, pundit, buff (*informal*), maestro, virtuoso,

boffin (*Brit. informal*), hotshot (*informal*), past master, dab hand (*Brit. informal*), wonk (*informal*), maven (*U.S.*)

funds PLURAL NOUN *The concert will raise funds for medical research.* = **money**, capital, cash, finance, means, savings, necessary (*informal*), resources, assets, silver, bread (*slang*), wealth, tin (*slang*), brass (*Northern English, dialect*), dough (*slang*), rhino (*Brit. slang*), the ready (*informal*), dosh (*Brit. & Austral. slang*), hard cash, the wherewithal, needful (*informal*), shekels (*informal*), dibs (*slang*), ready money, ackers (*slang*), spondulicks (*slang*)

funeral NOUN = **burial**, committal, laying to rest, cremation, interment, obsequies, entombment, inhumation

funereal ADJECTIVE = **gloomy**, dark, sad, grave, depressing, dismal, lamenting, solemn, dreary, sombre, woeful, mournful, lugubrious, sepulchral, dirge-like, deathlike

funk VERB = **chicken out of**, dodge, recoil from, take fright, flinch from, duck out of (*informal*), turn tail (*informal*)

funnel VERB **1** *This device funnels the water from a downpipe into a butt.* = **conduct**, direct, channel, convey, move, pass, pour, filter **2** *The centre will funnel money into research.* = **channel**, direct, pour, filter, convey

funny ADJECTIVE **1** *I'll tell you a funny story.* = **humorous**, amusing, comical, entertaining, killing (*informal*), rich, comic, silly, ridiculous, diverting, absurd, jolly, witty, hilarious, ludicrous, laughable, farcical, slapstick, riotous, droll, risible (*formal*), facetious, jocular, side-splitting, waggish, jocose (*old-fashioned*) ■ OPPOSITE: unfunny **2** *She could be funny when she wanted to be.* = **comic**, comical, a scream, a card (*informal*), a caution (*informal*) **3** *There's something funny about that pair.* = **peculiar**, odd, strange, unusual, remarkable, bizarre, puzzling, curious, weird, mysterious, suspicious, dubious, queer, rum (*Brit. slang*), quirky, perplexing **4** *My head ached and my stomach felt funny.* = **ill**, poorly (*informal*), queasy, sick, odd, crook (*Austral. & N.Z. informal*), ailing, queer, unhealthy, seedy (*informal*), unwell, out of sorts (*informal*), off-colour (*informal*), under the weather (*informal*)

furious ADJECTIVE **1** *He is furious at the way his family has been treated.* = **angry**, mad (*informal*), raging, boiling, fuming, choked, frantic, frenzied, infuriated, incensed, enraged, maddened, inflamed, very angry, cross, livid (*informal*), up in arms, incandescent, on the warpath (*informal*), foaming at the mouth, wrathful, in high dudgeon, wroth (*archaic*), fit to be tied (*slang*), beside yourself, tooshie (*Austral. slang*) ■ **OPPOSITE:** pleased **2** *A furious gunbattle ensued.* = **violent**, wild, intense, fierce, savage, turbulent, stormy, agitated, boisterous, tumultuous, vehement, unrestrained, tempestuous, impetuous, ungovernable

furnish VERB **1** *Many proprietors try to furnish their hotels with antiques.* = **decorate**, fit, fit out, appoint, provide, stock, supply, store, provision, outfit, equip, fit up, purvey **2** *They'll be able to furnish you with the details.* = **supply**, give, offer, provide, present, reveal, grant, afford, hand out, endow, bestow

furniture NOUN = **household goods**, furnishings, fittings, house fittings, goods, things (*informal*), effects, equipment, appointments, possessions, appliances, chattels, movable property, movables

furore or (*U.S.*) **furor** NOUN = **commotion**, to-do, stir, excitement, fury, disturbance, flap (*informal*), outburst, frenzy, outcry, uproar, brouhaha, hullabaloo

furrow NOUN **1** *Bike trails crisscrossed the grassy furrows.* = **groove**, line, channel, hollow, trench, seam, crease, fluting, rut, corrugation **2** *Deep furrows marked the corner of his mouth.* = **wrinkle**, line, crease, crinkle, crow's-foot, gather, fold, crumple, rumple, pucker, corrugation ▶ VERB *My boss furrowed his brow.* = **wrinkle**, knit, draw together, crease, seam, flute, corrugate

further ADVERB *Further, losing one day doesn't mean you won't win the next.* = **in addition**, moreover, besides, furthermore, also, yet, on top of, what's more, to boot, additionally, over and above, as well as, into the bargain ▶ ADJECTIVE *There was nothing further to be done.* = **additional**, more, new, other, extra, fresh, supplementary ▶ VERB *Education needn't only be about furthering your career.* = **promote**, help, develop, aid, forward, champion, push, encourage, speed, advance, work for, foster, contribute to, assist, plug (*informal*), facilitate, pave the way for, hasten, patronize, expedite, succour, lend support to ■ **OPPOSITE:** hinder

furthermore ADVERB = **moreover**, further, in addition, besides, too, as well, not to mention, what's more, to boot, additionally, into the bargain

furthest ADJECTIVE = **most distant**, extreme, ultimate, remotest, outermost, uttermost, furthermost, outmost

furtive ADJECTIVE = **sly**, secret, hidden, sneaking, covert, cloaked, behind someone's back, secretive, clandestine, sneaky, under-the-table, slinking, conspiratorial, skulking, underhand, surreptitious, stealthy ■ **OPPOSITE:** open

fury NOUN **1** *She screamed, her face distorted with fury.* = **anger**, passion, rage, madness (*informal*), frenzy, wrath, ire, red mist (*informal*), impetuosity ■ **OPPOSITE:** calmness **2** *We were lashed by the full fury of the elements.* = **violence**, force, power, intensity, severity, turbulence, ferocity, savagery, vehemence, fierceness, tempestuousness ■ **OPPOSITE:** peace

fuse VERB **1** *Conception occurs when a single sperm fuses with an egg.* = **join**, unite, combine, blend, integrate, merge, put together, dissolve, amalgamate, federate, coalesce, intermingle, meld, run together, commingle, intermix, agglutinate ■ **OPPOSITE:** separate **2** *They all fuse into a glassy state.* = **bond**, join, stick, melt, weld, smelt, solder

fusion NOUN = **merging**, uniting, union, merger, federation, mixture, blend, blending, integration, synthesis, amalgamation, coalescence, commingling, commixture

fuss NOUN **1** *I don't know what all the fuss is about.* = **commotion**, to-do, worry, upset, bother, stir, confusion, excitement, hurry, flap (*informal*), bustle, flutter, flurry, agitation, fidget, fluster, ado, hue and cry, palaver, storm in a teacup (*Brit.*), pother **2** *He gets down to work without any fuss.* = **bother**, trouble, struggle, hassle (*informal*), nuisance, inconvenience, hindrance **3** *We kicked up a fuss and got an apology.* = **complaint**, row, protest, objection, trouble, display, argument, difficulty, upset, bother, unrest, hassle (*informal*), squabble, furore, altercation ▶ VERB *She fussed about getting me a drink.* = **worry**, flap (*informal*), bustle, fret, niggle, fidget, chafe, take pains, make a meal of (*informal*), be agitated, labour over, get worked up, get in a stew (*informal*), make a thing of (*informal*)

fussy ADJECTIVE **1** *She's not fussy about her food.* = **particular**, difficult, exacting, discriminating, fastidious, dainty, squeamish, choosy (*informal*), picky (*informal*), nit-picking (*informal*), hard to please, finicky, pernickety, faddish, faddy, overparticular, nit-picky (*informal*) **2** *We are not keen on floral patterns and fussy designs.* = **overelaborate**, busy, cluttered, rococo, overdecorated, overembellished

futile ADJECTIVE **1** *a futile attempt to ward off the blow* = **useless**, vain, unsuccessful, pointless, empty, hollow, in vain, worthless, barren, sterile, fruitless, forlorn, unproductive, abortive, to no avail, ineffectual, unprofitable, valueless, unavailing, otiose, profitless, nugatory, without rhyme or reason, bootless ■ OPPOSITE: useful **2** *She doesn't want to comment. It's too futile.* = **trivial**, pointless, trifling, unimportant ■ OPPOSITE: important

futility NOUN **1** *the injustice and futility of terrorism* = **uselessness**, ineffectiveness, pointlessness, fruitlessness, emptiness, hollowness, spitting in the wind, bootlessness **2** *a sense of the emptiness and futility of life* = **triviality**, vanity, pointlessness, unimportance

future NOUN **1** *He made plans for the future.* = **time to come**, hereafter, what lies ahead **2** *She has a splendid future in the police force.* = **prospect**, expectation, outlook ▶ ADJECTIVE *the future King and Queen* = **forthcoming**, to be, coming, later, expected, approaching, to come, succeeding, fated, ultimate, subsequent, destined, prospective, eventual, ensuing, impending, unborn, in the offing ■ OPPOSITE: past

fuzz NOUN = **fluff**, down, hair, pile, fibre, nap, floss, lint

fuzzy ADJECTIVE **1** *He is a fierce bearded character with fuzzy hair.* = **frizzy**, fluffy, woolly, downy, flossy, down-covered, linty, napped **2** *a couple of fuzzy pictures* = **indistinct**, faint, blurred, vague, distorted, unclear, shadowy, bleary, unfocused, out of focus, ill-defined ■ OPPOSITE: distinct

Gg

gadget NOUN = **device**, thing, appliance, machine, tool, implement, invention, instrument, novelty, apparatus, gimmick, utensil, contraption (*informal*), gizmo (*slang*), contrivance

gaffe NOUN = **blunder**, mistake, error, indiscretion, lapse, boob (*Brit. slang*), slip-up (*informal*), slip, howler (*informal*), bloomer (*informal*), clanger (*informal*), faux pas, boo-boo (*informal*), solecism, gaucherie, barry or Barry Crocker (*Austral. slang*)

gag¹ NOUN *His captors had put a gag of thick leather in his mouth.* = **muzzle**, tie, restraint ▶ VERB **1** *a journalist who claimed he was gagged by his bosses* = **suppress**, silence, subdue, muffle, curb, stifle, muzzle, quieten **2** *I knelt by the toilet and gagged.* = **retch**, choke, heave

gag² NOUN *He made a gag about bald men.* = **joke**, crack (*slang*), funny (*informal*), quip, pun, jest, wisecrack (*informal*), sally, witticism

gaiety NOUN **1** *There was a bright, infectious gaiety in the children's laughter.* = **cheerfulness**, glee, good humour, buoyancy, happiness, animation, exuberance, high spirits, elation, exhilaration, hilarity, merriment, joie de vivre (*French*), good cheer, vivacity, jollity, liveliness, gladness, effervescence, light-heartedness, joyousness ■ **OPPOSITE:** misery **2** *The mood was one of laughter and gaiety.* = **merrymaking**, celebration, revels, festivity, fun, mirth, revelry, conviviality, jollification, carousal

gaily ADVERB **1** *She laughed gaily.* = **cheerfully**, happily, gleefully, brightly, blithely, merrily, joyfully, cheerily, jauntily, light-heartedly, chirpily (*informal*) **2** *gaily painted front doors* = **colourfully**, brightly, vividly, flamboyantly, gaudily, brilliantly, flashily, showily

gain VERB **1** *Students can gain valuable experience doing part-time work.* = **acquire**, get, receive, achieve, earn, pick up, win, secure, collect, gather, obtain, build up, attain, glean, procure **2** *The company didn't disclose how much it expects to gain from the deal.* = **profit**, make, earn, get, win, clear, land (*informal*), score (*slang*), achieve, net, bag, secure, collect, gather, realize, obtain, capture, acquire, bring in, harvest, attain, reap, glean, procure ■ **OPPOSITE:** lose **3** *Some people gain weight after they give up smoking.* = **put on**, increase in, gather, build up **4** *Passing exams is no longer enough to gain a place at university.* = **attain**, earn, get, achieve, win, reach, get to, secure, obtain, acquire, arrive at, procure ▶ NOUN **1** *House prices showed a gain of nearly 8% in June.* = **rise**, increase, growth, advance, improvement, upsurge, upturn, increment, upswing **2** *He buys art solely for financial gain.* = **profit**, income, earnings, proceeds, winnings, return, produce, benefit, advantage, yield, dividend, acquisition, attainment, lucre (*facetious*), emolument ■ **OPPOSITE:** loss ▶ PLURAL NOUN *Investors will have their gains taxed as income in future.* = **profits**, earnings, revenue, proceeds, winnings, takings, pickings, booty • **gain on something** or **someone** *The car began to gain on the van.* = **get nearer to**, close in on, approach, catch up with, narrow the gap on

gainful ADJECTIVE = **profitable**, rewarding, productive, lucrative, paying, useful, valuable, worthwhile, beneficial, fruitful, advantageous, expedient, remunerative, moneymaking

gainsay VERB = **deny**, dispute, disagree with, contradict, contravene, rebut, controvert ■ **OPPOSITE:** confirm

gait NOUN = **walk**, step, bearing, pace, stride, carriage, tread, manner of walking

gala NOUN *a gala at the Royal Opera House* = **festival**, party, fête, celebration, carnival, festivity, pageant, jamboree ▶ ADJECTIVE *I want to make her birthday a gala occasion.* = **festive**, merry, joyous, joyful, celebratory, convivial, gay, festal

galaxy NOUN = **star system**, solar system, nebula ■ **RELATED WORD:** *adjective* galactic

gale NOUN **1** *forecasts of fierce gales over the next few days* = **storm**, hurricane, tornado, cyclone, whirlwind, blast, gust, typhoon, tempest (*literary*), squall **2** *gales of laughter from the audience* = **outburst**, scream, roar, fit, storm, shout, burst, explosion, outbreak, howl, shriek, eruption, peal, paroxysm

gall NOUN *The mites live within the galls that are formed on the plant.* = **growth**, lump, excrescence ▶ VERB *It was their smugness that galled her most.* = **annoy**, provoke, irritate, aggravate (*informal*), get (*informal*), trouble, bother, disturb, plague, madden, ruffle, exasperate, nettle, vex, displease, irk, rile (*informal*), peeve (*informal*), get under your skin (*informal*), get on your nerves (*informal*), nark (*Brit., Austral. & N.Z. slang*), get up your nose (*informal*), make your blood boil, rub up the wrong way, get on your wick (*Brit. slang*), get your back up, put your back up, hack you off (*informal*)

gallant ADJECTIVE **1** *gallant soldiers who gave their lives* = **brave**, daring, bold, heroic, courageous, dashing, noble, manly, gritty, fearless, intrepid, valiant, plucky, doughty (*old-fashioned*), dauntless, lion-hearted, valorous, manful, mettlesome ■ **OPPOSITE:** cowardly **2** *He was a thoughtful, gallant and generous man.* = **courteous**, mannerly, gentlemanly, polite, gracious, attentive, courtly, chivalrous ■ **OPPOSITE:** discourteous

gallantry NOUN **1** *He was awarded a medal for his gallantry.* = **bravery**, spirit, daring, courage, nerve, guts (*informal*), pluck, grit, heroism, mettle, boldness, manliness, valour, derring-do (*archaic*), fearlessness, intrepidity, valiance, courageousness, dauntlessness, doughtiness ■ **OPPOSITE:** cowardice **2** *He kissed her hand with old-fashioned gallantry.* = **courtesy**, politeness, chivalry, attentiveness, graciousness, courtliness, gentlemanliness, courteousness ■ **OPPOSITE:** discourtesy

galling ADJECTIVE = **annoying**, provoking, irritating, aggravating (*informal*), disturbing, humiliating, maddening, exasperating, vexing, displeasing, rankling, irksome, vexatious, nettlesome

gallop VERB **1** *The horses galloped away.* = **run**, race, shoot, career, speed, bolt, stampede **2** *They were galloping around the garden playing football.* = **dash**, run, race, shoot, fly, career, speed, tear, rush, barrel (along) (*informal, chiefly U.S. & Canad.*), sprint, dart, zoom

galore ADVERB = **in abundance**, everywhere, to spare, all over the place, aplenty, in great numbers, in profusion, in great quantity, à gogo (*informal*)

galvanize VERB = **stimulate**, encourage, inspire, prompt, move, fire, shock, excite, wake, stir, spur, provoke, startle, arouse, awaken, rouse, prod, jolt, kick-start, electrify, goad, impel, invigorate

gamble NOUN **1** *the President's risky gamble in calling an election* = **risk**, chance, venture, lottery, speculation, uncertainty, leap in the dark ■ **OPPOSITE:** certainty **2** *My father-in-law likes a drink and the odd gamble.* = **bet**, flutter (*informal*), punt (*chiefly Brit.*), wager ▶ VERB **1** (*often with* **on**) *Few firms will be prepared to gamble on new products.* = **take a chance**, back, speculate, take the

plunge, stick your neck out (*informal*), put your faith or trust in **2** *Are you prepared to gamble your career on this matter?* = **risk**, chance, stake, venture, hazard, wager **3** *John gambled heavily on the horses.* = **bet**, play, game, stake, speculate, back, punt (*chiefly Brit.*), wager, put money on, have a flutter (*informal*), try your luck, put your shirt on, lay or make a bet

game¹ NOUN **1** *the game of hide-and-seek* = **pastime**, sport, activity, entertainment, recreation, distraction, amusement, diversion ■ **OPPOSITE:** job **2** *We won three games against Australia.* = **match**, meeting, event, competition, tournament, clash, contest, round, head-to-head **3** *Some people simply regard life as a game.* = **amusement**, joke, entertainment, diversion, lark **4** *She's new to this game, so go easy on her.* = **activity**, business, line, situation, proceeding, enterprise, undertaking, occupation, pursuit **5** *men who shoot game for food* = **wild animals** or **birds**, prey, quarry **6** *All right, what's your little game?* = **scheme**, plan, design, strategy, trick, plot, tactic, manoeuvre, dodge, ploy, scam, stratagem, fastie (*Austral. slang*) ▶ ADJECTIVE **1** *He said he's game for a similar challenge next year.* = **willing**, prepared, ready, keen, eager, interested, inclined, disposed, up for it (*informal*), desirous **2** *They were the only ones game enough to give it a try.* = **brave**, courageous, dogged, spirited, daring, bold, persistent, gritty, fearless, feisty (*informal*), persevering, intrepid, valiant, plucky, unflinching, dauntless, (as) game as Ned Kelly (*Austral. slang*) ■ **OPPOSITE:** cowardly

game² ADJECTIVE *a horse with a game leg* = **lame**, injured, disabled, crippled, defective, bad, maimed, deformed, gammy (*Brit. slang*)

gamut NOUN = **range**, series, collection, variety, lot, field, scale, sweep, catalogue, scope, compass, assortment

gang NOUN = **group**, crowd, pack, company, party, lot, band, crew (*informal*), bunch, mob, horde

gangster NOUN = **hoodlum** (*chiefly U.S.*), crook (*informal*), thug, bandit, heavy (*slang*), tough, hood (*U.S. slang*), robber, gang member, mobster (*U.S. slang*), racketeer, desperado, ruffian, brigand, wise guy (*U.S.*), tsotsi (*S. African*)

gaol *see* **jail**

gap NOUN **1** *the wind tearing through gaps in the window frames* = **opening**, space, hole, break, split, divide, crack, rent, breach, slot, vent, rift, aperture, cleft, chink, crevice, fissure, cranny, perforation, interstice

2 *There followed a gap of four years.* = **interval**, pause, recess, interruption, respite, lull, interlude, breathing space, hiatus, intermission, lacuna, entr'acte **3** *the gap between the poor and the well-off* = **difference**, gulf, contrast, disagreement, discrepancy, inconsistency, disparity, divergence

gape VERB **1** *She stopped what she was doing and gaped at me.* = **stare**, wonder, goggle, gawp (*Brit. slang*), gawk **2** *A hole gaped in the roof.* = **open**, split, crack, yawn

gaping ADJECTIVE = **wide**, great, open, broad, vast, yawning, wide open, cavernous

garb NOUN = **clothes**, dress, clothing, gear (*slang*), wear, habit, get-up (*informal*), uniform, outfit, costume, threads (*slang*), array, ensemble, garments, robes, duds (*informal*), apparel, clobber (*Brit. slang*), attire, togs (*informal*), vestments, raiment (*archaic*), rigout (*informal*), bling (*slang*)

garbage NOUN **1** *rotting piles of garbage* = **junk**, rubbish, litter, trash (*chiefly U.S.*), refuse, waste, sweepings, scraps, debris, muck, filth, swill, slops, offal, detritus, dross, odds and ends, flotsam and jetsam, grot (*slang*), leavings, dreck (*slang, chiefly U.S.*), scourings, offscourings **2** *I personally think the story is complete garbage.* = **nonsense**, rot, crap (*slang*), trash, hot air (*informal*), tosh (*informal*), pap, bilge (*informal*), drivel, twaddle, tripe (*informal*), gibberish, malarkey, guff (*slang*), moonshine, claptrap (*informal*), hogwash, hokum (*slang, chiefly U.S. & Canad.*), codswallop (*Brit. slang*), piffle (*informal*), poppycock (*informal*), balderdash, bosh (*informal*), eyewash (*informal*), kak (*S. African slang*), stuff and nonsense, bunkum or buncombe, bizzo (*Austral. slang*), bull's wool (*Austral. & N.Z. slang*)

garbled ADJECTIVE = **jumbled**, confused, distorted, mixed up, muddled, incomprehensible, unintelligible

garden NOUN = **grounds**, park, plot, patch, lawn, allotment, yard (*U.S. & Canad.*), forest park (*N.Z.*) ■ **RELATED WORD:** *adjective* horticultural

gargantuan ADJECTIVE = **huge**, big, large, giant, massive, towering, vast, enormous, extensive, tremendous, immense, mega (*slang*), titanic, jumbo (*informal*), gigantic, monumental (*informal*), monstrous, mammoth, colossal, mountainous, prodigious, stupendous, elephantine, ginormous (*informal*), Brobdingnagian, humongous or humungous (*informal*)
■ **OPPOSITE:** tiny

> **USAGE** Some people think that *gargantuan* should only be used to describe things connected with food: *a gargantuan meal; his gargantuan appetite.* Nevertheless, the word is now widely used as a synonym of *colossal* or *massive.*

garish ADJECTIVE = **gaudy**, bright, glaring, vulgar, brilliant, flash (*informal*), loud, brash, tacky (*informal*), flashy, tasteless, naff (*Brit. slang*), jazzy (*informal*), tawdry, showy, brassy, raffish ■ **OPPOSITE:** dull

garland NOUN *They wore garlands of summer flowers in their hair.* = **wreath**, band, bays, crown, honours, loop, laurels, festoon, coronet, coronal, chaplet ▸ VERB *Players were garlanded with flowers.* = **adorn**, crown, deck, festoon, wreathe

garment NOUN (*often plural*) = **clothes**, wear, dress, clothing, gear (*slang*), habit, get-up (*informal*), uniform, outfit, costume, threads (*slang*), array, robes, duds (*informal*), apparel, clobber (*Brit. slang*), attire, garb, togs, vestments, articles of clothing, raiment (*archaic*), rigout (*informal*), habiliment

garnish NOUN *Reserve some watercress for garnish.* = **decoration**, ornament, embellishment, adornment, ornamentation, trimming, trim ▸ VERB *She had prepared the vegetables and was garnishing the roast.* = **decorate**, adorn, ornament, embellish, deck, festoon, trim, bedeck ■ **OPPOSITE:** strip

garrison NOUN **1** *a five-hundred-man garrison* = **troops**, group, unit, section, command, armed force, detachment **2** *The approaches to the garrison have been heavily mined.* = **fort**, fortress, camp, base, post, station, stronghold, fortification, encampment, fortified pa (*N.Z.*) ▸ VERB *No other soldiers were garrisoned there.* = **station**, position, post, mount, install, assign, put on duty

garrulous ADJECTIVE **1** *I fell in with a set of garrulous would-be intellectuals.* = **talkative**, gossiping, chattering, babbling, gushing, chatty, long-winded, effusive, gabby (*informal*), prattling, voluble, gossipy, loquacious, verbose, mouthy ■ **OPPOSITE:** taciturn **2** *boring, garrulous prose* = **rambling**, lengthy, diffuse, long-winded, wordy, discursive, windy, overlong, verbose, prolix, prosy ■ **OPPOSITE:** concise

gas NOUN **1** *Exhaust gases contain many toxins.* = **fumes**, vapour **2** (*U.S., Canad. & N.Z.*) *a tank of gas* = **petrol**, gasoline (*U.S., Canad. & N.Z.*)

gash NOUN *a long gash just above his right eye* = **cut**, tear, split, wound, rent, slash, slit, gouge, incision, laceration ▸ VERB *He gashed his leg while felling trees.* = **cut**, tear, split, wound, rend (*literary*), slash, slit, gouge, lacerate

gasp VERB *He gasped for air before being pulled under again.* = **pant**, blow, puff, choke, gulp, fight for breath, catch your breath ▶ NOUN *She gave a small gasp of pain.* = **pant**, puff, gulp, intake of breath, sharp intake of breath

gate NOUN = **barrier**, opening, door, access, port (*Scot.*), entrance, exit, gateway, portal (*literary*), egress

gather VERB **1** *In the evenings, we gathered round the fire and talked.* = **congregate**, assemble, get together, collect, group, meet, mass, rally, flock, come together, muster, convene, converge, rendezvous, foregather ■ **OPPOSITE:** scatter **2** *He called to her to gather the children together.* = **assemble**, group, collect, round up, marshal, bring together, muster, convene, call together ■ **OPPOSITE:** disperse **3** *She started gathering up her things.* = **collect**, assemble, accumulate, round up, mass, heap, marshal, bring together, muster, pile up, garner, amass, stockpile, hoard, stack up **4** *The people lived by fishing, gathering nuts and fruits, and hunting.* = **pick**, harvest, pluck, reap, garner, glean **5** *Storm clouds were gathering in the distance.* = **build up**, rise, increase, grow, develop, expand, swell, intensify, wax, heighten, deepen, enlarge, thicken **6** *I gather his report is highly critical of the project.* = **understand**, believe, hear, learn, assume, take it, conclude, presume, be informed, infer, deduce, surmise, be led to believe **7** *Gather the skirt at the waist.* = **fold**, tuck, pleat, ruffle, pucker, shirr

gathering NOUN *He spoke today before a large gathering of world leaders.* = **assembly**, group, crowd, meeting, conference, company, party, congress, mass, rally, convention, knot, flock, get-together (*informal*), congregation, muster, turnout, multitude, throng, hui (*N.Z.*), concourse, assemblage, conclave, convocation (*formal*), runanga (*N.Z.*)

gauche ADJECTIVE = **awkward**, clumsy, inept, unsophisticated, inelegant, graceless, unpolished, uncultured, maladroit, ill-bred, ill-mannered, lacking in social graces ■ **OPPOSITE:** sophisticated

gaudy ADJECTIVE = **garish**, bright (*informal*), glaring, vulgar, brilliant, flash (*informal*), loud, brash, tacky (*informal*), flashy, tasteless, jazzy (*informal*), tawdry, showy, gay, ostentatious, raffish ■ **OPPOSITE:** dull

gauge VERB **1** *He gauged the wind at over thirty knots.* = **measure**, calculate, evaluate, value, size, determine, count, weigh, compute, ascertain, quantify **2** *See if you can gauge his reaction to the offer.* = **judge**, estimate, guess, assess, evaluate, rate, appraise, reckon, adjudge ▶ NOUN *a temperature gauge* = **meter**, indicator, dial, measuring instrument

gaunt ADJECTIVE **1** *Looking gaunt and tired, he denied there was anything to worry about.* = **thin**, lean, skinny, skeletal, wasted, drawn, spare, pinched, angular, bony, lanky, haggard, emaciated, scrawny, skin and bone, scraggy, cadaverous, rawboned ■ **OPPOSITE:** plump **2** *a large, gaunt, grey house* = **bleak**, bare, harsh, forbidding, grim, stark, dismal, dreary, desolate, forlorn ■ **OPPOSITE:** inviting

gawky ADJECTIVE = **awkward**, clumsy, lumbering, ungainly, gauche, uncouth, loutish, graceless, clownish, oafish, maladroit, lumpish, ungraceful, unco (*Austral. slang*) ■ **OPPOSITE:** graceful

gay ADJECTIVE **1** *a programme in which six gay men talked about their lives* = **homosexual**, lesbian, pink (*informal*), same-sex, sapphic **2** *I am in good health, gay and cheerful.* = **cheerful**, happy, bright, glad, lively, sparkling, sunny, jolly, animated, merry, upbeat (*informal*), buoyant, cheery, joyous, joyful, carefree, jaunty, chirpy (*informal*), vivacious, jovial, gleeful, debonair, blithe, insouciant, full of beans (*informal*), light-hearted ■ **OPPOSITE:** sad **3** *I like gay, vibrant posters.* = **colourful**, rich, bright, brilliant, vivid, flamboyant, flashy, gaudy, garish, showy ■ **OPPOSITE:** drab

> **USAGE** By far the most common and up-to-date use of the word *gay* is in reference to being homosexual. Other senses of the word have become uncommon and dated.

gaze VERB *He gazed reflectively at the fire.* = **stare**, look, view, watch, regard, contemplate, gape, eyeball (*slang*), ogle, look fixedly ▶ NOUN *She felt uncomfortable under the woman's steady gaze.* = **stare**, look, fixed look

gazette NOUN = **newspaper**, paper, journal, organ, periodical, news-sheet

g'day or **gidday** INTERJECTION (*Austral. & N.Z.*) *Gidday, mate!* = **hello**, hi (*informal*), greetings, how do you do?, good morning, good evening, good afternoon, welcome, kia ora (*N.Z.*)

gear NOUN **1** *The boat's steering gear failed.* = **mechanism**, works, action, gearing, machinery, cogs, cogwheels, gearwheels **2** *fishing gear* = **equipment**, supplies, tackle, tools, instruments, outfit, rigging, rig, accessories, apparatus, trappings, paraphernalia, accoutrements, appurtenances, equipage **3** *They helped us put our gear in the van.* = **possessions**, things, effects, stuff, kit, luggage, baggage, belongings, paraphernalia, personal property, chattels **4** *I used to wear trendy gear but it just looked ridiculous.* = **clothing**, wear, dress, clothes, habit, outfit, costume, threads (*slang*), array, garments, apparel (*old-fashioned*), attire, garb, togs, rigout ▸ VERB (*with* **to** *or* **towards**) *Colleges are not always geared towards the needs of mature students.* = **equip**, fit, suit, adjust, adapt, rig, tailor

geek (*informal*) NOUN **1** *Geeks like me revel in small details.* = **nerd** or **nurd**, bore, obsessive, anorak (*informal*), trainspotter (*informal*), dork (*slang*), wonk (*informal*) **2** *Online communication was once the preserve of computer geeks.* = **techie**, nerd or nurd, programmer, whiz

gem NOUN **1** *The mask is inset with emeralds and other gems.* = **precious stone**, jewel, stone, semiprecious stone **2** *Castel Clara was a gem of a hotel.* = **treasure**, pick, prize, jewel, flower, pearl, masterpiece, paragon, humdinger (*slang*), taonga (N.Z.)

genealogy NOUN = **ancestry**, descent, pedigree, line, origin, extraction, lineage, family tree, parentage, derivation, blood line

general ADJECTIVE **1** *Contrary to general opinion, these plants do not need acidic soil.* = **widespread**, accepted, popular, public, common, broad, extensive, universal, prevailing, prevalent ■ **OPPOSITE:** individual **2** *His firm took over general maintenance of the park last summer.* = **overall**, complete, total, global, comprehensive, blanket, inclusive, all-embracing, overarching ■ **OPPOSITE:** restricted **3** *The figures represent a general decline in unemployment.* = **universal**, overall, widespread, collective, across-the-board, all-inclusive ■ **OPPOSITE:** exceptional **4** *chemicals called by the general description 'flavour enhancer'* = **vague**, broad, loose, blanket, sweeping, unclear, inaccurate, approximate, woolly, indefinite, hazy, imprecise, ill-defined, inexact, unspecific, undetailed ■ **OPPOSITE:** specific

generality NOUN **1** *He avoided this tricky question and talked in generalities.* = **generalization**, abstraction, sweeping statement, vague notion, loose statement **2** *There are problems with this definition, given its level of generality.* = **impreciseness**, vagueness, looseness, lack of detail,

inexactitude, woolliness, indefiniteness, approximateness, inexactness, lack of preciseness

generally ADVERB **1** *Ivan made a few mistakes but was generally happy with his form.* = **broadly**, mainly, mostly, principally, on the whole, predominantly, in the main, for the most part **2** *We generally say and feel too much about these things.* = **usually**, commonly, typically, regularly, normally, on average, on the whole, for the most part, almost always, in most cases, by and large, ordinarily, as a rule, habitually, conventionally, customarily ■ **OPPOSITE:** occasionally **3** *It is generally believed that eating green vegetables is beneficial.* = **commonly**, widely, publicly, universally, extensively, popularly, conventionally, customarily ■ **OPPOSITE:** individually

generate VERB = **produce**, create, make, form, cause, initiate, bring about, originate, give rise to, engender, whip up ■ **OPPOSITE:** end

generation NOUN **1** *He's the leading American playwright of his generation.* = **age group**, peer group **2** *The whole island could become a desert within a generation.* = **age**, period, era, time, days, lifetime, span, epoch

generic ADJECTIVE = **collective**, general, common, wide, sweeping, comprehensive, universal, blanket, inclusive, all-encompassing ■ **OPPOSITE:** specific

generosity NOUN **1** *There are many stories of his generosity.* = **liberality**, charity, bounty, munificence, beneficence, largesse or largess **2** *her moral decency and generosity of spirit* = **magnanimity**, goodness, kindness, benevolence, selflessness, charity, unselfishness, high-mindedness, nobleness

generous ADJECTIVE **1** *You're very generous with your money.* = **liberal**, lavish, free, charitable, free-handed, hospitable, prodigal, bountiful, open-handed, unstinting, beneficent, princely, bounteous, munificent, ungrudging ■ **OPPOSITE:** mean **2** *He was not generous enough to congratulate his successor.* = **magnanimous**, kind, noble, benevolent, good, big, high-minded, unselfish, big-hearted, ungrudging **3** *a room with a generous amount of storage space* = **plentiful**, lavish, ample, abundant, full, rich, liberal, overflowing, copious, bountiful, unstinting, profuse, bounteous (*literary*), plenteous ■ **OPPOSITE:** meagre

genesis NOUN = **beginning**, source, root, origin, start, generation, birth, creation, dawn (*literary*), formation, outset,

g

starting point, engendering, inception, commencement, propagation ■ **OPPOSITE: end**

genial ADJECTIVE = **friendly**, kind, kindly, pleasant, warm, cheerful, jolly, hearty, agreeable, cheery, amiable, cordial, affable, congenial, jovial, convivial, good-natured, warm-hearted ■ **OPPOSITE: unfriendly**

genitals PLURAL NOUN = **sex organs**, privates, loins, genitalia, private parts, reproductive organs, pudenda ■ **RELATED WORD:** *adjective* venereal

genius NOUN **1** *This is the mark of her genius as a designer.* = **brilliance**, ability, talent, capacity, gift, bent, faculty, excellence, endowment, flair, inclination, knack, propensity, aptitude, cleverness, creative power **2** *a 14-year-old mathematical genius* = **master**, expert, mastermind, brain (*informal*), buff (*informal*), intellect (*informal*), adept, maestro, virtuoso, whiz (*informal*), hotshot (*informal*), rocket scientist (*informal*), wonk (*informal*), brainbox, maven (*U.S.*), master-hand, fundi (*S. African*)

genre NOUN = **type**, group, school, form, order, sort, kind, class, style, character (*informal*), fashion, brand, species, category, stamp, classification, genus, subdivision

genteel ADJECTIVE = **refined**, cultured, mannerly, elegant, formal, gentlemanly, respectable, polite, cultivated, courteous, courtly, well-bred, ladylike, well-mannered ■ **OPPOSITE: unmannerly**

gentility NOUN **1** = **refinement**, culture, breeding, courtesy, elegance, formality, respectability, cultivation, politeness, good manners, courtliness **2** = **blue blood**, high birth, rank, good family, good breeding, gentle birth

gentle ADJECTIVE **1** *a quiet and gentle man who liked sports and enjoyed life* = **kind**, loving, kindly, peaceful, soft, quiet, pacific, tender, mild, benign, humane, compassionate, amiable, meek, lenient, placid, merciful, kind-hearted, sweet-tempered, tender-hearted ■ **OPPOSITE: unkind 2** *His movements were gentle and deliberate.* = **slow**, easy, slight, deliberate, moderate, gradual, imperceptible **3** *The wind had dropped to a gentle breeze.* = **moderate**, low, light, easy, soft, calm, slight, mild, soothing, clement, temperate, balmy ■ **OPPOSITE: violent**

gentlemanly ADJECTIVE = **chivalrous**, mannerly, obliging, refined, polite, civil, cultivated, courteous, gallant, genteel, suave, well-mannered

gentleness NOUN = **tenderness**, compassion, kindness, consideration, sympathy, sweetness, softness, mildness, kindliness

gentry NOUN = **nobility**, lords, elite, nobles, upper class, aristocracy, peerage, ruling class, patricians, upper crust (*informal*), gentility, gentlefolk

genuine ADJECTIVE **1** *They are convinced the painting is genuine.* = **authentic**, real, original, actual, sound, true, pure, sterling, valid, legitimate, honest, veritable, bona fide, dinkum (*Austral. & N.Z. informal*), the real McCoy ■ **OPPOSITE: counterfeit 2** *There was genuine joy in the room.* = **heartfelt**, sincere, honest, earnest, real, true, frank, unaffected, wholehearted, unadulterated, unalloyed, unfeigned ■ **OPPOSITE: affected 3** *She is a very caring and genuine person.* = **sincere**, straightforward, honest, natural, frank, candid, upfront (*informal*), dinkum (*Austral. & N.Z. informal*), artless, guileless ■ **OPPOSITE: hypocritical**

genus NOUN = **type**, sort, kind, group, set, order, race, class, breed, category, genre, classification

germ NOUN **1** *a germ that destroyed hundreds of millions of lives* = **microbe**, virus, bug (*informal*), bacterium, bacillus, microorganism **2** *The germ of an idea took root in her mind.* = **beginning**, root, seed, origin, spark, bud, embryo, rudiment

German NOUN ■ **RELATED WORDS:** *prefixes* Germano-, Teuto-

germinate VERB = **sprout**, grow, shoot, develop, generate, swell, bud, vegetate

gestation NOUN = **incubation**, development, growth, pregnancy, evolution, ripening, maturation

gesticulate VERB = **signal**, sign, wave, indicate, motion, gesture, beckon, make a sign

gesture NOUN *She made a menacing gesture with her fist.* = **sign**, action, signal, motion, indication, gesticulation ▶ VERB *I gestured towards the boathouse and he looked inside.* = **signal**, sign, wave, indicate, motion, beckon, gesticulate

get VERB **1** *The boys were getting bored.* = **become**, grow, turn, wax, come to be **2** *How did you get him to pose for this picture?* = **persuade**, convince, win over, induce, influence, sway, entice, coax, incite, impel, talk into, wheedle, prevail upon **3** *It was dark by the time she got home.* = **arrive**, come, reach, make it (*informal*) **4** *How did he get to be the boss of a major company?* = **manage**, fix, succeed, arrange, contrive, wangle (*informal*) **5** (*informal*) *What gets me is the*

attitude of these people. = **annoy**, upset,
anger, bother, disturb, trouble, bug
(informal), irritate, aggravate (informal),
gall, madden, exasperate, nettle, vex, irk,
rile, pique, get on your nerves (informal),
nark (Brit., Austral. & N.Z. slang), get up your
nose (informal), give someone grief (Brit. &
S. African), make your blood boil, get your
goat (slang), get on your wick (Brit. slang),
get your back up, hack you off (informal)
6 The problem was how to get enough food.
= **obtain**, receive, gain, acquire, win, land
(informal), score (slang), achieve, net, pick
up, bag, secure, attain, reap, get hold of,
come by, glean, procure, get your hands on,
come into possession of **7** Go and get your
Daddy for me. = **fetch**, bring, collect **8** You
don't seem to get the point. = **understand**,
follow, catch, see, notice, realize,
appreciate, be aware of, take in, perceive,
grasp, comprehend, fathom, apprehend,
suss (out) (slang), get the hang of (informal),
get your head round **9** When I was five I got
measles. = **catch**, develop, contract,
succumb to, fall victim to, go down with,
come down with, become infected with, be
afflicted with, be smitten by **10** The police
have got the killer. = **arrest**, catch, grab,
capture, trap, seize, take, nail (informal),
collar (informal), nab (informal), apprehend,
take prisoner, take into custody, lay hold of
11 We've been trying to get you on the phone all
day. = **contact**, reach, communicate with,
get hold of, get in touch with **12** No, I can't
answer that question – you've got me there.
= **puzzle**, confuse, baffle, bewilder,
confound, perplex, mystify, stump, beat
(slang), flummox, nonplus **13** (informal) I
don't know what it is about that song, it just gets
me. = **move**, touch, affect, excite, stir,
stimulate, arouse, have an impact on, have
an effect on, tug at (someone's)
heartstrings (often facetious) • **get across
something** When we got across the beach,
we saw some guys waiting for us. = **cross**,
negotiate, pass over, traverse, ford • **get at
someone 1** His mother didn't like me, and she
gets at me all the time. = **criticize**, attack,
blame, put down, knock (informal), carp,
have a go (at) (informal), taunt, nag, hassle
(informal), pick on, disparage, diss (slang),
find fault with, put the boot into (slang),
nark (Brit., Austral. & N.Z. slang), be on your
back (slang) **2** He claims these government
officials have been got at. = **corrupt**,
influence, bribe, tamper with, buy off, fix
(informal), suborn • **get at something**
1 The goat was on its hind legs trying to get at the
leaves. = **reach**, touch, grasp, get (a) hold of,

stretch to **2** We're only trying to get at the
truth. = **find out**, get, learn, reach, reveal,
discover, acquire, detect, uncover, attain,
get hold of, gain access to, come to grips
with **3** 'What are you getting at now?'
demanded Rick. = **imply**, mean, suggest,
hint, intimate, lead up to, insinuate • **get
away** They tried to stop him but he got away.
= **escape**, leave, disappear, flee, depart, fly,
slip away, abscond, decamp, hook it (slang),
do a runner (slang), slope off, do a bunk
(Brit. slang), fly the coop (U.S. & Canad.
informal), skedaddle (informal), take a
powder (U.S. & Canad. slang), make good
your escape, make your getaway, take it on
the lam (U.S. & Canad. slang), break free or
out, run away or off, do a Skase (Austral.
informal) • **get back** It was late when we got
back from the hospital. = **return**, arrive home,
come back or home • **get back at
someone** My wife had left me and I wanted to
get back at her. = **retaliate**, pay (someone)
back, hit back at, take revenge on, get even
with, strike back at, even the score with,
exact retribution on, get your own back on,
make reprisal with, be avenged on, settle
the score with, give (someone) a taste of
their own medicine, give tit for tat, take or
wreak vengeance on • **get by** I'm a survivor.
I'll get by. = **manage**, survive, cope, fare, get
through, exist, make out, get along, make
do, subsist, muddle through, keep your
head above water, make both ends meet
• **get in** Our flight got in late. = **arrive**, come
in, appear, land • **get off 1** He is likely to get
off with a small fine. = **be absolved**, be
acquitted, escape punishment, walk (slang,
chiefly U.S.) **2** I'd like to get off before it begins to
get dark. = **leave**, go, move, take off
(informal), depart, slope off, make tracks,
set out or off **3** We got off at the next stop.
= **descend**, leave, exit, step down, alight,
disembark, dismount • **get on 1** Do you get
on with your neighbours? = **be friendly**, agree,
get along, concur, be compatible, hit it off
(informal), harmonize, be on good terms
2 I asked how he was getting on. = **progress**,
manage, cope, fare, advance, succeed,
make out (informal), prosper, cut it
(informal), get along **3** The bus stopped to let
the passengers get on. = **board**, enter, mount,
climb, embark, ascend • **get out** I think we
should get out while we still can. = **leave**,
escape, withdraw, quit, take off (informal),
exit, go, break out, go away, depart,
evacuate, vacate, clear out (informal),
abscond, decamp, hook it (slang), free
yourself, do a bunk (Brit. slang), extricate
yourself, sling your hook (Brit. slang), rack

off (*Austral. & N.Z. slang*), do a Skase (*Austral. informal*) • **get out of something** *It's amazing what people will do to get out of paying taxes.* = **avoid**, dodge, evade, escape, shirk, body-swerve • **get over something 1** *It took me a very long time to get over the shock of her death.* = **recover from**, survive, get better from, come round, bounce back, mend, get well, recuperate, turn the corner, pull through, get back on your feet, feel yourself again, regain your health or strength **2** *How would they get over that problem, he wondered?* = **overcome**, deal with, solve, resolve, defeat, master, lick (*informal*), shake off, rise above, get the better of, surmount **3** *The travellers were trying to get over the river.* = **cross**, pass, pass over, traverse, get across, move across, ford, go across • **get round someone** *Max could always get round his mother.* = **win over**, persuade, charm, influence, convince, convert, sway, coax, cajole, wheedle, prevail upon, bring round, talk round • **get round something** *No one has found a way of getting round the problem.* = **overcome**, deal with, solve, resolve, defeat, master, bypass, lick (*informal*), shake off, rise above, get the better of, circumvent, surmount • **get something across** *I need a better way of getting my message across to people.* = **communicate**, publish, spread, pass on, transmit, convey, impart, get (something) through, disseminate, bring home, make known, put over, make clear or understood • **get something back** *You have 14 days in which to cancel and get your money back.* = **regain**, recover, retrieve, take back, recoup, repossess • **get something over** *We have got the message over to young people that smoking isn't cool.* = **communicate**, spread, pass on, convey, impart, make known, get or put across, make clear or understood • **get together** *This is the only forum where East and West can get together.* = **meet**, unite, join, collect, gather, rally, assemble, muster, convene, converge, congregate • **get up** *I got up and walked over to the door.* = **arise** (*old-fashioned*), stand (up), rise, get to your feet

getaway NOUN = **escape**, break, flight, break-out, decampment

get-together NOUN = **gathering**, meet-up, party, celebration, reception, meeting, social, function, bash (*informal*), rave (*Brit. slang*), festivity, do (*informal*), knees-up (*Brit. informal*), beano (*Brit. slang*), social gathering, shindig (*informal*), soirée, rave-up (*Brit. slang*), hooley or hoolie (*chiefly Irish & N.Z.*)

ghastly ADJECTIVE = **horrible**, shocking (*informal*), terrible (*informal*), awful, grim, dreadful, horrendous, hideous, from hell (*informal*), horrid (*informal*), repulsive, frightful, loathsome, godawful (*slang*)
■ **OPPOSITE:** lovely

ghost NOUN **1** *The village is said to be haunted by the ghosts of past inhabitants.* = **spirit**, soul, phantom, spectre, spook (*informal*), apparition, wraith, shade (*literary*), phantasm, atua (*N.Z.*), kehua (*N.Z.*), wairua (*N.Z.*) **2** *He gave the ghost of a smile.* = **trace**, shadow, suggestion, hint, suspicion, glimmer, semblance ■ **RELATED WORD:** adjective spectral

ghostly ADJECTIVE = **unearthly**, weird, phantom, eerie, supernatural, uncanny, spooky (*informal*), spectral, eldritch (*poetic*), phantasmal

ghoulish ADJECTIVE = **macabre**, sick (*informal*), disgusting, hideous, gruesome, grisly, horrid, morbid, unwholesome

giant ADJECTIVE *a giant oak table; a giant step towards unification* = **huge**, great, large, vast, enormous, extensive, tremendous, immense, titanic, jumbo (*informal*), gigantic, monumental (*informal*), monstrous, mammoth, colossal, mountainous, stellar (*informal*), prodigious, stupendous, gargantuan, elephantine, ginormous (*informal*), Brobdingnagian, humongous or humungous (*informal*), supersize ■ **OPPOSITE:** tiny ▶ NOUN *a Nordic saga of giants and monsters* = **ogre**, monster, titan, colossus, leviathan, behemoth

gibber VERB = **gabble**, chatter, babble, waffle (*informal, chiefly Brit.*), prattle, jabber, blab, rabbit on (*Brit. informal*), blather, blabber, earbash (*Austral. & N.Z. slang*)

gibberish NOUN = **nonsense**, crap (*slang*), garbage (*informal*), hot air (*informal*), tosh (*slang, chiefly Brit.*), babble, pap, bilge (*informal*), drivel, malarkey, twaddle, tripe (*informal*), guff (*slang*), prattle, mumbo jumbo, moonshine, jabber, gabble, gobbledegook (*informal*), hogwash, hokum (*slang, chiefly U.S. & Canad.*), blather, double talk, piffle (*informal*), all Greek (*informal*), poppycock (*informal*), balderdash, bosh (*informal*), yammer (*informal*), eyewash (*informal*), tommyrot, horsefeathers (*U.S. slang*), bunkum or buncombe, bizzo (*Austral. slang*), bull's wool (*Austral. & N.Z. slang*)

gibe see **jibe**

giddy ADJECTIVE **1** *He felt giddy and light-headed.* = **dizzy**, reeling, faint, unsteady, light-headed, vertiginous **2** *At our stage in life we are unlikely to become giddy spendthrifts.*

= **flighty**, silly, volatile, irresponsible, reckless, dizzy, careless, frivolous, impulsive, capricious, thoughtless, impetuous, skittish, heedless, scatterbrained, ditzy or ditsy (slang) ■ **OPPOSITE:** serious

gift NOUN **1** a gift of $50,000 = **donation**, offering, present, contribution, grant, legacy, hand-out, endowment, boon (archaic), bequest, gratuity, prezzie (informal), bonsela (S. African), largesse or largess, koha (N.Z.) **2** As a youth he discovered a gift for teaching. = **talent**, ability, capacity, genius, power, bent, faculty, capability, forte, flair, knack, aptitude

gifted ADJECTIVE = **talented**, able, skilled, expert, masterly, brilliant, capable, clever, accomplished, proficient, adroit ■ **OPPOSITE:** talentless

gigantic ADJECTIVE = **huge**, great, large, giant, massive, vast, enormous, extensive, tremendous, immense, titanic, jumbo (informal), monumental, monstrous, mammoth, colossal, mountainous, stellar (informal), prodigious, stupendous, gargantuan, herculean, elephantine, ginormous (informal), Brobdingnagian, humongous or humungous (informal), supersize ■ **OPPOSITE:** tiny

giggle VERB Both girls began to giggle. = **laugh**, chuckle, snigger, chortle, titter, twitter, tee-hee ▶ NOUN She gave a little giggle. = **laugh**, chuckle, snigger, chortle, titter, twitter

gimmick NOUN = **stunt**, trick, device, scheme, manoeuvre, dodge, ploy, gambit, stratagem, contrivance

gingerly ADVERB = **cautiously**, carefully, reluctantly, suspiciously, tentatively, warily, hesitantly, timidly, circumspectly, cagily (informal), charily ■ **OPPOSITE:** carelessly

gird VERB **1** The other knights urged Galahad to gird on his sword. = **girdle**, bind, belt **2** a proposal to gird the river with a series of small hydroelectric dams = **surround**, ring, pen, enclose, encompass, encircle, hem in, enfold, engird **3** They are girding themselves for battle against a new enemy. = **prepare**, ready, steel, brace, fortify, make or get ready

girdle NOUN These muscles hold in the waist like an invisible girdle. = **belt**, band, sash, waistband, cummerbund ▶ VERB The old town centre is girdled by a boulevard lined with trees. = **surround**, ring, bound, enclose, encompass, hem, encircle, fence in, gird

girl NOUN = **female child**, schoolgirl, lass, lassie (informal), miss (old-fashioned or derogatory), maiden (archaic), maid (archaic)

girlfriend NOUN = **sweetheart**, love, girl, lover, beloved, valentine, truelove, steady (informal), GF or gf (informal), bae (U.S. informal)

girth NOUN = **size**, measure, proportions, dimensions, bulk, measurement(s), circumference

gist NOUN = **essence**, meaning, point, idea, sense, import, core, substance, drift, significance, nub, pith, quintessence

give VERB **1** She stretched her arms out and gave a great yawn. = **perform**, do, carry out, execute **2** He gave no details of his plans. = **communicate**, announce, publish, transmit, pronounce, utter, emit, issue, be a source of, impart **3** Her visit gave great pleasure to the children. = **produce**, make, cause, occasion (formal), engender **4** This recipe was given to me years ago. = **present**, contribute, donate, provide, supply, award, grant, deliver, commit, administer, furnish, confer, bestow, entrust, consign, make over, hand over or out ■ **OPPOSITE:** take **5** My knees gave under me. = **collapse**, fall, break, sink, bend **6** You're a bright enough kid, I'll give you that. = **concede**, allow, grant **7** a memorial to a man who gave his life for his country = **surrender**, yield, devote, hand over, relinquish, part with, cede **8** The handout gives all the times of the performances. = **demonstrate**, show, offer, provide, evidence, display, indicate, manifest, set forth • **give in** My parents gave in and let me go to the camp. = **admit defeat**, yield, concede, collapse, quit, submit, surrender, comply, succumb, cave in (informal), capitulate • **give something away** They were giving away company secrets. = **reveal**, expose, leak, disclose, betray, uncover, let out, divulge, let slip, let the cat out of the bag (informal) • **give something off** or **out** Natural gas gives off less carbon dioxide than coal. = **emit**, produce, release, discharge, send out, throw out, vent, exude, exhale • **give something out 1** There were people at the entrance giving out leaflets. = **distribute**, issue, deliver, circulate, hand out, dispense, dole out, pass round **2** He wouldn't give out any information. = **make known**, announce, publish, broadcast, communicate, transmit, utter, notify, impart, disseminate, shout from the rooftops (informal) • **give something up 1** I'm trying to give up smoking. = **abandon**, stop, quit, kick (informal), cease, cut out, renounce, leave off, say goodbye to, desist, kiss (something) goodbye, forswear **2** She gave up her job to join the campaign. = **quit**, leave, resign, step down from (informal) **3** The government refused to give up any territory.

= **hand over**, yield, surrender, relinquish (*formal*), waive

given ADJECTIVE **1** *the number of accidents at this spot in a given period* = **specified**, particular, specific, designated, stated, predetermined **2** *I am not very given to emotional displays.* = **inclined**, addicted, disposed, prone, liable

glacial ADJECTIVE **1** *The air from the sea felt glacial.* = **icy**, biting, cold, freezing, frozen, bitter, raw, chill, piercing, arctic (*informal*), polar, chilly, frosty, wintry **2** *The Duchess gave him a glacial look and moved on.* = **unfriendly**, hostile, cold, icy, frosty, antagonistic, frigid, inimical

glad ADJECTIVE **1** *I'm glad I decided to go after all.* = **happy**, pleased, delighted, contented, cheerful, gratified, joyful, overjoyed, chuffed (*slang*), gleeful ■ **OPPOSITE:** unhappy **2** *the bringer of glad tidings* = **pleasing**, happy, cheering, pleasant, delightful, cheerful, merry, gratifying, cheery, joyous, felicitous

gladly ADVERB **1** *He gladly accepted my invitation.* = **happily**, cheerfully, gleefully, merrily, gaily, joyfully, joyously, jovially **2** *The counsellors will gladly baby-sit during their free time.* = **willingly**, freely, happily, readily, cheerfully, with pleasure, with (a) good grace ■ **OPPOSITE:** reluctantly

glamorous ADJECTIVE **1** *some of the world's most beautiful and glamorous women* = **attractive**, beautiful, lovely, charming, entrancing, elegant, dazzling, enchanting, captivating, alluring, bewitching ■ **OPPOSITE:** unglamorous **2** *his glamorous playboy lifestyle* = **exciting**, glittering, prestigious, glossy, glitzy (*slang*), bling (*slang*) ■ **OPPOSITE:** unglamorous

glamour NOUN **1** *Her air of mystery only added to her glamour.* = **charm**, appeal, beauty, attraction, fascination, allure, magnetism, enchantment, bewitchment **2** *the glamour of showbiz* = **excitement**, magic, thrill, romance, prestige, glitz (*slang*)

glance VERB **1** *He glanced at his watch.* = **peek**, look, view, check, clock (*Brit. informal*), gaze, glimpse, check out (*informal*), peep, take a dekko at (*Brit. slang*) ■ **OPPOSITE:** scrutinize **2** (*with* **over, through,** *etc.*) *I picked up the book and glanced through it.* = **scan**, browse, dip into, leaf through, flip through, thumb through, skim through, riffle through, run over or through, surf (*Computing*) ▶ NOUN *She stole a quick glance at her watch.* = **peek**, look, glimpse, peep, squint, butcher's (*Brit. slang*), quick look, gander (*informal*), brief look, dekko (*slang*), shufti (*Brit. slang*), gink (*N.Z. slang*) ■ **OPPOSITE:** good look

USAGE Care should be taken not to confuse *glance* and *glimpse*: *he caught a glimpse* (not *glance*) *of her making her way through the crowd; he gave a quick glance* (not *glimpse*) *at his watch.* A *glance* is a deliberate action, while a *glimpse* seems opportunistic.

glare VERB **1** *He glared and muttered something.* = **scowl**, frown, glower, look daggers, stare angrily, give a dirty look, lour or lower **2** *The light was glaring straight into my eyes.* = **dazzle**, blaze, flare, flame ▶ NOUN **1** *His glasses magnified his irritable glare.* = **scowl**, frown, glower, dirty look, black look, angry stare, lour or lower **2** *the glare of a car's headlights* = **dazzle**, glow, blaze, flare, flame, brilliance

glaring ADJECTIVE *I never saw such a glaring example of misrepresentation.* = **obvious**, open, outstanding, patent, visible, gross, outrageous, manifest, blatant, conspicuous, overt, audacious, flagrant, rank, egregious, unconcealed ■ **OPPOSITE:** inconspicuous

glassy ADJECTIVE **1** *glassy green pebbles* = **smooth**, clear, slick, shiny, glossy, transparent, slippery **2** *There was a remote, glassy look in his eyes.* = **expressionless**, cold, fixed, empty, dull, blank, glazed, vacant, dazed, lifeless

glaze NOUN *hand-painted tiles with decorative glazes* = **coat**, finish, polish, shine, gloss, varnish, enamel, lacquer, lustre, patina ▶ VERB *After the pots are fired, they are glazed in a variety of colours.* = **coat**, polish, gloss, varnish, enamel, lacquer, burnish, furbish (*formal*)

gleam VERB *His red sports car gleamed in the sun.* = **shine**, flash, glow, sparkle, glitter, flare, shimmer, glint, glimmer, glisten, scintillate ▶ NOUN **1** *the gleam of the headlights* = **glimmer**, flash, beam, glow, sparkle **2** *There was a gleam of hope for a peaceful settlement.* = **trace**, ray, suggestion, hint, flicker, glimmer, inkling

gleaming ADJECTIVE = **shining**, bright, brilliant, glowing, sparkling, glimmering, glistening, scintillating, burnished, lustrous ■ **OPPOSITE:** dull

glean VERB = **gather**, learn, pick up, collect, harvest, accumulate, reap, garner, amass, cull

glee NOUN = **delight**, joy, triumph, exuberance, elation, exhilaration, mirth, hilarity, merriment, exultation, gladness, joyfulness, joyousness ■ **OPPOSITE:** gloom

gleeful ADJECTIVE = **delighted**, happy, pleased, cheerful, merry, triumphant, gratified, exuberant, jubilant, joyous, joyful, elated, overjoyed, chirpy (*informal*), exultant, cock-a-hoop, mirthful, stoked (*Austral. & N.Z. informal*)

glib ADJECTIVE = **smooth**, easy, ready, quick, slick, plausible, slippery, fluent, suave, artful, insincere, fast-talking, smooth-tongued ■ OPPOSITE: sincere

glide VERB = **slip**, sail, slide, skim

glimmer VERB *The moon glimmered faintly through the mists.* = **gleam**, shine, glow, sparkle, glitter, blink, flicker, shimmer, twinkle, glisten ▶ NOUN 1 *In the east there is the faintest glimmer of light.* = **glow**, ray, sparkle, gleam, blink, flicker, shimmer, twinkle 2 *Our last glimmer of hope faded.* = **trace**, ray, suggestion, hint, grain, gleam, flicker, inkling

glimpse NOUN *The fans waited outside the hotel to get a glimpse of their heroine.* = **look**, sighting, sight, glance, peep, peek, squint, butcher's (*Brit. slang*), quick look, gander (*informal*), brief view, shufti (*Brit. slang*) ▶ VERB *She glimpsed a group of people standing on the bank of a river.* = **catch sight of**, spot, sight, view, clock (*Brit. informal*), spy, espy

glint VERB *The sea glinted in the sun.* = **gleam**, flash, shine, sparkle, glitter, twinkle, glimmer ▶ NOUN *glints of sunlight* = **gleam**, flash, shine, sparkle, glitter, twinkle, twinkling, glimmer

glisten VERB = **gleam**, flash, shine, sparkle, glitter, shimmer, twinkle, glint, glimmer, scintillate

glitch NOUN = **problem**, difficulty, fault, flaw, bug (*informal*), hitch, snag, uphill (*S. African*), interruption, blip, malfunction, kink, gremlin, fly in the ointment

glitter VERB *The palace glittered with lights.* = **shine**, flash, sparkle, flare, glare, gleam, shimmer, twinkle, glint, glimmer, glisten, scintillate ▶ NOUN 1 *all the glitter and glamour of a Hollywood premiere* = **glamour**, show, display, gilt, splendour, tinsel, pageantry, gaudiness, showiness 2 *the glitter of strobe lights and mirror balls* = **sparkle**, flash, shine, beam, glare, gleam, brilliance, sheen, shimmer, brightness, lustre, radiance, scintillation

gloat VERB = **relish**, triumph, glory, crow, revel in, vaunt, drool, exult, rub your hands

global ADJECTIVE 1 *a global ban on nuclear testing* = **worldwide**, world, international, universal, planetary 2 *a global vision of contemporary society* = **comprehensive**, general, total, thorough, unlimited, exhaustive, all-inclusive, all-encompassing, encyclopedic, unbounded ■ OPPOSITE: limited

globe NOUN = **planet**, world, earth, sphere, orb

gloom NOUN 1 *the gloom of a foggy November morning* = **darkness**, dark, shadow, cloud, shade, twilight, dusk (*poetic*), obscurity, blackness, dullness, murk, dimness, murkiness, cloudiness, gloominess, duskiness ■ OPPOSITE: light 2 *the deepening gloom over the economy* = **depression**, despair, misery, sadness, sorrow, blues, woe, melancholy, unhappiness, desolation, despondency, dejection, low spirits, downheartedness ■ OPPOSITE: happiness

gloomy ADJECTIVE 1 *Inside it's gloomy after all that sunshine.* = **dark**, dull, dim, dismal, black, grey, obscure, murky, dreary, sombre, shadowy, overcast, dusky ■ OPPOSITE: light 2 *He is gloomy about the fate of the economy.* = **miserable**, down, sad, dismal, low, blue, pessimistic, melancholy, glum, dejected, despondent, dispirited, downcast, joyless, downhearted, down in the dumps (*informal*), cheerless, down in the mouth, in low spirits ■ OPPOSITE: happy 3 *Officials say the outlook for next year is gloomy.* = **depressing**, bad, dismal, dreary, black, saddening, sombre, dispiriting, disheartening, funereal, cheerless, comfortless

glorify VERB 1 *the banning of songs glorifying war* = **praise**, celebrate, magnify, laud (*literary*), extol, crack up (*informal*), eulogize, sing or sound the praises of ■ OPPOSITE: condemn 2 *We are committed to serving the Lord and glorifying his name.* = **worship**, honour, bless, adore, revere, exalt, pay homage to, venerate, sanctify, immortalize ■ OPPOSITE: dishonour 3 *They've glorified his job with an impressive title.* = **enhance**, raise, elevate, adorn, dignify, magnify, augment, lift up, ennoble, add lustre to, aggrandize ■ OPPOSITE: degrade

glorious ADJECTIVE 1 *a glorious Edwardian opera house* = **splendid**, beautiful, bright, brilliant, shining, superb, divine (*informal*), gorgeous, dazzling, radiant, resplendent, splendiferous (*facetious*) ■ OPPOSITE: dull 2 *We opened the window and let in the glorious evening air.* = **delightful**, fine, wonderful, excellent, heavenly (*informal*), marvellous, splendid, gorgeous, pleasurable, splendiferous (*facetious*) 3 *He had a glorious career spanning more than six decades.* = **illustrious**, famous, celebrated, distinguished, noted, grand, excellent, honoured, magnificent, noble, renowned, elevated, eminent, triumphant, majestic, famed, sublime ■ OPPOSITE: ordinary

glory NOUN 1 *He had his moment of glory when he won the Berlin Marathon.* = **honour**, praise, fame, celebrity, distinction, acclaim, prestige, immortality, eminence, kudos,

g

renown, exaltation, illustriousness
■ **OPPOSITE:** shame **2** *the glory of the royal court* = **splendour**, majesty, greatness, grandeur, nobility, pomp, magnificence, pageantry, éclat, sublimity **3** *the glory of an autumn sunset* = **beauty**, brilliance, lustre, radiance, gorgeousness, resplendence **4** *Glory be to God.* = **worship**, praise, blessing, gratitude, thanksgiving, homage, adoration, veneration ▶ VERB *The workers were glorying in their new-found freedom.* = **triumph**, boast, relish, revel, crow, drool, gloat, exult, take delight, pride yourself

gloss¹ NOUN **1** *The rain produced a black gloss on the asphalt.* = **shine**, gleam, sheen, polish, brilliance, varnish, brightness, veneer, lustre, burnish, patina **2** *He tried to put a gloss of respectability on the horrors the regime perpetrated.* = **façade**, show, front (*informal*), surface, appearance, mask, semblance

gloss² NOUN *A gloss in the margin explains this unfamiliar word.* = **interpretation**, comment, note, explanation, commentary, translation, footnote, elucidation ▶ VERB *Earlier editors glossed 'drynke' as 'love-potion'.* = **interpret**, explain, comment, translate, construe, annotate, elucidate

glossy ADJECTIVE = **shiny**, polished, shining, glazed, bright (*informal*), brilliant, smooth, sleek, silky, burnished, glassy, silken, lustrous ■ **OPPOSITE:** dull

glow NOUN **1** *The rising sun cast a golden glow over the fields.* = **light**, gleam, splendour, glimmer, brilliance, brightness, radiance, luminosity, vividness, incandescence, phosphorescence ■ **OPPOSITE:** dullness **2** *The moisturiser gave my face a healthy glow that lasted all day.* = **colour**, bloom, flush, blush, reddening, rosiness ■ **OPPOSITE:** pallor ▶ VERB **1** *The night lantern glowed softly in the darkness.* = **shine**, burn, gleam, brighten, glimmer, smoulder **2** *Her freckled skin glowed with health.* = **be pink**, colour, flush, blush **3** *The expectant mothers positively glowed with pride.* = **be suffused**, thrill, radiate, tingle

glower VERB *He glowered at me but said nothing.* = **scowl**, glare, frown, look daggers, give a dirty look, lour or lower ▶ NOUN *His frown deepened into a glower of resentment.* = **scowl**, glare, frown, dirty look, black look, angry stare, lour or lower

glowing ADJECTIVE **1** *The premiere of his play received glowing reviews.* = **complimentary**, enthusiastic, rave (*informal*), ecstatic, rhapsodic, laudatory, adulatory
■ **OPPOSITE:** scathing **2** *stained glass in rich, glowing colours* = **bright**, vivid, vibrant, rich, warm, radiant, luminous ■ **OPPOSITE:** dull

glue NOUN *a tube of glue* = **adhesive**, cement, gum, paste ▶ VERB *Glue the fabric around the window.* = **stick**, fix, seal, cement, gum, paste, affix

glum ADJECTIVE = **gloomy**, miserable, dismal, down, low, melancholy, dejected, downcast, morose, doleful, downhearted, down in the dumps (*informal*), down in the mouth, in low spirits ■ **OPPOSITE:** cheerful

glut NOUN *There's a glut of agricultural products in Western Europe.* = **surfeit**, excess, surplus, plethora, saturation, oversupply, overabundance, superabundance
■ **OPPOSITE:** scarcity ▶ VERB **1** *Soldiers returning from war had glutted the job market.* = **saturate**, flood, choke, clog, overload, inundate, deluge, oversupply **2** *The pond was glutted with fish.* = **overfill**, fill, stuff, cram, satiate

glutinous ADJECTIVE = **sticky**, adhesive, cohesive, gooey, viscous, gummy, gluey, viscid

glutton NOUN = **gourmand**, gorger, gannet (*slang*), gobbler, pig (*informal*)

gluttonous ADJECTIVE = **greedy**, insatiable, voracious, ravenous, rapacious, piggish, hoggish

gluttony NOUN = **greed**, rapacity, voracity, greediness, voraciousness, piggishness

gnarled ADJECTIVE **1** *a garden full of ancient gnarled trees* = **twisted**, knotted, contorted, knotty **2** *an old man with gnarled hands* = **wrinkled**, rough, rugged, leathery

gnaw VERB **1** *Woodlice attack living plants and gnaw at the stems.* = **bite**, chew, nibble, munch **2** *Doubts were already gnawing away at the back of his mind.* = **distress**, worry, trouble, harry, haunt, plague, nag, fret **3** *This run of bad luck has gnawed away at his usually optimistic character.* = **erode**, consume, devour, eat away or into, wear away or down

go VERB **1** *It took us an hour to go three miles.* = **move**, travel, advance, journey, proceed, pass, fare (*archaic*), set off ■ **OPPOSITE:** stay **2** *Come on, let's go.* = **leave**, withdraw, depart, move out, decamp, slope off, make tracks **3** *There's a mountain road that goes from Blairstown to Millbrook Village.* = **lead**, run, reach (*informal*), spread, extend, stretch, connect, span, give access **4** *The week has gone so quickly!* = **elapse**, pass, flow, fly by, expire, lapse, slip away **5** *The money goes to projects chosen by the Board.* = **be given**, be spent, be awarded, be allotted **6** *I want you to have my jewellery after I've gone.* = **die**, perish, pass away, buy it (*U.S. slang*), expire, check out (*U.S. slang*), kick it (*slang*), croak (*slang*), give up the ghost, snuff it (*informal*), peg out (*informal*), kick the bucket (*slang*), peg it (*informal*), cark it (*Austral. & N.Z. slang*), pop your clogs (*informal*) **7** *She says everything is going smoothly.* = **proceed**, develop, turn out, work out, fare, fall out, pan out (*informal*) **8** *My car isn't going very well at the moment.* = **function**, work, run, move, operate, perform ■ **OPPOSITE:** fail **9** *That jacket and those trousers don't really go.* = **match**, blend, correspond, fit, suit, chime, harmonize **10** *It just goes to prove you can't trust anyone.* = **serve**, help, tend ▶ NOUN **1** *It took us two goes to get the colour right.* = **attempt**, try, effort, bid, shot (*informal*), crack (*informal*), essay, stab (*informal*), whirl (*informal*), whack (*informal*) **2** *Whose go is it next?* = **turn**, shot (*informal*), spell, stint **3** *Considering her age, she still has a lot of go in her.* = **energy**, life, drive, spirit, pep, vitality, vigour, verve, force, get-up-and-go (*informal*), oomph (*informal*), brio, vivacity • **go about something 1** *I want him back, but I just don't know how to go about it.* = **tackle**, begin, approach, undertake, set about **2** *We were simply going about our business when we were pounced on by the police.* = **engage in**, perform, conduct, pursue, practise, ply, carry on with, apply yourself to, busy or occupy yourself with • **go along with something** *Whatever the majority decision, I'm prepared to go along with it.* = **agree**, follow, cooperate, concur, assent, acquiesce • **go at something** *He went at this unpleasant task with grim determination.* = **set about**, start, begin, tackle, set to, get down to, wade into, get to work on, make a start on, get cracking on (*informal*), address yourself to, get weaving on (*informal*) • **go away** *I wish he'd just go away and leave me alone.* = **leave**, withdraw, exit, depart, move out, go to hell (*informal*), decamp, hook it (*slang*), slope off, pack your bags (*informal*), make tracks, get on your bike (*Brit. slang*), bog off (*Brit. slang*), sling your hook (*Brit. slang*), rack off (*Austral. & N.Z. slang*) • **go back** *I decided to go back to bed.* = **return** • **go back on something** *The budget crisis has forced the President to go back on his word.* = **repudiate**, break, forsake, retract, renege on, desert, back out of, change your mind about • **go by** *My grandmother was becoming more and more frail as time went by.* = **pass**, proceed, elapse, flow on, move onward • **go by something** *If they can prove that I'm wrong, then I'll go by what they say.* = **obey**, follow, adopt, observe, comply with, heed, submit to, be guided by, take as guide • **go down 1** *Crime has gone down 70 per cent.* = **fall**, drop,

decline, slump, decrease, fall off, dwindle, lessen, ebb, depreciate, become lower **2** *the glow left in the sky after the sun has gone down* = **set**, sink **3** *The ship went down during a training exercise.* = **sink**, founder, go under, be submerged • **go for someone 1** *I tend to go for large dark men.* = **prefer**, like, choose, favour, admire, be attracted to, be fond of, hold with **2** *Patrick went for him, grabbing him by the throat.* = **attack**, assault, assail, spring upon, rush upon, launch yourself at, set about or upon **3** *My mum went for me because I hadn't told her where I was going.* = **scold**, attack, blast, criticize, flame (*informal*), put down, tear into (*informal*), diss (*slang*), impugn, lambast(e) • **go in for something** *They go in for tennis and bowls.* = **participate in**, pursue, take part in, undertake, embrace, practise, engage in • **go into something 1** *I'd like to go into this matter in a bit more detail.* = **investigate**, consider, study, research, discuss, review, examine, pursue, probe, analyse, look into, delve into, work over, scrutinize, inquire into **2** *He has decided to go into the tourism business.* = **enter**, begin, participate in • **go off 1** *She just went off without saying a word to anyone.* = **depart**, leave, quit, go away, move out, decamp, hook it (*slang*), slope off, pack your bags (*informal*), rack off (*Austral. & N.Z. slang*) **2** *A gun went off somewhere in the distance.* = **explode**, fire, blow up, detonate **3** *The fire alarm went off.* = **sound**, ring, toll, chime, peal **4** *The meeting went off all right.* = **take place**, happen, occur, come off (*informal*), come about **5** *Don't eat that! It's gone off!* = **go bad**, turn, spoil, rot, go stale • **go on 1** *I don't know what's going on.* = **happen**, occur, take place **2** *the necessity for the war to go on* = **continue**, last, stay, proceed, carry on, keep going **3** *They're always going on about choice and market forces.* = **ramble on**, carry on, chatter, waffle (*informal, chiefly Brit.*), witter (on) (*informal*), rabbit on (*Brit. informal*), prattle, blether, earbash (*Austral. & N.Z. slang*) • **go on doing something** or **go on with something** *Go on with your work.* = **continue**, pursue, proceed, carry on, stick to, persist, keep on, keep at, persevere, stick at • **go out** *The bedroom light went out after a moment.* = **be extinguished**, die out, fade out • **go out with** *I've been going out with her for six weeks now.* = **see someone**, court, date (*informal*), woo, go steady with (*informal*), be romantically involved with, step out with (*informal*) • **go over something 1** *An accountant has gone over the books.*

= **examine**, study, review, revise, inspect, work over **2** *We went over our lines together before the show.* = **rehearse**, read, scan, reiterate, skim over, peruse • **go through something 1** *He was going through a very difficult time.* = **suffer**, experience, bear, endure, brave, undergo, tolerate, withstand *It was evident that someone had been going through my possessions.* = **search**, look through, rummage through, rifle through, hunt through, fossick through (*Austral. & N.Z.*), ferret about in **3** *Going through his list of customers is a massive job.* = **examine**, check, search, explore, look through, work over **4** *He goes through around £500 a week.* = **use up**, exhaust, consume, squander • **go through with something** *We pleaded with Belinda not to go through with the divorce.* = **carry on**, continue, pursue, keep on, persevere • **go together 1** *Red wine and oysters don't really go together.* = **harmonize**, match, agree, accord, fit, make a pair **2** *We met a month ago and we've been going together ever since.* = **go out**, court, date (*informal, chiefly U.S.*), go steady (*informal*) • **go under 1** *If one firm goes under it could provoke a cascade of bankruptcies.* = **fail**, die, sink, go down, fold (*informal*), founder, succumb, go bankrupt **2** *The ship went under, taking with her all her crew.* = **sink**, go down, founder, submerge • **go up** *Interest rates have gone up again.* = **increase**, rise, mount, soar, get higher • **go with something** *Does this tie go with this shirt?* = **match**, suit, blend, correspond with, agree with, fit, complement, harmonize • **go without something** *I have known what it is like to go without food for days.* = **be deprived of**, want, lack, be denied, do without, abstain, go short, deny yourself • **no go** *I tried to get him to change his mind, but it was no go.* = **impossible**, not on (*informal*), vain, hopeless, futile

goad NOUN *His distrust only acted as a goad to me to prove him wrong.* = **incentive**, urge, spur, motivation, pressure, stimulus, stimulation, impetus, incitement

go-ahead NOUN *Don't do any major repair work until you get the go-ahead from your insurers.* = **permission**, consent, green light, assent, leave, authorization, O.K. or okay (*informal*) ▶ ADJECTIVE *The estate is one of the most go-ahead wine producers in South Africa.* = **enterprising**, pioneering, ambitious, progressive, go-getting (*informal*), up-and-coming

goal NOUN = **aim**, end, target, purpose, object, intention, objective, ambition, destination, Holy Grail (*informal*)

goat NOUN ■ RELATED WORDS: *adjective* caprine; *name of male* billy, buck; *name of female* nanny; *name of young* kid, yeanling; *collective nouns* herd, tribe

gob NOUN = **piece**, lump, chunk, hunk, nugget, blob, wad, clod, wodge (*Brit. informal*)

gobble VERB = **devour**, swallow, gulp, guzzle, wolf, bolt, cram in, gorge on, pig out on (*slang*), stuff yourself with

go-between NOUN = **intermediary**, agent, medium, broker, factor (*Scot.*), dealer, liaison, mediator, middleman

god NOUN = **deity**, immortal, divinity, divine being, supreme being, atua (*N.Z.*)

godforsaken ADJECTIVE = **desolate**, abandoned, deserted, remote, neglected, lonely, bleak, gloomy, backward, dismal, dreary, forlorn, wretched

godless ADJECTIVE = **wicked**, depraved, profane, unprincipled, atheistic, ungodly, irreligious, impious, unrighteous

godlike ADJECTIVE = **divine**, heavenly, celestial, superhuman

godly ADJECTIVE = **devout**, religious, holy, righteous, pious, good, saintly, god-fearing

godsend NOUN = **blessing**, help, benefit, asset, boon

gogga NOUN (*S. African*) = **insect**, bug, creepy-crawly (*Brit. informal*)

goggle VERB = **stare**, gape, gawp (*slang*), gawk

going-over NOUN **1** *Michael was given a complete going-over and was diagnosed with hay fever.* = **examination**, study, check, review, survey, investigation, analysis, inspection, scrutiny, perusal **2** *The bouncers took him outside and gave him a thorough going-over.* = **thrashing**, attack, beating, whipping, thumping, pasting (*slang*), buffeting, drubbing (*informal*) **3** *Our manager gave us a right going-over in the changing room after the game.* = **dressing-down**, talking-to (*informal*), lecture, rebuke, reprimand, scolding, chiding, tongue-lashing, chastisement, castigation

golden ADJECTIVE **1** *She combed and arranged her golden hair.* = **yellow**, bright, brilliant, blonde, blond, flaxen ■ OPPOSITE: dark **2** *the golden age of American moviemaking* = **successful**, glorious, prosperous, best, rich, flourishing, halcyon ■ OPPOSITE: worst **3** *There's a golden opportunity for peace which must be seized.* = **promising**, excellent, valuable, favourable, advantageous, auspicious, opportune (*formal*), propitious ■ OPPOSITE: unfavourable **4** = **favourite**, favoured, most popular, best-loved

gone ADJECTIVE **1** *He's already been gone four hours!* = **missing**, lost, away, vanished, absent, astray **2** *After two years, all her money was gone.* = **used up**, spent, finished, consumed **3** *Those happy times are gone forever.* = **past**, over, ended, finished, elapsed

good ADJECTIVE **1** *You should read this book – it's really good.* = **excellent**, great (*informal*), fine, pleasing, capital (*old-fashioned*), choice, crucial (*slang*), acceptable, pleasant, worthy, first-class, divine, splendid, satisfactory, superb, enjoyable, awesome (*slang*), dope (*slang*), sick (*slang*), world-class, admirable, agreeable, super (*informal*), pleasurable, wicked (*slang*), bad (*slang*), first-rate, tiptop, bitchin' (*U.S. slang*), booshit (*Austral. slang*), exo (*Austral. slang*), sik (*Austral. slang*), rad (*informal*), phat (*slang*), schmick (*Austral. informal*), beaut (*informal*), barrie (*Scot. slang*), belting (*Brit. slang*), pearler (*Austral. slang*) ■ **OPPOSITE:** bad **2** *He is very good at his job.* = **proficient**, able, skilled, capable, expert, talented, efficient, clever, accomplished, reliable, first-class, satisfactory, competent, thorough, adept, first-rate, adroit, dexterous ■ **OPPOSITE:** bad **3** *Rain water was once considered to be good for the complexion.* = **beneficial**, useful, healthy, helpful, favourable, wholesome, advantageous, salutary, salubrious ■ **OPPOSITE:** harmful **4** *The president is a good man.* = **honourable**, moral, worthy, ethical, upright, admirable, honest, righteous, exemplary, right, virtuous, trustworthy, altruistic, praiseworthy, estimable ■ **OPPOSITE:** bad **5** *The children have been very good all day.* = **well-behaved**, seemly, mannerly, proper, polite, orderly, obedient, dutiful, decorous, well-mannered ■ **OPPOSITE:** naughty **6** *It's very good of you to help out at such short notice.* = **kind**, kindly, friendly, obliging, charitable, humane, gracious, benevolent, merciful, beneficent, well-disposed, kind-hearted ■ **OPPOSITE:** unkind **7** *She's been a good friend to me over the years.* = **true**, real, genuine, proper, reliable, dependable, sound, trustworthy, dinkum (*Austral. & N.Z. informal*) **8** *The film lasts a good two and a half hours.* = **full**, long, whole, complete, entire, solid, extensive ■ **OPPOSITE:** scant **9** *A good number of people agree with me.* = **considerable**, large, substantial, sufficient, adequate, ample **10** *Can you think of one good reason why I should tell you?* = **valid**, convincing, compelling, legitimate, authentic, persuasive, sound, bona fide ■ **OPPOSITE:** invalid **11** *Try not to*

get paint on your good clothes. = **best**, newest, special, finest, nicest, smartest, fancy, most valuable, most precious **12** *Is this fish still good, or has it gone off?* = **edible**, untainted, uncorrupted, eatable, fit to eat ■ **OPPOSITE:** bad **13** *Is this a good time for us to discuss our plans?* = **convenient**, timely, fitting, fit, appropriate, suitable, well-timed, opportune (*formal*) ■ **OPPOSITE:** inconvenient ▶ NOUN **1** *I'm only doing all this for your own good.* = **benefit**, interest, gain, advantage, use, service, profit, welfare, behalf, usefulness, wellbeing ■ **OPPOSITE:** disadvantage **2** *Good and evil may co-exist within one family.* = **virtue**, goodness, righteousness, worth, merit, excellence, morality, probity (*formal*), rectitude, uprightness ■ **OPPOSITE:** evil • **for good** *A few shots of this drug cleared up the disease for good.* = **permanently**, finally, for ever, once and for all, irrevocably, never to return, sine die (*Latin*)

goodbye NOUN *It was a very emotional goodbye.* = **farewell**, parting, leave-taking ▶ INTERJECTION *Well, goodbye and good luck.* = **farewell**, see you, see you later, ciao (*Italian*), cheerio, adieu, ta-ta, au revoir (*French*), auf Wiedersehen (*German*), adios (*Spanish*), haere ra (*N.Z.*)

good-humoured ADJECTIVE = **genial**, happy, pleasant, cheerful, amiable, affable, congenial, good-tempered

good-looking ADJECTIVE = **attractive**, pretty, fair, beautiful, lovely, handsome, gorgeous (*informal*), bonny (*Scot. & Northern English, dialect*), personable, comely (*old-fashioned*), well-favoured, hot (*informal*), fit (*Brit. informal*)

good-natured ADJECTIVE = **amiable**, kind, kindly, friendly, generous, helpful, obliging, tolerant, agreeable, benevolent, good-hearted, magnanimous, well-disposed, warm-hearted

goodness NOUN **1** *He retains his faith in human goodness.* = **virtue**, honour, merit, integrity, morality, honesty, righteousness, probity (*formal*), rectitude, uprightness ■ **OPPOSITE:** badness **2** *her total belief in the goodness of the human spirit* = **excellence**, value, quality, worth, merit, superiority **3** *drinks full of natural goodness* = **nutrition**, benefit, advantage, nourishment, wholesomeness, salubriousness **4** *performing actions of goodness towards the poor* = **kindness**, charity, humanity, goodwill, mercy, compassion, generosity, friendliness, benevolence, graciousness, beneficence, kindliness, humaneness, kind-heartedness

goods PLURAL NOUN **1** *a wide range of consumer goods* = **merchandise**, stock, products, stuff, commodities, wares **2** *You can give all your unwanted goods to charity.* = **property**, things, effects, gear, furniture, movables, possessions, furnishings, belongings, trappings, paraphernalia, chattels, appurtenances

goodwill NOUN = **friendliness**, favour, friendship, benevolence, amity (*formal*), kindliness

gooey ADJECTIVE **1** *a lovely gooey, sticky mess* = **sticky**, soft, tacky, viscous, glutinous, gummy, icky (*informal*), gluey, gloopy, gungy **2** *He wrote me a long, gooey love letter.* = **sentimental**, romantic, sloppy (*informal*), soppy (*Brit. informal*), maudlin, syrupy (*informal*), slushy (*informal*), mawkish, tear-jerking (*informal*), icky (*informal*)

gore¹ NOUN *films full of blood and gore* = **blood**, slaughter, bloodshed, carnage, butchery

gore² VERB *He was gored to death by a rhinoceros.* = **pierce**, wound, stab, spit, transfix, impale

gorge NOUN *a steep path into Crete's Samaria Gorge* = **ravine**, canyon, pass, clough (*dialect*), chasm, cleft, fissure, defile, gulch (*U.S. & Canad.*) ▶ VERB **1** *I could spend all day gorging on chocolate.* = **overeat**, bolt, devour, gobble, wolf, swallow, gulp, guzzle, pig out (*slang*) **2** (*usually reflexive*) *Three men were gorging themselves on grouse and watermelon.* = **stuff**, fill, feed, cram, glut, surfeit, satiate, sate

gorgeous ADJECTIVE **1** *Some of these Renaissance buildings are absolutely gorgeous.* = **magnificent**, grand, beautiful, superb, spectacular, splendid, glittering, dazzling, luxurious, sumptuous, opulent ■ OPPOSITE: shabby **2** *The cosmetics industry uses gorgeous models to sell its products.* = **beautiful**, attractive, lovely, stunning (*informal*), elegant, handsome, good-looking, exquisite, drop-dead (*slang*), ravishing, hot (*informal*), fit (*Brit. informal*), lush (*slang*) **3** *It's a gorgeous day.* = **fine**, glorious, sunny ■ OPPOSITE: dull

gory ADJECTIVE **1** *The film is full of gory death scenes.* = **grisly**, bloody, murderous, bloodthirsty **2** *The paramedic carefully stripped off his gory clothes.* = **bloody**, bloodstained, blood-soaked

gospel NOUN **1** *He visited the sick and preached the gospel.* = **doctrine**, news, teachings, message, revelation, creed, credo, tidings **2** *The results were not to be taken as gospel.* = **truth**, fact, certainty, the last word, verity

gossip NOUN **1** *There has been a lot of gossip about the reasons for his absence.* = **idle talk**, scandal, hearsay, tittle-tattle, buzz, dirt (*slang*), goss (*informal*), jaw (*slang*), gen (*Brit. informal*), small talk, chitchat, blether, scuttlebutt (*U.S. slang*), chinwag (*Brit. informal*) **2** *I bet the old gossips back home are really shocked.* = **busybody**, babbler, prattler, chatterbox (*informal*), blether, chatterer, scandalmonger, gossipmonger, tattletale (*chiefly U.S. & Canad.*) ▶ VERB *We gossiped well into the night.* = **chat**, chatter, blather, schmooze (*slang*), jaw (*slang*), dish the dirt (*informal*), blether, shoot the breeze (*slang, chiefly U.S.*), chew the fat or rag (*slang*)

gouge VERB *quarries which have gouged great holes in the hills* = **scoop**, cut, score, dig (out), scratch, hollow (out), claw, chisel, gash, incise ▶ NOUN *iron-rimmed wheels digging great gouges into the road's surface* = **gash**, cut, scratch, hollow, score, scoop, notch, groove, trench, furrow, incision

gourmet NOUN = **connoisseur**, foodie (*informal*), bon vivant (*French*), epicure, gastronome

govern VERB **1** *They go to the polls on Friday to choose the people they want to govern their country.* = **rule**, lead, control, command, manage, direct, guide, handle, conduct, order, reign over, administer, oversee, supervise, be in power over, call the shots, call the tune, hold sway over, superintend **2** *Marine insurance is governed by a strict series of rules and regulations.* = **determine**, decide, guide, rule, influence, underlie, sway **3** *Try to govern your temper.* = **restrain**, control, check, contain, master, discipline, regulate, curb, inhibit, tame, subdue, get the better of, bridle, hold in check, keep a tight rein on

government NOUN **1** *The Government has insisted that confidence is needed before the economy can improve.* = **administration**, executive, ministry, regime, governing body, powers-that-be, e-government or egovernment **2** *our system of government* = **rule**, state, law, authority, administration, sovereignty, governance, dominion, polity, statecraft

governmental ADJECTIVE = **administrative**, state, political, official, executive, ministerial, sovereign, bureaucratic

governor NOUN = **leader**, administrator, ruler, head, minister, director, manager, chief, officer, executive, boss (*informal*), commander, controller, supervisor, superintendent, mandarin, comptroller, functionary, overseer ■ RELATED WORD: *adjective* gubernatorial

gown NOUN = **dress**, costume, garment, robe, frock, garb, habit

grab VERB = **snatch**, catch, seize, capture, bag, grip, grasp, clutch, snap up, pluck, latch on to, catch or take hold of

grace NOUN 1 *He moved with the grace of a trained dancer.* = **elegance**, finesse, poise, ease, polish, refinement, fluency, suppleness, gracefulness ■ OPPOSITE: ungainliness 2 *She hadn't even the grace to apologize for what she'd done.* = **manners**, decency, cultivation, etiquette, breeding, consideration, propriety, tact, decorum, mannerliness ■ OPPOSITE: bad manners 3 *He was granted four days' grace to be with his family.* = **indulgence**, mercy, pardon, compassion, quarter, charity, forgiveness, reprieve, clemency, leniency 4 *It was only by the grace of God that no one died.* = **benevolence**, favour, goodness, goodwill, generosity, kindness, beneficence, kindliness ■ OPPOSITE: ill will 5 *Leo, will you say grace?* = **prayer**, thanks, blessing, thanksgiving, benediction 6 *The reasons for his fall from grace are not clear.* = **favour**, regard, respect, approval, esteem, approbation, good opinion ■ OPPOSITE: disfavour ▶ VERB 1 *the beautiful old Welsh dresser that graced this homely room* = **adorn**, enhance, decorate, enrich, set off, garnish, ornament, deck, embellish, bedeck, beautify 2 *He graced our ceremony with his distinguished presence.* = **honour**, favour, distinguish, elevate, dignify, glorify ■ OPPOSITE: insult

graceful ADJECTIVE *Her movements were so graceful they seemed effortless.* = **elegant**, easy, flowing, smooth, fine, pleasing, beautiful, agile, symmetrical, gracile (*rare*) ■ OPPOSITE: inelegant

graceless ADJECTIVE 1 *a graceless pirouette* = **inelegant**, forced, awkward, clumsy, ungainly, unco (*Austral. slang*) 2 *She couldn't stand his blunt, graceless manner.* = **ill-mannered**, crude, rude, coarse, vulgar, rough, improper, shameless, unsophisticated, gauche, barbarous, boorish, gawky, uncouth, loutish, indecorous, unmannerly

gracious ADJECTIVE *He is always a gracious host.* = **courteous**, polite, civil, accommodating, kind, kindly, pleasing, friendly, obliging, amiable, cordial, hospitable, courtly, chivalrous, well-mannered ■ OPPOSITE: ungracious

grade VERB *The college does not grade the children's work.* = **classify**, rate, order, class, group, sort, value, range, rank, brand, arrange, evaluate ▶ NOUN 1 *a good grade of* plywood = **class**, condition, quality, brand 2 *pressure on students to obtain good grades* = **mark**, degree (*archaic*), place, order 3 *Staff turnover is high among junior grades.* = **level**, position, rank, group, order, class, stage, step, station, category, rung, echelon • **make the grade** *She had a strong desire to be a dancer, but failed to make the grade.* = **succeed**, measure up, win through, pass muster, come up to scratch (*informal*), come through with flying colours, prove acceptable, measure up to expectations

gradient NOUN = **slope**, hill, rise, grade, incline, camber, bank

gradual ADJECTIVE = **steady**, even, slow, regular, gentle, moderate, progressive, piecemeal, unhurried ■ OPPOSITE: sudden

gradually ADVERB = **steadily**, slowly, moderately, progressively, gently, step by step, evenly, piecemeal, bit by bit, little by little, by degrees, piece by piece, unhurriedly, drop by drop

graduate VERB 1 *The dial is graduated from 1 to 10.* = **mark off**, grade, proportion, regulate, gauge, calibrate, measure out 2 *proposals to introduce an income tax which is graduated* = **classify**, rank, grade, group, order, sort, range, arrange, sequence

graft¹ NOUN *These plants are propagated by grafts, buds or cuttings.* = **shoot**, bud, implant, sprout, splice, scion ▶ VERB *Pear trees are grafted on quince root-stocks.* = **join**, insert, transplant, implant, splice, affix

graft² (*informal*) NOUN *His career has been one of hard graft.* = **labour**, work, industry, effort, struggle, sweat, toil, slog, exertion, blood, sweat, and tears (*informal*) ▶ VERB *I really don't enjoy grafting away in a stuffy office all day.* = **work**, labour, struggle, sweat (*informal*), grind (*informal*), slave, strive, toil, drudge

grain NOUN 1 *a grain of wheat* = **seed**, kernel, grist 2 *a bag of grain* = **cereal**, corn 3 *a grain of sand* = **bit**, piece, trace, spark, scrap, suspicion, molecule, particle, fragment, atom, ounce, crumb, mite, jot, speck, morsel, granule, modicum, mote, whit, iota 4 *Brush the paint over the wood in the direction of the grain.* = **texture**, pattern, surface, fibre, weave, nap

grammar NOUN = **syntax**, rules of language

grammatical ADJECTIVE = **syntactic**, linguistic

grand ADJECTIVE 1 *a grand building in the centre of town* = **impressive**, great, large, magnificent, striking, fine, princely, imposing, superb, glorious, noble, splendid, gorgeous, luxurious, eminent, majestic, regal, stately, monumental, sublime, sumptuous, grandiose, opulent, palatial, ostentatious, splendiferous (*facetious*) ■ **OPPOSITE:** unimposing **2** *He arrived in America full of grand schemes and lofty dreams.* = **ambitious**, great, glorious, lofty, grandiose, exalted, ostentatious **3** *She's too busy with her grand new friends to bother with us now.* = **superior**, great, lordly, noble, elevated, eminent, majestic, dignified, stately, lofty, august, illustrious, pompous, pretentious, haughty **4** *He was having a grand time meeting new people.* = **excellent**, great (*informal*), fine, wonderful, very good, brilliant, outstanding, smashing (*informal*), superb, first-class, divine (*informal*), marvellous (*informal*), terrific (*informal*), splendid, awesome (*slang*), world-class, admirable, super (*informal*), first-rate, splendiferous (*facetious*) ■ **OPPOSITE:** bad **5** *the federal grand jury* = **chief**, highest, lead, leading, head, main, supreme, principal, big-time (*informal*), major league (*informal*), pre-eminent ■ **OPPOSITE:** inferior

grandeur NOUN = **splendour**, glory, majesty, nobility, pomp, state, magnificence, sumptuousness, sublimity, stateliness

grandiose ADJECTIVE **1** *Not one of his grandiose plans has ever come to anything.* = **pretentious**, ambitious, extravagant, flamboyant, high-flown, pompous, showy, ostentatious, bombastic ■ **OPPOSITE:** unpretentious **2** *the grandiose building which housed the mayor's offices* = **imposing**, grand, impressive, magnificent, majestic, stately, monumental, lofty ■ **OPPOSITE:** humble

grant NOUN *My application for a grant has been rejected.* = **award**, allowance, donation, endowment, gift, concession, subsidy, hand-out, allocation, bounty, allotment, bequest, stipend ▸ VERB **1** *France has agreed to grant him political asylum.* = **give**, allow, present, award, accord, permit, assign, allocate, hand out, confer on, bestow on, impart, allot, vouchsafe (*old-fashioned*) **2** *The magistrates granted that the charity was justified in bringing the action.* = **accept**, allow, admit, acknowledge, concede, cede, accede

granule NOUN = **grain**, scrap, molecule, particle, fragment, atom, crumb, jot, speck, iota

graphic ADJECTIVE **1** *graphic descriptions of violence* = **vivid**, clear, detailed, striking, telling, explicit, picturesque, forceful, expressive, descriptive, illustrative, well-drawn ■ **OPPOSITE:** vague **2** *a graphic representation of how the chemical acts on the body* = **pictorial**, seen, drawn, visible, visual, representational, illustrative, diagrammatic ■ **OPPOSITE:** impressionistic

grapple VERB **1** *The economy is just one of the problems that the country is grappling with.* = **deal**, tackle, cope, face, fight, battle, struggle, take on, engage, encounter, confront, combat, contend, wrestle, tussle, get to grips, do battle, address yourself to **2** *He grappled desperately with Holmes for control of the weapon.* = **struggle**, fight, combat, wrestle, battle, clash, contend, strive, tussle, scuffle, come to grips

grasp VERB **1** *He grasped both my hands.* = **grip**, hold, catch, grab, seize, snatch, clutch, clinch, clasp, lay or take hold of **2** *The Government has not yet grasped the seriousness of the crisis.* = **understand**, realize, take in, get, see, follow, catch on (*informal*), comprehend, get the message about, get the picture about, catch or get the drift of ▸ NOUN **1** *She slipped her hand from his grasp.* = **grip**, hold, possession, embrace, clutches, clasp **2** *They have a good grasp of foreign languages.* = **understanding**, knowledge, grip, perception, awareness, realization, mastery, comprehension **3** *Peace is now within our grasp.* = **reach**, power, control, range, sweep, capacity, scope, sway, compass, mastery

grasping ADJECTIVE = **greedy**, acquisitive, rapacious, mean, selfish, stingy, penny-pinching (*informal*), venal, miserly, avaricious, niggardly, covetous, tightfisted, close-fisted, snoep (*S. African informal*) ■ **OPPOSITE:** generous

grate VERB **1** *Grate the cheese into a mixing bowl.* = **shred**, mince, pulverize **2** *His chair grated as he got to his feet.* = **scrape**, grind, rub, scratch, creak, rasp • **grate on** someone or **grate on someone's nerves** *His manner always grated on me.* = **annoy**, irritate, aggravate (*informal*), gall, exasperate, nettle, jar, vex, chafe, irk, rankle, peeve, get under your skin (*informal*), get up your nose (*informal*), get on your nerves (*informal*), nark (*Brit., Austral. & N.Z. slang*), set your teeth on edge, get on your wick (*Brit. slang*), rub you up the wrong way, hack you off (*informal*)

grateful ADJECTIVE = **thankful**, obliged, in (someone's) debt, indebted, appreciative, beholden

gratification NOUN **1** *Eventually they recognized him, much to his gratification.* = **satisfaction**, delight, pleasure, joy, thrill, relish, enjoyment, glee, kick or kicks (*informal*) ■ **OPPOSITE:** disappointment **2** *the gratification of his every whim* = **indulgence**, satisfaction, fulfilment ■ **OPPOSITE:** denial

g

gratify VERB = **please**, delight, satisfy, thrill, give pleasure, gladden

grating¹ NOUN *an open grating in the sidewalk* = **grille**, grid, grate, lattice, trellis, gridiron

grating² ADJECTIVE *I can't stand that grating voice of his.* = **irritating**, grinding, harsh, annoying, jarring, unpleasant, scraping, raucous, strident, squeaky, rasping, discordant, disagreeable, irksome ■ **OPPOSITE:** pleasing

gratitude NOUN = **thankfulness**, thanks, recognition, obligation, appreciation, indebtedness, sense of obligation, gratefulness ■ **OPPOSITE:** ingratitude

gratuitous ADJECTIVE = **unjustified**, unnecessary, needless, unfounded, unwarranted, superfluous, wanton, unprovoked, groundless, baseless, uncalled-for, unmerited, causeless ■ **OPPOSITE:** justifiable

gratuity NOUN = **tip**, present, gift, reward, bonus, donation, boon (*archaic*), bounty, recompense, perquisite, baksheesh, benefaction, pourboire (*French*), bonsela (*S. African*), largesse *or* largess

grave¹ NOUN *They used to visit her grave twice a year.* = **tomb**, vault, crypt, mausoleum, sepulchre, pit, last resting place, burying place ■ **RELATED WORD:** *adjective* sepulchral

grave² ADJECTIVE **1** *He says the situation in his country is very grave.* = **serious**, important, significant, critical, pressing, threatening, dangerous, vital, crucial (*informal*), acute, severe, urgent, hazardous, life-and-death, momentous, perilous, weighty, leaden, of great consequence ■ **OPPOSITE:** trifling **2** *She could tell by his grave expression that something terrible had happened.* = **solemn**, sober, gloomy, dull, thoughtful, subdued, sombre, dour, grim-faced, long-faced, unsmiling ■ **OPPOSITE:** carefree

graveyard NOUN = **cemetery**, churchyard, burial ground, charnel house, necropolis, boneyard (*informal*), God's acre (*literary*)

gravitas NOUN = **seriousness**, gravity, solemnity

gravitate VERB (*with* **to** *or* **towards**) = **be drawn**, move, tend, lean, be pulled, incline, be attracted, be influenced

gravity NOUN **1** *You don't seem to appreciate the gravity of this situation.* = **seriousness**, importance, consequence, significance, urgency, severity, acuteness, moment, weightiness, momentousness, perilousness, hazardousness ■ **OPPOSITE:** triviality **2** *There was an appealing gravity to everything she said.* = **solemnity**, gloom, seriousness, gravitas, thoughtfulness, grimness ■ **OPPOSITE:** frivolity

graze¹ VERB *cows grazing in a field* = **feed**, crop, browse, pasture

graze² VERB **1** *I had grazed my knees a little.* = **scratch**, skin, bark, scrape, chafe, abrade **2** *A bullet had grazed his arm.* = **touch**, brush, rub, scrape, shave, skim, kiss, glance off ▶ NOUN *He just has a slight graze.* = **scratch**, scrape, abrasion

greasy ADJECTIVE **1** *He propped his elbows upon the greasy counter.* = **fatty**, slick, slippery, oily, slimy (*Brit.*), oleaginous **2** *She called him 'a greasy little sycophant'.* = **sycophantic**, fawning, grovelling, ingratiating, smooth, slick, oily, unctuous, smarmy (*Brit. informal*), toadying

great ADJECTIVE **1** *a great hall as long and high as a church* = **large**, big, huge, vast, enormous, extensive, tremendous, immense, gigantic, mammoth, bulky, colossal, prodigious, stupendous, voluminous, elephantine, ginormous (*informal*), humongous *or* humungous (*informal*), supersize ■ **OPPOSITE:** small **2** *I'll take great care of it.* = **extreme**, considerable, excessive, high, decided, pronounced, extravagant, prodigious, inordinate **3** *the great cultural achievements of the past* = **major**, lead, leading, chief, main, capital, grand, primary, principal, prominent, superior, paramount, big-time (*informal*), major league (*informal*) **4** *his pronouncements on the great political matters of the age* = **important**, serious, significant, critical, crucial (*informal*), heavy, grave, momentous, weighty, consequential ■ **OPPOSITE:** unimportant **5** *the great American president, Abraham Lincoln* = **famous**, celebrated, outstanding, excellent, remarkable, distinguished, prominent, glorious, notable, renowned, eminent, famed, illustrious, exalted, noteworthy **6** *He was one of the West Indies' greatest cricketers.* = **expert**, skilled, talented, skilful, good, able, masterly, crack (*slang*), superb, world-class, adept, stellar (*informal*), superlative, proficient, adroit ■ **OPPOSITE:** unskilled **7** *It's a great film; you must see it.* = **excellent**, good, fine, wonderful, mean (*slang*), topping (*Brit. slang*), cracking (*Brit. informal*), superb, fantastic (*informal*), tremendous (*informal*), marvellous (*informal*), terrific (*informal*), mega (*slang*), sovereign, awesome (*slang*), dope (*slang*), sick (*slang*), admirable, first-rate, def (*informal*), brill (*informal*), boffo (*slang*), bitchin', chillin' (*U.S. slang*), booshit (*Austral. slang*), exo (*Austral. slang*), sik (*Austral. slang*), rad (*informal*), phat (*slang*), schmick (*Austral. informal*), beaut

g

(informal), barrie (*Scot. slang*), belting (*Brit. slang*), pearler (*Austral. slang*) ■ **OPPOSITE:** poor **8** *He gave me a great big smile.* = **very**, really, particularly, truly, extremely, awfully (*informal*), exceedingly **9** *I'm not a great fan of football.* = **enthusiastic**, keen, active, devoted, zealous

greatly ADVERB = **very much**, much, hugely, vastly, extremely, highly, seriously (*informal*), notably, considerably, remarkably, enormously, immensely, tremendously, markedly, powerfully, exceedingly, mightily, abundantly, by much, by leaps and bounds, to the nth degree

greatness NOUN **1** *the greatness of ancient Rome* = **grandeur**, glory, majesty, splendour, power, pomp, magnificence **2** *Our team has the potential to achieve greatness this season.* = **fame**, glory, celebrity, distinction, eminence, note, lustre, renown, illustriousness

greed or **greediness** NOUN **1** *He ate too much out of sheer greed.* = **gluttony**, voracity, insatiableness, ravenousness **2** *an insatiable greed for power* = **avarice**, longing, desire, hunger, craving, eagerness, selfishness, acquisitiveness, rapacity, cupidity (*formal*), covetousness, insatiableness ■ **OPPOSITE:** generosity

greedy ADJECTIVE **1** *a greedy little boy who ate too many sweets* = **gluttonous**, insatiable, voracious, ravenous, piggish, hoggish, hungry **2** *He attacked greedy bosses for awarding themselves big pay rises.* = **avaricious**, grasping, selfish, insatiable, acquisitive, rapacious, materialistic, desirous, covetous ■ **OPPOSITE:** generous

Greek ADJECTIVE *his extensive knowledge of Greek antiquity* = **Hellenic** ▶ NOUN *The ancient Greeks referred to themselves as Hellenes.* = **Hellene**

green ADJECTIVE **1** *The city has only thirteen square centimetres of green space for each inhabitant.* = **verdant** (*literary*), leafy, grassy **2** *trying to persuade governments to adopt greener policies* = **ecological**, conservationist, environment-friendly, ecologically sound, eco-friendly, ozone-friendly, non-polluting, sustainable, recyclable, green-collar **3** *Pick and ripen any green fruits in a warm dark place.* = **unripe**, fresh, raw, immature **4** *He was a young lad, very green and immature.* = **inexperienced**, new, innocent, raw, naive, ignorant, immature, gullible, callow, untrained, unsophisticated, credulous, ingenuous, unpolished, wet behind the ears (*informal*) **5** *Collectors worldwide will turn green with envy.*

= **jealous**, grudging, resentful, envious, covetous **6** *By the end of the race the runners would be green with sickness.* = **nauseous**, ill, sick, pale, unhealthy, wan, under the weather ▶ NOUN **1** (*with cap.*) *The Greens see themselves as a radical alternative to the two major parties.* = **environmentalist**, conservationist **2** *a pageant on the village green* = **lawn**, common, turf, sward, grassplot ■ **RELATED WORD:** *adjective* verdant

green light NOUN = **authorization**, sanction, approval, go-ahead (*informal*), blessing, permission, confirmation, clearance, imprimatur, O.K. or okay (*informal*)

greet VERB **1** *He greeted us with a smile.* = **salute**, hail, nod to, say hello to, address, accost, tip your hat to **2** *She was waiting at the door to greet her guests.* = **welcome**, meet, receive, karanga (*N.Z.*), mihi (*N.Z.*), haeremai (*N.Z.*) **3** *The European Court's decision has been greeted with dismay.* = **receive**, take, respond to, react to

greeting NOUN *His greeting was familiar and friendly.* = **welcome**, reception, hail, salute, address, salutation (*formal*), hongi (*N.Z.*), kia ora (*N.Z.*) ▶ PLURAL NOUN *They exchanged hearty greetings.* = **best wishes**, regards, respects, compliments, good wishes, salutations

gregarious ADJECTIVE = **outgoing**, friendly, social, cordial, sociable, affable, convivial, companionable ■ **OPPOSITE:** unsociable

grey ADJECTIVE **1** *It was a grey, wet April Sunday.* = **dull**, dark, dim, gloomy, cloudy, murky, drab, misty, foggy, overcast, sunless **2** *little grey men in suits* = **boring**, dull, anonymous, faceless, colourless, nondescript, characterless **3** *a grey old man* = **old**, aged, ancient, mature, elderly, venerable, hoary **4** *His face was grey with pain.* = **pale**, wan, livid, bloodless, colourless, pallid, ashen, like death warmed up (*informal*) **5** *The whole question of accountability is something of a grey area.* = **ambiguous**, uncertain, neutral, unclear, debatable

gridlock NOUN **1** *The streets are wedged solid with the traffic gridlock.* = **traffic jam** **2** *He agreed that these policies will lead to a gridlock in the future.* = **deadlock**, halt, stalemate, impasse, standstill, full stop

grief NOUN *Their grief soon gave way to anger.* = **sadness**, suffering, pain, regret, distress, misery, agony, mourning, sorrow, woe, anguish, remorse, bereavement, heartache, heartbreak, mournfulness ■ **OPPOSITE:** joy • **come to grief** *So many marriages have come to grief over lack of money.*

= **fail**, founder, break down, come unstuck, miscarry, fall flat on your face, meet with disaster

grievance NOUN = **complaint**, protest, beef (slang), gripe (informal), axe to grind, chip on your shoulder (informal)

grieve VERB **1** He's grieving over his dead wife and son. = **mourn**, suffer, weep, ache, lament, sorrow, wail **2** It grieved me to see him in such distress. = **sadden**, hurt, injure, distress, wound, crush, pain, afflict, upset, agonize, break the heart of, make your heart bleed ■ **OPPOSITE:** gladden

grievous ADJECTIVE **1** Their loss would be a grievous blow to our engineering industries. = **deplorable**, shocking, appalling, dreadful, outrageous, glaring, intolerable, monstrous, shameful, unbearable, atrocious, heinous, lamentable, egregious ■ **OPPOSITE:** pleasant **2** He survived in spite of suffering grievous injuries. = **severe**, damaging, heavy, wounding, grave, painful, distressing, dreadful, harmful, calamitous, injurious ■ **OPPOSITE:** mild

grim ADJECTIVE = **terrible**, shocking (informal), severe, harsh, forbidding, horrible, formidable, sinister, ghastly, hideous, gruesome (slang), grisly, horrid, frightful, godawful

grimace VERB She started to sit up, grimaced with pain, and sank back. = **scowl**, frown, sneer, wince, lour or lower, make a face or faces ▶ NOUN He took another drink of his coffee. 'Awful,' he said with a grimace. = **scowl**, frown, sneer, wince, face, wry face

grime NOUN = **dirt**, filth, soot, smut, grot (slang)

grimy ADJECTIVE = **dirty**, polluted, filthy, soiled, foul, grubby, sooty, unclean, grotty (slang), smutty, scuzzy (slang), begrimed, festy (Austral. slang)

grind VERB **1** Grind the pepper in a pepper mill. = **crush**, mill, powder, grate, pulverize, pound, kibble, abrade, granulate **2** He ground his cigarette under his heel. = **press**, push, crush, jam, mash, force down **3** If you grind your teeth at night, see your dentist. = **grate**, scrape, grit, gnash **4** The tip can be ground to a much sharper edge. = **sharpen**, file, polish, sand, smooth, whet ▶ NOUN Life continues to be a terrible grind for the ordinary person. = **hard work** (informal), labour, effort, task, sweat (informal), chore, toil, drudgery • **grind someone down** There will always be some bosses who want to grind you down. = **oppress**, suppress, harass, subdue, hound, bring down, plague, persecute, subjugate, trample underfoot, tyrannize (over)

grip VERB **1** She gripped his hand tightly. = **grasp**, hold, catch, seize, clutch, clasp, latch on to, take hold of **2** The whole nation was gripped by the dramatic story. = **engross**, fascinate, absorb, entrance, hold, catch up, compel, rivet, enthral, mesmerize, spellbind ▶ NOUN **1** I eased the bag from her grip. = **clasp**, hold, grasp, handclasp (U.S.) **2** The president maintains an iron grip on the country. = **control**, rule, influence, command, power, possession, sway, dominance, domination, mastery **3** a new kind of rubber which gives tyres a better grip = **hold**, purchase, friction, traction **4** He has lost his grip on reality. = **understanding**, sense, command, perception, awareness, grasp, appreciation, mastery, comprehension, discernment • **come** or **get to grips with something** The government's first task is to get to grips with the economy. = **tackle**, deal with, handle, take on, meet, encounter, cope with, confront, undertake, grasp, face up to, grapple with, close with, contend with

gripe VERB She started griping about the prices they were charging. = **complain**, moan (informal), groan (informal), grumble, beef (slang), carp, bitch (slang), nag, whine, grouse, bleat, grouch (informal), bellyache (slang), kvetch (U.S. slang) ▶ NOUN My only gripe is that just one main course and one dessert were available. = **complaint**, protest, objection, beef (slang), moan, grumble, grievance, grouse, grouch (informal)

gripping ADJECTIVE = **fascinating**, exciting, thrilling, entrancing, compelling, compulsive, riveting, enthralling, engrossing, spellbinding, unputdownable (informal)

grisly ADJECTIVE = **gruesome**, shocking, terrible, awful, terrifying, appalling, horrible, grim, dreadful, sickening, ghastly, hideous, macabre, horrid, frightful, abominable, hellacious (U.S. slang) ■ **OPPOSITE:** pleasant

USAGE Note the spelling of grisly (as in a grisly murder). It should be carefully distinguished from the word grizzly (as in a grizzly bear), which means 'greyish in colour'.

grit NOUN **1** She felt tiny bits of grit and sand peppering her knees. = **gravel**, sand, dust, pebbles **2** He showed grit and determination in his fight back to health. = **courage**, spirit, resolution, determination, nerve, guts (informal), balls (vulgar slang), pluck, backbone, fortitude, toughness, tenacity, perseverance, mettle, doggedness, hardihood ▶ VERB Gritting my teeth, I did my best to stifle a sharp retort. = **clench**, grind, grate, gnash

gritty ADJECTIVE **1** *She threw a handful of gritty dust into his eyes.* = **rough**, sandy, dusty, abrasive, rasping, grainy, gravelly, granular **2** *a gritty determination to get to the top* = **courageous**, game, dogged, determined, tough, spirited, brave, hardy, feisty (*informal*), resolute, tenacious, plucky, steadfast, mettlesome, (as) game as Ned Kelly (*Austral. slang*)

grizzle VERB = **whine**, fret, whimper, whinge (*informal*), snivel, girn (*Scot.*)

grizzled ADJECTIVE = **grey**, greying, grey-haired, grizzly, hoary, grey-headed

groan VERB **1** *The man on the floor began to groan with pain.* = **moan**, cry, sigh **2** *His parents were beginning to groan about the cost of it all.* = **complain**, object, moan (*informal*), grumble, gripe (*informal*), beef (*slang*), carp, bitch (*slang*), lament, whine, grouse, bemoan, whinge (*informal*), grouch (*informal*), bellyache (*slang*) ▶ NOUN **1** *She heard him let out a pitiful, muffled groan.* = **moan**, cry, sigh, whine **2** *I don't have time to listen to your moans and groans.* = **complaint**, protest, objection, grumble, beef (*slang*), grouse, gripe (*informal*), grouch (*informal*)

groggy ADJECTIVE = **dizzy**, faint, stunned, confused, reeling, shaky, dazed, wobbly, weak, unsteady, muzzy, stupefied, befuddled, punch-drunk, woozy (*informal*)

groom NOUN **1** *He worked as a groom at a stables on Dartmoor.* = **stableman**, stableboy, hostler or ostler (*archaic*) **2** *We toasted the bride and groom.* = **newly-wed**, husband, bridegroom, marriage partner ▶ VERB **1** *The horses were exercised and groomed with special care.* = **brush**, clean, tend, rub down, curry **2** *She always appeared perfectly groomed.* = **smarten up**, dress, clean, turn out, get up (*informal*), tidy, preen, spruce up, primp, gussy up (*slang, chiefly U.S.*) **3** *He was already being groomed for a top job.* = **train**, prime, prepare, coach, ready, educate, drill, nurture, make ready

groove NOUN = **indentation**, cut, hollow, score, channel, trench, flute, gutter, trough, furrow, rut

grope VERB = **feel**, search, fumble, flounder, fish, finger, scrabble, cast about, fossick (*Austral. & N.Z.*)

gross ADJECTIVE **1** *The company were found guilty of gross negligence.* = **flagrant**, obvious, glaring, blatant, serious, shocking, rank, plain, sheer, utter, outrageous, manifest, shameful, downright, grievous, unqualified, heinous, egregious, unmitigated, arrant ■ OPPOSITE: qualified **2** *That's a disgusting thing to say – you're so gross!* = **vulgar**, offensive, crude, rude, obscene, low, coarse, indecent, improper, unseemly, lewd, X-rated (*informal*), impure, smutty, ribald, indelicate ■ OPPOSITE: decent **3** *He is a gross and boorish individual.* = **coarse**, crass, tasteless, unsophisticated, ignorant, insensitive, callous, boorish, unfeeling, unrefined, uncultured, undiscriminating, imperceptive ■ OPPOSITE: cultivated **4** *The animals were gross from overfeeding.* = **fat**, obese, overweight, great, big, large, heavy, massive, dense, bulky, hulking, corpulent, lumpish ■ OPPOSITE: slim **5** *Gross sales in June totalled £270 million.* = **total**, whole, entire, aggregate, before tax, before deductions ■ OPPOSITE: net ▶ VERB *So far the films have grossed nearly £290 million.* = **earn**, make, take, bring in, rake in (*informal*)

grotesque ADJECTIVE **1** *statues of grotesque mythical creatures* = **unnatural**, bizarre, weird, odd, strange, fantastic, distorted, fanciful, deformed, outlandish, whimsical, freakish, misshapen, malformed ■ OPPOSITE: natural **2** *the grotesque disparities between the rich and the poor* = **absurd**, ridiculous, ludicrous, preposterous, incongruous ■ OPPOSITE: natural

grouch VERB *They grouched about how hard-up they were.* = **complain**, moan (*informal*), grumble, beef (*slang*), carp, bitch (*slang*), whine, grouse, gripe (*informal*), whinge (*informal*), bleat, find fault, bellyache (*slang*), kvetch (*U.S. slang*) ▶ NOUN **1** *I'm a grouch and I'm always complaining.* = **moaner**, complainer, grumbler, whiner, grouser, malcontent, curmudgeon, crosspatch (*informal*), crab (*informal*), faultfinder **2** *One of their biggest grouches is the new system of payment.* = **complaint**, protest, objection, grievance, moan (*informal*), grumble, beef (*slang*), grouse, gripe (*informal*)

grouchy ADJECTIVE = **bad-tempered**, cross, irritable, grumpy, discontented, grumbling, surly, petulant, sulky, ill-tempered, irascible, cantankerous, tetchy, ratty (*Brit. & N.Z. informal*), testy, querulous, peevish, huffy, liverish

ground NOUN **1** *We slid down the roof and dropped to the ground.* = **earth**, land, dry land, terra firma **2** *the city's football ground* = **arena**, pitch, stadium, park, field, enclosure ▶ PLURAL NOUN **1** *the palace grounds* = **estate**, holding, land, fields, gardens, property, district, territory, domain **2** *In the interview he gave some grounds for optimism.* = **reason**, cause, basis, argument, call, base, occasion, foundation, excuse, premise, motive, justification, rationale, inducement **3** *Place the coffee grounds in the bottom and pour hot water over them.* = **dregs**, lees, deposit, sediment ▶ VERB **1** *Her argument was grounded in fact.* = **base**, found, establish, set, settle, fix **2** *Make sure the children are properly grounded in the basics.* = **instruct**, train, prepare, coach, teach, inform, initiate, tutor, acquaint with, familiarize with

groundless ADJECTIVE = **baseless**, false, unfounded, unjustified, unproven, empty, unauthorized, unsubstantiated, unsupported, uncorroborated ■ OPPOSITE: well-founded

groundwork NOUN = **preliminaries**, basis, foundation, base, footing, preparation, fundamentals, cornerstone, underpinnings, spadework

group NOUN **1** *The trouble involved a small group of football supporters.* = **crowd**, company, party, band, troop, pack, gathering, gang, bunch (*informal*), congregation, posse (*slang*), bevy, assemblage **2** *a small group of islands off northern Japan* = formation, clump, aggregation ▶ VERB **1** *The fact sheets are grouped into seven sections.* = **arrange**, order, sort, class, range, gather, organize, assemble, put together, classify, marshal, bracket, assort **2** *We want to encourage them to group together as one big purchaser.* = **unite**, associate, gather, cluster, get together, congregate, band together

grouse VERB *'How come they never tell us what's going on?' he groused.* = **complain**, moan (*informal*), grumble, gripe (*informal*), beef (*slang*), carp, bitch (*slang*), whine, whinge (*informal*), bleat, find fault, grouch (*informal*), bellyache (*slang*), kvetch (*U.S. slang*) ▶ NOUN *There have been grouses about the economy, interest rates and house prices.* = **complaint**, protest, objection, moan (*informal*), grievance, grumble, gripe (*informal*), beef (*slang*), grouch (*informal*)

grove NOUN = **wood**, woodland, plantation, covert, thicket, copse, brake, coppice, spinney

grovel VERB = **humble yourself**, creep, crawl, flatter, fawn, pander, cower, toady, kowtow, bow and scrape, lick someone's boots, demean yourself, abase yourself ■ OPPOSITE: hold your head high

grow VERB **1** *We stop growing once we reach maturity.* = **develop**, fill out, get bigger, get taller ■ OPPOSITE: shrink **2** *The puddle under* the burst pipe was growing. = **get bigger**, spread, swell, extend, stretch, expand, widen, enlarge, multiply, thicken **3** *The station had roses growing at each end of the platform.* = **spring up**, shoot up, develop, flourish, sprout, germinate, vegetate **4** *I always grow a few red onions in my allotment.* = **cultivate**, produce, raise, farm, breed, nurture, propagate **5** *He's growing old.* = **become**, get, turn, come to be **6** *The idea for this book grew out of conversations with Philippa Brewster.* = **originate**, spring, arise, stem, issue **7** *The economy continues to grow.* = **improve**, advance, progress, succeed, expand, thrive, flourish, prosper

grown-up NOUN *Tell a grown-up if you're being bullied.* = **adult**, man, woman ▶ ADJECTIVE *Her grown-up children are all doing well in their chosen careers.* = **mature**, adult, of age, fully-grown

growth NOUN **1** *the unchecked growth of the country's population* = **increase**, development, expansion, extension, growing, heightening, proliferation, enlargement, multiplication ■ OPPOSITE: decline **2** *enormous economic growth* = **progress**, success, improvement, expansion, advance, prosperity, advancement ■ OPPOSITE: failure **3** *This helps to encourage new growth and makes the plant flower profusely.* = **vegetation**, development, production, sprouting, germination, shooting **4** *This type of surgery could even be used to extract cancerous growths.* = **tumour**, cancer, swelling, lump, carcinoma (*Pathology*), sarcoma (*Medical*), excrescence

grub NOUN **1** *The grubs do their damage by tunnelling through ripened fruit.* = **larva**, maggot, caterpillar **2** *Get yourself some grub and come and sit down.* = **food**, feed, rations, tack (*informal*), eats (*slang*), kai (*N.Z. informal*), sustenance, nosh (*slang*), victuals, nosebag (*slang*), vittles (*obsolete, dialect*) ▶ VERB **1** *grubbing through piles of paper for his address* = **search**, hunt, scour, ferret, rummage, forage, fossick (*Austral. & N.Z.*) **2** *chickens grubbing around in the dirt for food* = **dig**, search, root (*informal*), probe, burrow, rootle (*Brit.*)

grubby ADJECTIVE = **dirty**, soiled, filthy, squalid, messy, shabby, seedy, scruffy, sordid, untidy, grimy, unwashed, unkempt, mucky, smutty, grungy (*slang, chiefly U.S. & Canad.*), slovenly, manky (*Scot., dialect*), scuzzy (*slang*), scungy (*Austral. & N.Z.*), frowzy, besmeared, festy (*Austral. slang*)

grudge NOUN *It was an accident and I bear him no grudge.* = **resentment**, bitterness,

grievance, malice, hate, spite, dislike, animosity, aversion, venom, antipathy, enmity, rancour, hard feelings, ill will, animus, malevolence ■ **OPPOSITE:** goodwill
▶ VERB *Few seem to grudge him his good fortune.* = **resent**, mind, envy, covet, begrudge ■ **OPPOSITE:** welcome

gruelling ADJECTIVE = **exhausting**, demanding, difficult, tiring, trying, hard, taxing, grinding, severe, crushing, fierce, punishing, harsh, stiff, brutal, fatiguing, strenuous, arduous, laborious, backbreaking ■ **OPPOSITE:** easy

gruesome ADJECTIVE = **horrific**, shocking, terrible, awful, horrible, grim, horrifying, fearful (*informal*), obscene, horrendous, ghastly, hideous, from hell (*informal*), grisly, macabre, horrid, repulsive, repugnant, loathsome, abominable, spine-chilling, hellacious (*U.S. slang*) ■ **OPPOSITE:** pleasant

gruff ADJECTIVE **1** *I was expecting to hear the chief executive's gruff voice.* = **hoarse**, rough, harsh, rasping, husky, low, croaking, throaty, guttural ■ **OPPOSITE:** mellifluous **2** *His gruff exterior concealed a kind heart.* = **surly**, rough, rude, grumpy, blunt, crabbed, crusty, sullen, bad-tempered, curt, churlish, brusque, impolite, grouchy (*informal*), ungracious, discourteous, uncivil, ill-humoured, unmannerly, ill-natured ■ **OPPOSITE:** polite

grumble VERB **1** *'This is very inconvenient,' she grumbled.* = **complain**, moan (*informal*), gripe (*informal*), whinge (*informal*), beef (*slang*), carp, bitch (*slang*), whine, grouse, bleat, grouch (*informal*), bellyache (*slang*), kvetch (*U.S. slang*), repine **2** *My stomach grumbled loudly.* = **rumble**, growl, gurgle
▶ NOUN **1** *My grumble is with the structure and organization of the material.* = **complaint**, protest, objection, moan (*informal*), grievance, grouse, gripe (*informal*), grouch (*informal*), beef (*slang*) **2** *One could hear, far to the east, a grumble of thunder.* = **rumble**, growl, gurgle

grumpy ADJECTIVE = **irritable**, cross, bad-tempered, grumbling, crabbed, edgy, surly, petulant, ill-tempered, cantankerous, tetchy, ratty (*Brit. & N.Z. informal*), testy, grouchy (*informal*), querulous, peevish, huffy, crotchety (*informal*), liverish

guarantee VERB **1** *Surplus resources alone do not guarantee growth.* = **ensure**, secure, assure, warrant, insure, make certain **2** *We guarantee to refund your money if you are not delighted with your purchase.* = **promise**, pledge, undertake, swear ▶ NOUN **1** *We can give no guarantee that their demands will be met.* = **promise**, word, pledge, undertaking,

assurance, certainty, covenant, word of honour **2** *The goods were still under guarantee.* = **warranty**, contract, bond, guaranty

guarantor NOUN = **underwriter**, guarantee, supporter, sponsor, backer, surety, warrantor

guard VERB *Gunmen guarded homes near the cemetery.* = **protect**, watch, defend, secure, police, mind, cover, screen, preserve, shelter, shield, patrol, oversee, safeguard, watch over ▶ NOUN **1** *The prisoners overpowered their guards and locked them in a cell.* = **sentry**, warder, warden, custodian, watch, patrol, lookout, watchman, sentinel **2** *a heavily armed guard of police* = **escort**, patrol, convoy **3** *The heater should have a safety guard fitted.* = **shield**, security, defence, screen, protection, pad, safeguard, bumper, buffer, rampart, bulwark • **off guard** *The question had caught me off guard.* = **unprepared**, napping, unwary, unready, with your defences down • **on (your) guard** *Be on your guard against crooked car dealers.* = **vigilant**, cautious, wary, prepared, ready, alert, watchful, on the lookout, circumspect, on the alert, on the qui vive ■ **RELATED WORD:** *adjective* custodial

guarded ADJECTIVE = **cautious**, reserved, careful, suspicious, restrained, wary, discreet, prudent, reticent, circumspect, cagey (*informal*), leery (*slang*), noncommittal

guardian NOUN = **keeper**, champion, defender, guard, trustee, warden, curator, protector, warder, custodian, preserver

guerrilla NOUN = **freedom fighter**, partisan, irregular, underground fighter, member of the underground or resistance

guess VERB **1** *I can only guess what it cost her to tell you the truth.* = **estimate**, predict, work out, speculate, fathom, conjecture, postulate, surmise, hazard a guess, hypothesize ■ **OPPOSITE:** know **2** *I guess I'm just being paranoid.* = **suppose**, think, believe, suspect, judge, imagine, reckon (*informal*), fancy, conjecture, dare say
▶ NOUN **1** *He took her pulse and made a guess at her blood pressure.* = **estimate**, reckoning, speculation, judgment, hypothesis, conjecture, surmise, shot in the dark, ballpark figure (*informal*) ■ **OPPOSITE:** certainty **2** *My guess is that she's waiting for you to make the first move.* = **supposition**, feeling, idea, theory, notion, suspicion, hypothesis

guesswork NOUN = **speculation**, theory, presumption, conjecture, estimation, surmise, supposition

guest NOUN = **visitor**, company, caller, manu(w)hiri (*N.Z.*)

guff NOUN = **nonsense**, rubbish, malarkey, rot, crap (*slang*), garbage (*informal*), trash, hot air (*informal*), tosh (*slang, chiefly Brit.*), pap, bilge (*informal*), humbug, drivel, tripe (*informal*), moonshine, hogwash (*informal*), hokum (*slang, chiefly U.S. & Canad.*), piffle (*informal*), poppycock (*informal*), balderdash, bosh (*informal*), eyewash (*informal*), kak (*S. African vulgar slang*), empty talk, tommyrot, horsefeathers (*U.S. slang*), bunkum or buncombe, bizzo (*Austral. slang*), bull's wool (*Austral. & N.Z. slang*)

guidance NOUN = **advice**, direction, leadership, instruction, government, help, control, management, teaching, counsel, counselling, auspices

guide NOUN 1 *Our 10-page guide will help you change your life for the better.* = **handbook**, manual, guidebook, instructions, catalogue 2 *These restaurants are all highly rated in the guide.* = **directory**, street map 3 *With guides, the journey can be done in fourteen days.* = **escort**, leader, controller, attendant, usher, chaperon, torchbearer, dragoman 4 *Our only guide was the stars overhead.* = **pointer**, sign, signal, mark, key, clue, landmark, marker, beacon, signpost, guiding light, lodestar 5 *The checklist serves as a guide to students, teachers, and parents.* = **model**, example, standard, ideal, master, inspiration, criterion, paradigm, exemplar, lodestar ▶ VERB 1 *She took the bewildered man by the arm and guided him out.* = **lead**, direct, escort, conduct, pilot, accompany, steer, shepherd, convoy, usher, show the way 2 *She guided the plane down the runway and took off.* = **steer**, control, manage, direct, handle, command, manoeuvre 3 *He should have let his instinct guide him.* = **supervise**, train, rule, teach, influence, advise, counsel, govern, educate, regulate, instruct, oversee, sway, superintend

guild NOUN = **society**, union, league, association, company, club, order, organization, corporation, lodge, fellowship, fraternity (*U.S. & Canad.*), brotherhood, sisterhood

guile NOUN = **cunning**, craft, deception, deceit, trickery, duplicity, cleverness, art, gamesmanship (*informal*), craftiness, artfulness, slyness, trickiness, wiliness
■ **OPPOSITE:** honesty

guilt NOUN 1 *Her emotions went from anger to guilt in the space of a few seconds.* = **shame**, regret, remorse, contrition, guilty conscience, bad conscience, self-reproach, self-condemnation, guiltiness
■ **OPPOSITE:** pride 2 *You were never convinced of his guilt, were you?* = **culpability**, blame, responsibility, misconduct, delinquency, criminality, wickedness, iniquity, sinfulness, blameworthiness, guiltiness
■ **OPPOSITE:** innocence

guilty ADJECTIVE 1 *When she saw me, she looked extremely guilty.* = **ashamed**, sorry, rueful, sheepish, contrite, remorseful, regretful, shamefaced, hangdog, conscience-stricken
■ **OPPOSITE:** proud 2 *They were found guilty of manslaughter.* = **culpable**, responsible, convicted, to blame, offending, erring, at fault, reprehensible, iniquitous, felonious, blameworthy ■ **OPPOSITE:** innocent

guise NOUN 1 *He claimed the Devil had appeared to him in the guise of a goat.* = **form**, appearance, dress, fashion, shape, aspect, mode, semblance 2 *The workers are being dismissed under the guise of a reorganization.* = **pretence**, show, mask, disguise, face, front (*informal*), aspect, façade, semblance

gulch NOUN (*U.S. & Canad.*) = **ravine**, canyon, defile, gorge, gully, pass

gulf NOUN 1 *Hurricane Andrew was last night heading into the Gulf of Mexico.* = **bay**, bight, sea inlet 2 *the gulf between rural and urban life* = **chasm**, opening, split, gap, rent, breach, separation, void, rift, abyss, cleft

gullible ADJECTIVE = **trusting**, innocent, naive, unsuspecting, green, simple, silly, foolish, unsophisticated, credulous, born yesterday, wet behind the ears (*informal*), easily taken in, unsceptical, as green as grass ■ **OPPOSITE:** suspicious

gully NOUN = **ravine**, canyon, gorge, chasm, channel, fissure, defile, watercourse

gulp VERB 1 *She quickly gulped her tea.* = **swallow**, bolt, devour, gobble, knock back (*informal*), wolf, swig (*informal*), swill, guzzle, quaff 2 *He slumped back, gulping for air.* = **gasp**, swallow, choke ▶ NOUN *He drank half of his whisky in one gulp.* = **swallow**, draught, mouthful, swig (*informal*)

gum NOUN *a banknote that had been torn in half and stuck together with gum* = **glue**, adhesive, resin, cement, paste ▶ VERB *a mild infection in which the baby's eyelashes can become gummed together* = **stick**, glue, affix, cement, paste, clog

gun NOUN = **firearm**, shooter (*slang*), piece (*slang*), rod (*slang*), heater (*U.S. slang*), handgun

gunman or **gunwoman** NOUN = **armed man** or **woman** or **person**, hitman or woman (*slang*), gunslinger (*U.S. slang*)

gurgle VERB *a narrow channel along which water gurgles* = **ripple**, lap, bubble, splash, murmur, babble, burble, purl, plash

guru NOUN **1** *fashion gurus dictating crazy ideas* = **authority**, expert, leader, master, pundit, arbiter, Svengali, torchbearer, fundi (*S. African*) **2** *He set himself up as a faith healer and spiritual guru.* = **teacher**, mentor, sage, master, tutor, mahatma, guiding light, swami, maharishi

gush VERB **1** *Piping hot water gushed out of the tap.* = **flow**, run, rush, flood, pour, jet, burst, stream, cascade, issue, spurt, spout **2** *'Oh, you were just brilliant,' she gushed.* = **enthuse**, rave (*informal*), spout, overstate, rhapsodize, effuse ▶ NOUN *I heard a gush of water.* = **stream**, flow, rush, flood, jet, burst, issue, outburst, cascade, torrent, spurt, spout, outflow

gust NOUN **1** *A gust of wind drove down the valley.* = **blast**, blow, rush, breeze, puff, gale, flurry, squall **2** *A gust of laughter greeted him as he walked into the room.* = **surge**, fit, storm, burst, explosion, gale (*informal*), outburst, eruption, paroxysm ▶ VERB *strong winds gusting up to 164 miles an hour* = **blow**, blast, puff, squall

gusto NOUN = **relish**, enthusiasm, appetite, appreciation, liking, delight, pleasure, enjoyment, savour, zeal, verve, zest, fervour, exhilaration, brio, zing (*informal*)
■ **OPPOSITE:** apathy

gusty ADJECTIVE = **windy**, stormy, breezy, blustering, tempestuous, blustery, inclement, squally, blowy

gut NOUN *His gut sagged over his belt.* = **paunch** (*informal*), belly, spare tyre (*Brit. slang*), potbelly, puku (*N.Z.*) ▶ VERB **1** *It is not always necessary to gut the fish prior to freezing.*

= **disembowel**, draw, dress, clean, eviscerate **2** *The church had been gutted by vandals.* = **ravage**, strip, empty, sack, rifle, plunder, clean out, ransack, pillage, despoil (*formal*) ▶ ADJECTIVE *At first my gut reaction was to simply walk out of there.* = **instinctive**, natural, basic, emotional, spontaneous, innate, intuitive, hard-wired, involuntary, heartfelt, deep-seated, unthinking
■ **RELATED WORDS:** *technical name* viscera; *adjective* visceral

guts PLURAL NOUN **1** *The crew were standing ankle-deep in fish guts.* = **intestines**, insides (*informal*), stomach, belly, bowels, inwards, innards (*informal*), entrails **2** *The new Chancellor has the guts to push through unpopular tax increases.* = **courage**, spirit, nerve, daring, pluck, grit, backbone, willpower, bottle (*slang*), audacity, mettle, boldness, spunk (*informal*), forcefulness, hardihood

gutsy ADJECTIVE = **brave**, determined, spirited, bold, have-a-go (*informal*), courageous, gritty, staunch, feisty (*informal*), game (*informal*), resolute, gallant, plucky, indomitable, mettlesome, (as) game as Ned Kelly (*Austral. slang*)

gutter NOUN = **drain**, channel, tube, pipe, ditch, trench, trough, conduit, duct, sluice

guy NOUN = **man**, person, fellow (*old-fashioned*), lad, cat (*obsolete slang*), bloke (*Brit. informal*), chap

guzzle VERB = **devour**, drink, bolt, wolf, cram, gorge, gobble, knock back (*informal*), swill, quaff, tope, pig out on (*slang*), stuff yourself with

gyrate VERB = **rotate**, circle, spin, spiral, revolve, whirl, twirl, pirouette

Hh

habit NOUN **1** *He has an endearing habit of licking his lips.* = **mannerism**, custom, way, practice, manner, characteristic, tendency, quirk, propensity, foible, proclivity (*formal*) **2** *It had become a habit with her to annoy him.* = **custom**, rule, practice, tradition, routine, convention, mode, usage, wont, second nature **3** *After twenty years as a chain smoker, he has given up the habit.* = **addiction**, weakness, obsession, dependence, compulsion, fixation **4** *She emerged having changed into her riding habit.* = **dress**, costume, garment, apparel (*old-fashioned*), garb, habiliment, riding dress

habitat NOUN = **home**, environment, surroundings, element, territory, domain, terrain, locality, home ground, abode, habitation (*formal*), natural home

habitation NOUN **1** *20 percent of private-rented dwellings are unfit for human habitation.* = **occupation**, living in, residence, tenancy, occupancy, residency, inhabitance, inhabitancy **2** *Behind the habitations, the sandstone cliffs rose abruptly.* = **dwelling** (*formal, literary*), home, house, residence, quarters, lodging, pad (*slang*), abode, living quarters, domicile, dwelling house

habitual ADJECTIVE **1** *He soon recovered his habitual geniality.* = **customary**, normal, usual, common, standard, natural, traditional, fixed, regular, ordinary, familiar, routine, accustomed, wonted ■ **OPPOSITE:** unusual **2** *Three out of four of them would become habitual criminals.* = **persistent**, established, confirmed, constant, frequent, chronic, hardened, recurrent, ingrained, inveterate ■ **OPPOSITE:** occasional

hack¹ VERB **1** (*sometimes with* **away**) *He desperately hacked through the undergrowth.* = **cut**, chop, slash, mutilate, mangle, mangulate (*Austral. slang*), gash, hew, lacerate **2** *The patients splutter and hack.* = **cough**, bark, wheeze, rasp **3** (*a computer, phone, etc*) = **manipulate**, exploit, attack, hijack, access, spoof, bluejack, pharm, bluesnarf, phish, phreak, spear-phish ▶ NOUN *smoker's hack* = **cough**, bark, wheeze, rasp

hack² NOUN **1** *tabloid hacks, always eager to find a story* = **reporter**, writer, correspondent, journalist, scribbler, contributor, literary hack, penny-a-liner, Grub Street writer **2** *Party hacks from the old days still hold influential jobs.* = **yes-man**, lackey, toady, flunky ▶ ADJECTIVE *ill-paid lectureships and hack writing* = **unoriginal**, pedestrian, mediocre, poor, tired, stereotyped, banal, undistinguished, uninspired

hacker (*Computing*) NOUN = **fraudster**, black hat, white hat, cybercriminal, script kiddie, hacktivist (*informal*), intruder

hackles PLURAL NOUN • **raise someone's hackles** *or* **make someone's hackles rise** = **anger**, annoy, infuriate, cause resentment, rub someone up the wrong way, make someone see red (*informal*), get someone's dander up (*slang*), hack you off (*informal*)

hackneyed ADJECTIVE = **clichéd**, stock, tired, common, stereotyped, pedestrian, played out (*informal*), commonplace, worn-out, stale, overworked, banal, run-of-the-mill, threadbare, trite, unoriginal, timeworn ■ **OPPOSITE:** original

Hades NOUN = **underworld**, hell, nether regions, lower world, infernal regions, realm of Pluto, (the) inferno

haemorrhage NOUN = **drain**, outpouring, rapid loss ▶ VERB = **drain**, bleed (*informal*), flow rapidly

haggard ADJECTIVE = **gaunt**, wasted, drawn, thin, pinched, wrinkled, ghastly, wan, emaciated, shrunken, careworn, hollow-eyed ■ **OPPOSITE:** robust

haggle VERB **1** *Ella taught her how to haggle with used furniture dealers.* = **bargain**, barter, beat down, drive a hard bargain, dicker (*chiefly U.S.*), chaffer, palter, higgle **2** *As the politicians haggle, the violence worsens.* = **wrangle**, dispute, quarrel, squabble, bicker

hail¹ NOUN **1** *a short-lived storm with heavy hail* = **hailstones**, sleet, hailstorm, frozen rain **2** *The victim was hit by a hail of bullets.* = **shower**, rain, storm, battery, volley, barrage, bombardment, pelting, downpour, salvo, broadside ▶ VERB **1** *It started to hail, huge great stones.* = **rain**, shower, pelt **2** *Shellfire was hailing down on the city's edge.* = **batter**, rain, barrage, bombard, pelt, rain down on, beat down upon

hail² VERB **1** *She was hailed as the greatest violinist of her generation.* = **acclaim**, honour, acknowledge, cheer, applaud, glorify, exalt ■ **OPPOSITE:** condemn **2** *I saw him and hailed him.* = **salute**, call, greet, address, welcome, speak to, shout to, say hello to, accost, sing out, halloo ■ **OPPOSITE:** snub **3** *I hurried away to hail a taxi.* = **flag down**, summon, signal to, wave down • **hail from somewhere** *The band hail from Glasgow.* = **come from**, be born in, originate in, be a native of, have your roots in

hair NOUN *a girl with long blonde hair* = **locks**, mane, tresses, shock, mop, head of hair • **by a hair** = **by a narrow margin**, by a whisker, by a hair's-breadth, by a split second, by a fraction of an inch, by the skin of your teeth • **get in someone's hair** = **annoy**, plague, irritate, harass, hassle (*informal*), aggravate (*informal*), exasperate, pester, be on someone's back (*slang*), get on someone's nerves (*informal*), nark (*Brit., Austral. & N.Z. slang*), get up your nose (*informal*), piss you off (*slang*), get on your wick (*Brit. slang*), hack you off (*informal*) • **let your hair down** *a time when everyone really lets their hair down* = **let yourself go**, relax, chill out (*slang, chiefly U.S.*), let off steam (*informal*), let it all hang out (*informal*), mellow out (*informal*), veg out (*slang*), outspan (*S. African*) • **make someone's hair stand on end** = **terrify**, shock, scare, appal, horrify, make someone's hair curl, freeze someone's blood, scare the bejesus out of (*informal*) • **not turn a hair** *The man didn't turn a hair.* = **remain calm**, keep your cool (*slang*), not bat an eyelid, keep your hair on (*Brit. informal*) • **split hairs** *Don't split hairs. You know what I'm getting at.* = **quibble**, find fault, cavil, overrefine, pettifog, nit-pick (*informal*)

hairdresser NOUN = **stylist**, barber, coiffeur *or* coiffeuse, friseur, snipper (*informal*)

hair-raising ADJECTIVE = **frightening**, shocking, alarming, thrilling, exciting, terrifying, startling, horrifying, scary (*informal*), breathtaking, creepy (*informal*), petrifying, spine-chilling, bloodcurdling

hairstyle NOUN = **haircut**, hairdo, coiffure, cut, style

hairy ADJECTIVE **1** *I don't mind having a hairy chest, but the stuff on my back is really thick.* = **shaggy**, woolly, furry, stubbly, bushy, bearded, unshaven, hirsute (*formal*), fleecy, bewhiskered, pileous (*Biology*), pilose (*Biology*) **2** *His driving was a bit hairy.* = **dangerous**, scary (*informal*), risky, unpredictable, hazardous, perilous

halcyon ADJECTIVE **1** *It was all a far cry from those halcyon days in 1990.* = **happy**, golden, flourishing, prosperous, carefree, palmy **2** *The next day dawned sunny with a halcyon blue sky.* = **peaceful**, still, quiet, calm, gentle, mild, serene, tranquil, placid, pacific, undisturbed, unruffled

hale ADJECTIVE = **healthy**, well, strong, sound, fit, flourishing, blooming, robust, vigorous, hearty, in the pink, in fine fettle, right as rain (*Brit. informal*), able-bodied

half NOUN *A half of the voters have not made up their minds.* = **fifty per cent**, equal part ▶ ADJECTIVE *Children received only a half portion.* = **partial**, limited, fractional, divided, moderate, halved, incomplete ▶ ADVERB *The vegetables are only half cooked.* = **partially**, partly, incompletely, slightly, all but, barely, in part, inadequately, after a fashion, pretty nearly ■ RELATED WORDS: prefixes bi-, demi-, hemi-, semi-

half-baked ADJECTIVE = **stupid**, impractical, crazy (*informal*), silly, foolish, senseless, short-sighted, inane, loopy (*informal*), ill-conceived, crackpot (*informal*), ill-judged, brainless, unformed, poorly planned, harebrained, dumb-ass (*slang*), unthought out *or* through

half-hearted ADJECTIVE = **unenthusiastic**, indifferent, apathetic, cool, neutral, passive, lacklustre, lukewarm, uninterested, perfunctory, listless, spiritless ■ OPPOSITE: enthusiastic

halfway ADVERB **1** *He was halfway up the ladder.* = **midway**, to the midpoint, to or in the middle **2** *You need hard currency to get anything halfway decent.* = **partially**, partly, moderately, rather, nearly ▶ ADJECTIVE *He was third fastest at the halfway point.* = **midway**, middle, mid, central, intermediate, equidistant • **meet someone halfway** *The Democrats are willing to meet the president halfway.* = **compromise**, accommodate, come to terms, reach a compromise, strike a balance, trade off with, find the middle ground

hall NOUN **1** *The lights were on in the hall and in the bedroom.* = **passage**, lobby, corridor, hallway, foyer, entry, passageway, entrance hall, vestibule **2** *We filed into the lecture hall.* = **meeting place**, chamber, auditorium, concert hall, assembly room

hallmark NOUN **1** *a technique that has become the hallmark of their films* = **trademark**, indication, badge, emblem, sure sign, telltale sign **2** *He uses a hallmark on the base of his lamps to distinguish them.* = **mark**, sign, device, stamp, seal, symbol, signet, authentication

hallowed ADJECTIVE = **sanctified**, holy, blessed, sacred, honoured, dedicated, revered, consecrated, sacrosanct, inviolable, beatified

hallucinate VERB = **imagine**, trip (*informal*), envision, daydream, fantasize, freak out (*informal*), have hallucinations

hallucination NOUN = **illusion**, dream, vision, fantasy, delusion, mirage, apparition, phantasmagoria, figment of the imagination

hallucinogenic ADJECTIVE = **psychedelic**, mind-blowing (*informal*), psychoactive, hallucinatory, psychotropic, mind-expanding

halo NOUN = **ring of light**, aura, corona, radiance, nimbus, halation (*Photography*), aureole *or* aureola

halt VERB **1** *They halted at a short distance from the house.* = **stop**, draw up, pull up, break off, stand still, wait, rest, call it a day, belay (*Nautical*) ■ **OPPOSITE:** continue **2** *The flow of charitable donations has virtually halted.* = **come to an end**, stop, cease **3** *Striking workers halted production at the auto plant yesterday.* = **hold back**, end, check, block, arrest, stem, curb, terminate, obstruct, staunch, cut short, impede, bring to an end, stem the flow, nip in the bud ■ **OPPOSITE:** aid ▶ NOUN *Air traffic has been brought to a halt.* = **stop**, end, close, break, stand, arrest, pause, interruption, impasse, standstill, stoppage, termination ■ **OPPOSITE:** continuation

halting ADJECTIVE = **faltering**, stumbling, awkward, hesitant, laboured, stammering, imperfect, stuttering

halve VERB **1** *The work force has been halved in two years.* = **cut in half**, reduce by fifty per cent, decrease by fifty per cent, lessen by fifty per cent **2** *Halve the pineapple and scoop out the inside.* = **split in two**, cut in half, bisect, divide in two, share equally, divide equally

hammer VERB **1** *Hammer a wooden peg into the hole.* = **hit**, drive, knock, beat, strike, tap, bang **2** (*often with* **into**) *They hammered it into me that I had not become a bad goalkeeper.* = **impress upon**, repeat, drive home, drum into, grind into, din into, drub into **3** *He hammered the young left-hander in four straight sets.* = **defeat**, beat, thrash, stuff (*slang*), master, worst, tank (*slang*), lick (*informal*), trounce, clobber (*slang*), run rings around (*informal*), wipe the floor with (*informal*), blow out of the water (*slang*), drub

• **hammer away at something** *Dr Lalkaka kept hammering away at the report.* = **work**, keep on, persevere, grind, persist, stick at, plug away (*informal*), drudge, pound away, peg away (*chiefly Brit.*), beaver away (*Brit. informal*)

hamper VERB = **hinder**, handicap, hold up, prevent, restrict, frustrate, curb, slow down, restrain, hamstring, interfere with, cramp, thwart, obstruct, impede, hobble, fetter, encumber, trammel ■ **OPPOSITE:** help

hamstring VERB = **thwart**, stop, block, prevent, ruin, frustrate, handicap, curb, foil, obstruct, impede, balk, fetter

hamstrung ADJECTIVE *a hamstrung coalition government* = **incapacitated**, disabled, crippled, helpless, paralysed, at a loss, hors de combat (*French*)

hand NOUN **1** *I put my hand into my pocket.* = **palm**, fist, paw (*informal*), mitt (*slang*), hook, meathook (*slang*) **2** *Did you have a hand in his downfall?* = **influence**, part, share, agency (*old-fashioned*), direction, participation **3** *Come and give me a hand in the garden.* = **assistance**, help, aid, support, helping hand **4** *He now works as a farm hand.* = **worker**, employee, labourer, workman, operative, craftsman *or* woman *or* person, artisan, hired hand, hireling **5** *Let's give 'em a big hand.* = **round of applause**, clap, ovation, big hand **6** *written in the composer's own hand* = **writing**, script, handwriting, calligraphy, longhand, penmanship, chirography ▶ VERB **1** *She handed me a little rectangle of white paper.* = **give**, pass, hand over, present to, deliver **2** *He handed her into his old Alfa Romeo sports car.* = **help**, guide, conduct, lead, aid, assist, convey • **at** *or* **on hand** *Having the right equipment on hand is enormously helpful.* = **within reach**, nearby, handy, close, available, ready, on tap (*informal*), at your fingertips • **hand in glove** *They work hand in glove with the western intelligence agencies.* = **in association**, in partnership, in league, in collaboration, in cooperation, in cahoots (*informal*) • **hand over fist** *Investors would lose money hand over fist if a demerger went ahead.* = **swiftly**, easily, steadily, by leaps and bounds • **hand something down** *a family heirloom handed down from generation to generation* = **pass on** *or* **down**, pass, transfer, bequeath, will, give, grant, gift, endow • **hand something on** *His chauffeur-driven car will be handed on to his successor.* = **pass on** *or* **down**, pass, transfer, bequeath, will, give, grant, relinquish • **hand something out** = **distribute**, give out, issue, pass out, dish out, dole out, deal out, hand round, pass round, give round • **hand something** *or* **someone in** = **give**, turn in, turn over • **hand something** *or* **someone over 1** *He handed over a letter of apology.* = **give**, present, deliver, donate **2** *The American was formally handed over to the ambassador.* = **turn over**, release, transfer, deliver, yield, surrender • **hands down** *We should have won hands down.* = **easily**, effortlessly, with ease, comfortably, without difficulty, with no trouble, standing on your head, with one hand tied behind your back, with no contest, with your eyes closed or shut • **in hand 1** *I'll pay now as I have the money in hand.* = **in reserve**, ready, put by, available for use **2** *The organizers say that matters are well in hand.* = **under control**, in order, receiving attention • **lay hands on someone 1** *The crowd laid hands on him.* = **attack**, assault, set on, beat up, work over (*slang*), lay into (*informal*) **2** *The bishop laid hands on the sick.* = **bless** (*Christianity*), confirm, ordain, consecrate • **lay hands on something** *the ease with which prisoners can lay hands on drugs* = **get hold of**, get, obtain, gain, grab, acquire, seize, grasp ■ **RELATED WORD:** *adjective* manual

handbook NOUN = **guidebook**, guide, manual, instruction book, Baedeker, vade mecum

handcuff VERB *They tried to handcuff him but he fought his way free.* = **shackle**, secure, restrain, fetter, manacle ▶ PLURAL NOUN *He was led away to jail in handcuffs.* = **shackles**, cuffs (*informal*), fetters, manacles, bracelets (*slang*)

handful NOUN = **few**, sprinkling, small amount, small quantity, smattering, small number ■ **OPPOSITE:** a lot

handgun NOUN = **pistol**, automatic, revolver, shooter (*informal*), piece (*U.S. slang*), rod (*U.S. slang*), derringer

handicap NOUN **1** *Being a foreigner was not a handicap.* = **disadvantage**, block, barrier, restriction, obstacle, limitation, hazard, drawback, shortcoming, stumbling block, impediment, albatross, hindrance, encumbrance ■ **OPPOSITE:** advantage **2** *I see your handicap is down from 16 to 12.* = **advantage**, penalty, head start ▶ VERB *Greater levels of stress may seriously handicap some students.* = **hinder**, limit, restrict, burden, hamstring, hamper, hold back, retard, impede, hobble, encumber, place at a disadvantage ■ **OPPOSITE:** help

handicraft NOUN = **skill**, art, craft, handiwork

handily ADVERB **1** *He was handily placed to slip the ball home at the far post.* = **conveniently**, readily, suitably, helpfully, advantageously, accessibly **2** *In the November election Nixon won handily.* = **skilfully**, expertly, cleverly, deftly, adroitly, capably, proficiently, dexterously

handiwork NOUN = **creation**, product, production, achievement, result, design, invention, artefact, handicraft, handwork

handkerchief NOUN = **hanky**, tissue (*informal*), mouchoir, snot rag (*slang*), nose rag (*slang*)

handle NOUN *The handle of a cricket bat protruded from under his arm.* = **grip**, knob, hilt, haft, stock, handgrip, helve ▶ VERB **1** *I don't know if I can handle the job.* = **manage**, deal with, tackle, cope with **2** *She handled travel arrangements for the press corps.* = **deal with**, manage, take care of, administer, conduct, supervise **3** *One report said the aircraft would become difficult to handle.* = **control**, manage, direct, operate, guide, use, steer, manipulate, manoeuvre, wield **4** *Be careful when handling young animals.* = **hold**, feel, touch, pick up, finger, grasp, poke, paw (*informal*), maul, fondle **5** *He was charged with handling stolen electrical goods.* = **deal in**, market, sell, trade in, carry, stock, traffic in **6** *I think we should handle the story very sensitively.* = **discuss**, report, treat, review, tackle, examine, discourse on • **fly off the handle** *He flew off the handle at the slightest thing.* = **lose your temper**, explode, lose it (*informal*), lose the plot (*informal*), let fly (*informal*), go ballistic (*slang*), fly into a rage, have a tantrum, wig out (*slang*), lose your cool (*slang*), blow your top, flip your lid (*slang*), hit or go through the roof (*informal*)

handling NOUN = **management**, running, treatment, approach, administration, conduct, manipulation

hand-out NOUN **1** (*often plural*) *They depended on handouts from the state.* = **charity**, dole, alms, pogey (*Canad.*) **2** *Official handouts described the couple as elated.* = **press release**, bulletin, circular, mailshot, press kit **3** *lectures, handouts, slides and videos* = **leaflet**, literature (*informal*), bulletin, flyer, pamphlet, printed matter **4** *advertised with publicity handouts* = **giveaway**, freebie (*informal*), free gift, free sample

hand-picked ADJECTIVE = **selected**, chosen, choice, select, elect, elite, recherché ■ **OPPOSITE:** random

handsome ADJECTIVE **1** *a tall, dark, handsome farmer* = **good-looking**, attractive, gorgeous (*informal*), fine, stunning (*informal*), elegant, personable, nice-looking, dishy (*informal, chiefly Brit.*), comely (*old-fashioned*), fanciable, well-proportioned, hot (*informal*), fit (*Brit. informal*) ■ **OPPOSITE:** ugly **2** *They will make a handsome profit on the property.* = **generous**, large, princely, liberal, considerable, lavish, ample, abundant, plentiful, bountiful, sizable *or* sizeable ■ **OPPOSITE:** mean

handsomely ADVERB = **generously**, amply, richly, liberally, lavishly, abundantly, plentifully, bountifully, munificently

handwriting NOUN = **writing**, hand, script, fist, scrawl, calligraphy, longhand,

penmanship (*formal*), chirography
■ **RELATED WORD:** *noun* graphology

handy ADJECTIVE **1** *handy hints on looking after indoor plants* = **useful**, practical, helpful, neat, convenient, easy to use, manageable, user-friendly, serviceable ■ **OPPOSITE:** useless **2** *This lively town is handy for Londoners.* = **convenient**, close, near, available, nearby, accessible, on hand, at hand, within reach, just round the corner, at your fingertips ■ **OPPOSITE:** inconvenient **3** *Are you handy with a needle?* = **skilful**, skilled, expert, clever, adept, ready, deft, nimble, proficient, adroit, dexterous ■ **OPPOSITE:** unskilled

handyman *or* **handywoman** *or* **handyperson** NOUN = **odd-jobman**, odd-jobber, jack-of-all-trades, handy Andy (*informal*), DIY expert

hang VERB **1** *I was left hanging by my fingertips.* = **dangle**, swing, suspend, be pendent **2** *I hung the sheet out of the window at 6am.* = **lower**, suspend, dangle, let down, let droop **3** *He hung over the railing and kicked out with his feet.* = **lean**, incline, loll, bend forward, bow, bend downward **4** *the shawl hanging loose from her shoulders* = **droop**, drop, dangle, trail, sag **5** *The walls were hung with huge modern paintings.* = **decorate**, cover, fix, attach, deck, furnish, drape, fasten **6** *The five were expected to be hanged at 7 am on Tuesday.* = **execute**, lynch, string up (*informal*), gibbet, send to the gallows **7** *A haze of expensive perfume hangs around her.* = **hover**, float, drift, linger, remain • **get the hang of something** *It's a bit tricky at first till you get the hang of it.* = **grasp**, understand, learn, master, comprehend, catch on to, acquire the technique of, get the knack *or* technique • **hang about** *or* **around** *On Saturdays we hang about in the park.* = **loiter**, frequent, haunt, linger, roam, loaf, waste time, dally, dawdle, skulk, tarry, dilly-dally (*informal*) • **hang around with someone** *She used to hang around with the boys.* = **associate**, go around with, mix, hang (*informal, chiefly U.S.*), hang out (*informal*) • **hang back** *His closest advisors believe he should hang back no longer.* = **be reluctant**, hesitate, hold back, recoil, demur, be backward • **hang fire** *I've got to hang fire on that one.* = **put off**, delay, stall, be slow, vacillate, hang back, procrastinate • **hang on 1** *Hang on a sec. I'll come with you.* = **wait**, stop, hold on, hold the line, remain **2** *Manchester United hung on to take the Cup.* = **continue**, remain, go on, carry on, endure, hold on, persist, hold out, persevere, stay the course **3** *He hangs on* tightly, his arms around my neck. = **grasp**, grip, clutch, cling, hold fast • **hang on** *or* **upon something 1** *Much hangs on the success of the collaboration.* = **depend on**, turn on, rest on, be subject to, hinge on, be determined by, be dependent on, be conditional on, be contingent on **2** *a man who knew his listeners were hanging on his every word* = **listen attentively to**, pay attention to, be rapt, give ear to

hanger-on NOUN = **parasite**, follower, cohort (*chiefly U.S.*), leech, dependant, minion, lackey, sycophant, freeloader (*slang*), sponger (*informal*), ligger (*slang*), quandong (*Austral. slang*)

hanging ADJECTIVE = **suspended**, swinging, dangling, loose, flopping, flapping, floppy, drooping, unattached, unsupported, pendent (*literary*)

hang-out NOUN = **haunt**, joint (*slang*), resort, dive (*slang*), den

hangover NOUN = **aftereffects**, morning after (*informal*), head (*informal*), crapulence

hang-up NOUN = **preoccupation**, thing (*informal*), problem, block, difficulty, obsession, mania, inhibition, phobia, fixation

hank NOUN = **coil**, roll, length, bunch, piece, loop, clump, skein

hanker after *or* **hanker for** VERB = **desire**, want, long for, hope for, crave, covet, wish for, yearn for, pine for, lust after, eat your heart out, ache for, yen for (*informal*), itch for, set your heart on, hunger for *or* after, thirst for *or* after

hankering NOUN = **desire**, longing, wish, hope, urge, yen (*informal*), pining, hunger, ache, craving, yearning, itch, thirst

haphazard ADJECTIVE **1** *The investigation does seem haphazard.* = **unsystematic**, disorderly, disorganized, casual, careless, indiscriminate, aimless, slapdash, slipshod, hit or miss (*informal*), unmethodical ■ **OPPOSITE:** systematic **2** *She was trying to connect her life's seemingly haphazard events.* = **random**, chance, accidental, arbitrary, fluky (*informal*) ■ **OPPOSITE:** planned

hapless ADJECTIVE = **unlucky**, unfortunate, cursed, unhappy, miserable, jinxed, luckless, wretched, ill-starred, ill-fated

happen VERB **1** *We cannot say for sure what will happen.* = **occur**, take place, come about, follow, result, appear, develop, arise, come off (*informal*), ensue, crop up (*informal*), transpire (*informal*), materialize, present itself, come to pass, see the light of day, eventuate **2** *I looked in the nearest paper, which happened to be the Daily Mail.* = **chance**, turn out (*informal*), have the fortune to be **3** *It's the best thing that ever* happened to me. = **befall**, overtake, become of, betide • **happen on** or **upon something** *He just happened upon a charming guest house.* = **find**, encounter, run into, come upon, turn up, stumble on, hit upon, chance upon, light upon, blunder on, discover unexpectedly

happening NOUN = **event**, incident, occasion, case, experience, chance, affair, scene, accident, proceeding, episode, adventure, phenomenon, occurrence, escapade

happily ADVERB 1 *Happily, his neck injuries were not serious.* = **luckily**, fortunately, providentially, favourably, auspiciously, opportunely, propitiously, seasonably 2 *Mum was sitting opposite another woman, smiling happily.* = **joyfully**, cheerfully, gleefully, blithely, merrily, gaily, joyously, delightedly 3 *If I've caused any offence, I will happily apologize.* = **willingly**, freely, gladly, enthusiastically, heartily, with pleasure, contentedly, lief (*rare*)

happiness NOUN = **pleasure**, delight, joy, cheer, satisfaction, prosperity, ecstasy, enjoyment, bliss, felicity, exuberance, contentment, wellbeing, high spirits, elation, gaiety, jubilation, merriment, cheerfulness, gladness, beatitude, cheeriness, blessedness, light-heartedness ■ **OPPOSITE:** unhappiness

happy ADJECTIVE 1 *I'm just happy to be back running.* = **pleased**, delighted, content, contented, thrilled, glad, blessed, blest, sunny, cheerful, jolly, merry, ecstatic, gratified, jubilant, joyous, joyful, elated, over the moon (*informal*), overjoyed, blissful, rapt, blithe, on cloud nine (*informal*), cock-a-hoop, walking on air (*informal*), floating on air, stoked (*Austral. & N.Z. informal*) ■ **OPPOSITE:** sad 2 *We have a very happy marriage.* = **contented**, blest, joyful, blissful, blithe ■ **OPPOSITE:** unhappy 3 *a happy coincidence* = **fortunate**, lucky, timely, appropriate, convenient, favourable, auspicious, propitious, apt, befitting, advantageous, well-timed, opportune (*formal*), felicitous, seasonable ■ **OPPOSITE:** unfortunate

happy-go-lucky ADJECTIVE = **carefree**, casual, easy-going, irresponsible, unconcerned, untroubled, nonchalant, blithe, heedless, insouciant, devil-may-care, improvident, light-hearted ■ **OPPOSITE:** serious

harangue VERB *haranguing her furiously in words she didn't understand* = **rant at**, address, lecture, exhort, preach to, declaim, hold forth, spout at (*informal*)

▶ NOUN *a political harangue* = **rant**, address, speech, lecture, tirade, polemic, broadside, diatribe, homily, exhortation, oration, spiel (*informal*), declamation, philippic

harass VERB = **annoy**, trouble, bother, worry, harry, disturb, devil (*informal*), plague, bait, hound, torment, hassle (*informal*), badger, persecute, exasperate, pester, vex, breathe down someone's neck, chivvy (*Brit.*), give someone grief (*Brit. & S. African*), be on your back (*slang*), beleaguer

harassed ADJECTIVE = **hassled** (*informal*), worried, troubled, strained, harried, under pressure, plagued, tormented, distraught, vexed, under stress, careworn

harassment NOUN = **hassle** (*informal*), trouble, bother, grief (*informal*), torment, irritation, persecution, nuisance, badgering, annoyance, pestering, aggravation (*informal*), molestation, vexation, bedevilment

harbinger NOUN = **sign**, indication, herald (*literary*), messenger, omen, precursor, forerunner, portent, foretoken

harbour NOUN 1 *The ship was allowed to tie up in the harbour.* = **port**, haven, dock, mooring, marina, pier, wharf, anchorage, jetty, pontoon, slipway 2 *a safe harbour for music rejected by the mainstream* = **sanctuary**, haven, shelter, retreat, asylum, refuge, oasis, covert, safe haven, sanctum ▶ VERB 1 *He might have been murdered by someone harbouring a grudge.* = **hold**, bear, maintain, nurse, retain, foster, entertain, nurture, cling to, cherish, brood over 2 *harbouring terrorist suspects* = **shelter**, protect, hide, relieve, lodge, shield, conceal, secrete, provide refuge, give asylum to

hard ADJECTIVE 1 *He stamped his feet on the hard floor.* = **tough**, strong, firm, solid, stiff, compact, rigid, resistant, dense, compressed, stony, impenetrable, inflexible, unyielding, rocklike ■ **OPPOSITE:** soft 2 *That's a very hard question.* = **difficult**, involved, complex, complicated, puzzling, tangled, baffling, intricate, perplexing, impenetrable, thorny, knotty, unfathomable, ticklish ■ **OPPOSITE:** easy 3 *Coping with three babies is very hard work.* = **exhausting**, tough, exacting, formidable, fatiguing, wearying, rigorous, uphill, gruelling, strenuous, arduous, laborious, burdensome, Herculean, backbreaking, toilsome ■ **OPPOSITE:** easy 4 *He gave me a hard push which toppled me backwards.* = **forceful**, strong, powerful, driving, heavy, sharp, violent, smart, tremendous, fierce, vigorous, hefty 5 *His father was a hard man.* = **harsh**, severe, strict, cold, exacting, cruel, grim, stern, ruthless, stubborn, unjust, callous, unkind, unrelenting, implacable, unsympathetic, pitiless, unfeeling, obdurate, unsparing, affectless, hardhearted ■ **OPPOSITE:** kind **6** *Those were hard times.* = **grim**, dark, painful, distressing, harsh, disastrous, unpleasant, intolerable, grievous, disagreeable, calamitous **7** *He wanted more hard evidence.* = **definite**, reliable, verified, cold, plain, actual, bare, undeniable, indisputable, verifiable, unquestionable, unvarnished ▶ ADVERB **1** *I'll work hard. I don't want to let him down.* = **strenuously**, steadily, persistently, earnestly, determinedly, doggedly, diligently, energetically, assiduously, industriously, untiringly, flatstick (*S. African slang*) **2** *You had to listen hard to hear him.* = **intently**, closely, carefully, sharply, keenly **3** *I kicked the bin very hard and broke my toe.* = **forcefully**, strongly, heavily, sharply, severely, fiercely, vigorously, intensely, violently, powerfully, forcibly, with all your might, with might and main ■ **OPPOSITE:** softly **4** *the hard won rights of the working woman* = **with difficulty**, painfully, laboriously

hard-bitten ADJECTIVE = **tough**, realistic, cynical, practical, shrewd, down-to-earth, matter-of-fact, hard-nosed (*informal*), hard-headed, unsentimental, hard-boiled (*informal*), case-hardened, badass (*slang, chiefly U.S.*) ■ **OPPOSITE:** idealistic

hard-boiled ADJECTIVE = **tough**, practical, realistic, cynical, shrewd, down-to-earth, matter-of-fact, hard-nosed (*informal*), hard-headed, hard-bitten (*informal*), unsentimental, case-hardened, badass (*slang, chiefly U.S.*) ■ **OPPOSITE:** idealistic

hard-core ADJECTIVE **1** *a hard-core group of right-wing senators* = **dyed-in-the-wool**, extreme, dedicated, rigid, staunch, die-hard, steadfast, obstinate, intransigent, swivel-eyed (*slang*) **2** *the availability of hard-core images online* = **explicit**, obscene, pornographic, X-rated (*informal*)

harden VERB **1** *Mould the mixture into shape before it hardens.* = **solidify**, set, freeze, cake, bake, clot, thicken, stiffen, crystallize, congeal, coagulate, anneal **2** *hardened by the rigours of the Siberian steppes* = **accustom**, season, toughen, train, brutalize, inure, habituate, case-harden **3** *Their action can only serve to harden the attitude of landowners.* = **reinforce**, strengthen, fortify, steel, nerve, brace, toughen, buttress, gird, indurate

hardened ADJECTIVE **1** *hardened criminals* = **habitual**, set, fixed, chronic, shameless,

inveterate, incorrigible, reprobate, irredeemable, badass (*slang, chiefly U.S.*) ■ **OPPOSITE:** occasional **2** *hardened politicians* = **seasoned**, experienced, accustomed, toughened, inured, habituated ■ **OPPOSITE:** naive

hard-headed ADJECTIVE = **shrewd**, tough, practical, cool, sensible, realistic, pragmatic, astute, hard-boiled (*informal*), hard-bitten, level-headed, unsentimental, badass (*slang, chiefly U.S.*) ■ **OPPOSITE:** idealistic

hard-hearted ADJECTIVE = **unsympathetic**, hard, cold, cruel, indifferent, insensitive, callous, stony, unkind, heartless, inhuman, merciless, intolerant, uncaring, pitiless, unfeeling, unforgiving, hard as nails, affectless ■ **OPPOSITE:** kind

hardly ADVERB **1** *Nick, on the sofa, hardly slept.* = **barely**, only just, scarcely, just, faintly, with difficulty, infrequently, with effort, at a push (*Brit. informal*), almost not ■ **OPPOSITE:** completely **2** *I could hardly see the garden for the fog.* = **only just**, just, only, barely, not quite, scarcely **3** *It's hardly surprising his ideas didn't catch on.* = **not at all**, not, no way, by no means

hard-nosed ADJECTIVE = **tough**, practical, realistic, shrewd, pragmatic, down-to-earth, hardline, uncompromising, businesslike, hard-headed, unsentimental, badass (*slang, chiefly U.S.*)

hard-pressed ADJECTIVE **1** *Hard-pressed consumers are spending less on luxuries.* = **under pressure**, pushed (*informal*), harried, in difficulties, up against it (*informal*), with your back to the wall **2** *This year the airline will be hard-pressed to make a profit.* = **pushed** (*informal*), in difficulties, up against it (*informal*)

hardship NOUN = **suffering**, want, need, trouble, trial, difficulty, burden, misery, torment, oppression, persecution, grievance, misfortune, austerity, adversity, calamity, affliction, discomfort, tribulation, privation (*formal*), destitution ■ **OPPOSITE:** ease

hard up ADJECTIVE = **poor**, broke (*informal*), short, bust (*informal*), bankrupt, impoverished, in the red (*informal*), cleaned out (*slang*), penniless, out of pocket, down and out, skint (*Brit. slang*), strapped for cash (*informal*), impecunious, dirt-poor (*informal*), on the breadline, flat broke (*informal*), on your uppers (*informal*), in queer street, without two pennies to rub together (*informal*), short of cash or funds ■ **OPPOSITE:** wealthy

hardy ADJECTIVE **1** *They grew up to be farmers, round-faced and hardy.* = **strong**, tough, robust, sound, fit, healthy, vigorous, rugged (*U.S. & Canad.*), sturdy, hale (*old-fashioned*), stout, stalwart, hearty, lusty, in fine fettle ■ **OPPOSITE:** frail **2** *A few hardy souls leapt into the encircling seas.* = **courageous**, brave, daring, bold, heroic, manly, gritty, feisty (*informal*), resolute, intrepid, valiant, plucky, valorous, stouthearted (*old-fashioned*) ■ **OPPOSITE:** feeble

hare NOUN ■ **RELATED WORDS:** *adjective* leporine; *name of male* buck; *name of female* doe; *name of young* leveret; *name of home* down, husk

harem NOUN = **women's quarters**, seraglio, zenana (*in eastern countries*), gynaeceum (*in ancient Greece*)

hark VERB *Hark. I hear the returning footsteps of my love.* = **listen**, attend, pay attention, hearken (*archaic*), give ear, hear, mark, notice, give heed • **hark back to something 1** *pitched roofs, which hark back to the Victorian era* = **recall**, recollect, call to mind, cause you to remember, cause you to recollect **2** *The result devastated me at the time. Even now I hark back to it.* = **return to**, remember, recall, revert to, look back to, think back to, recollect, regress to

harlot NOUN = **prostitute**, tart (*informal*), whore, slag (*Brit. slang*), pro (*slang*), call girl, slapper (*Brit. slang*), hussy, streetwalker, scrubber (*Brit. & Austral. slang*), strumpet

harm VERB **1** *The hijackers seemed anxious not to harm anyone.* = **injure**, hurt, wound, abuse, molest, ill-treat, maltreat, lay a finger on, ill-use ■ **OPPOSITE:** heal **2** *a warning that the product may harm the environment* = **damage**, hurt, ruin, mar, spoil, impair, blemish ▶ NOUN **1** *a release of radioactivity which would cause harm* = **injury**, suffering, damage, ill, hurt, distress **2** *It would probably do the economy more harm than good.* = **damage**, loss, ill, hurt, misfortune, mischief, detriment, impairment, disservice ■ **OPPOSITE:** good **3** *There was no harm in keeping the money.* = **sin**, wrong, evil, wickedness, immorality, iniquity, sinfulness, vice ■ **OPPOSITE:** goodness

harmful ADJECTIVE = **damaging**, dangerous, negative, evil, destructive, hazardous, unhealthy, detrimental, hurtful, toxic, pernicious (*formal*), noxious, baleful, deleterious (*formal*), injurious, unwholesome, disadvantageous, baneful, maleficent, toxic ■ **OPPOSITE:** harmless

harmless ADJECTIVE **1** *working at developing harmless substitutes for these gases* = **safe**, benign, wholesome, innocuous, not dangerous, nontoxic, innoxious ■ **OPPOSITE:** dangerous **2** *He seemed harmless enough.* = **inoffensive**, innocent, innocuous, gentle, tame, unobjectionable

harmonious ADJECTIVE **1** *the most harmonious European Community summit for some time* = **friendly**, amicable, cordial, sympathetic, compatible, agreeable, in harmony, in unison, fraternal, congenial, in accord, concordant, of one mind, en rapport (*French*) ■ **OPPOSITE:** unfriendly **2** *a harmonious blend of colours* = **compatible**, matching, coordinated, correspondent, agreeable, consistent, consonant, congruous ■ **OPPOSITE:** incompatible **3** *producing harmonious sounds* = **melodious**, musical, harmonic, harmonizing, tuneful, concordant, mellifluous, dulcet, sweet-sounding, euphonious, euphonic, symphonious (*literary*) ■ **OPPOSITE:** discordant

harmonize VERB **1** *The music had to harmonize with the seasons.* = **match**, accord, suit, blend, correspond, tally, chime, coordinate, go together, tone in, cohere, attune, be of one mind, be in unison **2** *members have progressed towards harmonizing their economies* = **coordinate**, match, agree, blend, tally, reconcile, attune

harmony NOUN **1** *a future in which humans live in harmony with nature* = **accord**, order, understanding, peace, agreement, friendship, unity, sympathy, consensus, cooperation, goodwill, rapport, conformity, compatibility, assent, unanimity, concord, amity (*formal*), amicability, like-mindedness ■ **OPPOSITE:** conflict **2** *singing in harmony* = **tune**, melody, unison, tunefulness, euphony, melodiousness ■ **OPPOSITE:** discord **3** *the ordered harmony of the universe* = **balance**, consistency, fitness, correspondence, coordination, symmetry, compatibility, suitability, concord, parallelism, consonance (*formal*), congruity ■ **OPPOSITE:** incongruity

harness VERB **1** *The firm is very big on harnessing the energy and enthusiasm of youth.* = **exploit**, control, channel, apply, employ, utilize, mobilize, make productive, turn to account, render useful **2** *The horses were harnessed to a heavy wagon.* = **put in harness**, couple, saddle, yoke, hitch up, span (*S. African*) ▶ NOUN *Always check that the straps of the harness are properly adjusted.* = **equipment**, tackle, gear, tack, trappings • **in harness 1** *Thomas was condemned to work in harness with his older brother.* = **working**, together, in a team **2** *The longing for work will*

return and you will be right back in harness.
= **at work**, working, employed, active, busy, in action

harp VERB = **go on**, reiterate (*formal*), dwell on, labour, press, repeat, rub in

harried ADJECTIVE = **harassed**, worried, troubled, bothered, anxious, distressed, plagued, tormented, hassled (*informal*), agitated, beset, hard-pressed, hag-ridden

harrowing ADJECTIVE = **distressing**, disturbing, alarming, frightening, painful, terrifying, chilling, traumatic, tormenting, heartbreaking, excruciating, agonizing, nerve-racking, heart-rending, gut-wrenching

harry VERB = **pester**, trouble, bother, disturb, worry, annoy, plague, tease, torment, harass, hassle (*informal*), badger, persecute, molest, vex, bedevil, breathe down someone's neck, chivvy (*Brit.*), give someone grief (*Brit. & S. African*), be on your back (*slang*), get in your hair (*informal*)

harsh ADJECTIVE **1** *Hundreds of political detainees were held under harsh conditions.* = **severe**, hard, tough, grim, stark, stringent, austere, Spartan, inhospitable, comfortless, bare-bones **2** *The weather grew harsh and unpredictable.* = **bleak**, cold, freezing, severe, bitter, icy **3** *the harsh experience of war* = **cruel**, savage, brutal, ruthless, relentless, unrelenting, barbarous, pitiless **4** *He said many harsh and unkind things.* = **hard**, sharp, severe, bitter, cruel, stern, unpleasant, abusive, unkind, pitiless, unfeeling ■ **OPPOSITE:** kind **5** *more harsh laws governing the behaviour and status of the citizens* = **drastic**, hard, severe, stringent, punitive, austere, Draconian, punitory **6** *He gave out a very loud and harsh laugh.* = **raucous**, rough, jarring, grating, strident, rasping, discordant, croaking, guttural, dissonant, unmelodious
■ **OPPOSITE:** soft

harshly ADVERB = **severely**, roughly, cruelly, strictly, grimly, sternly, brutally

harshness NOUN = **bitterness**, acrimony, ill-temper, sourness, asperity, acerbity

harvest NOUN **1** *300 million tons of grain in the fields at the start of the harvest* = **harvesting**, picking, gathering, collecting, reaping, harvest-time **2** *a bumper potato harvest* = **crop**, yield, year's growth, produce ▶ VERB **1** *Many farmers are refusing to harvest the sugar cane.* = **gather**, pick, collect, bring in, pluck, reap **2** *In his new career he has blossomed and harvested many awards.* = **collect**, get, gain, earn, acquire, accumulate, garner, amass

hash NOUN • **make a hash of** = **mess up**, muddle, bungle, botch, cock up (*Brit. slang*),

mishandle, mismanage, make a nonsense of (*informal*), bodge (*informal*), make a pig's ear of (*informal*), flub (*U.S. slang*)

hassle (*informal*) NOUN *I don't think it's worth the money or the hassle.* = **trouble**, problem, difficulty, upset, bother, grief (*informal*), trial, struggle, uphill (*S. African*), inconvenience ▶ VERB *My children started hassling me.* = **bother**, bug (*informal*), annoy, harry, hound, harass, badger, pester, get on your nerves (*informal*), be on your back (*slang*), get in your hair (*informal*), breath down someone's neck

hassled ADJECTIVE = **bothered**, pressured, worried, stressed, under pressure, hounded, uptight, browbeaten, hunted, hot and bothered

haste NOUN *Authorities appear to be moving with haste against the three dissidents.* = **speed**, rapidity, urgency, expedition, dispatch, velocity, alacrity, quickness, swiftness, briskness, nimbleness, fleetness, celerity, promptitude, rapidness
■ **OPPOSITE:** slowness

hasten VERB **1** *He may hasten the collapse of his own country.* = **hurry (up)**, speed (up), advance, urge, step up (*informal*), accelerate, press, dispatch, precipitate, quicken, push forward, expedite
■ **OPPOSITE:** slow down **2** *She hastened along the landing to her room.* = **rush**, run, race, fly, speed, tear (along), dash, hurry (up), barrel (along) (*informal, chiefly U.S. & Canad.*), sprint, bolt, beetle, scuttle, scurry, haste, burn rubber (*informal*), step on it (*informal*), make haste, get your skates on (*informal*)
■ **OPPOSITE:** dawdle

hastily ADVERB **1** *I said goodnight hastily.* = **quickly**, fast, rapidly, promptly, straightaway, speedily, apace (*literary*), pronto (*informal*), double-quick, hotfoot, pdq (*slang*), posthaste **2** *I decided that nothing should be done hastily.* = **hurriedly**, rashly, precipitately, recklessly, too quickly, on the spur of the moment, impulsively, impetuously, heedlessly

hasty ADJECTIVE **1** *They need to make a hasty escape.* = **speedy**, fast, quick, prompt, rapid, fleet, hurried, urgent, swift, brisk, expeditious ■ **OPPOSITE:** leisurely **2** *After the hasty meal, they took up their positions.* = **brief**, short, quick, passing, rushed, fleeting, superficial, cursory, perfunctory, transitory
■ **OPPOSITE:** long **3** *Let's not be hasty.* = **rash**, premature, reckless, precipitate, impulsive, headlong, foolhardy, thoughtless, impetuous, indiscreet, imprudent, heedless, incautious, unduly quick
■ **OPPOSITE:** cautious

hatch VERB **1** *I transferred the eggs to a hen canary to hatch and rear.* = **incubate**, breed, sit on, brood, bring forth **2** *accused of hatching a plot to assassinate the Pope* = **devise**, plan, design, project, scheme, manufacture, plot, invent, put together, conceive, brew, formulate, contrive, dream up (*informal*), concoct, think up, cook up (*informal*), trump up

hatchet NOUN = **axe**, machete, tomahawk, cleaver

hate VERB **1** *Most people hate him, but I don't.* = **detest**, loathe, despise, dislike, be sick of, abhor, be hostile to, recoil from, be repelled by, have an aversion to, abominate, not be able to bear, execrate ■ **OPPOSITE:** love **2** *She hated hospitals and dreaded the operation.* = **dislike**, detest, shrink from, recoil from, have no stomach for, not be able to bear ■ **OPPOSITE:** like **3** *I hate to admit it, but you were right.* = **be unwilling**, regret, be reluctant, hesitate, be sorry, be loath, feel disinclined ▶ NOUN *eyes that held a look of hate* = **dislike**, hostility, hatred, loathing, animosity, aversion, antagonism, antipathy, enmity, abomination, animus, abhorrence, odium (*formal*), detestation, execration ■ **OPPOSITE:** love

hateful ADJECTIVE = **horrible**, despicable, offensive, foul, disgusting, forbidding, revolting, obscene, vile, repellent, obnoxious, repulsive, heinous, odious, repugnant, loathsome, abhorrent, abominable, execrable, detestable

hatred NOUN = **hate**, dislike, animosity, aversion, revulsion, antagonism, antipathy, enmity, abomination, ill will, animus, repugnance, odium (*formal*), detestation, execration ■ **OPPOSITE:** love

haughty ADJECTIVE = **proud**, arrogant, lofty, high, stuck-up (*informal*), contemptuous, conceited, imperious, snooty (*informal*), scornful, snobbish, disdainful, supercilious, high and mighty (*informal*), overweening, hoity-toity (*informal*), on your high horse (*informal*), uppish (*Brit. informal*) ■ **OPPOSITE:** humble

haul VERB **1** *I hauled myself to my feet.* = **drag**, draw, pull, hale, heave **2** *A crane hauled the car out of the stream.* = **pull**, trail, convey, tow, move, carry, transport, tug, cart, hump (*Brit. slang*), lug ▶ NOUN *The haul was worth £4,000.* = **yield**, gain, spoils, find, catch, harvest, loot, takings, booty

haunt VERB **1** *The decision to leave her children now haunts her.* = **plague**, trouble, obsess, torment, come back to, possess, stay with, recur, beset, prey on, weigh on **2** *During the day she haunted the town's cinemas.* = **visit** (*old-fashioned*), hang around or about, frequent, linger in, resort to, patronize, repair to, spend time in, loiter in, be a regular in **3** *His ghost is said to haunt some of the rooms.* = **appear in**, materialize in ▶ NOUN *a favourite summer haunt for yachtsmen* = **meeting place**, resort, hangout (*informal*), den, rendezvous, stamping ground, gathering place

haunted ADJECTIVE **1** *a haunted castle* = **possessed**, ghostly, cursed, eerie, spooky (*informal*), jinxed **2** *She looked so haunted, I almost didn't recognise her.* = **preoccupied**, worried, troubled, plagued, obsessed, tormented

haunting ADJECTIVE = **evocative**, poignant, unforgettable, indelible

have VERB **1** *I want to have my own business.* = **own**, keep, possess, hold, retain, occupy, boast, be the owner of **2** *When can I have the new car?* = **get**, obtain, take, receive, accept, gain, secure, acquire, procure, take receipt of **3** *He might be having a heart attack.* = **suffer**, experience, undergo, sustain, endure, be suffering from **4** *My wife has just had a baby boy.* = **give birth to**, bear, deliver, bring forth, beget, bring into the world **5** *I'm not having any of that nonsense.* = **put up with** (*informal*), allow, permit, consider, think about, entertain, tolerate **6** *Did you have some trouble with your neighbours?* = **experience**, go through, undergo, meet with, come across, run into, be faced with • **have had it** *I've had it. Let's call it a day.* = **be exhausted**, be knackered (*Brit. informal*), be finished, be pooped (*U.S. slang*) • **have someone on** *I thought he was just having me on.* = **tease**, kid (*informal*), wind up (*Brit. slang*), trick, deceive, take the mickey, pull someone's leg, play a joke on, jerk or yank someone's chain (*informal*) • **have something on 1** *She had on new black shoes.* = **wear**, be wearing, be dressed in, be clothed in, be attired in **2** *We have a meeting on that day.* = **have something planned**, be committed to, be engaged to, have something on the agenda • **have to 1** *Now, you have to go into town.* = **must**, should, be forced, ought, be obliged, be bound, have got to, be compelled **2** *That has to be the biggest lie ever told.* = **have got to**, must

haven NOUN **1** *a real haven at the end of a busy working day* = **sanctuary**, shelter, retreat, asylum, refuge, oasis, sanctum **2** *She lay alongside in Largs Yacht Haven for a few days.* = **harbour**, port, anchorage, road (*Nautical*)

havoc NOUN **1** *Rioters caused havoc in the centre of the town.* = **devastation**, damage, destruction, waste, ruin, wreck, slaughter, ravages, carnage, desolation, rack and ruin, despoliation (*formal*) **2** *A single mare running loose could cause havoc among otherwise reliable stallions.* = **disorder**, confusion, chaos, disruption, mayhem, shambles • **play havoc with something** *Drug addiction soon played havoc with his career.* = **wreck**, destroy, devastate, disrupt, demolish, disorganize, bring into chaos

hawk VERB = **peddle**, market, sell, push, traffic, tout (*informal*), vend

hawker NOUN = **pedlar**, tout, vendor, travelling salesman, crier, huckster, barrow boy (*Brit.*), door-to-door salesperson

haywire ADJECTIVE **1** *The electrics in the house had gone haywire.* = **out of order**, out of commission, on the blink (*slang*), on the fritz (*slang*) **2** (*of a person*) *I went haywire in our first few weeks on holiday.* = **crazy**, wild, mad, potty (*Brit. informal*), berserk, bonkers (*slang, chiefly Brit.*), loopy (*informal*), mad as a hatter, berko (*Austral. slang*), off the air (*Austral. slang*), porangi (*N.Z.*)

hazard NOUN *a sole that reduces the hazard of slipping on slick surfaces* = **danger**, risk, threat, problem, menace, peril, jeopardy, pitfall, endangerment, imperilment ▶ VERB *He could not believe that the man would have hazarded his grandson.* = **jeopardize**, risk, endanger, threaten, expose, imperil, put in jeopardy • **hazard a guess** *I would hazard a guess that they'll do fairly well.* = **guess**, conjecture, suppose, speculate, presume, take a guess

hazardous ADJECTIVE = **dangerous**, risky, difficult, uncertain, unpredictable, insecure, hairy (*slang*), unsafe, precarious, perilous, parlous (*archaic, humorous*), dicey (*informal, chiefly Brit.*), fraught with danger, chancy (*informal*) ■ OPPOSITE: safe

haze NOUN = **mist**, film, cloud, steam, fog, obscurity, vapour, smog, dimness, smokiness

hazy ADJECTIVE **1** *The air was filled with hazy sunshine and frost.* = **misty**, faint, dim, dull, obscure, veiled, smoky, cloudy, foggy, overcast, blurry, nebulous ■ OPPOSITE: bright **2** *I have only a hazy memory of what he was like.* = **vague**, uncertain, unclear, muddled, fuzzy, indefinite, loose, muzzy, nebulous, ill-defined, indistinct ■ OPPOSITE: clear

head NOUN **1** *She turned her head away from him.* = **skull**, crown, pate, bean (*U.S. & Canad. slang*), nut (*slang*), loaf (*slang*), cranium, conk (*slang*), noggin, noddle (*informal, chiefly Brit.*) **2** *He was more inclined to use his head.* = **mind**, reasoning, understanding, thought, sense, brain, brains (*informal*), intelligence, wisdom, wits, common sense, loaf (*Brit. informal*), intellect, rationality, grey matter, brainpower, mental capacity **3** *I don't have a head for business.* = **ability**, mind, talent, capacity, faculty, flair, mentality, aptitude **4** *the head of the queue* = **front**, beginning, top, first place, fore, forefront **5** *his familiar position at the head of his field* = **forefront**, cutting edge, vanguard, van **6** *the head of the stairs* = **top**, crown, summit, height, peak, crest, pinnacle, apex, vertex **7** *full of admiration for the head and teachers* = **head teacher**, principal, headmaster or headmistress **8** *heads of government from more than 100 countries* = **leader**, president, director, manager, chief, boss (*informal*), captain, master, premier, commander, principal, supervisor, superintendent, chieftain, sherang (*Austral. & N.Z.*) **9** *These problems came to a head in September.* = **climax**, crisis, turning point, culmination, end, conclusion, tipping point **10** *the head of the river* = **source**, start, beginning, rise, origin, commencement, well head **11** *a ship off the beach head* = **headland**, point, cape, promontory, foreland ▶ ADJECTIVE *I had the head man out from the gas company.* = **chief**, main, leading, first, highest, front, prime, premier, supreme, principal, arch, foremost, pre-eminent, topmost ▶ VERB **1** *The parson, heading the procession, had just turned right.* = **lead**, precede, be the leader of, be or go first, be or go at the front of, lead the way **2** *Running a business heads the list of ambitions among interviewees.* = **top**, lead, crown, cap **3** *He heads the department's Office of Civil Rights.* = **be in charge of**, run, manage, lead, control, rule, direct, guide, command, govern, supervise • **go to your head 1** *That wine was strong, it went to your head.* = **intoxicate**, befuddle, inebriate, addle, stupefy, fuddle, put (someone) under the table (*informal*) **2** *not a man to let a little success go to his head* = **make someone conceited**, puff someone up, make someone full of themselves • **head for something** or **someone** *He headed for the bus stop.* = **make for**, aim for, set off for, go to, turn to, set out for, make a beeline for, start towards, steer for • **head over heels** *head over heels in love* = **completely**, thoroughly, utterly, intensely, wholeheartedly, uncontrollably • **head someone off** *He turned into the hallway and headed her off.* = **intercept**, divert, deflect, cut someone off, interpose, block someone off • **head something off** *good at spotting trouble on the way and heading it off* = **prevent**,

stop, avert, parry, fend off, ward off, forestall • **put your heads together** *Everyone put their heads together and reached an arrangement.* = **consult**, confer, discuss, deliberate, talk (something) over, powwow, confab (*informal*), confabulate
■ **RELATED WORDS:** *adjectives* capital, cephalic

headache NOUN **1** *I have had a terrible headache for the past two days.* = **migraine**, head (*informal*), neuralgia, cephalalgia (*Medical*) **2** (*informal*) *Their biggest headache is the increase in the price of fuel.* = **problem**, worry, trouble, bother, nuisance, inconvenience, bane, vexation

headfirst or **head first** ADVERB **1** *He has apparently fallen headfirst down the stairwell.* = **headlong**, head foremost **2** *On arrival he plunged head first into these problems.* = **recklessly**, rashly, hastily, precipitately, without thinking, carelessly, heedlessly, without forethought

heading NOUN **1** *helpful chapter headings* = **title**, name, caption, headline, rubric **2** *There, under the heading of wholesalers, he found it.* = **category**, class, section, division

headland NOUN = **promontory**, point, head, cape, cliff, bluff, mull (*Scot.*), foreland, bill

headlong ADVERB **1** *He ran headlong for the open door.* = **hastily**, hurriedly, helter-skelter, pell-mell, heedlessly **2** *She missed her footing and fell headlong down the stairs.* = **headfirst**, head-on, headforemost **3** *Do not leap headlong into decisions.* = **rashly**, wildly, hastily, precipitately, head first, thoughtlessly, impetuously, heedlessly, without forethought ▸ ADJECTIVE *a headlong rush for the exit* = **hasty**, reckless, precipitate, dangerous, impulsive, thoughtless, breakneck, impetuous, inconsiderate

headmaster or **headmistress** NOUN = **principal**, head (*informal*), head teacher, rector

> **USAGE** The general trend of nonsexist language is to find a term which can apply to both sexes equally, as in the use of *actor* to refer to both men and women. This being so, *head teacher* is usually preferable to the gender-specific terms *headmaster* and *headmistress*.

headstrong ADJECTIVE = **stubborn**, wilful, obstinate, contrary, perverse, unruly, intractable, stiff-necked, ungovernable, self-willed, pig-headed, mulish, froward (*archaic*) ■ **OPPOSITE:** manageable

headway NOUN = **progress**, ground, inroads, strides

heady ADJECTIVE **1** *in the heady days just after their marriage* = **exciting**, thrilling, stimulating, exhilarating, overwhelming, intoxicating **2** *The wine is a heady blend of claret and aromatic herbs.* = **intoxicating**, strong, potent, inebriating, spirituous

heal VERB **1** (*sometimes with* **up**) *The bruising had gone, but it was six months before it all healed.* = **mend**, get better, get well, regenerate, show improvement **2** *No doctor has ever healed a broken bone. They just set them.* = **cure**, restore, mend, make better, remedy, make good, make well ■ **OPPOSITE:** injure **3** *Sophie and her sister have healed the family rift.* = **patch up**, settle, reconcile, put right, harmonize, conciliate

healing ADJECTIVE *Get in touch with the body's own healing abilities.* = **restoring**, medicinal, therapeutic, remedial, restorative, curative, analeptic, sanative

health NOUN **1** *Although he's old, he's in good health.* = **condition**, state, form, shape, tone, constitution, fettle **2** *In hospital they nursed me back to health.* = **wellbeing**, strength, fitness, vigour, good condition, wellness, soundness, robustness, healthiness, salubrity, haleness ■ **OPPOSITE:** illness **3** *There's no way to predict the future health of the banking industry.* = **state**, condition, shape

healthful ADJECTIVE = **healthy**, beneficial, good for you, bracing, nourishing, wholesome, nutritious, invigorating, salutary, salubrious, health-giving

healthy ADJECTIVE **1** *She had a normal pregnancy and delivered a healthy child.* = **well**, sound, fit, strong, active, flourishing, hardy, blooming, robust, vigorous, sturdy, hale (*old-fashioned*), hearty, in good shape (*informal*), in good condition, in the pink, alive and kicking, fighting fit, in fine form, in fine fettle, hale and hearty, fit as a fiddle (*informal*), right as rain (*Brit. informal*), physically fit, in fine feather ■ **OPPOSITE:** ill **2** *a healthy diet* = **wholesome**, beneficial, nourishing, good for you, nutritious, salutary, hygienic, healthful, salubrious, health-giving ■ **OPPOSITE:** unwholesome **3** *a healthy outdoor pursuit* = **invigorating**, bracing, beneficial, good for you, salutary, healthful, salubrious

heap NOUN **1** *a heap of bricks* = **pile**, lot, collection, store, mountain, mass, stack, rick, mound, accumulation, stockpile, hoard, aggregation **2** (*often plural*) *You have heaps of time.* = **a lot**, lots, plenty, masses, load(s) (*informal*), ocean(s), great deal, quantities, tons (*informal*), stack(s), lashings (*Brit. informal*), abundance, oodles

(*informal*) ▶ VERB (*sometimes with* **up**) *They were heaping up wood for a bonfire.* = **pile**, store, collect, gather, stack, accumulate, mound, amass, stockpile, hoard, bank
• **heap something on someone** *He heaped scorn on both their methods and motives.* = **load with**, burden with, confer on, assign to, bestow on, shower upon

hear VERB **1** *She heard no further sounds.* = **overhear**, catch, detect **2** *You can hear commentary on the match in about half an hour.* = **listen to**, heed, attend to, eavesdrop on, listen in to, give attention to, hearken to (*archaic*), hark to, be all ears for (*informal*) **3** *He had to wait months before his case was heard.* = **try**, judge, examine, investigate **4** *He had heard that the trophy had been sold.* = **learn**, discover, find out, understand, pick up, gather, be informed, ascertain, be told of, get wind of (*informal*), hear tell (*dialect*)

hearing NOUN **1** *His mind still seemed clear and his hearing was excellent.* = **sense of hearing**, auditory perception, ear, aural faculty **2** *The judge adjourned the hearing until next Tuesday.* = **inquiry**, trial, investigation, industrial tribunal **3** *a means of giving a candidate a fair hearing* = **chance to speak**, interview, audience, audition **4** *No one spoke disparagingly of her father in her hearing.* = **earshot**, reach, range, hearing distance, auditory range ■ RELATED WORD: *adjective* audio

hearsay NOUN = **rumour**, talk, gossip, report, buzz, dirt (*slang*), goss (*informal*), word of mouth, tittle-tattle, talk of the town, scuttlebutt (*slang, chiefly U.S.*), idle talk, mere talk, on dit (*French*)

heart NOUN **1** *I phoned him up and poured out my heart.* = **emotions**, feelings, sentiments, love, affection **2** *She loved his brilliance and his generous heart.* = **nature**, character, soul, constitution, essence, temperament, inclination, disposition **3** *They are ruthless, formidable, without heart.* = **tenderness**, feeling(s), love, understanding, concern, sympathy, pity, humanity, affection, compassion, kindness, empathy, benevolence, concern for others **4** *The heart of the problem is supply and demand.* = **root**, core, essence, centre, nucleus, marrow, hub, kernel, crux, gist, central part, nitty-gritty (*informal*), nub, pith, quintessence **5** *I did not have the heart or spirit left to jog back to my hotel.* = **courage**, will, spirit, mind, purpose, bottle (*Brit. informal*), resolution, resolve, nerve, stomach, enthusiasm, determination, guts (*informal*), spine, pluck, bravery, backbone, fortitude, mettle, boldness, spunk (*informal*) • **at heart** = **fundamentally**,

essentially, basically, really, actually, in fact, truly, in reality, in truth, in essence, deep down, at bottom, au fond (*French*) • **by heart** *Mack knew this passage by heart.* = **from** or **by memory**, verbatim, word for word, pat, word-perfect, by rote, off by heart, off pat, parrot-fashion (*informal*)
• **from (the bottom of) your heart** *thanking you from the bottom of my heart* = **deeply**, heartily, fervently, heart and soul, devoutly, with all your heart • **from the heart** = **sincerely**, earnestly, in earnest, with all your heart, in all sincerity • **heart and soul** = **completely**, entirely, absolutely, wholeheartedly, to the hilt, devotedly • **lose heart** = **give up**, despair, lose hope, become despondent, give up the ghost (*informal*) • **take heart** *Investors failed to take heart from the stronger yen.* = **be encouraged**, be comforted, cheer up, perk up, brighten up, be heartened, buck up (*informal*), derive comfort ■ RELATED WORDS: *adjectives* cardiac, cardiothoracic

heartache NOUN = **sorrow**, suffering, pain, torture, distress, despair, grief, agony, torment, bitterness, anguish, remorse, heartbreak, affliction, heartsickness

heartbreak NOUN = **grief**, suffering, pain, despair, misery, sorrow, anguish, desolation

heartbreaking ADJECTIVE = **sad**, distressing, tragic, bitter, poignant, harrowing, desolating, grievous, pitiful, agonizing, heart-rending, gut-wrenching ■ OPPOSITE: happy

hearten VERB = **encourage**, inspire, cheer, comfort, assure, stimulate, reassure, animate, console, rouse, incite, embolden, buoy up, buck up (*informal*), raise someone's spirits, revivify, gee up, inspirit

heartfelt ADJECTIVE = **sincere**, deep, earnest, warm, genuine, profound, honest, ardent, devout, hearty, fervent, cordial, wholehearted, dinkum (*Austral. & N.Z. informal*), unfeigned ■ OPPOSITE: insincere

heartily ADVERB **1** *He laughed heartily.* = **sincerely**, feelingly, deeply, warmly, genuinely, profoundly, cordially, unfeignedly **2** *I heartily agree with her comments.* = **enthusiastically**, vigorously, eagerly, resolutely, earnestly, zealously **3** *We're all heartily sick of all the aggravation.* = **thoroughly**, very, completely, totally, absolutely

heartless ADJECTIVE = **cruel**, hard, callous, cold, harsh, brutal, unkind, inhuman, merciless, cold-blooded, uncaring, pitiless, unfeeling, cold-hearted, affectless, hardhearted ■ OPPOSITE: compassionate

heart-rending ADJECTIVE = **moving**, sad, distressing, affecting, tragic, pathetic, poignant, harrowing, heartbreaking, pitiful, gut-wrenching, piteous

heart-to-heart ADJECTIVE *I had a heart-to-heart talk with my mother.* = **intimate**, honest, candid, open, personal, sincere, truthful, unreserved ▸ NOUN *I've had a heart-to-heart with him.* = **tête-à-tête**, cosy chat, one-to-one, private conversation, private chat

heart-warming ADJECTIVE = **moving**, touching, affecting, pleasing, encouraging, warming, rewarding, satisfying, cheering, gratifying, heartening

hearty ADJECTIVE **1** *He was a hearty, bluff, athletic sort of guy.* = **friendly**, genial, warm, generous, eager, enthusiastic, ardent, cordial, affable, ebullient, jovial, effusive, unreserved, back-slapping ■ OPPOSITE: cool **2** *With the last sentiment, Arnold was in hearty agreement.* = **wholehearted**, sincere, heartfelt, real, true, earnest, genuine, honest, unfeigned ■ OPPOSITE: insincere **3** *The men ate a hearty breakfast.* = **substantial**, filling, ample, square, solid, nourishing, sizable or sizeable **4** *She was still hearty and strong at 92.* = **healthy**, well, strong, sound, active, hardy, robust, vigorous, energetic, hale (*old-fashioned*), alive and kicking, right as rain (*Brit. informal*) ■ OPPOSITE: frail

heat VERB **1** (*sometimes with* **up**) *Meanwhile, heat the tomatoes and oil in a pan.* = **warm (up)**, cook, boil, roast, reheat, make hot ■ OPPOSITE: chill **2** *The war of words continues to heat up.* = **intensify**, increase, heighten, deepen, escalate ▸ NOUN **1** *Leaves drooped in the fierce heat of the sun.* = **warmth**, hotness, temperature, swelter, sultriness, fieriness, torridity, warmness, calefaction ■ OPPOSITE: cold **2** *The heat is killing me.* = **hot weather**, warmth, closeness, high temperature, heatwave, warm weather, hot climate, hot spell, mugginess **3** *It was all done in the heat of the moment.* = **passion**, excitement, intensity, violence, fever, fury, warmth, zeal, agitation, fervour, ardour, vehemence, earnestness, impetuosity ■ OPPOSITE: calmness • **heat up** *In the summer her mobile home heats up like an oven.* = **warm up**, get hotter, become hot, rise in temperature, become warm, grow hot ■ RELATED WORD: *adjective* thermal

heated ADJECTIVE **1** *It was a very heated argument.* = **impassioned**, intense, spirited, excited, angry, violent, bitter, raging, furious, fierce, lively, passionate, animated, frenzied, fiery, stormy, vehement, tempestuous ■ OPPOSITE: calm **2** *People get a bit heated about issues like these.* = **wound up**, worked up, keyed up, het up (*informal*)

heathen NOUN **1** *the condescending air of missionaries seeking to convert the heathen* = **pagan**, infidel, unbeliever, idolater, idolatress **2** *She called us all heathens and hypocrites.* = **barbarian**, savage, philistine, oaf, ignoramus, boor ▸ ADJECTIVE **1** *a heathen temple* = **pagan**, infidel, godless, irreligious, idolatrous, heathenish **2** *to disappear into the cold heathen north* = **uncivilized**, savage, primitive, barbaric, brutish, unenlightened, uncultured

heave VERB **1** *He heaved Barney to his feet.* = **lift**, raise, pull (up), drag (up), haul (up), tug, lever, hoist, heft (*informal*) **2** *Heave a brick at the telly.* = **throw**, fling, toss, send, cast, pitch, hurl, sling (*informal*) **3** *The grey seas heaved.* = **surge**, rise, swell, billow **4** *She gasped and heaved and vomited.* = **vomit**, be sick, throw up (*informal*), chuck (up) (*slang, chiefly U.S.*), chuck (*Austral. & N.Z. informal*), gag, spew, retch, barf (*U.S. slang*), chunder (*slang, chiefly Austral.*), upchuck (*U.S. slang*), do a technicolour yawn (*slang*), toss your cookies (*U.S. slang*) **5** *Mr Collier heaved a sigh and got to his feet.* = **breathe**, sigh, puff, groan, sob, breathe heavily, suspire (*archaic*), utter wearily

heaven NOUN **1** *I believed that when I died I would go to heaven.* = **paradise**, next world, hereafter, nirvana (*Buddhism & Hinduism*), bliss, Zion (*Christianity*), Valhalla (*Norse myth*), Happy Valley, happy hunting ground (*Native American legend*), life to come, life everlasting, abode of God, Elysium or Elysian fields (*Greek myth*) **2** *My idea of heaven is drinking champagne with friends on a sunny day.* = **happiness**, paradise, ecstasy, bliss, felicity, utopia, contentment, rapture, enchantment, dreamland, seventh heaven, transport, sheer bliss • **the heavens** *a detailed map of the heavens* = **sky**, ether, firmament, celestial sphere, welkin (*archaic*), empyrean (*poetic*)

heavenly ADJECTIVE **1** *heavenly beings whose function it is to serve God* = **celestial**, holy, divine, blessed, blest, immortal, supernatural, angelic, extraterrestrial, superhuman, godlike, beatific, cherubic, seraphic, supernal (*literary*), empyrean (*poetic*), paradisaical ■ OPPOSITE: earthly **2** *The idea of spending two weeks with him seems heavenly.* = **wonderful**, lovely, delightful, beautiful, entrancing, divine (*informal*), glorious, exquisite, sublime, alluring, blissful, ravishing, rapturous ■ OPPOSITE: awful

heavily ADVERB **1** *Colonel Rall had been drinking heavily the night before.* = **excessively**, to excess, very much, a great deal, frequently, considerably, copiously, without restraint, immoderately, intemperately **2** *They can be found in grassy and heavily wooded areas.* = **densely**, closely, thickly, compactly **3** *A man stumbled heavily against the car.* = **hard**, clumsily, awkwardly, weightily

heaviness NOUN **1** *the heaviness of earthbound matter* = **weight**, gravity, ponderousness, heftiness **2** *a heaviness in his reply which discouraged further questioning* = **sadness**, depression, gloom, seriousness, melancholy, despondency, dejection, gloominess, glumness

heavy ADJECTIVE **1** *He was carrying a very heavy load.* = **weighty**, large, massive, hefty, bulky, ponderous ■ **OPPOSITE:** light **2** *Heavy fighting has been going on.* = **intensive**, severe, serious, concentrated, fierce, excessive, relentless **3** *There was a heavy amount of traffic on the roads.* = **considerable**, large, huge, substantial, abundant, copious, profuse ■ **OPPOSITE:** slight **4** *They bear a heavy burden of responsibility.* = **onerous**, hard, difficult, severe, harsh, tedious, intolerable, oppressive, grievous, burdensome, wearisome, vexatious ■ **OPPOSITE:** easy **5** *I struggle to raise eyelids still heavy with sleep.* = **sluggish**, slow, dull, wooden, stupid, inactive, inert, apathetic, drowsy, listless, indolent, torpid ■ **OPPOSITE:** alert **6** *They employ two full-timers to do the heavy work.* = **hard**, demanding, difficult, physical, strenuous, laborious **7** *The night sky was heavy with rain clouds.* = **overcast**, dull, gloomy, cloudy, leaden, louring or lowering **8** *My parents' faces were heavy with fallen hope.* = **sad**, depressed, gloomy, grieving, melancholy, dejected, despondent, downcast, sorrowful, disconsolate, crestfallen ■ **OPPOSITE:** happy **9** *I don't want any more of that heavy stuff.* = **serious**, grave, solemn, difficult, deep, complex, profound, weighty ■ **OPPOSITE:** trivial

heavy-handed ADJECTIVE **1** *heavy-handed police tactics* = **oppressive**, harsh, Draconian, autocratic, domineering, overbearing **2** *She tends to be a little heavy-handed.* = **clumsy**, awkward, bungling, inept, graceless, inexpert, maladroit, ham-handed (*informal*), like a bull in a china shop (*informal*), ham-fisted (*informal*) ■ **OPPOSITE:** skilful

heckle VERB = **jeer**, interrupt, shout down, disrupt, bait, barrack (*informal*), boo, taunt, pester

hectic ADJECTIVE = **frantic**, chaotic, frenzied, heated, wild, excited, furious, fevered, animated, turbulent, flurrying, frenetic, boisterous, feverish, tumultuous, flustering, riotous, rumbustious ■ **OPPOSITE:** peaceful

hector VERB = **bully**, harass, browbeat, worry, threaten, menace, intimidate, ride roughshod over, bullyrag

hedge NOUN *Gold is traditionally a hedge against inflation.* = **guard**, cover, protection, compensation, shield, safeguard, counterbalance, insurance cover ▶ VERB **1** *When asked about his involvement, he hedged.* = **prevaricate**, evade, sidestep, duck (*informal*), dodge, flannel (*Brit. informal*), waffle (*informal, chiefly Brit.*), quibble, beg the question, pussyfoot (*informal*), equivocate, temporize, be noncommittal **2** *sweeping lawns hedged with floribundas* = **enclose**, edge, border, surround, fence • **hedge against something** *You can hedge against redundancy or illness with insurance.* = **protect**, insure, guard, safeguard, shield, cover, fortify • **hedge someone in** *He was hedged in by his own shyness.* = **hamper**, restrict, handicap, hamstring, hinder, hem in • **hedge something in** *a steep and rocky footpath hedged in by the shadowy green forest* = **surround**, enclose, encompass, encircle, ring, fence in, girdle, hem in • **hedge something** *or* **someone about** *The offer was hedged about by conditions.* = **restrict**, confine, hinder, hem in, hem around, hem about

hedonism NOUN = **pleasure-seeking**, gratification, sensuality, self-indulgence, dolce vita, pursuit of pleasure, luxuriousness, sensualism, sybaritism, epicureanism, epicurism

hedonistic ADJECTIVE = **pleasure-seeking**, self-indulgent, luxurious, voluptuous, sybaritic, epicurean, bacchanalian

heed VERB *Few people at the conference heeded her warning.* = **pay attention to**, listen to, take notice of, follow, mark, mind, consider, note, regard, attend, observe, obey, bear in mind, be guided by, take to heart, give ear to ■ **OPPOSITE:** ignore ▶ NOUN *He pays too much heed these days to my nephew.* = **thought**, care, mind, note, attention, regard, respect, notice, consideration, watchfulness ■ **OPPOSITE:** disregard

heedless ADJECTIVE = **careless**, reckless, negligent, rash, precipitate, oblivious, foolhardy, thoughtless, unthinking, imprudent, neglectful, inattentive, incautious, unmindful, unobservant ■ **OPPOSITE:** careful

h

heel NOUN **1** *the heel of a loaf of bread* = **end**, stump, remainder, crust, rump, stub **2** *Suddenly I feel like a total heel.* = **swine**, cad (*Brit. informal*), scoundrel, scally (*Northwest English, dialect*), bounder (*Brit., old-fashioned slang*), rotter (*slang, chiefly Brit.*), scumbag (*slang*), blackguard, wrong 'un (*slang*) • **take to your heels** *He stood, for a moment, then took to his heels.* = **flee**, escape, run away *or* off, take flight, hook it (*slang*), turn tail, show a clean pair of heels, skedaddle (*informal*), vamoose (*slang, chiefly U.S.*)

hefty (*informal*) ADJECTIVE **1** *She was quite a hefty woman.* = **big**, strong, massive, strapping, robust, muscular, burly, husky (*informal*), hulking, beefy (*informal*), brawny ■ **OPPOSITE:** small **2** *Lambert gave him a hefty shove to send him on his way.* = **forceful**, heavy, powerful, vigorous (*slang*) ■ **OPPOSITE:** gentle **3** *The gritty foursome took turns shouldering the hefty load every five minutes.* = **heavy**, large, massive, substantial, tremendous, awkward, ample, bulky, colossal, cumbersome, weighty, unwieldy, ponderous ■ **OPPOSITE:** light **4** *Consumers often run up hefty bills without realizing they have done so.* = **large**, massive, substantial, excessive, inflated, sizeable, astronomical (*informal*), extortionate

height NOUN **1** *Her height is intimidating for some men.* = **tallness**, stature, highness, loftiness ■ **OPPOSITE:** shortness **2** *Build a wall up to a height of 2 metres.* = **altitude**, measurement, highness, elevation, tallness ■ **OPPOSITE:** depth **3** *From a height, it looks like a desert.* = **peak**, top, hill, mountain, crown, summit, crest, pinnacle, elevation, apex, apogee, vertex ■ **OPPOSITE:** valley **4** *He was struck down at the height of his career.* = **culmination**, climax, zenith, limit, maximum, ultimate, extremity, uttermost, ne plus ultra (*Latin*), utmost degree ■ **OPPOSITE:** low point ■ **RELATED WORD:** *phobia* acrophobia

heighten VERB = **intensify**, increase, add to, improve, strengthen, enhance, sharpen, aggravate, magnify, amplify, augment

heinous ADJECTIVE = **shocking**, evil, monstrous, grave, awful, vicious, outrageous, revolting, infamous, hideous, unspeakable, atrocious, flagrant, odious, hateful, abhorrent, abominable, villainous, nefarious, iniquitous, execrable

heir NOUN = **successor**, beneficiary, inheritor, heiress (*fem.*), scion, next in line, inheritress *or* inheritrix (*fem.*)

hell NOUN **1** *Don't worry about going to Hell, just be good.* = **the underworld**, the abyss, Hades (*Greek myth*), hellfire, the inferno, fire and brimstone, the bottomless pit, Gehenna (*New Testament & Judaism*), the nether world, the lower world, Tartarus (*Greek myth*), the infernal regions, the bad fire (*informal*), Acheron (*Greek myth*), Abaddon, the abode of the damned **2** *the hell of grief and lost love* = **torment**, suffering, agony, trial, nightmare, misery, ordeal, anguish, affliction, martyrdom, wretchedness • **hell for leather** *The first horse often goes hell for leather.* = **headlong**, speedily, quickly, swiftly, hurriedly, at the double, full-tilt, pell-mell, hotfoot, at a rate of knots, like a bat out of hell (*slang*), posthaste

hellbent ADJECTIVE = **intent** (*informal*), set, determined, settled, fixed, resolved, bent

hellish ADJECTIVE **1** *He was held for three years in hellish conditions.* = **atrocious**, terrible (*informal*), dreadful, cruel, vicious, monstrous, wicked, inhuman, barbarous, abominable, nefarious, accursed, execrable, detestable ■ **OPPOSITE:** wonderful **2** *They began to shout, making devilish gestures with a hellish noise.* = **devilish**, fiendish, diabolical, infernal (*informal*), damned (*slang*), damnable, demoniacal

hello INTERJECTION = **hi** (*informal*), greetings, how do you do?, good morning, good evening, good afternoon, welcome, kia ora (*N.Z.*), gidday *or* g'day (*Austral. & N.Z.*)

helm NOUN *I got into our dinghy while Willis took the helm.* = **tiller**, wheel, rudder, steering gear • **at the helm** *He has been at the helm of Lonrho for 31 years.* = **in charge**, in control, in command, directing, at the wheel, in the saddle, in the driving seat

help VERB **1** (*sometimes with* **out**) *If you're not willing to help me, I'll find somebody who will.* = **aid**, back, support, second, encourage, promote, assist, relieve, stand by, befriend, cooperate with, abet, lend a hand, succour, lend a helping hand, give someone a leg up (*informal*) ■ **OPPOSITE:** hinder **2** *A cosmetic measure which will do nothing to help the situation long term.* = **improve**, ease, heal, cure, relieve, remedy, facilitate, alleviate, mitigate, ameliorate ■ **OPPOSITE:** make worse **3** *Martin helped Tanya over the rail.* = **assist**, aid, support, give a leg up (*informal*) **4** *I can't help feeling sorry for the poor man.* = **resist**, refrain from, avoid, control, prevent, withstand, eschew, keep from, abstain from, forbear ▶ NOUN **1** *Thanks very much for your help.* = **assistance**, aid, support, service, advice, promotion, guidance, cooperation, helping hand

■ **OPPOSITE:** hindrance **2** *There is no help for him and no doctor on this earth could save him.* = **remedy**, cure, relief, corrective, balm, salve, succour, restorative **3** *a hired help* = **assistant**, hand, worker, employee, helper

helper NOUN = **assistant**, partner, ally, colleague, supporter, mate, deputy, second, subsidiary, aide, aider, attendant, collaborator, auxiliary, henchman or woman or person, right-hand man or woman or person, adjutant, helpmate, coadjutor, abettor

helpful ADJECTIVE **1** *The staff in the London office are helpful.* = **cooperative**, accommodating, kind, caring, friendly, neighbourly, sympathetic, supportive, benevolent, considerate, beneficent **2** *The catalogue includes helpful information.* = **useful**, practical, productive, profitable, constructive, serviceable **3** *It is often helpful to have someone with you when you get bad news.* = **beneficial**, advantageous, expedient, favourable

helpfulness NOUN **1** *The level of expertise and helpfulness is higher in small shops.* = **cooperation**, kindness, support, assistance, sympathy, friendliness, rallying round, neighbourliness, good neighbourliness **2** *the helpfulness of the information pack* = **usefulness**, benefit, advantage

helping NOUN = **portion**, serving, ration, piece, dollop (*informal*), plateful

helpless ADJECTIVE **1** *The children were left helpless.* = **vulnerable**, exposed, unprotected, defenceless, abandoned, dependent, stranded, wide open, forlorn, destitute ■ **OPPOSITE:** invulnerable **2** *We felt helpless in the face of the disaster.* = **powerless**, weak, incapable, paralysed, incompetent, unfit, feeble, debilitated, impotent, infirm ■ **OPPOSITE:** powerful

helplessness NOUN = **vulnerability**, weakness, impotence, powerlessness, infirmity, feebleness, forlornness, defencelessness

helter-skelter ADJECTIVE *another crisis in his helter-skelter existence* = **haphazard**, confused, disordered, random, muddled, jumbled, topsy-turvy, hit-or-miss, higgledy-piggledy (*informal*) ▶ ADVERB *a panic-stricken crowd running helter-skelter* = **wildly**, rashly, anyhow, headlong, recklessly, carelessly, pell-mell

hem NOUN *Cut a jagged edge along the hem to give a ragged look.* = **edge**, border, margin, trimming, fringe • **hem something** or **someone in 1** *Manchester is hemmed in by*

greenbelt countryside. = **surround**, edge, border, skirt, confine, enclose, shut in, hedge in, environ **2** *hemmed in by rigid, legal contracts* = **restrict**, confine, beset, circumscribe

hence ADVERB = **therefore**, thus, consequently, for this reason, in consequence, ergo, on that account

henceforth ADVERB = **from now on**, in the future, hereafter, hence, hereinafter, from this day forward

henchman or **henchwoman** or **henchperson** NOUN = **attendant**, supporter, heavy (*slang*), associate, aide, follower, subordinate, bodyguard, minder (*slang*), crony, sidekick (*slang*), cohort (*chiefly U.S.*), right-hand man or woman or person, minion, satellite, myrmidon

herald VERB **1** *Economists said the drop could herald a fall in consumer spending.* = **indicate**, promise, precede, pave the way, usher in, harbinger, presage, portend, foretoken **2** *Tonight's clash is being heralded as the match of the season.* = **announce**, publish, advertise, proclaim, broadcast, trumpet, publicize ▶ NOUN **1** *I welcome the report as the herald of more freedom, not less.* = **forerunner**, sign, signal, indication, token, omen, precursor, harbinger (*literary*) **2** *She hovered by the hearth while the herald delivered his news.* = **messenger**, courier, proclaimer, announcer, crier, town crier, bearer of tidings

herculean ADJECTIVE **1** *Finding a lawyer may seem like a Herculean task.* = **arduous**, hard, demanding, difficult, heavy, tough, exhausting, formidable, gruelling, strenuous, prodigious, onerous, laborious, toilsome (*literary*) **2** *His shoulders were Herculean with long arms.* = **strong**, muscular, powerful, athletic, strapping, mighty, rugged (*U.S. & Canad.*), sturdy, stalwart, husky (*informal*), sinewy, brawny, swole (*slang*), hench (*informal*)

herd NOUN **1** *large herds of elephant and buffalo* = **flock**, crowd, collection, mass, drove, crush, mob, swarm, horde, multitude, throng, assemblage, press **2** *They are individuals; they will not follow the herd.* = **mob**, the masses, rabble, populace, the hoi polloi, the plebs, riffraff ▶ VERB **1** *The group was herded onto a bus.* = **lead**, drive, force, direct, guide, shepherd **2** *A boy herded sheep down towards the lane.* = **drive**, lead, force, guide, shepherd

hereafter ADVERB *Hereafter for three years my name will not appear at all.* = **in future**, after this, from now on, henceforth, henceforward, hence • **the hereafter** *belief* *in the hereafter* = **afterlife**, next world, life after death, future life, the beyond

hereditary ADJECTIVE **1** *In men, hair loss is hereditary.* = **genetic**, inborn, inbred, transmissible, inheritable **2** *hereditary peerages* = **inherited**, handed down, passed down, willed, family, traditional, transmitted, ancestral, bequeathed, patrimonial

heredity NOUN = **genetics**, inheritance, genetic make-up, congenital traits

heresy NOUN = **unorthodoxy**, apostasy, dissidence, impiety, revisionism, iconoclasm, heterodoxy

heretic NOUN = **nonconformist**, dissident, separatist, sectarian, renegade, revisionist, dissenter, apostate, schismatic

heretical ADJECTIVE **1** *I made a heretical suggestion.* = **controversial**, unorthodox, revisionist, freethinking **2** *The Church regards spirit mediums as heretical.* = **unorthodox**, revisionist, iconoclastic, heterodox, impious, idolatrous, schismatic, freethinking

heritage NOUN = **inheritance**, legacy, birthright, lot, share, estate, tradition, portion, endowment, bequest, patrimony

hermit NOUN = **recluse**, monk, loner (*informal*), solitary, anchorite, anchoress, stylite, eremite

hero NOUN **1** *The hero of Doctor Zhivago dies in 1929.* = **protagonist**, leading man, lead actor, male lead, principal male character **2** *the goalscoring hero of the Indian hockey team* = **star**, champion, celebrity, victor, superstar, great man *or* woman, heart-throb (*Brit.*), conqueror, exemplar, celeb (*informal*), megastar (*informal*), popular figure **3** *I still remember my boyhood heroes.* = **idol**, favourite, pin-up (*slang*), fave (*informal*)

heroic ADJECTIVE **1** *The heroic sergeant risked his life to rescue 29 fishermen.* = **courageous**, brave, daring, bold, fearless, gallant, intrepid, valiant, doughty (*old-fashioned*), undaunted, dauntless, lion-hearted, valorous, stouthearted (*old-fashioned*) ■ **OPPOSITE:** cowardly **2** *another in an endless series of man's heroic myths of his own past* = **legendary**, classical, mythological, Homeric **3** *a heroic style, with a touch of antiquarian realism* = **epic**, grand, classic, extravagant, exaggerated, elevated, inflated, high-flown, grandiose ■ **OPPOSITE:** simple

heroine NOUN **1** *The heroine is a senior TV executive.* = **protagonist**, leading lady, diva, prima donna, female lead, lead actress, principal female character **2** *The heroine of the day was the winner of the Gold medal.*

= **star**, celebrity, goddess, celeb (*informal*), megastar (*informal*), woman of the hour **3** *I still remember my childhood heroines.* = **idol**, favourite, pin-up (*slang*), fave (*informal*)

> **USAGE** Note that the word *heroine*, meaning 'a female hero', has an *e* at the end. The drug *heroin* is spelled without a final *e*.

heroism NOUN = **bravery**, daring, courage, spirit, fortitude, boldness, gallantry, valour, fearlessness, intrepidity, courageousness

hero-worship NOUN = **admiration**, idolization, adulation, adoration, veneration, idealization, putting on a pedestal

hesitant ADJECTIVE = **uncertain**, reluctant, shy, halting, doubtful, sceptical, unsure, hesitating, wavering, timid, diffident, lacking confidence, vacillating, hanging back, irresolute, half-hearted ■ **OPPOSITE:** confident

hesitate VERB **1** *She hesitated, debating whether to answer the phone.* = **waver**, delay, pause, haver (*Brit.*), wait, doubt, falter, be uncertain, dither (*chiefly Brit.*), vacillate, equivocate, temporize, hum and haw, shillyshally (*informal*), swither (*Scot., dialect*) ■ **OPPOSITE:** be decisive **2** *I will not hesitate to take unpopular decisions.* = **be reluctant**, be unwilling, shrink from, think twice, boggle, scruple, demur, hang back, be disinclined, balk *or* baulk ■ **OPPOSITE:** be determined

hesitation NOUN **1** *After some hesitation, he answered her question.* = **delay**, pausing, uncertainty, stalling, dithering, indecision, hesitancy, doubt, vacillation, temporizing, shilly-shallying, irresolution, hemming and hawing, dubiety **2** *The board said it had no hesitation in rejecting the offer.* = **reluctance**, reservation(s), misgiving(s), ambivalence, qualm(s), unwillingness, scruple(s), compunction, demurral

heterogeneous ADJECTIVE = **varied**, different, mixed, contrasting, unlike, diverse, diversified, assorted, unrelated, disparate, miscellaneous, motley, incongruous, dissimilar, divergent, manifold (*formal*), discrepant

hew VERB **1** *He felled, peeled and hewed his own timber.* = **cut**, chop, axe, hack, split, lop **2** *medieval monasteries hewn out of the rockface* = **carve**, make, form, fashion, shape, model, sculpture, sculpt

heyday NOUN = **prime**, time, day, flowering, pink, bloom, high point, zenith, salad days, prime of life

hiatus NOUN = **pause**, break, interval, space, gap, breach, blank, lapse, interruption, respite, chasm, discontinuity, lacuna, entr'acte

hibernate VERB = **sleep**, lie dormant, winter, overwinter, vegetate, remain torpid, sleep snug

hidden ADJECTIVE **1** *Uncover hidden meanings and discover special messages.* = **secret**, veiled, dark, mysterious, obscure, mystical, mystic, shrouded, occult, latent, cryptic, ulterior, abstruse, recondite, hermetic *or* hermetical **2** *The pictures had obviously been taken by a hidden camera.* = **concealed**, covered, secret, covert, unseen, clandestine, secreted, under wraps, unrevealed

hide¹ VERB **1** *He hid the bicycle in the hawthorn hedge.* = **conceal**, stash (*informal*), secrete, cache, put out of sight ■ OPPOSITE: display **2** *They hid behind a tree.* = **go into hiding**, take cover, keep out of sight, hole up, lie low, go underground, go to ground, go to earth **3** *I have absolutely nothing to hide, I have done nothing wrong.* = **keep secret**, suppress, withhold, keep quiet about, hush up, draw a veil over, keep dark, keep under your hat ■ OPPOSITE: disclose **4** *The compound was hidden by trees and shrubs.* = **obscure**, cover, screen, bury, shelter, mask, disguise, conceal, eclipse, veil, cloak, shroud, camouflage, blot out ■ OPPOSITE: reveal

hide² NOUN *the process of tanning animal hides* = **skin**, fell, leather, pelt

hideaway NOUN = **hiding place**, haven, retreat, refuge, sanctuary, hide-out, nest, sequestered nook

hidebound ADJECTIVE = **conventional**, set, rigid, narrow, puritan, narrow-minded, strait-laced, brassbound, ultraconservative, set in your ways ■ OPPOSITE: broad-minded

hideous ADJECTIVE **1** *She saw a hideous face at the window and screamed.* = **ugly**, revolting, ghastly, monstrous, grotesque, gruesome, grisly, unsightly, repulsive ■ OPPOSITE: beautiful **2** *His family was subjected to a hideous attack.* = **terrifying**, shocking, terrible, awful, appalling, disgusting, horrible, dreadful, horrific, obscene, sickening, horrendous, macabre, horrid, odious, loathsome, abominable, detestable, godawful (*slang*)

hide-out NOUN = **hiding place**, shelter, den, hideaway, lair, secret place

hiding NOUN = **beating**, whipping, thrashing, tanning (*slang*), caning, licking (*informal*), flogging, spanking, walloping (*informal*), drubbing, lathering (*informal*), whaling, larruping (*Brit.*, *dialect*)

hierarchy NOUN = **grading**, ranking, social order, pecking order, class system, social stratum

higgledy-piggledy ADJECTIVE *books stacked in higgledy-piggledy piles on the floor* = **haphazard**, muddled, jumbled, indiscriminate, topsy-turvy, helter-skelter, pell-mell ▶ ADVERB *boulders tossed higgledy-piggledy as though by some giant* = **haphazardly**, all over the place, anyhow, topsy-turvy, helter-skelter, all over the shop (*informal*), pell-mell, confusedly, any old how

high ADJECTIVE **1** *A house with a high wall around it.* = **tall**, towering, soaring, steep, elevated, lofty ■ OPPOSITE: short **2** *Officials said casualties were high.* = **extreme**, great, acute, severe, extraordinary, excessive ■ OPPOSITE: low **3** *High winds have knocked down trees and power lines.* = **strong**, violent, extreme, blustery, squally, sharp **4** *I think it's a good buy overall, despite the high price.* = **expensive**, dear, steep (*informal*), costly, stiff, high-priced, exorbitant **5** *Every one of them is controlled by the families of high officials.* = **important**, leading, ruling, chief, powerful, significant, distinguished, prominent, superior, influential, notable, big-time (*informal*), eminent, major league (*informal*), exalted, consequential, skookum (*Canad.*) ■ OPPOSITE: lowly **6** *She has always had a high reputation for her excellent stories.* = **notable**, leading, famous, significant, celebrated, distinguished, renowned, eminent, pre-eminent **7** *Her high voice really irritated Maria.* = **high-pitched**, piercing, shrill, penetrating, treble, soprano, strident, sharp, acute, piping ■ OPPOSITE: deep **8** *Her spirits were high with the hope of seeing Nick.* = **cheerful**, excited, merry, exhilarated, exuberant, joyful, bouncy (*informal*), boisterous, elated, light-hearted, stoked (*Austral. & N.Z. informal*) ■ OPPOSITE: dejected **9** *He was too high on drugs and alcohol to remember them.* = **intoxicated**, stoned (*slang*), spaced out (*slang*), tripping (*informal*), turned on (*slang*), on a trip (*informal*), delirious, euphoric, freaked out (*informal*), hyped up (*slang*), zonked (*slang*), inebriated **10** *an emphatic contrast to his Park Avenue high life* = **luxurious**, rich, grand, lavish, extravagant, opulent, hedonistic ▶ ADVERB *on combat patrol flying high above the landing sites* = **way up**, aloft, far up, to a great height ▶ NOUN **1** *Sales of Russian vodka have reached an all-time high.* = **peak**, height, top, summit, crest, record level, apex **2** *The 'thrill' sought is said to be similar to a drug high.* = **intoxication**, trip (*informal*), euphoria, delirium, ecstasy • **high and dry** *You could be left high and dry in a strange town.* = **abandoned**, stranded, helpless, forsaken, bereft, destitute, in the lurch

• **high and mighty** *I think you're a bit too high and mighty yourself.* = **self-important**, superior, arrogant, stuck-up (*informal*), conceited, imperious, overbearing, haughty, snobbish, disdainful

highbrow ADJECTIVE *He presents his own highbrow literary programme.* = **intellectual**, cultured, sophisticated, deep, cultivated, brainy (*informal*), highbrowed, bookish ■ OPPOSITE: unintellectual ▶ NOUN *the sniggers of the highbrows* = **intellectual**, scholar, egghead (*informal*), brain (*informal*), mastermind, Brahmin (*U.S.*), aesthete, savant, brainbox (*slang*) ■ OPPOSITE: philistine

high-class ADJECTIVE = **high-quality**, top (*slang*), choice, select, exclusive, elite, superior, posh (*informal, chiefly Brit.*), classy (*slang*), top-flight, upper-class, swish (*informal, chiefly Brit.*), first-rate, up-market, top-drawer, ritzy (*slang*), tip-top, high-toned, A1 or A-one (*informal*) ■ OPPOSITE: inferior

higher-up NOUN = **superior**, senior, manager, director, executive, boss, gaffer (*informal, chiefly Brit.*), sherang (*Austral. & N.Z.*)

high-flown ADJECTIVE = **extravagant**, elaborate, pretentious, exaggerated, inflated, lofty, grandiose, overblown, florid, high-falutin (*informal*), arty-farty (*informal*), magniloquent ■ OPPOSITE: straightforward

high-handed ADJECTIVE = **dictatorial**, domineering, overbearing, arbitrary, oppressive, autocratic, bossy (*informal*), imperious, tyrannical, despotic, peremptory

highlight VERB *Two events have highlighted the tensions in recent days.* = **emphasize**, stress, accent, feature, set off, show up, underline, spotlight, play up, accentuate, flag, foreground, focus attention on, call attention to, give prominence to, bring to the fore ■ OPPOSITE: play down ▶ NOUN *one of the highlights of the tournament* = **high point**, peak, climax, feature, focus, best part, focal point, main feature, high spot, memorable part ■ OPPOSITE: low point

highly ADVERB **1** *He was a highly successful entrepreneur.* = **extremely**, very, greatly, seriously (*informal*), vastly, exceptionally, extraordinarily, immensely, decidedly, tremendously, supremely, eminently **2** *one of the most highly regarded chefs in the French capital* = **favourably**, well, warmly, enthusiastically, approvingly, appreciatively

highly-strung ADJECTIVE = **nervous**, stressed, tense, sensitive, wired (*slang*), restless, taut, edgy, temperamental, excitable, nervy (*Brit. informal*), twitchy (*informal*), on tenterhooks, easily upset, on pins and needles, adrenalized ■ OPPOSITE: relaxed

high-minded ADJECTIVE = **principled**, moral, worthy, noble, good, fair, pure, ethical, upright, elevated, honourable, righteous, idealistic, virtuous, magnanimous ■ OPPOSITE: dishonourable

high-powered ADJECTIVE = **dynamic**, driving, powerful, enterprising, effective, go-ahead, aggressive, vigorous, energetic, forceful, fast-track, go-getting (*informal*), high-octane (*informal*), highly capable

high-pressure ADJECTIVE = **forceful**, aggressive, compelling, intensive, persistent, persuasive, high-powered, insistent, bludgeoning, pushy (*informal*), in-your-face (*slang*), coercive, importunate (*formal*)

high-spirited ADJECTIVE = **lively**, spirited, vivacious, vital, daring, dashing, bold, energetic, animated, vibrant, exuberant, bouncy, boisterous, fun-loving, ebullient, sparky, effervescent, alive and kicking, full of life, spunky (*informal*), full of beans (*informal*), frolicsome, mettlesome

hijack or **highjack** VERB = **seize**, take over, commandeer, expropriate (*formal*), skyjack

hike NOUN *a hike around the cluster of hills* = **walk**, march, trek, ramble, tramp, traipse, journey on foot ▶ VERB *You could hike through the Fish River Canyon.* = **walk**, march, trek, ramble, tramp, leg it (*informal*), back-pack, hoof it (*slang*) • **hike something up** *He hiked up his trouser legs.* = **hitch up**, raise, lift, pull up, jack up

hiker NOUN = **walker**, rambler, backpacker, wayfarer, hillwalker

hilarious ADJECTIVE **1** *He had a fund of hilarious tales.* = **funny**, entertaining, amusing, hysterical (*informal*), humorous, exhilarating, comical, side-splitting **2** *Everyone had a hilarious time.* = **merry**, uproarious, happy, gay, noisy, jolly, joyous, joyful, jovial, rollicking, convivial, mirthful ■ OPPOSITE: serious

hilarity NOUN = **merriment**, high spirits, mirth, gaiety, laughter, amusement, glee, exuberance, exhilaration, cheerfulness, jollity, levity, conviviality, joviality, boisterousness, joyousness, jollification

hill NOUN **1** *They climbed to the top of the hill.* = **mount**, down (*archaic*), fell, height, mound, prominence, elevation, eminence, hilltop, tor, knoll, hillock, brae (*Scot.*), kopje or koppie (*S. African*) **2** *the shady street that led up the hill to the office building* = **slope**, incline, gradient, rise, climb, brae (*Scot.*), acclivity

hilly ADJECTIVE = **mountainous**, rolling, steep, undulating

hilt NOUN *the hilt of the small, sharp knife* = **handle**, grip, haft, handgrip, helve • **to the hilt** *James was overdrawn and mortgaged to the hilt.* = **fully**, completely, totally, entirely, wholly

hind ADJECTIVE = **back**, rear, hinder, posterior, caudal (*Anatomy*)

hinder VERB = **obstruct**, stop, check, block, prevent, arrest, delay, oppose, frustrate, handicap, interrupt, slow down, deter, hamstring, hamper, thwart, retard, impede, hobble, stymie, encumber, throw a spanner in the works, trammel, hold up *or* back ■ **OPPOSITE:** help

hindrance NOUN = **obstacle**, check, bar, block, difficulty, drag, barrier, restriction, handicap, limitation, hazard, restraint, hitch, drawback, snag, deterrent, interruption, obstruction, stoppage, stumbling block, impediment, encumbrance, trammel ■ **OPPOSITE:** help

hinge on VERB = **depend on**, be subject to, hang on, turn on, rest on, revolve around, be contingent on, pivot on

hint NOUN **1** *I'd dropped a hint about having an exhibition of his work.* = **clue**, mention, suggestion, implication, indication, reminder, tip-off, pointer, allusion, innuendo, inkling, intimation, insinuation, word to the wise **2** *I'm hoping to get some fashion hints.* = **advice**, help, tip(s), suggestion(s), pointer(s) **3** *I glanced at her and saw no hint of irony on her face.* = **trace**, touch, suggestion, taste, breath, dash, whisper, suspicion, tinge, whiff, speck, undertone, soupçon (*French*) ▶ VERB (*sometimes with* **at**) *The President hinted she might make some changes in the government.* = **suggest**, mention, indicate, imply, intimate, tip off, let it be known, insinuate, allude to the fact, tip the wink (*informal*)

hip ADJECTIVE = **trendy** (*Brit. informal*), on trend, with it (*old-fashioned, informal*), fashionable, in, aware, informed, wise (*slang*), clued-up (*informal*), funky

hippy *or* **hippie** NOUN = **flower child**, bohemian, dropout, free spirit, beatnik, basketweaver (*Austral., derogatory slang*)

hire VERB **1** *hired on short-term contracts* = **employ**, commission, take on, engage, appoint, sign up, enlist **2** *To hire a car you must produce a current driving licence.* = **rent**, charter, lease, let, engage ▶ NOUN **1** *Fishing tackle is available for hire.* = **rental**, hiring, rent, lease **2** *Surf board hire is $12 per day.* = **charge**, rental, price, cost, fee

hirsute ADJECTIVE = **hairy**, bearded, shaggy, unshaven, bristly, bewhiskered, hispid (*Biology*)

hiss VERB **1** *The air hissed out of the pipe.* = **whistle**, wheeze, rasp, whiz, whirr, sibilate **2** *The delegates booed and hissed him.* = **jeer**, mock, ridicule, deride, decry, revile ▶ NOUN *the hiss of a beer bottle opening* = **fizz**, buzz, hissing, fizzing, sibilance, sibilation

historian NOUN = **chronicler**, recorder, biographer, antiquarian, historiographer, annalist, chronologist

historic ADJECTIVE = **significant**, notable, momentous, famous, celebrated, extraordinary, outstanding, remarkable, ground-breaking, consequential, red-letter, epoch-making ■ **OPPOSITE:** unimportant

> **USAGE** Although *historic* and *historical* are similarly spelt they are very different in meaning and should not be used interchangeably. A distinction is usually made between *historic*, which means 'important' or 'significant', and *historical*, which means 'pertaining to history': *a historic decision; a historical perspective.*

historical ADJECTIVE = **factual**, real, documented, actual, authentic, chronicled, attested, archival, verifiable ■ **OPPOSITE:** contemporary

history NOUN **1** *Is history about to repeat itself?* = **the past**, the old days, antiquity, yesterday, the good old days, yesteryear, ancient history, olden days, days of old, days of yore, bygone times **2** *his magnificent history of broadcasting in Canada* = **chronicle**, record, story, account, relation, narrative, saga, recital, narration, annals, recapitulation

histrionic ADJECTIVE *Dorothea let out a histrionic groan.* = **theatrical**, affected, dramatic, forced, camp (*informal*), actorly, artificial, unnatural, melodramatic, actressy ▶ PLURAL NOUN *When I explained everything, there were no histrionics.* = **dramatics**, scene, tantrums, performance, temperament, theatricality, staginess, hissy fit (*informal*)

hit VERB **1** *She hit him hard across his left arm.* = **strike**, beat, knock, punch, belt (*informal*), deck (*slang*), bang, batter, clip (*informal*), slap, bash (*informal*), sock (*slang*), chin (*slang*), smack, thump, clout (*informal*), cuff, flog, whack, clobber (*slang*), smite (*archaic*), wallop (*informal*), swat, lay one on (*slang*), beat or knock seven bells out of (*informal*) **2** *The car hit a traffic sign before skidding out of control.* = **collide with**, run into, bump into, clash with, smash into, crash against, bang into, meet head-on **3** *The big cities have been*

hit by a wave of panic-buying. = **affect**, damage, harm, ruin, devastate, overwhelm, touch, impact on, impinge on, leave a mark on, make an impact or impression on **4** *Oil prices hit record levels yesterday.* = **reach**, strike, gain, achieve, secure, arrive at, accomplish, attain
▶ NOUN **1** *The house took a direct hit then the rocket exploded.* = **shot**, blow, impact, collision **2** *a hit on the head* = **blow**, knock, stroke, belt (*informal*), rap, slap, bump, smack, clout (*informal*), cuff, swipe (*informal*), wallop (*informal*) **3** *The song became a massive hit in 1945.* = **success**, winner, triumph, smash (*informal*), sensation, sellout, smasheroo (*informal*)
• **hit it off** *How well did you hit it off with one another?* = **get on (well) with**, take to, click (*slang*), warm to, be on good terms, get on like a house on fire (*informal*) • **hit on** or **upon something** *We finally hit on a solution.* = **think up**, discover, arrive at, guess, realize, invent, come upon, stumble on, chance upon, light upon, strike upon
• **hit out at someone** *The President hit out at perceived foreign interference.* = **attack**, condemn, denounce, lash out, castigate, rail against, assail, inveigh against (*formal*), strike out at

hit-and-miss or **hit-or-miss** ADJECTIVE = **haphazard**, random, uneven, casual, indiscriminate, cursory, perfunctory, aimless, disorganized, undirected, scattershot ■ OPPOSITE: systematic

hitch NOUN *The five-hour operation went without a hitch.* = **problem**, catch (*informal*), trouble, check, difficulty, delay, hold-up, obstacle, hazard, drawback, hassle (*informal*), snag, uphill (*S. African*), stoppage, mishap, impediment, hindrance
▶ VERB **1** *I hitched a lift into town.* = **hitchhike**, thumb a lift **2** *We hitched the horse to the cart.* = **fasten**, join, attach, unite, couple, tie, connect, harness, tether, yoke, make fast • **hitch something up** *He hitched his trousers up over his potbelly.* = **pull up**, tug, jerk, yank, hoick

hither ADVERB = **here**, over here, to this place, close, closer, near, nearer, nigh (*archaic*)

hitherto ADVERB = **previously**, so far, until now, thus far, up to now, till now, heretofore

hive NOUN **1** *the dance performed by honeybees as they returned to the hive* = **colony**, swarm **2** *In the morning the house was a hive of activity.* = **centre**, hub, powerhouse (*slang*)

hoard VERB *They've begun to hoard food and gasoline.* = **save**, store, collect, gather,

treasure, accumulate, garner, amass, stockpile, buy up, put away, hive, cache, lay up, put by, stash away (*informal*) ▶ NOUN *a hoard of silver and jewels* = **store**, fund, supply, reserve, mass, pile, heap, fall-back, accumulation, stockpile, stash, cache, treasure-trove

hoarse ADJECTIVE = **rough**, harsh, husky, grating, growling, raucous, rasping, gruff, throaty, gravelly, guttural, croaky
■ OPPOSITE: clear

hoary ADJECTIVE **1** *the hoary old myth that women are unpredictable* = **old**, aged, ancient, antique, venerable, antiquated **2** *hoary beards* = **white-haired**, white, grey, silvery, frosty, grey-haired, grizzled, hoar

hoax NOUN *His claim to have a bomb was a hoax.* = **trick**, joke, fraud, con (*informal*), deception, spoof (*informal*), prank, swindle, ruse, practical joke, canard, fast one (*informal*), imposture, fastie (*Austral. slang*)
▶ VERB *He recently hoaxed a number of celebrities.* = **deceive**, trick, fool, take in (*informal*), con (*slang*), wind up (*Brit. slang*), kid (*informal*), bluff, dupe, gull (*archaic*), delude, swindle, bamboozle (*informal*), gammon (*Brit. informal*), hoodwink, take (someone) for a ride (*informal*), prank, befool, hornswoggle (*slang*), scam (*slang*)

hobble VERB **1** *He got up slowly and hobbled over to the table.* = **limp**, stagger, stumble, shuffle, falter, shamble, totter, dodder, halt **2** *The poverty of 10 million citizens hobbles our economy.* = **restrict**, hamstring, shackle, fetter

hobby NOUN = **pastime**, relaxation, leisure pursuit, sideline, diversion, avocation (*formal*), favourite occupation, (leisure) activity

hobnob VERB = **socialize**, mix, associate, hang out (*informal*), mingle, consort, hang about, keep company, fraternize

hog VERB = **monopolize**, dominate, tie up, corner, corner the market in, be a dog in the manger

hoist VERB *He hoisted himself to a sitting position.* = **raise**, lift, erect, elevate, heave, upraise ▶ NOUN *It takes three nurses and a hoist to get me into this chair.* = **lift**, crane, elevator, winch, tackle

hold VERB **1** *Hold the baby while I load the car.* = **carry**, keep, grip, grasp, cling to, clasp **2** *Hold the weight with a straight arm above your head.* = **support**, take, bear, shoulder, sustain, prop, brace ■ OPPOSITE: give way **3** *I held the little baby close to me.* = **embrace**, grasp, clutch, hug, squeeze, cradle, clasp, enfold **4** *He was held in an arm lock.* = **restrain**, constrain, check, bind, curb,

hamper, hinder ■ **OPPOSITE:** release
5 *the return of two seamen held on spying charges* = **detain**, arrest, confine, imprison, impound, pound, hold in custody, put in jail ■ **OPPOSITE:** release **6** *The small bottles don't seem to hold much.* = **accommodate**, take, contain, seat, comprise, have a capacity for **7** *She holds that it is not admissible to ordain women.* = **consider**, think, believe, view, judge, regard, maintain, assume, reckon, esteem (*formal*), deem, presume, entertain the idea ■ **OPPOSITE:** deny **8** *She has never held a ministerial post.* = **occupy**, have, fill, maintain, retain, possess, hold down (*informal*) **9** *They held frequent consultations concerning technical problems.* = **conduct**, convene, have, call, run, celebrate, carry on, assemble, preside over, officiate at, solemnize ■ **OPPOSITE:** cancel
10 (*sometimes with* **up**) *Our luck couldn't hold for ever.* = **continue**, last, remain, stay, wear, resist, endure, persist, persevere **11** *Today, most people think that argument no longer holds.* = **apply**, exist, be the case, stand up, operate, be in force, remain true, hold good, remain valid ▶ NOUN **1** *He released his hold on the camera.* = **grip**, grasp, clutch, clasp **2** *The idea didn't really get a hold in this country.* = **foothold**, footing, purchase, leverage, vantage, anchorage **3** *It's always useful to have a hold over people.* = **control**, authority, influence, pull (*informal*), sway, dominance, clout (*informal*), mastery, dominion, ascendancy, mana (*N.Z.*) • **hold back** *She wanted to say something but held back.* = **desist**, forbear, hesitate, stop yourself, restrain yourself, refrain from doing something • **hold forth** *He is capable of holding forth with great eloquence.* = **speak**, go on, discourse, lecture, preach, spout (*informal*), harangue, declaim, spiel (*informal*), descant, orate, speechify, korero (*N.Z.*) • **hold off** *The hospital staff held off taking him in for an X-ray.* = **put off**, delay, postpone, defer, avoid, refrain, keep from • **hold on** *Hold on while I have a look.* = **wait (a minute)**, hang on (*informal*), sit tight (*informal*), hold your horses (*informal*), just a moment *or* second • **hold onto something** *or* **someone 1** *He was struggling to hold onto the rock above his head.* = **grab**, hold, grip, clutch, cling to **2** *to enable Spurs to hold onto their striker* = **retain**, keep, hang onto, not give away, keep possession of • **hold out** *He can only hold out for a few more weeks.* = **last**, continue, carry on, endure, hang on, persist, persevere, stay the course, stand fast • **hold out against something** *or* **someone** *They held out*

against two companies of troops. = **withstand**, resist, fend off, keep at bay, fight • **hold someone back** *Does her illness hold her back from making friends or enjoying life?* = **hinder**, prevent, restrain, check, hamstring, hamper, inhibit, thwart, obstruct, impede • **hold someone up** *Why were you holding everyone up?* = **delay**, slow down, hinder, stop, detain, retard, impede, set back • **hold something back 1** *Stagnation in home sales is holding back economic recovery.* = **restrain**, check, curb, control, suppress, rein (in), repress, stem the flow of **2** *You seem to be holding something back.* = **withhold**, hold in, suppress, stifle, repress, keep the lid on (*informal*), keep back • **hold something out** *Max held out his cup for a refill.* = **offer**, give, present, extend, proffer • **hold something over** *Further voting might be held over until tomorrow.* = **postpone**, delay, suspend, put off, defer, adjourn, waive, take a rain check on (*U.S. & Canad. informal*) • **hold something up 1** *Hold it up so we can see it.* = **display**, show, exhibit, flourish, show off, hold aloft, present **2** *Mills have iron pillars holding up the roof.* = **support**, prop, brace, bolster, sustain, shore up, buttress, jack up **3** *A thief ran off with hundreds of pounds after holding up a petrol station.* = **rob**, mug (*informal*), stick up (*slang, chiefly U.S.*), waylay • **hold something** *or* **someone off** *holding off a tremendous challenge* = **fend off**, repel, rebuff, stave off, repulse, keep off • **hold up** *Sales of children's clothes are holding up well.* = **last**, survive, endure, bear up, wear • **hold with something** *I don't hold with the way they do things nowadays.* = **approve of**, be in favour of, support, subscribe to, countenance, agree to *or* with, take kindly to

holder NOUN **1** *the holders of the Championship; the club has 73,500 season-ticket holders* = **owner**, bearer, possessor, keeper, purchaser, occupant, proprietor, custodian, incumbent **2** *a toothbrush holder* = **case**, cover, container, sheath, receptacle, housing

holding (*often plural*) NOUN = **property**, securities, investments, resources, estate, assets, possessions, stocks and shares, land interests

hold-up NOUN **1** *an armed hold-up at a National Australia bank* = **robbery**, theft, mugging (*informal*), stick-up (*slang, chiefly U.S.*) **2** *They arrived late due to a motorway hold-up.* = **delay**, wait, hitch, trouble, difficulty, setback, snag, traffic jam, obstruction, stoppage, bottleneck

hole NOUN **1** *He took a shovel, dug a hole, and buried his possessions.* = **cavity**, depression, pit, hollow, pocket, chamber, cave, shaft, cavern, excavation **2** *They got in through a hole in the wall.* = **opening**, split, crack, break, tear, gap, rent, breach, outlet, vent, puncture, aperture, fissure, orifice, perforation **3** *a rabbit hole* = **burrow**, nest, den, earth, shelter, retreat, covert, lair **4** *There were some holes in that theory.* = **fault**, error, flaw, defect, loophole, discrepancy, inconsistency, fallacy **5** *Why don't you leave this awful hole and come to live with me?* = **hovel**, dump (*informal*), dive (*slang*), slum, joint (*slang*) **6** *He admitted that the government was in 'a dreadful hole'.* = **predicament**, spot (*informal*), fix (*informal*), mess, jam (*informal*), dilemma, scrape (*informal*), tangle, hot water (*informal*), quandary, tight spot, imbroglio • **hole up** *The players holed up in their hotel, where they had been met by an angry crowd.* = **hide**, shelter, take refuge, go into hiding, take cover, go to earth

holiday NOUN **1** *I've just come back from a holiday in the United States.* = **vacation**, leave, break, time off, recess, away day, schoolie (*Austral.*), accumulated day off or ADO (*Austral.*), staycation or stacation (*informal*) **2** *New Year's Day is a public holiday throughout Britain.* = **festival**, bank holiday, festivity, public holiday, fête, celebration, anniversary, feast, red-letter day, name day, saint's day, gala

holiness NOUN = **sanctity**, spirituality, sacredness, purity, divinity, righteousness, piety, godliness, saintliness, blessedness, religiousness, devoutness, virtuousness

holler VERB (*sometimes with* out) *He hollered for help.* = **yell**, call, cry, shout, cheer, roar, hail, bellow, whoop, clamour, bawl, hurrah, halloo, huzzah (*archaic*) ▶ NOUN *The men were celebrating with drunken whoops and hollers.* = **yell**, call, cry, shout, cheer, roar, hail, bellow, whoop, clamour, bawl, hurrah, halloo, huzzah (*archaic*)

hollow ADJECTIVE **1** *a hollow cylinder* = **empty**, vacant, void, unfilled, not solid ■ **OPPOSITE:** solid **2** *hollow cheeks* = **sunken**, depressed, cavernous, indented, concave, deep-set ■ **OPPOSITE:** rounded **3** *Any threat to bring in the police is a hollow one.* = **worthless**, empty, useless, vain, meaningless, pointless, futile, fruitless, specious, Pyrrhic, unavailing ■ **OPPOSITE:** meaningful **4** *His hollow laugh had no mirth in it.* = **insincere**, false, artificial, cynical, hypocritical, hollow-hearted **5** *the hollow sound of a gunshot* = **dull**, low, deep, flat, rumbling,

muted, muffled, expressionless, sepulchral, toneless, reverberant ■ **OPPOSITE:** vibrant ▶ NOUN **1** *where water gathers in a hollow and forms a pond* = **cavity**, cup, hole, bowl, depression, pit, cave, den, basin, dent, crater, trough, cavern, excavation, indentation, dimple, concavity ■ **OPPOSITE:** mound **2** *Locals in the sleepy hollow peered out of their country cottages.* = **valley**, dale, glen, dell, dingle ■ **OPPOSITE:** hill ▶ VERB (*often followed by* out) *Someone had hollowed out a large block of stone.* = **scoop out**, dig out, excavate, gouge out, channel, groove, furrow

holocaust NOUN **1** *A nuclear holocaust seemed a very real possibility in the '50s.* = **devastation**, destruction, carnage, genocide, inferno, annihilation, conflagration **2** *a fund for survivors of the holocaust and their families* = **genocide**, massacre, carnage, mass murder, ethnic cleansing (*euphemistic*), annihilation, pogrom

holy ADJECTIVE **1** *To most of the islanders, this is a holy place.* = **sacred**, blessed, hallowed, dedicated, venerable, consecrated, venerated, sacrosanct, sanctified ■ **OPPOSITE:** unsanctified **2** *The Indians think of him as a holy man.* = **devout**, godly, religious, pure, divine, faithful, righteous, pious, virtuous, hallowed, saintly, god-fearing ■ **OPPOSITE:** sinful

homage NOUN **1** *two marvellous films that pay homage to our literary heritage* = **respect**, honour, worship, esteem, admiration, awe, devotion, reverence, duty, deference, adulation, adoration ■ **OPPOSITE:** contempt **2** *At his coronation he received the homage of kings.* = **allegiance**, service, tribute, loyalty, devotion, fidelity, faithfulness, obeisance, troth (*archaic*), fealty

home NOUN **1** *the allocation of land for new homes* = **dwelling** (*formal, literary*), house, residence, abode, habitation (*formal*), pad (*slang*), domicile, dwelling place **2** *She was told to leave home by her father.* = **birthplace**, household, homeland, home town, homestead, native land, Godzone (*Austral. informal*) **3** *threatening the home of the famous African mountain gorillas* = **territory**, environment, habitat, range, element, haunt, home ground, abode, habitation, stamping ground ▶ ADJECTIVE *Europe's software companies still have a growing home market.* = **domestic**, national, local, central, internal, native, inland • **at home 1** *Remember I'm not at home to callers.* = **in**, present, available **2** *We soon felt quite at home.*

= **at ease**, relaxed, comfortable, content, at peace • **at home in, on,** or **with** *Even beginners will feel at home with this camera within mere minutes.* = **familiar with**, experienced in, skilled in, proficient in, conversant with, au fait with, knowledgeable of, well-versed in • **bring something home to someone** *It was to bring home to Americans the immediacy of the crisis.* = **make clear**, emphasize, drive home, press home, impress upon

homeland NOUN = **native land**, birthplace, motherland, fatherland, country of origin, mother country, Godzone (*Austral. informal*)

homeless ADJECTIVE = **destitute**, exiled, displaced, dispossessed, unsettled, outcast, abandoned, down-and-out

homely ADJECTIVE **1** *We try and provide a very homely atmosphere.* = **comfortable**, welcoming, friendly, domestic, familiar, informal, cosy, comfy (*informal*), homespun, downhome (*slang, chiefly U.S.*), homelike, homy (*U.S.*) **2** *Scottish baking is homely, comforting and truly good.* = **plain**, simple, natural, ordinary, modest, everyday, down-to-earth, unaffected, unassuming, unpretentious, unfussy ■ **OPPOSITE:** elaborate **3** *The man was homely and overweight.* = **unattractive**, plain, ugly, not striking, unprepossessing, not beautiful, no oil painting (*informal*), ill-favoured

homespun ADJECTIVE = **unsophisticated**, homely, plain, rough, rude, coarse, home-made, rustic, artless, inelegant, unpolished

homicidal ADJECTIVE = **murderous**, deadly, lethal, maniacal, death-dealing

homicide NOUN = **murder**, killing, manslaughter, slaying, bloodshed

homily NOUN = **sermon**, talk, address, speech, lecture, preaching, discourse, oration, declamation

homogeneous or **homogenous** ADJECTIVE = **uniform**, similar, consistent, identical, alike, comparable, akin, analogous, kindred, unvarying, cognate ■ **OPPOSITE:** diverse

homosexual ADJECTIVE *a homosexual relationship* = **gay**, lesbian, queer (*informal, often offensive*), same-sex, homoerotic, sapphic ▶ NOUN *He was a homosexual in a society that disapproved of male relationships.* = **gay**, lesbian ■ **RELATED WORD:** *phobia* homophobia

homy or **homey** ADJECTIVE = **homely**, comfortable, welcoming, domestic, friendly, familiar, cosy, comfy (*informal*), homespun, downhome (*slang, chiefly U.S.*), homelike

hone VERB **1** *honing the skills of senior managers* = **improve**, better, polish, enhance, upgrade, refine, sharpen, augment, help **2** *four grinding wheels for honing fine-edged tools* = **sharpen**, point, grind, edge, file, polish, whet, strop

> **USAGE** *Hone* is sometimes wrongly used where *home* is meant: *this device makes it easier to home in on* (not *hone in on*) *the target.*

honest ADJECTIVE **1** *My dad was the most honest man I have ever met.* = **trustworthy**, decent, upright, reliable, ethical, honourable, conscientious, reputable, truthful, virtuous, law-abiding, trusty, scrupulous, high-minded, veracious ■ **OPPOSITE:** dishonest **2** *I was honest about what I was doing.* = **open**, direct, frank, plain, straightforward, outright, sincere, candid, forthright, upfront (*informal*), undisguised, round, ingenuous, unfeigned ■ **OPPOSITE:** secretive **3** *It was an honest mistake on his part.* = **genuine**, real, true, straight, fair, proper, authentic, equitable, impartial, on the level (*informal*), bona fide, dinkum (*Austral. & N.Z. informal*), above board, fair and square, on the up and up, honest to goodness ■ **OPPOSITE:** false

honestly ADVERB **1** *charged with failing to act honestly in his duties as an officer* = **ethically**, legitimately, legally, in good faith, on the level (*informal*), lawfully, honourably, by fair means, with clean hands **2** *It came as a shock to hear him talk so honestly about an old friend.* = **frankly**, plainly, candidly, straight (out), truthfully, to your face, in plain English, in all sincerity

honesty NOUN **1** *It's time for complete honesty from political representatives.* = **integrity**, honour, virtue, morality, fidelity, probity (*formal*), rectitude, veracity, faithfulness, truthfulness, trustworthiness, straightness, incorruptibility, scrupulousness, uprightness, reputability **2** *Good communication encourages honesty in a relationship.* = **frankness**, openness, sincerity, candour, bluntness, outspokenness, genuineness, plainness, straightforwardness

honeyed ADJECTIVE **1** *His gentle manner and honeyed tones reassured Andrew.* = **flattering**, sweet, soothing, enticing, mellow, seductive, agreeable, sweetened, cajoling, alluring, melodious, unctuous, dulcet **2** *I could smell the honeyed ripeness of melons and peaches.* = **sweet**, sweetened, luscious, sugary, syrupy, toothsome

honorary ADJECTIVE = **nominal**, unofficial, titular, ex officio, honoris causa (*Latin*), in name or title only

honour NOUN **1** *I can no longer serve with honour as a member of your government.* = **integrity**, principles, morality, honesty, goodness, fairness, decency, righteousness, probity (*formal*), rectitude, trustworthiness, uprightness ■ **OPPOSITE:** dishonour **2** *He brought honour and glory to his country.* = **prestige**, credit, reputation, glory, fame, distinction, esteem, dignity, elevation, eminence, renown, repute, high standing ■ **OPPOSITE:** disgrace **3** *The country's national honour was at stake.* = **reputation**, standing, prestige, image, status, stature, good name, kudos, cachet **4** *One old campaigner at least will be received with honour.* = **acclaim**, regard, respect, praise, recognition, compliments, homage, accolades, reverence, deference, adoration, commendation, veneration ■ **OPPOSITE:** contempt **5** *Five other cities had been competing for the honour of staging the Games.* = **privilege**, credit, favour, pleasure, compliment, source of pride or satisfaction ▶ VERB **1** *Two pioneering surgeons were honoured with the Nobel Prize.* = **acclaim**, celebrate, praise, decorate, compliment, commemorate, dignify, commend, glorify, exalt, laud (*literary*), lionize **2** *Honour your parents, that's what the Bible says.* = **respect**, value, esteem, prize, appreciate, admire, worship, adore, revere, glorify, reverence, exalt, venerate, hallow ■ **OPPOSITE:** scorn **3** *He had failed to honour his word.* = **fulfil**, keep, carry out, observe, discharge, live up to, be true to, be as good as (*informal*), be faithful to **4** *The bank refused to honour his cheque.* = **pay**, take, accept, clear, pass, cash, credit, acknowledge ■ **OPPOSITE:** refuse

honourable ADJECTIVE **1** *I believe she is an honourable person.* = **principled**, moral, ethical, just, true, fair, upright, honest, virtuous, trustworthy, trusty, high-minded, upstanding **2** *However, their intentions are honourable.* = **proper**, right, respectable, righteous, virtuous, creditable **3** *an honourable profession* = **prestigious**, great, noble, noted, distinguished, notable, renowned, eminent, illustrious, venerable

hoodoo NOUN = **jinx**, curse, bad luck, voodoo, nemesis, hex (*U.S. & Canad. informal*), evil eye, evil star

hoodwink VERB = **deceive**, trick, fool, cheat, con (*informal*), kid (*informal*), mislead, hoax, dupe, gull (*archaic*), delude, swindle, rook (*slang*), bamboozle (*informal*), take (someone) for a ride (*informal*), lead up the garden path (*informal*), sell a pup, pull a fast one (*informal*), cozen, befool, scam (*slang*)

hook NOUN *One of his jackets hung from a hook.* = **fastener**, catch, link, lock, holder, peg, clasp, hasp ▶ VERB **1** *one of those can openers you hook onto the wall* = **fasten**, fix, secure, catch, clasp, hasp **2** *Whenever one of us hooked a fish, we moved on.* = **catch**, land, trap, entrap • **by hook or by crook** *They intend to get their way, by hook or by crook.* = **by any means**, somehow, somehow or other, someway, by fair means or foul • **hook, line, and sinker** *We fell for it hook, line, and sinker.* = **completely**, totally, entirely, thoroughly, wholly, utterly, through and through, lock, stock and barrel • **off the hook** *Officials accused of bribery always seem to get off the hook.* = **let off**, cleared, acquitted, vindicated, in the clear, exonerated, under no obligation, allowed to walk (*slang, chiefly U.S.*)

hooked ADJECTIVE **1** *He was tall and thin, with a hooked nose.* = **bent**, curved, beaked, aquiline, beaky, hook-shaped, hamate (*rare*), hooklike, falcate (*Biology*), unciform (*Anatomy*), uncinate (*Biology*) **2** *Open this book and read a few pages and you will be hooked.* = **obsessed**, addicted, taken, devoted, turned on (*slang*), enamoured **3** *She spent a number of years hooked on amphetamine.* = **addicted**, dependent, using (*informal*), having a habit

hooligan NOUN = **delinquent**, tough, vandal, casual, ned (*Scot. slang*), rowdy, hoon (*Austral. & N.Z.*), hoodlum (*chiefly U.S.*), ruffian, lager lout, yob or yobbo (*Brit. slang*), cougan (*Austral. slang*), scozza (*Austral. slang*), bogan (*Austral. slang*), hoodie (*informal*)

hooliganism NOUN = **delinquency**, violence, disorder, vandalism, rowdiness, loutishness, yobbishness

hoop NOUN = **ring**, band, loop, wheel, round, girdle, circlet

hoot NOUN **1** *the hoots of night birds* = **cry**, shout, howl, scream, shriek, whoop **2** *He strode on, ignoring the car, in spite of a further warning hoot.* = **toot**, beep, honk **3** *Her confession was greeted with derisive hoots.* = **jeer**, yell, boo, catcall **4** *Jana's a hoot, a real character.* = **laugh** (*informal*), scream (*informal*), caution (*informal*), card (*informal*) ▶ VERB **1** *The protesters chanted, blew whistles and hooted.* = **jeer**, boo, howl, yell, catcall **2** *Out in the garden an owl hooted suddenly.* = **cry**, call, screech, tu-whit tu-whoo **3** *Somewhere in the distance a siren hooted.* = **toot**, sound, blast, blare, beep, honk **4** *Bev hooted with laughter.* = **shout**, cry, yell, scream, shriek, whoop

hop VERB *I hopped down three steps.* = **jump**,

spring, bound, leap, skip, vault, caper
▶ NOUN 'This is a catchy rhythm,' he added with a few hops. = **jump**, step, spring, bound, leap, bounce, skip, vault

hope VERB I hope that the police will take the strongest action against them. = **believe**, expect, trust, rely, look forward to, anticipate, contemplate, count on, foresee, keep your fingers crossed, cross your fingers ▶ NOUN Kevin hasn't given up hope of being fit. = **belief**, confidence, expectation, longing, dream, desire, faith, ambition, assumption, anticipation, expectancy, light at the end of the tunnel ■ **OPPOSITE:** despair

hopeful ADJECTIVE 1 Surgeons were hopeful of saving her sight. = **optimistic**, confident, assured, looking forward to, anticipating, buoyant, sanguine, expectant ■ **OPPOSITE:** despairing 2 hopeful forecasts that the economy will improve = **promising**, encouraging, bright, reassuring, cheerful, rosy, heartening, auspicious, propitious ■ **OPPOSITE:** unpromising

hopefully ADVERB 1 'Am I welcome?' he smiled hopefully. = **optimistically**, confidently, expectantly, with anticipation, sanguinely 2 (informal) Hopefully, you won't have any problems after reading this. = **it is hoped**, probably, all being well, God willing, conceivably, feasibly, expectedly

> **USAGE** Some people object to the use of hopefully as a synonym for the phrase 'it is hoped that' in a sentence such as hopefully I'll be able to attend the meeting. This use of the adverb first appeared in America in the 1960s, but it has rapidly established itself elsewhere. There are really no strong grounds for objecting to it, since we accept other sentence adverbials that fulfil a similar function, for example unfortunately, which means 'it is unfortunate that' in a sentence such as unfortunately I won't be able to attend the meeting.

hopeless ADJECTIVE 1 Even able pupils feel hopeless about job prospects. = **pessimistic**, desperate, despairing, forlorn, in despair, abject, dejected, wretched, despondent, demoralized, defeatist, disconsolate, downhearted ■ **OPPOSITE:** hopeful 2 I don't believe your situation is as hopeless as you think. = **impossible**, pointless, futile, useless, vain, forlorn, no-win, unattainable, impracticable, unachievable, not having a prayer 3 I'd be hopeless at working for somebody else. = **no good**, inadequate, useless (informal), poor, pants (informal), pathetic, inferior, incompetent, ineffectual 4 a hopeless mess = **incurable**, irreversible,

irreparable, lost, helpless, irremediable, past remedy, remediless ■ **OPPOSITE:** curable

hopelessly ADVERB 1 hopelessly in love = **without hope**, desperately, in despair, despairingly, irredeemably, irremediably, beyond all hope 2 The story is hopelessly confusing. = **completely**, totally, extremely, desperately, terribly, utterly, tremendously, awfully (informal), impossibly, frightfully

horde NOUN = **crowd**, mob, swarm, press, host, band, troop, pack, crew (informal), drove, gang, multitude, throng

horizon NOUN 1 The sun had already sunk below the horizon. = **skyline**, view, vista, field or range of vision 2 By embracing other cultures, we actually broaden our horizons. = **scope**, perspective, range, prospect, stretch, ken, sphere, realm, compass, ambit, purview

horizontal ADJECTIVE = **level**, flat, plane, parallel, supine

horrible ADJECTIVE 1 a horrible little boy = **dreadful**, terrible, awful, nasty, cruel, beastly (informal), mean, unpleasant, ghastly (informal), unkind, horrid (informal), disagreeable ■ **OPPOSITE:** wonderful 2 Still the horrible shrieking came out of his mouth. = **terrible**, awful, appalling, terrifying, shocking, grim, dreadful, revolting, fearful (informal), obscene, ghastly, hideous, shameful, gruesome, from hell (informal), grisly, horrid, repulsive, frightful, heinous, loathsome, abhorrent, abominable, hellacious (U.S. slang)

horrid ADJECTIVE 1 What a horrid smell! = **unpleasant**, terrible (informal), awful, offensive, nasty, disgusting, horrible, dreadful, obscene, disagreeable, yucky or yukky (slang), yucko (Austral. slang) 2 I must have been a horrid little girl. = **nasty**, dreadful, horrible (informal), mean (informal), unkind, cruel, beastly (informal)

horrific ADJECTIVE = **horrifying**, shocking (informal), appalling, frightening, awful, terrifying, grim, dreadful, horrendous, ghastly, from hell (informal), grisly, frightful, hellacious (U.S. slang)

horrify VERB 1 a crime trend that will horrify the community = **terrify**, alarm, frighten, scare, intimidate, petrify, terrorize, put the wind up (informal), make your hair stand on end, affright ■ **OPPOSITE:** comfort 2 When I saw these figures I was horrified. = **shock**, appal, disgust, dismay, sicken, outrage, gross out (U.S. slang) ■ **OPPOSITE:** delight

horror NOUN 1 I felt numb with horror. = **terror**, fear, alarm, panic, dread, dismay, awe, fright, apprehension, consternation, trepidation (*formal*) **2** *his horror of death* = **hatred**, disgust, loathing, aversion, revulsion, antipathy, abomination, abhorrence, repugnance, odium (*formal*), detestation ■ **OPPOSITE:** love

horse NOUN *A small man on a grey horse had appeared.* = **nag**, mount, mare, colt, filly, stallion, gelding, jade, pony, yearling, steed (*archaic, literary*), dobbin, moke (*Austral. slang*), hobby (*archaic, dialect*), yarraman or yarramin (*Austral.*), gee-gee (*slang*), cuddy or cuddie (*dialect, chiefly Scot.*), studhorse or stud • **horse around** or **about** *Later that day I was horsing around with Katie.* = **play around** or **about**, fool about or around, clown, misbehave, play the fool, roughhouse (*slang*), play the goat, monkey about or around, indulge in horseplay, lark about or around ■ **RELATED WORDS:** *adjectives* equestrian, equine, horsey; *noun* equitation; *name of male* stallion; *name of female* mare; *name of young* foal, colt, filly; *mania* hippomania; *phobia* hippophobia

horseman or **horsewoman** or **horseperson** NOUN = **rider**, equestrian

hospitable ADJECTIVE = **welcoming**, kind, friendly, liberal, generous, gracious, amicable, cordial, sociable, genial, bountiful ■ **OPPOSITE:** inhospitable

hospitality NOUN = **welcome**, warmth, kindness, friendliness, sociability, conviviality, neighbourliness, cordiality, heartiness, hospitableness

host¹ NOUN **1** *We were greeted by our host, a courteous man in a formal suit.* = **master** or **mistress of ceremonies**, proprietor, innkeeper, landlord or landlady **2** *I am host of a live radio programme.* = **presenter**, compere (*Brit.*), anchorman or anchorwoman ▶ VERB *She also hosts a show on St Petersburg Radio.* = **present**, introduce, compere (*Brit.*), front (*informal*)

host² NOUN **1** *a whole host of gadgets* = **multitude**, lot, load (*informal*), wealth, array, myriad, great quantity, large number **2** *A host of stars attended the awards ceremony.* = **crowd**, army, pack, drove, mob, herd, legion, swarm, horde, throng

hostage NOUN = **captive**, prisoner, pledge, pawn, security, surety

hostile ADJECTIVE **1** *hostile to the idea of foreign intervention* = **antagonistic**, anti (*informal*), opposed, opposite, contrary, inimical, ill-disposed **2** *The Governor faced hostile crowds when visiting the town.* = **unfriendly**, belligerent, antagonistic, unkind, malevolent, warlike, bellicose, inimical, rancorous, ill-disposed ■ **OPPOSITE:** friendly **3** *some of the most hostile climatic conditions in the world* = **inhospitable**, adverse, alien, uncongenial, unsympathetic, unwelcoming, unpropitious ■ **OPPOSITE:** hospitable

hostility NOUN **1** *She looked at Ron with open hostility.* = **unfriendliness**, hatred, animosity, spite, bitterness, malice, venom, antagonism, enmity, abhorrence, malevolence, detestation ■ **OPPOSITE:** friendliness **2** *hostility among traditionalists to this method of teaching history* = **opposition**, resentment, antipathy, aversion, antagonism, ill feeling, bad blood, ill-will, animus ■ **OPPOSITE:** approval ▶ PLURAL NOUN *Military chiefs agreed to cease hostilities throughout the country.* = **warfare**, war, fighting, conflict, combat, armed conflict, state of war ■ **OPPOSITE:** peace

hot ADJECTIVE **1** *Cook the meat quickly on a hot barbecue plate.* = **heated**, burning, boiling, steaming, flaming, roasting, searing, blistering, fiery, scorching, scalding, piping hot **2** *It was too hot even for a gentle stroll.* = **warm**, close, stifling, humid, torrid, sultry, sweltering, balmy, muggy ■ **OPPOSITE:** cold **3** *He loved hot curries.* = **spicy**, pungent, peppery, piquant, biting, sharp, acrid ■ **OPPOSITE:** mild **4** *The nature of Scottishness is a matter of hot debate in Scotland.* = **intense**, passionate, heated, spirited, excited, fierce, lively, animated, ardent, inflamed, fervent, impassioned, fervid **5** *If you hear any hot news, tell me, won't you?* = **new**, latest, fresh, recent, up to date, just out, up to the minute, bang up to date (*informal*), hot off the press ■ **OPPOSITE:** old **6** *a ticket for the hottest show in town* = **popular**, hip, fashionable, cool (*informal*), in demand, sought-after, must-see, in vogue ■ **OPPOSITE:** unpopular **7** = **attractive**, sexy (*informal*), fit (*Brit. informal*), good-looking, gorgeous (*informal*), lush (*slang*), drop-dead (*slang*) **8** *hot competition from abroad* = **fierce**, intense, strong, keen, competitive, cut-throat **9** *His hot temper was making it difficult for others to work with him.* = **fiery**, violent, raging, passionate, stormy, touchy, vehement, impetuous, irascible ■ **OPPOSITE:** calm

hot air NOUN = **empty talk**, rant, guff (*slang*), bombast, wind, gas (*informal*), verbiage, claptrap (*informal*), blather, bunkum, blether, bosh (*informal*), tall talk (*informal*)

hotbed NOUN = **breeding ground**, nest, den

hot-headed ADJECTIVE = **volatile**, rash, fiery, reckless, precipitate, hasty, unruly, foolhardy, impetuous, hot-tempered, quick-tempered

hothouse NOUN = **greenhouse**, conservatory, glasshouse, orangery

hotly ADVERB 1 *The bank hotly denies any wrongdoing.* = **fiercely**, passionately, angrily, vehemently, indignantly, with indignation, heatedly, impetuously 2 *He'd sneaked out of America hotly pursued by the CIA.* = **closely**, enthusiastically, eagerly, with enthusiasm, hotfoot

hound VERB 1 *hounded by the press* = **harass**, harry, bother, provoke, annoy, torment, hassle (*informal*), prod, badger, persecute, pester, goad, keep after 2 *hounded out of office* = **force**, drive, pressure, push, chase, railroad (*informal*), propel, impel, pressurize

house NOUN 1 *her parents' house in Warwickshire* = **home**, residence, dwelling (*formal, literary*), building, pad (*slang*), homestead, edifice, abode, habitation (*formal*), domicile, whare (*N.Z.*) 2 *If he set his alarm clock, it would wake the whole house.* = **household**, family, ménage 3 *the world's top fashion houses* = **firm**, company, business, concern, organization, partnership, establishment, outfit (*informal*) 4 *the joint sessions of the two parliamentary houses* = **assembly**, parliament, Commons, legislative body 5 *The house offers a couple of freshly prepared à la carte dishes.* = **restaurant**, inn, hotel, pub (*Brit. informal*), tavern, public house, hostelry 6 *the Saudi Royal House* = **dynasty**, line, race, tribe, clan, ancestry, lineage, family tree, kindred ▶ VERB 1 *Regrettably we have to house families in these inadequate flats.* = **accommodate**, board, quarter, take in, put up, lodge, harbour, billet, domicile 2 *The building houses a collection of motorcycles and cars.* = **contain**, keep, hold, cover, store, protect, shelter 3 *The building will house twelve boys and eight girls.* = **take**, accommodate, sleep, provide shelter for, give a bed to • **on the house** *He brought them glasses of champagne on the house.* = **free**, for free (*informal*), for nothing, free of charge, gratis, without expense

household NOUN *growing up in a male-only household* = **family**, home, house, ménage, family circle, ainga (*N.Z.*) ▶ MODIFIER *I always do the household chores first.* = **domestic**, family, domiciliary

householder NOUN = **occupant**, resident, tenant, proprietor, homeowner, freeholder, leaseholder

housekeeping NOUN = **household management**, homemaking (*U.S.*), home economy, housewifery, housecraft

housing NOUN 1 *a shortage of affordable housing* = **accommodation**, homes, houses, dwellings, domiciles 2 *Both housings are waterproof to a depth of two metres.* = **case**, casing, covering, cover, shell, jacket, holder, container, capsule, sheath, encasement

hovel NOUN = **hut**, hole, shed, cabin, den, slum, shack, shanty, whare (*N.Z.*)

hover VERB 1 *Beautiful butterflies hovered above the wild flowers.* = **float**, fly, hang, drift, be suspended, flutter, poise 2 *Judith was hovering in the doorway.* = **linger**, loiter, wait nearby, hang about or around (*informal*) 3 *We hover between great hopes and great fears.* = **waver**, alternate, fluctuate, haver (*Brit.*), falter, dither (*chiefly Brit.*), oscillate, vacillate, seesaw, swither (*Scot., dialect*)

however ADVERB = **but**, nevertheless, still, though, yet, even though, on the other hand, nonetheless, notwithstanding, anyhow, be that as it may

howl VERB 1 *A dog suddenly howled, baying at the moon.* = **bay**, cry, bark, yelp, quest (*of a hound*) 2 *The baby was howling for her 3am feed.* = **cry**, shout, scream, roar, weep, yell, cry out, wail, shriek, bellow, bawl, yelp ▶ NOUN 1 *It was the howl of an animal crying out in hunger.* = **baying**, cry, bay, bark, barking, yelp, yelping, yowl 2 *a howl of rage* = **cry**, scream, roar, bay, wail, outcry, shriek, bellow, clamour, hoot, bawl, yelp, yowl

howler NOUN = **mistake**, error, blunder, boob (*Brit. slang*), bloomer (*Brit. informal*), clanger (*informal*), malapropism, schoolboy howler, booboo (*informal*), barry or Barry Crocker (*Austral. slang*)

hub NOUN = **centre**, heart, focus, core, middle, focal point, pivot, nerve centre

hubbub NOUN 1 *a hubbub of excited conversation from over a thousand people* = **noise**, racket, din, uproar, cacophony, pandemonium, babel, tumult, hurly-burly 2 *the hubbub over the election* = **hue and cry**, confusion, disturbance, riot, disorder, clamour, rumpus, bedlam, brouhaha, ruction (*informal*), hullabaloo, ruckus (*informal*)

hubris NOUN = **pride**, vanity, arrogance, conceit, self-importance, haughtiness, conceitedness

huddle VERB 1 *She sat huddled on the side of the bed, weeping.* = **curl up**, crouch, hunch up, nestle, snuggle, make yourself small 2 *strangers huddling together for warmth* = **crowd**, press, gather, collect, squeeze, cluster, flock, herd, throng ▶ NOUN 1 *a huddle of bodies, gasping for air* = **crowd**, mass, bunch, cluster, heap, muddle, jumble 2 *He went into a huddle with his lawyers to* consider an appeal. = **discussion**, conference, meeting, hui (N.Z.), powwow, confab (informal), korero (N.Z.)

hue NOUN **1** The same hue will look different in different lights. = **colour**, tone, shade, dye, tint, tinge, tincture **2** a comeback of such theatrical hue = **aspect**, light, cast, complexion

huff NOUN I went into a huff because we lost the game. = **sulk**, temper, bad mood, passion, rage, pet, pique, foulie (Austral. slang)

hug VERB **1** They hugged each other like a couple of lost children. = **embrace**, hold (onto), cuddle, squeeze, cling, clasp, enfold, hold close, take in your arms **2** The road hugs the coast for hundreds of miles. = **follow closely**, keep close, stay near, cling to, follow the course of ▶ NOUN She leapt out of the seat, and gave him a hug. = **embrace**, squeeze, bear hug, clinch (slang), clasp

huge ADJECTIVE = **enormous**, great, giant, large, massive, vast, extensive, tremendous, immense, mega (slang), titanic, jumbo (informal), gigantic, monumental (informal), mammoth, bulky, colossal, mountainous, stellar (informal), prodigious, stupendous, gargantuan, elephantine, ginormous (informal), Brobdingnagian, humongous or humungous (informal) ■ **OPPOSITE:** tiny

hugely ADVERB = **immensely**, enormously, massively, prodigiously, monumentally, stupendously

hui NOUN (N.Z.) = **meeting**, gathering, assembly, meet, conference, congress, session, rally, convention, get-together (informal), reunion, congregation, conclave, convocation (formal), powwow

hulk NOUN = **wreck**, shell, hull, shipwreck, frame

hulking ADJECTIVE = **ungainly**, massive, lumbering, gross, awkward, clumsy, bulky, cumbersome, overgrown, unwieldy, ponderous, clunky (informal), oafish, lumpish, lubberly, unco (Austral. slang)

hull NOUN **1** The hull had suffered extensive damage to the starboard side. = **framework**, casing, body, covering, frame, skeleton **2** I soaked the hulls off lima beans. = **husk**, skin, shell, peel, pod, rind, shuck ▶ VERB Soak them in water with lemon juice for 30 minutes before hulling. = **trim**, peel, skin, shell, husk, shuck

hum VERB **1** We could hear a buzz, like a bee humming. = **drone**, buzz, murmur, throb, vibrate, purr, croon, thrum, whir **2** On Saturday morning, the town hums with activity. = **be busy**, buzz, bustle, move, stir, pulse, be active, vibrate, pulsate

human ADJECTIVE **1** the human body = **mortal**, anthropoid, manlike ■ **OPPOSITE:** nonhuman **2** Singapore has a human side too, beside the relentless efficiency. = **kind**, natural, vulnerable, kindly, understandable, humane, compassionate, considerate, approachable ■ **OPPOSITE:** inhuman ▶ NOUN The drug has not yet been tested on humans. = **human being**, person, individual, body (informal), creature, mortal, man or woman ■ **OPPOSITE:** nonhuman ■ **RELATED WORD:** prefix anthropo-

humane ADJECTIVE = **kind**, compassionate, good, kindly, understanding, gentle, forgiving, tender, mild, sympathetic, charitable, benign, clement, benevolent, lenient, merciful, good-natured, forbearing, kind-hearted ■ **OPPOSITE:** cruel

humanitarian ADJECTIVE **1** They will be released as a humanitarian act. = **compassionate**, charitable, humane, benevolent, altruistic, beneficent **2** a convoy of humanitarian aid = **charitable**, philanthropic, public-spirited ▶ NOUN I like to think of myself as a humanitarian. = **philanthropist**, benefactor, Good Samaritan, altruist

humanity NOUN **1** They face charges of committing crimes against humanity. = **the human race**, man, humankind, mankind, people, men and women, mortals, Homo sapiens **2** It made me feel deprived of my humanity. = **human nature**, mortality, humanness **3** The speech showed great humility and humanity. = **kindness**, charity, compassion, understanding, sympathy, mercy, tolerance, tenderness, philanthropy, benevolence, fellow feeling, benignity, brotherly love, kind-heartedness ▶ PLURAL NOUN The number of students majoring in the humanities has declined. = **arts**, liberal arts, classics, classical studies, literae humaniores

humble ADJECTIVE **1** Ashok was a humble, courteous and gentle man. = **modest**, meek, unassuming, unpretentious, submissive, self-effacing, unostentatious ■ **OPPOSITE:** proud **2** He came from a fairly humble, poor background. = **lowly**, common, poor, mean, low, simple, ordinary, modest, obscure, commonplace, insignificant, unimportant, unpretentious, undistinguished, plebeian, low-born ■ **OPPOSITE:** distinguished ▶ VERB the little car company that humbled the industry giants = **humiliate**, shame, disgrace, break, reduce, lower, sink, crush, put down (slang), bring down, subdue, degrade, demean, chagrin, chasten, mortify, debase, put (someone) in their place, abase, take down a peg (*informal*), abash ■ **OPPOSITE:** exalt

humbly ADVERB = **meekly**, modestly, respectfully, cap in hand, diffidently, deferentially, submissively, unassumingly, obsequiously, subserviently, on bended knee, servilely

humbug NOUN = **nonsense**, rubbish, trash, hypocrisy, cant, malarkey, baloney (*informal*), claptrap (*informal*), quackery, eyewash (*informal*), charlatanry

humdrum ADJECTIVE = **dull**, ordinary, boring, routine, commonplace, mundane, tedious, dreary, banal, tiresome, monotonous, uneventful, uninteresting, mind-numbing, ho-hum (*informal*), repetitious, wearisome, unvaried ■ **OPPOSITE:** exciting

humid ADJECTIVE = **damp**, sticky, moist, wet, steamy, sultry, dank, clammy, muggy ■ **OPPOSITE:** dry

humidity NOUN = **damp**, moisture, dampness, wetness, moistness, sogginess, dankness, clamminess, mugginess, humidness

humiliate VERB = **embarrass**, shame, humble, crush, disgrace, put down, subdue, degrade, chagrin, chasten, mortify, debase, discomfit, bring low, put (someone) in their place, take the wind out of someone's sails, abase, take down a peg (*informal*), abash, make (someone) eat humble pie ■ **OPPOSITE:** honour

humiliating ADJECTIVE = **embarrassing**, shaming, humbling, mortifying, crushing, disgracing, degrading, ignominious, toe-curling (*slang*), cringe-making (*Brit. informal*), cringeworthy (*Brit. informal*), barro (*Austral. slang*)

humiliation NOUN = **embarrassment**, shame, disgrace, humbling, put-down, degradation, affront, indignity, chagrin, ignominy, dishonour, mortification, loss of face, abasement, self-abasement

humility NOUN = **modesty**, diffidence, meekness, submissiveness, servility, self-abasement, humbleness, lowliness, unpretentiousness, lack of pride ■ **OPPOSITE:** pride

humorist NOUN = **comedian**, comic, wit, eccentric, wag, joker, card (*informal*), jester, dag (*N.Z. informal*), funny man or woman

humorous ADJECTIVE = **funny**, comic, amusing, entertaining, witty, merry, hilarious, ludicrous, laughable, farcical, whimsical, comical, droll, facetious, jocular, side-splitting, waggish, jocose (*old-fashioned*) ■ **OPPOSITE:** serious

humour NOUN **1** *She couldn't ignore the humour of the situation.* = **comedy**, funniness, fun, amusement, funny side, jocularity, facetiousness, ludicrousness, drollery, comical aspect ■ **OPPOSITE:** seriousness **2** *Could that have been the source of his good humour?* = **mood**, spirits, temper, disposition, frame of mind **3** *The film has lots of adult humour.* = **joking**, jokes, comedy, wit, gags (*informal*), farce, jesting, jests, wisecracks (*informal*), witticisms, wittiness ▶ VERB *Most of the time he humoured her for an easy life.* = **indulge**, accommodate, go along with, spoil, flatter, pamper, gratify, pander to, mollify, cosset, fawn on ■ **OPPOSITE:** oppose

humourless ADJECTIVE = **serious**, intense, solemn, straight, dry, dour, unfunny, po-faced, unsmiling, heavy-going, unamused, unamusing

hump NOUN *The path goes over a large hump by a tree.* = **lump**, bump, projection, bulge, mound, hunch, knob, protuberance, protrusion ▶ VERB *Charlie humped his rucksack up the stairs.* = **carry**, lug, heave, hoist, shoulder

hunch NOUN *I had a hunch that we would work well together.* = **feeling**, idea, impression, suspicion, intuition, premonition, inkling, presentiment ▶ VERB *He hunched over the map to read the small print.* = **crouch**, bend, stoop, curve, arch, huddle, draw in, squat, hump

hunger NOUN **1** *Hunger is the body's sign that blood sugar is too low.* = **appetite**, emptiness, voracity, hungriness, ravenousness **2** *Hundreds of people were dying of hunger every day.* = **starvation**, famine, malnutrition, undernourishment **3** *He has a hunger for success that seems bottomless.* = **desire**, appetite, craving, yen (*informal*), ache, lust, yearning, itch, thirst, greediness • **hunger for** or **after something** *He hungered for adventure.* = **want**, desire, crave, hope for, long for, wish for, yearn for, pine for, hanker after, ache for, thirst after, itch after

hungry ADJECTIVE **1** *My friend was hungry, so we went to get some food.* = **starving**, ravenous, famished, starved, empty (*informal*), hollow, voracious, peckish (*informal, chiefly Brit.*), famishing **2** *I was hungry to be an actor.* = **eager**, keen, craving, yearning, greedy, avid, desirous, covetous, athirst

hunk NOUN = **lump**, piece, chunk, block, mass, wedge, slab, nugget, wodge (*Brit. informal*), gobbet

hunt VERB *Police are hunting a large wildcat that was said to have escaped from the zoo.*

= **stalk**, track, chase, pursue, trail, hound, gun for ▶ NOUN *The couple had helped in the hunt for the lost hiker.* = **search**, hunting, investigation, chase, pursuit, quest • **hunt for something** or **someone** *A forensic team was hunting for clues.* = **search for**, look for, try to find, seek for, forage for, rummage for, scour for, look high and low, fossick for (*Austral. & N.Z.*), go in quest of, ferret about for

hunted ADJECTIVE = **harassed**, desperate, harried, tormented, stricken, distraught, persecuted, terror-stricken

hunter NOUN = **huntsman** or **woman**, Diana, Herne, Orion, Nimrod, jaeger (*rare*), Artemis, sportsman or sportswoman

hurdle NOUN **1** *The weather will be the biggest hurdle.* = **obstacle**, block, difficulty, barrier, handicap, hazard, complication, snag, uphill (*S. African*), obstruction, stumbling block, impediment, hindrance **2** *The horse dived at the hurdle and clipped the top.* = **fence**, wall, hedge, block, barrier, barricade

hurl VERB = **throw**, fling, chuck (*informal*), send, fire, project, launch, cast, pitch, shy, toss, propel, sling (*informal*), heave, let fly (with)

hurly-burly NOUN = **commotion**, confusion, chaos, turmoil, disorder, upheaval, furore, uproar, turbulence, pandemonium, bedlam, tumult, hubbub, brouhaha ■ **OPPOSITE:** order

hurricane NOUN = **storm**, gale, tornado, cyclone, typhoon, tempest (*literary*), twister (*U.S. informal*), windstorm, willy-willy (*Austral.*)

hurried ADJECTIVE **1** *They had a hurried breakfast, then left.* = **hasty**, quick, brief, rushed, short, swift, speedy, precipitate, quickie (*informal*), breakneck **2** *a hurried overnight redrafting of the text* = **rushed**, perfunctory, hectic, speedy, superficial, hasty, cursory, slapdash

hurriedly ADVERB = **hastily**, quickly, briskly, speedily, in a rush, at the double, hurry-scurry

hurry VERB **1** *Claire hurried along the road.* = **rush**, fly, dash, barrel (along) (*informal, chiefly U.S. & Canad.*), scurry, scoot, burn rubber (*informal*) ■ **OPPOSITE:** dawdle **2** *There was no longer any reason to hurry.* = **make haste**, rush, lose no time, get a move on (*informal*), step on it (*informal*), get your skates on (*informal*), crack on (*informal*) **3** (*sometimes with* **up**) *the President's attempt to hurry the process of independence* = **speed (up)**, accelerate, hasten, quicken, hustle, urge, push on, goad, expedite ■ **OPPOSITE:** slow down ▶ NOUN *the hurry of people*

wanting to get home = **rush**, haste, speed, urgency, bustle, flurry, commotion, precipitation, quickness, celerity (*formal*), promptitude ■ **OPPOSITE:** slowness

hurt VERB **1** *She had hurt her back in an accident.* = **injure**, damage, wound, cut, bruise, scrape, impair, gash ■ **OPPOSITE:** heal **2** *His collar bone only hurt when he lifted his arm.* = **ache**, be sore, be painful, burn, smart, sting, throb, be tender **3** *Did they hurt you?* = **harm**, injure, molest, ill-treat, maltreat, lay a finger on **4** *I'll go. I've hurt you enough.* = **upset**, distress, pain, wound, annoy, sting, grieve, afflict, sadden, cut to the quick, aggrieve ▶ NOUN **1** *I was full of jealousy and hurt.* = **distress**, suffering, pain, grief, misery, agony, sadness, sorrow, woe, anguish, heartache, wretchedness ■ **OPPOSITE:** happiness **2** *I am sorry for any hurt that it may have caused.* = **harm**, trouble, damage, wrong, loss, injury, misfortune, mischief, affliction ▶ ADJECTIVE **1** *They were dazed but did not seem to be badly hurt.* = **injured**, wounded, damaged, harmed, cut, scratched, bruised, scarred, scraped, grazed ■ **OPPOSITE:** healed **2** *He gave me a slightly hurt look.* = **upset**, pained, injured, wounded, sad, crushed, offended, aggrieved, miffed (*informal*), rueful, piqued, tooshie (*Austral. slang*) ■ **OPPOSITE:** calmed

hurtful ADJECTIVE = **unkind**, upsetting, distressing, mean, cutting, damaging, wounding, nasty, cruel, destructive, harmful, malicious, mischievous, detrimental, pernicious (*formal*), spiteful, prejudicial, injurious, disadvantageous, maleficent

hurtle VERB = **rush**, charge, race, shoot, fly, speed, tear, crash, plunge, barrel (along) (*informal, chiefly U.S. & Canad.*), scramble, spurt, stampede, scoot, burn rubber (*informal*), rush headlong, go hell for leather (*informal*)

husband NOUN **1** *I married my husband Jack in 2015.* = **partner**, man (*informal*), spouse, hubby (*informal*), mate, old man (*informal*), bridegroom, significant other (*informal, chiefly U.S.*), better half (*humorous*) ▶ VERB *Husbanding precious resources was part of rural life.* = **conserve**, budget, use sparingly, save, store, hoard, economize on, use economically, manage thriftily ■ **OPPOSITE:** squander

husbandry NOUN **1** *The current meagre harvest suggests poor husbandry.* = **farming**, agriculture, cultivation, land management, tillage, agronomy **2** *These people consider themselves adept at financial husbandry.* = **thrift**, economy, good housekeeping, frugality, careful management

hush VERB *She tried to hush her noisy father.* = **quieten**, still, silence, suppress, mute, muzzle, shush ▶ NOUN *A hush fell over the crowd.* = **quiet**, silence, calm, still (*poetic*), peace, tranquillity, stillness, peacefulness • **hush something up** *The authorities have tried to hush it up.* = **cover up**, conceal, suppress, sit on (*informal*), squash, smother, keep secret, sweep under the carpet (*informal*), draw a veil over, keep dark

hush-hush ADJECTIVE = **secret**, confidential, classified, top-secret, restricted, under wraps

husk NOUN = **rind**, shell, hull, covering, bark, chaff, shuck

husky ADJECTIVE **1** *His voice was husky with grief.* = **hoarse**, rough, harsh, raucous, rasping, croaking, gruff, throaty, guttural, croaky **2** *a very husky young man, built like a football player* = **muscular**, powerful, strapping, rugged (*U.S. & Canad.*), hefty, burly, stocky, beefy (*informal*), brawny, thickset

hustle VERB **1** *The guards hustled Harry out of the car.* = **jostle**, force, push, crowd (*informal*), rush, hurry, thrust, elbow, shove, jog, bustle, impel **2** *You'll have to hustle if you're to get home for supper.* = **hurry**, hasten, get a move on (*informal*)

hut NOUN **1** *a mud hut with no electricity, gas, or running water* = **cabin**, shack, shanty, hovel, whare (*N.Z.*) **2** *Never leave a garage or garden hut unlocked.* = **shed**, outhouse, lean-to, lockup

hybrid NOUN **1** *a hybrid between watermint and spearmint; best champion Mule or Hybrid* = **crossbreed**, cross, mixture, compound, composite, mule, amalgam, mongrel, half-breed, half-blood **2** *a hybrid of solid and liquid fuel* = **mixture**, compound, composite, amalgam

hygiene NOUN = **cleanliness**, sanitation, disinfection, sterility, sanitary measures, hygienics

hygienic ADJECTIVE = **clean**, healthy, sanitary, pure, sterile, salutary, disinfected, germ-free, aseptic ■ **OPPOSITE:** dirty

hymn NOUN **1** *Readings were accompanied by an old Irish hymn.* = **religious song**, song of praise, carol, chant, anthem, psalm, paean, canticle, doxology **2** *a hymn to freedom and rebellion* = **song of praise**, anthem, paean

hype NOUN = **publicity**, promotion, build-up, plugging (*informal*), puffing, racket, razzmatazz (*slang*), brouhaha, ballyhoo (*informal*)

hyperbole NOUN = **exaggeration**, hype (*informal*), overstatement, enlargement, magnification, amplification

hypnotic ADJECTIVE = **mesmeric**, soothing, narcotic, opiate, soporific, sleep-inducing, somniferous

hypnotize VERB **1** *The ability to hypnotize yourself can be learnt in a single session.* = **mesmerize**, put in a trance, put to sleep **2** *He's hypnotized by that black hair and that white face.* = **fascinate**, absorb, entrance, magnetize, spellbind

hypocrisy NOUN = **insincerity**, pretence, deceit, deception, cant, duplicity, dissembling, falsity, imposture, sanctimoniousness, phoniness (*informal*), deceitfulness, pharisaism, speciousness, two-facedness, phariseeism ■ **OPPOSITE:** sincerity

hypocrite NOUN = **fraud** (*informal*), deceiver, pretender, charlatan, impostor, pharisee, dissembler, Tartuffe, Pecksniff, Holy Willie, whited sepulchre, phoney *or* phony (*informal*)

hypocritical ADJECTIVE = **insincere**, false, fraudulent, hollow, deceptive, spurious, two-faced, deceitful, sanctimonious, specious, duplicitous, dissembling, canting, Janus-faced, pharisaical, phoney *or* phony (*informal*)

hypodermic NOUN = **syringe**, needle, works (*slang*)

hypothesis NOUN = **theory**, premise, proposition, assumption, thesis, postulate, supposition, premise

hypothetical ADJECTIVE = **theoretical**, supposed, academic, assumed, imaginary, speculative, putative (*formal*), conjectural ■ **OPPOSITE:** real

hysteria NOUN = **frenzy**, panic, madness, agitation, delirium, hysterics, unreason

hysterical ADJECTIVE **1** *When I told her the news she became hysterical.* = **frenzied**, frantic, raving, distracted, distraught, crazed, uncontrollable, berserk, overwrought, convulsive, beside yourself ■ **OPPOSITE:** calm **2** *a hysterical, satirical revue* = **hilarious**, uproarious, side-splitting, farcical, comical, wildly funny ■ **OPPOSITE:** serious

h

Ii

ice • **break the ice** *The main purpose of his trip was to break the ice.* = **kick off** (*informal*), lead the way, take the plunge (*informal*), make a start, begin a relationship, initiate the proceedings, start or set the ball rolling (*informal*) • **skate on thin ice** *I had skated on thin ice for long enough.* = **be at risk**, be vulnerable, be unsafe, be in jeopardy, be out on a limb, be open to attack, be sticking your neck out (*informal*)

icon NOUN 1 = **idol**, hero, superstar 2 = **representation**, image, likeness, avatar, favicon (*Computing*)

icy ADJECTIVE 1 *An icy wind blew across the moor.* = **cold**, freezing, bitter, biting, raw, chill, chilling, arctic (*informal*), chilly, frosty, glacial, ice-cold, frozen over, frost-bound ■ **OPPOSITE:** hot 2 *an icy road* = **slippery**, glassy, slippy (*informal, dialect*), like a sheet of glass, rimy 3 *Her response was icy.* = **unfriendly**, cold, distant, hostile, forbidding, indifferent, aloof, stony, steely, frosty, glacial, frigid, unwelcoming ■ **OPPOSITE:** friendly

idea NOUN 1 *It's a good idea to keep a stock of tins in the cupboard.* = **plan**, scheme, proposal, design, strategy, method, solution, suggestion, recommendation, proposition 2 *Some of his ideas about democracy are entirely his own.* = **notion**, thought, view, understanding, teaching, opinion, belief, conclusion, hypothesis, impression, conviction, judgment, interpretation, sentiment, doctrine, conception, viewpoint 3 *This graph will give you a rough idea of levels of ability.* = **impression**, estimate, guess, hint, notion, clue, conjecture, surmise, inkling, approximation, intimation, ballpark figure 4 *By the end of the week you will have a clearer idea of the system.* = **understanding**, thought, view, sense, opinion, concept, impression, judgment, perception, conception, abstraction, estimation 5 *The idea is to help lower-income families to buy their homes.* = **intention**, aim, purpose, object, end, plan, reason, goal, design, objective, motive

USAGE It is usually considered correct to say that someone has *the idea of doing something*, rather than *the idea to do something*. For example, you would say *he had the idea of taking a holiday*, not *he had the idea to take a holiday*.

ideal NOUN 1 (*often plural*) *The party has drifted too far from its socialist ideals.* = **principle**, standard, ideology, morals, conviction, integrity, scruples, probity (*formal*), moral value, rectitude, sense of duty, sense of honour, uprightness 2 *I didn't fit the American ideal of a leading man.* = **epitome**, standard, dream, pattern, perfection, last word, paragon, nonpareil, standard of perfection 3 *the ideal of beauty in those days* = **model**, example, criterion, prototype, paradigm, archetype, exemplar ▶ ADJECTIVE 1 *She decided I was the ideal person to take over this job.* = **perfect**, best, model, classic, supreme, ultimate, archetypal, exemplary, consummate, optimal, quintessential ■ **OPPOSITE:** imperfect 2 *Their ideal society collapsed around them in revolution.* = **imaginary**, impractical, Utopian, romantic, fantastic, fabulous, poetic, visionary, fairy-tale, mythical, unreal, fanciful, unattainable, ivory-towered, imagal (*Psychoanalysis*) ■ **OPPOSITE:** actual 3 *an ideal economic world* = **hypothetical**, academic, intellectual, abstract, theoretical, speculative, conceptual, metaphysical, transcendental, notional

idealist NOUN = **romantic**, visionary, dreamer, Utopian

idealistic ADJECTIVE = **perfectionist**, romantic, optimistic, visionary, Utopian, quixotic, impracticable, starry-eyed ■ **OPPOSITE:** realistic

idealize VERB = **romanticize**, glorify, exalt, worship, magnify, ennoble, deify, put on a pedestal, apotheosize

ideally ADVERB = **in a perfect world**, in theory, preferably, if possible, all things being equal, under the best of circumstances, if you had your way, in a Utopia

identical ADJECTIVE = **alike**, like, the same, matching, equal, twin, equivalent, corresponding, duplicate, synonymous, indistinguishable, analogous, interchangeable, a dead ringer (*slang*), the dead spit (*informal*), like two peas in a pod ■ **OPPOSITE:** different

identifiable ADJECTIVE = **recognizable**, noticeable, known, unmistakable, discernible, detectable, distinguishable, ascertainable

identification NOUN **1** *Early identification of the disease can prevent death.* = **discovery**, recognition, determining, establishment, diagnosis, confirmation, detection, divination **2** *Officials are awaiting positive identification before proceeding.* = **recognition**, naming, labelling, distinguishing, cataloguing, classifying, confirmation, pinpointing, establishment of identity **3** *There is a close identification of nationhood with language.* = **connection**, relationship, link, association, tie, partnership, affinity, familiarity, interconnection, interrelation **4** *She had an intense identification with animals.* = **understanding**, relationship, involvement, unity, sympathy, empathy, rapport, fellow feeling **5** *I'll need to see some identification.* = **ID**, papers, credentials, licence, warrant, identity card, proof of identity, photocard, letters of introduction, electronic signature

identify VERB **1** *I tried to identify her perfume.* = **recognize**, place, name, remember, spot, label, flag, catalogue, tag, diagnose, classify, make out, pinpoint, recollect, put your finger on (*informal*) **2** *Police have already identified around ten suspects.* = **establish**, spot, confirm, finger (*informal, chiefly U.S.*), demonstrate, pick out, single out, certify, verify, validate, mark out, substantiate, corroborate, flag up • **identify something or someone with something or someone** *Audiences identify her with roles depicting sweet, passive women.* = **equate with**, associate with, think of in connection with, put in the same category as • **identify with someone** *She would only play the role if she could identify with the character.* = **relate to**, understand, respond to, feel for, ally with, empathize with, speak the same language as, put yourself in the place or shoes of, see through another's eyes, be on the same wavelength as

identity NOUN = **individuality**, self, character, personality, existence, distinction, originality, peculiarity, uniqueness, oneness, singularity, separateness, distinctiveness, selfhood, particularity

ideology NOUN = **belief(s)**, ideas, principles, ideals, opinion, philosophy, doctrine, creed, dogma, tenets, world view, credence, articles of faith, Weltanschauung (*German*)

idiocy NOUN *the idiocy of subsidies for activities which damage the environment* = **foolishness**, insanity, lunacy, inanity, imbecility, senselessness, fatuity, abject stupidity, asininity, fatuousness ■ **OPPOSITE:** wisdom

idiom NOUN **1** *Proverbs and idioms may become worn with over-use.* = **phrase**, expression, turn of phrase, locution, set phrase **2** *I was irritated by his use of archaic idiom.* = **language**, talk, style, usage, jargon, vernacular, parlance, mode of expression

idiosyncrasy NOUN = **peculiarity**, habit, characteristic, foible, quirk, eccentricity, oddity, mannerism, affectation, trick, singularity, personal trait

idiosyncratic ADJECTIVE = **distinctive**, special, individual, typical, distinguishing, distinct, peculiar, individualistic

idiot NOUN *I knew I'd been an idiot to stay there.* = **fool**, jerk (*slang, chiefly U.S. & Canad.*), ass, plank (*Brit. slang*), charlie (*Brit. informal*), berk (*Brit. slang*), wally (*slang*), prat (*slang*), plonker (*slang*), twit (*informal, chiefly Brit.*), chump, oaf, airhead (*slang*), dimwit (*informal*), dork (*slang*), nitwit (*informal*), blockhead, divvy (*Brit. slang*), pillock (*Brit. slang*), halfwit, nincompoop, eejit (*Scot. & Irish*), dumb-ass (*slang*), dunderhead, numpty (*Scot. informal*), doofus (*slang, chiefly U.S.*), lamebrain (*informal*), mooncalf, numbskull or numskull, galah (*Austral. & N.Z. informal*), dorba or dorb (*Austral. slang*), dill (*Austral. & N.Z. informal*), mampara (*S. African informal*)

idiotic ADJECTIVE *What an idiotic thing to say!* = **foolish**, crazy, stupid, dumb (*informal*), daft (*informal*), senseless, foolhardy, inane, fatuous, loopy (*informal*), unintelligent, asinine, harebrained, dumb-ass (*slang*), halfwitted ■ **OPPOSITE:** wise

idle ADJECTIVE **1** *Employees have been idle for almost a month now.* = **unoccupied**, unemployed, redundant, jobless, out of work, out of action, inactive, at leisure, between jobs, unwaged, at a loose end ■ **OPPOSITE:** occupied **2** *Now the machine is lying idle.* = **unused**, stationary, inactive, out of order, ticking over, gathering dust, mothballed, out of service, out of action or operation **3** *I've never met such an idle bunch of workers!* = **lazy**, slow, slack, sluggish, lax, negligent, inactive, inert, lethargic, indolent, lackadaisical, good-for-nothing, remiss (*formal*), workshy, slothful (*formal*), shiftless ■ **OPPOSITE:** busy **4** *It would be idle to pretend the system is worthless.* = **useless**, vain, pointless, hopeless, unsuccessful, ineffective, worthless, futile, fruitless, unproductive, abortive, ineffectual, groundless, of no use, valueless, disadvantageous, unavailing, otiose, of no avail, profitless, bootless ■ **OPPOSITE:** useful **5** *He kept up the idle chatter for another five minutes.* = **trivial**, superficial, insignificant, frivolous, silly, unnecessary, irrelevant, foolish, unhelpful, flippant, puerile, flighty, ill-considered, empty-headed, nugatory ■ **OPPOSITE:** meaningful ▶ VERB (often with **away**) *He idled the time away in dreamy thought.* = **fritter**, while, waste, fool, lounge, potter, loaf, dally, loiter, dawdle, laze

idleness NOUN **1** *Idleness is a very bad thing for human nature.* = **inactivity**, unemployment, leisure, inaction, time on your hands **2** *Idleness and incompetence are not inbred in our workers.* = **loafing**, inertia, sloth, pottering, trifling, laziness, time-wasting, lazing, torpor, sluggishness, skiving (*Brit. slang*), vegetating, dilly-dallying (*informal*), shiftlessness

idly ADVERB = **lazily**, casually, passively, languidly, unthinkingly, sluggishly, languorously, lethargically, apathetically, indolently, inertly, lackadaisically, inactively, shiftlessly, slothfully ■ **OPPOSITE:** energetically

idol NOUN **1** *They cheered as they caught sight of their idol.* = **hero**, superstar, pin-up, favourite, pet, darling, beloved (*slang*), fave (*informal*) **2** *Some denounced them for worshipping idols.* = **graven image**, god, image, deity, pagan symbol

idolize VERB = **worship**, love, adore, admire, revere, glorify, exalt, look up to, venerate, hero-worship, deify, bow down before, dote upon, apotheosize, worship to excess

idyllic ADJECTIVE = **heavenly**, idealized, ideal, charming, peaceful, pastoral, picturesque, rustic, Utopian, halcyon, out of this world, unspoiled, arcadian

if CONJUNCTION **1** *If you want to apply for a refund, please go to our website.* = **provided**, assuming, given that, providing, allowing, admitting, supposing, granting, in case, presuming, on the assumption that, on condition that, as long as **2** *She gets very upset if I exclude her from anything.* = **when**, whenever, every time, any time **3** *He asked if I had left with you, and I said no.* = **whether** ▶ NOUN *This business is full of ifs.* = **doubt**, condition, uncertainty, provision, constraint, hesitation, vagueness, stipulation

iffy ADJECTIVE = **uncertain**, doubtful, unpredictable, conditional, undecided, up in the air, problematical, chancy (*informal*), in the lap of the gods

ignite VERB **1** *The blast was caused by pockets of methane gas which ignited.* = **catch fire**, burn, burst into flames, fire, inflame, flare up, take fire **2** *The bombs ignited a fire which*

destroyed some 60 houses. = **set fire to**, light, set alight, torch, kindle, touch off, put a match to (*informal*)

ignoble ADJECTIVE **1** *an ignoble episode from their country's past* = **dishonourable**, low, base, mean, petty, infamous, degraded, craven, disgraceful, shabby, vile, degenerate, abject, unworthy, shameless, despicable, heinous, dastardly (*old-fashioned*), contemptible, wretched **2** *They wanted to spare him the shame of an ignoble birth.* = **lowly**, mean, low, base, common, peasant, vulgar, plebeian, humble, lowborn (*rare*), baseborn (*archaic*)

ignominious ADJECTIVE = **humiliating**, disgraceful, shameful, sorry, scandalous, abject, despicable, mortifying, undignified, disreputable, dishonourable, inglorious, discreditable, indecorous ■ **OPPOSITE:** honourable

ignominy NOUN = **disgrace**, shame, humiliation, contempt, discredit, stigma, disrepute, dishonour, infamy, mortification, bad odour ■ **OPPOSITE:** honour

ignorance NOUN **1** *In my ignorance, I had never heard of R and B music.* = **lack of education**, stupidity, foolishness, blindness, illiteracy, benightedness, unenlightenment, unintelligence, mental darkness ■ **OPPOSITE:** knowledge **2** (*with* **of**) *a complete ignorance of non-European history* = **unawareness of**, inexperience of, unfamiliarity with, innocence of, unconsciousness of, greenness about, oblivion about, nescience of (*literary*)

ignorant ADJECTIVE **1** *They don't ask questions for fear of appearing ignorant.* = **uneducated**, unaware, naive, green, illiterate, inexperienced, innocent, untrained, unlearned, unread, untutored, uncultivated, wet behind the ears (*informal*), unlettered, untaught, unknowledgeable, uncomprehending, unscholarly, as green as grass ■ **OPPOSITE:** educated **2** *Some very ignorant people called me all kinds of names.* = **insensitive**, gross, crude, rude, shallow, superficial, crass **3** (*with* **of**) *Many people are worryingly ignorant of the facts.* = **uninformed of**, unaware of, oblivious to, blind to, innocent of, in the dark about, unconscious of, unschooled in, out of the loop of, inexperienced of, uninitiated about, unknowing of, unenlightened about ■ **OPPOSITE:** informed

ignore VERB **1** *She said her manager ignored her.* = **pay no attention to**, neglect, disregard, slight, overlook, scorn, spurn, rebuff, take no notice of, be oblivious to, dinghy (*Brit. slang*) ■ **OPPOSITE:** pay attention to **2** *Such arguments ignore the important issues.* = **overlook**, discount, disregard, reject, neglect, shrug off, pass over, brush aside, turn a blind eye to, turn a deaf ear to, shut your eyes to **3** *I kept sending letters and cards but he just ignored me.* = **snub**, cut (*informal*), slight, blank (*slang*), rebuff, cold-shoulder, turn your back on, give (someone) the cold shoulder, send (someone) to Coventry, give (someone) the brush-off, dinghy (*Brit. slang*)

ilk NOUN = **type**, sort, kind, class, style, character (*informal*), variety, brand, breed, stamp, description, kidney, disposition

> **USAGE** Some people object to the use of the phrase *of that ilk* to mean 'of that type or class', claiming that it arises from a misunderstanding of the original Scottish expression. The Scottish phrase *of that ilk* has a very specific meaning, indicating that the person mentioned is laird of an estate with the same name as his family, for example *Moncrieff of that ilk* (that is, 'Moncrieff, laird of Moncrieff estate'). The more general use is, however, well established and is now generally regarded as acceptable.

ill ADJECTIVE **1** *He was seriously ill with pneumonia.* = **unwell**, sick, poorly (*informal*), diseased, funny (*informal*), weak, crook (*Austral. & N.Z. slang*), ailing, queer, frail, feeble, unhealthy, seedy (*informal*), sickly, laid up (*informal*), queasy, infirm, out of sorts (*informal*), dicky (*Brit. informal*), nauseous, off-colour, under the weather (*informal*), at death's door, indisposed, peaky, on the sick list (*informal*), valetudinarian, green about the gills, not up to snuff (*informal*) ■ **OPPOSITE:** healthy **2** *ill effects from the contamination of the water* = **harmful**, bad, damaging, evil, foul, unfortunate, destructive, unlucky, vile, detrimental, hurtful, pernicious (*formal*), noxious, ruinous, deleterious (*formal*), injurious, iniquitous, disadvantageous, maleficent ■ **OPPOSITE:** favourable **3** *I bear no ill feelings towards you.* = **hostile**, malicious, acrimonious, cross, harsh, adverse, belligerent, unkind, hurtful, unfriendly, malevolent, antagonistic, hateful, bellicose, cantankerous, inimical, rancorous, ill-disposed ■ **OPPOSITE:** kind **4** *His absence preyed on her mind like an ill omen.* = **bad**, threatening, disturbing, menacing, unlucky, sinister, gloomy, dire, ominous, unhealthy, unfavourable, foreboding, unpromising, inauspicious,

unwholesome, unpropitious, bodeful
▶ NOUN **1** *She is responsible for many of the country's ills.* = **problem**, trouble, suffering, worry, trial, injury, pain, hurt, strain, harm, distress, misery, hardship, woe, misfortune, affliction, tribulation, unpleasantness **2** *I know it will be difficult for them but I wish them no ill.* = **harm**, suffering, damage, hurt, evil, destruction, grief, trauma, anguish, mischief, malice
■ **OPPOSITE:** good ▶ ADVERB **1** *This development may bode ill for the government.* = **badly**, unfortunately, unfavourably, inauspiciously **2** *We can ill afford another scandal.* = **hardly**, barely, scarcely, just, only just, by no means, at a push ■ **OPPOSITE:** well **3** *He used his ill-gotten gains to buy a new house.* = **illegally**, criminally, unlawfully, fraudulently, dishonestly, illicitly, illegitimately, unscrupulously, foully **4** *We were ill-prepared for last year's South Africa tour.* = **insufficiently**, badly, poorly, inadequately, imperfectly, deficiently

ill-advised ADJECTIVE = **misguided**, inappropriate, foolish, rash, reckless, unwise, short-sighted, unseemly, foolhardy, thoughtless, indiscreet, ill-judged, ill-considered, imprudent, wrong-headed, injudicious, incautious, impolitic, overhasty ■ **OPPOSITE:** wise

ill at ease ADJECTIVE = **uncomfortable**, nervous, tense, strange, wired (*slang*), disturbed, anxious, awkward, uneasy, unsettled, faltering, unsure, restless, out of place, self-conscious, hesitant, disquieted, edgy, on edge, twitchy (*informal*), on tenterhooks, fidgety, unquiet, like a fish out of water, antsy (*informal*), unrelaxed, on pins and needles (*informal*)
■ **OPPOSITE:** comfortable

ill-considered ADJECTIVE = **unwise**, rash, imprudent, careless, precipitate, hasty, heedless, injudicious, improvident, overhasty

ill-defined ADJECTIVE = **unclear**, vague, indistinct, blurred, dim, fuzzy, shadowy, woolly, nebulous ■ **OPPOSITE:** clear

illegal ADJECTIVE = **unlawful**, banned, forbidden, prohibited, criminal, outlawed, unofficial, illicit, unconstitutional, lawless, wrongful, off limits, unlicensed, under-the-table, unauthorized, proscribed, under-the-counter, actionable (*Law*), felonious ■ **OPPOSITE:** legal

illegality NOUN = **crime**, wrong, felony, criminality, lawlessness, illegitimacy, wrongness, unlawfulness, illicitness

illegible ADJECTIVE = **indecipherable**, unreadable, faint, crabbed, scrawled, hieroglyphic, hard to make out, undecipherable, obscure ■ **OPPOSITE:** legible

illegitimacy NOUN = **illegality**, unconstitutionality, unlawfulness, illicitness, irregularity

illegitimate ADJECTIVE **1** *Later, the news of his illegitimate child came out.* = **born out of wedlock**, natural, bastard (*archaic*), love, misbegotten (*literary*), baseborn (*archaic*) **2** *a ruthless and illegitimate regime* = **unlawful**, illegal, illicit, improper, unconstitutional, under-the-table, unauthorized, unsanctioned ■ **OPPOSITE:** legal **3** *It is not illegitimate to seek a parallel between the two events.* = **invalid**, incorrect, illogical, spurious, unsound

ill-fated ADJECTIVE = **doomed**, unfortunate, unlucky, unhappy, blighted, hapless, luckless, ill-starred, star-crossed, ill-omened

ill feeling NOUN = **hostility**, resentment, bitterness, offence, indignation, animosity, antagonism, enmity, rancour, bad blood, hard feelings, ill will, animus, dudgeon (*archaic*), chip on your shoulder ■ **OPPOSITE:** goodwill

ill-humoured ADJECTIVE = **bad-tempered**, cross, sharp, unpleasant, moody, impatient, irritable, snappy, grumpy, sullen, disagreeable, sulky

illiberal ADJECTIVE = **intolerant**, prejudiced, bigoted, narrow-minded, small-minded, reactionary, hidebound, uncharitable, ungenerous ■ **OPPOSITE:** tolerant

illicit ADJECTIVE **1** *information about the use of illicit drugs* = **illegal**, criminal, prohibited, unlawful, black-market, illegitimate, off limits, unlicensed, unauthorized, bootleg, contraband, felonious ■ **OPPOSITE:** legal **2** *It was claimed that Rice had conducted an illicit affair with the woman.* = **forbidden**, improper, immoral, wrong, guilty, clandestine, furtive

illiteracy NOUN = **lack of education**, ignorance, benightedness, illiterateness

illiterate ADJECTIVE = **uneducated**, ignorant, unlettered, unable to read and write, analphabetic ■ **OPPOSITE:** educated

ill-judged ADJECTIVE = **misguided**, foolish, rash, unwise, short-sighted, ill-advised, ill-considered, wrong-headed, injudicious, overhasty

ill-mannered ADJECTIVE = **rude**, impolite, discourteous, coarse, churlish, boorish, insolent, uncouth, loutish, uncivil, ill-bred, badly behaved, ill-behaved, unmannerly ■ **OPPOSITE:** polite

illness NOUN = **sickness**, ill health, malaise, attack, disease, complaint, infection, disorder, bug (*informal*), ailment, affliction, poor health, malady, infirmity, indisposition, lurgy (*informal*)

illogical ADJECTIVE = **irrational**, absurd, unreasonable, meaningless, incorrect, faulty, inconsistent, invalid, senseless, spurious, inconclusive, unsound, unscientific, specious, fallacious, untenable, sophistical ■ **OPPOSITE:** logical

ill-tempered ADJECTIVE = **cross**, irritable, grumpy, irascible, sharp, annoyed, impatient, touchy, bad-tempered, curt, spiteful, tetchy, ratty (*Brit. & N.Z. informal*), testy, chippy (*informal*), choleric, ill-humoured, liverish ■ **OPPOSITE:** good-natured

ill-treat VERB = **abuse**, injure, harm, wrong, damage, harry, harass, misuse, oppress, dump on (*slang, chiefly U.S.*), mishandle, maltreat, ill-use, handle roughly, knock about *or* around

ill-treatment NOUN = **abuse**, harm, mistreatment, damage, injury, misuse, ill-use, rough handling

illuminate VERB **1** *No streetlights illuminate the street.* = **light up**, light, brighten, irradiate, illumine (*literary*) ■ **OPPOSITE:** darken **2** *The instructors use games to illuminate the subject.* = **explain**, interpret, make clear, clarify, clear up, enlighten, shed light on, elucidate, explicate (*formal*), give insight into ■ **OPPOSITE:** obscure **3** *medieval illuminated manuscripts* = **decorate**, illustrate, adorn, ornament

illuminating ADJECTIVE = **informative**, revealing, enlightening, helpful, explanatory, instructive ■ **OPPOSITE:** confusing

illumination NOUN **1** *The only illumination came from a small window above.* = **light**, lighting, lights, ray, beam, lighting up, brightening, brightness, radiance **2** *No further illumination can be had from this theory.* = **enlightenment**, understanding, insight, perception, awareness, revelation, inspiration, clarification, edification ▶ PLURAL NOUN *the famous Blackpool illuminations* = **lights**, decorations, fairy lights

illusion NOUN **1** *No one really has any illusions about winning the war.* = **delusion**, misconception, misapprehension, fancy, deception, fallacy, self-deception, false impression, false belief, misbelief **2** *Floor-to-ceiling windows give the illusion of extra space.* = **false impression**, feeling, appearance, impression, fancy, deception, imitation, sham, pretence, semblance, fallacy ■ **OPPOSITE:** reality **3** *The rapid* *changes of lighting created an illusion of movement.* = **fantasy**, vision, hallucination, trick, spectre, mirage, semblance, daydream, apparition, chimera, figment of the imagination, phantasm, ignis fatuus, will-o'-the-wisp

illusory *or* **illusive** ADJECTIVE = **unreal**, false, misleading, untrue, seeming, mistaken, apparent, sham, deceptive, deceitful, hallucinatory, fallacious, chimerical, delusive ■ **OPPOSITE:** real

illustrate VERB **1** *The example of the United States illustrates this point.* = **demonstrate**, show, exhibit, emphasize, exemplify, explicate **2** *She illustrates her analysis with extracts from interviews and discussions.* = **explain**, describe, interpret, sum up, make clear, clarify, summarize, bring home, point up, make plain, elucidate **3** *He has illustrated the book with black-and-white photographs.* = **adorn**, ornament, embellish

illustrated ADJECTIVE = **pictured**, decorated, illuminated, embellished, pictorial, with illustrations

illustration NOUN **1** *These figures are an illustration of the country's dynamism.* = **example**, case, instance, sample, explanation, demonstration, interpretation, specimen, analogy, clarification, case in point, exemplar, elucidation, exemplification **2** *He made his illustrations of birds as he travelled in America.* = **picture**, drawing, painting, image, print, plate, figure, portrait, representation, sketch, decoration, portrayal, likeness, adornment

illustrative ADJECTIVE **1** *The following excerpt is illustrative of her interaction with students.* = **representative**, typical, descriptive, explanatory, interpretive, expository, explicatory, illustrational **2** *an illustrative guide to the daily activities of the football club* = **pictorial**, graphic, diagrammatic, delineative

illustrious ADJECTIVE = **famous**, great, noted, celebrated, signal, brilliant, remarkable, distinguished, prominent, glorious, noble, splendid, notable, renowned, eminent, famed, exalted ■ **OPPOSITE:** obscure

ill will NOUN = **hostility**, spite, dislike, hatred, envy, resentment, grudge, malice, animosity, aversion, venom, antagonism, antipathy, enmity, acrimony, rancour, bad blood, hard feelings, animus, malevolence, unfriendliness ■ **OPPOSITE:** goodwill

image NOUN **1** *The words 'Côte d'Azur' conjure up images of sun, sea and sand.* = **thought**, idea, vision, concept, impression, perception, conception, mental picture, conceptualization **2** *The images in the poem illustrate the poet's frame of mind.* = **figure of speech**, metaphor, simile, conceit (*archaic*), trope **3** *I peered at my image in the mirror.* = **reflection**, appearance, likeness, mirror image **4** *The polished stone bore the graven image of a snakebird.* = **figure**, idol, icon, fetish, talisman, avatar **5** *The boy is the image of his father.* = **replica**, copy, reproduction, counterpart, spit (*informal, chiefly Brit.*), clone, facsimile, spitting image (*informal*), similitude, Doppelgänger, (dead) ringer (*slang*), double **6** *All people want to see is an image on the TV screen.* = **picture**, photo, photograph, representation, reproduction, snapshot, TIFF, JPEG, avatar, thumbnail

imaginable ADJECTIVE = **possible**, conceivable, likely, credible, plausible, believable, under the sun, comprehensible, thinkable, within the bounds of possibility, supposable ■ **OPPOSITE:** unimaginable

imaginary ADJECTIVE = **fictional**, made-up, invented, supposed, imagined, assumed, ideal, fancied, legendary, visionary, shadowy, unreal, hypothetical, fanciful, fictitious, mythological, illusory, nonexistent, dreamlike, hallucinatory, illusive, chimerical, unsubstantial, phantasmal, suppositious, imagal (*Psychoanalysis*) ■ **OPPOSITE:** real

imagination NOUN **1** *He has a logical mind and a little imagination.* = **creativity**, vision, invention, ingenuity, enterprise, insight, inspiration, wit, originality, inventiveness, resourcefulness **2** *Long before I went there, the place was alive in my imagination.* = **mind's eye**, fancy (*old-fashioned, literary*)

imaginative ADJECTIVE = **creative**, original, inspired, enterprising, fantastic, clever, stimulating, vivid, ingenious, visionary, inventive, fanciful, dreamy, whimsical, poetical ■ **OPPOSITE:** unimaginative

imagine VERB **1** *He could not imagine a more peaceful scene.* = **envisage**, see, picture, plan, create, project, think of, scheme, frame, invent, devise, conjure up, envision, visualize, dream up (*informal*), think up, conceive of, conceptualize, fantasize about, see in the mind's eye, form a mental picture of, ideate **2** *I imagine you're referring to me.* = **believe**, think, suppose, assume, suspect, gather, guess (*informal, chiefly U.S. & Canad.*), realize, take it, reckon (*informal*), fancy, deem, speculate, presume, take for granted, infer, deduce, apprehend, conjecture, surmise

imbalance NOUN = **unevenness**, bias, inequality, unfairness, partiality, disproportion, lopsidedness, top-heaviness, lack of proportion

imbed see **embed**

imbibe VERB **1** *Tom had eaten a pie and imbibed some coffee.* = **drink**, consume, knock back (*informal*), sink (*informal*), swallow, suck, swig (*informal*), quaff **2** *He'd imbibed a set of mystical beliefs from the cradle.* = **absorb**, receive, take in, gain, gather, acquire, assimilate, ingest

imbue VERB = **instil**, infuse, steep, bathe, saturate, pervade, permeate, impregnate, inculcate

imitate VERB **1** *a precedent which may be imitated by other activists* = **copy**, follow, repeat, echo, emulate, ape, simulate, mirror, follow suit, duplicate, counterfeit, follow in the footsteps of, take a leaf out of (someone's) book **2** *He screwed up his face and imitated the Colonel.* = **do an impression of**, take off (*informal*), mimic, do (*informal*), affect, copy, mock, parody, caricature, send up (*Brit. informal*), spoof (*informal*), impersonate, burlesque, personate

imitation NOUN **1** *the most accurate imitation of Chinese architecture in Europe* = **replica**, fake, reproduction, sham, forgery, carbon copy (*informal*), counterfeit, counterfeiting, likeness, duplication **2** *She learned her golf by imitation.* = **copying**, echoing, resemblance, aping, simulation, mimicry **3** *I could do a pretty good imitation of him.* = **impression**, parody, mockery, takeoff (*informal*), impersonation ▶ ADJECTIVE *a set of novels bound in imitation leather* = **artificial**, mock, reproduction, dummy, synthetic, man-made, simulated, sham, pseudo (*informal*), ersatz, repro, phoney or phony (*informal*) ■ **OPPOSITE:** real

imitator NOUN = **impersonator**, mimic, impressionist, copycat, echo, follower, parrot (*informal*), copier, carbon copy (*informal*)

immaculate ADJECTIVE **1** *Her front room was kept immaculate.* = **clean**, impeccable, spotless, trim, neat, spruce, squeaky-clean, spick-and-span, neat as a new pin ■ **OPPOSITE:** dirty **2** *her immaculate reputation* = **pure**, perfect, innocent, impeccable, virtuous, flawless, faultless, squeaky-clean, guiltless, above reproach, sinless, incorrupt ■ **OPPOSITE:** corrupt **3** *My car's in absolutely immaculate condition.* = **perfect**, flawless, impeccable, stainless, faultless, unblemished, unsullied, uncontaminated, unpolluted, untarnished, unexceptionable, undefiled ■ **OPPOSITE:** tainted

immaterial ADJECTIVE = **irrelevant**, insignificant, unimportant, unnecessary, trivial, trifling, inconsequential, extraneous, inconsiderable, of no importance, of no consequence, inessential, a matter of indifference, of little account, inapposite ■ **OPPOSITE:** significant

immature ADJECTIVE **1** *The birds were in immature plumage.* = **young**, adolescent, undeveloped, green, raw, premature, unfinished, imperfect, untimely, unripe, unformed, unseasonable, unfledged **2** *You're just being childish and immature.* = **childish**, juvenile, infantile, puerile, callow, babyish, wet behind the ears (*informal*), jejune ■ **OPPOSITE:** adult

immaturity NOUN **1** *In spite of some immaturity of style, it showed real imagination.* = **rawness**, imperfection, greenness, unpreparedness, unripeness **2** *his immaturity and lack of social skills* = **childishness**, puerility, callowness, juvenility, babyishness

immeasurable ADJECTIVE = **incalculable**, vast, immense, endless, unlimited, infinite, limitless, boundless, bottomless, inexhaustible, unfathomable, unbounded, inestimable, measureless, illimitable ■ **OPPOSITE:** finite

immediate ADJECTIVE **1** *My immediate reaction was one of disgust.* = **instant**, prompt, instantaneous, quick, on-the-spot, split-second ■ **OPPOSITE:** later **2** *The immediate problem is not lack of food, but transportation.* = **current**, present, pressing, existing, actual, urgent, on hand, extant **3** *I was seated at his immediate left.* = **nearest**, next, direct, close, near, adjacent, contiguous (*formal*), proximate ■ **OPPOSITE:** far

immediately ADVERB = **at once**, now, instantly, straight away, directly, promptly, right now, right away, there and then, speedily, without delay, without hesitation, instantaneously, forthwith, pronto (*informal*), unhesitatingly, this instant, on the nail, this very minute, posthaste, tout de suite (*French*), before you could say Jack Robinson (*informal*)

immemorial ADJECTIVE = **age-old**, ancient, long-standing, traditional, fixed, rooted, archaic, time-honoured, of yore, olden (*archaic*)

immense ADJECTIVE = **huge**, great, massive, vast, large, giant, enormous, extensive, tremendous, mega (*slang*), titanic, infinite, jumbo (*informal*), very big, gigantic, monumental (*informal*), monstrous, mammoth, colossal, mountainous, stellar (*informal*), prodigious, interminable, stupendous, king-size, king-sized, immeasurable, elephantine, ginormous (*informal*), Brobdingnagian, illimitable, humongous or humungous (*informal*), supersize ■ **OPPOSITE:** tiny

immerse VERB **1** *I was able to immerse myself in family life.* = **engross**, involve, absorb, busy, occupy, engage **2** *The electrodes are immersed in liquid.* = **plunge**, dip, submerge, sink, duck, bathe, douse, dunk, submerse

immersed ADJECTIVE = **engrossed**, involved, absorbed, deep, busy, occupied, taken up, buried, consumed, wrapped up, bound up, rapt, spellbound, mesmerized, in a brown study

immersion NOUN **1** *long-term assignments that allowed them total immersion in their subjects* = **involvement**, concentration, preoccupation, absorption **2** *The wood had become swollen from prolonged immersion.* = **dipping**, submerging, plunging, ducking, dousing, dunking

immigrant NOUN = **settler**, incomer, alien, stranger, outsider, newcomer, migrant, emigrant

imminent ADJECTIVE = **near**, coming, close, approaching, threatening, gathering, on the way, in the air, forthcoming, looming, menacing, brewing, impending, at hand, upcoming, on the cards, on the horizon, in the pipeline, nigh (*archaic*), in the offing, fast-approaching, just round the corner, near-at-hand ■ **OPPOSITE:** remote

immobile ADJECTIVE = **motionless**, still, stationary, fixed, rooted, frozen, stable, halted, stiff, rigid, static, riveted, lifeless, inert, at rest, inanimate, immovable, immobilized, at a standstill, unmoving, stock-still, like a statue, immotile ■ **OPPOSITE:** mobile

immobility NOUN = **stillness**, firmness, steadiness, stability, fixity, inertness, immovability, motionlessness, absence of movement

immobilize VERB = **paralyse**, stop, freeze, halt, disable, cripple, bring to a standstill, put out of action, render inoperative

immoral ADJECTIVE = **wicked**, bad, wrong, abandoned, evil, corrupt, vicious, obscene, indecent, vile, degenerate, dishonest, pornographic, sinful, unethical, lewd, depraved, impure, debauched, unprincipled, nefarious, dissolute, iniquitous, reprobate, licentious, of easy virtue, unchaste ■ **OPPOSITE:** moral

immorality NOUN = **wickedness**, wrong, vice, evil, corruption, sin, depravity,

iniquity, debauchery, badness, licentiousness, turpitude (*formal*), dissoluteness ■ **OPPOSITE:** morality

immortal ADJECTIVE **1** *Wuthering Heights – that immortal love story* = **timeless**, eternal, everlasting, lasting, traditional, classic, constant, enduring, persistent, abiding, perennial, ageless, unfading ■ **OPPOSITE:** ephemeral **2** *They were considered gods and therefore immortal.* = **undying**, eternal, perpetual, indestructible, death-defying, imperishable, deathless ■ **OPPOSITE:** mortal ▶ NOUN **1** *I was in the presence of a sporting immortal.* = **hero**, genius, paragon, great **2** *In the legend, the fire is supposed to turn him into an immortal.* = **god**, goddess, deity, Olympian, divine being, immortal being, atua (*N.Z.*)

immortality NOUN **1** *belief in the immortality of the soul* = **eternity**, perpetuity, everlasting life, timelessness, incorruptibility, indestructibility, endlessness, deathlessness **2** *Some people want to achieve immortality through their works.* = **fame**, glory, celebrity, greatness, renown, glorification, gloriousness

immovable ADJECTIVE **1** *It was declared unsafe because the support bars were immovable.* = **fixed**, set, fast, firm, stuck, secure, rooted, stable, jammed, stationary, immutable, unbudgeable **2** *On one issue, however, she was immovable.* = **inflexible**, adamant, resolute, steadfast, constant, unyielding, unwavering, impassive, obdurate, unshakable, unchangeable, unshaken, stony-hearted, unimpressionable ■ **OPPOSITE:** flexible

immune ADJECTIVE • **immune from** *Members are immune from prosecution for corruption.* = **exempt from**, free from, let off (*informal*), not subject to, not liable to • **immune to 1** *The blood test will tell whether you are immune to the disease.* = **resistant to**, free from, protected from, safe from, not open to, spared from, secure against, invulnerable to, insusceptible to **2** *He never became immune to the sight of death.* = **unaffected by**, not affected by, invulnerable to, insusceptible to

immunity NOUN **1** *The police are offering immunity to witnesses who can help them.* = **exemption**, amnesty, indemnity, release, freedom, liberty, privilege, prerogative, invulnerability, exoneration **2** (*with* **to**) *immunity to airborne bacteria* = **resistance**, protection, resilience, inoculation, immunization ■ **OPPOSITE:** susceptibility

immunize VERB = **vaccinate**, inoculate, protect, safeguard

immutable ADJECTIVE = **unchanging**, fixed, permanent, stable, constant, enduring, abiding, perpetual, inflexible, steadfast, sacrosanct, immovable, ageless, invariable, unalterable, unchangeable, changeless

imp NOUN **1** *He sees the devil as a little imp with horns.* = **demon**, devil, sprite **2** *I didn't say that, you little imp!* = **rascal**, rogue, brat, urchin (*old-fashioned*), minx, scamp, pickle (*Brit. informal*), gamin, nointer (*Austral. slang*)

impact NOUN **1** *They expect the meeting to have a marked impact on the country's future.* = **effect**, influence, consequences, impression, repercussions, ramifications **2** *The pilot must have died on impact.* = **collision**, force, contact, shock, crash, knock, stroke, smash, bump, thump, jolt ▶ VERB *the sharp tinkle of metal impacting on stone* = **hit**, strike, crash, clash, crush, ram, smack, collide

impair VERB = **worsen**, reduce, damage, injure, harm, mar, undermine, weaken, spoil, diminish, decrease, blunt, deteriorate, lessen, hinder, debilitate, vitiate, enfeeble, enervate ■ OPPOSITE: improve

impaired ADJECTIVE = **damaged**, flawed, faulty, defective, imperfect, unsound

impale VERB = **pierce**, stick, run through, spike, lance, spear, skewer, spit, transfix

impart VERB **1** *the ability to impart knowledge and command respect* = **communicate**, pass on, convey, tell, reveal, discover, relate, disclose, divulge, make known **2** *She managed to impart great elegance to the dress she wore.* = **give**, accord, lend, bestow, offer, grant, afford, contribute, yield, confer

impartial ADJECTIVE = **neutral**, objective, detached, just, fair, equal, open-minded, equitable, disinterested, unbiased, even-handed, nonpartisan, unprejudiced, without fear or favour, nondiscriminating ■ OPPOSITE: unfair

impartiality NOUN = **neutrality**, equity, fairness, equality, detachment, objectivity, disinterest, open-mindedness, even-handedness, disinterestedness, dispassion, nonpartisanship, lack of bias ■ OPPOSITE: unfairness

impassable ADJECTIVE = **blocked**, closed, obstructed, impenetrable, unnavigable

impasse NOUN = **deadlock**, stalemate, standstill, dead end, standoff, blind alley (*informal*)

impassioned ADJECTIVE = **intense**, heated, passionate, warm, excited, inspired, violent, stirring, flaming, furious, glowing, blazing, vivid, animated, rousing, fiery, worked up, ardent, inflamed, fervent, ablaze, vehement, fervid ■ OPPOSITE: cool

impassive ADJECTIVE = **unemotional**, unmoved, emotionless, reserved, cool, calm, composed, indifferent, self-contained, serene, callous, aloof, stoical, unconcerned, apathetic, dispassionate, unfazed (*informal*), inscrutable, stolid, unruffled, phlegmatic, unfeeling, poker-faced (*informal*), imperturbable, insensible, impassible (*rare*), unexcitable, insusceptible, unimpressible

impatience NOUN **1** *There was a hint of impatience in his tone.* = **irritability**, shortness, edginess, intolerance, quick temper, snappiness, irritableness ■ OPPOSITE: patience **2** *She showed impatience to continue the climb.* = **eagerness**, longing, enthusiasm, hunger, yearning, thirst, zeal, fervour, ardour, vehemence, earnestness, keenness, impetuosity, heartiness, avidity, intentness, greediness **3** *They visited a fertility clinic in their impatience to have a child.* = **haste**, hurry, impetuosity, rashness, hastiness

impatient ADJECTIVE **1** *He becomes impatient as the hours pass.* = **cross**, tense, annoyed, irritated, prickly, edgy, touchy, bad-tempered, intolerant, petulant, ill-tempered, cantankerous, ratty (*Brit. & N.Z. informal*), chippy (*informal*), hot-tempered, quick-tempered, crotchety (*informal*), ill-humoured, narky (*Brit. slang*), out of humour **2** *Beware of being too impatient with others.* = **irritable**, fiery, abrupt, hasty, snappy, indignant, curt, vehement, brusque, irascible, testy ■ OPPOSITE: easy-going **3** *They are impatient for jobs and security.* = **eager**, longing, keen, hot, earnest, raring, anxious, hungry, intent, enthusiastic, yearning, greedy, restless, ardent, avid, fervent, zealous, chafing, vehement, fretful, straining at the leash, fervid, keen as mustard, like a cat on hot bricks (*informal*), athirst ■ OPPOSITE: calm

impeach VERB = **charge**, accuse, prosecute, blame, denounce, indict, censure, bring to trial, arraign

impeachment NOUN = **accusation**, prosecution, indictment, arraignment

impeccable ADJECTIVE = **faultless**, perfect, pure, exact, precise, exquisite, stainless, immaculate, flawless, squeaky-clean, unerring, unblemished, unimpeachable, irreproachable, sinless, incorrupt ■ OPPOSITE: flawed

impede VERB = **hinder**, stop, slow (down), check, bar, block, delay, hold up, brake, disrupt, curb, restrain, hamper, thwart, clog, obstruct, retard, encumber, cumber, throw a spanner in the works of (*Brit. informal*) ■ **OPPOSITE:** help

impediment NOUN = **obstacle**, barrier, check, bar, block, difficulty, hazard, curb, snag, obstruction, stumbling block, hindrance, encumbrance, fly in the ointment, millstone around your neck ■ **OPPOSITE:** aid

impel VERB = **force**, move, compel, drive, require, push, influence, urge, inspire, prompt, spur, stimulate, motivate, oblige, induce, prod, constrain, incite, instigate, goad, actuate ■ **OPPOSITE:** discourage

impending ADJECTIVE = **looming**, coming, approaching, near, nearing, threatening, forthcoming, brewing, imminent, hovering, upcoming, on the horizon, in the pipeline, in the offing

impenetrable ADJECTIVE **1** *The range forms an impenetrable barrier between Europe and Asia.* = **impassable**, solid, impervious, thick, dense, hermetic, impermeable, inviolable, unpierceable ■ **OPPOSITE:** passable **2** *His philosophical work is notoriously impenetrable.* = **incomprehensible**, obscure, baffling, dark, hidden, mysterious, enigmatic, arcane, inexplicable, unintelligible, inscrutable, unfathomable, indiscernible, cabbalistic, enigmatical ■ **OPPOSITE:** understandable

imperative ADJECTIVE = **urgent**, essential, pressing, vital, crucial (*informal*), compulsory, indispensable, obligatory, exigent ■ **OPPOSITE:** unnecessary

imperceptible ADJECTIVE = **undetectable**, slight, subtle, small, minute, fine, tiny, faint, invisible, gradual, shadowy, microscopic, indistinguishable, inaudible, infinitesimal, teeny-weeny, unnoticeable, insensible, impalpable (*formal*), indiscernible, teensy-weensy, inappreciable ■ **OPPOSITE:** perceptible

imperceptibly ADVERB = **invisibly**, slowly, subtly, little by little, unobtrusively, unseen, by a hair's-breadth, unnoticeably, indiscernibly, inappreciably

imperfect ADJECTIVE = **flawed**, impaired, faulty, broken, limited, damaged, partial, unfinished, incomplete, defective, patchy, immature, deficient, rudimentary, sketchy, undeveloped, inexact ■ **OPPOSITE:** perfect

imperfection NOUN **1** *Scanners locate imperfections in the cloth.* = **blemish**, fault, defect, flaw, stain **2** *He concedes that there are imperfections in the socialist system.* = **fault**, failing, weakness, defect, deficiency, flaw, shortcoming, inadequacy, frailty, foible,

weak point **3** *It is its imperfection that gives it its beauty.* = **incompleteness**, deficiency, inadequacy, frailty, insufficiency ■ **OPPOSITE:** perfection

imperial ADJECTIVE = **royal**, regal, kingly, queenly, princely, sovereign, majestic, monarchial, monarchal

imperil VERB = **endanger**, risk, hazard, jeopardize ■ **OPPOSITE:** protect

imperious ADJECTIVE = **domineering**, dictatorial, bossy (*informal*), haughty, lordly, commanding, arrogant, authoritative, autocratic, overbearing, tyrannical, magisterial, despotic, high-handed, overweening, tyrannous

impermanent ADJECTIVE = **temporary**, passing, brief, fleeting, elusive, mortal, short-lived, flying, fugitive, transient, momentary, ephemeral, transitory, perishable, fly-by-night (*informal*), evanescent, inconstant, fugacious, here today, gone tomorrow (*informal*)

impersonal ADJECTIVE **1** *a large impersonal orphanage* = **inhuman**, cold, remote, bureaucratic **2** *An executive announced the cuts in a curt and impersonal manner.* = **detached**, neutral, dispassionate, cold, formal, aloof, businesslike ■ **OPPOSITE:** intimate

impersonate VERB **1** *He was returned to prison for impersonating a police officer.* = **imitate**, pose as (*informal*), masquerade as, enact, ape, act out, pass yourself off as **2** *He was a brilliant mimic who could impersonate most of the staff.* = **mimic**, take off (*informal*), do (*informal*), ape, parody, caricature, do an impression of, personate

impersonation NOUN = **imitation**, impression, parody, caricature, takeoff (*informal*), mimicry

impertinent ADJECTIVE **1** *I don't like strangers who ask impertinent questions.* = **rude**, forward, cheeky (*informal*), saucy (*informal*), fresh (*informal*), bold, flip (*informal*), brazen, sassy (*U.S. informal*), pert, disrespectful, presumptuous, insolent, impolite, impudent, lippy (*U.S. & Canad. slang*), discourteous, uncivil, unmannerly ■ **OPPOSITE:** polite **2** *Since we already knew this, to tell us again seemed impertinent.* = **inappropriate**, irrelevant, incongruous, inapplicable ■ **OPPOSITE:** appropriate

imperturbable ADJECTIVE = **calm**, cool, collected, composed, complacent, serene, tranquil, sedate, undisturbed, unmoved, stoic, stoical, unfazed (*informal*), unflappable (*informal*), unruffled, self-possessed, nerveless, unexcitable, equanimous ■ **OPPOSITE:** agitated

impervious ADJECTIVE **1** *They are impervious to all suggestion of change.* = **unaffected**, immune, unmoved, closed, untouched, proof, invulnerable, unreceptive, unswayable **2** *The floorcovering will need to be impervious to water.* = **resistant**, sealed, impenetrable, invulnerable, impassable, hermetic, impermeable, imperviable

impetuous ADJECTIVE = **rash**, hasty, impulsive, violent, furious, fierce, eager, passionate, spontaneous, precipitate, ardent, impassioned, headlong, unplanned, unbridled, vehement, unrestrained, spur-of-the-moment, unthinking, unpremeditated, unreflecting ■ **OPPOSITE:** cautious

impetus NOUN **1** *She needed a new impetus for her talent.* = **incentive**, push, spur, motivation, impulse, stimulus, catalyst, goad, impulsion **2** *This decision will give renewed impetus to economic regeneration.* = **force**, power, energy, momentum

impinge VERB ● **impinge on** or **upon something** *If he were at home all the time he would impinge on my space.* = **invade**, violate, encroach on, trespass on, infringe on, make inroads on, obtrude on ● **impinge on** or **upon something** or **someone** *These cuts have impinged on the region's largest employers.* = **affect**, influence, relate to, impact on, touch, touch upon, have a bearing on, bear upon

impish ADJECTIVE = **mischievous**, devilish, roguish, rascally, elfin, puckish, waggish, sportive, prankish

implacable ADJECTIVE = **ruthless**, cruel, relentless, uncompromising, intractable, inflexible, unrelenting, merciless, unforgiving, inexorable, unyielding, remorseless, pitiless, unbending, unappeasable ■ **OPPOSITE:** merciful

implant VERB **1** *Doctors implanted an artificial heart into the 46-year-old man.* = **insert**, place, plant, fix, root, sow, graft, embed, ingraft **2** *His father had implanted in him an ambition to obtain an education.* = **instil**, sow, infuse, inculcate, infix

implausible ADJECTIVE = **improbable**, unlikely, weak, incredible, unbelievable, dubious, suspect, unreasonable, flimsy, unconvincing, far-fetched, cock-and-bull (*informal*)

implement VERB *The government promised to implement a new system to control loan institutions.* = **carry out**, effect, carry through, complete, apply, perform, realize, fulfil, enforce, execute, discharge, bring about, enact, put into action or effect ■ **OPPOSITE:** hinder ▶ NOUN

writing implements = **tool**, machine, device, instrument, appliance, apparatus, gadget, utensil, contraption (*informal*), contrivance, agent

implementation NOUN = **carrying out**, effecting, execution, performance, performing, discharge, enforcement, accomplishment, realization, fulfilment

implicate VERB *He didn't find anything in the notebooks to implicate her.* = **incriminate**, involve, compromise, embroil, entangle, inculpate (*formal*) ■ **OPPOSITE:** dissociate ● **implicate something** or **someone in something** *The lack of chromium is implicated in certain eye diseases.* = **involve in**, associate with, connect with, tie up with

implicated ADJECTIVE = **involved**, suspected, incriminated, under suspicion

implication NOUN **1** *The implication was obvious: vote for us or you'll be sorry.* = **suggestion**, hint, inference, meaning, conclusion, significance, presumption, overtone, innuendo, intimation, insinuation, signification **2** *Implication in a murder finally brought him to the gallows.* = **involvement**, association, connection, incrimination, entanglement **3** *He was acutely aware of the political implications of his decision.* = **consequence**, result, development, ramification, complication, upshot

implicit ADJECTIVE **1** *She wanted to make explicit in the film what was implicit in the play.* = **implied**, understood, suggested, hinted at, taken for granted, unspoken, inferred, tacit, undeclared, insinuated, unstated, unsaid, unexpressed ■ **OPPOSITE:** explicit **2** *Implicit in snobbery is a certain timidity.* = **inherent**, contained, underlying, intrinsic, latent, ingrained, inbuilt **3** *He had implicit faith in the noble intentions of the Emperor.* = **absolute**, full, complete, total, firm, fixed, entire, constant, utter, outright, consummate, unqualified, out-and-out, steadfast, wholehearted, unadulterated, unreserved, unshakable, unshaken, unhesitating

implicitly ADVERB = **absolutely**, completely, utterly, unconditionally, unreservedly, firmly, unhesitatingly, without reservation

implied ADJECTIVE = **suggested**, inherent, indirect, hinted at, implicit, unspoken, tacit, undeclared, insinuated, unstated, unexpressed

implore VERB = **beg**, beseech, entreat, conjure (*formal*), plead with, solicit, pray to, importune (*formal*), crave of, supplicate, go on bended knee to

imply VERB **1** *Are you implying that I had something to do with this?* = **suggest**, hint, insinuate, indicate, signal, intimate, signify, connote, give (someone) to understand **2** *The meeting in no way implies a resumption of contact with the terrorists.* = **involve**, mean, entail, include, require, indicate, import, point to, signify, denote, presuppose, betoken

impolite ADJECTIVE = **bad-mannered**, rude, disrespectful, rough, churlish, boorish, insolent, uncouth, unrefined, loutish, ungentlemanly, ungracious, discourteous, indelicate, uncivil, unladylike, indecorous, ungallant, ill-bred, unmannerly, ill-mannered ■ OPPOSITE: polite

import VERB *We spend much more on importing food than on selling abroad.* = **bring in**, buy in, ship in, land, introduce ▶ NOUN **1** *Such arguments are of little import.* = **significance**, concern, value, worth, weight, consequence, substance, moment, magnitude, usefulness, momentousness **2** *I have already spoken about the import of his speech.* = **meaning**, implication, significance, sense, message, bearing, intention, explanation, substance, drift, interpretation, thrust, purport, upshot, gist, signification

importance NOUN **1** *Safety is of paramount importance.* = **significance**, interest, concern, matter, moment, value, worth, weight, import (*formal*), consequence, substance, relevance, usefulness, momentousness **2** *He was too puffed up with his own importance to accept the verdict.* = **prestige**, standing, status, rule, authority, influence, distinction, esteem, prominence, supremacy, mastery, dominion, eminence, ascendancy, pre-eminence, mana (*N.Z.*)

important ADJECTIVE **1** *an important economic challenge to the government* = **significant**, critical, substantial, grave, urgent, serious, material, signal, primary, meaningful, far-reaching, momentous, seminal, weighty, of substance, salient, noteworthy ■ OPPOSITE: unimportant **2** (*often with* **to**) *Her sons are the most important thing in her life.* = **valued**, loved, prized, dear, essential, valuable, of interest, treasured, precious, esteemed, cherished, of concern, highly regarded **3** *an important figure in the media world* = **powerful**, leading, prominent, commanding, supreme, outstanding, high-level, dominant, influential, notable, big-time (*informal*), foremost, eminent, high-ranking, authoritative, major league (*informal*), of note, noteworthy, pre-eminent, skookum (*Canad.*)

impose VERB • **impose on someone** *I was afraid you'd think we were imposing on you.* = **intrude on**, exploit, take advantage of, use, trouble, abuse, bother, encroach on, horn in (*informal*), trespass on, gate-crash (*informal*), take liberties with, butt in on, presume upon, force yourself on, obtrude on • **impose something on** *or* **upon someone 1** *They impose fines on airlines who bring in illegal immigrants.* = **levy**, apply, introduce, put, place, set, charge, establish, lay, fix, institute, exact, decree, ordain (*formal*) **2** *Beware of imposing your own tastes on your children.* = **inflict**, force, enforce, visit, press, apply, thrust, dictate, saddle (someone) with, foist

imposing ADJECTIVE = **impressive**, striking, grand, august, powerful, effective, commanding, awesome, majestic, dignified, stately, forcible ■ OPPOSITE: unimposing

imposition NOUN **1** *the imposition of VAT on fuel bills* = **application**, introduction, levying, decree, laying on **2** *I know this is an imposition, but please hear me out.* = **intrusion**, liberty, presumption, cheek (*informal*), encroachment **3** *The American colonists rebelled over taxes and commercial impositions.* = **charge**, tax, duty, burden, levy

impossibility NOUN = **hopelessness**, inability, impracticability, inconceivability

impossible ADJECTIVE **1** *It was impossible to get in because no one knew the password.* = **not possible**, out of the question, impracticable, unfeasible, beyond the bounds of possibility **2** *You shouldn't promise what's impossible.* = **unachievable**, hopeless, out of the question, vain, unthinkable, inconceivable, far-fetched, unworkable, implausible, unattainable, unobtainable, beyond you, not to be thought of ■ OPPOSITE: possible **3** *The Government was now in an impossible situation.* = **absurd**, crazy (*informal*), ridiculous, unacceptable, outrageous, ludicrous, unreasonable, unsuitable, intolerable, preposterous, laughable, farcical, illogical, insoluble, unanswerable, inadmissible, ungovernable

impostor NOUN = **fraud** (*informal*), cheat, fake, impersonator, rogue, deceiver, sham, pretender, hypocrite, charlatan, quack, trickster, knave (*archaic*), phoney *or* phony (*informal*)

impotence NOUN = **powerlessness**, inability, helplessness, weakness, incompetence, inadequacy, paralysis, inefficiency, frailty, incapacity, infirmity, ineffectiveness, uselessness, feebleness, enervation, inefficacy ■ OPPOSITE: powerfulness

impotent ADJECTIVE = **powerless**, weak, helpless, unable, incapable, paralysed, frail, incompetent, ineffective, feeble, incapacitated, infirm, nerveless, enervated ■ **OPPOSITE:** powerful

impoverish VERB **1** *a society impoverished by wartime inflation* = **bankrupt**, ruin, beggar, break, pauperize **2** *Mint impoverishes the soil quickly.* = **deplete**, drain, exhaust, diminish, use up, sap, wear out, reduce

impoverished ADJECTIVE **1** *The goal is to lure businesses into impoverished areas.* = **poor**, needy, destitute, ruined, distressed, bankrupt, poverty-stricken, indigent (*formal*), impecunious, straitened, penurious, necessitous (*literary*), in reduced or straitened circumstances ■ **OPPOSITE:** rich **2** *Against the impoverished defence, he poached an early goal.* = **depleted**, spent, reduced, empty, drained, exhausted, played out, worn out, denuded

impracticable ADJECTIVE = **unfeasible**, impossible, out of the question, unworkable, unattainable, unachievable ■ **OPPOSITE:** practicable

impractical ADJECTIVE **1** *With regularly scheduled airlines, sea travel became impractical.* = **unworkable**, impracticable, unrealistic, inoperable, impossible, unserviceable, nonviable ■ **OPPOSITE:** practical **2** *He's full of wacky, weird and impractical ideas.* = **idealistic**, wild, romantic, unrealistic, visionary, unbusinesslike, starry-eyed ■ **OPPOSITE:** realistic

imprecise ADJECTIVE = **indefinite**, estimated, rough, vague, loose, careless, ambiguous, inaccurate, sloppy (*informal*), woolly, hazy, indeterminate, wide of the mark, equivocal, ill-defined, inexact, inexplicit, blurred round the edges ■ **OPPOSITE:** precise

impregnable ADJECTIVE = **invulnerable**, strong, secure, unbeatable, invincible, impenetrable, unassailable, indestructible, immovable, unshakable, unconquerable ■ **OPPOSITE:** vulnerable

impregnate VERB **1** *plastic impregnated with a light-absorbing dye* = **saturate**, soak, steep, fill, seep, pervade, infuse, permeate, imbue, suffuse, percolate, imbrue (*rare*) **2** *women impregnated by artificial insemination* = **inseminate**, fertilize, make pregnant, fructify, fecundate, get with child

impress VERB *What impressed him most was their speed.* = **excite**, move, strike, touch, affect, influence, inspire, grab (*informal*), amaze, overcome, stir, overwhelm, astonish, dazzle, sway, awe, overawe, make an impression on (*slang, chiefly U.S.*)

• **impress something on** or **upon someone** *I've impressed on them the need for professionalism.* = **stress**, bring home to, instil in, drum into, knock into, emphasize to, fix in, inculcate in, ingrain in

impression NOUN **1** *My impression is that they are totally out of control.* = **idea**, feeling, thought, sense, opinion, view, assessment, judgment, reaction, belief, concept, fancy, notion, conviction, suspicion, hunch, apprehension, inkling, funny feeling (*informal*) **2** *She gave no sign that his charm had made any impression on her.* = **effect**, influence, impact, sway **3** *He amused us doing impressions of film actors.* = **imitation**, parody, impersonation, mockery, send-up (*Brit. informal*), takeoff (*informal*) **4** *the world's oldest fossil impressions of plant life* = **mark**, imprint, stamp, stamping, depression, outline, hollow, dent, impress, indentation • **make an impression** *He's certainly made an impression on the interviewing board.* = **cause a stir**, stand out, make an impact, be conspicuous, find favour, make a hit (*informal*), arouse comment, excite notice

impressionable ADJECTIVE = **suggestible**, vulnerable, susceptible, open, sensitive, responsive, receptive, gullible, ingenuous ■ **OPPOSITE:** blasé

impressive ADJECTIVE = **grand**, striking, splendid, good, great (*informal*), fine, affecting, powerful, exciting, wonderful, excellent, dramatic, outstanding, stirring, superb, first-class, marvellous (*informal*), terrific (*informal*), awesome, world-class, admirable, first-rate, crash-hot (*Austral.*), forcible ■ **OPPOSITE:** unimpressive

imprint NOUN *the imprint of his little finger* = **mark**, print, impression, stamp, indentation ▶ VERB *a racket with the club's badge imprinted on the strings* = **engrave**, print, stamp, impress, etch, emboss

imprison VERB = **jail**, confine, detain, lock up, constrain, put away, intern, incarcerate, send down (*informal*), send to prison, impound, put under lock and key, immure (*archaic*) ■ **OPPOSITE:** free

imprisoned ADJECTIVE = **jailed**, confined, locked up, inside (*slang*), in jail, captive, behind bars, put away, interned, incarcerated, in irons, under lock and key, immured

imprisonment NOUN = **confinement**, custody, detention, captivity, incarceration, internment, duress

improbable ADJECTIVE **1** *It seems improbable that this year's figure will show a drop.* = **doubtful**, unlikely, uncertain, unbelievable, dubious, questionable, fanciful, far-fetched, implausible ■ **OPPOSITE:** probable **2** *Their marriage seems an improbable alliance.* = **unconvincing**, weak, unbelievable, preposterous ■ **OPPOSITE:** convincing

impromptu ADJECTIVE = **spontaneous**, improvised, unprepared, off-the-cuff (*informal*), offhand, ad-lib, unscripted, unrehearsed, unpremeditated, extempore, unstudied, extemporaneous, extemporized ■ **OPPOSITE:** rehearsed

improper ADJECTIVE **1** *I maintain that I have done nothing improper.* = **inappropriate**, unfit, unsuitable, out of place, unwarranted, incongruous, unsuited, ill-timed, uncalled-for, inopportune, inapplicable, unseasonable, inapt, infelicitous, inapposite, malapropos ■ **OPPOSITE:** appropriate **2** *Glover denied any improper behaviour with his wife's sister.* = **indecent**, vulgar, suggestive, unseemly, untoward, risqué, smutty, unbecoming, unfitting, impolite, off-colour, indelicate, indecorous ■ **OPPOSITE:** decent **3** *The improper use of medicine can lead to severe adverse reactions.* = **incorrect**, wrong, inaccurate, false, irregular, erroneous

impropriety NOUN **1** *She proudly recoiled from any suggestion of impropriety.* = **indecency**, vulgarity, immodesty, bad taste, incongruity, unsuitability, indecorum ■ **OPPOSITE:** propriety **2** *He resigned amid allegations of financial impropriety.* = **lapse**, mistake, slip, blunder, gaffe, bloomer (*Brit. informal*), faux pas, solecism, gaucherie

improve VERB **1** *He improved their house.* = **enhance**, better, add to, upgrade, amend, mend, augment, embellish, touch up, ameliorate, polish up ■ **OPPOSITE:** worsen **2** *The weather is beginning to improve.* = **get better**, pick up, look up (*informal*), develop, advance, perk up, take a turn for the better (*informal*) **3** *She had improved so much the doctor cut her dosage.* = **recuperate**, recover, rally, mend, make progress, turn the corner, gain ground, gain strength, convalesce, be on the mend, grow better, make strides, take on a new lease of life (*informal*)

improvement NOUN **1** *the dramatic improvements in conditions* = **enhancement**, increase, gain, boost, amendment, correction, heightening, advancement, enrichment, face-lift, embellishment, betterment, rectification, augmentation, amelioration **2** *The system we've just introduced has been a great improvement.* = **advance**, development, progress,

recovery, reformation, upswing, furtherance

improvisation NOUN **1** *Funds were not abundant, and clever improvisation was necessary.* = **invention**, spontaneity, ad-libbing, extemporizing **2** *an improvisation on 'Jingle Bells'* = **ad-lib**

improvise VERB **1** *If you don't have a wok, improvise one.* = **devise**, contrive, make do, concoct, throw together **2** *Take the story and improvise on it.* = **ad-lib**, invent, vamp, busk, wing it (*informal*), play it by ear (*informal*), extemporize, speak off the cuff (*informal*)

improvised ADJECTIVE = **unprepared**, spontaneous, makeshift, spur-of-the-moment, off-the-cuff (*informal*), ad-lib, unrehearsed, extempore, extemporaneous, extemporized

imprudent ADJECTIVE = **unwise**, foolish, rash, irresponsible, reckless, careless, ill-advised, foolhardy, indiscreet, unthinking, ill-judged, ill-considered, inconsiderate, heedless, injudicious, incautious, improvident, impolitic, overhasty, temerarious ■ **OPPOSITE:** prudent

impudence NOUN = **boldness**, nerve (*informal*), cheek (*informal*), face (*informal*), front, neck (*informal*), gall (*informal*), lip (*slang*), presumption, audacity, rudeness, chutzpah (*U.S. & Canad. informal*), insolence, impertinence, effrontery, brass neck (*Brit. informal*), shamelessness, sauciness, brazenness, sassiness (*U.S. informal*), pertness, bumptiousness

impudent ADJECTIVE = **bold**, rude, cheeky (*informal*), forward, fresh (*informal*), saucy (*informal*), cocky (*informal*), audacious, brazen, shameless, sassy (*U.S. informal*), pert, presumptuous, impertinent, insolent, lippy (*U.S. & Canad. slang*), bumptious, immodest, bold-faced ■ **OPPOSITE:** polite

impulse NOUN **1** *I resisted an impulse to smile.* = **urge**, longing, desire, drive, wish, fancy, notion, yen (*informal*), instinct, yearning, inclination, itch, whim, compulsion, caprice **2** *Their impulse of broadcasting was for human rights.* = **force**, pressure, push, movement, surge, motive, thrust, momentum, stimulus, catalyst, impetus • **on impulse** *After lunch she decided, on impulse, to take a bath.* = **impulsively**, of your own accord, freely, voluntarily, instinctively, impromptu, off the cuff (*informal*), in the heat of the moment, off your own bat, quite unprompted

impulsive ADJECTIVE = **instinctive**, emotional, unpredictable, quick, passionate, rash, spontaneous, precipitate, intuitive, hasty, headlong, impetuous, devil-may-care, unconsidered, unpremeditated ■ **OPPOSITE:** cautious

impunity NOUN = **immunity**, freedom, licence, permission, liberty, security, exemption, dispensation, nonliability

impure ADJECTIVE **1** *impure diamonds* = **unrefined**, mixed, alloyed, debased, adulterated, admixed **2** *They say such behaviour might lead to impure temptations.* = **immoral**, corrupt, obscene, indecent, gross, coarse, lewd, carnal, X-rated (*informal*), salacious, unclean, prurient, lascivious, smutty, lustful, ribald, immodest, licentious, indelicate, unchaste ■ **OPPOSITE:** moral **3** *They were warned against drinking the impure water from the stream.* = **unclean**, dirty, foul, infected, contaminated, polluted, filthy, tainted, sullied, defiled, unwholesome, vitiated, festy (*Austral. slang*) ■ **OPPOSITE:** clean

impurity NOUN **1** (*often plural*) *The air is filtered to remove impurities.* = **dirt**, pollutant, scum, grime, contaminant, dross, bits, foreign body, foreign matter **2** *The soap is boiled to remove all traces of impurity.* = **contamination**, infection, pollution, taint, filth, foulness, defilement, dirtiness, uncleanness, befoulment **3** *impurity, lust and evil desires* = **immorality**, corruption, obscenity, indecency, vulgarity, prurience, coarseness, licentiousness, immodesty, carnality, lewdness, grossness, salaciousness, lasciviousness, unchastity, smuttiness

impute VERB = **attribute**, assign, ascribe, credit, refer, accredit

inaccessible ADJECTIVE = **out-of-reach**, remote, out-of-the-way, unattainable, impassable, unreachable, unapproachable, un-get-at-able (*informal*) ■ **OPPOSITE:** accessible

inaccuracy NOUN **1** *He was disturbed by the inaccuracy of the answers.* = **imprecision**, unreliability, incorrectness, unfaithfulness, erroneousness, inexactness **2** *Guard against inaccuracies by checking with a variety of sources.* = **error**, mistake, slip, fault, defect, blunder, lapse, boob (*Brit. slang*), literal (*Printing*), howler (*informal*), miscalculation, typo (*informal, Printing*), erratum, corrigendum, barry *or* Barry Crocker (*Austral. slang*)

inaccurate ADJECTIVE = **incorrect**, wrong, mistaken, wild, faulty, careless, unreliable, defective, unfaithful, erroneous, unsound, imprecise, wide of the mark, out, inexact, off-base (*U.S. & Canad. informal*), off-beam (*informal*), discrepant, way off-beam (*informal*) ■ **OPPOSITE:** accurate

inaction NOUN = **inactivity**, inertia, idleness, immobility, torpor, dormancy, torpidity

inactive ADJECTIVE **1** *The satellite has been inactive since its launch two years ago.* = **unused**, idle, dormant, latent, inert, immobile, mothballed, out-of-service, inoperative, abeyant ■ **OPPOSITE:** used **2** *He has been inactive since last year.* = **idle**, unemployed, out of work, jobless, unoccupied, kicking your heels ■ **OPPOSITE:** employed **3** *They certainly were not politically inactive.* = **lazy**, passive, slow, quiet, dull, low-key (*informal*), sluggish, lethargic, sedentary, indolent, somnolent, torpid, slothful (*formal*) ■ **OPPOSITE:** active

inactivity NOUN = **immobility**, unemployment, inaction, passivity, hibernation, dormancy ■ **OPPOSITE:** mobility

inadequacy NOUN **1** *the inadequacy of the water supply* = **shortage**, poverty, dearth, paucity (*formal*), insufficiency, incompleteness, meagreness, skimpiness, scantiness, inadequateness **2** *a deep-seated sense of inadequacy* = **incompetence**, inability, deficiency, incapacity, ineffectiveness, incompetency, unfitness, inefficacy, defectiveness, inaptness, faultiness, unsuitableness **3** *We all make an effort to ignore our own inadequacies.* = **shortcoming**, failing, lack, weakness, shortage, defect, imperfection

inadequate ADJECTIVE **1** *Supplies of food and medicine are inadequate.* = **insufficient**, short, scarce, meagre, poor, lacking, incomplete, scant, sparse, skimpy, sketchy, insubstantial, scanty, niggardly, incommensurate ■ **OPPOSITE:** adequate **2** *She felt quite painfully inadequate in the crisis.* = **incapable**, incompetent, pathetic, faulty, unfitted, defective, unequal, deficient, imperfect, unqualified, not up to scratch (*informal*), inapt ■ **OPPOSITE:** capable

inadequately ADVERB = **insufficiently**, poorly, thinly, sparsely, scantily, imperfectly, sketchily, skimpily, meagrely

inadvertent ADJECTIVE = **unintentional**, accidental, unintended, chance, careless, negligent, unwitting, unplanned, thoughtless, unthinking, heedless, unpremeditated, unheeding

inadvertently ADVERB = **unintentionally**, accidentally, by accident, mistakenly, unwittingly, by mistake, involuntarily ■ **OPPOSITE:** deliberately

inalienable ADJECTIVE = **sacrosanct**, absolute, unassailable, inherent, entailed (*Law*), non-negotiable, inviolable, nontransferable, untransferable

inane ADJECTIVE = **senseless**, stupid, silly, empty, daft (*informal*), worthless, futile, trifling, frivolous, mindless, goofy (*informal*), idiotic, vacuous, fatuous, puerile, vapid, unintelligent, asinine, devoid of intelligence ■ **OPPOSITE:** sensible

inanimate ADJECTIVE = **lifeless**, inert, dead, cold, extinct, defunct, inactive, soulless, quiescent, spiritless, insensate, insentient ■ **OPPOSITE:** animate

inaugural ADJECTIVE = **first**, opening, initial, maiden, introductory, dedicatory

inaugurate VERB 1 *The new president will be inaugurated on January 20.* = **invest**, install, induct, instate 2 *A new centre for research was inaugurated today.* = **open**, commission, dedicate, ordain 3 *They inaugurated the first ever scheduled flights.* = **launch**, begin, introduce, institute, set up, kick off (*informal*), initiate, originate, commence, get under way, usher in, set in motion

inauguration NOUN 1 *the inauguration of the new Governor* = **investiture**, installation, induction 2 *They later attended the inauguration of the University.* = **opening**, launch, birth, inception, commencement 3 *the inauguration of monetary union* = **launch**, launching, setting up, institution, initiation

inborn ADJECTIVE = **natural**, inherited, inherent, hereditary, instinctive, innate, intuitive, ingrained, congenital, inbred, native, immanent, in your blood, connate

inbred ADJECTIVE = **innate**, natural, constitutional, native, ingrained, inherent, deep-seated, immanent

inbuilt ADJECTIVE = **integral**, built-in, incorporated, component

incalculable ADJECTIVE = **vast**, enormous, immense, countless, infinite, innumerable, untold, limitless, boundless, inestimable, numberless, uncountable, measureless, without number, incomputable

incandescent ADJECTIVE = **glowing**, brilliant, shining, red-hot, radiant, luminous, white-hot, Day-Glo, phosphorescent

incantation NOUN = **chant**, spell, charm, formula, invocation, hex (*U.S. & Canad. informal*), abracadabra, conjuration

incapacitate VERB = **immobilize**, paralyse, prostrate, put someone out of action (*informal*), lay someone up (*informal*)

incapacitated ADJECTIVE = **immobilized**, unfit, out of action (*informal*), laid up (*informal*), indisposed, hors de combat (*French*)

incapacity NOUN = **inability**, inadequacy, powerlessness, ineffectiveness, feebleness, incompetency, unfitness, incapability

incapsulate *see* **encapsulate**

incarcerate VERB = **imprison**, confine, detain, lock up, restrict, restrain, intern, send down (*Brit.*), impound, coop up, throw in jail, put under lock and key, immure (*archaic*), jail *or* gaol

incarceration NOUN = **confinement**, restraint, imprisonment, detention, captivity, bondage, internment

incarnate ADJECTIVE 1 *He referred to her as evil incarnate.* = **personified**, embodied, typified 2 *Why should God become incarnate as a male?* = **made flesh**, in the flesh, in human form, in bodily form

incarnation NOUN = **embodiment**, manifestation, epitome, type, impersonation, personification, avatar, exemplification, bodily form

incendiary ADJECTIVE = **inflammatory**, provocative, subversive, seditious, rabble-rousing, dissentious

incense¹ NOUN *an atmospheric place, pungent with incense* = **perfume**, scent, fragrance, bouquet, aroma, balm, redolence

incense² VERB *This proposal will incense conservation campaigners.* = **anger**, infuriate, enrage, excite, provoke, irritate, gall, madden, inflame, exasperate, rile (*informal*), raise the hackles of, nark (*Brit., Austral. & N.Z. slang*), make your blood boil (*informal*), rub you up the wrong way, make your hackles rise, get your hackles up, make you see red (*informal*)

incensed ADJECTIVE = **angry**, mad (*informal*), furious, cross, fuming, choked, infuriated, enraged, maddened, exasperated, indignant, irate, up in arms, incandescent, steamed up (*slang*), hot under the collar (*informal*), on the warpath (*informal*), wrathful, ireful (*literary*), tooshie (*Austral. slang*), off the air (*Austral. slang*)

incentive NOUN = **inducement**, motive, encouragement, urge, come-on (*informal*), spur, lure, bait, motivation, carrot (*informal*), impulse, stimulus, impetus, stimulant, goad, incitement, enticement ■ **OPPOSITE:** disincentive

inception NOUN = **beginning**, start, rise, birth, origin, dawn (*literary*), outset, initiation, inauguration, commencement, kickoff (*informal*) ■ **OPPOSITE:** end

incessant ADJECTIVE = **constant**, endless, continuous, persistent, eternal, relentless, perpetual, continual, unbroken, never-ending, interminable, unrelenting, everlasting, unending, ceaseless, unremitting, nonstop, unceasing ■ **OPPOSITE:** intermittent

incessantly ADVERB = **all the time**, constantly, continually, endlessly, persistently, eternally, perpetually, nonstop, ceaselessly, without a break, interminably, everlastingly

incidence NOUN = **prevalence**, frequency, occurrence, rate, amount, degree, extent

incident NOUN **1** *Safety chiefs are investigating the incident.* = **disturbance**, scene, clash, disorder, confrontation, brawl, uproar, skirmish, mishap, fracas, commotion, contretemps **2** *They have not based it on any incident from the past.* = **happening**, event, affair, business, fact, matter, occasion, circumstance, episode, occurrence, escapade **3** *The birth was not without incident.* = **adventure**, drama, excitement, crisis, spectacle, theatrics

incidental ADJECTIVE **1** *The playing of music proved to be incidental to the main business.* = **secondary**, subsidiary, subordinate, minor, occasional, ancillary, nonessential ■ OPPOSITE: essential **2** *At the bottom of the bill were various incidental expenses.* = **accompanying**, related, attendant, contingent, contributory, concomitant

incidentally ADVERB **1** *The tower, incidentally, dates from the twelfth century.* = **by the way**, in passing, en passant, parenthetically, by the bye **2** *In her denunciation, she incidentally shed some light on another mystery.* = **accidentally**, casually, by chance, coincidentally, fortuitously, by happenstance

incinerate VERB **1** *The government is trying to stop them incinerating their own waste.* = **burn up**, carbonize **2** *Some of the victims were incinerated.* = **cremate**, burn up, reduce to ashes, consume by fire

incipient ADJECTIVE = **beginning**, starting, developing, originating, commencing, embryonic, nascent, inchoate, inceptive

incision NOUN = **cut**, opening, slash, notch, slit, gash

incisive ADJECTIVE = **penetrating**, sharp, keen, acute, piercing, trenchant, perspicacious (*formal*) ■ OPPOSITE: dull

incite VERB = **provoke**, encourage, drive, excite, prompt, urge, spur, stimulate, set on, animate, rouse, prod, stir up, inflame, instigate, whip up, egg on, goad, impel, foment, put up to, agitate for or against ■ OPPOSITE: discourage

incitement NOUN = **provocation**, prompting, encouragement, spur, motive, motivation, impulse, stimulus, impetus, agitation, inducement, goad, instigation, clarion call

inclination NOUN **1** *He had neither the time nor the inclination to think about it.* = **desire**, longing, wish, need, aspiration, craving, yearning, hankering **2** *She set out to follow her artistic inclinations.* = **tendency**, liking, taste, turn, fancy, leaning, bent, stomach, prejudice, bias, affection, thirst, disposition, penchant, fondness, propensity, aptitude, predisposition, predilection, proclivity (*formal*), partiality, turn of mind, proneness ■ OPPOSITE: aversion **3** *a polite inclination of the head* = **bow**, bending, nod, bowing

incline VERB **1** *the factors which incline us towards particular beliefs* = **predispose**, influence, tend, persuade, prejudice, bias, sway, turn, dispose **2** *He inclined his head very slightly.* = **bend**, lower, nod, bow, stoop, nutate (*rare*) ▶ NOUN *I came to a halt at the edge of a steep incline.* = **slope**, rise, dip, grade, descent, ramp, ascent, gradient, declivity, acclivity

inclined ADJECTIVE **1** *She was inclined to self-pity.* = **disposed**, given, prone, likely, subject, liable, apt, predisposed, tending towards **2** *I am inclined to agree with Alan.* = **willing**, minded, ready, disposed, of a mind (*informal*)

inclose *see* **enclose**

include VERB **1** *The trip was extended to include a few other events.* = **contain**, involve, incorporate, cover, consist of, take in, embrace, comprise, take into account, embody, encompass, comprehend, subsume ■ OPPOSITE: exclude **2** *I had worked hard to be included in a project like this.* = **count**, introduce, make a part of, number among **3** *You should include details of all your benefits.* = **add**, enter, put in, insert

including PREPOSITION = **containing**, with, counting, plus, together with, as well as, inclusive of

inclusion NOUN = **addition**, incorporation, introduction, insertion ■ OPPOSITE: exclusion

inclusive ADJECTIVE = **comprehensive**, full, overall, general, global, sweeping, all-in, blanket, umbrella, across-the-board, all-together, catch-all, all-embracing, overarching, in toto (*Latin*) ■ OPPOSITE: limited

incognito ADJECTIVE = **in disguise**, unknown, disguised, unrecognized, under an assumed name

incoherent ADJECTIVE = **unintelligible**, wild, confused, disordered, wandering, muddled, rambling, inconsistent, jumbled, stammering, disconnected, stuttering, unconnected, disjointed, inarticulate, uncoordinated ■ OPPOSITE: coherent

income NOUN = **revenue**, gains, earnings, means, pay, interest, returns, profits, wages, rewards, yield, proceeds, salary, receipts, takings

incoming ADJECTIVE **1** *The airport was closed to incoming flights.* = **arriving**, landing, approaching, entering, returning, homeward ■ **OPPOSITE:** departing **2** *the problems confronting the incoming government* = **new**, next, succeeding, elected, elect

incomparable ADJECTIVE = **unequalled**, supreme, unparalleled, paramount, superlative, transcendent, unrivalled, inimitable, unmatched, peerless, matchless, beyond compare

incompatibility NOUN = **inconsistency**, conflict, discrepancy, antagonism, incongruity, irreconcilability, disparateness, uncongeniality

incompatible ADJECTIVE = **inconsistent**, conflicting, contradictory, unsuitable, disparate, incongruous, discordant, antagonistic, irreconcilable, unsuited, mismatched, discrepant, uncongenial, antipathetic, ill-assorted, inconsonant ■ **OPPOSITE:** compatible

incompetence NOUN = **ineptitude**, inability, inadequacy, incapacity, ineffectiveness, uselessness, insufficiency, ineptness, incompetency, unfitness, incapability, skill-lessness

incompetent ADJECTIVE = **inept**, useless (*informal*), incapable, unable, cowboy (*informal*), floundering, bungling, unfit, unfitted, ineffectual, incapacitated, inexpert, skill-less, unskilful ■ **OPPOSITE:** competent

incomplete ADJECTIVE = **unfinished**, partial, insufficient, wanting, short, lacking, undone, defective, deficient, imperfect, undeveloped, fragmentary, unaccomplished, unexecuted, half-pie (*N.Z. informal*) ■ **OPPOSITE:** complete

incomprehensible ADJECTIVE **1** *Her speech was almost incomprehensible.* = **unintelligible** ■ **OPPOSITE:** comprehensible **2** *incomprehensible mathematics puzzles* = **obscure**, puzzling, mysterious, baffling, enigmatic, perplexing, opaque, impenetrable, inscrutable, unfathomable, above your head, beyond comprehension, all Greek to you (*informal*), beyond your grasp ■ **OPPOSITE:** understandable

inconceivable ADJECTIVE = **unimaginable**, impossible, incredible, staggering (*informal*), unbelievable, unthinkable, out of the question, incomprehensible, unheard-of, mind-boggling (*informal*), beyond belief, unknowable, not to be thought of

■ **OPPOSITE:** conceivable

inconclusive ADJECTIVE = **uncertain**, vague, ambiguous, open, indecisive, unsettled, undecided, unconvincing, up in the air (*informal*), indeterminate

incongruity NOUN = **inappropriateness**, discrepancy, inconsistency, disparity, incompatibility, unsuitability, inaptness, inharmoniousness

incongruous ADJECTIVE = **inappropriate**, absurd, out of place, conflicting, contrary, contradictory, inconsistent, unsuitable, improper, incompatible, discordant, incoherent, extraneous, unsuited, unbecoming, out of keeping, inapt, disconsonant, paradoxical, ironic ■ **OPPOSITE:** appropriate

inconsequential ADJECTIVE = **unimportant**, trivial, insignificant, minor, petty, trifling, negligible, paltry, immaterial, measly (*informal*), inconsiderable, nickel-and-dime (*U.S. slang*), of no significance

inconsiderable ADJECTIVE = **insignificant**, small, slight, light, minor, petty, trivial, trifling, negligible, unimportant, small-time (*informal*), inconsequential, exiguous

inconsiderate ADJECTIVE = **selfish**, rude, insensitive, self-centred, careless, unkind, intolerant, thoughtless, unthinking, tactless, uncharitable, ungracious, indelicate ■ **OPPOSITE:** considerate

inconsistency NOUN **1** *Her worst fault was her inconsistency.* = **unreliability**, instability, unpredictability, fickleness, unsteadiness **2** *the alleged inconsistencies in her evidence* = **incompatibility**, paradox, discrepancy, disparity, disagreement, variance, divergence, incongruity, contrariety, inconsonance

inconsistent ADJECTIVE **1** *You are inconsistent and unpredictable.* = **changeable**, variable, unpredictable, unstable, irregular, erratic, uneven, fickle, capricious, unsteady, inconstant ■ **OPPOSITE:** consistent **2** *The outburst was inconsistent with the image he had cultivated.* = **incompatible**, conflicting, contrary, at odds, contradictory, in conflict, incongruous, discordant, incoherent, out of step, irreconcilable, at variance, discrepant, inconstant ■ **OPPOSITE:** compatible

inconsolable ADJECTIVE = **heartbroken**, devastated, despairing, desolate, wretched, heartsick, brokenhearted, sick at heart, prostrate with grief

inconspicuous ADJECTIVE **1** *I'll try to be as inconspicuous as possible.* = **unobtrusive**, hidden, unnoticeable, retiring, quiet, ordinary, plain, muted, camouflaged, insignificant, unassuming, unostentatious ■ **OPPOSITE:** noticeable **2** *The studio is an inconspicuous grey building.* = **plain**, ordinary, modest, unobtrusive, unnoticeable

incontrovertible ADJECTIVE
= **indisputable**, sure, certain, established, positive, undeniable, irrefutable, unquestionable, unshakable, beyond dispute, incontestable, indubitable, nailed-on (*slang*)

inconvenience NOUN **1** *We apologize for any inconvenience caused during the repairs.* = **trouble**, difficulty, bother, upset, fuss, disadvantage, disturbance, disruption, drawback, hassle (*informal*), nuisance, downside, annoyance, hindrance, awkwardness, vexation, uphill (*S. African*) **2** *You can change gear without the inconvenience of a clutch pedal.* = **awkwardness**, unfitness, unwieldiness, cumbersomeness, unhandiness, unsuitableness, untimeliness ► VERB *He promised not to inconvenience them any further.* = **trouble**, bother, disturb, upset, disrupt, put out, hassle (*informal*), irk, discommode, give (someone) bother or trouble, make (someone) go out of their way, put to trouble

inconvenient ADJECTIVE **1** *It's very inconvenient to have to wait so long.* = **troublesome**, annoying, awkward, embarrassing, disturbing, unsuitable, tiresome, untimely, bothersome, vexatious, inopportune, disadvantageous, unseasonable ■ **OPPOSITE:** convenient **2** *This must be the most inconvenient house ever built.* = **difficult**, awkward, unmanageable, cumbersome, unwieldy, unhandy

incorporate VERB **1** *The new cars will incorporate a number of major improvements.* = **include**, contain, take in, embrace, integrate, embody, encompass, assimilate, comprise of **2** *The agreement allowed the rebels to be incorporated into the police force.* = **integrate**, include, absorb, unite, merge, accommodate, knit, fuse, assimilate, amalgamate, subsume, coalesce, harmonize, meld **3** *Gradually incorporate the olive oil into the dough.* = **blend**, mix, combine, compound, consolidate, fuse, mingle, meld

incorporation NOUN = **merger**, federation, blend, integration, unifying, inclusion, fusion, absorption, assimilation, amalgamation, coalescence

incorrect ADJECTIVE = **false**, wrong, mistaken, flawed, faulty, unfitting, inaccurate, untrue, improper, erroneous, out, wide of the mark (*informal*), specious,

inexact, off-base (*U.S. & Canad. informal*), off-beam (*informal*), way off-beam (*informal*) ■ **OPPOSITE:** correct

incorrigible ADJECTIVE = **incurable**, hardened, hopeless, intractable, inveterate, unreformed, irredeemable

increase VERB **1** *The company has increased the price of its cars.* = **raise**, extend, boost, expand, develop, advance, add to, strengthen, enhance, step up (*informal*), widen, prolong, intensify, heighten, elevate, enlarge, multiply, inflate, magnify, amplify, augment, aggrandize, upscale ■ **OPPOSITE:** decrease **2** *The population continues to increase.* = **grow**, develop, spread, mount, expand, build up, swell, wax, enlarge, escalate, multiply, fill out, get bigger, proliferate, snowball, dilate ■ **OPPOSITE:** shrink ► NOUN *a sharp increase in productivity* = **growth**, rise, boost, development, gain, addition, expansion, extension, heightening, proliferation, enlargement, escalation, upsurge, upturn, increment, bounce, intensification, step-up (*informal*), augmentation, aggrandizement • **on the increase** *Crime is on the increase.* = **growing**, increasing, spreading, expanding, escalating, multiplying, developing, on the rise, proliferating

increasingly ADVERB = **progressively**, more and more, to an increasing extent, continuously more

incredible ADJECTIVE **1** *Thanks, I had an incredible time.* = **amazing**, great (*informal*), wonderful, brilliant, stunning (*informal*), extraordinary, overwhelming, ace (*informal*), astonishing, staggering, marvellous, sensational (*informal*), mega (*slang*), breathtaking, astounding, far-out (*slang*), eye-popping (*informal*), prodigious, awe-inspiring, superhuman, rad (*informal*) **2** *Do not dismiss as incredible the stories your children tell you.* = **unbelievable**, impossible, absurd, unthinkable, questionable, improbable, inconceivable, preposterous, unconvincing, unimaginable, outlandish, far-fetched, implausible, beyond belief, cock-and-bull (*informal*), not able to hold water

incredulity NOUN = **disbelief**, doubt, scepticism, distrust, unbelief

incredulous ADJECTIVE = **disbelieving**, doubting, sceptical, suspicious, doubtful, dubious, unconvinced, distrustful, mistrustful, unbelieving ■ **OPPOSITE:** credulous

increment NOUN = **increase**, gain, addition, supplement, step up, advancement, enlargement, accretion, accrual, augmentation, accruement

incriminate VERB = **implicate**, involve, accuse, blame, indict, point the finger at (*informal*), stigmatize, arraign, blacken the name of, inculpate (*formal*)

incumbent NOUN *The previous incumbent led the party for eleven years.* = **holder**, keeper, bearer, custodian ▶ ADJECTIVE *It is incumbent upon all of us to make an extra effort.* = **obligatory**, required, necessary, essential, binding, compulsory, mandatory, imperative

incur VERB = **sustain**, experience, suffer, gain, earn, collect, meet with, provoke, run up, induce, arouse, expose yourself to, lay yourself open to, bring upon yourself

incurable ADJECTIVE 1 *He is suffering from an incurable skin disease.* = **fatal**, terminal, inoperable, irrecoverable, irremediable, remediless 2 *He's an incurable romantic.* = **incorrigible**, hopeless, inveterate, dyed-in-the-wool

incursion NOUN = **foray**, raid, invasion, penetration, infiltration, inroad, irruption

indebted ADJECTIVE = **grateful**, obliged, in debt, obligated, beholden, under an obligation

indecency NOUN = **obscenity**, impurity, lewdness, impropriety, pornography, vulgarity, coarseness, crudity, licentiousness, foulness, outrageousness, immodesty, grossness, vileness, bawdiness, unseemliness, indelicacy, smuttiness, indecorum ■ OPPOSITE: decency

indecent ADJECTIVE 1 *She accused him of making indecent suggestions.* = **obscene**, lewd, dirty, blue, offensive, outrageous, inappropriate, rude, gross, foul, crude, coarse, filthy, vile, improper, pornographic, salacious, impure, ▶ smutty, immodest, licentious, scatological, indelicate ■ OPPOSITE: decent 2 *The legislation was drafted with indecent haste.* = **unbecoming**, unsuitable, vulgar, improper, tasteless, unseemly, undignified, disreputable, unrefined, discreditable, indelicate, indecorous, unbefitting ■ OPPOSITE: proper

indecision NOUN = **hesitation**, doubt, uncertainty, wavering, ambivalence, dithering (*chiefly Brit.*), hesitancy, indecisiveness, vacillation, shilly-shallying (*informal*), irresolution

indecisive ADJECTIVE 1 *He was criticised as a weak and indecisive leader.* = **hesitating**, uncertain, wavering, doubtful, faltering, tentative, undecided, dithering (*chiefly Brit.*), vacillating, in two minds (*informal*),

undetermined, pussyfooting (*informal*), irresolute ■ OPPOSITE: decisive 2 *An indecisive vote would force a second round of voting.* = **inconclusive**, unclear, undecided, indefinite, indeterminate ■ OPPOSITE: conclusive

indeed ADVERB 1 *'Did you know him?' 'I did indeed.'* = **certainly**, yes, definitely, surely, truly, absolutely, undoubtedly, positively, decidedly, without doubt, undeniably, without question, unequivocally, indisputably, assuredly, doubtlessly 2 *Later he admitted that the payments had indeed been made.* = **really**, actually, in fact, certainly, undoubtedly, genuinely, in reality, to be sure, in truth, categorically, verily (*archaic*), in actuality, in point of fact, veritably

indefatigable ADJECTIVE = **tireless**, dogged, persevering, patient, relentless, diligent, inexhaustible, unremitting, assiduous, unflagging, untiring, sedulous, pertinacious, unwearying, unwearied

indefensible ADJECTIVE = **unforgivable**, wrong, inexcusable, unjustifiable, untenable, unpardonable, insupportable, unwarrantable ■ OPPOSITE: defensible

indefinite ADJECTIVE 1 *The trial was adjourned for an indefinite period.* = **uncertain**, general, vague, unclear, unsettled, loose, unlimited, evasive, indeterminate, imprecise, undefined, equivocal, ill-defined, indistinct, undetermined, inexact, unfixed, oracular ■ OPPOSITE: settled 2 *a person of indefinite age* = **unclear**, unknown, uncertain, obscure, doubtful, ambiguous, indeterminate, imprecise, undefined, ill-defined, indistinct, undetermined, inexact, unfixed ■ OPPOSITE: specific

indefinitely ADVERB = **endlessly**, continually, for ever, ad infinitum, sine die (*Latin*), till the cows come home (*informal*)

indelible ADJECTIVE = **permanent**, lasting, enduring, ingrained, indestructible, ineradicable, ineffaceable, inexpungible, inextirpable ■ OPPOSITE: temporary

indemnify VERB 1 *They agreed to indemnify the taxpayers against any loss.* = **insure**, protect, guarantee, secure, endorse, underwrite 2 *They don't have the money to indemnify everybody.* = **compensate**, pay, reimburse, satisfy, repair, repay, requite, remunerate (*formal*)

indemnity NOUN 1 *They had failed to take out full indemnity cover.* = **insurance**, security, guarantee, protection 2 *The government paid the family an indemnity for the missing pictures.* = **compensation**, remuneration, reparation, satisfaction, redress, restitution, reimbursement, requital

3 *He was offered indemnity from prosecution in return for his evidence.* = **exemption**, immunity, impunity, privilege

indent VERB **1** *the country's heavily indented coastline* = **notch**, cut, score, mark, nick, pink, scallop, dint, serrate **2** *We had to indent for hatchets and torches.* = **order**, request, ask for, requisition

indentation NOUN = **notch**, cut, nick, depression, pit, dip, bash (*informal*), hollow, dent, jag, dimple

independence NOUN = **freedom**, liberty, autonomy, separation, sovereignty, self-determination, self-government, self-rule, self-sufficiency, self-reliance, home rule, autarchy, rangatiratanga (*N.Z.*) ■ **OPPOSITE:** subjugation

independent ADJECTIVE **1** *Two independent studies have been carried out.* = **separate**, unrelated, unconnected, unattached, uncontrolled, unconstrained ■ **OPPOSITE:** controlled **2** *There were benefits to being a single, independent woman.* = **self-sufficient**, free, liberated, unconventional, self-contained, individualistic, unaided, self-reliant, self-supporting **3** *a fully independent state* = **self-governing**, free, autonomous, separated, liberated, sovereign, self-determining, nonaligned, decontrolled, autarchic ■ **OPPOSITE:** subject

independently ADVERB = **separately**, alone, solo, on your own, by yourself, unaided, individually, autonomously, under your own steam

indescribable ADJECTIVE = **unutterable**, indefinable, beyond words, ineffable, inexpressible, beyond description, incommunicable, beggaring description

indestructible ADJECTIVE = **permanent**, durable, unbreakable, lasting, enduring, abiding, immortal, everlasting, indelible, incorruptible, imperishable, indissoluble, unfading, nonperishable ■ **OPPOSITE:** breakable

indeterminate ADJECTIVE = **uncertain**, indefinite, unspecified, vague, inconclusive, imprecise, undefined, undetermined, inexact, unfixed, unstipulated ■ **OPPOSITE:** fixed

index NOUN **1** *There's even a special subject index.* = **list**, listing, key, guide, register **2** *Weeds are an index to the character of the soil.* = **indication**, guide, sign, mark, note, evidence, signal, symptom, hint, clue, token

indicate VERB **1** *The survey indicated that most old people are independent.* = **show**, suggest, reveal, display, signal, demonstrate, point

to, imply, disclose, manifest, signify, denote, bespeak, make known, be symptomatic of, evince (*formal*), betoken, flag up **2** *She has indicated that she might resign.* = **imply**, suggest, hint, intimate, signify, insinuate, give someone to understand **3** *'Sit down,' he said, indicating a chair.* = **point to**, point out, specify, gesture towards, designate **4** *The gauge indicated that it was boiling.* = **register**, show, record, mark, read, express, display, demonstrate

indication NOUN = **sign**, mark, evidence, warning, note, signal, suggestion, symptom, hint, clue, manifestation, omen, inkling, portent, intimation, forewarning, wake-up call

indicative ADJECTIVE = **suggestive**, significant, symptomatic, pointing to, exhibitive, indicatory, indicial

indicator NOUN = **sign**, mark, measure, guide, display, index, signal, symbol, meter, gauge, marker, benchmark, pointer, signpost, barometer

indict VERB = **charge**, accuse, prosecute, summon, impeach, arraign, serve with a summons

indictment NOUN = **charge**, allegation, prosecution, accusation, impeachment, summons, arraignment

indifference NOUN **1** *his callous indifference to the plight of his son* = **disregard**, apathy, lack of interest, negligence, detachment, coolness, carelessness, coldness, nonchalance, callousness, aloofness, inattention, unconcern, absence of feeling, heedlessness ■ **OPPOSITE:** concern **2** *They regard dress as a matter of indifference.* = **irrelevance**, insignificance, triviality, unimportance

indifferent ADJECTIVE **1** *People have become indifferent to the suffering of others.* = **unconcerned**, distant, detached, cold, cool, regardless, careless, callous, aloof, unimpressed, unmoved, unsympathetic, impervious, uncaring, uninterested, apathetic, unresponsive, heedless, inattentive ■ **OPPOSITE:** concerned **2** *She had starred in several indifferent movies.* = **mediocre**, middling, average, fair, ordinary, moderate, insignificant, unimportant, so-so (*informal*), immaterial, passable, undistinguished, uninspired, of no consequence, no great shakes (*informal*), half-pie (*N.Z. informal*) ■ **OPPOSITE:** excellent

indigenous ADJECTIVE = **native**, original, aboriginal, home-grown, autochthonous

indigent ADJECTIVE = **destitute**, poor, impoverished, needy, penniless, poverty-stricken, down and out, in want, down at heel (*informal*), impecunious, dirt-poor, straitened, on the breadline, short, flat broke (*informal*), penurious, necessitous (*literary*) ■ **OPPOSITE:** wealthy

indigestion NOUN = **upset stomach**, heartburn, dyspepsia, dyspepsy

indignant ADJECTIVE = **resentful**, angry, mad (*informal*), heated, provoked, furious, annoyed, hacked (off) (*U.S. slang*), sore (*informal*), fuming (*informal*), choked, incensed, disgruntled, exasperated, irate, livid (*informal*), seeing red (*informal*), miffed (*informal*), riled, up in arms (*informal*), peeved (*informal*), in a huff, hot under the collar (*informal*), huffy (*informal*), wrathful, narked (*Brit., Austral. & N.Z. slang*), in high dudgeon, tooshie (*Austral. slang*), off the air (*Austral. slang*)

indignation NOUN = **resentment**, anger, rage, fury, wrath, ire (*literary*), exasperation, pique, umbrage, righteous anger

indignity NOUN = **humiliation**, abuse, outrage, injury, slight, insult, snub, reproach, affront, disrespect, dishonour, opprobrium, obloquy, contumely (*literary*)

indirect ADJECTIVE 1 *They are feeling the indirect effects of the recession elsewhere.* = **related**, accompanying, secondary, subsidiary, contingent, collateral, incidental, unintended, ancillary, concomitant 2 *The goods went by a rather indirect route.* = **circuitous**, winding, roundabout, curving, wandering, rambling, deviant, meandering, tortuous, zigzag, long-drawn-out, circumlocutory ■ **OPPOSITE:** direct

indirectly ADVERB 1 *Drugs are indirectly responsible for the violence.* = **by implication**, in a roundabout way, circumlocutorily 2 *She referred indirectly to the territorial dispute.* = **obliquely**, in a roundabout way, evasively, not in so many words, circuitously, periphrastically

indiscreet ADJECTIVE = **tactless**, foolish, rash, reckless, unwise, hasty, ill-advised, unthinking, ill-judged, ill-considered, imprudent, heedless, injudicious, incautious, undiplomatic, impolitic ■ **OPPOSITE:** discreet

indiscretion NOUN 1 *Occasionally they paid for their indiscretion with their lives.* = **folly**, foolishness, recklessness, imprudence, rashness, tactlessness, gaucherie 2 *rumours of his mother's youthful indiscretions* = **mistake**, slip, error, lapse, folly, boob (*Brit. slang*), gaffe, bloomer (*Brit. informal*), faux pas, barry or Barry Crocker (*Austral. slang*)

indiscriminate ADJECTIVE = **random**, general, wholesale, mixed, sweeping, confused, chaotic, careless, mingled, jumbled, miscellaneous, promiscuous, motley, haphazard, uncritical, aimless, desultory, hit or miss (*informal*), higgledy-piggledy (*informal*), undiscriminating, unsystematic, unselective, undistinguishable, unmethodical, scattershot ■ **OPPOSITE:** systematic

indispensable ADJECTIVE = **essential**, necessary, needed, key, vital, crucial (*informal*), imperative, requisite, needful, must-have ■ **OPPOSITE:** dispensable

indistinct ADJECTIVE 1 *The lettering is fuzzy and indistinct.* = **unclear**, confused, obscure, faint, blurred, vague, doubtful, ambiguous, fuzzy, shadowy, indefinite, misty, hazy, unintelligible, indistinguishable, indeterminate, bleary, undefined, out of focus, ill-defined, indiscernible ■ **OPPOSITE:** distinct 2 *the indistinct murmur of voices* = **muffled**, confused, faint, dim, weak, indistinguishable, indiscernible

indistinguishable ADJECTIVE = **identical**, the same, cut from the same cloth, like as two peas in a pod (*informal*)

individual ADJECTIVE 1 *waiting for the group to decide rather than making individual decisions* = **separate**, single, independent, isolated, lone, solitary, discrete ■ **OPPOSITE:** collective 2 *It was all part of her very individual personality.* = **unique**, special, fresh, novel, exclusive, distinct, singular, idiosyncratic, unorthodox ■ **OPPOSITE:** conventional ▶ NOUN *the rights and responsibilities of the individual* = **person**, being, human, party (*informal*), body (*informal*), type, unit, character (*informal*), soul, creature, human being, mortal, personage, living soul

individualism NOUN = **independence**, self-interest, originality, self-reliance, egoism, egocentricity, self-direction, freethinking

individualist NOUN = **maverick**, nonconformist, independent, original, loner (*informal*), lone wolf, freethinker

individuality NOUN = **character**, personality, uniqueness, distinction, distinctiveness, originality, peculiarity, singularity, separateness, discreteness

individually ADVERB = **separately**, independently, singly, one by one, one at a time, severally

indoctrinate VERB = **brainwash**, school, train, teach, drill, initiate, instruct, imbue

indoctrination NOUN = **brainwashing**, schooling, training, instruction, drilling, inculcation

indomitable ADJECTIVE = **invincible**, resolute, steadfast, set, staunch, unbeatable, unyielding, unflinching, unconquerable, untameable ■ **OPPOSITE:** weak

indorse *see* **endorse**

indorsement *see* **endorsement**

induce VERB **1** *an economic crisis induced by high oil prices* = **cause**, produce, create, begin, effect, lead to, occasion (*formal*), generate, provoke, motivate, set off, bring about, give rise to, precipitate, incite, instigate, engender, set in motion ■ **OPPOSITE:** prevent **2** *I would do anything to induce them to stay.* = **persuade**, encourage, influence, get, move, press, draw, convince, urge, prompt, sway, entice, coax, incite, impel, talk someone into, prevail upon, actuate ■ **OPPOSITE:** dissuade

inducement NOUN = **incentive**, motive, cause, influence, reward, come-on (*informal*), spur, consideration, attraction, lure, bait, carrot (*informal*), encouragement, impulse, stimulus, incitement, clarion call

induct VERB = **install**, admit, introduce, allow, swear, initiate, inaugurate

induction NOUN = **installation**, institution, introduction, initiation, inauguration, investiture

indulge VERB **1** *My success has let me indulge my love of expensive cars.* = **gratify**, satisfy, fulfil, feed, give way to, yield to, cater to, pander to, regale, gladden, satiate **2** *She did not agree with indulging children.* = **spoil**, pamper, cosset, baby, favour, humour, give in to, coddle, spoon-feed, mollycoddle, fawn on, overindulge • **indulge yourself** *You can indulge yourself without spending a fortune.* = **treat yourself**, splash out, spoil yourself, luxuriate in something, overindulge yourself

indulgence NOUN **1** *The car is one of my few indulgences.* = **luxury**, treat, extravagance, favour, privilege **2** *The king's indulgence towards his sons angered them.* = **leniency**, pampering, spoiling, kindness, fondness, permissiveness, partiality **3** *Sadly, constant indulgence can be a costly affair.* = **intemperance**, excess, extravagance, debauchery, dissipation, overindulgence, prodigality, immoderation, dissoluteness, intemperateness ■ **OPPOSITE:** temperance **4** *his indulgence of his gross appetites* = **gratification**, satisfaction, fulfilment, appeasement, satiation

indulgent ADJECTIVE = **lenient**, liberal, kind, kindly, understanding, gentle, tender, mild, fond, favourable, tolerant, gratifying, easy-going, compliant, permissive, forbearing ■ **OPPOSITE:** strict

industrialist NOUN = **capitalist**, tycoon, magnate, boss, producer, manufacturer, baron, financier, captain of industry, big businessperson

industrious ADJECTIVE = **hard-working**, diligent, active, busy, steady, productive, energetic, conscientious, tireless, zealous, laborious, assiduous, sedulous ■ **OPPOSITE:** lazy

industry NOUN **1** *countries where industry is developing rapidly* = **business**, production, manufacturing, trade, trading, commerce, commercial enterprise **2** *the textile industry* = **trade**, world, business, service, line, field, craft, profession, occupation **3** *No one doubted his industry or his integrity.* = **diligence**, effort, labour, hard work, trouble, activity, application, striving, endeavour, toil, vigour, zeal, persistence, assiduity, tirelessness

ineffable ADJECTIVE = **indescribable**, unspeakable, indefinable, beyond words, unutterable, inexpressible, incommunicable

ineffective ADJECTIVE **1** *Reform will continue to be painful and ineffective.* = **unproductive**, useless, futile, vain, unsuccessful, pointless, fruitless, to no avail, ineffectual, unprofitable, to no effect, unavailing, unfruitful, profitless, bootless, inefficacious ■ **OPPOSITE:** effective **2** *They are burdened with an ineffective leader.* = **inefficient**, inadequate, useless (*informal*), poor, weak, pathetic, powerless, unfit, feeble, worthless, inept, impotent, ineffectual

ineffectual ADJECTIVE **1** *the well-meaning but ineffectual jobs programs of the past* = **unproductive**, useless, ineffective, vain, unsuccessful, pointless, futile, fruitless, to no avail, unprofitable, to no effect, unavailing, unfruitful, profitless, bootless, inefficacious **2** *The mayor had become ineffectual in the war against drugs.* = **inefficient**, useless (*informal*), powerless, poor, weak, inadequate, pathetic, unfit, ineffective, feeble, worthless, inept, impotent

inefficiency NOUN = **incompetence**, slackness, sloppiness, disorganization, carelessness

inefficient ADJECTIVE **1** *the inefficient use of funds* = **wasteful**, uneconomical, profligate, ruinous, improvident, unthrifty, inefficacious **2** *Some people are very inefficient workers.* = **incompetent**, incapable, inept, weak, bungling, feeble, sloppy, ineffectual, disorganized, slipshod, inexpert ■ **OPPOSITE:** efficient

ineligible ADJECTIVE = **unqualified**, ruled out, unacceptable, disqualified, incompetent (*Law*), unfit, unfitted, unsuitable, undesirable, objectionable, unequipped

inept ADJECTIVE **1** *He was inept and lacked the intelligence to govern.* = **incompetent**, bungling, clumsy, cowboy (*informal*), awkward, bumbling, gauche, cack-handed (*informal*), inexpert, maladroit, unskilful, unhandy, unworkmanlike ■ **OPPOSITE:** competent **2** *The Government's inept response turned this into a crisis.* = **unsuitable**, inappropriate, out of place, ridiculous, absurd, meaningless, pointless, unfit, improper, inapt, infelicitous, malapropos ■ **OPPOSITE:** appropriate

ineptitude NOUN = **incompetence**, inefficiency, inability, incapacity, clumsiness, unfitness, gaucheness, inexpertness, unhandiness

inequality NOUN = **disparity**, prejudice, difference, bias, diversity, irregularity, unevenness, lack of balance, disproportion, imparity, preferentiality

inert ADJECTIVE *He covered the inert body with a blanket* = **inactive**, still, motionless, dead, passive, slack, static, dormant, lifeless, leaden, immobile, inanimate, unresponsive, unmoving, quiescent, torpid, unreactive, slumberous (*chiefly poetic*) ■ **OPPOSITE:** moving

inertia NOUN = **inactivity**, apathy, lethargy, passivity, stillness, laziness, sloth, idleness, stupor, drowsiness, dullness, immobility, torpor, sluggishness, indolence, lassitude, languor, listlessness, deadness, unresponsiveness ■ **OPPOSITE:** activity

inescapable ADJECTIVE = **unavoidable**, inevitable, certain, sure, fated, destined, inexorable, ineluctable, ineludible (*rare*)

inevitable ADJECTIVE = **unavoidable**, inescapable, inexorable, sure, certain, necessary, settled, fixed, assured, fated, decreed, destined, ordained, predetermined, predestined, preordained, ineluctable, unpreventable ■ **OPPOSITE:** avoidable

inevitably ADVERB = **unavoidably**, naturally, necessarily, surely, certainly, as a result, automatically, consequently, of necessity, perforce (*formal*), inescapably, as a necessary consequence

inexcusable ADJECTIVE = **unforgivable**, indefensible, unjustifiable, outrageous, unpardonable, unwarrantable, inexpiable ■ **OPPOSITE:** excusable

inexhaustible ADJECTIVE **1** *They seem to have an inexhaustible supply of ammunition.* = **endless**, infinite, never-ending, limitless, boundless, bottomless, unbounded, measureless, illimitable ■ **OPPOSITE:** limited **2** *the sound of his inexhaustible voice, still talking* = **tireless**, undaunted, indefatigable, unfailing, unflagging, untiring, unwearying, unwearied ■ **OPPOSITE:** tiring

inexorable ADJECTIVE = **unrelenting**, relentless, implacable, hard, severe, harsh, cruel, adamant, inescapable, inflexible, merciless, unyielding, immovable, remorseless, pitiless, unbending, obdurate, ineluctable, unappeasable ■ **OPPOSITE:** relenting

inexorably ADVERB = **relentlessly**, inevitably, irresistibly, remorselessly, implacably, unrelentingly

inexpensive ADJECTIVE = **cheap**, reasonable, low-priced, budget, bargain, modest, low-cost, economical ■ **OPPOSITE:** expensive

inexperience NOUN = **unfamiliarity**, ignorance, newness, rawness, greenness, callowness, unexpertness

inexperienced ADJECTIVE = **new**, unskilled, untrained, green, fresh, amateur, raw, unfamiliar, unused, callow, immature, unaccustomed, untried, unschooled, wet behind the ears (*informal*), unacquainted, unseasoned, unpractised, unversed, unfledged ■ **OPPOSITE:** experienced

inexplicable ADJECTIVE = **unaccountable**, strange, mysterious, baffling, enigmatic, incomprehensible, mystifying, unintelligible, insoluble, inscrutable, unfathomable, beyond comprehension ■ **OPPOSITE:** explicable

inextricably ADVERB = **inseparably**, totally, intricately, irretrievably, indissolubly, indistinguishably

infallibility NOUN **1** *exaggerated views of the infallibility of science* = **supremacy**, perfection, omniscience, impeccability, faultlessness, irrefutability, unerringness **2** *The technical infallibility of their systems is without doubt.* = **reliability**, safety, dependability, trustworthiness, sureness

infallible ADJECTIVE **1** *She had an infallible eye for style.* = **perfect**, impeccable, faultless, unerring, omniscient, unimpeachable ■ **OPPOSITE:** fallible **2** *She hit on an infallible way of staying sober amid a flood of toasts.* = **sure**, certain, reliable, unbeatable, dependable, trustworthy, foolproof, sure-fire (*informal*), unfailing ■ **OPPOSITE:** unreliable

infamous ADJECTIVE = **notorious**, base, shocking, outrageous, disgraceful, monstrous, shameful, vile, scandalous, wicked, atrocious, heinous, odious, hateful, loathsome, ignominious, disreputable, egregious, abominable, villainous, dishonourable, nefarious, iniquitous, detestable, opprobrious, ill-famed, flagitious ■ **OPPOSITE:** esteemed

infamy NOUN = **notoriety**, scandal, shame, disgrace, atrocity, discredit, stigma, disrepute, ignominy, dishonour, abomination, opprobrium, villainy, odium (*formal*), outrageousness, obloquy

infancy NOUN 1 *the development of the mind from infancy onwards* = **early childhood**, babyhood 2 *the infancy of printing* = **beginnings**, start, birth, roots, seeds, origins, dawn (*literary*), early stages, emergence, outset, cradle, inception ■ **OPPOSITE:** end

infant NOUN *young mums with infants in prams* = **baby**, child, babe, toddler, tot, wean (*Scot.*), little one, bairn (*Scot. & Northern English*), suckling, newborn child, babe in arms, sprog (*slang*), munchkin (*informal, chiefly U.S.*), neonate, rug rat (*slang*), littlie (*Austral. informal*), ankle-biter (*Austral. slang*), tacker (*Austral. slang*) ▶ ADJECTIVE *The infant company was based in Germany.* = **early**, new, developing, young, growing, initial, dawning, fledgling, newborn, immature, embryonic, emergent, nascent, unfledged

infantile ADJECTIVE = **childish**, immature, puerile, babyish, young, weak ■ **OPPOSITE:** mature

infatuated ADJECTIVE = **obsessed**, fascinated, captivated, possessed, carried away, inflamed, beguiled, smitten (*informal*), besotted, bewitched, intoxicated, crazy about (*informal*), spellbound, enamoured, enraptured, under the spell of, head over heels in love with, swept off your feet

infatuation NOUN = **obsession**, thing (*informal*), passion, crush (*informal*), madness, folly, fixation, foolishness

infect VERB 1 *A single mosquito can infect a large number of people.* = **contaminate**, transmit disease to, spread disease to or among 2 *The birds infect the milk.* = **pollute**, dirty, poison, foul, corrupt, contaminate, taint, defile, vitiate 3 *I was infected by her fear.* = **affect**, move, touch, influence, upset, overcome, stir, disturb

infection NOUN = **disease**, condition, complaint, illness, virus, disorder, corruption, poison, pollution, contamination, contagion, defilement, septicity

infectious ADJECTIVE = **catching**, spreading, contagious, communicable, poisoning, corrupting, contaminating, polluting, virulent, infective, vitiating, pestilential, transmittable

infer VERB = **deduce**, understand, gather, conclude, derive, presume, conjecture, surmise, read between the lines, put two and two together

> **USAGE** The use of *infer* to mean *imply* is becoming more and more common in both speech and writing. There is nevertheless a useful distinction between the two which many people would be in favour of maintaining. To *infer* means 'to deduce', and is used in the construction 'to infer something from something': *I inferred from what she said that she had not been well.* To *imply* means 'to suggest, to insinuate' and is normally followed by a clause: *are you implying that I was responsible for the mistake?*

inference NOUN = **deduction**, conclusion, assumption, reading, consequence, presumption, conjecture, surmise, corollary

inferior ADJECTIVE 1 *the inferior status of women in many societies* = **lower**, junior, minor, secondary, subsidiary, lesser, humble, subordinate, lowly, less important, menial ■ **OPPOSITE:** superior 2 *These recordings are of inferior quality.* = **substandard**, bad, poor, mean, worse, poorer, pants (*informal*), flawed, rotten (*informal*), dire, indifferent, duff (*Brit. informal*), mediocre, second-class, deficient, imperfect, second-rate, shoddy, low-grade, unsound, downmarket, low-rent (*informal, chiefly U.S.*), for the birds (*informal*), wretched, two-bit (*U.S. & Canad. slang*), crappy (*slang*), no great shakes (*informal*), poxy (*slang*), dime-a-dozen (*informal*), bush-league (*Austral. & N.Z. informal*), not much cop (*Brit. slang*), tinhorn (*U.S. slang*), half-pie (*N.Z. informal*), of a sort or of sorts, strictly for the birds (*informal*), bodger or bodgie (*Austral. slang*) ■ **OPPOSITE:** excellent ▶ NOUN *He was too proud to conceal his opinions from those he considered his inferiors.* = **underling** (*derogatory*), junior, subordinate, lesser, menial, minion

inferiority NOUN = **subservience**, subordination, lowliness, servitude, abasement, inferior status or standing ■ **OPPOSITE:** superiority

infernal ADJECTIVE 1 *The post office is shut, which is an infernal bore.* = **damned** (*slang*), malevolent, hellish, devilish, accursed, damnable (*informal*) 2 *the goddess of the infernal regions* = **hellish**, lower, underworld, nether, Stygian (*literary*), Hadean, Plutonian, chthonian, Tartarean (*literary*) ■ **OPPOSITE:** heavenly

infertile ADJECTIVE **1** *According to one survey, one woman in eight is infertile.* = **sterile**, barren (*old-fashioned*), infecund **2** *The waste is dumped, making the surrounding land infertile.* = **barren**, unproductive, nonproductive, unfruitful, infecund ■ **OPPOSITE:** fertile

infertility NOUN = **sterility**, barrenness, unproductiveness, unfruitfulness, infecundity

infest VERB = **overrun**, flood, invade, penetrate, ravage, swarm, throng, beset, permeate

infested ADJECTIVE = **overrun**, plagued, crawling, swarming, ridden, alive, ravaged, lousy (*slang*), beset, pervaded, teeming, buggy

infidel NOUN = **unbeliever**, sceptic, atheist, heretic, agnostic, heathen (*old-fashioned*), nonconformist, freethinker, nonbeliever

infidelity NOUN = **unfaithfulness**, cheating (*informal*), adultery, betrayal, duplicity, disloyalty, bad faith, perfidy (*literary*), falseness, faithlessness, false-heartedness

infiltrate VERB = **penetrate**, pervade, permeate, creep in, percolate, filter through to, make inroads into, sneak into (*informal*), insinuate yourself, work or worm your way into

infinite ADJECTIVE **1** *an infinite variety of landscapes* = **vast**, enormous, immense, wide, countless, innumerable, untold, stupendous, incalculable, immeasurable, inestimable, numberless, uncounted, measureless, uncalculable **2** *With infinite care, he shifted positions.* = **enormous**, total, supreme, absolute, all-embracing, unbounded **3** *There is an infinite number of atoms.* = **limitless**, endless, unlimited, eternal, perpetual, never-ending, interminable, boundless, everlasting, bottomless, unending, inexhaustible, immeasurable, without end, unbounded, numberless, measureless, illimitable, without number ■ **OPPOSITE:** finite

infinity NOUN = **eternity**, vastness, immensity, perpetuity, endlessness, infinitude, boundlessness

infirm ADJECTIVE **1** *my infirm husband* = **frail**, weak, feeble, failing, ailing, debilitated, decrepit, enfeebled, doddery, doddering ■ **OPPOSITE:** robust **2** *She has little patience with the 'infirm of purpose'.* = **irresolute**, weak, faltering, unstable, shaky, insecure, wavering, wobbly, indecisive, unsound, vacillating

inflame VERB **1** *They hold the rebels responsible for inflaming the villagers.* = **enrage**, stimulate, provoke, fire, heat, excite, anger, arouse, rouse, infuriate, ignite, incense, madden, agitate, kindle, rile, foment, intoxicate, make your blood boil, impassion ■ **OPPOSITE:** calm **2** *The shooting has only inflamed passions further.* = **aggravate**, increase, intensify, worsen, exacerbate, fan

inflamed ADJECTIVE = **swollen**, sore, red, hot, angry, infected, fevered, festering, chafing, septic

inflammable ADJECTIVE = **flammable**, explosive, volatile, incendiary, combustible

inflammation NOUN = **swelling**, soreness, burning, heat, sore, rash, tenderness, redness, painfulness

inflammatory ADJECTIVE = **provocative**, incendiary, explosive, fiery, inflaming, insurgent, anarchic, rabid, riotous, intemperate, seditious, rabble-rousing, demagogic, like a red rag to a bull, instigative

inflate VERB **1** *He jumped into the sea and inflated the liferaft.* = **blow up**, pump up, swell, balloon, dilate, distend, aerate, bloat, puff up *or* out ■ **OPPOSITE:** deflate **2** *Promotion can inflate a film's final cost.* = **increase**, boost, expand, enlarge, escalate, amplify ■ **OPPOSITE:** diminish **3** *Even his war record was fraudulently inflated.* = **exaggerate**, embroider, embellish, emphasize, enlarge, magnify, overdo, amplify, exalt, overstate, overestimate, overemphasize, blow out of all proportion, aggrandize, hyperbolize

inflated ADJECTIVE = **exaggerated**, excessive, swollen, amplified, hyped, exalted (*informal*), overblown

inflation NOUN = **increase**, expansion, extension, swelling, escalation, enlargement, intensification

inflection NOUN **1** *His voice was devoid of inflection.* = **intonation**, stress, emphasis, beat, measure, rhythm, cadence, modulation, accentuation **2** *At around 2 years, the child adds many grammatical inflections.* = **conjugation**, declension

inflexibility NOUN = **obstinacy**, persistence, intransigence, obduracy, fixity, steeliness

inflexible ADJECTIVE **1** *He was a man of unchanging habits and an inflexible routine.* = **fixed**, set, established, rooted, rigid, immovable, unadaptable **2** *They viewed him as stubborn, inflexible and dogmatic.* = **obstinate**, strict, relentless, firm, fixed, iron, adamant, rigorous, stubborn, stringent, uncompromising, resolute, steely, intractable, inexorable, implacable, steadfast, hard and fast, unyielding, immutable, immovable, unbending, obdurate, stiff-necked, dyed-in-the-wool, unchangeable, brassbound, set in your ways ■ **OPPOSITE:** flexible **3** *The boot is too inflexible to be comfortable.* = **stiff**, hard, rigid, hardened, taut, inelastic, nonflexible ■ **OPPOSITE:** pliable

inflict VERB = **impose**, exact, administer, visit, apply, deliver, levy, wreak, mete *or* deal out

influence NOUN **1** *As we grew older, I had less influence and couldn't control him.* = **control**, power, authority, direction, command, domination, supremacy, mastery, ascendancy, mana (*N.Z.*) **2** *They should continue to use their influence for the release of all hostages.* = **power**, force, authority, pull (*informal*), weight, strength, connections, importance, prestige, clout (*informal*), leverage, good offices **3** *I fell under the influence of a history master.* = **spell**, hold, power, rule, weight, magic, sway, allure, magnetism, enchantment ▶ VERB **1** *What you eat may influence your risk of getting cancer.* = **affect**, have an effect on, have an impact on, control, concern, direct, guide, impact on, modify, bear upon, impinge upon, act *or* work upon **2** *The conference influenced us to launch the campaign.* = **persuade**, move, prompt, urge, counsel, induce, incline, dispose, arouse, sway, rouse, entice, coax, incite, instigate, predispose, impel, prevail upon **3** *Her attempt to influence the Press rebounded.* = **carry weight with**, cut any ice with (*informal*), pull strings with (*informal*), bring pressure to bear upon, make yourself felt with

influential ADJECTIVE **1** *one of the most influential books ever written* = **important**, powerful, moving, telling, leading, strong, guiding, inspiring, prestigious, meaningful, potent, persuasive, authoritative, momentous, weighty ■ **OPPOSITE:** unimportant **2** *He had been influential in shaping economic policy.* = **instrumental**, important, significant, controlling, guiding, effective, crucial, persuasive, forcible, efficacious

influx NOUN = **arrival**, flow, rush, invasion, convergence, inflow, incursion, inundation, inrush

infold *see* **enfold**

inform VERB **1** *They would inform him of any progress they had made.* = **tell**, advise, let someone know, notify, brief, instruct, edify, enlighten, acquaint, leak to, communicate to, fill someone in, keep someone posted, apprise, clue someone in (*informal*), put someone in the picture (*informal*), tip someone off, send word to, give someone to understand, make someone conversant (with) **2** *All great songs are informed by a certain sadness and tension.* = **infuse**, characterize, permeate, animate, saturate, typify, imbue, suffuse • **inform on someone** *Somebody must have informed on us.* = **betray**, report, denounce, shop (*slang, chiefly Brit.*), peach (*slang*), give someone away, incriminate, tell on (*informal*), blow the whistle on (*informal*), grass on (*Brit. slang*), double-cross (*informal*), rat on (*informal*), spill the beans on (*informal*), stab someone in the back, nark (*Brit., Austral. & N.Z. slang*), blab about, squeal on (*slang*), snitch on (*slang*), put the finger on (*informal*), sell someone down the river (*informal*), blow the gaff on (*Brit. slang*), tell all on, inculpate, dob someone in (*Austral. & N.Z. slang*)

informal ADJECTIVE **1** *She is refreshingly informal.* = **natural**, relaxed, casual, familiar, unofficial, laid-back, easy-going, colloquial, unconstrained, unceremonious **2** *The house has an informal atmosphere.* = **relaxed**, easy, comfortable, simple, natural, casual, cosy, laid-back (*informal*), mellow, leisurely, easy-going ■ **OPPOSITE:** formal **3** *Most of the time she needs informal clothes.* = **casual**, comfortable, leisure, everyday, simple **4** *an informal meeting of EU ministers* = **unofficial**, irregular, unconstrained, unceremonious ■ **OPPOSITE:** official

informality NOUN = **familiarity**, naturalness, casualness, ease, relaxation, simplicity, lack of ceremony

information NOUN = **facts**, details, material, news, latest (*informal*), report, word, message, notice, advice, knowledge, data, intelligence, instruction, counsel, the score (*informal*), gen (*Brit. informal*), dope (*informal*), info (*informal*), inside story, blurb, lowdown (*informal*), tidings, drum (*Austral. informal*), heads up (*U.S. & Canad.*)

informative ADJECTIVE = **instructive**, revealing, educational, forthcoming, illuminating, enlightening, chatty, communicative, edifying, gossipy, newsy

informed ADJECTIVE = **knowledgeable**, up to date, enlightened, learned, primed, posted, expert, briefed, familiar, versed, acquainted, in the picture, up, abreast, in the know (*informal*), erudite, well-read, conversant, au fait (*French*), in the loop, genned up (*Brit. informal*), au courant (*French*), keeping your finger on the pulse

informer NOUN = **betrayer**, grass (*Brit. slang*), sneak, squealer (*slang*), Judas, accuser, stool pigeon, nark (*Brit., Austral. & N.Z. slang*), fizgig (*Austral. slang*)

infrequent ADJECTIVE = **occasional**, rare, uncommon, unusual, sporadic, few and far between, once in a blue moon
■ **OPPOSITE:** frequent

infringe VERB *The film exploited his image and infringed his copyright.* = **break**, violate, contravene (*formal*), disobey, transgress
• **infringe on** or **upon** *It's starting to infringe on our personal liberties.* = **intrude on**, compromise, undermine, limit, weaken, diminish, disrupt, curb, encroach on, trespass on

infringement NOUN = **contravention**, breach, violation, trespass, transgression, infraction, noncompliance, nonobservance

infuriate VERB = **enrage**, anger, provoke, irritate, incense, gall, madden, exasperate, rile, nark (*Brit., Austral. & N.Z. slang*), be like a red rag to a bull, make your blood boil, get your goat (*slang*), make your hackles rise, raise your hackles, get your back up, make you see red (*informal*), put your back up
■ **OPPOSITE:** soothe

infuriating ADJECTIVE = **annoying**, irritating, aggravating (*informal*), provoking, galling, maddening, exasperating, irksome, vexatious, pestilential

infuse VERB = **brew**, soak, steep, saturate, immerse, macerate

ingenious ADJECTIVE = **creative**, original, brilliant, clever, masterly, bright (*informal*), subtle, fertile, shrewd, inventive, skilful, crafty, resourceful, adroit, dexterous
■ **OPPOSITE:** unimaginative

ingenuity NOUN = **originality**, genius, inventiveness, skill, gift, faculty, flair, knack, sharpness, cleverness, resourcefulness, shrewdness, adroitness, ingeniousness ■ **OPPOSITE:** dullness

ingrained or **engrained** ADJECTIVE = **fixed**, rooted, deep-seated, fundamental, constitutional, inherent, hereditary, in the blood, intrinsic, deep-rooted, indelible, inveterate, inborn, inbred, inbuilt, ineradicable, brassbound

ingratiate VERB • **ingratiate yourself with someone** = **get on the right side of**, court, win over, flatter, pander to, crawl to, play up to, get in with, suck up to (*informal*), curry favour with, grovel to, keep someone sweet, lick someone's boots, fawn to, toady to, seek someone's favour, rub someone up the right way (*informal*), be a yes man to, insinuate yourself with

ingratiating ADJECTIVE = **sycophantic**, servile, obsequious, crawling, humble, flattering, fawning, unctuous, toadying, bootlicking (*informal*), timeserving

ingredient NOUN = **component**, part, element, feature, piece, unit, item, aspect, attribute, constituent

inhabit VERB = **live in**, people, occupy, populate, reside in, tenant, lodge in, dwell in, colonize, take up residence in, abide in, make your home in

inhabitant NOUN = **occupant**, resident, citizen, local, native, tenant, inmate, dweller, occupier, denizen, indigene, indweller

inhabited ADJECTIVE = **populated**, peopled, occupied, held, developed, settled, tenanted, colonized

inhalation NOUN = **breathing**, breath, inspiration, inhaling

inhale VERB = **breathe in**, gasp, draw in, suck in, respire ■ **OPPOSITE:** exhale

inherent ADJECTIVE = **intrinsic**, natural, basic, central, essential, native, fundamental, underlying, hereditary, instinctive, innate, ingrained, elemental, congenital, inborn, inbred, inbuilt, immanent, connate ■ **OPPOSITE:** extraneous

inherit VERB = **be left**, come into, be willed, accede to, succeed to, be bequeathed, fall heir to

inheritance NOUN = **legacy**, estate, heritage, provision, endowment, bequest, birthright, patrimony

inheritor NOUN = **heir**, successor, recipient, beneficiary, legatee

inhibit VERB **1** *buildings which inhibit the supply of light and air* = **hinder**, stop, prevent, check, bar, arrest, frustrate, curb, restrain, constrain, obstruct, impede, bridle, stem the flow of, throw a spanner in the works of, hold back or in ■ **OPPOSITE:** further **2** *The poor will be inhibited from getting the medical care they need.* = **prevent**, stop, bar, frustrate, forbid, prohibit, debar
■ **OPPOSITE:** allow

inhibited ADJECTIVE = **shy**, reserved, guarded, withdrawn, frustrated, subdued, repressed, constrained, self-conscious, reticent, uptight (*informal*) ■ **OPPOSITE:** uninhibited

inhibition NOUN **1** *They behave with a total lack of inhibition.* = **shyness**, reserve, restraint, hang-up (*informal*), modesty, nervousness, reticence, self-consciousness, timidity, diffidence, bashfulness, mental blockage, timidness **2** *A country's size is no inhibition to producing a top team.* = **obstacle**, check, bar, block, barrier, restriction, hazard, restraint, hitch, drawback, snag, deterrent, obstruction, stumbling block, impediment, hindrance, encumbrance, interdict

inhospitable ADJECTIVE **1** *the earth's most inhospitable regions* = **bleak**, empty, bare, hostile, lonely, forbidding, barren, sterile, desolate, unfavourable, uninhabitable, godforsaken **2** *Why does he employ such inhospitable, miserable staff?* = **unfriendly**, unwelcoming, uncongenial, cool, unkind, xenophobic, ungenerous, unsociable, unreceptive ■ **OPPOSITE:** hospitable

inhuman ADJECTIVE = **cruel**, savage, brutal, vicious, ruthless, barbaric, heartless, merciless, diabolical, cold-blooded, remorseless, barbarous, fiendish, pitiless, unfeeling, bestial ■ **OPPOSITE:** humane

inhumane ADJECTIVE = **cruel**, savage, brutal, severe, harsh, grim, unkind, heartless, atrocious, unsympathetic, hellish (*informal*), depraved, barbarous, pitiless, unfeeling, uncompassionate

inhumanity NOUN = **cruelty**, atrocity, brutality, ruthlessness, barbarism, viciousness, heartlessness, unkindness, brutishness, cold-bloodedness, pitilessness, cold-heartedness, hardheartedness

inimical ADJECTIVE = **hostile**, opposed, contrary, destructive, harmful, adverse, hurtful, unfriendly, unfavourable, antagonistic, injurious, unwelcoming, ill-disposed ■ **OPPOSITE:** helpful

inimitable ADJECTIVE = **unique**, unparalleled, unrivalled, incomparable, supreme, consummate, unmatched, peerless, unequalled, matchless, unsurpassable, nonpareil, unexampled

iniquity NOUN = **wickedness**, wrong, crime, evil, sin, offence, injustice, wrongdoing, misdeed, infamy, abomination, sinfulness, baseness, unrighteousness, heinousness, evildoing ■ **OPPOSITE:** goodness

initial ADJECTIVE = **opening**, first, early, earliest, beginning, primary, maiden, inaugural, commencing, introductory, embryonic, incipient, inchoate, inceptive ■ **OPPOSITE:** final

initially ADVERB = **at first**, first, firstly, originally, primarily, at the start, in the first place, to begin with, at the outset, in the beginning, in the early stages, at *or* in the beginning

initiate VERB **1** *They wanted to initiate a discussion on economics.* = **begin**, start, open, launch, establish, institute, pioneer, kick off (*informal*), bring about, embark on, originate, set about, get under way, instigate, kick-start, inaugurate, set in motion, trigger off, lay the foundations of, commence on, set going, break the ice on, set the ball rolling on **2** *She was initiated as a member of the secret society.* = **introduce**, admit, enlist, enrol, launch, establish, invest, recruit, induct, instate ▶ NOUN *He was an initiate of a Chinese spiritual discipline.* = **novice**, member, pupil, convert, amateur, newcomer, beginner, trainee, apprentice, entrant, learner, neophyte (*formal*), tyro, probationer, novitiate, proselyte • **initiate someone into something** *I was initiated into the darker side of the work.* = **instruct in**, train in, coach in, acquaint in, drill in, make aware of, teach about, tutor in, indoctrinate, prime in, familiarize with

initiation NOUN **1** *They announced the initiation of a rural development programme.* = **introduction**, installation, inauguration, inception, commencement **2** *This was my initiation into the peace movement.* = **entrance**, debut, introduction, admission, inauguration, induction, inception, enrolment, investiture, baptism of fire, instatement

initiative NOUN **1** *We have the initiative and we intend to keep it.* = **advantage**, start, lead, upper hand **2** *He was disappointed by her lack of initiative.* = **enterprise**, drive, push (*informal*), energy, spirit, resource, leadership, ambition, daring, enthusiasm, pep, vigour, zeal, originality, eagerness, dynamism, boldness, inventiveness, get-up-and-go (*informal*), resourcefulness, gumption (*informal*), adventurousness

inject VERB **1** *His son was injected with strong drugs.* = **vaccinate**, shoot (*informal*), administer, jab (*informal*), shoot up (*informal*), mainline (*informal*), inoculate **2** *She kept trying to inject a little fun into their relationship.* = **introduce**, bring in, insert, instil, infuse, breathe, interject

injection NOUN **1** *They gave me an injection to help me sleep.* = **vaccination**, shot (*informal*), jab (*informal*), dose, vaccine, booster, immunization, inoculation **2** *An injection of cash is needed to fund some of these projects.* = **introduction**, investment, insertion, advancement, dose, infusion, interjection

injunction NOUN = **order**, ruling, command, instruction, dictate, mandate, precept, exhortation (*formal*), admonition

injure VERB **1** *A bomb exploded, seriously injuring five people.* = **hurt**, wound, harm, break, damage, smash, crush, mar, disable, shatter, bruise, impair, mutilate, maim, mangle, mangulate (*Austral. slang*), incapacitate **2** *Too much stress can injure your health.* = **damage**, harm, ruin, wreck, weaken, spoil, impair, crool or cruel (*Austral. slang*) **3** *an attempt to injure another trader's business* = **undermine**, damage, mar, blight, tarnish, blacken, besmirch, vitiate

injured ADJECTIVE **1** *The injured man had a superficial stomach wound.* = **hurt**, damaged, wounded, broken, cut, crushed, weakened, bruised, scarred, crook (*Austral. & N.Z. slang*), fractured, mutilated, maimed, mangled **2** *As yet, there has been no complaint from the injured party.* = **wronged**, abused, harmed, insulted, offended, tainted, tarnished, blackened, maligned, vilified; mistreated, dishonoured, defamed, ill-treated, maltreated, ill-used **3** *compensation for injured feelings* = **upset**, hurt, wounded, troubled, bothered, undermined, distressed, unhappy, stung, put out, grieved, hassled (*informal*), disgruntled, displeased, reproachful, cut to the quick

injurious ADJECTIVE = **harmful**, bad, damaging, corrupting, destructive, adverse, unhealthy, detrimental, hurtful, toxic, pernicious (*formal*), noxious, ruinous, deleterious (*formal*), iniquitous, disadvantageous, baneful (*archaic*), maleficent, unconducive

injury NOUN **1** *Four police officers sustained serious injuries in the explosion.* = **wound**, cut, damage, slash, trauma (*Pathology*), sore, gash, lesion, abrasion, laceration **2** *The two other passengers escaped serious injury.* = **harm**, suffering, damage, ill, hurt, misfortune, affliction, impairment, disfigurement **3** *She was awarded compensation for the injury to her feelings.* = **wrong**, abuse, offence, insult, injustice, grievance, affront, detriment, disservice

injustice NOUN **1** *They will continue to fight injustice.* = **unfairness**, discrimination, prejudice, bias, inequality, oppression, intolerance, bigotry, favouritism, inequity, chauvinism, iniquity, partisanship, partiality, narrow-mindedness, one-sidedness, unlawfulness, unjustness
■ OPPOSITE: justice **2** *I don't want to do an injustice to what I've recorded.* = **wrong**, injury, crime, abuse, error, offence, sin, grievance, infringement, trespass, misdeed, transgression, infraction, bad or evil deed

inkling NOUN = **suspicion**, idea, hint, suggestion, notion, indication, whisper, clue, conception, glimmering, intimation, faintest or foggiest idea

inland ADJECTIVE = **interior**, internal, upcountry

inlet NOUN = **bay**, creek, cove, passage, entrance, fjord, bight, ingress, sea loch (*Scot.*), arm of the sea, firth or frith (*Scot.*)

innards PLURAL NOUN **1** *What happens to the innards of a carcass hung up for butchery?* = **intestines**, insides (*informal*), guts, entrails, viscera, vitals **2** *the delicate innards of a Swiss watch* = **works**, mechanism, guts (*informal*)

innate ADJECTIVE = **inborn**, natural, inherent, essential, native, constitutional, inherited, indigenous, instinctive, intuitive, intrinsic, ingrained, congenital, inbred, immanent, in your blood, connate
■ OPPOSITE: acquired

inner ADJECTIVE **1** *She got up and went into an inner office.* = **inside**, internal, interior, inward ■ OPPOSITE: outer **2** *I've always taught in inner London.* = **central**, middle, internal, interior **3** *He was part of the regime's inner circle.* = **intimate**, close, personal, near, private, friendly, confidential, cherished, bosom **4** *He loves studying chess and discovering its inner secrets.* = **hidden**, deep, secret, underlying, obscure, repressed, esoteric, unrevealed
■ OPPOSITE: obvious

innkeeper NOUN = **publican**, hotelier, mine host, host or hostess, landlord or landlady

innocence NOUN **1** *the sweet innocence of youth* = **naiveté**, simplicity, inexperience, freshness, credulity, gullibility, ingenuousness, artlessness, unworldliness, guilelessness, credulousness, simpleness, trustfulness, unsophistication, naiveness
■ OPPOSITE: worldliness **2** *He claims to have evidence which could prove his innocence.* = **blamelessness**, righteousness, clean hands, uprightness, sinlessness, irreproachability, guiltlessness ■ OPPOSITE: guilt **3** *She can still evoke the innocence of 14-year-old Juliet.* = **chastity**, virtue, purity, modesty, virginity, celibacy, continence, maidenhood, stainlessness **4** *'Maybe innocence is bliss,' he suggested.* = **ignorance**, oblivion, lack of knowledge, inexperience, unfamiliarity, greenness, unawareness, nescience (*literary*)

innocent ADJECTIVE **1** *The police knew from day one that I was innocent.* = **not guilty**, in the clear, blameless, clear, clean, honest, faultless, squeaky-clean, uninvolved, irreproachable, guiltless, unoffending
■ OPPOSITE: guilty **2** *They seemed so young and innocent.* = **naive**, open, trusting, simple, natural, frank, confiding, candid, unaffected, childlike, gullible, unpretentious,

unsophisticated, unworldly, credulous, artless, ingenuous, guileless, wet behind the ears (*informal*), unsuspicious ■ **OPPOSITE:** worldly **3** *It was probably an innocent question, but he got very flustered.* = **harmless**, innocuous, inoffensive, well-meant, unobjectionable, unmalicious, well-intentioned ■ **OPPOSITE:** malicious **4** *innocent children* = **pure**, stainless, immaculate, moral, virgin, decent, upright, impeccable, righteous, pristine, wholesome, spotless, demure, chaste, unblemished, virginal, unsullied, sinless, incorrupt ■ **OPPOSITE:** impure ▶ NOUN *He was a hopeless innocent in the world of politics.* = **child**, novice, greenhorn (*informal*), babe in arms (*informal*), ingénue or (*masc.*) ingénu • **innocent of** *She was completely natural and innocent of any airs and graces.* = **free from**, clear of, unaware of, ignorant of, untouched by, unfamiliar with, empty of, lacking, unacquainted with, nescient of

innocuous ADJECTIVE = **harmless**, safe, innocent, inoffensive, innoxious

innovation NOUN **1** *technological innovations of the industrial age* = **change**, revolution, departure, introduction, variation, transformation, upheaval, alteration **2** *We must promote originality and encourage innovation.* = **newness**, novelty, originality, freshness, modernism, modernization, uniqueness

innovative ADJECTIVE = **novel**, new, original, different, fresh, unusual, unfamiliar, uncommon, inventive, singular, ground-breaking, left-field (*informal*), transformational, variational

innovator NOUN = **modernizer**, introducer, inventor, changer, transformer

innuendo NOUN = **insinuation**, suggestion, hint, implication, whisper (*informal*), overtone, intimation, imputation, aspersion

innumerable ADJECTIVE = **countless**, many, numerous, infinite, myriad, untold, incalculable, numberless, unnumbered, multitudinous, beyond number ■ **OPPOSITE:** limited

inoculation NOUN = **injection**, shot (*informal*), jab (*informal*), vaccination, dose, vaccine, booster, immunization

inordinate ADJECTIVE = **excessive**, unreasonable, disproportionate, extravagant, undue, preposterous, unwarranted, exorbitant, unrestrained, intemperate, unconscionable, immoderate ■ **OPPOSITE:** moderate

inorganic ADJECTIVE = **artificial**, chemical, man-made, mineral

inquest NOUN = **inquiry**, investigation, probe, inquisition

inquire *or* **enquire** VERB *He inquired whether there had been any messages left for him.* = **ask**, question, query, quiz, seek information of, request information of • **inquire into** *Inspectors inquired into the affairs of the company.* = **investigate**, study, examine, consider, research, search, explore, look into, inspect, probe into, scrutinize, make inquiries into

inquiry *or* **enquiry** NOUN **1** *He made some inquiries and discovered she had gone abroad.* = **question**, query, investigation **2** *a murder inquiry* = **investigation**, hearing, study, review, search, survey, analysis, examination, probe, inspection, exploration, scrutiny, inquest **3** *The investigation has switched to a new line of inquiry.* = **research**, investigation, analysis, examination, inspection, exploration, scrutiny, interrogation

inquisition NOUN = **investigation**, questioning, examination, inquiry, grilling (*informal*), quizzing, inquest, cross-examination, third degree (*informal*)

inquisitive ADJECTIVE = **curious**, questioning, inquiring, peering, probing, intrusive, prying, snooping (*informal*), scrutinizing, snoopy (*informal*), nosy (*informal*), nosy-parkering (*informal*) ■ **OPPOSITE:** uninterested

insane ADJECTIVE *Listen, this is completely insane.* = **stupid**, foolish, daft (*informal*), bizarre, irresponsible, irrational, senseless, preposterous, impractical, idiotic, inane, fatuous, dumb-ass (*slang*) ■ **OPPOSITE:** reasonable

insanity NOUN *the final financial insanity of the decade* = **stupidity**, folly, lunacy, irresponsibility, senselessness, preposterousness ■ **OPPOSITE:** sense

insatiable ADJECTIVE = **unquenchable**, greedy, voracious, ravenous, rapacious, intemperate, gluttonous, unappeasable, insatiate, quenchless, edacious ■ **OPPOSITE:** satiable

inscribe VERB **1** *They read the words inscribed on the walls of the monument.* = **carve**, cut, etch, engrave, impress, imprint **2** *The book is inscribed: To John Arlott from Laurie Lee.* = **dedicate**, sign, address

inscription NOUN = **engraving**, words, lettering, label, legend, saying

inscrutable ADJECTIVE **1** *It is important to keep a straight face and remain inscrutable.* = **enigmatic**, blank, impenetrable, deadpan, unreadable, poker-faced (*informal*), sphinxlike ■ **OPPOSITE:**

transparent **2** *Even when opened the contents of the package were as inscrutable as ever.* = **mysterious**, incomprehensible, inexplicable, hidden, unintelligible, unfathomable, unexplainable, undiscoverable ■ **OPPOSITE:** comprehensible

insect NOUN = **bug**, creepy-crawly (*Brit. informal*), gogga (*S. African informal*)
■ **RELATED WORDS:** *adjective* entomic; *collective noun* swarm

insecure ADJECTIVE **1** *Many women are insecure about their performance as mothers.* = **unconfident**, worried, anxious, afraid, shy, uncertain, unsure, timid, self-conscious, hesitant, meek, self-effacing, diffident, unassertive ■ **OPPOSITE:** confident **2** *huge allowances paid to staff working in insecure environments* = **unsafe**, dangerous, exposed, vulnerable, hazardous, wide-open, perilous, unprotected, defenceless, unguarded, open to attack, unshielded, ill-protected ■ **OPPOSITE:** safe **3** *low-paid, insecure jobs* = **unreliable**, unstable, unsafe, precarious, unsteady, unsound ■ **OPPOSITE:** secure

insecurity NOUN **1** *She is always assailed by emotional insecurity.* = **anxiety**, fear, worry, uncertainty, unsureness ■ **OPPOSITE:** confidence **2** *The increase in crime has created feelings of insecurity.* = **vulnerability**, risk, danger, weakness, uncertainty, hazard, peril, defencelessness ■ **OPPOSITE:** safety **3** *the harshness and insecurity of agricultural life* = **instability**, uncertainty, unreliability, precariousness, weakness, shakiness, unsteadiness, dubiety, frailness ■ **OPPOSITE:** stability

insensitive ADJECTIVE *My husband is very insensitive about my problem.* = **unfeeling**, indifferent, unconcerned, uncaring, tough, hardened, callous, crass, unresponsive, thick-skinned, obtuse, tactless, imperceptive, unsusceptible ■ **OPPOSITE:** sensitive • **insensitive to** *He had become insensitive to cold.* = **unaffected by**, immune to, impervious to, dead to, unmoved by, proof against

inseparable ADJECTIVE **1** *The two girls were inseparable.* = **devoted**, close, intimate, bosom **2** *He believes liberty is inseparable from social justice.* = **indivisible**, inalienable, conjoined, indissoluble, inseverable

insert VERB = **put**, place, set, position, work in, slip, slide, slot, thrust, stick in, wedge, tuck in

insertion NOUN **1** *the first experiment involving the insertion of a new gene* = **inclusion**, introduction, interpolation **2** *The correction*

to the text may involve an insertion or a deletion. = **insert**, addition, inclusion, supplement, implant, inset

inside NOUN *Cut off the top and scoop out the inside with a teaspoon.* = **interior**, contents, core, nucleus, inner part, inner side
▶ PLURAL NOUN *My insides ached from eating too much.* = **stomach**, gut, guts, belly, bowels, internal organs, innards (*informal*), entrails, viscera, vitals ▶ ADJECTIVE **1** *four-berth inside cabins with en suite bathrooms* = **inner**, internal, interior, inward, innermost ■ **OPPOSITE:** outside **2** *The editor denies he had any inside knowledge.* = **confidential**, private, secret, internal, exclusive, restricted, privileged, classified
▶ ADVERB *They chatted briefly on the doorstep before going inside.* = **indoors**, in, within, under cover

insidious ADJECTIVE = **stealthy**, subtle, cunning, designing, smooth, tricky, crooked, sneaking, slick, sly, treacherous, deceptive, wily, crafty, disingenuous, Machiavellian, deceitful, surreptitious, duplicitous, guileful ■ **OPPOSITE:** straightforward

insight NOUN **1** *He was a man of considerable insight and diplomatic skills.* = **perception**, understanding, intelligence, sense, knowledge, vision, judgment, awareness, grasp, appreciation, intuition, penetration, comprehension, acumen, discernment, perspicacity (*formal*) **2** (*with* **into**) *The talk gave us some insight into the work they were doing.* = **understanding**, perception, awareness, experience, description, introduction, observation, judgment, revelation, comprehension, intuitiveness

insightful ADJECTIVE = **perceptive**, shrewd, discerning, understanding, wise, penetrating, knowledgeable, astute, observant, perspicacious (*formal*), sagacious (*formal*)

insignia NOUN = **badge**, symbol, decoration, crest, earmark, emblem, ensign, distinguishing mark

insignificance NOUN = **unimportance**, irrelevance, triviality, pettiness, worthlessness, meaninglessness, inconsequence, immateriality, paltriness, negligibility ■ **OPPOSITE:** importance

insignificant ADJECTIVE = **unimportant**, minor, irrelevant, petty, trivial, meaningless, trifling, meagre, negligible, flimsy, paltry, immaterial, inconsequential, nondescript, measly (*informal*), scanty, inconsiderable, of no consequence, nonessential, small potatoes, nickel-and-dime (*U.S. slang*), of no account, nugatory, unsubstantial, not worth mentioning, of no moment ■ **OPPOSITE:** important

insincere ADJECTIVE = **deceitful**, lying, false, pretended, hollow, untrue, dishonest, deceptive, devious, hypocritical, unfaithful, evasive, two-faced, disingenuous, faithless, double-dealing, duplicitous, dissembling, mendacious, perfidious (*literary*), untruthful, dissimulating, Janus-faced
■ **OPPOSITE:** sincere

insinuate VERB = **imply**, suggest, hint, indicate, intimate, allude

insipid ADJECTIVE 1 *It tasted bland and insipid, like warm cardboard.* = **tasteless**, bland, flavourless, watered down, watery, wishy-washy (*informal*), unappetizing, savourless ■ **OPPOSITE:** tasty 2 *She pretended to be meek and insipid so they would underestimate her.* = **bland**, boring, dull, flat, dry, weak, stupid, limp, tame, pointless, tedious, stale, drab, banal, tiresome, lifeless, prosaic, trite, unimaginative, colourless, uninteresting, anaemic, wishy-washy (*informal*), ho-hum (*informal*), vapid, wearisome, characterless, spiritless, jejune (*old-fashioned*), prosy ■ **OPPOSITE:** exciting

insist VERB 1 *I didn't want to join in, but he insisted.* = **persist**, press (someone), be firm, stand firm, stand your ground, lay down the law, put your foot down (*informal*), not take no for an answer, brook no refusal, take or make a stand 2 *I insisted that the fault be repaired.* = **demand**, order, urge, require, command, dictate, entreat 3 *He insisted that he was acting out of compassion.* = **assert**, state, maintain, hold, claim, declare, repeat, vow, swear, contend, affirm, reiterate, profess, avow, aver, asseverate (*formal*)

insistence NOUN 1 *She had attended an interview at his insistence.* = **demand**, urging, command, pressing, dictate, entreaty, importunity, insistency 2 *her insistence that she wanted to change her image* = **assertion**, claim, statement, declaration, contention, persistence, affirmation, pronouncement, reiteration, avowal, attestation

insistent ADJECTIVE 1 *He is most insistent on this point.* = **emphatic**, persistent, demanding, pressing, dogged, urgent, forceful, persevering, unrelenting, peremptory, importunate (*formal*), exigent 2 *the insistent rhythms of dance music* = **persistent**, repeated, constant, repetitive, incessant, unremitting

insolence NOUN = **rudeness**, cheek (*informal*), disrespect, front, abuse, sauce (*informal*), gall (*informal*), audacity,

boldness, chutzpah (*U.S. & Canad. informal*), insubordination, impertinence, impudence, effrontery, backchat (*informal*), incivility, sassiness (*U.S. informal*), pertness, contemptuousness ■ **OPPOSITE:** politeness

insolent ADJECTIVE = **rude**, cheeky, impertinent, fresh (*informal*), bold, insulting, abusive, saucy, contemptuous, pert, impudent, uncivil, insubordinate, brazen-faced ■ **OPPOSITE:** polite

insoluble ADJECTIVE = **inexplicable**, mysterious, baffling, obscure, mystifying, impenetrable, unaccountable, unfathomable, indecipherable, unsolvable
■ **OPPOSITE:** explicable

insolvency NOUN = **bankruptcy**, failure, ruin, liquidation

insolvent ADJECTIVE = **bankrupt**, ruined, on the rocks (*informal*), broke (*informal*), failed, gone bust (*informal*), in receivership, gone to the wall, in the hands of the receivers, in queer street (*informal*)

insomnia NOUN = **sleeplessness**, restlessness, wakefulness

insouciance NOUN = **nonchalance**, light-heartedness, jauntiness, airiness, breeziness, carefreeness

inspect VERB 1 *Cut the fruit in half and inspect the pips.* = **examine**, check, look at, view, eye, survey, observe, scan, check out (*informal*), look over, eyeball (*slang*), scrutinize, give (something or someone) the once-over (*informal*), take a dekko at (*Brit. slang*), go over or through 2 *Each hotel is inspected once a year.* = **check**, examine, investigate, study, look at, research, search, survey, assess, probe, audit, vet, oversee, supervise, check out (*informal*), look over, work over, superintend, give (something or someone) the once-over (*informal*), go over or through

inspection NOUN 1 *Closer inspection reveals that they are banded with yellow.* = **examination**, investigation, scrutiny, scan, look-over, once-over (*informal*) 2 *A routine inspection of the vessel turned up 50 kg of the drug.* = **check**, search, investigation, review, survey, examination, scan, scrutiny, supervision, surveillance, look-over, once-over (*informal*), checkup, recce (*slang*), superintendence

inspector NOUN = **examiner**, investigator, supervisor, monitor, superintendent, auditor, censor, surveyor, scrutinizer, checker, overseer, scrutineer

inspiration NOUN 1 *A good way of getting inspiration is by looking at others' work.* = **imagination**, creativity, ingenuity, talent, insight, genius, productivity, fertility, stimulation, originality, inventiveness, cleverness, fecundity, imaginativeness, inspo (*slang*) **2** *She was very impressive and a great inspiration to all.* = **motivation**, example, influence, model, boost, spur, incentive, revelation, encouragement, stimulus, catalyst, stimulation, inducement, incitement, instigation, afflatus, inspo (*slang*) ■ **OPPOSITE:** deterrent **3** *India's myths and songs are the inspiration for her books.* = **influence**, spur, stimulus, muse

inspire VERB **1** *What inspired you to change your name?* = **motivate**, move, cause, stimulate, encourage, influence, persuade, spur, be responsible for, animate, rouse, instil, infuse, hearten, enliven, imbue, spark off, energize, galvanize, gee up, inspirit, fire or touch the imagination of ■ **OPPOSITE:** discourage **2** *His legend would even inspire a well-known song.* = **give rise to**, cause, produce, result in, prompt, stir, spawn, engender

inspired ADJECTIVE **1** *She produced an inspired performance.* = **brilliant**, wonderful, impressive, exciting, outstanding, thrilling, memorable, dazzling, enthralling, superlative, of genius **2** *Garcia played like a man inspired.* = **stimulated**, possessed, aroused, uplifted, exhilarated, stirred up, enthused, exalted, elated, galvanized

inspiring ADJECTIVE = **uplifting**, encouraging, exciting, moving, affecting, stirring, stimulating, rousing, exhilarating, heartening ■ **OPPOSITE:** uninspiring

instability NOUN **1** *unpopular policies which resulted in political instability* = **uncertainty**, insecurity, weakness, imbalance, vulnerability, wavering, volatility, unpredictability, restlessness, fluidity, fluctuation, disequilibrium, transience, impermanence, precariousness, mutability, shakiness, unsteadiness, inconstancy ■ **OPPOSITE:** stability **2** *Caligula's inherent mental instability* = **imbalance**, weakness, volatility, variability, frailty, unpredictability, oscillation, vacillation, capriciousness, unsteadiness, flightiness, fitfulness, changeableness

install VERB **1** *They had installed wi-fi in the apartment.* = **set up**, put in, place, position, station, establish, lay, fix, locate, lodge **2** *A new Catholic bishop was installed yesterday.* = **institute**, establish, introduce, invest, ordain, inaugurate, induct, instate **3** *Before her husband's death she had installed herself in a modern villa.* = **settle**, position, plant, establish, lodge, ensconce

installation NOUN **1** *Lives could be saved if installation of alarms was stepped up.* = **setting up**, fitting, instalment, placing, positioning, establishment **2** *He invited her to attend his installation as chief of his tribe.* = **appointment**, ordination, inauguration, induction, investiture, instatement **3** *a secret military installation* = **base**, centre, post, station, camp, settlement, establishment, headquarters

instalment NOUN **1** *The first instalment is payable on application.* = **payment**, repayment, part payment **2** *The next instalment deals with the social impact of the war.* = **part**, section, chapter, episode, portion, division

instance NOUN **1** *a serious instance of corruption* = **example**, case, occurrence, occasion, sample, illustration, precedent, case in point, exemplification **2** *The meeting was organized at the instance of two senior ministers.* = **insistence**, demand, urging, pressure, stress, application, request, prompting, impulse, behest, incitement, instigation, solicitation, entreaty, importunity ▶ VERB *She could have instanced many women who fitted this description.* = **name**, mention, identify, point out, advance, quote, finger (*informal, chiefly U.S.*), refer to, point to, cite, specify, invoke, allude to, adduce, namedrop

instant NOUN **1** *The pain disappeared in an instant.* = **moment**, second, minute, shake (*informal*), flash, tick (*Brit. informal*), no time, twinkling, split second, jiffy (*informal*), trice, twinkling of an eye (*informal*), two shakes (*informal*), two shakes of a lamb's tail (*informal*), bat of an eye (*informal*) **2** *At the same instant, she flung open the car door.* = **time**, point, hour, moment, stage, occasion, phase, juncture ▶ ADJECTIVE **1** *I had taken an instant dislike to her.* = **immediate**, prompt, instantaneous, direct, quick, urgent, on-the-spot, split-second **2** *She was stirring instant coffee into two mugs of hot water.* = **ready-made**, fast, convenience, ready-mixed, ready-cooked, precooked

instantaneous ADJECTIVE = **immediate**, prompt, instant, direct, on-the-spot

instantaneously ADVERB = **immediately**, instantly, at once, straight away, promptly, on the spot, forthwith, in the same breath, then and there, pronto (*informal*), in the twinkling of an eye (*informal*), on the instant, in a fraction of a second, posthaste, quick as lightning, in the bat of an eye (*informal*)

instantly ADVERB = **immediately**, at once, straight away, now, directly, on the spot, right away, there and then, without delay, instantaneously, forthwith, this minute, pronto (*informal*), posthaste, instanter (*Law*), tout de suite (*French*)

instead ADVERB *Forget about dieting and eat normally instead.* = **rather**, alternatively, preferably, in preference, in lieu, on second thoughts • **instead of** *She had to spend four months away, instead of the usual two.* = **in place of**, rather than, in preference to, in lieu of, in contrast with, as an alternative or equivalent to

instigate VERB = **provoke**, start, encourage, move, influence, prompt, trigger, spur, stimulate, set off, initiate, bring about, rouse, prod, stir up, get going, incite, kick-start, whip up, impel, kindle, foment, actuate ■ **OPPOSITE:** suppress

instigation NOUN = **prompting**, urging, bidding, incentive, encouragement, behest, incitement

instigator NOUN = **ringleader**, inciter, motivator, leader, spur, goad, troublemaker, incendiary, firebrand, prime mover, fomenter, agitator, stirrer (*informal*), mischief-maker

instil *or* **instill** VERB = **introduce**, implant, engender, infuse, imbue, impress, insinuate, sow the seeds, inculcate, engraft, infix

instinct NOUN **1** *I didn't have a strong maternal instinct.* = **natural inclination**, feeling, urge, talent, tendency, faculty, inclination, intuition, knack, aptitude, predisposition, sixth sense, proclivity (*formal*), gut reaction (*informal*), second sight **2** *She has a natural instinct to perform.* = **talent**, skill, gift, capacity, bent, genius, faculty, knack, aptitude **3** *I should have gone with my first instinct.* = **intuition**, feeling, impulse, gut feeling (*informal*), sixth sense

instinctive ADJECTIVE = **natural**, inborn, automatic, unconscious, mechanical, native, inherent, spontaneous, reflex, innate, intuitive, subconscious, involuntary, visceral, unthinking, instinctual, unlearned, unpremeditated, intuitional ■ **OPPOSITE:** acquired

instinctively ADVERB = **intuitively**, naturally, automatically, without thinking, involuntarily, by instinct, in your bones

institute NOUN *a research institute devoted to software programming* = **establishment**, body, centre, school, university, society, association, college, institution, organization, foundation, academy, guild, conservatory, fellowship, seminary, seat of learning ▶ VERB *We will institute a number of methods to improve safety.* = **establish**, start,

begin, found, launch, set up, introduce, settle, fix, invest, organize, install, pioneer, constitute, initiate, originate, enact, commence, inaugurate, set in motion, bring into being, put into operation ■ **OPPOSITE:** end

institution NOUN **1** *Class size varies from one type of institution to another.* = **establishment**, body, centre, school, university, society, association, college, institute, organization, foundation, academy, guild, conservatory, fellowship, seminary, seat of learning **2** *I believe in the institution of marriage.* = **custom**, practice, tradition, law, rule, procedure, convention, ritual, fixture, rite **3** *the institution of the forty-hour week* = **creation**, introduction, establishment, investment, debut, foundation, formation, installation, initiation, inauguration, enactment, inception, commencement, investiture

institutional ADJECTIVE = **conventional**, accepted, established, formal, establishment (*informal*), organized, routine, orthodox, bureaucratic, procedural, societal

instruct VERB **1** *They have instructed solicitors to sue for compensation.* = **order**, tell, direct, charge (*formal*), bid, command, mandate, enjoin **2** *He instructs family members in nursing techniques.* = **teach**, school, train, direct, coach, guide, discipline, educate, drill, tutor, enlighten, give lessons in **3** *Instruct them that they've got three months to get it sorted out.* = **tell**, advise, inform, counsel, notify, brief, acquaint, apprise

instruction NOUN **1** *No reason for this instruction was given.* = **order**, ruling, command, rule, demand, direction, regulation, dictate, decree, mandate, directive, injunction, behest **2** *Each candidate is given instruction in safety.* = **teaching**, schooling, training, classes, grounding, education, coaching, lesson(s), discipline, preparation, drilling, guidance, tutoring, tuition, enlightenment, apprenticeship, tutorials, tutelage (*formal*) ▶ PLURAL NOUN *This book gives instructions for making a variety of hand creams.* = **information**, rules, advice, directions, recommendations, guidance, specifications

instructive ADJECTIVE = **informative**, revealing, useful, educational, helpful, illuminating, enlightening, instructional, cautionary, didactic, edifying

instructor NOUN = **teacher**, coach, guide, adviser, trainer, demonstrator, tutor, guru, mentor, educator, pedagogue, preceptor (*rare*), master or mistress, schoolmaster or schoolmistress

instrument NOUN **1** *a thin tube-like optical instrument* = **tool**, device, implement, mechanism, appliance, apparatus, gadget, utensil, contraption (*informal*), contrivance, waldo **2** *The veto is a traditional instrument for diplomacy.* = **agent**, means, force, cause, medium, agency (*old-fashioned*), factor (*Scot.*), channel, vehicle, mechanism, organ **3** *The Council was an instrument of Government.* = **puppet**, tool, pawn, toy, creature, dupe, stooge (*slang*), plaything, cat's-paw

instrumental ADJECTIVE = **active**, involved, influential, useful, helpful, conducive, contributory, of help or service

insubstantial ADJECTIVE **1** *Her limbs were insubstantial, almost transparent.* = **flimsy**, thin, weak, slight, frail, feeble, tenuous ■ **OPPOSITE:** substantial **2** *Their thoughts seemed as insubstantial as smoke.* = **imaginary**, unreal, fanciful, immaterial, ephemeral, illusory, incorporeal, chimerical

insufferable ADJECTIVE = **unbearable**, impossible, intolerable, dreadful, outrageous, unspeakable, detestable, insupportable, unendurable, past bearing, more than flesh and blood can stand, enough to test the patience of a saint, enough to try the patience of Job ■ **OPPOSITE:** bearable

insufficient ADJECTIVE = **inadequate**, incomplete, scant, meagre, short, sparse, deficient, lacking, unqualified, insubstantial, incommensurate ■ **OPPOSITE:** ample

insular ADJECTIVE = **narrow-minded**, prejudiced, provincial, closed, limited, narrow, petty, parochial, blinkered, circumscribed, inward-looking, illiberal, parish-pump ■ **OPPOSITE:** broad-minded

insulate VERB = **isolate**, protect, screen, defend, shelter, shield, cut off, cushion, cocoon, close off, sequester, wrap up in cotton wool

insult VERB *I didn't mean to insult you.* = **offend**, abuse, injure, wound, slight, outrage, put down, humiliate, libel, snub, slag (off) (*slang*), malign, affront, denigrate, disparage, revile, slander, displease, defame, hurt (someone's) feelings, call names, give offence to ■ **OPPOSITE:** praise ▸ NOUN **1** *Some of the officers shouted insults at prisoners on the roof.* = **jibe**, slight, put-down, abuse, snub, barb, affront, indignity, contumely, abusive remark, aspersion **2** *Their behaviour was an insult to the people they represented.* = **offence**, slight, outrage, snub, slur, affront, rudeness, slap in the face (*informal*), kick in the teeth (*informal*), insolence, aspersion

insulting ADJECTIVE = **offensive**, rude, abusive, slighting, degrading, affronting, contemptuous, disparaging, scurrilous, insolent ■ **OPPOSITE:** complimentary

insuperable ADJECTIVE = **insurmountable**, invincible, impassable, unconquerable ■ **OPPOSITE:** surmountable

insurance NOUN **1** *You are advised to take out insurance on your lenses.* = **assurance**, cover, security, protection, coverage, safeguard, indemnity, indemnification **2** *Put something away as insurance against failure of the business.* = **protection**, security, guarantee, provision, shelter, safeguard, warranty

insure VERB **1** *We automatically insure your furniture and belongings against fire.* = **assure**, cover, protect, guarantee, warrant, underwrite, indemnify **2** *He needs to insure himself against ambitious party rivals.* = **protect**, cover, safeguard

insurgent NOUN *The insurgents took control of the main military air base.* = **rebel**, revolutionary, revolter, rioter, resister, mutineer, revolutionist, insurrectionist ▸ ADJECTIVE *The insurgent leaders were publicly executed.* = **rebellious**, revolutionary, mutinous, revolting, riotous, seditious, disobedient, insubordinate, insurrectionary

insurmountable ADJECTIVE = **insuperable**, impossible, overwhelming, hopeless, invincible, impassable, unconquerable

insurrection NOUN = **rebellion**, rising, revolution, riot, coup, revolt, uprising, mutiny, insurgency, putsch, sedition

intact ADJECTIVE = **undamaged**, whole, complete, sound, perfect, entire, virgin, untouched, unscathed, unbroken, flawless, unhurt, faultless, unharmed, uninjured, unimpaired, undefiled, all in one piece, together, scatheless, unviolated ■ **OPPOSITE:** damaged

intangible ADJECTIVE = **abstract**, vague, invisible, dim, elusive, shadowy, airy, unreal, indefinite, ethereal, evanescent, incorporeal, impalpable (*formal*), unsubstantial

integral ADJECTIVE **1** *Rituals form an integral part of any human society.* = **essential**, basic, fundamental, necessary, component, constituent, indispensable, intrinsic, requisite, elemental ■ **OPPOSITE:** inessential **2** *This is meant to be an integral service.* = **whole**, full, complete, entire, intact, undivided ■ **OPPOSITE:** partial

integrate VERB = **join**, unite, combine, blend, incorporate, merge, accommodate, knit, fuse, mesh, assimilate, amalgamate,

coalesce, harmonize, meld, intermix
■ **OPPOSITE:** separate

integrity NOUN **1** *I have always regarded him
as a man of integrity.* = **honesty**, principle,
honour, virtue, goodness, morality, purity,
righteousness, probity (*formal*), rectitude,
truthfulness, trustworthiness,
incorruptibility, uprightness,
scrupulousness, reputability ■ **OPPOSITE:**
dishonesty **2** *Separatist movements are a
threat to the integrity of the nation.* = **unity**,
unification, cohesion, coherence,
wholeness, soundness, completeness
■ **OPPOSITE:** fragility

intellect NOUN **1** *Do the emotions develop in
parallel with the intellect?* = **intelligence**,
mind, reason, understanding, sense, brains
(*informal*), judgment **2** *My boss isn't a great
intellect.* = **thinker**, intellectual, genius,
mind, brain (*informal*), intelligence, rocket
scientist (*informal*), egghead (*informal*)

intellectual ADJECTIVE *They were very
intellectual and witty.* = **scholarly**, learned,
academic, lettered, intelligent, rational,
cerebral, erudite, scholastic, highbrow,
well-read, studious, bookish ■ **OPPOSITE:**
stupid ▶ NOUN *teachers, artists and other
intellectuals* = **academic**, expert, genius,
thinker, master, brain (*informal*),
mastermind, maestro, highbrow, rocket
scientist (*informal*), egghead (*informal*),
brainbox, bluestocking (*usually derogatory*),
pointy-head (*informal, chiefly U.S.*),
master-hand, fundi (*S. African*), acca
(*Austral. slang*)

intelligence NOUN **1** *She's a woman of
exceptional intelligence.* = **intellect**,
understanding, brains (*informal*), mind,
reason, sense, knowledge, capacity, smarts
(*slang, chiefly U.S.*), judgment, wit,
perception, awareness, insight,
penetration, comprehension, brightness
(*informal*), aptitude, acumen, nous (*Brit.
slang*), alertness, cleverness, quickness,
discernment, grey matter (*informal*), brain
power ■ **OPPOSITE:** stupidity **2** *a senior
officer involved in gathering intelligence*
= **information**, news, facts, report,
findings, word, notice, advice, knowledge,
data, disclosure, gen (*Brit. informal*), tip-off,
low-down (*informal*), notification, heads up
(*U.S. & Canad.*) ■ **OPPOSITE:** misinformation

intelligent ADJECTIVE = **clever**, bright
(*informal*), smart, knowing, quick, sharp,
acute, alert, rational, penetrating,
enlightened, apt, discerning, knowledgeable,
astute, well-informed, brainy (*informal*),
perspicacious, quick-witted, sagacious
(*formal*) ■ **OPPOSITE:** stupid

intelligentsia NOUN = **intellectuals**,
highbrows, literati, masterminds, the
learned, eggheads (*informal*), illuminati,
bloggerati (*informal*)

intelligible ADJECTIVE = **understandable**,
clear, distinct, lucid, comprehensible
■ **OPPOSITE:** unintelligible

intemperate ADJECTIVE = **excessive**,
extreme, over the top (*slang*), wild, violent,
severe, passionate, extravagant,
uncontrollable, self-indulgent, unbridled,
prodigal, unrestrained, tempestuous,
profligate, inordinate, incontinent,
ungovernable, immoderate, O.T.T. (*slang*)
■ **OPPOSITE:** temperate

intend VERB **1** *She intends to do A levels and go
to university.* = **plan**, mean, aim, determine,
scheme, propose, purpose, contemplate,
envisage, foresee, be resolved or
determined, have in mind or view **2** (*often
with* **for**) *This money is intended for the
development of the tourist industry.* = **destine**,
mean, design, earmark, consign, aim, mark
out, set apart

intended ADJECTIVE *He hoped the sarcasm
would have its intended effect.* = **planned**,
proposed ▶ NOUN *Meg is planning to marry
her intended on New Year's Day.* = **betrothed**,
fiancé or fiancée, future wife or husband,
husband- or wife-to-be

intense ADJECTIVE **1** *He was sweating from the
intense heat.* = **extreme**, great, severe,
fierce, serious (*informal*), deep, powerful,
concentrated, supreme, acute, harsh,
intensive, excessive, profound, exquisite,
drastic, forceful, protracted, unqualified,
agonizing, mother of all (*informal*)
■ **OPPOSITE:** mild **2** *The battle for third place
was intense.* = **fierce**, close, tough **3** *She is
more adult, and more intense than I had
imagined.* = **passionate**, burning, earnest,
emotional, keen, flaming, consuming,
fierce, eager, enthusiastic, heightened,
energetic, animated, ardent, fanatical,
fervent, heartfelt, impassioned, vehement,
forcible, fervid ■ **OPPOSITE:** indifferent

> **USAGE** *Intense* is sometimes wrongly
> used where *intensive* is meant: *the land is
> under intensive* (not *intense*) *cultivation*.
> *Intensely* is sometimes wrongly used
> where *intently* is meant: *he listened
> intently* (not *intensely*).

intensely ADVERB **1** *The fast-food business is
intensely competitive.* = **very**, highly,
extremely, greatly, strongly, severely,
terribly, ultra, utterly, unusually,
exceptionally, extraordinarily, markedly,
awfully (*informal*), acutely, exceedingly,
excessively, inordinately, uncommonly,

to the nth degree, to *or* in the extreme **2** *He sipped his drink, staring intensely at me.* = **intently**, deeply, seriously (*informal*), profoundly, passionately

intensify VERB **1** *They are intensifying their efforts to secure the release of the hostages.* = **increase**, boost, raise, extend, concentrate, add to, strengthen, enhance, compound, reinforce, step up (*informal*), emphasize, widen, heighten, sharpen, magnify, amplify, augment, redouble ■ **OPPOSITE:** decrease **2** *The conflict is almost bound to intensify.* = **escalate**, increase, extend, widen, heighten, deepen, quicken

intensity NOUN **1** *The attack was anticipated, but its intensity came as a shock.* = **force**, power, strength, severity, extremity, fierceness **2** *His intensity, and the ferocity of his feelings alarmed me.* = **passion**, emotion, fervour, force, power, fire, energy, strength, depth, concentration, excess, severity, vigour, potency, extremity, fanaticism, ardour, vehemence, earnestness, keenness, fierceness, fervency, intenseness

intensive ADJECTIVE = **concentrated**, thorough, exhaustive, full, demanding, detailed, complete, serious, concerted, intense, comprehensive, vigorous, all-out, in-depth, strenuous, painstaking, all-embracing, assiduous, thoroughgoing

intent ADJECTIVE *She looked from one intent face to another.* = **absorbed**, focused, fixed, earnest, committed, concentrated, occupied, intense, fascinated, steady, alert, wrapped up, preoccupied, enthralled, attentive, watchful, engrossed, steadfast, rapt, enrapt ■ **OPPOSITE:** indifferent ▶ NOUN *a statement of intent on arms control* = **intention**, aim, purpose, meaning, end, plan, goal, design, target, object, resolution, resolve, objective, ambition, aspiration ■ **OPPOSITE:** chance • **intent on something** *The rebels are obviously intent on stepping up the pressure.* = **set on**, committed to, eager to, bent on, fixated on, hellbent on (*informal*), insistent about, determined about, resolute about, inflexible about, resolved about • **to all intents and purposes** *To all intents and purposes he was my father.* = **in effect**, essentially, effectively, really, actually, in fact, virtually, in reality, in truth, in actuality, for practical purposes

intention NOUN = **aim**, plan, idea, goal, end, design, target, wish, scheme, purpose, object, objective, determination, intent

intentional ADJECTIVE = **deliberate**, meant, planned, studied, designed, purposed, intended, calculated, wilful, premeditated, prearranged, done on purpose, preconcerted ■ **OPPOSITE:** unintentional

intentionally ADVERB = **deliberately**, on purpose, wilfully, by design, designedly

intently ADVERB = **attentively**, closely, hard, keenly, steadily, fixedly, searchingly, watchfully

inter VERB = **bury**, lay to rest, entomb, sepulchre, consign to the grave, inhume, inurn

intercede VERB = **mediate**, speak, plead, intervene, arbitrate, advocate, interpose

intercept VERB = **catch**, take, stop, check, block, arrest, seize, cut off, interrupt, head off, deflect, obstruct

interchange NOUN *the interchange of ideas from different disciplines* = **exchange**, give and take, alternation, reciprocation ▶ VERB *She likes to interchange furniture at home with stock from the shop.* = **exchange**, switch, swap, alternate, trade, barter, reciprocate, bandy

interchangeable ADJECTIVE = **identical**, the same, equivalent, synonymous, reciprocal, exchangeable, transposable, commutable

intercourse NOUN **1** *DNA tests showed no evidence that intercourse had taken place.* = **sexual intercourse**, sex (*informal*), lovemaking, congress, sexual relations, sexual act, nookie (*slang*), copulation, rumpy-pumpy (*slang*), legover (*slang*) **2** *There was social intercourse between the old and the young.* = **contact**, relationships, communication, association, relations, trade, traffic, connection, truck, commerce (*literary*), dealings, correspondence, communion, converse, intercommunication

interest NOUN **1** *Food was of no interest to her at all.* = **importance**, concern, significance, moment, note, weight, import (*formal*), consequence, substance, relevance, momentousness ■ **OPPOSITE:** insignificance **2** *They will follow the political crisis with interest.* = **attention**, regard, curiosity, notice, suspicion, scrutiny, heed, absorption, attentiveness, inquisitiveness, engrossment ■ **OPPOSITE:** disregard **3** (*often plural*) *He developed a wide range of sporting interests.* = **hobby**, activity, pursuit, entertainment, relaxation, recreation, amusement, preoccupation, diversion, pastime, leisure activity **4** (*often plural*) *Did the Directors act in the best interests of their club?* = **advantage**, good, benefit, profit, gain, boot (*dialect*) **5** (*often plural*) *The family controls large dairy interests.* = **business**, concern, matter, affair **6** *The West has an interest in promoting democratic forces.*

= **stake**, investment ▶ VERB **1** *This part of the book interests me in particular.* = **arouse your curiosity**, engage, appeal to, fascinate, move, involve, touch, affect, attract, grip, entertain, absorb, intrigue, amuse, divert, rivet, captivate, catch your eye, hold the attention of, engross ■ **OPPOSITE:** bore **2** (*with* **in**) *In the meantime, can I interest you in a new car?* = **sell**, persuade to buy • **in the interest(s) of** *We must all work together in the interest of national stability.* = **for the sake of**, on behalf of, on the part of, to the advantage of

interested ADJECTIVE **1** *He did not look interested.* = **curious**, into (*informal*), moved, affected, attracted, excited, drawn, keen, gripped, fascinated, stimulated, intent, responsive, riveted, captivated, attentive ■ **OPPOSITE:** uninterested **2** *All the interested parties finally agreed to the idea.* = **involved**, concerned, affected, prejudiced, biased, partial, partisan, implicated, predisposed

interesting ADJECTIVE = **intriguing**, fascinating, absorbing, pleasing, appealing, attractive, engaging, unusual, gripping, stirring, entertaining, entrancing, stimulating, curious, compelling, amusing, compulsive, riveting, captivating, enthralling, beguiling, thought-provoking, engrossing, spellbinding ■ **OPPOSITE:** uninteresting

interface NOUN *the interface between bureaucracy and the working world* = **connection**, link, boundary, border, frontier ▶ VERB *the way we interface with the environment* = **connect**, couple, link, combine, join together

interfere VERB *Stop interfering and leave me alone!* = **meddle**, intervene, intrude, butt in, get involved, tamper, pry, encroach, intercede, stick your nose in (*informal*), stick your oar in (*informal*), poke your nose in (*informal*), intermeddle, put your two cents in (*U.S. slang*) • **interfere with something** *or* **someone** *Drug problems frequently interfered with his work.* = **conflict with**, affect, get in the way of, check, block, clash, frustrate, handicap, hamper, disrupt, cramp, inhibit, thwart, hinder, obstruct, impede, baulk, trammel, be a drag upon (*informal*)

interference NOUN = **intrusion**, intervention, meddling, opposition, conflict, obstruction, prying, impedance, meddlesomeness, intermeddling

interfering ADJECTIVE = **meddling**, intrusive, prying, obtrusive, meddlesome, interruptive

interim ADJECTIVE *an interim report*

= **temporary**, provisional, makeshift, acting, passing, intervening, caretaker, improvised, transient, stopgap, pro tem ▶ NOUN *He was to remain in jail in the interim.* = **interval**, meanwhile, meantime, respite, interregnum, entr'acte

interior NOUN **1** *The boat's interior badly needed painting.* = **inside**, centre, heart, middle, contents, depths, core, belly, nucleus, bowels, bosom, innards (*informal*) **2** *a 5-day hike into the interior* = **heartland**, centre, hinterland, upcountry ▶ ADJECTIVE **1** *He turned on the interior light and examined the map.* = **inside**, internal, inner ■ **OPPOSITE:** exterior **2** *the interior life of human beings* = **mental**, emotional, psychological, private, personal, secret, hidden, spiritual, intimate, inner, inward, instinctive, impulsive **3** *The French Interior Minister has intervened over the scandal.* = **domestic**, home, national, civil, internal

interject VERB = **interrupt with**, put in, interpose, introduce, throw in, interpolate

interjection NOUN = **exclamation**, cry, ejaculation (*literary*), interpolation, interposition

interloper NOUN = **trespasser**, intruder, gate-crasher (*informal*), uninvited guest, meddler, unwanted visitor, intermeddler

interlude NOUN = **interval**, break, spell, stop, rest, halt, episode, pause, respite, stoppage, breathing space, hiatus, intermission, entr'acte

intermediary NOUN = **mediator**, agent, middleman, broker, entrepreneur, go-between

intermediate ADJECTIVE = **middle**, mid, halfway, in-between (*informal*), midway, intervening, transitional, intermediary, median, interposed

interminable ADJECTIVE = **endless**, long, never-ending, dragging, unlimited, infinite, perpetual, protracted, limitless, boundless, everlasting, ceaseless, long-winded, long-drawn-out, immeasurable, wearisome, unbounded ■ **OPPOSITE:** limited

intermission NOUN = **interval**, break, pause, stop, rest, suspension, recess, interruption, respite, lull, stoppage, interlude, cessation, let-up (*informal*), breathing space, entr'acte

intermittent ADJECTIVE = **periodic**, broken, occasional, recurring, irregular, punctuated, sporadic, recurrent, stop-go (*informal*), fitful, spasmodic, discontinuous ■ **OPPOSITE:** continuous

intern VERB = **imprison**, hold, confine, detain, hold in custody

internal ADJECTIVE **1** *The country stepped up internal security.* = **domestic**, home, national, local, civic, in-house, intramural **2** *Some of the internal walls are made of plasterboard.* = **inner**, inside, interior
■ **OPPOSITE:** external **3** *The personal, internal battle is beautifully portrayed.* = **emotional**, mental, private, secret, subjective
■ **OPPOSITE:** revealed

international ADJECTIVE = **global**, world, worldwide, universal, cosmopolitan, planetary, intercontinental

internet NOUN • **the internet** = **the information superhighway**, the net (*informal*), the web (*informal*), the World Wide Web, cyberspace, the cloud, blogosphere, the interweb (*facetious*), blogostream, extranet, podosphere

interplay NOUN = **interaction**, give-and-take, reciprocity, reciprocation, meshing

interpret VERB **1** *The speech might be interpreted as a coded message.* = **take**, understand, read, explain, regard, construe **2** *She spoke little English, so her assistant interpreted.* = **translate**, convert, paraphrase, adapt, transliterate **3** *The judge has to interpret the law as it's being passed.* = **explain**, define, clarify, spell out, make sense of, decode, decipher, expound, elucidate, throw light on, explicate (*formal*) **4** *The pictures are often difficult to interpret.* = **understand**, read, explain, crack, solve, figure out (*informal*), comprehend, decode, deduce, decipher, suss out (*slang*) **5** *Shakespeare, marvellously interpreted by Orson Welles* = **portray**, present, perform, render, depict, enact, act out

interpretation NOUN **1** *The Opposition put a different interpretation on the figures.* = **explanation**, meaning, reading, understanding, sense, analysis, construction (*formal*), exposition, explication, elucidation, signification **2** *her full-bodied interpretation of the role of Micaela* = **performance**, portrayal, presentation, rendering, reading, execution, rendition, depiction **3** *the interpretation of the scriptures* = **reading**, study, review, version, analysis, explanation, examination, diagnosis, evaluation, exposition, exegesis, explication, elucidation

interpreter NOUN = **translator**, linguist, metaphrast, paraphrast

interrogate VERB = **question**, ask, examine, investigate, pump, grill (*informal*), quiz, cross-examine, cross-question, put the screws on (*informal*), catechize, give (someone) the third degree (*informal*)

interrogation NOUN = **questioning**, inquiry, examination, probing, grilling (*informal*), cross-examination, inquisition, third degree (*informal*), cross-questioning

interrupt VERB **1** *'Sorry to interrupt, Colonel.'* = **intrude**, disturb, intervene, interfere (with), break in, heckle, butt in, barge in (*informal*), break (someone's) train of thought **2** *We interrupted our holiday to return to London.* = **suspend**, break, stop, end, cut, stay, check, delay, cease, cut off, postpone, shelve, put off, defer, break off, adjourn, cut short, discontinue

interruption NOUN **1** *The sudden interruption stopped her in mid-flow.* = **disruption**, break, halt, obstacle, disturbance, hitch, intrusion, obstruction, impediment, hindrance **2** *interruptions in the supply of food and fuel* = **stoppage**, stop, pause, suspension, cessation, severance, hiatus, disconnection, discontinuance

intersect VERB = **cross**, meet, cut, divide, cut across, bisect, crisscross

intersection NOUN = **junction**, crossing, crossroads

intersperse VERB = **scatter**, sprinkle, intermix, pepper, interlard, bestrew

interval NOUN **1** *There was a long interval of silence.* = **period**, time, spell, term, season, space, stretch, pause, span **2** *During the interval, wine was served.* = **break**, interlude, intermission, rest, gap, pause, respite, lull, entr'acte **3** *the interval between her arrival and lunch* = **delay**, wait, gap, interim, hold-up, meanwhile, meantime, stoppage, hiatus **4** *figures separated by intervals of pattern and colour* = **stretch**, area, space, distance, gap

intervene VERB **1** *The situation calmed down when police intervened.* = **step in** (*informal*), interfere, mediate, intrude, intercede, arbitrate, interpose, take a hand (*informal*) **2** *She intervened and told me to stop it.* = **interrupt**, involve yourself, put your oar in, interpose yourself, put your two cents in (*U.S. slang*) **3** *The mailboat comes weekly unless bad weather intervenes.* = **happen**, occur, take place, follow, succeed, arise, ensue, befall, materialize, come to pass, supervene

intervention NOUN = **mediation**, involvement, interference, intrusion, arbitration, conciliation, intercession, interposition, agency (*old-fashioned*)

interview NOUN **1** *When I went for my first job interview I arrived extremely early.* = **meeting**, examination, evaluation, oral (examination), interrogation **2** *There'll be an interview with the Chancellor after the break.* = **audience**, talk, conference, exchange, dialogue, consultation, press conference ▸ VERB **1** *He was among three candidates interviewed for*

the job. = **examine**, talk to, sound out
2 *The police interviewed the driver, but they had no evidence to go on.* = **question**, interrogate, examine, investigate, ask, pump, grill (*informal*), quiz, cross-examine, cross-question, put the screws on (*informal*), catechize, give (someone) the third degree (*informal*)

interviewer NOUN = **questioner**, reporter, investigator, examiner, interrogator, interlocutor

intestinal ADJECTIVE = **abdominal**, visceral, duodenal, gut (*informal*), inner, coeliac, stomachic

intestine NOUN (*usually plural*) = **guts**, insides (*informal*), bowels, internal organs, innards (*informal*), entrails, vitals
■ **RELATED WORD:** *technical name* viscera

intimacy NOUN = **familiarity**, closeness, understanding, confidence, confidentiality, fraternization ■ **OPPOSITE:** aloofness

intimate¹ ADJECTIVE **1** *I discussed this only with my intimate friends.* = **close**, dear, loving, near, warm, friendly, familiar, thick (*informal*), devoted, confidential, cherished, bosom, inseparable, nearest and dearest
■ **OPPOSITE:** distant **2** *She wrote about the intimate details of her family life.* = **private**, personal, confidential, special, individual, particular, secret, exclusive, privy (*archaic*)
■ **OPPOSITE:** public **3** *He surprised me with his intimate knowledge of the situation.* = **detailed**, minute, full, experienced, personal, deep, particular, specific, immediate, comprehensive, exact, elaborate, profound, penetrating, thorough, in-depth, intricate, first-hand, exhaustive **4** *an intimate candlelit dinner for two* = **cosy**, relaxed, friendly, informal, harmonious, snug, comfy (*informal*), warm ▶ NOUN *They are to have an autumn wedding, an intimate of the couple confides.* = **friend**, close friend, buddy (*informal*), mate (*informal*), pal, comrade, chum (*informal*), mucker (*Brit. slang*), crony, main man (*slang, chiefly U.S.*), china (*Brit. slang*), homeboy (*slang, chiefly U.S.*), cobber (*Austral. & N.Z., old-fashioned, informal*), bosom friend, familiar, confidant or confidante, (constant) companion, E hoa (*N.Z.*) ■ **OPPOSITE:** stranger

intimate² VERB **1** *She intimated that she was contemplating leaving the company.* = **suggest**, indicate, hint, imply, warn, allude, let it be known, insinuate, give (someone) to understand, drop a hint, tip (someone) the wink (*Brit. informal*) **2** *He had intimated to them his readiness to come to a settlement.* = **announce**, state, declare, communicate, impart, make known

intimately ADVERB **1** *You have to be willing to get to know your partner intimately.* = **closely**, very well, personally, warmly, familiarly, tenderly, affectionately, confidentially, confidingly **2** *a golden age of musicians whose work she knew intimately* = **fully**, very well, thoroughly, in detail, inside out, to the core, through and through

intimation NOUN **1** *I did not have any intimation that he was going to resign.* = **hint**, warning, suggestion, indication, allusion, inkling, insinuation **2** *their first public intimation of how they will spend the budget* = **announcement**, notice, communication, declaration

intimidate VERB = **frighten**, pressure, threaten, alarm, scare, terrify, cow, bully, plague, menace, hound, awe, daunt, harass, subdue, oppress, persecute, lean on (*informal*), coerce, overawe, scare off (*informal*), terrorize, pressurize, browbeat, twist someone's arm (*informal*), tyrannize, dishearten, dispirit, affright (*archaic*), domineer

intimidation NOUN = **bullying**, pressure, threat(s), menaces, coercion, arm-twisting (*informal*), browbeating, terrorization

intonation NOUN **1** *His voice had a very slight German intonation.* = **tone**, inflection, cadence, modulation, accentuation **2** *They could hear strange music and chanting intonations.* = **incantation**, spell, charm, formula, chant, invocation, hex (*U.S. & Canad. informal*), conjuration

intone VERB = **chant**, sing, recite, croon, intonate

intoxicating ADJECTIVE **1** *intoxicating liquor* = **alcoholic**, strong, intoxicant, spirituous, inebriant **2** *The music is pulsating and the atmosphere intoxicating.* = **exciting**, thrilling, stimulating, sexy (*informal*), heady, exhilarating

intoxication NOUN **1** *Intoxication interferes with memory and thinking.* = **drunkenness**, inebriation, tipsiness, inebriety, insobriety **2** *the intoxication of greed and success* = **excitement**, euphoria, elation, exhilaration, infatuation, delirium, exaltation

intractable ADJECTIVE = **difficult**, contrary, awkward, wild, stubborn, perverse, wayward, unruly, uncontrollable, wilful, incurable, fractious, unyielding, obstinate, intransigent, headstrong, unmanageable, undisciplined, cantankerous, unbending, obdurate, uncooperative, stiff-necked, ungovernable, self-willed, refractory, pig-headed, bull-headed

intransigent ADJECTIVE = **uncompromising**, intractable, tough, stubborn, hardline, tenacious, unyielding, obstinate, immovable, unbending, obdurate, stiff-necked, inflexible, unbudgeable
■ **OPPOSITE:** compliant

intrenched *see* **entrenched**

intrepid ADJECTIVE = **fearless**, brave, daring, bold, heroic, game (*informal*), have-a-go (*informal*), courageous, stalwart, resolute, gallant, audacious, valiant, plucky, doughty (*old-fashioned*), undaunted, unafraid, unflinching, nerveless, dauntless, lion-hearted, valorous, stouthearted, (as) game as Ned Kelly (*Austral. slang*)
■ **OPPOSITE:** fearful

intricacy NOUN = **complexity**, involvement, complication, elaborateness, obscurity, entanglement, convolutions, involution, intricateness, knottiness

intricate ADJECTIVE = **complicated**, involved, complex, difficult, fancy, sophisticated, elaborate, obscure, tangled, baroque, perplexing, tortuous, Byzantine, convoluted, rococo, knotty, labyrinthine, daedal (*literary*) ■ **OPPOSITE:** simple

intrigue NOUN *the plots and intrigues in the novel* = **plot**, scheme, conspiracy, manoeuvre, manipulation, collusion, ruse, trickery, cabal, stratagem, double-dealing, chicanery, sharp practice, wile, knavery (*old-fashioned*), machination ▶ VERB
1 *The novelty of the situation intrigued him.* = **interest**, fascinate, arouse the curiosity of, attract, charm, rivet, titillate, pique, tickle your fancy **2** *The main characters spend their time intriguing for control.* = **plot**, scheme, manoeuvre, conspire, connive, machinate

intriguing ADJECTIVE = **interesting**, fascinating, absorbing, exciting, engaging, gripping, stirring, stimulating, curious, compelling, amusing, diverting, provocative, beguiling, thought-provoking, titillating, engrossing, tantalizing

intrinsic ADJECTIVE = **essential**, real, true, central, natural, basic, radical, native, genuine, fundamental, constitutional, built-in, underlying, inherent, elemental, congenital, inborn, inbred ■ **OPPOSITE:** extrinsic

intrinsically ADVERB = **essentially**, basically, fundamentally, constitutionally, as such, in itself, at heart, by definition, per se

introduce VERB **1** *The Government has introduced a number of other money-saving ideas.* = **bring in**, establish, set up, start, begin, found, develop, launch, institute, organize, pioneer, initiate, originate, commence, get going, instigate, phase in, usher in, inaugurate, set in motion, bring into being **2** *Someone introduced us and I sat next to him.* = **present**, acquaint, make known, familiarize, do the honours, make the introduction **3** *'Health Matters' is introduced by Dick Oliver on the World Service.* = **announce**, present, open, launch, precede, lead into, preface, lead off **4** *She does not abandon her responsibility to introduce new ideas.* = **suggest**, offer, air, table (*Brit.*), advance, propose, recommend, float, submit, bring up, put forward, set forth, ventilate, broach, moot **5** *I wish to introduce a note of cool reason to the discussion.* = **add**, insert, inject, throw in (*informal*), infuse, interpose, interpolate

introduction NOUN **1** *He is remembered for the introduction of the moving assembly line.* = **launch**, institution, establishment, start, opening, beginning, pioneering, presentation, initiation, inauguration, induction, commencement, instigation
■ **OPPOSITE:** elimination **2** *In her introduction to the book she provides a summary of the ideas.* = **opening**, prelude, preface, lead-in, preliminaries, overture, preamble, foreword, prologue, intro (*informal*), commencement, opening remarks, proem, opening passage, prolegomena, prolegomenon, exordium
■ **OPPOSITE:** conclusion **3** *the introduction of air bubbles into the veins* = **insertion**, addition, injection, interpolation
■ **OPPOSITE:** extraction

introductory ADJECTIVE **1** *an introductory course in religion and theology* = **preliminary**, elementary, first, early, initial, inaugural, preparatory, initiatory, prefatory, precursory ■ **OPPOSITE:** concluding **2** *out on the shelves at an introductory price of £2.99* = **starting**, opening, initial, early

introspection NOUN = **self-examination**, brooding, self-analysis, navel-gazing (*slang*), introversion, heart-searching

introspective ADJECTIVE = **inward-looking**, introverted, brooding, contemplative, meditative, subjective, pensive, inner-directed

introverted ADJECTIVE = **introspective**, withdrawn, inward-looking, self-contained, self-centred, indrawn, inner-directed

intrude VERB *He kept intruding with personal questions.* = **butt in**, encroach, push in, obtrude, thrust yourself in or forward, put your two cents in (*U.S. slang*) • **intrude on something** or **someone 1** *It's annoying when unforeseen events intrude on your day.*

= **interfere with**, interrupt, impinge on, encroach on, meddle with, infringe on **2** *They intruded on to the field of play.* = **trespass on**, invade, infringe on, obtrude on

intruder NOUN = **trespasser**, burglar, invader, squatter, prowler, interloper, infiltrator, gate-crasher (*informal*)

intrusion NOUN **1** *I hope you don't mind this intrusion.* = **interruption**, interference, infringement, trespass, encroachment **2** *I felt it was a grotesque intrusion into our lives.* = **invasion**, breach, infringement, infiltration, encroachment, infraction, usurpation

intrusive ADJECTIVE **1** *The cameras were not an intrusive presence.* = **interfering**, disturbing, invasive, unwanted, presumptuous, uncalled-for, importunate **2** *Her bodyguards were less than gentle with intrusive journalists.* = **pushy** (*informal*), forward, interfering, unwanted, impertinent, nosy (*informal*), officious, meddlesome

intrust *see* **entrust**

intuition NOUN **1** *Her intuition was telling her that something was wrong.* = **instinct**, perception, insight, sixth sense, discernment **2** *You can't make a case on intuitions, you know.* = **feeling**, idea, impression, suspicion, premonition, inkling, presentiment

intuitive ADJECTIVE = **instinctive**, spontaneous, innate, involuntary, instinctual, untaught, unreflecting

intuitively ADVERB = **instinctively**, automatically, spontaneously, involuntarily, innately, instinctually

intwine *see* **entwine**

inundate VERB **1** *Her office was inundated with requests for tickets.* = **overwhelm**, flood, swamp, engulf, overflow, overrun, glut **2** *Their neighbourhood is being inundated by the rising waters.* = **flood**, engulf, submerge, drown, overflow, immerse, deluge

invade VERB **1** *In 1944 the allies invaded the Italian mainland.* = **attack**, storm, assault, capture, occupy, seize, raid, overwhelm, violate, conquer, overrun, annex, march into, assail, descend upon, infringe on, burst in on, make inroads on **2** *Every so often the kitchen would be invaded by ants.* = **infest**, swarm, overrun, flood, infect, ravage, beset, pervade, permeate, overspread

invader NOUN = **attacker**, raider, plunderer, aggressor, looter, trespasser

invalid¹ NOUN *I hate being treated as an invalid.* = **patient**, sufferer, convalescent, valetudinarian

invalid² ADJECTIVE **1** *The trial was stopped and the results declared invalid.* = **null and void**, void, worthless, untrue, null, not binding, inoperative, nugatory ■ **OPPOSITE:** valid **2** *Those arguments are rendered invalid by the hard facts.* = **unfounded**, false, untrue, illogical, irrational, unsound, unscientific, baseless, fallacious, untenable, ill-founded ■ **OPPOSITE:** sound

invalidate VERB = **nullify**, cancel, annul, undermine, weaken, overthrow, undo, quash, overrule, rescind, abrogate, render null and void ■ **OPPOSITE:** validate

invalidity NOUN = **falsity**, fallacy, unsoundness, inconsistency, irrationality, illogicality, speciousness, sophism, fallaciousness

invaluable ADJECTIVE = **precious**, valuable, priceless, costly, inestimable, beyond price, worth your or its weight in gold ■ **OPPOSITE:** worthless

invariably ADVERB = **always**, regularly, constantly, every time, inevitably, repeatedly, consistently, ever, continually, aye (*Scot.*), eternally, habitually, perpetually, without exception, customarily, unfailingly, on every occasion, unceasingly, day in, day out

invasion NOUN **1** *seven years after the Roman invasion of Britain* = **attack**, assault, capture, takeover, raid, offensive, occupation, conquering, seizure, onslaught, foray, appropriation, sortie, annexation, incursion, expropriation (*formal*), inroad, irruption, arrogation **2** *Is reading someone's diary a gross invasion of privacy?* = **intrusion**, breach, violation, disturbance, disruption, infringement, overstepping, infiltration, encroachment, infraction, usurpation

invective NOUN = **abuse**, censure, tirade, reproach, berating, denunciation, diatribe, vilification, tongue-lashing, billingsgate, vituperation, castigation, obloquy, contumely (*literary*), philippic(s), revilement

invent VERB **1** *He invented the first electric clock.* = **create**, make, produce, develop, design, discover, imagine, manufacture, generate, come up with (*informal*), coin, devise, conceive, originate, formulate, spawn, contrive, improvise, dream up (*informal*), concoct, think up **2** *I stood there, trying to invent a plausible excuse.* = **make up**, devise, concoct, forge, fake, fabricate, feign, falsify, cook up (*informal*), trump up

invention NOUN **1** *It's been tricky marketing his new invention.* = **creation**, machine, device, design, development, instrument, discovery, innovation, gadget, brainchild (*informal*), contraption, contrivance

2 *fifty years after the invention of the printing press* = **development**, design, production, setting up, foundation, construction, constitution, creation, discovery, introduction, establishment, pioneering, formation, innovation, conception, masterminding, formulation, inception, contrivance, origination **3** *The story was undoubtedly pure invention.* = **fiction**, story (*informal*), fantasy, lie, yarn (*informal*), fabrication, concoction, falsehood, fib (*informal*), untruth, urban myth, prevarication, tall story (*informal*), urban legend, figment *or* product of (someone's) imagination **4** *powers of invention and mathematical ability* = **creativity**, vision, imagination, initiative, enterprise, inspiration, genius, brilliance, ingenuity, originality, inventiveness, resourcefulness, creativeness, ingeniousness, imaginativeness

inventive ADJECTIVE = **creative**, original, innovative, imaginative, gifted, inspired, fertile, ingenious, ground-breaking, resourceful ■ OPPOSITE: uninspired

inventor NOUN = **creator**, father, maker, author, framer, designer, architect, coiner, originator

inventory NOUN = **list**, record, catalogue, listing, account, roll, file, schedule, register, description, log, directory, tally, roster, stock book

inverse ADJECTIVE **1** *The tension grew in inverse proportion to the distance from their destination.* = **opposite**, reverse, reversed, contrary, inverted, converse, transposed **2** *The hologram can be flipped to show the inverse image.* = **reverse**, opposite, reversed, inverted, transposed

inversion NOUN = **reversal**, opposite, antithesis, transposition, contrary, contrariety, contraposition, transposal, antipode

invert VERB = **overturn**, upturn, turn upside down, upset, reverse, capsize, transpose, introvert, turn inside out, turn turtle, invaginate (*Pathology*), overset, intussuscept (*Pathology*)

invest VERB **1** *When people buy houses they're investing a lot of money.* = **spend**, expend, advance, venture, put in, devote, lay out, sink in, use up, plough in **2** *The buildings are invested with a nations's history.* = **charge**, fill, steep, saturate, endow, pervade, infuse, imbue, suffuse, endue **3** *The constitution had invested him with certain powers.* = **empower**, provide, charge, sanction, license, authorize, vest **4** *He was invested as a paramount chief of a district tribe.* = **install**, establish, ordain, crown, inaugurate, anoint, consecrate, adopt, induct, enthrone, instate • **invest in something** *Why don't you invest in an ice cream machine?* = **buy**, get, purchase, score (*slang*), pay for, obtain, acquire, procure

investigate VERB = **examine**, study, research, consider, go into, explore, search for, analyse, look into, inspect, look over, sift, probe into, work over, scrutinize, inquire into, make inquiries about, enquire into

investigation NOUN = **examination**, study, inquiry, hearing, research, review, search, survey, analysis, probe, inspection, exploration, scrutiny, inquest, fact finding, recce (*slang*)

investigative ADJECTIVE = **fact-finding**, researching, investigating, research, inspecting

investigator NOUN = **examiner**, researcher, inspector, monitor, detective, analyser, explorer, reviewer, scrutinizer, checker, inquirer, scrutineer

investment NOUN **1** *The government introduced tax incentives to encourage investment.* = **investing**, backing, funding, financing, contribution, speculation, transaction, expenditure, outlay **2** *an investment of £28 million* = **stake**, interest, share, concern, portion, ante (*informal*) **3** *Shoes that clip onto the pedals are a good investment for keen cyclists.* = **buy**, asset, acquisition, venture, risk, speculation, gamble

inveterate ADJECTIVE **1** *an inveterate gambler* = **chronic**, confirmed, incurable, hardened, established, long-standing, hard-core, habitual, obstinate, incorrigible, dyed-in-the-wool, ineradicable, deep-dyed **2** *the inveterate laziness of these boys* = **deep-rooted**, entrenched, ingrained, deep-seated, incurable, established **3** *the spirit of an inveterate Tory* = **staunch**, long-standing, dyed-in-the-wool, deep-dyed (*usually derogatory*)

invidious ADJECTIVE = **undesirable**, unpleasant, hateful, thankless ■ OPPOSITE: pleasant

invigorating ADJECTIVE = **refreshing**, stimulating, bracing, fresh, tonic, uplifting, exhilarating, rejuvenating, energizing, healthful, restorative, salubrious, rejuvenative

invincible ADJECTIVE = **unbeatable**, unassailable, indomitable, unyielding, indestructible, impregnable, insuperable, invulnerable, unconquerable, unsurmountable ■ OPPOSITE: vulnerable

invisible ADJECTIVE **1** *The lines were so fine as to be nearly invisible.* = **unseen**, imperceptible, indiscernible, unseeable, unperceivable ■ **OPPOSITE:** visible **2** *The problems of the poor are largely invisible.* = **hidden**, concealed, obscured, secret, disguised, inconspicuous, unobserved, unnoticeable, inappreciable

invitation NOUN **1** *He received an invitation to lunch.* = **request**, call, invite (*informal*), bidding, summons **2** *Don't leave your bag there – it's an invitation to a thief.* = **inducement**, come-on (*informal*), temptation, challenge, provocation, open door, overture, incitement, enticement, allurement

invite VERB **1** *She invited him to her birthday party.* = **ask**, bid, summon, request the pleasure of (someone's) company **2** *The Department is inviting applications from local groups.* = **request**, seek, look for, call for, ask for, bid for, appeal for, petition, solicit **3** *Their refusal to compromise will invite more criticism from the UN.* = **encourage**, attract, cause, draw, lead to, court, ask for (*informal*), generate, foster, tempt, provoke, induce, bring on, solicit, engender, allure, call forth, leave the door open to

inviting ADJECTIVE = **tempting**, appealing, attractive, pleasing, welcoming, warm, engaging, fascinating, intriguing, magnetic, delightful, enticing, seductive, captivating, beguiling, alluring, mouthwatering ■ **OPPOSITE:** uninviting

invocation NOUN **1** *an invocation for divine guidance* = **appeal**, request, petition, beseeching, solicitation, entreaty **2** *Please stand for the invocation.* = **prayer**, chant, supplication (*formal*), orison, karakia (*N.Z.*)

invoke VERB **1** *The judge invoked an international law that protects refugees.* = **apply**, use, implement, call in, initiate, resort to, put into effect **2** *The great magicians of old invoked their gods with sacrifice.* = **call upon**, appeal to, pray to, petition, conjure, solicit, beseech, entreat, adjure, supplicate

involuntary ADJECTIVE = **unintentional**, automatic, unconscious, spontaneous, reflex, instinctive, uncontrolled, unthinking, instinctual, blind, unconditioned ■ **OPPOSITE:** voluntary

involve VERB **1** *Running a kitchen involves a great deal of discipline and speed.* = **entail**, mean, demand, require, call for, occasion (*formal*), result in, imply, give rise to, encompass, necessitate **2** *The cover-up involved people at the very highest level.* = **include**, contain, take in, embrace, cover, incorporate, draw in, comprise, number among **3** *I seem to have involved myself in something I don't understand.* = **implicate**, tangle, mix up, embroil, link, entangle, incriminate, mire, stitch up (*slang*), enmesh, inculpate (*formal*) **4** *He started involving me in the more confidential aspects of the job.* = **concern**, draw in, associate, connect, bear on

involved ADJECTIVE *The operation can be quite involved, requiring special procedures.* = **complicated**, complex, intricate, hard, difficult, confused, confusing, sophisticated, elaborate, tangled, bewildering, jumbled, entangled, tortuous, Byzantine, convoluted, knotty, unfathomable, labyrinthine ■ **OPPOSITE:** straightforward

involvement NOUN *He has always felt a deep involvement with animals.* = **connection**, interest, relationship, concern, association, commitment, friendship, attachment

invulnerable ADJECTIVE = **safe**, secure, invincible, impenetrable, unassailable, indestructible, insusceptible ■ **OPPOSITE:** vulnerable

inward ADJECTIVE **1** *a sharp, inward breath like a gasp* = **incoming**, entering, penetrating, inbound, inflowing, ingoing, inpouring **2** *a glow of inward satisfaction* = **internal**, inner, private, personal, inside, secret, hidden, interior, confidential, privy (*archaic*), innermost, inmost ■ **OPPOSITE:** outward

inwardly ADVERB = **privately**, secretly, to yourself, within, inside, at heart, deep down, in your head, in your inmost heart

iota NOUN = **bit**, particle, atom, trace, hint, scrap, grain, mite, jot, speck, whit, tittle

irascible ADJECTIVE = **bad-tempered**, cross, irritable, crabbed, touchy, cantankerous, peppery, tetchy, ratty (*Brit. & N.Z. informal*), testy, chippy (*informal*), short-tempered, hot-tempered, quick-tempered, choleric, narky (*Brit. slang*)

irate ADJECTIVE = **angry**, cross, furious, angered, mad (*informal*), provoked, annoyed, irritated, fuming (*informal*), choked, infuriated, incensed, enraged, worked up, exasperated, indignant, livid, riled, up in arms, incandescent, hacked off (*informal*), piqued, hot under the collar (*informal*), wrathful, fit to be tied (*slang*), as black as thunder, tooshie (*Austral. slang*), off the air (*Austral. slang*)

ire NOUN (*Literary*) = **anger**, rage, fury, wrath, passion, indignation, annoyance, displeasure, exasperation, choler

iridescent ADJECTIVE = **shimmering**, pearly, opalescent, shot, opaline, prismatic, rainbow-coloured, polychromatic, nacreous

irk VERB = **irritate**, annoy, aggravate (*informal*), provoke, bug (*informal*), put out (*informal*), gall, ruffle, nettle, vex, rile, peeve (*informal*), get on your nerves (*informal*), nark (*Brit., Austral. & N.Z. slang*), miff (*informal*), be on your back (*slang*), get in your hair (*informal*), rub you up the wrong way (*informal*), put your nose out of joint (*informal*), get your back up, put your back up, hack you off (*informal*)

irksome ADJECTIVE = **irritating**, trying, annoying, aggravating (*informal*), troublesome, unwelcome, exasperating, tiresome, vexing, disagreeable, burdensome, wearisome, bothersome, vexatious ■ **OPPOSITE:** pleasant

iron MODIFIER *The huge iron gate was locked.* = **ferrous**, ferric, irony ▶ ADJECTIVE *a person of icy nerve and iron will* = **inflexible**, hard, strong, tough, steel, rigid, adamant, unconditional, steely, implacable, indomitable, unyielding, immovable, unbreakable, unbending, obdurate ■ **OPPOSITE:** weak • **iron something out** *The various groups had managed to iron out their differences.* = **settle**, resolve, sort out, eliminate, get rid of, reconcile, clear up, simplify, unravel, erase, eradicate, put right, straighten out, harmonize, expedite, smooth over ■ **RELATED WORDS:** *adjectives* ferric, ferrous; *prefix* ferro-

ironic or **ironical** ADJECTIVE **1** *At the most solemn moments he would make an ironic remark.* = **sarcastic**, dry, sharp, acid, bitter, stinging, mocking, sneering, scoffing, wry, scathing, satirical, tongue-in-cheek, sardonic, caustic, double-edged, acerbic, trenchant, mordant, mordacious **2** *It's ironic that the sort of people this film celebrates would never watch it.* = **paradoxical**, absurd, contradictory, puzzling, baffling, ambiguous, inconsistent, confounding, enigmatic, illogical, incongruous

irons PLURAL NOUN *These people need to be clapped in irons themselves.* = **chains**, shackles, fetters, manacles, bonds

irony NOUN **1** *She examined his face for a hint of irony, but found none.* = **sarcasm**, mockery, ridicule, bitterness, scorn, satire, cynicism, derision, causticity, mordancy **2** *Opposition parties wasted no time in stressing the irony of the situation.* = **paradox**, ambiguity, absurdity, incongruity, contrariness

irrational ADJECTIVE *an irrational fear of science* = **illogical**, crazy (*informal*), silly, absurd, foolish, unreasonable, unwise, preposterous, idiotic, nonsensical, unsound, unthinking, injudicious, unreasoning ■ **OPPOSITE:** rational

irrationality NOUN = **senselessness**, absurdity, lack of judgment, illogicality, unreasonableness, preposterousness, unsoundness

irreconcilable ADJECTIVE **1** *an irreconcilable clash of personalities* = **implacable**, uncompromising, inflexible, inexorable, intransigent, unappeasable **2** *their irreconcilable points of view* = **incompatible**, conflicting, opposed, inconsistent, incongruous, diametrically opposed

irrefutable ADJECTIVE = **undeniable**, sure, certain, irresistible, invincible, unassailable, indisputable, unanswerable, unquestionable, incontrovertible, beyond question, incontestable, indubitable, apodictic, irrefragable

irregular ADJECTIVE **1** *She was suffering from an irregular heartbeat.* = **variable**, inconsistent, erratic, shifting, occasional, random, casual, shaky, wavering, uneven, fluctuating, eccentric, patchy, sporadic, intermittent, haphazard, unsteady, desultory, fitful, spasmodic, unsystematic, inconstant, nonuniform, unmethodical, scattershot ■ **OPPOSITE:** steady **2** *He had bad teeth, irregular and discoloured.* = **uneven**, broken, rough, twisted, twisting, curving, pitted, ragged, crooked, unequal, jagged, bumpy, lumpy, serpentine, contorted, lopsided, craggy, indented, asymmetrical, serrated, holey, unsymmetrical ■ **OPPOSITE:** even **3** *The minister was accused of irregular business practices.* = **inappropriate**, unconventional, improper, unethical, odd, unusual, extraordinary, disorderly, exceptional, peculiar, unofficial, abnormal, queer, rum (*Brit. slang*), back-door, unsuitable, unorthodox, out-of-order, unprofessional, anomalous **4** *At least 17 irregular units are involved in the war.* = **unofficial**, underground, guerrilla, volunteer, resistance, partisan, rogue, paramilitary, mercenary

irregularity NOUN **1** *a dangerous irregularity in her heartbeat* = **inconsistency**, randomness, disorganization, unsteadiness, unpunctuality, haphazardness, disorderliness, lack of method, desultoriness **2** *treatment of irregularities of the teeth* = **unevenness**, deformity, asymmetry, crookedness, contortion, patchiness, lopsidedness, raggedness, lack of symmetry, spottiness, jaggedness

3 *charges arising from alleged financial irregularities* = **malpractice**, anomaly, breach, abnormality, deviation, oddity, aberration, malfunction, peculiarity, singularity, unorthodoxy, unconventionality

irregularly ADVERB = **erratically**, occasionally, now and again, intermittently, off and on, anyhow, unevenly, fitfully, haphazardly, eccentrically, spasmodically, jerkily, in snatches, out of sequence, by fits and starts, disconnectedly, unmethodically, unpunctually

irrelevance *or* **irrelevancy** NOUN = **inappropriateness**, inapplicability, inaptness, unconnectedness, pointlessness, non sequitur, inconsequence, extraneousness, inappositeness ■ **OPPOSITE:** relevance

irrelevant ADJECTIVE = **unconnected**, unrelated, unimportant, inappropriate, peripheral, insignificant, negligible, immaterial, extraneous, beside the point, impertinent, neither here nor there, inapplicable, inapt, inapposite, inconsequent ■ **OPPOSITE:** relevant

irreparable ADJECTIVE = **beyond repair**, irreversible, incurable, irretrievable, irrecoverable, irremediable

irreplaceable ADJECTIVE = **indispensable**, unique, invaluable, priceless

irrepressible ADJECTIVE = **unstoppable**, buoyant, uncontrollable, boisterous, ebullient, effervescent, unmanageable, unquenchable, bubbling over, uncontainable, unrestrainable, insuppressible

irresistible ADJECTIVE **1** *It proved an irresistible temptation to go back.* = **overwhelming**, compelling, overpowering, urgent, potent, imperative, compulsive, uncontrollable, overmastering **2** *The music is irresistible.* = **seductive**, inviting, tempting, enticing, provocative, fascinating, enchanting, captivating, beguiling, alluring, bewitching, ravishing **3** *They feel the case for change is irresistible.* = **inescapable**, inevitable, unavoidable, sure, certain, fated, destined, inexorable, ineluctable

irrespective of PREPOSITION = **despite**, in spite of, regardless of, discounting, notwithstanding, without reference to, without regard to

irresponsible ADJECTIVE = **thoughtless**, reckless, careless, wild, unreliable, giddy, untrustworthy, flighty, ill-considered, good-for-nothing, shiftless, harebrained, undependable, harum-scarum, scatterbrained, featherbrained ■ **OPPOSITE:** responsible

irreverence NOUN = **disrespect**, cheek (*informal*), impertinence, sauce (*informal*), mockery, derision, lack of respect, impudence, flippancy, cheekiness (*informal*)

irreverent ADJECTIVE = **disrespectful**, cheeky (*informal*), impertinent, fresh (*informal*), mocking, flip (*informal*), saucy, contemptuous, tongue-in-cheek, sassy (*U.S. informal*), flippant, iconoclastic, derisive, impudent ■ **OPPOSITE:** reverent

irreversible ADJECTIVE = **irrevocable**, incurable, irreparable, final, unalterable

irrevocable ADJECTIVE = **fixed**, settled, irreversible, fated, predetermined, immutable, invariable, irretrievable, predestined, unalterable, unchangeable, changeless, irremediable, unreversible

irrigate VERB = **water**, wet, moisten, flood, inundate, fertigate (*Austral.*)

irritability NOUN = **bad temper**, impatience, ill humour, prickliness, tetchiness, irascibility, peevishness, testiness, touchiness ■ **OPPOSITE:** good humour

irritable ADJECTIVE = **bad-tempered**, cross, snappy, hot, tense, crabbed, fiery, snarling, prickly, exasperated, edgy, touchy, petulant, ill-tempered, irascible, cantankerous, tetchy, ratty (*Brit. & N.Z. informal*), testy, chippy (*informal*), fretful, peevish, crabby, dyspeptic, choleric, crotchety (*informal*), oversensitive, snappish, ill-humoured, narky (*Brit. slang*), out of humour ■ **OPPOSITE:** even-tempered

irritate VERB **1** *Their attitude irritates me.* = **annoy**, anger, bother, provoke, offend, needle (*informal*), harass, infuriate, aggravate (*informal*), incense, fret, enrage, gall, ruffle, inflame, exasperate, nettle, pester, vex, irk, pique, rankle with, get under your skin (*informal*), get on your nerves (*informal*), nark (*Brit., Austral. & N.Z. slang*), drive you up the wall (*slang*), rub you up the wrong way (*informal*), get your goat (*slang*), try your patience, get in your hair (*informal*), get on your wick (*informal*), get your dander up (*informal*), raise your hackles, get your back up, get your hackles up, put your back up, hack you off (*informal*) ■ **OPPOSITE:** placate **2** *Chillies can irritate the skin.* = **inflame**, pain, rub, scratch, scrape, grate, graze, fret, gall, chafe, abrade

irritated ADJECTIVE = **annoyed**, cross, angry, bothered, put out, hacked (off)

(*U.S. slang*), harassed, impatient, ruffled, exasperated, irritable, nettled, vexed, displeased, flustered, peeved (*informal*), piqued, out of humour, tooshie (*Austral. slang*), hoha (*N.Z.*)

irritating ADJECTIVE = **annoying**, trying, provoking, infuriating, upsetting, disturbing, nagging, aggravating (*informal*), troublesome, galling, maddening, disquieting, displeasing, worrisome, irksome, vexatious, pestilential ■ **OPPOSITE:** pleasing

irritation NOUN **1** *For the first time he felt irritation at her methods.* = **annoyance**, anger, fury, resentment, wrath, gall, indignation, impatience, displeasure, exasperation, chagrin, pique, irritability, ill temper, shortness, vexation, ill humour, testiness, crossness, snappiness, infuriation ■ **OPPOSITE:** pleasure **2** *Don't allow a minor irritation to mar your ambitions.* = **nuisance**, annoyance, irritant, pain (*informal*), drag (*informal*), bother, plague (*informal*), menace (*informal*), tease, pest, hassle, provocation, gall, goad, aggravation (*informal*), pain in the neck (*informal*), thorn in your flesh

island NOUN = **isle**, inch (*Scot. & Irish*), atoll, holm (*dialect*), islet, ait *or* eyot (*dialect*), cay *or* key ■ **RELATED WORD:** adjective insular

isolate VERB **1** *This policy could isolate members from the UN security council.* = **separate**, break up, cut off, detach, split up, insulate, segregate, disconnect, divorce, sequester, set apart, disunite, estrange **2** *Patients will be isolated for one month after treatment.* = **quarantine**, separate, exclude, cut off, detach, keep in solitude

isolated ADJECTIVE *Many of the refugee areas are in isolated areas.* = **remote**, far, distant, lonely, out-of-the-way, hidden, retired, far-off, secluded, inaccessible, faraway, outlying, in the middle of nowhere, off the beaten track, backwoods, godforsaken, incommunicado, unfrequented

isolation NOUN = **separation**, withdrawal, loneliness, segregation, detachment, quarantine, solitude, exile, self-sufficiency, seclusion, remoteness, disconnection, insularity

issue NOUN **1** *Is it right for the Church to express a view on political issues?* = **topic**, point, matter, problem, business, case, question, concern, subject, affair, argument, theme, controversy, can of worms (*informal*) **2** *I wasn't earning much money, but that was not the issue.* = **point**, question, concern, bone of contention, matter of contention, point

in question **3** *The problem is underlined in the latest issue of the Lancet.* = **edition**, printing, copy, impression, publication, number, instalment, imprint, version **4** *He died without issue in 1946.* = **children**, young, offspring, babies, kids (*informal*), seed (*chiefly biblical*), successors, heirs, descendants, progeny, scions ■ **OPPOSITE:** parent **5** *the issue of supplies to refugees* = **distribution**, issuing, supply, supplying, delivery, publication, circulation, sending out, dissemination, dispersal, issuance ▶ VERB **1** *He issued a statement denying the allegations.* = **give out**, release, publish, announce, deliver, spread, broadcast, distribute, communicate, proclaim, put out, circulate, emit, impart, disseminate, promulgate, put in circulation **2** *A tinny voice issued from a speaker.* = **emerge**, come out, proceed, rise, spring, flow, arise, stem, originate, emanate, exude, come forth, be a consequence of • **at issue** *The problems of immigration were not the question at issue.* = **under discussion**, in question, in dispute, under consideration, to be decided, for debate • **take issue with something** *or* **someone** *She might take issue with you on that matter.* = **disagree with**, question, challenge, oppose, dispute, object to, argue with, take exception to, raise an objection to

itch VERB **1** *When you have hayfever, your eyes and nose stream and itch.* = **prickle**, tickle, tingle, crawl **2** *I was itching to get involved.* = **long**, ache, crave, burn, pine, pant, hunger, lust, yearn, hanker ▶ NOUN **1** *Scratch my back – I've got an itch.* = **irritation**, tingling, prickling, itchiness **2** *an insatiable itch to switch from channel to channel* = **desire**, longing, craving, passion, yen (*informal*), hunger, lust, yearning, hankering, restlessness

itchy ADJECTIVE = **impatient**, eager, restless, unsettled, edgy, restive, fidgety

item NOUN **1** *The most valuable item on show will be a Picasso.* = **article**, thing, object, piece, unit, component **2** *The other item on the agenda is the tour.* = **matter**, point, issue, case, question, concern, detail, subject, feature, particular, affair, aspect, entry, theme, consideration, topic **3** *There was an item in the paper about him.* = **report**, story, piece, account, note, feature, notice, article, paragraph, bulletin, dispatch, communiqué, write-up

itemize VERB = **list**, record, detail, count, document, instance, set out, specify, inventory, number, enumerate, particularize

itinerant ADJECTIVE = **wandering**,
travelling, journeying, unsettled, roaming,
roving, nomadic, migratory, vagrant,
peripatetic, vagabond, ambulatory,
wayfaring ■ **OPPOSITE:** settled

itinerary NOUN = **schedule**, line,
programme, tour, route, journey,
circuit, timetable

ivory tower NOUN = **seclusion**,
remoteness, unreality, retreat, refuge,
cloister, sanctum, splendid isolation,
world of your own

Jj

jab VERB *A needle was jabbed into the man's arm.* = **poke**, dig, punch, thrust, tap, stab, nudge, prod, lunge ▶ NOUN *He gave me a jab in the side.* = **poke**, dig, punch, thrust, stab, nudge, prod, lunge

jacket NOUN = **covering**, casing, case, cover, skin, shell, coat, wrapping, envelope, capsule, folder, sheath, wrapper, encasement, housing

jackpot NOUN = **prize**, winnings, award, pool, reward, pot, kitty, bonanza, pot of gold at the end of the rainbow

jack up VERB **1** *They jacked up the car.* = **hoist**, raise, elevate, winch up, lift, rear, uplift, lift up, heave, haul up, hike up, upraise **2** *The company would have to jack up its prices.* = **increase**, raise, put up, augment, advance, boost, expand, add to, enhance, step up (*informal*), intensify, enlarge, escalate, inflate, amplify

jaded ADJECTIVE **1** *We had both become jaded, disinterested and disillusioned.* = **tired**, bored, weary, worn out, done in (*informal*), clapped out (*Brit., Austral. & N.Z. informal*), spent, drained, exhausted, shattered (*informal*), dulled, fatigued, fed up, wearied, fagged (out) (*informal*), sapped, uninterested, listless, tired-out, enervated, zonked (*slang*), over-tired, ennuied, hoha (*N.Z.*) ■ OPPOSITE: fresh **2** *scrumptious little things to tickle my jaded palate* = **satiated**, sated, surfeited, cloyed, gorged, glutted

jagged ADJECTIVE = **uneven**, pointed, craggy, broken, toothed, rough, ragged, ridged, spiked, notched, barbed, cleft, indented, serrated, snaggy, denticulate ■ OPPOSITE: rounded

jail *or* **gaol** NOUN *Three prisoners escaped from a jail.* = **prison**, penitentiary (*U.S.*), jailhouse (*Southern U.S.*), penal institution, can (*slang*), inside, cooler (*slang*), confinement, dungeon, clink (*slang*), glasshouse (*Military informal*), brig (*chiefly U.S.*), borstal, calaboose (*U.S. informal*), choky (*slang*), pound, nick (*Brit. slang*), stir (*slang*), jug (*slang*), slammer (*slang*), lockup, reformatory, quod (*slang*), poky *or* pokey (*U.S. & Canad. slang*), boob (*Austral. slang*) ▶ VERB *He was jailed for twenty years.*

= **imprison**, confine, detain, lock up, constrain, put away, intern, incarcerate, send down, send to prison, impound, put under lock and key, immure

jailbird *or* **gaolbird** NOUN = **prisoner**, convict, con (*slang*), lag (*slang*), trusty, felon, malefactor, ticket-of-leave man (*archaic*)

jailer *or* **gaoler** NOUN = **guard**, keeper, warden (*U.S. & Canad.*), screw (*slang*), captor, warder, turnkey (*archaic*)

jam NOUN **1** *a nine-mile traffic jam* = **tailback**, queue, hold-up, bottleneck, snarl-up, line, chain, congestion, obstruction, stoppage, gridlock **2** *It could get the government out of a jam.* = **predicament**, tight spot, scrape (*informal*), corner, state, situation, trouble, spot (*informal*), hole (*slang*), fix (*informal*), bind, emergency, mess, dilemma, pinch, plight, strait, hot water, pickle (*informal*), deep water, quandary ▶ VERB **1** *He jammed his hands into his pockets.* = **pack**, force, press, stuff, squeeze, compact, ram, wedge, cram, compress **2** *In summer, the beach is jammed with day-trippers.* = **crowd**, cram, throng, crush, press, mass, surge, flock, swarm, congregate **3** *The phone lines are jammed. Everybody wants to talk about it.* = **congest**, block, clog, stick, halt, stall, obstruct

jamboree NOUN = **festival**, party, fête, celebration, blast (*U.S. slang*), rave (*Brit. slang*), carnival, spree, jubilee, festivity, beano (*Brit. slang*), merriment, revelry, carouse, rave-up (*Brit. slang*), carousal, frolic, hooley *or* hoolie (*chiefly Irish & N.Z.*)

jangle VERB *Her necklaces and bracelets jangled as she walked.* = **rattle**, ring, clash, clatter, chime, ping, vibrate, jingle, ding, clank ▶ NOUN *a jangle of bells* = **clash**, clang, cacophony, reverberation, rattle, jar, racket, din, dissonance, clangour ■ OPPOSITE: quiet

janitor NOUN = **caretaker**, porter (*Brit.*), custodian, concierge, doorkeeper

jar¹ NOUN *We saved each season's harvest in clear glass jars.* = **pot**, container, flask, receptacle, vessel, drum, vase, jug, pitcher, urn, crock, canister, repository, decanter, carafe, flagon

jar² VERB **1** (*usually with* **on**) *The least bit of discord seemed to jar on his nerves.* = **irritate**, grind, clash, annoy, offend, rattle, gall, nettle, jangle, irk, grate on, get on your nerves (*informal*), nark (*Brit., Austral. & N.Z. slang*), discompose **2** (*sometimes with* **with**) *They had always been complementary and their temperaments seldom jarred.* = **clash**, conflict, contrast, differ, disagree, interfere, contend, collide, oppose **3** *The impact jarred his arm, right up to the shoulder.* = **jolt**, rock, shake, disturb, bump, rattle, grate, agitate, vibrate, rasp, convulse

jargon NOUN = **parlance**, slang, idiom, patter, tongue, usage, dialect, cant, lingo (*informal*), patois, argot, leetspeak, l33tspeak *or* 1337speak (*Computing*), netspeak (*Computing*)

jaundiced ADJECTIVE = **cynical**, bitter, hostile, prejudiced, biased, suspicious, partial, jealous, distorted, sceptical, resentful, envious, bigoted, spiteful, preconceived ■ **OPPOSITE:** optimistic

jaunt NOUN = **outing**, tour, trip, stroll, expedition, excursion, ramble, promenade, airing

jaunty ADJECTIVE **1** *The novel is altogether jauntier than these quotations imply.* = **sprightly**, buoyant, carefree, high-spirited, gay, lively, airy, breezy, perky, sparky, self-confident ■ **OPPOSITE:** serious **2** *a jaunty little hat* = **smart**, trim, gay, dapper, spruce, showy

jaw PLURAL NOUN *He opens the jaws of the furnace with the yank of a lever.* = **opening**, gates, entrance, aperture, mouth, abyss, maw, orifice, ingress ▶ VERB *jawing for half an hour with the very affable waiter* = **talk**, chat, rabbit (on) (*Brit. informal*), gossip, chatter, spout (*informal*), babble, natter, schmooze (*slang*), shoot the breeze (*U.S. slang*), run off at the mouth (*slang*), chew the fat *or* rag (*slang*) ■ **RELATED WORDS:** technical names maxilla (*upper*), mandible (*lower*)

jealous ADJECTIVE **1** *She got insanely jealous and there was a terrible fight.* = **suspicious**, suspecting, guarded, protective, wary, doubtful, sceptical, attentive, anxious, apprehensive, vigilant, watchful, zealous, possessive, solicitous, distrustful, mistrustful, unbelieving ■ **OPPOSITE:** trusting **2** *I have never sought to make my readers jealous of my megastar lifestyle.* = **envious**, grudging, resentful, begrudging, green, intolerant, green-eyed, invidious, green with envy, desirous, covetous, emulous ■ **OPPOSITE:** satisfied

jealousy NOUN = **suspicion**, distrust, mistrust, possessiveness, doubt, spite, resentment, wariness, ill-will, dubiety

jeer VERB *His motorcade was jeered by angry residents.* = **mock**, hector, deride, heckle, knock (*informal*), barrack, ridicule, taunt, sneer, scoff, banter, flout, gibe, cock a snook at (*Brit.*), contemn (*formal*) ■ **OPPOSITE:** cheer ▶ NOUN *the heckling and jeers of his audience* = **mockery**, abuse, ridicule, taunt, sneer, hiss, boo, scoff, hoot, derision, gibe, catcall, obloquy, aspersion ■ **OPPOSITE:** applause

jeopardize VERB = **endanger**, threaten, put at risk, put in jeopardy, risk, expose, gamble, hazard, menace, imperil, put on the line

jeopardy NOUN = **danger**, risk, peril, vulnerability, venture, exposure, liability, hazard, insecurity, pitfall, precariousness, endangerment

jerk VERB *The car jerked to a halt.* = **jolt**, bang, bump, lurch, shake ▶ NOUN *He indicated the bedroom with a jerk of his head.* = **lurch**, movement, thrust, twitch, jolt, throw

jerky ADJECTIVE = **bumpy**, rough, jolting, jumpy, shaky, bouncy, uncontrolled, twitchy, fitful, spasmodic, convulsive, tremulous ■ **OPPOSITE:** smooth

jest NOUN *It was a jest rather than a reproach.* = **joke**, play, crack (*slang*), sally, gag (*informal*), quip, josh (*slang, chiefly U.S. & Canad.*), banter, hoax, prank, wisecrack (*informal*), pleasantry, witticism, jape, bon mot ▶ VERB *He enjoyed drinking and jesting with his cronies.* = **joke**, kid (*informal*), mock, tease, sneer, jeer, quip, josh (*slang, chiefly U.S. & Canad.*), scoff, banter, deride, chaff, gibe

jester NOUN *a chap dressed as a court jester* = **fool**, clown, harlequin, zany, madcap, prankster, buffoon, pantaloon, mummer

jet NOUN *benches equipped with water jets to massage your back and feet* = **stream**, current, spring, flow, rush, flood, burst, spray, fountain, cascade, gush, spurt, spout, squirt ▶ VERB **1** *They spend a great deal of time jetting around the world.* = **fly**, wing, cruise, soar, zoom **2** *A cloud of white smoke jetted out from the trees.* = **stream**, course, issue, shoot, flow, rush, surge, spill, gush, emanate, spout, spew, squirt

jet-black ADJECTIVE = **black**, jet, raven, ebony, sable, pitch-black, inky, coal-black

jet-setting ADJECTIVE = **fashionable**, rich, sophisticated, trendy (*Brit. informal*), cosmopolitan, well-off, high-society, ritzy (*slang*), trendsetting

jettison VERB **1** *The government seems to have jettisoned the plan.* = **abandon**, reject, desert, dump, shed, scrap, throw out, discard, throw away, relinquish, forsake, slough off, throw on the scrapheap **2** *The crew jettisoned excess fuel and made an emergency landing.* = **expel**, dump, unload, throw overboard, eject, heave

jetty NOUN = **pier**, dock, wharf, mole, quay, breakwater, groyne

jewel NOUN **1** *a golden box containing precious jewels* = **gemstone**, gem, precious stone, brilliant, ornament, trinket, sparkler (*informal*), rock (*slang*) **2** *Barbados is a perfect jewel of an island.* = **treasure**, wonder, prize, darling, pearl, gem, paragon, pride and joy, taonga (*N.Z.*)

jewellery NOUN = **jewels**, treasure, gems, trinkets, precious stones, ornaments, finery, regalia, bling (*slang*)

jibe *or* **gibe** NOUN *a cruel jibe about her weight* = **jeer**, sneer, dig (*informal*), crack, taunt, snide remark ▶ VERB *'What's the matter, can't you read?' she jibed.* = **jeer**, mock, sneer, taunt

jig VERB = **skip**, bob, prance, jiggle, shake, bounce, twitch, wobble, caper, wiggle, jounce

jiggle VERB **1** *He jiggled the doorknob noisily.* = **shake**, jerk, agitate, joggle **2** *He tapped his feet, hummed tunes and jiggled about.* = **jerk**, bounce, jog, fidget, shake, twitch, wiggle, jig, shimmy, joggle

jilt VERB = **reject**, drop, disappoint, abandon, desert, ditch (*slang*), betray, discard, deceive, forsake, throw over, coquette, leave (someone) in the lurch

jingle VERB *Her bracelets jingled like bells.* = **ring**, rattle, clatter, chime, jangle, tinkle, clink, clank, tintinnabulate ▶ NOUN **1** *the jingle of money in a man's pocket* = **rattle**, ringing, tinkle, clang, clink, reverberation, clangour **2** *advertising jingles* = **song**, tune, melody, ditty, chorus, slogan, verse, limerick, refrain, doggerel

jinx NOUN *Someone had put a jinx on him.* = **curse**, plague (*informal*), voodoo, nemesis, black magic, hoodoo (*informal*), hex (*U.S. & Canad. informal*), evil eye ▶ VERB *He's trying to rattle me, he said to himself, trying to jinx me so I can't succeed.* = **curse**, bewitch, hex (*U.S. & Canad. informal*)

jitters PLURAL NOUN = **nerves**, anxiety, butterflies (in your stomach) (*informal*), nervousness, the shakes (*informal*), fidgets, cold feet (*informal*), the willies (*informal*), tenseness, heebie-jeebies (*slang*)

jittery ADJECTIVE = **nervous**, anxious, jumpy, twitchy (*informal*), wired (*slang*), trembling, shaky, agitated, quivering, hyper (*informal*), fidgety, antsy (*informal*) ■ **OPPOSITE:** calm

job NOUN **1** *the pressure of being the first woman in the job* = **position**, post, function, capacity, work, posting, calling, place, business, office, trade, field, career, situation, activity, employment, appointment, craft, profession, occupation, placement, vocation, livelihood, métier **2** *Their main job is to* preserve health rather than treat illness. = **task**, concern, duty, charge, work, business, role, operation, affair, responsibility, function, contribution, venture, enterprise, undertaking, pursuit, assignment, stint, chore, errand

jobless ADJECTIVE = **unemployed**, redundant, out of work, on the dole (*Brit. informal*), inactive, out of a job, unoccupied, idle

jockey VERB = **manoeuvre**, manage, engineer, negotiate, trim, manipulate, cajole, insinuate, wheedle, finagle (*informal*)

jog VERB **1** *She could scarcely jog around the block that first day.* = **run**, trot, canter, lope, dogtrot **2** *Avoid jogging the camera.* = **nudge**, push, shake, prod **3** *Keep a card file on the books you have read to jog your memory later.* = **stimulate**, remind, prompt, stir, arouse, activate, nudge, prod

join VERB **1** *He joined the Army five years ago.* = **enrol in**, enter, sign up for, become a member of, enlist in **2** *The opened link is used to join the two ends of the chain.* = **connect**, unite, couple, link, marry, tie, combine, attach, knit, cement, adhere, fasten, annex, add, splice, yoke, append (*formal*) ■ **OPPOSITE:** detach **3** *Allahabad, where the Ganges and the Yamuna rivers join* = **meet**, touch, border, extend, butt, adjoin, conjoin, reach ■ **OPPOSITE:** part

joint ADJECTIVE *They came to a joint decision as to where they would live.* = **shared**, mutual, collective, communal, united, joined, allied, combined, corporate, concerted, consolidated, cooperative, reciprocal, collaborative ▶ NOUN *Cut the stem just below a leaf joint.* = **junction**, union, link, connection, knot, brace, bracket, seam, hinge, weld, linkage, intersection, node, articulation, nexus ■ **RELATED WORD:** *adjective* articular

jointly ADVERB = **collectively**, together, in conjunction, as one, in common, mutually, in partnership, in league, unitedly ■ **OPPOSITE:** separately

joke NOUN **1** *No one told worse jokes than Claus.* = **jest**, gag (*informal*), wisecrack (*informal*), witticism, crack (*informal*), sally, quip, josh (*slang, chiefly U.S. & Canad.*), pun, quirk, one-liner (*informal*), jape **2** *It was probably just a joke to them, but it wasn't funny to me.* = **laugh** (*informal*), jest, fun, josh (*slang, chiefly U.S. & Canad.*), lark, sport, frolic, whimsy, jape **3** *I thought she was playing a joke on me at first but she wasn't.* = **prank**, trick, practical joke, lark (*informal*), caper, frolic, escapade, antic, jape **4** *That man is* *just a complete joke.* = **laughing stock**, butt, clown, buffoon, simpleton ▶ VERB *Don't get defensive, Charlie. I was only joking.* = **jest**, kid (*informal*), fool, mock, wind up (*Brit. slang*), tease, ridicule, taunt, quip, josh (*slang, chiefly U.S. & Canad.*), banter, deride, frolic, chaff, gambol, play the fool, play a trick

joker NOUN = **comedian**, comic, wit, clown, wag, kidder (*informal*), jester, prankster, buffoon, trickster, humorist

jokey ADJECTIVE = **playful**, funny, amusing, teasing, humorous, mischievous, jesting, wisecracking, droll, facetious, waggish, prankish, nonserious ■ **OPPOSITE:** humourless

jolly ADJECTIVE = **happy**, bright, funny, lively, hopeful, sunny, cheerful, merry, vibrant, hilarious, festive, upbeat (*informal*), bubbly, gay, airy, playful, exuberant, jubilant, cheery, good-humoured, joyous, joyful, carefree, breezy, genial, ebullient, chirpy (*informal*), sprightly, jovial, convivial, effervescent, frolicsome, ludic (*literary*), mirthful, sportive, light-hearted, jocund, gladsome (*archaic*), blithesome ■ **OPPOSITE:** miserable

jolt VERB **1** *The train jolted into motion.* = **jerk**, push, shake, knock, jar, shove, jog, jostle **2** *He was momentarily jolted by the news.* = **surprise**, upset, stun, disturb, astonish, stagger, startle, perturb, discompose ▶ NOUN **1** *One tiny jolt could worsen her injuries.* = **jerk**, start, jump, shake, bump, jar, jog, lurch, quiver **2** *The campaign came at a time when America needed such a jolt.* = **surprise**, blow, shock, setback, reversal, bombshell, thunderbolt, whammy (*informal*), bolt from the blue

jostle VERB = **push**, press, crowd (*informal*), shake, squeeze, thrust, butt, elbow, bump, scramble, shove, jog, jolt, throng, hustle, joggle

jot VERB (*usually with* **down**) *Listen carefully to the instructions and jot them down.* = **note down**, record, list, note, register, tally, scribble ▶ NOUN *It doesn't affect my judgement one jot.* = **bit**, detail, ace, scrap, grain, particle, atom, fraction, trifle, mite, tad (*informal*), speck, morsel, whit, tittle, iota, scintilla, smidgen or smidgin (*informal, chiefly U.S. & Canad.*)

journal NOUN **1** *All our results are published in scientific journals.* = **magazine**, record, review, register, publication, bulletin, chronicle, gazette, periodical, zine (*informal*) **2** *He was a spokesperson for The New York Times and some other journals.* = **newspaper**, paper, daily, weekly, monthly, tabloid **3** *On the plane he wrote*

in his journal. = **diary**, record, history, log, notebook, chronicle, annals, yearbook, commonplace book, daybook, blog (*informal*)

journalist NOUN = **reporter**, writer, correspondent, newsman or newswoman, stringer, commentator, broadcaster, hack (*derogatory*), columnist, contributor, scribe (*informal*), pressman, journo (*slang*), newshound (*informal*), newspaperman or newspaperwoman

journey NOUN **1** *a journey from Manchester to Plymouth* = **trip**, drive, tour, flight, excursion, progress, cruise, passage, trek, outing, expedition, voyage, ramble, jaunt, peregrination, travel **2** *My films try to describe a journey of discovery.* = **progress**, passage, voyage, pilgrimage, odyssey ▶ VERB *She has journeyed on horseback through Africa and Turkey.* = **travel**, go, move, walk, fly, range, cross, tour, progress, proceed, fare, wander, trek, voyage, roam, ramble, traverse, rove, wend, go walkabout (*Austral.*), peregrinate

jovial ADJECTIVE = **cheerful**, happy, jolly, animated, glad (*archaic*), merry, hilarious, buoyant, airy, jubilant, cheery, cordial, convivial, blithe, gay, mirthful, jocund, jocose (*old-fashioned*) ■ **OPPOSITE:** solemn

joy NOUN **1** *Salter shouted with joy.* = **delight**, pleasure, triumph, satisfaction, happiness, ecstasy, enjoyment, bliss, transport, euphoria, festivity, felicity, glee, exuberance, rapture, elation, exhilaration, radiance, gaiety, jubilation, hilarity, exaltation, ebullience, exultation, gladness, joyfulness, ravishment ■ **OPPOSITE:** sorrow **2** *one of the joys of being a chef* = **treasure**, wonder, treat, prize, delight, pride, charm, thrill

joyful ADJECTIVE **1** *Giving birth to a child is both painful and joyful.* = **pleasing**, satisfying, engaging, charming, delightful, enjoyable, gratifying, agreeable, pleasurable **2** *We're a very joyful people.* = **delighted**, happy, satisfied, glad, jolly, merry, gratified, pleased, jubilant, elated, over the moon (*informal*), jovial, rapt, enraptured, on cloud nine (*informal*), cock-a-hoop, floating on air, light-hearted, jocund, gladsome (*archaic*), blithesome, stoked (*Austral. & N.Z. informal*)

joyless ADJECTIVE = **unhappy**, sad, depressing, miserable, gloomy, dismal, dreary, dejected, dispirited, downcast, down in the dumps (*informal*), cheerless

joyous ADJECTIVE = **joyful**, cheerful, merry, festive, heartening, rapturous, blithe

jubilant ADJECTIVE = **overjoyed**, excited, thrilled, glad, triumphant, rejoicing, exuberant, joyous, elated, over the moon (*informal*), euphoric, triumphal, enraptured, exultant, cock-a-hoop, rhapsodic, stoked (*Austral. & N.Z. informal*) ■ **OPPOSITE:** downcast

jubilation NOUN = **joy**, triumph, celebration, excitement, ecstasy, jubilee, festivity, elation, jamboree, exultation

jubilee NOUN = **celebration**, holiday, fête, festival, carnival, festivity, gala

judge NOUN **1** *The judge adjourned the hearing until next Tuesday.* = **magistrate**, justice, beak (*Brit. slang*), His, Her or Your Honour **2** *A panel of judges is now selecting the finalists.* = **referee**, expert, specialist, umpire, umpie (*Austral. slang*), mediator, examiner, connoisseur, assessor, arbiter, appraiser, arbitrator, moderator, adjudicator, evaluator, authority **3** *I'm a pretty good judge of character.* = **critic**, assessor, arbiter, appraiser, evaluator ▶ VERB **1** *Entries will be judged in two age categories.* = **adjudicate**, referee, umpire, mediate, officiate, adjudge, arbitrate **2** *It will take a few more years to judge the impact of these ideas.* = **evaluate**, rate, consider, appreciate, view, class, value, review, rank, examine, esteem (*formal*), criticize, ascertain, surmise **3** *It is important to judge the weight of your washing load.* = **estimate**, guess, assess, calculate, evaluate, gauge, appraise **4** *Players have been judged guilty of match-fixing.* = **find**, rule, pass, pronounce, decree, adjudge ■ **RELATED WORD:** adjective judicial

judgment NOUN **1** *In your judgment, what has changed over the past few years?* = **opinion**, view, estimate, belief, assessment, conviction, diagnosis, valuation, deduction, appraisal **2** *The Court is expected to give its judgment within the next ten days.* = **verdict**, finding, result, ruling, decision, sentence, conclusion, determination, decree, order, arbitration, adjudication, pronouncement **3** *Publication of the information was a serious error in judgment.* = **sense**, common sense, good sense, judiciousness, reason, understanding, taste, intelligence, smarts (*slang, chiefly U.S.*), discrimination, perception, awareness, wisdom, wit, penetration, prudence, sharpness, acumen, shrewdness, discernment, perspicacity (*formal*), sagacity, astuteness, percipience

judgmental ADJECTIVE = **condemnatory**, self-righteous, censorious, pharisaic, critical

judicial ADJECTIVE = **legal**, official, judiciary, juridical

judicious ADJECTIVE = **sensible**, considered, reasonable, discerning, sound, politic, acute, informed, diplomatic, careful, wise, cautious, rational, sober, discriminating, thoughtful, discreet, sage, enlightened, shrewd, prudent, sane, skilful, astute, expedient, circumspect, well-advised, well-judged, sagacious (*formal*), sapient (*used ironically*) ■ **OPPOSITE:** injudicious

jug NOUN = **container**, pitcher, urn, carafe, creamer (*U.S. & Canad.*), vessel, jar, crock, ewer

juggle VERB = **manipulate**, change, doctor (*informal*), fix (*informal*), alter, modify, disguise, manoeuvre, tamper with, misrepresent, falsify

juice NOUN **1** *the juice of about six lemons* = **liquid**, extract, fluid, liquor, sap, nectar **2** *the digestive juices of the human intestinal tract* = **secretion**, serum

juicy ADJECTIVE **1** *a thick, juicy steak* = **moist**, lush, watery, succulent, sappy **2** *It provided some juicy gossip for a few days.* = **interesting**, colourful, sensational, vivid, provocative, spicy (*informal*), suggestive, racy, risqué

jumble NOUN *a meaningless jumble of words* = **muddle**, mixture, mess, disorder, confusion, chaos, litter, clutter, disarray, medley, mélange (*French*), miscellany, mishmash, farrago, hotchpotch (*U.S.*), hodgepodge, gallimaufry, pig's breakfast (*informal*), disarrangement ▶ VERB *animals whose remains were jumbled together by scavengers and floods* = **mix**, mistake, confuse, disorder, shuffle, tangle, muddle, confound, entangle, ravel, disorganize, disarrange, dishevel

jumbo ADJECTIVE = **giant**, large, huge, immense, mega (*informal*), gigantic, oversized, elephantine, ginormous (*informal*), humongous or humungous (*informal*), supersize ■ **OPPOSITE:** tiny

jump VERB **1** *stamping their boots and jumping up and down to knock the snow off* = **leap**, dance, spring, bound, bounce, hop, skip, caper, prance, gambol **2** *He jumped the first fence beautifully.* = **vault**, clear, hurdle, go over, sail over, hop over **3** *She jumped to her feet and ran downstairs.* = **spring**, bound, leap, bounce **4** *The phone shrilled, making her jump.* = **recoil**, start, jolt, flinch, shake, jerk, quake, shudder, twitch, wince **5** *The number of crimes jumped by ten per cent last year.* = **increase**, rise, climb, escalate, gain, advance, boost, mount, soar, surge, spiral, hike (*informal*), ascend **6** *He refused to jump the queue for treatment at the local hospital.* = **miss**, avoid, skip (*informal*), omit, evade, digress ▶ NOUN **1** *With a few hops and a jump* they launched themselves into the air. = **leap**, spring, skip, bound, buck, hop, vault, caper **2** an eleven per cent jump in profits = **rise**, increase, escalation, upswing, advance, boost, elevation, upsurge, upturn, increment, augmentation **3** When Spider tapped on a window, Miguel gave an involuntary jump. = **jolt**, start, movement, shock, shake, jar, jerk, lurch, twitch, swerve, spasm **4** Hurdlers need to have unnaturally over-flexible knees to clear the jump. = **hurdle**, gate, barrier, fence, obstacle, barricade, rail

jumped-up ADJECTIVE = **conceited**, arrogant, pompous, stuck-up (informal), cocky, overbearing, puffed up, presumptuous, insolent, immodest, toffee-nosed, self-opinionated, too big for your boots or breeches

jumper NOUN = **sweater**, top, jersey, cardigan, woolly, pullover

jumpy ADJECTIVE = **nervous**, anxious, tense, shaky, restless, agitated, hyper (informal), apprehensive, jittery (informal), on edge, twitchy (informal), fidgety, timorous, antsy (informal), wired (slang) ■ **OPPOSITE:** calm

junction NOUN **1** Follow the road to a junction and turn left. = **crossroads**, crossing, intersection, interchange, T-junction **2** the junction between the nerve and muscle = **connection**, union, coupling, linking, joint, alliance, combination, seam, juncture

juncture NOUN = **moment**, time, point, crisis, occasion, emergency, strait, contingency, predicament, crux, exigency, conjuncture

junior ADJECTIVE **1** a junior minister attached to the prime minister's office = **minor**, lower, secondary, lesser, subordinate, inferior **2** junior pupils = **younger** ■ **OPPOSITE:** senior

junk NOUN = **rubbish**, refuse, waste, scrap, litter, debris, crap (slang), garbage (chiefly U.S.), trash, clutter, rummage, dross, odds and ends, space junk, oddments, flotsam and jetsam, leavings, dreck (slang, chiefly U.S.)

junta NOUN = **cabal**, council, faction, league, set, party, ring, camp, crew (informal), combination, assembly, gang, clique, coterie, schism, confederacy, convocation (formal)

jurisdiction NOUN **1** The British police have no jurisdiction over foreign bank accounts. = **authority**, say, power, control, rule, influence, command, sway, dominion, prerogative, mana (N.Z.) **2** matters which lie within his own jurisdiction = **range**, area, field, district, bounds, zone, province, circuit, scope, orbit, sphere, compass, dominion

just ADVERB **1** The two had only just met. = **recently**, lately, only now **2** It's just a suggestion. = **merely**, but, only, simply, solely, no more than, nothing but **3** He could just reach the man's head with his right hand. = **barely**, hardly, only just, scarcely, at most, by a whisker, at a push, by the skin of your teeth **4** Kiwi fruit are just the thing for a healthy snack. = **exactly**, really, quite, completely, totally, perfectly, entirely, truly, absolutely, precisely, altogether, positively ▶ ADJECTIVE **1** She fought honestly for a just cause and for freedom. = **fair**, good, legitimate, honourable, right, square, pure, decent, upright, honest, equitable, righteous, conscientious, impartial, virtuous, lawful, blameless, unbiased, fair-minded, unprejudiced ■ **OPPOSITE:** unfair **2** This cup final is a just reward for all the efforts they have put in. = **fitting**, due, correct, deserved, appropriate, justified, reasonable, suitable, decent, sensible, merited, proper, legitimate, desirable, apt, rightful, well-deserved, condign ■ **OPPOSITE:** inappropriate • **just about** He is just about the best golfer in the world. = **practically**, almost, nearly, close to, virtually, all but, not quite, well-nigh

> USAGE The expression just exactly is considered to be poor style because, since both words mean the same thing, only one or the other is needed. Use just – it's just what they want – or exactly – it's exactly what they want, but not both together.

justice NOUN **1** There is no justice in this world! = **fairness**, equity, integrity, honesty, decency, impartiality, rectitude, reasonableness, uprightness, justness, rightfulness, right ■ **OPPOSITE:** injustice **2** We must win people round to the justice of our cause. = **justness**, fairness, legitimacy, reasonableness, right, integrity, honesty, legality, rectitude, rightfulness **3** a justice on the Supreme Court = **judge**, magistrate, beak (Brit. slang), His, Her or Your Honour

justifiable ADJECTIVE = **reasonable**, right, sound, fit, acceptable, sensible, proper, valid, legitimate, understandable, lawful, well-founded, defensible, tenable, excusable, warrantable, vindicable ■ **OPPOSITE:** indefensible

justification NOUN = **reason**, grounds, defence, basis, excuse, approval, plea, warrant, apology, rationale, vindication, rationalization, absolution, exoneration, explanation, exculpation, extenuation

justify VERB = **explain**, support, warrant, bear out, legitimize, establish, maintain, confirm, defend, approve, excuse, sustain, uphold, acquit, vindicate, validate, substantiate, exonerate, legalize, absolve, exculpate

justly ADVERB = **justifiably**, rightly, correctly, properly, legitimately, rightfully, with good reason, lawfully

jut VERB = **stick out**, project, extend, protrude, poke, bulge, overhang, impend

juvenile NOUN *The number of juveniles in the general population has fallen.* = **child**, youth, minor, girl, boy, teenager, infant, adolescent ■ **OPPOSITE:** adult ▶ ADJECTIVE **1** *a scheme to rehabilitate juvenile offenders* = **young**, junior, adolescent, youthful, immature ■ **OPPOSITE:** adult **2** *As he gets older he becomes more juvenile.* = **immature**, childish, infantile, puerile, young, youthful, inexperienced, boyish, callow, undeveloped, unsophisticated, girlish, babyish, jejune (*formal*)

juxtaposition NOUN = **proximity**, adjacency, contact, closeness, vicinity, nearness, contiguity, propinquity

Kk

kai NOUN = **food**, grub (*slang*), provisions, fare, board, commons, eats (*slang*), feed, diet, meat, bread, tuck (*informal*), tucker (*Austral. & N.Z. informal*), rations, nutrition, tack (*informal*), refreshment, scoff (*slang*), nibbles, foodstuffs, nourishment, chow (*informal*), sustenance, nosh (*slang*), daily bread, victuals, edibles, comestibles, provender, nosebag (*slang*), pabulum (*rare*), nutriment, vittles (*obsolete, dialect*), viands, aliment, eatables (*slang*)

kak (*S. African vulgar slang*) NOUN **1** *His shoes were covered in kak.* = **faeces**, excrement, stool, muck, manure, dung, droppings, waste matter **2** *Now you're just talking kak.* = **rubbish**, nonsense, malarkey, garbage (*informal*), rot, crap (*slang*), drivel, tripe (*informal*), claptrap (*informal*), poppycock (*informal*), pants, bizzo (*Austral. slang*), bull's wool (*Austral. & N.Z. slang*)

kaleidoscopic ADJECTIVE **1** *a kaleidoscopic set of bright images* = **many-coloured**, multi-coloured, harlequin, psychedelic, motley, variegated, prismatic, varicoloured **2** *a kaleidoscopic world of complex relationships* = **changeable**, shifting, varied, mobile, variable, fluid, uncertain, volatile, unpredictable, unstable, fluctuating, indefinite, unsteady, protean, mutable, impermanent, inconstant **3** *a kaleidoscopic and fractured view of Los Angeles* = **complicated**, complex, confused, confusing, disordered, puzzling, unclear, baffling, bewildering, chaotic, muddled, intricate, jumbled, convoluted, disorganized, disarranged

kamikaze MODIFIER = **self-destructive**, suicidal, foolhardy

keel over VERB **1** *I keeled over and fell flat on my back.* = **collapse**, faint, pass out, black out (*informal*), swoon (*literary*) **2** *The vessel keeled over towards the murky water.* = **capsize**, list, upset, founder, overturn, turn over, lean over, tip over, topple over, turn turtle

keen¹ ADJECTIVE **1** *a keen amateur photographer* = **eager**, earnest, spirited, devoted, intense, fierce, enthusiastic, passionate, ardent, avid, fervent, impassioned, zealous, ebullient, wholehearted, fervid, bright-eyed and bushy-tailed (*informal*) ■ OPPOSITE: unenthusiastic **2** *a keen sense of loyalty* = **earnest**, fierce, intense, vehement, burning, flaming, consuming, eager, passionate, heightened, energetic, ardent, fanatical, fervent, impassioned, fervid **3** *a keen sense of humour* = **sharp**, satirical, incisive, trenchant, pointed, cutting, biting, edged, acute, acid, stinging, piercing, penetrating, searing, tart, withering, scathing, pungent, sarcastic, sardonic, caustic, astringent, vitriolic, acerbic, mordant, razor-like, finely honed ■ OPPOSITE: dull **4** *a person of keen intellect* = **perceptive**, quick, sharp, brilliant, acute, smart, wise, clever, subtle, piercing, penetrating, discriminating, shrewd, discerning, ingenious, astute, intuitive, canny, incisive, insightful, observant, perspicacious (*formal*), sapient ■ OPPOSITE: obtuse **5** *a keen eye for detail* = **penetrating**, clear, powerful, sharp, acute, sensitive, piercing, discerning, perceptive, observant **6** *Competition is keen for these awards.* = **intense**, strong, fierce, relentless, cut-throat

keen² VERB *He tossed back his head and keened.* = **lament**, cry, weep, sob, mourn, grieve, howl, sorrow, wail, whine, whimper, bewail

keep VERB **1** (*usually with* **from**) *Embarrassment has kept me from doing all sorts of things.* = **prevent**, hold back, deter, inhibit, block, stall, restrain, hamstring, hamper, withhold, hinder, retard, impede, shackle, keep back **2** (*sometimes with* **on**) *I turned back after a while, but he kept walking.* = **continue**, go on, carry on, persist in, persevere in, remain **3** *We want to keep as many players as we can.* = **hold on to**, maintain, retain, keep possession of, save, preserve, nurture, cherish, conserve ■ OPPOSITE: lose **4** *She kept her money under the mattress.* = **store**, put, place, house, hold, deposit, pile, stack, heap, amass, stow **5** *The shop keeps specialized books on various aspects of the collection.* = **carry**, stock, have, hold, sell, supply, handle, trade in, deal in **6** *I'm hoping you'll keep your promise to come for a long visit.* = **comply with**, carry out, honour, fulfil, hold, follow, mind, respect, observe, respond to, embrace, execute, obey, heed, conform to, adhere to, abide by, act upon ■ OPPOSITE: disregard **7** *She could just about afford to keep her five kids.* = **support**, maintain, sustain, provide for, mind, fund, board, finance, feed, look after, foster, shelter, care for, take care of, nurture, safeguard, cherish, nourish, subsidize **8** *This eccentric writer kept a lobster as a pet.* = **raise**, own, maintain, tend, farm, breed, look after, rear, care for, bring up, nurture, nourish **9** *His father kept a village shop.* = **manage**, run, administer, be in charge (of), rule, direct, handle, govern, oversee, supervise, preside over, superintend **10** *'Sorry to keep you, Jack.'* = **delay**, detain, hinder, impede, stop, limit, check, arrest, curb, constrain, obstruct, retard, set back ■ OPPOSITE: release **11** *I don't like the company you keep.* = **associate with**, mix with, mingle with, hang out with (*informal*), hang with (*informal, chiefly U.S.*), be friends with, consort with, run around with (*informal*), hobnob with, socialize with, hang about with, fraternize with ▶ NOUN **1** *I need to give my parents money for my keep.* = **board**, food, maintenance, upkeep, means, living, support, nurture, livelihood, subsistence, kai (*N.Z. informal*), nourishment, sustenance **2** *the parts of the keep open to visitors* = **tower**, castle, stronghold, dungeon, citadel, fastness, donjon • **keep at it** *'Keep at it!' Thade encouraged me.* = **persist**, continue, carry on, keep going, stick with it, stay with it, be steadfast, grind it out, persevere, remain with it • **keep something back 1** *Roughly chop the vegetables, and keep back a few for decoration.* = **hold back**, hold, save, set aside, husband, store, retain, preserve, hang on to, conserve, stockpile, hoard, lay up, put by **2** *Neither of them is telling the whole truth. They're both keeping something back.* = **suppress**, hide, reserve, conceal, restrain, cover up, withhold, stifle, censor, repress, smother, muffle, muzzle, keep something under your hat **3** *I can no longer keep back my tears.* = **restrain**, control, limit, check, delay, restrict, curb, prohibit, withhold, hold back, constrain, retard, keep a tight rein on • **keep something up 1** *They can no longer keep up the repayments.* = **continue**, make, maintain, carry on, persist in, persevere with **2** *keeping up the pressure against the government* = **maintain**, sustain, uphold, perpetuate, retain, preserve, prolong • **keep up** *Things are changing so fast, it's hard to keep up.* = **keep pace**, match, compete, contend, emulate, persevere

keeper NOUN *the keeper of the library at the V&A* = **curator**, guardian, steward, superintendent (*U.S.*), attendant, caretaker, overseer, preserver

keeping NOUN *It has been handed over for safe keeping.* = **care**, keep, charge, trust, protection, possession, maintenance, custody, patronage, guardianship, safekeeping • **in keeping with** *His office was in keeping with his station and experience.* = **in agreement with**, consistent with, in harmony with, in accord with, in compliance with, in conformity with, in balance with, in correspondence with, in proportion with, in congruity with, in observance with

keepsake NOUN = **souvenir**, symbol, token, reminder, relic, remembrance, emblem, memento, favour

keg NOUN = **barrel**, drum, vat, cask, firkin, tun, hogshead

ken NOUN • **beyond someone's ken** = **beyond the knowledge of**, beyond the comprehension of, beyond the understanding of, beyond the acquaintance of, beyond the awareness of, beyond the cognizance of

kernel NOUN = **essence**, core, substance, gist, grain, marrow, germ, nub, pith

key NOUN **1** *She reached for her coat and car keys.* = **opener**, door key, latchkey **2** *The key to success is to be ready from the start.* = **answer**, means, secret, solution, path, formula, passage, clue, cue, pointer, sign ▶ MODIFIER *He is expected to be the key witness at the trial.* = **essential**, leading, major, main, important, chief, necessary, basic, vital, crucial, principal, fundamental, decisive, indispensable, pivotal, must-have ■ OPPOSITE: minor

keynote NOUN = **heart**, centre, theme, core, substance, essence, marrow, kernel, gist, pith

keystone NOUN = **basis**, principle, core, crux, ground, source, spring, root, motive, cornerstone, lynchpin, mainspring, fundament, quoin

kia ora INTERJECTION (*N.Z.*) = **hello**, hi (*informal*), greetings, gidday or g'day (*Austral. & N.Z.*), how do you do?, good morning, good evening, good afternoon, welcome

kick VERB **1** *Sabrina kicked me in the shin under the table.* = **boot**, strike, knock, punt, put the boot in(to) (*slang*) **2** (*informal*) *She's kicked her drug habit.* = **give up**, break, stop, abandon, quit, cease, eschew, leave off, desist from, end ▶ NOUN **1** (*informal*) *I got a kick out of seeing my name in print.* = **thrill**, glow, buzz (*slang*), tingle, high (*informal*), sensation **2** (*informal*) *The coffee had more of a kick than it seemed on first tasting.* = **pungency**, force, power, edge, strength, snap (*informal*), punch, intensity, pep, sparkle, vitality, verve, zest, potency, tang, piquancy • **kick someone out** *They kicked five foreign journalists out of the country.* = **dismiss**, remove, reject, get rid of, discharge, expel, oust, eject, evict, toss out, give the boot (*slang*), sack (*informal*), kiss off (*slang, chiefly U.S. & Canad.*), give (someone) their marching orders, give the push, give the bum's rush (*slang*), show someone the door, throw someone out on their ear (*informal*), kennet (*Austral. slang*), jeff (*Austral. slang*) • **kick something off** *We kicked off the meeting with a song.* = **begin**, start, open, commence, launch, initiate, get under way, kick-start, get on the road

kickback NOUN = **bribe**, payoff, backhander (*slang*), enticement, share, cut (*informal*), payment, gift, reward, incentive, graft (*informal*), sweetener (*slang*), inducement, sop, recompense, hush money (*slang*), payola (*informal*), allurement

kick-off NOUN = **start**, opening, beginning, commencement, outset, starting point, inception

kid[1] NOUN = **child**, girl, boy, baby, lad, teenager, youngster, infant, adolescent, juvenile, toddler, tot, lass, wean (*Scot.*), little one, bairn (*Scot. & Northern English*), stripling, sprog (*slang*), munchkin (*informal, chiefly U.S.*), rug rat (*U.S. & Canad. informal*), littlie (*Austral. informal*), ankle-biter (*Austral. slang*), tacker (*Austral. slang*)

kid[2] VERB *I'm just kidding.* = **tease**, joke, trick, fool, pretend, mock, rag (*Brit.*), wind up (*Brit. slang*), ridicule, hoax, beguile, gull (*archaic*), delude, jest, bamboozle, hoodwink, cozen (*literary*), jerk or yank someone's chain (*informal*)

kidnap VERB = **abduct**, remove, steal, capture, seize, snatch (*slang*), hijack, run off with, run away with, make off with, hold to ransom

kill VERB 1 *More than 1,000 people have been killed by the armed forces.* = **slay**, murder, execute, slaughter, destroy, waste (*informal*), do in (*slang*), take out (*slang*), massacre, butcher, wipe out (*informal*), dispatch, cut down, erase, assassinate, eradicate, whack (*informal*), do away with, blow away (*slang, chiefly U.S.*), obliterate, knock off (*slang*), liquidate, decimate, annihilate, neutralize, exterminate, terminate (*slang*), croak, mow down, take (someone's) life, bump off (*slang*), extirpate, wipe from the face of the earth (*informal*) 2 *Public opinion may yet kill the proposal.* = **destroy**, defeat, crush, scotch, still, stop, total (*slang*), ruin, halt, cancel, wreck, shatter, veto, suppress, dismantle, stifle,

trash (*slang*), ravage, eradicate, smother, quash, quell, extinguish, annihilate, put paid to

killer NOUN = **murderer**, slaughterer, slayer, hitman or woman (*slang*), butcher, gunman or woman, assassin, destroyer, liquidator, terminator, executioner, exterminator, genocidaire

killing NOUN *This is a brutal killing.* = **murder**, massacre, slaughter, execution, dispatch, manslaughter, elimination, slaying, homicide, bloodshed, carnage, fatality, liquidation, extermination, annihilation, eradication, butchery ▸ ADJECTIVE 1 *He covered the last 300 metres in around 41 seconds, a killing pace.* = **tiring**, hard, testing, taxing, difficult, draining, exhausting, punishing, crippling, fatiguing, gruelling, sapping, debilitating, strenuous, arduous, laborious, enervating, backbreaking 2 *Diphtheria was a killing disease.* = **deadly**, deathly, dangerous, fatal, destructive, lethal, mortal, murderous, death-dealing • **make a killing** *They have made a killing on the deal.* = **profit**, gain, clean up (*informal*), be lucky, be successful, make a fortune, strike it rich (*informal*), make a bomb (*slang*), rake it in (*informal*), have a windfall

killjoy NOUN = **spoilsport** (*informal*), dampener, damper, wet blanket (*informal*)

kin NOUN = **family**, people, relations, relatives, connections, kindred, kinsmen, kith, kinsfolk, ainga (*N.Z.*), rellies (*Austral. slang*)

kind[1] ADJECTIVE *He was a very kind man, full of common sense.* = **considerate**, good, loving, kindly, understanding, concerned, friendly, neighbourly, gentle, generous, mild, obliging, sympathetic, charitable, thoughtful, benign, humane, affectionate, compassionate, clement, gracious, indulgent, benevolent, attentive, amiable, courteous, amicable, lenient, cordial, congenial, philanthropic, unselfish, propitious, beneficent, kind-hearted, bounteous, tender-hearted
■ OPPOSITE: unkind

kind[2] NOUN 1 *They developed a new kind of film-making.* = **class**, sort, type, variety, brand, grade, category, genre, classification, league 2 *I hate Lewis and his kind just as much as you do.* = **sort**, set, type, ilk, family, race, species, breed, genus 3 *Donations came in from all kinds of people.* = **nature**, sort, type, manner, style, quality, character, make-up, habit, stamp, description, mould, essence, temperament, persuasion, calibre, disposition

USAGE It is common in informal speech to combine singular and plural in sentences like *children enjoy those kind of stories*. However, this is not acceptable in careful writing, where the plural must be used consistently: *children enjoy those kinds of stories*.

kind-hearted ADJECTIVE = **sympathetic**, kind, generous, helpful, tender, humane, compassionate, gracious, amicable, considerate, altruistic, good-natured, tender-hearted ■ **OPPOSITE:** hard-hearted

kindle VERB **1** *These poems have helped kindle the imagination of generations of children.* = **arouse**, excite, inspire, stir, thrill, stimulate, provoke, induce, awaken, animate, rouse, sharpen, inflame, incite, foment, bestir, enkindle **2** *I came in and kindled a fire in the stove.* = **light**, start, ignite, fire, spark, torch, inflame, set fire to, set a match to ■ **OPPOSITE:** extinguish

kindly ADJECTIVE *He was a stern critic but an extremely kindly man.* = **benevolent**, kind, caring, nice, warm, gentle, helpful, pleasant, mild, sympathetic, beneficial, polite, favourable, benign, humane, compassionate, hearty, cordial, considerate, genial, affable, good-natured, beneficent, well-disposed, kind-hearted, warm-hearted ■ **OPPOSITE:** cruel ▶ ADVERB *She kindly carried our picnic in her rucksack.* = **benevolently**, politely, generously, thoughtfully, tenderly, lovingly, cordially, affectionately, helpfully, graciously, obligingly, agreeably, indulgently, selflessly, unselfishly, compassionately, considerately ■ **OPPOSITE:** unkindly

kindness NOUN **1** *We have been treated with such kindness by everybody.* = **goodwill**, understanding, charity, grace, humanity, affection, patience, tolerance, goodness, compassion, hospitality, generosity, indulgence, decency, tenderness, clemency, gentleness, philanthropy, benevolence, magnanimity, fellow-feeling, amiability, beneficence, kindliness ■ **OPPOSITE:** malice **2** *It would be a kindness to leave her alone.* = **good deed**, help, service, aid, favour, assistance, bounty, benefaction

kindred NOUN *The offender made proper restitution to the victim's kindred.* = **family**, relations, relatives, connections, flesh, kin, lineage, kinsmen, kinsfolk, ainga (N.Z.), rellies (*Austral. slang*) ▶ ADJECTIVE **1** *I recall discussions with her on these and kindred topics.* = **similar**, like, related, allied, corresponding, affiliated, akin, kin, cognate, matching **2** *We're sort of kindred spirits.* = **like-minded**, similar, compatible, understanding, similar, friendly, sympathetic, responsive, agreeable, in tune, congenial, like, companionable

king NOUN = **ruler**, monarch, sovereign, crowned head, leader, lord, prince, Crown, emperor, majesty, head of state, consort, His Majesty, overlord ■ **RELATED WORDS:** *adjectives* royal, regal, monarchical

kingdom NOUN **1** *the Kingdom of Denmark* = **country**, state, nation, land, division, territory, province, empire, commonwealth, realm, domain, tract, dominion, sovereign state **2** *nature study trips to the kingdom of the polar bear* = **domain**, territory, province, realm, area, department (*informal*), field, zone, arena, sphere

kink NOUN **1** *a tiny black kitten with tufted ears and a kink in her tail* = **twist**, bend, wrinkle, knot, tangle, coil, corkscrew, entanglement, crimp, frizz **2** *What kink did he have in his character?* = **quirk**, eccentricity, foible, idiosyncrasy, whim, fetish, vagary, singularity, crotchet **3** *working out the kinks of a potential trade agreement* = **flaw**, difficulty, defect, complication, tangle, knot, hitch, imperfection

kinky ADJECTIVE **1** *kinky behaviour* = **weird**, odd, strange, bizarre, peculiar, eccentric, queer, quirky, unconventional, off-the-wall (*slang*), outlandish, oddball (*informal*), outré **2** *He had red kinky hair.* = **twisted**, curled, curly, frizzy, tangled, coiled, crimped, frizzled

kinship NOUN **1** *the ties of kinship* = **relationship**, kin, family ties, consanguinity (*formal*), ties of blood, blood relationship **2** *She evidently felt a sense of kinship with the woman.* = **similarity**, relationship, association, bearing, connection, alliance, correspondence, affinity

kinsman *or* **kinswoman** *or* **kinsperson** NOUN = **relative**, relation, blood relative, fellow tribesperson, fellow clansperson, rellie (*Austral. slang*)

kiosk NOUN = **booth**, stand, counter, stall, newsstand, bookstall

kiss VERB **1** *She kissed me on the cheek.* = **peck** (*informal*), osculate, snog (*Brit. slang*), neck (*informal*), smooch (*informal*), canoodle (*slang*) **2** *The wheels of the aircraft kissed the runway.* = **brush**, touch, shave, scrape, graze, caress, glance off, stroke ▶ NOUN *I put my arms around her and gave her a kiss.* = **peck** (*informal*), snog (*Brit. slang*), smacker (*slang*), smooch (*informal*), French kiss, osculation

kit NOUN **1** *The kit consisted of about twenty cosmetic items.* = **equipment**, supplies, materials, tackle, tools, instruments, provisions, implements, rig, apparatus, trappings, utensils, paraphernalia, accoutrements, appurtenances **2** *I forgot my gym kit.* = **gear**, things, effects, dress, clothes, clothing, stuff, equipment, uniform, outfit, rig, costume, garments, baggage, equipage • **kit something or someone out** or **up** *kitted out with warm winter coats and jumpers* = **equip**, fit, supply, provide with, arm, stock, outfit, costume, furnish, fix up, fit out, deck out, accoutre

kitchen NOUN = **cookhouse**, galley, kitchenette, scullery

knack NOUN = **skill**, art, ability, facility, talent, gift, capacity, trick, bent, craft, genius, expertise, forte, flair, competence, ingenuity, propensity, aptitude, dexterity, cleverness, quickness, adroitness, expertness, handiness, skilfulness
■ **OPPOSITE:** ineptitude

knackered ADJECTIVE **1** = **exhausted**, worn out, tired out, drained, beat (*slang*), done in (*informal*), all in (*slang*), debilitated, prostrated, enervated, ready to drop, dog-tired (*informal*), zonked (*slang*), dead tired, dead beat (*slang*) **2** = **broken**, not working, out of order, not functioning, done in (*informal*), ruined, worn out, on the blink (*slang*), on its last legs

knavish ADJECTIVE = **dishonest**, tricky, fraudulent, deceptive, unscrupulous, rascally, scoundrelly, deceitful, villainous, unprincipled, dishonourable, roguish
■ **OPPOSITE:** honourable

knead VERB = **squeeze**, work, massage, manipulate, form, press, shape, stroke, blend, rub, mould

kneel VERB = **genuflect**, bow, stoop, curtsy or curtsey, bow down, kowtow, get down on your knees, make obeisance

knell NOUN = **ring**, sound, toll, chime, clang, peal

knickers PLURAL NOUN = **underwear**, smalls, briefs, drawers, panties, bloomers

knife NOUN *a knife and fork* = **blade**, carver, cutter, cutting tool ▶ VERB *She was knifed in the back six times.* = **cut**, wound, stab, slash, thrust, gore, pierce, spear, jab, bayonet, impale, lacerate

knit VERB **1** *Sport knits the whole family close together.* = **join**, unite, link, tie, bond, ally, combine, secure, bind, connect, merge, weave, fasten, meld **2** *broken bones that have failed to knit* = **heal**, unite, join, link, bind, connect, loop, mend, fasten, intertwine, interlace **3** *They knitted their brows and started to grumble.* = **furrow**, tighten, knot, wrinkle, crease, screw up, pucker, scrunch up

knob NOUN = **ball**, stud, nub, protuberance, boss, bunch, swell, knot, bulk, lump, bump, projection, snag, hump, protrusion, knurl

knock VERB **1** *Knock at my window at eight o'clock and I'll be ready.* = **bang**, beat, strike, tap, rap, bash (*informal*), thump, buffet, pummel **2** *He was mucking around and he knocked her in the stomach.* = **hit**, strike, punch, belt (*informal*), slap, chin (*slang*), smack, thump, clap, cuff, smite (*archaic*), thwack, lay one on (*slang*), beat or knock seven bells out of (*informal*) **3** (*informal*) *I'm not knocking them: if they want to do it, it's up to them.* = **criticize**, condemn, put down, run down, abuse, blast, pan (*informal*), slam (*slang*), slate (*informal*), have a go (at) (*informal*), censure, slag (off) (*slang*), denigrate, belittle, disparage, deprecate, diss (*slang*), throw shade (at) (*slang*), find fault with, carp at, lambast(e), pick holes in, cast aspersions on, cavil at, pick to pieces, give (someone or something) a bad press, nit-pick (*informal*) ▶ NOUN **1** *They heard a knock at the front door.* = **knocking**, pounding, beating, tap, hammering, bang, banging, rap, thump, thud **2** *The bags have tough exterior materials to protect against knocks.* = **bang**, blow, impact, jar, collision, jolt, smash **3** *He had taken a knock on the head in training.* = **blow**, hit, punch, crack (*informal*), belt (*informal*), clip, slap, bash, smack, thump, clout (*informal*), cuff, box **4** (*informal*) *The art market has suffered some severe knocks.* = **setback**, check, defeat, blow, upset, reverse, disappointment, hold-up, hitch, reversal, misfortune, rebuff, whammy (*informal*), bummer (*slang*)
• **knock about** or **around** *reporters who knock around in troubled parts of the world* = **wander**, travel, roam, rove, range, drift, stray, ramble, straggle, traipse, go walkabout (*Austral.*), stravaig (*Scot. & Northern English, dialect*) • **knock about** or **around with someone** *I used to knock about with all the lads.* = **mix with**, associate with, mingle with, hang out with (*informal*), hang with (*informal, chiefly U.S.*), be friends with, consort with, run around with (*informal*), hobnob with, socialize with, accompany, hang about with, fraternize with • **knock off** (*informal*) *What time do you knock off?* = **stop work**, get out, conclude, shut down, terminate, call it a day (*informal*), finish work, clock off, clock out • **knock someone about** or **around** *He started knocking me around.* = **hit**, attack, beat, strike, damage, abuse, hurt, injure, wound,

assault, harm, batter, slap, bruise, thrash, beat up (informal), buffet, maul, work over (slang), clobber (slang), mistreat, manhandle, maltreat, lambast(e), slap around (informal), beat or knock seven bells out of (informal) • **knock someone down** He was admitted to hospital after being knocked down by a car. = **run over**, hit, run down, knock over, mow down • **knock someone off** Several people had a motive to knock her off. = **kill**, murder, do in (slang), slaughter, destroy, waste (informal), take out (slang), execute, massacre, butcher, wipe out (informal), dispatch, cut down, erase, assassinate, slay, eradicate, whack (informal), do away with, blow away (slang, chiefly U.S.), obliterate, liquidate, decimate, annihilate, neutralize, exterminate, croak, mow down, take (someone's) life, bump off (slang), extirpate, wipe from the face of the earth (informal) • **knock someone out** 1 He had never been knocked out in a professional fight. = **floor**, knock unconscious, knock senseless, render unconscious, level, stun, daze 2 We were knocked out in the quarter-finals. = **eliminate**, beat, defeat, trounce, vanquish (literary) 3 That performance knocked me out. = **impress**, move, strike, touch, affect, influence, excite, inspire, grab (informal), stir, overwhelm, sway, make an impression on • **knock something down** Why don't they just knock the wall down? = **demolish**, destroy, flatten, tear down, level, total (slang), fell, ruin, dismantle, trash (slang), bulldoze, raze, pulverize, kennet (Austral. slang), jeff (Austral. slang) • **knock something off** 1 Cars can be stolen almost as easily as knocking off a bike. = **steal**, take, nick (slang, chiefly Brit.), thieve, rob, pinch (Brit. informal), cabbage (Brit. slang), blag (slang), pilfer, purloin (formal), filch 2 I'll knock off another £100 if you pay in cash. = **remove**, take away, deduct, debit, subtract

knockabout ADJECTIVE = **boisterous**, riotous, rollicking, rough-and-tumble, rumbustious, rambunctious (informal), harum-scarum, farcical, slapstick

knockout NOUN 1 a first-round knockout in Las Vegas = **killer blow**, coup de grâce (French), kayo (slang), KO or K.O. (slang) 2 The first story is a knockout. = **success**, hit, winner, triumph, smash (informal), sensation, smash hit, stunner (informal), smasheroo (informal) ■ OPPOSITE: failure

knoll NOUN = **hillock**, hill, mound

knot NOUN 1 One lace had broken and been tied in a knot. = **connection**, tie, bond, joint, bow, loop, braid, splice, rosette, ligature 2 A little knot of men stood clapping. = **group**, company, set, band, crowd, pack, squad, circle, crew (informal), gang, mob, clique, assemblage ▶ VERB He knotted the bandanna around his neck. = **tie**, secure, bind, weave, loop, knit, tether, entangle

knotty ADJECTIVE 1 The new management team faces some knotty problems. = **puzzling**, hard, difficult, complex, complicated, tricky, baffling, intricate, troublesome, perplexing, mystifying, thorny, problematical 2 the knotty trunk of a hawthorn tree = **knotted**, rough, rugged, bumpy, gnarled, knobby, nodular

know VERB 1 I don't know the name of the place. = **have knowledge of**, see, understand, recognize, perceive, be aware of, be conscious of 2 Do you two know each other? = **be acquainted with**, recognize, associate with, be familiar with, be friends with, be friendly with, have knowledge of, have dealings with, socialize with, fraternize with, be pals with ■ OPPOSITE: be unfamiliar with 3 (sometimes with **about** or **of**) Hire someone with experience, someone who knows about real estate. = **be familiar with**, experience, understand, ken (Scot.), comprehend, fathom, apprehend, have knowledge of, be acquainted with, feel certain of, have dealings in, be versed in ■ OPPOSITE: be ignorant of 4 Would she know you if she saw you on the street? = **recognize**, remember, identify, recall, place, spot, notice, distinguish, perceive, make out, discern, differentiate, recollect

know-all NOUN = **smart aleck**, wise guy (informal), smarty (informal), clever-clogs (informal), clever Dick (informal), smarty-pants (informal), smartarse (slang), wiseacre, smarty-boots (informal)

know-how NOUN = **expertise**, experience, ability, skill, knowledge, facility, talent, command, craft, grasp, faculty, capability, flair, knack, ingenuity, aptitude, proficiency, dexterity, cleverness, deftness, savoir-faire, adroitness, ableness

knowing ADJECTIVE = **meaningful**, significant, expressive, eloquent, enigmatic, suggestive

knowingly ADVERB = **deliberately**, purposely, consciously, intentionally, on purpose, wilfully, wittingly

knowledge NOUN 1 the quest for scientific knowledge = **understanding**, sense, intelligence, judgment, perception, awareness, insight, grasp, appreciation, penetration, comprehension, discernment 2 She didn't intend to display her knowledge, at least not yet. = **learning**, schooling, education,

k

science, intelligence, instruction, wisdom, scholarship, tuition, enlightenment, erudition ■ **OPPOSITE:** ignorance **3** *taken without my knowledge or consent* = **consciousness**, recognition, awareness, apprehension, cognition, discernment ■ **OPPOSITE:** unawareness **4** *She disclaims any knowledge of her husband's business concerns.* = **acquaintance**, information, notice, intimacy, familiarity, cognizance ■ **OPPOSITE:** unfamiliarity

knowledgeable ADJECTIVE **1** *school-age children who were very knowledgeable about soccer* = **well-informed**, acquainted, conversant, au fait (*French*), experienced, understanding, aware, familiar, conscious, in the know (*informal*), cognizant, in the loop, au courant (*French*), clued-up

(*informal*), across, down with, leet (*Computing slang*) **2** *He was a knowledgeable and well-read man.* = **intelligent**, lettered, learned, educated, scholarly, erudite

known ADJECTIVE = **famous**, well-known, celebrated, popular, common, admitted, noted, published, obvious, familiar, acknowledged, recognized, plain, confessed, patent, manifest, avowed ■ **OPPOSITE:** unknown

koppie *or* **kopje** NOUN (*S. African*) = **hill**, down (*archaic*), fell, mount, height, mound, prominence, elevation, eminence, hilltop, tor, knoll, hillock, brae (*Scot.*)

kudos NOUN = **prestige**, regard, honour, praise, glory, fame, distinction, esteem, acclaim, applause, plaudits, renown, repute, notability, laudation

k

Ll

label NOUN **1** *He peered at the label on the bottle.* = **tag**, ticket, tab, marker, flag, tally, sticker, docket (*chiefly Brit.*) **2** *Her treatment of her husband earned her the label of the most hated woman in America.* = **epithet**, description, classification, characterization **3** *designer labels* = **brand**, company, mark, trademark, brand name, trade name ▶ VERB **1** *The produce was labelled 'Made in China'.* = **tag**, mark, stamp, ticket, flag, tab, tally, sticker, docket (*chiefly Brit.*) **2** *Too often the press are labelled as irresponsible.* = **brand**, classify, describe, class, call, name, identify, define, designate, characterize, categorize, pigeonhole

laborious ADJECTIVE **1** *Keeping the garden tidy all year round can be a laborious task.* = **hard**, difficult, tiring, exhausting, wearing, tough, fatiguing, uphill, strenuous, arduous, tiresome, onerous, burdensome, herculean, wearisome, backbreaking, toilsome (*literary*) ■ OPPOSITE: easy **2** *He was gentle and kindly, living a laborious life in his Paris flat.* = **industrious**, hard-working, diligent, tireless, persevering, painstaking, indefatigable, assiduous, unflagging, sedulous **3** (*of a literary style*) *a laborious prose style* = **forced**, laboured, strained, ponderous, not fluent ■ OPPOSITE: natural

labour NOUN **1** *the labour of seeding, planting and harvesting* = **toil**, effort, industry, grind (*informal*), pains, sweat (*informal*), slog (*informal*), exertion, drudgery, travail, donkey-work ■ OPPOSITE: leisure **2** *The country lacked skilled labour.* = **workers**, employees, workforce, labourers, hands, workmen **3** *Every man should receive a fair price for the product of his labour.* = **work**, effort, employment, toil, industry **4** *By the time she realised she was in labour, it was too late.* = **childbirth**, birth, delivery, contractions, pains, throes, travail, labour pains, parturition **5** *The chef looked up from his labours.* = **chore**, job, task, undertaking ▶ VERB **1** *peasants labouring in the fields* = **work**, toil, strive, work hard, grind (*informal*), sweat (*informal*), slave, endeavour, plod away, drudge, travail, slog away (*informal*), exert yourself,

peg along *or* away (*chiefly Brit.*), plug along *or* away (*informal*) ■ OPPOSITE: rest **2** *For years he laboured to build a religious community.* = **struggle**, work, strain, work hard, strive, go for it (*informal*), grapple, toil, make an effort, make every effort, do your best, exert yourself, work like a Trojan **3** *I don't want to labour the point, but there it is.* = **overemphasize**, stress, elaborate, exaggerate, strain, dwell on, overdo, go on about, make a production (out) of (*informal*), make a federal case of (*U.S. informal*) **4** (*usually with* **under**) *She laboured under the illusion that I knew what I was doing.* = **be disadvantaged by**, suffer from, be a victim of, be burdened by

laboured ADJECTIVE **1** *From his slow walk and laboured breathing, she realized he was not well.* = **difficult**, forced, strained, heavy, awkward **2** *The prose of his official communications was so laboured, pompous and verbose.* = **contrived**, studied, affected, awkward, unnatural, overdone, ponderous, overwrought

labourer NOUN = **worker**, workman *or* woman *or* person, working man *or* woman *or* person, manual worker, hand, blue-collar worker, drudge, unskilled worker, navvy (*Brit. informal*), labouring man

labyrinth NOUN = **maze**, jungle, tangle, coil, snarl, entanglement

labyrinthine ADJECTIVE = **mazelike**, winding, tangled, intricate, tortuous, convoluted, mazy

lace NOUN **1** *a plain white lace bedspread* = **netting**, net, filigree, tatting, meshwork, openwork **2** *He was sitting on the bed, tying the laces of an old pair of running shoes.* = **cord**, tie, string, lacing, thong, shoelace, bootlace ▶ VERB **1** *No matter how tightly I lace these shoes, my ankles wobble.* = **fasten**, tie, tie up, do up, secure, bind, close, attach, thread **2** *The food was laced with sleeping pills.* = **mix**, drug, doctor, add to, spike, contaminate, fortify, adulterate **3** *He took to lacing his fingers together in an attempt to keep his hands still.* = **intertwine**, interweave, entwine, twine, interlink

lacerate VERB **1** *Its claws lacerated his thighs.* = **tear**, cut, wound, rend (*literary*), rip, slash, claw, maim, mangle, mangulate (*Austral. slang*), gash, jag **2** *He was born into a family already lacerated with tensions and divisions.* = **hurt**, wound, rend, torture, distress, torment, afflict, harrow

laceration NOUN = **cut**, injury, tear, wound, rent, rip, slash, trauma (*Pathology*), gash, mutilation

lack NOUN *Despite his lack of experience, he got the job.* = **shortage**, want, absence, deficiency, need, shortcoming, deprivation, inadequacy, scarcity, dearth, privation (*formal*), shortness, destitution, insufficiency, scantiness, debt ■ **OPPOSITE:** abundance
▶ VERB *It lacked the power of the Italian cars.* = **miss**, want, need, require, not have, be without, be short of, be in need of, be deficient in ■ **OPPOSITE:** have

lackey NOUN = **hanger-on**, fawner, pawn, attendant, tool, instrument, parasite, cohort (*chiefly U.S.*), valet, menial, minion, footman, sycophant, yes-man, manservant, toady, flunky, flatterer, varlet (*archaic*)

lacking ADJECTIVE = **deficient**, wanting, needing, missing, inadequate, minus (*informal*), flawed, impaired, sans (*archaic*)

lacklustre ADJECTIVE = **flat**, boring, dull, dim, dry, muted, sombre, drab, lifeless, prosaic, leaden, unimaginative, uninspired, unexciting, vapid, lustreless

laconic ADJECTIVE = **terse**, short, brief, clipped, to the point, crisp, compact, concise, curt, succinct, pithy, monosyllabic, sententious ■ **OPPOSITE:** long-winded

lacy ADJECTIVE = **filigree**, open, fine, sheer, delicate, frilly, gossamer, gauzy, net-like, lace-like, meshy

lad NOUN = **boy**, kid (*informal*), guy (*informal*), youth, fellow (*old-fashioned*), youngster, chap (*informal*), juvenile, shaver (*informal*), nipper (*informal*), laddie (*Scot.*), stripling

laden ADJECTIVE = **loaded**, burdened, hampered, weighted, full, charged, taxed, oppressed, fraught, weighed down, encumbered

lady NOUN **1** *the very noble lady whom I have the honour of calling patroness* = **gentlewoman**, duchess, noble, dame, baroness, countess, aristocrat, viscountess, noblewoman, peeress **2** *She's a very sweet old lady.* = **woman**, female, girl, miss (*old-fashioned or derogatory*), maiden (*archaic*), maid (*archaic*), lass, damsel (*archaic, poetic*), lassie (*informal*), charlie (*Austral., old-fashioned slang*), chook (*Austral. slang, sometimes derogatory*), wahine (*N.Z.*)

ladylike ADJECTIVE = **refined**, cultured, sophisticated, elegant, proper, respectable, polite, genteel, courtly, decorous ■ **OPPOSITE:** unladylike

lag VERB **1** *The boys crept forward, Roger lagging a little.* = **hang back**, delay, drag (behind), trail, linger, be behind, idle, saunter, loiter, straggle, dawdle, tarry, drag your feet (*informal*) **2** *Trade has lagged since the embargo.* = **drop**, fail, diminish, decrease, flag, fall off, wane, ebb, slacken, lose strength

laggard NOUN = **straggler**, lounger, lingerer, piker (*Austral. & N.Z. slang*), snail, saunterer, loafer, loiterer, dawdler, skiver (*Brit. slang*), idler, slowcoach (*Brit. informal*), sluggard, bludger (*Austral. & N.Z. informal*), slowpoke (*U.S. & Canad. informal*)

laid-back ADJECTIVE = **relaxed**, calm, casual, together (*slang*), at ease, easy-going, unflappable (*informal*), unhurried, free and easy, easy-peasy (*slang*), chilled (*informal*) ■ **OPPOSITE:** tense

lair NOUN **1** *a fox's lair* = **nest**, den, hole, burrow, resting place **2** *The village was once a pirate's lair.* = **hide-out** (*informal*), retreat, refuge, den, sanctuary

laissez faire *or* **laisser faire** NOUN = **nonintervention**, free trade, individualism, free enterprise, live and let live

lake NOUN = **pond**, pool, reservoir, loch (*Scot.*), lagoon, mere, lough (*Irish*), tarn

lame ADJECTIVE **1** *She had to pull out of the championships when her horse went lame.* = **crippled**, limping, hobbling, game, halt (*archaic*) **2** *He mumbled some lame excuse about having gone to sleep.* = **unconvincing**, poor, pathetic, inadequate, thin, weak, insufficient, feeble, unsatisfactory, flimsy

lament VERB *Ken began to lament the death of his only son.* = **bemoan**, grieve, mourn, weep over, complain about, regret, wail about, deplore, bewail ▶ NOUN **1** *The lament that politicians only care about power and privilege is heard constantly.* = **complaint**, moaning, moan, keening, wail, wailing, lamentation, plaint, ululation **2** *a lament for the late, great Buddy Holly* = **dirge**, requiem, elegy, threnody (*formal*), monody, coronach (*Scot. & Irish*)

lamentable ADJECTIVE **1** *This lamentable state of affairs lasted until 1947.* = **regrettable**, distressing, tragic, unfortunate, harrowing, grievous, woeful, deplorable, mournful, sorrowful, gut-wrenching **2** *He admitted he was partly to blame for England's lamentable performance.* = **disappointing**, poor, miserable, unsatisfactory, mean, low quality, meagre, pitiful, wretched, not much cop (*Brit. slang*)

lamentation NOUN = **sorrow**, grief, weeping, mourning, moan, grieving, sobbing, keening, lament, wailing, dirge, plaint, ululation

laminated ADJECTIVE = **covered**, coated, overlaid, veneered, faced

lampoon VERB *He was lampooned for his short stature and political views.* = **ridicule**, mock, mimic, parody, caricature, send up (*Brit. informal*), take off (*informal*), make fun of, squib, burlesque, satirize, pasquinade, take the piss (out of) (*informal*) ▶ NOUN *his scathing lampoons of consumer culture* = **satire**, parody, caricature, send-up (*Brit. informal*), takeoff (*informal*), skit, squib, burlesque, pasquinade, piss-take (*informal*)

land NOUN 1 *It isn't clear whether the plane went down over land or sea.* = **ground**, earth, dry land, terra firma 2 *a small piece of grazing land* = **soil**, ground, earth, clay, dirt, sod, loam 3 *Living off the land was hard enough at the best of times.* = **countryside**, farming, farmland, rural districts 4 (*Law*) *Good agricultural land is in short supply.* = **property**, grounds, estate, acres, real estate, realty, acreage, real property, homestead (*U.S. & Canad.*) 5 *America, land of opportunity* = **country**, nation, region, state, district, territory, province, kingdom, realm, tract, motherland, fatherland ▶ VERB 1 *The jet landed after a flight of just under three hours.* = **arrive**, dock, put down, moor, berth, alight, touch down, disembark, come to rest, debark 2 (*informal*) *She landed a place on the graduate training scheme.* = **gain**, get, win, score (*slang*), secure, obtain, acquire • **land up** *We landed up at the Las Vegas at about 6.30.* = **end up**, arrive, turn up, wind up, finish up, fetch up (*informal*) ■ **RELATED WORD:** *adjective* terrestrial

landing NOUN 1 *I had to make a controlled landing into the sea.* = **coming in**, arrival, touchdown, disembarkation, disembarkment 2 *Take the bus to the landing.* = **platform**, jetty, quayside, landing stage

landlord NOUN 1 *His landlord doubled the rent.* = **owner**, landowner, proprietor, freeholder, lessor, landholder 2 *the landlord of the Dog and Duck* = **innkeeper**, host, hotelier, hotel-keeper

landmark NOUN 1 *The Ambassador Hotel is a Los Angeles landmark.* = **feature**, spectacle, monument 2 *a landmark in world history* = **milestone**, turning point, watershed, critical point, tipping point 3 *an abandoned landmark on top of Townsville's Castle Hill* = **boundary marker**, cairn, benchmark, signpost, milepost

landscape NOUN = **scenery**, country, view, land, scene, prospect, countryside, outlook, terrain, panorama, vista

landslide NOUN = **landslip**, avalanche, mudslide, rockfall

lane NOUN = **road**, street, track, path, strip, way, passage, trail, pathway, footpath, passageway, thoroughfare

language NOUN 1 *the English language* = **tongue**, speech, vocabulary, dialect, idiom, vernacular, patter, lingo (*informal*), patois, lingua franca 2 *Students examined how children acquire language.* = **speech**, communication, expression, speaking, talk, talking, conversation, discourse, interchange, utterance, parlance, vocalization, verbalization 3 *a booklet summarising it in plain language* = **style**, wording, expression, phrasing, vocabulary, usage, parlance, diction, phraseology

languid ADJECTIVE = **inactive**, lazy, indifferent, lethargic, weary, sluggish, inert, uninterested, listless, unenthusiastic, languorous, lackadaisical, torpid, spiritless ■ **OPPOSITE:** energetic

languish VERB 1 *He continues to languish in prison.* = **decline**, waste away, fade away, wither away, flag, weaken, wilt, sicken ■ **OPPOSITE:** flourish 2 *New products languish on the drawing board.* = **waste away**, suffer, rot, be abandoned, be neglected, be disregarded ■ **OPPOSITE:** thrive 3 (*often with for*) *a bride languishing for a kiss that never comes* = **pine**, want, long, desire, sigh, hunger, yearn, hanker, eat your heart out over, suspire

languishing ADJECTIVE = **fading**, failing, declining, flagging, sinking, weakening, deteriorating, withering, wilting, sickening, drooping, droopy, wasting away

lank ADJECTIVE 1 *She ran her fingers through her hair; it felt lank and dirty.* = **limp**, lifeless, long, dull, straggling, lustreless 2 *a lank youth with a ponytail* = **thin**, lean, slim, slender, skinny, spare, gaunt, lanky, emaciated, scrawny, attenuated, scraggy, rawboned

lanky ADJECTIVE = **gangling**, thin, tall, spare, angular, gaunt, bony, weedy (*informal*), scrawny, rangy, scraggy, rawboned, loose-jointed ■ **OPPOSITE:** chubby

lap¹ NOUN *the last lap of the race* = **circuit**, course, round, tour, leg, distance, stretch, circle, orbit, loop

lap² VERB 1 *the water that lapped against the pillars of the pier* = **ripple**, wash, splash, slap, swish, gurgle, slosh, purl, plash 2 *The kitten lapped milk from a dish.* = **drink**, sip, lick, swallow, gulp, sup • **lap something up** *They're eager to learn, so they lap it up.* = **relish**, like, enjoy, appreciate, delight in, savour, revel in, wallow in, accept eagerly

lapse NOUN 1 *His behaviour showed neither decency or dignity. It was an uncommon lapse.* = **decline**, fall, drop, descent, deterioration, relapse, backsliding, downturn 2 *The incident was being seen as a serious security lapse.* = **mistake**, failing, fault, failure, error, slip, negligence, omission, oversight, indiscretion 3 *the time lapse between pulling*

the seat handle and the parachute deploying
= **interval**, break, gap, passage, pause,
interruption, lull, breathing space,
intermission ▶ VERB **1** *Teenagers occasionally
find it all too much to cope with and lapse into
bad behaviour.* = **slip**, fall, decline, sink, drop,
slide, deteriorate, degenerate **2** *Her
membership of the party has lapsed.* = **end**,
stop, run out, expire, terminate, become
obsolete, become void

lapsed ADJECTIVE **1** *He returned to the Party
after years of lapsed membership.* = **expired**,
ended, finished, run out, invalid, out of
date, discontinued, unrenewed **2** *She calls
herself a lapsed Catholic.* = **backsliding**,
uncommitted, lacking faith, nonpractising

large ADJECTIVE **1** *He was a large man with a
thick square head.* = **big**, great, huge, heavy,
giant, massive, vast, enormous, tall,
considerable, substantial, strapping,
immense, hefty, gigantic, monumental,
bulky, burly, colossal, hulking,
goodly, man-size, brawny, elephantine,
thickset, ginormous (*informal*), humongous
or humungous (*informal*), sizable or sizeable,
supersize ■ OPPOSITE: small **2** *In a large
room about a dozen children are sitting on the
carpet.* = **massive**, great, big, huge, giant,
vast, enormous, considerable, substantial,
immense, tidy (*informal*), jumbo (*informal*),
gigantic, monumental (*informal*),
mammoth, colossal, gargantuan, stellar
(*informal*), king-size, ginormous (*informal*),
humongous or humungous (*U.S. slang*),
sizable or sizeable, supersize ■ OPPOSITE:
small **3** *The gang finally left with a large amount
of cash and jewellery.* = **plentiful**, full, grand,
liberal, sweeping, broad, comprehensive,
extensive, generous, lavish, ample,
spacious, abundant, grandiose, copious,
roomy, bountiful, capacious, profuse
■ OPPOSITE: scanty • **at large 1** *The public at
large does not seem to want any change.* = **in
general**, generally, chiefly, mainly, as a
whole, in the main **2** *The man who tried to have
her killed is still at large.* = **free**, roaming, on
the run, fugitive, at liberty, on the loose,
unchained, unconfined • **by and large**
*By and large, the papers greet the government's
new policy with scepticism.* = **on the whole**,
generally, mostly, in general, all things
considered, predominantly, in the main,
for the most part, all in all, as a rule, taking
everything into consideration

largely ADVERB = **mainly**, generally, chiefly,
widely, mostly, principally, primarily,
considerably, predominantly, extensively,
by and large, as a rule, to a large extent,
to a great extent

large-scale ADJECTIVE = **wide-ranging**,
global, sweeping, broad, wide, vast,
extensive, wholesale, far-reaching

largesse or **largess** NOUN **1** *his most recent
act of largesse* = **generosity**, charity, bounty,
philanthropy, munificence, liberality,
alms-giving, benefaction, open-
handedness **2** *The president has been
travelling around the country distributing
largesse.* = **gift**, present, grant, donation,
endowment, bounty, bequest

lark NOUN *The children thought it was a great
lark.* = **prank**, game, fun, fling, romp, spree,
revel, mischief, caper, frolic, escapade,
skylark, gambol, antic, jape, rollick • **lark
about** *They complained about me larking about
when they were trying to concentrate.* = **fool
around**, play around, romp around, have
fun, caper, frolic, cavort, gambol, muck
around, make mischief, lark around, rollick,
cut capers

lascivious ADJECTIVE **1** *The man was
lascivious, sexually perverted and insatiable.*
= **lustful**, sensual, immoral, randy
(*informal, chiefly Brit.*), horny (*slang*),
voluptuous, lewd, wanton, salacious,
prurient, lecherous, libidinous, licentious,
unchaste **2** *their lewd and lascivious talk*
= **bawdy**, dirty, offensive, crude, obscene,
coarse, indecent, blue, vulgar, immoral,
pornographic, suggestive, X-rated
(*informal*), scurrilous, smutty, ribald

lash[1] VERB **1** *The rain was absolutely lashing
down.* = **pound**, beat, strike, hammer,
drum, smack (*dialect*) **2** *The report lashes
police commanders for failing to act on
intelligence information.* = **censure**, attack,
blast, put down, criticize, slate (*informal,
chiefly Brit.*), ridicule, scold, berate,
castigate, lampoon, tear into (*informal*),
flay, upbraid, satirize, lambast(e),
belabour **3** *They snatched up whips and
lashed the backs of those who had fallen.*
= **whip**, beat, thrash, birch, flog, lam
(*slang*), scourge, chastise, lambast(e),
flagellate, horsewhip ▶ NOUN *They
sentenced him to five lashes for stealing a ham
from his neighbour.* = **blow**, hit, strike, stroke,
stripe, swipe (*informal*)

lash[2] VERB *Secure the anchor by lashing it to the
rail.* = **fasten**, join, tie, secure, bind, rope,
strap, make fast

lass NOUN = **girl**, young woman, miss
(*old-fashioned or derogatory*), maiden, maid
(*archaic*), damsel (*archaic, poetic*), colleen
(*Irish*), lassie (*informal*), wench (*facetious*),
charlie (*Austral., old-fashioned slang*)

last[1] ADJECTIVE **1** *Much has changed since my
last visit.* = **most recent**, latest, previous

2 *She said it was the very last house on the road.*
= **hindmost**, furthest, final, at the end,
remotest, furthest behind, most distant,
rearmost, aftermost ■ **OPPOSITE:** foremost
3 *the last three pages of the chapter* = **final**,
closing, concluding, ultimate, utmost
■ **OPPOSITE:** first ▶ ADVERB *I testified last.*
= **in** or **at the end**, after, behind, in the rear,
bringing up the rear ▶ NOUN *a thriller with
plenty of twists to keep you guessing to the last*
= **end**, ending, close, finish, conclusion,
completion, finale, termination • **at last**
'All right,' he said at last. 'You may go.' = **finally**,
eventually, in the end, ultimately, at the
end of the day, at length, at long last, in
conclusion, in the fullness of time • **the
last word 1** *She likes to have the last word in
any discussion.* = **final decision**, final say,
final statement, conclusive comment **2** *a
venue that is the last word in cool* = **leading**,
best, first, highest, finest, cream, supreme,
elite, first-class, foremost, first-rate,
superlative, pre-eminent, unsurpassed,
the crème de la crème, most excellent

> USAGE Since *last* can mean either *after
> all others* or *most recent*, it is better to
> avoid using this word where ambiguity
> might arise, as in *her last novel*. *Final* or
> *latest* should be used as alternatives in
> such contexts to avoid any possible
> confusion.

last² VERB *You only need a very small amount,
so the tube lasts for ages.* = **continue**, keep,
remain, survive, wear, carry on, endure,
hold on, persist, keep on, hold out, abide
■ **OPPOSITE:** end
last-ditch ADJECTIVE = **final**, frantic,
desperate, struggling, straining, heroic,
all-out (*informal*)
lasting ADJECTIVE = **continuing**, long-term,
permanent, enduring, remaining, eternal,
abiding, long-standing, perennial, lifelong,
durable, perpetual, long-lasting, deep-
rooted, indelible, unending, undying,
unceasing ■ **OPPOSITE:** passing
lastly CONJUNCTION = **finally**, to conclude,
at last, in the end, ultimately, all in all, to
sum up, in conclusion
latch NOUN *You left the latch off the gate and
the dog escaped.* = **fastening**, catch, bar,
lock, hook, bolt, clamp, hasp, sneck (*dialect*)
▶ VERB *He latched the door, tested it and turned
round to speak to us.* = **fasten**, bar, secure,
lock, bolt, make fast, sneck (*dialect*)
late ADJECTIVE **1** *A few late arrivals were still
straggling in.* = **overdue**, delayed, last-
minute, belated, tardy, behind time,
unpunctual, behindhand ■ **OPPOSITE:** early
2 *my late husband* = **dead**, deceased,

departed (*euphemistic*), passed on, old,
former, previous, preceding, defunct
■ **OPPOSITE:** alive **3** *some late news just in
for the people of Merseyside* = **recent**, new,
advanced, fresh ■ **OPPOSITE:** old ▶ ADVERB
The talks began some fifteen minutes late.
= **behind time**, belatedly, tardily,
behindhand, dilatorily, unpunctually
■ **OPPOSITE:** early
lately ADVERB = **recently**, of late, just now,
in recent times, not long ago, latterly
lateness NOUN = **delay**, late date,
retardation, tardiness, unpunctuality,
belatedness, advanced hour
latent ADJECTIVE = **hidden**, secret,
concealed, invisible, lurking, veiled,
inherent, unseen, dormant, undeveloped,
quiescent, immanent, unrealized,
unexpressed ■ **OPPOSITE:** obvious
later ADVERB *I'll join you later.* = **afterwards**,
after, next, eventually, in time,
subsequently, later on, thereafter, in a
while, in due course, at a later date, by and
by, at a later time ▶ ADJECTIVE *at a later news
conference* = **subsequent**, next, following,
ensuing
lateral ADJECTIVE = **sideways**, side,
flanking, edgeways, sideward
latest ADJECTIVE = **up-to-date**, current,
fresh, newest, happening (*informal*),
modern, most recent, up-to-the-minute
lather NOUN **1** *I wiped off the lather with a
towel.* = **froth**, soap, bubbles, foam, suds,
soapsuds **2** *'I'm not going to get into a lather
over this defeat,' said the manager.* = **fluster**,
state (*informal*), sweat, fever, fuss, flap
(*informal*), stew (*informal*), dither (*chiefly
Brit.*), twitter (*informal*), tizzy (*informal*),
pother ▶ VERB *The shampoo lathers so much
it's difficult to rinse it all out.* = **froth**, soap,
foam
latitude NOUN = **scope**, liberty, indulgence,
freedom, play, room, space, licence,
leeway, laxity, elbowroom,
unrestrictedness
latter NOUN *He tracked down his cousin and
uncle. The latter was sick.* = **second**, last,
last-mentioned, second-mentioned
▶ ADJECTIVE *The latter part of the debate
concentrated on housing.* = **last**, later, latest,
ending, closing, final, concluding
■ **OPPOSITE:** earlier

> USAGE The *latter* should only be used to
> specify the second of two items, for
> example in *if I had to choose between the
> hovercraft and the ferry, I would opt for the
> latter*. Where there are three or more
> items, the last can be referred to as *the
> last-named*, but not *the latter*.

latterly ADVERB = **recently**, lately, of late, hitherto

lattice NOUN = **grid**, network, web, grating, mesh, grille, trellis, fretwork, tracery, latticework, openwork, reticulation

laud VERB = **praise**, celebrate, honour, acclaim, approve, magnify (*archaic*), glorify, extol, sing or sound the praises of

laudable ADJECTIVE = **praiseworthy**, excellent, worthy, admirable, of note, commendable, creditable, meritorious, estimable ■ **OPPOSITE:** blameworthy

laugh VERB *He laughed with pleasure when people said he looked like his Dad.* = **chuckle**, giggle, snigger, crack up (*informal*), cackle, chortle, guffaw, titter, roar, bust a gut (*informal*), be convulsed (*informal*), be in stitches, crease up (*informal*), split your sides, be rolling in the aisles (*informal*)
▶ NOUN **1** *She gave a throaty laugh at her own joke.* = **chortle**, giggle, chuckle, snigger, guffaw, titter, belly laugh, roar, shriek **2** *Working there's great. It's quite a good laugh actually.* = **joke**, scream (*informal*), hoot (*informal*), lark, prank **3** *He was a good laugh and great to have in the dressing room.* = **clown**, character (*informal*), scream (*informal*), comic, caution (*informal*), wit, comedian, entertainer, card (*informal*), wag, joker, hoot (*informal*), humorist • **laugh at something** or **someone** *I thought people were laughing at me because I was ugly.* = **make fun of**, mock, tease, ridicule, taunt, jeer, deride, scoff at, belittle, lampoon, take the mickey out of (*informal*), pour scorn on, make a mock of • **laugh something off** *While I used to laugh it off, I'm now getting irritated by it.* = **disregard**, ignore, dismiss, overlook, shrug off, minimize, brush aside, make light of, pooh-pooh

laughable ADJECTIVE **1** *She claimed that the allegations were 'laughable'.* = **ridiculous**, absurd, ludicrous, preposterous, farcical, nonsensical, derisory, risible (*formal*), derisive, worthy of scorn ⊳ *Groucho's laughable view of human pomp* = **funny**, amusing, hilarious, humorous, diverting, comical, droll, mirthful

laughing stock NOUN = **figure of fun**, target, victim, butt, fair game, Aunt Sally (*Brit.*), everybody's fool

laughter NOUN **1** *Their laughter filled the corridor.* = **chuckling**, laughing, giggling, chortling, guffawing, tittering, cachinnation **2** *She was a woman who brought laughter to millions.* = **amusement**, entertainment, humour, glee, fun, mirth, hilarity, merriment

launch VERB **1** *The rocket was launched early this morning.* = **propel**, fire, dispatch, discharge, project, send off, set in motion, send into orbit **2** *The police have launched an investigation into the incident.* = **begin**, start, open, initiate, introduce, found, set up, originate, commence, get under way, instigate, inaugurate, embark upon
▶ NOUN **1** *This morning's launch has been delayed.* = **propelling**, projection, sendoff **2** *the launch of a campaign to restore law and order* = **beginning**, start, introduction, initiation, opening, founding, setting-up, inauguration, commencement, instigation • **launch into something** *He launched into a speech about the importance of new products.* = **start enthusiastically**, begin, initiate, embark on, instigate, inaugurate, embark upon

launder VERB **1** *She wore a freshly laundered and starched white shirt.* = **wash**, clean, dry-clean, tub, wash and iron, wash and press **2** *The House voted today to crack down on banks that launder drug money.* = **process**, doctor, manipulate

laurel NOUN • **rest on your laurels** = **sit back**, relax, take it easy, relax your efforts

lavatory NOUN = **toilet**, bathroom, loo (*Brit. informal*), bog (*slang*), can (*U.S. & Canad. slang*), john (*slang, chiefly U.S. & Canad.*), head(s) (*Nautical slang*), throne (*informal*), closet, privy (*obsolete*), cloakroom (*Brit.*), urinal, latrine, washroom, powder room, ablutions (*Military informal*), crapper (*vulgar slang*), water closet, khazi (*slang*), pissoir (*French*), Gents or Ladies, little boy's room or little girl's room (*informal*), (public) convenience, W.C., dunny (*Austral. & N.Z., old-fashioned, informal*), bogger (*Austral. slang*), brasco (*Austral. slang*)

lavish ADJECTIVE **1** *a lavish party to celebrate his fiftieth birthday* = **grand**, magnificent, splendid, lush, abundant, sumptuous, exuberant, opulent, copious, luxuriant, profuse ■ **OPPOSITE:** stingy **2** *Critics attack his lavish spending and flamboyant style.* = **extravagant**, wild, excessive, exaggerated, unreasonable, wasteful, prodigal, unrestrained, intemperate, immoderate, improvident, thriftless ■ **OPPOSITE:** thrifty **3** *American reviewers are lavish in their praise of this book.* = **generous**, free, liberal, bountiful, effusive, open-handed, unstinting, munificent ■ **OPPOSITE:** stingy ▶ VERB *The emperor promoted the general and lavished him with gifts.* = **shower**, pour, heap, deluge, dissipate ■ **OPPOSITE:** stint

law NOUN **1** *Obscene and threatening phone calls are against the law.* = **constitution**, code, legislation, charter, jurisprudence **2** *The law was passed on a second vote.* = **statute**, act, bill, rule, demand, order, command, code, regulation, resolution, decree, canon, covenant, ordinance, commandment, enactment, edict **3** *inflexible moral laws* = **principle**, standard, code, formula, criterion, canon, precept, axiom, kaupapa (N.Z.) **4** *a career in law* = **the legal profession**, the bar, barristers • **lay down the law** *traditional parents who believed in laying down the law for their offspring* = **be dogmatic**, call the shots (*informal*), pontificate, rule the roost, crack the whip, boss around, dogmatize, order about or around ■ **RELATED WORDS:** *adjectives* legal, judicial

law-abiding ADJECTIVE = **obedient**, good, peaceful, honourable, orderly, honest, lawful, compliant, dutiful, peaceable

lawful ADJECTIVE = **legal**, constitutional, just, proper, valid, warranted, legitimate, authorized, rightful, permissible, legalized, allowable, licit ■ **OPPOSITE:** unlawful

lawless ADJECTIVE = **disorderly**, wild, unruly, rebellious, chaotic, reckless, insurgent, anarchic, riotous, unrestrained, seditious, mutinous, insubordinate, ungoverned ■ **OPPOSITE:** law-abiding

lawlessness NOUN = **anarchy**, disorder, chaos, reign of terror, mob rule, mobocracy, ochlocracy

lawsuit NOUN = **case**, cause, action, trial, suit, argument, proceedings, dispute, contest, prosecution, legal action, indictment, litigation, industrial tribunal, legal proceedings

lawyer NOUN = **legal adviser**, attorney, solicitor, counsel, advocate, barrister, counsellor, legal representative

lax ADJECTIVE = **slack**, casual, careless, sloppy (*informal*), easy-going, negligent, lenient, slapdash, neglectful, slipshod, remiss (*formal*), easy-peasy (*slang*), overindulgent ■ **OPPOSITE:** strict

laxative NOUN = **purgative**, salts, purge, cathartic, physic (*rare*), aperient

lay¹ VERB **1** *Lay a sheet of newspaper on the floor.* = **place**, put, set, spread, plant, establish, settle, leave, deposit, put down, set down, posit **2** *They were laying a trap for the kidnapper.* = **devise**, plan, design, prepare, work out, plot, hatch, contrive, concoct **3** *Freezing weather hampered the hen's ability to lay eggs.* = **produce**, bear, deposit **4** *The organisers meet in March to lay plans.* = **arrange**, prepare, make, organize, position, locate, set out, devise, put together, dispose, draw up **5** *She refused to lay the blame on any one party.* = **attribute**, charge, assign, allocate, allot, ascribe, impute **6** *Police have decided not to lay charges over allegations of phone tapping.* = **put forward**, offer, present, advance, lodge, submit, bring forward **7** *I wouldn't lay bets on his remaining manager after the spring.* = **bet**, stake, venture, gamble, chance, risk, hazard, wager, give odds • **lay into someone** *The model allegedly spat at a policeman and then laid into him with her fists.* = **attack**, hit, set about, hit out at, assail, tear into, pitch into (*informal*), go for the jugular, lambast(e), belabour, lash into, let fly at • **lay off** *He went on attacking her until other passengers arrived and told him to lay off.* = **stop**, give up, quit, cut it out, leave alone, pack in, abstain, leave off, give over (*informal*), let up, get off someone's back (*informal*), give it a rest (*informal*) • **lay someone off** *100,000 federal workers will be laid off to reduce the deficit.* = **dismiss**, fire (*informal*), release, drop, sack (*informal*), pay off, discharge, oust, let go, make redundant, give notice to, give the boot to (*slang*), give the sack to (*informal*), give someone their cards, kennet (*Austral. slang*), jeff (*Austral. slang*) • **lay someone out** *He turned round, marched over to the man, and just laid him out.* = **knock out**, fell, floor, knock unconscious, knock for six, kayo (*slang*) • **lay someone up** *He was recovering from a knee injury that laid him up for six months.* = **confine (to bed)**, hospitalize, incapacitate • **lay something aside** *All animosities were laid aside for the moment.* = **abandon**, reject, dismiss, postpone, shelve, put off, renounce, put aside, cast aside • **lay something bare** *The clearing out of disused workshops laid bare thousands of glazed tiles.* = **reveal**, show, expose, disclose, unveil, divulge • **lay something down 1** *The Companies Act lays down a set of minimum requirements.* = **stipulate**, state, establish, prescribe, assume, formulate, affirm, ordain (*formal*), set down, postulate **2** *The drug traffickers have offered to lay down their arms.* = **sacrifice**, give up, yield, surrender, turn over, relinquish • **lay something in** *They began to lay in extensive stores of food supplies.* = **store (up)**, collect, build up, accumulate, buy in, amass, stockpile, hoard, stock up, heap up • **lay something on** *They laid on a superb meal.* = **provide**, prepare, supply, organize, give, cater (for), furnish, purvey • **lay something out 1** *She took a deck of cards and* began to lay them out. = **arrange**, order, design, display, exhibit, put out, spread out **2** *You won't have to lay out a fortune for this dining table.* = **spend**, pay, invest, fork out (*slang*), expend, shell out (*informal*), disburse

> **USAGE** In standard English, the verb *to lay* (meaning 'to put something somewhere') always takes an object, for example *the Queen laid a wreath*. By contrast, the verb *to lie* is always used without an object, for example *he was just lying there*.

lay² ADJECTIVE **1** *He is a Methodist lay preacher and social worker.* = **nonclerical**, secular, non-ordained, laic, laical **2** *It is difficult for a lay person to gain access to medical libraries.* = **nonspecialist**, amateur, unqualified, untrained, inexpert, nonprofessional

layer NOUN **1** *A fresh layer of snow covered the street.* = **covering**, film, cover, sheet, coating, coat, blanket, mantle **2** *Critics and the public puzzle out the layers of meaning in his photos.* = **tier**, level, seam, stratum

layman or **laywoman** or **layperson** NOUN = **nonprofessional**, amateur, outsider, non-expert, nonspecialist

lay-off NOUN = **unemployment**, firing (*informal*), sacking (*informal*), dismissal, discharge

layout NOUN = **arrangement**, design, draft, outline, format, plan, formation, geography

laze VERB **1** *Fred lazed in an easy chair.* = **idle**, lounge, hang around, loaf, stand around, loll **2** (*often with* **away**) *She lazed away most of the morning.* = **kill time**, waste time, fritter away, pass time, while away the hours, veg out (*slang*), fool away

laziness NOUN = **idleness**, negligence, inactivity, slowness, sloth, sluggishness, slackness, indolence, tardiness, dilatoriness, slothfulness, do-nothingness, faineance

lazy ADJECTIVE **1** *I was too lazy to learn how to read music.* = **idle**, inactive, indolent, slack, negligent, inert, remiss (*formal*), workshy, slothful (*formal*), shiftless ■ **OPPOSITE:** industrious **2** *We would have a lazy lunch and then lie on the beach in the sun.* = **lethargic**, languorous, slow-moving, languid, sleepy, sluggish, drowsy, somnolent, torpid ■ **OPPOSITE:** quick

leach VERB = **extract**, strain, drain, filter, seep, percolate, filtrate, lixiviate (*Chemistry*)

lead VERB **1** *Tom was leading, a rifle slung over his back.* = **go in front (of)**, head, be in front, be at the head (of), walk in front (of) **2** *He led him into the house.* = **guide**, conduct,

steer, escort, precede, usher, pilot, show the way **3** *the doors that led to the yard* = **connect to**, link, open onto **4** *So far she leads by five games to two.* = **be ahead (of)**, be first, exceed, be winning, excel, surpass, come first, transcend, outstrip, outdo, blaze a trail **5** *He led the country between 1949 and 1984.* = **command**, rule, govern, preside over, head, control, manage, direct, supervise, be in charge of, head up **6** *She led a normal happy life with her sister and brother.* = **live**, have, spend, experience, pass, undergo **7** *A pay rise will only lead to job cuts.* = **result in**, cause, produce, contribute, generate, bring about, bring on, give rise to, conduce **8** *It was not as straightforward as we were led to believe.* = **cause**, prompt, persuade, move, draw, influence, motivate, prevail, induce, incline, dispose ▶ NOUN **1** *The Social Democrats are still in the lead in the opinion polls.* = **first place**, winning position, primary position, vanguard, van **2** *He now has a lead of 30 points.* = **advantage**, start, advance, edge, margin, winning margin **3** *the need for the president to give a moral lead* = **example**, direction, leadership, guidance, model, pattern **4** *The inquiry team is following up possible leads.* = **clue**, tip, suggestion, trace, hint, guide, indication, pointer, tip-off **5** *Two dancers from the Bolshoi Ballet dance the leads.* = **leading role**, principal, protagonist, title role, star part, principal part **6** *He came out with a little dog on a lead.* = **leash**, line, cord, rein, tether ▶ ADJECTIVE *Cossiga's reaction is the lead story in the Italian press.* = **main**, prime, top, leading, first, head, chief, premier, primary, most important, principal, foremost • **lead off** *Whenever there was a dance he and I led off.* = **begin**, start, open, set out, kick off (*informal*), initiate, commence, get going, get under way, inaugurate, start the ball rolling (*informal*) • **lead someone on** *Don't allow yourself to be led on.* = **entice**, tempt, lure, mislead, draw on, seduce, deceive, beguile, delude, hoodwink, inveigle, string along (*informal*) • **lead up to something** *I'm leading up to something quite important.* = **introduce**, approach, prepare for, intimate, pave the way for, prepare the way, make advances, make overtures, work round to

leaden ADJECTIVE **1** *The weather was bitterly cold, with leaden skies.* = **grey**, dingy, overcast, sombre, lacklustre, dark grey, greyish, lustreless, louring or lowering **2** *a leaden English translation from the Latin* = **laboured**, wooden, stiff, sluggish, plodding, stilted, humdrum **3** *the leaden* *boredom of the Victorian marriage* = **lifeless**, dull, gloomy, dismal, dreary, languid, listless, spiritless **4** *The dull, leaden sickly feeling returned.* = **heavy**, crushing, oppressive, cumbersome, inert, onerous, burdensome

leader NOUN = **principal**, president, head, chief, boss (*informal*), director, manager, chairperson, captain, chair, premier, governor, commander, superior, ruler, conductor, controller, counsellor, supervisor, superintendent, big name, big gun (*informal*), chieftain, bigwig (*informal*), ringleader, big shot (*informal*), overseer, big cheese (*slang, old-fashioned*), big noise (*informal*), big hitter (*informal*), torchbearer, number one, sherang (*Austral. & N.Z.*)
■ **OPPOSITE:** follower

leadership NOUN **1** *He praised her leadership during the crisis.* = **authority**, control, influence, command, premiership, captaincy, governance, headship, superintendency **2** *What most people want to see is determined, decisive action and firm leadership.* = **guidance**, government, authority, management, administration, direction, supervision, domination, directorship, superintendency

leading ADJECTIVE = **principal**, top, major, main, first, highest, greatest, ruling, chief, prime, key, primary, supreme, most important, outstanding, governing, superior, dominant, foremost, pre-eminent, unsurpassed, number one
■ **OPPOSITE:** minor

leaf NOUN **1** *The leaves of the horse chestnut had already fallen.* = **frond**, flag, needle, pad, blade, bract, cotyledon, foliole **2** *He flattened the wrappers and put them between the leaves of his book.* = **page**, sheet, folio • **leaf through something** (*a book, magazine, etc*) *Most patients derive enjoyment from leafing through old picture albums.* = **skim**, glance, scan, browse, look through, dip into, flick through, flip through, thumb through, riffle • **turn over a new leaf** *She realized she was in the wrong and promised to turn over a new leaf.* = **reform**, change, improve, amend, make a fresh start, begin anew, change your ways, mend your ways

leaflet NOUN = **booklet**, notice, advert (*Brit.*), brochure, bill, circular, flyer, tract, pamphlet, handout, mailshot, handbill

leafy ADJECTIVE = **green**, leaved, leafed, shaded, shady, summery, verdant (*literary*), bosky (*literary*), springlike, in foliage

league NOUN **1** *the League of Nations* = **association**, union, alliance, coalition, group, order, band, corporation, combination, partnership, federation, compact, consortium, guild, confederation, fellowship, fraternity (*U.S. & Canad.*), confederacy **2** *Her success has taken her out of my league.* = **class**, group, level, category, ability group • **in league with someone** *He accused the President of being in league with the terrorists.* = **collaborating with**, leagued with, allied with, conspiring with, working together with, in cooperation with, in cahoots with (*informal*), hand in glove with

leak VERB **1** *The pool's sides had cracked and the water had leaked out.* = **escape**, pass, spill, release, discharge, drip, trickle, ooze, seep, exude, percolate **2** *He revealed who had leaked a confidential police report.* = **disclose**, tell, reveal, pass on, give away, make public, divulge, let slip, make known, spill the beans (*informal*), blab (*informal*), let the cat out of the bag, blow wide open (*slang*)
▶ NOUN **1** *It's thought a gas leak may have caused the blast.* = **leakage**, leaking, discharge, drip, oozing, seepage, percolation **2** *a leak in the radiator* = **hole**, opening, crack, puncture, aperture, chink, crevice, fissure, perforation **3** *Serious leaks involving national security are likely to be investigated.* = **disclosure**, exposé, exposure, admission, revelation, uncovering, betrayal, unearthing, divulgence

leaky ADJECTIVE = **leaking**, split, cracked, punctured, porous, waterlogged, perforated, holey, not watertight

lean[1] VERB **1** *He leaned forward to give her a kiss.* = **bend**, tip, slope, incline, tilt, heel, slant **2** *She was feeling tired and was glad to lean against him.* = **rest**, prop, be supported, recline, repose **3** *Politically, I lean towards the right.* = **tend**, prefer, favour, incline, be prone to, gravitate, be disposed to, have a propensity to • **lean on someone** *She leaned on him to help her solve her problems.* = **depend on**, trust, rely on, cling to, count on, confide in, have faith in

lean[2] ADJECTIVE *She watched the tall, lean figure step into the car.* = **thin**, slim, slender, skinny, angular, trim, spare, gaunt, bony, lanky, wiry, emaciated, scrawny, svelte, lank, rangy, scraggy, macilent (*rare*)
■ **OPPOSITE:** fat

leaning NOUN = **tendency**, liking for, bias, inclination, taste, bent, disposition, penchant, propensity, aptitude, predilection, proclivity (*formal*), partiality, proneness

leap VERB **1** *The newsreels show him leaping into the air.* = **jump**, spring, bound, bounce, hop, skip, caper, cavort, frisk, gambol **2** *He leapt over a wall brandishing a weapon.* = **vault**, clear, jump, bound, spring ▶ NOUN **1** *He took the silver medal with a leap of 2.37 metres.* = **jump**, spring, bound, hop, skip, vault, caper, frisk **2** *The result has been a giant leap in productivity.* = **rise**, change, increase, soaring, surge, escalation, upsurge, upswing • **leap at something** *They leapt at the chance of a cheap holiday in Italy.* = **accept eagerly**, seize on, jump at

learn VERB **1** *Their children were going to learn English.* = **master**, grasp, acquire, pick up, take in, attain, become able, familiarize yourself with **2** *It was only after his death that she learned of his affair.* = **discover**, hear, understand, gain knowledge, find out about, become aware, discern, ascertain, come to know, suss (out) (*slang*) **3** *He learned this song as an inmate in a Texas prison.* = **memorize**, commit to memory, learn by heart, learn by rote, get (something) word-perfect, learn parrot-fashion, get off pat, con (*archaic*)

learned ADJECTIVE = **scholarly**, experienced, lettered, cultured, skilled, expert, academic, intellectual, versed, literate, well-informed, erudite, highbrow, well-read ■ **OPPOSITE:** uneducated

learner NOUN = **student**, pupil, scholar, novice, beginner, trainee, apprentice, disciple, neophyte (*formal*), tyro
■ **OPPOSITE:** expert

learning NOUN = **knowledge**, study, education, schooling, research, scholarship, tuition, enlightenment, e-learning or elearning

lease VERB = **hire**, rent, let, loan, charter, rent out, hire out

leash NOUN **1** *All dogs should be on a leash.* = **lead**, line, restraint, cord, rein, tether **2** *They have kept the company on a tight leash.* = **restraint**, hold, control, check, curb ▶ VERB *Make sure your dog is leashed and muzzled.* = **tether**, control, secure, restrain, tie up, hold back, fasten

least ADJECTIVE *If you like cheese, go for the ones with the least fat.* = **smallest**, meanest, fewest, minutest, lowest, tiniest, minimum, slightest, minimal • **at least** *Aim to have at least half a pint of milk a day.* = **at the minimum**, at the very least, not less than

leathery ADJECTIVE = **tough**, hard, rough, hardened, rugged, wrinkled, durable, leathern (*archaic*), coriaceous, leatherlike

leave¹ VERB **1** *Just pack your bags and leave.* = **depart from**, withdraw from, go from, escape from, desert, quit, flee, exit, pull out of, retire from, move out of, disappear from, run away from, forsake, flit (*informal*),

set out from, go away from, hook it (*slang*), pack your bags (*informal*), make tracks, abscond from, decamp from, sling your hook (*Brit. slang*), slope off from, take your leave of, do a bunk from (*Brit. slang*), take yourself off from (*informal*) ■ **OPPOSITE:** arrive **2** *I left school with no qualifications.* = **quit**, give up, get out of, resign from, drop out of **3** *He left me for another woman.* = **give up**, abandon, desert, dump (*informal*), drop, surrender, ditch (*informal*), chuck (*informal*), discard, relinquish, renounce, jilt (*informal*), cast aside, forbear, leave in the lurch
■ **OPPOSITE:** stay with **4** *For the moment, I leave you to make all the decisions.* = **entrust**, commit, delegate, refer, hand over, assign, consign, allot, cede, give over **5** *He died two years later, leaving everything to his wife.* = **bequeath**, will, transfer, endow, transmit, confer, hand down, devise (*Law*), demise **6** *I'd left my raincoat in the restaurant.* = **forget**, lay down, leave behind, mislay **7** *Abuse always leaves emotional scars.* = **cause**, produce, result in, generate, deposit
• **leave off something** *We all left off eating and stood about with bowed heads.* = **stop**, end, finish, give up, cease, halt, break off, refrain from, abstain from, discontinue, knock off (*informal*), give over (*informal*), kick (*informal*), desist, keep off, belay (*Nautical*) • **leave something** or **someone out** *If you prefer mild flavours, leave out the chilli.* = **omit**, exclude, miss out, forget, except, reject, ignore, overlook, neglect, skip, disregard, bar, cast aside, count out

leave² NOUN **1** *Why don't you take a few days' leave?* = **holiday**, break, vacation, time off, sabbatical, leave of absence, furlough, schoolie (*Austral.*), accumulated day off or ADO (*Austral.*) **2** *an application for leave to appeal against the judge's order* = **permission**, freedom, sanction, liberty, concession, consent, allowance, warrant, authorization, dispensation ■ **OPPOSITE:** refusal **3** *He thanked them for the pleasure of their company and took his leave.* = **departure**, parting, withdrawal, goodbye, farewell, retirement, leave-taking, adieu, valediction
■ **OPPOSITE:** arrival

leave-taking NOUN = **departure**, going, leaving, parting, goodbye, farewell, valediction, sendoff (*informal*)

lecherous ADJECTIVE = **lustful**, randy (*informal, chiefly Brit.*), raunchy (*informal*), lewd, wanton, carnal, salacious, prurient, lascivious, libidinous, licentious, lubricious (*literary*), concupiscent, goatish (*archaic, literary*), unchaste, ruttish ■ **OPPOSITE:** puritanical

lechery NOUN = **lustfulness**, lust, licentiousness, salaciousness, sensuality, profligacy, debauchery, prurience, womanizing, carnality, lewdness, wantonness, lasciviousness, libertinism, concupiscence, randiness (*informal, chiefly Brit.*), leching (*informal*), rakishness, lubricity (*literary*), libidinousness, lecherousness

lecture NOUN **1** *In his lecture he covered an enormous variety of topics.* = **talk**, address, speech, lesson, instruction, presentation, discourse, sermon, exposition, harangue, oration, disquisition, webinar **2** *Our captain gave us a stern lecture on safety.* = **telling-off** (*informal*), rebuke, reprimand, talking-to (*informal*), heat (*slang, chiefly U.S. & Canad.*), going-over (*informal*), wigging (*Brit. slang*), censure, scolding, chiding, dressing-down (*informal*), reproof, castigation ▶ VERB **1** *She has lectured and taught all over the world.* = **talk**, speak, teach, address, discourse, spout (*informal*), expound, harangue, give a talk, hold forth, expatiate **2** *He used to lecture me about getting too much sun.* = **tell off** (*informal*), berate, scold, reprimand, carpet (*informal*), censure, castigate, chide, admonish, tear into (*informal*), read the riot act, reprove, bawl out (*informal*), chew out (*U.S. & Canad. informal*), tear (someone) off a strip (*Brit. informal*), give a rocket (*Brit. & N.Z. informal*), give someone a talking-to (*informal*), give someone a dressing-down (*informal*), give someone a telling-off (*informal*)

ledge NOUN = **shelf**, step, ridge, projection, mantle, sill

lee NOUN = **shelter**, cover, screen, protection, shadow, shade, shield, refuge

leech NOUN = **parasite**, hanger-on, sycophant, freeloader (*slang*), sponger (*informal*), ligger (*slang*), bloodsucker (*informal*), quandong (*Austral. slang*)

leer VERB *They passed a man who turned and leered at them.* = **grin**, eye, stare, wink, squint, goggle, smirk, drool, gloat, ogle ▶ NOUN *When I asked the clerk for my room key, he gave it to me with a leer.* = **grin**, stare, wink, squint, smirk, drool, gloat, ogle

leery ADJECTIVE = **wary**, cautious, uncertain, suspicious, doubting, careful, shy, sceptical, dubious, unsure, distrustful, on your guard, chary

lees PLURAL NOUN = **sediment**, grounds, refuse, deposit, precipitate, dregs, settlings

leeway NOUN = **room**, play, space, margin, scope, latitude, elbowroom

left ADJECTIVE **1** *She had a pain in her chest, on the left side.* = **left-hand**, port, larboard (*Nautical*) **2** (*politics*) *The play offers a new perspective on left politics.* = **socialist**, liberal, radical, progressive, left-wing, leftist

■ **RELATED WORDS:** *adjectives* sinister, sinistral

leftover NOUN *Refrigerate any leftovers.* = **remnant**, leaving, remains, scrap, oddment ▶ ADJECTIVE *Leftover chicken makes a wonderful salad.* = **surplus**, remaining, extra, excess, unwanted, unused, uneaten

left-wing ADJECTIVE = **socialist**, communist, red (*informal*), radical, leftist, liberal, revolutionary, militant, Marxist, Bolshevik, Leninist, collectivist, Trotskyite

left-winger NOUN = **socialist**, communist, red (*informal*), pinko (*derogatory, chiefly U.S.*), radical, revolutionary, militant, Marxist, Bolshevik, Leninist, Trotskyite

leg NOUN **1** *He was tapping his walking stick against his leg.* = **limb**, member, shank, lower limb, pin (*informal*), stump (*informal*) **2** *His ankles were tied to the legs of the chair.* = **support**, prop, brace, upright **3** *The first leg of the journey was by boat.* = **stage**, part, section, stretch, lap, segment, portion • **a leg up** = **boost**, help, support, push, assistance, helping hand • **leg it** *He was legging it across the field.* = **run**, walk, escape, flee, hurry, run away, make off, make tracks, hotfoot, go on foot, skedaddle (*informal*) • **not have a leg to stand on** *It's only my word against his, so I don't have a leg to stand on.* = **have no basis**, be vulnerable, be undermined, be invalid, be illogical, be defenceless, lack support, be full of holes • **on its** *or* **your last legs** *By the mid-1980s the copper industry in the US was on its last legs.* = **worn out**, dying, failing, exhausted, giving up the ghost, at death's door, about to collapse, about to fail, about to break down • **pull someone's leg** *Of course I won't tell them; I was only pulling your leg.* = **tease**, joke, trick, fool, kid (*informal*), have (someone) on, rag, rib (*informal*), wind up (*Brit. slang*), deceive, hoax, make fun of, poke fun at, twit, chaff, lead up the garden path, jerk *or* yank someone's chain (*informal*) • **shake a leg** *Come on, shake a leg! We've got loads to do today.* = **hurry**, rush, move it, hasten, get cracking (*informal*), get a move on (*informal*), look lively (*informal*), stir your stumps (*informal*) • **stretch your legs** *Take regular breaks to stretch your legs.* = **take a walk**, exercise, stroll, promenade, move about, go for a walk, take the air

legacy NOUN = **bequest**, inheritance, endowment, gift, estate, devise (*Law*), heirloom

legal ADJECTIVE **1** *the Canadian legal system* = **judicial**, judiciary, forensic, juridical, jurisdictive **2** *What I did was perfectly legal.* = **lawful**, allowed, sanctioned, constitutional, proper, valid, legitimate, authorized, rightful, permissible, legalized, allowable, within the law, licit

legalistic ADJECTIVE = **hairsplitting**, narrow, strict, contentious, literal, narrow-minded, polemical, litigious, disputatious

legality NOUN = **lawfulness**, validity, legitimacy, accordance with the law, permissibility, rightfulness, admissibleness

legalize VERB = **permit**, allow, approve, sanction, license, legitimate, authorize, validate, legitimize, make legal, decriminalize

legal tender NOUN = **currency**, money, medium, payment, specie

legend NOUN **1** *the legends of ancient Greece* = **myth**, story, tale, fiction, narrative, saga, fable, folk tale, urban myth, urban legend, folk story **2** *the blues legend, B.B. King* = **celebrity**, star, phenomenon, genius, spectacle, wonder, big name, marvel, prodigy, luminary, celeb (*informal*), megastar (*informal*) **3** *a banner bearing the following legend* = **inscription**, title, caption, device, motto, rubric

legendary ADJECTIVE **1** *His political skill is legendary.* = **famous**, celebrated, well-known, acclaimed, renowned, famed, immortal, illustrious ■ **OPPOSITE:** unknown **2** *The hill is supposed to be the resting place of the legendary King Lud.* = **mythical**, fabled, traditional, romantic, fabulous, fanciful, fictitious, storybook, apocryphal ■ **OPPOSITE:** factual

legible ADJECTIVE = **readable**, clear, plain, bold, neat, distinct, easy to read, easily read, decipherable

legion NOUN **1** *The last of the Roman legions left Britain in AD 410.* = **army**, company, force, division, troop, brigade **2** *His sense of humour won him a legion of friends.* = **multitude**, host, mass, drove, number, horde, myriad, throng ▶ ADJECTIVE *Books on this subject are legion.* = **very many**, numerous, countless, myriad, numberless, multitudinous

legislate VERB = **make laws**, establish laws, prescribe, enact laws, pass laws, ordain (*formal*), codify laws, put laws in force

legislation NOUN **1** *legislation to protect women's rights* = **law**, act, ruling, rule, bill, measure, regulation, charter, statute **2** *This can be put right through positive legislation.* = **lawmaking**, regulation, prescription, enactment, codification

legislative ADJECTIVE = **law-making**, parliamentary, congressional, judicial, ordaining, law-giving, juridical, jurisdictive

legislator NOUN = **lawmaker**, parliamentarian, lawgiver

legislature NOUN = **parliament**, house, congress, diet, senate, assembly, chamber, law-making body

legitimate ADJECTIVE **1** *They have demanded the restoration of the legitimate government.* = **lawful**, real, true, legal, acknowledged, sanctioned, genuine, proper, authentic, statutory, authorized, rightful, kosher (*informal*), dinkum (*Austral. & N.Z. informal*), legit (*slang*), licit ■ **OPPOSITE:** unlawful **2** *That's a perfectly legitimate fear.* = **reasonable**, just, correct, sensible, valid, warranted, logical, justifiable, well-founded, admissible ■ **OPPOSITE:** unreasonable ▶ VERB *We want to legitimate this process by passing a law.* = **legitimize**, allow, permit, sanction, authorize, legalize, give the green light to, legitimatize, pronounce lawful

legitimize VERB = **legalize**, permit, sanction, legitimate, authorize, give the green light to, pronounce lawful

leisure NOUN *I was working constantly, with little or no leisure.* = **spare time**, free time, rest, holiday, quiet, ease, retirement, relaxation, vacation, recreation, time off, breathing space, spare moments ■ **OPPOSITE:** work • **at one's leisure** *He could read through all the national papers at his leisure.* = **in your own (good) time**, in due course, at your convenience, unhurriedly, when it suits you, without hurry, at an unhurried pace, when you get round to it (*informal*)

leisurely ADJECTIVE *Lunch was a leisurely affair.* = **unhurried**, relaxed, slow, easy, comfortable, gentle, lazy, laid-back (*informal*), restful ■ **OPPOSITE:** hurried ▶ ADVERB *We walked leisurely into the hotel.* = **unhurriedly**, slowly, easily, comfortably, lazily, at your leisure, at your convenience, lingeringly, indolently, without haste ■ **OPPOSITE:** hurriedly

lekker ADJECTIVE = **delicious**, tasty, luscious, choice, savoury, palatable, dainty, delectable, mouthwatering, yummy (*slang*), scrumptious (*informal*), appetizing, toothsome, ambrosial, yummo (*Austral. slang*)

lemon NOUN ■ **RELATED WORDS:** *adjectives* citric, citrine, citrous

lend VERB 1 *Sometimes he'd lend me the price of a haircut.* = **loan**, advance, sub (*Brit. informal*), accommodate one with 2 *He attended the news conference to lend his support.* = **give**, provide, add, present, supply, grant, afford, contribute, hand out, furnish, confer, bestow, impart • **lend itself to something** *The room lends itself well to summer eating with its light airy atmosphere.* = **be appropriate for**, suit, be suitable for, fit, be appropriate to, be adaptable to, present opportunities for, be serviceable for

length NOUN 1 *It is about a metre in length.* = **distance**, reach, measure, extent, span, longitude 2 *His film is over two hours in length.* = **duration**, term, period, space, stretch, span, expanse 3 *a 30ft length of rope* = **piece**, measure, section, segment, portion 4 *Don't be discouraged by the length of this recipe.* = **lengthiness**, extent, elongation, wordiness, verbosity, prolixity, long-windedness, extensiveness, protractedness • **at length** 1 *At length, my father went into the house.* = **at last**, finally, eventually, in time, in the end, at long last 2 *They spoke at length, reviewing the entire incident.* = **for a long time**, completely, fully, thoroughly, for hours, in detail, for ages, in depth, to the full, exhaustively, interminably

lengthen VERB 1 *The runway had to be lengthened.* = **extend**, continue, increase, stretch, expand, elongate, make longer ■ **OPPOSITE:** shorten 2 *They want to lengthen the school day.* = **protract**, extend, prolong, draw out, spin out, make longer ■ **OPPOSITE:** cut down

lengthy ADJECTIVE 1 *the lengthy process of filling out forms* = **protracted**, long, prolonged, very long, tedious, lengthened, diffuse, drawn-out, interminable, long-winded, long-drawn-out, overlong, verbose, prolix 2 *a lengthy article in the newspaper* = **very long**, rambling, interminable, long-winded, wordy, discursive, extended, overlong, verbose, prolix ■ **OPPOSITE:** brief

leniency *or* **lenience** NOUN = **mercy**, compassion, clemency, quarter, pity, tolerance, indulgence, tenderness, moderation, gentleness, forbearance, mildness, lenity

lenient ADJECTIVE = **merciful**, sparing, gentle, forgiving, kind, tender, mild, tolerant, compassionate, clement, indulgent, forbearing ■ **OPPOSITE:** severe

leper NOUN = **outcast**, reject, untouchable, pariah, lazar (*archaic*)

lesbian ADJECTIVE = **homosexual**, gay, sapphic, tribadic ▶ NOUN = **homosexual**, gay

lesion NOUN = **injury**, hurt, wound, bruise, trauma (*Pathology*), sore, impairment, abrasion, contusion (*formal*)

less ADJECTIVE *Eat less fat to reduce the risk of heart disease.* = **smaller**, shorter, slighter, not so much ▶ ADVERB *We are eating more and exercising less.* = **to a smaller extent**, little, barely, not much, not so much, meagrely ▶ PREPOSITION *Company car drivers will pay ten percent, less tax.* = **minus**, without, lacking, excepting, subtracting
■ USAGE *Less* should not be confused with *fewer*. *Less* refers strictly only to quantity and not to number: *there is less water than before*. *Fewer* means smaller in number: *there are fewer people than before.*

lessen VERB 1 *Keep immunisations up to date to lessen the risk of serious illness.* = **reduce**, lower, diminish, decrease, relax, ease, narrow, moderate, dial down, weaken, erode, impair, degrade, minimize, curtail, lighten, wind down, abridge, de-escalate ■ **OPPOSITE:** increase 2 *The attention she gives him will certainly lessen once the baby is born.* = **grow less**, diminish, decrease, contract, ease, weaken, shrink, slow down, dwindle, lighten, wind down, die down, abate, slacken

lesser ADJECTIVE = **lower**, slighter, secondary, subsidiary, subordinate, inferior, less important ■ **OPPOSITE:** greater

lesson NOUN 1 *She took piano lessons.* = **class**, schooling, period, teaching, coaching, session, instruction, lecture, seminar, tutoring, tutorial 2 *There is one lesson to be learned from this crisis.* = **example**, warning, model, message, moral, deterrent, precept, exemplar 3 *Now let's look at lesson one.* = **exercise**, reading, practice, task, lecture, drill, assignment, homework, recitation 4 *The Rev. Nicola Judd read the lesson.* = **Bible reading**, reading, text, Bible passage, Scripture passage

let VERB 1 *They let him talk.* = **enable**, make, allow, cause, grant, permit 2 *Mum didn't let us have sweets very often.* = **allow**, grant, permit, warrant, authorize, give the go-ahead, give permission, suffer (*archaic*), give the green light, give leave, give the O.K. or okay (*informal*) 3 *The reasons for letting a house, or part of one, are varied.* = **lease**, hire, rent, rent out, hire out, sublease • **let on** (*informal*) 1 *He knows who the culprit is, but he is not letting on.* = **reveal**, disclose, say, tell, admit, give away, divulge, let slip, make known, let the cat out of the bag (*informal*) 2 *I let on that I knew more than I really did.* = **pretend**, make out, feign, simulate, affect, profess, counterfeit, make believe, dissemble, dissimulate • **let someone down** *Don't worry, I won't let you down.* = **disappoint**, fail, abandon, desert, disillusion, fall short, leave stranded, leave in the lurch, disenchant, dissatisfy • **let someone off** *The police let him off with a warning.* = **excuse**, release, discharge, pardon, spare, forgive, exempt, dispense, exonerate, absolve, grant an amnesty to • **let something down** *I let the tyres down on his car.* = **deflate**, empty, exhaust, flatten, puncture • **let something off** 1 *He had let off fireworks to celebrate the Revolution.* = **fire**, explode, set off, discharge, detonate 2 *They must do it without letting off any fumes.* = **emit**, release, leak, exude, give off • **let something out** 1 *He let out his breath in a long sigh.* = **release**, discharge 2 *When she saw him, she let out a cry of horror.* = **emit**, make, produce, give vent to 3 *She let out that she had seen him the night before.* = **reveal**, tell, make known, let slip, leak, disclose, betray, let fall, take the wraps off • **let something** or **someone in** *The lattice-work lets in air, but not light.* = **admit**, include, receive, welcome, greet, take in, incorporate, give access to, allow to enter • **let up** *The rain had let up.* = **stop**, diminish, decrease, subside, relax, ease (up), moderate, lessen, abate, slacken

letdown NOUN = **disappointment**, disillusionment, frustration, anticlimax, setback, washout (*informal*), comedown (*informal*), disgruntlement

lethal ADJECTIVE = **deadly**, terminal, fatal, deathly, dangerous, devastating, destructive, mortal, murderous, poisonous, toxic, virulent, pernicious (*formal*), noxious, baneful ■ **OPPOSITE:** harmless

lethargic ADJECTIVE = **sluggish**, slow, lazy, sleepy, heavy, dull, indifferent, debilitated, inactive, inert, languid, apathetic, drowsy, listless, comatose, stupefied, unenthusiastic, somnolent, torpid, slothful (*formal*), enervated, unenergetic ■ **OPPOSITE:** energetic

lethargy NOUN = **sluggishness**, inertia, inaction, slowness, indifference, apathy, sloth, stupor, drowsiness, dullness, torpor, sleepiness, lassitude, languor, listlessness, torpidity, hebetude (*rare*) ■ **OPPOSITE:** energy

letter NOUN 1 *I had received a letter from a very close friend.* = **message**, line, answer, note, reply, communication, dispatch, acknowledgment, billet (*archaic*), missive, epistle, email *or* e-mail 2 *the letters of the alphabet* = **character**, mark, sign, symbol,

glyph (*Computing*) • **to the letter** *She obeyed his instructions to the letter.* = **precisely**, strictly, literally, exactly, faithfully, accurately, word for word, punctiliously ■ **RELATED WORD:** *adjective* epistolary

letters PLURAL NOUN *bon viveur, man of letters and long-time party supporter* = **learning**, education, culture, literature, humanities, scholarship, erudition, belles-lettres

let-up NOUN = **lessening**, break, pause, interval, recess, respite, lull, cessation, remission, breathing space, slackening, abatement

level NOUN 1 *in order according to their level of difficulty* = **position**, standard, degree (*archaic*), grade, standing, stage, rank, status 2 *The water came up to her chin and the bubbles were at eye level.* = **height**, altitude, elevation, vertical position 3 *The horse showed good form on the level.* = **flat surface**, plane, horizontal ▶ ADJECTIVE 1 *She knelt down so that their eyes were level.* = **equal**, in line, aligned, balanced, on a line, at the same height 2 *a plateau of level ground* = **horizontal**, even, flat, plane, smooth, uniform, as flat as a pancake ■ **OPPOSITE:** slanted 3 *The teams were level at the end of extra time.* = **even**, tied, equal, drawn, neck and neck, all square, level pegging ▶ VERB 1 *They got two goals to level the score.* = **equalize**, balance, even up 2 *Further tremors could level yet more buildings.* = **destroy**, devastate, wreck, demolish, flatten, knock down, pull down, tear down, bulldoze, raze, lay waste to, kennet (*Austral. slang*), jeff (*Austral. slang*) ■ **OPPOSITE:** build 3 *The soldiers level guns at each other along the border.* = **direct**, point, turn, train, aim, focus, beam 4 *I'd been levelling off the ground before putting up the shed.* = **flatten**, plane, smooth, make flat, even off or out • **level with someone** *Levelling with you, I was in two minds before this happened.* = **be honest**, be open, be frank, come clean (*informal*), be straightforward, be up front (*slang*), be above board, keep nothing back • **on the level** *There were moments where you wondered if anyone was on the level.* = **honest**, genuine, sincere, open, straight, fair, square, straightforward, up front (*slang*), dinkum (*Austral. & N.Z. informal*), above board

level-headed ADJECTIVE = **calm**, balanced, reasonable, composed, together (*slang*), cool, collected, steady, sensible, sane, dependable, unflappable (*informal*), self-possessed, even-tempered, grounded

lever NOUN *Robert leaned lightly on the lever and the rock groaned.* = **handle**, bar, crowbar, jemmy, handspike ▸ VERB *Neighbours eventually levered the door open with a crowbar.* = **prise**, move, force, raise, pry (*U.S.*), jemmy

leverage NOUN **1** *My position affords me the leverage to get things done.* = **influence**, authority, pull (*informal*), weight, rank, clout (*informal*), purchasing power, ascendancy **2** *The spade and fork have longer shafts, providing better leverage.* = **force**, hold, pull, strength, grip, grasp

leviathan NOUN = **monster**, whale, mammoth, Titan, hulk, colossus, behemoth

levy NOUN *an annual motorway levy on all drivers* = **tax**, fee, toll, tariff, duty, assessment, excise, imposition, impost, exaction ▸ VERB *Taxes should not be levied without the authority of Parliament.* = **impose**, charge, tax, collect, gather, demand, exact

lewd ADJECTIVE = **indecent**, obscene, vulgar, dirty, blue, loose (*old-fashioned*), vile, pornographic, wicked, wanton, X-rated (*informal*), profligate, bawdy, salacious, impure, lascivious, smutty, lustful, libidinous, licentious, unchaste

lexicon NOUN = **vocabulary**, dictionary, glossary, word list, wordbook

liabilities PLURAL NOUN *The company had liabilities of $250 million.* = **debts**, expenditure, debit, arrears, obligations, accounts payable

liability NOUN **1** *What was once a vote-catching policy is now a political liability.* = **disadvantage**, burden, drawback, inconvenience, drag (*informal*), handicap, minus (*informal*), nuisance, impediment, albatross, hindrance, millstone, encumbrance **2** *They admit liability, but dispute the amount of his claim.* = **responsibility**, accountability, culpability, obligation, onus, answerability

liable ADJECTIVE **1** *James is liable to make costly mistakes.* = **likely**, tending, inclined, disposed, prone, apt **2** *These women are particularly liable to depression.* = **vulnerable**, subject, exposed, prone, susceptible, open, at risk of **3** *The airline's insurer is liable for damages.* = **responsible**, accountable, amenable, answerable, bound, obligated, chargeable

> **USAGE** In the past, it was considered incorrect to use *liable* to mean 'probable' or 'likely', as in *it's liable to happen soon*. However, this usage is now generally considered acceptable.

liaise VERB = **communicate**, link up, connect, intermediate, mediate, interchange, hook up, keep contact

liaison NOUN **1** *Liaison between the police and the art world is vital to combat art crime.* = **contact**, communication, connection, interchange **2** *She acts as a liaison between patients and staff.* = **intermediary**, contact, hook-up, go-between **3** *She embarked on a liaison with a noted society figure.* = **affair**, romance, intrigue, fling, love affair, amour, entanglement, illicit romance

liar NOUN = **falsifier**, storyteller (*informal*), perjurer, fibber, fabricator, prevaricator

libel NOUN *She sued them for libel over the remarks.* = **defamation**, slander, misrepresentation, denigration, smear, calumny, vituperation, obloquy, aspersion ▸ VERB *The newspaper which libelled him had already offered him compensation.* = **defame**, smear, slur, blacken, malign, denigrate, revile, vilify, slander, traduce (*formal*), derogate, calumniate, drag (someone's) name through the mud

liberal ADJECTIVE **1** *She is known to have liberal views on social issues.* = **tolerant**, enlightened, open-minded, permissive, advanced, catholic, humanitarian, right-on (*informal*), indulgent, easy-going, unbiased, high-minded, broad-minded, unprejudiced, unbigoted, politically correct or PC ■ **OPPOSITE:** intolerant **2** *a liberal democracy with a multiparty political system* = **progressive**, radical, reformist, libertarian, advanced, right-on (*informal*), forward-looking, humanistic, free-thinking, latitudinarian, politically correct or PC ■ **OPPOSITE:** conservative **3** *She made liberal use of her older sister's make-up and clothes.* = **abundant**, generous, handsome, lavish, ample, rich, plentiful, copious, bountiful, profuse, munificent ■ **OPPOSITE:** limited **4** *They thanked him for his liberal generosity.* = **generous**, kind, charitable, extravagant, free-handed, prodigal, altruistic, open-hearted, bountiful, magnanimous, open-handed, unstinting, beneficent, bounteous ■ **OPPOSITE:** stingy **5** *a liberal translation* = **flexible**, general, broad, rough, free, loose, lenient, not close, inexact, not strict, not literal ■ **OPPOSITE:** strict

liberalism NOUN = **progressivism**, radicalism, humanitarianism, libertarianism, freethinking, latitudinarianism

liberalize VERB = **relax**, ease, moderate, modify, stretch, soften, broaden, loosen, mitigate, slacken, ameliorate

liberate VERB = **free**, release, rescue, save, deliver, discharge, redeem, let out, set free, let loose, untie, emancipate, unchain, unbind, manumit ■ **OPPOSITE:** imprison

liberator NOUN = **deliverer**, saviour, rescuer, redeemer, freer, emancipator, manumitter

liberty NOUN **1** *Such a system would be a blow to the liberty of the people.* = **independence**, sovereignty, liberation, autonomy, immunity, self-determination, emancipation, self-government, self-rule **2** *Three convictions meant three months' loss of liberty.* = **freedom**, liberation, redemption, emancipation, deliverance, manumission, enfranchisement, unshackling, unfettering ■ **OPPOSITE:** restraint • **at liberty 1** *There is no confirmation that he is at liberty.* = **free**, escaped, unlimited, at large, not confined, untied, on the loose, unchained, unbound **2** *I'm not at liberty to say where it is, because the deal hasn't gone through yet.* = **able**, free, allowed, permitted, entitled, authorized • **take liberties** or **a liberty** *She knew she was taking a big liberty in doing this for him without his knowledge.* = **not show enough respect**, show disrespect, act presumptuously, behave too familiarly, behave impertinently

libretto NOUN = **words**, book, lines, text, script, lyrics

licence NOUN **1** *The painting was returned on a temporary import licence.* = **certificate**, document, permit, charter, warrant **2** *Fiction gives her licence to go where the traditional biographer would not dare to tread.* = **permission**, the right, authority, leave, sanction, liberty, privilege, immunity, entitlement, exemption, prerogative, authorization, dispensation, a free hand, carte blanche, blank cheque ■ **OPPOSITE:** denial **3** *All that stuff about catching a giant fish was just a bit of poetic licence.* = **freedom**, creativity, latitude, independence, liberty, deviation, leeway, free rein, looseness ■ **OPPOSITE:** restraint **4** *a world of licence and corruption* = **laxity**, abandon, disorder, excess, indulgence, anarchy, lawlessness, impropriety, irresponsibility, profligacy, licentiousness, unruliness, immoderation ■ **OPPOSITE:** moderation

license VERB = **permit**, commission, enable, sanction, allow, entitle, warrant, authorize, empower, certify, accredit, give a blank cheque to ■ **OPPOSITE:** forbid

lick VERB **1** *The dog licked the man's hand excitedly.* = **taste**, lap, tongue, touch, wash, brush **2** *He might be able to lick us all in a fair fight.* = **beat**, defeat, overcome, best, top, stuff (*slang*), tank (*slang*), undo, rout, excel, surpass, outstrip, outdo, trounce, clobber

(*slang*), vanquish, run rings around (*informal*), wipe the floor with (*informal*), blow out of the water (*slang*) **3** *(flames) The fire sent its red tongues licking into the hallway.* = **flicker**, touch, flick, dart, ripple, ignite, play over, kindle ▶ NOUN **1** *It could do with a lick of paint to brighten up its premises.* = **dab**, little (bit), touch, taste, sample, stroke, brush, speck **2** *an athletic cyclist travelling at a fair lick* = **pace**, rate, speed, clip (*informal*)

licking NOUN = **thrashing**, beating, hiding (*informal*), whipping, tanning (*slang*), flogging, spanking, drubbing

lie¹ NOUN *I've had enough of your lies.* = **falsehood**, deceit, fabrication, fib, fiction, invention, deception, untruth, porky (*Brit. slang*), pork pie (*Brit. slang*), white lie, falsification, prevarication, falsity, mendacity ▶ VERB *If asked, he lies about his age.* = **fib**, fabricate, invent, misrepresent, falsify, tell a lie, prevaricate, perjure, not tell the truth, equivocate, dissimulate, tell untruths, not speak the truth, say something untrue, forswear yourself • **give the lie to something** *This survey gives the lie to the idea that Britain is moving towards economic recovery.* = **disprove**, expose, discredit, contradict, refute, negate, invalidate, rebut, make a nonsense of, prove false, controvert, confute ■ **RELATED WORD:** *adjective* mendacious

lie² VERB **1** *He was lying motionless on his back.* = **recline**, rest, lounge, couch, sprawl, stretch out, be prone, loll, repose, be prostrate, be supine, be recumbent **2** *a newspaper lying on a nearby couch* = **be placed**, be, rest, exist, extend, be situated **3** *The islands lie at the southern end of the mountain range.* = **be situated**, sit, be located, be positioned **4** *(usually with* **in***) The problem lay in the large amounts spent on defence.* = **exist**, be present, consist, dwell (*formal, literary*), reside, pertain, inhere **5** *Here lies Catin, son of Magarus.* = **be buried**, remain, rest, be, be found, belong, be located, be interred, be entombed **6** *(usually with* **on** *or* **upon***) The pain of losing his younger brother still lies heavy on his mind.* = **weigh**, press, rest, burden, oppress

liege NOUN = **feudal lord**, master, superior, sovereign, chieftain, overlord, seigneur, suzerain

lieu NOUN • **in lieu of** = **instead of**, in place of

life NOUN **1** *a newborn baby's first minutes of life* = **being**, existence, breath, entity, vitality, animation, viability, sentience **2** *Is there life on Mars?* = **living things**, creatures, wildlife, organisms, living beings **3** *He spent*

the last fourteen years of his life in retirement.
= **existence**, being, lifetime, time, days,
course, span, duration, continuance **4** *How
did you adjust to college life?* = **way of life**,
situation, conduct, behaviour, lifestyle
5 *The town itself was full of life and character.*
= **liveliness**, activity, energy, spirit, go
(*informal*), pep, sparkle, vitality, animation,
vigour, verve, zest, high spirits, get-up-and-
go (*informal*), oomph (*informal*), brio,
vivacity **6** *It was his aim to write a life of John
Paul Jones.* = **biography**, story, history,
career, profile, confessions, autobiography,
memoirs, life story **7** *He's sucked the life out of
the group.* = **spirit**, heart, soul, essence,
core, lifeblood, moving spirit, vital spark,
animating spirit, élan vital (*French*)
8 *a war in which thousands of lives were lost*
= **person**, human, individual, soul, human
being, mortal ■ **RELATED WORDS:** *adjectives*
animate, vital

lifeblood NOUN = **animating force**, life,
heart, inspiration, guts (*informal*), essence,
stimulus, driving force, vital spark

lifeless ADJECTIVE **1** *There was no breathing or
pulse and he was lifeless.* = **dead**, unconscious,
extinct, deceased, cold, defunct, inert,
inanimate, comatose, out cold, out for the
count, insensible, in a faint, insensate,
dead to the world (*informal*) ■ **OPPOSITE:**
alive **2** *They may appear lifeless, but they
provide a valuable habitat for plants and
animals.* = **barren**, empty, desert, bare,
waste, sterile, unproductive, uninhabited
3 *His novels are shallow and lifeless.* = **dull**,
cold, flat, hollow, heavy, slow, wooden,
stiff, passive, static, pointless, sluggish,
lacklustre, lethargic, colourless, listless,
torpid, spiritless ■ **OPPOSITE:** lively

lifelike ADJECTIVE = **realistic**, faithful,
authentic, natural, exact, graphic, vivid,
photographic, true-to-life, undistorted

lifelong ADJECTIVE = **long-lasting**,
enduring, lasting, permanent, constant,
lifetime, for life, persistent, long-standing,
perennial, deep-rooted, for all your life

lifetime NOUN = **existence**, time, day(s),
course, period, span, life span, your natural
life, all your born days

lift VERB **1** *Curious shoppers lifted their children
to take a closer look at the parade.* = **raise**, pick
up, hoist, draw up, elevate, uplift, heave
up, buoy up, raise high, bear aloft, upheave,
upraise ■ **OPPOSITE:** lower **2** *The Commission
has urged them to lift their ban on imports.*
= **revoke**, end, remove, withdraw, stop,
relax, cancel, terminate, rescind, annul,
countermand ■ **OPPOSITE:** impose **3** *A brisk
walk in the fresh air can lift your mood.* = **exalt**,

raise, improve, advance, promote,
boost, enhance, upgrade, elevate, dignify,
cheer up, perk up, ameliorate, buoy up
■ **OPPOSITE:** depress **4** *The fog had lifted and
revealed a warm sunny day.* = **disappear**,
clear, vanish, disperse, dissipate, rise, be
dispelled **5** *a cartoonish device lifted from a
Laurel and Hardy sequence* = **steal**, take, copy,
appropriate, nick (*slang, chiefly Brit.*),
pocket, pinch (*informal*), pirate, cabbage
(*Brit. slang*), crib (*informal*), half-inch
(*old-fashioned slang*), blag (*slang*), pilfer,
purloin (*formal*), plagiarize, thieve ▶ NOUN
1 *My selection for the team has given me a
tremendous lift.* = **boost**, encouragement,
stimulus, reassurance, uplift, pick-me-up,
fillip, shot in the arm (*informal*), gee-up
■ **OPPOSITE:** blow **2** *They took the lift to the
fourth floor.* = **elevator** (*chiefly U.S.*), hoist,
paternoster **3** *He had a car and often gave me a
lift home.* = **ride**, run, drive, transport, hitch
(*informal*), car ride • **lift off** *The plane lifted
off and climbed steeply into the night sky.* = **take
off**, be launched, blast off, take to the air

light[1] NOUN **1** *Cracks of light filtered through the
shutters.* = **brightness**, illumination,
luminosity, luminescence, ray of light, flash
of light, shining, glow, blaze, sparkle, glare,
gleam, brilliance, glint, lustre, radiance,
incandescence, phosphorescence,
scintillation, effulgence, lambency,
refulgence ■ **OPPOSITE:** dark **2** *You get into
the music and lights, and the people around you.*
= **lamp**, bulb, torch, candle, flare, beacon,
lighthouse, lantern, taper **3** *Have you got a
light, anybody?* = **match**, spark, flame,
lighter **4** *He has worked hard to portray New
York in a better light.* = **aspect**, approach,
attitude, context, angle, point of view,
interpretation, viewpoint, slant,
standpoint, vantage point **5** *At last the light
dawned. He was going to get married!*
= **understanding**, knowledge, awareness,
insight, information, explanation,
illustration, enlightenment,
comprehension, illumination, elucidation
■ **OPPOSITE:** mystery **6** *Three hours before
first light, he gave orders for the evacuation of the
camp.* = **daybreak**, morning, dawn, sun,
sunrise, sunshine, sunlight, daylight,
daytime, sunbeam, morn (*poetic*),
cockcrow, broad day ▶ ADJECTIVE **1** *Her
house is light and airy, crisp and clean.* = **bright**,
brilliant, shining, glowing, sunny,
illuminated, luminous, well-lighted,
well-lit, lustrous, aglow, well-illuminated
■ **OPPOSITE:** dark **2** *The walls are light in
colour.* = **pale**, fair, faded, blonde, blond,
bleached, pastel, light-coloured, whitish,

light-toned, light-hued ■ **OPPOSITE:** dark
▶ VERB **1** *The giant moon lit the road brightly.*
= **illuminate**, light up, brighten, lighten,
put on, turn on, clarify, switch on,
floodlight, irradiate, illumine, flood with
light ■ **OPPOSITE:** darken **2** *He hunched down
to light a cigarette.* = **ignite**, inflame, fire,
torch, kindle, touch off, set alight, set a
match to ■ **OPPOSITE:** put out • **bring
something to light** *The truth is unlikely to be
brought to light by this enquiry.* = **reveal**,
expose, unveil, show, discover, disclose,
show up, uncover, unearth, lay bare
• **come to light** *Nothing about this sum has
come to light.* = **be revealed**, appear, come
out, turn up, be discovered, become
known, become apparent, be disclosed,
transpire • **in the light of something** *In
the light of this information, we can now identify
a number of issues.* = **considering**, because
of, taking into account, bearing in mind, in
view of, taking into consideration, with
knowledge of • **light up 1** *Sue's face lit up
with surprise.* = **cheer**, shine, blaze, sparkle,
animate, brighten, lighten, irradiate
2 *a security camera that lights up when you press
the bell at the gate* = **shine**, flash, beam,
blaze, sparkle, flare, glare, gleam, flicker

light² ADJECTIVE **1** *Try to wear light, loose
clothes.* = **insubstantial**, thin, delicate,
lightweight, easy, slight, portable,
buoyant, airy, flimsy, underweight, not
heavy, transportable, lightsome,
imponderous ■ **OPPOSITE:** heavy
2 *a light breeze* = **weak**, soft, gentle,
moderate, slight, mild, faint, indistinct
■ **OPPOSITE:** strong **3** *light, tropical soils*
= **crumbly**, loose, sandy, porous, spongy,
friable ■ **OPPOSITE:** hard **4** *wine and cheese or
other light refreshment* = **digestible**, small,
restricted, modest, frugal, not rich, not
heavy ■ **OPPOSITE:** substantial **5** *He was on
the training field for some light work yesterday.*
= **undemanding**, easy, simple, moderate,
manageable, effortless, cushy (*informal*),
untaxing, unexacting ■ **OPPOSITE:**
strenuous **6** *She confessed her astonishment
at her light sentence.* = **insignificant**, small,
minute, tiny, slight, petty, trivial, trifling,
inconsequential, inconsiderable,
unsubstantial ■ **OPPOSITE:** serious **7** *a light
entertainment programme* = **light-hearted**,
pleasing, funny, entertaining, amusing,
diverting, witty, trivial, superficial,
humorous, gay, trifling, frivolous, unserious
■ **OPPOSITE:** serious **8** *to finish on a lighter
note* = **carefree**, happy, bright, lively, sunny,
cheerful, animated, merry, gay, airy,
frivolous, cheery, untroubled, blithe,

light-hearted **9** *the light steps of a ballet
dancer* = **nimble**, graceful, airy, deft, agile,
sprightly, lithe, limber, lissom(e), light-
footed, sylphlike ■ **OPPOSITE:** clumsy
10 *Her head felt light, and a serene confidence
came over her.* = **dizzy**, reeling, faint, volatile,
giddy, unsteady, light-headed • **light on** or
upon something 1 *Her eyes lit on the brandy
that he had dropped on the floor.* = **settle**, land,
perch, alight **2** *the kind of thing that
philosophers lighted upon* = **come across**,
find, discover, encounter, stumble on, hit
upon, happen upon • **light out** *I lit it out of
the door and never went back again.* = **run
away**, escape, depart, make off, abscond,
quit, do a runner (*slang*), scarper (*Brit.
slang*), do a bunk (*Brit. slang*), fly the coop
(*U.S. & Canad. informal*), skedaddle
(*informal*), take a powder (*U.S. & Canad.
slang*), take it on the lam (*U.S. & Canad.
slang*), do a Skase (*Austral. informal*)

lighten¹ VERB *The sky began to lighten.*
= **brighten**, flash, shine, illuminate, gleam,
light up, irradiate, become light, make
bright

lighten² VERB **1** *He felt the need to lighten the
atmosphere.* = **ease**, relieve, alleviate, allay,
reduce, facilitate, lessen, mitigate, assuage
■ **OPPOSITE:** intensify **2** *Here's a little
something to lighten your spirits.* = **cheer**, lift,
revive, brighten, hearten, perk up, buoy up,
gladden, elate ■ **OPPOSITE:** depress
3 *Blending with a food processor lightens the
mixture.* = **make lighter**, ease, disburden,
reduce in weight

light-headed ADJECTIVE **1** *Your blood pressure
will drop and you may feel light-headed.* = **faint**,
dizzy, hazy, giddy, delirious, unsteady,
vertiginous, woozy (*informal*) **2** *a light-
headed girl* = **frivolous**, silly, shallow,
foolish, superficial, trifling, inane, flippant,
flighty, bird-brained (*informal*),
featherbrained, rattlebrained (*slang*)

light-hearted ADJECTIVE = **carefree**,
happy, bright, glad, sunny, cheerful, jolly,
merry, upbeat (*informal*), playful, joyous,
joyful, genial, chirpy (*informal*), jovial,
untroubled, gleeful, happy-go-lucky, gay,
effervescent, blithe, insouciant, frolicsome,
ludic (*literary*), jocund, blithesome (*literary*)
■ **OPPOSITE:** gloomy

lightly ADVERB **1** *a small and lightly armed UN
contingent* = **moderately**, thinly, slightly,
sparsely, sparingly ■ **OPPOSITE:** heavily
2 *He kissed her lightly on the mouth.* = **gently**,
softly, slightly, faintly, delicately, gingerly,
airily, timidly ■ **OPPOSITE:** forcefully **3** *'Once
a detective always a detective,' he said lightly.*
= **carelessly**, indifferently, breezily,

thoughtlessly, flippantly, frivolously, heedlessly, slightingly ■ **OPPOSITE:** seriously **4** *These allegations cannot be dismissed lightly.* = **easily**, simply, readily, effortlessly, unthinkingly, without thought, flippantly, heedlessly ■ **OPPOSITE:** with difficulty

lightweight ADJECTIVE **1** *lightweight denim* = **thin**, fine, delicate, sheer, flimsy, gossamer, diaphanous, filmy, unsubstantial **2** *Some of the discussion in the book is lightweight and unconvincing.* = **unimportant**, shallow, trivial, insignificant, slight, petty, worthless, trifling, flimsy, paltry, inconsequential, undemanding, insubstantial, nickel-and-dime (*U.S. slang*), of no account ■ **OPPOSITE:** significant

like[1] ADJECTIVE *She's a great friend; we are like sisters.* = **similar to**, same as, allied to, equivalent to, parallel to, resembling, identical to, alike, corresponding to, comparable to, akin to, approximating, analogous to, cognate to ■ **OPPOSITE:** different ▶ NOUN *We are dealing with an epidemic the like of which we have never seen.* = **equal**, equivalent, parallel, match, twin, counterpart ■ **OPPOSITE:** opposite

> **USAGE** The use of *like* to mean 'such as' was in the past considered undesirable in formal writing, but has now become acceptable, for example in *I enjoy team sports like football and rugby*. However, the common use of *look like* and *seem like* to mean 'look or seem as if' is thought by many people to be incorrect or nonstandard. You might say *it looks as if* (or *as though*) *he's coming*, but it is still wise to avoid *it looks like he's coming*, particularly in formal or written contexts.

like[2] VERB **1** *He likes baseball.* = **enjoy**, love, adore (*informal*), delight in, go for, dig (*slang*), relish, savour, revel in, be fond of, be keen on, be partial to, have a preference for, have a weakness for ■ **OPPOSITE:** dislike **2** *I like the way this book is set out.* = **admire**, approve of, appreciate, prize, take to, esteem, cherish, hold dear, take a shine to (*informal*), think well of ■ **OPPOSITE:** dislike **3** *Would you like to come back for coffee?* = **wish**, want, choose, prefer, desire, select, fancy (*Brit. informal*), care, feel inclined ▶ NOUN (*usually plural*) *I know all her likes and dislikes, and her political viewpoints.* = **liking**, favourite, preference, cup of tea (*informal*), predilection, partiality

likelihood NOUN = **probability**, chance, possibility, prospect, liability, good chance, strong possibility, reasonableness, likeliness

likely ADJECTIVE **1** *People are more likely to accept change if they understand it.* = **inclined**, disposed, prone, liable, tending, apt **2** *A 'yes' vote is the likely outcome.* = **probable**, expected, anticipated, odds-on, on the cards, to be expected **3** *It's likely that he still loves her.* = **plausible**, possible, reasonable, credible, feasible, believable, verisimilar **4** *He seemed a likely candidate to become Prime Minister.* = **appropriate**, promising, pleasing, fit, fair, favourite, qualified, suitable, acceptable, proper, hopeful, agreeable, up-and-coming, befitting ▶ ADVERB *Very likely he'd told them of his business interest.* = **probably**, no doubt, presumably, in all probability, like enough (*informal*), doubtlessly, like as not (*informal*)

> **USAGE** When using *likely* as an adverb, it is usual to precede it by another, intensifying, adverb such as *very* or *most*, for example *it will most likely rain*. The use of *likely* as an adverb without an intensifier, for example *it will likely rain*, is considered nonstandard in British English, though it is common in colloquial U.S. English.

like-minded ADJECTIVE = **agreeing**, compatible, harmonious, in harmony, unanimous, in accord, of one mind, of the same mind, en rapport (*French*)

liken VERB = **compare**, match, relate, parallel, equate, juxtapose, mention in the same breath, set beside

likeness NOUN **1** *These stories have a startling likeness to one another.* = **resemblance**, similarity, correspondence, affinity, similitude **2** *The museum displays wax likenesses of every U.S. president.* = **portrait**, study, picture, model, image, photograph, copy, counterpart, representation, reproduction, replica, depiction, facsimile, effigy, delineation **3** *a disservice in the likeness of a favour* = **appearance**, form, guise, semblance

likewise ADVERB **1** *All their attempts were spurned. Similar offers from the right were likewise rejected.* = **also**, too, as well, further, in addition, moreover, besides, furthermore **2** *He made donations and encouraged others to do likewise.* = **similarly**, the same, in the same way, in similar fashion, in like manner

liking NOUN = **fondness**, love, taste, desire, bent, stomach, attraction, weakness, tendency, preference, bias, affection, appreciation, inclination, thirst, affinity, penchant, propensity, soft spot, predilection, partiality, proneness ■ **OPPOSITE:** dislike

lilt NOUN = **rhythm**, intonation, cadence, beat, pitch, swing, sway

limb NOUN **1** *She stretched out her cramped limbs.* = **part**, member, arm, leg, wing, extension, extremity, appendage **2** *the limb of an enormous leafy tree* = **branch**, spur, projection, offshoot, bough

limber ADJECTIVE *He bent at the waist to show how limber his long back was.* = **pliant**, flexible, supple, agile, plastic, graceful, elastic, lithe, pliable, lissom(e), loose-jointed, loose-limbed • **limber up** *The dancers were limbering up at the back of the hall.* = **loosen up**, prepare, exercise, warm up, get ready

limelight NOUN = **publicity**, recognition, fame, the spotlight, attention, prominence, stardom, public eye, public notice, glare of publicity

limit NOUN **1** *Her love for him was being tested to its limits.* = **end**, bound, ultimate, deadline, utmost, breaking point, termination, extremity, greatest extent, the bitter end, end point, cutoff point, furthest bound **2** *the city limits* = **boundary**, end, edge, border, extent, pale, confines, frontier, precinct, perimeter, periphery **3** *He outlined the limits of British power.* = **limitation**, maximum, restriction, ceiling, restraint ▶ VERB *He limited payments on the country's foreign debt.* = **restrict**, control, check, fix, bound, confine, specify, curb, restrain, ration, hinder, circumscribe, hem in, demarcate, delimit, put a brake on, keep within limits, straiten • **the limit** *Really, Mark, you are the limit!* = **the end**, it (*informal*), enough, the last straw, the straw that broke the camel's back

limitation NOUN **1** *There is to be no limitation on the number of opposition parties.* = **restriction**, control, check, block, curb, restraint, constraint, obstruction, impediment **2** *This drug has one important limitation.* = **weakness**, failing, qualification, reservation, defect, disadvantage, flaw, drawback, shortcoming, snag, imperfection

limited ADJECTIVE **1** *They have a limited amount of time to get their point across.* = **restricted**, controlled, fixed, defined, checked, bounded, confined, curbed, hampered, constrained, finite, circumscribed ■ **OPPOSITE:** unlimited **2** *The shop has a very limited selection.* = **narrow**, little, small, restricted, slight, inadequate, minimal, insufficient, unsatisfactory, scant

limitless ADJECTIVE = **infinite**, endless, unlimited, never-ending, vast, immense, countless, untold, boundless, unending, inexhaustible, undefined, immeasurable, unbounded, numberless, measureless, illimitable, uncalculable

limp[1] VERB *He limped off with a leg injury.* = **hobble**, stagger, stumble, shuffle, halt (*archaic*), hop, falter, shamble, totter, dodder, hirple (*Scot.*) ▶ NOUN *A stiff knee forced her to walk with a limp.* = **lameness**, hobble, hirple (*Scot.*)

limp[2] ADJECTIVE **1** *The residue can leave the hair limp and dull looking.* = **floppy**, soft, relaxed, loose, flexible, slack, lax, drooping, flabby, limber, pliable, flaccid ■ **OPPOSITE:** stiff **2** *Her body lay limp where she fell.* = **weak**, tired, exhausted, worn out, spent, debilitated, lethargic, enervated ■ **OPPOSITE:** strong

limpid ADJECTIVE **1** *limpid rock-pools* = **clear**, bright, pure, transparent, translucent, crystal-clear, crystalline, pellucid **2** *The speech was a model of its kind – limpid and unaffected.* = **understandable**, clear, lucid, unambiguous, comprehensible, intelligible, perspicuous (*literary*)

line[1] NOUN **1** *Draw a line down the centre of the page.* = **stroke**, mark, rule, score, bar, band, channel, dash, scratch, slash, underline, streak, stripe, groove **2** *He has a large, generous face with deep lines.* = **wrinkle**, mark, crease, furrow, crow's-foot **3** *Children clutching empty bowls form a line.* = **row**, queue, rank, file, series, column, sequence, convoy, procession, crocodile (*Brit.*) **4** *a piece of fishing line* = **string**, cable, wire (*old-fashioned*), strand, rope, thread, cord, filament, wisp **5** *Walk in a straight line.* = **trajectory**, way, course, track, channel, direction, route, path, axis **6** *a dress that follows the line of the body* = **outline**, shape, figure, style, cut, features, appearance, profile, silhouette, configuration, contour **7** *the California state line* = **boundary**, mark, limit, edge, border, frontier, partition, borderline, demarcation **8** *the fortification they called the Maginot Line* = **formation**, front, position, front line, trenches, firing line **9** *The government promised to take a hard line on terrorism.* = **approach**, policy, position, way, course, practice, scheme, method, technique, procedure, tactic, avenue, ideology, course of action **10** *What was your father's line of business?* = **occupation**, work, calling, interest, business, job, area, trade, department (*informal*), field, career, activity, bag (*slang*), employment, province, profession, pursuit, forte, vocation, specialization **11** *We were part of a long line of artists.* = **lineage**, family, breed, succession, race, stock, strain, descent, ancestry, parentage **12** *Drop me a line if I can be of any use to you.* = **note**, message, letter, memo, report, word, card, email *or* e-mail, postcard, text ▶ VERB **1** *Thousands of people lined the streets as the procession went by.* = **border**, edge, bound, fringe, rank, skirt, verge, rim **2** *Her face was lined with concern.* = **mark**, draw, crease, furrow, cut, rule, score, trace, underline, inscribe • **draw the line at something** *I will eat pretty much anything, but I do draw the line at offal.* = **object to**, prohibit, stop short at, set a limit at, put your foot down over • **in line for** *She must be in line for a place in the Guinness Book of Records.* = **due for**, being considered for, a candidate for, shortlisted for, in the running for, on the short list for, next in succession to • **in line with** *This is in line with medical opinion.* = **in accord**, in agreement, in harmony, in step, in conformity • **line something up 1** *He lined the glasses up behind the bar.* = **align**, order, range, arrange, sequence, array, regiment, dispose, marshal, straighten, straighten up, put in a line **2** *She's lining up a two-week tour for the New Year.* = **prepare**, schedule, organize, secure, obtain, come up with, assemble, get together, lay on, procure, jack up (*N.Z. informal*) • **line up** *The senior leaders lined up behind him in orderly rows.* = **queue up**, file, fall in, form a queue, form ranks

line² VERB *They line their dens with leaves or grass.* = **fill**, face, cover, reinforce, encase, inlay, interline, ceil

lineage NOUN = **descent**, family, line, succession, house, stock, birth, breed, pedigree, extraction, ancestry, forebears, progeny, heredity, forefathers, genealogy

lined ADJECTIVE **1** *His lined face was that of an old man.* = **wrinkled**, worn, furrowed, wizened **2** *Take a piece of lined paper.* = **ruled**, feint

lines PLURAL NOUN *so-called autonomous republics based on ethnic lines* = **principle**, plan, example, model, pattern, procedure, convention

line-up NOUN = **arrangement**, team, row, selection, array

linger VERB **1** *The guilty feelings lingered.* = **continue**, last, remain, stay, carry on, endure, persist, abide **2** *He lingered for weeks in a coma.* = **hang on**, last, survive, cling to life, die slowly **3** *Customers are welcome to linger over coffee until midnight.* = **stay**, remain, stop, wait, delay, lag, hang around, idle, dally, loiter, take your time, wait around, dawdle, hang in the air, procrastinate, tarry, drag your feet *or* heels

lingering ADJECTIVE = **slow**, prolonged, protracted, long-drawn-out, remaining, dragging, persistent

lingo NOUN = **language**, jargon, dialect, talk, speech, tongue, idiom, vernacular, patter, cant, patois, argot

link NOUN **1** *the link between smoking and lung cancer* = **connection**, relationship, association, tie-up, affinity, affiliation, vinculum **2** *They hope to cement close links with Moscow.* = **relationship**, association, tie, bond, connection, attachment, liaison, affinity, affiliation **3** *Seafood is the first link in a chain of contaminations.* = **component**, part, piece, division, element, constituent ▶ VERB **1** *Liver cancer is linked to the hepatitis B virus.* = **associate**, relate, identify, connect, bracket **2** *the Channel Tunnel linking Britain and France* = **connect**, join, unite, couple, tie, bind, attach, fasten, yoke ■ OPPOSITE: separate

lion NOUN = **hero**, champion, fighter, warrior, conqueror, lionheart, brave person ■ RELATED WORDS: *adjective* leonine; *name of female* lioness; *name of young* cub; *collective nouns* pride, troop

lip NOUN **1** *the lip of the jug* = **edge**, rim, brim, margin, brink, flange **2** *Enough of that lip if you want me to help you!* = **impudence**, rudeness, insolence, impertinence, sauce (*informal*), cheek (*informal*), effrontery, backchat (*informal*), brass neck (*informal*) • **pay lip service to something** *or* **someone** = **pretend to support**, support insincerely, support hypocritically • **smack** *or* **lick your lips** *They licked their lips in anticipation.* = **gloat**, drool, slaver ■ RELATED WORD: *adjective* labial

liquefy VERB = **melt**, dissolve, thaw, liquidize, run, fuse, flux, deliquesce

liquid NOUN *Drink plenty of liquid.* = **fluid**, solution, juice, liquor, sap ▶ ADJECTIVE **1** *Wash in warm water with liquid detergent.* = **fluid**, running, flowing, wet, melted, thawed, watery, molten, runny, liquefied, aqueous **2** *a mosaic of liquid cobalts and greens* = **clear**, bright, brilliant, shining, transparent, translucent, limpid **3** *He had a deep liquid voice.* = **smooth**, clear, soft, flowing, sweet, pure, melting, fluent, melodious, dulcet, mellifluent **4** (*assets*) *The bank had sufficient liquid assets to continue operating.* = **convertible**, disposable, negotiable, realizable

liquidate VERB **1** *A unanimous vote was taken to liquidate the company.* = **dissolve**, cancel, abolish, terminate, annul **2** *The company closed down operations and began liquidating its assets.* = **convert to cash**, cash, realize, sell off, sell up **3** *They have not hesitated in the past to liquidate their rivals.* = **kill**, murder, remove, destroy, do in (*slang*), silence, eliminate (*slang*), take out (*slang*), get rid of, wipe out (*informal*), dispatch, finish off, do away with, blow away (*slang, chiefly U.S.*), annihilate, exterminate, bump off (*slang*), rub out (*U.S. slang*)

liquor NOUN **1** *The room was filled with cases of liquor.* = **alcohol**, drink, spirits, booze (*informal*), grog, hard stuff (*informal*), strong drink, Dutch courage (*informal*), intoxicant, juice (*informal*), hooch or hootch (*informal, chiefly U.S. & Canad.*) **2** *Drain the oysters and retain the liquor.* = **juice**, stock, liquid, extract, gravy, infusion, broth

list¹ NOUN *There were six names on the list.* = **inventory**, record, listing, series, roll, file, schedule, index, register, catalogue, directory, tally, invoice, syllabus, tabulation, leet (*Scot.*) ▶ VERB *The students were asked to list their favourite sports.* = **itemize**, record, note, enter, file, schedule, index, register, catalogue, write down, enrol, set down, enumerate, note down, tabulate

list² VERB *The ship listed again, and she was thrown back across the bunk.* = **lean**, tip, heel, incline, tilt, cant, heel over, careen ▶ NOUN *The ship's list was so strong that she stumbled.* = **tilt**, leaning, slant, cant

listen VERB **1** *She spent her time listening to the radio.* = **hear**, attend, pay attention, hark, be attentive, be all ears, lend an ear, hearken (*archaic*), prick up your ears, give ear, keep your ears open, pin back your ears (*informal*) **2** *When I asked him to stop, he wouldn't listen.* = **pay attention**, observe, obey, mind, concentrate, heed, take notice, take note of, take heed of, do as you are told, give heed to

listless ADJECTIVE = **languid**, sluggish, lifeless, lethargic, heavy, limp, vacant, indifferent, languishing, inert, apathetic, lymphatic, impassive, supine, indolent, torpid, inattentive, enervated, spiritless, mopish ■ **OPPOSITE:** energetic

litany NOUN **1** *She listened to the litany of complaints against her client.* = **recital**, list, tale, catalogue, account, repetition, refrain, recitation, enumeration **2** *She recited a litany in an unknown tongue.* = **prayer**, petition, invocation, supplication (*formal*), set words

literacy NOUN = **education**, learning, knowledge, scholarship, cultivation, proficiency, articulacy, ability to read and write, articulateness

literal ADJECTIVE **1** *a literal translation* = **exact**, close, strict, accurate, faithful, verbatim, word for word **2** *He is a very literal person.* = **unimaginative**, boring, dull, down-to-earth, matter-of-fact, factual, prosaic, colourless, uninspired, prosy **3** *He was saying no more than the literal truth.* = **actual**, real, true, simple, plain, genuine, gospel, bona fide, unvarnished, unexaggerated

literally ADVERB = **exactly**, really, closely, actually, simply, plainly, truly, precisely, strictly, faithfully, to the letter, verbatim, word for word

literary ADJECTIVE = **well-read**, lettered, learned, formal, intellectual, scholarly, literate, erudite, bookish

literate ADJECTIVE = **educated**, lettered, learned, cultured, informed, scholarly, cultivated, knowledgeable, well-informed, erudite, well-read

literature NOUN **1** *classic works of literature* = **writings**, letters, compositions, lore, creative writing, written works, belles-lettres **2** (*informal*) *I'm sending you literature from two other companies.* = **information**, publicity, leaflet, brochure, circular, pamphlet, handout, mailshot, handbill

lithe ADJECTIVE = **supple**, flexible, agile, limber, pliable, pliant, lissom(e), loose-jointed, loose-limbed

litigant NOUN = **claimant**, party, plaintiff, contestant, litigator, disputant

litigation NOUN = **lawsuit**, case, action, process, disputing, prosecution, contending

litigious ADJECTIVE = **contentious**, belligerent, argumentative, quarrelsome, disputatious

litter NOUN **1** *If you see litter in the corridor, pick it up.* = **rubbish**, refuse, waste, fragments, junk, debris, shreds, garbage (*chiefly U.S.*), trash, muck, detritus, grot (*slang*) **2** *He pushed aside the litter of books.* = **jumble**, mess, disorder, confusion, scatter, tangle, muddle, clutter, disarray, untidiness **3** *a litter of puppies* = **brood**, family, young, offspring, progeny **4** *The birds scratch through leaf litter on the forest floor.* = **bedding**, couch, mulch, floor cover, straw-bed **5** *The Colonel winced as the porters jolted the litter.* = **stretcher**, palanquin ▶ VERB **1** *Glass from broken bottles litters the pavement.* = **clutter**, mess up, clutter up, be scattered about, disorder, disarrange, derange, muss (*U.S. & Canad.*) **2** *Concrete holiday resorts are littered across the mountainside.* = **scatter**, spread, shower, strew

little ADJECTIVE **1** *I had little money and little free time.* = **not much**, small, insufficient, scant, meagre, sparse, skimpy, measly

(*informal*), hardly any ■ **OPPOSITE:** ample
2 *We sat round a little table.* = **small**, minute,
short, tiny, mini, wee, compact, miniature,
dwarf, slender, diminutive, petite, dainty,
elfin, bijou, infinitesimal, teeny-weeny,
Lilliputian, munchkin (*informal, chiefly U.S.*),
teensy-weensy, pygmy or pigmy
■ **OPPOSITE:** big **3** *When I was little, I was
hyperactive.* = **young**, small, junior, infant,
immature, undeveloped, babyish **4** *He
found himself getting angry over little things.*
= **unimportant**, minor, petty, trivial,
trifling, insignificant, negligible, paltry,
inconsiderable ■ **OPPOSITE:** important
5 *I won't play your little mind-games.* = **mean**,
base, cheap (*informal*), petty, narrow-
minded, small-minded, illiberal ▶ ADVERB
1 *On the way back they spoke very little.*
= **hardly**, barely, not quite, not much, only
just, scarcely ■ **OPPOSITE:** much **2** *We go
there very little nowadays.* = **rarely**, seldom,
scarcely, not often, infrequently, hardly
ever ■ **OPPOSITE:** always ▶ NOUN *Don't give
me too much. Just a little.* = **bit**, touch, spot
(*Brit.*), trace, hint, dash, particle, fragment,
pinch, small amount, dab, trifle, tad
(*informal*), snippet, speck, modicum
■ **OPPOSITE:** lot • **a little** *I'm getting a little
tired of having to correct your mistakes.* = **to a
small extent**, slightly, to some extent, to a
certain extent, to a small degree
liturgical ADJECTIVE = **ceremonial**, ritual,
solemn, sacramental, formal, eucharistic
liturgy NOUN = **ceremony**, service, ritual,
services, celebration, formula, worship,
rite, sacrament, form of worship
live¹ VERB **1** *She has lived here for 10 years.*
= **dwell** (*formal, literary*), board, settle,
lodge, occupy, abide, inhabit, hang out
(*informal*), stay (*chiefly Scot.*), reside, have as
your home, have your home in **2** *He's got a
terrible disease and will not live long.* = **exist**,
last, prevail, be, have being, breathe,
persist, be alive, have life, draw breath,
remain alive **3** *the last indigenous people to live
by hunting* = **survive**, remain alive, feed
yourself, get along, make a living, earn a
living, make ends meet, subsist, eke out a
living, support yourself, maintain yourself
4 *My friends told me to get out and live a bit.*
= **thrive**, be happy, flourish, prosper, have
fun, enjoy life, enjoy yourself, luxuriate, live
life to the full, make the most of life
live² ADJECTIVE **1** *tests on live animals* = **living**,
alive, breathing, animate, existent, vital,
quick (*archaic*) **2** *A live bomb had earlier been
defused.* = **active**, connected, switched on,
unexploded **3** *Directors' remuneration looks set
to become a live issue.* = **topical**, important,

pressing, current, hot, burning, active,
vital, controversial, unsettled, prevalent,
pertinent • **live wire** *My sister's a real live
wire, and full of fun.* = **dynamo**, hustler (*U.S.
& Canad. slang*), ball of fire (*informal*), life and
soul of the party, go-getter (*informal*),
self-starter
livelihood NOUN = **occupation**, work,
employment, means, living, job,
maintenance, subsistence, bread and
butter (*informal*), sustenance, (means of)
support, (source of) income
lively ADJECTIVE **1** *She had a sweet, lively
personality.* = **animated**, spirited, quick,
keen, active, alert, dynamic, sparkling,
vigorous, cheerful, energetic, outgoing,
merry, upbeat (*informal*), brisk, bubbly,
nimble, agile, perky, chirpy (*informal*),
sparky, sprightly, vivacious, frisky, gay, alive
and kicking, spry, chipper (*informal*), blithe,
full of beans (*informal*), frolicsome, full of
pep (*informal*), blithesome, bright-eyed and
bushy-tailed ■ **OPPOSITE:** dull **2** *lively streets
full of bars and cafés* = **busy**, crowded,
stirring, buzzing, bustling, moving,
eventful ■ **OPPOSITE:** slow **3** *toys made with
bright and lively colours* = **vivid**, strong,
striking, bright (*informal*), exciting,
stimulating, bold, colourful, refreshing,
forceful, racy, invigorating ■ **OPPOSITE:** dull
4 *The newspapers showed a lively interest in
European developments.* = **enthusiastic**,
strong, keen, stimulating, eager,
formidable, vigorous, animated, weighty
liven up VERB **1** *He livened up after midnight,
relaxing a little.* = **stir**, brighten, hot up
(*informal*), cheer up, perk up, buck up
(*informal*) **2** *How could we decorate the room to
liven it up?* = **cheer up**, animate, rouse,
enliven, perk up, brighten up, pep up, buck
up (*informal*), put life into, vitalize, vivify
livery NOUN = **costume**, dress, clothing,
suit, uniform, attire, garb, regalia,
vestments, raiment (*archaic, poetic*)
livid ADJECTIVE **1** *I am absolutely livid about it.*
= **angry**, cross, furious, outraged, mad
(*informal*), boiling, fuming, choked,
infuriated, incensed, enraged, exasperated,
indignant, incandescent, hot under the
collar (*informal*), fit to be tied (*slang*), beside
yourself, as black as thunder, tooshie
(*Austral. slang*), off the air (*Austral. slang*)
■ **OPPOSITE:** delighted **2** *The scarred side of
his face was a livid red.* = **discoloured**, angry,
purple, bruised, black-and-blue, contused
living NOUN **1** *He earns his living doing all kinds
of things.* = **livelihood**, work, job,
maintenance, occupation, subsistence,
bread and butter (*informal*), sustenance,

(means of) support, (source of) income **2** *the stresses of modern living* = **lifestyle**, ways, situation, conduct, behaviour, customs, way of life, mode of living
▸ ADJECTIVE **1** *All things, whether living or dead, are believed to influence each other.* = **alive**, existing, moving, active, vital, breathing, lively, vigorous, animated, animate, alive and kicking, in the land of the living (*informal*), quick (*archaic*) ■ OPPOSITE: dead **2** *a living language* = **current**, continuing, present, developing, active, contemporary, persisting, ongoing, operative, in use, extant ■ OPPOSITE: obsolete

load VERB **1** *The three men had finished loading the truck.* = **fill**, stuff, pack, pile, stack, heap, cram, freight, lade **2** *I knew how to load and handle a gun.* = **make ready**, charge, prime, prepare to fire ▸ NOUN **1** *He drove by with a big load of hay.* = **cargo**, lading, delivery, haul, shipment, batch, freight, bale, consignment **2** *High blood pressure imposes an extra load on the heart.* = **oppression**, charge, pressure, worry, trouble, weight, responsibility, burden, affliction, onus, albatross, millstone, encumbrance, incubus • **load someone down** *I'm loaded down with work at the moment.* = **burden**, worry, trouble, hamper, oppress, weigh down, saddle with, encumber, snow under

loaded ADJECTIVE **1** *shoppers loaded with bags* = **laden**, full, charged, filled, weighted, burdened, freighted **2** *He allowed himself to be caught red-handed with a loaded gun.* = **charged**, armed, primed, at the ready, ready to shoot or fire **3** *That's a loaded question.* = **tricky**, charged, sensitive, delicate, manipulative, emotive, insidious, artful, prejudicial, tendentious **4** *The press is loaded in favour of the government.* = **biased**, weighted, rigged, distorted **5** *Her new boyfriend's absolutely loaded.* = **rich**, wealthy, affluent, well off, rolling (*slang*), flush (*informal*), well-heeled (*informal*), well-to-do, moneyed, minted (*Brit. slang*)

loaf¹ NOUN **1** *a loaf of crusty bread* = **lump**, block, cake, cube, slab **2** *You've got to use your loaf in this game.* = **head**, mind, sense, common sense, block (*informal*), nous (*Brit. slang*), chump (*Brit. slang*), gumption (*Brit. informal*), noddle (*informal, chiefly Brit.*)

loaf² VERB *She studied, and I just loafed around.* = **idle**, hang around, take it easy, lie around, loiter, loll, laze, lounge around, veg out (*slang*), be indolent

loafer NOUN = **idler**, lounger, bum (*informal*), piker (*Austral. & N.Z. slang*), drone (*Brit.*), shirker, couch potato (*slang*), time-waster, layabout, skiver (*Brit. slang*), ne'er-do-well, wastrel, bludger (*Austral. & N.Z. informal*), lazybones (*informal*)

loan NOUN *They want to make it easier for people to get a loan.* = **advance**, credit, mortgage, accommodation, allowance, touch (*slang*), overdraft ▸ VERB *They asked us to loan our boat to them.* = **lend**, allow, credit, advance, accommodate, let out

loath *or* **loth** ADJECTIVE = **unwilling**, against, opposed, counter, resisting, reluctant, backward, averse, disinclined, indisposed ■ OPPOSITE: willing

loathe VERB = **hate**, dislike, despise, detest, abhor, abominate, have a strong aversion to, find disgusting, execrate, feel repugnance towards, not be able to bear or abide

loathing NOUN = **hatred**, hate, horror, disgust, aversion, revulsion, antipathy, abomination, repulsion, abhorrence, repugnance, odium (*formal*), detestation, execration

loathsome ADJECTIVE = **hateful**, offensive, nasty, disgusting, horrible, revolting, obscene, vile, obnoxious, repulsive, nauseating, odious, repugnant, abhorrent, abominable, execrable, detestable, yucky or yukky (*slang*), yucko (*Austral. slang*) ■ OPPOSITE: delightful

lob VERB = **throw**, launch, toss, hurl, lift, pitch, shy (*informal*), fling, loft

lobby VERB *Gun control advocates are lobbying hard for new laws.* = **campaign**, press, pressure, push, influence, promote, urge, persuade, appeal, petition, pull strings (*Brit. informal*), exert influence, bring pressure to bear, solicit votes ▸ NOUN **1** *Agricultural interests are some of the most powerful lobbies there.* = **pressure group**, group, camp, faction, lobbyists, interest group, special-interest group, ginger group, public-interest group (*U.S. & Canad.*) **2** *I met her in the lobby of the museum.* = **corridor**, hall, passage, entrance, porch, hallway, foyer, passageway, entrance hall, vestibule

lobola NOUN (*S. African*) = **dowry**, portion, marriage settlement, dot (*archaic*)

local ADJECTIVE **1** *I was going to pop up to the local library.* = **community**, district, regional, provincial, parish, neighbourhood, small-town (*chiefly U.S.*), parochial, parish pump **2** *The blockage caused a local infection.* = **confined**, limited, narrow, restricted ▸ NOUN *That's what the locals call the place.* = **resident**, native, inhabitant, character (*informal*), local yokel (*derogatory*)

locale NOUN = **site**, place, setting, position, spot, scene, location, venue, locality, locus

locality NOUN **1** *Details of the drinking water quality in your locality can be obtained.*
= **neighbourhood**, area, region, district, vicinity, neck of the woods (*informal*) **2** *Such a locality is popularly referred to as a 'hot spot'.*
= **site**, place, setting, position, spot, scene, location, locale

localize VERB = **restrict**, limit, contain, concentrate, confine, restrain, circumscribe, delimit

locate VERB **1** *We've simply been unable to locate him.* = **find**, discover, detect, come across, track down, pinpoint, unearth, pin down, lay your hands on, run to earth or ground **2** *It was voted the best city to locate a business.* = **place**, put, set, position, seat, site, establish, settle, fix, situate

location NOUN = **place**, point, setting, position, situation, spot, venue, whereabouts, locus, locale

lock¹ VERB **1** *Are you sure you locked the front door?* = **fasten**, close, secure, shut, bar, seal, bolt, latch, sneck (*dialect*) **2** *She locked her fingers behind her head.* = **unite**, join, link, engage, mesh, clench, entangle, interlock, entwine **3** *She locked him in a passionate clinch.* = **embrace**, press, grasp, clutch, hug, enclose, grapple, clasp, encircle
▶ NOUN *He heard her key turning in the lock.*
= **fastening**, catch, bolt, clasp, padlock
• **lock someone out** *My husband's locked me out.* = **shut out**, bar, ban, exclude, keep out, debar, refuse admittance to • **lock someone up** *You're mad. You should be locked up.* = **imprison**, jail, confine, cage, detain, shut up, incarcerate, send down (*informal*), send to prison, put behind bars

lock² NOUN *She brushed a lock of hair off his forehead.* = **strand**, curl, tuft, tress, ringlet

lodge NOUN **1** *a ski lodge* = **cabin**, house, shelter, cottage, hut, chalet, gatehouse, hunting lodge **2** *My father would occasionally go to his Masonic lodge.* = **society**, group, club, association, section, wing, chapter, branch, assemblage ▶ VERB **1** *He has four weeks in which to lodge an appeal.* = **register**, put, place, set, lay, enter, file, deposit, submit, put on record **2** *She lodged with a farming family.* = **stay**, room, stop (*Brit. informal*), board, reside (*formal*), sojourn **3** *They questioned me, then lodged me in a children's home.* = **accommodate**, house, shelter, put up, entertain, harbour, quarter, billet **4** *The bullet lodged in the sergeant's leg.* = **stick**, remain, catch, implant, come to rest, become fixed, imbed

lodger NOUN = **tenant**, roomer, guest, resident, boarder, paying guest

lodging NOUN (*often plural*)
= **accommodation**, rooms, boarding, apartments, quarters, digs (*Brit. informal*), shelter, residence, dwelling (*formal, literary*), abode, habitation (*formal*), bachelor apartment (*Canad.*)

lofty ADJECTIVE **1** *Amid the chaos, he had lofty aims.* = **noble**, grand, distinguished, superior, imposing, renowned, elevated, majestic, dignified, stately, sublime, illustrious, exalted ■ OPPOSITE: humble **2** *a light, lofty apartment* = **high**, raised, towering, tall, soaring, elevated, sky-high
■ OPPOSITE: low **3** *the lofty disdain he often expresses for his profession* = **haughty**, lordly, proud, arrogant, patronizing, condescending, snooty (*informal*), disdainful, supercilious, high and mighty (*informal*), toffee-nosed (*slang, chiefly Brit.*)
■ OPPOSITE: modest

log NOUN **1** *He dumped the logs on the big stone hearth.* = **stump**, block, branch, chunk, trunk, bole, piece of timber **2** *The complaint was recorded in the ship's log.* = **record**, listing, account, register, journal, chart, diary, tally, logbook, daybook, blog (*informal*)
▶ VERB *Details of the crime are logged in the computer.* = **record**, report, enter, book, note, register, chart, put down, tally, set down, make a note of

loggerhead NOUN • **at loggerheads**
= **quarrelling**, opposed, feuding, at odds, estranged, in dispute, at each other's throats, at daggers drawn, at enmity

logic NOUN **1** *Students learn philosophy and logic.* = **science of reasoning**, deduction, dialectics, argumentation, ratiocination, syllogistic reasoning **2** *I don't follow the logic of your argument.* = **connection**, rationale, coherence, relationship, link, chain of thought **3** *The plan was based on sound commercial logic.* = **reason**, reasoning, sense, good reason, good sense, sound judgment

logical ADJECTIVE **1** *a logical argument* = **rational**, clear, reasoned, reasonable, sound, relevant, consistent, valid, coherent, pertinent, well-organized, cogent, well-reasoned, deducible
■ OPPOSITE: illogical **2** *There was a logical explanation.* = **reasonable**, obvious, sensible, most likely, natural, necessary, wise, plausible, judicious
■ OPPOSITE: unlikely

logistics NOUN = **organization**, management, strategy, engineering, plans, masterminding, coordination, orchestration

loiter VERB = **linger**, idle, loaf, saunter, delay, stroll, lag, dally, loll, dawdle, skulk, dilly-dally (*informal*), hang about or around

loll VERB **1** *He lolled back in his comfortable chair.* = **lounge**, relax, lean, slump, flop, sprawl, loaf, slouch, recline, outspan (*S. African*) **2** *his tongue lolling out of the side of his mouth* = **droop**, drop, hang, flop, flap, dangle, sag, hang loosely

lone ADJECTIVE **1** *a lone woman motorist* = **solitary**, single, separate, one, only, sole, by yourself, unaccompanied **2** *a lone tree on a hill* = **isolated**, deserted, remote, secluded, lonesome (*chiefly U.S. & Canad.*), godforsaken

loneliness NOUN = **solitude**, isolation, desolation, seclusion, aloneness, dreariness, solitariness, forlornness, lonesomeness (*chiefly U.S. & Canad.*), desertedness

lonely ADJECTIVE **1** *lonely people who just want to talk* = **solitary**, alone, isolated, abandoned, lone, withdrawn, single, estranged, outcast, forsaken, forlorn, destitute, by yourself, lonesome (*chiefly U.S. & Canad.*), friendless, companionless ■ **OPPOSITE:** accompanied **2** *dark, lonely streets* = **desolate**, deserted, remote, isolated, solitary, out-of-the-way, secluded, uninhabited, sequestered, off the beaten track (*informal*), godforsaken, unfrequented ■ **OPPOSITE:** crowded

loner NOUN = **individualist**, outsider, solitary, maverick, hermit, recluse, misanthrope, lone wolf

lonesome ADJECTIVE = **lonely**, deserted, isolated, lone, gloomy, dreary, desolate, forlorn, friendless, cheerless, companionless

long¹ ADJECTIVE **1** *Her legs were long and thin.* = **elongated**, extended, stretched, expanded, extensive, lengthy, far-reaching, spread out ■ **OPPOSITE:** short **2** *This is a long film, three hours and seven minutes.* = **prolonged**, slow, dragging, sustained, lengthy, lingering, protracted, interminable, spun out, long-drawn-out ■ **OPPOSITE:** brief

long² VERB *He longed for the good old days.* = **desire**, want, wish, burn, dream of, pine, hunger, ache, lust, crave, yearn, covet, itch, hanker, set your heart on, eat your heart out over

long-drawn-out ADJECTIVE = **prolonged**, marathon, lengthy, protracted, interminable, spun out, dragged out, overlong, overextended

longing NOUN *He felt a longing for the familiar.* = **desire**, hope, wish, burning, urge, ambition, hunger, yen (*informal*), hungering, aspiration, ache, craving, yearning, coveting, itch, thirst, hankering ■ **OPPOSITE:** indifference ▶ ADJECTIVE *sharp intakes of breath and longing looks* = **yearning**, anxious, eager, burning, hungry, pining, craving, languishing, ardent, avid, wishful, wistful, desirous ■ **OPPOSITE:** indifferent

long-lived ADJECTIVE = **long-lasting**, enduring, full of years, old as Methuselah, longevous (*rare*)

long-standing ADJECTIVE = **established**, fixed, enduring, abiding, long-lasting, long-lived, long-established, time-honoured

long-suffering ADJECTIVE = **uncomplaining**, patient, resigned, forgiving, tolerant, easy-going, stoical, forbearing

long-winded ADJECTIVE = **rambling**, prolonged, lengthy, tedious, diffuse, tiresome, wordy, long-drawn-out, garrulous, discursive, repetitious, overlong, verbose, prolix ■ **OPPOSITE:** brief

look VERB **1** *She turned to look at him.* = **see**, view, consider, watch, eye, study, check, regard, survey, clock (*Brit. slang*), examine, observe, stare, glance, gaze, scan, check out (*informal*), inspect, gape, peep, behold (*archaic*), goggle, eyeball (*slang*), scrutinize, ogle, gawp (*Brit. slang*), gawk, recce (*slang*), get a load of (*informal*), take a gander at (*informal*), rubberneck (*slang*), take a dekko at (*Brit. slang*), feast your eyes upon **2** *Have you looked on the piano?* = **search**, seek, hunt, forage, fossick (*Austral. & N.Z.*) **3** *Next term we'll be looking at the Second World War period.* = **consider**, contemplate **4** *The terrace looks onto the sea.* = **face**, overlook, front on, give onto **5** *We're not looking to make a fortune.* = **hope**, expect, await, anticipate, reckon on **6** *She was looking miserable.* = **seem**, appear, display, seem to be, look like, exhibit, manifest, strike you as ▶ NOUN **1** *She took a last look in the mirror.* = **glimpse**, view, glance, observation, review, survey, sight, examination, gaze, inspection, peek, squint (*informal*), butcher's (*Brit. slang*), gander (*informal*), once-over (*informal*), recce (*slang*), eyeful (*informal*), look-see (*slang*), shufti (*Brit. slang*) **2** *They've opted for a rustic look in the kitchen.* = **appearance**, effect, bearing, face, air, style, fashion, cast, aspect, manner, expression, impression, complexion, guise, countenance (*literary*), semblance, demeanour, mien (*literary*) • **look after something** or **someone** *I love looking after the children.* = **take care of**, mind, watch, protect, tend, guard, nurse, care for, supervise, sit with, attend to, keep an eye on, take charge of • **look down on** or **upon someone** *I wasn't successful, so they looked down on me.* = **disdain**, despise, scorn, sneer at, spurn, hold in contempt, treat with contempt, turn your nose up (at) (*informal*), contemn (*formal*), look down your nose at (*informal*), misprize • **look forward to something** *He was looking forward to working with the new Prime Minister.* = **anticipate**, expect, look for, wait for, await, hope for, long for, count on, count the days until, set your heart on • **look out for something** *What are the symptoms to look out for?* = **be careful of**, beware, watch out for, pay attention to, be wary of, be alert to, be vigilant about, keep an eye out for, be on guard for, keep your eyes open for, keep your eyes peeled for, keep your eyes skinned for, be on the qui vive for • **look over something** *He could have looked over the papers in less than ten minutes.* = **examine**, view, check, monitor, scan, check out (*informal*), inspect, look through, eyeball (*slang*), work over, flick through, peruse, cast an eye over, take a dekko at (*Brit. slang*) • **look someone up** *She looked up some friends of bygone years.* = **visit**, call on, go to see, pay a visit to, drop in on (*informal*), look in on • **look something up** *More people use the internet to look up phone numbers.* = **research**, find, search for, hunt for, track down, seek out • **look up** *Things are looking up in the computer industry.* = **improve**, develop, advance, pick up, progress, come along, get better, shape up (*informal*), perk up, ameliorate, show improvement • **look up to someone** *A lot of the younger girls look up to you.* = **respect**, honour, admire, esteem, revere, defer to, have a high opinion of, regard highly, think highly of

lookalike NOUN = **double**, twin, clone, replica, spit (*informal, chiefly Brit.*), ringer (*slang*), spitting image (*informal*), dead ringer (*slang*), living image, exact match, spit and image (*informal*)

lookout NOUN **1** *One committed the burglary and the other acted as lookout.* = **watchman**, guard, sentry, sentinel, vedette (*Military*) **2** *He denied that he had failed to keep a proper lookout during the night.* = **watch**, guard, vigil, qui vive **3** *Troops tried to set up a lookout post inside a refugee camp.* = **watchtower**, post, tower, beacon, observatory, citadel, observation post **4** *It was your lookout if you put your life in danger.* = **concern**, business, worry, funeral (*informal*), pigeon (*Brit. informal*)

loom VERB **1** *the bleak mountains that loomed out of the blackness* = **appear**, emerge, hover, take shape, threaten, bulk, menace, come into view, become visible **2** *He loomed over me.* = **overhang**, rise, mount, dominate, tower, soar, overshadow, hang over, rise up, overtop

loop NOUN *She reached for a loop of garden hose.* = **curve**, ring, circle, bend, twist, curl, spiral, hoop, coil, loophole, twirl, kink, noose, whorl, eyelet, convolution ▸ VERB *He looped the rope over the wood.* = **twist**, turn, join, roll, circle, connect, bend, fold, knot, curl, spiral, coil, braid, encircle, wind round, curve round

loophole NOUN = **let-out**, escape, excuse, plea, avoidance, evasion, pretence, pretext, subterfuge, means of escape

loose ADJECTIVE **1** *A page came loose and floated onto the tiles.* = **free**, detached, insecure, unfettered, released, floating, wobbly, unsecured, unrestricted, untied, unattached, movable, unfastened, unbound, unconfined **2** *Wear loose clothes as they're more comfortable.* = **slack**, easy, hanging, relaxed, loosened, not fitting, sloppy, baggy, slackened, loose-fitting, not tight ■ OPPOSITE: tight **3** *loose morals* = **promiscuous**, fast, abandoned, immoral, dissipated, lewd, wanton, profligate, disreputable, debauched, dissolute, libertine, licentious, unchaste ■ OPPOSITE: chaste **4** *We came to some sort of loose arrangement before he went home.* = **vague**, random, inaccurate, disordered, rambling, diffuse, indefinite, disconnected, imprecise, ill-defined, indistinct, inexact ■ OPPOSITE: precise ▸ VERB *He loosed his grip on the rifle.* = **free**, release, ease, liberate, detach, unleash, let go, undo, loosen, disconnect, set free, slacken, untie, disengage, unfasten, unbind, unloose, unbridle ■ OPPOSITE: fasten

loosen VERB *He loosened the scarf around his neck.* = **untie**, undo, release, separate, detach, let out, unstick, slacken, unbind, work free, work loose, unloose • **loosen up** *Relax, smile; loosen up in mind and body.* = **relax**, chill (*slang*), soften, unwind, go easy (*informal*), lighten up (*slang*), hang loose (*slang*), outspan (*S. African*), ease up or off

loot VERB *Gangs began breaking windows and looting shops.* = **plunder**, rob, raid, sack, rifle, ravage, ransack, pillage, despoil (*formal*) ▸ NOUN *They steal in order to sell their loot for cash.* = **plunder**, goods, prize, haul, spoils, booty, swag (*slang*)

lop VERB = **cut**, crop, chop, trim, clip, dock, hack, detach, prune, shorten, sever, curtail, truncate

lope VERB = **stride**, spring, bound, gallop, canter, lollop

lopsided ADJECTIVE = **crooked**, one-sided, tilting, warped, uneven, unequal, disproportionate, squint, unbalanced, off balance, awry, askew, out of shape, asymmetrical, cockeyed (*informal*), out of true, skewwhiff (*Brit. informal*)

lord NOUN **1** *She married a lord and lives in a huge house in the country.* = **peer**, nobleman, count, duke, gentleman, earl, noble, baron, aristocrat, viscount, childe (*archaic*) **2** *It was the home of the powerful lords of Baux.* = **ruler**, leader, chief, king, prince, master, governor, commander, superior, monarch, sovereign, liege, overlord, potentate, seigneur • **lord it over someone** *Alex seemed to enjoy lording it over the rest of us.* = **boss around** or **about** (*informal*), order around, threaten, bully, menace, intimidate, hector, bluster, browbeat, ride roughshod over, pull rank on, tyrannize, put on airs, be overbearing, act big (*slang*), overbear, play the lord, domineer • **the Lord** or **Our Lord** = **Jesus Christ**, God, Christ, Messiah, Jehovah, the Almighty, the Galilean, the Good Shepherd, the Nazarene

lore NOUN = **traditions**, sayings, experience, saws, teaching, beliefs, wisdom, doctrine, mythos, folk-wisdom, traditional wisdom

lose VERB **1** *The government lost the argument over the pace of reform.* = **be defeated**, be beaten, lose out, be worsted, come to grief, come a cropper (*informal*), be the loser, suffer defeat, get the worst of, take a licking (*informal*), crash out **2** *I lost my keys.* = **mislay**, miss, drop, forget, displace, be deprived of, fail to keep, lose track of, suffer loss, misplace **3** *He lost his licence.* = **forfeit**, miss, fail, yield, default, be deprived of, pass up (*informal*), lose out on (*informal*) **4** *He stands to lose millions of pounds.* = **waste**, consume, squander, drain, exhaust, lavish, deplete, use up, dissipate, expend, misspend **5** *The men lost their way in a sandstorm.* = **stray from**, miss, confuse, wander from **6** *I couldn't lose him, but he couldn't overtake.* = **escape from**, pass, leave behind, evade, lap, duck (*informal*), dodge, shake off, elude, slip away from, outstrip, throw off, outrun, outdistance, give someone the slip

loser NOUN = **failure**, flop (*informal*), underdog, also-ran, no-hoper (*Austral. slang*), dud (*informal*), lemon (*slang*), clinker (*slang, chiefly U.S.*), washout (*informal*), non-achiever, luser (*Computing slang*)

loss NOUN **1** *The loss of income is about £250 million.* = **losing**, waste, disappearance,

deprivation, squandering, drain, forfeiture ■ **OPPOSITE:** gain **2** (*sometimes plural*) *The company will cease operating due to continued losses.* = **deficit**, debt, deficiency, debit, depletion, shrinkage, losings ■ **OPPOSITE:** gain **3** *His death is a great loss to us.* = **damage**, cost, injury, hurt, harm, disadvantage, detriment, impairment ■ **OPPOSITE:** advantage ▶ PLURAL NOUN *Enemy losses were said to be high.* = **casualties**, dead, victims, death toll, fatalities, number killed, number wounded • **at a loss** *I was at a loss for what to do next.* = **confused**, puzzled, baffled, bewildered, stuck (*informal*), helpless, stumped, perplexed, mystified, nonplussed, at your wits' end

lost ADJECTIVE **1** *a lost book* = **missing**, missed, disappeared, vanished, strayed, wayward, forfeited, misplaced, mislaid **2** *I feel lost and lonely in a strange town.* = **bewildered**, confused, puzzled, baffled, helpless, ignorant, perplexed, mystified, clueless (*slang*) **3** *a lost opportunity* = **wasted**, consumed, neglected, misused, squandered, forfeited, dissipated, misdirected, frittered away, misspent, misapplied **4** *The sense of community is lost.* = **gone**, finished, destroyed, vanished, extinct, defunct, died out **5** *the relics of a lost civilization* = **past**, former, gone, dead, forgotten, lapsed, extinct, obsolete, out-of-date, bygone, unremembered **6** *She was silent for a while, lost in thought.* = **engrossed**, taken up, absorbed, entranced, abstracted, absent, distracted, preoccupied, immersed, dreamy, rapt, spellbound **7** *without honour, without heart ... a lost soul* = **fallen**, corrupt, depraved, wanton, abandoned, damned, profligate, dissolute, licentious, unchaste, irreclaimable

lot NOUN **1** *We've just sacked one lot of builders.* = **bunch** (*informal*), group, crowd, crew (*informal*), set, band, quantity, assortment, consignment **2** *Young people are usually less contented with their lot.* = **destiny**, situation, circumstances, fortune, chance, accident, fate, portion, doom, hazard, plight **3** *The receivers are keen to sell the stores as one lot.* = **share**, group, set, piece, collection, portion, parcel, batch • **a lot** or **lots 1** *A lot of our land is used to grow crops.* = **plenty**, scores, masses (*informal*), load(s) (*informal*), ocean(s), wealth, piles (*informal*), a great deal, quantities, stack(s), heap(s), a good deal, large amount, abundance, reams (*informal*), oodles (*informal*) **2** *They went out a lot when they lived in the city.* = **often**, regularly, a great deal, frequently, a good deal • **draw lots** *Two names were selected by drawing lots.* = **choose**, pick, select, toss up, draw straws (*informal*), throw dice, spin a coin • **throw in your lot with someone** *He has decided to throw in his lot with the far-right groups.* = **join with**, support, join forces with, make common cause with, align yourself with, ally *or* align yourself with, join fortunes with

lotion NOUN = **cream**, solution, balm, salve, liniment, embrocation

lottery NOUN **1** *the national lottery* = **raffle**, draw, lotto (*Brit., N.Z. & S. African*), sweepstake **2** *Which judges are assigned to a case is always a bit of a lottery.* = **gamble**, chance, risk, venture, hazard, toss-up (*informal*)

loud ADJECTIVE **1** *Suddenly there was a loud bang.* = **noisy**, strong, booming, roaring, piercing, thundering, forte (*Music*), turbulent, resounding, deafening, thunderous, rowdy, blaring, strident, boisterous, tumultuous, vociferous, vehement, sonorous, ear-splitting, obstreperous, stentorian, clamorous, ear-piercing, high-sounding ■ **OPPOSITE:** quiet **2** *He liked to shock with his earrings and loud clothes.* = **garish**, bold, glaring, flamboyant, vulgar, brash, tacky (*informal*), flashy, lurid, tasteless, naff (*Brit. slang*), gaudy, tawdry, showy, ostentatious, brassy ■ **OPPOSITE:** sombre **3** *I'm just not a loud person. I'm not a look-at-me type.* = **loud-mouthed**, offensive, crude, coarse, vulgar, brash, crass, raucous, brazen (*informal*) ■ **OPPOSITE:** quiet

loudly ADVERB = **noisily**, vigorously, vehemently, vociferously, uproariously, lustily, shrilly, fortissimo (*Music*), at full volume, deafeningly, at the top of your voice, clamorously

lounge VERB *They ate and drank and lounged in the shade.* = **relax**, pass time, hang out (*informal*), idle, loaf, potter, sprawl, lie about, waste time, recline, take it easy, saunter, loiter, loll, dawdle, laze, kill time, make yourself at home, veg out (*slang*), outspan (*S. African*), fritter time away ▶ NOUN *They sat before a roaring fire in the lounge.* = **sitting room** (*Brit.*), living room, parlour (*old-fashioned*), drawing room, front room, reception room, television room

louring *or* **lowering** ADJECTIVE **1** *a heavy, louring sky* = **darkening**, threatening, forbidding, menacing, black, heavy, dark, grey, clouded, gloomy, ominous, cloudy, overcast, foreboding **2** *We walked in fear of his lowering temperament.* = **glowering**, forbidding, grim, frowning, brooding, scowling, sullen, surly

lousy ADJECTIVE **1** *The menu is limited and the food is lousy.* = **inferior**, bad, poor, terrible, awful, no good, miserable, rotten (*informal*), duff (*Brit. informal*), second-rate, shoddy, low-rent (*informal, chiefly U.S.*), for the birds (*informal*), two-bit (*U.S. & Canad. slang*), slovenly, poxy (*slang*), dime-a-dozen (*informal*), bush-league (*Austral. & N.Z. informal*), not much cop (*Brit. slang*), tinhorn (*U.S. slang*), of a sort *or* of sorts, strictly for the birds (*informal*), bodger *or* bodgie (*Austral. slang*) **2** *This is just lousy, cheap, fraudulent behaviour from the government.* = **mean**, low, base, dirty, vicious, rotten (*informal*), vile, despicable, hateful, contemptible **3** (*with* **with**) *a hotel lousy with fleas* = **well-supplied with**, rolling in (*slang*), not short of, amply supplied with

lout NOUN = **oaf**, boor, bear, ned (*Scot. slang*), yahoo, hoon (*Austral. & N.Z. slang*), clod, bumpkin, gawk, dolt, churl, lubber, lummox (*informal*), clumsy idiot, yob *or* yobbo (*Brit. slang*), cougan (*Austral. slang*), scozza (*Austral. slang*), bogan (*Austral. slang*)

lovable *or* **loveable** ADJECTIVE = **endearing**, attractive, engaging, charming, winning, pleasing, sweet, lovely, fetching (*informal*), delightful, cute, enchanting, captivating, cuddly, amiable, adorable, winsome, likable *or* likeable ■ **OPPOSITE:** detestable

love VERB **1** *We love each other, and we want to spend our lives together.* = **adore**, care for, treasure, cherish, prize, worship, be devoted to, be attached to, be in love with, dote on, hold dear, think the world of, idolize, feel affection for, have affection for, adulate ■ **OPPOSITE:** hate **2** *We loved the food so much, especially the fish dishes.* = **enjoy**, like, desire, fancy (*informal*), appreciate, relish, delight in, savour, take pleasure in, have a soft spot for, be partial to, have a weakness for ■ **OPPOSITE:** dislike **3** *the loving and talking that marked an earlier stage of the relationship* = **cuddle**, neck (*informal*), kiss, pet (*informal*), embrace, caress, fondle, canoodle (*slang*) ▶ NOUN **1** *Our love for each other has been increased by what we've been through together.* = **passion**, liking, regard, friendship, affection, warmth, attachment, intimacy, devotion, tenderness, fondness, rapture, adulation, adoration, infatuation, ardour, endearment, aroha (*N.Z.*), amity ■ **OPPOSITE:** hatred **2** *a love of literature* = **liking**, taste, delight in, bent for, weakness for, relish for, enjoyment, devotion to, penchant for, inclination for, zest for, fondness for, soft spot for, partiality to **3** *Don't cry, my love.* = **beloved**, dear, dearest, sweet, lover, angel (*informal*), darling, honey, loved one, sweetheart, truelove, dear one, leman (*archaic*), inamorata or inamorato, bae (*U.S. informal*) ■ **OPPOSITE:** enemy **4** *a manifestation of his love for his fellow men* = **sympathy**, understanding, heart, charity, pity, humanity, warmth, mercy, sorrow, kindness, tenderness, friendliness, condolence, commiseration, fellow feeling, soft-heartedness, tender-heartedness, aroha (*N.Z.*) • **fall in love with someone** *I fell in love with him the moment I saw him.* = **lose your heart to**, fall for, be taken with, take a shine to (*informal*), become infatuated with, fall head over heels in love with, be swept off your feet by, bestow your affections on • **for love** *She does it for love – not money.* = **without payment**, freely, for nothing, free of charge, gratis, pleasurably • **for love or money** *Replacement parts couldn't be found for love or money.* = **by any means**, ever, under any conditions • **in love** *She had never before been in love.* = **enamoured**, charmed, captivated, smitten, wild (*informal*), mad (*informal*), crazy (*informal*), enthralled, besotted, infatuated, enraptured • **make love** = **have sexual intercourse**, have sex, go to bed, sleep together, have sexual relations, have it off (*slang*) ■ **RELATED WORD:** *adjective* amatory

love affair NOUN *a love affair with a married man* = **romance**, relationship, affair, intrigue, liaison, amour, affaire de coeur (*French*)

loveless ADJECTIVE **1** *She is in a loveless relationship.* = **unloving**, hard, cold, icy, insensitive, unfriendly, heartless, frigid, unresponsive, unfeeling, cold-hearted **2** *trapped by her social position into a lonely, loveless life* = **unloved**, disliked, forsaken, lovelorn, friendless, unappreciated, unvalued, uncherished

lovelorn ADJECTIVE = **lovesick**, mooning, slighted, pining, yearning, languishing, spurned, jilted, moping, unrequited, crossed in love

lovely ADJECTIVE **1** *You look lovely.* = **beautiful**, appealing, attractive, charming, winning, pretty, sweet, handsome, good-looking, exquisite, admirable, enchanting, graceful, captivating, amiable, adorable, comely, fit (*Brit. informal*) ■ **OPPOSITE:** ugly **2** *What a lovely surprise!* = **wonderful**, pleasing, nice, pleasant, engaging, marvellous, delightful, enjoyable, gratifying, agreeable ■ **OPPOSITE:** horrible

lovemaking NOUN = **sexual intercourse**, intercourse, intimacy, sexual relations, the other (*informal*), mating, nookie (*slang*), copulation, coitus, act of love, carnal knowledge, rumpy-pumpy (*slang*), coition, sexual union or congress, rumpo (*slang*)

lover NOUN = **sweetheart**, beloved, loved one, beau (*old-fashioned*), flame (*informal*), mistress, admirer, suitor, swain (*archaic*), woman friend, lady or gentleman friend, man or woman friend, toy boy, paramour (*old-fashioned*), leman (*archaic*), fancy bit (*slang*), boyfriend or girlfriend, bae (*U.S. informal*), fancy man or fancy woman (*slang*), fiancé or fiancée, inamorata or inamorato

loving ADJECTIVE **1** *a loving husband and father* = **affectionate**, kind, warm, dear, friendly, devoted, tender, fond, ardent, cordial, doting, amorous, solicitous, demonstrative, warm-hearted ■ **OPPOSITE:** cruel **2** *The house has been restored with loving care.* = **tender**, kind, caring, warm, gentle, sympathetic, considerate

low[1] ADJECTIVE **1** *She put it down on the low table.* = **small**, little, short, stunted, squat, fubsy (*archaic, dialect*) ■ **OPPOSITE:** tall **2** *The sun was low in the sky.* = **low-lying**, deep, depressed, shallow, subsided, sunken, ground-level ■ **OPPOSITE:** high **3** *The low prices and friendly service made for a pleasant evening out.* = **inexpensive**, cheap, reasonable, bargain, moderate, modest, cut-price, economical, bargain-basement **4** *They are having to live on very low incomes.* = **meagre**, little, small, reduced, depleted, scant, trifling, insignificant, sparse, paltry, measly (*informal*) ■ **OPPOSITE:** significant **5** *They criticised staff for the low standard of care.* = **inferior**, bad, poor, inadequate, pathetic, worthless, unsatisfactory, mediocre, deficient, second-rate, shoddy, low-grade, puny, substandard, low-rent (*informal, chiefly U.S.*), half-pie (*N.Z. informal*), bodger or bodgie (*Austral. slang*) **6** *Her voice was so low he had to strain to catch it.* = **quiet**, soft, gentle, whispered, muted, subdued, hushed, muffled ■ **OPPOSITE:** loud **7** *'I didn't ask for this job, you know,' he tells friends when he is low.* = **dejected**, down, blue, sad, depressed, unhappy, miserable, fed up, moody, gloomy, dismal, forlorn, glum, despondent, downcast, morose, disheartened, downhearted, down in the dumps (*informal*), sick as a parrot (*informal*), cheesed off (*informal*), brassed off (*Brit. slang*) ■ **OPPOSITE:** happy **8** *The film's low comedy is never unlikeable.* = **coarse**, common, rough, gross, crude, rude, obscene, disgraceful, vulgar, undignified, disreputable, unbecoming, unrefined, dishonourable, ill-bred **9** *That was a really low trick.* = **contemptible**, mean, base, nasty, cowardly, degraded, vulgar, vile, sordid, abject, unworthy, despicable, depraved, menial, reprehensible, dastardly (*old-fashioned*), scurvy (*old-fashioned*), servile, unprincipled, dishonourable, ignoble ■ **OPPOSITE:** honourable **10** *a man of low birth and no breeding* = **lowly**, poor, simple, plain, peasant, obscure, humble, meek, unpretentious, plebeian, lowborn **11** *She's still feeling a bit low after having flu.* = **ill**, weak, exhausted, frail, dying, reduced, sinking, stricken, feeble, debilitated, prostrate ■ **OPPOSITE:** strong • **lie low** *Far from lying low, he became more outspoken than ever.* = **hide**, lurk, hole up, hide away, keep a low profile, hide out, go underground, skulk, go into hiding, take cover, keep out of sight, go to earth, conceal yourself

low² VERB *Cattle were lowing in the barns.* = **moo**, bellow

low-down NOUN *We want you to give us the low-down on your team-mates.* = **information**, intelligence, info (*informal*), inside story, gen (*Brit. informal*), dope (*informal*) ▶ ADJECTIVE *They will stoop to every low-down trick.* = **mean**, low, base, cheap (*informal*), nasty, ugly, despicable, reprehensible, contemptible, underhand, scurvy (*old-fashioned*)

lower ADJECTIVE **1** *the lower ranks of council officers* = **subordinate**, under, smaller, junior, minor, secondary, lesser, low-level, inferior, second-class **2** *You may get it at a slightly lower price.* = **reduced**, cut, diminished, decreased, lessened, curtailed, pared down ■ **OPPOSITE:** increased ▶ VERB **1** *They lowered the coffin into the grave.* = **drop**, sink, depress, let down, submerge, take down, let fall, make lower ■ **OPPOSITE:** raise **2** *a drug which lowers cholesterol levels* = **lessen**, cut, reduce, moderate, diminish, slash, decrease, prune, minimize, curtail, abate ■ **OPPOSITE:** increase **3** *Don't lower yourself. Don't be the way they are.* = **demean**, humble, disgrace, humiliate, degrade, devalue, downgrade, belittle, condescend, debase, deign, abase **4** *He moved closer, lowering his voice.* = **quieten**, soften, hush, tone down

lowering *see* **louring**

low-key ADJECTIVE = **subdued**, quiet, restrained, muted, played down, understated, muffled, toned down, low-pitched

lowly ADJECTIVE **1** *lowly bureaucrats pretending to be senators* = **lowborn**, obscure, subordinate, inferior, mean, proletarian, ignoble, plebeian **2** *He started out as a lowly photographer.* = **unpretentious**, common, poor, average, simple, ordinary, plain, modest, homespun

low-tech ADJECTIVE = **unsophisticated**, simple, basic, elementary ■ **OPPOSITE:** high-tech *or* hi-tech

loyal ADJECTIVE = **faithful**, true, devoted, dependable, constant, attached, patriotic, staunch, trustworthy, trusty, steadfast, dutiful, unwavering, true-blue, immovable, unswerving, tried and true, true-hearted ■ **OPPOSITE:** disloyal

loyalty NOUN = **faithfulness**, commitment, devotion, allegiance, reliability, fidelity, homage, patriotism, obedience, constancy, dependability, trustworthiness, steadfastness, troth (*archaic*), fealty, staunchness, trueness, trustiness, true-heartedness

lozenge NOUN = **tablet**, pastille, troche, cough drop, jujube

lubricate VERB = **oil**, grease, smear, smooth the way, oil the wheels, make smooth, make slippery

lucid ADJECTIVE **1** *His prose is always lucid and compelling.* = **clear**, obvious, plain, evident, distinct, explicit, transparent, clear-cut, crystal clear, comprehensible, intelligible, limpid, pellucid ■ **OPPOSITE:** vague **2** *He wasn't very lucid; he didn't quite know where he was.* = **clear-headed**, sound, reasonable, sensible, rational, sober, all there, sane, compos mentis (*Latin*), in your right mind ■ **OPPOSITE:** confused

luck NOUN **1** *I knew I needed a bit of luck to win.* = **good fortune**, success, advantage, prosperity, break (*informal*), stroke of luck, blessing, windfall, good luck, fluke, godsend, serendipity **2** *The goal owed more to luck than good planning.* = **fortune**, lot, stars, chance, accident, fate, hazard, destiny, hap (*archaic*), twist of fate, fortuity

luckily ADVERB = **fortunately**, happily, by chance, as luck would have it, fortuitously, opportunely, as it chanced

luckless ADJECTIVE = **unlucky**, unfortunate, unsuccessful, hapless, unhappy, disastrous, cursed, hopeless, jinxed, calamitous, ill-starred, star-crossed, unpropitious, ill-fated

lucky ADJECTIVE **1** *I consider myself the luckiest man on the face of the earth.* = **fortunate**, successful, favoured, charmed, blessed, prosperous, jammy (*Brit. slang*), serendipitous ■ **OPPOSITE:** unlucky **2** *They are now desperate* *for a lucky break.* = **fortuitous**, timely, fortunate, auspicious, opportune (*formal*), propitious, providential, adventitious ■ **OPPOSITE:** unlucky

lucrative ADJECTIVE = **profitable**, rewarding, productive, fruitful, paying, high-income, well-paid, money-making, advantageous, gainful, remunerative

ludicrous ADJECTIVE = **ridiculous**, crazy (*informal*), absurd, preposterous, odd, funny, comic, silly, laughable, farcical, outlandish, incongruous, comical, zany, nonsensical, droll, burlesque, cockamamie (*slang, chiefly U.S.*) ■ **OPPOSITE:** sensible

lug VERB = **drag**, carry, pull, haul, tow, yank, hump (*Brit. slang*), heave

luggage NOUN = **baggage**, things, cases, bags, gear, trunks, suitcases, paraphernalia, impedimenta

lugubrious ADJECTIVE = **gloomy**, serious, sad, dismal, melancholy, dreary, sombre, woeful, mournful, morose, sorrowful, funereal, doleful, woebegone, dirgelike

lukewarm ADJECTIVE 1 *Wash your face with lukewarm water.* = **tepid**, warm, blood-warm 2 *The study received a lukewarm response from the Home Secretary.* = **half-hearted**, cold, cool, indifferent, unconcerned, uninterested, apathetic, unresponsive, phlegmatic, unenthusiastic, laodicean

lull NOUN *a lull in the conversation* = **respite**, pause, quiet, silence, calm, hush, tranquillity, stillness, let-up (*informal*), calmness ▶ VERB *It is easy to be lulled into a false sense of security.* = **calm**, soothe, subdue, still, quiet, compose, hush, quell, allay, pacify, lullaby, tranquillize, rock to sleep

lullaby NOUN = **cradlesong**, berceuse

lumber[1] VERB *She was lumbered with a bill for about £90.* = **burden**, land, load, saddle, impose upon, encumber ▶ NOUN *The wheels had been consigned to the loft as useless lumber.* = **junk**, refuse, rubbish, discards, trash (*U.S. & Canad.*), clutter, jumble, white elephants, castoffs, trumpery

lumber[2] VERB *He turned and lumbered back to his chair.* = **plod**, shuffle, shamble, trudge, stump, clump, waddle, trundle, lump along

lumbering ADJECTIVE = **awkward**, heavy, blundering, bumbling, hulking, unwieldy, ponderous, ungainly, elephantine, heavy-footed, lubberly

luminary NOUN = **celebrity**, star, expert, somebody, lion, worthy, notable, big name, dignitary, leading light, celeb (*informal*), personage, megastar (*informal*), fundi (*S. African*), V.I.P.

luminous ADJECTIVE *The luminous dial on the clock showed five minutes to seven.* = **bright**, lighted, lit, brilliant, shining, glowing, vivid, illuminated, radiant, resplendent, lustrous, luminescent

lump[1] NOUN 1 *a lump of wood* = **piece**, group, ball, spot, block, mass, cake, bunch, cluster, chunk, wedge, dab, hunk, nugget, gob, clod, gobbet 2 *I've got a lump on my shoulder.* = **swelling**, growth, bump, tumour, bulge, hump, protuberance, protrusion, tumescence ▶ VERB *These people do not deserve to be lumped together with criminals.* = **group**, throw, mass, combine, collect, unite, pool, bunch, consolidate, aggregate, batch, conglomerate, coalesce, agglutinate

lump[2] VERB • **lump it** *He was going to kick up a fuss, but he realized he'd have to lump it.* = **put up with it**, take it, stand it, bear it, suffer it, hack it (*slang*), tolerate it, endure it, brook it

lumpy ADJECTIVE = **bumpy**, clotted, uneven, knobbly, grainy, curdled, granular, full of lumps

lunacy NOUN *the lunacy of the tax system* = **foolishness**, madness, folly, stupidity, absurdity, aberration, idiocy, craziness, tomfoolery, imbecility, foolhardiness, senselessness ■ **OPPOSITE:** sense

lunatic ADJECTIVE *the operation of the market taken to lunatic extremes* = **mad**, crazy, insane, irrational, nuts (*slang*), barking (*slang*), daft, barmy (*slang*), deranged, bonkers (*slang, chiefly Brit.*), loopy (*informal*), crackpot (*informal*), barking mad (*slang*), crackbrained

lunge VERB *I lunged forward to try to hit him.* = **pounce**, charge, bound, dive, leap, plunge, dash, thrust, poke, jab ▶ NOUN *He knocked on the door and made a lunge for her when she opened it.* = **thrust**, charge, pounce, pass, spring, swing, jab, swipe (*informal*)

lurch VERB 1 *As the car sped over a pothole, she lurched forward.* = **tilt**, roll, pitch, list, rock, lean, heel 2 *Two old men struggled to their feet and lurched out onto the veranda.* = **stagger**, reel, stumble, weave, sway, totter

lure VERB *They did not realise that they were being lured into a trap.* = **tempt**, draw, attract, invite, trick, seduce, entice, beckon, lead on, allure, decoy, ensnare, inveigle ▶ NOUN *The lure of rural life is proving as strong as ever.* = **temptation**, attraction, incentive, bait, carrot (*informal*), magnet, inducement, decoy, enticement, siren song, allurement

lurid ADJECTIVE 1 *lurid accounts of deaths and mutilations* = **sensational**, shocking, disgusting, graphic, violent, savage, startling, grim, exaggerated, revolting, explicit, vivid, ghastly, gruesome, grisly, macabre, melodramatic, yellow (*of journalism*), gory, unrestrained, shock-horror (*facetious*) ■ **OPPOSITE:** mild **2** *She always painted her toenails a lurid red or orange.* = **glaring**, bright, bloody, intense, flaming, vivid, fiery, livid, sanguine, glowering, overbright ■ **OPPOSITE:** pale

lurk VERB = **hide**, sneak, crouch, prowl, snoop, lie in wait, slink, skulk, conceal yourself, move with stealth, go furtively

luscious ADJECTIVE **1** *those luscious lips* = **sexy**, attractive, arousing, erotic, inviting, provocative, seductive, cuddly, sensuous, alluring, voluptuous, kissable, beddable **2** *luscious fruit* = **delicious**, sweet, juicy, rich, honeyed (*poetic*), savoury, succulent, palatable, mouth-watering, delectable, yummy (*slang*), scrumptious (*informal*), appetizing, toothsome, yummo (*Austral. slang*)

lush ADJECTIVE **1** *the lush green meadows* = **abundant**, green, flourishing, lavish, dense, prolific, rank, teeming, overgrown, verdant (*literary*) **2** *The hotel is lush, plush and very non-backpacker.* = **luxurious**, grand, elaborate, lavish, extravagant, sumptuous, plush (*informal*), ornate, opulent, palatial, ritzy (*slang*) **3** *an unusual combination of vegetables and lush fruits* = **succulent**, fresh, tender, ripe, juicy

lust NOUN **1** *His lust grew until it was overpowering.* = **lechery**, sensuality, licentiousness, carnality, the hots (*slang*), libido, lewdness, wantonness, salaciousness, lasciviousness, concupiscence, randiness (*informal, chiefly Brit.*), pruriency **2** *It was his lust for glitz and glamour that was driving them apart.* = **desire**, longing, passion, appetite, craving, greed, thirst, cupidity (*formal*), covetousness, avidity, appetence • **lust for** or **after someone** or **something** *I instinctively sensed he was not to be lusted after.* = **desire**, want, crave, need, yearn for, covet, slaver over, lech after (*informal*), be consumed with desire for, hunger for or after

lustful ADJECTIVE = **lascivious**, sexy (*informal*), passionate, erotic, craving, sensual, randy (*informal, chiefly Brit.*), raunchy (*informal*), horny (*slang*), hankering, lewd, wanton, carnal, prurient, lecherous, hot-blooded, libidinous, licentious, concupiscent, unchaste

lustre NOUN **1** *Gold retains its lustre for far longer than other metals.* = **sparkle**, shine, glow, glitter, dazzle, gleam, gloss,

brilliance, sheen, shimmer, glint, brightness, radiance, burnish, resplendence, lambency, luminousness **2** *The team is relying too much on names that have lost their lustre.* = **glory**, honour, fame, distinction, prestige, renown, illustriousness

lustrous ADJECTIVE = **shining**, bright, glowing, sparkling, dazzling, shiny, gleaming, glossy, shimmering, radiant, luminous, glistening, burnished

lusty ADJECTIVE = **vigorous**, strong, powerful, healthy, strapping, robust, rugged (*U.S. & Canad.*), energetic, sturdy, hale (*old-fashioned*), stout, stalwart, hearty, virile, red-blooded (*informal*), brawny

luxuriant ADJECTIVE **1** *wide spreading branches and luxuriant foliage* = **lush**, rich, dense, abundant, excessive, thriving, flourishing, rank, productive, lavish, ample, fertile, prolific, overflowing, plentiful, exuberant, fruitful, teeming, copious, prodigal, riotous, profuse, fecund, superabundant, plenteous ■ **OPPOSITE:** sparse **2** *luxuriant draperies and soft sofas* = **elaborate**, fancy, decorated, extravagant, flamboyant, baroque, sumptuous, ornate, festooned, flowery, rococo, florid, corinthian ■ **OPPOSITE:** plain

luxuriate VERB **1** *Lie back and luxuriate in the scented oil.* = **enjoy**, delight, indulge, relish, revel, bask, wallow **2** *He retired to luxuriate in Hollywood.* = **live in luxury**, take it easy, live the life of Riley, have the time of your life, be in clover

luxurious ADJECTIVE **1** *a luxurious hotel* = **sumptuous**, expensive, comfortable, magnificent, costly, splendid, lavish, plush (*informal*), opulent, ritzy (*slang*), de luxe, well-appointed **2** *She had come to enjoy this luxurious lifestyle.* = **self-indulgent**, pleasure-loving, sensual, pampered, voluptuous, sybaritic, epicurean ■ **OPPOSITE:** austere

> **USAGE** *Luxurious* is sometimes wrongly used where *luxuriant* is meant: *he had a luxuriant (not luxurious) moustache; the walls were covered with a luxuriant growth of wisteria.*

luxury NOUN **1** *She was brought up in an atmosphere of luxury and wealth.* = **opulence**, splendour, richness, extravagance, affluence, hedonism, a bed of roses, voluptuousness, the life of Riley, sumptuousness ■ **OPPOSITE:** poverty **2** *We never had money for little luxuries.* = **extravagance**, treat, extra, indulgence, frill, nonessential ■ **OPPOSITE:** necessity **3** *Relax in the luxury of a Roman-style bath.*

= **pleasure**, delight, comfort, satisfaction, enjoyment, bliss, indulgence, gratification, wellbeing ■ **OPPOSITE:** discomfort

lyric ADJECTIVE **1** (*of poetry*) *His splendid short stories and lyric poetry.* = **songlike**, musical, lyrical, expressive, melodic **2** (*of a voice*) *her fresh, beautiful, lyric voice* = **melodic**, clear, light, flowing, graceful, mellifluous, dulcet

lyrical ADJECTIVE = **enthusiastic**, emotional, inspired, poetic, carried away, ecstatic, expressive, impassioned, rapturous, effusive, rhapsodic

Mm

macabre ADJECTIVE = **gruesome**, grim, ghastly, frightening, ghostly, weird, dreadful, unearthly, hideous, eerie, grisly, horrid, morbid, frightful, ghoulish ■ **OPPOSITE:** delightful

Machiavellian ADJECTIVE = **scheming**, cynical, shrewd, cunning, designing, intriguing, sly, astute, unscrupulous, wily, opportunist, crafty, artful, amoral, foxy, deceitful, underhand, double-dealing, perfidious (*literary*)

machine NOUN **1** *I put a coin in the machine and pulled the lever.* = **appliance**, device, apparatus, engine (*obsolete*), tool, instrument, mechanism, gadget, contraption (*informal*), gizmo (*informal*), contrivance **2** *He has put the party publicity machine behind another candidate.* = **system**, agency, structure, organization, machinery, setup (*informal*)

machinery NOUN **1** *Farmers import most of their machinery and materials.* = **equipment**, gear, instruments, apparatus, works, technology, tackle, tools, mechanism(s), gadgetry **2** *the government machinery and administrative procedures* = **administration**, system, organization, agency, machine, structure, channels, procedure

macho ADJECTIVE = **manly**, masculine, butch (*slang*), two-fisted, tough, chauvinist, virile, he-man

mad ADJECTIVE **1** *Isn't that a rather mad idea?* = **foolish**, absurd, wild, stupid, daft (*informal*), ludicrous, unreasonable, irrational, unsafe, senseless, preposterous, foolhardy, nonsensical, unsound, inane, imprudent, asinine ■ **OPPOSITE:** sensible **2** *I'm pretty mad about it, I can tell you.* = **angry**, cross, furious, irritated, fuming, choked, infuriated, raging, ape (*slang*), incensed, enraged, exasperated, irate, livid (*informal*), berserk, seeing red (*informal*), incandescent, wrathful, fit to be tied (*slang*), in a wax (*informal, chiefly Brit.*), berko (*Austral. slang*), tooshie (*Austral. slang*), off the air (*Austral. slang*) ■ **OPPOSITE:** calm **3** (*usually with* **about**) *He's mad about you.* = **enthusiastic**, wild, crazy (*informal*), nuts (*slang*), keen, hooked,

devoted, in love with, fond, daft (*informal*), ardent, fanatical, avid, impassioned, zealous, infatuated, dotty (*slang, chiefly Brit.*), enamoured ■ **OPPOSITE:** nonchalant **4** *The game is a mad dash against the clock.* = **frenzied**, wild, excited, energetic, abandoned, agitated, frenetic, uncontrolled, boisterous, full-on (*informal*), ebullient, gay, riotous, unrestrained

madcap ADJECTIVE *They flitted from one madcap scheme to another.* = **reckless**, rash, impulsive, ill-advised, wild, crazy (*informal*), foolhardy, thoughtless, crackpot (*informal*), hot-headed, imprudent, heedless, hare-brained ▶ NOUN *Madcap Mark Roberts can be seen doing dangerous stunts in the countryside.* = **daredevil**, tearaway, wild person, hothead

madden VERB = **infuriate**, irritate, incense, enrage, upset, provoke, annoy, aggravate (*informal*), gall, craze, inflame, exasperate, vex, unhinge, drive you crazy, nark (*Brit., Austral. & N.Z. slang*), drive you round the bend (*Brit. slang*), make your blood boil, drive you to distraction (*informal*), get your goat (*slang*), drive you round the twist (*Brit. slang*), get your dander up (*informal*), make your hackles rise, raise your hackles, drive you off your head (*slang*), drive you out of your mind, get your back up, get your hackles up, make you see red (*informal*), put your back up, hack you off (*informal*) ■ **OPPOSITE:** calm

made-up ADJECTIVE **1** *heavily made-up face* = **painted**, powdered, rouged, done up **2** *It looks like a made-up word to me.* = **false**, invented, imaginary, fictional, untrue, mythical, unreal, fabricated, make-believe, trumped-up, specious

madly ADVERB **1** *She has fallen madly in love with him.* = **passionately**, wildly, desperately, intensely, exceedingly, extremely, excessively, to distraction, devotedly **2** *This seemed madly dangerous.* = **foolishly**, wildly, absurdly, ludicrously, unreasonably, irrationally, senselessly, nonsensically **3** *Children ran madly around the tables, shouting and playing.* = **energetically**, quickly, wildly, rapidly, hastily, furiously, excitedly, hurriedly, recklessly, speedily, like mad (*informal*), hell for leather, like lightning, hotfoot, like the clappers (*Brit. informal*), like nobody's business (*informal*), like greased lightning (*informal*)

madness NOUN **1** *It is political madness.* = **foolishness**, nonsense, folly, absurdity, idiocy, wildness, daftness (*informal*), foolhardiness, preposterousness **2** *The country was in a state of madness.* = **frenzy**, riot, furore, uproar, abandon, excitement, agitation, intoxication, unrestraint

maelstrom NOUN **1** *a maelstrom of surf and confused seas* = **whirlpool**, swirl, eddy, vortex, Charybdis (*literary*) **2** *Inside, she was a maelstrom of churning emotions.* = **turmoil**, disorder, confusion, chaos, upheaval, uproar, pandemonium, bedlam, tumult

maestro NOUN = **master**, expert, genius, virtuoso, wonk (*informal*), fundi (*S. African*)

magazine NOUN = **journal**, paper, publication, supplement, rag (*informal*), issue, glossy (*informal*), pamphlet, periodical, fanzine (*informal*), ezine or e-zine

magic NOUN **1** *Legends say that Merlin raised the stones by magic.* = **sorcery**, wizardry, witchcraft, enchantment, occultism, black art, spells, necromancy, sortilege, theurgy **2** *His secret hobby: performing magic.* = **conjuring**, illusion, trickery, sleight of hand, hocus-pocus, jiggery-pokery (*informal, chiefly Brit.*), legerdemain, prestidigitation, jugglery **3** *The singer believes he can still regain some of his old magic.* = **charm**, power, glamour, fascination, magnetism, enchantment, allurement, mojo (*slang*) ▶ ADJECTIVE *Then came those magic moments in the rose-garden.* = **miraculous**, entrancing, charming, fascinating, marvellous, magical, magnetic, enchanting, bewitching, spellbinding, sorcerous

magician NOUN **1** *It was like watching a magician showing you how he performs a trick.* = **conjuror**, illusionist, prestidigitator **2** *Uther called on Merlin the magician to help him.* = **sorcerer**, witch, wizard, illusionist, warlock, necromancer, thaumaturge (*rare*), theurgist, archimage (*rare*), enchanter or enchantress **3** *He was a magician with words.* = **miracle-worker**, genius, marvel, wizard, virtuoso, wonder-worker, spellbinder

magisterial ADJECTIVE = **authoritative**, lordly, commanding, masterful, imperious ■ OPPOSITE: subservient

magistrate NOUN = **judge**, justice, provost (*Scot.*), bailie (*Scot.*), justice of the peace, J.P. ■ RELATED WORD: *adjective* magisterial

magnanimous ADJECTIVE = **generous**, kind, noble, selfless, big, free, kindly, handsome, charitable, high-minded, bountiful, unselfish, open-handed, big-hearted, unstinting, beneficent, great-hearted, munificent, ungrudging ■ OPPOSITE: petty

magnate NOUN = **tycoon**, leader, chief, fat cat (*slang*), baron, notable, mogul, bigwig (*informal*), grandee, big shot (*informal*), captain of industry, big wheel (*slang*), big cheese (*slang, old-fashioned*), plutocrat, big noise (*informal*), big hitter (*informal*), magnifico, heavy hitter (*informal*), nabob (*informal*), Mister Big (*slang, chiefly U.S.*), V.I.P.

magnetic ADJECTIVE = **attractive**, irresistible, seductive, captivating, charming, fascinating, entrancing, charismatic, enchanting, hypnotic, alluring, mesmerizing ■ OPPOSITE: repulsive

magnetism NOUN = **charm**, appeal, attraction, power, draw (*informal*), pull, spell, magic, fascination, charisma, attractiveness, allure, enchantment, hypnotism, drawing power, seductiveness, mesmerism, captivatingness

magnification NOUN **1** *a magnification of the human eye* = **enlargement**, increase, inflation, boost, expansion, blow-up (*informal*), intensification, amplification, dilation, augmentation **2** *the magnification of this character on the screen* = **exaggeration**, build-up, heightening, deepening, enhancement, aggrandizement

magnificence NOUN = **splendour**, glory, majesty, grandeur, brilliance, nobility, gorgeousness, sumptuousness, sublimity, resplendence

magnificent ADJECTIVE **1** *a magnificent country house in wooded grounds* = **splendid**, striking, grand, impressive, august, rich, princely, imposing, elegant, divine (*informal*), glorious, noble, gorgeous, lavish, elevated, luxurious, majestic, regal, stately, sublime, sumptuous, grandiose, exalted, opulent, transcendent, resplendent, splendiferous (*facetious*) ■ OPPOSITE: ordinary **2** *She is magnificent at making you feel able to talk.* = **brilliant**, fine, excellent, outstanding, superb, superior, splendid

magnify VERB **1** *The telescope magnifies images over 11 times.* = **enlarge**, increase, boost, expand, intensify, blow up (*informal*), heighten, amplify, augment, dilate ■ OPPOSITE: reduce **2** *Poverty and human folly magnify natural disasters.* = **make worse**, exaggerate, intensify, worsen, heighten, deepen, exacerbate, aggravate, increase, inflame, fan the flames of **3** *spend their time magnifying ridiculous details* = **exaggerate**, overdo, overstate, build up, enhance, blow up, inflate, overestimate, dramatize, overrate, overplay, overemphasize, blow up out of all proportion, aggrandize, make a production (out) of (*informal*), make a federal case of (*U.S. informal*) ■ OPPOSITE: understate

magnitude NOUN **1** *An operation of this magnitude is going to be difficult.*
= **importance**, consequence, significance, mark, moment, note, weight, proportion, dimension, greatness, grandeur, eminence ■ **OPPOSITE:** unimportance **2** *the magnitude of the task confronting them* = **immensity**, size, extent, enormity (*informal*), strength, volume, vastness, bigness, largeness, hugeness ■ **OPPOSITE:** smallness **3** *a quake with a magnitude exceeding 5* = **intensity**, measure, capacity, amplitude

maid NOUN **1** *A maid brought me breakfast at half past eight.* = **servant**, chambermaid, housemaid, menial, handmaiden (*archaic*), maidservant, female servant, domestic (*archaic*), parlourmaid, serving-maid **2** *But can he win back the heart of this fair maid?* = **girl**, maiden (*archaic, literary*), lass, miss (*old-fashioned or derogatory*), nymph (*poetic*), damsel, lassie (*informal*)

maiden NOUN *stories of brave princes and beautiful maidens* = **girl**, maid (*archaic, literary*), lass, damsel (*archaic, poetic*), miss (*old-fashioned or derogatory*), virgin, nymph (*poetic*), lassie (*informal*)
▶ MODIFIER **1** *The Titanic sank on its maiden voyage.* = **first**, initial, inaugural, introductory, initiatory **2** *An elderly maiden aunt had left him £1000.* = **unmarried**, pure, virgin, intact, chaste, virginal, unwed, undefiled

mail NOUN **1** *She looked through the mail.* = **letters**, post, packages, parcels, correspondence **2** *The parcel is in the mail.* = **postal service**, post, postal system
▶ VERB **1** *He mailed me the contract.* = **post**, send, forward, dispatch, send by mail *or* post **2** *You can write or mail your CV to us.* = **email** *or* **e-mail**, send, forward

maim VERB = **cripple**, hurt, injure, wound, disable, hamstring, impair, lame, mutilate, incapacitate, put out of action

main ADJECTIVE *My main concern now is to protect the children.* = **chief**, leading, major, prime, head, special, central, particular, necessary, essential, premier, primary, vital, critical, crucial, supreme, outstanding, principal, cardinal, paramount, foremost, predominant, pre-eminent, must-have ■ **OPPOSITE:** minor ▶ PLURAL NOUN **1** *the water supply from the mains* = **pipeline**, channel, pipe, conduit, duct **2** *amplifiers which plug into the mains* = **cable**, line, electricity supply, mains supply • **in the main** *In the main, children are taboo in the workplace.* = **on the whole**, generally, mainly, mostly, in general, for the most part

mainly ADVERB = **chiefly**, mostly, largely, generally, usually, principally, in general, primarily, above all, substantially, on the whole, predominantly, in the main, for the most part, most of all, first and foremost, to the greatest extent

mainstay NOUN = **pillar**, backbone, bulwark, prop, anchor, buttress, lynchpin, chief support

mainstream ADJECTIVE = **conventional**, general, established, received, accepted, central, current, core, prevailing, orthodox, lamestream (*informal*) ■ **OPPOSITE:** unconventional

maintain VERB **1** *You should always maintain your friendships.* = **continue**, retain, preserve, sustain, carry on, keep, keep up, prolong, uphold, nurture, conserve, perpetuate ■ **OPPOSITE:** end **2** *Prosecutors maintain that no deal was made.* = **assert**, state, hold, claim, insist, declare, allege, contend, affirm, profess, avow, aver, asseverate (*formal*) ■ **OPPOSITE:** disavow **3** *The house costs a fortune to maintain.* = **look after**, care for, take care of, finance, conserve, keep in good condition

maintenance NOUN **1** *the maintenance of government buildings* = **upkeep**, keeping, care, supply, repairs, provision, conservation, nurture, preservation **2** *Absent fathers must pay maintenance for their children.* = **allowance**, living, support, keep, food, livelihood, subsistence, upkeep, sustenance, alimony, aliment **3** *the maintenance of peace and stability* = **continuation**, carrying-on, continuance, support, perpetuation, prolongation, sustainment, retainment

majestic ADJECTIVE = **grand**, magnificent, impressive, superb, kingly, royal, august, princely, imposing, imperial, noble, splendid, elevated, awesome, dignified, regal, stately, monumental, sublime, lofty, pompous, grandiose, exalted, splendiferous (*facetious*) ■ **OPPOSITE:** modest

majesty NOUN = **grandeur**, glory, splendour, magnificence, dignity, nobility, sublimity, loftiness, impressiveness, awesomeness, exaltedness
■ **OPPOSITE:** triviality

major ADJECTIVE **1** *Exercise has a major part to play in combating disease.* = **important**, vital, critical, significant, great, serious, radical, crucial (*informal*), outstanding, grave, extensive, notable, weighty, pre-eminent **2** *We heard extracts from three of his major works.* = **main**, higher, greater, bigger, lead, leading, head, larger, better, chief, senior,

supreme, superior, elder, uppermost
- **OPPOSITE:** minor

majority NOUN **1** *The majority of our customers come from out of town.* = **most**, more, mass, bulk, best part, better part, lion's share, preponderance, plurality, greater number **2** *Once you reach your majority, you can do what you please.* = **adulthood**, maturity, age of consent, seniority, manhood *or* womanhood

> **USAGE** The majority of should always refer to a countable number of things or people. If you are talking about an amount or quantity, rather than a countable number, use *most of*, as in *most of the harvest was saved* (not *the majority of the harvest was saved*).

make VERB **1** *The crash made a noise like a building coming down.* = **produce**, cause, create, effect, lead to, occasion (*formal*), generate, bring about, give rise to, engender, beget (*old-fashioned*) **2** *I made a gesture at him and turned away.* = **perform**, do, act out, effect, carry out, engage in, execute, prosecute **3** *You can't make me do anything.* = **force**, cause, press, compel, drive, require, oblige, induce, railroad (*informal*), constrain, coerce, impel, dragoon, pressurize, prevail upon **4** *They made him transport minister.* = **appoint**, name, select, elect, invest, install, nominate, assign, designate, hire as, cast as, employ as, ordain, vote in as, recruit as, engage as, enlist as **5** *They now make cars at two plants in Europe.* = **create**, build, produce, manufacture, form, model, fashion, shape, frame, construct, assemble, compose, forge, mould, put together, originate, fabricate **6** *The only person who makes rules in this house is me.* = **enact**, form, pass, establish, fix, institute, frame, devise, lay down, draw up **7** *How much money did we make?* = **earn**, get, gain, net, win, clear, secure, realize, obtain, acquire, bring in, take in, fetch **8** *They are adding three aircraft carriers. That makes six in all.* = **amount to**, total, constitute, add up to, count as, tot up to (*informal*) **9** *We made the train, jumping aboard just as it was pulling out.* = **get to**, reach, catch, arrive at, meet, arrive in time for **10** *I make the total for the year £69,599.* = **calculate**, judge, estimate, determine, think, suppose, reckon, work out, compute, gauge, count up, put a figure on ▶ NOUN *What make of car did he rent?* = **brand**, sort, style, model, build, form, mark, kind, type, variety, construction, marque • **make as if** *He made as if to chase me.* = **pretend**, affect, give the impression

that, feign, feint, make a show of, act as if *or* though • **make away** *or* **off with something** *They tied her up and made away with £2000.* = **steal**, nick (*slang, chiefly Brit.*), pinch (*informal*), nab (*informal*), carry off, swipe (*slang*), knock off (*slang*), pilfer, cart off (*slang*), purloin, filch • **make believe** *He made believe he didn't understand what I was saying.* = **pretend**, play, enact, feign, play-act, act as if *or* though • **make do** *It's not going to be easy but I can make do.* = **manage**, cope, improvise, muddle through, get along *or* by, scrape along *or* by • **make for something 1** *He rose from his seat and made for the door.* = **head for**, aim for, head towards, set out for, be bound for, make a beeline for, steer (a course) for, proceed towards **2** *A happy parent makes for a happy child.* = **contribute to**, produce, further, forward, advance, promote, foster, facilitate, be conducive to • **make it 1** *I have the talent to make it.* = **succeed**, be successful, prosper, be a success, arrive (*informal*), get on, make good, cut it (*informal*), get ahead, make the grade (*informal*), crack it (*informal*), make it big, get somewhere, distinguish yourself **2** *The nurses didn't think he was going to make it.* = **get better**, survive, recover, rally, come through, pull through • **make off** *They broke free and made off in a stolen car.* = **flee**, clear out (*informal*), abscond, fly, bolt, decamp, hook it (*slang*), do a runner (*slang*), run for it (*informal*), slope off, cut and run (*informal*), beat a hasty retreat, fly the coop (*U.S. & Canad. informal*), make away, skedaddle (*informal*), take a powder (*U.S. & Canad. slang*), take to your heels, run away *or* off • **make out** *He wondered how they were making out.* = **fare**, manage, do, succeed, cope, get on, proceed, thrive, prosper • **make something out 1** *I could just make out a tall pale figure.* = **see**, observe, distinguish, perceive, recognize, detect, glimpse, pick out, discern, catch sight of, espy, descry **2** *It's hard to make out what criteria are used.* = **understand**, see, work out, grasp, perceive, follow, realize, comprehend, fathom, decipher, suss (out) (*slang*), get the drift of **3** *I'll make out a receipt for you.* = **write out**, complete, draft, draw up, inscribe, fill in *or* out **4** *They were trying to make out that I'd done it.* = **pretend**, claim, suggest, maintain, declare, allege, hint, imply, intimate, assert, insinuate, let on, make as if **5** *You could certainly make out a case for this point of view.* = **prove**, show, describe, represent, demonstrate, justify • **make something up** *She made up stories about him.*

= **invent**, create, construct, compose, write, frame, manufacture, coin, devise, hatch, originate, formulate, dream up, fabricate, concoct, cook up (*informal*), trump up • **make up** *She came back and they made up.* = **settle your differences**, shake hands, make peace, bury the hatchet, call it quits, forgive and forget, mend fences, become reconciled, declare a truce, be friends again • **make up for something** *The compensation is intended to make up for stress caused.* = **compensate for**, redress, make amends for, atone for, balance out, offset, expiate (*formal*), requite, make reparation for, make recompense for • **make up something 1** *Women should make up 50 per cent of the membership.* = **form**, account for, constitute, compose, comprise **2** *Some of the money they receive is in grants; loans make up the rest.* = **complete**, meet, supply, fill, round off • **make up to someone** *I watched my best friend make up to the man I myself loved.* = **flirt with**, be all over, come on to, chase after, court, pursue, woo, run after, chat up (*informal*), curry favour with, make overtures to, make eyes at

make-believe NOUN *She squandered her millions on a life of make-believe.* = **fantasy**, imagination, pretence, charade, unreality, dream, play-acting ■ **OPPOSITE:** reality ▶ ADJECTIVE *Children withdraw at times into a make-believe world.* = **imaginary**, dream, imagined, made-up, fantasy, pretend, pretended, mock, sham, unreal, fantasized ■ **OPPOSITE:** real

maker NOUN = **manufacturer**, producer, builder, constructor, fabricator

Maker NOUN = **God**, Creator, Prime Mover

makeshift ADJECTIVE = **temporary**, provisional, make-do, substitute, jury (*chiefly Nautical*), expedient, rough and ready, stopgap

make-up NOUN **1** *Normally she wore little make-up, but this evening was clearly an exception.* = **cosmetics**, paint (*informal*), powder, face (*informal*), greasepaint (*Theatre*), war paint (*informal*), maquillage (*French*) **2** *He became convinced that there was some fatal flaw in his make-up.* = **nature**, character, constitution, temperament, make, build, figure, stamp, temper, disposition, frame of mind, cast of mind **3** *the chemical make-up of the atmosphere* = **structure**, organization, arrangement, form, construction, assembly, c onstitution, format, formation, composition, configuration

making NOUN *a book about the making of the movie* = **creation**, production, manufacture, construction, assembly, forging, composition, fabrication ▶ PLURAL NOUN *He had the makings of a successful journalist.* = **beginnings**, qualities, potential, stuff, basics, materials, capacity, ingredients, essence, capability, potentiality • **in the making** *Her drama teacher says she is a star in the making.* = **budding**, potential, up and coming, emergent, coming, growing, developing, promising, burgeoning, nascent, incipient

malady NOUN = **disease**, complaint, illness, disorder, sickness, ailment, affliction, infirmity, ill, indisposition, lurgy (*informal*)

malaise NOUN = **unease**, illness, depression, anxiety, weakness, sickness, discomfort, melancholy, angst, disquiet, doldrums, lassitude, enervation

malcontent NOUN *Five years ago, a band of malcontents seized power.* = **troublemaker**, rebel, complainer, grumbler, grouser, agitator, stirrer (*informal*), mischief-maker, grouch (*informal*), fault-finder ▶ ADJECTIVE *The film follows three malcontent teenagers around Paris.* = **discontented**, unhappy, disgruntled, dissatisfied, disgusted, rebellious, resentful, disaffected, restive, unsatisfied, ill-disposed, factious

male ADJECTIVE = **masculine**, manly, macho, virile, manlike, manful

malevolent ADJECTIVE = **spiteful**, hostile, vicious, malicious, malign, malignant, vindictive, pernicious (*formal*), vengeful, hateful, baleful, rancorous, evil-minded, maleficent, ill-natured ■ **OPPOSITE:** benevolent

malfunction VERB *Radiation can cause microprocessors to malfunction.* = **break down**, fail, go wrong, play up (*Brit. informal*), stop working, be defective, conk out (*informal*), develop a fault, crash (*a computer*) ▶ NOUN *There must have been a computer malfunction.* = **fault**, failure, breakdown, defect, flaw, impairment, glitch

malice NOUN = **spite**, animosity, enmity, hate, hatred, bitterness, venom, spleen, rancour, bad blood, ill will, animus, malevolence, vindictiveness, evil intent, malignity, spitefulness, vengefulness, maliciousness

malicious ADJECTIVE = **spiteful**, malevolent, malignant, vicious, bitter, resentful, pernicious (*formal*), vengeful, bitchy (*informal*), hateful, baleful, injurious, rancorous, catty (*informal*), shrewish, ill-disposed, evil-minded, ill-natured ■ **OPPOSITE:** benevolent

malign VERB *We maligned him dreadfully, assuming the very worst about him.*
= **disparage**, abuse, run down, libel, knock (*informal*), injure, rubbish (*informal*), smear, blacken (someone's name), slag (off) (*slang*), denigrate, revile, vilify, slander, defame, bad-mouth (*slang*), traduce, speak ill of, derogate, do a hatchet job on (*informal*), calumniate, asperse ■ **OPPOSITE:** praise ▶ ADJECTIVE *the malign influence jealousy had on their lives* = **evil**, bad, destructive, harmful, hostile, vicious, malignant, wicked, hurtful, pernicious (*formal*), malevolent, baleful, deleterious (*formal*), injurious, baneful, maleficent
■ **OPPOSITE:** good

malignant ADJECTIVE **1** *a malignant breast tumour* = **uncontrollable**, dangerous, evil, fatal, deadly, cancerous, virulent, irremediable **2** *a malignant minority indulging in crime and violence* = **hostile**, harmful, bitter, vicious, destructive, malicious, malign, hurtful, pernicious (*formal*), malevolent, spiteful, baleful, injurious, inimical, maleficent, of evil intent
■ **OPPOSITE:** benign

malleable ADJECTIVE **1** *She was young enough to be malleable.* = **manageable**, adaptable, compliant, impressionable, pliable, tractable, biddable, governable, like putty in your hands **2** *Silver is the most malleable of all metals.* = **workable**, soft, plastic, tensile, ductile

malpractice NOUN = **misconduct**, abuse, negligence, mismanagement, misbehaviour, dereliction

mammoth ADJECTIVE = **colossal**, huge, giant, massive, vast, enormous, mighty, immense, titanic, jumbo (*informal*), gigantic, monumental (*informal*), mountainous, stellar (*informal*), prodigious, stupendous, gargantuan, elephantine, ginormous (*informal*), Brobdingnagian, humongous or humungous (*informal*), supersize ■ **OPPOSITE:** tiny

man NOUN **1** *I had not expected the young man to reappear before evening.* = **male**, guy (*informal*), fellow (*informal*), gentleman, bloke (*Brit. informal*), chap (*Brit. informal*), dude (*U.S. informal*), geezer (*informal*), adult male **2** *a possible step to sending a man back to the moon* = **human**, human being, body (*informal*), person, individual, adult, being, somebody, soul, personage **3** *Anxiety is modern man's natural state.* = **humankind**, humanity, mankind, people, mortals, human race, Homo sapiens **4** *Does your man cuddle you enough?* = **partner**, boy, husband, lover, mate, boyfriend, old man (*informal*),

groom, spouse, sweetheart, beau (*old-fashioned*), significant other (*informal, chiefly U.S.*) ▶ VERB *Soldiers manned roadblocks in the city.* = **staff**, people, fill, crew, occupy, garrison, furnish with men • **to a man** *Economists, almost to a man, were sceptical.*
= **without exception**, as one, every one, unanimously, each and every one, one and all, bar none ■ **RELATED WORDS:** *adjectives* anthropic, anthropoid, anthropoidal

mana NOUN (*N.Z.*) = **authority**, influence, power, might, force, weight, strength, domination, sway, standing, status, importance, esteem, stature, eminence

manacle NOUN *He had a steel-reinforced cell with manacles fixed to the walls.* = **handcuff**, bond, chain, shackle, tie, iron, fetter, gyve (*archaic*) ▶ VERB *His hands were manacled behind his back.* = **handcuff**, bind, confine, restrain, check, chain, curb, hamper, inhibit, constrain, shackle, fetter, tie someone's hands, put in chains, clap or put in irons

manage VERB **1** *Within two years, he was managing the store.* = **be in charge of**, run, handle, rule, direct, conduct, command, govern, administer, oversee, supervise, preside over, be head of, call the shots in, superintend, call the tune in **2** *Managing your time is increasingly important.* = **organize**, use, handle, govern, regulate **3** *How did your mother manage when he left?* = **cope**, survive, shift, succeed, get on, carry on, fare, get through, make out, cut it (*informal*), get along, make do, get by (*informal*), crack it (*informal*), muddle through **4** *those who can only manage a few hours of work* = **perform**, do, deal with, achieve, carry out, undertake, cope with, accomplish, contrive, finish off, bring about or off **5** *Her daughter couldn't manage the horse.*
= **control**, influence, guide, handle, master, dominate, manipulate **6** *managing a car well in bad conditions* = **steer**, operate, pilot

manageable ADJECTIVE = **easy**, convenient, handy, user-friendly, wieldy
■ **OPPOSITE:** difficult

management NOUN **1** *the responsibility for its day-to-day management* = **administration**, control, rule, government, running, charge, care, operation, handling, direction, conduct, command, guidance, supervision, manipulation, governance, superintendence **2** *The management is doing its best to control the situation.* = **directors**, board, executive(s), bosses (*informal*), administration, employers, directorate

manager NOUN = **supervisor**, head, director,

executive, boss (*informal*), governor, administrator, conductor, controller, superintendent, gaffer (*informal, chiefly Brit.*), proprietor, organizer, comptroller, overseer, sherang (*Austral. & N.Z.*)

mandate NOUN = **command**, order, charge, authority, commission, sanction, instruction, warrant, decree, bidding, canon, directive, injunction, fiat, edict, authorization, precept

mandatory ADJECTIVE = **compulsory**, required, binding, obligatory, requisite ■ **OPPOSITE:** optional

manfully ADVERB = **bravely**, boldly, vigorously, stoutly, hard, strongly, desperately, courageously, stalwartly, powerfully, resolutely, determinedly, heroically, valiantly, nobly, gallantly, like the devil, to the best of your ability, like a Trojan, intrepidly, like one possessed, with might and main

mangle VERB = **crush**, mutilate, maim, deform, cut, total (*slang*), tear, destroy, ruin, mar, rend, wreck, spoil, butcher, cripple, hack, distort, trash (*slang*), maul, disfigure, lacerate, mangulate (*Austral. slang*)

manhandle VERB **1** *Foreign journalists were manhandled by the police.* = **rough up**, pull, push, paw (*informal*), maul, handle roughly, knock about or around **2** *The three of us manhandled the dinghy out of the shed.* = **haul**, carry, pull, push, lift, manoeuvre, tug, shove, hump (*Brit. slang*), heave

manhood NOUN = **manliness**, masculinity, spirit, strength, resolution, courage, determination, maturity, bravery, fortitude, mettle, firmness, virility, valour, hardihood, manfulness

mania NOUN *They had a mania for travelling.* = **obsession**, passion, thing (*informal*), desire, rage, enthusiasm, craving, preoccupation, craze, fad (*informal*), fetish, fixation, partiality

maniac NOUN *big-spending football maniacs* = **fanatic**, fan, enthusiast, freak (*informal*), fiend (*informal*)

manifest ADJECTIVE *cases of manifest injustice* = **obvious**, apparent, patent, evident, open, clear, plain, visible, bold, distinct, glaring, noticeable, blatant, conspicuous, unmistakable, palpable, salient ■ **OPPOSITE:** concealed ▶ VERB *He's only convincing when that inner fury manifests itself.* = **display**, show, reveal, establish, express, prove, declare, demonstrate, expose, exhibit, set forth, make plain, evince (*formal*) ■ **OPPOSITE:** conceal

manifestation NOUN **1** *Different animals have different manifestations of the disease.* = **sign**, symptom, indication, mark, example, evidence, instance, proof, token, testimony **2** *the manifestation of grief* = **display**, show, exhibition, expression, demonstration, appearance, exposure, revelation, disclosure, materialization

manifold ADJECTIVE = **numerous**, many, various, varied, multiple, diverse, multiplied, diversified, abundant, assorted, copious, multifarious, multitudinous, multifold

manipulate VERB **1** *He's a very difficult character. He manipulates people.* = **influence**, control, direct, guide, conduct, negotiate, exploit, steer, manoeuvre, do a number on (*chiefly U.S.*), twist around your little finger **2** *complex tasks such as hanging 90 feet in the air trying to manipulate a mechanical arm* = **work**, use, operate, handle, employ, wield

mankind NOUN = **people**, man, humanity, human race, humankind, Homo sapiens

> **USAGE** Some people object to the use of *mankind* to refer to all human beings on the grounds that it is sexist. A preferable term is *humankind*, which refers to both men and women.

manliness NOUN = **virility**, masculinity, manhood, machismo, courage, bravery, vigour, heroism, mettle, boldness, firmness, valour, fearlessness, intrepidity, hardihood

manly ADJECTIVE = **virile**, male, masculine, macho, butch (*slang*), red-blooded (*informal*), manful

man-made ADJECTIVE = **artificial**, manufactured, plastic (*slang*), mock, synthetic, ersatz

manner NOUN **1** *The manner in which young children are spoken to depends on who is present.* = **style**, way, fashion, method, means, form, process, approach, practice, procedure, habit, custom, routine, mode, genre, tack, tenor, usage, wont **2** *His manner was self-assured and brusque.* = **behaviour**, look, air, bearing, conduct, appearance, aspect, presence, tone, demeanour, deportment, mien (*literary*), comportment **3** *What manner of place is this?* = **type**, form, sort, kind, nature, variety, brand, breed, category ▶ PLURAL NOUN **1** *She dresses well and has impeccable manners.* = **conduct**, bearing, behaviour, breeding, carriage, demeanour, deportment, comportment **2** *That should teach you some manners.* = **politeness**, courtesy, etiquette, refinement, polish, decorum, p's and q's **3** *the morals and manners of a society*

m

= **protocol**, ceremony, customs, formalities, good form, proprieties, the done thing, social graces, politesse

mannered ADJECTIVE = **affected**, put-on, posed, artificial, pseudo (*informal*), pretentious, stilted, arty-farty (*informal*) ■ OPPOSITE: natural

mannerism NOUN = **habit**, characteristic, trait, quirk, peculiarity, foible, idiosyncrasy

manoeuvre VERB **1** *We attempted to manoeuvre the canoe closer to him.* = **steer**, direct, guide, pilot, work, move, drive, handle, negotiate, jockey, manipulate, navigate **2** *He manoeuvred his way to the top.* = **scheme**, plot, plan, intrigue, wangle (*informal*), machinate **3** *You manoeuvred things in similar situations in the past.* = **manipulate**, arrange, organize, devise, manage, set up, engineer, fix (*informal*), orchestrate, contrive, stage-manage ▶ NOUN **1** *manoeuvres to block the electoral process* = **stratagem**, move, plan, action, movement, scheme, trick, plot, tactic, intrigue, dodge, ploy, ruse, artifice, subterfuge, machination **2** (*often plural*) *The camp was used for military manoeuvres.* = **movement**, operation, exercise, deployment, war game

mansion NOUN = **residence**, manor, hall, villa, dwelling (*formal, literary*), abode, habitation (*formal*), seat

mantle NOUN **1** *The park looked grim under a mantle of soot and ash.* = **covering**, cover, screen, cloud, curtain, envelope, blanket, veil, shroud, canopy, pall **2** *flaxen hair that hung round her shoulders like a silken mantle* = **cloak**, wrap, cape, hood, shawl ▶ VERB *Many of the peaks were already mantled with snow.* = **cover**, hide, blanket, cloud, wrap, screen, mask, disguise, veil, cloak, shroud, envelop, overspread

manual ADJECTIVE **1** *semi-skilled and unskilled manual work* = **physical**, human, done by hand **2** *There is a manual pump to get rid of water.* = **hand-operated**, hand, non-automatic ▶ NOUN *the instruction manual* = **handbook**, guide, instructions, bible, guidebook, workbook

manufacture VERB **1** *The first three models are being manufactured at our factory in Manchester.* = **make**, build, produce, construct, form, create, process, shape, turn out, assemble, compose, forge, mould, put together, fabricate, mass-produce **2** *He said the allegations were manufactured on the flimsiest evidence.* = **concoct**, make up, invent, devise, hatch, fabricate, think up, cook up (*informal*), trump up ▶ NOUN *the manufacture of*

nuclear weapons = **making**, production, construction, assembly, creation, produce, fabrication, mass-production

manufacturer NOUN = **maker**, producer, builder, creator, industrialist, factory-owner, constructor, fabricator

manure NOUN = **compost**, muck, fertilizer, dung, droppings, excrement, ordure

many ADJECTIVE *He had many books and papers on the subject.* = **numerous**, various, varied, countless, abundant, myriad, innumerable, sundry, copious, manifold (*formal*), umpteen (*informal*), profuse, multifarious, multitudinous, multifold, divers (*archaic*) ▶ PRONOUN *Many had avoided the delays after receiving text alerts.* = **a lot**, lots (*informal*), plenty, a mass, scores, piles (*informal*), tons (*informal*), heaps (*informal*), large numbers, a multitude, umpteen (*informal*), a horde, a thousand and one, a gazillion (*informal*)
• **the many** *It gave power to a few to change the world for the many.* = **the masses**, the people, the crowd, the majority, the rank and file, the multitude, (the) hoi polloi

mar VERB **1** *A number of problems marred the smooth running of the event.* = **harm**, damage, hurt, spoil, stain, blight, taint, tarnish, blot, sully, vitiate, put a damper on **2** *The scar didn't mar his self-confidence at all.* = **ruin**, injure, spoil, scar, flaw, impair, mutilate, detract from, maim, deform, blemish, mangle, disfigure, deface ■ OPPOSITE: improve

marauder NOUN = **raider**, outlaw, bandit, pirate, robber, ravager, plunderer, pillager, buccaneer, brigand, corsair, sea wolf, freebooter, reiver (*dialect*)

march VERB **1** *A Scottish battalion was marching down the street.* = **parade**, walk, file, pace, stride, tread, tramp, swagger, footslog **2** *She marched in without even knocking.* = **walk**, strut, storm, sweep, stride, stalk, flounce ▶ NOUN **1** *After a short march, the column entered the village.* = **walk**, trek, hike, tramp, slog, yomp (*Brit. informal*), routemarch **2** *Organisers expect up to 3000 people to join the march.* = **demonstration**, parade, procession, demo (*informal*) **3** *the relentless march of technology* = **progress**, development, advance, evolution, progression

margin NOUN **1** *There is very little margin for error in the way the money is collected.* = **room**, space, surplus, allowance, scope, play, compass, latitude, leeway, extra room, elbowroom **2** *These islands are on the margins of human habitation.* = **edge**, side, limit, border, bound, boundary, confine, verge (*Brit.*), brink, rim, brim, perimeter, periphery

marginal ADJECTIVE **1** *This is a marginal improvement on October.* = **insignificant**, small, low, minor, slight, minimal, negligible **2** *The poor are forced to cultivate marginal lands higher up the mountain.* = **borderline**, bordering, on the edge, peripheral

marijuana NOUN = **cannabis**, pot (*slang*), weed (*slang*), dope (*slang*), blow (*slang*), smoke (*informal*), stuff (*slang*), leaf (*slang*), tea (*U.S. slang*), grass (*slang*), chronic (*U.S. slang*), hemp, hash (*slang*), gage (*U.S., obsolete slang*), hashish, mary jane (*U.S. slang*), ganja, bhang, kif, wacky baccy (*slang*), sinsemilla, dagga (*S. African*), charas

marine ADJECTIVE = **nautical**, sea, maritime, oceanic, naval, saltwater, seafaring, ocean-going, seagoing, pelagic, thalassic

mariner NOUN = **sailor**, seaman *or* woman, sea dog, seafarer, hand, salt, tar, navigator, gob (*U.S. slang*), matelot (*slang, chiefly Brit.*), Jack Tar, seafaring man *or* woman *or* person, bluejacket

marital ADJECTIVE = **matrimonial**, married, wedded, nuptial, conjugal, spousal, connubial (*formal*)

maritime ADJECTIVE **1** *the largest maritime museum of its kind* = **nautical**, marine, naval, sea, oceanic, seafaring **2** *The country has a temperate, maritime climate.* = **coastal**, seaside, littoral

mark NOUN **1** *The dogs rub against the walls and make dirty marks.* = **spot**, stain, streak, smudge, line, nick, impression, scratch, bruise, scar, dent, blot, blemish, blotch, pock, splotch, smirch **2** *The mark of a civilized society is that it looks after its weakest members.* = **characteristic**, feature, symptom, standard, quality, measure, stamp, par, attribute, criterion, norm, trait, badge, hallmark (*Brit.*), yardstick, peculiarity **3** *Shopkeepers closed their shutters as a mark of respect.* = **indication**, sign, note, evidence, symbol, proof, token **4** *Each book was adorned with the publisher's mark at the bottom of the spine.* = **brand**, impression, label, stamp, print, device, flag, seal, symbol, token, earmark, emblem, insignia, signet, handprint **5** *A religious upbringing had left its mark on him.* = **impression**, effect, influence, impact, trace, imprint, vestiges **6** *The second shot missed its mark completely.* = **target**, goal, aim, purpose, end, object, objective ▶ VERB **1** *How do you stop the horses marking the turf?* = **scar**, scratch, dent, imprint, nick, brand, impress, stain, bruise, streak, blot, smudge, blemish, blotch, splotch, smirch **2** *I added a code to mark the document as genuine.* = **label**, identify, brand, flag, stamp, characterize **3** *He was marking essays in his study.* = **grade**, correct, assess, evaluate, appraise **4** *the river which marks the border* = **distinguish**, show, illustrate, exemplify, denote, evince (*formal*), betoken **5** *Mark my words. He won't last.* = **observe**, mind, note, regard, notice, attend to, pay attention to, pay heed to, hearken to (*archaic*) • **make your mark** *She made her mark in the film industry in the 1960s.* = **succeed**, make it (*informal*), make good, prosper, be a success, achieve recognition, get on in the world, make something of yourself, find a place in the sun, make a success of yourself

marked ADJECTIVE = **noticeable**, clear, decided, striking, noted, obvious, signal, dramatic, considerable, outstanding, remarkable, apparent, prominent, patent, evident, distinct, pronounced, notable, manifest, blatant, conspicuous, salient ■ **OPPOSITE:** imperceptible

markedly ADVERB = **noticeably**, greatly, clearly, obviously, seriously (*informal*), signally, patently, notably, considerably, remarkably, evidently, manifestly, distinctly, decidedly, strikingly, conspicuously, to a great extent, outstandingly

market NOUN *Many traders in the market have special offers today.* = **fair**, mart, bazaar, souk (*Arabic*) ▶ VERB *The drink has been marketed here since 1993.* = **sell**, promote, retail, peddle, vend, offer for sale

marketable ADJECTIVE = **sought after**, wanted, in demand, saleable, merchantable, vendible

marksman *or* **markswoman** NOUN = **sharpshooter**, good shot, crack shot (*informal*), dead shot (*informal*), deadeye (*informal, chiefly U.S.*)

maroon VERB = **abandon**, leave, desert, strand, leave high and dry (*informal*), cast away, cast ashore

marriage NOUN **1** *When did the marriage take place?* = **wedding**, match, nuptials, wedlock, wedding ceremony, matrimony, espousal (*old-fashioned*), nuptial rites **2** *The merger is an audacious marriage between old and new.* = **union**, coupling, link, association, alliance, merger, confederation, amalgamation ■ **RELATED WORDS:** *adjectives* conjugal, connubial, marital, nuptial

married ADJECTIVE **1** *We have been married for 14 years.* = **wedded**, one, united, joined, wed, hitched (*slang*), spliced (*informal*) **2** *the first ten years of married life* = **marital**, wifely, husbandly, nuptial, matrimonial, conjugal, spousal, connubial (*formal*)

marry VERB **1** *They married a month after they met.* = **tie the knot** (*informal*), wed, take the plunge (*informal*), walk down the aisle (*informal*), get hitched (*slang*), get spliced (*informal*), plight your troth (*old-fashioned*) **2** *It will be difficult to marry his two interests – cooking and sport.* = **unite**, match, join, link, tie, bond, ally, merge, knit, unify, splice, yoke

marsh NOUN = **swamp**, moss (*Scot. & Northern English, dialect*), bog, slough, fen, quagmire, morass, muskeg (*Canad.*)

marshal VERB **1** *He was marshalling the visitors, showing them where to go.* = **conduct**, take, lead, guide, steer, escort, shepherd, usher **2** *The government marshalled its economic resources.* = **arrange**, group, order, collect, gather, line up, organize, assemble, deploy, array, dispose, draw up, muster, align

martial ADJECTIVE = **military**, soldierly, brave, heroic, belligerent, warlike, bellicose

martyrdom NOUN = **persecution**, suffering, torture, agony, ordeal, torment, anguish ■ **OPPOSITE:** bliss

marvel VERB *Her fellow workers marvelled at her limitless energy.* = **be amazed**, wonder, gaze, gape, goggle, be awed, be filled with surprise ▶ NOUN **1** *A new technological marvel was invented there – the electron microscope.* = **wonder**, phenomenon, miracle, portent **2** *Her death is a great tragedy. She really was a marvel.* = **genius**, whizz (*informal*), prodigy

marvellous ADJECTIVE = **excellent**, great (*informal*), mean (*slang*), topping (*Brit. slang*), wonderful, brilliant, bad (*slang*), cracking (*Brit. informal*), amazing, crucial (*slang*), extraordinary, remarkable, smashing (*informal*), superb, spectacular, fantastic (*informal*), magnificent, astonishing, fabulous (*informal*), divine (*informal*), glorious, terrific (*informal*), splendid, sensational (*informal*), mega (*slang*), sovereign, awesome (*slang*), breathtaking, phenomenal, astounding, singular, miraculous, colossal, super (*informal*), wicked (*informal*), def (*slang*), sick (*slang*), prodigious, wondrous (*archaic, literary*), brill (*informal*), stupendous, jaw-dropping, eye-popping, bodacious (*slang, chiefly U.S.*), boffo (*slang*), jim-dandy (*slang*), chillin' (*U.S. slang*), booshit (*Austral. slang*), exo (*Austral. slang*), sik (*Austral. slang*), rad (*informal*), phat (*slang*), schmick (*Austral. informal*) ■ **OPPOSITE:** terrible

sculine ADJECTIVE **1** *masculine* *racteristics such as a deep voice and facial* **male**, manly, mannish, manlike, ~anful **2** *an aggressive, masculine image*

= **strong**, powerful, bold, brave, strapping, hardy, robust, vigorous, muscular, macho, butch (*slang*), resolute, gallant, well-built, red-blooded (*informal*), stout-hearted, two-fisted

mask NOUN **1** *a gunman wearing a mask* = **disguise**, visor, vizard (*archaic*), stocking mask, false face, domino (*rare*) **2** *His mask cracked, and she saw an angry and violent man.* = **façade**, disguise, show, front (*informal*), cover, screen, blind, cover-up, veil, cloak, guise, camouflage, veneer, semblance, concealment ▶ *A thick grey cloud masked the sun.* = **disguise**, hide, conceal, obscure, cover (up), screen, blanket, veil, cloak, mantle, camouflage, enshroud

masquerade VERB *He masqueraded as a doctor and fooled everyone.* = **pose**, pretend to be, impersonate, profess to be, pass yourself off, simulate, disguise yourself ▶ NOUN **1** *She claimed that the elections would be a masquerade.* = **pretence**, disguise, deception, front (*informal*), cover, screen, put-on (*slang*), mask, cover-up, cloak, guise, subterfuge, dissimulation, imposture **2** *A woman was injured at the Christmas masquerade.* = **masked ball**, revel, mummery, fancy dress party, costume ball, masked party

mass NOUN **1** *On the desk is a mass of books and papers.* = **lot**, collection, load (*informal*), combination, pile, quantity, bunch, stack, heap, rick, batch, accumulation, stockpile, assemblage, aggregation, conglomeration **2** *Cut it up before it cools and sets into a solid mass.* = **piece**, block, lump, chunk, hunk, concretion **3** *The Second World War involved the mass of the population.* = **majority**, body, bulk, best part, greater part, almost all, lion's share, preponderance **4** *A mass of excited people clogged the street.* = **crowd**, group, body, pack, lot, army, host, band, troop, drove, crush, bunch (*informal*), mob, flock, herd, number, horde, multitude, throng, rabble, assemblage **5** *Pluto and Triton have nearly the same mass and density.* = **size**, matter, weight, extent, dimensions, bulk, magnitude, greatness ▶ ADJECTIVE *ideas on combating mass unemployment* = **large-scale**, general, popular, widespread, extensive, universal, wholesale, indiscriminate, pandemic ▶ VERB *Shortly after the announcement, police began to mass at the shipyard.* = **gather**, assemble, accumulate, collect, rally, mob, muster, swarm, amass, throng, congregate, foregather • **the masses** *His music is commercial. It is aimed at the masses.* = **the multitude**, the crowd, the mob, the common people, the great unwashed (*derogatory*), the hoi polloi, the commonalty

massacre NOUN *She lost her mother in the massacre.* = **slaughter**, killing, murder, holocaust, carnage, extermination, annihilation, butchery, mass slaughter, blood bath ▶ VERB *Troops indiscriminately massacred the defenceless population.* = **slaughter**, kill, murder, butcher, take out (*slang*), wipe out, slay (*archaic*, *literary*), blow away (*slang*, *chiefly U.S.*), annihilate, exterminate, mow down, cut to pieces

massage NOUN *Massage isn't a long-term cure for stress.* = **rub-down**, rubbing, manipulation, kneading, reflexology, shiatsu, acupressure, chiropractic treatment, palpation ▶ VERB 1 *She massaged her foot, which was bruised and aching.* = **rub down**, rub, manipulate, knead, pummel, palpate 2 *efforts to massage the unemployment figures* = **manipulate**, alter, distort, doctor, cook (*informal*), fix (*informal*), rig, fiddle (*informal*), tamper with, tinker with, misrepresent, fiddle with, falsify

massive ADJECTIVE = **huge**, great, big, heavy, imposing, vast, enormous, solid, impressive, substantial, extensive, monster, immense, hefty, titanic, gigantic, monumental (*informal*), whacking (*informal*), mammoth, bulky, colossal, whopping (*informal*), weighty, stellar (*informal*), hulking, ponderous, gargantuan, elephantine, ginormous (*informal*), humongous *or* humungous (*informal*), supersize ■ **OPPOSITE:** tiny

master NOUN 1 *My master ordered me to deliver the message.* = **lord**, ruler, commander, chief, director, manager, boss (*informal*), head, owner, captain, governor, employer, principal, skipper (*informal*), controller, superintendent, overlord, overseer ■ **OPPOSITE:** servant 2 *He is a master at blocking progress.* = **expert**, maestro, pro (*informal*), ace (*informal*), genius, wizard, adept, virtuoso, grandmaster, doyen, past master, dab hand (*Brit. informal*), wonk (*informal*), maven (*U.S.*), fundi (*S. African*) ■ **OPPOSITE:** amateur 3 *a retired maths master* = **teacher**, tutor, instructor, schoolmaster, pedagogue, preceptor ■ **OPPOSITE:** student ▶ ADJECTIVE *There's a Georgian four-poster in the master bedroom.* = **main**, principal, chief, prime, grand, great, foremost, predominant ■ **OPPOSITE:** lesser ▶ VERB 1 *Students are expected to master a second language.* = **learn**, understand, pick up, acquire, grasp, get the hang of (*informal*), become proficient in, know inside out, know backwards 2 *She needs to*

master her fears of becoming ill. = **overcome**, defeat, suppress, conquer, check, curb, tame, lick (*informal*), subdue, overpower, quash, quell, triumph over, bridle, vanquish (*literary*), subjugate ■ **OPPOSITE:** give in to 3 *His genius alone has mastered every crisis.* = **control**, manage, direct, dominate, rule, command, govern, regulate

masterful ADJECTIVE 1 *a masterful performance of boxing* = **skilful**, skilled, expert, finished, fine, masterly, excellent, crack (*informal*), supreme, clever, superior, world-class, exquisite, adept, consummate, first-rate, deft, superlative, adroit, dexterous ■ **OPPOSITE:** unskilled 2 *Successful businesses need bold, masterful managers.* = **domineering**, authoritative, dictatorial, bossy (*informal*), arrogant, imperious, overbearing, tyrannical, magisterial, despotic, high-handed, peremptory, overweening, self-willed ■ **OPPOSITE:** meek

> **USAGE** In current usage there is a lot of overlap between the meanings of *masterful* and *masterly*. According to some, the first should only be used where there is a connotation of power and domination, the second where the connotations are of great skill. Nevertheless, as the Bank of English shows, the majority of uses of *masterful* these days relate to the second meaning, as in *musically, it was a masterful display of the folk singer's art*. Anyone wishing to observe the distinction would use only *masterly* in the context just given, and *masterful* in contexts such as: *his need to be masterful with women was extreme*; *Alec was so masterful that he surprised himself*.

masterly ADJECTIVE = **skilful**, skilled, expert, finished, fine, excellent, crack (*informal*), supreme, clever, superior, world-class, exquisite, adept, consummate, first-rate, superlative, masterful, adroit, dexterous

mastermind VERB *The finance minister will continue to mastermind economic reform.* = **plan**, manage, direct, organize, devise, conceive, be the brains behind (*informal*) ▶ NOUN *She was the mastermind behind the plan.* = **organizer**, director, manager, authority, engineer, brain(s) (*informal*), architect, genius, planner, intellect (*informal*), virtuoso, rocket scientist (*informal*), brainbox

masterpiece NOUN = **classic**, tour de force (*French*), pièce de résistance (*French*), magnum opus, master work, jewel, chef-d'oeuvre (*French*)

mastery NOUN **1** *He demonstrated his mastery of political manoeuvring.* = **understanding**, knowledge, comprehension, ability, skill, know-how (*informal*), command, grip, grasp, expertise, prowess, familiarity, attainment, finesse, proficiency, virtuosity, dexterity, cleverness, deftness, acquirement **2** *a region where humans have gained mastery over the major rivers* = **control**, authority, command, rule, victory, triumph, sway, domination, superiority, conquest, supremacy, dominion, upper hand, ascendancy, pre-eminence, mana (*N.Z.*), whip hand

match NOUN **1** *He was watching a football match.* = **game**, test, competition, trial, tie, contest, fixture, bout, head-to-head **2** *Moira was a perfect match for him.* = **companion**, mate, equal, equivalent, counterpart, fellow, complement **3** *He asked his assistant to look for a match of the vase he broke.* = **replica**, double, copy, twin, equal, spit (*informal, chiefly Brit.*), duplicate, lookalike, ringer (*slang*), spitting image (*informal*), dead ringer (*slang*), spit and image (*informal*) **4** *Hollywood's favourite love match foundered on the rocks.* = **marriage**, union, couple, pair, pairing, item (*informal*), alliance, combination, partnership, duet, affiliation **5** *I was no match for a man with such power.* = **equal**, rival, equivalent, peer, competitor, counterpart ▶ VERB **1** *These shoes match your dress.* = **correspond with**, suit, go with, complement, fit with, accompany, team with, blend with, tone with, harmonize with, coordinate with **2** *You don't have to match your lipstick to your outfit.* = **tailor**, fit, suit, adapt **3** *Their strengths in memory and spatial skills matched.* = **correspond**, agree, accord, square, coincide, tally, conform, match up, be compatible, harmonize, be consonant **4** *It can take time and money to match buyers and sellers.* = **pair**, unite, join, couple, link, marry, ally, combine, mate, yoke **5** *We matched them in every department of the game.* = **rival**, equal, compete with, compare with, emulate, contend with, measure up to • **match something** or **someone against something** or **someone** *The finals begin today, matching the United States against France.* = **pit against**, set against, play off against, put in opposition to

matching ADJECTIVE = **identical**, like, ~~me~~, double, paired, equal, toning, twin, ~~valent~~, parallel, corresponding, ~~arable~~, duplicate, coordinating, ~~us~~ ■ OPPOSITE: different ~~~~ ADJECTIVE = **unequalled**,

unique, unparalleled, unrivalled, perfect, supreme, exquisite, consummate, superlative, inimitable, incomparable, unmatched, peerless, unsurpassed ■ OPPOSITE: average

mate NOUN **1** *A mate of mine used to play soccer for Liverpool.* = **friend**, pal (*informal*), companion, buddy (*informal*), china (*Brit. slang*), cock (*Brit. informal*), comrade, chum (*informal*), mucker (*Brit. informal*), crony, blood or blud (*Brit. slang*), main man (*slang, chiefly U.S.*), homeboy (*slang, chiefly U.S.*), cobber (*Austral. & N.Z., old-fashioned, informal*), E hoa (*N.Z.*) **2** *He has found his ideal mate.* = **partner**, lover, companion, spouse, consort, significant other (*informal, chiefly U.S.*), better half (*humorous*), helpmeet, husband or wife **3** *The guest cabin is a mirror image of its mate.* = **double**, match, fellow, twin, counterpart, companion **4** *The electrician's mate ignored the red-lettered warning signs.* = **assistant**, subordinate, apprentice, helper, accomplice, sidekick (*informal*) **5** *He celebrated with work mates in the pub.* = **colleague**, associate, companion, co-worker, fellow-worker, compeer ▶ VERB **1** *They want the males to mate with wild females.* = **pair**, couple, breed, copulate **2** *We want to mate well so that our offspring will flourish.* = **marry**, match, wed, get married, shack up (*informal*) **3** *The film tries very hard to mate modern with old.* = **join**, match, couple, pair, yoke

material NOUN **1** *the decomposition of organic material* = **substance**, body, matter, stuff, elements, constituents **2** *the thick material of her skirt* = **cloth**, stuff, fabric, textile **3** *In my version of the story, I added some new material.* = **information**, work, details, facts, notes, evidence, particulars, data, info (*informal*), subject matter, documentation ▶ ADJECTIVE **1** *the material world* = **physical**, worldly, solid, substantial (*formal*), concrete, fleshly, bodily, tangible, palpable, corporeal, nonspiritual **2** *The company failed to disclose material information.* = **relevant**, important, significant, essential, vital, key, serious, grave, meaningful, applicable, indispensable, momentous, weighty, pertinent, consequential, apposite, apropos, germane

materialize VERB **1** *None of the anticipated difficulties materialized.* = **occur**, happen, take place, turn up, come about, take shape, come into being, come to pass **2** *He materialized at her side, notebook at the ready.* = **appear**, arrive, emerge, surface, turn up, loom, show up (*informal*), pop up (*informal*), put in an appearance

materially ADVERB = **significantly**, much, greatly, considerably, essentially, seriously, gravely, substantially ■ **OPPOSITE:** insignificantly

maternal ADJECTIVE = **motherly**, protective, nurturing, maternalistic

maternity NOUN = **motherhood**, parenthood, motherliness

matey ADJECTIVE = **friendly**, intimate, comradely, thick (*informal*), pally (*informal*), amiable, sociable, chummy (*informal*), free-and-easy, companionable, clubby, buddy-buddy (*slang, chiefly U.S. & Canad.*), hail-fellow-well-met, palsy-walsy (*informal*)

matrimonial ADJECTIVE = **marital**, married, wedding, wedded, nuptial, conjugal, spousal, connubial (*formal*), hymeneal

matrimony NOUN = **marriage**, nuptials, wedlock, wedding ceremony, marital rites

matted ADJECTIVE = **tangled**, knotted, unkempt, knotty, tousled, ratty, uncombed

matter NOUN **1** *It was a private matter.* = **situation**, thing, issue, concern, business, question, event, subject, affair, incident, proceeding, episode, topic, transaction, occurrence **2** *A proton is an elementary particle of matter.* = **substance**, material, body, stuff **3** *This conflict forms the matter of the play.* = **content**, sense, subject, argument, text, substance, burden, thesis, purport, gist, pith **4** *If the wound starts to produce yellow matter, see your doctor.* = **pus**, discharge, secretion, suppuration, purulence **5** *Forget it; it's of no matter.* = **importance**, interest, moment, note, weight, import (*formal*), consequence, significance ▶ VERB *It doesn't matter how long you take.* = **be important**, make a difference, count, be relevant, make any difference, mean anything, have influence, carry weight, cut any ice (*informal*), be of consequence, be of account

matter-of-fact ADJECTIVE = **unsentimental**, flat, dry, plain, dull, sober, down-to-earth, mundane, lifeless, prosaic, deadpan, unimaginative, unvarnished, emotionless, unembellished

mature VERB *young girls who have not yet matured* = **develop**, grow up, bloom, blossom, come of age, become adult, age, reach adulthood, maturate ▶ ADJECTIVE **1** *Grate some mature cheddar cheese.* = **matured**, seasoned, ripe, mellow, ripened **2** *Here is the voice of a mature man, expressing sorrow for a lost ideal.* = **grown-up**, adult, grown, of age, full-blown, fully fledged, fully-developed, full-grown ■ **OPPOSITE:** immature

maturity NOUN **1** *Humans experience a delayed maturity compared with other mammals.* = **adulthood**, majority, completion, puberty, coming of age, fullness, full bloom, full growth, pubescence, manhood *or* womanhood ■ **OPPOSITE:** immaturity **2** *the dried seeds of peas that have been picked at maturity* = **ripeness**, perfection, maturation

maudlin ADJECTIVE = **sentimental**, tearful, mushy (*informal*), soppy (*Brit. informal*), weepy (*informal*), slushy (*informal*), mawkish, lachrymose, icky (*informal*), overemotional

maul VERB **1** *He had been mauled by a bear.* = **mangle**, claw, lacerate, tear, mangulate (*Austral. slang*) **2** *The troops were severely mauled before evacuating the island.* = **ill-treat**, beat, abuse, batter, thrash, beat up (*informal*), molest, work over (*slang*), pummel, manhandle, rough up, handle roughly, knock about *or* around, beat *or* knock seven bells out of (*informal*)

maverick NOUN *He was too much of a maverick to hold high office.* = **rebel**, radical, dissenter, individualist, protester, eccentric, heretic, nonconformist, iconoclast, dissentient ■ **OPPOSITE:** traditionalist ▶ ADJECTIVE *Her maverick behaviour precluded any chance of promotion.* = **rebel**, radical, dissenting, individualistic, eccentric, heretical, iconoclastic, nonconformist

maw NOUN = **mouth**, crop, throat, jaws, gullet, craw

maxim NOUN = **saying**, motto, adage, proverb, rule, saw (*old-fashioned*), gnome, dictum, axiom, aphorism, byword, apophthegm

maximum ADJECTIVE *The maximum height for a fence here is 2 metres.* = **greatest**, highest, supreme, paramount, utmost, most, maximal, topmost ■ **OPPOSITE:** minimal ▶ NOUN *The law provides for a maximum of two years in prison.* = **top**, most, peak, ceiling, crest, utmost, upper limit, uttermost ■ **OPPOSITE:** minimum

maybe ADVERB = **perhaps**, possibly, it could be, conceivably, perchance (*archaic*), mayhap (*archaic*), peradventure (*archaic*)

mayhem NOUN = **chaos**, trouble, violence, disorder, destruction, confusion, havoc (*informal*), fracas, commotion

maze NOUN *a maze of dimly-lit corridors* = **web**, puzzle, confusion, tangle, snarl, mesh, labyrinth, imbroglio, convolutions, complex network

meadow NOUN = **field**, pasture, grassland, ley, lea (*poetic*)

meagre ADJECTIVE = **insubstantial**, little, small, poor, spare, slight, inadequate, pathetic, slender, scant, sparse, deficient, paltry, skimpy, puny, measly (*informal*), scanty, exiguous (*formal*), scrimpy

mean¹ VERB **1** *The red signal means that you can shoot.* = **signify**, say, suggest, indicate, represent, express, stand for, convey, spell out, purport, symbolize, denote, connote, betoken **2** *What do you think he means by that?* = **imply**, suggest, intend, indicate, refer to, intimate, get at (*informal*), hint at, have in mind, drive at (*informal*), allude to, insinuate **3** *An enlarged prostate does not necessarily mean cancer.* = **presage**, promise, herald, foreshadow, augur, foretell, portend, betoken, adumbrate **4** *Trade and product discounts can mean big savings.* = **result in**, cause, produce, effect, lead to, involve, bring about, give rise to, entail, engender, necessitate **5** *I didn't mean to hurt you.* = **intend**, want, plan, expect, design, aim, wish, think, propose, purpose, desire, set out, contemplate, aspire, have plans, have in mind **6** *He said that we were meant to be together.* = **destine**, make, design, suit, fate, predestine, preordain

> **USAGE** In standard British English, *mean* should not be followed by *for* when expressing intention. *I didn't mean this to happen* is acceptable, but not *I didn't mean for this to happen*.

mean² ADJECTIVE **1** *Don't be mean with the fabric, or the curtains will end up looking skimpy.* = **miserly**, stingy, parsimonious, niggardly, close (*informal*), near (*informal*), tight, selfish, beggarly, mercenary, skimpy, penny-pinching, ungenerous, penurious, tight-fisted, mingy (*Brit. informal*), snoep (*S. African informal*) ■ **OPPOSITE:** generous **2** *Upstaging the bride was a particularly mean trick.* = **dishonourable**, base, petty, degraded, disgraceful, shameful, shabby, vile, degenerate, callous, sordid, abject, despicable, narrow-minded, contemptible, wretched, scurvy (*old-fashioned*), ignoble, hard-hearted, scungy (*Austral. & N.Z.*), low-minded ■ **OPPOSITE:** honourable **3** *The prison officer described him as the meanest man he'd ever met.* = **malicious**, hostile, nasty, sour, unpleasant, rude, unfriendly, bad-tempered, disagreeable, churlish, ill-tempered, cantankerous ■ **OPPOSITE:** kind **4** *He was raised in the mean streets of the central market district.* = **shabby**, poor, miserable, rundown, beggarly, seedy, ⸺ffy, sordid, paltry, squalid, tawdry, ⸺ent (*informal, chiefly U.S.*), ⸺ptible, wretched, down-at-heel, ⸺slang, chiefly U.S.), scuzzy (*slang,* ⸺) ■ **OPPOSITE:** superb **5** *southern*

opportunists of mean origins = **lowly**, low, common, ordinary, modest, base, obscure, humble, inferior, vulgar, menial, proletarian, undistinguished, servile, ignoble, plebeian, lowborn, baseborn (*archaic*) ■ **OPPOSITE:** noble

mean³ NOUN *Take a hundred and twenty values and calculate the mean.* = **average**, middle, balance, norm, median, midpoint
▸ ADJECTIVE *the mean score for 26-year-olds* = **average**, middle, middling, standard, medium, normal, intermediate, median, medial

meander VERB **1** *The river meandered in lazy curves.* = **wind**, turn, snake, zigzag **2** *We meandered along the Irish country roads.* = **wander**, stroll, stray, drift, ramble, stravaig (*Scot. & Northern English, dialect*)

meandering ADJECTIVE = **winding**, wandering, snaking, tortuous, convoluted, serpentine, circuitous ■ **OPPOSITE:** straight

meaning NOUN **1** *I became more aware of the symbols and their meanings.* = **significance**, message, explanation, substance, value, import, implication, drift, interpretation, essence, purport, connotation, upshot, gist, signification **2** *arguing over the exact meaning of this word or that* = **definition**, sense, interpretation, explication, elucidation, denotation **3** *Unsure of the meaning of this remark, he remained silent.* = **purpose**, point, end, idea, goal, design, aim, object, intention **4** *a challenge that gives meaning to life* = **force**, use, point, effect, value, worth, consequence, thrust, validity, usefulness, efficacy ▸ ADJECTIVE *She nodded and gave me a meaning look.* = **expressive**, meaningful, pointed, revealing, significant, speaking, pregnant, suggestive, telltale

meaningful ADJECTIVE **1** *a meaningful and constructive dialogue* = **significant**, important, serious, material, useful, relevant, valid, worthwhile, purposeful ■ **OPPOSITE:** trivial **2** *The two exchanged a quick, meaningful look.* = **expressive**, suggestive, meaning, pointed, speaking, pregnant

meaningless ADJECTIVE = **nonsensical**, senseless, inconsequential, inane, insubstantial ■ **OPPOSITE:** worthwhile

meanness NOUN **1** *This careful attitude to money can border on meanness.* = **miserliness**, parsimony (*formal*), stinginess, tight-fistedness, niggardliness, selfishness, minginess (*Brit. informal*), penuriousness **2** *Their meanness of spirit is embarrassing.* = **pettiness**, degradation, degeneracy, wretchedness, narrow-mindedness, shabbiness, baseness, vileness, sordidness, shamefulness, scurviness, abjectness, low-mindedness, ignobility, despicableness, disgracefulness, dishonourableness **3** *There was always a certain amount of cruelty, meanness and villainy.* = **malice**, hostility, bad temper, rudeness, nastiness, unpleasantness, ill temper, sourness, unfriendliness, maliciousness, cantankerousness, churlishness, disagreeableness **4** *the meanness of our surroundings* = **shabbiness**, squalor, insignificance, pettiness, wretchedness, seediness, tawdriness, sordidness, scruffiness, humbleness, poorness, paltriness, beggarliness, contemptibleness

means PLURAL NOUN **1** *We do not have the means to fight such a crimewave.* = **method**, way, course, process, medium, measure, agency, channel, instrument, avenue, mode, expedient **2** *He did not have the means to compensate her.* = **money**, funds, capital, property, riches, income, resources, estate, fortune, wealth, substance, affluence, wherewithal • **by all means** *'Can I come and see your house?' 'Yes, by all means.'* = **certainly**, surely, of course, definitely, absolutely, positively, doubtlessly • **by means of** *a course taught by means of lectures and seminars* = **by way of**, using, through, via, utilizing, with the aid of, by dint of • **by no means** *This is by no means out of the ordinary.* = **in no way**, no way, not at all, definitely not, not in the least, on no account, not in the slightest, not the least bit, absolutely not

meantime *or* **meanwhile** ADVERB = **at the same time**, in the meantime, simultaneously, for the present, concurrently, in the meanwhile

meanwhile *or* **meantime** ADVERB = **for now**, in the meantime, for the moment, in the interim, for then, in the interval, in the meanwhile, in the intervening time

measly ADJECTIVE = **meagre**, miserable, pathetic, paltry, mean, poor, petty, beggarly, pitiful, skimpy, puny, stingy, contemptible, scanty, miserly, niggardly, ungenerous, mingy (*Brit. informal*), snoep (*S. African informal*)

measurable ADJECTIVE **1** *Both leaders expect measurable progress.* = **perceptible**, material, significant, distinct, palpable, discernible, detectable **2** *measurable quantities such as the number of jobs* = **quantifiable**, material, quantitative, assessable, determinable, computable, gaugeable, mensurable

measure VERB *Measure the length and width of the gap.* = **quantify**, rate, judge, determine, value, size, estimate, survey, assess, weigh, calculate, evaluate, compute, gauge, mark

out, appraise, calibrate ▶ NOUN **1** *The colonies were claiming a larger measure of self-government.* = **quantity**, share, amount, degree, reach, range, size, capacity, extent, proportion, allowance, portion, scope, quota, ration, magnitude, allotment, amplitude **2** *The local elections were seen as a measure of the government's success.* = **standard**, example, model, test, par, criterion, norm, benchmark, barometer, yardstick, touchstone, litmus test **3** *He said stern measures would be taken against the rioters.* = **action**, act, step, procedure, means, course, control, proceeding, initiative, manoeuvre, legal action, deed, expedient **4** *a tape measure* = **gauge**, rule, scale, metre, ruler, yardstick **5** *They passed a measure that would give small businesses more benefits.* = **law**, act, bill, legislation, resolution, statute, enactment • **for good measure** *For good measure, a few details of hotels were included.* = **in addition**, as well, besides, to boot, as an extra, into the bargain, as a bonus • **measure up** *I was informed that I didn't measure up.* = **come up to standard**, be fit, be adequate, be capable, be suitable, make the grade (*informal*), be suited, be satisfactory, come up to scratch (*informal*), cut the mustard (*slang*), fulfil the expectations, fit *or* fill the bill • **measure up to something** *or* **someone** *It was tiring, always trying to measure up to her high standards.* = **achieve**, meet, match, rival, equal, compare to, come up to, be equal to, vie with, be on a level with

measured ADJECTIVE **1** *They have to proceed at a measured pace.* = **steady**, even, slow, regular, dignified, stately, solemn, leisurely, sedate, unhurried **2** *Her more measured approach will appeal to voters.* = **considered**, planned, reasoned, studied, calculated, deliberate, sober, premeditated, well-thought-out **3** *Is the difference in measured intelligence genetic or environmental?* = **quantified**, standard, exact, regulated, precise, gauged, verified, predetermined, modulated

measurement NOUN **1** *Some of the measurements are doubtless inaccurate.* = **size**, length, dimension, area, amount, weight, volume, capacity, extent, height, depth, width, magnitude, amplitude **2** *Measurement of blood pressure can be undertaken by the practice nurse.* = **calculation**, assessment, evaluation, estimation, survey, judgment, valuation, appraisal, computation, calibration, mensuration, metage

m

meat NOUN **1** *They gave meat and drink to the poor.* = **food**, provisions, nourishment, sustenance, eats (*slang*), fare, flesh, rations, grub (*slang*), subsistence, kai (*N.Z. informal*), chow (*informal*), nosh (*slang*), victuals, comestibles, provender, nutriment, viands **2** *The real meat of the conference was the attempt to agree on minimum standards.* = **gist**, point, heart, core, substance, essence, nucleus, marrow, kernel, nub, pith

meaty ADJECTIVE **1** *a lasagne with a meaty sauce* = **substantial**, rich, nourishing, hearty **2** *a pleasant chap with meaty arms* = **brawny**, muscular, heavy, solid, strapping, sturdy, burly, husky (*informal*), fleshy, beefy (*informal*), heavily built **3** *This time she has been given a more meaty role in the film.* = **interesting**, rich, significant, substantial, profound, meaningful, pithy

mechanical ADJECTIVE **1** *a small mechanical device that taps out the numbers* = **automatic**, automated, mechanized, power-driven, motor-driven, machine-driven ■ **OPPOSITE:** manual **2** *His retort was mechanical.* = **unthinking**, routine, automatic, matter-of-fact, cold, unconscious, instinctive, lacklustre, involuntary, impersonal, habitual, cursory, perfunctory, unfeeling, machine-like, emotionless, spiritless ■ **OPPOSITE:** conscious

mechanism NOUN **1** *the locking mechanism* = **workings**, motor, gears, works, action, components, machinery, innards (*informal*) **2** *the clumsy mechanism of price controls* = **process**, workings, way, means, system, performance, operation, medium, agency (*old-fashioned*), method, functioning, technique, procedure, execution, methodology **3** *The heat-producing mechanism will switch itself on automatically.* = **machine**, system, structure, device, tool, instrument, appliance, apparatus, contrivance

meddle VERB = **interfere**, intervene, tamper, intrude, pry, butt in, interpose, stick your nose in (*informal*), put your oar in, intermeddle, put your two cents in (*U.S. slang*)

mediate VERB = **intervene**, moderate, step in (*informal*), intercede, settle, referee, resolve, umpire, reconcile, arbitrate, interpose, conciliate, make peace, restore harmony, act as middleman, bring to terms, bring to an agreement

mediation NOUN = **arbitration**, intervention, reconciliation, conciliation, good offices, intercession, interposition

mediator NOUN = **negotiator**, arbitrator, referee, advocate, umpire, intermediary, middleman, arbiter, peacemaker, go-between, moderator, interceder, honest broker

medicinal ADJECTIVE = **therapeutic**, medical, healing, remedial, restorative, curative, analeptic, roborant, sanative

medicine NOUN = **remedy**, drug, cure, prescription, medication, nostrum, physic, medicament

medieval ADJECTIVE = **old-fashioned**, antique, primitive, obsolete, out-of-date, archaic, prehistoric, antiquated, anachronistic, antediluvian, unenlightened, out of the ark

mediocre ADJECTIVE = **second-rate**, average, ordinary, indifferent, middling, pedestrian, inferior, commonplace, vanilla (*slang*), insignificant, so-so (*informal*), banal, tolerable (*informal*), run-of-the-mill, passable, undistinguished, uninspired, bog-standard (*Brit. & Irish slang*), no great shakes (*informal*), half-pie (*N.Z. informal*), fair to middling (*informal*), meh (*slang*) ■ **OPPOSITE:** excellent

mediocrity NOUN **1** *She lamented the mediocrity of contemporary literature.* = **insignificance**, indifference, inferiority, meanness, ordinariness, unimportance, poorness **2** *Surrounded by mediocrities, she seemed a towering intellectual.* = **nonentity**, nobody, lightweight (*informal*), second-rater, cipher

meditate VERB *I was meditating, and reached a higher state of consciousness.* = **reflect**, think, consider, contemplate, deliberate, muse, ponder, ruminate, cogitate, be in a brown study • **meditate on something** *I meditated on the problem.* = **consider**, study, contemplate, ponder, reflect on, mull over, think over, chew over, deliberate on, weigh, turn something over in your mind

meditation NOUN = **reflection**, thought, concentration, study, musing, pondering, contemplation, reverie, ruminating, rumination, cogitation, cerebration, a brown study

meditative ADJECTIVE = **reflective**, thoughtful, contemplative, studious, pensive, deliberative, ruminative, cogitative

medium ADJECTIVE *foods which contain only medium levels of sodium* = **average**, mean, middle, middling, fair, intermediate, midway, mediocre, median, medial ■ **OPPOSITE:** extraordinary ▶ NOUN **1** *Going to see a medium provided a starting point for her.* = **spiritualist**, seer, clairvoyant, fortune teller, spiritist, channeller **2** *It's difficult to strike a happy medium.* = **middle**, mean, centre, average, compromise, middle ground, middle way, midpoint, middle course, middle path

medley NOUN = **mixture**, confusion, jumble, assortment, patchwork, pastiche, mixed bag (*informal*), potpourri, mélange (*French*), miscellany, mishmash, farrago, hotchpotch, hodgepodge, salmagundi, olio, gallimaufry, omnium-gatherum

meek ADJECTIVE **1** *He was a meek, mild-mannered fellow.* = **submissive**, soft, yielding, gentle, peaceful, modest, mild, patient, humble, timid, long-suffering, compliant, unassuming, unpretentious, docile, deferential, forbearing, acquiescent ■ **OPPOSITE:** overbearing **2** *He may be self-effacing, but he certainly isn't meek.* = **spineless**, weak, tame, boneless, weak-kneed (*informal*), spiritless, unresisting, wussy (*slang*), wimpish *or* wimpy (*informal*)

meet VERB **1** *He's the kindest person I've ever met.* = **encounter**, come across, run into, happen on, find, contact, confront, bump into (*informal*), run across, chance on, come face to face with ■ **OPPOSITE:** avoid **2** *The commission met four times between 1988 and 1991.* = **gather**, collect, assemble, get together, rally, come together, muster, convene, congregate, foregather ■ **OPPOSITE:** disperse **3** *The current arrangements are inadequate to meet our needs.* = **fulfil**, match (up to), answer, perform, handle, carry out, equal, satisfy, cope with, discharge, comply with, come up to, conform to, gratify, measure up to ■ **OPPOSITE:** fall short of **4** *Never had she met such spite and pettiness.* = **experience**, face, suffer, bear, go through, encounter, endure, undergo **5** *a crossing where four paths meet* = **converge**, unite, join, cross, touch, connect, come together, link up, adjoin, intersect, abut ■ **OPPOSITE:** diverge

meeting NOUN **1** *I travel to London regularly for business meetings.* = **conference**, gathering, assembly, meet, congress, session, rally, convention, get-together (*informal*), meet-up, reunion, congregation, hui (*N.Z.*), conclave, convocation (*formal*), powwow **2** *Thirty-seven years after our first meeting I was back in her studio.* = **encounter**, introduction, confrontation, engagement, rendezvous, tryst, assignation **3** *the meeting of three streams* = **convergence**, union, crossing, conjunction, junction, intersection, concourse, confluence

melancholy ADJECTIVE *It was at this time of day that I felt most melancholy.* = **sad**, down, depressed, unhappy, low, blue, miserable,

moody, gloomy, dismal, sombre, woeful, glum, mournful, dejected, despondent, dispirited, melancholic, downcast, lugubrious, pensive, sorrowful, disconsolate, joyless, doleful, downhearted, heavy-hearted, down in the dumps (*informal*), woebegone, down in the mouth, low-spirited ■ **OPPOSITE:** happy ▶ NOUN *We watched the process with an air of melancholy.* = **sadness**, depression, misery, gloom, sorrow, woe, blues, unhappiness, despondency, the hump (*Brit. informal*), dejection, low spirits, gloominess, pensiveness ■ **OPPOSITE:** happiness

melee *or* **mêlée** NOUN = **fight**, fray, brawl, skirmish, tussle, scuffle, free-for-all (*informal*), fracas, set-to (*informal*), rumpus, broil, affray (*Law*), shindig (*informal*), donnybrook, ruction (*informal*), battle royal, ruckus (*informal*), scrimmage, stramash (*Scot.*), shindy (*informal*), bagarre (*French*), biffo (*Austral. slang*)

mellow ADJECTIVE **1** *the mellow background music* = **tuneful**, full, rich, soft, melodious, mellifluous, dulcet, well-tuned, euphonic **2** *a mellow, well-balanced wine* = **full-flavoured**, rounded, rich, sweet, smooth, delicate, juicy **3** *a mellow, creamy Somerset Brie* = **ripe**, perfect, mature, ripened, well-matured ■ **OPPOSITE:** unripe **4** *After a few glasses, he was feeling mellow.* = **relaxed**, happy, cheerful, jolly, elevated, merry (*Brit. informal*), expansive, cordial, genial, jovial ▶ VERB **1** *She has mellowed with age.* = **relax**, improve, settle, calm, mature, soften, sweeten **2** *Long cooking mellows the flavour beautifully.* = **season**, develop, improve, perfect, ripen

melodramatic ADJECTIVE = **theatrical**, actorly, extravagant, histrionic, sensational, hammy (*informal*), actressy, stagy, overemotional, overdramatic

melody NOUN **1** *a catchy melody with a frenetic beat* = **tune**, song, theme, refrain, air, music, strain, descant **2** *Her voice was full of melody.* = **tunefulness**, music, harmony, musicality, euphony, melodiousness

melt VERB **1** *The snow had melted.* = **dissolve**, run, soften, fuse, thaw, diffuse, flux, defrost, liquefy, unfreeze, deliquesce **2** (*often with* **away**) *When he heard these words, his inner doubts melted away.* = **disappear**, fade, vanish, dissolve, disperse, evaporate, evanesce (*formal*) **3** *Her smile is enough to melt anyone's heart.* = **soften**, touch, relax, disarm, mollify

member NOUN = **representative**, associate, supporter, fellow, subscriber, comrade, disciple

m

membership NOUN **1** *membership of the Communist Party* = **participation**, belonging, fellowship, enrolment **2** *the recent fall in party membership* = **members**, body, associates, fellows

memento NOUN = **souvenir**, trophy, memorial, token, reminder, relic, remembrance, keepsake

memoir NOUN = **account**, life, record, register, journal, essay, biography, narrative, monograph

memoirs PLURAL NOUN = **autobiography**, diary, life story, life, experiences, memories, journals, recollections, reminiscences

memorable ADJECTIVE = **noteworthy**, celebrated, impressive, historic, important, special, striking, famous, significant, signal, extraordinary, remarkable, distinguished, haunting, notable, timeless, unforgettable, momentous, illustrious, catchy, indelible, unfading ■ **OPPOSITE:** forgettable

memorandum NOUN = **note**, minute, message, communication, reminder, memo, jotting, email *or* e-mail

memorial NOUN **1** *Every village had its war memorial.* = **monument**, cairn, shrine, plaque, cenotaph **2** *a memorial to the Emperor written in characters of gold* = **petition**, address, statement, memorandum ▶ ADJECTIVE *A memorial service is being held at St Paul's Church.* = **commemorative**, remembrance, monumental

memorize VERB = **remember**, learn, commit to memory, learn by heart, learn by rote, get by heart, con (*archaic*)

memory NOUN **1** *She had a good memory for faces.* = **recall**, mind, retention, ability to remember, powers of recall, powers of retention **2** *He had happy memories of his father.* = **recollection**, reminder, reminiscence, impression, echo, remembrance **3** *They held a minute's silence in memory of those who had died.* = **commemoration**, respect, honour, recognition, tribute, remembrance, observance

menace NOUN **1** *In my view you are a menace to the public.* = **danger**, risk, threat, hazard, peril, jeopardy **2** *Don't be such a menace!* = **nuisance**, plague (*informal*), pest, annoyance, troublemaker, mischief-maker **3** *a pervading sense of menace* = **threat**, warning, intimidation, ill-omen, ominousness, commination ▶ VERB *She is being menaced by her sister's boyfriend.* = **bully**, threaten, intimidate, terrorize, alarm, frighten, scare, browbeat, utter threats to

menacing ADJECTIVE = **threatening**, dangerous, alarming, frightening, forbidding, looming, intimidating, ominous, baleful, intimidatory, minatory, bodeful, louring *or* lowering, minacious ■ **OPPOSITE:** encouraging

mend VERB **1** *They took a long time to mend the roof.* = **repair**, fix, restore, renew, patch up, renovate, refit, retouch **2** *cooking their meals, mending their socks* = **darn**, repair, patch, stitch, sew **3** *He must have an operation to mend torn knee ligaments.* = **heal**, improve, recover, cure, remedy, get better, be all right, be cured, recuperate, pull through, convalesce **4** *There will be disciplinary action if you do not mend your ways.* = **improve**, better, reform, correct, revise, amend, rectify, ameliorate, emend • **on the mend** *The baby had been poorly but was on the mend.* = **convalescent**, improving, recovering, getting better, recuperating, convalescing

menial ADJECTIVE *low-paid menial jobs such as cleaning* = **low-status**, degrading, lowly, unskilled, low, base, sorry, boring, routine, dull, humble, mean, vile, demeaning, fawning, abject, grovelling, humdrum, subservient, ignominious, sycophantic, servile, slavish, ignoble, obsequious ■ **OPPOSITE:** high ▶ NOUN *A number of polite and unobtrusive menials fetched and carried for us.* = **servant**, domestic, attendant, lackey, labourer, serf, underling (*derogatory*), drudge, vassal (*archaic*), dogsbody (*informal*), flunky, skivvy (*chiefly Brit.*), varlet (*archaic*) ■ **OPPOSITE:** master

menstruation NOUN = **period**, menstrual cycle, menses, courses (*Physiology*), flow (*informal*), monthly (*informal*), the curse (*informal*), catamenia (*Physiology*)

mental ADJECTIVE *the mental development of children* = **intellectual**, rational, theoretical, cognitive, brain, conceptual, cerebral

mentality NOUN = **attitude**, character, personality, psychology (*informal*), make-up, outlook, disposition, way of thinking, frame of mind, turn of mind, cast of mind

mentally ADVERB = **psychologically**, intellectually, rationally, inwardly, subjectively

mention VERB *She did not mention her mother's absence.* = **refer to**, point out, acknowledge, bring up, state, report, reveal, declare, cite, communicate, disclose, intimate, tell of, recount, hint at, impart, allude to, divulge, broach, call attention to, make known, touch upon, adduce, speak about *or* of

▶ NOUN **1** (*often with* **of**) *The statement made no mention of government casualties.* = **reference**, announcement, observation, indication, remark, notification, allusion **2** *Two of the losers deserve special mention.* = **acknowledgment**, recognition, tribute, citation, honourable mention • **not to mention** *It was both deliberate and malicious, not to mention sick.* = **to say nothing of**, besides, not counting, as well as

mentor NOUN = **guide**, teacher, coach, adviser, tutor, instructor, counsellor, guru

menu NOUN = **bill of fare**, tariff (*chiefly Brit.*), set menu, table d'hôte, carte du jour (*French*)

mercantile ADJECTIVE **1** *the emergence of a new mercantile class* = **commercial**, business, trade, trading, merchant **2** *the urban society and its mercantile values* = **profit-making**, money-orientated

mercenary NOUN *In the film he plays a brutish, trigger-happy mercenary.* = **hireling**, freelance (*History*), soldier of fortune, condottiere (*History*), free companion (*History*) ▶ ADJECTIVE **1** *Despite his mercenary motives, he is not a cynic.* = **greedy**, grasping, acquisitive, venal, avaricious, covetous, money-grubbing (*informal*), bribable ■ **OPPOSITE:** generous **2** *The mercenary soldier is not a valued creature.* = **hired**, paid, bought, venal

merchandise NOUN *25% off selected merchandise* = **goods**, produce, stock, products, truck, commodities, staples, wares, stock in trade, vendibles ▶ VERB *He advises shops on how to merchandise their wares.* = **trade**, market, sell, retail, distribute, deal in, buy and sell, traffic in, vend, do business in

merchant NOUN = **tradesperson**, dealer, trader, broker, retailer, supplier, seller, salesman *or* woman *or* person, vendor, shopkeeper, trafficker, wholesaler, purveyor

merciful ADJECTIVE = **compassionate**, forgiving, sympathetic, kind, liberal, soft, sparing, generous, mild, pitying, humane, clement, gracious, lenient, beneficent, forbearing, tender-hearted, benignant ■ **OPPOSITE:** merciless

merciless ADJECTIVE = **cruel**, ruthless, hard, severe, harsh, relentless, callous, heartless, unforgiving, fell (*archaic*), inexorable, implacable, unsympathetic, inhumane, barbarous, pitiless, unfeeling, unsparing, hard-hearted, unmerciful, unappeasable, unpitying

mercurial ADJECTIVE = **capricious**, volatile, unpredictable, erratic, variable, unstable, fickle, temperamental, impulsive, irrepressible, changeable, quicksilver, flighty, inconstant ■ **OPPOSITE:** consistent

mercy NOUN **1** *Neither side showed its prisoners any mercy.* = **compassion**, charity, pity, forgiveness, quarter, favour, grace, kindness, clemency, leniency, benevolence, forbearance ■ **OPPOSITE:** cruelty **2** *It was a mercy he'd gone so quickly in the end.* = **blessing**, relief, boon, godsend, piece of luck, benison (*archaic*) • **at the mercy of something** *or* **someone 1** *Buildings are left to decay at the mercy of vandals and bad weather.* = **defenceless against**, subject to, open to, exposed to, vulnerable to, threatened by, susceptible to, prey to, an easy target for, naked before, unprotected against **2** *Servants or slaves were at the mercy of their masters.* = **in the power of**, under the control of, in the clutches of, under the heel of

mere ADJECTIVE **1** *It proved to be a mere trick of fate.* = **simple**, merely, no more than, nothing more than, just, common, plain, pure, pure and simple, unadulterated, unmitigated, unmixed **2** *Cigarettes were a mere 2 cents a packet.* = **bare**, slender, trifling, meagre, just, only, basic, no more than, minimal, scant, paltry, skimpy, scanty

merge VERB **1** *The two countries merged into one.* = **combine**, blend, fuse, amalgamate, unite, join, mix, consolidate, mingle, converge, coalesce, melt into, meld, intermix ■ **OPPOSITE:** separate **2** *He wants to merge the two agencies.* = **join**, unite, combine, consolidate, fuse ■ **OPPOSITE:** separate **3** *His features merged into the darkness.* = **melt**, blend, incorporate, mingle, tone with, be swallowed up by, become lost in

merger NOUN = **union**, fusion, consolidation, amalgamation, combination, coalition, incorporation

merit NOUN *They have been persuaded of the merits of the scheme.* = **advantage**, value, quality, worth, strength, asset, virtue, good point, strong point, worthiness ▶ VERB *Such ideas merit careful consideration.* = **deserve**, warrant, be entitled to, earn, incur, have a right to, be worthy of, have a claim to

merited ADJECTIVE = **deserved**, justified, warranted, just, earned, appropriate, entitled, rightful, condign, rightly due

merriment NOUN = **fun**, amusement, glee, mirth, sport, laughter, festivity, frolic, gaiety, hilarity, revelry, jollity, levity, liveliness, conviviality, joviality, jocularity, merrymaking

m

merry ADJECTIVE **1** *He was much loved for his merry nature.* = **cheerful**, happy, upbeat (*informal*), carefree, glad, jolly, festive, joyous, joyful, genial, fun-loving, chirpy (*informal*), vivacious, rollicking, convivial, gleeful, blithe, frolicsome, mirthful, sportive, light-hearted, jocund, gay, blithesome ■ OPPOSITE: gloomy **2** *After a couple of glasses I was feeling a bit merry.* = **tipsy**, happy, elevated (*informal*), mellow, tiddly (*slang, chiefly Brit.*), squiffy (*Brit. informal*) • **make merry** *Neighbours went out into the streets and made merry together.* = **have fun**, celebrate, revel, have a good time, feast, frolic, enjoy yourself, carouse, make whoopee (*informal*)

mesh NOUN **1** *The ground-floor windows are obscured by wire mesh.* = **net**, netting, network, web, tracery **2** *He lures young talent into his mesh.* = **trap**, web, tangle, toils, snare, entanglement ▶ VERB **1** *Their senses of humour meshed perfectly.* = **engage**, combine, connect, knit, come together, coordinate, interlock, dovetail, fit together, harmonize **2** *Limes and plane trees meshed in unpruned disorder.* = **entangle**, catch, net, trap, tangle, snare, ensnare, enmesh

mesmerize VERB = **entrance**, fascinate, absorb, captivate, grip, enthral, hypnotize, magnetize, hold spellbound, spellbind

mess NOUN **1** *Linda can't stand mess.* = **untidiness**, disorder, confusion, chaos, turmoil, litter, clutter, disarray, jumble, disorganization, grot (*slang*), dirtiness **2** *I've made such a mess of my life.* = **shambles**, botch, hash, cock-up (*Brit. slang*), state, bodge (*informal*), pig's breakfast (*informal*), omnishambles (*Brit. informal*) **3** *I've got myself into a bit of a mess.* = **difficulty**, dilemma, plight, spot (*informal*), hole (*informal*), fix (*informal*), jam (*informal*), hot water (*informal*), stew (*informal*), mix-up, muddle, pickle (*informal*), uphill (*S. African*), predicament, deep water, perplexity, tight spot, imbroglio, fine kettle of fish (*informal*) • **mess about** or **around 1** *We were just messing around playing with paint.* = **potter about**, dabble, amuse yourself, footle (*informal*), fool about or around, muck about or around (*informal*), play about or around **2** *I'd like to know who's been messing about with the pram.* = **meddle**, play, interfere, toy, fiddle (*informal*), tamper, tinker, trifle, fool about or around • **mess something up 1** *If I messed it up, I would probably be fired.* = **botch**, bungle, make a hash of (*informal*), make a nonsense of, make a pig's ear of (*informal*), cock something up (*Brit. slang*), muck something

up (*Brit. slang*), muddle something up **2** *I hope they haven't messed up your house.* = **dirty**, foul, litter, pollute, clutter, besmirch, disarrange, befoul, dishevel • **mess with something** or **someone** *You are messing with people's religion and they don't like that.* = **interfere with**, play with, fiddle with (*informal*), tamper with, tinker with, meddle with

message NOUN **1** *Would you like to leave a message?* = **communication**, note, bulletin, word, letter, notice, memo, dispatch, memorandum, communiqué, missive, intimation, tidings, email or e-mail, text or text message, SMS, IMS, tweet (*on the Twitter website*), mention or @mention (*on the Twitter website*) **2** *The report's message was unequivocal.* = **point**, meaning, idea, moral, theme, import, purport ▶ VERB (*S.M.S. & Computing*) = **text**, send, communicate, email or e-mail, SMS, IM or instant message, DM or direct message, poke (*on the Facebook website*), tweet (*on the Twitter website*), chat (*Computing*) • **get the message** *I think they got the message that this attitude is wrong.* = **understand**, see, get it, catch on (*informal*), comprehend, twig (*Brit. informal*), get the point, take the hint

messenger NOUN = **courier**, agent, runner, carrier, herald, envoy, bearer, go-between, emissary, harbinger (*literary*), delivery boy, errand boy

messy ADJECTIVE **1** *She was a good, if messy, cook.* = **disorganized**, sloppy (*informal*), untidy, slovenly **2** *The work tends to be messy, so wear old clothes.* = **dirty**, grubby, grimy, scuzzy (*slang, chiefly U.S.*) **3** *Mum made me clean up my messy room.* = **untidy**, disordered, littered, chaotic, muddled, cluttered, shambolic (*informal*), disorganized, daggy (*Austral. & N.Z. informal*) ■ OPPOSITE: tidy **4** *She has very messy hair.* = **dishevelled**, ruffled, untidy, rumpled, bedraggled, unkempt, tousled, uncombed, daggy (*Austral. & N.Z. informal*) **5** *Life is a messy and tangled business.* = **confusing**, difficult, complex, confused, tangled, chaotic, tortuous

metamorphose VERB = **transform**, change, alter, remake, convert, remodel, mutate, reshape, be reborn, transmute, transfigure, transmogrify (*humorous*), transubstantiate

metamorphosis NOUN = **transformation**, conversion, alteration, change, mutation, rebirth, changeover, transfiguration, transmutation, transubstantiation, transmogrification (*humorous*)

metaphor NOUN = **figure of speech**, image, symbol, analogy, emblem, conceit (*literary*), allegory, trope, figurative expression

metaphorical ADJECTIVE = **figurative**, symbolic, emblematic, allegorical, emblematical, tropical (*Rhetoric*)

metaphysical ADJECTIVE 1 *metaphysical questions like personal responsibility for violence* = **abstract**, intellectual, theoretical, deep, basic, essential, ideal, fundamental, universal, profound, philosophical, speculative, high-flown, esoteric, transcendental, abstruse, recondite, oversubtle 2 *He was moved by a metaphysical sense quite alien to him.* = **supernatural**, spiritual, unreal, intangible, immaterial, incorporeal, impalpable, unsubstantial

meteoric ADJECTIVE = **spectacular**, sudden, overnight, rapid, fast, brief, brilliant, flashing, fleeting, swift, dazzling, speedy, transient, momentary, ephemeral ■ **OPPOSITE:** gradual

mete out VERB = **distribute**, portion, assign, administer, ration, dispense, allot, dole out, share out, apportion, deal out, measure out, parcel out, divide out

method NOUN 1 *new teaching methods* = **manner**, process, approach, technique, way, plan, course, system, form, rule, programme, style, practice, fashion, scheme, arrangement, procedure, routine, mode, modus operandi 2 *They go about their work with method and common sense.* = **orderliness**, planning, order, system, form, design, structure, purpose, pattern, organization, regularity

methodical ADJECTIVE = **orderly**, planned, ordered, structured, regular, disciplined, organized, efficient, precise, neat, deliberate, tidy, systematic, meticulous, painstaking, businesslike, well-regulated ■ **OPPOSITE:** haphazard

meticulous ADJECTIVE = **thorough**, detailed, particular, strict, exact, precise, microscopic, fussy, painstaking, perfectionist, scrupulous, fastidious, punctilious, nit-picky (*informal*) ■ **OPPOSITE:** careless

metropolis NOUN = **city**, town, capital, big city, municipality, conurbation, megalopolis

mettle NOUN 1 *It's the first real test of his mettle this season.* = **courage**, spirit, resolution, resolve, life, heart, fire, bottle (*Brit. slang*), nerve, daring, guts (*informal*), pluck, grit, bravery, fortitude, vigour, boldness, gallantry, ardour, valour, spunk (*informal*), indomitability, hardihood,

gameness 2 *He is of a different mettle from the others.* = **character**, quality, nature, make-up, stamp, temper, kidney, temperament, calibre, disposition

microbe NOUN = **microorganism**, virus, bug (*informal*), germ, bacterium, bacillus

microscopic ADJECTIVE = **tiny**, minute, invisible, negligible, minuscule, imperceptible, infinitesimal, teeny-weeny, teensy-weensy ■ **OPPOSITE:** huge

midday NOUN = **noon**, twelve o'clock, noonday, noontime, twelve noon, noontide

middle NOUN 1 *I was in the middle of the back row.* = **centre**, heart, inside, thick, core, midst, nucleus, hub, halfway point, midpoint, midsection 2 *At 53, I now have a few extra pounds around the middle.* = **waist**, gut, belly, tummy (*informal*), waistline, midriff, paunch, midsection ▶ ADJECTIVE 1 *that crucial middle point of the picture* = **central**, medium, inside, mid, intervening, inner, halfway, intermediate, median, medial 2 *the middle level of commanding officers* = **intermediate**, inside, intervening, inner

middle-class ADJECTIVE = **bourgeois**, traditional, conventional, suburban, petit-bourgeois

middleman NOUN = **intermediary**, broker, entrepreneur, distributor, go-between

middling ADJECTIVE 1 *They enjoyed only middling success until 1963.* = **mediocre**, all right, indifferent, so-so (*informal*), unremarkable, tolerable (*informal*), run-of-the-mill, passable, serviceable, unexceptional, half-pie (*N.Z. informal*), O.K. or okay (*informal*) 2 *a man of middling height* = **moderate**, medium, average, fair, ordinary, modest, adequate, bog-standard (*Brit. & Irish slang*)

midget ADJECTIVE *an accompaniment of midget roast potatoes* = **baby**, small, little, tiny, miniature, dwarf, diminutive, teeny-weeny, teensy-weensy

midnight NOUN = **twelve o'clock**, middle of the night, dead of night, twelve o'clock at night, the witching hour

midst NOUN *The organisation realised it had a traitor in its midst.* = **middle**, centre, heart, interior, thick, depths, core, hub, bosom • **in the midst of** 1 *We are in the midst of a recession.* = **during**, in the middle of, amidst 2 *I was sitting in the midst of a traffic jam.* = **among**, in the middle of, surrounded by, amidst, in the thick of, enveloped by

midway ADVERB = **halfway**, in the middle of, part-way, equidistant, at the midpoint, betwixt and between

m

miffed ADJECTIVE = **upset**, hurt, annoyed, offended, irritated, put out, hacked (off) (*U.S. slang*), resentful, nettled, aggrieved, vexed, displeased, irked, in a huff, piqued, narked (*Brit., Austral. & N.Z. slang*), tooshie (*Austral. slang*)

might NOUN *The might of the army could prove a decisive factor.* = **power**, force, energy, ability, strength, capacity, efficiency, capability, sway, clout (*informal*), vigour, prowess, potency, efficacy, valour, puissance, hard power

mightily ADVERB **1** *He had given a mightily impressive performance.* = **very**, highly, greatly, hugely, very much, seriously (*informal*), extremely, intensely, decidedly, exceedingly **2** *She strove mightily to put him from her thoughts.* = **powerfully**, vigorously, strongly, forcefully, energetically, with all your strength, with all your might and main

mighty ADJECTIVE **1** *a mighty young athlete* = **powerful**, strong, strapping, robust, hardy, vigorous, potent, sturdy, stout, forceful, stalwart, doughty, lusty, indomitable, manful, puissant ■ **OPPOSITE:** weak **2** *a land marked with vast lakes and mighty rivers* = **great**, large, huge, grand, massive, towering, vast, enormous, tremendous, immense, titanic, gigantic, monumental (*informal*), bulky, colossal, stellar (*informal*), prodigious, stupendous, elephantine, ginormous (*informal*), humongous *or* humungous (*informal*) ■ **OPPOSITE:** tiny

migrant NOUN *economic migrants and political refugees* = **wanderer**, immigrant, traveller, rover, transient, nomad, emigrant, itinerant, drifter, vagrant ▶ ADJECTIVE *migrant workers* = **itinerant**, wandering, drifting, roving, travelling, shifting, immigrant, transient, nomadic, migratory, vagrant

migrate VERB = **move**, travel, journey, wander, shift, drift, trek, voyage, roam, emigrate, rove

migration NOUN = **wandering**, journey, voyage, travel, movement, shift, trek, emigration, roving

migratory ADJECTIVE = **nomadic**, travelling, wandering, migrant, itinerant, unsettled, shifting, roving, transient, vagrant, peripatetic

mild ADJECTIVE **1** *He is a mild man, reasonable almost to the point of blandness.* = **gentle**, kind, easy, soft, pacific, calm, moderate, forgiving, tender, pleasant, mellow, compassionate, indulgent, serene, easy-going, amiable, meek, placid, docile, merciful, peaceable, forbearing, equable, easy-oasy (*slang*), chilled (*informal*) ■ **OPPOSITE:** harsh **2** *The area is famous for its mild winters.* = **temperate**, warm, calm, moderate, clement, tranquil, balmy ■ **OPPOSITE:** cold **3** *The cheese has a soft, mild flavour.* = **bland**, thin, smooth, tasteless, insipid, flavourless **4** *Wash your face thoroughly with a mild soap.* = **soothing**, mollifying, emollient, demulcent, lenitive

milieu NOUN = **surroundings**, setting, scene, environment, element, background, location, sphere, locale, mise en scène (*French*)

militant ADJECTIVE *one of the most active militant groups* = **aggressive**, warring, fighting, active, combating, contending, vigorous, two-fisted, assertive, in arms, embattled, belligerent, combative ■ **OPPOSITE:** peaceful ▶ NOUN *The militants were apparently planning a terrorist attack.* = **activist**, radical, fighter, partisan, belligerent, combatant

military ADJECTIVE *Military action may become necessary.* = **warlike**, armed, soldierly, martial, soldierlike • **the military** *Did you serve in the military?* = **the armed forces**, the forces, the services, the army

militate VERB • **militate against something** = **counteract**, conflict with, contend with, count against, oppose, counter, resist, be detrimental to, weigh against, tell against

militia NOUN = **reserve(s)**, National Guard (*U.S.*), Territorial Army (*Brit.*), yeomanry (*History*), fencibles (*History*), trainband (*History*)

milk VERB = **exploit**, use, pump, squeeze, drain, take advantage of, bleed (*informal*), impose on, wring, fleece, suck dry ■ **RELATED WORDS:** *adjectives* lactic, lacteal

milky ADJECTIVE = **white**, clouded, opaque, cloudy, alabaster, whitish, milk-white

mill NOUN **1** *a pepper mill* = **grinder**, crusher, quern **2** *a textile mill* = **factory**, works, shop, plant, workshop, foundry ▶ VERB *freshly milled black pepper* = **grind**, pound, press, crush, powder, grate, pulverize, granulate, comminute • **mill about** *or* **around** *Quite a few people were milling about.* = **swarm**, crowd, stream, surge, seethe, throng

millstone NOUN = **burden**, weight, load, albatross, drag, affliction, dead weight, encumbrance

mime NOUN *Students presented a mime and a puppet show.* = **dumb show**, gesture, pantomime, mummery ▶ VERB *She mimed getting up in the morning.* = **act out**, represent, gesture, simulate, pantomime

mimic VERB **1** *She could mimic anybody, reducing her friends to helpless laughter.*
= **imitate**, do (*informal*), take off (*informal*), ape, parody, caricature, impersonate
2 *Don't try to mimic anybody. Just be yourself.*
= **resemble**, look like, mirror, echo, simulate, take on the appearance of
▶ NOUN *He's a very good mimic.* = **imitator**, impressionist, copycat (*informal*), impersonator, caricaturist, parodist, parrot

mimicry NOUN = **imitation**, impression, impersonation, copying, imitating, mimicking, parody, caricature, mockery, burlesque, apery

mince VERB **1** *I'll buy some lean meat and mince it myself.* = **cut**, grind, crumble, dice, hash, chop up **2** *Orlando was flapping his arms like a bird and mincing around.* = **posture**, pose, ponce (*slang*), attitudinize **3** *The doctors didn't mince their words, and predicted the worst.* = **tone down**, spare, moderate, weaken, diminish, soften, hold back, extenuate, palliate, euphemize

mind NOUN **1** *I'm trying to clear my mind of all this.* = **brain**, head, imagination, psyche, subconscious **2** *He spent the next hour going over the trial in his mind.* = **memory**, recollection, remembrance, powers of recollection **3** *My mind was never on my work.* = **attention**, thinking, thoughts, concentration **4** *an excellent training for the young mind* = **intelligence**, reason, reasoning, understanding, sense, spirit, brain(s) (*informal*), wits, mentality, intellect, grey matter (*informal*), ratiocination **5** *She moved to London, meeting some of the best minds of her time.* = **thinker**, academic, intellectual, genius, brain (*informal*), scholar, sage, intellect (*informal*), rocket scientist (*informal*), brainbox, acca (*Austral. slang*) **6** *They could interpret it that way if they'd a mind to.* = **intention**, will, wish, desire, urge, fancy, purpose, leaning, bent, notion, tendency, inclination, disposition **7** *Sometimes I feel I'm losing my mind.* = **sanity**, reason, senses, judgment, wits, marbles (*informal*), rationality, mental balance
▶ VERB **1** *I hope you don't mind me calling in like this.* = **take offence at**, dislike, care about, object to, resent, disapprove of, be bothered by, look askance at, be affronted by **2** *Mind you don't burn those sausages.* = **be careful**, watch, take care, be wary, be cautious, be on your guard **3** *Mind you don't let the cat out.* = **be sure**, ensure, make sure, be careful, make certain **4** *Could you mind the shop while I'm out, please?* = **look after**, watch, protect, tend, guard, take care of, attend to, keep an eye on, have *or* take charge of **5** *You mind what I say now!* = **pay attention to**, follow, mark, watch, note, regard, respect, notice, attend to, listen to, observe, comply with, obey, heed, adhere to, take heed of, pay heed to • **in** *or* **of two minds** *I am in two minds about going.*
= **undecided**, uncertain, unsure, wavering, hesitant, dithering (*chiefly Brit.*), vacillating, swithering (*Scot.*), shillyshallying (*informal*)
• **make up your mind** *Once he made up his mind to do something, there was no stopping him.* = **decide**, choose, determine, resolve, reach a decision, come to a decision
• **mind out** *Mind out. We're coming in to land!*
= **be careful**, watch out, take care, look out, beware, pay attention, keep your eyes open, be on your guard ■ **RELATED WORD:** *adjective* mental

mindful ADJECTIVE (*with* **of**) = **aware**, careful, conscious, alert, sensible, wary, thoughtful, attentive, respectful, watchful, alive to, cognizant, chary, heedful, regardful ■ **OPPOSITE:** heedless

mindless ADJECTIVE **1** *blackmail, extortion and mindless violence* = **unthinking**, gratuitous, thoughtless, careless, oblivious, brutish, inane, witless, heedless, unmindful, dumb-ass (*slang*) ■ **OPPOSITE:** reasoning
2 *She wasn't at all the mindless fool they perceived her to be.* = **unintelligent**, stupid, foolish, careless, negligent, idiotic, thoughtless, inane, witless, forgetful, moronic, obtuse, neglectful, asinine, imbecilic, braindead (*informal*), dumb-ass (*slang*), dead from the neck up (*informal*) **3** *the mindless repetitiveness of some tasks* = **mechanical**, automatic, monotonous, mind-numbing, brainless

mind's eye NOUN • **in your mind's eye** = **in your imagination**, in your head, in your mind

mine NOUN **1** *an explosion at a coal mine* = **pit**, deposit, shaft, vein, colliery, excavation, coalfield, lode **2** *a mine of information* = **source**, store, fund, stock, supply, reserve, treasury, wealth, abundance, hoard ▶ VERB **1** *not enough coal to be mined economically* = **dig up**, extract, quarry, unearth, delve, excavate, hew, dig for **2** *The approaches to the garrison have been heavily mined.* = **lay mines in** *or* **under**, sow with mines

miner NOUN = **coalminer**, pitman (*Brit.*), collier (*Brit.*)

mingle VERB **1** *Cheers and applause mingled in a single roar.* = **mix**, combine, blend, merge, unite, join, marry, compound, alloy, interweave, coalesce, intermingle, meld,

commingle, intermix, admix ■ **OPPOSITE:**
separate **2** *Guests ate and mingled.*
= **associate**, circulate, hang out (*informal*),
consort, socialize, rub shoulders (*informal*),
hobnob, fraternize, hang about *or* around
■ **OPPOSITE:** dissociate

miniature ADJECTIVE = **small**, little, minute,
baby, reduced, tiny, pocket, toy, mini, wee,
dwarf, scaled-down, diminutive,
minuscule, midget, teeny-weeny,
Lilliputian, teensy-weensy, pygmy *or* pigmy
■ **OPPOSITE:** giant

minimal ADJECTIVE = **minimum**, smallest,
least, slightest, token, nominal, negligible,
least possible, littlest

minimize VERB **1** *You can minimize these
problems with sensible planning.* = **reduce**,
decrease, shrink, diminish, prune, curtail,
attenuate, downsize, miniaturize
■ **OPPOSITE:** increase **2** *Some have minimized
the importance of these factors.* = **play down**,
discount, underestimate, belittle,
disparage, decry, underrate, deprecate,
depreciate, make light *or* little of
■ **OPPOSITE:** praise

minimum ADJECTIVE *He was only five feet nine,
the minimum height for a policeman.* = **lowest**,
smallest, least, slightest, minimal, least
possible, littlest ■ **OPPOSITE:** maximum
▶ NOUN *She has cut her teaching hours to a
minimum.* = **lowest**, least, depth, slightest,
lowest level, nadir, bottom level

minion NOUN = **follower**, henchman *or*
woman *or* person, underling (*derogatory*),
lackey, favourite, pet, creature, darling,
parasite, cohort (*chiefly U.S.*), dependant,
hanger-on, sycophant, yes man, toady,
hireling, flunky, flatterer, lickspittle,
bootlicker (*informal*)

minister NOUN **1** *He concluded a deal with the
Danish minister in Washington.* = **official**,
ambassador, diplomat, delegate,
executive, administrator, envoy, cabinet
member, office-holder, plenipotentiary
2 *My father was a Baptist minister.*
= **clergyman** *or* **woman**, priest, divine,
vicar, parson, preacher, pastor, chaplain,
cleric, rector, curate, churchman *or* woman,
padre (*informal*), ecclesiastic • **minister to**
*For 44 years they had ministered to the poor and
the sick.* = **attend to**, serve, tend to, answer
to, accommodate, take care of, cater to,
pander to, administer to, be solicitous of

ministry NOUN **1** *the Ministry of Justice*
= **department**, office, bureau, government
department **2** *He disclosed that his ministry
gave funds to parties in Namibia.*
= **administration**, government, council,
cabinet **3** *So what prompted you to enter the*

ministry? = **the priesthood**, the church,
the cloth, the pulpit, holy orders

minor ADJECTIVE = **small**, lesser,
subordinate, smaller, light, slight,
secondary, petty, inferior, trivial, trifling,
insignificant, negligible, unimportant,
paltry, inconsequential, inconsiderable,
nickel-and-dime (*U.S. slang*)
■ **OPPOSITE:** major

minstrel NOUN = **musician**, singer, harper,
bard (*archaic, literary*), troubadour,
songstress, jongleur

mint VERB **1** *the right to mint coins* = **make**,
produce, strike, cast, stamp, punch, coin
2 *The book comprises a lexicon of freshly minted
descriptions.* = **invent**, produce, fashion,
make up, construct, coin, devise, forge,
fabricate, think up ▶ NOUN *They were worth
a mint.* = **fortune**, million, bomb (*Brit.
slang*), pile (*informal*), packet (*slang*), bundle
(*slang*), heap (*informal*), King's ransom, top
whack (*informal*) ▶ ADJECTIVE *a set of
Victorian stamps in mint condition* = **perfect**,
excellent, first-class, brand-new, fresh,
unmarked, undamaged, unblemished,
untarnished

minuscule ADJECTIVE = **tiny**, little, minute,
fine, very small, miniature, microscopic,
diminutive, infinitesimal, teeny-weeny,
Lilliputian, teensy-weensy

minute[1] NOUN **1** *A minute later she came to the
front door.* = **sixty seconds**, sixtieth of an
hour **2** *I'll be with you in a minute.* = **moment**,
second, bit, shake (*informal*), flash, instant,
tick (*Brit. informal*), sec (*informal*), short
time, little while, jiffy (*informal*), trice
• **up to the minute** *a big range of up-to-the-
minute appliances* = **latest**, in, newest, now
(*informal*), with it (*old-fashioned, informal*),
smart, stylish, trendiest, trendy (*Brit.
informal*), on trend, vogue, up to date,
modish, (most) fashionable, schmick
(*Austral. informal*)

minute[2] ADJECTIVE **1** *Only a minute amount is
needed.* = **small**, little, tiny, miniature,
slender, fine, microscopic, diminutive,
minuscule, infinitesimal, teeny-weeny,
Lilliputian, teensy-weensy ■ **OPPOSITE:**
huge **2** *gambling large sums on the minute
chance of a big win* = **negligible**, slight, petty,
trivial, trifling, unimportant, paltry, puny,
piddling (*informal*), inconsiderable,
picayune (*U.S.*) ■ **OPPOSITE:** significant
3 *We will have to pore over this report in minute
detail.* = **precise**, close, detailed, critical,
exact, meticulous, exhaustive, painstaking,
punctilious (*formal*) ■ **OPPOSITE:** imprecise

minutely ADVERB = **precisely**, closely,
exactly, in detail, critically, meticulously,

painstakingly, exhaustively, with a fine-tooth comb

minutes PLURAL NOUN *He'd been reading the minutes of the last meeting.* = **record**, notes, proceedings, transactions, transcript, memorandum

minutiae PLURAL NOUN = **details**, particulars, subtleties, trifles, trivia, niceties, finer points, ins and outs

miracle NOUN = **wonder**, phenomenon, sensation, marvel, amazing achievement, astonishing feat

miraculous ADJECTIVE = **wonderful**, amazing, extraordinary, incredible (*informal*), astonishing, marvellous, magical, unbelievable, phenomenal, astounding, eye-popping (*informal*), inexplicable, wondrous (*archaic, literary*), unaccountable, superhuman ■ OPPOSITE: ordinary

mirage NOUN = **illusion**, vision, hallucination, pipe dream, chimera, optical illusion, phantasm

mire VERB 1 *The party has been mired by allegations of sleaze.* = **soil**, dirty, muddy, besmirch, begrime, bespatter 2 *The minister still remains mired in the controversy of the affair.* = **entangle**, involve, mix up, catch up, bog down, tangle up, enmesh

mirror NOUN *He went into the bathroom and looked in the mirror.* = **looking-glass**, glass (*Brit.*), reflector, speculum ▶ VERB *His own shock was mirrored in her face.* = **reflect**, show, follow, match, represent, copy, repeat, echo, parallel, depict, reproduce, emulate

mirror image NOUN = **reflection**, double, image, copy, twin, representation, clone, replica, likeness, spitting image (*informal*), dead ringer (*informal*), exact likeness

mirth NOUN = **merriment**, amusement, fun, pleasure, laughter, rejoicing, festivity, glee, frolic, sport, gaiety, hilarity, cheerfulness, revelry, jollity, levity, gladness, joviality, jocularity, merrymaking, joyousness

misadventure NOUN = **misfortune**, accident, disaster, failure, reverse, setback, catastrophe, debacle, bad luck, calamity, mishap, bad break (*informal*), ill fortune, ill luck, mischance

misapprehension NOUN = **misunderstanding**, mistake, error, delusion, misconception, fallacy, misreading, false impression, misinterpretation, false belief, misconstruction, wrong idea *or* impression

misappropriate VERB = **steal**, embezzle, pocket, misuse, swindle, misspend, misapply, defalcate (*Law*)

misbehave VERB = **be naughty**, be bad, act up (*informal*), muck about (*Brit. slang*), get up to mischief (*informal*), carry on (*informal*), be insubordinate ■ OPPOSITE: behave

misbehaviour NOUN = **misconduct**, mischief, misdemeanour, shenanigans (*informal*), impropriety, acting up (*informal*), bad behaviour, misdeeds, rudeness, indiscipline, insubordination, naughtiness, monkey business (*informal*), incivility

miscalculate VERB 1 *He has badly miscalculated the mood of the people.* = **misjudge**, get something wrong, underestimate, underrate, overestimate, overrate 2 *The government seems to have miscalculated and bills are higher.* = **calculate wrongly**, blunder, make a mistake, get it wrong, err, slip up

miscarriage NOUN 1 *Her sister had a miscarriage earlier this month.* = **spontaneous abortion**, stillbirth 2 *The report concluded that no miscarriage of justice had taken place.* = **failure**, error, breakdown, mismanagement, undoing, thwarting, mishap, botch (*informal*), perversion, misfire, mischance, nonsuccess

miscarry VERB 1 *Many women who miscarry eventually have healthy babies.* = **have a miscarriage**, lose your baby, have a spontaneous abortion 2 *My career miscarried when I thought I had everything.* = **fail**, go wrong, fall through, come to nothing, misfire, go astray, go awry, come to grief, go amiss, go pear-shaped (*informal*), gang agley (*Scot.*)

miscellaneous ADJECTIVE = **mixed**, various, varied, diverse, confused, diversified, mingled, assorted, jumbled, sundry, motley, indiscriminate, manifold (*formal*), heterogeneous, multifarious, multiform

mischief NOUN 1 *The little lad was always up to some mischief.* = **misbehaviour**, trouble, naughtiness, pranks, shenanigans (*informal*), monkey business (*informal*), waywardness, devilment, impishness, roguishness, roguery 2 *The conference was a platform to cause political mischief.* = **harm**, trouble, damage, injury, hurt, evil, disadvantage, disruption, misfortune, detriment

mischievous ADJECTIVE 1 *She rocks back and forth on her chair like a mischievous child.* = **naughty**, bad, troublesome, wayward, exasperating, playful, rascally, impish, roguish, vexatious, puckish, frolicsome, arch, ludic (*literary*), sportive, badly behaved 2 *a mischievous campaign by the press* = **malicious**, damaging, vicious,

m

destructive, harmful, troublesome, malignant, detrimental, hurtful, pernicious (*formal*), spiteful, deleterious (*formal*), injurious

misconception NOUN = **delusion**, error, misunderstanding, fallacy, misapprehension, mistaken belief, wrong idea, wrong end of the stick, misconstruction

misconduct NOUN = **immorality**, wrongdoing, mismanagement, malpractice, misdemeanour, delinquency, impropriety, transgression, misbehaviour, dereliction, naughtiness, malfeasance (*Law*), unethical behaviour, malversation (*rare*)

misconstrue VERB = **misinterpret**, misunderstand, misjudge, misread, mistake, misapprehend, get a false impression of, misconceive, mistranslate, get your lines crossed about, make a wrong interpretation of

misdeed NOUN (*often plural*) = **offence**, wrong, crime, fault, sin, misconduct, trespass, misdemeanour, transgression, villainy

misdemeanour NOUN = **offence**, misconduct, infringement, trespass, misdeed, transgression, misbehaviour, peccadillo

miserable ADJECTIVE **1** *She went to bed, miserable and depressed.* = **sad**, down, low, depressed, distressed, gloomy, dismal, afflicted, melancholy, heartbroken, desolate, forlorn, mournful, dejected, broken-hearted, despondent, downcast, sorrowful, wretched, disconsolate, crestfallen, doleful, down in the dumps (*informal*), woebegone, down in the mouth (*informal*) ■ OPPOSITE: happy **2** *They have so far accepted only a miserable 1,100 refugees.* = **pathetic**, low, sorry, disgraceful, mean, shameful, shabby, abject, despicable, deplorable, lamentable, contemptible, scurvy (*old-fashioned*), pitiable, detestable, piteous ■ OPPOSITE: respectable

miserly ADJECTIVE = **mean**, stingy, penny-pinching (*informal*), parsimonious, close, near (*informal*), grasping, beggarly, illiberal, avaricious, niggardly, ungenerous, covetous, penurious, tightfisted, close-fisted, mingy (*Brit. informal*), snoep (*S. African informal*) ■ OPPOSITE: generous

misery NOUN **1** *All that money brought nothing but misery.* = **unhappiness**, distress, despair, grief, suffering, depression, torture, agony, gloom, sadness, discomfort, torment, hardship, sorrow, woe, anguish, melancholy, desolation, wretchedness

■ OPPOSITE: happiness **2** *An elite profited from the misery of the poor.* = **poverty**, want, need, squalor, privation (*formal*), penury, destitution, wretchedness, sordidness, indigence ■ OPPOSITE: luxury **3** *I'm not such a misery now. I've got things sorted out a bit.* = **moaner**, pessimist, killjoy, spoilsport (*informal*), grouch (*informal*), prophet of doom, wet blanket (*informal*), sourpuss (*informal*), wowser (*Austral. & N.Z. slang*) **4** *There is no point dwelling on the miseries of the past.* = **misfortune**, trouble, trial, disaster, load, burden, curse, ordeal, hardship, catastrophe, sorrow, woe, calamity, affliction, tribulation, bitter pill (*informal*)

misfire VERB = **fail**, go wrong, fall through, miscarry, go pear-shaped (*informal*), fail to go off, go phut (*informal*)

misfit NOUN = **nonconformist**, eccentric, flake (*slang, chiefly U.S.*), oddball (*informal*), fish out of water (*informal*), square peg (in a round hole) (*informal*)

misfortune NOUN **1** (*often plural*) *She seemed to enjoy the misfortunes of others.* = **bad luck**, adversity, hard luck, ill luck, infelicity, evil fortune, bad trot (*Austral. slang*) **2** *He had had his full share of misfortunes.* = **mishap**, loss, trouble, trial, blow, failure, accident, disaster, reverse, tragedy, harm, misery, setback, hardship, calamity, affliction, tribulation, whammy (*informal*), misadventure, bummer (*slang*), mischance, stroke of bad luck, evil chance ■ OPPOSITE: good luck

misgiving NOUN = **unease**, worry, doubt, anxiety, suspicion, uncertainty, reservation, hesitation, distrust, apprehension, qualm, trepidation (*formal*), scruple, dubiety

misguided ADJECTIVE = **unwise**, mistaken, foolish, misled, misplaced, deluded, ill-advised, imprudent, injudicious, labouring under a delusion or misapprehension

mishandle VERB = **mismanage**, bungle, botch, mess up (*informal*), screw (up) (*informal*), make a mess of, muff, make a hash of (*informal*), make a nonsense of, bodge (*informal*), flub (*U.S. slang*)

mishap NOUN = **accident**, disaster, misfortune, stroke of bad luck, adversity, calamity, misadventure, contretemps, mischance, infelicity, evil chance, evil fortune

misinform VERB = **mislead**, deceive, misdirect, misguide, give someone a bum steer (*informal, chiefly U.S.*)

misinterpret VERB = **misunderstand**, mistake, distort, misrepresent, misjudge, falsify, pervert, misread, misconstrue, get wrong, misapprehend, misconceive

misjudge VERB = **miscalculate**, be wrong about, underestimate, underrate, overestimate, overrate, get the wrong idea about

mislay VERB = **lose**, misplace, miss, be unable to find, lose track of, be unable to put or lay your hand on, forget the whereabouts of

mislead VERB = **deceive**, fool, delude, take someone in (informal), bluff, beguile, misdirect, misinform, hoodwink, lead astray, pull the wool over someone's eyes (informal), take someone for a ride (informal), misguide, give someone a bum steer (informal, chiefly U.S.)

misleading ADJECTIVE = **confusing**, false, ambiguous, deceptive, spurious, evasive, disingenuous, tricky (informal), deceitful, specious, delusive, delusory, sophistical, casuistical, unstraightforward
■ **OPPOSITE:** straightforward

mismatched ADJECTIVE = **incompatible**, clashing, irregular, disparate, incongruous, discordant, unsuited, ill-assorted, unreconcilable, misallied

misogynist ADJECTIVE = **chauvinist**, sexist, patriarchal ▶ NOUN = **woman-hater**, male chauvinist, anti-feminist, MCP (informal), male chauvinist pig (informal), male supremacist

misquote VERB = **misrepresent**, twist, distort, pervert, muddle, mangle, falsify, garble, misreport, misstate, quote or take out of context

misrepresent VERB = **distort**, disguise, pervert, belie, twist, misinterpret, falsify, garble, misstate

miss¹ VERB **1** It's the first thing you see. You can't miss it. = **fail to notice**, mistake, overlook, pass over **2** She seemed to have missed the point. = **misunderstand**, fail to appreciate **3** Your mum and I are going to miss you at Christmas. = **long for**, wish for, yearn for, want, need, hunger for, pine for, long to see, ache for, feel the loss of, regret the absence of **4** He missed the last bus home. = **be late for**, fail to catch or get **5** We missed our swimming lesson last week. = **not go to**, skip (informal), cut, omit, be absent from, fail to attend, skive off (informal), play truant from, bludge (Austral. & N.Z. informal), absent yourself from **6** We left early, hoping to miss the worst of the traffic. = **avoid**, beat, escape, skirt, duck (informal), cheat, bypass, dodge, evade, get round, elude, steer clear of, sidestep, circumvent (formal), find a way round, give a wide berth to

▶ NOUN After several more misses, they finally got two arrows into the target. = **mistake**, failure, fault, error, blunder, omission, oversight

miss² NOUN (old-fashioned or derogatory) a little miss of seven years of age = **girl**, maiden (archaic, literary), maid (archaic, literary), schoolgirl, young lady, lass, damsel (archaic, poetic), spinster, lassie (informal)

misshapen ADJECTIVE = **twisted**, crooked, warped, unsightly, contorted, malformed, ill-made, unshapely, ill-proportioned

missile NOUN = **projectile**, weapon, shell, rocket

missing ADJECTIVE = **lost**, misplaced, not present, gone, left behind, astray, unaccounted for, mislaid, nowhere to be found

mission NOUN **1** the most crucial stage of his latest peace mission = **assignment**, job, labour, operation, work, commission, trip, message (Scot.), task, undertaking, expedition, chore, errand **2** He viewed his mission in life as protecting the weak from evil. = **task**, work, calling, business, job, office, charge, goal, operation, commission, trust, aim, purpose, duty, undertaking, pursuit, quest, assignment, vocation, errand

missionary NOUN = **evangelist**, preacher, apostle, converter, propagandist, proselytizer

missive NOUN = **letter**, report, note, message, communication, dispatch, memorandum, epistle

mist NOUN Thick mist made flying impossible. = **fog**, cloud, steam, spray, film, haze, vapour, drizzle, smog, dew, condensation, haar (Eastern Brit.), smur or smir (Scot.)
• **mist over** or **up** The windscreen was misting over. = **steam (up)**, cloud, obscure, blur, fog, film, blear, becloud, befog

mistake NOUN **1** He says there must have been some mistake. = **error**, blunder, oversight, slip, misunderstanding, boob (Brit. slang), misconception, gaffe (informal), slip-up (informal), bloomer (Brit. informal), clanger (informal), miscalculation, error of judgment, faux pas, false move, boo-boo (informal), barry or Barry Crocker (Austral. slang) **2** Spelling mistakes are often just the result of haste. = **oversight**, error, slip, inaccuracy, fault, slip-up (informal), howler (informal), goof, solecism (formal), erratum, barry or Barry Crocker (Austral. slang)

▶ VERB No one should mistake how serious this issue is. = **misunderstand**, misinterpret, misjudge, misread, misconstrue, get wrong, misapprehend, misconceive

m

• **mistake something** or **someone for something** or **someone** Hayfever is often mistaken for a summer cold. = **confuse with**, accept as, take for, mix up with, misinterpret as, confound with

mistaken ADJECTIVE **1** I see I was mistaken about you. = **wrong**, incorrect, misled, in the wrong, misguided, off the mark, off target, wide of the mark, misinformed, off base (U.S. & Canad. informal), barking up the wrong tree (informal), off beam (informal), getting the wrong end of the stick (informal), way off beam (informal), labouring under a misapprehension ■ **OPPOSITE:** correct **2** She obviously had a mistaken view. = **inaccurate**, false, inappropriate, faulty, unfounded, erroneous, unsound, fallacious ■ **OPPOSITE:** accurate

mistakenly ADVERB = **incorrectly**, wrongly, falsely, by mistake, inappropriately, erroneously, in error, inaccurately, misguidedly, fallaciously

mistimed ADJECTIVE = **inopportune**, badly timed, inconvenient, untimely, ill-timed, unseasonable, unsynchronized

mistreat VERB = **abuse**, injure, harm, molest, misuse, maul, manhandle, wrong, rough up, ill-treat, brutalize, maltreat, ill-use, handle roughly, knock about or around

mistreatment NOUN = **abuse**, ill-treatment, maltreatment, injury, harm, misuse, mauling, manhandling, roughing up, molestation, unkindness, rough handling, brutalization, ill-usage

mistress NOUN **1** She had served her mistress with devotion for forty years. = **lady**, ruler, commander, chief, director, manager, boss (informal), head, owner, captain, governor, employer, principal, skipper (informal), controller, superintendent, overseer **2** I have put my relationship with my mistress on hold. = **lover**, girlfriend, concubine (old-fashioned), kept woman, paramour (old-fashioned), floozy (slang), fancy woman (slang), inamorata, doxy (archaic), fancy bit (slang), ladylove (old-fashioned)

mistrust NOUN There was mutual mistrust between the two men. = **suspicion**, scepticism, distrust, doubt, uncertainty, apprehension, misgiving, wariness, dubiety ▶ VERB I mistrust all journalists. = **be wary of**, suspect, beware, distrust, apprehend, have doubts about

misty ADJECTIVE = **foggy**, unclear, murky, fuzzy, obscure, blurred, vague, dim, opaque, cloudy, hazy, overcast, bleary, nebulous, indistinct ■ **OPPOSITE:** clear

misunderstand VERB **1** They simply misunderstood him. = **misinterpret**, misread, get the wrong idea (about), mistake, misjudge, misconstrue, mishear, misapprehend, be at cross-purposes with, misconceive **2** I think she simply misunderstood. = **miss the point**, get the wrong end of the stick, get your wires crossed, get your lines crossed

misunderstanding NOUN **1** Tell them what you want to avoid misunderstandings. = **mistake**, error, mix-up, misconception, misreading, misapprehension, false impression, misinterpretation, misjudgment, wrong idea, misconstruction **2** a misunderstanding between friends = **disagreement**, difference, conflict, argument, difficulty, breach, falling-out (informal), quarrel, rift, squabble, rupture, variance, discord, dissension

misunderstood ADJECTIVE = **misjudged**, misinterpreted, misread, misconstrued, unrecognized, misheard, unappreciated

misuse NOUN **1** the misuse of public funds = **waste**, embezzlement, squandering, dissipation, fraudulent use, misemployment, misusage **2** the misuse of power = **abuse**, corruption, exploitation **3** the misuse of drugs in sport = **misapplication**, abuse, illegal use, wrong use **4** Fundamentalism is a deplorable misuse of a faith. = **perversion**, distortion, desecration, profanation **5** his hilarious misuse of words = **misapplication**, solecism, malapropism, catachresis **6** the history of the misuse of indigenous peoples = **mistreatment**, abuse, harm, exploitation, injury, manhandling, ill-treatment, maltreatment, rough handling, inhumane treatment, cruel treatment, ill-usage ▶ VERB **1** She misused her position in the government. = **abuse**, misapply, misemploy, prostitute **2** The committee has cleared leaders of misusing funds. = **waste**, squander, dissipate, embezzle, misappropriate **3** His parents should not have misused him. = **mistreat**, abuse, injure, harm, exploit, wrong, molest, manhandle, ill-treat, brutalize, maltreat, ill-use, handle roughly ■ **OPPOSITE:** cherish **4** breaking a taboo, misusing a sacred ceremony = **profane**, corrupt, desecrate, pervert

mitigate VERB = **ease**, moderate, soften, check, quiet, calm, weaken, dull, diminish, temper, blunt, soothe, subdue, lessen, appease, lighten, remit, allay, placate, abate, tone down, assuage, pacify, mollify, take the edge off, extenuate, tranquillize, palliate, reduce the force of ■ **OPPOSITE:** intensify

USAGE *Mitigate is sometimes wrongly used where militate is meant: his behaviour militates (not mitigates) against his chances of promotion.*

mitigation NOUN **1** *In mitigation, the offences were at the lower end of the scale.* = **extenuation**, explanation, excuse **2** *the mitigation or cure of a physical or mental condition* = **relief**, moderation, allaying, remission, diminution, abatement, alleviation, easement, extenuation, mollification, palliation, assuagement

mix VERB **1** *Oil and water don't mix.* = **combine**, blend, merge, unite, join, cross, compound, incorporate, put together, fuse, mingle, jumble, alloy, amalgamate, interweave, coalesce, intermingle, meld, commingle, commix **2** *He mixes with people younger than himself.* = **socialize**, associate, hang out (*informal*), mingle, circulate, come together, consort, hobnob, fraternize, rub elbows (*informal*) **3** (*often with* **up**) *The plan was to mix up office and residential zones.* = **combine**, marry, blend, integrate, amalgamate, coalesce, meld, commix ▶ NOUN *a magical mix of fantasy and reality* = **mixture**, combination, blend, fusion, compound, jumble, assortment, alloy, medley, concoction, amalgam, mixed bag (*informal*), meld, mélange (*French*), miscellany • **mix someone up** *You're not helping at all, you're just mixing me up even more.* = **bewilder**, upset, confuse, disturb, puzzle, muddle, perplex, unnerve, fluster, throw into confusion • **mix someone up in something** (*usually passive*) *He could have got mixed up in the murder.* = **entangle**, involve, implicate, embroil, rope in • **mix something up 1** *Depressed people often mix up their words.* = **confuse**, scramble, muddle, confound **2** *Mix up the batter in advance.* = **blend**, beat, mix, stir, fold

mixed ADJECTIVE **1** *I came home from the meeting with mixed feelings.* = **uncertain**, conflicting, confused, doubtful, unsure, muddled, contradictory, ambivalent, indecisive, equivocal **2** *I found a very mixed group of individuals.* = **varied**, diverse, different, differing, diversified, cosmopolitan, assorted, jumbled, disparate, miscellaneous, motley, haphazard, manifold (*formal*), heterogeneous ■ **OPPOSITE:** homogeneous **3** *silver jewellery with mixed metals and semi-precious stones* = **combined**, blended, fused, alloyed, united, compound, incorporated, composite, mingled, amalgamated

mixed-up ADJECTIVE = **confused**, disturbed, puzzled, bewildered, at sea, upset, distraught, muddled, perplexed, maladjusted

mixture NOUN **1** *a mixture of spiced, grilled vegetables* = **blend**, mix, variety, fusion, assortment, combine, brew, jumble, medley, concoction, amalgam, amalgamation, mixed bag (*informal*), meld, potpourri, mélange (*French*), miscellany, conglomeration, hotchpotch, admixture, salmagundi **2** *a mixture of concrete and resin* = **composite**, union, compound, alloy **3** *a mixture between Reggae, Bhangra, and Soul fusion* = **cross**, combination, blend, association **4** *Prepare the mixture carefully.* = **concoction**, union, compound, blend, brew, composite, amalgam, conglomeration

mix-up NOUN = **confusion**, mistake, misunderstanding, mess, tangle, muddle, jumble, fankle (*Scot.*)

moan VERB **1** *'My head, my head,' she moaned.* = **groan**, sigh, sob, whine, keen, lament, deplore, bemoan, bewail **2** *I used to moan if I didn't get at least 8 hours' sleep.* = **grumble**, complain, groan (*informal*), whine, beef (*slang*), carp, bitch (*slang*), grouse, gripe (*informal*), whinge (*informal*), bleat, moan and groan, grouch (*informal*) ▶ NOUN **1** *She gave a low choking moan and began to tremble violently.* = **groan**, sigh, sob, lament, wail, grunt, whine, lamentation **2** *They have been listening to people's gripes and moans.* = **complaint**, protest, grumble, beef (*slang*), bitch (*slang*), whine, grouse, gripe (*informal*), grouch (*informal*), kvetch (*U.S. slang*)

mob NOUN **1** *a growing mob of demonstrators* = **crowd**, pack, collection, mass, body, press, host, gathering, drove, gang, flock, herd, swarm, horde, multitude, throng, assemblage **2** *If they continue like this, there is a danger of the mob taking over.* = **masses**, rabble (*derogatory*), hoi polloi, scum, great unwashed (*informal, derogatory*), riffraff, canaille (*French*), commonalty **3** *Can you stop your mob tramping all over the place?* = **gang**, company, group, set, lot, troop, crew (*informal*) ▶ VERB **1** *Her car was mobbed by the media.* = **surround**, besiege, overrun, jostle, fall on, set upon, crowd around, swarm around **2** *Demonstrators mobbed the streets.* = **crowd into**, fill, crowd, pack, jam, cram into, fill to overflowing

mobile ADJECTIVE **1** *a four-hundred-seat mobile theatre* = **movable**, moving, travelling, wandering, portable, locomotive, itinerant, peripatetic, ambulatory, motile

m

2 *She had a mobile, expressive face.*
= **changeable**, meaning, animated,
expressive, eloquent, suggestive,
ever-changing

mobilize VERB **1** *We must try to mobilize
international support.* = **rally**, organize,
stimulate, excite, prompt, marshal,
activate, awaken, animate, muster,
foment, put in motion **2** *The government has
mobilized troops to help.* = **deploy**, prepare,
ready, rally, assemble, call up, marshal,
muster, call to arms, get or make ready

mock VERB *I thought you were mocking me.*
= **laugh at**, insult, tease, ridicule, taunt,
scorn, sneer, scoff, deride, flout, make fun
of, wind someone up (*Brit. slang*), poke fun
at, chaff, take the mickey out of (*informal*),
jeer at, show contempt for, make a monkey
out of, laugh to scorn ■ **OPPOSITE:** respect
▶ ADJECTIVE *'It's tragic,' he swooned in mock
horror.* = **imitation**, pretended, artificial,
forged, fake, false, faked, dummy, bogus,
sham, fraudulent, pseudo (*informal*),
counterfeit, feigned, spurious, ersatz,
phoney or phony (*informal*) ■ **OPPOSITE:**
genuine ▶ NOUN *She found herself made a
mock of.* = **laughing stock**, fool, dupe,
sport, travesty, jest, Aunt Sally (*Brit.*)

mockery NOUN **1** *Was there a glint of mockery
in his eyes?* = **derision**, contempt, ridicule,
scorn, jeering, disdain, scoffing, disrespect,
gibes, contumely (*literary*) **2** *This action
makes a mockery of the government's plans.*
= **farce**, laughing stock, joke, apology
(*informal*), letdown

mocking ADJECTIVE = **scornful**, insulting,
taunting, scoffing, satirical,
contemptuous, irreverent, sarcastic,
sardonic, derisory, disrespectful, disdainful,
derisive, satiric, contumelious (*literary*)

mode NOUN **1** *the capitalist mode of production*
= **method**, way, plan, course, system,
form, state, process, condition, style,
approach, quality, practice, fashion,
technique, manner, procedure, custom,
vein **2** *Their designs were exterminated by the
mode for uncluttered space.* = **fashion**, style,
trend, rage, vogue, look, craze

model NOUN **1** *an architect's model of a wooden
house* = **representation**, image, copy,
miniature, dummy, replica, imitation,
duplicate, lookalike, facsimile, mock-up
2 *the Chinese model of economic reform*
= **pattern**, example, design, standard,
type, original, ideal, mould, norm, gauge,
prototype, paradigm, archetype, exemplar,
lodestar **3** *To keep the cost down, opt for a basic
model.* = **version**, form, kind, design, style,
type, variety, stamp, mode, configuration

4 *an artist's model* = **sitter**, subject, poser
5 *a top photographic model* = **mannequin**,
supermodel, fashion model, clothes horse
(*informal*) ▶ MODIFIER **1** *a model aeroplane*
= **imitation**, copy, toy, miniature, dummy,
duplicate, facsimile **2** *At school she was a
model pupil.* = **ideal**, perfect, impeccable,
exemplary, consummate, flawless,
faultless ■ **OPPOSITE:** imperfect **3** *The aim is
to develop a model farm from which farmers can
learn.* = **archetypal**, standard, typical,
illustrative, paradigmatic ▶ VERB **1** *She
asked if he had modelled the hero on anyone in
particular.* = **base**, shape, plan, found,
pattern, mould **2** *Two boys modelled a variety
of clothes.* = **show off** (*informal*), wear,
display, sport (*informal*) **3** *Sometimes she
carved wood or modelled clay.* = **shape**, form,
design, fashion, cast, stamp, carve, mould,
sculpt

moderate ADJECTIVE **1** *He was an easy-going
man of very moderate views.* = **mild**,
reasonable, controlled, limited, cool, calm,
steady, modest, restrained, deliberate,
sober, middle-of-the-road, temperate,
judicious, peaceable, equable ■ **OPPOSITE:**
extreme **2** *The drug offered only moderate
improvements.* = **average**, middling,
medium, fair, ordinary, indifferent,
mediocre, so-so (*informal*), passable,
unexceptional, fairish, half-pie (*N.Z.
informal*), fair to middling (*informal*) ▶ VERB
1 *They are hoping that she will be persuaded to
moderate her views.* = **soften**, control, calm,
temper, regulate, quiet, diminish, decrease,
curb, restrain, tame, subdue, play down,
lessen, repress, mitigate, tone down,
pacify, modulate, soft-pedal (*informal*)
2 *The crisis has moderated somewhat.* = **lessen**,
relax, ease, wane, abate ■ **OPPOSITE:**
intensify **3** *trying to moderate a quarrel
between the two states* = **arbitrate**, judge,
chair, referee, preside, mediate, take the
chair

moderation NOUN *He called on all parties to
show moderation.* = **restraint**, justice,
fairness, composure, coolness,
temperance, calmness, equanimity,
reasonableness, mildness, justness,
judiciousness, sedateness, moderateness
• **in moderation** *Many of us are able to drink
in moderation.* = **moderately**, within reason,
within limits, within bounds, in moderate
quantities

modern ADJECTIVE **1** *the problem of
materialism in modern society* = **current**,
present, contemporary, recent, late,
present-day, latter-day **2** *a more tailored and
modern style* = **up-to-date**, latest, fresh,

new, novel, with it (*old-fashioned*, *informal*), up-to-the-minute, newfangled, neoteric (*rare*) ■ **OPPOSITE:** old-fashioned

modernity NOUN = **novelty**, currency, innovation, freshness, newness, contemporaneity, recentness

modernize VERB = **update**, renew, revamp, remake, renovate, remodel, rejuvenate, make over, face-lift, bring up to date, rebrand

modest ADJECTIVE **1** *You don't get rich, but you can earn a modest living from it.* = **moderate**, small, limited, fair, ordinary, middling, meagre, frugal, scanty, unexceptional **2** *He's modest, as well as being a great player.* = **unpretentious**, simple, reserved, retiring, quiet, shy, humble, discreet, blushing, self-conscious, coy, meek, reticent, unassuming, self-effacing, demure, diffident, bashful, aw-shucks

modesty NOUN = **reserve**, decency, humility, shyness, propriety, reticence, timidity, diffidence, quietness, coyness, self-effacement, meekness, lack of pretension, bashfulness, humbleness, unpretentiousness, demureness, unobtrusiveness, discreetness
■ **OPPOSITE:** conceit

modicum NOUN = **little**, bit, drop, touch, inch, scrap, dash, grain, particle, fragment, atom, pinch, ounce, shred, small amount, crumb, tinge, mite, tad (*informal*), speck, iota

modification NOUN = **change**, restriction, variation, qualification, adjustment, revision, alteration, mutation, reformation, refinement, modulation

modify VERB **1** *They agreed to modify their recruitment policy.* = **change**, reform, vary, convert, transform, alter, adjust, adapt, revise, remodel, rework, tweak (*informal*), reorganize, recast, reshape, redo, refashion **2** *He had to modify his language considerably.* = **tone down**, limit, reduce, lower, qualify, relax, ease, restrict, moderate, temper, soften, restrain, lessen, abate

modish ADJECTIVE = **fashionable**, current, smart, stylish, trendy (*Brit. informal*), on trend, in, now (*informal*), with it (*old-fashioned, informal*), contemporary, hip (*slang*), vogue, chic, all the rage, up-to-the-minute, à la mode, voguish, schmick (*Austral. informal*), funky

modulate VERB = **adjust**, balance, vary, tone, tune, regulate, harmonize, inflect, attune

modus operandi NOUN = **procedure**, way, system, process, operation, practice, method, technique, praxis

mogul NOUN = **tycoon**, lord, baron, notable, magnate, big gun (*informal*), big shot (*informal*), personage, nob (*slang, chiefly Brit.*), potentate, big wheel (*slang*), big cheese (*slang, old-fashioned*), big noise (*informal*), big hitter (*informal*), heavy hitter (*informal*), nabob (*informal*), bashaw, V.I.P.

moist ADJECTIVE = **damp**, wet, dripping, rainy, soggy, humid, dank, clammy, dewy, not dry, drizzly, dampish, wettish

moisten VERB = **dampen**, water, wet, soak, damp, moisturize, humidify, bedew

moisture NOUN = **damp**, water, liquid, sweat, humidity, dew, perspiration, dampness, wetness, dankness, wateriness

molecule NOUN = **particle**, atom, mite, jot, speck, mote, iota

molest VERB **1** *He was accused of sexually molesting a colleague.* = **abuse**, attack, hurt, injure, harm, interfere with, assail, accost, manhandle, ill-treat, maltreat **2** *He disguised himself to avoid being molested in the street.* = **annoy**, worry, upset, harry, bother, disturb, bug (*informal*), plague, irritate, tease, torment, harass, afflict, badger, persecute, beset, hector, pester, vex

mollify VERB = **pacify**, quiet, calm, compose, soothe, appease, quell, sweeten, placate, conciliate, propitiate

mom NOUN (*U.S. & Canad.*) = **mum**, mother, ma

moment NOUN **1** *In a moment he was gone.* = **instant**, second, minute, flash, shake (*informal*), tick (*Brit. informal*), no time, twinkling, split second, jiffy (*informal*), trice, two shakes (*informal*), two shakes of a lamb's tail (*informal*), bat of an eye (*informal*) **2** *At this moment a car stopped outside the house.* = **time**, point, stage, instant, point in time, hour, juncture **3** *I was glad I had nothing of great moment to do that afternoon.* = **importance**, concern, value, worth, weight, import (*formal*), consequence, substance, significance, gravity, seriousness, weightiness

momentarily ADVERB = **briefly**, for a moment, temporarily, for a second, for a minute, for a short time, for an instant, for a little while, for a short while, for the nonce

momentary ADJECTIVE = **short-lived**, short, brief, temporary, passing, quick, fleeting, hasty, transitory ■ **OPPOSITE:** lasting

momentous ADJECTIVE = **significant**, important, serious, vital, critical, crucial (*informal*), grave, historic, decisive, pivotal, fateful, weighty, consequential, of moment, earth-shaking (*informal*)
■ **OPPOSITE:** unimportant

m

momentum NOUN = **impetus**, force, power, drive, push (*informal*), energy, strength, thrust, propulsion, go-forward

monarch NOUN = **ruler**, king or queen, sovereign, tsar, potentate, crowned head, emperor or empress, prince or princess

monarchy NOUN **1** *a debate on the future of the monarchy* = **sovereignty**, despotism, autocracy, kingship, absolutism, royalism, monocracy **2** *The country was a monarchy until 1973.* = **kingdom**, empire, realm, principality

monastery NOUN = **abbey**, house, convent, priory, cloister, religious community, nunnery, friary

monastic ADJECTIVE = **monkish**, secluded, cloistered, reclusive, withdrawn, austere, celibate, contemplative, ascetic, sequestered, hermit-like, conventual, cenobitic, coenobitic, cloistral, eremitic, monachal

monetary ADJECTIVE = **financial**, money, economic, capital, cash, fiscal, budgetary, pecuniary

money NOUN *A lot of money that you pay goes back to the distributor.* = **cash**, funds, capital, currency, hard cash, green (*slang*), readies (*informal*), riches, necessary (*informal*), silver, bread (*slang*), coin, tin (*slang*), brass (*Northern English, dialect*), loot (*informal*), dough (*slang*), the ready (*informal*), banknotes, dosh (*Brit. & Austral. slang*), lolly (*Brit. slang*), the wherewithal, legal tender, megabucks (*U.S. & Canad. slang*), needful (*informal*), specie, shekels (*informal*), dibs (*slang*), filthy lucre (*facetious*), moolah (*slang*), ackers (*slang*), gelt (*slang, chiefly U.S.*), spondulicks (*slang*), pelf (*archaic*), mazuma (*slang, chiefly U.S.*), kembla (*Austral. slang*) • **in the money** *If you are lucky, you could be in the money.* = **rich**, wealthy, prosperous, affluent, rolling (*slang*), loaded (*slang*), flush (*informal*), well-off, well-heeled (*informal*), well-to-do, on Easy Street (*informal*), in clover (*informal*), minted (*Brit. slang*) ■ **RELATED WORD:** *adjective* pecuniary

moneyed or **monied** ADJECTIVE = **rich**, loaded (*slang*), wealthy, flush (*informal*), prosperous, affluent, well-off, well-heeled (*informal*), well-to-do, minted (*Brit. slang*)

moneymaking ADJECTIVE = **profitable**, successful, lucrative, gainful, paying, thriving, remunerative

mongrel NOUN *They were walking their pet mongrel on the outskirts of the town when it happened.* = **hybrid**, cross, half-breed, crossbreed, mixed breed, bigener (*Biology*) ▶ ADJECTIVE *He was determined to save his mongrel puppy.* = **half-breed**, hybrid, crossbred, of mixed breed

monitor VERB *Officials had not been allowed to monitor the voting.* = **check**, follow, record, watch, survey, observe, scan, oversee, supervise, keep an eye on, keep tabs on ▶ NOUN **1** *Government monitors will continue to accompany reporters.* = **guide**, observer, supervisor, overseer, invigilator **2** *As a school monitor he set a good example.* = **prefect** (*Brit.*), head girl, head boy, senior boy, senior girl

monk NOUN = **friar**, brother, religious, novice, monastic, oblate ■ **RELATED WORD:** *adjective* monastic

monkey NOUN **1** *He walked on all fours like a monkey.* = **simian**, ape, primate, jackanapes (*archaic*) **2** *She's such a little monkey.* = **rascal**, horror (*informal*), devil, rogue, imp, tyke, scallywag, mischief maker, scamp, nointer (*Austral. slang*) ■ **RELATED WORDS:** *adjective* simian; *collective noun* troop

monolithic ADJECTIVE = **huge**, giant, massive, imposing, solid, substantial, gigantic, monumental (*informal*), colossal, impenetrable, intractable, immovable

monologue NOUN = **speech**, lecture, sermon, harangue, soliloquy, oration, spiel (*informal*)

monopolize VERB **1** *They are virtually monopolizing the market.* = **control**, corner, take over, dominate, exercise or have a monopoly of **2** *He monopolized her totally, to the exclusion of her brothers and sisters.* = **keep to yourself**, corner, hog (*slang*), engross

monotonous ADJECTIVE **1** *It's monotonous work, like most factory jobs.* = **tedious**, boring, dull, repetitive, uniform, all the same, plodding, tiresome, humdrum, unchanging, colourless, mind-numbing, soporific, ho-hum (*informal*), repetitious, wearisome, samey (*informal*), unvaried ■ **OPPOSITE:** interesting **2** *a monotonous voice* = **toneless**, flat, uniform, droning, unchanging, uninflected ■ **OPPOSITE:** animated

monotony NOUN = **tedium**, routine, boredom, dullness, sameness, uniformity, flatness, repetitiveness, tediousness, repetitiousness, colourlessness, tiresomeness

monster NOUN **1** *He said he'd hooked a real monster of a fish.* = **giant**, mammoth, titan, colossus, monstrosity, leviathan, behemoth **2** *You may sound like an absolute monster!* = **brute**, devil, savage, beast, demon, villain, barbarian, fiend, ogre, ghoul, bogeyman

monstrosity NOUN **1** *The towering figure looked like some monstrosity from a sci-fi movie.* = **freak**, horror (*informal*), monster, mutant, ogre, lusus naturae (*Latin*), miscreation, teratism **2** *the monstrosity of Nazism* = **hideousness**, horror, evil, atrocity, abnormality, obscenity, dreadfulness, frightfulness, heinousness, hellishness, loathsomeness

monstrous ADJECTIVE **1** *She endured his monstrous behaviour for years.* = **outrageous**, shocking, evil, horrifying, vicious, foul, cruel, infamous, intolerable, disgraceful, scandalous, atrocious, inhuman, diabolical, heinous, odious, loathsome, devilish, egregious, fiendish, villainous ■ OPPOSITE: decent **2** *They were erecting a monstrous edifice.* = **huge**, giant, massive, great, towering, vast, enormous, tremendous, immense, titanic, gigantic, mammoth, colossal, stellar (*informal*), prodigious, stupendous, gargantuan, elephantine, ginormous (*informal*), humongous or humungous (*informal*) ■ OPPOSITE: tiny **3** *the film's monstrous fantasy figure* = **unnatural**, terrible, horrible, dreadful, abnormal, obscene, horrendous, hideous, grotesque, gruesome, frightful, hellish (*informal*), freakish, fiendish, miscreated ■ OPPOSITE: normal

month NOUN = **four weeks**, thirty days, moon

monument NOUN **1** *He laid a wreath on a monument near Bayeux.* = **memorial**, cairn, statue, pillar, marker, shrine, tombstone, mausoleum, commemoration, headstone, gravestone, obelisk, cenotaph **2** *By her achievements she leaves a fitting monument to her beliefs.* = **testament**, record, witness, token, reminder, remembrance, memento

monumental ADJECTIVE **1** *a monumental work on Chinese astronomy* = **important**, classic, significant, outstanding, lasting, enormous, historic, enduring, memorable, awesome, majestic, immortal, unforgettable, prodigious, stupendous, awe-inspiring, epoch-making ■ OPPOSITE: unimportant **2** (*informal*) *It had been a monumental blunder to give him the assignment.* = **immense**, great, massive, terrible, tremendous, horrible, staggering, catastrophic, gigantic, colossal, whopping (*informal*), indefensible, unforgivable, egregious ■ OPPOSITE: tiny **3** *monumental architecture* = **commemorative**, memorial, monolithic, statuary, funerary

mood NOUN **1** *You are clearly in a good mood today.* = **state of mind**, spirit, humour, temper, vein, tenor, disposition, frame of mind **2** *She was obviously in a mood.* = **depression**, sulk, bad temper, blues, dumps (*informal*), wax (*informal, chiefly Brit.*), melancholy, doldrums, the hump (*Brit. informal*), bate (*Brit. slang*), fit of pique, low spirits, the sulks, grumps (*informal*), foulie (*Austral. slang*) • **in the mood** *After all that activity we were in the mood for a good meal.* = **inclined**, willing, interested, minded, keen, eager, disposed towards, in the (right) frame of mind, favourable towards

moody ADJECTIVE **1** *My friend was unstable and moody.* = **changeable**, volatile, unpredictable, unstable, erratic, fickle, temperamental, impulsive, mercurial, capricious, unsteady, fitful, flighty, faddish, inconstant ■ OPPOSITE: stable **2** *He is a moody man behind that jokey front.* = **sulky**, cross, wounded, angry, offended, irritable, crabbed, crusty, temperamental, touchy, curt, petulant, ill-tempered, irascible, cantankerous, tetchy, testy, chippy (*informal*), in a huff, short-tempered, waspish, piqued, crabby, huffy, splenetic, crotchety (*informal*), ill-humoured, huffish, tooshie (*Austral. slang*) ■ OPPOSITE: cheerful **3** *Don't go all moody on me!* = **gloomy**, sad, miserable, melancholy, frowning, dismal, dour, sullen, glum, introspective, in the doldrums, out of sorts (*informal*), downcast, morose, lugubrious, pensive, broody, crestfallen, doleful, down in the dumps (*informal*), saturnine, down in the mouth (*informal*), mopish, mopy ■ OPPOSITE: cheerful **4** *melancholy guitars and moody lyrics* = **sad**, gloomy, melancholy, sombre

moon NOUN *Neptune's large moon* = **satellite** ▶ VERB *She was mooning around all morning, doing nothing.* = **idle**, drift, loaf, languish, waste time, daydream, mope, mooch (*Brit. slang*) ■ RELATED WORD: *adjective* lunar

moor¹ NOUN *The small town is high up on the moors.* = **moorland**, fell (*Brit.*), heath, muir (*Scot.*)

moor² VERB *She had moored her boat on the right bank of the river.* = **tie up**, fix, secure, anchor, dock, lash, berth, fasten, make fast

moot VERB *When the theatre idea was first mooted, I had my doubts.* = **bring up**, propose, suggest, introduce, put forward, ventilate, broach ▶ ADJECTIVE *How long he'll be able to do so is a moot point.* = **debatable**, open, controversial, doubtful, unsettled, unresolved, undecided, at issue, arguable, open to debate, contestable, disputable

mop NOUN **1** *He was standing outside the door with a mop and bucket.* = **squeegee**, sponge,

m

swab **2** *He was dark-eyed with a mop of tight curls.* = **mane**, shock, mass, tangle, mat, thatch ▶ VERB *There was a woman mopping the stairs.* = **clean**, wash, wipe, sponge, swab, squeegee • **mop something up 1** *A waiter mopped up the mess as best he could.* = **clean up**, wash, sponge, mop, soak up, swab, wipe up, sop up **2** (*Military*) *The infantry divisions mopped up remaining centres of resistance.* = **finish off**, clear, account for, eliminate, round up, clean out, neutralize, pacify

mope VERB = **brood**, moon, pine, hang around, idle, fret, pout, languish, waste time, sulk, be gloomy, eat your heart out, be apathetic, be dejected, be down in the mouth (*informal*), have a long face, wear a long face, go about like a half-shut knife (*informal*)

moral ADJECTIVE **1** *the moral issues involved in 'playing God'* = **ethical**, social, behavioural **2** *He showed moral courage in defending his ideas.* = **psychological**, emotional, mental **3** *The committee members are moral, competent people.* = **good**, just, right, principled, pure, decent, innocent, proper, noble, ethical, upright, honourable, honest, righteous, virtuous, blameless, high-minded, chaste, upstanding, meritorious, incorruptible ■ **OPPOSITE:** immoral ▶ NOUN *The moral of the story is, let the buyer beware.* = **lesson**, meaning, point, message, teaching, import, significance, precept ▶ PLURAL NOUN *Western ideas and morals* = **morality**, standards, conduct, principles, behaviour, manners, habits, ethics, integrity, mores, scruples

morale NOUN = **confidence**, heart, spirit, temper, self-esteem, team spirit, mettle, esprit de corps

morality NOUN **1** *an effort to preserve traditional morality* = **virtue**, justice, principles, morals, honour, integrity, goodness, honesty, decency, fair play, righteousness, good behaviour, propriety, chastity, probity (*formal*), rectitude, rightness, uprightness **2** *aspects of Christian morality* = **ethics**, conduct, principles, ideals, morals, manners, habits, philosophy, mores, moral code **3** *the morality of blood sports* = **rights and wrongs**, ethics, ethicality

morass NOUN **1** *I tried to drag myself out of the morass of despair.* = **mess**, confusion, chaos, jam (*informal*), tangle, mix-up, muddle, quagmire **2** *a morass of gooey mud* = **marsh**, swamp, bog, slough, fen, moss (*Scot. & Northern English, dialect*), quagmire, marshland, muskeg (*Canad.*)

moratorium NOUN = **postponement**, stay, freeze, halt, suspension, respite, standstill

morbid ADJECTIVE **1** *Some people have a morbid fascination with crime.* = **gruesome**, sick (*informal*), dreadful, ghastly, hideous, unhealthy, grisly, macabre, horrid, ghoulish, unwholesome **2** *He was in no mood for any morbid introspection.* = **gloomy**, brooding, pessimistic, melancholy, sombre, grim, glum, lugubrious, funereal, low-spirited ■ **OPPOSITE:** cheerful **3** *Uraemia is a morbid condition.* = **diseased**, sick, infected, deadly, ailing, unhealthy, malignant, sickly, pathological, unsound ■ **OPPOSITE:** healthy

more DETERMINER *Give them a bit more information.* = **extra**, additional, spare, new, other, added, further, fresh, new-found, supplementary ▶ ADVERB **1** *When we are tired we feel pain more.* = **to a greater extent**, longer, better, further, some more **2** *They have the ability to argue that black is white, and more, to believe that black is white.* = **moreover**, also, in addition, besides, furthermore, what's more, on top of that, to boot, into the bargain, over and above that

moreover ADVERB = **furthermore**, also, further, in addition, too, as well, besides, likewise, what is more, to boot, additionally, into the bargain, withal (*literary*)

moribund ADJECTIVE = **declining**, weak, waning, standing still, stagnant, stagnating, on the way out, at a standstill, obsolescent, on its last legs, forceless

morning NOUN **1** *On Sunday morning he was woken by the telephone.* = **before noon**, forenoon, morn (*poetic*), a.m. **2** *I started to lose hope of ever seeing the morning.* = **dawn**, sunrise, morrow (*archaic*), first light, daybreak, break of day

moronic ADJECTIVE *It was wanton, moronic vandalism.* = **idiotic**, foolish, mindless, stupid, daft (*informal*), brainless, unintelligent, asinine, muttonheaded (*slang*)

morose ADJECTIVE = **sullen**, miserable, moody, gloomy, down, low, cross, blue, depressed, sour, crabbed, pessimistic, perverse, melancholy, dour, crusty, glum, surly, mournful, gruff, churlish, sulky, taciturn, ill-tempered, in a bad mood, grouchy (*informal*), down in the dumps (*informal*), crabby, saturnine, ill-humoured, ill-natured ■ **OPPOSITE:** cheerful

morsel NOUN = **piece**, bite, bit, slice, scrap, part, grain, taste, segment, fragment, fraction, snack, crumb, nibble, mouthful, tad (*informal*), titbit, soupçon (*French*)

mortal ADJECTIVE **1** *Man is designed to be mortal.* = **human**, worldly, passing, earthly, fleshly, temporal, transient, ephemeral, perishable, corporeal, impermanent, sublunary **2** *a mortal blow to terrorism* = **fatal**, killing, terminal, deadly, destructive, lethal, murderous, death-dealing **3** *He was forced to walk the plank by his mortal enemy, Cut-Throat Jake.* = **unrelenting**, bitter, sworn, deadly, relentless, to the death, implacable, out-and-out, irreconcilable, remorseless **4** *She lived in mortal fear that one day she would be found out.* = **great**, serious, terrible, enormous, severe, extreme, grave, intense, awful, dire, agonizing ▶ NOUN *impossible needs for any mere mortal to meet* = **human being**, being, man, woman, body (*informal*), person, human, individual, earthling

mortality NOUN **1** *The event served as a stark reminder of our mortality.* = **humanity**, transience, impermanence, ephemerality, temporality, corporeality, impermanency **2** *the nation's infant mortality rate* = **death**, dying, fatality, loss of life

mortified ADJECTIVE = **humiliated**, embarrassed, shamed, crushed, annoyed, humbled, horrified, put down, put out (*informal*), ashamed, confounded, deflated, vexed, affronted, displeased, chagrined, chastened, discomfited, abashed, put to shame, rendered speechless, made to eat humble pie (*informal*), given a showing-up (*informal*)

mortify VERB **1** *She mortified her family by leaving her husband.* = **humiliate**, disappoint, embarrass, shame, crush, annoy, humble, deflate, vex, affront, displease, chagrin, discomfit, abase, put someone to shame, abash **2** *The most austere of the Christians felt the need to mortify themselves.* = **discipline**, control, deny, subdue, chasten, abase

mortuary NOUN = **morgue**, funeral home (*U.S.*), funeral parlour

most PRONOUN = **nearly all**, the majority, the mass, almost all, the bulk, the lion's share, the preponderance

> USAGE *More* and *most* should be distinguished when used in comparisons. *More* applies to cases involving two people, objects, etc., *most* to cases involving three or more: *John is the more intelligent of the two; he is the most intelligent of the students.*

mostly ADVERB **1** *I am working with mostly highly motivated people.* = **mainly**, largely,

chiefly, principally, primarily, above all, on the whole, predominantly, for the most part, almost entirely **2** *We mostly go to clubs, or round to a friend's house.* = **generally**, usually, on the whole, most often, as a rule, customarily

mote NOUN = **speck**, spot, grain, particle, fragment, atom, mite

moth NOUN ■ RELATED WORDS: *name of young* caterpillar; *enthusiast* lepidopterist

mother NOUN *Mother and child form a close attachment.* = **female parent**, mum (*Brit. informal*), mom (*U.S. & Canad. informal*), mummy (*Brit. informal*), mommy (*U.S. & Canad. informal*), ma (*informal*), mater, dam, old woman (*informal*), old lady (*informal*), foster mother, birth mother, biological mother ▶ VERB **1** *She had dreamed of mothering a large family.* = **give birth to**, produce, bear, bring forth, drop **2** *She felt a great need to mother him.* = **nurture**, raise, protect, tend, nurse, rear, care for, cherish ▶ MODIFIER *He looks on Turkey as his mother country.* = **native**, natural, innate, inborn, connate ■ RELATED WORD: *adjective* maternal

motherly ADJECTIVE = **maternal**, loving, kind, caring, warm, comforting, sheltering, gentle, tender, protective, fond, affectionate

motif NOUN **1** *wallpaper with a rose motif* = **design**, form, shape, decoration, ornament **2** *the motif of magical apples in fairytales* = **theme**, idea, subject, concept, leitmotif, trope

motion NOUN **1** *the laws governing light, sound and motion* = **movement**, action, mobility, passing, travel, progress, flow, passage, locomotion, motility, kinesics **2** *He made a neat chopping motion with his hand.* = **gesture**, sign, wave, signal, gesticulation **3** *The conference is now debating the motion.* = **proposal**, suggestion, recommendation, proposition, submission ▶ VERB *She motioned for the doors to be opened.* = **gesture**, direct, wave, signal, nod, beckon, gesticulate • **in motion 1** *His job begins in earnest now that the World Cup is in motion.* = **in progress**, going on, under way, afoot, on the go (*informal*) **2** *Always stay seated while a bus is in motion.* = **moving**, going, working, travelling, functioning, under way, operational, on the move (*informal*) ■ RELATED WORD: *adjective* kinetic

motionless ADJECTIVE = **still**, static, stationary, standing, fixed, frozen, calm, halted, paralysed, lifeless, inert, unmoved, transfixed, at rest, immobile, inanimate, at a standstill, unmoving, stock-still ■ OPPOSITE: moving

motivate VERB **1** *His hard work was motivated by a need to achieve.* = **inspire**, drive, stimulate, provoke, lead, move, cause, prompt, stir, trigger, set off, induce, arouse, prod, get going, instigate, impel, actuate, give incentive to, inspirit **2** *How do you motivate people to work hard and efficiently?* = **stimulate**, drive, inspire, stir, arouse, get going, galvanize, incentivize

motivation NOUN **1** *Money is my motivation.* = **incentive**, inspiration, motive, stimulus, reason, spur, impulse, persuasion, inducement, incitement, instigation, carrot and stick **2** *The team may be lacking motivation for next week's game.* = **inspiration**, drive, desire, ambition, hunger, interest

motive NOUN *Police have ruled out robbery as a motive for the killing.* = **reason**, motivation, cause, ground(s), design, influence, purpose, object, intention, spur, incentive, inspiration, stimulus, rationale, inducement, incitement, mainspring, the why and wherefore ▸ ADJECTIVE *the motive power behind a boxer's punches* = **moving**, driving, motivating, operative, activating, impelling

motley ADJECTIVE = **miscellaneous**, mixed, varied, diversified, mingled, unlike, assorted, disparate, dissimilar, heterogeneous ■ OPPOSITE: homogeneous

mottled ADJECTIVE = **blotchy**, spotted, pied, streaked, marbled, flecked, variegated, chequered, speckled, freckled, dappled, tabby, stippled, piebald, brindled

motto NOUN = **saying**, slogan, maxim, rule, cry, formula, gnome, adage, proverb, dictum, precept, byword, watchword, tag-line

mould¹ NOUN **1** *the moulds for the foundry* = **cast**, form, die, shape, pattern, stamp, matrix **2** *At first sight, he is not cast in the leading man mould.* = **design**, line, style, fashion, build, form, cut, kind, shape, structure, pattern, brand, frame, construction, stamp, format, configuration **3** *every man of heroic mould who struggles up to eminence* = **nature**, character, sort, kind, quality, type, stamp, kidney, calibre, ilk ▸ VERB **1** *We moulded a statue out of mud.* = **shape**, make, work, form, create, model, fashion, cast, stamp, construct, carve, forge, sculpt **2** *The experience has moulded her personality.* = **influence**, make, form, control, direct, affect, shape

mould² NOUN *jars of jam with mould on them* = **fungus**, blight, mildew, mustiness, mouldiness

moulder VERB = **decay**, waste, break down, crumble, rot, disintegrate, perish, decompose

mouldy ADJECTIVE = **stale**, spoiled, rotting, decaying, bad, rotten, blighted, musty, fusty, mildewed

mound NOUN **1** *huge mounds of dirt* = **heap**, bing (*Scot.*), pile, drift, stack, rick **2** *We sat on a grassy mound and had our picnic.* = **hill**, bank, rise, dune, embankment, knoll, hillock, kopje or koppie (*S. African*) **3** *an ancient, man-made burial mound* = **barrow**, tumulus **4** *a rough double-moated mound earmarked as an ancient monument* = **earthwork**, rampart, bulwark, motte (*History*)

mount VERB **1** *a security operation mounted by the army* = **launch**, stage, prepare, deliver, set in motion **2** *For several hours, tension mounted.* = **increase**, build, grow, swell, intensify, escalate, multiply ■ OPPOSITE: decrease **3** *The uncollected garbage mounts in the streets.* = **accumulate**, increase, collect, gather, build up, pile up, amass, cumulate **4** *She was mounting the stairs to the tower.* = **ascend**, scale, climb (up), go up, clamber up, make your way up ■ OPPOSITE: descend **5** *He mounted his horse and rode away.* = **get (up) on**, jump on, straddle, climb onto, climb up on, hop on to, bestride, get on the back of, get astride ■ OPPOSITE: get off **6** *She mounts the work in a frame.* = **display**, set, frame, set off **7** *The fuel tank is mounted on the side of the truck.* = **fit**, place, set, position, set up, fix, secure, attach, install, erect, put in place, put in position, emplace **8** *mounting an exhibition of historical Tiffany jewellery* = **display**, present, stage, prepare, put on, organize, get up (*informal*), exhibit, put on display ▸ NOUN **1** *the number of owners who care for older mounts* = **horse**, steed (*literary*) **2** *Even on a solid mount, any movement nearby may shake the image.* = **backing**, setting, support, stand, base, mounting, frame, fixture, foil

mountain NOUN **1** *Ben Nevis, Britain's highest mountain* = **peak**, mount, height, ben (*Scot.*), horn, ridge, fell (*Brit.*), berg (*S. African*), alp, pinnacle, elevation, Munro, eminence **2** *They are faced with a mountain of bureaucracy.* = **heap**, mass, masses, pile, a great deal, ton, stack, abundance, mound, profusion, shedload (*Brit. informal*)

mountainous ADJECTIVE **1** *a mountainous region* = **high**, towering, soaring, steep (*informal*), rocky, highland, alpine, upland **2** *a plan designed to reduce the company's mountainous debt* = **huge**, great, enormous, mighty, immense, daunting, gigantic, monumental (*informal*), mammoth,

prodigious, hulking, ponderous
■ OPPOSITE: tiny

mourn VERB **1** (*often with* for) *She still mourned her father.* = **grieve for**, miss, lament, keen for, weep for, sorrow for, wail for, wear black for **2** *We mourned the loss of our cities.* = **bemoan**, rue (*literary*), deplore, bewail

mournful ADJECTIVE **1** *He looked mournful, even near to tears.* = **dismal**, sad, unhappy, miserable, gloomy, grieving, melancholy, sombre, heartbroken, desolate, woeful, rueful, heavy, downcast, grief-stricken, lugubrious, disconsolate, joyless, funereal, heavy-hearted, down in the dumps (*informal*), cheerless, brokenhearted
■ OPPOSITE: happy **2** *the mournful wail of bagpipes* = **sad**, distressing, unhappy, tragic, painful, afflicting, melancholy, harrowing, grievous, woeful, deplorable, lamentable, plaintive, calamitous, sorrowful, piteous
■ OPPOSITE: cheerful

mourning NOUN **1** *The period of mourning and bereavement may be long.* = **grieving**, grief, bereavement, weeping, woe, lamentation, keening **2** *Yesterday the whole country was in mourning.* = **black**, weeds, sackcloth and ashes, widow's weeds

mouth NOUN **1** *She clamped her hand against her mouth.* = **lips**, trap (*slang*), chops (*slang*), jaws, gob (*slang, esp. Brit.*), laughing gear (*Brit. & Austral. slang*), maw, yap (*slang*), cakehole (*Brit. slang*) **2** *the mouth of the tunnel* = **entrance**, opening, gateway, cavity, door, aperture, crevice, orifice **3** *a lit candle stuck in the bottle's mouth* = **opening**, lip, rim **4** *the mouth of the river* = **inlet**, outlet, estuary, firth, outfall, debouchment **5** *She is all mouth and no talent.* = **boasting**, gas (*informal*), bragging, hot air (*slang*), braggadocio, idle talk, empty talk **6** (*informal*) = **insolence**, lip (*slang*), sauce (*informal*), cheek (*informal*), rudeness, impudence, backchat (*informal*)
▶ VERB = **utter**, say, speak, voice, express, pronounce, articulate, enunciate, verbalize, vocalize, say insincerely, say for form's sake • **down in** *or* **at the mouth** = **depressed**, down, blue, sad, unhappy, miserable, melancholy, dejected, dispirited, downcast, disheartened, crestfallen, down in the dumps (*informal*), sick as a parrot (*informal*), in low spirits • **mouth off** = **rant**, rave, spout (*informal*), sound off, declaim, jabber ■ RELATED WORDS: *adjectives* oral, oscular

mouthful NOUN = **taste**, little, bite, bit, drop, sample, swallow, sip, sup, spoonful, morsel, forkful

mouthpiece NOUN **1** *Their mouthpiece is the vice-president.* = **spokesperson**, agent, representative, delegate, spokesman or woman or person **2** *The newspaper is regarded as a mouthpiece of the ministry.* = **publication**, journal, organ, periodical

movable ADJECTIVE = **portable**, mobile, transferable, detachable, not fixed, transportable, portative

move VERB **1** *She moved the sheaf of papers into position.* = **transfer**, change, carry, transport, switch, shift, transpose **2** *She waited for him to get up, but he didn't move.* = **go**, walk, march, advance, progress, shift, proceed, stir, budge, make a move, change position **3** *My home is in Yorkshire and I don't want to move.* = **relocate**, leave, remove, quit, go away, migrate, emigrate, move house, flit (*Scot. & Northern English, dialect*), decamp, up sticks (*Brit. informal*), pack your bags (*informal*), change residence **4** *The hearings moved me to come up with these suggestions.* = **drive**, lead, cause, influence, persuade, push, shift, inspire, prompt, stimulate, motivate, induce, shove, activate, propel, rouse, prod, incite, impel, set going ■ OPPOSITE: discourage **5** *These stories surprised and moved me.* = **touch**, affect, excite, impress, stir, agitate, disquiet, make an impression on, tug at your heartstrings (*often facetious*) **6** *I moved that the case be dismissed.* = **propose**, suggest, urge, recommend, request, advocate, submit, put forward
▶ NOUN **1** *My eyes followed her every move.* = **action**, act, step, movement, shift, motion, manoeuvre, deed **2** *The cut in interest rates was a wise move.* = **ploy**, action, measure, step, initiative, stroke, tactic, manoeuvre, deed, tack, ruse, gambit, stratagem **3** *He announced his move to Montparnasse in 1909.* = **transfer**, posting, shift, removal, migration, relocation, flit (*Scot. & Northern English, dialect*), flitting (*Scot. & Northern English, dialect*), change of address **4** *It's your move, chess fans tell Sports Minister.* = **turn**, go, play, chance, shot (*informal*), opportunity • **get a move on** *I'd better get a move on if I want to finish on time.* = **speed up**, hurry (up), get going, get moving, get cracking (*informal*), step on it (*informal*), make haste, shake a leg (*informal*), get your skates on (*informal*), stir yourself • **on the move 1** *My husband and I were always on the move.* = **in transit**, moving, travelling, journeying, on the road (*informal*), under way, voyaging, on the run, in motion, on the wing **2** *Many positive trends are showing that the country is on the move.*

= **active**, moving, developing, advancing, progressing, succeeding, stirring, going forward, astir

movement NOUN **1** *a nationalist movement that's gaining strength* = **group**, party, organization, grouping, front, camp, faction **2** *He contributed to the Movement for the Ordination of Women.* = **campaign**, drive, push (*informal*), crusade **3** *I could watch your every movement.* = **move**, act, action, operation, motion, gesture, manoeuvre **4** *There was movement behind the door.* = **activity**, moving, stirring, bustle, agitation **5** *the movement of the fish going up river* = **advance**, progress, flow, progression **6** *the movement of people, goods and services across borders* = **transfer**, transportation, displacement **7** *the movement towards democracy* = **trend**, flow, swing, current, tendency **8** *The meeting seems to have produced no movement on either side.* = **development**, change, shift, variation, fluctuation **9** *The participants believed movement forward was possible.* = **progression**, advance, progress, breakthrough **10** *the first movement of Beethoven's 7th symphony* = **section**, part, division, passage

movie NOUN *That was the first movie he ever made.* = **film**, picture, feature, flick (*slang*), motion picture, moving picture (*U.S.*), MP4, MPEG • **the movies** *I took them all to the movies.* = **the cinema**, a film, the pictures (*informal*), the flicks (*slang*), the silver screen (*informal*)

moving ADJECTIVE **1** *It was a moving moment for them.* = **emotional**, touching, affecting, exciting, inspiring, stirring, arousing, poignant, emotive, impelling ■ **OPPOSITE:** unemotional **2** *the moving parts in the engine* = **mobile**, running, active, going, operational, in motion, driving, kinetic, movable, motile, unfixed ■ **OPPOSITE:** stationary **3** *She has been a moving force in the world of art criticism.* = **motivating**, stimulating, dynamic, propelling, inspirational, impelling, stimulative

mow VERB *I mowed the lawn and did other routine chores.* = **cut**, crop, trim, shear, scythe • **mow something** or **someone down** *Gunmen mowed down 10 people in the attack.* = **massacre**, butcher, slaughter, cut down, shoot down, blow away (*slang, chiefly U.S.*), cut to pieces

much ADVERB **1** *My hairstyle has never changed much.* = **greatly**, a lot, considerably, decidedly, exceedingly, appreciably ■ **OPPOSITE:** hardly **2** *She didn't see her father much.* = **often**, a lot, regularly, routinely, a great deal, frequently, many times, habitually, on many occasions, customarily ▶ ADJECTIVE *They are grown in full sun, without much water.* = **great**, a lot of, plenty of, considerable, substantial, piles of (*informal*), ample, abundant, copious, oodles of (*informal*), plenteous, sizable or sizeable amount, shedful (*slang*) ■ **OPPOSITE:** little ▶ PRONOUN *There was so much to talk about.* = **a lot**, plenty, a great deal, lots (*informal*), masses (*informal*), loads (*informal*), tons (*informal*), heaps (*informal*), a good deal, an appreciable amount ■ **OPPOSITE:** little

muck NOUN **1** *This congealed muck was interfering with the filter.* = **dirt**, mud, filth, crap (*slang*), sewage, ooze, scum, sludge, mire, slime, slob (*Irish*), gunk (*informal*), gunge (*informal*), crud (*slang*), kak (*S. African vulgar slang*), grot (*slang*) **2** *He could smell muck and clean fresh hay.* = **manure**, crap (*slang*), dung, ordure • **muck something up** *At the 13th hole, I mucked it up.* = **ruin**, bungle, botch, make a mess of, blow (*slang*), mar, spoil, muff, make a nonsense of, bodge (*informal*), make a pig's ear of (*informal*), flub (*U.S. slang*), make a muck of (*slang*), mess something up, screw something up (*informal*), cock something up (*Brit. slang*), crool or cruel (*Austral. slang*)

mucky ADJECTIVE = **dirty**, soiled, muddy, filthy, messy, grimy, mud-caked, bespattered, begrimed, festy (*Austral. slang*)

mud NOUN = **dirt**, clay, ooze, silt, sludge, mire, slime, slob (*Irish*), gloop (*informal*)

muddle NOUN *My thoughts are all in a muddle.* = **confusion**, mess, disorder, chaos, plight, tangle, mix-up, clutter, disarray, daze, predicament, jumble, ravel, perplexity, disorganization, hotchpotch, hodgepodge (*U.S.*), pig's breakfast (*informal*), fankle (*Scot.*) ▶ VERB **1** *Already some people have begun to muddle the two names.* = **jumble**, confuse, disorder, scramble, tangle, mix up, make a mess of **2** *Don't talk all at once, you're muddling me.* = **confuse**, bewilder, daze, confound, perplex, disorient, stupefy, befuddle • **muddle along** or **through** *We will muddle through and just play it day by day.* = **scrape by**, make it, manage, cope, get along, get by (*informal*), manage somehow

muddled ADJECTIVE **1** *the muddled thinking of the Government's transport policy* = **incoherent**, confused, loose, vague, unclear, woolly, muddleheaded ■ **OPPOSITE:** clear **2** *I'm afraid I'm a little muddled. I don't know where to begin.*

= **bewildered**, confused, at sea, dazed, perplexed, disoriented, stupefied, befuddled **3** *a muddled pile of historical manuscripts* = **jumbled**, confused, disordered, scrambled, tangled, chaotic, messy, mixed-up, disorganized, higgledy-piggledy (*informal*), disarrayed
■ **OPPOSITE:** orderly

muddy ADJECTIVE **1** *a muddy track* = **boggy**, swampy, marshy, miry, quaggy **2** *muddy boots* = **dirty**, soiled, grimy, mucky, mud-caked, bespattered, clarty (*Scot. & Northern English, dialect*) **3** *The paper has turned a muddy colour.* = **dull**, flat, blurred, unclear, smoky, washed-out, dingy, lustreless **4** *He was up to his armpits in muddy water.* = **cloudy**, dirty, foul, opaque, impure, turbid **5** *Such muddy thinking is typical of those who have always had it easy.* = **confused**, vague, unclear, muddled, fuzzy, woolly, hazy, indistinct ▶ VERB *The clothes were all muddied.* = **smear**, soil, dirty, smirch, begrime, bespatter

muffle VERB **1** *I held a handkerchief over my mouth to muffle my voice.* = **deaden**, suppress, gag, stifle, silence, dull, soften, hush, muzzle, quieten **2** (*often with* **up**) *All of us were muffled up in several layers of clothing.* = **wrap up**, cover, disguise, conceal, cloak, shroud, swathe, envelop, swaddle

muffled ADJECTIVE = **indistinct**, suppressed, subdued, dull, faint, dim, muted, strangled, stifled

mug¹ NOUN *She had been drinking mugs of coffee to keep herself awake.* = **cup**, pot (*informal*), jug, beaker, tankard, stein, flagon, toby jug

mug² NOUN **1** *I managed to get my ugly mug on telly.* = **face**, features, countenance (*literary*), visage, clock (*Brit. slang*), kisser (*slang*), dial (*slang*), mush (*Brit. slang*), puss (*slang*), phiz *or* phizog (*Brit. slang*) **2** *I feel such a mug for signing the agreement.* = **fool**, innocent, sucker (*slang*), charlie (*Brit. informal*), gull (*archaic*), chump (*informal*), simpleton, putz (*U.S. slang*), weenie (*U.S. informal*), muggins (*Brit. slang*), easy *or* soft touch (*slang*), dorba *or* dorb (*Austral. slang*), bogan (*Austral. slang*) ▶ VERB *I was getting into my car when this guy tried to mug me.* = **attack**, assault, beat up, rob, steam (*informal*), hold up, do over (*Brit., Austral. & N.Z. slang*), work over (*slang*), assail, lay into (*informal*), put the boot in (*slang*), duff up (*Brit. slang*), set about *or* upon, beat *or* knock seven bells out of (*informal*) • **mug up (on) something** *It's advisable to mug up on your Spanish before you go.* = **study**, cram (*informal*), bone up on (*informal*), swot up on (*Brit. informal*), get up (*informal*)

mull over VERB = **ponder**, consider, study, think about, examine, review, weigh, contemplate, reflect on, think over, muse on, meditate on, ruminate on, deliberate on, turn something over in your mind

multiple ADJECTIVE = **many**, several, various, numerous, collective, sundry, manifold (*formal*), multitudinous

multiplicity NOUN = **number**, lot, host, mass, variety, load (*informal*), pile (*informal*), ton, stack, diversity, heap (*informal*), array, abundance, myriad, profusion

multiply VERB **1** *Her husband multiplied his demands on her time.* = **increase**, extend, expand, spread, build up, accumulate, augment, proliferate ■ **OPPOSITE:** decrease **2** *These creatures can multiply quickly.* = **reproduce**, breed, propagate

multitude NOUN **1** *Addiction to drugs can bring a multitude of other problems.* = **great number**, lot, host, collection, army, sea, mass, assembly, legion, horde, myriad, concourse, assemblage **2** *the multitudes that surround the Pope* = **crowd**, host, mass, mob, congregation, swarm, sea, horde, throng, great number **3** *The hideous truth was hidden from the multitude.* = **public**, mob, herd, populace, rabble (*derogatory*), proletariat, common people, hoi polloi, commonalty

mum ADJECTIVE = **silent**, quiet, dumb, mute, secretive, uncommunicative, unforthcoming, tight-lipped, closemouthed

mumbo jumbo NOUN **1** *It's all full of psychoanalytic mumbo jumbo.* = **gibberish**, nonsense, jargon, humbug, cant, Greek (*informal*), claptrap (*informal*), gobbledegook (*informal*), rigmarole, double talk **2** *We dabbled in all sorts of mumbo jumbo.* = **superstition**, magic, ritual, hocus-pocus

munch VERB = **chew**, champ, crunch, chomp, scrunch, masticate

mundane ADJECTIVE **1** *Be willing to do mundane tasks with good grace.* = **ordinary**, routine, commonplace, banal, everyday, day-to-day, vanilla (*slang*), prosaic, humdrum, workaday ■ **OPPOSITE:** extraordinary **2** *spiritual immortals who had transcended the mundane world* = **earthly**, worldly, human, material, fleshly, secular, mortal, terrestrial, temporal, sublunary ■ **OPPOSITE:** spiritual

municipal ADJECTIVE = **civic**, city, public, local, community, council, town, district, urban, metropolitan, borough

municipality NOUN = **town**, city, district, borough, township, burgh (*Scot.*), urban community, dorp (*S. African*)

murder NOUN **1** *The three accused are charged with attempted murder.* = **killing**, homicide, massacre, assassination, slaying, bloodshed, carnage, butchery **2** *I've taken three aspirins, but this headache's still absolute murder.* = **agony**, misery, hell (*informal*)
▶ VERB **1** *a thriller about two men who murder a third* = **kill**, massacre, slaughter, assassinate, hit (*slang*), destroy, waste (*informal*), do in (*informal*), eliminate (*slang*), take out (*slang*), terminate (*slang*), butcher, dispatch, slay, blow away (*slang, chiefly U.S.*), bump off (*slang*), rub out (*U.S. slang*), take the life of, do to death, murk (*slang*) **2** *She murdered the song.* = **ruin**, destroy, mar, spoil, butcher, mangle **3** *The front row murdered the Italians in the scrums.* = **beat decisively**, thrash, stuff (*slang*), cream (*slang, chiefly U.S.*), tank (*slang*), hammer (*informal*), slaughter, lick (*informal*), wipe the floor with (*informal*), make mincemeat of (*informal*), blow someone out of the water (*slang*), drub, defeat someone utterly, murk (*slang*)

murderer NOUN = **killer**, assassin, slayer, butcher, slaughterer, cut-throat, hitman or woman (*slang*)

murderous ADJECTIVE **1** *a series of murderous attacks* = **deadly**, savage, brutal, destructive, fell (*archaic*), bloody, devastating, cruel, lethal, withering, ferocious, cut-throat, bloodthirsty, barbarous, internecine, death-dealing, sanguinary **2** *Four games in six days is murderous and most unfair.* = **unpleasant**, difficult, dangerous, exhausting, sapping, harrowing, strenuous, arduous, hellish (*informal*), killing (*informal*)

murky ADJECTIVE **1** *Their plane crashed in murky weather.* = **dark**, gloomy, dismal, grey, dull, obscure, dim, dreary, cloudy, misty, impenetrable, foggy, overcast, dusky, nebulous, cheerless ■ **OPPOSITE:** bright **2** *the deep, murky waters of Loch Ness* = **dark**, obscure, cloudy, impenetrable

murmur VERB *He turned and murmured something to the professor.* = **mumble**, whisper, mutter, drone, purr, babble, speak in an undertone ▶ NOUN **1** *She spoke in a low murmur.* = **whisper**, whispering, mutter, mumble, drone, purr, babble, undertone **2** *She was so flattered she paid up without a murmur.* = **complaint**, word, moan (*informal*), grumble, beef (*slang*), grouse, gripe (*informal*)

muscle NOUN **1** *She has a strained thigh muscle.* = **tendon**, sinew, muscle tissue, thew **2** *The team showed more muscle than mental application.* = **strength**, might, force, power, weight, stamina, potency, brawn, sturdiness • **muscle in** *They complained that we were muscling in on their deal.* = **impose yourself**, encroach, butt in, force your way in, elbow your way in

muscular ADJECTIVE = **strong**, powerful, athletic, strapping, robust, vigorous, sturdy, stalwart, husky (*informal*), beefy (*informal*), swole (*slang*), hench (*informal*), lusty, sinewy, muscle-bound, brawny, powerfully built, thickset, well-knit

muse VERB = **ponder**, consider, reflect, contemplate, think, weigh up, deliberate, speculate, brood, meditate, mull over, think over, ruminate, cogitate, be lost in thought, be in a brown study

mush NOUN **1** *Over-ripe bananas will collapse into a mush in this recipe.* = **pulp**, paste, mash, purée, pap, slush, goo (*informal*) **2** *The lyrics are mush and the melodies banal.* = **sentimentality**, corn (*informal*), slush (*informal*), schmaltz (*slang*), mawkishness

mushroom VERB = **expand**, increase, spread, boom, flourish, sprout, burgeon, spring up, shoot up, proliferate, luxuriate, grow rapidly

mushy ADJECTIVE **1** *When the fruit is mushy and cooked, remove from the heat.* = **soft**, squidgy (*informal*), slushy, squashy, squelchy, pulpy, doughy, pappy, semi-liquid, paste-like, semi-solid **2** *Don't go getting all mushy and sentimental.* = **sentimental**, wet (*Brit. informal*), sloppy (*informal*), corny (*slang*), sugary, maudlin, weepy, saccharine, syrupy, slushy (*informal*), mawkish, schmaltzy (*slang*), icky (*informal*), three-hankie (*informal*)

musical ADJECTIVE = **melodious**, lyrical, harmonious, melodic, lilting, tuneful, dulcet, sweet-sounding, euphonious, euphonic ■ **OPPOSITE:** discordant

musing NOUN = **thinking**, reflection, meditation, abstraction, contemplation, introspection, reverie, dreaming, day-dreaming, rumination, navel gazing (*slang*), absent-mindedness, cogitation, brown study, cerebration, woolgathering

muskeg NOUN (*Canad.*) = **swamp**, bog, marsh, quagmire, moss (*Scot. & Northern English, dialect*), slough, fen, mire, morass, everglade(s) (*U.S.*), pakihi (*N.Z.*)

muss VERB = **mess (up)**, disarrange, dishevel, ruffle, rumple, make untidy, tumble

must¹ NOUN *A visit to the motor museum is a must.* = **necessity**, essential, requirement, duty, fundamental, obligation, imperative, requisite, prerequisite, sine qua non (*Latin*), necessary thing, must-have

must² NOUN *The air was heady with the smell of must.* = **mould**, rot, decay, mildew, mustiness, fustiness, fetor, mouldiness

muster VERB **1** *Mustering all her strength, she pulled hard on the oars.* = **summon up**, collect, call up, marshal **2** *The general had mustered his troops north of the border.* = **rally**, group, gather, assemble, round up, marshal, mobilize, call together **3** *They mustered in the open, well wrapped and saying little.* = **assemble**, meet, come together, convene, congregate, convoke (*formal*) ▸ NOUN *He called a general muster of all soldiers.* = **assembly**, meeting, collection, gathering, rally, convention, congregation, roundup, mobilization, hui (*N.Z.*), concourse, assemblage, convocation (*formal*), runanga (*N.Z.*) • **pass muster** *I could not pass muster in this language.* = **be acceptable**, qualify, measure up, make the grade, fill the bill (*informal*), be or come up to scratch

musty ADJECTIVE = **stale**, stuffy, airless, decayed, smelly, dank, mouldy, fusty, mildewed, frowsty, mildewy

mutation NOUN **1** *Scientists have found a genetic mutation that causes the disease.* = **anomaly**, variation, deviant, freak of nature **2** *the film's mutation from domestic drama into courtroom thriller* = **change**, variation, evolution, transformation, modification, alteration, deviation, metamorphosis, transfiguration

mute ADJECTIVE **1** *He was mute, distant and indifferent.* = **close-mouthed**, silent, taciturn, tongue-tied, tight-lipped, unspeaking **2** *I threw her a mute look of appeal.* = **silent**, dumb, unspoken, tacit, wordless, voiceless, unvoiced ▸ VERB **1** *They have muted some of their more extreme views.* = **tone down**, lower, moderate, subdue, dampen, soft-pedal **2** *The wooded hillside muted the sounds.* = **muffle**, subdue, moderate, lower, turn down, soften, dampen, tone down, deaden

mutilate VERB **1** *His arm was mutilated in an industrial accident.* = **maim**, damage, injure, disable, cripple, hack, cut up, mangle, dismember, disfigure, lacerate, cut to pieces **2** *The writer's verdict was that his screenplay had been mutilated.* = **distort**, cut, damage, mar, spoil, butcher, hack, censor, adulterate, expurgate, bowdlerize

mutiny NOUN *A series of mutinies in the armed forces destabilized the regime.* = **rebellion**, revolt, uprising, insurrection, rising, strike, revolution, riot, resistance, disobedience, insubordination, refusal to obey orders ▸ VERB *Units around the city mutinied after receiving no pay.* = **rebel**, revolt, rise up, disobey, strike, resist, defy authority, refuse to obey orders, be insubordinate

mutt NOUN *He was being harassed by a large, off-the-leash mutt.* = **mongrel**, dog, hound, tyke, pooch (*informal*), cur

mutter VERB = **grumble**, complain, murmur, rumble, whine, mumble, grouse, bleat, grouch (*informal*), talk under your breath

mutual ADJECTIVE = **shared**, common, joint, interactive, returned, communal, reciprocal, interchangeable, reciprocated, correlative, requited

> **USAGE** *Mutual* is sometimes used, as in *a mutual friend*, to mean 'common to or shared by two or more people'. This use has sometimes been frowned on in the past because it does not reflect the two-way relationship contained in the origins of the word, which comes from Latin *mutuus* meaning 'reciprocal'. However, this usage is very common and is now generally regarded as acceptable.

muzzle NOUN **1** *The dog presented its muzzle for scratching.* = **jaws**, mouth, nose, snout **2** *dogs that have to wear a muzzle* = **gag**, guard, restraint ▸ VERB *He complained of being muzzled by the chairman.* = **suppress**, silence, curb, restrain, choke, gag, stifle, censor

myopic ADJECTIVE **1** *The government still has a myopic attitude to spending.* = **narrow-minded**, short-sighted, narrow, unimaginative, small-minded, unadventurous, near-sighted **2** *Rhinos are thick-skinned, myopic and love to wallow in mud.* = **short-sighted**, near-sighted

myriad NOUN *They face a myriad of problems bringing up children.* = **multitude**, millions, scores, host, thousands, army, sea, mountain, flood, a million, a thousand, swarm, horde ▸ ADJECTIVE *pop culture in all its myriad forms* = **innumerable**, countless, untold, incalculable, immeasurable, a thousand and one, multitudinous

mysterious ADJECTIVE **1** *He died in mysterious circumstances.* = **strange**, unknown, puzzling, curious, secret, hidden, weird, concealed, obscure, baffling, veiled, mystical, perplexing, uncanny, incomprehensible, mystifying, impenetrable, arcane, inexplicable, cryptic, insoluble, unfathomable, abstruse, recondite ■ OPPOSITE: clear **2** *As for his job – well, he was very mysterious about it.* = **secretive**, enigmatic, evasive, discreet, covert, reticent, furtive, inscrutable, non-committal, surreptitious, cloak-and-dagger, sphinx-like

m

mystery NOUN **1** *The source of the gunshots still remains a mystery.* = **puzzle**, problem, question, secret, riddle, enigma, conundrum, teaser, poser (*informal*), closed book **2** *It is an elaborate ceremony, shrouded in mystery.* = **secrecy**, uncertainty, obscurity, mystique, darkness, ambiguity, ambiguousness

mystical *or* **mystic** ADJECTIVE = **supernatural**, mysterious, transcendental, esoteric, occult, arcane, metaphysical, paranormal, inscrutable, otherworldly, abstruse, cabalistic, preternatural, nonrational

mystify VERB = **puzzle**, confuse, baffle, bewilder, beat (*slang*), escape, stump, elude, confound, perplex, bamboozle (*informal*), flummox, be all Greek to (*informal*), nonplus, befog

mystique NOUN = **fascination**, spell, magic, charm, glamour, awe, charisma

myth NOUN **1** *a famous Greek myth* = **legend**, story, tradition, fiction, saga, fable, parable, allegory, fairy story, folk tale, urban myth, urban legend **2** *Several popular myths endure about art thieves.* = **illusion**, story, fancy, fantasy, imagination, invention, delusion, superstition, fabrication, falsehood, figment, tall story, cock and bull story (*informal*)

mythical ADJECTIVE **1** *the mythical beast that had seven or more heads* = **legendary**, storied, fabulous, imaginary, fairy-tale, fabled, mythological, storybook, allegorical, folkloric, chimerical **2** *They are trying to preserve a mythical sense of nationhood.* = **imaginary**, made-up, fantasy, invented, pretended, untrue, unreal, fabricated, fanciful, fictitious, make-believe, nonexistent

mythological ADJECTIVE = **legendary**, fabulous, fabled, traditional, invented, heroic, imaginary, mythical, mythic, folkloric

mythology NOUN = **legend**, myths, folklore, stories, tradition, lore, folk tales, mythos

m

Nn

nab VERB = **catch**, arrest, apprehend, seize, lift (*slang*), nick (*slang, chiefly Brit.*), grab, capture, nail (*informal*), collar (*informal*), snatch, catch in the act, feel your collar (*slang*)

nadir NOUN = **bottom**, depths, lowest point, rock bottom, all-time low
■ **OPPOSITE:** height

naff ADJECTIVE *This music is really naff.* = **bad**, poor, inferior, worthless, pants (*slang*), duff (*Brit. informal*), shabby, second-rate, shoddy, low-grade, low-quality, trashy, substandard, for the birds (*informal*), crappy (*slang*), valueless, rubbishy, poxy (*slang*), strictly for the birds (*informal*), twopenny-halfpenny, bodger or bodgie (*Austral. slang*)
■ **OPPOSITE:** excellent

nag¹ VERB *The more Sarah nagged her, the more stubborn Cissie became.* = **scold**, harass, badger, pester, worry, harry, plague, hassle (*informal*), vex, berate, breathe down someone's neck, upbraid, chivvy (*Brit.*), bend someone's ear (*informal*), be on your back (*slang*) ▶ NOUN *I get called a nag if I complain about anything.* = **complainer**, grumbler, moaner, fault-finder

nag² NOUN (*often derog.*) *a bedraggled knight riding a lame, flea-ridden old nag* = **horse**, hack, jade, plug

nagging ADJECTIVE **1** *He complained about a nagging pain between his shoulders.* = **continuous**, persistent, continual, niggling, repeated, constant, endless, relentless, perpetual, never-ending, interminable, unrelenting, incessant, unremitting **2** *He tried to ignore the screaming, nagging voice.* = **scolding**, complaining, critical, sharp-tongued, shrewish

nail NOUN **1** *A mirror hung on a nail above the washstand.* = **tack**, spike, rivet, hobnail, brad (*Technical*) **2** *Keep your nails short and your hands clean.* = **fingernail**, toenail, talon, thumbnail, claw ▶ VERB **1** *Frank put the first plank down and nailed it in place.* = **fasten**, fix, secure, attach, pin, hammer (*informal*), tack **2** *The police have been trying to nail him for years.* = **catch**, arrest, capture, apprehend, lift (*slang*), trap, nab (*informal*), snare, ensnare, entrap, feel your collar (*slang*)

naive, naïve *or* **naïf** ADJECTIVE = **gullible**, trusting, credulous, unsuspicious, green, simple, innocent, childlike, callow, unsophisticated, unworldly, artless, ingenuous, guileless, wet behind the ears (*informal*), jejune, as green as grass
■ **OPPOSITE:** worldly

naivety, naiveté *or* **naïveté** NOUN = **gullibility**, innocence, simplicity, inexperience, credulity, ingenuousness, artlessness, guilelessness, callowness

naked ADJECTIVE **1** *They stripped him naked.* = **nude**, stripped, exposed, bare, uncovered, undressed, in the raw (*informal*), starkers (*informal*), stark-naked, unclothed, in the buff (*informal*), in the altogether (*informal*), buck naked (*slang*), undraped, in your birthday suit (*informal*), without a stitch on (*informal*), in the bare scud (*Scot. slang*), naked as the day you were born (*informal*) ■ **OPPOSITE:** dressed **2** *Naked aggression could not go unchallenged.* = **undisguised**, open, simple, plain, patent, evident, stark, manifest, blatant, overt, unmistakable, unqualified, unadorned, unvarnished, unconcealed
■ **OPPOSITE:** disguised

nakedness NOUN **1** *He pulled the blanket over his body to hide his nakedness.* = **nudity**, undress, bareness, deshabille **2** *the nakedness of the emotion expressed in these songs* = **starkness**, simplicity, openness, plainness

name NOUN **1** *I don't even know if Sullivan is his real name.* = **title**, nickname, designation, appellation (*formal*), term, handle (*slang*), denomination, epithet, sobriquet, cognomen, moniker or monicker (*slang*) **2** *He had made a name for himself as a musician.* = **reputation**, character, honour, fame, distinction, esteem, eminence, renown, repute, note ▶ VERB **1** *My mother insisted on naming me Horace.* = **call**, christen, baptize, dub, term, style, label, entitle, denominate **2** *The Scots have yet to name their team.* = **nominate**, choose, commission, mention, identify, select, appoint, specify, designate ■ **RELATED WORD:** *adjective* nominal

named ADJECTIVE **1** *He was named John.* = **called**, christened, known as, dubbed, termed, styled, labelled, entitled, denominated, baptized **2** *She has been named Business Woman of the Year.* = **nominated**, chosen, picked, commissioned, mentioned, identified, selected, appointed, cited, specified, designated, singled out

n

nameless ADJECTIVE **1** *They had their cases rejected by nameless officials.* = **unnamed**, unknown, obscure, anonymous, unheard-of, undistinguished, untitled **2** *My source of information is a judge who wishes to remain nameless.* = **anonymous**, unknown, unnamed, incognito **3** *He was suddenly seized by a nameless dread.* = **horrible**, unspeakable, indescribable, abominable, ineffable, unutterable, inexpressible

namely ADVERB = **specifically**, that is to say, to wit, i.e., viz.

nap¹ VERB *I frequently nap during the day.* = **sleep**, rest, nod, drop off (*informal*), doze, kip (*Brit. slang*), snooze (*informal*), nod off (*informal*), catnap, drowse, zizz (*Brit. informal*) ▶ NOUN *I think I'll take a little nap for an hour or so.* = **sleep**, rest, kip (*Brit. slang*), siesta, catnap, forty winks (*informal*), shuteye (*slang*), zizz (*Brit. informal*), nana nap (*informal*)

nap² NOUN *She buried her face in the towel's soft nap.* = **pile**, down, fibre, weave, shag, grain

napkin NOUN = **serviette**, cloth

narcissism *or* **narcism** NOUN = **egotism**, vanity, self-love, self-admiration

narcotic NOUN *He appears to be under the influence of some sort of narcotic.* = **drug**, anaesthetic, painkiller, sedative, opiate, tranquillizer, anodyne, analgesic ▶ ADJECTIVE *drugs which have a narcotic effect* = **sedative**, calming, dulling, numbing, hypnotic, analgesic, stupefying, soporific, painkilling

narrate VERB = **tell**, recount, report, detail, describe, relate, unfold, chronicle, recite, set forth

narration NOUN **1** = **storytelling**, telling, reading, relation, explanation, description **2** = **account**, explanation, description, recital, voice-over (*in a film*)

narrative NOUN = **story**, report, history, detail, account, statement, tale, chronicle

narrator NOUN = **storyteller**, writer, author, reporter, commentator, chronicler, reciter, raconteur

narrow ADJECTIVE **1** *She drew beautiful bodies with elegant necks, narrow waists, and long legs.* = **thin**, fine, slim, pinched, slender, tapering, attenuated ■ **OPPOSITE:** broad **2** *He squeezed his way along the narrow space between the crates.* = **limited**, restricted, confined, tight, close, near, cramped, meagre, constricted, circumscribed, scanty, straitened, incapacious ■ **OPPOSITE:** wide **3** *a narrow and outdated view of family life* = **insular**, prejudiced, biased, partial, reactionary, puritan, bigoted, dogmatic, intolerant,

narrow-minded, small-minded, illiberal ■ **OPPOSITE:** broad-minded **4** *She achieved a fame that transcended the narrow world of avant-garde theatre.* = **exclusive**, limited, select, restricted, confined ▶ VERB **1** (*often with* **down**) *I don't want to narrow my options too early on.* = **restrict**, limit, reduce, diminish, constrict, circumscribe, straiten **2** *This sign means that the road narrows on both sides.* = **get narrower**, taper, shrink, tighten, constrict

narrowly ADVERB **1** *Five firefighters narrowly escaped death.* = **just**, barely, only just, scarcely, by the skin of your teeth, by a whisker or hair's-breadth **2** *He frowned and looked narrowly at his colleague.* = **closely**, keenly, carefully, intently, intensely, fixedly, searchingly

narrow-minded ADJECTIVE = **intolerant**, conservative, prejudiced, biased, provincial, petty, reactionary, parochial, short-sighted, bigoted, insular, opinionated, small-minded, hidebound, illiberal, strait-laced ■ **OPPOSITE:** broad-minded

narrows PLURAL NOUN = **channel**, sound, gulf, passage, straits

nastiness NOUN = **spite**, malice, venom, unpleasantness, meanness, bitchiness (*slang*), offensiveness, spitefulness

nasty ADJECTIVE **1** *This divorce could turn nasty.* = **unpleasant**, ugly, disagreeable ■ **OPPOSITE:** pleasant **2** *He's only nasty to me when there's no-one around to see it.* = **spiteful**, mean (*informal*), offensive, annoying, vicious, unpleasant, abusive, vile, malicious, bad-tempered, despicable, disagreeable ■ **OPPOSITE:** pleasant **3** *It's got a really nasty smell.* = **disgusting**, unpleasant, dirty, offensive, foul, horrible, polluted, filthy, sickening, vile, distasteful, repellent, obnoxious, objectionable, disagreeable, nauseating, odious, repugnant, loathsome, grotty (*slang*), malodorous, noisome, unappetizing, yucky *or* yukky (*slang*), festy (*Austral. slang*), yucko (*Austral. slang*) **4** *Lili had a nasty chest infection.* = **serious**, bad, dangerous, critical, severe, painful (*informal*) **5** *There's no need for such nasty language.* = **obscene**, blue, gross, foul, indecent, pornographic, lewd, impure, lascivious, smutty, ribald, licentious ■ **OPPOSITE:** clean

nation NOUN **1** *Such policies would require unprecedented cooperation between nations.* = **country**, state, commonwealth, realm, micronation **2** *It was a story that touched the nation's heart.* = **public**, people, community, society, population

national ADJECTIVE **1** *major national and international issues* = **nationwide**, state, public, civil, widespread, governmental, countrywide **2** *the national characteristics and history of the country* = **ethnic**, social ▶ NOUN *He is in fact a British national and passport holder.* = **citizen**, subject, resident, native, inhabitant

nationalism NOUN = **patriotism**, loyalty to your country, chauvinism, jingoism, nationality, allegiance, fealty

nationalistic ADJECTIVE = **patriotic**, xenophobic, chauvinistic, jingoistic, loyal to your country

nationality NOUN **1** *When asked his nationality, he said, 'British'.* = **citizenship**, birth **2** *the many nationalities that comprise Ethopia* = **race**, nation, ethnic group

nationwide ADJECTIVE = **national**, general, widespread, countrywide, overall

native ADJECTIVE **1** *a spokeswoman for native peoples around the world* = **indigenous**, local, aboriginal **2** *French is not my native tongue.* = **mother**, indigenous, vernacular **3** *Several native plants also provide edible berries.* = **domestic**, local, indigenous, home-made, home-grown, home ▶ NOUN (*usually with* **of**) *He was a native of France.* = **inhabitant**, national, resident, citizen, countryman, aborigine, dweller

Nativity NOUN = **birth of Christ**, manger scene

natter VERB *The pair would natter on the phone for hours.* = **gossip**, talk, rabbit (on) (*Brit. informal*), jaw (*slang*), chatter, witter (*informal*), prattle, jabber, gabble, blather, blether, shoot the breeze (*informal*), run off at the mouth (*slang*), prate, talk idly, chew the fat or rag (*slang*), earbash (*Austral. & N.Z. slang*) ▶ NOUN *We must get together some time for a good natter.* = **gossip**, talk, conversation, chat, jaw (*slang*), craic (*Irish informal*), gab (*informal*), prattle, jabber, gabble, palaver, blather, chitchat, blether, chinwag (*Brit. informal*), gabfest (*informal, chiefly U.S. & Canad.*), confabulation

natty ADJECTIVE = **smart**, sharp (*informal*), dashing (*old-fashioned*), elegant, trim, neat, fashionable, stylish, trendy (*Brit. informal*), chic, spruce, well-dressed, dapper, snazzy (*informal*), well-turned-out, crucial (*slang*), schmick (*Austral. informal*)

natural ADJECTIVE **1** *A period of depression is a natural response to bereavement.* = **logical**, reasonable, valid, legitimate **2** *It's just not natural to feel this anxious all the time.* = **normal**, common, regular, usual, ordinary, typical, everyday ■ OPPOSITE: abnormal **3** *He has a natural flair for business.*

= **innate**, native, characteristic, indigenous, inherent, instinctive, intuitive, congenital, inborn, immanent, in your blood, essential **4** *Jan's sister was as natural and friendly as the rest of the family.* = **unaffected**, open, frank, genuine, spontaneous, candid, unpretentious, unsophisticated, dinkum (*Austral. & N.Z. informal*), artless, ingenuous, real, simple, unstudied ■ OPPOSITE: affected **5** *He prefers to use high quality natural produce.* = **pure**, plain, organic, whole, unrefined, unbleached, unpolished, unmixed ■ OPPOSITE: processed

naturalism NOUN = **realism**, authenticity, plausibility, verisimilitude, factualism

naturalist NOUN = **biologist**, ecologist, botanist, zoologist

naturalistic ADJECTIVE **1** *These drawings are amongst his most naturalistic.* = **realistic**, photographic, kitchen sink, representational, lifelike, warts and all (*informal*), true-to-life, vérité, factualistic **2** *Research is needed under rather more naturalistic conditions.* = **lifelike**, realistic, real-life, true-to-life

naturally ADVERB **1** *We are naturally concerned about the future.* = **of course**, certainly, as a matter of course, as anticipated **2** *A study of yoga leads naturally to meditation.* = **typically**, simply, normally, spontaneously, customarily

nature NOUN **1** *man's ancient sense of kinship with nature* = **creation**, world, earth, environment, universe, cosmos, natural world **2** *an organization devoted to the protection of nature* = **flora and fauna**, country, landscape, countryside, scenery, natural history **3** *The protests had been non-political in nature.* = **quality**, character, make-up, constitution, attributes, essence, traits, complexion, features **4** *She trusted people. That was her nature.* = **temperament**, character, personality, disposition – outlook, mood, humour, temper **5** *This – and other books of a similar nature – are urgently needed.* = **kind**, sort, style, type, variety, species, category, description

naughty ADJECTIVE **1** *You naughty boy, you gave me such a fright.* = **disobedient**, bad, mischievous, badly behaved, wayward, playful, wicked, sinful, fractious, impish, roguish, refractory ■ OPPOSITE: good **2** *a comedy routine crammed with naughty innuendo* = **obscene**, blue, vulgar, improper, lewd, risqué, X-rated (*informal*), bawdy, smutty, off-colour, ribald ■ OPPOSITE: clean

nausea NOUN **1** *I was overcome with a feeling of nausea.* = **sickness**, vomiting, retching, squeamishness, queasiness, biliousness **2** *She spoke in a little-girl voice which brought on a palpable feeling of nausea.* = **disgust**, loathing, aversion, revulsion, abhorrence, repugnance, odium (*formal*)

nauseate VERB **1** *The smell of frying nauseated her.* = **sicken**, turn your stomach **2** *Ugliness nauseates me. I like to have beautiful things around me.* = **disgust**, offend, horrify, revolt, repel, repulse, gross out (*U.S. slang*)

nauseous ADJECTIVE **1** *The drugs make me feel nauseous.* = **sick**, crook (*Austral. & N.Z. informal*) **2** *The floor was deep with bat dung giving off a nauseous smell.* = **sickening**, offensive, disgusting, revolting, distasteful, repulsive, nauseating, repugnant, loathsome, abhorrent, detestable, yucky or yukky (*slang*), yucko (*Austral. slang*)

nautical ADJECTIVE = **maritime**, marine, yachting, naval, seafaring, seagoing

naval ADJECTIVE = **nautical**, marine, maritime

navel NOUN **1** *A small incision is made just below the navel.* = **bellybutton** (*informal*) **2** *The city was once the jewel in the navel of the Gold Coast.* = **centre**, middle, hub, central point ■ **RELATED WORDS:** technical name umbilicus; *adjective* umbilical

navigate VERB **1** *He was responsible for safely navigating the ship.* = **steer**, drive, direct, guide, handle, pilot, sail, skipper, manoeuvre **2** *She expertly navigated the plane through 45 minutes of fog.* = **manoeuvre**, drive, direct, guide, handle, pilot **3** *They navigated by the sun and stars.* = **plot a course**, sail, find your way, plan a course **4** *Such boats can be built locally and can navigate on the Nile.* = **sail**, cruise, manoeuvre, voyage

navigation NOUN = **sailing**, cruising, steering, voyaging, seamanship, helmsmanship

navigator NOUN = **helmsman** or **woman** or **person**, pilot, seaman or woman, mariner

navy NOUN = **fleet**, warships, flotilla, armada

near ADJECTIVE **1** *The town is very near.* = **close**, bordering, neighbouring, nearby, beside, adjacent, adjoining, close by, at close quarters, just round the corner, contiguous (*formal*), proximate, within sniffing distance (*informal*), a hop, skip and a jump away (*informal*) ■ **OPPOSITE:** far **2** *Departure time was near.* = **imminent**, forthcoming, approaching, looming, impending, upcoming, on the cards (*informal*), nigh, in the offing, near-at-hand, next ■ **OPPOSITE:** far-off **3** *I have no near relations.* = **intimate**,

close, related, allied, familiar, connected, attached, akin ■ **OPPOSITE:** distant **4** *They joked about him being so near with his money.* = **mean**, stingy, parsimonious, miserly, niggardly, ungenerous, tightfisted, close-fisted

nearby ADJECTIVE *At a nearby table a man was complaining in a loud voice.* = **neighbouring**, adjacent, adjoining ▶ ADVERB *He might easily have been seen by someone who lived nearby.* = **close at hand**, within reach, not far away, at close quarters, just round the corner, proximate, within sniffing distance (*informal*)

nearing ADJECTIVE = **approaching**, coming, advancing, imminent, impending, upcoming

nearly ADVERB **1** *The beach was nearly empty.* = **practically**, about, almost, virtually, all but, just about, not quite, as good as, well-nigh **2** *It was already nearly eight o'clock.* = **almost**, about, approaching, roughly, just about, approximately

neat ADJECTIVE **1** *Her house was neat and tidy and gleamingly clean.* = **tidy**, nice, straight, trim, orderly, spruce, uncluttered, shipshape, spick-and-span ■ **OPPOSITE:** untidy **2** *'It's not like Alf to leave a mess like that,' I remarked, 'He's always so neat.'* = **methodical**, tidy, systematic, fastidious ■ **OPPOSITE:** disorganized **3** *She always looked neat and well groomed.* = **smart**, trim, tidy, spruce, dapper, natty (*informal*), well-groomed, well-turned out **4** *He had the neat movements of a dancer.* = **graceful**, elegant, adept, nimble, agile, adroit, efficient ■ **OPPOSITE:** clumsy **5** *It was a neat solution to the problem.* = **clever**, efficient, handy, apt, well-judged ■ **OPPOSITE:** inefficient **6** *I've just had a really neat idea.* = **cool**, great (*informal*), excellent, brilliant, cracking (*Brit. informal*), smashing (*informal*), superb, fantastic (*informal*), tremendous, ace (*informal*), fabulous (*informal*), marvellous, terrific (*informal*), awesome (*slang*), mean (*slang*), super (*informal*), sick (*slang*), brill (*informal*), bodacious (*slang, chiefly U.S.*), boffo (*slang*), chillin' (*U.S. slang*), booshit (*Austral. slang*), exo (*Austral. slang*), sik (*Austral. slang*), rad (*informal*), phat (*slang*), schmick (*Austral. informal*), beaut (*informal*), barrie (*Scot. slang*), belting (*Brit. slang*), pearler (*Austral. slang*) ■ **OPPOSITE:** terrible **7** (*alcoholic drinks*) *He poured himself a glass of neat brandy.* = **undiluted**, straight, pure, unmixed

neatly ADVERB **1** *He took off his trousers and folded them neatly.* = **tidily**, nicely, smartly, systematically, methodically, fastidiously

2 *She was neatly dressed, her hair was tidy and she carried a shoulder-bag.* = **smartly**, elegantly, stylishly, tidily, nattily **3** *He sent the ball over the bar with a neatly executed header.* = **gracefully**, expertly, efficiently, adeptly, skilfully, nimbly, adroitly, dexterously, agilely **4** *She neatly summed up a common attitude among many teachers and parents.* = **cleverly**, precisely, accurately, efficiently, aptly, elegantly

neatness NOUN **1** *The grounds were a perfect balance between neatness and natural wildness.* = **order**, organization, harmony, tidiness, orderliness **2** *He was a paragon of neatness and efficiency.* = **tidiness**, niceness, orderliness, smartness, fastidiousness, trimness, spruceness **3** *neatness of movement* = **grace**, skill, efficiency, expertise, precision, elegance, agility, dexterity, deftness, nimbleness, adroitness, adeptness, daintiness, gracefulness, preciseness, skilfulness **4** *He appreciated the neatness of their plan.* = **cleverness**, efficiency, precision, elegance, aptness

nebulous ADJECTIVE **1** *the nebulous concept of 'spirit'* = **vague**, confused, uncertain, obscure, unclear, ambiguous, indefinite, hazy, indeterminate, imprecise, indistinct **2** *We glimpsed a nebulous figure through the mist.* = **obscure**, vague, dim, murky, shadowy, cloudy, misty, hazy, amorphous, indeterminate, shapeless, indistinct, unformed

necessarily ADVERB **1** *A higher price does not necessarily guarantee a better product.* = **automatically**, naturally, definitely, undoubtedly, accordingly, by definition, of course, certainly **2** *In any policy area, a number of ministries is necessarily involved.* = **inevitably**, of necessity, unavoidably, perforce (*formal*), incontrovertibly, nolens volens (*Latin*)

necessary ADJECTIVE **1** *Is your journey really necessary?* = **needed**, required, essential, vital, compulsory, mandatory, imperative, indispensable, obligatory, requisite, de rigueur (*French*), needful, must-have ■ **OPPOSITE:** unnecessary **2** *Wastage was no doubt a necessary consequence of war.* = **inevitable**, certain, unavoidable, inescapable ■ **OPPOSITE:** avoidable

necessitate VERB = **compel**, force, demand, require, call for, oblige, entail, constrain, impel, make necessary

necessity NOUN **1** *There is agreement on the necessity of reforms.* = **need**, demand, requirement, exigency, indispensability, needfulness **2** *Water is a basic necessity of life.* = **essential**, need, necessary, requirement,

fundamental, requisite, prerequisite, sine qua non (*Latin*), desideratum, want, must-have **3** *the ultimate necessity of death* = **inevitability**, certainty **4** *They were reduced to begging through economic necessity.* = **poverty**, need, privation (*formal*), penury, destitution, extremity, indigence **5** *They sometimes had to struggle to pay for necessities.* = **essential**, need, requirement, fundamental

necropolis NOUN = **cemetery**, graveyard, churchyard, burial ground

need VERB **1** *He desperately needed money.* = **want**, miss, require, lack, have to have, demand **2** *The building needs quite a few repairs.* = **require**, want, demand, call for, entail, necessitate, have occasion to or for **3** *You needn't bother, I'll do it myself.* = **have to**, be obliged to ▶ NOUN **1** *the special nutritional needs of children* = **requirement**, demand, essential, necessity, requisite, desideratum, must-have **2** *There's no need to call the police.* = **necessity**, call, demand, requirement, obligation **3** *In her moment of need, her mother was nowhere to be seen.* = **emergency**, want, necessity, urgency, exigency **4** *the state of need in the developing world* = **poverty**, deprivation, destitution, neediness, distress, extremity, privation (*formal*), penury, indigence, impecuniousness

needed ADJECTIVE = **necessary**, wanted, required, lacked, called for, desired

needle VERB = **irritate**, provoke, annoy, sting, bait, harass, taunt, nag, hassle (*informal*), aggravate (*informal*), prod, gall, ruffle, spur, prick, nettle, goad, irk, rile, get under your skin (*informal*), get on your nerves (*informal*), nark (*Brit., Austral. & N.Z. slang*), hack you off (*informal*), get in your hair (*informal*)

needless ADJECTIVE = **unnecessary**, excessive, pointless, gratuitous, useless, unwanted, redundant, superfluous, groundless, expendable, uncalled-for, dispensable, nonessential, undesired ■ **OPPOSITE:** essential

needlework NOUN = **embroidery**, tailoring, stitching, sewing, needlecraft

needy ADJECTIVE = **poor**, deprived, disadvantaged, impoverished, penniless, destitute, poverty-stricken, underprivileged, indigent (*formal*), down at heel (*informal*), impecunious, dirt-poor, on the breadline (*informal*) ■ **OPPOSITE:** wealthy

negate VERB **1** *These environmental protection laws could be negated if the EU decides they interfere with trade.* = **invalidate**, reverse, cancel, wipe out, void, repeal, revoke, retract, rescind, neutralize, annul, nullify, obviate, abrogate, countermand **2** *I can neither negate nor affirm this claim.* = **deny**, oppose, contradict, refute, disallow, disprove, rebut, gainsay (*archaic, literary*) ■ **OPPOSITE:** confirm

negation NOUN **1** *He repudiates liberty and equality as the negation of order and government.* = **opposite**, reverse, contrary, contradiction, converse, antithesis, inverse, antonym **2** *She shook her head in a gesture of negation.* = **denial**, refusal, rejection, contradiction, renunciation, repudiation, disavowal, veto

negative ADJECTIVE **1** *This will have a very serious negative effect on economic recovery.* = **neutralizing**, invalidating, annulling, nullifying, counteractive **2** *There's no point in going along to an interview with a negative attitude.* = **pessimistic**, cynical, unwilling, gloomy, antagonistic, jaundiced, uncooperative, contrary ■ **OPPOSITE:** optimistic **3** *Dr. Velayati gave a vague but negative response.* = **dissenting**, contradictory, refusing, denying, rejecting, opposing, resisting, contrary ■ **OPPOSITE:** assenting ▶ NOUN *We were fobbed off with a crisp negative.* = **denial**, no, refusal, rejection, contradiction

neglect VERB **1** *The couple denied that they had neglected their child.* = **disregard**, ignore, leave alone, turn your back on, fail to look after ■ **OPPOSITE:** look after **2** *If you don't keep an eye on them, children tend to neglect their homework.* = **shirk**, forget, overlook, omit, evade, pass over, skimp, procrastinate over, let slide, be remiss in or about **3** *She neglected to inform me of her change of plans.* = **fail**, forget, omit ▶ NOUN **1** *hundreds of orphans and old people, some of whom have since died of neglect* = **negligence**, inattention, unconcern ■ **OPPOSITE:** care **2** *her deliberate neglect of her professional duty* = **shirking**, failure, oversight, carelessness, dereliction, forgetfulness, slackness, laxity, laxness, slovenliness, remissness

neglected ADJECTIVE **1** *The fact that he is not coming today makes his grandmother feel neglected.* = **uncared-for**, abandoned, underestimated, disregarded, undervalued, unappreciated **2** *a neglected house with an overgrown garden* = **run down**, derelict, overgrown, uncared-for

negligence NOUN = **carelessness**, failure, neglect, disregard, shortcoming, omission, oversight, dereliction, forgetfulness, slackness, inattention, laxity, thoughtlessness, laxness, inadvertence, inattentiveness, heedlessness, remissness

negligent ADJECTIVE = **careless**, slack, thoughtless, unthinking, forgetful, slapdash, neglectful, heedless, slipshod, inattentive, remiss (*formal*), unmindful, disregardful ■ **OPPOSITE:** careful

negligible ADJECTIVE = **insignificant**, small, minute, minor, petty, trivial, trifling, unimportant, inconsequential, imperceptible, nickel-and-dime (*U.S. slang*) ■ **OPPOSITE:** significant

negotiable ADJECTIVE **1** *The manor is for sale at a negotiable price.* = **debatable**, flexible, unsettled, undecided, open to discussion, discussable *or* discussible **2** *The bonds may no longer be negotiable.* = **valid**, transferable, transactional

negotiate VERB **1** *The president may be willing to negotiate with the democrats.* = **bargain**, deal, contract, discuss, debate, consult, confer, mediate, hold talks, arbitrate, cut a deal, conciliate, parley, discuss terms **2** *The local government and the army have negotiated a truce.* = **arrange**, manage, settle, work out, bring about, transact **3** *I negotiated the corner on my motorbike.* = **get round**, clear, pass, cross, pass through, get over, get past, surmount

negotiation NOUN **1** *We have had meaningful negotiations and I believe we are close to a deal.* = **bargaining**, debate, discussion, transaction, dialogue, mediation, arbitration, wheeling and dealing (*informal*) **2** *They intend to take no part in the negotiation of a new treaty of union.* = **arrangement**, management, settlement, working out, transaction, bringing about

negotiator NOUN = **mediator**, ambassador, diplomat, delegate, intermediary, arbitrator, moderator, honest broker

neighbourhood *or* (*U.S.*) **neighborhood** NOUN **1** *It seemed like a good neighbourhood to raise my children.* = **district**, community, quarter, region, surroundings, locality, locale **2** *the loss of woodlands in the neighbourhood of large towns* = **vicinity**, confines, proximity, precincts, environs, purlieus

neighbouring *or* (*U.S.*) **neighboring** ADJECTIVE = **nearby**, next, near, bordering, surrounding, connecting, adjacent, adjoining, abutting, contiguous (*formal*), nearest ■ **OPPOSITE:** remote

neighbourly *or* (*U.S.*) **neighborly** ADJECTIVE = **helpful**, kind, social, civil, friendly, obliging, harmonious, amiable, considerate, sociable, genial, hospitable, companionable, well-disposed

nemesis (*sometimes cap.*) NOUN
= **retribution**, fate, destruction, destiny, vengeance

neophyte NOUN = **novice**, student, pupil, recruit, amateur, beginner, trainee, apprentice, disciple, learner, tyro, probationer, novitiate, proselyte, catechumen

nepotism NOUN = **favouritism**, bias, patronage, preferential treatment, partiality

nerd *or* **nurd** NOUN **1** (*slang*) *Football nerds who like nothing more than slavering over a spreadsheet of numbers.* = **bore**, obsessive, anorak (*informal*), geek (*informal*), trainspotter (*informal*), dork (*slang*), wonk (*informal*), techie (*informal*), alpha geek **2** *He is such a charmless little nerd.* = **weed**, drip (*informal*), sap (*slang*), wally (*slang*), sucker (*slang*), wimp (*informal*), booby, prat (*slang*), plonker (*slang*), twit (*informal, chiefly Brit.*), simpleton, dipstick (*Brit. slang*), schmuck (*U.S. slang*), divvy (*Brit. slang*), putz (*U.S. slang*), wuss (*slang*), eejit (*Scot. & Irish*), dumb-ass (*slang*), doofus (*slang, chiefly U.S.*), dorba *or* dorb (*Austral. slang*), bogan (*Austral. slang*)

nerve NOUN **1** *I never got up enough nerve to ask her out.* = **bravery**, courage, spirit, bottle (*Brit. slang*), resolution, daring, determination, guts (*informal*), pluck, grit, fortitude, vigour, coolness, balls (*vulgar slang*), mettle, firmness, spunk (*informal*), fearlessness, steadfastness, intrepidity, hardihood, gameness **2** *He had the nerve to ask me to prove who I was.* = **impudence**, face (*informal*), front, neck (*informal*), sauce (*informal*), cheek (*informal*), brass (*informal*), gall, audacity, boldness, temerity, chutzpah (*U.S. & Canad. informal*), insolence, impertinence, effrontery, brass neck (*Brit. informal*), brazenness, sassiness (*U.S. slang*)
▶ PLURAL NOUN *I just played badly. It wasn't nerves.* = **tension**, stress, strain, anxiety, butterflies (in your stomach) (*informal*), nervousness, cold feet (*informal*), heebie-jeebies (*slang*), worry • **get on someone's nerves** = **annoy**, provoke, bug (*informal*), needle (*informal*), plague, irritate, aggravate (*informal*), madden, ruffle, exasperate, nettle, irk, rile, peeve, get under your skin (*informal*), nark (*Brit., Austral. & N.Z. slang*), get up your nose (*informal*), make your blood boil, piss you off (*slang*), rub (someone) up the wrong way (*informal*), get your goat (*slang*), get in your hair (*informal*), get on your wick (*Brit. slang*), put your back up, hack you off (*informal*)
• **nerve yourself** *I nerved myself to face the pain.*
= **brace yourself**, prepare yourself, steel yourself, fortify yourself, gear yourself up, gee yourself up ■ **RELATED WORDS:** *technical name* neuron, neurone; *adjective* neural

nerve-racking *or* **nerve-wracking** ADJECTIVE = **tense**, trying, difficult, worrying, frightening, distressing, daunting, harassing, stressful, harrowing, gut-wrenching

nervous ADJECTIVE (*often with* **of**) = **apprehensive**, anxious, uneasy, edgy, worried, wired (*slang*), tense, fearful, shaky, hysterical, agitated, ruffled, timid, hyper (*informal*), jittery (*informal*), uptight (*informal*), flustered, on edge, excitable, nervy (*Brit. informal*), jumpy, twitchy (*informal*), fidgety, timorous (*literary*), highly strung, antsy (*informal*), toey (*Austral. slang*), adrenalized ■ **OPPOSITE:** calm

nervousness NOUN = **anxiety**, stress, tension, strain, unease, disquiet, agitation, trepidation (*formal*), timidity, excitability, perturbation, edginess, worry, jumpiness, antsiness (*informal*)

nervy ADJECTIVE = **anxious**, nervous, tense, agitated, wired (*slang*), restless, jittery (*informal*), on edge, excitable, jumpy, twitchy (*informal*), fidgety, adrenalized

nest NOUN **1** *The couple are desperate to buy a holiday love nest.* = **refuge**, resort, retreat, haunt, den, hideaway **2** *Biarritz was notorious in those days as a nest of spies.* = **hotbed**, den, breeding-ground

nest egg NOUN = **savings**, fund(s), store, reserve, deposit, fall-back, cache

nestle VERB (*often with* **up** *or* **down**) = **snuggle**, cuddle, huddle, curl up, nuzzle

nestling NOUN = **chick**, fledgling, baby bird

net¹ NOUN *the use of a net in greenhouses to protect crops against insects* = **mesh**, netting, network, web, lattice, lacework, openwork
▶ VERB *Poachers have been netting fish to sell on the black market.* = **catch**, bag, capture, trap, nab (*informal*), entangle, ensnare, enmesh

net² *or* **nett** ADJECTIVE **1** *At the year end, net assets were £18 million.* = **after taxes**, final, clear, take-home **2** *The party made a net gain of 210 seats.* = **final**, closing, ultimate, eventual, conclusive ▶ VERB *The state government expects to net about 1.46 billion rupees.* = **earn**, make, clear, gain, realize, bring in, accumulate, reap

nether ADJECTIVE = **lower**, bottom, beneath, underground, inferior, basal

nettle VERB = **irritate**, provoke, annoy, gall, sting, aggravate (*informal*), incense, ruffle, exasperate, vex, goad, pique, get on your nerves (*informal*), nark (*Brit., Austral. & N.Z. slang*), hack you off (*informal*)

n

network NOUN **1** *The uterus is supplied with a network of blood vessels and nerves.* = **web**, system, arrangement, grid, mesh, lattice, circuitry, nexus, plexus, interconnection, net **2** *Strasbourg, with its rambling network of medieval streets* = **maze**, warren, labyrinth

neurosis NOUN = **obsession**, phobia, anxiety

neuter VERB = **castrate**, doctor (*informal*), emasculate, spay, dress, fix (*informal*), geld

neutral ADJECTIVE **1** *Those who had decided to remain neutral now found themselves forced to take sides.* = **unbiased**, impartial, disinterested, even-handed, dispassionate, sitting on the fence, uninvolved, noncommittal, nonpartisan, unprejudiced, nonaligned, unaligned, noncombatant, nonbelligerent ■ **OPPOSITE:** biased **2** *He told her about the death, describing the events in as neutral a manner as he could.* = **expressionless**, dull, blank, deadpan, toneless **3** *Stick to talking about neutral subjects on your first meeting.* = **uncontroversial** or **noncontroversial**, safe, inoffensive **4** *I tend to wear neutral colours like grey and beige.* = **colourless**, achromatic

neutrality NOUN = **impartiality**, detachment, noninterference, nonpartisanship, noninvolvement, nonalignment, noninterventionism

neutralize VERB = **counteract**, cancel, offset, undo, compensate for, negate, invalidate, counterbalance, nullify

never ADVERB **1** *She was never really well after that.* = **at no time**, not once, not ever ■ **OPPOSITE:** always **2** *I would never do anything to hurt him.* = **under no circumstances**, no way, not at all, on no account, not on your life (*informal*), not on your nelly (*Brit. slang*), not for love nor money (*informal*), not ever

> USAGE *Never* is sometimes used in informal speech and writing as an emphatic form of *not*, with simple past tenses of certain verbs: *I never said that* – and in very informal speech as a denial in place of *did not*: *he says I hit him, but I never*. These uses of *never* should be avoided in careful writing.

never-never NOUN = **hire-purchase** (*Brit.*), H.P. (*Brit.*)

nevertheless SENTENCE CONNECTOR = **even so**, still, however, yet, regardless, nonetheless, notwithstanding, in spite of that, (even) though, but

new ADJECTIVE **1** *They opened a factory in India to manufacture this new invention.* = **modern**, recent, contemporary, up-to-date, latest, happening (*informal*), different, current, advanced, original, fresh, novel, topical, state-of-the-art, ground-breaking, modish, newfangled, modernistic, ultramodern, all-singing, all-dancing ■ **OPPOSITE:** old-fashioned **2** *There are many boats, new and used, for sale.* = **brand new**, unused **3** *Many are looking for a new source of income by taking on freelance work.* = **extra**, more, added, new-found, supplementary **4** *I had been in my new job only a few days.* = **unfamiliar**, unaccustomed, strange, unknown **5** *The treatment made him feel like a new man.* = **renewed**, changed, improved, restored, altered, rejuvenated, revitalized

newcomer NOUN **1** *He must be a newcomer to town.* = **new arrival**, incomer, immigrant, stranger, foreigner, alien, settler **2** *The candidates are all relative newcomers to politics.* = **beginner**, stranger, outsider, novice, new arrival, parvenu, Johnny-come-lately (*informal*), noob (*derogatory slang*)

newly ADVERB = **recently**, just, lately, freshly, anew, latterly

newness NOUN = **novelty**, innovation, originality, freshness, strangeness, unfamiliarity ■ **RELATED WORDS:** *prefix* neo-; *phobia* neophobia

news NOUN = **information**, latest (*informal*), report, word, story, release, account, statement, advice, exposé, intelligence, scandal, rumour, leak, revelation, buzz, gossip, dirt (*slang*), goss (*informal*), disclosure, bulletin, dispatch, gen (*Brit. informal*), communiqué, hearsay, tidings, news flash, scuttlebutt (*U.S. slang*)

newsworthy ADJECTIVE = **interesting**, important, arresting, significant, remarkable, notable, sensational, noteworthy

next ADJECTIVE **1** *I caught the next available flight.* = **following**, later, succeeding, subsequent **2** *The man in the next chair was asleep.* = **adjacent**, closest, nearest, neighbouring, adjoining ▶ ADVERB *I don't know what to do next.* = **afterwards**, then, later, following, subsequently, thereafter

nexus NOUN = **connection**, link, tie, bond, junction, joining

nibble VERB (*often with* **at**) *He started to nibble his biscuit.* = **bite**, eat, peck, pick at, nip, munch, gnaw ▶ NOUN *We each took a nibble of cheese.* = **snack**, bite, taste, peck, crumb, morsel, titbit, soupçon (*French*)

nice ADJECTIVE **1** *We had a nice meal with a bottle of champagne.* = **pleasant**, delightful, agreeable, good, attractive, charming, pleasurable, enjoyable ■ **OPPOSITE:** unpleasant **2** *It was nice of you to go to so*

much trouble. = **kind**, helpful, obliging, considerate ■ **OPPOSITE:** unkind
3 *I've met your father and I think he's really nice.* = **likable** *or* **likeable**, friendly, engaging, charming, pleasant, agreeable, amiable, prepossessing **4** *The kids are very well brought up and have nice manners.* = **polite**, cultured, refined, courteous, genteel, well-bred, well-mannered ■ **OPPOSITE:** vulgar
5 *As a politician, he drew a nice distinction between his own opinions and the wishes of the majority.* = **precise**, fine, careful, strict, accurate, exact, exacting, subtle, delicate, discriminating, rigorous, meticulous, scrupulous, fastidious ■ **OPPOSITE:** vague

nicely ADVERB **1** *She's just written a book, nicely illustrated and not too technical.* = **pleasantly**, well, delightfully, attractively, charmingly, agreeably, pleasingly, acceptably, pleasurably ■ **OPPOSITE:** unpleasantly
2 *He treated you very nicely and acted like a decent guy.* = **kindly**, politely, thoughtfully, amiably, courteously **3** *I think this sums up the problem very nicely.* = **precisely**, exactly, accurately, finely, carefully, strictly, subtly, delicately, meticulously, rigorously, scrupulously ■ **OPPOSITE:** carelessly
4 *She has a private income, so they manage very nicely.* = **satisfactorily**, well, adequately, acceptably, passably

nicety NOUN = **fine point**, distinction, subtlety, nuance, refinement, minutiae

niche NOUN **1** *There was a niche in the rock where the path ended.* = **recess**, opening, corner, hollow, nook, alcove **2** *Perhaps I will find my niche in a desk job.* = **position**, calling, place, slot (*informal*), vocation, pigeonhole (*informal*)

nick NOUN *The barbed wire had left only the tiniest nick below my right eye.* = **cut**, mark, scratch, score, chip, scar, notch, dent, snick
▶ VERB **1** *We used to nick biscuits from the kitchen.* = **steal**, pinch (*informal*), swipe (*slang*), pilfer, snitch (*slang*) **2** *A sharp blade is likely to nick the skin and draw blood.* = **cut**, mark, score, damage, chip, scratch, scar, notch, dent, snick

nickname NOUN = **pet name**, label, diminutive, epithet, sobriquet, familiar name, moniker *or* monicker (*slang*), handle (*slang*)

nifty ADJECTIVE **1** *The film features some nifty special effects.* = **slick**, excellent, sharp (*informal*), smart, clever, neat, stylish, schmick (*Austral. informal*) **2** *Knight displayed all the nifty legwork of a champion bowler.* = **agile**, quick, swift, skilful, deft

niggle VERB **1** *I realise now that the things which used to niggle me didn't really matter.* = **bother**, concern, worry, trouble, disturb, rankle **2** *I don't react any more when opponents try to niggle me.* = **criticize**, provoke, annoy, plague, irritate, hassle (*informal*), badger, find fault with, nag at, cavil, be on your back (*slang*) ▶ NOUN *The life we have built together is far more important than any minor niggle either of us might have.* = **complaint**, moan (*informal*), grievance, grumble, beef (*slang*), bitch (*slang*), lament, grouse, gripe (*informal*), grouch (*informal*)

niggling ADJECTIVE **1** *Both players have been suffering from niggling injuries.* = **irritating**, troubling, persistent, bothersome **2** *They started having tiffs about the most niggling little things.* = **petty**, minor, trifling, insignificant, unimportant, fussy, quibbling, picky (*informal*), piddling (*informal*), nit-picking (*informal*), finicky, pettifogging

nigh ADVERB *Accurate earthquake prediction is well nigh impossible.* = **almost**, about, nearly, close to, practically, approximately
▶ ADJECTIVE *The end of the world is nigh.* = **near**, next, close, imminent, impending, at hand, upcoming

night NOUN = **darkness**, dark, night-time, dead of night, night watches, hours of darkness ■ **RELATED WORD:** *adjective* nocturnal

nightfall NOUN = **evening**, sunset, twilight, dusk, sundown, eventide, gloaming (*Scot., poetic*), eve (*archaic*), evo (*Austral. slang*) ■ **OPPOSITE:** daybreak

nightly ADJECTIVE *One of the nurses came by on her nightly rounds.* = **nocturnal**, night-time
▶ ADVERB *She had prayed nightly for his safe return.* = **every night**, nights (*informal*), each night, night after night

nightmare NOUN **1** *Jane did not eat cheese because it gave her nightmares.* = **bad dream**, hallucination, night terror **2** *My years in prison were a nightmare.* = **ordeal**, trial, hell (*informal*), horror, torture, torment, tribulation, purgatory, hell on earth

nightmarish ADJECTIVE = **terrifying**, frightening, disturbing, appalling, horrible, horrific, ghastly, hideous, harrowing, frightful

nihilism NOUN *These disillusioned students embraced agnosticism, atheism, and nihilism.* = **negativity**, rejection, denial, scepticism, cynicism, pessimism, renunciation, atheism, repudiation, agnosticism, unbelief, abnegation

nil NOUN **1** *The score was two–nil.* = **nothing**, love, zero, zip (*U.S. slang*)
2 *The chances of success are virtually nil.* = **zero**, nothing, none, naught, zilch (*slang*), zip (*U.S. slang*)

nimble ADJECTIVE **1** *Lily, who was light and nimble on her feet, was learning to tap-dance.* = **agile**, active, lively, deft, proficient, sprightly, nippy (*Brit. informal*), spry, dexterous ∎ **OPPOSITE:** clumsy **2** *To keep your mind nimble, you must use it.* = **alert**, ready, bright (*informal*), sharp, keen, active, smart, quick-witted

nimbus NOUN = **halo**, atmosphere, glow, aura, ambience, corona, irradiation, aureole

nip¹ VERB **1** (*with* **along**, **up**, **out**, *etc*) *Could you nip down to the corner shop for some milk?* = **pop**, go, run, rush, dash **2** *She was patting the dog when it nipped her finger.* = **bite**, snap, nibble **3** *He gave Billy's cheek a nip between two rough fingers.* = **pinch**, catch, grip, squeeze, clip, compress, tweak • **nip something in the bud** *It is important to recognize jealousy and to nip it in the bud before it gets out of hand.* = **thwart**, check, frustrate

nip² NOUN *She had a habit of taking an occasional nip from a flask of cognac.* = **dram**, shot (*informal*), drop, taste, finger, swallow, portion, peg (*Brit.*), sip, draught, sup, mouthful, snifter (*informal*), soupçon (*French*)

nipper NOUN **1** *I couldn't have been much more than a nipper when you last saw me.* = **child**, girl, boy, baby, kid (*informal*), infant, tot, little one, sprog (*slang*), munchkin (*informal, chiefly U.S.*), rug rat (*slang*), littlie (*Austral. informal*), ankle-biter (*Austral. slang*), tacker (*Austral. slang*) **2** *Just inside the ragworm's mouth is a sharp, powerful pair of nippers.* = **pincer**, claw

nipple NOUN = **teat**, breast, udder, tit (*vulgar slang*), pap, papilla, mamilla

nippy ADJECTIVE **1** *It can get quite nippy in the evenings.* = **chilly**, biting, parky (*Brit. informal*) **2** *This nippy new car has fold-down rear seats.* = **fast** (*informal*), quick, speedy **3** *He's nippy, and well suited to badminton.* = **agile**, fast, quick, active, lively, nimble, sprightly, spry

nirvana NOUN = **paradise**, peace, joy, bliss, serenity, tranquillity

nitty-gritty NOUN = **basics**, facts, reality, essentials, core, fundamentals, substance, essence, bottom line, crux, gist, nuts and bolts, heart of the matter, ins and outs, brass tacks (*informal*)

no SENTENCE SUBSTITUTE *'Any problems?' – 'No, everything's fine.'* = **not at all**, certainly not, of course not, absolutely not, never, no way, nay ∎ **OPPOSITE:** yes ▶ NOUN **1** *My answer to that is an emphatic no.* = **refusal**, rejection, denial, negation, veto ∎ **OPPOSITE:** consent **2** *According to the latest poll, the noes*

have 50 per cent and the yeses 35 per cent. = **objector**, protester, dissident, dissenter

nob NOUN = **aristocrat**, fat cat (*slang*), toff (*Brit. slang*), bigwig (*informal*), celeb (*informal*), big shot (*informal*), big hitter (*informal*), aristo (*informal*), heavy hitter (*informal*), nabob (*informal*), V.I.P.

nobble VERB **1** *The trial was stopped after allegations of attempts to nobble the jury.* = **influence**, square, win over, pay off (*informal*), corrupt, intimidate, bribe, get at, buy off, suborn, grease the palm or hand of (*slang*) **2** *the drug used to nobble two horses at Doncaster last week* = **disable**, handicap, weaken, incapacitate **3** *Their plans were nobbled by jealous rivals.* = **thwart**, check, defeat, frustrate, snooker, foil, baffle, balk, prevent

nobility NOUN **1** *They married into the nobility and entered the highest ranks of society.* = **aristocracy**, lords, elite, nobles, upper class, peerage, ruling class, patricians, high society **2** *I found Mr. Mandela supremely courteous, with a genuine nobility of bearing.* = **dignity**, majesty, greatness, grandeur, magnificence, stateliness, nobleness **3** *There can be no doubt about the remarkable strength and nobility of her character.* = **integrity**, honour, virtue, goodness, honesty, righteousness, probity (*formal*), rectitude, worthiness, incorruptibility, uprightness

noble ADJECTIVE **1** *He was an upright and noble man.* = **worthy**, generous, upright, honourable, virtuous, magnanimous ∎ **OPPOSITE:** despicable **2** *She was described by contemporaries as possessing a noble bearing and excellent manners.* = **dignified**, great, august, imposing, impressive, distinguished, magnificent, splendid, stately ∎ **OPPOSITE:** lowly **3** *Although he was of noble birth he lived as a poor man.* = **aristocratic**, lordly, titled, gentle (*archaic*), patrician, blue-blooded, highborn (*old-fashioned*) ∎ **OPPOSITE:** humble ▶ NOUN *In those days, many of the nobles and landowners were a law unto themselves.* = **lord** or **lady**, peer, aristocrat, nobleman or woman, aristo (*informal*) ∎ **OPPOSITE:** commoner

nobody PRONOUN *They were shut away in a little room where nobody could overhear.* = **no-one** ▶ NOUN *A man in my position has nothing to fear from a nobody like you.* = **nonentity**, nothing (*informal*), lightweight (*informal*), zero, no-mark (*Brit. slang*), cipher ∎ **OPPOSITE:** celebrity

nocturnal ADJECTIVE = **nightly**, night, of the night, night-time

nod VERB **1** '*Are you okay?*' *I asked. She nodded and smiled.* = **agree**, concur, assent, show agreement **2** *She nodded her head in understanding.* = **incline**, bob, bow, duck, dip **3** *He lifted his end of the canoe, nodding to me to take up mine.* = **signal**, indicate, motion, gesture **4** *All the girls nodded and said 'Hi'.* = **salute**, acknowledge ▶ NOUN **1** *Then, at a nod from their leader, they all sat.* = **signal**, sign, motion, gesture, indication **2** *I gave him a quick nod of greeting and slipped into the nearest chair.* = **salute**, greeting, acknowledgment

node NOUN = **nodule**, growth, swelling, knot, lump, bump, bud, knob, protuberance

noise NOUN = **sound**, talk, row, racket, outcry, clamour, din, clatter, uproar, babble, blare, fracas, commotion, pandemonium, rumpus, cry, tumult, hubbub ■ **OPPOSITE:** silence

noisy ADJECTIVE **1** *a noisy group of revellers* = **rowdy**, chattering, strident, boisterous, vociferous, riotous, uproarious, obstreperous, clamorous ■ **OPPOSITE:** quiet **2** *It may be necessary to ask a neighbour to turn down noisy music.* = **loud**, piercing, deafening, tumultuous, ear-splitting, cacophonous, clamorous ■ **OPPOSITE:** quiet

nomad NOUN = **wanderer**, migrant, rover, rambler, itinerant, drifter, vagabond

nomadic ADJECTIVE = **wandering**, travelling, roaming, migrant, roving, itinerant, migratory, vagrant, peripatetic

nomenclature NOUN = **terminology**, vocabulary, classification, taxonomy, phraseology, locution

nominal ADJECTIVE **1** *As he was still not allowed to run a company, his wife became its nominal head.* = **titular**, formal, purported, in name only, supposed, so-called, pretended, theoretical, professed, ostensible **2** *The ferries carry bicycles for a nominal charge.* = **token**, small, symbolic, minimal, trivial, trifling, insignificant, inconsiderable

nominate VERB **1** *The public will be able to nominate candidates for the awards.* = **propose**, suggest, recommend, submit, put forward **2** *It is legally possible for an elderly person to nominate someone to act for them.* = **appoint**, name, choose, commission, select, elect, assign, designate, empower

nomination NOUN **1** *a list of nominations for senior lectureships* = **proposal**, suggestion, recommendation **2** *On Leo's death there were two main candidates for nomination as his replacement.* = **appointment**, election, selection, designation, choice

nominee NOUN = **candidate**, applicant, entrant, contestant, aspirant, runner

nonaligned ADJECTIVE = **neutral**, impartial, uninvolved, nonpartisan, noncombatant, nonbelligerent

nonchalance NOUN = **indifference**, insouciance, detachment, unconcern, cool (*slang*), calm, apathy, composure, carelessness, equanimity, casualness, sang-froid, self-possession, dispassion, imperturbability

nonchalant ADJECTIVE = **indifferent**, cool, calm, casual, detached, careless, laid-back (*informal*), airy, unconcerned, apathetic, dispassionate, unfazed (*informal*), unperturbed, blasé, offhand, unemotional, insouciant, imperturbable ■ **OPPOSITE:** concerned

noncommittal ADJECTIVE = **evasive**, politic, reserved, guarded, careful, cautious, neutral, vague, wary, discreet, tentative, ambiguous, indefinite, circumspect, tactful, equivocal, temporizing, unrevealing

nonconformist NOUN = **dissenter**, rebel, radical, protester, eccentric, maverick, heretic, individualist, iconoclast, dissentient ■ **OPPOSITE:** traditionalist

nondescript ADJECTIVE = **undistinguished**, ordinary, dull, commonplace, unremarkable, run-of-the-mill, uninspiring, indeterminate, uninteresting, featureless, insipid, unexceptional, common or garden (*informal*), mousy, characterless, unmemorable, vanilla (*informal*), nothing to write home about ■ **OPPOSITE:** distinctive

none PRONOUN **1** *I turned to bookshops and libraries seeking information and found none.* = **not any**, nothing, zero, not one, nil, no part, not a bit, zilch (*slang*), diddly (*U.S. slang*) **2** *None of us knew what to say to her.* = **no-one**, nobody, not one

nonentity NOUN = **nobody**, lightweight (*informal*), mediocrity, cipher, small fry, unimportant person

nonetheless SENTENCE CONNECTOR = **nevertheless**, however, yet, even so, despite that, in spite of that

nonevent NOUN = **flop** (*informal*), failure, disappointment, fiasco, dud (*informal*), washout, clunker (*informal*)

nonexistent ADJECTIVE = **imaginary**, imagined, fancied, fictional, mythical, unreal, hypothetical, illusory, insubstantial, hallucinatory ■ **OPPOSITE:** real

nonplussed ADJECTIVE = **taken aback**, stunned, confused, embarrassed, puzzled, astonished, stumped, dismayed, baffled,

n

bewildered, astounded, confounded, perplexed, disconcerted, mystified, fazed, dumbfounded, discomfited, flummoxed, discountenanced

nonsense NOUN **1** *Most orthodox doctors, however, dismiss this theory as complete nonsense.* = **rubbish**, hot air (*informal*), waffle (*informal, chiefly Brit.*), twaddle, pants (*slang*), rot, crap (*slang*), garbage (*informal*), trash, bunk (*informal*), tosh (*slang, chiefly Brit.*), rhubarb, pap, foolishness, bilge (*informal*), drivel, tripe (*informal*), gibberish, guff (*slang*), bombast, moonshine, claptrap (*informal*), hogwash, hokum (*slang, chiefly U.S. & Canad.*), blather, double Dutch (*Brit. informal*), piffle (*informal*), poppycock (*informal*), balderdash, bosh (*informal*), eyewash (*informal*), stuff and nonsense, tommyrot, horsefeathers (*U.S. slang*), bunkum or buncombe, bizzo (*Austral. slang*), bull's wool (*Austral. & N.Z. slang*) ■ **OPPOSITE:** sense **2** *Surely it is an economic nonsense to deplete the world of natural resources.* = **idiocy**, folly, stupidity, absurdity, silliness, inanity, senselessness, ridiculousness, ludicrousness, fatuity

nonsensical ADJECTIVE = **senseless**, crazy (*informal*), silly, ridiculous, absurd, foolish, ludicrous, meaningless, irrational, incomprehensible, inane, asinine, cockamamie (*slang, chiefly U.S.*)

nonstarter NOUN = **dead loss**, dud (*informal*), washout (*informal*), no-hoper (*informal*), turkey (*informal*), lemon (*informal*), loser, waste of space or time

non-stop ADJECTIVE *The training was non-stop and continued for three days.* = **continuous**, constant, relentless, uninterrupted, steady, endless, unbroken, interminable, incessant, unending, ceaseless, unremitting, unfaltering ■ **OPPOSITE:** occasional
▶ ADVERB *The snow fell non-stop for 24 hours.* = **continuously**, constantly, steadily, endlessly, relentlessly, perpetually, incessantly, unremittingly, uninterruptedly, unendingly, unfalteringly, unbrokenly

nook NOUN = **niche**, corner, recess, cavity, crevice, alcove, cranny, inglenook (*Brit.*), cubbyhole, opening

noon NOUN *The long day of meetings started at noon.* = **midday**, high noon, noonday, noontime, twelve noon, noontide

norm NOUN *Their actions departed from what she called the commonly accepted norms of behaviour.* = **standard**, rule, model, pattern, mean, type, measure, average, par, criterion, benchmark, yardstick

normal ADJECTIVE *The two countries have resumed normal diplomatic relations.* = **usual**, common, standard, average, natural, regular, ordinary, acknowledged, typical, conventional, routine, accustomed, habitual, run-of-the-mill ■ **OPPOSITE:** unusual

normality or (*U.S.*) **normalcy** NOUN *A semblance of normality has returned to the city after the attack.* = **regularity**, order, routine, ordinariness, naturalness, conventionality, usualness

normally ADVERB **1** *Normally, the transportation system carries a million passengers a day.* = **usually**, generally, commonly, regularly, typically, ordinarily, as a rule, habitually **2** *the failure of the blood to clot normally* = **as usual**, naturally, properly, conventionally, in the usual way

normative ADJECTIVE = **standardizing**, controlling, regulating, prescriptive, normalizing, regularizing

north ADJECTIVE *on the north side of the mountain; a bitterly cold north wind* = **northern**, polar, arctic, boreal, northerly
▶ ADVERB *The hurricane which had destroyed Honolulu was moving north.* = **northward(s)**, in a northerly direction

North Star NOUN = **Pole Star**, Polaris, lodestar

nose NOUN **1** *She had sunscreen on her nose.* = **snout**, bill, beak (*slang*), hooter (*slang*), snitch (*slang*), conk (*slang*), neb (*archaic, dialect*), proboscis, schnozzle (*slang, chiefly U.S.*) **2** *My mother has always had a nose for a bargain.* = **instinct**, feeling, intuition, sixth sense ▶ VERB *The car nosed forward out of the drive.* = **ease forward**, push, edge, shove, nudge • **by a nose** = **only just**, just, hardly, barely, scarcely, by the skin of your teeth • **get up someone's nose** = **irritate**, annoy, anger, madden, get (*informal*), bug (*informal*), aggravate (*informal*), gall, exasperate, nettle, vex, irk, rile, peeve, get under someone's skin (*informal*), get someone's back up, piss someone off (*slang*), put someone's back up, nark (*Brit., Austral. & N.Z. slang*), get someone's goat (*slang*), make someone's blood boil, get someone's dander up (*informal*), hack someone off (*informal*) • **nose around** or **about** = **search**, examine, investigate, explore, inspect, work over, fossick (*Austral. & N.Z.*) • **nose something out** = **detect**, smell, scent, sniff out • **poke** or **stick your nose into something** = **pry**, interfere, meddle, intrude, snoop (*informal*), be inquisitive ■ **RELATED WORDS:** *adjectives* nasal, rhinal

nose dive NOUN **1** *The catamaran sailed over the precipice and plunged into a nosedive.* = **drop**, plunge, dive, plummet, sharp fall **2** *My career has taken a nosedive in the past year or two.* = **sharp fall**, plunge, drop, dive, plummet ▶ VERB **1** *The cockpit was submerged as the plane nosedived into the water.* = **drop**, plunge, dive, plummet, fall sharply **2** *The value of the shares nosedived by £2.6 billion.* = **fall sharply**, drop, plunge, dive, plummet

nosey *or* **nosy** ADJECTIVE = **inquisitive**, curious, intrusive, prying, eavesdropping, snooping (*informal*), busybody, interfering, meddlesome

nosh NOUN **1** *a restaurant which serves fine wines and posh nosh* = **food**, eats (*slang*), fare, grub (*slang*), feed, tack (*informal*), scoff (*slang*), kai (*N.Z. informal*), chow (*informal*), sustenance, victuals, comestibles, nosebag (*slang*), vittles (*obsolete, dialect*), viands **2** *We went for a nosh at our local Indian restaurant.* = **meal**, repast ▶ VERB *Guests mingled in the gardens, sipped wine, and noshed at cabaret tables.* = **eat**, consume, scoff (*slang*), devour, feed on, munch, gobble, partake of, wolf down

nostalgia NOUN = **reminiscence**, longing, regret, pining, yearning, remembrance, homesickness, wistfulness

nostalgic ADJECTIVE = **sentimental**, longing, emotional, homesick, wistful, maudlin, regretful

notable ADJECTIVE **1** *The most notable architectural feature of the town is its castle.* = **remarkable**, marked, striking, unusual, extraordinary, outstanding, evident, pronounced, memorable, noticeable, uncommon, conspicuous, salient, noteworthy ■ OPPOSITE: imperceptible **2** *the notable occultist, Madame Blavatsky* = **prominent**, famous, celebrated, distinguished, well-known, notorious, renowned, eminent, pre-eminent ■ OPPOSITE: unknown ▶ NOUN *The notables attending included five Senators, two Supreme Court judges and three State Governors.* = **celebrity**, worthy, big name, dignitary, luminary, celeb (*informal*), personage, megastar (*informal*), notability, V.I.P.

notably ADVERB *a notably brave officer who had served under Wolfe at Quebec* = **remarkably**, unusually, distinctly, extraordinarily, markedly, noticeably, strikingly, conspicuously, singularly, outstandingly, uncommonly, pre-eminently, signally

notation NOUN **1** *The dot in musical notation symbolizes an abrupt or staccato quality.* = **signs**, system, characters, code, symbols, script **2** *He was checking the readings and making notations on a clipboard.* = **note**, record, noting, jotting

notch NOUN **1** *Average earnings in the economy moved up another notch in August.* = **level**, step, degree, grade, cut (*informal*) **2** *The blade had a hole through the middle and a notch on one side.* = **cut**, nick, incision, indentation, mark, score, cleft ▶ VERB *a bamboo walking stick with a notched handle* = **cut**, mark, score, nick, scratch, indent

note NOUN **1** *Stevens wrote him a note asking him to come to his apartment.* = **message**, letter, communication, memo, memorandum, epistle, email *or* e-mail, text **2** *I made a note of his address.* = **record**, reminder, memo, memorandum, jotting, minute **3** *See note 16 on page 223.* = **annotation**, comment, remark, gloss **4** *In the eyes of the law, signing a delivery note is seen as 'accepting' the goods.* = **document**, form, record, certificate **5** *He has never been able to read or transcribe musical notes.* = **symbol**, mark, sign, indication, token **6** *I detected a note of bitterness in his voice.* = **tone**, touch, trace, hint, sound ▶ VERB **1** *Suddenly I noted that the rain had stopped.* = **notice**, see, observe, perceive **2** *Please note that there are a limited number of tickets.* = **bear in mind**, be aware, take into account **3** *The report noted a sharp drop in new cases.* = **mention**, record, mark, indicate, register, remark **4** *A police officer was noting the number plates of passing cars.* = **write down**, record, scribble, take down, set down, jot down, put in writing, put down in black and white • **of note 1** *Besides being an artist of great note, he can also be a fascinating conversationalist.* = **famous**, prestigious, eminent, renowned, of standing, of character, of reputation, of consequence, celebrated **2** *She has published nothing of note in the last ten years.* = **important**, consequential, significant, of distinction • **take note of something** *or* **someone** *Take note of the weather conditions.* = **notice**, note, regard, observe, heed, pay attention to

notebook NOUN = **notepad**, record book, exercise book, jotter, journal, diary, Filofax®, memorandum book

noted ADJECTIVE = **famous**, celebrated, recognized, distinguished, well-known, prominent, notorious, acclaimed, notable, renowned, eminent, conspicuous, illustrious ■ OPPOSITE: unknown

noteworthy ADJECTIVE = **remarkable**, interesting, important, significant, extraordinary, outstanding, exceptional, notable ■ OPPOSITE: ordinary

nothing PRONOUN **1** *I know nothing of these matters.* = **nought**, zero, nil, naught, not a thing, zilch (*slang*), sod all (*slang*), damn all (*slang*), zip (*U.S. slang*) **2** *'Thanks for all your help.' 'It was nothing.'* = **a trifle**, no big deal, a mere bagatelle **3** *philosophical ideas of the void, the nothing and the 'un-thought'* = **void**, emptiness, nothingness, nullity, nonexistence ▸ NOUN *I went from being a complete nothing to having people call me a star.* = **nobody**, cipher, nonentity

nothingness NOUN **1** *There might be something beyond the grave, you know, and not just nothingness.* = **oblivion**, nullity, nonexistence, nonbeing **2** *the banal lyrics, clichéd song structures and light, fluffy nothingness of her latest album* = **insignificance**, triviality, worthlessness, meaninglessness, unimportance

notice NOUN **1** *I saw a little notice advertising an open day at a nearby estate.* = **sign**, advertisement, poster, placard, warning, bill **2** *Unions are requested to give seven days' notice of industrial action.* = **notification**, warning, advice, intimation, news, communication, intelligence, announcement, instruction, advance warning, wake-up call, heads up (*U.S. & Canad.*) **3** *She got some good notices for her performance last night.* = **review**, comment, criticism, evaluation, critique, critical assessment **4** *Nothing that went on in the hospital escaped her notice.* = **attention**, interest, note, regard, consideration, observation, scrutiny, heed, cognizance ■ OPPOSITE: oversight **5** *They predicted that many teachers would be given their notice by the end of next term.* = **the sack** (*informal*), dismissal, discharge, the boot (*slang*), the push (*slang*), marching orders (*informal*), the (old) heave-ho (*informal*), your books or cards (*informal*) ▸ VERB *People should not hesitate to contact the police if they notice anything suspicious.* = **observe**, see, mind, note, spot, remark, distinguish, perceive, detect, heed, discern, behold (*archaic, literary*), mark, eyeball (*slang*) ■ OPPOSITE: overlook

noticeable ADJECTIVE = **obvious**, clear, striking, plain, bold, evident, distinct, manifest, conspicuous, unmistakable, salient, observable, perceptible, appreciable

notification NOUN = **announcement**, declaration, notice, statement, telling, information, warning, message, advice, intelligence, publication, notifying, heads up (*U.S. & Canad.*)

notify VERB = **inform**, tell, advise, alert to, announce, warn, acquaint with, make known to, apprise of

notion NOUN **1** *the notion that musical ability is present from birth; He has a realistic notion of his capabilities.* = **idea**, view, opinion, belief, concept, impression, judgment, sentiment, conception, apprehension, inkling, mental image or picture, picture **2** *I had a whimsical notion to fly off to Rio that night.* = **whim**, wish, desire, fancy, impulse, inclination, caprice

notional ADJECTIVE = **hypothetical**, ideal, abstract, theoretical, imaginary, speculative, conceptual, unreal, fanciful ■ OPPOSITE: actual

notoriety NOUN = **infamy**, discredit, disrepute, dishonour, bad reputation, opprobrium, ill repute, obloquy

notorious ADJECTIVE = **infamous**, disreputable, opprobrious

notoriously ADVERB = **infamously**, disreputably

notwithstanding PREPOSITION *He despised Pitt, notwithstanding the similar views they both held.* = **despite**, in spite of, regardless of ▸ SENTENCE CONNECTOR *He doesn't want me there, but I'm going, notwithstanding.* = **nevertheless**, however, though, nonetheless

nought (*archaic, literary*)**, naught, ought** or **aught** NOUN **1** *Properties are graded from nought to ten for energy efficiency.* = **zero**, nothing, nil **2** *All our efforts came to nought.* = **nothing**, zip (*U.S. slang*), nothingness, nada, zilch, sod all (*slang*), damn all (*slang*)

nourish VERB **1** *The food the mother eats nourishes both her and her baby.* = **feed**, supply, sustain, nurture **2** *This attitude has been carefully nourished by a small group of journalists and scholars.* = **encourage**, support, maintain, promote, sustain, foster, cultivate

nourishing ADJECTIVE = **nutritious**, beneficial, wholesome, healthful, health-giving, nutritive

nourishment NOUN = **food**, nutrition, sustenance, nutriment, tack (*informal*), kai (*N.Z. informal*), victuals, vittles (*obsolete, dialect*)

novel¹ NOUN *He had all but finished writing a first novel.* = **story**, tale, fiction, romance, narrative

novel² ADJECTIVE *Clubs are always looking at novel ways to raise cash.* = **new**, different, original, fresh, unusual, innovative, uncommon, singular, ground-breaking, left-field (*informal*) ■ OPPOSITE: ordinary

novelist NOUN = **author**, writer

novelty NOUN **1** *The radical puritanism of Conceptual art and Minimalism had lost its novelty.* = **newness**, originality, freshness, innovation, surprise, uniqueness, strangeness, unfamiliarity **2** *In those days a motor car was still a novelty.* = **curiosity**, marvel, rarity, oddity, wonder **3** *At Easter, we give them plastic eggs filled with small toys, novelties and coins.* = **trinket**, souvenir, memento, bauble, bagatelle, gimcrack, trifle, gewgaw, knick-knack

novice NOUN *I'm a novice at these things. You're the professional.* = **beginner**, pupil, amateur, newcomer, trainee, apprentice, learner, neophyte (*formal*), tyro, probationer, proselyte ■ **OPPOSITE:** expert

now ADVERB **1** *Most of our revenue now comes from overseas clients.* = **nowadays**, at the moment, these days **2** *Please tell him I need to talk to him now.* = **immediately**, presently (*Scot. & U.S.*), promptly, instantly, at once, straightaway • **now and then** or **again** *Now and then he would pay us a brief visit.* = **occasionally**, sometimes, at times, from time to time, on and off, on occasion, once in a while, intermittently, infrequently, sporadically

nowadays ADVERB = **now**, today, at the moment, these days, in this day and age

noxious ADJECTIVE = **harmful**, deadly, poisonous, toxic, unhealthy, hurtful, pernicious (*formal*), injurious, unwholesome, noisome, pestilential, insalubrious, foul ■ **OPPOSITE:** harmless

nuance NOUN = **subtlety**, degree, distinction, graduation, refinement, nicety, gradation

nub NOUN = **gist**, point, heart, core, essence, nucleus, kernel, crux, pith

nubile ADJECTIVE = **attractive**, sexy (*informal*), desirable, marriageable

nucleus NOUN = **centre**, heart, focus, basis, core, pivot, kernel, nub

nude ADJECTIVE = **naked**, stripped, exposed, bare, uncovered, undressed, stark-naked, in the raw (*informal*), disrobed, starkers (*informal*), unclothed, in the buff (*informal*), au naturel (*French*), in the altogether (*informal*), buck naked (*slang*), unclad, undraped, in your birthday suit (*informal*), without a stitch on (*informal*), in the bare scud (*Scot. slang*), naked as the day you were born (*informal*) ■ **OPPOSITE:** dressed

nudge VERB **1** *'Stop it,' he said, and nudged me in the ribs.* = **push**, touch, dig, jog, prod, elbow, shove, poke **2** *Bit by bit Bob nudged Fritz into selling his controlling interest.* = **prompt**, influence, urge, persuade, spur, prod, coax, prevail upon ▶ NOUN **1** *She slipped her arm under his and gave him a nudge.* = **push**, touch, dig, elbow, bump, shove, poke, jog, prod **2** *The challenge appealed to him. All he needed was a little nudge.* = **prompting**, push, encouragement, prod

nudity NOUN = **nakedness**, undress, nudism, bareness, deshabille

nugget NOUN = **lump**, piece, mass, chunk, clump, hunk

nuisance NOUN = **trouble**, problem, trial, bore, drag (*informal*), bother, plague (*informal*), pest, irritation, hassle (*informal*), inconvenience, annoyance, pain (*informal*), pain in the neck (*informal*), pain in the backside (*informal*), pain in the butt (*informal*) ■ **OPPOSITE:** benefit

null ADJECTIVE • **null and void** = **invalid**, useless, void, worthless, ineffectual, valueless, inoperative

nullify VERB **1** *He used his broad executive powers to nullify decisions by local government.* = **invalidate**, quash, revoke, render null and void, abolish, void, repeal, rescind, annul, abrogate ■ **OPPOSITE:** validate **2** *This, of course, would nullify the effect of the move.* = **cancel out**, counteract, negate, neutralize, obviate (*formal*), countervail, bring to naught

numb ADJECTIVE **1** *His legs felt numb and his toes ached.* = **unfeeling**, dead, frozen, paralysed, insensitive, deadened, immobilized, torpid, insensible ■ **OPPOSITE:** sensitive **2** *The mother, numb with grief, had trouble speaking.* = **stupefied**, deadened, unfeeling, insensible ▶ VERB **1** *For a while the shock of his letter numbed her.* = **stun**, knock out, paralyse, daze, stupefy **2** *The cold numbed my fingers.* = **deaden**, freeze, dull, paralyse, immobilize, benumb

number NOUN **1** *None of the doors have numbers on them.* = **numeral**, figure, character, digit, integer **2** *I have had an enormous number of letters from concerned parents.* = **amount**, quantity, collection, total, count, sum, aggregate ■ **OPPOSITE:** shortage **3** *People turned out to vote in huge numbers.* = **crowd**, horde, multitude, throng **4** *We had a stag night for one of our number who had decided to get married.* = **group**, company, set, band, crowd, gang, coterie **5** *an article which appeared in the summer number of the magazine* = **issue**, copy, edition, imprint, printing ▶ VERB **1** *They told me that their village numbered 100 or so.* = **amount to**, come to, total, add up to **2** *One widely cited report numbered the dead at over 10,000.* = **calculate**, account, reckon, compute, enumerate ■ **OPPOSITE:** guess **3** *He numbered*

n

several Americans among his friends. = **include**, count

numbered ADJECTIVE **1** *Their army is officially numbered at eight thousand strong.* = **reckoned**, totalled, counted **2** *Her days as leader are numbered.* = **limited**, restricted, limited in number

numbness NOUN **1** *I have recently been suffering from numbness in my fingers and toes.* = **deadness**, paralysis, insensitivity, dullness, torpor, insensibility **2** *She swung from emotional numbness to overwhelming fear and back again.* = **torpor**, deadness, dullness, stupefaction

numeral NOUN = **number**, figure, digit, character, symbol, cipher, integer

numerous ADJECTIVE = **many**, several, countless, lots, abundant, plentiful, innumerable, copious, manifold (*formal*), umpteen (*informal*), profuse, thick on the ground ■ OPPOSITE: few

nuptial ADJECTIVE = **marital**, wedding, wedded, bridal, matrimonial, conjugal, connubial (*formal*), hymeneal (*poetic*)

nuptials PLURAL NOUN (*sometimes singular*) = **wedding**, marriage, matrimony, espousal (*archaic*)

nurse VERB **1** *All the years he was sick my mother had nursed him.* = **look after**, treat, tend, care for, take care of, minister to **2** *He nursed an ambition to lead his own orchestra.* = **harbour**, have, maintain, preserve, entertain, cherish, keep alive **3** *She did not have enough*

milk to nurse the infant. = **breast-feed**, feed, nurture, nourish, suckle, wet-nurse

nursery NOUN = **crèche**, kindergarten, playgroup, play-centre (*N.Z.*)

nurture NOUN *The human organism learns partly by nature, partly by nurture.* = **upbringing**, training, education, instruction, rearing, development ▶ VERB *Parents want to know the best way to nurture and raise their children to adulthood.* = **bring up**, raise, look after, rear, care for, develop ■ OPPOSITE: neglect

nut NOUN **1** *Nuts are a good source of vitamin E.* = **kernel**, stone, seed, pip **2** *Kit shot up, hitting his nut on the roof.* = **head**, skull, noggin

nutrition NOUN = **food**, nourishment, sustenance, nutriment

nutritious ADJECTIVE = **nourishing**, beneficial, wholesome, healthful, health-giving, nutritive

nuts • nuts and bolts = **essentials**, basics, fundamentals, nitty-gritty (*informal*), practicalities, ins and outs, details

nuzzle VERB = **snuggle**, cuddle, nudge, burrow, nestle

nymph NOUN **1** *In the depths of a river, the three water nymphs – the Rhinemaidens – play and sing.* = **sylph**, dryad, naiad, hamadryad, Oceanid (*Greek myth*), oread **2** *They had one daughter, an exquisite nymph named Jacqueline.* = **girl**, lass, maiden (*archaic, literary*), maid (*archaic, literary*), damsel (*archaic, poetic*)

n

Oo

oasis NOUN **1** *The province was largely a wasteland with an occasional oasis.* = **watering hole 2** *an oasis of peace in a troubled world* = **haven**, retreat, refuge, sanctuary, island, resting place, sanctum

oath NOUN **1** *a solemn oath by members to help each other* = **promise**, bond, pledge, vow, word, compact, covenant, affirmation, sworn statement, avowal, word of honour **2** *Weller let out a foul oath and hurled himself upon him.* = **swear word**, curse, obscenity, blasphemy, expletive, four-letter word, cuss (*informal*), profanity, strong language, imprecation (*formal*), malediction

obedience NOUN = **compliance**, yielding, submission, respect, conformity, reverence, deference, observance, subservience, submissiveness, docility, complaisance, tractability, dutifulness, conformability ■ **OPPOSITE:** disobedience

obedient ADJECTIVE = **submissive**, yielding, compliant, under control, respectful, law-abiding, well-trained, amenable, docile, dutiful, subservient, deferential, tractable, acquiescent, biddable, accommodating, passive, meek, ingratiating, malleable, pliant, unresisting, bootlicking (*informal*), obeisant, duteous ■ **OPPOSITE:** disobedient

obese ADJECTIVE = **fat**, overweight, heavy, solid, gross, plump, stout, fleshy, beefy (*informal*), tubby, portly, outsize, roly-poly, rotund, podgy, corpulent, elephantine, paunchy, well-upholstered (*informal*), Falstaffian ■ **OPPOSITE:** thin

obesity *or* **obeseness** NOUN = **fatness**, flab, heaviness, a weight problem, grossness, corpulence, beef (*informal*), embonpoint (*French*), rotundity, fleshiness, stoutness, portliness, bulkiness, podginess, tubbiness ■ **OPPOSITE:** thinness

obey VERB **1** *Cissie obeyed her mother without question.* = **submit to**, surrender (to), give way to, succumb to, bow to, give in to, yield to, serve, cave in to (*informal*), take orders from, do what you are told by ■ **OPPOSITE:** disobey **2** *If you love me, you will obey.* = **submit**, yield, surrender, give in, give way, succumb, cave in, toe the line, knuckle under (*informal*), do what is expected, come to heel, get into line **3** *The commander refused to obey an order.* = **carry out**, follow, perform, respond to, implement, fulfil, execute, discharge, act upon, carry through ■ **OPPOSITE:** disregard **4** *Most people obey the law.* = **abide by**, keep, follow, comply with, observe, mind, embrace, hold to, heed, conform to, keep to, adhere to, be ruled by

object¹ NOUN **1** *an object the shape of a coconut* = **thing**, article, device, body, item, implement, entity, gadget, contrivance **2** *The object of the exercise is to raise money for charity.* = **purpose**, aim, end, point, plan, idea, reason, goal, design, target, principle, function, intention, objective, intent, motive, end in view, end purpose, the why and wherefore **3** *She was an object of pity among her friends.* = **target**, victim, focus, butt, recipient

object² VERB **1** *(often with* **to***) A lot of people objected to the plan.* = **protest against**, oppose, say no to, kick against (*informal*), argue against, draw the line at, take exception to, raise objections to, cry out against, complain against, take up the cudgels against, expostulate against ■ **OPPOSITE:** accept **2** *We objected strongly.* = **disagree**, demur, remonstrate (*formal*), expostulate, express disapproval ■ **OPPOSITE:** agree

objection NOUN = **protest**, opposition, complaint, doubt, exception, dissent, outcry, censure, disapproval, niggle (*informal*), protestation, scruple, demur, formal complaint, counter-argument, cavil, remonstrance (*formal*), demurral ■ **OPPOSITE:** agreement

objectionable ADJECTIVE = **offensive**, annoying, irritating, unacceptable, unpleasant, rude, intolerable, undesirable, distasteful, obnoxious, deplorable, displeasing, unseemly, disagreeable, repugnant, abhorrent, beyond the pale, insufferable, detestable, discourteous, uncivil, unmannerly, exceptionable, dislikable *or* dislikeable ■ **OPPOSITE:** pleasant

objective ADJECTIVE **1** *He has no objective evidence to support his claim.* = **factual**, real, circumstantial **2** *I would like your objective opinion on this.* = **unbiased**, detached, just, fair, judicial, open-minded, equitable, impartial, impersonal, disinterested, even-handed, dispassionate, unemotional, uninvolved, unprejudiced, uncoloured ■ **OPPOSITE:** subjective ▶ NOUN *His objective was to play golf and win.* = **purpose**, aim, goal, end, plan, hope, idea, design, target, wish, scheme, desire, object, intention, ambition, aspiration, Holy Grail (*informal*), end in view, why and wherefore

objectively ADVERB = **impartially**, neutrally, fairly, justly, without prejudice, dispassionately, with an open mind, equitably, without fear or favour, even-handedly, without bias, disinterestedly, with objectivity *or* impartiality

objectivity NOUN = **impartiality**, detachment, neutrality, equity, fairness, disinterest, open-mindedness, even-handedness, impersonality, disinterestedness, dispassion, nonpartisanship, lack of bias, equitableness ■ **OPPOSITE:** subjectivity

obligation NOUN **1** *Students usually feel an obligation to attend lectures.* = **duty**, compulsion **2** *I feel that's my obligation, to do whatever is possible.* = **task**, job, duty, work, calling, business, charge, role, function, mission, province, assignment, pigeon (*informal*), chore **3** *I have an ethical and moral obligation to my client.* = **responsibility**, duty, liability, accountability, culpability, answerability, accountableness

obligatory ADJECTIVE **1** *Third-party insurance is obligatory when driving in Italy.* = **compulsory**, required, necessary, essential, binding, enforced, mandatory, imperative, unavoidable, requisite, coercive, de rigueur (*French*) ■ **OPPOSITE:** optional **2** *This hotel has every facility, including the obligatory swimming-pool.* = **customary**, regular, usual, popular, normal, familiar, conventional, fashionable, bog-standard (*Brit. & Irish slang*)

oblige VERB **1** *This decree obliges unions to delay strikes.* = **compel**, make, force, require, bind, railroad (*informal*), constrain, necessitate, coerce, impel, dragoon, obligate **2** *He is always ready to oblige journalists with information.* = **help**, assist, serve, benefit, please, favour, humour, accommodate, indulge, gratify, do someone a service, put yourself out for, do (someone) a favour *or* a kindness, meet the wants *or* needs of ■ **OPPOSITE:** bother

obliged ADJECTIVE **1** *I was obliged to answer their questions.* = **forced**, required, bound, compelled, obligated, duty-bound, under an obligation, under compulsion, without any option **2** *I am extremely obliged to you.* = **grateful**, in (someone's) debt, thankful, indebted, appreciative, beholden

obliging ADJECTIVE = **accommodating**, kind, helpful, willing, civil, friendly, polite, cooperative, agreeable, amiable, courteous, considerate, hospitable, unselfish, good-natured, eager to please, complaisant ■ **OPPOSITE:** unhelpful

oblique ADJECTIVE **1** *It was an oblique reference to his time in prison.* = **indirect**, implied, roundabout, backhanded, evasive, elliptical, circuitous, circumlocutory, inexplicit, periphrastic ■ **OPPOSITE:** direct **2** *The mountain ridge runs at an oblique angle to the coastline.* = **slanting**, angled, sloped, sloping, inclined, tilted, tilting, slanted, diagonal, at an angle, asymmetrical, canted, aslant, slantwise, atilt, cater-cornered (*U.S. informal*) **3** *She gave him an oblique glance.* = **sidelong**, sideways, covert, indirect, furtive, surreptitious

obliquely ADVERB **1** *He referred obliquely to a traumatic event in her past.* = **indirectly**, evasively, not in so many words, circuitously, in a roundabout manner *or* way **2** *The muscle runs obliquely downwards inside the abdominal cavity.* = **at an angle**, sideways, diagonally, sidelong, aslant, slantwise, aslope

obliterate VERB **1** *Whole villages were obliterated by the fire.* = **destroy**, eliminate, devastate, waste, wreck, wipe out, demolish, ravage, eradicate, desolate, annihilate, put paid to, raze, blow to bits, extirpate, blow sky-high, destroy root and branch, kennet (*Austral. slang*), jeff (*Austral. slang*), wipe from *or* off the face of the earth ■ **OPPOSITE:** create **2** *I would like to obliterate the memory of what just occurred.* = **eradicate**, remove, eliminate, cancel, get rid of, wipe out, erase, excise, delete, extinguish, root out, efface, blot out, expunge (*formal*), extirpate

oblivion NOUN = **neglect**, anonymity, insignificance, obscurity, limbo, nothingness, unimportance

oblivious ADJECTIVE (*usually with of or to*) = **unaware**, unconscious, ignorant, regardless, careless, negligent, blind to, unaffected by, impervious to, forgetful, deaf to, unconcerned about, neglectful, heedless, inattentive, insensible, unmindful, unobservant, disregardful, incognizant ■ **OPPOSITE:** aware

> **USAGE** It was formerly considered incorrect to use *oblivious* and *unaware* as synonyms, but this use is now acceptable. When employed with this meaning, *oblivious* should be followed either by *to* or *of*, *to* being much the commoner.

obnoxious ADJECTIVE = **loathsome**, offensive, nasty, foul, disgusting, unpleasant, revolting, obscene, sickening, vile, horrid (*informal*), repellent, repulsive, objectionable, disagreeable, nauseating, odious, hateful, repugnant, reprehensible, abhorrent, abominable, insufferable, execrable, detestable, hateable, dislikable or dislikeable, yucky or yukky (*slang*), yucko (*Austral. slang*) ■ **OPPOSITE:** pleasant

obscene ADJECTIVE **1** *I'm no prude, but I think these photos are obscene.* = **indecent**, dirty, offensive, gross, foul, coarse, filthy, vile, improper, immoral, pornographic, suggestive, blue, loose (*old-fashioned*), shameless, lewd, depraved, X-rated (*informal*), bawdy, salacious, prurient, impure, lascivious, smutty, ribald, unwholesome, scabrous, immodest, licentious, indelicate, unchaste ■ **OPPOSITE:** decent **2** *It was obscene to spend millions producing unwanted food.* = **offensive**, shocking, evil, disgusting, outrageous, revolting, sickening, vile, wicked, repellent, atrocious, obnoxious, heinous, nauseating, odious, loathsome, abominable, detestable

obscenity NOUN **1** *He justified the use of obscenity on the grounds that it was art.* = **indecency**, pornography, impurity, impropriety, vulgarity, smut, prurience, coarseness, crudity, licentiousness, foulness, outrageousness, blueness, immodesty, suggestiveness, lewdness, dirtiness, grossness, vileness, filthiness, bawdiness, unseemliness, indelicacy, smuttiness, salacity ■ **OPPOSITE:** decency **2** *They shouted obscenities at us as we passed.* = **swear word**, curse, oath, expletive, four-letter word, cuss (*informal*), profanity, vulgarism

obscure ADJECTIVE **1** *The hymn was written by an obscure Greek composer.* = **unknown**, minor, little-known, humble, unfamiliar, out-of-the-way, unseen, lowly, unimportant, unheard-of, unsung, nameless, undistinguished, inconspicuous, unnoted, unhonoured, unrenowned ■ **OPPOSITE:** famous **2** *The contract is written in obscure language.* = **abstruse**, involved, complex, confusing, puzzling, subtle, mysterious, deep, vague, unclear, doubtful, mystical, intricate, ambiguous, enigmatic, esoteric, perplexing, occult, opaque, incomprehensible, arcane, cryptic, unfathomable, recondite, clear as mud (*informal*) ■ **OPPOSITE:** straightforward **3** *The word is of obscure origin.* = **unclear**, hidden, uncertain, confused, mysterious, concealed, doubtful, indefinite, indeterminate ■ **OPPOSITE:** well-known **4** *The hills were just an obscure shape in the mist.*

= **indistinct**, vague, blurred, dark, clouded, faint, dim, gloomy, veiled, murky, fuzzy, shadowy, cloudy, misty, hazy, indistinguishable, indeterminate, dusky, undefined, out of focus, ill-defined, obfuscated, indiscernible, tenebrous ■ **OPPOSITE:** clear ▸ VERB **1** *Trees obscured his vision.* = **obstruct**, hinder, block out **2** *The building is almost completely obscured by a huge banner.* = **hide**, cover (up), screen, mask, disguise, conceal, veil, cloak, shroud, camouflage, envelop, encase, enshroud ■ **OPPOSITE:** expose

obscurity NOUN **1** *His later life was spent in obscurity and loneliness.* = **insignificance**, oblivion, unimportance, non-recognition, inconsequence, lowliness, inconspicuousness, namelessness, ingloriousness **2** *Hunt was irritated by the obscurity of his reply.* = **vagueness**, complexity, ambiguity, intricacy, incomprehensibility, inexactitude, woolliness, abstruseness, impreciseness, impenetrableness, reconditeness, lack of preciseness ■ **OPPOSITE:** clarity **3** *the vast branches vanished into deep indigo obscurity above my head* = **darkness**, dark, shadows, shade, gloom, haze, blackness, murk, dimness, murkiness, haziness, duskiness, shadiness, shadowiness, indistinctness

observable ADJECTIVE = **noticeable**, clear, obvious, open, striking, apparent, visible, patent, evident, distinct, manifest, blatant, conspicuous, unmistakable, discernible, salient, recognizable, detectable, perceptible, appreciable, perceivable

observance NOUN **1** *(with of) Councils should ensure strict observance of laws.* = **carrying out of**, attention to, performance of, respect for, notice of, honouring of, observation of, compliance with, adherence to, fulfilment of, discharge of, obedience to, keeping of, heeding of, conformity to ■ **OPPOSITE:** disregard for **2** *Numerous religious observances set the rhythm of the day.* = **ceremony**, rite, procedure, service, form, act, practice, tradition, celebration, custom, ritual, formality, ceremonial, ordinance, liturgy

observant ADJECTIVE **1** *An observant doctor can detect depression from expression and posture.* = **attentive**, quick, alert, perceptive, concentrating, careful, vigilant, mindful, watchful, wide-awake, sharp-eyed, eagle-eyed, keen-eyed, on your toes, heedful ■ **OPPOSITE:** unobservant **2** *This is a profoundly observant Islamic country.*
= **devout**, godly, holy, orthodox, pious, obedient, reverent

observation NOUN **1** *careful observation of the movement of the planets* = **watching**, study, survey, review, notice, investigation, monitoring, attention, consideration, examination, inspection, scrutiny, surveillance, contemplation, cognition, perusal **2** *This book contains observations about the nature of addiction.* = **comment**, finding, thought, note, statement, opinion, remark, explanation, reflection, exposition, utterance, pronouncement, annotation, elucidation, obiter dictum (*Latin*) **3** *Is that a criticism or just an observation?* = **remark**, thought, comment, statement, opinion, reflection, assertion, utterance, animadversion **4** (*with* **of**) *strict observation of oil quotas* = **observance of**, attention to, compliance with, notice of, honouring of, adherence to, fulfilment of, discharge of, heeding of, carrying out of

observe VERB **1** *He studies and observes the behaviour of babies.* = **watch**, study, view, look at, note, check, regard, survey, monitor, contemplate, check out (*informal*), look on, keep an eye on (*informal*), gaze at, pay attention to, keep track of, scrutinize, keep tabs on (*informal*), recce (*slang*), keep under observation, watch like a hawk, take a dekko at (*Brit. slang*) **2** *In 1664 Hooke observed a reddish spot on the surface of the planet.* = **notice**, see, note, mark, discover, spot, regard, witness, clock (*Brit. slang*), distinguish, perceive, detect, discern, behold (*archaic, literary*), eye, eyeball (*slang*), peer at, espy, get a load of (*informal*) **3** *'I like your hair that way,' he observed.* = **remark**, say, comment, state, note, reflect, mention, declare, opine (*formal*), pass comment, animadvert **4** *Forcing motorists to observe speed restrictions is difficult.* = **comply with**, keep, follow, mind, respect, perform, carry out, honour, fulfil, discharge, obey, heed, conform to, adhere to, abide by
■ **OPPOSITE:** disregard

observer NOUN **1** *A casual observer would have assumed they were lovers.* = **witness**, viewer, spectator, looker-on, watcher, onlooker, eyewitness, bystander, spotter, fly on the wall, beholder **2** *Political observers believe there may be a general election soon.* = **commentator**, commenter, reporter, special correspondent **3** *A UN observer should attend the conference.* = **monitor**, inspector, watchdog, supervisor, overseer, scrutineer

obsess VERB = **preoccupy**, dominate, grip, absorb, possess, consume, rule, haunt, plague, hound, torment, bedevil, monopolize, be on your mind, engross, prey on your mind, be uppermost in your thoughts

obsessed ADJECTIVE (*often with* **with** *or* **by**) = **absorbed**, dominated, gripped, caught up, haunted, distracted, hung up (*slang*), preoccupied, immersed, beset, in the grip, infatuated, fixated, having a one-track mind ■ **OPPOSITE:** indifferent

obsession NOUN = **preoccupation**, thing (*informal*), complex, enthusiasm, addiction, hang-up (*informal*), mania, phobia, fetish, fixation, infatuation, ruling passion, pet subject, hobbyhorse, idée fixe (*French*), bee in your bonnet (*informal*)

obsessive ADJECTIVE = **compulsive**, fixed, gripping, consuming, haunting, tormenting, irresistible, neurotic, besetting, uncontrollable, obsessional

obsolete ADJECTIVE = **outdated**, old, passé, ancient, antique, old-fashioned, dated, discarded, extinct, past it (*informal*), out of date, archaic, disused, out of fashion, out, antiquated, anachronistic, outmoded, musty, old hat, behind the times, superannuated, antediluvian, outworn, démodé (*French*), out of the ark (*informal*), vieux jeu (*French*) ■ **OPPOSITE:** up-to-date

obstacle NOUN **1** *She had to navigate her way round trolleys and other obstacles.* = **obstruction**, block, barrier, hurdle, hazard, snag, impediment, blockage, hindrance **2** *Overcrowding remains a large obstacle to improving conditions.* = **hindrance**, check, bar, block, difficulty, barrier, handicap, hurdle, hitch, drawback, snag, deterrent, uphill (*S. African*), obstruction, stumbling block, impediment ■ **OPPOSITE:** help

obstinacy NOUN = **stubbornness**, persistence, tenacity, perseverance, resolution, intransigence, firmness, single-mindedness, inflexibility, obduracy, doggedness, relentlessness, wilfulness, resoluteness, pig-headedness, pertinacity, tenaciousness, mulishness ■ **OPPOSITE:** flexibility

obstinate ADJECTIVE = **stubborn**, dogged, determined, persistent, firm, perverse, intractable, inflexible, wilful, tenacious, recalcitrant, steadfast, unyielding, opinionated, intransigent, immovable, headstrong, unmanageable, cussed, strong-minded, unbending, obdurate, stiff-necked, unshakable, self-willed, refractory, pig-headed, bull-headed, mulish, contumacious, pertinacious ■ **OPPOSITE:** flexible

obstruct VERB **1** *Lorries obstructed the road completely.* = **block**, close, bar, cut off, plug, choke, clog, barricade, shut off, stop up, bung up (*informal*) **2** *Drivers who park illegally obstruct the flow of traffic.* = **hold up**, stop, check, bar, block, prevent, arrest, restrict, interrupt, slow down, hamstring, interfere with, hamper, inhibit, clog, hinder, retard, impede, get in the way of, bring to a standstill, cumber **3** *The authorities are obstructing the investigation.* = **impede**, prevent, frustrate, hold up, slow down, hamstring, interfere with, hamper, hold back, thwart, hinder, retard, get in the way of, trammel, cumber ■ **OPPOSITE:** help **4** *She positioned herself so as not to obstruct his view.* = **obscure**, screen, cut off, cover, hide, mask, shield

obstruction NOUN **1** *drivers parking near his house and causing an obstruction* = **obstacle**, bar, block, difficulty, barrier, hazard, barricade, snag, impediment, hindrance **2** *The boy was suffering from a bowel obstruction.* = **blockage**, stoppage, occlusion **3** *Americans viewed the army as an obstruction to legitimate economic development.* = **hindrance**, stop, check, bar, block, difficulty, barrier, restriction, handicap, obstacle, restraint, deterrent, stumbling block, impediment, trammel ■ **OPPOSITE:** help

obstructive ADJECTIVE = **unhelpful**, difficult, awkward, blocking, delaying, contrary, stalling, inhibiting, restrictive, hindering, uncooperative, disobliging, unaccommodating ■ **OPPOSITE:** helpful

obtain VERB **1** *Evans was trying to obtain a false passport.* = **get**, gain, acquire, land (*informal*), net, pick up, bag, secure, get hold of, come by, procure, get your hands on, score (*slang*), come into possession of ■ **OPPOSITE:** lose **2** *The perfect body has always been difficult to obtain.* = **achieve**, get, gain, realize, accomplish, attain **3** *The longer this situation obtains, the bigger the problems will be.* = **prevail**, hold, stand, exist, be the case, abound, predominate, be in force, be current, be prevalent

obtainable ADJECTIVE **1** *This herb is obtainable from health food shops.* = **available**, to be had, procurable **2** *That's new information that isn't obtainable by other means.* = **attainable**, accessible, achievable, at your fingertips, at your disposal, reachable, realizable, gettable, accomplishable

obtuse ADJECTIVE = **stupid**, simple, slow, thick, dull, dim (*informal*), dense, dumb (*informal*), sluggish, simple-minded, dozy (*Brit. informal*), witless, stolid, dopey (*informal*), brainless, uncomprehending,

unintelligent, half-witted, slow on the uptake (*informal*), dumb-ass (*informal*), doltish, boneheaded (*slang*), thickheaded, imperceptive, muttonheaded (*slang*), thick as mince (*Scot. informal*), woodenheaded (*informal*) ■ **OPPOSITE:** clever

obviate VERB = **avert**, avoid, remove, prevent, counter, do away with, preclude, counteract, ward off, stave off, forestall, render unnecessary

obvious ADJECTIVE = **clear**, open, plain, apparent, visible, bold, patent, evident, distinct, pronounced, straightforward, explicit, manifest, transparent, noticeable, blatant, conspicuous, overt, unmistakable, palpable, unequivocal, undeniable, salient, recognizable, unambiguous, self-evident, indisputable, perceptible, much in evidence, unquestionable, open-and-shut, cut-and-dried (*informal*), undisguised, incontrovertible, self-explanatory, unsubtle, unconcealed, clear as a bell, staring you in the face (*informal*), right under your nose (*informal*), sticking out a mile (*informal*), plain as the nose on your face (*informal*) ■ **OPPOSITE:** unclear

obviously ADVERB **1** *There are obviously exceptions to this.* = **clearly**, of course, certainly, needless to say, without doubt, assuredly **2** *She's obviously cleverer than I am.* = **plainly**, patently, undoubtedly, evidently, manifestly, markedly, without doubt, unquestionably, undeniably, beyond doubt, palpably, indubitably, incontrovertibly, irrefutably, incontestably

occasion NOUN **1** *I often think fondly of an occasion some years ago.* = **time**, moment, point, stage, incident, instance, occurrence, juncture **2** *It will be a unique family occasion.* = **function**, event, affair, do (*informal*), happening, experience, gathering, celebration, occurrence, social occasion **3** *It is always an occasion for setting out government policy.* = **opportunity**, chance, time, opening, window **4** *You had no occasion to speak to him like that.* = **reason**, cause, call, ground(s), basis, excuse, incentive, motive, warrant, justification, provocation, inducement ▶ VERB *The incident occasioned a full-scale parliamentary row.* = **cause**, begin, produce, create, effect, lead to, inspire, result in, generate, prompt, provoke, induce, bring about, originate, evoke, give rise to, precipitate, elicit, incite, engender

occasional ADJECTIVE = **infrequent**, odd, rare, casual, irregular, sporadic, intermittent, few and far between, desultory, periodic ■ **OPPOSITE:** constant

o

occasionally ADVERB = **sometimes**, at times, from time to time, on and off, now and then, irregularly, on occasion, now and again, periodically, once in a while, every so often, at intervals, off and on, (every) now and then ■ **OPPOSITE:** constantly

occult ADJECTIVE *organizations which campaign against paganism and occult practices* = **supernatural**, dark, magical, mysterious, psychic, mystical, mystic, unearthly, unnatural, esoteric, uncanny, arcane, paranormal, abstruse, recondite, preternatural, cabbalistic, supranatural • **the occult** *his unhealthy fascination with the occult* = **magic**, witchcraft, sorcery, wizardry, enchantment, occultism, black art, necromancy, theurgy

occultism NOUN = **black magic**, magic, witchcraft, wizardry, sorcery, the black arts, necromancy, diabolism, theurgy, supernaturalism

occupancy NOUN = **occupation**, use, residence, holding, term, possession, tenure, tenancy, habitation, inhabitancy

occupant NOUN = **occupier**, resident, tenant, user, holder, inmate, inhabitant, incumbent, dweller, denizen, addressee, lessee, indweller

occupation NOUN **1** *I was looking for an occupation which would allow me to travel.* = **job**, work, calling, business, line (of work), office, trade, position, post, career, situation, activity, employment, craft, profession, pursuit, vocation, livelihood, walk of life **2** *Hang-gliding is a dangerous occupation.* = **hobby**, pastime, diversion, relaxation, sideline, leisure pursuit, (leisure) activity **3** *The site dates back to the Roman occupation of Britain.* = **invasion**, seizure, conquest, incursion, subjugation, foreign rule **4** *She is seeking an order for 'sole use and occupation' of the house.* = **occupancy**, use, residence, holding, control, possession, tenure, tenancy, habitation, inhabitancy

occupied ADJECTIVE **1** *three beds, two of which were occupied* = **in use**, taken, full, engaged, unavailable **2** *The house was occupied by successive generations of farmers.* = **inhabited**, peopled, lived-in, settled, tenanted ■ **OPPOSITE:** uninhabited **3** *I forgot about it because I was so occupied with other things.* = **busy**, engaged, employed, working, active, tied up (*informal*), engrossed, hard at work, in harness, hard at it (*informal*), rushed off your feet

occupy VERB **1** *the couple who occupy the flat above mine* = **inhabit**, own, live in, stay in (*Scot.*), be established in, dwell in, be in residence in, establish yourself in, ensconce

yourself in, tenant, reside in, lodge in, take up residence in, make your home, abide in ■ **OPPOSITE:** vacate **2** *Alexandretta had been occupied by the French in 1918.* = **invade**, take over, capture, seize, conquer, keep, hold, garrison, overrun, annex, take possession of, colonize, cybersquat (*Computing*) ■ **OPPOSITE:** withdraw **3** *Men still occupy more positions of power than women.* = **hold**, control, dominate, possess **4** *Her parliamentary career has occupied all of her time.* = **take up**, consume, tie up, use up, monopolize, keep busy *or* occupied **5** (*often passive*) *I had other matters to occupy me that day.* = **engage**, interest, involve, employ, busy, entertain, absorb, amuse, divert, preoccupy, immerse, hold the attention of, engross, keep busy *or* occupied **6** *The tombs occupy two thirds of the church.* = **fill**, take up, cover, fill up, utilize, pervade, permeate, extend over

occur VERB **1** *The deaths occurred when troops tried to disperse the demonstrators.* = **happen**, take place, come about, follow, result, chance, arise, turn up (*informal*), come off (*informal*), ensue, crop up (*informal*), transpire (*informal*), befall, materialize, come to pass (*archaic*), betide, eventuate **2** *The disease occurs in all age groups.* = **exist**, appear, be found, develop, obtain (*formal*), turn up, be present, be met with, manifest itself, present itself, show itself • **occur to someone** *It didn't occur to me to check my insurance policy.* = **come to mind**, strike someone, dawn on someone, come to someone, spring to mind, cross someone's mind, present itself to someone, enter someone's head, offer itself to someone, suggest itself to someone

> **USAGE** It is usually regarded as incorrect to talk of pre-arranged events *occurring* or *happening*. For this meaning a synonym such as *take place* would be more appropriate: *the wedding took place* (not *occurred* or *happened*) *in the afternoon*.

occurrence NOUN **1** *Traffic jams are now a daily occurrence.* = **incident**, happening, event, fact, matter, affair, proceeding, circumstance, episode, adventure, phenomenon, transaction **2** *the greatest occurrence of heart disease in the over-65s* = **existence**, instance, appearance, manifestation, materialization

odd ADJECTIVE **1** *She'd always been odd, but not to this extent.* = **peculiar**, strange, unusual, different, funny, extraordinary, bizarre, weird, exceptional, eccentric, abnormal, queer, rum (*Brit. slang*), deviant, unconventional, far-out (*slang*), quaint, kinky (*informal*), off-the-wall (*slang*), outlandish, whimsical, oddball (*informal*), out of the ordinary, offbeat, left-field (*informal*), freakish, freaky (*slang*), wacky (*informal*), outré, daggy (*Austral. & N.Z. informal*) **2** *Something odd began to happen.* = **unusual**, different, strange, rare, funny (*slang*), extraordinary, remarkable, bizarre, fantastic, curious, weird, exceptional, peculiar, abnormal, queer, irregular, uncommon, singular, uncanny, outlandish, out of the ordinary, freakish, atypical, freaky (*slang*) ■ **OPPOSITE:** normal **3** *I did various odd jobs around the place.* = **occasional**, various, varied, random, casual, seasonal, irregular, periodic, miscellaneous, sundry, incidental, intermittent, infrequent ■ **OPPOSITE:** regular **4** *I found an odd sock in the washing machine.* = **spare**, remaining, extra, surplus, single, lone, solitary, uneven, leftover, unmatched, unpaired ■ **OPPOSITE:** matched • **odd man out** *or* **odd one out** *All my family wear glasses apart from me – I'm the odd man out.* = **misfit**, exception, outsider, freak (*informal*), eccentric, maverick, oddball (*informal*), nonconformist, fish out of water (*informal*), square peg in a round hole (*informal*)

oddity NOUN **1** *He's a bit of an oddity, but quite harmless.* = **misfit**, eccentric, crank (*informal*), maverick, flake (*slang, chiefly U.S.*), oddball (*informal*), loose cannon, nonconformist, odd man out, screwball (*slang, chiefly U.S. & Canad.*), card (*informal*), fish out of water, square peg (in a round hole) (*informal*), odd fish (*Brit. informal*), odd bird (*informal*), rara avis (*Latin*), weirdo *or* weirdie (*informal*) **2** *I was struck by the oddity of this question.* = **strangeness**, abnormality, peculiarity, eccentricity, weirdness, singularity, incongruity, oddness, unconventionality, queerness, unnaturalness, bizarreness, freakishness, extraordinariness, outlandishness **3** *the oddities of the Welsh legal system* = **irregularity**, phenomenon, anomaly, freak, abnormality, rarity, quirk, eccentricity, kink, peculiarity, idiosyncrasy, singularity, unorthodoxy, unconventionality

odds PLURAL NOUN *What are the odds of that happening?* = **probability**, chances, likelihood • **at odds 1** *He was at odds with his neighbour.* = **in conflict**, arguing, quarrelling, in opposition to, at loggerheads, in disagreement, at daggers drawn, on bad terms **2** *Her inexperience is at odds with the tale she tells.* = **at variance**, conflicting, contrary to, at odds, out of line, out of step, at sixes and sevens (*informal*), not in keeping, out of harmony • **odds and ends** *She packed her clothes and a few other odds and ends.* = **scraps**, bits, pieces, remains, rubbish, fragments, litter, debris, shreds, remnants, bits and pieces, bric-a-brac, bits and bobs, oddments, odds and sods, leavings, miscellanea, sundry *or* miscellaneous items

odious ADJECTIVE = **offensive**, nasty, foul, disgusting, horrible, unpleasant, revolting, obscene, sickening, vile, horrid, repellent, unsavoury, obnoxious, unpalatable, repulsive, disagreeable, nauseating, hateful, repugnant, loathsome, abhorrent, abominable, execrable, detestable, yucky *or* yukky (*slang*), yucko (*Austral. slang*) ■ **OPPOSITE:** delightful

odour *or* (*U.S.*) **odor** NOUN **1** *the faint odour of garlic on his breath* = **smell**, scent, perfume, fragrance, stink, bouquet, aroma, whiff, stench, pong (*Brit. informal*), niff (*Brit. slang*), redolence, malodour, fetor **2** *a tantalising odour of scandal* = **atmosphere**, feeling, air, quality, spirit, tone, climate, flavour, aura, vibe (*slang*)

odyssey NOUN (*sometimes cap.*) = **journey**, tour, trip, passage, quest, trek, expedition, voyage, crusade, excursion, pilgrimage, jaunt, peregrination

of PREPOSITION = **about**, on, concerning, regarding, with respect to, as regards

> **USAGE** *Of* is sometimes used instead of *have* in phrases such as *should have*, *could have*, and *might have*. This is because, when people are speaking, they often drop the *h* at the beginning of *have*, making the word's pronunciation very similar to that of *of*. Using *of* in this way is, however, regarded as nonstandard, and in writing it should definitely be avoided.

off ADVERB **1** *He went off on his own.* = **away**, out, apart, elsewhere, aside, hence, from here **2** *She was off sick 27 days last year.* = **absent**, gone, unavailable, not present, inoperative, nonattendant ▶ ADJECTIVE **1** *Today's game is off.* = **cancelled**, abandoned, postponed, shelved **2** *Food starts to smell when it goes off.* = **bad**, rotten, rancid, mouldy, high, turned, spoiled, sour, decayed, decomposed, putrid **3** *Playing your music that loud – it's a bit off, isn't it?* = **unacceptable**, poor, unsatisfactory, disappointing, inadequate, second-rate, shoddy, displeasing, below par, mortifying, substandard, disheartening • **off and on** *We lived together, off and on, for two years.*

= **occasionally**, sometimes, at times, from time to time, on and off, now and then, irregularly, on occasion, now and again, periodically, once in a while, every so often, intermittently, at intervals, sporadically, every once in a while, (every) now and again

offbeat ADJECTIVE = **unusual**, odd, strange, novel, extraordinary, bizarre, weird, way-out (*informal*), eccentric, queer, rum (*Brit. slang*), uncommon, Bohemian, unconventional, far-out (*slang*), idiosyncratic, kinky (*informal*), off-the-wall (*slang*), unorthodox, oddball (*informal*), out of the ordinary, left-field (*informal*), freaky (*slang*), wacky (*informal*), outré, daggy (*Austral. & N.Z. informal*) ■ **OPPOSITE:** conventional

offence or (*U.S.*) **offense** NOUN **1** *It is a criminal offence to sell goods which are unsafe.* = **crime**, wrong, sin, lapse, fault, violation, wrongdoing, trespass, felony, misdemeanour, delinquency, misdeed, transgression, peccadillo, unlawful act, breach of conduct **2** *The book might be published without creating offence.* = **outrage**, shock, anger, trouble, bother, grief (*informal*), resentment, irritation, hassle (*informal*), wrath, indignation, annoyance, ire (*literary*), displeasure, pique, aggravation (*informal*), hard feelings, umbrage, vexation, wounded feelings **3** *Your behaviour is an offence to your hosts.* = **insult**, injury, slight, hurt, harm, outrage, put-down (*slang*), injustice, snub, affront, indignity, displeasure, rudeness, slap in the face (*informal*), insolence • **take offence** *You're very quick to take offence today.* = **be offended**, resent, be upset, be outraged, be put out (*informal*), be miffed (*informal*), be displeased, take umbrage, be disgruntled, be affronted, be piqued, take the needle (*informal*), get riled, take the huff, go into a huff, be huffy

offend VERB **1** *I had no intention of offending the community.* = **distress**, upset, outrage, pain, wound, slight, provoke, insult, annoy, irritate, put down, dismay, snub, aggravate (*informal*), gall, agitate, ruffle, disconcert, vex, affront, displease, rile, pique, give offence, hurt (someone's) feelings, nark (*Brit., Austral. & N.Z. slang*), cut to the quick, miff (*informal*), tread on (someone's) toes (*informal*), put (someone's) nose out of joint, put (someone's) back up, disgruntle, get (someone's) goat (*slang*), hack someone off (*informal*) ■ **OPPOSITE:** please **2** *The smell of cigar smoke offends me.* = **disgust**, revolt, turn (someone) off (*informal*), put off,

sicken, repel, repulse, nauseate, gross out (*U.S. slang*), make (someone) sick, turn someone's stomach, be disagreeable to, fill with loathing **3** *alleged criminals who offend while on bail* = **break the law**, sin, err, do wrong, fall, fall from grace, go astray

offended ADJECTIVE = **upset**, pained, hurt, bothered, disturbed, distressed, outraged, stung, put out (*informal*), grieved, disgruntled, agitated, ruffled, resentful, affronted, miffed (*informal*), displeased, in a huff, piqued, huffy, tooshie (*Austral. slang*)

offender NOUN = **criminal**, convict, con (*slang*), crook, lag (*slang*), villain, culprit, sinner, delinquent, felon, jailbird, wrongdoer, miscreant, malefactor, evildoer, transgressor, lawbreaker, perp (*U.S. & Canad. informal*)

offensive ADJECTIVE **1** *offensive remarks about minority groups* = **insulting**, rude, abusive, embarrassing, slighting, annoying, irritating, degrading, affronting, contemptuous, disparaging, displeasing, objectionable, disrespectful, scurrilous, detestable, discourteous, uncivil, unmannerly ■ **OPPOSITE:** respectful **2** *the offensive smell of manure* = **disgusting**, gross, nasty, foul, unpleasant, revolting, stinking, sickening, vile, repellent, unsavoury, obnoxious, unpalatable, objectionable, disagreeable, nauseating, odious, repugnant, loathsome, abominable, grotty (*slang*), detestable, noisome, yucky or yukky (*slang*), festy (*Austral. slang*), yucko (*Austral. slang*) ■ **OPPOSITE:** pleasant **3** *The troops were in an offensive position.* = **attacking**, threatening, aggressive, striking, hostile, invading, combative ■ **OPPOSITE:** defensive ▶ NOUN *The armed forces have launched an offensive to recapture lost ground.* = **attack**, charge, campaign, strike, push (*informal*), rush, assault, raid, drive, invasion, onslaught, foray, incursion

offer VERB **1** *Rhys offered him an apple.* = **present with**, give, hand, hold out to **2** *Western governments have offered aid.* = **provide**, present, furnish, make available, afford, place at (someone's) disposal ■ **OPPOSITE:** withhold **3** *Peter offered to help us.* = **volunteer**, come forward, offer your services, be at (someone's) service **4** *They offered no suggestion as to how it might be done.* = **propose**, suggest, advance, extend, submit, put forward, put forth **5** *His mother and sister rallied round offering comfort.* = **give**, show, bring, provide, render, impart **6** *The house is being offered at 1.5 million pounds.* = **put up for sale**, sell, put

on the market, put under the hammer
7 *We offered a fair price for the land.* = **bid**,
submit, propose, extend, tender, proffer
▶ NOUN **1** *She has refused all offers of help.*
= **proposal**, suggestion, proposition,
submission, attempt, endeavour, overture
2 *We've made an offer for the house.* = **bid**,
tender, bidding price

offering NOUN **1** *funds from local church
offerings* = **contribution**, gift, donation,
present, subscription, hand-out, stipend,
widow's mite **2** *a Shinto ritual in which
offerings are made to the great Sun* = **sacrifice**,
tribute, libation, burnt offering, oblation
(*in religious contexts*)

offhand ADJECTIVE *Consumers found the
attitude of its staff offhand.* = **casual**,
informal, indifferent, careless, abrupt,
cavalier, aloof, unconcerned, curt,
uninterested, glib, cursory, couldn't-care-
less, apathetic, perfunctory, blasé,
brusque, take-it-or-leave-it (*informal*),
nonchalant, lackadaisical, unceremonious,
offhanded ■ OPPOSITE: attentive ▶ ADVERB
*I couldn't tell you offhand how long he's worked
here.* = **off the cuff** (*informal*),
spontaneously, impromptu, just like that
(*informal*), ad lib, extempore, off the top of
your head (*informal*), without preparation,
extemporaneously

office NOUN **1** *He had an office just big enough
for a desk and chair.* = **place of work**,
workplace, base, workroom, place of
business **2** *Downing Street's press office*
= **branch**, department, division, section,
wing, subdivision, subsection **3** *the honour
and dignity of the office of President* = **post**,
place, role, work, business, service,
charge, situation, commission, station,
responsibility, duty, function, employment,
capacity, appointment, occupation
▶ PLURAL NOUN *Thanks to his good offices, a
home has been found for the birds.* = **support**,
help, backing, aid, favour, assistance,
intervention, recommendation, patronage,
mediation, advocacy, auspices, aegis,
moral support, intercession, espousal

officer NOUN **1** *a local education authority
officer* = **official**, executive, agent,
representative, bureaucrat, public servant,
appointee, dignitary, functionary,
office-holder, office bearer **2** *an officer in the
West Midlands police force* = **police officer**,
detective, PC, police constable, policeman,
policewoman

official ADJECTIVE **1** *An official announcement is
expected later today.* = **authorized**, approved,
formal, sanctioned, licensed, proper,
endorsed, warranted, legitimate,

authentic, ratified, certified, authoritative,
accredited, bona fide, signed and sealed, ex
officio, ex cathedra, straight from the
horse's mouth (*informal*) ■ OPPOSITE:
unofficial **2** *his official duties* = **formal**,
prescribed, bureaucratic, ceremonial,
solemn, ritualistic ▶ NOUN *a senior UN
official* = **officer**, executive, agent,
representative, bureaucrat, public servant,
appointee, dignitary, functionary,
office-holder, office bearer

officiate VERB *Bishop Silvester officiated at
the funeral.* = **preside**, conduct, celebrate
2 *He has been chosen to officiate at the cup final.*
= **superintend**, supervise, be in charge,
run, control, serve, manage, direct, handle,
chair, look after, overlook, oversee, preside,
take charge, adjudicate, emcee (*informal*)

offing NOUN • **in the offing** *A general
amnesty for political prisoners may be in the
offing.* = **imminent**, coming, close, near,
coming up, gathering, on the way, in the
air, forthcoming, looming, brewing,
hovering, impending, at hand, upcoming,
on the cards, on the horizon, in the wings,
in the pipeline, nigh (*archaic*), in prospect,
close at hand, fast-approaching, in the
immediate future, just round the corner

off-key ADJECTIVE = **cacophonous**, harsh,
jarring, grating, shrill, jangling, discordant,
dissonant, inharmonious, unmelodious

off-load VERB *Prices have been cut by developers
anxious to offload unsold apartments.* = **get rid
of**, shift, dump, dispose of, unload,
dispense with, jettison, foist, see the back
of, palm off

off-putting ADJECTIVE = **discouraging**,
upsetting, disturbing, frustrating, nasty,
formidable, intimidating, dismaying,
unsettling, daunting, dampening,
unnerving, disconcerting, unfavourable,
dispiriting, discomfiting

offset VERB = **cancel out**, balance, set off,
make up for, compensate for, redeem,
counteract, neutralize, counterbalance,
nullify, obviate, balance out, counterpoise,
countervail

offshoot NOUN = **by-product**,
development, product, branch,
supplement, complement, spin-off,
auxiliary, adjunct, appendage, outgrowth,
appurtenance

offspring NOUN **1** *She was less anxious about
her offspring than she had been.* = **child**, baby,
kid (*informal*), youngster, infant, successor,
babe, toddler, heir, issue, tot, descendant,
wean (*Scot.*), little one, brat, bairn (*Scot. &
Northern English*), nipper (*informal*), chit,
scion, babe in arms (*informal*), sprog (*slang*),

munchkin (*informal, chiefly U.S.*), rug rat (*slang*), littlie (*Austral. informal*), ankle-biter (*Austral. slang*), tacker (*Austral. slang*) ■ **OPPOSITE:** parent **2** *Characteristics are often passed from parents to offspring.* = **children**, kids (*informal*), young, family, issue, stock, seed (*chiefly biblical*), fry, successors, heirs, spawn (*derogatory*), descendants, brood, posterity, lineage, progeny, scions

often ADVERB = **frequently**, much, generally, commonly, repeatedly, again and again, very often, oft (*archaic, poetic*), over and over again, time and again, habitually, time after time, customarily, oftentimes (*archaic*), not infrequently, many a time, ofttimes (*archaic*) ■ **OPPOSITE:** never

ogle VERB = **leer at**, stare at, eye up (*informal*), gawp at (*Brit. slang*), give the once-over (*informal*), make sheep's eyes at (*informal*), give the glad eye (*informal*), lech *or* letch after (*informal*)

ogre NOUN **1** *I have been painted as this ogre who walked out on his family.* = **fiend**, monster, beast, villain, brute, bogeyman **2** *an ogre in a fairy tale* = **monster**, giant, devil, beast, demon, bogey, spectre, fiend, ghoul, bogeyman, bugbear

oil NOUN **1** *Her car had run out of oil.* = **lubricant**, grease, lubrication, fuel oil **2** *sun-tan oil* = **lotion**, cream, balm, salve, liniment, embrocation, solution ▶ VERB *A crew of assistants oiled the mechanism until it worked perfectly.* = **lubricate**, grease, make slippery

oily ADJECTIVE **1** *traces of an oily substance* = **greasy**, slick, slimy (*Brit.*), fatty, slippery, oleaginous, smeary **2** *He asked in an oily voice what he could do for them today.* = **sycophantic**, smooth, flattering, slick, plausible, hypocritical, fawning, grovelling, glib, ingratiating, fulsome, deferential, servile, unctuous, obsequious, smarmy (*Brit. informal*), mealy-mouthed, toadying

ointment NOUN = **salve**, dressing, cream, lotion, balm, lubricant, emollient, liniment, embrocation, unguent, cerate

OK, O.K. *or* **okay** SENTENCE SUBSTITUTE *'Shall I ring you later?' - 'OK.'* = **all right**, right, yes, agreed, very good, roger, very well, ya (*S. African*), righto (*Brit. informal*), okey-dokey (*informal*), chur (*N.Z. informal*), yebo (*S. African informal*) ▶ ADJECTIVE **1** *Is it OK if I bring a friend with me?* = **all right**, fine, fitting, fair, in order, correct, approved, permitted, suitable, acceptable, convenient, allowable ■ **OPPOSITE:** unacceptable **2** *'Did you enjoy the film?' - 'It was okay.'* = **fine**, good, average, middling, fair, all right, acceptable, adequate, satisfactory, not bad (*informal*),

so-so (*informal*), tolerable, up to scratch (*informal*), passable, unobjectionable ■ **OPPOSITE:** unsatisfactory **3** *Would you go and check the baby's OK?* = **well**, all right, safe, sound, healthy, hale (*old-fashioned*), unharmed, uninjured, unimpaired ▶ VERB *His doctor wouldn't OK the trip.* = **approve**, allow, pass, agree to, permit, sanction, second, endorse, authorize, ratify, go along with, consent to, validate, countenance, give the go-ahead, rubber-stamp (*informal*), say yes to, give the green light, assent to, give the thumbs up (*informal*), concur in, give your consent to, give your blessing to ▶ NOUN *She gave the okay to issue a new press release.* = **authorization**, agreement, sanction, licence, approval, go-ahead (*informal*), blessing, permission, consent, say-so (*informal*), confirmation, mandate, endorsement, green light, ratification, assent, seal of approval, approbation

old ADJECTIVE **1** *I was considered too old for the job.* = **aged**, elderly, ancient, getting on, grey, mature, past it (*informal*), venerable, patriarchal, grey-haired, antiquated, over the hill (*informal*), senile, grizzled, hoary, senescent, advanced in years, full of years, past your prime ■ **OPPOSITE:** young **2** *a dilapidated old farmhouse* = **tumbledown**, ruined, crumbling, decayed, shaky, disintegrating, worn-out, done, tottering, ramshackle, rickety, decrepit, falling to pieces **3** *Dress in old clothes for gardening.* = **worn**, ragged, shabby, frayed, cast-off, tattered, tatty (*Brit.*), threadbare **4** *They got rid of all their old, outdated office equipment.* = **out of date**, old-fashioned, dated, passé, antique, outdated, obsolete, archaic, unfashionable, antiquated, outmoded, behind the times, superannuated, out of style, antediluvian, out of the ark (*informal*), démodé (*French*) ■ **OPPOSITE:** up-to-date **5** *Mark was heartbroken when Jane returned to her old boyfriend.* = **former**, earlier, past, previous, prior, one-time, erstwhile, late, quondam, whilom (*archaic*), ex- **6** *He is an old enemy of mine.* = **long-standing**, established, fixed, enduring, abiding, long-lasting, long-established, time-honoured **7** *How did people manage in the old days before electricity?* = **early**, ancient, original, remote, of old, antique, aboriginal, primitive, archaic, gone by, bygone, undeveloped, primordial, primeval, immemorial, of yore, olden (*archaic*), pristine **8** *He trotted out all the same old excuses as before.* = **stale**, common, commonplace, worn-out, banal, threadbare, trite, old hat, insipid, hackneyed, overused, repetitious, unoriginal, platitudinous, cliché-ridden, timeworn **9** *She's an old campaigner at this game.* = **long-established**, seasoned, experienced, tried, tested, trained, professional, skilled, expert, master, qualified, familiar, capable, veteran, practised, accomplished, vintage, versed, hardened, competent, skilful, adept, knowledgeable, age-old, of long standing, well-versed **10** *They dance, and sing the old songs they sang at home.* = **customary**, established, traditional, conventional, historic, long-established, time-honoured, of long standing

old-fashioned ADJECTIVE **1** *She always wears such boring, old-fashioned clothes.* = **out of date**, ancient, dated, outdated, unfashionable, antiquated, outmoded, passé, old hat, behind the times, fusty, out of style, démodé (*French*), out of the ark (*informal*), not with it (*informal*), (old-) fogeyish ■ **OPPOSITE:** up-to-date **2** *She has some old-fashioned values.* = **oldfangled**, square (*informal*), outdated, old, past, dead, past it (*informal*), obsolete, old-time, archaic, unfashionable, superannuated, obsolescent, out of the ark (*informal*)

old man NOUN **1** *an old man of ninety* = **senior citizen**, grandfather, patriarch, old age pensioner, old person, old-timer (*U.S.*), elder, elder statesman, wrinkly (*informal*), old codger (*informal*), old stager, greybeard, oldster (*informal*), O.A.P. (*Brit.*), koro (*N.Z.*) **2** *My old man used to work down the mines.* = **father**, pop (*informal*), dad (*informal*), daddy (*informal*), pa (*informal*), old boy (*informal*), papa (*old-fashioned, informal*), pater (*old-fashioned*), paterfamilias **3** *Why's the old man got it in for you?* = **manager**, boss (*informal*), supervisor, governor (*informal*), ganger, superintendent, gaffer (*informal*), foreman, overseer

old person NOUN = **senior citizen**, senior, retired person, old age pensioner, elder, pensioner (*slang*), coffin-dodger (*slang*), elderly person, O.A.P. (*Brit.*)

> **USAGE** While not as offensive as *coffin-dodger* and some of the other synonyms listed here, phrases such as *old man, old woman, old person,* and *elderly person* may still cause offence. It is better to use *senior citizen* or *senior*.

old-time ADJECTIVE = **old-fashioned**, traditional, vintage, ancient, antique, old-style, bygone

old woman NOUN = **senior citizen**, old lady, pensioner, retired person, old age pensioner, elder, elderly person, old person, matriarch, O.A.P. (*Brit.*), kuia (*N.Z.*)

old-world ADJECTIVE = **traditional**, old-fashioned, picturesque, quaint, archaic, gentlemanly, courteous, gallant, courtly, chivalrous, ceremonious

Olympian ADJECTIVE = **majestic**, kingly, regal, royal, august, grand, princely, imperial, glorious, noble, splendid, elevated, awesome, dignified, regal, stately, sublime, lofty, pompous, grandiose, exalted, rarefied, godlike

omen NOUN = **portent**, sign, warning, threat, indication, foreshadowing, foreboding, harbinger (*literary*), presage, forewarning, writing on the wall, prognostication, augury, prognostic, foretoken

ominous ADJECTIVE = **threatening**, menacing, sinister, dark, forbidding, grim, fateful, foreboding, unpromising, portentous, baleful, inauspicious, premonitory, unpropitious, minatory, bodeful ■ **OPPOSITE:** promising

omission NOUN **1** *her omission from the guest list* = **exclusion**, removal, leaving out, elimination, deletion, excision, noninclusion ■ **OPPOSITE:** inclusion **2** *an injury occasioned by any omission of the defendant* = **failure**, neglect, default, negligence, oversight, carelessness, dereliction, forgetfulness, slackness, laxity, laxness, slovenliness, neglectfulness, remissness **3** *There is one noticeable omission in your article.* = **gap**, space, blank, exclusion, lacuna

omit VERB **1** *Our apologies for omitting your name from the article.* = **leave out**, miss (out), drop, exclude, eliminate, skip, give (something) a miss (*informal*) ■ **OPPOSITE:** include **2** *She had omitted to tell him she was married.* = **forget**, fail, overlook, neglect, pass over, lose sight of, leave (something) undone, let (something) slide

omnipotence NOUN *leaders who use violent discipline to assert their omnipotence* = **supremacy**, sovereignty, dominance, domination, mastery, primacy, ascendancy, pre-eminence, predominance, invincibility, supreme power, absolute rule, undisputed sway ■ **OPPOSITE:** powerlessness

omnipotent ADJECTIVE = **almighty**, supreme, invincible, all-powerful ■ **OPPOSITE:** powerless

once ADVERB **1** *I only met her once, very briefly.* = **on one occasion**, one time, one single time **2** *I lived there once, before I was married.* = **at one time**, in the past, previously, formerly, long ago, in the old days, once upon a time, in times past, in times gone by ▶ CONJUNCTION *Once she got inside the house,* *she slammed the door.* = **as soon as**, when, after, the moment, immediately, the instant • **at once 1** *I must go at once.* = **immediately**, now, right now, straight away, directly, promptly, instantly, right away, without delay, without hesitation, forthwith, this (very) minute, pronto (*informal*), this instant, straightway (*archaic*), posthaste, tout de suite (*French*) **2** *They all started talking at once.* = **simultaneously**, together, at the same time, all together, in concert, in unison, concurrently, in the same breath, in chorus, at or in one go (*informal*) • **once and for all** *We have to resolve this matter once and for all.* = **for the last time**, finally, completely, for good, positively, permanently, for ever, decisively, inexorably, conclusively, irrevocably, for all time, inescapably, with finality, beyond the shadow of a doubt • **once in a while** *He phones me once in a while.* = **occasionally**, sometimes, at times, from time to time, on and off, irregularly, on occasion, now and again, periodically, every now and then, every so often, at intervals, off and on

oncoming ADJECTIVE **1** *He skidded into the path of an oncoming car.* = **approaching**, advancing, looming, onrushing **2** *the oncoming storm* = **forthcoming**, coming, approaching, expected, threatening, advancing, gathering, imminent, impending, upcoming, fast-approaching

one-horse ADJECTIVE (*of a town*) = **small**, slow, quiet, minor, obscure, sleepy, unimportant, small-time (*informal*), backwoods, tinpot (*Brit. informal*)

onerous ADJECTIVE = **trying**, hard, taxing, demanding, difficult, heavy, responsible, grave, crushing, arduous, exhausting, exacting, formidable, troublesome, oppressive, weighty, laborious, burdensome, irksome, backbreaking, exigent ■ **OPPOSITE:** easy

one-sided ADJECTIVE **1** *It was a totally one-sided competition.* = **unequal**, unfair, uneven, unjust, unbalanced, lopsided, inequitable, ill-matched ■ **OPPOSITE:** equal **2** *She gave a very one-sided account of the affair.* = **biased**, prejudiced, weighted, twisted, coloured, unfair, partial, distorted, partisan, warped, slanted, unjust, discriminatory, lopsided ■ **OPPOSITE:** unbiased

one-time ADJECTIVE = **former**, previous, prior, sometime, late, erstwhile, quondam, ci-devant (*French*), ex-

ongoing ADJECTIVE = **in progress**, current, growing, developing, advancing, progressing, evolving, unfolding, unfinished, extant

onlooker NOUN = **spectator**, witness, observer, viewer, looker-on, watcher, eyewitness, bystander

only ADJECTIVE *She was the only applicant for the job.* = **sole**, one, single, individual, exclusive, unique, lone, solitary, one and only ▶ ADVERB **1** *At the moment it's only a theory.* = **just**, simply, purely, merely, no more than, nothing but, but, at most, at a push **2** *I only have enough money for one ticket.* = **hardly**, just, barely, only just, scarcely, at most, at a push **3** *Computers are only for use by class members.* = **exclusively**, entirely, purely, solely

onset NOUN = **beginning**, start, rise, birth, kick-off (*informal*), outbreak, starting point, inception, commencement ■ **OPPOSITE:** end

onslaught NOUN = **attack**, charge, campaign, strike, rush, assault, raid, invasion, offensive, blitz, onset, foray, incursion, onrush, inroad ■ **OPPOSITE:** retreat

onus NOUN = **burden**, weight, responsibility, worry, task, stress, load, obligation, liability

onwards or **onward** ADVERB = **forward**, on, forwards, ahead, beyond, in front, forth (*formal, old-fashioned*)

ooze[1] VERB **1** *Blood was still oozing from the wound.* = **seep**, well, drop, escape, strain, leak, drain, sweat, filter, bleed, weep, drip, trickle, leach, dribble, percolate **2** *The cut was oozing a clear liquid.* = **emit**, release, leak, sweat, bleed, discharge, drip, leach, give out, dribble, exude, give off, excrete, overflow with, pour forth **3** *Graham positively oozed confidence.* = **exude**, emit, radiate, display, exhibit, manifest, emanate, overflow with

ooze[2] NOUN *He thrust his hand into the ooze and brought out a large toad.* = **mud**, clay, dirt, muck, silt, sludge, mire, slime, slob (*Irish*), gloop (*informal*), alluvium

opaque ADJECTIVE **1** *The bathroom has an opaque glass window.* = **cloudy**, clouded, dull, dim, muddied, muddy, murky, hazy, filmy, turbid, lustreless ■ **OPPOSITE:** clear **2** *the opaque language of the official report* = **incomprehensible**, obscure, unclear, difficult, puzzling, baffling, enigmatic, perplexing, impenetrable, unintelligible, cryptic, unfathomable, abstruse, obfuscated, beyond comprehension ■ **OPPOSITE:** lucid

open ADJECTIVE **1** *an open door* = **unclosed**, unlocked, ajar, unfastened, yawning, gaping, unlatched, unbolted, partly open, unbarred, off the latch ■ **OPPOSITE:** closed **2** *an open carton of milk* = **unsealed**, unstoppered ■ **OPPOSITE:** unopened **3** *A newspaper lay open on the coffee table.* = **extended**, expanded, unfolded, stretched out, spread out, unfurled, straightened out, unrolled ■ **OPPOSITE:** shut **4** *She has an open, trusting nature.* = **frank**, direct, natural, plain, innocent, straightforward, sincere, transparent, honest, candid, truthful, upfront (*informal*), plain-spoken, above board, unreserved, artless, ingenuous, guileless, straight from the shoulder (*informal*) ■ **OPPOSITE:** sly **5** *their open dislike of each other* = **obvious**, clear, frank, plain, apparent, visible, patent, evident, distinct, pronounced, manifest, transparent, noticeable, blatant, conspicuous, downright, overt, unmistakable, palpable, recognizable, avowed, flagrant, perceptible, much in evidence, undisguised, unsubtle, barefaced, unconcealed ■ **OPPOSITE:** hidden **6** *He seems open to suggestions.* = **receptive**, welcoming, sympathetic, responsive, amenable **7** *They left themselves open to accusations of double standards.* = **susceptible**, subject, exposed, vulnerable, in danger, disposed, liable, wide open, unprotected, at the mercy of, left open, laid bare, an easy target for, undefended, laid open, defenceless against, unfortified ■ **OPPOSITE:** defended **8** *It is an open question how long his commitment will last.* = **unresolved**, unsettled, undecided, debatable, up in the air, moot, arguable, yet to be decided **9** *The emergency services will do their best to keep the highway open.* = **clear**, free, passable, uncluttered, unhindered, unimpeded, navigable, unobstructed, unhampered ■ **OPPOSITE:** obstructed **10** *Police will continue their search of nearby open ground.* = **unenclosed**, wide, rolling, sweeping, exposed, extensive, bare, spacious, wide-open, undeveloped, uncrowded, unfenced, not built-up, unsheltered ■ **OPPOSITE:** enclosed **11** *His jacket was open to the waist.* = **undone**, gaping, unbuttoned, unzipped, agape, unfastened ■ **OPPOSITE:** fastened **12** *There are a wide range of career opportunities open to young people.* = **available**, to hand, accessible, handy, vacant, on hand, obtainable, attainable, at your fingertips, at your disposal **13** *an open invitation* = **general**, public, free, catholic, broad, universal, blanket, unconditional, across-the-board, unqualified, all-inclusive,

unrestricted, overarching, free to all, nondiscriminatory, one-size-fits-all ■ **OPPOSITE:** restricted **14** *The job is still open.* = **vacant**, free, available, empty, up for grabs (*informal*), unoccupied, unfilled, unengaged **15** *the public's open and generous response to the appeal* = **generous**, kind, liberal, charitable, benevolent, prodigal, bountiful, open-handed, unstinting, beneficent, bounteous, munificent, ungrudging **16** *Ciabatta has a distinctive crisp crust and open texture.* = **gappy**, loose, lacy, porous, honeycombed, spongy, filigree, fretted, holey, openwork ▶ VERB **1** *He opened the window and looked out.* = **unfasten**, unlock, unclasp, throw wide, unbar, unclose, unzip (*a computer file*) ■ **OPPOSITE:** close **2** *The Inspector opened the parcel.* = **unwrap**, uncover, undo, unravel, untie, unstrap, unseal, unlace ■ **OPPOSITE:** wrap **3** *Let's open another bottle.* = **uncork**, crack (open) **4** *When you open the map, you will find it is divided into squares.* = **unfold**, spread (out), expand, stretch out, unfurl, unroll ■ **OPPOSITE:** fold **5** *Police have opened the road again after the crash.* = **clear**, unblock ■ **OPPOSITE:** block **6** *He opened his shirt to show me his scar.* = **undo**, loosen, unbutton, unfasten ■ **OPPOSITE:** fasten **7** *The new shopping complex opens tomorrow.* = **begin business 8** *They are now ready to open negotiations.* = **start**, begin, launch, trigger, kick off (*informal*), initiate, commence, get going, instigate, kick-start, inaugurate, set in motion, get (something) off the ground (*informal*), enter upon ■ **OPPOSITE:** end **9** *The service opened with a hymn.* = **begin**, start, commence ■ **OPPOSITE:** end

open-air MODIFIER = **outdoor**, outside, out-of-door(s), alfresco

open-and-shut ADJECTIVE = **straightforward**, simple, obvious, routine, clear-cut, foregone, noncontroversial

opening ADJECTIVE *the season's opening game* = **first**, early, earliest, beginning, premier, primary, initial, maiden, inaugural, commencing, introductory, initiatory ▶ NOUN **1** *the opening of peace talks* = **beginning**, start, launch, launching, birth, dawn (*literary*), outset, starting point, onset, overture, initiation, inauguration, inception, commencement, kickoff (*informal*), opening move ■ **OPPOSITE:** ending **2** *He squeezed through an opening in the fence.* = **hole**, break, space, tear, split, crack, gap, rent, breach, slot, outlet, vent, puncture, rupture, aperture, cleft, chink, fissure, orifice, perforation, interstice ■ **OPPOSITE:** blockage **3** *All she needed was an opening to show her capabilities.* = **opportunity**, chance, break (*informal*), time, place, moment, window, occasion, look-in (*informal*) **4** *We don't have any openings just now, but we'll call you.* = **job**, position, post, situation, opportunity, vacancy

openly ADVERB **1** *Many people want to talk openly about their experiences.* = **frankly**, plainly, in public, honestly, face to face, overtly, candidly, unreservedly, unhesitatingly, forthrightly, straight from the shoulder (*informal*) ■ **OPPOSITE:** privately **2** *He was openly gay.* = **blatantly**, publicly, brazenly, unashamedly, shamelessly, in full view, flagrantly, unabashedly, wantonly, undisguisedly, without pretence ■ **OPPOSITE:** secretly

open-minded ADJECTIVE = **unprejudiced**, liberal, free, balanced, catholic, broad, objective, reasonable, enlightened, tolerant, impartial, receptive, unbiased, even-handed, dispassionate, fair-minded, broad-minded, undogmatic ■ **OPPOSITE:** narrow-minded

openness NOUN = **frankness**, honesty, truthfulness, naturalness, bluntness, forthrightness, ingenuousness, artlessness, guilelessness, candidness, freeness, open-heartedness, absence of reserve, candour, sincerity *or* sincereness, unreservedness

operate VERB **1** *Until his death he owned and operated a huge company.* = **manage**, run, direct, handle, govern, oversee, supervise, preside over, be in charge of, call the shots in, superintend, call the tune in **2** *allowing commercial businesses to operate in the country* = **function**, work, act, be in business, be in action **3** *The men were trapped as they operated a tunnelling machine.* = **run**, work, use, control, drive, manoeuvre **4** *The machine operates at a pace of just 2 miles per hour.* = **work**, go, run, perform, function ■ **OPPOSITE:** break down **5** *The surgeons had to decide quickly whether or not to operate.* = **perform surgery**, carry out surgery, put someone under the knife (*informal*)

operation NOUN **1** *A major rescue operation is under way.* = **undertaking**, process, affair, organization, proceeding, procedure, coordination **2** *a full-scale military operation* = **manoeuvre**, campaign, movement, exercise, assault, deployment **3** *a nationwide retail operation with an exceptional record of growth* = **business**, concern, firm, organization, corporation, venture, enterprise **4** *an operation to reduce a bloodclot*

on the brain = **surgery**, surgical operation, surgical intervention **5** *Dials monitor every aspect of the operation of the aircraft.* = **performance**, working, running, action, movement, functioning, motion, manipulation **6** *This change is due to the operation of several factors.* = **effect**, force, activity, agency (*old-fashioned*), influence, impact, effectiveness, instrumentality
• **in operation** *The night-time curfew remains in operation.* = **in action**, current, effective, going, functioning, active, in effect, in business, operative, in force

operational ADJECTIVE = **working**, going, running, ready, functioning, operative, viable, functional, up and running, workable, usable, in working order ■ **OPPOSITE:** inoperative

operative ADJECTIVE **1** *The scheme was soon operative.* = **in force**, current, effective, standing, functioning, active, efficient, in effect, in business, operational, functional, in operation, workable, serviceable ■ **OPPOSITE:** inoperative **2** *Just stir it gently – 'gently' being the operative word.* = **relevant**, important, key, fitting, significant, appropriate, crucial, influential, apt, applicable, indicative, pertinent, apposite, germane ▶ NOUN **1** *In an automated car plant there is not a human operative to be seen.* = **worker**, hand, employee, mechanic, labourer, workman *or* woman *or* person, artisan, machinist, working man *or* woman *or* person **2** *The CIA wants to protect its operatives.* = **spy**, secret agent, double agent, secret service agent, undercover agent, mole, foreign agent, fifth columnist, nark (*Brit., Austral. & N.Z. slang*)

operator NOUN **1** *He first of all worked as a machine operator.* = **worker**, hand, driver, mechanic, operative, conductor, technician, handler, skilled employee **2** *the country's largest cable TV operator* = **contractor**, dealer, trader, administrator **3** *one of the shrewdest political operators in the Arab world* = **manipulator**, worker, mover, Machiavellian, mover and shaker, machinator, wheeler-dealer (*informal*), wirepuller

opiate NOUN = **narcotic**, drug, downer (*slang*), painkiller, sedative, tranquillizer, bromide, anodyne, analgesic, soporific, pacifier, nepenthe

opine VERB = **suggest**, say, think, believe, judge, suppose, declare, conclude, venture, volunteer, imply, intimate, presume, conjecture, surmise, ween (*poetic*), give as your opinion

opinion NOUN **1** *Most who expressed an opinion spoke favourably of her.* = **belief**, feeling, view, idea, theory, notion, conviction, point of view, sentiment, viewpoint, persuasion, conjecture **2** *That has improved my already favourable opinion of him.* = **estimation**, view, impression, assessment, judgment, evaluation, conception, appraisal, considered opinion • **be of the opinion** *Frank is of the opinion that there has been a cover-up.* = **believe**, think, hold, consider, judge, suppose, maintain, imagine, guess (*informal, chiefly U.S. & Canad.*), reckon, conclude, be convinced, speculate, presume, conjecture, postulate, surmise, be under the impression • **matter of opinion** *Whether or not it is a work of art is a matter of opinion.* = **debatable point**, debatable, open question, open to question, moot point, open for discussion, matter of judgment

opinionated ADJECTIVE = **dogmatic**, prejudiced, biased, arrogant, adamant, stubborn, assertive, uncompromising, single-minded, inflexible, bigoted, dictatorial, imperious, overbearing, obstinate, doctrinaire, obdurate, cocksure, pig-headed, self-assertive, bull-headed ■ **OPPOSITE:** open-minded

opponent NOUN **1** *Mrs Kennedy's opponent in the leadership contest* = **adversary**, rival, enemy, the opposition, competitor, challenger, foe (*formal, literary*), contestant, antagonist ■ **OPPOSITE:** ally **2** *She became an outspoken opponent of the old regime.* = **opposer**, dissident, objector, dissentient, disputant ■ **OPPOSITE:** supporter

opportune ADJECTIVE = **timely**, fitting, fit, welcome, lucky, appropriate, suitable, happy, proper, convenient, fortunate, favourable, apt, advantageous, auspicious, fortuitous, well-timed, propitious, heaven-sent, felicitous, providential, seasonable, falling into your lap ■ **OPPOSITE:** inopportune

opportunism NOUN = **expediency**, convenience, exploitation, realism, manipulation, pragmatism, capitalization, realpolitik, utilitarianism, making hay while the sun shines (*informal*), striking while the iron is hot (*informal*), unscrupulousness, Machiavellianism

opportunity NOUN = **chance**, opening, time, turn, hour, break (*informal*), moment, window, possibility, occasion, slot (*informal*), scope, look-in (*informal*)

oppose VERB = **be against**, fight (against), check, bar, block, prevent, take on, counter, contest, resist, confront, face, combat, defy, thwart, contradict, withstand, stand up to, hinder, struggle against, obstruct, fly in the face of, take issue with, be hostile to, counterattack, speak (out) against, be in opposition to, be in defiance of, strive against, set your face against, take or make a stand against ■ **OPPOSITE:** support

opposed ADJECTIVE **1** (*with* **to**) *I am utterly opposed to any form of terrorism.* = **against**, anti (*informal*), hostile, adverse, contra (*informal*), in opposition, averse, antagonistic, inimical, (*dead*) set against **2** *people with views almost diametrically opposed to his own* = **contrary**, opposite, conflicting, opposing, clashing, counter, adverse, contradictory, in opposition, incompatible, antithetical, antipathetic, dissentient

opposing ADJECTIVE **1** *I have a friend who holds the opposing view.* = **conflicting**, different, opposed, contrasting, opposite, differing, contrary, contradictory, incompatible, irreconcilable **2** *The leader said he still favoured a dialogue between the opposing sides.* = **rival**, warring, conflicting, clashing, competing, enemy, opposite, hostile, combatant, antagonistic, antipathetic

opposite ADJECTIVE **1** *the opposite side of the room* = **facing**, other, opposing **2** *Everything he does is opposite to what is considered normal behaviour.* = **different**, conflicting, opposed, contrasted, contrasting, unlike, differing, contrary, diverse, adverse, at odds, contradictory, inconsistent, dissimilar, divergent, irreconcilable, at variance, poles apart, diametrically opposed, antithetical, streets apart ■ **OPPOSITE:** alike **3** *They fought on opposite sides during the War of Independence.* = **rival**, conflicting, opposed, opposing, competing, hostile, antagonistic, inimical ▶ PREPOSITION (*often with* **to**) *She sat opposite her at breakfast.* = **facing**, face to face with, across from, eyeball to eyeball with (*informal*) ▶ NOUN *She's very shy, but her sister is quite the opposite.* = **reverse**, contrary, converse, antithesis, the other extreme, contradiction, inverse, the other side of the coin (*informal*), obverse

opposition NOUN **1** *Much of the opposition to this plan has come from the media.* = **hostility**, resistance, resentment, disapproval, obstruction, animosity, aversion, antagonism, antipathy, obstructiveness, counteraction, contrariety ■ **OPPOSITE:** support **2** *The team inflicted a crushing defeat on the opposition.* = **opponent(s)**, competition, rival(s), enemy, competitor(s), other side, challenger(s), foe, contestant(s), antagonist(s)

o

oppress VERB **1** *predatory lenders who oppress the poor* = **subjugate**, abuse, suppress, wrong, master, overcome, crush, overwhelm, put down, subdue, overpower, persecute, rule over, enslave, maltreat, hold sway over, trample underfoot, bring someone to heel, tyrannize over, rule with an iron hand, bring someone under the yoke ■ **OPPOSITE:** liberate **2** *The atmosphere in the room oppressed her.* = **depress**, burden, discourage, torment, daunt, harass, afflict, sadden, vex, weigh down, dishearten, cast someone down, dispirit, take the heart out of, deject, lie *or* weigh heavy upon, make someone despondent

oppressed ADJECTIVE = **downtrodden**, abused, exploited, subject, burdened, distressed, slave, disadvantaged, helpless, misused, enslaved, prostrate, underprivileged, subservient, subjugated, browbeaten, maltreated, tyrannized ■ **OPPOSITE:** liberated

oppression NOUN = **persecution**, control, suffering, abuse, injury, injustice, cruelty, domination, repression, brutality, suppression, severity, tyranny, authoritarianism, harshness, despotism, ill-treatment, subjugation, subjection, maltreatment ■ **OPPOSITE:** justice

oppressive ADJECTIVE **1** *The new laws will be as oppressive as those they replace.* = **tyrannical**, severe, harsh, heavy, overwhelming, cruel, brutal, authoritarian, unjust, repressive, Draconian, autocratic, inhuman, dictatorial, coercive, imperious, domineering, overbearing, burdensome, despotic, high-handed, peremptory, overweening, tyrannous ■ **OPPOSITE:** merciful **2** *The oppressive afternoon heat had quite tired me out.* = **stifling**, close, heavy, sticky, overpowering, suffocating, stuffy, humid, torrid, sultry, airless, muggy

oppressor NOUN = **persecutor**, tyrant, bully, scourge, tormentor, despot, autocrat, taskmaster, iron hand, slave-driver, harrier, intimidator, subjugator

opt VERB *Students can opt to stay in residence.* = **choose**, decide, prefer, select, elect, see fit, make a selection ■ **OPPOSITE:** reject
• **opt for something** *or* **someone** *You may wish to opt for one method or the other.* = **choose**, pick, select, take, adopt, go for, designate, decide on, single out, espouse, fix on, plump for, settle upon, exercise your discretion in favour of

optimistic ADJECTIVE **1** *Michael was in a jovial and optimistic mood.* = **hopeful**, positive, confident, encouraged, can-do (*informal*), bright, assured, cheerful, rosy, buoyant, idealistic, Utopian, sanguine, expectant, looking on the bright side, buoyed up, disposed to take a favourable view, seen through rose-coloured spectacles ■ **OPPOSITE:** pessimistic **2** *an optimistic forecast that the economy would pick up by the end of the year* = **encouraging**, promising, bright, good, cheering, reassuring, satisfactory, rosy, heartening, auspicious, propitious ■ **OPPOSITE:** discouraging

optimum ADJECTIVE = **ideal**, best, highest, finest, choicest, perfect, supreme, peak, outstanding, first-class, foremost, first-rate, flawless, superlative, pre-eminent, most excellent, A1 *or* A-one (*informal*), most favourable *or* advantageous ■ **OPPOSITE:** worst

option NOUN = **choice**, alternative, selection, preference, freedom of choice, power to choose, election

optional ADJECTIVE = **voluntary**, open, discretionary, possible, extra, elective, up to the individual, noncompulsory ■ **OPPOSITE:** compulsory

opulence *or* **opulency** NOUN **1** *the opulence of the hotel's sumptuous interior* = **luxury**, riches, wealth, splendour, prosperity, richness, affluence, voluptuousness, lavishness, sumptuousness, luxuriance **2** *He is surrounded by possessions which testify to his opulence.* = **wealth**, means, riches (*informal*), capital, resources, assets, fortune, substance, prosperity, affluence, easy circumstances, prosperousness ■ **OPPOSITE:** poverty

opulent ADJECTIVE **1** *an opulent lifestyle* = **luxurious**, expensive, magnificent, costly, splendid, lavish, sumptuous, plush (*informal*), ritzy (*slang*), de luxe, well-appointed **2** *the spoilt child of an opulent father* = **rich**, wealthy, prosperous, propertied, loaded (*slang*), flush (*informal*), affluent, well-off, well-heeled (*informal*), well-to-do, moneyed, filthy rich, stinking rich (*informal*), made of money (*informal*), minted (*Brit. slang*) ■ **OPPOSITE:** poor

opus NOUN = **work**, piece, production, creation, composition, work of art, brainchild, oeuvre (*French*)

oracle NOUN **1** *Ancient peoples consulted the oracle and the shaman for advice.* = **prophet**, diviner, sage, seer, clairvoyant, augur, soothsayer, sibyl, prophesier **2** *Aeneas had begged the Sibyl to speak her oracle in words.* = **prophecy**, vision, revelation, forecast, prediction, divination, prognostication, augury, divine utterance

oral ADJECTIVE = **spoken**, vocal, verbal, unwritten, viva voce

oration NOUN = **speech**, talk, address, lecture, discourse, harangue, homily, spiel (*informal*), disquisition, declamation, whaikorero (*N.Z.*)

orator NOUN = **public speaker**, speaker, lecturer, spokesman *or* woman *or* person, declaimer, rhetorician, Cicero, spieler (*informal*), word-spinner

oratory NOUN = **rhetoric**, eloquence, public speaking, speech-making, expressiveness, fluency, a way with words, declamation, speechifying, grandiloquence, spieling (*informal*), whaikorero (*N.Z.*)

orb NOUN = **sphere**, ball, circle, globe, round

orbit NOUN 1 *the point at which the planet's orbit is closest to the sun* = **path**, course, track, cycle, circle, revolution, passage, rotation, trajectory, sweep, ellipse, circumgyration 2 *Cora dazzled all who came within her orbit.* = **sphere of influence**, reach, range, influence, province, scope, sphere, domain, compass, ambit ▶ VERB *the first satellite to orbit the Earth* = **circle**, ring, go round, compass, revolve around, encircle, circumscribe, gird, circumnavigate

orchestrate VERB 1 *The colonel orchestrated the rebellion from inside his army jail.* = **organize**, plan, run, set up, arrange, be responsible for, put together, see to (*informal*), marshal, coordinate, concert, stage-manage 2 *She was orchestrating the first act of her opera.* = **score**, set, arrange, adapt

ordain VERB 1 *Her brother had been ordained as a priest.* = **appoint**, call, name, commission, select, elect, invest, install, nominate, anoint, consecrate, frock 2 *He ordained that women should be veiled in public.* = **order**, will, rule, demand, require, direct, establish, command, dictate, prescribe, pronounce, lay down, decree, instruct, enact, legislate, enjoin 3 *Their destiny was ordained right from the start.* = **predestine**, fate, intend, mark out, predetermine, foreordain, destine, preordain

ordeal NOUN = **hardship**, trial, difficulty, test, labour, suffering, trouble(s), nightmare, burden, torture, misery, agony, torment, anguish, toil, affliction, tribulation(s), baptism of fire ■ OPPOSITE: pleasure

order VERB 1 *Williams ordered him to leave.* = **command**, instruct, direct, charge (*formal*), demand, require, bid, compel, enjoin, adjure ■ OPPOSITE: forbid 2 *The President has ordered a full investigation.* = **decree**, rule, demand, establish, prescribe, pronounce, ordain (*formal*)

■ OPPOSITE: ban 3 *I often order goods over the Internet these days.* = **request**, ask (for), book, demand, seek, call for, reserve, engage, apply for, contract for, solicit, requisition, put in for, send away for 4 *Entries in the book are ordered alphabetically.* = **arrange**, group, sort, class, position, range, file, rank, line up, organize, set out, sequence, catalogue, sort out, classify, array, dispose, tidy, marshal, lay out, tabulate, systematize, neaten, put in order, set in order, put to rights ■ OPPOSITE: disarrange ▶ NOUN 1 *Mr North had been arrested on the orders of the Spanish government.* = **instruction**, ruling, demand, direction, command, say-so (*informal*), dictate, decree, mandate, directive, injunction, behest, stipulation 2 *The company say they can't supply our order.* = **request**, booking, demand, commission, application, reservation, requisition 3 *List the key headings and sort them in a logical order.* = **sequence**, grouping, ordering, line, series, structure, chain, arrangement, line-up, succession, disposal, array, placement, classification, layout, progression, disposition (*archaic*), setup (*informal*), categorization, codification 4 *The wish to impose order upon confusion is a kind of intellectual instinct.* = **organization**, system, method, plan, pattern, arrangement, harmony, symmetry, regularity, propriety, neatness, tidiness, orderliness ■ OPPOSITE: chaos 5 *He has the power to use force to maintain public order.* = **peace**, control, law, quiet, calm, discipline, law and order, tranquillity, peacefulness, lawfulness 6 *the Benedictine order of monks* = **society**, company, group, club, union, community, league, association, institute, organization, circle, corporation, lodge, guild, sect, fellowship, fraternity (*U.S. & Canad.*), brotherhood, sisterhood, sodality 7 *He maintained that the higher orders of society must rule the lower.* = **class**, set, rank, degree (*archaic*), grade, sphere, caste 8 *the order of insects Coleoptera, better known as beetles* = **kind**, group, class, family, form, sort, type, variety, cast, species, breed, strain, category, tribe, genre, classification, genus, ilk, subdivision, subclass, taxonomic group
• **in order** 1 *We tried to keep the room in order.* = **tidy**, ordered, neat, arranged, trim, orderly, spruce, well-kept, well-ordered, shipshape, spick-and-span, trig (*archaic, dialect*), in apple-pie order (*informal*) 2 *I think an apology would be in order.* = **appropriate**, right, fitting, seemly, called for, correct,

suitable, acceptable, proper, to the point, apt, applicable, pertinent, befitting, well-suited, well-timed, apposite, germane, to the purpose, meet (*archaic*), O.K. or okay (*informal*) • **out of order** 1 *The espresso machine is out of order.* = **not working**, broken, broken-down, ruined, bust (*informal*), defective, wonky (*Brit. slang*), not functioning, out of commission, on the blink (*slang*), on its last legs, inoperative, kaput (*informal*), in disrepair, gone haywire (*informal*), nonfunctional, on the fritz (*U.S. slang*), gone phut (*informal*) 2 *Don't you think that remark was a bit out of order?* = **improper**, wrong, unsuitable, not done, not on (*informal*), unfitting, vulgar, out of place, unseemly, untoward, unbecoming, impolite, off-colour, out of turn, uncalled-for, not cricket (*informal*), indelicate, indecorous

orderly ADJECTIVE 1 *The organizers guided them in orderly fashion out of the building.* = **well-behaved**, controlled, disciplined, quiet, restrained, law-abiding, nonviolent, peaceable, decorous ■ OPPOSITE: disorderly 2 *The vehicles were parked in orderly rows.* = **well-organized**, ordered, regular, in order, organized, trim, precise, neat, tidy, systematic, businesslike, methodical, well-kept, shipshape, systematized, well-regulated, in apple-pie order (*informal*) ■ OPPOSITE: disorganized

ordinance NOUN = **rule**, order, law, ruling, standard, guide, direction, principle, command, regulation, guideline, criterion, decree, canon, statute, fiat, edict, dictum, precept

ordinarily ADVERB = **usually**, generally, normally, commonly, regularly, routinely, in general, as a rule, habitually, customarily, in the usual way, as is usual, as is the custom, in the general run (of things) ■ OPPOSITE: seldom

ordinary ADJECTIVE 1 *It was just an ordinary day for us.* = **usual**, standard, normal, common, established, settled, regular, familiar, household, typical, conventional, routine, stock, everyday, prevailing, accustomed, customary, habitual, quotidian, wonted 2 *My life seems pretty ordinary compared to yours.* = **commonplace**, plain, modest, humble, stereotyped, pedestrian, mundane, vanilla (*slang*), stale, banal, unremarkable, prosaic, run-of-the-mill, humdrum, homespun, uninteresting, workaday, common or garden (*informal*), unmemorable 3 *The food here is cheap, but very ordinary.* = **average**, middling, fair, indifferent, not bad, mediocre, so-so

(*informal*), unremarkable, tolerable (*informal*), run-of-the-mill, passable, undistinguished, uninspired, unexceptional, bog-standard (*Brit. & Irish slang*), no great shakes (*informal*), dime-a-dozen (*informal*) ■ OPPOSITE: extraordinary • **out of the ordinary** *Have you noticed anything out of the ordinary about him?* = **unusual**, different, odd, important, special, striking, surprising, significant, strange, exciting, rare, impressive, extraordinary, outstanding, remarkable, bizarre, distinguished, unexpected, curious, exceptional, notable, unfamiliar, abnormal, queer, uncommon, singular, unconventional, noteworthy, atypical

ordnance NOUN = **weapons**, arms, guns, artillery, cannon, firearms, weaponry, big guns, armaments, munitions, materiel, instruments of war

organ NOUN 1 *damage to the muscles and internal organs* = **body part**, part of the body, member, element, biological structure 2 *the People's Daily, the official organ of the Chinese Commmunist Party* = **newspaper**, paper, medium, voice, agency (*old-fashioned*), channel, vehicle, journal, publication, rag (*informal*), gazette, periodical, mouthpiece

organic ADJECTIVE 1 *Oxygen is vital to all organic life on Earth.* = **natural**, biological, living, live, vital, animate, biotic 2 *City planning treats the city as an organic whole.* = **systematic**, ordered, structured, organized, integrated, orderly, standardized, methodical, well-ordered, systematized 3 *The history of Russia is an organic part of European history.* = **integral**, fundamental, constitutional, structural, inherent, innate, immanent

organism NOUN = **creature**, being, thing, body (*informal*), animal, structure, beast, entity, living thing, critter (*U.S., dialect*)

organization or **organisation** NOUN 1 *Most of the funds are provided by voluntary organizations.* = **group**, company, party, body, concern, league, association, band, institution, gathering, circle, corporation, federation, outfit (*informal*), faction, consortium, syndicate, combine, congregation, confederation 2 *the work that goes into the organization of this event* = **management**, running, planning, making, control, operation, handling, structuring, administration, direction, regulation, construction, organizing, supervision, governance, formulation, coordination, methodology, superintendence 3 *the internal organization* of the department = **structure**, grouping, plan, system, form, design, method, pattern, make-up, arrangement, construction, constitution, format, formation, framework, composition, chemistry, configuration, conformation, interrelation of parts

organize VERB **1** *We need someone to help organize our campaign.* = **arrange**, run, plan, form, prepare, establish, set up, shape, schedule, frame, look after, be responsible for, construct, constitute, devise, put together, take care of, see to (*informal*), get together, marshal, contrive, get going, coordinate, fix up, straighten out, lay the foundations of, lick into shape, jack up (N.Z. *informal*) ■ **OPPOSITE:** disrupt **2** *He began to organize his papers.* = **put in order**, arrange, group, list, file, index, catalogue, classify, codify, pigeonhole, tabulate, inventory, systematize, dispose ■ **OPPOSITE:** muddle

orgy NOUN **1** *a drunken orgy* = **party**, celebration, rave (*Brit. slang*), revel, festivity, bender (*informal*), debauch, revelry, carouse, Saturnalia, bacchanal, rave-up (*Brit. slang*), bacchanalia, carousal, hooley or hoolie (*chiefly Irish & N.Z.*) **2** *He blew the money in a six-month orgy of spending.* = **spree**, fit, spell, run, session, excess, bout, indulgence, binge (*informal*), splurge, surfeit, overindulgence

orient or **orientate** VERB *It will take some time to orient yourself to this new way of thinking.* = **adjust**, settle, adapt, tune, convert, alter, compose, accommodate, accustom, reconcile, align, harmonize, familiarize, acclimatize, find your feet (*informal*) • **orient yourself** *She lay still for a few seconds, trying to orient herself.* = **get your bearings**, get the lie of the land, establish your location

orientation NOUN **1** *The party is liberal and democratic in orientation.* = **inclination**, tendency, bias, leaning, bent, disposition, predisposition, predilection, proclivity (*formal*), partiality, turn of mind **2** *the company's policy on recruiting and orientation* = **induction**, introduction, breaking in, adjustment, settling in, adaptation, initiation, assimilation, familiarization, acclimatization **3** *The orientation of the church is such that the front faces the square.* = **position**, situation, location, site, bearings, direction, arrangement, whereabouts, disposition, coordination

orifice NOUN = **opening**, space, hole, split, mouth, gap, rent, breach, vent, pore, rupture, aperture, cleft, chink, fissure, perforation, interstice

origin NOUN **1** *theories about the origin of life* = **beginning**, start, birth, source, launch, foundation, creation, dawning, early stages, emergence, outset, starting point, onset, genesis, initiation, inauguration, inception, font (*poetic*), commencement, fountain, fount, origination, fountainhead, mainspring ■ **OPPOSITE:** end **2** *What is the origin of the word 'honeymoon'?* = **root**, source, basis, beginnings, base, cause, spring, roots, seed, foundation, nucleus, germ, provenance, derivation, wellspring, fons et origo (*Latin*) **3** *people of Asian origin* = **ancestry**, family, race, beginnings, stock, blood, birth, heritage, ancestors, descent, pedigree, extraction, lineage, forebears, antecedents, parentage, forefathers, genealogy, derivation, progenitors, stirps

original ADJECTIVE **1** *The Dayaks were the original inhabitants of Borneo.* = **first**, earliest, early, initial, aboriginal, primitive, pristine, primordial, primeval, autochthonous **2** *Let's stick to the original plan.* = **initial**, first, starting, opening, primary, inaugural, commencing, introductory ■ **OPPOSITE:** final **3** *The company specializes in selling original movie posters.* = **authentic**, real, actual, genuine, legitimate, first generation, bona fide, the real McCoy ■ **OPPOSITE:** copied **4** *an original idea* = **new**, fresh, novel, different, unusual, unknown, unprecedented, innovative, unfamiliar, unconventional, seminal, ground-breaking, untried, innovatory, newfangled ■ **OPPOSITE:** unoriginal **5** *a chef with an original touch and a measure of inspiration* = **creative**, inspired, imaginative, artistic, fertile, ingenious, visionary, inventive, resourceful ▶ NOUN **1** *Photocopy the form and send the original to your employer.* = **prototype**, master, pattern ■ **OPPOSITE:** copy **2** *He's an original, this one, and a good storyteller.* = **character**, eccentric, case (*informal*), card (*informal*), flake (*slang, chiefly U.S.*), anomaly, oddity, oddball (*informal*), nonconformist, odd bod (*informal*), queer fish (*Brit. informal*), weirdo or weirdie (*informal*)

originality NOUN = **novelty**, imagination, creativity, innovation, new ideas, individuality, ingenuity, freshness, uniqueness, boldness, inventiveness, cleverness, resourcefulness, break with tradition, newness, unfamiliarity, creative spirit, unorthodoxy, unconventionality, creativeness, innovativeness, imaginativeness ■ **OPPOSITE:** conventionality

originally ADVERB = **initially**, first, firstly, at first, primarily, at the start, in the first place, to begin with, at the outset, in the beginning, in the early stages

originate VERB 1 *The dish originated in North Africa.* = **begin**, start, emerge, come, issue, happen, rise, appear, spring, flow, be born, proceed, arise, dawn, stem, derive, commence, emanate, crop up (*informal*), come into being, come into existence ■ **OPPOSITE:** end 2 *No-one knows who originated this story.* = **invent**, produce, create, form, develop, design, launch, set up, introduce, imagine, institute, generate, come up with (*informal*), pioneer, evolve, devise, initiate, conceive, bring about, formulate, give birth to, contrive, improvise, dream up (*informal*), inaugurate, think up, set in motion

originator NOUN = **creator**, father, mother, parent, founder, author, maker, framer, designer, architect, pioneer, generator, inventor, innovator, prime mover, initiator, begetter

ornament NOUN 1 *Christmas tree ornaments* = **decoration**, trimming, accessory, garnish, frill, festoon, trinket, bauble, flounce, gewgaw, knick-knack, furbelow, falderal 2 *Her dress was plain and without ornament.* = **embellishment**, trimming, decoration, embroidery, elaboration, adornment, ornamentation ▶ VERB *The Egyptians ornamented their mirrors with carved handles of ivory, gold, or wood.* = **decorate**, trim, adorn, enhance, deck, array, dress up, enrich, brighten, garnish, gild, do up (*informal*), embellish, emblazon, festoon, bedeck, beautify, prettify, bedizen (*archaic*), engarland

ornamental ADJECTIVE = **decorative**, pretty, attractive, fancy, enhancing, for show, embellishing, showy, beautifying, nonfunctional

ornamentation NOUN = **decoration**, trimming, frills, garnishing, embroidery, enrichment, elaboration, embellishment, adornment, beautification, ornateness

ornate ADJECTIVE = **elaborate**, fancy, decorated, detailed, beautiful, complex, busy, complicated, elegant, extravagant, baroque, ornamented, fussy, flowery, showy, ostentatious, rococo, florid, bedecked, overelaborate, high-wrought, aureate ■ **OPPOSITE:** plain

orthodox ADJECTIVE 1 *These ideas are now being incorporated into orthodox medical treatment.* = **established**, official, accepted, received, common, popular, traditional, normal, regular, usual, ordinary, approved, familiar, acknowledged, conventional, routine, customary, well-established, kosher (*informal*) ■ **OPPOSITE:** unorthodox 2 *orthodox Jews* = **conformist**, conservative, traditional, strict, devout, observant, doctrinal ■ **OPPOSITE:** nonconformist

orthodoxy NOUN 1 *He departed from prevailing orthodoxies and broke new ground.* = **doctrine**, teaching, opinion, principle, belief, convention, canon, creed, dogma, tenet, precept, article of faith 2 *a return to political orthodoxy* = **conformity**, received wisdom, traditionalism, inflexibility, conformism, conventionality ■ **OPPOSITE:** nonconformity

oscillate VERB 1 *The needle indicating volume was oscillating wildly.* = **fluctuate**, swing, vary, sway, waver, veer, rise and fall, vibrate, undulate, go up and down, seesaw 2 *She oscillated between elation and despair.* = **waver**, change, swing, shift, vary, sway, alternate, veer, ebb and flow, vacillate, seesaw ■ **OPPOSITE:** settle

oscillation NOUN 1 *a slight oscillation in world temperature* = **fluctuation**, swing, variation, instability, imbalance, wavering, volatility, variability, unpredictability, seesawing, disequilibrium, capriciousness, mutability, inconstancy, changeableness 2 *his oscillation between scepticism and credulity* = **wavering**, swing, shift, swaying, alteration, veering, seesawing, vacillation

ostensible ADJECTIVE = **apparent**, seeming, supposed, alleged, so-called, pretended, exhibited, manifest, outward, superficial, professed, purported, avowed, specious

ostensibly ADVERB = **apparently**, seemingly, supposedly, outwardly, on the surface, on the face of it, superficially, to all intents and purposes, professedly, speciously, for the ostensible purpose of

ostentatious ADJECTIVE = **pretentious**, extravagant, flamboyant, flash (*informal*), loud, dashing, inflated, conspicuous, vulgar, brash, high-flown, flashy, pompous, flaunted, flaunting, grandiose, crass, gaudy, showy, swanky (*informal*), snobbish, puffed up, specious, boastful, obtrusive, highfalutin (*informal*), arty-farty (*informal*), magniloquent, bling (*slang*) ■ **OPPOSITE:** modest

ostracism NOUN = **exclusion**, boycott, isolation, exile, rejection, expulsion, avoidance, cold-shouldering, renunciation, banishment ■ **OPPOSITE:** acceptance

other DETERMINER 1 *No other details are available at the moment.* = **additional**, more, further, new, added, extra, fresh, spare, supplementary, auxiliary 2 *Try to find other* words and phrases to give variety to your writing. = **different**, alternative, contrasting, distinct, diverse, dissimilar, separate, alternative, substitute, alternate, unrelated, variant **3** *The other pupils were taken to an exhibition.* = **remaining**, left-over, residual, extant

otherwise SENTENCE CONNECTOR *Write it down, otherwise you'll forget it.* = **or else**, or, if not, or then ▶ ADVERB **1** *a caravan slightly dented but otherwise in good condition* = **apart from that**, in other ways, in (all) other respects **2** *I believed he would be home soon – I had no reason to think otherwise.* = **differently**, any other way, in another way, contrarily, contrastingly, in contrary fashion

ounce NOUN = **shred**, bit, drop, trace, scrap, grain, particle, fragment, atom, crumb, snippet, speck, whit, iota

oust VERB = **expel**, turn out, dismiss, exclude, exile, discharge, throw out, relegate, displace, topple, banish, eject, depose, evict, dislodge, unseat, dispossess, send packing, turf out (*informal*), disinherit, drum out, show someone the door, give the bum's rush (*slang*), throw out on your ear (*informal*)

out ADJECTIVE **1** *I tried to phone you last night, but you were out.* = **not in**, away, elsewhere, outside, gone, abroad, from home, absent, not here, not there, not at home **2** *There was an occasional spark but the fire was out.* = **extinguished**, ended, finished, dead, cold, exhausted, expired, used up, doused, at an end ■ OPPOSITE: alight **3** *The daffodils are out now.* = **in bloom**, opening, open, flowering, blooming, in flower, in full bloom **4** *Their new album is out next week.* = **available**, on sale, in the shops, at hand, to be had, purchasable, procurable **5** *Drinking is bad enough, but smoking is right out.* = **not allowed**, banned, forbidden, ruled out, vetoed, not on (*informal*), unacceptable, prohibited, taboo, verboten (*German*) ■ OPPOSITE: allowed **6** *Romance is making a comeback. Cynicism is out.* = **out of date**, dead, square (*informal*), old-fashioned, dated, outdated, unfashionable, antiquated, outmoded, passé, old hat, behind the times, out of style, démodé (*French*), not with it (*informal*) ■ OPPOSITE: fashionable **7** *Our calculations were only slightly out.* = **inaccurate**, wrong, incorrect, faulty, off the mark, erroneous, off target, wide of the mark ■ OPPOSITE: accurate **8** *The secret about his tax affairs is out.* = **revealed**, exposed, common knowledge, public knowledge, (out) in the open ■ OPPOSITE: kept secret ▶ VERB *She was outed as a spy.* = **expose**, uncover, unmask

out-and-out ADJECTIVE = **absolute**, complete, total, perfect, sheer, utter, outright, thorough, downright, consummate, unqualified, unmitigated, dyed-in-the-wool, thoroughgoing, unalloyed, arrant, deep-dyed

outbreak NOUN **1** *an outbreak of violence involving hundreds of youths; This outbreak of flu is no worse than normal.* = **eruption**, burst, explosion, epidemic, rash, outburst, flare-up, flash, spasm, upsurge **2** *On the outbreak of war he expected to be called up.* = **onset**, beginning, outset, opening, dawn (*literary*), commencement

outburst NOUN **1** = **explosion**, surge, outbreak, eruption, flare-up **2** = **fit**, storm, attack, gush, flare-up, eruption, spasm, outpouring, paroxysm

outcast NOUN = **pariah**, exile, outlaw, undesirable, untouchable, leper, vagabond, wretch, persona non grata (*Latin*)

outclass VERB = **surpass**, top, beat, cap (*informal*), exceed, eclipse, overshadow, excel, transcend, outstrip, outdo, outshine, leave standing (*informal*), tower above, go one better than (*informal*), be a cut above (*informal*), run rings around (*informal*), outdistance, outrank, leave *or* put in the shade

outcome NOUN = **result**, end, consequence, conclusion, end result, payoff (*informal*), upshot

outcry NOUN = **protest**, complaint, objection, cry, dissent, outburst, disapproval, clamour, uproar, commotion, protestation, exclamation, formal complaint, hue and cry, hullaballoo, demurral

outdated ADJECTIVE = **old-fashioned**, dated, obsolete, out of date, passé, antique, archaic, unfashionable, antiquated, outmoded, behind the times, out of style, obsolescent, démodé (*French*), out of the ark (*informal*), oldfangled ■ OPPOSITE: modern

outdo VERB = **surpass**, best, top, beat, overcome, exceed, eclipse, overshadow, excel, transcend, outstrip, get the better of, outclass, outshine, tower above, outsmart, outmanoeuvre, go one better than (*informal*), run rings around (*informal*), outfox, outdistance, be one up on, score points off, put in the shade, outjockey

outdoor ADJECTIVE = **open-air**, outside, out-of-door(s), alfresco ■ OPPOSITE: indoor

outer ADJECTIVE **1** *Peel away the outer skin of the onion.* = **external**, outside, outward, exterior, exposed, outermost ■ **OPPOSITE:** inner **2** *Our preoccupation with appearance goes much deeper than the outer image.* = **surface**, external, outward, exterior, superficial **3** *the outer suburbs of the city* = **outlying**, remote, distant, provincial, out-of-the-way, peripheral, far-flung ■ **OPPOSITE:** central

outfit NOUN **1** *She was wearing an outfit we'd bought the previous day.* = **costume**, dress, clothes, clothing, suit, gear (*informal*), get-up (*informal*), kit, ensemble, apparel (*old-fashioned*), attire, garb, togs (*informal*), threads (*slang*), schmutter (*slang*), rigout (*informal*) **2** *He works for a private security outfit.* = **group**, company, team, set, party, firm, association, unit, crowd, squad, organization, crew, gang, corps, setup (*informal*), galère (*French*) ▶ VERB **1** *Homes can be outfitted with security lights for a few hundred dollars.* = **equip**, stock, supply, turn out, appoint, provision, furnish, fit out, deck out, kit out, fit up, accoutre **2** *The travel company outfitted their staff in coloured jerseys.* = **dress**, clothe, attire, deck out, kit out, rig out

outfitter NOUN = **clothier**, tailor, couturier, dressmaker, seamstress, haberdasher (*U.S.*), costumier, garment maker, modiste

outflow NOUN **1** *an increasing outflow of refugees from the country* = **stream**, issue, flow, rush, emergence, spate, deluge, outpouring, effusion, emanation, efflux **2** *an outflow of fresh water from a river* = **discharge**, flow, jet, cascade, ebb, gush, drainage, torrent, deluge, spurt, spout, outpouring, outfall, efflux, effluence, debouchment

outgoing ADJECTIVE **1** *the outgoing director of the Edinburgh International Festival* = **leaving**, last, former, past, previous, retiring, withdrawing, prior, departing, erstwhile, late, ex- ■ **OPPOSITE:** incoming **2** *She is very friendly and outgoing.* = **sociable**, open, social, warm, friendly, accessible, expansive, cordial, genial, affable, extrovert, approachable, gregarious, communicative, convivial, demonstrative, unreserved, companionable
■ **OPPOSITE:** reserved

outgoings PLURAL NOUN = **expenses**, costs, payments, expenditure, overheads, outlay

outgrowth NOUN **1** *Her first book is an outgrowth of an art project she began ten years ago.* = **product**, result, development, fruit, consequence, outcome, legacy, emergence, derivative, spin-off, by-product, end result, offshoot, upshot

2 *A new organism develops as an outgrowth or bud.* = **offshoot**, shoot, branch, limb, projection, sprout, node, outcrop, appendage, scion, protuberance, excrescence

outing NOUN = **journey**, run, trip, tour, expedition, excursion, spin (*informal*), ramble, jaunt, pleasure trip

outlandish ADJECTIVE = **strange**, odd, extraordinary, wonderful, funny, bizarre, fantastic, astonishing, eye-popping (*informal*), curious, weird, foreign, alien, exotic, exceptional, peculiar, eccentric, abnormal, out-of-the-way, queer, irregular, singular, grotesque, far-out (*slang*), unheard-of, preposterous, off-the-wall (*slang*), left-field (*informal*), freakish, barbarous, outré, daggy (*Austral. & N.Z. informal*) ■ **OPPOSITE:** normal

outlast VERB = **outlive**, survive, live after, outstay, live on after, endure beyond, outwear, remain alive after

outlaw NOUN *a band of desperate outlaws* = **bandit**, criminal, thief, crook (*informal*), robber, fugitive, outcast, delinquent, felon, highwayman *or* woman, desperado, marauder, brigand, lawbreaker, footpad (*archaic*) ▶ VERB **1** *The new government has outlawed some extremist groups.* = **ban**, bar, veto, forbid, condemn, exclude, embargo, suppress, prohibit, banish, disallow, proscribe, make illegal, interdict
■ **OPPOSITE:** legalize **2** *He should be outlawed for his crimes against the state.* = **banish**, excommunicate, ostracize, put a price on (someone's) head

outlay NOUN = **expenditure**, cost, spending, charge, investment, payment, expense(s), outgoings, disbursement

outlet NOUN **1** *the largest retail outlet in the city* = **shop**, store, supermarket, market, mart, boutique, emporium (*old-fashioned*), hypermarket **2** *He found an outlet for his emotions in his music.* = **channel**, release, medium, avenue, vent, conduit, safety valve, means of expression **3** *The leak was caused by a fracture in the cooling water outlet.* = **pipe**, opening, channel, passage, tube, exit, canal, way out, funnel, conduit, duct, orifice, egress (*formal*)

outline NOUN **1** *There follows an outline of the survey findings.* = **summary**, review, résumé, abstract, summing-up, digest, rundown, compendium, main features, synopsis, rough idea, précis, bare facts, thumbnail sketch, recapitulation, abridgment **2** *an outline of a plan to reduce the country's national debt* = **draft**, plan, drawing, frame, tracing, rough, framework, sketch, skeleton,

layout, delineation, preliminary form
3 *She could see only the hazy outline of the trees.*
= **shape**, lines, form, figure, profile,
silhouette, configuration, contour(s),
delineation, lineament(s) ▶ VERB **1** *The
methods outlined in this book are only
suggestions.* = **summarize**, review, draft,
plan, trace, sketch (in), sum up,
encapsulate, delineate, rough out,
adumbrate **2** *The building was a beautiful
sight, outlined against the starry sky.*
= **silhouette**, etch, delineate

outlive VERB = **survive**, outlast, live on
after, endure beyond, remain alive after

outlook NOUN **1** *The illness had a profound
effect on his outlook.* = **attitude**, views,
opinion, position, approach, mood,
perspective, point of view, stance,
viewpoint, disposition, standpoint, frame
of mind **2** *The economic outlook is one of rising
unemployment.* = **prospect(s)**, future,
expectations, forecast, prediction,
projection, probability, prognosis **3** *The
house has an expansive southern outlook over the
valley.* = **view**, prospect, scene, aspect,
perspective, panorama, vista

outlying ADJECTIVE = **remote**, isolated,
distant, outer, provincial, out-of-the-way,
peripheral, far-off, secluded, far-flung,
faraway, in the middle of nowhere, off the
beaten track, backwoods, godforsaken

outmanoeuvre or (U.S.) **outmaneuver**
VERB = **outwit**, outdo, get the better of,
circumvent, outflank, outsmart, steal a
march on (*informal*), put one over on
(*informal*), outfox, run rings round
(*informal*), outthink, outgeneral, outjockey

outmoded ADJECTIVE = **old-fashioned**,
passé, dated, out, dead, square (*informal*),
ancient, antique, outdated, obsolete,
out-of-date, old-time, archaic,
unfashionable, superseded, bygone,
antiquated, anachronistic, olden (*archaic*),
behind the times, superannuated,
fossilized, out of style, antediluvian,
outworn, obsolescent, démodé (*French*),
out of the ark (*informal*), not with it
(*informal*), oldfangled ■ **OPPOSITE:** modern

out of date ADJECTIVE **1** *processes using
out-of-date technology and very old equipment*
= **old-fashioned**, ancient, dated,
discarded, extinct, outdated, stale,
obsolete, démodé (*French*), archaic,
unfashionable, superseded, antiquated,
outmoded, passé, old hat, behind the
times, superannuated, out of style,
outworn, obsolescent, out of the ark
(*informal*), oldfangled ■ **OPPOSITE:** modern
2 *These tax records are now out of date.*

= **invalid**, expired, lapsed, void,
superseded, elapsed, null and void,
dead (*data*)

out of the way ADJECTIVE **1** *I like travelling to
out-of-the-way places.* = **remote**, far, distant,
isolated, lonely, obscure, far-off, secluded,
inaccessible, far-flung, faraway, outlying,
in the middle of nowhere, off the beaten
track, backwoods, godforsaken,
unfrequented ■ **OPPOSITE:** nearby **2** *He did
not seem to think her behaviour at all out of the
way.* = **unusual**, surprising, odd, strange,
extraordinary, remarkable, bizarre,
unexpected, curious, exceptional, notable,
peculiar, abnormal, queer, uncommon,
singular, unconventional, outlandish, out
of the ordinary, left-field (*informal*), atypical

outpouring NOUN = **outburst**, storm,
stream, explosion, surge, outbreak, deluge,
eruption, spasm, paroxysm, effusion, issue

output NOUN = **production**, manufacture,
manufacturing, yield, productivity,
outturn (*rare*)

outrage NOUN **1** *The decision has provoked
outrage from human rights groups.*
= **indignation**, shock, anger, rage, fury,
hurt, resentment, scorn, wrath, ire
(*literary*), exasperation, umbrage, righteous
anger **2** *The terrorists' latest outrage is a bomb
attack on a busy station.* = **atrocity**, crime,
horror, evil, cruelty, brutality, enormity,
barbarism, inhumanity, abomination,
barbarity, villainy, act of cruelty ▶ VERB
*Many people have been outraged by these
comments.* = **offend**, shock, upset, pain,
wound, provoke, insult, infuriate, incense,
gall, madden, vex, affront, displease, rile,
scandalize, give offence, nark (*Brit., Austral.
& N.Z. slang*), cut to the quick, make your
blood boil, put (someone's) nose out of
joint, put (someone's) back up, disgruntle

outrageous ADJECTIVE **1** *I must apologize for
my friend's outrageous behaviour.* = **atrocious**,
shocking, terrible, violent, offensive,
appalling, cruel, savage, horrible, beastly,
horrifying, vicious, ruthless, infamous,
disgraceful, scandalous, wicked, barbaric,
unspeakable, inhuman, diabolical,
heinous, flagrant, egregious, abominable,
infernal, fiendish, villainous, nefarious,
iniquitous, execrable, godawful (*slang*),
hellacious (*U.S. slang*) ■ **OPPOSITE:** mild
2 *The prices these places charge are absolutely
outrageous.* = **unreasonable**, unfair,
excessive, steep (*informal*), shocking, over
the top (*slang*), extravagant, too great,
scandalous, preposterous, unwarranted,
exorbitant, extortionate, immoderate,
O.T.T. (*slang*) ■ **OPPOSITE:** reasonable

o

outright ADJECTIVE **1** *He told me an outright lie.* = **absolute**, complete, total, direct, perfect, pure, sheer, utter, thorough, wholesale, unconditional, downright, consummate, unqualified, undeniable, out-and-out, unadulterated, unmitigated, thoroughgoing, unalloyed, arrant, deep-dyed **2** *She failed to win an outright victory.* = **definite**, clear, certain, straight, flat, absolute, black-and-white, decisive, straightforward, clear-cut, unmistakable, unequivocal, unqualified, unambiguous, cut-and-dried (*informal*), incontrovertible, uncontestable ▶ ADVERB **1** *Why are you being so mysterious? Why can't you just tell me outright?* = **openly**, frankly, plainly, face to face, explicitly, overtly, candidly, unreservedly, unhesitatingly, forthrightly, straight from the shoulder (*informal*) **2** *His plan was rejected outright.* = **absolutely**, completely, totally, fully, entirely, thoroughly, wholly, utterly, to the full, without hesitation, to the hilt, one hundred per cent, straightforwardly, without restraint, unmitigatedly, lock, stock and barrel **3** *The driver was killed outright in the crash.* = **instantly**, immediately, at once, straight away, cleanly, on the spot, right away, there and then, instantaneously

outset NOUN = **beginning**, start, opening, early days, starting point, onset, inauguration, inception, commencement, kickoff (*informal*) ■ OPPOSITE: finish

outside ADJECTIVE **1** *Cracks are beginning to appear on the outside wall.* = **external**, outer, exterior, surface, extreme, outdoor, outward, superficial, extraneous, outermost, extramural ■ OPPOSITE: inner **2** *I thought I had an outside chance of winning.* = **remote**, small, unlikely, slight, slim, poor, distant, faint, marginal, doubtful, dubious, slender, meagre, negligible, inconsiderable ▶ ADVERB *I went outside and sat on the steps.* = **outdoors**, out, out of the house, out-of-doors ▶ NOUN *the outside of the building; Grill until the outsides are browned.* = **exterior**, face, front, covering, skin, surface, shell, coating, finish, façade, topside

> USAGE The use of *outside of* and *inside of*, although fairly common, is generally thought to be incorrect or nonstandard: *She waits outside* (not *outside of*) *the school*.

outsider NOUN = **stranger**, incomer, visitor, foreigner, alien, newcomer, intruder, new arrival, unknown, interloper, odd one out, nonmember, outlander

outsize *or* **outsized** ADJECTIVE **1** *An outsize teddy bear sat on the bed.* = **huge**, great, large, giant, massive, enormous, monster, immense, mega (*slang*), jumbo (*informal*), gigantic, monumental (*informal*), mammoth, bulky, colossal, mountainous, oversized, stupendous, gargantuan, elephantine, ginormous (*informal*), Brobdingnagian, humongous *or* humungous (*informal*) ■ OPPOSITE: tiny **2** *Often outsize clothes are made from cheap fabric.* = **extra-large**, large, generous, ample, roomy

outskirts PLURAL NOUN = **edge**, borders, boundary, suburbs, fringe, perimeter, vicinity, periphery, suburbia, environs, purlieus, faubourgs

outsmart VERB = **outwit**, trick, take in (*informal*), cheat, deceive, defraud, dupe, gull (*archaic*), get the better of, swindle, circumvent, outperform, make a fool of (*informal*), outmanoeuvre, go one better than (*informal*), put one over on (*informal*), outfox, run rings round (*informal*), pull a fast one on (*informal*), outthink, outjockey

outspan VERB (*S. African*) = **relax**, chill out (*slang, chiefly U.S.*), take it easy, loosen up, laze, lighten up (*slang*), put your feet up, hang loose (*slang*), let yourself go (*informal*), let your hair down (*informal*), mellow out (*informal*), make yourself at home

outspoken ADJECTIVE = **forthright**, open, free, direct, frank, straightforward, blunt, explicit, downright, candid, upfront (*informal*), unequivocal, undisguised, plain-spoken, unreserved, unconcealed, unceremonious, free-spoken, straight from the shoulder (*informal*), undissembling ■ OPPOSITE: reserved

outstanding ADJECTIVE **1** *an outstanding tennis player* = **excellent**, good, great (*informal*), important, special, fine, noted, champion, celebrated, brilliant, impressive, superb, distinguished, well-known, prominent, superior, first-class, exceptional, notable, world-class, exquisite, admirable, eminent, exemplary, first-rate, stellar (*informal*), superlative, top-notch (*informal*), mean (*slang*), sick (*slang*), pre-eminent, meritorious, estimable, tiptop, A1 *or* A-one (*informal*), booshit (*Austral. slang*), exo (*Austral. slang*), sik (*Austral. slang*), rad (*informal*), phat (*slang*), schmick (*Austral. informal*), beaut (*informal*), barrie (*Scot. slang*), belting (*Brit. slang*), pearler (*Austral. slang*) ■ OPPOSITE: mediocre **2** *an area of outstanding natural beauty* = **conspicuous**, marked, striking, arresting, signal, remarkable, memorable, notable, eye-catching, salient, noteworthy

3 *The total debt outstanding is $70 billion.*
= **unpaid**, remaining, due, owing, ongoing,
pending, payable, unsettled, unresolved,
uncollected **4** *Complete any work outstanding
from yesterday.* = **undone**, left, not done,
omitted, unfinished, incomplete, passed
over, unfulfilled, not completed,
unperformed, unattended to

outstrip VERB **1** *In recent years demand has
outstripped supply.* = **exceed**, eclipse,
overtake, top, cap (*informal*), go beyond,
surpass, outdo **2** *In pursuing her ambition she
outstripped everyone else.* = **surpass**, beat,
leave behind, eclipse, overtake, best, top,
better, overshadow, outdo, outclass,
outperform, outshine, leave standing
(*informal*), tower above, get ahead of, go
one better than (*informal*), run rings
around, knock spots off (*informal*), put in
the shade **3** *He soon outstripped the other
runners.* = **outdistance**, shake off, outrun,
outpace

outward ADJECTIVE = **apparent**, seeming,
outside, surface, external, outer,
superficial, ostensible ■ **OPPOSITE:** inward

outwardly ADVERB = **apparently**,
externally, seemingly, it seems that, on the
surface, it appears that, ostensibly, on the
face of it, superficially, to the eye, to all
intents and purposes, to all appearances,
as far as you can see, professedly

outweigh VERB = **override**, cancel (out),
eclipse, offset, make up for, compensate
for, redeem, supersede, neutralize,
counterbalance, nullify, take precedence
over, prevail over, obviate, balance out,
preponderate, outbalance

outwit VERB = **outsmart**, get the better of,
circumvent, outperform, outmanoeuvre,
go one better than (*informal*), put one over
on (*informal*), outfox, run rings round
(*informal*), pull a fast one on (*informal*),
outthink, outjockey

oval ADJECTIVE = **elliptical**, egg-shaped,
ovoid, ovate, ellipsoidal, oviform

ovation NOUN = **applause**, hand, cheering,
cheers, praise, tribute, acclaim, clapping,
accolade, plaudits, big hand, commendation,
hand-clapping, acclamation, laudation
■ **OPPOSITE:** derision

over PREPOSITION **1** *She looked at herself in the
mirror over the fireplace.* = **above**, on top of,
atop **2** *His coat was thrown over a chair.* = **on
top of**, on, across, upon **3** *a room with a
wonderful view over the river* = **across**, past,
(looking) onto **4** *Over a million people were
seeking shelter.* = **more than**, above,
exceeding, in excess of, upwards of **5** *You're
making a lot of fuss over nothing.* = **about**,

regarding, relating to, with respect to, re,
concerning, apropos of, anent (*Scot.*)
▶ ADVERB **1** *Planes flew over every 15 minutes or
so.* = **above**, overhead, in the sky, on high,
aloft, up above **2** *There were two for each of us,
and one over.* = **extra**, more, other, further,
beyond, additional, in addition, surplus, in
excess, left over, unused, supplementary,
auxiliary ▶ ADJECTIVE *I think the worst is over
now.* = **finished**, by, done (with), through,
ended, closed, past, completed, complete,
gone, in the past, settled, concluded,
accomplished, wrapped up (*informal*),
bygone, at an end, ancient history
(*informal*), over and done with • **over and
above** *Costs have gone up 7% over and above
inflation.* = **in addition to**, added to, on top
of, besides, plus, let alone, not to mention,
as well as, over and beyond • **over and
over (again)** *He plays the same song over and
over again.* = **repeatedly**, frequently, again
and again, often, many times, time and
(time) again, time after time, ad nauseam
■ **RELATED WORDS:** prefixes hyper-, super-,
supra-, sur-

overall ADJECTIVE *Cut down your overall intake
of calories.* = **total**, full, whole, general,
complete, long-term, entire, global,
comprehensive, gross, blanket, umbrella,
long-range, inclusive, all-embracing,
overarching ▶ ADVERB *Overall, I was
disappointed with the result.* = **in general**,
generally, mostly, all things considered, on
average, in (the) large, on the whole,
predominantly, in the main, in the long
term, by and large, all in all, on balance,
generally speaking, taking everything into
consideration

overawed ADJECTIVE = **intimidated**,
threatened, alarmed, frightened, scared,
terrified, cowed, put off, daunted,
unnerved

overbearing ADJECTIVE = **domineering**,
lordly, superior, arrogant, authoritarian,
oppressive, autocratic, masterful,
dictatorial, coercive, bossy (*informal*),
imperious, haughty, tyrannical,
magisterial, despotic, high-handed,
peremptory, supercilious, officious,
overweening, iron-handed ■ **OPPOSITE:**
submissive

overblown ADJECTIVE **1** *The reporting of the
story was fair, though a little overblown.*
= **excessive**, exaggerated, over the top
(*slang*), too much, inflated, extravagant,
overdone, disproportionate, undue,
fulsome, intemperate, immoderate, O.T.T.
(*slang*) **2** *The book contains a heavy dose of
overblown lyrical description.* = **inflated**,

rhetorical, high-flown, pompous, pretentious, flowery, florid, turgid, bombastic, windy, grandiloquent, fustian, magniloquent, aureate, euphuistic

overcast ADJECTIVE = **cloudy**, grey, dull, threatening, dark, clouded, dim, gloomy, dismal, murky, dreary, leaden, clouded over, sunless, louring or lowering ■ **OPPOSITE:** bright

overcharge VERB = **cheat**, con (informal), do (slang), skin (slang), stiff (slang), sting (informal), rip off (slang), fleece, defraud, surcharge, swindle, stitch up (slang), rook (slang), short-change, diddle (informal), take for a ride (informal), cozen

overcome VERB 1 the satisfaction of overcoming a rival = **defeat**, beat, conquer, master, tank (slang), crush, overwhelm, overthrow, lick (informal), undo, subdue, rout, overpower, quell, triumph over, best, get the better of, trounce, worst, clobber (slang), stuff (slang), vanquish, surmount, subjugate, prevail over, wipe the floor with (informal), make mincemeat of (informal), blow (someone) out of the water (slang), come out on top of (informal), bring (someone) to their knees (informal), render incapable, render powerless, be victorious over, render helpless 2 I have fought to overcome my fear of spiders. = **conquer**, beat, master, survive, weather, curb, suppress, subdue, rise above, quell, triumph over, get the better of, vanquish (literary)

overdo VERB He overdid his usually quite funny vitriol. = **exaggerate**, overstate, overuse, overplay, do to death (informal), belabour, carry or take too far, make a production (out) of (informal), lay (something) on thick (informal) ■ **OPPOSITE:** minimize • **overdo it** When you start your running programme, don't be tempted to overdo it. = **overwork**, go too far, go overboard, strain or overstrain yourself, burn the midnight oil, burn the candle at both ends (informal), wear yourself out, bite off more than you can chew, have too many irons in the fire, overtire yourself, drive yourself too far, overburden yourself, overload yourself, overtax your strength, work your fingers to the bone

overdone ADJECTIVE 1 The meat was overdone and the vegetables disappointing. = **overcooked**, burnt, spoiled, dried up, charred, burnt to a crisp or cinder 2 In fact, all the panic about the drought in Britain was overdone. = **excessive**, too much, unfair, unnecessary, exaggerated, over the top (slang), needless, unreasonable, disproportionate, undue, hyped,

preposterous, inordinate, fulsome, immoderate, overelaborate, beyond all bounds, O.T.T. (slang) ■ **OPPOSITE:** minimized

overdue ADJECTIVE 1 I'll go and pay an overdue visit to my mother. = **delayed**, belated, late, late in the day, long delayed, behind schedule, tardy, not before time (informal), behind time, unpunctual, behindhand ■ **OPPOSITE:** early 2 a strike aimed at forcing the government to pay overdue salaries = **unpaid**, owing

overflow VERB 1 I was concerned that the soup might overflow onto the carpet. = **spill over**, discharge, well over, run over, pour over, pour out, bubble over, brim over, surge over, slop over, teem over 2 The river has overflowed its banks in several places. = **flood**, swamp, submerge, cover, drown, soak, immerse, inundate, deluge, pour over ▶ NOUN 1 Carpeting is damaged from the overflow of water from a bathtub. = **flood**, flooding, spill, discharge, spilling over, inundation 2 Tents have been set up next to hospitals to handle the overflow. = **surplus**, extra, excess, overspill, inundation, overabundance, additional people or things

overflowing ADJECTIVE = **full**, abounding, swarming, rife, plentiful, thronged, teeming, copious, bountiful, profuse, brimful, overfull, superabundant ■ **OPPOSITE:** deficient

overhang VERB = **project (over)**, extend (over), loom (over), stand out (over), bulge (over), stick out (over), protrude (over), jut (over), impend (over)

overhaul VERB 1 The plumbing was overhauled a year ago. = **check**, service, maintain, examine, restore, tune (up), repair, go over, inspect, fine tune, do up (informal), re-examine, recondition 2 Beattie led for several laps before he was overhauled by Itoh. = **overtake**, pass, leave behind, catch up with, get past, outstrip, get ahead of, draw level with, outdistance ▶ NOUN The study says there must be a complete overhaul of air traffic control systems. = **check**, service, examination, going-over (informal), inspection, once-over (informal), checkup, reconditioning

overhead ADJECTIVE people who live under or near overhead cables = **raised**, suspended, elevated, aerial, overhanging ▶ ADVERB planes passing overhead = **above**, in the sky, on high, aloft, up above ■ **OPPOSITE:** underneath

overheads PLURAL NOUN = **running costs**, expenses, outgoings, operating costs, oncosts

overjoyed ADJECTIVE = **delighted**, happy, pleased, thrilled, ecstatic, jubilant, joyous, joyful, elated, over the moon (*informal*), euphoric, rapturous, rapt, only too happy, gladdened, on cloud nine (*informal*), transported, cock-a-hoop, blissed out, in raptures, tickled pink (*informal*), deliriously happy, in seventh heaven, floating on air, stoked (*Austral. & N.Z. informal*)
■ **OPPOSITE:** heartbroken

overlay VERB *The floor was overlaid with rugs of Turkish design.* = **cover**, coat, blanket, adorn, mantle, ornament, envelop, veneer, encase, inlay, superimpose, laminate, overspread ▸ NOUN *Silver overlay is bonded to the entire surface.* = **covering**, casing, wrapping, decoration, veneer, adornment, ornamentation, appliqué

overlook VERB **1** *The rooms overlooked the garden.* = **look over** or **out on**, have a view of, command a view of, front on to, give upon, afford a view of **2** *We overlook all sorts of warning signals about our health.* = **miss**, forget, neglect, omit, disregard, pass over, fail to notice, leave undone, slip up on, leave out of consideration ■ **OPPOSITE:** notice **3** *satisfying relationships that enable them to overlook each other's faults* = **ignore**, excuse, forgive, pardon, disregard, condone, turn a blind eye to, wink at, blink at, make allowances for, let someone off with, let pass, let ride, discount, pass over, take no notice of, be oblivious to, pay no attention to, turn a deaf ear to, shut your eyes to

overly ADVERB = **too**, very, extremely, exceedingly, unduly, excessively, unreasonably, inordinately, immoderately, over-

overpower VERB **1** *It took four police officers to overpower him.* = **overcome**, master, overwhelm, overthrow, subdue, quell, get the better of, subjugate, prevail over, immobilize, bring (someone) to their knees (*informal*), render incapable, render powerless, render helpless, get the upper hand over **2** *Britain's tennis No.1 yesterday overpowered his American rival.* = **defeat**, beat, tank (*slang*), crush, lick (*informal*), triumph over, best, clobber (*slang*), stuff (*slang*), vanquish, be victorious (over), wipe the floor with (*informal*), make mincemeat of (*informal*), worst **3** *I was so overpowered by shame that I was unable to speak.* = **overwhelm**, overcome, bowl over (*informal*), stagger

overpowering ADJECTIVE **1** *The desire for revenge can be overpowering.* = **overwhelming**, powerful, extreme, compelling, irresistible, breathtaking, compulsive, invincible, uncontrollable **2** *There was an overpowering smell of garlic.* = **strong**, marked, powerful, distinct, sickening, unbearable, suffocating, unmistakable, nauseating **3** *his overpowering manner* = **forceful**, powerful, overwhelming, dynamic, compelling, persuasive, overbearing

overrate VERB = **overestimate**, glorify, overvalue, oversell, make too much of, rate too highly, assess too highly, overpraise, exaggerate the worth of, overprize, think or expect too much of, think too highly of, attach too much importance to

override VERB **1** *My work frequently overrides all other considerations.* = **outweigh**, overcome, eclipse, supersede, take precedence over, prevail over, outbalance **2** *The senate failed by one vote to override the President's veto.* = **overrule**, reverse, cancel, overturn, set aside, repeal, quash, revoke, disallow, rescind, upset, rule against, invalidate, annul, nullify, ride roughshod over, outvote, countermand, trample underfoot, make null and void **3** *He overrode all opposition to his plans.* = **ignore**, reject, discount, overlook, set aside, disregard, pass over, take no notice of, take no account of, pay no attention to, turn a deaf ear to

overriding ADJECTIVE = **major**, chief, main, prime, predominant, leading, controlling, final, ruling, determining, primary, supreme, principal, ultimate, dominant, compelling, prevailing, cardinal, sovereign, paramount, prevalent, pivotal, top-priority, overruling, preponderant, number one ■ **OPPOSITE:** minor

overrule VERB = **reverse**, alter, cancel, recall, discount, overturn, set aside, override, repeal, quash, revoke, disallow, rescind, rule against, invalidate, annul, nullify, outvote, countermand, make null and void ■ **OPPOSITE:** approve

overrun VERB **1** *A group of rebels overran the port.* = **overwhelm**, attack, assault, occupy, raid, invade, penetrate, swamp, rout, assail, descend upon, run riot over **2** *The flower beds were overrun with weeds.* = **spread over**, overwhelm, choke, swamp, overflow, infest, inundate, permeate, spread like wildfire, swarm over, surge over, overgrow **3** *Costs overran the budget by about 30%.* = **exceed**, go beyond, surpass, overshoot, outrun, run over or on

overseer NOUN = **supervisor**, manager, chief, boss (*informal*), master, inspector, superior, administrator, steward, superintendent, gaffer (*informal, chiefly Brit.*), foreman or woman or person, super (informal)

overshadow VERB **1** Her mother's illness overshadowed her childhood. = **spoil**, ruin, mar, wreck, scar, blight, crool or cruel (Austral. slang), mess up, take the edge off, put a damper on, cast a gloom upon, take the pleasure or enjoyment out of **2** She overshadows all the other members of the cast. = **outshine**, eclipse, surpass, dwarf, rise above, take precedence over, tower above, steal the limelight from, leave or put in the shade, render insignificant by comparison, throw into the shade **3** one of the towers that overshadow the square = **shade**, cloud, eclipse, darken, overcast, adumbrate

oversight NOUN **1** By an unfortunate oversight, full instructions do not come with the product. = **mistake**, error, slip, fault, misunderstanding, blunder, lapse, omission, boob (Brit. slang), gaffe, slip-up (informal), delinquency, inaccuracy, carelessness, howler (informal), goof (informal), bloomer (Brit. informal), clanger (informal), miscalculation, error of judgment, faux pas, inattention, laxity, boo-boo (informal), erratum, barry or Barry Crocker (Austral. slang) **2** I had the oversight of their collection of manuscripts. = **supervision**, keeping, control, charge, care, management, handling, administration, direction, custody, stewardship, superintendence

overt ADJECTIVE = **open**, obvious, plain, public, clear, apparent, visible, patent, evident, manifest, noticeable, blatant, downright, avowed, flagrant, observable, undisguised, barefaced, unconcealed ■ **OPPOSITE:** hidden

overtake VERB **1** He overtook the truck and pulled into the inside lane. = **pass**, leave behind, overhaul, catch up with, get past, draw level with, outdistance, go by or past **2** China overtook Japan to become the world's second-biggest economy. = **outdo**, top, exceed, eclipse, surpass, outstrip, get the better of, outclass, outshine, best, go one better than (informal), outdistance, be one up on **3** Tragedy was about to overtake him. = **befall** (archaic, literary), hit, happen to, come upon, take by surprise, catch off guard, catch unawares, catch unprepared **4** A sudden flood of panic overtook me. = **engulf**, overwhelm, hit, strike, consume, swamp, envelop, swallow up

overthrow VERB The government was overthrown in a military coup three years ago. = **defeat**, beat, master, overcome, crush, overwhelm, conquer, bring down, oust, lick (informal), topple, subdue, rout, overpower, do away with, depose, trounce, unseat, vanquish (literary), subjugate, dethrone ■ **OPPOSITE:** uphold ▶ NOUN They were charged with plotting the overthrow of the state. = **downfall**, end, fall, defeat, collapse, ruin, destruction, breakdown, ousting, undoing, rout, suppression, displacement, subversion, deposition, unseating, subjugation, dispossession, disestablishment, dethronement ■ **OPPOSITE:** preservation

overtone NOUN (often plural) = **connotation**, association, suggestion, sense, hint, flavour, implication, significance, nuance, colouring, innuendo, undercurrent, intimation

overture NOUN the William Tell Overture = **prelude**, opening, introduction, introductory movement ■ **OPPOSITE:** finale

overtures PLURAL NOUN He had begun to make clumsy yet endearing overtures of friendship. = **approach**, offer, advance, proposal, appeal, invitation, tender, proposition, opening move, conciliatory move ■ **OPPOSITE:** rejection

overturn VERB **1** The lorry went out of control, overturned and smashed into a wall. = **tip over**, spill, topple, upturn, capsize, upend, keel over, overbalance **2** Alex jumped up so violently that he overturned the table. = **knock over** or **down**, upset, upturn, tip over, upend **3** The Russian parliament overturned his decision. = **reverse**, change, alter, cancel, abolish, overthrow, set aside, repeal, quash, revoke, overrule, override, negate, rescind, invalidate, annul, nullify, obviate, countermand, declare null and void, overset **4** He accused his opponents of wanting to overturn the government. = **overthrow**, defeat, destroy, overcome, crush, bring down, oust, topple, do away with, depose, unseat, dethrone

overweight ADJECTIVE = **fat**, heavy, stout, huge, massive, solid, gross, hefty, ample, plump, bulky, chunky, chubby, obese, fleshy, beefy (informal), tubby (informal), portly, outsize, buxom, roly-poly, rotund, podgy, corpulent, elephantine, well-padded (informal), well-upholstered (informal), broad in the beam (informal), on the plump side ■ **OPPOSITE:** underweight

overwhelm VERB **1** He was overwhelmed by a longing for times past. = **overcome**, overpower, devastate (informal), stagger, get the better of, bowl over (informal), prostrate, knock (someone) for six (informal), render speechless, render incapable, render powerless, render helpless, sweep (someone) off their feet, take (someone's) breath away **2** *One massive assault would overwhelm the weakened enemy.* = **destroy**, beat, defeat, overcome, smash, crush, massacre, conquer, wipe out, overthrow, knock out, lick (*informal*), subdue, rout, eradicate, overpower, quell, annihilate, put paid to, vanquish (*literary*), subjugate, immobilize, make mincemeat of (*informal*), cut to pieces **3** *The small Pacific island could be overwhelmed by rising sea levels.* = **swamp**, bury, flood, crush, engulf, submerge, beset, inundate, deluge, snow under

overwhelming ADJECTIVE **1** *She felt an overwhelming desire to have another child.* = **overpowering**, strong, powerful, towering, vast, stunning, extreme, crushing, devastating, shattering, compelling, irresistible, breathtaking, compulsive, forceful, unbearable, uncontrollable ■ OPPOSITE: negligible **2** *An overwhelming majority of small businesses fail within the first two years.* = **vast**, huge, massive, enormous, tremendous, immense, very large, astronomic, humongous *or* humungous (*informal*) ■ OPPOSITE: insignificant

overwork VERB **1** *You've been overworking – you need a holiday.* = **wear yourself out**, burn the midnight oil, burn the candle at both ends, bite off more than you can chew, strain yourself, overstrain yourself, work your fingers to the bone, overtire yourself, drive yourself too far, overburden yourself, overload yourself, overtax yourself **2** *They overwork their staff.* = **exploit**, exhaust, fatigue, weary, oppress, wear out, prostrate, overtax, drive into the ground, be a slave-driver *or* hard taskmaster to

overwrought ADJECTIVE **1** *When I'm feeling overwrought, I try to take some time out to relax.* = **distraught**, upset, excited, desperate, wired (*slang*), anxious, distressed, tense, distracted, frantic, in a state, hysterical, wound up (*informal*), worked up (*informal*), agitated, uptight (*informal*), on edge, strung out (*informal*), out of your mind, keyed up, overexcited, in a tizzy (*informal*), at the end of your tether, wrought-up, beside yourself, in a twitter (*informal*), tooshie (*Austral. slang*), adrenalized ■ OPPOSITE: calm **2** *He writes pretentious, overwrought poetry.* = **overelaborate**, contrived, overdone, flamboyant, baroque, high-flown, ornate, fussy, flowery, busy, rococo, florid, grandiloquent, euphuistic, overembellished, overornate

owe VERB = **be in debt (to)**, be in arrears (to), be overdrawn (by), be beholden to, be under an obligation to, be obligated *or* indebted (to)

owing ADJECTIVE = **unpaid**, due, outstanding, owed, payable, unsettled, overdue • **owing to** = **because of**, thanks to, as a result of, on account of, by reason of

own DETERMINER *She insisted on having her own room.* = **personal**, special, private, individual, particular, exclusive ▸ VERB *Her parents own a local café.* = **possess**, have, keep, hold, enjoy, retain, be responsible for, be in possession of, have to your name
• **hold your own** *Placed in brilliant company, she more than held her own.* = **keep going**, compete, get on, get along, stand your ground, keep your head above water, keep your end up, maintain your position
• **on your own 1** *I need some time on my own.* = **alone**, by yourself, all alone, unaccompanied, on your tod (*Brit. slang*) **2** *I work best on my own.* = **independently**, alone, singly, single-handedly, by yourself, unaided, without help, unassisted, left to your own devices, under your own steam, off your own bat, by your own efforts, (standing) on your own two feet

owner NOUN = **possessor**, holder, proprietor, freeholder, titleholder, proprietress, proprietrix, landlord *or* landlady, master *or* mistress, deed holder

ownership NOUN = **possession**, occupation, tenure, dominion, occupancy, proprietorship, proprietary rights, right of possession

Pp

pace NOUN **1** *driving at a steady pace* = **speed**, rate, momentum, tempo, progress, motion, clip (*informal*), lick (*informal*), velocity **2** *Their pace quickened as they approached their cars.* = **step**, walk, stride, tread, gait **3** *I took a pace backwards.* = **footstep**, step, stride ▶ VERB *I paced the room nervously.* = **stride**, walk, pound, patrol, walk up and down, march up and down, walk back and forth

pacific ADJECTIVE **1** *a country with a pacific policy* = **nonaggressive**, pacifist, nonviolent, friendly, gentle, peace-loving, peaceable, dovish, nonbelligerent, dovelike ■ **OPPOSITE:** aggressive **2** *She spoke in a pacific voice.* = **peacemaking**, diplomatic, appeasing, conciliatory, placatory, propitiatory, irenic, pacificatory

pacifist NOUN = **peace lover**, dove, conscientious objector, peacenik (*informal*), conchie (*informal*), peacemonger, satyagrahi (*rare*), passive resister

pacify VERB *Is this just something to pacify the critics?* = **calm (down)**, appease, placate, still, content, quiet, moderate, compose, soften, soothe, allay, assuage, make peace with, mollify, ameliorate, conciliate, propitiate, tranquillize, smooth someone's ruffled feathers, clear the air with, restore harmony to

pack VERB **1** *They offered me a job packing goods in a warehouse.* = **package**, load, store, bundle, batch, stow **2** *All her possessions were packed into the back of her car.* = **cram**, charge, crowd, press, fill, stuff, jam, compact, mob, ram, wedge, compress, throng, tamp ▶ NOUN **1** *a pack of cigarettes* = **packet**, box, package, carton **2** *I hid the money in my pack.* = **bundle**, kit, parcel, load, burden, bale, rucksack, truss, knapsack, back pack, kitbag, fardel (*archaic*) **3** *a pack of journalists who wanted to interview him* = **group**, crowd, collection, company, set, lot, band, troop, crew (*informal*), drove, gang, deck, bunch (*informal*), mob, flock, herd, assemblage

• **pack someone off** *The children were packed off to bed.* = **send away**, dismiss, send packing (*informal*), bundle out, hustle out

• **pack something in 1** *I've just packed in my job.* = **resign from**, leave, give up, quit (*informal*), chuck (*informal*), jack in (*informal*) **2** *She's trying to pack in smoking.* = **stop**, give up, kick (*informal*), cease, chuck (*informal*), leave off, jack in (*informal*), desist from

• **pack something up 1** *I began packing up my things.* = **put away**, store, tidy up **2** *He's packed up coaching and retired.* = **stop**, finish, give up, pack in (*Brit. informal*), call it a day (*informal*), call it a night (*informal*) • **pack up** *Our car packed up.* = **break down**, stop, fail, stall, give out, conk out (*informal*)

• **send someone packing** *They were sent packing in disgrace.* = **send away**, dismiss, discharge, give someone the bird (*informal*), give someone the brushoff (*slang*), send someone about their business, send someone away with a flea in their ear (*informal*)

package NOUN **1** *I tore open the package.* = **parcel**, box, container, packet, carton **2** *A complete package of teaching aids, course notes and case studies had been drawn up.* = **collection**, lot, unit, combination, compilation ▶ VERB *The coffee beans are ground and packaged for sale.* = **pack**, box, wrap up, parcel (up), batch

packaging NOUN = **wrapping**, casing, covering, cover, box, packing, wrapper

packed ADJECTIVE = **filled**, full, crowded, jammed, crammed, swarming, overflowing, overloaded, seething, congested, jam-packed, chock-full, bursting at the seams, cram-full, brimful, chock-a-block, packed like sardines, hoatching (*Scot.*), loaded or full to the gunwales ■ **OPPOSITE:** empty

packet NOUN **1** *He wrote the number on the back of a cigarette packet.* = **container**, box, package, wrapping, poke (*dialect*), carton, wrapper **2** *the cost of sending letters and packets abroad* = **package**, parcel **3** *You could save yourself a packet.* = **a fortune**, lot(s), pot(s) (*informal*), a bomb (*Brit. slang*), a pile (*informal*), big money, a bundle (*slang*), big bucks (*informal, chiefly U.S.*), a small fortune, a mint, a wad (*U.S. & Canad. slang*), megabucks (*U.S. & Canad. slang*), an arm and a leg (*informal*), a bob or two (*Brit. informal*), a tidy sum (*informal*), a king's ransom (*informal*), a pretty penny (*informal*), top whack (*informal*)

pact NOUN = **agreement**, contract, alliance, treaty, deal (*informal*), understanding, league, bond, arrangement, bargain, convention, compact, protocol, covenant, concord, concordat

pad¹ NOUN **1** *He placed a pad of cotton wool over the cut.* = **wad**, dressing, pack, padding, compress, wadding **2** *seat-pad covers which tie to the backs of your chairs* = **cushion**, filling, stuffing, pillow, bolster, upholstery **3** *Have a pad and pencil ready.* = **notepad**, block, tablet, notebook, jotter, writing pad **4** *She wants to buy a pad near Sydney's Bondi Beach.* = **home**, flat, apartment (*chiefly U.S.*), place, room, quarters, hang-out (*informal*), bachelor apartment (*Canad.*) **5** *My cat has an infection in the pad of its foot.* = **paw**, foot, sole ▶ VERB *Pad the seat with a pillow.* = **pack**, line, fill, protect, shape, stuff, cushion
• **pad something out** *He padded out his article with a lot of quotations.* = **lengthen**, stretch, elaborate, inflate, fill out, amplify, augment, spin out, flesh out, eke out, protract

pad² VERB *He padded around in his slippers.* = **sneak**, creep, steal, pussyfoot (*informal*), go barefoot

padding NOUN **1** *the chair's foam rubber padding* = **filling**, stuffing, packing, wadding **2** *Politicians fill their speeches with a lot of padding.* = **waffle** (*informal, chiefly Brit.*), hot air (*informal*), verbiage, wordiness, verbosity, prolixity

paddle¹ NOUN *He used a piece of driftwood as a paddle.* = **oar**, sweep, scull ▶ VERB *paddling around the South Pacific in a kayak* = **row**, pull, scull

paddle² VERB *The children were paddling in the stream.* = **wade**, splash (about), slop, plash

paddy NOUN = **temper**, tantrum, bad mood, passion, rage, pet, fit of pique, fit of temper, foulie (*Austral. slang*), hissy fit (*informal*), strop (*informal*)

paean or (*sometimes U.S.*) **pean** NOUN = **eulogy**, tribute, panegyric, hymn of praise, encomium

pagan NOUN *He has been a practising pagan for years.* = **heathen** (*old-fashioned*), infidel, unbeliever, polytheist, idolater ▶ ADJECTIVE *Britain's ancient pagan heritage* = **heathen**, infidel, irreligious, polytheistic, idolatrous, heathenish

page¹ NOUN **1** *Turn to page four of your books.* = **folio**, side, leaf, sheet **2** *a new page in the country's history* = **period**, chapter, phase, era, episode, time, point, event, stage, incident, epoch

page² NOUN **1** *He worked as a page in a hotel.* = **attendant**, bellboy (*U.S.*), pageboy, footboy **2** *He served as page to a noble lord.* = **servant**, attendant, squire, pageboy, footboy ▶ VERB *She was paged repeatedly as the flight was boarding.* = **call**, seek, summon, call out for, send for

pageant NOUN *a traditional Christmas pageant* = **show**, display, parade, ritual, spectacle, procession, extravaganza, tableau

pageantry NOUN = **spectacle**, show, display, drama, parade, splash (*informal*), state, glitter, glamour, grandeur, splendour, extravagance, pomp, magnificence, theatricality, showiness

pain NOUN **1** *a disease that causes excruciating pain* = **suffering**, discomfort, trouble, hurt, irritation, tenderness, soreness **2** *I felt a sharp pain in my lower back.* = **ache**, smarting, stinging, aching, cramp, throb, throbbing, spasm, pang, twinge, shooting pain **3** *Her eyes were filled with pain.* = **sorrow**, suffering, torture, distress, despair, grief, misery, agony, sadness, torment, hardship, bitterness, woe, anguish, heartache, affliction, tribulation, desolation, wretchedness ▶ PLURAL NOUN *He got little thanks for his pains.* = **trouble**, labour, effort, industry, care, bother, diligence, special attention, assiduousness ▶ VERB **1** *It pains me to think of an animal being in distress.* = **distress**, worry, hurt, wound, torture, grieve, torment, afflict, sadden, disquiet, vex, agonize, cut to the quick, aggrieve **2** *My ankle still pained me.* = **hurt**, chafe, cause pain to, cause discomfort to

pained ADJECTIVE = **distressed**, worried, hurt, injured, wounded, upset, unhappy, stung, offended, aggrieved, anguished, miffed (*informal*), reproachful

painful ADJECTIVE **1** *Her glands were swollen and painful.* = **sore**, hurting, smarting, aching, raw, tender, throbbing, inflamed, excruciating ■ **OPPOSITE:** painless **2** *His remark brought back painful memories.* = **distressing**, unpleasant, harrowing, saddening, grievous, distasteful, agonizing, disagreeable, afflictive ■ **OPPOSITE:** pleasant **3** *the long and painful process of getting divorced* = **difficult**, arduous, trying, hard, severe, troublesome, laborious, vexatious ■ **OPPOSITE:** easy **4** *The interview was painful to watch.* = **terrible** (*informal*), awful, dreadful, dire, excruciating, abysmal, gut-wrenching, eye-watering, godawful, extremely bad

painfully ADVERB = **distressingly**, clearly, sadly, unfortunately, markedly, excessively, alarmingly, woefully, dreadfully, deplorably

painkiller NOUN = **analgesic**, drug, remedy, anaesthetic, sedative, palliative, anodyne

painless ADJECTIVE **1** *The operation is a brief, painless procedure.* = **pain-free**, without pain **2** *There are no painless solutions to the problem.* = **simple**, easy, fast, quick, no trouble, effortless, trouble-free

p

painstaking ADJECTIVE =**thorough**, careful, meticulous, earnest, exacting, strenuous, conscientious, persevering, diligent, scrupulous, industrious, assiduous, thoroughgoing, punctilious (*formal*), sedulous ■ **OPPOSITE:** careless

paint NOUN *a pot of red paint* = **colouring**, colour, stain, dye, tint, pigment, emulsion ▶ VERB **1** *They painted the walls yellow.* = **colour**, cover, coat, decorate, stain, whitewash, daub, distemper, apply paint to **2** *He was painting a portrait of his wife.* = **depict**, draw, portray, figure, picture, represent, sketch, delineate, catch a likeness **3** *The report paints a grim picture of life in the city.* = **describe**, capture, portray, depict, evoke, recount, bring to life, make you see, conjure up a vision, put graphically, tell vividly • **paint the town red** *Thousands of football fans painted the town red after the match.* = **celebrate**, revel, carouse, live it up (*informal*), make merry, make whoopee (*informal*), go on a binge (*informal*), go on a spree, go on the town

pair NOUN **1** *a pair of socks* = **set**, match, combination, doublet, matched set, two of a kind **2** *A pair of teenage boys were arrested.* = **couple**, brace, duo, twosome ▶ VERB (*often with* **off**) *Each trainee is paired with an experienced worker.* = **team**, match (up), join, couple, marry, wed, twin, put together, bracket, yoke, pair off

> USAGE Like other collective nouns, *pair* takes a singular or a plural verb according to whether it is seen as a unit or as a collection of two things: *the pair are said to dislike each other; a pair of good shoes is essential.*

pal NOUN = **friend**, companion, mate (*informal*), buddy (*informal*), comrade, chum (*informal*), crony, cock (*Brit. informal*), blood or blud (*Brit. slang*), main man (*slang, chiefly U.S.*), homeboy (*slang, chiefly U.S.*), cobber (*Austral. & N.Z., old-fashioned, informal*), boon companion, E hoa (*N.Z.*)

palatable ADJECTIVE **1** *flavourings designed to make the food more palatable* = **delicious**, tasty, luscious, savoury, delectable, mouthwatering, appetizing, toothsome, yummo (*Austral. slang*) ■ **OPPOSITE:** unpalatable **2** *There is no palatable way of sacking someone.* = **acceptable**, pleasant, agreeable, fair, attractive, satisfactory, enjoyable

palate NOUN = **taste**, heart, stomach, appetite

> USAGE This word is occasionally confused with *palette*: *I have a sweet palate* (not *palette*).

palatial ADJECTIVE = **magnificent**, grand, imposing, splendid, gorgeous, luxurious, spacious, majestic, regal, stately, sumptuous, plush (*informal*), illustrious, grandiose, opulent, de luxe, splendiferous (*facetious*)

pale¹ ADJECTIVE **1** *a pale blue dress* = **light**, soft, faded, subtle, muted, bleached, pastel, light-coloured **2** *A pale light seeped through the window.* = **dim**, weak, faint, feeble, thin, wan, watery **3** *She looked pale and tired.* = **white**, pasty, bleached, washed-out, wan, bloodless, colourless, pallid, anaemic, ashen, sallow, whitish, ashy, like death warmed up (*informal*) ■ **OPPOSITE:** rosy-cheeked **4** *a pale imitation of the real thing* = **poor**, weak, inadequate, pathetic, feeble ▶ VERB **1** *My problems paled in comparison with his.* = **fade**, dull, diminish, decrease, dim, lessen, grow dull, lose lustre **2** *Her face paled at the news.* = **become pale**, blanch, whiten, go white, lose colour

pale² NOUN *the pales of the fence* = **post**, stake, paling, upright, picket, slat, palisade • **beyond the pale** *His behaviour was beyond the pale.* = **unacceptable**, not done, forbidden, irregular, indecent, unsuitable, improper, barbaric, unspeakable, out of line, unseemly, inadmissible

pall¹ NOUN **1** *A pall of black smoke drifted over the cliff-top.* = **cloud**, shadow, veil, mantle, shroud **2** *His depression cast a pall on the proceedings.* = **gloom**, damp, dismay, melancholy, damper, check

pall² VERB (*often with* **on**) *The glamour of her job soon palled.* = **become boring**, become dull, become tedious, become tiresome, jade, cloy, become wearisome

pallid ADJECTIVE *His thin, pallid face broke into a smile.* = **pale**, wan, pasty, colourless, anaemic, ashen, sallow, whitish, cadaverous, waxen, ashy, like death warmed up (*informal*), wheyfaced

pallor NOUN = **paleness**, whiteness, lack of colour, wanness, bloodlessness, ashen hue, pallidness

palm NOUN *I wiped my sweaty palm.* = **hand**, hook, paw (*informal*), mitt (*slang*), meathook (*slang*) • **in the palm of your hand** *She had the board of directors in the palm of her hand.* = **in your power**, in your control, in your clutches, at your mercy • **palm someone off** *Mario was palmed off with a series of excuses.* = **fob off**, dismiss, disregard, pooh-pooh (*informal*) • **palm something off on someone** *They palm a lot of junk off on the tourists.* = **foist on**, force upon, impose upon, pass off, thrust upon, unload upon

palpable ADJECTIVE = **obvious**, apparent, patent, clear, plain, visible, evident, manifest, open, blatant, conspicuous, unmistakable, salient

paltry ADJECTIVE **1** *He was fined the paltry sum of $50.* = **meagre**, petty, trivial, trifling, beggarly, derisory, measly (*informal*), piddling (*informal*), inconsiderable ■ **OPPOSITE:** considerable **2** *She had no interest in such paltry concerns.* = **insignificant**, trivial, worthless, unimportant, small, low, base, minor, slight, petty, trifling, Mickey Mouse (*slang*), piddling (*informal*), toytown (*slang*), poxy (*slang*), nickel-and-dime (*U.S. slang*), picayune (*U.S.*), twopenny-halfpenny (*Brit. informal*) ■ **OPPOSITE:** important

pamper VERB = **spoil**, indulge, gratify, baby, pet, humour, pander to, fondle, cosset, coddle, mollycoddle, wait on (someone) hand and foot, cater to your every whim

pamphlet NOUN = **booklet**, leaflet, brochure, circular, tract, folder

pan¹ NOUN *Heat the butter in a large pan.* = **pot**, vessel, container, saucepan ▶ VERB **1** *His first movie was panned by the critics.* = **criticize**, knock (*informal*), blast, hammer (*Brit. informal*), slam (*slang*), rubbish (*informal*), roast (*informal*), put down, slate (*informal*), censure, slag (off) (*slang*), tear into (*informal*), flay, lambast(e), throw brickbats at (*informal*) **2** *People came westward in the 1800s to pan for gold in Sierra Nevada.* = **sift out**, look for, wash, search for • **pan out** *None of his ideas panned out.* = **work out**, happen, result, come out, turn out, culminate, come to pass (*archaic*), eventuate

pan² VERB *A television camera panned the crowd.* = **move along** or **across**, follow, track, sweep, scan, traverse, swing across

panacea NOUN = **cure-all**, elixir, nostrum, heal-all, sovereign remedy, universal cure

panache NOUN = **style**, spirit, dash, flair (*informal*), verve, swagger, swag (*slang*), flourish, élan, flamboyance, brio

pandemonium NOUN = **uproar**, confusion, chaos, turmoil, racket, clamour, din, commotion, rumpus, bedlam, babel, tumult, hubbub, ruction (*informal*), hullabaloo, hue and cry, ruckus (*informal*) ■ **OPPOSITE:** order

pander VERB • **pander to something** or **someone** = **indulge**, please, satisfy, gratify, cater to, play up to (*informal*), fawn on

pang NOUN **1** *pangs of hunger* = **pain**, stab, sting, stitch, ache, wrench, prick, spasm, twinge, throe (*rare*) **2** *She felt a pang of guilt about the way she was treating him.* = **twinge**, stab, prick, spasm, qualm, gnawing

panic NOUN *The earthquake has caused panic among the population.* = **fear**, alarm, horror, terror, anxiety, dismay, hysteria, fright, agitation, consternation, trepidation (*formal*), a flap (*informal*) ▶ VERB **1** *The guests panicked and screamed when the bomb went off.* = **go to pieces**, overreact, become hysterical, have kittens (*informal*), lose your nerve, be terror-stricken, lose your bottle (*Brit. slang*) **2** *The dogs were panicked by the noise.* = **alarm**, scare, terrify, startle, unnerve

panicky ADJECTIVE = **frightened**, worried, afraid, nervous, distressed, fearful, frantic, frenzied, hysterical, worked up, windy (*slang*), agitated, jittery (*informal*), in a flap (*informal*), antsy (*informal*), in a tizzy (*informal*) ■ **OPPOSITE:** calm

panic-stricken or **panic-struck** ADJECTIVE = **frightened**, alarmed, scared, terrified, startled, horrified, fearful, frenzied, hysterical, agitated, unnerved, petrified, aghast, panicky, scared stiff, in a cold sweat (*informal*), frightened to death, terror-stricken, horror-stricken, frightened out of your wits

panoply NOUN **1** *The film features a vast panoply of special effects.* = **array**, range, display, collection **2** *all the panoply of a royal wedding* = **trappings**, show, dress, get-up (*informal*), turnout, attire, garb, insignia, regalia, raiment (*archaic*, *poetic*)

panorama NOUN **1** *He looked out over a panorama of hills and valleys.* = **view**, prospect, scenery, vista, bird's-eye view, scenic view **2** *The play presents a panorama of the history of communism.* = **survey**, perspective, overview, overall picture

panoramic ADJECTIVE **1** *I had a panoramic view of the city.* = **wide**, overall, extensive, scenic, bird's-eye **2** *the panoramic sweep of his work* = **comprehensive**, general, extensive, sweeping, inclusive, far-reaching, all-embracing

pant VERB *He was panting with the effort of the climb.* = **puff**, blow, breathe, gasp, throb, wheeze, huff, heave, palpitate ▶ NOUN *His breath was coming in short pants.* = **gasp**, puff, wheeze, huff • **pant for something** *They left the audience panting for more.* = **long for**, want, desire, crave for, covet, yearn for, thirst for, hunger for, pine for, hanker after, ache for, sigh for, set your heart on, eat your heart out over, suspire for (*archaic*, *poetic*)

panting ADJECTIVE **1** *She collapsed, panting, at the top of the stairs.* = **out of breath**, winded, gasping, puffed, puffing, breathless, puffed out, short of breath, out of puff, out of whack (informal) **2** He came down here panting to be rescued from the whole ghastly mess. = **eager**, raring, anxious, impatient, champing at the bit (informal), all agog

pants PLURAL NOUN **1** a matching set of bra and pants = **underpants**, briefs, drawers, knickers, panties, boxer shorts, Y-fronts®, broekies (S. African), underdaks (Austral. slang) **2** (U.S.) He was wearing brown corduroy pants and a white shirt. = **trousers**, slacks

pap NOUN = **rubbish**, trash, trivia, drivel

paper NOUN **1** The story is in all the papers. = **newspaper**, news, daily, journal, organ, rag (informal), tabloid, gazette, broadsheet **2** He has just written a paper on the subject. = **essay**, study, article, analysis, script, composition, assignment, thesis, critique, treatise, dissertation, monograph **3** the applied mathematics paper = **examination**, test, exam **4** a new government paper on European policy = **report**, study, survey, inquiry ▶ PLURAL NOUN **1** After her death, her papers were collected and published. = **letters**, records, documents, file, diaries, archive, paperwork, dossier **2** people who were trying to leave the country with forged papers = **documents**, records, certificates, identification, deeds, identity papers, I.D. (informal) ▶ VERB We have papered this room in grey. = **wallpaper**, line, hang, paste up, cover with paper • **on paper 1** It is important to get something down on paper. = **in writing**, written down, on (the) record, in print, in black and white **2** On paper, she is the best person for the job. = **in theory**, ideally, theoretically, in the abstract

parable NOUN = **lesson**, story, fable, allegory, moral tale, exemplum

parade NOUN **1** A military parade marched slowly through the streets. = **procession**, march, ceremony, pageant, train, review, column, spectacle, tattoo, motorcade, cavalcade, cortège **2** A glittering parade of celebrities attended the event. = **show**, display, exhibition, spectacle, array ▶ VERB **1** More than four thousand people paraded down the Champs Elysées. = **march**, process, file, promenade **2** He was a modest man who never paraded his wealth. = **flaunt**, show, display, exhibit, show off (informal), air, draw attention to, brandish, vaunt, make a show of **3** They love to parade around in designer clothes. = **strut**, show off (informal), swagger, swank

paradigm NOUN = **model**, example, original, pattern, ideal, norm, prototype, archetype, exemplar

paradise NOUN **1** They believe they will go to paradise when they die. = **heaven**, Promised Land, Zion, City of God, Elysian fields, garden of delights, divine abode, heavenly kingdom **2** Adam and Eve's expulsion from Paradise = **Garden of Eden**, Eden **3** This job is paradise compared to my last one. = **bliss**, delight, heaven (informal), felicity, utopia, seventh heaven

paradox NOUN = **contradiction**, mystery, puzzle, ambiguity, anomaly, inconsistency, enigma, oddity, absurdity

paradoxical ADJECTIVE = **contradictory**, inconsistent, incongruous, ironic, impossible, puzzling, absurd, baffling, riddling, ambiguous, improbable, confounding, enigmatic, illogical, equivocal, oracular

paragon NOUN = **model**, standard, pattern, ideal, criterion, norm, jewel, masterpiece, prototype, paradigm, archetype, epitome, exemplar, apotheosis, quintessence, nonesuch (archaic), nonpareil, best or greatest thing since sliced bread (informal), cynosure

paragraph NOUN = **section**, part, notice, item, passage, clause, portion, subdivision

parallel NOUN **1** It is an ecological disaster with no parallel in the modern era. = **equivalent**, counterpart, match, equal, twin, complement, duplicate, analogue, likeness, corollary ■ OPPOSITE: opposite **2** Detectives realised there were parallels between the two murders. = **similarity**, correspondence, correlation, comparison, analogy, resemblance, likeness, parallelism ■ OPPOSITE: difference ▶ VERB **1** Her remarks paralleled those of the president. = **correspond to**, compare with, agree with, complement, conform to, be alike, chime with, correlate to ■ OPPOSITE: differ from **2** His achievements have never been paralleled. = **match**, equal, duplicate, keep pace (with), measure up to ▶ ADJECTIVE **1** an epidemic parallel to that of AIDS = **matching**, correspondent, corresponding, like, similar, uniform, resembling, complementary, akin, analogous ■ OPPOSITE: different **2** seventy-two ships, drawn up in two parallel lines = **equidistant**, alongside, aligned, side by side, coextensive ■ OPPOSITE: divergent

paralyse or **paralyze** VERB **1** He was paralysed with fear. = **freeze**, stun, numb, petrify, transfix, stupefy, halt, stop dead, immobilize, anaesthetize, benumb **2** The strike has virtually paralysed the country. = **immobilize**, freeze, halt, disable, cripple, arrest, incapacitate, bring to a standstill

paralysis NOUN **1** paralysis of the legs = **immobility**, palsy, paresis (Pathology) **2** The unions have brought about a total *paralysis of trade.* = **standstill**, breakdown, stoppage, shutdown, halt, stagnation, inactivity

parameter NOUN (*usually plural*) = **limit**, constant, restriction, guideline, criterion, framework, limitation, specification

paramount ADJECTIVE = **principal**, prime, first, chief, main, capital, primary, supreme, outstanding, superior, dominant, cardinal, foremost, eminent, predominant, pre-eminent ■ OPPOSITE: secondary

paranoid ADJECTIVE *We live in an increasingly paranoid and fearful society.* = **suspicious**, worried, nervous, fearful, apprehensive, antsy (*informal*)

paraphernalia NOUN = **equipment**, things, effects, material, stuff, tackle, gear, baggage, apparatus, belongings, clobber (*Brit. slang*), accoutrements, impedimenta, appurtenances, equipage

paraphrase VERB *Baxter paraphrased the contents of the press release.* = **reword**, interpret, render, restate, rehash, rephrase, express in other words or your own words ▶ NOUN *The following is a paraphrase of his remarks.* = **rewording**, version, interpretation, rendering, translation, rendition, rehash, restatement, rephrasing

parasite NOUN = **sponger** (*informal*), sponge (*informal*), drone (*Brit.*), leech, hanger-on, scrounger (*informal*), bloodsucker (*informal*), cadger, quandong (*Austral. slang*)

parasitic or **parasitical** ADJECTIVE = **scrounging** (*informal*), sponging (*informal*), cadging, bloodsucking (*informal*), leechlike

parcel NOUN **1** *They sent parcels of food and clothing.* = **package**, case, box, pack, packet, bundle, carton **2** *These small parcels of land were sold to the local people.* = **plot**, area, property, section, patch, tract, allotment, piece of land **3** *He described them, quite rightly, as a parcel of rogues.* = **group**, crowd, pack, company, lot, band, collection, crew (*informal*), gang, bunch (*informal*), batch ▶ VERB (*often with* **up**) *We parcelled up our unwanted clothes to take to the charity shop.* = **wrap**, pack, package, tie up, do up, gift-wrap, box up, fasten together • **parcel something out** *The inheritance was parcelled out equally among the three brothers.* = **distribute**, divide, portion, allocate, split up, dispense, allot, carve up, mete out, dole out, share out, apportion, deal out

parched ADJECTIVE **1** *Showers poured down upon the parched earth.* = **dried out** or **up**, dry, withered, scorched, arid, torrid, shrivelled, dehydrated, waterless **2** *After all that exercise, I was parched.* = **thirsty**, dry, dehydrated, drouthy (*Scot.*)

pardon VERB *Hundreds of political prisoners were pardoned and released.* = **acquit**, free, release, liberate, reprieve, remit, amnesty, let off (*informal*), exonerate, absolve, exculpate ■ OPPOSITE: punish ▶ NOUN **1** *He asked God's pardon for his sins.* = **forgiveness**, mercy, indulgence, absolution, grace ■ OPPOSITE: condemnation **2** *They lobbied the government on his behalf and he was granted a pardon.* = **acquittal**, release, discharge, amnesty, reprieve, remission, exoneration ■ OPPOSITE: punishment • **pardon me** *Pardon me for asking, but what business is it of yours?* = **forgive me**, excuse me

pare VERB **1** *Pare the rind thinly from the lemon.* = **peel**, cut, skin, trim, clip, shave **2** *Local authorities must pare down their budgets.* = **cut back**, cut, reduce, crop, decrease, dock, prune, shear, lop, retrench

parent NOUN **1** *Both her parents were born in Sri Lanka.* = **father** or **mother**, sire, progenitor, begetter, procreator, old (*Austral. & N.Z. informal*), oldie (*Austral. informal*), patriarch **2** *He is regarded as one of the parents of modern classical music.* = **source**, cause, author, root, origin, architect, creator, prototype, forerunner, originator, wellspring

parentage NOUN = **family**, birth, origin, descent, line, race, stock, pedigree, extraction, ancestry, lineage, paternity, derivation

parenthood NOUN = **fatherhood** or **motherhood**, parenting, rearing, bringing up, nurturing, upbringing, child rearing, baby or child care, fathering or mothering

pariah NOUN = **outcast**, exile, outlaw, undesirable, untouchable, leper, unperson

parings PLURAL NOUN = **peelings**, skins, slices, clippings, peel, fragments, shavings, shreds, flakes, rind, snippets, slivers

parish NOUN **1** *the vicar of a small parish in a West Country town* = **district**, community **2** *The whole parish will object if he is appointed as priest.* = **community**, fold, flock, church, congregation, parishioners, churchgoers ■ RELATED WORD: *adjective* parochial

parity NOUN = **equality**, correspondence, consistency, equivalence, quits (*informal*), par, unity, similarity, likeness, uniformity, equal terms, sameness, parallelism, congruity

park NOUN **1** *We went for a brisk walk round the park.* = **recreation ground**, garden, playground, pleasure garden, playpark, domain (*N.Z.*), forest park (*N.Z.*) **2** *a manor house in six acres of park and woodland* = **parkland**, grounds, estate (*Brit.*), lawns,

p

woodland, grassland **3** *Chris was the best player on the park.* = **field**, pitch, playing field ▶ VERB **1** *He found a place to park the car.* = **leave**, stop, station, position **2** *Just park your bag on the floor.* = **put (down)**, leave, place, stick (*informal*), deposit, dump, shove, plonk (*informal*)

parlance NOUN = **language**, talk, speech, tongue, jargon, idiom, lingo (*informal*), phraseology, manner of speaking

parliament NOUN **1** *The Bangladesh parliament has approved the policy.* = **assembly**, council, congress, senate, convention, legislature, talking shop (*informal*), convocation **2** *The legislation will be passed in the next parliament.* = **sitting**, diet **3** (*with cap.*) *Questions have been raised in Parliament regarding this issue.* = **Houses of Parliament**, the House, Westminster, Mother of Parliaments, the House of Commons and the House of Lords, House of Representatives (*N.Z.*)

parliamentary ADJECTIVE = **governmental**, congressional, legislative, law-making, law-giving, deliberative

parlour *or* (*U.S.*) **parlor** NOUN **1** (*old-fashioned*) *The guests were shown into the parlour.* = **sitting room** (*Brit.*), lounge, living room, drawing room, front room, reception room, best room **2** *a funeral parlour* = **establishment**, shop, store, salon

parlous ADJECTIVE = **dangerous**, difficult, desperate, risky, dire, hazardous, hairy (*slang*), perilous, chancy (*informal*)

parochial ADJECTIVE = **provincial**, narrow, insular, limited, restricted, petty, narrow-minded, inward-looking, small-minded, parish-pump ■ OPPOSITE: cosmopolitan

parody NOUN **1** *a parody of a well-known soap opera* = **takeoff** (*informal*), imitation, satire, caricature, send-up (*Brit. informal*), spoof (*informal*), lampoon, skit, burlesque, piss-take (*informal*) **2** *His trial was a parody of justice.* = **travesty**, farce, caricature, mockery, apology for ▶ VERB *It was easy to parody his rather pompous manner of speaking.* = **take off** (*informal*), mimic, caricature, send up (*Brit. informal*), spoof (*informal*), travesty, lampoon, poke fun at, burlesque, satirize, do a takeoff of (*informal*)

paroxysm NOUN = **outburst**, attack, fit, seizure, flare-up (*informal*), eruption, spasm, convulsion

parrot VERB = **repeat**, echo, imitate, copy, reiterate (*formal*), mimic

parry VERB **1** *He parried questions about his involvement in the affair.* = **evade**, avoid, fence off, dodge, duck (*informal*), shun, sidestep, circumvent (*formal*), fight shy of

2 *My opponent parried every blow I got close enough to attempt.* = **ward off**, block, deflect, repel, rebuff, fend off, stave off, repulse, hold at bay

parsimonious ADJECTIVE = **mean**, stingy, penny-pinching (*informal*), miserly, near (*informal*), saving, sparing, grasping, miserable, stinting, frugal, niggardly, penurious, tightfisted, close-fisted, mingy (*Brit. informal*), cheeseparing, skinflinty, snoep (*S. African informal*) ■ OPPOSITE: extravagant

parson NOUN = **clergyman**, minister, priest, vicar, divine, incumbent, reverend (*informal*), preacher, pastor, cleric, rector, curate, churchman, man of God, man of the cloth, ecclesiastic

part NOUN **1** *A large part of his earnings went to repaying the bank loan.* = **piece**, share, proportion, percentage, lot, bit, section, sector, slice, scrap, particle, segment, portion, fragment, lump, fraction, chunk, wedge ■ OPPOSITE: entirety **2** (*often plural*) *It's a beautiful part of the country.* = **region**, area, district, territory, neighbourhood, quarter, vicinity, neck of the woods (*informal*), airt (*Scot.*) **3** *The engine only has three moving parts.* = **component**, bit, piece, unit, element, ingredient, constituent, module **4** *He works in a different part of the company.* = **branch**, department, division, office, section, wing, subdivision, subsection **5** *hands, feet, and other body parts* = **organ**, member, limb **6** *the actor who played the part of the doctor in the soap* = **role**, representation, persona, portrayal, depiction, character part **7** *She's having a lot of trouble learning her part.* = **lines**, words, script, dialogue **8** *He felt a sense of relief now that his part in this business was over.* = **duty**, say, place, work, role, hand, business, share, charge, responsibility, task, function, capacity, involvement, participation **9** *There's no hurry on my part.* = **side**, behalf ▶ VERB **1** *The clouds parted and a shaft of sunlight broke through.* = **divide**, separate, break, tear, split, rend (*literary*), detach, sever, disconnect, cleave, come apart, disunite, disjoin ■ OPPOSITE: join **2** *We parted on bad terms.* = **part company**, separate, break up, split up, say goodbye, go (their) separate ways ■ OPPOSITE: meet • **for the most part** *For the most part, they try to keep out of local disputes.* = **mainly**, largely, generally, chiefly, mostly, principally, on the whole, in the main • **in good part** *She took their jokes in good part.* = **good-naturedly**, well, cheerfully, cordially, without offence • **in part** *His*

reaction was due, in part, to his fear of rejection.
= **partly**, a little, somewhat, slightly,
partially, to some degree, to a certain
extent, in some measure • **on the part of**
There was a change of mood on the part of the
government. = **by**, in, from, made by, carried
out by • **part with something** He was
reluctant to part with his money, even in such a
good cause. = **give up**, abandon, yield,
sacrifice, surrender, discard, relinquish,
renounce, let go of, forgo • **take part in**
Thousands of students have taken part in the
demonstrations. = **participate in**, be
involved in, join in, play a part in, be
instrumental in, have a hand in, partake in,
take a hand in, associate yourself with, put
your twopence-worth in

partake VERB • **partake in something** Do
you partake in dangerous sports? = **participate
in**, share in, take part in, engage in, enter
into • **partake of something 1** They were
happy to partake of our food and drink.
= **consume**, take, share, receive, eat
2 These groups generally partake of a common
characteristic. = **display**, exhibit, evoke, hint
at, be characterized by

> **USAGE** The phrase partake of is
> sometimes inappropriately used as if it
> were a synonym of eat or drink. In strict
> usage, you can only partake of food or
> drink which is available for several
> people to share.

partial ADJECTIVE **1** Their policy only met with
partial success. = **incomplete**, limited,
unfinished, imperfect, fragmentary,
uncompleted ■ **OPPOSITE:** complete **2** Some
of the umpiring in the tournament was partial.
= **biased**, prejudiced, discriminatory,
partisan, influenced, unfair, one-sided,
unjust, predisposed, tendentious
■ **OPPOSITE:** unbiased

partially ADVERB = **partly**, somewhat,
moderately, in part, halfway (informal),
piecemeal, not wholly, fractionally,
incompletely, to a certain extent or degree

participant NOUN = **participator**, party,
member, player, associate, shareholder,
contributor, stakeholder, partaker

participate VERB = **take part**, be involved,
engage, perform, join, enter, partake, have
a hand, get in on the act, be a party to, be a
participant, come to the party ■ **OPPOSITE:**
refrain from

participation NOUN = **taking part**,
contribution, partnership, involvement,
assistance, sharing in, joining in, partaking

particle NOUN = **bit**, piece, scrap, grain,
molecule, atom, shred, crumb, mite, jot,
speck, mote, whit, tittle, iota

particular ADJECTIVE **1** What particular
aspects of the job are you interested in?
= **specific**, special, express, exact, precise,
distinct, peculiar ■ **OPPOSITE:** general
2 This is a question of particular importance for
us. = **special**, exceptional, notable,
uncommon, marked, unusual, remarkable,
singular, noteworthy, especial (formal)
3 Ted was very particular about the colours he
used. = **fussy**, demanding, critical, exacting,
discriminating, meticulous, fastidious,
dainty, choosy (informal), picky (informal),
finicky, pernickety (informal), overnice,
nit-picky (informal) ■ **OPPOSITE:**
indiscriminate **4** a very particular account of
the history of sociology = **detailed**, minute,
precise, thorough, selective, painstaking,
circumstantial, itemized, blow-by-blow
▶ NOUN (usually plural) The nurses at the
admission desk asked for her particulars.
= **detail**, fact, feature, item, circumstance,
specification • **in particular** Why should he
have noticed me in particular? = **especially**,
particularly, expressly, specifically, exactly,
distinctly

particularly ADVERB **1** I particularly asked for
a seat by the window. = **specifically**,
expressly, explicitly, especially, in particular,
distinctly **2** The pollen count has been
particularly high. = **especially**, surprisingly,
notably, unusually, exceptionally,
decidedly, markedly, peculiarly, singularly,
outstandingly, uncommonly

parting NOUN **1** It was a dreadfully emotional
parting. = **farewell**, departure, goodbye,
leave-taking, adieu, valediction **2** Through a
parting in the mist, we saw a huddle of buildings.
= **division**, breaking, split, separation, rift,
partition, detachment, rupture, divergence
▶ MODIFIER Her parting words made him feel
empty and alone. = **farewell**, last, final,
departing, valedictory

partisan ADJECTIVE **1** He is too partisan to be a
referee. = **prejudiced**, one-sided, biased,
partial, sectarian, factional, tendentious
■ **OPPOSITE:** unbiased **2** the hide-out of a
partisan leader = **underground**, resistance,
guerrilla, irregular ▶ NOUN **1** At first the
young poet was a partisan of the Revolution.
= **supporter**, champion, follower, backer,
disciple, stalwart, devotee, adherent,
upholder, votary ■ **OPPOSITE:** opponent
2 He was rescued by some Italian partisans.
= **underground fighter**, guerrilla,
irregular, freedom fighter, resistance
fighter

partition NOUN **1** offices divided only by a glass
partition = **screen**, wall, barrier, divider,
room divider **2** the fighting which followed the

P

partition of India = **division**, splitting, dividing, separation, segregation, severance ▸ VERB **1** *Two rooms have been created by partitioning a single larger room.* = **separate**, screen, divide, fence off, wall off **2** *Korea was partitioned in 1945.* = **divide**, separate, segment, split up, share, section, portion, cut up, apportion, subdivide, parcel out

partly ADVERB = **partially**, relatively, somewhat, slightly, in part, halfway (*informal*), not fully, in some measure, incompletely, up to a certain point, to a certain degree or extent ■ OPPOSITE: completely

> **USAGE** *Partly* and *partially* are to some extent interchangeable, but *partly* should be used when referring to a part or parts of something: *the building is partly* (not *partially*) *made of stone*, while *partially* is preferred for the meaning *to some extent*: *his mother is partially* (not *partly*) *sighted*.

partner NOUN **1** *Wanting other friends doesn't mean you don't love your partner.* = **spouse**, consort, bedfellow, significant other (*informal*, *chiefly U.S.*), mate, better half (*Brit. informal*), helpmate, husband or wife, plus-one (*informal*) **2** *They were partners in crime.* = **companion**, collaborator, accomplice, ally, colleague, associate, mate, team-mate, participant, comrade, confederate, bedfellow, copartner **3** *He is a partner in a Chicago law firm.* = **associate**, colleague, collaborator, copartner

partnership NOUN **1** *the partnership between Germany's banks and its businesses* = **cooperation**, association, alliance, sharing, union, connection, participation, copartnership **2** *As the partnership prospered, the employees shared in the benefits.* = **company**, firm, corporation, house, interest, society (*old-fashioned*), conglomerate, cooperative

party NOUN **1** *opposing political parties* = **faction**, association, alliance, grouping, set, side, league, camp, combination, coalition, clique, coterie, schism, confederacy, cabal **2** *We threw a huge birthday party.* = **get-together** (*informal*), celebration, do (*informal*), social, at-home, gathering, function, reception, bash (*informal*), rave (*Brit. slang*), festivity, knees-up (*Brit. informal*), beano (*Brit. slang*), social gathering, shindig (*informal*), soirée, wrap party, rave-up (*Brit. slang*), afterparty, hooley or hoolie (*chiefly Irish & N.Z.*) **3** *a party of explorers* = **group**, team, band, company, body, unit, squad, gathering, crew, gang, bunch (*informal*), detachment (*Military*) **4** *It has to be proved that he is the guilty party.* = **litigant**, defendant, participant, contractor (*Law*), plaintiff

pass VERB **1** *A car passed me going quite fast.* = **go by** or **past**, overtake, drive past, lap, leave behind, pull ahead of ■ OPPOSITE: stop **2** *I passed through the doorway to ward B.* = **go**, move, travel, roll, progress, flow, proceed, move onwards **3** *She passed a hand through her hair.* = **run**, move, stroke **4** *I passed the books to the librarian.* = **give**, hand, send, throw, exchange, transfer, deliver, toss, transmit, convey, chuck (*informal*), let someone have **5** *His mother's estate passed to him after her death.* = **be left**, come, be bequeathed, be inherited by **6** *Their team passed the ball better than ours did.* = **kick**, hit, loft, head, lob **7** *As the years passed, they grew discontented.* = **elapse**, progress, go by, lapse, wear on, go past, tick by **8** *This crisis will pass eventually.* = **end**, go, die, disappear, fade, cease, vanish, dissolve, expire, terminate, dwindle, evaporate, wane, ebb, melt away, blow over **9** *The children passed the time playing in the streets.* = **spend**, use (up), kill, fill, waste, employ, occupy, devote, beguile, while away **10** *They were the first company in their field to pass the £2 billion turnover mark.* = **exceed**, beat, overtake, go beyond, excel, surpass, transcend, outstrip, outdo, surmount **11** *Kevin has just passed his driving test.* = **be successful in**, qualify (in), succeed (in), graduate (in), get through, do, pass muster (in), come up to scratch (in) (*informal*), gain a pass (in) ■ OPPOSITE: fail **12** *The Senate passed the bill by a vote of seventy-three to twenty-four.* = **approve**, accept, establish, adopt, sanction, decree, enact, authorize, ratify, ordain (*formal*), validate, legislate (for) ■ OPPOSITE: ban **13** *Passing sentence, the judge described the crime as odious.* = **pronounce**, deliver, issue, set forth **14** *We passed a few remarks about the weather.* = **utter**, speak, voice, express, declare **15** *The first symptom is extreme pain when passing urine.* = **discharge**, release, expel, evacuate, emit, let out, eliminate (*rare*) ▸ NOUN **1** *Can I see your boarding pass, please?* = **licence**, ticket, permit, permission, passport, warrant, identification, identity card, authorization **2** *The monastery is in a remote mountain pass.* = **gap**, route, canyon, col, gorge, ravine, defile **3** *Things have come to a pretty pass when people are afraid to go out after dark.* = **predicament**, condition, situation, state, stage, pinch, plight, straits, state of affairs, juncture • **make a**

pass at someone *Was he just being friendly, or was he making a pass at me?* = **make advances to**, proposition, hit on (*U.S. & Canad. slang*), come on to (*informal*), make a play for (*informal*), make an approach to, make sexual overtures to • **pass as** or **for something** or **someone** *She was trying to pass as one of the locals.* = **be mistaken for**, be taken for, impersonate, be accepted as, be regarded as • **pass away** or **on** *He unfortunately passed away last year.* = **die**, pass on, depart (this life), buy it (*U.S. slang*), expire, check out (*U.S. slang*), pass over, kick it (*slang*), croak (*slang*), go belly-up (*slang*), snuff it (*informal*), peg out (*informal*), kick the bucket (*slang*), buy the farm (*U.S. slang*), peg it (*informal*), decease, shuffle off this mortal coil, cark it (*Austral. & N.Z. informal*), pop your clogs (*informal*) • **pass off 1** *The event passed off without any major incidents.* = **take place**, happen, occur, turn out, go down (*U.S. & Canad.*), be completed, go off, fall out, be finished, pan out **2** *The effects of the anaesthetic gradually passed off.* = **come to an end**, disappear, vanish, die away, fade out or away • **pass out** *She got drunk and passed out.* = **faint**, drop, black out (*informal*), swoon (*literary*), lose consciousness, keel over (*informal*), flake out (*informal*), become unconscious • **pass someone over** *She claimed she was repeatedly passed over for promotion.* = **overlook**, ignore, discount, pass by, disregard, not consider, take no notice of, not take into consideration, pay no attention to • **pass something out** *They were passing out leaflets in the street.* = **hand out**, distribute, dole out, deal out • **pass something over** *Let's pass over that subject.* = **disregard**, forget, ignore, skip, omit, pass by, not dwell on • **pass something up** *It's too good a chance to pass up.* = **miss**, ignore, let slip, refuse, decline, reject, neglect, forgo, abstain from, let (something) go by, give (something) a miss (*informal*) • **pass something** or **someone off as something** or **someone** *horse meat being passed off as ground beef* = **misrepresent**, palm something or someone off, falsely represent, disguise something or someone, dress something or someone up

USAGE The past participle of *pass* is sometimes wrongly spelt *past: the time for recriminations has passed* (not *past*).

passable ADJECTIVE **1** *The meal was passable, but nothing special.* = **adequate**, middling, average, fair, all right, ordinary, acceptable, moderate, fair enough, mediocre, so-so (*informal*), tolerable, not too bad, allowable, presentable, admissible, unexceptional, half-pie (*N.Z. informal*) ■ **OPPOSITE:** unsatisfactory **2** *muddy mountain roads that are barely passable* = **clear**, open, navigable, unobstructed, traversable, crossable ■ **OPPOSITE:** impassable

passage NOUN **1** *The toilets are up the stairs and along the passage to your right.* = **corridor**, hallway, passageway, hall, lobby, entrance, exit, doorway, aisle, entrance hall, vestibule **2** *I spotted someone lurking in the passage between the two houses.* = **alley**, way, opening, close (*Brit.*), course, road, channel, route, path, lane, avenue, thoroughfare **3** *He read a passage from the Bible.* = **extract**, reading, piece, section, sentence, text, clause, excerpt, paragraph, verse, quotation **4** *the passage of troops through Spain* = **movement**, passing, advance, progress, flow, motion, transit, progression **5** *the passage from school to college* = **transition**, change, move, development, progress, shift, conversion, progression, metamorphosis **6** *a long speech to prevent the passage of a bill* = **establishment**, passing, legislation, sanction, approval, acceptance, adoption, ratification, enactment, authorization, validation, legalization **7** *We arrived after a 10-hour passage by ship.* = **journey**, crossing, tour, trip, trek, voyage **8** *They were granted safe passage to Baghdad.* = **safe-conduct**, right to travel, freedom to travel, permission to travel, authorization to travel

passageway NOUN = **corridor**, passage, hallway, hall, lane, lobby, entrance, exit, alley, aisle, wynd (*Scot.*)

passé ADJECTIVE = **out-of-date**, old-fashioned, dated, outdated, obsolete, unfashionable, antiquated, outmoded, old hat, outworn, démodé (*French*)

passenger NOUN = **traveller**, rider, fare, commuter, hitchhiker, pillion rider, fare payer

passer-by NOUN = **bystander**, witness, observer, viewer, spectator, looker-on, watcher, onlooker, eyewitness

passing ADJECTIVE **1** *people who dismissed mobile phones as a passing fad* = **momentary**, fleeting, short-lived, transient, ephemeral, short, brief, temporary, transitory, evanescent (*formal*), fugacious (*rare*) **2** *He only gave us a passing glance.* = **superficial**, short, quick, slight, glancing, casual, summary, shallow, hasty, cursory, perfunctory, desultory ▶ NOUN **1** *the passing of an era* = **end**, finish, loss, vanishing, disappearance, termination, dying out,

P

expiry, expiration **2** *His passing will be mourned by many people.* = **death**, demise (*euphemistic*), decease (*formal*), passing on or away • **in passing** *She only mentioned you in passing.* = **incidentally**, on the way, by the way, accidentally, en passant, by the bye

passion NOUN **1** *Romeo's passion for Juliet* = **love**, desire, affection, lust, the hots (*slang*), attachment, fondness, adoration, infatuation, ardour, keenness, concupiscence (*formal*) **2** *Her eyes were blazing with passion.* = **emotion**, feeling, fire, heat, spirit, transport, joy, excitement, intensity, warmth, animation, zeal, zest, fervour, eagerness, rapture, ardour ■ **OPPOSITE:** indifference **3** *She has a passion for gardening.; Mountaineering is his passion.* = **mania**, fancy, enthusiasm, obsession, bug (*informal*), craving, fascination, craze, infatuation **4** *Sam flew into a passion at the suggestion.* = **rage**, fit, storm, anger, fury, resentment, outburst, frenzy, wrath, indignation, flare-up (*informal*), ire, vehemence, paroxysm

passionate ADJECTIVE **1** *He made a passionate speech about his commitment to peace.* = **emotional**, excited, eager, enthusiastic, animated, strong, warm, wild, intense, flaming, fierce, frenzied, ardent, fervent, heartfelt, impassioned, zealous, impulsive, vehement, impetuous, fervid ■ **OPPOSITE:** unemotional **2** *a passionate embrace* = **loving**, sensual, ardent, steamy (*informal*), amorous, lustful, desirous ■ **OPPOSITE:** cold

passionately ADVERB **1** *He spoke passionately about the country's moral crisis.* = **emotionally**, eagerly, enthusiastically, vehemently, excitedly, strongly, warmly, wildly, fiercely, intensely, fervently, impulsively, ardently, zealously, animatedly, with all your heart, frenziedly, impetuously, fervidly ■ **OPPOSITE:** unemotionally **2** *She kissed him passionately.* = **lovingly**, with passion, erotically, ardently, sexily (*informal*), sensually, lustfully, amorously, libidinously, desirously ■ **OPPOSITE:** coldly

passive ADJECTIVE **1** *their passive acceptance of the new regime* = **submissive**, resigned, compliant, receptive, lifeless, docile, nonviolent, quiescent, acquiescent, unassertive, unresisting ■ **OPPOSITE:** spirited **2** *He took a passive role in the interview.* = **inactive**, inert, uninvolved, non-participating ■ **OPPOSITE:** active

password NOUN = **watchword**, key word, magic word (*informal*), open sesame

past NOUN **1** *In the past, things were very different.* = **former times**, history, long ago, antiquity, the good old days, yesteryear (*literary*), times past, the old times, days gone by, the olden days, days of yore ■ **OPPOSITE:** future **2** *shocking revelations about his past* = **background**, life, experience, history, past life, life story, career to date ▶ ADJECTIVE **1** *a return to the turbulence of past centuries* = **former**, late, early, recent, previous, ancient, prior, long-ago, preceding, foregoing, erstwhile, bygone, olden ■ **OPPOSITE:** future **2** *My past life seems like a dream now.* = **previous**, former, one-time, sometime, erstwhile, quondam, ex- **3** *the events of the past few days* = **last**, recent, previous, preceding **4** *The great age of exploration is past.* = **over**, done, ended, spent, finished, completed, gone, forgotten, accomplished, extinct, elapsed, over and done with ▶ PREPOSITION **1** *It's well past your bedtime.* = **after**, beyond, later than, over, outside, farther than, in excess of, subsequent to **2** *She dashed past me and ran out of the room.* = **by**, across, in front of ▶ ADVERB *The ambulance drove past.* = **on**, by, along

▌ **USAGE** The past participle of *pass* is sometimes wrongly spelt *past*: *the time for recrimination has passed* (not *past*).

paste NOUN **1** *wallpaper paste* = **adhesive**, glue, cement, gum, mucilage **2** *tomato paste* = **purée**, pâté, spread ▶ VERB *pasting labels on bottles* = **stick**, fix, glue, cement, gum, fasten

pastel ADJECTIVE = **pale**, light, soft, delicate, muted, soft-hued ■ **OPPOSITE:** bright

pastiche NOUN **1** *The world menu may be a pastiche of dishes from many countries.* = **medley**, mixture, blend, motley, mélange (*French*), miscellany, farrago, hotchpotch, gallimaufry **2** *a pastiche of Botticelli's Birth of Venus* = **parody**, take-off, imitation

pastime NOUN = **activity**, game, sport, entertainment, leisure, hobby, relaxation, recreation, distraction, amusement, diversion

pastor NOUN = **clergyman** *or* **woman**, minister, priest, vicar, divine, parson, rector, curate, churchman *or* woman, ecclesiastic

pastoral ADJECTIVE **1** *the pastoral duties of bishops* = **ecclesiastical**, priestly, ministerial, clerical **2** *a tranquil pastoral scene* = **rustic**, country, simple, rural, idyllic, bucolic, Arcadian, georgic (*literary*), agrestic

pasture NOUN = **grassland**, grass, meadow, grazing, lea (*poetic*), grazing land, pasturage, shieling (*Scot.*)

p

pasty ADJECTIVE = **pale**, unhealthy, wan, sickly, pallid, anaemic, sallow, like death warmed up (*informal*), wheyfaced

pat¹ VERB *She patted me on the knee.* = **stroke**, touch, tap, pet, slap, dab, caress, fondle ▶ NOUN **1** *He gave her an encouraging pat on the shoulder.* = **tap**, stroke, slap, clap, dab, light blow **2** *a pat of butter* = **lump**, cake, portion, dab, small piece

pat² ADJECTIVE *There's no pat answer to your question.* = **glib**, easy, ready, smooth, automatic, slick, simplistic, facile • **off pat** *He doesn't have the answer off pat.* = **perfectly**, precisely, exactly, flawlessly, faultlessly

patch NOUN **1** *a damp patch on the carpet* = **spot** (*Brit.*), bit, stretch, scrap, shred, small piece **2** *the little vegetable patch in her backyard* = **plot**, area, ground, land, tract **3** *jackets with patches on the elbows* = **reinforcement**, piece of fabric, piece of cloth, piece of material, piece sewn on ▶ VERB **1** (*often with* **up**) *elaborately patched blue jeans* = **sew (up)**, mend, repair, reinforce, stitch (up) **2** (*often with* **up**) *They patched the barn roof.* = **mend**, cover, fix, reinforce • **patch things up** *They're trying to patch things up with their neighbours.* = **settle**, make friends, placate, bury the hatchet, conciliate, settle differences, smooth something over

patchwork NOUN = **mixture**, confusion, jumble, medley, hash, pastiche, mishmash, hotchpotch

patchy ADJECTIVE **1** *Bottle tans can make your legs look a patchy orange colour.* = **uneven**, irregular, variegated, spotty, mottled, dappled ■ **OPPOSITE:** even **2** *The response to the strike call has been patchy.* = **irregular**, varying, variable, random, erratic, uneven, sketchy, fitful, bitty, inconstant, scattershot ■ **OPPOSITE:** constant

patent NOUN *He had a number of patents for his inventions.* = **copyright**, licence, franchise, registered trademark ▶ ADJECTIVE *This was a patent lie.* = **obvious**, apparent, evident, blatant, open, clear, glaring, manifest, transparent, conspicuous, downright, unmistakable, palpable, unequivocal, flagrant, indisputable, unconcealed

paternal ADJECTIVE **1** *He has always taken a paternal interest in her.* = **fatherly**, concerned, protective, benevolent, vigilant, solicitous, fatherlike **2** *my paternal grandparents* = **patrilineal**, patrimonial

paternity NOUN = **fatherhood**, fathership (*rare*)

path NOUN **1** *We followed the path along the clifftops.* = **way**, road, walk, track, trail,

avenue, pathway, footpath, walkway (*chiefly U.S.*), towpath, footway, berm (*N.Z.*) **2** *A group of reporters blocked his path.* = **route**, way, course, direction, passage **3** *The country is on the path to economic recovery.* = **course**, way, road, track, route, procedure

pathetic ADJECTIVE **1** *It was a pathetic sight, watching the people queue for food.* = **sad**, moving, touching, affecting, distressing, tender, melting, poignant, harrowing, heartbreaking, plaintive, heart-rending, gut-wrenching, pitiable ■ **OPPOSITE:** funny **2** *That's the most pathetic excuse I've ever heard.* = **inadequate**, useless, feeble, poor, sorry, wet (*Brit. informal*), pants (*informal*), miserable, petty, worthless, meagre, pitiful, woeful, deplorable, lamentable, trashy, measly (*informal*), crummy (*slang*), crappy (*slang*), rubbishy, poxy (*slang*)

pathfinder NOUN = **pioneer**, guide, scout, explorer, discoverer, trailblazer

pathos NOUN = **sadness**, poignancy, plaintiveness, pitifulness, pitiableness

patience NOUN **1** *She lost her patience and shrieked, 'Just shut up, will you?'* = **forbearance**, tolerance, composure, serenity, cool (*slang*), restraint, calmness, equanimity, toleration, sufferance, even temper, imperturbability ■ **OPPOSITE:** impatience **2** *a burden which he has borne with great patience* = **endurance**, resignation, submission, fortitude, persistence, long-suffering, perseverance, stoicism, constancy

patient NOUN *She specializes in the treatment of cancer patients.* = **sick person**, case, sufferer, invalid ▶ ADJECTIVE **1** *She was endlessly kind and patient with children.* = **forbearing**, understanding, forgiving, mild, accommodating, tolerant, indulgent, lenient, even-tempered ■ **OPPOSITE:** impatient **2** *years of patient devotion to her family* = **long-suffering**, resigned, calm, enduring, quiet, composed, persistent, philosophical, serene, persevering, stoical, submissive, self-possessed, uncomplaining, untiring

patois NOUN **1** *In France patois was spoken in rural regions.* = **dialect**, vernacular **2** *people from the ghetto who speak street patois* = **jargon**, slang, vernacular, patter, cant, lingo (*informal*), argot

patriarch NOUN = **father**, old man, elder, grandfather, sire, paterfamilias, greybeard

patrician NOUN *He was a patrician, born to wealth.* = **aristocrat**, peer, noble, nobleman or woman, aristo (*informal*) ▶ ADJECTIVE *a member of a patrician German family*

= **aristocratic**, noble, lordly, high-class, blue-blooded, highborn (*old-fashioned*)

patriot NOUN = **nationalist**, loyalist, chauvinist, flag-waver (*informal*), lover of your country

patriotic ADJECTIVE = **nationalistic**, loyal, flag-waving (*informal*), chauvinistic, jingoistic

patriotism NOUN = **nationalism**, loyalty, flag-waving (*informal*), jingoism, love of your country

patrol VERB *Prison officers continued to patrol the grounds.* = **police**, guard, keep watch (on), pound, range (over), cruise, inspect, safeguard, make the rounds (of), keep guard (on), walk *or* pound the beat (of) ▶ NOUN *Gunmen opened fire after they were challenged by a patrol.* = **guard**, watch, garrison, watchman, sentinel, patrolman

patron NOUN 1 *Catherine the Great was a patron of the arts and sciences.* = **supporter**, friend, champion, defender, sponsor, guardian, angel (*informal*), advocate, backer, helper, protagonist, protector, benefactor, philanthropist 2 *Like so many of its patrons, he could not resist the food at the Savoy.* = **customer**, client, buyer, frequenter, shopper, habitué

patronage NOUN = **support**, promotion, sponsorship, backing, help, aid, championship, assistance, encouragement, espousal, benefaction

patronize VERB 1 *doctors who do not patronize their patients* = **talk down to**, look down on, treat as inferior, treat like a child, be lofty with, treat condescendingly 2 *Some believe it is not the job of the government to patronize the arts.* = **support**, promote, sponsor, back, help, fund, maintain, foster, assist, subscribe to, befriend 3 *the record stores he patronized* = **be a customer** *or* **client of**, deal with, frequent, buy from, trade with, shop at, do business with

patronizing ADJECTIVE = **condescending**, superior, stooping, lofty, gracious, contemptuous, haughty, snobbish, disdainful, supercilious, toffee-nosed (*slang, chiefly Brit.*) ■ **OPPOSITE:** respectful

patter¹ VERB *All night the sleet pattered on the tin roof.* = **tap**, beat, pat, pelt, spatter, rat-a-tat, pitter-patter, pitapat ▶ NOUN *the patter of the driving rain on the window* = **tapping**, pattering, pitter-patter, pitapat

patter² NOUN 1 *Don't be taken in by the sales patter.* = **spiel** (*informal*), line, pitch, monologue 2 *the cheery patter of DJs* = **chatter**, prattle, nattering, jabber, gabble, yak (*slang*) 3 *the famous Glasgow*

patter = **jargon**, slang, vernacular, cant, lingo (*informal*), patois, argot

pattern NOUN 1 *All three attacks followed the same pattern.* = **order**, plan, system, method, arrangement, sequence, orderliness 2 *curtains in a light floral pattern* = **design**, arrangement, motif, figure, device, decoration, ornament, decorative design 3 *a sewing pattern* = **plan**, design, original, guide, instructions, diagram, stencil, template 4 *the ideal pattern of a good society* = **model**, example, standard, original, guide, par, criterion, norm, prototype, paradigm, archetype, paragon, exemplar, cynosure

paucity NOUN = **scarcity**, lack, poverty, shortage, deficiency, rarity, dearth, smallness, insufficiency, slenderness, sparseness, slightness, sparsity, meagreness, paltriness, scantiness

paunch NOUN = **belly**, beer-belly (*informal*), spread (*informal*), corporation (*informal*), pot, spare tyre (*Brit. slang*), middle-age spread (*informal*), potbelly, large abdomen, muffin top (*informal*), puku (*N.Z.*)

pauper NOUN = **down-and-out**, have-not, bankrupt, beggar, insolvent, indigent, poor person, mendicant

pause VERB *He paused briefly before answering.* = **stop briefly**, delay, hesitate, break, wait, rest, halt, cease, interrupt, deliberate, waver, take a break, discontinue, desist, have a breather (*informal*) ■ **OPPOSITE:** continue ▶ NOUN *There was a brief pause in the conversation.* = **stop**, break, delay, interval, hesitation, stay, wait, rest, gap, halt, interruption, respite, lull, stoppage, interlude, cessation, let-up (*informal*), breathing space, breather (*informal*), intermission, discontinuance, entr'acte, caesura ■ **OPPOSITE:** continuance

pave VERB = **cover**, floor, surface, flag, concrete, tile, tar, asphalt, macadamize

paw (*informal*) VERB = **manhandle**, grab, maul, molest, handle roughly

pawn¹ VERB *He pawned his wedding ring.* = **hock** (*informal, chiefly U.S.*), pop (*Brit. informal*), stake, mortgage, deposit, pledge, hazard, wager

pawn² NOUN *They are being used as political pawns.* = **tool**, instrument (*informal*), toy, creature, puppet, dupe, stooge (*slang*), plaything, cat's-paw

pay VERB 1 *They are paid well for doing such a difficult job.* = **reward**, compensate, reimburse, recompense, requite, remunerate (*formal*), front up 2 *I was prepared to pay anything for that car.* = **spend**, offer, give, fork out (*informal*), remit, cough up (*informal*), shell out (*informal*) **3** *If you cannot pay your debts, you can file for bankruptcy.* = **settle**, meet, clear, foot, honour, discharge, liquidate, square up **4** *This job pays $1000 a week.* = **bring in**, earn, return, net, yield **5** *She took over the family restaurant and made it pay.* = **be profitable**, make money, make a return, provide a living, be remunerative **6** *It pays to invest in protective clothing.* = **benefit**, serve, repay, be worthwhile, be advantageous **7** *He never pays me compliments or says he loves me.* = **give**, extend, present with, grant, render, hand out, bestow, proffer ▶ NOUN *the workers' complaints about pay and conditions* = **wages**, income, payment, earnings, fee, reward, hire, salary, compensation, allowance, remuneration, takings, reimbursement, hand-outs, recompense, stipend, emolument, vacation pay (*Canad.*), meed (*archaic*) • **pay off** *Her persistence paid off in the end.* = **succeed**, work, be successful, be effective, be profitable • **pay someone back** *It was her chance to pay him back for humiliating her.* = **get even with** (*informal*), punish, repay, retaliate, hit back at, reciprocate, recompense, get revenge on, settle a score with, get your own back on, revenge yourself on, avenge yourself for • **pay someone off 1** *corrupt societies where officials have to be paid off* = **bribe**, corrupt, oil (*informal*), get at, buy off, suborn, grease the palm of (*slang*) **2** *Most of the staff are being paid off at the end of the month.* = **dismiss**, fire (*informal*), sack (*informal*), discharge, let go, lay off, kennet (*Austral. slang*), jeff (*Austral. slang*) • **pay something back** *I'll pay you back that money tomorrow.* = **repay**, return, square, refund, reimburse, settle up • **pay something off** *It would take him the rest of his life to pay off that loan.* = **settle**, clear, square, discharge, liquidate, pay in full • **pay something out** *football clubs who pay out millions of pounds for players* = **spend**, lay out (*informal*), expend, cough up (*informal*), shell out (*informal*), disburse, fork out or over or up (*slang*) • **pay up** *We claimed a refund, but the company wouldn't pay up.* = **pay**, fork out (*informal*), stump up (*Brit. informal*), make payment, pay in full, settle up, come up with the money

payable ADJECTIVE = **due**, outstanding, owed, owing, mature, to be paid, obligatory, receivable

payment NOUN **1** *an initial deposit, followed by twelve monthly payments* = **remittance**, advance, deposit, premium, portion, instalment, e-payment **2** *He sought payment of a sum which he claimed was owed to him.*

= **settlement**, paying, discharge, outlay, remittance, defrayal **3** *It is reasonable to expect proper payment for this work.* = **wages**, fee, reward, hire, remuneration

payoff NOUN **1** *payoffs from drugs exporters* = **bribe**, incentive, cut (*informal*), payment, sweetener (*informal*), bung (*Brit. informal*), inducement, kick-back (*informal*), backhander (*informal*), hush money (*informal*) **2** *an eye-wateringly huge divorce payoff* = **settlement**, payment, reward, payout, recompense **3** *The payoff of the novel is patently predictable.* = **outcome**, result, consequence, conclusion, climax, finale, culmination, the crunch (*informal*), upshot, moment of truth, clincher (*informal*), punch line

peace NOUN **1** *They hope the treaty will bring peace to the troubled region.* = **truce**, ceasefire, treaty, armistice, pacification, conciliation, cessation of hostilities ■ OPPOSITE: war **2** *All I want is a bit of peace and quiet.* = **stillness**, rest, quiet, silence, calm, hush, tranquillity, seclusion, repose, calmness, peacefulness, quietude, restfulness **3** *People always felt a sense of peace in her company.* = **serenity**, calm, relaxation, composure, contentment, repose, equanimity, peacefulness, placidity, harmoniousness **4** *a period of relative peace in the country's industrial relations* = **harmony**, accord, agreement, concord, amity (*formal*)

peaceable ADJECTIVE = **peace-loving**, friendly, gentle, peaceful, mild, conciliatory, amiable, pacific, amicable, placid, inoffensive, dovish, unwarlike, nonbelligerent

peaceful ADJECTIVE **1** *Their relations with most of these people were peaceful.* = **friendly**, at peace, harmonious, amicable, cordial, nonviolent, without hostility, free from strife, on friendly or good terms ■ OPPOSITE: hostile **2** *warriors who killed or enslaved the peaceful farmers* = **peace-loving**, conciliatory, peaceable, placatory, irenic, pacific, unwarlike ■ OPPOSITE: belligerent **3** *a peaceful scene* = **calm**, still, quiet, gentle, pleasant, soothing, tranquil, placid, restful, chilled (*informal*) ■ OPPOSITE: agitated **4** *I felt relaxed and peaceful.* = **serene**, placid, undisturbed, untroubled, unruffled

peacemaker NOUN = **mediator**, appeaser, arbitrator, conciliator, pacifier, peacemonger

peak NOUN **1** *Her career was at its peak when she died.* = **high point**, crown, climax, culmination, zenith, maximum point, apogee, acme, ne plus ultra (*Latin*) **2** *the snow-covered peaks of the Alps* = **point**, top, tip, summit, brow, crest, pinnacle, apex, aiguille ▶ VERB *Temperatures have peaked at over 30 degrees Celsius.* = **culminate**, climax, come to a head, be at its height, reach its highest point, reach the zenith

peal VERB *The church bells pealed at the stroke of midnight.* = **ring**, sound, toll, resound, chime, resonate, tintinnabulate ▶ NOUN **1** *the great peals of the Abbey bells* = **ring**, sound, ringing, clamour, chime, clang, carillon, tintinnabulation **2** *great peals of thunder* = **clap**, sound, crash, blast, roar, rumble, resounding, reverberation **3** *She burst into peals of laughter.* = **roar**, fit, shout, scream, gale (*informal*), howl, shriek, hoot

pearly ADJECTIVE **1** *a suit covered with pearly buttons* = **iridescent**, mother-of-pearl, opalescent, nacreous, margaric, margaritic **2** *pearly white teeth* = **ivory**, creamy, milky, silvery

peasant NOUN **1** *land given to peasants for food production* = **rustic**, countryman, hind (*obsolete*), swain (*archaic*), son of the soil, churl (*archaic*) **2** *Why should I let a lot of peasants traipse over my property?* = **boor**, provincial, hick (*informal, chiefly U.S. & Canad.*), lout, yokel, country bumpkin, hayseed (*U.S. & Canad. informal*), churl (*archaic*)

peck VERB **1** *The crow pecked his hand.* = **pick**, bite, hit, strike, tap, poke, jab, prick, nibble **2** *She walked up to him and pecked him on the cheek.* = **kiss**, plant a kiss, give someone a smacker, give someone a peck or kiss ▶ NOUN *He gave me a peck on the lips.* = **kiss**, smacker, osculation (*rare*)

peculiar ADJECTIVE **1** *She has a very peculiar sense of humour.* = **odd**, strange, unusual, bizarre, funny, extraordinary, curious, weird, exceptional, eccentric, abnormal, out-of-the-way, queer, uncommon, singular, unconventional, far-out (*slang*), quaint, off-the-wall (*slang*), outlandish, offbeat, freakish, wacky (*informal*), outré, daggy (*Austral. & N.Z. informal*) ■ OPPOSITE: ordinary **2** *We have our own peculiar way of doing things.* = **special**, private, individual, personal, particular, unique, characteristic, distinguishing, distinct, idiosyncratic ■ OPPOSITE: common **3** (*with* **to**) *surnames peculiar to this area* = **specific to**, restricted to, appropriate to, endemic to

peculiarity NOUN **1** *the peculiarity of her behaviour* = **oddity**, abnormality, eccentricity, weirdness, queerness, bizarreness, freakishness **2** *He had many little peculiarities.* = **quirk**, caprice, mannerism, whimsy, foible, idiosyncrasy,

odd trait **3** *a strange peculiarity of the university system* = **characteristic**, mark, feature, quality, property, attribute, trait, speciality, singularity, distinctiveness, particularity

pecuniary ADJECTIVE = **monetary**, economic, financial, capital, commercial, fiscal, budgetary

pedantic ADJECTIVE **1** *all their pedantic quibbles about grammar* = **hairsplitting**, particular, formal, precise, fussy, picky (*informal*), nit-picking (*informal*), punctilious, priggish, pedagogic, overnice **2** *Her lecture was pedantic and uninteresting.* = **academic**, pompous, schoolmasterly, stilted, erudite, scholastic, didactic, bookish, abstruse, donnish, sententious

peddle VERB = **sell**, trade, push (*informal*), market, hawk, flog (*slang*), vend, huckster, sell door to door

peddler *or* **pedlar** NOUN = **seller**, vendor, hawker, duffer (*dialect*), huckster, door-to-door salesperson, cheap-jack (*informal*), colporteur

pedestal NOUN *a bronze statue on a granite pedestal* = **support**, stand, base, foot, mounting, foundation, pier, plinth, dado (*Architecture*) • **put someone on a pedestal** *Since childhood, I put my parents on a pedestal.* = **worship**, dignify, glorify, exalt, idealize, ennoble, deify, apotheosize

pedestrian NOUN *In Los Angeles, a pedestrian is a rare spectacle.* = **walker**, foot-traveller, footslogger ■ OPPOSITE: driver ▶ ADJECTIVE *His style is so pedestrian that the book is really boring.* = **dull**, flat, ordinary, boring, commonplace, mundane, mediocre, plodding, banal, prosaic, run-of-the-mill, humdrum, unimaginative, uninteresting, uninspired, ho-hum (*informal*), no great shakes (*informal*), half-pie (*N.Z. informal*) ■ OPPOSITE: exciting

pedigree MODIFIER *Two families have become locked in a custody battle over a pedigree dog.* = **purebred**, thoroughbred, full-blooded ▶ NOUN *a countess of impeccable pedigree* = **lineage**, family, line, race, stock, blood, breed, heritage, descent, extraction, ancestry, family tree, genealogy, derivation

pedlar *see* **peddler**

peek VERB *She peeked at him through a crack in the wall.* = **glance**, look, peer, spy, take a look, peep, eyeball (*slang*), sneak a look, keek (*Scot.*), snatch a glimpse, take *or* have a gander (*informal*) ▶ NOUN *I had a quick peek into the bedroom.* = **glance**, look, glimpse, blink, peep, butcher's (*Brit. slang*), gander (*informal*), look-see (*slang*), shufti (*Brit. slang*), keek (*Scot.*)

peel NOUN *grated lemon peel* = **rind**, skin, peeling, epicarp, exocarp ▸ VERB *I sat down and began peeling potatoes.* = **skin**, scale, strip, pare, shuck, flake off, decorticate (*rare*), take the skin or rind off

peep VERB **1** *Now and then she peeped to see if they were paying attention.* = **peek**, look, peer, spy, eyeball (*slang*), sneak a look, steal a look, keek (*Scot.*), look surreptitiously, look from hiding **2** *Purple and yellow flowers peeped between the rocks.* = **appear briefly**, emerge, pop up, spring up, issue from, peer out, peek from, show partially ▸ NOUN *He took a peep at his watch.* = **look**, glimpse, peek, butcher's (*Brit. slang*), gander (*informal*), look-see (*slang*), shufti (*Brit. slang*), keek (*Scot.*)

peer¹ NOUN **1** *The author is a life peer and the former M.P.* = **noble**, lord, count, duke, earl, baron, aristocrat, viscount, marquess, marquis, nobleman or woman, aristo (*informal*) **2** *Her personality made her popular with her peers.* = **equal**, like, match, fellow, contemporary, coequal, compeer

peer² VERB *She peered at him sleepily over the bedclothes.* = **squint**, look, spy, gaze, scan, inspect, peep, peek, snoop, scrutinize, look closely

peerage NOUN = **aristocracy**, peers, nobility, lords and ladies, titled classes

peerless ADJECTIVE = **unequalled**, excellent, unique, outstanding, unparalleled, superlative, unrivalled, second to none, incomparable, unmatched, unsurpassed, matchless, beyond compare, nonpareil
■ **OPPOSITE:** mediocre

peeved ADJECTIVE = **irritated**, upset, annoyed, put out, hacked off (*informal*), sore, galled, exasperated, nettled, vexed, irked, riled, piqued, tooshie (*Austral. slang*)

peg NOUN *He builds furniture using wooden pegs instead of nails.* = **pin**, spike, rivet, skewer, dowel, spigot ▸ VERB **1** *trying to peg a sheet on to the washing line* = **fasten**, join, fix, secure, attach, make fast **2** *The bank wants to peg interest rates at 9%.* = **fix**, set, control, limit, freeze

pejorative ADJECTIVE = **derogatory**, negative, slighting, unpleasant, belittling, disparaging, debasing, deprecatory, uncomplimentary, depreciatory, detractive, detractory

pelt¹ VERB **1** *Crowds started to pelt police cars with stones.* = **shower**, beat, strike, pepper, batter, thrash, bombard, wallop (*informal*), assail, pummel, hurl at, cast at, belabour, sling at **2** *It's pelting down with rain out there.* = **pour**, teem, rain hard, bucket down (*informal*), rain cats and dogs (*informal*) **3** *She pelted down the stairs in her nightgown.* = **rush**, charge, shoot, career, speed, tear, belt (*slang*), dash, hurry, barrel (along) (*informal, chiefly U.S. & Canad.*), whizz (*informal*), stampede, run fast, burn rubber (*informal*)

pelt² NOUN *mink which had been bred for their pelts* = **coat**, fell, skin, hide

pen¹ VERB *She penned a short memo to his private secretary.* = **write (down)**, draft, compose, pencil, draw up, scribble, take down, inscribe, scrawl, jot down, dash off, commit to paper

pen² NOUN *a holding pen for sheep* = **enclosure**, pound, fold, cage, coop, hutch, corral (*chiefly U.S. & Canad.*), sty ▸ VERB *The cattle had been milked and penned for the night.* = **enclose**, confine, cage, pound, mew (up), fence in, impound, hem in, coop up, hedge in, shut up or in

penal ADJECTIVE = **disciplinary**, punitive, corrective, penalizing, retributive

penalize VERB **1** *Players who break the rules will be penalized.* = **punish**, discipline, correct, handicap, award a penalty against (*Sport*), impose a penalty on **2** *Old people are being penalized for being pensioners.* = **put at a disadvantage**, handicap, cause to suffer, unfairly disadvantage, inflict a handicap on

penalty NOUN = **punishment**, price, fine, handicap, forfeit, retribution, forfeiture

penance NOUN = **atonement**, punishment, penalty, reparation, expiation (*formal*), sackcloth and ashes, self-punishment, self-mortification

penchant NOUN = **liking**, taste, tendency, turn, leaning, bent, bias, inclination, affinity, disposition, fondness, propensity, predisposition, predilection, proclivity (*formal*), partiality, proneness

pending ADJECTIVE **1** *The cause of death was listed as pending.* = **undecided**, unsettled, in the balance, up in the air, undetermined **2** *Customers have been inquiring about the pending price rises.* = **forthcoming**, imminent, prospective, impending, in the wind, in the offing ▸ PREPOSITION *The judge has suspended the ban, pending a full inquiry.* = **awaiting**, until, waiting for, till

penetrate VERB **1** *The needle penetrated the skin.* = **pierce**, enter, go through, bore, probe, stab, prick, perforate, impale **2** *A cool breeze penetrated the mosquito netting.* = **pervade**, enter, permeate, filter through, suffuse, seep through, get in through, percolate through **3** *They had managed to penetrate Soviet defences.* = **infiltrate**, enter, get in to, make inroads into, sneak in to

p

(*informal*), work or worm your way into **4** *long answers that were often difficult to penetrate* = **grasp**, understand, work out, figure out (*informal*), unravel, discern, comprehend, fathom, decipher, suss (out) (*slang*), get to the bottom of

penetrating ADJECTIVE **1** *Her voice was nasal and penetrating.* = **sharp**, harsh, piercing, carrying, piping, loud, intrusive, strident, shrill, high-pitched, ear-splitting ■ OPPOSITE: sweet **2** *a most wonderful penetrating smell and taste* = **pungent**, biting, strong, powerful, sharp, heady, pervasive, aromatic **3** *A raw, penetrating wind was blowing in off the plain.* = **piercing**, cutting, biting, sharp, freezing, fierce, stinging, frosty, bitterly cold, arctic (*informal*) **4** *a penetrating mind* = **intelligent**, quick, sharp, keen, critical, acute, profound, discriminating, shrewd, discerning, astute, perceptive, incisive, sharp-witted, perspicacious (*formal*), sagacious (*formal*) ■ OPPOSITE: dull **5** *a penetrating stare* = **perceptive**, searching, sharp, keen, alert, probing, discerning ■ OPPOSITE: unperceptive

penetration NOUN **1** *the penetration of eggs by more than one sperm* = **piercing**, entry, entrance, invasion, puncturing, incision, perforation **2** *penetration of foreign export markets* = **entry**, entrance, inroad

pennant NOUN = **flag**, jack, banner, ensign, streamer, burgee (*Nautical*), pennon, banderole

penniless ADJECTIVE = **poor**, broke (*informal*), bankrupt, impoverished, short, ruined, strapped (*slang*), needy, cleaned out (*slang*), destitute, poverty-stricken, down and out, skint (*Brit. slang*), indigent, down at heel, impecunious, dirt-poor (*informal*), on the breadline, flat broke (*informal*), penurious, on your uppers, stony-broke (*Brit. slang*), necessitous, in queer street, moneyless, without two pennies to rub together (*informal*), without a penny to your name ■ OPPOSITE: rich

penny-pinching ADJECTIVE = **mean**, close, near (*informal*), frugal, stingy, scrimping, miserly, niggardly, tightfisted, Scrooge-like, mingy (*Brit. informal*), cheeseparing, snoep (*S. African informal*) ■ OPPOSITE: generous

pension NOUN = **allowance**, benefit, welfare, annuity, superannuation

pensioner NOUN = **senior citizen**, retired person, retiree (*U.S.*), old-age pensioner, O.A.P.

pensive ADJECTIVE = **thoughtful**, serious, sad, blue (*informal*), grave, sober, musing, preoccupied, melancholy, solemn, reflective, dreamy, wistful, mournful, contemplative, meditative, sorrowful, ruminative, in a brown study (*informal*), cogitative ■ OPPOSITE: carefree

pent-up ADJECTIVE = **suppressed**, checked, curbed, inhibited, held back, stifled, repressed, smothered, constrained, bridled, bottled-up

penury NOUN = **poverty**, want, need, privation (*formal*), destitution, straitened circumstances, beggary, indigence, pauperism

people PLURAL NOUN **1** *People should treat the planet with respect.* = **humankind**, persons, humans, individuals, folk (*informal*), men and women, human beings, humanity, mankind, mortals, the human race, Homo sapiens **2** *the will of the people* = **the public**, the crowd, the masses, the general public, the mob, the herd, the grass roots, the rank and file, the multitude, the populace, the proletariat, the rabble, the plebs, the proles (*derogatory slang, chiefly Brit.*), the commonalty, (the) hoi polloi **3** *the people of Rome* = **nation**, public, community, subjects, population, residents, citizens, folk, inhabitants, electors, populace, tax payers, citizenry, (general) public **4** *the native peoples of Central and South America* = **race**, tribe, ethnic group **5** *My people still live in Ireland.* = **family**, parents, relations, relatives, folk, folks (*informal*), clan, kin, next of kin, kinsmen or women, nearest and dearest, kith and kin, your own flesh and blood, rellies (*Austral. slang*) ▶ VERB *a small town peopled by workers and families* = **inhabit**, occupy, settle, populate, colonize

pep NOUN *They need something to put the pep back in their lives.* = **energy**, life, spirit, zip (*informal*), vitality, animation, vigour, verve, high spirits, gusto, get-up-and-go (*informal*), brio, vivacity, liveliness, vim • **pep something** or **someone up** *A drizzle of its delicate flavour will pep up even the simplest of suppers.* = **enliven**, inspire, stimulate, animate, exhilarate, quicken, invigorate, jazz up (*informal*), vitalize, vivify

pepper NOUN *Season the mixture with salt and pepper.* = **seasoning**, flavour, spice ▶ VERB **1** *He was peppered with shrapnel.* = **pelt**, hit, shower, scatter, blitz, riddle, rake, bombard, assail, strafe, rain down on **2** *The road was peppered with glass.* = **sprinkle**, spot, scatter, dot, stud, fleck, intersperse, speck, spatter, freckle, stipple, bespatter

peppery ADJECTIVE = **hot**, fiery, spicy, pungent, highly seasoned, piquant ■ OPPOSITE: mild

perceive VERB **1** *I perceived a number of changes.* = **see**, notice, note, identify, discover, spot, observe, remark, recognize, distinguish, glimpse, make out, pick out, discern, behold (*archaic*, *literary*), catch sight of, espy, descry **2** *He was beginning to perceive the true nature of their relationship.* = **understand**, sense, gather, get (*informal*), know, see, feel, learn, realize, conclude, appreciate, grasp, comprehend, get the message about, deduce, apprehend, suss (out) (*slang*), get the picture about **3** *How real do you perceive this threat to be?* = **consider**, believe, judge, suppose, rate, deem, adjudge

perceptible ADJECTIVE = **noticeable**, clear, obvious, apparent, visible, evident, distinct, tangible, blatant, conspicuous, palpable, discernible, recognizable, detectable, observable, appreciable, perceivable ■ OPPOSITE: imperceptible

perception NOUN **1** *how our perception of death affects the way we live* = **awareness**, understanding, sense, impression, feeling, idea, taste, notion, recognition, observation, consciousness, grasp, sensation, conception, apprehension **2** *It did not require a great deal of perception to realise what he meant.* = **understanding**, intelligence, observation, discrimination, insight, sharpness, cleverness, keenness, shrewdness, acuity, discernment, perspicacity (*formal*), astuteness, incisiveness, perceptiveness, quick-wittedness, perspicuity

perceptive ADJECTIVE = **observant**, acute, intelligent, discerning, quick, aware, sharp, sensitive, alert, penetrating, discriminating, shrewd, responsive, astute, intuitive, insightful, percipient, perspicacious (*formal*) ■ OPPOSITE: obtuse

perch VERB **1** *She perched on the corner of the desk.* = **sit**, rest, balance, settle **2** *Her glasses were perched precariously on her head.* = **place**, put, rest, balance **3** *A blackbird perched on the parapet outside the window.* = **land**, alight, roost ▶ NOUN *The canary fell off its perch.* = **resting place**, post, branch, pole, roost

percolate VERB **1** *These truths begin to percolate through our minds.* = **penetrate**, filter, seep, pervade, permeate, transfuse (*literary*) **2** *the machine I use to percolate my coffee* = **filter**, brew, perk (*informal*) **3** *Water cannot percolate through the clay.* = **seep**, strain, drain, filter, penetrate, drip, leach, ooze, pervade, permeate, filtrate

perennial ADJECTIVE = **continual**, lasting, continuing, permanent, constant, enduring, chronic, persistent, abiding, lifelong, perpetual, recurrent, never-ending, incessant, unchanging, inveterate

perfect ADJECTIVE **1** = **faultless**, correct, pure, accurate, faithful, impeccable, exemplary, flawless, foolproof, blameless ■ OPPOSITE: deficient **2** *This is a perfect time to buy a house.* = **excellent**, ideal, supreme, superb, splendid, sublime, superlative **3** *The car is in perfect condition.* = **immaculate**, impeccable, flawless, spotless, unblemished, untarnished, unmarred ■ OPPOSITE: flawed **4** *She behaved like a perfect fool.* = **complete**, absolute, sheer, utter, consummate, out-and-out, unadulterated, unmitigated, unalloyed ■ OPPOSITE: partial **5** *She spoke in a perfect imitation of her father's voice.* = **exact**, true, accurate, precise, right, close, correct, strict, faithful, spot-on (*Brit. informal*), on the money (*informal*), unerring ▶ VERB *He worked hard to perfect his drawing technique.* = **improve**, develop, polish, elaborate, refine, cultivate, hone ■ OPPOSITE: mar

USAGE For most of its meanings, the adjective *perfect* describes an absolute state, so that something either is or is not *perfect*, and cannot be referred to in terms of degree - thus, one thing should not be described as *more perfect* or *less perfect* than another thing. However, when *perfect* is used in the sense of 'excellent in all respects', *more* and *most* are acceptable, for example *the next day the weather was even more perfect*.

perfection NOUN **1** *the quest for physical perfection* = **excellence**, integrity, superiority, purity, wholeness, sublimity, exquisiteness, faultlessness, flawlessness, perfectness, immaculateness **2** *She seems to be perfection itself.* = **the ideal**, the crown, the last word, one in a million (*informal*), a paragon, the crème de la crème, the acme, a nonpareil, the beau idéal **3** *the woman credited with the perfection of this technique* = **accomplishment**, achieving, achievement, polishing, evolution, refining, completion, realization, fulfilment, consummation

perfectionist NOUN = **stickler**, purist, formalist, precisionist, precisian

perfectly ADVERB **1** *These mushrooms are perfectly safe to eat.* = **completely**, totally, entirely, absolutely, quite, fully, altogether, thoroughly, wholly, utterly, consummately, every inch ■ OPPOSITE: partially **2** *The system worked perfectly.* = **flawlessly**, ideally, wonderfully, superbly, admirably, supremely, to perfection, exquisitely, superlatively, impeccably, like a dream, faultlessly ■ OPPOSITE: badly

perforate VERB = **pierce**, hole, bore, punch, drill, penetrate, puncture, honeycomb

perform VERB **1** *people who have performed outstanding acts of bravery* = **do**, achieve, carry out, effect, complete, satisfy, observe, fulfil, accomplish, execute, bring about, pull off, act out, transact **2** *Each part of the engine performs a different function.* = **fulfil**, carry out, execute, discharge **3** *students performing Shakespeare's Macbeth* = **present**, act (out), stage, play, produce, represent, put on, render, depict, enact, appear as **4** *He began performing in the early fifties.* = **appear on stage**, act

performance NOUN **1** *They are giving a performance of Bizet's Carmen.* = **presentation**, playing, acting (out), staging, production, exhibition, interpretation, representation, rendering, portrayal, rendition **2** *The band did three performances at the Royal Albert Hall.* = **show**, appearance, concert, gig (*informal*), recital **3** *The study looked at the performance of 18 surgeons.* = **work**, acts, conduct, exploits, feats **4** *What is the car's performance like?* = **functioning**, running, operation, working, action, behaviour, capacity, efficiency, capabilities **5** *the performance of his duties* = **carrying out**, practice, achievement, discharge, execution, completion, accomplishment, fulfilment, consummation **6** *She made a big performance of cooking the dinner.* = **carry-on** (*informal, chiefly Brit.*), business, to-do, act, scene, display, bother, fuss, pantomime (*informal, chiefly Brit.*), song and dance (*informal*), palaver, rigmarole, pother (*literary*)

performer NOUN = **artiste**, player, Thespian, trouper, play-actor, actor *or* actress

perfume NOUN **1** *The room smelled of her mother's perfume.* = **fragrance**, scent, essence, incense, cologne, eau de toilette, eau de cologne, attar **2** *the perfume of roses* = **scent**, smell, fragrance, bouquet, aroma, odour, sweetness, niff (*Brit. slang*), redolence, balminess

perfunctory ADJECTIVE = **offhand**, routine, wooden, automatic, stereotyped, mechanical, indifferent, careless, superficial, negligent, sketchy, unconcerned, cursory, unthinking, slovenly, heedless, slipshod, inattentive ■ **OPPOSITE:** thorough

perhaps ADVERB = **maybe**, possibly, it may be, it is possible (that), conceivably, as the case may be, perchance (*archaic*), feasibly, for all you know, happen (*Northern English, dialect*)

peril NOUN **1** *sailors in peril on the sea* = **danger**, risk, threat, hazard, menace, jeopardy, perilousness **2** (*often plural*) *the perils of starring in a TV commercial* = **pitfall**, problem, risk, hazard ■ **OPPOSITE:** safety

perilous ADJECTIVE = **dangerous**, threatening, exposed, vulnerable, risky, unsure, hazardous, hairy (*slang*), unsafe, precarious, parlous (*archaic*), fraught with danger, chancy (*informal*)

perimeter NOUN = **boundary**, edge, border, bounds, limit, margin, confines, periphery, borderline, circumference, ambit ■ **OPPOSITE:** centre

period NOUN **1** *a period of a few months* = **time**, term, season, space, run, stretch, spell, phase, patch (*Brit. informal*), interval, span **2** *the Victorian period* = **age**, generation, years, time, days, term, stage, date, cycle, era, epoch, aeon

periodic ADJECTIVE = **recurrent**, regular, repeated, occasional, periodical, seasonal, cyclical, sporadic, intermittent, every so often, infrequent, cyclic, every once in a while, spasmodic, at fixed intervals

periodical NOUN *The walls were lined with books and periodicals.* = **publication**, paper, review, magazine, journal, weekly, monthly, organ, serial, quarterly, zine (*informal*) ▶ ADJECTIVE *periodical fits of depression* = **recurrent**, regular, repeated, occasional, seasonal, cyclical, sporadic, intermittent, every so often, infrequent, cyclic, every once in a while, spasmodic, at fixed intervals

peripheral ADJECTIVE **1** *That information is peripheral to the main story.* = **secondary**, beside the point, minor, marginal, irrelevant, superficial, unimportant, incidental, tangential, inessential **2** *development in the peripheral areas of large towns* = **outermost**, outside, external, outer, exterior, borderline, perimetric

periphery NOUN = **boundary**, edge, border, skirt, fringe, verge (*Brit.*), brink, outskirts, rim, hem, brim, perimeter, circumference, outer edge, ambit

perish VERB **1** *the ferry disaster in which 193 passengers perished* = **die**, be killed, be lost, expire, pass away, lose your life, decease, cark it (*Austral. & N.Z. slang*) **2** *Civilizations do eventually decline and perish.* = **be destroyed**, fall, decline, collapse, disappear, vanish, go under **3** *The rubber lining had perished.* = **rot**, waste away, break down, decay, wither, disintegrate, decompose, moulder

perishable ADJECTIVE = **short-lived**, biodegradable, easily spoilt, decomposable, liable to rot ■ **OPPOSITE:** non-perishable

perjury NOUN = **lying under oath**, false statement, forswearing, bearing false witness, giving false testimony, false oath, oath breaking, false swearing, violation of an oath, wilful falsehood

perk NOUN = **bonus**, benefit, extra, plus (*informal*), dividend, icing on the cake, fringe benefit, perquisite (*formal*)

perk up VERB *She perked up and began to laugh.* = **cheer up**, recover, rally, revive, look up, brighten, take heart, recuperate, buck up (*informal*) • **perk something** or **someone up** *A brisk stroll will perk you up.* = **liven someone up**, revive someone, cheer someone up, pep someone up

perky ADJECTIVE = **lively**, spirited, bright, sunny, cheerful, animated, upbeat (*informal*), buoyant, bubbly, cheery, bouncy, genial, jaunty, chirpy (*informal*), sprightly, vivacious, in fine fettle, full of beans (*informal*), gay, bright-eyed and bushy-tailed (*informal*)

permanence NOUN = **continuity**, survival, stability, duration, endurance, immortality, durability, finality, perpetuity, constancy, continuance, dependability, permanency, fixity, indestructibility, fixedness, lastingness, perdurability (*rare*)

permanent ADJECTIVE **1** *Wear earplugs to avoid causing permanent damage.* = **lasting**, fixed, constant, enduring, persistent, eternal, abiding, perennial, durable, perpetual, everlasting, unchanging, immutable, indestructible, immovable, invariable, imperishable, unfading ■ OPPOSITE: temporary **2** *a permanent job* = **long-term**, established, secure, stable, steady, long-lasting ■ OPPOSITE: temporary

permanently ADVERB = **for ever**, constantly, continually, always, invariably, perennially, persistently, eternally, perpetually, steadfastly, indelibly, in perpetuity, enduringly, unwaveringly, immutably, lastingly, immovably, abidingly, unchangingly, unfadingly ■ OPPOSITE: temporarily

permeable ADJECTIVE = **penetrable**, porous, absorbent, spongy, absorptive, pervious

permeate VERB **1** *Bias against women permeates every level of the judicial system.* = **infiltrate**, fill, pass through, pervade, filter through, spread through, diffuse throughout **2** *The water will eventually permeate through the surrounding concrete.* = **pervade**, saturate, charge, fill, pass through, penetrate, infiltrate, imbue, filter through, spread through, impregnate, seep through, percolate, soak through, diffuse throughout

permissible ADJECTIVE = **permitted**, acceptable, legitimate, legal, all right, sanctioned, proper, authorized, lawful, allowable, kosher (*informal*), admissible, legit (*slang*), licit, O.K. or okay (*informal*) ■ OPPOSITE: forbidden

permission NOUN = **authorization**, sanction, licence, approval, leave, freedom, permit, go-ahead (*informal*), liberty, consent, allowance, tolerance, green light, assent, dispensation, carte blanche, blank cheque, sufferance ■ OPPOSITE: prohibition

permissive ADJECTIVE = **tolerant**, liberal, open-minded, indulgent, easy-going, free, lax, lenient, forbearing, acquiescent, latitudinarian, easy-oasy (*slang*) ■ OPPOSITE: strict

permit VERB **1** *I was permitted to bring my camera into the concert.* = **allow**, admit, grant, sanction, let, suffer, agree to, entitle, endure, license, endorse, warrant, tolerate, authorize, empower, consent to, give the green light to, give leave or permission ■ OPPOSITE: forbid **2** *This method of cooking permits the heat to penetrate evenly.* = **enable**, let, allow, cause ▶ NOUN *He has to apply for a permit before looking for a job.* = **licence**, pass, document, certificate, passport, visa, warrant, authorization ■ OPPOSITE: prohibition

permutation NOUN = **transformation**, change, shift, variation, modification, alteration, mutation, transmutation, transposition

pernicious ADJECTIVE = **wicked**, bad, damaging, dangerous, evil, offensive, fatal, deadly, destructive, harmful, toxic, poisonous, malicious, malign, malignant, detrimental, hurtful, malevolent, noxious, venomous, ruinous, baleful, deleterious (*formal*), injurious, noisome, baneful (*archaic*), pestilent, maleficent

perpendicular ADJECTIVE **1** *the perpendicular wall of sandstone* = **upright**, straight, vertical, plumb, on end **2** *The left wing dipped until it was perpendicular to the ground.* = **at right angles**, at 90 degrees

perpetrate VERB = **commit**, do, perform, carry out, effect, be responsible for, execute, inflict, bring about, enact, wreak

> USAGE *Perpetrate* and *perpetuate* are sometimes confused: *he must answer for the crimes he has perpetrated* (not *perpetuated*); *the book helped to perpetuate* (not *perpetrate*) *some of the myths surrounding his early life.*

P

perpetual ADJECTIVE **1** *the regions of perpetual night at the lunar poles* = **everlasting**, permanent, endless, eternal, lasting, enduring, abiding, perennial, infinite, immortal, never-ending, unending, unchanging, undying, sempiternal (*literary*) ■ OPPOSITE: temporary **2** *her perpetual complaints* = **continual**, repeated, constant, endless, continuous, persistent, perennial, recurrent, never-ending, uninterrupted, interminable, incessant, ceaseless, unremitting, unfailing, unceasing ■ OPPOSITE: brief

perpetuate VERB = **maintain**, preserve, sustain, keep up, keep going, continue, keep alive, immortalize, eternalize ■ OPPOSITE: end

perplex VERB = **puzzle**, confuse, stump, baffle, bewilder, muddle, confound, beset, mystify, faze, befuddle, flummox, bemuse, dumbfound, nonplus, mix you up

perplexing ADJECTIVE = **puzzling**, complex, confusing, complicated, involved, hard, taxing, difficult, strange, weird, mysterious, baffling, bewildering, intricate, enigmatic, mystifying, inexplicable, thorny, paradoxical, unaccountable, knotty, labyrinthine

perplexity NOUN **1** *There was utter perplexity in both their expressions.* = **puzzlement**, confusion, bewilderment, incomprehension, bafflement, mystification, stupefaction **2** (*usually plural*) *the perplexities of quantum mechanics* = **complexity**, difficulty, mystery, involvement, puzzle, paradox, obscurity, enigma, intricacy, inextricability

per se ADVERB = **in itself**, essentially, as such, in essence, by itself, of itself, by definition, intrinsically, by its very nature

persecute VERB **1** *They have been persecuted for their beliefs.* = **victimize**, hunt, injure, pursue, torture, hound, torment, martyr, oppress, pick on, molest, ill-treat, maltreat ■ OPPOSITE: mollycoddle **2** *He described his first wife as constantly persecuting him.* = **harass**, bother, annoy, bait, tease, worry, hassle (*informal*), badger, pester, vex, be on your back (*slang*) ■ OPPOSITE: leave alone

perseverance NOUN = **persistence**, resolution, determination, dedication, stamina, endurance, tenacity, diligence, constancy, steadfastness, doggedness, purposefulness, pertinacity, indefatigability, sedulity

persevere VERB = **keep going**, continue, go on, carry on, endure, hold on (*informal*), hang on, persist, stand firm, plug away (*informal*), hold fast, remain firm, stay the course, keep your hand in, pursue your goal, be determined or resolved, keep on or at, stick at or to ■ OPPOSITE: give up

persist VERB **1** *Consult your doctor if the symptoms persist.* = **continue**, last, remain, carry on, endure, keep up, linger, abide **2** *He urged them to persist with their efforts to bring about peace.* = **persevere**, continue, go on, carry on, hold on (*informal*), keep on, keep going, press on, not give up, stand firm, soldier on (*informal*), stay the course, plough on, be resolute, stick to your guns (*informal*), show determination, crack on (*informal*)

persistence NOUN = **determination**, resolution, pluck, stamina, grit, endurance, tenacity, diligence, perseverance, constancy, steadfastness, doggedness, pertinacity, indefatigability, tirelessness

persistent ADJECTIVE **1** *flooding caused by persistent rain* = **continuous**, constant, relentless, lasting, repeated, endless, perpetual, continual, never-ending, interminable, unrelenting, incessant, unremitting ■ OPPOSITE: occasional **2** *He phoned again this morning – he's very persistent.* = **determined**, dogged, fixed, steady, enduring, stubborn, persevering, resolute, tireless, tenacious, steadfast, obstinate, indefatigable, immovable, assiduous, obdurate, stiff-necked, unflagging, pertinacious ■ OPPOSITE: irresolute

person NOUN *Sam's the only person who can do the job.* = **individual**, being, body (*informal*), human, soul, creature, human being, mortal, living soul, man or woman • **in person 1** *She collected the award in person.* = **personally**, yourself **2** *It was the first time she had seen him in person.* = **in the flesh**, actually, physically, bodily

persona NOUN = **personality**, part, face, front (*informal*), role, character, mask, façade, public face, assumed role

personable ADJECTIVE = **pleasant**, pleasing, nice, attractive, charming, handsome, good-looking, winning, agreeable, amiable, affable, presentable, likable or likeable ■ OPPOSITE: unpleasant

personage NOUN = **personality**, celebrity, big name, somebody, worthy, notable, public figure, dignitary, luminary, celeb (*informal*), big shot (*informal*), megastar (*informal*), big noise (*informal*), well-known person, V.I.P.

personal ADJECTIVE **1** *That's my personal property!* = **own**, special, private, individual, particular, peculiar, privy (*archaic*) **2** *I'll give it my personal attention.* = **individual**, special, particular, exclusive **3** *prying into his* *personal life* = **private**, intimate, confidential **4** *a series of personal comments about my family* = **offensive**, critical, slighting, nasty, insulting, rude, belittling, disparaging, derogatory, disrespectful, pejorative **5** *personal hygiene* = **physical**, intimate, bodily, corporal, corporeal

personality NOUN **1** *She has such a kind, friendly personality.* = **nature**, character, make-up, identity, temper, traits, temperament, psyche, disposition, individuality **2** *a woman of great personality and charm* = **character**, charm, attraction, charisma, attractiveness, dynamism, magnetism, pleasantness, likableness *or* likeableness **3** *a radio and television personality* = **celebrity**, star, big name, notable, household name, famous name, celeb (*informal*), personage, megastar (*informal*), well-known face, well-known person

personalized ADJECTIVE = **customized**, special, private, individual, distinctive, tailor-made, individualized, monogrammed

personally ADVERB **1** *Personally, I think it's a waste of time.* = **in your opinion**, for yourself, in your book, for your part, from your own viewpoint, in your own view **2** *The minister will answer the allegations personally.* = **by yourself**, alone, independently, solely, on your own, in person, in the flesh **3** *This topic interests me personally.* = **individually**, specially, subjectively, individualistically **4** *Personally he was quiet, modest and unobtrusive.* = **privately**, in private, off the record

personification NOUN = **embodiment**, image, representation, re-creation, portrayal, incarnation, likeness, semblance, epitome

personify VERB = **embody**, represent, express, mirror, exemplify, symbolize, typify, incarnate, image (*rare*), epitomize, body forth

personnel NOUN = **employees**, people, members, staff, workers, men and women, workforce, human resources, helpers, liveware

perspective NOUN **1** *The death of my mother gave me a new perspective on life.* = **outlook**, attitude, context, angle, overview, way of looking, frame of reference, broad view **2** *helping her to get her problems into perspective* = **objectivity**, proportion, relation, relativity, relative importance **3** *stretching away along the perspective of a tree-lined, wide avenue* = **view**, scene, prospect, outlook, panorama, vista

perspiration NOUN = **sweat**, moisture, wetness, exudation

perspire VERB = **sweat**, glow, swelter, drip with sweat, break out in a sweat, pour with sweat, secrete sweat, be damp *or* wet *or* soaked with sweat, exude sweat

persuade VERB **1** *My husband persuaded me to come.* = **talk (someone) into**, urge, advise, prompt, influence, counsel, win (someone) over, induce, sway, entice, coax, incite, prevail upon, inveigle, bring (someone) round (*informal*), twist (someone's) arm, argue (someone) into ■ OPPOSITE: dissuade **2** *the event which persuaded the United States to enter the war* = **cause**, prompt, lead, move, influence, motivate, induce, incline, dispose, impel, actuate **3** *Derek persuaded me of the feasibility of the idea.* = **convince**, satisfy, assure, prove to, convert to, cause to believe

persuasion NOUN **1** *It took all her powers of persuasion to induce them to stay.* = **urging**, influencing, conversion, inducement, exhortation (*formal*), wheedling, enticement, cajolery, blandishment, soft power, inveiglement **2** *people who are of a different political persuasion* = **belief**, views, opinion, party, school, side, camp, faith, conviction, faction, cult, sect, creed, denomination, tenet, school of thought, credo, firm belief, certitude, fixed opinion

persuasive ADJECTIVE = **convincing**, telling, effective, winning, moving, sound, touching, impressive, compelling, influential, valid, inducing, logical, credible, plausible, forceful, eloquent, weighty, impelling, cogent ■ OPPOSITE: unconvincing

pertain to VERB = **relate to**, concern, refer to, regard, be part of, belong to, apply to, bear on, befit, be relevant to, be appropriate to, appertain to

pertinent ADJECTIVE = **relevant**, fitting, fit, material, appropriate, pat, suitable, proper, to the point, apt, applicable, apposite, apropos, admissible, germane, to the purpose, ad rem (*Latin*)
■ OPPOSITE: irrelevant

perturb VERB = **disturb**, worry, trouble, upset, alarm, bother, unsettle, agitate, ruffle, unnerve, disconcert, disquiet, vex, fluster, faze, discountenance, discompose

perturbed ADJECTIVE = **disturbed**, worried, troubled, shaken, upset, alarmed, nervous, anxious, uncomfortable, uneasy, fearful, restless, flurried, agitated, disconcerted, disquieted, flustered, ill at ease, antsy (*informal*) ■ OPPOSITE: relaxed

peruse VERB = **read**, study, scan, check, examine, inspect, browse, look through, eyeball (*slang*), work over, scrutinize, run your eye over, surf (*Computing*)

pervade VERB = **spread through**, fill, affect, penetrate, infuse, permeate, imbue, suffuse, percolate, extend through, diffuse through, overspread

pervasive ADJECTIVE = **widespread**, general, common, extensive, universal, prevalent, ubiquitous, rife, pervading, permeating, inescapable, omnipresent

perverse ADJECTIVE 1 *You're just being perverse.* = **stubborn**, contrary, unreasonable, dogged, contradictory, troublesome, rebellious, wayward, delinquent, intractable, wilful, unyielding, obstinate, intransigent, headstrong, unmanageable, cussed (*informal*), obdurate, stiff-necked, disobedient, wrong-headed, refractory, pig-headed, miscreant, mulish, cross-grained, contumacious ■ OPPOSITE: cooperative 2 *He seems to take a perverse pleasure in being disagreeable.* = **ill-natured**, cross, surly, petulant, crabbed, fractious, spiteful, churlish, ill-tempered, stroppy (*Brit. slang*), cantankerous, peevish, shrewish ■ OPPOSITE: good-natured 3 *perverse sexual practices* = **abnormal**, incorrect, unhealthy, improper, deviant, depraved

perversion NOUN 1 *a tale of dynastic backstabbing spiced up with various kinds of perversion* = **deviation**, vice, abnormality, aberration, kink (*informal*), wickedness, depravity, immorality, debauchery, unnaturalness, kinkiness (*slang*), vitiation 2 *a monstrous perversion of justice* = **distortion**, twisting, corruption, misuse, misrepresentation, misinterpretation, falsification

perversity NOUN = **contrariness**, intransigence, obduracy, waywardness, contradictoriness, wrong-headedness, refractoriness, contumacy, contradictiveness, frowardness (*archaic*)

pervert VERB 1 *attempting to pervert the course of justice* = **distort**, abuse, twist, misuse, warp, misinterpret, misrepresent, falsify, misconstrue 2 *He was accused of perverting the nation's youth.* = **corrupt**, degrade, subvert, deprave, debase (*formal*), desecrate, debauch, lead astray ▶ NOUN *You're nothing but a sick pervert.* = **deviant**, degenerate, sicko (*informal*), sleazeball (*slang*), debauchee, weirdo or weirdie (*informal*)

perverted ADJECTIVE = **unnatural**, sick, corrupt, distorted, abnormal, evil, twisted, impaired, warped, misguided, unhealthy, immoral, deviant, wicked, kinky (*slang*), depraved, debased, debauched, aberrant, vitiated, pervy (*slang*), sicko (*slang*)

pessimism NOUN = **gloominess**, depression, despair, gloom, cynicism, melancholy, hopelessness, despondency, dejection, glumness

pessimist NOUN = **defeatist**, cynic, melancholic, worrier, killjoy, prophet of doom, misanthrope, wet blanket (*informal*), gloom merchant (*informal*), doomster

pessimistic ADJECTIVE = **gloomy**, dark, despairing, bleak, resigned, sad, depressed, cynical, hopeless, melancholy, glum, dejected, foreboding, despondent, morose, fatalistic, distrustful, downhearted, misanthropic ■ OPPOSITE: optimistic

pest NOUN 1 *all kinds of pests like flies and mosquitoes; bacterial, fungal, and viral pests of the plants themselves* = **infection**, bug, insect, plague, epidemic, blight, scourge, bane, pestilence, gogga (*S. African informal*) 2 *My neighbour's a real pest.* = **nuisance**, bore, trial, pain (*informal*), drag (*informal*), bother, irritation, gall, annoyance, bane, pain in the neck (*informal*), vexation, thorn in your flesh

pester VERB = **annoy**, worry, bother, disturb, bug (*informal*), plague, torment, get at, harass, nag, hassle (*informal*), harry, aggravate (*informal*), fret, badger, pick on, irk, bedevil, chivvy (*Brit.*), get on your nerves (*informal*), bend someone's ear (*informal*), drive you up the wall (*slang*), be on your back (*slang*), get in your hair (*informal*)

pestilence NOUN = **plague**, epidemic, visitation, pandemic

pet ADJECTIVE 1 *The proceeds will be split between her pet charities.* = **favourite**, chosen, special, personal, particular, prized, preferred, favoured, dearest, cherished, fave (*informal*), dear to your heart 2 *One in four households owns a pet dog.* = **tame**, trained, domestic, house, domesticated, house-trained (*Brit.*), house-broken ▶ NOUN *They taunted her about being the teacher's pet.* = **favourite**, treasure, darling, jewel, idol, fave (*informal*), apple of your eye, blue-eyed boy or girl (*Brit. informal*) ▶ VERB 1 *A woman sat petting a cocker spaniel.* = **fondle**, pat, stroke, caress 2 *She had petted her son all his life.* = **pamper**, spoil, indulge, cosset, baby, dote on, coddle, mollycoddle, wrap in cotton wool 3 *They were kissing and petting on the couch.* = **cuddle**, kiss, snog (*Brit. slang*), smooch (*informal*), neck (*informal*), canoodle (*slang*)

peter out VERB = **die out**, stop, fail, run out, fade, dwindle, evaporate, wane, give out, ebb, come to nothing, run dry, taper off

petite ADJECTIVE = **small**, little, slight, delicate, dainty, dinky (*Brit. informal*), elfin

petition NOUN **1** *We presented the government with a petition signed by 4,500 people.* = **appeal**, round robin, list of signatures **2** *a humble petition to Saint Anthony* = **entreaty**, appeal, address, suit, application, request, prayer, plea, invocation, solicitation, supplication (*formal*) ▶ VERB *She is petitioning to regain custody of the child.* = **appeal**, press, plead, call (upon), ask, urge, sue, pray, beg, crave (*informal*), solicit, beseech, entreat, adjure, supplicate

petrified ADJECTIVE **1** *He was petrified at the thought of having to make a speech.* = **terrified**, horrified, shocked, frozen, stunned, appalled, numb, dazed, speechless, aghast, dumbfounded, stupefied, scared stiff, terror-stricken **2** *a block of petrified wood* = **fossilized**, ossified, rocklike

petrify VERB **1** *His story petrified me.* = **terrify**, horrify, amaze, astonish, stun, appal, paralyse, astound, confound, transfix, stupefy, immobilize, dumbfound **2** *Bird and bat guano petrifies into a mineral called taranakite.* = **fossilize**, set, harden, solidify, ossify, turn to stone, calcify

petty ADJECTIVE **1** *Rows would start over petty things.* = **trivial**, inferior, insignificant, little, small, slight, trifling, negligible, unimportant, paltry, measly (*informal*), contemptible, piddling (*informal*), inconsiderable, inessential, nickel-and-dime (*U.S. slang*) ■ **OPPOSITE:** important **2** *I think that attitude is a bit petty.* = **small-minded**, mean, cheap (*informal*), grudging, shabby, spiteful, stingy, ungenerous, mean-minded ■ **OPPOSITE:** broad-minded **3** *Wilson was not a man who dealt with petty officials.* = **minor**, lower, junior, secondary, lesser, subordinate, inferior

petulance NOUN = **sulkiness**, bad temper, irritability, spleen, pique, sullenness, ill-humour, peevishness, querulousness, crabbiness, waspishness, pettishness

petulant ADJECTIVE = **sulky**, cross, moody, sour, crabbed, impatient, pouting, perverse, irritable, crusty, sullen, bad-tempered, ratty (*Brit. & N.Z. informal*), fretful, waspish, querulous, peevish, ungracious, cavilling, huffy, fault-finding, snappish, ill-humoured, captious ■ **OPPOSITE:** good-natured

phantom NOUN = **spectre**, ghost, spirit, shade (*literary*), spook (*informal*), apparition, wraith, revenant, phantasm

phase NOUN *The crisis is entering a crucial phase.* = **stage**, time, state, point, position, step, development, condition, period, chapter, aspect, juncture • **phase something in** *Reforms will be phased in over the next three years.* = **introduce**, incorporate, ease in, start • **phase something out** *The present system of military conscription should be phased out.* = **eliminate**, close, pull, remove, replace, withdraw, pull out, axe (*informal*), wind up, run down, terminate, wind down, ease off, taper off, deactivate, dispose of gradually

phenomenal ADJECTIVE = **extraordinary**, outstanding, remarkable, fantastic (*informal*), unique, unusual, marvellous, exceptional, notable, sensational (*informal*), uncommon, singular, miraculous, stellar (*informal*), prodigious, unparalleled, wondrous (*archaic*, *literary*) ■ **OPPOSITE:** unremarkable

phenomenon NOUN **1** *scientific explanations of this natural phenomenon* = **occurrence**, happening, fact, event, incident, circumstance, episode **2** *The Loch Ness monster is not the only bizarre phenomenon that bookmakers take bets on.* = **wonder**, sensation, spectacle, sight, exception, miracle, marvel, prodigy, rarity, nonpareil, black swan

> **USAGE** Although *phenomena* is often treated as a singular, this is not grammatically correct. *Phenomenon* is the singular form of this word, and *phenomena* the plural; so *several new phenomena were recorded in his notes* is correct, but *that is an interesting phenomena* is not.

philanthropic ADJECTIVE = **humanitarian**, generous, charitable, benevolent, kind, humane, gracious, altruistic, public-spirited, beneficent, kind-hearted, munificent, almsgiving, benignant ■ **OPPOSITE:** selfish

philanthropist NOUN = **humanitarian**, patron, benefactor, giver, donor, contributor, altruist, almsgiver

philanthropy NOUN = **humanitarianism**, charity, generosity, patronage, bounty, altruism, benevolence, munificence, beneficence, liberality, public-spiritedness, benignity, almsgiving, brotherly love, charitableness, kind-heartedness, generousness, open-handedness, largesse *or* largess

philistine NOUN *The man's a total philistine when it comes to the arts.* = **boor**, barbarian, yahoo, lout, bourgeois, hoon (*Austral. & N.Z.*), ignoramus, lowbrow, vulgarian, cougan (*Austral. slang*), scozza (*Austral. slang*), bogan (*Austral. slang*) ▶ ADJECTIVE *the country's philistine, consumerist mentality* = **uncultured**, ignorant, crass, tasteless, bourgeois, uneducated, boorish, unrefined, uncultivated, anti-intellectual, lowbrow, inartistic

philosopher NOUN = **thinker**, theorist, sage, wise man, logician, metaphysician, dialectician, seeker after truth

philosophical *or* **philosophic** ADJECTIVE 1 *a philosophical discourse* = **theoretical**, abstract, learned, wise, rational, logical, thoughtful, erudite, sagacious ■ **OPPOSITE:** practical 2 *He was remarkably philosophical about his failure.* = **stoical**, calm, composed, patient, cool, collected, resigned, serene, tranquil, sedate, impassive, unruffled, imperturbable ■ **OPPOSITE:** emotional

philosophy NOUN 1 *He studied philosophy and psychology at Cambridge.* = **thought**, reason, knowledge, thinking, reasoning, wisdom, logic, metaphysics 2 *his philosophy of non-violence* = **outlook**, values, principles, convictions, thinking, beliefs, doctrine, ideology, viewpoint, tenets, world view, basic idea, attitude to life, Weltanschauung (*German*)

phlegm NOUN = **mucus**, catarrh, sputum, mucous secretion

phlegmatic ADJECTIVE = **unemotional**, indifferent, cold, heavy, dull, sluggish, matter-of-fact, placid, stoical, lethargic, bovine, apathetic, frigid, lymphatic, listless, impassive, stolid, unfeeling, undemonstrative ■ **OPPOSITE:** emotional

phobia NOUN = **fear**, horror, terror, thing about (*informal*), obsession, dislike, dread, hatred, loathing, distaste, revulsion, aversion to, repulsion, irrational fear, detestation, overwhelming anxiety about ■ **OPPOSITE:** liking

phone NOUN 1 *I spoke to her on the phone only yesterday.* = **telephone**, blower (*informal*), dog and bone (*slang*), smartphone, mobile (phone), landline, iPhone®, cellphone or cellular phone (*U.S. & Canad.*), camera phone, handset, Blackberry, picture phone 2 *If you need anything, give me a phone.* = **call**, ring (*informal, chiefly Brit.*), bell (*Brit. slang*), buzz (*informal*), tinkle (*Brit. informal*) ▶ VERB *I got more and more angry as I waited for her to phone.* = **call**, telephone, ring (up) (*informal, chiefly Brit.*), give someone a call, give someone a ring (*informal, chiefly Brit.*), make a call, give someone a buzz (*informal*), give someone a bell (*Brit. slang*), conference call, Skype®, video call, get on the blower (*informal*), give someone a tinkle (*Brit. informal*), video phone

phoney ADJECTIVE 1 *He used a phoney accent.* = **fake**, affected, assumed, trick, put-on, false, forged, imitation, sham, pseudo (*informal*), counterfeit, feigned, spurious ■ **OPPOSITE:** genuine 2 *phoney 'experts'* = **bogus**, false, fake, pseudo (*informal*), ersatz ▶ NOUN 1 *He was a liar, a cheat, and a phoney.* = **faker**, fraud (*informal*), fake, pretender, humbug (*old-fashioned*), impostor, pseud (*informal*) 2 *This passport is a phoney.* = **fake**, sham, forgery, counterfeit

photograph NOUN *He wants to take some photographs of the house.* = **picture**, photo (*informal*), shot, image, print, slide, snap (*informal*), snapshot, selfie (*informal*), transparency, likeness, JPEG, thumbnail, avatar ▶ VERB *I hate being photographed.* = **take a picture of**, record, film, shoot, snap (*informal*), take (someone's) picture, capture on film, get a shot of

photographic ADJECTIVE 1 *The bank is able to use photographic evidence of who used the machine.* = **pictorial**, visual, graphic, cinematic, filmic 2 *a photographic memory* = **accurate**, minute, detailed, exact, precise, faithful, retentive

phrase NOUN *the Latin phrase, 'mens sana in corpore sano'* = **expression**, saying, remark, motto, construction, tag, quotation, maxim, idiom, utterance, adage, dictum, way of speaking, group of words, locution ▶ VERB *The speech was carefully phrased.* = **express**, say, word, put, term, present, voice, frame, communicate, convey, utter, couch, formulate, put into words

physical ADJECTIVE 1 *the physical problems caused by the illness* = **corporal**, fleshly, bodily, carnal, somatic, corporeal 2 *They were still aware of the physical world around them.* = **earthly**, fleshly, mortal, incarnate, unspiritual 3 *There is no physical evidence to support the story.* = **material**, real, substantial (*formal*), natural, solid, visible, sensible, tangible, palpable

physician NOUN = **doctor**, specialist, doc (*informal*), healer, medic (*informal*), general practitioner, medical practitioner, medico (*informal*), doctor of medicine, sawbones (*slang*), G.P., M.D.

physique NOUN = **build**, form, body, figure, shape, structure, make-up, frame, constitution

pick VERB 1 *He had picked ten people to interview for the jobs.* = **select**, choose, identify, elect, nominate, sort out, specify, opt for, single out, mark out, plump for, hand-pick, decide upon, cherry-pick, fix upon, settle on *or* upon, sift out, flag up ■ **OPPOSITE:** reject 2 *He helped his mother pick fruit.* = **gather**, cut, pull, collect, take in, harvest, pluck, garner, cull **3** *He picked a fight with a waiter and landed in jail.* = **provoke**, start, cause, stir up, incite, instigate, foment **4** *He picked the lock, and rifled through the papers in each drawer.* = **open**, force, crack (*informal*), break into, break open, prise open, jemmy (*informal*) ▶ NOUN **1** *We had the pick of winter coats from the shop.* = **choice**, decision, choosing, option, selection, preference **2** *These boys are the pick of the under-15 cricketers in the country.* = **best**, prime, finest, tops (*slang*), choicest, flower, prize, elect, pride, elite, cream, jewel in the crown, the crème de la crème • **pick at something** *She picked at her breakfast.* = **nibble (at)**, peck at, have no appetite for, play or toy with, push round the plate, eat listlessly • **pick on someone 1** *Bullies pick on smaller children.* = **torment**, bully, bait, tease, get at (*informal*), badger, persecute, hector, goad, victimize, have it in for (*informal*), tyrannize, have a down on (*informal*) **2** *He needed to confess to someone – he just happened to pick on me.* = **choose**, select, prefer, elect, single out, fix on, settle upon • **pick someone up** *The police picked him up within the hour.* = **arrest**, nick (*slang, chiefly Brit.*), bust (*informal*), do (*slang*), lift (*slang*), run in (*slang*), nail (*informal*), collar (*informal*), pinch (*informal*), pull in (*Brit. slang*), nab (*informal*), apprehend, take someone into custody, feel your collar (*slang*) • **pick something** or **someone out 1** *He wasn't difficult to pick out when the bus drew in.* = **identify**, notice, recognize, distinguish, perceive, discriminate, make someone or something out, tell someone or something apart, single someone or something out **2** *Pick out a painting you think she'd like.* = **select**, choose, decide on, take, sort out, opt for, cull, plump for, hand-pick • **pick something up 1** *Where did you pick up your English?* = **learn**, master, acquire, get the hang of (*informal*), become proficient in **2** *Auctions can be great places to pick up a bargain.* = **obtain**, get, find, buy, score (*slang*), discover, purchase, acquire, locate, come across, come by, unearth, garner, stumble across, chance upon, happen upon • **pick something** or **someone up 1** *He picked his cap up from the floor.* = **lift**, raise, gather, take up, grasp, uplift, hoist **2** *We drove to the airport to pick her up.; He went to Miami where he had arranged to pick up the money.* = **collect**, get, call for, go for, go to get, fetch, uplift (*Scot.*), go and get, give someone a lift or a ride • **pick up 1** *Industrial production is beginning to pick up.* = **improve**, recover, rally, get better, bounce back, make progress, make a comeback (*informal*), perk up, turn the corner, gain ground, take a turn for the better, be on the road to recovery **2** *A good dose of tonic will help you to pick up.* = **recover**, improve, rally, get better, mend, perk up, turn the corner, be on the mend, take a turn for the better • **pick your way** *I picked my way among the rubble.* = **tread carefully**, work through, move cautiously, walk tentatively, find or make your way

picket VERB *The miners went on strike and picketed the power station.* = **blockade**, boycott, demonstrate outside ▶ NOUN **1** *Demonstrators have set up a twenty-four-hour picket.* = **demonstration**, blockade **2** *Ten hotels were damaged by pickets in the weekend strike.* = **protester**, demonstrator, picketer, flying picket **3** *Troops are still manning pickets and patrolling the area.* = **lookout**, watch, guard, patrol, scout, spotter, sentry, sentinel, vedette (*Military*) **4** *The area was fenced in with pickets to keep out the animals.* = **stake**, post, pale, paling, peg, upright, palisade, stanchion

pickings PLURAL NOUN = **profits**, returns, rewards, earnings, yield, proceeds, spoils, loot, plunder, gravy (*slang*), booty, ill-gotten gains

pickle VERB *Herrings can be salted, smoked and pickled.* = **preserve**, marinade, keep, cure, steep ▶ NOUN **1** *jars of pickle* = **chutney**, relish, piccalilli **2** *Connie had got herself into a real pickle this time.* = **predicament**, spot (*informal*), fix (*informal*), difficulty, bind (*informal*), jam (*informal*), dilemma, scrape (*informal*), hot water (*informal*), uphill! (*S. African*), quandary, tight spot

pick-me-up NOUN = **tonic**, drink, pick-up (*slang*), bracer (*informal*), refreshment, stimulant, shot in the arm (*informal*), restorative

pick-up NOUN = **improvement**, recovery, rise, gain, rally, strengthening, revival, upturn, change for the better, upswing

picky ADJECTIVE = **fussy**, particular, critical, carping, fastidious, dainty, choosy (*informal*), finicky, cavilling, pernickety (*informal*), fault-finding, captious, nit-picky (*informal*)

picnic NOUN **1** *We're going on a picnic tomorrow.* = **excursion**, fête champêtre (*French*), barbecue, barbie (*informal*), cookout (*U.S. & Canad.*), alfresco meal, déjeuner sur l'herbe (*French*), clambake (*U.S. & Canad.*), outdoor meal, outing **2** (*used in negative constructions*) *Emigrating is no picnic.* = **walkover** (*informal*), breeze (*informal*),

p

pushover (*slang*), snap (*informal*), child's play (*informal*), piece of cake (*Brit. informal*), cinch (*slang*), cakewalk (*informal*), duck soup (*U.S. slang*)

pictorial ADJECTIVE = **graphic**, striking, illustrated, vivid, picturesque, expressive, scenic, representational

picture NOUN **1** *drawing a small picture with coloured chalks* = **representation**, drawing, painting, portrait, image, print, illustration, sketch, portrayal, engraving, likeness, effigy, delineation, similitude, avatar **2** *I saw his picture in the paper.* = **photograph**, photo, still, shot, selfie (*informal*), image, print, frame, slide, snap, exposure, portrait, snapshot, transparency, enlargement, JPEG, thumbnail **3** *a director of epic pictures* = **film**, movie (*U.S. informal*), flick (*slang*), feature film, motion picture **4** *I'm trying to get a picture of what kind of person you are.* = **idea**, vision, concept, impression, notion, visualization, mental picture, mental image **5** *I want to give you a clear picture of what we are trying to do.* = **description**, impression, explanation, report, account, image, sketch, depiction, re-creation **6** *Six years after the operation, he remains a picture of health.* = **personification**, model, embodiment, soul, essence, archetype, epitome, perfect example, exemplar, quintessence, living example, avatar ▶ VERB **1** *She pictured herself working with animals.* = **imagine**, see, envision, visualize, conceive of, fantasize about, conjure up an image of, see in the mind's eye **2** *The goddess Demeter is pictured holding an ear of wheat.* = **represent**, show, describe, draw, paint, illustrate, portray, sketch, render, depict, delineate **3** *Betty is pictured here with her award.* = **show**, photograph, capture on film ■ **RELATED WORD:** *adjective* pictorial

picturesque ADJECTIVE **1** *the Algarve's most picturesque village* = **interesting**, pretty, beautiful, attractive, charming, scenic, quaint ■ **OPPOSITE:** unattractive **2** *Every inn had a quaint and picturesque name.* = **vivid**, striking, graphic, colourful, memorable ■ **OPPOSITE:** dull

piddling ADJECTIVE = **trivial**, little, petty, worthless, insignificant, pants (*informal*), useless, fiddling, trifling, unimportant, paltry, Mickey Mouse (*slang*), puny, derisory, measly (*informal*), crappy (*slang*), toytown (*slang*), piffling, poxy (*slang*), nickel-and-dime (*U.S. slang*) ■ **OPPOSITE:** significant

piece NOUN **1** *a piece of wood* = **bit**, section, slice, part, share, division, block, length,

quantity, scrap, segment, portion, fragment, fraction, chunk, wedge, shred, slab, mouthful, morsel, wodge (*Brit. informal*) **2** *The equipment was taken down the shaft in pieces.* = **component**, part, section, bit, unit, segment, constituent, module **3** *a highly complex piece of legislation* = **instance**, case, example, sample, specimen, occurrence **4** *There was a piece about him on television.* = **item**, report, story, bit (*informal*), study, production, review, article **5** *an orchestral piece* = **composition**, work, production, opus **6** *The cabinets display a wide variety of porcelain pieces.* = **work of art**, work, creation **7** *They got a small piece of the net profits.* = **share**, cut (*informal*), slice, percentage, quantity, portion, quota, fraction, allotment, subdivision • **go** or **fall to pieces** *I went to pieces when my parents died.* = **break down**, fall apart, disintegrate, lose control, crumple, crack up (*informal*), have a breakdown, lose your head • **of a piece (with)** *These essays are of a piece with his earlier work.* = **like**, the same (as), similar (to), consistent (with), identical (to), analogous (to), of the same kind (as)

piecemeal ADJECTIVE *piecemeal changes to the constitution* = **unsystematic**, interrupted, partial, patchy, intermittent, spotty, fragmentary ▶ ADVERB *It was built piecemeal over some 130 years.* = **bit by bit**, slowly, gradually, partially, intermittently, at intervals, little by little, fitfully, by degrees, by fits and starts

pied ADJECTIVE = **variegated**, spotted, streaked, irregular, flecked, motley, mottled, dappled, multicoloured, piebald, parti-coloured, varicoloured

pier NOUN **1** *The lifeboats were moored at the pier.* = **jetty**, wharf, quay, promenade, landing place **2** *the cross-beams bracing the piers of the jetty* = **pillar**, support, post, column, pile, piling, upright, buttress

pierce VERB **1** *Pierce the skin of the potato with a fork.* = **penetrate**, stab, spike, enter, bore, probe, drill, run through, lance, puncture, prick, transfix, stick into, perforate, impale **2** *Her words pierced Lydia's heart like an arrow.* = **hurt**, cut, wound, strike, touch, affect, pain, move, excite, stir, thrill, sting, rouse, cut to the quick

piercing ADJECTIVE **1** *(of a sound) a piercing whistle* = **penetrating**, sharp, loud, shattering, shrill, high-pitched, ear-splitting ■ **OPPOSITE:** low **2** *He fixes you with a piercing stare.* = **perceptive**, searching, aware, bright (*informal*), sharp, keen, alert, probing, penetrating, shrewd,

perspicacious (*formal*), quick-witted
■ **OPPOSITE:** unperceptive **3** *I felt a piercing pain in my abdomen.* = **sharp**, shooting, powerful, acute, severe, intense, painful, stabbing, fierce, racking, exquisite, excruciating, agonizing **4** (*of weather*) *a piercing wind* = **cold**, biting, keen, freezing, bitter, raw, arctic (*informal*), nipping, numbing, frosty, wintry, nippy

piety NOUN = **holiness**, duty, faith, religion, grace, devotion, reverence, sanctity, veneration, godliness, devoutness, dutifulness, piousness

pig NOUN **1** *He keeps poultry, pigs and goats.* = **hog** (*U.S.*), sow, boar, piggy, swine, grunter, piglet, porker, shoat **2** *He's just a greedy pig.* = **slob**, hog (*informal*), guzzler (*slang*), glutton, gannet (*informal*), sloven, greedy guts (*slang*) **3** *The whole incident just confirms what a pig he has become.* = **brute**, monster, scoundrel (*old-fashioned*), animal, beast, rogue, swine, rotter (*old-fashioned*), boor ■ **RELATED WORDS:** *adjective* porcine; *name of male* boar; *name of female* sow; *name of young* piglet; *collective noun* litter; *name of home* sty

pigeon NOUN = **squab**, bird, dove, culver (*archaic*) ■ **RELATED WORDS:** *name of young* squab; *collective nouns* flock, flight

pigment NOUN = **colour**, colouring, paint, stain, dye, tint, tincture, colouring matter, colorant, dyestuff

piker NOUN = **slacker**, shirker, skiver (*Brit. slang*), loafer, layabout, idler, passenger, do-nothing, dodger, good-for-nothing, bludger (*Austral. & N.Z. informal*), gold brick (*U.S. slang*), scrimshanker (*Brit. Military slang*)

pile¹ NOUN **1** *a pile of books* = **heap**, collection, mountain, mass, stack, rick, mound, accumulation, stockpile, hoard, assortment, assemblage **2** (*often plural*) *I've got piles of questions for you.* = **lot(s)**, mountain(s), load(s) (*informal*), oceans, wealth, great deal, stack(s), abundance, large quantity, oodles (*informal*), shedload (*Brit. informal*) **3** *a stately pile in the country* = **mansion**, building, residence, manor, country house, seat, big house, stately home, manor house **4** *He made a pile in various business ventures.* = **fortune**, bomb (*Brit. slang*), pot, packet (*slang*), mint, big money, wad (*U.S. & Canad. slang*), big bucks (*informal, chiefly U.S.*), megabucks (*U.S. & Canad. slang*), tidy sum (*informal*), pretty penny (*informal*), top whack (*informal*)
▶ VERB **1** *He was piling clothes into the case.* = **load**, stuff, pack, stack, charge, heap, cram, lade **2** *They all piled into the car.* = **crowd**, pack, charge, rush, climb, flood, stream, crush, squeeze, jam, flock, shove
• **pile something up 1** *Bulldozers piled up huge mounds of dirt.* = **gather (up)**, collect, assemble, stack (up), mass, heap (up), load up **2** *Their aim is to pile up the points and aim for a qualifying place.* = **collect**, accumulate, gather in, pull in, amass, hoard, stack up, store up, heap up • **pile up** *Her mail had piled up inside the front door.* = **accumulate**, collect, gather (up), build up, amass

pile² NOUN *wooden houses set on piles along the shore* = **foundation**, support, post, column, piling, beam, upright, pier, pillar

pile³ NOUN *the carpet's thick pile* = **nap**, fibre, down, hair, surface, fur, plush, shag, filament

piles PLURAL NOUN *More women than men suffer from piles.* = **haemorrhoids**

pile-up NOUN = **collision**, crash, accident, smash, smash-up (*informal*), multiple collision

pilfer VERB = **steal**, take, rob, lift (*informal*), nick (*slang, chiefly Brit.*), appropriate, rifle, pinch (*informal*), swipe (*slang*), embezzle, blag (*slang*), walk off with, snitch (*slang*), purloin, filch, snaffle (*Brit. informal*), thieve

pilgrim NOUN = **traveller**, crusader, wanderer, devotee, palmer, haji (*Islam*), wayfarer

pilgrimage NOUN = **journey**, tour, trip, mission, expedition, crusade, excursion, hajj (*Islam*)

pill NOUN *a sleeping pill* = **tablet**, capsule, pellet, bolus, pilule • **a bitter pill (to swallow)** *You're too old to be given a job. That's a bitter pill to swallow.* = **trial**, pain (*informal*), bore, drag (*informal*), pest, nuisance, pain in the neck (*informal*)

pillage VERB *Soldiers went on a rampage, pillaging stores and shooting.* = **plunder**, strip, sack, rob, raid, spoil (*archaic*), rifle, loot, ravage, ransack, despoil (*formal*), maraud, reive (*dialect*), depredate (*rare*), freeboot, spoliate ▶ NOUN *There were no signs of violence or pillage.* = **plundering**, sacking, robbery, plunder, sack, devastation, marauding, depredation, rapine, spoliation

pillar NOUN **1** *the pillars supporting the roof* = **support**, post, column, piling, prop, shaft, upright, pier, obelisk, stanchion, pilaster **2** *My father had been a pillar of the community.* = **supporter**, leader, rock, worthy, mainstay, leading light (*informal*), tower of strength, upholder, torchbearer

pillory VERB = **ridicule**, denounce, stigmatize, brand, lash, show someone up, expose someone to ridicule, cast a slur on, heap or pour scorn on, hold someone up to shame

p

pilot NOUN **1** *He spent seventeen years as an airline pilot.* = **airman**, captain, flyer (*old-fashioned*), aviator, aeronaut **2** *The pilot steered the ship safely inside the main channel.* = **helmsman**, guide, navigator, leader, director, conductor, coxswain, steersman or woman or person ▶ VERB **1** *the first person to pilot an aircraft across the Pacific* = **fly**, control, operate, be at the controls of **2** *Local fishermen piloted the boats.* = **navigate**, drive, manage, direct, guide, handle, conduct, steer **3** *We are piloting the strategy through Parliament.* = **direct**, lead, manage, conduct, steer ▶ MODIFIER *a pilot show for a new TV series* = **trial**, test, model, sample, experimental

pimple NOUN = **spot**, boil, swelling, pustule, zit (*slang*), papule (*Pathology*), plook (*Scot.*)

pin NOUN **1** *Use pins to keep the material in place as you work.* = **tack**, nail, needle, safety pin **2** *the steel pin holding his left leg together* = **peg**, rod, brace, bolt ▶ VERB **1** *They pinned a notice to the door.* = **fasten**, stick, attach, join, fix, secure, nail, clip, staple, tack, affix **2** *I pinned him against the wall.* = **hold fast**, hold down, press, restrain, constrain, immobilize, pinion • **pin someone down** *She couldn't pin him down to a decision.* = **force**, pressure, compel, put pressure on, pressurize, nail someone down, make someone commit themselves • **pin something down 1** *It has taken until now to pin down its exact location.* = **determine**, identify, locate, name, specify, designate, pinpoint, home in on **2** *The wreckage of the cockpit had pinned down my legs.* = **trap**, confine, constrain, bind, squash, tie down, nail down, immobilize

pinch VERB **1** *She pinched his arm as hard as she could.* = **nip**, press, squeeze, grasp, compress, tweak **2** *shoes which pinch our toes* = **hurt**, crush, squeeze, pain, confine, cramp, chafe **3** *pickpockets who pinched his wallet* = **steal**, rob, snatch, lift (*informal*), nick (*slang, chiefly Brit.*), swipe (*slang*), knock off (*slang*), blag (*slang*), pilfer, snitch (*slang*), purloin, filch, snaffle (*Brit. informal*) ▶ NOUN **1** *She gave him a little pinch.* = **nip**, squeeze, tweak **2** *a pinch of salt* = **dash**, bit, taste, mite, jot, speck, small quantity, smidgen (*informal*), soupçon (*French*) **3** *I'd trust her in a pinch.* = **emergency**, crisis, difficulty, plight, scrape (*informal*), strait, uphill (*S. African*), predicament, extremity, hardship

pinched ADJECTIVE = **thin**, starved, worn, drawn, gaunt, haggard, careworn, peaky ■ OPPOSITE: plump

pine VERB *While away from her children, she pined dreadfully.* = **waste**, decline, weaken,
sicken, sink, flag, fade, decay, dwindle, wither, wilt, languish, droop • **pine for something** or **someone 1** *He was pining for his children.* = **long**, ache, crave, yearn, sigh, carry a torch, eat your heart out over, suspire (*archaic, poetic*) **2** *pining for a mythical past* = **hanker after**, crave, covet, wish for, yearn for, thirst for, hunger for, lust after

pink ADJECTIVE *his pink face* = **rosy**, rose, salmon, flushed, reddish, roseate ▶ NOUN *the pink of perfection* = **best**, summit, height, peak, perfection, acme • **in the pink** *A glass of red wine a day will keep you in the pink.* = **in good health**, strong, blooming, very healthy, in fine fettle, in perfect health, in excellent shape, hale and hearty, fit as a fiddle

pinnacle NOUN **1** *This castle sits on a rocky pinnacle.* = **summit**, top, height, peak, eminence **2** *He had reached the pinnacle of his career.* = **height**, top, crown, crest, meridian, zenith, apex, apogee, acme, vertex

pinpoint VERB **1** *It was impossible to pinpoint the cause of death.* = **identify**, discover, spot, define, distinguish, put your finger on **2** *trying to pinpoint his precise location* = **locate**, find, spot, identify, home in on, zero in on, get a fix on

pint NOUN = **beer**, jar (*Brit. informal*), jug (*Brit. informal*), ale

pint-sized ADJECTIVE = **small**, little, tiny, wee, pocket-sized, miniature, diminutive, midget, teeny-weeny, teensy-weensy, pygmy or pigmy

pioneer NOUN **1** *one of the pioneers in embryology work* = **founder**, leader, developer, innovator, founding father, trailblazer **2** *abandoned settlements of early European pioneers* = **settler**, explorer, colonist, colonizer, frontiersman or frontierswoman ▶ VERB *the scientist who invented and pioneered DNA tests* = **develop**, create, launch, establish, start, prepare, discover, institute, invent, open up, initiate, originate, take the lead on, instigate, map out, show the way on, lay the groundwork on

pious ADJECTIVE **1** *He was brought up by pious female relatives.* = **religious**, godly, devoted, spiritual, holy, dedicated, righteous, devout, saintly, God-fearing, reverent ■ OPPOSITE: irreligious **2** *They were derided as pious, self-righteous bores.* = **self-righteous**, hypocritical, sanctimonious, goody-goody, unctuous, holier-than-thou, pietistic, religiose ■ OPPOSITE: humble

pipe NOUN **1** *The liquid is conveyed along a pipe.* = **tube**, drain, canal, pipeline, line, main, passage, cylinder, hose, conduit, duct, conveyor **2** *He gave up cigarettes and started smoking a pipe.* = **clay (pipe)**, briar, calabash (*rare*), meerschaum, hookah (*rare*) **3** *Pan is often pictured playing a reed pipe.* = **whistle**, horn, recorder, fife, flute, wind instrument, penny whistle ▶ VERB *The gas is piped through a coil surrounded by water.* = **convey**, channel, supply, conduct, bring in, transmit, siphon • **pipe down** *Just pipe down and I'll tell you what I want.* = **be quiet**, shut up (*informal*), hush, stop talking, quieten down, shush, button it (*slang*), belt up (*slang*), shut your mouth, hold your tongue, put a sock in it (*Brit. slang*), button your lip (*slang*) • **pipe up** *'That's right, mister,' another child piped up.* = **speak**, volunteer, speak up, have your say, raise your voice, make yourself heard, put your oar in

pipe dream NOUN = **daydream**, dream, notion, fantasy, delusion, vagary, reverie, chimera, castle in the air

pipeline NOUN *a natural-gas pipeline* = **tube**, passage, pipe, line, conduit, duct, conveyor • **in the pipeline** *A 2.9 per cent pay increase is already in the pipeline.* = **on the way**, expected, coming, close, near, being prepared, anticipated, forthcoming, under way, brewing, imminent, in preparation, in production, in process, in the offing

piquant ADJECTIVE **1** *a mixed salad with a piquant dressing* = **spicy**, biting, sharp, stinging, tart, savoury, pungent, tangy, highly-seasoned, peppery, zesty, with a kick (*informal*), acerb ■ **OPPOSITE:** mild **2** *There was a piquant novelty about her books.* = **interesting**, spirited, stimulating, lively, sparkling, provocative, salty, racy, scintillating ■ **OPPOSITE:** dull

pique NOUN *In a fit of pique, he threw down his bag.* = **resentment**, offence, irritation, annoyance, huff, displeasure, umbrage, hurt feelings, vexation, wounded pride ▶ VERB **1** *This phenomenon piqued Dr. Acharya's interest.* = **arouse**, excite, stir, spur, stimulate, provoke, rouse, goad, whet, kindle, galvanize **2** *She was piqued by his lack of enthusiasm.* = **displease**, wound, provoke, annoy, get (*informal*), sting, offend, irritate, put out, incense, gall, nettle, vex, affront, mortify, irk, rile, peeve (*informal*), nark (*Brit., Austral. & N.Z. slang*), put someone's nose out of joint (*informal*), miff (*informal*), hack off (*informal*)

piracy NOUN **1** *Seven of the fishermen have been formally charged with piracy.* = **robbery**, stealing, theft, hijacking, infringement, buccaneering, rapine, freebooting **2** *Video piracy is a criminal offence.* = **illegal copying**, bootlegging, plagiarism, copyright

infringement, illegal reproduction

pirate NOUN *In the nineteenth century, pirates roamed the seas.* = **buccaneer**, raider, rover, filibuster, marauder, corsair, sea wolf, freebooter, sea robber, sea rover ▶ VERB *pirating copies of music tapes* = **copy**, steal, reproduce, bootleg, lift (*informal*), appropriate, borrow, poach, crib (*informal*), plagiarize

pirouette NOUN *a ballerina famous for her pirouettes* = **spin** (*informal*), turn, whirl, pivot, twirl ▶ VERB *She pirouetted in front of the mirror.* = **spin**, turn, whirl, pivot, twirl

pit NOUN **1** *Up to ten pits and ten thousand jobs could be lost.* = **coal mine**, mine, shaft, colliery, mine shaft **2** *He lost his footing and began to slide into the pit.* = **hole**, gulf, depression, hollow, trench, crater, trough, cavity, abyss, chasm, excavation, pothole ▶ VERB *The plaster was pitted and the paint scuffed.* = **scar**, mark, hole, nick, notch, dent, gouge, indent, dint, pockmark • **pit something** or **someone against something** or **someone** *You will be pitted against people as good as you are.* = **set against**, oppose, match against, measure against, put in competition with, put in opposition to

pitch NOUN **1** *a cricket pitch* = **sports field**, ground, stadium, arena, park, field of play **2** *He raised his voice to a higher pitch.* = **tone**, sound, key, frequency, timbre, modulation **3** *Tensions have reached such a pitch in the area that the army have been called in.* = **level**, point, degree, summit, extent, height, intensity, high point **4** *He was impressed with her hard sales pitch.* = **talk**, line, patter, spiel (*informal*) ▶ VERB **1** *Simon pitched the empty bottle into the lake.* = **throw**, launch, cast, toss, hurl, fling, chuck (*informal*), sling, lob (*informal*), bung (*Brit. slang*), heave **2** *He pitched head-first over the low wall.* = **fall**, drop, plunge, dive, stagger, tumble, topple, plummet, fall headlong, (take a) nosedive **3** *He had pitched his tent in the yard.* = **set up**, place, station, locate, raise, plant, settle, fix, put up, erect **4** *The ship was pitching and rolling as if in mid-ocean.* = **toss (about)**, roll, plunge, flounder, lurch, wallow, welter, make heavy weather • **pitch in** *Everyone pitched in to help.* = **help**, contribute, participate, join in, cooperate, chip in (*informal*), get stuck in (*Brit. informal*), lend a hand, muck in (*Brit. informal*), do your bit, lend a helping hand

pitch-black or **pitch-dark** ADJECTIVE = **dark**, black, jet, raven, ebony, sable, unlit, jet-black, inky, Stygian (*literary*), pitchy, unilluminated

pitfall NOUN (*usually plural*) = **danger**, difficulty, peril, catch (*informal*), trap, hazard, drawback, snag, uphill (*S. African*), banana skin (*informal*)

pithy ADJECTIVE = **succinct**, pointed, short, brief, to the point, compact, meaningful, forceful, expressive, concise, terse, laconic, trenchant, cogent, epigrammatic, finely honed ■ **OPPOSITE:** long-winded

pitiful ADJECTIVE **1** *It was the most pitiful sight I had ever seen.* = **pathetic**, distressing, miserable, harrowing, heartbreaking, grievous, sad, woeful, deplorable, lamentable, heart-rending, gut-wrenching, wretched, pitiable, piteous ■ **OPPOSITE:** funny **2** *Many of them work as farm labourers for pitiful wages.* = **inadequate**, mean, low, miserable, dismal, beggarly, shabby, insignificant, paltry, despicable, measly (*informal*), contemptible ■ **OPPOSITE:** adequate **3** *a pitiful performance* = **worthless**, base, sorry, vile, abject, scurvy (*old-fashioned*) ■ **OPPOSITE:** admirable

pitiless ADJECTIVE = **merciless**, ruthless, heartless, harsh, cruel, brutal, relentless, callous, inhuman, inexorable, implacable, unsympathetic, cold-blooded, uncaring, unfeeling, cold-hearted, unmerciful, hardhearted ■ **OPPOSITE:** merciful

pittance NOUN = **peanuts** (*slang*), trifle, modicum, drop, mite, chicken feed (*slang*), slave wages, small allowance

pitted ADJECTIVE = **scarred**, marked, rough, scratched, dented, riddled, blemished, potholed, indented, eaten away, holey, pockmarked, rutty

pity NOUN **1** *He felt a sudden tender pity for her.* = **compassion**, understanding, charity, sympathy, distress, sadness, sorrow, kindness, tenderness, condolence, commiseration, fellow feeling ■ **OPPOSITE:** mercilessness **2** *It's a pity you couldn't come.* = **shame**, crime (*informal*), sin (*informal*), misfortune, bad luck, sad thing, bummer (*slang*), crying shame, source of regret **3** *a killer who had no pity for his victims* = **mercy**, kindness, clemency, leniency, forbearance, quarter ▶ VERB *I don't know whether to hate him or pity him.* = **feel sorry for**, feel for, sympathize with, grieve for, weep for, take pity on, empathize with, bleed for, commiserate with, have compassion for, condole with • **take pity on something** or **someone** *She took pity on him because he was homeless.* = **have mercy on**, spare, forgive, pity, pardon, reprieve, show mercy to, feel compassion for, put out of your misery, relent against

pivot NOUN **1** *A large group of watercolours forms the pivot of the exhibition.* = **hub**, centre, heart, hinge, focal point, kingpin **2** *The pedal had sheared off at the pivot.* = **axis**, swivel, axle, spindle, fulcrum ▶ VERB *The boat pivoted on its central axis.* = **turn**, spin, revolve, rotate, swivel, twirl

pivotal ADJECTIVE = **crucial**, central, determining, vital, critical, decisive, focal, climactic

pixie NOUN = **elf**, fairy, brownie, sprite, peri

placard NOUN = **notice**, bill, advertisement, poster, sticker, public notice, affiche (*French*)

placate VERB = **calm**, satisfy, humour, soothe, appease, assuage, pacify, mollify, win someone over, conciliate, propitiate

place NOUN **1** *the place where the temple actually stood* = **spot**, point, position, site, area, situation, station, location, venue, whereabouts, locus **2** *the opportunity to visit new places* = **region**, city, town, quarter, village, district, neighbourhood, hamlet, vicinity, locality, locale, dorp (*S. African*) **3** *He returned the album to its place on the shelf.* = **position**, point, spot, location **4** *There was a single empty place left at the table.* = **space**, position, seat, chair **5** *All the candidates won places on the ruling council.* = **job**, position, post, situation, office, employment, appointment, berth (*informal*), billet (*informal*) **6** *Let's all go back to my place!* = **home**, house, room, property, seat, flat, apartment (*chiefly U.S.*), accommodation, pad (*slang*), residence, mansion, dwelling (*formal, literary*), manor, abode, domicile, bachelor apartment (*Canad.*) **7** *It is not my place to comment.* = **duty**, right, job, charge, concern, role, affair, responsibility, task, function, prerogative ▶ VERB **1** *Chairs were placed in rows for the parents.* = **lay (down)**, leave, put (down), set (down), stand, sit, position, rest, plant, station, establish, stick (*informal*), settle, fix, arrange, lean, deposit, locate, set out, install, prop, dispose, situate, stow, bung (*Brit. slang*), plonk (*informal*), array **2** *Children place their trust in us.* = **put**, lay, set, invest, pin **3** *Red meat was placed in the category below this.* = **classify**, class, group, put, order, sort, rank, arrange, grade, assign, categorize **4** *The twins were placed in a foster home.* = **entrust to**, give to, assign to, appoint to, allocate to, find a home for **5** *I know we've met, but I can't place you.* = **identify**, remember, recognize, pin someone down, put your finger on, put a name to, set someone in context • **in place of** *Cooked kidney beans can be used in place of*

French beans. = **instead of**, rather than, in exchange for, as an alternative to, taking the place of, in lieu of, as a substitute for, as a replacement for • **in your/his/her/their place** *If I were in your place I'd see a lawyer as soon as possible.* = **situation**, position, circumstances, shoes (*informal*) • **know one's place** *a society where everyone knows their place* = **know one's rank**, know one's standing, know one's position, know one's footing, know one's station, know one's status, know one's grade, know one's niche • **put someone in their place** *She put him in his place with just a few words.* = **humble**, humiliate, deflate, crush, mortify, take the wind out of someone's sails, cut someone down to size (*informal*), take someone down a peg (*informal*), make someone eat humble pie, bring someone down to size (*informal*), make someone swallow their pride, settle someone's hash (*informal*) • **take place** *Similar demonstrations also took place elsewhere.* = **happen**, occur, go on, go down (*U.S. & Canad.*), arise, come about, crop up, transpire (*informal*), befall, materialize, come to pass (*archaic*), betide

placement NOUN **1** *The treatment involves the placement of electrodes in the inner ear.* = **positioning**, stationing, arrangement, location, ordering, distribution, locating, installation, deployment, disposition (*archaic*), emplacement **2** *He had a six-month work placement with the Japanese government.* = **appointment**, employment, engagement, assignment

placid ADJECTIVE **1** *She was a placid child who rarely cried.* = **calm**, cool, quiet, peaceful, even, collected, gentle, mild, composed, serene, tranquil, undisturbed, unmoved, untroubled, unfazed (*informal*), unruffled, self-possessed, imperturbable, equable, even-tempered, unexcitable, chilled (*informal*) ■ OPPOSITE: excitable **2** *the placid waters of Lake Erie* = **still**, quiet, calm, peaceful, serene, tranquil, undisturbed, halcyon, unruffled ■ OPPOSITE: rough

plagiarism NOUN = **copying**, borrowing, theft, appropriation, infringement, piracy, lifting (*informal*), cribbing (*informal*)

plague NOUN **1** *A cholera plague had killed many prisoners of war.* = **disease**, infection, epidemic, contagion, pandemic, pestilence, lurgy (*informal*) **2** *The city is under threat from a plague of rats.* = **infestation**, invasion, epidemic, influx, host, swarm, multitude **3** *the cynicism which is the plague of our generation* = **bane**, trial, cancer, evil, curse, torment, blight, calamity, scourge, affliction **4** *Those children can be a real plague*

at times. = **nuisance**, problem, pain (*informal*), bother, pest, hassle (*informal*), annoyance, irritant, aggravation (*informal*), vexation, thorn in your flesh ▶ VERB **1** *She was plagued by weakness, fatigue, and dizziness.* = **torment**, trouble, pain, torture, haunt, afflict **2** *I'm not going to plague you with a lot of questions.* = **pester**, trouble, bother, disturb, annoy, tease, harry, harass, hassle, fret, badger, persecute, molest, vex, bedevil, get on your nerves (*informal*), give someone grief (*Brit. & S. African*), be on your back (*slang*), get in your hair (*informal*)

plain ADJECTIVE **1** *a plain grey stone house, distinguished by its unspoilt simplicity; Her dress was plain, but it hung well on her.* = **unadorned**, simple, basic, severe, pure, bare, modest, stark, restrained, muted, discreet, austere, spartan, unfussy, unvarnished, unembellished, unornamented, unpatterned, bare-bones ■ OPPOSITE: ornate **2** *It was plain to me that he was having a nervous breakdown.* = **clear**, obvious, patent, evident, apparent, visible, distinct, understandable, manifest, transparent, overt, unmistakable, lucid, unambiguous, comprehensible, legible ■ OPPOSITE: hidden **3** *his reputation for plain speaking* = **straightforward**, open, direct, frank, bold, blunt, sincere, outspoken, honest, downright, candid, forthright, upfront (*informal*), artless, ingenuous, guileless ■ OPPOSITE: roundabout **4** *a shy, rather plain girl with a pale complexion* = **ugly**, ordinary, unattractive, homely (*U.S. & Canad.*), not striking, unlovely, unprepossessing, not beautiful, no oil painting (*informal*), ill-favoured, unalluring ■ OPPOSITE: attractive **5** *We are just plain people.* = **ordinary**, homely, common, simple, modest, everyday, commonplace, lowly, unaffected, unpretentious, frugal, workaday ■ OPPOSITE: sophisticated ▶ NOUN *Once there were 70 million buffalo on the plains.* = **flatland**, plateau, prairie, grassland, mesa, lowland, steppe, open country, pampas, tableland, veld, llano

plain-spoken ADJECTIVE = **blunt**, direct, frank, straightforward, open, explicit, outright, outspoken, downright, candid, forthright, upfront (*informal*), unequivocal ■ OPPOSITE: tactful

plaintive ADJECTIVE = **sorrowful**, sad, pathetic, melancholy, grievous, pitiful, woeful, wistful, mournful, heart-rending, rueful, grief-stricken, disconsolate, doleful, woebegone, piteous

plan NOUN **1** *She met her creditors to propose a plan for making repayments.* = **scheme**, system, design, idea, programme, project, proposal, strategy, method, suggestion, procedure, plot, device, scenario, proposition, contrivance **2** *Draw a plan of the garden.* = **diagram**, map, drawing, chart, illustration, representation, sketch, blueprint, layout, delineation, scale drawing ▶ VERB **1** *I had been planning a trip to the West Coast.* = **devise**, arrange, prepare, scheme, frame, plot, draft, organize, outline, invent, formulate, contrive, think out, concoct **2** *The rebel soldiers plan to strike again.* = **intend**, aim, mean, propose, purpose, contemplate, envisage, foresee **3** *The company is planning a theme park on the site.* = **design**, outline, draw up a plan of

plane NOUN **1** *He had plenty of time to catch his plane.* = **aeroplane**, aircraft, jet, airliner, jumbo jet **2** *a building with angled planes* = **flat surface**, the flat, horizontal, level surface **3** *life on a higher plane of existence* = **level**, position, stage, footing, condition, standard, degree (*archaic*), rung, stratum, echelon ▶ ADJECTIVE *a plane surface* = **level**, even, flat, regular, plain, smooth, uniform, flush, horizontal ▶ VERB *The boats planed across the lake with the greatest of ease.* = **skim**, sail, skate, glide

plant¹ NOUN *Water each plant as often as required.* = **flower**, bush, vegetable, herb, weed, shrub ▶ VERB **1** *He intends to plant fruit and vegetables.* = **sow**, scatter, set out, transplant, implant, put in the ground **2** *They are going to plant the area with grass and trees.* = **seed**, sow, implant **3** *She planted her feet wide and bent her knees slightly.* = **place**, put, set, settle, fix **4** *So far no-one has admitted to planting the bomb in the hotel.* = **hide**, put, place, conceal **5** *Sir Eric had evidently planted the idea in her mind.* = **place**, put, establish, found, fix, institute, root, lodge, insert, sow the seeds of, imbed

■ RELATED WORD: *mania* florimania

plant² NOUN **1** *The plant provides forty per cent of the country's electricity.* = **factory**, works, shop, yard, mill, foundry **2** *Firms may invest in plant and equipment abroad where costs are cheaper.* = **machinery**, equipment, gear, apparatus

plaque NOUN = **plate**, panel, medal, tablet, badge, slab, brooch, medallion, cartouch(e)

plaster NOUN **1** *a sculpture in plaster by Rodin* = **mortar**, stucco, gypsum, plaster of Paris, gesso **2** *Put a piece of plaster on the graze.* = **bandage**, dressing, sticking plaster, Elastoplast®, adhesive plaster ▶ VERB *She gets sunburn even when she plasters herself in lotion.* = **cover**, spread, coat, smear, overlay, daub, besmear, bedaub

plastic ADJECTIVE **1** *When girls wear too much make-up, they look plastic.* = **false**, artificial, synthetic, superficial, sham, pseudo (*informal*), spurious, specious, meretricious, phoney or phony (*informal*) ■ OPPOSITE: natural **2** *The mud is as soft and plastic as butter.* = **pliant**, soft, flexible, supple, pliable, tensile, ductile, mouldable, fictile ■ OPPOSITE: rigid

plate NOUN **1** *Scott piled his plate with food.* = **platter**, dish, dinner plate, salver, trencher (*archaic*) **2** *a huge plate of bacon and eggs* = **helping**, course, serving, dish, portion, platter, plateful **3** *The beam is strengthened by a steel plate 6 millimetres thick.* = **layer**, panel, sheet, slab **4** *The book has 55 colour plates.* = **illustration**, picture, photograph, print, engraving, lithograph ▶ VERB *small steel balls plated with chrome or gold* = **coat**, gild, laminate, face, cover, silver, nickel, overlay, electroplate, anodize, platinize

plateau NOUN **1** *a high, flat plateau of cultivated land* = **upland**, table, highland, mesa, tableland **2** *The economy is stuck on a plateau of slow growth.* = **levelling off**, level, stage, stability

platform NOUN **1** *Nick finished his speech and jumped down from the platform.* = **stage**, stand, podium, rostrum, dais, pulpit, soapbox **2** *The party has announced a platform of economic reforms.* = **policy**, programme, principle, objective(s), manifesto, tenet(s), party line

platitude NOUN = **cliché**, stereotype, commonplace, banality, truism, bromide, verbiage, inanity, trite remark, hackneyed saying

platonic ADJECTIVE (*sometimes cap.*) = **nonphysical**, ideal, intellectual, spiritual, idealistic, transcendent

platoon NOUN = **squad**, company, group, team, outfit (*informal*), patrol, squadron

platter NOUN = **plate**, dish, tray, charger, salver, trencher (*archaic*)

plaudits PLURAL NOUN = **approval**, acclaim, applause, praise, clapping, ovation, kudos, congratulation, round of applause, commendation, approbation, acclamation

plausible ADJECTIVE **1** *That explanation seems entirely plausible to me.* = **believable**, possible, likely, reasonable, credible, probable, persuasive, conceivable, tenable, colourable, verisimilar ■ OPPOSITE: unbelievable **2** *He was so plausible he conned us all.* = **glib**, smooth, specious, smooth-talking, smooth-tongued, fair-spoken

play VERB **1** *The children played in the garden.*
= **amuse yourself**, have fun, frolic, sport,
fool, romp, revel, trifle, caper, frisk, gambol,
entertain yourself, engage in games **2** *I used
to play basketball.* = **take part in**, be involved
in, engage in, participate in, compete in, be
in a team for **3** *Northern Ireland will play
Latvia tomorrow.* = **compete against**,
challenge, take on, rival, oppose, vie with,
contend against **4** *Someone had played a trick
on her.* = **perform**, carry out, execute **5** *His
ambition is to play the part of Dracula.* = **act**,
portray, represent, perform, impersonate,
act the part of, take the part of, personate
6 *Do you play the guitar?* = **perform on**,
strum, make music on **7** (*often with* **about**
or **around**) *He's not working, he's just playing
around.* = **fool around**, toy, fiddle, trifle,
mess around, take something lightly
▶ NOUN **1** *Try to strike a balance between work
and play.* = **amusement**, pleasure, leisure,
games, sport, fun, entertainment,
relaxation, a good time, recreation,
enjoyment, romping, larks, capering,
frolicking, junketing, fun and games,
revelry, skylarking, living it up (*informal*),
gambolling, horseplay, merrymaking,
me-time **2** *The company put on a Shakespeare
play.* = **drama**, show, performance, piece,
comedy, entertainment, tragedy, farce,
soap opera, soapie *or* soapy (*Austral. slang*),
pantomime, stage show, television drama,
radio play, masque, dramatic piece • **in
play** *It was done only in play, but they got a
ticking off from the police.* = **in** *or* **for fun**, for
sport, for a joke, for a lark (*informal*), as a
prank, for a jest • **play around** *married
people who play around* = **philander**, have an
affair, carry on (*informal*), fool around, dally,
sleep around (*informal*), womanize, play
away from home (*informal*) • **play at
something** *rich people just playing at being
farmers* = **pretend to be**, pose as,
impersonate, make like (*U.S. & Canad.
informal*), profess to be, assume the role of,
give the appearance of, masquerade as,
pass yourself off as • **play on** *or* **upon
something** *I felt as if I was playing on her
generosity.* = **take advantage of**, abuse,
exploit, impose on, trade on, misuse, milk,
make use of, utilize, profit by, capitalize on,
turn to your account • **play something
down** *Western diplomats have played down the
significance of the reports.* = **minimize**, make
light of, gloss over, talk down, underrate,
underplay, pooh-pooh (*informal*), soft-pedal
(*informal*), make little of, set no store by
• **play something up** *This increase in crime is
definitely being played up by the media.*

= **emphasize**, highlight, underline,
magnify, stress, accentuate, point up, call
attention to, turn the spotlight on, bring to
the fore • **play up 1** *My bad back is playing up
again.* = **hurt**, be painful, bother you,
trouble you, be sore, pain you, give you
trouble, give you gyp (*Brit. & N.Z. slang*)
2 *The engine has started playing up.*
= **malfunction**, not work properly, be on
the blink (*slang*), be wonky (*Brit. slang*)
3 *The kids always play up in his class.* = **be
awkward**, misbehave, give trouble, be
disobedient, give someone grief (*Brit. &
S. African*), be stroppy (*Brit. slang*), be bolshie
(*Brit. informal*) • **play up to someone** *She
plays up to journalists in the media.* = **butter
up**, flatter, pander to, crawl to, get in with,
suck up to (*informal*), curry favour with,
toady, fawn over, keep someone sweet,
bootlick (*informal*), ingratiate yourself to
or with

playboy NOUN = **womanizer**, philanderer,
rake, man about town, pleasure seeker,
roué, ladies' man

player NOUN **1** *top chess players* = **sportsman**
or **sportswoman**, competitor, participant,
contestant, team member **2** *a professional
trumpet player* = **musician**, artist, performer,
virtuoso, instrumentalist, music maker
3 *Oscar nominations went to all five leading
players.* = **performer**, entertainer, Thespian,
trouper, actor *or* actress

playful ADJECTIVE **1** *She gave her husband a
playful slap.* = **joking**, humorous, jokey,
arch, teasing, coy, tongue-in-cheek,
jesting, flirtatious, good-natured, roguish,
waggish **2** *They tumbled around like playful
children.* = **lively**, spirited, cheerful, merry,
mischievous, joyous, sprightly, vivacious,
rollicking, impish, frisky, puckish, coltish,
kittenish, frolicsome, ludic (*literary*),
sportive, gay, larkish (*informal*)
■ OPPOSITE: sedate

playmate NOUN = **friend**, companion,
comrade, chum (*informal*), pal (*informal*),
cobber (*Austral. & N.Z., old-fashioned,
informal*), playfellow

plaything NOUN = **toy**, amusement, game,
pastime, trifle, trinket, bauble, gimcrack,
gewgaw

playwright NOUN = **dramatist**,
scriptwriter, tragedian, dramaturge,
dramaturgist

plea NOUN **1** *an impassioned plea to mankind
to act to save the planet* = **appeal**, request,
suit, prayer, begging, petition, overture,
entreaty, intercession, supplication (*formal*)
2 *We will enter a plea of not guilty.* = **suit**,
cause, action, allegation **3** *Evidence is being*

P

invoked in support of pleas of diminished responsibility. = **excuse**, claim, defence, explanation, justification, pretext, vindication, extenuation

plead VERB **1** *He was kneeling on the floor pleading for mercy.* = **appeal**, ask, request, beg, petition, crave (*informal*), solicit, implore, beseech, entreat, importune (*formal*), supplicate **2** *The guards pleaded that they were only obeying orders.* = **allege**, claim, argue, maintain, assert, put forward, adduce, use as an excuse

pleasant ADJECTIVE **1** *a pleasant surprise* = **pleasing**, nice, welcome, satisfying, fine, lovely, acceptable, amusing, refreshing, delightful, enjoyable, gratifying, agreeable, pleasurable, delectable, lekker (*S. African slang*) ■ **OPPOSITE:** horrible **2** *He was most anxious to seem agreeable and pleasant.* = **friendly**, nice, agreeable, likable or likeable, engaging, charming, cheerful, cheery, good-humoured, amiable, genial, affable, congenial ■ **OPPOSITE:** disagreeable

pleasantry NOUN (*usually plural*) = **comment**, remark, casual remark, polite remark

please VERB *This comment pleased her immensely.* = **delight**, entertain, humour, amuse, suit, content, satisfy, charm, cheer, indulge, tickle, gratify, gladden, give pleasure to, tickle someone pink (*informal*) ■ **OPPOSITE:** annoy

pleased ADJECTIVE = **happy**, delighted, contented, satisfied, thrilled, glad, tickled, gratified, over the moon (*informal*), chuffed (*Brit. slang*), euphoric, rapt, in high spirits, tickled pink (*informal*), pleased as punch (*informal*)

pleasing ADJECTIVE **1** *a pleasing view* = **enjoyable**, satisfying, attractive, charming, entertaining, delightful, gratifying, agreeable, pleasurable ■ **OPPOSITE:** unpleasant **2** *a pleasing personality* = **likable** or **likeable**, attractive, engaging, charming, winning, entertaining, amusing, delightful, polite, agreeable, amiable ■ **OPPOSITE:** disagreeable

pleasurable ADJECTIVE = **enjoyable**, pleasant, diverting, good, nice, welcome, fun, lovely, entertaining, delightful, gratifying, agreeable, congenial

pleasure NOUN **1** *We exclaimed with pleasure when we saw them.* = **happiness**, delight, satisfaction, enjoyment, bliss, gratification, contentment, gladness, delectation (*formal*) ■ **OPPOSITE:** displeasure **2** *Watching TV is our only pleasure.* = **amusement**, joy, recreation, diversion, solace, jollies (*slang*), beer and skittles (*informal*) ■ **OPPOSITE:**

duty **3** *Let me get you a drink. What's your pleasure?* = **wish**, choice, desire, will, mind, option, preference, inclination

pledge NOUN **1** *a pledge to step up cooperation between the states* = **promise**, vow, assurance, word, undertaking, warrant, oath, covenant, word of honour **2** *items held in pledge for loans* = **guarantee**, security, deposit, bail, bond, collateral, earnest (*old-fashioned*), pawn, gage, surety ▶ VERB **1** *I pledge that by next year we will have the problem solved.* = **promise**, vow, vouch, swear, contract, engage, undertake, give your word, give your word of honour, give your oath **2** *He asked her to pledge the house as security for the loan.* = **bind**, guarantee, mortgage, engage, gage (*archaic*)

plenary ADJECTIVE **1** (*of an assembly, council, etc*) *a plenary session of the Central Committee* = **full**, open, general, whole, complete, entire **2** *The president has plenary power in some areas of foreign policy.* = **complete**, full, sweeping, absolute, thorough, unlimited, unconditional, unqualified, unrestricted

plentiful ADJECTIVE **1** *a plentiful supply* = **abundant**, liberal, generous, lavish, complete, ample, infinite, overflowing, copious, inexhaustible, bountiful, profuse, thick on the ground, bounteous (*literary*), plenteous ■ **OPPOSITE:** scarce **2** *a celebration that gives thanks for a plentiful harvest* = **productive**, bumper, fertile, prolific, fruitful, luxuriant, plenteous

plenty NOUN **1** *You are fortunate to be growing up in a time of peace and plenty.* = **abundance**, wealth, luxury, prosperity, fertility, profusion, affluence, opulence, plenitude, fruitfulness, copiousness, plenteousness, plentifulness **2** (*usually with of*) *There was still plenty of time.* = **lots of** (*informal*), enough, a great deal of, masses of, quantities of, piles of (*informal*), mountains of, a good deal of, stacks of, heaps of (*informal*), a mass of, a volume of, an abundance of, a plethora of, a quantity of, a fund of, oodles of (*informal*), a store of, a mine of, a sufficiency of

plethora NOUN = **excess**, surplus, glut, profusion, surfeit, overabundance, superabundance, superfluity ■ **OPPOSITE:** shortage

pliable ADJECTIVE **1** *The baskets are made with young, pliable spruce roots.* = **flexible**, plastic, supple, lithe, limber, malleable, pliant, tensile, bendy, ductile, bendable ■ **OPPOSITE:** rigid **2** *His young queen was pliable and easily influenced.* = **compliant**, susceptible, responsive, manageable, receptive, yielding, adaptable, docile, impressionable, easily led, pliant, tractable, persuadable, influenceable, like putty in your hands ■ **OPPOSITE:** stubborn

plight NOUN = **difficulty**, condition, state, situation, trouble, circumstances, dilemma, straits, predicament, extremity, perplexity

plod VERB **1** *He plodded slowly up the hill.* = **trudge**, drag, tread, clump, lumber, tramp, stomp (*informal*), slog **2** *He is still plodding away at the same job.* = **slog away**, labour, grind away (*informal*), toil, grub, persevere, soldier on, plough through, plug away (*informal*), drudge, peg away

plot[1] NOUN **1** *a plot to overthrow the government* = **plan**, scheme, intrigue, conspiracy, cabal, stratagem, machination, covin (*Law*) **2** *the plot of a cheap spy novel* = **story**, action, subject, theme, outline, scenario, narrative, thread, story line ▶ VERB **1** *They are awaiting trial for plotting against the state.* = **plan**, scheme, conspire, intrigue, manoeuvre, contrive, collude, cabal, hatch a plot, machinate **2** *a meeting to plot the survival strategy of the party* = **devise**, design, project, lay, imagine, frame, conceive, brew, hatch, contrive, concoct, cook up (*informal*) **3** *We were trying to plot the course of the submarine.* = **chart**, mark, draw, map, draft, locate, calculate, outline, compute

plot[2] NOUN *a small plot of land for growing vegetables* = **patch**, lot, area, ground, parcel, tract, allotment

plotter NOUN = **conspirator**, architect, intriguer, planner, conspirer, strategist, conniver, Machiavellian, schemer, cabalist

plough or (*U.S.*) **plow** VERB *They ploughed 100,000 acres of virgin moorland.* = **turn over**, dig, till, ridge, cultivate, furrow, break ground • **plough into something** or **someone** *The car veered off the road and ploughed into a culvert.* = **plunge into**, crash into, smash into, career into, shove into, hurtle into, bulldoze into • **plough through something** *Mr Dambar watched her plough through the grass.* = **forge**, cut, drive, press, push, plunge, surge, stagger, wade, flounder, trudge, plod

ploy NOUN = **tactic**, move, trick, device, game, scheme, manoeuvre, dodge, ruse, gambit, subterfuge, stratagem, contrivance, wile

pluck VERB **1** *I plucked a lemon from the tree.* = **pull out** or **off**, pick, draw, collect, gather, harvest **2** *He plucked the cigarette from his mouth.* = **tug**, catch, snatch, clutch, jerk, yank, tweak, pull at **3** *Nell was plucking a harp.* = **strum**, pick, finger, twang, thrum, plunk ▶ NOUN *Cynics might sneer at him but*

you have to admire his pluck. = **courage**, nerve, heart, spirit, bottle (*Brit. slang*), resolution, determination, guts (*informal*), grit, bravery, backbone, mettle, boldness, spunk (*informal*), intrepidity, hardihood

plucky ADJECTIVE = **courageous**, spirited, brave, daring, bold, game, hardy, heroic, gritty, feisty (*informal*), gutsy (*slang*), intrepid, valiant, doughty (*old-fashioned*), undaunted, unflinching, spunky (*informal*), ballsy (*slang*), mettlesome, (as) game as Ned Kelly (*Austral. slang*) ■ **OPPOSITE:** cowardly

plug NOUN **1** *A plug had been inserted in the drill hole.* = **stopper**, cork, bung, spigot, stopple **2** (*informal*) *The show was little more than a plug for her new film.* = **mention**, advertisement, advert (*Brit.*), push, promotion, publicity, puff, hype, good word ▶ VERB **1** *Crews are working to plug a major oil leak.* = **seal**, close, stop, fill, cover, block, stuff, pack, cork, choke, stopper, bung, stop up, stopple **2** (*informal*) *If I hear another actor plugging his latest book I will scream.* = **mention**, push, promote, publicize, advertise, build up, puff, hype, write up • **plug away** *I just keep plugging away at this job, although I hate it.* = **slog away**, labour, toil away, grind away (*informal*), peg away, plod away, drudge away

plum MODIFIER = **choice**, prize, first-class

plumb VERB *her attempts to plumb my innermost emotions* = **delve into**, measure, explore, probe, sound out, search, go into, penetrate, gauge, unravel, fathom ▶ ADVERB *The hotel is set plumb in the middle of the High Street.* = **exactly**, precisely, bang, slap, spot-on (*Brit. informal*)

plume NOUN = **feather**, crest, quill, pinion, aigrette

plummet VERB **1** *Share prices have plummeted.* = **drop**, fall, crash, nosedive, descend rapidly **2** *The car plummeted off a cliff.* = **plunge**, fall, drop, crash, tumble, swoop, stoop, nosedive, descend rapidly

plummy ADJECTIVE (*of a voice*) = **deep**, posh (*informal, chiefly Brit.*), refined, upper-class, fruity, resonant

plump[1] ADJECTIVE *Maria was small and plump with a mass of curly hair.* = **chubby**, fat, stout, full, round, burly, obese, fleshy, beefy (*informal*), tubby, portly, buxom, dumpy, roly-poly, well-covered, rotund, podgy, corpulent, well-upholstered (*informal*) ■ **OPPOSITE:** scrawny

plump[2] VERB *Breathlessly, she plumped down next to Katrina.* = **flop**, fall, drop, sink, dump, slump • **plump for something** or **someone** *Most people plumped for the more expensive* _option_. = **choose**, favour, go for, back, support, opt for, side with, come down in favour of

plunder VERB **1** _They plundered and burned the town._ = **loot**, strip, sack, rob, raid, devastate, spoil, rifle, ravage, ransack, pillage, despoil (_formal_) **2** _a settlement to recover money plundered from government coffers_ = **steal**, rob, take, nick (_informal_), pinch (_informal_), embezzle, pilfer, thieve ▶ NOUN **1** _a guerrilla group infamous for torture and plunder_ = **pillage**, sacking, robbery, marauding, rapine, spoliation **2** _Pirates swarmed the seas in search of easy plunder._ = **loot**, spoils, prey, booty, swag (_slang_), ill-gotten gains

plunge VERB **1** _50 people died when a bus plunged into a river._ = **descend**, fall, drop, crash, pitch, sink, go down, dive, tumble, plummet, nosedive **2** _I plunged forward, calling her name._ = **hurtle**, charge, career, jump, tear, rush, dive, dash, swoop, lurch **3** _She plunged her face into a bowl of cold water._ = **submerge**, sink, duck, dip, immerse, douse, dunk **4** _conflicts which threaten to plunge the country into chaos_ = **throw**, cast, pitch, propel **5** _Net profits plunged 73% last year._ = **fall steeply**, drop, crash (_informal_), go down, slump, plummet, take a nosedive (_informal_) ▶ NOUN **1** _the stock market plunge_ = **fall**, crash (_informal_), slump, drop, tumble **2** _a refreshing plunge into cold water_ = **dive**, jump, duck, swoop, descent, immersion, submersion

plurality NOUN = **multiplicity**, variety, diversity, profusion, numerousness

plus PREPOSITION _We have one copy of the game to give away, plus ten posters for runners-up._ = **and**, with, added to, coupled with, with the addition of ▶ NOUN _A big plus is that the data can be stored on a PC._ = **advantage**, benefit, asset, gain, extra, bonus, perk (_Brit. informal_), good point, icing on the cake ▶ ADJECTIVE _Accessibility is the other plus point of the borough._ = **additional**, added, extra, positive, supplementary, add-on

USAGE When you have a sentence with more than one subject linked by _and_, this makes the subject plural and means it should take a plural verb: _the doctor and all the nurses were_ (not _was_) _waiting for the patient_. However, where the subjects are linked by _plus_, _together with_, or _along with_, the number of the verb remains just as it would have been if the extra subjects had not been mentioned. Therefore you would say _the doctor, together with all the nurses, was_ (not _were_) _waiting for the patient_.

plush ADJECTIVE = **luxurious**, luxury, costly, lavish, rich, sumptuous, opulent, palatial, ritzy (_slang_), de luxe ■ OPPOSITE: cheap

ply¹ VERB **1** _Elsie plied her with food and drink._ = **provide**, supply, shower, lavish, regale **2** _Giovanni plied him with questions._ = **bombard**, press, harass, besiege, beset, assail, importune (_formal_) **3** _streetmarkets with stallholders plying their trade_ = **work at**, follow, exercise, pursue, carry on, practise **4** _The brightly-coloured boats ply between the islands._ = **travel**, go, ferry, shuttle **5** _With startling efficiency, the chef plied his knives._ = **use**, handle, employ, swing, manipulate, wield, utilize

ply² NOUN _The plastic surfaces are covered with teak ply._ = **thickness**, leaf, sheet, layer, fold, strand

poach VERB **1** _Many national parks are invaded by people poaching game._ = **steal**, rob, plunder, hunt or fish illegally **2** _allegations that it had poached members from other unions_ = **take**, steal, appropriate, snatch (_informal_), nab (_informal_), purloin

pocket NOUN _a canvas container with customised pockets for each tool_ = **pouch**, bag, sack, hollow, compartment, receptacle ▶ MODIFIER _a pocket dictionary_ = **small**, compact, miniature, portable, little, potted (_informal_), concise, pint-size(d) (_informal_), abridged ▶ VERB _He pocketed a wallet from the bedside of a dead man._ = **steal**, take, lift (_informal_), appropriate, pilfer, purloin (_formal_), filch, help yourself to, snaffle (_Brit. informal_)

pod NOUN = **shell**, case, hull, husk, shuck

podcast NOUN = **broadcast**, webcast, vlog, vodcast, mobcast, webisode, webinar ▶ VERB = **upload**, broadcast, vlog, webcast, vodcast, mobcast, update

podium NOUN = **platform**, stand, stage, rostrum, dais

poem NOUN = **verse**, song, lyric, rhyme, sonnet, ode, verse composition

poet NOUN = **bard** (_archaic, literary_), rhymer, lyricist, lyric poet, versifier, maker (_archaic_), elegist

poetic ADJECTIVE **1** _Heidegger's interest in the poetic, evocative uses of language_ = **figurative**, creative, lyric, symbolic, lyrical, rhythmic, rhythmical, songlike **2** _There's a very rich poetic tradition in Gaelic._ = **lyrical**, lyric, rhythmic, elegiac, rhythmical, metrical

poetry NOUN = **verse**, poems, rhyme, rhyming, poesy (_archaic_), verse composition, metrical composition

po-faced ADJECTIVE = **humourless**, disapproving, solemn, prim, puritanical, narrow-minded, stolid, prudish, strait-laced

pogey NOUN (*Canad.*) = **benefits**, the dole (*Brit. & Austral.*), welfare, social security, unemployment benefit, state benefit, allowance

poignancy NOUN = **sadness**, emotion, sentiment, intensity, feeling, tenderness, pathos, emotionalism, plaintiveness, evocativeness, piteousness

poignant ADJECTIVE = **moving**, touching, affecting, upsetting, sad, bitter, intense, painful, distressing, pathetic, harrowing, heartbreaking, agonizing, heart-rending, gut-wrenching

point NOUN 1 *You have missed the main point of my argument.* = **essence**, meaning, subject, question, matter, heart, theme, import, text, core, burden, drift, thrust, proposition, marrow, crux, gist, main idea, nub, pith 2 *What's the point of all these questions?* = **purpose**, aim, object, use, end, reason, goal, design, intention, objective, utility, intent, motive, usefulness 3 *The most interesting point about the village is its religion.* = **aspect**, detail, feature, side, quality, property, particular, respect, item, instance, characteristic, topic, attribute, trait, facet, peculiarity, nicety 4 *The town square is a popular meeting point for tourists.* = **place**, area, position, station, site, spot, location, locality, locale 5 *At this point, Diana arrived.* = **moment**, time, stage, period, phase, instant, juncture, moment in time, very minute 6 *It got to the point where he had to leave.* = **stage**, level, position, condition, degree, pitch, circumstance, extent 7 *the point of a knife* = **end**, tip, sharp end, top, spur, spike, apex, nib, tine, prong 8 *Sort the answers out and add up the points.* = **score**, tally, mark 9 *a long point of land reaching southwards into the sea* = **headland**, head, bill, cape, ness (*archaic*), promontory, foreland 10 *a point of light in an otherwise dark world* = **pinpoint**, mark, spot, dot, fleck, speck ▶ VERB 1 (*usually followed by* at *or* to) *A man pointed a gun at them and pulled the trigger.* = **aim**, level, train, direct 2 *He controlled the car until it was pointing forwards again.* = **face**, look, direct • **beside the point** *Brian didn't like it, but that was beside the point.* = **irrelevant**, inappropriate, pointless, peripheral, unimportant, incidental, unconnected, immaterial, inconsequential, nothing to do with it, extraneous, neither here nor there, off the subject, inapplicable, not to the point, inapposite, without connection, inconsequent, not pertinent, not germane, not to the purpose • **point at** *or* **to something** *or* **someone** *I pointed at the boy*

sitting nearest me. = **indicate**, show, signal, point to, point out, specify, designate, gesture towards • **point of view** 1 *His point of view is that money isn't everything.* = **opinion**, view, attitude, belief, feeling, thought, idea, approach, judgment, sentiment, viewpoint, way of thinking, way of looking at it 2 *Try to look at it from my point of view.* = **perspective**, side, position, stance, stand, angle, outlook, orientation, viewpoint, slant, standpoint, frame of reference • **point something** *or* **someone out** 1 *She pointed him out to me as we drove past.* = **identify**, show, point to, indicate, finger (*informal, chiefly U.S.*), single out, call attention to, draw *or* call attention to, flag up 2 *We all too easily point out other people's failings.* = **allude to**, reveal, mention, identify, indicate, bring up, specify, draw *or* call attention to, flag up • **point something up** *Politicians pointed up the differences between the two countries.* = **emphasize**, stress, highlight, underline, make clear, accent, spotlight, draw attention to, flag up, underscore, play up, accentuate, foreground, focus attention on, give prominence to, turn the spotlight on, bring to the fore, put emphasis on • **point to something** 1 *All the evidence pointed to his guilt.* = **denote**, reveal, indicate, show, suggest, evidence, signal, signify, be evidence of, bespeak (*literary*) 2 *The coach pointed to their bowling as the key to their success.* = **refer to**, mention, indicate, specify, single out, touch on, call attention to • **to the point** *The description he gave was brief and to the point.* = **relevant**, appropriate, apt, pointed, short, fitting, material, related, brief, suitable, applicable, pertinent, terse, pithy, apposite, apropos, germane

point-blank ADJECTIVE *He gave a point-blank refusal.* = **direct**, plain, blunt, explicit, abrupt, express, downright, categorical, unreserved, straight-from-the-shoulder ▶ ADVERB *Mr Patterson was asked point-blank if he would resign.* = **directly**, openly, straight, frankly, plainly, bluntly, explicitly, overtly, candidly, brusquely, straightforwardly, forthrightly

pointed ADJECTIVE 1 *the pointed end of the chisel* = **sharp**, edged, acute, barbed 2 *a pointed remark* = **cutting**, telling, biting, sharp, keen, acute, accurate, penetrating, pertinent, incisive, trenchant

pointer NOUN 1 *Here are a few pointers to help you make a choice.* = **hint**, tip, suggestion, warning, recommendation, caution, piece of information, piece of advice 2 *The pointer* _indicates the pressure on the dial._ = **indicator**, hand, guide, needle, arrow

pointless ADJECTIVE = **senseless**, meaningless, futile, fruitless, unproductive, stupid, silly, useless, absurd, irrelevant, in vain, worthless, ineffectual, unprofitable, nonsensical, aimless, inane, unavailing, without rhyme or reason ■ **OPPOSITE:** worthwhile

poise NOUN **1** _It took a moment for Mark to recover his poise._ = **composure**, cool (_slang_), presence, assurance, dignity, equilibrium, serenity, coolness, aplomb, calmness, equanimity, presence of mind, sang-froid, savoir-faire, self-possession **2** _Ballet classes are important for poise._ = **grace**, balance, equilibrium, elegance

poised ADJECTIVE **1** _US forces are poised for a massive air, land and sea assault._ = **ready**, waiting, prepared, standing by, on the brink, in the wings, all set **2** _Rachel appeared poised and calm._ = **composed**, calm, together (_informal_), collected, dignified, graceful, serene, suave, urbane, self-confident, unfazed (_informal_), debonair, unruffled, nonchalant, self-possessed ■ **OPPOSITE:** agitated

poison NOUN **1** _Poison from the weaver fish causes paralysis and swelling._ = **toxin**, venom, bane (_archaic_) **2** _the poison of crime and violence spreading through the city_ = **contamination**, corruption, contagion, cancer, virus, blight, bane, malignancy, miasma, canker ▶ VERB **1** _There were rumours that she had poisoned her husband._ = **give someone poison**, murder, kill, administer poison to **2** _The land has been completely poisoned by chemicals._ = **contaminate**, foul, infect, spoil, pollute, blight, taint, adulterate, envenom, befoul **3** _ill-feeling that will poison further negotiations_ = **corrupt**, colour, undermine, bias, sour, pervert, warp, taint, subvert, embitter, deprave, defile, jaundice, vitiate, envenom

poisonous ADJECTIVE **1** _All parts of the yew tree are poisonous._ = **toxic**, fatal, deadly, lethal, mortal, virulent, noxious, venomous, baneful (_archaic_), mephitic **2** _poisonous attacks on the Church_ = **evil**, vicious, malicious, corrupting, pernicious (_formal_), baleful, baneful (_archaic_), pestiferous

poke VERB **1** _Lindy poked him in the ribs._ = **jab**, hit, push, stick, dig, punch, stab, thrust, butt, elbow, shove, nudge, prod **2** _His fingers poked through the worn tips of his gloves._ = **protrude**, stick, thrust, jut ▶ NOUN _John smiled and gave Rashid a playful poke._ = **jab**, hit, dig, punch, thrust, butt, nudge, prod

polar ADJECTIVE = **opposite**, opposed, contrary, contradictory, antagonistic, antithetical, diametric, antipodal

polarity NOUN = **opposition**, contradiction, paradox, ambivalence, dichotomy, duality, contrariety

pole¹ NOUN _The sign hung at the top of a large pole._ = **rod**, post, support, staff, standard, bar, stick, stake, paling, shaft, upright, pillar, mast, picket, spar, stave

pole² NOUN _The two mayoral candidates represent opposite poles of the political spectrum._ = **extremity**, limit, terminus, antipode • **poles apart** _Her views on Europe are poles apart from those of her successor._ = **at opposite extremes**, incompatible, irreconcilable, worlds apart, miles apart, like chalk and cheese (_Brit._), like night and day, widely separated, completely different, at opposite ends of the earth

polemic NOUN = **argument**, attack, debate, dispute, controversy, rant, tirade, diatribe, invective, philippic (_rare_)

polemics NOUN = **dispute**, debate, argument, discussion, controversy, contention, wrangling, disputation, argumentation

police NOUN _The police have arrested twenty people following the disturbances._ = **the law** (_informal_), police force, constabulary, the fuzz (_slang_), law enforcement agency, boys in blue (_informal_), the Old Bill (_slang_), the rozzers (_slang_) ▶ VERB **1** _the UN force whose job it is to police the border_ = **control**, patrol, guard, watch, protect, regulate, keep the peace, keep in order **2** _the body which polices the investment management business_ = **monitor**, check, observe, oversee, supervise

police officer NOUN = **cop** (_slang_), officer, pig (_offensive slang_), bobby (_informal_), copper (_slang_), constable, peeler (_Irish & Brit., obsolete slang_), gendarme (_slang_), fuzz (_slang_), woodentop (_slang_), bizzy (_informal_), flatfoot (_slang_), rozzer (_slang_), policeman or policewoman

policy NOUN **1** _plans which include changes in foreign policy_ = **procedure**, plan, action, programme, practice, scheme, theory, code, custom, stratagem **2** _significant changes in Britain's policy on global warming_ = **line**, rules, approach, guideline, protocol

polish NOUN **1** _The air smelt of furniture polish._ = **varnish**, wax, glaze, lacquer, japan **2** _I admired the high polish of his boots._ = **sheen**, finish, sparkle, glaze, gloss, brilliance, brightness, veneer, lustre, smoothness **3** _She was enormously popular for her charm and polish._ = **style**, class (_informal_), finish, breeding, grace, elegance, refinement, finesse, urbanity, suavity, politesse ▶ VERB **1** *Every morning he polished his shoes.* = **shine**, wax, clean, smooth, rub, buff, brighten, burnish, furbish **2** (*often with* **up**) *Polish up your writing skills on a one-week course.* = **perfect**, improve, enhance, refine, finish, correct, cultivate, brush up, touch up, emend • **polish someone off** *a chance to polish off their bitter local rivals* = **eliminate**, take out (*slang*), get rid of, dispose of, do away with, blow away (*slang, chiefly U.S.*), beat someone once and for all • **polish something off** *He polished off the whole box of truffles on his own.* = **finish**, down (*informal*), shift (*informal*), wolf, consume, put away, eat up, swill

polished ADJECTIVE **1** *Nic is polished, charming and articulate.* = **elegant**, sophisticated, refined, polite, cultivated, civilized, genteel, suave, finished, urbane, courtly, well-bred ■ **OPPOSITE:** unsophisticated **2** *a polished performance* = **accomplished**, professional, masterly, fine, expert, outstanding, skilful, adept, impeccable, flawless, superlative, faultless ■ **OPPOSITE:** amateurish **3** *a highly polished surface* = **shining**, bright (*informal*), smooth, gleaming, glossy, slippery, burnished, glassy, furbished ■ **OPPOSITE:** dull

polite ADJECTIVE **1** *He was a quiet and very polite young man.* = **mannerly**, civil, courteous, affable, obliging, gracious, respectful, well-behaved, deferential, complaisant, well-mannered ■ **OPPOSITE:** rude **2** *Certain words are not acceptable in polite society.* = **refined**, cultured, civilized, polished, sophisticated, elegant, genteel, urbane, courtly, well-bred ■ **OPPOSITE:** uncultured

politeness NOUN = **courtesy**, decency, correctness, etiquette, deference, grace, civility, graciousness, common courtesy, complaisance, courteousness, respectfulness, mannerliness, obligingness

politic ADJECTIVE = **wise**, diplomatic, sensible, discreet, prudent, advisable, expedient, judicious, tactful, sagacious (*formal*), in your best interests

political ADJECTIVE **1** *a democratic political system* = **governmental**, government, state, parliamentary, constitutional, administrative, legislative, civic, ministerial, policy-making, party political **2** *I'm not political, I take no interest in politics.* = **factional**, party, militant, partisan

politician NOUN = **statesman** or **woman** or **person**, representative, senator (*U.S.*), Member of Parliament (*Brit.*), congressman or woman or person (*U.S.*), legislator, public servant, politico (*informal, chiefly U.S.*), lawmaker, office bearer, M.P., elected official

politics NOUN **1** *He quickly involved himself in politics.* = **affairs of state**, government, government policy, public affairs, civics **2** *My politics are well to the left of centre.* = **political beliefs**, party politics, political allegiances, political leanings, political sympathies **3** *He studied politics and medieval history.* = **political science**, polity, statesmanship, civics, statecraft **4** *He doesn't know how to handle office politics.* = **power struggle**, machinations, opportunism, realpolitik, Machiavellianism

poll NOUN **1** *Polls show that the party is losing support.* = **survey**, figures, count, sampling, returns, ballot, tally, census, canvass, Gallup Poll, (public) opinion poll **2** *In 1945, Churchill was defeated at the polls.* = **election**, vote, voting, referendum, ballot, plebiscite ▶ VERB **1** *More than 18,000 people were polled.* = **question**, interview, survey, sample, ballot, canvass **2** *He had polled enough votes to force a second ballot.* = **gain**, return, record, register, tally

pollute VERB **1** *beaches polluted by sewage pumped into the sea* = **contaminate**, dirty, mar, poison, soil, foul, infect, spoil, stain, taint, adulterate, make filthy, smirch, befoul ■ **OPPOSITE:** decontaminate **2** *a man accused of polluting the minds of children* = **defile**, violate, corrupt, sully, deprave, debase, profane, desecrate, dishonour, debauch, besmirch ■ **OPPOSITE:** honour

pollution NOUN **1** *environmental pollution* = **contamination**, dirtying, corruption, taint, adulteration, foulness, defilement, uncleanness, vitiation, carbon footprint **2** *the level of pollution in the river* = **waste**, poisons, dirt, impurities

pomp NOUN **1** *the pomp and splendour of the English aristocracy* = **ceremony**, grandeur, splendour, state, show, display, parade, flourish, pageant, magnificence, solemnity, pageantry, ostentation, éclat **2** *The band have trawled new depths of pomp and self-indulgence.* = **show**, pomposity, grandiosity, vainglory

pompous ADJECTIVE **1** *What a pompous little man he is.* = **self-important**, affected, arrogant, pretentious, bloated, grandiose, imperious, showy, overbearing, ostentatious, puffed up, portentous, magisterial, supercilious, pontifical, vainglorious ■ **OPPOSITE:** unpretentious **2** *She winced at his pompous phraseology.* = **grandiloquent**, high-flown, inflated, windy, overblown, turgid, bombastic, boastful, flatulent, arty-farty (*informal*), fustian, orotund, magniloquent ■ **OPPOSITE:** simple

pond NOUN = **pool**, tarn, small lake, fish pond, duck pond, millpond, lochan (*Scot.*), dew pond

ponder VERB = **think about**, consider, study, reflect on, examine, weigh up, contemplate, deliberate about, muse on, brood on, meditate on, mull over, puzzle over, ruminate on, give thought to, cogitate on, rack your brains about, excogitate

ponderous ADJECTIVE **1** *He had a dense, ponderous writing style.* = **dull**, laboured, pedestrian, dreary, heavy, tedious, plodding, tiresome, lifeless, stilted, stodgy, pedantic, long-winded, verbose, prolix **2** *He strolled about with a ponderous, heavy gait.* = **clumsy**, awkward, lumbering, laborious, graceless, elephantine, heavy-footed, unco (*Austral. slang*) ■ **OPPOSITE:** graceful

pontificate VERB = **expound**, preach, sound off, pronounce, declaim, lay down the law, hold forth, dogmatize, pontify

pool¹ NOUN **1** *a heated indoor pool* = **swimming pool**, lido, swimming bath(s) (*Brit.*), bathing pool (*archaic*) **2** *Beautiful gardens filled with pools and fountains.* = **pond**, lake, mere, tarn **3** *There were pools of water on the gravel drive.* = **puddle**, drop, patch, splash

pool² NOUN **1** *the available pool of manpower* = **supply**, reserve, fall-back **2** *a reserve pool of cash* = **kitty**, bank, fund, stock, store, pot, jackpot, stockpile, hoard, cache ▶ VERB *We pooled our savings to start up a new business.* = **combine**, share, merge, put together, amalgamate, lump together, join forces on

poor ADJECTIVE **1** *He was one of thirteen children from a poor family.* = **impoverished**, broke (*informal*), badly off, hard up (*informal*), short, in need, needy, on the rocks, penniless, destitute, poverty-stricken, down and out, skint (*Brit. slang*), in want, indigent (*formal*), down at heel, impecunious, dirt-poor (*informal*), on the breadline, flat broke (*informal*), penurious, on your uppers, stony-broke (*Brit. slang*), necessitous, in queer street, without two pennies to rub together (*informal*), on your beam-ends ■ **OPPOSITE:** rich **2** *I feel sorry for that poor child.* = **unfortunate**, pathetic, miserable, unlucky, hapless, pitiful, luckless, wretched, ill-starred, pitiable, ill-fated ■ **OPPOSITE:** fortunate **3** *The wine is very poor.; He was a poor actor.* = **inferior**, unsatisfactory, mediocre, second-rate,

sorry, weak, pants (*informal*), rotten (*informal*), faulty, feeble, worthless, shabby, shoddy, low-grade, below par, substandard, low-rent (*informal*), crappy (*slang*), valueless, no great shakes (*informal*), rubbishy, poxy (*slang*), not much cop (*Brit. slang*), half-pie (*N.Z. informal*), bodger or bodgie (*Austral. slang*) ■ **OPPOSITE:** excellent **4** *poor wages and terrible working conditions; A poor crop has sent vegetable prices spiralling.* = **meagre**, inadequate, insufficient, reduced, lacking, slight, miserable, pathetic, incomplete, scant, sparse, deficient, skimpy, measly (*informal*), scanty, pitiable, niggardly, straitened, exiguous ■ **OPPOSITE:** ample **5** *Mix in some planting compost to improve poor soil when you dig.* = **unproductive**, barren, fruitless, bad, bare, exhausted, depleted, impoverished, sterile, infertile, unfruitful ■ **OPPOSITE:** productive

poorly ADVERB *poorly built houses* = **badly**, incompetently, inadequately, crudely, inferiorly, unsuccessfully, insufficiently, shabbily, unsatisfactorily, inexpertly ■ **OPPOSITE:** well ▶ ADJECTIVE *I've just phoned Julie and she's still poorly.* = **ill**, sick, ailing, unwell, crook (*Austral. & N.Z. informal*), seedy (*informal*), below par, out of sorts, off colour, under the weather (*informal*), indisposed, feeling rotten (*informal*) ■ **OPPOSITE:** healthy

pop NOUN **1** *He still visits the village shop for buns and fizzy pop.* = **soft drink**, ginger (*Scot.*), soda (*U.S. & Canad.*), fizzy drink, cool drink (*S. African*) **2** *Each corn kernel will make a loud pop when cooked.* = **bang**, report, crack, noise, burst, explosion ▶ VERB **1** *The champagne cork popped and shot to the ceiling.* = **burst**, crack, snap, bang, explode, report, go off (with a bang) **2** *My eyes popped at the sight of so much food.* = **protrude**, bulge, stick out **3** *He plucked a grape from the bunch and popped it into his mouth.* = **put**, insert, push, stick, slip, thrust, tuck, shove **4** (*often with in, out, etc*) *Wendy popped in for a quick visit on Monday night.* = **call**, visit, appear, drop in (*informal*), leave quickly, come or go suddenly, nip in or out (*Brit. informal*)

pope NOUN = **Holy Father**, pontiff, His Holiness, Bishop of Rome, Vicar of Christ ■ **RELATED WORD:** *adjective* papal

populace NOUN = **people**, crowd, masses, mob, inhabitants, general public, multitude, throng, rabble (*derogatory*), hoi polloi, Joe Public (*slang*), Joe Six-Pack (*U.S. slang*), commonalty

popular ADJECTIVE **1** *This is the most popular game ever devised.* = **well-liked**, liked, favoured, celebrated, in, accepted, favourite, famous, approved, in favour, fashionable, trending, in demand, sought-after, fave (*informal*) ■ **OPPOSITE:** unpopular **2** *the popular misconception that dinosaurs were all lumbering giants* = **common**, general, standard, widespread, prevailing, stock, current, public, conventional, universal, prevalent, ubiquitous ■ **OPPOSITE:** rare

popularity NOUN **1** *His authority and popularity have declined.* = **favour**, fame, esteem, acclaim, regard, reputation, approval, recognition, celebrity, vogue, adoration, renown, repute, idolization, lionization **2** *This theory has enjoyed tremendous popularity among sociologists.* = **currency**, acceptance, circulation, vogue, prevalence

popularize VERB **1** *the first person to popularize rock 'n' roll in China* = **make something popular**, spread the word about, disseminate, universalize, give mass appeal to **2** *a magazine devoted to popularizing science* = **simplify**, make available to all, give currency to, give mass appeal to

popularly ADVERB = **generally**, commonly, widely, usually, regularly, universally, traditionally, ordinarily, conventionally, customarily

populate VERB **1** *the native people who populate areas around the city* = **inhabit**, people, live in, occupy, reside in, dwell in (*formal*) **2** *the time when Europe was populated by modern humans* = **settle**, people, occupy, pioneer, colonize

population NOUN = **inhabitants**, people, community, society, residents, natives, folk, occupants, populace, denizens, citizenry

populous ADJECTIVE = **populated**, crowded, packed, swarming, thronged, teeming, heavily populated, overpopulated

pore¹ VERB **1** (*followed by* **over**) *We spent whole afternoons poring over travel brochures.* = **study**, read, examine, go over, scrutinize, peruse **2** (*followed by* **over**, **on**, *or* **upon**) *One day historians will pore over these strange months.* = **contemplate**, ponder, brood, dwell on, work over

pore² NOUN *microscopic pores in the plant's leaves* = **opening**, hole, outlet, orifice, stoma

pornographic ADJECTIVE = **obscene**, erotic, indecent, blue, dirty, offensive, rude, sexy, filthy, lewd, risqué, X-rated (*informal*), salacious, prurient, smutty

pornography NOUN = **obscenity**, porn (*informal*), erotica, dirt, filth, indecency, porno (*informal*), smut

porous ADJECTIVE = **permeable**, absorbent, spongy, absorptive, penetrable, pervious ■ **OPPOSITE:** impermeable

port NOUN = **harbour**, haven, anchorage, seaport, roadstead

portable ADJECTIVE = **light**, compact, convenient, handy, lightweight, manageable, movable, easily carried, portative

portal NOUN = **doorway**, door, entry, way in, entrance, gateway, entrance way

portent NOUN = **omen**, sign, warning, threat, indication, premonition, foreshadowing, foreboding, harbinger (*literary*), presage, forewarning, prognostication, augury, presentiment, prognostic

portentous ADJECTIVE **1** *There was nothing portentous or solemn about him.* = **pompous**, solemn, ponderous, self-important, pontifical **2** *portentous prophecies of doom* = **significant**, alarming, sinister, ominous, important, threatening, crucial (*informal*), forbidding, menacing, momentous, fateful, minatory, bodeful

porter¹ NOUN *A porter slammed the baggage compartment doors.* = **baggage attendant**, carrier, bearer, baggage-carrier

porter² NOUN *a porter at the block of flats* = **doorman**, caretaker, janitor, concierge, gatekeeper

portion NOUN **1** *I have spent a large portion of my life here.* = **part**, bit, piece, section, scrap, segment, fragment, fraction, chunk, wedge, hunk, morsel **2** *a large portion of green vegetables* = **helping**, serving, piece, plateful **3** *his portion of the inheritance* = **share**, division, allowance, lot, measure, quantity, quota, ration, allocation, allotment

portly ADJECTIVE = **stout**, fat, overweight, plump, large, heavy, ample, bulky, burly, obese, fleshy, beefy (*informal*), tubby (*informal*), rotund, corpulent

portrait NOUN **1** *oversize portraits of royal ancestors* = **picture**, painting, image, photograph, representation, sketch, likeness, portraiture **2** *a beautifully written and sensitive portrait of a great woman* = **description**, account, profile, biography, portrayal, depiction, vignette, characterization, thumbnail sketch

portray VERB **1** *He portrayed the king in a revival of 'Camelot'.* = **play**, take the role of, act the part of, represent, personate (*rare*) **2** *The novelist accurately portrays provincial domestic life.* = **describe**, present, depict, evoke, delineate, put in words **3** *the landscape as portrayed by painters such as*

P

Poussin = **represent**, draw, paint, illustrate, sketch, figure, picture, render, depict, delineate **4** *complaints about the way women are portrayed in adverts* = **characterize**, describe, represent, depict, paint a mental picture of

portrayal NOUN **1** *She was much admired for her portrayals of assertive women.* = **performance**, interpretation, enacting, take (*informal, chiefly U.S.*), acting, impersonation, performance as, characterization, personation (*rare*) **2** *a near-monochrome portrayal of a wood infused with silvery light* = **depiction**, picture, representation, sketch, rendering, delineation **3** *an often funny portrayal of a friendship between two boys* = **description**, account, representation **4** *The media persists in its portrayal of us as muggers and dope sellers.* = **characterization**, representation, depiction

pose VERB **1** *His ill health poses serious problems.* = **present**, cause, produce, create, lead to, result in, constitute, give rise to **2** *When I posed the question 'Why?', he merely shrugged.* = **ask**, state, advance, put, set, submit, put forward, posit, propound **3** *The six foreign ministers posed for photographs.* = **position yourself**, sit, model, strike a pose, arrange yourself **4** *He criticized them for posing pretentiously.* = **put on airs**, affect, posture, show off (*informal*), strike an attitude, attitudinize ▸ NOUN **1** *We have had several sittings in various poses.* = **posture**, position, bearing, attitude, stance, mien (*literary*) **2** *In many writers modesty is a pose, but in him it seems to be genuine.* = **act**, role, façade, air, front, posturing, pretence, masquerade, mannerism, affectation, attitudinizing • **pose as something** or **someone** *The team posed as drug dealers to trap the ringleaders.* = **impersonate**, pretend to be, sham, feign, profess to be, masquerade as, pass yourself off as

poser[1] NOUN = **show-off** (*informal*), poseur, posturer, masquerader, hot dog (*chiefly U.S.*), impostor, exhibitionist, self-publicist, mannerist, attitudinizer

poser[2] NOUN = **puzzle**, problem, question, riddle, enigma, conundrum, teaser, tough one, vexed question, brain-teaser (*informal*), knotty point

posh (*chiefly Brit. informal*) ADJECTIVE **1** *I took her to a posh hotel for a cocktail.* = **smart**, grand, exclusive, luxury, elegant, fashionable, stylish, luxurious, classy (*slang*), swish (*informal, chiefly Brit.*), up-market, swanky (*informal*), ritzy (*slang*), schmick (*Austral. informal*) **2** *He sounded very*

posh on the phone. = **upper-class**, high-class, top-drawer, plummy, high-toned, la-di-da (*informal*)

posit VERB = **put forward**, advance, submit, state, assume, assert, presume, predicate, postulate (*formal*), propound

position NOUN **1** *The ship's position was reported to the coastguard.* = **location**, place, point, area, post, situation, site, spot, bearings, reference, orientation, whereabouts, locality, locale **2** *He had raised himself into a sitting position.* = **posture**, attitude, arrangement, pose, stance, disposition (*archaic*) **3** *their changing role and position in society* = **status**, place, standing, class, footing, station, rank, reputation, importance, consequence, prestige, caste, stature, eminence, repute **4** *He took up a position with the Arts Council.* = **job**, place, post, opening, office, role, situation, duty, function, employment, capacity, occupation, berth (*informal*), billet (*informal*) **5** *The players resumed their battle for the no. 1 position.* = **place**, standing, rank, status **6** *He's going to be in a difficult position if things go badly.* = **situation**, state, condition, set of circumstances, plight, strait(s), predicament **7** *He usually takes a moderate position.* = **attitude**, view, perspective, point of view, standing, opinion, belief, angle, stance, outlook, posture, viewpoint, slant, way of thinking, standpoint ▸ VERB *Position trailing plants near the edges of the basket.* = **place**, put, set, stand, stick (*informal*), settle, fix, arrange, locate, sequence, array, dispose, lay out

positive ADJECTIVE **1** *Working abroad should be a positive experience.* = **beneficial**, effective, useful, practical, helpful, progressive, productive, worthwhile, constructive, pragmatic, efficacious ■ OPPOSITE: harmful **2** *I'm positive she said she'd be here.* = **certain**, sure, convinced, confident, satisfied, assured, free from doubt ■ OPPOSITE: uncertain **3** *There was no positive evidence.* = **definite**, real, clear, firm, certain, direct, express, actual, absolute, concrete, decisive, explicit, affirmative, clear-cut, unmistakable, conclusive, unequivocal, indisputable, categorical, incontrovertible, nailed-on (*slang*) ■ OPPOSITE: inconclusive **4** *He was in a positive fury.* = **absolute**, complete, perfect, right (*Brit. informal*), real, total, rank, sheer, utter, thorough, downright, consummate, veritable, unqualified, out-and-out, unmitigated, thoroughgoing, unalloyed

positively ADVERB **1** *This is positively the worst thing I can imagine.* = **definitely**, surely, firmly, certainly, absolutely, emphatically, unquestionably, undeniably, categorically, unequivocally, unmistakably, with certainty, assuredly, without qualification **2** *He was positively furious.* = **really**, completely, simply, plain (*informal*), absolutely, thoroughly, utterly, downright

possess VERB **1** *He is said to possess a huge fortune.* = **own**, have, hold, be in possession of, be the owner of, have in your possession, have to your name **2** *individuals who possess the qualities of sense and discretion* = **be endowed with**, have, enjoy, benefit from, be born with, be blessed with, be possessed of, be gifted with **3** *Absolute terror possessed her.* = **control**, influence, dominate, consume, obsess, bedevil, mesmerize, eat someone up, fixate, put under a spell **4** *It was as if the spirit of his father possessed him.* = **seize**, hold, control, dominate, occupy, haunt, take someone over, bewitch, take possession of, have power over, have mastery over

possessed ADJECTIVE = **crazed**, haunted, cursed, obsessed, raving, frenzied, consumed, enchanted, maddened, frenetic, berserk, bewitched, bedevilled, under a spell, hag-ridden

possession NOUN **1** *These documents are now in the possession of the authorities.* = **ownership**, control, custody, hold, hands, tenure, occupancy, proprietorship **2** *All of these countries were once French possessions.* = **province**, territory, colony, dominion, protectorate ▶ PLURAL NOUN *People had lost their homes and all their possessions.* = **property**, things, effects, estate, assets, wealth, belongings, chattels, goods and chattels

possessive ADJECTIVE **1** *Danny could be very jealous and possessive of me.* = **jealous**, controlling, dominating, domineering, proprietorial, overprotective **2** *He's very possessive about his toys.* = **selfish**, grasping, acquisitive

possibility NOUN **1** *a debate about the possibility of political reform* = **feasibility**, likelihood, plausibility, potentiality, practicability, workableness **2** *There is still a possibility of unrest in the country.* = **likelihood**, chance, risk, odds, prospect, liability, hazard, probability **3** (*often plural*) *This situation has great possibilities.* = **potential**, promise, prospects, talent, capabilities, potentiality

possible ADJECTIVE **1** *Everything is possible if we want it enough.* = **feasible**, viable, workable, achievable, within reach, on (*informal*), practicable, attainable, doable,

realizable ■ OPPOSITE: unfeasible **2** *One possible solution is to take legal action.* = **likely**, potential, anticipated, probable, odds-on, on the cards ■ OPPOSITE: improbable **3** *It's just possible that he was trying to put me off the trip.* = **conceivable**, likely, credible, plausible, hypothetical, imaginable, believable, thinkable ■ OPPOSITE: inconceivable **4** *a possible presidential contender* = **aspiring**, would-be, promising, hopeful, prospective, wannabe (*informal*)

> USAGE Although it is very common to talk about something's being *very possible* or *more possible*, many people object to such uses, claiming that *possible* describes an absolute state, and therefore something can only be either *possible* or *not possible*. If you want to refer to different degrees of probability, a word such as *likely* or *easy* may be more appropriate than *possible*, for example *it is very likely that he will resign* (not *very possible*).

possibly ADVERB **1** *Exercise may possibly protect against heart attacks.* = **perhaps**, maybe, God willing, perchance (*archaic*), mayhap (*archaic*), peradventure (*archaic*), haply (*archaic*) **2** *I couldn't possibly answer that.* = **at all**, in any way, conceivably, by any means, under any circumstances, by any chance

post¹ NOUN *Eight wooden posts were driven into the ground.* = **support**, stake, pole, stock, standard, column, pale, shaft, upright, pillar, picket, palisade, newel ▶ VERB *Officials began posting warning notices.* = **put up**, announce, publish, display, advertise, proclaim, publicize, promulgate, affix, stick something up, make something known, pin something up

post² NOUN **1** *Sir Peter has held several senior military posts.* = **job**, place, office, position, situation, employment, appointment, assignment, berth (*informal*), billet (*informal*) **2** *Quick, men, back to your posts!* = **position**, place, base, beat, station ▶ VERB *After training she was posted to Brixton.* = **station**, assign, put, place, position, establish, locate, situate, put on duty

post³ NOUN **1** *You'll receive your book through the post.* = **mail**, collection, delivery, postal service, snail mail (*informal*) **2** *He flipped through the post without opening any of it.* = **correspondence**, letters, cards, mail ▶ VERB *I'll post a card to her tonight.* = **send (off)**, forward, mail, get off, transmit, dispatch, consign • **keep someone posted** *Keep me posted on your progress.* = **notify**, brief, advise, inform, report to, keep someone informed, keep someone up to date, apprise, fill someone in on (*informal*)

poster NOUN = **notice**, bill, announcement, advertisement, sticker, placard, public notice, affiche (*French*)

posterior NOUN *Sit down on your posterior!* = **bottom** (*informal*), behind (*informal*), bum (*Brit. slang*), seat, rear (*informal*), tail (*informal*), butt (*U.S. & Canad. informal*), buns (*U.S. slang*), buttocks, backside (*informal*), rump, rear end, derrière (*euphemistic*), tush (*U.S. slang*), fundament, jacksy (*Brit. slang*) ▶ ADJECTIVE *the posterior lobe of the pituitary gland* = **rear**, back, hinder, hind

posterity NOUN = **the future**, future generations, succeeding generations

postpone VERB = **put off**, delay, suspend, adjourn, table, shelve, defer, put back, hold over, put on ice (*informal*), put on the back burner (*informal*), take a rain check on (*U.S. & Canad. informal*) ■ OPPOSITE: go ahead with

postponement NOUN = **delay**, stay, suspension, moratorium, respite, adjournment, deferment, deferral

postscript NOUN = **P.S.**, addition, supplement, appendix, afterthought, afterword

postulate VERB = **presuppose**, suppose, advance, propose, assume, put forward, take for granted, predicate, theorize, posit, hypothesize

posture NOUN **1** *She walked haltingly and her posture was stooped.* = **bearing**, set, position, attitude, pose, stance, carriage, disposition, mien (*literary*) **2** *None of the banks changed their posture on the deal as a result of the inquiry.* = **attitude**, feeling, mood, point of view, stance, outlook, inclination, disposition, standpoint, frame of mind ▶ VERB = **show off** (*informal*), pose, affect, hot-dog (*chiefly U.S.*), make a show, put on airs, try to attract attention, attitudinize, do something for effect

posy NOUN = **bouquet**, spray, buttonhole, corsage, nosegay, boutonniere

pot NOUN **1** *metal cooking pots; Use a large terracotta pot or a wooden tub.* = **container**, bowl, pan, vessel, basin, vase, jug, cauldron, urn, utensil, crock, skillet **2** *The pot for this Saturday's draw stands at over £18 million.* = **jackpot**, bank, prize, stakes, purse **3** *If there is more money in the pot, all the members will benefit proportionally.* = **kitty**, funds, pool **4** *He's already developing a pot from all the beer he drinks.* = **paunch**, beer belly or gut (*informal*), spread (*informal*), corporation (*informal*), gut, bulge, spare tyre (*Brit. slang*), potbelly

pot-bellied ADJECTIVE = **fat**, overweight, bloated, obese, distended, corpulent, paunchy

pot belly NOUN = **paunch**, beer belly or gut (*informal*), spread (*informal*), corporation (*informal*), pot, gut, spare tyre (*Brit. slang*), middle-age spread (*informal*), puku (*N.Z.*)

potency NOUN **1** *the extraordinary potency of his personality* = **influence**, might, force, control, authority, energy, potential, strength, capacity, mana (*N.Z.*) **2** *Her remarks have added potency given the current situation.* = **persuasiveness**, force, strength, muscle, effectiveness, sway, forcefulness, cogency, impressiveness **3** *The potency of the wine increases with time.* = **power**, force, strength, effectiveness, efficacy

potent ADJECTIVE **1** *a potent political force* = **powerful**, commanding, dynamic, dominant, influential, authoritative **2** *a potent electoral message* = **persuasive**, telling, convincing, effective, impressive, compelling, forceful, cogent ■ OPPOSITE: unconvincing **3** *The drug is extremely potent, but can have unpleasant side-effects.* = **strong**, powerful, mighty, vigorous, forceful, efficacious, puissant ■ OPPOSITES: weak, impotent

potentate NOUN = **ruler**, king, prince, emperor, monarch, sovereign, mogul, overlord

potential ADJECTIVE **1** *potential customers* = **possible**, future, likely, promising, budding, embryonic, undeveloped, unrealized, probable **2** *We are aware of the potential dangers.* = **hidden**, possible, inherent, dormant, latent ▶ NOUN *The boy has potential.* = **ability**, possibilities, capacity, capability, the makings, what it takes (*informal*), aptitude, wherewithal, potentiality

potion NOUN = **concoction**, mixture, brew, tonic, cup, dose, draught, elixir, philtre

potter VERB (*usually with* **around** *or* **about**) = **mess about**, fiddle (*informal*), tinker, dabble, fritter, footle (*informal*), poke along, fribble

pottery NOUN = **ceramics**, terracotta, crockery, earthenware, stoneware

potty ADJECTIVE *a wild, potty scheme* = **crazy**, eccentric, crackers (*Brit. slang*), barmy (*slang*), silly, foolish, daft (*informal*), off-the-wall (*slang*), off the rails, dotty (*slang, chiefly Brit.*), loopy (*informal*), crackpot (*informal*), dippy (*slang*), gonzo (*slang*), doolally (*slang*), porangi (*N.Z.*), daggy (*Austral. & N.Z. informal*)

p

pouch NOUN = **bag**, pocket, sack, container, purse (U.S.), poke (dialect)

pounce VERB (often followed by **on** or **upon**) Before I could get to the pigeon, the cat pounced. = **attack**, strike, jump, leap, swoop

pound¹ VERB **1** (sometimes with **on**) He pounded the table with his fist. = **beat**, strike, hammer (informal), batter, thrash, thump, pelt, clobber (slang), pummel, belabour, beat or knock seven bells out of (informal), beat the living daylights out of **2** She paused as she pounded the maize grains. = **crush**, powder, bruise, bray (dialect), pulverize **3** I'm sweating and my heart is pounding. = **pulsate**, beat, pulse, throb, palpitate, pitapat **4** (often with **out**) A group of tribal drummers pounded out an unrelenting beat. = **thump**, beat, hammer, bang **5** I pounded up the stairs to my room and slammed the door. = **stomp**, tramp, march, thunder (informal), clomp

pound² NOUN The dog has been sent to the pound. = **enclosure**, yard, pen, compound, kennels, corral (chiefly U.S. & Canad.)

pour VERB **1** Pour a small amount of water into a glass. = **let flow**, spill, splash, dribble, drizzle, slop (informal), slosh (informal), decant **2** Blood was pouring from his broken nose. = **flow**, stream, run, course, rush, emit, cascade, gush, spout, spew **3** It has been pouring all week. = **rain**, sheet, pelt (down), teem, bucket down (informal), rain cats and dogs (informal), come down in torrents, rain hard or heavily **4** The northern forces poured across the border. = **stream**, crowd, flood, swarm, gush, throng, teem

> USAGE The spelling of pour (as in she poured cream on her strudel) should be carefully distinguished from that of pore over or through (as in she pored over the manuscript).

pout VERB He whined and pouted like a kid when he didn't get what he wanted. = **sulk**, glower, mope, look sullen, purse your lips, look petulant, pull a long face, lour or lower, make a moue, turn down the corners of your mouth ▶ NOUN She jutted her lower lip out in a pout. = **sullen look**, glower, long face, moue (French)

poverty NOUN **1** Many people in the region still live in absolute poverty. = **pennilessness**, want, need, distress, necessity, hardship, insolvency, privation (formal), penury, destitution, hand-to-mouth existence, beggary, indigence, pauperism, necessitousness ■ OPPOSITE: wealth **2** a poverty of ideas = **scarcity**, lack, absence, want, deficit, shortage, deficiency, inadequacy, dearth, paucity (formal),

insufficiency, sparsity ■ OPPOSITE: abundance **3** the poverty of the soil = **barrenness**, deficiency, infertility, sterility, aridity, bareness, poorness, meagreness, unfruitfulness ■ OPPOSITE: fertility

poverty-stricken ADJECTIVE = **penniless**, broke (informal), bankrupt, impoverished, short, poor, distressed, beggared, needy, destitute, down and out, skint (Brit. slang), indigent, down at heel, impecunious, dirt-poor (informal), on the breadline, flat broke (informal), penurious, on your uppers, stony-broke (Brit. slang), in queer street, without two pennies to rub together (informal), on your beam-ends

powder NOUN a fine white powder = **dust**, pounce (rare), talc, fine grains, loose particles ▶ VERB **1** Powder the puddings with icing sugar. = **dust**, cover, scatter, sprinkle, strew, dredge **2** Mix all the powdered ingredients together. = **grind**, crush, pound, pestle, pulverize, granulate

powdery ADJECTIVE = **fine**, dry, sandy, dusty, loose, crumbling, grainy, chalky, crumbly, granular, pulverized, friable

power NOUN **1** women who have reached positions of great power and influence = **control**, authority, influence, command, sovereignty, sway, dominance, domination, supremacy, mastery, dominion, ascendancy, mana (N.Z.) **2** He was so drunk that he had lost the power of speech. = **ability**, capacity, faculty, property, potential, capability, competence, competency ■ OPPOSITE: inability **3** The Prime Minister has the power to dismiss senior ministers. = **authority**, right, licence, privilege, warrant, prerogative, authorization **4** He had no power in his left arm. = **strength**, might, energy, weight, muscle, vigour, potency, brawn, hard power ■ OPPOSITE: weakness **5** the power of his rhetoric = **forcefulness**, force, strength, punch (informal), intensity, potency, eloquence, persuasiveness, cogency, powerfulness

powerful ADJECTIVE **1** You're a powerful woman – people will listen to you. = **influential**, dominant, controlling, commanding, supreme, prevailing, sovereign, authoritative, puissant, skookum (Canad.) ■ OPPOSITE: powerless **2** a big, powerful man = **strong**, strapping, mighty, robust, vigorous, potent, energetic, sturdy, stalwart ■ OPPOSITE: weak **3** a powerful drama about a corrupt city leader = **persuasive**, convincing, effective, telling, moving, striking, storming,

P

dramatic, impressive, compelling, authoritative, forceful, weighty, forcible, cogent, effectual

powerfully ADVERB = **strongly**, hard, vigorously, forcibly, forcefully, mightily, with might and main

powerless ADJECTIVE *political systems that keep women poor and powerless* = **defenceless**, vulnerable, dependent, subject, tied, ineffective, unarmed, disenfranchised, over a barrel (*informal*), disfranchised

practicable ADJECTIVE = **feasible**, possible, viable, workable, achievable, attainable, doable, within the realm of possibility, performable ■ **OPPOSITE:** unfeasible

practical ADJECTIVE **1** *practical suggestions on how to improve your diet* = **functional**, efficient, realistic, pragmatic ■ **OPPOSITE:** impractical **2** *theories based on practical knowledge* = **empirical**, real, applied, actual, hands-on, in the field, experimental, factual ■ **OPPOSITE:** theoretical **3** *She is always so practical and full of common sense.* = **sensible**, ordinary, realistic, down-to-earth, mundane, matter-of-fact, no-nonsense, businesslike, hard-headed, workaday, grounded ■ **OPPOSITE:** impractical **4** *We do not yet have any practical way to prevent cancer.* = **feasible**, possible, sound, viable, constructive, workable, practicable, doable ■ **OPPOSITE:** impractical **5** *clothes which are practical as well as stylish* = **useful**, ordinary, appropriate, sensible, everyday, functional, utilitarian, serviceable **6** *people with practical experience of running businesses* = **skilled**, working, seasoned, trained, experienced, qualified, veteran, efficient, accomplished, proficient ■ **OPPOSITE:** inexperienced

> USAGE A distinction is usually made between *practical* and *practicable*. *Practical* refers to a person, idea, project, etc, as being more concerned with or relevant to practice than theory: *he is a very practical person; the idea had no practical application*. *Practicable* refers to a project or idea as being capable of being done or put into effect: *the plan was expensive, yet practicable*.

practically ADVERB **1** *He'd known the old man practically all his life.* = **almost**, nearly, close to, essentially, virtually, basically, fundamentally, all but, just about, in effect, very nearly, to all intents and purposes, well-nigh **2** *'Let me help you to bed,' Helen said, practically.* = **sensibly**, reasonably, matter-of-factly, realistically, rationally, pragmatically, with common sense, unsentimentally

practice NOUN **1** *a public inquiry into bank practices* = **custom**, use, way, system, rule, method, tradition, habit, routine, mode, usage, wont, praxis, usual procedure, tikanga (*N.Z.*) **2** *netball practice* = **training**, study, exercise, work-out, discipline, preparation (*old-fashioned*), drill, rehearsal, repetition **3** *improving his skills in the practice of medicine* = **profession**, work, business, career, occupation, pursuit, vocation **4** *He worked in a small legal practice.* = **business**, company, office, firm, enterprise, partnership, outfit (*informal*) **5** *They advocate self-knowledge through the practice of yoga.* = **use**, experience, action, effect, operation, application, enactment

practise VERB **1** *Lauren practises the concerto every day.* = **rehearse**, study, prepare, perfect, repeat, go through, polish, go over, refine, run through **2** *practising for a gym display* = **do**, train, exercise, work out, drill, warm up, keep your hand in **3** *Astronomy continued to be practised in Byzantium.* = **carry out**, follow, apply, perform, observe, engage in, live up to, put into practice **4** *He practised as a lawyer for thirty years.* = **work at**, pursue, carry on, undertake, specialize in, ply your trade

practised ADJECTIVE = **skilled**, trained, experienced, seasoned, able, expert, qualified, accomplished, versed, proficient ■ **OPPOSITE:** inexperienced

pragmatic ADJECTIVE = **practical**, efficient, sensible, realistic, down-to-earth, matter-of-fact, utilitarian, businesslike, hard-headed ■ **OPPOSITE:** idealistic

praise VERB **1** *Many praised him for taking a strong stand.* = **acclaim**, approve of, honour, cheer, admire, applaud, compliment, congratulate, pay tribute to, laud, extol, sing the praises of, pat someone on the back, cry someone up, big up (*slang*), eulogize, take your hat off to, crack someone up (*informal*) ■ **OPPOSITE:** criticize **2** *She asked the congregation to praise God.* = **give thanks to**, bless, worship, adore, magnify (*archaic*), glorify, exalt, pay homage to ▶ NOUN **1** *I have nothing but praise for the police.* = **approval**, acclaim, applause, cheering, tribute, compliment, congratulations, ovation, accolade, good word, kudos, eulogy, commendation, approbation, acclamation, panegyric, encomium, plaudit, laudation ■ **OPPOSITE:** criticism **2** *Hindus were singing hymns in praise of the god Rama.* = **thanks**, glory, worship, devotion, homage, adoration

prance VERB **1** *The cheerleaders pranced on the far side of the pitch.* = **dance**, bound, leap, trip, spring, jump, skip, romp, caper, cavort, frisk, gambol, cut a rug (*informal*) **2** *models prancing around on the catwalk* = **strut**, parade, stalk, show off (*informal*), swagger, swank (*informal*)

prank NOUN = **trick**, lark (*informal*), caper, frolic, escapade, practical joke, skylarking (*informal*), antic, jape

prattle VERB *She prattled on until I wanted to scream.* = **chatter**, babble, waffle (*informal, chiefly Brit.*), run on, rabbit on (*Brit. informal*), witter on (*informal*), patter, drivel, clack, twitter, jabber, gabble, rattle on, blather, blether, run off at the mouth (*slang*), earbash (*Austral. & N.Z. slang*) ▶ NOUN *I had had enough of his mindless prattle.* = **chatter**, talk, babble, waffle (*informal*), rambling, wittering (*informal*), prating, drivel, jabber, gabble, blather, blether (*Scot.*)

pray VERB **1** *He spent his time in prison praying and studying.* = **say your prayers**, offer a prayer, recite the rosary **2** *They prayed for help.* = **beg**, ask, plead, petition, urge, request, sue, crave (*informal*), invoke, call upon, cry, solicit, implore, beseech, entreat, importune (*formal*), adjure, supplicate

prayer NOUN **1** *The night was spent in prayer and meditation.* = **supplication**, devotion, communion **2** *prayers of thanksgiving* = **orison**, litany, invocation, intercession **3** *Say a quick prayer I don't get stopped for speeding.* = **plea**, appeal, suit, request, petition, entreaty, supplication (*formal*)

preach VERB **1** (*often with* **to**) *The bishop preached to a huge crowd.* = **deliver a sermon**, address, exhort, evangelize, preach a sermon, orate **2** *The movement preaches revolution.* = **urge**, teach, champion, recommend, advise, counsel, advocate, exhort

preacher NOUN = **clergyman** or **woman**, minister, parson, missionary, evangelist, revivalist

preamble NOUN = **introduction**, prelude, preface, foreword, overture, opening move, proem, prolegomenon, exordium, opening statement or remarks

precarious ADJECTIVE **1** *Our financial situation had become precarious.* = **insecure**, dangerous, uncertain, tricky, risky, doubtful, dubious, unsettled, dodgy (*Brit., Austral. & N.Z. informal*), unstable, unsure, hazardous, shaky, hairy (*slang*), perilous, touch and go, dicey (*informal, chiefly Brit.*), chancy (*informal*), built on sand, shonky (*Austral. & N.Z. informal*) ■ OPPOSITE: secure **2** *They crawled up a precarious rope ladder.*

= **dangerous**, unstable, shaky, slippery, insecure, unsafe, unreliable, unsteady ■ OPPOSITE: stable

precaution NOUN *This is purely a safety precaution.* = **safeguard**, insurance, protection, provision, safety measure, preventative measure, belt and braces (*informal*)

precede VERB **1** *Intensive negotiations preceded the vote.* = **go before**, introduce, herald, pave the way for, usher in, antedate, antecede, forerun **2** *Alice preceded them from the room.* = **go ahead of**, lead, head, go before, take precedence **3** *the information that precedes the paragraph in question* = **preface**, introduce, go before, launch, prefix

precedence NOUN = **priority**, lead, rank, preference, superiority, supremacy, seniority, primacy, pre-eminence, antecedence

precedent NOUN = **instance**, example, authority, standard, model, pattern, criterion, prototype, paradigm, antecedent, exemplar, previous example

preceding ADJECTIVE **1** *Please refer back to the preceding chapter.* = **previous**, earlier, former, above, foregoing, aforementioned, anterior, aforesaid **2** *the student revolution of the preceding years* = **past**, earlier, former, prior, foregoing

precept NOUN **1** *the precepts of Buddhism* = **rule**, order, law, direction, principle, command, regulation, instruction, decree, mandate, canon, statute, ordinance, commandment, behest, dictum **2** *the precept, 'If a job's worth doing, it's worth doing well'* = **maxim**, saying, rule, principle, guideline, motto, dictum, axiom, byword

precinct NOUN *a pedestrian precinct* = **area**, quarter, section, sector, district, zone ▶ PLURAL NOUN *No-one carrying arms is allowed within the precincts of the temple.* = **district**, limits, region, borders, bounds, boundaries, confines, neighbourhood, milieu, surrounding area, environs, purlieus

precious ADJECTIVE **1** *jewellery and precious objects belonging to her mother* = **valuable**, expensive, rare, fine, choice, prized, dear, costly, high-priced, exquisite, invaluable, priceless, recherché, inestimable ■ OPPOSITE: worthless **2** *her most precious possession* = **loved**, valued, favourite, prized, dear, dearest, treasured, darling, beloved, adored, cherished, fave (*informal*), idolized, worth your or its weight in gold **3** *Actors, he decided, were all precious and neurotic.* = **affected**, artificial, fastidious, twee (*Brit. informal*), chichi, overrefined, overnice

precipice NOUN = **cliff**, crag, rock face, cliff face, height, brink, bluff, sheer drop, steep cliff, scarp

precipitate VERB 1 *The killings in the city have precipitated the worst crisis yet.* = **quicken**, trigger, accelerate, further, press, advance, hurry, dispatch, speed up, bring on, hasten, push forward, expedite 2 *Dust was precipitated into the air.* = **throw**, launch, cast, discharge, hurl, fling, let fly, send forth ▶ ADJECTIVE 1 *I don't think we should make any precipitate decisions.* = **hasty**, hurried, frantic, rash, reckless, impulsive, madcap, ill-advised, precipitous, impetuous, indiscreet, heedless, harum-scarum 2 *the precipitate collapse of European communism* = **sudden**, quick, brief, rushing, violent, plunging, rapid, unexpected, swift, abrupt, without warning, headlong, breakneck

precipitous ADJECTIVE 1 *a steep, precipitous cliff* = **sheer**, high, steep, dizzy, abrupt, perpendicular, falling sharply 2 *the stock market's precipitous drop* = **hasty**, sudden, hurried, precipitate, abrupt, harum-scarum
> USAGE Some people think the use of *precipitous* to mean 'hasty' is incorrect, and that *precipitate* should be used instead.

precise ADJECTIVE 1 *We will never know the precise details of his death.* = **exact**, specific, actual, particular, express, fixed, correct, absolute, accurate, explicit, definite, clear-cut, literal, unequivocal, surgical ■ OPPOSITE: vague 2 *They speak very precise English.* = **strict**, particular, exact, nice, formal, careful, stiff, rigid, meticulous, inflexible, scrupulous, fastidious, prim, puritanical, finicky, punctilious (*formal*), ceremonious ■ OPPOSITE: inexact

precisely ADVERB 1 *The meeting began at precisely 4.00 p.m.* = **exactly**, bang on, squarely, correctly, absolutely, strictly, accurately, plumb (*informal*), slap on (*informal*), square on, on the dot, smack on (*informal*) 2 *'Is that what you meant?' – 'Precisely.'* = **just so**, yes, absolutely, exactly, quite so, you bet (*informal*), without a doubt, on the button (*informal*), indubitably 3 *That is precisely what I suggested.* = **just**, entirely, absolutely, altogether, exactly, in all respects 4 *Please repeat precisely what she said.* = **word for word**, literally, exactly, to the letter, neither more nor less

precision NOUN = **exactness**, care, accuracy, fidelity, correctness, rigour, nicety, particularity, exactitude, meticulousness, definiteness, dotting the i's and crossing the t's, preciseness

preclude VERB 1 *At 84, John feels his age precludes much travelling.* = **rule out**, put a stop to, obviate (*formal*), make impossible, make impracticable 2 *Poor English precluded them from ever finding a job.* = **prevent**, stop, check, exclude, restrain, prohibit, inhibit, hinder, forestall, debar

precocious ADJECTIVE = **advanced**, developed, forward, quick, bright (*informal*), smart

preconceived ADJECTIVE = **presumed**, premature, predetermined, presupposed, prejudged, forejudged

preconception NOUN = **preconceived idea** or **notion**, notion, prejudice, bias, presumption, predisposition, presupposition, prepossession

precondition NOUN = **necessity**, essential, requirement, prerequisite, must, sine qua non (*Latin*), must-have

precursor NOUN 1 *Real tennis, a precursor of the modern game, originated in the eleventh century.* = **forerunner**, pioneer, predecessor, forebear, antecedent, originator 2 *The deal should not be seen as a precursor to a merger.* = **herald** (*literary*), usher, messenger, vanguard, forerunner, harbinger (*literary*)

predatory ADJECTIVE 1 *predatory birds like the eagle* = **hunting**, ravening, carnivorous, rapacious, raptorial, predacious 2 *predatory gangs* = **plundering**, ravaging, pillaging, marauding, thieving, despoiling 3 *predatory business practices* = **rapacious**, greedy, voracious, vulturous, vulturine

predecessor NOUN 1 *He learned everything he knew from his predecessor.* = **previous job holder**, precursor, forerunner, antecedent, former job holder, prior job holder 2 *opportunities our predecessors never had* = **ancestor**, forebear, antecedent, forefather, tupuna or tipuna (*N.Z.*)

predetermined ADJECTIVE 1 *our predetermined fate* = **fated**, predestined, preordained, meant, doomed, foreordained, pre-elected, predestinated 2 *The capsules release the drug at a predetermined time.* = **prearranged**, set, agreed, set up, settled, fixed, cut and dried (*informal*), preplanned, decided beforehand, arranged in advance

predicament NOUN = **fix** (*informal*), state, situation, spot (*informal*), corner, hole (*slang*), emergency, mess, jam (*informal*), dilemma, pinch, plight, scrape (*informal*), hot water (*informal*), pickle (*informal*), how-do-you-do (*informal*), quandary, tight spot

predict VERB = **foretell**, forecast, divine, foresee, prophesy, call, augur, presage, portend, prognosticate, forebode, soothsay, vaticinate (*rare*)

predictable ADJECTIVE = **likely**, expected, sure, certain, anticipated, reliable, foreseen, on the cards, foreseeable, sure-fire (*informal*), calculable
■ **OPPOSITE:** unpredictable

prediction NOUN = **prophecy**, forecast, prognosis, divination, prognostication, augury, soothsaying, sortilege

predilection NOUN = **liking**, love, taste, weakness, fancy, leaning, tendency, preference, bias, inclination, penchant, fondness, propensity, predisposition, proclivity (*formal*), partiality, proneness

predispose VERB = **incline**, influence, prepare, prompt, lead, prime, affect, prejudice, bias, induce, dispose, sway, make you of a mind to

predisposed ADJECTIVE **1** *Franklin was predisposed to believe him.* = **inclined**, willing, given, minded, ready, agreeable, amenable **2** *Some people are genetically predisposed to diabetes.* = **susceptible**, subject, prone, liable

predisposition NOUN **1** *the predisposition to behave in a certain way* = **inclination**, tendency, disposition, bent, bias, willingness, likelihood, penchant, propensity, predilection, proclivity (*formal*), potentiality, proneness **2** *a hereditary predisposition to the disease* = **susceptibility**, tendency, proneness

predominance NOUN **1** *An interesting note was the predominance of London club players.* = **prevalence**, weight, preponderance, greater number **2** *their economic predominance* = **dominance**, hold, control, edge, leadership, sway, supremacy, mastery, dominion, upper hand, ascendancy, paramountcy

predominant ADJECTIVE **1** *Amanda's predominant emotion was one of confusion.* = **main**, chief, prevailing, notable, paramount, prevalent, preponderant **2** *He played a predominant role in shaping French economic policy.* = **principal**, leading, important, prime, controlling, ruling, chief, capital, primary, supreme, prominent, superior, dominant, sovereign, top-priority, ascendant ■ **OPPOSITE:** minor

predominantly ADVERB = **mainly**, largely, chiefly, mostly, generally, principally, primarily, on the whole, in the main, for the most part, to a great extent, preponderantly

predominate VERB **1** *All nationalities were represented, but the English and American predominated.* = **be in the majority**, dominate, prevail, stand out, be predominant, be most noticeable, preponderate **2** *a society where Islamic principles predominate* = **prevail**, rule, reign, hold sway, get the upper hand, carry weight

pre-eminence NOUN = **superiority**, distinction, excellence, supremacy, prestige, prominence, transcendence, renown, predominance, paramountcy

pre-eminent ADJECTIVE = **outstanding**, supreme, paramount, chief, excellent, distinguished, superior, renowned, foremost, consummate, predominant, transcendent, unrivalled, incomparable, peerless, unsurpassed, unequalled, matchless

preen VERB **1** (*often reflexive*) *He spent half an hour preening in front of the mirror.* = **smarten**, admire, dress up, doll up (*slang*), trim, array, deck out, spruce up, prettify, primp, trig (*archaic, dialect*), titivate, prink **2** (*of a bird*) *The linnet shook herself and preened a few feathers on her breast.* = **clean**, smooth, groom, tidy, plume • **preen yourself** *His only negative feature is the desire to brag and preen himself over his abilities.* = **pride yourself**, congratulate yourself, give yourself a pat on the back, pique yourself, plume yourself

preface NOUN *the preface to the English edition of the novel* = **introduction**, preliminary, prelude, preamble, foreword, prologue, proem, prolegomenon, exordium ▶ VERB *I will preface what I am going to say with a few lines from Shakespeare.* = **introduce**, precede, open, begin, launch, lead up to, prefix

prefer VERB **1** *Do you prefer a particular sort of music?* = **like better**, favour, go for, pick, select, adopt, fancy (*Brit. informal*), opt for, single out, plump for, incline towards, be partial to **2** *I prefer to go on self-catering holidays.* = **choose**, elect, opt for, pick, wish, desire, would rather, would sooner, incline towards

> **USAGE** Normally, *to* (not *than*) is used after *prefer* and *preferable*. Therefore, you would say *I prefer skating to skiing*, and *a small income is preferable to no income at all*. However, when expressing a preference between two activities stated as infinitive verbs, for example *to skate* and *to ski*, use *than*, as in *I prefer to skate than to ski*.

preferable ADJECTIVE = **better**, best, chosen, choice, preferred, recommended, favoured, superior, worthier, more suitable, more desirable, more eligible
■ **OPPOSITE:** undesirable

> **USAGE** Since *preferable* already means 'more desirable', it is better when writing not to say something is *more preferable* or *most preferable*.

preferably ADVERB = **ideally**, if possible, rather, sooner, much rather, by choice, much sooner, as a matter of choice, in or for preference

preference NOUN 1 *Whatever your preference, we have a product to suit you.* = **liking**, wish, taste, desire, bag (*slang*), leaning, bent, bias, cup of tea (*informal*), inclination, penchant, fondness, predisposition, predilection, proclivity (*formal*), partiality 2 *He enjoys all styles of music, but his preference is opera.* = **first choice**, choice, favourite, election, pick, option, selection, top of the list, fave (*informal*) 3 *Candidates with the right qualifications should be given preference.* = **priority**, first place, precedence, advantage, favouritism, pride of place, favoured treatment

preferential ADJECTIVE = **privileged**, favoured, superior, better, special, partial, partisan, advantageous

prefigure VERB = **foreshadow**, suggest, indicate, intimate, presage, portend, shadow forth, adumbrate, foretoken

pregnancy NOUN = **gestation**, gravidity
■ **RELATED WORDS:** *adjectives* antenatal, postnatal, maternity

pregnant ADJECTIVE 1 *Tina was pregnant with their first child.* = **expectant**, expecting (*informal*), with child (*archaic*), in the club (*Brit. slang*), up the duff (*Brit. slang*), in the family way (*informal*), gravid, preggers (*Brit. informal*), enceinte, in the pudding club (*slang*), big or heavy with child (*archaic*) 2 *There was a long, pregnant silence.* = **meaningful**, pointed, charged, significant, telling, loaded, expressive, eloquent, weighty, suggestive 3 (*with* **with**) *The songs are pregnant with irony and insight.* = **full of**, rich in, fraught with, teeming with, replete with, abounding in, abundant in, fecund with

prehistoric ADJECTIVE = **earliest**, early, primitive, primordial, primeval

prejudice NOUN 1 *a victim of racial prejudice* = **discrimination**, racism, injustice, sexism, intolerance, bigotry, unfairness, chauvinism, narrow-mindedness, faith hate 2 *the deep cultural prejudices I inherited as a child* = **bias**, preconception, partiality, preconceived notion, warp, jaundiced eye, prejudgment 3 *I feel sure it can be done without prejudice to anybody's principles.* = **harm**, damage, hurt, disadvantage, loss, mischief, detriment, impairment

▶ VERB 1 *I think your upbringing has prejudiced you.* = **bias**, influence, colour, poison, distort, sway, warp, slant, predispose, jaundice, prepossess 2 *He claimed that the media coverage had prejudiced his chance of a fair trial.* = **harm**, damage, hurt, injure, mar, undermine, spoil, impair, hinder, crool or cruel (*Austral. slang*)

prejudiced ADJECTIVE = **biased**, influenced, unfair, one-sided, conditioned, partial, partisan, discriminatory, bigoted, intolerant, opinionated, narrow-minded, jaundiced, prepossessed ■ **OPPOSITE:** unbiased

prejudicial ADJECTIVE = **harmful**, damaging, undermining, detrimental, hurtful, unfavourable, counterproductive, deleterious (*formal*), injurious, inimical, disadvantageous

preliminary ADJECTIVE 1 *Preliminary talks began yesterday.* = **first**, opening, trial, initial, test, pilot, prior, introductory, preparatory, exploratory, initiatory, prefatory, precursory 2 *the last match of the preliminary rounds* = **qualifying**, eliminating ▶ NOUN *Today's survey is a preliminary to a more detailed one.* = **introduction**, opening, beginning, foundation, start, preparation, first round, prelude, preface, overture, initiation, preamble, groundwork, prelims

prelude NOUN 1 *The protests are now seen as the prelude to last year's uprising.* = **introduction**, beginning, preparation, preliminary, start, commencement, curtain-raiser 2 *the third-act Prelude of Parsifal* = **overture**, opening, introduction, introductory movement

premature ADJECTIVE 1 *a twenty-four-year-old man suffering from premature baldness* = **early**, untimely, before time, unseasonable 2 *It now seems their optimism was premature.* = **hasty**, rash, too soon, precipitate, impulsive, untimely, ill-considered, jumping the gun, ill-timed, inopportune, overhasty 3 *a greater risk of having a premature baby* = **preterm**, prem (*informal*), preemie (*U.S. & Canad. informal*)

prematurely ADVERB 1 *Danny was born prematurely.* = **too early**, too soon, before your time, preterm 2 *He may have spoken just a little prematurely.* = **overhastily**, rashly, too soon, precipitately, too hastily, half-cocked, at half-cock

premeditated ADJECTIVE = **planned**, calculated, deliberate, considered, studied, intended, conscious, contrived, intentional, wilful, aforethought, prepense ■ **OPPOSITE:** unplanned

premier NOUN *the premier of Western Australia*
= **head of government**, prime minister,
chancellor, chief minister, P.M. ▶ ADJECTIVE
the country's premier opera company = **chief**,
leading, top, first, highest, head, main,
prime, primary, principal, arch, foremost

premiere NOUN = **first night**, opening,
debut, first showing, first performance

premise NOUN *the premise that men and
women are on equal terms in this society*
= **assumption**, proposition, thesis, ground,
argument, hypothesis, assertion,
postulate, supposition, presupposition,
postulation

premises PLURAL NOUN = **building(s)**,
place, office, property, site, establishment

premium NOUN **1** *an increase in insurance
premiums* = **fee**, charge, payment,
instalment **2** *Customers are not willing to pay
a premium.* = **surcharge**, extra charge,
additional fee or charge **3** *Shareholders did
not receive a premium on the price of their shares.*
= **bonus**, reward, prize, percentage
(*informal*), perk (*Brit. informal*), boon,
bounty, remuneration, recompense,
perquisite (*formal*) • **at a premium** *Tickets
to the game are at a premium.* = **in great
demand**, valuable, expensive, rare, costly,
scarce, in short supply, hard to come by, like
gold dust, beyond your means, not to be
had for love or money

premonition NOUN = **feeling**, idea,
intuition, suspicion, hunch, apprehension,
misgiving, foreboding, funny feeling
(*informal*), presentiment, feeling in your
bones

preoccupation NOUN **1** *Her main
preoccupation from an early age was boys.*
= **obsession**, concern, hang-up (*informal*),
fixation, pet subject, hobbyhorse, idée fixe
(*French*), bee in your bonnet **2** *He kept sinking
back into gloomy preoccupation.* = **absorption**,
musing, oblivion, abstraction, daydreaming,
immersion, reverie, absent-mindedness,
brown study, inattentiveness, absence of
mind, pensiveness, engrossment,
prepossession, woolgathering

preoccupied ADJECTIVE **1** *They were
preoccupied with their own concerns.*
= **absorbed**, taken up, caught up, lost,
intent, wrapped up, immersed, engrossed,
rapt **2** *He was too preoccupied to notice what
was going on.* = **lost in thought**, abstracted,
distracted, unaware, oblivious, faraway,
absent-minded, heedless, distrait, in a
brown study

preparation NOUN **1** *Behind any successful
event lies months of preparation.* = **groundwork**,
development, preparing, arranging,
devising, getting ready, thinking-up,
putting in order **2** *a military build-up in
preparation for war* = **readiness**, expectation,
provision, safeguard, precaution,
anticipation, foresight, preparedness,
alertness **3** (*usually plural*) *Final preparations
are under way for the celebration.*
= **arrangement**, plan, measure, provision
4 *a specially formulated natural skin preparation*
= **mixture**, cream, medicine, compound,
composition, lotion, concoction, amalgam,
ointment, tincture

preparatory ADJECTIVE *At least a year's
preparatory work will be needed.*
= **introductory**, preliminary, opening,
basic, primary, elementary, prefatory,
preparative • **preparatory to** *Sloan cleared
his throat preparatory to speaking.* = **before**,
prior to, in preparation for, in advance of,
in anticipation of

prepare VERB **1** *He said the government must
prepare an emergency plan for evacuation.*
= **make** *or* **get ready**, arrange, draw up,
form, fashion, get up (*informal*), construct,
assemble, contrive, put together, make
provision, put in order, jack up (*N.Z.
informal*) **2** *The crew has been preparing the ship
for storage.* = **equip**, fit, adapt, adjust, outfit,
furnish, fit out, accoutre **3** *It is a school's job
to prepare students for university studies.*
= **train**, guide, prime, direct, coach, brief,
discipline, groom, put someone in the
picture **4** *She found him in the kitchen,
preparing dinner.* = **make**, cook, put together,
get, produce, assemble, muster, concoct,
fix up, dish up, rustle up (*informal*) **5** *They
were not given enough time to prepare for the
election battle.* = **get ready**, plan, anticipate,
make provision, lay the groundwork, make
preparations, arrange things, get
everything set **6** *giving the players a chance to
prepare for the match* = **practise**, get ready,
train, exercise, warm up, get into shape

prepared ADJECTIVE **1** *Are you prepared to take
industrial action?* = **willing**, minded, able,
ready, inclined, disposed, in the mood,
predisposed, of a mind **2** *I was prepared for a
long wait.* = **ready**, set, all set **3** *The country is
fully prepared for war.* = **fit**, primed, in order,
arranged, in readiness, all systems go
(*informal*)

preparedness NOUN = **readiness**, order,
preparation, fitness, alertness

preponderance NOUN **1** *the huge
preponderance of males among homeless people*
= **predominance**, predominate, dominance,
prevalence **2** *The preponderance of the
evidence strongly supports his guilt.* = **greater
part**, mass, bulk, weight, lion's share,

greater numbers, extensiveness **3** *In 1965, the preponderance of West Germany over East had become even greater.* = **domination**, power, sway, superiority, supremacy, dominion, ascendancy

preposterous ADJECTIVE = **ridiculous**, bizarre, incredible, outrageous, shocking, impossible, extreme, crazy (*informal*), excessive, absurd, foolish, ludicrous, extravagant, unthinkable, unreasonable, irrational, monstrous, senseless, out of the question, laughable, exorbitant, nonsensical, risible (*formal*), asinine, cockamamie (*slang, chiefly U.S.*)

prerequisite NOUN *Good self-esteem is a prerequisite for a happy life.* = **requirement**, must, essential, necessity, condition, qualification, imperative, precondition, requisite, sine qua non (*Latin*), must-have ▶ ADJECTIVE *Young children can be taught the prerequisite skills necessary to learn to read.* = **required**, necessary, essential, called for, vital, mandatory, imperative, indispensable, obligatory, requisite, of the essence, needful

prerogative NOUN = **right**, choice, claim, authority, title, due, advantage, sanction, liberty, privilege, immunity, exemption, birthright, droit, perquisite

presage VERB *Diplomats fear the incidents presage a new chapter in the conflict.* = **portend**, point to, warn of, signify, omen, bode, foreshadow, augur, betoken, adumbrate, forebode, foretoken ▶ NOUN *Soldiers used to believe a raven was a presage of coming battle.* = **omen**, sign, warning, forecast, prediction, prophecy, portent, harbinger (*literary*), intimation, forewarning, prognostication, augury, prognostic, auspice

prescient ADJECTIVE = **foresighted**, psychic, prophetic, divining, discerning, perceptive, clairvoyant, far-sighted, divinatory, mantic

prescribe VERB **1** *Our doctor prescribed antibiotics for her throat infection.* = **specify**, order, direct, stipulate, write a prescription for **2** *The judge said he was passing the sentence prescribed by law.* = **ordain** (*formal*), set, order, establish, rule, require, fix, recommend, impose, appoint, command, define, dictate, assign, lay down, decree, stipulate, enjoin

prescription NOUN **1** *These drugs are freely available without a prescription.* = **instruction**, direction, formula, script (*informal*), recipe **2** *I'm not sleeping, even with that new prescription the doctor gave me.* = **medicine**, drug, treatment, preparation, cure, mixture, dose, remedy

prescriptive ADJECTIVE = **dictatorial**, rigid, authoritarian, legislating, dogmatic, didactic, preceptive

presence NOUN **1** *His presence in the village could only stir up trouble.* = **being**, existence, company, residence, attendance, showing up, companionship, occupancy, habitation, inhabitance **2** *conscious of being in the presence of a great man* = **proximity**, closeness, vicinity, nearness, neighbourhood, immediate circle, propinquity **3** *Hendrix's stage presence appealed to thousands of teenage rebels.* = **personality**, bearing, appearance, aspect, air, ease, carriage, aura, poise, demeanour, self-assurance, mien (*literary*), comportment **4** *The house was haunted by shadows and unseen presences.* = **spirit**, ghost, manifestation, spectre, apparition, shade (*literary*), wraith, supernatural being, revenant, eidolon, atua (*N.Z.*), wairua (*N.Z.*)
• **presence of mind** *Someone had the presence of mind to call for an ambulance.* = **level-headedness**, assurance, composure, poise, cool (*slang*), wits, countenance, coolness, aplomb, alertness, calmness, equanimity, self-assurance, phlegm, quickness, sang-froid, self-possession, unflappability, imperturbability, quick-wittedness, self-command, collectedness

present¹ ADJECTIVE **1** *the government's present economic difficulties* = **current**, existing, immediate, contemporary, instant, present-day, existent, extant **2** *The whole family was present.* = **here**, there, near, available, ready, nearby, accounted for, to hand, at hand, in attendance ■ OPPOSITE: absent **3** *This vitamin is naturally present in breast milk.* = **in existence**, existing, existent, extant • **at present** *At present, children under 14 are not permitted in bars.* = **just now**, now, presently, currently, at the moment, right now, nowadays, at this time, at the present time, in this day and age • **for the present** *The ministers agreed that sanctions should remain in place for the present.* = **for now**, for a while, in the meantime, temporarily, for the moment, for the time being, provisionally, not for long, for the nonce • **the present** *his struggle to reconcile the past with the present* = **now**, today, the time being, here and now, this day and age, the present moment

present² NOUN *The vase was a wedding present.* = **gift**, offering, grant, favour, donation, hand-out, endowment, boon (*archaic*), bounty, gratuity, prezzie (*informal*), benefaction, bonsela (*S. African*), koha (*N.Z.*), largesse or largess ▶ VERB **1** *The queen presented the prizes to the winning captain.* = **give**, award, hand over, offer, grant, donate, hand out, furnish, confer, bestow, entrust, proffer, put at someone's disposal **2** *We presented three options to the unions for discussion.* = **put forward**, offer, suggest, raise, state, produce, introduce, advance, relate, declare, extend, pose, submit, tender, hold out, recount, expound, proffer, adduce **3** *The theatre is presenting a new production of 'Hamlet'.* = **put on**, stage, perform, give, show, mount, render, put before the public **4** *presenting a new product or service to the market-place* = **launch**, display, demonstrate, parade, exhibit, unveil **5** *Fox stepped forward and presented him to Jack.* = **introduce**, make known, acquaint someone with

presentable ADJECTIVE **1** *She managed to make herself presentable in time for work.* = **tidy**, elegant, well groomed, becoming, trim, spruce, dapper, natty (*informal*), smartly dressed, fit to be seen ■ **OPPOSITE:** unpresentable **2** *His score had reached a presentable total.* = **satisfactory**, suitable, decent, acceptable, proper, good enough, respectable, not bad (*informal*), tolerable, passable, O.K. or okay (*informal*) ■ **OPPOSITE:** unsatisfactory

presentation NOUN **1** *at the presentation ceremony* = **giving**, award, offering, donation, investiture, bestowal, conferral **2** *Keep the presentation of the dish simple.* = **appearance**, look, display, packaging, arrangement, layout **3** *Scottish Opera's presentation of Das Rheingold* = **performance**, staging, production, show, arrangement, representation, portrayal, rendition

present-day ADJECTIVE = **current**, modern, present, recent, contemporary, up-to-date, latter-day, newfangled

presently ADVERB **1** *The island is presently uninhabited.* = **at present**, currently, now, today, these days, nowadays, at the present time, in this day and age, at the minute (*Brit. informal*) **2** *Just take it easy and you'll feel better presently.* = **soon**, shortly, directly, before long, momentarily (*U.S. & Canad.*), in a moment, in a minute, pretty soon (*informal*), anon (*archaic*), by and by, in a short while, in a jiffy (*informal*), erelong (*archaic, poetic*)

preservation NOUN **1** *the preservation of the status quo* = **upholding**, keeping, support, security, defence, maintenance, perpetuation **2** *the preservation of buildings of historic interest* = **protection**, safety,

maintenance, conservation, salvation, safeguarding, safekeeping **3** *the preparation, cooking and preservation of food* = **storage**, smoking, drying, bottling, freezing, curing, chilling, candying, pickling, conserving, tinning

preserve VERB **1** *We will do everything we can to preserve peace.* = **maintain**, keep, continue, retain, sustain, keep up, prolong, uphold, conserve, perpetuate, keep alive ■ **OPPOSITE:** end **2** *We need to preserve the rainforests.* = **protect**, keep, save, maintain, guard, defend, secure, shelter, shield, care for, safeguard, conserve ■ **OPPOSITE:** attack **3** *ginger preserved in syrup* = **keep**, save, store, can, dry, bottle, salt, cure, candy, pickle, conserve ▶ NOUN **1** (*often plural*) *jars of pear and blackberry preserves* = **jam**, jelly, conserve, marmalade, confection, sweetmeat, confiture **2** *The conduct of foreign policy is largely the preserve of the president.* = **area**, department (*informal*), field, territory, province, arena, orbit, sphere, realm, domain, specialism **3** *one of the world's great wildlife preserves* = **reserve**, reservation, sanctuary, game reserve

preside VERB *He presided at the closing ceremony.* = **officiate**, chair, moderate, be chairperson • **preside over something** or **someone** *The question of who should preside over the next full commission was being debated.* = **run**, lead, head, control, manage, direct, conduct, govern, administer, supervise, be at the head of, be in authority

press VERB **1** *her hands pressing down on the desk; He pressed a button and the door closed.* = **push (down)**, depress, lean on, bear down, press down, force down **2** *He pressed his back against the door.* = **push**, squeeze, jam, thrust, ram, wedge, shove **3** *I pressed my child closer to my heart and shut my eyes.* = **hug**, squeeze, embrace, clasp, crush, encircle, enfold, hold close, fold in your arms **4** *The trade unions are pressing him to stand firm.* = **urge**, force, beg, petition, sue, enforce, insist on, compel, constrain, exhort (*formal*), implore, enjoin, pressurize, entreat, importune (*formal*), supplicate **5** *mass strikes and demonstrations to press their demands* = **plead**, present, lodge, submit, tender, advance insistently **6** *He would shine his father's shoes and press his shirts.* = **iron**, steam, finish, smooth, flatten, put the creases in **7** *The grapes are hand-picked and pressed.* = **compress**, grind, reduce, mill, crush, pound, squeeze, tread, pulp, mash, trample, condense, pulverize, tamp, macerate **8** *As the music stopped, the crowd pressed forward.* = **crowd**, push, gather, rush, surge, mill, hurry, cluster, flock, herd, swarm, hasten, seethe, throng • **the press** **1** *Today the press is full of articles on the subject.* = **newspapers**, the papers, journalism, news media, Fleet Street, fourth estate **2** *He looked relaxed and calm as he faced the press.* = **journalists**, correspondents, reporters, photographers, columnists, pressmen, presswomen, newsmen, newswomen, journos (*slang*)

pressing ADJECTIVE = **urgent**, serious, burning, vital, crucial (*informal*), imperative, important, constraining, high-priority, now or never, importunate (*formal*), exigent ■ **OPPOSITE:** unimportant

pressure NOUN **1** *The pressure of his fingers had relaxed.* = **force**, crushing, squeezing, compressing, weight, compression, heaviness **2** *He may be putting pressure on her to agree.* = **power**, influence, force, obligation, constraint, sway, compulsion, coercion **3** *The pressures of modern life are great.* = **stress**, demands, difficulty, strain, press, heat, load, burden, distress, hurry, urgency, hassle (*informal*), uphill (*S. African*), adversity, affliction, exigency

pressurize VERB = **force**, drive, compel, intimidate, coerce, dragoon, breathe down someone's neck, browbeat, press-gang, twist someone's arm (*informal*), turn on the heat (*informal*), put the screws on (*slang*)

prestige NOUN = **status**, standing, authority, influence, credit, regard, weight, reputation, honour, importance, fame, celebrity, distinction, esteem, stature, eminence, kudos, cachet, renown, Brownie points, mana (*N.Z.*)

prestigious ADJECTIVE = **celebrated**, respected, prominent, great, important, imposing, impressive, influential, esteemed, notable, renowned, eminent, illustrious, reputable, exalted ■ **OPPOSITE:** unknown

presumably ADVERB = **it would seem**, probably, likely, apparently, most likely, seemingly, doubtless, on the face of it, in all probability, in all likelihood, doubtlessly

presume VERB **1** *I presume you're here on business.* = **believe**, think, suppose, assume, guess (*informal, chiefly U.S. & Canad.*), take it, take for granted, infer, conjecture, postulate (*formal*), surmise, posit, presuppose **2** *I wouldn't presume to question your judgement.* = **dare**, venture, undertake, go so far as, have the audacity, take the liberty, make bold, make so bold as • **presume on something** or **someone** *He's presuming on your good nature.* = **depend on**, rely on, exploit, take advantage of,

count on, bank on, take liberties with, trust in or to

presumption NOUN **1** *the presumption that a defendant is innocent until proved guilty* = **assumption**, opinion, belief, guess, hypothesis, anticipation, conjecture, surmise, supposition, presupposition, premise **2** *He had the presumption to answer me back.* = **cheek** (*informal*), front, neck (*informal*), nerve (*informal*), assurance, brass (*informal*), gall (*informal*), audacity, boldness, temerity, chutzpah (*U.S. & Canad. informal*), insolence, impudence, effrontery, brass neck (*Brit. informal*), sassiness (*U.S. informal*), presumptuousness, forwardness

presumptuous ADJECTIVE = **pushy** (*informal*), forward, bold, arrogant, presuming, rash, audacious, conceited, foolhardy, insolent, overweening, overconfident, overfamiliar, bigheaded (*informal*), uppish (*Brit. informal*), too big for your boots ■ **OPPOSITE:** shy

presuppose VERB = **presume**, consider, accept, suppose, assume, take it, imply, take for granted, postulate (*formal*), posit, take as read

presupposition NOUN = **assumption**, theory, belief, premise, hypothesis, presumption, preconception, supposition, preconceived idea

pretence NOUN **1** *struggling to keep up the pretence that all was well* = **deception**, invention, sham, fabrication, acting, faking, simulation, deceit, feigning, charade, make-believe, trickery, falsehood, subterfuge, fakery ■ **OPPOSITE:** candour **2** *She was completely without guile or pretence.* = **show**, posturing, artifice, affectation, display, appearance, posing, façade, veneer, pretentiousness, hokum (*slang, chiefly U.S. & Canad.*) ■ **OPPOSITE:** reality **3** *He claimed the police beat him up under the pretence that he was resisting arrest.* = **pretext**, claim, excuse, show, cover, mask, veil, cloak, guise, façade, masquerade, semblance, ruse, garb, wile

pretend VERB **1** *He pretended to be asleep.* = **feign**, affect, assume, allege, put on, fake, make out, simulate, profess, sham, counterfeit, falsify, impersonate, dissemble, dissimulate, pass yourself off as **2** *She can sunbathe and pretend she's in Spain.* = **make believe**, suppose, imagine, play, act, make up, play the part of **3** *I cannot pretend to understand the problem.* = **lay claim**, claim, allege, aspire, profess, purport

pretended ADJECTIVE = **feigned**, alleged, so-called, phoney or phony (*informal*), false, pretend (*informal*), fake, imaginary, bogus,

professed, sham, purported, pseudo
(*informal*), counterfeit, spurious, fictitious,
avowed, ostensible

pretender NOUN **1** = **claimant**, claimer,
aspirant **2** = **impostor**

pretension NOUN **1** *We liked him for his
honesty and lack of pretension.* = **affectation**,
hypocrisy, conceit, show, airs, vanity,
snobbery, pomposity, self-importance,
ostentation, pretentiousness,
snobbishness, vainglory, showiness
2 (*usually plural*) *one of the few fashion
designers who does not have pretensions to be an
artist* = **aspiration**, claim, demand,
profession, assumption, assertion,
pretence

pretentious ADJECTIVE = **affected**,
mannered, exaggerated, pompous,
assuming, hollow, inflated, extravagant,
high-flown, flaunting, grandiose,
conceited, showy, ostentatious, snobbish,
puffed up, bombastic, specious,
grandiloquent, vainglorious, high-
sounding, highfalutin (*informal*),
overambitious, arty-farty (*informal*),
magniloquent ■ **OPPOSITE:** unpretentious

pretext NOUN = **guise**, excuse, veil, show,
cover, appearance, device, mask, ploy,
cloak, simulation, pretence, semblance,
ruse, red herring, alleged reason

pretty ADJECTIVE **1** *She's a charming and pretty
girl.* = **attractive**, appealing, beautiful,
sweet, lovely, charming, fair, fetching
(*informal*), good-looking, cute, graceful,
bonny (*Scot. & Northern English, dialect*),
personable, comely (*old-fashioned*),
prepossessing, fit (*Brit. informal*)
■ **OPPOSITE:** plain **2** *comfortable sofas covered
in a pretty floral print* = **pleasant**, fine,
pleasing, nice, elegant, trim, delicate, neat,
tasteful, dainty, bijou ▶ ADVERB *I had a
pretty good idea what she was going to do.*
= **fairly**, rather, quite, kind of (*informal*),
somewhat, moderately, reasonably

prevail VERB **1** *We hoped that common sense
would prevail.* = **win**, succeed, triumph,
overcome, overrule, be victorious,
carry the day, prove superior, gain mastery
2 *A similar situation prevails in America.* = **be
widespread**, abound, predominate, be
current, be prevalent, preponderate, exist
generally • **prevail on** or **upon someone**
Do you think she can be prevailed upon to do it?
= **persuade**, influence, convince, prompt,
win over, induce, incline, dispose, sway,
talk into, bring round

prevailing ADJECTIVE **1** *individuals who have
gone against the prevailing opinion*
= **widespread**, general, established,

popular, common, set, current, usual,
ordinary, fashionable, in style, customary,
prevalent, in vogue **2** *the prevailing weather
conditions in the area* = **predominating**,
ruling, main, existing, principal

prevalence NOUN = **commonness**,
frequency, regularity, currency, universality,
ubiquity, common occurrence,
pervasiveness, extensiveness, widespread
presence, rampancy, rifeness

prevalent ADJECTIVE = **common**, accepted,
established, popular, general, current,
usual, widespread, extensive, universal,
frequent, everyday, rampant, customary,
commonplace, ubiquitous, rife, habitual
■ **OPPOSITE:** rare

prevent VERB *We took steps to prevent it
happening.* = **stop**, avoid, frustrate, restrain,
check, bar, block, anticipate, hamper, foil,
inhibit, head off, avert, thwart, intercept,
hinder, obstruct, preclude, impede,
counteract, ward off, balk, stave off,
forestall, defend against, obviate (*formal*),
nip in the bud ■ **OPPOSITE:** help

prevention NOUN = **elimination**,
safeguard, precaution, anticipation,
thwarting, avoidance, deterrence,
forestalling, prophylaxis, preclusion,
obviation

preventive or **preventative** ADJECTIVE
1 *They accused the police of failing to take
adequate preventive measures.*
= **precautionary**, protective, hampering,
hindering, deterrent, impeding, pre-
emptive, obstructive, inhibitory
2 *preventive medicine* = **prophylactic**,
protective, precautionary,
counteractive

> **USAGE** In all contexts, *preventive* is
> commoner than, and generally used in
> preference to, *preventative*.

preview NOUN *He had gone to see a preview of
the play.* = **sample**, sneak preview, trailer,
sampler, taster, foretaste, advance
showing ▶ VERB *We preview this season's
collections from Paris.* = **sample**, taste,
give a foretaste of

previous ADJECTIVE **1** *He had a daughter from
a previous marriage.* = **earlier**, former, past,
prior, one-time, preceding, sometime,
erstwhile, antecedent, anterior, quondam,
ex- ■ **OPPOSITE:** later **2** *He recalled what Bob
had told him the previous night.* = **preceding**,
past, prior, foregoing

previously ADVERB = **before**, earlier, once,
in the past, formerly, back then, until now,
at one time, hitherto (*formal*), beforehand,
a while ago, heretofore, in days or years
gone by

prey NOUN 1 *These animals were the prey of hyenas.* = **quarry**, game, kill 2 *Old people are easy prey for conmen.* = **victim**, target, mark, mug (*Brit. slang*), dupe, fall guy (*informal*) • **prey on something** or **someone** 1 *The larvae prey on small aphids.* = **hunt**, live off, eat, seize, devour, feed upon 2 *unscrupulous men who preyed on young runaways* = **victimize**, bully, intimidate, exploit, take advantage of, bleed (*informal*), blackmail, terrorize 3 *This was the question that preyed on his mind.* = **worry**, trouble, burden, distress, haunt, hang over, oppress, weigh down, weigh heavily

price NOUN 1 *a sharp increase in the price of petrol; What's the price on that one?* = **cost**, value, rate, charge, bill, figure, worth, damage (*informal*), amount, estimate, fee, payment, expense, assessment, expenditure, valuation, face value, outlay, asking price 2 *He's paying the price for pushing his body so hard.* = **consequences**, penalty, cost, result, sacrifice, toll, forfeit 3 *He is still at large despite the high price on his head.* = **reward**, bounty, compensation, premium, recompense ▶ VERB *The shares are priced at 330p.* = **evaluate**, value, estimate, rate, cost, assess, put a price on • **at any price** *We want the hostages home at any price.* = **whatever the cost**, regardless, no matter what the cost, anyhow, cost what it may, expense no object

priceless ADJECTIVE = **valuable**, expensive, precious, invaluable, rich, prized, dear, rare, treasured, costly, cherished, incomparable, irreplaceable, incalculable, inestimable, beyond price, worth a king's ransom, worth your or its weight in gold ■ OPPOSITE: worthless

pricey or **pricy** ADJECTIVE = **expensive**, dear, steep (*informal*), costly, high-priced, exorbitant, over the odds (*Brit. informal*), extortionate

prick VERB 1 *She pricked her finger with a needle.* = **pierce**, stab, puncture, bore, pink, punch, lance, jab, perforate, impale 2 *Most were sympathetic once we had pricked their consciences.* = **move**, trouble, touch, pain, wound, distress, grieve ▶ NOUN 1 *She felt a prick on the back of her neck.* = **pang**, smart, sting, spasm, gnawing, twinge, prickle 2 *a tiny hole no bigger than a pin prick* = **puncture**, cut, hole, wound, gash, perforation, pinhole • **prick up** *The dog's ears pricked up at the sound.* = **raise**, point, rise, stand erect

prickle VERB 1 *His scalp prickled under his wig.* = **tingle**, smart, sting, twitch, itch 2 *The pine needles prickled her skin.* = **prick**, stick

into, nick, jab ▶ NOUN 1 *A prickle at the nape of my neck reminds me of my fears.* = **tingling**, smart, chill, tickle, tingle, pins and needles (*informal*), goose bumps, goose flesh 2 *an erect stem covered at the base with prickles* = **spike**, point, spur, needle, spine, thorn, barb

prickly ADJECTIVE 1 *The grass was prickly and damp.* = **spiny**, barbed, thorny, bristly, brambly, briery 2 *a hot prickly feeling at the back of her eyes* = **itchy**, sharp, smarting, stinging, crawling, pricking, tingling, scratchy, prickling 3 *You know how prickly she can be.* = **irritable**, edgy, grumpy, touchy, bad-tempered, fractious, petulant, stroppy (*Brit. slang*), cantankerous, tetchy, ratty (*Brit. & N.Z. informal*), chippy (*informal*), waspish, shirty (*slang, chiefly Brit.*), peevish, snappish, liverish, pettish 4 *The issue is likely to prove a prickly one.* = **difficult**, complicated, tricky, trying, involved, intricate, troublesome, thorny, knotty, ticklish

pride NOUN 1 *the sense of pride in a job well done* = **satisfaction**, achievement, fulfilment, delight, content, pleasure, joy, gratification 2 *Her rejection was a severe blow to his pride.* = **self-respect**, honour, ego, dignity, self-esteem, self-image, self-worth, amour-propre (*French*) 3 *His pride may still be his downfall.* = **conceit**, vanity, arrogance, pretension, presumption, snobbery, morgue (*French*), hubris, smugness, self-importance, egotism, self-love, hauteur, pretentiousness, haughtiness, loftiness, vainglory, superciliousness, bigheadedness (*informal*) ■ OPPOSITE: humility 4 *This glittering dress is the pride of her collection.* = **elite**, pick, best, choice, flower, prize, cream, glory, boast, treasure, jewel, gem, pride and joy • **pride yourself on something** *He prides himself on being able to organize his own life.* = **be proud of**, revel in, boast of, glory in, vaunt, take pride in, brag about, crow about, exult in, congratulate yourself on, flatter yourself, pique yourself, plume yourself

priest NOUN = **clergyman** or **woman**, minister, father, divine, vicar, pastor, cleric, curate, churchman, padre (*informal*), holy man or woman or person, man or woman or person of God, man or woman or person of the cloth, ecclesiastic

priestly ADJECTIVE = **ecclesiastic**, pastoral, clerical, canonical, hieratic, sacerdotal, priestlike

prim ADJECTIVE = **prudish**, particular, formal, proper, precise, stiff, fussy, fastidious, puritanical, demure, starchy (*informal*), prissy (*informal*), strait-laced, priggish, niminy-piminy ■ **OPPOSITE:** liberal

primacy NOUN = **supremacy**, leadership, command, dominance, superiority, dominion, ascendancy, pre-eminence

prima donna NOUN = **diva**, star, leading lady, female lead

primal ADJECTIVE **1** *the most primal of human fears* = **basic**, prime, central, first, highest, greatest, major, chief, main, most important, principal, paramount **2** *Yeats's remarks about folklore and the primal religion* = **earliest**, prime, original, primary, first, initial, primitive, pristine, primordial

primarily ADVERB **1** *Public order is primarily an urban problem.* = **chiefly**, largely, generally, mainly, especially, essentially, mostly, basically, principally, fundamentally, above all, on the whole, for the most part **2** *These machines were primarily intended for use in editing.* = **at first**, originally, initially, in the first place, in the beginning, first and foremost, at or from the start

primary ADJECTIVE **1** *His primary aim in life is to be happy.* = **chief**, leading, main, best, first, highest, greatest, top, prime, capital, principal, dominant, cardinal, paramount ■ **OPPOSITE:** subordinate **2** *our primary needs of air, food and water* = **basic**, essential, radical, fundamental, ultimate, underlying, elemental, bog-standard (*informal*)

prime ADJECTIVE **1** *Political stability is a prime concern.* = **main**, leading, chief, central, major, ruling, key, senior, primary, supreme, principal, ultimate, cardinal, paramount, overriding, foremost, predominant, pre-eminent, number-one (*informal*) **2** *It was one of the City's prime locations.* = **best**, top, select, highest, capital, quality, choice, selected, excellent, superior, first-class, first-rate, grade-A **3** *A prime cause of deforestation was the burning of charcoal to melt ore into iron.* = **fundamental**, original, basic, primary, underlying ▶ NOUN *She was in her intellectual prime.* = **peak**, flower, bloom, maturity, height, perfection, best days, heyday, zenith, full flowering ▶ VERB **1** *The press corps has been primed to avoid this topic.* = **inform**, tell, train, coach, brief, fill in (*informal*), groom (*informal*), notify, clue in (*informal*), gen up (*Brit. informal*), give someone the lowdown, clue up (*informal*) **2** *They had primed the bomb to go off in an hour's time.* = **prepare**, set up, load, equip, get ready, make ready

primeval *or* **primaeval** ADJECTIVE **1** *a vast expanse of primeval swamp* = **earliest**, old, original, ancient, primitive, first, early, pristine, primal, prehistoric, primordial

2 *a primeval urge* = **primal**, primitive, natural, basic, inherited, inherent, hereditary, instinctive, innate, congenital, primordial, inborn, inbred

primitive ADJECTIVE **1** *studies of primitive societies* = **uncivilized**, savage, barbarian, barbaric, undeveloped, uncultivated ■ **OPPOSITE:** civilized **2** *primitive birds from the dinosaur era* = **early**, first, earliest, original, primary, elementary, pristine, primordial, primeval ■ **OPPOSITE:** modern **3** *primitive art* = **simple**, naive, childlike, untrained, undeveloped, unsophisticated, untutored ■ **OPPOSITE:** sophisticated **4** *primitive tools* = **crude**, simple, rough, rude, rudimentary, unrefined ■ **OPPOSITE:** elaborate

primordial ADJECTIVE **1** *Twenty million years ago this was dense primordial forest.* = **primeval**, primitive, first, earliest, pristine, primal, prehistoric **2** *primordial particles generated by the Big Bang* = **fundamental**, original, basic, radical, elemental

prince NOUN = **ruler**, lord, monarch, sovereign, crown prince, liege, potentate, prince regent, crowned head, dynast

princely ADJECTIVE **1** *It cost them the princely sum of seventy-five pounds.* = **substantial**, considerable, goodly, large, huge, massive, enormous, tidy (*informal*), whopping (*great*) (*informal*), sizable *or* sizeable **2** *the embodiment of princely magnificence* = **regal**, royal, imposing, magnificent, august, grand, imperial, noble, sovereign, majestic, dignified, stately, lofty, high-born

princess NOUN = **ruler**, lady, monarch, sovereign, liege, crowned head, crowned princess, dynast, princess regent

principal ADJECTIVE *Their principal concern is that of winning the next election.* = **main**, leading, chief, prime, first, highest, controlling, strongest, capital, key, essential, primary, most important, dominant, arch, cardinal, paramount, foremost, pre-eminent ■ **OPPOSITE:** minor ▶ NOUN **1** *the principal of the local high school* = **headmaster** *or* **headmistress**, head (*informal*), director, dean, head teacher, rector, master *or* mistress **2** *the principal of the company* = **boss**, head, leader, director, chief (*informal*), master, ruler, superintendent, sherang (*Austral. & N.Z.*) **3** *soloists and principals of The Scottish Ballet orchestra* = **star**, lead, leader, prima ballerina, first violin, leading man *or* lady, coryphée **4** *Use the higher premiums to pay the interest and principal on the debt.* = **capital**, money, assets, working capital, capital funds

P

principally ADVERB = **mainly**, largely, chiefly, especially, particularly, mostly, primarily, above all, predominantly, in the main, for the most part, first and foremost

principle NOUN **1** *He would never compromise his principles.* = **morals**, standards, ideals, honour, virtue, ethics, integrity, conscience, morality, decency, scruples, probity (*formal*), rectitude, moral standards, sense of duty, moral law, sense of honour, uprightness, kaupapa (*N.Z.*) **2** *a violation of the basic principles of Marxism* = **belief**, rule, standard, attitude, code, notion, criterion, ethic, doctrine, canon, creed, maxim, dogma, tenet, dictum, credo, axiom **3** *the principles of quantum theory* = **rule**, idea, law, theory, basis, truth, concept, formula, fundamental, assumption, essence, proposition, verity, golden rule, precept • **in principle 1** *I agree with this plan in principle.* = **in general**, generally, all things considered, on the whole, in the main, by and large, in essence, all in all, on balance **2** *In principle, it should be possible.* = **in theory**, ideally, on paper, theoretically, in an ideal world, en principe (*French*)

> USAGE *Principle* and *principal* are often confused: *the principal* (not *principle*) *reason for his departure; the plan was approved in principle* (not *principal*).

principled ADJECTIVE = **moral**, ethical, upright, honourable, just, correct, decent, righteous, conscientious, virtuous, scrupulous, right-minded, high-minded

print VERB **1** *He produces corporate brochures and prints books.* = **run off**, publish, copy, reproduce, issue, engrave, go to press, put to bed (*informal*) **2** *a questionnaire printed in the magazine* = **publish**, release, circulate, issue, disseminate **3** *printed with a paisley pattern* = **mark**, impress, stamp, imprint ▸ NOUN **1** *a black and white print of the children* = **photograph**, photo, snap **2** *Hogarth's famous series of prints* = **picture**, plate, etching, engraving, lithograph, woodcut, linocut **3** *There was a huge print of 'Le Déjeuner Sur l'Herbe' on the wall.* = **copy**, photo (*informal*), picture, reproduction, replica **4** *columns of tiny print* = **type**, lettering, letters, characters, face, font, fount, typeface • **in print 1** *the appearance of his poems in print* = **published**, printed, on the streets, on paper, in black and white, out **2** *The book has been in print for over 40 years.* = **available**, current, on the market, in the shops, on the shelves, obtainable • **out of print** *The book is now out of print,*

but can be found in libraries. = **unavailable**, unobtainable, no longer published, o.p.

prior ADJECTIVE *He claimed he had no prior knowledge of the protest.* = **earlier**, previous, former, preceding, foregoing, antecedent, aforementioned, pre-existing, anterior, pre-existent • **prior to** *A man was seen in the area prior to the shooting.* = **before**, preceding, earlier than, in advance of, previous to

priority NOUN **1** *The government's priority should be better health care.* = **prime concern**, first concern, primary issue, most pressing matter **2** *The school gives priority to science and maths.* = **precedence**, preference, greater importance, primacy, predominance **3** *the premise that economic development has priority over the environment* = **supremacy**, rank, the lead, superiority, precedence, prerogative, seniority, right of way, pre-eminence

priory NOUN = **monastery**, abbey, convent, cloister, nunnery, religious house

prise or **prize** VERB **1** *He tried to prise the dog's jaws open.* = **force**, pull, lever **2** *We had to prise the story out of him.* = **drag**, force, draw, wring, extort

prison NOUN = **jail**, confinement, can (*slang*), pound, nick (*Brit. slang*), stir (*slang*), cooler (*slang*), jug (*slang*), dungeon, clink (*slang*), glasshouse (*Military informal*), gaol, penitentiary (*U.S.*), slammer (*slang*), lockup, quod (*slang*), penal institution, calaboose (*U.S. informal*), choky (*slang*), poky or pokey (*U.S. & Canad. slang*), boob (*Austral. slang*)

prisoner NOUN **1** *the large number of prisoners sharing cells* = **convict**, con (*slang*), lag (*slang*), jailbird **2** *wartime hostages and concentration-camp prisoners* = **captive**, hostage, detainee, internee

prissy ADJECTIVE = **prim**, precious, fussy, fastidious, squeamish, prudish, finicky, strait-laced, niminy-piminy, overnice, prim and proper

pristine ADJECTIVE = **new**, pure, virgin, immaculate, untouched, unspoiled, virginal, unsullied, uncorrupted, undefiled

> USAGE The use of *pristine* to mean 'fresh, clean, and unspoiled' used to be considered incorrect by some people, but it is now generally accepted.

privacy NOUN = **seclusion**, isolation, solitude, retirement, retreat, separateness, sequestration, privateness

private ADJECTIVE **1** *a joint venture with private industry* = **nonpublic**, independent, commercial, privatised, private-enterprise, denationalized, closed (*of data or programming language*) **2** *He has had to sell his private plane.* = **exclusive**, individual, privately owned, own, special, particular,

reserved ■ **OPPOSITE:** public **3** *He held a private meeting with the country's political party leaders.* = **secret**, confidential, covert, inside, closet, unofficial, privy (*archaic*), clandestine, off the record, hush-hush (*informal*), in camera ■ **OPPOSITE:** public **4** *I've always kept my private and professional life separate.* = **personal**, individual, secret, intimate, undisclosed, unspoken, innermost, unvoiced **5** *It was the only reasonably private place they could find to talk.* = **secluded**, secret, separate, isolated, concealed, retired, sequestered, not overlooked ■ **OPPOSITE:** busy **6** *Gould was an intensely private individual.* = **solitary**, reserved, retiring, withdrawn, discreet, secretive, self-contained, reclusive, reticent, insular, introvert, uncommunicative ■ **OPPOSITE:** sociable
▶ NOUN *The rest of the gunners in the battery were privates.* = **enlisted man** (*U.S.*), tommy (*Brit. informal*), private soldier, Tommy Atkins (*Brit. informal*), squaddie or squaddy (*Brit. slang*) • **in private** *I think we should discuss this in private.* = **in secret**, privately, personally, behind closed doors, in camera, between ourselves, confidentially

privation NOUN = **want**, poverty, need, suffering, loss, lack, distress, misery, necessity, hardship, penury, destitution, neediness, indigence

privilege NOUN = **right**, benefit, due, advantage, claim, freedom, sanction, liberty, concession, franchise, entitlement, prerogative, birthright

privileged ADJECTIVE **1** *They were a wealthy and privileged elite.* = **special**, powerful, advantaged, favoured, ruling, honoured, entitled, elite, indulged **2** *This data is privileged information.* = **confidential**, special, inside, exceptional, privy (*archaic*), off the record, not for publication

privy NOUN *an outside privy* = **lavatory**, closet, bog (*slang*), latrine, outside toilet, earth closet, pissoir (*French*), bogger (*Austral. slang*), brasco (*Austral. slang*)
▶ ADJECTIVE (**with to**) *Only three people were privy to the facts.* = **informed of**, aware of, in on, wise to (*slang*), hip to (*slang*), in the loop, apprised of, cognizant of, in the know about (*informal*)

prize¹ NOUN **1** *He won a prize in the Leeds Piano Competition.* = **reward**, cup, award, honour, premium, medal, trophy, accolade **2** *A single winner is in line for the jackpot prize.* = **winnings**, haul, jackpot, stakes, purse, windfall **3** *A settlement of the dispute would be a great prize.* = **goal**, hope, gain, aim, desire, ambition, conquest, Holy Grail (*informal*)

▶ MODIFIER *a prize bull* = **champion**, best, winning, top, outstanding, award-winning, first-rate, top-notch (*informal*)

prize² VERB *These items are greatly prized by collectors.* = **value**, appreciate, treasure, esteem, cherish, hold dear, regard highly, set store by

prize³ *see* **prise**

probability NOUN **1** *There is a high probability of success.* = **likelihood**, prospect, chance, odds, expectation, liability, presumption, likeliness **2** *the probability of life on other planets* = **chance**, odds, possibility, likelihood

probable ADJECTIVE = **likely**, possible, apparent, reasonable to think, most likely, presumed, credible, plausible, feasible, odds-on, on the cards, presumable
■ **OPPOSITE:** unlikely

probably ADVERB = **likely**, perhaps, maybe, possibly, presumably, most likely, doubtless, in all probability, in all likelihood, perchance (*archaic*), as likely as not

probation NOUN = **trial period**, test, trial, examination, apprenticeship, initiation, novitiate

probe VERB **1** (*often with* **into**) *The more they probed into his background, the more suspicious they became.* = **examine**, research, go into, investigate, explore, test, sound, search, look into, query, verify, sift, analyze, dissect, delve into, work over, scrutinize **2** *A doctor probed deep in his shoulder wound for shrapnel.* = **explore**, examine, poke, prod, feel around ▶ NOUN *a federal grand-jury probe into corruption within the FDA* = **investigation**, study, research, inquiry, analysis, examination, exploration, scrutiny, inquest, scrutinization

probity NOUN = **integrity**, worth, justice, honour, equity, virtue, goodness, morality, honesty, fairness, fidelity, sincerity, righteousness, rectitude, truthfulness, trustworthiness, uprightness

problem NOUN **1** *the economic problems of the inner city* = **difficulty**, trouble, dispute, plight, obstacle, dilemma, headache (*informal*), disagreement, complication, predicament, quandary **2** *a mathematical problem* = **puzzle**, question, riddle, enigma, conundrum, teaser, poser, brain-teaser (*informal*), bitch (*slang*) ▶ MODIFIER *Sometimes a problem child is placed in a special school.* = **difficult**, disturbed, troublesome, unruly, delinquent, uncontrollable, intractable, recalcitrant, intransigent, unmanageable, disobedient, ungovernable, refractory, maladjusted

problematic ADJECTIVE = **tricky**, puzzling, uncertain, doubtful, dubious, unsettled, questionable, enigmatic, debatable, moot, problematical, chancy (*informal*), open to doubt ■ OPPOSITE: clear

procedure NOUN = **method**, policy, process, course, system, form, action, step, performance, operation, practice, scheme, strategy, conduct, formula, custom, routine, transaction, plan of action, modus operandi (*Latin*)

proceed VERB 1 *I had no idea how to proceed.* = **begin**, go ahead, get going, make a start, get under way, set something in motion 2 *The defence is not yet ready to proceed with the trial.* = **continue**, go on, progress, carry on, go ahead, get on, press on, crack on (*informal*) ■ OPPOSITE: discontinue 3 *She proceeded along the hallway.* = **go on**, continue, advance, progress, carry on, go ahead, move on, move forward, press on, push on, make your way, crack on (*informal*) ■ OPPOSITE: stop 4 *Does Othello's downfall proceed from a flaw in his character?* = **arise**, come, follow, issue, result, spring, flow, stem, derive, originate, ensue, emanate

proceeding NOUN = **action**, process, procedure, move, act, step, measure, venture, undertaking, deed, occurrence, course of action

proceeds PLURAL NOUN = **income**, profit, revenue, returns, produce, products, gain, earnings, yield, receipts, takings

process NOUN 1 *The best way to find out is by a process of elimination.* = **procedure**, means, course, system, action, performance, operation, measure, proceeding, manner, transaction, mode, course of action 2 *the evolutionary process of Homo sapiens* = **development**, growth, progress, course, stage, step, movement, advance, formation, evolution, unfolding, progression 3 *the cost of the production process* = **method**, system, practice, technique, procedure 4 *steps in the impeachment process against the president* = **action**, case, trial, suit ▶ VERB 1 *facilities to process the beans before export; Silicon chips process electrical signals.* = **prepare**, treat, convert, transform, alter, refine 2 *A number of applications are being processed at the moment.* = **handle**, manage, action, deal with, fulfil, take care of, dispose of

procession NOUN *a funeral procession* = **parade**, train, march, file, column, motorcade, cavalcade, cortege

proclaim VERB 1 *He continues to proclaim his innocence.* = **announce**, declare, advertise, show, publish, indicate, blaze (abroad), herald, circulate, trumpet, affirm, give out, profess, promulgate, make known, enunciate, blazon (abroad), shout from the housetops (*informal*) ■ OPPOSITE: keep secret 2 *He launched a coup and proclaimed himself president.* = **pronounce**, announce, declare

proclamation NOUN 1 *A formal proclamation of independence was issued eight days ago.* = **declaration**, notice, announcement, decree, manifesto, edict, pronouncement, pronunciamento 2 *his proclamation of the good news* = **publishing**, broadcasting, announcement, publication, declaration, notification, pronouncement, promulgation

proclivity NOUN = **tendency**, liking, leaning, inclination, bent, weakness, bias, disposition, penchant, propensity, kink, predisposition, predilection, partiality, proneness, liableness

procrastinate VERB = **delay**, stall, postpone, prolong, put off, defer, adjourn, retard, dally, play for time, gain time, temporize, play a waiting game, protract, drag your feet (*informal*), be dilatory ■ OPPOSITE: hurry (up)

procrastination NOUN = **delay**, hesitation, slowness, slackness, dilatoriness, temporization

procure VERB = **obtain**, get, find, buy, win, land (*informal*), score (*slang*), gain, earn, pick up, purchase, secure, appropriate, acquire, manage to get, get hold of, come by, lay hands on

prod VERB 1 *He prodded Murray with the broom.* = **poke**, push, dig, shove, propel, nudge, jab, prick 2 *a tactic to prod the government into spending more on education* = **prompt**, move, urge, motivate, spur, stimulate, rouse, stir up, incite, egg on, goad, impel, put a bomb under (*informal*) ▶ NOUN 1 *He gave the donkey a prod in the backside.* = **poke**, push, boost, dig, elbow, shove, nudge, jab 2 *She won't do it without a prod from you.* = **prompt**, boost, signal, cue, reminder, stimulus 3 *a cattle prod* = **goad**, stick, spur, poker

prodigal ADJECTIVE 1 *his prodigal habits* = **extravagant**, excessive, reckless, squandering, wasteful, wanton, profligate, spendthrift, intemperate, immoderate, improvident ■ OPPOSITE: thrifty 2 (*often with of*) *You are prodigal of both your toil and your talent.* = **lavish**, bountiful, unstinting, unsparing, bounteous, profuse ■ OPPOSITE: generous

prodigious ADJECTIVE 1 *This business generates cash in prodigious amounts.* = **huge**, giant, massive, vast, enormous, tremendous, immense, gigantic, monumental (*informal*), monstrous, mammoth, colossal, stellar (*informal*), stupendous, inordinate, immeasurable ■ **OPPOSITE:** tiny 2 *He impressed everyone with his prodigious memory.* = **wonderful**, striking, amazing, unusual, dramatic, impressive, extraordinary, remarkable, fantastic (*informal*), fabulous, staggering, marvellous, startling, exceptional, abnormal, phenomenal, astounding, miraculous, stupendous, flabbergasting (*informal*) ■ **OPPOSITE:** ordinary

prodigy NOUN = **genius**, talent, wizard, mastermind, whizz (*informal*), whizz kid (*informal*), wunderkind, brainbox, child genius, wonder child, up-and-comer (*informal*)

produce VERB 1 *The drug is known to produce side-effects.* = **cause**, lead to, result in, effect, occasion (*formal*), generate, trigger, make for, provoke, set off, induce, bring about, give rise to, engender 2 *The company produces circuitry for communications systems.* = **make**, build, create, develop, turn out, manufacture, construct, invent, assemble, put together, originate, fabricate, mass-produce 3 *So far he has produced only one composition he deems suitable for performance.* = **create**, develop, write, turn out, compose, originate, churn out (*informal*) 4 *The plant produces sweet fruit with deep red flesh.* = **yield**, provide, grow, bear, give, supply, afford, render, furnish 5 *Some species of snake produce live young.* = **bring forth**, bear, deliver, breed, give birth to, beget (*old-fashioned*), bring into the world 6 *They challenged him to produce evidence to support his allegations.* = **show**, provide, present, advance, demonstrate, offer, come up with, exhibit, put forward, furnish, bring forward, set forth, bring to light 7 *You must produce your passport upon re-entering the country.* = **display**, show, present, proffer 8 *I'm going to produce the show and write the scripts.* = **present**, stage, direct, put on, do, show, mount, exhibit, put before the public ▸ NOUN *I buy organic produce whenever possible.* = **fruit and vegetables**, goods, food, products, crops, yield, harvest, greengrocery (*Brit.*)

producer NOUN 1 *a freelance film producer* = **director**, promoter, impresario, régisseur (*French*) 2 *producers of precision instruments and electrical equipment* = **maker**, manufacturer, builder, creator, fabricator 3 *They are producers of high-quality wines.* = **grower**, farmer

product NOUN 1 *Try to get the best products at the lowest price.* = **goods**, produce, production, creation, commodity, invention, merchandise, artefact, concoction 2 *The company is the product of a merger.* = **result**, fruit, consequence, yield, returns, issue, effect, outcome, legacy, spin-off, end result, offshoot, upshot

production NOUN 1 *two companies involved in the production of the steel pipes* = **producing**, making, manufacture, manufacturing, construction, assembly, preparation, formation, fabrication, origination 2 *the apparent lack of skill in the production of much new modern art* = **creation**, development, fashioning, composition, origination 3 *the story behind the show's production* = **management**, administration, direction 4 *a critically acclaimed production of Othello* = **presentation**, staging, mounting

productive ADJECTIVE 1 *fertile and productive soil* = **fertile**, rich, producing, prolific, plentiful, fruitful, teeming, generative, fecund ■ **OPPOSITE:** barren 2 *a highly productive writer of fiction* = **creative**, dynamic, vigorous, energetic, inventive 3 *a productive relationship* = **useful**, rewarding, valuable, profitable, effective, worthwhile, beneficial, constructive, gratifying, fruitful, advantageous, gainful ■ **OPPOSITE:** useless

productivity NOUN = **output**, production, capacity, yield, efficiency, mass production, work rate, productive capacity, productiveness

profane ADJECTIVE 1 *a hard-drinking, profane Irishman* = **sacrilegious**, wicked, irreverent, sinful, disrespectful, heathen, impure, godless, ungodly, irreligious, impious, idolatrous ■ **OPPOSITE:** religious 2 *a campaign against suggestive and profane lyrics in country songs* = **crude**, foul, obscene, abusive, coarse, filthy, vulgar, blasphemous 3 *Churches should not be used for profane or secular purposes.* = **secular**, lay, temporal, unholy, worldly, unconsecrated, unhallowed, unsanctified ▸ VERB *They have profaned the traditions of the Church.* = **desecrate**, violate, abuse, prostitute, contaminate, pollute, pervert, misuse, debase, defile, vitiate, commit sacrilege

profess VERB 1 *'I don't know,' he replied, professing innocence.* = **claim**, allege, pretend, fake, make out, sham, purport, feign, act as if, let on, dissemble 2 *He professed that he was content with the arrangements.* = **state**, admit, announce, maintain, own, confirm, declare, acknowledge, confess, assert, proclaim, affirm, certify, avow, vouch, aver, asseverate (*formal*)

professed ADJECTIVE **1** *their professed concern for justice* = **supposed**, would-be, alleged, so-called, apparent, pretended, purported, self-styled, ostensible, soi-disant (*French*) **2** *He was a professed anarchist.* = **declared**, confirmed, confessed, proclaimed, certified, self-confessed, avowed, self-acknowledged

profession NOUN = **occupation**, calling, business, career, employment, line, office, position, sphere, vocation, walk of life, line of work, métier

professional ADJECTIVE **1** *professional people like doctors and engineers* = **qualified**, trained, skilled, white-collar **2** *She told me we'd done a really professional job.* = **expert**, experienced, finished, skilled, masterly, efficient, crack (*slang*), polished, practised, ace (*informal*), accomplished, slick, competent, adept, proficient ■ **OPPOSITE:** amateurish ▶ NOUN *a dedicated professional* = **expert**, authority, master, pro (*informal*), specialist, guru, buff (*informal*), wizard, adept, whizz (*informal*), maestro, virtuoso, hotshot (*informal*), past master, dab hand (*Brit. informal*), wonk (*informal*), maven (*U.S.*), fundi (*S. African*)

professor NOUN = **don** (*Brit.*), fellow (*Brit.*), prof (*informal*), head of faculty

proffer VERB **1** *He proffered a box of cigarettes.* = **offer**, hand over, present, extend, hold out **2** *They have not yet proffered an explanation of how the accident happened.* = **suggest**, propose, volunteer, submit, tender, propound

proficiency NOUN = **skill**, ability, know-how (*informal*), talent, facility, craft, expertise, competence, accomplishment, mastery, knack, aptitude, dexterity, expertness, skilfulness

proficient ADJECTIVE = **skilled**, trained, experienced, qualified, able, expert, masterly, talented, gifted, capable, efficient, clever, accomplished, versed, competent, apt, skilful, adept, conversant ■ **OPPOSITE:** unskilled

profile NOUN **1** *His handsome profile was turned away from us.* = **outline**, lines, form, figure, shape, silhouette, contour, side view **2** *The newspaper published comparative profiles of the candidates.* = **biography**, sketch, vignette, characterization, thumbnail sketch, character sketch **3** *a profile of the hospital's catchment area* = **analysis**, study, table, review, survey, chart, examination, diagram, graph

profit NOUN **1** (*often plural*) *The bank made pre-tax profits of £3.5 million.* = **earnings**, winnings, return, revenue, gain, boot (*dialect*), yield, proceeds, percentage

(*informal*), surplus, receipts, bottom line, takings, emoluments ■ **OPPOSITE:** loss **2** *They saw little profit in risking their lives to capture the militants.* = **benefit**, good, use, interest, value, gain, advantage, advancement, mileage (*informal*), avail ■ **OPPOSITE:** disadvantage ▶ VERB **1** *The dealers profited shamelessly at my family's expense.* = **make money**, clear up, gain, earn, clean up (*informal*), rake in (*informal*), make a killing (*informal*), make a good thing of (*informal*) **2** *So far the French alliance has profited the rebels very little.* = **benefit**, help, serve, aid, gain, promote, contribute to, avail, be of advantage to

profitable ADJECTIVE **1** *Drug manufacturing is the most profitable business in America.* = **money-making**, lucrative, paying, commercial, rewarding, worthwhile, cost-effective, fruitful, gainful, remunerative **2** *a profitable exchange of ideas* = **beneficial**, useful, rewarding, valuable, productive, worthwhile, fruitful, advantageous, expedient, serviceable ■ **OPPOSITE:** useless

profligacy NOUN = **extravagance**, excess, squandering, waste, recklessness, wastefulness, lavishness, prodigality, improvidence

profligate ADJECTIVE = **extravagant**, reckless, squandering, wasteful, prodigal, spendthrift, immoderate, improvident

profound ADJECTIVE **1** *The overwhelming feeling is profound shock and anger.* = **sincere**, acute, intense, great, keen, extreme, hearty, heartfelt, abject, deeply felt, heartrending ■ **OPPOSITE:** insincere **2** *a book full of profound and challenging insights* = **wise**, learned, serious, deep, skilled, subtle, penetrating, philosophical, thoughtful, sage, discerning, weighty, insightful, erudite, abstruse, recondite, sagacious (*formal*) ■ **OPPOSITE:** uninformed **3** *A profound silence fell.* = **complete**, intense, absolute, serious (*informal*), total, extreme, pronounced, utter, consummate, unqualified, out-and-out ■ **OPPOSITE:** slight **4** *the profound changes brought about by World War I* = **radical**, extensive, thorough, far-reaching, exhaustive, thoroughgoing

profoundly ADVERB = **greatly**, very, deeply, seriously (*informal*), keenly, extremely, thoroughly, sincerely, intensely, acutely, heartily, to the core, abjectly, to the nth degree, from the bottom of your heart

profundity NOUN = **insight**, intelligence, depth, wisdom, learning, penetration, acumen, erudition, acuity, perspicacity (*formal*), sagacity, perceptiveness, perspicuity

profuse ADJECTIVE **1** *This plant produces profuse bright-blue flowers.* = **plentiful**, ample, prolific, abundant, overflowing, teeming, copious, bountiful, luxuriant ■ OPPOSITE: sparse **2** *Helena's profuse thanks were met with only a nod.* = **extravagant**, liberal, generous, excessive, lavish, exuberant, prodigal, fulsome, open-handed, unstinting, immoderate ■ OPPOSITE: moderate

profusion NOUN = **abundance**, wealth, excess, quantity, surplus, riot, multitude, bounty, plethora, exuberance, glut, extravagance, cornucopia, oversupply, plenitude, superabundance, superfluity, lavishness, luxuriance, prodigality, copiousness

progenitor NOUN **1** *the Arabian stallions which were the progenitors of all modern thoroughbreds* = **ancestor**, parent, forebear, forefather, begetter, procreator, primogenitor **2** *the man who is considered the progenitor of modern drama* = **originator**, source, predecessor, precursor, forerunner, antecedent, instigator

progeny NOUN **1** *They set aside funds to ensure the welfare of their progeny.* = **children**, family, young, issue, offspring, descendants **2** *They claimed to be the progeny of Genghis Khan.* = **race**, stock, breed, posterity (*archaic*), seed (*chiefly biblical*), lineage, scions

prognosis NOUN = **forecast**, prediction, diagnosis, expectation, speculation, projection, surmise, prognostication

programme NOUN **1** *the programme for reform outlined by the Soviet President* = **plan**, scheme, strategy, procedure, project, plan of action **2** *the programme of events for the forthcoming year* = **schedule**, plan, agenda, timetable, listing, list, line-up, calendar, order **3** *a detailed ten-step programme of study with attainment targets* = **course**, curriculum, syllabus **4** *a series of TV programmes on global warming* = **show**, performance, production, broadcast, episode, presentation, transmission, telecast, podcast ▶ VERB **1** *His homework is more manageable now because it is programmed into his schedule.* = **schedule**, plan, timetable, book, bill, list, design, arrange, work out, line up, organize, lay on, formulate, map out, itemize, prearrange **2** *Many parents were reliant on their children to programme the machine.* = **set**, fix

progress NOUN **1** *The two sides made little progress towards agreement.* = **development**, increase, growth, advance, gain, improvement, promotion, breakthrough, step forward, advancement, progression,

headway, betterment, amelioration ■ OPPOSITE: regression **2** *The road was too rough for further progress in the car.* = **movement forward**, passage, advancement, progression, course, advance, headway, onward movement ■ OPPOSITE: movement backward ▶ VERB **1** *He progressed slowly along the coast in an easterly direction.* = **move on**, continue, travel, advance, proceed, go forward, gain ground, forge ahead, make inroads (into), make headway, make your way, cover ground, make strides, gather way, crack on (*informal*) ■ OPPOSITE: move back **2** *He came round to see how our work was progressing.* = **develop**, improve, advance, better, increase, grow, gain, get on, come on, mature, blossom, ameliorate ■ OPPOSITE: get behind • **in progress** *The game was already in progress when we took our seats.* = **going on**, happening, continuing, being done, occurring, taking place, proceeding, under way, ongoing, being performed, in operation

progression NOUN **1** *Both drugs slow the progression of the disease.* = **progress**, advance, advancement, gain, headway, furtherance, movement forward **2** *the steady progression of events in my life* = **sequence**, course, order, series, chain, cycle, string, succession

progressive ADJECTIVE **1** *The children go to a progressive school.* = **enlightened**, liberal, modern, advanced, radical, enterprising, go-ahead, revolutionary, dynamic, avant-garde, reformist, up-and-coming, forward-looking **2** *One symptom of the disease is a progressive loss of memory.* = **growing**, continuing, increasing, developing, advancing, accelerating, ongoing, continuous, intensifying, escalating

prohibit VERB **1** *the law which prohibits trading on Sunday* = **forbid**, ban, rule out, veto, outlaw, disallow, proscribe, debar, interdict ■ OPPOSITE: permit **2** *The contraption prohibited any movement.* = **prevent**, restrict, rule out, stop, hamper, hinder, constrain, obstruct, preclude, impede, make impossible ■ OPPOSITE: allow

prohibited ADJECTIVE = **forbidden**, barred, banned, illegal, not allowed, vetoed, taboo, off limits, proscribed, verboten (*German*)

prohibition NOUN = **ban**, boycott, embargo, bar, veto, prevention, exclusion, injunction, disqualification, interdiction, interdict, proscription, disallowance, forbiddance, restraining order (*U.S. Law*)

prohibitive ADJECTIVE **1** *The cost of private treatment can be prohibitive.* = **exorbitant**, excessive, steep (*informal*), high-priced, preposterous, sky-high, extortionate, beyond your means **2** *prohibitive regulations* = **prohibiting**, forbidding, restraining, restrictive, repressive, suppressive, proscriptive

project NOUN **1** *a local development project* = **scheme**, plan, job, idea, design, programme, campaign, operation, activity, proposal, venture, enterprise, undertaking, occupation, proposition, plan of action **2** *Students complete their projects at their own pace.* = **assignment**, task, homework, piece of research ▶ VERB **1** *The country's population is projected to double in the next fifty years.* = **forecast**, expect, estimate, predict, reckon, calculate, gauge, extrapolate, predetermine **2** *His projected visit to Washington had to be postponed.* = **plan**, propose, design, scheme, purpose, frame, draft, outline, devise, contemplate, contrive, map out **3** *The hardware can be used for projecting nuclear missiles.* = **launch**, shoot, throw, cast, transmit, discharge, hurl, fling, propel **4** *A piece of metal projected out from the side.* = **stick out**, extend, stand out, bulge, beetle, protrude, overhang, jut

projectile NOUN = **missile**, shell, bullet, rocket

projection NOUN = **forecast**, estimate, reckoning, prediction, calculation, estimation, computation, extrapolation

proletarian ADJECTIVE *the issue of proletarian world solidarity* = **working-class**, common, cloth-cap (*informal*), plebeian, blue-singlet (*Austral. slang*) ▶ NOUN *The proletarians have nothing to lose but their chains.* = **worker**, commoner, Joe Bloggs (*Brit. informal*), pleb, plebeian, prole (*derogatory slang, chiefly Brit.*)

proletariat NOUN = **working class**, the masses, lower classes, commoners, the herd, wage-earners, lower orders, the common people, hoi polloi, plebs, the rabble, the great unwashed (*derogatory*), labouring classes, proles (*derogatory slang, chiefly Brit.*), commonalty ■ **OPPOSITE:** ruling class

proliferate VERB = **increase**, expand, breed, mushroom, escalate, multiply, burgeon, snowball, run riot, grow rapidly

proliferation NOUN = **multiplication**, increase, spread, build-up, concentration, expansion, extension, step-up (*informal*), escalation, intensification

prolific ADJECTIVE **1** *a prolific writer of novels and short stories* = **productive**, creative, fertile, inventive, copious **2** *Closer planting will give you a more prolific crop.* = **fruitful**, fertile, abundant, rich, rank, teeming,

bountiful, luxuriant, generative, profuse, fecund ■ **OPPOSITE:** unproductive

prologue NOUN = **introduction**, preliminary, prelude, preface, preamble, foreword, proem, exordium

prolong VERB = **lengthen**, continue, perpetuate, draw out, extend, delay, stretch out, carry on, spin out, drag out, make longer, protract ■ **OPPOSITE:** shorten

promenade NOUN **1** *a fine promenade running past the boathouses* = **walkway**, parade, boulevard, prom, esplanade, public walk **2** *Take a tranquil promenade along a stretch of picturesque coastline.* = **stroll**, walk, turn, airing, constitutional, saunter ▶ VERB **1** *People came out to promenade along the front.* = **stroll**, walk, saunter, take a walk, perambulate, stretch your legs **2** *attracting attention as he promenaded up and down the street in his flashy clothes* = **parade**, strut, swagger, flaunt

prominence NOUN **1** *He came to prominence during the last World Cup.* = **fame**, name, standing, rank, reputation, importance, celebrity, distinction, prestige, greatness, eminence, pre-eminence, notability, outstandingness **2** *Many papers give prominence to reports of the latest violence.* = **conspicuousness**, weight, precedence, top billing, specialness, salience, markedness **3** *Birds have a prominence on the breast bone called a keel.* = **protrusion**, swelling, projection, bulge, jutting, protuberance

prominent ADJECTIVE **1** *a prominent member of the Law Society* = **famous**, leading, top, chief, important, main, noted, popular, respected, celebrated, outstanding, distinguished, well-known, notable, renowned, big-time (*informal*), foremost, eminent, major league (*informal*), pre-eminent, well-thought-of ■ **OPPOSITE:** unknown **2** *the lighthouses that are still a prominent feature of the Scottish coast* = **noticeable**, striking, obvious, outstanding, remarkable, pronounced, blatant, conspicuous, to the fore, unmistakable, eye-catching, salient, in the foreground, easily seen, obtrusive ■ **OPPOSITE:** inconspicuous **3** *a low forehead and prominent eyebrows* = **jutting**, projecting, standing out, bulging, hanging over, protruding, protuberant, protrusive ■ **OPPOSITE:** indented

promiscuity NOUN = **licentiousness**, profligacy, sleeping around (*informal*), permissiveness, abandon, incontinence, depravity, immorality, debauchery, laxity, dissipation, looseness, amorality, lechery, laxness, wantonness, libertinism, promiscuousness

promiscuous ADJECTIVE = **licentious**, wanton, profligate, debauched, fast, wild, abandoned, loose (old-fashioned), immoral, lax, dissipated, unbridled, dissolute, libertine, of easy virtue, unchaste
■ **OPPOSITE:** chaste

promise VERB **1** They promised they would deliver it on Friday. = **guarantee**, pledge, vow, swear, contract, assure, undertake, warrant, plight (old-fashioned), stipulate, vouch, take an oath, give an undertaking to, cross your heart, give your word **2** The seminar promises to be most instructive. = **seem likely**, look like, hint at, show signs of, bespeak, augur, betoken, lead you to expect, hold out hopes of, give hope of, bid fair, hold a probability of ▶ NOUN **1** If you make a promise, you should keep it.
= **guarantee**, word, bond, vow, commitment, pledge, undertaking, assurance, engagement, compact, oath, covenant, word of honour **2** He first showed promise as an athlete in grade school.
= **potential**, ability, talent, capacity, capability, flair, aptitude

promising ADJECTIVE **1** a new and promising stage in the negotiations = **encouraging**, likely, bright, reassuring, hopeful, favourable, rosy, auspicious, propitious, full of promise ■ **OPPOSITE:** unpromising **2** one of the school's brightest and most promising pupils = **talented**, able, gifted, rising, likely, up-and-coming

promontory NOUN = **point**, cape, head, spur, ness (archaic), headland, foreland

promote VERB **1** His country will do everything possible to promote peace. = **help**, back, support, further, develop, aid, forward, champion, encourage, advance, work for, urge, boost, recommend, sponsor, foster, contribute to, assist, advocate, stimulate, endorse, prescribe, speak for, nurture, push for, espouse, popularize, gee up
■ **OPPOSITE:** impede **2** He has announced a full British tour to promote his new album.
= **advertise**, sell, hype, publicize, push, plug (informal), puff, call attention to, beat the drum for (informal) **3** I was promoted to editor and then editorial director. = **raise**, upgrade, elevate, honour, dignify, exalt, kick upstairs (informal), aggrandize
■ **OPPOSITE:** demote

promoter NOUN **1** one of the top boxing promoters in Britain = **organizer**, arranger, entrepreneur, impresario **2** Aaron Copland was a most energetic promoter of American music. = **supporter**, champion, advocate,

campaigner, helper, proponent, stalwart, mainstay, upholder

promotion NOUN **1** rewarding outstanding employees with promotion = **rise**, upgrading, move up, advancement, elevation, exaltation, preferment, aggrandizement, ennoblement **2** The company spent a lot of money on advertising and promotion.
= **publicity**, advertising, hype, pushing, plugging (informal), propaganda, advertising campaign, hard sell, media hype, ballyhoo (informal), puffery (informal), boosterism **3** dedicated to the promotion of new ideas and research = **encouragement**, backing, support, development, progress, boosting, advancement, advocacy, cultivation, espousal, furtherance, boosterism

prompt VERB **1** The recession has prompted consumers to cut back on buying cars. = **cause**, move, inspire, stimulate, occasion (formal), urge, spur, provoke, motivate, induce, evoke, give rise to, elicit, incite, instigate, impel, call forth ■ **OPPOSITE:** discourage **2** 'What was that you were saying about a guided tour?' he prompted her. = **remind**, assist, cue, help out, prod, jog the memory, refresh the memory ▶ ADJECTIVE **1** an inflammation of the eyeball which needs prompt treatment = **immediate**, quick, rapid, instant, timely, early, swift, on time, speedy, instantaneous, punctual, pdq (slang), unhesitating ■ **OPPOSITE:** slow **2** I was impressed by the prompt service I received.
= **quick**, ready, efficient, eager, willing, smart, alert, brisk, responsive, expeditious
■ **OPPOSITE:** inefficient ▶ ADVERB The invitation specifies eight o'clock prompt.
= **exactly**, sharp, promptly, on the dot, punctually ▶ NOUN Her blushes were saved by a prompt from her host. = **reminder**, hint, cue, help, spur, stimulus, jog, prod, jolt

promptly ADVERB **1** She lay down and promptly fell asleep. = **immediately**, instantly, swiftly, directly, quickly, at once, speedily, by return, pronto (informal), unhesitatingly, hotfoot, pdq (slang), posthaste **2** We left the hotel promptly at seven. = **punctually**, on time, spot on (informal), bang on (informal), on the dot, on the button (U.S.), on the nail

promulgate VERB **1** Such behaviour promulgates a negative image of the British.
= **make known**, issue, announce, publish, spread, promote, advertise, broadcast, communicate, proclaim, circulate, notify, make public, disseminate **2** Only the Pope has the authority to promulgate a decree.
= **make official**, pass, declare, decree

prone ADJECTIVE **1** *For all her experience, she was still prone to nerves.* = **liable**, given, subject, inclined, tending, bent, disposed, susceptible, apt, predisposed ■ **OPPOSITE:** disinclined **2** *Bob slid from his chair and lay prone on the floor.* = **face down**, flat, lying down, horizontal, prostrate, recumbent, procumbent ■ **OPPOSITE:** face up

pronounce VERB **1** *Have I pronounced your name correctly?* = **say**, speak, voice, stress, sound, utter, articulate, enunciate, vocalize **2** *A specialist has pronounced him fully fit.* = **declare**, announce, judge, deliver, assert, proclaim, decree, affirm

pronounced ADJECTIVE = **noticeable**, clear, decided, strong, marked, striking, obvious, broad, evident, distinct, definite, conspicuous, unmistakable, salient ■ **OPPOSITE:** imperceptible

pronouncement NOUN = **announcement**, statement, declaration, judgment, decree, manifesto, proclamation, notification, edict, dictum, promulgation, pronunciamento

pronunciation NOUN = **intonation**, accent, speech, stress, articulation, inflection, diction, elocution, enunciation, accentuation

> **USAGE** The *-un-* in *pronunciation* should be written and pronounced in the same way as the *-un-* in *unkind*. It is incorrect to add an *o* before the *u* to make this word look and sound more like *pronounce*.

proof NOUN **1** *You must have proof of residence in the state.* = **evidence**, demonstration, testimony, confirmation, verification, certification, corroboration, authentication, substantiation, attestation **2** *I'm correcting the proofs of the Spanish edition right now.* = **trial print**, pull, slip, galley, page proof, galley proof, trial impression ▶ ADJECTIVE *The fortress was proof against attack.* = **impervious**, strong, tight, resistant, impenetrable, repellent

prop VERB **1** *He propped his bike against the fence.* = **lean**, place, set, stand, position, rest, lay, balance, steady **2** *(often with* **up***) Plaster ceilings are propped with scaffolding.* = **support**, maintain, sustain, shore, hold up, brace, uphold, bolster, truss, buttress ▶ NOUN **1** *The timber is reinforced with three steel props on a concrete foundation.* = **support**, stay, brace, mainstay, truss, buttress, stanchion **2** *The army is one of the main props of the government.* = **mainstay**, support, sustainer, anchor, backbone, cornerstone, upholder • **prop something** or **someone up** *World leaders were scrambling for ways to*

prop up the euro. = **subsidize**, support, fund, finance, maintain, underwrite, shore up, buttress, bolster up

propaganda NOUN = **information**, advertising, promotion, publicity, hype, brainwashing, disinformation, ballyhoo *(informal)*, agitprop, newspeak, boosterism

propagandist NOUN = **publicist**, advocate, promoter, proponent, evangelist, proselytizer, pamphleteer, indoctrinator

propagate VERB **1** *They propagated subversive political doctrines.* = **spread**, publish, promote, broadcast, proclaim, transmit, circulate, diffuse, publicize, disseminate, promulgate, make known ■ **OPPOSITE:** suppress **2** *The easiest way to propagate a vine is to take cuttings.* = **produce**, generate, engender, increase **3** *Tomatoes rot in order to transmit their seed and propagate the species.* = **reproduce**, breed, multiply, proliferate, beget, procreate *(formal)*

propagation NOUN **1** *working towards the propagation of true Buddhism* = **spreading**, spread, promotion, communication, distribution, circulation, transmission, diffusion, dissemination, promulgation **2** *the successful propagation of a batch of new plants* = **reproduction**, generation, breeding, increase, proliferation, multiplication, procreation

propel VERB **1** *The rocket is designed to propel the spacecraft.* = **drive**, launch, start, force, send, shoot, push, thrust, shove, set in motion ■ **OPPOSITE:** stop **2** *He is propelled by the need to avenge his father.* = **impel**, drive, push, prompt, spur, motivate ■ **OPPOSITE:** hold back

propensity NOUN = **tendency**, leaning, weakness, inclination, bent, liability, bias, disposition, penchant, susceptibility, predisposition, proclivity *(formal)*, proneness, aptness

proper ADJECTIVE **1** *Two out of five people do not have a proper job.* = **real**, actual, genuine, true, bona fide, kosher *(informal)*, dinkum *(Austral. & N.Z. informal)* **2** *Please ensure that the proper procedures are followed.* = **correct**, accepted, established, appropriate, right, formal, conventional, accurate, exact, precise, legitimate, orthodox, apt ■ **OPPOSITE:** improper **3** *In those days it was not thought proper for a woman to be on the stage.* = **polite**, right, becoming, seemly, fitting, fit, mannerly, suitable, decent, gentlemanly, refined, respectable, befitting, genteel, de rigueur *(French)*, ladylike, meet *(archaic)*, decorous, punctilious, comme il faut *(French)* ■ **OPPOSITE:** unseemly **4** *Make sure everything* *is in its proper place.* = **characteristic**, own, special, individual, personal, particular, specific, peculiar, respective

properly ADVERB 1 *The debate needs to be conducted properly.* = **correctly**, rightly, fittingly, appropriately, legitimately, accurately, suitably, aptly, deservedly, as intended, in the true sense, in the accepted or approved manner ■ OPPOSITE: incorrectly 2 *It's about time that brat learned to behave properly.* = **politely**, respectfully, ethically, decently, respectably, decorously, punctiliously ■ OPPOSITE: badly

property NOUN 1 *Security forces confiscated weapons and stolen property.* = **possessions**, goods, means, effects, holdings, capital, riches, resources, estate, assets, wealth, belongings, chattels 2 *He inherited a family property near Stamford.* = **land**, holding, title, estate, acres, real estate, freehold, realty, real property 3 *A radio signal has both electrical and magnetic properties.* = **quality**, feature, characteristic, mark, ability, attribute, virtue, trait, hallmark, peculiarity, idiosyncrasy

prophecy NOUN 1 *Nostradamus's prophecy of the end of the world* = **prediction**, forecast, revelation, prognosis, foretelling, prognostication, augury, sortilege, vaticination (*rare*) 2 *a child born with the gift of prophecy* = **second sight**, divination, augury, telling the future, soothsaying

prophesy VERB = **predict**, forecast, divine, foresee, augur, presage, foretell, forewarn, prognosticate, soothsay, vaticinate (*rare*)

prophet *or* **prophetess** NOUN = **soothsayer**, forecaster, diviner, oracle, seer, clairvoyant, augur, sibyl, prognosticator, prophesier

prophetic ADJECTIVE = **predictive**, foreshadowing, presaging, prescient, divinatory, oracular, sibylline, prognostic, mantic, vatic (*rare*), augural, fatidic (*rare*)

propitious ADJECTIVE = **favourable**, timely, promising, encouraging, bright, lucky, fortunate, prosperous, rosy, advantageous, auspicious, opportune (*formal*), full of promise

proponent NOUN = **supporter**, friend, champion, defender, advocate, patron, enthusiast, subscriber, backer, partisan, exponent, apologist, upholder, vindicator, spokesman *or* woman *or* person

proportion NOUN 1 *A proportion of the rent is met by the city council.* = **part**, share, cut (*informal*), amount, measure, division, percentage, segment, quota, fraction 2 *the proportion of women in the profession; the proportion of length to breadth*

= **relative amount**, relationship, distribution, ratio 3 *an artist with a special feel for colour and proportion* = **balance**, agreement, harmony, correspondence, symmetry, concord, congruity ▶ PLURAL NOUN *In the tropics, plants grow to huge proportions.* = **dimensions**, size, volume, capacity, extent, range, bulk, scope, measurements, magnitude, breadth, expanse, amplitude

proportional *or* **proportionate** ADJECTIVE = **correspondent**, equivalent, corresponding, even, balanced, consistent, comparable, compatible, equitable, in proportion, analogous, commensurate ■ OPPOSITE: disproportionate

proposal NOUN = **suggestion**, plan, programme, scheme, offer, terms, design, project, bid, motion, recommendation, tender, presentation, proposition, overture

propose VERB 1 *We are about to propose some changes to the system.* = **put forward**, present, suggest, advance, come up with, submit, tender, proffer, propound 2 *I propose to spend my entire life travelling.* = **intend**, mean, plan, aim, design, scheme, purpose, have in mind, have every intention 3 *He was proposed for renomination as party chairman.* = **nominate**, name, present, introduce, invite, recommend, put up 4 *I proposed to my partner on bended knee.* = **offer marriage**, pop the question (*informal*), ask for someone's hand (in marriage), pay suit

proposition NOUN 1 *Designing his own flat was quite a different proposition to designing for clients.* = **task**, problem, activity, job, affair, venture, undertaking 2 *the proposition that monarchs derived their authority by divine right* = **theory**, idea, argument, concept, thesis, hypothesis, theorem, premise, postulation 3 *I want to make you a business proposition.* = **proposal**, plan, suggestion, scheme, bid, motion, recommendation 4 *unwanted sexual propositions* = **advance**, pass (*informal*), proposal, overture, improper suggestion, come-on (*informal*) ▶ VERB *I felt uncomfortable when he propositioned me.* = **make a pass at**, solicit, accost, make an indecent proposal to, make an improper suggestion to

propound VERB = **put forward**, present, advance, propose, advocate, submit, suggest, lay down, contend, postulate (*formal*), set forth

proprietor *or* **proprietress** NOUN = **owner**, landowner, freeholder, possessor, titleholder, deed holder, landlord *or* landlady

propriety NOUN **1** *Their sense of social propriety is eroded.* = **decorum**, manners, courtesy, protocol, good form, decency, breeding, delicacy, modesty, respectability, etiquette, refinement, politeness, good manners, rectitude, punctilio, seemliness ■ **OPPOSITE:** indecorum **2** *They questioned the propriety of the corporation's use of public money.* = **correctness**, fitness, appropriateness, rightness, aptness, seemliness, suitableness • **the proprieties** *respectable couples who observe the proprieties but loathe each other* = **etiquette**, the niceties, the civilities, the amenities, the done thing, the social graces, the rules of conduct, the social conventions, social code, accepted conduct, kawa (*N.Z.*), tikanga (*N.Z.*)

propulsion NOUN = **power**, pressure, push, thrust, momentum, impulse, impetus, motive power, impulsion, propelling force

prosaic ADJECTIVE = **dull**, ordinary, boring, routine, flat, dry, everyday, tame, pedestrian, commonplace, mundane, matter-of-fact, stale, banal, uninspiring, humdrum, trite, unimaginative, hackneyed, workaday, vapid ■ **OPPOSITE:** exciting

proscribe VERB **1** *They are proscribed by federal law from owning guns.* = **prohibit**, ban, forbid, boycott, embargo, interdict ■ **OPPOSITE:** permit **2** *Slang is reviled and proscribed by pedants and purists.* = **condemn**, reject, damn, denounce, censure **3** *He was proscribed in America, where his estate was put up for sale.* = **outlaw**, exclude, exile, expel, banish, deport, expatriate, excommunicate, ostracize, blackball, attaint (*archaic*)

prosecute VERB **1** *The police have decided not to prosecute him.* = **take someone to court**, try, sue, summon, indict, do (*slang*), arraign, seek redress, put someone on trial, litigate, bring suit against, bring someone to trial, put someone in the dock, bring action against, prefer charges against **2** *To prosecute this war is costing the country fifteen million pounds a day.* = **conduct**, continue, manage, direct, pursue, work at, carry on, practise, engage in, discharge, persist, see through, follow through, persevere, carry through

prospect NOUN **1** *There is little prospect of having these questions answered.* = **likelihood**, chance, possibility, plan, hope, promise, proposal, odds, expectation, probability, anticipation, presumption **2** *the pleasant prospect of a quiet night in* = **idea**, thought, outlook, contemplation **3** *The windows overlooked the superb prospect of the hills.* = **view**, perspective, landscape, scene, sight, vision, outlook, spectacle, panorama, vista ▶ PLURAL NOUN *I chose to work abroad to improve my career prospects.* = **possibilities**, openings, chances, future, potential, expectations, outlook, scope ▶ VERB *The companies are prospecting for oil not far from here.* = **look**, search, seek, survey, explore, drill, go after, dowse

prospective ADJECTIVE **1** *The story is a warning to other prospective buyers.* = **potential**, possible, to come, about to be, upcoming, soon-to-be **2** *The terms of the prospective deal are spelled out clearly.* = **expected**, coming, future, approaching, likely, looked-for, intended, awaited, hoped-for, anticipated, forthcoming, imminent, destined, eventual, on the cards

prospectus NOUN = **catalogue**, plan, list, programme, announcement, outline, brochure, handbook, syllabus, synopsis, conspectus (*formal*)

prosper VERB = **succeed**, advance, progress, thrive, make it (*informal*), flower, get on, do well, flourish, bloom, make good, be fortunate, grow rich, fare well

prosperity NOUN = **success**, riches, plenty, ease, fortune, wealth, boom, luxury, well-being, good times, good fortune, the good life, affluence, life of luxury, life of Riley (*informal*), prosperousness ■ **OPPOSITE:** poverty

prosperous ADJECTIVE **1** *the youngest son of a prosperous family* = **wealthy**, rich, affluent, well-off, in the money (*informal*), blooming, opulent, well-heeled (*informal*), well-to-do, moneyed, in clover (*informal*), minted (*Brit. slang*) ■ **OPPOSITE:** poor **2** *She has developed a prosperous business.* = **successful**, booming, thriving, flourishing, doing well, prospering, on a roll, on the up and up (*Brit.*), palmy ■ **OPPOSITE:** unsuccessful

prostitute NOUN = **sex worker**, call girl, courtesan (*History*), hooker (*U.S. slang, derogatory*), pro (*slang*), camp follower, fille de joie (*French*) ▶ VERB *His friends said that he had prostituted his talents.* = **cheapen**, sell out, pervert, degrade, devalue, squander, demean, debase, profane, misapply

prostitution NOUN = **sex work**, the game (*slang*), vice, the oldest profession, streetwalking, harlot's trade (*old-fashioned*), Mrs. Warren's profession

prostrate ADJECTIVE **1** *Percy was lying prostrate with his arms outstretched.* = **prone**, fallen, flat, horizontal, abject, bowed low, kowtowing, procumbent **2** *After my*

mother's death, I was prostrate with grief.
= **exhausted**, overcome, depressed, drained, spent, worn out, desolate, dejected, inconsolable, at a low ebb, fagged out (*informal*) **3** *Gaston was prostrate on his sickbed.* = **helpless**, overwhelmed, disarmed, paralysed, powerless, reduced, impotent, defenceless, brought to your knees ▶ VERB *patients who have been prostrated by fatigue* = **exhaust**, tire, drain, fatigue, weary, sap, wear out, fag out (*informal*) • **prostrate yourself** *They prostrated themselves before the king in awe and fear.* = **bow down**, submit, kneel, cringe, grovel, fall at someone's feet, bow, kowtow, bend the knee, abase yourself, cast yourself, fall on your knees

protagonist NOUN **1** *an active protagonist of his country's membership of the EU* = **supporter**, leader, champion, advocate, exponent, mainstay, prime mover, standard-bearer, moving spirit, torchbearer **2** *the protagonist of J.D. Salinger's novel* = **leading character**, lead, principal, central character, hero *or* heroine

protean ADJECTIVE = **changeable**, variable, volatile, versatile, temperamental, ever-changing, mercurial, many-sided, mutable, polymorphous, multiform

protect VERB = **keep someone safe**, defend, keep, support, save, guard, secure, preserve, look after, foster, shelter, shield, care for, harbour, safeguard, watch over, stick up for (*informal*), cover up for, chaperon, give someone sanctuary, take someone under your wing, mount *or* stand guard over ■ **OPPOSITE:** endanger

protection NOUN **1** *The primary duty of parents is the protection of their children.* = **safety**, charge, care, defence, protecting, security, guarding, custody, safeguard, preservation, aegis, guardianship, safekeeping **2** *Innocence is no protection from the evils in our society.* = **safeguard**, cover, guard, shelter, screen, barrier, shield, refuge, buffer, bulwark **3** *Riot shields acted as protection against the attack.* = **armour**, cover, screen, barrier, shelter, shield, bulwark

protective ADJECTIVE **1** *Protective gloves reduce the absorption of chemicals through the skin.* = **protecting**, covering, sheltering, shielding, safeguarding, insulating **2** *He is very protective towards his sisters.* = **caring**, defensive, motherly, fatherly, warm, careful, maternal, vigilant, watchful, paternal, possessive

protector NOUN **1** *Many mothers see their son as a protector and provider.* = **defender**, champion, guard, guardian, counsel, advocate, patron, safeguard, bodyguard, benefactor, guardian angel, tower of strength, knight in shining armour **2** *Ear protectors must be worn when operating this equipment.* = **guard**, screen, protection, shield, pad, cushion, buffer

protégé *or* **protégée** NOUN = **charge**, student, pupil, ward, discovery, dependant

protest VERB **1** *Women took to the streets to protest against the arrests.* = **object**, demonstrate, oppose, complain, disagree, cry out, disapprove, say no to, demur, take exception, remonstrate (*formal*), kick against (*informal*), expostulate, take up the cudgels, express disapproval **2** *'I never said that,' he protested.* = **assert**, argue, insist, maintain, declare, vow, testify, contend, affirm, profess, attest, avow, asseverate (*formal*) ▶ NOUN **1** *The opposition staged a protest against the government.* = **demonstration**, march, rally, sit-in, demo (*informal*), hikoi (*N.Z.*) **2** *a protest against people's growing economic hardship* = **objection**, complaint, declaration, dissent, outcry, disapproval, protestation, demur, formal complaint, remonstrance, demurral

protestation NOUN = **declaration**, pledge, vow, oath, profession, affirmation, avowal, asseveration (*formal*)

protester NOUN **1** *anti-abortion protesters* = **demonstrator**, rebel, dissident, dissenter, agitator, picketer, protest marcher **2** *Protesters say the government is corrupt.* = **objector**, opposer, complainer, opponent, dissident, dissenter

protocol NOUN **1** *He is a stickler for royal protocol.* = **code of behaviour**, manners, courtesies, conventions, customs, formalities, good form, etiquette, propriety, decorum, rules of conduct, politesse, p's and q's **2** *the Montreal Protocol to phase out use and production of CFCs* = **agreement**, contract, treaty, convention, pact, compact, covenant, concordat

prototype NOUN = **original**, model, precedent, first, example, standard, paradigm, archetype, mock-up

protracted ADJECTIVE = **extended**, long, prolonged, lengthy, time-consuming, never-ending, drawn-out, interminable, spun out, dragged out, long-drawn-out, overlong

protrude VERB = **stick out**, start (from), point, project, pop (*of an eye*), extend, come through, stand out, bulge, shoot out, jut, stick out like a sore thumb, obtrude

p

proud ADJECTIVE **1** *I am proud to be a Scot.*
= **satisfied**, pleased, content, contented,
honoured, thrilled, glad, gratified, joyful,
appreciative, well-pleased ■ **OPPOSITE:**
dissatisfied **2** *My daughter's graduation was a
proud moment for me.* = **glorious**, rewarding,
memorable, pleasing, satisfying,
illustrious, gratifying, exalted, red-letter
3 *the indignity and degradation inflicted on a
proud people* = **distinguished**, great, grand,
imposing, magnificent, noble, august,
splendid, eminent, majestic, stately,
illustrious ■ **OPPOSITE:** lowly **4** *She has a
reputation for being proud and arrogant.*
= **conceited**, vain, arrogant, stuck-up
(*informal*), lordly, imperious, narcissistic,
overbearing, snooty (*informal*), haughty,
snobbish, egotistical, self-satisfied,
disdainful, self-important, presumptuous,
boastful, supercilious, high and mighty
(*informal*), toffee-nosed (*slang, chiefly Brit.*),
too big for your boots *or* breeches
■ **OPPOSITE:** humble

prove VERB **1** *In the past this process has proved
difficult.* = **turn out**, come out, end up, be
found to be **2** *new evidence that could prove
their innocence* = **verify**, establish,
determine, show, evidence, confirm,
demonstrate, justify, ascertain, bear out,
attest, substantiate, corroborate,
authenticate, evince (*formal*), show clearly
■ **OPPOSITE:** disprove

proven ADJECTIVE = **established**, accepted,
proved, confirmed, tried, tested, checked,
reliable, valid, definite, authentic, certified,
verified, attested, undoubted, dependable,
trustworthy

provenance NOUN = **origin**, source,
birthplace, derivation

proverb NOUN = **saying**, saw (*old-fashioned*),
maxim, gnome, adage, dictum, aphorism,
byword, apophthegm

proverbial ADJECTIVE = **conventional**,
accepted, traditional, famous,
acknowledged, typical, well-known,
legendary, notorious, customary, famed,
archetypal, time-honoured, self-evident,
unquestioned, axiomatic

provide VERB **1** *I will be happy to provide you
with a copy of the report.* = **supply**, give,
contribute, provision, distribute, outfit,
equip, accommodate, donate, furnish,
dispense, part with, fork out (*informal*),
stock up, cater to, purvey ■ **OPPOSITE:**
withhold **2** *The summit will provide an
opportunity for discussions on the crisis.*
= **give**, bring, add, produce, present,
serve, afford, yield, lend, render, impart
3 *Russian law provides that marital assets are*
divided equally on divorce. = **stipulate**, state,
require, determine, specify, lay down
• **provide for someone** *He can't even provide
for his family.* = **support**, look after, care for,
keep, maintain, sustain, take care of, fend
for • **provide for** *or* **against something**
James had provided for just such an emergency.
= **take precautions against**, plan for,
prepare for, anticipate, arrange for,
get ready for, make plans for, make
arrangements for, plan ahead for, take
measures against, forearm for

providence NOUN = **fate**, fortune, destiny,
God's will, divine intervention,
predestination

provider NOUN **1** *the world's largest provider of
foreign aid* = **supplier**, giver, source, donor,
benefactor **2** *I have always tried to be a good
provider for my family.* = **breadwinner**,
supporter, earner, mainstay, wage earner

providing *or* **provided** CONJUNCTION (*often
with* **that**) = **on condition that**, if, subject
to, given that, on the assumption that, in
the event that, with the proviso that,
contingent upon, with the understanding
that, as long as, if and only if, upon these
terms

province NOUN **1** *the Algarve, Portugal's
southernmost province* = **region**, section,
county, district, territory, zone, patch,
colony, domain, dependency, tract **2** *Opera
remained largely the province of the aristocracy.*
= **area**, business, concern, responsibility,
part, line, charge, role, post, department
(*informal*), field, duty, function,
employment, capacity, orbit, sphere, turf
(*slang*), pigeon (*Brit. informal*)

provincial ADJECTIVE **1** *The local and provincial
elections take place in June.* = **regional**, state,
local, county, district, territorial, parochial
2 *My accent gave away my provincial roots.*
= **rural**, country, local, home-grown, rustic,
homespun, hick (*informal, chiefly U.S. &
Canad.*), backwoods ■ **OPPOSITE:** urban
3 *The audience was dull and very provincial.*
= **parochial**, insular, narrow-minded,
unsophisticated, limited, narrow,
small-town (*chiefly U.S.*), uninformed,
inward-looking, small-minded, parish-
pump, upcountry ■ **OPPOSITE:**
cosmopolitan ▶ NOUN *French provincials
looking for work in Paris* = **yokel**, hick
(*informal, chiefly U.S. & Canad.*), rustic,
country cousin, hayseed (*U.S. & Canad.
informal*)

provision NOUN **1** *the provision of military
supplies to the Khmer Rouge* = **supplying**,
giving, providing, supply, delivery,
distribution, catering, presentation,

equipping, furnishing, allocation, fitting out, purveying, accoutrement **2** *There is no provision for funding performance-related pay increases.* = **arrangement**, plan, planning, preparation, precaution, contingency, prearrangement **3** *Special provision should be made for single mothers.* = **facilities**, services, funds, resources, means, opportunities, arrangements, assistance, concession(s), allowance(s), amenities **4** *a provision that would allow existing regulations to be reviewed* = **condition**, term, agreement, requirement, demand, rider, restriction, qualification, clause, reservation, specification, caveat, proviso, stipulation ▶ PLURAL NOUN *On board were enough provisions for two weeks.* = **food**, supplies, stores, feed, fare, rations, eats (*slang*), groceries, tack (*informal*), grub (*slang*), foodstuff, kai (*N.Z. informal*), sustenance, victuals (*old-fashioned*), edibles, comestibles, provender, nosebag (*slang*), vittles (*obsolete, dialect*), viands, eatables

provisional ADJECTIVE **1** *the possibility of setting up a provisional coalition government* = **temporary**, interim, transitional, stopgap, pro tem ■ OPPOSITE: permanent **2** *The times stated are provisional and subject to confirmation.* = **conditional**, limited, qualified, contingent, tentative, provisory ■ OPPOSITE: definite

proviso NOUN = **condition**, requirement, strings, rider, restriction, qualification, clause, reservation, limitation, stipulation

provocation NOUN **1** *The soldiers fired without provocation.* = **cause**, reason, grounds, motivation, justification, stimulus, inducement, incitement, instigation, casus belli (*Latin*) **2** *They kept their tempers in the face of severe provocation.* = **offence**, challenge, insult, taunt, injury, dare, grievance, annoyance, affront, indignity, red rag, vexation

provocative ADJECTIVE **1** *Their behaviour was called provocative and antisocial.* = **offensive**, provoking, insulting, challenging, disturbing, stimulating, annoying, outrageous, aggravating (*informal*), incensing, galling, goading **2** *sexually provocative behaviour* = **suggestive**, tempting, stimulating, exciting, inviting, sexy (*informal*), arousing, erotic, seductive, alluring, tantalizing

provoke VERB **1** *I didn't want to do anything to provoke him.* = **anger**, insult, annoy, offend, irritate, infuriate, hassle (*informal*), aggravate (*informal*), incense, enrage, gall, put someone out, madden, exasperate, vex, affront, chafe, irk, rile, pique, get on someone's nerves (*informal*), get someone's back up, put someone's back up, try someone's patience, nark (*Brit., Austral. & N.Z. slang*), make someone's blood boil, get in someone's hair (*informal*), rub someone up the wrong way, hack someone off (*informal*) ■ OPPOSITE: pacify **2** *His comments have provoked a shocked reaction.* = **rouse**, cause, produce, lead to, move, fire, promote, occasion (*formal*), excite, inspire, generate, prompt, stir, stimulate, motivate, induce, bring about, evoke, give rise to, precipitate, elicit, inflame, incite, instigate, kindle, foment, call forth, draw forth, bring on or down ■ OPPOSITE: curb

prowess NOUN **1** *He's always bragging about his prowess as a cricketer.* = **skill**, ability, talent, expertise, facility, command, genius, excellence, accomplishment, mastery, attainment, aptitude, dexterity, adroitness, adeptness, expertness ■ OPPOSITE: inability **2** *a race of people noted for their fighting prowess* = **bravery**, daring, courage, heroism, mettle, boldness, gallantry, valour, fearlessness, intrepidity, hardihood, valiance, dauntlessness, doughtiness ■ OPPOSITE: cowardice

prowl VERB = **move stealthily**, hunt, patrol, range, steal, cruise, stalk, sneak, lurk, roam, rove, scavenge, slink, skulk, nose around

proximity NOUN = **nearness**, closeness, vicinity, neighbourhood, juxtaposition, contiguity, propinquity, adjacency

proxy NOUN = **representative**, agent, deputy, substitute, factor (*Scot.*), attorney, delegate, surrogate

prudence NOUN **1** *He urged prudence rather than haste on any new resolution.* = **caution**, care, discretion, vigilance, wariness, circumspection, canniness, heedfulness **2** *acting with prudence and judgment* = **wisdom**, common sense, good sense, good judgment, sagacity, judiciousness **3** *A lack of prudence may lead to financial problems.* = **thrift**, economy, planning, saving, precaution, foresight, providence, preparedness, good management, husbandry, frugality, forethought, economizing, far-sightedness, careful budgeting

prudent ADJECTIVE **1** *He is taking a prudent and cautious approach.* = **cautious**, careful, wary, discreet, canny, vigilant, circumspect ■ OPPOSITE: careless **2** *We believed ours was the prudent and responsible course of action.* = **wise**, politic, sensible, sage, shrewd, discerning, judicious, sagacious (*formal*)

p

■ **OPPOSITE:** unwise **3** *In private, she is prudent and even frugal.* = **thrifty**, economical, sparing, careful, canny, provident, frugal, far-sighted
■ **OPPOSITE:** extravagant

prudish ADJECTIVE = **prim**, formal, proper, stuffy, puritanical, demure, squeamish, narrow-minded, starchy (*informal*), prissy (*informal*), strait-laced, Victorian, priggish, niminy-piminy, overmodest, overnice
■ **OPPOSITE:** broad-minded

prune VERB **1** *You have to prune the bushes if you want fruit.* = **cut**, trim, clip, dock, shape, cut back, shorten, snip, lop, pare down **2** *Economic hard times are forcing the company to prune their budget.* = **reduce**, cut, cut back, trim, cut down, pare down, make reductions in

prurient ADJECTIVE **1** *our prurient fascination with sexual scandals* = **lecherous**, longing, lewd, salacious, lascivious, itching, hankering, voyeuristic, lustful, libidinous, desirous, concupiscent **2** *the film's harshly prurient and cynical sex scenes* = **indecent**, dirty, erotic, obscene, steamy (*informal*), pornographic, X-rated (*informal*), salacious, smutty

pry VERB = **be inquisitive**, peer, interfere, poke, peep, meddle, intrude, snoop (*informal*), nose into, be nosy (*informal*), be a busybody, ferret about, poke your nose in or into (*informal*)

prying ADJECTIVE = **inquisitive**, spying, curious, interfering, meddling, intrusive, eavesdropping, snooping (*informal*), snoopy (*informal*), impertinent, nosy (*informal*), meddlesome

psalm NOUN = **hymn**, carol, chant, paean, song of praise

pseudonym NOUN = **false name**, alias, incognito, stage name, pen name, assumed name, nom de guerre, nom de plume, professional name

psyche NOUN = **soul**, mind, self, spirit, personality, individuality, subconscious, true being, anima, essential nature, pneuma (*Philosophy*), innermost self, inner man or woman or person, wairua (*N.Z.*)

psychedelic ADJECTIVE **1** *experimenting with psychedelic drugs* = **hallucinogenic**, mind-blowing (*informal*), psychoactive, hallucinatory, mind-bending (*informal*), psychotropic, mind-expanding, consciousness-expanding, psychotomimetic **2** *psychedelic patterns* = **multicoloured**, wild, crazy (*informal*), freaky (*slang*), kaleidoscopic

psychiatrist NOUN = **psychotherapist**, analyst, therapist, psychologist, shrink (*slang*), psychoanalyst, psychoanalyser, headshrinker (*slang*)

psychic ADJECTIVE **1** *Trevor helped police by using his psychic powers.* = **supernatural**, mystic, occult, clairvoyant, telepathic, extrasensory, preternatural, telekinetic **2** *He declared his total disbelief in psychic phenomena.* = **mystical**, spiritual, magical, other-worldly, paranormal, preternatural **3** *the psychic trauma of losing a twin* = **psychological**, emotional, mental, spiritual, inner, psychiatric, cognitive, psychogenic ▶ NOUN *a natural psychic who used Tarot as a focus for his intuition* = **clairvoyant**, fortune teller

psychological ADJECTIVE **1** *the treatment of psychological disorders* = **mental**, emotional, intellectual, inner, cognitive, cerebral **2** *My GP dismissed my back pains as purely psychological.* = **imaginary**, psychosomatic, unconscious, subconscious, subjective, irrational, unreal, all in the mind

psychology NOUN **1** *He is Professor of Psychology at Bedford Community College.* = **behaviourism**, study of personality, science of mind **2** *a fascination with the psychology of serial killers* = **way of thinking**, attitude, behaviour, temperament, mentality, thought processes, mental processes, what makes you tick, mental make-up

pub or **public house** NOUN = **tavern**, bar, inn, local (*Brit. informal*), saloon, watering hole (*facetious slang*), boozer (*Brit., Austral. & N.Z. informal*), beer parlour (*Canad.*), beverage room (*Canad.*), roadhouse, hostelry (*archaic, facetious*), alehouse (*archaic*), taproom

puberty NOUN = **adolescence**, teenage, teens, young adulthood, pubescence, awkward age, juvenescence

public NOUN *The poll is a test of the public's confidence in the government.* = **people**, society, country, population, masses, community, nation, everyone, citizens, voters, electorate, multitude, populace, hoi polloi, Joe Public (*slang*), Joe Six-Pack (*U.S. slang*), Main Street (*U.S. & Canad.*), commonalty ▶ ADJECTIVE **1** *a substantial part of public spending* = **civic**, government, state, national, local, official, community, social, federal, civil, constitutional, municipal **2** *Parliament's decision was in line with public opinion.* = **general**, popular, national, shared, common, widespread, universal, collective **3** *a public library* = **open**, community, accessible, communal, open to the public, unrestricted, free to all, not private ■ **OPPOSITE:** private **4** *He hit out at* *public figures who evade taxes.* = **well-known**, leading, important, respected, famous, celebrated, recognized, distinguished, prominent, influential, notable, renowned, eminent, famed, noteworthy, in the public eye **5** *She was reluctant to make her views public.* = **known**, published, exposed, open, obvious, acknowledged, recognized, plain, patent, notorious, overt, in circulation ■ **OPPOSITE:** secret

publication NOUN **1** *expensively produced glossy publications* = **pamphlet**, book, newspaper, magazine, issue, title, leaflet, brochure, booklet, paperback, hardback, periodical, zine (*informal*), handbill, blog (*informal*) **2** *We have no comment regarding the publication of these photographs.* = **publishing**, announcement, broadcasting, reporting, airing, appearance, declaration, advertisement, disclosure, proclamation, notification, dissemination, promulgation

publicity NOUN **1** *Much advance publicity was given to the talks.* = **advertising**, press, promotion, hype, boost, build-up, plug (*informal*), puff, ballyhoo (*informal*), puffery (*informal*), boosterism **2** *The case has generated enormous publicity.* = **attention**, exposure, fame, celebrity, fuss, public interest, limelight, notoriety, media attention, renown, public notice

publicize VERB **1** *The author appeared on TV to publicize her latest book.* = **advertise**, promote, plug (*informal*), hype, push, spotlight, puff, play up, write up, spread about, beat the drum for (*informal*), give publicity to, bring to public notice **2** *He never publicized his plans.* = **make known**, report, reveal, publish, broadcast, leak, disclose, proclaim, circulate, make public, divulge ■ **OPPOSITE:** keep secret

public-spirited ADJECTIVE = **altruistic**, generous, humanitarian, charitable, philanthropic, unselfish, community-minded

publish VERB **1** *His latest book will be published in May.* = **put out**, issue, produce, print, bring out **2** *The paper did not publish his name for legal reasons.* = **announce**, reveal, declare, spread, advertise, broadcast, leak, distribute, communicate, disclose, proclaim, circulate, impart, publicize, divulge, promulgate, shout from the rooftops (*informal*), blow wide open (*slang*)

pucker VERB *She puckered her lips and kissed him on the nose.* = **wrinkle**, tighten, purse, pout, contract, gather, knit, crease, compress, crumple, ruffle, furrow, screw up, crinkle, draw together, ruck up, ruckle ▶ NOUN *small puckers in the material* = **wrinkle**, fold, crease, crumple, ruck, crinkle, ruckle

pudding NOUN = **dessert**, afters (*Brit. informal*), sweet, pud (*informal*), second course, last course

puerile ADJECTIVE = **childish**, juvenile, naive, weak, silly, ridiculous, foolish, petty, trivial, irresponsible, immature, infantile, inane, babyish, jejune (*formal*) ■ **OPPOSITE:** mature

puff VERB **1** *He gave a wry smile as he puffed on his cigarette.* = **smoke**, draw, drag (*slang*), suck, inhale, pull at or on **2** *I could see he was unfit, because he was puffing.* = **breathe heavily**, pant, exhale, blow, gasp, gulp, wheeze, fight for breath, puff and pant **3** *TV correspondents puffing the new digital channels* = **promote**, push, plug (*informal*), hype, publicize, advertise, praise, crack up (*informal*), big up (*slang*), overpraise ▶ NOUN **1** *She was taking quick puffs at her cigarette.* = **drag**, pull (*slang*), smoke **2** *an occasional puff of air stirring the brittle leaves* = **blast**, breath, flurry, whiff, draught, gust, emanation **3** *an elaborate puff for his magazine* = **advertisement**, ad (*informal*), promotion, plug (*informal*), good word, commendation, sales talk, favourable mention, piece of publicity • **puff out** or **up** *His chest puffed out with pride.* = **swell**, expand, enlarge, inflate, stick out, dilate, distend, bloat

puffy ADJECTIVE = **swollen**, enlarged, inflated, inflamed, bloated, puffed up, distended

pugnacious ADJECTIVE = **aggressive**, contentious, irritable, belligerent, combative, petulant, antagonistic, argumentative, bellicose, irascible, quarrelsome, hot-tempered, choleric, disputatious, aggro (*Austral. & N.Z.*), aggers (*Austral. slang*), biffo (*Austral. slang*) ■ **OPPOSITE:** peaceful

puke VERB = **vomit**, be sick, throw up (*informal*), spew, heave, regurgitate, disgorge, retch, be nauseated, chuck (*Austral. & N.Z. informal*), barf (*U.S. slang*), chunder (*slang, chiefly Austral.*), upchuck (*U.S. slang*), do a technicolour yawn (*slang*), toss your cookies (*U.S. slang*)

pull VERB **1** *I helped pull him out of the water.* = **draw**, haul, drag, trail, tow, tug, jerk, yank, prise, wrench, lug, wrest ■ **OPPOSITE:** push **2** *Wes was in the yard pulling weeds when we drove up.* = **extract**, pick, remove, gather, take out, weed, pluck, cull, uproot, draw out ■ **OPPOSITE:** insert **3** *The organizers have to employ performers to pull a crowd.* = **attract**,

P

draw, bring in, tempt, lure, interest, entice, pull in, magnetize ■ **OPPOSITE:** repel
4 *Dave pulled a back muscle and could hardly move.* = **strain**, tear, stretch, rend (*literary*), rip, wrench, dislocate, sprain ▶ NOUN
1 *The tooth must be removed with a firm, straight pull.* = **tug**, jerk, yank, twitch, heave ■ **OPPOSITE:** shove **2** *No matter how much you feel the pull of the past, try to look to the future.* = **attraction**, appeal, lure, fascination, force, draw (*informal*), influence, magnetism, enchantment, drawing power, enticement, allurement **3** *the pull of gravity* = **force**, exertion, magnetism, forcefulness **4** *He took a deep pull of his cigarette.* = **puff**, drag (*slang*), inhalation **5** *Using all his pull in parliament, he obtained the necessary papers.* = **influence**, power, authority, say, standing, weight, advantage, muscle, sway, prestige, clout (*informal*), leverage, kai (*N.Z. informal*) • **pull a fast one on someone** *Someone had pulled a fast one on her over a procedural matter.* = **trick**, cheat, con (*informal*), take advantage of, deceive, defraud, swindle, bamboozle (*informal*), hoodwink, take for a ride (*informal*), put one over on (*informal*) • **pull in** *He pulled in at the side of the road.* = **draw in**, stop, park, arrive, come in, halt, draw up, pull over, come to a halt • **pull out (of)** **1** *An injury forced him to pull out of the race.* = **withdraw**, retire from, abandon, quit, step down from, back out, bow out, stop participating in **2** *The troops prepared to pull out of the country.* = **leave**, abandon, get out, quit, retreat from, depart (*U.S.*), evacuate • **pull someone in** *The police pulled him in for questioning.* = **arrest**, nail (*informal*), bust (*informal*), lift (*slang*), run in (*slang*), collar (*informal*), pinch (*informal*), nab (*informal*), take someone into custody, feel someone's collar (*slang*) • **pull someone up** *My boss pulled me up about my timekeeping.* = **reprimand**, lecture, rebuke, reproach, carpet (*informal*), censure, scold, berate, castigate, admonish, chastise, tear into (*informal*), read the riot act to, tell someone off (*informal*), reprove, upbraid, take someone to task, tick someone off (*informal*), read someone the riot act, bawl someone out (*informal*), dress someone down (*informal*), lambaste, give someone an earful, chew someone out (*U.S. & Canad. informal*), tear someone off a strip (*Brit. informal*), haul someone over the coals, give someone a dressing down, give someone a rocket (*Brit. & N.Z. informal*), slap someone on the wrist, rap someone over the knuckles • **pull something apart** *or* **to pieces**

1 *You'll have to pull it apart and start all over again.* = **dismantle**, strip down, disassemble, take something apart, break something up, take something to bits **2** *The critics pulled his new book to pieces.* = **criticize**, attack, blast, pan (*informal*), slam (*slang*), put down, run down, slate (*informal*), tear into (*informal*), lay into (*informal*), flay, diss (*slang*), find fault with, lambast(e), pick holes in • **pull something down** *They'd pulled the school down.* = **demolish**, level, destroy, dismantle, remove, flatten, knock down, take down, tear down, bulldoze, raze, lay waste, raze to the ground, kennet (*Austral. slang*), jeff (*Austral. slang*) • **pull something in** **1** *his ability to pull in a near capacity crowd for a match* = **attract**, draw, pull (*informal*), bring in, lure **2** *As a social worker I don't pull in a huge salary.* = **earn**, make, clear, gain, net, collect, be paid, pocket, bring in, gross, take home, rake in • **pull something off** **1** (*informal*) *The team is looking to pull off its third victory in a row.* = **succeed in**, manage, establish, effect, complete, achieve, engineer, carry out, crack (*informal*), fulfil, accomplish, execute, discharge, clinch, bring about, carry off, perpetrate, bring off **2** *He pulled off his shirt.* = **remove**, detach, rip off, tear off, doff, wrench off • **pull something out** *He pulled out a gun and threatened us.* = **produce**, draw, bring out, draw out • **pull something up** *Pull up weeds by hand and put them on the compost heap.* = **uproot**, raise, lift, weed, dig up, dig out, rip up • **pull through** *Everyone waited to see whether he would pull through or not.* = **survive**, improve, recover, rally, come through, get better, be all right, recuperate, turn the corner, pull round, get well again • **pull up** *The cab pulled up and the driver jumped out.* = **stop**, park, halt, arrive, brake, draw up, come to a halt, reach a standstill • **pull yourself together** *He pulled himself together and got back to work.* = **get a grip on yourself**, recover, get over it, buck up (*informal*), snap out of it (*informal*), get your act together, regain your composure

pulp NOUN **1** *The olives are crushed to a pulp by stone rollers.* = **paste**, mash, pap, mush, semisolid, pomace, semiliquid **2** *Use the whole fruit, including the pulp, which is high in fibre.* = **flesh**, meat, marrow, soft part ▶ MODIFIER *lurid '50s pulp fiction* = **cheap**, sensational, lurid, mushy (*informal*), trashy, rubbishy ▶ VERB *Onions can be boiled and pulped to a puree.* = **crush**, squash, mash, pulverize
pulsate VERB = **throb**, pound, beat, hammer, pulse, tick, thump, quiver, vibrate, thud, palpitate

pulse NOUN *the repetitive pulse of the music* = **beat**, rhythm, vibration, beating, stroke, throb, throbbing, oscillation, pulsation ▶ VERB *Her feet pulsed with pain.* = **beat**, tick, throb, vibrate, pulsate

pummel VERB = **beat**, punch, pound, strike, knock, belt (*informal*), hammer, bang, batter, thump, clobber (*slang*), lambast(e), beat the living daylights out of, rain blows upon, beat or knock seven bells out of (*informal*)

pump VERB **1** *drill rigs that are busy pumping natural gas* = **drive out**, empty, drain, force out, bail out, siphon, draw off **2** *The government must pump more money into community care.* = **supply**, send, pour, inject **3** *He ran in every five minutes to pump me for details.* = **interrogate**, probe, quiz, cross-examine, grill (*informal*), worm out of, give someone the third degree, question closely • **pump something up** *I was trying to pump up my back tyre.* = **inflate**, blow up, fill up, dilate, puff up, aerate

pun NOUN = **play on words**, quip, double entendre, witticism, paronomasia (*Rhetoric*), equivoque

punch¹ VERB *After punching him on the chin, she hit him over the head.* = **hit**, strike, box, smash, belt (*informal*), slam, plug (*slang*), bash (*informal*), sock (*slang*), clout (*informal*), slug, swipe (*informal*), biff (*slang*), bop (*informal*), wallop (*informal*), pummel ▶ NOUN **1** *He's asking for a punch on the nose.* = **blow**, hit, knock, bash (*informal*), plug (*slang*), sock (*slang*); thump, clout (*informal*), jab, swipe (*informal*), biff (*slang*), bop (*informal*), wallop (*informal*) **2** *The film lacks punch and pace.* = **effectiveness**, force, bite, impact, point, drive, vigour, verve, forcefulness

punch² VERB *I took a pen and punched holes in the carton.* = **pierce**, cut, bore, drill, pink, stamp, puncture, prick, perforate

punch-up NOUN = **fight**, row, argument, set-to (*informal*), scrap (*informal*), brawl, free-for-all (*informal*), dust-up (*informal*), shindig (*informal*), battle royal, stand-up fight (*informal*), dingdong, shindy (*informal*), bagarre (*French*), biffo (*Austral. slang*)

punchy ADJECTIVE = **effective**, spirited, dynamic, lively, storming (*informal*), aggressive, vigorous, forceful, incisive, in-your-face (*slang*)

punctual ADJECTIVE = **on time**, timely, early, prompt, strict, exact, precise, in good time, on the dot, seasonable ■ OPPOSITE: late

punctuality NOUN = **promptness**, readiness, regularity, promptitude

punctuate VERB = **interrupt**, break, pepper, sprinkle, intersperse, interject

puncture NOUN **1** *Someone helped me to mend the puncture.* = **flat tyre**, flat, flattie (N.Z.) **2** *an instrument used to make a puncture in the abdominal wall* = **hole**, opening, break, cut, nick, leak, slit, rupture, perforation ▶ VERB **1** *The bullet punctured his stomach.* = **pierce**, cut, nick, penetrate, prick, rupture, perforate, impale, bore a hole (in) **2** *The tyre is guaranteed never to puncture.* = **deflate**, go down, go flat **3** *a witty column which punctures celebrity egos* = **humble**, discourage, disillusion, flatten, deflate, take down a peg (*informal*)

pundit NOUN = **expert**, guru, maestro, buff (*informal*), wonk (*informal*), fundi (*S. African*), one of the cognoscenti, (self-appointed) expert or authority

pungent ADJECTIVE **1** *The more herbs you use, the more pungent the sauce will be.* = **strong**, hot, spicy, seasoned, sharp, acid, bitter, stinging, sour, tart, aromatic, tangy, acrid, peppery, piquant, highly flavoured, acerb ■ OPPOSITE: mild **2** *He enjoyed the play's shrewd and pungent social analysis.* = **cutting**, pointed, biting, acute, telling, sharp, keen, stinging, piercing, penetrating, poignant, stringent, scathing, acrimonious, barbed, incisive, sarcastic, caustic, vitriolic, trenchant, mordant, mordacious ■ OPPOSITE: dull

punish VERB = **discipline**, correct, castigate, chastise, beat, sentence, whip, lash, cane, flog, scourge, chasten, penalize, bring to book, slap someone's wrist, throw the book at, rap someone's knuckles, give someone the works (*slang*), give a lesson to

punishable ADJECTIVE = **culpable**, criminal, chargeable, indictable, blameworthy, convictable

punishing ADJECTIVE = **hard**, taxing, demanding, grinding, wearing, tiring, exhausting, uphill, gruelling, strenuous, arduous, burdensome, backbreaking ■ OPPOSITE: easy

punishment NOUN **1** *The man is guilty and he deserves punishment.* = **penalizing**, discipline, correction, retribution, what for (*informal*), chastening, just deserts, chastisement, punitive measures **2** *The usual punishment is a fine.* = **penalty**, reward, sanction, penance, comeuppance (*slang*) **3** *He took a lot of punishment in the first few rounds of the fight.* = **beating**, abuse, torture, pain, victimization, manhandling, maltreatment, rough treatment **4** *This bike isn't designed to take that kind of punishment.* = **rough treatment**, abuse, maltreatment

punitive ADJECTIVE = **retaliatory**, in retaliation, vindictive, in reprisal, revengeful, retaliative, punitory

punt VERB (*chiefly Brit.*) *He punted the lot on Little Nell in the third race.* = **bet**, back, stake, gamble, lay, wager ▶ NOUN (*chiefly Brit.*) *I like to take the odd punt on the stock exchange.* = **bet**, stake, gamble, wager

punter NOUN **1** *Punters are expected to gamble on the race in record numbers.* = **gambler**, better, backer, punt (*chiefly Brit.*) **2** *The last-minute cancellation left 1200 irate punters standing on the pavement.* = **customer**, guest, client, patron, member of the audience **3** *Most of these artists are not known to the ordinary punter.* = **person**, guy (*informal*), fellow, bloke (*Brit. informal*), man in the street

puny ADJECTIVE **1** *Our Kevin has always been a puny lad.* = **feeble**, weak, frail, little, tiny, weakly, stunted, diminutive, sickly, undeveloped, pint-sized (*informal*), undersized, underfed, dwarfish, pygmy or pigmy ■ **OPPOSITE:** strong **2** *the puny resources at our disposal* = **insignificant**, minor, petty, inferior, trivial, worthless, trifling, paltry, inconsequential, piddling (*informal*)

pup or **puppy** NOUN = **whippersnapper**, braggart, whelp, jackanapes, popinjay

pupil NOUN **1** *a school with over 1,000 pupils* = **student**, scholar, schoolboy or schoolgirl, schoolchild ■ **OPPOSITE:** teacher **2** *Goldschmidt became a pupil of the composer Franz Schreker.* = **learner**, student, follower, trainee, novice, beginner, apprentice, disciple, protégé, neophyte (*formal*), tyro, catechumen ■ **OPPOSITE:** instructor

puppet NOUN **1** *The show features huge inflatable puppets.* = **marionette**, doll, glove puppet, sock puppet, finger puppet **2** *The ministers have denied that they are puppets of a foreign government.* = **pawn**, tool, instrument (*informal*), creature, dupe, gull (*archaic*), figurehead, mouthpiece, stooge (*slang*), cat's-paw

purchase VERB *She purchased a tuna sandwich and a carton of orange juice.* = **buy**, pay for, obtain, get, score (*slang*), gain, pick up, secure, acquire, invest in, shop for, get hold of, come by, procure, make a purchase ■ **OPPOSITE:** sell ▶ NOUN **1** *She opened the bag and looked at her purchases.* = **acquisition**, buy, investment, property, gain, asset, possession **2** *I got a purchase on the rope and pulled.* = **grip**, hold, support, footing, influence, edge, advantage, grasp, lever, leverage, foothold, toehold

purchaser NOUN = **buyer**, customer, consumer, vendee (*Law*) ■ **OPPOSITE:** seller

pure ADJECTIVE **1** *The ancient alchemists tried to transmute base metals into pure gold.* = **unmixed**, real, clear, true, simple, natural, straight, perfect, genuine, neat, authentic, flawless, unalloyed ■ **OPPOSITE:** adulterated **2** *demands for pure and clean river water* = **clean**, immaculate, sterile, wholesome, sanitary, spotless, sterilized, squeaky-clean, unblemished, unadulterated, untainted, disinfected, uncontaminated, unpolluted, pasteurized, germ-free ■ **OPPOSITE:** contaminated **3** *Physics isn't just about pure science with no practical applications.* = **theoretical**, abstract, philosophical, speculative, academic, conceptual, hypothetical, conjectural, non-practical ■ **OPPOSITE:** practical **4** *The old man turned to give her a look of pure surprise.* = **complete**, total, perfect, absolute, mere, sheer, patent, utter, outright, thorough, downright, palpable, unqualified, out-and-out, unmitigated ■ **OPPOSITE:** qualified **5** *pure and chaste thoughts* = **innocent**, virgin, modest, good, true, moral, maidenly, upright, honest, immaculate, impeccable, righteous, virtuous, squeaky-clean, blameless, chaste, virginal, unsullied, guileless, uncorrupted, unstained, undefiled, unspotted ■ **OPPOSITE:** corrupt

purely ADVERB = **absolutely**, just, only, completely, simply, totally, entirely, exclusively, plainly, merely, solely, wholly

purgatory NOUN = **torment**, agony, murder (*informal*), hell (*informal*), torture, misery, hell on earth

purge VERB **1** *They voted to purge the party of 'hostile and anti-party elements'.* = **rid**, clear, cleanse, strip, empty, void **2** *They have purged thousands from the upper levels of the civil service.* = **get rid of**, kill, remove, dismiss, axe (*informal*), expel, wipe out, oust, eradicate, eject, do away with, liquidate, exterminate, sweep out, rout out, wipe from the face of the earth, rid somewhere of **3** *He lay still, trying to purge his mind of anxiety.* = **cleanse**, clear, purify, wash, clean out, expiate ▶ NOUN *a thorough purge of people associated with the late ruler* = **removal**, elimination, crushing, expulsion, suppression, liquidation, cleanup, witch hunt, eradication, ejection

purify VERB **1** *Plants can filter and purify the air in your office.* = **clean**, filter, cleanse, refine, clarify, disinfect, fumigate, decontaminate, sanitize, detoxify ■ **OPPOSITE:** contaminate **2** *They believe that bathing in the Ganges at*

certain holy places purifies the soul.
= **absolve**, cleanse, redeem, exonerate,
sanctify, exculpate, shrive, lustrate
■ **OPPOSITE:** sully

purist NOUN = **stickler**, traditionalist,
perfectionist, classicist, pedant, formalist,
literalist

puritan NOUN He delighted in dealing with
subjects that enraged puritans. = **moralist**,
fanatic, zealot, prude, pietist, rigorist
▶ ADJECTIVE Paul has always had a puritan
streak. = **strict**, austere, puritanical,
narrow, severe, intolerant, ascetic,
narrow-minded, moralistic, prudish,
hidebound, strait-laced

puritanical ADJECTIVE = **strict**, forbidding,
puritan, stuffy, narrow, severe, proper,
stiff, rigid, disapproving, austere, fanatical,
bigoted, prim, ascetic, narrow-minded,
prudish, strait-laced ■ **OPPOSITE:** liberal

puritanism NOUN = **strictness**, austerity,
severity, zeal, piety, rigidity, fanaticism,
narrowness, asceticism, moralism,
prudishness, rigorism, piousness

purity NOUN **1** the purity of the air in your
working environment = **cleanness**, clarity,
cleanliness, brilliance, genuineness,
wholesomeness, fineness, clearness,
pureness, faultlessness, immaculateness,
untaintedness ■ **OPPOSITE:** impurity **2** The
American Female Reform Society promoted
sexual purity. = **innocence**, virtue, integrity,
honesty, decency, sincerity, virginity, piety,
chastity, rectitude, guilelessness,
virtuousness, chasteness, blamelessness
■ **OPPOSITE:** immorality

purport VERB = **claim**, allege, proclaim,
maintain, declare, pretend, assert, pose as,
profess

purpose NOUN **1** The purpose of the occasion
was to raise money for charity. = **reason**, point,
idea, goal, grounds, design, aim, basis,
principle, function, object, intention,
objective, motive, motivation, justification,
impetus, the why and wherefore **2** They are
prepared to go to any lengths to achieve their
purpose. = **aim**, end, plan, hope, view, goal,
design, project, target, wish, scheme,
desire, object, intention, objective,
ambition, aspiration, Holy Grail (informal)
3 The teachers are enthusiastic and have a sense
of purpose. = **determination**, commitment,
resolve, will, resolution, initiative,
enterprise, ambition, conviction,
motivation, persistence, tenacity,
firmness, constancy, single-mindedness,
steadfastness **4** Talking about it will serve
no purpose. = **use**, good, return, result,
effect, value, benefit, profit, worth, gain,

advantage, outcome, utility, merit, mileage
(informal), avail, behoof (archaic) • **on
purpose** Was it an accident, or did she do it on
purpose? = **deliberately**, purposely,
consciously, intentionally, knowingly,
wilfully, by design, wittingly, calculatedly,
designedly

> **USAGE** The two concepts purposeful
> and on purpose should be carefully
> distinguished. On purpose and purposely
> have roughly the same meaning, and
> imply that a person's action is
> deliberate, rather than accidental.
> However, purposeful and its related
> adverb purposefully refer to the way that
> someone acts as being full of purpose
> or determination.

purposeful ADJECTIVE = **determined**,
resolved, resolute, decided, firm, settled,
positive, fixed, deliberate, single-minded,
tenacious, strong-willed, steadfast,
immovable, unfaltering ■ **OPPOSITE:**
undecided

purposely ADVERB = **deliberately**,
expressly, consciously, intentionally,
knowingly, with intent, on purpose,
wilfully, by design, calculatedly, designedly
■ **OPPOSITE:** accidentally

purse NOUN **1** I dug the money out of my purse.
= **pouch**, wallet, money-bag, e-wallet or
eWallet **2** (U.S.) She reached into her purse for
her cigarettes. = **handbag**, bag, shoulder
bag, pocket book, clutch bag **3** The money
will go into the public purse, helping to lower
taxes. = **funds**, means, money, resources,
treasury, wealth, exchequer, coffers,
wherewithal **4** She is tipped to win the biggest
purse in women's pro volleyball history. = **prize**,
winnings, award, gift, reward ▶ VERB She
pursed her lips in disapproval. = **pucker**, close,
contract, tighten, knit, wrinkle, pout, press
together

pursue VERB **1** Japan would continue to pursue
the policies laid down at the summit. = **engage
in**, follow, perform, conduct, wage, tackle,
take up, work at, carry on, practise,
participate in, prosecute, ply, go in for,
apply yourself to **2** Mr Menendez has
aggressively pursued success. = **try for**, seek,
desire, search for, aim for, aspire to, work
towards, strive for, have as a goal **3** If your
request is denied, don't be afraid to pursue the
matter. = **continue**, maintain, carry on,
keep on, hold to, see through, adhere to,
persist in, proceed in, persevere in
4 She pursued the man who had stolen her bag.
= **follow**, track, hunt, chase, dog, attend,
shadow, accompany, harry, tail (informal),
haunt, plague, hound, stalk, harass,

P

go after, run after, hunt down, give chase to ■ **OPPOSITE:** flee **5** *He had pursued her, and within weeks they had become lovers.* = **court**, woo, pay attention to, make up to (*informal*), chase after, pay court to, set your cap at ■ **OPPOSITE:** fight shy of

pursuit NOUN **1** *individuals in pursuit of their dreams; the pursuit of happiness* = **quest**, seeking, search, aim, aspiration, striving towards **2** *Police had obstructed justice by hindering the pursuit of terrorists.* = **pursuing**, seeking, tracking, search, hunt, hunting, chase, trail, trailing **3** *They both love outdoor pursuits.* = **occupation**, activity, interest, line, pleasure, hobby, pastime, vocation

push VERB **1** *They pushed him into the car.* = **shove**, force, press, thrust, drive, knock, sweep, plunge, elbow, bump, ram, poke, propel, nudge, prod, jostle, hustle, bulldoze (*informal*), impel, manhandle ■ **OPPOSITE:** pull **2** *He got into the lift and pushed the button for the second floor.* = **press**, operate, depress, squeeze, activate, hold down **3** *I pushed through the crowds and on to the escalator.* = **make** or **force your way**, move, shoulder, inch, squeeze, thrust, elbow, shove, jostle, work your way, thread your way **4** *Her parents kept her in school and pushed her to study.* = **urge**, encourage, persuade, spur, drive, press, influence, prod, constrain, incite, coerce, egg on, impel, browbeat, exert influence on, inspan (*S. African*) ■ **OPPOSITE:** discourage **5** *Advertisers often use scientific doublespeak to push their products.* = **promote**, advertise, hype, publicize, boost, plug (*informal*), puff, make known, propagandize, cry up
▶ NOUN **1** *He gave me a sharp push.* = **shove**, thrust, butt, elbow, poke, nudge, prod, jolt ■ **OPPOSITE:** pull **2** *All that was needed was one final push, and the enemy would be vanquished once and for all.* = **effort**, charge, attack, campaign, advance, assault, raid, offensive, sally, thrust, blitz, onset **3** *He lacked the push to succeed in his chosen vocation.* = **drive**, go (*informal*), energy, initiative, enterprise, ambition, determination, pep, vitality, vigour, dynamism, get-up-and-go (*informal*), gumption (*informal*) • **push off** *Do me a favour and push off, will you?* = **go away**, leave, get lost (*informal*), clear off (*informal*), take off (*informal*), depart, beat it (*slang*), light out (*informal*), hit the road (*slang*), hook it (*slang*), slope off, pack your bags (*informal*), make tracks, buzz off (*informal*), hop it (*informal*), shove off (*informal*), skedaddle (*informal*), naff off (*informal*), be off with you, sling your hook (*informal*), make yourself scarce (*informal*),

voetsek (*S. African, offensive*), rack off (*Austral. & N.Z. slang*) • **the push** *Two cabinet ministers also got the push.* = **dismissal**, the sack (*informal*), discharge, the boot (*slang*), your cards (*informal*), your books (*informal*), your marching orders (*informal*), the kiss-off (*slang, chiefly U.S. & Canad.*), the (old) heave-ho (*informal*), the order of the boot (*slang*)

pushed ADJECTIVE (*often with* **for**) = **short of**, pressed, rushed, tight, hurried, under pressure, in difficulty, up against it (*informal*)

pushover NOUN **1** *He's a tough negotiator – you won't find him a pushover.* = **sucker** (*slang*), mug (*Brit. slang*), stooge (*slang*), soft touch (*slang*), chump (*informal*), walkover (*informal*), easy game (*informal*), easy or soft mark (*informal*) **2** *You might think Hungarian is a pushover to learn, but it isn't.* = **piece of cake** (*Brit. informal*), breeze (*informal*), picnic (*informal*), child's play (*informal*), plain sailing (*informal*), doddle (*Brit. slang*), walkover (*informal*), cinch (*slang*), cakewalk (*informal*), duck soup (*U.S. slang*) ■ **OPPOSITE:** challenge

pushy ADJECTIVE = **forceful**, aggressive, assertive, brash, loud, offensive, ambitious, bold, obnoxious, presumptuous, obtrusive, officious, bumptious, self-assertive ■ **OPPOSITE:** shy

put VERB **1** *She put her bag on the floor.* = **place**, leave, set, position, rest, park (*informal*), plant, establish, lay, stick (*informal*), settle, fix, lean, deposit, dump (*informal*), prop, lay down, put down, situate, set down, stow, bung (*informal*), plonk (*informal*) **2** *She was put in prison for her beliefs.* = **consign to**, place, commit to, doom to, condemn to **3** *The government has put a big tax on beer, wine and spirits.* = **impose**, subject, levy, inflict **4** *To put it bluntly, he doesn't give a damn.* = **express**, state, word, phrase, set, pose, utter **5** *He sat there listening as we put our suggestions to him.* = **present**, suggest, advance, propose, offer, forward, submit, tender, bring forward, proffer, posit, set before, lay before • **put someone away** *He's a murderer! He should be put away for life.* = **imprison**, commit, confine, cage (*informal*), certify, institutionalize, incarcerate, put in prison, put behind bars, lock up or away • **put someone down** *She's always putting her husband down in public.* = **humiliate**, shame, crush, show up, reject, dismiss, condemn, slight, criticize, snub, have a go at (*informal*), deflate, denigrate, belittle, disparage, deprecate, mortify, diss (*slang*) • **put someone off**

1 *We tried to visit the abbey but were put off by the queues.* = **discourage**, intimidate, deter, daunt, dissuade, demoralize, scare off, dishearten **2** *All this noise is putting me off.* = **disconcert**, confuse, unsettle, throw (*informal*), distress, rattle (*informal*), dismay, perturb, faze, discomfit, take the wind out of someone's sails, nonplus, abash • **put someone out 1** *Thanks for the offer, but I couldn't put you out like that.* = **inconvenience**, trouble, upset, bother, disturb, impose upon, discomfit, discommode, incommode **2** *They were quite put out to find me in charge.* = **annoy**, anger, provoke, irritate, disturb, harass, confound, exasperate, disconcert, nettle, vex, perturb, irk, put on the spot, take the wind out of someone's sails, discountenance, discompose • **put someone up 1** *She asked if I could put her up for a few days.* = **accommodate**, house, board, lodge, quarter, entertain, take someone in, billet, give someone lodging **2** *The new party is putting up 15 candidates for 22 seats.* = **nominate**, put forward, offer, present, propose, recommend, float, submit • **put someone up to something** *How do you know he asked me out? Did you put him up to it?* = **encourage**, urge, persuade, prompt, incite, egg on, goad, put the idea into someone's head • **put something across** *or* **over** *The opposition parties were hampered from putting across their message.* = **communicate**, explain, clarify, express, get through, convey, make clear, spell out, get across, make yourself understood • **put something aside** *or* **by 1** *Encourage children to put some money aside each week.* = **save**, store, stockpile, deposit, hoard, cache, lay by, stow away, salt away, keep in reserve, squirrel away **2** *We should put aside our differences and discuss this sensibly.* = **disregard**, forget, ignore, bury, discount, set aside, pay no heed to • **put something away 1** *She began putting away the dishes.* = **store away**, replace, put back, tidy up, clear away, tidy away, return to its place **2** *He had been able to put away money, to insure against old age.* = **save**, set aside, put aside, keep, deposit, put by, stash away, store away **3** (*informal*) *The food was superb, and we put away a fair amount of it.* = **consume**, devour, eat up, demolish (*informal*), gobble, guzzle, polish off (*informal*), gulp down, wolf down, pig out on (*informal*) • **put something down 1** *Never put anything down on paper which might be used in evidence.* = **record**, write down, list, enter, log, take down, inscribe, set down, transcribe, put in

black and white **2** *Soldiers went in to put down a rebellion.* = **repress**, crush, suppress, check, silence, overthrow, squash, subdue, quash, quell, stamp out **3** *Magistrates ordered that the dog should be put down at once.* = **put to sleep**, kill, destroy, do away with, put away, put out of its misery • **put something down to something** *You may be a sceptic and put it down to coincidence.* = **attribute**, blame, ascribe, set down, impute, chalk up • **put something forward** *He has put forward new peace proposals.* = **recommend**, present, suggest, introduce, advance, propose, press, submit, tender, nominate, prescribe, move for, proffer • **put something off** *The Association has put the event off until December.* = **postpone**, delay, defer, adjourn, put back, hold over, reschedule, put on ice, put on the back burner (*informal*), take a rain check on (*U.S. & Canad. informal*) • **put something on 1** *She put on her coat and went out.* = **don**, dress in, slip into, pull on, climb into, change into, throw on, get dressed in, fling on, pour yourself into, doll yourself up in **2** *The band are putting on a UK show before the end of the year.* = **present**, stage, perform, do, show, produce, mount **3** *I've put on a stone since I stopped training.* = **add**, gain, increase by **4** *They put £20 on Ahmed scoring the first goal.* = **bet**, back, place, chance, risk, lay, stake, hazard, wager **5** *Anything becomes funny if you put on an American accent.* = **fake**, affect, assume, simulate, feign, make believe, play-act • **put something out 1** *The French news agency put out a statement from the Trade Minister.* = **issue**, release, publish, broadcast, bring out, circulate, make public, make known **2** *Firefighters tried to free the injured and put out the blaze.* = **extinguish**, smother, blow out, stamp out, douse, snuff out, quench • **put something up 1** *He was putting up a new fence round the garden.* = **build**, raise, set up, construct, erect, fabricate **2** *In the end they surrendered without putting up any resistance.* = **offer**, present, mount, put forward **3** *The state agreed to put up the money to start his company.* = **provide**, advance, invest, contribute, give, pay up, supply, come up with, pledge, donate, furnish, fork out (*informal*), cough up (*informal*), shell out (*informal*) • **put up with something** *or* **someone** *I won't put up with this kind of behaviour from you.* = **stand**, suffer, bear, take, wear (*Brit. informal*), stomach, endure, swallow, brook, stand for, lump (*informal*), tolerate, hack (*slang*), abide, countenance • **put upon someone**

p

Don't allow people to put upon you or take you for granted. = **take advantage of**, trouble, abuse, harry, exploit, saddle, take for granted, put someone out, inconvenience, beset, overwork, impose upon, take for a fool

putative ADJECTIVE = **supposed**, reported, assumed, alleged, presumed, reputed, imputed, presumptive, commonly believed

put-down NOUN = **humiliation**, slight, snub, knock (*informal*), dig, sneer, rebuff, barb, sarcasm, kick in the teeth (*slang*), gibe, disparagement, one in the eye (*informal*)

puzzle VERB *What puzzles me is why nobody has complained before now.* = **perplex**, beat (*slang*), confuse, baffle, stump, bewilder, confound, mystify, faze, flummox, bemuse, nonplus ▸ NOUN **1** *a word puzzle* = **problem**, riddle, maze, labyrinth, question, conundrum, teaser, poser, brain-teaser (*informal*) **2** *the puzzle of why there are no Stone Age cave paintings in Britain* = **mystery**, problem, paradox, enigma, conundrum • **puzzle over something** *puzzling over the complexities of Shakespeare's verse* = **think about**, study, wonder about, mull over, muse on, think hard about, ponder on, brood over, ask yourself about, cudgel or rack your brains • **puzzle something out** *I stared at the symbols, trying to puzzle out their meaning.* = **solve**, work out, figure out, unravel, see, get, crack, resolve, sort out, clear up, decipher, think through, suss (out)

(*slang*), get the answer of, find the key to, crack the code of

puzzled ADJECTIVE = **perplexed**, beaten, confused, baffled, lost, stuck (*informal*), stumped, doubtful, at sea, bewildered, mixed up, at a loss, mystified, clueless, nonplussed, flummoxed, in a fog, without a clue

puzzlement NOUN = **perplexity**, questioning, surprise, doubt, wonder, confusion, uncertainty, bewilderment, disorientation, bafflement, mystification, doubtfulness

puzzling ADJECTIVE = **perplexing**, baffling, bewildering, hard, involved, misleading, unclear, ambiguous, enigmatic, incomprehensible, mystifying, inexplicable, unaccountable, knotty, unfathomable, labyrinthine, full of surprises, abstruse, beyond you, oracular ■ OPPOSITE: simple

pygmy *or* **pigmy** MODIFIER *The pygmy hippopotamus is less than 6 ft long.* = **small**, miniature, dwarf, tiny, wee, stunted, diminutive, minuscule, midget, elfin, undersized, teeny-weeny, Lilliputian, dwarfish, teensy-weensy, pygmean ▸ NOUN **1** *an encounter with the Ituri Forest pygmies* = **midget**, dwarf, shrimp (*informal*), Lilliputian, Tom Thumb, munchkin (*informal, chiefly U.S.*), homunculus, manikin **2** *He saw the politicians of his day as pygmies, not as giants.* = **nonentity**, nobody, lightweight (*informal*), mediocrity, cipher, small fry, pipsqueak (*informal*)

P

Qq

quack MODIFIER *Why do intelligent people find quack remedies so appealing?* = **fake**, fraudulent, phoney or phony (*informal*), pretended, sham, counterfeit

quaff VERB = **drink**, gulp, swig (*informal*), have, down (*informal*), swallow, slug, guzzle, imbibe (*formal*), partake of

quagmire NOUN **1** *a political quagmire* = **predicament**, difficulty, quandary, pass, fix (*informal*), jam (*informal*), dilemma, pinch, plight, scrape (*informal*), muddle, pickle (*informal*), impasse, entanglement, imbroglio **2** *Overnight rain had turned the grass airstrip into a quagmire.* = **bog**, marsh, swamp, slough, fen, mire, morass, quicksand, muskeg (*Canad.*)

quail VERB = **shrink**, cringe, flinch, shake, faint, tremble, quake, shudder, falter, droop, blanch, recoil, cower, blench, have cold feet (*informal*)

quaint ADJECTIVE **1** *When visiting restaurants, be prepared for some quaint customs.* = **unusual**, odd, curious, original, strange, bizarre, fantastic, old-fashioned, peculiar, eccentric, queer, rum (*Brit. slang*), singular, fanciful, whimsical, droll ■ OPPOSITE: ordinary **2** *a quaint relic of a previous age* = **old-fashioned**, charming, picturesque, antique, gothic, old-world, antiquated ■ OPPOSITE: modern

quake VERB = **shake**, tremble, quiver, move, rock, shiver, throb, quake, wobble, waver, vibrate, pulsate, quail, totter, convulse

qualification NOUN **1** *That time with him is my qualification to write the book.* = **eligibility**, quality, ability, skill, capacity, fitness, attribute, capability, endowment(s), accomplishment, achievement, aptitude, suitability, suitableness **2** *The empirical evidence is subject to many qualifications.* = **condition**, restriction, proviso, requirement, rider, exception, criterion, reservation, allowance, objection, limitation, modification, exemption, prerequisite, caveat, stipulation

qualified ADJECTIVE **1** *Demand has far outstripped supply of qualified teachers.* = **capable**, trained, experienced, seasoned, able, fit, expert, talented, chartered, efficient, practised, licensed, certificated, equipped, accomplished, eligible, competent, skilful, adept, knowledgeable, proficient ■ OPPOSITE: untrained **2** *He answers both questions with a qualified yes.* = **restricted**, limited, provisional, conditional, reserved, guarded, bounded, adjusted, moderated, adapted, confined, modified, tempered, cautious, refined, amended, contingent, tentative, hesitant, circumscribed, equivocal ■ OPPOSITE: unconditional

qualify VERB **1** *The course does not qualify you to practise as a therapist.* = **certify**, equip, empower, train, ground, condition, prepare, fit, commission, ready, permit, sanction, endow, capacitate ■ OPPOSITE: disqualify **2** *13 percent of households qualify as poor.* = **be described**, count, be considered as, be named, be counted, be eligible, be characterized, be designated, be distinguished **3** *I would qualify that by putting it into context.* = **restrict**, limit, reduce, vary, ease, moderate, adapt, modify, regulate, diminish, temper, soften, restrain, lessen, mitigate, abate, tone down, assuage, modulate, circumscribe

quality NOUN **1** *high quality paper and plywood* = **standard**, standing, class, condition, value, rank, grade, merit, classification, calibre **2** *a college of quality* = **excellence**, status, merit, position, value, worth, distinction, virtue, superiority, calibre, eminence, pre-eminence **3** *He wanted to introduce mature people with leadership qualities.* = **characteristic**, feature, attribute, point, side, mark, property, aspect, streak, trait, facet, quirk, peculiarity, idiosyncrasy **4** *The pretentious quality of the poetry.* = **nature**, character, constitution, make, sort, kind, worth, description, essence

qualm NOUN = **misgiving**, doubt, uneasiness, regret, anxiety, uncertainty, reluctance, hesitation, remorse, apprehension, disquiet, remorse, compunction, twinge or pang of conscience

quandary NOUN = **difficulty**, dilemma, predicament, puzzle, uncertainty, embarrassment, plight, strait, impasse, bewilderment, perplexity, delicate situation, cleft stick

quantity NOUN **1** *a vast quantity of food* = **amount**, lot, total, sum, part, portion, quota, aggregate, number, allotment **2** *the sheer quantity of data can cause problems.* = **size**, measure, mass, volume, length, capacity, extent, bulk, magnitude, greatness, expanse

USAGE The use of a plural noun after *quantity of*, as in *a large quantity of bananas*, used to be considered incorrect, the objection being that the word *quantity* should only be used to refer to an uncountable amount, which was grammatically regarded as a singular concept. Nowadays, however, most people consider the use of *quantity* with a plural noun to be acceptable.

quarrel NOUN *I had a terrible quarrel with my other brothers.* = **disagreement**, fight, row, difference (of opinion), argument, dispute, controversy, breach, scrap (*informal*), disturbance, misunderstanding, contention, feud, fray, brawl, spat, squabble, strife, wrangle, skirmish, vendetta, discord, fracas, commotion, tiff, altercation, broil, tumult, dissension, affray, shindig (*informal*), disputation, dissidence, shindy (*informal*), bagarre (*French*), biffo (*Austral. slang*) ■ **OPPOSITE:** accord ▶ VERB *My brother quarrelled with my father.* = **disagree**, fight, argue, row, clash, dispute, scrap (*informal*), differ, fall out (*informal*), brawl, squabble, spar, wrangle, bicker, be at odds, lock horns, cross swords, fight like cat and dog, go at it hammer and tongs, altercate ■ **OPPOSITE:** get on *or* along (with)

quarrelsome ADJECTIVE = **argumentative**, belligerent, pugnacious, cross, contentious, irritable, combative, fractious, petulant, ill-tempered, irascible, cantankerous, litigious, querulous, peevish, choleric, disputatious ■ **OPPOSITE:** easy-going

quarry NOUN = **prey**, victim, game, goal, aim, prize, objective

quarter NOUN **1** *He wandered through the Chinese quarter.* = **district**, region, neighbourhood, place, point, part, side, area, position, station, spot, territory, zone, location, province, colony, locality **2** *It is bloody brutal work, with no quarter given.* = **mercy**, pity, compassion, favour, charity, sympathy, tolerance, kindness, forgiveness, indulgence, clemency, leniency, forbearance, lenity ▶ VERB *Our soldiers are quartered in Peredelkino.* = **accommodate**, house, lodge, place, board, post, station, install, put up, billet, give accommodation, provide with accommodation

quarters PLURAL NOUN = **lodgings**, rooms, accommodation, post, station, chambers, digs (*Brit. informal*), shelter, lodging, residence, dwelling, barracks, abode, habitation, billet, domicile, cantonment (*Military*)

quash VERB **1** *The Appeal Court has quashed the convictions.* = **annul**, overturn, reverse, cancel, overthrow, set aside, void, revoke, overrule, rescind, invalidate, nullify, declare null and void **2** *an attempt to quash regional violence* = **suppress**, crush, put down, beat, destroy, overthrow, squash, subdue, repress, quell, extinguish, quench, extirpate

quaver VERB = **tremble**, shake, quiver, thrill, quake, shudder, flicker, flutter, waver, vibrate, pulsate, oscillate, trill, twitter

queasy ADJECTIVE **1** *He was prone to sickness and already felt queasy.* = **sick**, ill, nauseous, squeamish, upset, uncomfortable, crook (*Austral. & N.Z. informal*), queer, unwell, giddy, nauseated, groggy (*informal*), off colour, bilious, indisposed, green about the gills (*informal*), sickish **2** *Some people feel queasy about how their names and addresses have been obtained.* = **uneasy**, concerned, worried, troubled, disturbed, anxious, uncertain, restless, ill at ease, fidgety

queen NOUN **1** *the time she met the Queen* = **sovereign**, ruler, monarch, leader, Crown, princess, majesty, head of state, Her Majesty, empress, crowned head **2** *the queen of crime writing* = **leading light**, star, favourite, celebrity, darling, mistress, idol, big name, doyenne

queer ADJECTIVE **1** *If you ask me, there's something queer going on.* = **strange**, odd, funny, unusual, extraordinary, remarkable, curious, weird, peculiar, abnormal, rum (*Brit. slang*), uncommon, erratic, singular, eerie, unnatural, unconventional, uncanny, disquieting, unorthodox, outlandish, left-field (*informal*), anomalous, droll, atypical, outré ■ **OPPOSITE:** normal **2** *Wine before beer and you'll feel queer.* = **faint**, dizzy, giddy, queasy, light-headed, reeling

quell VERB **1** *Troops eventually quelled the unrest.* = **suppress**, crush, put down, defeat, overcome, conquer, subdue, stifle, overpower, quash, extinguish, stamp out, vanquish (*literary*), squelch **2** *He is trying to quell fears of a looming crisis.* = **calm**, quiet, silence, moderate, dull, soothe, alleviate, appease, allay, mitigate, assuage, pacify, mollify, deaden

quench VERB **1** *He stopped to quench his thirst at a stream.* = **satisfy**, appease, allay, satiate, slake, sate **2** *Fire crews struggled to quench the fire.* = **put out**, extinguish, douse, end, check, destroy, crush, suppress, stifle, smother, snuff out, squelch

query NOUN **1** *If you have any queries, please contact us.* = **question**, inquiry, enquiry, problem, demand **2** *I read the query in the* guide's eyes. = **doubt**, suspicion, reservation, objection, hesitation, scepticism ▶ VERB **1** No one queried my decision. = **question**, challenge, doubt, suspect, dispute, object to, distrust, mistrust, call into question, disbelieve, feel uneasy about, throw doubt on, harbour reservations about **2** 'Is there something else?' he queried. = **ask**, inquire or enquire, question

quest NOUN **1** his quest to find true love = **search**, hunt, mission, enterprise, undertaking, exploration, crusade **2** Sir Guy the Seeker came on his quest to Dunstanburgh Castle. = **expedition**, journey, adventure, voyage, pilgrimage

question NOUN **1** He refused to answer further questions on the subject. = **inquiry**, enquiry, query, investigation, examination, interrogation ■ OPPOSITE: answer **2** There's no question about their success. = **difficulty**, problem, doubt, debate, argument, dispute, controversy, confusion, uncertainty, query, contention, misgiving, can of worms (informal), dubiety **3** The whole question of aid is a tricky political one. = **issue**, point, matter, subject, problem, debate, proposal, theme, motion, topic, proposition, bone of contention, point at issue ▶ VERB **1** A man is being questioned by police. = **interrogate**, cross-examine, interview, examine, investigate, pump (informal), probe, grill (informal), quiz, ask questions, sound out, catechize **2** It never occurs to them to question the doctor's decisions. = **dispute**, challenge, doubt, suspect, oppose, query, distrust, mistrust, call into question, disbelieve, impugn (formal), cast aspersions on, cast doubt upon, controvert ■ OPPOSITE: accept • **in question** The film in question detailed allegations about party corruption. = **under discussion**, at issue, under consideration, in doubt, on the agenda, to be discussed, for debate, open to debate • **out of the question** Is a tax increase still out of the question? = **impossible**, unthinkable, inconceivable, not on (informal), hopeless, unimaginable, unworkable, unattainable, unobtainable, not feasible, impracticable, unachievable, unrealizable, not worth considering, not to be thought of

questionable ADJECTIVE = **dubious**, suspect, doubtful, controversial, uncertain, suspicious, dodgy (Brit., Austral. & N.Z. informal), unreliable, shady (informal), debatable, unproven, fishy (informal), moot, arguable, iffy (informal), equivocal, problematical, disputable, controvertible, dubitable, shonky (Austral. & N.Z. informal) ■ OPPOSITE: indisputable

questionnaire NOUN = **set of questions**, form, survey form, question sheet

queue NOUN = **line**, row, file, train, series, chain, string, column, sequence, succession, procession, crocodile (Brit. informal), progression, cavalcade, concatenation (formal)

quibble VERB Let's not quibble. = **split hairs**, carp, cavil, prevaricate, beat about the bush, equivocate, nit-pick (informal) ▶ NOUN These are minor quibbles. = **objection**, complaint, niggle, protest, criticism, nicety, equivocation, prevarication, cavil, quiddity, sophism

quick ADJECTIVE **1** Europe has moved a long way at a quick pace. = **fast**, swift, speedy, express, active, cracking (Brit. informal), smart, rapid, fleet, brisk, hasty, headlong, nippy (informal), pdq (slang) ■ OPPOSITE: slow **2** I just popped in for a quick chat. = **brief**, passing, hurried, flying, fleeting, summary, lightning, short-lived, hasty, cursory, perfunctory ■ OPPOSITE: long **3** The President has admitted there is no quick end in sight. = **immediate**, instant, prompt, sudden, abrupt, instantaneous, expeditious **4** She had inherited her father's quick temper. = **excitable**, passionate, impatient, abrupt, hasty, irritable, touchy, curt, petulant, irascible, testy ■ OPPOSITE: calm **5** The older adults are not as quick in their thinking. = **intelligent**, bright (informal), alert, sharp, acute, smart, clever, all there (informal), shrewd, discerning, astute, receptive, perceptive, quick-witted, quick on the uptake (informal), nimble-witted ■ OPPOSITE: stupid

quicken VERB **1** He quickened his pace a little. = **speed up**, hurry, accelerate, hasten, gee up (informal) **2** Thank you for quickening my spiritual understanding. = **stimulate**, inspire, arouse, excite, strengthen, revive, refresh, activate, animate, rouse, incite, resuscitate, energize, revitalize, kindle, galvanize, invigorate, reinvigorate, vitalize, vivify

quickly ADVERB **1** She turned and ran quickly up the stairs to the flat above. = **swiftly**, rapidly, hurriedly, speedily, fast, quick, hastily, briskly, at high speed, apace (literary), at full speed, hell for leather (informal), like lightning, at the speed of light, at full tilt, hotfoot, at a rate of knots (informal), like the clappers (Brit. informal), pdq (slang), like nobody's business (informal), with all speed, posthaste, lickety-split (U.S. informal), like greased lightning (informal), at or on the double, latstick (S. African slang) ■ OPPOSITE: slowly **2** You can become fitter quickly and easily. = **soon**, speedily, as soon as possible, momentarily (U.S.), instantaneously, pronto (informal), a.s.a.p. (informal) **3** The meeting quickly adjourned. = **immediately**, instantly, at once, directly, promptly, abruptly, without delay, expeditiously

quick-witted ADJECTIVE = **clever**, bright (informal), sharp, keen, smart, alert, shrewd, astute, perceptive

quid pro quo NOUN = **exchange**, interchange, tit for tat, equivalent, compensation, retaliation, reprisal, substitution

quiet ADJECTIVE **1** A quiet murmur passed through the classroom. = **soft**, low, muted, lowered, whispered, faint, suppressed, stifled, hushed, muffled, inaudible, indistinct, low-pitched ■ **OPPOSITE:** loud **2** She was received in a small, quiet office. = **peaceful**, silent, hushed, soundless, noiseless ■ **OPPOSITE:** noisy **3** I just want a quiet life. = **calm**, peaceful, tranquil, contented, gentle, mild, serene, pacific, placid, restful, untroubled, chilled (informal) ■ **OPPOSITE:** exciting **4** a look of quiet satisfaction = **still**, motionless, calm, peaceful, tranquil, untroubled ■ **OPPOSITE:** troubled **5** a quiet rural backwater = **undisturbed**, isolated, secluded, private, secret, retired, sequestered, unfrequented ■ **OPPOSITE:** crowded **6** I told them to be quiet and go to sleep. = **silent**, still **7** He's a nice quiet man. = **reserved**, retiring, shy, collected, gentle, mild, composed, serene, sedate, meek, placid, docile, unflappable (informal), phlegmatic, peaceable, imperturbable, equable, even-tempered, unexcitable ■ **OPPOSITE:** excitable **8** They dress in quiet colours. = **subdued**, conservative, plain, sober, simple, modest, restrained, unassuming, unpretentious, unobtrusive ■ **OPPOSITE:** bright ▶ NOUN He wants some peace and quiet. = **peace**, rest, tranquillity, ease, silence, solitude, serenity, stillness, repose, calmness, quietness, peacefulness, restfulness ■ **OPPOSITE:** noise

quieten VERB **1** She tried to quieten her breathing. = **silence**, subdue, stifle, still, stop, quiet, mute, hush, quell, muffle, shush (informal) **2** It took a long time to quieten the paranoia of the West. = **soothe**, calm, allay, dull, blunt, alleviate, appease, lull, mitigate, assuage, mollify, deaden, tranquillize, palliate ■ **OPPOSITE:** provoke

quietly ADVERB **1** She closed the door quietly. = **noiselessly**, silently **2** 'This is goodbye, isn't it?' she said quietly. = **softly**, in hushed tones,

in a low voice or whisper, inaudibly, in an undertone, under your breath **3** quietly planning their next move = **privately**, secretly, confidentially **4** She sat quietly watching all that was going on around her. = **calmly**, serenely, placidly, patiently, mildly, meekly, contentedly, dispassionately, undemonstratively **5** Amy stood quietly in the door watching him. = **silently**, in silence, mutely, without talking, dumbly **6** They are quietly confident about the magazine's chances. = **modestly**, humbly, unobtrusively, diffidently, unpretentiously, unassumingly, unostentatiously

quilt NOUN = **bedspread**, duvet, comforter (U.S.), downie (informal), coverlet, eiderdown, counterpane, doona (Austral.), continental quilt

quintessential ADJECTIVE = **ultimate**, essential, typical, fundamental, definitive, archetypal, prototypical

quip NOUN = **joke**, sally, jest, riposte, wisecrack (informal), retort, counter, pleasantry, repartee, gibe, witticism, bon mot, badinage

quirk NOUN = **peculiarity**, eccentricity, mannerism, foible, idiosyncrasy, habit, fancy, characteristic, trait, whim, oddity, caprice, fetish, aberration, kink, vagary, singularity, idée fixe (French)

quirky ADJECTIVE = **odd**, unusual, eccentric, idiosyncratic, curious, peculiar, unpredictable, rum (Brit. slang), singular, fanciful, whimsical, capricious, offbeat

quit VERB **1** He figured he would quit his job before he was fired. = **resign (from)**, leave, retire (from), pull out (of), surrender, chuck (informal), step down (from) (informal), relinquish, renounce, pack in (informal), abdicate **2** I was trying to quit smoking at the time. = **stop**, give up, cease, end, drop, abandon, suspend, halt, discontinue, belay (Nautical) ■ **OPPOSITE:** continue **3** Police were called when he refused to quit the building. = **leave**, depart from, go out of, abandon, desert, exit, withdraw from, forsake, go away from, pull out from, decamp from

quite ADVERB **1** I was doing quite well, but I wasn't earning a lot of money. = **somewhat**, rather, fairly, reasonably, kind of (informal), pretty (informal), relatively, moderately, to some extent, comparatively, to some degree, to a certain extent **2** It is quite clear that we were firing in self defence. = **absolutely**, perfectly, completely, totally, fully, entirely, precisely, considerably, wholly, in all respects, without reservation

quiver VERB His bottom lip quivered and big tears rolled down his cheeks. = **shake**, tremble,

q

shiver, quake, shudder, agitate, vibrate,
pulsate, quaver, convulse, palpitate
▶ NOUN *I felt a quiver of panic.* = **shake**,
tremble, shiver, throb, shudder, tremor,
spasm, vibration, tic, convulsion,
palpitation, pulsation

quixotic ADJECTIVE = **unrealistic**, idealistic,
romantic, absurd, imaginary, visionary,
fanciful, impractical, dreamy, Utopian,
impulsive, fantastical, impracticable,
chivalrous, unworldly, chimerical

quiz NOUN *Man faces quiz over knife death.*
= **examination**, questioning,
interrogation, interview, investigation,
grilling (*informal*), cross-examination,
cross-questioning, the third degree
(*informal*) ▶ VERB *Detectives quizzed them for
four hours before they were released.*
= **question**, ask, interrogate, examine,
investigate, pump (*informal*), grill (*informal*),
catechize

quizzical ADJECTIVE = **mocking**,
questioning, inquiring, curious, arch,
teasing, bantering, sardonic, derisive,
supercilious

quota NOUN = **share**, allowance, ration,
allocation, part, cut (*informal*), limit,
proportion, slice, quantity, portion,
assignment, whack (*informal*),
dispensation

quotation NOUN **1** *He illustrated his argument
with quotations from Pasternak.* = **passage**,
quote (*informal*), excerpt, cutting, selection,
reference, extract, citation **2** *Get several
written quotations and check exactly what's
included in the cost.* = **estimate**, price,
tender, rate, cost, charge, figure, quote
(*informal*), bid price

quote VERB **1** *Then suddenly he quoted a line
from the play.* = **repeat**, recite, reproduce,
recall, echo, extract, excerpt, proclaim,
parrot, paraphrase, retell **2** *Most newspapers
quote the warning.* = **refer to**, cite, give,
name, detail, relate, mention, instance,
specify, spell out, recount, recollect, make
reference to, adduce

Rr

rabble NOUN **1** *a rabble of gossip columnists* = **mob**, crowd, herd, swarm, horde, throng, canaille **2** *They are forced to socialise with the rabble.* = **commoners**, proletariat, common people, riffraff, crowd, masses, trash (*chiefly U.S. & Canad.*), scum, lower classes, populace, peasantry, dregs, hoi polloi, the great unwashed (*derogatory*), canaille, lumpenproletariat, commonalty
■ **OPPOSITE:** upper classes

rabid ADJECTIVE **1** *the rabid state media* = **fanatical**, extreme, irrational, fervent, zealous, bigoted, intolerant, narrow-minded, intemperate, swivel-eyed (*slang*)
■ **OPPOSITE:** moderate **2** *The tablets gave him the look of a rabid dog.* = **crazed**, wild, violent, mad (*informal*), raging, furious, frantic, frenzied, infuriated, berserk, maniacal, berko (*Austral. slang*)

race¹ NOUN **1** *a running race across the Sahara desert* = **competition**, contest, chase, dash, pursuit, contention **2** *the race for the White House* = **contest**, competition, rivalry, contention ▸ VERB **1** *They may even have raced each other.* = **compete against**, run against **2** *He, too, will be racing here again soon.* = **compete**, run, contend, take part in a race **3** *They raced away out of sight.* = **run**, fly, career, speed, tear, dash, hurry, barrel (along) (*informal, chiefly U.S. & Canad.*), dart, gallop, zoom, hare (*Brit. informal*), hasten, burn rubber (*informal*), go like a bomb (*Brit. & N.Z. informal*), run like mad (*informal*)

race² NOUN *We welcome students of all races, faiths and nationalities.* = **people**, ethnic group, nation, blood, house, family, line, issue, stock, type, seed (*chiefly biblical*), breed, folk, tribe, offspring, clan, kin, lineage, progeny, kindred

racial ADJECTIVE = **ethnic**, ethnological, national, folk, genetic, tribal, genealogical

rack NOUN *a luggage rack* = **frame**, stand, structure, framework ▸ VERB *a teenager racked with guilt* = **torture**, distress, torment, harass, afflict, oppress, harrow, crucify, agonize, pain, excruciate

▌ **USAGE** The use of the spelling *wrack* rather than *rack* in sentences such as *she was wracked by grief* or *the country was wracked by civil war* is very common, but is thought by many people to be incorrect.

racket NOUN **1** *The racket went on past midnight.* = **noise**, row, shouting, fuss, disturbance, outcry, clamour, din, uproar, commotion, pandemonium, rumpus, babel, tumult, hubbub, hullabaloo, ballyhoo (*informal*) **2** *a drugs racket* = **fraud**, scheme, criminal activity, illegal enterprise

racy ADJECTIVE **1** *Her novels may be racy but they don't fight shy of larger issues.* = **risqué**, naughty, indecent, bawdy, blue, broad, spicy (*informal*), suggestive, smutty, off colour, immodest, indelicate, near the knuckle (*informal*) **2** *very high-quality wines with quite a racy character* = **lively**, spirited, exciting, dramatic, entertaining, stimulating, sexy (*informal*), sparkling, vigorous, energetic, animated, heady, buoyant, exhilarating, zestful

radiance NOUN **1** *There was a new radiance about her.* = **happiness**, delight, pleasure, joy, warmth, rapture, gaiety **2** *The dim bulb cast a soft radiance over his face.* = **brightness**, light, shine, glow, glitter, glare, gleam, brilliance, lustre, luminosity, incandescence, resplendence, effulgence

radiant ADJECTIVE **1** *On her wedding day the bride looked truly radiant.* = **happy**, glowing, ecstatic, joyful, sent (*informal*), gay, delighted, beaming, joyous, blissful, rapturous, rapt, on cloud nine (*informal*), beatific, blissed out (*informal*), floating on air ■ **OPPOSITE:** miserable **2** *Out on the bay the morning is radiant.* = **bright**, brilliant, shining, glorious, beaming, glowing, sparkling, sunny, glittering, gleaming, luminous, resplendent, incandescent, lustrous, effulgent ■ **OPPOSITE:** dull

radiate VERB **1** *Thermal imagery will show up objects radiating heat.* = **emit**, spread, send out, disseminate, pour, shed, scatter, glitter, gleam **2** *From here contaminated air radiates out to the open countryside.* = **emanate**, shine, be diffused **3** *She radiates happiness and health.* = **show**, display, demonstrate, exhibit, emanate, give off or out **4** *the narrow streets which radiate from the Cathedral Square* = **spread out**, diverge, branch out

radiation NOUN = **emission**, rays, emanation

radical ADJECTIVE **1** *periods of radical change* = **extreme**, complete, entire, sweeping, violent, severe, excessive, thorough, drastic **2** *political tension between radical and conservative politicians* = **revolutionary**, extremist, fanatical, swivel-eyed (*slang*)

3 *the radical differences between them*
= **fundamental**, natural, basic, essential,
native, constitutional, organic, profound,
innate, deep-seated, thoroughgoing
■ **OPPOSITE:** superficial ▶ NOUN *a former
left-wing radical who was involved with the civil
rights movement* = **extremist**, revolutionary,
militant, fanatic ■ **OPPOSITE:** conservative

raffle NOUN = **draw**, lottery, sweepstake,
sweep

rage NOUN **1** *I flew into a rage.* = **fury**, temper,
frenzy, rampage, tantrum, foulie (*Austral.
slang*), hissy fit (*informal*), strop (*Brit.
informal*), paddy (*Brit. slang*) ■ **OPPOSITE:**
calmness **2** *The people are full of fear and rage.*
= **anger**, violence, passion, obsession,
madness, raving, wrath, mania, agitation,
ire, vehemence, high dudgeon **3** *the latest
technological rage* = **craze**, fashion,
enthusiasm, vogue, fad (*informal*), latest
thing ▶ VERB **1** *The war rages on and the time
has come to take sides.* = **be at its height**,
surge, rampage, be uncontrollable, storm
2 *He raged at me for being late.* = **be furious**,
rave, blow up (*informal*), fume, lose it
(*informal*), fret, seethe, crack up (*informal*),
see red (*informal*), chafe, lose the plot
(*informal*), go ballistic (*slang*), rant and rave,
foam at the mouth, lose your temper, blow
a fuse (*slang, chiefly U.S.*), fly off the handle
(*informal*), be incandescent, go off the deep
end (*informal*), throw a fit (*informal*), wig out
(*slang*), go up the wall (*slang*), blow your
top, lose your rag (*slang*), be beside
yourself, flip your lid (*slang*) ■ **OPPOSITE:**
stay calm

ragged ADJECTIVE **1** *I am usually happiest in
ragged jeans and a t-shirt.* = **tatty** (*Brit.*),
worn, poor, torn, rent, faded, neglected,
rundown, frayed, shabby, worn-out, seedy,
scruffy, in tatters, dilapidated, tattered,
threadbare, unkempt, in rags, down at
heel, the worse for wear, in holes, having
seen better days, scraggy ■ **OPPOSITE:**
smart **2** *She tore her tights on the ragged edge of
a desk.* = **rough**, fragmented, crude, rugged,
notched, irregular, unfinished, uneven,
jagged, serrated

raging ADJECTIVE = **furious**, mad (*informal*),
raving, fuming, frenzied, infuriated,
incensed, enraged, seething, fizzing (*Scot.*),
incandescent, foaming at the mouth, fit to
be tied (*slang*), boiling mad (*informal*),
beside yourself, doing your nut (*Brit. slang*),
off the air (*Austral. slang*)

raid VERB **1** *The guerrillas raided banks and
destroyed a police barracks.* = **steal from**,
break into, plunder, pillage, sack
2 *8th century Vikings set off to raid the coasts*

of Europe. = **attack**, invade, assault, rifle,
forage (*Military*), fall upon, swoop down
upon, reive (*dialect*) **3** *Fraud squad officers
raided the firm's offices.* = **make a search of**,
search, bust (*informal*), descend on, make a
raid on, make a swoop on ▶ NOUN **1** *The
rebels attempted a surprise raid on a military
camp.* = **attack**, invasion, seizure, onset,
foray, sortie, incursion, surprise attack,
hit-and-run attack, sally, inroad, irruption
2 *a raid on a house by thirty armed police* = **bust**
(*informal*), swoop, descent, surprise search

raider NOUN = **attacker**, thief, robber,
plunderer, invader, forager (*Military*),
marauder, reiver (*dialect*)

rail VERB = **complain**, attack, abuse, blast,
put down, criticize, censure, scold,
castigate, revile, tear into (*informal*),
fulminate, inveigh, upbraid, lambast(e),
vituperate, vociferate

railing NOUN = **fence**, rails, barrier, paling,
balustrade

rain NOUN **1** *You'll get soaked standing out in
the rain.* = **rainfall**, fall, showers, deluge,
drizzle, downpour, precipitation, raindrops,
cloudburst **2** *A rain of stones descended on the
police.* = **shower**, flood, stream, hail, volley,
spate, torrent, deluge ▶ VERB **1** *It rained the
whole weekend.* = **pour**, pelt (down), teem,
bucket down (*informal*), fall, shower,
drizzle, rain cats and dogs (*informal*),
come down in buckets (*informal*) **2** *Rockets,
mortars and artillery rained on buildings.* = **fall**,
shower, be dropped, sprinkle, be deposited
3 *Banks rained money on commercial real estate
developers.* = **bestow**, pour, shower, lavish
■ **RELATED WORDS:** *adjectives* pluvial, pluvious

rainy ADJECTIVE = **wet**, damp, drizzly,
showery ■ **OPPOSITE:** dry

raise VERB **1** *He raised his hand to wave.* = **lift**,
move up, elevate, uplift, heave **2** *She raised
herself on one elbow.* = **set upright**, lift,
elevate **3** *Two incidents in recent days have
raised the level of concern.* = **increase**,
reinforce, intensify, heighten, advance,
boost, strengthen, enhance, put up,
exaggerate, hike (up) (*informal*), enlarge,
escalate, inflate, aggravate, magnify,
amplify, augment, jack up ■ **OPPOSITE:**
reduce **4** *Don't you raise your voice to me!*
= **make louder**, heighten, amplify, louden
5 *events held to raise money* = **collect**, get,
gather, obtain **6** *Landed nobles provided courts
of justice and raised troops.* = **mobilize**, form,
mass, rally, recruit, assemble, levy, muster
7 *a joke that raised a smile* = **cause**, start,
produce, create, occasion (*formal*), provoke,
bring about, originate, give rise to, engender
8 *He had been consulted and had raised no*

r

objections. = **put forward**, suggest, introduce, advance, bring up, broach, moot **9** *the house where she was raised* = **bring up**, develop, rear, nurture **10** *They raise 2,000 acres of wheat and hay.* = **grow**, produce, rear, cultivate, propagate **11** *She raised chickens and pigs.* = **breed**, keep **12** *They raised a church in the shape of a boat.* = **build**, construct, put up, erect ■ **OPPOSITE:** demolish **13** *She was to be raised to the rank of ambassador.* = **promote**, upgrade, elevate, advance, prefer, exalt, aggrandize
■ **OPPOSITE:** demote

rake¹ VERB **1** *The beach is raked and cleaned daily.* = **scrape**, break up, scratch, scour, harrow, hoe **2** *I watched the men rake leaves into heaps.* = **gather**, collect, scrape together, scrape up, remove **3** *The caravan was raked with bullets.* = **strafe**, pepper, enfilade **4** *Ragged fingernails raked her skin.* = **graze**, scratch, scrape **5** (*with* **through**) *Many can only survive by raking through dustbins.* = **search**, hunt, examine, scan, comb, scour, ransack, forage, scrutinize, fossick (*Austral. & N.Z.*)

rake² NOUN *As a young man I was a rake.* = **libertine**, playboy, swinger (*slang*), profligate, lecher, roué, sensualist, voluptuary, debauchee, rakehell (*archaic*), dissolute man, lech or letch (*informal*)
■ **OPPOSITE:** puritan

rakish ADJECTIVE = **dashing** (*old-fashioned*), smart, sporty, flashy, breezy, jaunty, dapper, natty (*informal*), debonair, snazzy (*informal*), raffish, devil-may-care

rally NOUN **1** *They held a rally to mark international human rights day.* = **gathering**, mass meeting, convention, convocation (*formal*), meeting, conference, congress, assembly, congregation, muster, hui (*N.Z.*) **2** *After a brief rally, shares returned to 126p.* = **recovery**, improvement, comeback (*informal*), revival, renewal, resurgence, recuperation, turn for the better
■ **OPPOSITE:** relapse ▶ VERB **1** *He rallied his own supporters for a fight.* = **gather together**, unite, bring together, regroup, reorganize, reassemble, re-form **2** *He rallied enough to thank his doctor.* = **recover**, improve, pick up, revive, get better, come round, perk up, recuperate, turn the corner, pull through, take a turn for the better, regain your strength, get your second wind
■ **OPPOSITE:** get worse

ram VERB **1** *They used a lorry to ram the main gate.* = **hit**, force, drive into, strike, crash, impact, smash, slam, dash, run into, butt, collide with **2** *He rammed the key into the lock and kicked the front door open.* = **cram**, pound,

force, stuff, pack, hammer (*informal*), jam, thrust, tamp

ramble NOUN *an hour's ramble through the woods* = **walk**, tour, trip, stroll, hike, roaming, excursion, roving, saunter, traipse (*informal*), peregrination, perambulation ▶ VERB **1** *freedom to ramble across the moors* = **walk**, range, drift, wander, stroll, stray, roam, rove, amble, saunter, straggle, traipse (*informal*), go walkabout (*Austral.*), perambulate, stravaig (*Scot. & Northern English, dialect*), peregrinate **2** (*often with* **on**) *Sometimes she tended to ramble.* = **babble**, wander, rabbit (on) (*Brit. informal*), chatter, waffle (*informal, chiefly Brit.*), digress, rattle on, maunder, witter on (*informal*), expatiate, run off at the mouth (*slang*)

rambler NOUN = **walker**, roamer, wanderer, rover, hiker, drifter, stroller, wayfarer

rambling ADJECTIVE **1** *that rambling house with its bizarre contents* = **sprawling**, spreading, trailing, irregular, straggling **2** *He wrote a rambling letter to his wife.* = **long-winded**, incoherent, disjointed, prolix, irregular, diffuse, disconnected, desultory, wordy, circuitous, discursive, digressive, periphrastic ■ **OPPOSITE:** concise

ramification NOUN (*usually plural*) = **consequences**, results, developments, complications, sequel, upshot

ramp NOUN = **slope**, grade, incline, gradient, inclined plane, rise

rampage VERB *He used a sword to defend his shop from a rampaging mob.* = **go berserk**, tear, storm, rage, run riot, run amok, run wild, go ballistic (*slang*), go ape (*slang*) • **on the rampage** *a bull that went on the rampage* = **berserk**, wild, violent, raging, destructive, out of control, rampant, amok, riotous, berko (*Austral. slang*)

rampant ADJECTIVE **1** *the rampant corruption of the administration* = **widespread**, rank, epidemic, prevalent, rife, exuberant, uncontrolled, unchecked, unrestrained, luxuriant, profuse, spreading like wildfire **2** *rampant civil and military police atrocities* = **unrestrained**, wild, violent, raging, aggressive, dominant, excessive, outrageous, out of control, rampaging, out of hand, uncontrollable, flagrant, unbridled, vehement, wanton, riotous, on the rampage, ungovernable **3** *a shield with a lion rampant* = **upright**, standing, rearing, erect

rampart NOUN = **defence**, wall, parapet, fortification, security, guard, fence, fort, barricade, stronghold, bastion, embankment, bulwark, earthwork, breastwork

ramshackle ADJECTIVE = **rickety**, broken-down, crumbling, shaky, unsafe, derelict, flimsy, tottering, dilapidated, decrepit, unsteady, tumbledown, jerry-built ■ OPPOSITE: stable

rancid ADJECTIVE = **rotten**, sour, foul, bad, off, rank, tainted, stale, musty, fetid, putrid, fusty, strong-smelling, frowsty ■ OPPOSITE: fresh

rancour NOUN = **hatred**, hate, spite, hostility, resentment, bitterness, grudge, malice, animosity, venom, antipathy, spleen, enmity, ill feeling, bad blood, ill will, animus, malevolence, malignity, chip on your shoulder (*informal*), resentfulness

random ADJECTIVE **1** *The competitors will be subject to random drug testing.* = **chance**, spot, casual, stray, accidental, arbitrary, incidental, indiscriminate, haphazard, unplanned, fortuitous, aimless, desultory, hit or miss, purposeless, unpremeditated, adventitious ■ OPPOSITE: planned **2** *random violence against innocent children* = **casual**, arbitrary, indiscriminate, unplanned, aimless, purposeless, unpremeditated • **at random** *We received several answers and we picked one at random.* = **haphazardly**, randomly, arbitrarily, casually, accidentally, irregularly, by chance, indiscriminately, aimlessly, willy-nilly, unsystematically, purposelessly, adventitiously

randy ADJECTIVE = **lustful**, hot, sexy (*informal*), turned-on (*slang*), aroused, raunchy (*informal*), horny (*slang*), amorous, lascivious, lecherous, sexually excited, concupiscent, satyric

range NOUN **1** *The two men discussed a range of issues.* = **series**, variety, selection, assortment, lot, collection, gamut **2** *The average age range is between 35 and 55.* = **limits**, reach, distance, sweep, extent, pale, confines, parameters (*informal*), ambit **3** *The trees on the mountain within my range of vision had all been felled.* = **scope**, area, field, bounds, province, orbit, span, domain, compass, latitude, radius, amplitude, purview, sphere **4** *the massive mountain ranges to the north* = **row**, series, line, file, rank, chain, string, sequence, tier ▶ VERB **1** *offering merchandise ranging from the everyday to the esoteric* = **vary**, run, reach (*informal*), extend, go, stretch, fluctuate **2** *More than 1,500 police are ranged against them.* = **arrange**, order, line up, sequence, array, dispose, draw up, align **3** *They range widely in search of carrion.* = **roam**, explore, wander, rove, sweep, cruise, stroll, ramble, traverse **4** *The pots are all ranged in neat rows.* = **group**, class, file, rank, arrange, grade, catalogue,

classify, bracket, categorize, pigeonhole

rank[1] NOUN **1** *He eventually rose to the rank of captain.* = **status**, level, position, grade, order, standing, sort, quality, type, station, division, degree (*archaic*), classification, echelon **2** *Each rank of the peerage was respected.* = **class**, dignity, caste, nobility, stratum **3** *Ranks of police in riot gear stood nervously by.* = **row**, line, file, column, group, range, series, formation, tier ▶ VERB **1** *Universities were ranked according to marks scored in seven areas.* = **order**, class, grade, classify, dispose **2** *Daffodils were ranked along a crazy paving path.* = **arrange**, sort, position, range, line up, locate, sequence, array, marshal, align • **rank and file 1** *There was widespread support for him among the rank and file.* = **general public**, body, majority, mass, masses, Joe (and Eileen) Public (*slang*), Joe Six-Pack (*U.S. slang*) **2** *the rank and file of the Red Army* = **lower ranks**, men, troops, soldiers, other ranks, private soldiers

rank[2] ADJECTIVE **1** *He accused his rival of rank hypocrisy.* = **absolute**, complete, total, gross, sheer, excessive, utter, glaring, thorough, extravagant, rampant, blatant, downright, flagrant, egregious, unmitigated, undisguised, arrant **2** *the rank smell of unwashed clothes* = **foul**, off, bad, offensive, disgusting, revolting, stinking, stale, pungent, noxious, disagreeable, musty, rancid, fetid, putrid, fusty, strong-smelling, gamey, noisome, mephitic, olid, yucky *or* yukky (*slang*), festy (*Austral. slang*) **3** *brambles and rank grass* = **abundant**, flourishing, lush, luxuriant, productive, vigorous, dense, exuberant, profuse, strong-growing

rankle VERB = **annoy**, anger, irritate, gall, fester, embitter, chafe, irk, rile, get on your nerves (*informal*), get your goat (*slang*), hack you off (*informal*)

ransack VERB **1** *Why should they be allowed to ransack your bag?* = **search**, go through, rummage through, rake through, explore, comb, scour, forage, turn inside out, fossick (*Austral. & N.Z.*) **2** *Demonstrators ransacked and burned the house where he was staying.* = **plunder**, raid, loot, pillage, strip, sack, gut, rifle, ravage, despoil (*formal*)

ransom NOUN **1** *The demand for the ransom was made by telephone.* = **payment**, money, price, payoff **2** *the eventual ransom of the victim* = **release**, rescue, liberation, redemption, deliverance ▶ VERB *The same system was used for ransoming or exchanging captives.* = **buy the freedom of**, release, deliver, rescue, liberate, buy (someone) out

r

(*informal*), redeem, set free, obtain or pay for the release of

rant VERB *I don't rant and rave or throw tea cups.* = **shout**, roar, yell, rave, bellow, cry, spout (*informal*), bluster, declaim, vociferate
▶ NOUN *As the boss began his rant, I stood up and went out.* = **tirade**, rhetoric, bluster, diatribe, harangue, bombast, philippic, vociferation, fanfaronade (*rare*)

rap VERB **1** *A guard raps his stick on a metal hand rail.* = **hit**, strike, knock, crack (*informal*), tap **2** *The minister rapped the banks over their treatment of small businesses.* = **reprimand**, knock (*informal*), blast, pan (*informal*), carpet (*informal*), criticize, censure, scold, tick off (*informal*), castigate, read the riot act, lambast(e), chew out (*U.S. & Canad. informal*), give a rocket (*Brit. & N.Z. informal*) **3** *Today we're going to rap about relationships.* = **talk**, chat, discourse, converse, shoot the breeze (*slang, chiefly U.S.*), confabulate
▶ NOUN **1** *There was a light rap on the door.* = **blow**, knock, crack (*informal*), tap, clout (*informal*) **2** *You'll be facing a federal rap for aiding and abetting an escaped convict.* = **rebuke**, sentence, blame, responsibility, punishment, censure, chiding

rapacious ADJECTIVE = **greedy**, grasping, insatiable, ravenous, preying, plundering, predatory, voracious, marauding, extortionate, avaricious, wolfish, usurious

rape VERB = **sexually assault**, violate, abuse ▶ NOUN **1** *Ninety per cent of all rapes and violent assaults went unreported.* = **sexual assault**, violation **2** *the rape of the environment* = **plundering**, pillage, depredation, despoliation (*formal*), rapine, spoliation, despoilment, sack

rapid ADJECTIVE **1** *the country's rapid economic growth* = **sudden**, prompt, speedy, precipitate, express, fleet, swift, quickie (*informal*), expeditious ■ OPPOSITE: gradual **2** *He walked at a rapid pace along Charles Street.* = **quick**, fast, hurried, swift, brisk, hasty, flying, pdq (*slang*) ■ OPPOSITE: slow

rapidity NOUN = **speed**, swiftness, promptness, speediness, rush, hurry, expedition, dispatch, velocity, haste, alacrity, quickness, briskness, fleetness, celerity (*formal*), promptitude, precipitateness

rapidly ADVERB = **quickly**, fast, swiftly, briskly, promptly, hastily, precipitately, in a hurry, at speed, hurriedly, speedily, apace (*literary*), in a rush, in haste, like a shot, pronto (*informal*), hell for leather, like lightning, expeditiously, hotfoot, like the clappers (*Brit. informal*), pdq (*slang*), like nobody's business (*informal*), posthaste, with dispatch, like greased lightning (*informal*)

rapport NOUN = **bond**, understanding, relationship, link, tie, sympathy, harmony, affinity, empathy, interrelationship

rapprochement NOUN = **reconciliation**, softening, reunion, détente, reconcilement, restoration of harmony ■ OPPOSITE: dissension

rapt ADJECTIVE **1** *I noticed that everyone was watching me with rapt attention.* = **spellbound**, entranced, enthralled, engrossed; held, gripped, fascinated, absorbed, intent, preoccupied, carried away ■ OPPOSITE: uninterested **2** *He played to a rapt audience.* = **rapturous**, enchanted, captivated, bewitched, sent, transported, delighted, charmed, ecstatic, blissful, ravished, enraptured, blissed out

rapture NOUN = **ecstasy**, delight, enthusiasm, joy, transport, spell, happiness, bliss, euphoria, felicity, rhapsody, exaltation, cloud nine (*informal*), seventh heaven, delectation (*formal*), beatitude, ravishment

rapturous ADJECTIVE = **ecstatic**, delighted, enthusiastic, rapt, sent (*informal*), happy, transported, joyous, exalted, joyful, over the moon (*informal*), overjoyed, blissful, ravished, euphoric, on cloud nine (*informal*), blissed out (*informal*), rhapsodic, in seventh heaven, floating on air

rare[1] ADJECTIVE **1** *She collects rare plants.* = **priceless**, rich, precious, invaluable **2** *I think big families are extremely rare nowadays.* = **uncommon**, unusual, exceptional, out of the ordinary, few, strange, scarce, singular, sporadic, sparse, infrequent, thin on the ground, recherché ■ OPPOSITE: common **3** *She has a rare ability to record her observations on paper.* = **superb**, great (*informal*), fine, excellent, extreme, exquisite, admirable, superlative, choice, incomparable, peerless

rare[2] ADJECTIVE *Waiter, I specifically asked for this steak rare.* = **underdone**, bloody, undercooked, half-cooked, half-raw

rarefied ADJECTIVE = **exclusive**, select, esoteric, cliquish, private, occult, clannish

rarely ADVERB = **seldom**, hardly, almost never, hardly ever, little, once in a while, infrequently, on rare occasions, once in a blue moon (*informal*), only now and then, scarcely ever ■ OPPOSITE: often

USAGE Since the meaning of *rarely* is 'hardly ever', the combination *rarely ever* is repetitive and should be avoided in careful writing, even though you may sometimes hear this phrase used in informal speech.

raring ADJECTIVE • **raring to** = **eager to**, impatient to, longing to, yearning to, willing to, ready to, keen to, desperate to, enthusiastic to, avid to, champing at the bit to (*informal*), keen as mustard to, athirst to

rarity NOUN **1** *Other rarities include an interview with Presley.* = **curio**, find, treasure, pearl, one-off, curiosity, gem, collector's item **2** *This indicates the rarity of such attacks.* = **uncommonness**, scarcity, infrequency, unusualness, shortage, strangeness, singularity, sparseness

rascal NOUN = **rogue**, devil, villain, scoundrel (*old-fashioned*), disgrace, rake, pickle (*Brit. informal*), imp, scally (*Northwest English, dialect*), wretch, knave (*archaic*), ne'er-do-well, reprobate, scallywag (*informal*), good-for-nothing, miscreant, scamp, wastrel, bad egg (*old-fashioned, informal*), blackguard, varmint (*informal*), rapscallion, caitiff (*archaic*), wrong 'un (*slang*), nointer (*Austral. slang*)

rash¹ ADJECTIVE *Don't do anything rash until the feelings subside.* = **reckless**, hasty, impulsive, imprudent, premature, adventurous, careless, precipitate, brash, audacious, headlong, madcap, ill-advised, foolhardy, unwary, thoughtless, unguarded, headstrong, impetuous, indiscreet, unthinking, helter-skelter, ill-considered, hot-headed, heedless, injudicious, incautious, venturesome, harebrained, harum-scarum ■ **OPPOSITE:** cautious

rash² NOUN **1** *I noticed a rash on my leg.* = **outbreak of spots**, (skin) eruption **2** *a rash of internet-related companies* = **spate**, series, wave, flood, succession, plague, outbreak, epidemic

rasp VERB = **scrape**, grind, rub, scour, excoriate, abrade

rasping *or* **raspy** ADJECTIVE = **harsh**, rough, hoarse, gravelly, jarring, grating, creaking, husky, croaking, gruff, croaky

rat NOUN **1** *He was known as 'The Rat', even before the bribes had come to light.* = **traitor**, grass (*Brit. informal*), betrayer, deceiver, informer, defector, deserter, double-crosser, quisling, stool pigeon, nark (*Brit., Austral. & N.Z. slang*), snake in the grass, two-timer (*informal*), fizgig (*Austral. slang*) **2** *What did you do with the gun you took from that little rat?* = **rogue**, scoundrel (*old-fashioned*), heel (*slang*), cad (*old-fashioned, informal, Brit.*), bounder (*old-fashioned slang, Brit.*), rotter (*slang, chiefly Brit.*), bad lot, shyster (*informal, chiefly U.S.*), ratfink (*slang, chiefly U.S. & Canad.*), wrong 'un (*slang*) • **rat on someone** *They were accused of encouraging*

children to rat on their parents. = **betray**, denounce, tell on, shop (*slang, chiefly Brit.*), grass (*Brit. slang*), peach (*slang*), squeal (*slang*), incriminate (*informal*), blow the whistle on (*informal*), spill the beans (*informal*), snitch (*slang*), blab, let the cat out of the bag, blow the gaff (*Brit. slang*), nark (*Brit., Austral. & N.Z. slang*), put the finger on (*informal*), spill your guts (*slang*), inculpate, clype (*Scot.*), dob in (*Austral. slang*)

rate NOUN **1** *The rate at which hair grows can be agonisingly slow.* = **speed**, pace, tempo, velocity, time, measure, gait, frequency **2** *bank accounts paying above the average rate of interest* = **degree**, standard, scale, proportion, percentage, ratio **3** *specially reduced rates* = **charge**, price, cost, fee, tax, figure, dues, duty, hire, toll, tariff ▶ VERB **1** *The film was rated excellent by 90 per cent of children.* = **evaluate**, consider, rank, reckon, class, value, measure, regard, estimate, count, grade, assess, weigh, esteem (*formal*), classify, appraise, adjudge **2** *Her attire did not rate a second glance.* = **deserve**, merit, be entitled to, be worthy of • **at any rate** *Well, at any rate, let me thank you for all you did.* = **in any case**, anyway, nevertheless, anyhow, at all events

rather ADVERB **1** *I'd rather stay at home than fight against the holiday crowds.* = **preferably**, sooner, instead, more readily, more willingly **2** *I'm afraid it's rather a long story.* = **to some extent**, quite, sort of (*informal*), kind of (*informal*), a little, a bit, pretty (*informal*), fairly, relatively, somewhat, slightly, moderately, to some degree

> **USAGE** It is acceptable to use either *would rather* or *had rather* in sentences such as I *would rather* (or *had rather*) *see a film than a play*. *Had rather*, however, is less common than *would rather*, and sounds a little old-fashioned nowadays.

ratify VERB = **approve**, sign, establish, confirm, bind, sanction, endorse, uphold, authorize, affirm, certify, consent to, validate, bear out, corroborate, authenticate ■ **OPPOSITE:** annul

rating NOUN = **position**, evaluation, classification, placing, rate, order, standing, class, degree (*archaic*), estimate, rank, status, grade, designation

ratio NOUN = **proportion**, rate, relationship, relation, arrangement, percentage, equation, fraction, correspondence, correlation

ration NOUN *The meat ration was down to one pound per person per week.* = **allowance**, quota, allotment, provision, helping, part, share, measure, dole, portion ▶ VERB

r

1 *Staples such as bread, rice and tea are already being rationed.* = **limit**, control, restrict, save, budget, conserve **2** *I had a flask so I rationed out cups of tea.* = **distribute**, issue, deal, dole, allocate, give out, allot, mete, apportion, measure out, parcel out

rational ADJECTIVE **1** *a rational decision* = **sensible**, sound, wise, reasonable, intelligent, realistic, logical, enlightened, sane, lucid, judicious, sagacious, grounded **2** *Man, as a rational being, may act against his impulses.* = **reasoning**, thinking, cognitive, cerebral, ratiocinative **3** *Rachel looked calmer and more rational now.* = **sane**, balanced, normal, all there (*informal*), lucid, of sound mind, compos mentis (*Latin*), in your right mind

rationale NOUN = **reason**, grounds, theory, principle, philosophy, logic, motivation, exposition, raison d'être (*French*)

rationalize VERB **1** *the trend to rationalize our failings by blaming our upbringing* = **justify**, excuse, account for, vindicate, explain away, make allowances for, make excuses for, extenuate **2** *an attempt to rationalize my feelings* = **reason out**, resolve, think through, elucidate, apply logic to **3** *They have been unable or unwilling to modernize and rationalize the business.* = **streamline**, trim, make more efficient, make cuts in

rattle VERB **1** *She slams the kitchen door so hard I hear dishes rattle.* = **clatter**, bang, jangle **2** *He gently rattled the cage and whispered to the canary.* = **shake**, jiggle, jolt, vibrate, bounce, jar, jounce **3** *She refused to be rattled by his lawyer.* = **fluster**, shake, upset, frighten, scare, disturb, disconcert, perturb, faze, discomfit, discountenance, put (someone) off their stride, discompose, put (someone) out of countenance • **rattle on** *I listened in silence as Sam rattled on.* = **prattle**, rabbit (on) (*Brit. informal*), chatter, witter (*informal*), cackle, yak (away) (*slang*), gibber, jabber, gabble, blether, prate, run on, earbash (*Austral. & N.Z. slang*) • **rattle something off** *He could rattle off yards of poetry.* = **recite**, list, run through, rehearse, reel off, spiel off (*informal*)

ratty ADJECTIVE = **irritable**, cross, angry, annoyed, crabbed, impatient, snappy, touchy, tetchy, testy, short-tempered, tooshie (*Austral. slang*)

raucous ADJECTIVE = **harsh**, rough, loud, noisy, grating, strident, rasping, husky, hoarse ■ **OPPOSITE:** quiet

raunchy ADJECTIVE = **sexy**, sexual, steamy (*informal*), earthy, suggestive, lewd, lusty, bawdy, salacious, smutty, lustful, lecherous, ribald, coarse

ravage VERB *The soldiers had ravaged the village.* = **destroy**, ruin, devastate, wreck, shatter, gut, spoil, loot, demolish, plunder, desolate, sack, ransack, pillage, raze, lay waste, wreak havoc on, despoil (*formal*), leave in ruins ▶ NOUN (*often plural*) *the ravages of a cold, wet climate* = **damage**, destruction, devastation, desolation, waste, ruin, havoc, demolition, plunder, pillage, depredation, ruination, rapine, spoliation

rave VERB **1** *She cried and raved for weeks.* = **rant**, rage, roar, thunder, fume, go mad (*informal*), babble, splutter, storm, be delirious, talk wildly **2** *She raved about the new foods she ate while she was there.* = **enthuse**, praise, gush, be delighted by, be mad about (*informal*), big up (*slang*), rhapsodize, be wild about (*informal*), cry up ▶ NOUN *an all-night rave* = **party**, rave-up (*Brit. slang*), do (*informal*), affair, celebration, bash (*informal*), blow-out (*slang*), beano (*Brit. slang*), hooley or hoolie (*chiefly Irish & N.Z.*) ▶ MODIFIER *The show has drawn rave reviews from the critics.* = **enthusiastic**, excellent, favourable, ecstatic, laudatory

ravenous ADJECTIVE **1** *a pack of ravenous animals* = **starving**, starved, very hungry, famished, esurient ■ **OPPOSITE:** sated **2** *He had moderated his ravenous appetite.* = **greedy**, insatiable, avaricious, covetous, grasping, insatiate

ravine NOUN = **canyon**, pass, gap (*U.S.*), gorge, clough (*dialect*), gully, defile, linn (*Scot.*), gulch (*U.S. & Canad.*), flume

raving ADJECTIVE = **mad**, wild, raging, crazy, furious, frantic, frenzied, hysterical, irrational, crazed, berserk, delirious, rabid

ravish VERB = **enchant**, transport, delight, charm, fascinate, entrance, captivate, enrapture, spellbind, overjoy

ravishing ADJECTIVE = **enchanting**, beautiful, lovely, stunning (*informal*), charming, entrancing, gorgeous (*informal*), dazzling, delightful, radiant, drop-dead (*slang*), bewitching

raw ADJECTIVE **1** *two ships carrying raw sugar* = **unrefined**, natural, crude, unprocessed, basic, rough, organic, coarse, unfinished, untreated, unripe ■ **OPPOSITE:** refined **2** *a popular dish made of raw fish* = **uncooked**, natural, fresh, bloody (*of meat*), undressed, unprepared ■ **OPPOSITE:** cooked **3** *the drag of the rope against the raw flesh of my shoulder* = **sore**, open, skinned, sensitive, tender, scratched, grazed, chafed, abraded **4** *the raw passions of nationalism* = **frank**, plain, bare, naked, realistic, brutal, blunt, candid, unvarnished, unembellished ■ **OPPOSITE:** embellished **5** *He is still raw but his potential shows.* = **inexperienced**, new, green, ignorant, immature, unskilled, callow, untrained, untried, undisciplined, unseasoned, unpractised ■ **OPPOSITE:** experienced **6** *a raw December morning* = **chilly**, biting, cold, freezing, bitter, wet, chill, harsh, piercing, damp, unpleasant, bleak, parky (*Brit. informal*)

ray NOUN **1** *The first rays of light spread over the horizon.* = **beam**, bar, flash, shaft, gleam **2** *I can offer you a slender ray of hope.* = **trace**, spark, flicker, glimmer, hint, indication, scintilla

raze VERB = **destroy**, level, remove, ruin, demolish, flatten, knock down, pull down, tear down, throw down, bulldoze, kennet (*Austral. slang*), jeff (*Austral. slang*)

re PREPOSITION = **concerning**, about, regarding, respecting, with regard to, on the subject of, in respect of, with reference to, apropos, anent (*Scot.*)

> USAGE In contexts such as *re your letter, your remarks have been noted* or *he spoke to me re your complaint*, *re* is common in business or official correspondence. In spoken and in general written English *with reference to* is preferable in the former case and *about* or *concerning* in the latter. Even in business correspondence, the use of *re* is often restricted to the letter heading.

reach VERB **1** *He did not stop until he reached the door.* = **arrive at**, get to, get as far as, make, attain, land at **2** *We're told the figure could reach 100,000 next year.* = **amount to**, attain, get to **3** *Can you reach your toes with your fingertips?* = **touch**, grasp, extend to, get (a) hold of, stretch to, go as far as, contact **4** *I'll tell her you've been trying to reach her.* = **contact**, get in touch with, get through to, make contact with, get, find, communicate with, get hold of, establish contact with **5** *a nightshirt that reached to his knees* = **come to**, move to, rise to, fall to, drop to, sink to **6** *They are meeting in Lusaka in an attempt to reach a compromise.* = **achieve**, come to, arrive at ▸ NOUN **1** *The clothes they model are in easy reach of every woman.* = **grasp**, range, distance, stretch, sweep, capacity, extent, extension, scope **2** *The elite are no longer beyond the reach of the law.* = **jurisdiction**, power, influence, command, compass, mastery, ambit

react VERB = **respond**, act, proceed, behave, conduct yourself

reaction NOUN **1** *He showed no reaction when the judge pronounced his sentence.* = **response**, acknowledgment, feedback, answer, reply **2** *All new fashion starts out as a reaction against existing convention.* = **counteraction**, compensation, backlash, recoil, counterbalance, counterpoise **3** *their victory against the forces of reaction and conservatism* = **conservatism**, the right, counter-revolution, obscurantism

> USAGE Some people say that *reaction* should always refer to an instant response to something (as in *his reaction was one of amazement*), and that this word should not be used to refer to a considered response given in the form of a statement (as in *the Minister gave his reaction to the court's decision*). Use *response* instead.

reactionary ADJECTIVE *narrow and reactionary ideas about family life* = **conservative**, right-wing, counter-revolutionary, obscurantist, blimpish ■ **OPPOSITE:** radical ▸ NOUN *Critics viewed him as a reactionary, even a monarchist.* = **conservative**, die-hard, right-winger, rightist, counter-revolutionary, obscurantist, Colonel Blimp ■ **OPPOSITE:** radical

read VERB **1** *He read through the pages slowly and carefully.* = **scan**, study, look at, refer to, glance at, pore over, peruse, run your eye over, follow (*a blog or microblog*) **2** *Jay reads poetry so beautifully.* = **recite**, deliver, utter, declaim, speak, announce **3** *He could read words at 18 months.* = **understand**, interpret, comprehend, construe, decipher, perceive the meaning of, see, discover **4** *The sign on the bus read 'Private: Not in Service'.* = **register**, show, record, display, indicate

readable ADJECTIVE **1** *This is an impeccably researched and very readable book.* = **enjoyable**, interesting, gripping, entertaining, pleasant, enthralling, easy to read, worth reading ■ **OPPOSITE:** dull **2** *a typewritten and readable script* = **legible**, clear, plain, understandable, comprehensible, intelligible, decipherable ■ **OPPOSITE:** illegible

readily ADVERB **1** *When I was invited to the party, I readily accepted.* = **willingly**, freely, quickly, gladly, eagerly, voluntarily, cheerfully, with pleasure, with good grace, lief (*rare*) ■ **OPPOSITE:** reluctantly **2** *I don't readily make friends.* = **promptly**, quickly, easily, smoothly, at once, straight away, right away, effortlessly, in no time, speedily, without delay, without hesitation, without difficulty, unhesitatingly, hotfoot, without demur, pdq (*slang*) ■ **OPPOSITE:** with difficulty

r

readiness NOUN **1** *their readiness to co-operate with the new US envoy* = **willingness**, inclination, eagerness, keenness, aptness, gameness (*informal*) **2** *a constant state of readiness for war* = **preparedness**, preparation, fitness, maturity, ripeness **3** *the warmth of his personality and the readiness of his wit* = **promptness**, facility, ease, skill, dexterity, rapidity, quickness, adroitness, handiness, promptitude • **in readiness** *Everything was in readiness for the President's arrival.* = **prepared**, set, waiting, primed, ready, all set, waiting in the wings, at the ready, at or on hand, fit

reading NOUN **1** *This knowledge makes the second reading as enjoyable as the first.* = **perusal**, study, review, examination, inspection, scrutiny **2** *a man of great imagination, of wide reading and deep learning* = **learning**, education, knowledge, scholarship, erudition, edification, book-learning **3** *a poetry reading* = **recital**, performance, rendering, rendition, lesson, lecture, sermon, homily **4** *There is a reading of this situation which upsets people.* = **interpretation**, take (*informal, chiefly U.S.*), understanding, treatment, version, construction (*formal*), impression, grasp, conception

ready ADJECTIVE **1** *It took her a long time to get ready for church.* = **prepared**, set, primed, organized, all set, in readiness ■ **OPPOSITE:** unprepared **2** *Everything's ready for the family to move in.* = **completed**, arranged **3** *In a few days' time the sprouts will be ready to eat.* = **mature**, ripe, mellow, ripened, fully developed, fully grown, seasoned **4** *She was always ready to give interviews.* = **willing**, happy, glad, disposed, game (*informal*), minded, keen, eager, inclined, prone, have-a-go (*informal*), apt, agreeable, predisposed ■ **OPPOSITE:** reluctant **5** *I didn't have a ready answer for this dilemma.* = **prompt**, smart, quick, bright (*informal*), sharp, keen, acute, rapid, alert, clever, intelligent, handy, apt, skilful, astute, perceptive, expert, deft, resourceful, adroit, quick-witted, dexterous ■ **OPPOSITE:** slow **6** *I'm afraid I don't have much ready cash.* = **available**, handy, at the ready, at your fingertips, present, near, accessible, convenient, on call, on tap (*informal*), close to hand, at or on hand ■ **OPPOSITE:** unavailable **7** (*with* **to**) *She looked ready to cry.* = **on the point of**, close to, about to, on the verge of, likely to, in danger of, liable to, on the brink of ▶ VERB *John's soldiers were readying themselves for the final assault.* = **prepare**, get set, organize, get ready,

order, arrange, equip, fit out, make ready, jack up (*N.Z. informal*)

real ADJECTIVE **1** *No, it wasn't a dream. It was real.* = **true**, genuine, sincere, honest, factual, existent, dinkum (*Austral. & N.Z. informal*), unfeigned **2** *the smell of real leather* = **genuine**, authentic, bona fide, dinkum (*Austral. & N.Z. informal*) ■ **OPPOSITE:** fake **3** *his first real girlfriend* = **proper**, true, valid, legitimate **4** *This was the real reason for her call.* = **actual**, true **5** *Their expressions of regret did not smack of real sorrow.* = **sincere**, true, genuine, unaffected, dinkum (*Austral. & N.Z. informal*), unfeigned **6** *You must think I'm a real idiot.* = **complete**, right, total, perfect, positive (*informal*), absolute, utter, thorough, veritable, out-and-out

realistic ADJECTIVE **1** *a realistic view of what we can afford* = **practical**, real, sensible, rational, common-sense, sober, pragmatic, down-to-earth, matter-of-fact, businesslike, level-headed, hard-headed, unsentimental, unromantic, grounded ■ **OPPOSITE:** impractical **2** *Establish deadlines that are more realistic.* = **attainable**, reasonable, sensible **3** *The language is foul and the violence horribly realistic.* = **lifelike**, true to life, authentic, naturalistic, true, natural, genuine, graphic, faithful, truthful, representational, vérité

reality NOUN **1** *Fiction and reality were increasingly blurred.* = **fact**, truth, certainty, realism, validity, authenticity, verity, actuality, materiality, genuineness, verisimilitude, corporeality **2** *the harsh reality of top international competition* = **truth**, fact, actuality • **in reality** *He came across as streetwise, but in reality he was not.* = **in fact**, really, actually, in truth, as a matter of fact, in actuality, in point of fact

realization NOUN **1** *There is a growing realization that things cannot go on like this for much longer.* = **awareness**, understanding, recognition, perception, imagination, consciousness, grasp, appreciation, conception, comprehension, apprehension, cognizance, aha moment (*informal*), light bulb moment (*informal*) **2** *the realization of his worst fears* = **achievement**, carrying-out, completion, accomplishment, fulfilment, consummation, effectuation

realize VERB **1** *As soon as we realized what was going on, we moved the children away.* = **become aware of**, understand, recognize, appreciate, take in, grasp, conceive, catch on (*informal*), comprehend, twig (*Brit. informal*), get the message, apprehend, become conscious of, be cognizant of **2** *Realize your dreams! Pursue your passions!* = **fulfil**, achieve, accomplish, make real **3** *The kaleidoscopic quality of the book is brilliantly realized on stage.* = **achieve**, do, effect, complete, perform, fulfil, accomplish, bring about, consummate, incarnate, bring off, make concrete, bring to fruition, actualize, make happen, effectuate, reify, carry out or through **4** *A selection of correspondence from P.G. Wodehouse realized £1,232.* = **sell for**, go for, bring or take in, make, get, clear, produce, gain, net, earn, obtain, acquire

really ADVERB **1** *I really do feel that some people are being unfair.* = **certainly**, absolutely, undoubtedly, genuinely, positively, categorically, without a doubt, assuredly, verily, surely **2** *My father didn't really love her.* = **truly**, actually, in fact, indeed, in reality, in actuality

realm NOUN **1** *the realm of politics* = **field**, world, area, province, sphere, department (*informal*), region, branch, territory, zone, patch, orbit, turf (*slang*) **2** *Defence of the realm is crucial.* = **kingdom**, state, country, empire, monarchy, land, province, domain, dominion, principality

reap VERB **1** *We are not in this to reap immense financial rewards.* = **get**, win, gain, obtain, acquire, derive **2** *a group of peasants reaping a harvest of fruit and vegetables* = **collect**, gather, bring in, harvest, garner, cut

rear¹ NOUN **1** *He settled back in the rear of the taxi.* = **back part**, back ■ OPPOSITE: front **2** *Musicians played at the front and rear of the procession.* = **back**, end, tail, rearguard, tail end, back end ▶ MODIFIER *the rear end of a tractor* = **back**, aft, hind, hindmost, after (*Nautical*), last, following, trailing ■ OPPOSITE: front

rear² VERB **1** *I was reared in east Texas.* = **bring up**, raise, educate, care for, train, nurse, foster, nurture **2** *She spends a lot of time rearing animals.* = **breed**, keep **3** (*often with* **up** *or* **over**) *The exhibition hall reared above me behind a high fence.* = **rise**, tower, soar, loom

reason NOUN **1** *There is a reason for every important thing that happens.* = **cause**, grounds, purpose, motive, end, goal, design, target, aim, basis, occasion, object, intention, incentive, warrant, impetus, inducement, why and wherefore (*informal*) **2** *I hope you have a good reason for your behaviour.* = **justification**, case, grounds, defence, argument, explanation, excuse, apology, rationale, exposition, vindication, apologia **3** *a conflict between emotion and reason* = **sense**, mind, reasoning, understanding, brains, judgment, logic,

mentality, intellect, comprehension, apprehension, sanity, rationality, soundness, sound mind, ratiocination ■ OPPOSITE: emotion ▶ VERB *I reasoned that changing my diet would lower my cholesterol level.* = **deduce**, conclude, work out, solve, resolve, make out, infer, draw conclusions, think, ratiocinate, syllogize • **in** *or* **within reason** *I will take any job that comes along, within reason.* = **within limits**, within reasonable limits, within bounds • **reason with someone** *All he wanted was to reason with one of them.* = **persuade**, debate with, remonstrate with, bring round, urge, win over, argue with, dispute with, dissuade, prevail upon (*formal*), expostulate with, show (someone) the error of their ways, talk into or out of

> USAGE Many people object to the expression *the reason is because*, on the grounds that it is repetitive. It is therefore advisable to use either *this is because* or *the reason is that*.

reasonable ADJECTIVE **1** *He's a reasonable sort of chap.* = **sensible**, reasoned, sound, practical, wise, intelligent, rational, logical, sober, credible, plausible, sane, judicious, grounded ■ OPPOSITE: irrational **2** *a perfectly reasonable decision* = **fair**, just, right, acceptable, moderate, equitable, justifiable, well-advised, well-thought-out, tenable ■ OPPOSITE: unfair **3** *It seems reasonable to expect rapid urban growth.* = **within reason**, fit, proper ■ OPPOSITE: impossible **4** *His fees were quite reasonable.* = **low**, cheap, competitive, moderate, modest, inexpensive, tolerable **5** *The boy answered him in reasonable French.* = **average**, fair, moderate, modest, tolerable (*informal*), O.K. or okay (*informal*)

reasoned ADJECTIVE = **sensible**, clear, logical, systematic, judicious, well-thought-out, well-presented, well-expressed

reasoning NOUN **1** *the reasoning behind the decision* = **thinking**, thought, reason, analysis, logic, deduction, cogitation, ratiocination **2** *She was not really convinced by their line of reasoning.* = **argument**, proof, interpretation, hypothesis, exposition, train of thought

reassure VERB = **encourage**, comfort, bolster, hearten, cheer up, buoy up, gee up, restore confidence to, inspirit, relieve (someone) of anxiety, put or set your mind at rest

rebate NOUN = **refund**, discount, reduction, bonus, allowance, deduction

rebel NOUN **1** *fighting between rebels and*

r

government forces = **revolutionary**, resistance fighter, insurgent, secessionist, mutineer, insurrectionary, revolutionist **2** *She had been a rebel at school.* = **nonconformist**, dissenter, heretic, apostate, schismatic ▶ VERB **1** *Poverty-stricken citizens could rise up and rebel.* = **revolt**, resist, rise up, mutiny, take to the streets, take up arms, man the barricades **2** *The child who rebels against his parents is unlikely to be overlooked.* = **defy**, dissent, disobey, come out against, refuse to obey, dig your heels in (*informal*) **3** *His free spirit rebelled at this demand.* = **recoil**, shrink, shy away, flinch, show repugnance ▶ MODIFIER *Many soldiers in this rebel platoon joined as teenagers.* = **rebellious**, revolutionary, insurgent, mutinous, insubordinate, insurrectionary

rebellion NOUN **1** *They soon put down the rebellion.* = **resistance**, rising, revolution, revolt, uprising, mutiny, insurrection, insurgency, insurgence **2** *He engaged in a small act of rebellion against his heritage.* = **nonconformity**, dissent, defiance, heresy, disobedience, schism, insubordination, apostasy

rebellious ADJECTIVE **1** *a rebellious teenager* = **defiant**, difficult, resistant, intractable, recalcitrant, obstinate, unmanageable, incorrigible, refractory, contumacious (*literary*) ■ OPPOSITE: obedient **2** *a rebellious and dissident territory* = **revolutionary**, rebel, disorderly, unruly, turbulent, disaffected, insurgent, recalcitrant, disloyal, seditious, mutinous, disobedient, ungovernable, insubordinate, insurrectionary ■ OPPOSITE: obedient

rebirth NOUN = **revival**, restoration, renaissance, renewal, resurrection, reincarnation, regeneration, resurgence, new beginning, revitalization, renascence

rebound VERB **1** *His shot rebounded from a post.* = **bounce**, ricochet, spring back, return, resound, recoil **2** *Mia realised her trick had rebounded on her.* = **misfire**, backfire, recoil, boomerang

rebuff VERB *He wanted to go out with with Julie but she rebuffed him.* = **reject**, decline, refuse, turn down, cut (*informal*), check, deny, resist, slight, discourage, put off, snub, spurn, knock back (*slang*), brush off (*slang*), repulse, cold-shoulder ■ OPPOSITE: encourage ▶ NOUN *The results of the poll dealt a humiliating rebuff to Mr Jones.* = **rejection**, defeat, snub, knock-back, check, opposition, slight, refusal, denial, brush-off (*slang*), repulse, thumbs down, cold shoulder, slap in the face (*informal*),

kick in the teeth (*slang*), discouragement ■ OPPOSITE: encouragement

rebuke VERB *They have been seriously rebuked.* = **scold**, censure, reprimand, reproach, blame, lecture, carpet (*informal*), berate, tick off (*informal*), castigate, chide, dress down (*informal*), admonish, tear into (*informal*), tell off (*informal*), take to task, read the riot act, reprove, upbraid, bawl out (*informal*), haul (someone) over the coals (*informal*), chew out (*U.S. & Canad. informal*), tear (someone) off a strip (*informal*), give a rocket (*Brit. & N.Z. informal*), reprehend ■ OPPOSITE: praise ▶ NOUN *'Silly little boy' was his favourite expression of rebuke.* = **scolding**, censure, reprimand, reproach, blame, row, lecture, wigging (*Brit. slang*), ticking-off (*informal*), dressing-down (*informal*), telling-off (*informal*), admonition, tongue-lashing, reproof, castigation, reproval ■ OPPOSITE: praise

rebut VERB = **disprove**, defeat, overturn, quash, refute, negate, invalidate, prove wrong, confute

rebuttal NOUN = **disproof**, negation, refutation, invalidation, confutation, defeat

recalcitrant ADJECTIVE = **disobedient**, contrary, unwilling, defiant, stubborn, wayward, unruly, uncontrollable, intractable, wilful, obstinate, unmanageable, ungovernable, refractory, insubordinate, contumacious (*literary*) ■ OPPOSITE: obedient

recall VERB **1** *I recalled the way they had been dancing together.* = **recollect**, remember, call up, evoke, reminisce about, call to mind, look or think back to, mind (*dialect*) **2** *Parliament was recalled from its summer recess.* = **call back 3** *The order was recalled.* = **annul**, withdraw, call in, take back, cancel, repeal, call back, revoke, retract, rescind, nullify, countermand, abjure ▶ NOUN **1** *He had a total recall of her spoken words.* = **recollection**, memory, remembrance **2** *The appellant sought a recall of the order.* = **annulment**, withdrawal, repeal, cancellation, retraction, revocation, nullification, rescission, rescindment

recant VERB = **withdraw**, take back, retract, disclaim, deny, recall, renounce, revoke, repudiate, renege, disown, disavow, forswear, abjure, unsay, apostatize ■ OPPOSITE: maintain

recede VERB **1** *As she receded into the distance he waved goodbye.* = **fall back**, withdraw, retreat, draw back, return, go back, retire, back off, regress, retrogress, retrocede **2** *The illness began to recede.* = **lessen**, decline, subside, abate, sink, fade, shrink, diminish, dwindle, wane, ebb

receipt NOUN **1** *I wrote her a receipt for the money.* = **sales slip**, proof of purchase, voucher, stub, acknowledgment, counterfoil **2** *the receipt of your order* = **receiving**, delivery, reception, acceptance, recipience ▶ PLURAL NOUN *He was tallying the day's receipts.* = **takings**, return, profits, gains, income, gate, proceeds

receive VERB **1** *I received your letter.* = **get**, accept, be given, pick up, collect, obtain, acquire, take, derive, be in receipt of, accept delivery of **2** *He received a blow to the head.* = **experience**, suffer, bear, go through, encounter, meet with, sustain, undergo, be subjected to **3** *The following evening the duchess was again receiving guests.* = **greet**, meet, admit, welcome, entertain, take in, accommodate, be at home to

recent ADJECTIVE = **new**, modern, contemporary, up-to-date, late, young, happening (*informal*), current, fresh, novel, latter, present-day, latter-day ■ OPPOSITE: old

recently ADVERB = **not long ago**, newly, lately, currently, freshly, of late, latterly

receptacle NOUN = **container**, holder, repository

reception NOUN **1** *a glittering wedding reception* = **party**, gathering, get-together, social gathering, do (*informal*), social, function, entertainment, celebration, bash (*informal*), festivity, knees-up (*Brit. informal*), shindig (*informal*), soirée, levee, rave-up (*Brit. slang*) **2** *He received a cool reception to his speech.* = **response**, reaction, acknowledgment, recognition, treatment, welcome, greeting **3** *the production, distribution and reception of medical knowledge* = **receiving**, admission, acceptance, receipt, recipience

receptive ADJECTIVE *The voters had seemed receptive to his ideas.* = **open**, sympathetic, favourable, amenable, interested, welcoming, friendly, accessible, susceptible, open-minded, hospitable, approachable, open to suggestions ■ OPPOSITE: narrow-minded

recess NOUN **1** *Parliament returns to work today after its summer recess.* = **break**, rest, holiday, closure, interval, vacation, respite, intermission, cessation of business, schoolie (*Austral.*) **2** *a discreet recess next to a fireplace* = **alcove**, corner, bay, depression, hollow, niche, cavity, nook, oriel, indentation **3** (*often plural*) *He emerged from the dark recesses of the garage.* = **depths**,

reaches, heart, retreats, bowels, innards (*informal*), secret places, innermost parts, penetralia

recession NOUN = **depression**, drop, decline, credit crunch, slump, downturn ■ OPPOSITE: boom

recherché ADJECTIVE = **refined**, rare, exotic, esoteric, arcane, far-fetched, choice

recipe NOUN *I can give you the recipe for these biscuits.* = **directions**, instructions, ingredients, receipt (*obsolete*) • **a recipe for something** *Large-scale inflation is a recipe for disaster.* = **method**, formula, prescription, process, programme, technique, procedure, modus operandi

reciprocal ADJECTIVE = **mutual**, corresponding, reciprocative, reciprocatory, exchanged, equivalent, alternate, complementary, interchangeable, give-and-take, interdependent, correlative ■ OPPOSITE: unilateral

reciprocate VERB = **return**, requite, feel in return, match, respond, equal, retaliate, return the compliment

recital NOUN **1** *a solo recital* = **performance**, rendering, rehearsal, reading **2** *It was a depressing recital of childhood abuse.* = **account**, telling, story, detailing, statement, relation, tale, description, narrative, narration, enumeration, recapitulation **3** *The album features a recital of 13th century Latin prayers.* = **recitation**, repetition

recitation NOUN = **recital**, reading, performance, piece, passage, lecture, rendering, narration, telling

recite VERB = **perform**, relate, deliver, repeat, rehearse, declaim, recapitulate, do your party piece (*informal*)

reckless ADJECTIVE = **careless**, wild, rash, irresponsible, precipitate, hasty, mindless, negligent, headlong, madcap, ill-advised, regardless, foolhardy, daredevil, thoughtless, indiscreet, imprudent, heedless, devil-may-care, inattentive, incautious, harebrained, harum-scarum, overventuresome ■ OPPOSITE: cautious

reckon VERB **1** *He reckoned he was still fond of her.* = **think**, believe, suppose, imagine, assume, guess (*informal, chiefly U.S. & Canad.*), fancy, conjecture, surmise, be of the opinion **2** *The sale has been held up because the price is reckoned to be too high.* = **consider**, hold, rate, account, judge, think of, regard, estimate, count, evaluate, esteem (*formal*), deem, gauge, look upon, appraise **3** *The 'normal' by-election swing against a government is reckoned at about*

r

5 per cent. = **count**, figure, total, calculate, compute, add up, tally, number, enumerate
• **reckon on** or **upon something** She reckons on being world champion one day. = **rely on**, count on, bank on, depend on, hope for, calculate, trust in, take for granted
• **reckon with something** or **someone** (used in negative constructions) He had not reckoned with the strength of her feelings for him. = **take into account**, expect, plan for, anticipate, be prepared for, bear in mind, foresee, bargain for, take cognizance of
• **to be reckoned with** This act was a signal that she was someone to be reckoned with. = **powerful**, important, strong, significant, considerable, influential, weighty, consequential, skookum (Canad.)

reckoning NOUN **1** By my reckoning we were seven or eight kilometres away. = **count**, working, estimate, calculation, adding, counting, addition, computation, summation **2** the day of reckoning = **day of retribution**, doom, judgment day, last judgment

reclaim VERB **1** I've come to reclaim my property. = **retrieve**, get or take back, rescue, regain, reinstate **2** The Netherlands has been reclaiming farmland from water. = **regain**, restore, salvage, recapture, regenerate **3** Education was to reclaim him. = **rescue**, reform, redeem

recline VERB = **lean**, lie (down), stretch out, rest, lounge, sprawl, loll, repose, be recumbent ■ **OPPOSITE:** stand up

recluse NOUN = **hermit**, solitary, ascetic, anchoress, monk, anchorite, eremite

reclusive ADJECTIVE = **solitary**, retiring, withdrawn, isolated, secluded, cloistered, monastic, recluse, ascetic, sequestered, hermit-like, hermitic, eremitic
■ **OPPOSITE:** sociable

recognition NOUN **1** He searched for a sign of recognition on her face. = **identification**, recall, recollection, discovery, detection, remembrance **2** They welcomed his recognition of the recession. = **acceptance**, acknowledgment, understanding, admission, perception, awareness, concession, allowance, confession, realization, avowal **3** His government did not receive full recognition until July. = **acknowledgment**, approval **4** At last, her father's work has received popular recognition. = **approval**, honour, appreciation, salute, gratitude, acknowledgment

recognize VERB **1** The receptionist recognized him at once. = **identify**, know, place, remember, spot, notice, recall, make out, recollect, know again, put your finger on **2** I

recognize my own shortcomings.
= **acknowledge**, see, allow, understand, accept, admit, grant, realize, concede, perceive, confess, be aware of, take on board, avow ■ **OPPOSITE:** ignore **3** Eisenhower recognized the Castro government at once.
= **approve**, acknowledge, appreciate, greet, honour **4** He had the insight to recognize their talents. = **appreciate**, respect, notice, salute

recoil VERB **1** I recoiled in horror. = **jerk back**, kick, react, rebound, spring back, resile **2** People used to recoil from the idea of getting into debt. = **draw back**, shrink, falter, shy away, flinch, quail, balk at ▶ NOUN **1** His reaction was as much a rebuff as a physical recoil. = **jerking back**, reaction, springing back **2** The police officer fires again, tensed against the recoil. = **kickback**, kick

recollect VERB = **remember**, mind (dialect), recall, reminisce, summon up, call to mind, place

recollection NOUN = **memory**, recall, impression, remembrance, reminiscence, mental image

recommend VERB **1** Ask your doctor to recommend a suitable treatment. = **advocate**, suggest, propose, approve, endorse, commend ■ **OPPOSITE:** disapprove of **2** He recommended me for a promotion. = **put forward**, approve, endorse, commend, vouch for, praise, big up (slang), speak well of, put in a good word for **3** I recommend that you consult your doctor. = **advise**, suggest, advance, propose, urge, counsel, advocate, prescribe, put forward, exhort (formal), enjoin **4** It was his enthusiasm that recommended him to the archbishop. = **make attractive**, make interesting, make appealing, make acceptable

recommendation NOUN **1** The committee's recommendations are unlikely to be made public. = **advice**, proposal, suggestion, counsel, urging **2** The best way of finding a solicitor is by personal recommendation. = **commendation**, reference, praise, sanction, approval, blessing, plug (informal), endorsement, advocacy, testimonial, good word, approbation, favourable mention

recompense NOUN He demands no financial recompense for his troubles. = **compensation**, pay, payment, satisfaction, amends, repayment, remuneration, reparation, indemnity, restitution, damages, emolument, indemnification, requital
▶ VERB If they succeed in court, they will be fully recompensed for their loss. = **compensate**, reimburse, redress, repay, pay for, satisfy, make good, make up for, make amends for, indemnify, requite, make restitution for

reconcile VERB 1 *It is possible to reconcile these apparently opposing perspectives.* = **resolve**, settle, square, adjust, compose, rectify, patch up, harmonize, put to rights 2 *He never believed he and Susan would be reconciled.* = **reunite**, bring back together, make peace between, pacify, conciliate 3 *my attempt to reconcile him and Toby* = **make peace between**, reunite, propitiate, bring to terms, restore harmony between, re-establish friendly relations between • **reconcile yourself to something** (*often passive*) *She reconciled herself to never seeing him again.* = **accept**, resign yourself to, get used to, put up with (*informal*), submit to, yield to, make the best of, accommodate yourself to

reconciliation NOUN 1 *The couple have separated but he wants a reconciliation.* = **reunion**, conciliation, rapprochement (*French*), appeasement, détente, pacification, propitiation, understanding, reconcilement ■ OPPOSITE: separation 2 *the reconciliation of our differences* = **accommodation**, settlement, compromise

reconnaissance NOUN = **inspection**, survey, investigation, observation, patrol, scan, exploration, scouting, scrutiny, recce (*slang*), reconnoitring

reconsider VERB = **rethink**, review, revise, think again, think twice, reassess, re-examine, have second thoughts, change your mind, re-evaluate, think over, think better of, take another look at

reconstruct VERB 1 *The government must reconstruct the shattered economy.* = **rebuild**, reform, restore, recreate, remake, renovate, remodel, re-establish, regenerate, reorganize, reassemble 2 *Elaborate efforts were made to reconstruct what had happened.* = **build up a picture of**, build up, piece together, deduce

record NOUN 1 *Keep a record of all the payments.* = **document**, file, register, log, report, minute, account, entry, journal, diary, memorial, archives, memoir, chronicle, memorandum, annals, blog (*informal*) 2 *There's no record of any marriage or children.* = **evidence**, trace, documentation, testimony, witness, memorial, remembrance 3 *This is one of my favourite records.* = **disc** (*old-fashioned*), recording, single, release, album, waxing (*informal*), LP, vinyl, EP, forty-five, platter (*U.S. slang*), seventy-eight, gramophone record, black disc 4 *His record reveals a tough streak.* = **background**, history, performance, career, track record (*informal*), curriculum

vitae ▶ VERB 1 *In her letters she records the domestic and social details of life in China.* = **set down**, report, minute, note, enter, document, register, preserve, log, put down, chronicle, write down, enrol, take down, inscribe, transcribe, chalk up (*informal*), put on record, put on file 2 *She recorded a new album in Nashville.* = **make a recording of**, cut, video, tape, lay down (*slang*), wax (*informal*), video-tape, tape-record, put on wax (*informal*) 3 *The test records the electrical activity of the brain.* = **register**, show, read, contain, indicate, give evidence of • **off the record** 1 *May I speak off the record?* = **confidentially**, in private, in confidence, unofficially, sub rosa, under the rose 2 *Those remarks were supposed to be off the record.* = **confidential**, private, unofficial, not for publication

recorder NOUN = **chronicler**, archivist, historian, scorer, clerk, registrar, scribe, diarist, scorekeeper, annalist

recording NOUN = **record**, video, tape, disc (*old-fashioned*), gramophone record, cut (*informal*)

recount VERB = **tell**, report, detail, describe, relate, repeat, portray, depict, rehearse, recite, tell the story of, narrate, delineate, enumerate, give an account of

recoup VERB = **regain**, recover, make good, retrieve, redeem, win back

recourse NOUN = **option**, choice, alternative, resort, appeal, resource, remedy, way out, refuge, expedient, backstop

recover VERB 1 *He is recovering after sustaining a knee injury.* = **get better**, improve, get well, recuperate, pick up, heal, revive, come round, bounce back, mend, turn the corner, pull through, convalesce, be on the mend, take a turn for the better, get back on your feet, feel yourself again, regain your health or strength ■ OPPOSITE: relapse 2 *The stock market index fell by 80% before it began to recover.* = **rally** 3 *Rescue teams recovered a few more survivors from the rubble.* = **save**, rescue, retrieve, salvage, reclaim ■ OPPOSITE: abandon 4 *Legal action is being taken to try and recover the money.* = **recoup**, restore, repair, get back, regain, make good, retrieve, reclaim, redeem, recapture, win back, take back, repossess, retake, find again ■ OPPOSITE: lose

recovery NOUN 1 *He made a remarkable recovery from a shin injury.* = **improvement**, return to health, rally, healing, revival, mending, recuperation, convalescence, turn for the better 2 *In many sectors of the economy the recovery has started.* = **revival**,

r

improvement, rally, restoration, rehabilitation, upturn, betterment, amelioration **3** *the recovery of a painting by Turner* = **retrieval**, repossession, reclamation, restoration, repair, redemption, recapture

recreation NOUN = **leisure**, play, sport, exercise, fun, relief, pleasure, entertainment, relaxation, enjoyment, distraction, amusement, diversion, refreshment, beer and skittles (*informal*), me-time

recrimination NOUN = **bickering**, retaliation, counterattack, mutual accusation, retort, quarrel, squabbling, name-calling, countercharge

recruit VERB **1** *He helped to recruit volunteers to serve the meals.* = **gather**, take on, obtain, engage, round up, enrol, procure, proselytize **2** *He's managed to recruit an army of crooks.* = **assemble**, raise, levy, muster, mobilize **3** *He had the forlorn job of trying to recruit soldiers.* = **enlist**, draft, impress, enrol ■ **OPPOSITE:** dismiss ▶ NOUN *A new recruit could well arrive later this week.* = **beginner**, trainee, apprentice, novice, convert, initiate, rookie (*informal*), helper, learner, neophyte (*formal*), tyro, greenhorn (*informal*), proselyte

rectify VERB = **correct**, right, improve, reform, square, fix, repair, adjust, remedy, amend, make good, mend, redress, put right, set the record straight, emend

rectitude NOUN **1** *people of the utmost rectitude* = **morality**, principle, honour, virtue, decency, justice, equity, integrity, goodness, honesty, correctness, righteousness, probity (*formal*), incorruptibility, scrupulousness, uprightness ■ **OPPOSITE:** immorality **2** *Has the rectitude of this principle ever been formally contested?* = **correctness**, justice, accuracy, precision, verity, rightness, soundness, exactness

recuperate VERB = **recover**, improve, pick up, get better, mend, turn the corner, convalesce, be on the mend, get back on your feet, regain your health

recur VERB = **happen again**, return, come back, repeat, persist, revert, reappear, come and go, come again

recurrent ADJECTIVE = **periodic**, continued, regular, repeated, frequent, recurring, repetitive, cyclical, habitual ■ **OPPOSITE:** one-off

recycle VERB = **reprocess**, reuse, salvage, reclaim, save

red NOUN **1** *a deep shade of red* = **crimson**, scarlet, ruby, vermilion, rose, wine, pink, cherry, cardinal, coral, maroon, claret, carmine **2** (*informal*) = **communist**, socialist, revolutionary, militant, Marxist, leftist, left-winger, lefty (*informal*), Trotskyite ▶ ADJECTIVE **1** *a red coat* = **crimson**, scarlet, ruby, vermilion, rose, wine, pink, cherry, cardinal, coral, maroon, claret, carmine **2** *She was red with shame.* = **flushed**, embarrassed, blushing, suffused, florid, shamefaced, rubicund (*old-fashioned*) **3** (*hair*) *Her red hair flowed out in the wind.* = **chestnut**, flaming, reddish, flame-coloured, bay, sandy, foxy, Titian, carroty, ginger **4** *He rubbed his red eyes.* = **bloodshot**, inflamed, red-rimmed **5** *rosy red cheeks* = **rosy**, healthy, glowing, blooming (*informal*), ruddy, roseate • **in the red** *The theatre is in the red.* = **in debt**, bankrupt, on the rocks, insolvent, in arrears, overdrawn, owing money, in deficit, showing a loss, in debit • **see red** *I didn't mean to break his nose. I just saw red.* = **lose your temper**, boil, lose it (*informal*), seethe, go mad (*informal*), crack up (*informal*), lose the plot (*informal*), go ballistic (*slang*), blow a fuse (*slang, chiefly U.S.*), fly off the handle (*informal*), become enraged, go off the deep end (*informal*), wig out (*slang*), go up the wall (*slang*), blow your top, lose your rag (*slang*), be beside yourself with rage (*informal*), be or get very angry, go off your head (*slang*) ■ **RELATED WORDS:** *adjectives* rubicund, ruddy

red-blooded ADJECTIVE = **vigorous**, lusty, virile, strong, vital, robust, hearty

redden VERB = **flush**, colour (up), blush, crimson, suffuse, go red, go beetroot (*informal*)

redeem VERB **1** *He had realized the mistake he had made and wanted to redeem himself.* = **reinstate**, absolve, restore to favour, rehabilitate **2** *Work is the way people seek to redeem their sins.* = **make up for**, offset, make good, compensate for, outweigh, redress, atone for, make amends for, defray **3** *The voucher will be redeemed for one toy.* = **trade in**, cash (in), exchange, change **4** *the date upon which you plan to redeem the item* = **buy back**, recover, regain, retrieve, reclaim, win back, repossess, repurchase, recover possession of **5** *a new female spiritual force to redeem the world* = **save**, free, deliver, rescue, liberate, ransom, set free, extricate, emancipate, buy the freedom of, pay the ransom of **6** *They must redeem that pledge.* = **fulfil**, meet, keep, carry out, satisfy, discharge, make good, hold to, acquit, adhere to, abide by, keep faith with, be faithful to, perform

redemption NOUN **1** *trying to make some redemption for his actions* = **compensation**, amends, reparation, atonement, expiation (*formal*) **2** *offering redemption from our sins* = **salvation**, release, rescue, liberation, ransom, emancipation, deliverance **3** *redemption of the loan* = **paying-off**, paying back **4** *cash redemptions and quota payments* = **trade-in**, recovery, retrieval, repurchase, repossession, reclamation, quid pro quo

red-handed ADJECTIVE = **in the act**, with your pants down (*U.S. slang*), (in) flagrante delicto, with your fingers or hand in the till (*informal*), bang to rights (*slang*)

red-hot ADJECTIVE **1** = **very hot**, burning, heated, steaming, searing, scorching, scalding, piping hot **2** = **exciting**, inspiring, sensational (*informal*), electrifying **3** = **passionate**, thrilling, sexy, arousing, titillating

redolent ADJECTIVE **1** *a sad tale, redolent with regret* = **reminiscent**, evocative, suggestive, remindful **2** *The air was redolent of cinnamon and apple.* = **scented**, perfumed, fragrant, aromatic, sweet-smelling, odorous

redoubtable ADJECTIVE = **formidable**, strong, powerful, terrible, awful, mighty, dreadful, fearful (*informal*), fearsome, resolute, valiant, doughty (*old-fashioned*)

redress VERB **1** *Victims are turning to litigation to redress wrongs done to them.* = **make amends for**, pay for, make up for, compensate for, put right, recompense for, make reparation for, make restitution for **2** *to redress the economic imbalance* = **put right**, reform, balance, square, correct, ease, repair, relieve, adjust, regulate, remedy, amend, mend, rectify, even up, restore the balance ▶ NOUN *a legal battle to seek some redress from the government* = **amends**, payment, compensation, reparation, restitution, atonement, recompense, requital, quittance

reduce VERB **1** *Consumption is being reduced by 25 per cent.* = **lessen**, cut, contract, lower, depress, moderate, dial down, weaken, diminish, turn down, decrease, slow down, cut down, shorten, dilute, impair, curtail, wind down, abate, tone down, debase, truncate, abridge, downsize, downscale, kennet (*Austral. slang*), jeff (*Austral. slang*) ■ OPPOSITE: increase **2** *They wanted the army reduced to a police force.* = **degrade**, downgrade, demote, lower in rank, break, humble, humiliate, bring low, take down a peg (*informal*), lower the status of ■ OPPOSITE: promote **3** *He was reduced to begging for a living.* = **drive**, force, bring, bring to the point of **4** *Companies should*

reduce prices today. = **cheapen**, cut, lower, discount, slash, mark down, bring down the price of **5** = **impoverish**, ruin, bankrupt, pauperize • **in reduced circumstances** *living in reduced circumstances* = **impoverished**, broke (*informal*), badly off, hard up (*informal*), short, in need, needy, on the rocks, penniless, destitute, poverty-stricken, down and out, skint (*Brit. slang*), in want, indigent (*formal*), down at heel, impecunious, dirt-poor (*informal*), on the breadline, flat broke (*informal*), penurious, on your uppers, stony-broke (*Brit. slang*), necessitous, in queer street, without two pennies to rub together (*informal*), on your beam-ends

redundancy NOUN **1** *They hope to avoid future redundancies.* = **layoff**, sacking, dismissal **2** *Thousands of employees are facing redundancy.* = **unemployment**, the sack (*informal*), the axe (*informal*), joblessness **3** *the redundancy of its two main exhibits* = **superfluity**, surplus, surfeit, superabundance

redundant ADJECTIVE **1** *the conversion of redundant buildings to residential use* = **superfluous**, extra, surplus, excessive, unnecessary, unwanted, inordinate, inessential, supernumerary, de trop (*French*), supererogatory ■ OPPOSITE: essential **2** *The last couplet collapses into redundant adjectives.* = **tautological**, wordy, repetitious, verbose, padded, diffuse, prolix, iterative, periphrastic, pleonastic

reek VERB **1** *Your breath reeks.* = **stink**, smell, pong (*Brit. informal*), smell to high heaven, hum (*slang*) **2** (*with* **of**) *The whole thing reeks of hypocrisy.* = **be redolent of**, suggest, smack of, testify to, be characterized by, bear the stamp of, be permeated by, be suggestive or indicative of ▶ NOUN *He smelt the reek of whisky.* = **stink**, smell, odour, stench, pong (*Brit. informal*), effluvium, niff (*Brit. slang*), malodour, mephitis, fetor

reel VERB **1** *He lost his balance and reeled back.* = **stagger**, rock, roll, pitch, stumble, sway, falter, lurch, wobble, waver, totter **2** *The room reeled and I jammed my head down.* = **whirl**, swim, spin, revolve, swirl, twirl, go round and round

refer VERB **1** *He could refer the matter to the high court.* = **pass on**, transfer, deliver, commit, hand over, submit, turn over, consign **2** *He referred me to a book on the subject.* = **direct**, point, send, guide, recommend • **refer to something** or **someone 1** *She referred to a recent trip to Canada.* = **allude to**, mention, cite, speak of, bring up, invoke, hint at, touch on, make reference to, make

r

mention of **2** *The term 'electronics' refers to electrically-induced action.* = **relate to**, concern, apply to, pertain to, be relevant to **3** *He referred briefly to his notebook.* = **consult**, go, apply, turn to, look up, have recourse to, seek information from

> USAGE It is usually unnecessary to add *back* to the verb *refer*, since the sense of *back* is already contained in the *re-* part of this word. For example, you might say *This refers to* (not *refers back to*) *what has already been said*. *Refer back* is only considered acceptable when used to mean 'return a document or question to the person it came from for further consideration', as in *he referred the matter back to me*.

referee NOUN *The referee stopped the fight.* = **umpire**, umpie (*Austral. slang*), judge, ref (*informal*), arbiter, arbitrator, adjudicator ▶ VERB *He has refereed in two World Cups.* = **umpire**, judge, mediate, adjudicate, arbitrate

reference NOUN **1** *He summed up his philosophy, with reference to Calvin.* = **allusion**, note, mention, remark, quotation **2** *I would have found a brief list of references useful.* = **citation 3** *The firm offered to give her a reference.* = **testimonial**, recommendation, credentials, endorsement, certification, good word, character reference

referendum NOUN = **public vote**, popular vote, plebiscite

refine VERB **1** *Oil is refined so as to remove naturally occurring impurities.* = **purify**, process, filter, cleanse, clarify, distil, rarefy **2** *Surgical techniques are constantly being refined.* = **improve**, perfect, polish, temper, elevate, hone

refined ADJECTIVE **1** *refined sugar* = **purified**, processed, pure, filtered, clean, clarified, distilled ■ OPPOSITE: unrefined **2** *His speech and manner are refined.* = **cultured**, civil, polished, tasteful, sophisticated, gentlemanly, elegant, polite, cultivated, gracious, civilized, genteel, urbane, courtly, well-bred, ladylike, well-mannered ■ OPPOSITE: coarse **3** *refined tastes* = **discerning**, fine, nice, sensitive, exact, subtle, delicate, precise, discriminating, sublime, fastidious, punctilious (*formal*)

refinement NOUN **1** *the refinements of the game* = **subtlety**, nuance, nicety, fine point **2** *a girl who possessed both dignity and refinement* = **sophistication**, finish, style, culture, taste, breeding, polish, grace, discrimination, courtesy, civilization, precision, elegance, delicacy, cultivation, finesse, politeness, good manners, civility,

gentility, good breeding, graciousness, urbanity, fastidiousness, fineness, courtliness, politesse **3** *the refinement of crude oil* = **purification**, processing, filtering, cleansing, clarification, distillation, rectification, rarefaction

reflect VERB **1** *Concern was reflected in the government's budget.* = **show**, reveal, express, display, indicate, demonstrate, exhibit, communicate, manifest, bear out, bespeak, evince (*formal*) **2** *The glass appears to reflect light naturally.* = **throw back**, return, mirror, echo, reproduce, imitate, give back **3** (*usually followed by* **on**) *I reflected on the child's future.* = **consider**, think, contemplate, deliberate, muse, ponder, meditate, mull over, ruminate, cogitate, wonder

reflection NOUN **1** *Meg stared at her reflection in the mirror.* = **image**, echo, counterpart, mirror image **2** *Infection with head lice is no reflection on personal hygiene.* = **criticism**, censure, slur, reproach, imputation, derogation, aspersion **3** *After days of reflection she decided to write back.* = **consideration**, thinking, pondering, deliberation, thought, idea, view, study, opinion, impression, observation, musing, meditation, contemplation, rumination, perusal, cogitation, cerebration

reflective ADJECTIVE = **thoughtful**, contemplative, meditative, pensive, reasoning, pondering, deliberative, ruminative, cogitating

reform NOUN *a programme of economic reform* = **improvement**, amendment, correction, rehabilitation, renovation, betterment, rectification, amelioration ▶ VERB **1** *his plans to reform the country's economy* = **improve**, better, correct, restore, repair, rebuild, amend, reclaim, mend, renovate, reconstruct, remodel, rectify, rehabilitate, regenerate, reorganize, reconstitute, revolutionize, ameliorate, emend **2** *Under such a system where is the incentive to reform?* = **mend your ways**, go straight (*informal*), shape up (*informal*), get it together (*informal*), turn over a new leaf, get your act together (*informal*), clean up your act (*informal*), pull your socks up (*Brit. informal*), get back on the straight and narrow (*informal*)

refrain¹ VERB *She refrained from making any comment.* = **stop**, avoid, give up, cease, do without, renounce, abstain, eschew, leave off, desist, forbear, kick (*informal*)

refrain² NOUN *a refrain from an old song* = **chorus**, song, tune, melody

refresh VERB **1** *The lotion cools and refreshes*

the skin. = **revive**, cool, freshen, revitalize, cheer, stimulate, brace, rejuvenate, kick-start (*informal*), enliven, breathe new life into, invigorate, revivify, reanimate, inspirit **2** *She appeared, her make-up refreshed.* = **replenish**, restore, repair, renew, top up, renovate **3** *Allow me to refresh your memory.* = **stimulate**, prompt, renew, jog, prod, brush up (*informal*)

refreshing ADJECTIVE **1** *refreshing new ideas* = **new**, different, original, novel **2** *Herbs have been used for centuries to make refreshing drinks.* = **stimulating**, fresh, cooling, bracing, invigorating, revivifying, thirst-quenching, inspiriting
■ **OPPOSITE:** tiring

refreshment NOUN **1** *a place where city dwellers come to find spiritual refreshment* = **revival**, restoration, renewal, stimulation, renovation, freshening, reanimation, enlivenment, repair **2** (*plural*) *Some refreshments would be nice.* = **food and drink**, drinks, snacks, titbits, kai (*N.Z. informal*)

refrigerate VERB = **cool**, freeze, chill, keep cold

refrigerator NOUN = **fridge**, chiller, cooler, ice-box (*U.S. & Canad.*)

refuge NOUN **1** *They took refuge in a bomb shelter.* = **protection**, security, shelter, harbour, asylum **2** *We climbed up a winding track towards a mountain refuge.* = **haven**, resort, retreat, sanctuary, hide-out, bolt hole

refugee NOUN = **exile**, émigré, displaced person, runaway, fugitive, escapee

refund NOUN *They plan to demand a refund.* = **repayment**, reimbursement, return ▶ VERB *She will refund you the purchase price.* = **repay**, return, restore, make good, pay back, reimburse, give back

refurbish VERB = **renovate**, restore, repair, clean up, overhaul, revamp, mend, remodel, do up (*informal*), refit, fix up (*informal, chiefly U.S. & Canad.*), spruce up, pimp up, pimp out, re-equip, set to rights

refusal NOUN *a refusal of planning permission* = **rejection**, denial, defiance, rebuff, knock-back (*slang*), thumbs down, repudiation, kick in the teeth (*slang*), negation, no • **first refusal** *A tenant may have a right of first refusal if a property is offered for sale.* = **option**, choice, opportunity, consideration

refuse¹ VERB **1** *I could hardly refuse his invitation.* = **decline**, reject, turn down, say no to, repudiate **2** *She was refused access to her children.* = **deny**, decline, withhold
■ **OPPOSITE:** allow

refuse² NOUN *a weekly collection of refuse* = **rubbish**, waste, sweepings, junk (*informal*), litter, garbage (*chiefly U.S.*), trash, sediment, scum, dross, dregs, leavings, dreck (*slang, chiefly U.S.*), offscourings, lees

refute VERB = **disprove**, counter, discredit, prove false, silence, overthrow, negate, rebut, give the lie to, blow out of the water (*slang*), confute ■ **OPPOSITE:** prove

> **USAGE** The use of *refute* to mean *deny* as in *I'm not refuting the fact that* is thought by some people to be incorrect. In careful writing it may be advisable to use *refute* only where there is an element of disproving something through argument and evidence, as in *we haven't got evidence to refute their hypothesis.*

regain VERB **1** *Troops have regained control of the city.* = **recover**, get back, retrieve, redeem, recapture, win back, take back, recoup, repossess, retake **2** *We cannot regain our road.* = **get back to**, return to, reach again, reattain

regal ADJECTIVE = **royal**, majestic, kingly or queenly, noble, princely, proud, magnificent, sovereign, fit for a king or queen

regale VERB **1** *He was constantly regaled with amusing stories.* = **entertain**, delight, amuse, divert, gratify **2** *On Sunday evenings we were usually regaled with a roast dinner.* = **serve**, refresh, ply

regalia PLURAL NOUN = **trappings**, gear, decorations, finery, apparatus, emblems, paraphernalia, garb, accoutrements, rigout (*informal*), bling (*slang*)

regard VERB **1** *I regard creativity as both a gift and a skill.* = **consider**, see, hold, rate, view, value, account, judge, treat, think of, esteem (*formal*), deem, look upon, adjudge **2** *She regarded him curiously for a moment.* = **look at**, view, eye, watch, observe, check, notice, clock (*Brit. slang*), remark, check out (*informal*), gaze at, behold (*archaic, literary*), eyeball (*U.S. slang*), scrutinize, get a load of (*informal*), take a dekko at (*Brit. slang*) ▶ NOUN **1** *I have a very high regard for him and what he has achieved.* = **respect**, esteem, deference, store, thought, love, concern, care, account, note, reputation, honour, consideration, sympathy, affection, attachment, repute **2** *This gave a look of calculated menace to his regard.* = **look**, gaze, scrutiny, stare, glance **3** (*plural*) *Give my regards to your family.* = **good wishes**, respects, greetings, compliments, best wishes, salutations, devoirs • **as regards** *As regards the war, he believed in victory at any price.* = **concerning**, regarding, relating to,

r

pertaining to • **in this regard** *In this regard nothing has changed.* = **on this point**, on this matter, on this detail, in this respect • **with regard to** *The UN has urged sanctions with regard to trade in arms.* = **concerning**, regarding, relating to, with respect to, as regards

> **USAGE** The word *regard* in the expression *with regard to* is singular, and has no *s* at the end. People often make the mistake of saying *with regards to*, perhaps being influenced by the phrase *as regards*.

regarding PREPOSITION = **concerning**, about, as to, on the subject of, re, respecting, in respect of, as regards, with reference to, in re, in the matter of, apropos, in *or* with regard to

regardless ADVERB *Despite her recent surgery she has been carrying on regardless.* = **in spite of everything**, anyway, nevertheless, nonetheless, in any case, no matter what, for all that, rain or shine, despite everything, come what may ▶ ADJECTIVE (*with* **of**) *It takes in anybody regardless of religion, colour or creed.* = **irrespective of**, disregarding, unconcerned about, heedless of, unmindful of

regenerate VERB = **renew**, restore, revive, renovate, change, reproduce, uplift, reconstruct, re-establish, rejuvenate, kick-start (*informal*), breathe new life into, invigorate, reinvigorate, reawaken, revivify, give a shot in the arm, inspirit ■ **OPPOSITE:** degenerate

regime NOUN **1** *the collapse of the fascist regime* = **government**, rule, management, administration, leadership, establishment, reign **2** *a drastic regime of economic reform* = **plan**, course, system, policy, programme, scheme, regimen

region NOUN *a remote mountain region* = **area**, country, place, part, land, quarter, division, section, sector, district, territory, zone, province, patch, turf (*slang*), tract, expanse, locality

regional ADJECTIVE = **local**, district, provincial, parochial, sectional, zonal

register NOUN *registers of births, deaths and marriages* = **list**, record, roll, file, schedule, diary, catalogue, log, archives, chronicle, memorandum, roster, ledger, annals ▶ VERB **1** *Have you come to register at the school?* = **enrol**, sign on *or* up, enlist, list, note, enter, check in, inscribe, set down **2** *We registered his birth.* = **record**, catalogue, chronicle, take down **3** *The meter registered loads of 9 and 10 kg.* = **indicate**, show, record, read **4** *Many people registered no symptoms*

when they became infected. = **show**, mark, record, reflect, indicate, betray, manifest, bespeak **5** *Workers stopped work to register their protest.* = **express**, say, show, reveal, display, exhibit **6** *What I said sometimes didn't register in her brain.* = **have an effect**, get through, sink in, make an impression, tell, impress, come home, dawn on

regress VERB = **revert**, deteriorate, return, go back, retreat, lapse, fall back, wane, recede, ebb, degenerate, relapse, lose ground, turn the clock back, backslide, retrogress, retrocede, fall away *or* off ■ **OPPOSITE:** progress

regret VERB **1** *She regrets having given up her home.* = **be** *or* **feel sorry about**, feel remorse about, be upset about, rue (*literary*), deplore, bemoan, repent (of), weep over, bewail, cry over spilt milk ■ **OPPOSITE:** be satisfied with **2** *I regret the passing of the old era.* = **mourn**, miss, grieve for *or* over ▶ NOUN **1** *He has no regrets about retiring.* = **remorse**, compunction, self-reproach, pang of conscience, bitterness, repentance, contrition, penitence, ruefulness **2** *He expressed great regret.* = **sorrow**, disappointment, grief, lamentation ■ **OPPOSITE:** satisfaction

regretful ADJECTIVE = **sorry**, disappointed, sad, ashamed, apologetic, mournful, rueful, contrite, sorrowful, repentant, remorseful, penitent

> **USAGE** *Regretful* and *regretfully* are sometimes wrongly used where *regrettable* and *regrettably* are meant. A simple way of making the distinction is that when you regret something YOU have done, you are *regretful*: *he gave a regretful smile; he smiled regretfully.* In contrast, when you are sorry about an occurrence you did not yourself cause, you view the occurrence as *regrettable*: *this is a regrettable* (not *regretful*) *mistake; regrettably* (not *regretfully*, i.e. because of circumstances beyond my control) *I shall be unable to attend.*

regrettable ADJECTIVE = **unfortunate**, wrong, disappointing, sad, distressing, unhappy, shameful, woeful, deplorable, ill-advised, lamentable, pitiable

regular ADJECTIVE **1** *Take regular exercise.* = **frequent**, daily **2** *Children are encouraged to make reading a regular routine.* = **normal**, common, established, usual, ordinary, typical, routine, everyday, customary, commonplace, habitual, unvarying ■ **OPPOSITE:** infrequent **3** *a very regular beat* = **steady**, consistent **4** *regular rows of wooden huts* = **even**, level, balanced, straight, flat, fixed, smooth, uniform, symmetrical ■ **OPPOSITE:** uneven **5** *an unfailingly regular procedure* = **methodical**, set, ordered, formal, steady, efficient, systematic, orderly, standardized, dependable, consistent ■ **OPPOSITE:** inconsistent **6** *The regular method is to take your cutting, and insert it into the compost.* = **official**, standard, established, traditional, classic, correct, approved, formal, sanctioned, proper, prevailing, orthodox, time-honoured, bona fide

regulate VERB **1** *a powerful body to regulate the stock market* = **control**, run, order, rule, manage, direct, guide, handle, conduct, arrange, monitor, organize, govern, administer, oversee, supervise, systematize, superintend **2** *He breathed deeply, trying to regulate the pound of his heartbeat.* = **moderate**, control, modulate, settle, fit, balance, tune, adjust

regulation NOUN **1** *new safety regulations* = **rule**, order, law, direction, procedure, requirement, dictate, decree, canon, statute, ordinance, commandment, edict, precept, standing order **2** *They also have responsibility for the regulation of nurseries.* = **control**, government, management, administration, direction, arrangement, supervision, governance, rule ▶ MODIFIER *He wears the regulation dark suit of corporate America.* = **conventional**, official, standard, required, normal, usual, prescribed, mandatory, customary

regurgitate VERB = **disgorge**, throw up (*informal*), chuck up (*slang, chiefly U.S.*), puke up (*slang*), sick up (*informal*), spew out or up

rehabilitate VERB **1** *Considerable efforts have been made to rehabilitate patients.* = **reintegrate 2** *a program for rehabilitating low-income housing* = **restore**, convert, renew, adjust, change, rebuild, make good, mend, renovate, reconstruct, reinstate, re-establish, fix up (*informal, chiefly U.S. & Canad.*), reconstitute, recondition, reinvigorate

rehash NOUN *It was a rehash of an old script.* = **reworking**, rewrite, new version, rearrangement ▶ VERB *The tour seems to rely heavily on rehashed old favourites.* = **rework**, rewrite, rearrange, change, alter, reshuffle, make over, reuse, rejig (*informal*), refashion

rehearsal NOUN = **practice**, rehearsing, practice session, run-through, reading, preparation, drill (*informal*), going-over (*informal*)

rehearse VERB **1** *A group of actors are rehearsing a play about Joan of Arc.* = **practise**, prepare, run through, go over, train, act,

study, ready, repeat, drill, try out, recite **2** *Anticipate any tough questions and rehearse your answers.* = **recite**, practise, go over, run through, tell, list, detail, describe, review, relate, depict, spell out, recount, narrate, trot out (*informal*), delineate, enumerate

reign VERB **1** *A relative calm reigned over the city.* = **be supreme**, prevail, predominate, hold sway, be rife, be rampant **2** *Henry II, who reigned from 1154 to 1189* = **rule**, govern, be in power, occupy or sit on the throne, influence, command, administer, hold sway, wear the crown, wield the sceptre ▶ NOUN *Queen Victoria's reign* = **rule**, sovereignty, supremacy, power, control, influence, command, empire, monarchy, sway, dominion, hegemony, ascendancy

USAGE The words rein and reign should not be confused; note the correct spellings in *he gave full rein to his feelings* (not *reign*); and it will be necessary to rein in *public spending* (not *reign in*).

reimburse VERB = **pay back**, refund, repay, recompense, return, restore, compensate, indemnify, remunerate (*formal*)

rein NOUN *He wrapped his horse's reins round his left wrist.* = **control**, harness, bridle, hold, check, restriction, brake, curb, restraint • **give (a) free rein to something** *or* **someone** *They gave him a free rein with time to mould a decent side.* = **give a free hand (to)**, give carte blanche (to), give a blank cheque (to), remove restraints (from), indulge, let go, give way (to), give (someone) their head • **rein something in** *or* **back** *He promised the government would rein back inflation.* = **check**, control, limit, contain, master, curb, restrain, hold back, constrain, bridle, keep in check

reincarnation NOUN = **rebirth**, metempsychosis, transmigration of souls

reinforce VERB **1** *They had to reinforce the walls with exterior beams.* = **support**, strengthen, fortify, toughen, stress, prop, supplement, emphasize, underline, harden, bolster, stiffen, shore up, buttress **2** *Troops and police have been reinforced.* = **increase**, extend, add to, strengthen, supplement, augment

reinforcement NOUN **1** *the reinforcement of peace and security around the world* = **strengthening**, increase, supplement, enlargement, fortification, amplification, augmentation **2** *There are reinforcements on all doors.* = **support**, stay, shore, prop, brace, buttress **3** (*plural*) *troop reinforcements* = **reserves**, support, auxiliaries, additional or fresh troops

reinstate VERB = **restore**, recall, bring back, re-establish, return, rehabilitate

reiterate VERB = **repeat**, restate, say again, retell, do again, recapitulate, iterate

reject VERB **1** *people who have been rejected by their lovers* = **rebuff**, drop, jilt, desert, turn down, ditch (*slang*), break with, spurn, refuse, say no to, repulse, throw over, unfollow, unfriend ■ **OPPOSITE:** accept **2** *Paloma has rejected the values of her rich parents.* = **deny**, decline, abandon, exclude, veto, discard, relinquish, renounce, spurn, eschew, leave off, throw off, disallow, forsake, retract, repudiate, cast off, disown, forgo, disclaim, forswear, swear off, wash your hands of ■ **OPPOSITE:** approve **3** *Seventeen publishers rejected the manuscript.* = **discard**, decline, eliminate, scrap, bin, jettison, cast aside, throw away or out ■ **OPPOSITE:** accept ► NOUN **1** *a hat that looks like a reject from an army patrol* = **castoff**, second, discard, flotsam, clunker (*informal*) ■ **OPPOSITE:** treasure **2** *I'm an outsider, a reject, a social failure.; a reject of Real Madrid* = **failure**, loser, flop (*informal*)

rejection NOUN **1** *his rejection of our values* = **denial**, veto, dismissal, exclusion, abandonment, spurning, casting off, disowning, thumbs down, renunciation, repudiation, eschewal ■ **OPPOSITE:** approval **2** *These feelings of rejection and hurt remain.* = **rebuff**, refusal, knock-back (*slang*), kick in the teeth (*slang*), bum's rush (*slang*), the (old) heave-ho (*informal*), brushoff (*slang*) ■ **OPPOSITE:** acceptance

rejoice VERB = **be glad**, celebrate, delight, be happy, joy, triumph, glory, revel, be overjoyed, exult, jump for joy, make merry ■ **OPPOSITE:** lament

rejoicing NOUN = **happiness**, delight, joy, triumph, celebration, cheer, festivity, elation, gaiety, jubilation, revelry, exultation, gladness, merrymaking

rejoin VERB = **reply**, answer, respond, retort, come back with, riposte, return

rejuvenate VERB = **revitalize**, restore, renew, refresh, regenerate, breathe new life into, reinvigorate, revivify, give new life to, reanimate, make young again, restore vitality to

relapse VERB **1** *He was relapsing into his usual gloom.* = **lapse**, revert, degenerate, slip back, fail, weaken, fall back, regress, backslide, retrogress **2** *In 90 per cent of cases the patient will relapse within six months.* = **worsen**, deteriorate, sicken, weaken, fail, sink, fade ■ **OPPOSITE:** recover ► NOUN **1** *a relapse into the nationalism of the nineteenth century* = **lapse**, regression, fall from grace, reversion, backsliding, recidivism, retrogression **2** *The sufferer can experience frequent relapses.* = **worsening**, setback, deterioration, recurrence, turn for the worse, weakening ■ **OPPOSITE:** recovery

relate VERB *He was relating a story he had once heard.* = **tell**, recount, report, present, detail, describe, chronicle, rehearse, recite, impart, narrate, set forth, give an account of • **relate to something** or **someone 1** *papers relating to the children* = **concern**, refer to, apply to, have to do with, pertain to, be relevant to, bear upon, appertain to, have reference to **2** *how language relates to particular cultural codes* = **connect with**, associate with, link with, couple with, join with, ally with, correlate to, coordinate with

related ADJECTIVE **1** *equipment and accessories for diving and related activities* = **associated**, linked, allied, joint, accompanying, connected, affiliated, akin, correlated, interconnected, concomitant, cognate, agnate ■ **OPPOSITE:** unconnected **2** *He is related by marriage to some of the complainants.* = **akin**, kin, kindred, cognate, consanguineous, agnate ■ **OPPOSITE:** unrelated

relation NOUN **1** *This theory bears no relation to reality.* = **similarity**, link, bearing, bond, application, comparison, tie-in, correlation, interdependence, pertinence, connection **2** *I call him Uncle though he's no relation.* = **relative**, kin, kinsman or woman or person, rellie (*Austral. slang*) ► PLURAL NOUN **1** *The company has a track record of good employee relations.* = **dealings**, relationship, rapport, communications, meetings, terms, associations, affairs, contact, connections, interaction, intercourse, liaison **2** *All my relations come from Wales.* = **family**, relatives, tribe, clan, kin, kindred, kinsfolk, ainga (*N.Z.*), rellies (*Austral. slang*)

relationship NOUN **1** *Money problems place great stress on close family relationships.* = **association**, bond, communications, connection, conjunction, affinity, rapport, kinship **2** *She likes to have a relationship with her leading men.* = **affair**, romance, liaison, amour, intrigue **3** *the relationship between culture and power* = **connection**, link, proportion, parallel, ratio, similarity, tie-up, correlation, read-across

relative NOUN *Do relatives of yours still live in Siberia?* = **relation**, connection, kinsman or woman or person, member of your or the family, cuzzie or cuzzie-bro (*N.Z.*), rellie (*Austral. slang*) ► ADJECTIVE **1** *a period of relative calm* = **comparative 2** *the relative importance of education in 50 countries* = **corresponding**, respective, reciprocal

3 (*with* **to**) *The satellite remains in one spot relative to the earth's surface.* = **in proportion to**, corresponding to, proportionate to, proportional to

relatively ADVERB = **comparatively**, rather, somewhat, to some extent, in or by comparison

relax VERB **1** *I ought to relax and stop worrying about it.* = **be** or **feel at ease**, chill out (*slang, chiefly U.S.*), take it easy, loosen up, laze, lighten up (*slang*), put your feet up, hang loose (*slang*), let yourself go (*informal*), let your hair down (*informal*), mellow out (*informal*), make yourself at home, outspan (*S. African*), take your ease ■ **OPPOSITE:** be alarmed **2** *Do something that you know relaxes you.* = **calm down**, calm, unwind, loosen up, tranquillize **3** *Massage is used to relax muscles.* = **make less tense**, soften, loosen up, unbend, rest **4** *He gradually relaxed his grip on the arms of the chair.* = **lessen**, reduce, ease, relieve, weaken, loosen, let up, slacken ■ **OPPOSITE:** tighten **5** *Rules governing student conduct have been relaxed in recent years.* = **moderate**, ease, relieve, weaken, diminish, mitigate, slacken ■ **OPPOSITE:** tighten up

relaxation NOUN **1** *You should be able to find the odd moment for relaxation.* = **leisure**, rest, fun, pleasure, entertainment, recreation, enjoyment, amusement, refreshment, beer and skittles (*informal*), me-time **2** *There will be no relaxation of army pressure.* = **lessening**, easing, reduction, weakening, moderation, let-up (*informal*), slackening, diminution, abatement

relaxed ADJECTIVE **1** *Try to adopt a more relaxed manner.* = **easy-going**, easy, casual, informal, laid-back (*informal*), mellow, leisurely, downbeat (*informal*), unhurried, nonchalant, free and easy, mild, insouciant, untaxing, chilled (*informal*) **2** *The atmosphere at lunch was relaxed.* = **comfortable**, easy-going, casual, laid-back (*informal*), informal, chilled (*informal*)

relay VERB = **broadcast**, carry, spread, communicate, transmit, send out, stream

release VERB **1** *He was released from custody the next day.* = **set free**, free, discharge, liberate, drop, deliver, loose, let go, undo, let out, extricate, untie, disengage, emancipate, unchain, unfasten, turn loose, unshackle, unloose, unfetter, unbridle, manumit ■ **OPPOSITE:** imprison **2** *He wants to be released from any promise between us.* = **acquit**, excuse, exempt, let go, dispense, let off, exonerate, absolve **3** *They're not releasing any more details yet.* = **issue**, publish, make public, make known, break, present,

launch, distribute, unveil, put out, circulate, disseminate ■ **OPPOSITE:** withhold ▶ NOUN **1** *the secret negotiations necessary to secure the release of the hostages* = **liberation**, freedom, delivery, liberty, discharge, emancipation, deliverance, manumission, relief ■ **OPPOSITE:** imprisonment **2** *a blessed release from the obligation to work* = **acquittal**, exemption, let-off (*informal*), dispensation, absolution, exoneration, acquittance **3** *a meeting held after the release of the report* = **issue**, announcement, publication, proclamation, offering

relegate VERB **1** *Other newspapers relegated the item to the middle pages.* = **demote**, degrade, downgrade, declass **2** *a team about to be relegated to the second division* = **banish**, exile, expel, throw out, oust, deport, eject, expatriate

relent VERB **1** *Finally his mother relented.* = **be merciful**, yield, give in, soften, give way, come round, capitulate, acquiesce, change your mind, unbend, forbear, show mercy, have pity, melt, give quarter ■ **OPPOSITE:** show no mercy **2** *If the bad weather relents the game will be finished today.* = **ease**, die down, let up, fall, drop, slow, relax, weaken, slacken ■ **OPPOSITE:** intensify

relentless ADJECTIVE **1** *He was the most relentless enemy I have ever known.* = **merciless**, hard, fierce, harsh, cruel, grim, ruthless, uncompromising, unstoppable, inflexible, unrelenting, unforgiving, inexorable, implacable, unyielding, remorseless, pitiless, undeviating ■ **OPPOSITE:** merciful **2** *The pressure now was relentless.* = **unremitting**, sustained, punishing, persistent, unstoppable, unbroken, unrelenting, incessant, unabated, nonstop, unrelieved, unflagging, unfaltering

relevant ADJECTIVE = **significant**, appropriate, proper, related, fitting, material, suited, relative, to the point, apt, applicable, pertinent, apposite, admissible, germane, to the purpose, appurtenant, ad rem (*Latin*) ■ **OPPOSITE:** irrelevant

reliable ADJECTIVE **1** *She was efficient and reliable.* = **dependable**, trustworthy, honest, responsible, sure, sound, true, certain, regular, stable, faithful, predictable, upright, staunch, reputable, trusty, unfailing, tried and true ■ **OPPOSITE:** unreliable **2** *They have a reputation for building some of the most reliable cars on the road.* = **safe**, dependable **3** *There is no reliable evidence.* = **definitive**, sound, dependable, trustworthy

reliance NOUN 1 *the country's increasing reliance on foreign aid* = **dependency**, dependence 2 *If you respond immediately, you will guarantee people's reliance on you.* = **trust**, confidence, belief, faith, assurance, credence, credit

relic NOUN = **remnant**, vestige, memento, trace, survival, scrap, token, fragment, souvenir, remembrance, keepsake

relief NOUN 1 *The news will come as a great relief.* = **ease**, release, comfort, cure, remedy, solace, balm, deliverance, mitigation, abatement, alleviation, easement, palliation, assuagement 2 *a self-help programme which can give lasting relief* = **rest**, respite, let-up (*informal*), relaxation, break, diversion, refreshment (*informal*), remission, breather (*informal*) 3 *famine relief* = **aid**, help, support, assistance, sustenance, succour

relieve VERB 1 *Drugs can relieve much of the pain.* = **ease**, soothe, alleviate, allay, relax, comfort, calm, cure, dull, diminish, soften, console, appease, solace, mitigate, abate, assuage, mollify, salve, palliate ■ **OPPOSITE:** intensify 2 *He felt relieved of a burden.* = **free**, release, deliver, discharge, exempt, unburden, disembarrass, disencumber 3 *At seven o'clock the night nurse came in to relieve her.* = **take over from**, substitute for, stand in for, take the place of, give (someone) a break or rest 4 *a programme to relieve poor countries* = **help**, support, aid, sustain, assist, succour, bring aid to

religion NOUN = **belief**, faith, theology, creed

religious ADJECTIVE 1 *different religious beliefs* = **spiritual**, holy, sacred, divine, theological, righteous, sectarian, doctrinal, devotional, scriptural 2 *The clientele turned up, with religious regularity, every night.* = **conscientious**, exact, faithful, rigid, rigorous, meticulous, scrupulous, fastidious, unerring, unswerving, punctilious (*formal*)

relinquish VERB = **give up**, leave, release, drop, abandon, resign, desert, quit, yield, hand over, surrender, withdraw from, let go, retire from, renounce, waive, vacate, say goodbye to, forsake, cede, repudiate, cast off, forgo, abdicate, kiss (something) goodbye, lay aside

relish VERB 1 *He ate quietly, relishing his meal.* = **enjoy**, like, prefer, taste, appreciate, savour, revel in, luxuriate in ■ **OPPOSITE:** dislike 2 *She is not relishing the prospect of another spell in prison.* = **look forward to**, fancy (*informal*), delight in, lick your lips over ▸ NOUN 1 *The three men ate with relish.* = **enjoyment**, liking, love, taste, fancy, stomach, appetite, appreciation, penchant, zest, fondness, gusto, predilection, zing (*informal*), partiality ■ **OPPOSITE:** distaste 2 *pots of spicy relish* = **condiment**, seasoning, sauce, appetizer

reluctance NOUN = **unwillingness**, dislike, loathing, distaste, aversion, backwardness, hesitancy, disinclination, repugnance, indisposition, disrelish

reluctant ADJECTIVE = **unwilling**, slow, backward, grudging, hesitant, averse, recalcitrant, loath, disinclined, unenthusiastic, indisposed ■ **OPPOSITE:** willing

> **USAGE** *Reticent* is quite commonly used nowadays as a synonym of *reluctant* and followed by *to* and a verb. In careful writing it is advisable to avoid this use, since many people would regard it as mistaken.

rely on VERB 1 *They relied heavily on the advice of their advisors.* = **depend on**, lean on 2 *I know I can rely on you to sort it out.* = **be confident of**, bank on, trust, count on, bet on, reckon on, lean on, be sure of, have confidence in, swear by, repose trust in

remain VERB 1 *The three men remained silent.* = **stay**, continue, go on, stand, dwell (*formal, literary*), bide 2 *He remained at home with his family.* = **stay behind**, wait, delay, stay put, tarry ■ **OPPOSITE:** go 3 *There remains deep mistrust of his government.* = **continue**, be left, endure, persist, linger, hang in the air, stay

remainder NOUN = **rest**, remains, balance, trace, excess, surplus, butt, remnant, relic, residue, stub, vestige(s), tail end, dregs, oddment, leavings, residuum

remaining ADJECTIVE 1 *Stir in the remaining ingredients.* = **left-over**, surviving, outstanding, lingering, unfinished, residual 2 *They wanted to purge remaining memories of his reign.* = **surviving**, lasting, persisting, abiding, extant

remains PLURAL NOUN 1 *the remains of their picnic* = **remnants**, leftovers, remainder, scraps, rest, pieces, balance, traces, fragments, debris, residue, crumbs, vestiges, detritus, dregs, odds and ends, oddments, leavings 2 *There are Roman remains all around us.* = **relics** 3 *The remains of a man had been found.* = **corpse**, body, carcass, cadaver

remark VERB 1 *I remarked that I would go shopping that afternoon.* = **comment**, say, state, reflect, mention, declare, observe, pass comment, animadvert 2 *Everyone has* remarked what a lovely person she is. = **notice**, note, observe, perceive, see, mark, regard, make out, heed, espy, take note or notice of ▶ NOUN **1** She has made outspoken remarks on the issue. = **comment**, observation, reflection, statement, thought, word, opinion, declaration, assertion, utterance **2** He had never found the situation worthy of remark. = **notice**, thought, comment, attention, regard, mention, recognition, consideration, observation, heed, acknowledgment

remarkable ADJECTIVE = **extraordinary**, striking, outstanding, famous, odd, strange, wonderful, signal, rare, unusual, impressive, surprising, distinguished, prominent, notable, phenomenal, uncommon, conspicuous, singular, miraculous, noteworthy, pre-eminent ■ **OPPOSITE:** ordinary

remedy NOUN **1** a remedy for economic ills = **solution**, relief, redress, antidote, corrective, panacea, countermeasure **2** natural remedies to overcome winter infections = **cure**, treatment, specific, medicine, therapy, antidote, panacea, restorative, relief, nostrum, physic (rare), medicament, counteractive ▶ VERB **1** A great deal has been done to remedy the situation. = **put right**, redress, rectify, reform, fix, correct, solve, repair, relieve, ameliorate, set to rights **2** He's been remedying a hamstring injury. = **cure**, treat, heal, help, control, ease, restore, relieve, soothe, alleviate, mitigate, assuage, palliate

remember VERB **1** He was remembering the old days. = **recall**, think back to, recollect, reminisce about, retain, recognize, call up, summon up, call to mind ■ **OPPOSITE:** forget **2** Remember that each person reacts differently. = **bear in mind**, keep in mind **3** He is remembered for being bad at games. = **look back (on)**, commemorate

remembrance NOUN **1** They wore black in remembrance of those who had died. = **commemoration**, memorial, testimonial **2** As a remembrance, he left a photo album. = **souvenir**, token, reminder, monument, relic, remembrancer (archaic), memento, keepsake **3** He had clung to the remembrance of things past. = **memory**, recollection, thought, recall, recognition, retrospect, reminiscence, anamnesis

remind VERB Can you remind me to buy a bottle of milk? = **jog your memory**, prompt, refresh your memory, make you remember • **remind someone of something** or **someone** She reminds me of the wife of the pilot. = **bring to mind**, call to mind, put in

mind, awaken memories of, call up, bring back to

reminisce VERB = **recall**, remember, look back, hark back, review, think back, recollect, live in the past, go over in the memory

reminiscences PLURAL NOUN = **recollections**, memories, reflections, retrospections, reviews, recalls, memoirs, anecdotes, remembrances

reminiscent ADJECTIVE = **suggestive**, evocative, redolent, remindful, similar

remission NOUN **1** The disease is in remission. = **lessening**, abatement, abeyance, lull, relaxation, ebb, respite, moderation, let-up (informal), alleviation, amelioration **2** It had been raining hard all day, without remission. = **reduction**, lessening, suspension, decrease, diminution **3** I've got 10 years and there's no remission for drug offenders. = **pardon**, release, discharge, amnesty, forgiveness, indulgence, exemption, reprieve, acquittal, absolution, exoneration, excuse

remit NOUN That issue is not within the remit of the group. = **instructions**, brief, guidelines, authorization, terms of reference, orders ▶ VERB **1** Many immigrants regularly remit money to their families. = **send**, post, forward, mail, transmit, dispatch **2** Every creditor shall remit the claim that is held against a neighbour. = **cancel**, stop, halt, repeal, rescind, desist, forbear **3** an episode of 'baby blues' which eventually remitted = **lessen**, diminish, abate, ease up, reduce, relax, moderate, weaken, decrease, soften, dwindle, alleviate, wane, fall away, mitigate, slacken

remittance NOUN = **payment**, fee, consideration, allowance

remnant NOUN = **remainder**, remains, trace, fragment, end, bit, rest, piece, balance, survival, scrap, butt, shred, hangover, residue, rump, leftovers, stub, vestige, tail end, oddment, residuum

remonstrate VERB = **protest**, challenge, argue, take issue, object, complain, dispute, dissent, take exception, expostulate

remorse NOUN = **regret**, shame, guilt, pity, grief, compassion, sorrow, anguish, repentance, contrition, compunction, penitence, self-reproach, pangs of conscience, ruefulness, bad or guilty conscience

remorseless ADJECTIVE = **pitiless**, hard, harsh, cruel, savage, ruthless, callous, merciless, unforgiving, implacable, inhumane, unmerciful, hardhearted, uncompassionate

r

remote ADJECTIVE **1** *a remote farm in the hills* = **distant**, far, isolated, lonely, out-of-the-way, far-off, secluded, inaccessible, faraway, outlying, in the middle of nowhere, off the beaten track, backwoods, godforsaken ■ **OPPOSITE:** nearby **2** *particular events in the remote past* = **far**, distant, obscure, far-off **3** *The chances of his surviving are pretty remote.* = **slight**, small, outside, poor, unlikely, slim, faint, doubtful, dubious, slender, meagre, negligible, implausible, inconsiderable ■ **OPPOSITE:** strong **4** *She looked so remote.* = **aloof**, cold, removed, reserved, withdrawn, distant, abstracted, detached, indifferent, faraway, introspective, uninterested, introverted, uninvolved, unapproachable, uncommunicative, standoffish ■ **OPPOSITE:** outgoing

removal NOUN **1** *the removal of a small lump* = **extraction**, stripping, withdrawal, purging, abstraction, uprooting, displacement, eradication, erasure, subtraction, dislodgment, expunction, taking away *or* off *or* out **2** *His removal from power was illegal.* = **dismissal**, expulsion, elimination, ejection, dispossession **3** *Home removals are best done in cool weather.* = **move**, transfer, departure, relocation, flitting (*Scot. & Northern English, dialect*)

remove VERB **1** *Remove the cake from the oven.* = **take out**, withdraw, extract, abstract ■ **OPPOSITE:** insert **2** *He removed his jacket.* = **take off**, doff ■ **OPPOSITE:** put on **3** *This treatment removes the most stubborn stains.* = **erase**, eliminate, take out **4** *The senate voted to remove him.* = **dismiss**, eliminate, get rid of, discharge, abolish, expel, throw out, oust, relegate, purge, eject, do away with, depose, unseat, see the back of, dethrone, show someone the door, give the bum's rush (*slang*), throw out on your ear (*informal*) ■ **OPPOSITE:** appoint **5** *Most of her fears have been removed.* = **get rid of**, wipe out, erase, eradicate, blow away (*slang, chiefly U.S.*), blot out, expunge **6** *They tried to remove the barricades which had been erected.* = **take away**, move, pull, transfer, detach, displace, do away with, dislodge, cart off (*slang*), carry off *or* away ■ **OPPOSITE:** put back **7** *They intend to remove up to 100 offensive words.* = **delete**, shed, get rid of, erase, excise, strike out, efface, expunge (*formal*) **8** *They removed to America.* = **move**, transfer, transport, shift, quit, depart, move away, relocate, vacate, flit (*Scot. & Northern English, dialect*) **9** *If someone irritates you, remove him, destroy him.* = **kill**, murder, do in (*slang*), eliminate, take out (*slang*), get rid

of, execute, wipe out, dispose of, assassinate, do away with, liquidate, bump off (*slang*), wipe from the face of the earth

remuneration NOUN = **payment**, income, earnings, salary, pay, return, profit, fee, wages, reward, compensation, repayment, reparation, indemnity, retainer, reimbursement, recompense, stipend, emolument, meed (*archaic*)

renaissance *or* **renascence** NOUN = **rebirth**, revival, restoration, renewal, awakening, resurrection, regeneration, resurgence, reappearance, new dawn, re-emergence, reawakening, new birth

rend VERB = **tear**, break, split, rip, pull, separate, divide, crack, burst, smash, disturb, shatter, pierce, fracture, sever, wrench, splinter, rupture, cleave, lacerate, rive, tear to pieces, sunder (*literary*), dissever

render VERB **1** *It has so many errors as to render it useless.* = **make**, cause to become, leave **2** *Any assistance you can render him will be helpful.* = **provide**, give, show, pay, present, supply, deliver, contribute, yield, submit, tender, hand out, furnish, turn over, make available **3** *The Board was slow to render its verdict.* = **deliver**, give, return, announce, pronounce **4** *150 Psalms rendered into English* = **translate**, put, explain, interpret, reproduce, transcribe, construe, restate **5** (*sometimes followed by* **up**) *I render up my soul to God.* = **give up**, give, deliver, yield, hand over, surrender, turn over, relinquish, cede **6** *a powerful, bizarre, and beautifully rendered story* = **represent**, interpret, portray, depict, do, give, play, act, present, perform

rendezvous NOUN **1** *I had decided to keep my rendezvous with him.* = **appointment**, meeting, date, engagement, tryst (*archaic*), assignation **2** *Their rendezvous would be the hotel at the airport.* = **meeting place**, venue, gathering point, place of assignation, trysting-place (*archaic*) ▶ VERB *The plan was to rendezvous on Sunday afternoon.* = **meet**, assemble, get together, come together, collect, gather, rally, muster, converge, join up, be reunited

rendition NOUN **1** *The musicians broke into a rousing rendition of the song.* = **performance**, arrangement, interpretation, rendering, take (*informal, chiefly U.S.*), reading, version, delivery, presentation, execution, portrayal, depiction **2** *a rendition of the works of Conrad* = **translation**, reading, version, construction (*formal*), explanation, interpretation, transcription

renegade NOUN *He was a renegade – a traitor.*
= **deserter**, rebel, betrayer, dissident,
outlaw, runaway, traitor, defector,
mutineer, turncoat, apostate, backslider,
recreant (*archaic*) ▶ MODIFIER *The renegade
police officer supplied details of the murder.*
= **traitorous**, rebel, dissident, outlaw,
runaway, rebellious, unfaithful, disloyal,
backsliding, mutinous, apostate, recreant
(*archaic*)

renege VERB = **break your word**, go back,
welsh (*slang*), default, back out, repudiate,
break a promise

renew VERB **1** *He renewed his attack on
government policy.* = **recommence**,
continue, extend, repeat, resume, prolong,
reopen, recreate, reaffirm, re-establish,
rejuvenate, regenerate, restate, begin
again, revitalize, bring up to date
2 *They renewed their friendship.* = **reaffirm**,
resume, breathe new life into, recommence
3 *Cells are constantly renewed.* = **replace**,
refresh, replenish, restock **4** *the cost of
renewing the buildings* = **restore**, repair,
transform, overhaul, mend, refurbish,
renovate, refit, fix up (*informal, chiefly
U.S. & Canad.*), modernize

renounce VERB **1** *She renounced terrorism.*
= **disown**, reject, abandon, quit, discard,
spurn, eschew, leave off, throw off,
forsake, retract, repudiate, cast off,
abstain from, recant, forswear, abjure,
swear off, wash your hands of **2** *He
renounced his claim to the throne.* = **disclaim**,
deny, decline, give up, resign, relinquish,
waive, renege, forgo, abdicate, abjure,
abnegate ■ **OPPOSITE:** assert

renovate VERB = **restore**, repair, refurbish,
do up (*informal*), reform, renew, overhaul,
revamp, recreate, remodel, rehabilitate,
refit, fix up (*informal, chiefly U.S. & Canad.*),
modernize, reconstitute, recondition

renown NOUN = **fame**, note, distinction,
repute, mark, reputation, honour, glory,
celebrity, acclaim, stardom, eminence,
lustre, illustriousness

renowned ADJECTIVE = **famous**, noted,
celebrated, well-known, distinguished,
esteemed, acclaimed, notable, eminent,
famed, illustrious ■ **OPPOSITE:** unknown

rent¹ VERB **1** *He rented a car.* = **hire**, lease
2 *She rented rooms to university students.* = **let**,
lease ▶ NOUN *She worked to pay the rent.*
= **hire**, rental, lease, tariff, fee, payment

rent² NOUN **1** *a small rent in the silk* = **tear**,
split, rip, slash, slit, gash, perforation,
hole **2** *welling up from a rent in the ground*
= **opening**, break, hole, crack, breach,
flaw, chink

renunciation NOUN **1** *a renunciation of
terrorism* = **rejection**, giving up, denial,
abandonment, spurning, abstention,
repudiation, forswearing, disavowal,
abnegation, eschewal, abjuration
2 *the renunciation of territory* = **giving up**,
resignation, surrender, waiver, disclaimer,
abdication, relinquishment, abjuration

repair¹ VERB **1** *He has repaired the roof.*
= **mend**, fix, recover, restore, heal, renew,
patch, make good, renovate, patch up, put
back together, restore to working order
■ **OPPOSITE:** damage **2** *They needed to repair
the damage done by the interview.* = **put right**,
make up for, compensate for, rectify,
square, retrieve, redress ▶ NOUN **1** *Many of
the buildings are in need of repair.* = **mending**,
restoration, overhaul, adjustment **2** *She
spotted a couple of obvious repairs in the dress.*
= **darn**, mend, patch **3** *The road was in bad
repair.* = **condition**, state, form, shape
(*informal*), nick (*informal*), fettle

repair² VERB *We repaired to the pavilion for
lunch.* = **go**, retire, withdraw, head for,
move, remove, leave for, set off for, betake
yourself

reparation NOUN = **compensation**,
damages, repair, satisfaction, amends,
renewal, redress, indemnity, restitution,
atonement, recompense, propitiation,
requital

repay VERB **1** *It will take 30 years to repay the
loan.* = **pay back**, refund, settle up, return,
square, restore, compensate, reimburse,
recompense, requite, remunerate (*formal*)
2 *How can I ever repay such kindness?*
= **reward**, make restitution

repeal VERB *The government has just repealed
that law.* = **abolish**, reverse, revoke, annul,
recall, withdraw, cancel, set aside, rescind,
invalidate, nullify, obviate, abrogate,
countermand, declare null and void
■ **OPPOSITE:** pass ▶ NOUN *a repeal of the age
of consent law* = **abolition**, withdrawal,
cancellation, rescinding, annulment,
revocation, nullification, abrogation,
rescission, invalidation, rescindment
■ **OPPOSITE:** passing

repeat VERB **1** *He repeated that he had been
misquoted.* = **reiterate** (*formal*), restate,
recapitulate, iterate **2** *I repeated the story to
a delighted audience.* = **retell**, relate, quote,
renew, echo, replay, reproduce, rehearse,
recite, duplicate, redo, rerun, reshow
▶ NOUN **1** *a repeat of Wednesday's massive
protests* = **repetition**, echo, duplicate,
reiteration, recapitulation **2** *There's nothing
except repeats on TV.* = **rerun**, replay,
reproduction, reshowing

r

USAGE Since the sense of *again* is already contained within the *re-* part of the word *repeat*, it is unnecessary to say that something is *repeated again*.

repeatedly ADVERB = **over and over**, often, frequently, many times, again and again, time and (time) again, time after time, many a time and oft (*archaic, poetic*)

repel VERB **1** *troops ready to repel an attack* = **drive off**, fight, refuse, check, decline, reject, oppose, resist, confront, parry, hold off, rebuff, ward off, beat off, repulse, keep at arm's length, put to flight ■ **OPPOSITE:** submit to **2** *excitement which frightened and repelled her* = **disgust**, offend, revolt, sicken, nauseate, put you off, make you sick, gross you out (*U.S. slang*), turn you off (*informal*), make you shudder, turn your stomach, give you the creeps (*informal*) ■ **OPPOSITE:** delight

repellent ADJECTIVE **1** *She still found the place repellent.* = **disgusting**, offensive, revolting, obscene, sickening, distasteful, horrid (*informal*), obnoxious, repulsive, noxious, nauseating, odious, hateful, repugnant, off-putting (*Brit. informal*), loathsome, abhorrent, abominable, cringe-making (*Brit. informal*), yucky *or* yukky (*slang*), yucko (*Austral. slang*), discouraging **2** *a shower repellent jacket* = **proof**, resistant, repelling, impermeable

repent VERB = **regret**, lament, rue (*literary*), sorrow, be sorry about, deplore, be ashamed of, relent, atone for, be contrite about, feel remorse about, reproach yourself for, see the error of your ways, show penitence

repentance NOUN = **regret**, guilt, grief, sorrow, remorse, contrition, compunction, penitence, self-reproach, sackcloth and ashes, sorriness

repercussion NOUN (*often plural*) = **consequences**, result, side effects, backlash, sequel

repertoire NOUN = **range**, list, stock, supply, store, collection, repertory, repository

repertory NOUN = **repertoire**, list, range, stock, supply, store, collection, repository

repetition NOUN **1** *He wants to avoid repetition of the confusion.* = **recurrence**, repeating, reappearance, duplication, echo **2** *He could have cut much of the repetition and saved pages.* = **repeating**, redundancy, replication, duplication, restatement, iteration, reiteration, tautology, recapitulation, repetitiousness

repetitive ADJECTIVE = **monotonous**, boring, dull, mechanical, tedious, recurrent, unchanging, samey (*informal*), unvaried

replace VERB **1** *the man who deposed and replaced him* = **take the place of**, follow, succeed, oust, take over from, supersede, supplant, stand in lieu of, fill (someone's) shoes *or* boots, step into (someone's) shoes *or* boots **2** *Replace that liquid with salt, sugar and water.* = **substitute**, change, exchange, switch, swap, commute **3** *Replace the caps on the bottles.* = **put back**, restore

replacement NOUN **1** *the replacement of damaged or lost books* = **replacing** **2** *a replacement for the injured player* = **successor**, double, substitute, stand-in, fill-in, proxy, surrogate, understudy

replenish VERB **1** *He went to replenish her glass.* = **fill**, top up, refill, replace, renew, furnish ■ **OPPOSITE:** empty **2** *stock to replenish the shelves* = **refill**, provide, stock, supply, fill, make up, restore, top up, reload, restock, refresh

replete ADJECTIVE **1** *The harbour was replete with boats.* = **filled**, stuffed, jammed, crammed, abounding, brimming, teeming, glutted, well-stocked, jam-packed, well-provided, chock-full, brimful, full to bursting, charged ■ **OPPOSITE:** empty **2** *replete after a heavy lunch* = **sated**, full, gorged, full up, satiated ■ **OPPOSITE:** hungry

replica NOUN **1** *It was a replica, for display only.* = **reproduction**, model, copy, imitation, facsimile, carbon copy ■ **OPPOSITE:** original **2** *The child was a replica of her mother.* = **duplicate**, copy, carbon copy

replicate VERB = **copy**, follow, repeat, reproduce, recreate, ape, mimic, duplicate, reduplicate

reply VERB *He replied that this was absolutely impossible.* = **answer**, respond, retort, return, come back, counter, acknowledge, react, echo, rejoin, retaliate, write back, reciprocate, riposte, make an answer ▶ NOUN *They went ahead without waiting for a reply.* = **answer**, response, reaction, counter, echo, comeback (*informal*), retort, retaliation, acknowledgment, riposte, counterattack, return, rejoinder, reciprocation

report VERB **1** *I reported the theft to the police.* = **inform of**, communicate, announce, mention, declare, recount, give an account of, bring word on **2** (*often with* **on**) *Several newspapers reported the decision.* = **communicate**, publish, record, announce, tell, state, air, detail, describe, note, cover, document, give an account of, relate, broadcast, post, tweet, pass on, proclaim, circulate, relay, recite, narrate, write up **3** *None of them had reported for duty.* = **present yourself**, come, appear, arrive, turn up, be present, show up (*informal*), clock in or on ▶ NOUN **1** *Press reports vary dramatically.* = **article**, story, dispatch, piece, message, communiqué, write-up **2** *a full report of what happened here tonight* = **account**, record, detail, note, statement, relation, version, communication, tale, description, declaration, narrative, summary, recital **3** (*often plural*) *There were no reports of casualties.* = **news**, word, information, announcement, tidings **4** *There was a loud report as the fuel tanks exploded.* = **bang**, sound, crash, crack, noise, blast, boom, explosion, discharge, detonation, reverberation **5** *According to report, she made an impact at the party.* = **rumour**, talk, buzz, gossip, goss (*informal*), hearsay, scuttlebutt (*U.S. slang*) **6** *He is true, manly, and of good report.* = **repute**, character, regard, reputation, fame, esteem, eminence

reporter NOUN = **journalist**, writer, correspondent, newscaster, hack (*derogatory*), pressman or presswoman, journo (*slang*), newshound (*informal*), newspaperman or newspaperwoman

repose¹ NOUN **1** *He had a still, almost blank, face in repose.* = **rest**, relaxation, inactivity, restfulness **2** *The atmosphere is one of repose.* = **peace**, rest, quiet, ease, relaxation, respite, tranquillity, stillness, inactivity, quietness, quietude, restfulness **3** *She has a great deal of natural repose.* = **composure**, dignity, peace of mind, poise, serenity, tranquillity, aplomb, calmness, equanimity, self-possession

repose² VERB *Little trust can be reposed in such promises.* = **place**, put, store, invest, deposit, lodge, confide (*formal*), entrust

repository NOUN *The church became a repository for police files.* = **store**, archive, storehouse, depository, magazine, treasury, warehouse, vault, depot, emporium (*old-fashioned*), receptacle

reprehensible ADJECTIVE = **blameworthy**, bad, disgraceful, shameful, delinquent, errant, unworthy, objectionable, culpable, ignoble, discreditable, remiss, erring, opprobrious, condemnable, censurable ■ OPPOSITE: praiseworthy

represent VERB **1** *the lawyers representing the victims* = **act for**, speak for **2** *He will represent the president at ceremonies.* = **stand for**, substitute for, play the part of, assume the role of, serve as **3** *Circle the letter that represents the sound.* = **express**, equal, correspond to, symbolize, equate with, mean, betoken **4** *He represents everything that is wrong with the modern world.* = **exemplify**, embody, symbolize, typify, personify, epitomize **5** *The cartoonist represents him as an old man in a dressing gown.* = **depict**, show, describe, picture, express, illustrate, outline, portray, sketch, render, designate, reproduce, evoke, denote, delineate • **represent someone as something** or **someone** *They tend to represent him as a guru.* = **make out to be**, describe as

representation NOUN **1** *They have no representation in congress.* = **body of representatives**, committee, embassy, delegates, delegation **2** *a life-like representation of Christ* = **picture**, model, image, portrait, illustration, sketch, resemblance, likeness **3** *the representation of women in film and literature* = **portrayal**, depiction, account, relation, description, narrative, narration, delineation **4** (*often plural*) *We have made representations to ministers.* = **statement**, argument, explanation, exposition, remonstrance, expostulation, account

representative NOUN **1** *trade union representatives* = **delegate**, member, agent, deputy, commissioner, councillor, proxy, depute (*Scot.*), spokesman or woman or person **2** *the representative for Eastleigh* = **member**, congressman or woman or person (*U.S.*), member of parliament, Member of Congress (*U.S.*), M.P. **3** *She was a sales representative.* = **agent**, salesperson, rep, traveller, commercial traveller ▶ ADJECTIVE **1** *a representative government* = **chosen**, elected, delegated, elective **2** *fairly representative groups of adults* = **typical**, characteristic, archetypal, exemplary, illustrative ■ OPPOSITE: uncharacteristic **3** *images chosen as representative of English life* = **symbolic**, evocative, emblematic, typical

repress VERB **1** *People who repress their emotions risk having nightmares.* = **control**, suppress, hold back, bottle up, check, master, hold in, overcome, curb, restrain, inhibit, overpower, keep in check ■ OPPOSITE: release **2** *I couldn't repress a sigh of admiration.* = **hold back**, suppress, stifle, smother, silence, swallow, muffle **3** *They have been repressed for decades.* = **subdue**, abuse, crush, quash, wrong, persecute, quell, subjugate, maltreat, trample underfoot, tyrannize over, rule with an iron hand ■ OPPOSITE: liberate

repression NOUN **1** *a society conditioned by violence and repression* = **subjugation**, control, constraint, domination, censorship, tyranny, coercion, authoritarianism, despotism **2** *extremely violent repression of opposition* = **suppression**, crushing, prohibition, quashing, dissolution **3** *the repression of intense feelings* = **inhibition**, control, holding in, restraint, suppression, bottling up

repressive ADJECTIVE = **oppressive**, tough, severe, absolute, harsh, authoritarian, dictatorial, coercive, tyrannical, despotic ■ OPPOSITE: democratic

reprieve VERB *Fourteen people, waiting to be hanged, have been reprieved.* = **grant a stay of execution to**, pardon, let off the hook (*slang*), postpone or remit the punishment of ▶ NOUN *a reprieve for eight people waiting to be hanged* = **stay of execution**, suspension, amnesty, pardon, remission, abeyance, deferment, postponement of punishment

reprimand VERB *He was reprimanded by a teacher.* = **blame**, censure, rebuke, reproach, check, lecture, carpet (*informal*), scold, tick off (*informal*), castigate, chide, dress down (*informal*), admonish, tear into (*informal*), tell off (*informal*), take to task, read the riot act, tongue-lash, reprove, upbraid, slap on the wrist (*informal*), bawl out (*informal*), rap over the knuckles, haul over the coals (*informal*), chew out (*U.S. & Canad. informal*), tear (someone) off a strip (*Brit. informal*), give (someone) a rocket (*Brit. & N.Z. informal*), reprehend, give (someone) a row (*informal*), send (someone) away with a flea in their ear (*informal*) ■ OPPOSITE: praise ▶ NOUN *He has been given a severe reprimand.* = **blame**, talking-to (*informal*), row, lecture, wigging (*Brit. slang*), censure, rebuke, reproach, ticking-off (*informal*), dressing-down (*informal*), telling-off (*informal*), admonition, tongue-lashing, reproof, castigation, reprehension, flea in your ear (*informal*) ■ OPPOSITE: praise

reprisal NOUN = **retaliation**, revenge, vengeance, retribution, an eye for an eye, counterstroke, requital

reproach VERB *She is quick to reproach anyone.* = **blame**, criticize, rebuke, reprimand, abuse, blast, condemn, carpet (*informal*), discredit, censure, have a go at (*informal*), scold, disparage, chide, tear into (*informal*), diss (*slang*), defame, find fault with, take to task, read the riot act to, reprove, upbraid, lambast(e), bawl out (*informal*), chew out (*U.S. & Canad. informal*), tear (someone) off a strip (*Brit. informal*), give a rocket (*Brit. & N.Z. informal*), reprehend ▶ NOUN **1** *Her reproach was automatic.* = **rebuke**, lecture, wigging (*Brit. slang*), censure, reprimand, scolding, ticking-off (*informal*), dressing-down (*informal*), telling-off (*informal*), admonition, tongue-lashing, reproof, castigation, reproval **2** *He looked at her with reproach.* = **censure**, blame, abuse, contempt, condemnation, scorn, disapproval, opprobrium, odium (*formal*), obloquy **3** *The shootings were a reproach to all of us.* = **disgrace**, shame, slight, stain, discredit, stigma, slur, disrepute, blemish, indignity, ignominy, dishonour

reproduce VERB **1** *The effect has proved hard to reproduce.* = **copy**, recreate, replicate, duplicate, match, represent, mirror, echo, parallel, imitate, emulate **2** *permission to reproduce this article* = **print**, copy, transcribe **3** *The animals were unable to reproduce when the vitamin was missing from their diet.* = **breed**, produce young, procreate (*formal*), generate, multiply, spawn, propagate, proliferate

reproduction NOUN **1** *a reproduction of a religious painting* = **copy**, picture, print, replica, imitation, duplicate, facsimile ■ OPPOSITE: original **2** *what doctors call 'assisted human reproduction'* = **breeding**, procreation, propagation, increase, generation, proliferation, multiplication

repudiate VERB **1** *He repudiated any form of nationalism.* = **reject**, renounce, retract, disown, abandon, desert, reverse, cut off, discard, revoke, forsake, cast off, rescind, disavow, turn your back on, abjure, wash your hands of ■ OPPOSITE: assert **2** *He repudiated the charges.* = **deny**, oppose, disagree with, rebuff, refute, disprove, rebut, disclaim, gainsay (*archaic, literary*)

repugnant ADJECTIVE **1** *His actions were improper and repugnant.* = **distasteful**, offensive, foul, disgusting, revolting, sickening, vile, horrid (*informal*), repellent, obnoxious, objectionable, nauseating, odious, hateful, loathsome, abhorrent, abominable, yucky or yukky (*slang*), yucko (*Austral. slang*) ■ OPPOSITE: pleasant **2** *It is repugnant to the values of our society.* = **incompatible**, opposed, hostile, adverse, contradictory, inconsistent, averse, antagonistic, inimical, antipathetic ■ OPPOSITE: compatible

repulse NOUN **1** *the repulse of invaders in 1785* = **defeat**, check **2** *If he meets with a repulse he will not be cast down.* = **rejection**, refusal, snub, spurning, rebuff, knock-back (*slang*), cold shoulder, kick in the teeth (*slang*), the (old) heave-ho (*informal*)

USAGE Some people think that the use of *repulse* in sentences such as *he was repulsed by what he saw* is incorrect and that the correct word is *repel*.

repulsive ADJECTIVE = **disgusting**, offensive, foul, ugly, forbidding, unpleasant, revolting, obscene, sickening, hideous, vile, distasteful, horrid (*informal*), repellent, obnoxious, objectionable, disagreeable, nauseating, odious, hateful, loathsome, abhorrent, abominable, yucky or yukky (*slang*), yucko (*Austral. slang*)
■ **OPPOSITE:** delightful

reputable ADJECTIVE = **respectable**, good, excellent, reliable, worthy, legitimate, upright, honourable, honoured, trustworthy, creditable, estimable, well-thought-of, of good repute
■ **OPPOSITE:** disreputable

reputation NOUN = **name**, standing, credit, character, honour, fame, distinction, esteem, stature, eminence, renown, repute

repute NOUN **1** *The UN's repute has risen immeasurably.* = **reputation**, standing, fame, celebrity, distinction, esteem, stature, eminence, estimation, renown **2** *a house of ill-repute* = **name**, character, reputation

reputed ADJECTIVE **1** *a man reputed to be in his nineties* = **supposed**, said, seeming, held, believed, thought, considered, accounted, regarded, estimated, alleged, reckoned, rumoured, deemed **2** *They booked the ballroom for a reputed $15,000 last year.* = **apparent**, supposed, putative (*formal*), ostensible

reputedly ADVERB = **supposedly**, apparently, allegedly, seemingly, ostensibly

request VERB **1** *I requested a copy of the form.* = **ask for**, apply for, appeal for, put in for, demand, desire (*formal*), pray for, beg for, requisition, beseech **2** *They requested him to leave.* = **invite**, call for, beg, petition, beseech, entreat, supplicate **3** *the right to request a divorce* = **seek**, ask (for), sue for, solicit ▶ NOUN **1** *They agreed to his request for help.* = **appeal**, call, demand, plea, desire, application, prayer, petition, requisition, solicitation, entreaty, supplication (*formal*), suit **2** *At his request, they attended some of the meetings.* = **asking**, plea, begging

require VERB **1** *A baby requires warmth and physical security.* = **need**, crave, depend upon, have need of, want, miss, lack, wish, desire, stand in need of **2** *This requires thought, effort, and a certain ruthlessness.* = **demand**, take, involve, call for, entail, necessitate **3** *The rules require employers to provide safety training.* = **order**, demand,

direct, command, compel, exact, oblige, instruct, call upon, constrain, insist upon **4** *She was required to take to the stage.* = **ask**, enjoin

USAGE The use of *require to* as in *I require to see the manager* or *you require to complete a special form* is thought by many people to be incorrect. Useful alternatives are: *I need to see the manager* and *you are required to complete a special form*.

required ADJECTIVE = **obligatory**, prescribed, compulsory, mandatory, needed, set, demanded, necessary, called for, essential, recommended, vital, unavoidable, requisite, de rigueur (*French*)
■ **OPPOSITE:** optional

requirement NOUN = **necessity**, demand, specification, stipulation, want, need, must, essential, qualification, precondition, requisite, prerequisite, sine qua non (*Latin*), desideratum, must-have

requisite ADJECTIVE *She filled in the requisite paperwork.* = **necessary**, needed, required, called for, essential, vital, mandatory, indispensable, obligatory, prerequisite, needful ▶ NOUN *a major requisite for the work of the analysts* = **necessity**, condition, requirement, precondition, need, must, essential, prerequisite, sine qua non (*Latin*), desideratum, must-have

requisition VERB **1** *The vessel was requisitioned by the navy.* = **take over**, appropriate, occupy, seize, commandeer, take possession of **2** *the task of requisitioning men and supplies* = **demand**, call for, request, apply for, put in for ▶ NOUN *a requisition for a replacement typewriter* = **demand**, request, call, application, summons **2** *They are against the requisition of common land.* = **takeover**, occupation, seizure, appropriation, commandeering

rescind VERB = **annul**, recall, reverse, cancel, overturn, set aside, void, repeal, quash, revoke, retract, invalidate, obviate, abrogate, countermand, declare null and void ■ **OPPOSITE:** confirm

rescue VERB **1** *Helicopters rescued nearly 20 people.* = **save**, get out, save the life of, extricate, free, release, deliver, recover, liberate, set free, save (someone's) bacon (*Brit. informal*) ■ **OPPOSITE:** desert **2** *He rescued a 14th century barn from demolition.* = **salvage**, deliver, redeem, come to the rescue of ▶ NOUN *the rescue of the crew of a ship* = **saving**, salvage, deliverance, extrication, release, relief, recovery, liberation, salvation, redemption

research NOUN *His groundbreaking research will be vital in future developments.*

= **investigation**, study, inquiry, analysis, examination, probe, exploration, scrutiny, experimentation, delving, groundwork, fact-finding ▶ VERB *They research the needs of both employers and staff.* = **investigate**, study, examine, experiment, explore, probe, analyse, look into, work over, scrutinize, make inquiries, do tests, consult the archives

resemblance NOUN = **similarity**, correspondence, conformity, semblance, image, comparison, parallel, counterpart, analogy, affinity, closeness, parity, likeness, kinship, facsimile, sameness, comparability, similitude ■ **OPPOSITE:** dissimilarity

resemble VERB = **be like**, look like, favour (*informal*), mirror, echo, parallel, be similar to, duplicate, take after, remind you of, bear a resemblance to, put you in mind of

resent VERB = **be bitter about**, dislike, object to, grudge, begrudge, take exception to, be offended by, be angry about, take offence at, take umbrage at, harbour a grudge against, take as an insult, bear a grudge about, be in a huff about, take amiss to, have hard feelings about ■ **OPPOSITE:** be content with

resentful ADJECTIVE = **bitter**, hurt, wounded, angry, offended, put out, jealous, choked, incensed, grudging, exasperated, aggrieved, indignant, irate, miffed (*informal*), embittered, unforgiving, peeved (*informal*), in a huff, piqued, huffy, in high dudgeon, revengeful, huffish, tooshie (*Austral. slang*) ■ **OPPOSITE:** content

resentment NOUN = **bitterness**, indignation, ill feeling, ill will, hurt, anger, rage, fury, irritation, grudge, wrath, malice, animosity, huff, ire, displeasure, pique, rancour, bad blood, umbrage, vexation, chip on your shoulder (*informal*)

reservation NOUN **1** (*often plural*) *Their demands were met with some reservations.* = **doubt**, scepticism, scruples, demur, hesitancy **2** *a Navaho from a North American reservation* = **reserve**, territory, preserve, homeland, sanctuary, tract, enclave, rez (*U.S. & Canad. slang*)

reserve VERB **1** *I'll reserve a table for five.* = **book**, prearrange, pre-engage, engage, bespeak **2** *Ask your newsagent to reserve your copy today.* = **put by**, secure, retain **3** *Strain and reserve the cooking liquor.* = **keep**, hold, save, husband, store, retain, preserve, set aside, withhold, hang on to, conserve, stockpile, hoard, lay up, put by, keep back **4** *The Court has reserved its judgement.* = **delay**, postpone, withhold, put off, defer,

keep back ▶ NOUN **1** *The country's reserves of petrol are running very low.* = **store**, fund, savings, stock, capital, supply, reservoir, fall-back, stockpile, hoard, backlog, cache **2** *monkeys at the wildlife reserve* = **park**, reservation, preserve, sanctuary, tract, forest park (*N.Z.*) **3** *I hope you'll overcome your reserve.* = **shyness**, silence, restraint, constraint, reluctance, formality, modesty, reticence, coolness, aloofness, secretiveness, taciturnity **4** *I committed myself without reserve.* = **reservation**, doubt, delay, uncertainty, indecision, hesitancy, vacillation, irresolution, dubiety **5** *In this sport, you always have to have reserves.* = **substitute**, extra, spare, alternative, fall-back, auxiliary

reserved ADJECTIVE **1** *He was unemotional and reserved.* = **uncommunicative**, cold, cool, retiring, formal, silent, modest, shy, cautious, restrained, secretive, aloof, reticent, prim, demure, taciturn, unresponsive, unapproachable, unsociable, undemonstrative, standoffish, close-mouthed, unforthcoming ■ **OPPOSITE:** uninhibited **2** *Three coaches were reserved for us boys.* = **set aside**, taken, kept, held, booked, retained, engaged, restricted, spoken for

reservoir NOUN **1** *Torrents of water gushed into the reservoir.* = **lake**, pond, basin **2** *It was on his desk next to the ink reservoir.* = **repository**, store, tank, holder, container, receptacle **3** *the body's short-term reservoir of energy* = **store**, stock, source, supply, reserves, fund, pool, accumulation, stockpile

reside VERB **1** *She resides with her invalid mother.* = **live**, lodge, dwell (*formal, literary*), have your home, remain, stay, settle, abide, hang out (*informal*), sojourn ■ **OPPOSITE:** visit **2** *Happiness does not reside in money.* = **be present**, lie, exist, consist, dwell, abide, rest with, be intrinsic to, inhere, be vested

residence NOUN **1** *There was a stabbing at a residence next door.* = **home**, house, household, dwelling (*formal, literary*), place, quarters, flat, lodging, pad (*slang*), abode, habitation (*formal*), domicile **2** *She's staying at her country residence.* = **mansion**, seat, hall, palace, villa, manor **3** *He returned to his place of residence.* = **stay**, tenancy, occupancy, occupation, sojourn

resident NOUN **1** *Ten per cent of residents live below the poverty line.* = **inhabitant**, citizen, denizen, indweller, local ■ **OPPOSITE:** nonresident **2** *council house residents purchasing their own homes* = **tenant**, occupant, lodger **3** *Bar closed on Sunday except to hotel residents.* = **guest**, lodger

▶ ADJECTIVE **1** *He had been resident in Brussels for ten years.* = **inhabiting**, living, settled, dwelling ■ **OPPOSITE:** nonresident **2** *The resident population of the inner city has risen.* = **local**, neighbourhood

residual ADJECTIVE = **remaining**, net, unused, leftover, vestigial, nett, unconsumed

residue NOUN = **remainder**, remains, remnant, leftovers, rest, extra, balance, excess, surplus, dregs, residuum

resign VERB **1** *He has resigned after only ten weeks in office.* = **quit**, leave, step down (*informal*), vacate, abdicate, call it a day or night, give or hand in your notice **2** *He has resigned his seat in parliament.* = **give up**, abandon, yield, hand over, surrender, turn over, relinquish, renounce, forsake, cede, forgo • **resign yourself to something** *I simply resigned myself to staying indoors.* = **accept**, reconcile yourself to, succumb to, submit to, bow to, give in to, yield to, acquiesce to

resignation NOUN **1** *He has withdrawn his letter of resignation.* = **leaving**, notice, retirement, departure, surrender, abandonment, abdication, renunciation, relinquishment **2** *He sighed with profound resignation.* = **acceptance**, patience, submission, compliance, endurance, fortitude, passivity, acquiescence, forbearing, sufferance, nonresistance ■ **OPPOSITE:** resistance

resigned ADJECTIVE = **stoical**, patient, subdued, long-suffering, compliant, submissive, acquiescent, unresisting, unprotesting

resilient ADJECTIVE **1** *some resilient plastic material* = **flexible**, plastic, elastic, supple, bouncy, rubbery, pliable, springy, whippy ■ **OPPOSITE:** rigid **2** *I'm a resilient kind of person.* = **tough**, strong, hardy, buoyant, feisty (*informal*), bouncy, irrepressible, quick to recover ■ **OPPOSITE:** weak

resist VERB **1** *They resisted our attempts to modernize distribution.* = **oppose**, fight, battle against, refuse, check, weather, dispute, confront, combat, defy, curb, thwart, stand up to, hinder, contend with, counteract, hold out against, put up a fight (against), countervail ■ **OPPOSITE:** accept **2** *He tried to resist arrest.* = **fight against**, fight, struggle against, put up a fight (against) **3** *Try to resist giving him advice.* = **refrain from**, refuse, avoid, turn down, leave alone, keep from, forgo, abstain from, forbear, prevent yourself from ■ **OPPOSITE:** indulge in **4** *bodies trained to resist the cold* = **withstand**, repel, be proof against

resistance NOUN **1** *In remote villages there is a resistance to change.* = **opposition**, hostility, aversion **2** *The protesters offered no resistance.* = **fighting**, fight, battle, struggle, combat, contention, defiance, obstruction, impediment, intransigence, hindrance, counteraction

Resistance NOUN = **freedom fighters**, underground, guerrillas, partisans, irregulars, maquis

resistant ADJECTIVE **1** *Some people are resistant to the idea of exercise.* = **opposed**, hostile, dissident, unwilling, defiant, intractable, combative, recalcitrant, antagonistic, intransigent **2** *The body may be less resistant if it is cold.* = **impervious**, hard, strong, tough, unaffected, unyielding, insusceptible

resolute ADJECTIVE = **determined**, set, firm, dogged, fixed, constant, bold, relentless, stubborn, stalwart, staunch, persevering, inflexible, purposeful, tenacious, undaunted, strong-willed, steadfast, obstinate, unwavering, immovable, unflinching, unbending, unshakable, unshaken ■ **OPPOSITE:** irresolute

resolution NOUN **1** *The UN had passed two major resolutions.* = **declaration**, motion, verdict, judgment **2** *It had been her resolution to lose weight.* = **decision**, resolve, intention, aim, purpose, determination, intent **3** *He implemented policy with resolution and single-mindedness.* = **determination**, energy, purpose, resolve, courage, dedication, fortitude, sincerity, tenacity, perseverance, willpower, boldness, firmness, staying power, stubbornness, constancy, earnestness, obstinacy, steadfastness, doggedness, relentlessness, resoluteness, staunchness **4** *a peaceful resolution to the crisis* = **solution**, end, settlement, outcome, finding, answer, working out, solving, sorting out, unravelling, upshot

resolve VERB **1** *We must find a way to resolve these problems.* = **work out**, answer, solve, find the solution to, clear up, crack, fathom, suss (out) (*slang*), elucidate **2** *She resolved to report the matter.* = **decide**, determine, undertake, make up your mind, agree, design, settle, purpose, intend, fix, conclude **3** *The spirals of light resolved into points.* = **change**, convert, transform, alter, metamorphose, transmute **4** *Many years of doubt were finally resolved.* = **dispel**, explain, remove, clear up, banish ▶ NOUN **1** *He doesn't weaken in his resolve.* = **determination**, resolution, courage, willpower, boldness, firmness, earnestness, steadfastness, resoluteness ■ **OPPOSITE:** indecision

2 *the resolve to enforce a settlement using troops* = **decision**, resolution, undertaking, objective, design, project, purpose, conclusion, intention

resonant ADJECTIVE **1** *He responded with a resonant laugh.* = **sonorous**, full, rich, ringing, booming, vibrant **2** *a hall, resonant with the sound of violins* = **echoing**, resounding, reverberating, reverberant

resort NOUN **1** *a genteel resort on the south coast* = **holiday centre**, spot, retreat, haunt, refuge, tourist centre, watering place (*Brit.*) **2** (*with* **to**) *without resort to illegal methods* = **recourse to**, reference to • **resort to something** *We were forced to resort to violence.* = **have recourse to**, turn to, fall back on, bring into play, use, exercise, employ, look to, make use of, utilize, avail yourself of

resound VERB **1** *The soldiers' boots resounded in the street.* = **echo**, resonate, reverberate, fill the air, re-echo **2** *The whole place resounded with music.* = **ring**

resounding ADJECTIVE = **echoing**, full, sounding, rich, ringing, powerful, booming, vibrant, reverberating, resonant, sonorous

resource NOUN **1** *a great resource of teaching materials* = **supply**, source, reserve, stockpile, hoard **2** *The directory is a valuable resource.* = **facility 3** *She is willing to use every resource to win an argument.* = **means**, course, resort, device, expedient ▶ PLURAL NOUN **1** *They do not have the resources to feed themselves properly.* = **funds**, means, holdings, money, capital, wherewithal, riches, materials, assets, wealth, property **2** *We are overpopulated, straining the earth's resources.* = **reserves**, supplies, stocks

resourceful ADJECTIVE = **ingenious**, able, bright (*informal*), talented, sharp, capable, creative, clever, imaginative, inventive, quick-witted ■ **OPPOSITE:** unimaginative

respect VERB **1** *I want him to respect me as a career woman.* = **think highly of**, value, regard, honour, recognize, appreciate, admire, esteem, adore, revere, reverence, look up to, defer to, venerate, set store by, have a good *or* high opinion of **2** *Trying to respect her wishes, I said I'd leave.* = **show consideration for**, regard, notice, honour, observe, heed, attend to, pay attention to **3** *It's about time they respected the law.* = **abide by**, follow, observe, comply with, obey, heed, keep to, adhere to ■ **OPPOSITE:** disregard ▶ NOUN **1** *I have tremendous respect for him.* = **regard**, honour, recognition, esteem, appreciation, admiration, reverence, estimation, veneration,

approbation, props (*U.S. slang*) ■ **OPPOSITE:** contempt **2** *They should be treated with respect.* = **consideration**, kindness, deference, friendliness, tact, thoughtfulness, solicitude, kindliness, considerateness **3** *He's simply wonderful in every respect.* = **particular**, way, point, matter, sense, detail, feature, aspect, characteristic, facet ▶ PLURAL NOUN *He visited the hospital to pay his respects to her.* = **greetings**, regards, compliments, good wishes, salutations, devoirs • **in respect of** *or* **with respect to** *The system is not working in respect of training.* = **concerning**, in relation to, in connection with, with regard to, with reference to, apropos of

respectable ADJECTIVE **1** *He came from a respectable middle-class family.* = **honourable**, good, respected, decent, proper, worthy, upright, admirable, honest, dignified, venerable, reputable, decorous, estimable ■ **OPPOSITE:** disreputable **2** *At last I have something respectable to wear.* = **decent**, neat, tidy (*informal*), spruce **3** *respectable and highly attractive rates of return* = **reasonable**, considerable, substantial, fair, tidy (*informal*), ample, tolerable (*informal*), presentable, appreciable, fairly good, sizable *or* sizeable, goodly ■ **OPPOSITE:** small

respectful ADJECTIVE = **polite**, civil, mannerly, humble, gracious, courteous, obedient, submissive, self-effacing, dutiful, courtly, deferential, reverential, solicitous, reverent, regardful, well-mannered

respective ADJECTIVE = **specific**, own, several (*formal*), individual, personal, particular, various, separate, relevant, corresponding

respite NOUN **1** *I rang home during a brief respite at work.* = **pause**, break, rest, relief, halt, interval, relaxation, recess, interruption, lull, cessation, let-up (*informal*), breathing space, breather (*informal*), hiatus, intermission **2** *Devaluation would only give the economy brief respite.* = **reprieve**, stay, delay, suspension, moratorium, postponement, adjournment

resplendent ADJECTIVE = **brilliant**, radiant, splendid, glorious, bright, shining, beaming, glittering, dazzling, gleaming, luminous, lustrous, refulgent (*literary*), effulgent, irradiant

respond VERB **1** *'Of course,' she responded scornfully.* = **answer**, return, reply, come back, counter, acknowledge, retort, rejoin ■ **OPPOSITE:** remain silent **2** (*often with* **to**) *He was quick to respond to questions.* = **reply to**, answer **3** *He responded to the attacks by* *exacting suitable retribution.* = **react**, retaliate, reciprocate, take the bait, rise to the bait, act in response

response NOUN = **answer**, return, reply, reaction, comeback (*informal*), feedback, retort, acknowledgment, riposte, counterattack, rejoinder, counterblast

responsibility NOUN **1** *The 600 properties were his responsibility.* = **duty**, business, job, role, task, accountability, answerability **2** *They have admitted responsibility for the accident.* = **fault**, blame, liability, guilt, culpability, burden **3** *This helps employees balance work and family responsibilities.* = **obligation**, duty, liability, charge, care **4** *a better-paying job with more responsibility* = **authority**, power, importance, mana (*N.Z.*) **5** *I'm glad it's not my responsibility to be their guardian.* = **job**, task, function, role, pigeon (*informal*) **6** *I think she's shown responsibility.* = **level-headedness**, stability, maturity, reliability, rationality, dependability, trustworthiness, conscientiousness, soberness, sensibleness

responsible ADJECTIVE **1** *He felt responsible for her death.* = **to blame**, guilty, at fault, culpable **2** *the minister responsible for the environment* = **in charge**, in control, at the helm, in authority, carrying the can (*informal*) **3** *I'm responsible to my board of directors.* = **accountable**, subject, bound, liable, amenable, answerable, duty-bound, chargeable, under obligation ■ OPPOSITE: unaccountable **4** *He's a very responsible sort of person.* = **sensible**, sound, adult, stable, mature, reliable, rational, sober, conscientious, dependable, trustworthy, level-headed ■ OPPOSITE: unreliable **5** *demoted to less responsible jobs* = **authoritative**, high, important, executive, decision-making

responsive ADJECTIVE = **sensitive**, open, aware, sharp, alive, forthcoming, sympathetic, awake, susceptible, receptive, reactive, perceptive, impressionable, quick to react
■ OPPOSITE: unresponsive

rest¹ VERB **1** *He has been advised to rest for two weeks.* = **relax**, sleep, take it easy, lie down, idle, nap, be calm, doze, sit down, slumber, kip (*Brit. slang*), snooze (*informal*), laze, lie still, be at ease, put your feet up, take a nap, drowse, mellow out (*informal*), have a snooze (*informal*), refresh yourself, outspan (*S. African*), zizz (*Brit. informal*), have forty winks (*informal*), take your ease
■ OPPOSITE: work **2** *They rested only once that morning.* = **stop**, have a break, break off, take a breather (*informal*), stay, halt, cease,

discontinue, knock off (*informal*), desist, come to a standstill ■ OPPOSITE: keep going **3** *Such a view rests on incorrect assumptions.* = **depend**, turn, lie, be founded, hang, be based, rely, hinge, reside **4** *He rested his arms on the back of the chair.* = **place**, lay, repose, stretch out, stand, sit, lean, prop **5** *Matt's elbow rested on the table.* = **be placed**, sit, lie, be supported, recline ▶ NOUN **1** *Go home and have a rest.* = **sleep**, snooze (*informal*), lie-down, nap, doze, slumber, kip (*Brit. slang*), siesta, forty winks (*informal*), zizz (*Brit. informal*) **2** *I feel in need of some rest.* = **relaxation**, repose, leisure, idleness, me-time ■ OPPOSITE: work **3** *He took a rest from teaching.* = **pause**, break, breather (*informal*), time off, stop, holiday, halt, interval, vacation, respite, lull, interlude, cessation, breathing space (*informal*), intermission **4** *some rest from the intense concentration* = **refreshment**, release, relief, ease, comfort, cure, remedy, solace, balm, deliverance, mitigation, abatement, alleviation, easement, palliation, assuagement **5** *The plane came to rest in a field.* = **inactivity**, a halt, a stop, a standstill, motionlessness **6** *Keep your elbow on the arm rest.* = **support**, stand, base, holder, shelf, prop, trestle **7** *a remote part of the valley for those seeking rest and relaxation* = **calm**, tranquillity, stillness, somnolence • **at rest 1** *When you are at rest you breathe with your tummy muscles.* = **motionless**, still, stopped, at a standstill, unmoving **2** *with your mind at rest* = **calm**, still, cool, quiet, pacific, peaceful, composed, serene, tranquil, at peace, sedate, placid, undisturbed, restful, untroubled, unperturbed, unruffled, unexcited **3** *She is at rest; don't disturb her.* = **asleep**, resting, sleeping, napping, dormant, crashed out (*slang*), dozing, slumbering, snoozing (*informal*), fast asleep, sound asleep, out for the count, dead to the world (*informal*)

rest² NOUN *The rest is thrown away.* = **remainder**, remains, excess, remnants, others, balance, surplus, residue, rump, leftovers, residuum ▶ VERB *Of one thing we may rest assured.* = **continue being**, keep being, remain, stay, be left, go on being

restaurant NOUN = **café**, diner (*chiefly U.S. & Canad.*), bistro, cafeteria, trattoria, tearoom, eatery *or* eaterie

restful ADJECTIVE = **relaxing**, quiet, relaxed, comfortable, pacific, calm, calming, peaceful, soothing, sleepy, serene, tranquil, placid, undisturbed, languid, unhurried, tranquillizing, chilled (*informal*) ■ OPPOSITE: busy

r

restitution NOUN **1** *The victims are demanding full restitution.* = **compensation**, satisfaction, amends, refund, repayment, redress, remuneration, reparation, indemnity, reimbursement, recompense, indemnification, requital **2** *the restitution of their equal rights as citizens* = **return**, return, replacement, restoration, reinstatement, re-establishment, reinstallation

restive ADJECTIVE = **restless**, nervous, uneasy, impatient, agitated, unruly, edgy, jittery (*informal*), recalcitrant, on edge, fractious, ill at ease, jumpy, fretful, fidgety, refractory, unquiet, antsy (*informal*) ■ OPPOSITE: calm

restless ADJECTIVE **1** *My father seemed very restless and excited.* = **unsettled**, worried, troubled, nervous, disturbed, anxious, uneasy, agitated, unruly, edgy, fidgeting, on edge, ill at ease, restive, jumpy, fitful, fretful, fidgety, unquiet, antsy (*informal*) ■ OPPOSITE: relaxed **2** *He had spent a restless few hours on the plane.* = **sleepless**, disturbed, wakeful, unsleeping, insomniac, tossing and turning **3** *He led a restless life.* = **moving**, active, wandering, unsettled, unstable, bustling, turbulent, hurried, roving, transient, nomadic, unsteady, changeable, footloose, irresolute, inconstant, having itchy feet ■ OPPOSITE: settled

restlessness NOUN **1** *increasing sounds of restlessness* = **movement**, activity, turmoil, unrest, instability, bustle, turbulence, hurry, transience, inconstancy, hurry-scurry, unsettledness **2** *She complained of hyperactivity and restlessness.* = **restiveness**, anxiety, disturbance, nervousness, disquiet, agitation, insomnia, jitters (*informal*), uneasiness, edginess, heebie-jeebies (*slang*), jumpiness, fretfulness, ants in your pants (*slang*), fitfulness, inquietude, worriedness

restoration NOUN **1** *the restoration of diplomatic relations* = **reinstatement**, return, revival, restitution, re-establishment, reinstallation, replacement ■ OPPOSITE: abolition **2** *I specialized in the restoration of old houses.* = **repair**, recovery, reconstruction, renewal, rehabilitation, refurbishing, refreshment, renovation, rejuvenation, revitalization ■ OPPOSITE: demolition

restore VERB **1** *The army has been brought in to restore order.* = **reinstate**, re-establish, reintroduce, reimpose, re-enforce, reconstitute ■ OPPOSITE: abolish **2** *We will restore her to health.* = **revive**, build up, strengthen, bring back, refresh, rejuvenate, revitalize, revivify, reanimate ■ OPPOSITE: make worse **3** *Civil rights were* restored in a matter of days. = **re-establish**, replace, reinstate, give back, reinstall, retrocede **4** *They partly restored a local castle.* = **repair**, refurbish, renovate, reconstruct, fix (up), recover, renew, rebuild, mend, rehabilitate, touch up, recondition, retouch, set to rights ■ OPPOSITE: demolish **5** *Their horses and goods were restored.* = **return**, replace, recover, bring back, send back, hand back

restrain VERB **1** *He grabbed my arm, partly to restrain me.* = **hold back**, hold, control, check, contain, prevent, restrict, handicap, confine, curb, hamper, rein, harness, subdue, hinder, constrain, curtail, bridle, debar, keep under control, have on a tight leash, straiten ■ OPPOSITE: encourage **2** *She was unable to restrain her desperate anger.* = **control**, keep in, limit, govern, suppress, inhibit, repress, muzzle, keep under control **3** *Police restrained her on July 28.* = **imprison**, hold, arrest, jail, bind, chain, confine, detain, tie up, lock up, fetter, manacle, pinion ■ OPPOSITE: release

restrained ADJECTIVE **1** *He felt he'd been very restrained.* = **controlled**, reasonable, moderate, self-controlled, soft, calm, steady, mild, muted, reticent, temperate, undemonstrative ■ OPPOSITE: hot-headed **2** *Her black suit was restrained and expensive.* = **unobtrusive**, discreet, subdued, tasteful, quiet ■ OPPOSITE: garish

restraint NOUN **1** *Criminals could cross into the country without restraint.* = **limitation**, limit, check, ban, boycott, embargo, curb, rein, taboo, bridle, disqualification, interdict, restraining order (*U.S. Law*) ■ OPPOSITE: freedom **2** *They behaved with more restraint than I'd expected.* = **self-control**, self-discipline, self-restraint, self-possession, pulling your punches ■ OPPOSITE: self-indulgence **3** *A Bill of Rights would act as a restraint on judicial power.* = **constraint**, limitation, inhibition, moderation, hold, control, restriction, prevention, suppression, hindrance, curtailment

restrict VERB **1** *a move to restrict the number of students on campus at any one time* = **limit**, fix, regulate, specify, curb, ration, keep within bounds or limits ■ OPPOSITE: widen **2** *The shoulder straps restrict movement.* = **hamper**, impede, handicap, restrain, cramp, inhibit, straiten

restriction NOUN **1** *the relaxation of travel restrictions* = **control**, rule, condition, check, regulation, curb, restraint, constraint, confinement, containment, demarcation, stipulation **2** *the restrictions of urban living* = **limitation**, handicap, inhibition

result NOUN **1** *This is the result of eating too much fatty food.* = **consequence**, effect, outcome, end result, issue, event, development, product, reaction, fruit, sequel, upshot ■ **OPPOSITE:** cause **2** *They were surprised by the result of their trials.* = **outcome**, conclusion, end, decision, termination ▶ VERB *(often followed by* **from***) Many hair problems result from what you eat.* = **arise**, follow, issue, happen, appear, develop, spring, flow, turn out, stem, derive, ensue, emanate, eventuate • **result in something** *Fifty per cent of road accidents result in head injuries.* = **end in**, bring about, cause, lead to, wind up, finish with, culminate in, terminate in

resume VERB **1** *They are expected to resume the search early today.* = **begin again**, continue, go on with, proceed with, carry on, reopen, restart, recommence, reinstitute, take up *or* pick up where you left off ■ **OPPOSITE:** discontinue **2** *After the war he resumed his duties at the college.* = **take up again**, assume again **3** *She resumed her seat.* = **occupy again**, take back, reoccupy

résumé NOUN **1** *I will leave you a résumé of his speech.* = **summary**, synopsis, abstract, précis, review, digest, epitome, rundown, recapitulation **2** *(U.S.) I mailed him my résumé this week.* = **curriculum vitae**, CV, career history, details, biography

resumption NOUN = **continuation**, carrying on, reopening, renewal, restart, resurgence, new beginning, re-establishment, fresh outbreak

resurgence NOUN = **revival**, return, renaissance, resurrection, resumption, rebirth, re-emergence, recrudescence, renascence

resurrect VERB **1** *Attempts to resurrect the ceasefire have failed.* = **revive**, renew, bring back, kick-start *(informal)*, reintroduce, breathe new life into **2** *the archaic myth of the god who is wounded, dies, and is finally resurrected* = **restore to life**, raise from the dead

resurrection NOUN **1** *This is a resurrection of an old story.* = **revival**, restoration, renewal, resurgence, return, comeback *(informal)*, renaissance, rebirth, reappearance, resuscitation, renascence ■ **OPPOSITE:** killing off **2** *the Resurrection of Jesus Christ* = **raising** *or* **rising from the dead**, return from the dead ■ **OPPOSITE:** demise

resuscitate VERB **1** *A paramedic tried to resuscitate her.* = **give artificial respiration to**, save, quicken, bring to life, bring round, give the kiss of life to **2** *his promise to resuscitate the failing economy* = **revive**, rescue, restore, renew, resurrect, revitalize, breathe new life into, revivify, reanimate

retain VERB **1** *He retains a deep respect for the profession.* = **maintain**, keep, reserve, preserve, keep up, uphold, nurture, continue to have, hang *or* hold onto **2** *They want to retain a strip 33ft wide on the eastern shore.* = **keep**, keep possession of, hang *or* hold onto, save ■ **OPPOSITE:** let go **3** *She needs tips on how to retain facts.* = **remember**, recall, bear in mind, keep in mind, memorize, recollect, impress on the memory ■ **OPPOSITE:** forget

retainer NOUN **1** *Clients would pay a retainer to ensure she did not work for their rivals.* = **fee**, advance, deposit **2** *the ever-faithful family retainer* = **servant**, domestic, attendant, valet, supporter, dependant, henchman *or* woman *or* person, footman, lackey, vassal, flunky

retaliate VERB = **pay someone back**, hit back, strike back, reciprocate, take revenge, get back at someone, get even with *(informal)*, even the score, get your own back *(informal)*, wreak vengeance, exact retribution, give as good as you get *(informal)*, take an eye for an eye, make reprisal, give (someone) a taste of their own medicine, give tit for tat, return like for like ■ **OPPOSITE:** turn the other cheek

retaliation NOUN = **revenge**, repayment, vengeance, reprisal, retribution, tit for tat, an eye for an eye, reciprocation, counterstroke, requital, counterblow, a taste of your own medicine

retard VERB = **slow down**, check, arrest, delay, handicap, stall, brake, detain, defer, clog, hinder, obstruct, impede, set back, encumber, decelerate, hold back *or* up ■ **OPPOSITE:** speed up

retch VERB = **gag**, be sick, vomit, regurgitate, chuck *(Austral. & N.Z. informal)*, throw up *(informal)*, spew, heave, puke *(slang)*, disgorge, barf *(U.S. slang)*, chunder *(slang, chiefly Austral.)*, upchuck *(U.S. slang)*, do a technicolour yawn *(slang)*, toss your cookies *(U.S. slang)*

reticence NOUN = **silence**, reserve, restraint, quietness, secretiveness, taciturnity, uncommunicativeness, unforthcomingness

reticent ADJECTIVE = **uncommunicative**, reserved, secretive, unforthcoming, quiet, silent, restrained, taciturn, tight-lipped, unspeaking, close-lipped, mum ■ **OPPOSITE:** communicative

retinue NOUN = **attendants**, entourage, escort, servants, following, train, suite, aides, followers, cortege

retire VERB **1** *Parker will retire as chief executive in November.* = **stop working**, give up work, be pensioned off, be put out to grass (*informal*) **2** *He retired from the room with his colleagues.* = **withdraw**, leave, remove, exit, go away, depart, absent yourself, betake yourself **3** *She retires early most nights.* = **go to bed**, turn in (*informal*), go to sleep, hit the sack (*slang*), go to your room, kip down (*Brit. slang*), hit the hay (*slang*) **4** *He was wounded, but did not retire from the field.* = **retreat**, withdraw, pull out, give way, recede, pull back, back off, decamp, give ground

retirement NOUN = **withdrawal**, retreat, privacy, loneliness, obscurity, solitude, seclusion

retiring ADJECTIVE = **shy**, reserved, quiet, modest, shrinking, humble, timid, coy, meek, reclusive, reticent, unassuming, self-effacing, demure, diffident, bashful, aw-shucks, timorous (*literary*), unassertive ■ **OPPOSITE:** outgoing

retort VERB *'Who do you think you're talking to?' she retorted.* = **reply**, return, answer, respond, counter, rejoin, retaliate, come back with, riposte, answer back ▶ NOUN *His sharp retort made an impact.* = **reply**, answer, response, comeback, riposte, rejoinder

retract VERB **1** *He hurriedly sought to retract the statement.* = **withdraw**, take back, revoke, disown, deny, recall, reverse, cancel, repeal, renounce, go back on, repudiate, rescind, renege on, back out of, disavow, recant, disclaim, abjure, eat your words, unsay **2** *A cat in ecstasy will extend and retract his claws.* = **draw in**, pull in, pull back, reel in, sheathe

retreat VERB *They were forced to retreat.* = **withdraw**, retire, back off, draw back, leave, go back, shrink, depart, fall back, recede, pull back, back away, recoil, give ground, turn tail ■ **OPPOSITE:** advance ▶ NOUN **1** *The army was in full retreat.* = **flight**, retirement, departure, withdrawal, evacuation ■ **OPPOSITE:** advance **2** *He spent yesterday in his country retreat.* = **refuge**, haven, resort, retirement, shelter, haunt, asylum, privacy, den, sanctuary, hideaway, seclusion

retrenchment NOUN = **cutback**, cuts, economy, reduction, pruning, contraction, cost-cutting, rundown, curtailment, tightening your belt ■ **OPPOSITE:** expansion

retribution NOUN = **punishment**, retaliation, reprisal, redress, justice, reward, reckoning, compensation, satisfaction, revenge, repayment, vengeance, Nemesis, recompense, an eye for an eye, requital

retrieve VERB **1** *She retrieved her jacket from the seat.* = **get back**, regain, repossess, fetch back, recall, recover, restore, recapture **2** *He could retrieve the situation.* = **redeem**, save, rescue, repair, salvage, win back, recoup

retro ADJECTIVE = **old-time**, old, former, past, period, antique, old-fashioned, nostalgic, old-world, bygone, of yesteryear

retrograde ADJECTIVE = **deteriorating**, backward, regressive, retrogressive, declining, negative, reverse, retreating, worsening, downward, waning, relapsing, inverse, degenerative

retrospect NOUN = **hindsight**, review, afterthought, re-examination, survey, recollection, remembrance, reminiscence ■ **OPPOSITE:** foresight

return VERB **1** *More than 350,000 people have returned home.* = **come back**, go back, repair, retreat, turn back, revert, reappear ■ **OPPOSITE:** depart **2** *The car was not returned on time.* = **put back**, replace, restore, render, transmit, convey, send back, reinstate, take back, give back, carry back, retrocede ■ **OPPOSITE:** keep **3** *They promised to return the money.* = **give back**, repay, refund, pay back, remit, reimburse, recompense ■ **OPPOSITE:** keep **4** *Her feelings are not returned.* = **reciprocate**, requite, feel in return, respond to **5** *The pain returned in waves.* = **recur**, come back, repeat, persist, revert, happen again, reappear, come and go, come again **6** *They returned a verdict of not guilty.* = **announce**, report, come to, deliver, arrive at, bring in, submit, render **7** *The business returned a handsome profit.* = **earn**, make, net, yield, bring in, repay ■ **OPPOSITE:** lose **8** *He has been returned as leader of the party.* = **elect**, choose, pick, vote in ▶ NOUN **1** *his sudden return to London* = **reappearance** ■ **OPPOSITE:** departure **2** *Their demand was for the return of acres of forest.* = **restoration**, replacement, reinstatement, re-establishment ■ **OPPOSITE:** removal **3** *It was like the return of his youth.* = **recurrence**, repetition, reappearance, reversion, persistence **4** *They have seen no return on their investment.* = **profit**, interest, benefit, gain, income, advantage, revenue, yield, proceeds, takings, boot (*dialect*) **5** *What do I get in return for taking part in your experiment?* = **repayment**, reward, compensation, reparation, reimbursement, recompense, reciprocation, requital, retaliation, meed (*archaic*) **6** *a new analysis of the census returns* = **statement**, report, form, list, account, summary

revamp VERB = **renovate**, restore, overhaul, refurbish, rehabilitate, do up (*informal*), patch up, refit, repair, fix up (*informal, chiefly U.S. & Canad.*), recondition, give a face-lift to

reveal VERB **1** *She has refused to reveal her daughter's whereabouts.* = **make known**, disclose, give away, make public, tell, announce, publish, broadcast, leak, communicate, proclaim, betray, give out, let out, impart, divulge, let slip, let on, take the wraps off (*informal*), blow wide open (*slang*), get off your chest (*informal*) ■ **OPPOSITE:** keep secret **2** *A grey carpet was removed to reveal the pine floor.* = **show**, display, bare, exhibit, unveil, uncover, manifest, unearth, unmask, lay bare, bring to light, expose to view ■ **OPPOSITE:** hide

revel VERB *I'm afraid I revelled the night away.* = **celebrate**, rave (*Brit. slang*), carouse, live it up (*informal*), push the boat out (*Brit. informal*), whoop it up (*informal*), make merry, paint the town red (*informal*), go on a spree, roister ▶ NOUN (*often plural*) *The revels often last until dawn.* = **merrymaking**, party, celebration, rave (*Brit. slang*), gala, spree, festivity, beano (*Brit. slang*), debauch, saturnalia, bacchanal, rave-up (*Brit. slang*), jollification, carousal, hooley *or* hoolie (*chiefly Irish & N.Z.*), carouse • **revel in something** *She revelled in her freedom.* = **enjoy**, relish, indulge in, delight in, savour, thrive on, bask in, wallow in, lap up, take pleasure in, drool over, luxuriate in, crow about, rejoice over, gloat about, rub your hands

revelation NOUN **1** *revelations about his private life* = **disclosure**, discovery, news, broadcast, exposé, announcement, publication, exposure, leak, uncovering, confession, divulgence **2** *the revelation of his private life* = **exhibition**, telling, communication, broadcasting, discovery, publication, exposure, leaking, unveiling, uncovering, manifestation, unearthing, giveaway, proclamation, exposition

reveller NOUN = **merrymaker**, carouser, pleasure-seeker, partygoer, roisterer, celebrator

revelry NOUN = **merrymaking**, partying, fun, celebration, rave (*Brit. slang*), spree, festivity, beano (*Brit. slang*), debauch, debauchery, carouse, jollity, saturnalia, roistering, rave-up (*Brit. slang*), jollification, carousal, hooley *or* hoolie (*chiefly Irish & N.Z.*)

revenge NOUN *in revenge for the murder of her lover* = **retaliation**, satisfaction, vengeance, reprisal, retribution, vindictiveness, an eye for an eye, requital ▶ VERB *The relatives wanted to revenge the dead man's murder.* = **avenge**, repay, vindicate, pay (someone) back, take revenge for, requite, even the score for, get your own back for (*informal*), make reprisal for, take an eye for an eye for

revenue NOUN = **income**, interest, returns, profits, gain, rewards, yield, proceeds, receipts, takings ■ **OPPOSITE:** expenditure

reverberate VERB = **echo**, ring, resound, vibrate, re-echo

reverberation NOUN = **echo**, ringing, resonance, resounding, vibration, re-echoing

revere VERB = **be in awe of**, respect, honour, worship, adore, reverence, exalt, look up to, defer to, venerate, have a high opinion of, put on a pedestal, think highly of ■ **OPPOSITE:** despise

reverence NOUN *in mutual support and reverence for the dead* = **respect**, honour, worship, admiration, awe, devotion, homage, deference, adoration, veneration, high esteem ■ **OPPOSITE:** contempt ▶ VERB *Some men even seem to reverence them.* = **revere**, respect, honour, admire, worship, adore, pay homage to, venerate, be in awe of, hold in awe

reverent ADJECTIVE = **respectful**, awed, solemn, deferential, loving, humble, adoring, devout, pious, meek, submissive, reverential ■ **OPPOSITE:** disrespectful

reverie NOUN = **daydream**, musing, preoccupation, trance, abstraction, daydreaming, inattention, absent-mindedness, brown study, woolgathering, castles in the air *or* Spain

reverse VERB **1** *They have made it clear they will not reverse the decision.* = **change**, alter, cancel, overturn, overthrow, set aside, undo, repeal, quash, revoke, overrule, retract, negate, rescind, invalidate, annul, obviate, countermand, declare null and void, overset, upset ■ **OPPOSITE:** implement **2** *The curve of the spine may be reversed under such circumstances.* = **turn round**, turn over, turn upside down, upend **3** *He reversed the position of the two stamps.* = **transpose**, change, move, exchange, transfer, switch, shift, alter, swap, relocate, rearrange, invert, interchange, reorder **4** *He reversed and drove away.* = **go backwards**, retreat, back up, turn back, backtrack, move backwards, back ■ **OPPOSITE:** go forward ▶ NOUN **1** *There is absolutely no evidence. Quite the reverse.* = **opposite**, contrary, converse, antithesis, inverse, contradiction **2** *They have suffered a major reverse.* = **misfortune**, check, defeat, blow, failure, disappointment, setback, hardship, reversal, adversity, mishap, affliction, repulse, trial, misadventure, vicissitude **3** *on the reverse of the coin* = **back**, rear, other side, wrong side, underside, flip side, verso ■ **OPPOSITE:** front ▶ ADJECTIVE **1** *The wrong attitude will have the reverse effect.* = **opposite**, contrary, converse, inverse **2** *We will take them in reverse order.* = **backward**, inverted, back to front

revert VERB **1** *He reverted to smoking heavily.* = **go back**, return, come back, resume, lapse, recur, relapse, regress, backslide, take up where you left off **2** *The property reverts to the freeholder.* = **return**

> **USAGE** Since the concept *back* is already contained in the *re-* part of the word *revert*, it is unnecessary to say that someone *reverts back* to a particular type of behaviour.

review NOUN **1** *She has announced a review of adoption laws.* = **re-examination**, revision, rethink, retrospect, another look, reassessment, fresh look, second look, reconsideration, re-evaluation, recapitulation **2** *a review on the training and education of over-16s* = **survey**, report, study, analysis, examination, scrutiny, perusal **3** *We've never had a good review in the press.* = **critique**, commentary, evaluation, critical assessment, study, notice, criticism, judgment **4** *an early morning review of the troops* = **inspection**, display, parade, procession, march past **5** *He was recruited to write for the Edinburgh Review.* = **magazine**, journal, periodical, zine (*informal*) ▶ VERB **1** *The next day we reviewed the previous day's work.* = **reconsider**, revise, rethink, run over, reassess, re-examine, re-evaluate, think over, take another look at, recapitulate, look at again, go over again **2** *I see that no papers have reviewed my book.* = **assess**, write a critique of, study, judge, discuss, weigh, evaluate, criticize, read through, give your opinion of **3** *He reviewed the troops.* = **inspect**, check, survey, examine, vet, check out (*informal*), scrutinize, give (something or someone) the once-over (*informal*) **4** *Review all the information you need.* = **look back on**, remember, recall, reflect on, summon up, recollect, call to mind

reviewer NOUN = **critic**, judge, commentator, connoisseur, arbiter, essayist

revile VERB = **malign**, abuse, knock (*informal*), rubbish (*informal*), run down, smear, libel, scorn, slag (off) (*slang*), reproach, denigrate, vilify, slander, defame, bad-mouth (*slang*), traduce, calumniate, vituperate, asperse

revise VERB **1** *He soon came to revise his opinion.* = **change**, review, modify, reconsider, re-examine **2** *Three editors handled revising the articles.* = **edit**, correct, alter, update, amend, rewrite, revamp, rework, redo, emend **3** *I have to revise maths tonight.* = **study**, go over, run through, cram (*informal*), memorize, reread, swot up on (*Brit. informal*)

revision NOUN **1** *The phase of writing that is important is revision.* = **emendation**, editing, updating, correction, rewriting **2** *The government will make a number of revisions.* = **change**, review, amendment, modification, alteration, re-examination **3** *They prefer to do their revision at home.* = **studying**, cramming (*informal*), memorizing, swotting (*Brit. informal*), rereading, homework

revitalize VERB = **reanimate**, restore, renew, refresh, resurrect, rejuvenate, breathe new life into, bring back to life, revivify

revival NOUN **1** *There is no chance of a revival in car sales.* = **resurgence** ■ **OPPOSITE:** decline **2** *a revival of nationalism and the rudiments of democracy* = **reawakening**, restoration, renaissance, renewal, awakening, resurrection, refreshment, quickening, rebirth, resuscitation, revitalization, recrudescence, reanimation, renascence, revivification

revive VERB **1** *an attempt to revive the economy* = **revitalize**, restore, rally, renew, renovate, rekindle, kick-start (*informal*), breathe new life into, invigorate, reanimate **2** *They tried in vain to revive him.* = **bring round**, awaken, animate, rouse, resuscitate, bring back to life **3** *After three days in a coma, he revived.* = **come round**, recover, quicken, spring up again **4** *Superb food and drink revived our little band.* = **refresh**, restore, comfort, cheer, renew, resurrect, rejuvenate, revivify ■ **OPPOSITE:** exhaust

revoke VERB = **cancel**, recall, withdraw, reverse, abolish, set aside, repeal, renounce, quash, take back, call back, retract, repudiate, negate, renege, rescind, invalidate, annul, nullify, recant, obviate, disclaim, abrogate, countermand, declare null and void ■ **OPPOSITE:** endorse

revolt NOUN *a revolt by ordinary people against the leaders* = **uprising**, rising, revolution, rebellion, mutiny, defection, insurrection, insurgency, putsch, sedition ▶ VERB **1** *The townspeople revolted.* = **rebel**, rise up, resist, defect, mutiny, take to the streets, take up

arms (against) **2** *He entirely revolts me.*
= **disgust**, offend, turn off (*informal*),
sicken, repel, repulse, nauseate, gross out
(*U.S. slang*), shock, turn your stomach,
make your flesh creep, give you the creeps
(*informal*)

revolting ADJECTIVE = **disgusting**,
shocking, offensive, appalling, nasty, foul,
horrible, obscene, sickening, distasteful,
horrid (*informal*), repellent, obnoxious,
repulsive, nauseating, repugnant,
loathsome, abhorrent, abominable,
nauseous, cringe-making (*Brit. informal*),
noisome, yucky or yukky (*slang*), yucko
(*Austral. slang*) ■ OPPOSITE: delightful

revolution NOUN **1** *after the French Revolution*
= **revolt**, rising, coup, rebellion, uprising,
mutiny, insurgency, coup d'état, putsch
2 *a revolution in ship design and propulsion*
= **transformation**, shift, innovation,
upheaval, reformation, metamorphosis,
sea change, drastic or radical change **3** *The
gear drives a wheel 1/10th revolution per cycle.*
= **rotation**, turn, cycle, circle, wheel, spin,
lap, circuit, orbit, whirl, gyration, round

revolutionary ADJECTIVE **1** *Do you know
anything about the revolutionary movement?*
= **rebel**, radical, extremist, subversive,
insurgent, seditious, mutinous,
insurrectionary ■ OPPOSITE: reactionary
2 *His trumpet-playing was quite revolutionary.*
= **innovative**, new, different, novel,
radical, fundamental, progressive,
experimental, drastic, avant-garde,
ground-breaking, thoroughgoing
■ OPPOSITE: conventional ▶ NOUN
The revolutionaries laid down their arms.
= **rebel**, insurgent, mutineer,
insurrectionary, revolutionist,
insurrectionist ■ OPPOSITE: reactionary

revolutionize VERB = **transform**, reform,
revamp, modernize, metamorphose, break
with the past

revolve VERB **1** *The satellite revolves around
the earth.* = **go round**, circle, orbit, gyrate
2 *The entire circle revolved slowly.* = **rotate**,
turn, wheel, spin, twist, whirl **3** *He revolved
the new notion dizzily in his mind.* = **consider**,
study, reflect, think about, deliberate,
ponder, turn over (in your mind), meditate,
mull over, think over, ruminate

revulsion NOUN = **disgust**, loathing,
distaste, aversion, recoil, abomination,
repulsion, abhorrence, repugnance, odium
(*formal*), detestation ■ OPPOSITE: liking

reward NOUN **1** *He earned his reward for
contributions to the struggle.* = **prize 2** *He'll get
his reward before long.* = **punishment**, desert,
retribution, comeuppance (*slang*), just

deserts, requital **3** *They last night offered a
£10,000 reward.* = **payment**, return, benefit,
profit, gain, prize, wages, honour,
compensation, bonus, premium, merit,
repayment, bounty, remuneration,
recompense, meed (*archaic*), requital
■ OPPOSITE: penalty ▶ VERB *Their generosity
will be rewarded.* = **compensate**, pay,
honour, repay, recompense, requite,
remunerate (*formal*), make it worth your
while ■ OPPOSITE: penalize

rewarding ADJECTIVE = **satisfying**,
fulfilling, gratifying, edifying, economic
(*Brit.*), pleasing, valuable, profitable,
productive, worthwhile, beneficial,
enriching, fruitful, advantageous, gainful,
remunerative ■ OPPOSITE: unrewarding

rewrite VERB = **revise**, correct, edit, recast,
touch up, redraft, emend

rhetoric NOUN **1** *a torrent of warlike rhetoric*
= **hyperbole**, rant, hot air (*informal*),
pomposity, bombast, wordiness, verbosity,
fustian, grandiloquence, magniloquence
2 *the noble institutions, such as political rhetoric*
= **oratory**, eloquence, public speaking,
speech-making, elocution, declamation,
speechifying, grandiloquence, spieling
(*informal*), whaikorero (*N.Z.*)

rhetorical ADJECTIVE **1** *a rhetorical device used
to emphasize moments in the text* = **oratorical**,
verbal, linguistic, stylistic **2** *He disgorges a
stream of rhetorical flourishes.* = **high-flown**,
flamboyant, windy, flashy, pompous,
pretentious, flowery, showy, florid,
bombastic, hyperbolic, verbose, oratorical,
grandiloquent, high-sounding,
declamatory, arty-farty (*informal*),
silver-tongued, magniloquent

rhyme NOUN *He has taught her a little rhyme.*
= **poem**, song, verse, ode • **rhyme or
reason** (*used in negative constructions*) *He
picked people without rhyme or reason.* = **sense**,
meaning, plan, planning, system, method,
pattern, logic

rhythm NOUN **1** *His music fused the rhythms
of jazz and classical music.* = **beat**, swing,
accent, pulse, tempo, cadence, lilt **2** *the
rhythm and rhyme inherent in nursery rhymes*
= **metre**, time, measure (*Prosody*) **3** *This is
the rhythm of the universe.* = **pattern**,
movement, flow, periodicity

rhythmic *or* **rhythmical** ADJECTIVE
= **cadenced**, throbbing, periodic,
pulsating, flowing, musical, harmonious,
lilting, melodious, metrical

rich ADJECTIVE **1** *You're going to be a very rich
man.* = **wealthy**, affluent, well-off, opulent,
propertied, rolling (*slang*), loaded (*slang*),
flush (*informal*), prosperous, well-heeled

(*informal*), well-to-do, moneyed, filthy rich, stinking rich (*informal*), made of money (*informal*), minted (*Brit. slang*) ■ **OPPOSITE:** poor **2** *a rich supply of fresh, clean water* = **well-stocked**, full, productive, ample, abundant, plentiful, copious, well-provided, well-supplied, plenteous ■ **OPPOSITE:** scarce **3** *the hearty rich foods of Gascony* = **full-bodied**, heavy, sweet, delicious, fatty, tasty, creamy, spicy, juicy, luscious, savoury, succulent, flavoursome, highly-flavoured ■ **OPPOSITE:** bland **4** *Farmers grow rice in the rich soil.* = **fruitful**, productive, fertile, prolific, fecund ■ **OPPOSITE:** barren **5** *The bees buzzed around a garden rich with flowers.* = **abounding**, full, luxurious, lush, abundant, exuberant, well-endowed **6** *He spoke in that deep rich voice which made them all swoon.* = **resonant**, full, deep, mellow, mellifluous, dulcet ■ **OPPOSITE:** high-pitched **7** *an attractive, glossy rich red colour* = **vivid**, strong, deep, warm, bright, intense, vibrant, gay ■ **OPPOSITE:** dull **8** *This is a Baroque church with a rich interior.* = **costly**, fine, expensive, valuable, superb, elegant, precious, elaborate, splendid, gorgeous, lavish, exquisite, sumptuous, priceless, palatial, beyond price ■ **OPPOSITE:** cheap **9** *That's rich, coming from him.* = **funny**, amusing, ridiculous, hilarious, ludicrous, humorous, laughable, comical, risible (*formal*), side-splitting

riches PLURAL NOUN **1** *Some people want fame or riches.* = **wealth**, money, property, gold, assets, plenty, fortune, substance, treasure, abundance, richness, affluence, opulence, top whack (*informal*) ■ **OPPOSITE:** poverty **2** *Russia's vast natural riches* = **resources**, treasures

richly ADVERB **1** *The rooms are richly decorated.* = **elaborately**, lavishly, elegantly, splendidly, exquisitely, expensively, luxuriously, gorgeously, sumptuously, opulently, palatially **2** *He achieved the success he so richly deserved.* = **fully**, well, thoroughly, amply, appropriately, properly, suitably, in full measure

rickety ADJECTIVE = **shaky**, broken, weak, broken-down, frail, insecure, feeble, precarious, derelict, flimsy, wobbly, imperfect, tottering, ramshackle, dilapidated, decrepit, unsteady, unsound, infirm, jerry-built

rid VERB *an attempt to rid the country of corruption* = **free**, clear, deliver, relieve, purge, lighten, unburden, disabuse, make free, disembarrass, disencumber, disburden
• **get rid of something** *or* **someone**

The owner needs to get rid of the car. = **dispose of**, throw away or out, dispense with, dump, remove, eliminate, expel, unload, shake off, eject, do away with, jettison, weed out, see the back of, wipe from the face of the earth, give the bum's rush to (*slang*)

riddle¹ NOUN **1** *Tell me a riddle.* = **puzzle**, problem, conundrum, teaser, poser, rebus, brain-teaser (*informal*), Chinese puzzle **2** *a riddle of modern architecture* = **enigma**, question, secret, mystery, puzzle, conundrum, teaser, problem

riddle² VERB **1** *Attackers riddled two homes with gunfire.* = **pierce**, pepper, puncture, perforate, honeycomb **2** *The report was riddled with errors.* = **pervade**, fill, spread through, mar, spoil, corrupt, impair, pervade, infest, permeate

ride VERB **1** *I saw a girl riding a horse.* = **control**, handle, sit on, manage **2** *I was riding on the back of a friend's bicycle.* = **travel**, be carried, be supported, be borne, go, move, sit, progress, journey ▶ NOUN *Would you like to go for a ride?* = **journey**, drive, trip, lift, spin (*informal*), outing, whirl (*informal*), jaunt

ridicule VERB *I admire her for allowing them to ridicule her.* = **laugh at**, mock, make fun of, make a fool of, humiliate, taunt, sneer at, parody, caricature, jeer at, scoff at, deride, send up (*Brit. informal*), lampoon, poke fun at, chaff, take the mickey out of (*informal*), satirize, pooh-pooh, laugh out of court, make a monkey out of, make someone a laughing stock, laugh to scorn ▶ NOUN *He was subjected to public ridicule.* = **mockery**, scorn, derision, laughter, irony, rib, taunting, sneer, satire, jeer, banter, sarcasm, chaff, gibe, raillery

ridiculous ADJECTIVE = **laughable**, stupid, incredible, silly, outrageous, absurd, foolish, unbelievable, hilarious, ludicrous, preposterous, farcical, comical, zany, nonsensical, derisory, inane, risible (*formal*), contemptible, cockamamie (*slang, chiefly U.S.*) ■ **OPPOSITE:** sensible

rife ADJECTIVE **1** *Speculation is rife that he'll be sacked.* = **widespread**, abundant, plentiful, rampant, general, common, current, raging, universal, frequent, prevailing, epidemic, prevalent, ubiquitous **2** (*usually with* with) *Hollywood soon became rife with rumours.* = **abounding**, seething, teeming

rifle VERB **1** *The men rifled through his clothing.* = **rummage**, go, rake, fossick (*Austral. & N.Z.*) **2** *The child rifled the till while her mother distracted the postmistress.* = **ransack**, rob, burgle, loot, strip, sack, gut, plunder, pillage, despoil (*formal*)

rift NOUN **1** *They hope to heal the rift with their father.* = **breach**, difference, division, split, separation, falling out (*informal*), disagreement, quarrel, alienation, schism, estrangement **2** *In the open bog are many rifts and potholes.* = **split**, opening, space, crack, gap, break, fault, breach, fracture, flaw, cleavage, cleft, chink, crevice, fissure, cranny

rig VERB **1** *She accused her opponents of rigging the vote.* = **fix** (*informal*), doctor, engineer (*informal*), arrange, fake, manipulate, juggle, tamper with, fiddle with (*informal*), falsify, trump up, gerrymander **2** *He had rigged the dinghy for a sail.* = **equip**, fit out, kit out, outfit, supply, turn out, provision, furnish, accoutre • **rig something up** *I rigged up a shelter with a tarpaulin.* = **set up**, build, construct, put up, arrange, assemble, put together, erect, improvise, fix up, throw together, cobble together

right ADJECTIVE **1** *That's absolutely right!* = **correct**, true, genuine, accurate, exact, precise, valid, authentic, satisfactory, spot-on (*Brit. informal*), factual, on the money (*informal*), unerring, admissible, dinkum (*Austral. & N.Z. informal*), veracious, sound ■ **OPPOSITE:** wrong **2** *Make sure you approach it in the right way.* = **proper**, done, becoming, seemly, fitting, fit, appropriate, suitable, desirable, comme il faut (*French*) ■ **OPPOSITE:** inappropriate **3** *at the right time in the right place* = **favourable**, due, ideal, convenient, rightful, advantageous, opportune (*formal*), propitious ■ **OPPOSITE:** disadvantageous **4** *It's not right, leaving her like this.* = **just**, good, fair, moral, proper, ethical, upright, honourable, honest, equitable, righteous, virtuous, lawful ■ **OPPOSITE:** unfair **5** *I think he's not right in the head actually.* = **sane**, sound, balanced, normal, reasonable, rational, all there (*informal*), lucid, unimpaired, compos mentis (*Latin*) **6** *He just didn't look right.* = **healthy**, well, fine, fit, in good health, in the pink, up to par ■ **OPPOSITE:** unwell ▶ ADVERB **1** *He guessed right about some things.* = **correctly**, truly, precisely, exactly, genuinely, accurately, factually, aright ■ **OPPOSITE:** wrongly **2** *They made sure I did everything right.* = **suitably**, fittingly, appropriately, properly, aptly, satisfactorily, befittingly ■ **OPPOSITE:** improperly **3** *It caught me right in the middle of the forehead.* = **exactly**, squarely, precisely, bang, slap-bang (*informal*) **4** *It was taken right there on a conveyor belt.* = **directly**, straight, precisely, exactly, unswervingly, without deviation, by the shortest route, in a beeline **5** *The candle had burned right down.* = **all the way**, completely, totally, perfectly, entirely, absolutely, altogether, thoroughly, wholly, utterly, quite **6** *She'll be right down.* = **straight**, directly, immediately, quickly, promptly, instantly, straightaway, without delay ■ **OPPOSITE:** indirectly **7** *If you're not treated right, let us know.* = **properly**, fittingly, fairly, morally, honestly, justly, ethically, honourably, righteously, virtuously **8** *I hope things will turn out right.* = **favourably**, well, fortunately, for the better, to advantage, beneficially, advantageously ■ **OPPOSITE:** badly ▶ NOUN **1** *a woman's right to choose* = **prerogative**, interest, business, power, claim, authority, title, due, freedom, licence, permission, liberty, privilege **2** *a fight between right and wrong* = **justice**, good, reason, truth, honour, equity, virtue, integrity, goodness, morality, fairness, legality, righteousness, propriety, rectitude, lawfulness, uprightness ■ **OPPOSITE:** injustice ▶ VERB *We've made progress in righting the wrongs of the past.* = **rectify**, settle, fix, correct, repair, sort out, compensate for, straighten, redress, vindicate, put right • **by rights** *Negotiations should, by rights, have been conducted by him.* = **in fairness**, properly, justly, equitably • **put something to rights** *He decided to put matters to rights.* = **order**, arrange, straighten out

right away ADVERB = **immediately**, now, directly, promptly, instantly, at once, right off, straightaway, without delay, without hesitation, straight off (*informal*), forthwith, pronto (*informal*), this instant, posthaste

righteous ADJECTIVE = **virtuous**, good, just, fair, moral, pure, ethical, upright, honourable, honest, equitable, law-abiding, squeaky-clean, blameless ■ **OPPOSITE:** wicked

righteousness NOUN = **virtue**, justice, honour, equity, integrity, goodness, morality, honesty, purity, probity (*formal*), rectitude, faithfulness, uprightness, blamelessness, ethicalness

rightful ADJECTIVE = **lawful**, just, real, true, due, legal, suitable, proper, valid, legitimate, authorized, bona fide, de jure

right-wing ADJECTIVE = **conservative**, Tory, reactionary ■ **OPPOSITE:** left-wing

rigid ADJECTIVE **1** *Hospital routines for nurses are very rigid.* = **strict**, set, fixed, exact, rigorous, stringent, austere, severe ■ **OPPOSITE:** flexible **2** *My father is very rigid in his thinking.* = **inflexible**, harsh, stern, adamant, uncompromising, unrelenting, unyielding, intransigent, unbending, invariable, unalterable, undeviating **3** *rigid plastic containers* = **stiff**, inflexible, inelastic ■ **OPPOSITE:** pliable

rigorous ADJECTIVE **1** *rigorous military training* = **strict**, hard, firm, demanding, challenging, tough, severe, exacting, harsh, stern, rigid, stringent, austere, inflexible ■ **OPPOSITE:** soft **2** *He is rigorous in his control of expenditure.* = **thorough**, meticulous, painstaking, scrupulous, nice, accurate, exact, precise, conscientious, punctilious (*formal*) ■ **OPPOSITE:** careless

rigour NOUN **1** (*often plural*) *the rigours of childbirth* = **ordeal**, suffering, trial, hardship, privation (*formal*) **2** *We need to address such challenging issues with rigour.* = **strictness**, austerity, rigidity, firmness, hardness, harshness, inflexibility, stringency, asperity, sternness **3** *His work is built round academic rigour and years of insight.* = **thoroughness**, accuracy, precision, exactitude, exactness, conscientiousness, meticulousness, punctiliousness, preciseness

rile VERB = **anger**, upset, provoke, bug (*informal*), annoy, irritate, aggravate (*informal*), gall, nettle, vex, irk, pique, peeve (*informal*), get under your skin (*informal*), get on your nerves (*informal*), nark (*Brit., Austral. & N.Z. slang*), get your goat (*slang*), try your patience, rub you up the wrong way, get *or* put your back up, hack you off (*informal*)

rim NOUN **1** *She looked at him over the rim of her glass.* = **edge**, lip, brim, flange **2** *a round mirror with white metal rim* = **border**, edge, trim, circumference **3** *round the eastern rim of the Mediterranean* = **margin**, border, verge (*Brit.*), brink

rind NOUN **1** *grated lemon rind* = **skin**, peel, outer layer, epicarp **2** *Cut off the rind of the cheese.* = **crust**, husk, integument

ring¹ NOUN **1** *a ring of blue smoke* = **circle**, round, band, circuit, loop, hoop, halo **2** *The fight continued in the ring.* = **arena**, enclosure, circus, rink **3** *investigation of an international crime ring* = **gang**, group, association, band, cell, combine, organization, circle, crew (*informal*), knot, mob, syndicate, cartel, junta, clique, coterie, cabal ▶ VERB *The area is ringed by troops.* = **encircle**, surround, enclose, encompass, seal off, girdle, circumscribe, hem in, gird

ring² VERB **1** *He rang me at my mother's.* = **phone**, call, telephone, buzz (*informal, chiefly Brit.*) **2** *He heard the school bell ring.* = **chime**, sound, toll, resound, resonate, reverberate, clang, peal **3** *The whole place was ringing with music.* = **reverberate**, resound, resonate ▶ NOUN **1** *We'll give him a ring as soon as we get back.* = **call**, phone call, buzz (*informal, chiefly Brit.*) **2** *There was a ring of the bell.* = **chime**, knell, peal

> **USAGE** *Rang* is the past tense of the verb *ring*, as in *he rang the bell*. *Rung* is the past participle, as in *he has already rung the bell*, and care should be taken not to use it as if it were a variant form of the past tense.

rinse VERB *After washing always rinse the hair in clear water.* = **wash**, clean, wet, dip, splash, cleanse, bathe, wash out ▶ NOUN *plenty of lather followed by a rinse with cold water* = **wash**, wetting, dip, splash, bath

riot NOUN **1** *Twelve inmates have been killed during a riot.* = **disturbance**, row, disorder, confusion, turmoil, quarrel, upheaval, fray, strife, uproar, turbulence, commotion, lawlessness, street fighting, tumult, donnybrook, mob violence **2** *The garden was a riot of colour.* = **display**, show, splash, flourish, extravaganza, profusion **3** *It was a riot when I introduced my two cousins!* = **laugh** (*informal*), joke, scream (*informal*), blast (*U.S. slang*), hoot (*informal*), lark ▶ VERB *They rioted in protest against the government.* = **rampage**, take to the streets, run riot, go on the rampage, fight in the streets, raise an uproar • **run riot 1** *Rampaging prisoners ran riot through the jail.* = **rampage**, go wild, be out of control, raise hell, let yourself go, break *or* cut loose, throw off all restraint **2** *Virginia creeper ran riot up the walls.* = **grow profusely**, luxuriate, spread like wildfire, grow like weeds

riotous ADJECTIVE **1** *They wasted their lives in riotous living.* = **reckless**, wild, outrageous, lavish, rash, luxurious, extravagant, wanton, unrestrained, intemperate, heedless, immoderate **2** *Dinner was often a riotous affair.* = **unrestrained**, wild, loud, noisy, boisterous, rollicking, uproarious, orgiastic, side-splitting, rambunctious (*informal*), saturnalian, roisterous **3** *a riotous mob of hooligans* = **unruly**, violent, disorderly, rebellious, rowdy, anarchic, tumultuous, lawless, mutinous, ungovernable, uproarious, refractory, insubordinate, rampageous ■ **OPPOSITE:** orderly

rip VERB **1** *I tried not to rip the paper.* = **tear**, cut, score, split, burst, rend (*literary*), slash, hack, claw, slit, gash, lacerate **2** *I felt the banner rip as we were pushed in opposite directions.* = **be torn**, tear, split, burst, be rent ▶ NOUN *She looked at the rip in her new dress.* = **tear**, cut, hole, split, rent, slash, slit, cleavage, gash, laceration • **rip someone off** *Ticket touts ripped them off.* = **cheat**, trick, rob, con (*informal*), skin (*slang*), stiff (*slang*), steal from, fleece, defraud, dupe, swindle, diddle (*informal*), do the dirty on (*Brit. informal*), gyp (*slang*), cozen, scam (*slang*)

ripe ADJECTIVE **1** *Always choose firm but ripe fruit.* = **ripened**, seasoned, ready, mature, mellow, fully developed, fully grown ■ **OPPOSITE:** unripe **2** *Conditions are ripe for an outbreak of cholera.* = **right**, suitable **3** *He lived to the ripe old age of 65.* = **mature** **4** *The time is ripe for high-level dialogue.* = **suitable**, timely, ideal, favourable, auspicious, opportune (*formal*) ■ **OPPOSITE:** unsuitable **5** (*with* **for**) *Do you feel ripe for the journey?* = **ready for**, prepared for, eager for, in readiness for

ripen VERB = **mature**, season, develop, get ready, burgeon, come of age, come to fruition, grow ripe, make ripe

rip-off *or* **ripoff** NOUN = **cheat**, con (*informal*), scam (*slang*), con trick (*informal*), fraud, theft, sting (*informal*), robbery, exploitation, swindle, daylight robbery (*informal*)

riposte NOUN *He glanced at her, expecting a cheeky riposte.* = **retort**, return, answer, response, reply, sally, comeback (*informal*), counterattack, repartee, rejoinder ▶ VERB *'You look kind of funny,' she riposted blithely.* = **retort**, return, answer, reply, respond, come back, rejoin, reciprocate

ripple NOUN **1** *the ripples on the sea's calm surface* = **wave**, tremor, oscillation, undulation **2** *The news sent a ripple of excitement through the Security Council.* = **flutter**, thrill, tremor, tingle, vibration, frisson

rise VERB **1** *He rose slowly from his chair.* = **get up**, stand up, get to your feet **2** *He had risen early and gone to work.* = **arise** (*old-fashioned*), surface, get out of bed, rise and shine **3** *The sun had risen high in the sky.* = **go up**, climb, move up, ascend ■ **OPPOSITE:** descend **4** *The building rose before him.* = **loom**, tower **5** *the slope of land that rose from the house* = **get steeper**, mount, climb, ascend, go uphill, slope upwards ■ **OPPOSITE:** drop **6** *We need to increase our charges in order to meet rising costs.* = **increase**, mount ■ **OPPOSITE:** decrease **7** *His voice rose almost to a scream.* = **grow**, go up, intensify **8** *The people wanted to rise against the oppression.* = **rebel**, resist, revolt, mutiny, take up arms, mount the barricades **9** *She has risen to the top of her organization.* = **advance**, progress, get on, be promoted, prosper, go places (*informal*), climb the ladder, work your way up ▶ NOUN

1 *I climbed to the top of the rise.* = **upward slope**, incline, elevation, ascent, hillock, rising ground, acclivity, kopje or koppie (*S. African*) **2** *the prospect of another rise in interest rates* = **increase**, climb, upturn, upswing, advance, improvement, ascent, upsurge, bounce, upward turn ■ **OPPOSITE:** decrease **3** *He will get a rise of nearly £4,000.* = **pay increase**, raise (*U.S.*), increment **4** *They celebrated the regime's rise to power.* = **advancement**, progress, climb, promotion, aggrandizement • **give rise to something** *The picture gave rise to speculation.* = **cause**, produce, effect, result in, provoke, bring about, bring on

risible ADJECTIVE = **ridiculous**, ludicrous, laughable, farcical, funny, amusing, absurd, hilarious, humorous, comical, droll, side-splitting, rib-tickling (*informal*)

risk NOUN **1** *There is a small risk of brain damage.* = **danger**, chance, possibility, speculation, uncertainty, hazard **2** *This was one risk that paid off.* = **gamble**, chance, venture, speculation, leap in the dark **3** *He would not put their lives at risk.* = **peril**, jeopardy ▶ VERB **1** *Those who fail to register risk severe penalties.* = **stand a chance of** **2** *She risked her life to help a woman.* = **dare**, endanger, jeopardize, imperil, venture, gamble, hazard, take a chance on, put in jeopardy, expose to danger

risky ADJECTIVE = **dangerous**, hazardous, unsafe, perilous, uncertain, tricky, dodgy (*Brit., Austral. & N.Z. informal*), precarious, touch-and-go, dicey (*informal, chiefly Brit.*), fraught with danger, chancy (*informal*), shonky (*Austral. & N.Z. informal*) ■ **OPPOSITE:** safe

risqué ADJECTIVE = **suggestive**, blue, daring, naughty, improper, racy, bawdy, off colour, ribald, immodest, indelicate, near the knuckle (*informal*), Rabelaisian

rite NOUN = **ceremony**, custom, ritual, act, service, form, practice, procedure, mystery, usage, formality, ceremonial, communion, ordinance, observance, sacrament, liturgy, solemnity

ritual NOUN **1** *This is the most ancient and holiest of the rituals.* = **ceremony**, rite, ceremonial, sacrament, service, mystery, communion, observance, liturgy, solemnity **2** *Italian culture revolves around the ritual of eating.* = **custom**, tradition, routine, convention, form, practice, procedure, habit, usage, protocol, formality, ordinance, tikanga (*N.Z.*), lockstep (*U.S. & Canad.*) ▶ ADJECTIVE *Here, the conventions required me to make the ritual noises.* = **ceremonial**, formal, conventional, routine, prescribed, stereotyped, customary, procedural, habitual, ceremonious

ritzy ADJECTIVE = **luxurious**, grand, luxury, elegant, glittering, glamorous, stylish, posh (*informal, chiefly Brit.*), sumptuous, plush (*informal*), high-class, opulent, swanky (*informal*), de luxe, schmick (*Austral. informal*)

rival NOUN **1** *He finished two seconds ahead of his rival.* = **opponent**, competitor, contender, challenger, contestant, adversary, antagonist, emulator
■ **OPPOSITE:** supporter **2** *He is a pastry chef without rival.* = **equal**, match, fellow, equivalent, peer, compeer ▶ VERB *London cannot rival the glamour of Barcelona or Madrid.* = **compete with**, match, equal, oppose, compare with, contend, come up to, emulate, vie with, measure up to, be a match for, bear comparison with, seek to displace ▶ MODIFIER *It would be no use having two rival companies.* = **competing**, conflicting, opposed, opposing, competitive, emulating

rivalry NOUN = **competition**, competitiveness, vying, opposition, struggle, conflict, contest, contention, duel, antagonism, emulation

river NOUN **1** *boating on the river* = **stream**, brook, creek (*U.S., Canad., Austral. & N.Z.*), beck, waterway, tributary, rivulet, watercourse, burn (*Scot.*) **2** *A river of lava was flowing down the mountainside towards the village.* = **flow**, rush, flood, spate, torrent
■ **RELATED WORD:** *adjective* fluvial

riveting ADJECTIVE = **enthralling**, arresting, gripping, fascinating, absorbing, captivating, hypnotic, engrossing, spellbinding

road NOUN **1** *There was very little traffic on the roads.* = **roadway**, street, highway, motorway, track, direction, route, path, lane, avenue, pathway, thoroughfare, course, ice road (*Canad.*) **2** *on the road to recovery* = **way**, path

roam VERB = **wander**, walk, range, travel, drift, stroll, stray, ramble, meander, rove, stravaig (*Scot. & Northern English, dialect*), peregrinate

roar VERB **1** *the roaring waters of Niagara Falls* = **thunder**, crash, rumble **2** *He threw back his head and roared.* = **guffaw**, laugh heartily, hoot, crack up (*informal*), bust a gut (*informal*), split your sides (*informal*) **3** *'I'll kill you for that,' he roared.* = **cry**, shout, yell, howl, bellow, clamour, bawl, bay, vociferate ▶ NOUN **1** *the roar of traffic* = **rumble**, thunder **2** *There were roars of*

laughter as he stood up. = **guffaw**, hoot, belly laugh (*informal*) **3** *the roar of lions in the distance* = **cry**, crash, shout, yell, howl, outcry, bellow, clamour

rob VERB **1** *Police said he had robbed a man hours earlier.* = **steal from**, hold up, rifle, mug (*informal*), stiff (*slang*) **2** *A man who tried to rob a bank was sentenced yesterday.* = **raid**, hold up, sack, loot, plunder, burgle, ransack, pillage **3** *I was robbed by a used-car dealer.* = **dispossess**, con (*informal*), rip off (*slang*), skin (*slang*), cheat, defraud, swindle, despoil (*formal*), gyp (*slang*) **4** *I can't forgive her for robbing me of an Olympic gold.* = **deprive**, strip, do out of (*informal*)

robber NOUN = **thief**, raider, burglar, looter, stealer, fraud (*informal*), cheat, pirate, bandit, plunderer, mugger (*informal*), highwayman *or* woman, conman *or* woman (*informal*), fraudster, swindler, brigand, grifter (*slang, chiefly U.S. & Canad.*), footpad (*archaic*), rogue trader

robbery NOUN **1** *The gang committed dozens of armed robberies.* = **burglary**, raid, hold-up, rip-off (*slang*), stick-up (*slang, chiefly U.S.*), home invasion (*Austral. & N.Z.*) **2** *The twins were convicted of robbery.* = **theft**, stealing, fraud, steaming (*informal*), mugging (*informal*), plunder, swindle, pillage, embezzlement, larceny, depredation, filching, thievery, rapine, spoliation

robe NOUN **1** *a fur-lined robe of green silk* = **gown**, costume, vestment, habit **2** *She put on a robe and went down to the kitchen.* = **dressing gown**, wrapper, bathrobe, negligée, housecoat, peignoir

robot NOUN = **machine**, automaton, android, mechanical man *or* woman

robust ADJECTIVE **1** *His robust physique counts for much in the modern game.* = **strong**, tough, powerful, athletic, well, sound, fit, healthy, strapping, hardy, rude, vigorous, rugged (*U.S. & Canad.*), muscular, swole (*slang*), hench (*informal*), sturdy, hale (*old-fashioned*), stout, staunch, hearty, husky (*informal*), in good health, lusty, alive and kicking, fighting fit, sinewy, brawny, in fine fettle, thickset, fit as a fiddle (*informal*), able-bodied ■ **OPPOSITE:** weak **2** *a robust sense of humour* = **rough**, raw, rude, coarse, raunchy (*informal*), earthy, boisterous, rollicking, unsubtle, indecorous, roisterous
■ **OPPOSITE:** refined **3** *the local police's robust attitude to troublemakers* = **straightforward**, practical, sensible, realistic, pragmatic, down-to-earth, hard-headed, common-sensical

rock¹ NOUN **1** *She sat cross-legged on the rock.* = **stone**, boulder **2** *She was the rock of the* family. = **tower of strength**, foundation, cornerstone, mainstay, support, protection, anchor, bulwark

rock² VERB **1** *His body rocked from side to side.* = **sway**, pitch, swing, reel, toss, lurch, wobble, roll **2** *His death rocked the fashion business.* = **shock**, surprise, shake, stun, astonish, stagger, jar, astound, daze, dumbfound, set you back on your heels (*informal*)

rocky¹ ADJECTIVE *The paths are often very rocky.* = **rough**, rugged, stony, craggy, pebbly, boulder-strewn

rocky² ADJECTIVE *Their relationship had gotten off to a rocky start.* = **unstable**, weak, uncertain, doubtful, shaky, unreliable, wobbly, rickety, unsteady, undependable

rod NOUN **1** *reinforced with steel rods* = **stick**, bar, pole, shaft, switch, crook, cane, birch, dowel **2** *It was a witch-doctor's rod.* = **staff**, baton, mace, wand, sceptre

rogue NOUN **1** *He wasn't a rogue at all.* = **scoundrel** (*old-fashioned*), crook (*informal*), villain, fraudster, sharper, fraud (*informal*), cheat, devil, deceiver, charlatan, conman *or* woman (*informal*), swindler, knave (*archaic*), ne'er-do-well, reprobate, scumbag (*slang*), blackguard, mountebank, grifter (*slang, chiefly U.S. & Canad.*), skelm (*S. African*), rorter (*Austral. slang*), wrong 'un (*slang*) **2** *a loveable rogue* = **scamp**, rascal, scally (*Northwest English, dialect*), rapscallion, nointer (*Austral. slang*)

role NOUN **1** *His role in the events has been pivotal.* = **job**, part, position, post, task, duty, function, capacity **2** *Shakespearean women's roles* = **part**, character, representation, portrayal, impersonation

roll VERB **1** *The car went off the road and rolled over into a ditch.* = **turn**, wheel, spin, reel, go round, revolve, rotate, whirl, swivel, pivot, twirl, gyrate **2** *The lorry slowly rolled forward.* = **trundle**, go, move **3** *Tears rolled down her cheeks.* = **flow**, run, course, slide, glide, purl **4** (*often with* **up**) *He took off his sweater and rolled it into a pillow.* = **wind**, bind, wrap, twist, curl, coil, swathe, envelop, entwine, furl, enfold **5** (*often with* **out**) *Rub in and roll out the pastry.* = **level**, even, press, spread, smooth, flatten **6** *The ship was still rolling in the troughs.* = **toss**, rock, lurch, reel, tumble, sway, wallow, billow, swing, welter **7** *guns firing, drums rolling, cymbals clashing* = **rumble**, boom, echo, drum, roar, thunder, grumble, resound, reverberate **8** *They rolled about in hysterics.* = **sway**, reel, stagger, lurch, lumber, waddle, swagger **9** *The years roll by and look at us now.* = **pass**, go past, elapse ▶ NOUN **1** *a roll of blue insulated wire* = **reel**, ball, bobbin, cylinder **2** *They heard the roll of drums.* = **rumble**, boom, drumming, roar, thunder, grumble, resonance, growl, reverberation **3** *A new electoral roll should be drawn up.* = **register**, record, list, table, schedule, index, catalogue, directory, inventory, census, chronicle, scroll, roster, annals **4** *despite the roll of the boat* = **tossing**, rocking, rolling, pitching, swell, lurching, wallowing **5** *Control the roll of the ball.* = **turn**, run, spin, rotation, cycle, wheel, revolution, reel, whirl, twirl, undulation, gyration

rollicking¹ ADJECTIVE *outrageous, and a rollicking good read* = **boisterous**, spirited, lively, romping, merry, hearty, playful, exuberant, joyous, carefree, jaunty, cavorting, sprightly, jovial, swashbuckling, frisky, rip-roaring (*informal*), devil-may-care, full of beans (*informal*), frolicsome, sportive ■ **OPPOSITE:** sedate

rollicking² NOUN *Whoever was responsible got a rollicking.* = **scolding**, lecture, reprimand, telling-off, roasting (*informal*), wigging (*Brit. slang*), ticking off (*informal*), dressing-down (*informal*), tongue-lashing (*informal*)

romance NOUN **1** *a holiday romance* = **love affair**, relationship, affair, intrigue, attachment, liaison, amour, affair of the heart, affaire (du coeur) (*French*) **2** *He still finds time for romance.* = **love 3** *We want to recreate the romance of old train journeys.* = **excitement**, colour, charm, mystery, adventure, sentiment, glamour, fascination, nostalgia, exoticness **4** *Her taste in fiction was for historical romances.* = **story**, novel, tale, fantasy, legend, fiction, fairy tale, love story, melodrama, idyll, tear-jerker (*informal*)

romantic ADJECTIVE **1** *They enjoyed a romantic dinner for two.* = **loving**, tender, passionate, fond, sentimental, sloppy (*informal*), amorous, mushy (*informal*), soppy (*Brit. informal*), lovey-dovey, icky (*informal*) ■ **OPPOSITE:** unromantic **2** *He has a romantic view of rural society.* = **idealistic**, unrealistic, visionary, high-flown, impractical, dreamy, utopian, whimsical, quixotic, starry-eyed ■ **OPPOSITE:** realistic **3** *romantic images from travel brochures* = **exciting**, charming, fascinating, exotic, mysterious, colourful, glamorous, picturesque, nostalgic ■ **OPPOSITE:** unexciting **4** *Both figures have become the stuff of romantic legends.* = **fictitious**, made-up, fantastic, fabulous, legendary, exaggerated, imaginative, imaginary, extravagant, unrealistic, improbable, fairy-tale, idyllic, fanciful, wild, chimerical ■ **OPPOSITE:** realistic

r

▶ NOUN *You're a hopeless romantic.* = **idealist**, romancer, visionary, dreamer, utopian, Don Quixote, sentimentalist

romp VERB *Dogs romped happily in the garden.* = **frolic**, sport, skip, have fun, revel, caper, cavort, frisk, gambol, make merry, rollick, roister, cut capers ▶ NOUN *a romp in the snow and slush* = **frolic**, lark (*informal*), caper • **romp home** *or* **in** *He romped home with 141 votes.* = **win easily**, walk it (*informal*), win hands down, run away with it, win by a mile (*informal*)

room NOUN **1** *He excused himself and left the room.* = **chamber**, office **2** *There wasn't enough room for all the gear.* = **space**, area, territory, volume, capacity, extent, expanse, elbowroom **3** *There's a lot of room for you to express yourself.* = **opportunity**, scope, leeway, play, chance, range, occasion, margin, allowance, compass, latitude

roomy ADJECTIVE = **spacious**, large, wide, broad, extensive, generous, ample, capacious, commodious, sizable *or* sizeable ■ **OPPOSITE:** cramped

root¹ NOUN **1** *the twisted roots of an apple tree* = **stem**, tuber, rhizome, radix, radicle **2** *We got to the root of the problem.* = **source**, cause, heart, bottom, beginnings, base, seat, occasion, seed, foundation, origin, core, fundamental, essence, nucleus, starting point, germ, crux, nub, derivation, fountainhead, mainspring ▶ PLURAL NOUN *I am proud of my Brazilian roots.* = **sense of belonging**, origins, heritage, birthplace, home, family, cradle • **root and branch 1** *in need of root and branch reform* = **complete**, total, entire, radical, thorough **2** *They want to deal with the problem root and branch.* = **completely**, finally, totally, entirely, radically, thoroughly, wholly, utterly, without exception, to the last man • **root something** *or* **someone out 1** *The generals have to root out traitors.* = **get rid of**, remove, destroy, eliminate, abolish, cut out, erase, eradicate, do away with, uproot, weed out, efface, exterminate, extirpate, wipe from the face of the earth **2** *It shouldn't take long to root out the cause of the problem.* = **discover**, find, expose, turn up, uncover, unearth, bring to light, ferret out ■ **RELATED WORD:** *adjective* radical

root² VERB *She rooted through the bag.* = **dig**, hunt, nose, poke, burrow, delve, ferret, pry, rummage, forage, rootle

rooted ADJECTIVE = **deep-seated**, firm, deep, established, confirmed, fixed, radical, rigid, entrenched, ingrained, deeply felt

rootless ADJECTIVE = **footloose**, homeless, roving, transient, itinerant, vagabond

rope NOUN *He tied the rope around his waist.* = **cord**, line, cable, strand, hawser ▶ VERB *I roped myself to the chimney.* = **tie**, bind, moor, lash, hitch, fasten, tether, pinion, lasso • **know the ropes** *She got to know the ropes.* = **be experienced**, know the score (*informal*), be knowledgeable, know what's what, be an old hand, know your way around, know where it's at (*slang*), know all the ins and outs • **rope someone in** *or* **into something** *I got roped into helping.* = **persuade**, involve, engage, enlist, talk into, drag in, inveigle

roster NOUN = **rota**, listing, list, table, roll, schedule, register, agenda, catalogue, inventory, scroll

rostrum NOUN = **stage**, stand, platform, podium, dais

rosy ADJECTIVE **1** *She had bright, rosy cheeks.* = **glowing**, fresh, blooming, flushed, blushing, radiant, reddish, ruddy, healthy-looking, roseate, rubicund ■ **OPPOSITE:** pale **2** *Is the future really so rosy?* = **promising**, encouraging, bright, reassuring, optimistic, hopeful, sunny, cheerful, favourable, auspicious, rose-coloured, roseate ■ **OPPOSITE:** gloomy **3** *the rosy brick buildings* = **pink**, red, rose-coloured, roseate

rot VERB **1** *The grain will start rotting in the silos.* = **decay**, break down, spoil, corrupt, deteriorate, taint, perish, degenerate, fester, decompose, corrode, moulder, go bad, putrefy (*formal*) **2** *It is not true to say that this wood never rots.* = **crumble**, disintegrate, become rotten **3** *I was left to rot nine years for a crime I didn't commit.* = **deteriorate**, decline, languish (*literary*), degenerate, wither away, waste away ▶ NOUN **1** *Investigations revealed rot in the beams.* = **decay**, disintegration, corrosion, decomposition, corruption, mould, blight, deterioration, canker, putrefaction, putrescence **2** *You do talk rot!* = **nonsense**, rubbish, drivel, twaddle, malarkey, pants (*slang*), crap (*slang*), garbage (*chiefly U.S.*), trash, bunk (*informal*), hot air (*informal*), tosh (*slang, chiefly Brit.*), pap, bilge (*informal*), tripe (*informal*), guff (*slang*), moonshine, claptrap (*informal*), hogwash, hokum (*slang, chiefly U.S. & Canad.*), codswallop (*Brit. slang*), piffle (*informal*), poppycock (*informal*), balderdash, bosh (*informal*), eyewash (*informal*), stuff and nonsense, flapdoodle (*slang*), tommyrot, horsefeathers (*U.S. slang*), bunkum *or* buncombe, bizzo (*Austral. slang*), bull's wool (*Austral. & N.Z. slang*) ■ **RELATED WORD:** *adjective* putrid

rotary ADJECTIVE = **revolving**, turning, spinning, rotating, rotational, gyratory, rotatory

rotate VERB **1** *The earth rotates round the sun.* = **revolve**, turn, wheel, spin, reel, go round, swivel, pivot, gyrate, pirouette **2** *The members of the club can rotate.* = **follow in sequence**, switch, alternate, interchange, take turns

rotation NOUN **1** *the daily rotation of the earth upon its axis* = **revolution**, turning, turn, wheel, spin, spinning, reel, orbit, pirouette, gyration **2** *crop rotation and integration of livestock* = **sequence**, switching, cycle, succession, interchanging, alternation

rotten ADJECTIVE **1** *The smell is like rotten eggs.* = **decaying**, bad, rank, foul, corrupt, sour, stinking, tainted, perished, festering, decomposed, decomposing, mouldy, mouldering, fetid, putrid, putrescent (*formal*), festy (*Austral. slang*) ■ **OPPOSITE:** fresh **2** *The bay window is rotten.* = **crumbling**, decayed, disintegrating, perished, corroded, unsound **3** *What rotten luck!* = **bad**, disappointing, unfortunate, unlucky, regrettable, deplorable **4** *You rotten swine!* = **despicable**, mean, base, dirty, nasty, unpleasant, filthy, vile, wicked, disagreeable, contemptible, scurrilous **5** *I felt rotten with the flu.* = **unwell**, poorly (*informal*), ill, sick, rough (*informal*), bad, crook (*Austral. & N.Z. informal*), below par, off colour, under the weather (*informal*), ropey or ropy (*Brit. informal*) **6** *I thought it was a rotten idea.* = **inferior**, poor, sorry, inadequate, unacceptable, punk, duff (*Brit. informal*), unsatisfactory, lousy (*slang*), low-grade, substandard, ill-considered, crummy (*slang*), ill-thought-out, poxy (*slang*), of a sort or of sorts, ropey or ropy (*Brit. informal*), bodger or bodgie (*Austral. slang*) **7** *There was something rotten in our legal system.* = **corrupt**, immoral, deceitful, untrustworthy, bent (*slang*), crooked (*informal*), vicious, degenerate, mercenary, treacherous, dishonest, disloyal, faithless, venal, dishonourable, perfidious (*literary*) ■ **OPPOSITE:** honourable

rotund ADJECTIVE **1** *A rotund gentleman appeared.* = **plump**, rounded, heavy, fat, stout, chubby, obese, fleshy, tubby, portly, roly-poly, podgy, corpulent ■ **OPPOSITE:** skinny **2** *writing rotund passages of purple prose* = **pompous**, orotund, magniloquent, full **3** *rotund towers, moats and drawbridges* = **round**, rounded, spherical, bulbous, globular, orbicular **4** *the wonderfully rotund*

tones of the presenter = **sonorous**, round, rich, resonant, orotund

rough ADJECTIVE **1** *She made her way across the rough ground.* = **uneven**, broken, rocky, rugged, irregular, jagged, bumpy, stony, craggy ■ **OPPOSITE:** even **2** *people who looked rough and stubbly* = **coarse**, disordered, tangled, hairy, fuzzy, bushy, shaggy, dishevelled, uncut, unshaven, tousled, bristly, unshorn ■ **OPPOSITE:** smooth **3** *Rugby's a rough game.* = **boisterous**, hard, tough, rugged, arduous **4** *He was rough and common.* = **ungracious**, blunt, rude, coarse, bluff, curt, churlish, bearish, brusque, uncouth, unrefined, inconsiderate, impolite, loutish, untutored, discourteous, unpolished, indelicate, uncivil, uncultured, unceremonious, ill-bred, unmannerly, ill-mannered ■ **OPPOSITE:** refined **5** *Women have a rough time in our society.* = **unpleasant**, hard, difficult, tough, uncomfortable, drastic, unjust ■ **OPPOSITE:** easy **6** (*informal*) *The lad is still feeling a bit rough.* = **unwell**, poorly (*informal*), ill, upset, sick, crook (*Austral. & N.Z. informal*), rotten (*informal*), below par, off colour, under the weather (*informal*), not a hundred per cent (*informal*), ropey or ropy (*Brit. informal*) **7** *We were only able to make a rough estimate.* = **approximate**, estimated ■ **OPPOSITE:** exact **8** *I've got a rough idea of what he looks like.* = **vague**, general, sketchy, imprecise, hazy, foggy, amorphous, inexact **9** *Make a rough plan of the space.* = **basic**, quick, raw, crude, unfinished, incomplete, hasty, imperfect, rudimentary, sketchy, cursory, shapeless, rough-and-ready, unrefined, formless, rough-hewn, untutored, unpolished ■ **OPPOSITE:** complete **10** *a rough wooden table* = **rough-hewn**, crude, uncut, unpolished, raw, undressed, unprocessed, unhewn, unwrought **11** *The ships collided in rough seas.* = **stormy**, wild, turbulent, agitated, choppy, tempestuous, inclement, squally ■ **OPPOSITE:** calm **12** '*Wait!' a rough voice commanded.* = **grating**, harsh, jarring, raucous, rasping, husky, discordant, gruff, cacophonous, unmusical, inharmonious ■ **OPPOSITE:** soft **13** *I was a bit rough with you this morning.* = **harsh**, tough, sharp, severe, nasty, cruel, rowdy, curt, unfeeling ■ **OPPOSITE:** gentle ▶ NOUN **1** *Editors are always saying that the roughs are better.* = **outline**, draft, mock-up, preliminary sketch, suggestion **2** (*informal*) *The roughs of the town are out.* = **thug**, tough, casual, rowdy, hoon (*Austral. & N.Z.*), bully boy, bruiser (*informal*), ruffian, lager lout, roughneck (*slang*), ned (*Scot. slang*), cougan

r

(*Austral. slang*), scozza (*Austral. slang*), bogan (*Austral. slang*) • **rough and ready 1** *Here is a rough and ready measurement.* = **makeshift**, adequate, crude, provisional, improvised, sketchy, thrown together, cobbled together, stopgap **2** *The soldiers were a bit rough and ready.* = **unrefined**, shabby, untidy, unkempt, unpolished, ungroomed, ill-groomed, daggy (*Austral. & N.Z. informal*) • **rough and tumble 1** *the rough and tumble of political combat* = **fight**, struggle, scrap (*informal*), brawl, scuffle, punch-up (*Brit. informal*), fracas, affray (*Law*), dust-up (*informal*), shindig (*informal*), donnybrook, scrimmage, roughhouse (*slang*), shindy (*informal*), melee *or* mêlée, biffo (*Austral. slang*) **2** *He enjoys rough and tumble play.* = **disorderly**, rough, scrambled, scrambling, irregular, rowdy, boisterous, haphazard, indisciplined • **rough someone up** *They roughed him up a bit.* = **beat up**, batter, thrash, do over (*Brit., Austral. & N.Z. slang*), work over (*slang*), mistreat, manhandle, maltreat, bash up (*informal*), beat the living daylights out of (*informal*), knock about *or* around, beat *or* knock seven bells out of (*informal*) • **rough something out** *He roughed out a framework for their story.* = **outline**, plan, draft, sketch, suggest, block out, delineate, adumbrate

round NOUN **1** *This is the latest round of job cuts.* = **series**, session, cycle, sequence, succession, bout **2** *in the third round of the cup* = **stage**, turn, level, period, division, session, lap **3** *small fresh rounds of goat's cheese* = **sphere**, ball, band, ring, circle, disc, globe, orb **4** *The consultant did his morning round.* = **course**, turn, tour, circuit, beat, series, schedule, routine, compass, ambit **5** *live rounds of ammunition* = **bullet**, shot, shell, discharge, cartridge ▶ ADJECTIVE **1** *the round church known as The New Temple* = **spherical**, rounded, bowed, curved, circular, cylindrical, bulbous, rotund, globular, curvilinear, ball-shaped, ring-shaped, disc-shaped, annular, discoid, orbicular **2** *a round dozen* = **complete**, full, whole, entire, solid, unbroken, undivided **3** *She was a small, round person in her early sixties.* = **plump**, full, rounded, ample, fleshy, roly-poly, rotund, full-fleshed ▶ VERB *The boats rounded the Cape.* = **go round**, circle, skirt, flank, bypass, encircle, turn, circumnavigate • **round on someone** *He has rounded on his critics.* = **attack**, abuse, turn on, retaliate against, have a go at (*Brit. slang*), snap at, wade into, lose your temper with, bite (someone's) head off (*informal*) • **round something off** *A fireworks display*

rounded off the day. = **complete**, close, settle, crown, cap, conclude, finish off, put the finishing touch to, bring to a close • **round something** *or* **someone up** *The police rounded up a number of suspects.* = **gather**, assemble, bring together, muster, group, drive, collect, rally, herd, marshal

roundabout ADJECTIVE **1** *a roundabout route* = **indirect**, meandering, devious, tortuous, circuitous, evasive, discursive, circumlocutory ■ OPPOSITE: direct **2** *indirect or roundabout language* = **oblique**, implied, indirect, evasive, circuitous, circumlocutory, periphrastic

roundly ADVERB = **thoroughly**, sharply, severely, bitterly, fiercely, bluntly, intensely, violently, vehemently, rigorously, outspokenly, frankly

roundup NOUN **1** *a roundup of the day's news* = **summary**, survey, collation **2** *What keeps a cowboy ready for another roundup?* = **muster**, collection, rally, assembly, herding

rouse VERB **1** *She roused him at 8.30.* = **wake up**, call, wake, awaken **2** *He did more to rouse the crowd than anybody else.* = **excite**, move, arouse, stir, disturb, provoke, anger, startle, animate, prod, exhilarate, get going, agitate, inflame, incite, whip up, galvanize, bestir **3** *It roused a feeling of rebellion in her.* = **stimulate**, provoke, arouse, incite, instigate

rousing ADJECTIVE = **lively**, moving, spirited, exciting, inspiring, stirring, stimulating, vigorous, brisk, exhilarating, inflammatory, electrifying ■ OPPOSITE: dull

rout VERB *The Norman army routed the English opposition.* = **defeat**, beat, overthrow, thrash, stuff (*slang*), worst, destroy, chase, tank (*slang*), crush, scatter, conquer, lick (*informal*), dispel, drive off, overpower, clobber (*slang*), wipe the floor with (*informal*), cut to pieces, put to flight, drub, put to rout, throw back in confusion ▶ NOUN *The retreat turned into a rout.* = **defeat**, beating, hiding (*informal*), ruin, overthrow, thrashing, licking (*informal*), pasting (*slang*), shambles, debacle, drubbing, overwhelming defeat, headlong flight, disorderly retreat

route NOUN **1** *the most direct route to the town centre* = **way**, course, road, direction, path, journey, passage, avenue, itinerary **2** *They would go out on his route and check him.* = **beat**, run, round, circuit ▶ VERB **1** *Approaching cars will be routed into two lanes.* = **direct**, lead, guide, steer, convey **2** *plans to route every emergency call through three exchanges* = **send**, forward, dispatch

USAGE When adding *-ing* to the verb *route* to form the present participle, it is more conventional, and clearer, to keep the final *e* from the end of the verb stem: *routeing*. The spelling *routing* in this sense is also possible, but keeping the *e* distinguishes it from *routing*, which is the participle formed from the verb *rout* meaning 'to defeat'.

routine NOUN **1** *The players had to change their daily routine.* = **procedure**, programme, way, order, practice, method, pattern, formula, custom, usage, wont, lockstep (*U.S. & Canad.*) **2** *the mundane routine of her life* = **grind** (*informal*), monotony, banality, groove, boredom, chore, the doldrums, dullness, sameness, ennui (*literary*), drabness, deadness, dreariness, tediousness, lifelessness ▸ ADJECTIVE **1** *a series of routine medical tests* = **usual**, standard, normal, customary, ordinary, familiar, typical, conventional, everyday, habitual, workaday, wonted ■ **OPPOSITE:** unusual **2** *So many days are routine and uninteresting.* = **boring**, dull, predictable, tedious, tiresome, run-of-the-mill, humdrum, unimaginative, clichéd, uninspired, mind-numbing, hackneyed, unoriginal

rove VERB = **wander**, range, cruise, drift, stroll, stray, roam, ramble, meander, traipse (*informal*), gallivant, gad about, stravaig (*Scot. & Northern English, dialect*)

rover NOUN = **wanderer**, traveller, roamer, rolling stone, rambler, transient, nomad, itinerant, ranger, drifter, vagrant, stroller, bird of passage, gadabout (*informal*)

row¹ NOUN *a row of pretty little cottages* = **line**, bank, range, series, file, rank, string, column, sequence, queue, tier • **in a row** *They have won five championships in a row.* = **consecutively**, running, in turn, one after the other, successively, in sequence

row² NOUN **1** *A man was stabbed to death in a family row.* = **quarrel**, dispute, argument, squabble, tiff, trouble, controversy, scrap (*informal*), fuss, falling-out (*informal*), fray, brawl, fracas, altercation, slanging match (*Brit.*), shouting match (*informal*), shindig (*informal*), ruction (*informal*), ruckus (*informal*), shindy (*informal*), bagarre (*French*) **2** *'Whatever is that row?' she demanded.* = **disturbance**, noise, racket, uproar, commotion, rumpus, tumult **3** *I can't give you a row for scarpering off.* = **telling-off**, talking-to (*informal*), lecture, reprimand,

ticking-off (*informal*), dressing-down (*informal*), rollicking (*Brit. informal*), tongue-lashing, reproof, castigation, flea in your ear (*informal*) ▸ VERB *They rowed all the time.* = **quarrel**, fight, argue, dispute, scrap (*informal*), brawl, squabble, spar, wrangle, go at it hammer and tongs

rowdy ADJECTIVE *He has complained about rowdy neighbours.* = **disorderly**, rough, loud, noisy, unruly, boisterous, loutish, wild, uproarious, obstreperous ■ **OPPOSITE:** orderly ▸ NOUN *The owner kept a baseball bat to deal with rowdies.* = **hooligan**, tough, rough (*informal*), casual, ned (*Scot. slang*), brawler, yahoo, lout, troublemaker, tearaway (*Brit.*), ruffian, lager lout, yob or yobbo (*Brit. slang*), cougan (*Austral. slang*), scozza (*Austral. slang*), bogan (*Austral. slang*)

royal ADJECTIVE **1** *an invitation to a royal garden party* = **regal**, kingly or queenly, princely, imperial, sovereign, monarchical, kinglike or queenlike **2** *She was given a royal welcome on her first visit to Britain.* = **splendid**, august, grand, impressive, superb, magnificent, superior, majestic, stately

rub VERB **1** *He rubbed his arms and stiff legs.* = **stroke**, smooth, massage, caress, knead **2** *She took off her glasses and rubbed them.* = **polish**, clean, shine, wipe, scour **3** *He rubbed oil into my aching back.* = **spread**, put, apply, smear **4** *Smear cream on to prevent it from rubbing.* = **chafe**, scrape, grate, abrade ▸ NOUN **1** *She sometimes asks if I want a back rub.* = **massage**, caress, kneading **2** *Give them a rub with a clean, dry cloth.* = **polish**, stroke, shine, wipe • **rub something out** *She began rubbing out the pencilled marks.* = **erase**, remove, cancel, wipe out, excise, delete, obliterate, efface, expunge (*formal*) • **the rub** *And therein lies the rub.* = **difficulty**, problem, catch (*informal*), trouble, obstacle, hazard, hitch, drawback, snag, uphill (*S. African*), impediment, hindrance

rubbish NOUN **1** *unwanted household rubbish* = **waste**, refuse, scrap, junk (*informal*), litter, debris, crap (*slang*), garbage (*chiefly U.S.*), trash, lumber (*Brit.*), offal, dross, dregs, flotsam and jetsam, grot (*slang*), dreck (*slang, chiefly U.S.*), offscourings **2** *He's talking rubbish.* = **nonsense**, garbage (*chiefly U.S.*), drivel, malarkey, twaddle, pants (*slang*), rot, crap (*slang*), trash, hot air (*informal*), tosh (*slang, chiefly Brit.*), pap, bilge (*informal*), tripe (*informal*), gibberish, guff (*slang*), havers (*Scot.*), moonshine, claptrap (*informal*), hogwash, hokum (*slang, chiefly U.S. & Canad.*), codswallop (*Brit. slang*), piffle (*informal*), poppycock (*informal*), balderdash, bosh (*informal*), wack (*U.S. slang*), eyewash (*informal*), s tuff and nonsense, flapdoodle (*slang*), tommyrot, horsefeathers (*U.S. slang*), bunkum *or* buncombe, bizzo (*Austral. slang*), bull's wool (*Austral. & N.Z. slang*)

ruddy ADJECTIVE **1** *He had a naturally ruddy complexion.* = **rosy**, red, fresh, healthy, glowing, blooming, flushed, blushing, radiant, reddish, sanguine, florid, sunburnt, rosy-cheeked, rubicund ■ **OPPOSITE:** pale **2** *barges, with their sails ruddy brown* = **red**, pink, scarlet, ruby, crimson, reddish, roseate

rude ADJECTIVE **1** *He's rude to her friends.* = **impolite**, insulting, cheeky, abrupt, short, blunt, abusive, curt, churlish, disrespectful, brusque, offhand, impertinent, insolent, inconsiderate, peremptory, impudent, discourteous, uncivil, unmannerly, ill-mannered ■ **OPPOSITE:** polite **2** *a rude barbarian* = **uncivilized**, low, rough, savage, ignorant, coarse, illiterate, uneducated, brutish, barbarous, scurrilous, boorish, uncouth, unrefined, loutish, untutored, graceless, ungracious, unpolished, oafish, uncultured **3** *He made a rude gesture with his finger.* = **vulgar**, gross, crude ■ **OPPOSITE:** refined **4** *It came as a rude shock.* = **unpleasant**, sharp, violent, sudden, harsh, startling, abrupt **5** *He had already constructed a rude cabin.* = **roughly-made**, simple, rough, raw, crude, primitive, makeshift, rough-hewn, artless, inelegant, inartistic ■ **OPPOSITE:** well-made

rudiment NOUN (*often plural*) = **basics**, elements, essentials, fundamentals, beginnings, foundation, nuts and bolts, first principles

rudimentary ADJECTIVE **1** *It had been extended into a kind of rudimentary kitchen.* = **primitive**, undeveloped **2** *He had only a rudimentary knowledge of French.* = **basic**, fundamental, elementary, early, primary, initial, introductory **3** *a rudimentary backbone called a notochord* = **undeveloped**, embryonic, vestigial ■ **OPPOSITE:** complete

rue VERB = **regret**, mourn, grieve, lament, deplore, bemoan, repent, be sorry for, weep over, sorrow for, bewail, kick yourself for, reproach yourself for

rueful ADJECTIVE = **regretful**, sad, dismal, melancholy, grievous, pitiful, woeful, sorry, mournful, plaintive, lugubrious, contrite,

sorrowful, repentant, doleful, remorseful, penitent, pitiable, woebegone, conscience-stricken, self-reproachful ■ **OPPOSITE:** unrepentant

ruffle VERB **1** *She let the wind ruffle her hair.* = **disarrange**, disorder, wrinkle, mess up, rumple, tousle, derange, discompose, dishevel, muss (*U.S. & Canad.*) **2** *My refusal to let him ruffle me infuriated him.* = **annoy**, worry, trouble, upset, confuse, stir, disturb, rattle (*informal*), irritate, put out, unsettle, shake up (*informal*), harass, hassle (*informal*), agitate, unnerve, disconcert, disquiet, nettle, vex, fluster, perturb, faze, peeve (*informal*), hack off (*informal*) ■ **OPPOSITE:** calm

rugged ADJECTIVE **1** *a rugged mountainous terrain* = **rocky**, broken, rough, craggy, difficult, ragged, stark, irregular, uneven, jagged, bumpy ■ **OPPOSITE:** even **2** *A look of disbelief crossed his rugged face.* = **strong-featured**, lined, worn, weathered, wrinkled, furrowed, leathery, rough-hewn, weather-beaten ■ **OPPOSITE:** delicate **3** *this rugged all-steel design* = **well-built**, strong, tough, robust, sturdy **4** *He's rugged and durable, but not the best technical boxer.* = **tough**, strong, hardy, robust, vigorous, muscular, swole (*slang*), hench (*informal*), sturdy, hale (*old-fashioned*), burly, husky (*informal*), beefy (*informal*), brawny ■ **OPPOSITE:** delicate **5** *a fairly rugged customer* = **stern**, hard, severe, rough, harsh, sour, rude, crabbed, austere, dour, surly, gruff

ruin VERB **1** *Roads have been destroyed and crops ruined.* = **destroy**, devastate, wreck, trash (*slang*), break, total (*slang*), defeat, smash, crush, overwhelm, shatter, overturn, overthrow, bring down, demolish, raze, l ay waste, lay in ruins, wreak havoc upon, bring to ruin, bring to nothing, kennet (*Austral. slang*), jeff (*Austral. slang*) ■ **OPPOSITE:** create **2** *She accused him of ruining her financially.* = **bankrupt**, break, impoverish, beggar, pauperize **3** *The original decor was all ruined during renovation.* = **spoil**, damage, mar, mess up, blow (*slang*), injure, undo, screw up (*informal*), botch, mangle, cock up (*Brit. slang*), disfigure, make a mess of, bodge (*informal*), crool *or* cruel (*Austral. slang*) ■ **OPPOSITE:** improve ▶ NOUN **1** *Recent inflation has driven them to the brink of ruin.* = **bankruptcy**, insolvency, destitution **2** *The vineyards were falling into ruin.* = **disrepair**, decay, disintegration, ruination, wreckage **3** *It is the ruin of society.* = **destruction**, fall, the end, breakdown, damage, defeat, failure, crash, collapse, wreck, overthrow, undoing, havoc, Waterloo, downfall, devastation, dissolution, subversion, nemesis, crackup (*informal*) ■ **OPPOSITE:** preservation

ruinous ADJECTIVE **1** *the ruinous effects of the conflict* = **destructive**, devastating, shattering, fatal, deadly, disastrous, dire, withering, catastrophic, murderous, pernicious (*formal*), noxious, calamitous, baleful, deleterious (*formal*), injurious, baneful (*archaic*) **2** *They passed by the ruinous building.* = **ruined**, broken-down, derelict, ramshackle, dilapidated, in ruins, decrepit

rule NOUN **1** *the rule against retrospective prosecution* = **regulation**, order, law, ruling, guide, direction, guideline, decree, ordinance, dictum **2** *An important rule is to drink plenty of water.* = **precept**, principle, criterion, canon, maxim, tenet, axiom **3** *according to the rules of quantum theory* = **procedure**, policy, standard, method, way, course, formula **4** *The usual rule is to start as one group.* = **custom**, procedure, practice, routine, form, condition, tradition, habit, convention, wont, order or way of things **5** *the winding-up of British rule over the territory* = **government**, power, control, authority, influence, administration, direction, leadership, command, regime, empire, reign, sway, domination, jurisdiction, supremacy, mastery, dominion, ascendancy, mana (*N.Z.*) ▸ VERB **1** *the feudal lord who ruled this land* = **govern**, lead, control, manage, direct, guide, regulate, administer, oversee, preside over, have power over, reign over, command over, have charge of **2** *She ruled for eight years.* = **reign**, govern, be in power, hold sway, wear the crown, be in authority, be number one (*informal*) **3** *Fear can rule our lives.* = **control**, dominate, monopolize, tyrannize, be pre-eminent, have the upper hand over **4** *The court ruled that laws passed by the assembly remained valid.* = **decree**, find, decide, judge, establish, determine, settle, resolve, pronounce, lay down, adjudge **5** *A ferocious form of anarchy ruled here.* = **be prevalent**, prevail, predominate, hold sway, be customary, preponderate, obtain (*formal*) • **as a rule** *As a rule, these tourists take far too many souvenirs with them.* = **usually**, generally, mainly, normally, on the whole, for the most part, ordinarily, customarily • **rule someone out** *a suspension which ruled him out of the grand final* = **exclude**, eliminate, disqualify, ban, prevent, reject, dismiss, forbid, prohibit, leave out, preclude, proscribe, obviate

(*formal*), debar • **rule something out** *Local detectives have ruled out foul play.* = **reject**, exclude, eliminate

ruler NOUN **1** *He was an indecisive ruler.* = **governor**, leader, lord, commander, controller, monarch, sovereign, head of state, potentate, crowned head, emperor or empress, king or queen, prince or princess **2** *taking measurements with a ruler* = **measure**, rule, yardstick, straight edge

ruling ADJECTIVE **1** *the domination of the ruling class* = **governing**, upper, reigning, controlling, leading, commanding, dominant, regnant **2** *a ruling passion for liberty and equality* = **predominant**, dominant, prevailing, preponderant, chief, main, current, supreme, principal, prevalent, pre-eminent, regnant ■ **OPPOSITE:** minor ▸ NOUN *He tried to have the court ruling overturned.* = **decision**, finding, resolution, verdict, judgment, decree, adjudication, pronouncement

rum ADJECTIVE = **strange**, odd, suspect, funny, unusual, curious, weird, suspicious, peculiar, dodgy (*Brit., Austral. & N.Z. informal*), queer, singular, shonky (*Austral. & N.Z. informal*)

ruminate VERB = **ponder**, think, consider, reflect, contemplate, deliberate, muse, brood, meditate, mull over things, chew over things, cogitate, rack your brains, turn over in your mind

rummage VERB = **search**, hunt, root, explore, delve, examine, ransack, forage, fossick (*Austral. & N.Z.*), rootle

rumour NOUN *There's a strange rumour going around.* = **story**, news, report, talk, word, whisper (*informal*), buzz, gossip, dirt (*slang*), goss (*informal*), hearsay, canard, tidings, scuttlebutt (*U.S. slang*), bush telegraph, bruit (*archaic*) • **be rumoured** *It was rumoured that he'd been interned in an asylum.* = **be said**, be told, be reported, be published, be circulated, be whispered, be passed around, be put about, be noised abroad

rump NOUN = **buttocks**, bottom (*informal*), rear (*informal*), backside (*informal*), tail (*informal*), seat, butt (*U.S. & Canad. informal*), bum (*Brit. slang*), buns (*U.S. slang*), rear end, posterior, haunch, hindquarters, derrière (*euphemistic*), croup, jacksy (*Brit. slang*)

rumple VERB = **ruffle**, crush, disorder, dishevel, wrinkle, crease, crumple, screw up, mess up, pucker, crinkle, scrunch, tousle, derange, muss (*U.S. & Canad.*)

rumpus NOUN = **commotion**, row, noise, confusion, fuss, disturbance, disruption, furore, uproar, tumult, brouhaha, shindig (*informal*), hue and cry, kerfuffle (*informal*), shindy (*informal*)

run VERB **1** *I excused myself and ran back to the telephone.* = **race**, speed, rush, dash, hurry, career, barrel (along) (*informal, chiefly U.S. & Canad.*), sprint, scramble, bolt, dart, gallop, hare (*Brit. informal*), jog, scud, hasten, scurry, stampede, scamper, leg it (*informal*), lope, hie, hotfoot ■ **OPPOSITE:** dawdle **2** *As they closed in on him, he turned and ran.* = **flee**, escape, take off (*informal*), depart, bolt, clear out, beat it (*slang*), leg it (*informal*), make off, abscond, decamp, take flight, do a runner (*slang*), scarper (*Brit. slang*), slope off, cut and run (*informal*), make a run for it, fly the coop (*U.S. & Canad. informal*), beat a retreat, show a clean pair of heels, skedaddle (*informal*), take a powder (*U.S. & Canad. slang*), take it on the lam (*U.S. & Canad. slang*), take to your heels ■ **OPPOSITE:** stay **3** *I was running in the marathon.* = **take part**, compete **4** *the trail which ran through the beech woods* = **continue**, go, stretch, last, reach, lie, range, extend, proceed ■ **OPPOSITE:** stop **5** *He announced he would run for president.* = **compete**, stand, contend, be a candidate, put yourself up for, take part, challenge, re-offer (*Canad.*) **6** *His father ran a prosperous business.* = **manage**, lead, direct, be in charge of, own, head, control, boss (*informal*), operate, handle, conduct, look after, carry on, regulate, take care of, administer, oversee, supervise, mastermind, coordinate, superintend **7** *the staff who have kept the bank running* = **go**, work, operate, perform, function, be in business, be in action, tick over **8** *He ran a lot of tests.* = **perform**, carry out **9** *The tape recorder was still running.* = **work**, go, operate, function **10** *I ran a 1960 Rover 100.* = **drive 11** *A shuttle bus runs frequently.* = **operate**, go **12** *Can you run me to work?* = **give a lift to**, drive, carry, transport, convey, bear, manoeuvre, propel **13** *He winced as he ran his hand over his ribs.* = **pass**, go, move, roll, slide, glide, skim **14** *cisterns to catch rainwater as it ran off the walls* = **flow**, pour, stream, cascade, go, move, issue, proceed, leak, spill, discharge, gush, spout, course **15** *The ink had run on the wet paper.* = **spread**, mix, bleed, be diffused, lose colour **16** *A buzz of excitement ran through the crowd.* = **circulate**, spread, creep, go round **17** *The paper ran a series of scathing editorials.* = **publish**, feature, display, print **18** *The pitch between the planks of the deck melted and ran.* = **melt**, dissolve, liquefy, go soft, turn

to liquid **19** *ladders in your tights gradually running all the way up your leg* = **unravel**, tear, ladder, come apart, come undone **20** *I started running guns again.* = **smuggle**, deal in, traffic in, bootleg, ship, sneak

▶ NOUN **1** *a six mile run* = **race**, rush, dash, sprint, gallop, jog, spurt **2** *Take them for a run in the car.* = **ride**, drive, trip, lift, journey, spin (*informal*), outing, excursion, jaunt, joy ride (*informal*) **3** *Their run of luck is holding.* = **sequence**, period, stretch, spell, course, season, round, series, chain, cycle, string, passage, streak **4** *outside the common run of professional athletes* = **type**, sort, kind, class, variety, category, order **5** *She had a huge run in her tights.* = **tear**, rip, ladder, snag **6** *My mother had a little chicken run.* = **enclosure**, pen, coop **7** *The only try came against the run of play.* = **direction**, way, course, current, movement, progress, flow, path, trend, motion, passage, stream, tendency, drift, tide, tenor **8** (*with on*) *A run on sterling has killed hopes of a rate cut.* = **sudden demand for**, pressure for, rush for • **in the long run** *Things could get worse in the long run.* = **in the end**, eventually, in time, ultimately, at the end of the day, in the final analysis, when all is said and done, in the fullness of time • **on the run 1** *Some of the gang members are still on the run.* = **escaping**, fugitive, in flight, at liberty, on the loose, on the lam (*U.S. & Canad. slang*) **2** *I knew I had him on the run.* = **in retreat**, defeated, fleeing, retreating, running away, falling back, in flight **3** *We ate lunch on the run.* = **hurrying**, hastily, in a hurry, at speed, hurriedly, in a rush, in haste • **run across something** or **someone** *We ran across some old friends.* = **meet**, encounter, meet with, come across, run into, bump into, come upon, chance upon • **run away** *I ran away from home when I was sixteen.* = **flee**, escape, take off, bolt, run off, clear out, beat it (*slang*), abscond, decamp, take flight, hook it (*slang*), do a runner (*slang*), scarper (*Brit. slang*), cut and run (*informal*), make a run for it, turn tail, do a bunk (*Brit. slang*), scram (*informal*), fly the coop (*U.S. & Canad. informal*), show a clean pair of heels, skedaddle (*informal*), take a powder (*U.S. & Canad. slang*), take it on the lam (*U.S. & Canad. slang*), take to your heels, do a Skase (*Austral. informal*) • **run away with something** or **someone 1** *She ran away with a man called Allen.* = **abscond with**, run off with, elope with **2** *She ran away with the gold medal.* = **win easily**, walk it (*informal*), romp home, win hands down, win by a mile (*informal*) • **run into someone** *He ran into* him in the corridor. = **meet**, encounter, bump into, run across, chance upon, come across or upon • **run into something** *They ran into financial problems.* = **be beset by**, encounter, meet with, come across or upon, face, experience, be confronted by, happen on or upon **2** *The driver ran into a tree.* = **collide with**, hit, strike, ram, bump into, crash into, dash against • **run off** *He then ran off towards a nearby underground railway station.* = **flee**, escape, bolt, run away, clear out, make off, decamp, take flight, hook it (*slang*), do a runner (*slang*), scarper (*Brit. slang*), cut and run (*informal*), turn tail, fly the coop (*U.S. & Canad. informal*), show a clean pair of heels, skedaddle (*informal*), take a powder (*U.S. & Canad. slang*), take it on the lam (*U.S. & Canad. slang*), take to your heels • **run off with someone** *He ran off with a younger woman.* = **run away with**, elope with, abscond with • **run off with something** *Who ran off with the money?* = **steal**, take, lift (*informal*), nick (*slang, chiefly Brit.*), pinch (*informal*), swipe (*slang*), run away with, make off with, embezzle, misappropriate, purloin (*formal*), filch, walk or make off with • **run out** *Supplies are running out.* = **be used up**, dry up, give out, peter out, fail, finish, cease, be exhausted **2** *the day my visa ran out* = **expire**, end, terminate • **run out of something** *The plane ran out of fuel.* = **exhaust your supply of**, be out of, be cleaned out, have no more, have none left, have no remaining • **run out on someone** *You can't run out on your wife and children like that.* = **desert**, abandon, strand, run away from, forsake, rat on (*informal*), leave high and dry, leave holding the baby, leave in the lurch • **run over** *Water ran over the sides and trickled down on to the floor.* = **overflow**, spill over, brim over • **run over something** *Phase one has run over budget.* = **exceed**, overstep, go over the top of, go beyond the bounds of, go over the limit of **2** *Let's run over the instructions again.* = **review**, check, survey, examine, go through, go over, run through, rehearse, reiterate • **run over something** or **someone** *He was nearly run over by a car.* = **knock down**, hit, strike, run down, knock over • **run someone in** *They had run him in on a petty charge.* = **arrest**, apprehend, pull in (*Brit. slang*), take into custody, lift (*slang*), pick up, jail, nail (*informal*), bust (*informal*), collar (*informal*), pinch (*informal*), nab (*informal*), throw in jail, take to jail, feel your collar (*slang*) • **run something in** *I was running in a new pair of shoes.* = **break in gently**, run gently • **run something off**

They ran off some copies for me. = **produce**, print, duplicate, churn out (*informal*) • **run something** or **someone down 1** *He was running down state schools.* = **criticize**, denigrate, belittle, revile, knock (*informal*), rubbish (*informal*), put down, slag (off) (*slang*), disparage, decry, vilify, diss (*slang*), defame, bad-mouth (*slang*), speak ill of, asperse **2** *The property business could be sold or run down.* = **downsize**, cut, drop, reduce, trim, decrease, cut back, curtail, pare down, kennet (*Austral. slang*), jeff (*Austral. slang*) **3** *He was in the roadway and I nearly ran him down.* = **knock down**, hit, strike, run into, run over, knock over • **run through something 1** *I ran through the options with him.* = **review**, check, survey, examine, go through, look over, run over **2** *I ran through the handover procedure.* = **rehearse**, read, practise, go over, run over **3** *The country had run through its public food stocks.* = **squander**, waste, exhaust, throw away, dissipate, fritter away, spend like water, blow (*slang*)

runaway ADJECTIVE **1** *a runaway success* = **easily won**, easy, effortless **2** *The runaway car careered into a bench.* = **out of control**, uncontrolled **3** *a runaway horse* = **escaped**, wild, fleeing, loose, fugitive ▶ NOUN *a teenage runaway* = **fugitive**, escaper, refugee, deserter, truant, escapee, absconder

rundown or **run-down** ADJECTIVE **1** *She started to feel rundown last December.* = **exhausted**, weak, tired, drained, fatigued, weary, unhealthy, worn-out, debilitated, below par, under the weather (*informal*), enervated, out of condition, peaky ■ OPPOSITE: fit **2** *a rundown block of flats* = **dilapidated**, broken-down, shabby, worn-out, seedy, ramshackle, dingy, decrepit, tumbledown ▶ NOUN *Here's a rundown of the options.* = **summary**, review, briefing, résumé, outline, sketch, run-through, synopsis, recap (*informal*), précis

run-in NOUN (*informal*) = **fight**, row, argument, dispute, set-to (*informal*), encounter, brush, confrontation, quarrel, skirmish, tussle, altercation, face-off (*slang*), dust-up (*informal*), contretemps, biffo (*Austral. slang*)

runner NOUN **1** *a marathon runner* = **athlete**, miler, sprinter, harrier, jogger **2** *a bookie's runner* = **messenger**, courier, errand boy, dispatch bearer **3** *strawberry runners* = **stem**, shoot, sprout, sprig, offshoot, tendril, stolon (*Botany*)

running NOUN **1** *in charge of the day-to-day running of the party* = **management**, control, administration, direction, conduct, charge, leadership, organization, regulation, supervision, coordination, superintendency **2** *the smooth running of the machine* = **working**, performance, operation, functioning, maintenance

▶ ADJECTIVE **1** *The song turned into a running joke between them.* = **continuous**, constant, perpetual, uninterrupted, incessant, unceasing **2** *She never seems the same woman two days running.* = **in succession**, together, unbroken, on the trot (*informal*) **3** *Wash the lentils under cold, running water.* = **flowing**, moving, streaming, coursing

runny ADJECTIVE = **flowing**, liquid, melted, fluid, diluted, watery, streaming, liquefied

run-of-the-mill ADJECTIVE = **ordinary**, middling, average, fair, modest, commonplace, common, vanilla (*informal*), mediocre, banal, tolerable (*informal*), passable, undistinguished, unimpressive, unexciting, unexceptional, bog-standard (*Brit. & Irish slang*), no great shakes (*informal*), dime-a-dozen (*informal*) ■ **OPPOSITE:** exceptional

run-up NOUN = **time leading up to**, approach, build-up, preliminaries

rupture NOUN **1** *a rupture of the abdominal aorta* = **hernia** (*Medical*) **2** *a major rupture between the two countries* = **breach**, split, hostility, falling-out (*informal*), disagreement, contention, feud, disruption, quarrel, rift, break, bust-up (*informal*), dissolution, altercation, schism, estrangement **3** *ruptures in a 60-mile pipeline on the island* = **break**, tear, split, crack, rent, burst, breach, fracture, cleavage, cleft, fissure ▶ VERB **1** *Tanks can rupture and burn in a collision.* = **break**, separate, tear, split, crack, burst, rend (*literary*), fracture, sever, puncture, cleave **2** *an accident which ruptured the bond between them* = **cause a breach**, split, divide, disrupt, break off, come between, dissever

rural ADJECTIVE **1** *These plants grow in the more rural areas.* = **agricultural**, country, agrarian, upcountry, agrestic **2** *the old rural way of life* = **rustic**, country, hick (*informal, chiefly U.S. & Canad.*), pastoral, bucolic, sylvan, Arcadian, countrified ■ **OPPOSITE:** urban

ruse NOUN = **trick**, deception, ploy, hoax, device, manoeuvre, dodge, sham, artifice, blind, subterfuge, stratagem, wile, imposture (*formal*)

rush VERB **1** *Someone inside the building rushed out.* = **hurry**, run, race, shoot, fly, career, speed, tear, dash, sprint, scramble, bolt, dart, hasten, scurry, stampede, lose no time, make short work of, burn rubber (*informal*), make haste, hotfoot ■ **OPPOSITE:** dawdle **2** *The Act was rushed through after a legal loophole was discovered.* = **push**, hurry, accelerate, dispatch, speed up, quicken, press, hustle, expedite **3** *They rushed the entrance.* = **attack**, storm, capture, overcome, charge at, take by storm

▶ NOUN **1** *The explosion caused panic and a mad rush for the doors.* = **dash**, charge, race, scramble, stampede, expedition, speed, dispatch **2** *the rush not to be late for school* = **hurry**, urgency, bustle, haste, hustle, helter-skelter, hastiness **3** *A rush of affection swept over him.* = **surge**, flow, gush **4** *Throw something noisy and feign a rush at him.* = **attack**, charge, push (*informal*), storm, assault, surge, onslaught ▶ ADJECTIVE *I guess you could call it a rush job.* = **hasty**, fast, quick, hurried, emergency, prompt, rapid, urgent, swift, brisk, cursory, expeditious ■ **OPPOSITE:** leisurely

rust NOUN **1** *a decaying tractor, red with rust* = **corrosion**, oxidation **2** *canker, rust, mildew or insect attack* = **mildew**, must, mould, rot, blight ▶ VERB **1** *The bolt on the door had rusted.* = **corrode**, tarnish, oxidize **2** *If you rest, you rust.* = **deteriorate**, decline, decay, stagnate, atrophy, go stale

rustic ADJECTIVE **1** *the rustic charms of a country lifestyle* = **rural**, country, pastoral, bucolic, sylvan, Arcadian, countrified, upcountry, agrestic ■ **OPPOSITE:** urban **2** *wonderfully rustic old log cabins* = **simple**, homely, plain, homespun, unsophisticated, unrefined, artless, unpolished ■ **OPPOSITE:** grand ▶ NOUN *rustics in from the country* = **yokel**, peasant, hick (*informal, chiefly U.S. & Canad.*), bumpkin, swain (*archaic*), hillbilly, country boy, clod, boor, country cousin, hayseed (*U.S. & Canad. informal*), clodhopper (*informal*), son of the soil, clown, countryman or countrywoman ■ **OPPOSITE:** sophisticate

rustle VERB *The leaves rustled in the wind.* = **crackle**, whisper, swish, whoosh, crinkle, whish, crepitate, susurrate (*literary*) ▶ NOUN *with a rustle of her frilled petticoats* = **crackle**, whisper, rustling, crinkling, crepitation, susurration or susurrus (*literary*)

rusty ADJECTIVE **1** *travelling around in a rusty old van* = **corroded**, rusted, oxidized, rust-covered **2** *Your French is a bit rusty.* = **out of practice**, weak, impaired, sluggish, stale, deficient, not what it was, unpractised **3** *Her hair was rusty brown.* = **reddish-brown**, chestnut, reddish, russet, coppery, rust-coloured

4 *his mild, rusty voice* = **croaking**, cracked, creaking, hoarse, croaky

rut NOUN **1** *I don't like being in a rut.* = **habit**, routine, dead end, humdrum existence, system, pattern, groove **2** *deep ruts left by the truck's heavy wheels* = **groove**, score, track, trough, furrow, gouge, pothole, indentation, wheel mark

ruthless ADJECTIVE = **merciless**, hard, severe, fierce, harsh, cruel, savage, brutal, stern, relentless, adamant, ferocious, callous, heartless, unrelenting, inhuman, inexorable, remorseless, barbarous, pitiless, unfeeling, hard-hearted, without pity, unmerciful, unpitying ■ OPPOSITE: merciful

rutted ADJECTIVE = **grooved**, cut, marked, scored, holed, furrowed, gouged, indented

r

Ss

sable ADJECTIVE **1** *thick sable lashes* = **black**, jet, raven, jetty, ebony, ebon (*poetic*) **2** *Night enveloped me in its sable mantle.* = **dark**, black, dim, gloomy, dismal, dreary, sombre, shadowy

sabotage VERB **1** *The main pipeline was sabotaged by rebels.* = **damage**, destroy, wreck, undermine, disable, disrupt, cripple, subvert, incapacitate, vandalize, throw a spanner in the works (*Brit. informal*) **2** *the extremists who are trying to sabotage any chance of peace* = **disrupt**, ruin, wreck, spoil, interrupt, interfere with, obstruct, intrude, crool or cruel (*Austral. slang*) ▶ NOUN **1** *The bombing was a spectacular act of sabotage.* = **damage**, destruction, wrecking, vandalism, deliberate damage **2** *political sabotage of government policy* = **disruption**, ruining, wrecking, spoiling, interference, intrusion, interruption, obstruction

saboteur NOUN = **demonstrator**, rebel, dissident, hooligan, vandal, delinquent, dissenter, agitator, protest marcher

sac NOUN = **pouch**, bag, pocket, bladder, pod, cyst, vesicle

saccharine ADJECTIVE = **sickly**, honeyed (*poetic*), sentimental, sugary, nauseating, soppy (*Brit. informal*), cloying, maudlin, syrupy (*informal*), mawkish, icky (*informal*), treacly, oversweet

sack[1] NOUN *a sack of potatoes* = **bag**, pocket, poke (*Scot.*), sac, pouch, receptacle ▶ VERB *They were sacked for financial mismanagement.* = **dismiss**, fire (*informal*), axe (*informal*), discharge, kick out (*informal*), give (someone) the boot (*slang*), give (someone) their marching orders, kiss off (*slang, chiefly U.S. & Canad.*), give (someone) the push (*informal*), give (someone) the bullet (*Brit. slang*), give (someone) their books (*informal*), give (someone) the elbow, give (someone) their cards, kennet (*Austral. slang*), jeff (*Austral. slang*) • **hit the sack** *I hit the sack early.* = **go to bed**, retire, turn in (*informal*), bed down, hit the hay (*slang*) • **the sack** *People who make mistakes can be given the sack the same day.* = **dismissal**, discharge, the boot (*slang*), the axe (*informal*), the chop (*Brit. slang*), the push

(*slang*), the (old) heave-ho (*informal*), termination of employment, the order of the boot (*slang*)

sack[2] VERB *Imperial troops sacked the French ambassador's residence in Rome.* = **plunder**, loot, pillage, destroy, strip, rob, raid, ruin, devastate, spoil, rifle, demolish, ravage, lay waste, despoil (*formal*), maraud, depredate (*rare*) ▶ NOUN *the sack of Troy* = **plundering**, looting, pillage, waste, rape, ruin, destruction, ravage, plunder, devastation, depredation, despoliation (*formal*), rapine

sacred ADJECTIVE **1** *shrines and sacred places* = **holy**, hallowed, consecrated, blessed, divine, revered, venerable, sanctified ■ **OPPOSITE:** secular **2** *the awe-inspiring sacred art of the Renaissance masters* = **religious**, holy, ecclesiastical, hallowed, venerated ■ **OPPOSITE:** unconsecrated **3** *My memories are sacred.* = **inviolable**, protected, sacrosanct, secure, hallowed, inalienable, invulnerable, inviolate, unalterable

sacrifice VERB **1** *The priest sacrificed a chicken.* = **offer**, offer up, immolate (*literary*) **2** *She sacrificed family life when her career took off.* = **give up**, abandon, relinquish, lose, surrender, let go, do without, renounce, forfeit, forego, say goodbye to ▶ NOUN **1** *animal sacrifices to the gods* = **offering**, immolation (*literary*), oblation, hecatomb **2** *They have not suffered any sacrifice of identity.* = **surrender**, loss, giving up, resignation, rejection, waiver, abdication, renunciation, repudiation, forswearing, relinquishment, eschewal, self-denial

sacrificial ADJECTIVE = **propitiatory**, atoning, reparative, expiatory, oblatory

sacrilege NOUN = **desecration**, violation, blasphemy, mockery, heresy, irreverence, profanity, impiety, profanation, profaneness ■ **OPPOSITE:** reverence

sacrosanct ADJECTIVE = **inviolable**, sacred, inviolate, untouchable, hallowed, sanctified, set apart

sad ADJECTIVE **1** *The loss left me feeling sad and empty.* = **unhappy**, down, low, blue, depressed, gloomy, grieved, dismal, melancholy, sombre, glum, wistful, mournful, dejected, downcast, grief-stricken, tearful, lugubrious, pensive, disconsolate, doleful, heavy-hearted, down in the dumps (*informal*), cheerless, lachrymose, woebegone, down in the mouth (*informal*), low-spirited, triste (*archaic*), sick at heart ■ **OPPOSITE:** happy **2** *the sad news of the destruction of a historic building* = **tragic**, moving, upsetting, dark, sorry, depressing, disastrous, dismal, pathetic, poignant, harrowing, grievous, pitiful, calamitous, heart-rending, pitiable **3** *It's a sad truth that children are the biggest victims of passive smoking.* = **deplorable**, bad, sorry, terrible, distressing, unfortunate, miserable, dismal, shabby, heartbreaking, regrettable, lamentable, wretched, to be deplored ■ **OPPOSITE:** good **4** *a sad state of affairs* = **regrettable**, disappointing, distressing, unhappy, unfortunate, unsatisfactory, woeful, deplorable, lamentable ■ **OPPOSITE:** fortunate

sadden VERB = **upset**, depress, distress, grieve, desolate, cast down, bring tears to your eyes, make sad, dispirit, make your heart bleed, aggrieve, deject, cast a gloom upon

saddle VERB = **burden**, load, lumber (*Brit. informal*), charge, tax, task, encumber

sadism NOUN = **cruelty**, savagery, brutality, severity, ferocity, spite, ruthlessness, depravity, harshness, inhumanity, barbarity, callousness, viciousness, bestiality, heartlessness, brutishness, spitefulness, bloodthirstiness, murderousness, mercilessness, fiendishness, hard-heartedness

sadistic ADJECTIVE = **cruel**, savage, brutal, beastly (*informal*), vicious, ruthless, perverted, perverse, inhuman, barbarous, fiendish

sadness NOUN = **unhappiness**, sorrow, grief, tragedy, depression, the blues, misery, melancholy, poignancy, despondency, bleakness, heavy heart, dejection, wretchedness, gloominess, mournfulness, dolour (*poetic*), dolefulness, cheerlessness, sorrowfulness ■ **OPPOSITE:** happiness

safe ADJECTIVE **1** *Keep your camera safe from sand.* = **protected**, secure, in safety, impregnable, out of danger, safe and sound, in safe hands, out of harm's way, free from harm ■ **OPPOSITE:** endangered **2** *Where is Sophie? Is she safe?* = **all right**, fine, intact, unscathed, unhurt, unharmed, undamaged, out of the woods, O.K. or okay (*informal*) **3** *I shall conceal myself at a safe distance from the battlefield.* = **cautious**, prudent, sure, conservative, reliable, realistic, discreet, dependable, trustworthy, circumspect, on the safe side, unadventurous, tried and true ■ **OPPOSITE:** risky **4** *We are assured by our engineers that the building is safe.* = **risk-free**, sound, secure, certain, impregnable, riskless **5** *a clean, inexpensive and safe fuel* = **harmless**, wholesome, innocuous, pure, tame, unpolluted, nontoxic, nonpoisonous ■ **OPPOSITE:** dangerous ▶ NOUN *The files are now in a safe.* = **strongbox**, vault, coffer, repository, deposit box, safe-deposit box

safeguard VERB *international action to safeguard the ozone layer* = **protect**, guard, defend, save, screen, secure, preserve, look after, shield, watch over, keep safe ▶ NOUN *A system like ours lacks adequate safeguards for civil liberties.* = **protection**, security, defence, guard, shield, armour, aegis, bulwark, surety

safely ADVERB = **in safety**, securely, with impunity, without risk, with safety, safe and sound

safety NOUN **1** *The report makes recommendations to improve safety on aircraft.* = **security**, protection, safeguards, assurance, precautions, immunity, safety measures, impregnability ■ **OPPOSITE:** risk **2** *the safety of your own home* = **shelter**, haven, protection, cover, retreat, asylum, refuge, sanctuary

sag VERB **1** *The shirt's cuffs won't sag and lose their shape after washing.* = **sink**, bag, droop, fall, drop, seat (*of a skirt, etc*), settle, slump, dip, give way, bulge, swag, hang loosely, fall unevenly **2** *He shrugged and sagged into a chair.* = **drop**, sink, slump, flop, droop, loll **3** *Some of the tension he builds up begins to sag.* = **decline**, fall, slip, tire, slide, flag, slump, weaken, wilt, wane, cave in, droop

saga NOUN **1** *I'll tell you the whole saga of how I got the part.* = **carry-on** (*informal*), to-do, performance (*informal*), rigmarole, soap opera, pantomime (*informal*) **2** *a Nordic saga of giants and trolls* = **epic**, story, tale, legend, adventure, romance, narrative, chronicle, yarn (*informal*), fairy tale, folk tale, roman-fleuve (*French*)

sage NOUN *ancient Chinese sages* = **wise man**, philosopher, guru, authority, expert, master, elder, pundit, Solomon, mahatma, Nestor, savant, Solon, man of learning, tohunga (*N.Z.*) ▶ ADJECTIVE *My parents were always on hand to offer sage advice.* = **wise**, learned, intelligent, sensible, politic, acute, discerning, prudent, canny, judicious, perspicacious (*formal*), sagacious (*formal*), sapient (*used ironically*)

sail NOUN *The white sails billow with the breezes they catch.* = **sheet**, canvas ▶ VERB **1** *We sailed upstream.* = **go by water**, cruise, voyage, ride the waves, go by sea **2** *The boat is due to sail tonight.* = **set sail**, embark, get under way, put to sea, put off, leave port, hoist sail, cast or weigh anchor **3** *I shall get myself a little boat and sail her around the world.* = **pilot**, steer, navigate, captain, skipper **4** *We got into the lift and sailed to the top floor.*

S

= **glide**, sweep, float, shoot, fly, wing, soar, drift, skim, scud, skirr • **sail through something** *She sailed through her maths exams.* = **cruise through**, walk through, romp through, pass easily, succeed easily at • **set sail** *He loaded his vessel with another cargo and set sail.* = **put to sea**, embark, get under way, put off, leave port, hoist sail, cast or weigh anchor

sailor NOUN = **mariner**, marine, seaman or woman, salt, tar (*informal*), hearty (*informal*), navigator, sea dog, seafarer, matelot (*slang, chiefly Brit.*), Jack Tar, seafaring man, lascar, leatherneck (*slang*)

saintly ADJECTIVE = **virtuous**, godly, holy, religious, sainted, blessed, worthy, righteous, devout, pious, angelic, blameless, god-fearing, beatific, sinless, saintlike, full of good works

sake NOUN *For the sake of historical accuracy, permit us to state the true facts.* = **purpose**, interest, cause, reason, end, aim, principle, objective, motive • **for someone's sake** *I trust you to do a good job for Stan's sake.* = **in someone's interests**, to someone's advantage, on someone's account, for the benefit of, for the good of, for the welfare of, out of respect for, out of consideration for, out of regard for

salacious ADJECTIVE = **obscene**, indecent, pornographic, blue, erotic, steamy (*informal*), lewd, X-rated (*informal*), bawdy, smutty, lustful, ribald, ruttish

salary NOUN = **pay**, income, wage, fee, payment, wages, earnings, allowance, remuneration, recompense, stipend, emolument

sale NOUN **1** *Efforts were made to limit the sale of junk food.* = **selling**, marketing, dealing, trading, transaction, disposal, vending **2** *The Old Master was bought at the Christie's sale.* = **auction**, fair, mart, bazaar

salient ADJECTIVE = **prominent**, outstanding, important, marked, striking, arresting, signal, remarkable, pronounced, noticeable, conspicuous

saliva NOUN = **spit**, dribble, drool, slaver, spittle, sputum

sallow ADJECTIVE = **wan**, pale, sickly, pasty, pallid, unhealthy, yellowish, anaemic, bilious, jaundiced-looking, peely-wally (*Scot.*) ■ **OPPOSITE:** rosy

sally NOUN *She had thus far succeeded in fending off my conversational sallies.* = **witticism**, joke, quip, crack (*informal*), retort, jest, riposte, wisecrack (*informal*), bon mot, smart remark ▶ VERB *She would sally out on a bitter night to keep her appointments.* = **go forth**, set out, rush, issue, surge, erupt

salon NOUN **1** *a beauty salon* = **shop**, store, establishment, parlour, boutique **2** *His apartment was the most famous literary salon in Russia.* = **sitting room** (*Brit.*), lounge, living room, parlour (*old-fashioned*), drawing room, front room, reception room, morning room

salt NOUN **1** *a pinch of salt* = **seasoning**, sodium chloride, table salt, rock salt **2** *'Did he look like an old sea salt?' I asked, laughing.* = **sailor**, marine, seaman or woman, mariner, tar (*informal*), hearty (*informal*), navigator, sea dog, seafarer, matelot (*slang, chiefly Brit.*), Jack Tar, seafaring man or woman or person, lascar, leatherneck (*slang*) ▶ ADJECTIVE *Put a pan of salt water on to boil.* = **salty**, salted, saline, brackish, briny • **rub salt into the wound** *I had no intention of rubbing salt into his wounds.* = **make something worse**, add insult to injury, fan the flames, aggravate matters, magnify a problem • **with a grain** or **pinch of salt** *You have to take these findings with a pinch of salt.* = **sceptically**, suspiciously, cynically, doubtfully, with reservations, disbelievingly, mistrustfully

salty ADJECTIVE = **salt**, salted, saline, brackish, briny, over-salted, brak (*S. African*)

salubrious ADJECTIVE *your salubrious lochside hotel* = **healthy**, beneficial, good for you, wholesome, invigorating, salutary, healthful, health-giving

salutary ADJECTIVE = **beneficial**, useful, valuable, helpful, profitable, good, practical, good for you, advantageous

salute VERB **1** *He stepped out and saluted the general.* = **greet**, welcome, acknowledge, address, kiss, hail, salaam, accost, pay your respects to, doff your cap to, mihi (*N.Z.*) **2** *The statement salutes the changes of the past year.* = **honour**, acknowledge, recognize, take your hat off to (*informal*), pay tribute or homage to ▶ NOUN *He raised his hand in salute.* = **greeting**, recognition, salutation (*formal*), address, kiss, salaam, obeisance

salvage VERB *They studied flight recorders salvaged from the wreckage.* = **save**, recover, rescue, restore, repair, get back, retrieve, redeem, glean, repossess, fetch back ▶ NOUN **1** *The salvage of the ship went on.* = **rescue**, saving, recovery, release, relief, liberation, salvation, deliverance, extrication **2** *They climbed up on the rock with their salvage.* = **scrap**, remains, waste, junk, offcuts

salvation NOUN **1** *those whose marriages are beyond salvation* = **saving**, rescue, recovery, restoration, salvage, redemption, deliverance ■ **OPPOSITE:** ruin **2** *I consider books my salvation.* = **lifeline**, escape, relief, preservation

salve VERB *I give myself treats and justify them to salve my conscience.* = **ease**, soothe, appease, still, allay, pacify, mollify, tranquillize, palliate ▶ NOUN *a soothing salve for sore, dry lips* = **balm**, cream, medication, lotion, lubricant, ointment, emollient, liniment, dressing, unguent

salvo NOUN = **barrage**, storm, bombardment, strafe, cannonade

same ADJECTIVE **1** *The houses were all the same.* = **identical**, similar, alike, equal, twin, equivalent, corresponding, comparable, duplicate, indistinguishable, interchangeable ■ **OPPOSITE:** different **2** *Bernard works at the same institution as Arlette.* = **the very same**, very, one and the same, selfsame **3** *an invoice for two wristwatches and inscription of same* = **aforementioned**, aforesaid, selfsame **4** *Always taking the ingredients from here means the beers stay the same.* = **unchanged**, consistent, constant, uniform, unaltered, unfailing, invariable, unvarying, changeless ■ **OPPOSITE:** altered • **all the same 1** *She didn't understand the joke but laughed all the same.* = **nevertheless**, still, regardless, nonetheless, after all, in any case, for all that, notwithstanding, in any event, anyhow, just the same, be that as it may **2** *It's all the same to me whether he goes or not.* = **unimportant**, insignificant, immaterial, inconsequential, of no consequence, of little account, not worth mentioning

> **USAGE** The use of *same* as in *If you send us your order for the materials, we will deliver same tomorrow* is common in business and official English. In general English, however, this use of the word is best avoided, as it may sound rather stilted: *May I borrow your book? I will return it* (not *same*) *tomorrow.*

sameness NOUN = **similarity**, resemblance, uniformity, likeness, oneness, standardization, indistinguishability, identicalness

sample NOUN **1** *We're giving away 2000 free samples.* = **specimen**, example, model, pattern, instance, representative, indication, illustration, exemplification **2** *We based our analysis on a random sample of more than 200 males.* = **cross section**, test, sampling ▶ VERB *We sampled a selection of different bottled waters.* = **test**, try, check out (*informal*), experience, taste, examine, evaluate, inspect, experiment with, appraise, partake of

sanctify VERB **1** *Their marriage has not been sanctified in a place of worship.* = **consecrate**, bless, anoint, set apart, hallow, make sacred **2** *May the God of peace sanctify you entirely.* = **cleanse**, redeem, purify, absolve

sanctimonious ADJECTIVE = **pious**, smug, hypocritical, pi (*Brit. slang*), too good to be true, self-righteous, self-satisfied, goody-goody (*informal*), unctuous, holier-than-thou, priggish, pietistic, canting, pharisaical

sanction VERB *He may seem ready to sanction the use of force.* = **permit**, back, support, allow, approve, entitle, endorse, authorize, countenance, vouch for, lend your name to ■ **OPPOSITE:** forbid ▶ NOUN **1** (*often plural*) *He expressed his opposition to lifting the sanctions.* = **ban**, restriction, boycott, embargo, exclusion, penalty, deterrent, prohibition, coercive measures ■ **OPPOSITE:** permission **2** *The king could not enact laws without the sanction of parliament.* = **permission**, backing, support, authority, approval, allowance, confirmation, endorsement, countenance, ratification, authorization, approbation, O.K. or okay (*informal*), stamp or seal of approval ■ **OPPOSITE:** ban

sanctity NOUN = **sacredness**, inviolability, inalienability, hallowedness, sacrosanctness

sanctuary NOUN **1** *Some of them have sought sanctuary in the church.* = **protection**, shelter, refuge, haven, retreat, asylum **2** *a bird sanctuary* = **reserve**, park, preserve, reservation, national park, tract, nature reserve, conservation area

sanctum NOUN **1** *His bedroom is his inner sanctum.* = **refuge**, retreat, den, private room **2** *the inner sanctum of the mosque* = **sanctuary**, shrine, altar, holy place, Holy of Holies

sand NOUN *miles of golden sands* = **beach**, shore, strand (*literary*), dunes

sane ADJECTIVE **1** *He seemed perfectly sane.* = **rational**, normal, lucid, of sound mind, compos mentis (*Latin*), in your right mind, mentally sound, in possession of all your faculties **2** *a sane and safe energy policy* = **sensible**, sound, reasonable, balanced, moderate, sober, judicious, level-headed, grounded ■ **OPPOSITE:** foolish

sanguine ADJECTIVE = **cheerful**, confident, optimistic, assured, hopeful, buoyant, in good heart ■ **OPPOSITE:** gloomy

sanitary ADJECTIVE = **hygienic**, clean, healthy, wholesome, salubrious, unpolluted, germ-free

S

sanitation NOUN = **hygiene**, cleanliness, sewerage

sanity NOUN **1** *They finally had to move, just to preserve their sanity.* = **reason**, rationality, stability, normality, saneness **2** *He's been looking at ways of introducing some sanity into the market.* = **common sense**, sense, good sense, rationality, level-headedness, judiciousness, soundness of judgment ■ **OPPOSITE:** stupidity

sap¹ NOUN **1** *The leaves, bark and sap are common ingredients of herbal remedies.* = **juice**, essence, vital fluid, secretion, lifeblood, plant fluid **2** *her poor sap of a husband* = **fool**, idiot, noodle, wally (*slang*), wet (*Brit. informal*), charlie (*Brit. informal*), drip (*informal*), gull (*archaic*), prat (*slang*), plonker (*slang*), noddy, twit (*informal*), chump (*informal*), oaf, nitwit (*informal*), ninny, nincompoop, dweeb (*U.S. slang*), wuss (*slang*), Simple Simon, weenie (*U.S. informal*), muggins (*Brit. slang*), eejit (*Scot. & Irish*), dumb-ass (*slang*), numpty (*Scot. informal*), doofus (*slang, chiefly U.S.*), numskull or numbskull, dorba or dorb (*Austral. slang*)

sap² VERB *I was afraid the sickness had sapped my strength.* = **weaken**, drain, undermine, rob, exhaust, bleed (*informal*), erode, deplete, wear down, enervate, devitalize

sarcasm NOUN = **irony**, satire, cynicism, contempt, ridicule, bitterness, scorn, sneering, mockery, venom, derision, vitriol, mordancy, causticness

sarcastic ADJECTIVE = **ironical**, cynical, satirical, cutting, biting, sharp, acid, mocking, taunting, sneering, acrimonious, backhanded, contemptuous, disparaging, sardonic, caustic, bitchy (*informal*), vitriolic, acerbic, derisive, ironic, mordant, sarky (*Brit. informal*), mordacious, acerb

sardonic ADJECTIVE = **mocking**, cynical, dry, bitter, sneering, jeering, malicious, wry, sarcastic, derisive, ironical, mordant, mordacious

sash NOUN = **belt**, girdle, waistband, cummerbund

Satan NOUN = **The Devil**, Lucifer, Prince of Darkness, Lord of the Flies, Mephistopheles, Beelzebub, Old Nick (*informal*), The Evil One, Apollyon, Old Scratch (*informal*)

satanic ADJECTIVE = **evil**, demonic, hellish, black, malignant, wicked, inhuman, malevolent, devilish, infernal (*informal*), fiendish, accursed, iniquitous, diabolic, demoniac, demoniacal ■ **OPPOSITE:** godly

sate VERB = **satisfy**, satiate, slake, indulge to the full

satellite NOUN **1** *The rocket launched two satellites.* = **spacecraft**, communications satellite, sputnik, space capsule **2** *the satellites of Jupiter* = **moon**, secondary planet

satire NOUN **1** *It's an easy target for satire.* = **mockery**, wit, irony, ridicule, sarcasm **2** *a sharp satire on the American political process* = **parody**, mockery, caricature, send-up (*Brit. informal*), spoof (*informal*), travesty, takeoff (*informal*), lampoon, skit, burlesque

satirical *or* **satiric** ADJECTIVE = **mocking**, ironical, cynical, cutting, biting, bitter, taunting, pungent, incisive, sarcastic, sardonic, caustic, vitriolic, burlesque, mordant, Rabelaisian, mordacious

satisfaction NOUN **1** *She felt a small glow of satisfaction.* = **fulfilment**, pleasure, achievement, joy, relish, glee, gratification, pride, complacency ■ **OPPOSITE:** dissatisfaction **2** *Buyers have the right to go to court and demand satisfaction.* = **compensation**, damages, justice, amends, settlement, redress, remuneration, reparation, vindication, restitution, reimbursement, atonement, recompense, indemnification, requital ■ **OPPOSITE:** injury **3** *a state of satisfaction* = **contentment**, content, comfort, ease, pleasure, well-being, happiness, enjoyment, peace of mind, gratification, satiety, repletion, contentedness ■ **OPPOSITE:** discontent

satisfactory ADJECTIVE = **adequate**, acceptable, good enough, average, fair, all right, suitable, sufficient, competent, up to scratch, passable, up to standard, up to the mark ■ **OPPOSITE:** unsatisfactory

satisfied ADJECTIVE **1** *our satisfied customers* = **contented**, happy, content, pacified, pleased ■ **OPPOSITE:** dissatisfied **2** *People must be satisfied that the treatment is safe.* = **sure**, smug, convinced, positive, easy in your mind

satisfy VERB **1** *The pace of change has not been quick enough to satisfy everyone.* = **content**, please, indulge, fill, feed, appease, gratify, pander to, assuage, pacify, quench, mollify, surfeit, satiate, slake, sate ■ **OPPOSITE:** dissatisfy **2** *He has to satisfy us that real progress will be made.* = **convince**, persuade, assure, reassure, dispel (someone's) doubts, put (someone's) mind at rest ■ **OPPOSITE:** dissuade **3** *The procedures should satisfy certain basic requirements.* = **comply with**, meet, fulfil, answer, serve, fill, observe, obey, conform to ■ **OPPOSITE:** fail to meet

satisfying ADJECTIVE = **satisfactory**, pleasing, gratifying, pleasurable, cheering

saturate VERB 1 *Both sides are saturating the airwaves.* = **flood**, overwhelm, swamp, overrun, deluge, glut 2 *If the filter has been saturated with motor oil, discard it.* = **soak**, steep, drench, seep, imbue, douse, impregnate, suffuse, ret (*flax, etc*), wet through, waterlog, souse, drouk (*Scot.*)

saturated ADJECTIVE = **soaked**, soaking (wet), drenched, sodden, dripping, waterlogged, sopping (wet), wet through, soaked to the skin, wringing wet, droukit or drookit (*Scot.*)

sauce NOUN = **dressing**, dip, relish, condiment

saucy ADJECTIVE = **impudent**, cheeky (*informal*), impertinent, forward, fresh (*informal*), flip (*informal*), pert, disrespectful, flippant, presumptuous, insolent, lippy (*U.S. & Canad. slang*), smart-alecky (*informal*)

saunter VERB *We watched our fellow students saunter into the building.* = **stroll**, wander, amble, roam, ramble, meander, rove, take a stroll, mosey (*informal*), stravaig (*Scot. & Northern English, dialect*) ▶ NOUN *She began a slow saunter towards the bonfire.* = **stroll**, walk, amble, turn, airing, constitutional, ramble, promenade, breather, perambulation

sausage NOUN = **banger**

savage ADJECTIVE 1 *This was a savage attack.* = **cruel**, brutal, vicious, bloody, fierce, harsh, beastly (*informal*), ruthless, ferocious, murderous, ravening, sadistic, inhuman, merciless, diabolical, brutish, devilish, bloodthirsty, barbarous, pitiless, bestial ■ OPPOSITE: gentle 2 *a strange and savage animal encountered at the zoo* = **wild**, fierce, ferocious, unbroken, feral, untamed, undomesticated ■ OPPOSITE: tame 3 *a savage people* = **primitive**, undeveloped, uncultivated, uncivilized, in a state of nature, nonliterate 4 *stunning images of a wild and savage land* = **uncultivated**, rugged, unspoilt, uninhabited, waste, rough, uncivilized, unfrequented ■ OPPOSITE: cultivated ▶ NOUN 1 *The Romans viewed the people they conquered as savages.* = **barbarian**, primitive person 2 *The kids in the orchestra are a right bunch of savages!* = **lout**, yob (*Brit. slang*), brute, bear, monster, beast, barbarian, fiend, yahoo, hoon (*Austral. & N.Z.*), yobbo (*Brit. slang*), roughneck (*slang*), boor, cougan (*Austral. slang*), scozza (*Austral. slang*), bogan (*Austral. slang*) ▶ VERB 1 *A man was taken to hospital after being savaged by a dog.* = **maul**, tear, claw, attack, mangle, lacerate, mangulate (*Austral. slang*) 2 *The show had already been savaged by the critics.* = **criticize**, attack, knock (*informal*), blast, pan (*informal*), slam (*slang*), put down, slate (*informal*), have a go (at) (*informal*), disparage, tear into (*informal*), find fault with, lambast(e), pick holes in, pick to pieces, give (someone or something) a bad press ■ OPPOSITE: praise

savagery NOUN = **cruelty**, brutality, ferocity, ruthlessness, sadism, inhumanity, barbarity, viciousness, bestiality, fierceness, bloodthirstiness

save VERB 1 *She could have saved him from this final disaster.* = **rescue**, free, release, deliver, recover, get out, liberate, salvage, redeem, bail out, come to someone's rescue, set free, save the life of, extricate, save someone's bacon (*Brit. informal*)
■ OPPOSITE: endanger 2 *I thought we were saving money for a holiday.* = **keep**, reserve, set aside, store, collect, gather, hold, hoard, hide away, lay by, put by, salt away, treasure up, keep up your sleeve (*informal*), put aside for a rainy day ■ OPPOSITE: spend 3 *a final attempt to save 40,000 jobs* = **protect**, keep, guard, preserve, look after, take care of, safeguard, salvage, conserve, keep safe 4 *The majority of people intend to save.* = **budget**, be economical, economize, scrimp and save, retrench, be frugal, make economies, be thrifty, tighten your belt (*informal*) 5 *Scraps of material were saved, cut up and pieced together for quilts.* = **put aside**, keep, reserve, collect, retain, set aside, amass, put by 6 *This will save the expense and trouble of buying two pairs.* = **prevent**, avoid, spare, rule out, avert, obviate (*formal*)

saving NOUN *Use these vouchers for some great savings on holidays.* = **economy**, discount, reduction, bargain, cut ▶ PLURAL NOUN *Many people lost all their savings when the bank collapsed.* = **nest egg**, fund, store, reserves, resources, fall-back, provision for a rainy day

saviour NOUN = **rescuer**, deliverer, defender, guardian, salvation, protector, liberator, Good Samaritan, redeemer, preserver, knight in shining armour, friend in need

Saviour NOUN = **Christ**, Jesus, the Messiah, the Redeemer

savour VERB 1 *We won't pretend we savour the prospect of a month in prison.* = **relish**, like, delight in, revel in, luxuriate in, gloat over 2 *Savour the flavour of each mouthful.* = **enjoy**, appreciate, relish, delight in, revel in, partake of, drool over, luxuriate in, enjoy to

S

the full, smack your lips over ▶ NOUN
1 *The rich savour of the beans give this dish its character.* = **flavour**, taste, smell, relish, smack, zest, tang, zing (*informal*), piquancy
2 *Life without Anna had no savour.* = **zest**, interest, spice, excitement, salt, flavour

savoury ADJECTIVE **1** *Italian cooking is best known for its savoury dishes.* = **spicy**, rich, delicious, tasty, luscious, palatable, tangy, dainty, delectable, mouthwatering, piquant, full-flavoured, scrumptious (*informal*), appetizing, toothsome, yummo (*Austral. slang*) ■ OPPOSITE: tasteless **2** *He does not have a particularly savoury reputation.* = **wholesome**, decent, respectable, honest, reputable, apple-pie (*informal*)
■ OPPOSITE: disreputable ▶ PLURAL NOUN *I'll make some cheese straws or savouries.* = **appetizers**, nibbles, apéritifs, canapés, titbits, hors d'oeuvres

savvy NOUN *He is known for his political savvy.* = **understanding**, perception, grasp, ken, comprehension, apprehension ▶ ADJECTIVE *She was a pretty savvy woman.* = **shrewd**, sharp, astute, knowing, fly (*slang*), keen, smart, clever, intelligent, discriminating, discerning, canny, perceptive, artful, far-sighted, far-seeing, long-headed, perspicacious (*formal*), sagacious (*formal*)

say VERB **1** *She said she was very impressed.* = **state**, declare, remark, add, announce, maintain, mention, assert, affirm, asseverate (*formal*) **2** *I hope you didn't say anything about me.* = **speak**, utter, voice, express, pronounce, come out with (*informal*), put into words, give voice or utterance to **3** *I must say that that rather shocked me, too.* = **make known**, reveal, disclose, divulge, answer, reply, respond, give as your opinion **4** *That says a lot about the power of their marketing people.* = **suggest**, express, imply, communicate, disclose, give away, convey, divulge **5** *Say you lived in Boston, Massachusetts.* = **suppose**, supposing, imagine, assume, presume **6** *I don't know how long it lasted but I'd say it was about a quarter of an hour.* = **estimate**, suppose, guess, conjecture, surmise, dare say, hazard a guess **7** *How am I going to go on and say those lines tonight?* = **recite**, perform, deliver, do, read, repeat, render, rehearse, orate **8** *He says he did it after the police pressured him.* = **allege**, report, claim, hold, suggest, insist, maintain, rumour, assert, uphold, profess, put about that ▶ NOUN
1 *The students wanted more say in the running of the university.* = **influence**, power, control, authority, weight, sway, clout (*informal*), predominance, mana (*N.Z.*) **2** *Let him have*

his say. = **chance to speak**, vote, voice, crack (*informal*), opportunity to speak, turn to speak • **to say the least** *The result was, to say the least, fascinating.* = **at the very least**, without any exaggeration, to put it mildly

saying NOUN *that old saying: 'Charity begins at home'* = **proverb**, maxim, adage, saw (*old-fashioned*), slogan, gnome, dictum, axiom, aphorism, byword, apophthegm
• **go without saying** *It should go without saying that you shouldn't smoke.* = **be obvious**, be understood, be taken for granted, be accepted, be self-evident, be taken as read, be a matter of course

say-so NOUN = **assertion**, authority, agreement, word, guarantee, sanction, permission, consent, assurance, assent, authorization, dictum, asseveration (*formal*), O.K. or okay (*informal*)

scalding ADJECTIVE = **burning**, boiling, searing, blistering, piping hot

scale[1] NOUN *a thing with scales all over its body* = **flake**, plate, layer, lamina

scale[3] NOUN **1** *He underestimates the scale of the problem.* = **degree**, size, range, spread, extent, dimensions, scope, magnitude, breadth **2** *an earthquake measuring five-point-five on the Richter scale* = **system of measurement**, register, measuring system, graduated system, calibration, calibrated system **3** *This has become a reality for increasing numbers across the social scale.* = **ranking**, ladder, spectrum, hierarchy, series, sequence, progression, pecking order (*informal*) **4** *The map, on a scale of 1:10,000, shows over 5,000 individual paths.* = **ratio**, proportion, relative size ▶ VERB *The men scaled a wall and climbed down scaffolding on the other side.* = **climb up**, mount, go up, ascend, surmount, scramble up, clamber up, escalade • **scale something down** *The air rescue operation has now been scaled down.* = **reduce**, cut, moderate, slow down, cut down, wind down, tone down, downsize, kennet (*Austral. slang*), jeff (*Austral. slang*) • **scale something up** *Simply scaling up a size 10 garment often leads to disaster.* = **expand**, extend, blow up, enlarge, lengthen, magnify, amplify, augment

scaly ADJECTIVE **1** *The brown rat has prominent ears and a long scaly tail.* = **squamous**, squamate, lamellose, lamelliform **2** *If your skin becomes red, sore or very scaly, consult your doctor.* = **flaky**, scabrous, scurfy, furfuraceous (*Medical*), squamous or squamose (*Biology*), squamulose

scamper VERB = **run**, dash, dart, fly, hurry, sprint, romp, beetle, hasten, scuttle, scurry, scoot

scan VERB 1 *She scanned the advertisement pages of the newspaper.* = **glance over**, skim, look over, eye, check, clock (*Brit. slang*), examine, check out (*informal*), run over, eyeball (*slang*), size up (*informal*), get a load of (*informal*), look someone up and down, run your eye over, take a dekko at (*Brit. slang*), surf (*Computing*) 2 *The officer scanned the room.* = **survey**, search, investigate, sweep, con (*archaic*), scour, scrutinize, take stock of, recce (*slang*) ▶ NOUN 1 *I've had a quick scan through your book again.* = **look**, glance, skim, browse, flick, squint, butcher's (*Brit. slang*), brief look, dekko (*Brit. slang*), shufti (*Brit. slang*) 2 *He was rushed to hospital for a brain scan.* = **examination**, scanning, ultrasound

scandal NOUN 1 *a financial scandal* = **disgrace**, crime, offence, sin, embarrassment, wrongdoing, skeleton in the cupboard, dishonourable behaviour, discreditable behaviour 2 *He loved gossip and scandal.* = **gossip**, goss (*informal*), talk, rumours, dirt (*informal*), slander, tattle, dirty linen (*informal*), calumny, backbiting, aspersion 3 *She braved the scandal of her husband's infidelity.* = **shame**, offence, disgrace, stigma, infamy, opprobrium, obloquy 4 *It is a scandal that a person can be stopped for no reason by the police.* = **outrage**, shame, insult, disgrace, injustice, crying shame

scandalous ADJECTIVE 1 *They would be sacked for criminal or scandalous behaviour.* = **shocking**, disgraceful, outrageous, offensive, appalling, foul, dreadful, horrifying, obscene, monstrous, unspeakable, atrocious (*informal*), frightful, abominable ■ OPPOSITE: decent 2 *Newspaper columns were full of scandalous tales.* = **slanderous**, gossiping, scurrilous, untrue, defamatory, libellous ■ OPPOSITE: laudatory 3 *a scandalous waste of money* = **outrageous**, shocking, infamous, disgraceful, monstrous, shameful, atrocious, unseemly, odious, disreputable, opprobrious, highly improper ■ OPPOSITE: proper

scant ADJECTIVE 1 *There is scant evidence of strong economic growth to come.* = **inadequate**, insufficient, meagre, sparse, little, limited, bare, minimal, deficient, barely sufficient ■ OPPOSITE: adequate 2 *The hole was a scant 0.23 inches in diameter.* = **small**, limited, inadequate, insufficient, meagre, measly (*informal*), scanty, inconsiderable

scanty ADJECTIVE 1 *So far, what scanty evidence we have points to two subjects.* = **meagre**,

sparse, poor, thin, narrow, sparing, restricted, bare, inadequate, pathetic, insufficient, slender, scant, deficient, exiguous (*formal*) 2 *a model in scanty clothing* = **skimpy**, short, brief, tight, thin

scapegoat NOUN = **fall guy**, whipping boy

scar NOUN 1 *He had a scar on his forehead.* = **mark**, injury, wound, trauma (*Pathology*), blemish, cicatrix 2 *emotional scars that come from having been abused* = **trauma**, suffering, pain, strain, torture, disturbance, anguish ▶ VERB *He was scarred for life during a pub fight.* = **mark**, disfigure, damage, brand, mar, mutilate, maim, blemish, deface, traumatize, disfeature

scarce ADJECTIVE 1 *Food was scarce and expensive.* = **in short supply**, wanting, insufficient, deficient, at a premium, thin on the ground ■ OPPOSITE: plentiful 2 *I'm unemployed, so luxuries are scarce.* = **rare**, few, unusual, uncommon, few and far between, infrequent, thin on the ground ■ OPPOSITE: common

scarcely ADVERB 1 *He could scarcely breathe.* = **hardly**, barely, only just, scarce (*archaic*) 2 *It can scarcely be coincidence.* = **by no means**, hardly, not at all, definitely not, under no circumstances, on no account

> USAGE Since *scarcely*, *hardly*, and *barely* already have negative force, it is unnecessary to use another negative word with them. Therefore, say *he had hardly had time to think* (not *he hadn't hardly had time to think*); and *there was scarcely any bread left* (not *there was scarcely no bread left*). When *scarcely*, *hardly*, and *barely* are used at the beginning of a sentence, as in *scarcely had I arrived*, the following clause should start with *when*: *scarcely had I arrived when I was asked to chair a meeting*. The word *before* can be used in place of *when* in this context, but the word *than* used in the same way is considered incorrect by many people, though this use is becoming increasingly common.

scarcity NOUN = **shortage**, lack, deficiency, poverty, want, dearth, paucity (*formal*), insufficiency, infrequency, undersupply, rareness ■ OPPOSITE: abundance

scare VERB *She's just trying to scare me.* = **frighten**, alarm, terrify, panic, shock, startle, intimidate, dismay, daunt, terrorize, put the wind up (someone) (*informal*), give (someone) a fright, give (someone) a turn (*informal*), affright (*archaic*) ▶ NOUN 1 *We got a bit of a scare.* = **fright**, shock, start 2 *an apparently endless series of public health scares* = **panic**, hysteria

3 *a security scare over a suspect package* = **alert**, warning, alarm

scared ADJECTIVE = **afraid**, alarmed, frightened, terrified, shaken, cowed, startled, fearful, unnerved, petrified, panicky, terrorized, panic-stricken, scared stiff, terror-stricken

scarf NOUN = **muffler**, stole, headscarf, comforter, cravat, neckerchief, headsquare

scary ADJECTIVE = **frightening**, alarming, terrifying, shocking, chilling, horrifying, intimidating, horrendous, hairy (*slang*), unnerving, spooky (*informal*), creepy (*informal*), hair-raising, spine-chilling, bloodcurdling

scathing ADJECTIVE = **critical**, cutting, biting, harsh, savage, brutal, searing, withering, belittling, sarcastic, caustic, scornful, vitriolic, trenchant, mordant, mordacious

scatter VERB **1** *He began by scattering seed and putting in plants.* = **throw about**, spread, sprinkle, strew, broadcast, shower, fling, litter, sow, diffuse, disseminate ■ OPPOSITE: gather **2** *After dinner, everyone scattered.* = **disperse**, separate, break up, dispel, disband, dissipate, disunite, put to flight ■ OPPOSITE: assemble

scattering NOUN = **sprinkling**, few, handful, scatter, smattering, smatter

scavenge VERB = **search**, hunt, forage, rummage, root about, fossick (*Austral. & N.Z.*), scratch about

scenario NOUN **1** *That apocalyptic scenario cannot be ruled out.* = **situation**, sequence of events, chain of events, course of events, series of developments **2** *I will write an outline of the scenario.* = **story line**, résumé, outline, sketch, summary, rundown, synopsis

scene NOUN **1** *the opening scene* = **act**, part, division, episode **2** *The lights go up, revealing a scene of chaos.* = **setting**, set, background, location, backdrop, mise en scène (*French*) **3** *There were emotional scenes as the refugees enjoyed their first breath of freedom.* = **incident**, happening, event, episode **4** *Riot vans were on the scene in minutes.* = **site**, place, setting, area, position, stage, situation, spot, whereabouts, locality **5** *the local music scene; Sport just isn't my scene.* = **world**, business, environment, preserve, arena, realm, domain, milieu, thing, field of interest **6** *James Lynch's country scenes* = **view**, prospect, panorama, vista, landscape, tableau, outlook **7** *I'm sorry I made such a scene.* = **fuss**, to-do, row, performance (*informal*), upset, drama, exhibition, carry-on (*informal, chiefly Brit.*),

confrontation, tantrum, commotion, hue and cry, display of emotion, hissy fit (*informal*) **8** *She was told to cut some scenes from her new series.* = **section**, part, sequence, segment, clip

scenery NOUN **1** *Sometimes they just drive slowly down the lane enjoying the scenery.* = **landscape**, view, surroundings, terrain, vista **2** *There was a break while the scenery was changed.* = **set**, setting, backdrop, flats, décor, stage set

scenic ADJECTIVE = **picturesque**, beautiful, spectacular, striking, grand, impressive, breathtaking, panoramic

scent NOUN **1** *She could smell the scent of her mother's lacquer.* = **fragrance**, smell, perfume, bouquet, aroma, odour, niff (*Brit. slang*), redolence **2** *A police dog picked up the murderer's scent.* = **trail**, track, spoor **3** *a bottle of scent* = **perfume**, fragrance, cologne, eau de toilette (*French*), eau de cologne (*French*), toilet water ▶ VERB *dogs which scent the hidden birds* = **smell**, sense, recognize, detect, sniff, discern, sniff out, nose out, get wind of (*informal*), be on the track or trail of

scented ADJECTIVE = **fragrant**, perfumed, aromatic, sweet-smelling, redolent, ambrosial, odoriferous

sceptic NOUN **1** *He was a born sceptic.* = **doubter**, cynic, scoffer, disbeliever, Pyrrhonist **2** *a lifelong religious sceptic* = **agnostic**, doubter, unbeliever, doubting Thomas

sceptical ADJECTIVE = **doubtful**, cynical, dubious, questioning, doubting, hesitating, scoffing, unconvinced, disbelieving, incredulous, quizzical, mistrustful, unbelieving ■ OPPOSITE: convinced

scepticism NOUN = **doubt**, suspicion, disbelief, cynicism, incredulity

schedule NOUN **1** *He has been forced to adjust his schedule.* = **plan**, programme, agenda, calendar, timetable, itinerary, list of appointments **2** *a detailed written schedule* = **list**, catalogue, inventory, syllabus ▶ VERB *No new talks are scheduled.* = **plan**, set up, book, programme, arrange, organize, timetable

schematic ADJECTIVE = **graphic**, representational, illustrative, diagrammatic, diagrammatical

scheme NOUN **1** *a private pension scheme* = **plan**, programme, strategy, system, design, project, theory, proposal, device, tactics, course of action, contrivance **2** *a quick money-making scheme* = **plot**, dodge, ploy, ruse, game (*informal*), shift, intrigue, conspiracy, manoeuvre, machinations, subterfuge, stratagem ▸ VERB *Everyone's always scheming and plotting.* = **plot**, plan, intrigue, manoeuvre, conspire, contrive, collude, wheel and deal, machinate

scheming ADJECTIVE = **calculating**, cunning, sly, designing, tricky, slippery, wily, artful, conniving, Machiavellian, foxy, deceitful, underhand, duplicitous ■ **OPPOSITE:** straightforward

schism NOUN = **division**, break, split, breach, separation, rift, splintering, rupture, discord, disunion

schmick ADJECTIVE **1** *The band launch their schmick new CD next week.* = **excellent**, outstanding, good, great (*informal*), fine, prime, capital, noted, choice, champion, cool (*informal*), select, brilliant, very good, cracking (*Brit. informal*), crucial (*slang*), mean (*slang*), superb, distinguished, fantastic (*informal*), magnificent, superior, sterling, worthy, first-class, marvellous, exceptional, terrific (*informal*), splendid, notable, mega (*slang*), dope (*slang*), sick (*slang*), world-class, exquisite, admirable, exemplary, wicked (*slang*), first-rate, superlative, top-notch (*informal*), brill (*informal*), A1 or A-one (*informal*), booshit (*Austral. slang*), exo (*Austral. slang*), sik (*Austral. slang*), rad (*informal*), beaut (*informal*) ■ **OPPOSITE:** terrible **2** *the city's schmick new restaurant* = **stylish**, smart, chic, polished, fashionable, trendy (*Brit. informal*), classy (*slang*), in fashion, snappy, in vogue, dapper, natty (*informal*), snazzy (*informal*), modish, well turned-out, dressy (*informal*), à la mode, voguish, funky ■ **OPPOSITE:** scruffy

scholar NOUN **1** *The library attracts thousands of scholars and researchers.* = **intellectual**, academic, man *or* woman of letters, bookworm, egghead (*informal*), savant, bluestocking (*usually derogatory*), acca (*Austral. slang*) **2** *She could be a good scholar if she didn't let her mind wander so much.* = **student**, pupil, learner, schoolboy *or* schoolgirl

scholarly ADJECTIVE = **learned**, academic, intellectual, lettered, erudite, scholastic, well-read, studious, bookish, swotty (*Brit. informal*) ■ **OPPOSITE:** uneducated

scholarship NOUN **1** *scholarships for young students* = **grant**, award, payment, exhibition, endowment, fellowship, bursary **2** *I want to take advantage of your lifetime of scholarship.* = **learning**, education, culture, knowledge, wisdom, accomplishments, attainments, lore, erudition, academic study, book-learning

scholastic ADJECTIVE = **learned**, academic, scholarly, lettered, literary, bookish

school NOUN **1** *a boy who was in my class at school* = **academy**, college, institution, institute, discipline, seminary, educational institution, centre of learning, alma mater **2** *the Chicago school of economists* = **group**, set, circle, following, class, faction, followers, disciples, sect, devotees, denomination, clique, adherents, schism **3** *He was never a member of any school.* = **way of life**, creed, faith, outlook, persuasion, school of thought ▸ VERB *He is schooled to spot trouble.* = **train**, prime, coach, prepare, discipline, educate, drill, tutor, instruct, verse, indoctrinate

schooling NOUN **1** *Normal schooling has been severely disrupted.* = **teaching**, education, tuition, formal education, book-learning **2** *the schooling of horses* = **training**, coaching, instruction, grounding, preparation, drill, guidance

schoolteacher NOUN = **schoolmaster** *or* **schoolmistress**, instructor, pedagogue, schoolmarm (*informal*), dominie (*Scot.*)

science NOUN = **discipline**, body of knowledge, branch of knowledge

scientific ADJECTIVE **1** *scientific research* = **technological**, technical, chemical, biological, empirical, factual **2** *an engineer who takes a scientific approach to the sport* = **systematic**, accurate, exact, precise, controlled, mathematical

scientist NOUN = **researcher**, inventor, boffin (*informal*), technophile

scintillating ADJECTIVE = **brilliant**, exciting, stimulating, lively, sparkling, bright, glittering, dazzling, witty, animated

scion NOUN = **descendant**, child, offspring, successor, heir

scoff¹ VERB *At first I scoffed at the notion.* = **scorn**, mock, laugh at, ridicule, knock (*informal*), taunt, despise, sneer, jeer, deride, slag (off) (*slang*), flout, belittle, revile, make light of, poke fun at, twit, gibe, pooh-pooh, make sport of

scoff² VERB *I scoffed the lot!* = **gobble (up)**, wolf, devour, bolt, cram, put away, guzzle, gulp down, gorge yourself on, gollop, stuff yourself with, cram yourself on, make a pig of yourself on (*informal*)

scold VERB = **reprimand**, censure, rebuke, rate, blame, lecture, carpet (*informal*), slate (*informal, chiefly Brit.*), nag, go on at, reproach, berate, tick off (*informal*), castigate, chide, tear into (*informal*), tell off (*informal*), find fault with, remonstrate with, bring (someone) to book, take (someone) to task, read the riot act,

S

reprove, upbraid, bawl out (*informal*), give (someone) a talking-to (*informal*), haul (someone) over the coals (*informal*), chew out (*U.S. & Canad. informal*), give (someone) a dressing-down (*informal*), tear (someone) off a strip (*Brit. informal*), give a rocket (*Brit. & N.Z. informal*), vituperate, give (someone) a row, have (someone) on the carpet (*informal*) ■ **OPPOSITE:** praise

scolding NOUN = **ticking-off**, row, lecture, wigging (*Brit. slang*), rebuke (*informal*), dressing-down (*informal*), telling-off (*informal*), tongue-lashing, piece of your mind, (good) talking-to (*informal*)

scoop VERB *films which scooped awards around the world* = **win**, get, receive, land (*informal*), gain, achieve, net, earn, pick up, bag (*informal*), secure, collect, obtain, procure, come away with ▶ NOUN **1** *a small ice-cream scoop* = **ladle**, spoon, dipper **2** *She gave him an extra scoop of clotted cream.* = **spoonful**, lump, dollop (*informal*), ball, ladleful **3** *one of the biggest scoops in the history of newspapers* = **exclusive**, exposé, coup, revelation, sensation, inside story • **scoop something out 1** *Cut a marrow in half and scoop out the seeds.* = **take out**, empty, dig out, scrape out, spoon out, bail or bale out **2** *A hole had been scooped out next to the house.* = **dig**, shovel, excavate, gouge, hollow out • **scoop something** or **someone up** *He began to scoop his things up frantically.* = **gather up**, lift, pick up, take up, sweep up or away

scoot VERB = **dash**, run, dart, sprint, bolt, zip, scuttle, scurry, scamper, skitter, skedaddle (*informal*), skirr

scope NOUN **1** *He believed in giving his staff scope for initiative.* = **opportunity**, room, freedom, space, liberty, latitude, elbowroom, leeway **2** *the scope of a novel* = **range**, capacity, reach, area, extent, outlook, orbit, span, sphere, ambit, purview, field of reference

scorch VERB = **burn**, sear, char, roast, blister, wither, blacken, shrivel, parch, singe

scorching ADJECTIVE = **burning**, boiling, baking, flaming, tropical, roasting, searing, fiery, sizzling, red-hot, torrid, sweltering, broiling, unbearably hot

score VERB **1** *They scored 282 runs in their first innings.* = **gain**, win, achieve, make, get, net, bag, obtain, bring in, attain, amass, notch up (*informal*), chalk up (*informal*) **2** *He told them he had scored with the girl.* = **go down well with (someone)**, impress, triumph, make a hit (*informal*), make a point, gain an advantage, put yourself across, make an impact *or* impression **3** *He scored a piece for a chamber music ensemble.* = **arrange**, set, orchestrate, adapt **4** *Lightly score the surface of the steaks with a sharp cook's knife.* = **cut**, scratch, nick, mark, mar, slash, scrape, notch, graze, gouge, deface, indent, crosshatch ▶ NOUN **1** *low maths scores* = **rating**, mark, grade, percentage **2** *The final score was 4-1.* = **points**, result, total, outcome **3** *the composer of classic film scores* = **composition**, soundtrack, arrangement, orchestration **4** *They had a score to settle with each other.* = **grievance**, wrong, injury, injustice, grudge, bone of contention, bone to pick **5** *So what is the score anyway?* = **charge**, bill, account, total, debt, reckoning, tab (*informal*), tally, amount due ▶ PLURAL NOUN *Campaigners lit scores of bonfires.* = **lots**, loads, many, millions, gazillions (*informal*), hundreds, hosts, crowds, masses, droves, an army, legions, swarms, multitudes, myriads, very many, a flock, a throng, a great number • **score something out** or **through** *Words and sentences had been scored out and underlined.* = **cross out**, delete, strike out, cancel, obliterate, put a line through

scorn NOUN *They greeted the proposal with scorn.* = **contempt**, disdain, mockery, derision, despite, slight, sneer, sarcasm, disparagement, contumely (*literary*), contemptuousness, scornfulness ■ **OPPOSITE:** respect ▶ VERB *people who scorned traditional methods* = **despise**, reject, disdain, slight, snub, shun, be above, spurn, rebuff, deride, flout, look down on, scoff at, make fun of, sneer at, hold in contempt, turn up your nose at (*informal*), contemn, curl your lip at, consider beneath you ■ **OPPOSITE:** respect

scornful ADJECTIVE = **contemptuous**, insulting, mocking, defiant, withering, sneering, slighting, jeering, scoffing, scathing, sarcastic, sardonic, haughty, disdainful, insolent, derisive, supercilious, contumelious (*literary*)

scornfully ADVERB = **contemptuously**, with contempt, dismissively, disdainfully, with disdain, scathingly, witheringly, with a sneer, slightingly, with lip curled

scotch VERB = **put an end to**, destroy, smash, devastate, wreck, thwart, scupper (*Brit. slang*), extinguish, put paid to, nip in the bud, bring to an end, put the lid on, put the kibosh on

Scots ADJECTIVE = **Scottish**, Caledonian

scoundrel NOUN (*old-fashioned*) = **rogue**, cad (*old-fashioned, informal*), villain, heel (*slang*), cheat, swine, rascal, scally

(*Northwest English*, *dialect*), wretch, incorrigible, knave (*archaic*), rotter (*slang*, *chiefly Brit.*), ne'er-do-well, reprobate, scumbag (*slang*), good-for-nothing, miscreant, scamp, bad egg (*old-fashioned*, *informal*), blackguard, scapegrace, caitiff (*archaic*), dastard (*archaic*), skelm (*S. African*), wrong 'un (*slang*)

scour¹ VERB *He decided to scour the sink.* = **scrub**, clean, polish, rub, cleanse, buff, burnish, whiten, furbish (*formal*), abrade

scour² VERB *We scoured the telephone directory for clues.* = **search**, hunt, comb, ransack, forage, look high and low, go over with a fine-tooth comb

scourge NOUN **1** *Drugs are a scourge that is devastating our society.* = **affliction**, plague (*informal*), curse, terror, pest, torment, misfortune, visitation, bane, infliction ■ OPPOSITE: benefit **2** *a heavy scourge with a piece of iron lashed into its knot* = **whip**, lash, thong, switch, strap, cat-o'-nine-tails ▶ VERB **1** *Economic anarchy scourged the post-war world.* = **afflict**, plague, curse, torment, harass, terrorize, excoriate **2** *They were scourging him severely.* = **whip**, beat, lash, thrash, discipline, belt (*informal*), leather, punish, whale, cane, flog, trounce, castigate, wallop (*informal*), chastise, lather (*informal*), horsewhip, tan (someone's) hide (*slang*), take a strap to

scout NOUN *They set off, two men out in front as scouts.* = **vanguard**, lookout, precursor, outrider, reconnoitrer, advance guard ▶ VERB *I have people scouting the hills already.* = **reconnoitre**, investigate, check out, case (*slang*), watch, survey, observe, spy, probe, recce (*slang*), spy out, make a reconnaissance, see how the land lies • **scout around** or **round** *They scouted around for more fuel.* = **search**, look for, hunt for, fossick (*Austral. & N.Z.*), cast about or around, ferret about or around

scowl VERB *She scowled at the two men as they entered the room.* = **glower**, frown, look daggers, grimace, lour or lower ▶ NOUN *He met the remark with a scowl.* = **glower**, frown, dirty look, black look, grimace

scrabble VERB = **scrape**, scratch, scramble, dig, claw, paw, grope, clamber

scramble VERB **1** *He scrambled up a steep bank.* = **struggle**, climb, clamber, push, crawl, swarm, scrabble, move with difficulty **2** *More than a million fans are expected to scramble for tickets.* = **strive**, rush, contend, vie, run, push, hasten, jostle, jockey for position, make haste **3** *The latest machines scramble the messages.* = **jumble**, mix up, muddle, shuffle, entangle, disarrange ▶ NOUN **1** *the scramble to the top of the cliffs* = **clamber**, ascent **2** *the scramble for jobs* = **race**, competition, struggle, rush, confusion, hustle, free-for-all (*informal*), commotion, melee or mêlée

scrap¹ NOUN **1** *a fire fuelled by scraps of wood* = **piece**, fragment, bit, trace, grain, particle, portion, snatch, part, atom, remnant, crumb, mite, bite, mouthful, snippet, sliver, morsel, modicum, iota **2** *cut up for scrap* = **waste**, junk, off cuts ▶ PLURAL NOUN *My dog begs for scraps of food.* = **leftovers**, remains, bits, scrapings, leavings ▶ VERB *We should scrap nuclear and chemical weapons.* = **get rid of**, drop, abandon, shed, break up, ditch (*slang*), junk (*informal*), chuck (*informal*), discard, write off, demolish, trash (*slang*), dispense with, jettison, toss out, throw on the scrapheap, throw away or out ■ OPPOSITE: bring back

scrap² (*informal*) NOUN *He has never been one to avoid a scrap.* = **fight**, battle, row, argument, dispute, set-to (*informal*), disagreement, quarrel, brawl, squabble, wrangle, scuffle, tiff, dust-up (*informal*), shindig (*informal*), scrimmage, shindy (*informal*), bagarre (*French*), biffo (*Austral. slang*) ▶ VERB *They are always scrapping.* = **fight**, argue, row, fall out (*informal*), barney (*informal*), squabble, spar, wrangle, bicker, have words, come to blows, have a shouting match (*informal*)

scrape VERB **1** *She went round the car scraping the frost off the windows.* = **rake**, sweep, drag, brush **2** *The only sound is that of knives and forks scraping against china.* = **grate**, grind, scratch, screech, squeak, rasp **3** *She stumbled and fell, scraping her palms and knees.* = **graze**, skin, scratch, bark, scuff, rub, abrade **4** *She scraped food off the plates into the bin.* = **clean**, remove, scour ▶ NOUN *We got into terrible scrapes.* = **predicament**, trouble, difficulty, spot (*informal*), fix (*informal*), mess, distress, dilemma, plight, tight spot, awkward situation, pretty pickle (*informal*) • **scrape something together** *They only just managed to scrape the money together.* = **collect**, save, muster, get hold of, amass, hoard, glean, dredge up, rake up or together

scrapheap NOUN • **on the scrapheap** = **discarded**, ditched (*slang*), redundant, written off, jettisoned, put out to grass (*informal*)

scrappy ADJECTIVE = **incomplete**, sketchy, piecemeal, disjointed, perfunctory, thrown together, fragmentary, bitty

scratch VERB **1** *The old man lifted his cardigan to scratch his side.* = **rub**, scrape, claw at **2** *Knives will scratch the worktop.* = **mark**, cut, score, damage, grate, graze, etch, lacerate, incise, make a mark on ▸ NOUN *I pointed to a number of scratches on the tile floor.* = **mark**, scrape, graze, blemish, gash, laceration, claw mark • **scratch something out** *She scratched out the word 'frightful'.* = **erase**, eliminate, delete, cancel, strike off, annul, cross out • **not up to scratch** *This work just isn't up to scratch.* = **inadequate**, unacceptable, unsatisfactory, incapable, insufficient, incompetent, not up to standard, not up to snuff (*informal*)

scrawl VERB *graffiti scrawled on school walls* = **scribble**, doodle, squiggle ▸ NOUN *a hasty, barely decipherable scrawl* = **scribble**, doodle, squiggle

scrawny ADJECTIVE = **thin**, lean, skinny, angular, gaunt, skeletal, bony, lanky, undernourished, skin-and-bones (*informal*), scraggy, rawboned, macilent (*rare*)

scream VERB *If I hear one more joke about my hair, I shall scream.* = **cry**, yell, shriek, screech, squeal, shrill, bawl, howl, holler (*informal*), sing out ▸ NOUN **1** *Hilda let out a scream.* = **cry**, yell, howl, wail, outcry, shriek, screech, yelp **2** *He's a scream, isn't he?* = **laugh** (*informal*), card (*informal*), riot (*slang*), comic, character (*informal*), caution (*informal*), sensation, wit, comedian, entertainer, wag, joker, hoot (*informal*)

screech NOUN *The figure gave a screech.* = **cry**, scream, shriek, squeal, squawk, yelp

screen NOUN *They put a screen in front of me.* = **cover**, guard, shade, shelter, shield, hedge, partition, cloak, mantle, shroud, canopy, awning, concealment, room divider ▸ VERB **1** *The series is likely to be screened in January.* = **broadcast**, show, put on, present, air, cable, beam, transmit, stream, relay, televise, put on the air **2** *The road is screened by a block of flats.* = **cover**, hide, conceal, shade, mask, veil, cloak, shroud, shut out **3** *They need to screen everyone at risk of contracting the illness.* = **investigate**, test, check, examine, scan **4** *It was their job to screen information for their bosses.* = **process**, sort, examine, grade, filter, scan, evaluate, gauge, sift **5** *They deliberately screened him from knowledge of their operations.* = **protect**, guard, shield, defend, shelter, safeguard

screw NOUN *Each bracket is fixed to the wall with just three screws.* = **nail**, pin, tack, rivet, fastener, spike ▸ VERB **1** *I like the sort of shelving that you screw on the wall.* = **fasten**, fix, attach, bolt, clamp, rivet **2** *Screw down the lid fairly tightly.* = **turn**, twist, tighten, work in **3** *He screwed his face into an expression of mock pain.* = **contort**, twist, distort, contract, wrinkle, warp, crumple, deform, pucker **4** *We've been screwed.* = **cheat**, do (*slang*), rip (someone) off (*slang*), skin (*slang*), trick, con, stiff (*slang*), sting (*informal*), deceive, fleece, dupe, overcharge, rook (*slang*), bamboozle (*informal*), diddle (*informal*), take (someone) for a ride (*informal*), put one over on (someone) (*informal*), pull a fast one (on someone) (*informal*), take to the cleaners (*informal*), sell a pup (to) (*slang*), hornswoggle (*slang*) **5** (*often with* **out of**) *rich nations screwing money out of poor nations* = **squeeze**, wring, extract, wrest, bleed someone of something • **put the screws on someone** *They had to put the screws on Harper to get the information they needed.* = **coerce**, force, compel, drive, squeeze, intimidate, constrain, oppress, pressurize, browbeat, press-gang, bring pressure to bear on, hold a knife to someone's throat • **screw something up 1** *She screwed up her eyes.* = **contort**, contract, wrinkle, knot, knit, distort, crumple, pucker **2** *Get out. Haven't you screwed things up enough already?* = **bungle**, botch, mess up, spoil, queer (*informal*), cock up (*Brit. slang*), mishandle, make a mess of (*slang*), mismanage, make a hash of (*informal*), make a nonsense of, bodge (*informal*), flub (*U.S. slang*), louse up (*slang*), crool or cruel (*Austral. slang*)

scribble VERB = **scrawl**, write, jot, pen, scratch, doodle, dash off

scribe NOUN = **secretary**, clerk, scrivener (*archaic*), notary (*archaic*), amanuensis, copyist

script NOUN **1** *Jenny's writing a film script.* = **text**, lines, words, book, copy, dialogue, manuscript, libretto **2** *She wrote the letter in an elegant script.* = **handwriting**, writing, hand, letters, calligraphy, longhand, penmanship (*formal*) ▸ VERB *I scripted and directed both films.* = **write**, draft, compose, author

scripture NOUN = **The Bible**, The Word, The Gospels, The Scriptures, The Word of God, The Good Book, Holy Scripture, Holy Writ, Holy Bible, The Book of Books

Scrooge NOUN = **miser**, penny-pincher (*informal*), skinflint, cheapskate (*informal*), tightwad (*U.S. & Canad. slang*), niggard, money-grubber (*informal*), meanie or meany (*informal, chiefly Brit.*)

scrounge VERB = **cadge**, beg, sponge (*informal*), bum (*informal*), touch (someone) for (*slang*), blag (*slang*), wheedle, mooch (*slang*), forage for, hunt around (for), sorn (*Scot.*), freeload (*slang*), bludge (*Austral. & N.Z. informal*)

scrounger NOUN = **parasite**, freeloader (*slang*), sponger (*informal*), bum (*informal*), cadger, bludger (*Austral. & N.Z. informal*), sorner (*Scot.*), quandong (*Austral. slang*)

scrub VERB **1** *The corridors are scrubbed clean.* = **scour**, clean, polish, rub, wash, cleanse, buff, exfoliate **2** *The whole thing had to be scrubbed.* = **cancel**, drop, give up, abandon, abolish, forget about, call off, delete, do away with, discontinue

scruff NOUN = **nape**, scrag (*informal*)

scruffy ADJECTIVE = **shabby**, untidy, ragged, rundown, messy, sloppy (*informal*), seedy, squalid, tattered, tatty (*Brit.*), unkempt, disreputable, scrubby (*Brit. informal*), grungy, slovenly, mangy, sluttish, slatternly, ungroomed, frowzy, ill-groomed, draggletailed (*archaic*), daggy (*Austral. & N.Z. informal*) ■ OPPOSITE: neat

scrumptious ADJECTIVE = **delicious**, delectable, inviting, magnificent, exquisite, luscious, succulent, mouthwatering, yummy (*slang*), appetizing, moreish (*informal*), yummo (*Austral. slang*)

scrunch VERB = **crumple**, crush, squash, crunch, mash, ruck up

scruple NOUN = **misgiving**, hesitation, qualm, doubt, difficulty, caution, reluctance, second thoughts, uneasiness, perplexity, compunction, squeamishness, twinge of conscience

scrupulous ADJECTIVE **1** *I have been scrupulous about telling them the truth.* = **moral**, principled, upright, honourable, conscientious ■ OPPOSITE: unscrupulous **2** *scrupulous attention to detail* = **careful**, strict, precise, minute, nice, exact, rigorous, meticulous, painstaking, fastidious, punctilious (*formal*) ■ OPPOSITE: careless

scrutinize VERB = **examine**, study, inspect, research, search, investigate, explore, probe, analyse, scan, sift, dissect, work over, pore over, peruse, inquire into, go over with a fine-tooth comb

scrutiny NOUN = **examination**, study, investigation, search, inquiry, analysis, inspection, exploration, sifting, once-over (*informal*), perusal, close study

scud VERB = **fly**, race, speed, shoot, blow, sail, skim

scuffle NOUN *Violent scuffles broke out.* = **fight**, set-to (*informal*), scrap (*informal*), disturbance, fray, brawl, barney (*informal*), ruck (*slang*), skirmish, tussle, commotion, rumpus, affray (*Law*), shindig (*informal*), ruction (*informal*), ruckus (*informal*), scrimmage, shindy (*informal*), bagarre (*French*), biffo (*Austral. slang*) ▶ VERB *Police*

scuffled with some of the protesters. = **fight**, struggle, clash, contend, grapple, jostle, tussle, come to blows, exchange blows

sculpture NOUN *a collection of 20th-century sculptures* = **statue**, figure, model, bust, effigy, figurine, statuette ▶ VERB *He sculptured the figure in marble.* = **carve**, form, cut, model, fashion, shape, mould, sculpt, chisel, hew (*old-fashioned*), sculp

scum NOUN **1** *I think people who hurt animals are scum.* = **rabble** (*derogatory*), trash (*chiefly U.S. & Canad.*), riffraff, rubbish, dross, lowest of the low, dregs of society, canaille (*French*), ragtag and bobtail **2** *scum around the bath* = **impurities**, film, crust, froth, scruff, dross, offscourings

scungy ADJECTIVE *He was living in some scungy flat on the outskirts of town.* = **sordid**, seedy, sleazy, squalid, mean, dirty, foul, filthy, unclean, wretched, seamy, slovenly, skanky (*slang*), slummy, festy (*Austral. slang*)

scupper VERB = **destroy**, ruin, wreck, defeat, overwhelm, disable, overthrow, demolish, undo, torpedo, put paid to, discomfit

scurrilous ADJECTIVE = **slanderous**, scandalous, defamatory, low, offensive, gross, foul, insulting, infamous, obscene, abusive, coarse, indecent, vulgar, foul-mouthed, salacious, ribald, vituperative, scabrous, Rabelaisian

scurry VERB *The attack began, sending residents scurrying for cover.* = **hurry**, race, dash, fly, sprint, dart, whisk, skim, beetle, scud, scuttle, scoot, scamper ■ OPPOSITE: amble ▶ NOUN *a mad scurry for a suitable venue* = **flurry**, race, bustle, whirl, scampering

scuttle VERB = **run**, scurry, scamper, rush, hurry, scramble, hare (*Brit. informal*), bustle, beetle, scud, hasten, scoot, scutter (*Brit. informal*)

sea NOUN **1** *Most of the kids have never seen the sea.* = **ocean**, the deep, the waves, the drink (*informal*), the briny (*informal*), main **2** *Down below them was the sea of upturned faces.* = **mass**, lot, lots (*informal*), army, host, crowd, collection, sheet, assembly, mob, congregation, legion, abundance, swarm, horde, multitude, myriad, throng, expanse, plethora, profusion, concourse, assemblage, vast number, great number ▶ MODIFIER *a sea vessel* = **marine**, ocean, maritime, aquatic, oceanic, saltwater, ocean-going, seagoing, pelagic, briny, salt • **at sea** *I'm totally at sea with popular culture.* = **bewildered**, lost, confused, puzzled, uncertain, baffled, adrift, perplexed, disconcerted, at a loss, mystified, disoriented, bamboozled (*informal*),

S

flummoxed, at sixes and sevens ■ **RELATED WORDS:** *adjectives* marine, maritime

seafaring ADJECTIVE = **nautical**, marine, naval, maritime, oceanic

seal VERB *The group has sealed a deal to sell its products in China.* = **settle**, clinch, conclude, consummate, finalize, shake hands on (*informal*) ▶ NOUN **1** *Wet the edges where the two crusts join, to form a seal.* = **sealant**, sealer, adhesive **2** *the President's seal of approval* = **authentication**, stamp, confirmation, assurance, ratification, notification, insignia, imprimatur, attestation • **set the seal on something** *Such a visit may set the seal on a new relationship between them.* = **confirm**, establish, assure, stamp, ratify, validate, attest, authenticate

seam NOUN **1** *The seam of her tunic was split from armpit to hem.* = **joint**, closure, suture (*Surgery*) **2** *The average UK coal seam is one metre thick.* = **layer**, vein, stratum, lode

sear VERB = **wither**, burn, blight, brand, scorch, sizzle, shrivel, cauterize, desiccate, dry up *or* out

search VERB *Armed troops searched the hospital yesterday.* = **examine**, check, investigate, explore, probe, inspect, comb, inquire, sift, scour, ferret, pry, ransack, forage, scrutinize, turn upside down, rummage through, frisk (*informal*), cast around, rifle through, leave no stone unturned, turn inside out, fossick (*Austral. & N.Z.*), go over with a fine-tooth comb ▶ NOUN *There was no chance of him being found alive and the search was abandoned.* = **hunt**, look, inquiry, investigation, examination, pursuit, quest, going-over (*informal*), inspection, exploration, scrutiny, rummage, Google (*Computing*), googlewhack (*Computing informal*) • **search for something** *or* **someone** *The security forces have started searching for the missing men.* = **look for**, seek, hunt for, pursue, go in search of, cast around for, go in pursuit of, go in quest of, ferret around for, look high and low for

searching ADJECTIVE = **keen**, sharp, probing, close, severe, intent, piercing, penetrating, thorough, quizzical ■ **OPPOSITE:** superficial

searing ADJECTIVE **1** *She woke to a searing pain in her feet.* = **acute**, sharp, intense, shooting, violent, severe, painful, distressing, stabbing, fierce, stinging, piercing, sore, excruciating, gut-wrenching **2** *They have long been subject to searing criticism.* = **cutting**, biting, severe, bitter, harsh, scathing, acrimonious, barbed, hurtful, sarcastic, sardonic, caustic, vitriolic, trenchant, mordant, mordacious, acerb

season NOUN *birds arriving for the breeding season* = **period**, time, term, spell, time of year ▶ VERB **1** *Season the meat with salt and pepper.* = **flavour**, salt, spice, lace, salt and pepper, enliven, pep up, leaven **2** *Ensure that the new wood has been seasoned.* = **mature**, age, condition, prime, prepare, temper, mellow, ripen, acclimatize **3** *Both actors seem to have been seasoned by experience.* = **make experienced**, train, mature, prepare, discipline, harden, accustom, toughen, inure, habituate, acclimatize, anneal

seasoned ADJECTIVE = **experienced**, veteran, mature, practised, old, weathered, hardened, long-serving, battle-scarred, time-served, well-versed ■ **OPPOSITE:** inexperienced

seasoning NOUN = **flavouring**, spice, salt and pepper, condiment

seat NOUN **1** *Stephen returned to his seat.* = **chair**, bench, stall, throne, stool, pew, settle **2** *He lost his seat to the Tories.* = **membership**, place, constituency, chair, incumbency **3** *Gunfire broke out around the seat of government.* = **centre**, place, site, heart, capital, situation, source, station, location, headquarters, axis, cradle, hub **4** *her family's ancestral seat in Scotland* = **mansion**, house, residence, abode, ancestral hall ▶ VERB **1** *He waved towards a chair, and seated himself at the desk.* = **sit**, place, settle, set, fix, deposit, locate, install **2** *The theatre seats 570.* = **hold**, take, accommodate, sit, contain, cater for, have room *or* capacity for

seating NOUN = **accommodation**, room, places, seats, chairs

secede VERB = **withdraw**, leave, resign, separate, retire, quit, pull out, break with, split from, disaffiliate, apostatize

secession NOUN = **withdrawal**, break, split, defection, seceding, apostasy, disaffiliation

secluded ADJECTIVE = **private**, sheltered, isolated, remote, lonely, cut off, solitary, out-of-the-way, tucked away, cloistered, sequestered, off the beaten track, unfrequented ■ **OPPOSITE:** public

seclusion NOUN = **privacy**, isolation, solitude, hiding, retirement, shelter, retreat, remoteness, ivory tower, concealment, purdah

second¹ ADJECTIVE **1** *the second day of his visit to Delhi* = **next**, following, succeeding, subsequent, sophomore (*U.S. & Canad.*) **2** *Her second attempt proved disastrous.*

= **additional**, other, further, extra, alternative, repeated **3** *The suitcase contained clean shirts and a second pair of shoes.* = **spare**, duplicate, alternative, additional, back-up **4** *They have to rely on their second string strikers.* = **inferior**, secondary, subordinate, supporting, lower, lesser ▶ NOUN *He shouted to his seconds, 'I did it!'* = **supporter**, assistant, aide, partner, colleague, associate, backer, helper, collaborator, henchman *or* woman *or* person, right-hand man *or* woman *or* person, cooperator ▶ VERB *He seconded the motion against fox hunting.* = **support**, back, endorse, forward, promote, approve, go along with, commend, give moral support to

second² NOUN = **moment**, minute, instant, flash, tick (*Brit. informal*), sec (*informal*), twinkling, split second, jiffy (*informal*), trice, twinkling of an eye, two shakes of a lamb's tail (*informal*), bat of an eye (*informal*)

secondary ADJECTIVE **1** *Refugee problems remained of secondary importance.* = **subordinate**, minor, lesser, lower, inferior, unimportant, second-rate ■ **OPPOSITE:** main **2** *There was evidence of secondary tumours.* = **resultant**, resulting, contingent, derived, derivative, indirect, second-hand, consequential ■ **OPPOSITE:** original

second-class ADJECTIVE **1** *Too many airlines treat our children as second-class citizens.* = **inferior**, lesser, second-best, unimportant, second-rate, low-class **2** *a second-class education* = **mediocre**, second-rate, mean, middling, ordinary, inferior, indifferent, commonplace, insignificant, so-so (*informal*), outclassed, uninspiring, undistinguished, uninspired, bog-standard (*Brit. & Irish slang*), no great shakes (*informal*), déclassé, half-pie (*N.Z. informal*), fair to middling (*informal*)

second-hand ADJECTIVE = **used**, old, handed down, hand-me-down (*informal*), nearly new, reach-me-down (*informal*), preloved (*slang*)

secondly ADVERB = **next**, second, moreover, furthermore, also, in the second place

second-rate ADJECTIVE = **inferior**, mediocre, poor, cheap, pants (*slang*), commonplace, tacky (*informal*), shoddy, low-grade, tawdry, low-quality, substandard, low-rent (*informal, chiefly U.S.*), (strictly) for the birds (*informal*), two-bit (*U.S. & Canad. slang*), end-of-the-pier (*Brit. informal*), no great shakes (*informal*), cheap and nasty (*informal*),

rubbishy, dime-a-dozen (*informal*), bush-league (*Austral. & N.Z. informal*), not much cop (*Brit. slang*), tinhorn (*U.S. slang*), bodger *or* bodgie (*Austral. slang*) ■ **OPPOSITE:** first-rate

secrecy NOUN **1** *He shrouded his business dealings in secrecy.* = **mystery**, stealth, concealment, furtiveness, cloak and dagger, secretiveness, huggermugger (*archaic*), clandestineness, covertness **2** *the secrecy of the confessional* = **confidentiality**, privacy **3** *These problems had to be dealt with in the secrecy of your own cell.* = **privacy**, silence, retirement, solitude, seclusion

secret ADJECTIVE **1** *Soldiers have been training at a secret location.* = **undisclosed**, unknown, confidential, underground, undercover, unpublished, under wraps, unrevealed **2** *It has a secret compartment hidden behind the magical mirror.* = **concealed**, hidden, disguised, covered, camouflaged, unseen ■ **OPPOSITE:** unconcealed **3** *I was heading on a secret mission that made my flesh crawl.* = **undercover**, covert, furtive, shrouded, behind someone's back, conspiratorial, hush-hush (*informal*), surreptitious, cloak-and-dagger, backstairs ■ **OPPOSITE:** open **4** *the secret man behind the masks* = **secretive**, reserved, withdrawn, close, deep, discreet, enigmatic, reticent, cagey (*informal*), unforthcoming ■ **OPPOSITE:** frank **5** *a secret code* = **mysterious**, cryptic, abstruse, classified, esoteric, occult, clandestine, arcane, recondite, cabbalistic ■ **OPPOSITE:** straightforward ▶ NOUN **1** *I can't tell you; it's a secret.* = **private affair**, confidence, skeleton in the cupboard **2** *The secret of success is honesty and fair dealing.* = **key**, answer, formula, recipe • **in secret** *Dan found out that I'd been meeting my ex-boyfriend in secret.* = **secretly**, surreptitiously, slyly, behind closed doors, incognito, by stealth, in camera, huggermugger (*archaic*) ■ **RELATED WORD:** *adjective* cryptic

secret agent NOUN = **spy**, undercover agent, spook (*U.S. & Canad. informal*), nark (*Brit., Austral. & N.Z. slang*), cloak-and-dagger man

secrete¹ VERB *The sweat glands secrete water.* = **give off**, emit, emanate, exude, extrude

secrete² VERB *She secreted the gun in the kitchen cabinet.* = **hide**, conceal, stash (*informal*), cover, screen, secure, bury, harbour, disguise, veil, shroud, stow, cache, stash away (*informal*) ■ **OPPOSITE:** display

secretion NOUN = **discharge**, emission, excretion, exudation, extravasation (*Medical*)

secretive ADJECTIVE = **reticent**, reserved, withdrawn, close, deep, enigmatic, cryptic, cagey (*informal*), uncommunicative, unforthcoming, tight-lipped, playing your cards close to your chest, clamlike ■ **OPPOSITE:** open

secretly ADVERB = **in secret**, privately, surreptitiously, quietly, covertly, behind closed doors, in confidence, in your heart, furtively, in camera, confidentially, on the fly (*slang, chiefly Brit.*), stealthily, under the counter, clandestinely, unobserved, on the sly, in your heart of hearts, behind (someone's) back, in your innermost thoughts, on the q.t. (*informal*)

sect NOUN = **group**, division, faction, party, school, camp, wing, denomination, school of thought, schism, splinter group

sectarian ADJECTIVE *sectarian religious groups* = **narrow-minded**, partisan, fanatic, fanatical, limited, exclusive, rigid, parochial, factional, bigoted, dogmatic, insular, doctrinaire, hidebound, clannish, cliquish ■ **OPPOSITE:** tolerant ▶ NOUN *He remains a sectarian.* = **bigot**, extremist, partisan, disciple, fanatic, adherent, zealot, true believer, dogmatist

section NOUN 1 *a geological section of a rock* = **part**, piece, portion, division, sample, slice, passage, component, segment, fragment, fraction, instalment, cross section, subdivision 2 *Kolonarai is a lovely residential section of Athens.* = **district**, area, region, sector, zone

sectional ADJECTIVE = **regional**, local, separate, divided, exclusive, partial, separatist, factional, localized

sector NOUN 1 *the nation's manufacturing sector* = **part**, division, category, stratum, subdivision 2 *Officers were going to retake sectors of the city.* = **area**, part, region, district, zone, quarter

secular ADJECTIVE = **worldly**, state, lay, earthly, civil, temporal, profane, laic, nonspiritual, laical ■ **OPPOSITE:** religious

secure VERB 1 *His achievements helped him to secure the job.* = **obtain**, get, acquire, land (*informal*), score (*slang*), gain, pick up, get hold of, come by, procure, make sure of, win possession of ■ **OPPOSITE:** lose 2 *The frames are secured by horizontal rails to the back wall.* = **attach**, stick, fix, bind, pin, lash, glue, fasten, rivet ■ **OPPOSITE:** detach 3 *The loan is secured against your home.* = **guarantee**, insure, ensure, assure ■ **OPPOSITE:** endanger ▶ ADJECTIVE 1 *We shall make sure our home is as secure as possible.* = **safe**, protected, shielded, sheltered, immune, unassailable, impregnable

■ **OPPOSITE:** unprotected 2 *Shelves are only as secure as their fixings.* = **fast**, firm, fixed, tight, stable, steady, fortified, fastened, dependable, immovable ■ **OPPOSITE:** insecure 3 *demands for secure wages and employment* = **reliable**, definite, solid, absolute, conclusive, in the bag (*informal*) 4 *She felt secure and protected when she was with him.* = **confident**, sure, easy, certain, assured, reassured ■ **OPPOSITE:** uneasy

security NOUN 1 *under pressure to tighten airport security* = **precautions**, defence, safeguards, guards, protection, surveillance, safety measures 2 *He loves the security of a happy home life.* = **assurance**, confidence, conviction, certainty, reliance, sureness, positiveness, ease of mind, freedom from doubt ■ **OPPOSITE:** insecurity 3 *The banks will pledge the land as security.* = **pledge**, insurance, guarantee, hostage, collateral, pawn, gage, surety 4 *He could not remain long in a place of security.* = **protection**, cover, safety, retreat, asylum, custody, refuge, sanctuary, immunity, preservation, safekeeping ■ **OPPOSITE:** vulnerability

sedate ADJECTIVE 1 *She took them to visit her sedate, elderly cousins.* = **calm**, collected, quiet, seemly, serious, earnest, cool, grave, proper, middle-aged, composed, sober, dignified, solemn, serene, tranquil, placid, staid, demure, unflappable (*informal*), unruffled, decorous, imperturbable ■ **OPPOSITE:** wild 2 *We set off again at a more sedate pace.* = **unhurried**, easy, relaxed, comfortable, steady, gentle, deliberate, leisurely, slow-moving, chilled (*informal*)

sedative ADJECTIVE *Amber bath oil has a sedative effect.* = **calming**, relaxing, soothing, allaying, anodyne, soporific, sleep-inducing, tranquillizing, calmative, lenitive ▶ NOUN *They use opium as a sedative.* = **tranquillizer**, narcotic, sleeping pill, opiate, anodyne, calmative, downer or down (*slang*)

sedentary ADJECTIVE = **inactive**, sitting, seated, desk, motionless, torpid, desk-bound ■ **OPPOSITE:** active

sediment NOUN = **dregs**, grounds, residue, lees, deposit, precipitate, settlings

sedition NOUN = **rabble-rousing**, treason, subversion, agitation, disloyalty, incitement to riot

seduce VERB 1 *The view of the lake and plunging cliffs seduces visitors.* = **tempt**, attract, lure, entice, mislead, deceive, beguile, allure, decoy, ensnare, lead astray, inveigle 2 *a young lacemaker seduced by an aristocrat* = **corrupt**, ruin (*archaic*), betray, deprave, dishonour, debauch, deflower

seduction NOUN **1** *The seduction of the show is the fact that the kids are in it.* = **temptation**, lure, snare, allure, enticement **2** *the attempted seduction of a passing waiter* = **corruption**, ruin (*archaic*), defloration

seductive ADJECTIVE = **tempting**, inviting, attractive, sexy (*informal*), irresistible, siren, enticing, provocative, captivating, beguiling, alluring, bewitching, ravishing, flirtatious, come-to-bed (*informal*), come-hither (*informal*), hot (*informal*)

see VERB **1** *I saw a man making his way towards me.* = **perceive**, note, spot, notice, mark, view, eye, check, regard, identify, sight, witness, clock (*Brit. slang*), observe, recognize, distinguish, glimpse, check out (*informal*), make out, heed, discern, behold (*archaic, literary*), eyeball (*slang*), catch a glimpse of, catch sight of, espy, get a load of (*slang*), descry, take a dekko at (*Brit. slang*), lay *or* clap eyes on (*informal*) **2** *Oh, I see what you're saying.* = **understand**, get, follow, realize, know, appreciate, take in, grasp, make out, catch on (*informal*), comprehend, fathom, get the hang of (*informal*), get the drift of **3** *We can see a day when all people live side by side.* = **foresee**, picture, imagine, anticipate, divine, envisage, visualize, foretell **4** *I'd better go and see if she's all right.* = **find out**, learn, discover, determine, investigate, verify, ascertain, make inquiries **5** *We'll see what we can do, Miss.* = **consider**, decide, judge, reflect, deliberate, mull over, think over, make up your mind, give some thought to **6** *See that you take care of him.* = **make sure**, mind, ensure, guarantee, take care, make certain, see to it **7** *He didn't offer to see her to her car.* = **accompany**, show, escort, lead, walk, attend, usher **8** *The doctor can see you now.* = **speak to**, receive, interview, consult, confer with **9** *I saw her last night at Monica's.* = **meet**, encounter, come across, run into, happen on, bump into, run across, chance on **10** *I've been seeing someone else.* = **go out with**, court, date (*informal*), walk out with (*obsolete*), keep company with, go steady with (*informal*), consort *or* associate with, step out with (*informal*) • **see about something** *I must see about selling the house.* = **take care of**, deal with, look after, see to, attend to • **see something through** *He will not be credited with seeing the project through.* = **persevere (with)**, keep at, persist, stick out (*informal*), see out, stay to the bitter end • **see through something** *or* **someone** *I saw through your little ruse from the start.* = **be undeceived by**, penetrate,

be wise to (*informal*), fathom, get to the bottom of, not fall for, have (someone's) number (*informal*), read (someone) like a book • **see to something** *or* **someone** *Franklin saw to the luggage.* = **take care of**, manage, arrange, look after, organize, be responsible for, sort out, attend to, take charge of, do • **seeing as** *Seeing as he is a doctor, I would assume he has a modicum of intelligence.* = **since**, as, in view of the fact that, inasmuch as

> **USAGE** It is common to hear *seeing as how*, as in *Seeing as how the bus is always late, I don't need to hurry.* However, the use of *how* here is considered incorrect or nonstandard, and should be avoided.

seed NOUN **1** *a packet of cabbage seed* = **grain**, pip, germ, kernel, egg, embryo, spore, ovum, egg cell, ovule **2** *His questions were meant to plant seeds of doubt in our minds.* = **beginning**, start, suspicion, germ, inkling **3** *the seed of an idea* = **origin**, source, nucleus **4** *a curse on my seed* = **offspring**, children, descendants, issue, race, successors, heirs, spawn (*derogatory*), progeny, scions • **go** *or* **run to seed** *If unused, winter radishes run to seed in spring.* = **decline**, deteriorate, degenerate, decay, go downhill (*informal*), go to waste, go to pieces, let yourself go, go to pot, go to rack and ruin, retrogress

seedy ADJECTIVE **1** *a seedy hotel* = **shabby**, rundown, scruffy, old, worn, faded, decaying, grubby, dilapidated, tatty (*Brit.*), unkempt, grotty (*slang*), crummy (*slang*), down at heel, slovenly, mangy, manky (*Scot., dialect*), scungy (*Austral. & N.Z.*) ■ OPPOSITE: smart **2** *All right, are you? Not feeling seedy?* = **unwell**, ill, poorly (*informal*), crook (*Austral. & N.Z. informal*), ailing, sickly, out of sorts, off colour, under the weather (*informal*), peely-wally (*Scot.*)

seek VERB **1** *They have had to seek work as labourers.* = **look for**, pursue, search for, be after, hunt, go in search of, go in pursuit of, go gunning for, go in quest of **2** *The couple have sought help from marriage guidance counsellors.* = **request**, invite, ask for, petition, plead for, solicit, beg for, petition for **3** *He also denied that he would seek to annex the country.* = **try**, attempt, aim, strive, endeavour, essay (*formal*), aspire to, have a go at (*informal*)

seem VERB = **appear**, give the impression of being, look, look to be, sound as if you are, look as if you are, look like you are, strike you as being, have the *or* every appearance of being

S

seeming ADJECTIVE = **apparent**, appearing, outward, surface, illusory, ostensible, specious, quasi-

seemingly ADVERB = **apparently**, outwardly, on the surface, ostensibly, on the face of it, to all intents and purposes, to all appearances, as far as anyone could tell

seep VERB = **ooze**, well, leak, soak, bleed, weep, trickle, leach, exude, permeate, percolate

seer NOUN = **prophet**, augur, predictor, soothsayer, sibyl

seesaw VERB = **alternate**, swing, fluctuate, teeter, oscillate, go from one extreme to the other

seethe VERB **1** *Under the surface she was seething.* = **be furious**, storm, rage, fume, simmer, be in a state (*informal*), see red (*informal*), be incensed, be livid, go ballistic (*slang*), foam at the mouth, be incandescent, get hot under the collar (*informal*), wig out (*slang*), breathe fire and slaughter **2** *a seething cauldron of broth* = **boil**, bubble, foam, churn, fizz, ferment, froth

segment NOUN = **section**, part, piece, division, slice, portion, wedge, compartment

segregate VERB = **set apart**, divide, separate, isolate, single out, discriminate against, dissociate ■ **OPPOSITE:** unite

segregation NOUN = **separation**, discrimination, apartheid, isolation

seize VERB **1** *an otter seizing a fish* = **grab**, grip, grasp, take, snatch, clutch, snap up, pluck, fasten, latch on to, lay hands on, catch *or* take hold of ■ **OPPOSITE:** let go **2** *Troops have seized the airport and radio stations.* = **take by storm**, take over, acquire, occupy, conquer, annex, usurp **3** *Police were reported to have seized all copies of the newspaper.* = **confiscate**, appropriate, commandeer, impound, take possession of, requisition, sequester, expropriate (*formal*), sequestrate ■ **OPPOSITE:** hand back **4** *Men carrying sub-machine guns seized the five soldiers.* = **capture**, catch, arrest, get, nail (*informal*), grasp, collar (*informal*), hijack, abduct, nab (*informal*), apprehend, take captive ■ **OPPOSITE:** release

seizure NOUN **1** *I was prescribed drugs to control seizures.* = **attack**, fit, spasm, convulsion, paroxysm **2** *the seizure of territory through force* = **taking**, grabbing, annexation, confiscation, commandeering **3** *a mass seizure of hostages* = **capture**, arrest, apprehension, abduction

seldom ADVERB = **rarely**, occasionally, not often, infrequently, once in a blue moon (*informal*), hardly ever, scarcely ever ■ **OPPOSITE:** often

select VERB *They selected only bright pupils.* = **choose**, take, pick, prefer, opt for, decide on, adopt, single out, fix on, cherry-pick, settle upon ■ **OPPOSITE:** reject ▶ ADJECTIVE **1** *a select group of French cheeses* = **choice**, special, prime, picked, selected, excellent, rare, superior, first-class, posh (*informal, chiefly Brit.*), first-rate, hand-picked, top-notch (*informal*), recherché ■ **OPPOSITE:** ordinary **2** *a meeting of a very select club* = **exclusive**, elite, privileged, limited, cliquish ■ **OPPOSITE:** indiscriminate

selection NOUN **1** *Make your selection from the list.* = **choice**, choosing, pick, option, preference **2** *this selection of popular songs* = **anthology**, collection, medley, choice, line-up, mixed bag (*informal*), potpourri, miscellany

selective ADJECTIVE = **particular**, discriminating, critical, careful, discerning, astute, discriminatory, tasteful, fastidious ■ **OPPOSITE:** indiscriminate

self-assurance NOUN = **confidence**, self-confidence, poise, nerve, swag (*slang*), assertiveness, self-possession, positiveness

self-centred ADJECTIVE = **selfish**, narcissistic, self-absorbed, inward looking, self-seeking, egotistic, wrapped up in yourself

self-confidence NOUN = **self-assurance**, confidence, poise, nerve, swag (*slang*), self-respect, aplomb, self-reliance, high morale

self-confident ADJECTIVE = **self-assured**, confident, assured, secure, poised, fearless, self-reliant, sure of yourself

self-conscious ADJECTIVE = **embarrassed**, nervous, uncomfortable, awkward, insecure, diffident, ill at ease, sheepish, bashful, aw-shucks, shamefaced, like a fish out of water, out of countenance

self-control NOUN = **willpower**, restraint, self-discipline, cool (*slang*), coolness, calmness, self-restraint, self-mastery, strength of mind *or* will

self-denial NOUN = **self-sacrifice**, renunciation, asceticism, abstemiousness, selflessness, unselfishness, self-abnegation

self-esteem NOUN = **self-respect**, confidence, courage, vanity, boldness, self-reliance, self-assurance, self-regard, self-possession, amour-propre (*French*), faith in yourself, pride in yourself

self-evident ADJECTIVE = **obvious**, clear, undeniable, inescapable, written all over (something), cut-and-dried (*informal*), incontrovertible, axiomatic, manifestly *or* patently true

self-government NOUN = **independence**, democracy, sovereignty, autonomy, devolution, self-determination, self-rule, home rule

self-important ADJECTIVE = **conceited**, arrogant, pompous, strutting, swaggering, cocky, pushy (*informal*), overbearing, presumptuous, bumptious, swollen-headed, bigheaded, full of yourself

self-indulgence NOUN = **extravagance**, excess, incontinence, dissipation, self-gratification, intemperance, sensualism

selfish ADJECTIVE = **self-centred**, self-interested, greedy, mercenary, self-seeking, ungenerous, egoistic *or* egoistical, egotistic *or* egotistical, looking out for number one (*informal*) ■ OPPOSITE: unselfish

selfless ADJECTIVE = **unselfish**, generous, altruistic, self-sacrificing, magnanimous, self-denying, ungrudging

self-reliant ADJECTIVE = **independent**, capable, self-sufficient, self-supporting, able to stand on your own two feet (*informal*) ■ OPPOSITE: dependent

self-respect NOUN = **pride**, dignity, self-esteem, morale, amour-propre (*French*), faith in yourself

self-restraint NOUN = **self-control**, self-discipline, willpower, patience, forbearance, abstemiousness, self-command

self-righteous ADJECTIVE = **sanctimonious**, smug, pious, superior, complacent, hypocritical, pi (*Brit. slang*), too good to be true, self-satisfied, goody-goody (*informal*), holier-than-thou, priggish, pietistic, pharisaic

self-sacrifice NOUN = **selflessness**, altruism, self-denial, generosity, self-abnegation

self-satisfied ADJECTIVE = **smug**, complacent, proud of yourself, well-pleased, puffed up, self-congratulatory, flushed with success, pleased with yourself, like a cat that has swallowed the canary, too big for your boots *or* breeches

self-styled ADJECTIVE = **so-called**, would-be, professed, self-appointed, soi-disant (*French*), quasi-

sell VERB **1** *I sold everything I owned except for my car and books.* = **trade**, dispose of, exchange, barter, put up for sale ■ OPPOSITE: buy **2** *It sells everything from hair ribbons to oriental rugs.* = **deal in**, market, trade in, stock, handle, retail, hawk, merchandise, peddle, traffic in, vend, be in the business of ■ OPPOSITE: buy **3** *She is hoping she can sell the idea to clients.*

= **promote**, put across, gain acceptance for • **sell out of something** *Hardware stores have sold out of water pumps and tarpaulins.* = **run out of**, be out of stock of

seller NOUN = **dealer**, merchant, vendor, agent, representative, rep, retailer, traveller, supplier, shopkeeper, purveyor, tradesman *or* woman *or* person, salesman *or* woman *or* person

semblance NOUN = **appearance**, show, form, air, figure, front, image, bearing, aspect, mask, similarity, resemblance, guise, façade, pretence, veneer, likeness, mien (*literary*)

seminal ADJECTIVE = **influential**, important, ground-breaking, original, creative, productive, innovative, imaginative, formative

send VERB **1** *He sent a basket of exotic fruit and a card.* = **dispatch**, forward, direct, convey, consign, remit **2** *The space probe sent back pictures of Triton.* = **transmit**, broadcast, communicate **3** *He let me go with a thrust of his wrist that sent me flying.* = **propel**, hurl, fling, shoot, fire, deliver, cast, let fly • **send something** *or* **someone up** *a spoof that sends up the macho world of fighter pilots* = **mock**, mimic, parody, spoof (*informal*), imitate, take off (*informal*), make fun of, lampoon, burlesque, take the mickey out of (*informal*), satirize

sendoff NOUN = **farewell**, departure, leave-taking, valediction, going-away party

send-up NOUN = **parody**, take-off (*informal*), satire, mockery, spoof (*informal*), imitation, skit, mickey-take (*informal*)

senile ADJECTIVE = **in your dotage**, failing, infirm

> **USAGE** Words such as *senile* and *geriatric* are only properly used as medical terms. They are very insulting when used loosely to describe a person of advanced years.

senility NOUN = **dotage**, infirmity, senescence, caducity

senior ADJECTIVE **1** *Television and radio needed many more women in senior jobs.* = **higher ranking**, superior ■ OPPOSITE: subordinate **2** *Carlton Jones Senior* = **the elder**, major (*Brit.*) ■ OPPOSITE: junior

senior citizen NOUN = **pensioner**, retired person, old age pensioner, O.A.P., elder, old *or* elderly person

seniority NOUN = **superiority**, rank, priority, precedence, longer service

sensation NOUN **1** *A sensation of burning or tingling may be felt in the hands.* = **feeling**, sense, impression, perception, awareness, consciousness **2** *She caused a sensation at the Montreal Olympics.* = **excitement**, surprise, thrill, stir, scandal, furore, agitation, commotion **3** *the film that turned her into an overnight sensation* = **hit**, wow (*slang, chiefly U.S.*), crowd puller (*informal*)

sensational ADJECTIVE **1** *The world champions suffered a sensational defeat.* = **amazing**, dramatic, thrilling, revealing, spectacular, eye-popping (*informal*), staggering, startling, horrifying, breathtaking, astounding, lurid, electrifying, hair-raising ■ **OPPOSITE:** dull **2** *sensational tabloid newspaper reports* = **shocking**, scandalous, exciting, yellow (*of the press*), melodramatic, shock-horror (*facetious*), sensationalistic ■ **OPPOSITE:** unexciting **3** *Her voice is sensational.* = **excellent**, brilliant, superb, mean (*slang*), topping (*Brit. slang*), cracking (*Brit. informal*), crucial (*slang*), impressive, smashing (*informal*), fabulous (*informal*), first class, marvellous, exceptional, mega (*slang*), sick (*slang*), sovereign, awesome (*slang*), def (*slang*), brill (*informal*), out of this world (*informal*), mind-blowing (*informal*), bodacious (*slang, chiefly U.S.*), boffo (*slang*), jim-dandy (*slang*), chillin' (*U.S. slang*), booshit (*Austral. slang*), exo (*Austral. slang*), sik (*Austral. slang*), rad (*informal*), phat (*slang*), schmick (*Austral. informal*), beaut (*informal*), barrie (*Scot. slang*), belting (*Brit. slang*), pearler (*Austral. slang*), funky ■ **OPPOSITE:** ordinary

sense NOUN **1** *a keen sense of smell* = **faculty**, sensibility **2** *There is no sense of urgency on either side.* = **feeling**, impression, perception, awareness, consciousness, atmosphere, aura, intuition, premonition, presentiment **3** *He has an impeccable sense of timing.* = **understanding**, awareness, appreciation **4** (*sometimes plural*) *When he was younger he had a bit more sense.* = **intelligence**, reason, understanding, brains (*informal*), smarts (*slang, chiefly U.S.*), judgment, discrimination, wisdom, wit(s), common sense, sanity, sharpness, tact, nous (*Brit. slang*), cleverness, quickness, discernment, gumption (*Brit. informal*), sagacity, clear-headedness, mother wit ■ **OPPOSITE:** foolishness **5** *There's no sense in pretending this doesn't happen.* = **point**, good, use, reason, value, worth, advantage, purpose, logic **6** *a noun which has two senses* = **meaning**, definition, interpretation, significance, message, import, substance, implication, drift, purport, nuance, gist, signification, denotation ▸ VERB *He had sensed what might happen.* = **perceive**, feel, understand, notice, pick up, suspect,

realize, observe, appreciate, grasp, be aware of, divine, discern, just know, have a (funny) feeling (*informal*), get the impression, apprehend, have a hunch ■ **OPPOSITE:** be unaware of

senseless ADJECTIVE **1** *acts of senseless violence* = **pointless**, mad, crazy (*informal*), stupid, silly, ridiculous, absurd, foolish, daft (*informal*), ludicrous, meaningless, unreasonable, irrational, inconsistent, unwise, mindless, illogical, incongruous, idiotic, nonsensical, inane, fatuous, moronic, unintelligent, asinine, imbecilic, dumb-ass (*slang*), without rhyme or reason, halfwitted ■ **OPPOSITE:** sensible **2** *Then I saw him lying senseless on the floor.* = **unconscious**, stunned, insensible, out, cold, numb, numbed, deadened, unfeeling, out cold, anaesthetized, insensate ■ **OPPOSITE:** conscious

sensibility NOUN **1** *Everything he writes demonstrates the depths of his sensibility.* = **awareness**, insight, intuition, taste, appreciation, delicacy, discernment, perceptiveness ■ **OPPOSITE:** lack of awareness **2** (*often plural*) *The challenge offended their sensibilities.* = **feelings**, emotions, sentiments, susceptibilities, moral sense

sensible ADJECTIVE **1** *It might be sensible to get a solicitor.* = **wise**, practical, prudent, shrewd, well-informed, judicious, well-advised ■ **OPPOSITE:** foolish **2** *She was a sensible girl and did not panic.* = **intelligent**, practical, reasonable, rational, sound, realistic, sober, discriminating, discreet, sage, shrewd, down-to-earth, matter-of-fact, prudent, sane, canny, judicious, far-sighted, sagacious, grounded ■ **OPPOSITE:** senseless

sensitive ADJECTIVE **1** *He was always so sensitive and caring.* = **thoughtful**, kind, kindly, concerned, patient, attentive, tactful, unselfish **2** *gentle cosmetics for sensitive skin* = **delicate**, tender **3** *My eyes are overly sensitive to bright light.* = **susceptible**, responsive, reactive, easily affected **4** *Young people are very sensitive about their appearance.* = **touchy**, oversensitive, easily upset, easily offended, easily hurt, umbrageous (*rare*) ■ **OPPOSITE:** insensitive **5** *an extremely sensitive microscope* = **precise**, fine, acute, keen, responsive, perceptive ■ **OPPOSITE:** imprecise

sensitivity NOUN **1** *the sensitivity of cells to chemotherapy* = **susceptibility**, responsiveness, reactivity, receptiveness, sensitiveness, reactiveness **2** *concern and sensitivity for each other's feelings*

= **consideration**, patience, thoughtfulness **3** *an atmosphere of extreme sensitivity over the situation* = **touchiness**, oversensitivity **4** *the sensitivity of the detector* = **responsiveness**, precision, keenness, acuteness

sensual ADJECTIVE **1** *He was a very sensual person.* = **sexual**, sexy (*informal*), erotic, randy (*informal, chiefly Brit.*), steamy (*informal*), raunchy (*informal*), lewd, lascivious, lustful, lecherous, libidinous, licentious, unchaste **2** *sensual pleasure* = **physical**, bodily, voluptuous, animal, luxurious, fleshly, carnal, epicurean, unspiritual

sensuality NOUN = **eroticism**, sexiness (*informal*), voluptuousness, prurience, licentiousness, carnality, lewdness, salaciousness, lasciviousness, animalism, libidinousness, lecherousness

sensuous ADJECTIVE = **pleasurable**, pleasing, sensory, gratifying

sentence NOUN **1** *He was given a four-year sentence.* = **punishment**, prison term, condemnation **2** *When she heard of the sentence, she said: 'Is that all?'* = **verdict**, order, ruling, decision, judgment, decree, pronouncement ▶ VERB **1** *A military court sentenced him to death in his absence.* = **condemn**, doom **2** *They sentenced him for punching a police officer.* = **convict**, condemn, penalize, pass judgment on, mete out justice to

sentient ADJECTIVE = **feeling**, living, conscious, live, sensitive, reactive

sentiment NOUN **1** *The Foreign Secretary echoed this sentiment.* = **feeling**, thought, idea, view, opinion, attitude, belief, judgment, persuasion, way of thinking **2** *Laura kept that letter out of sentiment.* = **sentimentality**, emotion, tenderness, romanticism, sensibility, slush (*informal*), emotionalism, tender feeling, mawkishness, soft-heartedness, overemotionalism

sentimental ADJECTIVE = **romantic**, touching, emotional, tender, pathetic, nostalgic, sloppy (*informal*), tearful, corny (*slang*), impressionable, mushy (*informal*), maudlin, simpering, weepy (*informal*), slushy (*informal*), mawkish, tear-jerking (*informal*), drippy (*informal*), schmaltzy (*slang*), icky (*informal*), gushy (*informal*), soft-hearted, overemotional, dewy-eyed, three-hankie (*informal*) ■ OPPOSITE: unsentimental

sentimentality NOUN = **romanticism**, nostalgia, tenderness, gush (*informal*), pathos, slush (*informal*), mush (*informal*), schmaltz (*slang*), sloppiness (*informal*),

emotionalism, bathos, mawkishness, corniness (*slang*), play on the emotions, sob stuff (*informal*)

sentinel NOUN = **guard**, watch, lookout, sentry, picket, watchman

separate ADJECTIVE **1** *The two things are separate and mutually irrelevant.* = **unconnected**, individual, particular, divided, divorced, isolated, detached, disconnected, discrete, unattached, disjointed ■ OPPOSITE: connected **2** *We both live our separate lives.* = **individual**, independent, apart, distinct, autonomous ■ OPPOSITE: joined ▶ VERB **1** *Police moved in to separate the two groups.* = **divide**, detach, disconnect, come between, disentangle, keep apart, disjoin ■ OPPOSITE: combine **2** *The nose section separates from the fuselage.* = **come apart**, split, break off, come away ■ OPPOSITE: connect **3** *Separate the garlic into cloves.* = **sever**, disconnect, break apart, split in two, divide in two, uncouple, bifurcate ■ OPPOSITE: join **4** *Her parents separated when she was very young.* = **split up**, part, divorce, break up, part company, get divorced, be estranged, go different ways **5** *What separates terrorism from other acts of violence?* = **distinguish**, mark, single out, set apart, make distinctive, set at variance or at odds ■ OPPOSITE: link

separated ADJECTIVE **1** *Most single parents are either separated or divorced.* = **estranged**, parted, split up, separate, apart, broken up, disunited, living apart or separately **2** *They're trying their best to bring together separated families.* = **disconnected**, parted, divided, separate, disassociated, disunited, sundered, put asunder

separately ADVERB **1** *Chris had insisted that we went separately to the club.* = **alone**, independently, apart, personally, not together, severally ■ OPPOSITE: together **2** *Cook the stuffing separately.* = **individually**, singly, one by one, one at a time

separation NOUN **1** *a permanent separation from his son* = **division**, break, segregation, detachment, severance, disengagement, dissociation, disconnection, disjunction, disunion, disconnect **2** *They agreed to a trial separation.* = **split-up**, parting, split, divorce, break-up, farewell, rift, estrangement, leave-taking

septic ADJECTIVE = **infected**, poisoned, toxic, festering, pussy, putrid, putrefying, suppurating, putrefactive

sequel NOUN **1** *She is currently writing a sequel.* = **follow-up**, continuation, development **2** *The arrests were a direct sequel to the investigations.* = **consequence**, result, outcome, conclusion, end, issue, payoff (*informal*), upshot

sequence NOUN **1** *the sequence of events that led to the murder* = **succession**, course, series, order, chain, cycle, arrangement, procession, progression **2** *The chronological sequence gives the book an element of structure.* = **order**, structure, arrangement, ordering, placement, layout, progression

serene ADJECTIVE = **calm**, peaceful, tranquil, composed, sedate, placid, undisturbed, untroubled, unruffled, imperturbable, chilled (*informal*) ■ **OPPOSITE:** troubled

serenity NOUN = **calm**, peace, tranquillity, composure, peace of mind, stillness, calmness, quietness, peacefulness, quietude, placidity

serf NOUN = **vassal**, servant, slave, thrall, bondsman, varlet (*archaic*), helot, villein, liegeman

series NOUN **1** *a series of explosions* = **sequence**, course, chain, succession, run, set, line, order, train, arrangement, string, progression **2** *the award for the year's best drama series* = **drama**, serial, soap (*informal*), sitcom (*informal*), soap opera, soapie *or* soapy (*Austral. slang*), situation comedy

serious ADJECTIVE **1** *His condition was serious but stable.* = **grave**, bad, critical, worrying, dangerous, acute, alarming, severe, extreme, grievous **2** *I regard this as a serious matter.* = **important**, crucial (*informal*), urgent, pressing, difficult, worrying, deep, significant, grim, far-reaching, momentous, fateful, weighty, no laughing matter, of moment *or* consequence ■ **OPPOSITE:** unimportant **3** *It was a question which deserved serious consideration.* = **thoughtful**, detailed, careful, deep, profound, in-depth **4** *a serious novel* = **deep**, sophisticated, highbrowed **5** *He's quite a serious person.* = **solemn**, earnest, grave, stern, sober, thoughtful, sedate, glum, staid, humourless, long-faced, pensive, unsmiling ■ **OPPOSITE:** light-hearted **6** *You really are serious about this, aren't you?* = **sincere**, determined, earnest, resolved, genuine, deliberate, honest, resolute, in earnest ■ **OPPOSITE:** insincere

seriously ADVERB **1** *Seriously, though, something must be done about it.* = **truly**, no joking (*informal*), in earnest, all joking aside **2** *Three people were seriously injured in the blast.* = **badly**, severely, gravely, critically, acutely, sorely, dangerously, distressingly, grievously

seriousness NOUN **1** *the seriousness of the crisis* = **importance**, gravity, urgency,

moment, weight, danger, significance **2** *They had shown a commitment and a seriousness of purpose.* = **solemnity**, gravity, earnestness, sobriety, gravitas, sternness, humourlessness, staidness, sedateness

sermon NOUN = **homily**, address, exhortation (*formal*)

serpentine ADJECTIVE = **twisting**, winding, snaking, crooked, coiling, meandering, tortuous, sinuous, twisty, snaky

serrated ADJECTIVE = **notched**, toothed, sawtoothed, serrate, serrulate, sawlike, serriform (*Biology*)

servant NOUN = **attendant**, domestic, slave, maid, help, helper, retainer, menial, drudge, lackey, vassal, skivvy (*chiefly Brit.*), servitor (*archaic*), varlet (*archaic*), liegeman

serve VERB **1** *soldiers who have served their country well* = **work for**, help, aid, assist, be in the service of **2** *He had served an apprenticeship as a bricklayer.* = **perform**, do, complete, go through, fulfil, pass, discharge **3** *This little book should serve.* = **be adequate**, do, suffice, answer, suit, content, satisfy, be good enough, be acceptable, fill the bill (*informal*), answer the purpose **4** *Serve it with French bread.* = **present**, provide, supply, deliver, arrange, set out, distribute, dish up, purvey • **serve as something** *or* **someone** *She ushered me into the front room, which served as her office.* = **act as**, function as, do the work of, do duty as

service NOUN **1** *a campaign for better social services* = **facility**, system, resource, utility, amenity **2** *The President was attending the morning service.* = **ceremony**, worship, rite, function, observance **3** *If a young woman did not have a dowry, she went into domestic service.* = **work**, labour, employment, business, office, duty, employ **4** *The car needs a service.* = **check**, servicing, maintenance check ▶ VERB *Make sure that all gas fires are serviced annually.* = **overhaul**, check, maintain, tune (up), repair, go over, fine tune, recondition

serviceable ADJECTIVE = **useful**, practical, efficient, helpful, profitable, convenient, operative, beneficial, functional, durable, usable, dependable, advantageous, utilitarian, hard-wearing ■ **OPPOSITE:** useless

servile ADJECTIVE = **subservient**, cringing, grovelling, mean, low, base, humble, craven, fawning, abject, submissive, menial, sycophantic, slavish, unctuous, obsequious, toadying, bootlicking (*informal*), toadyish

serving NOUN = **portion**, helping, plateful

servitude NOUN = **slavery**, bondage,

enslavement, bonds, chains, obedience, thrall, subjugation, serfdom, vassalage, thraldom

session NOUN = **meeting**, hearing, sitting, term, period, conference, congress, discussion, assembly, seminar, get-together (*informal*)

set¹ VERB 1 *He took the case out of her hand and set it on the floor.* = **put**, place, lay, park (*informal*), position, rest, plant, station, stick (*informal*), deposit, locate, lodge, situate, plump, plonk 2 *I forgot to set my alarm and I overslept.* = **switch on**, turn on, activate, programme 3 *He set his watch, then waited for five minutes.* = **adjust**, regulate, coordinate, rectify, synchronize 4 *a gate set in a high wall* = **embed**, fix, mount, install, fasten 5 *A date will be set for a future meeting.* = **arrange**, decide (upon), settle, name, establish, determine, fix, schedule, appoint, specify, allocate, designate, ordain, fix up, agree upon 6 *We will train you first before we set you a task.* = **assign**, give, allot, prescribe 7 *Lower the heat and allow the omelette to set on the bottom.* = **harden**, stiffen, condense, solidify, cake, thicken, crystallize, congeal, jell, gelatinize 8 *The sun sets at about 4pm in winter.* = **go down**, sink, dip, decline, disappear, vanish, subside 9 *She had set the table and was drinking coffee at the hearth.* = **prepare**, lay, spread, arrange, make ready ▶ ADJECTIVE 1 *A set period of fasting is supposed to bring us closer to godliness.* = **established**, planned, decided, agreed, usual, arranged, rigid, definite, inflexible, hard and fast, immovable 2 *They have very set ideas about how to get the message across.* = **strict**, firm, rigid, hardened, stubborn, entrenched, inflexible, hidebound ■ OPPOSITE: flexible 3 *Use the subjunctive in some set phrases and idioms.* = **conventional**, stock, standard, traditional, formal, routine, artificial, stereotyped, rehearsed, hackneyed, unspontaneous ▶ NOUN 1 *a movie set* = **scenery**, setting, scene, stage setting, stage set, mise-en-scène (*French*) 2 *the set of his shoulders* = **position**, bearing, attitude, carriage, turn, fit, hang, posture • **set on** or **upon something** *She was set on going to an all-girls school.* = **determined**, intent on, bent on, resolute about • **set about someone** *Several thugs set about him with clubs.* = **assault**, attack, mug (*informal*), assail, sail into (*informal*), lambast(e), belabour • **set about something** *He set about proving she was completely wrong.* = **begin**, start, get down to, attack, tackle, set to, get to work, sail into (*informal*), take

the first step, wade into, get cracking (*informal*), make a start on, roll up your sleeves, get weaving (*informal*), address yourself to, put your shoulder to the wheel (*informal*) • **set off** *I set off, full of optimism.* = **leave**, set out, depart, embark, start out, sally forth • **set on** or **upon someone** *We were set upon by three youths.* = **attack**, beat up, assault, turn on, mug (*informal*), set about, ambush, go for, sic, pounce on, fly at, work over (*slang*), assail, sail into (*informal*), fall upon, lay into (*informal*), put the boot in (*slang*), pitch into (*informal*), let fly at, beat or knock seven bells out of (*informal*) • **set out** *When setting out on a long walk, always wear suitable boots.* = **embark**, set off, start out, begin, get under way, hit the road (*slang*), take to the road, sally forth • **set someone against someone** *The case has set neighbour against neighbour in the village.* = **alienate**, oppose, divide, drive a wedge between, disunite, estrange, set at odds, make bad blood between, make mischief between, set at cross purposes, set by the ears (*informal*), sow dissension amongst • **set someone up 1** *Grandfather set them up in a grocery business.* = **finance**, back, fund, establish, promote, build up, subsidize 2 *The win set us up perfectly for the match in Belgium.* = **prepare**, prime, warm up, dispose, make ready, put in order, put in a good position • **set something against something** *a considerable sum when set against the maximum wage* = **balance**, compare, contrast, weigh, juxtapose • **set something aside 1** *£130 million would be set aside for repairs to schools.* = **reserve**, keep, save, separate, select, single out, earmark, keep back, set apart, put on one side 2 *The decision was set aside because one of the judges had links with the defendant.* = **reject**, dismiss, reverse, cancel, overturn, discard, quash, overrule, repudiate, annul, nullify, abrogate, render null and void • **set something back** *a risk of public protest that could set back reforms* = **hold up**, slow, delay, hold back, hinder, obstruct, retard, impede, slow up • **set off 1** *Who set off the bomb?* = **detonate**, trigger (off), explode, ignite, light, set in motion, touch off 2 *It set off a storm of speculation.* = **cause**, start, produce, generate, prompt, trigger (off), provoke, bring about, give rise to, spark off, set in motion 3 *Blue suits you – it sets off the colour of your hair.* = **enhance**, show off, throw into relief, bring out the highlights in • **set something out 1** *Set out the cakes attractively.* = **arrange**, present, display, lay out, exhibit, array, dispose, set forth,

S

expose to view **2** *He has written a letter setting out his views.* = **explain**, list, describe, detail, elaborate, recount, enumerate, elucidate, itemize, particularize • **set something up 1** *an organization that sets up meetings* = **arrange**, organize, prepare, make provision for, prearrange **2** *He set up the company four years ago.* = **establish**, begin, found, institute, install, initiate **3** *The activists set up a peace camp at the border.* = **build**, raise, construct, put up, assemble, put together, erect, elevate **4** *I set up the computer so that they could work from home.* = **assemble**, put up

set² NOUN **1** *Only she and Mr Cohen had complete sets of keys to the shop.* = **series**, collection, assortment, kit, outfit, batch, compendium, assemblage, coordinated group, ensemble **2** *the popular watering hole for the literary set* = **group**, company, crowd, circle, class, band, crew (*informal*), gang, outfit (*informal*), faction, sect, posse (*informal*), clique, coterie, schism

setback NOUN = **hold-up**, check, defeat, blow, upset, reverse, disappointment, hitch, misfortune, rebuff, whammy (*informal*), bummer (*slang*), bit of trouble

setting NOUN = **surroundings**, site, location, set, scene, surround, background, frame, context, perspective, backdrop, scenery, locale, mise en scène (*French*)

settle VERB **1** *They agreed to try and settle their dispute by negotiation.* = **resolve**, work out, put an end to, straighten out, set to rights **2** *I settled the bill for my coffee and his two glasses of wine.* = **pay**, clear, square (up), discharge **3** *He visited Paris and eventually settled there.* = **move to**, take up residence in, live in, dwell in, inhabit, reside in, set up home in, put down roots in, make your home in **4** *This was one of the first areas to be settled by Europeans.* = **colonize**, populate, people, pioneer **5** *Alberto settled himself on the sofa.* = **make comfortable**, bed down **6** *Once its impurities had settled, the oil could be graded.* = **subside**, fall, sink, decline **7** *The birds settled less than two hundred paces away.* = **land**, alight, descend, light, come to rest **8** *They needed a win to settle their nerves.* = **calm**, quiet, relax, relieve, reassure, compose, soothe, lull, quell, allay, sedate, pacify, quieten, tranquillize ■ **OPPOSITE:** disturb • **settle on** or **upon something** or **someone** *We finally settled on a Mercedes estate.* = **decide on**, choose, pick, select, adopt, agree on, opt for, fix on, elect for

settlement NOUN **1** *Our objective must be to secure a peace settlement.* = **agreement**, arrangement, resolution, working out,

conclusion, establishment, adjustment, confirmation, completion, disposition, termination **2** *ways to delay the settlement of debts* = **payment**, clearing, discharge, clearance, defrayal **3** *a Muslim settlement* = **colony**, community, outpost, peopling, hamlet, encampment, colonization, kainga or kaika (*N.Z.*)

settler NOUN = **colonist**, immigrant, pioneer, colonizer

setup NOUN = **arrangement**, system, structure, organization, conditions, circumstances, regime

sever VERB **1** *Oil was still gushing from the severed fuel line.* = **cut**, separate, split, part, divide, rend (*literary*), detach, disconnect, cleave, bisect, disunite, cut in two, sunder, disjoin ■ **OPPOSITE:** join **2** *He was able to sever all emotional bonds to his family.* = **discontinue**, terminate, break off, abandon, dissolve, put an end to, dissociate ■ **OPPOSITE:** continue

several ADJECTIVE *one of several failed attempts* = **various**, different, diverse, divers (*archaic*), assorted, disparate, indefinite, sundry

severe ADJECTIVE **1** *a business with severe cash flow problems* = **serious**, critical, terrible, desperate, alarming, extreme, awful, distressing, appalling, drastic, catastrophic, woeful, ruinous **2** *He woke up blinded and in severe pain.* = **acute**, extreme, intense, burning, violent, piercing, racking, searing, tormenting, exquisite, harrowing, unbearable, agonizing, insufferable, torturous, unendurable **3** *He had faced an appallingly severe task in the jungle.* = **tough**, hard, difficult, taxing, demanding, fierce, punishing, exacting, rigorous, stringent, arduous, unrelenting ■ **OPPOSITE:** easy **4** *This was a dreadful crime and a severe sentence is necessary.* = **strict**, hard, harsh, cruel, rigid, relentless, drastic, oppressive, austere, Draconian, unrelenting, inexorable, pitiless, unbending, iron-handed ■ **OPPOSITE:** lenient **5** *He had a severe look that disappeared when he smiled.* = **grim**, serious, grave, cold, forbidding, stern, sober, disapproving, dour, unsmiling, flinty, strait-laced, tight-lipped ■ **OPPOSITE:** genial **6** *wearing her felt hats and severe grey suits* = **plain**, simple, austere, classic, restrained, functional, Spartan, ascetic, unadorned, unfussy, unembellished, bare-bones ■ **OPPOSITE:** fancy **7** *The team has suffered severe criticism from influential figures.* = **harsh**, cutting, biting, scathing, satirical, caustic, astringent, vitriolic, mordant, unsparing, mordacious ■ **OPPOSITE:** kind

severely ADVERB **1** *the severely depressed construction industry* = **seriously**, badly, extremely, gravely, hard, sorely, dangerously, critically, acutely **2** *They should punish these drivers more severely.* = **strictly**, harshly, sternly, rigorously, sharply, like a ton of bricks (*informal*), with an iron hand, with a rod of iron

severity NOUN = **strictness**, seriousness, harshness, austerity, rigour, toughness, hardness, stringency, sternness, severeness

sew VERB = **stitch**, tack (*Brit.*), seam, hem

sex NOUN **1** *a campaign to help parents talk about sex with their children* = **facts of life**, sexuality, reproduction, the birds and the bees (*informal*) **2** *The entire film revolves around sex and drugs.* = **lovemaking**, sexual relations, copulation, intimacy, going to bed (with someone), nookie (*slang*), fornication, coitus, rumpy-pumpy (*slang*), legover (*slang*), rumpo (*slang*), cybersex

sex appeal NOUN = **desirability**, attractiveness, allure, glamour, sensuality, magnetism, sexiness (*informal*), oomph (*informal*), it (*informal*), voluptuousness, seductiveness

sexual ADJECTIVE **1** *sexual fantasies* = **carnal**, erotic, intimate, of the flesh, coital **2** *exchanging sexual glances* = **sexy**, erotic, sensual, inviting, bedroom, provoking, arousing, naughty, provocative, seductive, sensuous, suggestive, voluptuous, slinky, titillating, flirtatious, come-hither (*informal*), kissable, beddable

sexual intercourse NOUN = **copulation**, sex (*informal*), coupling, congress, mating, commerce (*archaic*), intimacy, nookie (*slang*), consummation, bonking (*informal*), coitus, carnal knowledge, rumpy-pumpy (*slang*), legover (*slang*)

sexuality NOUN = **desire**, lust, eroticism, sensuality, virility, sexiness (*informal*), voluptuousness, carnality, bodily appetites

sexy ADJECTIVE = **erotic**, sensual, seductive, inviting, bedroom, provoking, arousing, naughty, provocative, sensuous, suggestive, voluptuous, slinky, titillating, flirtatious, come-hither (*informal*), kissable, beddable, hot (*informal*)

shabby ADJECTIVE **1** *His clothes were old and shabby.* = **tatty** (*Brit.*), worn, ragged, scruffy, faded, frayed, worn-out, tattered, threadbare, down at heel, the worse for wear, having seen better days ■ **OPPOSITE:** smart **2** *a rather shabby Naples hotel* = **rundown**, seedy, mean, neglected, dilapidated **3** *It was hard to know why the man deserved such shabby treatment.* = **mean**, low,

rotten (*informal*), cheap, dirty, shameful, low-down (*informal*), shoddy, unworthy, despicable, contemptible, scurvy (*old-fashioned*), dishonourable, ignoble, ungentlemanly ■ **OPPOSITE:** fair

shack NOUN = **hut**, cabin, shanty, lean-to, dump (*informal*), hovel, shiel (*Scot.*), shieling (*Scot.*), whare (*N.Z.*)

shackle VERB **1** *The trade unions are shackled by the law.* = **hamper**, limit, restrict, restrain, hamstring, inhibit, constrain, obstruct, impede, encumber, tie (someone's) hands **2** *She was shackled to a wall.* = **fetter**, chain, handcuff, secure, bind, hobble, manacle, trammel, put in irons ▶ NOUN (*often plural*) *He unbolted the shackles on Billy's hands.* = **fetter**, chain, iron, bond, handcuff, hobble, manacle, leg-iron, gyve (*archaic*)

shade NOUN **1** *The walls were painted in two shades of green.* = **hue**, tone, colour, tint **2** *Exotic trees provide welcome shade.* = **shadow**, screen, shadows, coolness, shadiness **3** *There was a shade of irony in her voice.* = **dash**, trace, hint, suggestion, suspicion, small amount, semblance **4** *the capacity to convey subtle shades of meaning* = **nuance**, difference, degree, graduation, subtlety **5** *She left the shades down and the lights off.* = **screen**, covering, cover, blind, curtain, shield, veil, canopy **6** *His writing benefits from the shade of Lincoln hovering over his shoulder.* = **ghost**, spirit, shadow, phantom, spectre, manes, apparition, eidolon, kehua (*N.Z.*) ▶ VERB **1** *a health resort whose beaches are shaded by palm trees* = **darken**, shadow, cloud, dim, cast a shadow over, shut out the light **2** *You've got to shade your eyes or close them altogether.* = **cover**, protect, screen, hide, shield, conceal, obscure, veil, mute

shadow NOUN **1** *All he could see was his shadow.* = **silhouette**, shape, outline, profile **2** *Most of the lake was in shadow.* = **shade**, dimness, darkness, gloom, cover, protection, shelter, dusk (*poetic*), obscurity, gloaming (*Scot., poetic*), gathering darkness ▶ VERB **1** *The hood shadowed her face.* = **shade**, screen, shield, darken, overhang, cast a shadow over **2** *shadowed by a large and highly visible body of police* = **follow**, dog, tail (*informal*), trail, stalk, spy on

shadowy ADJECTIVE **1** *I watched him from a shadowy corner.* = **dark**, shaded, dim, gloomy, shady, obscure, murky, dusky, funereal, crepuscular, tenebrous, tenebrious **2** *the shadowy shape of a big barge loaded with logs* = **vague**, indistinct, faint, ghostly, obscure, dim, phantom, imaginary, unreal, intangible, illusory, spectral, undefined, nebulous, dreamlike, impalpable (*formal*), unsubstantial, wraithlike

shady ADJECTIVE **1** *After flowering, place the pot in a shady spot.* = **shaded**, cool, shadowy, dim, leafy, bowery, bosky (*literary*), umbrageous ■ **OPPOSITE:** sunny **2** *Be wary of people who try to talk you into shady deals.* = **crooked** (*informal*), dodgy (*Brit., Austral. & N.Z. informal*), unethical, suspect, suspicious, dubious, slippery, questionable, unscrupulous, fishy (*informal*), shifty, disreputable, untrustworthy, shonky (*Austral. & N.Z. informal*) ■ **OPPOSITE:** honest

shaft NOUN **1** *old mine shafts* = **tunnel**, hole, passage, burrow, passageway, channel **2** *a drive shaft* = **handle**, staff, pole, rod, stem, upright, baton, shank **3** *A brilliant shaft of sunlight burst through the doorway.* = **ray**, beam, gleam, streak

shaggy ADJECTIVE = **unkempt**, rough, tousled, hairy, long-haired, hirsute (*formal*), unshorn ■ **OPPOSITE:** smooth

shake VERB **1** *Shake the rugs well and hang them out.* = **jiggle**, agitate, joggle **2** *I stood there, crying and shaking with fear.* = **tremble**, shiver, quake, shudder, quiver **3** *The plane shook frighteningly as it hit the high, drenching waves.* = **rock**, sway, shudder, wobble, waver, totter, oscillate **4** *They shook clenched fists.* = **wave**, wield, flourish, brandish **5** *The news of his escape had shaken them all.* = **upset**, shock, frighten, disturb, distress, move, rattle (*informal*), intimidate, unnerve, discompose, traumatize **6** *It won't shake the football world if we beat them.* = **undermine**, threaten, disable, weaken, impair, sap, debilitate, subvert, pull the rug out from under (*informal*) ▶ NOUN *blurring of photos caused by camera shake* = **vibration**, trembling, quaking, shock, jar, disturbance, jerk, shiver, shudder, jolt, tremor, agitation, convulsion, pulsation, jounce • **shake someone off** *He had shaken off his pursuers.* = **leave behind**, lose, get rid of, get away from, elude, get rid of, throw off, get shot of (*slang*), rid yourself of, give the slip • **shake someone up** *She was shaken up when she was thrown from her horse.* = **upset**, shock, frighten, disturb, distress, rattle (*informal*), unsettle, unnerve, discompose • **shake something off** *I just can't shake off this cough.* = **get rid of**, lose, recuperate from • **shake something up** *Directors and shareholders are preparing to shake things up.* = **restructure**, reorganize, mix, overturn, churn (up), turn upside down

shaky ADJECTIVE **1** *Our house will remain on shaky foundations unless the architect sorts out the basement.* = **unstable**, weak, precarious, tottering, rickety ■ **OPPOSITE:** stable **2** *Even small operations can leave you feeling a bit shaky.* = **unsteady**, faint, trembling, faltering, wobbly, tremulous, quivery, all of a quiver (*informal*) **3** *We knew we may have to charge them on shaky evidence.* = **uncertain**, suspect, dubious, questionable, unreliable, unsound, iffy (*informal*), unsupported, undependable ■ **OPPOSITE:** reliable

shallow ADJECTIVE = **superficial**, surface, empty, slight, foolish, idle, trivial, meaningless, flimsy, frivolous, skin-deep ■ **OPPOSITE:** deep

sham NOUN *Their promises were exposed as a hollow sham.* = **fraud** (*informal*), imitation, hoax, pretence, forgery, counterfeit, pretender, humbug, impostor, feint, pseud (*informal*), wolf in sheep's clothing, imposture, phoney or phony (*informal*) ■ **OPPOSITE:** the real thing ▶ ADJECTIVE *a sham marriage* = **false**, artificial, bogus, pretended, mock, synthetic, imitation, simulated, pseudo (*informal*), counterfeit, feigned, spurious, ersatz, pseud (*informal*), phoney or phony (*informal*) ■ **OPPOSITE:** real

shambles NOUN **1** *The economy is a shambles.* = **chaos**, mess, disorder, confusion, muddle, havoc (*informal*), anarchy, disarray, madhouse (*informal*), disorganization, omnishambles (*Brit. informal*) **2** *The boat's interior was an utter shambles.* = **mess**, state, jumble, untidiness

shambling ADJECTIVE = **clumsy**, awkward, shuffling, lurching, lumbering, unsteady, ungainly, unco (*Austral. slang*)

shambolic ADJECTIVE = **disorganized**, disordered, chaotic, confused, muddled, inefficient, anarchic, topsy-turvy, at sixes and sevens, in total disarray, unsystematic

shame NOUN **1** *I was, to my shame, a coward.* = **embarrassment**, humiliation, chagrin, ignominy, compunction, mortification, loss of face, abashment ■ **OPPOSITE:** shamelessness **2** *I don't want to bring shame on the family name.* = **disgrace**, scandal, discredit, contempt, smear, degradation, disrepute, reproach, derision, dishonour, infamy, opprobrium, odium (*formal*), ill repute, obloquy ■ **OPPOSITE:** honour ▶ VERB **1** *Her son's affair had humiliated and shamed her.* = **embarrass**, disgrace, humiliate, humble, disconcert, mortify, take (someone) down a peg (*informal*), abash ■ **OPPOSITE:** make proud **2** *I wouldn't shame my family by trying that.* = **dishonour**, discredit, degrade, stain, smear, blot, debase, defile ■ **OPPOSITE:** honour • **put something** or **someone to shame**

His playing really puts me to shame. = **show up**, disgrace, eclipse, surpass, outstrip, outclass

shameful ADJECTIVE = **disgraceful**, outrageous, scandalous, mean, low, base, infamous, indecent, degrading, vile, wicked, atrocious, unworthy, reprehensible, ignominious, dastardly (*old-fashioned*), unbecoming, dishonourable ■ **OPPOSITE**: admirable

shameless ADJECTIVE = **brazen**, audacious, flagrant, abandoned, corrupt, hardened, indecent, brash, improper, depraved, wanton, unabashed, profligate, unashamed, incorrigible, insolent, unprincipled, impudent, dissolute, reprobate, immodest, barefaced, unblushing

shanty NOUN = **shack**, shed, cabin, hut, lean-to, hovel, shiel (*Scot.*), bothy (*Scot.*), shieling (*Scot.*)

shape NOUN **1** *The glass bottle is the shape of a woman's torso.* = **appearance**, form, aspect, guise, likeness, semblance **2** *the shapes of the trees against the sky* = **form**, profile, outline, lines, build, cut, figure, silhouette, configuration, contours **3** *Carefully cut round the shape of the design you wish to use.* = **pattern**, model, frame, mould **4** *He was still in better shape than many young men.* = **condition**, state, health, trim, kilter, fettle ▶ VERB **1** *Like it or not, our families shape our lives.* = **form**, make, produce, create, model, fashion, mould **2** *Cut the dough in half and shape each half into a loaf.* = **mould**, form, make, fashion, model, frame

shapeless ADJECTIVE = **formless**, irregular, amorphous, unstructured, misshapen, asymmetrical ■ **OPPOSITE**: well-formed

shapely ADJECTIVE = **well-formed**, elegant, trim, neat, graceful, well-turned, curvaceous (*informal*), sightly, comely (*old-fashioned*), well-proportioned

share NOUN *I have had more than my share of adventures.* = **part**, portion, quota, ration, lot, cut (*informal*), due, division, contribution, proportion, allowance, whack (*informal*), allotment ▶ VERB **1** *the small income he has shared with his brother* = **divide**, split, distribute, assign, apportion, parcel out, divvy up (*informal*) **2** *Share the cost of the flowers.* = **go halves on**, go fifty-fifty on (*informal*), go Dutch on (*informal*)

sharp ADJECTIVE **1** *Using a sharp knife, cut away the pith and peel from both fruits.* = **keen**, cutting, sharpened, honed, jagged, knife-edged, razor-sharp, serrated, knifelike ■ **OPPOSITE**: blunt **2** *He is very sharp*

and swift with repartee. = **quick-witted**, clever, astute, knowing, ready, quick, bright (*informal*), alert, subtle, penetrating, apt, discerning, on the ball (*informal*), perceptive, observant, long-headed ■ **OPPOSITE**: dim **3** *'Don't criticize your mother,' was his sharp reprimand.* = **cutting**, biting, severe, bitter, harsh, scathing, acrimonious, barbed, hurtful, sarcastic, sardonic, caustic, vitriolic, trenchant, mordant, mordacious, acerb ■ **OPPOSITE**: gentle **4** *There's been a sharp rise in the rate of inflation.* = **sudden**, marked, abrupt, extreme, distinct ■ **OPPOSITE**: gradual **5** *All the footmarks are quite sharp and clear.* = **clear**, distinct, clear-cut, well-defined, crisp ■ **OPPOSITE**: indistinct **6** *a colourless, almost odourless liquid with a sharp, sweetish taste* = **sour**, tart, pungent, hot, burning, acid, acerbic, acrid, piquant, acetic, vinegary, acerb ■ **OPPOSITE**: bland **7** *Now politics is all about the right haircut and a sharp suit.* = **stylish**, smart, fashionable, trendy (*informal*), chic, classy (*slang*), snappy, natty (*informal*), dressy, schmick (*Austral. informal*) **8** *I felt a sharp pain in my lower back.* = **acute**, violent, severe, intense, painful, shooting, distressing, stabbing, fierce, stinging, piercing, sore, excruciating, gut-wrenching ▶ ADVERB *She planned to unlock the store at 8.00 sharp.* = **promptly**, precisely, exactly, on time, on the dot, punctually ■ **OPPOSITE**: approximately

sharpen VERB = **make sharp**, hone, whet, grind, edge, strop, put an edge on

shatter VERB **1** *Safety glass won't shatter if it's broken.* = **smash**, break, burst, split, crack, crush, explode, demolish, shiver, implode, pulverize, crush to smithereens **2** *Something like that really shatters your confidence.* = **destroy**, ruin, wreck, blast, disable, overturn, demolish, impair, blight, torpedo, bring to nought **3** *the tragedy which had shattered him* = **devastate** (*informal*), shock, stun, crush, overwhelm, upset, break (someone's) heart, knock the stuffing out of (someone) (*informal*), traumatize

shattered ADJECTIVE **1** *I am absolutely shattered to hear the news.* = **devastated**, crushed, upset, gutted (*slang*) **2** *He was shattered and too tired to concentrate.* = **exhausted**, drained, worn out, spent, done in (*informal*), all in (*slang*), wiped out (*informal*), weary, knackered (*slang*), clapped out (*Brit., Austral. & N.Z. informal*), tired out, ready to drop, dog-tired (*informal*), zonked (*slang*), dead tired (*informal*), dead beat (*informal*), shagged out (*Brit. slang*), jiggered (*informal*)

shattering ADJECTIVE = **devastating**, stunning (*informal*), severe, crushing, overwhelming, paralysing

shave VERB 1 *It's a pity you shaved your moustache off.* = **trim**, crop 2 *I set the log on the ground and shaved off the bark.* = **scrape**, plane, trim, shear, pare 3 *The ball shaved the goalpost.* = **brush past**, touch, graze

shed¹ NOUN *a garden shed* = **hut**, shack, lean-to, outhouse, lockup, bothy (*chiefly Scot.*), whare (*N.Z.*)

shed² VERB 1 *Some of the trees were already beginning to shed their leaves.* = **drop**, spill, scatter 2 *a snake who has shed its skin* = **cast off**, discard, moult, slough off, exuviate 3 *as dawn sheds its first light* = **give out**, cast, emit, give, throw, afford, radiate, diffuse, pour forth

sheen NOUN = **shine**, gleam, gloss, polish, brightness, lustre, burnish, patina, shininess

sheepish ADJECTIVE = **embarrassed**, uncomfortable, ashamed, silly, foolish, self-conscious, chagrined, mortified, abashed, shamefaced ■ **OPPOSITE:** unembarrassed

sheer ADJECTIVE 1 *acts of sheer desperation* = **total**, complete, absolute, utter, rank, pure, downright, unqualified, out-and-out, unadulterated, unmitigated, thoroughgoing, unalloyed, arrant ■ **OPPOSITE:** moderate 2 *There was a sheer drop just outside my window.* = **steep**, abrupt, perpendicular, precipitous ■ **OPPOSITE:** gradual 3 *sheer black tights* = **fine**, thin, transparent, see-through, gossamer, diaphanous, gauzy ■ **OPPOSITE:** thick

sheet NOUN 1 *I was able to fit it all on one sheet.* = **page**, leaf, folio, piece of paper 2 *a cracked sheet of glass* = **plate**, piece, panel, slab, pane 3 *a sheet of ice* = **coat**, film, layer, membrane, surface, stratum, veneer, overlay, lamina 4 *Sheets of rain slanted across the road.* = **expanse**, area, stretch, sweep, covering, blanket

shell NOUN 1 *They cracked the nuts and removed their shells.* = **husk**, case, pod, shuck 2 *The baby tortoise tucked his head in his shell.* = **carapace**, armour 3 *The solid feel of the car's shell is impressive.* = **frame**, structure, hull, framework, skeleton, chassis ▶ VERB 1 *She shelled and ate a few nuts.* = **remove the shells from**, husk, shuck (*U.S.*) 2 *The rebels shelled the densely-populated suburbs near the port.* = **bomb**, barrage, bombard, attack, strike, blitz, strafe • **shell something out** *You won't have to shell out a fortune for it.* = **pay out**, fork out (*slang*), expend, give, hand over, lay out (*informal*), disburse, ante up (*informal, chiefly U.S.*)

shelter NOUN 1 *a bus shelter* = **cover**, screen, awning, shiel (*Scot.*) 2 *the hut where they were given food and shelter* = **protection**, safety, refuge, cover, security, defence, sanctuary 3 *a shelter for homeless women* = **refuge**, haven, sanctuary, retreat, asylum ▶ VERB 1 *a man sheltering in a doorway* = **take shelter**, hide, seek refuge, take cover 2 *A neighbour sheltered the boy for seven days.* = **protect**, shield, harbour, safeguard, cover, hide, guard, defend, take in ■ **OPPOSITE:** endanger

sheltered ADJECTIVE 1 *a shallow-sloping beach next to a sheltered bay* = **screened**, covered, protected, shielded, secluded ■ **OPPOSITE:** exposed 2 *She had a sheltered upbringing.* = **protected**, screened, shielded, quiet, withdrawn, isolated, secluded, cloistered, reclusive, ensconced, hermitic, conventual

shelve VERB = **postpone**, put off, defer, table (*U.S.*), dismiss, freeze, suspend, put aside, hold over, mothball, pigeonhole, lay aside, put on ice, put on the back burner (*informal*), hold in abeyance, take a rain check on (*U.S. & Canad. informal*)

shepherd NOUN *The shepherd was filled with terror.* = **drover**, stockman, herdsman or woman (*Brit.*), herder, grazier ▶ VERB *She was shepherded by her guards up the rear ramp of the aircraft.* = **guide**, conduct, steer, convoy, herd, marshal, usher ■ **RELATED WORD:** adjective pastoral

sherang NOUN (*Austral. & N.Z.*) = **boss**, manager, head, leader, director, chief, executive, owner, master, governor (*informal*), employer, administrator, supervisor, superintendent, gaffer (*informal, chiefly Brit.*), foreman or woman or person, overseer, kingpin, big cheese (*old-fashioned slang*), numero uno (*informal*), Mister Big (*slang, chiefly U.S.*)

shield NOUN 1 *innocents used as a human shield against attack* = **protection**, cover, defence, screen, guard, ward (*archaic*), shelter, safeguard, aegis, rampart, bulwark 2 *a warrior with sword and shield* = **buckler**, escutcheon (*Heraldry*), targe (*archaic*) ▶ VERB *He shielded his head from the sun with an old sack.* = **protect**, cover, screen, guard, defend, shelter, safeguard

shift VERB 1 *The entire pile shifted and slid, thumping onto the floor.* = **move**, drift, move around, veer, budge, swerve, change position 2 *We shifted the vans and used the area for skateboarding.* = **remove**, move, transfer, displace, relocate, rearrange, transpose, reposition ▶ NOUN 1 *a shift in policy* = **change**, switch, shifting, modification, alteration, displacement, about-turn, permutation, fluctuation **2** *There has been a shift of the elderly to this state.* = **move**, transfer, removal, veering, rearrangement

shifty ADJECTIVE = **untrustworthy**, sly, devious, scheming, tricky, slippery, contriving, wily, crafty, evasive, furtive, deceitful, underhand, unprincipled, duplicitous, fly-by-night (*informal*) ■ **OPPOSITE:** honest

shimmer VERB *The lights shimmered on the water.* = **gleam**, twinkle, glimmer, dance, glisten, scintillate ▶ NOUN *a shimmer of starlight* = **gleam**, glimmer, iridescence, unsteady light

shine VERB **1** *It is a mild morning and the sun is shining.* = **gleam**, flash, beam, glow, sparkle, glitter, glare, shimmer, radiate, twinkle, glimmer, glisten, emit light, give off light, scintillate **2** *Let him dust and shine the furniture.* = **polish**, buff, burnish, brush, rub up **3** *He conspicuously failed to shine academically.* = **be outstanding**, stand out, excel, star, be distinguished, steal the show, be conspicuous, be pre-eminent, stand out in a crowd ▶ NOUN **1** *The wood has been recently polished to bring back the shine.* = **polish**, gloss, sheen, glaze, lustre, patina **2** *There was a sparkle about her, a shine of anticipation.* = **brightness**, light, sparkle, radiance

shining ADJECTIVE **1** *She is a shining example to us all.* = **outstanding**, glorious, splendid, leading, celebrated, brilliant, distinguished, eminent, conspicuous, illustrious **2** *shining brass buttons* = **bright**, brilliant, gleaming, beaming, sparkling, glittering, shimmering, radiant, luminous, glistening, resplendent, aglow, effulgent, incandescent

shiny ADJECTIVE = **bright**, gleaming, glossy, glistening, polished, burnished, lustrous, satiny, sheeny, agleam

ship NOUN = **vessel**, boat, craft

shirk VERB **1** *We will not shirk the task of considering the need for further action.* = **dodge**, avoid, evade, get out of, duck (out of) (*informal*), shun, sidestep, body-swerve, bob off (*Brit. slang*), scrimshank (*Brit. Military slang*) **2** *He was sacked for shirking.* = **skive** (*Brit. slang*), slack, idle, malinger, swing the lead, gold-brick (*U.S. slang*), bob off (*Brit. slang*), bludge (*Austral. & N.Z. informal*), scrimshank (*Brit. Military slang*)

shiver VERB *He shivered in the cold.* = **shudder**, shake, tremble, quake, quiver, palpitate ▶ NOUN *Alice gave a shiver of delight.* = **tremble**, shudder, quiver, thrill, trembling, flutter, tremor, frisson (*French*)

• **the shivers** *My boss gives me the shivers.* = **the shakes**, a chill (*informal*), goose pimples, goose flesh, chattering teeth

shock NOUN **1** *The extent of the violence came as a shock.* = **upset**, blow, trauma, bombshell, turn (*informal*), distress, disturbance, consternation, whammy (*informal*), state of shock, rude awakening, bolt from the blue, prostration **2** *Steel barriers can bend and absorb the shock.* = **impact**, blow, jolt, clash, encounter, jarring, collision **3** *It gave me quite a shock to see his face on the screen.* = **start**, scare, fright, turn (*informal*), jolt ▶ VERB **1** *Relief workers were shocked by what they saw.* = **shake**, stun, stagger, jar, shake up (*informal*), paralyse, numb, jolt, stupefy, shake out of your complacency **2** *They were easily shocked in those days.* = **horrify**, appal, disgust, outrage, offend, revolt, unsettle, sicken, agitate, disquiet, nauseate, raise someone's eyebrows, scandalize, gross out (*U.S. slang*), traumatize, give (someone) a turn (*informal*)

shocking ADJECTIVE **1** *I must have been in a shocking state last night.* = **terrible**, appalling, dreadful, bad, fearful (*informal*), dire, horrendous, ghastly, from hell (*informal*), deplorable, abysmal, frightful, godawful (*slang*) **2** *This was a shocking invasion of privacy.* = **appalling**, outrageous, disgraceful, offensive, distressing, disgusting, horrible, dreadful, horrifying, revolting, obscene, sickening, ghastly, hideous, monstrous, scandalous, disquieting, unspeakable, atrocious (*informal*), repulsive, nauseating, odious, loathsome, abominable, stupefying, hellacious (*U.S. slang*) ■ **OPPOSITE:** wonderful

shoddy ADJECTIVE = **inferior**, poor, second-rate, cheap, tacky (*informal*), tawdry, tatty, trashy, low-rent (*informal, chiefly U.S.*), slipshod, cheapo (*informal*), rubbishy, junky (*informal*), cheap-jack (*informal*), bodger or bodgie (*Austral. slang*) ■ **OPPOSITE:** excellent

shoemaker NOUN = **cobbler**, bootmaker, souter (*Scot.*)

shoot VERB **1** *The police had orders to shoot anyone who attacked them.* = **open fire on**, blast (*slang*), hit, kill, bag, plug (*slang*), bring down, blow away (*slang, chiefly U.S.*), zap (*slang*), pick off, pump full of lead (*slang*) **2** *He shot an arrow into the air.* = **fire**, launch, discharge, project, hurl, fling, propel, emit, let fly **3** *They had almost reached the boat when a figure shot past them.* = **speed**, race, rush, charge, fly, spring, tear, flash, dash, barrel

S

(along) (*informal, chiefly U.S. & Canad.*), bolt, streak, dart, whisk, whizz (*informal*), hurtle, scoot, burn rubber (*informal*) ▶ NOUN *This week saw the first pink shoots of the new season's crop.* = **sprout**, branch, bud, twig, sprig, offshoot, scion, slip

shop NOUN = **store**, market, supermarket, mart, boutique, emporium (*old-fashioned*), hypermarket, dairy (N.Z.)

shore NOUN = **beach**, coast, sands, strand (*poetic*), lakeside, waterside, seaboard (*chiefly U.S.*), foreshore, seashore

shore up VERB = **support**, strengthen, reinforce, prop, brace, underpin, augment, buttress

short ADJECTIVE 1 *We had a short meeting.* = **brief**, fleeting, short-term, short-lived, momentary ■ **OPPOSITE**: long 2 *This is a short note to say thank you.* = **concise**, brief, succinct, clipped, summary, compressed, curtailed, terse, laconic, pithy, abridged, compendious, sententious ■ **OPPOSITE**: lengthy 3 *I'm tall and thin and he's short and fat.* = **small**, little, wee, squat, diminutive, petite, dumpy, knee high to a grasshopper, fubsy (*archaic, dialect*), knee high to a gnat ■ **OPPOSITE**: tall 4 *She was definitely short with me.* = **abrupt**, sharp, terse, curt, blunt, crusty, gruff, brusque, offhand, testy, impolite, discourteous, uncivil ■ **OPPOSITE**: polite 5 *a crisp short pastry* = **crumbly**, crisp, brittle, friable 6 *Money was short in those days.* = **scarce**, wanting, low, missing, limited, lacking, tight, slim, inadequate, insufficient, slender, scant, meagre, sparse, deficient, scanty ■ **OPPOSITE**: plentiful ▶ ADVERB *He had no insurance and was caught short when his house was burgled.* = **abruptly**, suddenly, unaware, by surprise, without warning ■ **OPPOSITE**: gradually

shortage NOUN = **deficiency**, want, lack, failure, deficit, poverty, shortfall, inadequacy, scarcity, dearth, paucity (*formal*), insufficiency ■ **OPPOSITE**: abundance

shortcoming NOUN = **failing**, fault, weakness, defect, flaw, drawback, imperfection, frailty, foible, weak point

shorten VERB 1 *The day surgery will help to shorten waiting lists.* = **cut**, reduce, decrease, cut down, trim, diminish, dock, cut back, prune, lessen, curtail, abbreviate, truncate, abridge, downsize ■ **OPPOSITE**: increase 2 *It's a simple matter to shorten trouser legs.* = **turn up**, trim

short-lived ADJECTIVE = **brief**, short, temporary, fleeting, passing, transient, ephemeral, transitory, impermanent

shortly ADVERB 1 *Their trial will begin shortly.* = **soon**, presently, before long, anon (*archaic*), in a little while, any minute now, erelong (*archaic, poetic*) 2 *'I don't know you,' he said shortly, 'and I'm in a hurry.'* = **curtly**, sharply, abruptly, tartly, tersely, succinctly, briefly, concisely, in a few words

short-sighted ADJECTIVE 1 *Testing showed her to be very short-sighted.* = **near-sighted**, myopic 2 *I think we're being very short-sighted.* = **imprudent**, injudicious, ill-advised, unthinking, careless, impractical, ill-considered, improvident, impolitic, seeing no further than (the end of) your nose

shot NOUN 1 *Guards at the training base heard the shots.* = **discharge**, report, gunfire, crack, blast, explosion, bang 2 *These guns are lighter and take more shot for their size.* = **ammunition**, bullet, slug, pellet, projectile, lead, ball 3 *He was not a particularly good shot because of his eyesight.* = **marksman** or **woman**, shooter 4 *They had only one shot at goal.* = **strike**, throw, lob 5 *He will be given a shot at the world title.* = **attempt**, go (*informal*), try, turn, chance, effort, opportunity, crack (*informal*), essay, stab (*informal*), endeavour • **a shot in the arm** *A win would provide a much-needed shot in the arm for the team.* = **boost**, lift, encouragement, stimulus, impetus, fillip, geeing-up *Why don't you have* **have a shot** *a shot at it?* = **make an attempt**, have a go, try, have a crack (*informal*), try your luck, have a stab (*informal*), have a bash (*informal*), tackle • **like a shot** *I heard the key in the front door and I was out of bed like a shot.* = **at once**, immediately, in a flash, quickly, eagerly, unhesitatingly, like a bat out of hell (*slang*)

shoulder VERB 1 *He has to shoulder the consequences of his father's mistakes.* = **bear**, carry, take on, accept, assume, be responsible for, take upon yourself 2 *He shouldered past her and opened the door.* = **push**, thrust, elbow, shove, jostle, press • **give someone the cold shoulder** (*informal*) *He was given the cold shoulder by his former friends.* = **snub**, ignore, blank (*slang*), put down, shun, rebuff, kick in the teeth (*slang*), ostracize, send someone to Coventry, cut (*informal*) • **rub shoulders with someone** *I was destined to rub shoulders with the most unexpected people.* = **mix with**, associate with, consort with, hobnob with, socialize with, fraternize with • **shoulder to shoulder** 1 *walking shoulder to shoulder with their heads bent against the rain* = **side by side**, abreast, next to each other 2 *My party* will stand shoulder to shoulder with the Prime Minister and her government. = **together**, united, jointly, as one, in partnership, in cooperation, in unity

shout VERB We began to shout for help. = **cry (out)**, call (out), yell, scream, roar, shriek, bellow, bawl, holler (informal), raise your voice ▸ NOUN I heard a distant shout. = **cry**, call, yell, scream, roar, shriek, bellow
• **shout someone down** The hecklers began to shout down the speakers. = **drown out**, overwhelm, drown, silence

shove VERB He shoved her out of the way. = **push**, shoulder, thrust, elbow, drive, press, crowd (informal), propel, jostle, impel ▸ NOUN She gave Gracie a shove in the back. = **push**, knock, thrust, elbow, bump, nudge, jostle • **shove off** Why don't you just shove off and leave me alone? = **go away**, leave, clear off (informal), depart, go to hell (informal), push off (informal), slope off, pack your bags (informal), scram (informal), get on your bike (Brit. slang), take yourself off, vamoose (slang, chiefly U.S.), sling your hook (Brit. slang), rack off (Austral. & N.Z. slang)

shovel NOUN She dug the foundation with a pick and shovel. = **spade**, scoop ▸ VERB 1 He had to get out and shovel snow. = **move**, scoop, dredge, shift, load, heap 2 shovelling food into his mouth = **stuff**, spoon, ladle

show VERB 1 These figures show an increase in unemployment. = **indicate**, demonstrate, prove, reveal, display, evidence, point out, manifest, testify to, evince, flag up ◼ **OPPOSITE:** disprove 2 What made you decide to show your paintings? = **display**, exhibit, put on display, present, put on show, put before the public 3 Let me show you to my study. = **guide**, lead, conduct, accompany, direct, steer, escort 4 Claire showed us how to make a chocolate roulade. = **demonstrate**, describe, explain, teach, illustrate, instruct 5 I'd driven both ways down this road, but the tracks didn't show. = **be visible**, be seen ◼ **OPPOSITE:** be invisible 6 She had enough time to show her gratitude. = **express**, display, reveal, indicate, register, demonstrate, disclose, manifest, divulge, make known, evince ◼ **OPPOSITE:** hide 7 There was always a chance he wouldn't show. = **turn up**, come, appear, arrive, attend, show up (informal), put in or make an appearance 8 The drama will be shown on American TV. = **broadcast**, transmit, air, beam, relay, televise, put on the air, podcast ▸ NOUN 1 Spring brings a lovely show of green and yellow striped leaves. = **display**, view, sight, spectacle, array 2 the Chelsea

flower show = **exhibition**, fair, display, parade, expo (informal), exposition, pageant, pageantry 3 The change in government is more for show than for real. = **appearance**, display, pose, profession, parade, ostentation 4 We need to make a show of acknowledging their expertise. = **pretence**, appearance, semblance, illusion, pretext, likeness, affectation 5 I had my own TV show. = **programme**, broadcast, presentation, production 6 How about going to see a show in London? = **entertainment**, performance, play, production, drama, musical, presentation, theatrical performance • **show off** He had been showing off at the poker table. = **boast**, brag, blow your own trumpet, swagger, hot-dog (chiefly U.S.), strut your stuff (informal), make a spectacle of yourself
• **show someone up** We wanted to teach them a lesson for showing us up. = **embarrass**, shame, let down, mortify, put to shame, show in a bad light • **show something off** She was showing off her engagement ring. = **exhibit**, display, parade, advertise, demonstrate, spread out, flaunt • **show something up** The awards showed up the fact that TV has been a washout this year. = **reveal**, expose, highlight, pinpoint, unmask, lay bare, put the spotlight on

showdown NOUN = **confrontation**, crisis, clash, moment of truth, face-off (slang)

shower NOUN 1 a shower of rain = **deluge**, downpour 2 They were reunited in a shower of kisses and tears. = **profusion**, plethora ▸ VERB 1 They were showered with rice in the traditional manner. = **cover**, dust, spray, sprinkle 2 She showered gifts on us. = **inundate**, load, heap, lavish, pour, deluge

showing NOUN 1 a private showing of the hit film = **display**, staging, presentation, exhibition, demonstration 2 On this showing he has a big job ahead of him. = **performance**, demonstration, track record, show, appearance, impression, account of yourself

showman or **show-woman** or **showperson** NOUN = **performer**, entertainer, artiste, player, Thespian, trouper, play-actor, actor or actress

show-off NOUN = **exhibitionist**, boaster, swaggerer, hot dog (chiefly U.S.), poseur, egotist, braggart, braggadocio, peacock, figjam (Austral. slang)

showy ADJECTIVE = **ostentatious**, flamboyant, flashy, flash (informal), loud, over the top (informal), brash, pompous, pretentious, gaudy, garish, tawdry, splashy (informal), tinselly ◼ **OPPOSITE:** tasteful

S

shred NOUN **1** *Cut the cabbage into fine long shreds.* = **strip**, bit, piece, scrap, fragment, rag, ribbon, snippet, sliver, tatter **2** *There is not a shred of truth in this story.* = **particle**, trace, scrap, grain, atom, jot, whit, iota

shrewd ADJECTIVE = **astute**, clever, sharp, knowing, fly (*slang*), keen, acute, smart, calculated, calculating, intelligent, discriminating, cunning, discerning, sly, canny, perceptive, wily, crafty, artful, far-sighted, far-seeing, long-headed, perspicacious (*formal*), sagacious (*formal*) ■ **OPPOSITE:** naive

shrewdly ADVERB = **astutely**, perceptively, cleverly, knowingly, artfully, cannily, with consummate skill, sagaciously, far-sightedly, perspicaciously, with all your wits about you

shriek VERB *She shrieked and leapt from the bed.* = **scream**, cry, yell, howl, wail, whoop, screech, squeal, holler ▶ NOUN *a shriek of joy* = **scream**, cry, yell, howl, wail, whoop, screech, squeal, holler

shrill ADJECTIVE = **piercing**, high, sharp, acute, piping, penetrating, screeching, high-pitched, ear-splitting, ear-piercing ■ **OPPOSITE:** deep

shrink VERB = **decrease**, dwindle, lessen, grow or get smaller, contract, narrow, diminish, fall off, shorten, wrinkle, wither, drop off, deflate, shrivel, downsize ■ **OPPOSITE:** grow

shrivel VERB = **wither**, dry (up), wilt, shrink, wrinkle, dwindle, dehydrate, desiccate, wizen

shrivelled ADJECTIVE = **withered**, dry, dried up, wrinkled, shrunken, wizened, desiccated, sere (*archaic*)

shroud NOUN **1** *a burial shroud* = **winding sheet**, grave clothes, cerecloth, cerement **2** *a parked car huddled under a shroud of grey snow* = **covering**, veil, mantle, screen, cloud, pall ▶ VERB *Mist shrouded the outline of the palace.* = **conceal**, cover, screen, hide, blanket, veil, cloak, swathe, envelop

shudder VERB *She shuddered with cold.* = **shiver**, shake, tremble, quake, quiver, convulse ▶ NOUN *She recoiled with a shudder.* = **shiver**, trembling, tremor, quiver, spasm, convulsion

shuffle VERB **1** *She shuffled across the kitchen.* = **shamble**, stagger, stumble, dodder **2** *He shuffled his feet along the gravel path.* = **scuffle**, drag, scrape, scuff **3** *The silence lengthened as he unnecessarily shuffled some papers.* = **rearrange**, jumble, mix, shift, disorder, disarrange, intermix

shun VERB = **avoid**, steer clear of, keep away from, evade, eschew, shy away from,

cold-shoulder, have no part in, fight shy of, give (someone or something) a wide berth, body-swerve

shut VERB *Just make sure you shut the gate after you.* = **close**, secure, fasten, bar, seal, slam, push to, draw to ■ **OPPOSITE:** open ▶ ADJECTIVE *A smell of burning came from behind the shut door.* = **closed**, fastened, sealed, locked ■ **OPPOSITE:** open • **shut down** *Smaller constructors had been forced to shut down.* = **stop work**, halt work, cease operating, close down, cease trading, discontinue • **shut someone out** *I was set to shut out anyone else who came knocking.* = **exclude**, bar, keep out, black, lock out, ostracize, debar, blackball • **shut someone up 1** (*informal*) *A sharp put-down was the only way he knew of shutting her up.* = **silence**, gag, hush, muzzle, fall silent, button it (*slang*), pipe down (*slang*), hold your tongue, put a sock in it (*Brit. slang*), keep your trap shut (*slang*), cut the cackle (*informal*), button your lip (*slang*) **2** *They shut him up in a windowless tower.* = **confine**, cage, imprison, keep in, box in, intern, incarcerate, coop up, immure (*archaic*) • **shut something in** *The door enables us to shut the birds in in bad weather.* = **confine**, cage, enclose, imprison, impound, pound, wall off or up • **shut something out** *I shut out the memory that was too painful to dwell on.* = **block out**, screen, hide, cover, mask, veil

shuttle VERB = **go back and forth**, commute, go to and fro, alternate, ply, shunt, seesaw

shy ADJECTIVE **1** *He is painfully shy when it comes to talking to women.* = **timid**, self-conscious, bashful, reserved, retiring, nervous, modest, aw-shucks, shrinking, backward, coy, reticent, self-effacing, diffident, mousy ■ **OPPOSITE:** confident **2** *You should not be shy of having your say.* = **cautious**, wary, hesitant, suspicious, reticent, distrustful, chary ■ **OPPOSITE:** reckless ▶ VERB (*sometimes with* **off** *or* **away**) *The horse shied as the wind sent sparks flying.* = **recoil**, flinch, draw back, start, rear, buck, wince, swerve, balk, quail, take fright

shyness NOUN = **timidity**, self-consciousness, bashfulness, modesty, nervousness, lack of confidence, reticence, diffidence, timorousness, mousiness, timidness

sick ADJECTIVE **1** *She's very sick.* = **unwell**, ill, poorly (*informal*), diseased, weak, crook (*Austral. & N.Z. informal*), under par (*informal*), ailing, feeble, laid up (*informal*), under the weather (*informal*), indisposed,

on the sick list (*informal*) ■ **OPPOSITE:** well
2 *The very thought of food made him feel sick.*
= **nauseous**, ill, queasy, nauseated, green
about the gills (*informal*), qualmish **3** *I am
sick of hearing all these people moaning.* = **tired**,
bored, fed up, weary, jaded, blasé, satiated
4 *a sick joke about a cat* = **morbid**, cruel,
sadistic, black, macabre, ghoulish

sicken VERB **1** *What he saw there sickened him,
despite years of police work.* = **disgust**, revolt,
nauseate, repel, gross out (*U.S. slang*), turn
your stomach, make your gorge rise
2 *Many of them sickened and died.* = **fall ill**,
take sick, ail (*literary*), go down with
something, contract something, be
stricken by something

sickening ADJECTIVE = **disgusting**,
revolting, vile, offensive, foul, distasteful,
repulsive, nauseating, loathsome,
nauseous, gut-wrenching, putrid,
stomach-turning (*informal*), cringe-making
(*Brit. informal*), noisome, yucky or yukky
(*slang*), yucko (*Austral. slang*) ■ **OPPOSITE:**
delightful

sickly ADJECTIVE **1** *He had been a sickly child.*
= **unhealthy**, weak, delicate, ailing, feeble,
infirm, in poor health, indisposed **2** *his pale,
sickly face and woebegone expression* = **pale**,
wan, pasty, bloodless, pallid, sallow,
ashen-faced, waxen, peaky **3** *the sickly smell
of rum* = **nauseating**, revolting (*informal*),
cloying, icky (*informal*) **4** *a sickly sequel to the
flimsy series* = **sentimental**, romantic,
sloppy (*informal*), corny (*slang*), mushy
(*informal*), weepy (*informal*), slushy
(*informal*), mawkish, tear-jerking (*informal*),
schmaltzy (*slang*), gushy (*informal*)

sickness NOUN **1** *a sickness that affects children*
= **illness**, disorder, ailment, disease,
complaint, bug (*informal*), affliction,
malady, infirmity, indisposition, lurgy
(*informal*) **2** *He felt a great rush of sickness.*
= **nausea**, queasiness **3** *Symptoms include
sickness and diarrhoea.* = **vomiting**, nausea,
upset stomach, throwing up (*informal*),
puking (*slang*), retching, barfing (*U.S. slang*)

side NOUN **1** *Park at the side of the road.*
= **border**, margin, boundary, verge (*Brit.*),
flank, rim, perimeter, periphery, edge
■ **OPPOSITE:** middle **2** *The copier only copies
onto one side of the paper.* = **face**, surface,
facet **3** *the right side of your face* = **half**, part
4 *He lives on the south side of Edinburgh.*
= **district**, area, region, quarter, sector,
neighbourhood, vicinity, locality, locale,
neck of the woods (*informal*) **5** *Both sides
appealed for a new ceasefire.* = **party**, camp,
faction, cause **6** *those with the ability to see all
sides of a question* = **point of view**,

viewpoint, position, opinion, angle, slant,
standpoint **7** *Italy were the better side.*
= **team**, squad, crew, line-up **8** *He is in
charge of the civilian side of the UN mission.*
= **aspect**, feature, angle, facet ▶ ADJECTIVE
The refugees were treated as a side issue.
= **subordinate**, minor, secondary,
subsidiary, lesser, marginal, indirect,
incidental, ancillary ■ **OPPOSITE:** main
• **side with someone** *They side with the
forces of evil.* = **support**, back, champion,
agree with, stand up for, second, favour,
defend, team up with (*informal*), go along
with, befriend, join with, sympathize with,
be loyal to, take the part of, associate
yourself with, ally yourself with
■ **RELATED WORD:** *adjective* lateral

sidestep VERB = **avoid**, dodge, evade, duck
(*informal*), skirt, skip, bypass, elude,
circumvent (*formal*), find a way round,
body-swerve

sidetrack VERB = **distract**, divert, lead off
the subject, deflect

sidewalk NOUN (*U.S. & Canad.*) = **pavement**,
footpath (*Austral. & N.Z.*)

sideways ADVERB **1** *He glanced sideways at
her.* = **indirectly**, obliquely **2** *They moved
sideways, their arms still locked together.* = **to
the side**, laterally, crabwise ▶ ADJECTIVE
Alfred shot him a sideways glance. = **sidelong**,
side, slanted, oblique

sidle VERB = **edge**, steal, slink, inch, creep,
sneak

siege NOUN = **blockade**, encirclement,
besiegement

siesta NOUN = **nap**, rest, sleep, doze, kip
(*Brit. slang*), snooze (*informal*), catnap, forty
winks (*informal*), zizz (*Brit. informal*)

sieve NOUN *Press the raspberries through a fine
sieve to form a puree.* = **strainer**, sifter,
colander, screen, riddle, tammy cloth
▶ VERB *Sieve the icing sugar into the bowl.*
= **sift**, filter, strain, separate, pan, bolt,
riddle

sift VERB **1** *Sift the flour and baking powder into
a medium-sized mixing bowl.* = **sieve**, filter,
strain, separate, pan, bolt, part, riddle
2 *He has sifted the evidence and summarized it
clearly.* = **examine**, investigate, go through,
research, screen, probe, analyse, work over,
pore over, scrutinize

sigh VERB **1** *Dad sighed and stood up.* = **breathe
out**, exhale, moan, suspire (*archaic*)
2 *'Everyone forgets,' she sighed.* = **moan**,
complain, groan (*informal*), grieve, lament,
sorrow • **sigh for something** *or* **someone**
sighing for the good old days = **long for**, yearn
for, pine for, mourn for, languish over, eat
your heart out over

S

sight NOUN **1** *My sight is failing and I can't see to read any more.* = **vision**, eyes, eyesight, seeing, eye **2** *Among the most spectacular sights are the great sea-bird colonies.* = **spectacle**, show, scene, display, exhibition, vista, pageant **3** *The Queen's carriage came into sight.* = **view**, field of vision, range of vision, eyeshot, viewing, ken, visibility **4** *She looked a sight in the street-lamps.* = **eyesore**, mess, spectacle, fright (*informal*), monstrosity, blot on the landscape (*informal*) ▶ VERB *A fleet of ships was sighted in the North Sea.* = **spot**, see, observe, distinguish, perceive, make out, discern, behold (*archaic*, *literary*) ■ **RELATED WORDS:** *adjectives* optical, visual

sign NOUN **1** *Equations are generally written with a two-bar equals sign.* = **symbol**, mark, character, figure, device, representation, logo, badge, emblem, ensign, cipher **2** *The priest made the sign of the cross over him.* = **figure**, form, shape, outline **3** *They gave him the thumbs-up sign.* = **gesture**, signal, motion, indication, cue, gesticulation **4** *a sign saying that the highway was closed* = **notice**, board, warning, signpost, placard **5** *His face and movements rarely betrayed any sign of nerves.* = **indication**, evidence, trace, mark, note, signal, suggestion, symptom, hint, proof, gesture, clue, token, manifestation, giveaway, vestige, spoor **6** *It is a sign of things to come.* = **omen**, warning, portent, foreboding, presage, forewarning, writing on the wall, augury, auspice, wake-up call ▶ VERB **1** *She signed to me to go out.* = **gesture**, indicate, signal, wave, beckon, gesticulate, use sign language **2** *I got him to sign my copy of his book.* = **autograph**, initial, inscribe, subscribe, set your hand to • **sign someone up** *Spalding wants to sign you up.* = **engage**, recruit, employ, take on, hire, contract, take on board (*informal*), put on the payroll, take into service • **sign something away** *The Duke signed away his inheritance.* = **give up**, relinquish, renounce, lose, transfer, abandon, surrender, dispose of, waive, forgo • **sign up** *He signed up as a steward.* = **enlist**, join, volunteer, register, enrol, join up

signal NOUN **1** *They fired three distress signals.* = **flare**, rocket, beam, beacon, smoke signal, signal fire **2** *You mustn't fire without my signal.* = **cue**, sign, nod, prompting, go-ahead (*informal*), reminder, green light **3** *The event was seen as a signal of support.* = **sign**, gesture, indication, mark, note, evidence, expression, proof, token, indicator, manifestation ▶ VERB *She signalled a passing taxi.* = **gesture**, sign, wave, indicate, nod, motion, beckon, gesticulate, give a sign to

significance NOUN = **importance**, import (*formal*), consequence, matter, moment, weight, consideration, gravity, relevance, magnitude, impressiveness

significant ADJECTIVE **1** *It is the first drug that seems to have a significant effect on this disease.* = **important**, notable, serious, material, vital, critical, considerable, momentous, weighty, noteworthy ■ **OPPOSITE:** insignificant **2** *The old woman gave her a significant glance.* = **meaningful**, expressive, eloquent, knowing, meaning, expressing, pregnant, indicative, suggestive ■ **OPPOSITE:** meaningless

signify VERB = **indicate**, show, mean, matter, suggest, announce, evidence, represent, express, imply, exhibit, communicate, intimate, stand for, proclaim, convey, be a sign of, symbolize, denote, connote, portend, betoken, flag up

silence NOUN **1** *They stood in silence.* = **quiet**, peace, calm, hush, lull, stillness, quiescence, noiselessness ■ **OPPOSITE:** noise **2** *The court ruled that his silence should be entered as a plea of not guilty.* = **reticence**, dumbness, taciturnity, speechlessness, muteness, uncommunicativeness ■ **OPPOSITE:** speech ▶ VERB *The shock silenced her completely.* = **quieten**, still, quiet, cut off, subdue, stifle, cut short, quell, muffle, deaden, strike dumb ■ **OPPOSITE:** make louder

silent ADJECTIVE **1** *They both fell silent.* = **mute**, dumb, speechless, wordless, mum, struck dumb, voiceless, unspeaking ■ **OPPOSITE:** noisy **2** *He was a serious, silent man.* = **uncommunicative**, quiet, taciturn, tongue-tied, unspeaking, nonvocal, not talkative **3** *The heavy guns have again fallen silent.* = **quiet**, still, hushed, soundless, noiseless, muted, stilly (*poetic*) ■ **OPPOSITE:** loud **4** *He watched with silent contempt.* = **unspoken**, implied, implicit, tacit, understood, unexpressed

silently ADVERB **1** *as silently as a mouse* = **quietly**, in silence, soundlessly, noiselessly, inaudibly, without a sound **2** *He could no longer stand by silently while these rumours persisted.* = **mutely**, dumbly, in silence, wordlessly, speechlessly

silhouette NOUN *the dark silhouette of the castle ruins* = **outline**, form, shape, profile, delineation ▶ VERB *firefighters silhouetted against the burning wreckage* = **outline**, delineate, etch

silky ADJECTIVE = **smooth**, soft, sleek, velvety, silken

silly ADJECTIVE **1** *That's a silly thing to say.* = **stupid**, ridiculous, absurd, daft, inane, childish, immature, senseless, frivolous, preposterous, giddy, goofy (*informal*), idiotic, dozy (*Brit. informal*), fatuous, witless, puerile, brainless, asinine, dumb-ass (*slang*), dopy (*slang*) ■ OPPOSITE: clever **2** *Don't go doing anything silly, now, will you?* = **foolish**, stupid, unwise, inappropriate, rash, irresponsible, reckless, foolhardy, idiotic, thoughtless, imprudent, inadvisable ■ OPPOSITE: sensible ▸ NOUN *Come on, silly, we'll miss all the fun.* = **fool**, twit (*informal*), goose (*informal*), clot (*Brit. informal*), wally (*slang*), prat (*slang*), plonker (*slang*), duffer (*informal*), nitwit (*informal*), ninny, silly-billy (*informal*), dweeb (*U.S. slang*), putz (*U.S. slang*), eejit (*Scot. & Irish*), doofus (*slang, chiefly U.S.*), dorba or dorb (*Austral. slang*)

silt NOUN *The lake was almost solid with silt and vegetation.* = **sediment**, deposit, residue, ooze, sludge, alluvium • **silt something up** *The soil washed from the hills is silting up the dams.* = **clog up**, block up, choke up, obstruct, stop up, jam up, dam up, bung up, occlude (*formal*), congest

silver NOUN *He beat the rugs and polished the silver.* = **silverware**, silver plate ▸ ADJECTIVE *He had thick silver hair which needed cutting.* = **snowy**, white, grey, silvery, greyish-white, whitish-grey

similar ADJECTIVE **1** *The sisters looked very similar.* = **alike**, uniform, resembling, corresponding, comparable, much the same, homogeneous, of a piece, homogenous, cut from the same cloth, congruous ■ OPPOSITE: different **2** (*with to*) *The accident was similar to one that happened in 1973.* = **like**, much the same as, comparable to, analogous to, close to, cut from the same cloth as

> USAGE As should not be used after similar - so *Wilson held a similar position to Jones* is correct, but not *Wilson held a similar position as Jones*; and *The system is similar to the one in France* is correct, but not *The system is similar as in France.*

similarity NOUN = **resemblance**, likeness, sameness, agreement, relation, correspondence, analogy, affinity, closeness, concordance, congruence, comparability, point of comparison, similitude ■ OPPOSITE: difference

similarly ADVERB **1** *Most of the men who now gathered round him were similarly dressed.* = **in the same way**, the same, identically, in a similar fashion, uniformly, homogeneously, undistinguishably **2** *Similarly a baby's cry is instantly identified by the mother.* = **likewise**, in the same way, by the same token, correspondingly, in like manner

simmer VERB **1** *Turn the heat down so the sauce simmers gently.* = **bubble**, stew, boil gently, seethe, cook gently **2** *He simmered with rage.* = **fume**, seethe, smoulder, burn, smart, rage, boil, be angry, see red (*informal*), be tense, be agitated, be uptight (*informal*) • **simmer down** *After an hour or so, she finally managed to simmer down.* = **calm down**, grow quieter, control yourself, unwind (*informal*), contain yourself, collect yourself, cool off or down, get down off your high horse (*informal*)

simper VERB = **smile coyly**, smirk, smile self-consciously, smile affectedly

simpering ADJECTIVE = **coy**, affected, flirtatious, coquettish, kittenish

simple ADJECTIVE **1** *simple pictures and diagrams* = **uncomplicated**, clear, plain, understandable, coherent, lucid, recognizable, unambiguous, comprehensible, intelligible, uninvolved ■ OPPOSITE: complicated **2** *The job itself had been simple enough.* = **easy**, straightforward, not difficult, light, elementary, manageable, effortless, painless, uncomplicated, undemanding, easy-peasy (*slang*) **3** *She's shunned Armani for a simple blouse and jeans.* = **plain**, natural, basic, classic, severe, Spartan, uncluttered, unadorned, unfussy, unembellished, bare-bones ■ OPPOSITE: elaborate **4** *His refusal to talk was simple stubbornness.* = **pure**, mere, sheer, unalloyed **5** *He was as simple as a child.* = **artless**, innocent, naive, natural, frank, green, sincere, simplistic, unaffected, childlike, unpretentious, unsophisticated, ingenuous, guileless ■ OPPOSITE: sophisticated **6** *It was a simple home.* = **unpretentious**, modest, humble, homely, lowly, rustic, uncluttered, unfussy, unembellished ■ OPPOSITE: fancy

simplicity NOUN **1** *The apparent simplicity of his plot is deceptive.* = **straightforwardness**, ease, clarity, obviousness, easiness, clearness, absence of complications, elementariness ■ OPPOSITE: complexity **2** *fussy details that ruin the simplicity of the design* = **plainness**, restraint, purity, clean lines, naturalness, lack of adornment ■ OPPOSITE: elaborateness

simplify VERB = **make simpler**, facilitate, streamline, disentangle, dumb down, make intelligible, reduce to essentials, declutter

simplistic ADJECTIVE = **oversimplified**, shallow, facile, naive, oversimple

> USAGE Since *simplistic* already has 'too' as part of its meaning, some people object to something being referred to as *too simplistic* or *oversimplistic*, and it is best to avoid such uses in serious writing.

simply ADVERB **1** *The table is simply a chipboard circle on a base.* = **just**, only, merely, purely, solely **2** *He's simply wonderful in every respect.* = **totally**, really, completely, absolutely, altogether, wholly, utterly, unreservedly **3** *The book is clearly and simply written.* = **clearly**, straightforwardly, directly, plainly, intelligibly, unaffectedly **4** *He dressed simply and led a quiet family life.* = **plainly**, naturally, modestly, with restraint, unpretentiously, without any elaboration **5** *It was simply the greatest night any of us ever had.* = **without doubt**, surely, certainly, definitely, unquestionably, undeniably, unmistakably, beyond question, beyond a shadow of (a) doubt

simulate VERB = **pretend**, act, feign, affect, assume, put on, reproduce, imitate, sham, fabricate, counterfeit, make believe

simulated ADJECTIVE **1** *He performed a simulated striptease.* = **pretended**, put-on, feigned, assumed, artificial, make-believe, insincere, phoney *or* phony (*informal*) **2** *a necklace of simulated pearls* = **synthetic**, artificial, fake, substitute, mock, imitation, man-made, sham, pseudo (*informal*)

simultaneous ADJECTIVE = **coinciding**, concurrent, contemporary, coincident, synchronous, happening at the same time

simultaneously ADVERB = **at the same time**, together, all together, in concert, in unison, concurrently, in the same breath, in chorus

sin NOUN **1** *Sin can be forgiven, but never condoned.* = **wickedness**, wrong, evil, crime, error, trespass, immorality, transgression, iniquity, sinfulness, unrighteousness, ungodliness **2** *Was it a sin to have believed too much in themselves?* = **crime**, offence, misdemeanour, error, wrongdoing, misdeed, transgression, act of evil, guilt ▶ VERB *They charged him with sinning against God and man.* = **transgress**, offend, lapse, err, trespass (*archaic*), fall from grace, go astray, commit a sin, do wrong

sincere ADJECTIVE = **honest**, genuine, real, true, serious, natural, earnest, frank, open, straightforward, candid, unaffected, no-nonsense, heartfelt, upfront (*informal*), bona fide, wholehearted, dinkum (*Austral. & N.Z. informal*), artless, guileless, unfeigned ■ OPPOSITE: false

sincerely ADVERB = **honestly**, really, truly, genuinely, seriously, earnestly, wholeheartedly, in good faith, in earnest, in all sincerity, from the bottom of your heart

sincerity NOUN = **honesty**, truth, candour, frankness, seriousness, good faith, probity (*formal*), bona fides (*Law*), genuineness, straightforwardness, artlessness, guilelessness, wholeheartedness

sinewy ADJECTIVE = **muscular**, strong, powerful, athletic, robust, wiry, brawny

sinful ADJECTIVE = **wicked**, bad, criminal, guilty, corrupt, immoral, erring, unholy, depraved, iniquitous, ungodly, irreligious, unrighteous, morally wrong ■ OPPOSITE: virtuous

sing VERB **1** *Go on, then, sing us a song!* = **croon**, carol, chant, warble, yodel, pipe, vocalize **2** *Birds were already singing in the garden.* = **trill**, chirp, warble, make melody • **sing out** *'See you,' Jeff sang out.* = **call (out)**, cry (out), shout, yell, holler (*informal*), halloo

> USAGE *Sang* is the past tense of the verb *sing*, as in *she sang sweetly*. *Sung* is the past participle, as in *we have sung our song*, and care should be taken not to use it as if it were a variant form of the past tense.

singe VERB = **burn**, sear, scorch, char

singer NOUN = **vocalist**, divo, diva (*fem.*), crooner, minstrel, soloist, cantor, troubadour, chorister, chanteuse (*fem.*), balladeer, songster *or* songstress

single ADJECTIVE **1** *A single shot rang out.* = **one**, sole, lone, solitary, only, only one, unique, singular **2** *Every single house had been damaged.* = **individual**, particular, separate, distinct **3** *The last I heard she was still single, still out there.* = **unmarried**, free, unattached, unwed **4** *I booked a single room at the hotel.* = **separate**, individual, exclusive, undivided, unshared **5** *single malt whisky* = **simple**, unmixed, unblended, uncompounded • **single something** *or* **someone out** *He singled me out for special attention.* = **pick**, choose, select, separate, distinguish, fix on, set apart, winnow, put on one side, pick on *or* out, flag up

single-handed ADVERB = **unaided**, on your own, by yourself, alone, independently, solo, without help, unassisted, under your own steam

single-minded ADJECTIVE = **determined**, dogged, fixed, dedicated, stubborn, tireless, steadfast, unwavering, unswerving, hellbent (*informal*), undeviating, monomaniacal

singly ADVERB = **one by one**, individually, one at a time, separately, one after the other

singular ADJECTIVE **1** *The pronoun 'you' can be singular or plural.* = **single**, individual **2** *a smile of singular sweetness* = **remarkable**, unique, extraordinary, outstanding, exceptional, rare, notable, eminent, uncommon, conspicuous, prodigious, unparalleled, noteworthy ■ **OPPOSITE:** ordinary **3** *He was without doubt a singular character.* = **unusual**, odd, strange, extraordinary, puzzling, curious, peculiar, eccentric, out-of-the-way, queer, oddball (*informal*), atypical, outré, daggy (*Austral. & N.Z. informal*) ■ **OPPOSITE:** conventional

singularity NOUN = **oddity**, abnormality, eccentricity, peculiarity, strangeness, idiosyncrasy, irregularity, particularity, oddness, queerness, extraordinariness, curiousness

singularly ADVERB = **remarkably**, particularly, exceptionally, especially, seriously (*informal*), surprisingly, notably, unusually, extraordinarily, conspicuously, outstandingly, uncommonly, prodigiously

sinister ADJECTIVE = **threatening**, evil, menacing, forbidding, dire, ominous, malign, disquieting, malignant, malevolent, baleful, injurious, bodeful ■ **OPPOSITE:** reassuring

sink NOUN *The sink was full of dirty dishes.* = **basin**, washbasin, hand basin, wash-hand basin ▶ VERB **1** *In a naval battle your aim is to sink the enemy's ship.* = **scupper**, scuttle **2** *The boat was beginning to sink fast.* = **go down**, founder, go under, submerge, capsize **3** *Kate laughed, and sank down again to her seat.* = **slump**, drop, flop, collapse, droop **4** *Pay increases have sunk to around seven per cent.* = **fall**, drop, decline, slip, plunge, plummet, subside, relapse, abate, retrogress **5** *Her voice had sunk to a whisper.* = **drop**, fall **6** *You know who you are, be proud of it and don't sink to his level.* = **stoop**, descend, be reduced to, succumb, lower yourself, debase yourself, demean yourself **7** *He's still alive, but sinking fast.* = **decline**, die, fade, fail, flag, weaken, diminish, decrease, deteriorate, decay, worsen, dwindle, lessen, degenerate, depreciate, go downhill (*informal*) ■ **OPPOSITE:** improve **8** *the site where Stephenson sank his first mineshaft* = **dig**, bore, drill, drive, lay, put down, excavate

sinner NOUN = **wrongdoer**, offender, evildoer, trespasser (*archaic*), reprobate, miscreant, malefactor, transgressor

sinuous ADJECTIVE = **curving**, winding, meandering, crooked, coiling, tortuous, undulating, serpentine, curvy, lithe, twisty, mazy

sip VERB *Jessica sipped her drink thoughtfully.* = **drink**, taste, sample, sup ▶ NOUN *Tariq took a sip of water.* = **swallow**, mouthful, swig, drop, taste, thimbleful

siren NOUN **1** *It sounds like an air raid siren.* = **alert**, warning, signal, alarm **2** *famous screen sirens such as Rita Hayworth* = **seductress**, vamp (*informal*), femme fatale (*French*), witch, charmer, temptress, Lorelei, Circe

sissy or **cissy** NOUN *They were rough kids and thought we were sissies.* = **wimp** (*informal*), softie (*informal*), weakling, baby, wet (*Brit. informal*), coward (*informal*), jessie (*Scot. slang*), mummy's boy, mollycoddle, namby-pamby, wuss (*slang*), milksop, milquetoast (*U.S.*), sisspot (*informal*) ▶ ADJECTIVE *Far from being sissy, it takes a real man to admit he's not perfect.* = **wimpish** or **wimpy** (*informal*), soft (*informal*), weak, wet (*Brit. informal*), cowardly, feeble, namby-pamby, wussy (*slang*)

sit VERB **1** *Eva pulled up a chair and sat beside her husband.* = **take a seat**, perch, settle down, be seated, take the weight off your feet **2** *She found her chair and sat it in the usual spot.* = **place**, set, put, position, rest, lay, settle, deposit, situate **3** *He was asked to sit on numerous committees.* = **be a member of**, serve on, have a seat on, preside on **4** *Parliament sits for only 28 weeks out of 52.* = **convene**, meet, assemble, officiate, be in session

site NOUN **1** *He became a hod carrier on a building site.* = **area**, ground, plot, patch, tract **2** *the site of Moses' tomb* = **location**, place, setting, point, position, situation, spot, whereabouts, locus ▶ VERB *He said chemical weapons had never been sited in Germany.* = **locate**, put, place, set, position, establish, install, situate

sitting NOUN **1** *Dinner was in two sittings.* = **session**, period **2** *the recent emergency sittings* = **meeting**, hearing, session, congress, consultation, get-together (*informal*)

situation NOUN **1** *We are in a difficult financial situation.* = **position**, state, case, condition, circumstances, equation, plight, status quo, state of affairs, ball game (*informal*), kettle of fish (*informal*) **2** *They looked at each other and weighed up the situation.* = **scenario**, the picture (*informal*), the score (*informal*), state of affairs, lie of the land **3** *The garden is in a beautiful situation.* = **location**, place, setting, position, seat, site, spot, locality, locale

S

USAGE It is common to hear the word *situation* used in sentences such as *the company is in a crisis situation*. This use of *situation* is considered bad style and the word should be left out, since it adds nothing to the sentence's meaning.

sixth sense NOUN = **intuition**, second sight, clairvoyance

size NOUN *books of various sizes* = **dimensions**, extent, measurement(s), range, amount, mass, length, volume, capacity, proportions, bulk, width, magnitude, greatness, vastness, immensity, bigness, largeness, hugeness • **size something** or **someone up** *He spent the evening sizing me up intellectually.* = **assess**, evaluate, appraise, take stock of, eye up, get the measure of, get (something) taped (*Brit. informal*)

sizeable or **sizable** ADJECTIVE = **large**, considerable, substantial, goodly, decent, respectable, tidy (*informal*), decent-sized, largish

sizzle VERB = **hiss**, spit, crackle, sputter, fry, frizzle

skeletal ADJECTIVE = **emaciated**, wasted, gaunt, skin-and-bone (*informal*), cadaverous, hollow-cheeked, lantern-jawed, fleshless, worn to a shadow

skeleton NOUN **1** *a human skeleton* = **bones**, bare bones **2** *Only skeletons of buildings remained in the area.* = **frame**, shell, framework, basic structure **3** *a skeleton of policy guidelines* = **plan**, structure, frame, draft, outline, framework, sketch, abstract, blueprint, main points ▶ MODIFIER *Only a skeleton staff remains to see anyone interested around the site.* = **minimum**, reduced, minimal, essential

sketch NOUN **1** *a sketch of a soldier* = **drawing**, design, draft, delineation **2** *I had a basic sketch of a plan.* = **draft**, outline, framework, plan, frame, rough, skeleton, layout, lineament(s) **3** *a five-minute humorous sketch* = **skit**, piece, scene, turn, act, performance, item, routine (*informal*), number ▶ VERB *I sketched the scene with my pen and paper.* = **draw**, paint, outline, represent, draft, portray, depict, delineate, rough out

sketchy ADJECTIVE = **incomplete**, rough, vague, slight, outline, inadequate, crude, superficial, unfinished, skimpy, scrappy, cursory, perfunctory, cobbled together, bitty ■ **OPPOSITE:** complete

skid VERB = **slide**, slip, slither, coast, glide, skim, veer, toboggan

skilful ADJECTIVE = **expert**, deft, skilled, masterly, trained, experienced, able, professional, quick, clever, practised, accomplished, handy, competent, apt, adept, proficient, adroit, dexterous ■ **OPPOSITE:** clumsy

skill NOUN = **expertise**, ability, proficiency, experience, art, technique, facility, talent, intelligence, craft, competence, readiness, accomplishment, knack, ingenuity, finesse, aptitude, dexterity, cleverness, quickness, adroitness, expertness, handiness, skilfulness ■ **OPPOSITE:** clumsiness

skilled ADJECTIVE = **expert**, professional, accomplished, trained, experienced, able, masterly, practised, skilful, proficient, a dab hand at (*Brit. informal*) ■ **OPPOSITE:** unskilled

skim VERB **1** *Skim off the fat.* = **remove**, separate, cream, take off **2** *seagulls skimming over the waves* = **glide**, fly, coast, sail, float, brush, dart **3** (*usually with* **over** or **through**) *I only had time to skim over the script before I came here.* = **scan**, glance, run your eye over, thumb or leaf through

skimp VERB = **stint**, scrimp, be sparing with, pinch, withhold, scant, cut corners, scamp, be mean with, be niggardly, tighten your belt ■ **OPPOSITE:** be extravagant

skimpy ADJECTIVE = **inadequate**, insufficient, scant, meagre, short, tight, thin, sparse, scanty, miserly, niggardly, exiguous (*formal*)

skin NOUN **1** *His skin is clear and smooth.* = **complexion**, colouring, skin tone **2** *That was real crocodile skin.* = **hide**, fleece, pelt, fell, integument, tegument **3** *banana skins* = **peel**, rind, husk, casing, outside, crust **4** *Stir the custard occasionally to prevent a skin forming.* = **film**, coating, coat, membrane ▶ VERB **1** *two tomatoes, skinned, peeled and chopped* = **peel**, pare, hull **2** *He fell down and skinned his knee.* = **scrape**, graze, bark, flay, excoriate, abrade • **by the skin of one's teeth** *He won, but only by the skin of his teeth.* = **narrowly**, only just, by a whisker (*informal*), by a narrow margin, by a hair's-breadth • **get under your skin** *Her mannerisms can just get under your skin and needle you.* = **annoy**, irritate, aggravate (*informal*), needle (*informal*), nettle, irk, grate on, get on your nerves (*informal*), get in your hair (*informal*), rub you up the wrong way, hack you off (*informal*)

skin-deep ADJECTIVE = **superficial**, surface, external, artificial, shallow, on the surface, meaningless

skinny ADJECTIVE = **thin**, lean, scrawny, skeletal, emaciated, twiggy, undernourished, skin-and-bone (*informal*), scraggy ■ **OPPOSITE:** fat

skip VERB **1** *She was skipping along the pavement.* = **hop**, dance, bob, trip, bounce, caper, prance, cavort, frisk, gambol **2** *It is important not to skip meals.* = **miss out**, omit, leave out, overlook, pass over, eschew, forgo, skim over, give (something) a miss **3** *Her daughter started skipping school.* = **miss**, cut (*informal*), bunk off (*slang*), play truant from, wag (*dialect*), dog it or dog off (*dialect*)

skirmish NOUN *Border skirmishes are common.* = **fight**, battle, conflict, incident, clash, contest, set-to (*informal*), encounter, brush, combat, scrap (*informal*), engagement, spat, tussle, fracas, affray (*Law*), dust-up (*informal*), scrimmage, biffo (*Austral. slang*), boilover (*Austral.*) ▶ VERB *Police skirmished with youths on a council estate last Friday.* = **fight**, clash, come to blows, scrap (*informal*), collide, grapple, wrangle, tussle, lock horns, cross swords

skirt VERB **1** *We raced across a large field that skirted the slope of the hill.* = **border**, edge, lie alongside, line, fringe, flank **2** (*often with* **around** *or* **round**) *She skirted around the edge of the room to the door.* = **go round**, bypass, walk round, circumvent **3** (*often with* **around** *or* **round**) *They have, until now, skirted around the issue.* = **avoid**, evade, steer clear of, sidestep, circumvent (*formal*), detour, body-swerve ▶ NOUN (*often plural*) *the skirts of the hill* = **border**, edge, margin, fringe, outskirts, rim, hem, periphery, purlieus

skit NOUN = **parody**, spoof (*informal*), travesty, takeoff (*informal*), burlesque, turn, sketch

skittish ADJECTIVE = **nervous**, lively, excitable, jumpy, restive, fidgety, highly strung, antsy (*informal*) ■ **OPPOSITE**: calm

skookum ADJECTIVE (*Canad.*) = **powerful**, influential, big, dominant, controlling, commanding, supreme, prevailing, sovereign, authoritative, puissant

skulduggery NOUN = **trickery**, swindling, machinations, duplicity, double-dealing, fraudulence, shenanigan(s) (*informal*), unscrupulousness, underhandedness

skulk VERB **1** *He skulked off.* = **creep**, sneak, slink, pad, prowl **2** *skulking in the safety of the car* = **lurk**, hide, lie in wait, loiter

sky NOUN = **heavens**, firmament, upper atmosphere, azure (*poetic*), welkin (*archaic*), vault of heaven, rangi (*N.Z.*) ■ **RELATED WORD:** *adjective* celestial

slab NOUN = **piece**, slice, lump, chunk, wedge, hunk, portion, nugget, wodge (*Brit. informal*)

slack ADJECTIVE **1** *The electronic pads work slack muscles to astounding effect.* = **limp**, relaxed, loose, lax, flaccid, not taut **2** *The wind had* gone, leaving the sails slack. = **loose**, hanging, flapping, baggy ■ **OPPOSITE**: taut **3** *busy times and slack periods* = **slow**, quiet, inactive, dull, sluggish, slow-moving ■ **OPPOSITE**: busy **4** *Many publishers have simply become far too slack.* = **negligent**, lazy, lax, idle, easy-going, inactive, tardy, slapdash, neglectful, slipshod, inattentive, remiss (*formal*), asleep on the job (*informal*) ■ **OPPOSITE**: strict ▶ NOUN **1** *Buying-to-let could stimulate the housing market by reducing the slack.* = **surplus**, excess, overflow, leftover, glut, surfeit, overabundance, superabundance, superfluity **2** *He cranked in the slack, and the ship was moored.* = **room**, excess, leeway, give (*informal*), play, looseness ▶ VERB *He had never let a foreman see him slacking.* = **shirk**, idle, relax, flag, neglect, dodge, skive (*Brit. slang*), bob off (*Brit. slang*), bludge (*Austral. & N.Z. informal*)

slacken VERB (*often with* **off**) = **lessen**, reduce, decrease, ease (off), moderate, diminish, slow down, drop off, abate, let up, slack off

slacker NOUN = **layabout**, shirker, loafer, skiver (*Brit. slang*), idler, passenger, do-nothing, piker (*Austral. & N.Z. slang*), dodger, good-for-nothing, bludger (*Austral. & N.Z. informal*), gold brick (*U.S. slang*), scrimshanker (*Brit. Military slang*)

slag • **slag something** *or* **someone off** *People keep slagging me off.* = **criticize**, abuse, malign, slam (*slang*), insult, mock, slate (*Brit. informal*), slang, throw shade (at) (*slang*), deride, berate, slander, diss (*slang*), lambast(e), flame (*informal*)

slam VERB **1** *She slammed the door and locked it behind her.* = **bang**, crash, smash, thump, shut with a bang, shut noisily **2** *They slammed him up against a wall.* = **throw**, dash, hurl, fling **3** *The director slammed the claims as an outrageous lie.* = **criticize**, attack, blast, pan (*informal*), damn, slate (*informal*), shoot down (*informal*), castigate, vilify, pillory, tear into (*informal*), diss (*slang*), lambast(e), excoriate (*literary*)

slander NOUN *He is now suing the company for slander.* = **defamation**, smear, libel, scandal, misrepresentation, calumny, backbiting, muckraking, obloquy, aspersion, detraction ■ **OPPOSITE**: praise ▶ VERB *He has been questioned on suspicion of slandering the politician.* = **defame**, smear, libel, slur, malign, detract, disparage, decry, vilify, traduce (*formal*), backbite, blacken (someone's) name, calumniate, muckrake ■ **OPPOSITE**: praise

slang NOUN = **colloquialisms**, jargon, idioms, argot, informal language

slant VERB 1 *The morning sun slanted through the glass roof.* = **slope**, incline, tilt, list, bend, lean, heel, shelve, skew, cant, bevel, angle off 2 *The coverage was deliberately slanted to make the home team look good.* = **bias**, colour, weight, twist, angle, distort ▶ NOUN 1 *The house is on a slant.* = **slope**, incline, tilt, gradient, pitch, ramp, diagonal, camber, declination 2 *They give a slant to every single news item that's put on the air.* = **bias**, emphasis, prejudice, angle, leaning, point of view, viewpoint, one-sidedness

slanting ADJECTIVE = **sloping**, angled, inclined, tilted, tilting, sideways, slanted, bent, diagonal, oblique, at an angle, canted, on the bias, aslant, slantwise, atilt, cater-cornered (*U.S. informal*)

slap VERB 1 *My yoga instructor turned up and slapped me on the shoulder.* = **smack**, hit, strike, beat, bang, clap, clout (*informal*), cuff, whack, swipe (*informal*), spank, clobber (*slang*), wallop (*informal*), lay one on (*slang*) 2 *We now routinely slap sunscreen on ourselves before venturing out.* = **plaster**, apply, spread, daub ▶ NOUN *He reached forward and gave me a slap.* = **smack**, blow, whack, wallop (*informal*), bang, clout (*informal*), cuff, swipe (*informal*), spank
• **a slap in the face** *They treated any pay rise of less than 5% as a slap in the face.* = **insult**, humiliation, snub, affront, blow, rejection, put-down, rebuke, rebuff, repulse

slapstick NOUN = **farce**, horseplay, buffoonery, knockabout comedy

slap-up ADJECTIVE = **luxurious**, lavish, sumptuous, princely, excellent, superb, magnificent, elaborate, splendid, first-rate, no-expense-spared, fit for a king

slash VERB 1 *He nearly bled to death after slashing his wrists.* = **cut**, slit, gash, lacerate, score, rend (*literary*), rip, hack 2 *Everyone agrees that subsidies have to be slashed.* = **reduce**, cut, decrease, drop, lower, moderate, diminish, cut down, lessen, curtail ▶ NOUN *deep slashes in the meat* = **cut**, slit, gash, rent, rip, incision, laceration

slate VERB = **criticize**, blast, pan (*informal*), slam (*slang*), blame, roast (*informal*), censure, rebuke, slang, scold, berate, castigate, rail against, tear into (*informal*), lay into (*informal*), pitch into (*informal*), take to task, lambast(e), flame (*informal*), excoriate, haul over the coals (*informal*), tear (someone) off a strip (*informal*), rap (someone's) knuckles

slaughter VERB 1 *Thirty-four people were slaughtered while queueing up to cast their votes.* = **kill** (*informal*), murder, massacre, destroy, do in (*slang*), execute, dispatch, assassinate, blow away (*slang, chiefly U.S.*), annihilate, bump off (*slang*) 2 *Whales and dolphins are still being slaughtered for commercial gain.* = **butcher**, kill, slay (*archaic, literary*), destroy, massacre, exterminate 3 *He slaughtered his opponent in three sets.* = **defeat**, thrash, vanquish (*literary*), stuff (*slang*), tank (*slang*), hammer (*informal*), crush, overwhelm, lick (*informal*), undo, rout, trounce, wipe the floor with (*informal*), blow out of the water (*slang*) ▶ NOUN *The annual slaughter of wildlife is horrific.* = **slaying**, killing, murder, massacre, holocaust, bloodshed, carnage, liquidation, extermination, butchery, blood bath

slaughterhouse NOUN = **abattoir**, butchery, shambles

slave NOUN 1 *still living as slaves in the desert* = **servant**, serf, vassal, bondsman, slavey (*Brit. informal*), varlet (*archaic*), villein, bondservant 2 *wage slaves stuck in offices* = **drudge**, skivvy (*chiefly Brit.*), scullion (*archaic*) ▶ VERB *slaving over a hot stove* = **toil**, labour, grind (*informal*), drudge, sweat, graft, slog, skivvy (*Brit.*), work your fingers to the bone

slaver VERB = **dribble**, drool, salivate, slobber

slavery NOUN = **enslavement**, servitude, subjugation, captivity, bondage, thrall, serfdom, vassalage, thraldom
■ **OPPOSITE:** freedom

slavish ADJECTIVE 1 *a slavish follower of fashion* = **imitative**, unimaginative, unoriginal, conventional, second-hand, uninspired
■ **OPPOSITE:** original 2 *slavish devotion* = **servile**, cringing, abject, submissive, grovelling, mean, low, base, fawning, despicable, menial, sycophantic, obsequious ■ **OPPOSITE:** rebellious

slay VERB 1 *the hill where he slew the dragon* = **kill** (*informal*), destroy, slaughter, eliminate, massacre, butcher, dispatch, annihilate, exterminate 2 *Two Australian tourists were slain.* = **murder**, kill, assassinate, do in (*slang*), eliminate, massacre, slaughter, do away with, exterminate, mow down, rub out (*U.S. slang*)

sleaze NOUN = **corruption**, fraud, dishonesty, fiddling (*informal*), bribery, extortion, venality, shady dealings (*informal*), crookedness (*informal*), unscrupulousness

sleazy ADJECTIVE = **squalid**, seedy, sordid, low, rundown, tacky (*informal*), disreputable, crummy (*slang*), scungy (*Austral. & N.Z.*)

sleek ADJECTIVE = **glossy**, shiny, lustrous, smooth, silky, velvety, well-groomed ■ OPPOSITE: shaggy

sleep NOUN *Try and get some sleep.* = **slumber(s)**, rest, nap, doze, kip (*Brit. slang*), snooze (*informal*), repose, hibernation, siesta, dormancy, beauty sleep (*informal*), forty winks (*informal*), shuteye (*slang*), zizz (*Brit. informal*) ▶ VERB *I've not been able to sleep for the last few nights.* = **slumber**, drop off (*informal*), doze, kip (*Brit. slang*), snooze (*informal*), snore, hibernate, nod off (*informal*), take a nap, catnap, drowse, go out like a light, take forty winks (*informal*), zizz (*Brit. informal*), be in the land of Nod, rest in the arms of Morpheus

sleepless ADJECTIVE 1 *I have sleepless nights worrying about her.* = **wakeful**, disturbed, restless, insomniac, unsleeping 2 *his sleepless vigilance* = **alert**, vigilant, watchful, wide awake, unsleeping

sleepwalking NOUN = **somnambulism**, noctambulation, noctambulism, somnambulation

sleepy ADJECTIVE 1 *I was beginning to feel amazingly sleepy.* = **drowsy**, sluggish, lethargic, heavy, dull, inactive, somnolent, torpid ■ OPPOSITE: wide-awake 2 *How long we spent there in that sleepy heat, I don't know.* = **soporific**, hypnotic, somnolent, sleep-inducing, slumberous 3 *a sleepy little town* = **quiet**, peaceful, dull, tranquil, inactive ■ OPPOSITE: busy

slender ADJECTIVE 1 *He gazed at her slender neck.* = **slim**, narrow, slight, lean, svelte, willowy, sylphlike ■ OPPOSITE: chubby 2 *the first slender hope of peace* = **faint**, slight, remote, slim, thin, weak, fragile, feeble, flimsy, tenuous ■ OPPOSITE: strong 3 *the Government's slender 21-seat majority* = **meagre**, little, small, inadequate, insufficient, scant, scanty, inconsiderable ■ OPPOSITE: large

sleuth NOUN = **detective**, private eye (*informal*), (private) investigator, tail (*informal*), dick (*slang, chiefly U.S.*), gumshoe (*U.S. slang*), sleuthhound (*informal*)

slice NOUN *water flavoured with a slice of lemon* = **piece**, segment, portion, wedge, sliver, helping, share, cut (*informal*) ▶ VERB *She sliced the cake.* = **cut**, divide, carve, segment, sever, dissect, cleave

slick ADJECTIVE 1 *His style is slick and visually exciting.* = **efficient**, professional, smart, smooth, streamlined, masterly, sharp, deft, well-organized, adroit 2 *a slick change* = **skilful**, deft, adroit, dextrous, dexterous, professional, polished ■ OPPOSITE: clumsy

3 *a slick, suit-wearing detective* = **glib**, smooth, sophisticated, plausible, polished, specious, meretricious ▶ VERB *She had slicked her hair.* = **smooth**, oil, grease, sleek, plaster down, make glossy, smarm down (*Brit. informal*)

slide VERB *She slipped and slid downhill on her backside.* = **slip**, slither, glide, skim, coast, toboggan, glissade • **let something slide** *The company had let environmental standards slide.* = **neglect**, forget, ignore, pass over, turn a blind eye to, gloss over, push to the back of your mind, let ride

slight ADJECTIVE 1 *It's only made a slight difference.* = **small**, minor, insignificant, negligible, weak, modest, trivial, superficial, feeble, trifling, meagre, unimportant, paltry, measly (*informal*), insubstantial, scanty, inconsiderable ■ OPPOSITE: large 2 *a man of slight build* = **slim**, small, delicate, spare, fragile, lightly-built ■ OPPOSITE: sturdy ▶ VERB *They felt slighted by not being adequately consulted.* = **snub**, insult, ignore, rebuff, affront, neglect, put down, despise, scorn, disdain, disparage, cold-shoulder, treat with contempt, show disrespect for, give offence or umbrage to ■ OPPOSITE: compliment ▶ NOUN *a child weeping over an imagined slight* = **insult**, snub, affront, contempt, disregard, indifference, disdain, rebuff, disrespect, slap in the face (*informal*), inattention, discourtesy, (the) cold shoulder ■ OPPOSITE: compliment

slightly ADVERB = **a little**, a bit, somewhat, moderately, marginally, a shade, to some degree, on a small scale, to some extent or degree

slim ADJECTIVE 1 *She is pretty, of slim build, with blue eyes.* = **slender**, slight, trim, thin, narrow, lean, svelte, willowy, sylphlike ■ OPPOSITE: chubby 2 *a slim chance* = **slight**, remote, faint, distant, slender ■ OPPOSITE: strong ▶ VERB *Some people will gain weight no matter how hard they try to slim.* = **lose weight**, diet, get thinner, get into shape, slenderize (*chiefly U.S.*) ■ OPPOSITE: put on weight

slimy ADJECTIVE 1 *Her hand touched something cold and slimy.* = **viscous**, clammy, glutinous, muddy, mucous, gloopy (*informal*), oozy, miry 2 *his slimy business partner* = **obsequious**, creepy, unctuous, smarmy (*Brit. informal*), oily, grovelling, soapy (*slang*), sycophantic, servile, toadying

sling VERB 1 *She slung her coat over the desk chair.* = **throw**, cast, toss, hurl, fling, chuck (*informal*), lob (*informal*), heave, shy

2 *We slept in hammocks slung beneath the roof.* = **hang**, swing, suspend, string, drape, dangle ▶ NOUN *She was back at work with her arm in a sling.* = **harness**, support, bandage, strap

slink VERB = **creep**, steal, sneak, slip, prowl, skulk, pussyfoot (*informal*)

slinky ADJECTIVE = **figure-hugging**, clinging, sleek, close-fitting, skintight

slip¹ VERB **1** *Be careful not to slip.* = **fall**, trip (over), slide, skid, lose your balance, miss *or* lose your footing **2** *The hammer slipped out of her grasp.* = **slide**, fall, drop, slither **3** *She slipped downstairs and out of the house.* = **sneak**, creep, steal, insinuate yourself ▶ NOUN *There must be no slips.* = **mistake**, failure, error, blunder, lapse, omission, boob (*Brit. slang*), oversight, slip-up (*informal*), indiscretion, bloomer (*Brit. informal*), faux pas, slip of the tongue, imprudence, barry *or* Barry Crocker (*Austral. slang*) • **give someone the slip** *He gave reporters the slip by leaving by the back door at midnight.* = **escape from**, get away from, evade, shake (someone) off, elude, lose (someone), flee, dodge, outwit, slip through someone's fingers • **let something slip** *I bet he'd let slip that I'd gone to America.* = **give away**, reveal, disclose, divulge, leak, come out with (*informal*), let out (*informal*), blurt out, let the cat out of the bag • **slip away** *He slipped away in the early hours to exile in France.* = **get away**, escape, disappear, break away, break free, get clear of, take French leave • **slip up** *You will see exactly where you are slipping up.* = **make a mistake**, go wrong, blunder, mistake, boob (*Brit. slang*), err, misjudge, miscalculate, drop a brick *or* clanger (*informal*)

slip² NOUN *little slips of paper* = **strip**, piece, sliver

slippery ADJECTIVE **1** *The floor was wet and slippery.* = **smooth**, icy, greasy, glassy, slippy (*informal, dialect*), unsafe, lubricious (*rare*), skiddy (*informal*) **2** *a slippery customer* = **untrustworthy**, tricky, cunning, false, treacherous, dishonest, devious, crafty, evasive, sneaky, two-faced, shifty (*informal*), foxy, duplicitous

slit VERB *They say somebody slit her throat.* = **cut (open)**, rip, slash, knife, pierce, lance, gash, split open ▶ NOUN **1** *Make a slit in the stem.* = **cut**, gash, incision, tear, rent, fissure **2** *She watched them through a slit in the curtain.* = **opening**, split, crack, aperture, chink, space

slither VERB = **slide**, slip, glide, snake, undulate, slink, skitter

sliver NOUN = **shred**, fragment, splinter, slip, shaving, flake, paring

slob NOUN = **layabout**, lounger, loafer, couch potato (*slang*), idler, good-for-nothing

slog VERB **1** *While slogging at your work, have you neglected your marriage?* = **work**, labour, toil, slave, plod, persevere, plough through, sweat blood (*informal*), apply yourself to, work your fingers to the bone, peg away at, keep your nose to the grindstone **2** *The men had to slog up a muddy incline.* = **trudge**, tramp, plod, trek, hike, traipse (*informal*), yomp, walk heavily, footslog ▶ NOUN **1** *There is little to show for two years of hard slog.* = **work**, labour, toil, industry, grind (*informal*), effort, struggle, pains, sweat (*informal*), painstaking, exertion, donkey-work, blood, sweat, and tears (*informal*) **2** *a slog through heather and bracken* = **trudge**, tramp, trek, hike, traipse (*informal*), yomp, footslog

slogan NOUN = **catch phrase**, motto, jingle, rallying cry, tag-line, catchword, catchcry (*Austral.*)

slop VERB = **spill**, splash, overflow, splatter, spatter, slosh (*informal*)

slope NOUN *a mountain slope* = **inclination**, rise, incline, tilt, descent, downgrade (*chiefly U.S.*), slant, ramp, gradient, camber, brae (*Scot.*), scarp, declination, declivity ▶ VERB *The garden sloped quite steeply.* = **slant**, incline, drop away, fall, rise, pitch, lean, tilt • **slope off** *She sloped off quietly on Saturday afternoon.* = **slink away**, slip away, steal away, skulk, creep away, make yourself scarce

sloping ADJECTIVE = **slanting**, leaning, inclined, inclining, oblique, atilt

sloppy ADJECTIVE **1** *I won't accept sloppy work from my students.* = **careless**, slovenly, slipshod, messy, clumsy, untidy, amateurish, hit-or-miss (*informal*), inattentive **2** *some sloppy love-story* = **sentimental**, mushy (*informal*), soppy (*Brit. informal*), slushy (*informal*), wet (*Brit. informal*), gushing, banal, trite, mawkish, icky (*informal*), overemotional, three-hankie (*informal*) **3** *sloppy foods* = **wet**, watery, slushy, splashy, sludgy

slosh VERB **1** *The water sloshed around the bridge.* = **splash**, wash, slop, break, plash **2** *We sloshed through the mud together.* = **wade**, splash, flounder, paddle, dabble, wallow, swash

slot NOUN **1** *He dropped a coin in the slot and dialled.* = **opening**, hole, groove, vent, slit, aperture, channel **2** *Visitors can book a time slot a week or more in advance.* = **place**, time, space, spot, opening, position, window, vacancy, niche ▶ VERB *She slotted a fresh filter into the machine.* = **fit**, slide, insert, put, place

sloth NOUN = **laziness**, inactivity, idleness, inertia, torpor, sluggishness, slackness, indolence

slouch VERB = **lounge**, slump, flop, sprawl, stoop, droop, loll, lean

slouching ADJECTIVE = **shambling**, lumbering, ungainly, awkward, uncouth, loutish

slow ADJECTIVE **1** *He moved in a slow, unhurried way.* = **unhurried**, sluggish, leisurely, easy, measured, creeping, deliberate, lagging, lazy, plodding, slow-moving, loitering, ponderous, leaden, dawdling, laggard, lackadaisical, tortoise-like, sluggardly ■ **OPPOSITE:** quick **2** *The distribution of passports has been a slow process.* = **prolonged**, time-consuming, protracted, long-drawn-out, lingering, gradual **3** *He was not slow to take up the offer.* = **unwilling**, reluctant, loath, averse, hesitant, disinclined, indisposed **4** *My watch is slow.* = **late**, unpunctual, behindhand, behind, tardy **5** *Island life is too slow for her liking.* = **dull**, quiet, boring, dead, tame, slack, sleepy, sluggish, tedious, stagnant, unproductive, inactive, one-horse (*informal*), uneventful, uninteresting, wearisome, dead-and-alive (*Brit.*), unprogressive ■ **OPPOSITE:** exciting ▶ VERB **1** (*often with* **down**) *The car slowed down as they passed customs.* = **decelerate**, brake, lag **2** (*often with* **down**) *Damage to the turbine slowed the work down.* = **delay**, hold up, hinder, check, restrict, handicap, detain, curb, retard, rein in ■ **OPPOSITE:** speed up

slowly ADVERB = **gradually**, steadily, by degrees, unhurriedly, taking your time, at your leisure, at a snail's pace, in your own (good) time, ploddingly, inchmeal ■ **OPPOSITE:** quickly

sludge NOUN = **sediment**, ooze, silt, mud, muck, residue, slop, mire, slime, slush, slob (*Irish*), dregs, gloop (*informal*)

sluggish ADJECTIVE = **inactive**, slow, lethargic, listless, heavy, dull, lifeless, inert, slow-moving, unresponsive, phlegmatic, indolent, torpid, slothful (*formal*) ■ **OPPOSITE:** energetic

sluice VERB = **drain**, cleanse, flush, drench, wash out, wash down

slum NOUN = **hovel**, ghetto, shanty

slumber NOUN *He had fallen into exhausted slumber.* = **sleep**, nap, doze, rest, kip (*Brit. informal*), snooze (*informal*), siesta, catnap, forty winks (*informal*) ▶ VERB *The older three girls are still slumbering peacefully.* = **sleep**, nap, doze, kip (*Brit. slang*), snooze (*informal*), lie dormant, drowse, zizz (*Brit. informal*)

slump VERB **1** *Net profits slumped.* = **fall**, decline, sink, plunge, crash, collapse, slip, deteriorate, fall off, plummet, go downhill (*informal*) ■ **OPPOSITE:** increase **2** *I closed the door and slumped into a chair.* = **sag**, bend, hunch, droop, slouch, loll ▶ NOUN **1** *a slump in property prices* = **fall**, drop, decline, crash, collapse, reverse, lapse, falling-off, downturn, depreciation, trough, meltdown (*informal*) ■ **OPPOSITE:** increase **2** *Even in the slump, some jobs were being created.* = **recession**, depression, stagnation, inactivity, hard or bad times

slur NOUN *yet another slur on the integrity of the police* = **insult**, stain, smear, stigma, disgrace, discredit, blot, affront, innuendo, calumny, insinuation, aspersion ▶ VERB *He repeated himself and slurred his words more than usual.* = **mumble**, stammer, stutter, stumble over, falter, mispronounce, garble, speak unclearly

sly ADJECTIVE **1** *His lips were spread in a sly smile.* = **roguish**, knowing, arch, mischievous, impish **2** *She is devious, sly and manipulative.* = **cunning**, scheming, devious, secret, clever, subtle, tricky, covert, astute, wily, insidious, crafty, artful, furtive, conniving, Machiavellian, shifty (*informal*), foxy, underhand, stealthy, guileful ■ **OPPOSITE:** open **3** *They were giving each other sly looks across the room.* = **secret**, furtive, surreptitious, stealthy, sneaking, covert, clandestine • **on the sly** *Was she meeting some guy on the sly?* = **secretly**, privately, covertly, surreptitiously, under the counter (*informal*), on the quiet, behind (someone's) back, like a thief in the night, underhandedly, on the q.t. (*informal*)

smack VERB **1** *She smacked me on the side of the head.* = **slap**, hit, strike, pat, tap, sock (*slang*), clap, cuff, swipe (*informal*), box, spank **2** *He smacked the ball against the post.* = **drive**, hit, strike, thrust, impel ▶ NOUN *I end up shouting at him or giving him a smack.* = **slap**, blow, whack, clout (*informal*), cuff, crack (*informal*), swipe (*informal*), spank, wallop (*informal*) ▶ ADVERB *smack in the middle of the city* = **directly**, right, straight, squarely, precisely, exactly, slap (*informal*), plumb, point-blank • **smack of something** *His comments smacked of racism.* = **be suggestive** or **indicative of**, suggest, smell of, testify to, reek of, have all the hallmarks of, betoken, be redolent of, bear the stamp of

S

small ADJECTIVE **1** *She is small for her age.*
= **little**, minute, tiny, slight, mini,
miniature, minuscule, diminutive, petite,
teeny (*informal*), puny, pint-sized (*informal*),
pocket-sized, undersized, teeny-weeny,
Lilliputian, teensy-weensy, pygmy or pigmy
■ **OPPOSITE:** big **2** *a small select group of
friends* = **intimate**, close, private **3** *What
were you like when you were small?* = **young**,
little, growing up, junior, wee, juvenile,
youthful, immature, unfledged, in the
springtime of life **4** *No detail was too small to
escape her attention.* = **unimportant**, minor,
trivial, insignificant, little, lesser, petty,
trifling, negligible, paltry, piddling (*informal*)
■ **OPPOSITE:** important **5** *shops, restaurants
and other small businesses* = **modest**,
small-scale, humble, unpretentious
■ **OPPOSITE:** grand **6** *a very small voice* = **soft**,
low, inaudible, low-pitched, noiseless
7 *a diet of one small meal a day* = **meagre**,
inadequate, insufficient, scant, measly
(*informal*), scanty, limited, inconsiderable
■ **OPPOSITE:** ample

small-minded ADJECTIVE = **petty**, mean,
rigid, grudging, envious, bigoted,
intolerant, narrow-minded, hidebound,
ungenerous ■ **OPPOSITE:** broad-minded

small-time ADJECTIVE = **minor**,
insignificant, unimportant, petty,
no-account (*U.S. informal*), piddling
(*informal*), of no consequence, of no
account

smart ADJECTIVE **1** *I was dressed in a smart
navy-blue suit.* = **chic**, trim, neat,
fashionable, stylish, fine, elegant, trendy
(*Brit. informal*), spruce, snappy, natty
(*informal*), modish, well turned-out,
schmick (*Austral. informal*) ■ **OPPOSITE:**
scruffy **2** *He thinks he's much smarter than
Sarah.* = **clever**, bright (*informal*),
intelligent, quick, sharp, keen, acute,
shrewd, apt, ingenious, astute, canny,
quick-witted **3** *smart dinner parties*
= **fashionable**, stylish, chic, genteel, in
vogue, voguish (*informal*) **4** *We set off at a
smart pace.* = **brisk**, quick, lively, vigorous,
spirited, cracking (*informal*), spanking,
jaunty ▶ VERB *My eyes smarted from the
smoke.* = **sting**, burn, tingle, pain, hurt,
throb

smarten VERB (*often with* **up**) = **tidy**, spruce
up, groom, beautify, put in order, put to
rights, gussy up (*slang, chiefly U.S.*)

smash VERB **1** *A crowd of youths started
smashing windows.* = **break**, crush, shatter,
crack, demolish, shiver, disintegrate,
pulverize, crush to smithereens **2** *The bottle
smashed against a wall.* = **shatter**, break,

disintegrate, split, crack, explode, splinter
3 *The train smashed into the car at 40 mph.*
= **collide**, crash, meet head-on, clash, come
into collision **4** *The authorities were trying to
smash a smuggling ring.* = **destroy**, ruin,
wreck, total (*slang*), defeat, overthrow,
trash (*slang*), lay waste ▶ NOUN **1** *It is the
public who decide if a film is a smash or a flop.*
= **success**, hit, winner, triumph (*informal*),
belter (*slang*), sensation, smash hit, sellout
2 *He was near to death after a car smash.*
= **collision**, crash, accident, pile-up
(*informal*), smash-up (*informal*) **3** *the smash
of falling crockery* = **crash**, smashing, clatter,
clash, bang, thunder, racket, din,
clattering, clang

smashing ADJECTIVE = **excellent**, mean
(*slang*), great (*informal*), wonderful, topping
(*Brit. slang*), brilliant (*informal*), cracking
(*Brit. informal*), crucial (*slang*), superb,
fantastic (*informal*), magnificent, fabulous
(*informal*), first-class, marvellous, terrific
(*informal*), sensational (*informal*), mega
(*slang*), sick (*slang*), sovereign, awesome
(*slang*), world-class, exhilarating, fab
(*informal, chiefly Brit.*), super (*informal*),
first-rate, def (*slang*), superlative, brill
(*informal*), stupendous, out of this world
(*informal*), bodacious (*slang, chiefly U.S.*),
boffo (*slang*), jim-dandy (*slang*), chillin' (*U.S.
slang*), booshit (*Austral. slang*), exo (*Austral.
slang*), sik (*Austral. slang*), rad (*informal*),
phat (*slang*), schmick (*Austral. informal*)
■ **OPPOSITE:** awful

smattering NOUN = **modicum**, dash,
rudiments, bit, elements, sprinkling,
passing acquaintance, nodding
acquaintance, smatter

smear VERB **1** *Smear a little olive oil over the
inside of the salad bowl.* = **spread over**, daub,
rub on, cover, coat, plaster, bedaub **2** *a
crude attempt to smear her* = **slander**, tarnish,
malign, vilify, blacken, sully, besmirch,
traduce (*formal*), calumniate, asperse, drag
(someone's) name through the mud **3** *a face
covered by a heavy beard, smeared with dirt*
= **smudge**, soil, dirty, stain, sully, besmirch,
smirch ▶ NOUN **1** *a smear of gravy* = **smudge**,
daub, streak, blot, blotch, splotch, smirch
2 *a smear by his rivals* = **slander**, libel,
defamation, vilification, whispering
campaign, calumny, mudslinging

smell NOUN **1** *the smell of freshly baked bread*
= **odour**, scent, fragrance, perfume,
bouquet, aroma, whiff, niff (*Brit. slang*),
redolence **2** *horrible smells* = **stink**, stench,
reek, pong (*Brit. informal*), niff (*Brit. slang*),
malodour, fetor ▶ VERB **1** *Do my feet smell?*
= **stink**, reek, pong (*Brit. informal*), hum

(slang), whiff (Brit. slang), stink to high heaven (informal), niff (Brit. slang), be malodorous **2** We could smell the gas. = **sniff**, scent, get a whiff of, nose ■ **RELATED WORD:** adjective olfactory

smelly ADJECTIVE = **stinking**, reeking, fetid, foul-smelling, high, strong, foul, putrid, strong-smelling, stinky (informal), malodorous, evil-smelling, noisome, whiffy (Brit. slang), pongy (Brit. informal), mephitic, niffy (Brit. slang), olid, festy (Austral. slang) ■ **OPPOSITE:** fragrant

smile VERB He smiled and waved. = **grin**, beam, smirk, twinkle, grin from ear to ear ▶ NOUN She gave a wry smile. = **grin**, beam, smirk

smirk NOUN Wipe that smirk off your face! = **smug smile**, grin, simper ▶ VERB = **give a smug look**, grin, simper

smitten ADJECTIVE **1** They were totally smitten with each other. = **infatuated**, charmed, captivated, beguiled, bewitched, bowled over (informal), enamoured, swept off your feet **2** smitten with yellow fever = **afflicted**, struck, beset, laid low, plagued

smoke VERB **1** = **smoulder**, fume **2** = **puff on**, draw on, inhale, vape

smoky ADJECTIVE = **thick**, murky, hazy

smooth ADJECTIVE **1** a smooth surface = **even**, level, flat, plane, plain, flush, horizontal, unwrinkled ■ **OPPOSITE:** uneven **2** The flagstones were worn smooth by centuries of use. = **sleek**, polished, shiny, glossy, silky, velvety, glassy, mirror-like ■ **OPPOSITE:** rough **3** This makes the flavour much smoother. = **mellow**, pleasant, mild, soothing, bland, agreeable **4** This exercise is done in one smooth motion. = **flowing**, steady, fluent, regular, uniform, rhythmic **5** This was only a brief upset in their smooth lives. = **calm**, peaceful, serene, tranquil, undisturbed, unruffled, equable ■ **OPPOSITE:** troubled **6** A number of problems marred the smooth running of this event. = **easy**, effortless, untroubled, well-ordered **7** Twelve extremely good-looking, smooth entrants have been picked as finalists. = **suave**, slick, persuasive, urbane, silky, glib, facile, ingratiating, debonair, unctuous, smarmy (Brit. informal) ▶ VERB **1** She stood up and smoothed down her frock. = **flatten**, level, press, plane, iron **2** smoothing the path towards a treaty = **ease**, aid, assist, facilitate, pave the way, make easier, help along, iron out the difficulties of ■ **OPPOSITE:** hinder

smoothness NOUN **1** The lawn was rich, weed-free, and trimmed to smoothness. = **evenness**, regularity, levelness, flushness, unbrokenness **2** the strength and smoothness of his movements = **fluency**, finish, flow, ease, polish, rhythm, efficiency, felicity, smooth running, slickness, effortlessness **3** the smoothness of her skin = **sleekness**, softness, smooth texture, silkiness, velvetiness **4** His cleverness, smoothness even, made his relationships uneasy. = **suavity**, urbanity, oiliness, glibness, smarminess (Brit. informal)

smother VERB **1** They tried to smother the flames. = **extinguish**, put out, stifle, snuff **2** He had attempted to smother the child. = **suffocate**, choke, strangle, stifle **3** She tried to smother her feelings of panic. = **suppress**, stifle, repress, hide, conceal, muffle, keep back **4** He smothered her with kisses. = **overwhelm**, cover, shower, surround, heap, shroud, inundate, envelop, cocoon **5** trying to smother our giggles = **stifle**, suppress, hold in, restrain, hold back, repress, muffle, bottle up, keep in check **6** Luckily, it wasn't smothered in creamy sauce. = **smear**, cover, spread

smoulder VERB **1** Whole blocks had been turned into smouldering rubble. = **smoke**, burn slowly **2** He smouldered as he drove home for lunch. = **seethe**, rage, fume, burn, boil, simmer, fester, be resentful, smart

smudge NOUN smudges of blood = **smear**, blot, smut, smutch ▶ VERB **1** Smudge the outline using a cotton-wool bud. = **smear**, blur, blot **2** She kissed me, careful not to smudge me with her fresh lipstick. = **mark**, soil, dirty, daub, smirch

smug ADJECTIVE = **self-satisfied**, superior, complacent, conceited, self-righteous, holier-than-thou, priggish, self-opinionated

smuggler NOUN = **trafficker**, runner, bootlegger, moonshiner (U.S.), rum-runner, contrabandist

snack NOUN = **light meal**, bite, refreshment(s), nibble, titbit, bite to eat, elevenses (Brit. informal)

snag NOUN A police crackdown hit a snag when villains stole one of their cars. = **difficulty**, hitch, problem, obstacle, catch (informal), hazard, disadvantage, complication, drawback, inconvenience, downside, stumbling block, the rub ▶ VERB He snagged his suit. = **catch**, tear, rip, hole

snake NOUN He was caught with his pet snake in his pocket. = **serpent** ▶ VERB The road snaked through the forested mountains. = **wind**, twist, curve, turn, bend, ramble, meander, deviate, zigzag ■ **RELATED WORD:** adjective serpentine

snap VERB **1** The brake pedal had just snapped. = **break**, split, crack, separate, fracture,

S

give way, come apart **2** *He snapped the cap on his ballpoint.* = **pop**, click, crackle **3** *I'm sorry, I didn't mean to snap at you.* = **speak sharply**, bark, lash out at, flash, retort, snarl, growl, fly off the handle at (*informal*), jump down (someone's) throat (*informal*) **4** *The poodle yapped and snapped at our legs.* = **bite at**, bite, nip ▸ NOUN **1** *Every minute or so I could hear a snap, a crack and a crash as another tree went down.* = **crack**, pop, crash, report, burst, explosion, clap **2** *He shut the book with a snap and stood up.* = **pop**, crack (*informal*), smack, whack ▸ MODIFIER *I think this is too important for a snap decision.* = **instant**, immediate, sudden, abrupt, spur-of-the-moment, unpremeditated • **snap out of it** (*informal*) *Come on, snap out of it!* = **get over it**, recover, cheer up, perk up, liven up, pull yourself together (*informal*), get a grip on yourself • **snap something up** *a queue of people waiting to snap up the bargains* = **grab**, seize, take advantage of, swoop down on, pounce upon, avail yourself of

snappy ADJECTIVE **1** *snappy sports jackets* = **smart**, fashionable, stylish, trendy (*Brit. informal*), chic, dapper, up-to-the-minute, natty (*informal*), modish, voguish, schmick (*Austral. informal*) **2** *He wasn't irritable or snappy.* = **irritable**, cross, bad-tempered, tart, impatient, edgy, touchy, tetchy, ratty (*Brit. & N.Z. informal*), testy, waspish, quick-tempered, snappish, like a bear with a sore head (*informal*), apt to fly off the handle (*informal*) • **make it snappy** *Look at the pamphlets, and make it snappy.* = **hurry (up)**, be quick, get a move on (*informal*), buck up (*informal*), make haste, look lively, get your skates on

snare NOUN *an animal caught in a snare* = **trap**, net, wire, gin, pitfall, noose, springe ▸ VERB *He'd snared a rabbit earlier in the day.* = **trap**, catch, net, wire, seize, entrap, springe

snarl¹ VERB **1** *The dogs snarled at the intruders.* = **growl**, show its teeth (*of an animal*) **2** *'Call that a good performance?' he snarled.* = **snap**, bark, lash out, speak angrily, jump down someone's throat, speak roughly

snarl² • **snarl something up** *The group had succeeded in snarling up rush-hour traffic throughout the country.* = **tangle**, complicate, muddle, embroil, entangle, entwine, ravel, enmesh

snatch VERB **1** *He snatched the telephone from me.* = **grab**, seize, wrench, wrest, take, grip, grasp, clutch, take hold of **2** *He snatched her bag and ran away at high speed.* = **steal**, take, nick (*slang, chiefly Brit.*), pinch (*informal*), swipe (*slang*), lift (*informal*), pilfer, filch, shoplift, thieve, walk or make off with

3 *They snatched a third goal.* = **win**, take, score, gain, secure, obtain **4** *He was snatched from the jaws of death at the last minute.* = **save**, free, rescue, pull, recover, get out, salvage, extricate ▸ NOUN *I heard snatches of the conversation.* = **bit**, part, fragment, piece, spell, snippet, smattering

snazzy ADJECTIVE = **stylish**, smart, dashing (*old-fashioned*), with it (*old-fashioned, informal*), attractive, sophisticated, flamboyant, sporty, flashy, jazzy (*informal*), showy, ritzy (*slang*), raffish, schmick (*Austral. informal*)

sneak VERB **1** *Don't sneak away and hide.* = **slink**, slip, steal, pad, sidle, skulk **2** *He snuck me a cigarette.* = **slip**, smuggle, spirit ▸ NOUN *He is disloyal, distrustful and a sneak.* = **informer**, grass (*Brit. slang*), betrayer, telltale, squealer (*slang*), Judas, accuser, stool pigeon, snake in the grass, nark (*Brit., Austral. & N.Z. slang*), fizgig (*Austral. slang*) ▸ MODIFIER *We can give you this exclusive sneak preview.* = **secret**, quick, clandestine, furtive, stealthy

sneaking ADJECTIVE **1** *a sneaking suspicion* = **nagging**, worrying, persistent, niggling, uncomfortable **2** *a sneaking admiration* = **secret**, private, hidden, suppressed, unexpressed, unvoiced, unavowed, unconfessed, undivulged

sneaky ADJECTIVE = **sly**, dishonest, devious, mean, low, base, nasty, cowardly, slippery, unreliable, malicious, unscrupulous, furtive, disingenuous, shifty (*informal*), snide, deceitful, contemptible, untrustworthy, double-dealing

sneer VERB **1** *There is too great a readiness to sneer at anything they do.* = **scorn**, mock, ridicule, laugh, jeer, disdain, scoff, deride, look down on, snigger, sniff at, gibe, hold in contempt, hold up to ridicule, turn up your nose (*informal*) **2** *'I wonder what you people do with your lives,' he sneered.* = **say contemptuously**, snigger ▸ NOUN **1** *Best-selling authors may have to face the sneers of the literati.* = **scorn**, ridicule, mockery, derision, jeer, disdain, snigger, gibe, snidery **2** *His mouth twisted in a contemptuous sneer.* = **contemptuous smile**, snigger, curl of the lip

snide *or* **snidey** ADJECTIVE = **nasty**, sneering, malicious, mean (*informal*), cynical, unkind, hurtful, sarcastic, disparaging, spiteful, insinuating, scornful, shrewish, ill-natured, snarky (*informal*)

sniff VERB **1** *She wiped her face and sniffed loudly.* = **breathe in**, inhale, snuffle, snuff **2** *Suddenly, he stopped and sniffed the air.* = **smell**, nose, breathe in, scent, get a whiff of **3** *He'd been sniffing glue.* = **inhale**, breathe in, suck in, draw in

sniffy ADJECTIVE = **contemptuous**, superior, condescending, haughty, scornful, disdainful, supercilious

snigger VERB *The tourists snigger at the locals' outdated ways and dress.* = **laugh**, giggle, sneer, snicker, titter ▸ NOUN *trying to suppress a snigger* = **laugh**, giggle, sneer, snicker, titter

snip VERB *Snip the corners off the card.* = **cut**, nick, clip, crop, trim, dock, notch, nip off ▸ NOUN *a snip at £74.25* = **bargain**, steal (*informal*), good buy, giveaway

snipe VERB = **criticize**, knock (*informal*), put down, carp, bitch (*slang*), have a go (at) (*informal*), throw shade (at) (*slang*), jeer, denigrate, disparage

snippet NOUN = **piece**, scrap, fragment, part, particle, snatch, shred

snob NOUN = **elitist**, highbrow, social climber

snobbery NOUN = **arrogance**, airs, pride, pretension, condescension, snobbishness, snootiness (*informal*), side (*Brit. slang*), uppishness (*Brit. informal*)

snobbish ADJECTIVE = **superior**, arrogant, stuck-up (*informal*), patronizing, condescending, snooty (*informal*), pretentious, uppity (*informal*), high and mighty (*informal*), toffee-nosed (*slang, chiefly Brit.*), hoity-toity (*informal*), high-hat (*informal, chiefly U.S.*), uppish (*Brit. informal*) ■ OPPOSITE: humble

snoop VERB **1** *He's been snooping around the place.* = **investigate**, explore, have a good look at, prowl around, nose around, peer into **2** *Governments have been known to snoop into innocent citizens' lives.* = **spy**, poke your nose in, nose, interfere, pry (*informal*) ▸ NOUN *He had a snoop around.* = **look**, search, nose, prowl, investigation

snooty ADJECTIVE = **snobbish**, superior, aloof, pretentious, stuck-up (*informal*), condescending, proud, haughty, disdainful, snotty, uppity (*informal*), supercilious, high and mighty (*informal*), toffee-nosed (*slang, chiefly Brit.*), hoity-toity (*informal*), high-hat (*informal, chiefly U.S.*), uppish (*Brit. informal*), toplofty (*informal*) ■ OPPOSITE: humble

snooze NOUN *The bird is enjoying a snooze.* = **doze**, nap, kip (*Brit. slang*), siesta, catnap, forty winks (*informal*) ▸ VERB *He snoozed in front of the television.* = **doze**, drop off (*informal*), nap, kip (*Brit. slang*), nod off (*informal*), catnap, drowse, take forty winks (*informal*)

snub VERB *He snubbed her in public and made her feel an idiot.* = **insult**, slight, put down, humiliate, cut (*informal*), shame, humble, rebuff, mortify, cold-shoulder, kick in the teeth (*slang*), give (someone) the cold shoulder, give (someone) the brush-off (*slang*), cut dead (*informal*) ▸ NOUN *He took it as a snub.* = **insult**, put-down, humiliation, affront, slap in the face (*informal*), brush-off (*slang*)

snug ADJECTIVE **1** *a snug log cabin* = **cosy**, warm, comfortable, homely, sheltered, intimate, comfy (*informal*) **2** *a snug black T-shirt and skin-tight black jeans* = **tight**, close, trim, neat

snuggle VERB = **nestle**, cuddle up

so SENTENCE CONNECTOR = **therefore**, thus, hence, consequently, then, as a result, accordingly, for that reason, whence, thence, ergo

soak VERB **1** *Soak the beans for two hours.* = **steep**, immerse, submerge, infuse, marinate (*Cookery*), dunk, submerse **2** *Soak the soil around each bush with at least 4 gallons of water.* = **wet**, damp, saturate, drench, douse, moisten, suffuse, wet through, waterlog, souse, drouk (*Scot.*) **3** *Rain had soaked into the sand.* = **penetrate**, pervade, permeate, enter, get in, infiltrate, diffuse, seep, suffuse, make inroads (into) • **soak something up** *Wrap in absorbent paper after frying to soak up excess oil.* = **absorb**, suck up, take in or up, drink in, assimilate

soaking ADJECTIVE = **soaked**, dripping, saturated, drenched, sodden, waterlogged, streaming, sopping, wet through, soaked to the skin, wringing wet, like a drowned rat, droukit or drookit (*Scot.*)

soar VERB **1** *soaring unemployment* = **rise**, increase, grow, mount, climb, go up, rocket, swell, escalate, shoot up **2** *Buzzards soar overhead at a great height.* = **fly**, rise, wing, climb, ascend, fly up ■ OPPOSITE: plunge **3** *The steeple soars skyward.* = **tower**, rise, climb, go up

sob VERB *She began to sob again, burying her face in the pillow.* = **cry**, weep, blubber, greet (*Scot.*), howl, bawl, snivel, shed tears, boohoo ▸ NOUN *Her body was racked by violent sobs.* = **cry**, whimper, howl

sober ADJECTIVE **1** *He was dour and uncommunicative when stone sober.* = **abstinent**, temperate, abstemious, moderate, on the wagon (*informal*) ■ OPPOSITE: drunk **2** *We are now far more sober and realistic.* = **serious**, practical, realistic, sound, cool, calm, grave, reasonable, steady, composed, rational, solemn, lucid, sedate, staid, level-headed, dispassionate, unruffled, clear-headed, unexcited, grounded ■ OPPOSITE: frivolous

S

3 *He dresses in sober grey suits.* = **plain**, dark, sombre, quiet, severe, subdued, drab ■ **OPPOSITE:** bright

sobriety NOUN **1** *the boredom of a lifetime of sobriety* = **abstinence**, temperance, abstemiousness, moderation, self-restraint, soberness, nonindulgence **2** *the values society depends upon, such as honesty, sobriety and trust* = **seriousness**, gravity, steadiness, restraint, composure, coolness, calmness, solemnity, reasonableness, level-headedness, staidness, sedateness

so-called ADJECTIVE = **alleged**, supposed, professed, pretended, self-styled, ostensible, soi-disant (*French*)

sociability NOUN = **friendliness**, conviviality, cordiality, congeniality, neighbourliness, affability, gregariousness, companionability, social intelligence

sociable ADJECTIVE = **friendly**, social, outgoing, warm, neighbourly, accessible, cordial, genial, affable, approachable, gregarious, convivial, companionable, conversable ■ **OPPOSITE:** unsociable

social ADJECTIVE **1** *the tightly woven social fabric of small towns* = **communal**, community, collective, group, public, general, common, societal **2** *We ought to organize more social events.* = **sociable**, friendly, companionable, neighbourly **3** *social insects like bees and ants* = **organized**, gregarious ▶ NOUN *church socials* = **get-together** (*informal*), party, gathering, function, do (*informal*), reception, bash (*informal*), social gathering

socialize VERB = **mix**, interact, mingle, be sociable, meet, go out, entertain, get together, fraternize, be a good mixer, get about or around

society NOUN **1** *This reflects attitudes and values prevailing in society.* = **the community**, social order, people, the public, the population, humanity, civilization, humankind, mankind, the general public, the world at large **2** *those responsible for destroying our society* = **culture**, community, population **3** *the historical society* = **organization**, group, club, union, league, association, institute, circle, corporation, guild, fellowship, fraternity (*U.S. & Canad.*), brotherhood or sisterhood **4** *The couple tried to secure themselves a position in society.* = **upper classes**, gentry, upper crust (*informal*), elite, the swells (*informal*), high society, the top drawer, polite society, the toffs (*Brit. slang*), the smart set, beau monde (*slang*), the nobs (*slang*), the country set, haut monde (*French*) **5** *I largely withdrew from the society of others.* = **companionship**, company, fellowship, friendship, camaraderie

sodden ADJECTIVE = **soaked**, saturated, sopping, drenched, soggy, waterlogged, marshy, boggy, miry, droukit or drookit (*Scot.*)

sofa NOUN = **couch**, settee, divan, chaise longue, chesterfield, ottoman

soft ADJECTIVE **1** *Regular use of a body lotion will keep the skin soft and supple.* = **velvety**, smooth, silky, furry, feathery, downy, fleecy, like a baby's bottom (*informal*) ■ **OPPOSITE:** rough **2** *She lay down on the soft, comfortable bed.* = **yielding**, flexible, pliable, cushioned, elastic, malleable, spongy, springy, cushiony ■ **OPPOSITE:** hard **3** *The horse didn't handle the soft ground very well.* = **soggy**, swampy, marshy, boggy, squelchy, quaggy **4** *a simple bread made with a soft dough* = **squashy**, sloppy, mushy, spongy, squidgy (*Brit. informal*), squishy, gelatinous, squelchy, pulpy, doughy **5** *Aluminium is a soft metal.* = **pliable**, flexible, supple, malleable, plastic, elastic, tensile, ductile (*of a metal*), bendable, mouldable, impressible **6** *When he woke again he could hear soft music.* = **quiet**, low, gentle, sweet, whispered, soothing, murmured, muted, subdued, mellow, understated, melodious, mellifluous, dulcet, soft-toned ■ **OPPOSITE:** loud **7** *He says the measure is soft and weak on criminals.* = **lenient**, easy-going, lax, liberal, weak, indulgent, permissive, spineless, boneless, overindulgent ■ **OPPOSITE:** harsh **8** *a very soft and sensitive heart* = **kind**, tender, sentimental, compassionate, sensitive, gentle, pitying, sympathetic, tenderhearted, touchy-feely (*informal*) **9** *a soft option* = **easy**, comfortable, undemanding, cushy (*informal*), easy-peasy (*slang*) **10** *The room was tempered by the soft colours.* = **pale**, light, subdued, pastel, pleasing, bland, mellow ■ **OPPOSITE:** bright **11** *His skin looked golden in the soft light.* = **dim** (*informal*), faint, dimmed ■ **OPPOSITE:** bright **12** *a soft breeze* = **mild**, delicate, caressing, temperate, balmy

soften VERB **1** *Soften the butter mixture in a small saucepan.* = **melt**, tenderize **2** *He could not think how to soften the blow of what he had to tell her.* = **lessen**, moderate, diminish, temper, lower, relax, ease, calm, modify, cushion, soothe, subdue, alleviate, lighten, quell, muffle, allay, mitigate, abate, tone down, assuage

software NOUN = **computer program**, operating system, application, system, product, app, program, platform, network

soggy ADJECTIVE = **sodden**, saturated, moist, heavy, soaked, dripping, waterlogged, sopping, mushy, spongy, pulpy

soil¹ NOUN **1** *regions with sandy soils* = **earth**, ground, clay, dust, dirt, loam **2** *the first World Cup finals to be held on African soil* = **territory**, country, land, region, turf (*slang*), terrain

soil² VERB *Young people don't want to do things that soil their hands.* = **dirty**, foul, stain, smear, muddy, pollute, tarnish, spatter, sully, defile, besmirch, smirch, bedraggle, befoul, begrime ■ **OPPOSITE:** clean

sojourn NOUN = **stay**, visit, stop, rest, stopover

solace NOUN *I found solace in writing when my father died.* = **comfort**, consolation, help, support, relief, succour, alleviation, assuagement ▶ VERB *They solaced themselves with their fan mail.* = **comfort**, console, soothe

soldier NOUN = **fighter**, serviceman *or* servicewoman, trooper, warrior, Tommy (*Brit. informal*), GI (*U.S. informal*), military man *or* woman, redcoat, enlisted man (*U.S.*), man-at-arms, squaddie *or* squaddy (*Brit. slang*)

sole ADJECTIVE = **only**, one, single, individual, alone, exclusive, solitary, singular, one and only

solely ADVERB = **only**, completely, entirely, exclusively, alone, singly, merely, single-handedly

solemn ADJECTIVE **1** *His solemn little face broke into smiles.* = **serious**, earnest, grave, sober, thoughtful, sedate, glum, staid, portentous ■ **OPPOSITE:** cheerful **2** *This is a solemn occasion.* = **formal**, august, grand, imposing, impressive, grave, majestic, dignified, ceremonial, stately, momentous, awe-inspiring, ceremonious ■ **OPPOSITE:** informal **3** *a solemn religious ceremony* = **sacred**, religious, holy, ritual, venerable, hallowed, sanctified, devotional, reverential ■ **OPPOSITE:** irreligious

solemnity NOUN **1** *the solemnity of the occasion* = **seriousness**, gravity, formality, grandeur, gravitas, earnestness, portentousness, momentousness, impressiveness **2** (*often plural*) *the constitutional solemnities* = **ritual**, proceedings, ceremony, rite, formalities, ceremonial, observance, celebration

solicit VERB **1** *He's already solicited their support on health care reform.* = **request**, seek, ask for, petition, crave (*informal*), pray for, plead for, canvass, beg for **2** *She was soliciting a donation from a rich tycoon.* = **appeal to**, ask, call on, lobby, press, beg, petition, plead with, implore, beseech, entreat, importune (*formal*), supplicate

solicitous ADJECTIVE = **concerned**, caring, attentive, careful

solid ADJECTIVE **1** *a tunnel carved through soft of solid rock* = **firm**, hard, compact, dense, massed, concrete ■ **OPPOSITE:** unsubstantial **2** *I stared up at the square, solid house.* = **strong**, stable, sturdy, sound, substantial, unshakable ■ **OPPOSITE:** unstable **3** *The taps appeared to be made of solid gold.* = **pure**, unalloyed, unmixed, complete **4** *a solid line* = **continuous**, unbroken, uninterrupted **5** *a good, solid member of the community* = **reliable**, decent, dependable, upstanding, serious, constant, sensible, worthy, upright, sober, law-abiding, trusty, level-headed, estimable ■ **OPPOSITE:** unreliable **6** *Some solid evidence was what was required.* = **sound**, real, reliable, good, genuine, dinkum (*Austral. & N.Z. informal*) ■ **OPPOSITE:** unsound

solidarity NOUN = **unity**, harmony, unification, accord, stability, cohesion, team spirit, camaraderie, unanimity, soundness, concordance, esprit de corps, community of interest, singleness of purpose, like-mindedness, kotahitanga (*N.Z.*)

solidify VERB = **harden**, set, congeal, cake, jell, coagulate, cohere

soliloquy NOUN = **monologue**, address, speech, aside, oration, dramatic monologue

> **USAGE** Although *soliloquy* and *monologue* are close in meaning, you should take care when using one as a synonym of the other. Both words refer to a long speech by one person, but a *monologue* can be addressed to other people, whereas in a *soliloquy* the speaker is always talking to himself or herself.

solitary ADJECTIVE **1** *Paul was a shy, pleasant, solitary man.* = **unsociable**, retiring, reclusive, unsocial, isolated, lonely, cloistered, lonesome (*U.S. & Canad.*), friendless, companionless ■ **OPPOSITE:** sociable **2** *His evenings were spent in solitary drinking.* = **lone**, alone **3** *a boy of eighteen in a solitary house in the Ohio countryside* = **isolated**, remote, out-of-the-way, desolate, hidden, sequestered, unvisited, unfrequented ■ **OPPOSITE:** busy

solitude NOUN **1** *Imagine long golden beaches where you can wander in solitude.* = **isolation**, privacy, seclusion, retirement, loneliness, ivory tower, reclusiveness **2** *travelling by yourself in these vast solitudes* = **wilderness**, waste, desert, emptiness, wasteland

S

solution NOUN **1** *the ability to sort out effective solutions to practical problems* = **answer**, resolution, key, result, solving, explanation, unfolding, unravelling, clarification, explication, elucidation **2** *a warm solution of liquid detergent* = **mixture**, mix, compound, blend, suspension, solvent, emulsion

solve VERB = **answer**, work out, resolve, explain, crack, interpret, unfold, clarify, clear up, unravel, decipher, expound, suss (out) (*slang*), get to the bottom of, disentangle, elucidate

solvent ADJECTIVE = **financially sound**, secure, in the black, solid, profit-making, in credit, debt-free, unindebted

sombre ADJECTIVE **1** *The pair were in sombre mood.* = **gloomy**, sad, sober, grave, dismal, melancholy, mournful, lugubrious, joyless, funereal, doleful, sepulchral ■ **OPPOSITE:** cheerful **2** *a worried official in sombre black* = **dark**, dull, gloomy, sober, drab ■ **OPPOSITE:** bright

somebody NOUN = **celebrity**, big name, public figure, name, star, heavyweight (*informal*), notable, superstar, household name, dignitary, luminary, bigwig (*informal*), celeb (*informal*), big shot (*informal*), personage, megastar (*informal*), big wheel (*slang*), big noise (*informal*), big hitter (*informal*), heavy hitter (*informal*), person of note, V.I.P., someone, muckymuck (*Canad. informal*) ■ **OPPOSITE:** nobody

someday ADVERB = **one day**, eventually, ultimately, sooner or later, one of these (fine) days, in the fullness of time

somehow ADVERB = **one way or another**, come what may, come hell or high water (*informal*), by fair means or foul, by hook or (by) crook, by some means or other

sometime ADVERB *Why don't you come and see me sometime?* = **some day**, one day, at some point in the future, sooner or later, one of these days, by and by ▶ ADJECTIVE *She was in her early thirties, a sometime actress, dancer and singer.* = **former**, one-time, erstwhile, ex-, late, past, previous

> **USAGE** *Sometime* as a single word should only be used to refer to an unspecified point in time. When referring to a considerable length of time, you should use *some time*. Compare: *It was some time after, that the rose garden was planted*, i.e. after a considerable period of time, with *It was sometime after the move that the rose garden was planted*, i.e. at some unspecified point after the move, but not necessarily a long time after.

sometimes ADVERB = **occasionally**, at times, now and then, from time to time, on occasion, now and again, once in a while, every now and then, every so often, off and on ■ **OPPOSITE:** always

son NOUN = **male child**, boy, lad (*informal*), descendant, son and heir ■ **RELATED WORD:** *adjective* filial

song NOUN = **ballad**, air, tune, lay, strain, carol, lyric, chant, chorus, melody, anthem, number, hymn, psalm, shanty, pop song, ditty, canticle, canzonet, choon (*slang*), waiata (*N.Z.*)

song and dance NOUN = **fuss**, to-do, flap (*informal*), performance (*informal*), stir, pantomime (*informal*), commotion, ado, shindig (*informal*), kerfuffle (*informal*), hoo-ha, pother (*literary*), shindy (*informal*)

soon ADVERB = **before long**, shortly, in the near future, in a minute, anon (*archaic*), in a short time, in a little while, any minute now, betimes (*archaic*), in two shakes of a lamb's tail, erelong (*archaic, poetic*), in a couple of shakes

sooner ADVERB **1** *I thought she would have recovered sooner.* = **earlier**, before, already, beforehand, ahead of time **2** *They would sooner die than stay in London.* = **rather**, more readily, by preference, more willingly

> **USAGE** *When* is sometimes used instead of *than* after *no sooner*, but this use is generally regarded as incorrect: *no sooner had he arrived than* (not *when*) *the telephone rang*.

soothe VERB **1** *He would take her in his arms and soothe her.* = **calm**, still, quiet, hush, settle, calm down, appease, lull, mitigate, pacify, mollify, smooth down, tranquillize ■ **OPPOSITE:** upset **2** *Lemon tisanes with honey can soothe sore throats.* = **relieve**, ease, alleviate, dull, diminish, assuage ■ **OPPOSITE:** irritate

soothing ADJECTIVE **1** *Put on some nice soothing music.* = **calming**, relaxing, peaceful, quiet, calm, restful **2** *Cold tea is very soothing for burns.* = **emollient**, palliative, balsamic, demulcent, easeful, lenitive

sophisticated ADJECTIVE **1** *a large and sophisticated new telescope* = **complex**, advanced, complicated, subtle, delicate, elaborate, refined, intricate, multifaceted, highly-developed ■ **OPPOSITE:** simple **2** *Recently her tastes have become more sophisticated.* = **cultured**, refined, cultivated, worldly, cosmopolitan, urbane, jet-set, world-weary, citified, worldly-wise ■ **OPPOSITE:** unsophisticated

S

sophistication NOUN = **poise**, worldliness, savoir-faire, urbanity, finesse, savoir-vivre (*French*), worldly wisdom

soporific ADJECTIVE = **sleep-inducing**, hypnotic, sedative, sleepy, somnolent, tranquillizing, somniferous (*rare*)

soppy ADJECTIVE = **sentimental**, corny (*slang*), slushy (*informal*), soft (*informal*), silly, daft (*informal*), weepy (*informal*), mawkish, drippy (*informal*), lovey-dovey, schmaltzy (*slang*), icky (*informal*), gushy (*informal*), overemotional, three-hankie (*informal*)

sorcerer *or* **sorceress** NOUN = **magician**, witch, wizard, magus, warlock, mage (*archaic*), enchanter, necromancer

sorcery NOUN = **black magic**, witchcraft, black art, necromancy, spell, magic, charm, wizardry, enchantment, divination, incantation, witchery

sordid ADJECTIVE 1 *He put his head in his hands as his sordid life was exposed.* = **base**, degraded, shameful, low, vicious, shabby, vile, degenerate, despicable, disreputable, debauched ■ OPPOSITE: honourable 2 *the attic windows of their sordid little rooms* = **dirty**, seedy, sleazy, squalid, mean, foul, filthy, unclean, wretched, seamy, slovenly, slummy, scungy (*Austral. & N.Z.*), festy (*Austral. slang*) ■ OPPOSITE: clean

sore ADJECTIVE 1 *My chest is still sore from the surgery.* = **painful**, smarting, raw, tender, burning, angry, sensitive, irritated, inflamed, chafed, reddened 2 *The result of it is that they are all feeling very sore at you.* = **annoyed**, cross, angry, pained, hurt, upset, stung, irritated, grieved, resentful, aggrieved, vexed, irked, peeved (*informal*), tooshie (*Austral. slang*), hoha (*N.Z.*) 3 *Timing is frequently a sore point.* = **annoying**, distressing, troublesome, harrowing, grievous 4 *The prime minister is in sore need of friends.* = **urgent**, desperate, extreme, dire, pressing, critical, acute ▶ NOUN *All of us had long sores on our backs.* = **abscess**, boil, ulcer, inflammation, gathering

sorrow NOUN 1 *It was a time of great sorrow.* = **grief**, sadness, woe, regret, distress, misery, mourning, anguish, unhappiness, heartache, heartbreak, affliction ■ OPPOSITE: joy 2 *the joys and sorrows of family life* = **hardship**, trial, tribulation, affliction, worry, trouble, blow, woe, misfortune, bummer (*slang*) ■ OPPOSITE: good fortune ▶ VERB *She was lamented by a large circle of sorrowing friends and acquaintances.* = **grieve**, mourn, lament, weep, moan, be sad, bemoan, agonize, eat your heart out, bewail ■ OPPOSITE: rejoice

sorrowful ADJECTIVE = **sad**, unhappy, miserable, sorry, depressed, painful, distressed, grieving, dismal, afflicted, melancholy, tearful, heartbroken, woeful, mournful, dejected, rueful, lugubrious, wretched, disconsolate, doleful, heavy-hearted, down in the dumps (*informal*), woebegone, piteous, sick at heart

sorry ADJECTIVE 1 *She was very sorry about all the trouble she'd caused.* = **regretful**, apologetic, contrite, repentant, guilt-ridden, remorseful, penitent, shamefaced, conscience-stricken, in sackcloth and ashes, self-reproachful ■ OPPOSITE: unapologetic 2 *I am very sorry for the family.* = **sympathetic**, moved, full of pity, pitying, compassionate, commiserative ■ OPPOSITE: unsympathetic 3 *What he must not do is sit around at home feeling sorry for himself.* = **sad**, distressed, unhappy, grieved, melancholy, mournful, sorrowful, disconsolate ■ OPPOSITE: happy 4 *She is in a sorry state.* = **wretched**, miserable, pathetic, mean, base, poor, sad, distressing, dismal, shabby, vile, paltry, pitiful, abject, deplorable, pitiable, piteous

sort NOUN *What sort of person is he?* = **kind**, type, class, make, group, family, order, race, style, quality, character, nature, variety, brand, species, breed, category, stamp, description, denomination, genus, ilk ▶ VERB *He sorted the materials into their folders.* = **arrange**, group, order, class, separate, file, rank, divide, grade, distribute, catalogue, classify, categorize, tabulate, systematize, put in order • **out of sorts** 1 *Lack of sleep can leave us feeling jaded and out of sorts.* = **irritable**, cross, edgy, tense, crabbed, snarling, prickly, snappy, touchy, bad-tempered, petulant, ill-tempered, irascible, cantankerous, tetchy, ratty (*Brit. & N.Z. informal*), testy, fretful, grouchy (*informal*), peevish, crabby, dyspeptic, choleric, crotchety (*informal*), oversensitive, snappish, ill-humoured, narky (*Brit. slang*), out of humour 2 *You are feeling out of sorts and unable to see the wood for the trees.* = **depressed**, miserable, in low spirits, down, low, blue, sad, unhappy, gloomy, melancholy, mournful, dejected, despondent, dispirited, downcast, long-faced, sorrowful, disconsolate, crestfallen, down in the dumps (*informal*), down in the mouth (*informal*), mopy 3 *At times, he has seemed lifeless and out of sorts.* = **unwell**, ill, sick, poorly (*informal*), funny (*informal*), crook (*Austral. & N.Z. informal*), ailing, queer, unhealthy, seedy (*informal*), laid up (*informal*), queasy, infirm, dicky (*Brit.*

S

informal), off colour, under the weather (*informal*), at death's door, indisposed, on the sick list (*informal*), not up to par, valetudinarian, green about the gills (*informal*), not up to snuff (*informal*)

• **sort of** *I sort of made my own happiness.*
= **rather**, somewhat, as it were, slightly, moderately, in part, reasonably

> **USAGE** It is common in informal speech to combine singular and plural in sentences like *These sort of distinctions are becoming blurred.* This is not acceptable in careful writing, where the plural must be used consistently: *These sorts of distinctions are becoming blurred.*

SO-SO ADJECTIVE = **average**, middling, fair, ordinary, moderate, adequate, respectable, indifferent, not bad (*informal*), tolerable, run-of-the-mill, passable, undistinguished, fair to middling (*informal*), O.K. or okay (*informal*)

soul NOUN **1** *Such memories stirred in his soul.* = **spirit**, essence, psyche, life, mind, reason, intellect, vital force, animating principle, wairua (*N.Z.*) **2** *With such celebrated clients, she necessarily remains the soul of discretion.* = **embodiment**, essence, incarnation, epitome, personification, quintessence, type **3** *a tiny village of only 100 souls* = **person**, being, human, individual, body, creature, mortal, man or woman **4** *an ice goddess without soul* = **feeling**, force, energy, vitality, animation, fervour, ardour, vivacity

soulful ADJECTIVE = **expressive**, sensitive, eloquent, moving, profound, meaningful, heartfelt, mournful

soulless ADJECTIVE **1** *a clean but soulless hotel* = **characterless**, dull, bland, mundane, ordinary, grey, commonplace, dreary, mediocre, drab, uninspiring, colourless, featureless, unexceptional **2** *He was big and brawny with soulless eyes.* = **unfeeling**, dead, cold, lifeless, inhuman, harsh, cruel, callous, unkind, unsympathetic, spiritless

sound¹ NOUN **1** *Peter heard the sound of gunfire.* = **noise**, racket, din, report, tone, resonance, hubbub, reverberation **2** *Here's a new idea we like the sound of.* = **idea**, impression, implication(s), drift **3** *She didn't make a sound.* = **cry**, noise, peep, squeak **4** *the soulful sound of the violin* = **tone**, music, note, chord **5** *I was born and bred within the sound of the cathedral bells.* = **earshot**, hearing, hearing distance ▸ VERB **1** *A young man sounds the bell to start the Sunday service.* = **toll**, set off **2** *A silvery bell sounded somewhere.* = **resound**, echo, go off, toll, set off, chime, resonate, reverberate, clang, peal **3** *She sounded a bit worried.* = **seem**,

seem to be, appear to be, give the impression of being, strike you as being

■ **RELATED WORDS:** *adjectives* sonic, acoustic

sound² ADJECTIVE **1** *His body was still sound.* = **fit**, healthy, robust, firm, perfect, intact, vigorous, hale (*old-fashioned*), unhurt, undamaged, uninjured, unimpaired, hale and hearty ■ **OPPOSITE:** frail **2** *a perfectly sound building* = **sturdy**, strong, solid, stable, substantial, durable, stout, well-constructed **3** *a sound financial proposition* = **safe**, secure, reliable, proven, established, recognized, solid, stable, solvent, reputable, tried and true
■ **OPPOSITE:** unreliable **4** *They are trained nutritionists who can give sound advice on diets.* = **sensible**, wise, reasonable, right, true, responsible, correct, proper, reliable, valid, orthodox, rational, logical, prudent, trustworthy, well-founded, level-headed, right-thinking, well-grounded, grounded
■ **OPPOSITE:** irresponsible **5** *She has woken me out of a sound sleep.* = **deep**, peaceful, unbroken, undisturbed, untroubled
■ **OPPOSITE:** troubled

sound³ • **sound someone out** *Sound him out gradually.* = **question**, interview, survey, poll, examine, investigate, pump (*informal*), inspect, canvass, test the opinion of
• **sound something out** *They are discreetly sounding out blue-chip American banks.* = **investigate**, research, examine, probe, look into, test the water, put out feelers to, see how the land lies, carry out an investigation of

sound⁴ NOUN *a blizzard blasting great drifts of snow across the sound* = **channel**, passage, strait, inlet, fjord, voe, arm of the sea

sour ADJECTIVE **1** *The stewed apple was sour even with honey.* = **sharp**, acid, tart, bitter, unpleasant, pungent, acetic, acidulated, acerb ■ **OPPOSITE:** sweet **2** *tiny fridges full of sour milk* = **rancid**, turned, gone off, fermented, unsavoury, curdled, unwholesome, gone bad, off ■ **OPPOSITE:** fresh **3** *He became a sour, lonely man.* = **bitter**, cynical, crabbed, tart, discontented, grudging, acrimonious, embittered, disagreeable, churlish, ill-tempered, jaundiced, waspish, grouchy (*informal*), ungenerous, peevish, ill-natured
■ **OPPOSITE:** good-natured ▸ VERB *The experience, she says, has soured her.*
= **embitter**, disenchant, alienate, envenom

source NOUN **1** *This gave me a clue as to the source of the problem.* = **cause**, origin, derivation, beginning, author **2** *a major source of information about the arts* = **informant**, authority, documentation

3 *the source of the Tiber* = **origin**, spring, fount, fountainhead, wellspring, rise

souvenir NOUN = **keepsake**, token, reminder, relic, remembrancer (*archaic*), memento

sovereign ADJECTIVE **1** *No contract can absolutely restrain a sovereign power.* = **supreme**, ruling, absolute, chief, royal, principal, dominant, imperial, unlimited, paramount, regal, predominant, monarchal, kingly *or* queenly **2** *wild garlic, a sovereign remedy in any healer's chest* = **excellent**, efficient, efficacious, effectual ▶ NOUN *the first British sovereign to set foot on Spanish soil* = **monarch**, ruler, king *or* queen, chief, shah, potentate, supreme ruler, emperor *or* empress, prince *or* princess, tsar *or* tsarina

sovereignty NOUN = **supreme power**, domination, supremacy, primacy, sway, ascendancy, kingship, suzerainty, rangatiratanga (*N.Z.*)

sow VERB = **scatter**, plant, seed, lodge, implant, disseminate, broadcast, inseminate

space NOUN **1** *The furniture proved impractical because it took up too much space.* = **room**, volume, capacity, extent, margin, extension, scope, play, expanse, leeway, amplitude, spaciousness, elbowroom **2** *The space underneath could be used as a storage area.* = **gap**, opening, interval, gulf, cavity, aperture **3** *They've come a long way in a short space of time.* = **period**, interval, time, while, span, duration, time frame, timeline **4** *launching satellites into space* = **outer space**, the universe, the galaxy, the solar system, the cosmos **5** *Affix your stamps on the space provided.* = **blank**, gap, interval ■ RELATED WORD: *adjective* spatial

spaceman *or* **spacewoman** NOUN = **astronaut**, cosmonaut, space cadet, space traveller

spacious ADJECTIVE = **roomy**, large, huge, broad, vast, extensive, ample, expansive, capacious, uncrowded, commodious, comfortable, sizable *or* sizeable ■ OPPOSITE: cramped

span NOUN **1** *The batteries had a life span of six hours.* = **period**, term, duration, spell **2** *The bridge has a span of 579 feet.* = **extent**, reach, spread, length, distance, stretch ▶ VERB *the humped iron bridge spanning the railway* = **extend across**, cross, bridge, cover, link, vault, traverse, range over, arch across

spank VERB = **smack**, slap, whack, belt (*informal*), tan (*slang*), slipper (*informal*), cuff, wallop (*informal*), give (someone) a hiding (*informal*), put (someone) over your knee

spanking¹ NOUN *Andrea gave her son a sound spanking.* = **smacking**, hiding (*informal*), whacking, slapping, walloping (*informal*)

spanking² ADJECTIVE **1** *a spanking new car* = **smart**, brand-new, fine, gleaming **2** *The film moves along at a spanking pace.* = **fast**, quick, brisk, lively, smart, vigorous, energetic, snappy

spar VERB = **argue**, row, squabble, dispute, scrap (*informal*), fall out (*informal*), spat, wrangle, skirmish, bicker, have a tiff

spare ADJECTIVE **1** *He could have taken a spare key.* = **back-up**, reserve, second, extra, relief, emergency, additional, substitute, fall-back, auxiliary, in reserve **2** *They don't have a lot of spare cash.* = **extra**, surplus, leftover, over, free, odd, unwanted, in excess, unused, superfluous, supernumerary ■ OPPOSITE: necessary **3** *In her spare time she raises funds for charity.* = **free**, leisure, unoccupied **4** *She was thin and spare, with a shapely intelligent face.* = **thin**, lean, slim, slender, slight, meagre, gaunt, wiry, lank ■ OPPOSITE: plump **5** *The two rooms were spare and neat, stripped bare of ornaments.* = **meagre**, sparing, modest, economical, frugal, scanty ▶ VERB **1** *He suggested that his country could not spare the troops.* = **afford**, give, grant, do without, relinquish, part with, allow, bestow, dispense with, manage without, let someone have **2** *Not a soul was spared.* = **have mercy on**, pardon, have pity on, leave, release, excuse, let off (*informal*), go easy on (*informal*), be merciful to, grant pardon to, deal leniently with, refrain from hurting, save (from harm) ■ OPPOSITE: show no mercy to

sparing ADJECTIVE = **economical**, frugal, thrifty, saving, careful, prudent, cost-conscious, chary, money-conscious ■ OPPOSITE: lavish

spark NOUN **1** *Sparks flew in all directions.* = **flicker**, flash, gleam, glint, spit, flare, scintillation **2** *Even Oliver felt a tiny spark of excitement.* = **trace**, hint, scrap, atom, jot, vestige, scintilla ▶ VERB (*often with* **off**) *What was it that sparked your interest in horses?* = **start**, stimulate, provoke, excite, inspire, stir, trigger (off), set off, animate, rouse, prod, precipitate, kick-start, set in motion, kindle, touch off

sparkle VERB *His bright eyes sparkled.* = **glitter**, flash, spark, shine, beam, glow, gleam, wink, shimmer, twinkle, dance, glint, glisten, glister (*archaic*), scintillate ▶ NOUN **1** *There was a sparkle in her eye that could not be hidden.* = **glitter**, flash, gleam, spark, dazzle, flicker, brilliance, twinkle,

S

glint, radiance **2** *There was little sparkle in their performance.* = **vivacity**, life, spirit, dash, zip (*informal*), vitality, animation, panache, gaiety, élan, brio, liveliness, vim

sparse ADJECTIVE = **scattered**, scarce, meagre, sporadic, few and far between, scanty ■ **OPPOSITE:** thick

Spartan ADJECTIVE = **austere**, severe, frugal, ascetic, plain, disciplined, extreme, strict, stern, bleak, rigorous, stringent, abstemious, self-denying, bare-bones

spasm NOUN **1** *A lack of magnesium causes muscles to go into spasm.* = **convulsion**, contraction, paroxysm, twitch, throe (*rare*) **2** *He felt a spasm of fear.* = **burst**, fit, outburst, seizure, frenzy, eruption, access

spasmodic ADJECTIVE = **sporadic**, irregular, erratic, intermittent, jerky, fitful, convulsive

spat NOUN = **quarrel**, dispute, squabble, controversy, contention, bickering, tiff, altercation

spate NOUN **1** = **flood**, flow, torrent, rush, deluge, outpouring **2** = **series**, sequence, course, chain, succession, run, train, string

spatter VERB = **splash**, spray, sprinkle, soil, dirty, scatter, daub, speckle, splodge, bespatter, bestrew

spawn VERB *His novels spawned both movies and television shows.* = **generate**, produce, give rise to, start, prompt, provoke, set off, bring about, spark off, set in motion

speak VERB **1** *The President spoke of the need for territorial compromise.* = **talk**, say something **2** *The very act of speaking the words gave him comfort.* = **articulate**, say, voice, pronounce, utter, tell, state, talk, express, communicate, make known, enunciate **3** *It was very emotional when we spoke again.* = **converse**, talk, chat, discourse, confer, commune, exchange views, shoot the breeze (*slang, chiefly U.S. & Canad.*), korero (*N.Z.*) **4** *Last month I spoke in front of two thousand people in Birmingham.* = **lecture**, talk, discourse, spout (*informal*), make a speech, pontificate, give a speech, declaim, hold forth, spiel (*informal*), address an audience, deliver an address, speechify
• **speak for something** or **someone**
1 *It was the job of the church to speak for the underprivileged.* = **represent**, act for or on behalf of, appear for, hold a brief for, hold a mandate for **2** *a role in which he would be seen as speaking for the Government* = **support**, back, champion, defend, promote, advocate, fight for, uphold, commend, espouse, stick up for (*informal*)

speaker NOUN = **orator**, public speaker, lecturer, spokesman or woman or person,

mouthpiece, spieler (*informal*), word-spinner

spearhead VERB = **lead**, head, pioneer, launch, set off, initiate, lead the way, set in motion, blaze the trail, be in the van, lay the first stone

special ADJECTIVE **1** *I usually reserve these outfits for special occasions.* = **exceptional**, important, significant, particular, unique, unusual, extraordinary, distinguished, memorable, gala, festive, uncommon, momentous, out of the ordinary, one in a million, red-letter, especial (*formal*) ■ **OPPOSITE:** ordinary **2** *He is a special correspondent for Newsweek magazine.* = **major**, chief, main, primary **3** *It requires a very special brand of courage to fight dictators.* = **specific**, particular, distinctive, certain, individual, appropriate, characteristic, precise, peculiar, specialized, especial ■ **OPPOSITE:** general

specialist NOUN = **expert**, authority, professional, master, consultant, guru, buff (*informal*), whizz (*informal*), connoisseur, boffin (*Brit. informal*), hotshot (*informal*), wonk (*informal*), maven (*U.S.*), fundi (*S. African*)

speciality NOUN **1** *His speciality was creating rich, creamy sauces.* = **forte**, strength, special talent, métier, specialty, bag (*slang*), claim to fame, pièce de résistance (*French*), distinctive or distinguishing feature **2** *His speciality was the history of Germany.* = **special subject**, specialty (*chiefly U.S. & Canad.*), field of study, branch of knowledge, area of specialization

species NOUN = **kind**, sort, type, group, class, variety, breed, category, description, genus

specific ADJECTIVE **1** *the specific needs of the individual* = **particular**, special, characteristic, distinguishing, peculiar, definite, especial ■ **OPPOSITE:** general **2** *I asked him to be more specific.* = **precise**, exact, explicit, definite, limited, express, clear-cut, unequivocal, unambiguous ■ **OPPOSITE:** vague **3** *Send your résumé with a covering letter that is specific to that particular job.* = **peculiar**, appropriate, individual, particular, personal, unique, restricted, idiosyncratic, endemic

specification NOUN = **requirement**, detail, particular, stipulation, condition, qualification

specify VERB = **state**, designate, spell out, stipulate, name, detail, mention, indicate, define, cite, individualize, enumerate, itemize, be specific about, particularize

specimen NOUN **1** *a perfect specimen of a dinosaur fossil* = **sample**, example, individual, model, type, pattern, instance, representative, exemplar, exemplification **2** *a fine specimen of manhood* = **example**, model, exhibit, embodiment, type

specious ADJECTIVE = **fallacious**, misleading, deceptive, plausible, unsound, sophistic, sophistical, casuistic

speck NOUN **1** *There is a speck of blood by his ear.* = **mark**, spot, dot, stain, blot, fleck, speckle, mote **2** *He leaned forward and brushed a speck of dust off his shoes.* = **particle**, bit, grain, dot, atom, shred, mite, jot, modicum, whit, tittle, iota

speckled ADJECTIVE = **flecked**, spotted, dotted, sprinkled, spotty, freckled, mottled, dappled, stippled, brindled, speckledy

spectacle NOUN **1** *a director passionate about music and spectacle* = **show**, display, exhibition, event, performance, sight, parade, extravaganza, pageant **2** *the bizarre spectacle of an actor desperately demanding an encore* = **sight**, wonder, scene, phenomenon, curiosity, marvel, laughing stock

spectacles PLURAL NOUN = **glasses**, specs (*informal*), eyeglasses (*U.S.*), eyewear

spectacular ADJECTIVE *The results have been spectacular.* = **impressive**, striking, dramatic, stunning (*informal*), marked, grand, remarkable, fantastic (*informal*), magnificent, staggering, splendid, dazzling, sensational, breathtaking, eye-catching ■ OPPOSITE: unimpressive ▶ NOUN *a television spectacular* = **show**, display, spectacle, extravaganza

spectator NOUN = **onlooker**, observer, viewer, witness, looker-on, watcher, eyewitness, bystander, beholder ■ OPPOSITE: participant

spectral ADJECTIVE = **ghostly**, unearthly, eerie, supernatural, weird, phantom, shadowy, uncanny, spooky (*informal*), insubstantial, incorporeal, wraithlike

spectre NOUN = **ghost**, spirit, phantom, presence, vision, shadow, shade (*literary*), apparition, wraith, kehua (*N.Z.*)

speculate VERB **1** *The reader can speculate about what will happen next.* = **conjecture**, consider, wonder, guess, contemplate, deliberate, muse, meditate, surmise, theorize, hypothesize, cogitate **2** *They speculated in property whose value has now dropped.* = **gamble**, risk, venture, hazard, have a flutter (*informal*), take a chance with, play the market

speculation NOUN **1** *I had published my speculations about the future of the universe.*

= **theory**, opinion, hypothesis, conjecture, guess, consideration, deliberation, contemplation, surmise, guesswork, supposition **2** *speculation on the Stock Exchange* = **gamble**, risk, gambling, hazard

speculative ADJECTIVE **1** *He has written a speculative biography of Christopher Marlowe.* = **hypothetical**, academic, theoretical, abstract, tentative, notional, conjectural, suppositional **2** *a speculative venture* = **risky**, uncertain, hazardous, unpredictable, dicey (*informal, chiefly Brit.*), chancy (*informal*)

speech NOUN **1** *the development of speech in children* = **communication**, talk, conversation, articulation, discussion, dialogue, intercourse **2** *His speech became increasingly thick and nasal.* = **diction**, pronunciation, articulation, delivery, fluency, inflection, intonation, elocution, enunciation **3** *the way common letter clusters are pronounced in speech* = **language**, tongue, utterance, jargon, dialect, idiom, parlance, articulation, diction, lingo (*informal*), enunciation **4** *He delivered his speech in French.* = **talk**, address, lecture, discourse, harangue, homily, oration, spiel (*informal*), disquisition, whaikorero (*N.Z.*)

speechless ADJECTIVE = **dumb**, dumbfounded, lost for words, dumbstruck, astounded, shocked, mum, amazed, silent, mute, dazed, aghast, inarticulate, tongue-tied, wordless, thunderstruck, unable to get a word out (*informal*)

speed NOUN **1** *He drove off at high speed.* = **rate**, pace, momentum, tempo, velocity **2** *Speed is the essential ingredient of all athletics.* = **velocity**, swiftness, acceleration, precipitation, rapidity, quickness, fastness, briskness, speediness, precipitateness **3** *I was amazed at his speed of working.* = **swiftness**, rush, hurry, expedition, haste, rapidity, quickness, fleetness, celerity (*formal*) ■ OPPOSITE: slowness ▶ VERB **1** *The engine noise rises only slightly as I speed along.* = **race**, rush, hurry, zoom, career, bomb (along), tear, flash, belt (along) (*slang*), barrel (along) (*informal, chiefly U.S. & Canad.*), sprint, gallop, hasten, press on, quicken, lose no time, get a move on (*informal*), burn rubber (*informal*), bowl along, put your foot down (*informal*), step on it (*informal*), make haste, go hell for leather (*informal*), exceed the speed limit, go like a bomb (*Brit. & N.Z. informal*), go like the wind, go like a bat out of hell ■ OPPOSITE: crawl **2** *Invest in low-cost language courses to speed your progress.* = **help**, further, advance, aid, promote, boost, assist, facilitate, impel, expedite

■ **OPPOSITE:** hinder • **speed something up** *Excessive drinking will speed up the ageing process.* = **accelerate**, promote, hasten, help along, further, forward, advance

> **USAGE** The past tense of *speed up* is *speeded up* (not *sped up*), for example *I speeded up to overtake the lorry*. The past participle is also *speeded up*, for example *I had already speeded up when I spotted the police car*.

speedy ADJECTIVE = **quick**, fast, rapid, swift, express, winged, immediate, prompt, fleet, hurried, summary, precipitate, hasty, headlong, quickie (*informal*), expeditious, fleet of foot, pdq (*slang*) ■ **OPPOSITE:** slow

spell¹ VERB *The report spells more trouble.* = **indicate**, mean, signify, suggest, promise, point to, imply, amount to, herald, augur, presage, portend • **spell something out** *How many times do I have to spell it out?* = **make clear** or **plain**, specify, make explicit, clarify, elucidate, explicate (*formal*)

spell² NOUN **1** *Vile witch! She cast a spell on me!* = **incantation**, charm, sorcery, exorcism, abracadabra, witchery, conjuration, makutu (*N.Z.*) **2** *The King also falls under her spell.* = **enchantment**, magic, fascination, glamour, allure, bewitchment

spell³ NOUN *There has been a spell of dry weather.* = **period**, time, term, stretch, turn, course, season, patch, interval, bout, stint

spellbound ADJECTIVE = **entranced**, gripped, fascinated, transported, charmed, hooked, possessed, bemused, captivated, enthralled, bewitched, transfixed, rapt, mesmerized, under a spell

spelling NOUN = **orthography**

spend VERB **1** *They have spent £23m on new players.* = **pay out**, fork out (*slang*), expend, lay out, splash out (*Brit. informal*), shell out (*informal*), disburse ■ **OPPOSITE:** save **2** *This energy could be much better spent taking some positive action.* = **apply**, use, employ, concentrate, invest, put in, devote, lavish, exert, bestow **3** *We spent the night in a hotel.* = **pass**, fill, occupy, while away **4** *My stepson was spending money like it grew on trees.* = **use up**, waste, squander, blow (*slang*), empty, drain, exhaust, consume, run through, deplete, dissipate, fritter away

■ **OPPOSITE:** save

spendthrift NOUN *I was a natural spendthrift when I was single.* = **squanderer**, spender, profligate, prodigal, big spender, waster, wastrel ■ **OPPOSITE:** miser ▶ ADJECTIVE *his father's spendthrift ways* = **wasteful**, extravagant, prodigal, profligate, improvident ■ **OPPOSITE:** economical

spent ADJECTIVE **1** *The money was spent.* = **used up**, finished, gone, consumed, expended **2** *After all that exertion, we were completely spent.* = **exhausted**, drained, worn out, bushed (*informal*), all in (*slang*), shattered (*informal*), weakened, wiped out (*informal*), wearied, weary, played out (*informal*), burnt out, fagged (out) (*informal*), whacked (*Brit. informal*), debilitated, knackered (*slang*), prostrate, clapped out (*Brit., Austral. & N.Z. informal*), tired out, ready to drop (*informal*), dog-tired (*informal*), zonked (*informal*), dead beat (*informal*), shagged out (*Brit. slang*), done in or up (*informal*)

spew VERB **1** *An oil tanker spewed its cargo into the sea.* = **shed**, discharge, send out, issue, throw out, eject, diffuse, emanate, exude, cast out **2** *Let's get out of his way before he starts spewing.* = **vomit**, throw up (*informal*), puke (*slang*), chuck (*Austral. & N.Z. informal*), spit out, regurgitate, disgorge, barf (*U.S. slang*), chunder (*slang, chiefly Austral.*), belch forth, upchuck (*U.S. slang*), do a technicolour yawn (*slang*), toss your cookies (*U.S. slang*)

sphere NOUN **1** *The cactus will form a large sphere crested with golden thorns.* = **ball**, globe, orb, globule, circle **2** *the sphere of international politics* = **field**, range, area, department (*informal*), function, territory, capacity, province, patch, scope, turf (*slang*), realm, domain, compass, walk of life **3** *life outside academic spheres of society* = **rank**, class, station, status, stratum

spherical ADJECTIVE = **round**, globular, globe-shaped, rotund, orbicular

spice NOUN **1** *herbs and spices* = **seasoning**, condiment **2** *The spice of danger will add to the lure.* = **excitement**, kick (*informal*), zest, colour, pep, zip (*informal*), tang, zap (*slang*), gusto, zing (*informal*), piquancy

spicy ADJECTIVE **1** *Thai food is hot and spicy.* = **hot**, seasoned, pungent, aromatic, savoury, tangy, piquant, flavoursome **2** *spicy anecdotes* = **risqué**, racy, off-colour, ribald, hot (*informal*), broad, improper, suggestive, unseemly, titillating, indelicate, indecorous

spider NOUN ■ **RELATED WORD:** *phobia* arachnophobia

spiel NOUN = **patter**, speech, pitch, recital, harangue, sales talk, sales patter

spike NOUN *a 15-foot wall topped with iron spikes* = **point**, stake, spur, pin, nail, spine, barb, tine, prong ▶ VERB **1** *drinks spiked with tranquillizers* = **drug**, lace, dope, cut, contaminate, adulterate **2** *My foot kept getting spiked by the runners in front.* = **impale**, spit, spear, stick

spill VERB **1** *He always spilled the drinks.* = **tip over**, upset, overturn, capsize, knock over, topple over **2** *A number of bags had split and were spilling their contents.* = **shed**, scatter, discharge, throw off, disgorge, spill or run over **3** *It doesn't matter if red wine spills on this floor.* = **slop**, flow, pour, run, overflow, slosh, splosh **4** *When the bell rings, more than 1,000 children spill from the classrooms.* = **emerge**, flood, pour, mill, stream, surge, swarm, crowd, teem ▶ NOUN *An oil spill could be devastating for wildlife.* = **spillage**, flood, leak, leakage, overspill

spin VERB **1** *The Earth spins on its own axis.* = **revolve**, turn, rotate, wheel, twist, reel, whirl, twirl, gyrate, pirouette, birl (*Scot.*) **2** *My head was spinning from the wine.* = **reel**, swim, whirl, be giddy, be in a whirl, grow dizzy **3** *She had spun a story that was too good to be true.* = **tell**, relate, recount, develop, invent, unfold, concoct, narrate ▶ NOUN **1** *Think twice about going for a spin by the light of the silvery moon.* = **drive**, ride, turn, hurl (*Scot.*), whirl, joy ride (*informal*) **2** *a spin of the roulette wheel* = **revolution**, roll, whirl, twist, gyration • **spin something out** *They will try to spin out the conference into next autumn.* = **prolong**, extend, lengthen, draw out, drag out, delay, amplify, pad out, protract, prolongate

spindly ADJECTIVE = **lanky**, gangly, spidery, leggy, twiggy, attenuated, gangling, spindle-shanked

spine NOUN **1** *fractures of the hip and spine* = **backbone**, vertebrae, spinal column, vertebral column **2** *Carry a pair of thick gloves to protect you from hedgehog spines.* = **barb**, spur, needle, spike, ray, quill **3** *If you had any spine, you wouldn't let her walk all over you like that.* = **determination**, resolution, backbone, resolve, drive, conviction, fortitude, persistence, tenacity, perseverance, willpower, firmness, constancy, single-mindedness, steadfastness, doggedness, resoluteness, indomitability

spine-chilling ADJECTIVE = **frightening**, terrifying, horrifying, scary (*informal*), eerie, spooky (*informal*), hair-raising, bloodcurdling

spineless ADJECTIVE = **weak**, soft, cowardly, ineffective, feeble, yellow (*informal*), inadequate, pathetic, submissive, squeamish, vacillating, boneless, gutless (*informal*), weak-willed, weak-kneed (*informal*), faint-hearted, irresolute, spiritless, lily-livered, without a will of your own ■ **OPPOSITE:** brave

spiral ADJECTIVE *a spiral staircase* = **coiled**, winding, corkscrew, circular, scrolled, whorled, helical, cochlear, voluted, cochleate (*Biology*) ▶ NOUN *Larks were rising in spirals from the ridge.* = **coil**, helix, corkscrew, whorl, screw, curlicue

spirit¹ NOUN **1** *The human spirit is virtually indestructible.* = **soul**, life, psyche, essential being **2** *His spirit left him during the night.* = **life force**, vital spark, breath, mauri (*N.Z.*) **3** *Do you believe in the existence of evil spirits?* = **ghost**, phantom, spectre, vision, shadow, shade (*literary*), spook (*informal*), apparition, sprite, atua (*N.Z.*), kehua (*N.Z.*) **4** *She was a very brave girl and everyone admired her spirit.* = **courage**, guts (*informal*), grit, balls (*vulgar slang*), backbone, spunk (*informal*), gameness, ballsiness (*slang*), dauntlessness, stoutheartedness **5** *They played with spirit.* = **liveliness**, energy, vigour, life, force, fire, resolution, enterprise, enthusiasm, sparkle, warmth, animation, zest, mettle, ardour, earnestness, brio **6** *They approached the talks in a conciliatory spirit.* = **attitude**, character, quality, humour, temper, outlook, temperament, complexion, ethos, disposition **7** *the real spirit of the revolutionary movement* = **heart**, sense, nature, soul, core, substance, essence, lifeblood, quintessence, fundamental nature **8** *the spirit of the treaty* = **intention**, meaning, purpose, substance, intent, essence, purport, gist **9** *I appreciate the sounds, smells and the spirit of the place.* = **feeling**, atmosphere, character, feel, quality, tone, mood, flavour, tenor, ambience, vibes (*slang*) **10** *It takes a lot of spirit to win with 10 men.* = **resolve**, will, drive, resolution, conviction, motivation, dedication, backbone, fortitude, persistence, tenacity, perseverance, willpower, firmness, constancy, single-mindedness, steadfastness, doggedness, resoluteness, indomitability **11** (*plural*) *A bit of exercise will help lift his spirits.* = **mood**, feelings, morale, humour, temper, tenor, disposition, state of mind, frame of mind

spirit² NOUN (*often plural*) = **strong alcohol**, liquor, the hard stuff (*informal*), firewater, strong liquor

spirited ADJECTIVE = **lively**, vigorous, energetic, animated, game, active, bold, sparkling, have-a-go (*informal*), courageous, ardent, feisty (*informal*), plucky, high-spirited, sprightly, vivacious, spunky (*informal*), mettlesome, (as) game as Ned Kelly (*Austral. slang*) ■ **OPPOSITE:** lifeless

S

spiritual ADJECTIVE **1** *She lived entirely by spiritual values.* = **nonmaterial**, immaterial, incorporeal ■ OPPOSITE: material **2** *A man in priestly clothes offered spiritual guidance.* = **sacred**, religious, holy, divine, ethereal, devotional, otherworldly

spit VERB **1** *They spat at me and taunted me.* = **expectorate**, sputter, flob (*Brit. informal*) **2** *I spat it on to my plate.* = **eject**, discharge, throw out ▶ NOUN *When he took a corner kick he was showered with spit.* = **saliva**, dribble, spittle, drool, slaver, sputum

spite NOUN *Never had she met such spite and pettiness.* = **malice**, malevolence, ill will, hate, hatred, gall, animosity, venom, spleen, pique, rancour, bitchiness (*slang*), malignity, spitefulness ■ OPPOSITE: kindness ▶ VERB *He was giving his art collection away for nothing, to spite them.* = **annoy**, hurt, injure, harm, provoke, offend, needle (*informal*), put out, gall, nettle, vex, pique, discomfit, put someone's nose out of joint (*informal*), hack someone off (*informal*) ■ OPPOSITE: benefit • **in spite of** *Their love of life comes in spite of considerable hardship.* = **despite**, regardless of, notwithstanding, in defiance of, (even) though

spiteful ADJECTIVE = **malicious**, nasty, vindictive, cruel, malignant, barbed, malevolent, venomous, bitchy (*informal*), snide, rancorous, catty (*informal*), splenetic, shrewish, ill-disposed, ill-natured

spitting image NOUN = **double**, lookalike, (dead) ringer (*slang*), picture, spit (*informal, chiefly Brit.*), clone, replica, likeness, living image, spit and image (*informal*)

splash VERB **1** *A lot of people were in the water, splashing about.* = **paddle**, plunge, bathe, dabble, wade, wallow **2** *He closed his eyes tight, and splashed the water on his face.* = **scatter**, shower, spray, sprinkle, spread, wet, strew, squirt, spatter, slop, slosh (*informal*) **3** *The carpet was splashed with beer stains.* = **spatter**, mark, stain, smear, speck, speckle, blotch, splodge, bespatter **4** *waves splashing against the side of the boat* = **dash**, break, strike, wash, batter, surge, smack, buffet, plop, plash ▶ NOUN **1** *I would sit alone and listen to the splash of water on the rocks.* = **splashing**, dashing, plash, beating, battering, swashing **2** *Add a splash of lemon juice to flavour the butter.* = **dash**, touch, spattering, splodge **3** *splashes of colour* = **spot** (*Brit.*), burst, patch, stretch, spurt **4** *splashes of ink over a glowing white surface* = **blob**, spot, smudge, stain, smear, fleck, speck • **make a splash** *He knows how to make a splash in the House of Lords.*

= **cause a stir**, make an impact, cause a sensation, cut a dash, be ostentatious

spleen NOUN = **spite**, anger, bitterness, hostility, hatred, resentment, wrath, gall, malice, animosity, venom, bile, bad temper, acrimony, pique, rancour, ill will, animus, malevolence, vindictiveness, malignity, spitefulness, ill humour, peevishness

splendid ADJECTIVE **1** *The book includes a wealth of splendid photographs.* = **excellent**, wonderful, marvellous, mean (*slang*), great (*informal*), topping (*Brit. slang*), fine, cracking (*Brit. informal*), crucial (*slang*), fantastic (*informal*), first-class, glorious, mega (*slang*), sick (*slang*), sovereign, awesome (*slang*), def (*slang*), brill (*informal*), bodacious (*slang, chiefly U.S.*), boffo (*slang*), chillin' (*U.S. slang*), booshit (*Austral. slang*), exo (*Austral. slang*), sik (*Austral. slang*), rad (*informal*), phat (*slang*), schmick (*Austral. informal*), beaut (*informal*), barrie (*Scot. slang*), belting (*Brit. slang*), pearler (*Austral. slang*) ■ OPPOSITE: poor **2** *a splendid Victorian mansion* = **magnificent**, grand, imposing, impressive, rich, superb, costly, gorgeous, dazzling, lavish, luxurious, sumptuous, ornate, resplendent, splendiferous (*facetious*) ■ OPPOSITE: squalid **3** *a splendid career in publishing* = **glorious**, superb, magnificent, grand, brilliant, rare, supreme, outstanding, remarkable, sterling, exceptional, renowned, admirable, sublime, illustrious ■ OPPOSITE: ignoble

splendour NOUN *They met in the splendour of the hotel.* = **magnificence**, glory, grandeur, show, display, ceremony, luxury, spectacle, majesty, richness, nobility, pomp, opulence, solemnity, éclat, gorgeousness, sumptuousness, stateliness, resplendence, luxuriousness ■ OPPOSITE: squalor

splice VERB = **join**, unite, graft, marry, wed, knit, mesh, braid, intertwine, interweave, yoke, plait, entwine, interlace, intertwist

splinter NOUN *a splinter in the finger* = **sliver**, fragment, chip, needle, shaving, flake, paring ▶ VERB *The ruler cracked and splintered into pieces.* = **shatter**, split, fracture, shiver, disintegrate, break into fragments

split VERB **1** *In a severe gale the ship split in two.* = **break**, crack, burst, snap, break up, open, give way, splinter, gape, come apart, come undone **2** *He started on the main course while she split the avocados.* = **cut**, break, crack, snap, chop, cleave, hew **3** *It is feared they could split the government.* = **divide**, separate, disunite, disrupt, disband, cleave, pull apart, set at odds, set at variance **4** *that* place where the road split in two = **diverge**, separate, branch, fork, part, go separate ways **5** The seat of his short grey trousers split. = **tear**, rend (literary), rip, slash, slit **6** Split the wages between you. = **share out**, divide, distribute, halve, allocate, partition, allot, carve up, dole out, apportion, slice up, parcel out, divvy up (informal) ▶ NOUN **1** a split in the party = **division**, break, breach, rift, difference, disruption, rupture, discord, divergence, schism, estrangement, dissension, disunion **2** The split from her husband was acrimonious. = **separation**, break, divorce, break-up, split-up, disunion **3** The seat had a few small splits around the corners. = **crack**, tear, rip, damage, gap, rent, breach, slash, slit, fissure ▶ ADJECTIVE **1** The government is deeply split in its approach to foreign policy. = **divided**, ambivalent, bisected **2** a split finger nail = **broken**, cracked, snapped, fractured, splintered, ruptured, cleft • **split on someone** If I wanted to tell, I'd have split on you before now. = **betray**, tell on, shop (slang, chiefly Brit.), sing (slang, chiefly U.S.), grass (Brit. slang), give away, squeal (slang), inform on, spill your guts (slang), dob in (Austral. slang) • **split up** I was beginning to think that we would never split up. = **break up**, part, separate, divorce, disband, part company, go separate ways

spoil VERB **1** It is important not to let mistakes spoil your life. = **ruin**, destroy, wreck, damage, total (slang), blow (slang), injure, upset, harm, mar, scar, undo, trash (slang), impair, mess up, blemish, disfigure, debase, deface, put a damper on, crool or cruel (Austral. slang) ■ OPPOSITE: improve **2** Grandparents are often tempted to spoil their grandchildren. = **overindulge**, indulge, pamper, baby, cosset, coddle, spoon-feed, mollycoddle, kill with kindness ■ OPPOSITE: deprive **3** Spoil yourself with a new perfume this summer. = **indulge**, treat, pamper, satisfy, gratify, pander to, regale **4** Fats spoil by becoming tainted. = **go bad**, turn, go off (Brit. informal), rot, decay, decompose, curdle, mildew, addle, putrefy (formal), become tainted

spoils PLURAL NOUN Competing warlords and foreign powers scrambled for political spoils. = **booty**, loot, plunder, gain, prizes, prey, pickings, pillage, swag (slang), boodle (slang, chiefly U.S.), rapine

spoken ADJECTIVE written and spoken communication skills = **verbal**, voiced, expressed, uttered, oral, said, told, unwritten, phonetic, by word of mouth, put into words, viva voce • **spoken for** **1** The top jobs in the party are already spoken for. = **reserved**, booked, claimed, chosen, selected, set aside **2** Both my son and daughter are spoken for. = **engaged**, taken, going out with someone, betrothed (archaic), going steady

spokesperson NOUN = **speaker**, official, spokesman or woman, voice, spin doctor (informal), mouthpiece

spongy ADJECTIVE = **porous**, light, absorbent, springy, cushioned, elastic, cushiony

sponsor VERB They are sponsoring a major pop art exhibition. = **back**, fund, finance, promote, subsidize, patronize, put up the money for, lend your name to ▶ NOUN the new sponsors of the world championships = **backer**, patron, promoter, angel (informal), guarantor

spontaneous ADJECTIVE = **unplanned**, impromptu, unprompted, willing, free, natural, voluntary, instinctive, impulsive, unforced, unbidden, unconstrained, unpremeditated, extempore, uncompelled ■ OPPOSITE: planned

spontaneously ADVERB = **voluntarily**, freely, instinctively, impromptu, off the cuff (informal), on impulse, impulsively, in the heat of the moment, extempore, off your own bat, of your own accord, quite unprompted

spoof NOUN = **parody**, takeoff (informal), satire, caricature, mockery, send-up (Brit. informal), travesty, lampoon, burlesque

spook NOUN She woke up to see a spook hovering over her bed. = **ghost**, spirit, phantom, spectre, soul, shade (literary), manes, apparition, wraith, revenant, phantasm, eidolon, kehua (N.Z.) ▶ VERB But was it the wind that spooked her? = **frighten**, alarm, scare, terrify, startle, intimidate, daunt, unnerve, petrify, scare (someone) stiff, put the wind up (someone) (informal), scare the living daylights out of (someone) (informal), make your hair stand on end (informal), get the wind up, make your blood run cold, throw into a panic, scare the bejesus out of (informal), affright (archaic), freeze your blood, make (someone) jump out of their skin (informal), throw into a fright

spooky (informal) ADJECTIVE = **eerie**, frightening, chilling, ghostly, weird, mysterious, scary (informal), unearthly, supernatural, uncanny, creepy (informal), spine-chilling

sporadic ADJECTIVE = **intermittent**, occasional, scattered, isolated, random, on and off, irregular, infrequent, spasmodic, scattershot ■ OPPOSITE: steady

S

sport NOUN **1** *I'd say football is my favourite sport.* = **game**, exercise, recreation, play, entertainment, amusement, diversion, pastime, physical activity **2** *Had themselves a bit of sport first, didn't they?* = **fun**, kidding (*informal*), joking, teasing, ridicule, joshing (*slang, chiefly U.S. & Canad.*), banter, frolic, jest, mirth, merriment, badinage, raillery ▸ VERB *He was fat-faced, heavily-built and sported a red moustache.* = **wear**, display, flaunt, boast, exhibit, flourish, show off, vaunt

sporting ADJECTIVE = **fair**, sportsmanlike, game (*informal*), gentlemanly ■ **OPPOSITE:** unfair

sporty ADJECTIVE **1** *He would go to the ballgames with his sporty friends.* = **athletic**, outdoor, energetic, hearty **2** *The moustache gave him a certain sporty air.* = **casual**, stylish, jazzy (*informal*), loud, informal, trendy (*Brit. informal*), flashy, jaunty, showy, snazzy (*informal*), raffish, rakish, gay, schmick (*Austral. informal*)

spot NOUN **1** *The floorboards were covered with white spots.* = **mark**, stain, speck, scar, flaw, taint, blot, smudge, blemish, daub, speckle, blotch, discoloration **2** *Never squeeze blackheads, spots or pimples.* = **pimple**, blackhead, pustule, zit (*slang*), plook (*Scot.*), acne **3** *We've given all the club members tea, coffee and a spot of lunch.* = **bit**, little, drop, bite, splash, small amount, tad, morsel **4** *They returned to the remote spot where they had left him.* = **place**, situation, site, point, position, scene, location, locality **5** *In a tight spot there is no one I would sooner see than Frank.* = **predicament**, trouble, difficulty, mess, plight, hot water (*informal*), quandary, tight spot ▸ VERB **1** *He left the party seconds before smoke was spotted coming up the stairs.* = **see**, observe, catch sight of, identify, sight, recognize, detect, make out, pick out, discern, behold (*archaic, literary*), espy, descry **2** *a brown shoe spotted with paint* = **mark**, stain, dot, soil, dirty, scar, taint, tarnish, blot, fleck, spatter, sully, speckle, besmirch, splodge, splotch, mottle, smirch

spotless ADJECTIVE **1** *Every morning cleaners make sure everything is spotless.* = **clean**, immaculate, impeccable, white, pure, virgin, shining, gleaming, snowy, flawless, faultless, unblemished, virginal, unsullied, untarnished, unstained ■ **OPPOSITE:** dirty **2** *He was determined to leave a spotless record behind him.* = **blameless**, squeaky-clean, unimpeachable, innocent, chaste, irreproachable, above reproach ■ **OPPOSITE:** reprehensible

spotlight NOUN **1** *the light of a powerful spotlight from a police helicopter* = **search light**, headlight, floodlight, headlamp, foglamp **2** *Webb is back in the spotlight.* = **attention**, limelight, public eye, interest, fame, notoriety, public attention ▸ VERB *a new book spotlighting female entrepreneurs* = **highlight**, feature, draw attention to, focus attention on, accentuate, point up, give prominence to, throw into relief

spot-on ADJECTIVE = **accurate**, exact, precise, right, correct, on the money (*informal*), unerring, punctual (to the minute), hitting the nail on the head (*informal*), on the bull's-eye (*informal*)

spotted ADJECTIVE = **speckled**, dotted, flecked, pied, specked, mottled, dappled, polka-dot

spotty ADJECTIVE **1** *She was rather fat, and her complexion was muddy and spotty.* = **pimply**, pimpled, blotchy, poor-complexioned, plooky-faced (*Scot.*) **2** *His attendance record was spotty.* = **inconsistent**, irregular, erratic, uneven, fluctuating, patchy, sporadic

spouse NOUN = **partner**, mate, husband or wife, companion, consort, significant other (*informal, chiefly U.S.*), better half (*humorous*), her indoors (*Brit. slang*), helpmate

spout VERB **1** *In a storm, water spouts out of the blowhole just like a whale.* = **stream**, shoot, gush, spurt, jet, spray, surge, discharge, erupt, emit, squirt **2** *She would go red in the face and start to spout.* = **hold forth**, talk, rant, go on (*informal*), rabbit (on) (*Brit. informal*), ramble (on), pontificate, declaim, spiel (*informal*), expatiate, orate, speechify

sprawl VERB = **loll**, slump, lounge, flop, slouch

spray¹ NOUN **1** *The moon was casting a rainbow through the spray of the waterfall.* = **droplets**, moisture, fine mist, drizzle, spindrift, spoondrift **2** *an insect-repellent spray* = **aerosol**, sprinkler, atomizer ▸ VERB *A shower of seeds sprayed into the air and fell on the grass.* = **scatter**, shower, sprinkle, diffuse

spray² NOUN *a small spray of freesias* = **sprig**, floral arrangement, branch, bough, shoot, corsage

spread VERB **1** *He spread his coat over the bed.* = **open (out)**, extend, stretch, unfold, sprawl, unfurl, fan out, unroll **2** *He stepped back and spread his hands wide.* = **extend**, open, stretch **3** *Spread the bread with the cream cheese.* = **coat**, cover, smear, smother **4** *Spread the cream over the skin and allow it to remain for 12 hours.* = **smear**, apply, rub, put, smooth, plaster, daub **5** *The sense of fear is spreading in residential neighbourhoods.* = **grow**, increase, develop, expand, widen, mushroom, escalate, proliferate, multiply, broaden **6** *The course is spread over a five-week period.* = **space out**, stagger **7** *Someone has been spreading rumours about us.* = **circulate**, publish, broadcast, advertise, distribute, scatter, proclaim, transmit, make public, publicize, propagate, disseminate, promulgate, make known, blazon, bruit ■ **OPPOSITE:** suppress **8** *The overall flaring tends to spread light.* = **diffuse**, cast, shed, radiate ▶ NOUN **1** *The greatest hope for reform is the gradual spread of information.* = **increase**, development, advance, spreading, expansion, transmission, proliferation, advancement, escalation, diffusion, dissemination, dispersal, suffusion **2** *The rhododendron grows to 18 inches with a spread of 24 inches.* = **extent**, reach, span, stretch, sweep, compass **3** *They put on a spread of sandwiches for us.* = **feast**, banquet, blowout (*slang*), repast, array

spree NOUN **1** *They went on a spending spree.* = **fling**, binge (*informal*), orgy, splurge **2** *They attacked two London shops after a drinking spree.* = **binge**, bender (*informal*), orgy, revel (*informal*), jag (*slang*), junketing, beano (*Brit. slang*), debauch, carouse, bacchanalia, carousal

sprightly ADJECTIVE = **lively**, spirited, active, energetic, animated, brisk, nimble, agile, jaunty, gay, perky, vivacious, spry, bright-eyed and bushy-tailed ■ **OPPOSITE:** inactive

spring NOUN **1** *It is the first day of spring, and sunlight streams through the windows.* = **springtime**, springtide (*literary*) **2** *the hidden springs of consciousness* = **source**, root, origin, well, beginning, cause, fount, fountainhead, wellspring **3** *Put some spring back into your old sofa.* = **flexibility**, give (*informal*), bounce, resilience, elasticity, recoil, buoyancy, springiness, bounciness ▶ VERB **1** *The lion roared once and sprang.* = **jump**, bound, leap, bounce, hop, rebound, vault, recoil **2** (*usually followed by* **from**) *The art springs from the country's Muslim heritage.* = **originate**, come, derive, start, issue, grow, emerge, proceed, arise, stem, descend, be derived, emanate, be descended ▶ ADJECTIVE *Walking carefree through the fresh spring rain.* = **vernal**, springlike ■ **RELATED WORD:** *adjective* vernal

springy ADJECTIVE = **flexible**, elastic, resilient, bouncy, rubbery, spongy

sprinkle VERB = **scatter**, dust, strew, pepper, shower, spray, powder, dredge

sprinkling NOUN = **scattering**, dusting, scatter, few, dash, handful, sprinkle, smattering, admixture

sprint VERB = **run**, race, shoot, tear, dash, barrel (along) (*informal, chiefly U.S. & Canad.*), dart, hare (*Brit. informal*), whizz (*informal*), scamper, hotfoot, go like a bomb (*Brit. & N.Z. informal*), put on a burst of speed, go at top speed

sprite NOUN = **spirit**, fairy, elf, nymph, brownie, pixie, apparition, imp, goblin, leprechaun, peri, dryad, naiad, sylph, Oceanid (*Greek myth*), atua (*N.Z.*)

sprout VERB **1** *It only takes a few days for beans to sprout.* = **germinate**, bud, shoot, push, spring, vegetate **2** *Leaf-shoots were beginning to sprout on the hawthorn.* = **grow**, develop, blossom, ripen

spruce ADJECTIVE = **smart**, trim, neat, elegant, dainty, dapper, natty (*informal*), well-groomed, well turned out, trig (*archaic, dialect*), as if you had just stepped out of a bandbox, soigné *or* soignée ■ **OPPOSITE:** untidy

spry ADJECTIVE = **active**, sprightly, quick, brisk, supple, nimble, agile, nippy (*Brit. informal*) ■ **OPPOSITE:** inactive

spur VERB *His friend's plight had spurred him into taking part.* = **incite**, drive, prompt, press, urge, stimulate, animate, prod, prick, goad, impel ▶ NOUN *Redundancy is the spur for many to embark on new careers.* = **stimulus**, incentive, impetus, motive, impulse, inducement, incitement, kick up the backside (*informal*) • **on the spur of the moment** *They admitted they had taken a vehicle on the spur of the moment.* = **on impulse**, without thinking, impulsively, on the spot, impromptu, unthinkingly, without planning, impetuously, unpremeditatedly

spurious ADJECTIVE = **false**, bogus, sham, pretended, artificial, forged, fake, mock, imitation, simulated, contrived, pseudo (*informal*), counterfeit, feigned, ersatz, specious, unauthentic, phoney *or* phony (*informal*) ■ **OPPOSITE:** genuine

spurn VERB = **reject**, slight, scorn, rebuff, put down, snub, disregard, despise, disdain, repulse, cold-shoulder, kick in the teeth (*slang*), turn your nose up at (*informal*), contemn (*formal*) ■ **OPPOSITE:** accept

spurt VERB *I saw flames spurt from the roof.* = **gush**, shoot, burst, jet, surge, erupt, spew, squirt ▶ NOUN **1** *A spurt of diesel came from one valve and none from the other.* = **gush**,

S

jet, burst, spray, surge, eruption, squirt **2** *I flushed bright red as a spurt of anger flashed through me.* = **burst**, rush, surge, fit, access, spate

spy NOUN *He was jailed for five years as an alleged spy.* = **undercover agent**, secret agent, double agent, secret service agent, foreign agent, mole, fifth columnist, nark (*Brit., Austral. & N.Z. slang*) ▶ VERB **1** *I never agreed to spy for the United States.* = **be a spy**, snoop (*informal*), gather intelligence **2** (*usually followed by* **on**) *He had his wife spied on for evidence in a divorce case.* = **watch**, follow, shadow, tail (*informal*), trail, keep watch on, keep under surveillance **3** *He was walking down the street when he spied an old friend.* = **catch sight of**, see, spot, notice, sight, observe, glimpse, behold (*archaic, literary*), set eyes on, espy, descry

spying NOUN = **espionage**, reconnaissance, infiltration, undercover work

squabble VERB *Mother is devoted to Dad although they squabble all the time.* = **quarrel**, fight, argue, row, clash, dispute, scrap (*informal*), fall out (*informal*), brawl, spar, wrangle, bicker, have words, fight like cat and dog, go at it hammer and tongs ▶ NOUN *There have been minor squabbles about phone bills.* = **quarrel**, fight, row, argument, dispute, set-to (*informal*), scrap (*informal*), disagreement, barney (*informal*), spat, difference of opinion, tiff, bagarre (*French*)

squad NOUN = **team**, group, band, company, force, troop, crew, gang

squalid ADJECTIVE **1** *The migrants have been living in squalid conditions.* = **dirty**, filthy, seedy, sleazy, sordid, low, nasty, foul, disgusting, rundown, decayed, repulsive, poverty-stricken, unclean, fetid, slovenly, skanky (*slang*), slummy, yucky or yukky (*slang*), yucko (*Austral. slang*), festy (*Austral. slang*) ■ OPPOSITE: hygienic **2** *the squalid pursuit of profit* = **unseemly**, sordid, inappropriate, unsuitable, out of place, improper, undignified, disreputable, unbecoming, unrefined, out of keeping, discreditable, indelicate, in poor taste, indecorous, unbefitting

squalor NOUN = **filth**, wretchedness, sleaziness, decay, foulness, slumminess, squalidness, meanness ■ OPPOSITE: luxury

squander VERB = **waste**, spend, fritter away, blow (*slang*), consume, scatter, run through, lavish, throw away, misuse, dissipate, expend, misspend, be prodigal with, frivol away, spend like water ■ OPPOSITE: save

square NOUN **1** *The house is located in one of Pimlico's prettiest squares.* = **town square**,

close, quad, market square, quadrangle, village square **2** *I'm a square, man. I adore Steely Dan.* = **conservative**, dinosaur, traditionalist, die-hard, stick-in-the-mud (*informal*), fuddy-duddy (*informal*), old buffer (*Brit. informal*), antediluvian, back number (*informal*), (old) fogey ▶ ADJECTIVE **1** *We are asking for a square deal.* = **fair**, just, straight, genuine, decent, ethical, straightforward, upright, honest, equitable, upfront (*informal*), on the level (*informal*), kosher (*informal*), dinkum (*Austral. & N.Z. informal*), above board, fair and square, on the up and up **2** *I felt so square in my three-piece suit.* = **old-fashioned**, straight (*slang*), conservative, conventional, dated, bourgeois, out of date, stuffy, behind the times, strait-laced, out of the ark (*informal*), Pooterish ■ OPPOSITE: fashionable ▶ VERB (*often followed by* **with**) *His dreams did not square with reality.* = **agree**, match, fit, accord, correspond, tally, conform, reconcile, harmonize

squash VERB **1** *She made clay models and squashed them flat again.* = **crush**, press, flatten, mash, pound, smash, distort, pulp, compress, stamp on, trample down **2** *The troops would stay in position to squash the first murmur of trouble.* = **suppress**, put down (*slang*), quell, silence, sit on (*informal*), crush, quash, annihilate **3** *Worried managers would be sacked or simply squashed.* = **embarrass**, put down, humiliate, shame, disgrace, degrade, mortify, debase, discomfit, take the wind out of someone's sails, put (someone) in their place, take (someone) down a peg (*informal*)

squawk VERB **1** *I threw pebbles at the hens, and that made them jump and squawk.* = **cry**, crow, screech, hoot, yelp, cackle **2** *He squawked that the deal was a double cross.* = **complain**, protest, squeal (*informal, chiefly Brit.*), kick up a fuss (*informal*), raise Cain (*slang*) ▶ NOUN **1** *rising steeply into the air with an angry squawk* = **cry**, crow, screech, hoot, yelp, cackle **2** *She gave a loud squawk when the water was poured on her.* = **scream**, cry, yell, wail, shriek, screech, squeal, yelp, yowl

squeak VERB = **squeal**, pipe, peep, shrill, whine, yelp

squeal VERB **1** *Jennifer squealed with delight and hugged me.* = **scream**, yell, shriek, screech, yelp, wail, yowl **2** *They went squealing to the European Commission.* = **complain**, protest, moan (*informal*), squawk (*informal*), kick up a fuss (*informal*) **3** *There was no question of squealing to the police.* = **inform on**, grass (*Brit. slang*), betray, shop (*slang, chiefly Brit.*), sing (*slang,* chiefly U.S.), peach (slang), tell all, spill the beans (informal), snitch (slang), blab, rat on (informal), sell (someone) down the river (informal), blow the gaff (Brit. slang), spill your guts (slang), dob in (Austral. slang) ▶ NOUN the squeal of piglets; At that moment there was a squeal of brakes. = **scream**, shriek, screech, yell, scream, wail, yelp, yowl

squeamish ADJECTIVE **1** I feel squeamish at the sight of blood. = **queasy**, sick, nauseous, queer, sickish, qualmish ■ **OPPOSITE:** strong-stomached **2** A meeting with this man is not for the socially squeamish. = **fastidious**, particular, delicate, nice (rare), scrupulous, prudish, prissy (informal), finicky, strait-laced, punctilious (formal) ■ **OPPOSITE:** coarse

squeeze VERB **1** Dip the bread in the water and squeeze it dry. = **press**, crush, squash, pinch **2** He squeezed her arm reassuringly. = **clutch**, press, grip, crush, pinch, squash, nip, compress, wring **3** Joe squeezed some juice from the oranges. = **extract**, force, press, express **4** Somehow they managed to squeeze into the tight space. = **cram**, press, crowd, force, stuff, pack, jam, thrust, ram, wedge, jostle **5** The investigators are accused of squeezing the residents for information. = **pressurize**, lean on (informal), bring pressure to bear on, milk, bleed (informal), oppress, wrest, extort, put the squeeze on (informal), put the screws on (informal) **6** He scooped up the puppy and squeezed it. = **hug**, embrace, cuddle, clasp, enfold, hold tight ▶ NOUN **1** = **press**, grip, clasp, crush, pinch, squash, nip, wring **2** The lift holds six people, but it's a bit of a squeeze. = **crush**, jam, squash, press, crowd, congestion **3** She gave her teddy bear a squeeze. = **hug**, embrace, cuddle, hold, clasp, handclasp

squint VERB The girl squinted at the photograph. = **peer**, screw up your eyes, narrow your eyes, look through narrowed eyes ▶ NOUN She had a bad squint in her right eye. = **cross eyes**, strabismus

squirm VERB = **wriggle**, twist, writhe, shift, flounder, wiggle, fidget

squirt VERB a splat of cream that squirts from a plastic container = **spurt**, shoot, gush, burst, jet, surge, erupt, spew ▶ NOUN a squirt of air freshener = **spurt**, jet, burst, gush, surge, eruption

stab VERB Somebody stabbed him in the stomach. = **pierce**, cut, gore, run through, stick, injure, wound, knife, thrust, spear, jab, puncture, bayonet, transfix, impale, spill blood ▶ NOUN **1** Several times tennis stars have had a stab at acting. = **attempt**, go (informal), try, shot (informal), crack

(informal), essay, endeavour **2** a stab of pain just above his eye = **twinge**, prick, pang, ache • **stab someone in the back** She has been stabbed in the back by her supposed 'friends'. = **betray**, double-cross (informal), sell out (informal), sell, let down, inform on, do the dirty on (Brit. slang), break faith with, play false, give the Judas kiss to, dob in (Austral. slang)

stability NOUN = **firmness**, strength, soundness, durability, permanence, solidity, constancy, steadiness, steadfastness ■ **OPPOSITE:** instability

stable ADJECTIVE **1** a stable marriage = **secure**, lasting, strong, sound, fast, sure, established, permanent, constant, steady, enduring, reliable, abiding, durable, deep-rooted, well-founded, steadfast, immutable, unwavering, invariable, unalterable, unchangeable ■ **OPPOSITE:** insecure **2** Their characters are fully formed and they are both very stable children. = **well-balanced**, balanced, sensible, reasonable, rational, mentally sound **3** This structure must be stable. = **solid**, firm, secure, fixed, substantial, sturdy, durable, well-made, well-built, immovable, built to last ■ **OPPOSITE:** unstable

stack NOUN **1** There were stacks of books on the bedside table and floor. = **pile**, heap, mountain, mass, load (informal), cock, rick, clamp (Brit. Agriculture), mound **2** If the job's that good, you'll have stacks of money. = **lot**, mass, load (informal), ton (informal), heap (informal), large quantity, great amount ▶ VERB They are stacked neatly in piles of three. = **pile**, heap up, load, assemble, accumulate, amass, stockpile, bank up

staff NOUN **1** The staff were very good. = **workers**, employees, personnel, workforce, team, organization **2** We carried a staff that was notched at various lengths. = **stick**, pole, rod, prop, crook, cane, stave, wand, sceptre

stage NOUN the final stage of the tour = **step**, leg, phase, point, level, period, division, length, lap, juncture ▶ VERB **1** She staged her first play at the Edinburgh Festival. = **present**, produce, perform, put on, do, give, play **2** In the middle of this year the government staged a huge military parade. = **organize**, mount, arrange, lay on, orchestrate, engineer

stagger VERB **1** He was staggering and had to lean on the bar. = **totter**, reel, sway, falter, lurch, wobble, waver, teeter **2** The whole thing staggers me. = **astound**, amaze, stun, surprise, shock, shake, overwhelm, astonish, confound, take (someone) aback,

S

bowl over (*informal*), stupefy, strike (someone) dumb, throw off balance, give (someone) a shock, dumbfound, nonplus, flabbergast (*informal*), take (someone's) breath away

stagnant ADJECTIVE **1** *Mosquitoes have been thriving in stagnant water on building sites.* = **stale**, still, standing, quiet, sluggish, motionless, brackish ■ OPPOSITE: flowing **2** *Mass movements are often a factor in the awakening of stagnant societies.* = **inactive**, declining, stagnating, slow, depressed, sluggish, slow-moving

stagnate VERB *His career had stagnated.* = **vegetate**, decline, deteriorate, rot, decay, idle, rust, languish, stand still, fester, go to seed, lie fallow

staid ADJECTIVE = **sedate**, serious, sober, quiet, calm, grave, steady, composed, solemn, demure, decorous, self-restrained, set in your ways ■ OPPOSITE: wild

stain NOUN **1** *a black stain* = **mark**, spot, blot, blemish, discoloration, smirch **2** *a stain on the honour of its war dead* = **stigma**, shame, disgrace, slur, reproach, blemish, dishonour, infamy, blot on the escutcheon **3** *Give each surface two coats of stain.* = **dye**, colour, tint ▶ VERB **1** *Some foods can stain teeth, as of course can smoking.* = **mark**, soil, discolour, dirty, tarnish, tinge, spot, blot, blemish, smirch **2** *a technique biologists use to stain proteins* = **dye**, colour, tint **3** *It was too late. Their reputation had been stained.* = **disgrace**, taint, blacken, sully, corrupt, contaminate, deprave, defile, besmirch, drag through the mud

stake[1] NOUN *Drive in a stake before planting the tree.* = **pole**, post, spike, stick, pale, paling, picket, stave, palisade ▶ VERB *The plants are susceptible to wind, and should be well staked.* = **support**, secure, prop, brace, tie up, tether • **stake something out** *The time has come for us to stake out a claim to our homeland.* = **lay claim to**, define, outline, mark out, demarcate, delimit

stake[2] NOUN **1** *The game was usually played for high stakes between two large groups.* = **bet**, ante, wager, chance, risk, venture, hazard **2** *a stake in the plot* = **interest**, share, involvement, claim, concern, investment ▶ VERB *He has staked his reputation on the outcome.* = **bet**, gamble, wager, chance, risk, venture, hazard, jeopardize, imperil, put on the line • **at stake** *The tension was naturally high for a game with so much at stake.* = **to lose**, at risk, being risked

stale ADJECTIVE **1** *a lump of stale bread* = **old**, hard, dry, decayed, fetid ■ OPPOSITE: fresh **2** *the smell of stale sweat* = **musty**, stagnant,

fusty **3** *The place smelled of stale beer and dusty carpets.* = **tasteless**, flat, sour, insipid **4** *repeating stale jokes to kill the time* = **unoriginal**, banal, trite, common, flat, stereotyped, commonplace, worn-out, antiquated, threadbare, old hat, insipid, hackneyed, overused, repetitious, platitudinous, cliché-ridden ■ OPPOSITE: original

stalemate NOUN = **deadlock**, draw, tie, impasse, standstill

stalk VERB **1** *He stalks his victims like a hunter after a deer.* = **pursue**, follow, track, hunt, shadow, tail (*informal*), haunt, creep up on **2** *If his patience is tried at meetings he has been known to stalk out.* = **march**, pace, stride, strut, flounce

stall[1] VERB *The engine stalled.* = **stop dead**, jam, seize up, catch, stick, stop short ▶ NOUN **1** *market stalls selling local fruits* = **stand**, table, counter, booth, kiosk **2** *mucking out the animal stalls* = **enclosure**, pen, coop, corral, sty

stall[2] VERB **1** *an attempt to stall the negotiations* = **hinder**, obstruct, impede, block, check, arrest, halt, slow down, hamper, thwart, sabotage **2** *Tomas had spent all week stalling over a decision.* = **play for time**, delay, hedge, procrastinate, stonewall, beat about the bush (*informal*), temporize, drag your feet **3** *The shop manager stalled the man until the police arrived.* = **hold up**, delay, detain, divert, distract

stalwart ADJECTIVE **1** *a stalwart supporter of the colonial government* = **loyal**, faithful, strong, firm, true, constant, resolute, dependable, steadfast, true-blue, tried and true **2** *I was never in any danger with my stalwart bodyguard around me.* = **strong**, strapping, robust, athletic, vigorous, rugged (*U.S. & Canad.*), manly, hefty (*informal*), muscular, sturdy, stout, husky (*informal*), beefy (*informal*), lusty, sinewy, brawny ■ OPPOSITE: puny

stamina NOUN = **staying power**, endurance, resilience, force, power, energy, strength, resistance, grit, vigour, tenacity, power of endurance, indefatigability, lustiness

stammer VERB *She stammered her way through an introduction.* = **stutter**, falter, splutter, pause, hesitate, hem and haw, stumble over your words ▶ NOUN *A speech-therapist cured his stammer.* = **speech impediment**, stutter, speech defect

stamp NOUN **1** *You may live only where the stamp in your passport says you may.* = **imprint**, mark, brand, cast, mould, signature, earmark, hallmark **2** *the stamp of feet on the*

stairs = **stomp** (*informal*), stump, clump,
tramp, clomp **3** *Monty is a man of a very
different stamp.* = **type**, sort, kind, form, cut,
character (*informal*), fashion, cast, breed,
description ▶ VERB **1** *'Eat before July 14' was
stamped on the label.* = **print**, mark, fix,
impress, mould, imprint, engrave, inscribe
2 *She stamped her feet on the pavement to keep
out the cold.* = **stomp** (*informal*), stump,
clump, tramp, clomp **3** *He received a ban last
week after stamping on the referee's foot.*
= **trample**, step, tread, crush **4** *They had
stamped me as a bad woman.* = **identify**,
mark, brand, label, reveal, exhibit, betray,
pronounce, show to be, categorize,
typecast • **stamp something out**
on-the-spot fines to stamp the problems out
= **eliminate**, destroy, eradicate, crush,
suppress, put down, put out, scotch, quell,
extinguish, quench, extirpate

stampede NOUN *There was a stampede for the
exit.* = **rush**, charge, flight, scattering, rout
▶ VERB *The crowd stampeded and many were
crushed or trampled underfoot.* = **bolt**, run,
charge, race, career, rush, dash

stance NOUN **1** *They have maintained a
consistently neutral stance.* = **attitude**, stand,
position, viewpoint, standpoint **2** *The
woman detective shifted her stance from one foot
to the other.* = **posture**, carriage, bearing,
deportment

stand VERB **1** *She was standing beside my bed
staring down at me.* = **be upright**, be erect,
be vertical **2** *Becker stood and shook hands
with Ben.* = **get to your feet**, rise, stand up,
straighten up **3** *The house stands alone on top
of a small hill.* = **be located**, be, sit, perch,
nestle, be positioned, be sited, be perched,
be situated or located **4** *The supreme court
says the convictions still stand.* = **be valid**, be
in force, continue, stay, exist, prevail,
remain valid **5** *Stand the plant in the open in a
sunny, sheltered place.* = **put**, place, position,
set, mount **6** *The salad improves if made in the
open and left to stand.* = **sit**, rest, mellow,
maturate **7** *Ancient wisdom has stood the test
of time.* = **resist**, endure, withstand, wear
(*Brit. slang*), weather, undergo, defy,
tolerate, stand up to, hold out against,
stand firm against **8** *He hates vegetables and
can't stand curry.* = **tolerate**, bear, abide,
suffer, stomach, endure, brook, hack
(*slang*), submit to, thole (*dialect*) **9** *I can't
stand any more. I'm going to run away.* = **take**,
bear, handle, cope with, experience,
sustain, endure, undergo, put up with
(*informal*), withstand, countenance
▶ NOUN **1** *His tough stand won some grudging
admiration.* = **position**, attitude, stance,

opinion, determination, standpoint, firm
stand **2** *She bought a hot dog from a stand on a
street corner.* = **stall**, booth, kiosk, table
3 *The people in the stands are cheering with all
their might.* = **grandstand 4** *The teapot came
with a stand to catch the drips.* = **support**,
base, platform, place, stage, frame, rack,
bracket, tripod, dais, trivet • **stand by**
1 *Stand by for details.* = **be prepared**, wait,
stand ready, prepare yourself, wait in the
wings **2** *The police just stood by and watched as
the missiles rained down on us.* = **look on**,
watch, not lift a finger, wait, turn a blind
eye • **stand by something** *The decision has
been made and I have got to stand by it.*
= **support**, maintain, defend, champion,
justify, sustain, endorse, assert, uphold,
vindicate, stand up for, espouse, speak up
for, stick up for (*informal*) • **stand by
someone** *I wouldn't break the law for a friend,
but I would stand by her if she did.* = **support**,
back, champion, defend, take (someone's)
part, uphold, befriend, be loyal to, stick up
for (*informal*) • **stand for something**
1 *What does NATO stand for?* = **represent**,
mean, signify, denote, indicate, exemplify,
symbolize, betoken **2** *It's outrageous, and we
won't stand for it any more.* = **tolerate**, suffer,
bear, endure, put up with, wear (*Brit.
informal*), brook, lie down under (*informal*)
• **stand in for someone** *I had to stand in for
her on Tuesday when she didn't show up.* = **be a
substitute for**, represent, cover for, take
the place of, replace, understudy, hold the
fort for, do duty for, deputize for • **stand
out 1** *Every tree, wall and fence stood out
against dazzling white fields.* = **be
conspicuous**, be striking, be prominent, be
obvious, be highlighted, attract attention,
catch the eye, be distinct, stick out like a
sore thumb (*informal*), stare you in the face
(*informal*), be thrown into relief, bulk large,
stick out a mile (*informal*), leap to the eye
2 *Her hair stood out in spikes.* = **project**,
protrude, bristle • **stand up for
something** or **someone** *They stood up for
what they believed to be right.* = **support**,
champion, defend, uphold, side with, stick
up for (*informal*), come to the defence of
• **stand up to something** or **someone 1** *Is
this building going to stand up to the strongest
gales?* = **withstand**, take, bear, weather,
cope with, resist, endure, tolerate, hold out
against, stand firm against **2** *Women are now
aware of their rights and are prepared to stand up
to their employers.* = **resist**, oppose, confront,
tackle, brave, defy

standard NOUN **1** *There will be new standards
of hospital cleanliness.* = **level**, grade

2 *systems that were by later standards absurdly primitive* = **criterion**, measure, guideline, example, model, average, guide, pattern, sample, par, norm, gauge, benchmark, yardstick, touchstone **3** *(often plural) My father has always had high moral standards.* = **principles**, ideals, morals, rule, ethics, canon, moral principles, code of honour **4** *a gleaming limousine bearing the royal standard* = **flag**, banner, pennant, colours, ensign, pennon ▸ ADJECTIVE **1** *It was standard practice for them to advise in cases of murder.* = **usual**, normal, customary, set, stock, average, popular, basic, regular, typical, prevailing, orthodox, staple, one-size-fits-all ■ OPPOSITE: unusual **2** *a standard text in several languages* = **accepted**, official, established, classic, approved, recognized, definitive, authoritative ■ OPPOSITE: unofficial

standardize VERB = **bring into line**, stereotype, regiment, assimilate, mass-produce, institutionalize

stand-in NOUN = **substitute**, deputy, replacement, reserve, surrogate, understudy, locum, stopgap

standing NOUN **1** *He has improved his country's standing abroad.* = **status**, position, station, footing, condition, credit, rank, reputation, eminence, estimation, repute **2** *My girlfriend of long standing left me.* = **duration**, existence, experience, continuance ▸ ADJECTIVE **1** *a standing offer* = **permanent**, lasting, fixed, regular, repeated, perpetual **2** *standing stones* = **upright**, erect, vertical, rampant *(Heraldry)*, perpendicular, upended

standpoint NOUN = **point of view**, position, angle, viewpoint, stance, vantage point

staple ADJECTIVE = **principal**, chief, main, key, basic, essential, primary, fundamental, predominant

star NOUN **1** *The nights were pure with cold air and lit with stars.* = **heavenly body**, sun, celestial body **2** *Not all football stars are ill-behaved louts.* = **celebrity**, big name, celeb *(informal)*, megastar *(informal)*, name, draw, idol, luminary, leading man or lady, lead, hero or heroine, principal, main attraction ▸ PLURAL NOUN *There was nothing in my stars to say I'd have problems.* = **horoscope**, forecast, astrological chart ▸ VERB *He's starred in dozens of films.* = **play the lead**, appear, feature, perform ■ RELATED WORDS: *adjectives* astral, sidereal, stellar

starchy ADJECTIVE = **formal**, stiff, stuffy, conventional, precise, prim, punctilious *(formal)*, ceremonious

stare VERB = **gaze**, look, goggle, watch, gape, eyeball *(slang)*, ogle, gawp *(Brit. slang)*, gawk, rubberneck *(slang)*

stark ADJECTIVE **1** *The stark truth is that we are paying more now than we ever were.* = **plain**, simple, harsh, basic, bare, grim, straightforward, blunt, bald **2** *in stark contrast* = **sharp**, clear, striking, distinct, clear-cut **3** *the stark, white, characterless fireplace in the drawing room* = **austere**, severe, plain, bare, harsh, unadorned, bare-bones **4** *a stark landscape of concrete, wire and utility equipment* = **bleak**, grim, barren, hard, cold, depressing, dreary, desolate, forsaken, godforsaken, drear *(literary)* **5** *They are motivated, he said, by stark fear.* = **absolute**, pure, sheer, utter, downright, patent, consummate, palpable, out-and-out, flagrant, unmitigated, unalloyed, arrant ▸ ADVERB *I gasped again. He must have gone stark staring mad.* = **absolutely**, quite, completely, clean, entirely, altogether, wholly, utterly

start VERB **1** *She started counting up the coins.* = **set about**, begin, proceed, embark upon, take the plunge *(informal)*, take the first step, make a beginning, put your hand to the plough *(informal)* ■ OPPOSITE: stop **2** *The fire is thought to have started in an upstairs room.* = **begin**, arise, originate, issue, appear, commence, get under way, come into being, come into existence, first see the light of day ■ OPPOSITE: end **3** *Who started the fight?* = **set in motion**, initiate, instigate, open, trigger, kick off *(informal)*, originate, get going, engender, kick-start, get (something) off the ground *(informal)*, enter upon, get or set or start the ball rolling ■ OPPOSITE: stop **4** *Now is probably as good a time as any to start a business.* = **establish**, begin, found, father, create, launch, set up, introduce, institute, pioneer, initiate, inaugurate, lay the foundations of ■ OPPOSITE: terminate **5** *He started the car, which hummed smoothly.* = **start up**, activate, get something going ■ OPPOSITE: turn off **6** *Rachel started at his touch.* = **jump**, shy, jerk, twitch, flinch, recoil ▸ NOUN **1** *She demanded to know why she had not been told from the start.* = **beginning**, outset, opening, birth, foundation, dawn *(literary)*, first step(s), onset, initiation, inauguration, inception, commencement, kickoff *(informal)*, opening move ■ OPPOSITE: end **2** *He gave a start of surprise and astonishment.* = **jump**, jerk, twitch, spasm, convulsion

startle VERB = **surprise**, shock, alarm, frighten, scare, agitate, take (someone) aback, make (someone) jump, give (someone) a turn (*informal*)

startling ADJECTIVE = **surprising**, shocking, alarming, extraordinary, sudden, unexpected, staggering, unforeseen, jaw-dropping

starving ADJECTIVE = **hungry**, starved, ravenous, famished, hungering, sharp-set, esurient, faint from lack of food, ready to eat a horse (*informal*)

stash VERB *He had stashed money away in secret offshore bank accounts.* = **store**, stockpile, save up, hoard, hide, secrete, stow, cache, lay up, salt away, put aside for a rainy day ▶ NOUN *A large stash of drugs had been found aboard the yacht.* = **hoard**, supply, store, stockpile, cache, collection

state NOUN **1** *Mexico is a secular state.* = **country**, nation, land, republic, territory, federation, commonwealth, kingdom, body politic **2** *Leaders of the Southern States are meeting in Louisville.* = **province**, region, district, area, territory, federal state **3** *The state does not collect enough revenue to cover its expenditure.* = **government**, ministry, administration, executive, regime, powers-that-be **4** *When we moved here the walls and ceiling were in an awful state.* = **condition**, shape, state of affairs **5** *When you left our place, you weren't in a fit state to drive.* = **frame of mind**, condition, spirits, attitude, mood, humour **6** *Nelson's body lay in state in the Painted Hall after the battle of Trafalgar.* = **ceremony**, glory, grandeur, splendour, dignity, majesty, pomp **7** *You shouldn't be lifting heavy things in your state.* = **circumstances**, situation, position, case, pass, mode, plight, predicament ▶ VERB *Clearly state your address and telephone number.* = **say**, report, declare, specify, put, present, explain, voice, express, assert, utter, articulate, affirm, expound, enumerate, propound, aver, asseverate (*formal*) • **in a state 1** *I was in a state because nobody could understand why I had this illness.* = **distressed**, upset, agitated, disturbed, anxious, ruffled, uptight (*informal*), flustered, panic-stricken, het up, all steamed up (*slang*) **2** *The living room was in a state.* = **untidy**, disordered, messy, muddled, cluttered, jumbled, in disarray, topsy-turvy, higgledy-piggledy (*informal*)

stately ADJECTIVE = **grand**, majestic, dignified, royal, august, imposing, impressive, elegant, imperial, noble, regal, solemn, lofty, pompous, ceremonious ■ OPPOSITE: lowly

statement NOUN **1** *He now disowns that statement, saying he was depressed when he* made it. = **announcement**, declaration, communication, explanation, communiqué, proclamation, utterance **2** *statements from witnesses to the event* = **account**, report, testimony, evidence

state-of-the-art ADJECTIVE = **latest**, newest, up-to-date, up-to-the-minute ■ OPPOSITE: old-fashioned

static ADJECTIVE = **stationary**, still, motionless, fixed, constant, stagnant, inert, immobile, unmoving, stock-still, unvarying, changeless ■ OPPOSITE: moving

station NOUN **1** *She went with him to the station to see him off.* = **railway station**, stop, stage, halt, terminal, train station, terminus **2** *He was taken to the police station for questioning.* = **headquarters**, base, depot (*U.S. & Canad.*) **3** *Which radio station do you usually listen to?* = **channel**, wavelength, broadcasting company **4** *The vast majority knew their station in life and kept to it.* = **position**, rank, status, standing, post, situation, grade, sphere **5** *Police said the bomb was buried in the sand near a lifeguard station.* = **post**, place, location, position, situation, seat ▶ VERB *I was stationed there just after the war.* = **assign**, post, locate, set, establish, fix, install, garrison

stationary ADJECTIVE = **motionless**, standing, at a standstill, parked, fixed, moored, static, inert, unmoving, stock-still ■ OPPOSITE: moving

> **USAGE** This word, which is always an adjective, is occasionally wrongly used where 'paper products' are meant: *in the stationery (not stationary) cupboard.*

statuesque ADJECTIVE = **well-proportioned**, stately, Junoesque, imposing, majestic, dignified, regal

stature NOUN **1** *She was a little short in stature.* = **height**, build, size **2** *This club has grown in stature over the last 20 years.* = **importance**, standing, prestige, size, rank, consequence, prominence, eminence, high station

status NOUN **1** *promoted to the status of foreman* = **position**, rank, grade, degree (*archaic*) **2** *She cheated banks to satisfy her desire for money and status.* = **prestige**, standing, authority, influence, weight, reputation, honour, importance, consequence, fame, distinction, eminence, renown, mana (*N.Z.*) **3** *Please keep us informed of the status of this project.* = **state of play**, development, progress, condition, evolution, progression

statute NOUN = **law**, act, rule, regulation, decree, ordinance, enactment, edict

staunch ADJECTIVE = **loyal**, faithful, stalwart, sure, strong, firm, sound, true, constant, reliable, stout, resolute, dependable, trustworthy, trusty, steadfast, true-blue, immovable, tried and true

stay VERB **1** *Hundreds of people defied army orders to stay at home.* = **remain**, continue to be, linger, stand, stop, wait, settle, delay, halt, pause, hover, abide, hang around (*informal*), reside, stay put, bide, loiter, hang in the air, tarry, put down roots, establish yourself ■ **OPPOSITE:** go **2** (*often with* **at**) *He tried to stay at the hotel a few days every year.* = **lodge**, visit, sojourn (*literary*), put up at, be accommodated at **3** *Nothing stays the same for long.* = **continue**, remain, go on, survive, endure **4** *The finance ministry stayed the execution to avoid upsetting a nervous market.* = **suspend**, put off, defer, adjourn, hold over, hold in abeyance, prorogue ▶ NOUN **1** *An experienced Italian guide is provided during your stay.* = **visit**, stop, holiday, stopover, sojourn (*literary*) **2** *The court dismissed defence appeals for a permanent stay of execution.* = **postponement**, delay, suspension, stopping, halt, pause, reprieve, remission, deferment

staying power NOUN = **endurance**, strength, stamina, toughness

steadfast ADJECTIVE **1** *a steadfast friend* = **loyal**, faithful, stalwart, staunch, constant, steady, dedicated, reliable, persevering, dependable ■ **OPPOSITE:** undependable **2** *He remained steadfast in his belief that he had done the right thing.* = **resolute**, firm, fast, fixed, stable, intent, single-minded, unwavering, immovable, unflinching, unswerving, unfaltering ■ **OPPOSITE:** irresolute

steady ADJECTIVE **1** *the steady beat of the drums* = **continuous**, even, regular, constant, consistent, persistent, rhythmic, unbroken, habitual, uninterrupted, incessant, ceaseless, unremitting, unwavering, nonstop, unvarying, unfaltering, unfluctuating ■ **OPPOSITE:** irregular **2** *Make sure the camera is steady.* = **stable**, fixed, secure, firm, safe, immovable, on an even keel ■ **OPPOSITE:** unstable **3** *a steady boyfriend* = **regular**, established **4** *He was firm and steady, unlike other men she knew.* = **dependable**, sensible, reliable, balanced, settled, secure, calm, supportive, sober, staunch, serene, sedate, staid, steadfast, level-headed, serious-minded, imperturbable, equable, unchangeable, having both feet on the ground ■ **OPPOSITE:** undependable

steal VERB **1** *Anybody could walk in here and steal stuff.* = **take**, nick (*slang, chiefly Brit.*), pinch (*informal*), lift (*informal*), cabbage

(*Brit. slang*), swipe (*slang*), half-inch (*old-fashioned slang*), heist (*U.S. slang*), embezzle, blag (*slang*), pilfer, misappropriate, snitch (*slang*), purloin, filch, prig (*Brit. slang*), shoplift, thieve, be light-fingered, peculate (*literary*), walk or make off with **2** *They solved the problem by stealing an idea from nature.* = **copy**, take, plagiarize, appropriate, pinch (*informal*), pirate, poach, rip (*Computing*) **3** *They can steal away at night and join us.* = **sneak**, slip, creep, flit, tiptoe, slink, insinuate yourself

stealth NOUN = **secrecy**, furtiveness, slyness, sneakiness, unobtrusiveness, stealthiness, surreptitiousness

stealthy ADJECTIVE = **secret**, secretive, furtive, sneaking, covert, sly, clandestine, sneaky, skulking, underhand, surreptitious

steamy ADJECTIVE **1** *He'd had a steamy affair with an office colleague.* = **erotic**, hot (*slang*), sexy (*informal*), sensual, raunchy (*informal*), lewd, carnal, titillating, prurient, lascivious, lustful, lubricious (*formal, literary*) **2** *a steamy café* = **muggy**, damp, humid, sweaty, like a sauna

steep¹ ADJECTIVE **1** *a narrow, steep-sided valley* = **sheer**, precipitous, perpendicular, abrupt, headlong, vertical ■ **OPPOSITE:** gradual **2** *Unemployment has shown a steep rise.* = **sharp**, sudden, abrupt, marked, extreme, distinct **3** *The annual premium can be a little steep.* = **high**, excessive, exorbitant, extreme, stiff, unreasonable, overpriced, extortionate, uncalled-for ■ **OPPOSITE:** reasonable

steep² VERB *green beans steeped in olive oil* = **soak**, immerse, marinate (*Cookery*), damp, submerge, drench, moisten, macerate, souse, imbrue (*rare*)

steeped ADJECTIVE = **saturated**, pervaded, permeated, filled, infused, imbued, suffused

steer VERB **1** *What is it like to steer a ship of this size?* = **drive**, control, direct, handle, conduct, pilot, govern, be in the driver's seat **2** *Nick steered them into the nearest seats.* = **direct**, lead, guide, conduct, escort, show in or out • **steer clear of something** or **someone** *A lot of people steer clear of these sensitive issues.* = **avoid**, evade, fight shy of, shun, eschew, circumvent (*formal*), body-swerve, give a wide berth to, sheer off

stem¹ NOUN *He cut the stem for her with his knife and handed her the flower.* = **stalk**, branch, trunk, shoot, stock, axis, peduncle • **stem from something** *Much of the instability stems from the economic effects of the war.* = **originate from**, be caused by, derive from, arise from, flow from, emanate from, develop from, be generated by, be brought about by, be bred by, issue forth from

stem² VERB *He was still conscious, trying to stem the bleeding with his right hand.* = **stop**, hold back, staunch, stay (*archaic*), check, contain, dam, curb, restrain, bring to a standstill, stanch

stench NOUN = **stink**, whiff (*Brit. slang*), reek, pong (*Brit. informal*), foul smell, niff (*Brit. slang*), malodour, mephitis, noisomeness

step NOUN **1** *I took a step towards him.* = **pace**, stride, footstep **2** *He heard steps in the corridor.* = **footfall 3** *He slowly climbed the steps.* = **stair**, tread, rung **4** *He greeted the agreement as the first step towards peace.* = **move**, measure, action, means, act, proceeding, procedure, manoeuvre, deed, expedient **5** *Aristotle took the scientific approach a step further.* = **stage**, point, phase **6** *He quickened his step.* = **gait**, walk **7** *This is the final step in the career ladder.* = **level**, rank, remove, degree ▶ VERB *the first man to step on the moon* = **walk**, pace, tread, move • **in step** *Now they are more in step and more in love with each other.* = **in agreement**, in harmony, in unison, in line, coinciding, conforming, in conformity • **mind** or **watch your step** *Hey! she thought. Watch your step, girl!* = **be careful**, take care, look out, be cautious, be discreet, take heed, tread carefully, be canny, be on your guard, mind how you go, have your wits about you, mind your p's and q's • **out of step** *They jogged in silence a while, faces lowered, out of step.* = **in disagreement**, out of line, out of phase, out of harmony, incongruous, pulling different ways • **step down** or **aside** *Many would prefer to see him step aside in favour of his rival.* = **resign**, retire, quit, leave, give up, pull out, bow out, abdicate • **step in** *If no agreement was reached, the army would step in.* = **intervene**, take action, become involved, chip in (*informal*), intercede, take a hand • **step something up** *Security is being stepped up to deal with the increase in violence.* = **increase**, boost, intensify, up, raise, accelerate, speed up, escalate, augment • **take steps** *They agreed to take steps to avoid confrontation.* = **take action**, act, intervene, move in, take the initiative, take measures

stereotype NOUN *Accents can reinforce a stereotype.* = **formula**, cliché, pattern, mould, received idea ▶ VERB *He was stereotyped by some as a renegade.* = **categorize**, typecast, pigeonhole, dub, standardize, take to be, ghettoize, conventionalize

stereotyped ADJECTIVE = **unoriginal**, stock, standard, tired, conventional, played out, stale, banal, standardized, mass-produced, corny (*slang*), threadbare, trite, hackneyed, overused, platitudinous, cliché-ridden

sterile ADJECTIVE **1** *He always made sure that any cuts were protected by sterile dressings.* = **germ-free**, antiseptic, sterilized, disinfected, aseptic ■ **OPPOSITE:** unhygienic **2** *a sterile male* = **barren**, infertile, unproductive, infecund ■ **OPPOSITE:** fertile

sterilize VERB *Sulphur is also used to sterilize equipment.* = **disinfect**, purify, fumigate, decontaminate, autoclave, sanitize

sterling ADJECTIVE = **excellent**, sound, fine, first-class, superlative

stern ADJECTIVE **1** *He said stern measures would be taken against the killers.* = **strict**, harsh, rigorous, hard, cruel, grim, rigid, relentless, drastic, authoritarian, austere, inflexible, unrelenting, unyielding, unsparing ■ **OPPOSITE:** lenient **2** *Her father was stern and hard to please.* = **severe**, serious, forbidding, steely, boot-faced (*informal*), flinty ■ **OPPOSITE:** friendly

stew NOUN *She served him a bowl of beef stew.* = **hash**, casserole, goulash, ragout ▶ VERB *Stew the apple and blackberries to make a thick pulp.* = **braise**, boil, simmer, casserole • **in a stew** *Highly charged emotions have you in a stew.* = **troubled**, concerned, anxious, worried, fretting, in a panic, in a lather (*informal*)

stick¹ NOUN **1** *people carrying bundles of dry sticks to sell for firewood* = **twig**, branch, birch, offshoot **2** *Crowds armed with sticks and stones took to the streets.* = **cane**, staff, pole, rod, stake, switch, crook, baton, wand, sceptre **3** *It's not motorists who give you the most stick, it's the general public.* = **abuse**, criticism, flak (*informal*), blame, knocking (*informal*), hostility, slagging (*slang*), denigration, critical remarks, fault-finding

stick² VERB **1** *He folded the papers and stuck them in a drawer.* = **put**, place, set, position, drop, plant, store, lay, stuff, fix, deposit, install, plonk **2** *They stuck a needle in my back.* = **poke**, dig, stab, insert, thrust, pierce, penetrate, spear, prod, jab, transfix **3** *Stick down any loose bits of flooring.* = **fasten**, fix, bind, hold, bond, attach, hold on, glue, fuse, paste, adhere, affix **4** *The soil sticks to the blade and blocks the plough.* = **adhere**, cling, cleave, become joined, become cemented, become welded **5** *That song has stuck in my head for years.* = **stay**, remain, linger, persist **6** *The dagger stuck tightly in the*

S

silver scabbard. = **catch**, lodge, jam, stop, clog, snag, be embedded, be bogged down, come to a standstill, become immobilized **7** *How long did you stick that abuse for?* = **tolerate**, take, stand, stomach, endure, hack (*slang*), abide, bear up under • **stick out** *Your label's sticking out.* = **protrude**, stand out, jut out, show, project, bulge, obtrude • **stick something out 1** *He stuck his hand out in welcome.* = **offer**, present, extend, hold out, advance, reach out, stretch out, proffer **2** (*informal*) *I know the job's tough, but try to stick it out a bit longer.* = **endure**, bear, put up with (*informal*), weather, take it (*informal*), see through, soldier on, last out, grin and bear it (*informal*) • **stick to something 1** *Stick to well-lit roads.* = **keep to**, persevere in, cleave to **2** *We must stick to the rules.* = **adhere to**, honour, hold to, keep to, abide by, stand by • **stick up for someone** *Thanks for sticking up for me.* = **defend**, support, champion, uphold, stand up for, take the part or side of

stickler NOUN = **fanatic**, nut (*slang*), maniac (*informal*), purist, perfectionist, pedant, martinet, hard taskmaster, fusspot (*Brit. informal*)

sticky ADJECTIVE **1** *Peel away the sticky paper.* = **adhesive**, gummed, adherent, grippy **2** *a weakness for rich meat dishes and sticky puddings* = **gooey**, tacky (*informal*), syrupy, viscous, glutinous, gummy, icky (*informal*), gluey, clinging, claggy (*dialect*), viscid **3** *He found himself in a not inconsiderably sticky situation.* = **difficult**, awkward, tricky, embarrassing, painful, nasty, delicate, unpleasant, discomforting, hairy (*slang*), thorny, barro (*Austral. slang*) **4** *sticky days in the middle of August* = **humid**, close, sultry, oppressive, sweltering, clammy, muggy

stiff ADJECTIVE **1** *The film is crammed with corsets, bustles and stiff collars.* = **inflexible**, rigid, unyielding, hard, firm, tight, solid, tense, hardened, brittle, taut, solidified, unbending, inelastic ■ **OPPOSITE:** flexible **2** *I'm stiff all over right now.* = **unsupple**, arthritic, creaky (*informal*), rheumaticky ■ **OPPOSITE:** supple **3** *They always seemed a little awkward with each other, a bit stiff and formal.* = **formal**, constrained, forced, laboured, cold, mannered, wooden, artificial, uneasy, chilly, unnatural, austere, pompous, prim, stilted, starchy (*informal*), punctilious, priggish, standoffish, ceremonious, unrelaxed ■ **OPPOSITE:** informal **4** *The film faces stiff competition for the nomination.* = **vigorous**, great, strong **5** *stiff anti-drugs laws* = **severe**, strict, harsh, hard, heavy, sharp, extreme, cruel, drastic,

rigorous, stringent, oppressive, austere, inexorable, pitiless **6** *a stiff breeze rustling the trees* = **strong**, fresh, powerful, vigorous, brisk **7** *the stiff climb to the finish* = **difficult**, hard, tough, exacting, formidable, trying, fatiguing, uphill, arduous, laborious

stifle VERB **1** *Critics have accused them of trying to stifle debate.* = **suppress**, repress, prevent, stop, check, silence, curb, restrain, cover up, gag, hush, smother, extinguish, muffle, choke back **2** *She makes no attempt to stifle a yawn.* = **restrain**, suppress, repress, smother

stigma NOUN = **disgrace**, shame, dishonour, mark, spot, brand, stain, slur, blot, reproach, imputation, smirch

stigmatize VERB = **brand**, label, denounce, mark, discredit, pillory, defame, cast a slur upon

still ADJECTIVE **1** *He sat very still for several minutes.* = **motionless**, stationary, at rest, calm, smooth, peaceful, serene, tranquil, lifeless, placid, undisturbed, inert, restful, unruffled, unstirring ■ **OPPOSITE:** moving **2** *The night air was very still.* = **silent**, quiet, hushed, noiseless, stilly (*poetic*) ■ **OPPOSITE:** noisy ▶ VERB *Her crying slowly stilled.* = **quieten**, calm, subdue, settle, quiet, silence, soothe, hush, alleviate, lull, tranquillize ■ **OPPOSITE:** get louder ▶ NOUN *It was the only noise in the still of the night.* = **stillness**, peace, quiet, silence, hush, tranquillity ■ **OPPOSITE:** noise ▶ ADVERB *I still dream of home.* = **yet**, even now, up until now, up to this time ▶ SENTENCE CONNECTOR *It won't be easy. Still, I'll do my best.* = **however**, but, yet, nevertheless, for all that, notwithstanding

stilted ADJECTIVE = **stiff**, forced, wooden, laboured, artificial, inflated, constrained, unnatural, high-flown, pompous, pretentious, pedantic, bombastic, grandiloquent, high-sounding, arty-farty (*informal*), fustian ■ **OPPOSITE:** natural

stimulant NOUN = **pick-me-up** (*informal*), tonic, restorative, upper (*slang*), reviver, bracer (*informal*), energizer, pep pill (*informal*), excitant, analeptic ■ **OPPOSITE:** sedative

stimulate VERB = **encourage**, inspire, prompt, galvanize, fire, fan, urge, spur, provoke, arouse, animate, rouse, prod, quicken, inflame, incite, instigate, goad, whet, impel, foment, gee up

stimulating ADJECTIVE = **exciting**, inspiring, stirring, provoking, intriguing, rousing, provocative, exhilarating, thought-provoking, galvanic ■ **OPPOSITE:** boring

stimulus NOUN = **incentive**, spur, encouragement, impetus, provocation, inducement, goad, incitement, fillip, shot in the arm (*informal*), clarion call, geeing-up

sting VERB **1** *The nettles stung their legs.* = **hurt**, burn, wound **2** *His cheeks were stinging from the icy wind.* = **smart**, burn, pain, hurt, tingle **3** *Some of the criticism has really stung him.* = **anger**, provoke, infuriate, incense, gall, inflame, nettle, rile, pique

stingy ADJECTIVE **1** *My dad was stingy with pocket money.* = **mean**, penny-pinching (*informal*), miserly, near (*informal*), parsimonious, scrimping, illiberal, avaricious, niggardly, ungenerous, penurious, tightfisted, tight, close-fisted, mingy (*Brit. informal*), cheeseparing, snoep (*S. African informal*) **2** *Many people may consider this a rather stingy amount.* = **insufficient**, inadequate, meagre, small, pathetic, scant, skimpy, measly (*informal*), scanty, on the small side

stink VERB **1** *We all stank and nobody minded.* = **reek**, pong (*Brit. informal*), whiff (*Brit. slang*), stink to high heaven (*informal*), offend the nostrils **2** *I think their methods stink.* = **be bad**, be no good, be rotten, be offensive, be abhorrent, have a bad name, be detestable, be held in disrepute ▶ NOUN **1** *The stink was overpowering.* = **stench**, pong (*Brit. informal*), foul smell, foulness, malodour, fetor, noisomeness **2** *The family's making a hell of a stink.* = **fuss**, to-do, row, upset, scandal, stir, disturbance, uproar, commotion, rumpus, hubbub, brouhaha, deal of trouble (*informal*)

stinker NOUN = **scoundrel** (*old-fashioned*), heel (*slang*), sod (*slang*), cad (*Brit. informal*), swine, bounder (*Brit., old-fashioned slang*), cur, rotter (*slang, chiefly Brit.*), nasty piece of work (*informal*), dastard (*archaic*), wrong 'un (*slang*)

stinking ADJECTIVE **1** *I had a stinking cold.* = **rotten** (*informal*), disgusting, unpleasant, vile, contemptible, wretched **2** *They were locked up in a stinking cell.* = **foul-smelling**, smelly, reeking, fetid, malodorous, noisome, whiffy (*Brit. slang*), pongy (*Brit. informal*), mephitic, ill-smelling, niffy (*Brit. slang*), olid, festy (*Austral. slang*), yucko (*Austral. slang*)

stint NOUN *a five-year stint in Hong Kong* = **term**, time, turn, bit, period, share, tour, shift, stretch, spell, quota, assignment ▶ VERB *He didn't stint on the special effects.* = **be mean**, hold back, be sparing, scrimp, skimp on, save, withhold, begrudge, economize, be frugal, be parsimonious, be mingy (*Brit. informal*), spoil the ship for a ha'porth of tar

stipulate VERB = **specify**, agree, require, promise, contract, settle, guarantee, engage, pledge, lay down, covenant, postulate, insist upon, lay down *or* impose conditions

stipulation NOUN = **condition**, requirement, provision, term, contract, agreement, settlement, rider, restriction, qualification, clause, engagement, specification, precondition, prerequisite, proviso, sine qua non (*Latin*)

stir VERB **1** *Stir the soup for a few seconds.* = **mix**, beat, agitate **2** *The two women lay on their backs, not stirring.* = **move**, change position **3** *Stir yourself! We've got a visitor.* = **get moving**, move, get a move on (*informal*), hasten, budge, make an effort, be up and about (*informal*), look lively (*informal*), shake a leg (*informal*), exert yourself, bestir yourself **4** *I was intrigued by him, stirred by his intellect.* = **stimulate**, move, excite, fire, raise, touch, affect, urge, inspire, prompt, spur, thrill, provoke, arouse, awaken, animate, rouse, prod, quicken, inflame, incite, instigate, electrify, kindle ■ OPPOSITE: inhibit **5** *The sight of them stirred him into action.* = **spur**, drive, prompt, stimulate, prod, press, urge, animate, prick, incite, goad, impel ▶ NOUN *His film has caused a stir in America.* = **commotion**, to-do, excitement, activity, movement, disorder, fuss, disturbance, bustle, flurry, uproar, ferment, agitation, ado, tumult

stirring ADJECTIVE = **exciting**, dramatic, thrilling, moving, spirited, inspiring, stimulating, lively, animating, rousing, heady, exhilarating, impassioned, emotive, intoxicating

stock NOUN **1** *Stock prices have dropped.* = **shares**, holdings, securities, investments, bonds, equities **2** *The Fisher family holds 40% of the stock.* = **property**, capital, assets, funds **3** *We took a decision to withdraw a quantity of stock from sale.* = **goods**, merchandise, wares, range, choice, variety, selection, commodities, array, assortment **4** *a stock of ammunition* = **supply**, store, reserve, fund, reservoir, stockpile, hoard, cache **5** *We are both from working-class stock.* = **lineage**, descent, extraction, ancestry, house, family, line, race, type, variety, background, breed, strain, pedigree, forebears, parentage, line of descent **6** *I am carefully selecting the breeding stock.* = **livestock**, cattle, beasts, domestic animals ▶ VERB **1** *The shop stocks everything from cigarettes to recycled loo paper.* = **sell**, supply, handle, keep, trade in, deal in **2** *I worked stocking shelves in a grocery store.*

S

= **fill**, supply, provide with, provision, equip, furnish, fit out, kit out ▶ ADJECTIVE **1** *National security is the stock excuse for keeping things confidential.* = **hackneyed**, standard, usual, set, routine, stereotyped, staple, commonplace, worn-out, banal, run-of-the-mill, trite, overused **2** *They supply stock sizes outside the middle range.* = **regular**, traditional, usual, basic, ordinary, conventional, staple, customary • **stock up with something** *New Yorkers have been stocking up with bottled water.* = **store (up)**, lay in, hoard, save, gather, accumulate, amass, buy up, put away, replenish supplies of • **take stock** *It was time to take stock of my life.* = **review the situation**, weigh up, appraise, estimate, size up (*informal*), see how the land lies

stocky ADJECTIVE = **thickset**, solid, sturdy, chunky, stubby, dumpy, stumpy, mesomorphic

stodgy ADJECTIVE **1** *He was disgusted by the stodgy pizzas on sale in London.* = **heavy**, filling, substantial, leaden, starchy ■ OPPOSITE: light **2** *stodgy old fogies* = **dull**, boring, stuffy, formal, tedious, tiresome, staid, unimaginative, turgid, uninspired, unexciting, ho-hum, heavy going, fuddy-duddy (*informal*), dull as ditchwater ■ OPPOSITE: exciting

stoical ADJECTIVE = **resigned**, long-suffering, phlegmatic, philosophic, cool, calm, indifferent, stoic, dispassionate, impassive, stolid, imperturbable

stoicism NOUN = **resignation**, acceptance, patience, indifference, fortitude, long-suffering, calmness, fatalism, forbearance, stolidity, dispassion, impassivity, imperturbability

stolen ADJECTIVE = **hot** (*slang*), bent (*slang*), hooky (*slang*)

stolid ADJECTIVE = **apathetic**, unemotional, dull, heavy, wooden, stupid, bovine, dozy (*Brit. informal*), obtuse, lumpish, doltish ■ OPPOSITE: lively

stomach NOUN **1** *My stomach is completely full.* = **belly**, inside(s) (*informal*), gut (*informal*), abdomen, tummy (*informal*), puku (*N.Z.*) **2** *This exercise strengthens the stomach, buttocks and thighs.* = **tummy** (*informal*), pot, spare tyre (*informal*), paunch, breadbasket (*slang*), potbelly **3** *They have no stomach for a fight.* = **inclination**, taste, desire, appetite, relish, mind ▶ VERB *I could never stomach the cruelty involved in the wounding of animals.* = **bear**, take, tolerate, suffer, endure, swallow, hack (*slang*), abide, put up with (*informal*), submit to, reconcile or resign

yourself to ■ RELATED WORD: *adjective* gastric

stone NOUN **1** *He could not tell if the floor was wood or stone.* = **masonry**, rock **2** *The crowd began throwing stones.* = **rock**, pebble **3** *Old men sat beneath the plane trees and spat cherry stones at my feet.* = **pip**, seed, pit, kernel

stony ADJECTIVE **1** *a stony track* = **rocky**, rough, gritty, gravelly, rock-strewn, pebble **2** *The stony look he was giving her made it hard to think.* = **cold**, icy, hostile, hard, harsh, blank, adamant, indifferent, chilly, callous, heartless, merciless, unforgiving, inexorable, frigid, expressionless, unresponsive, pitiless, unfeeling, obdurate

stooge NOUN = **pawn**, puppet, fall guy (*informal*), butt, foil, patsy (*slang, chiefly U.S. & Canad.*), dupe, henchman *or* woman *or* person, lackey

stoop VERB **1** *She was taller than he was and stooped slightly.* = **hunch**, be bowed *or* round-shouldered **2** *He stooped to pick up the carrier bag of groceries.* = **bend**, lean, bow, duck, descend, incline, kneel, crouch, squat ▶ NOUN *He was a tall, thin fellow with a slight stoop.* = **slouch**, slump, droop, sag, bad posture, round-shoulderedness • **stoop to something** *How could anyone stoop to doing such a thing?* = **resort to**, sink to, descend to, deign to, condescend to, demean yourself by, lower yourself by

stop VERB **1** *I've been told to lose weight and stop smoking.* = **quit**, cease, refrain, break off, put an end to, pack in (*Brit. informal*), discontinue, leave off, call it a day (*informal*), desist, belay (*Nautical*), bring *or* come to a halt *or* standstill ■ OPPOSITE: start **2** *I think she really would have liked to stop everything right there.* = **prevent**, suspend, cut short, close, break, check, bar, arrest, silence, frustrate, axe (*informal*), interrupt, restrain, hold back, intercept, hinder, repress, impede, rein in, forestall, nip (something) in the bud ■ OPPOSITE: facilitate **3** *The music stopped and the lights were turned up.* = **end**, conclude, finish, be over, cut out (*informal*), terminate, come to an end, peter out ■ OPPOSITE: continue **4** *His heart stopped three times.* = **cease**, shut down, discontinue, desist ■ OPPOSITE: continue **5** *The car failed to stop at an army checkpoint.* = **halt**, pause, stall, draw up, pull up ■ OPPOSITE: keep going **6** *She doesn't stop to think about what she's saying.* = **pause**, wait, rest, hesitate, deliberate, take a break, have a breather (*informal*), stop briefly **7** *He insisted we stop at a small restaurant just outside Atlanta.* = **stay**, rest, put up, lodge, sojourn (*literary*), tarry, break your journey

▶ NOUN **1** *He slowed the car almost to a stop.*
= **halt**, standstill **2** *They waited at a bus stop.*
= **station**, stage, halt, destination, depot
(*U.S. & Canad.*), termination, terminus
3 *The last stop in his lengthy tour was Paris.*
= **stay**, break, visit, rest, stopover,
sojourn (*literary*)

stopgap NOUN *It is not an acceptable long term
solution, just a stopgap.* = **makeshift**,
improvisation, temporary expedient, shift,
resort, substitute ▶ MODIFIER *It was only
ever intended as a stopgap solution.*
= **makeshift**, emergency, temporary,
provisional, improvised, impromptu,
rough-and-ready

stoppage NOUN **1** *a seven-hour stoppage by
air-traffic controllers* = **stopping**, halt,
standstill, close, arrest, lay-off, shutdown,
cutoff, abeyance, discontinuance **2** *The
small traffic disturbance will soon grow into a
complete stoppage.* = **blockage**, obstruction,
stopping up, occlusion

store NOUN **1** *The company owns two stores in
Manchester.* = **shop**, outlet, department
store, market, supermarket, mart,
emporium (*old-fashioned*), chain store,
hypermarket **2** *I handed over my store of
chocolate biscuits.* = **supply**, stock, reserve,
lot, fund, mine, plenty, provision, wealth,
quantity, reservoir, abundance,
accumulation, stockpile, hoard, plethora,
cache **3** *a grain store* = **repository**,
warehouse, depot, storehouse, depository,
storeroom ▶ VERB **1** (*often with* **away** *or* **up**)
*storing away cash that will come in useful later
on* = **put by**, save, hoard, keep, stock,
husband, reserve, deposit, accumulate,
garner, stockpile, put aside, stash
(*informal*), salt away, keep in reserve, put
aside for a rainy day, lay by or in **2** *Some types
of garden furniture must be stored inside in the
winter.* = **put away**, put in storage, put in
store, lock away **3** *chips for storing data*
= **keep**, hold, preserve, maintain, retain,
conserve • **set great store by something**
*a retail group that sets great store by traditional
values* = **value**, prize, esteem, appreciate,
hold in high regard, think highly of

storm NOUN **1** *the violent storms which whipped
America's East Coast* = **tempest** (*literary*),
blast, hurricane, gale, tornado, cyclone,
blizzard, whirlwind, gust, squall **2** *The
photos caused a storm when they were first
published.* = **outburst**, row, stir, outcry,
furore, violence, anger, passion, outbreak,
turmoil, disturbance, strife, clamour,
agitation, commotion, rumpus, tumult,
hubbub **3** *His speech was greeted with a storm
of applause.* = **roar**, thunder, clamour, din

4 *a storm of missiles* = **barrage**, volley, salvo,
rain, shower, spray, discharge, fusillade
▶ VERB **1** *After a bit of an argument, he stormed
out.* = **rush**, stamp, flounce, fly, stalk,
stomp (*informal*) **2** *'It's a fiasco,' he stormed.*
= **rage**, fume, rant, complain, thunder,
rave, scold, bluster, go ballistic (*slang*), fly
off the handle (*informal*), wig out (*slang*)
3 *The refugees decided to storm the embassy.*
= **attack**, charge, rush, assault, beset,
assail, take by storm

stormy ADJECTIVE **1** *the long stormy winter of
1942* = **wild**, rough, tempestuous, raging,
dirty, foul, turbulent, windy, blustering,
blustery, gusty, inclement, squally **2** *the
stormy waters that surround the British Isles*
= **rough**, wild, turbulent, tempestuous,
raging **3** *The letter was read at a stormy
meeting.* = **angry**, heated, fierce,
passionate, fiery, impassioned, tumultuous

story NOUN **1** *a popular love story with a happy
ending* = **tale**, romance, narrative, record,
history, version, novel, legend, chronicle,
yarn (*informal*), recital, narration, urban
myth, urban legend, fictional account
2 *The parents all shared interesting stories about
their children.* = **anecdote**, account, tale,
report, detail, relation **3** *He invented some
story about a cousin.* = **lie**, falsehood, fib,
fiction, untruth, porky (*Brit. slang*), pork pie
(*Brit. slang*), white lie **4** *Those are some of the
top stories in the news.* = **report**, news,
article, feature, scoop, news item

storyteller NOUN = **raconteur**, author,
narrator, romancer, novelist, chronicler,
bard, fabulist, spinner of yarns, anecdotist

stout ADJECTIVE **1** *Poirot, a stout detective with
a moustache* = **fat**, big, heavy, overweight,
plump, bulky, substantial, burly, obese,
fleshy, tubby, portly, rotund, corpulent,
on the large or heavy side ■ **OPPOSITE:** slim
2 *a great stout fellow, big in brawn and bone*
= **strong**, strapping, muscular, tough,
substantial, athletic, hardy, robust,
vigorous, sturdy, stalwart, husky (*informal*),
hulking, beefy (*informal*), lusty, brawny,
thickset, able-bodied ■ **OPPOSITE:** puny
3 *The invasion was held up by unexpectedly stout
resistance.* = **brave**, bold, courageous,
fearless, resolute, gallant, intrepid, valiant,
plucky, doughty (*old-fashioned*),
indomitable, dauntless, lion-hearted,
valorous ■ **OPPOSITE:** timid

stow VERB = **pack**, load, put away, store,
stuff, deposit, jam, tuck, bundle, cram,
stash (*informal*), secrete

straggle VERB = **trail**, drift, wander,
range, lag, stray, roam, ramble, rove,
loiter, string out

S

straggly ADJECTIVE = **spread out**, spreading, rambling, untidy, loose, drifting, random, straying, irregular, aimless, disorganized, straggling

straight ADJECTIVE **1** *Keep the boat in a straight line.* = **direct**, unswerving, undeviating ■ **OPPOSITE:** indirect **2** *There wasn't a single straight wall in the building.* = **level**, even, right, square, true, smooth, in line, aligned, horizontal ■ **OPPOSITE:** crooked **3** *a straight answer to a straight question* = **frank**, plain, straightforward, blunt, outright, honest, downright, candid, forthright, bold, point-blank, upfront (*informal*), unqualified ■ **OPPOSITE:** evasive **4** *They'd won twelve straight games before they lost.* = **successive**, consecutive, continuous, through, running, solid, sustained, uninterrupted, nonstop, unrelieved ■ **OPPOSITE:** discontinuous **5** *Dorothy was described as a very straight woman.* = **conventional**, conservative, orthodox, traditional, square (*informal*), bourgeois, Pooterish ■ **OPPOSITE:** fashionable **6** *You need to be straight with them to gain their respect.* = **honest**, just, fair, decent, reliable, respectable, upright, honourable, equitable, law-abiding, trustworthy, above board, fair and square ■ **OPPOSITE:** dishonest **7** *a large straight whisky* = **undiluted**, pure, neat, unadulterated, unmixed **8** *We need to get the house straight again before they come home.* = **in order**, organized, arranged, sorted out, neat, tidy, orderly, shipshape, put to rights ■ **OPPOSITE:** untidy ▶ ADVERB **1** *Straight ahead were the low cabins of the motel.* = **directly**, precisely, exactly, as the crow flies, unswervingly, by the shortest route, in a beeline **2** *As always, we went straight to the experts for advice.* = **immediately**, directly, promptly, instantly, at once, straightaway, without delay, without hesitation, forthwith, unhesitatingly, before you could say Jack Robinson (*informal*) **3** *I told him straight that I had been looking for another job.* = **frankly**, honestly, point-blank, candidly, pulling no punches (*informal*), in plain English, with no holds barred

straightaway ADVERB = **immediately**, now, at once, directly, instantly, on the spot, right away, there and then, this minute, straightway (*archaic*), without more ado, without any delay

straighten VERB *She looked in the mirror and straightened her hair.* = **neaten**, arrange, tidy (up), order, spruce up, smarten up, put in order, set *or* put to rights • **straighten**

something out *My sister had come in with her common sense and straightened things out.* = **sort out**, resolve, put right, settle, correct, work out, clear up, rectify, disentangle, unsnarl

straightforward ADJECTIVE **1** *The question seemed straightforward enough.* = **simple**, easy, uncomplicated, routine, elementary, clear-cut, undemanding, easy-peasy (*slang*) ■ **OPPOSITE:** complicated **2** *I was impressed by his straightforward intelligent manner.* = **honest**, open, direct, genuine, sincere, candid, truthful, forthright, upfront (*informal*), dinkum (*Austral. & N.Z. informal*), above board, guileless ■ **OPPOSITE:** devious

strain[1] NOUN **1** *The prison service is already under considerable strain.* = **pressure**, stress, difficulty, demands, burden, adversity **2** *She was tired and under great strain.* = **stress**, pressure, anxiety, difficulty, distress, nervous tension **3** *the strain of being responsible for the mortgage* = **worry**, effort, struggle, tension; hassle ■ **OPPOSITE:** ease **4** *Place your hands under your buttocks to take some of the strain off your back.* = **burden**, tension **5** *a groin strain* = **injury**, wrench, sprain, pull, tension, tautness, tensity (*rare*) **6** *She could hear the tinny strains of a chamber orchestra.* = **tune**, air, melody, measure (*poetic*), lay, song, theme ▶ VERB **1** *Resources will be further strained by new demands for housing.* = **stretch**, test, tax, overtax, push to the limit **2** *He strained his back during a practice session.* = **injure**, wrench, sprain, damage, pull, tear, hurt, twist, rick **3** *Several thousand supporters strained to catch a glimpse of the new president.* = **strive**, struggle, endeavour, labour, go for it (*informal*), bend over backwards (*informal*), go for broke (*slang*), go all out for (*informal*), bust a gut (*informal*), give it your best shot (*informal*), make an all-out effort (*informal*), knock yourself out (*informal*), do your damnedest (*informal*), give it your all (*informal*), break your back *or* neck (*informal*), rupture yourself (*informal*) ■ **OPPOSITE:** relax **4** *Strain the stock and put it back in the pan.* = **sieve**, filter, sift, screen, separate, riddle, purify

strain[2] NOUN **1** *There was a strain of bitterness in his voice.* = **trace**, suggestion, suspicion, tendency, streak, trait **2** *a particularly beautiful strain of Swiss pansies* = **breed**, type, stock, family, race, blood, descent, pedigree, extraction, ancestry, lineage

strained ADJECTIVE **1** *a period of strained relations* = **tense**, difficult, uncomfortable, awkward, embarrassed, stiff, uneasy, constrained, self-conscious, unrelaxed

■ **OPPOSITE:** relaxed **2** *His laughter seemed a little strained.* = **forced**, put on, false, artificial, unnatural, laboured
■ **OPPOSITE:** natural

strait NOUN *(often plural) Thousands of vessels pass through the straits annually.* = **channel**, sound, narrows, stretch of water, sea passage ▶ PLURAL NOUN *If we had a child, we'd be in really dire straits.* = **difficulty**, crisis, mess, pass, hole (*slang*), emergency, distress, dilemma, embarrassment, plight, hardship, uphill (*S. African*), predicament, extremity, perplexity, panic stations (*informal*), pretty or fine kettle of fish (*informal*)

strand NOUN = **filament**, fibre, thread, length, lock, string, twist, rope, wisp, tress

stranded ADJECTIVE **1** *He returned to his stranded vessel yesterday afternoon.* = **beached**, grounded, marooned, ashore, shipwrecked, aground, cast away **2** *He left me stranded by the side of the road.* = **helpless**, abandoned, high and dry, left in the lurch

strange ADJECTIVE **1** *There was something strange about the flickering blue light.* = **odd**, unusual, curious, weird, wonderful, rare, funny, extraordinary, remarkable, bizarre, fantastic (*informal*), astonishing, marvellous, exceptional, peculiar, eccentric, abnormal, out-of-the-way, queer, irregular, rum (*Brit. slang*), uncommon, singular, perplexing, uncanny, mystifying, unheard-of, off-the-wall (*slang*), oddball (*informal*), unaccountable, left-field (*informal*), outré, curiouser and curiouser, daggy (*Austral. & N.Z. informal*)
■ **OPPOSITE:** ordinary **2** *I felt strange in his office, realizing how absurd it was.* = **out of place**, lost, uncomfortable, awkward, bewildered, disoriented, ill at ease, like a fish out of water ■ **OPPOSITE:** comfortable **3** *I ended up alone in a strange city.* = **unfamiliar**, new, unknown, foreign, novel, alien, exotic, untried, unexplored, outside your experience ■ **OPPOSITE:** familiar

stranger NOUN **1** *Sometimes I feel like I'm living with a stranger.* = **unknown person 2** *Being a stranger in town can be a painful experience.* = **newcomer**, incomer, foreigner, guest, visitor, unknown, alien, new arrival, outlander • **a stranger to something** *He is no stranger to controversy.* = **unaccustomed to**, new to, unused to, ignorant of, inexperienced in, unversed in, unpractised in, unseasoned in ■ **RELATED WORD:** phobia xenophobia

strangle VERB **1** *He was almost strangled by his parachute harness straps.* = **throttle**, choke, asphyxiate, garrotte, strangulate, smother, suffocate **2** *His creative drive has been strangled by his sense of guilt.* = **suppress**, inhibit, subdue, stifle, gag, repress, overpower, quash, quell, quench

strap NOUN *Nancy gripped the strap of her beach bag.* = **tie**, thong, leash, belt ▶ VERB *She strapped the gun belt around her waist.* = **fasten**, tie, secure, bind, lash, buckle, truss

strapping ADJECTIVE = **well-built**, big, powerful, robust, hefty (*informal*), sturdy, stalwart, burly, husky (*informal*), hulking, beefy (*informal*), brawny, well set-up

stratagem NOUN = **trick**, scheme, manoeuvre, plan, plot, device, intrigue, dodge, ploy, ruse, artifice, subterfuge, feint, wile, tactic

strategic ADJECTIVE **1** *a strategic plan for reducing the rate of infant mortality* = **tactical**, calculated, deliberate, planned, politic, diplomatic **2** *an operation to take the strategic island* = **crucial**, important, key, vital, critical, decisive, cardinal

strategy NOUN **1** *Community involvement is now integral to company strategy.* = **policy**, procedure, planning, programme, approach, scheme, manoeuvring, grand design **2** *the basic principles of my strategy* = **plan**, approach, scheme, manoeuvring, grand design

stratum NOUN **1** *It was an enormous task that affected every stratum of society.* = **class**, group, level, station, estate, rank, grade, category, bracket, caste **2** *The rock strata show that the region was intensely dry 15,000 years ago.* = **layer**, level, seam, table, bed, vein, tier, stratification, lode

> **USAGE** The word *strata* is the plural form of *stratum*, and should not be used as if it is a singular form: so you would say *This stratum of society is often disregarded*, or *These strata of society are often disregarded*, but not *This strata of society is often disregarded*.

stray VERB **1** *A railway line crosses the park so children must not be allowed to stray.* = **wander**, roam, go astray, range, drift, meander, rove, straggle, lose your way, be abandoned or lost **2** *She could not keep her eyes from straying towards him.* = **drift**, wander, roam, meander, rove **3** *Anyway, as usual, we seem to have strayed from the point.* = **digress**, diverge, deviate, ramble, get sidetracked, go off at a tangent, get off the point ▶ MODIFIER *A stray dog came up to him.* = **lost**, abandoned, homeless, roaming, vagrant ▶ ADJECTIVE *He was struck in the face by a stray boot.* = **random**, chance, freak, accidental, odd, scattered, erratic, scattershot

streak NOUN **1** *There are these dark streaks on the surface of the moon.* = **band**, line, strip, stroke, layer, slash, vein, stripe, smear **2** *He's still got a mean streak.* = **trace**, touch, element, strain, dash, vein ▸ VERB **1** *Rain had begun to streak the window panes.* = **fleck**, smear, daub, band, slash, stripe, striate **2** *A meteorite streaked across the sky.* = **speed**, fly, tear, sweep, flash, barrel (along) (*informal, chiefly U.S. & Canad.*), whistle, sprint, dart, zoom, whizz (*informal*), hurtle, burn rubber (*informal*), move like greased lightning (*informal*)

stream NOUN **1** *a mountain stream* = **river**, brook, creek (*U.S.*), burn (*Scot.*), beck, tributary, bayou, rivulet, rill, freshet **2** *a continuous stream of lava* = **flow**, current, rush, run, course, drift, surge, tide, torrent, outpouring, tideway **3** *a never-ending stream of jokes* = **succession**, series, flood, chain, battery, volley, avalanche, barrage, torrent ▸ VERB **1** *Tears streamed down their faces.* = **flow**, run, pour, course, issue, flood, shed, spill, emit, glide, cascade, gush, spout **2** *The traffic streamed past him.* = **rush**, fly, speed, tear, flood, pour

streamer NOUN = **banner**, flag, pennant, standard, colours, ribbon, ensign, pennon

streamlined ADJECTIVE = **efficient**, organized, modernized, rationalized, smooth, slick, sleek, well-run, time-saving, smooth-running

street NOUN = **road**, lane, avenue, terrace, row, boulevard, roadway, thoroughfare • **up one's street** *She loved it, this was right up her street.* = **to one's liking**, to one's taste, one's cup of tea (*informal*), pleasing, familiar, suitable, acceptable, compatible, congenial

strength NOUN **1** *He threw it forward with all his strength.* = **might**, muscle, brawn, sinew, brawniness ■ **OPPOSITE:** weakness **2** *Something gave me the strength to overcome the difficulty.* = **will**, spirit, resolution, resolve, courage, character, nerve, determination, pluck, stamina, grit, backbone, fortitude, toughness, tenacity, willpower, mettle, firmness, strength of character, steadfastness, moral fibre **3** *It'll take a while before you regain full strength.* = **health**, fitness, vigour, lustiness **4** *He was my strength during that terrible time.* = **mainstay**, anchor, tower of strength, security, succour **5** *He checked the strength o f the cables.* = **toughness**, soundness, robustness, sturdiness, stoutness **6** *He was surprised at the strength of his own feeling.*

= **force**, power, intensity, energy, vehemence, intenseness ■ **OPPOSITE:** weakness **7** *maximum-strength migraine tablets* = **potency**, effectiveness, concentration, efficacy **8** *Take into account your own strengths and weaknesses.* = **strong point**, skill, asset, advantage, talent, forte, speciality, aptitude ■ **OPPOSITE:** failing

strengthen VERB **1** *Such antagonism, he has asserted, strengthened his resolve.* = **fortify**, encourage, harden, toughen, consolidate, stiffen, hearten, gee up, brace up, give new energy to ■ **OPPOSITE:** weaken **2** *Research would strengthen the case for socialist reform.* = **reinforce**, support, confirm, establish, justify, enhance, intensify, bolster, substantiate, buttress, corroborate, give a boost to **3** *Any experience can teach and strengthen you.* = **bolster**, harden, reinforce, give a boost to **4** *Every day of sunshine strengthens the feeling of optimism.* = **heighten**, intensify **5** *Yoga can be used to strengthen the immune system.* = **make stronger**, build up, invigorate, restore, nourish, rejuvenate, give strength to **6** *The builders will have to strengthen the existing joists with additional timber.* = **support**, brace, steel, reinforce, consolidate, harden, bolster, augment, buttress **7** *As it strengthened, the wind was veering southerly.* = **become stronger**, intensify, heighten, gain strength

strenuous ADJECTIVE **1** *Avoid strenuous exercise in the evening.* = **demanding**, hard, tough, exhausting, taxing, uphill, arduous, laborious, Herculean, tough going, toilsome (*literary*), unrelaxing ■ **OPPOSITE:** easy **2** *Strenuous efforts have been made to improve conditions in the jail.* = **tireless**, determined, zealous, strong, earnest, spirited, active, eager, bold, persistent, vigorous, energetic, resolute

stress VERB **1** *He stressed the need for new measures.* = **emphasize**, highlight, underline, repeat, draw attention to, dwell on, underscore, accentuate, point up, rub in, flag up, harp on, belabour **2** *She stresses the syllables as though teaching a child.* = **place the emphasis on**, emphasize, give emphasis to, place the accent on, lay emphasis upon ▸ NOUN **1** *schools that put more stress on practical activities* = **emphasis**, importance, significance, force, weight, urgency **2** *Katy could not think clearly when under stress.* = **strain**, pressure, worry, tension, burden, anxiety, trauma, oppression, hassle (*informal*), nervous tension **3** *the misplaced stress on the first syllable* = **accent**, beat, emphasis, accentuation, ictus

stressful ADJECTIVE = **worrying**, anxious, tense, taxing, demanding, tough, draining, exhausting, exacting, traumatic, agitating, nerve-racking

stretch VERB **1** *an artificial reef stretching the length of the coast* = **extend**, cover, spread, reach, unfold, put forth, unroll **2** *Protests stretched into their second week.* = **last**, continue, go on, extend, carry on, reach (*informal*) **3** *The cables are designed not to stretch.* = **expand**, lengthen, be elastic, be stretchy **4** *Make sure you don't stretch the pastry as you ease it into the corners.* = **pull**, distend, pull out of shape, strain, swell, tighten, rack, inflate, lengthen, draw out, elongate **5** *She stretched out her hand and slowly led him upstairs.* = **hold out**, offer, present, extend, proffer ▶ NOUN **1** *It's a very dangerous stretch of road.* = **expanse**, area, tract, spread, distance, sweep, extent **2** *He would study for eight- to ten-hour stretches.* = **period**, time, spell, stint, run, term, bit, space

strew VERB = **scatter**, spread, litter, toss, sprinkle, disperse, bestrew

stricken ADJECTIVE = **affected**, hit, afflicted, struck, injured, struck down, smitten, laid low

strict ADJECTIVE **1** *French privacy laws are very strict.* = **severe**, harsh, stern, firm, rigid, rigorous, stringent, austere ■ OPPOSITE: easy-going **2** *My parents were very strict.* = **stern**, firm, severe, harsh, authoritarian, austere, no-nonsense **3** *the strictest sense of the word* = **exact**, accurate, precise, close, true, particular, religious, faithful, meticulous, scrupulous **4** *a strict Catholic* = **devout**, religious, orthodox, pious, pure, reverent, prayerful **5** *Your enquiry will be handled in strict confidence.* = **absolute**, complete, total, perfect, utter

stricture NOUN = **criticism**, censure, stick (*slang*), blame, rebuke, flak (*informal*), bad press, animadversion

strident ADJECTIVE = **harsh**, jarring, grating, clashing, screeching, raucous, shrill, rasping, jangling, discordant, clamorous, unmusical, stridulant, stridulous ■ OPPOSITE: soft

strife NOUN = **conflict**, battle, struggle, row, clash, clashes, contest, controversy, combat, warfare, rivalry, contention, quarrel, friction, squabbling, wrangling, bickering, animosity, discord, dissension

strike NOUN *a call for a strike* = **walkout**, industrial action, mutiny, revolt, stop-work or stop-work meeting (*Austral.*) ▶ VERB **1** *their recognition of the worker's right to strike* = **walk out**, take industrial action, down tools, revolt, mutiny **2** *She took two steps forward and struck him across the mouth.* = **hit**, smack, thump, pound, beat, box, knock, punch, hammer, deck (*slang*), slap, sock (*slang*), chin (*slang*), buffet, clout (*informal*), cuff, clump (*slang*), swipe, clobber (*slang*), smite, wallop (*informal*), lambast(e), lay a finger on (*informal*), lay one on (*slang*), beat or knock seven bells out of (*informal*) **3** *He struck the ball straight into the hospitality tents.* = **drive**, propel, force, hit, smack, wallop (*informal*) **4** *The car skidded and struck a wall.* = **collide with**, hit, run into, bump into, touch, smash into, come into contact with, knock into, be in collision with **5** *He fell and struck his head on the stone floor.* = **knock**, bang, smack, thump, beat, smite **6** *He was suddenly struck with a sense of loss.* = **affect**, move, hit, touch, devastate (*informal*), overwhelm, leave a mark on, make an impact or impression on **7** *The killer says he will strike again.* = **attack**, assault someone, fall upon someone, set upon someone, lay into someone (*informal*) **8** *At this point, it suddenly struck me that I was wasting my time.* = **occur to**, hit, come to, register (*informal*), come to the mind of, dawn on or upon **9** *He struck me as a very serious but friendly person.* = **seem to**, appear to, look to, give the impression to **10** *She was struck by his simple, spellbinding eloquence.* = **move**, touch, impress, hit, affect, overcome, stir, disturb, perturb, make an impact on **11** *You have to strike a balance between sleep and homework.* = **achieve**, arrive at, attain, reach, effect, arrange **12** (*sometimes with* **upon**) *He realized he had just struck oil.* = **discover**, find, come upon or across, reach, encounter, turn up, uncover, unearth, hit upon, light upon, happen or chance upon, stumble upon or across • **strike out** *They left the car and struck out along the muddy track.* = **set out**, set off, start out, sally forth • **strike someone down** *a great sporting hero, struck down at 49* = **kill** (*informal*), destroy, slay (*archaic, literary*), ruin, afflict, smite, bring low, deal a deathblow to • **strike something out** or **off** or **through** *The censor struck out the next two lines.* = **score out**, delete, cross out, remove, cancel, erase, excise, efface, expunge (*formal*)

striking ADJECTIVE **1** *He bears a striking resemblance to Lenin.* = **distinct**, noticeable, conspicuous, clear, obvious, evident, manifest, unmistakable, observable, perceptible, appreciable **2** *She was a striking woman with long blonde hair.* = **impressive**, dramatic, stunning (*informal*), wonderful, extraordinary, outstanding, astonishing, memorable, dazzling, noticeable, conspicuous, drop-dead (*slang*), out of the ordinary, forcible, jaw-dropping, eye-popping (*informal*) ■ **OPPOSITE:** unimpressive

string NOUN **1** *He held out a small bag tied with string.* = **cord**, yarn, twine, strand, fibre, thread **2** *The landscape is broken only by a string of villages.* = **series**, line, row, file, sequence, queue, succession, procession **3** *The incident was the latest in a string of attacks.* = **sequence**, run, series, chain, succession, streak ▶ PLURAL NOUN **1** *The strings provided a melodic background.* = **stringed instruments** **2** *an offer made in good faith, with no strings attached* = **conditions**, catches (*informal*), provisos, stipulations, requirements, riders, obligations, qualifications, complications, prerequisites ▶ VERB *He had strung a banner across the wall.* = **hang**, stretch, suspend, sling, thread, loop, festoon • **string along with someone** *Can I string along with you for a while?* = **accompany**, go with, go along with, chaperon • **string someone along** *She was stringing him along even after they were divorced.* = **deceive**, fool, take (someone) for a ride (*informal*), kid (*informal*), bluff, hoax, dupe, put one over on (someone) (*informal*), play fast and loose with (someone) (*informal*), play (someone) false

stringent ADJECTIVE = **strict**, tough, rigorous, demanding, binding, tight, severe, exacting, rigid, inflexible ■ **OPPOSITE:** lax

stringy ADJECTIVE = **fibrous**, tough, chewy, sinewy, gristly, wiry

strip[1] VERB **1** *Women residents stripped naked in protest.* = **undress**, disrobe, unclothe, uncover yourself **2** *The soldiers have stripped the civilians of their passports.* = **plunder**, rob, loot, empty, sack, deprive, ransack, pillage, divest, denude

strip[2] NOUN **1** *Serve with strips of fresh raw vegetables.* = **piece**, shred, bit, band, slip, belt, tongue, ribbon, fillet, swathe **2** *a short boat ride across a narrow strip of water* = **stretch**, area, tract, expanse, extent

striped ADJECTIVE = **banded**, stripy, barred, striated

stripy or **stripey** ADJECTIVE = **banded**, striped, streaky

strive VERB = **try**, labour, struggle, fight, attempt, compete, strain, contend, endeavour, go for it (*informal*), try hard, toil, make every effort, go all out (*informal*), bend over backwards (*informal*), do your best, go for broke (*slang*), leave no stone unturned, bust a gut (*informal*), do all you can, give it your best shot (*informal*), jump through hoops (*informal*), break your neck (*informal*), exert yourself, make an all-out effort (*informal*), knock yourself out (*informal*), do your utmost, do your damnedest (*informal*), give it your all (*informal*), rupture yourself (*informal*)

stroke VERB *She was smoking a cigarette and stroking her cat.* = **caress**, rub, fondle, pat, pet ▶ NOUN **1** *He had a minor stroke, which left him partly paralysed.* = **apoplexy**, fit, seizure, attack, shock, collapse **2** *Fill in gaps by using short, upward strokes of the pencil.* = **mark**, line, slash **3** *I turned and swam a few strokes further out to sea.* = **movement**, action, motion **4** *He was sending the ball into the net with each stroke.* = **blow**, hit, knock, pat, rap, thump, swipe (*informal*) **5** *At the time, his appointment seemed a stroke of genius.* = **feat**, move, achievement, accomplishment, movement

stroll VERB *We strolled back, put the kettle on and settled down.* = **walk**, ramble, amble, wander, promenade, saunter, stooge (*slang*), take a turn, toddle, make your way, mooch (*slang*), mosey (*informal*), stretch your legs ▶ NOUN *After dinner, I took a stroll around the city.* = **walk**, promenade, turn, airing, constitutional, excursion, ramble, breath of air

strong ADJECTIVE **1** *I'm not strong enough to carry him.* = **powerful**, muscular, tough, capable, athletic, strapping, hardy, sturdy, stout, stalwart, burly, beefy (*informal*), virile, Herculean, sinewy, brawny, swole (*slang*), hench (*informal*) ■ **OPPOSITE:** weak **2** *It took me a long while to feel well and strong again.* = **fit**, sound, healthy, robust, hale (*old-fashioned*), in good shape, in good condition, lusty, fighting fit, fit as a fiddle **3** *Eventually I felt strong enough to look at him.* = **self-confident**, determined, tough, brave, aggressive, courageous, high-powered, forceful, resilient, feisty (*informal*), resolute, resourceful, tenacious, plucky, hard-nosed (*informal*), steadfast, unyielding, hard as nails, self-assertive, stout-hearted, two-fisted, firm in spirit ■ **OPPOSITE:** timid **4** *Around its summit, a strong wall had been built.* = **durable**, substantial, sturdy, reinforced, heavy-duty, well-built, well-armed, hard-wearing, well-protected, on a firm foundation ■ **OPPOSITE:** flimsy **5** *A strong current seemed to be moving the whole boat.* = **forceful**, powerful, intense, vigorous **6** *She is known to hold strong views on Cuba.* = **extreme**, radical, drastic, strict, harsh, rigid, forceful, uncompromising, Draconian, unbending

7 *The government will take strong action against any further strikes.* = **decisive**, firm, forceful, decided, determined, severe, resolute, incisive **8** *The evidence that such investment promotes growth is strong.* = **persuasive**, convincing, compelling, telling, great, clear, sound, effective, urgent, formidable, potent, well-established, clear-cut, overpowering, weighty, well-founded, redoubtable, trenchant, cogent **9** *strong aftershave* = **pungent**, powerful, concentrated, pure, undiluted ■ **OPPOSITE:** bland **10** *It's a good strong flavour, without being overpowering.* = **highly-flavoured**, hot, spicy, piquant, biting, sharp, heady, overpowering, intoxicating, highly-seasoned **11** *He has a strong interest in paintings and owns a fine collection.* = **keen**, deep, acute, eager, fervent, zealous, vehement **12** *Having strong unrequited feelings for someone is hard.* = **intense**, deep, passionate, ardent, fierce, profound, forceful, fervent, deep-rooted, vehement, fervid **13** *The Deputy Prime Minister is a strong supporter of the plan.* = **staunch**, firm, keen, dedicated, fierce, ardent, eager, enthusiastic, passionate, fervent **14** *She spoke English with a strong French accent.* = **distinct**, marked, clear, unmistakable ■ **OPPOSITE:** slight **15** *strong colours* = **bright** (*informal*), brilliant, dazzling, loud, bold, stark, glaring ■ **OPPOSITE:** dull

strong-arm MODIFIER = **bullying**, threatening, aggressive, violent, terror, forceful, high-pressure, coercive, terrorizing, thuggish

stronghold NOUN **1** *The seat was a stronghold of the Labour Party.* = **bastion**, fortress, bulwark, fastness **2** *Shetland is the last stronghold of otters in the British Isles.* = **refuge**, haven, retreat, sanctuary, hide-out, bolt hole

strong-minded ADJECTIVE = **determined**, resolute, strong-willed, firm, independent, uncompromising, iron-willed, unbending

strong point NOUN = **forte**, strength, speciality, advantage, asset, strong suit, métier, long suit (*informal*)

stroppy ADJECTIVE = **awkward**, difficult, obstreperous, destructive, perverse, unhelpful, cantankerous, bloody-minded (*Brit. informal*), quarrelsome, litigious, uncooperative

structure NOUN **1** *The chemical structure of this particular molecule is very unusual.* = **arrangement**, form, make-up, make, design, organization, construction, fabric, formation, configuration, conformation, interrelation of parts **2** *The house was a* handsome four-storey brick structure. = **building**, construction, erection, edifice, pile ▶ VERB *You have begun to structure your time.* = **arrange**, organize, design, shape, build up, assemble, put together

struggle VERB **1** *They had to struggle against all kinds of adversity.* = **strive**, labour, toil, work, strain, go for it (*informal*), make every effort, go all out (*informal*), bend over backwards (*informal*), go for broke (*slang*), bust a gut (*informal*), give it your best shot (*informal*), break your neck (*informal*), exert yourself, make an all-out effort (*informal*), work like a Trojan, knock yourself out (*informal*), do your damnedest (*informal*), give it your all (*informal*), rupture yourself (*informal*) **2** *We were struggling for the gun when it went off.* = **fight**, battle, wrestle, grapple, compete, contend, scuffle, lock horns **3** *The company is struggling to find visitors.* = **have trouble**, have problems, have difficulties, fight, come unstuck ▶ NOUN **1** *Life became a struggle.* = **problem**, battle, effort, trial, strain **2** *a young lad's struggle to support his poverty-stricken family* = **effort**, labour, toil, work, grind (*informal*), pains, scramble, long haul, exertion **3** *He died in a struggle with prison officers.* = **fight**, battle, conflict, clash, contest, encounter, brush, combat, hostilities, strife, skirmish, tussle, biffo (*Austral. slang*)

strut VERB = **swagger**, parade, stalk, peacock, prance

stub NOUN **1** *an ashtray of cigarette stubs* = **butt**, end, stump, tail (*informal*), remnant, tail end, fag end (*informal*), dog-end (*informal*) **2** *Those who still have their ticket stubs, please contact the arena.* = **counterfoil**

stubborn ADJECTIVE = **obstinate**, dogged, inflexible, fixed, persistent, intractable, wilful, tenacious, recalcitrant, unyielding, headstrong, unmanageable, unbending, obdurate, stiff-necked, unshakeable, self-willed, refractory, pig-headed, bull-headed, mulish, cross-grained, contumacious ■ **OPPOSITE:** compliant

stubby ADJECTIVE = **stumpy**, short, squat, stocky, chunky, dumpy, thickset, fubsy (*archaic, dialect*)

stuck ADJECTIVE **1** *She had got something stuck between her teeth.* = **fastened**, fast, fixed, joined, glued, cemented **2** *I don't want to get stuck in another job like that.* = **trapped**, caught, ensnared **3** *Many people are now stuck with fixed-rate mortgages.* = **burdened**, saddled, lumbered, landed, loaded, encumbered **4** *They will be there to help if you're stuck.* = **baffled**, stumped, at a loss, beaten, nonplussed, at a standstill, bereft of ideas, up against a brick wall (*informal*), at your wits' end • **be stuck on something** or **someone** *She's still stuck on him after all this time.* = **infatuated with**, obsessed with, keen on, enthusiastic about, mad about, wild about (*informal*), hung up on (*slang*), crazy about, for, or over (*informal*) • **get stuck into something** *The sooner we get stuck into this, the sooner we'll finish.* = **set about**, tackle, get down to, make a start on, take the bit between your teeth

stuck-up ADJECTIVE = **snobbish**, arrogant, conceited, proud, patronizing, condescending, snooty (*informal*), haughty, uppity (*informal*), high and mighty (*informal*), toffee-nosed (*slang, chiefly Brit.*), hoity-toity (*informal*), swollen-headed, bigheaded (*informal*), uppish (*Brit. informal*)

student NOUN **1** *a 23-year-old medical student* = **undergraduate**, scholar **2** *She's a former student of the school.* = **pupil**, scholar, schoolchild, schoolboy or schoolgirl **3** *a passionate student of history* = **learner**, observer, trainee, apprentice, disciple

studied ADJECTIVE = **planned**, calculated, deliberate, conscious, intentional, wilful, purposeful, premeditated, well-considered ■ **OPPOSITE:** unplanned

studio NOUN = **workshop**, shop, workroom, atelier

studious ADJECTIVE **1** *I was a very quiet, studious little girl.* = **scholarly**, academic, intellectual, serious, earnest, hard-working, thoughtful, reflective, diligent, meditative, bookish, assiduous, sedulous ■ **OPPOSITE:** unacademic **2** *He had a look of studious concentration on his face.* = **intent**, attentive, watchful, listening, concentrating, careful, regardful ■ **OPPOSITE:** careless **3** *the studious refusal of most of these firms to get involved in politics* = **deliberate**, planned, conscious, calculated, considered, studied, thoughtful, intentional, wilful, purposeful, premeditated, prearranged

study VERB **1** *The rehearsals make it difficult for her to study for her law exams.* = **learn**, cram (*informal*), swot (up) (*Brit. informal*), read up, hammer away at, bone up on (*informal*), burn the midnight oil, mug up (*Brit. slang*) **2** *Debbie studied her friend's face for a moment.* = **examine**, survey, look at, scrutinize, peruse **3** *I invite every citizen to carefully study the document.* = **contemplate**, read, examine, consider, go into, con (*archaic*), pore over, apply yourself (to) ▶ NOUN **1** *the use of maps and visual evidence in the study of local history* = **examination**, investigation, analysis, consideration, inspection, scrutiny, contemplation, perusal, cogitation **2** *the first study of English children's attitudes* = **piece of research**, survey, report, paper, review, article, inquiry, investigation **3** *She hopes to work full-time after she finishes her studies.* = **learning**, lessons, school work, academic work, reading, research, cramming (*informal*), swotting (*Brit. informal*), book work **4** *I went through the papers in his study.* = **office**, room, studio, workplace, den, place of work, workroom

stuff NOUN **1** *He pointed to a duffle bag. 'That's my stuff.'* = **things**, gear, possessions, effects, materials, equipment, objects, tackle, kit, junk, luggage, belongings, trappings, bits and pieces, paraphernalia, clobber (*Brit. slang*), impedimenta, goods and chattels **2** *Don't tell me you believe in all that stuff.* = **nonsense**, rubbish, rot (*informal*), trash, bunk (*informal*), foolishness, humbug, twaddle, tripe (*informal*), baloney (*informal*), verbiage, claptrap (*informal*), malarkey (*informal*), bunkum, poppycock (*informal*), balderdash, pants (*slang*), bosh (*informal*), stuff and nonsense, tommyrot, bizzo (*Austral. slang*), bull's wool (*Austral. & N.Z. slang*) **3** *The idea that we can be what we want has become the stuff of TV commercials.* = **substance**, material, essence, matter, staple, pith, quintessence ▶ VERB **1** *His trousers were stuffed inside the tops of his boots.* = **shove**, force, push, squeeze, jam, ram, wedge, compress, stow **2** *wallets stuffed with dollars* = **cram**, fill, pack, load, crowd

stuffing NOUN **1** *a stuffing for turkey, guinea fowl or chicken* = **filling**, forcemeat **2** *She made a wig from pillow stuffing.* = **wadding**, filling, packing, quilting, kapok

stuffy ADJECTIVE **1** *stuffy attitudes* = **staid**, conventional, dull, old-fashioned, deadly (*informal*), dreary, pompous, formal, prim, stilted, musty, stodgy, uninteresting, humourless, fusty, strait-laced, priggish, as dry as dust, old-fogeyish, niminy-piminy, prim and proper **2** *It was hot and stuffy in the classroom.* = **airless**, stifling, oppressive, close, heavy, stale, suffocating, sultry, fetid, muggy, unventilated, fuggy, frowsty ■ **OPPOSITE:** airy

stumble VERB **1** *The smoke was so thick that I stumbled on the first step.* = **trip**, fall, slip, reel, stagger, falter, flounder, lurch, come a cropper (*informal*), lose your balance, blunder about **2** *It was dark by the time they stumbled into the farmyard.* = **totter**, reel, stagger, blunder, falter, lurch, wobble, teeter **3** *His voiced wavered and he stumbled* over his words. = **falter**, hesitate, stammer, stutter, fluff (*informal*) • **stumble across** or **on** or **upon something** or **someone** *History relates that they stumbled on a magnificent waterfall.* = **discover**, find, come across, encounter, run across, chance upon, happen upon, light upon, blunder upon

stumbling block NOUN = **obstacle**, difficulty, bar, barrier, hurdle, hazard, snag, uphill (*S. African*), obstruction, impediment, hindrance

stump NOUN *The tramp produced a stump of candle from his pocket.* = **tail end**, end, remnant, remainder ▶ VERB **1** *Well, maybe I stumped you on that one.* = **baffle**, confuse, puzzle, snooker, foil, bewilder, confound, perplex, mystify, outwit, stymie, flummox, bring (someone) up short, dumbfound, nonplus **2** *The marshal stumped out of the room.* = **stamp**, clump, stomp (*informal*), trudge, plod, clomp • **stump something up** (*a sum of money*) *Customers do not have to stump up cash for at least four weeks.* = **pay**, fork out (*slang*), shell out (*informal*), contribute, hand over, donate, chip in (*informal*), cough up (*informal*), come across with (*informal*)

stumped ADJECTIVE = **baffled**, perplexed, at a loss, floored (*informal*), at sea, stymied, nonplussed, flummoxed, brought to a standstill, uncertain which way to turn, at your wits' end

stun VERB **1** *Many cinema-goers were stunned by the film's violent and tragic end.* = **overcome**, shock, amaze, confuse, astonish, stagger, bewilder, astound, overpower, confound, stupefy, strike (someone) dumb, knock (someone) for six (*informal*), dumbfound, flabbergast (*informal*), hit (someone) like a ton of bricks (*informal*), take (someone's) breath away **2** *He stood his ground and took a heavy blow that stunned him.* = **daze**, knock out, stupefy, numb, benumb

stung ADJECTIVE = **hurt**, wounded, angered, roused, incensed, exasperated, resentful, nettled, goaded, piqued

stunned ADJECTIVE = **staggered**, shocked, devastated, numb, astounded, bowled over (*informal*), gobsmacked (*Brit. slang*), dumbfounded, flabbergasted (*informal*), struck dumb, at a loss for words

stunner NOUN = **beauty**, looker (*informal*), lovely (*slang*), dish (*informal*), sensation, honey (*informal*), good-looker, dazzler, peach (*informal*), wow (*slang, chiefly U.S.*), knockout (*informal*), heart-throb, charmer, eyeful (*informal*), smasher (*informal*), humdinger (*slang*), glamour puss, beaut (*Austral. & N.Z. slang*)

stunning ADJECTIVE = **wonderful**, beautiful, impressive, great (*informal*), striking, brilliant, dramatic, lovely, remarkable, smashing (*informal*), heavenly, devastating (*informal*), spectacular, marvellous, splendid, gorgeous (*informal*), dazzling, sensational (*informal*), drop-dead (*slang*), ravishing, out of this world (*informal*), jaw-dropping, eye-popping (*informal*) ■ **OPPOSITE:** unimpressive

stunt NOUN = **feat**, act, trick, exploit, deed, tour de force (*French*)

stunted ADJECTIVE = **undersized**, dwarfed, little, small, tiny, diminutive, dwarfish

stupefy VERB = **astound**, shock, amaze, astonish, stun, stagger, bewilder, numb, daze, confound, knock senseless, dumbfound

stupendous ADJECTIVE **1** *This stupendous novel keeps you gripped to the end.* = **wonderful**, brilliant, amazing, stunning (*informal*), superb, overwhelming, fantastic (*informal*), tremendous (*informal*), fabulous (*informal*), surprising, staggering, marvellous, sensational (*informal*), breathtaking, phenomenal, astounding, prodigious, wondrous (*archaic, literary*), mind-boggling (*informal*), out of this world (*informal*), mind-blowing (*informal*), jaw-dropping, surpassing belief ■ **OPPOSITE:** unremarkable **2** *a stupendous amount of money* = **huge**, vast, enormous, mega (*slang*), gigantic, colossal ■ **OPPOSITE:** tiny

stupid ADJECTIVE **1** *I'm not stupid, you know.* = **unintelligent**, thick, dumb (*informal*), dull, dim (*informal*), dense, sluggish, deficient, gullible, dozy (*Brit. informal*), witless, stolid, dopey (*informal*), obtuse, brainless, slow on the uptake (*informal*), dumb-ass (*slang*), doltish, thickheaded, Boeotian, woodenheaded (*informal*) ■ **OPPOSITE:** intelligent **2** *I wouldn't call it art. It's just stupid and tasteless.* = **silly**, foolish, daft (*informal*), rash, trivial, ludicrous, meaningless, irresponsible, pointless, futile, senseless, mindless, laughable, short-sighted, ill-advised, idiotic, fatuous, nonsensical, half-baked (*informal*), inane, crackpot (*informal*), unthinking, puerile, crass, unintelligent, asinine, crackbrained ■ **OPPOSITE:** sensible **3** *She worked herself stupid.* = **senseless**, dazed, groggy, punch-drunk, insensate, semiconscious, into a daze

stupidity NOUN *I can't get over the stupidity of their decision.* = **silliness**, folly, foolishness, idiocy, madness, absurdity, futility, irresponsibility, pointlessness, inanity, rashness, impracticality, foolhardiness, senselessness, bêtise (*rare*), ludicrousness, puerility, fatuousness, fatuity

stupor NOUN = **daze**, numbness, unconsciousness, trance, coma, inertia, lethargy, torpor, stupefaction, insensibility

sturdy ADJECTIVE **1** *She was a short, sturdy woman in her early sixties.* = **robust**, hardy, vigorous, powerful, athletic, muscular, swole (*slang*), hench (*informal*), stalwart, staunch, hearty, lusty, brawny, thickset ■ **OPPOSITE:** puny **2** *The camera was mounted on a sturdy tripod.* = **substantial**, secure, solid, durable, well-made, well-built, built to last ■ **OPPOSITE:** flimsy

stutter NOUN *He spoke with a pronounced stutter.* = **stammer**, falter, speech impediment, speech defect, hesitance ▶ VERB *I was trembling so hard, I thought I would stutter when I spoke.* = **stammer**, stumble, falter, hesitate, splutter, speak haltingly

style NOUN **1** *Our children's different learning styles created many problems.* = **manner**, way, method, approach, technique, custom, mode **2** *She has not lost her grace and style.* = **elegance**, taste, chic, flair (*informal*), polish, grace, dash, sophistication, refinement, panache, flamboyance, élan, cosmopolitanism, savoir-faire, smartness, urbanity, stylishness, bon ton (*French*), fashionableness, dressiness (*informal*) **3** *Several styles of hat were available.* = **design**, form, cut **4** *six scenes in the style of a classical Greek tragedy* = **type**, sort, kind, spirit, pattern, variety, appearance, tone, strain, category, characteristic, genre, tenor **5** *The longer length of skirt is the style at the moment.* = **fashion**, trend, mode, vogue, rage **6** *The £17 million settlement allowed her to live in style to the end.* = **luxury**, ease, comfort, elegance, grandeur, affluence, gracious living **7** *The author's style is wonderfully anecdotal.* = **mode of expression**, phrasing, turn of phrase, wording, treatment, expression, vein, diction, phraseology ▶ VERB **1** *classically styled clothes* = **design**, cut, tailor, fashion, shape, arrange, adapt **2** *people who would like to style themselves as arms dealers* = **call**, name, term, address, label, entitle, dub, designate, christen, denominate

stylish ADJECTIVE = **smart**, chic, polished, fashionable, trendy (*Brit. informal*), classy (*slang*), in fashion, on trend, snappy, in vogue, dapper, natty (*informal*), snazzy (*informal*), modish, well turned-out, dressy (*informal*), à la mode, voguish, schmick

(*Austral. informal*), bling (*slang*), funky ■ **OPPOSITE:** scruffy

stymie VERB = **frustrate**, defeat, foil, thwart, puzzle, stump, snooker, hinder, confound, mystify, balk, flummox, throw a spanner in the works (*Brit. informal*), nonplus, spike (someone's) guns

suave ADJECTIVE = **smooth**, charming, urbane, debonair, worldly, cool (*informal*), sophisticated, polite, gracious, agreeable, courteous, affable, smooth-tongued

subconscious NOUN *the hidden power of the subconscious* = **mind**, psyche ▶ ADJECTIVE *a subconscious cry for affection* = **hidden**, inner, suppressed, repressed, intuitive, latent, innermost, subliminal ■ **OPPOSITE:** conscious

subdue VERB **1** *They admit they have not been able to subdue the rebels.* = **overcome**, defeat, master, break, control, discipline, crush, humble, put down, conquer, tame, overpower, overrun, trample, quell, triumph over, get the better of, vanquish (*literary*), beat down, get under control, get the upper hand over, gain ascendancy over **2** *He forced himself to subdue and overcome his fears.* = **moderate**, control, check, suppress, soften, repress, mellow, tone down, quieten down ■ **OPPOSITE:** arouse

subdued ADJECTIVE **1** *He faced the press, initially, in a somewhat subdued mood.* = **quiet**, serious, sober, sad, grave, restrained, repressed, solemn, chastened, dejected, downcast, crestfallen, repentant, down in the mouth, sadder and wiser, out of spirits ■ **OPPOSITE:** lively **2** *The conversation around them was resumed, but in subdued tones.* = **hushed**, soft, quiet, whispered, murmured, muted ■ **OPPOSITE:** loud **3** *The lighting was subdued.* = **dim** (*informal*), soft, subtle, muted, shaded, low-key, understated, toned down, unobtrusive ■ **OPPOSITE:** bright

subject NOUN **1** *It was I who first raised the subject of plastic surgery.* = **topic**, question, issue, matter, point, business, affair, object, theme, substance, subject matter, field of inquiry or reference **2** *a tutor in maths and science subjects* = **branch of study**, area, field, discipline, speciality, branch of knowledge **3** *Subjects in the study were forced to follow a modified diet.* = **participant**, case, patient, victim, client, guinea pig (*informal*) **4** *Roughly half of them are British subjects.* = **citizen**, resident, native, inhabitant, national **5** *His subjects regard him as a great and wise monarch.* = **dependant**, subordinate, vassal, liegeman ▶ ADJECTIVE *colonies and other subject territories* = **subordinate**, dependent, satellite, inferior, captive, obedient, enslaved, submissive, subservient, subjugated ▸ VERB *The police subjected her to some tough questioning.* = **put through**, expose, submit, lay open, make liable • **subject to 1** *Prices may be subject to alteration.* = **liable to**, open to, exposed to, vulnerable to, prone to, susceptible to, disposed to **2** *It could not be subject to another country's laws.* = **bound by**, under the control of, constrained by **3** *The merger is subject to certain conditions.* = **dependent on**, contingent on, controlled by, conditional on

subjective ADJECTIVE = **personal**, emotional, prejudiced, biased, instinctive, intuitive, idiosyncratic, nonobjective ■ **OPPOSITE:** objective

subjugate VERB = **conquer**, master, overcome, defeat, crush, suppress, put down, overthrow, tame, lick (*informal*), subdue, overpower, quell, rule over, enslave, vanquish (*literary*), hold sway over, bring to heel, bring (someone) to their knees, bring under the yoke

sublimate VERB = **channel**, transfer, divert, redirect, turn

sublime ADJECTIVE = **noble**, magnificent, glorious, high, great, grand, imposing, elevated, eminent, majestic, lofty, exalted, transcendent ■ **OPPOSITE:** lowly

subliminal ADJECTIVE = **subconscious**, unconscious

submerge VERB **1** *The river burst its banks, submerging an entire village.* = **flood**, swamp, engulf, drown, overflow, inundate, deluge **2** *Submerge the pieces of fish in the poaching liquid and simmer.* = **immerse**, plunge, dip, duck, dunk **3** *Just as I shot at it, the crocodile submerged again.* = **sink**, plunge, go under water **4** *He was suddenly submerged in an avalanche of scripts and offers.* = **overwhelm**, swamp, engulf, overload, inundate, deluge, snow under, overburden

submerged ADJECTIVE = **immersed**, sunk, underwater, drowned, submarine, sunken, undersea, subaqueous, submersed, subaquatic

submission NOUN **1** *The army intends to take the city or force it into submission.* = **surrender**, yielding, giving in, cave-in (*informal*), capitulation, acquiescence **2** *the submission of a dissertation* = **presentation**, submitting, handing in, entry, tendering **3** *A written submission has to be prepared.* = **proposal**, argument, contention **4** *She nodded her head in submission.* = **compliance**, obedience, submissiveness, meekness, resignation, deference, passivity, docility, tractability, unassertiveness

submissive ADJECTIVE = **meek**, passive, obedient, compliant, patient, resigned, yielding, accommodating, humble, subdued, lowly, abject, amenable, docile, dutiful, ingratiating, malleable, deferential, pliant, obsequious, uncomplaining, tractable, acquiescent, biddable, unresisting, bootlicking (*informal*), obeisant ■ **OPPOSITE:** obstinate

submit VERB **1** *If I submitted to their demands, they would not press the allegations.* = **surrender**, yield, give in, agree, bend, bow, endure, tolerate, comply, put up with (*informal*), succumb, defer, stoop, cave in (*informal*), capitulate, accede, acquiesce, toe the line, knuckle under, resign yourself, lay down arms, hoist the white flag, throw in the sponge **2** *They submitted their reports to the Chancellor yesterday.* = **present**, hand in, tender, put forward, table (*Brit.*), commit, refer, proffer **3** *I submit that you knew exactly what you were doing.* = **suggest**, claim, argue, propose, state, put, move, advance, volunteer, assert, contend, propound

subordinate NOUN *Nearly all her subordinates adored her.* = **inferior**, junior, assistant, aide, second, attendant, dependant, underling, subaltern ■ **OPPOSITE:** superior ▸ ADJECTIVE **1** *Sixty of his subordinate officers followed his example.* = **inferior**, lesser, lower, junior, subject, minor, secondary, dependent, subservient ■ **OPPOSITE:** superior **2** *It was an art in which words were subordinate to images.* = **subsidiary**, supplementary, auxiliary, ancillary

subordination NOUN = **inferiority**, servitude, subjection, inferior or secondary status

subscribe to VERB **1** *I've personally never subscribed to the view.* = **support**, agree with, advocate, consent to, endorse, countenance, acquiesce with **2** *I subscribe to a few favourable charities.* = **contribute to**, give to, donate to, chip in to (*informal*)

subscription NOUN = **membership fee**, charge, dues, annual payment

subsequent ADJECTIVE = **following**, later, succeeding, after, successive, ensuing, consequent ■ **OPPOSITE:** previous

subsequently ADVERB = **later**, afterwards, in the end, consequently, in the aftermath (of), at a later date

subservient ADJECTIVE **1** *Her willingness to be subservient to her children isolated her.* = **servile**, submissive, deferential, subject, inferior, abject, sycophantic, slavish, obsequious, truckling, bootlicking (*informal*) ■ **OPPOSITE:** domineering **2** *The individual's needs are seen as subservient to the* *group's.* = **subordinate**, subsidiary, accessory, auxiliary, conducive, ancillary

subside VERB **1** *The pain had subsided during the night.* = **decrease**, diminish, lessen, ease, moderate, dwindle, wane, recede, ebb, abate, let up, peter out, slacken, melt away, quieten, level off, de-escalate ■ **OPPOSITE:** increase **2** *Does that mean that the whole house is subsiding?* = **collapse**, sink, cave in, drop, lower, settle **3** *Local officials say the flood waters have subsided.* = **drop**, fall, decline, ebb, descend

subsidence NOUN = **sinking**, settling, collapse, settlement

subsidiary NOUN *a subsidiary of the American multinational* = **branch**, division, section, office, department, wing, subdivision, subsection, local office ▶ ADJECTIVE *a subsidiary position* = **secondary**, lesser, subordinate, minor, supplementary, auxiliary, supplemental, contributory, ancillary, subservient ■ **OPPOSITE:** main

subsidize VERB = **fund**, finance, support, promote, sponsor, underwrite, put up the money for

subsidy NOUN = **aid**, help, support, grant, contribution, assistance, allowance, financial aid, stipend, subvention

subsist VERB = **stay alive**, survive, keep going, make ends meet, last, live, continue, exist, endure, eke out an existence, keep your head above water, sustain yourself

subsistence NOUN = **living**, maintenance, upkeep, keep, support, existence, survival, livelihood

substance NOUN **1** *The substance that causes the problem comes from the barley.* = **material**, body, stuff, element, fabric, texture **2** *It is questionable whether anything of substance has been achieved.* = **importance**, significance, concreteness **3** *The substance of his discussions doesn't really matter.* = **meaning**, main point, gist, matter, subject, theme, import, significance, essence, pith, burden, sum and substance **4** *There is no substance in any of these allegations.* = **truth**, fact, reality, certainty, validity, authenticity, verity, verisimilitude **5** *mature men of substance* = **wealth**, means, property, assets, resources, estate, affluence

substandard ADJECTIVE = **inferior**, inadequate, unacceptable, damaged, imperfect, second-rate, shoddy

substantial ADJECTIVE **1** *That is a very substantial improvement in the current situation.* = **big**, significant, considerable, goodly, large, important, generous, worthwhile, tidy (*informal*), ample, sizable *or* sizeable ■ **OPPOSITE:** small **2** *those fortunate enough to have a fairly substantial property to sell* = **solid**, sound, sturdy, strong, firm, massive, hefty, durable, bulky, well-built ■ **OPPOSITE:** insubstantial

substantially ADVERB **1** *The price was substantially higher than had been expected.* = **considerably**, significantly, very much, greatly, seriously (*informal*), remarkably, markedly, noticeably, appreciably **2** *He checked the details given and found them substantially correct.* = **essentially**, largely, mainly, materially, in the main, in essence, to a large extent, in substance, in essentials

substantiate VERB = **support**, prove, confirm, establish, affirm, verify, validate, bear out, corroborate, attest to, authenticate ■ **OPPOSITE:** disprove

substitute VERB **1** *They were substituting violence for dialogue.* = **replace**, exchange, swap, change, switch, commute, interchange **2** (*with* **for**) *Her parents are trying to be supportive but they can't substitute for Jackie as a mother.* = **stand in for**, cover for, take over from, relieve, act for, double for, fill in for, hold the fort for, be in place of, deputize for ▶ NOUN *She is seeking a substitute for the man who broke her heart.* = **replacement**, reserve, equivalent, surrogate, deputy, relief, representative, sub, temporary, stand-by, makeshift, proxy, temp (*informal*), expedient, locum, depute (*Scot.*), stopgap, locum tenens

> **USAGE** Although *substitute* and *replace* have the same meaning, the structures they are used in are different. You replace A *with* B, while you substitute B *for* A. Accordingly, *he replaced the worn tyre with a new one*, and *he substituted a new tyre for the worn one* are both correct ways of saying the same thing.

substitution NOUN = **replacement**, exchange, switch, swap, change, interchange

subterfuge NOUN = **trick**, dodge, ploy, shift, manoeuvre, deception, evasion, pretence, pretext, ruse, artifice, duplicity, stratagem, deviousness, machination

subtle ADJECTIVE **1** *a subtle hint* = **faint**, slight, implied, delicate, indirect, understated, insinuated ■ **OPPOSITE:** obvious **2** *He is a subtle character, you know.* = **crafty**, cunning, sly, designing, scheming, intriguing, shrewd, ingenious, astute, devious, wily, artful, Machiavellian ■ **OPPOSITE:** straightforward **3** *subtle shades of brown* = **muted**, soft, subdued, low-key, toned down **4** *There was, however, a subtle distinction between the two lawsuits.* = **fine**, minute, narrow, tenuous, hair-splitting

S

subtlety NOUN **1** *All those linguistic subtleties get lost when a book goes into translation.* = **fine point**, refinement, nicety, sophistication, delicacy, intricacy, discernment **2** *She analyses herself with great subtlety.* = **skill**, acumen, astuteness, ingenuity, guile, cleverness, deviousness, sagacity, acuteness, craftiness, artfulness, slyness, wiliness **3** *They had obviously been hoping to approach the topic with more subtlety.* = **sensitivity**, diplomacy, discretion, delicacy, understanding, skill, consideration, judgment, perception, finesse, thoughtfulness, discernment, savoir-faire, adroitness

subtract VERB = **take away**, take off, deduct, remove, withdraw, diminish, take from, detract ■ OPPOSITE: add

suburb NOUN = **residential area**, neighbourhood, outskirts, precincts, suburbia, environs, purlieus, dormitory area (*Brit.*), faubourgs

subversive ADJECTIVE *The play was promptly banned as subversive and possibly treasonous.* = **seditious**, inflammatory, incendiary, underground, undermining, destructive, overthrowing, riotous, insurrectionary, treasonous, perversive ▶ NOUN *Agents regularly rounded up suspected subversives.* = **dissident**, terrorist, saboteur, insurrectionist, quisling, fifth columnist, deviationist, seditionary, seditionist

subvert VERB **1** *an alleged plot to subvert the state* = **overturn**, destroy, undermine, upset, ruin, wreck, demolish, sabotage **2** *an attempt to subvert culture from within* = **corrupt**, pervert, deprave, poison, contaminate, confound, debase, demoralize, vitiate

succeed VERB **1** *Some people will succeed in their efforts to stop smoking.* = **triumph**, win, prevail **2** *a move which would make any future talks even more unlikely to succeed* = **work out**, work, be successful, come off (*informal*), do the trick (*informal*), turn out well, go like a bomb (*Brit. & N.Z. informal*), go down a bomb (*informal, chiefly Brit.*), do the business (*informal*) **3** *the skills and qualities needed to succeed* = **make it** (*informal*), do well, be successful, arrive (*informal*), triumph, thrive, flourish, make good, prosper, cut it (*informal*), make the grade (*informal*), get to the top, crack it (*informal*), hit the jackpot (*informal*), bring home the bacon (*informal*), make your mark (*informal*), gain your end, carry all before you, do all right for yourself ■ OPPOSITE: fail **4** *She expects her Norwegian rival to succeed her as the best in the world.* = **take over from**, replace, assume the office of, fill (someone's) boots, step into (someone's) boots **5** (*with* **to**) *She eventually succeeded to the post in 1998.* = **take over**, assume, attain, acquire, come into, inherit, accede to, come into possession of **6** *He succeeded Trajan as emperor in AD 117.* = **follow**, come after, follow after, replace, be subsequent to, supervene ■ OPPOSITE: precede

success NOUN **1** *the success of European business in building a stronger partnership* = **victory**, triumph, positive result, favourable outcome ■ OPPOSITE: failure **2** *Nearly all of them believed work was the key to success.* = **prosperity**, fortune, luck, fame, eminence, ascendancy **3** *We hope it will be a commercial success.* = **hit** (*informal*), winner, smash (*informal*), triumph, sensation, wow (*slang*), best seller, market leader, smash hit (*informal*) ■ OPPOSITE: flop (*informal*) **4** *Everyone who knows her says she will be a great success.* = **big name**, star, hit (*informal*), somebody, celebrity, sensation, megastar (*informal*), V.I.P. ■ OPPOSITE: nobody

successful ADJECTIVE **1** *The successful candidate will be announced in June.* = **triumphant**, victorious, lucky, fortunate **2** *One of the keys to successful business is careful planning.* = **thriving**, profitable, productive, paying, effective, rewarding, booming, efficient, flourishing, unbeaten, lucrative, favourable, fruitful, efficacious, moneymaking ■ OPPOSITE: unprofitable **3** *She is a successful lawyer.* = **top**, prosperous, acknowledged, wealthy, out in front (*informal*), going places, at the top of the tree

successfully ADVERB = **well**, favourably, in triumph, with flying colours, famously (*informal*), swimmingly, victoriously

succession NOUN **1** *He took a succession of jobs which have stood him in good stead.* = **series**, run, sequence, course, order, train, flow, chain, cycle, procession, continuation, progression **2** *She is now seventh in line of succession to the throne.* = **taking over**, assumption, inheritance, elevation, accession, entering upon • **in succession** *They needed to reach the World Cup final for the third time in succession.* = **one after the other**, running, successively, consecutively, on the trot (*informal*), one behind the other

successive ADJECTIVE = **consecutive**, following, succeeding, in a row, in succession, sequent

succinct ADJECTIVE = **brief**, to the point, concise, compact, summary, condensed, terse, laconic, pithy, gnomic, compendious, in a few well-chosen words ■ OPPOSITE: rambling

S

succour NOUN *Have you offered comfort and succour to your friend?* = **help**, support, aid, relief, comfort, assistance ▸ VERB *The money would be used to succour evicted families.* = **help**, support, aid, encourage, nurse, comfort, foster, assist, relieve, minister to, befriend, render assistance to, give aid and encouragement to

succulent ADJECTIVE = **juicy**, moist, luscious, rich, lush, mellow, mouthwatering

succumb VERB **1** (*often with* **to**) *Don't succumb to the temptation to have just one cigarette.* = **surrender (to)**, yield (to), submit (to), give in (to), give way (to), go under (to), cave in (to) (*informal*), capitulate (to), knuckle under (to) ■ **OPPOSITE:** beat **2** (*with* **to**) (*an illness*) *I was determined not to succumb to the virus.* = **catch**, fall victim to, fall ill with

suck VERB **1** *They waited in silence and sucked their drinks through straws.* = **drink**, sip, draw **2** *The air is sucked out by a high-powered fan.* = **take**, draw, pull, extract • **suck up to someone** *She kept sucking up to the teachers.* = **ingratiate yourself with**, play up to (*informal*), curry favour with, flatter, pander to, toady, butter up, keep in with (*informal*), fawn on, truckle, lick someone's boots, dance attendance on, get on the right side of, worm yourself into (someone's) favour

sucker NOUN = **fool**, mug (*Brit. slang*), dupe, victim, butt, sap (*slang*), pushover (*slang*), sitting duck (*informal*), sitting target, putz (*U.S. slang*), cat's paw, easy game *or* mark (*informal*), nerd *or* nurd (*slang*), dorba *or* dorb (*Austral. slang*), bogan (*Austral. slang*)

sudden ADJECTIVE = **quick**, rapid, unexpected, swift, hurried, abrupt, hasty, impulsive, unforeseen ■ **OPPOSITE:** gradual

suddenly ADVERB = **abruptly**, all of a sudden, all at once, unexpectedly, out of the blue (*informal*), without warning, on the spur of the moment

sue VERB **1** *The company could be sued for damages.* = **take (someone) to court**, prosecute, bring an action against (someone), charge, summon, indict, have the law on (someone) (*informal*), prefer charges against (someone), institute legal proceedings against (someone) **2** *He realized that suing for peace was the only option.* = **appeal for**, plead, beg, petition, solicit, beseech, entreat, supplicate

suffer VERB **1** *Can you assure me that my father is not suffering?* = **be in pain**, hurt, ache, be racked, have a bad time, go through a lot (*informal*), go through the mill (*informal*), feel wretched **2** *I realized he was suffering from*

shock. = **be affected**, have trouble with, be afflicted, be troubled with **3** *The peace process has suffered a serious blow now.* = **undergo**, experience, sustain, feel, bear, go through, endure **4** *I'm not surprised that your studies are suffering.* = **deteriorate**, decline, get worse, fall off, be impaired **5** *She doesn't suffer fools gladly and, in her view, most people are fools.* = **tolerate**, stand, put up with (*informal*), support, bear, endure, hack (*Brit. informal*), abide

suffering NOUN = **pain**, torture, distress, agony, misery, ordeal, discomfort, torment, hardship, anguish, affliction, martyrdom

suffice VERB = **be enough**, do, be sufficient, be adequate, answer, serve, content, satisfy, fill the bill (*informal*), meet requirements, tick all the boxes

sufficient ADJECTIVE = **adequate**, enough, ample, satisfactory, enow (*archaic*) ■ **OPPOSITE:** insufficient

suffocate VERB **1** *They were suffocated as they slept.* = **choke**, stifle, smother, asphyxiate **2** *He either suffocated, or froze to death.* = **be choked**, be stifled, be smothered, be asphyxiated

suffuse VERB = **spread through** *or* **over**, flood, infuse, cover, steep, bathe, mantle, pervade, permeate, imbue, overspread, transfuse (*literary*)

suggest VERB **1** *I suggest you ask him some specific questions about his past.* = **recommend**, propose, advise, move, advocate, prescribe, put forward, offer a suggestion **2** *The figures suggest that their success is conditional on this restriction.* = **indicate**, lead you to believe **3** *What exactly are you suggesting?* = **hint at**, imply, insinuate, intimate, get at, drive at (*informal*) **4** *Its hairy body suggests a mammal.* = **bring to mind**, evoke, remind you of, connote, make you think of, put you in mind of

suggestion NOUN **1** *I have lots of suggestions for the park's future.* = **recommendation**, proposal, proposition, plan, motion **2** *There is absolutely no suggestion of any mainstream political party involvement.* = **hint**, implication, insinuation, intimation **3** *that fashionably faint suggestion of a tan* = **trace**, touch, hint, breath, indication, whisper, suspicion, intimation

suggestive ADJECTIVE *An employee claimed he made suggestive remarks.* = **smutty**, rude, indecent, improper, blue, provocative, spicy (*informal*), racy, unseemly, titillating, risqué, bawdy, prurient, off colour, ribald, immodest, indelicate • **suggestive of** *These headaches were most suggestive of raised* *blood pressure.* = **reminiscent of**, indicative of, redolent of, evocative of

suit NOUN **1** *a smart suit and tie* = **outfit**, costume, ensemble, dress, clothing, habit **2** *The judge dismissed the suit.* = **lawsuit**, case, trial, proceeding, cause, action, prosecution, industrial tribunal ▶ VERB **1** *They will only release information if it suits them.* = **be acceptable to**, please, satisfy, do, answer, gratify **2** *I don't think a sedentary life would altogether suit me.* = **agree with**, become, match, go with, correspond with, conform to, befit, harmonize with • **follow suit** *The Dutch seem set to follow suit.* = **copy someone**, emulate someone, accord with someone, take your cue from someone, run with the herd

suitability NOUN = **appropriateness**, fitness, rightness, aptness

suitable ADJECTIVE **1** *She had no other dress suitable for the occasion.* = **appropriate**, right, fitting, fit, suited, acceptable, becoming, satisfactory, apt, befitting ■ **OPPOSITE:** inappropriate **2** *Was it really suitable behaviour for someone who wants to be taken seriously?* = **seemly**, fitting, becoming, due, proper, correct ■ **OPPOSITE:** unseemly **3** *a resort where the slopes are more suitable for young children* = **suited**, appropriate, in keeping with, in character, cut out for ■ **OPPOSITE:** out of keeping **4** *Give a few people an idea of suitable questions to ask.* = **pertinent**, relevant, applicable, fitting, appropriate, to the point, apt, apposite, germane ■ **OPPOSITE:** irrelevant **5** *He could think of no less suitable moment to mention the idea.* = **convenient**, timely, appropriate, well-timed, opportune *(formal)*, commodious ■ **OPPOSITE:** inopportune

suite NOUN **1** *a suite at the Paris Hilton* = **rooms**, apartment, set of rooms, living quarters **2** *We will run a suite of checks.* = **set**, series, collection **3** *Fox and his suite sat there, looking uncertain.* = **attendants**, escorts, entourage, train, followers, retainers, retinue

suitor NOUN = **admirer**, young man, beau *(old-fashioned)*, follower *(obsolete)*, swain *(archaic)*, wooer

sulk VERB = **be sullen**, brood, be in a huff, pout, be put out, have the hump *(Brit. informal)*

sulky ADJECTIVE = **huffy**, sullen, petulant, cross, put out, moody, perverse, disgruntled, aloof, resentful, vexed, churlish, morose, querulous, ill-humoured, in the sulks

sullen ADJECTIVE = **morose**, cross, moody, sour, gloomy, brooding, dour, surly,

glowering, sulky, unsociable, out of humour ■ **OPPOSITE:** cheerful

sully VERB **1** *Reputations are easily sullied and business lost.* = **dishonour**, ruin, disgrace, besmirch, smirch **2** *I felt loath to sully the gleaming brass knocker by handling it.* = **defile**, dirty, stain, spot, spoil, contaminate, pollute, taint, tarnish, blemish, befoul

sultry ADJECTIVE **1** *The climax came one sultry August evening.* = **humid**, close, hot, sticky, stifling, oppressive, stuffy, sweltering, muggy ■ **OPPOSITE:** cool **2** *a role reserved for sultry models and actors* = **seductive**, sexy *(informal)*, sensual, voluptuous, passionate, erotic, provocative, amorous, come-hither *(informal)*

sum NOUN **1** *Large sums of money were lost.* = **amount**, quantity, volume **2** *I can't do my sums.* = **calculation**, figures, arithmetic, problem, numbers, reckonings, mathematics, maths *(Brit. informal)*, math *(U.S. informal)*, arithmetical problem **3** *The sum of all the angles of a triangle is 180 degrees.* = **total**, aggregate, entirety, sum total **4** *A group is more than the sum of the individuals in it.* = **totality**, whole • **sum something** *or* **someone up** *My mother probably summed her up better than I ever could.* = **size up**, estimate *(informal)*, get the measure of, form an opinion of

summarily ADVERB = **immediately**, promptly, swiftly, on the spot, speedily, without delay, arbitrarily, at short notice, forthwith, expeditiously, peremptorily, without wasting words

summarize VERB = **sum up**, recap, review, outline, condense, encapsulate, epitomize, abridge, précis, recapitulate, give a rundown of, put in a nutshell, give the main points of

summary NOUN *Here's a summary of the day's news.* = **synopsis**, résumé, précis, recapitulation, review, outline, extract, essence, abstract, summing-up, digest, epitome, rundown, compendium, abridgment ▶ ADJECTIVE **1** *The four men were killed after a summary trial.* = **hasty**, cursory, perfunctory, arbitrary **2** *a summary profit and loss statement* = **concise**, brief, compact, condensed, laconic, succinct, pithy, compendious

summit NOUN **1** *a NATO summit held in Rome* = **meeting**, talks, conference, discussion, negotiation, dialogue **2** *the first man to reach the summit of Mount Everest* = **peak**, top, tip, pinnacle, apex, head, crown, crest ■ **OPPOSITE:** base **3** *This is just a molehill on the way to the summit of her ambitions.*

S

= **height**, pinnacle, culmination, peak, high point, zenith, acme, crowning point
■ OPPOSITE: depths

summon VERB **1** *Howe summoned a doctor and hurried over.* = **send for**, call, bid, invite, rally, assemble, convene, call together, convoke (*formal*) **2** (*often with* **up**) *We couldn't even summon up the energy to open the envelope.* = **gather**, muster, draw on, invoke, mobilize, call into action

sumptuous ADJECTIVE = **luxurious**, rich, grand, expensive, superb, magnificent, costly, splendid, posh (*informal, chiefly Brit.*), gorgeous, lavish, extravagant, plush (*informal*), opulent, palatial, ritzy (*slang*), de luxe, splendiferous (*facetious*)
■ OPPOSITE: plain

sun NOUN *The sun was now high in the southern sky.* = **Sol** (*Roman myth*), Helios (*Greek myth*), Phoebus (*Greek myth*), daystar (*poetic*), eye of heaven, Phoebus Apollo (*Greek myth*)
• **sun yourself** *She was last seen sunning herself in a riverside park.* = **sunbathe**, tan, bask ■ RELATED WORD: *adjective* solar

sundry DETERMINER = **various**, several, varied, assorted, some, different, divers (*archaic*), miscellaneous

sunk ADJECTIVE = **ruined**, lost, finished, done for (*informal*), on the rocks, all washed up (*informal*), up the creek without a paddle (*informal*)

sunken ADJECTIVE **1** *Try diving for sunken treasure.* = **submerged**, immersed, submersed **2** *Steps led down to the sunken bath.* = **lowered**, buried, depressed, recessed, below ground, at a lower level **3** *an elderly man with sunken cheeks* = **hollow**, drawn, haggard, hollowed, concave

sunny ADJECTIVE **1** *The weather was surprisingly warm and sunny.* = **bright**, clear, fine, brilliant, radiant, luminous, sunlit, summery, unclouded, sunshiny, without a cloud in the sky ■ OPPOSITE: dull **2** *The staff wear big sunny smiles.* = **cheerful**, happy, cheery, smiling, beaming, pleasant, optimistic, buoyant, joyful, genial, chirpy (*informal*), blithe, light-hearted
■ OPPOSITE: gloomy

sunrise NOUN = **dawn**, daybreak, break of day, daylight, aurora (*poetic*), sunup, cockcrow, dayspring (*poetic*)

sunset NOUN = **nightfall**, dusk, sundown, eventide, gloaming (*Scot., poetic*), close of (the) day

super ADJECTIVE = **excellent**, wonderful, marvellous, mean (*slang*), topping (*Brit. slang*), cracking (*Brit. informal*), crucial (*slang*), outstanding, smashing (*informal*), superb, magnificent, glorious, terrific (*informal*), sensational (*informal*), mega (*slang*), sovereign, awesome (*slang*), sick (*slang*), def (*slang*), top-notch (*informal*), brill (*informal*), incomparable, out of this world (*informal*), peerless, matchless, boffo (*slang*), jim-dandy (*slang*), chillin' (*U.S. slang*), booshit (*Austral. slang*), exo (*Austral. slang*), sik (*Austral. slang*), rad (*informal*), phat (*slang*), schmick (*Austral. informal*)

superb ADJECTIVE **1** *a superb 18-hole golf course* = **splendid**, excellent, magnificent, topping (*Brit. slang*), fine, choice, grand, superior, divine (*informal*), marvellous, gorgeous, mega (*slang*), sick (*slang*), awesome (*slang*), world-class, exquisite, breathtaking, first-rate, superlative, unrivalled, brill (*informal*), bodacious (*slang, chiefly U.S.*), boffo (*slang*), splendiferous (*facetious*), of the first water, chillin' (*U.S. slang*), booshit (*Austral. slang*), exo (*Austral. slang*), sik (*Austral. slang*), rad (*informal*), phat (*slang*), schmick (*Austral. informal*) ■ OPPOSITE: inferior **2** *With superb skill he managed to make a perfect landing.* = **magnificent**, superior, marvellous, exquisite, breathtaking, admirable, superlative, unrivalled, splendiferous (*facetious*) ■ OPPOSITE: terrible

superficial ADJECTIVE **1** *a superficial yuppie with no intellect whatsoever* = **shallow**, frivolous, empty-headed, empty, silly, lightweight, trivial ■ OPPOSITE: serious **2** *He only gave it a superficial glance through.* = **hasty**, cursory, perfunctory, passing, nodding, hurried, casual, sketchy, facile, desultory, slapdash, inattentive
■ OPPOSITE: thorough **3** *It may well look different but the changes are only superficial.* = **slight**, surface, external, cosmetic, on the surface, exterior, peripheral, skin-deep
■ OPPOSITE: profound

superficially ADVERB = **at first glance**, apparently, on the surface, ostensibly, externally, at face value, to the casual eye

superfluous ADJECTIVE = **excess**, surplus, redundant, remaining, extra, spare, excessive, unnecessary, in excess, needless, left over, on your hands, surplus to requirements, uncalled-for, unneeded, residuary, supernumerary, superabundant, pleonastic (*Rhetoric*), unrequired, supererogatory ■ OPPOSITE: necessary

superhuman ADJECTIVE = **heroic**, phenomenal, prodigious, stupendous, herculean

superintend VERB = **supervise**, run, oversee, control, manage, direct, handle, look after, overlook, administer, inspect

superintendent NOUN **1** *superintendent of the bank's East African branches* = **supervisor**, director, manager, chief, governor, inspector, administrator, conductor, controller, overseer **2** *a building superintendent* = **warden**, caretaker, curator, keeper, porter (*Brit.*), custodian, watchman, janitor, concierge

superior ADJECTIVE **1** *She was greatly superior in education.* = **better**, higher, greater, grander, preferred, prevailing, paramount, surpassing, more advanced, predominant, unrivalled, more extensive, more skilful, more expert, a cut above (*informal*), streets ahead (*informal*), running rings around (*informal*) ■ **OPPOSITE:** inferior **2** *He's got a superior car, and it's easy to win races that way.* = **first-class**, excellent, first-rate, good, fine, choice, exclusive, distinguished, exceptional, world-class, good quality, admirable, high-class, high-calibre, de luxe, of the first order, sick (*slang*), booshit (*Austral. slang*), exo (*Austral. slang*), sik (*Austral. slang*), rad (*informal*), phat (*slang*), schmick (*Austral. informal*) ■ **OPPOSITE:** average **3** *negotiations between mutineers and their superior officers* = **higher-ranking**, senior, higher-level, upper-level **4** *Finch gave a superior smile.* = **supercilious**, patronizing, condescending, haughty, disdainful, lordly, lofty, airy, pretentious, stuck-up (*informal*), snobbish, on your high horse (*informal*) ▶ NOUN *my immediate superior* = **boss**, senior, director, manager, chief (*informal*), principal, supervisor, sherang (*Austral. & N.Z.*) ■ **OPPOSITE:** subordinate

> USAGE *Superior* should not be used with *than: He is a better* (not *a superior*) *poet than his brother; His poetry is superior to* (not *than*) *his brother's.*

superiority NOUN = **supremacy**, lead, advantage, excellence, prevalence, ascendancy, pre-eminence, preponderance, predominance

superlative ADJECTIVE = **supreme**, excellent, outstanding, highest, greatest, crack (*slang*), magnificent, surpassing, consummate, stellar (*informal*), unparalleled, transcendent, unrivalled, peerless, unsurpassed, matchless, of the highest order, of the first water ■ **OPPOSITE:** average

supernatural ADJECTIVE = **paranormal**, mysterious, unearthly, uncanny, dark, hidden, ghostly, psychic, phantom, abnormal, mystic, miraculous, unnatural, occult, spectral, preternatural, supranatural

supersede VERB = **replace**, displace, usurp, supplant, remove, take over, oust, take the place of, fill or step into (someone's) boots

supervise VERB **1** *He supervised and trained more than 400 volunteers.* = **observe**, guide, monitor, oversee, keep an eye on **2** *One of his jobs was supervising the dining room.* = **oversee**, run, manage, control, direct, handle, conduct, look after, be responsible for, administer, inspect, preside over, keep an eye on, be on duty, superintend, have or be in charge of

supervision NOUN = **superintendence**, direction, instruction, control, charge, care, management, administration, guidance, surveillance, oversight, auspices, stewardship

supervisor NOUN = **boss** (*informal*), manager, superintendent, chief, inspector, administrator, steward, gaffer (*informal, chiefly Brit.*), foreman or woman or person, overseer

supervisory ADJECTIVE = **managerial**, administrative, overseeing, superintendent, executive

supine ADJECTIVE **1** *a statue of a supine dog* = **flat on your back**, flat, horizontal, recumbent ■ **OPPOSITE:** prone **2** *a willing and supine executive* = **lethargic**, passive, lazy, idle, indifferent, careless, sluggish, negligent, inert, languid, uninterested, apathetic, lymphatic, listless, indolent, heedless, torpid, slothful (*formal*), spiritless

supplant VERB = **replace**, oust, displace, supersede, remove, take over, undermine, overthrow, unseat, take the place of

supple ADJECTIVE **1** *The leather is supple and sturdy enough to last for years.* = **pliant**, flexible, pliable, plastic, bending, elastic ■ **OPPOSITE:** rigid **2** *Paul was incredibly supple and strong.* = **flexible**, lithe, limber, lissom(e), loose-limbed ■ **OPPOSITE:** stiff

supplement VERB I *suggest supplementing your diet with vitamins E and A.* = **add to**, reinforce, complement, augment, extend, top up, fill out ▶ NOUN **1** *a special supplement to a monthly financial magazine* = **pull-out**, insert, magazine section, added feature, sidebar **2** *the supplement to the Encyclopedia Britannica* = **appendix**, sequel, add-on, complement, postscript, addendum, codicil, sidebar **3** *I had to pay a single room supplement.* = **addition**, extra, surcharge

supplementary ADJECTIVE = **additional**, extra, complementary, accompanying, secondary, auxiliary, add-on, supplemental, ancillary

supply VERB **1** *an agreement not to supply chemical weapons to these countries* = **provide**,

S

give, furnish, produce, stock, store, grant, afford, contribute, yield, come up with, outfit, endow, purvey, victual **2** *a pipeline which will supply the city with natural gas* = **furnish**, provide, equip, endow **3** *a society that looks to the government to supply their needs* = **meet**, provide for, fill, satisfy, fulfil, be adequate for, cater to or for ▶ NOUN *The brain requires a constant supply of oxygen.* = **store**, fund, stock, source, reserve, quantity, reservoir, stockpile, hoard, cache ▶ PLURAL NOUN *The country's only supplies are those it can import by lorry.* = **provisions**, necessities, stores, food, materials, items, equipment, rations, foodstuff, provender

support VERB **1** *He supported the hardworking people.* = **help**, back, champion, second, aid, forward, encourage, defend, promote, take (someone's) part, strengthen, assist, advocate, uphold, side with, go along with, stand up for, espouse, stand behind, hold (someone's) hand, stick up for (*informal*), succour, buoy up, boost (someone's) morale, take up the cudgels for, be a source of strength to ■ **OPPOSITE:** oppose **2** *I have children to support, and a home to be maintained.* = **provide for**, maintain, look after, keep, fund, finance, sustain, foster, take care of, subsidize ■ **OPPOSITE:** live off **3** *The evidence does not support the argument.* = **bear out**, confirm, verify, substantiate, corroborate, document, endorse, attest to, authenticate, lend credence to ■ **OPPOSITE:** refute **4** *the thick wooden posts that supported the ceiling* = **bear**, hold up, carry, sustain, prop (up), reinforce, hold, brace, uphold, bolster, underpin, shore up, buttress ▶ NOUN **1** *They are prepared to resort to violence in support of their views.* = **furtherance**, backing, promotion, championship, approval, assistance, encouragement, espousal **2** *We hope to continue to have her close support and friendship.* = **help**, protection, comfort, friendship, assistance, blessing, loyalty, patronage, moral support, succour ■ **OPPOSITE:** opposition **3** *a proposal to cut agricultural support* = **aid**, help, benefits, relief, assistance **4** *Rats had been gnawing at the supports of the house.* = **prop**, post, foundation, back, lining, stay, shore, brace, pillar, underpinning, stanchion, stiffener, abutment **5** *Andrew is terrific. He's been such a support to me.* = **supporter**, prop, mainstay, tower of strength, second, stay, backer, backbone, comforter ■ **OPPOSITE:** antagonist **6** *He failed to send child support.* = **upkeep**, maintenance, keep, livelihood, subsistence, sustenance

supporter NOUN = **follower**, fan, advocate, friend, champion, ally, defender, sponsor, patron, helper, protagonist, adherent, henchman *or* woman *or* person, apologist, upholder, well-wisher ■ **OPPOSITE:** opponent

supportive ADJECTIVE = **helpful**, caring, encouraging, understanding, reassuring, sympathetic ■ **RELATED WORD:** *prefix* pro-

suppose VERB **1** *Where do you suppose he's got to?* = **imagine**, believe, consider, conclude, fancy, conceive, conjecture, postulate (*formal*), hypothesize **2** *The problem was more complex than he supposed.* = **think**, imagine, expect, judge, assume, guess (*informal, chiefly U.S. & Canad.*), calculate (*U.S., dialect*), presume, take for granted, infer, conjecture, surmise, dare say, opine (*formal*), presuppose, take as read

supposed ADJECTIVE **1** (*usually with* **to**) *He produced a handwritten list of nine men he was supposed to kill.* = **meant**, expected, required, obliged **2** *What is it his son is supposed to have said?* = **presumed**, alleged, professed, reputed, accepted, assumed, rumoured, hypothetical, putative (*formal*), presupposed

supposedly ADVERB = **presumably**, allegedly, ostensibly, theoretically, by all accounts, purportedly, avowedly, hypothetically, at a guess, professedly ■ **OPPOSITE:** actually

supposition NOUN = **belief**, idea, notion, view, theory, speculation, assumption, hypothesis, presumption, conjecture, surmise, guesswork

suppress VERB **1** *drug traffickers who flourish despite attempts to suppress them* = **stamp out**, stop, check, crush, conquer, overthrow, subdue, put an end to, overpower, quash, crack down on, quell, extinguish, clamp down on, snuff out, quench, beat down, trample on, drive underground ■ **OPPOSITE:** encourage **2** *strong evidence that ultraviolet light can suppress immune responses* = **check**, inhibit, subdue, stop, quell, quench **3** *Liz thought of Barry and suppressed a smile.* = **restrain**, cover up, withhold, stifle, contain, silence, conceal, curb, repress, smother, keep secret, muffle, muzzle, hold in check, hold in *or* back **4** *At no time did they try to persuade me to suppress the information.* = **conceal**, hide, keep secret, hush up, stonewall, sweep under the carpet, draw a veil over, keep silent about, keep dark, keep under your hat (*informal*)

suppression NOUN **1** *They were imprisoned after the suppression of pro-democracy protests.*

= **elimination**, crushing, crackdown, check, extinction, prohibition, quashing, dissolution, termination, clampdown **2** *suppression of the immune system* = **inhibition**, blocking, restriction, restraint, smothering **3** *A mother's suppression of her own feelings can cause problems.* = **concealment**, covering, hiding, disguising, camouflage **4** *suppression of official documents* = **hiding**, hushing up, stonewalling

supremacy NOUN = **domination**, dominance, ascendancy, sovereignty, sway, lordship, mastery, dominion, primacy, pre-eminence, predominance, supreme power, absolute rule, paramountcy

supreme ADJECTIVE **1** *The group conspired to seize supreme power.* = **paramount**, surpassing, superlative, prevailing, sovereign, predominant, incomparable, mother of all (*informal*), unsurpassed, matchless ■ **OPPOSITE:** least **2** *He proposes to make himself the supreme overlord.* = **chief**, leading, principal, first, highest, head, top, prime, cardinal, foremost, pre-eminent, peerless ■ **OPPOSITE:** lowest **3** *Many young men made the supreme sacrifice during that war.* = **ultimate**, highest, greatest, utmost, final, crowning, extreme, culminating

supremo NOUN = **head**, leader, boss (*informal*), director, master, governor, commander, principal, ruler

sure ADJECTIVE **1** *She was no longer sure how she felt about him.* = **certain**, positive, clear, decided, convinced, persuaded, confident, satisfied, assured, definite, free from doubt ■ **OPPOSITE:** uncertain **2** *Another victory is now sure.* = **inevitable**, guaranteed, bound, assured, in the bag (*slang*), inescapable, irrevocable, ineluctable, nailed-on (*slang*) ■ **OPPOSITE:** unsure **3** *a sure sign of rain* = **reliable**, accurate, dependable, effective, precise, honest, unmistakable, undoubted, undeniable, trustworthy, never-failing, trusty, foolproof, infallible, indisputable, sure-fire (*informal*), unerring, well-proven, unfailing, tried and true ■ **OPPOSITE:** unreliable **4** *A doctor's sure hands may perform surgery.* = **secure**, firm, steady, fast, safe, solid, stable

surely ADVERB **1** *If I can accept this situation, surely you can?* = **it must be the case that**, assuredly **2** *He knew that under the surgeon's knife he would surely die.* = **undoubtedly**, certainly, definitely, inevitably, doubtless, for certain, without doubt, unquestionably, inexorably, come what may, without fail, indubitably, doubtlessly, beyond the shadow of a doubt

surety NOUN **1** *a surety of £2,500* = **security**, guarantee, deposit, insurance, bond, safety, pledge, bail, warranty, indemnity **2** *I agreed to stand surety for Arthur to be bailed out.* = **guarantor**, sponsor, hostage, bondsman, mortgagor

surface NOUN **1** *The road surface had started breaking up.* = **covering**, face, exterior, side, top, skin, plane, facet, veneer **2** *A much wider controversy was bubbling under the surface.* = **façade**, outward appearance ▶ MODIFIER *Doctors believed it was just a surface wound.* = **superficial**, external, outward, exterior ▶ VERB **1** *He surfaced, gasping for air.* = **emerge**, come up, come to the surface **2** *The emotions will surface at some point in life.* = **appear**, emerge, arise, come to light, crop up (*informal*), transpire, materialize • **on the surface** *On the surface the elections appear to be democratic.* = **at first glance**, apparently, outwardly, seemingly, ostensibly, superficially, to all appearances, to the casual eye

surfeit NOUN = **excess**, plethora, glut, satiety, overindulgence, superabundance, superfluity ■ **OPPOSITE:** shortage

surge NOUN **1** *a new surge of interest in Dylan's work* = **rush**, flood, upsurge, sudden increase, uprush **2** *The bridge was destroyed in a tidal surge during a storm.* = **flow**, wave, rush, roller, breaker, gush, upsurge, outpouring, uprush **3** *the beating and surge of the sea* = **tide**, roll, rolling, swell, swirling, billowing **4** *He was overcome by a sudden surge of jealousy.* = **wave**, rush, storm, outburst, torrent, eruption ▶ VERB **1** *The crowd surged out from the church.* = **rush**, pour, stream, rise, swell, spill, swarm, seethe, gush, well forth **2** *Fish and seaweed rose, caught motionless in the surging water.* = **roll**, rush, billow, heave, swirl, eddy, undulate **3** *Panic surged through her.* = **sweep**, rush, storm

surly ADJECTIVE = **ill-tempered**, cross, churlish, crabbed, perverse, crusty, sullen, gruff, bearish, sulky, morose, brusque, testy, grouchy (*informal*), curmudgeonly, ungracious, uncivil, shrewish ■ **OPPOSITE:** cheerful

surmise VERB *She surmised that they had discovered one of the illegal streets.* = **guess**, suppose, imagine, presume, consider, suspect, conclude, fancy, speculate, infer, deduce, come to the conclusion, conjecture, opine (*formal*), hazard a guess ▶ NOUN *Her surmise proved correct.* = **guess**, speculation, assumption, thought, idea, conclusion, notion, suspicion, hypothesis, deduction, inference, presumption, conjecture, supposition

S

surmount VERB = **overcome**, master, conquer, pass, exceed, surpass, overpower, triumph over, vanquish (*literary*), prevail over

surpass VERB = **outdo**, top, beat, best, cap (*informal*), exceed, eclipse, overshadow, excel, transcend, outstrip, outshine, tower above, go one better than (*informal*), put in the shade

surpassing ADJECTIVE = **supreme**, extraordinary, outstanding, exceptional, rare, phenomenal, stellar (*informal*), transcendent, unrivalled, incomparable, matchless

surplus NOUN *The country suffers from a surplus of lawyers.* = **excess**, surfeit, superabundance, superfluity ■ **OPPOSITE:** shortage ▸ ADJECTIVE *Few people have large sums of surplus cash.* = **extra**, spare, excess, remaining, odd, in excess, left over, unused, superfluous ■ **OPPOSITE:** insufficient

surprise NOUN **1** *It is perhaps no surprise to see her attempting a comeback.* = **shock**, start, revelation, jolt, bombshell, eye-opener (*informal*), bolt from the blue, turn-up for the books (*informal*) **2** *To my surprise I am in a room where I see one of my mother's sisters.* = **amazement**, astonishment, wonder, incredulity, stupefaction ▸ VERB **1** *We'll solve the case ourselves and surprise everyone.* = **amaze**, astonish, astound, stun, startle, stagger, disconcert, take aback, bowl over (*informal*), leave open-mouthed, nonplus, flabbergast (*informal*), take (someone's) breath away **2** *The army surprised their enemy near the village of Blenheim.* = **catch unawares** or **off-guard**, catch napping, catch on the hop (*informal*), burst in on, spring upon, catch in the act or red-handed, come down on like a bolt from the blue

surprised ADJECTIVE = **amazed**, astonished, startled, disconcerted, at a loss, taken aback, speechless, incredulous, open-mouthed, nonplussed, thunderstruck, unable to believe your eyes

surprising ADJECTIVE = **amazing**, remarkable, incredible (*informal*), astonishing, wonderful, unusual, extraordinary, unexpected, staggering, marvellous, startling, astounding, jaw-dropping, eye-popping (*informal*), unlooked-for

surrender VERB **1** *We'll never surrender to the terrorists.* = **give in**, yield, submit, give way, quit, succumb, cave in (*informal*), capitulate, throw in the towel, lay down arms, give yourself up, show the white flag ■ **OPPOSITE:** resist **2** *She had to surrender all rights to her property.* = **give up**, abandon, relinquish, resign, yield, concede, part with, renounce, waive, forgo, cede, deliver up ▸ NOUN *the unconditional surrender of the rebels* = **submission**, yielding, cave-in (*informal*), capitulation, resignation, renunciation, relinquishment

surreptitious ADJECTIVE = **secret**, clandestine, furtive, sneaking, veiled, covert, sly, fraudulent, unauthorized, underhand, stealthy ■ **OPPOSITE:** open

surrogate NOUN = **substitute**, deputy, representative, stand-in, proxy

surround VERB **1** *The church was surrounded by a rusted wrought-iron fence.* = **enclose**, ring, encircle, encompass, envelop, close in on, fence in, girdle, hem in, environ, enwreath **2** *When the car stopped it was surrounded by police and militiamen.* = **besiege**, beset, lay siege to, invest (*rare*)

surrounding ADJECTIVE *Aerial bombing of the surrounding area is continuing.* = **nearby**, neighbouring

surroundings PLURAL NOUN *a peaceful holiday home in beautiful surroundings* = **environment**, setting, background, location, neighbourhood, milieu, environs

surveillance NOUN = **observation**, watch, scrutiny, supervision, control, care, direction, inspection, vigilance, superintendence, dataveillance

survey NOUN **1** *According to the survey, overall world trade has also slackened.* = **poll**, study, research, review, inquiry, investigation, opinion poll, questionnaire, census **2** *He sniffed the perfume she wore, then gave her a quick survey.* = **examination**, inspection, scrutiny, overview, once-over (*informal*), perusal **3** *a structural survey undertaken by a qualified surveyor* = **valuation**, estimate, assessment, appraisal ▸ VERB **1** *Only 18 percent of those surveyed opposed the idea.* = **interview**, question, poll, study, research, investigate, sample, canvass **2** *He pushed himself to his feet and surveyed the room.* = **look over**, view, scan, examine, observe, contemplate, supervise, inspect, eyeball (*slang*), scrutinize, size up, take stock of, eye up, recce (*slang*), reconnoitre **3** *Geological experts were commissioned to survey the land.* = **measure**, estimate, prospect, assess, appraise, triangulate

survive VERB **1** *Drugs that dissolve blood clots can help heart-attack victims survive.* = **remain alive**, live, pull through, last, exist, live on, endure, hold out, subsist, keep body and soul together (*informal*), be extant, fight for your life, keep your head above water **2** *Rejected by the people, can the organization survive at all?* = **continue**, last, live on, pull

S

through **3** *Most women will survive their spouses.* = **live longer than**, outlive, outlast

susceptibility NOUN = **vulnerability**, weakness, liability, propensity, predisposition, proneness

susceptible ADJECTIVE **1** *He was unusually susceptible to flattery.* = **responsive**, sensitive, receptive, alive to, impressionable, easily moved, suggestible ■ **OPPOSITE:** unresponsive **2** *(usually with to) Walking with weights makes the shoulders susceptible to injury.* = **liable**, inclined, prone, given, open, subject, vulnerable, disposed, predisposed ■ **OPPOSITE:** resistant

suspect VERB **1** *I suspect they were right.* = **believe**, feel, guess, consider, suppose, conclude, fancy, speculate, conjecture, surmise, hazard a guess, have a sneaking suspicion, think probable ■ **OPPOSITE:** know **2** *You don't really think he suspects you, do you?* = **distrust**, doubt, mistrust, smell a rat *(informal)*, harbour suspicions about, have your doubts about ■ **OPPOSITE:** trust ▶ ADJECTIVE *Delegates evacuated the building when a suspect package was found.* = **dubious**, doubtful, dodgy *(Brit., Austral. & N.Z. informal)*, questionable, fishy *(informal)*, iffy *(informal)*, open to suspicion, shonky *(Austral. & N.Z. informal)* ■ **OPPOSITE:** innocent

suspend VERB **1** *The union suspended strike action this week.* = **postpone**, delay, put off, arrest, cease, interrupt, shelve, withhold, defer, adjourn, hold off, cut short, discontinue, lay aside, put in cold storage ■ **OPPOSITE:** continue **2** *Julie was suspended from her job shortly after the incident.* = **remove**, expel, eject, debar ■ **OPPOSITE:** reinstate **3** *chandeliers suspended on heavy chains from the ceiling* = **hang**, attach, dangle, swing, append *(formal)*

suspense NOUN *a writer who holds the suspense throughout her tale* = **uncertainty**, doubt, tension, anticipation, expectation, anxiety, insecurity, expectancy, apprehension

suspension NOUN = **postponement**, delay, break, stay, breaking off, interruption, moratorium, respite, remission, adjournment, abeyance, deferment, discontinuation, disbarment

suspicion NOUN **1** *Police had suspicions that it was not a natural death.* = **feeling**, theory, impression, intuition, conjecture, surmise, funny feeling *(informal)*, presentiment **2** *Our culture harbours deep suspicions of big-time industry.* = **distrust**, scepticism, mistrust, doubt, misgiving, qualm, lack of confidence, wariness, bad vibes *(slang)*, dubiety, chariness **3** *I have a sneaking suspicion that they are going to succeed.* = **idea**, notion, hunch, guess, impression, conjecture, surmise, gut feeling *(informal)*, supposition **4** *large blooms of white with a suspicion of pale pink* = **trace**, touch, hint, shadow, suggestion, strain, shade, streak, tinge, glimmer, soupçon *(French)* • **above suspicion** *He was a respected academic and above suspicion* = **blameless**, unimpeachable, above reproach, pure, honourable, virtuous, sinless, like Caesar's wife

suspicious ADJECTIVE **1** *He has his father's suspicious nature.* = **distrustful**, suspecting, sceptical, doubtful, apprehensive, leery *(slang)*, mistrustful, unbelieving, wary ■ **OPPOSITE:** trusting **2** *two suspicious-looking characters* = **suspect**, dubious, questionable, funny, doubtful, dodgy *(Brit., Austral. & N.Z. informal)*, queer, irregular, shady *(informal)*, fishy *(informal)*, of doubtful honesty, open to doubt or misconstruction, shonky *(Austral. & N.Z. informal)* ■ **OPPOSITE:** beyond suspicion **3** *Four people have died in suspicious circumstances.* = **odd**, strange, mysterious, dark, dubious, irregular, questionable, murky *(informal)*, shady *(informal)*, fishy

sustain VERB **1** *He has sustained his fierce social conscience.* = **maintain**, continue, keep up, prolong, keep going, keep alive, protract **2** *Every aircraft in there has sustained some damage.* = **suffer**, experience, undergo, feel, bear, endure, withstand, bear up under **3** *I am sustained by letters of support.* = **help**, aid, comfort, foster, assist, relieve, nurture **4** *not enough food to sustain a mouse* = **keep alive**, nourish, provide for **5** *The magnets have lost the capacity to sustain the weight.* = **support**, carry, bear, keep up, uphold, keep from falling **6** *The court sustained his objection.* = **uphold**, confirm, endorse, approve, ratify, verify, validate

sustained ADJECTIVE = **continuous**, constant, steady, prolonged, perpetual, unremitting, nonstop ■ **OPPOSITE:** periodic

sustenance NOUN **1** *The state provided a basic quantity of food for daily sustenance.* = **nourishment**, food, provisions, rations, refreshments, kai *(N.Z. informal)*, daily bread, victuals, edibles, comestibles, provender, aliment, eatables, refection **2** *everything that is necessary for the sustenance of the offspring* = **support**, maintenance, livelihood, subsistence

svelte ADJECTIVE = **slender**, lithe, willowy, graceful, slinky, lissom(e), sylphlike

S

swagger VERB **1** *The burly brute swaggered forward, towering over me, and shouted.* = **stride**, parade, strut, prance **2** *It's bad manners to swagger about how rich you are.* = **show off**, boast, brag, hot-dog (*chiefly U.S.*), bluster, swank (*informal*), gasconade (*rare*) ▶ NOUN **1** *He walked with something of a swagger.* = **strut 2** *What he needed was confidence and a bit of swagger.* = **ostentation**, show, display, swag (*slang*), showing off (*informal*), bluster, swashbuckling, swank (*informal*), braggadocio, gasconade (*rare*)

swallow VERB **1** *Polly took a bite of the apple, chewed and swallowed it.* = **eat**, down (*informal*), consume, devour, absorb, swig (*informal*), swill, wash down, ingest **2** *He took a glass of Scotch and swallowed it down.* = **gulp**, drink **3** *I too found this story a little hard to swallow.* = **believe**, accept, buy (*slang*), fall for, take (something) as gospel **4** *Gordon swallowed the anger he felt.* = **suppress**, hold in, restrain, contain, hold back, stifle, repress, bottle up, bite back, choke back • **swallow something** or **someone up 1** *Weeds had swallowed up the garden.* = **engulf**, overwhelm, overrun, consume **2** *Wage costs swallow up two-thirds of the turnover.* = **absorb**, assimilate, envelop

swamp NOUN *Much of the land is desert or swamp.* = **bog**, marsh, quagmire, moss (*Scot. & Northern English, dialect*), slough, fen, mire, morass, everglade(s) (*U.S.*), pakihi (*N.Z.*), muskeg (*Canad.*) ▶ VERB **1** *The river burst its banks, swamping a mobile home park.* = **flood**, engulf, submerge, inundate, deluge **2** *We swamp them with praise, make them think that they are important.* = **overload**, overwhelm, inundate, besiege, beset, snow under

swampy ADJECTIVE = **boggy**, waterlogged, marshy, wet, fenny, miry, quaggy, marish (*obsolete*)

swank VERB *I never swank about the things I have been lucky enough to win.* = **show off**, swagger, give yourself airs, posture (*informal*), hot-dog (*chiefly U.S.*), put on side (*Brit. slang*) ▶ NOUN *There was no swank in Martin.* = **boastfulness**, show, ostentation, display, swagger, vainglory

swanky ADJECTIVE = **ostentatious**, grand, posh (*informal, chiefly Brit.*), rich, expensive, exclusive, smart, fancy, flash (*informal*), fashionable, glamorous, stylish, gorgeous, lavish, luxurious, sumptuous, plush (*informal*), flashy, swish (*informal, chiefly Brit.*), glitzy (*slang*), showy, ritzy (*slang*), de luxe, swank (*informal*), plushy (*informal*), schmick (*Austral. informal*)
■ OPPOSITE: modest

swap or **swop** VERB = **exchange**, trade, switch, traffic, interchange, barter

swarm NOUN *A swarm of people encircled the hotel.* = **multitude**, crowd, mass, army, host, drove, flock, herd, horde, myriad, throng, shoal, concourse, bevy ▶ VERB **1** *People swarmed to the shops, buying up everything in sight.* = **crowd**, flock, throng, mass, stream, congregate **2** *Within minutes the area was swarming with officers.* = **teem**, crawl, be alive, abound, bristle, be overrun, be infested

swashbuckling ADJECTIVE = **dashing**, spirited, bold, flamboyant, swaggering, gallant, daredevil, mettlesome, roisterous

swath or **swathe** NOUN *On May 1st the army took over another swathe of territory.* = **area**, section, stretch, patch, tract

swathe VERB *She swathed her enormous body in thin black fabrics.* = **wrap**, drape, envelop, bind, lap, fold, bandage, cloak, shroud, swaddle, furl, sheathe, enfold, bundle up, muffle up, enwrap

sway VERB **1** *The people swayed back and forth with arms linked.* = **move from side to side**, rock, wave, roll, swing, bend, lean, incline, lurch, oscillate, move to and fro **2** *Don't ever be swayed by fashion.* = **influence**, control, direct, affect, guide, dominate, persuade, govern, win over, induce, prevail on ▶ NOUN *How can mothers keep daughters under their sway?* = **power**, control, influence, government, rule, authority, command, sovereignty, jurisdiction, clout (*informal*), dominion, predominance, ascendency • **hold sway** *Here, a completely different approach seems to hold sway.* = **prevail**, rule, predominate, reign

swear VERB **1** *It is wrong to swear and shout.* = **curse**, cuss (*informal*), blaspheme, turn the air blue (*informal*), be foul-mouthed, take the Lord's name in vain, utter profanities, imprecate **2** *Alan swore that he would do everything in his power to help us.* = **vow**, promise, take an oath, warrant, testify, depose, attest, avow, give your word, state under oath, pledge yourself **3** *I swear I've told you all I know.* = **declare**, assert, affirm, swear blind, asseverate (*formal*) • **swear by something** *Many people swear by vitamin C's ability to ward off colds.* = **believe in**, trust, depend on, rely on, have confidence in

swearing NOUN = **bad language**, cursing, profanity, blasphemy, cussing (*informal*), foul language, imprecations, malediction

swearword NOUN = **oath**, curse, obscenity, expletive, four-letter word, cuss (*informal*), profanity

sweat NOUN 1 *He wiped the sweat off his face and looked around.* = **perspiration**, moisture, dampness 2 *She was in a sweat about the exam.* = **panic**, anxiety, state (*informal*), worry, distress, flap (*informal*), agitation, fluster, lather (*informal*), tizzy (*informal*), state of anxiety ▸ VERB 1 *Already they were sweating as the sun beat down upon them.* = **perspire**, swelter, break out in a sweat, exude moisture, glow 2 *It gives sales chiefs something to sweat about.* = **worry**, fret, agonize, lose sleep over, be on tenterhooks, torture yourself, be on pins and needles (*informal*) • **sweat something out** *I just had to sweat it out and hope.* = **endure**, see (something) through, stick it out (*informal*), stay the course

sweaty ADJECTIVE = **perspiring**, sweating, sticky, clammy, bathed *or* drenched *or* soaked in perspiration, glowing

sweep VERB 1 *She was in the kitchen sweeping the floor.* = **brush**, clean 2 *I swept rainwater off the flat top of a gravestone.* = **clear**, remove, brush, clean 3 *The car swept past the gate house.* = **sail**, pass, fly, tear, zoom, glide, skim, scud, hurtle 4 *She swept into the conference room.* = **swagger**, sail, breeze, stride, stroll, glide, flounce ▸ NOUN 1 *She indicated the garden with a sweep of her hand.* = **movement**, move, swing, stroke, gesture 2 *the great sweep of the bay* = **arc**, bend, curve 3 *the whole sweep of German social and political history* = **extent**, range, span, stretch, scope, compass

sweeping ADJECTIVE 1 *sweeping generalizations about gender based on gender* = **indiscriminate**, blanket, across-the-board, wholesale, exaggerated, overstated, unqualified, overdrawn 2 *sweeping economic reforms* = **wide-ranging**, global, comprehensive, wide, broad, radical, extensive, all-inclusive, all-embracing, overarching, thoroughgoing ■ OPPOSITE: limited

sweet ADJECTIVE 1 *a mug of sweet tea* = **sugary**, sweetened, cloying, honeyed (*poetic*), saccharine, syrupy, icky (*informal*), treacly ■ OPPOSITE: sour 2 *the sweet smell of a summer garden* = **fragrant**, perfumed, aromatic, redolent, sweet-smelling ■ OPPOSITE: stinking 3 *I gulped a breath of sweet air.* = **fresh**, clean, pure, wholesome 4 *the sweet sounds of Mozart* = **melodious**, musical, harmonious, soft, mellow, silvery, tuneful, dulcet, sweet-sounding, euphonious, silver-toned, euphonic ■ OPPOSITE: harsh 5 *He was a sweet man but he was hopeless with money.* = **charming**, kind, gentle, tender, affectionate,

agreeable, amiable, sweet-tempered ■ OPPOSITE: nasty 6 *a sweet little baby girl* = **delightful**, appealing, cute, taking, winning, fair, beautiful, attractive, engaging, lovable, winsome, cutesy (*informal*), likable *or* likeable ■ OPPOSITE: unpleasant 7 *my dear, sweet mother* = **beloved**, dear, darling, dearest, pet, treasured, precious, cherished ▸ NOUN 1 (*usually plural*) *They've always enjoyed fish and chips – and sweets and cakes.* = **confectionery**, candy (*U.S.*), sweetie, lolly (*Austral. & N.Z.*), sweetmeat, bonbon 2 *The sweet was a mousse flavoured with whisky.* = **dessert**, pudding, afters (*Brit. informal*), sweet course • **sweet on** *It was rumoured that she was sweet on him.* = **in love with**, keen on, infatuated with, gone on (*slang*), fond of, taken with, enamoured of, head over heels in love with, obsessed *or* bewitched by, wild *or* mad about (*informal*)

sweeten VERB 1 *He liberally sweetened his coffee.* = **sugar** 2 *They sweetened the deal with a rather generous cash payment.* = **soften**, ease, alleviate, relieve, temper, cushion, mellow, make less painful 3 *He is likely to try to sweeten them with pledges of fresh aid.* = **mollify**, appease, soothe, pacify, soften up, sugar the pill

sweetheart NOUN 1 *Happy birthday, sweetheart!* = **dearest**, beloved, sweet, angel (*informal*), treasure, honey, dear, sweetie (*informal*) 2 *I married my childhood sweetheart, in Liverpool.* = **love**, boyfriend *or* girlfriend, beloved, lover, steady (*informal*), flame (*informal*), darling, follower (*obsolete*), valentine, admirer, suitor, beau (*old-fashioned*), swain (*archaic*), truelove, leman (*archaic*), inamorata *or* inamorato, bae (*U.S. informal*)

swell VERB 1 *The human population swelled as migrants moved south.* = **increase**, rise, grow, mount, expand, accelerate, escalate, multiply, grow larger ■ OPPOSITE: decrease 2 *The limbs swell to an enormous size.* = **expand**, increase, grow, rise, extend, balloon, belly, enlarge, bulge, protrude, well up, billow, fatten, dilate, puff up, round out, be inflated, become larger, distend, bloat, tumefy, become bloated *or* distended ■ OPPOSITE: shrink ▸ NOUN *the swell of the incoming tide* = **wave**, rise, surge, billow

swelling NOUN = **enlargement**, lump, puffiness, bump, blister, bulge, inflammation, dilation, protuberance, distension, tumescence ■ RELATED WORD: *adjective* tumescent

sweltering ADJECTIVE = **hot**, burning, boiling, steaming, baking, roasting, stifling, scorching, oppressive, humid, torrid, sultry, airless

swerve VERB = **veer**, turn, swing, shift, bend, incline, deflect, depart from, skew, diverge, deviate, turn aside, sheer off

swift ADJECTIVE **1** *We need to make a swift decision.* = **quick**, immediate, prompt, rapid, instant, abrupt, ready, expeditious **2** *a swift runner* = **fast**, quick, rapid, flying, express, winged, sudden, fleet, hurried, speedy, spanking, nimble, quickie (*informal*), nippy (*Brit. informal*), fleet-footed ■ OPPOSITE: slow

swiftly ADVERB **1** *They have acted swiftly and decisively.* = **quickly**, rapidly, speedily, without losing time **2** *Lenny moved swiftly and silently across the front lawn.* = **fast**, promptly, hurriedly, apace (*literary*), pronto (*informal*), double-quick, hell for leather, like lightning, hotfoot, like the clappers (*Brit. informal*), posthaste, like greased lightning (*informal*), nippily (*Brit. informal*), in less than no time, as fast as your legs can carry you, (at) full tilt, pdq (*slang*)

swill VERB **1** *A crowd of men were standing around swilling beer.* = **drink**, gulp, swig (*informal*), guzzle, drain, consume, swallow, imbibe, quaff, bevvy (*dialect*), toss off, bend the elbow (*informal*), pour down your gullet **2** (*often with* **out**) *He swilled out the mug and left it on the draining board.* = **rinse**, wash out, sluice, flush, drench, wash down ▶ NOUN *The porker ate swill from a trough.* = **waste**, slops, mash, mush, hogwash, pigswill, scourings

swindle VERB *He swindled investors out of millions of pounds.* = **cheat**, do (*slang*), con, skin (*slang*), trick, stiff (*slang*), sting (*informal*), rip (someone) off (*slang*), deceive, fleece, defraud, dupe, overcharge, rook (*slang*), bamboozle (*informal*), diddle (*informal*), take (someone) for a ride (*informal*), put one over on (someone) (*informal*), pull a fast one (on someone) (*informal*), bilk (of), take to the cleaners (*informal*), sell a pup (to) (*slang*), cozen, hornswoggle (*slang*), scam (*slang*) ▶ NOUN *He fled to Switzerland rather than face trial for a tax swindle.* = **fraud**, fiddle (*Brit. informal*), rip-off (*slang*), racket, scam (*slang*), sting (*informal*), deception, imposition, deceit, trickery, double-dealing, con trick (*informal*), sharp practice, swizzle (*Brit. informal*), knavery, swizz (*Brit. informal*), roguery, fastie (*Austral. slang*)

swing VERB **1** *She was swinging a bottle by its neck.* = **brandish**, wave, shake, flourish, wield, dangle **2** *The sail of the little boat swung from one side to the other.* = **sway**, rock, wave, veer, vibrate, oscillate, move back and forth, move to and fro **3** (*usually with* **round**) *The canoe found the current and swung around.* = **turn**, veer, swivel, twist, curve, rotate, pivot, turn on your heel **4** *The two men were swinging wildly at each other.* = **hit out**, strike, swipe (*informal*), lash out at, slap **5** *Within moments of arriving, Jingo was climbing and swinging from a tyre.* = **hang**, dangle, be suspended, suspend, move back and forth ▶ NOUN **1** *a woman walking with a slight swing to her hips* = **swaying**, sway **2** *Dieters can suffer from violent mood swings.* = **fluctuation**, change, shift, switch, variation • **in full swing** *The international rugby season was in full swing.* = **at its height**, under way, on the go (*informal*)

swingeing ADJECTIVE = **severe**, heavy, drastic, huge, punishing, harsh, excessive, daunting, stringent, oppressive, Draconian, exorbitant

swipe VERB **1** *She swiped at him as though he were a fly.* = **hit out**, strike, slap, lash out at **2** *People kept trying to swipe my copy of the New York Times.* = **steal**, nick (*slang, chiefly Brit.*), pinch (*informal*), lift (*informal*), appropriate, cabbage (*Brit. slang*), make off with, pilfer, purloin (*formal*), filch, snaffle (*Brit. informal*) ▶ NOUN *He gave Andrew a swipe on the ear.* = **blow**, slap, smack, clip (*informal*), thump, clout (*informal*), cuff, clump (*slang*), wallop (*informal*)

swirl VERB = **whirl**, churn, spin, twist, boil, surge, agitate, eddy, twirl

swish ADJECTIVE = **smart**, grand, posh (*informal, chiefly Brit.*), exclusive, elegant, swell (*informal*), fashionable, sumptuous, ritzy (*slang*), de luxe, plush or plushy (*informal*)

switch NOUN **1** *a light switch* = **control**, button, lever, on/off device **2** *New technology made the switch to oil possible.* = **change**, shift, transition, conversion, reversal, alteration, about-turn, change of direction ▶ VERB **1** *I'm switching to a new gas supplier.* = **change**, shift, convert, divert, deviate, change course **2** *The ballot boxes have been switched.* = **exchange**, trade, swap, replace, substitute, rearrange, interchange • **switch something off** *She switched off the coffee-machine.* = **turn off**, shut off, deactivate, cut • **switch something on** *He pointed the light at his feet and tried to switch it on.* = **turn on**, put on, set off, activate, set in motion

swivel VERB = **turn**, spin, revolve, rotate, pivot, pirouette, swing round

S

swollen ADJECTIVE = **enlarged**, bloated, puffy, inflamed, puffed up, distended, tumescent, oedematous, dropsical, tumid, edematous

swoop VERB **1** *The terror ended when armed police swooped on the car.* = **pounce**, attack, charge, rush, descend **2** *The hawk swooped and soared away carrying something.* = **drop**, plunge, dive, sweep, descend, plummet, pounce, stoop ▶ NOUN *a swoop on a German lorry* = **raid**, attack, assault, surprise search

swop *see* **swap**

sword NOUN *The stubby sword used by ancient Roman gladiators.* = **blade**, brand (*archaic*), trusty steel

swot VERB = **study**, revise, cram (*informal*), work, get up (*informal*), pore over, bone up on (*informal*), burn the midnight oil, mug up (*Brit. slang*), toil over, apply yourself to, lucubrate (*rare*)

sycophant NOUN = **crawler**, yes man, toady, slave, parasite, cringer, fawner, hanger-on, sponger (*informal*), flatterer, truckler, lickspittle, apple polisher (*U.S. slang*), bootlicker (*informal*), toadeater (*rare*), suckhole (*Austral. slang*)

sycophantic ADJECTIVE = **obsequious**, grovelling, ingratiating, servile, crawling, flattering, cringing, fawning, slimy (*Brit.*), slavish, unctuous, smarmy (*Brit. informal*), toadying, parasitical, bootlicking (*informal*), timeserving

syllabus NOUN = **course of study**, curriculum

symbol NOUN **1** *To them the monarchy is a special symbol of nationhood.* = **metaphor**, image, sign, representation, token **2** *The artist uses the oak tree as a symbol of strength.* = **representation**, sign, figure, mark, type, image, token, logo, badge, emblem **3** = **character**, hieroglyph, emoticon

symbolic ADJECTIVE **1** *The move today was largely symbolic.* = **representative**, token, emblematic, allegorical **2** *symbolic representations of landscape* = **figurative**, representative

symbolize VERB = **represent**, signify, stand for, mean, exemplify, denote, typify, personify, connote, betoken, body forth

symmetrical ADJECTIVE = **balanced**, regular, proportional, in proportion, well-proportioned ■ **OPPOSITE:** unbalanced

symmetry NOUN = **balance**, proportion, regularity, form, order, harmony, correspondence, evenness

sympathetic ADJECTIVE **1** *It may be that he sees you only as a sympathetic friend.* = **caring**, kind, understanding, concerned, feeling, interested, kindly, warm, tender, pitying, supportive, responsive, affectionate, compassionate, commiserating, warm-hearted, condoling ■ **OPPOSITE:** uncaring **2** *They were sympathetic to our cause.* = **supportive**, encouraging, pro, approving of, friendly to, in sympathy with, well-disposed towards, favourably disposed towards **3** *She sounds a most sympathetic character.* = **like-minded**, compatible, agreeable, friendly, responsive, appreciative, congenial, companionable, well-intentioned ■ **OPPOSITE:** uncongenial

sympathetically ADVERB = **feelingly**, kindly, understandingly, warmly, with interest, with feeling, sensitively, with compassion, appreciatively, perceptively, responsively, warm-heartedly

sympathizer NOUN = **supporter**, partisan, protagonist, fellow traveller, well-wisher

sympathize with VERB **1** *I must tell you how much I sympathize with you for your loss.* = **feel for**, pity, empathize with, commiserate with, bleed for, have compassion for, grieve with, offer consolation for, condole with, share another's sorrow, feel your heart go out to ■ **OPPOSITE:** have no feelings for **2** *Some Europeans sympathize with the Americans over the issue.* = **agree with**, support, side with, understand, identify with, go along with, be in accord with, be in sympathy with ■ **OPPOSITE:** disagree with

sympathy NOUN **1** *We expressed our sympathy for her loss.* = **compassion**, understanding, pity, empathy, tenderness, condolence(s), thoughtfulness, commiseration, aroha (*N.Z.*) ■ **OPPOSITE:** indifference **2** *I still have sympathy with this point of view.* = **affinity**, agreement, rapport, union, harmony, warmth, correspondence, fellow feeling, congeniality ■ **OPPOSITE:** opposition

symptom NOUN **1** *patients with flu symptoms* = **sign**, mark, indication, warning **2** *Your problem with sleep is just a symptom of a larger problem.* = **manifestation**, sign, indication, mark, evidence, expression, proof, token

symptomatic ADJECTIVE = **indicative**, characteristic, suggestive

synonymous with ADJECTIVE = **equivalent to**, the same as, identical to, similar to, identified with, equal to, tantamount to, interchangeable with, one and the same as

synopsis NOUN = **summary**, review, résumé, outline, abstract, digest, epitome, rundown, condensation, compendium, précis, aperçu (*French*), abridgment, conspectus (*formal*), outline sketch

synthesis NOUN = **combining**, integration, amalgamation, unification, welding, coalescence

S

synthetic ADJECTIVE = **artificial**, manufactured, fake, man-made, mock, simulated, sham, pseudo (*informal*), ersatz ■ **OPPOSITE:** real

system NOUN **1** *a multi-party system of government* = **arrangement**, structure, organization, scheme, combination, classification, coordination, setup (*informal*) **2** *a news channel on a local cable system* = **network**, organization, web, grid, set of channels **3** *the decimal system of metric weights and measures* = **method**, practice, technique, procedure, routine, theory, usage, methodology, frame of reference, modus operandi, fixed order

systematic ADJECTIVE = **methodical**, organized, efficient, precise, orderly, standardized, businesslike, well-ordered, systematized ■ **OPPOSITE:** unmethodical

S

Tt

tab NOUN = **flap**, tag, label, ticket, flag, marker, sticker

table NOUN **1** *I placed his drink on the small table.* = **counter**, bench, stand, board, surface, slab, work surface **2** *Consult the table on page 104.* = **list**, chart, tabulation, record, roll, index, register, digest, diagram, inventory, graph, synopsis, itemization **3** *They always keep a marvellous table.* = **food**, spread (*informal*), board, diet, fare, kai (*N.Z. informal*), victuals ▶ VERB *They've tabled a motion criticizing the government for inaction.* = **submit**, propose, put forward, move, suggest, enter, file, lodge, moot

tableau NOUN = **picture**, scene, representation, arrangement, spectacle

taboo *or* **tabu** ADJECTIVE *Cancer is a taboo subject.* = **forbidden**, banned, prohibited, ruled out, not allowed, unacceptable, outlawed, unthinkable, not permitted, disapproved of, anathema, off limits, frowned on, proscribed, beyond the pale, unmentionable ■ OPPOSITE: permitted ▶ NOUN *a cultural taboo against eating fish* = **prohibition**, ban, restriction, disapproval, anathema, interdict, proscription, tapu (*N.Z.*)

tacit ADJECTIVE = **implied**, understood, implicit, silent, taken for granted, unspoken, inferred, undeclared, wordless, unstated, unexpressed ■ OPPOSITE: stated

taciturn ADJECTIVE = **uncommunicative**, reserved, reticent, unforthcoming, quiet, withdrawn, silent, distant, dumb, mute, aloof, antisocial, tight-lipped, close-lipped ■ OPPOSITE: communicative

tack NOUN *Use a staple gun or upholstery tacks.* = **nail**, pin, stud, staple, rivet, drawing pin, thumbtack (*U.S.*), tintack ▶ VERB **1** *He had tacked this note to the door.* = **fasten**, fix, attach, pin, nail, staple, affix **2** *Tack the cord around the cushion.* = **stitch**, sew, hem, bind, baste • **tack something on to something** *The childcare bill is to be tacked on to the budget plan.* = **append** (*formal*), add, attach, tag, annex

tackle NOUN **1** *a tackle by a full-back* = **block**, stop, challenge **2** *I finally hoisted him up with a block and tackle.* = **rig**, rigging, apparatus

▶ VERB **1** *We need to tackle these problems and save people's lives.* = **deal with**, take on, set about, wade into, get stuck into (*informal*), sink your teeth into, apply yourself to, come *or* get to grips with, step up to the plate (*informal*) **2** *She is quite good at DIY and wants to tackle the job herself.* = **undertake**, deal with, attempt, try, begin, essay (*formal*), engage in, embark upon, get stuck into (*informal*), turn your hand to, have a go *or* stab at (*informal*) **3** *He tackled the quarter-back.* = **intercept**, block, bring down, stop, challenge

tacky[1] ADJECTIVE *If the finish is still tacky, leave to harden.* = **sticky**, wet, adhesive, gummy, icky (*informal*), gluey

tacky[2] (*informal*) ADJECTIVE **1** *tacky red sunglasses* = **vulgar**, cheap (*informal*), tasteless, nasty, sleazy, naff (*Brit. slang*) **2** *The whole thing is dreadfully tacky.* = **seedy**, shabby, shoddy

tact NOUN = **diplomacy**, understanding, consideration, sensitivity, delicacy, skill, judgment, perception, discretion, finesse, thoughtfulness, savoir-faire, adroitness ■ OPPOSITE: tactlessness

tactful ADJECTIVE = **diplomatic**, politic, discreet, prudent, understanding, sensitive, polished, careful, subtle, delicate, polite, thoughtful, perceptive, considerate, judicious ■ OPPOSITE: tactless

tactic NOUN *His tactic to press on paid off.* = **policy**, approach, course, way, means, move, line, scheme, plans, method, trick, device, manoeuvre, tack, ploy, stratagem

tactical ADJECTIVE = **strategic**, politic, shrewd, smart, diplomatic, clever, cunning, skilful, artful, foxy, adroit ■ OPPOSITE: impolitic

tactician NOUN = **strategist**, campaigner, planner, mastermind, general, director, brain (*informal*), coordinator, schemer

tactics PLURAL NOUN *guerrilla tactics* = **strategy**, campaigning, manoeuvres, generalship

tag NOUN *Staff wore name tags and called inmates by their first names.* = **label**, tab, sticker, note, ticket, slip, flag, identification, marker, flap, docket (*Brit.*) ▶ VERB **1** *Important trees were tagged to protect them from machinery.* = **label**, mark, flag, ticket, identify, earmark **2** *The critics still tagged him with his old name.* = **name**, call, label, term, style, dub, nickname, christen

tail NOUN **1** *The cattle were swinging their tails to disperse the flies.* = **extremity**, appendage, brush, rear end, hindquarters, hind part, empennage **2** *a comet tail* = **train**, end, trail, tailpiece **3** *He desperately needs a kick in the* tail. = **buttocks**, behind (*informal*), bottom, butt (*U.S. & Canad. informal*), bum (*Brit. slang*), rear (*informal*), buns (*U.S. slang*), backside (*informal*), rump, rear end, posterior, derrière (*euphemistic*), jacksy (*Brit. slang*) **4** (*of hair*) *She wore bleached denims with her golden tail of hair swinging.* = **ponytail**, braid, plait, tress, pigtail ▶ VERB *Officers had tailed the gang in an undercover inquiry.* = **follow**, track, shadow, trail, stalk, keep an eye on, dog the footsteps of • **turn tail** *I turned tail and fled in the direction of the house.* = **run away**, flee, run off, escape, take off (*informal*), retreat, make off, hook it (*slang*), run for it (*informal*), scarper (*Brit. slang*), cut and run, show a clean pair of heels, skedaddle (*informal*), take to your heels

■ RELATED WORD: *adjective* caudal

tailor NOUN *a tailor who specialized in making ceremonial uniforms* = **outfitter** (*old-fashioned*), couturier, dressmaker, seamstress, clothier, costumier, garment maker ▶ VERB *scripts tailored to American comedy audiences* = **adapt**, adjust, modify, cut, style, fit, fashion, shape, suit, convert, alter, accommodate, mould, customize

■ RELATED WORD: *adjective* sartorial

tailor-made ADJECTIVE **1** *This job was tailor-made for me.* = **perfect**, right, ideal, suitable, just right, right up your street (*informal*), up your alley **2** *his expensive tailor-made shirt* = **made-to-measure**, fitted, cut to fit, made to order

taint VERB **1** *They said that the elections had been tainted by corruption.* = **disgrace**, shame, dishonour, brand, ruin, blacken, stigmatize **2** *Rancid oil will taint the flavour.* = **spoil**, ruin, contaminate, damage, soil, dirty, poison, foul, infect, stain, corrupt, smear, muddy, pollute, blight, tarnish, blot, blemish, sully, defile, adulterate, besmirch, vitiate, smirch ■ OPPOSITE: purify

take VERB **1** *He took her by the shoulders and shook her.* = **grip**, grab, seize, catch, grasp, clutch, get hold of, clasp, take hold of, lay hold of **2** *I'll take these papers home and read them.* = **carry**, bring, bear, transport, ferry, haul, convey, fetch, cart, tote (*informal*)
■ OPPOSITE: send **3** *She was taken to hospital.* = **accompany**, lead, bring, guide, conduct, escort, convoy, usher **4** *He took a handkerchief from his pocket.* = **remove**, draw, pull, fish, withdraw, extract, abstract **5** *The burglars took just about anything they could carry.* = **steal**, nick (*slang, chiefly Brit.*), appropriate, pocket, pinch (*informal*), carry off, swipe (*slang*), run off with, blag (*slang*), walk off with, misappropriate, cart off (*slang*), purloin, filch, help yourself to, gain

possession of ■ OPPOSITE: return **6** *Marines went in and took 15 prisoners.* = **capture**, arrest, seize, abduct, take into custody, ensnare, entrap, lay hold of ■ OPPOSITE: release **7** *His rudeness was becoming hard to take.* = **tolerate**, stand, bear, suffer, weather, go through, brave, stomach, endure, undergo, swallow, brook, hack (*slang*), abide, put up with (*informal*), withstand, submit to, countenance, pocket, thole (*Scot.*) ■ OPPOSITE: avoid **8** *Walking across the room took all her strength.* = **require**, need, involve, demand, call for, entail, necessitate **9** *When I took the job, I thought I could change the system.* = **accept**, assume, take on, undertake, adopt, take up, enter upon ■ OPPOSITE: reject **10** *They've turned sensible, if you take my meaning.* = **understand**, follow, comprehend, get, see, grasp, apprehend **11** *My wife and I have taken the cottage for a month.* = **hire**, book, rent, lease, reserve, pay for, engage, make a reservation for **12** *She took her driving test last week.* = **perform**, have, do, make, effect, accomplish, execute **13** *She's been taking sleeping pills.* = **ingest**, consume, swallow, inhale **14** *She took tea with Nanny every day.* = **consume**, have, drink, eat, imbibe (*formal*) **15** *The place could just about take 2000 people.* = **have room for**, hold, contain, accommodate, accept **16** *If the cortisone doesn't take, I may have to have surgery.* = **work**, succeed, do the trick (*informal*), have effect, be efficacious ■ OPPOSITE: fail ▶ NOUN (*informal*) *It added another $11.8 million to the take.* = **takings**, profits, revenue, return, gate, yield, proceeds, haul, receipts • **take it** *I take it you're a friend of theirs.* = **assume**, suppose, presume, expect, imagine, guess (*informal, chiefly U.S. & Canad.*) • **take off 1** *We eventually took off at 11am and arrived in Venice at 1.30pm.* = **lift off**, leave the ground, take to the air, become airborne **2** *He took off at once and headed home.* = **depart**, go, leave, split (*slang*), disappear, set out, strike out, beat it (*slang*), hit the road (*slang*), abscond, decamp, hook it (*slang*), slope off, pack your bags (*informal*) • **take on** *Please don't take on so. I'll help you.* = **get upset**, get excited, make a fuss, break down, give way • **take someone for something** *Do you take me for an idiot?* = **regard as**, see as, believe to be, consider to be, think of as, deem to be, perceive to be, hold to be, judge to be, reckon to be, presume to be, look on as • **take someone in 1** *The monastery has taken in 26 refugees.* = **let in**, receive, admit, board, welcome, harbour, accommodate, take care of, put up, billet **2** *He was a real charmer who totally took me in.* = **deceive**, fool, con (*informal*), do (*slang*), trick, cheat, mislead, dupe, gull (*archaic*), swindle, hoodwink, pull the wool over someone's eyes (*informal*), bilk, cozen, scam (*slang*) • **take someone off** *He can take off his father to perfection.* = **parody**, imitate, mimic, mock, ridicule, ape, caricature, send up (*Brit. informal*), spoof (*informal*), travesty, impersonate, lampoon, burlesque, satirize • **take someone on 1** *I knew I couldn't take him on if it came to a fight.* = **compete against**, face, contend with, fight, oppose, vie with, pit yourself against, enter the lists against, match yourself against **2** *A publishing firm agreed to take him on.* = **engage**, employ, hire, retain, enlist, enrol • **take something back 1** *I'm going to take it back and ask for a refund.* = **return**, bring back, send back, hand back **2** *Take back what you said about Jeremy!* = **retract**, withdraw, renounce, renege on, disavow, recant, disclaim, unsay **3** *The government took back control of the city.* = **regain**, get back, reclaim, recapture, repossess, retake, reconquer • **take something down 1** *He went to the bookcase and took down a volume.* = **remove**, take off, extract **2** *They took down the barricades that had been erected.* = **dismantle**, demolish, take apart, disassemble, level, tear down, raze, take to pieces **3** *I took down his comments in shorthand.* = **make a note of**, record, write down, minute, note, set down, transcribe, put on record • **take something in 1** *She seemed to take in all he said.* = **understand**, absorb, grasp, digest, comprehend, assimilate, get the hang of (*informal*) **2** *The constituency takes in a population of more than 4 million people.* = **include**, contain, comprise, cover, embrace, encompass • **take something off** *She took off her spectacles.* = **remove**, discard, strip off, drop, peel off, doff, divest yourself of • **take something on 1** *No one was able or willing to take on the job.* = **accept**, tackle, undertake, shoulder, have a go at (*informal*), agree to do, address yourself to, step up to the plate (*informal*) **2** *His writing took on a feverish intensity.* = **acquire**, assume, come to have • **take something over** *They took over the company to eliminate competition.* = **gain control of**, take command of, assume control of, come to power in, become leader of • **take something up 1** *He didn't want to take up a competitive sport.* = **start**, begin, engage in, assume, adopt, become involved in **2** *I don't*

want to take up too much of your time. = **occupy**, absorb, consume, use up, cover, fill, waste, squander, extend over **3** *His wife takes up the story.* = **resume**, continue, go on with, pick up, proceed with, restart, carry on with, recommence, follow on with, begin something again • **take to someone** *Did the children take to him?* = **like**, get on with, warm to, be taken with, be pleased by, become friendly with, conceive an affection for • **take to something 1** *They had taken to aimlessly wandering through the streets.* = **start**, resort to, make a habit of, have recourse to **2** *They took to the roof when the police officers came round.* = **head for**, make for, run for, flee to

takeoff NOUN **1** *The aircraft crashed soon after takeoff.* = **departure**, launch, liftoff **2** *an inspired takeoff of the two sisters* = **parody**, imitation, send-up (*Brit. informal*), mocking, satire, caricature, spoof (*informal*), travesty, lampoon, piss-take (*informal*)

takeover NOUN = **merger**, coup, change of leadership, incorporation

tale NOUN **1** *a collection of poems and folk tales* = **story**, narrative, anecdote, account, relation, novel, legend, fiction, romance, saga, short story, yarn (*informal*), fable, narration, conte (*French*), spiel (*informal*), urban myth, urban legend **2** *He's always ready to spin a tall tale about the one that got away.* = **lie**, fabrication, falsehood, fib, untruth, spiel (*informal*), tall story (*informal*), rigmarole, cock-and-bull story (*informal*)

talent NOUN = **ability**, gift, aptitude, power, skill, facility, capacity, bent, genius, expertise, faculty, endowment, forte, flair, knack

talented ADJECTIVE = **gifted**, able, expert, master, masterly, brilliant, ace (*informal*), artistic, consummate, first-rate, top-notch (*informal*), adroit

talisman NOUN = **charm**, mascot, amulet, lucky charm, fetish, juju

talk VERB **1** *The boys all began to talk at once.* = **speak**, chat, chatter, converse, communicate, rap (*slang*), articulate, witter (*informal*), gab (*informal*), express yourself, prattle, natter, shoot the breeze (*U.S. slang*), prate, run off at the mouth (*slang*), earbash (*Austral. & N.Z. slang*) **2** *Let's talk about these new ideas of yours.* = **discuss**, confer, hold discussions, negotiate, palaver, parley, confabulate, have a confab (*informal*), chew the rag or fat (*slang*), korero (*N.Z.*) **3** *They'll talk; they'll implicate me.* = **inform**, shop (*slang, chiefly Brit.*), grass (*Brit. slang*), sing (*slang, chiefly U.S.*), squeal (*slang*), squeak (*informal*), tell all, spill the

t

beans (*informal*), give the game away, blab, let the cat out of the bag, reveal information, spill your guts (*slang*) ▶ NOUN **1** *The guide gave us a brief talk on the history of the site.* = **speech**, lecture, presentation, report, address, seminar, discourse, sermon, symposium, dissertation, harangue, oration, disquisition, whaikorero (*N.Z.*) **2** *I think it's time we had a talk.* = **discussion**, tête-à-tête, conference, dialogue, consultation, heart-to-heart, confabulation, confab (*informal*), powwow, korero (*N.Z.*) **3** *We had a long talk about her father.* = **conversation**, chat, natter, crack (*Scot. & Irish*), rap (*slang*), jaw (*slang*), chatter, gab (*informal*), chitchat, blether, blather **4** *There has been a lot of talk about me getting married.* = **gossip**, rumour, hearsay, tittle-tattle, goss (*informal*) **5** *children babbling on in baby talk* = **language**, words, speech, jargon, slang, dialect, lingo (*informal*), patois, argot **6** (*often plural*) *Talks between strikers and government have broken down.* = **meeting**, conference, discussions, negotiations, congress, summit, mediation, arbitration, conciliation, conclave, palaver, parley, hui (*N.Z.*) • **talk big** *people who talk big and drive fast cars* = **boast**, exaggerate, brag, crow, vaunt, bluster, blow your own trumpet • **talk someone into something** *He talked me into marrying him.* = **persuade**, convince, win someone over, sway, bring round (*informal*), sweet-talk someone into, prevail on *or* upon

talkative ADJECTIVE = **loquacious**, chatty, garrulous, long-winded, big-mouthed (*slang*), wordy, effusive, gabby (*informal*), voluble, gossipy, verbose, mouthy, prolix ■ OPPOSITE: reserved

talker NOUN = **speaker**, lecturer, orator, conversationalist, chatterbox, speechmaker

talking-to NOUN = **reprimand**, lecture, rebuke, scolding, row, criticism, wigging (*Brit. slang*), slating (*informal*), reproach, ticking-off (*informal*), dressing-down (*informal*), telling-off (*informal*), reproof, rap on the knuckles ■ OPPOSITE: praise

tall ADJECTIVE **1** *Being tall can make you incredibly self-confident.* = **lofty**, big, giant, long-legged, lanky, leggy **2** *a lawn of tall, waving grass* = **high**, towering, soaring, steep, elevated, lofty ■ OPPOSITE: short

tally VERB **1** *The figures didn't seem to tally.* = **agree**, match, accord, fit, suit, square, parallel, coincide, correspond, conform, concur, harmonize ■ OPPOSITE: disagree **2** *When the final numbers are tallied, sales will*

probably have fallen. = **count up**, total, compute, keep score ▶ NOUN *They do not keep a tally of visitors to the palace.* = **record**, score, total, count, reckoning, running total

tame ADJECTIVE **1** *tame animals at a children's zoo or farm* = **domesticated**, unafraid, docile, broken, gentle, fearless, obedient, amenable, tractable, used to human contact ■ OPPOSITE: wild **2** *a tame and gullible newspaper journalist* = **submissive**, meek, compliant, subdued, manageable, obedient, docile, spiritless, unresisting ■ OPPOSITE: stubborn **3** *The report was pretty tame stuff.* = **unexciting**, boring, dull, bland, tedious, flat, tiresome, lifeless, prosaic, uninspiring, humdrum, uninteresting, insipid, vapid, wearisome ■ OPPOSITE: exciting ▶ VERB **1** *They were the first to tame horses.* = **domesticate**, train, break in, gentle, pacify, house-train, make tame ■ OPPOSITE: make fiercer **2** *Two regiments were called out to tame the crowds.* = **subdue**, suppress, master, discipline, curb, humble, conquer, repress, bridle, enslave, subjugate, bring to heel, break the spirit of ■ OPPOSITE: arouse

tamper (*usually with* **with**) VERB **1** *He found his computer had been tampered with.* = **interfere with**, tinker with, meddle with, alter, fiddle with (*informal*), mess about with, muck about with (*Brit. slang*), monkey around with, fool about with (*informal*) **2** *I don't want to be accused of tampering with the evidence.* = **influence**, fix (*informal*), rig, corrupt, manipulate

tang NOUN **1** *She could smell the salty tang of the sea.* = **scent**, smell, odour, perfume, fragrance, aroma, reek, redolence **2** *Some liked its strong, fruity tang.* = **taste**, bite, flavour, edge, relish, smack, savour, zest, sharpness, piquancy, spiciness, zestiness **3** *His criticism seemed to have acquired a tang of friendliness.* = **trace**, touch, tinge, suggestion, hint, whiff, smattering

tangible ADJECTIVE = **definite**, real, positive, solid, material, physical, actual, substantial (*formal*), objective, concrete, evident, manifest, palpable, discernible, tactile, perceptible, corporeal, touchable ■ OPPOSITE: intangible

tangle NOUN **1** *a tangle of wires* = **knot**, mass, twist, web, jungle, mat, coil, snarl, mesh, ravel, entanglement **2** *I was thinking what a tangle we had got ourselves into.* = **mess**, jam (*informal*), fix (*informal*), confusion, complication, maze, mix-up, shambles, labyrinth, entanglement, imbroglio ▶ VERB **1** *a huge mass of hair, all tangled together*

= **twist**, knot, mat, coil, snarl, mesh, entangle, interlock, kink, interweave, ravel, interlace, enmesh, intertwist ■ **OPPOSITE:** disentangle **2** (*sometimes with* **up**) *Animals get tangled in fishing nets and drown.* = **entangle**, catch, ensnare, entrap **3** *Themes get tangled in his elliptical storytelling.* = **confuse**, mix up, muddle, jumble, scramble • **tangle with someone** *They are not the first bank to tangle with the taxman recently.* = **come into conflict with**, come up against, cross swords with, dispute with, contend with, contest with, lock horns with

tangled ADJECTIVE **1** *tugging a comb through her tangled hair* = **knotted**, twisted, matted, messy, snarled, jumbled, entangled, knotty, tousled **2** *His personal life has become more tangled than ever.* = **complicated**, involved, complex, confused, messy, mixed-up, convoluted, knotty

tangy ADJECTIVE = **sharp**, tart, piquant, biting, fresh, spicy, pungent, briny, acerb

tantalize VERB = **torment**, tease, taunt, torture, provoke, entice, lead on, titillate, make someone's mouth water, keep someone hanging on

tantamount ADJECTIVE • **tantamount to** = **equivalent to**, equal to, as good as, synonymous with, the same as, commensurate with

tantrum NOUN = **outburst**, temper, hysterics, fit, storm, paddy (*Brit. informal*), wax (*informal, chiefly Brit.*), flare-up, paroxysm, bate (*Brit. slang*), ill humour, foulie (*Austral. slang*), hissy fit (*informal*), strop (*Brit. informal*)

tap[1] VERB *Tap the egg lightly with a teaspoon.* = **knock**, strike, pat, rap, beat, touch, drum ▶ NOUN *A tap on the door interrupted him.* = **knock**, pat, rap, beat, touch, drumming, light blow

tap[2] NOUN **1** *She turned on the taps.* = **valve**, spout, faucet (*U.S. & Canad.*), spigot, stopcock **2** *Ministers are not subject to phone taps.* = **bug** (*informal*), listening device, wiretap, bugging device, hidden microphone ▶ VERB *laws allowing the police to tap telephones* = **listen in on**, monitor, bug (*informal*), spy on, eavesdrop on, wiretap • **on tap 1** (*informal*) *He's already got surveyors on tap to measure for the road.* = **available**, ready, standing by, to hand, on hand, at hand, in reserve **2** *They only have one beer on tap.* = **on draught**, cask-conditioned, from barrels, not bottled or canned

tape NOUN *The books were all tied up with tape.* = **binding**, strip, band, string, ribbon ▶ VERB **1** *She has just taped an interview.* = **record**, video, tape-record, make a recording of **2** (*sometimes with* **up**) *I taped the base of the feather onto the velvet.* = **bind**, secure, stick, seal, wrap

taper VERB *The trunk doesn't taper very much.* = **narrow**, thin, attenuate, come to a point, become thinner, become narrow • **taper off** *The fighting is beginning to taper off.* = **decrease**, dwindle, lessen, reduce, fade, weaken, wane, subside, wind down, die out, die away, thin out

tardy ADJECTIVE **1** *He was as tardy as ever for our appointment.* = **late**, overdue, unpunctual, belated, dilatory, behindhand **2** *the agency's tardy response to the hurricane* = **slow**, belated, delayed

target NOUN **1** *We threw knives at targets.* = **mark**, goal, bull's-eye **2** *school leavers who fail to reach their targets* = **goal**, aim, objective, end, mark, object, intention, ambition, Holy Grail (*informal*) **3** *In the past they have been the targets of racist abuse.* = **victim**, butt, prey, quarry, scapegoat

tariff NOUN **1** *America wants to eliminate tariffs on items such as electronics.* = **tax**, rate, duty, toll, levy, excise, impost, assessment **2** *electricity tariffs and telephone charges* = **price list**, charges, schedule

tarnish VERB **1** *It never rusts or tarnishes.* = **stain**, dull, discolour, spot, soil, dim, rust, darken, blot, blemish, befoul, lose lustre or shine ■ **OPPOSITE:** brighten **2** *His image was tarnished by the savings and loans scandal.* = **damage**, taint, blacken, sully, drag through the mud, smirch ■ **OPPOSITE:** enhance ▶ NOUN *The tarnish lay thick on the inside of the ring.* = **stain**, taint, discoloration, spot, rust, blot, blemish

tarry VERB = **linger**, remain, loiter, wait, delay, pause, hang around (*informal*), lose time, bide, dally, take your time, dawdle, drag your feet or heels ■ **OPPOSITE:** hurry

tart[1] NOUN *a slice of home-made tart* = **pie**, pastry, pasty, tartlet, patty

tart[2] ADJECTIVE **1** *a slightly tart wine* = **sharp**, acid, sour, bitter, pungent, tangy, astringent, piquant, vinegary, acidulous, acerb ■ **OPPOSITE:** sweet **2** *The words were more tart than she had intended.* = **cutting**, biting, sharp, short, wounding, nasty, harsh, scathing, acrimonious, barbed, hurtful, caustic, astringent, vitriolic, trenchant, testy, mordant, snappish, mordacious ■ **OPPOSITE:** kind

task NOUN *He had the unenviable task of breaking the bad news.* = **job**, duty, assignment, work, business, charge, labour, exercise, mission, employment, enterprise, undertaking, occupation, chore, toil ▶ VERB *The minister was tasked with checking that aid was spent wisely.* = **charge** (*formal*), assign to, entrust • **take someone to task** *The country's intellectuals are being taken to task.* = **criticize**, blame, blast, lecture, carpet (*informal*), censure, rebuke, reprimand, reproach, scold, tear into (*informal*), tell off (*informal*), diss (*slang*), read the riot act to, reprove, upbraid, lambast(e), bawl out (*informal*), chew out (*U.S. & Canad. informal*), tear (someone) off a strip (*Brit. informal*), give a rocket to (*Brit. & N.Z. informal*)

taste NOUN **1** *Nettles have a surprisingly sweet taste.* = **flavour**, savour, relish, smack, tang ■ **OPPOSITE:** blandness **2** *He took another small taste.* = **bit**, bite, drop, swallow, sip, mouthful, touch, sample, dash, nip, spoonful, morsel, titbit, soupçon (*French*) **3** *She developed a taste for journeys to hazardous regions.* = **liking**, preference, penchant, fondness, partiality, desire, fancy, leaning, bent, appetite, relish, inclination, palate, predilection ■ **OPPOSITE:** dislike **4** *She has very good taste in clothes.* = **refinement**, style, judgment, culture, polish, grace, discrimination, perception, appreciation, elegance, sophistication, cultivation, discernment ■ **OPPOSITE:** lack of judgment **5** *I do not feel your actions were in good taste.* = **propriety**, discretion, correctness, delicacy, tact, politeness, nicety, decorum, tactfulness ■ **OPPOSITE:** impropriety ▶ VERB **1** (*often with* **of**) *The drink tastes like chocolate.* = **have a flavour of**, smack of, savour of **2** *Cut off a small piece of meat and taste it.* = **sample**, try, test, relish, sip, savour, nibble **3** *You can taste the chilli in the dish.* = **distinguish**, perceive, discern, differentiate **4** *He had tasted outdoor life, and didn't want to come home.* = **experience**, know, undergo, partake of, feel, encounter, meet with, come up against, have knowledge of ■ **OPPOSITE:** miss ■ **RELATED WORD:** *noun* gustation

tasteful ADJECTIVE = **refined**, stylish, elegant, cultured, beautiful, smart, charming, polished, delicate, artistic, handsome, cultivated, discriminating, exquisite, graceful, harmonious, urbane, fastidious, aesthetically pleasing, in good taste ■ **OPPOSITE:** tasteless

tasteless ADJECTIVE **1** *spectacularly tasteless objets d'art* = **gaudy**, cheap, vulgar, tacky (*informal*), flashy, naff (*Brit. slang*), garish, inelegant, tawdry ■ **OPPOSITE:** tasteful **2** *a tasteless remark* = **vulgar**, crude, improper, low, gross, rude, coarse, crass, unseemly, indiscreet, tactless, uncouth, impolite, graceless, indelicate, indecorous **3** *The fish was mushy and tasteless.* = **insipid**, bland, flat, boring, thin, weak, dull, mild, tame, watered-down, uninteresting, uninspired, vapid, flavourless ■ **OPPOSITE:** tasty

tasty ADJECTIVE = **delicious**, luscious, palatable, delectable, good-tasting, savoury, full-flavoured, yummy (*slang*), flavoursome, scrumptious (*informal*), appetizing, toothsome, flavourful, sapid, lekker (*S. African slang*), yummo (*Austral. slang*) ■ **OPPOSITE:** bland

tattletale NOUN = **gossip**, busybody, babbler, prattler, chatterbox (*informal*), blether, chatterer, bigmouth (*slang*), scandalmonger, gossipmonger

tatty ADJECTIVE = **shabby**, seedy, scruffy, worn, poor, neglected, ragged, run-down, frayed, worn out, dilapidated, tattered, tawdry, threadbare, rumpled, bedraggled, unkempt, down at heel, the worse for wear, having seen better days ■ **OPPOSITE:** smart

taunt VERB *Other youths taunted him about his clothes.* = **jeer**, mock, tease, ridicule, provoke, insult, torment, sneer, deride, revile, twit, guy (*informal*), gibe ▶ NOUN *For years they suffered taunts about their looks.* = **jeer**, dig, insult, ridicule, cut, teasing, provocation, barb, derision, sarcasm, gibe

taut ADJECTIVE **1** *When muscles are taut or cold, there is more chance of injury.* = **tense**, rigid, tight, stressed, stretched, strained, flexed ■ **OPPOSITE:** relaxed **2** *The clothes line is pulled taut and secured.* = **tight**, stretched, rigid, tightly stretched ■ **OPPOSITE:** slack

tavern NOUN = **inn**, bar, pub (*informal, chiefly Brit.*), public house, watering hole (*facetious slang*), boozer (*Brit., Austral. & N.Z. informal*), beer parlour (*Canad.*), beverage room (*Canad.*), hostelry, alehouse (*archaic*), taproom

tawdry ADJECTIVE = **vulgar**, cheap, tacky (*informal*), flashy, tasteless, plastic (*slang*), glittering, naff (*Brit. slang*), gaudy, tatty, showy, tinsel, raffish, gimcrack, meretricious, tinselly, cheap-jack (*informal*) ■ **OPPOSITE:** stylish

tax NOUN **1** *a cut in tax on new cars* = **charge**, rate, duty, toll, levy, tariff, excise, contribution, assessment, customs, tribute, imposition, tithe, impost **2** *less of a tax on her bodily resources* = **strain**, demand, burden, pressure, weight, load, drain ▶ VERB **1** *The government taxes profits of corporations at a high rate.* = **charge** (*formal*), impose a tax on, levy a tax on, rate, demand, assess, extract, exact, tithe

2 *Overcrowding has taxed the city's ability to deal with waste.* = **strain**, push, stretch, try, test, task, load, burden, drain, exhaust, weaken, weary, put pressure on, sap, wear out, weigh heavily on, overburden, make heavy demands on, enervate **3** *Writers to the letters column taxed me with shallowness.* = **accuse**, charge, blame, confront, impeach, incriminate, arraign, impugn, lay at your door ■ **OPPOSITE:** acquit

taxing ADJECTIVE = **demanding**, trying, wearing, heavy, tough, tiring, punishing, exacting, stressful, sapping, onerous, burdensome, wearisome, enervating ■ **OPPOSITE:** easy

teach VERB **1** *a programme to teach educational skills; She taught me to read.* = **instruct**, train, coach, school, direct, advise, inform, discipline, educate, drill, tutor, enlighten, impart, instil, inculcate, edify, give lessons in **2** *(often with how)* *George had taught him how to ride a horse.* = **show**, train, demonstrate

teacher NOUN = **instructor**, coach, tutor, don, guide, professor, trainer, lecturer, guru, mentor, educator, handler, schoolteacher, pedagogue, dominie (*Scot.*), master *or* mistress, schoolmaster *or* schoolmistress

team NOUN **1** *The team failed to qualify for the final.* = **side**, squad, troupe **2** *Mr Hunter and his management team* = **group**, company, set, body, band, crew (*informal*), gang, line-up, bunch (*informal*), posse (*informal*) **3** *Ploughing is no longer done with a team of oxen.* = **pair**, span, yoke • **team up** *He suggested that we team up for a working holiday in France.* = **join**, unite, work together, cooperate, couple, link up, get together, yoke, band together, collaborate, join forces

teamwork NOUN = **cooperation**, collaboration, unity, concert, harmony, fellowship, coordination, joint action, esprit de corps

tear VERB **1** *She very nearly tore my overcoat.* = **rip**, split, rend (*literary*), shred, rupture, sunder **2** *Too fine a material may tear.* = **run**, rip, ladder, snag **3** *He'd torn his skin trying to do it barehanded.* = **scratch**, cut (open), gash, lacerate, injure, mangle, cut to pieces, cut to ribbons, mangulate (*Austral. slang*) **4** *Canine teeth are for tearing flesh.* = **pull apart**, claw, lacerate, sever, mutilate, mangle, mangulate (*Austral. slang*) **5** *The door flew open and she tore into the room.* = **rush**, run, charge, race, shoot, fly, career, speed, belt (*slang*), dash, hurry, barrel (along) (*informal, chiefly U.S. & Canad.*),

sprint, bolt, dart, gallop, zoom, burn rubber (*informal*) **6** *(often with away or from)* *She tore the windscreen wipers from his car.* = **pull**, seize, rip, grab, snatch, pluck, yank, wrench, wrest ▶ NOUN *I peered through a tear in the van's curtains.* = **hole**, split, rip, run, rent, snag, rupture

tearaway NOUN = **hooligan**, delinquent, tough, rough (*informal*), rowdy, ruffian, roughneck (*slang*), good-for-nothing

tearful ADJECTIVE **1** *She was tearful when asked to talk about it.* = **weeping**, crying, sobbing, in tears, whimpering, blubbering, weepy (*informal*), lachrymose **2** *a tearful farewell* = **sad**, pathetic, poignant, upsetting, distressing, harrowing, pitiful, woeful, mournful, lamentable, sorrowful, pitiable, dolorous

tears PLURAL NOUN *She was very near to tears.* = **crying**, weeping, sobbing, wailing, whimpering, blubbering, lamentation • **in tears** *He was in tears at the funeral.* = **weeping**, crying, sobbing, whimpering, blubbering, visibly moved ■ **RELATED WORDS:** *adjectives* lacrimal, lachrymal, lacrymal

tease VERB **1** *He teased me mercilessly about going there.* = **mock**, bait, wind up (*Brit. slang*), worry, bother, provoke, annoy, needle (*informal*), plague (*informal*), rag, rib (*informal*), torment, ridicule, taunt, aggravate (*informal*), badger, pester, vex, goad, bedevil, take the mickey out of (*informal*), twit, chaff, guy (*informal*), gibe, pull someone's leg (*informal*), make fun of **2** *When did you last flirt with him or tease him?* = **tantalize**, lead on, flirt with, titillate

technical ADJECTIVE = **scientific**, technological, skilled, specialist, specialized, hi-tech *or* high-tech

technique NOUN **1** *tests performed using a new technique* = **method**, way, system, approach, means, course, style, fashion, manner, procedure, mode, MO, modus operandi **2** *He went abroad to improve his tennis technique.* = **skill**, art, performance, craft, touch, know-how (*informal*), facility, delivery, execution, knack, artistry, craftsmanship, proficiency, adroitness

tedious ADJECTIVE = **boring**, dull, dreary, monotonous, tiring, annoying, fatiguing, drab, banal, tiresome, lifeless, prosaic, laborious, humdrum, uninteresting, long-drawn-out, mind-numbing, irksome, unexciting, soporific, ho-hum (*informal*), vapid, wearisome, deadly dull, prosy, dreich (*Scot.*) ■ **OPPOSITE:** exciting

tedium NOUN = **boredom**, monotony, dullness, routine, the doldrums, banality, sameness, ennui (*literary*), drabness, deadness, dreariness, tediousness, lifelessness ■ **OPPOSITE:** excitement

teem¹ VERB *The forest below him seethed and teemed with life.* = **be full of**, abound, swarm, bristle, brim, overflow, be abundant, burst at the seams, be prolific, be crawling, pullulate

teem² VERB (*often with* **down** *or* **with rain**) *The wedding was supposed to be outside but it teemed with rain.* = **pour**, lash, pelt (down), sheet, stream, belt (*slang*), bucket down (*informal*), rain cats and dogs (*informal*)

teeming¹ ADJECTIVE *The area is usually teeming with tourists.* = **full**, packed, crowded, alive, thick, bursting, numerous, crawling, swarming, abundant, bristling, brimming, overflowing, fruitful, replete, chock-full, brimful, chock-a-block ■ **OPPOSITE:** lacking

teeming² ADJECTIVE *I arrived early to find it teeming with rain.* = **pouring**, lashing, pelting, sheeting, streaming, belting (*slang*), bucketing down (*informal*)

teenage ADJECTIVE = **youthful**, adolescent, juvenile, immature

teenager NOUN = **youth**, minor, adolescent, juvenile, girl, boy

teeny ADJECTIVE = **tiny**, minute, wee, miniature, microscopic, diminutive, minuscule, teeny-weeny, teensy-weensy

teeter VERB = **wobble**, rock, totter, balance, stagger, sway, tremble, waver, pivot, seesaw

telegram NOUN = **cable**, wire (*informal*), telegraph, telex, radiogram

telegraph VERB = **cable**, wire (*informal*), transmit, telex, send

telepathy NOUN = **mind-reading**, ESP, sixth sense, clairvoyance, extrasensory perception, psychometry, thought transference

telephone NOUN *They usually exchanged messages by telephone.* = **phone**, blower (*informal*), mobile, mobile phone *or* (*informal*) moby, cellphone *or* cellular phone (*U.S.*), handset, landline, dog and bone (*slang*), iPhone®, smartphone, Blackberry, camera phone, picture phone ▶ VERB *I had to telephone him to say I was sorry.* = **call**, phone, ring (*chiefly Brit.*), buzz (*informal*), dial, call up, give someone a call, give someone a ring (*informal, chiefly Brit.*), give someone a buzz (*informal*), give someone a bell (*Brit. slang*), put a call through to, give someone a tinkle (*Brit. informal*), get on the blower to (*informal*)

telescope NOUN *The telescope enables us to see deeper into the universe than ever.* = **glass**, scope (*informal*), spyglass ▶ VERB *Film*

naturally tends to telescope time.* = **shorten**, contract, compress, cut, trim, shrink, tighten, condense, abbreviate, abridge, capsulize ■ **OPPOSITE:** lengthen

television NOUN = **TV**, telly (*Brit. informal*), small screen (*informal*), the box (*Brit. informal*), receiver, the tube (*slang*), TV set, gogglebox (*Brit. slang*), idiot box (*slang*)

tell VERB **1** *I called her to tell her how spectacular it looked.* = **inform**, notify, make aware, say to, state to, warn, reveal to, express to, brief, advise, disclose to, proclaim to, fill in, speak about to, confess to, impart, alert to, divulge, announce to, acquaint with, communicate to, mention to, make known to, apprise, utter to, get off your chest (*informal*), let know, flag up **2** *He told his story to a national newspaper.* = **describe**, relate, recount, report, portray, depict, chronicle, rehearse, narrate, give an account of **3** *She told me to come and help clean the house.* = **instruct**, order, command, direct, bid, enjoin **4** *It was impossible to tell where the bullet had entered.* = **see**, make out, discern, understand, discover, be certain, comprehend **5** *I can't really tell the difference between their policies and ours.* = **distinguish**, discriminate, discern, differentiate, identify **6** *The pressure began to tell as rain closed in after 20 laps.* = **have** *or* **take effect**, register (*informal*), weigh, have force, count, take its toll, carry weight, make its presence felt

• **tell someone off** *He never listened to us when we told him off.* = **reprimand**, rebuke, scold, lecture, carpet (*informal*), censure, reproach, berate, chide, tear into (*informal*), read the riot act to, reprove, upbraid, take to task, tick off (*informal*), bawl out (*informal*), chew out (*U.S. & Canad. informal*), tear off a strip (*Brit. informal*), give a piece of your mind to, haul over the coals (*informal*), give a rocket to (*Brit. & N.Z. informal*)

telling ADJECTIVE = **effective**, significant, considerable, marked, striking, powerful, solid, impressive, influential, decisive, potent, forceful, weighty, forcible, trenchant, effectual ■ **OPPOSITE:** unimportant

temerity NOUN = **audacity**, nerve (*informal*), cheek, gall (*informal*), front, assurance, pluck, boldness, recklessness, chutzpah (*U.S. & Canad. informal*), impudence, effrontery, impulsiveness, rashness, brass neck (*Brit. informal*), foolhardiness, sassiness (*U.S. informal*), forwardness, heedlessness

temper NOUN **1** *I hope he can control his temper.* = **irritability**, anger, irascibility, passion, resentment, irritation, annoyance, petulance, surliness, ill humour, peevishness, hot-headedness ■ **OPPOSITE:** good humour **2** *He's known for his placid temper.* = **frame of mind**, character, nature, attitude, mind, mood, constitution, humour, vein, temperament, tenor, disposition **3** *She was still in a temper when I arrived.* = **rage**, fury, bad mood, passion, paddy (*Brit. informal*), wax (*informal, chiefly Brit.*), tantrum, bate (*Brit. slang*), fit of pique, foulie (*Austral. slang*), hissy fit (*informal*), strop (*Brit. informal*) **4** *I've never seen him lose his temper.* = **self-control**, composure, cool (*slang*), calm, good humour, tranquillity, coolness, calmness, equanimity ■ **OPPOSITE:** anger ▶ VERB **1** *He had to learn to temper his enthusiasm.* = **moderate**, restrain, tone down, calm, soften, soothe, lessen, allay, mitigate, abate, assuage, mollify, soft-pedal (*informal*), palliate, admix ■ **OPPOSITE:** intensify **2** *a new way of tempering glass* = **strengthen**, harden, toughen, anneal ■ **OPPOSITE:** soften

temperament NOUN *His impulsive temperament regularly got him into difficulties.* = **nature**, character, personality, quality, spirit, make-up, soul, constitution, bent, stamp, humour, tendencies, tendency, temper, outlook, complexion, disposition, frame of mind, mettle, cast of mind

temperamental ADJECTIVE **1** *given to temperamental outbursts and paranoia* = **moody**, emotional, touchy, sensitive, explosive, passionate, volatile, fiery, impatient, erratic, irritable, mercurial, excitable, capricious, petulant, hot-headed, hypersensitive, highly strung, easily upset, unstable ■ **OPPOSITE:** even-tempered **2** *The machine guns could be temperamental.* = **unreliable**, unpredictable, undependable, inconsistent, erratic, inconstant, unstable ■ **OPPOSITE:** reliable **3** *Some temperamental qualities are not easily detected by parents.* = **natural**, inherent, innate, constitutional, ingrained, congenital, inborn

temperance NOUN **1** *a reformed alcoholic extolling the joys of temperance* = **teetotalism**, abstinence, sobriety, abstemiousness **2** *The age of hedonism was replaced by a new era of temperance.* = **moderation**, restraint, self-control, self-discipline, continence, self-restraint, forbearance ■ **OPPOSITE:** excess

temperate ADJECTIVE **1** *The valley keeps a temperate climate throughout the year.* = **mild**, moderate, balmy, fair, cool, soft, calm, gentle, pleasant, clement, agreeable

■ **OPPOSITE:** extreme **2** *His final report was more temperate than earlier ones.* = **moderate**, dispassionate, self-controlled, calm, stable, reasonable, sensible, mild, composed, equable, even-tempered, self-restrained ■ **OPPOSITE:** unrestrained

tempest NOUN **1** *torrential rain and howling tempest* = **storm**, hurricane, gale, tornado, cyclone, typhoon, squall **2** *I hadn't foreseen the tempest my request would cause.* = **uproar**, storm, furore, disturbance, upheaval, ferment, commotion, tumult ■ **OPPOSITE:** calm

tempestuous ADJECTIVE **1** *the couple's tempestuous relationship* = **passionate**, intense, turbulent, heated, wild, excited, emotional, violent, flaming, hysterical, stormy, impassioned, uncontrolled, boisterous, feverish ■ **OPPOSITE:** peaceful **2** *adverse winds and tempestuous weather* = **stormy**, turbulent, inclement, raging, windy, boisterous, blustery, gusty, squally

temple NOUN = **shrine**, church, sanctuary, holy place, place of worship, house of God

tempo NOUN = **pace**, time, rate, beat, measure (*Prosody*), speed, metre, rhythm, cadence, pulse

temporal ADJECTIVE **1** *Clergy should not be preoccupied with temporal matters.* = **secular**, worldly, lay, earthly, mundane, material, civil, fleshly, mortal, terrestrial, carnal, profane, sublunary **2** *The temporal gifts that Fortune grants in this world are finally worthless.* = **temporary**, passing, transitory, fleeting, short-lived, fugitive, transient, momentary, evanescent (*formal*), impermanent, fugacious

temporarily ADVERB = **briefly**, for the moment, for the time being, momentarily, for a moment, for a short time, for a little while, fleetingly, for a short while, pro tem, for the nonce

temporary ADJECTIVE **1** *a temporary loss of memory* = **impermanent**, passing, transitory, brief, fleeting, interim, short-lived, fugitive, transient, momentary, ephemeral, evanescent (*formal*), pro tem, here today and gone tomorrow, pro tempore (*Latin*), fugacious ■ **OPPOSITE:** permanent **2** *She was working as a temporary teacher at a Belfast school.* = **short-term**, acting, interim, supply, stand-in, fill-in, caretaker, provisional, stopgap, pop-up

tempt VERB **1** *Can I tempt you with a little puff pastry?* = **attract**, draw, appeal to, allure, whet the appetite of, make your mouth water **2** *Don't let credit tempt you to buy something you can't afford.* = **entice**, lure, lead on, invite, woo, seduce, coax, decoy,

inveigle ■ **OPPOSITE:** discourage **3** *As soon as
you talk about never losing, it's tempting fate.*
= **provoke**, try, test, risk, dare, bait, fly in
the face of

temptation NOUN **1** *the many temptations to
which they will be exposed* = **enticement**,
lure, inducement, pull, come-on (*informal*),
invitation, bait, coaxing, snare, seduction,
decoy, allurement, tantalization **2** *The thrill
and the temptation of crime is very strong.*
= **appeal**, draw (*informal*), attraction,
attractiveness

tempting ADJECTIVE = **inviting**, enticing,
seductive, alluring, attractive,
mouthwatering, appetizing
■ **OPPOSITE:** uninviting

tenacious ADJECTIVE **1** *He is regarded as a
persistent and tenacious interviewer.*
= **stubborn**, dogged, determined,
persistent, sure, firm, adamant, staunch,
resolute, inflexible, strong-willed,
steadfast, unyielding, obstinate,
intransigent, immovable, unswerving,
obdurate, stiff-necked, pertinacious
■ **OPPOSITE:** irresolute **2** *a tenacious belief*
= **firm**, dogged, persistent, unyielding,
unswerving **3** *He has a particularly tenacious
grip on life.* = **strong**, firm, fast, iron, tight,
clinging, forceful, immovable, unshakeable
4 *her analytical mind and tenacious memory*
= **retentive**, good, photographic,
unforgetful **5** *tenacious catarrh in the nasal
passages and lungs* = **adhesive**, clinging,
sticky, glutinous, gluey, mucilaginous

tenacity NOUN = **perseverance**,
resolution, determination, application,
resolve, persistence, diligence,
intransigence, firmness, stubbornness,
inflexibility, obstinacy, steadfastness,
obduracy, doggedness, strength of will,
strength of purpose, resoluteness,
pertinacity, staunchness

tenancy NOUN **1** *Check the terms of your
tenancy closely.* = **lease**, residence,
occupancy, holding, renting, possession,
occupation **2** *his tenancy as Ryder Cup captain*
= **period of office**, tenure, incumbency,
time in office

tenant NOUN = **leaseholder**, resident,
renter, occupant, holder, inhabitant,
occupier, lodger, boarder, lessee

tend¹ VERB *Lighter cars tend to be noisy.* = **be
inclined**, be likely, be liable, have a
tendency, be apt, be prone, trend, lean,
incline, be biased, be disposed, gravitate,
have a leaning, have an inclination

tend² VERB **1** *For years he tended her in her
illness.* = **take care of**, look after, care for,
keep, watch, serve, protect, feed, handle,

attend, guard, nurse, see to, nurture,
minister to, cater for, keep an eye on, wait
on, watch over ■ **OPPOSITE:** neglect **2** *The
woman dug and tended her garden.*
= **maintain**, take care of, nurture,
cultivate, manage ■ **OPPOSITE:** neglect

tendency NOUN **1** *the government's tendency
towards secrecy in recent years* = **trend**, drift,
movement, turning, heading, course, drive,
bearing, direction, bias **2** *He has a tendency
towards snobbery.* = **inclination**, leaning,
bent, liability, readiness, disposition,
penchant, propensity, susceptibility,
predisposition, predilection, proclivity
(*formal*), partiality, proneness

tender¹ ADJECTIVE **1** *tender, loving care*
= **gentle**, loving, kind, caring, warm,
sympathetic, fond, sentimental, humane,
affectionate, compassionate, benevolent,
considerate, merciful, amorous, warm-
hearted, tenderhearted, softhearted,
touchy-feely (*informal*) ■ **OPPOSITE:** harsh
2 *a tragic, tender love story* = **romantic**,
moving, touching, emotional, sentimental,
poignant, evocative, soppy (*Brit. informal*)
3 *He had become attracted to the game at the
tender age of seven.* = **vulnerable**, young,
sensitive, new, green, raw, youthful,
inexperienced, immature, callow,
impressionable, unripe, wet behind the
ears (*informal*) ■ **OPPOSITE:** experienced
4 *My tummy felt very tender.* = **sensitive**,
painful, sore, smarting, raw, bruised,
irritated, aching, inflamed **5** *The newborn
looked so fragile and tender.* = **fragile**, delicate,
frail, soft, weak, feeble, breakable **6** *Even his
continuing presence remains a tender issue.*
= **difficult**, sensitive, tricky, dangerous,
complicated, risky, touchy, ticklish

tender² VERB *She quickly tendered her
resignation.* = **offer**, present, submit, give,
suggest, propose, extend, volunteer, hand
in, put forward, proffer ▸ NOUN *Builders will
be asked to submit a tender for the work.* = **offer**,
bid, estimate, proposal, suggestion,
submission, proffer

tenderness NOUN **1** *She smiled, politely, rather
than with tenderness.* = **gentleness**, love,
affection, liking, care, consideration,
sympathy, pity, humanity, warmth, mercy,
attachment, compassion, devotion,
kindness, fondness, sentimentality,
benevolence, humaneness, amorousness,
warm-heartedness, softheartedness,
tenderheartedness ■ **OPPOSITE:** harshness
2 *There is still some tenderness on her tummy.*
= **soreness**, pain, sensitivity, smart,
bruising, ache, aching, irritation,
inflammation, rawness, sensitiveness,

painfulness **3** *the vulnerability and tenderness he brings to the role* = **fragility**, vulnerability, weakness, sensitivity, softness, feebleness, sensitiveness, frailness, delicateness

tenet NOUN = **principle**, rule, doctrine, creed, view, teaching, opinion, belief, conviction, canon, thesis, maxim, dogma, precept, article of faith, kaupapa (*N.Z.*)

tenor NOUN = **meaning**, trend, drift, way, course, sense, aim, purpose, direction, path, theme, substance, burden, tendency, intent, purport

tense ADJECTIVE **1** *the tense atmosphere of the talks* = **strained**, uneasy, stressful, fraught (*informal*), charged, difficult, worrying, exciting, uncomfortable, knife-edge, nail-biting, nerve-racking **2** *He had been very tense, but he finally relaxed.* = **nervous**, wound up (*informal*), edgy, strained, wired (*slang*), anxious, under pressure, restless, apprehensive, jittery (*informal*), uptight (*informal*), on edge, jumpy, twitchy (*informal*), overwrought, strung up (*informal*), on tenterhooks, fidgety, keyed up, antsy (*informal*), wrought up, adrenalized ■ OPPOSITE: calm **3** *She lay, eyes shut, body tense.* = **rigid**, strained, taut, stretched, tight ■ OPPOSITE: relaxed ▶ VERB *His stomach muscles tensed.* = **tighten**, strain, brace, tauten, stretch, flex, stiffen ■ OPPOSITE: relax

tension NOUN **1** *Smiling relieves tension and stress.* = **strain**, stress, nervousness, pressure, anxiety, unease, apprehension, suspense, restlessness, the jitters (*informal*), edginess ■ OPPOSITE: calmness **2** *The tension between the two countries is likely to remain.* = **friction**, hostility, unease, antagonism, antipathy, enmity, ill feeling **3** *Slowly, the tension in his face dispersed.* = **rigidity**, tightness, stiffness, pressure, stress, stretching, straining, tautness

tentative ADJECTIVE **1** *They have reached a tentative agreement to hold talks next month.* = **unconfirmed**, provisional, indefinite, test, trial, pilot, preliminary, experimental, unsettled, speculative, pencilled in, exploratory, to be confirmed, TBC, conjectural ■ OPPOSITE: confirmed **2** *My first attempts at complaining were very tentative.* = **hesitant**, cautious, uncertain, doubtful, backward, faltering, unsure, timid, undecided, diffident, iffy (*informal*) ■ OPPOSITE: confident

tenuous ADJECTIVE **1** *Links between the provinces were seen to be tenuous.* = **slight**, weak, dubious, shaky, doubtful, questionable, insignificant, flimsy, sketchy,

insubstantial, nebulous ■ OPPOSITE: strong **2** *She was holding onto life by a tenuous thread.* = **fine**, slim, delicate, attenuated, gossamer

tenure NOUN **1** *Lack of security of tenure meant that many became homeless.* = **occupancy**, holding, occupation, residence, tenancy, possession, proprietorship **2** *his short tenure of the party leadership* = **term of office**, incumbency, period in office, time

tepid ADJECTIVE **1** *She bent to the tap and drank the tepid water.* = **lukewarm**, warmish, slightly warm **2** *His nomination has received tepid support in the Senate.* = **unenthusiastic**, half-hearted, indifferent, cool, lukewarm, apathetic ■ OPPOSITE: enthusiastic

term NOUN **1** *What's the medical term for a heart attack?* = **word**, name, expression, title, label, phrase, denomination, designation, appellation (*formal*), locution **2** *the summer term* = **session**, course, quarter (*U.S.*), semester, trimester (*U.S.*) **3** *a 12-month term of service* = **period**, time, spell, while, season, space, interval, span, duration, incumbency **4** *They all successfully carried the babies to term.* = **conclusion**, end, close, finish, culmination, fruition ▶ VERB *He had been termed a temporary employee.* = **call**, name, label, style, entitle, tag, dub, designate, describe as, denominate

terminal ADJECTIVE **1** *terminal cancer* = **fatal**, deadly, lethal, killing, mortal, incurable, inoperable, untreatable **2** *Endowments pay a terminal bonus at maturity.* = **final**, last, closing, finishing, concluding, ultimate, terminating ■ OPPOSITE: initial ▶ NOUN *Only the original ochre facade of the nearby railway terminal remains.* = **terminus**, station, depot (*U.S. & Canad.*), end of the line

terminate VERB **1** *Her next remark abruptly terminated the conversation.* = **end**, stop, conclude, finish, complete, axe (*informal*), cut off, wind up, put an end to, discontinue, pull the plug on (*informal*), belay (*Nautical*), bring or come to an end ■ OPPOSITE: begin **2** *His contract terminates at the end of the season.* = **cease**, end, close, finish, run out, expire, lapse **3** *She finally decided to terminate the pregnancy.* = **abort**, end

termination NOUN **1** *a dispute which led to the abrupt termination of trade* = **ending**, end, close, finish, conclusion, wind-up, completion, cessation, expiry, cut-off point, finis, discontinuation ■ OPPOSITE: beginning **2** *You should have a medical after the termination of a pregnancy.* = **abortion**, ending, discontinuation

t

terminology NOUN = **language**, terms, vocabulary, jargon, cant, lingo (*informal*), nomenclature, patois, phraseology, argot

terminus NOUN = **end of the line**, terminal, station, depot (*U.S. & Canad.*), last stop, garage

terms PLURAL NOUN **1** *The video explains in simple terms how the tax works.* = **language**, terminology, phraseology, manner of speaking **2** *the terms of the Helsinki agreement* = **conditions**, particulars, provisions, provisos, stipulations, qualifications, premises (*Law*), specifications **3** *We shook hands and parted on good terms.* = **relationship**, standing, footing, relations, position, status **4** *They provide favourable terms to shops that invest in their services.* = **price**, rates, charges, fee, payment • **come to terms** *Even if they came to terms, investors would object to the merger.* = **come to an agreement**, reach agreement, come to an understanding, conclude agreement • **come to terms with something** *She had come to terms with the fact that she would always be ill.* = **learn to live with**, come to accept, be reconciled to, reach acceptance of

> USAGE Many people object to the use of *in terms of* as an all-purpose preposition replacing phrases such as 'as regards', 'about', and so forth in a context such as the following: *In terms of trends in smoking habits, there is good news.* They would maintain that in strict usage it should be used to specify a relationship, as in: *Obesity is defined in terms of body mass index, which involves a bit of cumbersome maths.* Nevertheless, despite objections, it is very commonly used as a linking phrase, particularly in speech.

terrain NOUN = **ground**, country, land, landscape, topography, going

terrestrial ADJECTIVE = **earthly**, worldly, global, mundane, sublunary, tellurian, terrene

terrible ADJECTIVE **1** *Thousands suffered terrible injuries in the disaster.* = **awful**, shocking (*informal*), appalling, terrifying, horrible, dreadful, horrifying, dread (*literary*), dreaded, fearful (*informal*), horrendous, monstrous, harrowing, gruesome, horrid (*informal*), unspeakable, frightful, hellacious (*U.S. slang*) **2** *I have the most terrible nightmares.* = **bad**, awful, dreadful, beastly (*informal*), dire, abysmal, abhorrent, poor, offensive, foul, unpleasant, revolting, rotten (*informal*), obscene, hideous, vile, from hell (*informal*), obnoxious, repulsive,

frightful, odious, hateful, loathsome, godawful (*slang*) ■ **OPPOSITE:** wonderful **3** *He claimed that he had a terrible pain in his head.* = **serious**, desperate, severe, extreme, bad, dangerous, insufferable ■ **OPPOSITE:** mild

terribly ADVERB **1** *He has suffered terribly in losing his best friend.* = **very much**, greatly, very, much, dreadfully, seriously, extremely, gravely, desperately, thoroughly, decidedly, awfully (*informal*), exceedingly **2** *I'm terribly sorry to bother you at this hour.* = **extremely**, very, much, greatly, dreadfully, seriously (*informal*), desperately, thoroughly, decidedly, awfully (*informal*), exceedingly

terrific ADJECTIVE **1** *What a terrific idea!* = **excellent**, great (*informal*), wonderful, mean (*slang*), topping (*Brit. slang*), fine, brilliant, very good, cracking (*Brit. informal*), amazing, outstanding, smashing (*informal*), superb, fantastic (*informal*), ace (*informal*), magnificent, fabulous (*informal*), marvellous, sensational (*informal*), sovereign, awesome (*slang*), breathtaking, super (*informal*), brill (*informal*), sick (*slang*), stupendous, bodacious (*slang, chiefly U.S.*), boffo (*slang*), jim-dandy (*slang*), chillin' (*U.S. slang*), booshit (*Austral. slang*), exo (*Austral. slang*), sik (*Austral. slang*), ka pai (*N.Z.*), rad (*informal*), phat (*slang*), schmick (*Austral. informal*), beaut (*informal*), barrie (*Scot. slang*), belting (*Brit. slang*), pearler (*Austral. slang*) ■ **OPPOSITE:** awful **2** *There was a terrific bang and a great cloud of smoke.* = **intense**, great, huge, terrible, enormous, severe, extreme, awful, tremendous (*informal*), fierce, harsh, excessive, dreadful, horrific, fearful (*informal*), awesome, gigantic, monstrous

terrified ADJECTIVE = **frightened**, scared, petrified, alarmed, intimidated, awed, panic-stricken, scared to death, scared stiff, terror-stricken, horror-struck, frightened out of your wits

terrify VERB = **frighten**, scare, petrify, alarm, intimidate, terrorize, scare to death, put the fear of God into, make your hair stand on end, fill with terror, make your flesh creep, make your blood run cold, frighten out of your wits

territory NOUN = **district**, area, land, region, state, country, sector, zone, province, patch, turf (*slang*), domain, terrain, tract, bailiwick

terror NOUN **1** *I shook with terror whenever I flew in an aeroplane.* = **fear**, alarm, dread, fright, panic, anxiety, intimidation, fear and trembling **2** *the many obscure terrors that haunted the children of that period*

= **nightmare**, monster, bogeyman, devil, fiend, bugbear, scourge

terrorize VERB **1** *In his childhood he liked to terrorize his young siblings.* = **bully**, menace, intimidate, threaten, oppress, coerce, strong-arm (*informal*), browbeat **2** *The government had the helicopter gunships to terrorize the population.* = **terrify**, alarm, frighten, scare, intimidate, petrify, scare to death, strike terror into, put the fear of God into, fill with terror, frighten out of your wits, inspire panic in

terse ADJECTIVE **1** *His tone was terse as he asked the question.* = **curt**, abrupt, brusque, short, rude, tart, snappy, gruff ■ OPPOSITE: polite **2** *He issued a terse statement, saying the decision will be made on Monday.* = **concise**, short, brief, clipped, neat, to the point, crisp, compact, summary, condensed, incisive, elliptical, laconic, succinct, pithy, monosyllabic, gnomic, epigrammatic, aphoristic, sententious ■ OPPOSITE: lengthy

test VERB **1** *Test the temperature of the water with your wrist.* = **check**, try, investigate, assess, research, prove, analyse, experiment with, try out, verify, assay, put something to the proof, put something to the test, run something up the flagpole **2** *He tested him on verbs and gave him a forfeit for each one he got wrong.* = **examine**, put someone to the test, put someone through their paces ▶ NOUN **1** *High levels of dioxin were confirmed by scientific tests.* = **trial**, research, check, investigation, attempt, analysis, assessment, proof, examination, evaluation, acid test **2** *Only 922 pupils passed the test.* = **examination**, paper, assessment, evaluation

testament NOUN **1** *His house is a testament to his Gothic tastes.* = **proof**, evidence, testimony, witness, demonstration, tribute, attestation, exemplification **2** *a codicil to my will and testament* = **will**, last wishes

testify VERB = **bear witness**, state, swear, certify, declare, witness, assert, affirm, depose (*Law*), attest, corroborate, vouch, evince, give testimony, asseverate (*formal*) ■ OPPOSITE: disprove

testimonial NOUN = **reference**, recommendation, credential, character, tribute, certificate, endorsement, commendation

> USAGE *Testimonial* is sometimes wrongly used where *testimony* is meant: *His re-election is a testimony* (not *a testimonial*) *to his popularity with his constituents.*

testimony NOUN **1** *His testimony was an important element of the case.* = **evidence**, information, statement, witness, profession, declaration, confirmation, submission, affirmation, affidavit, deposition, corroboration, avowal, attestation **2** *Her living room piled with documents is a testimony to her dedication to her work.* = **proof**, evidence, demonstration, indication, support, manifestation, verification, corroboration

testing ADJECTIVE = **difficult**, trying, demanding, taxing, challenging, searching, tough, exacting, formidable, rigorous, strenuous, arduous ■ OPPOSITE: undemanding

testy ADJECTIVE = **irritable**, cross, grumpy, crabbed, impatient, snappy, sullen, touchy, bad-tempered, petulant, irascible, cantankerous, peppery, tetchy, ratty (*Brit. & N.Z. informal*), quarrelsome, fretful, short-tempered, waspish, peevish, quick-tempered, splenetic, snappish, liverish, captious

tetchy ADJECTIVE = **irritable**, cross, grumpy, crabbed, impatient, snappy, sullen, touchy, bad-tempered, petulant, irascible, cantankerous, peppery, ratty (*Brit. & N.Z. informal*), testy, quarrelsome, fretful, short-tempered, waspish, peevish, quick-tempered, splenetic, snappish, liverish, captious

tether NOUN *The eagle sat on a tether, looking fierce.* = **leash**, rope, lead, bond, chain, restraint, fastening, shackle, fetter, halter ▶ VERB *He dismounted, tethering his horse to a tree.* = **tie**, secure, bind, chain, rope, restrain, fasten, shackle, leash, fetter, manacle • **at the end of your tether** *She was emotionally at the end of her tether.* = **exasperated**, exhausted, at your wits' end, finished, out of patience, at the limit of your endurance

text NOUN **1** *The photographs enhance the clarity of the text.* = **contents**, words, content, wording, body, matter, subject matter, main body **2** *The output might be just one line of characters or several hundred pages of text.* = **words**, wording **3** *the text of Dr. Zuckermann's speech* = **transcript**, script **4** *reluctant readers of GCSE set texts* = **reference book**, textbook, source, reader **5** *I'll read the text aloud first.* = **passage**, extract, line, sentence, paragraph, verse **6** *His work served as the text of secret debates.* = **subject**, matter, topic, argument, theme, thesis, motif **7** = **text message**, SMS, MMS ▶ VERB = **text message**, SMS, MMS, message

texture NOUN = **feel**, quality, character, consistency, structure, surface, constitution, fabric, tissue, grain, weave, composition

thank VERB = **say thank you to**, express gratitude to, show gratitude to, show your appreciation to

thankful ADJECTIVE = **grateful**, pleased, relieved, obliged, in (someone's) debt, indebted, appreciative, beholden ■ **OPPOSITE:** ungrateful

thankless ADJECTIVE = **unrewarding**, unappreciated ■ **OPPOSITE:** rewarding

thanks PLURAL NOUN *They accepted their certificates with words of thanks.* = **gratitude**, appreciation, thanksgiving, credit, recognition, acknowledgment, gratefulness • **thanks to** *Thanks to recent research, effective treatment is available.* = **because of**, through, due to, as a result of, owing to, by reason of

thaw VERB = **melt**, dissolve, soften, defrost, warm, liquefy, unfreeze ■ **OPPOSITE:** freeze

theatrical ADJECTIVE **1** *major theatrical productions* = **dramatic**, stage, Thespian, dramaturgical **2** *In a theatrical gesture he clamped his hand over his eyes.* = **exaggerated**, dramatic, melodramatic, histrionic, affected, camp (*informal*), mannered, artificial, overdone, unreal, pompous, stilted, showy, ostentatious, hammy (*informal*), ceremonious, stagy, actorly or actressy ■ **OPPOSITE:** natural

theft NOUN = **stealing**, robbery, thieving, fraud, rip-off (*slang*), swindling, embezzlement, pilfering, larceny, purloining, thievery

theme NOUN **1** *The need to strengthen the family has become a recurrent theme.* = **motif**, leitmotif, recurrent image, unifying idea, trope **2** *The novel's central theme is the ideal of social justice.* = **subject**, idea, topic, matter, argument, text, burden, essence, thesis, subject matter, keynote, gist, through-line (*Austral., U.S. & Canad.*)

theological ADJECTIVE = **religious**, ecclesiastical, doctrinal, divine

theorem NOUN = **proposition**, statement, formula, rule, principle, thesis, hypothesis, deduction, dictum

theoretical *or* **theoretic** ADJECTIVE **1** *theoretical physics* = **abstract**, pure, speculative, ideal, impractical ■ **OPPOSITE:** practical **2** *There is a theoretical risk, but there is seldom a problem.* = **hypothetical**, academic, notional, unproven, conjectural, nominal, postulatory

theorize VERB = **speculate**, conjecture,

hypothesize, project, suppose, guess, formulate, propound, blue-sky

theory NOUN **1** *He produced a theory about historical change.* = **hypothesis**, philosophy, system of ideas, plan, system, science, scheme, proposal, principles, ideology, thesis ■ **OPPOSITE:** fact **2** *There was a theory that he wanted to marry her.* = **belief**, feeling, speculation, assumption, guess, hunch, presumption, conjecture, surmise, supposition

therapeutic ADJECTIVE = **beneficial**, healing, restorative, good, corrective, remedial, salutary, curative, salubrious, ameliorative, analeptic, sanative ■ **OPPOSITE:** harmful

therapist NOUN = **psychologist**, analyst, psychiatrist, shrink (*informal*), counsellor, healer, psychotherapist, psychoanalyst, trick cyclist (*informal*)

therapy NOUN = **remedy**, treatment, cure, healing, method of healing, remedial treatment

therefore ADVERB = **consequently**, so, thus, as a result, hence, accordingly, for that reason, whence, thence, ergo

thesaurus NOUN = **wordbook**, wordfinder

thesis NOUN **1** *This thesis does not stand up to close inspection.* = **proposition**, theory, hypothesis, idea, view, opinion, proposal, contention, line of argument **2** *He was awarded his PhD for a thesis on industrial robots.* = **dissertation**, paper, treatise, essay, composition, monograph, disquisition **3** *His central thesis is that crime is up because children do not learn self-control.* = **premise**, subject, statement, proposition, theme, topic, assumption, postulate, surmise, supposition

thick ADJECTIVE **1** *He folded his thick arms across his chest.* = **bulky**, broad, big, large, fat, solid, substantial, hefty, plump, sturdy, stout, chunky, stocky, meaty, beefy (*informal*), thickset ■ **OPPOSITE:** thin **2** *The folder was two inches thick.* = **wide**, across, deep, broad, in extent *or* diameter **3** *He led the rescuers through the thick undergrowth.* = **dense**, close, heavy, deep, compact, impenetrable, lush **4** *She wore a thick tartan skirt.* = **heavy**, heavyweight, dense, chunky, bulky, woolly **5** *The smoke was blueish-black and thick.* = **opaque**, heavy, dense, impenetrable **6** *The sauce is thick and rich.* = **viscous**, concentrated, stiff, condensed, clotted, coagulated, gelatinous, semi-solid, viscid ■ **OPPOSITE:** runny **7** *The area is so thick with people that the police close the streets.* = **crowded**, full, packed, covered, filled, bursting, jammed, crawling, choked, crammed, swarming, abundant, bristling, brimming, overflowing, seething, thronged, teeming, congested, replete, chock-full, bursting at the seams, chock-a-block ■ **OPPOSITE:** empty **8** *His voice was thick with bitterness.* = **husky**, rough, hoarse, distorted, muffled, croaking, inarticulate, throaty, indistinct, gravelly, guttural, raspy, croaky ■ **OPPOSITE:** clear **9** *He answered questions in a thick accent.* = **strong**, marked, broad, decided, rich, distinct, pronounced ■ **OPPOSITE:** slight **10** *How could she have been so thick?* = **stupid**, dull, dense, insensitive, dozy (*Brit. informal*), dopey (*informal*), obtuse, brainless, blockheaded, dumb-ass (*informal*), thickheaded, dim-witted (*informal*), slow-witted ■ **OPPOSITE:** clever **11** *You're thick with the girl, aren't you?* = **friendly**, close, intimate, familiar, pally (*informal*), devoted, well in (*informal*), confidential, inseparable, on good terms, chummy (*informal*), hand in glove, buddy-buddy (*slang, chiefly U.S. & Canad.*), palsy-walsy (*informal*), matey or maty (*Brit. informal*) ■ **OPPOSITE:** unfriendly ▶ NOUN *I enjoy being in the thick of things.* = **middle**, centre, heart, focus, core, midst, hub

thicken VERB = **set**, condense, congeal, cake, gel, clot, jell, coagulate, inspissate (*archaic*) ■ **OPPOSITE:** thin

thicket NOUN = **wood**, grove, woodland, brake, clump, covert, hurst (*archaic*), copse, coppice, spinney (*Brit.*)

thick-skinned ADJECTIVE = **insensitive**, tough, callous, hardened, hard-boiled (*informal*), impervious, stolid, unfeeling, case-hardened, unsusceptible
■ **OPPOSITE:** sensitive

thief NOUN = **robber**, crook (*informal*), burglar, stealer, bandit, plunderer, mugger (*informal*), shoplifter, embezzler, pickpocket, pilferer, swindler, purloiner, housebreaker, footpad (*archaic*), cracksman (*slang*), larcenist

thin ADJECTIVE **1** *A thin cable carries the signal to a computer.* = **narrow**, fine, attenuate, attenuated, threadlike ■ **OPPOSITE:** thick **2** *a tall, thin man with grey hair* = **slim**, spare, lean, slight, slender, skinny, light, meagre, skeletal, bony, lanky, emaciated, spindly, underweight, scrawny, lank, undernourished, skin and bone, scraggy, thin as a rake ■ **OPPOSITE:** fat **3** *The soup was thin and clear.* = **watery**, weak, diluted, dilute, runny, rarefied, wishy-washy (*informal*) ■ **OPPOSITE:** viscous **4** *The crowd had been thin for the first half of the match.*

= **meagre**, sparse, scanty, poor, scattered, inadequate, insufficient, deficient, paltry ■ **OPPOSITE:** plentiful **5** *Her gown was thin and she shivered from the cold.* = **fine**, delicate, flimsy, sheer, transparent, see-through, translucent, skimpy, gossamer, diaphanous, filmy, unsubstantial ■ **OPPOSITE:** thick **6** *The evidence is thin, and to some extent, ambiguous.* = **unconvincing**, inadequate, feeble, poor, weak, slight, shallow, insufficient, superficial, lame, scant, flimsy, scanty, unsubstantial ■ **OPPOSITE:** convincing **7** *She had pale thin yellow hair.* = **wispy**, thinning, sparse, scarce, scanty ▶ VERB **1** *It would have been better to thin the trees over several winters.* = **prune**, trim, cut back, weed out **2** *Aspirin thins the blood, letting it flow more easily.* = **dilute**, water down, weaken, attenuate

thing NOUN **1** *What's that thing in the middle of the fountain?* = **object**, article, implement, machine, device, tool, instrument, mechanism, apparatus, gadget, gizmo (*informal*), contrivance, whatsit (*informal*), doo-dah (*informal*), thingummy (*informal*), thingummyjig (*informal*) **2** *The Earth is mainly made of iron and silicon and things like that.* = **substance**, stuff, element, being, body, material, fabric, texture, entity **3** *Literacy isn't the same thing as intelligence.* = **concept**, idea, notion, conception **4** *There were far more serious things on my mind.* = **matter**, issue, subject, thought, concern, worry, topic, preoccupation **5** *This war thing is upsetting me.* = **affair**, situation, state of affairs, state, circumstance, scenario **6** *The first thing parents want to know is what sex the baby is.* = **fact**, detail, particular, point, factor, piece of information **7** *If you could change one thing about yourself, what would it be?* = **feature**, point, detail, something, particular, factor, item, aspect, facet **8** *A strange thing happened.* = **happening**, event, incident, proceeding, phenomenon, occurrence, eventuality **9** *I have a thing about spiders.* = **phobia**, fear, complex (*informal*), horror, terror, hang-up (*informal*), aversion, bee in your bonnet (*informal*) **10** *He's got a thing about red hair.* = **obsession**, liking, preoccupation, mania, quirk, fetish, fixation, soft spot, predilection, idée fixe (*French*) **11** *No, some things are better left unsaid.* = **remark**, comment, statement, observation, declaration, utterance, pronouncement **12** (*often plural*) *She told him to take his things and not come back.* = **possessions**, stuff, gear, belongings, goods, effects, clothes, luggage, baggage, bits and pieces, paraphernalia, clobber

(*Brit. slang*), odds and ends, chattels, impedimenta **13** *He forgot his shaving things.* = **equipment**, gear, tool, stuff, tackle, implement, kit, apparatus, utensil, accoutrement **14** *Everyone agrees things are getting better.* = **circumstances**, the situation, the state of affairs, matters, life, affairs

think VERB **1** *I think there should be a ban on tobacco advertising.* = **believe**, hold that, be of the opinion, conclude, esteem, conceive, be of the view **2** *I think he'll do a great job for us.* = **anticipate**, expect, figure (*U.S. informal*), suppose, imagine, guess (*informal, chiefly U.S. & Canad.*), reckon (*informal*), presume, envisage, foresee, surmise **3** *She thought he was about seventeen years old.* = **judge**, consider, estimate, reckon, deem, regard as **4** *She closed her eyes for a moment, trying to think.* = **ponder**, reflect, contemplate, deliberate, brood, meditate, ruminate, cogitate, rack your brains, be lost in thought, cerebrate **5** *I was trying to think what else we had to do.* = **remember**, recall, recollect, review, think back to, bring to mind, call to mind ▶ NOUN (*informal*) *I'll have a think about that.* = **ponder**, consideration, muse, assessment, reflection, deliberation, contemplation • **think something over** *She says she needs time to think it over.* = **consider**, contemplate, ponder, reflect upon, give thought to, consider the pros and cons of, weigh up, rack your brains about, chew over (*informal*), mull over, turn over in your mind • **think something up** '*Where did you get that idea?*' – '*I just thought it up.*' = **devise**, create, imagine, manufacture, come up with, invent, contrive, improvise, visualize, concoct, dream up, trump up

thinker NOUN = **philosopher**, intellect (*informal*), wise man, sage, brain (*informal*), theorist, mastermind, mahatma

thinking NOUN *There was a strong theoretical dimension to his thinking.* = **reasoning**, thoughts, philosophy, idea, view, position, theory, opinion, conclusions, assessment, judgment, outlook, conjecture ▶ ADJECTIVE *Thinking people on both sides will applaud this book.* = **thoughtful**, intelligent, cultured, reasoning, sophisticated, rational, philosophical, reflective, contemplative, meditative, ratiocinative

third-rate ADJECTIVE = **mediocre**, bad, inferior, indifferent, poor, duff (*Brit. informal*), shoddy, poor-quality, low-grade, no great shakes (*informal*), not much cop (*informal*), cheap-jack, half-pie (*N.Z.*

informal), of a sort or of sorts, ropey or ropy (*Brit. informal*), bodger or bodgie (*Austral. slang*)

thirst NOUN **1** *Instead of tea or coffee, drink water to quench your thirst.* = **dryness**, thirstiness, drought, craving to drink **2** *their ever-growing thirst for cash* = **craving**, hunger, appetite, longing, desire, passion, yen (*informal*), ache, lust, yearning, eagerness, hankering, keenness ■ **OPPOSITE:** aversion

thirsty ADJECTIVE **1** *If a baby is thirsty, it feeds more often.* = **parched**, dry, dehydrated **2** (*with* **for**) *People should understand how thirsty for revenge they are.* = **eager for**, longing for, hungry for, dying for, yearning for, lusting for, craving for, thirsting for, burning for, hankering for, itching for, greedy for, desirous of, avid for, athirst for

thorn NOUN *Roses will always have thorns, but with care they can be avoided.* = **prickle**, spike, spine, barb • **thorn in your side** *You're a real thorn in my side.* = **irritation**, nuisance, annoyance, trouble, bother, torture, plague (*informal*), curse, pest, torment, hassle (*informal*), scourge, affliction, irritant, bane

thorny ADJECTIVE **1** *thorny hawthorn trees* = **prickly**, spiky, spiny, pointed, sharp, barbed, bristly, spinous, bristling with thorns **2** *the thorny issue of immigration policy* = **troublesome**, difficult, problematic(al), trying, hard, worrying, tough, upsetting, awkward, unpleasant, sticky (*informal*), harassing, irksome, ticklish, vexatious

thorough ADJECTIVE **1** *We are making a thorough investigation.* = **comprehensive**, full, complete, sweeping, intensive, in-depth, exhaustive, all-inclusive, all-embracing, leaving no stone unturned ■ **OPPOSITE:** cursory **2** *The men were expert, thorough and careful.* = **careful**, conscientious, painstaking, efficient, meticulous, exhaustive, scrupulous, assiduous ■ **OPPOSITE:** careless **3** *I was a thorough little academic snob.* = **complete**, total, absolute, utter, perfect, entire, pure, sheer, outright, downright, unqualified, out-and-out, unmitigated, arrant, deep-dyed ■ **OPPOSITE:** partial

thoroughbred ADJECTIVE = **purebred**, pedigree, pure-blooded, blood, full-blooded, of unmixed stock ■ **OPPOSITE:** mongrel

thoroughfare NOUN **1** = **road**, way, street, highway, roadway, passageway, avenue **2** = **access**, way, passage

thoroughly ADVERB **1** *a thoroughly researched and illuminating biography* = **carefully**, completely, fully, comprehensively, sweepingly, efficiently, inside out, meticulously, painstakingly, scrupulously, assiduously, intensively, from top to bottom, conscientiously, exhaustively, leaving no stone unturned ■ **OPPOSITE:** carelessly **2** *Food must be reheated thoroughly.* = **fully**, completely, throughout, inside out, through and through **3** *We returned home thoroughly contented.* = **completely**, quite, totally, perfectly, entirely, absolutely, utterly, to the full, downright, to the hilt, without reservation ■ **OPPOSITE:** partly

though CONJUNCTION *He's very attractive, though he certainly isn't a ladykiller.* = **although**, while, even if, despite the fact that, allowing, granted, even though, albeit, notwithstanding, even supposing, tho' ▶ ADVERB *I like him. He makes me angry sometimes, though.* = **nevertheless**, still, however, yet, nonetheless, all the same, for all that, notwithstanding

thought NOUN **1** *After much thought I decided to end my marriage.* = **thinking**, consideration, reflection, deliberation, regard, musing, meditation, contemplation, introspection, rumination, navel-gazing (*slang*), cogitation, brainwork, cerebration **2** *It is my thought that the situation will be resolved.* = **opinion**, view, belief, idea, thinking, concept, conclusion, assessment, notion, conviction, judgment, conception, conjecture, estimation **3** *He had given some thought to what she had told him.* = **consideration**, study, attention, care, regard, scrutiny, heed **4** *They had no thought of surrendering.* = **intention**, plan, idea, design, aim, purpose, object, notion **5** *He had now banished all thought of retirement.* = **hope**, expectation, dream, prospect, aspiration, anticipation **6** *They had no thought for others who might get hurt.* = **concern**, care, regard, anxiety, sympathy, compassion, thoughtfulness, solicitude, attentiveness

thoughtful ADJECTIVE **1** *He was looking very thoughtful.* = **reflective**, pensive, contemplative, meditative, thinking, serious, musing, wistful, introspective, rapt, studious, lost in thought, deliberative, ruminative, in a brown study ■ **OPPOSITE:** shallow **2** *a thoughtful and caring man* = **considerate**, kind, caring, kindly, helpful, attentive, unselfish, solicitous ■ **OPPOSITE:** inconsiderate

thoughtless ADJECTIVE **1** *a minority of thoughtless and inconsiderate people* = **inconsiderate**, rude, selfish, insensitive, unkind, uncaring, indiscreet, tactless, impolite, undiplomatic

■ **OPPOSITE:** considerate **2** *It was thoughtless of her to mention it.* = **unthinking**, stupid, silly, careless, regardless, foolish, rash, reckless, mindless, negligent, inadvertent, ill-considered, tactless, absent-minded, imprudent, slapdash, neglectful, heedless, slipshod, inattentive, injudicious, remiss (*formal*), unmindful, unobservant, ditsy or ditzy (*slang*) ■ **OPPOSITE:** wise

thrall NOUN = **slavery**, bondage, servitude, enslavement, subjugation, serfdom, subjection, vassalage, thraldom

thrash VERB **1** *They thrashed their opponents 5-0.* = **defeat**, beat, hammer (*informal*), stuff (*slang*), tank (*slang*), crush, overwhelm, slaughter (*informal*), lick (*informal*), paste (*slang*), rout, maul, trounce, clobber (*slang*), run rings around (*informal*), wipe the floor with (*informal*), make mincemeat of (*informal*), blow someone out of the water (*slang*), drub, beat someone hollow (*Brit. informal*) **2** *He was thrashed with a cane until his skin turned red.* = **beat**, wallop, whip, hide (*informal*), belt (*informal*), leather, tan (*slang*), cane, lick (*informal*), paste (*slang*), birch, flog, scourge, spank, clobber (*slang*), lambast(e), flagellate, horsewhip, give someone a (good) hiding (*informal*), drub, take a stick to, beat or knock seven bells out of (*informal*) **3** *He collapsed on the floor, thrashing his legs about.* = **thresh**, flail, jerk, plunge, toss, squirm, writhe, heave, toss and turn • **thrash something out** *an effort to thrash out differences about which they have strong feelings* = **settle**, resolve, discuss, debate, solve, argue out, have out, talk over

thrashing NOUN **1** *She dropped only eight points in her thrashing of the former champion.* = **defeat**, beating, hammering (*informal*), hiding (*informal*), pasting (*slang*), rout, mauling, trouncing, drubbing **2** *She knew if she was caught she would get a thrashing.* = **beating**, hiding (*informal*), belting (*informal*), whipping, tanning (*slang*), lashing, caning, pasting (*slang*), flogging, drubbing, chastisement

thread NOUN **1** *a hat embroidered with golden threads* = **strand**, fibre, yarn, filament, line, string, cotton, twine **2** *the thread running through the book* = **theme**, motif, train of thought, course, direction, strain, plot, drift, tenor, story line ▶ VERB *She threaded her way back through the crowd.* = **move**, pass, inch, ease, thrust, meander, squeeze through, pick your way

threadbare ADJECTIVE **1** *She sat cross-legged on a square of threadbare carpet.* = **shabby**, worn, frayed, old, ragged, worn-out,

t

scruffy, tattered, tatty (*Brit.*), down at heel ■ **OPPOSITE:** new **2** *the government's threadbare domestic policies* = **hackneyed**, common, tired, stale, corny (*slang*), stock, familiar, conventional, stereotyped, commonplace, well-worn, trite, clichéd, overused, cliché-ridden ■ **OPPOSITE:** original

threat NOUN **1** *the threat of tropical storms* = **danger**, risk, hazard, menace, peril **2** *He may be forced to carry out his threat to resign.* = **threatening remark**, menace, commination, intimidatory remark **3** *The people who lived there felt a permanent sense of threat.* = **warning**, foreshadowing, foreboding

threaten VERB **1** *If you threaten me verbally or physically, then you will be prosecuted.* = **intimidate**, bully, menace, terrorize, warn, cow, lean on (*slang*), pressurize, browbeat, make threats to ■ **OPPOSITE:** defend **2** *The newcomers directly threaten the livelihood of current workers.* = **endanger**, jeopardize, put at risk, imperil, put in jeopardy, put on the line ■ **OPPOSITE:** protect **3** *Plants must be covered with a leaf mould if frost threatens.* = **be imminent**, hang over, be in the air, loom, be in the offing, hang over someone's head, impend

threatening ADJECTIVE **1** *The police should have charged them with threatening behaviour.* = **menacing**, bullying, intimidatory, terrorizing, minatory, comminatory **2** *a threatening atmosphere of rising tension and stress* = **ominous**, sinister, forbidding, grim, baleful, inauspicious, bodeful ■ **OPPOSITE:** promising

threesome NOUN = **trio**, trinity, trilogy, triplet, triad, triumvirate, troika, triptych, triplex, trine, triune

threshold NOUN **1** *He stopped at the threshold of the bedroom.* = **entrance**, doorway, door, doorstep, sill, doorsill **2** *We are on the threshold of a new era in astronomy.* = **start**, beginning, opening, dawn (*literary*), verge, brink, outset, starting point, inception ■ **OPPOSITE:** end **3** *She has a low threshold of boredom, and needs constant stimulation.* = **limit**, margin, starting point, minimum

thrift NOUN = **economy**, prudence, frugality, saving, parsimony, carefulness, good husbandry, thriftiness ■ **OPPOSITE:** extravagance

thrifty ADJECTIVE = **economical**, prudent, provident, frugal, saving, sparing, careful, parsimonious ■ **OPPOSITE:** extravagant

thrill NOUN **1** *I remember the thrill of opening presents on Christmas morning.* = **pleasure**, charge (*slang*), kick (*informal*), glow,

sensation, buzz (*slang*), high, stimulation, tingle, titillation, flush of excitement ■ **OPPOSITE:** tedium **2** *He felt a thrill of fear, of adrenaline.* = **trembling**, throb, shudder, flutter, fluttering, tremor, quiver, vibration ▶ VERB *The electric atmosphere both thrilled and terrified him.* = **excite**, stimulate, arouse, move, send (*slang*), stir, flush, tingle, electrify, titillate, give someone a kick

thrilling ADJECTIVE = **exciting**, gripping, stimulating, stirring, sensational, rousing, riveting, electrifying, hair-raising, rip-roaring (*informal*) ■ **OPPOSITE:** boring

thrive VERB = **prosper**, do well, flourish, increase, grow, develop, advance, succeed, get on, boom, bloom, wax, burgeon, grow rich ■ **OPPOSITE:** decline

thriving ADJECTIVE = **successful**, doing well, flourishing, growing, developing, healthy, booming, wealthy, blooming, prosperous, burgeoning, going strong ■ **OPPOSITE:** unsuccessful

throaty ADJECTIVE = **hoarse**, husky, gruff, low, deep, thick, guttural

throb VERB **1** *His head throbbed.* = **pulsate**, pound, beat, pulse, thump, palpitate **2** *The engines throbbed.* = **vibrate**, pulse, resonate, pulsate, reverberate, shake, judder (*informal*) ▶ NOUN **1** *The bruise on his stomach ached with a steady throb.* = **pulse**, pounding, beat, thump, thumping, pulsating, palpitation **2** *His head jerked up at the throb of the engine.* = **vibration**, pulse, throbbing, resonance, reverberation, judder (*informal*), pulsation

throes PLURAL NOUN *The animal twitched in its final death throes.* = **pains**, spasms, pangs, fit, stabs, convulsions, paroxysm • **in the throes of something** *The country is in the throes of a general election.* = **in the midst of**, in the process of, suffering from, struggling with, wrestling with, toiling with, anguished by, in the pangs of

throng NOUN *An official pushed through the throng.* = **crowd**, mob, horde, press, host, pack, mass, crush, jam, congregation, swarm, multitude, concourse, assemblage ▶ VERB **1** *the multitudes that throng around the Pope* = **crowd**, flock, congregate, troop, bunch, herd, cram, converge, hem in, mill around, swarm around ■ **OPPOSITE:** disperse **2** *They throng the beaches in July and August.* = **pack**, fill, crowd, press, jam

throttle VERB **1** *The strap of his haversack was twisted round his throat and was in danger of throttling him.* = **strangle**, choke, garrotte, strangulate **2** *The over-valuation of sterling is throttling industry.* = **suppress**, inhibit, stifle, control, silence, gag

through PREPOSITION **1** *The path continues through a tunnel of trees.* = **via**, by way of, by, between, past, in and out of, from end to end of, from one side to the other of **2** *the thought of someone suffering through a mistake of mine* = **because of**, by way of, by means of, by virtue of, with the assistance of, as a consequence or result of **3** *I got it cheap through a friend in the trade.* = **using**, via, by way of, by means of, by virtue of, with the assistance of **4** *trips at home and abroad all through the year* = **during**, throughout, in the middle of, for the duration of, in ▶ ADJECTIVE **1** (*with* **with**) *I'm through with women.* = **finished with**, done with, having had enough of **2** *It would guarantee employment once her schooling was through.* = **completed**, done, finished, ended, terminated • **through and through** *People assume they know me through and through as soon as we meet.* = **completely**, totally, fully, thoroughly, entirely, altogether, wholly, utterly, to the core, unreservedly

throughout PREPOSITION **1** *The same themes are repeated throughout the film.* = **right through**, all through, everywhere in, for the duration of, during the whole of, through the whole of, from end to end of **2** *He now runs projects throughout Africa.* = **all over**, all through, everywhere in, through the whole of, over the length and breadth of ▶ ADVERB **1** *The concert wasn't bad, but people talked throughout.* = **from start to finish**, right through, the whole time, all the time, from the start, all through, from beginning to end **2** *Throughout, the walls are white.* = **all through**, right through, in every nook and cranny

throw VERB **1** *He spent hours throwing a tennis ball against a wall.* = **hurl**, toss, fling, send, project, launch, cast, pitch, shy, chuck (*informal*), propel, sling, lob (*informal*), heave, put **2** *He threw his jacket onto the back seat.* = **toss**, fling, chuck (*informal*), cast, hurl, sling (*informal*), heave, put **3** *The horse reared, throwing its rider.* = **dislodge**, unseat, upset, overturn, hurl to the ground **4** *He threw me by asking if I went in for martial arts.* = **confuse**, baffle, faze, astonish, confound, unnerve, disconcert, perturb, throw you out, throw you off, dumbfound, discompose, put you off your stroke, throw you off your stride, unsettle ▶ NOUN *One of the judges thought it was a foul throw.* = **toss**, pitch, fling, put, cast, shy, sling, lob (*informal*), heave • **throw someone off 1** *I lost my first serve in the first set; it threw me off a bit.* = **disconcert**, unsettle, faze, throw (*informal*), upset, confuse, disturb, put you

off your stroke, throw you off your stride **2** *He threw off his pursuers by pedalling across the state line.* = **escape from**, lose, leave behind, get away from, evade, shake off, elude, outrun, outdistance, give someone the slip, show a clean pair of heels to • **throw someone out** *I wanted to kill him, but instead I just threw him out.* = **expel**, eject, evict, dismiss, get rid of, oust, kick out (*informal*), show the door to, turf out (*Brit. informal*), give the bum's rush to (*slang*), kiss off (*slang, chiefly U.S. & Canad.*) • **throw something away 1** *I never throw anything away.* = **discard**, dump (*informal*), get rid of, reject, scrap, axe (*informal*), bin (*informal*), ditch (*slang*), junk (*informal*), chuck (*informal*), throw out, dispose of, dispense with, jettison, cast off **2** *Failing to tackle the problem would be throwing away an opportunity.* = **waste**, lose, blow (*slang*), squander, fritter away, fail to make use of, make poor use of • **throw something off** *a country ready to throw off the shackles of its colonial past* = **cast off**, shake off, rid yourself of, free yourself of, drop, abandon, discard • **throw something out 1** *Never throw out milk that is about to go off.* = **discard**, dump (*informal*), get rid of, reject, scrap, bin (*informal*), ditch (*slang*), junk (*informal*), chuck (*informal*), throw away, dispose of, dispense with, jettison, cast off **2** *a workshop throwing out a pool of light* = **emit**, radiate, give off, diffuse, disseminate, put forth • **throw something up 1** *Scrap metal dwellings are thrown up in any available space.* = **throw together**, jerry-build, run up, slap together **2** *These studies have thrown up some interesting results.* = **produce**, reveal, bring to light, bring forward, bring to the surface, bring to notice **3** *He threw up his job as party chairman.* = **give up**, leave, abandon, quit, chuck (*informal*), resign from, relinquish, renounce, step down from (*informal*), jack in • **throw up** *He threw up over a seat next to me.* = **vomit**, be sick, spew, puke (*slang*), chuck (*Austral. & N.Z. informal*), heave, regurgitate, disgorge, retch, barf (*U.S. slang*), chunder (*slang, chiefly Austral.*), upchuck (*U.S. slang*), do a technicolour yawn (*slang*), toss your cookies (*U.S. slang*)

throwaway ADJECTIVE **1** *Now they are producing throwaway razors.* = **disposable**, one-use, expendable **2** *a throwaway remark she later regretted* = **casual**, passing, offhand, careless, understated, unthinking, ill-considered

thrust VERB **1** *They thrust him into the back of a jeep.* = **push**, force, shove, drive, press, plunge, jam, butt, ram, poke, propel, prod, impel **2** *She thrust her way into the crowd.* = **shove**, push, shoulder, lunge, jostle, elbow or shoulder your way **3** (*often with* **through** *or* **into**) *How can I thrust a knife into my son's heart?* = **stab**, stick, jab, pierce ▶ NOUN **1** *Two of the knife thrusts were fatal.* = **stab**, pierce, lunge **2** *a thrust of his hand that sent the lad reeling* = **push**, shove, poke, prod **3** *It provides the thrust that makes the craft move forward.* = **momentum**, impetus, drive, motive power, motive force, propulsive force

thud NOUN *She tripped and fell with a sickening thud.* = **thump**, crash, knock, smack, clump, wallop (*informal*), clunk, clonk ▶ VERB *She ran upstairs, her bare feet thudding on the wood.* = **thump**, crash, knock, smack, clump, wallop (*informal*), clunk, clonk

thug NOUN = **ruffian**, hooligan, tough, heavy (*slang*), killer, murderer, robber, gangster, assassin, bandit, mugger (*informal*), cut-throat, bully boy, bruiser (*informal*), tsotsi (*S. African*)

thumb NOUN *She bit her thumb, not looking at me.* = **digit** ▶ VERB **1** *a well-thumbed copy of Who's Who* = **handle**, finger, mark, soil, maul, mess up, dog-ear **2** *Thumbing a lift once had a carefree image.* = **hitch** (*informal*), request (*informal*), signal for, hitchhike • **all thumbs** *Can you open this? I'm all thumbs.* = **clumsy**, inept, cack-handed (*informal*), maladroit, butterfingered (*informal*), ham-fisted (*informal*), unco (*Austral. slang*) • **thumbs down** *Brokers have given the firm the thumbs down.* = **disapproval**, refusal, rejection, no, rebuff, negation • **thumbs up** *The film got a general thumbs up from the critics.* = **approval**, go-ahead (*informal*), acceptance, yes, encouragement, green light, affirmation, O.K. or okay (*informal*) • **thumb through something** *He had the drawer open and was thumbing through files.* = **flick through**, browse through, leaf through, glance at, turn over, flip through, skim through, riffle through, scan the pages of, run your eye over

thumbnail ADJECTIVE = **brief**, short, concise, quick, compact, succinct, pithy

thump NOUN **1** *He felt a thump on his shoulder.* = **blow**, knock, punch, rap, smack, clout (*informal*), whack, swipe (*informal*), wallop (*informal*) **2** *There was a loud thump as the horse crashed into the van.* = **thud**, crash, bang, clunk, thwack ▶ VERB **1** *He thumped me, nearly knocking me over.* = **strike**, hit, punch, pound, beat, knock, deck (*slang*), batter, rap, chin (*slang*), smack, thrash, clout (*informal*), whack, swipe, clobber (*slang*), wallop (*informal*), lambast(e),

belabour, lay one on (*slang*), beat or knock seven bells out of (*informal*) **2** *She thumped her hand on the witness box.* = **thud**, crash, bang, thwack **3** *My heart was thumping wildly.* = **throb**, pound, beat, pulse, pulsate, palpitate

thumping ADJECTIVE = **huge**, massive, enormous, great, impressive, tremendous, excessive, terrific, thundering (*slang*), titanic, gigantic, monumental (*informal*), mammoth, colossal, whopping (*informal*), stellar (*informal*), exorbitant, gargantuan, elephantine, humongous or humungous (*informal*) ■ **OPPOSITE:** insignificant

thunder NOUN *the thunder of the sea on the rocks* = **rumble**, crash, crashing, boom, booming, explosion, rumbling, pealing, detonation, cracking ▶ VERB **1** *the sound of the guns thundering in the fog* = **rumble**, crash, blast, boom, explode, roar, clap, resound, detonate, reverberate, crack, peal **2** *'It's your money. Ask for it!' she thundered.* = **shout**, roar, yell, bark, bellow, declaim **3** *He started thundering about the election result.* = **rail**, curse, fulminate

thunderous ADJECTIVE = **loud**, noisy, deafening, booming, roaring, resounding, tumultuous, ear-splitting

thus ADVERB **1** *She explained her mistake thus.* = **in this way**, so, like this, as follows, like so, in this manner, in this fashion, to such a degree **2** *getting access to the basic means of production, and thus to political power* = **therefore**, so, hence, consequently, accordingly, for this reason, ergo, on that account

thwart VERB = **frustrate**, stop, foil, check, defeat, prevent, oppose, snooker, baffle, hinder, obstruct, impede, balk, outwit, stymie, cook someone's goose (*informal*), put a spoke in someone's wheel (*informal*) ■ **OPPOSITE:** assist

tic NOUN = **twitch**, jerk, spasm

tick NOUN **1** *Place a tick in the appropriate box.* = **check mark**, mark, line, stroke, dash **2** *He sat listening to the tick of the grandfather clock.* = **click**, tap, tapping, clicking, clack, ticktock **3** *I'll be back in a tick.* = **moment**, second, minute, shake (*informal*), flash, instant, sec (*informal*), twinkling, split second, jiffy (*informal*), trice, half a mo (*Brit. informal*), two shakes of a lamb's tail (*informal*), bat of an eye (*informal*) ▶ VERB **1** *Please tick here if you do not want to receive such mailings.* = **mark**, indicate, mark off, check off, choose, select **2** *A clock ticked busily from the kitchen counter.* = **click**, tap, clack, ticktock • **tick someone off** (*informal*) *His mum ticked him off when they* *got home.* = **scold**, rebuke, tell off (*informal*), lecture, carpet (*informal*), censure, reprimand, reproach, berate, chide, tear into (*informal*), reprove, upbraid, take to task, read the riot act to, bawl out (*informal*), chew out (*U.S. & Canad. informal*), tear off a strip (*Brit. informal*), haul over the coals (*informal*), give a rocket to (*Brit. & N.Z. informal*) • **tick something off** *He ticked off my name on a piece of paper.* = **mark off**, check off, put a tick at

ticket NOUN **1** *They were queueing to get tickets for the football match.* = **voucher**, pass, coupon, card, slip, certificate, token, chit **2** *a price ticket* = **label**, tag, marker, sticker, card, slip, tab, docket (*Brit.*)

tickle VERB = **amuse**, delight, entertain, please, divert, gratify, titillate ■ **OPPOSITE:** bore

tide NOUN **1** *They used to sail with the tide.* = **current**, flow, stream, course, ebb, undertow, tideway **2** *They talked of reversing the tide of events.* = **course**, direction, trend, current, movement, tendency, drift • **tide someone over** *He wanted to borrow some money to tide him over.* = **keep you going**, see you through, keep the wolf from the door, keep your head above water, bridge the gap for

tidings PLURAL NOUN = **news**, report, word, message, latest (*informal*), information, communication, intelligence, bulletin, gen (*Brit. informal*)

tidy ADJECTIVE **1** *Having a tidy desk can sometimes seem impossible.* = **neat**, orderly, ordered, clean, trim, systematic, spruce, businesslike, well-kept, well-ordered, shipshape, spick-and-span, trig (*archaic, dialect*), in apple-pie order (*informal*) ■ **OPPOSITE:** untidy **2** *She wasn't a tidy person.* = **organized**, neat, fastidious, methodical, smart, efficient, spruce, businesslike, well-groomed, well turned out **3** *The opportunities are there to make a tidy profit.* = **considerable**, large, substantial, good, goodly, fair, healthy, generous, handsome, respectable, ample, largish, sizable or sizeable ■ **OPPOSITE:** small ▶ VERB *She made her bed and tidied her room.* = **neaten**, straighten, put in order, order, clean, groom, spruce up, put to rights, put in trim ■ **OPPOSITE:** disorder

tie VERB **1** *He tied the ends of the plastic bag together.* = **fasten**, bind, join, unite, link, connect, attach, knot, truss, interlace ■ **OPPOSITE:** unfasten **2** *She tied her horse to a fence post.* = **tether**, secure, rope, moor, lash, make fast **3** *I wouldn't like to be tied to catching the last train home.* = **restrict**, limit,

confine, hold, bind, restrain, hamper, hinder ■ **OPPOSITE:** free **4** *Both teams had tied on points and goal difference.* = **draw**, be even, be level, be neck and neck, match, equal ▶ NOUN **1** *little empire-line coats with ribbon ties* = **fastening**, binding, link, band, bond, joint, connection, string, rope, knot, cord, fetter, ligature **2** *She had family ties in France.* = **bond**, relationship, connection, duty, commitment, obligation, liaison, allegiance, affinity, affiliation, kinship **3** *The first game ended in a tie.* = **draw**, dead heat, deadlock, stalemate **4** *They'll meet the winners of the first-round tie.* = **match**, game, contest, fixture, meeting, event, trial, bout **5** *It's a bit of a tie, going there every Sunday.* = **encumbrance**, restriction, limitation, check, handicap, restraint, hindrance, bind (*informal*) • **tie in with something 1** *subjects which tie in with whatever you enjoy about painting* = **link**, relate to, connect, be relevant to, come in to, have a bearing on **2** *Our wedding date had to tie in with Dave's leaving the army.* = **fit in with**, coincide with, coordinate with, harmonize with, occur simultaneously with • **tie something up 1** *I had tied the boat up in the marina and furled my sail.* = **secure**, lash, tether, make fast, moor, attach, rope **2** *They hope to tie up a deal within the next few weeks.* = **conclude**, settle, wrap up (*informal*), end, wind up, terminate, finish off, bring to a close • **tie something** or **someone up** *Don't you think we should tie him up and put a guard over him?* = **bind**, restrain, pinion, truss up

tie in or **tie-in** NOUN = **link**, connection, relation, relationship, association, tie-up, liaison, coordination, hook-up

tier NOUN = **row**, bank, layer, line, order, level, series, file, rank, storey, stratum, echelon

tie-up NOUN = **link**, association, connection, relationship, relation, liaison, tie-in, coordination, hook-up, linkup

tiff NOUN = **quarrel**, row, disagreement, words, difference, dispute, scrap (*informal*), falling-out (*informal*), squabble, petty quarrel

tight ADJECTIVE **1** *His jeans were too tight.* = **close-fitting**, narrow, cramped, snug, constricted, close ■ **OPPOSITE:** loose **2** *Keep a tight grip on my hand.* = **secure**, firm, fast, fixed **3** *Pull the elastic tight and knot the ends.* = **taut**, stretched, tense, rigid, stiff ■ **OPPOSITE:** slack **4** *tight control of media coverage* = **strict**, stringent, severe, tough, harsh, stern, rigid, rigorous, uncompromising, inflexible, unyielding ■ **OPPOSITE:** easy-going **5** *Cover with foil and* the lid to ensure a tight seal. = **sealed**, watertight, impervious, sound, proof, hermetic ■ **OPPOSITE:** open **6** It was a very tight match. = **close**, even, well-matched, near, hard-fought, evenly-balanced ■ **OPPOSITE:** uneven **7** Are you so tight you won't even spend a few quid? = **miserly**, mean, stingy, close, sparing, grasping, parsimonious, niggardly, penurious, tightfisted ■ **OPPOSITE:** generous **8** They teach you to use your head and get out of a tight spot. = **difficult**, tough, dangerous, tricky, sticky (informal), hazardous, troublesome, problematic, precarious, perilous, worrisome, ticklish **9** He laughed loudly. There was no doubt he was tight. = **drunk**, intoxicated, flying (slang), bombed (slang), stoned (slang), wasted (slang), smashed (slang), steaming (slang), wrecked (slang), out of it (slang), plastered (slang), blitzed (slang), lit up (slang), stewed (slang), pickled (informal), bladdered (slang), under the influence (informal), tipsy, legless (informal), paralytic (informal), sozzled (informal), steamboats (Scot. slang), tiddly (slang, chiefly Brit.), half cut (Brit. slang), zonked (slang), blotto (slang), inebriated, out to it (Austral. & N.Z. slang), three sheets to the wind (slang), in your cups, half seas over (Brit. informal), bevvied (dialect), pie-eyed (slang) ■ **OPPOSITE:** sober

tighten VERB **1** He answered by tightening his grip on her shoulder. = **close**, narrow, strengthen, squeeze, harden, constrict ■ **OPPOSITE:** slacken **2** He flung his whole weight back, tightening the rope. = **stretch**, strain, tense, tauten, stiffen, rigidify ■ **OPPOSITE:** slacken **3** I used my thumbnail to tighten the screw. = **fasten**, secure, screw, fix ■ **OPPOSITE:** unfasten

tight-lipped ADJECTIVE = **secretive**, reticent, uncommunicative, reserved, quiet, silent, mute, taciturn, close-mouthed, unforthcoming, close-lipped

till¹ see **until**

till² VERB freshly tilled fields = **cultivate**, dig, plough, work, turn over

till³ NOUN He checked the register. There was money in the till. = **cash register**, cash box, cash drawer

tilt VERB The boat instantly tilted, filled and sank. = **slant**, tip, slope, list, lean, heel, incline, cant ▶ NOUN **1** the tilt of the earth's axis = **slope**, angle, inclination, list, pitch, incline, slant, cant, camber, gradient **2** The crowd cheered and the tilt began. = **joust**, fight, tournament, lists, clash, set-to (informal), encounter, combat, duel, tourney

timber NOUN **1** a bird nesting in the timbers of the roof = **beams**, boards, planks **2** These forests have been exploited for timber since Saxon times. = **wood**, logs

timbre NOUN = **tone**, sound, ring, resonance, colour, tonality, tone colour, quality of sound

time NOUN **1** For a long time I didn't tell anyone. = **period**, while, term, season, space, stretch, spell, phase, interval, span, period of time, stint, duration, length of time, time frame, timeline **2** It seemed like a good time to tell her. = **occasion**, point, moment, stage, instance, point in time, juncture **3** The design has remained unchanged since the time of the pharaohs. = **age**, days, era, year, date, generation, duration, epoch, chronology, aeon **4** A reel is in four-four time. = **tempo**, beat, rhythm, measure, metre **5** I wouldn't change anything if I had my time again. = **lifetime**, day, life, season, duration, life span, allotted span **6** He was a very good jockey in his time. = **heyday**, prime, peak, hour, springtime, salad days, best years or days ▶ VERB **1** He timed each performance with a stopwatch. = **measure**, judge, clock, count **2** We had timed our visit for March 7. = **schedule**, set, plan, book, programme, set up, fix, arrange, line up, organize, timetable, slate (U.S.), fix up, prearrange **3** an alarm timed to go off every hour on the hour = **regulate**, control, calculate • **at one time** At one time, 400 people lived in the village. = **once**, previously, formerly, for a while, hitherto (formal), once upon a time • **at times** The debate was highly emotional at times. = **sometimes**, occasionally, from time to time, now and then, on occasion, once in a while, every now and then, every so often • **for the time being** The situation is calm for the time being. = **for now**, meanwhile, meantime, in the meantime, temporarily, for the moment, for the present, pro tem, for the nonce • **from time to time** Her daughters visited her from time to time. = **occasionally**, sometimes, now and then, at times, on occasion, once in a while, every now and then, every so often • **in good time 1** We always make sure we're home in good time for the programme. = **on time**, early, ahead of schedule, ahead of time, with time to spare **2** Ninety-three per cent of the students received their loans in good time. = **promptly**, quickly, rapidly, swiftly, speedily, with dispatch • **in no time** At his age he'll heal in no time. = **quickly**, rapidly, swiftly, in a moment, in a flash, speedily, in an instant, apace (literary), before you know it, in a trice, in a jiffy (informal), in two shakes of a lamb's tail (*informal*), before you can say Jack Robinson • **in time 1** *I arrived in time for my flight to London.* = **on time**, on schedule, in good time, at the appointed time, early, with time to spare **2** *He would sort out his own problems in time.* = **eventually**, one day, ultimately, sooner or later, someday, in the fullness of time, by and by • **on time** *Don't worry, she'll be on time.* = **punctual(ly)**, prompt(ly), on schedule, in good time, on the dot • **time and again** *Time and again political parties have failed to tackle this issue.* = **over and over again**, repeatedly, time after time

■ **RELATED WORD:** *adjective* temporal

time-honoured ADJECTIVE = **long-established**, traditional, customary, old, established, fixed, usual, ancient, conventional, venerable, age-old

timeless ADJECTIVE = **eternal**, lasting, permanent, enduring, abiding, immortal, everlasting, ceaseless, immutable, indestructible, undying, ageless, imperishable, deathless, changeless

■ **OPPOSITE:** temporary

timely ADJECTIVE = **opportune** (*formal*), appropriate, well-timed, prompt, suitable, convenient, at the right time, judicious, punctual, propitious, seasonable

■ **OPPOSITE:** untimely

timetable NOUN **1** *The timetable was hopelessly optimistic.* = **schedule**, programme, agenda, list, diary, calendar, order of the day **2** *Latin was not included on the timetable.* = **syllabus**, course, curriculum, programme, teaching programme

timid ADJECTIVE = **nervous**, shy, retiring, modest, shrinking, fearful, cowardly, apprehensive, coy, diffident, bashful, mousy, timorous (*literary*), pusillanimous (*formal*), faint-hearted, irresolute

■ **OPPOSITE:** bold

tincture NOUN = **tinge**, trace, hint, colour, touch, suggestion, shade, flavour, dash, stain, smack, aroma, tint, hue, soupçon (*French*)

tinge NOUN **1** *His skin had an unhealthy greyish tinge.* = **tint**, colour, shade, cast, wash, stain, dye, tincture **2** *Could there have been a slight tinge of envy in her voice?* = **trace**, bit, drop, touch, suggestion, dash, pinch, smack, sprinkling, smattering, soupçon (*French*) ▶ VERB *The living room was tinged yellow by the sunlight.* = **tint**, colour, shade, stain, dye

tingle VERB *The backs of her thighs tingled.* = **prickle**, sting, itch, tickle, have goose pimples ▶ NOUN *I felt a sudden tingle in my fingers.* = **prickling**, stinging, itch, itching, tickle, tickling, pins and needles (*informal*)

tinker VERB = **meddle**, play, toy, monkey, potter, fiddle (*informal*), dabble, mess about, muck about (*Brit. slang*)

tinsel ADJECTIVE = **showy**, flashy, gaudy, cheap, plastic (*slang*), superficial, sham, tawdry, ostentatious, trashy, specious, gimcrack, meretricious, pinchbeck

tint NOUN **1** *Its large leaves often show a delicate purple tint.* = **shade**, colour, tone, hue, cast **2** *You've had a tint on your hair.* = **dye**, wash, stain, rinse, tinge, tincture **3** *His words had more than a tint of truth to them.* = **hint**, touch, trace, suggestion, shade, tinge ▶ VERB *Eyebrows can be tinted with the same dye.* = **dye**, colour, stain, rinse, tinge, tincture

tiny ADJECTIVE = **small**, little, minute, slight, mini, wee, miniature, trifling, insignificant, negligible, microscopic, diminutive, petite, puny, pint-sized (*informal*), infinitesimal, teeny-weeny, Lilliputian, dwarfish, teensy-weensy, pygmy *or* pigmy

■ **OPPOSITE:** huge

tip¹ NOUN **1** *She poked and shifted things with the tip of her walking stick.* = **end**, point, head, extremity, sharp end, nib, prong **2** *After dusk, the tip of the cone will light up.* = **peak**, top, summit, pinnacle, crown, cap, zenith, apex, spire, acme, vertex ▶ VERB *a missile tipped with three warheads* = **cap**, top, crown, surmount (*formal*), finish

tip² VERB **1** *She took the plate and tipped the contents into the bin.* = **pour**, drop, empty, dump, drain, spill, discharge, unload, jettison, offload, slop (*informal*), slosh (*informal*), decant **2** *the costs of tipping rubbish in landfills* = **dump**, empty, ditch (*slang*), unload, pour out ▶ NOUN *I took a load of rubbish and grass cuttings to the tip.* = **dump**, midden, rubbish heap, refuse heap • **tip off** *He tipped police off on his carphone.* = **advise**, warn, caution, forewarn, give a clue to, give a hint to, tip someone the wink (*Brit. informal*)

tip³ NOUN **1** *I gave the barber a tip.* = **gratuity**, gift, reward, present, sweetener (*informal*), perquisite, baksheesh, pourboire (*French*) **2** *A good tip is to buy the most expensive lens you can afford.* = **hint**, suggestion, piece of information, piece of advice, gen (*Brit. informal*), pointer, piece of inside information, heads up (*U.S. & Canad.*) ▶ VERB **1** *Do you think it's customary to tip the waiters?* = **reward**, remunerate (*formal*), give a tip to, sweeten (*informal*) **2** *He was widely tipped for success.* = **predict**, back, recommend, think of

t

tip-off NOUN = **hint**, word, information, warning, suggestion, clue, pointer, inside information, word of advice, heads up (U.S. & Canad.)

tipple VERB *You may be tempted to tipple unobserved.* = **drink**, imbibe (formal), tope, indulge (informal), swig, quaff, take a drink, bevvy (dialect), bend the elbow (informal) ▶ NOUN *My favourite tipple is a glass of port.* = **alcohol**, drink, booze (informal), poison (informal), liquor, John Barleycorn

tipsy ADJECTIVE = **tiddly** (slang, chiefly Brit.), fuddled, slightly drunk, happy (informal), merry (Brit. informal), mellow, woozy (slang, chiefly Brit.)

tirade NOUN = **outburst**, diatribe, harangue, abuse, lecture, denunciation, invective, fulmination, philippic

tire VERB **1** *If driving tires you, take the train.* = **exhaust**, drain, fatigue, weary, fag (informal), whack (Brit. informal), wear out, wear down, take it out of (informal), knacker (slang), enervate ■ OPPOSITE: refresh **2** *He tired easily, and was unable to sleep well at night.* = **flag**, become tired, fail, droop

tired ADJECTIVE **1** *He is tired and he has to rest after his long trip.* = **exhausted**, fatigued, weary, spent, done in (informal), flagging, all in (slang), drained, sleepy, fagged (informal), whacked (Brit. informal), worn out, drooping, knackered (slang), drowsy, clapped out (Brit., Austral. & N.Z. informal), enervated, ready to drop, dog-tired (informal), zonked (slang), dead beat (informal), tuckered out (Austral. & N.Z. informal), asleep or dead on your feet (informal), leggy ■ OPPOSITE: energetic **2** *I was tired of being a bookkeeper.* = **bored**, fed up, weary, sick (informal), annoyed, irritated, exasperated, irked, hoha (N.Z.) ■ OPPOSITE: enthusiastic about **3** *I didn't want to hear one of his tired excuses.* = **hackneyed**, stale, well-worn, old, stock, familiar, conventional, corny (slang), threadbare, trite, clichéd, outworn ■ OPPOSITE: original

tireless ADJECTIVE = **energetic**, vigorous, industrious, determined, resolute, indefatigable, unflagging, untiring, unwearied ■ OPPOSITE: exhausted

tiresome ADJECTIVE = **boring**, annoying, irritating, trying, wearing, dull, tedious, exasperating, monotonous, laborious, uninteresting, irksome, wearisome, vexatious ■ OPPOSITE: interesting

tiring ADJECTIVE = **exhausting**, demanding, wearing, tough, exacting, fatiguing, wearying, strenuous, arduous, laborious, enervative

tissue NOUN **1** *As we age we lose muscle tissue.* = **matter**, material, substance, stuff, structure **2** *a box of tissues* = **paper**, wipe, paper handkerchief, wrapping paper **3** *It was all a tissue of lies which ended in his resignation.* = **series**, pack, collection, mass, network, chain, combination, web, accumulation, fabrication, conglomeration, concatenation (formal)

titan NOUN = **giant**, superman or woman, colossus, leviathan

titanic ADJECTIVE = **gigantic**, huge, giant, massive, towering, vast, enormous, mighty, immense, jumbo (informal), monstrous, mammoth, colossal, mountainous, stellar (informal), prodigious, stupendous, herculean, elephantine, humongous or humungous (informal)

titbit or (esp. U.S.) **tidbit** NOUN = **delicacy**, goody, dainty, morsel, treat, snack, choice item, juicy bit, bonne bouche (French)

tit for tat NOUN *a dangerous game of tit for tat* = **retaliation**, like for like, measure for measure, an eye for an eye, a tooth for a tooth, blow for blow, as good as you get

tithe NOUN = **tax**, levy, duty, assessment, tribute, toll, tariff, tenth, impost

titillate VERB = **excite**, arouse, interest, thrill, provoke, turn on (slang), tease, tickle, tantalize

titillating ADJECTIVE = **exciting**, stimulating, interesting, thrilling, arousing, sensational, teasing, provocative, lurid, suggestive, lewd

title NOUN **1** *The book was first published under the title 'A Place for Us'.* = **heading**, name, caption, label, legend, inscription **2** *Lady Mary hates being referred to by her title.* = **name**, designation, epithet, term, handle (slang), nickname, denomination, pseudonym, appellation (formal), sobriquet, nom de plume, moniker or monicker (slang) **3** *He has retained his title as world chess champion.* = **championship**, trophy, laurels, bays, crown, honour **4** *He never had title to the property.* = **ownership**, right, claim, privilege, entitlement, tenure, prerogative, freehold ▶ VERB *a new book titled 'The Golden Thirteen'* = **name**, call, term, style, label, tag, designate

titter VERB = **snigger**, laugh, giggle, chuckle, chortle (informal), tee-hee, te-hee

toad NOUN ■ RELATED WORDS: adjective batrachian; name of young tadpole

toast¹ VERB **1** *Toast the bread lightly on both sides.* = **brown**, grill, crisp, roast **2** *a bar with an open fire for toasting feet after a day skiing* = **warm (up)**, heat (up), thaw, bring back to life

toast² NOUN **1** *We drank a toast to Miss Jacobs.*
= **tribute**, drink, compliment, salute,
health, pledge, salutation (*formal*) **2** *She was
the toast of Paris.* = **favourite**, celebrity,
darling, talk, pet, focus of attention, hero *or*
heroine, blue-eyed boy *or* girl (*Brit. informal*)
▶ VERB *They toasted her with champagne.*
= **drink to**, honour, pledge to, salute, drink
(to) the health of

to-do NOUN = **fuss**, performance (*informal*),
disturbance, bother, stir, turmoil, unrest,
flap (*informal*), quarrel, upheaval, bustle,
furore, uproar, agitation, commotion,
rumpus, tumult, brouhaha, ruction
(*informal*), hue and cry, hoo-ha

together ADVERB **1** *Together they swam to the
ship.* = **collectively**, jointly, closely, as one,
with each other, in conjunction, side by
side, mutually, hand in hand, as a group, in
partnership, in concert, in unison, shoulder
to shoulder, cheek by jowl, in cooperation,
in a body, hand in glove ■ **OPPOSITE:**
separately **2** *'Yes,' they said together.* = **at the
same time**, simultaneously, in unison, as
one, (all) at once, en masse, concurrently,
contemporaneously, with one accord, at
one fell swoop ▶ ADJECTIVE *She was very
headstrong, and very together.* = **self-
possessed**, calm, composed, well-
balanced, cool, stable, well-organized,
well-adjusted, grounded

toil NOUN *It is only toil which gives meaning to
things.* = **hard work**, industry, labour,
effort, pains, application, sweat, graft
(*informal*), slog, exertion, drudgery, travail,
donkey-work, elbow grease (*informal*),
blood, sweat and tears (*informal*)
■ **OPPOSITE:** idleness ▶ VERB **1** *Boys toiled in
the hot sun to finish the wall.* = **labour**, work,
struggle, strive, grind (*informal*), sweat
(*informal*), slave, graft (*informal*), go for it
(*informal*), slog, grub, bend over backwards
(*informal*), drudge, go for broke (*slang*), push
yourself, bust a gut (*informal*), give it your
best shot (*informal*), break your neck
(*informal*), work like a dog, make an all-out
effort (*informal*), work like a Trojan, knock
yourself out (*informal*), do your damnedest
(*informal*), give it your all (*informal*), work
your fingers to the bone, rupture yourself
(*informal*) **2** *He had his head down as he toiled
up the hill.* = **struggle**, trek, slog, trudge,
push yourself, fight your way, drag yourself,
footslog

toilet NOUN **1** *She made him flush the pills down
the toilet.* = **lavatory**, bathroom, loo (*Brit.
informal*), bog (*slang*), gents *or* ladies, can
(*U.S. & Canad. slang*), john (*slang, chiefly U.S.
& Canad.*), head(s) (*Nautical slang*), throne

(*informal*), closet, privy (*obsolete*),
cloakroom (*Brit.*), urinal, latrine,
washroom, powder room, ablutions
(*Military informal*), dunny (*Austral. & N.Z.,
old-fashioned, informal*), water closet, khazi
(*slang*), pissoir (*French*), little boy's room *or*
little girl's room (*informal*), (public)
convenience, W.C., bogger (*Austral. slang*),
brasco (*Austral. slang*) **2** *I ran to the toilet,
vomiting.* = **bathroom**, washroom, gents *or*
ladies (*Brit. informal*), privy, outhouse,
latrine, powder room, water closet, pissoir
(*French*), ladies' room, little boy's *or* little
girl's room, W.C.

token NOUN *He sent her a gift as a token of his
appreciation.* = **symbol**, mark, sign, note,
evidence, earnest (*old-fashioned*), index,
expression, demonstration, proof,
indication, clue, representation, badge,
manifestation ▶ ADJECTIVE *weak token
gestures with no real consequences* = **nominal**,
symbolic, minimal, hollow, superficial,
perfunctory

tolerable ADJECTIVE **1** *He described their
living conditions as tolerable.* = **bearable**,
acceptable, allowable, supportable,
endurable, sufferable ■ **OPPOSITE:**
intolerable **2** *Is there anywhere tolerable to
eat in town?* = **fair**, O.K. *or* okay (*informal*),
middling, average, all right, ordinary,
acceptable, reasonable, good enough,
adequate, indifferent, not bad (*informal*),
mediocre, so-so (*informal*), run-of-the-mill,
passable, unexceptional, fairly good, fair
to middling ■ **OPPOSITE:** dreadful

tolerance NOUN **1** *his tolerance and
understanding of diverse human nature*
= **broad-mindedness**, charity, sympathy,
patience, indulgence, forbearance,
permissiveness, magnanimity, open-
mindedness, sufferance, lenity ■ **OPPOSITE:**
intolerance **2** *She has a high tolerance for pain.*
= **endurance**, resistance, stamina,
fortitude, resilience, toughness, staying
power, hardness, hardiness **3** *Your body will
build up a tolerance to most drugs.*
= **resistance**, immunity, resilience,
non-susceptibility

tolerant ADJECTIVE = **broad-minded**,
understanding, sympathetic, open-
minded, patient, fair, soft, catholic,
charitable, indulgent, easy-going,
long-suffering, lax, lenient, permissive,
magnanimous, free and easy, forbearing,
kind-hearted, unprejudiced, complaisant,
latitudinarian, unbigoted, easy-oasy (*slang*)
■ **OPPOSITE:** intolerant

tolerate VERB **1** *She can no longer tolerate the
position that she's in.* = **endure**, stand, suffer,

t

bear, take, stomach, undergo, swallow, hack (*slang*), abide, put up with (*informal*), submit to, thole (*Scot.*) **2** *I will not tolerate breaches of the code of conduct.* = **allow**, accept, permit, sanction, take, receive, admit, brook, indulge, put up with (*informal*), condone, countenance, turn a blind eye to, wink at ■ **OPPOSITE:** forbid

toleration NOUN **1** *society's continuing toleration of many forms of inequality* = **acceptance**, endurance, indulgence, sanction, allowance, permissiveness, sufferance, condonation **2** *his views on religious toleration, education and politics* = **religious freedom**, freedom of conscience, freedom of worship

toll¹ VERB **1** *Church bells tolled and black flags fluttered.* = **ring**, sound, strike, chime, knell, clang, peal **2** *The station clock tolled the midnight hour.* = **announce**, call, signal, warn of ▸ NOUN *the insistent toll of the bell in the church tower* = **ringing**, ring, tolling, chime, knell, clang, peal

toll² NOUN **1** *Opponents of motorway tolls say they would force cars onto smaller roads.* = **charge**, tax, fee, duty, rate, demand, payment, assessment, customs, tribute, levy, tariff, impost **2** *There are fears that the death toll may be higher.* = **damage**, cost, loss, roll, penalty, sum, number, roster, inroad **3** *Winter takes its toll on your health.* = **adverse effects**, price, cost, suffering, damage, penalty, harm

tomb NOUN = **grave**, vault, crypt, mausoleum, sarcophagus, catacomb, sepulchre, burial chamber

tombstone NOUN = **gravestone**, memorial, monument, marker, headstone

tome NOUN = **book**, work, title, volume, opus, publication

tone NOUN **1** *He spoke in a low tone to her.* = **pitch**, stress, volume, accent, force, strength, emphasis, inflection, intonation, timbre, modulation, tonality **2** *the clear tone of the bell* = **volume**, timbre, tonality **3** *The tone of the letter was very friendly.* = **character**, style, approach, feel, air, effect, note, quality, spirit, attitude, aspect, frame, manner, mood, drift, grain, temper, vein, tenor **4** *Each brick also varies slightly in tone.* = **colour**, cast, shade, tint, tinge, hue ▸ VERB *Her sister toned with her in a turquoise print dress.* = **harmonize**, match, blend, suit, go well with • **tone something down 1** *He toned down his militant statement after the meeting.* = **moderate**, temper, soften, restrain, subdue, play down, dampen, mitigate, subdue, modulate, soft-pedal (*informal*) **2** *He was asked to tone down the spices and*

garlic in his recipes. = **reduce**, moderate, soften, lessen • **tone something up** *Regular exercise will tone up your stomach muscles.* = **get into condition**, trim, shape up, freshen, tune up, sharpen up, limber up, invigorate, get in shape

tongue NOUN **1** *They feel passionately about their native tongue.* = **language**, speech, vernacular, talk, dialect, idiom, parlance, lingo (*informal*), patois, argot **2** *her sharp wit and quick tongue* = **utterance**, voice, speech, articulation, verbal expression ■ **RELATED WORD:** *adjective* lingual

tongue-tied ADJECTIVE = **speechless**, inarticulate, dumbstruck, struck dumb, at a loss for words ■ **OPPOSITE:** talkative

tonic NOUN = **stimulant**, boost, bracer (*informal*), refresher, cordial, pick-me-up (*informal*), fillip, shot in the arm (*informal*), restorative, livener, analeptic, roborant

too ADVERB **1** *Depression may be expressed physically too.* = **also**, as well, further, in addition, moreover, besides, likewise, to boot, into the bargain **2** *I'm afraid you're too late; she's gone.* = **excessively**, very, extremely, overly, unduly, unreasonably, inordinately, exorbitantly, immoderately, over-

tool NOUN **1** *The best tool for the purpose is a pair of shears.* = **implement**, device, appliance, apparatus, machine, instrument, gadget, utensil, contraption (*informal*), contrivance **2** *The video has become an invaluable teaching tool.* = **means**, agency (*old-fashioned*), vehicle, medium, agent, intermediary, wherewithal **3** *He became the tool of the security services.* = **puppet**, creature, pawn, dupe, stooge (*slang*), jackal, minion, lackey, flunkey, hireling, cat's-paw ▸ VERB *We have a beautifully tooled glass replica of it.* = **make**, work, cut, shape, chase, decorate, ornament

top NOUN **1** *I came down alone from the top of the mountain.* = **peak**, summit, head, crown, height, ridge, brow, crest, high point, pinnacle, culmination, meridian, zenith, apex, apogee, acme, vertex ■ **OPPOSITE:** bottom **2** *the plastic tops from aerosol containers* = **lid**, cover, cap, cork, plug, stopper, bung **3** *The US will be at the top of the medals table.* = **first place**, head, peak, lead, highest rank, high point ▸ ADJECTIVE **1** *Our new flat was on the top floor.* = **highest**, upper, loftiest, furthest up, uppermost, topmost **2** *He was the top student in physics.* = **leading**, best, first, highest, greatest, lead, head, prime, finest, crowning, crack (*informal*), elite, superior, dominant, foremost, pre-eminent ■ **OPPOSITE:** lowest

3 *I need to have the top people in this company work together.* = **chief**, most important, principal, most powerful, highest, lead, head, ruling, leading, main, commanding, prominent, notable, sovereign, eminent, high-ranking, illustrious **4** *a candlelit dinner at a top restaurant* = **prime**, best, select, first-class, capital (*old-fashioned*), quality, choice, excellent, premier, superb, elite, superior, top-class, A1 (*informal*), top-quality, first-rate, top-notch (*informal*), grade A, top-grade ▶ VERB **1** *What happens if the socialists top the poll?* = **lead**, head, command, be at the top of, be first in **2** *To serve, top the fish with cooked leeks.* = **cover**, coat, garnish, finish, crown, cap, overspread **3** *How are you ever going to top that?* = **surpass**, better, beat, improve on, cap, exceed, best, eclipse, go beyond, excel, transcend, outstrip, outdo, outshine ■ **OPPOSITE:** not be as good as **4** *As they topped the hill he saw the town in the distance.* = **reach the top of**, scale, mount, climb, conquer, crest, ascend, surmount • **over the top** *The special effects are a bit over the top, but I enjoyed it.* = **excessive**, too much, going too far, inordinate, over the limit, a bit much (*informal*), uncalled-for, immoderate • **top something up 1** *He topped her glass up, complaining that she was a slow drinker.* = **fill (up)**, refresh, recharge, refill, replenish, freshen **2** *The bank topped up their loan to £5000.* = **supplement**, boost, add to, enhance, augment

topic NOUN = **subject**, point, question, issue, matter, theme, text, thesis, subject matter

topical ADJECTIVE = **current**, popular, contemporary, up-to-date, up-to-the-minute, newsworthy

topple VERB **1** *He released his hold and toppled slowly backwards.* = **fall over**, fall, collapse, tumble, overturn, capsize, totter, tip over, keel over, overbalance, fall headlong **2** *Wind and rain toppled trees and electricity lines.* = **knock over**, upset, knock down, tip over **3** *the revolution which toppled the regime* = **overthrow**, overturn, bring down, oust, unseat, bring low

topsy-turvy ADJECTIVE = **confused**, upside-down, disorderly, chaotic, messy, mixed-up, jumbled, inside-out, untidy, disorganized, disarranged ■ **OPPOSITE:** orderly

torment VERB **1** *At times, memories returned to torment her.* = **torture**, pain, distress, afflict, rack, harrow, crucify, agonize, excruciate ■ **OPPOSITE:** comfort **2** *My older brother used to torment me by singing it to me.* = **tease**,

annoy, worry, trouble, bother, provoke, devil (*informal*), harry, plague, irritate, hound, harass, hassle (*informal*), aggravate (*informal*), persecute, pester, vex, bedevil, chivvy (*Brit.*), give someone grief (*Brit. & S. African*), lead someone a merry dance (*Brit. informal*) ▶ NOUN **1** *He spent days in torment while he waited for news.* = **suffering**, distress, misery, pain, hell (*informal*), torture, agony, anguish ■ **OPPOSITE:** bliss **2** *the torments of being a writer* = **trouble**, worry, bother, plague (*informal*), irritation, hassle (*informal*), nuisance, annoyance, bane, pain in the neck (*informal*)

torn ADJECTIVE **1** *a torn photograph* = **cut**, split, rent, ripped, ragged, slit, lacerated **2** *I know the administration was very torn on this subject.* = **undecided**, divided, uncertain, split, unsure, wavering, vacillating, in two minds (*informal*), irresolute

tornado NOUN = **whirlwind**, storm, hurricane, gale, cyclone, typhoon, tempest (*literary*), squall, twister (*U.S. informal*), windstorm

torpor NOUN = **inactivity**, apathy, inertia, lethargy, passivity, laziness, numbness, sloth, stupor, drowsiness, dullness, sluggishness, indolence, languor, listlessness, somnolence, inertness, stagnancy, accidie (*Theology*), inanition, torpidity ■ **OPPOSITE:** vigour

torrent NOUN **1** *A torrent of water rushed into the reservoir.* = **stream**, flow, rush, flood, tide, spate, cascade, gush, effusion, inundation **2** *The rain came down in torrents.* = **downpour**, flood, shower, deluge, rainstorm **3** *He directed a torrent of abuse at me.* = **outburst**, stream, barrage, hail, spate, outpouring, effusion

torrid ADJECTIVE **1** *the torrid heat of a Spanish summer* = **hot**, tropical, burning, dry, boiling, flaming, blistering, stifling, fiery, scorched, scorching, sizzling, arid, sultry, sweltering, parched, parching, broiling **2** *He is locked in a torrid affair with a mystery lover.* = **passionate**, intense, sexy (*informal*), hot, flaming, erotic, ardent, steamy (*informal*), fervent

tortuous ADJECTIVE **1** *a tortuous mountain route* = **winding**, twisting, meandering, bent, twisted, curved, crooked, indirect, convoluted, serpentine, zigzag, sinuous, circuitous, twisty, mazy **2** *long and tortuous negotiations* = **complicated**, involved, misleading, tricky, indirect, ambiguous, roundabout, deceptive, devious, convoluted, mazy ■ **OPPOSITE:** straightforward

t

USAGE The adjective *tortuous* is sometimes confused with *torturous*. A *tortuous* road is one that winds or twists, while a *torturous* experience is one that involves pain, suffering, or discomfort.

torture VERB **1** *Police are convinced she was tortured and killed.* = **torment**, abuse, persecute, afflict, martyr, scourge, molest, crucify, mistreat, ill-treat, maltreat, put on the rack ■ **OPPOSITE:** comfort **2** *He would not torture her further by arguing.* = **distress**, torment, worry, trouble, pain, rack, afflict, harrow, agonize, give someone grief (*Brit. & S. African*), inflict anguish on ▶ NOUN **1** *alleged cases of torture and murder by security forces* = **ill-treatment**, abuse, torment, persecution, martyrdom, maltreatment, harsh treatment **2** *Waiting for the result was torture.* = **agony**, suffering, misery, anguish, hell (*informal*), distress, torment, heartbreak ■ **OPPOSITE:** bliss

toss VERB **1** *He screwed the paper up and tossed it into the fire.* = **throw**, pitch, hurl, fling, project, launch, cast, shy, chuck (*informal*), flip, propel, sling (*informal*), lob (*informal*) **2** *Toss the apple slices in the mixture.* = **shake**, turn, mix, stir, tumble, agitate, jiggle **3** *The small boat tossed about in the high seas like a cork.* = **heave**, labour, rock, roll, pitch, lurch, jolt, wallow **4** *I felt as though I'd been tossing and turning all night.* = **thrash (about)**, twitch, wriggle, squirm, writhe ▶ NOUN *Decisions are almost made with the toss of a die.* = **throw**, cast, pitch, shy, fling, lob (*informal*)

tot NOUN **1** *They may hold a clue to the missing tot.* = **infant**, child, baby, toddler, mite, wean (*Scot.*), bairn (*Scot. & Northern English*), little one, sprog (*slang*), munchkin (*informal, chiefly U.S.*), rug rat (*slang*), littlie (*Austral. informal*), ankle-biter (*Austral. slang*), tacker (*Austral. slang*) **2** *a tot of dark rum* = **measure**, shot (*informal*), finger, nip, slug, dram, snifter (*informal*), toothful • **tot something up** *Now tot up the points you've scored.* = **add up**, calculate, sum (up), total, reckon, compute, tally, enumerate, count up

total NOUN *The companies have a total of 1,776 employees.* = **sum**, mass, entirety, grand total, whole, amount, aggregate, totality, full amount, sum total ■ **OPPOSITE:** part ▶ ADJECTIVE *The car was in a total mess.* = **complete**, absolute, utter, whole, perfect, entire, sheer, outright, all-out, thorough, unconditional, downright, undisputed, consummate, unqualified, out-and-out, undivided, overarching, unmitigated, thoroughgoing, arrant, deep-dyed ■ **OPPOSITE:** partial ▶ VERB

1 *Their exports will total £85 million this year.* = **amount to**, make, come to, reach, equal, run to, number, add up to, correspond to, work out as, mount up to, tot up to **2** *They haven't totalled the exact figures.* = **add up**, work out, sum up, compute, reckon, tot up ■ **OPPOSITE:** subtract

totalitarian ADJECTIVE = **dictatorial**, authoritarian, one-party, oppressive, undemocratic, monolithic, despotic, tyrannous ■ **OPPOSITE:** democratic

totality NOUN *He did not want to reform the system in its totality.* = **entirety**, unity, fullness, wholeness, completeness, entireness **2** *We must take into consideration the totality of the evidence.* = **aggregate**, whole, entirety, all, total, sum, sum total

totally ADVERB = **completely**, entirely, absolutely, quite, perfectly, fully, comprehensively, thoroughly, wholly, utterly, consummately, wholeheartedly, unconditionally, to the hilt, one hundred per cent, unmitigatedly ■ **OPPOSITE:** partly

totter VERB **1** *He tottered to the fridge to get another beer.* = **stagger**, stumble, reel, sway, falter, lurch, wobble, walk unsteadily **2** *The balconies begin to tremble and totter in the smoke and fumes.* = **shake**, sway, rock, tremble, quake, shudder, lurch, waver, quiver, vibrate, teeter, judder

touch VERB **1** *Her tiny hand gently touched my face.* = **feel**, handle, finger, stroke, brush, make contact with, graze, caress, fondle, lay a finger on, palpate **2** *Their knees were touching.* = **come into contact**, meet, contact, border, brush, come together, graze, adjoin, converge, be in contact, abut, impinge upon **3** *As the aeroplane came down, the wing touched a pile of rubble.* = **tap**, hit, strike, push, pat **4** *a guilt that in some way touches everyone* = **affect**, mark, involve, strike, get to (*informal*), influence, inspire, impress, get through to, have an effect on, make an impression on **5** *He doesn't drink much, and he never touches drugs.* = **consume**, take, drink, eat, partake of **6** *It has touched me deeply to see how these people live.* = **move**, upset, stir, disturb, melt, soften, tug at someone's heartstrings (*often facetious*), leave an impression on **7** *No one can touch these girls for professionalism.* = **match**, rival, equal, compare with, parallel, come up to, come near, be on a par with, be a match for, hold a candle to (*informal*), be in the same league as **8** *These days no sports will touch tobacco advertising.* = **get involved in**, use, deal with, handle, have to do with, utilize, be a party to, concern yourself with **9** *The winds had touched storm-force the day before.*

= **reach**, hit (*informal*), come to, rise to, arrive at, attain, get up to ▶ NOUN **1** *Even a light touch on the face can trigger this pain.* = **contact**, push, stroke, brush, press, tap, poke, nudge, prod, caress, fondling **2** *Our sense of touch is programmed to diminish with age.* = **feeling**, feel, handling, physical contact, palpation, tactility **3** *She thought she might have a touch of flu.* = **bit**, spot (*Brit.*), trace, drop, taste, suggestion, hint, dash, suspicion, pinch, smack, small amount, tinge, whiff, jot, speck, smattering, intimation, tincture **4** *The striker was unable to find his scoring touch.* = **style**, approach, method, technique, way, manner, characteristic, trademark, handiwork **5** *They've lost touch with what is happening in the country.* = **awareness**, understanding, acquaintance, familiarity **6** *In my job one tends to lose touch with friends.* = **communication**, contact, association, connection, correspondence **7** *You don't want to lose your touch. You should get some practice.* = **skill**, ability, flair, art, facility, command, craft, mastery, knack, artistry, virtuosity, deftness, adroitness **8** *This place is crying out for a woman's touch.* = **influence**, hand, effect, management, direction
• **touch and go** *It was touch and go whether we'd go bankrupt.* = **risky**, close, near, dangerous, critical, tricky, sticky (*informal*), hazardous, hairy (*slang*), precarious, perilous, nerve-racking, parlous (*archaic, humorous*) • **touch on** or **upon something** *The film touches on these issues, but only superficially.* = **refer to**, cover, raise, deal with, mention, bring in, speak of, hint at, allude to, broach, make allusions to
• **touch something off 1** *The massacre touched off a new round of violence.* = **trigger (off)**, start, begin, cause, provoke, set off, initiate, arouse, give rise to, ignite, stir up, instigate, spark off, set in motion, foment **2** *set enormous fuel fires raging, or touch off explosions* = **ignite**, light, fire, set off, detonate, put a match to • **touch something up 1** *He got up regularly to touch up the painting.* = **enhance**, revamp, renovate, patch up, brush up, gloss over, polish up, retouch, titivate, give a face-lift to **2** *Use these tips to touch up your image.* = **improve**, perfect, round off, enhance, dress up, finish off, embellish, put the finishing touches to ■ **RELATED WORDS:** *adjectives* haptic, tactile, tactual

touched ADJECTIVE *I was touched to hear that he finds me engaging.* = **moved**, affected, upset, impressed, stirred, disturbed, melted, softened, swayed

touching ADJECTIVE = **moving**, affecting, sad, stirring, tender, melting, pathetic, poignant, heartbreaking, emotive, pitiful, pitiable, piteous

touchstone NOUN = **standard**, measure, par, criterion, norm, gauge, yardstick

touchy ADJECTIVE **1** *She is very touchy about her past.* = **oversensitive**, irritable, bad-tempered, cross, crabbed, grumpy, surly, petulant, irascible, tetchy, ratty (*Brit. & N.Z. informal*), testy, thin-skinned, grouchy (*informal*), querulous, peevish, quick-tempered, splenetic, easily offended, captious, pettish, toey (*N.Z. slang*) ■ **OPPOSITE:** thick-skinned **2** *a touchy subject* = **delicate**, sensitive, tricky, risky, sticky (*informal*), thorny, knotty, ticklish

tough ADJECTIVE **1** *She is tough and ambitious.* = **strong**, determined, aggressive, high-powered, feisty (*informal*), hard-nosed (*informal*), self-confident, unyielding, hard as nails, two-fisted, self-assertive, badass (*slang, chiefly U.S.*) ■ **OPPOSITE:** weak **2** *He's small, but he's tough, and I expect him to do well in the match.* = **hardy**, strong, seasoned, fit, strapping, hardened, vigorous, sturdy, stout, stalwart, resilient, brawny, hard as nails **3** *He has the reputation of being a tough guy.* = **violent**, rough, vicious, ruthless, pugnacious, hard-bitten, ruffianly, two-fisted **4** *He announced tough measures to limit the money supply.* = **strict**, severe, stern, hard, firm, exacting, adamant, resolute, draconian, intractable, inflexible, merciless, unforgiving, unyielding, unbending ■ **OPPOSITE:** lenient **5** *Whoever wins the election is going to have a tough job.* = **hard**, difficult, exhausting, troublesome, uphill, strenuous, arduous, thorny, laborious, irksome **6** *tough leather boots and trousers* = **resilient**, hard, resistant, durable, strong, firm, solid, stiff, rigid, rugged (*U.S. & Canad.*), sturdy, inflexible, cohesive, tenacious, leathery, hard-wearing, robust ■ **OPPOSITE:** fragile ▶ NOUN *Three burly toughs elbowed their way to the front.* = **ruffian**, heavy (*slang*), rough (*informal*), bully, thug, hooligan, brute, rowdy, bravo, bully boy, bruiser (*informal*), roughneck (*slang*), tsotsi (*S. African*)

tour NOUN **1** *a cricket tour of the West Indies* = **circuit**, course, round **2** *week five of my tour of European cities* = **journey**, expedition, excursion, trip, progress, outing, jaunt, junket, peregrination ▶ VERB **1** *A few years ago they toured the country in a roadshow.* = **travel round**, holiday in, travel through, journey round, trek round, go on a trip through **2** *You can tour the site in modern* *coaches fitted with videos.* = **visit**, explore, go round, inspect, walk round, drive round, sightsee

tourist NOUN = **traveller**, journeyer, voyager, tripper (*Brit.*), globetrotter, holiday-maker, sightseer, excursionist

tournament NOUN **1** *Here is a player capable of winning a world tournament.* = **competition**, meeting, match, event, series, contest **2** *a medieval tournament with displays of archery, armour and combat* = **joust**, the lists, tourney

tousled ADJECTIVE = **dishevelled**, disordered, tangled, ruffled, messed up, rumpled, disarranged, disarrayed

tout VERB **1** *the advertising practice of using performers to tout products* = **recommend**, promote, endorse, support, tip, urge, approve, praise, commend, speak well of **2** *He visited several foreign countries to tout for business.* = **solicit**, canvass, drum up, bark (*U.S. informal*), spiel ▶ NOUN *a ticket tout* = **seller**, solicitor, barker, canvasser, spieler

tow VERB = **drag**, draw, pull, trail, haul, tug, yank, hale, trawl, lug

towards PREPOSITION **1** *She walked down the corridor towards the foyer.* = **in the direction of**, to, for, on the way to, on the road to, en route for **2** *You must develop your own attitude towards religion.* = **regarding**, about, concerning, respecting, in relation to, with regard to, with respect to, apropos **3** *There's a forecast of cooler weather towards the end of the week.* = **just before**, nearing, close to, coming up to, almost at, getting on for, shortly before

tower NOUN **1** *an eleventh-century house with 120-foot high towers* = **column**, pillar, turret, belfry, steeple, obelisk **2** *troops occupied the first two floors of the tower* = **stronghold**, castle, fort, refuge, keep, fortress, citadel, fortification ▶ VERB (*often with* **over**) *He stood up and towered over her.* = **rise**, dominate, loom, top, mount, rear, soar, overlook, surpass, transcend, ascend, be head and shoulders above, overtop

towering ADJECTIVE **1** *towering cliffs of black granite* = **tall**, high, great, soaring, elevated, gigantic, lofty, colossal **2** *a towering figure in British politics* = **impressive**, imposing, supreme, striking, extraordinary, outstanding, magnificent, superior, paramount, surpassing, sublime, stellar (*informal*), prodigious, transcendent **3** *I saw her in a towering rage only once.* = **intense**, violent, extreme, excessive, burning, passionate, mighty, fiery, vehement, inordinate, intemperate, immoderate

toxic ADJECTIVE = **poisonous**, deadly, lethal, harmful, pernicious (*formal*), noxious, septic, pestilential, baneful (*archaic*)
■ **OPPOSITE:** harmless

toy NOUN *He was really too old for children's toys.* = **plaything**, game, doll • **toy with something** *He toyed with the idea of going to China.* = **play with**, consider, trifle with, flirt with, dally with, entertain the possibility of, amuse yourself with, think idly of

trace NOUN **1** *Wash them in cold water to remove all traces of sand.* = **bit**, drop, touch, shadow, suggestion, hint, dash, suspicion, tinge, trifle, whiff, jot, tincture, iota **2** *The church has traces of fifteenth-century frescoes.* = **remnant**, remains, sign, record, mark, evidence, indication, token, relic, vestige, footprint, electronic footprint **3** *He disappeared mysteriously without a trace.* = **track**, trail, footstep, path, slot, footprint, spoor, footmark, electronic footprint ▶ VERB **1** *I first went there to trace my roots.* = **search for**, follow, seek out, track, determine, pursue, unearth, ascertain, hunt down **2** *Police are anxious to trace a man seen leaving the house.* = **find**, track (down), discover, trail, detect, unearth, hunt down, ferret out, locate **3** *I traced the course of the river on the map.* = **outline**, chart, sketch, draw, map out, depict, mark out, delineate **4** *She learnt to draw by tracing pictures from story books.* = **copy**, map, draft, outline, sketch, reproduce, draw over

track NOUN **1** *We set off once more, over a rough mountain track.* = **path**, way, road, route, trail, pathway, footpath **2** *following the track of a hurricane* = **course**, line, path, orbit, trajectory, flight path **3** *A woman fell onto the railway track.* = **line**, rail, tramline ▶ VERB *He thought he had better track this creature and kill it.* = **follow**, pursue, chase, trace, tail (*informal*), dog, shadow, trail, stalk, hunt down, follow the trail of • **keep track of something** *or* **someone** *It's hard to keep track of time here.* = **keep up with**, follow, monitor, watch, keep an eye on, keep in touch with, keep up to date with • **lose track of something** *or* **someone** *It's so easy to lose track of who's playing who and when.* = **lose**, lose sight of, misplace • **track something** *or* **someone down** *They are doing all they can to track down terrorists.* = **find**, catch, capture, apprehend, discover, expose, trace, unearth, dig up, hunt down, sniff out, bring to light, ferret out, run to earth or ground

tracks PLURAL NOUN *He suddenly noticed tyre tracks on the bank ahead.* = **trail**, marks, impressions, traces, imprints, prints

t

tract¹ NOUN *A vast tract of land is ready for development.* = **area**, lot, region, estate (*Brit.*), district, stretch, quarter, territory, extent, zone, plot, expanse

tract² NOUN *They produced a tract on the dangers of ignoring climate change.* = **treatise**, essay, leaflet, brochure, booklet, pamphlet, dissertation, monograph, homily, disquisition, tractate

traction NOUN = **grip**, resistance, friction, adhesion, purchase

trade NOUN **1** *The ministry has control over every aspect of foreign trade.* = **commerce**, business, transactions, buying and selling, dealing, exchange, traffic, truck, barter **2** *He was a jeweller by trade.* = **job**, employment, calling, business, line, skill, craft, profession, occupation, pursuit, line of work, métier, avocation **3** *It wouldn't exactly have been a fair trade.* = **exchange**, deal, swap, interchange ▸ VERB **1** *They had years of experience trading with the west.* = **deal**, do business, buy and sell, exchange, traffic, truck, bargain, peddle, barter, transact, cut a deal, have dealings **2** *They traded land for goods and money.* = **exchange**, switch, swap, barter **3** *The company is thought to be trading at a loss.* = **operate**, run, deal, do business ■ RELATED WORD: *adjective* mercantile

trader NOUN = **dealer**, marketer, buyer, broker, supplier, merchant, seller, purveyor, merchandiser

tradesman *or* **tradeswoman** *or* **tradesperson** NOUN = **craftsman** *or* **woman** *or* **person**, workman *or* woman *or* person, artisan, journeyman, skilled worker

tradition NOUN **1** *a country steeped in tradition* = **customs**, institution, ritual, folklore, lore, praxis, tikanga (*N.Z.*) **2** *She has carried on the family tradition of giving away plants.* = **established practice**, custom, convention, habit, ritual, unwritten law

traditional ADJECTIVE **1** *Traditional teaching methods can put students off learning.* = **old-fashioned**, old, established, conventional, fixed, usual, transmitted, accustomed, customary, ancestral, long-established, unwritten, time-honoured ■ OPPOSITE: revolutionary **2** *traditional Indian music* = **folk**, old, historical

traffic NOUN **1** *There was heavy traffic on the roads.* = **transport**, movement, vehicles, transportation, freight, coming and going **2** *traffic in illicit drugs* = **trade**, dealing, commerce, buying and selling, business, exchange, truck, dealings, peddling, barter, doings ▸ VERB (*often with* **in**) *Anyone who trafficked in illegal drugs was brought to justice.*

= **trade**, market, deal, exchange, truck, bargain, do business, buy and sell, peddle, barter, cut a deal, have dealings, have transactions

tragedy NOUN = **disaster**, catastrophe, misfortune, adversity, calamity, affliction, whammy (*informal*), bummer (*slang*), grievous blow ■ OPPOSITE: fortune

tragic *or* **tragical** ADJECTIVE **1** *the tragic loss of so many lives* = **distressing**, shocking, sad, awful, appalling, fatal, deadly, unfortunate, disastrous, dreadful, dire, catastrophic, grievous, woeful, lamentable, ruinous, calamitous, wretched, ill-starred, ill-fated ■ OPPOSITE: fortunate **2** *She is a tragic figure.* = **sad**, miserable, dismal, pathetic, heartbreaking, anguished, mournful, heart-rending, sorrowful, doleful, pitiable ■ OPPOSITE: happy

trail NOUN **1** *He was following a broad trail through the trees.* = **path**, track, route, way, course, road, pathway, footpath, beaten track, singletrack **2** *They would take no action except that of following her trail.* = **tracks**, path, mark, marks, wake, trace, scent, footsteps, footprints, spoor **3** *the high vapour trail of an aircraft* = **wake**, stream, tail, slipstream ▸ VERB **1** *Two detectives were trailing him.* = **follow**, track, chase, pursue, dog, hunt, shadow, trace, tail (*informal*), hound, stalk, keep an eye on, keep tabs on (*informal*), run to ground **2** *She came down the stairs, trailing the coat behind her.* = **drag**, draw, pull, sweep, stream, haul, tow, dangle, droop **3** *I spent a long afternoon trailing behind him.* = **lag**, follow, drift, wander, linger, trudge, fall behind, plod, meander, amble, loiter, straggle, traipse (*informal*), dawdle, hang back, tag along (*informal*), bring up the rear, drag yourself • **trail away** *or* **off** *'But he of all men...' her voice trailed away.* = **fade away** *or* **out**, sink, weaken, diminish, decrease, dwindle, shrink, lessen, subside, fall away, peter out, die away, tail off, taper off, grow weak, grow faint

train VERB **1** *We train them in bricklaying and other building techniques.* = **instruct**, school, prepare, improve, coach, teach, guide, discipline, rear, educate, drill, tutor, rehearse **2** *They have spent a year training for the race.* = **exercise**, prepare, work out, practise, do exercise, get into shape **3** *She trained her binoculars on the horizon.* = **aim**, point, level, position, direct, focus, sight, line up, turn on, fix on, zero in, bring to bear

trainer NOUN = **coach**, manager, guide, adviser, tutor, instructor, counsellor, guru, handler

training NOUN *He had no formal training as a decorator.* = **instruction**, practice, schooling, grounding, education, preparation, exercise, working out, body building, tutelage (*formal*)

traipse VERB *I traipsed from one doctor to another.* = **trudge**, trail, tramp, slouch, drag yourself, footslog ▶ NOUN *It's rather a long traipse from here. Let's take a bus.* = **trudge**, trek, tramp, slog, long walk

trait NOUN = **characteristic**, feature, quality, attribute, quirk, peculiarity, mannerism, idiosyncrasy, lineament

traitor NOUN = **betrayer**, deserter, turncoat, deceiver, informer, renegade, defector, Judas, double-crosser (*informal*), quisling, apostate, miscreant, fifth columnist, snake in the grass (*informal*), back-stabber, fizgig (*Austral. slang*) ■ **OPPOSITE:** loyalist

trajectory NOUN = **path**, line, course, track, flight, route, flight path

tramp VERB **1** *They put on their coats and tramped through the fallen snow.* = **trudge**, march, stamp, stump, toil, plod, traipse (*informal*), walk heavily **2** *He spent a month tramping in the hills around Balmoral.* = **hike**, walk, trek, roam, march, range, ramble, slog, rove, yomp, footslog ▶ NOUN **1** *an old tramp who slept rough in our neighbourhood* = **vagrant**, bum (*informal*), derelict, drifter, down-and-out, hobo (*chiefly U.S.*), vagabond, bag lady (*chiefly U.S.*), dosser (*Brit. slang*), derro (*Austral. slang*) **2** *the slow, heavy tramp of feet on the staircase* = **tread**, stamp, footstep, footfall **3** *He had just come from a day-long tramp on some wild moor.* = **hike**, march, trek, ramble, slog

trample VERB (*often with* **on**, **upon**, *or* **over**) = **stamp**, crush, squash, tread, flatten, run over, walk over

trance NOUN = **daze**, dream, spell, ecstasy, muse, abstraction, rapture, reverie, stupor, unconsciousness, hypnotic state

tranquil ADJECTIVE **1** *The place was tranquil and appealing.* = **peaceful**, quiet, calm, serene, still, cool, pacific, composed, at peace, sedate, placid, undisturbed, restful, untroubled, unperturbed, unruffled, unexcited, chilled (*informal*) **2** *She settled into a life of tranquil celibacy.* = **calm**, quiet, peaceful, serene, still, cool, pacific, composed, sedate, placid, undisturbed, restful, untroubled, unperturbed, unruffled, unexcited, chilled (*informal*) ■ **OPPOSITE:** troubled

tranquillity or (*sometimes U.S.*) **tranquility** NOUN **1** *The hotel is a haven of peace and tranquillity.* = **peace**, calm, quiet, hush, composure, serenity, stillness, coolness, repose, rest, calmness, equanimity, quietness, peacefulness, quietude, placidity, restfulness, sedateness **2** *He has a tranquillity and maturity that I desperately need.* = **calm**, peace, composure, serenity, stillness, coolness, repose, calmness, equanimity, quietness, peacefulness, quietude, placidity, imperturbability, restfulness, sedateness ■ **OPPOSITE:** agitation

tranquillizer or (*U.S.*) **tranquilizer** NOUN = **sedative**, opiate, barbiturate, downer (*slang*), red (*slang*), bromide

transact VERB = **carry out**, handle, conduct, do, manage, perform, settle, conclude, negotiate, carry on, accomplish, execute, take care of, discharge, see to, prosecute, enact

transaction NOUN **1** *plans to disclose their latest business transaction* = **deal** (*informal*), matter, affair, negotiation, business, action, event, proceeding, enterprise, bargain, coup, undertaking, deed, occurrence **2** (*plural*) *the transactions of the Metallurgical Society of Great Britain* = **records**, minutes, affairs, proceedings, goings-on (*informal*), annals, doings

transcend VERB = **surpass**, exceed, go beyond, rise above, leave behind, eclipse, excel, outstrip, outdo, outshine, overstep, go above, leave in the shade (*informal*), outrival, outvie

transcendence or **transcendency** NOUN = **greatness**, excellence, superiority, supremacy, ascendancy, pre-eminence, sublimity, paramountcy, incomparability, matchlessness

transcendent ADJECTIVE = **unparalleled**, unique, extraordinary, superior, exceeding, sublime, consummate, unrivalled, second to none, pre-eminent, transcendental, incomparable, peerless, unequalled, matchless

transcribe VERB **1** *Every telephone call will be recorded and transcribed.* = **write out**, reproduce, take down, copy out, note, transfer, set out, rewrite **2** *He decided to transcribe the work for piano.* = **translate**, interpret, render, transliterate

transcript NOUN = **copy**, record, note, summary, notes, version, carbon, log, translation, manuscript, reproduction, duplicate, transcription, carbon copy, transliteration, written version

transfer VERB *The person can be transferred from wheelchair to seat with relative ease.* = **move**, carry, remove, transport, shift, transplant, displace, relocate, transpose, change, download, upload ▶ NOUN *Arrange for the transfer of medical records to your new doctor.* = **transference**, move, removal, handover, change, shift, transmission, translation, displacement, relocation, transposition

transfix VERB = **stun**, hold, fascinate, paralyse, petrify, mesmerize, hypnotize, stop dead, root to the spot, engross, rivet the attention of, spellbind, halt or stop in your tracks ■ **OPPOSITE:** bore

transform VERB **1** *the speed at which your body transforms food into energy* = **change**, convert, alter, translate, reconstruct, metamorphose, transmute, renew, transmogrify (*humorous*) **2** *A cheap table can be transformed by an attractive cover.* = **make over**, overhaul, revamp, remake, renovate, remodel, revolutionize, redo, transfigure, restyle

transformation NOUN **1** *the transformation of an attic room into a study* = **change**, conversion, alteration, metamorphosis, transmutation, renewal, transmogrification (*humorous*) **2** *He has undergone a personal transformation.* = **revolution**, radical change, sea change, revolutionary change, transfiguration

transgress VERB **1** *We should be confident that justice is done to those who transgress.* = **misbehave**, sin, offend, break the law, err, lapse, fall from grace, go astray, be out of order, do or go wrong **2** *He had transgressed the boundaries of good taste.* = **go beyond**, exceed, infringe, overstep, break, defy, violate, trespass, contravene (*formal*), disobey, encroach upon

transgression NOUN = **crime**, wrong, fault, error, offence, breach, sin, lapse, violation, wrongdoing, infringement, trespass, misdemeanour, misdeed, encroachment, misbehaviour, contravention, iniquity, peccadillo, infraction

transient ADJECTIVE = **brief**, passing, short-term, temporary, short, flying, fleeting, short-lived, fugitive, momentary, ephemeral, transitory, evanescent (*formal*), impermanent, here today and gone tomorrow, fugacious ■ **OPPOSITE:** lasting

transit NOUN *They halted transit of EU livestock.* = **movement**, transfer, transport, passage, travel, crossing, motion, transportation, carriage, shipment, traverse, conveyance, portage ▶ VERB *They have been allowed back into Kuwait by transiting through Baghdad.* = **pass**, travel, cross, journey, traverse, move • **in transit** *We cannot be held responsible for goods lost in transit.* = **en route**, on the way, on the road, on the move, in motion, on the go (*informal*), on the journey, while travelling, during transport, during passage

transition NOUN = **change**, passing, development, shift, passage, conversion, evolution, transit, upheaval, alteration, progression, flux, metamorphosis, changeover, transmutation, metastasis

transitional ADJECTIVE **1** *a transitional period following a decade of civil war* = **changing**, passing, fluid, intermediate, unsettled, developmental, transitionary **2** *a meeting to set up a transitional government* = **temporary**, working, acting, short-term, interim, fill-in, caretaker, provisional, makeshift, make-do, stopgap, pro tem

transitory ADJECTIVE = **short-lived**, short, passing, brief, short-term, temporary, fleeting, transient, flying, momentary, ephemeral, evanescent (*formal*), impermanent, here today and gone tomorrow, fugacious ■ **OPPOSITE:** lasting

translate VERB **1** *Only a small number of his books have been translated into English.* = **render**, put, change, convert, interpret, decode, transcribe, construe (*old-fashioned*), paraphrase, decipher, transliterate **2** *Translating IT jargon is the key to the IT director's role.* = **put in plain English**, explain, make clear, clarify, spell out, simplify, gloss, unravel, decode, paraphrase, decipher, elucidate, rephrase, reword, state in layperson's terms **3** *Your decision must be translated into specific actions.* = **convert**, change, turn, transform, alter, render, metamorphose, transmute, transfigure **4** *The bishop was later translated to the diocese of Carlisle.* = **transfer**, move, send, relocate, carry, remove, transport, shift, convey, transplant, transpose

translation NOUN **1** *his excellent English translation of 'Faust'* = **interpretation**, version, rendering, gloss, rendition, decoding, transcription, paraphrase, transliteration **2** *the translation of these goals into classroom activities* = **conversion**, change, rendering, transformation, alteration, metamorphosis, transfiguration, transmutation

translator NOUN = **interpreter**, transcriber, paraphraser, decipherer, linguist, metaphrast, paraphrast, transliterator

translucent ADJECTIVE = **semitransparent**, clear, limpid, lucent, diaphanous, pellucid

transmission NOUN **1** *the transmission of knowledge and skills* = **transfer**, spread, spreading, communication, passing on, circulation, dispatch, relaying, mediation, imparting, diffusion, transference, dissemination, conveyance, channelling **2** *The transmission of the programme was brought forward.* = **broadcasting**, showing, putting out, relaying, sending **3** *A webcast is a transmission using the internet.* = **programme**, broadcast, show, production, telecast, podcast

transmit VERB **1** *letters begging them to transmit the programme daily* = **broadcast**, put on the air, televise, relay, send, air, radio, send out, disseminate, beam out, stream, podcast **2** *mosquitoes that transmit disease to humans* = **pass on**, carry, spread, communicate, take, send, forward, bear, transfer, transport, hand on, convey, dispatch, hand down, diffuse, remit, impart, disseminate

transmute VERB = **transform**, change, convert, alter, metamorphose, transfigure, alchemize

transparency NOUN **1** *The first colour photo was a transparency of a tartan ribbon.* = **photograph**, slide, exposure, photo, picture, image, print, plate, still **2** *It is a condition that affects the transparency of the lenses.* = **clarity**, translucency, translucence, clearness, limpidity, transparence, diaphaneity, filminess, diaphanousness, gauziness, limpidness, pellucidity, pellucidness, sheerness ■ **OPPOSITE:** opacity **3** *openness and transparency in the government's decision-making* = **frankness**, openness, candour, directness, forthrightness, straightforwardness ■ **OPPOSITE:** ambiguity

transparent ADJECTIVE **1** *a sheet of transparent coloured plastic* = **clear**, sheer, see-through, lucid, translucent, crystal clear, crystalline, limpid, lucent, diaphanous, gauzy, filmy, pellucid ■ **OPPOSITE:** opaque **2** *striving to establish a transparent parliamentary democracy* = **frank**, open, direct, straight, straightforward, candid, forthright, unequivocal, unambiguous, plain-spoken ■ **OPPOSITE:** unclear **3** *The meaning of their actions is transparent.* = **obvious**, plain, apparent, visible, bold, patent, evident, distinct, explicit, easy, understandable, manifest, recognizable, unambiguous, undisguised, as plain as the nose on your face (*informal*), perspicuous ■ **OPPOSITE:** uncertain

transpire VERB **1** *It transpired that he had left his driving licence at home.* = **become known**, emerge, come out, be discovered, come to light, be disclosed, be made public **2** *Nothing is known about what transpired at the*

meeting. = **happen**, occur, take place, arise, turn up, come about, come to pass (*archaic*)

■ **USAGE** It is sometimes maintained that *transpire* should not be used to mean 'happen' or 'occur', as in *the event transpired late in the evening*, and that the word is properly used to mean 'become known', as in *it transpired later that the thief had been caught*. The word is, however, widely used in the first sense, especially in spoken English.

transplant VERB **1** *The operation to transplant a kidney is now fairly routine.* = **implant**, transfer, graft **2** *Marriage had transplanted her from London to Manchester.* = **transfer**, take, bring, carry, remove, transport, shift, convey, fetch, displace, relocate, uproot

transport VERB **1** *There's no petrol so it's difficult to transport goods.* = **convey**, take, run, move, bring, send, carry, bear, remove, ship, transfer, deliver, conduct, shift, ferry, haul, fetch **2** *I have never seen any man so completely transported by excitement.* = **enrapture**, move, delight, entrance, enchant, carry away, captivate, electrify, ravish, spellbind **3** *He was transported to Italy and interned.* = **exile**, banish, deport, sentence to transportation ▶ NOUN **1** *Have you got your own transport?* = **vehicle**, wheels (*informal*), transportation, conveyance (*old-fashioned*) **2** *Safety rules had been breached during transport of radioactive fuel.* = **transference**, carrying, shipping, delivery, distribution, removal, transportation, carriage, shipment, freight, haulage, conveyance, freightage **3** (*often plural*) *transports of joy* = **ecstasy**, delight, heaven (*informal*), happiness, bliss, euphoria, rapture, enchantment, cloud nine (*informal*), seventh heaven, ravishment ■ **OPPOSITE:** despondency

transpose VERB **1** *Genetic engineers transpose bits of material from one organism to another.* = **transplant**, move, transfer, shift, displace, relocate, reposition **2** *Many people inadvertently transpose the digits of the code.* = **interchange**, switch, swap, reorder, change, move, exchange, substitute, alter, rearrange

transverse ADJECTIVE = **crossways**, diagonal, oblique, crosswise, athwart

trap NOUN **1** *He came across a bird caught in a trap.* = **snare**, net, booby trap, gin, toils (*old-fashioned*), pitfall, noose, springe **2** *He failed to keep the appointment after sensing a police trap.* = **ambush**, set-up (*informal*), device, lure, bait, honey trap, ambuscade (*old-fashioned*) **3** *He was trying to decide whether the question was a trap.* = **trick**, set-up (*informal*), deception, ploy, ruse, artifice, trickery, subterfuge, stratagem, wile, device ▶ VERB **1** *The locals were trying to trap and kill the birds.* = **catch**, snare, ensnare, entrap, take, corner, bag, lay hold of, enmesh, lay a trap for, run to earth or ground **2** *Were you trying to trap her into making an admission?* = **trick**, fool, cheat, lure, seduce, deceive, dupe, beguile, gull, cajole, ensnare, hoodwink, wheedle, inveigle **3** *To trap the killer they had to play him at his own game.* = **capture**, catch, arrest, seize, take, lift (*slang*), secure, nail (*informal*), collar (*informal*), nab (*informal*), apprehend, take prisoner, take into custody

trapped ADJECTIVE = **caught**, cornered, snared, ensnared, stuck (*informal*), netted, surrounded, cut off, at bay, in a tight corner, in a tight spot, with your back to the wall

trappings PLURAL NOUN = **accessories**, trimmings, paraphernalia, finery, things, fittings, dress, equipment, gear, fixtures, decorations, furnishings, ornaments, livery, adornments, panoply, accoutrements, fripperies, bells and whistles, raiment (*archaic, poetic*), bling (*slang*)

trash NOUN **1** *Don't read that awful trash.* = **nonsense**, rubbish, garbage (*informal*), rot, pants (*slang*), crap (*slang*), hot air (*informal*), tosh (*slang, chiefly Brit.*), pap, bilge (*informal*), drivel, twaddle, tripe (*informal*), guff (*slang*), moonshine, hogwash (*informal*), malarkey, hokum (*slang, chiefly U.S. & Canad.*), piffle (*informal*), poppycock (*informal*), inanity, balderdash, bosh (*informal*), eyewash (*informal*), kak (*S. African vulgar slang*), trumpery, tommyrot, foolish talk, horsefeathers (*U.S. slang*), bunkum or buncombe, bizzo (*Austral. slang*), bull's wool (*Austral. & N.Z. slang*) ■ OPPOSITE: sense **2** *The yards are overgrown and cluttered with trash.* = **litter**, refuse, waste, rubbish, sweepings, junk (*informal*), garbage, dross, dregs, dreck (*slang, chiefly U.S.*), offscourings

trashy ADJECTIVE = **worthless**, cheap, inferior, shabby, flimsy, shoddy, tawdry, tinsel, thrown together, crappy (*slang*), meretricious, rubbishy, poxy (*slang*), catchpenny, cheap-jack (*informal*), of a sort or of sorts ■ OPPOSITE: excellent

trauma NOUN **1** *I'd been through the trauma of losing a house.* = **shock**, suffering, worry, pain, stress, upset, strain, torture, distress, misery, disturbance, ordeal, anguish, upheaval, jolt **2** *spinal trauma* = **injury**, damage, hurt, wound, agony

traumatic ADJECTIVE = **shocking**, upsetting, alarming, awful, disturbing, devastating, painful, distressing, terrifying, scarring, harrowing ■ OPPOSITE: calming

travel VERB **1** *You can travel to Helsinki tomorrow.* = **go**, journey, proceed, make a journey, move, walk, cross, tour, progress, wander, trek, voyage, roam, ramble, traverse, rove, take a trip, make your way, wend your way **2** *Light travels at around 300 million metres per second.* = **be transmitted**, move, advance, proceed, get through ▶ NOUN (*usually plural*) *He collects things for the house on his travels.* = **journey**, wandering, expedition, globetrotting, walk, tour, touring, movement, trip, passage, voyage, excursion, ramble, peregrination ■ RELATED WORD: *adjective* itinerant

traveller NOUN **1** *Many air travellers suffer puffy ankles during long flights.* = **voyager**, tourist, passenger, journeyer, explorer, hiker, tripper (*Brit.*), globetrotter, holiday-maker, wayfarer, excursionist **2** *My father was a commercial traveller who migrated from Scotland.* = **travelling salesperson**, representative, rep, salesperson, sales rep, commercial traveller, agent

travelling ADJECTIVE = **itinerant**, moving, touring, mobile, wandering, unsettled, roaming, migrant, restless, roving, nomadic, migratory, peripatetic, wayfaring

traverse VERB **1** *I traversed the narrow pedestrian bridge.* = **cross**, go across, travel over, make your way across, cover, range, bridge, negotiate, wander, go over, span, roam, ply **2** *a steep-sided valley traversed by streams* = **cut across**, pass over, stretch across, extend across, lie across

travesty NOUN = **mockery**, distortion, parody, caricature, sham, send-up (*Brit. informal*), spoof (*informal*), perversion, takeoff (*informal*), lampoon, burlesque

treacherous ADJECTIVE **1** *The President spoke of the treacherous intentions of the enemy.* = **disloyal**, deceitful, untrustworthy, duplicitous, false, untrue, unreliable, unfaithful, faithless, double-crossing (*informal*), double-dealing, perfidious (*literary*), traitorous, treasonable, recreant (*archaic*) ■ OPPOSITE: loyal **2** *The current of the river is fast-flowing and treacherous.* = **dangerous**, tricky, risky, unstable, hazardous, icy, slippery, unsafe, unreliable, precarious, deceptive, perilous, slippy (*informal, dialect*) ■ OPPOSITE: safe

treachery NOUN = **betrayal**, infidelity, treason, duplicity, disloyalty, double-cross (*informal*), double-dealing, stab in the back, perfidy (*literary*), faithlessness, perfidiousness ■ OPPOSITE: loyalty

tread VERB *She trod casually, enjoying the sensation of bare feet on grass.* = **step**, walk, march, pace, stamp, stride, hike, tramp, trudge, plod ▶ NOUN *We could hear their heavy tread and an occasional coarse laugh.* = **step**, walk, pace, stride, footstep, gait, footfall • **tread on something 1** *Oh sorry, I didn't mean to tread on your foot.* = **crush underfoot**, step on, stamp on, trample (on), stomp on, squash, flatten **2** *Paid lawyers would tread on the farmers' interests.* = **repress**, crush, suppress, subdue, oppress, quell, bear down on, subjugate, ride roughshod over

treason NOUN = **disloyalty**, mutiny, treachery, subversion, disaffection, duplicity, sedition, perfidy (*literary*), lese-majesty, traitorousness
■ **OPPOSITE:** loyalty

treasure NOUN **1** *It was here, the buried treasure, she knew it was.* = **riches**, money, gold, fortune, wealth, valuables, jewels, funds, cash **2** *Charlie? Oh he's a treasure, loves children.* = **angel**, darling, find, star (*informal*), prize, pearl, something else (*informal*), jewel, gem, paragon, one in a million (*informal*), one of a kind (*informal*), nonpareil ▶ VERB *She treasures her memories of those joyous days.* = **prize**, value, worship, esteem, adore, cherish, revere, venerate, hold dear, love, idolize, set great store by, dote upon, place great value on

treasury NOUN **1** *reconciling accounts with the central bank and its treasury* = **funds**, money, capital, finances, resources, assets, revenues, exchequer, coffers **2** *He had been compiling a treasury of jokes.* = **storehouse**, bank, store, vault, hoard, cache, repository

treat VERB **1** *He treated most women with indifference.* = **behave towards**, deal with, handle, act towards, use, consider, serve, manage, regard, look upon **2** *An experienced nurse treats all minor injuries.* = **take care of**, minister to, attend to, give medical treatment to, doctor (*informal*), nurse, care for, medicate, prescribe medicine for, apply treatment to **3** (*often with* **to**) *She was always treating him to ice cream.* = **provide**, give, buy, stand (*informal*), pay for, entertain, feast, lay on, regale, wine and dine, take out for, foot *or* pay the bill **4** *They assumed we were treating with the rebels.* = **negotiate**, bargain, consult, have talks, confer, come to terms, parley, make a bargain, make terms
▶ NOUN **1** *a birthday treat* = **entertainment**, party, surprise, gift, celebration, feast, outing, excursion, banquet, refreshment **2** *It's a real treat to see someone doing justice to the film.* = **pleasure**, delight, joy, thrill,

satisfaction, enjoyment, gratification, source of pleasure, fun • **treat of something** *part of Christian theology that treats of the afterlife* = **deal with**, discuss, go into, be concerned with, touch upon, discourse upon

treatise NOUN = **paper**, work, writing, study, essay, thesis, tract, pamphlet, exposition, dissertation, monograph, disquisition

treatment NOUN **1** *Many patients are not getting the treatment they need.* = **care**, medical care, nursing, medicine, surgery, therapy, healing, medication, therapeutics, ministrations **2** *a new treatment for eczema* = **cure**, remedy, medication, medicine **3** (*often with* **of**) *She was shocked at his treatment of her.* = **handling**, dealings with, behaviour towards, conduct towards, management, reception, usage, manipulation, action towards

treaty NOUN = **agreement**, pact, contract, bond, alliance, bargain, convention, compact, covenant, entente, concordat

trek NOUN **1** *It's a bit of a trek, but it's worth it.* = **slog**, tramp, long haul, footslog **2** *He is on a trek through the South Gobi desert.* = **journey**, hike, expedition, safari, march, odyssey
▶ VERB **1** *trekking through the jungles* = **journey**, march, range, hike, roam, tramp, rove, go walkabout (*Austral.*) **2** *They trekked from shop to shop looking for knee-length socks.* = **trudge**, plod, traipse (*informal*), footslog, slog

tremble VERB **1** *He began to tremble all over.* = **shake**, shiver, quake, shudder, quiver, teeter, totter, quake in your boots, shake in your boots *or* shoes **2** *He felt the earth tremble under him.* = **vibrate**, rock, shake, quake, wobble, oscillate ▶ NOUN *I'll never forget the tremble in his hand.* = **shake**, shiver, quake (*informal*), shudder, wobble, tremor, quiver, vibration, oscillation

tremendous ADJECTIVE **1** *I felt a tremendous pressure on my chest.* = **huge**, great, towering, vast, enormous, terrific, formidable, immense, awesome, titanic, gigantic, monstrous, mammoth, colossal, whopping (*informal*), stellar (*informal*), prodigious, stupendous, gargantuan
■ **OPPOSITE:** tiny **2** *I thought it was absolutely tremendous.* = **excellent**, great (*informal*), wonderful, brilliant, mean (*slang*), topping (*Brit. slang*), cracking (*Brit. informal*), amazing, extraordinary, fantastic (*informal*), ace (*informal*), incredible, fabulous (*informal*), marvellous, exceptional, terrific (*informal*), sensational (*informal*), sovereign, awesome (*slang*), sick

(slang), super (informal), brill (informal), bodacious (slang, chiefly U.S.), boffo (slang), jim-dandy (slang), chillin' (U.S. slang), booshit (Austral. slang), exo (Austral. slang), sik (Austral. slang), rad (informal), phat (slang), schmick (Austral. informal), beaut (informal), barrie (Scot. slang), belting (Brit. slang), pearler (Austral. slang) ■ **OPPOSITE:** terrible

tremor NOUN **1** He felt a tremor in his arm. = **shake**, shaking, tremble, trembling, shiver, quaking, wobble, quiver, quivering, agitation, vibration, quaver **2** The minute-long tremor measured 6.8 on the Richter Scale. = **earthquake**, shock, quake (informal), temblor (U.S. informal)

trench NOUN = **ditch**, cut, channel, drain, pit, waterway, gutter, trough, furrow, excavation, earthwork, fosse, entrenchment

trenchant ADJECTIVE **1** He was shattered by the trenchant criticism. = **scathing**, pointed, cutting, biting, sharp, keen, acute, severe, acid, penetrating, tart, pungent, incisive, hurtful, sarcastic, caustic, astringent, vitriolic, acerbic, piquant, mordant, acidulous, mordacious ■ **OPPOSITE:** kind **2** His comment was trenchant and perceptive. = **clear**, driving, strong, powerful, effective, distinct, crisp, explicit, vigorous, potent, energetic, clear-cut, forceful, emphatic, unequivocal, salient, well-defined, effectual, distinctly defined ■ **OPPOSITE:** vague

trend NOUN **1** a trend towards part-time employment = **tendency**, swing, drift, inclination, current, direction, flow, leaning, bias **2** The record may well start a trend. = **fashion**, craze, fad (informal), mode, look, thing, style, rage, vogue, mania ▶ VERB Unemployment is still trending down. = **tend**, turn, head, swing, flow, bend, lean, incline, veer, run

trendy (Brit. informal) ADJECTIVE a trendy London nightclub = **fashionable**, in (slang), now (informal), latest, with it (old-fashioned, informal), flash (informal), stylish, in fashion, in vogue, on trend, up to the minute, modish, voguish, schmick (Austral. informal), funky ▶ NOUN an example of what happens when you get a few trendies in power = **poser** (informal), pseud (informal)

trepidation NOUN = **anxiety**, fear, worry, alarm, emotion, excitement, dread, butterflies (informal), shaking, disturbance, dismay, trembling, fright, apprehension, tremor, quivering, nervousness, disquiet, agitation, consternation, jitters (informal), cold feet (informal), uneasiness, palpitation,

cold sweat (informal), perturbation, the heebie-jeebies (slang) ■ **OPPOSITE:** composure

trespass VERB **1** They were trespassing on private property. = **intrude**, infringe, encroach, enter without permission, invade, poach, obtrude **2** (often with **against**) (archaic) Forgive those who trespass against us. = **sin**, offend, transgress, commit a sin ▶ NOUN **1** You could be prosecuted for trespass. = **intrusion**, infringement, encroachment, unlawful entry, invasion, poaching, wrongful entry **2** Forgive us our trespasses. = **sin**, crime, fault, error, offence, breach, misconduct, wrongdoing, misdemeanour, delinquency, misdeed, transgression, misbehaviour, iniquity, infraction, evildoing, injury

tress NOUN (often plural) = **hair**, lock, curl, braid, plait, pigtail, ringlet

triad NOUN = **threesome**, triple, trio, trinity, trilogy, triplet, triumvirate, triptych, trine, triune

trial NOUN **1** New evidence showed that he lied at the trial. = **hearing**, case, court case, inquiry, contest, tribunal, lawsuit, appeal, litigation, industrial tribunal, court martial, legal proceedings, judicial proceedings, judicial examination **2** They have been treated with drugs in clinical trials. = **test**, testing, experiment, evaluation, check, examination, audition, assay, dry run (informal), assessment, proof, probation, appraisal, try-out, test-run, pilot study, dummy run **3** the trials of adolescence = **hardship**, suffering, trouble, pain, load, burden, distress, grief, misery, ordeal, hard times, woe, unhappiness, adversity, affliction, tribulation, wretchedness, vexation, cross to bear **4** The whole affair has been a terrible trial for us all. = **nuisance**, drag (informal), bother, plague (informal), pest, irritation, hassle (informal), bane, pain in the neck (informal), vexation, thorn in your flesh or side ▶ ADJECTIVE a trial period = **experimental**, probationary, testing, pilot, provisional, exploratory

tribe NOUN = **race**, ethnic group, people, family, class, stock, house, division, blood, seed (chiefly biblical), sept, gens, clan, caste, dynasty, hapu (N.Z.), iwi (N.Z.)

tribulation NOUN = **trouble**, care, suffering, worry, trial, blow, pain, burden, distress, grief, misery, curse, ordeal, hardship, sorrow, woe, hassle (informal), misfortune, bad luck, unhappiness, heartache, adversity, affliction, bummer (slang), wretchedness, vexation, ill fortune, cross to bear ■ **OPPOSITE:** joy

tribunal NOUN = **hearing**, court, trial, bar, bench, industrial tribunal, judgment seat, judicial examination

tribute NOUN = **accolade**, testimonial, eulogy, recognition, respect, gift, honour, praise, esteem, applause, compliment, gratitude, acknowledgment, commendation, panegyric, encomium, laudation ■ **OPPOSITE:** criticism

trick NOUN **1** *We are playing a trick on a man who keeps bothering me.* = **joke**, put-on (*slang*), gag (*informal*), stunt, spoof (*informal*), caper, prank, frolic, practical joke, antic, jape, leg-pull (*Brit. informal*), cantrip (*Scot.*) **2** *That was a really mean trick.* = **deception**, trap, fraud, con (*slang*), sting (*informal*), manoeuvre, dodge, ploy, scam (*slang*), imposition, gimmick, device, hoax, deceit, swindle, ruse, artifice, subterfuge, canard, feint, stratagem, wile, imposture, fastie (*Austral. slang*) **3** *He shows me card tricks.* = **sleight of hand**, device, feat, stunt, juggle, legerdemain **4** *She showed me all the tricks of the trade.* = **secret**, skill, device, knack, art, hang (*informal*), technique, know-how (*informal*), gift, command, craft, expertise **5** *all her little tricks and funny voices* = **mannerism**, habit, characteristic, trait, quirk, peculiarity, foible, idiosyncrasy, practice, crotchet ▶ VERB *He'll be upset when he finds out how you tricked him.* = **deceive**, trap, have someone on, take someone in (*informal*), fool, cheat, con (*informal*), kid (*informal*), stiff (*slang*), sting (*informal*), mislead, hoax, defraud, dupe, gull (*archaic*), delude, swindle, impose upon, bamboozle (*informal*), hoodwink, put one over on (*informal*), pull the wool over someone's eyes, pull a fast one on (*informal*), scam (*slang*) • **do the trick** *Sometimes a few choice words will do the trick.* = **work**, fit the bill, have effect, achieve the desired result, produce the desired result, take care of the problem, be effective or effectual, do the business (*informal*)

trickery NOUN = **deception**, fraud, cheating, con (*informal*), hoax, pretence, deceit, dishonesty, swindling, guile, double-dealing, skulduggery (*informal*), chicanery, hanky-panky (*informal*), hokum (*slang, chiefly U.S. & Canad.*), monkey business (*informal*), funny business, jiggery-pokery (*informal, chiefly Brit.*), imposture ■ **OPPOSITE:** honesty

trickle VERB *A tear trickled down his cheek.* = **dribble**, run, drop, stream, creep, crawl, drip, ooze, seep, exude, percolate ▶ NOUN *There was not so much as a trickle of water.* = **dribble**, drip, seepage, thin stream

trickster NOUN = **deceiver**, fraud (*informal*), cheat, joker, hoaxer, pretender, hustler (*U.S. informal*), conman or woman (*informal*), con artist (*informal*), impostor, fraudster, swindler, practical joker, grifter (*slang, chiefly U.S. & Canad.*), chiseller (*informal*), rorter (*Austral. slang*), rogue trader

tricky ADJECTIVE **1** *This could be a very tricky problem.* = **difficult**, sensitive, complicated, delicate, risky, sticky (*informal*), hairy (*informal*), problematic, thorny, touch-and-go, knotty, dicey (*informal*), ticklish ■ **OPPOSITE:** simple **2** *They could encounter some tricky political manoeuvring.* = **crafty**, scheming, subtle, cunning, slippery, sly, deceptive, devious, wily, artful, foxy, deceitful ■ **OPPOSITE:** open

trifle NOUN *He had no money to spare on trifles.* = **knick-knack**, nothing, toy, plaything, bauble, triviality, bagatelle, gewgaw • **a trifle** *He found both locations just a trifle disappointing.* = **slightly**, a little, a bit, somewhat, rather, moderately, marginally, a shade, to some degree, on a small scale, to some extent or degree

trifling ADJECTIVE = **insignificant**, small, tiny, empty, slight, silly, shallow, petty, idle, trivial, worthless, negligible, unimportant, frivolous, paltry, minuscule, puny, measly, piddling (*informal*), inconsiderable, valueless, nickel-and-dime (*U.S. slang*), footling (*informal*) ■ **OPPOSITE:** significant

trigger VERB = **bring about**, start, cause, produce, generate, prompt, provoke, set off, activate, give rise to, elicit, spark off, set in motion ■ **OPPOSITE:** prevent

trim ADJECTIVE **1** *The neighbour's gardens were trim and neat.* = **neat**, nice, smart, compact, tidy, orderly, spruce, dapper, natty (*informal*), well-groomed, well-ordered, well turned-out, shipshape, spick-and-span, trig (*archaic, dialect*), soigné or soignée ■ **OPPOSITE:** untidy **2** *The driver was a trim young woman of about thirty.* = **slender**, fit, slim, sleek, streamlined, shapely, svelte, willowy, lissom(e) ▶ VERB **1** *My friend trims my hair every eight weeks.* = **cut**, crop, clip, dock, shave, barber, tidy, prune, shear, pare, lop, even up, neaten **2** *jackets trimmed with crocheted flowers* = **decorate**, dress, array, adorn, embroider, garnish, ornament, embellish, deck out, bedeck, beautify, trick out ▶ NOUN **1** *a white satin scarf with black trim* = **decoration**, edging, border, piping, trimming, fringe, garnish, frill, embellishment, adornment, ornamentation **2** *He is already getting in trim for the big day.* = **condition**, form, health, shape (informal), repair, fitness, wellness, order, fettle **3** *His hair needed a trim.* = **cut**, crop, trimming, clipping, shave, pruning, shearing, tidying up

trimming NOUN *the lace trimming on her satin nightgown* = **decoration**, edging, border, piping, fringe, garnish, braid, frill, festoon, embellishment, adornment, ornamentation ▶ PLURAL NOUN **1** *a Thanksgiving dinner of turkey and all the trimmings* = **extras**, accessories, garnish, ornaments, accompaniments, frills, trappings, paraphernalia, appurtenances **2** *Use any pastry trimmings to decorate the apples.* = **clippings**, ends, cuttings, shavings, brash, parings

trinity NOUN = **threesome**, triple, trio, trilogy, triplet, triad, triumvirate, triptych, trine, triune

trinket NOUN = **ornament**, bauble, knick-knack, piece of bric-a-brac, nothing, toy, trifle, bagatelle, gimcrack, gewgaw, bibelot, kickshaw

trio NOUN = **threesome**, triple, trinity, trilogy, triplet, triad, triumvirate, triptych, trine, triune

trip NOUN **1** *On the Thursday we went out on a day trip.* = **journey**, outing, excursion, day out, run, drive, travel, tour, spin (informal), expedition, voyage, ramble, foray, jaunt, errand, junket (informal) **2** *Slips, trips and falls were monitored using a daily calendar.* = **stumble**, fall, slip, blunder, false move, misstep, false step ▶ VERB **1** *(often with* **up***) She tripped and broke her hip.* = **stumble**, fall, fall over, slip, tumble, topple, stagger, misstep, lose your balance, make a false move, lose your footing, take a spill **2** *They tripped along without a care in the world.* = **skip**, dance, spring, hop, caper, flit, frisk, gambol, tread lightly **3** *(informal) One night I was tripping on acid.* = **take drugs**, get high (informal), get stoned (slang), turn on (slang) **4** *He set the timer, then tripped the switch.* = **activate**, turn on, flip, release, pull, throw, engage, set off, switch on • **trip someone up** *Your own lies will trip you up.* = **catch out**, trap, confuse, unsettle, disconcert, throw you off, wrongfoot, put you off your stride

tripe NOUN = **nonsense**, rot (informal), trash, twaddle, rubbish, pants (slang), crap (slang), garbage (informal), hot air (informal), tosh (slang, chiefly Brit.), pap, bilge (informal), drivel, guff (slang), moonshine, claptrap (informal), hogwash, hokum (slang, chiefly U.S. & Canad.), piffle (informal), poppycock (informal), inanity, balderdash, bosh (informal), eyewash (informal),

trumpery, tommyrot, foolish talk, horsefeathers (U.S. slang), bunkum or buncombe, bizzo (Austral. slang), bull's wool (Austral. & N.Z. slang)

triple ADJECTIVE **1** *The kitchen is triple the size it used to be.* = **treble**, three times, three times as much as **2** *Germany, Austria and Italy formed the Triple Alliance.* = **three-way**, threefold, tripartite ▶ VERB *I got a great new job and my salary tripled.* = **treble**, triplicate, increase threefold

triplet NOUN = **threesome**, triple, trio, trinity, trilogy, triad, triumvirate, trine, triune

tripper NOUN = **tourist**, holiday-maker, sightseer, excursionist, journeyer, voyager

trite ADJECTIVE = **unoriginal**, worn, common, stock, ordinary, tired, routine, dull, stereotyped, hack, pedestrian, commonplace, stale, banal, corny (slang), run-of-the-mill, threadbare, clichéd, uninspired, hackneyed, bromidic ■ OPPOSITE: original

triumph NOUN **1** *Cataract operations are a triumph of modern surgery.* = **success**, victory, accomplishment, mastery, hit (informal), achievement, smash (informal), coup, sensation, feat, conquest, attainment, smash hit (informal), tour de force (French), walkover (informal), feather in your cap, smasheroo (slang) ■ OPPOSITE: failure **2** *Her sense of triumph was short-lived.* = **joy**, pride, happiness, rejoicing, elation, jubilation, exultation ▶ VERB **1** *(often with* **over***) a symbol of good triumphing over evil* = **succeed**, win, overcome, prevail, best, dominate, overwhelm, thrive, flourish, subdue, prosper, get the better of, vanquish (literary), come out on top (informal), carry the day, take the honours ■ OPPOSITE: fail **2** *the euphoria, the sense of triumphing together as a nation* = **rejoice**, celebrate, glory, revel, swagger, drool, gloat, exult, jubilate, crow

triumphant ADJECTIVE **1** *the triumphant team* = **victorious**, winning, successful, dominant, conquering, undefeated ■ OPPOSITE: defeated **2** *his triumphant return home* = **celebratory**, rejoicing, jubilant, triumphal, proud, glorious, swaggering, elated, exultant, boastful, cock-a-hoop

trivia NOUN = **minutiae**, details, trifles, trivialities, petty details ■ OPPOSITE: essentials

trivial ADJECTIVE = **unimportant**, little, small, minor, slight, everyday, petty, meaningless, commonplace, worthless, trifling, insignificant, negligible, frivolous, paltry, incidental, puny, inconsequential, trite, inconsiderable, valueless, nickel-and-dime (U.S. slang) ■ OPPOSITE: important

triviality NOUN **1** *news items of quite astonishing triviality* = **insignificance**, frivolity, smallness, pettiness, worthlessness, meaninglessness, unimportance, littleness, slightness, triteness, paltriness, inconsequentiality, valuelessness, negligibility, much ado about nothing ■ OPPOSITE: importance **2** *He accused me of making a great fuss about trivialities.* = **trifle**, nothing, detail, technicality, petty detail, no big thing, no great matter ■ OPPOSITE: essential

troop NOUN **1** *She was aware of a little troop of travellers watching them.* = **group**, company, team, body, unit, band, crowd, pack, squad, gathering, crew (*informal*), drove, gang, bunch (*informal*), flock, herd, contingent, swarm, horde, multitude, throng, posse (*informal*), bevy, assemblage **2** (*plural*) *the deployment of more than 35,000 troops from a dozen countries* = **soldiers**, armed forces, service personnel, fighters, military, army, soldiery ▶ VERB *The VIPs trooped into the hall and sat down.* = **flock**, march, crowd, stream, parade, swarm, throng, traipse (*informal*)

trophy NOUN **1** *They could win a trophy this year.* = **prize**, cup, award, bays, laurels **2** *lines of stuffed animal heads, trophies of his hunting hobby* = **souvenir**, spoils, relic, memento, booty, keepsake

tropical ADJECTIVE = **hot**, stifling, lush, steamy, humid, torrid, sultry, sweltering ■ OPPOSITE: cold

trot VERB *I trotted down the steps and out to the shed.* = **run**, jog, scamper, lope, go briskly, canter ▶ NOUN *He walked briskly, but without breaking into a trot.* = **run**, jog, lope, brisk pace, canter • **on the trot** *She lost five games on the trot.* = **one after the other**, in a row, in succession, without break, without interruption, consecutively • **trot something out** *Was it really necessary to trot out the same old stereotypes?* = **repeat**, relate, exhibit, bring up, reiterate (*formal*), recite, come out with, bring forward, drag up

troubadour NOUN = **minstrel**, singer, poet, balladeer, lyric poet, jongleur

trouble NOUN **1** *You've caused a lot of trouble.* = **bother**, problems, concern, worry, stress, difficulty, anxiety, distress, grief (*Brit. & S. African*), irritation, hassle (*informal*), strife, inconvenience, unease, disquiet, annoyance, agitation, commotion, unpleasantness, vexation **2** (*often plural*) *She tells me her troubles. I tell mine.* = **distress**, problem, suffering, worry, pain, anxiety, grief, torment, hardship, sorrow, woe, irritation, hassle (*informal*),

misfortune, heartache, disquiet, annoyance, agitation, tribulation, bummer (*slang*), vexation ■ OPPOSITE: pleasure **3** *He had never before had any heart trouble.* = **ailment**, disease, failure, complaint, upset, illness, disorder, defect, malfunction **4** *Riot police are being deployed to prevent any trouble.* = **disorder**, fighting, row, conflict, bother, grief (*Brit. & S. African*), unrest, disturbance, to-do (*informal*), discontent, dissatisfaction, furore, uproar, scuffling, discord, fracas, commotion, rumpus, breach of the peace, tumult, affray (*Law*), brouhaha, ructions, hullabaloo (*informal*), kerfuffle (*Brit. informal*), hoo-ha (*informal*), biffo (*Austral. slang*), boilover (*Austral.*) ■ OPPOSITE: peace **5** *He's no trouble at all, but his brother is rude and selfish.* = **problem**, bother, concern, pest, irritation, hassle (*informal*), nuisance, inconvenience, irritant, cause of annoyance **6** *You've saved us a lot of trouble by helping.* = **effort**, work, thought, care, labour, struggle, pains, bother, grief (*Brit. & S. African*), hassle (*informal*), inconvenience, exertion ■ OPPOSITE: convenience **7** *a charity that helps women in trouble with the law* = **difficulty**, hot water (*informal*), predicament, deep water (*informal*), spot (*informal*), danger, mess, dilemma, scrape (*informal*), pickle (*informal*), dire straits, tight spot ▶ VERB *Is anything troubling you?* = **bother**, worry, upset, disturb, distress, annoy, plague, grieve, torment, harass, hassle (*informal*), afflict, pain, fret, agitate, sadden, perplex, disconcert, disquiet, pester, vex, perturb, faze, give someone grief (*Brit. & S. African*), discompose, put or get someone's back up, hack you off (*informal*) ■ OPPOSITE: please **2** *The ulcer had been troubling her for several years.* = **afflict**, hurt, bother, cause discomfort to, pain, grieve **3** *'Good morning. I'm sorry to trouble you.'* = **inconvenience**, disturb, burden, put out, impose upon, discommode, incommode ■ OPPOSITE: relieve **4** *He yawns, not troubling to cover his mouth.* = **take pains**, take the time, make an effort, go to the effort of, exert yourself ■ OPPOSITE: avoid

troublemaker NOUN = **mischief-maker**, firebrand, instigator, agitator, bad apple (*informal*), rabble-rouser, agent provocateur (*French*), stirrer (*informal*), incendiary, rotten apple (*Brit. informal*), meddler, stormy petrel ■ OPPOSITE: peace-maker

troublesome ADJECTIVE **1** *The economy has become a troublesome problem for the party.* = **bothersome**, trying, taxing, demanding, difficult, worrying, upsetting, annoying, irritating, tricky, harassing, oppressive, arduous, tiresome, inconvenient, laborious, burdensome, hard, worrisome, irksome, wearisome, vexatious, importunate, pestilential, plaguy (*informal*) ■ **OPPOSITE: simple 2** *Parents may find that a troublesome teenager becomes unmanageable.* = **disorderly**, violent, turbulent, rebellious, unruly, rowdy, recalcitrant, undisciplined, uncooperative, refractory, insubordinate ■ **OPPOSITE:** well-behaved

trough NOUN = **manger**, crib, water trough

trounce VERB = **defeat someone heavily** *or* **utterly**, beat, thrash, slaughter (*informal*), stuff (*slang*), tank (*slang*), hammer (*informal*), crush, overwhelm, lick (*informal*), paste (*slang*), rout, walk over (*informal*), clobber (*slang*), run rings around (*informal*), wipe the floor with (*informal*), make mincemeat of, blow someone out of the water (*slang*), give someone a hiding (*informal*), drub, beat someone hollow (*Brit. informal*), give someone a pasting (*slang*)

troupe NOUN = **company**, group, band, cast, ensemble

truancy NOUN = **absence**, shirking, skiving (*Brit. slang*), malingering, absence without leave

truant NOUN *She became a truant at the age of ten.* = **absentee**, skiver (*Brit. slang*), shirker, dodger, runaway, delinquent, deserter, straggler, malingerer ▶ ADJECTIVE *Neither the parents nor the truant students showed up at court.* = **absent**, missing, skiving (*Brit. slang*), absent without leave, A.W.O.L. ▶ VERB *In his fourth year he was truanting regularly.* = **absent yourself**, play truant, skive (*Brit. slang*), bunk off (*slang*), desert, run away, dodge, wag (*dialect*), go missing, shirk, malinger, bob off (*Brit. slang*)

truce NOUN = **ceasefire**, break, stay, rest, peace, treaty, interval, moratorium, respite, lull, cessation, let-up (*informal*), armistice, intermission, cessation of hostilities

truculent ADJECTIVE = **hostile**, defiant, belligerent, bad-tempered, cross, violent, aggressive, fierce, contentious, combative, sullen, scrappy (*informal*), antagonistic, pugnacious, ill-tempered, bellicose, obstreperous, itching *or* spoiling for a fight (*informal*), aggro (*Austral. & N.Z.*), aggers (*Austral. slang*) ■ **OPPOSITE:** amiable

trudge VERB *We had to trudge up the track back to the station.* = **plod**, trek, tramp, traipse (*informal*), march, stump, hike, clump, lumber, slog, drag yourself, yomp, walk heavily, footslog ▶ NOUN *We were reluctant*

to start the long trudge home. = **tramp**, march, haul, trek, hike, slog, traipse (*informal*), yomp, footslog

true ADJECTIVE **1** *Everything I had heard about him was true.* = **correct**, right, accurate, exact, precise, valid, legitimate, factual, truthful, veritable, bona fide, veracious ■ **OPPOSITE:** false **2** *I allowed myself to acknowledge my true feelings.* = **actual**, real, natural, pure, genuine, proper, authentic, dinkum (*Austral. & N.Z. informal*), dinky-di (*Austral. & N.Z. informal*) **3** *He was always true to his wife.* = **faithful**, loyal, devoted, dedicated, firm, fast, constant, pure, steady, reliable, upright, sincere, honourable, honest, staunch, trustworthy, trusty, dutiful, true-blue, unswerving ■ **OPPOSITE:** unfaithful **4** *The score is usually a true reflection of events on the pitch.* = **exact**, perfect, correct, accurate, proper, precise, spot-on (*Brit. informal*), on target, unerring ■ **OPPOSITE:** inaccurate ▶ ADVERB **1** *Does the lad speak true?* = **truthfully**, honestly, veritably, veraciously, rightly **2** *Most of the bullets hit true.* = **precisely**, accurately, on target, perfectly, correctly, properly, unerringly

true-blue ADJECTIVE = **staunch**, confirmed, constant, devoted, dedicated, loyal, faithful, orthodox, uncompromising, trusty, unwavering, dyed-in-the-wool

truism NOUN = **cliché**, commonplace, platitude, axiom, stock phrase, trite saying

truly ADVERB **1** *a truly democratic system* = **genuinely**, really, correctly, truthfully, rightly, in fact, precisely, exactly, legitimately, accurately, in reality, in truth, beyond doubt, without a doubt, authentically, beyond question, factually, in actuality, veritably, veraciously ■ **OPPOSITE:** falsely **2** *a truly splendid man* = **really**, very, greatly, indeed, seriously (*informal*), extremely, to be sure, exceptionally, verily **3** *He truly loved his children.* = **faithfully**, firmly, constantly, steadily, honestly, sincerely, staunchly, dutifully, loyally, honourably, devotedly, with all your heart, with dedication, with devotion, confirmedly

trump VERB *The Socialists tried to trump this with their slogan.* = **outdo**, top, cap (*informal*), surpass, score points off, excel • **trump something up** *He insists that charges against him have been trumped up.* = **invent**, create, make up, manufacture, fake, contrive, fabricate, concoct, cook up (*informal*)

trumped up ADJECTIVE = **invented**, made-up, manufactured, false, fake, contrived, untrue, fabricated, concocted, falsified, cooked-up (*informal*), phoney or phony (*informal*) ■ **OPPOSITE:** genuine

trumpet NOUN **1** *Picking up his trumpet, he gave it a quick blow.* = **horn**, clarion, bugle **2** *The elephant gave a loud trumpet.* = **roar**, call, cry, bay, bellow ▶ VERB *He is trumpeted as the greatest talent of his generation.* = **proclaim**, advertise, extol, tout (*informal*), announce, publish, broadcast, crack up (*informal*), sound loudly, shout from the rooftops, noise abroad

■ **OPPOSITE:** keep secret • **blow your own trumpet** *The camera crew have good reason to blow their own trumpets.* = **boast**, crow, brag, vaunt, sing your own praises, big yourself up (*slang, chiefly Caribbean*)

truncate VERB = **shorten**, cut, crop, trim, clip, dock, prune, curtail, cut short, pare, lop, abbreviate ■ **OPPOSITE:** lengthen

truncheon NOUN = **club**, staff, stick, baton, cudgel, mere (*N.Z.*), patu (*N.Z.*)

trunk NOUN **1** *toadstools growing on fallen tree trunks* = **stem**, stock, stalk, bole **2** *He had left most of his records in a trunk in the attic.* = **chest**, case, box, crate, bin, suitcase, locker, coffer, casket, portmanteau, kist (*Scot. & Northern English, dialect*) **3** *Simultaneously, raise your trunk six inches above the ground.* = **body**, torso **4** *It could exert the suction power of an elephant's trunk.* = **snout**, nose, proboscis

truss VERB (*often with* **up**) *She trussed him with the bandage and gagged his mouth.* = **tie**, secure, bind, strap, fasten, tether, pinion, make fast ▶ NOUN **1** *For a hernia he introduced the simple solution of a truss.* = **support**, pad, bandage **2** *the bridge's arched, lightweight steel truss* = **joist**, support, stay, shore, beam, prop, brace, strut, buttress, stanchion

trust NOUN **1** *There's a feeling of warmth and trust here.* = **confidence**, credit, belief, faith, expectation, conviction, assurance, certainty, reliance, credence, certitude

■ **OPPOSITE:** distrust **2** *She held a position of trust, which was generously paid.* = **responsibility**, duty, obligation **3** *The British Library holds its collection in trust for the nation.* = **custody**, care, guard, protection, guardianship, safekeeping, trusteeship ▶ VERB **1** *'I trust you completely,' he said.* = **believe in**, have faith in, depend on, count on, bank on, lean on, rely upon, swear by, take at face value, take as gospel, place reliance on, place your trust in, pin your faith on, place or have confidence in

■ **OPPOSITE:** distrust **2** *I'd been willing to trust my life to him.* = **entrust**, commit, assign,

confide (*formal*), consign, put into the hands of, allow to look after, hand over, turn over, sign over, delegate **3** *We trust that they are considering our suggestion.* = **expect**, believe, hope, suppose, assume, guess (*informal*), take it, presume, surmise, think likely ■ **RELATED WORD:** *adjective* fiducial

trustful *or* **trusting** ADJECTIVE = **unsuspecting**, simple, innocent, optimistic, naive, confiding, gullible, unwary, unguarded, credulous, unsuspicious ■ **OPPOSITE:** suspicious

trustworthy ADJECTIVE = **dependable**, responsible, principled, mature, sensible, reliable, ethical, upright, true, honourable, honest, staunch, righteous, reputable, truthful, trusty, steadfast, level-headed, to be trusted ■ **OPPOSITE:** untrustworthy

trusty ADJECTIVE = **reliable**, dependable, trustworthy, responsible, solid, strong, firm, true, steady, faithful, straightforward, upright, honest, staunch ■ **OPPOSITE:** unreliable

truth NOUN **1** *Is it possible to separate truth from fiction?* = **reality**, fact(s), real life, actuality ■ **OPPOSITE:** unreality **2** *There is no truth in this story.* = **truthfulness**, fact, accuracy, honesty, precision, validity, legitimacy, authenticity, correctness, sincerity, verity, candour, veracity, rightness, genuineness, exactness, factuality, factualness

■ **OPPOSITE:** inaccuracy **3** *It's a universal truth that we all die eventually.* = **fact**, law, reality, certainty, maxim, verity, axiom, truism, proven principle **4** *His mission is to uphold truth, justice and the American way.* = **honesty**, principle, honour, virtue, integrity, goodness, righteousness, candour, frankness, probity (*formal*), rectitude, incorruptibility, uprightness

■ **OPPOSITE:** dishonesty ■ **RELATED WORDS:** *adjectives* veritable, veracious

truthful ADJECTIVE **1** *We are all fairly truthful about our personal lives.* = **honest**, frank, candid, upfront (*informal*), true, straight, reliable, faithful, straightforward, sincere, forthright, trustworthy, plain-spoken, veracious ■ **OPPOSITE:** dishonest **2** *They had not given a truthful account of what actually happened.* = **true**, correct, accurate, exact, realistic, precise, literal, veritable, naturalistic ■ **OPPOSITE:** untrue

try VERB **1** *He secretly tried to block her advancement in the Party.* = **attempt**, seek, aim, undertake, essay (*formal*), strive, struggle, endeavour, have a go, go for it (*informal*), make an effort, have a shot (*informal*), have a crack (*informal*), bend over backwards (*informal*), do your best, go for

broke (*slang*), make an attempt, move heaven and earth, bust a gut (*informal*), give it your best shot (*informal*), have a stab (*informal*), break your neck (*informal*), exert yourself, make an all-out effort (*informal*), knock yourself out (*informal*), have a whack (*informal*), do your damnedest (*informal*), give it your all (*informal*), front up, rupture yourself (*informal*) **2** *It's best not to try a new recipe on such an important occasion.*
= **experiment with**, try out, put to the test, test, taste, examine, investigate, sample, evaluate, check out, inspect, appraise **3** *The case was tried in Tampa, a changed venue with an all-white jury.* = **judge**, hear, consider, examine, adjudicate, adjudge, pass judgement on **4** *She really tried my patience.* = **tax**, test, trouble, pain, stress, upset, tire, strain, drain, exhaust, annoy, plague, irritate, weary, afflict, sap, inconvenience, wear out, vex, irk, make demands on, give someone grief (*Brit. & S. African*) ▶ NOUN *I didn't really expect anything, but it was worth a try.* = **attempt**, go (*informal*), shot (*informal*), effort, crack (*informal*), essay, stab (*informal*), bash (*informal*), endeavour, whack (*informal*) • **try something out** *She knew I wanted to try the boat out at the weekend.* = **test**, experiment with, appraise, put to the test, taste, sample, evaluate, check out, inspect, put into practice

trying ADJECTIVE = **annoying**, hard, taxing, difficult, tough, upsetting, irritating, fatiguing, stressful, aggravating (*informal*), troublesome, exasperating, arduous, tiresome, vexing, irksome, wearisome, bothersome ■ **OPPOSITE:** straightforward

tsar or **czar** NOUN *the government's new mental health tsar* = **head**, chief, boss, big cheese (*informal*), head honcho (*informal*), sherang (*Austral. & N.Z.*)

tubby ADJECTIVE = **fat**, overweight, plump, stout, chubby, obese, portly, roly-poly, podgy, corpulent, paunchy

tuck VERB *He tried to tuck his shirt inside his trousers.* = **push**, stick, stuff, slip, ease, insert, pop (*informal*) ▶ NOUN **1** *The wags from the rival house were ready to snaffle his tuck.* = **food**, eats (*slang*), tack (*informal*), scoff (*slang*), grub (*slang*), kai (*N.Z. informal*), nosh (*slang*), victuals, comestibles, nosebag (*slang*), vittles (*obsolete, dialect*) **2** *a tapered tuck used to take in fullness and control shape in a garment* = **fold**, gather, pleat, pinch • **tuck in** *Tuck in, it's the last hot food you'll get for a while.* = **eat up**, get stuck in (*informal*), eat heartily, fall to, chow down (*slang*) • **tuck someone in** *I read her a story and tucked her in.*

= **make snug**, wrap up, put to bed, bed down, swaddle

tuft NOUN = **clump**, bunch, shock, collection, knot, cluster, tussock, topknot

tug VERB **1** *A little boy tugged at her sleeve excitedly.* = **pull**, drag, pluck, jerk, yank, wrench, lug **2** *She tugged him along by his arm.* = **drag**, pull, haul, tow, lug, heave, draw ▶ NOUN *My head was snapped backwards by a tug on my air hose.* = **pull**, jerk, yank, wrench, drag, haul, tow, traction, heave

tuition NOUN = **training**, schooling, education, teaching, lessons, instruction, tutoring, tutelage (*formal*)

tumble VERB *The dog had tumbled down the cliff.* = **fall**, drop, topple, plummet, roll, pitch, toss, stumble, flop, trip up, fall head over heels, fall headlong, fall end over end ▶ NOUN *He injured his knee in a tumble from his horse.* = **fall**, drop, roll, trip, collapse, plunge, spill (*informal*), toss, stumble, flop, headlong fall

tummy NOUN = **stomach**, belly, abdomen, corporation (*informal*), pot, gut (*informal*), paunch, tum (*informal*), spare tyre (*informal*), breadbasket (*slang*), potbelly

tumour or (*U.S.*) **tumor** NOUN = **growth**, cancer, swelling, lump, carcinoma (*Pathology*), sarcoma (*Medical*), neoplasm (*Medical*)

tumult NOUN **1** *the recent tumult in global financial markets* = **disturbance**, trouble, chaos, turmoil, storms, upset, stir, disorder, excitement, unrest, upheaval, havoc (*informal*), mayhem, strife, disarray, turbulence, ferment, agitation, convulsions, bedlam **2** *Round one ended to a tumult of whistles, screams and shouts.* = **clamour**, row, outbreak, racket, din, uproar, fracas, commotion, pandemonium, babel, hubbub, hullabaloo ■ **OPPOSITE:** silence

tumultuous ADJECTIVE **1** *the tumultuous changes in Eastern Europe* = **turbulent**, exciting, confused, disturbed, hectic, stormy, agitated ■ **OPPOSITE:** quiet **2** *Delegates greeted the news with tumultuous applause.* = **wild**, excited, riotous, unrestrained, violent, raging, disorderly, fierce, passionate, noisy, restless, unruly, rowdy, boisterous, full-on (*informal*), lawless, vociferous, rumbustious, uproarious, obstreperous, clamorous

tune NOUN **1** *She was humming a merry little tune.* = **melody**, air, song, theme, strain(s), motif, jingle, ditty, choon (*slang*), melody line **2** *It was an ordinary voice, but he sang in tune.* = **harmony**, pitch, euphony ▶ VERB **1** *They were quietly tuning their instruments.*

= **tune up**, adjust, bring into harmony **2** *He will rapidly be tuned to the keynote of his new associates.* = **regulate**, adapt, modulate, harmonize, attune, pitch

tuneful ADJECTIVE = **melodious**, musical, pleasant, harmonious, melodic, catchy, consonant (*Music*), symphonic, mellifluous, easy on the ear (*informal*), euphonious, euphonic ■ **OPPOSITE:** discordant

tunnel NOUN *two new railway tunnels through the Alps* = **passage**, underpass, passageway, subway, channel, hole, shaft
▶ VERB *The rebels tunnelled out of a maximum security jail.* = **dig**, dig your way, burrow, mine, bore, drill, excavate

turbulence NOUN = **confusion**, turmoil, unrest, instability, storm, boiling, disorder, upheaval, agitation, commotion, pandemonium, tumult, roughness
■ **OPPOSITE:** peace

turbulent ADJECTIVE **1** *six turbulent years of rows and reconciliations* = **wild**, violent, disorderly, agitated, rebellious, unruly, rowdy, boisterous, anarchic, tumultuous, lawless, unbridled, riotous, undisciplined, seditious, mutinous, ungovernable, uproarious, refractory, obstreperous, insubordinate **2** *I had to have a boat that could handle turbulent seas.* = **stormy**, rough, raging, tempestuous, boiling, disordered, furious, unsettled, foaming, unstable, agitated, tumultuous, choppy, blustery
■ **OPPOSITE:** calm

turf NOUN **1** *They shuffled slowly down the turf towards the cliff's edge.* = **grass**, green, sward **2** *Lift the turfs carefully – they can be reused elsewhere.* = **sod**, divot, clod • **the turf** *He has sent out only three winners on the turf this year.* = **horse-racing**, the flat, racecourse, racetrack, racing • **turf someone out** *stories of people being turfed out and ending up on the streets* = **throw out**, evict, cast out, kick out (*informal*), fire (*informal*), dismiss, sack (*informal*), bounce (*slang*), discharge, expel, oust, relegate, banish, eject, dispossess, chuck out (*informal*), fling out, kiss off (*slang, chiefly U.S. & Canad.*), show someone the door, give someone the sack (*informal*), give someone the bum's rush (*slang*), kennet (*Austral. slang*), jeff (*Austral. slang*)

turgid ADJECTIVE = **pompous**, inflated, windy, high-flown, pretentious, grandiose, flowery, overblown, stilted, ostentatious, fulsome, bombastic, grandiloquent, arty-farty (*informal*), fustian, orotund, magniloquent, sesquipedalian, tumid

turmoil NOUN = **confusion**, trouble, violence, row, noise, stir, disorder, chaos, disturbance, upheaval, bustle, flurry, strife, disarray, uproar, turbulence, ferment, agitation, commotion, pandemonium, bedlam, tumult, hubbub, brouhaha
■ **OPPOSITE:** peace

turn VERB **1** (*sometimes with* **round**) *He turned abruptly and walked away.* = **change course**, swing round, wheel round, veer, move, return, go back, switch, shift, reverse, swerve, change position **2** *As the wheel turned, the potter shaped the clay.* = **rotate**, spin, go round (and round), revolve, roll, circle, wheel, twist, spiral, whirl, swivel, pivot, twirl, gyrate, go round in circles, move in a circle **3** *The taxi turned the corner of the lane and stopped.* = **go round**, come round, negotiate, pass, corner, pass around, take a bend **4** (*with* **into**) *She turned the house into a beautiful home.* = **change**, transform, fashion, shape, convert, alter, adapt, mould, remodel, form, mutate, refit, metamorphose, transmute, transfigure **5** *finely-turned metal* = **shape**, form, fashion, cast, frame, construct, execute, mould, make **6** *The true facts will turn your stomach.* = **sicken**, upset, nauseate **7** *milk starting to turn in the refrigerator* = **go bad**, go off (*Brit. informal*), curdle, go sour, become rancid **8** *Warm temperatures can turn milk.* = **make rancid**, spoil, sour, taint ▶ NOUN **1** *The rear sprocket will turn only twice for one turn of the pedals.* = **rotation**, turning, cycle, circle, revolution, spin, twist, reversal, whirl, swivel, pivot, gyration **2** *You can't do a right-hand turn here.* = **change of direction**, bend, curve, change of course, shift, departure, deviation **3** *The scandal took a new turn today.* = **direction**, course, tack, swing, tendency, drift, bias **4** *Let each child have a turn at fishing.* = **opportunity**, go, spell, shot (*informal*), time, try, round, chance, period, shift, crack (*informal*), succession, fling, stint, whack (*informal*) **5** *I think I'll just go up and take a turn round the deck.* = **stroll**, airing, walk, drive, ride, spin (*informal*), circuit, constitutional, outing, excursion, promenade, jaunt, saunter **6** *He did you a good turn by resigning.* = **deed**, service, act, action, favour, gesture **7** *It gave me quite a turn.* = **shock**, start, surprise, scare, jolt, fright **8** *She has a turn for gymnastic exercises.* = **inclination**, talent, gift, leaning, bent, bias, flair, affinity, knack, propensity, aptitude • **by turns** *His tone was by turns angry and aggrieved.* = **alternately**, in succession, turn and turn about, reciprocally • **to a turn** *sweet tomatoes roasted to a turn* = **perfectly**, correctly, precisely, exactly, just right

• **turn off** He turned off only to find that he was trapped in the main square. = **branch off**, leave, quit, depart from, deviate, change direction, take a side road, take another road • **turn on someone** The demonstrators turned on the police. = **attack**, assault, fall on, round on, lash out at, assail, lay into (informal), let fly at, lose your temper with • **turn on something** It all turns on what his real motives are. = **depend on**, hang on, rest on, hinge on, be decided by, balance on, be contingent on, pivot on • **turn out 1** It turned out that I knew the person who got shot. = **prove to be**, transpire, become apparent, happen, emerge, become known, develop, come to light, crop up (informal) **2** Things don't always turn out the way we expect. = **end up**, happen, result, work out, evolve, come to be, come about, transpire (informal), pan out (informal), eventuate **3** Thousands of people turned out for the funeral. = **come**, be present, turn up, show up (informal), go, appear, attend, gather, assemble, put in an appearance • **turn over** The buggy turned over and she was thrown out. = **overturn**, tip over, flip over, upend, be upset, reverse, capsize, keel over • **turn someone off** Rude people turn me off completely. = **repel**, bore, put someone off, disgust, offend, irritate, alienate, sicken, displease, nauseate, gross someone out (U.S. slang), disenchant, lose your interest • **turn someone on** What turns me on is helping people achieve greater things. = **arouse**, attract, excite, thrill, stimulate, please, press someone's buttons (slang), work someone up, titillate, ring someone's bell (U.S. slang), arouse someone's desire • **turn someone out** It was a monastery but the authorities turned all the monks out. = **expel**, drive out, evict, throw out, fire (informal), dismiss, sack (informal), axe (informal), discharge, oust, relegate, banish, deport, put out, cashier, unseat, dispossess, kick out (informal), cast out, drum out, show the door, turf out (Brit. informal), give someone the sack (informal), give someone the bum's rush (slang), kiss off (slang, chiefly U.S. & Canad.), kennet (Austral. slang), jeff (Austral. slang) • **turn something down 1** I thanked him for the offer but turned it down. = **refuse**, decline, reject, spurn, rebuff, say no to, repudiate, abstain from, throw something out **2** The police told the DJs to turn down the music. = **lower**, soften, reduce the volume of, mute, lessen, muffle, quieten, diminish • **turn something in** He told her to turn in her library books. = **hand in**, return, deliver, give back, give up, hand over, submit, surrender,

tender • **turn something off** She had turned off the light to go to sleep. = **switch off**, turn out, put out, stop, kill (informal), cut out, shut down, unplug, flick off • **turn something on** Why haven't you turned the lights on? = **switch on**, put on, activate, start, start up, ignite, kick-start, set in motion, energize • **turn something out 1** I'll read till they come round to turn the lights out. = **turn off**, put out, switch off, extinguish, disconnect, unplug, flick off **2** They have been turning out great furniture for 400 years. = **produce**, make, process, finish, manufacture, assemble, put together, put out, bring out, fabricate, churn out • **turn something over 1** She was turning over the pages of the directory. = **flip over**, flick through, leaf through **2** You could see her turning things over in her mind. = **consider**, think about, contemplate, ponder, reflect on, wonder about, mull over, think over, deliberate on, give thought to, ruminate about, revolve **3** The lawyer turned over the release papers. = **hand over**, transfer, deliver, commit, give up, yield, surrender, pass on, render, assign, commend (formal), give over **4** I squeezed into the seat and turned the engine over. = **start up**, warm up, activate, switch on, crank, set something in motion, set something going, switch on the ignition of • **turn something up 1** Investigations have never turned up any evidence. = **find**, reveal, discover, expose, come up with, disclose, unearth, dig up, bring to light **2** I turned the volume up. = **increase**, raise, boost, enhance, intensify, amplify, increase the volume of, make louder • **turn up 1** He turned up on Christmas Day with a friend. = **arrive**, come, appear, show up (informal), show (informal), attend, put in an appearance, show your face **2** The rare spoon turned up in an old house in Devon. = **come to light**, be found, show up, pop up, materialize, appear

turning NOUN **1** Take the next turning on the right. = **turn-off**, turn, junction, crossroads, side road, exit **2** = **bend**, turn, curve

turning point NOUN = **crossroads**, critical moment, decisive moment, change, crisis, crux, moment of truth, point of no return, moment of decision, climacteric, tipping point

turn-off NOUN = **turning**, turn, branch, exit, side road

turnout NOUN = **attendance**, crowd, audience, gate, assembly, congregation, number, throng, assemblage

turnover NOUN **1** The company had a turnover of £3.8 million. = **output**, business, production, flow, volume, yield, productivity, outturn (*rare*) **2** *Short-term contracts increase staff turnover.* = **movement**, replacement, coming and going, change

tussle VERB *They ended up tussling with the security staff.* = **fight**, battle, struggle, scrap (*informal*), contend, wrestle, vie, brawl, grapple, scuffle ▶ NOUN *The referee booked him for a tussle with the goalie.* = **fight**, scrap (*informal*), brawl, scuffle, battle, competition, struggle, conflict, contest, set-to (*informal*), bout, contention, fray, punch-up (*Brit. informal*), fracas, shindig (*informal*), scrimmage, shindy (*informal*), bagarre (*French*), biffo (*Austral. slang*)

tutelage NOUN = **guidance**, education, instruction, preparation, schooling, charge, care, teaching, protection, custody, tuition, dependence, patronage, guardianship, wardship

tutor NOUN *He surprised his tutors by failing the exam.* = **teacher**, coach, instructor, educator, guide, governor, guardian, lecturer, guru, mentor, preceptor, master *or* mistress, schoolmaster *or* schoolmistress ▶ VERB *She was at home, being tutored with her brothers.* = **teach**, educate, school, train, coach, guide, discipline, lecture, drill, instruct, edify, direct

tutorial NOUN *Methods of study include lectures, tutorials and practical work.* = **seminar**, lesson, individual instruction ▶ ADJECTIVE *Students may seek tutorial guidance.* = **teaching**, coaching, guiding, instructional

TV NOUN = **television**, telly (*Brit. informal*), the box (*Brit. informal*), receiver, the tube (*slang*), television set, TV set, small screen (*informal*), gogglebox (*Brit. slang*), idiot box (*slang*)

twaddle NOUN = **nonsense**, rubbish, rot (*informal*), garbage (*informal*), pants (*slang*), gossip, crap (*slang*), trash, hot air (*informal*), tosh (*slang, chiefly Brit.*), waffle (*informal, chiefly Brit.*), pap, bilge (*informal*), drivel, tripe (*informal*), guff (*slang*), tattle, moonshine, verbiage, gabble, claptrap (*informal*), gobbledegook (*informal*), hogwash, hokum (*slang, chiefly U.S. & Canad.*), rigmarole, blather, piffle (*informal*), poppycock (*informal*), inanity, balderdash, bosh (*informal*), eyewash (*informal*), trumpery, tommyrot, foolish talk, horsefeathers (*U.S. slang*), bunkum *or* buncombe (*informal*), bizzo (*Austral. slang*), bull's wool (*Austral. & N.Z. slang*)

tweak VERB *He tweaked my ear roughly.* = **twist**, pull, pinch, jerk, squeeze, nip, twitch ▶ NOUN *a tweak on the ear* = **twist**, pull, squeeze, pinch, jerk, nip, twitch

twee ADJECTIVE **1** *twee musical boxes shaped like cottages* = **sweet**, pretty, cute, sentimental, quaint, dainty, cutesy (*informal*), bijou, precious **2** *Although twee at times, the script is well-constructed.* = **sentimental**, over-sentimental, soppy (*Brit. informal*), mawkish, affected, precious

twiddle VERB = **fiddle with**, adjust, finger, play with, juggle, wiggle (*informal*), twirl, jiggle, monkey with (*informal*)

twig[1] NOUN *There was a slight sound of a twig breaking underfoot.* = **branch**, stick, sprig, offshoot, shoot, spray, withe

twig[2] VERB *By the time she'd twigged what it was all about, it was too late.* = **understand**, get, see, find out, grasp, make out, rumble (*Brit. informal*), catch on (*informal*), comprehend, fathom, tumble to (*informal*)

twilight NOUN **1** *They returned at twilight and set off for the bar.* = **dusk**, evening, sunset, early evening, nightfall, sundown, gloaming (*Scot., poetic*), close of day, evo (*Austral. slang*) ■ OPPOSITE: dawn **2** *the deepening autumn twilight* = **half-light**, gloom, dimness, semi-darkness **3** *Now they are both in the twilight of their careers.* = **decline**, last years, final years, closing years, autumn, downturn, ebb, last phase ■ OPPOSITE: height ▶ ADJECTIVE **1** *the summer twilight sky* = **evening**, dim, darkening, evo (*Austral. slang*) **2** *the twilight years of the Hapsburg Empire* = **declining**, last, final, dying, ebbing

twin NOUN *the twin of the chair she had at the cottage* = **double**, counterpart, mate, match, fellow, clone, duplicate, lookalike, likeness, ringer (*slang*), corollary ▶ VERB *The borough is twinned with Kasel in Germany.* = **pair**, match, join, couple, link, yoke ▶ ADJECTIVE *the twin spires of the cathedral* = **identical**, matched, matching, double, paired, parallel, corresponding, dual, duplicate, twofold, geminate

twine NOUN *a ball of twine* = **string**, cord, yarn, strong thread ▶ VERB **1** *He twined his fingers into hers.* = **twist together**, weave, knit, braid, splice, interweave, plait, entwine, interlace, twist **2** *These strands of molecules twine around each other.* = **coil**, wind, surround, bend, wrap, twist, curl, loop, spiral, meander, encircle, wreathe

twinge NOUN **1** *I would have twinges of guilt occasionally.* = **pang**, twitch, tweak, throe (*rare*), twist **2** *the occasional twinge of indigestion* = **pain**, sharp pain, gripe, stab, bite, twist, stitch, pinch, throb, twitch, prick, spasm, tweak, tic

twinkle VERB *At night, lights twinkle in distant villages across the valleys.* = **sparkle**, flash, shine, glitter, gleam, blink, flicker, wink, shimmer, glint, glisten, scintillate, coruscate ▶ NOUN **1** *A kindly twinkle came into his eyes.* = **sparkle**, light, flash, spark, shine, glittering, gleam, blink, flicker, wink, shimmer, glimmer, glistening, scintillation, coruscation **2** *Hours can pass in a twinkle.* = **moment**, second, shake (*informal*), flash, instant, tick (*Brit. informal*), twinkling, split second, jiffy (*informal*), trice, two shakes of a lamb's tail (*informal*)

twinkling or **twink** NOUN = **moment**, second, flash, instant, tick (*Brit. informal*), twinkle, split second, jiffy (*informal*), trice, two shakes of a lamb's tail (*informal*), shake (*informal*), bat of an eye (*informal*)

twirl VERB **1** *She twirled an empty glass in her fingers.* = **twiddle**, turn, rotate, wind, spin, twist, revolve, whirl **2** *Several hundred people twirl around the dance floor.* = **turn**, whirl, wheel, spin, twist, pivot, gyrate, pirouette, turn on your heel ▶ NOUN *with a twirl of his silver-handled cane* = **turn**, spin, rotation, whirl, wheel, revolution, twist, pirouette, gyration

twist VERB **1** *She twisted her hair into a bun.* = **coil**, curl, wind, plait, wrap, screw, twirl **2** *The fibres are twisted together during spinning.* = **intertwine**, wind, weave, braid, interweave, plait, entwine, twine, wreathe, interlace **3** *The car was left a mess of twisted metal.* = **distort**, screw up, contort, mangle, mangulate (*Austral. slang*) ■ **OPPOSITE:** straighten **4** *He fell and twisted his ankle.* = **sprain**, turn, rick, wrench **5** *It's a shame the way the media can twist your words.* = **misrepresent**, distort, misquote, alter, change, pervert, warp, falsify, garble **6** *He tried to twist out of my grasp.* = **squirm**, wriggle, writhe ▶ NOUN **1** *This little story has a twist in its tail.* = **surprise**, change, turn (*informal*), development, revelation, reveal **2** *The political debate took on a new twist.* = **development**, emphasis, variation, slant **3** *The bag is resealed with a simple twist of the valve.* = **wind**, turn, spin, swivel, twirl **4** *the bare bulb hanging from a twist of flex* = **coil**, roll, curl, hank, twine **5** *the twists and turns of the existing track* = **curve**, turn, bend, loop, arc, kink, zigzag, convolution, dog-leg, undulation **6** *If only she could alter this personality twist.* = **trait**, fault, defect, peculiarity, bent, characteristic, flaw, deviation, quirk, eccentricity, oddity, aberration, imperfection, kink, foible, idiosyncrasy, proclivity (*formal*), crotchet **7** *A twist of the ankle denied him a place on the* substitutes' bench. = **sprain**, turn, pull, jerk, wrench

twit NOUN = **fool**, idiot, jerk (*slang, chiefly U.S. & Canad.*), charlie (*Brit. informal*), dope (*informal*), clown, ass, plank (*Brit. slang*), berk (*Brit. slang*), wally (*slang*), prat (*slang*), plonker (*slang*), chump (*informal*), oaf, simpleton, airhead (*slang*), dipstick (*Brit. slang*), schmuck (*U.S. slang*), dork (*slang*), nitwit (*informal*), blockhead, ninny, divvy (*Brit. slang*), pillock (*Brit. slang*), halfwit, silly-billy (*informal*), nincompoop, dweeb (*U.S. slang*), putz (*U.S. slang*), weenie (*U.S. informal*), eejit (*Scot. & Irish*), dumb-ass (*slang*), numpty (*Scot. informal*), doofus (*slang, chiefly U.S.*), juggins (*Brit. informal*), numbskull or numskull, twerp or twirp (*informal*), dorba or dorb (*Austral. slang*)

twitch VERB **1** *His left eyelid twitched involuntarily.* = **jerk**, blink, flutter, jump, squirm **2** *He twitched his curtains to check on callers.* = **pull (at)**, snatch (at), tug (at), pluck (at), yank (at) ▶ NOUN *He developed a nervous twitch.* = **jerk**, tic, spasm, twinge, jump, blink, flutter, tremor

twitter VERB **1** *There were birds twittering in the trees.* = **chirrup**, whistle, chatter, trill, chirp, warble, cheep, tweet **2** *They were twittering excitedly about their new dresses.* = **chatter**, chat, rabbit (on) (*Brit. informal*), gossip, babble, gab (*informal*), prattle, natter, jabber, blather, prate ▶ NOUN *She would waken to the twitter of birds.* = **chirrup**, call, song, cry, whistle, chatter, trill, chirp, warble, cheep, tweet

two-faced ADJECTIVE = **hypocritical**, false, deceiving, treacherous, deceitful, untrustworthy, insincere, double-dealing, duplicitous, dissembling, perfidious (*literary*), Janus-faced ■ **OPPOSITE:** honest

tycoon NOUN = **magnate**, capitalist, baron, industrialist, financier, fat cat (*slang*), mogul, captain of industry, potentate, wealthy businessperson, big cheese (*slang, old-fashioned*), plutocrat, big noise (*informal*), merchant prince

type NOUN **1** *There are various types of the disease.* = **kind**, sort, class, variety, group, form, order, style, species, breed, strain, category, stamp, kidney, genre, classification, ilk, subdivision **2** *The correction has already been set in type.* = **print**, printing, face, case, characters, font, fount

typhoon NOUN = **storm**, tornado, cyclone, tempest (*literary*), squall, tropical storm

typical ADJECTIVE **1** *such typical schoolgirl pastimes as horse-riding and reading* = **archetypal**, standard, model, normal, classic, stock, essential, representative, usual, conventional, regular, characteristic, orthodox, indicative, illustrative, archetypal, stereotypical ■ **OPPOSITE:** unusual **2** *That's just typical of you, isn't it?* = **characteristic**, in keeping, in character, true to type **3** *not exactly your typical Sunday afternoon stroll* = **average**, normal, usual, conventional, routine, regular, orthodox, predictable, run-of-the-mill, bog-standard (*Brit. & Irish slang*)

typify VERB = **represent**, illustrate, sum up, characterize, embody, exemplify, personify, incarnate, epitomize

tyrannical *or* **tyrannic** ADJECTIVE = **oppressive**, cruel, authoritarian, dictatorial, severe, absolute, unreasonable, arbitrary, unjust, autocratic, inhuman, coercive, imperious, domineering, overbearing, magisterial, despotic, high-handed, peremptory, overweening, tyrannous ■ **OPPOSITE:** liberal

tyranny NOUN = **oppression**, cruelty, dictatorship, authoritarianism, reign of terror, despotism, autocracy, absolutism, coercion, high-handedness, harsh discipline, unreasonableness, imperiousness, peremptoriness ■ **OPPOSITE:** liberality

tyrant NOUN = **dictator**, bully, authoritarian, oppressor, despot, autocrat, absolutist, martinet, slave-driver

tyro *or* **tiro** NOUN = **beginner**, novice, apprentice, learner, neophyte (*formal*), rookie (*informal*), greenhorn (*informal*), catechumen

t

Uu

ubiquitous ADJECTIVE = **ever-present**, pervasive, omnipresent, all-over, everywhere, universal

ugly ADJECTIVE **1** *She makes me feel dowdy and ugly.* = **unattractive**, homely (*chiefly U.S.*), plain, unsightly, unlovely, unprepossessing, not much to look at, no oil painting (*informal*), ill-favoured, hard-featured, hard-favoured ■ OPPOSITE: beautiful **2** *an ugly scene* = **unpleasant**, shocking, terrible (*informal*), offensive, nasty, disgusting, revolting, obscene, hideous, monstrous, vile, distasteful, horrid (*informal*), repulsive, frightful, objectionable, disagreeable, repugnant ■ OPPOSITE: pleasant **3** *He's in an ugly mood today.* = **bad-tempered**, nasty, sullen, surly, threatening, dangerous, angry, forbidding, menacing, sinister, ominous, malevolent, spiteful, baleful, bodeful ■ OPPOSITE: good-natured

ulcer NOUN = **sore**, abscess, gathering (*informal*), peptic ulcer, gumboil

ulterior ADJECTIVE = **hidden**, secret, concealed, personal, secondary, selfish, covert, undisclosed, unexpressed ■ OPPOSITE: obvious

ultimate ADJECTIVE **1** *He said it is still not possible to predict the ultimate outcome.* = **final**, eventual, conclusive, last, end, furthest, extreme, terminal, decisive **2** *the ultimate cause of what's happened* = **fundamental**, basic, primary, radical, elemental **3** *Of course the ultimate authority remained the presidency.* = **supreme**, highest, greatest, maximum, paramount, most significant, superlative, topmost **4** *Treachery was the ultimate sin.* = **worst**, greatest, utmost, extreme **5** *the ultimate luxury foods* = **best**, greatest, supreme, optimum, quintessential ▶ NOUN *This hotel is the ultimate in luxury.* = **epitome**, height, greatest, summit, peak, extreme, perfection, the last word

ultimately ADVERB **1** *a tough but ultimately worthwhile struggle* = **finally**, eventually, in the end, after all, at last, at the end of the day, sooner or later, in the fullness of time, in due time **2** *Ultimately, Bismarck's revisionism scarcely affected British interests.*

= **fundamentally**, essentially, basically, primarily, at heart, deep down

ultra-modern ADJECTIVE = **advanced**, progressive, avant-garde, futuristic, ahead of its time, modernistic, neoteric (*rare*)

umbrella NOUN **1** *Harry held an umbrella over Dawn.* = **brolly** (*Brit. informal*), parasol, sunshade, gamp **2** *under the moral umbrella of the United Nations* = **cover**, protection, guardianship, backing, support, charge, care, agency, responsibility, guidance, patronage, auspices, aegis, safe keeping, protectorship

umpire NOUN *The umpire's decision is final.* = **referee**, judge, ref (*informal*), arbiter, arbitrator, moderator, adjudicator, umpie (*Austral. slang*) ▶ VERB *He umpired for school football matches.* = **referee**, judge, adjudicate, arbitrate, call (*Sport*), moderate, mediate

umpteen ADJECTIVE = **very many**, numerous, countless, millions, gazillions (*informal*), considerable, a good many, a thousand and one, ever so many

unable ADJECTIVE (*with* **to**) = **incapable**, inadequate, powerless, unfit, unfitted, not able, impotent, not up to, unqualified, ineffectual, not equal to ■ OPPOSITE: able

unaccountable ADJECTIVE **1** *He had an unaccountable change of mind.* = **inexplicable**, mysterious, baffling, odd, strange, puzzling, peculiar, incomprehensible, inscrutable, unfathomable, unexplainable ■ OPPOSITE: understandable **2** *Economic policy should not be run by an unaccountable committee.* = **not answerable**, exempt, not responsible, free, unliable

unaccustomed ADJECTIVE **1** *He comforted me with unaccustomed gentleness.* = **unfamiliar**, unusual, unexpected, new, special, surprising, strange, remarkable, unprecedented, uncommon, out of the ordinary, unwonted ■ OPPOSITE: familiar **2** (*with* **to**) *They were unaccustomed to such military setbacks.* = **not used to**, unfamiliar with, unused to, not given to, a newcomer to, a novice at, inexperienced at, unversed in, unpractised in ■ OPPOSITE: used to

unaffected[1] ADJECTIVE *this unaffected, charming couple* = **natural**, genuine, unpretentious, simple, plain, straightforward, naive, sincere, honest, unassuming, unspoilt, unsophisticated, dinkum (*Austral. & N.Z. informal*), artless, ingenuous, without airs, unstudied ■ OPPOSITE: pretentious

unaffected[2] ADJECTIVE (*often with* **by**) *She seemed totally unaffected by what she'd drunk.* = **impervious to**, unchanged, untouched,

u

unimpressed, unmoved, unaltered, not influenced, unresponsive to, unstirred ■ **OPPOSITE:** affected

unanimity NOUN = **agreement**, accord, consensus, concert, unity, harmony, chorus, unison, assent, concord, one mind, concurrence, like-mindedness ■ **OPPOSITE:** disagreement

unanimous ADJECTIVE **1** *Editors were unanimous in their condemnation of the proposals.* = **agreed**, united, in agreement, agreeing, at one, harmonious, like-minded, concordant, of one mind, of the same mind, in complete accord ■ **OPPOSITE:** divided **2** *the unanimous vote for Hungarian membership* = **united**, common, concerted, solid, consistent, harmonious, undivided, congruent, concordant, unopposed ■ **OPPOSITE:** split

unanimously ADVERB = **without exception**, by common consent, without opposition, with one accord, unitedly, nem. con.

unarmed ADJECTIVE = **defenceless**, helpless, unprotected, without arms, unarmoured, weaponless ■ **OPPOSITE:** armed

unassailable ADJECTIVE *His legal position is unassailable.* = **undeniable**, indisputable, irrefutable, sound, proven, positive, absolute, conclusive, incontrovertible, incontestable ■ **OPPOSITE:** doubtful

unassuming ADJECTIVE = **modest**, quiet, humble, meek, simple, reserved, retiring, unpretentious, unobtrusive, self-effacing, diffident, unassertive, unostentatious ■ **OPPOSITE:** conceited

unattached ADJECTIVE **1** *Those who are unattached may find that a potential mate is very close.* = **single**, available, unmarried, on your own, by yourself, a free agent, not spoken for, left on the shelf, footloose and fancy-free, unengaged **2** (*often with* **to**) *There's one nursery which is unattached to any school.* = **independent (from)**, unaffiliated (to), nonaligned (to), free (from), autonomous (from), uncommitted (to) ■ **OPPOSITE:** attached (to)

unavoidable ADJECTIVE = **inevitable**, inescapable, inexorable, sure, certain, necessary, fated, compulsory, obligatory, bound to happen, ineluctable

unaware ADJECTIVE = **ignorant**, unconscious, oblivious, in the dark (*informal*), unsuspecting, uninformed, unknowing, heedless, unenlightened, unmindful, not in the loop (*informal*), incognizant ■ **OPPOSITE:** aware

unawares ADVERB **1** *The suspect was taken unawares.* = **by surprise**, unprepared, off guard, suddenly, unexpectedly, abruptly, aback, without warning, on the hop (*Brit. informal*), caught napping ■ **OPPOSITE:** prepared **2** *It is quite easy to trip over one of the birds unawares.* = **unknowingly**, unwittingly, unconsciously ■ **OPPOSITE:** knowingly

unbalanced ADJECTIVE **1** *unbalanced and unfair reporting* = **biased**, one-sided, prejudiced, unfair, partial, partisan, unjust, inequitable **2** *unbalanced and uncontrolled diets* = **irregular**, not balanced, lacking **3** *The plane was notoriously unbalanced.* = **shaky**, unstable, wobbly ■ **OPPOSITE:** stable

unbearable ADJECTIVE = **intolerable**, insufferable, unendurable, too much (*informal*), unacceptable, oppressive, insupportable ■ **OPPOSITE:** tolerable

unbeatable ADJECTIVE **1** *These resorts remain unbeatable in terms of price.* = **unsurpassed**, matchless, unsurpassable **2** *The opposition was unbeatable.* = **invincible**, unstoppable, indomitable, unconquerable

unbeaten ADJECTIVE = **undefeated**, winning, triumphant, victorious, unsurpassed, unbowed, unvanquished, unsubdued

unbelievable ADJECTIVE **1** *His guitar solos are just unbelievable.* = **wonderful**, excellent, superb, fantastic (*informal*), mean (*slang*), great (*informal*), topping (*Brit. slang*), bad (*slang*), cracking (*Brit. informal*), crucial (*slang*), smashing (*informal*), magnificent, fabulous (*informal*), divine (*informal*), glorious, terrific (*informal*), splendid, sensational (*informal*), mega (*slang*), sick (*slang*), sovereign, awesome (*slang*), colossal, super (*informal*), wicked (*informal*), def (*slang*), brill (*informal*), stupendous, bodacious (*slang, chiefly U.S.*), boffo (*slang*), jim-dandy (*slang*), chillin' (*U.S. slang*), booshit (*Austral. slang*), exo (*Austral. slang*), sik (*Austral. slang*), rad (*informal*), phat (*slang*), schmick (*Austral. informal*), beaut (*informal*), barrie (*Scot. slang*), belting (*Brit. slang*), pearler (*Austral. slang*) ■ **OPPOSITE:** terrible **2** *I find it unbelievable that people can accept this sort of behaviour.* = **incredible**, impossible, unthinkable, astonishing, staggering, questionable, improbable, inconceivable, preposterous, unconvincing, unimaginable, outlandish, far-fetched, implausible, beyond belief, jaw-dropping, eye-popping (*informal*), cock-and-bull (*informal*) ■ **OPPOSITE:** believable

u

unbeliever NOUN = **atheist**, sceptic, disbeliever, agnostic, infidel, doubting Thomas

unborn ADJECTIVE = **expected**, awaited, embryonic, in utero (*Latin*)

unbridled ADJECTIVE = **unrestrained**, uncontrolled, unchecked, violent, excessive, rampant, unruly, full-on (*informal*), wanton, riotous, intemperate, ungovernable, unconstrained, licentious, ungoverned, uncurbed

unbroken ADJECTIVE **1** *Against all odds her glasses remained unbroken after the explosion.* = **intact**, whole, undamaged, complete, total, entire, solid, untouched, unscathed, unspoiled, unimpaired ■ OPPOSITE: broken **2** *The ruling party has governed the country for an unbroken thirty years.* = **continuous**, uninterrupted, constant, successive, endless, progressive, incessant, ceaseless, unremitting ■ OPPOSITE: interrupted **3** *We maintained an almost unbroken silence.* = **undisturbed**, uninterrupted, sound, fast, deep, profound, untroubled, unruffled **4** *The car plunged like an unbroken horse.* = **untamed**, wild, undomesticated

unburden VERB **1** *He had to unburden his soul to somebody.* = **reveal**, confide, disclose, lay bare, unbosom **2** *The human touch is one of the surest ways of unburdening stresses.* = **unload**, relieve, discharge, lighten, disencumber, disburden, ease the load of • **unburden yourself** *Many came to unburden themselves of emotional problems.* = **confess**, come clean about (*informal*), get something off your chest (*informal*), tell all about, empty yourself, spill your guts about (*slang*), make a clean breast of something

uncanny ADJECTIVE **1** *I had this uncanny feeling that Alice was warning me.* = **weird**, strange, mysterious, queer, unearthly, eerie, supernatural, unnatural, spooky (*informal*), creepy (*informal*), eldritch (*poetic*), preternatural **2** *The hero bears an uncanny resemblance to Kirk Douglas.* = **extraordinary**, remarkable, incredible (*informal*), unusual, fantastic, astonishing, exceptional, astounding, singular, miraculous, unheard-of, prodigious

uncertain ADJECTIVE **1** *He stopped, uncertain how to put the question tactfully.* = **unsure**, undecided, at a loss, vague, unclear, doubtful, dubious, ambivalent, hazy, hesitant, vacillating, in two minds, undetermined, irresolute ■ OPPOSITE: sure **2** *Students all over the country are facing an uncertain future.* = **doubtful**, undetermined, unpredictable, insecure, questionable, ambiguous, unreliable, precarious, indefinite, indeterminate, incalculable, iffy (*informal*), changeable, indistinct, chancy (*informal*), unforeseeable, unsettled, unresolved, in the balance, unconfirmed, up in the air, unfixed, conjectural, sketchy (*informal*) ■ OPPOSITE: decided

uncertainty NOUN **1** *a period of political uncertainty* = **unpredictability**, precariousness, state of suspense, ambiguity, unreliability, fickleness, inconclusiveness, chanciness, changeableness ■ OPPOSITE: predictability **2** *The magazine ignores all the uncertainties males currently face.* = **doubt**, confusion, dilemma, misgiving, qualm, bewilderment, quandary, puzzlement, perplexity, mystification ■ OPPOSITE: confidence **3** *There was a hint of uncertainty in his voice.* = **hesitancy**, hesitation, indecision, lack of confidence, vagueness, irresolution

uncharted ADJECTIVE = **unexplored**, unknown, undiscovered, strange, virgin, unfamiliar, unplumbed, not mapped

> **USAGE** *Unchartered* is sometimes mistakenly used where *uncharted* is meant: *We did not want to pioneer in completely uncharted* (not *unchartered*) *territory.*

unclean ADJECTIVE **1** *By bathing in unclean water, they expose themselves to contamination.* = **dirty**, soiled, foul, contaminated, polluted, nasty, filthy, defiled, impure, scuzzy (*slang, chiefly U.S.*) ■ OPPOSITE: clean **2** *unclean thoughts* = **immoral**, corrupt, impure, evil, dirty, nasty, foul, polluted, filthy, scuzzy (*slang, chiefly U.S.*)

uncomfortable ADJECTIVE **1** *The request for money made them feel uncomfortable.* = **uneasy**, troubled, disturbed, embarrassed, distressed, awkward, out of place, self-conscious, disquieted, ill at ease, discomfited, like a fish out of water ■ OPPOSITE: comfortable **2** *Wigs are hot and uncomfortable to wear constantly.* = **painful**, awkward, irritating, hard, rough, troublesome, disagreeable, causing discomfort

uncommitted ADJECTIVE = **undecided**, uninvolved, nonpartisan, nonaligned, free, floating, neutral, not involved, unattached, free-floating, (sitting) on the fence

uncommon ADJECTIVE **1** *Certain types of flu are relatively uncommon.* = **rare**, unusual, odd, novel, strange, bizarre, curious, peculiar, unfamiliar, scarce, queer, singular, few and far between, out of the ordinary, infrequent, thin on the ground ■ OPPOSITE: common **2** *Both are blessed with an uncommon ability to fix things.*

u

= **extraordinary**, rare, remarkable, special, outstanding, superior, distinctive, exceptional, unprecedented, notable, singular, unparalleled, noteworthy, inimitable, incomparable
■ **OPPOSITE:** ordinary

uncommonly ADVERB **1** *Mary was uncommonly good at tennis.* = **exceptionally**, very, extremely, remarkably, particularly, strangely, seriously (*informal*), unusually, peculiarly, to the nth degree **2** (*used in negative constructions*) *Not uncommonly, family strains may remain hidden behind complaints.* = **rarely**, occasionally, seldom, not often, infrequently, hardly ever, only now and then, scarcely ever

uncompromising ADJECTIVE = **inflexible**, strict, rigid, decided, firm, tough, stubborn, hardline, die-hard, inexorable, steadfast, unyielding, obstinate, intransigent, unbending, obdurate, stiff-necked

unconcerned ADJECTIVE = **untroubled**, relaxed, unperturbed, nonchalant, easy, careless, not bothered, serene, callous, carefree, unruffled, blithe, insouciant, unworried, not giving a toss (*informal*)
■ **OPPOSITE:** concerned

unconditional ADJECTIVE = **absolute**, full, complete, total, positive (*informal*), entire, utter, explicit, outright, unlimited, downright, unqualified, unrestricted, out-and-out, plenary, categorical, unreserved ■ **OPPOSITE:** qualified

unconscious ADJECTIVE **1** *By the time ambulancemen arrived he was unconscious.* = **senseless**, knocked out, out cold (*informal*), out, stunned, numb, dazed, blacked out (*informal*), in a coma, comatose, stupefied, asleep, out for the count (*informal*), insensible, dead to the world (*informal*) ■ **OPPOSITE:** awake **2** *Mr Battersby was apparently quite unconscious of their presence.* = **unaware**, ignorant, oblivious, unsuspecting, lost to, blind to, in ignorance, unknowing ■ **OPPOSITE:** aware **3** *'You're well out of it,' he said with unconscious brutality.* = **unintentional**, unwitting, unintended, inadvertent, accidental, unpremeditated ■ **OPPOSITE:** intentional **4** *an unconscious desire expressed solely during sleep* = **subconscious**, automatic, suppressed, repressed, inherent, reflex, instinctive, innate, involuntary, latent, subliminal, unrealized, gut (*informal*)

unconventional ADJECTIVE **1** *He was known for his unconventional behaviour.* = **unusual**, unorthodox, odd, eccentric, different, individual, original, bizarre, way-out (*informal*), informal, irregular, bohemian,

far-out (*slang*), idiosyncratic, off-the-wall (*slang*), oddball (*informal*), individualistic, out of the ordinary, offbeat, left-field (*informal*), freakish, atypical, nonconformist, wacky (*informal*), outré, uncustomary, daggy (*Austral. & N.Z. informal*) ■ **OPPOSITE:** conventional **2** *The vaccine had been produced by an unconventional technique.* = **unorthodox**, original, unusual, irregular, atypical, different, uncustomary
■ **OPPOSITE:** normal

uncover VERB **1** *Auditors said they had uncovered evidence of fraud.* = **reveal**, find, discover, expose, encounter, turn up, detect, disclose, unveil, come across, unearth, dig up, divulge, chance on, root out, unmask, lay bare, make known, blow the whistle on (*informal*), bring to light, smoke out, take the wraps off, blow wide open (*slang*), stumble on *or* across
■ **OPPOSITE:** conceal **2** *When the seedlings sprout, uncover the tray.* = **open**, unveil, unwrap, show, strip, expose, bare, lay bare, lift the lid, lay open

undaunted ADJECTIVE = **undeterred**, unflinching, not discouraged, not put off, brave, bold, courageous, gritty, fearless, resolute, gallant, intrepid, steadfast, indomitable, dauntless, undismayed, unfaltering, nothing daunted, undiscouraged, unshrinking

undecided ADJECTIVE **1** *She was still undecided as to what career she wanted to pursue.* = **unsure**, uncertain, uncommitted, torn, doubtful, dubious, wavering, hesitant, ambivalent, dithering (*chiefly Brit.*), in two minds, irresolute, swithering (*Scot.*)
■ **OPPOSITE:** sure **2** *The release date for his record is still undecided.* = **unsettled**, open, undetermined, vague, pending, tentative, in the balance, indefinite, debatable, up in the air, moot, iffy (*informal*), unconcluded
■ **OPPOSITE:** settled

undeniable ADJECTIVE = **certain**, evident, undoubted, incontrovertible, clear, sure, sound, proven, obvious, patent, manifest, beyond (a) doubt, unassailable, indisputable, irrefutable, unquestionable, beyond question, incontestable, indubitable ■ **OPPOSITE:** doubtful

under PREPOSITION **1** *A path runs under the trees.* = **below**, beneath, underneath, on the bottom of ■ **OPPOSITE:** over **2** *I am the new manager and you will be working under me.* = **subordinate to**, subject to, reporting to, directed by, governed by, inferior to, secondary to, subservient to, junior to **3** *under section 4 of the Family Law Reform Act* = **included in**, belonging to, subsumed

under, comprised in ▶ ADVERB *A hand came from behind and pushed his head under.*
= **below**, down, beneath, downward, to the bottom ■ OPPOSITE: up

■ RELATED WORD: *prefix* sub-

undercover ADJECTIVE = **secret**, covert, clandestine, private, hidden, intelligence, underground, spy, concealed, confidential, hush-hush (*informal*), surreptitious

■ OPPOSITE: open

undercurrent NOUN **1** *There is a strong undercurrent of sadness in the film.*
= **undertone**, feeling, atmosphere, sense, suggestion, trend, hint, flavour, tendency, drift, murmur, tenor, aura, tinge, vibes (*slang*), vibrations, overtone, hidden feeling **2** *He tried to swim after him but the strong undercurrent swept them apart.* = **undertow**, tideway, riptide, rip, rip current, crosscurrent, underflow

undercut VERB = **underprice**, sell cheaply, sell at a loss, undersell, sacrifice, undercharge

underdog NOUN = **weaker party**, victim, loser, little fellow (*informal*), outsider, fall guy (*informal*)

underestimate VERB **1** *Never underestimate what you can learn from a group of like-minded people.* = **undervalue**, understate, underrate, diminish, play down, minimize, downgrade, miscalculate, trivialize, rate too low, underemphasize, hold cheap, misprize ■ OPPOSITE: overestimate **2** *The first lesson I learnt was never to underestimate the enemy.* = **underrate**, undervalue, belittle, sell short (*informal*), not do justice to, rate too low, set no store by, hold cheap, think too little of ■ OPPOSITE: overrate

> USAGE *Underestimate* is sometimes wrongly used where *overestimate* is meant: *The importance of his work cannot be overestimated* (not *cannot be underestimated*).

undergo VERB = **experience**, go through, be subjected to, stand, suffer, bear, weather, sustain, endure, withstand, submit to

underground ADJECTIVE **1** *a rundown shopping area with an underground car park*
= **subterranean**, basement, lower-level, sunken, covered, buried, below the surface, below ground, subterrestrial **2** *accused of organizing and financing an underground youth movement* = **secret**, undercover, covert, hidden, guerrilla, revolutionary, concealed, confidential, dissident, closet, subversive, clandestine, renegade, insurgent, hush-hush (*informal*), surreptitious, cloak-and-dagger, hugger-mugger,

insurrectionist, hole-and-corner (*informal*), radical • **the underground 1** *The underground is ideal for getting to work in Milan.* = **the tube** (*Brit.*), the subway, the metro **2** *US dollars were smuggled into the country to aid the underground.* = **the Resistance**, partisans, freedom fighters, the Maquis

undergrowth NOUN = **scrub**, brush, underwood, bracken, brambles, briars, underbrush, brushwood, underbush

underhand ADJECTIVE = **sly**, secret, crooked (*informal*), devious, sneaky, secretive, fraudulent, treacherous, dishonest, deceptive, clandestine, unscrupulous, crafty, unethical, furtive, deceitful, surreptitious, stealthy, dishonourable, below the belt (*informal*), underhanded

■ OPPOSITE: honest

underline VERB **1** *The report underlined his concern that standards were at risk.*
= **emphasize**, stress, highlight, bring home, accentuate, point up, give emphasis to, call *or* draw attention to ■ OPPOSITE: minimize **2** *Take two pens and underline the positive and negative words.* = **underscore**, mark, italicize, rule a line under

underling NOUN = **subordinate**, inferior, minion, servant, slave, cohort (*chiefly U.S.*), retainer, menial, nonentity, lackey, hireling, flunky, understrapper

underlying ADJECTIVE **1** *To stop a problem you have to understand its underlying causes.*
= **fundamental**, basic, essential, root, prime, primary, radical, elementary, intrinsic, basal **2** *hills with the hard underlying rock poking through the turf* = **hidden**, concealed, lurking, veiled, latent

undermine VERB = **weaken**, sabotage, subvert, compromise, disable, debilitate

■ OPPOSITE: reinforce

underpinning NOUN = **support**, base, foundation, footing, groundwork, substructure

underprivileged ADJECTIVE
= **disadvantaged**, poor, deprived, in need, impoverished, needy, badly off, destitute, in want, on the breadline

underrate VERB = **underestimate**, discount, undervalue, belittle, disparage, fail to appreciate, not do justice to, set (too) little store by, misprize ■ OPPOSITE: overestimate

understand VERB **1** *I think you understand my meaning.* = **comprehend**, get, take in, perceive, grasp, know, see, follow, realize, recognize, appreciate, be aware of, penetrate, make out, discern, twig (*Brit. informal*), fathom, savvy (*slang*), apprehend, conceive of, suss (*Brit. informal*), get to the

u

bottom of, get the hang of (*informal*), tumble to (*informal*), catch on to (*informal*), cotton on to (*informal*), make head or tail of (*informal*), get your head round **2** *Trish had not exactly understood his feelings.*
= **sympathize with**, appreciate, be aware of, be able to see, take on board (*informal*), empathize with, commiserate with, show compassion for **3** *I understand you've heard about David.* = **believe**, hear, learn, gather, think, see, suppose, notice, assume, take it, conclude, fancy, presume, be informed, infer, surmise, hear tell, draw the inference

understandable ADJECTIVE = **reasonable**, natural, normal, justified, expected, inevitable, legitimate, logical, predictable, accountable, on the cards (*informal*), foreseeable, to be expected, justifiable, unsurprising, excusable, pardonable

understanding NOUN **1** *They have to have a basic understanding of computers.*
= **perception**, knowledge, grasp, sense, know-how (*informal*), intelligence, judgment, awareness, appreciation, insight, skill, penetration, mastery, comprehension, familiarity with, discernment, proficiency ■ **OPPOSITE:** ignorance **2** *We had not set a date but there was an understanding between us.*
= **agreement**, deal (*informal*), promise, arrangement, accord, contract, bond, pledge, bargain, pact, compact, concord, gentlemen's agreement ■ **OPPOSITE:** disagreement **3** *It is my understanding that this has been going on for many years.* = **belief**, view, opinion, impression, interpretation, feeling, idea, conclusion, notion, conviction, judgment, assumption, point of view, perception, suspicion, viewpoint, hunch, way of thinking, estimation, supposition, sneaking suspicion, funny feeling ▶ ADJECTIVE *Her boss, who was very understanding, gave her time off.*
= **sympathetic**, kind, compassionate, considerate, kindly, accepting, patient, sensitive, forgiving, discerning, tolerant, responsive, perceptive, forbearing ■ **OPPOSITE:** unsympathetic

understood ADJECTIVE **1** *The management is understood to be very unwilling to agree.*
= **assumed**, presumed, accepted, taken for granted **2** *The technical equality of all officers was understood.* = **implied**, implicit, unspoken, inferred, tacit, unstated

understudy NOUN = **stand-in**, reserve, substitute, double, sub, replacement, fill-in

undertake VERB **1** *She undertook the arduous task of monitoring the elections.* = **take on**, embark on, set about, commence, try, begin, attempt, tackle, enter upon, endeavour to do **2** *He undertook to edit the text himself.* = **agree**, promise, contract, guarantee, engage, pledge, covenant, commit yourself, take upon yourself

undertaker NOUN = **funeral director**, mortician (*U.S.*)

undertaking NOUN **1** *Organizing the show has been a massive undertaking.* = **task**, business, operation, project, game, attempt, effort, affair, venture, enterprise, endeavour **2** *The new owners gave an undertaking that the factory would remain open.* = **promise**, commitment, pledge, word, vow, assurance, word of honour, solemn word

undertone NOUN **1** *Well-dressed clients were talking in polite undertones as they ate.*
= **murmur**, whisper, low tone, subdued voice **2** *The sobbing voice had an undertone of anger.* = **undercurrent**, suggestion, trace, hint, feeling, touch, atmosphere, flavour, tinge, vibes (*slang*)

undervalue VERB = **underrate**, underestimate, minimize, look down on, misjudge, depreciate, make light of, set no store by, hold cheap, misprize ■ **OPPOSITE:** overrate

underwater ADJECTIVE = **submerged**, submarine, immersed, sunken, undersea, subaqueous, subaquatic

under way ADJECTIVE = **in progress**, going on, started, begun, in business, in motion, in operation, afoot

underwear NOUN = **underclothes**, lingerie, undies (*informal*), smalls (*informal*), undergarments, unmentionables (*humorous*), underclothing, underthings, underlinen, brookies (*S. African informal*), underdaks (*Austral. slang*)

underweight ADJECTIVE = **skinny**, puny, emaciated, undernourished, skin and bone (*informal*), undersized, half-starved, underfed

underworld NOUN **1** *a wealthy businessman with connections to the underworld*
= **criminals**, gangsters, organized crime, gangland (*informal*), criminal element **2** *Persephone, goddess of the underworld*
= **nether world**, hell, Hades, the inferno, nether regions, infernal region, abode of the dead

underwrite VERB = **finance**, back, fund, guarantee, sponsor, insure, ratify, subsidize, bankroll (*informal*), provide security, provide capital for

undesirable ADJECTIVE = **unwanted**, unwelcome, disagreeable, objectionable, offensive, disliked, unacceptable, dreaded, unpopular, unsuitable, out of place, unattractive, distasteful, unsavoury, obnoxious, repugnant, unpleasing, unwished-for ■ **OPPOSITE:** desirable

undo VERB **1** *I managed to undo a corner of the parcel.* = **open**, unfasten, loose, loosen, unlock, unwrap, untie, disengage, unbutton, disentangle, unstrap, unclasp **2** *It would be difficult to undo the damage that had been done.* = **reverse**, cancel, offset, wipe out, neutralize, invalidate, annul, nullify **3** *Our hopes of a victory were undone by an error from the goalkeeper.* = **ruin**, defeat, destroy, wreck, shatter, upset, mar, undermine, overturn, quash, subvert, bring to naught

undoing NOUN = **downfall**, weakness, curse, trouble, trial, misfortune, blight, affliction, the last straw, fatal flaw

undone¹ ADJECTIVE *She left nothing undone that needed attention.* = **unfinished**, left, outstanding, not done, neglected, omitted, incomplete, passed over, unfulfilled, not completed, unperformed, unattended to ■ **OPPOSITE:** finished

undone² ADJECTIVE *He is undone by his lack of inner substance.* = **ruined**, destroyed, overcome, hapless, forlorn, prostrate, wretched

undoubted ADJECTIVE = **certain**, sure, definite, confirmed, positive, obvious, acknowledged, patent, evident, manifest, transparent, clear-cut, undisputed, indisputable, unquestioned, unquestionable, incontrovertible, indubitable, nailed-on (*slang*)

undoubtedly ADVERB = **certainly**, definitely, undeniably, surely, of course, doubtless, without doubt, unquestionably, unmistakably, assuredly, beyond question, beyond a shadow of (a) doubt

undress VERB *She went out, leaving Rachel to undress and have her shower.* = **strip**, strip naked, disrobe, take off your clothes, peel off, doff your clothes ▶ NOUN *Every cover showed a woman in a state of undress.* = **nakedness**, nudity, disarray, deshabille

undue ADJECTIVE = **excessive**, too much, inappropriate, extreme, unnecessary, extravagant, needless, unsuitable, improper, too great, disproportionate, unjustified, unwarranted, unseemly, inordinate, undeserved, intemperate, uncalled-for, overmuch, immoderate ■ **OPPOSITE:** appropriate

undulate VERB = **wave**, roll, surge, swell, ripple, rise and fall, billow, heave

unduly ADVERB = **excessively**, overly, too much, unnecessarily, disproportionately, improperly, unreasonably, extravagantly,

out of all proportion, inordinately, unjustifiably, overmuch, immoderately ■ **OPPOSITE:** reasonably

undying ADJECTIVE = **eternal**, everlasting, perpetual, continuing, permanent, constant, perennial, infinite, unending, indestructible, undiminished, imperishable, deathless, inextinguishable, unfading, sempiternal (*literary*) ■ **OPPOSITE:** short-lived

unearth VERB **1** *No evidence has yet been unearthed.* = **discover**, find, reveal, expose, turn up, uncover, bring to light, ferret out, root up **2** *Fossil hunters have unearthed the bones of an elephant.* = **dig up**, excavate, exhume, dredge up (*informal*)

unearthly ADJECTIVE **1** *The sound was so serene that it seemed unearthly.* = **eerie**, strange, supernatural, ghostly, weird, phantom, uncanny, spooky (*informal*), nightmarish, spectral, eldritch (*poetic*), preternatural **2** *They arranged to meet at the unearthly hour of seven in the morning.* = **unreasonable**, ridiculous, absurd, strange, extraordinary, abnormal, unholy (*informal*), ungodly (*informal*)

uneasiness NOUN = **anxiety**, apprehension, misgiving, worry, doubt, alarm, suspicion, nervousness, disquiet, agitation, qualms, trepidation (*formal*), perturbation, apprehensiveness, dubiety ■ **OPPOSITE:** ease

uneasy ADJECTIVE **1** *He looked uneasy and refused to answer questions.* = **anxious**, worried, troubled, upset, wired (*slang*), nervous, disturbed, uncomfortable, unsettled, impatient, restless, agitated, apprehensive, edgy, jittery (*informal*), perturbed, on edge, ill at ease, restive, twitchy (*informal*), like a fish out of water, antsy (*informal*), discomposed ■ **OPPOSITE:** relaxed **2** *An uneasy calm has settled over the city.* = **precarious**, strained, uncomfortable, tense, awkward, unstable, shaky, insecure, constrained **3** *This is an uneasy book.* = **disturbing**, upsetting, disquieting, worrying, troubling, bothering, dismaying

uneconomic ADJECTIVE = **unprofitable**, loss-making, non-profit-making, nonpaying, nonviable ■ **OPPOSITE:** profitable

unemployed ADJECTIVE = **out of work**, redundant, laid off, jobless, idle, on the dole (*Brit. informal*), out of a job, workless, resting (*of an actor*) ■ **OPPOSITE:** working

unequal ADJECTIVE **1** *the unequal division of wealth in many countries throughout the world* = **disproportionate**, uneven, unbalanced,

u

unfair, irregular, unjust, inequitable, ill-matched **2** *These pipes appear to me to be all of unequal length.* = **different**, differing, dissimilar, unlike, varying, variable, disparate, unmatched, not uniform
■ **OPPOSITE:** identical **3** (*with* **to**) *Her critics say that she has proved unequal to the task.* = **not up to**, not qualified for, inadequate for, insufficient for, found wanting in, not cut out for (*informal*), incompetent at

unequalled *or* (*U.S.*) **unequaled** ADJECTIVE = **incomparable**, supreme, unparalleled, paramount, transcendent, unrivalled, second to none, pre-eminent, inimitable, unmatched, peerless, unsurpassed, matchless, beyond compare, without equal, nonpareil

unequivocal ADJECTIVE = **clear**, absolute, definite, certain, direct, straight, positive, plain, evident, black-and-white, decisive, explicit, manifest, clear-cut, unmistakable, unambiguous, cut-and-dried (*informal*), incontrovertible, indubitable, uncontestable, nailed-on (*slang*)
■ **OPPOSITE:** vague

unerring ADJECTIVE = **accurate**, sure, certain, perfect, exact, impeccable, faultless, infallible, unfailing

uneven ADJECTIVE **1** *He staggered on the uneven surface of the car park.* = **rough**, bumpy, not flat, not level, not smooth
■ **OPPOSITE:** level **2** *He could hear that her breathing was uneven.* = **irregular**, unsteady, fitful, variable, broken, fluctuating, patchy, intermittent, jerky, changeable, spasmodic, inconsistent **3** *It was an uneven contest.* = **unequal**, unfair, one-sided, ill-matched **4** *a flat head accentuated by a short, uneven crew-cut* = **lopsided**, unbalanced, asymmetrical, odd, out of true, not parallel

uneventful ADJECTIVE = **humdrum**, ordinary, routine, quiet, boring, dull, commonplace, tedious, monotonous, unremarkable, uninteresting, unexciting, unexceptional, ho-hum (*informal*), unmemorable, unvaried ■ **OPPOSITE:** exciting

unexpected ADJECTIVE = **unforeseen**, surprising, unanticipated, chance, sudden, astonishing, startling, unpredictable, accidental, abrupt, out of the blue, unannounced, fortuitous, unheralded, unlooked-for, not bargained for
■ **OPPOSITE:** expected

unfailing ADJECTIVE **1** *He continued to appear in the office with unfailing regularity.* = **continuous**, endless, persistent, unlimited, continual, never-failing, boundless, bottomless, ceaseless, inexhaustible, unflagging **2** *I would like to thank on Erika for her unfailing care and support.* = **reliable**, constant, dependable, sure, true, certain, loyal, faithful, staunch, infallible, steadfast, tried and true
■ **OPPOSITE:** unreliable

unfair ADJECTIVE **1** *Some have been sentenced to long prison terms after unfair trials.* = **biased**, prejudiced, unjust, one-sided, partial, partisan, arbitrary, discriminatory, bigoted, inequitable **2** *nations involved in unfair trade practices* = **unscrupulous**, crooked (*informal*), dishonest, unethical, wrongful, unprincipled, dishonourable, unsporting
■ **OPPOSITE:** ethical

unfaithful ADJECTIVE **1** *a woman of who dumps her unfaithful partner and proceeds to lead her own life* = **faithless**, untrue, two-timing (*informal*), adulterous, fickle, inconstant, unchaste ■ **OPPOSITE:** faithful **2** *They denounced him as unfaithful to the traditions of the Society.* = **disloyal**, false, treacherous, deceitful, faithless, perfidious (*literary*), traitorous, treasonable, false-hearted, recreant (*archaic*) ■ **OPPOSITE:** loyal

unfamiliar ADJECTIVE **1** *She grew many plants that were unfamiliar to me.* = **strange**, new, unknown, different, novel, unusual, curious, alien, out-of-the-way, uncommon, little known, unaccustomed, beyond your ken ■ **OPPOSITE:** familiar **2** (*with* **with**) *She speaks no Japanese and is unfamiliar with Japanese culture.* = **unacquainted with**, a stranger to, unaccustomed to, inexperienced in, uninformed about, unversed in, uninitiated in, unskilled at, unpractised in, unconversant with
■ **OPPOSITE:** acquainted with

unfathomable ADJECTIVE **1** *How unfathomable and odd is life!* = **baffling**, incomprehensible, inexplicable, deep, profound, esoteric, impenetrable, unknowable, abstruse, indecipherable **2** *Her eyes were black, unfathomable pools.* = **immeasurable**, bottomless, unmeasured, unplumbed, unsounded

unfavourable *or* (*U.S.*) **unfavorable** ADJECTIVE *Unfavourable economic conditions were blocking a recovery.* = **adverse**, bad, unfortunate, disadvantageous, threatening, contrary, unlucky, ominous, untimely, untoward, unpromising, unsuited, inauspicious, ill-suited, inopportune, unseasonable, unpropitious, infelicitous

unfinished ADJECTIVE **1** *Jane Austen's unfinished novel* = **incomplete**, uncompleted, half-done, lacking, undone, in the making, imperfect, unfulfilled, unaccomplished **2** *unfinished wood ready for you to varnish or paint* = **natural**, rough, raw, bare, crude, unrefined, unvarnished, unpolished ■ **OPPOSITE:** polished

unfit ADJECTIVE **1** *Many children are so unfit they are unable to do basic exercises.* = **out of shape**, feeble, unhealthy, debilitated, flabby, decrepit, in poor condition, out of trim, out of kilter ■ **OPPOSITE:** healthy **2** *They were utterly unfit to govern America.* = **incapable**, inadequate, incompetent, no good, useless (*informal*), not up to, unprepared, ineligible, unqualified, untrained, ill-equipped, not equal, not cut out ■ **OPPOSITE:** capable **3** *I can show them plenty of houses unfit for human habitation.* = **unsuitable**, inadequate, inappropriate, useless, not fit, not designed, unsuited, ill-adapted ■ **OPPOSITE:** suitable

unflappable ADJECTIVE = **imperturbable**, cool, collected, calm, composed, level-headed, unfazed (*informal*), impassive, unruffled, self-possessed, not given to worry ■ **OPPOSITE:** excitable

unflinching ADJECTIVE = **determined**, firm, steady, constant, bold, stalwart, staunch, resolute, steadfast, unwavering, immovable, unswerving, unshaken, unfaltering, unshrinking ■ **OPPOSITE:** wavering

unfold VERB **1** *The outcome depends on conditions as well as how events unfold.* = **develop**, happen, progress, grow, emerge, occur, take place, expand, work out, mature, evolve, blossom, transpire (*informal*), bear fruit **2** *Mr Wills unfolds his story with evident enjoyment.* = **reveal**, tell, present, show, describe, explain, illustrate, disclose, uncover, clarify, divulge, narrate, make known **3** *He quickly unfolded the blankets and spread them on the mattress.* = **open**, spread out, undo, expand, flatten, straighten, stretch out, unfurl, unwrap, unroll

unfortunate ADJECTIVE **1** *Through some unfortunate accident, the information reached me a day late.* = **disastrous**, calamitous, inopportune, adverse, untimely, unfavourable, untoward, ruinous, ill-starred, infelicitous, ill-fated ■ **OPPOSITE:** opportune **2** *the unfortunate incident of the upside-down Canadian flag* = **regrettable**, deplorable, lamentable, inappropriate, unsuitable, ill-advised, unbecoming ■ **OPPOSITE:** becoming **3** *charity days to raise money for unfortunate people* = **unlucky**, poor, unhappy, doomed, cursed, hopeless, unsuccessful, hapless,

luckless, out of luck, wretched, star-crossed, unprosperous ■ **OPPOSITE:** fortunate

unfounded ADJECTIVE = **groundless**, false, unjustified, unproven, unsubstantiated, idle, fabricated, spurious, trumped up, baseless, without foundation, without basis ■ **OPPOSITE:** justified

unfriendly ADJECTIVE **1** *She spoke in a loud, rather unfriendly voice.* = **hostile**, cold, distant, sour, chilly, aloof, surly, antagonistic, disagreeable, quarrelsome, unsociable, ill-disposed, unneighbourly ■ **OPPOSITE:** friendly **2** *We got an unfriendly reception from the hotel-owner.* = **unfavourable**, hostile, inhospitable, alien, inauspicious, inimical, uncongenial, unpropitious, unkind ■ **OPPOSITE:** congenial

ungainly ADJECTIVE = **awkward**, clumsy, inelegant, lumbering, slouching, gawky, uncouth, gangling, loutish, uncoordinated, ungraceful, lubberly, unco (*Austral. slang*) ■ **OPPOSITE:** graceful

unguarded ADJECTIVE **1** *The U-boat entered in through a narrow unguarded eastern entrance.* = **unprotected**, vulnerable, defenceless, undefended, open to attack, unpatrolled **2** *He was tricked by a reporter into an unguarded comment.* = **careless**, rash, unwary, foolhardy, thoughtless, indiscreet, unthinking, ill-considered, imprudent, heedless, incautious, undiplomatic, impolitic, uncircumspect ■ **OPPOSITE:** cautious

unhappiness NOUN *There was a lot of unhappiness in my adolescence.* = **sadness**, depression, misery, gloom, sorrow, melancholy, heartache, despondency, blues, dejection, wretchedness, low spirits

unhappy ADJECTIVE **1** *Her marriage is in trouble and she is desperately unhappy.* = **sad**, depressed, miserable, down, low, blue, gloomy, melancholy, mournful, dejected, despondent, dispirited, downcast, long-faced, sorrowful, disconsolate, crestfallen, down in the dumps (*informal*) ■ **OPPOSITE:** happy **2** *I have already informed your unhappy father of your expulsion.* = **unlucky**, unfortunate, hapless, luckless, cursed, wretched, ill-omened, ill-fated ■ **OPPOSITE:** fortunate **3** *The legislation represents in itself an unhappy compromise.* = **inappropriate**, awkward, clumsy, unsuitable, inept, ill-advised, tactless, ill-timed, injudicious, infelicitous, malapropos, untactful ■ **OPPOSITE:** apt

unhealthy ADJECTIVE **1** *the unhealthy environment of a coal mine* = **harmful**,

detrimental, unwholesome, noxious, toxic, deleterious (*formal*), insanitary, noisome, insalubrious ■ **OPPOSITE:** beneficial
2 *a poorly dressed, unhealthy looking fellow with a poor complexion* = **sick**, sickly, unwell, poorly (*informal*), weak, delicate, crook (*Austral. & N.Z. informal*), ailing, frail, feeble, invalid, unsound, infirm, in poor health ■ **OPPOSITE:** well **3** *a clear sign of an unhealthy economy* = **weak**, unsound, ailing ■ **OPPOSITE:** strong **4** *an unhealthy obsession with secrecy* = **unwholesome**, morbid, bad, negative, corrupt, corrupting, degrading, undesirable, demoralizing, baneful (*archaic*) ■ **OPPOSITE:** wholesome

unheard-of ADJECTIVE **1** *In those days, it was unheard-of for a woman to work after marriage.* = **unprecedented**, inconceivable, undreamed of, new, novel, unique, unusual, unbelievable, singular, ground-breaking, never before encountered, unexampled **2** *They achieved the then unheard-of speed of sixty miles per hour.* = **shocking**, extreme, outrageous, offensive, unacceptable, unthinkable, disgraceful, preposterous, outlandish **3** *an unheard-of comic waiting for his big break to come along* = **obscure**, unknown, undiscovered, unfamiliar, little known, unsung, unremarked, unregarded

unhinge VERB = **unbalance**, confuse, derange, disorder, unsettle, madden, craze, confound, distemper (*archaic*), dement, drive you out of your mind

unholy ADJECTIVE **1** *The economy is still in an unholy mess.* = **shocking** (*informal*), awful, appalling, dreadful, outrageous, horrendous, unearthly, ungodly (*informal*) **2** *He screamed unholy things at me.* = **evil**, vile, wicked, base, corrupt, immoral, dishonest, sinful, heinous, depraved, profane, iniquitous, ungodly, irreligious ■ **OPPOSITE:** holy

unification NOUN = **union**, uniting, alliance, combination, coalition, merger, federation, confederation, fusion, amalgamation, coalescence

uniform NOUN **1** *He was dressed in his uniform for parade.* = **regalia**, suit, livery, colours, habit, regimentals **2** *dressed in the uniform of the anti-Establishment business class* = **outfit**, dress, costume, attire, gear (*informal*), get-up (*informal*), ensemble, garb ▶ ADJECTIVE **1** *Chips should be cut into uniform size and thickness.* = **consistent**, unvarying, similar, even, same, matching, regular, constant, equivalent, identical, homogeneous, unchanging, equable, undeviating ■ **OPPOSITE:** varying

2 *Along each wall stretched uniform green metal filing cabinets.* = **alike**, similar, identical, like, same, equal, selfsame

uniformity NOUN **1** *Caramel was used to maintain uniformity of colour in the brandy.* = **regularity**, similarity, sameness, constancy, homogeneity, evenness, invariability **2** *the dull uniformity of the houses* = **monotony**, sameness, tedium, dullness, flatness, drabness, lack of diversity

unify VERB = **unite**, join, combine, merge, consolidate, bring together, fuse, confederate, amalgamate, federate ■ **OPPOSITE:** divide

uninterested ADJECTIVE = **indifferent**, unconcerned, apathetic, bored, distant, listless, impassive, blasé, unresponsive, uninvolved, incurious ■ **OPPOSITE:** concerned

union NOUN **1** *Norway's union with Denmark in the late fourteenth century* = **joining**, uniting, unification, combination, coalition, merger, mixture, blend, merging, integration, conjunction, fusion, synthesis, amalgamating, amalgam, amalgamation **2** *the question of which countries should join the currency union* = **alliance**, league, association, coalition, federation, confederation, confederacy, Bund **3** *Even Louis began to think their union was not blessed.* = **marriage**, match, wedlock, matrimony

unique ADJECTIVE **1** *The area has its own unique language, Catalan.* = **distinct**, special, exclusive, peculiar, only, single, lone, solitary, one and only, sui generis **2** *She was a woman of unique talent and determination.* = **unparalleled**, unrivalled, incomparable, inimitable, unmatched, peerless, unequalled, matchless, without equal, nonpareil, unexampled

> **USAGE** *Unique* with the meaning 'being the only one' or 'having no equal' describes an absolute state: *a case unique in British law*. In this use it cannot therefore be qualified; something is either *unique* or *not unique*. However, *unique* is also very commonly used in the sense of 'remarkable' or 'exceptional', particularly in the language of advertising, and in this meaning it can be used with qualifying words such as *rather*, *quite*, etc. Since many people object to this use, it is best avoided in formal and serious writing.

unit NOUN **1** *Agriculture was based in the past on the family as a unit.* = **entity**, whole, item, feature, piece, portion, module **2** *a secret military unit* = **section**, company, group, force, detail, division, cell, squad, crew, outfit (*informal*), faction, corps, brigade, regiment, battalion, legion, contingent, squadron, garrison, detachment, platoon **3** *The liver can only burn up one unit of alcohol in an hour.* = **measure**, quantity, measurement **4** *designed for teachers to plan a study unit on marine mammals* = **part**, section, segment, class, element, component, constituent, tutorial

unite VERB **1** *They have agreed to unite their efforts to bring peace.* = **join**, link, combine, couple, marry, wed, blend, incorporate, merge, consolidate, unify, fuse, amalgamate, coalesce, meld ■ **OPPOSITE:** separate **2** *The two parties have been trying to unite since the New Year.* = **cooperate**, ally, join forces, league, band, associate, pool, collaborate, confederate, pull together, join together, close ranks, club together ■ **OPPOSITE:** split

united ADJECTIVE **1** *Every party is united on the need for parliamentary democracy.* = **in agreement**, agreed, unanimous, one, like-minded, in accord, of like mind, of one mind, of the same opinion **2** *the warm and fuzzy message of a united Africa* = **combined**, leagued, allied, unified, pooled, concerted, collective, affiliated, in partnership, banded together

unity NOUN **1** *the future of European economic unity* = **union**, unification, coalition, federation, integration, confederation, amalgamation **2** *The deer represents the unity of the universe.* = **wholeness**, integrity, oneness, union, unification, entity, singleness, undividedness ■ **OPPOSITE:** disunity **3** *Speakers at the rally mouthed sentiments of unity.* = **agreement**, accord, consensus, peace, harmony, solidarity, unison, assent, unanimity, concord, concurrence ■ **OPPOSITE:** disagreement

universal ADJECTIVE **1** *proposals for universal health care* = **widespread**, general, common, whole, total, entire, catholic, unlimited, ecumenical, omnipresent, all-embracing, overarching, one-size-fits-all **2** *universal diseases* = **global**, worldwide, international, pandemic

> USAGE The use of *more universal* as in *his writings have long been admired by fellow scientists, but his latest book should have more universal appeal* is acceptable in modern English usage.

universality NOUN = **comprehensiveness**, generalization, generality, totality, completeness, ubiquity, all-inclusiveness

universally ADVERB = **without exception**, uniformly, everywhere, always, invariably, across the board, in all cases, in every instance

universe NOUN = **cosmos**, space, creation, everything, nature, heavens, the natural world, macrocosm, all existence

unjust ADJECTIVE = **unfair**, prejudiced, biased, wrong, one-sided, partial, partisan, unjustified, wrongful, undeserved, inequitable, unmerited ■ **OPPOSITE:** fair

unkempt ADJECTIVE **1** *His hair was unkempt and filthy.* = **uncombed**, tousled, shaggy, ungroomed **2** *an unkempt look* = **untidy**, scruffy, dishevelled, disordered, messy, sloppy (*informal*), shabby, rumpled, bedraggled, slovenly, blowsy, sluttish, slatternly, disarranged, ungroomed, disarrayed, frowzy, daggy (*Austral. & N.Z. informal*) ■ **OPPOSITE:** tidy

unkind ADJECTIVE = **cruel**, mean (*informal*), nasty, spiteful, harsh, malicious, insensitive, unfriendly, inhuman, unsympathetic, uncaring, thoughtless, unfeeling, inconsiderate, uncharitable, unchristian, hardhearted ■ **OPPOSITE:** kind

unknown ADJECTIVE **1** *a perilous expedition, through unknown terrain* = **strange**, new, undiscovered, uncharted, unexplored, virgin, remote, alien, exotic, outlandish, unmapped, untravelled, beyond your ken **2** *Unknown thieves had forced their way into the apartment.* = **unidentified**, mysterious, anonymous, unnamed, nameless, incognito **3** *He was an unknown writer.* = **obscure**, little known, minor, humble, unfamiliar, insignificant, lowly, unimportant, unheard-of, unsung, inconsequential, undistinguished, unrenowned ■ **OPPOSITE:** famous

unleash VERB = **release**, let go, let loose, free, untie, unloose, unbridle

unlike PREPOSITION **1** *She was unlike him in every way except her eyes.* = **different from**, dissimilar to, not resembling, far from, not like, distinct from, incompatible with, unrelated to, distant from, unequal to, far apart from, divergent from, not similar to, as different as chalk and cheese from (*informal*) ■ **OPPOSITE:** similar to **2** *Unlike aerobics, walking entails no expensive fees.* = **contrasted with**, not like, in contradiction to, in contrast with or to, as opposed to, differently from, opposite to

unlikely ADJECTIVE **1** *A military coup seems unlikely.* = **improbable**, doubtful, remote, slight, faint, not likely, unimaginable ■ **OPPOSITE:** probable **2** *I smiled sincerely, to encourage him to buy this unlikely story.* = **unbelievable**, incredible, unconvincing, implausible, questionable, cock-and-bull (*informal*) ■ **OPPOSITE:** believable

unlimited ADJECTIVE **1** *An unlimited number of copies can be made from the original.* = **infinite**, endless, countless, great, vast, extensive, immense, stellar (*informal*), limitless, boundless, incalculable, immeasurable, unbounded, illimitable ■ **OPPOSITE:** finite **2** *You'll also have unlimited access to the swimming pool.* = **total**, full, complete, absolute, unconditional, unqualified, unfettered, unrestricted, all-encompassing, unconstrained
■ **OPPOSITE:** restricted

unload VERB **1** *Unload everything from the boot and clean it thoroughly.* = **empty**, clear, unpack, dump, discharge, off-load, disburden, unlade **2** *He unloaded the horse where the track dead-ended.* = **unburden**, relieve, lighten, disburden

unlock VERB = **open**, undo, unfasten, release, unbolt, unlatch, unbar

unlucky ADJECTIVE **1** *Argentina's unlucky defeat by Ireland* = **unfortunate**, unhappy, disastrous ■ **OPPOSITE:** fortunate **2** *13 was to prove an unlucky number.* = **ill-fated**, doomed, inauspicious, ominous, untimely, unfavourable, cursed, ill-starred, ill-omened

unmask VERB = **reveal**, expose, uncover, discover, disclose, unveil, show up, lay bare, bring to light, uncloak

unmistakable ADJECTIVE = **clear**, certain, positive, decided, sure, obvious, plain, patent, evident, distinct, pronounced, glaring, manifest, blatant, conspicuous, palpable, unequivocal, unambiguous, indisputable ■ **OPPOSITE:** doubtful

unmitigated ADJECTIVE **1** *She leads a life of unmitigated misery.* = **unrelieved**, relentless, unalleviated, intense, harsh, grim, persistent, oppressive, unbroken, unqualified, unabated, undiminished, unmodified, unredeemed **2** *A senior police officer had called him an unmitigated liar.* = **complete**, absolute, utter, perfect, rank, sheer, total, outright, thorough, downright, consummate, out-and-out, thoroughgoing, arrant, deep-dyed

unnatural ADJECTIVE **1** *The altered landscape looks unnatural and weird.* = **abnormal**, odd, strange, unusual, extraordinary, bizarre, perverted, queer, irregular, perverse, supernatural, uncanny, outlandish, unaccountable, anomalous, freakish, aberrant ■ **OPPOSITE:** normal **2** *She gave him a bright, determined smile which seemed unnatural.* = **false**, forced, artificial, studied, laboured, affected, assumed, mannered, strained, stiff, theatrical, contrived, self-conscious, feigned, stilted, insincere, factitious, stagy, phoney or phony (*informal*)

■ **OPPOSITE:** genuine **3** *Murder is an unnatural act.* = **inhuman**, evil, monstrous, wicked, savage, brutal, ruthless, callous, heartless, cold-blooded, fiendish, unfeeling
■ **OPPOSITE:** humane

unnecessary ADJECTIVE = **needless**, excessive, unwarranted, useless, pointless, not needed, redundant, wasteful, gratuitous, superfluous, wanton, expendable, surplus to requirements, uncalled-for, dispensable, unneeded, nonessential, inessential, unmerited, to no purpose, unrequired, supererogatory
■ **OPPOSITE:** essential

unnerve VERB = **shake**, upset, disconcert, disturb, intimidate, frighten, rattle (*informal*), discourage, dismay, daunt, disarm, confound, fluster, faze, unman, demoralize, unhinge, psych out (*informal*), throw off balance, dishearten, dispirit
■ **OPPOSITE:** strengthen

unoccupied ADJECTIVE **1** *The house was unoccupied at the time of the explosion.* = **empty**, vacant, uninhabited, untenanted, tenantless **2** *Portraits of unoccupied youths and solitary females predominate.* = **idle**, unemployed, inactive, disengaged, at leisure, at a loose end

unofficial ADJECTIVE **1** *Unofficial estimates speak of at least two hundred dead.* = **unconfirmed**, off the record, unsubstantiated, private, personal, unauthorized, undocumented, uncorroborated **2** *Rail workers have voted to continue their unofficial strike.* = **unauthorized**, informal, unsanctioned, casual, wildcat

unparalleled ADJECTIVE = **unequalled**, exceptional, unprecedented, rare, unique, singular, consummate, superlative, unrivalled, incomparable, unmatched, peerless, unsurpassed, matchless, beyond compare, without equal

unpleasant ADJECTIVE **1** *They tolerated what they felt was an unpleasant situation.* = **nasty**, bad, horrid (*informal*), distressing, annoying, irritating, miserable, troublesome, distasteful, obnoxious, unpalatable, displeasing, repulsive, objectionable, disagreeable, abhorrent, irksome, unlovely, execrable, eye-watering
■ **OPPOSITE:** nice **2** *He was very unpleasant indeed.* = **obnoxious**, disagreeable, vicious, malicious, rude, mean (*informal*), cruel, poisonous, unattractive, unfriendly, vindictive, venomous, mean-spirited, inconsiderate, impolite, unloveable, ill-natured, unlikable or unlikeable
■ **OPPOSITE:** likable or likeable

unpleasantness NOUN 1 *Most offices are riddled with sniping and general unpleasantness.* = **hostility**, animosity, antagonism, bad feeling, malice, rudeness, offensiveness, abrasiveness, argumentativeness, unfriendliness, quarrelsomeness, ill humour or will ■ **OPPOSITE:** friendliness 2 *the unpleasantness of surgery and chemotherapy* = **nastiness**, awfulness, grimness, trouble, misery, woe, ugliness, unacceptability, dreadfulness, disagreeableness, horridness ■ **OPPOSITE:** pleasantness

unpopular ADJECTIVE = **disliked**, rejected, unwanted, avoided, shunned, unwelcome, undesirable, unattractive, detested, out of favour, unloved, out in the cold, cold-shouldered, not sought out, sent to Coventry (*Brit.*) ■ **OPPOSITE:** popular

unprecedented ADJECTIVE 1 *Such a move is unprecedented.* = **unparalleled**, unheard-of, exceptional, new, original, novel, unusual, abnormal, singular, ground-breaking, unrivalled, freakish, unexampled 2 *The scheme has been hailed as an unprecedented success.* = **extraordinary**, amazing, remarkable, outstanding, fantastic (*informal*), marvellous, exceptional, phenomenal, uncommon

unprofessional ADJECTIVE 1 *He was fined for unprofessional conduct.* = **unethical**, unfitting, improper, lax, negligent, unworthy, unseemly, unprincipled 2 *He rubbished his team for another unprofessional performance.* = **amateurish**, amateur, incompetent, inefficient, cowboy (*informal*), inexperienced, untrained, slapdash, slipshod, inexpert ■ **OPPOSITE:** skilful

unqualified ADJECTIVE 1 *She was unqualified for the job.* = **unfit**, incapable, incompetent, not up to, unprepared, ineligible, ill-equipped, not equal to 2 *The event was an unqualified success.* = **unconditional**, complete, total, absolute, utter, outright, thorough, downright, consummate, unrestricted, out-and-out, categorical, unmitigated, unreserved, thoroughgoing, without reservation, arrant, deep-dyed

unquestionable ADJECTIVE = **certain**, undeniable, indisputable, clear, sure, perfect, absolute, patent, definite, manifest, unmistakable, conclusive, flawless, unequivocal, faultless, self-evident, irrefutable, incontrovertible, incontestable, indubitable, beyond a shadow of doubt, nailed-on (*slang*) ■ **OPPOSITE:** doubtful

unravel VERB 1 *She wanted to unravel the mystery of her husband's disappearance.* = **solve**, explain, work out, resolve, interpret, figure out (*informal*), make out, clear up, suss (out) (*slang*), get to the bottom of, get straight, puzzle out 2 *He could unravel knots that others could not even attempt.* = **undo**, separate, disentangle, free, unwind, extricate, straighten out, untangle, unknot

unreadable ADJECTIVE 1 *Most computer ads used to be unreadable.* = **turgid**, heavy going, badly written, dry as dust 2 *She scribbled an unreadable address on the receipt.* = **illegible**, undecipherable, crabbed

unreal ADJECTIVE = **imaginary**, make-believe, illusory, fabulous, visionary, mythical, fanciful, fictitious, intangible, immaterial, storybook, insubstantial, nebulous, dreamlike, impalpable, chimerical, phantasmagoric

unreasonable ADJECTIVE 1 *The strikers were being unreasonable in their demands.* = **biased**, arbitrary, irrational, illogical, blinkered, opinionated, headstrong ■ **OPPOSITE:** open-minded 2 *unreasonable increases in the price of petrol* = **excessive**, steep (*informal*), exorbitant, unfair, absurd, extravagant, unjust, too great, undue, preposterous, unwarranted, far-fetched, extortionate, uncalled-for, immoderate ■ **OPPOSITE:** moderate

unrelenting ADJECTIVE 1 *in the face of severe opposition and unrelenting criticism* = **merciless**, tough, ruthless, relentless, cruel, stern, inexorable, implacable, intransigent, remorseless, pitiless, unsparing 2 *an unrelenting downpour of rain* = **steady**, constant, continuous, endless, perpetual, continual, unbroken, incessant, unabated, ceaseless, unremitting, unwavering

unremitting ADJECTIVE = **constant**, continuous, relentless, perpetual, continual, unbroken, incessant, diligent, unabated, unwavering, indefatigable, remorseless, assiduous, unceasing, sedulous, unwearied

unrest NOUN = **discontent**, rebellion, dissatisfaction, protest, turmoil, upheaval, strife, agitation, discord, disaffection, sedition, tumult, dissension ■ **OPPOSITE:** peace

unrivalled ADJECTIVE = **unparalleled**, incomparable, unsurpassed, supreme, unmatched, peerless, unequalled, matchless, beyond compare, without equal, nonpareil, unexcelled

unruffled ADJECTIVE **1** *Anne had remained unruffled, very cool and controlled.* = **calm**, cool, collected, peaceful, composed, serene, tranquil, sedate, placid, undisturbed, unmoved, unfazed (*informal*), unperturbed, unflustered **2** *the unruffled surface of the pool* = **smooth**, even, level, flat, unbroken

unruly ADJECTIVE = **uncontrollable**, wild, unmanageable, disorderly, turbulent, boisterous, rebellious, wayward, rowdy, intractable, wilful, lawless, fractious, riotous, headstrong, mutinous, disobedient, ungovernable, refractory, obstreperous, insubordinate ■ OPPOSITE: manageable

unsafe ADJECTIVE = **dangerous**, risky, hazardous, threatening, uncertain, unstable, insecure, unreliable, precarious, treacherous, perilous, unsound ■ OPPOSITE: safe

unsavoury ADJECTIVE **1** *The sport has long been associated with unsavoury characters.* = **unpleasant**, nasty, obnoxious, offensive, revolting, distasteful, repellent, repulsive, objectionable, repugnant **2** *unsavoury school meals* = **unappetizing**, unpalatable, distasteful, sickening, disagreeable, nauseating ■ OPPOSITE: appetizing

unscathed ADJECTIVE = **unharmed**, unhurt, uninjured, whole, sound, safe, untouched, unmarked, in one piece, unscarred, unscratched

unscrupulous ADJECTIVE = **unprincipled**, corrupt, crooked (*informal*), ruthless, improper, immoral, dishonest, unethical, exploitative, dishonourable, roguish, unconscionable, knavish (*archaic*), conscienceless, unconscientious ■ OPPOSITE: honourable

unseat VERB **1** *It is not clear who was behind the attempt to unseat the President.* = **depose**, overthrow, oust, remove, dismiss, discharge, displace, dethrone **2** *She was unseated on her first ride.* = **throw**, unsaddle, unhorse

unseemly ADJECTIVE = **improper**, inappropriate, unsuitable, out of place, undignified, disreputable, unbecoming, unrefined, out of keeping, discreditable, indelicate, in poor taste, indecorous, unbefitting ■ OPPOSITE: proper

unseen ADJECTIVE **1** *I can now accept that there are unseen forces at work.* = **unobserved**, undetected, unperceived, lurking, unnoticed, unobtrusive **2** *playing computer games against unseen opponents* = **hidden**, concealed, invisible, veiled, obscure

unselfish ADJECTIVE = **generous**, selfless, noble, kind, liberal, devoted, humanitarian, charitable, disinterested, altruistic, self-sacrificing, magnanimous, self-denying

unsettle VERB = **disturb**, trouble, upset, throw (*informal*), bother, confuse, disorder, rattle (*informal*), agitate, ruffle, unnerve, disconcert, unbalance, fluster, perturb, faze, throw into confusion, throw off balance, discompose, throw into disorder, throw into uproar

unsettled ADJECTIVE **1** *The unsettled political scene worries some investors.* = **unstable**, shaky, insecure, disorderly, unsteady **2** *To tell the truth, I'm a bit unsettled tonight.* = **restless**, tense, uneasy, troubled, shaken, confused, wired (*slang*), disturbed, anxious, agitated, unnerved, flustered, perturbed, on edge, restive, adrenalized **3** *They were in the process of resolving all the unsettled issues.* = **unresolved**, undecided, undetermined, open, doubtful, debatable, up in the air, moot **4** *Despite the unsettled weather, we had a marvellous weekend.* = **inconstant**, changing, unpredictable, variable, uncertain, changeable **5** *Liabilities related to unsettled transactions are recorded.* = **owing**, due, outstanding, pending, payable, in arrears

unsightly ADJECTIVE = **ugly**, unattractive, repulsive, unpleasant, revolting (*informal*), hideous, horrid, disagreeable, unprepossessing ■ OPPOSITE: attractive

unskilled ADJECTIVE = **unprofessional**, inexperienced, unqualified, untrained, uneducated, amateurish, cowboy (*informal*), untalented ■ OPPOSITE: skilled

unsophisticated ADJECTIVE **1** *music of a crude kind which unsophisticated audiences enjoyed* = **simple**, plain, uncomplicated, straightforward, unrefined, uninvolved, unspecialized, uncomplex ■ OPPOSITE: advanced **2** *She was quite unsophisticated in the ways of the world.* = **naive**, innocent, inexperienced, unworldly, unaffected, childlike, natural, artless, ingenuous, guileless

unsound ADJECTIVE **1** *The thinking is muddled and fundamentally unsound.* = **flawed**, faulty, weak, false, shaky, unreliable, invalid, defective, illogical, erroneous, specious, fallacious, ill-founded **2** *The church was structurally unsound.* = **unstable**, shaky, insecure, unsafe, unreliable, flimsy, wobbly, tottering, rickety, unsteady, not solid ■ OPPOSITE: stable **3** *He was rejected as an army conscript as being of unsound mind.* = **unhealthy**, unstable, unbalanced, diseased, ill, weak, delicate, ailing, frail, defective, unwell, deranged, unhinged

unspeakable ADJECTIVE = **dreadful**, shocking, appalling, evil, awful, overwhelming, horrible, unbelievable, monstrous, from hell (*informal*), inconceivable, unimaginable, repellent, abysmal, frightful, heinous, odious, indescribable, loathsome, abominable, ineffable, beyond words, execrable, unutterable, inexpressible, beyond description, hellacious (*U.S. slang*), too horrible for words

unstable ADJECTIVE **1** *The situation is unstable and potentially dangerous.* = **changeable**, volatile, unpredictable, variable, fluctuating, unsteady, fitful, inconstant ■ **OPPOSITE:** constant **2** *a house built on unstable foundations* = **insecure**, shaky, precarious, unsettled, wobbly, tottering, rickety, unsteady, not fixed **3** *He was emotionally unstable.* = **unpredictable**, irrational, erratic, inconsistent, unreliable, temperamental, capricious, changeable, untrustworthy, vacillating ■ **OPPOSITE:** level-headed

unsteady ADJECTIVE **1** *a slightly unsteady item of furniture* = **unstable**, shaky, insecure, unsafe, precarious, treacherous, rickety, infirm **2** *The boy was unsteady, staggering around the room.* = **reeling**, wobbly, tottering **3** *She knew the impact an unsteady parent could have on a young girl.* = **erratic**, unpredictable, volatile, unsettled, wavering, unreliable, temperamental, changeable, vacillating, flighty, inconstant

unsung ADJECTIVE = **unacknowledged**, unrecognized, unappreciated, unknown, neglected, anonymous, disregarded, unnamed, uncelebrated, unhonoured, unacclaimed, unhailed

unswerving ADJECTIVE = **firm**, staunch, steadfast, constant, true, direct, devoted, steady, dedicated, resolute, single-minded, unwavering, unflagging, untiring, unfaltering, undeviating

untangle VERB **1** *trying to untangle several reels of film* = **disentangle**, unravel, sort out, extricate, straighten out, untwist, unsnarl ■ **OPPOSITE:** entangle **2** *Lawyers began trying to untangle the complex affairs of the bank.* = **solve**, clear up, straighten out, understand, explain, figure out (*informal*), clarify, unravel, fathom, get to the bottom of, elucidate, suss out (*informal*), puzzle out ■ **OPPOSITE:** complicate

untenable ADJECTIVE = **unsustainable**, indefensible, unsound, groundless, weak, flawed, shaky, unreasonable, illogical, fallacious, insupportable, invalid ■ **OPPOSITE:** justified

unthinkable ADJECTIVE **1** *Returning to live with my parents would have been unthinkable.* = **impossible**, out of the question, inconceivable, unlikely, not on (*informal*), absurd, unreasonable, improbable, preposterous, illogical **2** *Monday's unthinkable tragedy* = **inconceivable**, incredible, unbelievable, unimaginable, beyond belief, beyond the bounds of possibility

unthinking ADJECTIVE **1** *He doesn't say those silly things that unthinking people say.* = **thoughtless**, insensitive, tactless, rude, blundering, inconsiderate, undiplomatic **2** *Bruce was no unthinking vandal.* = **impulsive**, senseless, unconscious, mechanical, rash, careless, instinctive, oblivious, negligent, unwitting, witless, inadvertent, heedless, unmindful ■ **OPPOSITE:** deliberate

untidy ADJECTIVE **1** *Clothes were thrown in the luggage in an untidy heap.* = **messy**, disordered, chaotic, littered, muddled, cluttered, jumbled, rumpled, shambolic (*informal*), bedraggled, unkempt, topsy-turvy, higgledy-piggledy (*informal*), mussy (*U.S. informal*), muddly, disarrayed ■ **OPPOSITE:** neat **2** *a thin man with untidy hair* = **unkempt**, dishevelled, tousled, disordered, messy, ruffled, scruffy, rumpled, bedraggled, ratty (*informal*), straggly, windblown, disarranged, mussed up (*informal*), daggy (*Austral. & N.Z. informal*) **3** *I'm untidy in most ways.* = **sloppy** (*informal*), messy (*informal*), slovenly, slipshod, slatternly (*old-fashioned*) ■ **OPPOSITE:** methodical

untie VERB = **undo**, free, release, loosen, unfasten, unbind, unstrap, unclasp, unlace, unknot, unmoor, unbridle

until PREPOSITION **1** = **till**, up to, up till, up to the time, as late as **2** = **before**, up to, prior to, in advance of, previous to, pre-
▶ CONJUNCTION **1** = **till**, up to, up till, up to the time, as late as **2** = **before**, up to, prior to, in advance of, previous to

> USAGE The use of *until such time as* (as in *Industrial action will continue until such time as our demands are met*) is unnecessary and should be avoided: *Industrial action will continue until our demands are met.* The use of *up* before *until* is also redundant and should be avoided: *the talks will continue until* (not *up until*) *23rd March.*

untimely ADJECTIVE **1** *His mother's untimely death had a catastrophic effect on him.* = **early**, premature, before time, unseasonable ■ **OPPOSITE:** timely **2** *Your readers would have* *seen the article as at best untimely.* = **ill-timed**, inappropriate, badly timed, inopportune, unfortunate, awkward, unsuitable, inconvenient, mistimed, inauspicious ■ **OPPOSITE:** well-timed

untold ADJECTIVE **1** *This might do untold damage to her health.* = **indescribable**, unthinkable, unimaginable, unspeakable, undreamed of, unutterable, inexpressible **2** *the glittering prospect of untold riches* = **countless**, incalculable, innumerable, myriad, numberless, uncounted, uncountable, unnumbered, measureless **3** *the untold story of children's suffering* = **undisclosed**, unknown, unrevealed, private, secret, hidden, unrelated, unpublished, unrecounted

untoward ADJECTIVE = **unfavourable**, unfortunate, disastrous, adverse, contrary, annoying, awkward, irritating, unlucky, inconvenient, untimely, inauspicious, inimical, ill-timed, vexatious, inopportune

untrue ADJECTIVE **1** *The allegations were completely untrue.* = **false**, lying, wrong, mistaken, misleading, incorrect, inaccurate, sham, dishonest, deceptive, spurious, erroneous, fallacious, untruthful ■ **OPPOSITE:** true **2** *untrue to the basic tenets of socialism* = **unfaithful**, disloyal, deceitful, treacherous, two-faced, faithless, false, untrustworthy, perfidious (*literary*), forsworn, traitorous, inconstant ■ **OPPOSITE:** faithful

untruth NOUN *The Authority accused estate agents of using blatant untruths.* = **lie**, fabrication, falsehood, fib, story (*informal*), tale, fiction, deceit, whopper (*informal*), porky (*Brit. slang*), pork pie (*Brit. slang*), falsification, prevarication

unused ADJECTIVE **1** *unused containers of food and drink* = **new**, untouched, remaining, fresh, intact, immaculate, pristine **2** *Throw away any unused cream when it has reached the expiry date.* = **remaining**, leftover, unconsumed, left, available, extra, unutilized **3** (*with* **to**) *Mother was entirely unused to such hard work.* = **unaccustomed to**, new to, unfamiliar with, not up to, not ready for, a stranger to, inexperienced in, unhabituated to

unusual ADJECTIVE **1** *rare and unusual plants* = **rare**, odd, strange, extraordinary, different, surprising, novel, bizarre, unexpected, curious, weird (*informal*), unfamiliar, abnormal, queer, phenomenal, uncommon, out of the ordinary, left-field (*informal*), unwonted ■ **OPPOSITE:** common **2** *He was an unusual man with great business talents.* = **extraordinary**, unique,

remarkable, exceptional, notable, phenomenal, uncommon, singular, unconventional, out of the ordinary, atypical ■ **OPPOSITE:** average

unveil VERB = **reveal**, publish, launch, introduce, release, display, broadcast, demonstrate, expose, bare, parade, exhibit, disclose, uncover, bring out, make public, flaunt, divulge, lay bare, make known, bring to light, put on display, lay open, put on show, put on view ■ **OPPOSITE:** conceal

unwarranted ADJECTIVE = **unnecessary**, unjustified, indefensible, wrong, unreasonable, unjust, gratuitous, unprovoked, inexcusable, groundless, uncalled-for

unwary ADJECTIVE = **careless**, rash, reckless, hasty, thoughtless, unguarded, indiscreet, imprudent, heedless, incautious, uncircumspect, unwatchful ■ **OPPOSITE:** cautious

unwell ADJECTIVE = **ill**, poorly (*informal*), sick, crook (*Austral. & N.Z. informal*), ailing, unhealthy, sickly, out of sorts, off colour, under the weather (*informal*), in poor health, at death's door, indisposed, green about the gills ■ **OPPOSITE:** well

unwieldy ADJECTIVE **1** *They came panting up to his door with their unwieldy baggage.* = **bulky**, massive, hefty, clumsy, weighty, ponderous, ungainly, clunky (*informal*) **2** *His firm must contend with the unwieldy Russian bureaucracy.* = **awkward**, cumbersome, inconvenient, burdensome, unmanageable, unhandy

unwilling ADJECTIVE **1** *Initially the government was unwilling to accept the defeat.* = **disinclined**, reluctant, averse, loath, slow, opposed, resistant, not about, not in the mood, indisposed ■ **OPPOSITE:** willing **2** *He finds himself an unwilling participant in school politics.* = **reluctant**, grudging, unenthusiastic, resistant, involuntary, averse, demurring, laggard (*rare*) ■ **OPPOSITE:** eager

unwind VERB **1** *It helps them to unwind after a busy day at work.* = **relax**, wind down, take it easy, slow down, sit back, calm down, take a break, loosen up, quieten down, let yourself go, mellow out (*informal*), make yourself at home, outspan (*S. African*) **2** *One of them unwound a length of rope from around his waist.* = **unravel**, undo, uncoil, slacken, disentangle, unroll, unreel, untwist, untwine

unwise ADJECTIVE = **foolish**, stupid, silly, rash, irresponsible, reckless, senseless, short-sighted, ill-advised, foolhardy, inane, indiscreet, ill-judged, ill-considered, imprudent, inadvisable, asinine, injudicious, improvident, impolitic ■ **OPPOSITE:** wise

unwitting ADJECTIVE **1** *It had been an unwitting blunder on his part.* = **unintentional**, involuntary, inadvertent, chance, accidental, unintended, unplanned, undesigned, unmeant ■ **OPPOSITE:** deliberate **2** *We're unwitting victims of the system.* = **unknowing**, innocent, unsuspecting, unconscious, unaware, ignorant ■ **OPPOSITE:** knowing

unworthy ADJECTIVE **1** *You may feel unworthy of the attention and help people offer you.* = **undeserving**, not good enough, not fit, not worth, ineligible, not deserving ■ **OPPOSITE:** deserving **2** *Aren't you amazed by how loving the father is to his unworthy son?* = **dishonourable**, base, contemptible, degrading, disgraceful, shameful, disreputable, ignoble, discreditable ■ **OPPOSITE:** commendable **3** (*with* **of**) *His accusations are unworthy of a prime minister.* = **unbefitting**, beneath, unfitting to, unsuitable for, inappropriate to, improper to, out of character with, out of place with, unbecoming to

unwritten ADJECTIVE **1** *the unwritten stories of his infancy and childhood* = **oral**, word-of-mouth, unrecorded, vocal **2** *They obey the one unwritten rule that binds them all – no talking.* = **understood**, accepted, tacit, traditional, conventional, silent, customary, implicit, unformulated

up NOUN • **ups and downs** = **fluctuations**, changes, vicissitudes, moods, ebb and flow

up-and-coming ADJECTIVE = **promising**, ambitious, go-getting (*informal*), pushing, eager

upbeat ADJECTIVE = **cheerful**, positive, optimistic, promising, encouraging, looking up, hopeful, favourable, rosy, buoyant, heartening, cheery, forward-looking

upbringing NOUN = **education**, training, breeding, rearing, care, raising, tending, bringing-up, nurture, cultivation

update VERB = **bring up to date**, improve, correct, renew, revise, upgrade, amend, overhaul, streamline, modernize, rebrand, refresh (*a webpage*)

upgrade VERB **1** *Medical facilities are being reorganized and upgraded.* = **improve**, better, update, reform, add to, enhance, refurbish, renovate, remodel, make better, modernize, spruce up, ameliorate **2** *He was upgraded to security guard.* = **promote**, raise, advance, boost, move up, elevate, kick

upstairs (*informal*), give promotion to ■ **OPPOSITE:** demote

upheaval NOUN = **disturbance**, revolution, disorder, turmoil, overthrow, disruption, eruption, cataclysm, violent change

uphill ADJECTIVE **1** *a long, uphill journey* = **ascending**, rising, upward, mounting, climbing ■ **OPPOSITE:** descending **2** *It had been an uphill struggle to achieve what she wanted.* = **arduous**, hard, taxing, difficult, tough, exhausting, punishing, gruelling, strenuous, laborious, wearisome, Sisyphean

uphold VERB **1** *upholding the artist's right to creative freedom* = **support**, back, defend, aid, champion, encourage, maintain, promote, sustain, advocate, stand by, stick up for (*informal*) **2** *The crown court upheld the magistrate's decision.* = **confirm**, support, sustain, endorse, approve, justify, hold to, ratify, vindicate, validate

upkeep NOUN **1** *The money will be used for the estate's upkeep.* = **maintenance**, running, keep, subsistence, support, repair, conservation, preservation, sustenance **2** *subsidies for the upkeep of kindergartens and orphanages* = **running costs**, expenses, overheads, expenditure, outlay, operating costs, oncosts (*Brit.*)

uplift VERB *Art was created to uplift the mind and the spirit.* = **improve**, better, raise, advance, inspire, upgrade, refine, cultivate, civilize, ameliorate, edify ▶ NOUN *literature intended for the uplift of the soul* = **improvement**, enlightenment, advancement, cultivation, refinement, enhancement, enrichment, betterment, edification

upper ADJECTIVE **1** *There is a smart restaurant on the upper floor.* = **topmost**, top ■ **OPPOSITE:** bottom **2** *the muscles of the upper back and chest* = **higher**, high ■ **OPPOSITE:** lower **3** *the upper echelons of the Army* = **superior**, senior, higher-level, greater, top, important, chief, most important, elevated, eminent, higher-ranking ■ **OPPOSITE:** inferior

upper-class ADJECTIVE = **aristocratic**, noble, high-class, patrician, top-drawer, blue-blooded, highborn (*old-fashioned*)

uppermost ADJECTIVE **1** *John was on the uppermost floor of the three-storey gatehouse.* = **top**, highest, topmost, upmost, loftiest, most elevated ■ **OPPOSITE:** bottom **2** *Protection of sites is of uppermost priority.* = **supreme**, greatest, chief, leading, main, primary, principal, dominant, paramount, foremost, predominant, pre-eminent ■ **OPPOSITE:** least

u

upright ADJECTIVE **1** *He moved into an upright position.* = **vertical**, straight, standing up, erect, on end, perpendicular, bolt upright ■ OPPOSITE: horizontal **2** *a very upright, trustworthy man* = **honest**, good, principled, just, true, faithful, ethical, straightforward, honourable, righteous, conscientious, virtuous, trustworthy, high-minded, above board, incorruptible, unimpeachable ■ OPPOSITE: dishonourable

uprising NOUN = **rebellion**, rising, revolution, outbreak, revolt, disturbance, upheaval, mutiny, insurrection, putsch, insurgence

uproar NOUN **1** *The announcement caused uproar in the crowd.* = **commotion**, noise, racket, riot, confusion, turmoil, brawl, mayhem, clamour, din, turbulence, pandemonium, rumpus, hubbub, hurly-burly, brouhaha, ruction (*informal*), hullabaloo, ruckus (*informal*), bagarre (*French*) **2** *The announcement could cause an uproar in the United States.* = **protest**, outrage, complaint, objection, fuss, stink (*informal*), outcry, furore, hue and cry

uproot VERB **1** *the trauma of uprooting them from their homes* = **displace**, remove, exile, disorient, deracinate **2** *fallen trees which have been uprooted by the storm* = **pull up**, dig up, root out, weed out, rip up, grub up, extirpate, deracinate, pull out by the roots

upset ADJECTIVE **1** *They are terribly upset by the breakup of their parents' marriage.* = **distressed**, shaken, disturbed, worried, troubled, hurt, bothered, confused, unhappy, gutted (*Brit. informal*), put out, dismayed, choked (*informal*), grieved, frantic, hassled (*informal*), agitated, ruffled, cut up (*informal*), disconcerted, disquieted, overwrought, discomposed **2** *Larry is suffering from an upset stomach.* = **sick**, queasy, bad, poorly (*informal*), ill, gippy (*slang*) ▶ VERB **1** *She warned me not to say anything to upset him.* = **distress**, trouble, disturb, worry, alarm, bother, dismay, grieve, hassle (*informal*), agitate, ruffle, unnerve, disconcert, disquiet, fluster, perturb, faze, throw someone off balance, give someone grief (*Brit. & S. African*), discompose **2** *bumping into him, and almost upsetting the ginger ale* = **tip over**, overturn, capsize, knock over, spill, topple over **3** *I was wondering whether that might upset my level of concentration.* = **mess up**, spoil, disturb, change, confuse, disorder, unsettle, mix up, disorganize, turn topsy-turvy, put out of order, throw into disorder ▶ NOUN **1** *a source of continuity in times of worry and upset* = **distress**, worry,

trouble, shock, bother, disturbance, hassle (*informal*), disquiet, agitation, discomposure **2** *She caused a major upset when she beat last year's finalist.* = **reversal**, surprise, shake-up (*informal*), defeat, sudden change **3** *Paul was unwell last night with a stomach upset.* = **illness**, complaint, disorder, bug (*informal*), disturbance, sickness, malady, queasiness, indisposition

upshot NOUN = **result**, consequence, outcome, end, issue, event, conclusion, sequel, finale, culmination, end result, payoff (*informal*)

upside down *or* **upside-down** ADVERB *The painting was hung upside down.* = **wrong side up**, bottom up, on its head ▶ ADJECTIVE **1** *Tony had an upside-down map of Britain on his wall.* = **inverted**, overturned, upturned, on its head, bottom up, wrong side up **2** *the upside-down sort of life that we've had* = **confused**, disordered, chaotic, muddled, jumbled, in disarray, in chaos, topsy-turvy, in confusion, higgledy-piggledy (*informal*), in disorder

upstanding ADJECTIVE = **honest**, principled, upright, honourable, good, moral, ethical, trustworthy, incorruptible, true ■ OPPOSITE: immoral

upstart NOUN = **social climber**, nobody, nouveau riche (*French*), parvenu, arriviste, status seeker

uptight ADJECTIVE = **tense**, wired (*slang*), anxious, uneasy, prickly, edgy, on the defensive, on edge, nervy (*Brit. informal*), adrenalized

up-to-date ADJECTIVE = **modern**, fashionable, trendy (*Brit. informal*), in, newest, now (*informal*), happening (*informal*), current, with it (*old-fashioned, informal*), stylish, in vogue, on trend, all the rage, up-to-the-minute, having your finger on the pulse ■ OPPOSITE: out-of-date

upturn NOUN = **rise**, increase, boost, improvement, recovery, revival, advancement, upsurge, upswing

urban ADJECTIVE = **civic**, city, town, metropolitan, municipal, dorp (*S. African*), inner-city

urbane ADJECTIVE = **sophisticated**, cultured, polished, civil, mannerly, smooth, elegant, refined, cultivated, cosmopolitan, civilized, courteous, suave, well-bred, debonair, well-mannered ■ OPPOSITE: boorish

urchin NOUN = **ragamuffin**, waif, guttersnipe, brat, mudlark (*slang*), gamin, young rogue

urge VERB **1** *They urged parliament to approve plans for their reform programme.* = **beg**, appeal to, exhort (*formal*), press, prompt, plead, put pressure on, lean on, solicit, goad, implore, enjoin, beseech, pressurize, entreat, twist someone's arm (*informal*), put the heat on (*informal*), put the screws on (*informal*) **2** *He urged restraint on the security forces.* = **advocate**, suggest, recommend, advise, back, support, champion, counsel, insist on, endorse, push for ■ **OPPOSITE:** discourage ▶ NOUN *He had an urge to open a shop of his own.* = **impulse**, longing, wish, desire, fancy, drive, yen (*informal*), hunger, appetite, craving, yearning, itch (*informal*), thirst, compulsion, hankering ■ **OPPOSITE:** reluctance • **urge someone on** *She had a strong and supportive sister who urged her on.* = **drive on**, push, encourage, force, press, prompt, stimulate, compel, induce, propel, hasten, constrain, incite, egg on, goad, spur on, impel, gee up

urgency NOUN = **importance**, need, necessity, gravity, pressure, hurry, seriousness, extremity, exigency, imperativeness

urgent ADJECTIVE **1** *There is an urgent need for food and water.* = **crucial** (*informal*), desperate, pressing, great, important, crying, critical, immediate, acute, grave, instant, compelling, imperative, top-priority, now or never, exigent, not to be delayed ■ **OPPOSITE:** unimportant **2** *His mother leaned forward and spoke to him in urgent undertones.* = **insistent**, earnest, determined, intense, persistent, persuasive, resolute, clamorous, importunate (*formal*) ■ **OPPOSITE:** casual

urinate VERB = **pee**, wee (*informal*), leak (*slang*), tinkle (*Brit. informal*), piddle (*informal*), spend a penny (*Brit. informal*), make water, pass water, wee-wee (*informal*), micturate, take a whizz (*slang, chiefly U.S.*)

usable ADJECTIVE = **serviceable**, working, functional, available, current, practical, valid, at your disposal, ready for use, in running order, fit for use, utilizable

usage NOUN **1** *Parts of the motor wore out because of constant usage.* = **use**, operation, employment, running, control, management, treatment, handling **2** *a fruitful convergence with past usage and custom* = **practice**, method, procedure, form, rule, tradition, habit, regime, custom, routine, convention, mode, matter of course, wont

use VERB **1** *Officials used loud-hailers to call for calm.* = **employ**, utilize, make use of, work, apply, operate, exercise, practise, resort to, exert, wield, ply, put to use, bring into play,

find a use for, avail yourself of, turn to account, call into play **2** (*sometimes with* **up**) *You used all the ice cubes and didn't put the ice trays back.* = **consume**, go through, exhaust, spend, waste, get through, run through, deplete, dissipate, expend, fritter away **3** *Be careful she's not just using you.* = **take advantage of**, exploit, manipulate, abuse, milk, profit from, impose on, misuse, make use of, cash in on (*informal*), walk all over (*informal*), take liberties with ▶ NOUN **1** *research related to microcomputers and their use in classrooms* = **usage**, employment, utilization, operation, application **2** *Holes had developed, the result of many years of use.* = **service**, handling, wear and tear, treatment, practice, exercise **3** *You will no longer have a use for the car.* = **purpose**, call, need, end, point, cause, reason, occasion, object, necessity **4** *There's no use you asking me any more questions about that.* = **good**, point, help, service, value, benefit, profit, worth, advantage, utility, mileage (*informal*), avail, usefulness • **use something up** *They aren't the ones who use up the world's resources.* = **consume**, drain, exhaust, finish, waste, absorb, run through, deplete, squander, devour, swallow up, burn up, fritter away

used ADJECTIVE = **second-hand**, worn, not new, cast-off, hand-me-down (*informal*), nearly new, shopsoiled, reach-me-down (*informal*), preloved (*slang*) ■ **OPPOSITE:** new

used to ADJECTIVE = **accustomed to**, familiar with, in the habit of, given to, at home in, attuned to, tolerant of, wont to, inured to, hardened to, habituated to

useful ADJECTIVE = **helpful**, effective, valuable, practical, of use, profitable, of service, worthwhile, beneficial, of help, fruitful, advantageous, all-purpose, salutary, general-purpose, serviceable ■ **OPPOSITE:** useless

usefulness NOUN = **helpfulness**, value, worth, use, help, service, benefit, profit, utility, effectiveness, convenience, practicality, efficacy

useless ADJECTIVE **1** *He realised that their money was useless in this country.* = **worthless**, of no use, valueless, pants (*slang*), ineffective, impractical, fruitless, unproductive, ineffectual, unworkable, disadvantageous, unavailing, bootless, unsuitable ■ **OPPOSITE:** useful **2** *She knew it was useless to protest.* = **pointless**, hopeless, futile, vain, idle, profitless ■ **OPPOSITE:** worthwhile **3** *He was useless at any game with a ball.* = **inept**, no good, hopeless (*informal*), weak, stupid, pants (*slang*), incompetent, ineffectual

u

usher VERB *They were quickly ushered away.*
= **escort**, lead, direct, guide, conduct, pilot, steer, show ▶ NOUN *He did part-time work as an usher in a theatre.* = **attendant**, guide, doorman, usherette, escort, doorkeeper
• **usher something in** *a unique opportunity to usher in a new era of stability in Europe* = **introduce**, launch, bring in, precede, initiate, herald, pave the way for, ring in, open the door to, inaugurate

usual ADJECTIVE = **normal**, customary, regular, expected, general, common, stock, standard, fixed, ordinary, familiar, typical, constant, routine, everyday, accustomed, habitual, bog-standard (*Brit. & Irish slang*), wonted ■ **OPPOSITE:** unusual

usually ADVERB = **normally**, generally, mainly, commonly, regularly, mostly, routinely, on the whole, in the main, for the most part, by and large, most often, ordinarily, as a rule, habitually, as is usual, as is the custom

usurp VERB = **seize**, take over, assume, take, appropriate, wrest, commandeer, arrogate, infringe upon, lay hold of

utility NOUN = **usefulness**, use, point, benefit, service, profit, fitness, convenience, mileage (*informal*), avail, practicality, efficacy, advantageousness, serviceableness

utilize VERB = **use**, employ, deploy, take advantage of, resort to, make the most of, make use of, put to use, bring into play, have recourse to, avail yourself of, turn to account

utmost ADJECTIVE **1** *Security matters are treated with the utmost seriousness.*
= **greatest**, highest, maximum, supreme, extreme, paramount, pre-eminent **2** *The break-up tested our resolve to its utmost limits.*
= **farthest**, extreme, last, final, outermost, uttermost, farthermost ▶ NOUN *I'm going to do my utmost to climb as fast and as far as I can.*

= **best**, greatest, maximum, most, highest, hardest

utopia NOUN = **paradise**, heaven (*informal*), Eden, bliss, perfect place, Garden of Eden, Shangri-la, Happy Valley, seventh heaven, ideal life, Erewhon

utopian ADJECTIVE *He was pursuing a utopian dream of world prosperity.* = **perfect**, ideal, romantic, dream, fantasy, imaginary, visionary, airy, idealistic, fanciful, impractical, illusory, chimerical ▶ NOUN *Kennedy had no patience with dreamers or liberal utopians.* = **dreamer**, visionary, idealist, Don Quixote, romanticist

utter[1] VERB *They departed without uttering a word.* = **say**, state, speak, voice, express, deliver, declare, mouth, breathe, pronounce, articulate, enunciate, put into words, verbalize, vocalize

utter[2] ADJECTIVE *A look of utter confusion swept across his handsome face.* = **absolute**, complete, total, perfect, positive (*informal*), pure, sheer, stark, outright, all-out, thorough, downright, real, consummate, veritable, unqualified, out-and-out, unadulterated, unmitigated, thoroughgoing, arrant, deep-dyed

utterance NOUN **1** *the Queen's public utterances* = **speech**, words, statement, comment, opinion, remark, expression, announcement, observation, declaration, reflection, pronouncement **2** *the simple utterance of a few platitudes* = **speaking**, voicing, expression, breathing, delivery, ejaculation, articulation, enunciation, vocalization, verbalization, vociferation

utterly ADVERB = **totally**, completely, absolutely, just, really, quite, perfectly, fully, entirely, extremely, altogether, thoroughly, wholly, downright, categorically, to the core, one hundred per cent, in all respects, to the nth degree, unqualifiedly

u

Vv

vacancy NOUN **1** *They had a vacancy for a temporary secretary.* = **opening**, job, post, place, position, role, situation, opportunity, slot (*informal*), berth (*informal*), niche, job opportunity, vacant position, situation vacant **2** *The hotel only has a few vacancies left.* = **room**, space, available accommodation, unoccupied room

vacant ADJECTIVE **1** *They came upon a vacant house.* = **empty**, free, available, abandoned, deserted, to let, for sale, on the market, void, up for grabs, disengaged, uninhabited, unoccupied, not in use, unfilled, untenanted ■ OPPOSITE: occupied **2** *The post has been vacant for some time.* = **unfilled**, unoccupied ■ OPPOSITE: taken **3** *a dreamy, vacant look* = **blank**, vague, dreamy, dreaming, empty, abstracted, idle, thoughtless, vacuous, inane, expressionless, unthinking, absent-minded, incurious, ditzy or ditsy (*slang*) ■ OPPOSITE: thoughtful

vacate VERB **1** *I vacated the flat and went back to stay with my parents.* = **leave**, quit, move out of, give up, withdraw from, evacuate, depart from, go away from, leave empty, relinquish possession of **2** *She recently vacated her post as Finance Director.* = **quit**, leave, resign from, give up, withdraw from, chuck (*informal*), retire from, relinquish, renounce, walk out on, pack in (*informal*), abdicate, step down from (*informal*), stand down from

vacuous ADJECTIVE = **vapid**, stupid, inane, blank, vacant, unintelligent

vacuum NOUN **1** *The collapse of the army left a vacuum in the area.* = **gap**, lack, absence, space, deficiency, void **2** *The spinning turbine creates a vacuum.* = **emptiness**, space, void, gap, empty space, nothingness, vacuity

vagabond NOUN *He had lived as a vagabond, begging for food.* = **vagrant**, tramp, bum (*informal*), drifter, migrant, rolling stone, wanderer, beggar, outcast, rover, nomad, itinerant, down-and-out, hobo (*chiefly U.S.*), bag lady (*chiefly U.S.*), wayfarer, dosser (*Brit. slang*), knight of the road, person of no fixed address, derro (*Austral. slang*) ▶ MODIFIER *his impoverished, vagabond existence*

= **vagrant**, drifting, wandering, homeless, journeying, unsettled, roaming, idle, roving, nomadic, destitute, itinerant, down and out, rootless, footloose, fly-by-night (*informal*), shiftless

vagary NOUN (*usually plural*) = **whim**, caprice, unpredictability, sport, urge, fancy, notion, humour, impulse, quirk, conceit (*archaic*), whimsy, crotchet, sudden notion

vagrant NOUN *He lived on the street as a vagrant.* = **drifter**, tramp, bum (*informal*), vagabond, rolling stone, wanderer, beggar, derelict, itinerant, down-and-out, hobo (*U.S.*), bag lady (*chiefly U.S.*), dosser (*Brit. slang*), person of no fixed address, derro (*Austral. slang*) ▶ ADJECTIVE *the terrifying subculture of vagrant alcoholics* = **vagabond**, drifting, wandering, homeless, journeying, unsettled, roaming, idle, roving, nomadic, destitute, itinerant, down and out, rootless, footloose, fly-by-night (*informal*), shiftless ■ OPPOSITE: settled

vague ADJECTIVE **1** *Her description of her attacker was very vague.* = **unclear**, indefinite, hazy, confused, loose, uncertain, doubtful, unsure, superficial, incomplete, woolly, imperfect, sketchy, cursory ■ OPPOSITE: clear **2** *His answer was deliberately vague.* = **imprecise**, unspecified, generalized, rough, loose, ambiguous, hazy, equivocal, ill-defined, non-specific, inexact, obfuscatory, inexplicit **3** *She had married a charming but rather vague Englishman.* = **absent-minded**, absorbed, abstracted, distracted, unaware, musing, vacant, preoccupied, bemused, oblivious, dreamy, daydreaming, faraway, unthinking, heedless, inattentive, unheeding **4** *He could just make out a vague shape in the distance.* = **indistinct**, blurred, unclear, dim, fuzzy, unknown, obscure, faint, shadowy, indefinite, misty, hazy, indistinguishable, amorphous, indeterminate, bleary, nebulous, out of focus, ill-defined, indiscernible ■ OPPOSITE: distinct

vaguely ADVERB **1** *The voice was vaguely familiar.* = **slightly**, rather, sort of (*informal*), kind of (*informal*), a little, a bit, somewhat, moderately, faintly, dimly, to some extent, kinda (*informal*) **2** *'What did you talk about?' 'Oh, this and that,' she replied vaguely.* = **absent-mindedly**, evasively, abstractedly, obscurely, vacantly, inattentively **3** *'She's back there,' he said, waving vaguely behind him.* = **roughly**, loosely, indefinitely, carelessly, in a general way, imprecisely

vagueness NOUN **1** *the vagueness of the language used in the text* = **impreciseness**, ambiguity, obscurity, looseness, inexactitude, woolliness, undecidedness, lack of preciseness ■ **OPPOSITE:** preciseness **2** *her deliberately affected vagueness* = **absent-mindedness**, abstraction, forgetfulness, confusion, inattention, disorganization, giddiness, dreaminess, befuddlement, empty-headedness

vain ADJECTIVE **1** *They worked all night in a vain attempt to finish on schedule.* = **futile**, useless, pointless, unsuccessful, empty, hollow, idle, trivial, worthless, trifling, senseless, unimportant, fruitless, unproductive, abortive, unprofitable, time-wasting, unavailing, nugatory ■ **OPPOSITE:** successful **2** *She's a shallow, vain and self-centred woman.* = **conceited**, narcissistic, proud, arrogant, inflated, swaggering, stuck-up (*informal*), cocky, swanky (*informal*), ostentatious, egotistical, self-important, overweening, vainglorious, swollen-headed (*informal*), pleased with yourself, bigheaded (*informal*), peacockish ■ **OPPOSITE:** modest
• **in vain 1** *All her complaints were in vain.* = **useless**, to no avail, unsuccessful, fruitless, wasted, vain, ineffectual, without success, to no purpose, bootless **2** *He hammered the door, trying in vain to attract her attention.* = **uselessly**, to no avail, unsuccessfully, fruitlessly, vainly, ineffectually, without success, to no purpose, bootlessly

valiant ADJECTIVE = **brave**, heroic, courageous, bold, worthy, fearless, gallant, intrepid, plucky, doughty (*old-fashioned*), indomitable, redoubtable, dauntless, lion-hearted, valorous, stouthearted (*old-fashioned*) ■ **OPPOSITE:** cowardly

valid ADJECTIVE **1** *Both sides have made valid points.* = **sound**, good, reasonable, just, telling, powerful, convincing, substantial, acceptable, sensible, rational, logical, viable, credible, sustainable, plausible, conclusive, weighty, well-founded, cogent, well-grounded ■ **OPPOSITE:** unfounded **2** *For foreign holidays you will need a valid passport.* = **legal**, official, legitimate, correct, genuine, proper, in effect, authentic, in force, lawful, bona fide, legally binding, signed and sealed ■ **OPPOSITE:** invalid

validate VERB **1** *The evidence has been validated by historians.* = **confirm**, prove, certify, substantiate, corroborate **2** *Give the retailer your winning ticket to validate.* = **authorize**, endorse, ratify, legalize, authenticate, make legally binding, set your seal on or to

validity NOUN **1** *Some people deny the validity of this claim.* = **soundness**, force, power, grounds, weight, strength, foundation, substance, point, cogency **2** *They now want to challenge the validity of the vote.* = **legality**, authority, legitimacy, right, lawfulness

valley NOUN = **hollow**, dale, glen, vale, depression, dell, dingle, strath (*Scot.*), cwm (*Welsh*), coomb

valour or (*U.S.*) **valor** NOUN = **bravery**, courage, heroism, spirit, boldness, gallantry, derring-do (*archaic*), fearlessness, intrepidity, doughtiness, lion-heartedness ■ **OPPOSITE:** cowardice

valuable ADJECTIVE **1** *The experience was very valuable.* = **useful**, important, profitable, worthwhile, beneficial, valued, helpful, worthy, of use, of help, invaluable, serviceable, worth its weight in gold ■ **OPPOSITE:** useless **2** *She was a valuable friend and an excellent teacher.* = **treasured**, esteemed, cherished, prized, precious, held dear, estimable, worth your weight in gold **3** *valuable old books* = **precious**, expensive, costly, dear, high-priced, priceless, irreplaceable ■ **OPPOSITE:** worthless
▶ PLURAL NOUN *Leave your valuables in the hotel safe.* = **treasures**, prized possessions, precious items, heirlooms, personal effects, costly articles

value NOUN **1** *Studies are needed to see if these therapies have any value.* = **importance**, use, benefit, worth, merit, point, help, service, sense, profit, advantage, utility, significance, effectiveness, mileage (*informal*), practicality, usefulness, efficacy, desirability, serviceableness ■ **OPPOSITE:** worthlessness **2** *The value of his investment has risen by more than 100%.* = **cost**, price, worth, rate, equivalent, market price, face value, asking price, selling price, monetary worth ▶ PLURAL NOUN *a return to traditional family values* = **principles**, morals, ethics, mores, standards of behaviour, code of behaviour, (moral) standards ▶ VERB **1** *Do you value your best friend enough?* = **appreciate**, rate (*slang*), prize, regard highly, respect, admire, treasure, esteem, cherish, think much of, hold dear, have a high opinion of, set store by, hold in high regard or esteem ■ **OPPOSITE:** undervalue **2** (*often with* **at**) *I have had my jewellery valued for insurance purposes.* = **evaluate**, price, estimate, rate, cost, survey, assess, set at, appraise, put a price on

valued ADJECTIVE = **appreciated**, prized, esteemed, highly regarded, loved, dear, treasured, cherished

vandal NOUN = **hooligan**, ned (*Scot. slang*),

delinquent, rowdy, lager lout, graffiti artist, yob or yobbo (Brit. *slang*), cougan (*Austral. slang*), scozza (*Austral. slang*), bogan (*Austral. slang*)

vanguard NOUN = **forefront**, front line, cutting edge, leaders, front, van, spearhead, forerunners, front rank, trailblazers, advance guard, trendsetters ■ **OPPOSITE:** rearguard

vanish VERB **1** *The aircraft vanished without trace.* = **disappear**, become invisible, be lost to sight, dissolve, evaporate, fade away, melt away, disappear from sight, exit, evanesce (*formal*) ■ **OPPOSITE:** appear **2** *Dinosaurs vanished from the earth millions of years ago.* = **die out**, disappear, pass away, end, fade, dwindle, cease to exist, become extinct, disappear from the face of the earth

vanity NOUN **1** *Men who use steroids are motivated by sheer vanity.* = **pride**, arrogance, conceit, airs, showing off (*informal*), pretension, narcissism, egotism, self-love, ostentation, vainglory, self-admiration, affected ways, bigheadedness (*informal*), conceitedness, swollen-headedness (*informal*) ■ **OPPOSITE:** modesty **2** *the futility of human existence and the vanity of wealth* = **futility**, uselessness, worthlessness, emptiness, frivolity, unreality, triviality, hollowness, pointlessness, inanity, unproductiveness, fruitlessness, unsubstantiality, profitlessness ■ **OPPOSITE:** value

vanquish VERB = **defeat**, beat, conquer, reduce, stuff (*slang*), master, tank (*slang*), overcome, crush, overwhelm, put down, lick (*informal*), undo, subdue, rout, repress, overpower, quell, triumph over, clobber (*slang*), subjugate, run rings around (*informal*), wipe the floor with (*informal*), blow out of the water (*slang*), put to flight, get the upper hand over, put to rout

vapour or (U.S.) **vapor** NOUN = **mist**, fog, haze, smoke, breath, steam, fumes, dampness, miasma, exhalation

variable ADJECTIVE = **changeable**, unstable, fluctuating, shifting, flexible, wavering, uneven, fickle, temperamental, mercurial, capricious, unsteady, protean, vacillating, fitful, mutable, inconstant, chameleonic ■ **OPPOSITE:** constant

variance NOUN • **at variance** *Many of his statements are at variance with the facts.* = **in disagreement**, conflicting, at odds, in opposition, out of line, at loggerheads, at sixes and sevens (*informal*), out of harmony

variant ADJECTIVE *There are so many variant spellings of this name.* = **different**,

alternative, modified, derived, exceptional, divergent ▶ NOUN *The device is a variant of a conventional phone.* = **variation**, form, version, development, alternative, adaptation, revision, modification, permutation, transfiguration, aberration, derived form

variation NOUN **1** *This delicious variation on an omelette is easy to prepare.* = **alternative**, variety, modification, departure, innovation, variant **2** *Every day without variation my grandfather ate a plate of ham.* = **variety**, change, deviation, difference, diversity, diversion (*Brit.*), novelty, alteration, discrepancy, diversification, departure from the norm, break in routine ■ **OPPOSITE:** uniformity

varied ADJECTIVE = **different**, mixed, various, diverse, assorted, miscellaneous, sundry, motley, manifold (*formal*), heterogeneous ■ **OPPOSITE:** unvarying

variegated ADJECTIVE = **mottled**, pied, streaked, motley, many-coloured, parti-coloured, varicoloured

variety NOUN **1** *people who like variety in their lives and enjoy trying new things* = **diversity**, change, variation, difference, diversification, heterogeneity, many-sidedness, multifariousness ■ **OPPOSITE:** uniformity **2** *a store selling a wide variety of goods* = **range**, selection, assortment, mix, collection, line-up, mixture, array, cross section, medley, multiplicity, mixed bag (*informal*), miscellany, motley collection, intermixture **3** *She grows 12 varieties of old-fashioned roses.* = **type**, sort, kind, make, order, class, brand, species, breed, strain, category

various DETERMINER *He plans to spread his capital between various bank accounts.* = **different**, assorted, miscellaneous, varied, differing, distinct, diverse, divers (*archaic*), diversified, disparate, sundry, heterogeneous ■ **OPPOSITE:** similar ▶ ADJECTIVE *The methods employed are many and various.* = **many**, numerous, countless, several, abundant, innumerable, sundry, manifold (*formal*), profuse

┃ **USAGE** The use of *different* after *various*, ┃ which seems to be most common in ┃ speech, is unnecessary and should be ┃ avoided in serious writing: *The disease* ┃ *exists in various forms* (not in various ┃ *different forms*).

varnish NOUN *The varnish comes in six natural shades.* = **lacquer**, polish, glaze, japan, gloss, shellac ▶ VERB **1** *The painting still has to be varnished.* = **lacquer**, polish, glaze, japan, gloss, shellac **2** *The floors have all been*

V

varnished. = **polish**, decorate, glaze, adorn, gild, lacquer, embellish

vary VERB **1** *As the rugs are all handmade, each one varies slightly.* = **differ**, be different, be dissimilar, disagree, diverge, be unlike **2** *people whose moods vary according to the time of year* = **change**, shift, swing, transform, alter, fluctuate, oscillate, see-saw **3** *Try to vary your daily diet to include all the major food groups.* = **alternate**, mix, diversify, reorder, intermix, bring variety to, permutate, variegate **4** *The colour can be varied by adding filters.* = **modify**, change, alter, adjust

varying ADJECTIVE **1** *Reporters gave varying figures on the number of casualties.* = **different**, contrasting, inconsistent, varied, distinct, diverse, assorted, disparate, dissimilar, distinguishable, discrepant, streets apart **2** *The green table lamp flickered with varying intensity.* = **changing**, variable, irregular, inconsistent, fluctuating ■ OPPOSITE: unchanging

vassal NOUN = **serf**, slave, bondsman, subject, retainer, thrall, varlet (*archaic*), bondservant, liegeman

vast ADJECTIVE = **huge**, massive, enormous, great, wide, sweeping, extensive, tremendous, immense, mega (*slang*), unlimited, gigantic, astronomical, monumental (*informal*), monstrous, mammoth, colossal, never-ending, prodigious, limitless, boundless, voluminous, immeasurable, unbounded, elephantine, ginormous (*informal*), vasty (*archaic*), measureless, illimitable, humongous or humungous (*informal*) ■ OPPOSITE: tiny

vault[1] NOUN **1** *The money was in storage in bank vaults.* = **strongroom**, repository, depository **2** *He ordered that Matilda's body should be buried in the family vault.* = **crypt**, tomb, catacomb, cellar, mausoleum, charnel house, undercroft **3** *the vault of a magnificent cathedral* = **arch**, roof, ceiling, span

vault[2] VERB *Ned vaulted over the low wall.* = **jump**, spring, leap, clear, bound, hurdle

vaunted ADJECTIVE = **boasted about**, flaunted, paraded, shown off, made much of, bragged about, crowed about, exulted in, made a display of, prated about

veer VERB = **change direction**, turn, swerve, shift, sheer, tack, be deflected, change course

vehemence NOUN = **forcefulness**, force, violence, fire, energy, heat, passion, emphasis, enthusiasm, intensity, warmth, vigour, zeal, verve, fervour, eagerness, ardour, earnestness, keenness, fervency ■ OPPOSITE: indifference

vehement ADJECTIVE = **strong**, fierce, forceful, earnest, powerful, violent, intense, flaming, eager, enthusiastic, passionate, ardent, emphatic, fervent, impassioned, zealous, forcible, fervid ■ OPPOSITE: half-hearted

vehicle NOUN **1** *a vehicle which was somewhere between a tractor and a truck* = **conveyance** (*old-fashioned*), machine, motor vehicle, means of transport **2** *Her art became a vehicle for her political beliefs.* = **medium**, means, channel, mechanism, organ, apparatus, means of expression

veil NOUN **1** *She swathed her face in a veil of decorative muslin.* = **mask**, cover, shroud, film, shade, curtain, cloak **2** *the chilling facts behind this veil of secrecy* = **screen**, mask, disguise, blind **3** *He recognized the coast of England through the veil of mist.* = **film**, cover, curtain, cloak, shroud ▶ VERB *Her hair swept across her face, as if to veil it.* = **cover**, screen, hide, mask, shield, disguise, conceal, obscure, dim, cloak, mantle ■ OPPOSITE: reveal

veiled ADJECTIVE = **disguised**, implied, hinted at, covert, masked, concealed, suppressed

vein NOUN **1** *Many veins are found just under the skin.* = **blood vessel** **2** *He also wrote several works in a lighter vein.* = **mood**, style, spirit, way, turn, note, key, character, attitude, atmosphere, tone, manner, bent, stamp, humour, tendency, mode, temper, temperament, tenor, inclination, disposition, frame of mind **3** *The song has a vein of black humour running through it.* = **streak**, element, thread, suggestion, strain, trace, hint, dash, trait, sprinkling, nuance, smattering **4** *a rich deep vein of copper in the rock* = **seam**, layer, stratum, course, current, bed, deposit, streak, stripe, lode ■ RELATED WORD: *adjective* venous

velocity NOUN = **speed**, pace, rapidity, quickness, swiftness, fleetness, celerity (*formal*)

velvety ADJECTIVE = **soft**, smooth, downy, delicate, mossy, velvet-like

venal ADJECTIVE = **corrupt**, bent (*slang*), crooked (*informal*), prostituted, grafting (*informal*), mercenary, sordid, rapacious, unprincipled, dishonourable, corruptible, purchasable ■ OPPOSITE: honest

vendetta NOUN = **feud**, dispute, quarrel, enmity, bad blood, blood feud

veneer NOUN **1** *He was able to fool people with his veneer of intellectuality.* = **mask**, show, façade, front (*informal*), appearance, guise, pretence, semblance, false front **2** *bath panels fitted with a mahogany veneer* = **layer**, covering, finish, facing, film, gloss, patina, laminate, cladding, lamination

venerable ADJECTIVE = **respected**, august, sage, revered, honoured, wise, esteemed, reverenced

venerate VERB = **respect**, honour, esteem, revere, worship, adore, reverence, look up to, hold in awe ■ **OPPOSITE:** scorn

veneration NOUN = **respect**, esteem, reverence, worship, awe, deference, adoration

vengeance NOUN *She wanted vengeance for the loss of her daughter.* = **revenge**, retaliation, reprisal, retribution, avenging, an eye for an eye, settling of scores, requital, lex talionis ■ **OPPOSITE:** forgiveness • **with a vengeance** *The problem has returned with a vengeance.* = **to the utmost**, greatly, extremely, to the full, and no mistake, to the nth degree, with no holds barred

vengeful ADJECTIVE = **unforgiving**, relentless, avenging, vindictive, punitive, implacable, spiteful, retaliatory, rancorous, thirsting for revenge, revengeful

venom NOUN **1** *There was no mistaking the venom in his voice.* = **malice**, hate, spite, bitterness, grudge, gall, acidity, spleen, acrimony, rancour, ill will, malevolence, virulence, pungency, malignity, spitefulness, maliciousness ■ **OPPOSITE:** benevolence **2** *snake handlers who grow immune to snake venom* = **poison**, toxin, bane

venomous ADJECTIVE **1** *He made a venomous personal attack on his opponent.* = **malicious**, vindictive, spiteful, hostile, savage, vicious, malignant, virulent, baleful, rancorous ■ **OPPOSITE:** benevolent **2** *The adder is Britain's only venomous snake.* = **poisonous**, poison, toxic, virulent, noxious, baneful (*archaic*), envenomed, mephitic ■ **OPPOSITE:** harmless

vent NOUN *There was a small air vent in the ceiling.* = **outlet**, opening, hole, split, aperture, duct, orifice ▶ VERB *She telephoned her best friend to vent her frustration.* = **express**, release, voice, air, empty, discharge, utter, emit, come out with, pour out, give vent to, give expression to ■ **OPPOSITE:** hold back

ventilate VERB **1** *The pit is ventilated by a steel fan.* = **aerate**, fan, cool, refresh, air-condition, freshen, oxygenate **2** *Following a bereavement, people need a safe place to ventilate their feelings.* = **discuss**, air, bring out into the open, talk about, debate, examine, broadcast, sift, scrutinize, make known

venture VERB **1** *Few Europeans had ventured beyond the Himalayas.* = **go**, travel, journey, set out, wander, stray, plunge into, rove, set forth **2** *Each time I ventured to speak, I was ignored.* = **dare**, presume, have the courage to, be brave enough, hazard, go out on a limb (*informal*), take the liberty, stick your neck out (*informal*), go so far as, make so bold as, have the temerity or effrontery or nerve **3** *We were warned not to make fools of ourselves by venturing an opinion.* = **put forward**, offer, suggest, present, air, table (*Brit.*), advance, propose, volunteer, submit, bring up, postulate (*formal*), proffer, broach, posit, moot, propound, dare to say ▶ NOUN *a Russian-American joint venture* = **undertaking**, project, enterprise, chance, campaign, risk, operation, activity, scheme, task, mission, speculation, gamble, adventure, exploit, pursuit, fling, hazard, crusade, endeavour

veracity NOUN **1** *We have total confidence in the veracity of our research.* = **accuracy**, truth, credibility, precision, exactitude **2** *He was shocked to find his veracity being questioned.* = **truthfulness**, integrity, honesty, candour, frankness, probity (*formal*), rectitude, trustworthiness, uprightness

verbal ADJECTIVE **1** = **spoken**, oral, word-of-mouth, unwritten **2** = **verbatim**, literal

verbally ADVERB = **orally**, vocally, in words, in speech, by word of mouth

verbatim ADVERB *The president's speeches are reproduced verbatim in the state-run newspapers.* = **exactly**, to the letter, word for word, closely, precisely, literally, faithfully, rigorously, in every detail, letter for letter ▶ ADJECTIVE *He gave me a verbatim report of the entire conversation.* = **word for word**, exact, literal, close, precise, faithful, line by line, unabridged, unvarnished, undeviating, unembellished

verdant ADJECTIVE = **green**, lush, leafy, grassy, fresh, flourishing

verdict NOUN = **decision**, finding, judgment, opinion, sentence, conclusion, conviction, adjudication, pronouncement

verge NOUN **1** *Carole was on the verge of tears.* = **brink**, point, edge, threshold **2** *The car pulled over on to the verge off the road.* = **border**, edge, margin, limit, extreme, lip, boundary, threshold, roadside, brim • **verge on something** *a fury that verges on madness* = **come near to**, approach, border on, resemble, incline to, be similar to, touch on, be more or less, tantamount to, tend towards, be not far from, incline towards

V

verification NOUN = **proof**, confirmation, validation, corroboration, authentication, substantiation

verify VERB **1** *A clerk simply verifies that the payment and invoice amount match.* = **check**, confirm, make sure, examine, monitor, check out (*informal*), inspect **2** *The government has not verified any of these reports.* = **confirm**, prove, substantiate, support, validate, bear out, attest, corroborate, attest to, authenticate ■ **OPPOSITE:** disprove

vernacular NOUN (*with* **the**) *To use the vernacular of the day, Peter was square.* = **speech**, jargon, idiom, parlance, cant, native language, dialect, patois, argot, vulgar tongue ▶ ADJECTIVE *dialects such as black vernacular English* = **colloquial**, popular, informal, local, common, native, indigenous, vulgar

versatile ADJECTIVE **1** *He stood out as one of the game's most versatile athletes.* = **adaptable**, flexible, all-round, resourceful, protean, multifaceted, many-sided, all-singing, all-dancing ■ **OPPOSITE:** unadaptable **2** *a versatile piece of equipment* = **all-purpose**, handy, functional, variable, adjustable, all-singing, all-dancing ■ **OPPOSITE:** limited

versed ADJECTIVE (*with* **in**) = **knowledgeable**, experienced, skilled, seasoned, qualified, familiar, practised, accomplished, competent, acquainted, well-informed, proficient, well up (*informal*), conversant ■ **OPPOSITE:** ignorant

version NOUN **1** *Ludo is a version of an ancient Indian racing game.* = **form**, variety, variant, sort, kind, class, design, style, model, type, brand, genre **2** *The English version is far inferior to the original French text.* = **adaptation**, edition, interpretation, form, reading, copy, rendering, translation, reproduction, portrayal **3** *She went public with her version of events.* = **account**, report, side, description, record, reading, story, view, understanding, history, statement, analysis, take (*informal, chiefly U.S.*), construction, tale, impression, explanation, interpretation, rendering, narrative, chronicle, rendition, narration, construal

vertical ADJECTIVE = **upright**, sheer, perpendicular, straight (up and down), erect, plumb, on end, precipitous, vertiginous, bolt upright ■ **OPPOSITE:** horizontal

vertigo NOUN = **dizziness**, giddiness, light-headedness, fear of heights, loss of balance, acrophobia, loss of equilibrium, swimming of the head

verve NOUN = **enthusiasm**, energy, spirit, life, force, punch (*informal*), dash, pep, sparkle, zip (*informal*), vitality, animation, vigour, zeal, gusto, get-up-and-go (*informal*), élan, brio, vivacity, liveliness, vim ■ **OPPOSITE:** indifference

very ADVERB *I am very grateful to you for all your help.* = **extremely**, highly, greatly, really, deeply, particularly, seriously (*informal*), truly, absolutely, terribly, remarkably, unusually, jolly (*Brit.*), wonderfully, profoundly, decidedly, awfully (*informal*), acutely, exceedingly, excessively, noticeably, eminently, superlatively, uncommonly, surpassingly ▶ ADJECTIVE **1** *Those were his very words to me.* = **exact**, actual, precise, same, real, express, identical, unqualified, selfsame **2** *the very person we need for the job* = **ideal**, perfect, right, fitting, appropriate, suitable, spot on (*Brit. informal*), apt, just the job (*Brit. informal*)

> **USAGE** In strict usage, adverbs of degree such as *very*, *too*, *quite*, *really*, and *extremely* are used only to qualify adjectives: *he is very happy; she is too sad.* By this rule, these words should not be used to qualify past participles that follow the verb *to be*, since they would then be technically qualifying verbs. With the exception of certain participles, such as *tired* or *disappointed*, that have come to be regarded as adjectives, all other past participles are qualified by adverbs such as *much*, *greatly*, *seriously*, or *excessively*: *he has been much* (not *very*) *inconvenienced; she has been excessively* (not *too*) *criticized.*

vessel NOUN **1** *a Moroccan fishing vessel* = **ship**, boat, craft, barque (*poetic*) **2** *plastic storage vessels* = **container**, receptacle, can, bowl, tank, pot, drum, barrel, butt, vat, bin, jar, basin, tub, jug, pitcher, urn, canister, repository, cask

vest VERB • **vest in something** *or* **someone** (*usually passive*) *All the authority was vested in one man.* = **place**, invest, entrust, settle, lodge, confer, endow, bestow, consign, put in the hands of, be devolved upon • **vest with something** (*usually passive*) *The mass media has been vested with considerable power.* = **endow with**, furnish with, entrust with, empower with, authorize with

vestibule NOUN = **hall**, lobby, foyer, porch, entrance hall, portico, anteroom

vestige NOUN = **trace**, sign, hint, scrap, evidence, indication, suspicion, glimmer

vet NOUN = **veterinary surgeon**, veterinarian (*U.S.*), animal doctor ▶ VERB = **check**, examine, investigate, check out, review, scan, look over, appraise, scrutinize, size up (*informal*), give the once-over (*informal*), pass under review

veteran NOUN *At 24 she was already the veteran of five Grand Slam finals.* = **old hand**, master, pro (*informal*), old-timer, past master, trouper, warhorse (*informal*), old stager ■ **OPPOSITE:** novice ▶ MODIFIER *a veteran political commentator* = **long-serving**, seasoned, experienced, old, established, expert, qualified, mature, practised, hardened, adept, proficient, well trained, battle-scarred, worldly-wise

veto NOUN *congressmen who tried to override the president's veto of the bill* = **ban**, dismissal, rejection, vetoing, boycott, embargo, prohibiting, prohibition, suppression, knock-back (*informal*), interdict, declination, preclusion, nonconsent ■ **OPPOSITE:** ratification ▶ VERB *De Gaulle vetoed Britain's application to join the EEC.* = **ban**, block, reject, rule out, kill (*informal*), negative, turn down, forbid, boycott, prohibit, disallow, put a stop to, refuse permission to, interdict, give the thumbs down to, put the kibosh on (*slang*) ■ **OPPOSITE:** pass

vex VERB = **annoy**, bother, irritate, worry, trouble, upset, disturb, distress, provoke, bug (*informal*), offend, needle (*informal*), plague, put out, tease, torment, harass, hassle (*informal*), aggravate (*informal*), afflict, fret, gall, agitate, exasperate, nettle, pester, displease, rile, pique, peeve (*informal*), grate on, get on your nerves (*informal*), nark (*Brit., Austral. & N.Z. slang*), give someone grief (*Brit. & S. African*), get your back up, put your back up, hack you off (*informal*) ■ **OPPOSITE:** soothe

vexed ADJECTIVE **1** *He was vexed by the art establishment's rejection of his work.* = **annoyed**, upset, irritated, worried, troubled, bothered, confused, disturbed, distressed, provoked, put out, fed up, tormented, harassed, aggravated (*informal*), afflicted, agitated, ruffled, exasperated, perplexed, nettled, miffed (*informal*), displeased, riled, peeved (*informal*), hacked off (*informal*), out of countenance, tooshie (*Austral. slang*), hoha (*N.Z.*) **2** *Later the minister raised the vexed question of refugees.* = **controversial**, disputed, contested, moot, much debated

viable ADJECTIVE = **workable**, practical, feasible, suitable, realistic, operational, applicable, usable, practicable, serviceable, operable, within the bounds of possibility ■ **OPPOSITE:** unworkable

vibes (*sometimes singular*) PLURAL NOUN **1** *I don't like the guy – I have bad vibes about him.* = **feelings**, emotions, response, reaction **2** *a club with really good vibes* = **atmosphere**, aura, vibrations, feeling, emanation

vibrant ADJECTIVE **1** *Tom was drawn to her by her vibrant personality.* = **energetic**, dynamic, sparkling, vivid, spirited, storming, alive, sensitive, colourful, vigorous, animated, responsive, electrifying, vivacious, full of pep (*informal*) **2** *His shirt was a vibrant shade of green.* = **vivid**, bright, brilliant, intense, clear, rich, glowing, colourful, highly-coloured

vibrate VERB **1** *Her whole body seemed to vibrate with terror.* = **shake**, tremble, shiver, fluctuate, quiver, oscillate, judder (*informal*) **2** *The noise vibrated through the whole house.* = **throb**, pulse, resonate, pulsate, reverberate

vibration NOUN **1** *The vibration dislodged the pins from the plane's rudder.* = **shaking**, shake, trembling, quake, quaking, shudder, shuddering, quiver, oscillation, judder (*informal*) **2** *They heard a distant low vibration in the distance.* = **throbbing**, pulse, thumping, hum, humming, throb, resonance, tremor, drone, droning, reverberation, pulsation

vicarious ADJECTIVE = **indirect**, substitute, surrogate, by proxy, empathetic, at one remove

vice NOUN **1** *Having the odd flutter on the horses is his only vice.* = **fault**, failing, weakness, limitation, defect, deficiency, flaw, shortcoming, blemish, imperfection, frailty, foible, weak point, infirmity ■ **OPPOSITE:** good point **2** *offences connected with vice, gaming and drugs* = **wickedness**, evil, corruption, sin, depravity, immorality, iniquity, profligacy, degeneracy, venality, turpitude (*formal*), evildoing ■ **OPPOSITE:** virtue

vice versa ADVERB = **the other way round**, conversely, in reverse, contrariwise

vicinity NOUN = **neighbourhood**, area, district, precincts, locality, environs, neck of the woods (*informal*), purlieus

vicious ADJECTIVE **1** *He suffered a vicious attack by a gang of youths.* = **savage**, brutal, violent, bad, dangerous, foul, cruel, ferocious, monstrous, vile, atrocious, diabolical, heinous, abhorrent, barbarous, fiendish ■ **OPPOSITE:** gentle **2** *a vicious criminal incapable of remorse* = **depraved**, corrupt, wicked, infamous, degraded, worthless, degenerate, immoral, sinful, debased,

V

profligate, unprincipled ■ **OPPOSITE:** virtuous **3** *a vicious attack on an innocent woman's character* = **malicious**, vindictive, spiteful, mean, cruel, venomous, bitchy (*informal*), defamatory, rancorous, backbiting, slanderous ■ **OPPOSITE:** complimentary

vicissitude NOUN (*often plural*) = **variation**, change, shift, change of fortune, life's ups and downs (*informal*)

victim NOUN **1** *an organization representing victims of the accident* = **casualty**, sufferer, injured party, fatality ■ **OPPOSITE:** survivor **2** *the victim of a particularly cruel hoax* = **prey**, patsy (*slang, chiefly U.S. & Canad.*), sucker (*slang*), dupe, gull (*archaic*), stooge, sitting duck (*informal*), sitting target, innocent ■ **OPPOSITE:** culprit **3** *A sacrificial victim was thrown to the judicial authorities.* = **scapegoat**, sacrifice, martyr, fall guy (*informal*), whipping boy

victimize VERB = **persecute**, bully, pick on, abuse, harass, discriminate against, lean on, have it in for (*informal*), push around, give a hard time, demonize, have a down on (*informal*), have your knife into

victor NOUN = **winner**, champion, conqueror, first, champ (*informal*), vanquisher, top dog (*informal*), prizewinner, conquering hero ■ **OPPOSITE:** loser

victorious ADJECTIVE = **winning**, successful, triumphant, first, champion, conquering, vanquishing, prizewinning ■ **OPPOSITE:** losing

victory NOUN = **win**, success, triumph, the prize, superiority, conquest, laurels, mastery, walkover (*informal*) ■ **OPPOSITE:** defeat

vie VERB (*with* **with** *or* **for**) = **compete**, struggle, contend, contest, strive, be rivals, match yourself against

view NOUN **1** (*sometimes plural*) *You should make your views known to your local M.P.* = **opinion**, thought, idea, belief, thinking, feeling, attitude, reckoning, impression, notion, conviction, judgment, point of view, sentiment, viewpoint, persuasion, way of thinking, standpoint **2** *The view from our window was one of beautiful countryside.* = **scene**, picture, sight, prospect, aspect, perspective, landscape, outlook, spectacle, panorama, vista **3** *A group of riders came into view.* = **vision**, sight, visibility, perspective, eyeshot, range *or* field of vision **4** *a concise but comprehensive view of basic economics* = **study**, review, survey, assessment, examination, scan, inspection, look, scrutiny, contemplation ▸ VERB **1** *America was viewed as a land of golden opportunity.* = **regard**, see, consider, judge, perceive, treat, estimate, reckon, deem, look on, adjudge, think about *or* of **2** *The mourners filed past to view the body.* = **look at**, see, inspect, gaze at, eye, watch, check, regard, survey, witness, clock (*Brit. slang*), examine, observe, explore, stare at, scan, contemplate, check out (*informal*), behold (*archaic, literary*), eyeball (*slang*), gawp at, recce (*slang*), get a load of (*informal*), spectate, take a dekko at (*Brit. slang*) • **with a view to** *She joined a dating agency with a view to finding a husband.* = **with the aim** *or* **intention of**, in order to, so as to, in the hope of

viewer NOUN = **watcher**, observer, spectator, onlooker, couch potato (*informal*), TV watcher, one of an audience

viewpoint NOUN = **point of view**, perspective, angle, position, attitude, stance, slant, belief, conviction, feeling, opinion, way of thinking, standpoint, vantage point, frame of reference

vigilance NOUN = **watchfulness**, alertness, caution, observance, circumspection, attentiveness, carefulness

vigilant ADJECTIVE = **watchful**, alert, on the lookout, careful, cautious, attentive, circumspect, wide awake, on the alert, on your toes, wakeful, on your guard, on the watch, on the qui vive, keeping your eyes peeled *or* skinned (*informal*) ■ **OPPOSITE:** inattentive

vigorous ADJECTIVE **1** *Avoid vigorous exercise for a few weeks.* = **strenuous**, energetic, arduous, hard, taxing, active, intense, exhausting, rigorous, brisk **2** *The choir and orchestra gave a vigorous performance of Haydn's oratorio.* = **spirited**, lively, energetic, active, intense, dynamic, sparkling, animated, forceful, feisty (*informal*), spanking, high-spirited, sprightly, vivacious, forcible, effervescent, full of energy, zippy (*informal*), spunky (*informal*) ■ **OPPOSITE:** lethargic **3** *He was a vigorous, handsome young man.* = **strong**, powerful, robust, sound, healthy, vital, lively, flourishing, hardy, hale (*old-fashioned*), hearty, lusty, virile, alive and kicking, red-blooded (*informal*), fighting fit, full of energy, full of beans (*informal*), hale and hearty, fit as a fiddle (*informal*) ■ **OPPOSITE:** weak

vigorously ADVERB **1** *She shivered and rubbed her arms vigorously.* = **energetically**, hard, forcefully, strongly, all out, eagerly, with a vengeance, strenuously, like mad (*slang*), lustily, hammer and tongs, with might and main **2** *The police vigorously denied that* excessive force had been used. = **forcefully**, strongly, vehemently, strenuously

vigour or (U.S.) **vigor** NOUN = **energy**, might, force, vitality, power, activity, spirit, strength, snap (informal), punch (informal), dash, pep, zip (informal), animation, verve, gusto, dynamism, oomph (informal), brio, robustness, liveliness, vim, forcefulness ■ **OPPOSITE:** weakness

vile ADJECTIVE **1** a vile and despicable crime = **wicked**, base, evil, mean, bad, low, shocking, appalling, ugly, corrupt, miserable, vicious, humiliating, perverted, coarse, degrading, worthless, disgraceful, vulgar, degenerate, abject, sinful, despicable, depraved, debased, loathsome, contemptible, impure, wretched, nefarious, ignoble ■ **OPPOSITE:** honourable **2** the vile smell of his cigar smoke = **disgusting**, foul, revolting, offensive, nasty, obscene, sickening, horrid (informal), repellent, repulsive, noxious, nauseating, repugnant, loathsome, yucky or yukky (slang), yucko (Austral. slang) ■ **OPPOSITES:** pleasant, agreeable

vilification NOUN = **denigration**, abuse, defamation, invective, calumny, mudslinging, disparagement, vituperation, contumely, aspersion, scurrility, calumniation

vilify VERB = **malign**, abuse, denigrate, knock (informal), rubbish (informal), run down, smear, slag (off) (slang), berate, disparage, decry, revile, slander, dump on (slang, chiefly U.S.), debase, defame, bad-mouth (slang), traduce, speak ill of, pull to pieces (informal), calumniate, vituperate, asperse ■ **OPPOSITE:** praise

villain NOUN **1** As a copper, I've spent my life putting villains like him away. = **evildoer**, criminal, rogue, profligate, scoundrel (old-fashioned), wretch, libertine, knave (archaic), reprobate, miscreant, malefactor, blackguard, rapscallion, caitiff (archaic), wrong 'un (slang) **2** Darth Vader, the villain of the Star Wars trilogy = **baddy** (informal), antihero ■ **OPPOSITE:** hero

villainous ADJECTIVE = **wicked**, evil, depraved, mean, bad, base, criminal, terrible, cruel, vicious, outrageous, infamous, vile, degenerate, atrocious, inhuman, sinful, diabolical, heinous, debased, hateful, scoundrelly, fiendish, ruffianly, nefarious, ignoble, detestable, blackguardly, thievish ■ **OPPOSITES:** virtuous, noble

vindicate VERB **1** The director said he had been vindicated by the expert's report. = **clear**, acquit, exonerate, absolve, let off the hook,

exculpate, free from blame ■ **OPPOSITE:** condemn **2** Subsequent events vindicated his policy. = **support**, uphold, ratify, defend, excuse, justify, substantiate

vindication NOUN **1** He insisted on a complete vindication from the libel jury. = **exoneration**, pardon, acquittal, dismissal, discharge, amnesty, absolution, exculpating, exculpation **2** He called the success a vindication of his party's economic policy. = **support**, defence, ratification, excuse, apology, justification, assertion, substantiation

vindictive ADJECTIVE = **vengeful**, malicious, spiteful, relentless, resentful, malignant, unrelenting, unforgiving, implacable, venomous, rancorous, revengeful, full of spleen ■ **OPPOSITE:** merciful

vintage NOUN **1** (wine) This wine is from one of the best vintages of the decade. = **harvest**, year, crop, yield **2** a Jeep of World War Two vintage = **era**, period, origin, sort, type, generation, stamp, epoch, ilk, time of origin ▶ ADJECTIVE **1** (wines) Gourmet food and vintage wines are also part of the service. = **high-quality**, best, prime, quality, choice, select, rare, superior **2** vintage, classic and racing cars; This is vintage comedy at its best. = **classic**, old, veteran, historic, heritage, enduring, antique, timeless, old-world, age-old, ageless

violate VERB **1** They violated the ceasefire agreement. = **break**, infringe, disobey, transgress, ignore, defy, disregard, flout, rebel against, contravene (formal), fly in the face of, overstep, not comply with, take no notice of, encroach upon, pay no heed to, infract ■ **OPPOSITE:** obey **2** These journalists were violating her family's privacy. = **invade**, infringe on, disturb, upset, shatter, disrupt, impinge on, encroach on, intrude on, trespass on, obtrude on **3** Police are still searching for the people who violated the graves. = **desecrate**, profane, defile, abuse, outrage, pollute, deface, dishonour, vandalize, treat with disrespect, befoul ■ **OPPOSITE:** honour

violation NOUN **1** This is a flagrant violation of state law. = **breach**, abuse, infringement, contravention, trespass, transgression, infraction **2** Legal action will be initiated for defamation and violation of privacy. = **invasion**, intrusion, trespass, breach, disturbance, disruption, interruption, encroachment **3** This violation of the church is not the first such incident. = **desecration**, sacrilege, defilement, profanation, spoliation

V

violence NOUN **1** *Twenty people were killed in the violence.* = **brutality**, bloodshed, savagery, fighting, terrorism, frenzy, thuggery, destructiveness, bestiality, strong-arm tactics (*informal*), rough handling, bloodthirstiness, murderousness **2** *I staggered back due to the violence of the blow.* = **force**, power, strength, might, ferocity, brute force, fierceness, forcefulness, powerfulness **3** *'There's no need,' she snapped with sudden violence.* = **intensity**, passion, fury, force, cruelty, severity, fervour, sharpness, harshness, vehemence **4** *The house was destroyed in the violence of the storm.* = **power**, turbulence, wildness, raging, tumult, roughness, boisterousness, storminess

violent ADJECTIVE **1** *He was a violent man with a drink and drugs problem.* = **brutal**, aggressive, savage, wild, rough, fierce, bullying, cruel, vicious, destructive, ruthless, murderous, maddened, berserk, merciless, bloodthirsty, homicidal, pitiless, hot-headed, thuggish, maniacal, hot-tempered ■ OPPOSITE: gentle **2** *The next moment she felt a violent blow underneath her chin.* = **sharp**, hard, powerful, forceful, strong, fierce, fatal, savage, deadly, brutal, vicious, lethal, hefty, ferocious, death-dealing **3** *He had violent stomach pains.* = **intense**, acute, severe, biting, sharp, extreme, painful, harsh, excruciating, agonizing, inordinate **4** *his violent, almost pathological jealousy* = **passionate**, intense, extreme, strong, wild, consuming, uncontrollable, vehement, unrestrained, tempestuous, ungovernable **5** *I had a violent temper and was always in fights.* = **fiery**, raging, fierce, flaming, furious, passionate, peppery, ungovernable **6** *That night a violent storm arose and wrecked most of the ships.* = **powerful**, wild, devastating, strong, storming, raging, turbulent, tumultuous, tempestuous, gale force, blustery, ruinous, full of force ■ OPPOSITE: mild

VIP NOUN = **celebrity**, big name, public figure, star, somebody, lion, notable, luminary, bigwig (*informal*), leading light (*informal*), big shot (*informal*), personage, big noise (*informal*), big hitter (*informal*), heavy hitter (*informal*), man or woman of the hour

virgin NOUN *I was a virgin until I was twenty-four years old.* = **maiden** (*archaic, literary*), maid (*archaic*), damsel (*archaic*), girl (*archaic*), celibate, vestal, virgo intacta ▶ ADJECTIVE **1** *Within 40 years there will be no virgin forest left.* = **untouched**, immaculate, fresh, new, pure, unused, pristine, flawless, unblemished, unadulterated, unsullied ■ OPPOSITE: spoiled **2** *a society in which virgin brides are still prized* = **pure**, maidenly, chaste, immaculate, virginal, unsullied, vestal, uncorrupted, undefiled ■ OPPOSITE: corrupted

virginal ADJECTIVE **1** *the virginal saints of religious legend* = **chaste**, pure, maidenly, virgin, immaculate, celibate, uncorrupted, undefiled **2** *linen tablecloths of virginal white* = **immaculate**, fresh, pristine, white, pure, untouched, snowy, undisturbed, spotless

virginity NOUN = **chastity**, maidenhead, maidenhood

virile ADJECTIVE = **manly**, masculine, macho, male, red-blooded (*informal*), manlike

virility NOUN = **masculinity**, manhood, potency, vigour, machismo

virtual ADJECTIVE = **practical**, near, essential, implied, indirect, implicit, tacit, near enough, unacknowledged, in all but name

virtually ADVERB = **practically**, almost, nearly, in effect, in essence, as good as, to all intents and purposes, in all but name, for all practical purposes, effectually

virtue NOUN **1** *His mother was held up to the family as a paragon of virtue.* = **goodness**, honour, integrity, worth, dignity, excellence, morality, honesty, decency, respectability, nobility, righteousness, propriety, probity (*formal*), rectitude, worthiness, high-mindedness, incorruptibility, uprightness, virtuousness, ethicalness ■ OPPOSITE: vice **2** *His chief virtue is patience.* = **merit**, strength, asset, plus (*informal*), attribute, good quality, good point, strong point ■ OPPOSITE: failing **3** *There is no virtue in overexercising.* = **advantage**, benefit, merit, credit, usefulness, efficacy **4** *His many attempts on her virtue were all unavailing.* = **chastity**, honour (*old-fashioned*), virginity, innocence, purity, maidenhood, chasteness ■ OPPOSITE: unchastity • **by virtue of** *Mr Olaechea has British residency by virtue of his marriage.* = **because of**, in view of, on account of, based on, thanks to, as a result of, owing to, by reason of, by dint of

virtuosity NOUN = **mastery**, skill, brilliance, polish, craft, expertise, flair, panache, éclat

virtuoso NOUN *China's foremost piano virtuoso* = **master**, artist, genius, maestro, magician, grandmaster, maven (*U.S.*), master hand ▶ MODIFIER *a virtuoso performance by a widely respected musician*

= **masterly**, brilliant, dazzling, bravura (*Music*)

virtuous ADJECTIVE **1** *The president is portrayed as a virtuous family man.* = **good**, moral, ethical, upright, honourable, excellent, pure, worthy, honest, righteous, exemplary, squeaky-clean, blameless, praiseworthy, incorruptible, high-principled ■ **OPPOSITE:** corrupt **2** *a prince who falls in love with a beautiful and virtuous maiden* = **chaste**, pure, innocent, celibate, spotless, virginal, clean-living ■ **OPPOSITE:** promiscuous

virulent ADJECTIVE **1** *A virulent personal campaign is being waged against him.* = **vicious**, vindictive, bitter, hostile, malicious, resentful, acrimonious, malevolent, spiteful, venomous, rancorous, splenetic, envenomed ■ **OPPOSITE:** benign **2** *A virulent form of the disease has appeared in Belgium.* = **deadly**, lethal, toxic, poisonous, malignant, pernicious (*formal*), venomous, septic, infective, injurious, baneful (*archaic*) ■ **OPPOSITE:** harmless

viscous ADJECTIVE = **thick**, sticky, gooey (*informal*), adhesive, tenacious, clammy, syrupy, glutinous, gummy, gelatinous, icky (*informal*), gluey, treacly, mucilaginous, viscid

visible ADJECTIVE = **perceptible**, noticeable, observable, clear, obvious, plain, apparent, bold, patent, to be seen, evident, manifest, in sight, in view, conspicuous, unmistakable, palpable, discernible, salient, detectable, not hidden, distinguishable, unconcealed, perceivable, discoverable, anywhere to be seen ■ **OPPOSITE:** invisible

vision NOUN **1** *I have a vision of a society free of exploitation and injustice.* = **image**, idea, dream, plans, hopes, prospect, ideal, concept, fancy, fantasy, conception, delusion, daydream, reverie, flight of fancy, mental picture, pipe dream, imago (*Psychoanalysis*), castle in the air, fanciful notion **2** *She heard voices and saw visions of her ancestors.* = **hallucination**, illusion, apparition, revelation, ghost, phantom, delusion, spectre, mirage, wraith, chimera, phantasm, eidolon **3** *The disease causes blindness or serious loss of vision.* = **sight**, seeing, eyesight, view, eyes, perception **4** *The government's lack of vision could have profound economic consequences.* = **foresight**, imagination, perception, insight, awareness, inspiration, innovation, creativity, intuition, penetration, inventiveness, shrewdness, discernment,

prescience (*formal*), perceptiveness, farsightedness, breadth of view **5** *The girl was a vision in crimson organza.* = **picture**, dream, sight, delight, beauty, joy, sensation, spectacle, knockout (*informal*), beautiful sight, perfect picture, feast for the eyes, sight for sore eyes, pearler (*Austral. slang*), beaut (*Austral. & N.Z. slang*)

visionary ADJECTIVE **1** *His ideas were dismissed as mere visionary speculation.* = **idealistic**, romantic, unrealistic, utopian, dreaming, speculative, impractical, dreamy, unworkable, quixotic, starry-eyed, with your head in the clouds ■ **OPPOSITE:** realistic **2** *visionary experiences and contact with spirit beings* = **prophetic**, mystical, divinatory, predictive, oracular, sibylline, mantic, vatic (*rare*), fatidic (*rare*) **3** *the visionary worlds created by fantasy writers* = **imaginary**, fantastic, unreal, fanciful, ideal, idealized, illusory, imaginal (*Psychoanalysis*), chimerical, delusory ■ **OPPOSITE:** real ▶ NOUN **1** *Visionaries see the world not as it is but as it could be.* = **idealist**, romantic, dreamer, daydreamer, utopian, enthusiast (*archaic*), theorist, zealot, Don Quixote ■ **OPPOSITE:** realist **2** *shamans, mystics and religious visionaries* = **prophet**, diviner, mystic, seer, soothsayer, sibyl, scryer, spaewife (*Scot.*)

visit VERB **1** = **call on**, go to see, drop in on (*informal*), stop by, look up, call in on, pop in on (*informal*), pay a call on, go see (*U.S.*), swing by (*informal*) **2** *I want to visit my relatives in Scotland.* = **stay at**, stay with, spend time with, pay a visit to, be the guest of **3** *He'll be visiting four cities, including Cagliari in Sardinia.* = **stay in**, see, tour, explore, take in (*informal*), holiday in, go to see, stop by, spend time in, vacation in (*U.S.*), stop over in ▶ NOUN **1** *Helen recently paid me a visit.* = **call**, social call **2** *the Pope's visit to Canada* = **trip**, stop, stay, break, tour, holiday, vacation, stopover, sojourn

visitation NOUN **1** *He claims to have had a visitation from the Virgin Mary.* = **apparition**, vision, manifestation, appearance, materialization **2** *the bishop's annual visitation of the diocese* = **inspection**, survey, examination, visit, review, scrutiny

visitor NOUN = **guest**, caller, company, visitant, manu(w)hiri (*N.Z.*)

vista NOUN = **view**, scene, prospect, landscape, panorama, perspective

visual ADJECTIVE **1** *the way our brain processes visual information* = **optical**, optic, ocular **2** *There was no visual evidence to support his claim.* = **observable**, visible, perceptible, discernible ■ **OPPOSITE:** imperceptible

V

visualize VERB = **picture**, imagine, think about, envisage, contemplate, conceive of, see in the mind's eye, conjure up a mental picture of

vital ADJECTIVE **1** *a blockade which could cut off vital oil and gas supplies* = **essential**, important, necessary, key, basic, significant, critical, radical, crucial (*informal*), fundamental, urgent, decisive, cardinal, imperative, indispensable, requisite, life-or-death, must-have
■ **OPPOSITE:** unnecessary **2** *It is tragic to see how the disease has diminished a once vital person.* = **lively**, vigorous, energetic, spirited, dynamic, animated, vibrant, forceful, sparky, vivacious, full of beans (*informal*), zestful, full of the joy of living
■ **OPPOSITE:** lethargic

vitality NOUN = **energy**, vivacity, sparkle, go (*informal*), life, strength, pep, stamina, animation, vigour, exuberance, brio, robustness, liveliness, vim, lustiness, vivaciousness ■ **OPPOSITE:** lethargy

vitriolic ADJECTIVE = **venomous**, scathing, malicious, acid, bitter, destructive, withering, virulent, sardonic, caustic, bitchy (*informal*), acerbic, envenomed, dripping with malice

vivacious ADJECTIVE = **lively**, spirited, vital, gay, bubbling, sparkling, cheerful, jolly, animated, merry, upbeat (*informal*), high-spirited, ebullient, chirpy (*informal*), sparky, scintillating, sprightly, effervescent, full of life, full of beans (*informal*), frolicsome, sportive, light-hearted
■ **OPPOSITE:** dull

vivid ADJECTIVE **1** *Last night I had a vivid dream which really upset me.* = **clear**, detailed, realistic, telling, moving, strong, affecting, arresting, powerful, sharp, dramatic, stirring, stimulating, haunting, graphic, distinct, lively, memorable, unforgettable, evocative, lucid, lifelike, true to life, sharply-etched ■ **OPPOSITE:** vague **2** *a vivid blue sky* = **bright**, brilliant, intense, clear, rich, glowing, colourful, highly-coloured
■ **OPPOSITE:** dull **3** *one of the most vivid personalities in tennis* = **lively**, strong, dynamic, striking, spirited, powerful, quick, storming, active, vigorous, energetic, animated, vibrant, fiery, flamboyant, expressive, vivacious, zestful ■ **OPPOSITE:** quiet

viz ADVERB = **namely**, that is to say, to wit, videlicet

vocabulary NOUN **1** *Children need to read to improve their vocabularies.* = **language**, words, lexicon, word stock, word hoard **2** *I could not find this word in my small Italian-English vocabulary.* = **wordbook**, dictionary, glossary, lexicon

vocal ADJECTIVE **1** *He has been very vocal in his displeasure over the decision.* = **outspoken**, frank, blunt, forthright, strident, vociferous, noisy, articulate, expressive, eloquent, plain-spoken, clamorous, free-spoken ■ **OPPOSITE:** quiet **2** *a child's ability to imitate rhythms and vocal sounds* = **spoken**, voiced, uttered, oral, said, articulate, put into words

vocation NOUN = **profession**, calling, job, business, office, trade, role, post, career, mission, employment, pursuit, life work, métier

vociferous ADJECTIVE = **outspoken**, vocal, strident, noisy, shouting, loud, ranting, vehement, loudmouthed (*informal*), uproarious, obstreperous, clamorous
■ **OPPOSITE:** quiet

vogue NOUN *the new vogue for herbal medicines* = **fashion**, trend, craze, style, the latest, the thing (*informal*), mode, last word, the rage, passing fancy, dernier cri (*French*)
▶ ADJECTIVE *The word 'talisman' has become a vogue word in sports writing.* = **fashionable**, trendy (*Brit. informal*), in, now (*informal*), popular, with it (*old-fashioned, informal*), prevalent, up-to-the-minute, modish, voguish • **in vogue** *Pale colours are in vogue this season.* = **popular**, big, fashionable, all the rage, happening, accepted, current, cool (*informal*), in favour, stylish, on trend, up to date, in use, prevalent, up to the minute, modish, trendsetting, schmick (*Austral. informal*)

voice NOUN **1** *Miriam's voice was strangely calm.* = **tone**, sound, language, articulation, power of speech **2** *The crowd gave voice to their anger.* = **utterance**, expression, words, airing, vocalization, verbalization **3** *the voice of the opposition* = **opinion**, will, feeling, wish, desire **4** *Our employees have no voice in how our company is run.* = **say**, part, view, decision, vote, comment, input **5** *He claims to be the voice of the people.* = **instrument**, medium, spokesman or woman or person, agency (*old-fashioned*), channel, vehicle, organ, intermediary, mouthpiece ▶ VERB *Scientists have voiced concern that the disease could be passed to humans.* = **express**, say, declare, air, raise, table, reveal, mention, mouth, assert, pronounce, utter, articulate, come out with (*informal*), divulge, ventilate, enunciate, put into words, vocalize, give expression or utterance to ■ **RELATED WORD:** *adjective* vocal

void ADJECTIVE **1** *The elections were declared void by the former military ruler.* = **invalid**, null and void, inoperative, useless, ineffective, worthless, ineffectual, unenforceable, nonviable **2** (*with of*) *His face was void of emotion as he left the room.* = **devoid of**, without, lacking, free from, wanting, bereft of, empty of, bare of, destitute of, vacant of ▶ NOUN **1** *His death has created a void which will never be filled.* = **gap**, space, lack, want, hole, blank, emptiness **2** *the limitless void of outer space* = **emptiness**, space, vacuum, oblivion, blankness, nullity, vacuity ▶ VERB *The Supreme Court voided his conviction for murder.* = **invalidate**, nullify, cancel, withdraw, reverse, undo, repeal, quash, revoke, disallow, retract, repudiate, negate, rescind, annul, abrogate, countermand, render invalid, abnegate

volatile ADJECTIVE **1** *There have been riots before and the situation is volatile.* = **changeable**, shifting, variable, unsettled, unstable, explosive, unreliable, unsteady, inconstant ■ OPPOSITE: stable **2** *She has a volatile temperament.* = **temperamental**, erratic, mercurial, up and down (*informal*), fickle, whimsical, giddy, flighty, over-emotional, inconstant ■ OPPOSITE: calm

volition NOUN = **free will**, will, choice, election, choosing, option, purpose, resolution, determination, preference, discretion

volley NOUN = **barrage**, blast, burst, explosion, shower, hail, discharge, bombardment, salvo, fusillade, cannonade

voluble ADJECTIVE = **talkative**, garrulous, loquacious, forthcoming, articulate, fluent, glib, blessed with the gift of the gab ■ OPPOSITE: reticent

volume NOUN **1** *the sheer volume of traffic on our motorways* = **amount**, quantity, level, body, total, measure, degree, mass, proportion, bulk, aggregate **2** *When water is frozen it increases in volume.* = **capacity**, size, mass, extent, proportions, dimensions, bulk, measurements, magnitude, compass, largeness, cubic content **3** *a slim volume of English poetry* = **book**, work, title, opus, publication, manual, tome, treatise, almanac, compendium **4** *He came round to complain about the volume of the music.* = **loudness**, sound, amplification ■ RELATED WORD: *adjective* cubical

voluminous ADJECTIVE **1** *She was swathed in a voluminous cloak.* = **large**, big, full, massive, vast, ample, bulky, billowing, roomy, cavernous, capacious ■ OPPOSITE: small **2** *this author's voluminous writings and correspondence* = **copious**, extensive, prolific, abundant, plentiful, profuse ■ OPPOSITE: scanty

voluntarily ADVERB = **willingly**, freely, by choice, without being asked, without prompting, lief (*rare*), on your own initiative, of your own free will, off your own bat, of your own accord, of your own volition

voluntary ADJECTIVE **1** *a voluntary act undertaken in full knowledge of the consequences* = **intentional**, intended, deliberate, planned, studied, purposed, calculated, wilful, done on purpose ■ OPPOSITE: unintentional **2** *The extra course in Commercial French is voluntary.* = **optional**, discretionary, up to the individual, open, unforced, unconstrained, unenforced, at your discretion, discretional, open to choice, uncompelled ■ OPPOSITE: obligatory **3** *In her spare time she does voluntary work for the homeless.* = **unpaid**, volunteer, free, willing, honorary, gratuitous, pro bono (*Law*)

volunteer VERB **1** *Aunt Mary volunteered to clean up the kitchen.* = **offer**, step forward, offer your services, propose, let yourself in for (*informal*), need no invitation, present your services, proffer your services, put yourself at someone's disposal ■ OPPOSITE: refuse **2** *His wife volunteered an ingenious suggestion.* = **suggest**, advance, put forward, venture, tender

voluptuous ADJECTIVE **1** *a voluptuous, well-rounded woman with glossy red hair* = **buxom**, shapely, curvaceous (*informal*), erotic, ample, enticing, provocative, seductive (*informal*), well-stacked (*Brit., derogatory slang*), full-bosomed **2** *a life of voluptuous decadence* = **sensual**, luxurious, self-indulgent, hedonistic, sybaritic, epicurean, licentious, bacchanalian, pleasure-loving ■ OPPOSITE: abstemious

vomit VERB **1** *Any dairy product made him vomit.* = **be sick**, throw up (*informal*), spew, chuck (*Austral. & N.Z. informal*), heave (*slang*), puke (*slang*), retch, barf (*U.S. slang*), chunder (*slang, chiefly Austral.*), belch forth, upchuck (*U.S. slang*), do a technicolour yawn (*slang*), toss your cookies (*U.S. slang*) **2** (*often with* **up**) *She vomited up all she had just eaten.* = **bring up**, throw up, regurgitate, chuck (up) (*slang, chiefly U.S.*), emit, eject, puke (*slang*), disgorge, sick up (*informal*), spew out *or* up

voracious ADJECTIVE **1** *For their size, stoats are voracious predators.* = **gluttonous**, insatiable, ravenous, hungry, greedy, ravening, devouring **2** *He was a voracious reader.* = **avid**, prodigious, insatiable, uncontrolled, rapacious, unquenchable ■ OPPOSITE: moderate

V

vortex NOUN = **whirlpool**, eddy, maelstrom, gyre, countercurrent

vote NOUN **1** *They took a vote and decided not to do it.* = **poll**, election, ballot, referendum, popular vote, plebiscite, straw poll, show of hands **2** *Before that, women did not even have the vote.* = **right to vote**, franchise, voting rights, suffrage, say, voice, enfranchisement ▸ VERB **1** *Over half of the electorate did not vote in the last general election.* = **cast your vote**, go to the polls, mark your ballot paper **2** *They voted him Player of the Year.* = **judge**, declare, pronounce, decree, adjudge • **vote someone in** *The Prime Minister was voted in by a huge majority.* = **elect**, choose, select, appoint, return, pick, opt for, designate, decide on, settle on, fix on, plump for, put in power

voucher NOUN = **ticket**, token, coupon, pass, slip, chit, docket

vouch for VERB **1** *Kim's mother agreed to vouch for Maria and get her a job.* = **guarantee**, back, certify, answer for, swear to, stick up for (*informal*), stand witness, give assurance of, asseverate, go bail for **2** *I cannot vouch for the accuracy of the story.* = **confirm**, support, affirm, attest to, assert, uphold

vow NOUN *Most people still take their marriage vows seriously.* = **promise**, commitment, pledge, oath, profession, troth (*archaic*), avowal ▸ VERB *She vowed that some day she would return to live in France.* = **promise**, pledge, swear, commit, engage, affirm, avow, bind yourself, undertake solemnly

voyage NOUN *He aims to follow Columbus's voyage to the West Indies.* = **journey**, travels, trip, passage, expedition, crossing, sail, cruise, excursion ▸ VERB *The boat is currently voyaging through the Barents Sea.* = **travel**, journey, tour, cruise, steam, take a trip, go on an expedition

vulgar ADJECTIVE **1** *The decor is ugly, tasteless and vulgar.* = **tasteless**, common, flashy, low, gross, nasty, gaudy, tawdry, cheap and nasty, common as muck ■ **OPPOSITE:** tasteful **2** *vulgar jokes* = **crude**, dirty, rude, low, blue, nasty, naughty, coarse, indecent, improper, suggestive, tasteless, risqué, off colour, ribald, indelicate, indecorous **3** *He was a vulgar old man, but he never swore in front of women.* = **uncouth**, boorish, unrefined, impolite, ill-bred, unmannerly ■ **OPPOSITE:** refined **4** *translated from Latin into the vulgar tongue* = **vernacular**, common, general, ordinary

vulgarity NOUN **1** *I hate the vulgarity of this room.* = **tastelessness**, bad taste, grossness, tawdriness, gaudiness, lack of refinement ■ **OPPOSITE:** tastefulness **2** *a comedian famous for his vulgarity and irreverence* = **crudeness**, rudeness, coarseness, crudity, ribaldry, suggestiveness, indelicacy, indecorum ■ **OPPOSITE:** decorum **3** *For all his apparent vulgarity, Todd had a certain raw charm.* = **coarseness**, roughness, boorishness, rudeness, loutishness, oafishness, uncouthness ■ **OPPOSITE:** refinement

vulnerable ADJECTIVE **1** *criminals who prey on the more vulnerable members of our society* = **susceptible**, helpless, unprotected, defenceless, exposed, weak, sensitive, tender, unguarded, thin-skinned ■ **OPPOSITE:** immune **2** *Their tanks would be vulnerable to attack from the air.* = **exposed**, open, unprotected, defenceless, accessible, wide open, open to attack, assailable ■ **OPPOSITE:** well-protected

Ww

wacky ADJECTIVE = **unusual**, odd, wild, strange, crazy, silly, weird, way-out (*informal*), eccentric, unpredictable, daft (*informal*), irrational, erratic, Bohemian, unconventional, far-out (*slang*), off-the-wall (*slang*), unorthodox, nutty (*slang*), oddball, zany, goofy (*informal*), offbeat, freaky (*slang*), outré, gonzo (*slang*), screwy (*informal*), off the air (*Austral. slang*)

wad NOUN **1** *a wad of banknotes* = **bundle**, roll, bankroll (*informal*), pocketful **2** *a wad of cotton wool* = **mass**, ball, lump, hunk, piece, block, plug, chunk

waddle VERB = **shuffle**, shamble, totter, toddle, rock, stagger, sway, wobble

wade VERB **1** *The boys were wading in the cold pool nearby.* = **paddle**, splash, splash about, slop **2** *We had to wade the river and then climb out of the valley.* = **walk through**, cross, ford, pass through, go across, travel across, make your way across • **wade in** *I waded in to help, but I got pushed aside.* = **move in**, pitch in, dive in (*informal*), set to work, advance, set to, get stuck in (*informal*), buckle down • **wade into someone** *The troops waded into the protesters with batons.* = **launch yourself at**, charge at, attack, rush, storm, tackle, go for, set about, strike at, assail, tear into (*informal*), fall upon, set upon, lay into (*informal*), light into (*informal*) • **wade into something** *The Stock Exchange yesterday waded into the debate on stamp duty.* = **get involved in**, tackle, pitch in, interfere in, dive in, plunge in, get stuck into • **wade through something** *scientists who have to wade through tons of data* = **plough through**, trawl through, labour at, work your way through, toil at, drudge at, peg away at

waffle VERB (*often followed by* **on**) *some guy on TV waffling about political correctness* = **chatter**, rabbit (on) (*Brit. informal*), babble, drivel, prattle, jabber, gabble, rattle on, verbalize, blather, witter on (*informal*), blether, run off at the mouth (*slang*), prate, earbash (*Austral. & N.Z. slang*) ▶ NOUN *I'm tired of his smug, sanctimonious waffle.* = **prattle**, nonsense, hot air (*informal*), twaddle, padding, prating, gibberish, jabber, verbiage, blather, wordiness, verbosity, prolixity, bunkum *or* buncombe, bizzo (*Austral. slang*), bull's wool (*Austral. & N.Z. slang*)

waft VERB **1** *The scent of roses wafted through the open window.* = **drift**, float, be carried, be transported, coast, flow, stray, glide, be borne, be conveyed **2** *A slight breeze wafted the heavy scent of flowers past her.* = **transport**, bring, carry, bear, guide, conduct, transmit, convey ▶ NOUN *A waft of perfume reached Ingrid's nostrils.* = **current**, breath, puff, whiff, draught, breeze

wag¹ VERB **1** *The dog was barking and wagging its tail wildly.* = **wave**, shake, swing, waggle, stir, sway, flutter, waver, quiver, vibrate, wiggle, oscillate **2** *He wagged a disapproving finger at me.* = **waggle**, wave, shake, flourish, brandish, wobble, wiggle **3** *She wagged her head in agreement.* = **shake**, bob, nod ▶ NOUN **1** *The dog gave a responsive wag of his tail.* = **wave**, shake, swing, toss, sway, flutter, waver, quiver, vibration, wiggle, oscillation, waggle **2** *a wag of the head* = **nod**, bob, shake

wag² NOUN *My dad's always been a bit of a wag.* = **joker**, comic, wit, comedian, clown, card (*informal*), kidder (*informal*), jester, dag (*N.Z. informal*), prankster, buffoon, trickster, humorist, joculator *or* (*fem.*) joculatrix

wage NOUN (*often plural*) *efforts to set a minimum wage well above the poverty line* = **payment**, pay, earnings, remuneration, fee, reward, compensation, income, allowance, recompense, stipend, emolument ▶ VERB *the three factions that had been waging a civil war* = **engage in**, conduct, pursue, carry on, undertake, practise, prosecute, proceed with

wager VERB *People had wagered a good deal of money on his winning the championship.* = **bet**, chance, risk, stake, lay, venture, put on, pledge, gamble, hazard, speculate, punt (*chiefly Brit.*) ▶ NOUN *punters placing wagers on the day's racing* = **bet**, stake, pledge, gamble, risk, flutter (*Brit. informal*), ante, punt (*chiefly Brit.*), long shot

waggle VERB = **wag**, wiggle, wave, shake, flutter, wobble, oscillate

waif NOUN = **stray**, orphan, outcast, urchin (*old-fashioned*), foundling

wail VERB *The woman began to wail for her lost child.* = **cry**, weep, grieve, lament, keen, greet (*Scot., archaic*), howl, whine, deplore, bemoan, bawl, bewail, yowl, ululate ▶ NOUN *Wails of grief were heard as visitors filed past the site of the disaster.* = **cry**, moan, sob, howl, keening, lament, bawl, lamentation, yowl, ululation

wait VERB **1** *I waited at the corner for the lights to go green.* = **stay**, remain, stop, pause, rest, delay, linger, hover, hang around (*informal*), dally, loiter, tarry ■ **OPPOSITE:** go **2** *Let's wait and see what happens.* = **stand by**, delay, hold on (*informal*), hold back, wait in the wings, mark time, hang fire, bide your time, kick your heels, cool your heels **3** *I want to talk to you but it can wait.* = **be postponed**, be suspended, be delayed, be put off, be put back, be deferred, be put on hold (*informal*), be shelved, be tabled, be held over, be put on ice (*informal*), be put on the back burner (*informal*) ▶ NOUN *After a long wait, someone finally picked up the phone.* = **delay**, gap, pause, interval, stay, rest, halt, hold-up, lull, stoppage, hindrance, hiatus, entr'acte • **wait for** *or* **on something** *or* **someone** *I'm still waiting for a reply from him.* = **await**, expect, look forward to, hope for, anticipate, look for • **wait on** *or* **upon someone** *The owner of the restaurant himself waited on us.* = **serve**, tend to, look after, take care of, minister to, attend to, cater to • **wait up** *I waited up for you till three in the morning.* = **stay awake**, stay up, keep vigil

waiter NOUN = **attendant**, server, flunkey, steward, servant

waitress NOUN = **attendant**, server, stewardess, servant

waive VERB **1** *He pled guilty to the charges and waived his right to appeal.* = **give up**, relinquish, renounce, forsake, drop, abandon, resign, yield, surrender, set aside, dispense with, cede, forgo ■ **OPPOSITE:** claim **2** *The council has agreed to waive certain statutory planning regulations.* = **disregard**, ignore, discount, overlook, set aside, pass over, dispense with, brush aside, turn a blind eye to, forgo

waiver NOUN = **renunciation**, surrender, remission, abdication, giving up, resignation, denial, setting aside, abandonment, disclaimer, disavowal, relinquishment, eschewal, abjuration

wake¹ VERB **1** *It was still dark when I woke.* = **awake**, stir, awaken, come to, arise, get up, rouse, get out of bed, waken, bestir, rouse from sleep, bestir yourself ■ **OPPOSITE:** fall asleep **2** *She went upstairs at once to wake the children.* = **awaken**, arouse, rouse, waken, rouse someone from sleep **3** *Seeing him again upset her, because it woke painful memories.* = **evoke**, recall, excite, renew, stimulate, revive, induce, arouse, call up, awaken, rouse, give rise to, conjure up, stir up, rekindle, summon up, reignite ▶ NOUN *A funeral wake was in progress.* = **vigil**, watch, funeral, deathwatch, tangi (*N.Z.*) • **wake someone up** *He needs a shock to wake him up a bit.* = **activate**, stimulate, enliven, galvanize, fire, excite, provoke, motivate, arouse, awaken, animate, rouse, mobilize, energize, kindle, switch someone on, stir someone up

> USAGE Both *wake* and its synonym *waken* can be used either with or without an object: *I woke/wakened my sister*, and also *I woke/wakened (up) at noon*. *Wake*, *wake up*, and occasionally *waken*, can also be used in a figurative sense, for example *Seeing him again woke painful memories*; and *It's time he woke up to his responsibilities*. The verbs *awake* and *awaken* are more commonly used in the figurative than the literal sense, for example *He awoke to the danger he was in*.

wake² NOUN *Dolphins sometimes play in the wake of the boats.* = **slipstream**, wash, trail, backwash, train, track, waves, path • **in the wake of** *The move comes in the wake of new measures brought in by the government.* = **in the aftermath of**, following, because of, as a result of, on account of, as a consequence of

waken VERB **1** *Have a cup of coffee to waken you.* = **awaken**, wake, stir, wake up, stimulate, revive, awake, arouse, activate, animate, rouse, enliven, galvanize **2** *I dozed off and I only wakened when she came in.* = **wake up**, come to, get up, awake, awaken, be roused, come awake ■ **OPPOSITE:** fall asleep

Wales NOUN = **Cymru** (*Welsh*), Cambria (*Latin*)

walk VERB **1** *They walked in silence for a while.* = **stride**, wander, stroll, trudge, go, move, step, march, advance, pace, trek, hike, tread, ramble, tramp, promenade, amble, saunter, take a turn, traipse (*informal*), toddle, make your way, mosey (*informal*), plod on, perambulate, footslog **2** *When I was your age I walked five miles to school.* = **travel on foot**, go on foot, hoof it (*slang*), foot it, go by shanks's pony (*informal*) **3** *He offered to walk me home.* = **escort**, take, see, show, partner, guide, conduct, accompany, shepherd, convoy, usher, chaperon ▶ NOUN **1** *He often took long walks in the hills.* = **stroll**, hike, ramble, tramp, turn, march, constitutional, trek, outing, trudge, promenade, amble, saunter, traipse (*informal*), breath of air, perambulation **2** *Despite his gangling walk, George was a good dancer.* = **gait**, manner of walking, step, bearing, pace, stride, carriage, tread **3** *a covered walk consisting of a*

roof supported by columns = **path**, pathway, footpath (*Austral. & N.Z.*), track, way, road, lane, trail, avenue, pavement, alley, aisle, sidewalk (*chiefly U.S.*), walkway (*chiefly U.S.*), promenade, towpath, esplanade, footway, berm (*N.Z.*) • **walk of life** *In this job you meet people from all walks of life.* = **area**, calling, business, line, course, trade, class, field, career, rank, employment, province, profession, occupation, arena, sphere, realm, domain, caste, vocation, line of work, métier
• **walk out 1** *Mr Mason walked out during the performance.* = **leave suddenly**, storm out, get up and go, flounce out, vote with your feet, make a sudden departure, take off (*informal*) **2** *Industrial action began this week, when most of the staff walked out.* = **go on strike**, strike, revolt, mutiny, stop work, take industrial action, down tools, withdraw your labour • **walk out on someone** *a father who walked out on his three children* = **abandon**, leave, desert, strand, betray, chuck (*informal*), run away from, forsake, jilt, run out on (*informal*), throw over, leave high and dry, leave in the lurch

walker NOUN = **hiker**, rambler, backpacker, wayfarer, footslogger, pedestrian

walkout NOUN = **strike**, protest, revolt, stoppage, industrial action

wall NOUN **1** *We're going to knock down the dividing wall to give us one big room.* = **partition**, divider, room divider, screen, panel, barrier, enclosure **2** *The Romans breached the city walls and captured the city.* = **barricade**, rampart, fortification, bulwark, blockade, embankment, parapet, palisade, stockade, breastwork **3** *I appealed for help but met the usual wall of silence.* = **barrier**, obstacle, barricade, obstruction, check, bar, block, fence, impediment, hindrance • **drive someone up the wall** *That tuneless humming of his drives me up the wall.* = **infuriate**, madden, exasperate, get on your nerves (*informal*), anger, provoke, annoy, irritate, aggravate (*informal*), incense, enrage, gall, rile, drive you crazy (*informal*), nark (*Brit., Austral. & N.Z. slang*), be like a red rag to a bull, make your blood boil, get your goat (*slang*), drive you insane, make your hackles rise, raise your hackles, send you off your head (*slang*), get your back up, make you see red (*informal*), put your back up, hack you off (*informal*) • **go to the wall** *Even big companies are going to the wall these days.* = **fail**, close down, go under, go out of business, fall, crash, collapse, fold (*informal*), be ruined, go bust (*informal*), go bankrupt, go broke (*informal*), go into

receivership, become insolvent ■ **RELATED WORD:** *adjective* mural

wallet NOUN = **purse**, pocketbook, notecase, pouch, case, holder, moneybag, e-wallet *or* eWallet

wallop VERB **1** *Once she walloped me over the head with a frying pan.* = **hit**, beat, strike, knock, belt (*informal*), deck (*slang*), bang, batter, bash (*informal*), pound, chin (*slang*), smack, thrash, thump, paste (*slang*), buffet, clout (*informal*), slug, whack, swipe, clobber (*slang*), pummel, tonk (*slang*), lambast(e), lay one on (*slang*), beat *or* knock seven bells out of (*informal*) **2** *England were walloped by Brazil in the finals.* = **beat**, defeat, slaughter, thrash, best, stuff (*slang*), worst, tank (*slang*), hammer (*informal*), crush, overwhelm, lick (*informal*), paste (*slang*), rout, walk over (*informal*), trounce, clobber (*slang*), vanquish, run rings around (*informal*), wipe the floor with (*informal*), make mincemeat of, blow out of the water (*slang*), drub, beat hollow (*Brit. informal*), defeat heavily *or* utterly ▸ NOUN *With one brutal wallop, Clarke sent him flying.* = **blow**, strike, punch, thump, belt (*informal*), bash, sock (*slang*), smack, clout (*informal*), slug, whack, swipe (*informal*), thwack, haymaker (*slang*)

wallow VERB **1** *All he wants to do is wallow in self-pity.* = **revel**, indulge, relish, savour, delight, glory, thrive, bask, take pleasure, luxuriate, indulge yourself ■ **OPPOSITE:** refrain from **2** *Hippos love to wallow in mud.* = **roll about**, lie, tumble, wade, slosh, welter, splash around

wan ADJECTIVE **1** *He looked wan and tired.* = **pale**, white, washed out, pasty, faded, bleached, ghastly, sickly, bloodless, colourless, pallid, anaemic, discoloured, ashen, sallow, whitish, cadaverous, waxen, like death warmed up (*informal*), wheyfaced ■ **OPPOSITE:** glowing **2** *The lamp cast a wan light through the swirls of fog.* = **dim**, weak, pale, faint, feeble

wand NOUN = **stick**, rod, cane, baton, stake, switch, birch, twig, sprig, withe, withy

wander VERB *He wandered aimlessly around the garden.* = **roam**, walk, drift, stroll, range, cruise, stray, ramble, prowl, meander, rove, straggle, traipse (*informal*), mooch around (*slang*), stravaig (*Scot. & Northern English, dialect*), knock about *or* around, peregrinate ▸ NOUN *Let's go for a wander round the shops.* = **excursion**, turn, walk, stroll, cruise, ramble, meander, promenade, traipse (*informal*), mosey (*informal*), peregrination • **wander off** *The child wandered off and got lost.* = **stray**, roam, go astray, lose your way,

w

drift, depart, rove, straggle • **wander off something** *He has a tendency to wander off the point when he's talking.* = **deviate**, diverge, veer, swerve, digress, go off at a tangent, go off course, lapse

wanderer NOUN = **traveller**, rover, nomad, drifter, ranger, journeyer, roamer, explorer, migrant, rolling stone, rambler, voyager, tripper, itinerant, globetrotter, vagrant, stroller, vagabond, wayfarer, bird of passage

wandering ADJECTIVE = **itinerant**, travelling, journeying, roving, drifting, homeless, strolling, voyaging, unsettled, roaming, rambling, nomadic, migratory, vagrant, peripatetic, vagabond, rootless, wayfaring

wane VERB **1** *His interest in her began to wane.* = **decline**, flag, weaken, diminish, fall, fail, drop, sink, fade, decrease, dim, dwindle, wither, lessen, subside, ebb, wind down, die out, fade away, abate, draw to a close, atrophy, taper off ■ **OPPOSITE:** grow **2** *The sliver of a waning moon was high in the sky.* = **diminish**, decrease, dwindle
■ **OPPOSITE:** wax • **on the wane** *My career prospects were clearly on the wane.*
= **declining**, dropping, fading, weakening, dwindling, withering, lessening, subsiding, ebbing, dying out, on the way out, on the decline, tapering off, obsolescent, on its last legs, at its lowest ebb

want VERB **1** *My husband really wants a new car.* = **wish for**, desire, fancy, long for, crave, covet, hope for, yearn for, thirst for, hunger for, pine for, hanker after, set your heart on, feel a need for, have a yen for (*informal*), have a fancy for, eat your heart out over, would give your eyeteeth for
■ **OPPOSITE:** have **2** *The grass wants cutting.* = **need**, demand, require, call for, have need of, stand in need of **3** *You want to look where you're going, mate.* = **should**, need, must, ought **4** *Come on, darling. I want you.*
= **desire**, fancy (*informal*), long for, crave, wish for, yearn for, thirst for, hanker after, burn for **5** *Our team still wants one more player.* = **lack**, need, require, be short of, miss, deficient in, be without, fall short in
▶ NOUN **1** *The men were daily becoming weaker for want of rest.* = **lack**, need, absence, shortage, deficiency, famine, default, shortfall, inadequacy, scarcity, dearth, paucity (*formal*), shortness, insufficiency, non-existence, scantiness ■ **OPPOSITE:** abundance **2** *He said they were fighting for freedom from want.* = **poverty**, need, hardship, privation (*formal*), penury, destitution, neediness, hand-to-mouth

existence, indigence, pauperism, pennilessness, distress ■ **OPPOSITE:** wealth **3** *The company needs to respond to the wants of our customers.* = **wish**, will, need, demand, desire, requirement, fancy, yen (*informal*), longing, hunger, necessity, appetite, craving, yearning, thirst, whim, hankering

wanting ADJECTIVE **1** *He examined her work and found it wanting.* = **deficient**, poor, disappointing, inadequate, pathetic, inferior, insufficient, faulty, not good enough, defective, patchy, imperfect, sketchy, unsound, substandard, leaving much to be desired, not much cop (*Brit. slang*), not up to par, not up to expectations, bodger or bodgie (*Austral. slang*) ■ **OPPOSITE:** adequate **2** *I feel as if something important is wanting in my life.*
= **lacking**, missing, absent, incomplete, needing, short, shy ■ **OPPOSITE:** complete

wanton ADJECTIVE **1** *the unnecessary and wanton destruction of our environment* = **wilful**, needless, senseless, unjustified, willed, evil, cruel, vicious, deliberate, arbitrary, malicious, wicked, purposeful, gratuitous, malevolent, spiteful, unprovoked, groundless, unjustifiable, uncalled-for, motiveless ■ **OPPOSITE:** justified **2** *His eldest son was a wanton youth and a disappointment to him.* = **promiscuous**, immoral, shameless, licentious, fast, wild, abandoned, loose (*old-fashioned*), dissipated, lewd, profligate, debauched, lustful, lecherous, dissolute, libertine, libidinous, of easy virtue, unchaste ■ **OPPOSITE:** puritanical

war NOUN **1** *matters of war and peace* = **conflict**, drive, attack, fighting, fight, operation, battle, movement, push, struggle, clash, combat, offensive, hostilities, hostility, warfare, expedition, crusade, strife, bloodshed, jihad, enmity, armed conflict ■ **OPPOSITE:** peace **2** *the war against organized crime* = **campaign**, drive, attack, operation, movement, push (*informal*), mission, offensive, crusade, cyberwar ▶ VERB *The two tribes warred to gain new territory.* = **fight**, battle, clash, wage war, campaign, struggle, combat, contend, go to war, do battle, make war, take up arms, bear arms, cross swords, conduct a war, engage in hostilities, carry on hostilities ■ **OPPOSITE:** make peace
■ **RELATED WORDS:** *adjectives* belligerent, martial

warble VERB *A flock of birds was warbling in the trees.* = **sing**, trill, chirp, twitter, chirrup, make melody, peep, quaver ▶ NOUN *the soft warble of her speaking voice* = **song**, trill, quaver, twitter, call, cry, chirp, chirrup

ward NOUN 1 *A toddler was admitted to the emergency ward.* = **room**, department, unit, quarter, division, section, apartment (*U.S.*), cubicle 2 *Canvassers are focusing on marginal wards in this election.* = **district**, constituency, area, division, zone, parish, precinct 3 *Richard became his legal ward and took his name by deed poll.* = **dependant**, charge, pupil, minor, protégé • **ward someone off** *She may have tried to ward off her assailant.* = **drive off**, resist, confront, fight off, block, oppose, thwart, hold off, repel, fend off, beat off, keep someone at bay, keep someone at arm's length • **ward something off** 1 *A rowan cross was hung over the door to ward off evil.* = **avert**, turn away, fend off, stave off, avoid, block, frustrate, deflect, repel, forestall 2 *He lifted his hands as if to ward off a blow.* = **parry**, avert, deflect, fend off, avoid, block, repel, turn aside

warden NOUN 1 *He was a warden at the local parish church.* = **steward**, guardian, administrator, superintendent (*U.S.*), caretaker, curator, warder, custodian, watchman, janitor 2 *The prisoners seized three wardens.* = **jailer**, prison officer, guard, screw (*slang*), keeper, captor, turnkey (*archaic*), gaoler 3 *A new warden took over the prison.* = **governor**, head, leader, director, manager, chief, executive, boss (*informal*), commander, ruler, controller, overseer 4 *a safari park warden* = **ranger**, keeper, guardian, protector, custodian, official

warder *or* **wardress** (*chiefly Brit.*) NOUN = **jailer**, guard, screw (*slang*), warden, prison officer, keeper, captor, custodian, turnkey (*archaic*), gaoler

wardrobe NOUN 1 *Hang your dress up in the wardrobe.* = **clothes cupboard**, cupboard, closet (*U.S.*), clothes-press, cabinet 2 *splurging on an expensive new wardrobe of clothes* = **clothes**, outfit, apparel (*old-fashioned*), clobber (*Brit. slang*), attire, collection of clothes

warehouse NOUN = **store**, depot, storehouse, repository, depository, stockroom

wares PLURAL NOUN = **goods**, produce, stock, products, stuff, commodities, merchandise, lines

warfare NOUN = **war**, fighting, campaigning, battle, struggle, conflict, combat, hostilities, strife, bloodshed, jihad, armed struggle, discord, enmity, armed conflict, clash of arms, passage of arms ■ **OPPOSITE:** peace

warily ADVERB 1 *He backed warily away from the animal.* = **cautiously**, carefully, discreetly, with care, tentatively, gingerly,

guardedly, circumspectly, watchfully, vigilantly, cagily (*informal*), heedfully ■ **OPPOSITE:** carelessly 2 *The two men eyed each other warily.* = **suspiciously**, uneasily, guardedly, sceptically, cagily (*informal*), distrustfully, mistrustfully, charily

wariness NOUN 1 *Extreme wariness is the safest policy when dealing with these substances.* = **caution**, care, attention, prudence, discretion, deliberation, foresight, vigilance, alertness, forethought, circumspection, mindfulness, watchfulness, carefulness, caginess (*informal*), heedfulness ■ **OPPOSITE:** carelessness 2 *the country's obsessive wariness of foreigners* = **suspicion**, scepticism, distrust, mistrust

warlike ADJECTIVE = **belligerent**, military, aggressive, hostile, martial, combative, unfriendly, antagonistic, pugnacious, argumentative, bloodthirsty, hawkish, bellicose, quarrelsome, militaristic, inimical, sabre-rattling, jingoistic, warmongering, aggers (*Austral. slang*), biffo (*Austral. slang*) ■ **OPPOSITE:** peaceful

warm ADJECTIVE 1 *The weather was so warm I had to take off my jacket.* = **balmy**, mild, temperate, pleasant, fine, bright, sunny, agreeable, sultry, summery, moderately hot ■ **OPPOSITE:** cool 2 *Nothing beats coming home to a warm house.* = **cosy**, snug, toasty (*informal*), comfortable, homely, comfy (*informal*) 3 *A warm bath will help to relax you.* = **moderately hot**, heated ■ **OPPOSITE:** cool 4 *Some people can't afford warm clothes.* = **thermal**, winter, thick, chunky, woolly ■ **OPPOSITE:** cool 5 *The basement hallway is painted a warm yellow.* = **mellow**, relaxing, pleasant, agreeable, restful 6 *We were instantly attracted by his warm personality.* = **affable**, kindly, friendly, affectionate, loving, happy, tender, pleasant, cheerful, hearty, good-humoured, amiable, amicable, cordial, sociable, genial, congenial, hospitable, approachable, amorous, good-natured, likable *or* likeable ■ **OPPOSITE:** unfriendly 7 *Am I getting warm? Am I right?* = **near**, close, hot, near to the truth ▶ VERB *She went to warm her hands by the fire.* = **warm up**, heat, thaw (out), heat up ■ **OPPOSITE:** cool down • **warm something** *or* **someone up** 1 *He blew on his hands to warm them up.* = **heat**, thaw, heat up 2 *They went on before us to warm up the audience.* = **rouse**, stimulate, stir up, animate, interest, excite, provoke, turn on (*slang*), arouse, awaken, exhilarate, incite, whip up, galvanize, put some life into, get something *or* someone going, make something *or* someone enthusiastic

warm-hearted ADJECTIVE = **kindly**, loving, kind, warm, gentle, generous, tender, pleasant, mild, sympathetic, affectionate, compassionate, hearty, cordial, genial, affable, good-natured, kind-hearted, tender-hearted ■ **OPPOSITE:** cold-hearted

warmth NOUN 1 *She went in, drawn by the warmth of the fire.* = **heat**, snugness, warmness, comfort, homeliness, hotness ■ **OPPOSITE:** coolness 2 *He greeted us both with warmth.* = **affection**, feeling, love, goodwill, kindness, tenderness, friendliness, cheerfulness, amity (*formal*), cordiality, affability, kindliness, heartiness, amorousness, hospitableness, fondness ■ **OPPOSITE:** hostility

warn VERB 1 *They warned him of the dangers of sailing alone.* = **notify**, tell, remind, inform, alert, tip off, give notice, make someone aware, forewarn, apprise, give fair warning 2 *My mother warned me not to interfere.* = **advise**, urge, recommend, counsel, caution, commend, exhort (*formal*), admonish, put someone on their guard

warning NOUN 1 *health warnings on cigarette packets* = **caution**, information, advice, injunction, notification, caveat, word to the wise 2 *The soldiers opened fire without warning.* = **notice**, notification, word, sign, threat, tip, signal, alarm, announcement, hint, alert, tip-off (*informal*), heads up (*U.S. & Canad.*) 3 *a warning of impending doom* = **omen**, sign, forecast, indication, token, prediction, prophecy, premonition, foreboding, portent, presage, augury, foretoken, rahui (*N.Z.*) 4 *He was given a severe warning from the referee.* = **reprimand**, talking-to (*informal*), caution, censure, counsel, carpeting (*Brit. informal*), rebuke, reproach, scolding, berating, ticking-off (*informal*), chiding, dressing down (*informal*), telling-off (*informal*), admonition, upbraiding, reproof, remonstrance (*formal*) ▶ ADJECTIVE *Pain can act as a warning signal that something is wrong.* = **cautionary**, threatening, ominous, premonitory, admonitory, monitory, bodeful

warp VERB 1 *Rainwater had warped the door's timber.* = **distort**, bend, twist, buckle, deform, disfigure, contort, misshape, malform 2 *Plastic can warp in the sun.* = **become distorted**, bend, twist, contort, become deformed, become misshapen 3 *Their minds have been warped by their experiences.* = **pervert**, twist, corrupt, degrade, deprave, debase, desecrate, debauch, lead astray ▶ NOUN *small warps in the planking* = **twist**, turn, bend, defect, flaw, distortion, deviation, quirk, imperfection, kink, contortion, deformation

warrant VERB *The allegations are serious enough to warrant an investigation.* = **call for**, demand, require, merit, rate, commission, earn, deserve, permit, sanction, excuse, justify, license, authorize, entail, necessitate, be worthy of, give ground for ▶ NOUN *Police have issued a warrant for his arrest.* = **authorization**, permit, licence, permission, security, authority, commission, sanction, pledge, warranty, carte blanche

warranty NOUN = **guarantee**, promise, contract, bond, pledge, certificate, assurance, covenant

warring ADJECTIVE = **hostile**, fighting, conflicting, opposed, contending, at war, embattled, belligerent, combatant, antagonistic, warlike, bellicose, ill-disposed

warrior NOUN = **soldier**, combatant, fighter, gladiator, champion, brave, trooper, military man *or* woman, fighter, man-at-arms

wary ADJECTIVE 1 *My mother always told me to be wary of strangers.* = **suspicious**, sceptical, mistrustful, suspecting, guarded, apprehensive, cagey (*informal*), leery (*slang*), distrustful, on your guard, chary, heedful 2 *Keep a wary eye on children when they are playing near water.* = **watchful**, careful, alert, cautious, prudent, attentive, vigilant, circumspect, heedful ■ **OPPOSITE:** careless

wash VERB 1 *He got a job washing dishes in a pizza parlour.* = **clean**, scrub, sponge, rinse, scour, cleanse 2 *The colours will fade a little each time you wash the shirt.* = **launder**, clean, wet, rinse, dry-clean, moisten 3 *It took a long time to wash the mud out of his hair.* = **rinse**, clean, scrub, lather 4 *There was a sour smell about him, as if he had not washed for days.* = **bathe**, bath, shower, take a bath *or* shower, clean yourself, soak, sponge, douse, freshen up, lave (*archaic*), soap, scrub yourself down 5 *The sea washed against the shore.* = **lap**, break, dash, roll, flow, surge, splash, slap, ripple, swish, splosh 6 *A wave of despair washed over him.* = **move**, overcome, touch, upset, stir, disturb, perturb, surge through, tug at someone's heartstrings (*often facetious*) 7 (*used in negative constructions*) *All those excuses simply won't wash with me.* = **be plausible**, stand up, hold up, pass muster, hold water, stick, carry weight, be convincing, bear scrutiny ▶ NOUN 1 *That coat could do with a good wash.* = **laundering**, cleaning, clean, cleansing 2 *She had a wash*

and changed her clothes. = **bathe** (*Brit.*), bath, shower, dip, soak, scrub, shampoo, rinse, ablution **3** *The wash from a passing ship overturned their dinghy.* = **backwash**, slipstream, path, trail, train, track, waves, aftermath **4** *The steady wash of waves on the shore calmed me.* = **splash**, roll, flow, sweep, surge, swell, rise and fall, ebb and flow, undulation **5** *He painted a wash of colour over the entire surface.* = **coat**, film, covering, layer, screen, coating, stain, overlay, suffusion • **wash something away** *The topsoil is washed away by flood rains.* = **erode**, corrode, eat into, wear something away, eat something away • **wash something or someone away** *Flood waters washed him away.* = **sweep away**, carry off, bear away

washed out ADJECTIVE **1** *The room was now dull and flat with washed-out colours.* = **pale**, light, flat, mat, muted, drab, lacklustre, watery, lustreless **2** *She tried to hide her washed-out face behind large, dark glasses.* = **wan**, drawn, pale, pinched, blanched, haggard, bloodless, colourless, pallid, anaemic, ashen, chalky, peaky, deathly pale **3** *a washed-out blue denim jacket* = **faded**, bleached, blanched, colourless, stonewashed **4** *She looked washed-out and listless.* = **exhausted**, drained, worn-out, tired-out, spent, drawn, done in (*informal*), all in (*slang*), fatigued, wiped out (*informal*), weary, knackered (*slang*), clapped out (*Austral. & N.Z. informal*), dog-tired (*informal*), zonked (*slang*), dead on your feet (*informal*) ■ **OPPOSITE:** lively

washout NOUN **1** *The concert was a total washout.* = **failure**, disaster, disappointment, flop (*informal*), mess, fiasco, dud (*informal*), clunker (*informal*) ■ **OPPOSITE:** success **2** *As a husband, he's a complete washout.* = **loser**, failure, incompetent, no-hoper

waste VERB **1** *We can't afford to waste money on another holiday.* = **squander**, throw away, blow (*slang*), run through, lavish, misuse, dissipate, fritter away, frivol away (*informal*) ■ **OPPOSITE:** save **2** (*often followed by* **away**) *a cruel disease which wastes the muscles* = **wear out**, wither, deplete, debilitate, drain, undermine, exhaust, consume, gnaw, eat away, corrode, enfeeble, sap the strength of, emaciate ▸ NOUN **1** *The whole project is a complete waste of time and resources.* = **squandering**, misuse, loss, expenditure, extravagance, frittering away, lost opportunity, dissipation, wastefulness, misapplication, prodigality, unthriftiness ■ **OPPOSITE:** saving **2** *This country produces 10 million tonnes of toxic waste every year.* = **rubbish**, refuse, debris, sweepings, scrap, litter, garbage, trash (*U.S. & Canad.*), leftovers, offal, dross, dregs, leavings, offscourings **3** (*usually plural*) *the barren wastes of the Sahara* = **desert**, wilds, wilderness, void, solitude (*poetic*), wasteland ▸ ADJECTIVE **1** *suitable locations for the disposal of waste products* = **unwanted**, useless, worthless, unused, leftover, superfluous, unusable, supernumerary ■ **OPPOSITE:** necessary **2** *Yarrow can be found growing wild on waste ground.* = **uncultivated**, wild, bare, barren, empty, devastated, dismal, dreary, desolate, unproductive, uninhabited ■ **OPPOSITE:** cultivated • **lay something waste** *The war has laid waste large regions of the country.* = **devastate**, destroy, ruin, spoil, total (*slang*), sack, undo, trash (*slang*), ravage, raze, kennet (*Austral. slang*), jeff (*Austral. slang*), despoil, wreak havoc upon, depredate (*rare*) • **waste away** *The plants are just wasting away in this heat.* = **decline**, dwindle, wither, perish, sink, fade, crumble, decay, wane, ebb, wear out, atrophy

> USAGE *Waste* and *wastage* are to some extent interchangeable, but many people think that *wastage* should not be used to refer to loss resulting from human carelessness, inefficiency, etc: *a waste* (not *a wastage*) *of time, money, effort,* etc.

wasteful ADJECTIVE = **extravagant**, lavish, prodigal, profligate, ruinous, uneconomical, improvident, unthrifty, thriftless ■ **OPPOSITE:** thrifty

wasteland NOUN = **wilderness**, waste, wild, desert, void

waster NOUN = **layabout**, loser, good-for-nothing, shirker, piker (*Austral. & N.Z. slang*), drone, loafer, skiver (*Brit. slang*), idler, ne'er-do-well, wastrel, malingerer, bludger (*Austral. & N.Z. informal*)

watch VERB **1** *The man was standing in the doorway watching him.* = **look at**, observe, regard, eye, see, mark, view, note, check, clock (*Brit. slang*), stare at, contemplate, check out (*informal*), look on, gaze at, pay attention to, eyeball (*slang*), peer at, leer at, get a load of (*informal*), feast your eyes on, take a butcher's at (*Brit. informal*), take a dekko at (*Brit. slang*) **2** *I had the feeling we were being watched.* = **spy on**, follow, track, monitor, keep an eye on, stake out, keep tabs on (*informal*), keep watch on, keep under observation, keep under surveillance **3** *Parents can't be expected to watch their children 24 hours a day.* = **guard**, keep, mind,

W

protect, tend, look after, shelter, take care of, safeguard, superintend ▶ NOUN **1** *He looked at his watch and checked the time.* = **wristwatch**, timepiece, pocket watch, clock, chronometer **2** *Keep a close watch on him while I'm gone.* = **guard**, eye, attention, supervision, surveillance, notice, observation, inspection, vigil, lookout, vigilance • **watch out** or **watch it** or **watch yourself** *Watch out if you're walking home after dark.* = **be careful**, look out, be wary, be alert, be on the lookout, be vigilant, take heed, have a care, be on the alert, watch yourself, keep your eyes open, be watchful, be on your guard, mind out, be on (the) watch, keep a sharp lookout, keep a weather eye open, keep your eyes peeled or skinned (*informal*), pay attention
• **watch out for something** or **someone** *We had to watch out for unexploded mines.* = **keep a sharp lookout for**, look out for, be alert for, be on the alert for, keep your eyes open for, be on your guard for, be on (the) watch for, be vigilant for, keep a weather eye open for, be watchful for, keep your eyes peeled or skinned for (*informal*)

watchdog NOUN **1** *the government's consumer watchdog* = **guardian**, monitor, inspector, protector, custodian, scrutineer **2** *A good watchdog can be a faithful friend as well as a deterrent to intruders.* = **guard dog**

watchful ADJECTIVE = **alert**, attentive, vigilant, observant, guarded, suspicious, wary, on the lookout, circumspect, wide awake, on your toes, on your guard, on the watch, on the qui vive, heedful ■ **OPPOSITE:** careless

watchman NOUN = **guard**, security guard, security man, custodian, caretaker

watchword NOUN = **motto**, slogan, maxim, byword, rallying cry, battle cry, catch phrase, tag-line, catchword, catchcry (*Austral.*)

water NOUN **1** *Could I have a glass of water, please?* = **liquid**, aqua, Adam's ale or wine, H₂O, wai (*N.Z.*) **2** (*often plural*) *the open waters of the Arctic Ocean* = **sea**, main, waves, ocean, depths, briny (*informal*) ▶ VERB **1** *Water the plants once a week.* = **sprinkle**, spray, soak, irrigate, damp, hose, dampen, drench, douse, moisten, souse, fertigate (*Austral.*) **2** *His eyes were watering from the smoke.* = **get wet**, cry, weep, become wet, exude water • **hold water** *This argument simply doesn't hold water.* = **be sound**, work, stand up, be convincing, hold up, make sense, be logical, ring true, be credible, pass the test, be plausible, be tenable, bear examination or scrutiny

• **water something down 1** *He always waters his whisky down before drinking it.* = **dilute**, add water to, put water in, weaken, water, doctor, thin, adulterate **2** *The government has no intention of watering down its social security reforms.* = **moderate**, weaken, temper, curb, soften, qualify, tame, mute, play down, mitigate, tone down, downplay, adulterate, soft-pedal
■ **RELATED WORDS:** *adjectives* aquatic, aqueous; *prefix* hydro-; *phobia* hydrophobia

waterfall NOUN = **cascade**, fall, cataract, chute, linn (*Scot.*), force (*Northern English, dialect*)

waterlogged ADJECTIVE = **soaked**, saturated, drenched, sodden, streaming, dripping, sopping, wet through, wringing wet, drookit or drookit (*Scot.*)

watertight ADJECTIVE **1** *The batteries are enclosed in a watertight compartment.* = **waterproof**, hermetically sealed, sealed, water-resistant, sound, coated, impermeable, weatherproof, water-repellent, damp-proof, rubberized ■ **OPPOSITE:** leaky **2** *The police had a watertight case against their suspect.* = **foolproof**, firm, sound, perfect, conclusive, flawless, undeniable, unassailable, airtight, indisputable, impregnable, irrefutable, unquestionable, incontrovertible ■ **OPPOSITE:** weak

watery ADJECTIVE **1** *A watery light began to show through the branches.* = **pale**, thin, weak, faint, feeble, washed-out, wan, colourless, anaemic, insipid, wishy-washy (*informal*) **2** *a plateful of watery cabbage soup* = **diluted**, thin, weak, dilute, watered-down, tasteless, runny, insipid, washy, adulterated, wishy-washy (*informal*), flavourless, waterish ■ **OPPOSITE:** concentrated **3** *a wide watery sweep of marshland* = **wet**, damp, moist, soggy, humid, marshy, squelchy **4** *There was a watery discharge from her ear.* = **liquid**, fluid, aqueous, hydrous **5** *Emma's eyes were red and watery.* = **tearful**, moist, weepy, lachrymose (*formal*), tear-filled, rheumy

wave VERB **1** *He waved to us from across the street.* = **signal**, sign, gesture, gesticulate **2** *The police officer waved to us to go on.* = **guide**, point, direct, indicate, signal, motion, gesture, nod, beckon, point in the direction **3** *The protesters were waving banners and shouting.* = **brandish**, swing, flourish, wield, wag, move something to and fro, shake **4** *Flags were waving gently in the breeze.* = **flutter**, flap, stir, waver, shake, swing, sway, ripple, wag, quiver, undulate, oscillate, move to and fro ▶ NOUN

1 *Paddy spotted Mary Anne and gave her a cheery wave.* = **gesture**, sign, signal, indication, gesticulation **2** *the sound of waves breaking on the shore* = **ripple**, breaker, sea surf, swell, ridge, roller, comber, billow **3** *the current wave of violence in schools* = **outbreak**, trend, rash, upsurge, sweep, flood, tendency, surge, groundswell **4** *The second wave of bombers began their attack.* = **stream**, flood, surge, spate, current, movement, flow, rush, tide, torrent, deluge, upsurge

waver VERB **1** *Some military commanders wavered over whether to support the coup.* = **hesitate**, dither (*chiefly Brit.*), vacillate, be irresolute, falter, fluctuate, seesaw, blow hot and cold (*informal*), be indecisive, hum and haw, be unable to decide, shillyshally (*informal*), be unable to make up your mind, swither (*Scot.*) ■ OPPOSITE: be decisive **2** *The shadows of the dancers wavered on the wall.* = **flicker**, wave, shake, vary, reel, weave, sway, tremble, wobble, fluctuate, quiver, undulate, totter

wax VERB **1** *Portugal and Spain had vast empires which waxed and waned.* = **increase**, rise, grow, develop, mount, expand, swell, enlarge, fill out, magnify, get bigger, dilate, become larger ■ OPPOSITE: wane **2** *One should plant seeds and cuttings when the moon is waxing.* = **become fuller**, become larger, enlarge, get bigger

way NOUN **1** *Freezing is a great way to preserve most foods.* = **method**, means, system, process, approach, practice, scheme, technique, manner, plan, procedure, mode, course of action **2** *He had a strange way of talking.* = **manner**, style, fashion, mode **3** *In some ways, we are better off than we were before.* = **aspect**, point, sense, detail, feature, particular, regard, respect, characteristic, facet **4** (*often plural*) *You'll have to get used to my mother's odd little ways.* = **custom**, manner, habit, idiosyncrasy, style, practice, nature, conduct, personality, characteristic, trait, usage, wont, tikanga (*N.Z.*) **5** *Can you tell me the way to the station?* = **route**, direction, course, road, path **6** *He came round the back way.* = **access**, street, road, track, channel, route, path, lane, trail, avenue, highway, pathway, thoroughfare **7** *She said she'd pick me up on her way to work.* = **journey**, approach, advance, progress, passage **8** *The ranks of soldiers parted and made way for her.* = **room**, opening, space, elbowroom **9** *We've a long way to go yet.* = **distance**, length, stretch, journey, trail **10** *He's in a bad way, but he'll live.* = **condition**, state, shape

(*informal*), situation, status, circumstances, plight, predicament, fettle **11** *It's bad for a child to get its own way all the time.* = **will**, demand, wish, desire, choice, aim, pleasure, ambition • **by the way** *By the way, how did your seminar go?* = **incidentally**, in passing, in parenthesis, en passant, by the bye • **give way 1** *The whole ceiling gave way and fell in on us.* = **collapse**, give, fall, crack, break down, subside, cave in, crumple, fall to pieces, go to pieces **2** *I knew he'd give way if I nagged enough.* = **concede**, yield, back down, make concessions, accede, acquiesce, acknowledge defeat • **give way to something** *The numbness gave way to anger.* = **be replaced by**, be succeeded by, be supplanted by • **under way** *A full-scale security operation is now under way.* = **in progress**, going, started, moving, begun, on the move, in motion, afoot, on the go (*informal*) • **ways and means** *discussing ways and means of improving productivity* = **capability**, methods, procedure, way, course, ability, resources, capacity, tools, wherewithal

way-out ADJECTIVE = **outlandish**, eccentric, unconventional, unorthodox, advanced, wild, crazy, bizarre, weird, progressive, experimental, avant-garde, far-out (*slang*), off-the-wall (*slang*), oddball (*informal*), offbeat, freaky (*slang*), outré, wacky (*informal*), off the air (*Austral. slang*)

wayward ADJECTIVE = **erratic**, unruly, wilful, unmanageable, disobedient, contrary, unpredictable, stubborn, perverse, rebellious, fickle, intractable, capricious, obstinate, headstrong, changeable, flighty, incorrigible, obdurate, ungovernable, self-willed, refractory, insubordinate, undependable, inconstant, mulish, cross-grained, contumacious (*literary*), froward (*archaic*) ■ OPPOSITE: obedient

weak ADJECTIVE **1** *I was too weak to move my arms and legs.* = **feeble**, exhausted, frail, debilitated, spent, wasted, weakly, tender, delicate, faint, fragile, shaky, sickly, languid, puny, decrepit, unsteady, infirm, anaemic, effete, enervated ■ OPPOSITE: strong **2** *His eyesight had always been weak.* = **deficient**, wanting, poor, lacking, inadequate, pathetic, faulty, substandard, under-strength ■ OPPOSITE: effective **3** *a clash between a weak minister and a domineering civil servant* = **ineffectual**, pathetic, cowardly, powerless, soft, impotent, indecisive, infirm, spineless, boneless, timorous (*literary*), weak-kneed (*informal*), namby-pamby, irresolute

W

■ **OPPOSITE:** firm **4** *He managed a weak smile and said, 'Don't worry about me.'* = **slight**, faint, feeble, pathetic, shallow, hollow **5** *Her voice was so weak we could hardly hear her.* = **faint**, soft, quiet, slight, small, low, poor, distant, dull, muffled, imperceptible ■ **OPPOSITE:** loud **6** *The animals escaped through a weak spot in the fence.* = **fragile**, brittle, flimsy, unsound, fine, delicate, frail, dainty, breakable **7** *The trade unions are in a very weak position.* = **unsafe**, exposed, vulnerable, helpless, wide open, unprotected, untenable, defenceless, unguarded ■ **OPPOSITE:** secure **8** *The evidence against him was too weak to hold up in court.* = **unconvincing**, unsatisfactory, lame, invalid, flimsy, inconclusive, pathetic ■ **OPPOSITE:** convincing **9** *a weak cup of tea* = **tasteless**, thin, diluted, watery, runny, insipid, wishy-washy (*informal*), under-strength, milk-and-water, waterish ■ **OPPOSITE:** strong

weaken VERB **1** *Her opponents believe that her authority has been fatally weakened.* = **reduce**, undermine, moderate, diminish, temper, impair, lessen, sap, mitigate, invalidate, soften up, take the edge off ■ **OPPOSITE:** boost **2** *The storm was finally beginning to weaken.* = **wane**, fail, diminish, dwindle, lower, flag, fade, give way, lessen, abate, droop, ease up ■ **OPPOSITE:** grow **3** *Malnutrition weakens the patient.* = **sap the strength of**, tire, exhaust, debilitate, depress, incapacitate, enfeeble, enervate ■ **OPPOSITE:** strengthen

weakness NOUN **1** *Symptoms of anaemia include weakness and fatigue.* = **frailty**, fatigue, exhaustion, fragility, infirmity, debility, feebleness, faintness, decrepitude, enervation ■ **OPPOSITE:** strength **2** *Carol has a great weakness for ice cream.* = **liking**, appetite, penchant, soft spot, passion, inclination, fondness, predilection, proclivity (*formal*), partiality, proneness ■ **OPPOSITE:** aversion **3** *People are always taking advantage of his weakness.* = **powerlessness**, vulnerability, impotence, meekness, irresolution, spinelessness, ineffectuality, timorousness, cravenness, cowardliness **4** *She was quick to spot the weakness in his argument.* = **inadequacy**, deficiency, transparency, lameness, hollowness, implausibility, flimsiness, unsoundness, tenuousness **5** *His main weakness was his violent temper.* = **failing**, fault, defect, deficiency, flaw, shortcoming, blemish, imperfection, Achilles' heel, chink in your armour, lack ■ **OPPOSITE:** strong point

wealth NOUN **1** *The discovery of oil brought untold wealth to the island.* = **riches**, fortune, prosperity, affluence, goods, means, money, funds, property, cash, resources, substance, possessions, big money, big bucks (*informal, chiefly U.S.*), opulence, megabucks (*U.S. & Canad. slang*), lucre, pelf (*archaic*) ■ **OPPOSITE:** poverty **2** *His personal wealth is estimated at over 50 million dollars.* = **property**, funds, capital, estate, assets, fortune, possessions **3** *The city boasts a wealth of beautiful churches* = **abundance**, store, plenty, richness, bounty, profusion, fullness, cornucopia, plenitude, copiousness ■ **OPPOSITE:** lack ■ **RELATED WORD:** *mania* plutomania

wealthy ADJECTIVE = **rich**, prosperous, affluent, well-off, loaded (*slang*), comfortable, flush (*informal*), in the money (*informal*), opulent, well-heeled (*informal*), well-to-do, moneyed, quids in (*slang*), filthy rich, rolling in it (*slang*), on Easy Street (*informal*), stinking rich (*slang*), made of money (*informal*), minted (*Brit. slang*) ■ **OPPOSITE:** poor

wear VERB **1** *He was wearing a dark green uniform.* = **be dressed in**, have on, dress in, be clothed in, carry, sport (*informal*), bear, put on, clothe yourself in **2** *Millson's face wore a smug expression.* = **show**, present, bear, display, assume, put on, exhibit **3** *The living room carpet is beginning to wear.* = **deteriorate**, fray, wear thin, become threadbare **4** *I asked if I could work part-time, but the company wouldn't wear it.* = **accept**, take, allow, permit, stomach, swallow (*informal*), brook, stand for, fall for, put up with (*informal*), countenance ▶ NOUN **1** *The shops stock an extensive range of beach wear.* = **clothes**, things, dress, gear (*informal*), attire, habit, outfit, costume, threads (*slang*), garments, apparel (*old-fashioned*), garb, raiments **2** *You'll get more wear out of a car if you look after it properly.* = **usefulness**, use, service, employment, utility, mileage (*informal*) **3** *a large, well-upholstered armchair which showed signs of wear* = **damage**, wear and tear, use, erosion, friction, deterioration, depreciation, attrition, corrosion, abrasion ■ **OPPOSITE:** repair
• **wear down** *Eventually the parts start to wear down.* = **be eroded**, erode, be consumed, wear away • **wear off 1** *Her initial excitement soon began to wear off.* = **subside**, disappear, fade, weaken, diminish, decrease, dwindle, wane, ebb, abate, peter out, lose strength, lose effect **2** *The paint is discoloured and little bits have worn off.* = **rub away**, disappear, fade,

abrade • **wear out** *Eventually the artificial joint wears out and has to be replaced.* = **deteriorate**, become worn, become useless, wear through, fray • **wear someone down** *his sheer persistence in wearing down the opposition* = **undermine**, reduce, chip away at (*informal*), fight a war of attrition against, overcome gradually • **wear someone out** *The past few days had really worn him out.* = **exhaust**, tire, fatigue, weary, impair, sap, prostrate, knacker (*slang*), frazzle (*informal*), fag someoné out (*informal*), enervate • **wear something down** *Rabbits wear down their teeth with constant gnawing.* = **erode**, grind down, consume, impair, corrode, rub away, abrade • **wear something out** *He wore his shoes out wandering around the streets.* = **erode**, go through, consume, use up, wear holes in, make worn

weariness NOUN = **tiredness**, fatigue, exhaustion, lethargy, drowsiness, lassitude, languor, listlessness, prostration, enervation ■ **OPPOSITE:** energy

wearing ADJECTIVE = **tiresome**, trying, taxing, tiring, exhausting, fatiguing, oppressive, exasperating, irksome, wearisome ■ **OPPOSITE:** refreshing

weary ADJECTIVE **1** *She sank to the ground, too weary to walk another step.* = **tired**, exhausted, drained, worn out, spent, done in (*informal*), flagging, all in (*slang*), fatigued, wearied, sleepy, fagged (*informal*), whacked (*Brit. informal*), jaded, drooping, knackered (*slang*), drowsy, clapped out (*Austral. & N.Z. informal*), enervated, ready to drop, dog-tired (*informal*), zonked (*slang*), dead beat (*informal*), asleep or dead on your feet (*informal*) ■ **OPPOSITE:** energetic **2** *I am growing weary of your constant complaints.* = **fed up**, bored, sick (*informal*), discontented, impatient, indifferent, jaded, sick and tired (*informal*), browned-off (*informal*) ■ **OPPOSITE:** excited **3** *a long, weary journey in search of food and water* = **tiring**, taxing, wearing, arduous, tiresome, laborious, irksome, wearisome, enervative ■ **OPPOSITE:** refreshing ▶ VERB **1** *He had wearied of teaching in state universities.* = **grow tired**, tire, sicken, have had enough, become bored **2** *Her boss's criticism wearied her so much that she left.* = **bore**, annoy, plague, sicken, jade, exasperate, vex, irk, try the patience of, make discontented ■ **OPPOSITE:** excite **3** *Her pregnancy wearied her to the point of exhaustion.* = **tire**, tax, burden, drain, fatigue, fag (*informal*), sap, wear out, debilitate, take it out of (*informal*), tire out, enervate ■ **OPPOSITE:** invigorate

weather NOUN *I don't like hot weather much.* = **climate**, conditions, temperature, forecast, outlook, meteorological conditions, elements ▶ VERB **1** *The stones have been weathered by centuries of wind and rain.* = **toughen**, season, wear, expose, harden **2** *The company has weathered the recession.* = **withstand**, stand, suffer, survive, overcome, resist, brave, endure, come through, get through, rise above, live through, ride out, make it through (*informal*), surmount, pull through, stick it out (*informal*), bear up against ■ **OPPOSITE:** surrender to • **under the weather** *I'm feeling a bit under the weather today.* = **ill**, unwell, poorly (*informal*), sick, rough (*informal*), crook (*Austral. & N.Z. informal*), ailing, not well, seedy (*informal*), below par, queasy, out of sorts, nauseous, off-colour (*Brit.*), indisposed, peaky, ropy (*Brit. informal*), wabbit (*Scot. informal*)

weave VERB **1** *She then weaves the fibres together to make the traditional Awatum basket.* = **knit**, twist, intertwine, plait, unite, introduce, blend, incorporate, merge, mat, fuse, braid, entwine, intermingle, interlace **2** *The cyclists wove in and out of the traffic.* = **zigzag**, wind, move in and out, crisscross, weave your way **3** *The author weaves a compelling tale of life in London during the war.* = **create**, tell, recount, narrate, make, build, relate, make up, spin (*informal*), construct, invent, put together, unfold, contrive, fabricate

web NOUN **1** *He was caught like a fly in a web.* = **cobweb**, spider's web **2** *a delicate web of fine lace* = **mesh**, net, netting, screen, webbing, weave, lattice, latticework, interlacing, lacework **3** *a complex web of financial dealings* = **tangle**, series, network, mass, chain, knot, maze, toils, nexus

wed VERB **1** *She wed her childhood sweetheart.* = **get married to**, espouse, get hitched to (*slang*), be united to, plight your troth to (*old-fashioned*), get spliced to (*informal*), take as your husband or wife ■ **OPPOSITE:** divorce **2** *The pair wed in a secret ceremony in front of just nine guests.* = **get married**, marry, be united, tie the knot (*informal*), take the plunge (*informal*), get hitched (*slang*), get spliced (*informal*), plight your troth (*old-fashioned*) ■ **OPPOSITE:** divorce **3** *a film which weds stunning visuals and a first-class score* = **unite**, combine, bring together, amalgamate, join, link, marry, ally, connect, blend, integrate, merge, unify, make one, fuse, weld, interweave, yoke, coalesce, commingle ■ **OPPOSITE:** divide

W

wedding NOUN = **marriage**, nuptials, wedding ceremony, marriage ceremony, marriage service, wedding service, nuptial rite, espousals

wedge VERB *He wedged himself between the door and the radiator.* = **squeeze**, force, lodge, jam, crowd, block, stuff, pack, thrust, ram, cram, stow ▶ NOUN *a wedge of cheese* = **block**, segment, lump, chunk, triangle, slab, hunk, chock, wodge (*Brit. informal*)

wedlock NOUN = **marriage**, matrimony, holy matrimony, married state, conjugal bond

wee ADJECTIVE = **little**, small, minute, tiny, miniature, insignificant, negligible, microscopic, diminutive, minuscule, teeny (*informal*), itsy-bitsy (*informal*), teeny-weeny, titchy (*Brit. informal*), teensy-weensy, pygmy *or* pigmy

weedy ADJECTIVE = **weak**, thin, frail, skinny, feeble, ineffectual, puny, undersized, weak-kneed (*informal*), namby-pamby, nerdy *or* nurdy (*slang*)

weekly ADJECTIVE *her weekly visit to her parents' house* = **once a week**, hebdomadal, hebdomadary ▶ ADVERB *The group meets weekly.* = **every week**, once a week, by the week, hebdomadally

weep VERB = **cry**, shed tears, sob, whimper, complain, keen, greet (*Scot.*), moan, mourn, grieve, lament, whinge (*informal*), blubber, snivel, blubbering, lachrymose, blub (*slang*), boohoo ■ **OPPOSITE:** rejoice

weepy ADJECTIVE *After her mother's death she was depressed and weepy for months.* = **tearful**, crying, weeping, sobbing, whimpering, close to tears, blubbering, lachrymose, on the verge of tears ▶ NOUN *The film is an old-fashioned weepy with fine performances by both stars.* = **tear-jerker** (*informal*)

weigh VERB **1** *He weighs about 13 stone.* = **have a weight of**, tip the scales at (*informal*) **2** *They counted and weighed the fruits.* = **measure the weight of**, put someone or something on the scales, measure how heavy someone or something is **3** *He is weighing the possibility of filing charges against the doctor.* = **consider**, study, examine, contemplate, evaluate, ponder, mull over, think over, eye up, reflect upon, give thought to, meditate upon, deliberate upon **4** *We must weigh the pros and cons of each method.* = **compare**, balance, contrast, juxtapose, place side by side **5** *His opinion doesn't weigh much with me, I'm afraid.* = **matter**, carry weight, cut any ice (*informal*), impress, tell, count, have influence, be influential • **weigh on someone**

The separation weighed on both of them. = **oppress**, burden, depress, distress, plague, prey, torment, hang over, bear down, gnaw at, cast down, take over • **weigh someone down 1** *The soldiers were weighed down by their heavy packs.* = **burden**, overload, encumber, overburden, tax, weight, strain, handicap, saddle, hamper **2** *He could not shake off the guilt that weighed him down.* = **oppress**, worry, trouble, burden, depress, haunt, plague, get down, torment, take control of, hang over, beset, prey on, bear down, gnaw at, cast down, press down on, overburden, weigh upon, lie heavy on • **weigh someone up** *As soon as I walked into his office I could see him weighing me up.* = **assess**, judge, gauge, appraise, eye someone up, size someone up (*informal*) • **weigh something out** *I weighed out portions of tea and sugar.* = **measure**, dole out, apportion, deal out

weight NOUN **1** *Try to reduce the weight of the load.* = **heaviness**, mass, burden, poundage, pressure, load, gravity, tonnage, heft (*informal*), avoirdupois **2** *Straining to lift heavy weights can cause back injury.* = **load** (*informal*), mass, ballast, heavy object **3** *That argument no longer carries much weight.* = **importance**, force, power, moment, value, authority, influence, bottom, impact, import (*formal*), muscle, consequence, substance, consideration, emphasis, significance, sway, clout (*informal*), leverage, efficacy, mana (*N.Z.*), persuasiveness **4** *He heaved a sigh of relief. 'That's a great weight off my mind.'* = **burden**, pressure, load, strain, oppression, albatross, millstone, encumbrance **5** *The weight of evidence suggests that he is guilty.* = **preponderance**, mass, bulk, main body, most, majority, onus, lion's share, greatest force, main force, best *or* better part ▶ VERB **1** (*often with* **down**) *The body was weighted down with bricks.* = **load**, ballast, make heavier **2** *The electoral law is still heavily weighted in favour of the ruling party.* = **bias**, load, slant, unbalance **3** *His life was a struggle, weighted with failures and disappointments.* = **burden**, handicap, oppress, impede, weigh down, encumber, overburden

weighty ADJECTIVE **1** *Surely such weighty matters merit a higher level of debate?* = **important**, serious, significant, critical, crucial, considerable, substantial, grave, solemn, momentous, forcible, consequential ■ **OPPOSITE:** unimportant **2** *Simon lifted a weighty volume from the shelf.* = **heavy**, massive, dense, hefty (*informal*), cumbersome, ponderous, burdensome **3** *the weighty responsibility of organizing the entire event* = **onerous**, taxing, demanding, difficult, worrying, crushing, exacting, oppressive, burdensome, worrisome, backbreaking

weird ADJECTIVE **1** *I had such a weird dream last night.* = **strange**, odd, unusual, bizarre, ghostly, mysterious, queer, unearthly, eerie, grotesque, supernatural, unnatural, far-out (*slang*), uncanny, spooky (*informal*), creepy (*informal*), eldritch (*poetic*) ■ **OPPOSITE:** normal **2** *I don't like that guy – he's really weird.* = **bizarre**, odd, strange, unusual, queer, grotesque, unnatural, creepy (*informal*), outlandish, freakish ■ **OPPOSITE:** ordinary

weirdo *or* **weirdie** NOUN = **eccentric**, freak (*informal*), crank (*informal*), oddball (*informal*), queer fish (*Brit. informal*)

welcome VERB **1** *Several people came out to welcome me.* = **greet**, meet, receive, embrace, hail, usher in, say hello to, roll out the red carpet for, offer hospitality to, receive with open arms, bid welcome, karanga (*N.Z.*), mihi (*N.Z.*), haeremai (*N.Z.*) ■ **OPPOSITE:** reject **2** *They welcomed the move but felt it did not go far enough.* = **accept gladly**, appreciate, embrace, approve of, be pleased by, give the thumbs up to (*informal*), be glad about, express pleasure or satisfaction at ▶ NOUN *There was a wonderful welcome waiting for him when he arrived.* = **greeting**, welcoming, entertainment, reception, acceptance, hail, hospitality, salutation (*formal*), haeremai (*N.Z.*) ■ **OPPOSITE:** rejection ▶ ADJECTIVE **1** *a welcome change from the usual routine* = **pleasing**, wanted, accepted, appreciated, acceptable, pleasant, desirable, refreshing, delightful, gratifying, agreeable, pleasurable, gladly received ■ **OPPOSITE:** unpleasant **2** *I was really made to feel welcome.* = **wanted**, at home, invited ■ **OPPOSITE:** unwanted **3** *Non-residents are welcome to use our facilities.* = **free**, invited

weld VERB **1** *It's possible to weld stainless steel to ordinary steel.* = **join**, link, bond, bind, connect, cement, fuse, solder, braze **2** *The miracle was that Rose had welded them into a team.* = **unite**, combine, blend, consolidate, unify, fuse, meld ▶ NOUN *The weld on the outlet pipe was visibly fractured.* = **joint**, bond, seam, juncture

welfare NOUN **1** *Above all we must consider the welfare of the children.* = **wellbeing**, good, interest, health, security, benefit, success, profit, safety, protection, fortune, comfort, happiness, prosperity, prosperousness

2 *proposed cuts in welfare* = **state benefit**, support, benefits, pensions, dole (*slang*), social security, unemployment benefit, state benefits, pogey (*Canad.*)

well¹ ADVERB **1** *All the team members played well.* = **skilfully**, expertly, adeptly, with skill, professionally, correctly, properly, effectively, efficiently, adequately, admirably, ably, conscientiously, proficiently ■ **OPPOSITE:** badly **2** *I thought the interview went very well.* = **satisfactorily**, nicely, smoothly, successfully, capitally, pleasantly, happily, famously (*informal*), splendidly, agreeably, like nobody's business (*informal*), in a satisfactory manner ■ **OPPOSITE:** badly **3** *Mix all the ingredients well.* = **thoroughly**, completely, fully, carefully, effectively, efficiently, rigorously **4** *How well do you know him?* = **intimately**, closely, completely, deeply, fully, personally, profoundly ■ **OPPOSITE:** slightly **5** *This is obviously a man who's studied his subject well.* = **carefully**, closely, minutely, fully, comprehensively, accurately, in detail, in depth, extensively, meticulously, painstakingly, rigorously, scrupulously, assiduously, intensively, from top to bottom, methodically, attentively, conscientiously, exhaustively **6** *He speaks very well of you.* = **favourably**, highly, kindly, warmly, enthusiastically, graciously, approvingly, admiringly, with admiration, appreciatively, with praise, glowingly, with approbation ■ **OPPOSITE:** unfavourably **7** *Franklin did not turn up until well after midnight.* = **considerably**, easily, very much, significantly, substantially, markedly **8** *I am well aware of how much she has suffered.* = **fully**, highly, greatly, completely, amply, very much, thoroughly, considerably, sufficiently, substantially, heartily, abundantly **9** *The murderer may well be someone who was close to the victim.* = **possibly**, probably, certainly, reasonably, conceivably, justifiably **10** *My parents always treated me well.* = **decently**, right, kindly, fittingly, fairly, easily, correctly, properly, readily, politely, suitably, generously, justly, in all fairness, genially, civilly, hospitably ■ **OPPOSITE:** unfairly **11** *We manage to live very well on our combined salaries.* = **prosperously**, comfortably, splendidly, in comfort, in (the lap of) luxury, flourishingly, without hardship ▶ ADJECTIVE **1** *I hope you're well.* = **healthy**, strong, sound, fit, blooming, robust, hale (*old-fashioned*), hearty, in good health, alive and kicking, fighting fit (*informal*), in fine fettle, up to par, fit as a fiddle, able-bodied, in good

W

condition ■ **OPPOSITE:** ill **2** *He was satisfied that all was well.* = **satisfactory**, good, right, fine, happy, fitting, pleasing, bright, useful, lucky, proper, thriving, flourishing, profitable, fortunate ■ **OPPOSITE:** unsatisfactory **3** *It would be well to check the facts before you speak out.* = **advisable**, useful, proper, prudent, agreeable ■ **OPPOSITE:** inadvisable • **as well** *I like the job, and the people I work with are very nice as well.* = **also**, too, in addition, moreover, besides, to boot, into the bargain • **as well as** *food and other goods, as well as energy supplies such as gas and oil* = **including**, along with, in addition to, not to mention, at the same time as, over and above

well² NOUN **1** *the cost of drilling an oil well* = **hole**, bore, pit, shaft **2** *I had to fetch water from the well.* = **waterhole**, source, spring, pool, fountain, fount **3** *a man with a well of experience and insight* = **source**, fund, mine, treasury, reservoir, storehouse, repository, fount, wellspring ▶ VERB **1** *Blood welled from a gash in his thigh.* = **flow**, trickle, seep, run, issue, spring, pour, jet, burst, stream, surge, discharge, trickle, gush, ooze, seep, exude, spurt, spout **2** *He could feel the anger welling inside him.* = **rise**, increase, grow, mount, surge, swell, intensify

well-balanced ADJECTIVE **1** *a sensible, well-balanced individual* = **sensible**, rational, level-headed, well-adjusted, together (*slang*), sound, reasonable, sober, sane, judicious, grounded **2** *Intervals of depth are essential to a well-balanced composition.* = **well-proportioned**, proportional, graceful, harmonious, symmetrical

well-bred ADJECTIVE **1** *She was too well-bred to make personal remarks.* = **polite**, ladylike, well-brought-up, well-mannered, cultured, civil, mannerly, polished, sophisticated, gentlemanly, refined, cultivated, courteous, gallant, genteel, urbane, courtly ■ **OPPOSITE:** ill-bred **2** *He was clearly of well-bred stock.* = **aristocratic**, gentle (*archaic*), noble, patrician, blue-blooded, well-born, highborn (*old-fashioned*)

well-groomed ADJECTIVE = **smart**, trim, neat, tidy, spruce, well-dressed, dapper, well turned out, soigné or soignée

well-heeled ADJECTIVE = **prosperous**, rich, wealthy, affluent, loaded (*slang*), comfortable, flush (*informal*), well-off, in the money (*informal*), opulent, well-to-do, moneyed, well-situated, in clover (*informal*), minted (*Brit. slang*)

well-informed ADJECTIVE = **educated**, aware, informed, acquainted, knowledgeable or knowledgable,

understanding, well-educated, in the know (*informal*), well-read, conversant, au fait (*French*), in the loop (*informal*), well-grounded, au courant (*French*), clued-up (*informal*), cognizant or cognisant, well-versed

well-known ADJECTIVE **1** *He liked to surround himself with attractive or well-known people.* = **famous**, important, celebrated, prominent, great, leading, noted, august, popular, familiar, distinguished, esteemed, acclaimed, notable, renowned, eminent, famed, illustrious, on the map, widely known **2** *It is a well-known fact that smoking can cause lung cancer.* = **familiar**, common, established, popular, everyday, widely known

well-mannered ADJECTIVE = **polite**, civil, mannerly, gentlemanly, gracious, respectful, courteous, genteel, urbane, ladylike

well-nigh ADVERB = **almost**, nearly, virtually, practically, next to, all but, just about, more or less

well-off ADJECTIVE **1** *My family was quite well-off.* = **rich**, wealthy, comfortable, affluent, loaded (*slang*), flush (*informal*), prosperous, well-heeled (*informal*), well-to-do, moneyed, minted (*Brit. slang*) ■ **OPPOSITE:** poor **2** *Compared to some of the people in my ward, I feel quite well off.* = **fortunate**, lucky, comfortable (*informal*), thriving, flourishing, successful

well-to-do ADJECTIVE = **rich**, wealthy, affluent, well-off, loaded (*slang*), comfortable, flush (*informal*), prosperous, well-heeled (*informal*), moneyed, minted (*Brit. slang*) ■ **OPPOSITE:** poor

well-worn ADJECTIVE **1** *To use a well-worn cliché, she does not suffer fools gladly.* = **stale**, tired, stereotyped, commonplace, banal, trite, hackneyed, overused, timeworn **2** *He was dressed casually in a sweater and well-worn jeans.* = **shabby**, worn, faded, ragged, frayed, worn-out, scruffy, tattered, tatty (*Brit.*), threadbare

welter NOUN = **jumble**, confusion, muddle, hotchpotch, web, mess, tangle

wend VERB • **wend your way** = **go**, move, travel, progress, proceed, make for, direct your course

wet ADJECTIVE **1** *He rubbed his wet hair with a towel.* = **damp**, soaked, soaking, dripping, saturated, moist, drenched, watery, soggy, sodden, waterlogged, moistened, dank, sopping, aqueous, wringing wet ■ **OPPOSITE:** dry **2** *It was a miserable wet day.* = **rainy**, damp, drizzly, showery, raining, pouring, drizzling, misty, teeming, humid,

dank, clammy ■ **OPPOSITE:** sunny
3 *I despised him for being so wet and spineless.*
= **feeble**, soft, weak, silly, foolish, ineffectual, weedy (*informal*), spineless, effete, boneless, timorous, namby-pamby, irresolute, wussy (*slang*), nerdy or nurdy (*slang*) ▶ VERB *Wet the fabric with a damp sponge before ironing.* = **moisten**, spray, damp, dampen, water, dip, splash, soak, steep, sprinkle, saturate, drench, douse, irrigate, humidify, fertigate (*Austral.*) ■ **OPPOSITE:** dry ▶ NOUN **1** *They had come in from the cold and the wet.* = **rain**, rains, damp, drizzle, wet weather, rainy season, rainy weather, damp weather ■ **OPPOSITE:** fine weather **2** *splashing around in the wet of the puddles* = **moisture**, water, liquid, damp, humidity, condensation, dampness, wetness, clamminess ■ **OPPOSITE:** dryness

whack (*informal*) VERB *Someone whacked him on the head with a baseball bat.* = **strike**, hit, beat, box, belt (*informal*), deck (*slang*), bang, rap, slap, bash (*informal*), sock (*slang*), chin (*slang*), smack, thrash, thump, buffet, clout (*informal*), slug, cuff, swipe (*informal*), clobber (*slang*), wallop (*informal*), thwack, lambast(e), lay one on (*slang*), beat or knock seven bells out of (*informal*) ▶ NOUN **1** *He gave the tree a powerful whack with the axe.* = **blow**, hit, box, stroke, belt (*informal*), bang, rap, slap, bash (*informal*), sock (*slang*), smack, thump, buffet, clout (*informal*), slug, cuff, swipe (*informal*), wallop (*informal*), wham, thwack **2** *I pay a sizeable whack of capital gains tax.* = **share**, part, cut (*informal*), bit, portion, quota, allotment **3** *Let me have a whack at trying to fix the car.* = **attempt**, go (*informal*), try, turn, shot (*informal*), crack (*informal*), stab (*informal*), bash (*informal*)

whacking ADJECTIVE = **huge**, big, large, giant, enormous, extraordinary, tremendous, gigantic, great, monstrous, mammoth, whopping (*informal*), prodigious, elephantine, humongous or humungous (*informal*)

whale NOUN ■ **RELATED WORDS:** *adjective* cetacean; *name of male bull*; *name of female* cow; *name of young calf*; *collective nouns* school, gam, run

wharf NOUN = **dock**, pier, berth, quay, jetty, landing stage

wheedle VERB = **coax**, talk, court, draw, persuade, charm, worm, flatter, entice, cajole, inveigle

wheel NOUN *a bicycle wheel* = **disc**, ring, hoop ▶ VERB **1** *He wheeled his bike into the alley beside the house.* = **push**, trundle, roll **2** *I wheeled around to face her.* = **turn**, swing, spin, revolve, rotate, whirl, swivel **3** *A flock of crows wheeled overhead.* = **circle**, orbit, go round, twirl, gyrate • **at** or **behind the wheel** *She insisted that she was at the wheel when the car crashed.* = **driving**, steering, in the driving seat, in the driver's seat

wheeze VERB *His chest problems made him wheeze constantly.* = **gasp**, whistle, cough, hiss, rasp, catch your breath, breathe roughly ▶ NOUN **1** *She puffed up the stairs, emitting a wheeze at every breath.* = **gasp**, whistle, cough, hiss, rasp **2** *She came up with a clever wheeze to get round the problem.* = **trick**, plan, idea, scheme, stunt, ploy, expedient, ruse

whereabouts PLURAL NOUN = **position**, situation, site, location

wherewithal NOUN = **resources**, means, money, funds, capital, supplies, ready (*informal*), essentials, ready money

whet VERB = **stimulate**, increase, excite, stir, enhance, provoke, arouse, awaken, animate, rouse, quicken, incite, kindle, pique ■ **OPPOSITE:** suppress

whiff NOUN **1** *He caught a whiff of her perfume.* = **smell**, hint, scent, sniff, aroma, odour, draught, niff (*Brit. slang*) **2** *the nauseating whiff of rotting flesh* = **stink**, stench, reek, pong (*Brit. informal*), niff (*Brit. slang*), malodour, hum (*slang*) **3** *Not a whiff of scandal has ever tainted his private life.* = **trace**, suggestion, hint, suspicion, bit, drop, note, breath, whisper, shred, crumb, tinge, jot, smidgen (*informal*), soupçon (*French*) **4** *At the first whiff of smoke, the alarm will go off.* = **puff**, breath, flurry, waft, rush, blast, draught, gust ▶ VERB *These socks whiff a bit, don't they?* = **stink**, stench, reek, pong (*Brit. informal*), niff (*Brit. slang*), hum (*slang*)

whim NOUN = **impulse**, sudden notion, caprice, fancy, sport, urge, notion, humour, freak, craze, fad (*informal*), quirk, conceit (*archaic*), vagary, whimsy, passing thought, crotchet

whimper VERB *She lay at the bottom of the stairs, whimpering in pain.* = **cry**, moan, sob, weep, whine, whinge (*informal*), grizzle (*informal, chiefly Brit.*), blubber, snivel, blub (*slang*), mewl ▶ NOUN *David's crying subsided to a whimper.* = **sob**, moan, whine, snivel

whimsical ADJECTIVE = **fanciful**, odd, funny, unusual, fantastic, curious, weird, peculiar, eccentric, queer, flaky (*slang, chiefly U.S.*), singular, quaint, playful, mischievous, capricious, droll, freakish, fantastical, crotchety, chimerical, waggish

whine VERB **1** *He could hear a child whining in the background.* = **cry**, sob, wail, whimper, sniffle, snivel, moan **2** *She's always calling me* to whine about her problems. = **complain**, grumble, gripe (*informal*), whinge (*informal*), moan, cry, beef (*slang*), carp, sob, wail, grouse, whimper, bleat, grizzle (*informal, chiefly Brit.*), grouch (*informal*), bellyache (*slang*), kvetch (*U.S. slang*) ▶ NOUN **1** *His voice became a pleading whine.* = **cry**, moan, sob, wail, whimper, plaintive cry **2** *the whine of air-raid sirens* = **drone**, note, hum **3** *endless whines about how shallow our society is* = **complaint**, moan (*informal*), grumble, grouse, gripe (*informal*), whinge (*informal*), grouch (*informal*), beef (*slang*)

whinge VERB *people who whinge about their alleged misfortunes* = **complain**, moan (*informal*), grumble, grouse, gripe (*informal*), beef (*slang*), carp, bleat, grizzle (*informal, chiefly Brit.*), grouch (*informal*), bellyache (*slang*), kvetch (*U.S. slang*) ▶ NOUN *It must be depressing having to listen to everyone's whinges.* = **complaint**, moan (*informal*), grumble, whine, grouse, gripe (*informal*), grouch (*informal*), beef (*slang*)

whip NOUN *Prisoners were regularly beaten with a whip.* = **lash**, cane, birch, switch, crop, scourge, thong, rawhide, riding crop, horsewhip, bullwhip, knout, cat-o'-nine-tails ▶ VERB **1** *He was whipped with a studded belt.* = **lash**, cane, flog, beat, switch, leather, punish, strap, tan (*slang*), thrash, lick (*informal*), birch, scourge, spank, castigate, lambast(e), flagellate, give a hiding (*informal*) **2** *I whipped into a parking space.* = **dash**, shoot, fly, tear, rush, dive, dart, whisk, flit **3** *Whip the cream until it is thick.* = **whisk**, beat, mix vigorously, stir vigorously **4** *an accomplished orator who could whip a crowd into hysteria* = **incite**, drive, push, urge, stir, spur, provoke, compel, hound, prod, work up, get going, agitate, prick, inflame, instigate, goad, foment **5** *Our school can whip theirs at football and rugby.* = **beat**, thrash, trounce, wipe the floor with (*informal*), best, defeat, stuff (*slang*), worst, overcome, hammer (*informal*), overwhelm, conquer, lick (*informal*), rout, overpower, outdo, clobber (*slang*), take apart (*slang*), run rings around (*informal*), blow out of the water (*slang*), make mincemeat out of (*informal*), drub • **whip someone up** *He tried to whip his side up into an emotional frenzy before every game.* = **rouse**, excite, provoke, arouse, stir up, work up, agitate, inflame • **whip something out** *Bob whipped out his notebook.* = **pull out**, produce, remove, jerk out, show, flash, seize, whisk out, snatch out

whipping NOUN = **beating**, lashing, thrashing, caning, hiding (*informal*),

punishment, tanning (*slang*), birching, flogging, spanking, the strap, flagellation, castigation, leathering

whirl VERB **1** *Hearing a sound behind her, she whirled round.* = **spin**, turn, circle, wheel, twist, reel, rotate, pivot, twirl **2** *The smoke whirled and grew into a monstrous column.* = **rotate**, roll, twist, revolve, swirl, twirl, gyrate, pirouette **3** *My head whirled in a giddiness like that of intoxication.* = **feel dizzy**, swim, spin, reel, go round ▶ NOUN **1** *the whirl of snowflakes in the wind* = **revolution**, turn, roll, circle, wheel, spin, twist, reel, swirl, rotation, twirl, pirouette, gyration, birl (*Scot.*) **2** *Her life is one long whirl of parties.* = **bustle**, round, series, succession, flurry, merry-go-round **3** *My thoughts are in a complete whirl.* = **confusion**, daze, dither (*chiefly Brit.*), giddiness **4** *I was caught up in a terrible whirl of emotion.* = **tumult**, spin (*informal*), stir, agitation, commotion, hurly-burly • **give something a whirl** *Why not give acupuncture a whirl?* = **attempt**, try, have a go at (*informal*), have a crack at (*informal*), have a shot at (*informal*), have a stab at (*informal*), have a bash at, have a whack at (*informal*)

whirlwind NOUN **1** *They scattered like leaves in a whirlwind.* = **tornado**, hurricane, cyclone, typhoon, twister (*U.S.*), dust devil, waterspout **2** *a whirlwind of frenzied activity* = **turmoil**, chaos, swirl, mayhem, uproar, maelstrom, welter, bedlam, tumult, hurly-burly, madhouse (*informal*)
▶ MODIFIER *He got married after a whirlwind romance.* = **rapid**, short, quick, swift, lightning, rash, speedy, hasty, impulsive, headlong, impetuous ▪ OPPOSITE: unhurried

whisk VERB **1** *I was whisked away in a police car.* = **rush**, sweep, hurry **2** *The waiter whisked our plates away.* = **pull**, whip (*informal*), snatch, take **3** *She whisked out of the room.* = **speed**, race, shoot, fly, career, tear, rush, sweep, dash, hurry, barrel (along) (*informal, chiefly U.S. & Canad.*), sprint, dart, hasten, burn rubber (*informal*), go like the clappers (*Brit. informal*), hightail it (*U.S. informal*), wheech (*Scot. informal*) **4** *The dog whisked its tail around in excitement.* = **flick**, whip, sweep, brush, wipe, twitch **5** *Whisk together the sugar and the egg yolks.* = **beat**, mix vigorously, stir vigorously, whip, fluff up
▶ NOUN **1** *With one whisk of its tail, the horse brushed the flies off.* = **flick**, sweep, brush, whip, wipe **2** *Using a whisk, beat the mixture until it thickens.* = **beater**, mixer, blender

whisky NOUN = **Scotch**, malt, rye, bourbon, firewater, John Barleycorn, usquebaugh (*Gaelic*), barley-bree (*Scot.*)

whisper VERB **1** *'Keep your voice down,'
I whispered.* = **murmur**, breathe, mutter,
mumble, purr, speak in hushed tones, say
softly, say sotto voce, utter under the
breath ■ **OPPOSITE:** shout **2** *People started
whispering that the pair were having an affair.*
= **gossip**, hint, intimate, murmur,
insinuate, spread rumours **3** *The leaves
whispered and rustled in the breeze.* = **rustle**,
sigh, moan, murmur, hiss, swish, sough,
susurrate (*literary*) ▶ NOUN **1** *Men were
talking in whispers in the corridor.* = **murmur**,
mutter, mumble, undertone, low voice,
soft voice, hushed tone **2** *I've heard a whisper
that he is planning to resign.* = **rumour**,
report, word, story, hint, buzz, gossip,
dirt (*slang*), goss (*informal*), innuendo,
insinuation, scuttlebutt (*U.S. slang*)
3 *the slight whisper of the wind in the grass*
= **rustle**, sigh, sighing, murmur, hiss,
swish, soughing, susurration *or* susurrus
(*literary*) **4** *There is a whisper of conspiracy
about the whole affair.* = **hint**, shadow,
suggestion, trace, breath, suspicion,
fraction, tinge, whiff

whit NOUN = **bit**, drop, piece, trace, scrap,
dash, grain, particle, fragment, atom,
pinch, shred, crumb, mite, jot, speck,
modicum, least bit, iota

white ADJECTIVE **1** *He turned white and began
to stammer.* = **pale**, grey, ghastly, wan,
pasty, bloodless, pallid, ashen, waxen, like
death warmed up (*informal*), wheyfaced
2 (*of hair*) *an old man with white hair* = **silver**,
grey, snowy, grizzled, hoary • **whiter than
white** = **immaculate**, innocent, virtuous,
saintly, clean, pure, worthy, noble,
stainless, impeccable, exemplary, spotless,
squeaky-clean, unblemished, untainted,
unsullied, irreproachable, uncorrupted

white-collar ADJECTIVE = **clerical**, office,
executive, professional, salaried,
nonmanual

whiten VERB **1** *His face whitened as he heard
the news.* = **pale**, blanch, go white, turn
pale, blench, fade, etiolate ■ **OPPOSITE:**
darken **2** *toothpastes that whiten the teeth*
= **bleach**, lighten ■ **OPPOSITE:** darken

whitewash VERB *The administration is
whitewashing the regime's actions.* = **cover up**,
conceal, suppress, camouflage, make light
of, gloss over, extenuate ■ **OPPOSITE:**
expose ▶ NOUN *The report's findings were
condemned as total whitewash.* = **cover-up**,
deception, camouflage, concealment,
extenuation

whittle VERB *Chitty sat in his rocking chair
whittling a piece of wood.* = **carve**, cut, hew
(*old-fashioned*), shape, trim, shave, pare

• **whittle something away** *I believe the
Government's aim is to whittle away the Welfare
State.* = **undermine**, reduce, destroy,
consume, erode, eat away, wear away, cut
down, cut, decrease, prune, scale down

whole NOUN **1** *Taken as a percentage of the
whole, it has to be a fairly minor part.* = **total**,
all, lot, everything, aggregate, sum total,
the entire amount **2** *The different components
combine to form a complete whole.* = **unit**,
body, piece, object, combination, unity,
entity, ensemble, entirety, fullness, totality
■ **OPPOSITE:** part ▶ ADJECTIVE **1** *I have now
read the whole book.* = **complete**, full, total,
entire, integral, uncut, undivided,
unabridged, unexpurgated, uncondensed
■ **OPPOSITE:** partial **2** *I struck the glass with
all my might, but it remained whole.*
= **undamaged**, intact, unscathed,
unbroken, good, sound, perfect, mint,
untouched, flawless, unhurt, faultless,
unharmed, in one piece, uninjured,
inviolate, unimpaired, unmutilated
■ **OPPOSITE:** damaged ▶ ADVERB *Snakes
swallow their prey whole.* = **in one piece**, in
one • **on the whole 1** *On the whole, I think
it's better if I don't come with you.* = **all in all**,
altogether, all things considered, by and
large, taking everything into consideration
2 *On the whole, women are having children
much later these days.* = **generally**, in
general, for the most part, as a rule, chiefly,
mainly, mostly, principally, on average,
predominantly, in the main, to a large
extent, as a general rule, generally
speaking

wholehearted ADJECTIVE = **sincere**,
complete, committed, genuine, real, true,
determined, earnest, warm, devoted,
dedicated, enthusiastic, emphatic, hearty,
heartfelt, zealous, unqualified, unstinting,
unreserved, unfeigned ■ **OPPOSITE:**
half-hearted

wholesale ADJECTIVE *the wholesale destruction
of life on this planet* = **extensive**, total, mass,
sweeping, broad, comprehensive,
wide-ranging, blanket, outright, far-
reaching, indiscriminate, all-inclusive
■ **OPPOSITE:** limited ▶ ADVERB *The army was
burning down houses and killing villagers
wholesale.* = **extensively**, comprehensively,
across the board, all at once,
indiscriminately, without exception, on a
large scale

wholesome ADJECTIVE **1** *It was all good,
wholesome fun.* = **moral**, nice, clean, pure,
decent, innocent, worthy, ethical,
respectable, honourable, uplifting,
righteous, exemplary, virtuous, apple-pie

W

(*informal*), squeaky-clean, edifying
■ **OPPOSITE:** corrupt **2** *The food was filling and wholesome.* = **healthy**, good, strengthening, beneficial, nourishing, nutritious, sanitary, invigorating, salutary, hygienic, healthful, health-giving
■ **OPPOSITE:** unhealthy

wholly ADVERB **1** *The accusation is wholly without foundation.* = **completely**, totally, perfectly, fully, entirely, comprehensively, altogether, thoroughly, utterly, heart and soul, one hundred per cent (*informal*), in every respect ■ **OPPOSITE:** partly **2** *societies which rely wholly on farming to survive* = **solely**, only, exclusively, without exception, to the exclusion of everything else

whoop VERB *The audience whooped and cheered with delight.* = **cry**, shout, scream, cheer, yell, shriek, hoot, holler (*informal*) ▶ NOUN *A wild frenzy of whoops and yells arose outside.* = **cry**, shout, scream, cheer, yell, shriek, hoot, holler (*informal*), hurrah, halloo

whopper NOUN **1** *He's been telling a load of whoppers about his acting skills.* = **big lie**, fabrication, falsehood, untruth, tall story (*informal*), fable **2** *As comets go, it is a whopper.* = **giant**, monster, jumbo (*informal*), mammoth, colossus, leviathan, crackerjack (*informal*)

whopping ADJECTIVE = **gigantic**, great, big, large, huge, giant, massive, enormous, extraordinary, tremendous, monstrous, whacking (*informal*), mammoth, prodigious, elephantine, humongous *or* humungous (*informal*)

whore NOUN = **prostitute**, hooker (*U.S. slang*), streetwalker, tom (*Brit. slang*), hustler (*U.S. & Canad. slang*), call girl, courtesan, harlot, lady of the night, cocotte

whorl NOUN = **swirl**, spiral, coil, twist, vortex, helix, corkscrew

wicked ADJECTIVE **1** *She flew at me, shouting how evil and wicked I was.* = **bad**, evil, corrupt, vile, guilty, abandoned, foul, vicious, worthless, shameful, immoral, scandalous, atrocious, sinful, heinous, depraved, debased, devilish, amoral, egregious, abominable, fiendish, villainous, unprincipled, nefarious, dissolute, iniquitous, irreligious, black-hearted, impious, unrighteous, maleficent, flagitious ■ **OPPOSITE:** virtuous **2** *She has a delightfully wicked sense of humour.*
= **mischievous**, playful, impish, devilish, arch, teasing, naughty, cheeky, rascally, incorrigible, raffish, roguish, rakish, tricksy, puckish, waggish ■ **OPPOSITE:** well-behaved

3 *A wicked pain shot through his injured elbow.*
= **agonizing**, terrible, acute, severe, intense, awful, painful (*informal*), fierce, mighty, dreadful, fearful (*informal*), gut-wrenching **4** *The wind gets so wicked you want to stay indoors while the sea rages.*
= **harmful**, terrible, intense, mighty, crashing, dreadful, destructive, injurious
■ **OPPOSITE:** harmless **5** *From what I have seen so far, she is going to be a wicked dancer.*
= **expert**, great (*informal*), strong, powerful, masterly, wonderful, outstanding, remarkable, ace (*informal*), first-class, marvellous, mighty, dazzling, skilful, A1 (*informal*), adept, deft, adroit

wide ADJECTIVE **1** *The doorway should be wide enough to allow wheelchair access.* = **spacious**, broad, extensive, ample, roomy, commodious ■ **OPPOSITE:** confined **2** *Wear the shirt loose over wide trousers.*
= **baggy**, full, loose, ample, billowing, roomy, voluminous, capacious, oversize, generously cut **3** *His eyes were wide with disbelief.* = **expanded**, dilated, fully open, distended ■ **OPPOSITE:** shut **4** *The brochure offers a wide choice of hotels and holiday homes.*
= **broad**, comprehensive, extensive, wide-ranging, large, catholic, expanded, sweeping, vast, immense, ample, inclusive, expansive, exhaustive, encyclopedic, far-ranging, compendious ■ **OPPOSITE:** restricted **5** *The case has attracted wide publicity.* = **extensive**, general, far-reaching, overarching **6** *the wide variation in the ages and backgrounds of the candidates*
= **large**, broad, vast, immense **7** *The shot was several feet wide.* = **distant**, off, away, remote, off course, off target ▶ ADVERB **1** *He opened his mouth wide.* = **fully**, completely, right out, as far as possible, to the furthest extent ■ **OPPOSITE:** partly **2** *The big striker fired wide and missed an easy goal.* = **off target**, nowhere near, astray, off course, off the mark

wide-eyed ADJECTIVE **1** *He told tall stories to a wide-eyed group of tourists.* = **naive**, green, trusting, credulous, simple, innocent, impressionable, unsophisticated, ingenuous, wet behind the ears (*informal*), unsuspicious, as green as grass **2** *She was wide-eyed in astonishment.* = **staring**, spellbound, gobsmacked (*Brit. slang*), dumbfounded, agog, agape, thunderstruck, goggle-eyed, awe-stricken

widen VERB **1** *He had an operation to widen an artery in his heart.* = **broaden**, expand, enlarge, dilate, spread, extend, stretch, open wide, open out *or* up ■ **OPPOSITE:** narrow **2** *The river widens considerably as it* *begins to turn east.* = **get wider**, spread, extend, expand, broaden, open wide, open out or up ■ **OPPOSITE:** narrow

wide open ADJECTIVE **1** *He came towards her with his arms wide open in welcome.* = **outspread**, spread, outstretched, splayed, fully open, fully extended, gaping **2** *The virus leaves the body wide open to infection.* = **unprotected**, open, exposed, vulnerable, at risk, in danger, susceptible, defenceless, in peril **3** *The match was still wide open at half-time.* = **uncertain**, unsettled, unpredictable, up for grabs (*informal*), indeterminate, anybody's guess (*informal*)

widespread ADJECTIVE = **common**, general, popular, sweeping, broad, extensive, universal, epidemic, wholesale, far-reaching, prevalent, rife, pervasive, far-flung ■ **OPPOSITE:** limited

width NOUN = **breadth**, extent, span, wideness, reach, range, measure, scope, diameter, compass, thickness, girth

wield VERB **1** *He was attacked by an assailant wielding a kitchen knife.* = **brandish**, flourish, manipulate, swing, use, manage, handle, employ, ply **2** *He remains chairman, but wields little power in the company.* = **exert**, hold, maintain, exercise, have, control, manage, apply, command, possess, make use of, utilize, put to use, be possessed of, have at your disposal

wife NOUN = **spouse**, woman (*informal*), partner, mate, bride, old woman (*informal*), old lady (*informal*), little woman (*informal*), significant other (*informal, chiefly U.S.*), better half (*humorous*), her indoors (*Brit. slang*), helpmate, helpmeet, (the) missis or missus (*informal*), femme, vrou (*S. African*), wahine (*N.Z.*), wifey (*informal*) ■ **RELATED WORD:** *adjective* uxorial

wiggle VERB **1** *She wiggled her fingers to attract his attention.* = **jerk**, shake, twitch, wag, jiggle, waggle **2** *A little worm was wiggling on the pavement.* = **squirm**, twitch, writhe, shimmy ▶ NOUN *Push the fork in with your foot and give it a wiggle to make the holes bigger.* = **jerk**, shake, twitch, wag, squirm, writhe, jiggle, waggle, shimmy

wild ADJECTIVE **1** *The organization is calling for a total ban on the trade of wild animals.* = **untamed**, fierce, savage, ferocious, unbroken, feral, undomesticated, free, warrigal (*Austral., literary*) ■ **OPPOSITE:** tame **2** *The lane was lined with wild flowers.* = **uncultivated**, natural, native, indigenous ■ **OPPOSITE:** cultivated **3** *one of the few wild areas remaining in the South East* = **desolate**, empty, desert, deserted, virgin,

lonely, uninhabited, godforsaken, uncultivated, uncivilized, trackless, unpopulated ■ **OPPOSITE:** inhabited **4** *The recent wild weather has caused millions of pounds' worth of damage.* = **stormy**, violent, rough, intense, raging, furious, howling, choppy, tempestuous, blustery **5** *The children were wild with excitement.* = **excited**, mad (*informal*), crazy (*informal*), eager, nuts (*slang*), enthusiastic, raving, frantic, daft (*informal*), frenzied, hysterical, avid, potty (*Brit. informal*), delirious, agog ■ **OPPOSITE:** unenthusiastic **6** *When drunk, he became wild and violent.* = **uncontrolled**, violent, rough, disorderly, noisy, chaotic, turbulent, wayward, unruly, rowdy, boisterous, lawless, unfettered, unbridled, riotous, unrestrained, unmanageable, impetuous, undisciplined, ungovernable, self-willed, uproarious ■ **OPPOSITE:** calm **7** *When I told him what I had done, he was wild.* = **mad** (*informal*), furious, fuming, infuriated, incensed, enraged, very angry, irate, livid (*informal*), in a rage, on the warpath (*informal*), hot under the collar (*informal*), beside yourself, tooshie (*Austral. slang*), off the air (*Austral. slang*) **8** *I was just a kid and full of wild ideas.* = **outrageous**, fantastic, foolish, rash, extravagant, reckless, preposterous, giddy, madcap, foolhardy, flighty, ill-considered, imprudent, impracticable ■ **OPPOSITE:** practical **9** *They were alarmed by his wild hair and staring eyes.* = **dishevelled**, disordered, untidy, unkempt, tousled, straggly, windblown, daggy (*Austral. & N.Z. informal*) **10** *She's just wild about him.* = **passionate**, mad (*informal*), ardent, fervent, zealous, fervid **11** *the wild tribes which still roam the northern plains with their horse herds* = **uncivilized**, fierce, savage, primitive, rude, ferocious, barbaric, brutish, barbarous ■ **OPPOSITE:** civilized • **the wilds** *They went canoeing in the wilds of Canada.* = **wilderness**, desert, wasteland, middle of nowhere (*informal*), backwoods, back of beyond (*informal*), uninhabited area • **run wild 1** *The front garden is running wild.* = **grow unchecked**, spread, ramble, straggle **2** *She lets her children run wild.* = **go on the rampage**, stray, rampage, run riot, cut loose, run free, kick over the traces, be undisciplined, abandon all restraint

wilderness NOUN **1** *He looked out over a wilderness of mountain, lake and forest.* = **wilds**, waste, desert, wasteland, uncultivated region **2** *The neglected cemetery was a wilderness of crumbling gravestones and parched grass.* = **tangle**, confusion, maze,

W

muddle, clutter, jumble, welter, congeries, confused mass

wildlife NOUN = **flora and fauna**, animals, fauna

wile NOUN *His wit and wile has made him one of the sharpest politicians in the Cabinet.* = **cunning**, craft, fraud, cheating, guile, artifice, trickery, chicanery, craftiness, artfulness, slyness ▶ PLURAL NOUN *Telling stories about encounters with less principled fingersmiths and con artists he shows how vulnerable we are to their sophisticated wiles.* = **ploys**, tricks, devices, lures, manoeuvres, dodges, ruses, artifices, subterfuges, stratagems, contrivances, impositions

wilful or (U.S.) **willful** ADJECTIVE 1 *Wilful neglect of the environment has caused this problem.* = **intentional**, willed, intended, conscious, voluntary, deliberate, purposeful, volitional ■ OPPOSITE: unintentional 2 *a spoilt and wilful teenager* = **obstinate**, dogged, determined, persistent, adamant, stubborn, perverse, uncompromising, intractable, inflexible, unyielding, intransigent, headstrong, obdurate, stiff-necked, self-willed, refractory, pig-headed, bull-headed, mulish, froward (*archaic*) ■ OPPOSITE: obedient

will NOUN 1 *He lacked the will to confront her.* = **determination**, drive, aim, purpose, commitment, resolution, resolve, intention, spine, backbone, tenacity, willpower, single-mindedness, doggedness, firmness of purpose 2 *He was forced to leave the country against his will.* = **wish**, mind, desire, pleasure, intention, fancy, preference, inclination 3 *the concept of free will* = **choice**, decision, option, prerogative, volition 4 *He has submitted himself to the will of God.* = **decree**, wish, desire, command, dictate, ordinance 5 *Attached to his will was a letter he had written just before his death.* = **testament**, declaration, bequest(s), last wishes, last will and testament ▶ VERB 1 *They believed they would win because God had willed it.* = **decree**, order, cause, effect, direct, determine, bid, intend, command, resolve, bring about, ordain (*formal*) 2 *Say what you will about him, but he's always been a good provider.* = **wish**, want, choose, prefer, desire, elect, opt, see fit 3 *She had willed all her money to her brother, Frank.* = **bequeath**, give, leave, transfer, gift, hand on, pass on, confer, hand down, settle on • **at will** *Some yoga practitioners can slow their heart rates down at will.* = **as you please**, at your discretion, as you think fit, at your pleasure, at your desire, at your whim, at your inclination, at your wish ■ RELATED WORDS: *adjectives* voluntary, volitive

willing ADJECTIVE 1 *There are some questions which they will not be willing to answer.* = **inclined**, prepared, happy, pleased, content, in favour, consenting, disposed, favourable, agreeable, in the mood, compliant, amenable, desirous, so-minded, nothing loath ■ OPPOSITE: unwilling 2 *He had plenty of willing volunteers to help him clear up.* = **ready**, game (*informal*), eager, enthusiastic ■ OPPOSITE: reluctant

willingly ADVERB = **readily**, freely, gladly, happily, eagerly, voluntarily, cheerfully, with pleasure, without hesitation, by choice, with all your heart, lief (*rare*), of your own free will, of your own accord ■ OPPOSITE: unwillingly

willingness NOUN = **inclination**, will, agreement, wish, favour, desire, enthusiasm, consent, goodwill, disposition, volition, agreeableness ■ OPPOSITE: reluctance

willowy ADJECTIVE = **slender**, slim, graceful, supple, lithe, limber, svelte, lissom(e), sylphlike

willpower NOUN = **self-control**, drive, resolution, resolve, determination, grit, self-discipline, single-mindedness, fixity of purpose, firmness of purpose or will, force or strength of will ■ OPPOSITE: weakness

willy-nilly ADVERB 1 *We were dragged willy-nilly into the argument.* = **whether you like it or not**, necessarily, of necessity, perforce (*formal*), whether or no, whether desired or not, nolens volens (*Latin*) 2 *The papers were just bundled into the drawers willy-nilly.* = **haphazardly**, at random, randomly, without order, without method, without planning, any old how (*informal*)

wilt VERB 1 *The roses wilted the day after she bought them.* = **droop**, wither, sag, shrivel, become limp or flaccid 2 *She began to wilt in the morning heat.* = **weaken**, sag, languish, droop 3 *Their resolution wilted in the face of such powerful opposition.* = **wane**, fail, sink, flag, fade, diminish, dwindle, wither, ebb, melt away, lose courage

wily ADJECTIVE = **cunning**, designing, scheming, sharp, intriguing, arch, tricky, crooked (*informal*), shrewd, sly, astute, deceptive, crafty, artful, shifty (*informal*), foxy, cagey (*informal*), deceitful, underhand, guileful, fly (*slang*) ■ OPPOSITE: straightforward

wimp NOUN = **weakling**, wet (*Brit. slang*), mouse, drip (*informal*), coward, jessie (*Scot. slang*), jellyfish (*informal*), sissy, doormat (*slang*), wuss (*slang*), milksop, softy or softie

w

win VERB **1** *He does not have any reasonable chance of winning the election.* = **be victorious in**, succeed in, prevail in, come first in, finish first in, be the victor in, gain victory in, achieve first place in ■ **OPPOSITE:** lose **2** *Our team is confident of winning again this year.* = **be victorious**, succeed, triumph, overcome, prevail, conquer, come first, finish first, carry the day, sweep the board, take the prize, gain victory, achieve mastery, achieve first place, carry all before you, topscore (*informal*) ■ **OPPOSITE:** lose **3** *The first correct entry will win the prize.* = **gain**, get, receive, land (*informal*), catch, achieve, net, earn, pick up, bag (*informal*), secure, collect, obtain, acquire, accomplish, attain, procure, come away with ■ **OPPOSITE:** forfeit ▸ NOUN *Arsenal's run of eight games without a win* = **victory**, success, triumph, conquest ■ **OPPOSITE:** defeat • **win someone over** or **round** *He had won over a significant number of his opponents.* = **convince**, influence, attract, persuade, convert, charm, sway, disarm, allure, prevail upon, bring or talk round

wince VERB *He tightened his grip on her arm until she winced in pain.* = **flinch**, start, shrink, cringe, quail, recoil, cower, draw back, blench ▸ NOUN *She gave a wince at the memory of their first date.* = **flinch**, start, cringe

wind¹ NOUN **1** *During the night the wind had blown down the fence.* = **air**, blast, breath, hurricane, breeze, draught, gust, zephyr, air-current, current of air **2** *tablets to treat trapped wind* = **flatulence**, gas, flatus **3** *A punch in the stomach knocked the wind out of me.* = **breath**, puff, respiration **4** *You're just talking a lot of wind.* = **nonsense**, talk, boasting, hot air, babble, bluster, humbug, twaddle (*informal*), gab (*informal*), verbalizing, blather, codswallop (*informal*), eyewash (*informal*), idle talk, empty talk, bizzo (*Austral. slang*), bull's wool (*Austral. & N.Z. slang*) • **get wind of something** *I don't want the press to get wind of our plans at this stage.* = **hear about**, learn of, find out about, become aware of, be told about, be informed of, be made aware of, hear tell of, have brought to your notice, hear on the grape vine (*informal*) • **in the wind** *By the mid-1980s, economic change was in the wind again.* = **imminent**, coming, near, approaching, on the way, looming, brewing, impending, on the cards (*informal*), in the offing, about to happen, close at hand • **put the wind up someone** *I had an anonymous letter that really put the wind up me.* = **scare**, alarm, frighten, panic, discourage, unnerve, scare off, frighten off

wind² VERB **1** *The Moselle winds through some 160 miles of tranquil countryside.* = **meander**, turn, bend, twist, curve, snake, ramble, twist and turn, deviate, zigzag **2** *She wound the sash round her waist.* = **wrap**, twist, reel, curl, loop, coil, twine, furl, wreathe **3** *The snake wound around my leg.* = **coil**, curl, spiral, encircle, twine • **wind down 1** *I need a drink to help me wind down.* = **calm down**, unwind, take it easy, unbutton (*informal*), put your feet up, de-stress (*informal*), outspan (*S. African*), cool down or off **2** *The relationship was winding down by more or less mutual agreement.* = **subside**, decline, diminish, come to an end, dwindle, tail off, taper off, slacken off • **wind someone up 1** *They kept winding me up by talking over me.* = **irritate**, excite, anger, annoy, exasperate, nettle, work someone up, pique, make someone nervous, put someone on edge, make someone tense, hack you off (*informal*) **2** *You're joking. Come on, you're just winding me up.* = **tease**, kid (*informal*), have someone on (*informal*), annoy, rag (*informal*), rib (*informal*), josh (*informal*), vex, make fun of, take the mickey out of (*informal*), send someone up (*informal*), pull someone's leg (*informal*), jerk or yank someone's chain (*informal*) • **wind something up 1** *The President is about to wind up his visit to Somalia.* = **end**, finish, settle, conclude, tie up, wrap up, finalize, bring to a close, tie up the loose ends of (*informal*) **2** *The bank seems determined to wind up the company.* = **close down**, close, dissolve, terminate, liquidate, put something into liquidation • **wind up** *You're going to wind up a bitter and lonely old man.* = **end up**, be left, find yourself, finish up, fetch up (*informal*), land up, end your days

winded ADJECTIVE = **out of breath**, panting, puffed, breathless, gasping for breath, puffed out, out of puff, out of whack (*informal*)

windfall NOUN = **godsend**, find, jackpot, bonanza, stroke of luck, manna from heaven, pot of gold at the end of the rainbow ■ **OPPOSITE:** misfortune

winding ADJECTIVE = **twisting**, turning, bending, curving, crooked, spiral, indirect, roundabout, meandering, tortuous, convoluted, serpentine, sinuous, circuitous, twisty, anfractuous, flexuous ■ **OPPOSITE:** straight

windy ADJECTIVE = **breezy**, wild, stormy, boisterous, blustering, windswept, tempestuous, blustery, gusty, inclement, squally, blowy ■ **OPPOSITE:** calm

W

wing NOUN **1** *The bird flapped its wings furiously.* = **organ of flight**, pinion (*poetic*), pennon (*poetic*) **2** *We were given an office in the empty west wing of the building.* = **annexe**, part, side, section, extension, adjunct, ell (*U.S.*) **3** *the liberal wing of the Democratic party* = **faction**, grouping, group, set, side, arm, section, camp, branch, circle, lobby, segment, caucus, clique, coterie, schism, cabal ▶ VERB **1** *Several birds broke cover and went winging over the lake.* = **fly**, soar, glide, take wing **2** *He was soon winging his way home to rejoin his family.* = **hurry**, fly, race, speed, streak, zoom, hasten, hurtle **3** *He shot at the bird but only managed to wing it.* = **wound**, hit, nick, clip, graze

wink VERB **1** *Brian winked an eye at me, giving me his seal of approval.* = **blink**, bat, flutter, nictate, nictitate **2** *From the hotel window, they could see lights winking on the bay.* = **twinkle**, flash, shine, sparkle, gleam, shimmer, glimmer ▶ NOUN **1** *Diana gave me a reassuring wink.* = **blink**, flutter, nictation, nictitation **2** *In the distance, he noticed the wink of a red light.* = **twinkle**, flash, sparkle, gleam, blink, glimmering, glimmer • **wink at something** *Corrupt police have been known to wink at crimes in return for bribes.* = **condone**, allow, ignore, overlook, tolerate, put up with (*informal*), disregard, turn a blind eye to, blink at, connive at, pretend not to notice, shut your eyes to

winner NOUN = **victor**, first, champion, master, champ (*informal*), conqueror, vanquisher, prizewinner, conquering hero ■ **OPPOSITE:** loser

winning ADJECTIVE **1** *The winning team returned home to a heroes' welcome.* = **victorious**, first, top, successful, unbeaten, conquering, triumphant, undefeated, vanquishing, top-scoring, unvanquished **2** *She had great charm and a winning personality.* = **charming**, taking, pleasing, sweet, attractive, engaging, lovely, fascinating, fetching (*informal*), delightful, cute, disarming, enchanting, endearing, captivating, amiable, alluring, bewitching, delectable, winsome, prepossessing, likable or likeable ■ **OPPOSITE:** unpleasant ▶ PLURAL NOUN *The poker player collected his winnings and left.* = **spoils**, profits, gains, prize, proceeds, takings, booty

winsome ADJECTIVE = **charming**, taking, winning, pleasing, pretty, fair, sweet, attractive, engaging, fascinating, pleasant, fetching (*informal*), cute, disarming, enchanting, endearing, captivating, agreeable, amiable, alluring, bewitching, delectable, comely (*old-fashioned*), likable or likeable, fit (*Brit. informal*)

wintry ADJECTIVE **1** *The wintry weather continues to sweep across the country.* = **cold**, freezing, frozen, harsh, icy, chilly, snowy, frosty, hibernal ■ **OPPOSITE:** warm **2** *Melissa gave him a wintry smile and walked on without a word.* = **unfriendly**, cold, cool, remote, distant, bleak, chilly, frigid, cheerless

wipe VERB **1** *She wiped her hands on the towel.* = **clean**, dry, polish, brush, dust, rub, sponge, mop, swab **2** *Gleb wiped the sweat from his face.* = **erase**, remove, take off, get rid of, take away, rub off, efface, clean off, sponge off ▶ NOUN *I'll give the surfaces a wipe with some disinfectant.* = **rub**, clean, polish, brush, lick, sponge, mop, swab • **wipe something** or **someone out** *a fanatic who is determined to wipe out anyone who opposes him* = **destroy**, eliminate (*slang*), take out (*slang*), massacre, slaughter, erase, eradicate, blow away (*slang, chiefly U.S.*), obliterate, liquidate (*informal*), annihilate, efface, exterminate, expunge (*formal*), extirpate, wipe from the face of the earth (*informal*), kill to the last man, kennet (*Austral. slang*), jeff (*Austral. slang*)

wiry ADJECTIVE **1** *a wiry and athletic young man* = **lean**, strong, tough, thin, spare, skinny, stringy, sinewy ■ **OPPOSITE:** flabby **2** *wiry black hair* = **stiff**, rough, coarse, curly, kinky, bristly

wisdom NOUN **1** *a man respected for his wisdom and insight* = **understanding**, learning, knowledge, intelligence, smarts (*slang, chiefly U.S.*), judgment, insight, enlightenment, penetration, comprehension, foresight, erudition, discernment, sagacity, sound judgment, sapience ■ **OPPOSITE:** foolishness **2** *Many have expressed doubts about the wisdom of the decision.* = **prudence**, reason, circumspection, judiciousness ■ **RELATED WORD:** *adjective* sagacious

wise ADJECTIVE **1** *She has the air of a wise woman.* = **sage**, knowing, understanding, aware, informed, clever, intelligent, sensible, enlightened, shrewd, discerning, perceptive, well-informed, erudite, sagacious (*formal*), sapient, clued-up (*informal*), grounded ■ **OPPOSITE:** foolish **2** *She had made a very wise decision.* = **sensible**, sound, politic, informed, reasonable, clever, intelligent, rational, logical, shrewd, prudent, judicious, well-advised ■ **OPPOSITE:** unwise

wisecrack NOUN = **joke**, sally, gag (*informal*), quip, jibe, barb, jest, witticism, smart remark, pithy remark, sardonic remark

wish NOUN **1** *Clearly she had no wish for his company.* = **desire**, liking, want, longing, hope, urge, intention, fancy (*informal*), ambition, yen (*informal*), hunger, aspiration, craving, lust, yearning, inclination, itch (*informal*), thirst, whim, hankering ■ **OPPOSITE:** aversion **2** *The decision was made against the wishes of the party leader.* = **request**, will, want, order, demand, desire, command, bidding, behest (*literary*) ▶ VERB **1** *We can dress as we wish nowadays.* = **want**, feel, choose, please, desire, think fit **2** *I will do as you wish.* = **require**, ask, order, direct, bid, desire (*formal*), command, instruct **3** *He wished me a good morning.* = **bid**, greet with • **wish for** *They both wished for a son to carry on the family business.* = **desire**, want, need, hope for, long for, crave, covet, aspire to, yearn for, thirst for, hunger for, hanker for, sigh for, set your heart on, desiderate

wisp NOUN = **piece**, twist, strand, thread, shred, snippet

wispy ADJECTIVE **1** *Grey wispy hair straggled down to her shoulders.* = **straggly**, fine, thin, frail, wisplike **2** *a wispy chiffon dress* = **thin**, light, fine, delicate, fragile, flimsy, ethereal, insubstantial, gossamer, diaphanous, wisplike

wistful ADJECTIVE = **melancholy**, longing, dreaming, sad, musing, yearning, thoughtful, reflective, dreamy, forlorn, mournful, contemplative, meditative, pensive, disconsolate

wit NOUN **1** *Bill was known for his biting wit.* = **humour**, fun, quips, banter, puns, pleasantry, repartee, wordplay, levity, witticisms, badinage, jocularity, facetiousness, drollery, raillery, waggishness, wittiness ■ **OPPOSITE:** seriousness **2** *a man who fancied himself as a great wit* = **humorist**, card (*informal*), comedian, wag, joker, dag (*N.Z. informal*), punster, epigrammatist **3** *The information is there for anyone with the wit to use it.* = **cleverness**, mind, reason, understanding, sense, brains, smarts (*slang, chiefly U.S.*), judgment, perception, wisdom, insight, common sense, intellect, comprehension, ingenuity, acumen, nous (*Brit. slang*), discernment, practical intelligence ■ **OPPOSITE:** stupidity

witch NOUN = **enchantress**, magician, hag, crone, occultist, sorceress, Wiccan, necromancer

witchcraft NOUN = **magic**, spell, witching, voodoo, the occult, wizardry, black magic, enchantment, occultism, sorcery, incantation, Wicca, the black art, witchery, necromancy, sortilege, makutu (*N.Z.*)

withdraw VERB **1** *Cassandra withdrew her hand from Roger's.* = **remove**, pull, take off, pull out, extract, take away, pull back, draw out, draw back **2** *They withdrew 100 dollars from their bank account.* = **take out**, extract, draw out **3** *Troops withdrew from the country last March.* = **retreat**, go, leave, retire, depart, pull out, fall back, pull back, back out, back off, cop out (*slang*), disengage from ■ **OPPOSITE:** advance **4** *The waiter poured the wine and then withdrew.* = **go**, leave, retire, retreat, depart, make yourself scarce, absent yourself **5** *The Nationalists threatened to withdraw from the talks.* = **pull out**, leave, drop out, secede, disengage, detach yourself, absent yourself **6** *He withdrew his remarks and said he had not intended to cause offence.* = **retract**, recall, take back, revoke, rescind, disavow, recant, disclaim, abjure, unsay

withdrawal NOUN **1** *the withdrawal of foreign aid* = **removal**, ending, stopping, taking away, abolition, elimination, cancellation, termination, extraction, discontinuation **2** *the withdrawal of troops from Eastern Europe* = **exit**, retirement, departure, pull-out, retreat, exodus, evacuation, disengagement **3** *her withdrawal from public life* = **departure**, retirement, exit, secession **4** *The charity insists on a withdrawal of the accusations.* = **retraction**, recall, disclaimer, repudiation, revocation, disavowal, recantation, rescission, abjuration

withdrawn ADJECTIVE = **uncommunicative**, reserved, retiring, quiet, silent, distant, shy, shrinking, detached, aloof, taciturn, introverted, timorous (*literary*), unforthcoming ■ **OPPOSITE:** outgoing

wither VERB **1** *Farmers have watched their crops wither because of the drought.* = **wilt**, dry, decline, shrink, decay, disintegrate, perish, languish, droop, shrivel, desiccate ■ **OPPOSITE:** flourish **2** *His leg muscles had withered from lack of use.* = **waste**, decline, shrink, shrivel, atrophy **3** *His dream of being a famous footballer withered and died.* = **fade**, decline, wane, perish ■ **OPPOSITE:** increase **4** *Mary withered me with a glance.* = **humiliate**, blast, shame, put down, snub, mortify, abash

withering ADJECTIVE = **scornful**, blasting, devastating, humiliating, snubbing, blighting, hurtful, mortifying

withhold VERB **1** *Police withheld the victim's name until her relatives had been informed.*

W

= **keep secret**, keep, refuse, hide, reserve, retain, sit on (*informal*), conceal, suppress, hold back, keep back ■ **OPPOSITE:** reveal **2** *She could not withhold a scornful comment as he passed.* = **hold back**, check, resist, suppress, restrain, repress, keep back ■ **OPPOSITE:** release

withstand VERB = **resist**, take, face, suffer, bear, weather, sustain, oppose, take on, cope with, brave, confront, combat, endure, defy, tolerate, put up with (*informal*), thwart, stand up to, hold off, grapple with, hold out against, stand firm against ■ **OPPOSITE:** give in to

witless ADJECTIVE *a witless piece of planning* = **foolish**, crazy (*informal*), stupid, silly, dull, daft (*informal*), senseless, goofy (*informal*), idiotic, dozy (*Brit. informal*), inane, loopy (*informal*), crackpot (*informal*), obtuse, unintelligent, empty-headed, asinine, dumb-ass (*slang*), halfwitted, rattlebrained (*slang*)

witness NOUN **1** *No witnesses of the crash have come forward.* = **observer**, viewer, spectator, looker-on, watcher, onlooker, eyewitness, bystander, beholder **2** *Eleven witnesses were called to testify.* = **testifier**, deponent, attestant ▶ VERB **1** *Anyone who witnessed the attack is urged to contact the police.* = **see**, mark, view, watch, note, notice, attend, observe, perceive, look on, be present at, behold (*archaic, literary*) **2** *Ask a friend to witness your signature on the application.* = **countersign**, sign, endorse, validate • **bear witness 1** *Many of his poems bear witness to the years he spent in India.* = **confirm**, show, prove, demonstrate, bear out, testify to, be evidence of, corroborate, attest to, be proof of, vouch for, evince (*formal*), betoken, be a monument to, constitute proof of **2** *His mother bore witness in court that he had been at home that night.* = **give evidence**, testify, depose, give testimony, depone ■ **RELATED WORD:** *adjective* testimonial

witter VERB = **chatter**, chat, rabbit (on) (*Brit. informal*), babble, waffle (*informal, chiefly Brit.*), cackle, twaddle, clack, burble, gab (*informal*), prattle, tattle, jabber, blab, gabble, blather, blether, prate, earbash (*Austral. & N.Z. slang*)

witty ADJECTIVE = **humorous**, gay, original, brilliant, funny, clever, amusing, lively, sparkling, ingenious, fanciful, whimsical, droll, piquant, facetious, jocular, epigrammatic, waggish ■ **OPPOSITE:** dull

wizard NOUN **1** *Merlin, the legendary wizard who worked magic for King Arthur* = **magician**, witch, shaman, sorcerer, occultist, magus,

conjuror, warlock, mage (*archaic*), enchanter, necromancer, thaumaturge (*rare*), tohunga (*N.Z.*) **2** *a mathematical wizard at Harvard University* = **genius**, star, expert, master, ace (*informal*), guru, buff (*informal*), adept, whizz (*informal*), prodigy, maestro, virtuoso, hotshot (*informal*), rocket scientist (*informal*), wiz (*informal*), whizz kid (*informal*), wonk (*informal*), maven (*U.S.*), fundi (*S. African*), up-and-comer (*informal*)

wizardry NOUN **1** *a piece of technical wizardry* = **expertise**, skill, know-how (*informal*), craft, mastery, cleverness, expertness **2** *Hogwarts School of Witchcraft and Wizardry* = **magic**, witching, witchcraft, voodoo, enchantment, occultism, sorcery, the black art, witchery, necromancy, conjuration, sortilege

wizened ADJECTIVE = **wrinkled**, lined, worn, withered, dried up, shrivelled, gnarled, shrunken, sere (*archaic*) ■ **OPPOSITE:** rounded

wobble VERB **1** *The ladder wobbled on the uneven ground.* = **shake**, rock, sway, tremble, quake, waver, teeter, totter, seesaw **2** *My voice wobbled with nerves.* = **tremble**, shake, vibrate **3** *He dithered and wobbled when questioned on his policies.* = **hesitate**, waver, fluctuate, dither (*chiefly Brit.*), be undecided, vacillate, shillyshally (*informal*), be unable to make up your mind, swither (*Scot.*) ▶ NOUN **1** *He rode off on his bicycle with only a slight wobble.* = **unsteadiness**, shake, tremble, quaking **2** *There was a distinct wobble in her voice when she replied.* = **unsteadiness**, shake, tremor, vibration

wobbly ADJECTIVE **1** *I was sitting on a wobbly plastic chair.* = **unstable**, shaky, unsafe, uneven, teetering, unbalanced, tottering, rickety, unsteady, wonky (*Brit. slang*) **2** *His legs felt wobbly after the long flight.* = **unsteady**, weak, unstable, shaky, quivery, all of a quiver (*informal*) **3** *'I want to go home,' she said in a wobbly voice.* = **shaky**, unsteady, tremulous

woe NOUN **1** *He listened to my tale of woe.* = **misery**, suffering, trouble, pain, disaster, depression, distress, grief, agony, gloom, sadness, hardship, sorrow, anguish, misfortune, unhappiness, heartache, heartbreak, adversity, dejection, wretchedness ■ **OPPOSITE:** happiness **2** *He did not tell his friends about all his woes.* = **problem**, trouble, trial, burden, grief, misery, curse, hardship, sorrow, misfortune, heartache, heartbreak, affliction, tribulation

w

woeful ADJECTIVE 1 *those woeful people to whom life had dealt a bad hand* = **wretched**, sad, unhappy, tragic, miserable, gloomy, grieving, dismal, pathetic, afflicted, pitiful, anguished, agonized, disconsolate, doleful, pitiable ■ OPPOSITE: happy 2 *a woeful ballad about lost love* = **sad**, distressing, tragic, miserable, gloomy, dismal, pathetic, harrowing, heartbreaking, grievous, mournful, plaintive, heart-rending, sorrowful, doleful, piteous ■ OPPOSITE: happy 3 *the team's recent woeful performance* = **pitiful**, mean, bad, poor, shocking (*informal*), sorry, disappointing, terrible, awful, appalling, disastrous, inadequate, dreadful, miserable, hopeless, rotten (*informal*), pathetic, catastrophic, duff (*Brit. informal*), feeble, disgraceful, lousy (*slang*), grievous, paltry, deplorable, abysmal, lamentable, calamitous, wretched, pitiable, godawful (*slang*), not much cop (*Brit. slang*)

wolf VERB (*often with* **down**) *I was in the changing room wolfing down tea and sandwiches.* = **devour**, stuff, bolt, cram, scoff (*slang*), gulp, gobble, pack away (*informal*), gorge on, gollop ■ OPPOSITE: nibble ■ RELATED WORDS: *adjective* lupine; *name of female* bitch; *name of young* cub, whelp; *collective nouns* pack, rout, herd

woman NOUN 1 *I asked the woman at the desk for an application form.* = **lady**, girl, miss (*old-fashioned or derogatory*), female (*sometimes derogatory*), dame (*slang, chiefly U.S. & Canad.*), sheila (*Austral. & N.Z. informal*), vrou (*S. African*), maiden (*archaic*), maid (*archaic*), gal (*slang*), lass, lassie (*informal*), wench (*facetious*), adult female, she, charlie (*Austral. slang, old-fashioned*), femme, wahine (*N.Z.*) ■ OPPOSITE: man 2 *I know my woman will never leave me.* = **girlfriend**, girl, wife, partner, mate, lover, bride, mistress, spouse, old lady (*informal*), sweetheart, significant other (*informal, chiefly U.S.*), ladylove (*old-fashioned*), wifey (*informal*) ■ RELATED WORDS: *prefixes* gyn-, gyno-, gynaeco-

womanly ADJECTIVE 1 *the womanly virtues so valued by nineteenth-century European society* = **feminine**, motherly, female, matronly, ladylike 2 *a womanly figure* = **curvaceous** (*informal*), ample, voluptuous, shapely, curvy (*informal*), busty (*informal*), buxom, full-figured, Rubenesque, Junoesque

wonder VERB 1 *I wonder what he's up to.* = **think**, question, doubt, puzzle, speculate, query, ponder, inquire, ask yourself, meditate, be curious, conjecture,

be inquisitive 2 *I wondered at the arrogance of the man.* = **be amazed**, stare, marvel, be astonished, gape, boggle, be awed, be flabbergasted (*informal*), gawk, be dumbstruck, stand amazed ▸ NOUN 1 *'How did you know that?' Bobby exclaimed in wonder.* = **amazement**, surprise, curiosity, admiration, awe, fascination, astonishment, bewilderment, wonderment, stupefaction 2 *a fascinating lecture on the wonders of nature* = **phenomenon**, sight, miracle, spectacle, curiosity, marvel, prodigy, rarity, portent, wonderment, nonpareil

wonderful ADJECTIVE 1 *I've always thought he was a wonderful actor.* = **excellent**, mean (*slang*), great (*informal*), topping (*Brit. slang*), brilliant, cracking (*Brit. informal*), outstanding, smashing (*informal*), superb, fantastic (*informal*), tremendous, ace (*informal*), magnificent, fabulous (*informal*), marvellous, terrific (*informal*), sensational (*informal*), sovereign, awesome (*slang*), sick (*slang*), admirable, super (*informal*), brill (*informal*), stupendous, out of this world (*informal*), tiptop, bodacious (*slang, chiefly U.S.*), boffo (*slang*), jim-dandy (*slang*), chillin' (*U.S. slang*), booshit (*Austral. slang*), exo (*Austral. slang*), sik (*Austral. slang*), rad (*informal*), phat (*slang*), schmick (*Austral. informal*) ■ OPPOSITE: terrible 2 *This is a wonderful achievement for one so young.* = **remarkable**, surprising, odd, strange, amazing, extraordinary, fantastic, incredible (*informal*), astonishing, staggering, eye-popping (*informal*), marvellous, startling, peculiar, awesome, phenomenal, astounding, miraculous, unheard-of, wondrous (*archaic, literary*), awe-inspiring, jaw-dropping ■ OPPOSITE: ordinary

wonky ADJECTIVE 1 *The wheels of the trolley kept going wonky.* = **askew**, squint (*informal*), awry, out of alignment, skewwhiff (*Brit. informal*) 2 *He's got a wonky knee.* = **shaky**, weak, wobbly, unsteady, infirm

wont ADJECTIVE *Both have made mistakes, as human beings are wont to do.* = **accustomed**, used, given, in the habit of ▸ NOUN *Keith woke early, as was his wont.* = **habit**, use, way, rule, practice, custom

woo VERB 1 *The bank wooed customers by offering low interest rates.* = **seek**, cultivate, try to attract, curry favour with, seek to win, solicit the goodwill of 2 *The penniless author successfully wooed and married Roxanne.* = **court**, chase, pursue, spark (*rare*), importune, seek to win, pay court to, seek the hand of, set your cap at (*old-fashioned*),

W

pay your addresses to, pay suit to, press your suit with

wood NOUN **1** *The floor is made of polished wood.* = **timber**, planks, planking, lumber (*U.S.*) **2** *We gathered wood for the fire.* = **firewood**, fuel, logs, kindling ▸ PLURAL NOUN *After dinner they went for a walk through the woods.* = **woodland**, trees, forest, grove, hurst (*archaic*), thicket, copse, coppice, bushland • **out of the wood(s)** (*used in negative constructions*) *The nation's economy is not out of the woods yet.* = **safe**, clear, secure, in the clear, out of danger, home and dry (*Brit. slang*), safe and sound ■ **RELATED WORDS:** *adjectives* ligneous, sylvan

wooded ADJECTIVE = **tree-covered**, forested, timbered, woody, sylvan (*poetic*), tree-clad

wooden ADJECTIVE **1** *the shop's bare brick walls and wooden floorboards* = **made of wood**, timber, woody, of wood, ligneous **2** *The film is marred by the wooden acting of the star.* = **awkward**, stiff, rigid, clumsy, lifeless, stilted, ungainly, gauche, gawky, inelegant, graceless, maladroit ■ **OPPOSITE:** graceful **3** *It's hard to tell from his wooden expression whether he's happy or sad.* = **expressionless**, empty, dull, blank, vacant, lifeless, deadpan, colourless, glassy, unresponsive, unemotional, emotionless, spiritless

wool NOUN **1** *These shawls are made from the wool of mountain goats.* = **fleece**, hair, coat **2** *a ball of wool* = **yarn** • **pull the wool over someone's eyes** *a phony psychic who pulled the wool over everyone's eyes* = **deceive**, kid (*informal*), trick, fool, take in (*informal*), con (*slang*), dupe, delude, bamboozle (*informal*), hoodwink, put one over on (*slang*), pull a fast one on someone (*informal*), lead someone up the garden path (*informal*)

woolly or (*sometimes U.S.*) **wooly** ADJECTIVE **1** *She wore a woolly hat with pompoms.* = **woollen**, fleecy, made of wool **2** *It is no good setting vague, woolly goals - we need a specific aim.* = **vague**, confused, clouded, blurred, unclear, muddled, fuzzy, indefinite, hazy, foggy, nebulous, ill-defined, indistinct ■ **OPPOSITE:** precise **3** *The plant has silvery, woolly leaves.* = **downy**, hairy, shaggy, flocculent ▸ NOUN *Bring a woolly - it can get cold here at night.* = **sweater**, jersey, jumper, pullover

word NOUN **1** *The word 'ginseng' comes from the Chinese word 'Shen-seng'.* = **term**, name, expression, designation, appellation (*formal*), locution, vocable **2** *James, could I have a quick word with you?* = **chat**, tête-à-tête, talk, discussion, consultation, chitchat, brief conversation, colloquy

(*formal*), confabulation, confab (*informal*), heart-to-heart, powwow (*informal*) **3** *I'd like to say a word of thanks to everyone who helped me.* = **comment**, remark, expression, declaration, utterance, brief statement **4** *There is no word from the authorities on the reported attack.* = **message**, news, latest (*informal*), report, information, account, notice, advice, communication, intelligence, bulletin, dispatch, gen (*Brit. informal*), communiqué, intimation, tidings, heads up (*U.S. & Canad.*) **5** *He simply cannot be trusted to keep his word.* = **promise**, guarantee, pledge, undertaking, vow, assurance, oath, parole, word of honour, solemn oath, solemn word **6** *I want nothing said about this until I give the word.* = **command**, will, order, go-ahead (*informal*), decree, bidding, commandment, edict, ukase (*rare*) ▸ VERB *If I had written the letter, I might have worded it differently.* = **express**, say, state, put, phrase, utter, couch, formulate • **in a word** *'Don't you like her?' 'In a word - no.'* = **briefly**, in short, in a nutshell, to sum up, succinctly, concisely, not to put too fine a point on it, to put it briefly • **the last word 1** *Our manager has the last word on all major decisions.* = **final say**, ultimatum **2** *We'll let this gentleman have the last word.* = **summation**, finis • **the last word in something** *The spa is the last word in luxury.* = **epitome**, newest, best, latest, crown, cream, rage, ultimate, vogue, perfection, mother of all (*informal*), quintessence, the crème de la crème, ne plus ultra (*French*), dernier cri (*French*) ■ **RELATED WORDS:** *adjectives* lexical, verbal

wording NOUN = **phraseology**, words, language, phrasing, terminology, choice of words, mode of expression

wordy ADJECTIVE = **long-winded**, rambling, windy, diffuse, garrulous, discursive, loquacious, verbose, prolix, pleonastic (*rare*) ■ **OPPOSITE:** brief

work VERB **1** *I want to work, I don't want to be on welfare.* = **be employed**, do business, have a job, earn a living, be in work, hold down a job **2** *My father worked hard all his life.* = **labour**, sweat, slave, toil, slog (away), drudge, peg away, exert yourself, break your back ■ **OPPOSITE:** relax **3** *The pump doesn't work and we have no running water.* = **function**, go, run, operate, perform, be in working order ■ **OPPOSITE:** be out of order **4** *Most of these diets don't work.* = **succeed**, work out, pay off (*informal*), be successful, be effective, do the trick (*informal*), do the business (*informal*), get results, turn out well, have the desired result, go as planned

5 *Modern medicine can work miracles.*
= **accomplish**, cause, create, effect, achieve, carry out, implement, execute, bring about, encompass, contrive
6 *a performer with the ability to work an audience* = **handle**, move, excite, manipulate, rouse, stir up, agitate, incite, whip up, galvanize **7** *Farmers worked the fertile valleys.* = **cultivate**, farm, dig, till, plough **8** *I learnt how to work the forklift.* = **operate**, use, move, control, drive, manage, direct, handle, manipulate, wield, ply **9** *Work the dough with your hands until it is very smooth.* = **manipulate**, make, form, process, fashion, shape, handle, mould, knead **10** *Rescuers were still working their way towards the trapped men.* = **progress**, move, force, manoeuvre, make your way **11** *His face was working in his sleep.* = **move**, twitch, writhe, convulse, be agitated **12** *Some clever people work it so that they never have to pay taxes.* = **contrive**, handle, fix (*informal*), swing (*informal*), arrange, exploit, manipulate, pull off, fiddle (*informal*), bring off ▶ NOUN **1** *What kind of work do you do?* = **employment**, calling, business, job, line, office, trade, duty, craft, profession, occupation, pursuit, livelihood, métier ■ OPPOSITE: play **2** *This needs time and a lot of hard work.* = **effort**, industry, labour, grind (*informal*), sweat, toil, slog, exertion, drudgery, travail (*literary*), elbow grease (*facetious*) ■ OPPOSITE: leisure **3** *I used to take work home, but I don't do it any more.* = **task**, jobs, projects, commissions, duties, assignments, chores, yakka (*Austral. & N.Z. informal*) **4** *Police say the bombing was the work of extremists.* = **handiwork**, doing, act, feat, deed **5** *In my opinion, this is Rembrandt's greatest work.* = **creation**, performance, piece, production, opus, achievement, composition, oeuvre (*French*), handiwork • **work out 1** *Things didn't work out as planned.* = **happen**, go, result, develop, come out, turn out, evolve, pan out (*informal*) **2** *I hope everything works out for you in your new job.* = **succeed**, flourish, go well, be effective, prosper, go as planned, prove satisfactory, do the business (*informal*) **3** *I work out at a gym twice a week.* = **exercise**, train, practise, drill, warm up, do exercises • **work out at something** *The price per pound works out at £7.20.* = **amount to**, come to, reach, add up to, reach a total of • **work someone up** *By now she had worked herself up so much that she couldn't sleep.* = **excite**, move, spur, wind up (*informal*), arouse, animate, rouse, stir up, agitate, inflame, incite, instigate, get someone all steamed up (*slang*) • **work something out 1** *It took me some time to work out what was going on.* = **solve**, find out, resolve, calculate, figure out, clear up, suss (out) (*slang*), puzzle out **2** *Negotiators are due to meet today to work out a compromise.* = **plan**, form, develop, arrange, construct, evolve, devise, elaborate, put together, formulate, contrive • **work something up** *Malcolm worked up the courage to ask his grandfather for help.* = **generate**, rouse, instigate, foment, enkindle

workable ADJECTIVE = **viable**, possible, practical, feasible, practicable, doable ■ OPPOSITE: unworkable

workaday ADJECTIVE = **ordinary**, common, familiar, practical, routine, everyday, commonplace, mundane, prosaic, run-of-the-mill, humdrum, bog-standard (*Brit. & Irish slang*) ■ OPPOSITE: extraordinary

worker NOUN = **employee**, hand, labourer, workman or woman or person, craftsman or woman or person, artisan, tradesperson, wage earner, proletarian, working man or woman or person

working ADJECTIVE **1** *Like most working women, I use a lot of convenience foods.* = **employed**, labouring, in work, in a job **2** *the oldest working steam engine in the world* = **functioning**, going, running, operating, active, operative, operational, functional, usable, serviceable, in working order **3** *I used to have a good working knowledge of French.* = **effective**, useful, practical, sufficient, adequate ▶ NOUN *computer systems which mimic the workings of the human brain* = **operation**, running, action, method, functioning, manner, mode of operation ▶ PLURAL NOUN *housing which was built over old mine workings* = **mine**, pit, shaft, quarry, excavations, diggings

workman or **workwoman** or **workperson** NOUN = **labourer**, hand, worker, employee, mechanic, operative, craftsman or woman or person, artisan, tradesperson, journeyman, artificer (*rare*)

workmanlike ADJECTIVE = **efficient**, professional, skilled, expert, masterly, careful, satisfactory, thorough, skilful, adept, painstaking, proficient ■ OPPOSITE: amateurish

workmanship NOUN = **skill**, work, art, technique, manufacture, craft, expertise, execution, artistry, craftsmanship, handiwork, handicraft

workout NOUN = **exercise**, training, drill, warm-up, training session, practice session, exercise session

W

works PLURAL NOUN **1** *the belching chimneys of the steel works* = **factory**, shop, plant, mill, workshop **2** *the complete works of Milton* = **writings**, productions, output, canon, oeuvre (*French*) **3** *a religious order who dedicated their lives to prayer and good works* = **deeds**, acts, actions, doings **4** *The box held what looked like the works of a large clock.* = **mechanism**, workings, parts, action, insides (*informal*), movement, guts (*informal*), machinery, moving parts, innards (*informal*)

workshop NOUN **1** *She runs a writing workshop for women.* = **seminar**, class, discussion group, study group, masterclass **2** *a small workshop for repairing secondhand motorcycles* = **factory**, works, shop, plant, mill **3** *He got a job in the workshop of a local tailor.* = **workroom**, studio, atelier

world NOUN **1** *It's a beautiful part of the world.* = **earth**, planet, globe, earthly sphere **2** *The world was shocked by this heinous crime.* = **humankind**, mankind, man, men, everyone, the public, everybody, humanity, human race, the race of man **3** *The publishing world had never seen an event quite like this.* = **sphere**, system, area, field, environment, province, kingdom, realm, domain **4** *Be happy, in this world and the next!* = **life**, nature, existence, creation, universe, cosmos **5** *conditions which would support life on other worlds* = **planet**, star, orb, heavenly body **6** *What was life like for the ordinary man in the medieval world?* = **period**, times, days, age, era, epoch • **a world of** *They may look alike but there's a world of difference between them.* = **a huge amount of**, a mountain of, a wealth of, a great deal of, a good deal of, an abundance of, an enormous amount of, a vast amount of • **for all the world** *He looked for all the world as if he was dead.* = **exactly**, just like, precisely, in every way, to all intents and purposes, just as if, in every respect • **on top of the world** *After his win, he was on top of the world.* = **overjoyed**, happy, ecstatic, elated, over the moon (*informal*), exultant, on cloud nine (*informal*), cock-a-hoop, in raptures, beside yourself with joy, stoked (*Austral. & N.Z. informal*) • **out of this world** *The food in this place is simply out of this world.* = **wonderful**, great (*informal*), excellent, superb, fantastic (*informal*), incredible, fabulous (*informal*), marvellous, unbelievable, awesome (*slang*), sick (*slang*), indescribable, bodacious (*slang, chiefly U.S.*), booshit (*Austral. slang*), exo (*Austral. slang*), sik (*Austral. slang*), rad (*informal*), phat (*slang*), schmick (*Austral. informal*)

worldly ADJECTIVE **1** *It is time you woke up and focused your thoughts on more worldly matters.* = **earthly**, lay, physical, fleshly, secular, mundane, terrestrial, temporal, carnal, profane, sublunary ■ **OPPOSITE:** spiritual **2** *He has repeatedly criticized Western churches as being too worldly.* = **materialistic**, grasping, selfish, greedy, avaricious, covetous, worldly-minded ■ **OPPOSITE:** nonmaterialistic **3** *He was worldly and sophisticated, quite unlike me.* = **worldly-wise**, knowing, experienced, politic, sophisticated, cosmopolitan, urbane, blasé, well versed in the ways of the world ■ **OPPOSITE:** naive

worldwide ADJECTIVE = **global**, general, international, universal, ubiquitous, omnipresent, pandemic ■ **OPPOSITE:** limited

worn ADJECTIVE **1** *an elderly man in well-cut but worn clothes* = **ragged**, shiny, frayed, shabby, tattered, tatty (*Brit.*), threadbare, the worse for wear **2** *A sudden smile lit up his worn face.* = **haggard**, lined, drawn, pinched, wizened, careworn **3** *She looked tired and worn.* = **exhausted**, spent, tired, fatigued, wearied, weary, played-out (*informal*), worn out, jaded, tired out

worn out ADJECTIVE **1** *Always replace worn out tyres with the same brand.* = **worn**, done, used, broken-down, ragged, useless, rundown, frayed, used-up, shabby, tattered, tatty (*Brit.*), threadbare, decrepit, clapped out (*Brit., Austral. & N.Z. informal*), moth-eaten **2** *I was exhausted – worn out by the strain I'd been under.* = **exhausted**, spent, done in (*informal*), tired, all in (*slang*), fatigued, wiped out (*informal*), weary, played-out, knackered (*slang*), prostrate, clapped out (*Austral. & N.Z. informal*), tired out, dog-tired (*informal*), zonked (*slang*), shagged out (*Brit. slang*), fit to drop, jiggered (*dialect*), dead or out on your feet (*informal*) ■ **OPPOSITE:** refreshed

worried ADJECTIVE = **anxious**, concerned, troubled, upset, afraid, bothered, frightened, wired (*slang*), nervous, disturbed, distressed, tense, distracted, uneasy, fearful, tormented, distraught, apprehensive, perturbed, on edge, ill at ease, overwrought, fretful, hot and bothered, unquiet, antsy (*informal*) ■ **OPPOSITE:** unworried

worrisome ADJECTIVE = **disturbing**, worrying, upsetting, distressing, troublesome, disquieting, vexing, perturbing, irksome, bothersome

worry VERB **1** *I worry about my daughter constantly.* = **be anxious**, be concerned, be worried, obsess, brood, fret, agonize, feel uneasy, get in a lather (*informal*), get in a sweat (*informal*), get in a tizzy (*informal*), get overwrought ■ **OPPOSITE:** be unconcerned **2** '*Why didn't you tell us?*' – '*Didn't want to worry you.*' = **trouble**, upset, harry, bother, disturb, distress, annoy, plague, irritate, tease, unsettle, torment, harass, hassle (*informal*), badger, hector, disquiet, pester, vex, perturb, tantalize, importune (*formal*), make anxious ■ **OPPOSITE:** soothe ▶ NOUN **1** *His last years were overshadowed by financial worry.* = **anxiety**, concern, care, fear, trouble, misery, disturbance, torment, woe, irritation, unease, apprehension, misgiving, annoyance, trepidation (*formal*), perplexity, vexation ■ **OPPOSITE:** peace of mind **2** *Robert's health had always been a worry to his wife.* = **problem**, care, trouble, trial, bother, plague (*informal*), pest, torment, irritation, hassle (*informal*), annoyance, vexation

worsen VERB **1** *The security forces had to intervene to prevent the situation from worsening.* = **deteriorate**, decline, sink, decay, get worse, degenerate, go downhill (*informal*), go from bad to worse, take a turn for the worse, retrogress ■ **OPPOSITE:** improve **2** *These options would actually worsen the economy and add to the deficit.* = **aggravate**, damage, exacerbate, make worse ■ **OPPOSITE:** improve

worship VERB **1** *people who still worship the pagan gods* = **revere**, praise, respect, honour, adore, glorify, reverence, exalt, laud (*literary*), pray to, venerate, deify, adulate ■ **OPPOSITE:** dishonour **2** *The children worship their father.* = **love**, adore, idolize, put on a pedestal ■ **OPPOSITE:** despise ▶ NOUN *The temple had been a centre of worship of the goddess Hathor.* = **reverence**, praise, love, regard, respect, honour, glory, prayer(s), devotion, homage, adulation, adoration, admiration, exaltation, glorification, deification, laudation

worth NOUN **1** *Buyers are usually prepared to spend about 1 per cent of their total worth on art.* = **value**, price, rate, cost, estimate, valuation ■ **OPPOSITE:** worthlessness **2** *She did not appreciate her husband's true worth until he was gone.* = **merit**, value, quality, importance, desert(s), virtue, excellence, goodness, estimation, worthiness ■ **OPPOSITE:** unworthiness **3** *The client has little means of judging the worth of the advice he is given.* = **usefulness**, value, benefit, quality, importance, utility, excellence, goodness ■ **OPPOSITE:** uselessness

worthless ADJECTIVE **1** *This piece of old junk is totally worthless.* = **valueless**, poor,

miserable, trivial, trifling, paltry, trashy, measly (*informal*), wretched, two a penny (*informal*), rubbishy, poxy (*slang*), nickel-and-dime (*U.S. slang*), a dime a dozen, nugatory, negligible ■ **OPPOSITE:** valuable **2** *Training is worthless unless there is proof that it works.* = **useless**, meaningless, pointless, futile, no use, insignificant, unimportant, ineffectual, unusable, unavailing, not much cop (*Brit. slang*), inutile, not worth a hill of beans (*chiefly U.S.*), negligible, pants (*slang*) ■ **OPPOSITE:** useful **3** *Murphy was an evil, worthless man.* = **good-for-nothing**, base, abandoned, useless, vile, abject, despicable, depraved, contemptible, ignoble ■ **OPPOSITE:** honourable

worthwhile ADJECTIVE = **useful**, good, valuable, helpful, worthy, profitable, productive, beneficial, meaningful, constructive, justifiable, expedient, gainful ■ **OPPOSITE:** useless

worthy ADJECTIVE *worthy members of the community* = **praiseworthy**, good, excellent, deserving, valuable, decent, reliable, worthwhile, respectable, upright, admirable, honourable, honest, righteous, reputable, virtuous, dependable, commendable, creditable, laudable, meritorious, estimable ■ **OPPOSITE:** disreputable ▶ NOUN *The event brought together worthies from many fields.* = **dignitary**, notable, luminary, bigwig (*informal*), big shot (*informal*), personage, big hitter (*informal*), heavy hitter (*informal*) ■ **OPPOSITE:** nobody

would-be ADJECTIVE = **budding**, potential, so-called, professed, dormant, self-styled, latent, wannabe (*informal*), unfulfilled, undeveloped, self-appointed, unrealized, manqué, soi-disant (*French*), quasi-

wound NOUN **1** *Six soldiers are reported to have died of their wounds.* = **injury**, cut, damage, hurt, harm, slash, trauma (*Pathology*), gash, lesion, laceration **2** (*often plural*) *Her experiences have left deep psychological wounds.* = **trauma**, injury, shock, pain, offence, slight, torture, distress, insult, grief, torment, anguish, heartbreak, pang, sense of loss ▶ VERB **1** *The driver of the bus was wounded by shrapnel.* = **injure**, cut, hit, damage, wing, hurt, harm, slash, pierce, irritate, gash, lacerate **2** *He was deeply wounded by the treachery of his closest friends.* = **offend**, shock, pain, hurt, distress, annoy, sting, grieve, mortify, cut to the quick, hurt the feelings of, traumatize

wounding ADJECTIVE = **hurtful**, pointed, cutting, damaging, acid, bitter, slighting,

W

offensive, distressing, insulting, cruel, savage, stinging, destructive, harmful, malicious, scathing, grievous, barbed, unkind, pernicious (*formal*), caustic, spiteful, vitriolic, trenchant, injurious, maleficent

wrangle VERB *The two parties are still wrangling over the timing of the election.* = **argue**, fight, row, dispute, scrap, disagree, fall out (*informal*), contend, quarrel, brawl, squabble, spar, bicker, have words, altercate ▶ NOUN *He was involved in a legal wrangle with the Health Secretary.* = **argument**, row, clash, dispute, contest, set-to (*informal*), controversy, falling-out (*informal*), quarrel, brawl, barney (*informal*), squabble, bickering, tiff, altercation, slanging match (*Brit.*), angry exchange, argy-bargy (*Brit. informal*), bagarre (*French*)

wrap VERB **1** *She wrapped the baby in a blanket.* = **cover**, surround, fold, enclose, roll up, cloak, shroud, swathe, muffle, envelop, encase, sheathe, enfold, bundle up ■ OPPOSITE: uncover **2** *Harry had wrapped some presents for the children.* = **pack**, package, parcel (up), tie up, gift-wrap ■ OPPOSITE: unpack **3** *She wrapped a handkerchief round her bleeding hand.* = **bind**, wind, fold, swathe ■ OPPOSITE: unwind ▶ NOUN *a model wearing a leopard-print wrap* = **cloak**, cape, stole, mantle (*archaic*), shawl • **wrap something up 1** *We spent the evening wrapping up presents.* = **giftwrap**, pack, package, enclose, bundle up, enwrap **2** (*informal*) *NATO defence ministers wrap up their meeting in Brussels today.* = **end**, conclude, wind up, terminate, finish off, round off, tidy up, polish off, bring to a close • **wrap up** *Make sure you wrap up warmly before you go out.* = **dress warmly**, muffle up, wear something warm, put warm clothes on

wrapper NOUN = **cover**, case, paper, packaging, wrapping, jacket, envelope, sleeve, sheath

wrath NOUN = **anger**, passion, rage, temper, fury, resentment, irritation, indignation, ire, displeasure, exasperation, choler ■ OPPOSITE: satisfaction

wreak VERB **1** *Violent storms wreaked havoc on the coast.* = **create**, work, cause, visit, effect, exercise, carry out, execute, inflict, bring about **2** *He wreaked vengeance on the men who had betrayed him.* = **unleash**, express, indulge, vent, gratify, give vent to, give free rein to

wreath NOUN = **garland**, band, ring, crown, loop, festoon, coronet, chaplet

wreathe VERB **1** *Cigarette smoke wreathed her face.* = **surround**, envelop, encircle, enfold, coil around, writhe around, enwrap **2** *The temple's huge columns were wreathed in laurels.* = **festoon**, wind, crown, wrap, twist, coil, adorn, intertwine, interweave, entwine, twine, engarland

wreck VERB **1** *Vandals wrecked the garden.* = **destroy**, break, total (*slang*), smash, ruin, devastate, mar, shatter, spoil, demolish, sabotage, trash (*slang*), ravage, dash to pieces, kennet (*Austral. slang*), jeff (*Austral. slang*) ■ OPPOSITE: build **2** *His life has been wrecked by the tragedy.* = **spoil**, blow (*slang*), ruin, devastate, shatter, undo, screw up (*informal*), cock up (*Brit. slang*), play havoc with, crool or cruel (*Austral. slang*) ■ OPPOSITE: save **3** *His ship was wrecked off the coast of Ireland.* = **run aground**, strand, shipwreck, run onto the rocks ▶ NOUN **1** *the wreck of a sailing ship* = **shipwreck**, derelict, hulk, sunken vessel **2** *a broken man contemplating the wreck of his life* = **ruin**, mess, destruction, overthrow, undoing, disruption, devastation, desolation ■ OPPOSITE: preservation **3** *He was killed in a car wreck.* = **accident**, smash, pile-up (*informal*)

wreckage NOUN = **remains**, pieces, ruin, fragments, debris, rubble, hulk, wrack

wrench VERB **1** *They wrenched open the passenger door and got into the car.* = **twist**, force, pull, tear, rip, tug, jerk, yank, wring, wrest **2** *He had wrenched his ankle badly in the fall.* = **sprain**, strain, rick, distort ▶ NOUN **1** *The rope stopped his fall with a wrench that broke his neck.* = **twist**, pull, rip, tug, jerk, yank **2** *We are hoping the injury is just a wrench.* = **sprain**, strain, twist **3** *I knew it would be a wrench to leave home.* = **blow**, shock, pain, ache, upheaval, uprooting, pang **4** *He took a wrench from his toolbox.* = **spanner**, adjustable spanner, shifting spanner

wrest VERB **1** *He has been trying to wrest control from the central government.* = **seize**, take, win, extract **2** *She wrested the suitcase from the chauffeur's grasp.* = **pull**, force, strain, seize, twist, extract, wrench, wring

wrestle VERB = **fight**, battle, struggle, combat, contend, strive, grapple, tussle, scuffle

wretch NOUN **1** *Before the wretch had time to reply, he was shot.* = **poor thing**, unfortunate, poor soul, poor devil (*informal*), miserable creature **2** *I think he's a mean-minded, vindictive old wretch.* = **scoundrel** (*old-fashioned*), rat (*informal*), worm, villain, rogue, outcast, swine, rascal, profligate, vagabond, ruffian, cur, rotter (*slang, chiefly Brit.*), scumbag (*slang*), good-for-nothing, miscreant, bad egg (*old-fashioned, informal*), blackguard, wrong 'un (*slang*)

wretched ADJECTIVE **1** *wretched people living in abject poverty* = **unfortunate**, poor, sorry, hapless, pitiful, luckless, star-crossed, pitiable **2** *What a wretched excuse!* = **worthless**, poor, sorry, miserable, pathetic, inferior, paltry, deplorable ■ OPPOSITE: excellent **3** *Politicians – I hate the whole wretched lot of them.* = **shameful**, mean, low, base, shabby, vile, low-down (*informal*), paltry, despicable, contemptible, scurvy (*old-fashioned*), crappy (*slang*), poxy (*slang*) ■ OPPOSITE: admirable **4** *The flu was making him feel absolutely wretched.* = **ill**, poorly (*informal*), sick, crook (*Austral. & N.Z. informal*), sickly, unwell, off colour (*Brit. informal*), under the weather (*informal*)

wriggle VERB **1** *The audience were fidgeting and wriggling in their seats.* = **jiggle**, turn, twist, jerk, squirm, writhe **2** *She pulled off her shoes and stockings and wriggled her toes.* = **wiggle**, jerk, wag, jiggle, waggle **3** *Bauman wriggled along the passage on his stomach.* = **crawl**, snake, worm, twist and turn, zigzag, slink ▶ NOUN *With a wriggle, he freed himself from her grasp and ran off.* = **twist**, turn, jerk, wag, squirm, wiggle, jiggle, waggle • **wriggle out of something** *The government is trying to wriggle out of its responsibilities.* = **twist**, avoid, duck (*informal*), dodge, extricate yourself from, talk your way out of, worm your way out of

wring VERB = **twist**, force, squeeze, extract, screw, wrench, coerce, wrest, extort

wrinkle NOUN **1** *His face was covered with wrinkles.* = **line**, fold, crease, furrow, pucker, crow's-foot, corrugation **2** *He noticed a wrinkle in the material.* = **crease**, gather, fold, crumple, furrow, rumple, pucker, crinkle, corrugation ▶ VERB *I wrinkled the velvet.* = **crease**, line, gather, fold, crumple, ruck, furrow, rumple, pucker, crinkle, corrugate ■ OPPOSITE: smooth

writ NOUN = **summons**, document, decree, indictment, court order, subpoena, arraignment

write VERB **1** *Write your name and address at the top of the page.* = **record**, copy, scribble, take down, inscribe, set down, transcribe, jot down, put in writing, commit to paper, indite, put down in black and white **2** *She wrote articles for magazines in Paris.* = **compose**, create, author, draft, pen, draw up **3** *Why didn't you write and let me know you were coming?* = **correspond**, get in touch, keep in touch, write a letter, drop a line, drop a note, email *or* e-mail • **write**

something off 1 *John's written off four cars. Now he sticks to public transport.* = **wreck**, total (*slang*), crash, destroy, trash (*slang*), smash up, damage beyond repair **2** *The banks agreed to write off the company's debts.* = **cancel**, shelve, forget about, cross out, score out, give up for lost • **write something** *or* **someone off** *He is fed up with people writing him off because of his age.* = **disregard**, ignore, dismiss, regard something *or* someone as finished, consider something *or* someone as unimportant

writer NOUN = **author**, novelist, hack, columnist, scribbler, scribe, essayist, penman *or* woman, wordsmith, man *or* woman of letters, penpusher, littérateur, penny-a-liner (*rare*)

writhe VERB = **squirm**, struggle, twist, toss, distort, thrash, jerk, wriggle, wiggle, contort, convulse, thresh

writing NOUN **1** *It's a little difficult to read your writing.* = **script**, hand, print, printing, fist (*informal*), scribble, handwriting, scrawl, calligraphy, longhand, penmanship (*formal*), chirography **2** *Althusser's writings are focused mainly on France.* = **document**, work, book, letter, title, opus, publication, literature, composition, belle-lettre

wrong ADJECTIVE **1** *Pain is the body's way of telling us that something is wrong.* = **amiss**, faulty, unsatisfactory, not right, defective, awry **2** *That was the wrong answer – try again.* = **incorrect**, mistaken, false, faulty, inaccurate, untrue, erroneous, off target, unsound, in error, wide of the mark, fallacious, off base (*U.S. & Canad. informal*), off beam (*informal*), way off beam (*informal*) **3** *I'm always embarrassing myself by saying the wrong thing.* = **inappropriate**, incorrect, unfitting, unsuitable, unhappy, not done, unacceptable, undesirable, improper, unconventional, incongruous, unseemly, unbecoming, indecorous, inapt, infelicitous, malapropos ■ OPPOSITE: correct **4** *It was wrong of you to leave her alone in the house.* = **bad**, criminal, illegal, evil, unfair, crooked (*informal*), unlawful, illicit, immoral, unjust, dishonest, wicked, sinful, unethical, wrongful, under-the-table, reprehensible, dishonourable, iniquitous, not cricket (*informal*), felonious, blameworthy ■ OPPOSITE: moral **5** *We think there's something wrong with the computer.* = **defective**, not working, faulty, out of order, awry, askew, out of commission **6** *Iron the T-shirt on the wrong side to prevent damage to the design.* = **opposite**, inside, reverse, inverse ▶ ADVERB **1** *You've spelled my name wrong.* = **incorrectly**, badly, wrongly,

mistakenly, erroneously, inaccurately
■ **OPPOSITE:** correctly **2** *Where did we go wrong with our children?* = **amiss**, astray, awry, askew ▶ NOUN **1** *He doesn't seem to know the difference between right and wrong.* = **wickedness**, injustice, unfairness, inequity, immorality, iniquity, sinfulness
■ **OPPOSITE:** morality **2** *I intend to right the wrong done to you.* = **offence**, injury, crime, abuse, error, sin, injustice, grievance, infringement, trespass, misdeed, transgression, infraction, bad *or* evil deed
■ **OPPOSITE:** good deed ▶ VERB *She felt she had been wronged.* = **mistreat**, abuse, hurt, injure, harm, cheat, take advantage of, discredit, oppress, malign, misrepresent, dump on (*slang*, *chiefly U.S.*), impose upon, dishonour, ill-treat, maltreat, ill-use
■ **OPPOSITE:** treat well • **go wrong 1** *Nearly everything that could go wrong has gone wrong.* = **fail**, flop (*informal*), fall through, come to nothing, miscarry, misfire, come to grief (*informal*), go pear-shaped (*informal*) **2** *I think*

I've gone wrong somewhere in my calculations. = **make a mistake**, boob (*Brit. slang*), err, slip up (*informal*), go astray **3** *If your DVD player goes wrong, you can have it repaired.* = **break down**, fail, malfunction, misfire, cease to function, conk out (*informal*), go on the blink (*slang*), go kaput (*informal*), go phut (*informal*) **4** *We condemn teenagers who go wrong and punish those who step out of line.* = **lapse**, sin, err, fall from grace, go astray, go to the bad, go off the straight and narrow (*informal*)

wrongful ADJECTIVE = **improper**, illegal, unfair, inappropriate, unlawful, illicit, immoral, unjust, illegitimate, unethical, groundless ■ **OPPOSITE:** rightful

wry ADJECTIVE **1** *a wry sense of humour* = **ironic**, dry, mocking, sarcastic, sardonic, droll, pawky (*Scot.*), mordacious **2** *She cast a wry grin in his direction.* = **contorted**, twisted, crooked, distorted, warped, uneven, deformed, awry, askew, aslant, skewwhiff (*Brit. informal*) ■ **OPPOSITE:** straight

W

Xmas NOUN = **Christmas**, Noel, festive
   season, Yule (*archaic*), Yuletide (*archaic*),
   Christmastime, Christmastide, Crimbo
   (*Brit. informal*)
X-ray NOUN = **radiograph**, X-ray image

Yy

yahoo NOUN = **philistine**, savage, lout, beast, barbarian, brute, rowdy, hoon (*Austral. & N.Z.*), roughneck (*slang*), boor, churl, yob or yobbo (*Brit. slang*), cougan (*Austral. slang*), scozza (*Austral. slang*), bogan (*Austral. slang*)

yak VERB = **gossip**, go on, gab (*informal*), rabbit (on) (*Brit. informal*), run on, jaw (*slang*), chatter, spout (*informal*), waffle (*informal, chiefly Brit.*), yap (*informal*), tattle, jabber, blather, chew the fat (*slang*), witter on (*informal*), run off at the mouth

yank VERB *She yanked the child back into the house.* = **pull**, tug, jerk, seize, snatch, pluck, hitch, wrench ▶ NOUN *Grabbing his ponytail, Shirley gave it a yank.* = **pull**, tug, jerk, snatch, hitch, wrench, tweak

yap VERB **1** *The little dog yapped frantically.* = **yelp**, bark, woof, yip (*chiefly U.S.*) **2** *She keeps yapping at me about Joe.* = **talk**, go on, rabbit (on) (*Brit. informal*), gossip, jaw (*slang*), chatter, spout (*informal*), babble, waffle (*informal, chiefly Brit.*), prattle, jabber, blather, run off at the mouth (*slang*), earbash (*Austral. & N.Z. slang*)

yardstick NOUN = **standard**, measure, criterion, gauge, benchmark, touchstone, par

yarn NOUN **1** *vegetable-dyed yarn* = **thread**, fibre, cotton, wool **2** *Doug has a yarn or two to tell me about his trips into the bush.* = **story**, tale, anecdote, account, narrative, fable, reminiscence, urban myth, tall story, urban legend, cock-and-bull story (*informal*)

yawning ADJECTIVE = **gaping**, wide, huge, vast, wide-open, cavernous

yearly ADJECTIVE *a yearly meeting* = **annual**, each year, every year, once a year ▶ ADVERB *Interest is paid yearly.* = **annually**, every year, by the year, once a year, per annum

yearn VERB (*often with* for) = **long**, desire, pine, pant, hunger, ache, lust, crave, covet, itch, languish, hanker after, have a yen for (*informal*), eat your heart out over, set your heart upon, suspire (*archaic, poetic*), would give your eyeteeth for

yell VERB *He was out there shouting and yelling.* = **scream**, shout, cry out, howl, call out, wail, shriek, screech, squeal, bawl, holler (*informal*), yelp, call at the top of your voice ■ OPPOSITE: whisper ▶ NOUN *He let out a yell.* = **scream**, cry, shout, roar, howl, shriek, whoop, screech, squeal, holler (*informal*), yelp, yowl ■ OPPOSITE: whisper

yellow NOUN = **lemon**, gold, amber ▶ ADJECTIVE (*informal*) = **cowardly**, spineless, gutless, chicken (*informal*), craven, faint-hearted, yellow-bellied (*informal*), lily-livered

yelp VERB *Her dog yelped and came to heel.* = **bark**, howl, yap, yip (*chiefly U.S.*), yowl ▶ NOUN *She gave a yelp of pain.* = **cry**, squeal

yen NOUN = **longing**, desire, craving, yearning, passion, hunger, ache, itch, thirst, hankering

yet ADVERB **1** *They haven't finished yet.* = **so far**, until now, up to now, still, as yet, even now, thus far, up till now, up to the present time **2** *Don't get up yet.* = **now**, right now, just now, so soon, already **3** *This weekend yet more uniformed soldiers were posted at official buildings.* = **still**, further, in addition, as well, moreover, besides, to boot, additionally, over and above, into the bargain ▶ CONJUNCTION *I don't eat much, yet I am a size 16.* = **nevertheless**, still, however, for all that, notwithstanding, just the same, be that as it may

yield VERB **1** *She yielded to general pressure.* = **bow**, submit, give in, surrender, give way, succumb, cave in (*informal*), capitulate, knuckle under, resign yourself **2** *He may yield control.* = **relinquish**, resign, hand over, surrender, turn over, part with, make over, cede, give over, bequeath, abdicate, deliver up ■ OPPOSITE: retain **3** *Their leader refused to yield.* = **surrender**, give up, give in, concede defeat, cave in (*informal*), throw in the towel, admit defeat, accept defeat, give up the struggle, knuckle under, raise the white flag, lay down your arms, cry quits **4** *400,000 acres of land yielded a crop worth $1.75 billion.* = **produce**, give, provide, pay, return, supply, bear, net, earn, afford, generate, bring in, furnish, bring forth ■ OPPOSITE: use up ▶ NOUN **1** *improving the yield of the crop* = **produce**, crop, harvest, output **2** *the yield on a bank's investment* = **profit**, return, income, revenue, earnings, takings ■ OPPOSITE: loss • **yield to something** *Television officials had yielded to demands.* = **comply with**, agree to, concede, allow, grant, permit, go along with, bow to, consent to, accede to

yielding ADJECTIVE **1** *the soft yielding cushions* = **soft**, pliable, springy, elastic, resilient, supple, spongy, unresisting, quaggy **2** *His personality was sometimes prickly, sometimes yielding.* = **submissive**, obedient, compliant, docile, easy (*informal*), flexible, accommodating, pliant, tractable, acquiescent, biddable ■ **OPPOSITE:** obstinate

yob *or* **yobbo** NOUN = **thug**, hooligan, lout, heavy (*slang*), tough, rough (*informal*), rowdy, yahoo, hoon (*Austral. & N.Z. slang*), hoodlum, ruffian, roughneck (*slang*), tsotsi (*S. African*), cougan (*Austral. slang*), scozza (*Austral. slang*), bogan (*Austral. slang*)

yoke NOUN **1** *People are suffering under the yoke of capitalism.* = **oppression**, slavery, bondage, servitude, service, burden, enslavement, serfdom, servility, vassalage, thraldom **2** *He put a yoke around his body and pulled along the cart.* = **harness**, coupling, tackle, chain, collar, tack ▶ VERB **1** *They are yoked by money and votes.* = **unite**, join, link, tie, bond, bind, connect **2** *a plough team of eight oxen yoked in pairs* = **harness**, join, couple, link, tie, connect, bracket, hitch, inspan (*S. African*)

young ADJECTIVE **1** *I was still too young to understand what was going on.* = **immature**, juvenile, youthful, little, growing, green, junior, infant, adolescent, callow, unfledged, in the springtime of life ■ **OPPOSITE:** old **2** *the larvae, the young stages of the worm* = **early**, new, undeveloped, fledgling, newish, not far advanced

■ **OPPOSITE:** advanced ▶ NOUN *The hen may not be able to feed its young.* = **offspring**, baby, litter, family, issue, brood, little ones, progeny ■ **OPPOSITE:** parent

youngster NOUN = **youth**, girl, boy, kid (*informal*), lad, teenager, juvenile, cub, young person, lass, young adult, pup (*informal, chiefly Brit.*), urchin, teenybopper (*slang*), young shaver (*informal*), young 'un (*informal*)

youth NOUN **1** *the comic books of my youth* = **immaturity**, adolescence, early life, young days, boyhood *or* girlhood, salad days, juvenescence ■ **OPPOSITE:** old age **2** *gangs of youths who broke windows and looted shops* = **boy**, lad, youngster, kid (*informal*), teenager, young man, adolescent, teen (*informal*), stripling, young shaver (*informal*) ■ **OPPOSITE:** adult **3** *He represents the opinions of the youth of today.* = **young people**, the young, the younger generation, teenagers, the rising generation ■ **OPPOSITE:** old people

youthful ADJECTIVE **1** *youthful enthusiasm and high spirits* = **young**, juvenile, childish, immature, boyish, pubescent, girlish, puerile ■ **OPPOSITE:** elderly **2** *I'm a very youthful 50.* = **vigorous**, fresh, active, young looking, young at heart, spry ■ **OPPOSITE:** tired

Zz

zany ADJECTIVE = **comical**, crazy, nutty (*slang*), funny, eccentric, wacky (*informal*), oddball (*informal*), madcap, goofy (*informal*), kooky (*U.S. informal*), clownish, wacky (*informal*), off the air (*Austral. slang*)

zeal NOUN = **enthusiasm**, passion, zest, fire, spirit, warmth, devotion, verve, fervour, eagerness, gusto, militancy, fanaticism, ardour, earnestness, keenness, fervency ■ **OPPOSITE:** apathy

zealot NOUN = **fanatic**, enthusiast, extremist, militant, maniac, fiend (*informal*), bigot

zealous ADJECTIVE = **enthusiastic**, passionate, earnest, burning, spirited, keen, devoted, eager, militant, ardent, fanatical, fervent, impassioned, rabid, fervid, swivel-eyed (*slang*) ■ **OPPOSITE:** apathetic

zenith NOUN = **height**, summit, peak, top, climax, crest, high point, pinnacle, meridian, apex, high noon, apogee, acme, vertex ■ **OPPOSITE:** lowest point

zero NOUN **1** *a scale ranging from zero to seven* = **nought**, nothing (*informal*), nil, naught, cipher (*obsolete*) **2** *My spirits were at zero.* = **rock bottom**, the bottom, an all-time low, a nadir, as low as you can get, the lowest point or ebb • **zero in on something 1** *He raised the binoculars again and zeroed in on an eleventh-floor room.* = **zoom in on**, focus on, aim at, train on, home in on **2** *Critics have zeroed in on his weakness.* = **focus on**, concentrate on, home in on, pinpoint, converge on

zest NOUN **1** *He has a zest for life and a quick intellect.* = **enjoyment**, love, appetite, relish, interest, joy, excitement, zeal, gusto, keenness, zing (*informal*), delectation ■ **OPPOSITE:** aversion **2** *Lemon oil adds zest to your cuppa.* = **flavour**, taste, savour, kick (*informal*), spice, relish, smack, tang, piquancy, pungency **3** *the zest and juice of the lemon* = **rind**, skin, peel, outer layer

zip VERB **1** *My craft zipped along the bay.* = **speed**, shoot, fly, tear, rush, flash, dash, hurry, barrel (along) (*informal, chiefly U.S. & Canad.*), buzz, streak, hare (*Brit. informal*), zoom, whizz (*informal*), hurtle, pelt, burn rubber (*informal*) **2** (*data*) = **compress** (*Computing*), archive (*Computing*) ■ **OPPOSITES:** unzip, decompress ▶ NOUN *He gave the choreography his usual class and zip.* = **energy**, go (*informal*), life, drive, spirit, punch (*informal*), pep, sparkle, vitality, vigour, verve, zest, gusto, get-up-and-go (*informal*), oomph (*informal*), brio, zing (*informal*), liveliness, vim, pizzazz or pizazz (*informal*) ■ **OPPOSITE:** lethargy

zone NOUN = **area**, region, section, sector, district, territory, belt, sphere, tract

zoom VERB = **speed**, shoot, fly, tear, rush, flash, dash, barrel (along) (*informal, chiefly U.S. & Canad.*), buzz, streak, hare (*Brit. informal*), zip (*informal*), whizz (*informal*), hurtle, pelt, burn rubber (*informal*)

WORDS FOR
CRYPTIC
CROSSWORDS

Cryptic crosswords

''

'Cryptic' means 'hidden', 'secret' or 'obscure'. Setters of cryptic crosswords are devious creatures who love to mislead solvers as much as possible, using phrases and sentences which appear to be straightforward English, but are in fact anything but!

You may not be familiar with all the terms used in this supplement, so here are some brief explanations to help you:

Setter	The person who produces the crossword puzzle (this person used to be known as the 'compiler' but 'setter' is now generally accepted).
Grid	The squared pattern into which solvers must write their answers.
Grid entry	The answer to a clue.
Clues	The sets of words that appear with the grid. They are numbered by their respective entries in the grid, and categorized as either across or down according to the direction of the entry.
Definition	The word or words which tell the solver the meaning of the answer to the clue. The definition is usually at the beginning or the end of a clue.
Wordplay	The main part of the clue which enables the solver to build a word (or words) that provides a satisfactory and unambiguous answer.
Devices	The methods used in the wordplay to help the solver arrive at the solution.
Linking words	The words which help the setter form an intelligible, readable sentence. They are not essential to the wordplay. Examples include 'and', 'in', 'giving', 'seeing' and 'offering'.
Anagram	A word or phrase with letters which can be rearranged to form another word or phrase.
Anagram indicator	A word or words indicating that the solver has to rearrange some of the letters in the clue to create another word to produce the correct answer.

Cryptic indicators

An 'indicator' is a word or phrase that tells a solver to do something with other words or phrases in a clue. Many of the words listed under the following headings are verbs: they are in their basic form (e.g. 'order'), present tense (e.g. 'orders', 'ordering') or past (e.g. 'ordered'). Where convenient, inflected and derived forms are indicated with round brackets (e.g. 'northern (erly)'). Limited space means we cannot include all possible forms of each verb, so only those that you are most likely to encounter are shown here.

Similarly, it would be impossible to include every little two- or three-word phrase that can be used with an indicator. For example, you will find 'reported' in the list headed 'homophone (sound device)', but the actual wording in a clue may be 'as reported'. Likewise, the indicator 'stripped' may appear as 'stripped of' in a real clue.

Anagram indicators

The words in this list tend to be concerned with movement and change, either directly, as in 'amended', 'different' and 'reordered', or indirectly, as in 'cuckoo', 'nervous' and 'off'. If you search the web for 'cryptic crossword anagram indicators' you will find thousands of sites, some of which list over 2000 words and phrases! Many entries in these lists are rather far-fetched and obscure, and editors and setters might not agree on which are acceptable and fair. It is important to become familiar with the commonest anagram indicators because anagram clues can be some of the easiest to solve.

abroad	becoming	busy	complex
acrobatically	befuddled	careering	complicated
adapted	bemused	careless	components
adjusted	bespoke	carved (up)	composed
affected	bewildered	cavorting	compounded
agitated	bizarre	changed	concocted
all at sea	blended	chaotic	confection
all over the place	blundering	chewed (up)	confounded
all-round	blurred	chopped (up)	confused
altered	bogus	choppy	constituents
amended	boiling	churned	contrived
annoyed	botched	circulating	converted
appalling	bothered	clobbered	convoluted
aroused	brewed	clumsy	convulsed
arranged	broadcast	cock up (cock-up)	corrected
assorted	broken	cocktail	corrupt
baffled	buckled	collapsing	could be
bamboozled	bumbling	collected	cracked (up)
bats	bungled	combustible	crackers
battered	bust	compiled	crackpot

crafted	doctored	free	leaping
cranky	dodgy	frenetic	liberal
crashed	dotty	fresh	lively
crazy	doubtful	frisky	loose
crooked	dreadful	frolicsome	malleable
crumbled	drifting	from	managed
crushed	drunk	fudged	mangled
cuckoo	dubious	funny	manipulated
cultivated	duff	gambolling	manoeuvred
damaged	dynamic	garbled	marred
dancing	eccentric	generated	marshalled
dashed	effervescent	giddy	mashed
dazed	elastic	groomed	masquerading
dealt out	emended	ground	massaged
decomposed	emerging from	haphazard	maybe
demolished	engineered	hash	mayhem
destabilized	entangled	havoc	meandering
destroyed	entwined	haywire	medley
deteriorating	erratic	head over heels	mélange
devastated	erroneous	hectic	mêlée
developed	erupting	helter-skelter	melting
deviating	evolving	higgledy-piggledy	merry
devious	exchanged	hotchpotch	messed
diabolical	excited	ill-assorted	metamorphosed
different	exploded	impaired	minced
disarranged	extraordinary	imperfect	mingled
disbanded	fabricated	improvised	mischievous
disconcerted	fake	in a mess	misconstrued
disguised	falsified	in disarray	misdirected
dishevelled	fashioned	in discord	misguided
disintegrated	fermented	in error	mishandled
disjointed	feverish	in motion	mishap
dislocated	fishy	incorrect	misinterpreted
dismantled	flailing	intoxicated	mismanaged
disordered	flawed	invalid	misplaced
disorganized	flexible	irregular	misprinted
disorientated	flighty	itinerant	misrepresented
dispersed	flitting	jazzy	misshapen
disrupted	floundering	jittery	misspelt
dissolute	flowing	jockeying	mistaken
distorted	fluctuating	jostled	mixed
distraught	fluid	juggled	mixture
distressed	fluttering	jumbled	mobile
distributed	flying	kind of	modelled
disturbed	forged	kneaded	modified
diverted	forming	lawless	mongrel
dizzy	frantic	lax	moulded

moving
muddled
mussed
mutilated
mysterious
negotiated
nervous
new
novel
odd
off
ordered
organized
otherwise
out of order
outrageous
pastiche
peculiar
perhaps
perturbed
phony
playing
ploughed
possibly
potentially
prancing
preposterous
processed
producing
providing
pummelled
quaking
quivering
rambling
ramshackle
random
realigned
rearranged
reassembled
rebuilt
recast
recollected
reconfigured
reconstituted
reconstructed
recreated
recycled

redeployed
redeveloped
rediscovered
redistributed
redrafted
refashioned
refined
reformed
regenerated
rehashed
rejigged
remade
remedied
remodelled
renewed
renovated
reordered
reorganized
repackaged
replaced
repositioned
represented
reprocessed
resettled
reshaped
reshuffled
resolved
resorted
restless
restored
revamped
revised
reworked
rewritten
rocked
rollicking
rotten
rough
roving
ruffled
ruined
rum
sabotaged
salad
scattered
scrambled
scuffled

sculpted
seething
shaken
sham
shattered
shifted
shivering
shuffled
slapdash
smashed
somehow
sort of
sorted
spattered
spilt
spinning
spoilt
sporting
spread
sprinkled
squirming
staggering
stew
stirring
strange
straying
stumbling
suffering
supple
suspect
swimming
swirling
tailored
terrible
thrown
tipsy
tottering
trained
transferred
transfigured
transformed
translated
transposed
trembling
tumbledown
turbulent
turmoil

tweaked
twirling
twisted
unbalanced
uncommon
unexpected
unfamiliar
unhappy
unlikely
unnatural
unorthodox
unravelled
unrestrained
unrestricted
unruly
unscrambled
unsteady
untidy
unusual
unwound
upset
vacillating
vagrant
vague
varied
vibrating
vigorous
volatile
wandering
warped
wavering
waving
weird
whirling
wild
wobbling
worked
wrecked
writhing
wrong
zany

Reverse direction

Some of these indicators should only appear in across clues, such as 'back', 'backing', 'going west' and 'turning'. Those found in down clues include 'rising', 'falling' and 'taken up'. Words such as 'reversed' and 'revolutionary' are widely used whether the entry is down or across.

about	climbing	going west	revolutionary
around	decscending	in recession	rising
ascending	downwards	lifted	southern (erly)
back(ing)	dropping	northern (erly)	taken up
backed up	elated	over(turned)	turning
(down clue)	elevated	reactionary	upwards
backward	falling	rearing	western
capsized	flipping	returning	

Hidden word

Clues in which the grid entry is concealed within the wordplay are usually easy to solve, so a working knowledge of these indicators can give you a good start in a crossword. Some more obvious examples of these are 'in', 'part of' and 'some', while others like 'boxing', 'bottles', 'parcels' and 'houses' are used with the intention of misleading you.

apparent in	emerges from	includes	restricts
bottles	encloses (ed by)	involves	shown in
cans	encompasses	parcels	slice of
comes from	found in	part of	some
contributing to	held by	partly	
covers	houses	resides in	
discovered in	in	restrained by	

Contracted forms

When we call a word a contracted form, we mean that it is a shortened version of a word or words, such as 'promo' for 'promotion' and 'kinda' for 'kind of'. Dictionaries sometimes call these short forms. They are not used very often in cryptic crosswords but it is useful to be able to recognize them when they occur. Then you will know that 'in brief' may be an indicator of a contracted form, and nothing to do with law or legal matters.

contracted (to)	in short
contracting	reduced (to)
contracts (to)	shortened (to)
in brief	

Moving letter

Wordplay sometimes indicates that a letter needs to be moved to provide the grid entry. 'Head dropping', for example, may suggest that the first letter of a word be moved to create the word to be written in the grid. As with the indicators for 'reverse direction', some indicators of moving letters apply only to down clues, for example 'rising', 'descending' and 'climbing'. This is also the case for 'boosted' which means 'raised'. Indicators like 'switching' and 'swapping' can be for across or down clues. 'Spooner's' indicates that the initial letters of two words should be swapped, as in 'sons of toil' for 'tons of soil'. The Reverend William Spooner, an English clergyman renowned for mistakenly swapping letters in this way, gave these verbal slips their name: spoonerisms.

boosted	dropping	rising	swapping
climbing	exchanging	slipping	switching
descending	falling	Spooner's	

Deletion

Deletion is the device that requires the solver to drop part of a word in order to create the grid entry. It is one of the easier devices to use and so it has many indicators. Some are easy to understand, for example 'scrapped', 'omitted' and 'taken away'. Others are more obscure, such as 'Manx', which means that the last letter of a word is to be removed, because Manx cats have no tail! Strictly speaking 'Manx' should start with a capital letter, which is not a problem when it is the first word in the clue. However, a little bit of 'setter's licence' would allow it to appear elsewhere in a clue without the initial capital letter.

abandoned	discarded	in Whitechapel	reduced
abridged	discounted	(no h)	scrapped
absconding	dismissed	incomplete	scratched
absent	dropped	left	scrubbed
away	East End (no h)	lopped	shelled
banned	eclipsed	lost	shorn
barred	ejected	Manx	short (ened)
binned	endless(ly)	masked	splits
blotted out	eschewed	mislaid	stripped
cast	evicted	missing	subtracted (ing)
chucked	excised	not allowed	taken away
clipped	excluded (ing)	obfuscated	topless
cockney	flees (ing)	obliterated	trashed
(missing h)	guillotined	obscured	unfinished
curtailed	gutted	off	veiled
deadheaded	headless	omitted	without
decaudated	heaved (ing)	out	
defaced	ignored	peeled	
departs (ed), (ing)	in Spitalfields (no h)	polled	

Substituted letter

Sometimes a letter suggested by the wordplay must be changed to form the grid entry. An example of this is 'Scour new opening for tomb', where changing the first letter of 'tomb' provides the answer 'comb'. Most of these indicators are self-explanatory, but it is worth mentioning 'afore' and 'inform'. These words can be broken up into pieces: 'afore' becomes 'a for e' and 'inform' becomes 'in for m'. These can be used as indicators of substituted letters in a clue: 'substitute the letter a for the letter e' (afore) and 'substitute the letters in for m' (inform). However, some setters and editors would consider these unfair, and would not accept any word that contains 'for' within it as an indicator of a substituted letter.

afore (a for e)	exchanged for	in place of	switched for
becomes	for	instead of	
change of	inform (in for m)	replaces	
changed to	in lieu of	swapped for	

Archaic indicator

Clues referring to words that are no longer in current usage are not very common, and tend to be confined to the hardest cryptic crosswords. Nevertheless, they do occasionally turn up in the 'dailies', so you need to be on your guard. Most of the indicators in this list are easy to understand, but there are one or two surprises. The best-known meaning of 'pristine', for example, is 'pure and unspoilt', but it can also mean 'original', 'former' and 'belonging to the earliest time'. 'Hoary', as in 'a hoary old chestnut' (meaning a joke that everyone has heard), also means 'ancient'. The French word 'passé', meaning 'out of date', has been imported into English. Accents are generally included in clues but ignored in grid entries.

ancient	(in) former (times)	old	Shakespearean
archaic	historic	old world	Spenser's
bygone	hoary	once	the Bard's
defunct	in olden times	outdated	(Shakespeare's)
disused	long gone	passé	veteran
Edmund's	lost	(in the) past	was
Ed's (Spenser)	no longer	previously	Will's
ere-now	obsolete	pristine	(Shakespeare's)
extinct	of yore	Shakespeare's	

Container and contents

Some words may not mean what they appear to mean. A good example of this is 'without', which can mean 'deprived of' but can also mean 'outside'. 'Bottles' is a very devious and misleading indicator, as on first reading it seems to indicate a plural noun. But 'bottle' can also be a verb meaning 'to enclose in a bottle', so 'bottles' can actually mean 'encloses'. Another indicator of a container and contents device is 'bandage', which indicates wrapping one object round another.

about	consuming	held by	parcelling
absorbing	containing	holds	ports
accommodating	contains	houses	restrains
adopting	conveying	hugging	restricts
around	covering	humping	retired (in bed)
bandages	digesting	imbibes	sandwiches
bearing	dividing	including	separating
besetting	dressing	inflated	splits
besieging	drinking	(containing air)	splitting
blocks	eating	ingesting	sporting
boarding	embracing	investing	stops
bottles	encasing	keeping	straddling
boxing	enfolds	limits	surrounded by
cans	engaging	lining	surrounding
captivating	ensnaring	necking	swallowing
carrying	entertaining	netting	takes in
carts	enthralling	obstructs	toting
cases	espousing	occupying	trapping
catching	filling	overdrawn	wearing
caught by	frames	(in red)	without
clipping	harnesses	packing	wrapping

Homophone (sound device)

A homophone is a word that sounds like another word, even though they are spelt differently, for example 'rein', 'rain' and 'reign'. There are many groups of two or three or even more homophones in English, and crossword setters love them! Homophone indicators can include any term that indicates the sound of a word, including potentially misleading ones such as 'pipe' and 'spout'. Both of these verbs can mean 'to speak' but that meaning is not the first one you would think of for either of them, so beware of 'piped' and 'spouted'.

articulated	listened to	piped	stated
breathed	mouthed	reported	sung
broadcast	noised	said	voiced
called	on the blower	so to speak	whispered
hear (d) (ing)	on the phone	sound	
in conversation	on the radio	spoken	
intoned	phonetically	spouted	

Initial and final letters

Setters often have to indicate one or more individual letters in wordplay. The following list contains some of the main ways of indicating these. When just one letter is required, something like 'initially' or 'finally' can be used for the first or last letter of either the preceding or following word. Strictly speaking, if the setter wishes to indicate a string of initials, the clue should include something like 'first of all'. However, this is not always the case. Any kind of opening or ending could be used, which is why 'overture' and 'bottom' are included. 'Overture' is the piece played at the beginning of an opera and 'bottom' can indicate the last letter in a down entry.

at last	finishes	margins
beginning of	first of all	onset of
borders	foremost	openings
bottom	foundation	origin (s)
bounds	front of	overture (s)
cap (s)	Gateshead	peripherally
crown (s)	head of	preliminaries
debut	initially	primary
determination of	intro	primes
edges	introduction	rims
end of	introductory	start(s) of
endings	last of	top of
eventually	last of all	ultimately
extremes	leader of	
finally	limits	

Regularly placed letters other than odd or even

Although straightforward alternate letters are those most likely to be indicated in standard cryptic crosswords of average difficulty, setters may often select every third or fourth letter, in which case 'intermittently' won't necessarily mean every odd or even letter.

found at intervals in	intermittently	taken regularly from
found regularly in	taken at intervals from	

Odd or even letters

'Odds' or 'evens' must mean every other letter. Watch out for 'odds' though, for it could relate to betting odds and actually be referring to 'SP' (which is an abbreviation for 'starting price'). Some indicators such as 'intermittently' may be used either for alternate letters or for other intervals between letters. It is for the solver to determine which is intended, by noting how many letters are needed for the grid entry.

alternately	intermittently	unevenly
at intervals	odd ones from/in	
even ones from/in	oddly (discarded)	
evenly (discarded)	odds	
every other from/in	regularly (discarded)	

Dialect and foreign words

Cockney pronunciation is often used in crosswords to indicate a dropped H at the start of a word and, less often, a missing G from the end of a word. Scots or Yorkshire terms both qualify as 'northern'. Simple words from other languages are often included, the most common being 'the French' which can represent LE, LA, or LES (which are all ways of writing 'the' in French). Less common are 'a German' (EIN or EINE, which are German for 'a'), 'the Italian' (IL, LO, LA, I, GLI or LE which are Italian words meaning 'the') and 'the Spanish' (EL, LA, LOS or LAS, all of which mean 'the').

cockney (missing h)	in Spitalfields (no h)	northern
East End (missing h)	in the country	Senor (man's name)
French	in Whitechapel (no h)	Senorita (girl's name)
German	Italian	Spanish
in places	locally	

Specifically placed letters

'Colin essentially' could indicate L or OLI. The essence of this is that you need to use the central letter or letters of the word, and you have to work out how many you need from the rest of the wordplay in the clue. 'Beethoven's ninth' refers to the letter N, the ninth letter in his name.

Beethoven's ninth (n)	essentially	nucleus of
centre of	heart of	second, third, fourth
core of	middle of	(etc.)

Shortened forms

Setters may sometimes indicate that a shortened form of a word is needed, such as 'lab' for 'laboratory' or 'labrador' (the dog). A devious setter may reverse this idea by using something like 'I expanded' where the entry required is 'independent'. 'I' is a common abbreviation for 'independent' and the setter is asking the solver to expand the abbreviation 'I' to its full form.

briefly	in brief	little	short (ened)

Misleading single word definitions

Crossword setters love to use tricky definitions within wordplay, and sometimes even like to include themselves in the clue. So a 'setter' appearing within a clue is not necessarily a dog. When indicating the creator of the puzzle, 'setter' may mean 'me' or 'I', or even the setter's name. Sometimes it might even be the name of another setter of that newspaper's puzzles, 'Phi' being the most popular. Another common device is the one-word definition of the answer. A 'swimmer' is almost always a fish and a 'banker', rather than someone who works for Barclays, is sometimes a river. A river, however, is more often a 'flower' (something that 'flows', not the thing you buy in bunches). Watch out for 'specs', which can indicate 'oo' (supposedly resembling the frames of a pair of glasses), and other indicators that depend on what the letters look like.

admission of (I'm)	flower (river)	rhino (money)
banker (river)	his (greetings)	scorer (composer)
bread (money)	lower (cattle)	setter (of puzzle – not
butter (ram, goat)	my (setter of puzzle)	a dog!)
claim by or of (I'm)	number (drug)	spec(tacle)s (oo)
declaration of (I'm)	pen (writer)	swimmer (fish)
empty (containing o)	potter (snooker player)	tin (money)
engagement (battle)	ready (money)	winger (bird)
flier (bird)	retired (in bed)	writer (setter of puzzle)

Entry direction in across clues

If the setter indicates that an across clue is 'going west', this could be a way of saying that there is a reversal involved. We write from left to right or, in terms of direction, from west to east. Therefore 'going west' can be a hint about reversing the order of something in the clue to find the grid entry.

about	backward	going west	western (ly)
around	forward	reverse	

Entry direction in down clues

'West' and 'western' won't work for a down clue because down answers are written from top to bottom. In down clues you are likely to find references to 'rising' and 'falling'.

ascending	dropping	going up
climbing	falling	northerly
descending	going down	southerly

Position of parts

Those letters or words that make up the required solution may be placed alongside each other, as in 'One playing recordings of a bird by a river' for DEEJAY ('Dee' is a river and 'jay' is a bird). In this clue 'by' is a linking word meaning 'at the side of'. The words in the following list are generally links like this, although they may be less obvious than 'by', 'on' or 'over'. In down clues, words indicating 'support' may be used when one part is to be placed on top of another. But be careful. 'River supports' could be a clue for TEES ('Tees' is a river and 'tees' are the pegs used to support golf balls). The word 'by' may indicate the letter X (as used in measurements, for example 6m x 10m). In a down clue, a word may be described as 'supporting' if it appears under another word. However, a word that is on top of another word may be considered to be an 'oppressor'.

above	below	in support of	over
alongside	beneath	on	supporting
bearing	by	oppressing	

Homonyms

|||||||||||||||||||||||||||||||||||||||||||||||||||||||||||

A homonym is a word that is spelled (and often pronounced) in the same way as another word, but has a different meaning, such as NOVEL (a book) and NOVEL (new). Homonyms are often used in word games and crossword puzzles; solvers of cryptic crosswords in particular should beware the use of homonyms designed to mislead the unwary. Typical homonym clues might appear to give two definitions for the 'same' word.

Here are some interesting examples:

APOSTROPHE	punctuation mark / digression
BARROW	wheelbarrow / mound of earth on prehistoric tomb
BEETLE	insect / to overhang
BLACKJACK	card game / truncheon
BLAZE	strong fire or flame / mark on tree indicating a path
BOWLER	hat / cricket player
BRAZIER	container for burning coal / worker in brass
BROGUE	sturdy shoe / strong Irish accent
BUNTING	decorative flags / songbird
BURDEN	heavy load / theme of a speech
CADDY	small container for tea / golfer's assistant
CASHIER	person who handles cash / to dismiss with dishonour
CHAR	to blacken by partial burning / cleaning woman / tea
CLAMP	mechanical device / mound of harvested crop
CLINK	metallic sound / prison
CLOBBER	to defeat utterly / clothes
CLUTCH	to seize / set of eggs laid at the same time
COPPER	metal / police officer
COS	lettuce / cosine
DOMINO	tile marked with dots used in game / hooded cloak with eye mask
DRILL	boring machine / cotton cloth / W African monkey
DUN	to demand payment / brownish-grey
ENTRANCE	way into a place / to delight
FEINT	sham attack / narrow lines on ruled paper
FETCH	to go after and bring back / ghost of a living person
FLUKE	stroke of luck / anchor's point / lobe of a whale's tail
FORTE	thing at which a person excels / loudly
FROG	tailless amphibian / military coat fastening / horny material on horse's foot
GOBBLE	to eat hastily and greedily / cry of the male turkey
GUDGEON	small fish / socket of a hinge
HARRIER	cross-country runner / bird of prey
HINDER	to get in the way of / situated at the back

HUSKY	slightly hoarse / Arctic sledge dog
JUNK	rubbish / narcotic drugs / Chinese sailing boat
KEEN	eager / lament for the dead
KITTY	name for a cat / communal fund
LASHINGS	floggings / ropes used for binding / large amounts
LEVEE	river embankment / formal reception held by sovereign after rising from bed
LIMBER	agile / part of a gun carriage
LING	fish / heather
MEW	cry of a cat / seagull
MOLE	skin spot / small mammal / unit of amount of substance / breakwater
MUST	essential thing / newly pressed grape juice
NAVE	long central part of a church / hub of a wheel
NIP	pinch or squeeze / sharp coldness / small drink of spirits
ORATORY	art of making speeches / small private chapel
PIANO	musical instrument / quietly
PIGEON	bird / victim / concern or responsibility
PLIGHT	difficult or dangerous situation / to promise
QUACK	sound made by a duck / unqualified person who claims medical knowledge
QUAIL	small game bird / to shrink back with fear
QUID	pound (sterling) / piece of tobacco for chewing
RIME	hoarfrost / rhyme
ROOK	bird of the crow family / castle-shaped chess piece
RUCK	rough crowd of common people / wrinkle or crease
SAKE	benefit / Japanese alcoholic drink made from rice
SERPENTINE	twisting like a snake / soft green or brownish-red mineral
SHANTY	small rough hut / rhythmic song
SMACK	to slap sharply / slight flavour or trace / heroin / small fishing boat
SPAR	pole used as a ship's mast / to box / crystalline mineral
TATTOO	pattern made on the body by staining the skin with inks / military display
TIDDLY	tiny / slightly drunk
TOPE	to drink lots of alcohol / small grey shark
TROLL	supernatural dwarf or giant / to fish by dragging a lure through water
TRUMP	card of the suit outranking the others / (sound of) a trumpet
VIOLA	stringed instrument / variety of pansy
VIVA	long live (a person or thing) / examination in the form of an interview
WEAL	raised mark on the skin produced by a blow / prosperity
WOOF	cross threads in weaving / a dog's barking noise
YEN	longing or desire / monetary unit of Japan

Homophones

Homophones are words that are pronounced identically but have different meanings, spellings, or both (such as DIE and DYE). Like homonyms, they afford excellent opportunities for wordplay, and often feature in word games and puzzles. Thinking of a pair of homophones, and creating clues to help others guess what they might be, can in itself be a simple and humorous game for two or more players on a long car journey. In cryptic crosswords, clues involving homophones are generally indicated by terms such as 'they say' or 'reportedly' (see page 9 for more homophone indicators). Some familiar homophones:

AID	AIDE	JAM	JAMB	ROOT	ROUTE
ALTER	ALTAR	KEY	QUAY	ROUGH	RUFF
ARC	ARK	LEAK	LEEK	SAIL	SALE
BAIL	BALE	LINKS	LYNX	SENT	SCENT
BARE	BEAR	LOAN	LONE	SHEAR	SHEER
BASE	BASS	MADE	MAID	SIGHT	SITE
BEACH	BEECH	MAIN	MANE	SLAY	SLEIGH
BOAR	BORE	MANNER	MANOR	SOLE	SOUL
BOUGH	BOW	MARSHAL	MARTIAL	SOME	SUM
BRAKE	BREAK	MEWS	MUSE	STAIR	STARE
CARAT	CARROT	MUSCLE	MUSSEL	STAKE	STEAK
CEREAL	SERIAL	NEED	KNEAD	STATIONARY	STATIONERY
CHUTE	SHOOT	NEW	KNEW	STEAL	STEEL
COUNCIL	COUNSEL	NIGHT	KNIGHT	STILE	STYLE
DEAR	DEER	PAIL	PALE	TAIL	TALE
DIE	DYE	PAIN	PANE	THEIR	THERE
DUAL	DUEL	PAIR	PEAR	THREW	THROUGH
EARN	URN	PEACE	PIECE	THYME	TIME
FEAT	FEET	PEAL	PEEL	TIRE	TYRE
FLEA	FLEE	PEER	PIER	VAIN	VANE
FLOUR	FLOWER	PLACE	PLAICE	VALE	VEIL
GAIT	GATE	PLAIN	PLANE	WAIL	WHALE
GRATE	GREAT	PLUM	PLUMB	WAIST	WASTE
GROAN	GROWN	PRAY	PREY	WAIT	WEIGHT
HAIR	HARE	PRINCIPAL	PRINCIPLE	WEAK	WEEK
HART	HEART	PRISE	PRIZE	WEATHER	WHETHER
HEAL	HEEL	PROFIT	PROPHET	WHICH	WITCH
HEAR	HERE	QUEUE	CUE	WHITHER	WITHER
HIM	HYMN	RAIN	REIGN	WON	ONE
HOARSE	HORSE	RAP	WRAP	WRY	RYE
IDLE	IDOL	READ	REED	YOLK	YOKE
ISLE	AISLE	RIGHT	WRITE		